**Department of Economic and Social Affairs**
Statistics Division

**Département des affaires économiques et sociales**
Division de statistique

# Statistical Yearbook
Fifty-second issue
Data available as of June 2008

# Annuaire statistique
Cinquante-deuxième édition
Données disponibles en juin 2008

United Nations | Nations Unies
New York, 2008

# Department of Economic and Social Affairs

The Department of Economic and Social Affairs of the United Nations Secretariat is a vital interface between global policies in the economic, social and environmental spheres and national action. The Department works in three main interlinked areas: (i) it compiles, generates and analyses a wide range of economic, social and environmental data and information on which States Members of the United Nations draw to review common problems and to take stock of policy options; (ii) it facilitates the negotiations of Member States in many intergovernmental bodies on joint courses of action to address ongoing or emerging global challenges; and (iii) it advises interested Governments on the ways and means of translating policy frameworks developed in United Nations conferences and summits into programmes at the country level and, through technical assistance, helps build national capacities.

## Note

The designations employed and the presentation of the material in this publication do not imply the expression of any opinion whatsoever on the part of the Secretariat of the United Nations concerning the legal status of any country, city or area, or of its authorities, or concerning the delimitation of its frontiers or boundaries.

In general, statistics contained in the present publication are those available to the United Nations Secretariat up to June 2008 and refer to 2007 or earlier. They therefore reflect the country nomenclature currently in use.

The term "country" as used in the text of this publication also refers, as appropriate, to territories or areas.

The designations "developed" and "developing" which appear in some tables are intended for statistical convenience and do not necessarily express a judgement about the stage reached by a particular country or area in the development process.

Symbols of United Nations documents are composed of capital letters combined with figures.

# Département des affaires économiques et sociales

Le Département des affaires économiques et sociales du Secrétariat de l'Organisation des Nations Unies assure le lien essentiel entre les politiques adoptées au plan international dans les domaines économique, social et écologique et les mesures prises au plan national. Il mène ses activités dans trois grands domaines interdépendants : i) il compile, produit et analyse une grande variété de données et d'informations économiques, sociales et écologiques dont les États Membres de l'ONU tirent parti pour examiner les problèmes communs et faire le point sur les possibilités d'action; ii) il facilite les négociations que les États Membres mènent dans un grand nombre d'organes intergouvernementaux sur les moyens d'action à employer conjointement pour faire face aux problèmes mondiaux existants ou naissants; et iii) il aide les gouvernements intéressés à traduire les orientations politiques établies lors des conférences et sommets de l'ONU en programmes nationaux et contribue à renforcer les capacités des pays en leur apportant une assistance technique.

## Note

Les appellations employées dans la présente publication et la présentation des données qui y figurent n'impliquent, de la part du Secrétariat de l'Organisation des Nations Unies, aucune prise de position quant au statut juridique des pays, territoires, villes ou zones, ou de leurs autorités, ni quant au tracé de leurs frontières ou limites.

En règle générale, les statistiques contenues dans la présente publication sont celles dont disposait le Secrétariat de l'Organisation des Nations Unies jusqu'à juin 2008 et portent sur la période finissant en 2007. Elles reflètent donc la nomenclature des pays en vigueur à l'époque.

Le terme « pays », tel qu'il est utilisé ci-après, peut également désigner des territoires ou des zones.

Les appellations « développées » et « en développement » qui figurent dans certains tableaux sont employées à des fins exclusivement statistiques et n'expriment pas nécessairement un jugement quant au niveau de développement atteint par tel pays ou telle région.

Les cotes des documents de l'Organisation des Nations Unies se composent de lettres majuscules et de chiffres.

ST/ESA/STAT/SER.S/28

UNITED NATIONS PUBLICATION
Sales No. E/F.08.XVII.1

ISBN 978-92-1-061247-0
ISSN 0082-8459

ST/ESA/STAT/SER.S/28

PUBLICATION DES NATIONS UNIES
Numéro de vente : E/F.08.XVII.1

ISBN 978-92-1-061247-0
ISSN 0082-8459

# Preface

This is the fifty-second issue of the United Nations *Statistical Yearbook*, prepared by the Statistics Division of the Department of Economic and Social Affairs. Ever since the compilation of data for the *Statistical Yearbook* series was initiated in 1948, it has consistently provided a wide range of internationally available statistics on social and economic conditions and activities at the national, regional and world levels.

The tables include series covering from one to ten years, depending upon data availability (as of 30 June 2008) and space constraints. The ten-year tables generally cover the years 1996 to 2005 or 1997 to 2006.

The *Yearbook* tables are based on data which have been compiled by the Statistics Division mainly from official national and international sources as these are more authoritative and comprehensive, more generally available as time series and more comparable among countries than other sources. These sources include the United Nations Statistics Division in the fields of national accounts, industry, energy and international trade, the United Nations Statistics Division and Population Division in the field of demographic statistics, and over 20 offices of the United Nations system and international organizations in other specialized fields. In some cases, official sources have been supplemented by other sources and estimates, where these have been subjected to professional scrutiny and debate and are consistent with other independent sources.

The United Nations agencies and other international, national and specialized organizations which furnished data are listed under "Statistical sources and references" at the end of the *Yearbook*. Acknowledgement is gratefully made for their generous and valuable cooperation in continually providing data.

The 68 tables of the *Yearbook* are organized in four parts. The first part presents key world and regional aggregates and totals. In the other three parts, the subject matter is generally presented by countries or areas, with world and regional aggregates shown in some cases only. Parts two, three and four cover, respectively, population and social topics, national economic activity and international economic relations. Each chapter ends with brief technical notes on statistical sources and methods for the tables it includes.

The three annexes contain information on country and area nomenclature and the conversion coefficients and factors used in the various tables, and list those tables which were added to or omitted from the last issue of the *Yearbook*.

\* \* \*

The *Statistical Yearbook* is prepared by the Statistical Dissemination Section, Statistical Services Branch of the Statistics Division, Department of Economic and Social

# Préface

La présente édition de *l'Annuaire statistique* des Nations Unies est la cinquante-deuxième, préparée par la Division de statistique du Département des affaires économiques et sociales. Depuis son instauration en 1948 comme outil de compilation des données statistiques internationales, *l'Annuaire statistique* s'efforce de constamment diffuser un large éventail de statistiques disponibles sur les activités et conditions économiques et sociales, aux niveaux national, régional et mondial.

Les tableaux présentent des séries qui couvrent d'un à dix ans, en fonction de la disponibilité des données (à la date du 30 juin 2008) et des contraintes d'espace. Les tableaux décennaux couvrent généralement les années 1996 à 2005 ou 1997 à 2006.

Les tableaux de *l'Annuaire* sont construits essentiellement à partir des données compilées par la Division de statistique et provenant de sources officielles, nationales et internationales; c'est en effet la meilleure source si l'on veut des données fiables, complètes et comparables, et si l'on a besoin de séries chronologiques. Ces sources sont: la Division de statistique du Secrétariat de l'Organisation des Nations Unies pour ce qui concerne la comptabilité nationale, l'industrie, l'énergie et le commerce extérieur, la Division de statistique et la Division de la population du Secrétariat de l'Organisation des Nations Unies pour les statistiques démographiques; et plus de 20 bureaux du système des Nations Unies et d'organisations internationales pour les autres domaines spécialisés. Dans quelques cas, les données officielles sont complétées par des informations et des estimations provenant d'autres sources qui ont été examinées par des spécialistes et confirmées par des sources indépendantes.

Les institutions spécialisées des Nations Unies et les autres organisations internationales, nationales et spécialisées qui ont fourni des données sont énumérées dans la section "Sources statistiques et références" figurant à la fin de l'ouvrage. Les auteurs de *l'Annuaire statistique* les remercient de leur précieuse et généreuse collaboration.

Les 68 tableaux de *l'Annuaire* sont regroupés en quatre parties. La première partie présente les principaux agrégats et totaux aux niveaux mondial et régional. Dans les trois parties suivantes, les thèmes sont généralement présentés par pays ou régions. Les agrégats mondiaux ou régionaux ne son indiqués que dans certains cas seulement. Les trois parties autres sont consacrées à la population et aux questions sociales (deuxième partie), à l'activité économique nationale (troisième partie) et aux relations économiques internationales (quatrième partie). Chaque chapitre termine par une brève note technique sur les sources et les méthodes statistiques utilisées pour les tableaux présentés.

Les trois annexes donnent des renseignements sur la

## Preface (*continued*)

Affairs of the United Nations Secretariat. The programme manager is Mary Jane Holupka and the chief editor is Jacob Assa. They are assisted by Anna Marie Scherning, David Carter, Aida Diawara and Weihua Ju. Bogdan Dragovic developed the software.

Comments on the present *Yearbook* and suggestions for its future evolution are welcome. They may be sent via e-mail to statistics@un.org or to the United Nations Statistics Division, Statistical Dissemination Section, New York, NY 10017, USA.

## Préface (*suite*)

nomenclature des pays et des zones, ainsi que sur les coefficients et facteurs de conversion employés dans les différents tableaux. Une liste des tableaux ajoutés et supprimés depuis la dernière édition de l'*Annuaire* y est également disponible.

\* \* \*

L'*Annuaire statistique* est préparé par la Section de la diffusion des statistiques, Service des services statistiques de la Division de statistique, Département des affaires économiques et sociales du Secrétariat de l'Organisation des Nations Unies. La responsable du programme est Mary Jane Holupka, et le rédacteur en chef est Jacob Assa. Ils sont secondés par Anna Marie Scherning, David Carter, Aida Diawara et Weihua Ju. Bogdan Dragovic est chargé des logiciels.

Les observations sur la présente édition de l'*Annuaire* et les suggestions de modification pour l'avenir seront reçues avec intérêt. Elles peuvent être envoyées par message électronique à statistics@un.org, ou adressées à la Division de statistique des Nations Unies, Section de la Diffusion Statistique, New York, N.Y. 10017 (États Unis d'Amérique).

## New features in the 52<sup>nd</sup> issue

Several improvements and changes have been made to this issue of the UN *Statistical Yearbook*:

### A new chapter

A brand new chapter has been added to the current yearbook. Chapter 5 - Gender – includes three tables based on the Millennium Development Goals (MDG) indicators:

- Table 10 - Women in national parliaments
- Table 11 - Share of women in wage employment in the non-agricultural sector
- Table 12 - Ratio of girls to boys in primary, secondary and tertiary education.

### New tables

Two new tables have been added:

- Table 20 - Implicit price deflators (in Chapter 7 - National accounts and industrial production)
- Table 64 - Reserves minus gold (in Chapter 19 - International finance).

### New series in existing tables

- A new data series – Chicken – has been added to table 40 – Meat – as this category of meat production is currently the second largest in terms of quantity.

### New features in existing tables

- The tables in Chapter 6 dealing with communications (Telephones, Cellular mobile telephone subscribers, Internet users) have a new column indicating the type of fiscal year used in those countries that do now follow the calendar year. This notation replaces the previous use of footnotes to denote fiscal years, and makes it easier to quickly identify which fiscal year is used by a given country
- In table 9, Selected indicators of life expectancy, childbearing and mortality, infant mortality rates are now shown separately for males and females; Child mortality has been replaced by under 5 mortality.

## Les nouveautés de la 52<sup>ème</sup> édition

Plusieurs améliorations et changements ont été apportés à cette édition de l'*Annuaire statistique* des Nations Unies :

### Un nouveau chapitre

Un nouveau chapitre, le Chapitre 5, a été ajouté. Il est consacré à la situation des femmes et comprend trois tableaux fondés sur les indicateurs des objectifs du Millénaire pour le développement :

- Tableau 10 – Femmes élues à l'assemblée nationale
- Tableau 11 – Proportion de femmes salariées dans le secteur non agricole
- Tableau 12 – Proportion de filles inscrites dans l'enseignement primaire, secondaire et tertiaire par rapport aux garçons.

### Nouveaux tableaux

Deux tableaux ont été ajoutés :

- Tableau 20 – Déflateurs implicites des prix (au Chapitre 7 – Comptabilités nationales et production industrielle)
- Tableau 64 – Réserves internationales, moins l'or (au Chapitre 19 – Finances internationales).

### Nouvelles séries de données dans des tableaux existants

- Une nouvelle série de données consacrée à la viande de poulet a été ajoutée au tableau 40 (Viande) puisque, en quantité, la production de ce type de viande se classe au deuxième rang.

### Des nouveautés dans les tableaux existants

- Les tableaux du Chapitre 6 concernant les communications (téléphones, abonnés au téléphone mobile et usagers d'Internet) comportent une nouvelle colonne indiquant l'année fiscale lorsque celle-ci ne correspond pas à l'année civile. Ce renseignement figurait précédemment dans les notes de bas de page et est désormais plus aisé à trouver
- Dans le tableau 9, une distinction est désormais faite entre les hommes et les femmes pour le taux de mortalité infantile; l'indicateur concernant la mortalité juvénile a été remplacé par un indicateur concernant la mortalité des enfants de moins de 5 ans.

# Contents

# Table des matières

# Contents (*continued*)

# Table des matières (*suite*)

# Contents (*continued*)

# Table des matières (*suite*)

# Contents (*continued*)

# Table des matières (*suite*)

\*\*    Asterisks preceding table names identify tables that were presented in
previous issues of the *Statistical Yearbook* which are not contained in
the present issue. These tables will be updated in future issues of the
*Yearbook* when new data become available.

\*\*    Ce symbole indique les tableaux publiés dans les éditions précédentes
de l'*Annuaire statistique* mais qui n'ont pas été repris dans la présente
édition. Ces tableaux seront actualisés dans les futures livraisons de
l'*Annuaire* à mesure que des données nouvelles deviendront disponibles.

# Explanatory notes

In general, the statistics presented in the present publication are based on information available to the Statistics Division of the United Nations Secretariat as of June 2008.

## Units of measurement

The metric system of weights and measures has been employed throughout the *Statistical Yearbook*. For conversion coefficients and factors, see annex II.

## Symbols and conventions used in the tables

| | |
|---|---|
| . | A point is used to indicate decimals. |
| - | A hyphen between years, e.g., 1998-1999, indicates the full period involved, including the beginning and end years. |
| / | A slash between years indicates a financial year, school year or crop year, e.g., 1998/99. |
| … | Data not available or not applicable. |
| * | Provisional or estimated figure. |
| # | Marked break in series. |
| ^0 | Not zero but less than half of the unit used. |

Please note that a space is used as a thousand separator, e.g. 1 000 is one thousand.

Details and percentages in the tables do not necessarily add to totals because of rounding.

# Notes explicatives

En général, les statistiques qui figurent dans la présente publication sont fondées sur les informations dont disposait la Division de statistique du Secrétariat de l'ONU en juin 2008.

## Unités de mesure

Le système métrique de poids et mesures a été utilisé dans tout l'*Annuaire statistique*. On trouvera à l'annexe II les coefficients et facteurs de conversion.

## Signes et conventions employés dans les tableaux

| | |
|---|---|
| . | Les décimales sont précédées d'un point. |
| - | Un tiret entre des années, par exemple "1998-1999", indique que la période est embrassée dans sa totalité, y compris la première et la dernière année. |
| / | Une barre oblique entre des années renvoie à un exercice financier, à une année scolaire ou à une campagne agricole, par exemple "1998/99". |
| … | Données non disponibles ou non applicables. |
| * | Chiffre provisoire ou estimatif. |
| # | Discontinuité notable dans la série. |
| ^0 | Non nul mais inférieur à la moitié de l'unité employée. |

Le séparateur utilisé pour les milliers est l'espace : par exemple, 1 000 correspond à un millier.

Les chiffres étant arrondis, les totaux ne correspondent pas toujours à la somme exacte des éléments ou pourcentages figurant dans les tableaux.

# Introduction

This is the fifty-second issue of the United Nations *Statistical Yearbook*, prepared by the Statistics Division, Department of Economic and Social Affairs, of the United Nations Secretariat. The tables include series covering from one to ten years, depending upon data availability and space constraints. The ten-year tables generally cover the years 1996 to 2005 or 1997 to 2006. For the most part, the statistics presented are those which were available to the Statistics Division as of 30 June 2008.

## Objective and content of the Statistical Yearbook

The main purpose of the *Statistical Yearbook* is to provide in a single volume a comprehensive compilation of internationally available statistics on social and economic conditions and activities, at world, regional and national levels, covering a ten-year period to the extent possible.

Most of the statistics presented in the *Yearbook* are extracted from more detailed, specialized databases prepared by the Statistics Division and by many other international statistical services. Thus, while the specialized databases concentrate on monitoring topics and trends in particular social and economic fields, the *Statistical Yearbook* tables aim to provide data for a more comprehensive, overall description of social and economic structures, conditions, changes and activities. The objective has been to collect, systematize, coordinate and present in a consistent way the most essential components of comparable statistical information which can give a broad picture of social and economic processes.

The content of the *Statistical Yearbook* is planned to serve a general readership. The *Yearbook* endeavours to provide information for various bodies of the United Nations system as well as for other international organizations, governments and non-governmental organizations, national statistical, economic and social policy bodies, scientific and educational institutions, libraries and the public. Data published in the *Statistical Yearbook* may also be of interest to companies and enterprises and to agencies engaged in market research. The *Statistical Yearbook* thus provides information on a wide range of social and economic issues which are of concern in the United Nations system and among the governments and peoples of the world. A particular value of the *Yearbook* is that it facilitates meaningful analysis of issues by systematizing and coordinating the data across many fields and shedding light on such interrelated issues as:

- General economic growth and related economic conditions;
- Progress towards the Millennium Development Goals;
- Population and urbanization, and their growth and impact;

# Introduction

La présente édition est la cinquante-deuxième de l'*Annuaire statistique* des Nations Unies, établi par la Division de statistique du Département des affaires économiques et sociales du Secrétariat de l'Organisation des Nations Unies. Les tableaux présentent des séries qui couvrent d'un à dix ans, en fonction de la disponibilité des données et des contraintes d'espace. Les tableaux décennaux couvrent généralement les années 1996 à 2005 ou 1997 à 2006. La majeure partie des statistiques présentées ici sont celles dont disposait la Division de Statistique à la date du 30 juin 2008.

## Objectif et contenu de l'Annuaire statistique

Le principal objectif de l'*Annuaire statistique* est de fournir en un seul volume un inventaire complet de statistiques internationales concernant la situation et les activités sociales et économiques aux niveaux mondial, régional et national, sur une période s'étalant, dans la mesure du possible, sur dix ans.

La plupart des données qui figurent dans l'*Annuaire statistique* proviennent de bases de données spécialisées davantage détaillées, préparées par la Division de statistique et par bien d'autres services statistiques internationaux. Tandis que les bases de données spécialisées se concentrent sur le suivi de domaines socioéconomiques particuliers, les données de l'*Annuaire* sont présentées de telle sorte qu'elles fournissent une description globale et exhaustive des structures, conditions, transformations et activités socioéconomiques. On a cherché à recueillir, systématiser, coordonner et présenter de manière cohérente les principales informations statistiques comparables, de manière à dresser un tableau général des processus socioéconomiques.

Le contenu de l'*Annuaire statistique* a été élaboré en vue d'un lectorat large. Les renseignements fournis devraient ainsi pouvoir être utilisés par les divers organismes du système des Nations Unies, mais aussi par d'autres organisations internationales, les gouvernements et les organisations non gouvernementales, les organismes nationaux de statistique et de politique économique et sociale, les institutions scientifiques et les établissements d'enseignement, les bibliothèques et les particuliers. Les données publiées dans l'*Annuaire* peuvent également intéresser les sociétés et entreprises, et les organismes spécialisés dans les études de marché. L'*Annuaire* présente des informations sur un large éventail de questions socioéconomiques liées aux préoccupations actuelles du système des Nations Unies, des gouvernements et des peuples du monde entier. Une qualité particulière de l'*Annuaire* est de faciliter une analyse approfondie de ces questions en systématisant et en articulant les données d'un domaine/secteur à l'autre, et en apportant un éclairage sur des sujets interdépendants, tels que :

- Employment, inflation and wages;
- Energy production and consumption and the development of new energy sources;
- Expansion of trade;
- Supply of food and alleviation of hunger;
- The financial situation of countries and external payments and receipts;
- Education, training and eradication of illiteracy;
- Improvement in general living conditions;
- Pollution and protection of the environment;
- Assistance provided to developing countries for social and economic development purposes.

## Organization of the Yearbook

The 68 tables of the *Yearbook* are grouped into four broad parts:
- Part One: World and Region Summary (chapter I, tables 1-7);
- Part Two: Population and Social Statistics (chapters II-V: tables 8-18);
- Part Three: Economic Activity (chapters VI-XIV: tables 19-54);
- Part Four: International Economic Relations (chapters XV-XIX: tables 55-68).

The more aggregated information shown in part one provides an overall picture of development at the world and region levels. More specific and detailed information for analysis concerning individual countries or areas is presented in the other three parts. Each of these parts is divided into chapters, by topic, and each chapter ends with a section on "Technical notes", which provides brief descriptions of major statistical concepts, definitions and classifications required for interpretation and analysis of the data. Information on the methodology used for the computation of the figures can be found in the publications on methodology of the United Nations and its agencies, listed in the section "Statistical sources and references" at the end of the *Yearbook*.

Part One, World and Region Summary, comprises seven tables highlighting the principal trends in the world as well as in each of the regions and in the major economic and social sectors. It contains global totals of important aggregate statistics needed for the analysis of economic growth, the structure of the world economy, major changes in world population and expansion of external merchandise trade. The global totals are, as a rule, subdivided into major geographical areas.

Part Two, Population and Social Statistics, comprises eleven tables which contain more detailed statistical series on population, as well as education, gender, culture, and communication.

Of the 36 tables in Part Three, Economic Activity, 21 provide data on national accounts, index numbers of industrial

- La croissance économique générale, et les conditions économiques qui lui sont liées;
- Les progrès accomplis dans la réalisation des Objectifs du Millénaire pour le Développement;
- La population et l'urbanisation, leur croissance et leur impact;
- L'emploi, l'inflation et les salaires;
- La production et la consommation d'énergie et le développement de nouvelles sources d'énergie;
- L'expansion des échanges;
- L'approvisionnement alimentaire et la lutte contre la faim;
- La situation financière, les paiements et recettes extérieurs des pays;
- L'éducation, la formation et l'élimination de l'analphabétisme;
- L'amélioration des conditions de vie;
- La pollution et la protection de l'environnement;
- L'assistance aux pays en développement à des fins socioéconomiques.

## Présentation de l'Annuaire

Les 68 tableaux de l'*Annuaire* sont groupés en quatre parties:
- La première partie : Aperçu mondial et régional (chapitre I, tableaux 1 à 7);
- La deuxième partie : Statistiques démographiques et sociales (chapitres II à V, tableaux 8 à 18);
- La troisième partie : Activité économique (chapitres VI à XIV, tableaux 19 à 54);
- La quatrième partie : Relations économiques internationales (chapitres XV à XIX, tableaux 55 à 68).

Les valeurs les plus agrégées qui figurent dans la première partie donnent un tableau global du développement à l'échelon mondial et régional, tandis que les trois autres parties contiennent des renseignements plus précis et détaillés qui se prêtent mieux à une analyse par pays ou par zones. Chacune de ces trois parties est divisée en chapitres portant sur des sujets donnés, et chaque chapitre comprend une section intitulée "Notes techniques" où l'on trouve une brève description des principales notions, définitions et classifications statistiques nécessaires pour interpréter et analyser les données. Les méthodes de calcul utilisées sont décrites dans les publications se référant à la méthodologie des Nations Unies et de leurs organismes, énumérées à la fin de l'*Annuaire* dans la section "Sources et références statistiques".

La première partie, intitulée "Aperçu mondial et régional", comprend sept tableaux présentant les principales tendances dans le monde et dans les régions ainsi que dans les principaux

production, interest rates, labour force, wages and prices, energy, environment and science and technology; 15 tables provide data on production in the major branches of the economy (using, in general, the *International Standard Industrial Classification*, ISIC), namely agriculture, hunting, forestry and fishing, and manufacturing. Consumption data are combined with the production data in tables on specific commodities, where feasible.

Part Four, International Economic Relations, comprises 14 tables on international merchandise trade, balance of payments, international tourism and transport, international finance and development assistance.

An index (in English only) is provided at the end of the *Yearbook*.

## Annexes and regional groupings of countries or areas

The annexes to the *Statistical Yearbook*, and the section "Explanatory notes" preceding the Introduction, provide additional essential information on the *Yearbook*'s contents and presentation of data.

Annex I provides information on countries or areas covered in the *Yearbook* tables and on their arrangement in geographical regions and economic or other groupings. The geographical groupings shown in the *Yearbook* are generally based on continental regions unless otherwise indicated. However, strict consistency in this regard is impossible. A wide range of classifications is used for different purposes in the various international agencies and other sources of statistics for the *Yearbook*. These classifications vary in response to administrative and analytical requirements.

Similarly, there is no common agreement in the United Nations system concerning the terms "developed" and "developing" when referring to the stage of development reached by any given country or area, and its corresponding classification in one or the other grouping. The *Yearbook* thus refers more generally to "developed" or "developing" regions on the basis of conventional practice. Following this practice, "developed" regions or areas comprise Canada and the United States in Northern America, Japan in Asia, Australia and New Zealand in Oceania, and Europe, while all of Africa and the remainder of the Americas, Asia and Oceania comprise the "developing regions". These designations are intended for statistical convenience and do not necessarily express a judgement about the stage reached by a particular country or area in the development process.

Annex II provides detailed information on conversion coefficients and factors used in various tables, and annex III provides a list of tables added and omitted in the present edition of the *Yearbook*. Tables for which a sufficient amount of new data is not available are not

secteurs économiques et sociaux. Elle fournit des chiffres mondiaux pour les principaux agrégats statistiques nécessaires pour analyser la croissance économique, la structure de l'économie mondiale, les principaux changements dans la population mondiale et l'expansion du commerce extérieur de marchandises. En règle générale, les chiffres mondiaux sont répartis par grandes régions géographiques.

La deuxième partie, intitulée "Population et statistiques sociales", comporte onze tableaux où figurent des séries plus détaillées concernant la population, l'éducation, la situation des femmes, la culture, et la communication.

La troisième partie, intitulée "Activité économique", comporte 36 tableaux, 21 qui présentent des statistiques concernant les comptes nationaux, les nombres indices relatifs à la production industrielle, les taux d'intérêt, la population active, les prix et les salaires, l'énergie, l'environnement, et la science et technologie; et 15 qui présentent des données sur la production des principales branches d'activité économique (en utilisant en général la *Classification internationale type, par industrie, de toutes les branches d'activité économique*): agriculture, chasse, sylviculture et pêche, et industries manufacturières. Les tableaux traitant de certains produits de base associent autant que possible les données relatives à la consommation aux valeurs concernant la production.

La quatrième partie, intitulée "Relations économiques internationales", comprend 14 tableaux relatifs au commerce international de marchandises, aux balances des paiements, au tourisme et transport internationaux, aux finances internationales, et à l'aide au développement.

Un index (en anglais seulement) figure à la fin de l'*Annuaire*.

## Annexes et groupements régionaux des pays et zones

Les annexes à l'*Annuaire statistique*, et la section intitulée "Notes explicatives" qui précède l'introduction, offrent d'importantes informations complémentaires quant à la teneur et à la présentation des données figurant dans le présent ouvrage.

L'annexe I donne des renseignements sur les pays ou zones couverts par les tableaux de l'*Annuaire* et sur leur regroupement en régions géographiques et groupements économiques ou autres. Sauf indication contraire, les groupements géographiques figurant dans l'*Annuaire* sont généralement fondés sur les régions continentales, mais une présentation absolument systématique est impossible à cet égard car les diverses institutions internationales et autres sources de statistiques employées pour la confection de l'*Annuaire* emploient, selon l'objet de l'exercice, des classifications fort différentes en réponse à diverses exigences d'ordre administratif ou analytique.

Il n'existe pas non plus dans le système des Nations Unies

being published in this *Yearbook*. Their titles nevertheless are still listed in the table of contents since it is planned that they will be published in a later issue as new data are compiled by the collecting agency.

## Data comparability, quality and relevance

The major challenge continuously facing the *Statistical Yearbook* is to present series which are as nearly comparable across countries as the available statistics permit. Considerable efforts have already been made among the international suppliers of data and by the staff of the *Statistical Yearbook* to ensure the compatibility of various series by coordinating time periods, base years, prices chosen for valuation, and so on. This is indispensable in relating various bodies of data to each other and in facilitating analysis across different sectors. Thus, for example, relating data on short-term interest rates to those on prices makes it possible to arrive at a general understanding about the inflation environment, and relating a country's data on tourism expenditure in other countries to those on its per capita GDP provides a gauge on that country's wealth status. In general, the data presented reflect the methodological recommendations of the United Nations Statistical Commission issued in various United Nations publications, and of other international bodies concerned with statistics. Publications containing these recommendations and guidelines are listed in the section "Statistical sources and references" at the end of the *Yearbook*. The use of international recommendations not only promotes international comparability of the data but also ensures a degree of compatibility regarding the underlying concepts, definitions and classifications relating to different series. However, much work remains to be done in this area and, for this reason, some tables can serve only as a first source of data, which require further adjustment before being used for more in-depth analytical studies. While on the whole, a significant degree of comparability has been achieved in international statistics, there will remain some limitations, for a variety of reasons.

One common cause of non-comparability of economic data is different valuations of statistical aggregates such as national income, wages and salaries, output of industries and so forth. Conversion of these and similar series originally expressed in national prices into a common currency, for example into United States dollars, through the use of exchange rates, is not always satisfactory owing to frequent wide fluctuations in market rates and differences between official rates and rates which would be indicated by unofficial markets or purchasing power parities. The use of different kinds of sources for obtaining data is another cause of incomparability. This is true, for example, in the case of employment and unemployment, where data are obtained from different sources, namely household and la-

de définition commune des termes "développé" et "en développement" pour décrire le niveau atteint en la matière par un pays ou une zone donnés ni pour les classifier dans l'un ou l'autre de ces groupes. Ainsi, dans l'*Annuaire*, on s'en remet à l'usage pour qualifier les régions de "développées" ou "en développement". Selon cet usage, les régions ou zones développées sont le Canada et les Etats-Unis dans l'Amérique septentrionale, le Japon dans l'Asie, l'Australie et la Nouvelle-Zélande dans l'Océanie, et l'Europe, alors que toute l'Afrique et le reste des Amériques, l'Asie et l'Océanie constituent les régions en développement. Ces appellations sont utilisées pour plus de commodité dans la présentation des statistiques et n'impliquent pas nécessairement un jugement quant au stade de développement auquel est parvenu tel pays ou telle zone.

L'annexe II fournit des renseignements sur les coefficients et facteurs de conversion employés dans les différents tableaux, et l'annexe III contient la liste de tableaux qui ont été ajoutés ou omis dans la présente édition de l'*Annuaire*. Les tableaux pour lesquels on ne dispose pas d'une quantité suffisante des données nouvelles, n'ont pas été publiés dans cet *Annuaire*. Comme ils seront repris dans une prochaine édition à mesure que des données nouvelles seront dépouillées par l'office statistique d'origine, ses titres figurent toujours dans la table des matières.

## Comparabilité, qualité et pertinence des statistiques

Le défi majeur auquel l'*Annuaire Statistique* fait continuellement face est de présenter des séries aussi comparables entre les pays que la disponibilité des statistiques le permettent. Les sources internationales de données et les auteurs de l'*Annuaire* ont réalisé des efforts considérables pour faire en sorte que diverses séries soient compatibles, en harmonisant les périodes de référence, les années de base, les prix utilisés pour les évaluations, etc. Cette démarche est indispensable si l'on veut rapprocher divers ensembles de données, et faciliter l'analyse intersectorielle de l'économie. Ainsi, lier les données concernant les taux d'intérêt à court terme à celles des prix permet d'arriver à une compréhension globale de l'environnement de l'inflation; lier les données de dépenses touristiques d'un pays dans d'autres pays à celles de son PIB par tête fournit un indicateur de la richesse de ce pays. De façon générale, les données sont présentées selon les recommandations méthodologiques formulées par la Commission de statistique des Nations Unies, et par les autres entités internationales impliquées dans les statistiques. Les titres des publications contenant ces recommandations et leurs lignes directrices figurent à la fin de l'*Annuaire*, dans la section "Sources et références statistiques". Le respect des recommandations internationales tend non seulement

bour force sample surveys, establishment censuses or surveys, official estimates, social insurance statistics and employment office statistics, which are not fully comparable in many cases. Non-comparability of data may also result from differences in the institutional patterns of countries. Certain variations in social and economic organization and institutions may have an impact on the comparability of the data even if the underlying concepts and definitions are identical. These and other causes of non-comparability of the data are briefly explained in the technical notes to each chapter.

A further set of challenges relate to timeliness, quality and relevance of the data contained in the *Yearbook*. Users generally demand the most up-to-date statistics. However, due to the different development stages of statistical capacity in different countries, data for the most recent years may only be available for a small number of countries. For a global print publication, therefore, a balance has to be struck between presenting the most updated information and satisfactory country coverage. Of course the UN Statistics Division's website offers greater flexibility in presenting continuously updated information and is therefore a useful complement to the annual print publication. Furthermore, as most of the information presented in this *Yearbook* is collected through specialized United Nations agencies and partners, the timeliness is continuously enhanced by improving the communication and data flow between countries and the specialized agencies on the one hand, and between the UN Statistics Division and the specialized agencies on the other. The development of new XML-based data transfer protocols will address this issue and is expected to make international data flows more efficient in the future.

Data quality at the international level is a function of the data quality at the national level. The UN Statistics Division in close cooperation with its partners in the UN agencies and the international statistical system continues to support countries' efforts to improve both the coverage and the quality of their data. Metadata, as for example reflected in the footnotes and technical notes of this publication, are an important service to the user to allow an informed assessment of the quality of the data. Given the wide variety of sources for the *Yearbook*, there is of course an equally wide variety of data formats and accompanying metadata. An important challenge for the UN Statistics Division and its partners for the future is to work further towards the standardization, or at least harmonization, of metadata.

The final challenge relates to maintaining the relevance of the series included in the *Yearbook*. As new policy concerns enter the developmental debate, the UN Statistics Division will need to introduce new series that describe concerns that have gained prominence as well as to prune outdated data

à promouvoir la comparabilité internationale des données, mais elle assure également une certaine comparabilité entre les concepts, les définitions et classifications utilisés. Mais comme il reste encore beaucoup à faire dans ce domaine, les données présentées dans certains tableaux n'ont qu'une valeur indicative, et nécessiteront des ajustements plus poussés avant de pouvoir servir à des analyses approfondies. Bien que l'on soit parvenu, dans l'ensemble, à un degré de comparabilité appréciable en matière de statistiques internationales, diverses raisons expliquent que subsistent encore de nombreuses limitations.

Une cause commune de non comparabilité des données économiques réside dans la diversité des méthodes d'évaluation employées pour comptabiliser des agrégats tels que le revenu national, les salaires et traitements, la production des différentes branches d'activité industrielle, etc. Il n'est pas toujours satisfaisant de ramener la valeur des séries de ce type—exprimée à l'origine en prix nationaux—à une monnaie commune (par exemple le dollar des États-Unis) car les taux de change du marché connaissent fréquemment de fortes fluctuations, et parce que les taux officiels ne coïncident pas avec ceux des marchés officieux ni avec les parités réelles de pouvoir d'achat. Le recours à des sources diverses pour la collecte des données est un autre facteur qui limite la comparabilité. C'est le cas, par exemple, des données d'emploi et de chômage, obtenues par des moyens aussi peu comparables que les sondages, le dépouillement des registres d'assurances sociales et les enquêtes auprès des entreprises. Dans certains cas, les données ne sont pas comparables en raison de différences entre les structures institutionnelles des pays. Des changements dans l'organisation et les institutions économiques et sociales peuvent affecter la comparabilité des données, même si les concepts et définitions sont fondamentalement identiques. Ces causes, et d'autres, de non comparabilité des données sont brièvement expliquées dans les notes techniques de chaque chapitre.

Un autre ensemble de défis à relever concerne la fraîcheur, la qualité et la pertinence des données présentées dans l'*Annuaire*. Les utilisateurs exigent généralement des données les plus récentes possibles. Toutefois, selon le niveau de développement de la capacité statistique des pays, les données pour les dernières années peuvent n'être disponibles que pour un nombre limité de pays. Dans le cadre d'une publication mondiale, un équilibre doit être trouvé entre la présentation de l'information la plus récente et une couverture géographique satisfaisante. Bien entendu, le site Internet de la Division de statistique des Nations Unies offre une plus grande flexibilité, puisqu'il propose une information actualisée au fil de l'eau, et constitue ainsi un complément utile à la publication papier annuelle.

and continue to update the recurrent *Yearbook* series that still address those issues which are most pertinent. Often choosing the appropriate moment when the statistical information on new topics has matured sufficiently so as to be able to disseminate meaningful global data can be challenging. Furthermore, a balance has to continuously be found between the ever-increasing amount of information available for dissemination and the space limitations of the print version of the *Statistical Yearbook*. International comparability, data availability and data quality will remain the key criteria to guide the UN Statistics Division in its selection.

Needless to say, more can always be done to improve the *Statistical Yearbook*'s scope, coverage, design, metadata and timeliness. The *Yearbook* team continually strives to improve upon each of these aspects and to make its publication as responsive as possible to its users' needs and expectations, while at the same time focusing on a manageable body of data and metadata. Since data disseminated in digital form have clear advantages over those in print, as much of the *Yearbook* information as possible will continue to be included in the Statistics Division's online databases. Still, the *Statistical Yearbook* will continue to claim its rightful place among the products of the Statistics Division as a useful, compact resource for a general understanding of the global social and economic situation.

Par ailleurs, étant donné que la plupart des informations présentées dans cet *Annuaire* sont collectées parmi les agences spécialisées des Nations Unies et autres partenaires, la fraîcheur des données est continuellement améliorée, grâce à une meilleure communication et un meilleur échange de données entre les pays et les agences spécialisées d'une part, et entre la Division de statistique des Nations Unies et les agences spécialisées d'autre part. Le développement de nouveaux protocoles de transfert de données basés sur le langage XML devrait contribuer à rendre, à l'avenir, les échanges de données internationales encore plus efficaces.

La qualité des données au niveau international est fonction de la qualité des données au niveau national. La Division de statistique des Nations Unies, en étroite collaboration avec ses partenaires dans les agences de l'ONU et dans le système statistique international, continue de soutenir les efforts des pays pour améliorer à la fois la couverture et la qualité de leurs données. Des métadonnées, comme l'illustrent les notes de bas de page et les notes techniques de cette publication, constituent un important service fourni à l'utilisateur pour lui permettre d'évaluer de manière avisée la qualité des données. Etant donné la grande variété des sources de l'*Annuaire*, il y a bien entendu une non moins grande variété de formats de données et de métadonnées associées. Un important défi que la Division de statistique des Nations Unies et ses partenaires doivent relever dans le futur est d'aboutir à la standardisation, ou au moins l'harmonisation, des métadonnées.

Le dernier défi concerne la constance de la pertinence des séries présentées dans l'*Annuaire*. Au fur et à mesure que de nouvelles préoccupations politiques pénètrent le débat lié au développement, la Division de statistique des Nations Unies doit introduire dans l'*Annuaire* de nouvelles séries qui leur sont liées, et, ce faisant, effectuer une coupe sombre parmi les données qui lui semblent dépassées, tout en s'assurant de continuer à actualiser les séries récurrentes de qui paraissent encore pertinentes. Souvent, choisir le moment idoine auquel les données statistiques sur de nouveaux thèmes sont suffisamment matures pour qu'elles puissent, au niveau mondial, être diffusées sans hésitation, est un défi en soi. Par ailleurs, un équilibre doit continuellement être trouvé entre le volume toujours croissant d'informations disponibles à la diffusion, et les contraintes d'espace de la version papier de l'*Annuaire statistique*. La comparabilité internationale, la disponibilité des données et leur qualité devront rester le principal critère à considérer par la Division de statistique des Nations Unies dans sa sélection.

Inutile de dire qu'il est toujours possible d'améliorer l'*Annuaire statistique* en ce qui concerne son champ, sa couverture, sa conception générale, ses métadonnées et sa

mise à jour. L'équipe en charge de l'*Annuaire* s'évertue en permanence à améliorer chacun de ces aspects, et de faire en sorte que cette publication réponde au plus près aux besoins et aux attentes de ses utilisateurs, sans toutefois oublier de mettre l'accent sur un corpus gérable de données et de métadonnées. Puisqu'il est avéré que les données diffusées de manière digitale ont des avantages comparés à celles diffusées sur papier, autant d'informations de l'*Annuaire* que possible continueront d'être inclues dans les bases de données électroniques de la Division de statistique. L'*Annuaire statistique* garde toujours une place de choix parmi les produits de la Division de statistique comme une ressource compact et utile pour une compréhension général de la situation sociale et économique globale

## PART ONE

# World and region summary

# Aperçu mondial et régional

## Chapter I    World and region summary (tables 1-7)

This part of the *Statistical Yearbook* presents selected aggregate series on principal economic and social topics for the world as a whole and for the major regions. The topics include population and surface area, agricultural and industrial production, external trade, government financial reserves, and energy production and consumption. More detailed data on individual countries and areas are provided in the subsequent parts of the present *Yearbook*. These comprise Part Two: Population and Social Statistics; Part Three: Economic Activity; and Part Four: International Economic Relations.

Regional totals between series may be incomparable owing to differences in definitions of regions and lack of data for particular regional components. General information on regional groupings is provided in annex I of the *Yearbook*. Supplementary information on regional groupings used in specific series is provided, as necessary, in table footnotes and in the technical notes at the end of chapter I.

## Chapitre I    Aperçu mondial et régional (tableaux 1 à 7)

Cette partie de l'*Annuaire statistique* présente, pour le monde entier et ses principales subdivisions, un choix d'agrégats ayant trait à des questions économiques et sociales essentielles: population et superficie, production agricole et industrielle, commerce extérieur, réserves financières publiques, et la production et la consommation d'énergie. Des statistiques plus détaillées pour divers pays ou zones figurent dans les parties ultérieures de l'*Annuaire*, c'est-à-dire dans les deuxième, troisième et quatrième parties intitulées respectivement: population et statistiques sociales, activités économiques et relations économiques internationales.

Les totaux régionaux peuvent être incomparables entre les séries en raison de différences dans la définition des régions et de l'absence de données sur tel ou tel élément régional. A l'annexe I de l'*Annuaire*, on trouvera des renseignements généraux sur les groupements régionaux. Des informations complémentaires sur les groupements régionaux pour certaines séries bien précises sont fournies, lorsqu'il y a lieu, dans les notes figurant au bas des tableaux et dans les notes techniques à la fin du chapitre I.

# 1

## World statistics: selected series
Population, production, external trade and finance

## Statistiques mondiales : séries principales
Population, production, commerce extérieur et finances

| Series | Unit or base | | | | | | | | | | |
|---|---|---|---|---|---|---|---|---|---|---|---|
| Séries | Unité ou base | 1997 | 1998 | 1999 | 2000 | 2001 | 2002 | 2003 | 2004 | 2005 | 2006 |
| **Population — Population** | | | | | | | | | | | |
| World population[1] Population mondiale[1] | million | 5 883 | 5 964 | 6 045 | 6 124 | 6 203 | 6 281 | 6 359 | 6 437 | 6 515 | 6 593 |
| **Output / production — Production** | | | | | | | | | | | |
| Gross domestic product — Produit intérieur brut | | | | | | | | | | | |
| GDP at current prices PIB aux prix courants | billion US $ milliard $ E.-U. | 30 152 | 29 907 | 31 018 | 31 850 | 31 640 | 32 930 | 37 019 | 41 610 | 44 923 | 48 598 |
| GDP per capita PIB par habitant | US $ $ E.-U. | 5 126 | 5 015 | 5 132 | 5 201 | 5 101 | 5 243 | 5 822 | 6 465 | 6 896 | 7 372 |
| GDP real rates of growth Taux de l'accroissement réels | % | 3.6 | 2.4 | 3.3 | 4.2 | 1.7 | 1.9 | 2.8 | 4.0 | 3.5 | 4.1 |
| Agriculture, forestry and fishing production — Production agricole, forestière et de la pêche | | | | | | | | | | | |
| Index numbers — Indices | | | | | | | | | | | |
| All commodities Tous produits | 1999-01 = 100 | 94.0 | 95.6 | 98.2 | 100.1 | 101.7 | 102.9 | 105.8 | 111.1 | 113.0 | 114.1 |
| Food Produits alimentaires | 1999-01 = 100 | 93.6 | 95.3 | 98.2 | 100.2 | 101.6 | 103.0 | 105.9 | 110.8 | 112.8 | 113.8 |
| Quantities — Quantités | | | | | | | | | | | |
| Cereals Céréales | million t. | 2 096 | 2 084 | 2 086 | 2 061 | 2 109 | 2 029 | 2 085 | 2 280 | 2 268 | 2 221 |
| Meat Viande | million t. | 216 | 224 | 229 | 235 | 239 | 247 | 253 | 260 | 268 | 273 |
| Roundwood Bois rond | million m³ | 3 306 | 3 225 | 3 334 | 3 395 | 3 303 | 3 332 | 3 384 | 3 447 | 3 551 | 3 536 |
| Fish production Production halieutique | million t. | 123 | 118 | 127 | 131 | 134 | 131 | 133 | 140 | 143 | 144 |
| **Industrial production — Production industrielle** | | | | | | | | | | | |
| Index numbers[2] — Indices[2] | | | | | | | | | | | |
| All commodities Tous produits | 2000 = 100 | 93.9 | 94.3 | 95.9 | 100.0 | 97.8 | 98.0 | 100.4 | 104.6 | 107.7 | 112.9 |
| Mining Mines | 2000 = 100 | 98.6 | 99.3 | 97.2 | 100.0 | 99.4 | 96.5 | 102.0 | 105.4 | 106.3 | 108.5 |
| Manufacturing Manufactures | 2000 = 100 | 93.6 | 93.8 | 95.6 | 100.0 | 97.2 | 97.5 | 99.4 | 103.8 | 107.2 | 113.2 |
| Quantities — Quantités | | | | | | | | | | | |
| Coal Houille | million t. | 3 491 | 3 289 | 3 266 | 3 294 | 3 475 | 3 525 | 3 836 | 4 213 | 4 513 | ... |
| Lignite and brown coal Lignite et charbon brun | million t. | 1 247 | 1 255 | 1 267 | 1 292 | 1 329 | 1 332 | 1 351 | 1 359 | 1 384 | ... |
| Crude petroleum Pétrole brut | million t. | 3 238 | 3 292 | 3 204 | 3 347 | 3 360 | 3 324 | 3 462 | 3 576 | 3 625 | ... |
| Natural gas Gaz naturel | petajoules pétajoules | 89 877 | 92 358 | 94 858 | 96 136 | 98 562 | 100 783 | 104 439 | 107 453 | 110 555 | ... |
| Electricity[3] Electricité[3] | billion kWh milliard kWh | 14 084 | 14 400 | 14 824 | 15 457 | 15 545 | 16 171 | 16 773 | 17 556 | 18 335 | ... |
| Sugar, raw Sucre, brut | million t. | 125 | 126 | 135 | 130 | 131 | 142 | 148 | 147 | 141 | 152 |

| Series / Séries | Unit or base / Unité ou base | 1997 | 1998 | 1999 | 2000 | 2001 | 2002 | 2003 | 2004 | 2005 | 2006 |
|---|---|---|---|---|---|---|---|---|---|---|---|
| Woodpulp / Pâte de bois | million t. | 163 | 160 | 164 | 172 | 166 | 168 | 171 | 176 | 175 | 178 |
| Sawnwood / Sciages | million m³ | 394 | 379 | 389 | 386 | 380 | 394 | 401 | 425 | 421 | 425 |
| **External trade — Commerce extérieur** | | | | | | | | | | | |
| Value — Valeur | | | | | | | | | | | |
| Imports, c.i.f. / Importations c.a.f. | billion US $ / milliard $ E.-U. | 5 289 | 5 245 | 5 461 | 6 157 | 5 937 | 6 154 | 7 168 | 8 745 | 9 912 | 11 341 |
| Exports, f.o.b. / Exportations f.o.b. | billion US $ / milliard $ E.-U. | 5 232 | 5 166 | 5 355 | 5 984 | 5 754 | 6 028 | 7 006 | 8 528 | 9 697 | 11 162 |
| Volume: index of exports — Volume : indice des exportations | | | | | | | | | | | |
| All commodities / Tous produits | 2000 = 100 | 79 | 83 | 88 | 100 | 99 | 103 | 108 | 120 | 131 | 145 |
| Manufactures / Produits manufacturés | 2000 = 100 | 80 | 83 | 88 | 100 | 100 | 103 | 111 | 116 | 126 | … |
| Unit value: index of exports[4] — Valeur unitaure : indice des exportations[4] | | | | | | | | | | | |
| All commodities / Tous produits | 2000 = 100 | 110 | 105 | 102 | 100 | 97 | 98 | 108 | 117 | 122 | 127 |
| Manufactures / Produits manufacturés | 2000 = 100 | 110 | 106 | 103 | 100 | 98 | 98 | 104 | 111 | 112 | … |
| **Finance — Finances** | | | | | | | | | | | |
| International reserves minus gold[5] — Réserves internationales moins l'or[5] | | | | | | | | | | | |
| All countries / Tous les pays | billion SDR / milliard DTS | 1 226.4 | 1 249.7 | 1 374.7 | 1 555.1 | 1 709.5 | 1 859.1 | 2 124.4 | 2 491.1 | 2 971.7 | 3 387.1 |
| Position in IMF / Disponibilité au FMI | billion SDR / milliard DTS | 47.1 | 60.6 | 54.8 | 47.4 | 56.9 | 66.1 | 66.5 | 55.8 | 28.6 | 17.5 |
| Foreign exchange / Devises | billion SDR / milliard DTS | 1 197.8 | 1 167.5 | 1 298.4 | 1 486.2 | 1 631.1 | 1 771.5 | 2 036.1 | 2 413.9 | 2 921.2 | 3 348.1 |
| SDR (special drawing rights) / DTS (droits de triage spéc.) | billion SDR / milliard DTS | 20.5 | 20.4 | 18.5 | 18.5 | 19.6 | 19.7 | 19.9 | 20.3 | 20.1 | 18.2 |

Source

Databases of the Food and Agriculture Organization of the United Nations (FAO), Rome; the International Monetary Fund (IMF), Washington, D.C.; and the United Nations Statistics Division, New York.

Notes

1 Mid-year estimates.
2 Excluding China and the countries of the former USSR (except Russian Federation and Ukraine).
3 Electricity generated by establishments for public or private use.

4 Indices computed in US dollars.
5 End of period.

Source

Les bases de données de l'Organisation des Nations Unies pour l'alimentation et l'agriculture (FAO), Rome ; du Fonds Monétaire International (FMI), Washington, D.C. ; et de la Division de statistique de l'Organisation de Nations Unies, New York.

Notes

1 Estimations au milieu de l'année.
2 Non compris la Chine et les pays de l'ancienne URSS (sauf la Fédération de Russie et Ukraine).
3 L'électricité produite par des enterprises d'utilisation publique ou privée.

4 Indice calculé en dollars des Etats-Unis.
5 Fin de la période.

# 2. Population, rate of increase, birth and death rates, surface area and density

## Population, taux d'accroissement, taux de natalité, taux de mortalité, superficie et densité

| Major areas and regions / Grandes régions | Mid-year population estimates (millions) / Estimations de population au milieu de l'année (millions) | | | | | | | Annual rate of increase Taux d'accroissement annuel % | Crude birth rate Taux bruts de natalité (p.1 000) | Crude death rate Taux bruts de mortalité (p.1 000) | Surface area Superficie (000 km²) | Density[1] Densité[1] |
|---|---|---|---|---|---|---|---|---|---|---|---|---|
| | 1950 | 1960 | 1970 | 1980 | 1990 | 2000 | 2005 | 2000 - 2005 | | | 2005 | 2005 |
| **World Monde** | **2 520** | **3 024** | **3 697** | **4 442** | **5 280** | **6 086** | **6 515** | **1.2** | **21** | **9** | **136 127** | **48** |
| Africa Afrique | 224 | 282 | 364 | 479 | 636 | 812 | 922 | 2.2 | 38 | 15 | 30 312 | 30 |
| Eastern Africa Afrique orientale | 65 | 82 | 109 | 146 | 198 | 256 | 292 | 2.4 | 41 | 17 | 6 361 | 46 |
| Middle Africa Afrique centrale | 26 | 32 | 41 | 54 | 73 | 96 | 112 | 2.6 | 46 | 20 | 6 613 | 17 |
| Northern Africa Afrique du Nord | 53 | 67 | 86 | 112 | 144 | 175 | 190 | 1.7 | 26 | 7 | 8 525 | 22 |
| Southern Africa Afrique australe | 16 | 20 | 26 | 33 | 42 | 52 | 55 | 0.7 | 24 | 17 | 2 675 | 21 |
| Western Africa Afrique occidentale | 64 | 80 | 102 | 134 | 178 | 234 | 272 | 2.4 | 42 | 18 | 6 138 | 44 |
| Northern America[2] Amérique septentrionale[2] | 172 | 204 | 232 | 256 | 283 | 315 | 332 | 1.0 | 14 | 8 | 21 776 | 15 |
| Latin America and the Caribbean Amérique latine et Caraïbes | 167 | 219 | 285 | 362 | 444 | 523 | 558 | 1.4 | 22 | 6 | 20 546 | 27 |
| Caribbean Caraïbes | 17 | 20 | 25 | 29 | 34 | 38 | 40 | 0.9 | 20 | 8 | 234 | 173 |
| Central America Amérique centrale | 37 | 50 | 68 | 91 | 113 | 136 | 144 | 1.6 | 24 | 5 | 2 480 | 58 |
| South America Amérique du sud | 113 | 148 | 192 | 242 | 297 | 349 | 374 | 1.4 | 21 | 6 | 17 832 | 21 |
| Asia[3] Asie[3] | 1 396 | 1 699 | 2 140 | 2 630 | 3 169 | 3 676 | 3 938 | 1.2 | 20 | 8 | 31 880 | 124 |
| Eastern Asia Asie orientale | 671 | 792 | 987 | 1 178 | 1 350 | 1 479 | 1 522 | 0.6 | 13 | 7 | 11 763 | 129 |
| South-central Asia Asie centrale et du Sud | 496 | 617 | 780 | 978 | 1 226 | 1 485 | 1 646 | 1.6 | 26 | 9 | 10 791 | 153 |
| South-eastern Asia Asie du Sud-Est | 178 | 223 | 286 | 358 | 440 | 519 | 558 | 1.4 | 21 | 7 | 4 495 | 124 |
| Western Asia Asie occidentale | 51 | 67 | 88 | 116 | 154 | 193 | 212 | 2.1 | 26 | 6 | 4 831 | 44 |
| Europe[3] Europe[3] | 547 | 604 | 656 | 692 | 721 | 728 | 731 | 0.0 | 10 | 12 | 23 049 | 32 |
| Eastern Europe Europe orientale | 220 | 254 | 276 | 295 | 311 | 305 | 298 | -0.5 | 10 | 14 | 18 814 | 16 |
| Northern Europe Europe septentrionale | 77 | 81 | 86 | 89 | 92 | 94 | 96 | 0.3 | 11 | 10 | 1 810 | 53 |
| Southern Europe Europe méridionale | 109 | 118 | 127 | 138 | 143 | 146 | 150 | 0.4 | 10 | 10 | 1 317 | 114 |
| Western Europe Europe occidentale | 141 | 152 | 166 | 170 | 176 | 184 | 187 | 0.2 | 10 | 10 | 1 108 | 168 |

| Major areas and regions Grandes régions | Mid-year population estimates (millions) Estimations de population au milieu de l'année (millions) | | | | | | | Annual rate of increase Taux d'accrois-sement annuel % | Crude birth rate Taux bruts de natalité (p.1 000) | Crude death rate Taux bruts de mortalité (p.1 000) | Surface area Superficie (000 km²) | Density[1] Densité[1] |
|---|---|---|---|---|---|---|---|---|---|---|---|---|
| | 1950 | 1960 | 1970 | 1980 | 1990 | 2000 | 2005 | 2000 - 2005 | | | 2005 | 2005 |
| Oceania[2] Océanie[2] | 13 | 16 | 20 | 23 | 27 | 31 | 33 | 1.3 | 17 | 7 | 8 564 | 4 |
| Australia and New Zealand Australie et Nouvelle-Zélande | 10 | 13 | 16 | 18 | 20 | 23 | 24 | 1.1 | 13 | 7 | 8 012 | 3 |
| Melanesia Mélanésie | 2 | 3 | 3 | 4 | 6 | 7 | 8 | 2.0 | 31 | 10 | 541 | 14 |
| Micronesia Micronésie | ^0 | ^0 | ^0 | ^0 | ^0 | 1 | 1 | 1.9 | 26 | 5 | 3 | 167 |
| Polynesia Polynésie | ^0 | ^0 | ^0 | 1 | 1 | 1 | 1 | 1.2 | 24 | 5 | 8 | 75 |

Source

United Nations Statistics Division, New York, "Demographic Yearbook 2005".

Notes

1 Population per square kilometre of surface area. Figures are merely the quotients of population divided by surface area and are not to be considered either as reflecting density in the urban sense or as indicating the supporting power of a territory's land and resources.

2 Hawaii, a state of the United States of America, is included in Northern America rather than Oceania.

3 The European portion of Turkey is included in Western Asia rather than Europe.

Source

Organisation des Nations Unies, Division de statistique, New York, "Annuaire démographique 2005".

Notes

1 Nombre d'habitants au kilomètre carré. Il s'agit simplement du quotient du chiffre de la population divisé par celui de la superficie: il ne faut pas y voir d'indication de la densité au sens urbain du terme ni de l'effectif de population que les terres et les ressources du territoire sont capables de nourrir.

2 Hawaii, un Etat des Etats-Unis d'Amérique, est comprise en Amérique septentrionale plutôt qu'en Océanie.

3 La partie européenne de la Turquie est comprise en Asie Occidentale plutôt qu'en Europe.

# 3

## Index numbers of total agricultural and food production
1999 – 2001 = 100

## Indices de la production agricole totale et de la production alimentaire
1999 – 2001 = 100

| Region — Région | 1997 | 1998 | 1999 | 2000 | 2001 | 2002 | 2003 | 2004 | 2005 | 2006 |
|---|---|---|---|---|---|---|---|---|---|---|
| **World — Monde** | | | | | | | | | | |
| **Total agricultural production — Production agricole totale** | **94.0** | **95.4** | **98.2** | **100.1** | **101.7** | **102.9** | **105.8** | **111.1** | **113.0** | **114.1** |
| **Food production — Production alimentaire** | **93.6** | **95.3** | **98.2** | **100.2** | **101.6** | **103.0** | **105.9** | **110.8** | **112.8** | **113.8** |
| Africa — Afrique | | | | | | | | | | |
| Total agricultural production — Production agricole totale | 91.4 | 95.3 | 98.6 | 99.8 | 101.6 | 104.5 | 109.4 | 112.3 | 116.4 | 118.8 |
| Food production — Production alimentaire | 90.8 | 95.0 | 98.6 | 99.8 | 101.6 | 104.8 | 110.3 | 113.1 | 117.3 | 119.9 |
| Northern America — Amérique septentrionale | | | | | | | | | | |
| Total agricultural production — Production agricole totale | 96.9 | 97.8 | 99.9 | 101.3 | 98.8 | 96.9 | 100.5 | 107.4 | 107.0 | 105.6 |
| Food production — Production alimentaire | 96.3 | 98.3 | 100.0 | 101.6 | 98.4 | 97.1 | 100.7 | 106.9 | 106.5 | 105.4 |
| Latin America and the Caribbean — Amérique latine et Caraïbes | | | | | | | | | | |
| Total agricultural production — Production agricole totale | 90.6 | 92.4 | 97.2 | 99.6 | 103.3 | 106.1 | 111.9 | 116.3 | 118.4 | 120.5 |
| Food production — Production alimentaire | 90.6 | 92.2 | 97.3 | 99.5 | 103.2 | 106.0 | 112.4 | 115.9 | 118.1 | 120.1 |
| Asia — Asie | | | | | | | | | | |
| Total agricultural production — Production agricole totale | 91.4 | 93.9 | 97.3 | 100.1 | 102.5 | 104.8 | 108.8 | 113.6 | 117.9 | 120.9 |
| Food production — Production alimentaire | 90.6 | 93.7 | 97.3 | 100.2 | 102.5 | 105.0 | 108.8 | 113.1 | 117.7 | 120.5 |
| Europe — Europe | | | | | | | | | | |
| Total agricultural production — Production agricole totale | 101.7 | 98.9 | 99.4 | 100.0 | 100.6 | 101.2 | 97.6 | 105.1 | 101.5 | 100.2 |
| Food production — Production alimentaire | 101.7 | 98.9 | 99.4 | 100.0 | 100.6 | 101.3 | 97.7 | 105.2 | 101.6 | 100.3 |
| Oceania — Océanie | | | | | | | | | | |
| Total agricultural production — Production agricole totale | 90.2 | 95.0 | 97.9 | 98.7 | 103.3 | 89.8 | 100.9 | 98.2 | 103.5 | 89.8 |
| Food production — Production alimentaire | 89.5 | 94.7 | 97.8 | 98.7 | 103.5 | 89.8 | 104.0 | 101.6 | 105.8 | 90.9 |

Source

Food and Agriculture Organization of the United Nations (FAO), Rome, FAOSTAT data, last accessed January 2008, http://faostat.fao.org.

Source

Organisation des Nations Unies pour l'alimentation et l'agriculture (FAO), Rome, données FAOSTAT, dernier accès janvier 2008, http://faostat.fao.org.

# Index numbers of per capita agricultural and food production
1999 – 2001 = 100

# Indices de la production agricole et de la production alimentaire par habitant
1999 – 2001 = 100

| Region — Région | 1997 | 1998 | 1999 | 2000 | 2001 | 2002 | 2003 | 2004 | 2005 | 2006 |
|---|---|---|---|---|---|---|---|---|---|---|
| **World — Monde** | | | | | | | | | | |
| **Per capita agricultural production — Production agricole par habitant** | **97.8** | **97.9** | **99.4** | **100.1** | **100.4** | **100.4** | **101.9** | **105.8** | **106.3** | **106.1** |
| **Per capita food production — Production alimentaire par habitant** | **97.3** | **97.8** | **99.5** | **100.2** | **100.4** | **100.5** | **102.1** | **105.5** | **106.2** | **105.9** |
| Africa — Afrique | | | | | | | | | | |
| Per capita agricultural production — Production agricole par habitant | 98.2 | 100.0 | 101.0 | 99.8 | 99.2 | 99.7 | 102.0 | 102.4 | 103.8 | 103.6 |
| Per capita food production — Production alimentaire par habitant | 97.6 | 99.6 | 101.0 | 99.8 | 99.2 | 100.0 | 102.9 | 103.1 | 104.5 | 104.6 |
| Northern America — Amérique septentrionale | | | | | | | | | | |
| Per capita agricultural production — Production agricole par habitant | 99.9 | 99.9 | 100.9 | 101.3 | 97.8 | 94.9 | 97.4 | 103.1 | 101.7 | 99.3 |
| Per capita food production — Production alimentaire par habitant | 99.3 | 100.4 | 101.0 | 101.5 | 97.4 | 95.1 | 97.6 | 102.6 | 101.2 | 99.1 |
| Latin America and the Caribbean — Amérique latine et Caraïbes | | | | | | | | | | |
| Per capita agricultural production — Production agricole par habitant | 94.8 | 95.2 | 98.6 | 99.6 | 101.8 | 103.3 | 107.5 | 110.4 | 111.0 | 111.6 |
| Per capita food production — Production alimentaire par habitant | 94.8 | 95.0 | 98.7 | 99.5 | 101.8 | 103.2 | 108.0 | 110.0 | 110.7 | 111.2 |
| Asia — Asie | | | | | | | | | | |
| Per capita agricultural production — Production agricole par habitant | 95.2 | 96.4 | 98.6 | 100.1 | 101.3 | 102.3 | 104.9 | 108.3 | 111.1 | 112.6 |
| Per capita food production — Production alimentaire par habitant | 94.3 | 96.2 | 98.6 | 100.2 | 101.2 | 102.4 | 104.9 | 107.8 | 110.9 | 112.3 |
| Europe — Europe | | | | | | | | | | |
| Per capita agricultural production — Production agricole par habitant | 101.7 | 98.9 | 99.4 | 100.0 | 100.6 | 101.1 | 97.4 | 104.8 | 101.2 | 99.8 |
| Per capita food production — Production alimentaire par habitant | 101.7 | 98.9 | 99.4 | 100.0 | 100.6 | 101.2 | 97.5 | 104.9 | 101.2 | 99.9 |
| Oceania — Océanie | | | | | | | | | | |
| Per capita agricultural production — Production agricole par habitant | 93.3 | 97.2 | 99.1 | 98.8 | 102.1 | 87.7 | 97.2 | 93.5 | 97.4 | 83.6 |
| Per capita food production — Production alimentaire par habitant | 92.5 | 96.9 | 99.0 | 98.7 | 102.3 | 87.6 | 100.3 | 96.8 | 99.6 | 84.6 |

Source

Food and Agriculture Organization of the United Nations (FAO), Rome, FAOSTAT data, last accessed January 2008, http://faostat.fao.org.

Source

Organisation des Nations Unies pour l'alimentation et l'agriculture (FAO), Rome, données FAOSTAT, dernier accès janvier 2008, http://faostat.fao.org.

# Index numbers of industrial production
2000 = 100

## Indices de la production industrielle
2000 = 100

| Region and industry [ISIC Rev. 3] / Région et industrie [CITI Rév. 3] | Weight (%) / Pondération (%) | 2000 | 2001 | 2002 | 2003 | 2004 | 2005 | 2006 |
|---|---|---|---|---|---|---|---|---|
| **World — Monde** | | | | | | | | |
| Total industry [CDE] — Total, industrie [CDE] | 100.0 | 100.0 | 97.8 | 98.0 | 100.4 | 104.6 | 107.7 | 112.9 |
| Total mining [C] — Total, industries extractives [C] | 10.4 | 100.0 | 99.4 | 96.5 | 102.0 | 105.4 | 106.3 | 108.5 |
| Coal — Houille | 0.8 | 100.0 | 103.6 | 103.1 | 106.1 | 110.3 | 119.5 | 124.7 |
| Crude petroleum and natural gas / Pétrole brut et gaz naturel | 8.0 | 100.0 | 99.3 | 95.8 | 101.6 | 105.0 | 105.5 | 107.5 |
| Metal ores — Minerais métalliques | 1.0 | 100.0 | 97.8 | 96.2 | 101.3 | 103.3 | 103.3 | 105.1 |
| Total manufacturing [D] / Total, industries manufacturières [D] | 80.1 | 100.0 | 97.2 | 97.5 | 99.4 | 103.8 | 107.2 | 113.2 |
| Food, beverages, tobacco / Industries alimentaires, boissons, tabac | 9.4 | 100.0 | 100.3 | 101.6 | 103.8 | 106.1 | 109.5 | 113.2 |
| Textiles — Textiles | 2.3 | 100.0 | 94.2 | 92.1 | 90.3 | 90.9 | 89.8 | 90.4 |
| Wearing apparel, leather and footwear / Articles d'habillement, cuir et chaussures | 2.2 | 100.0 | 93.2 | 84.2 | 80.3 | 78.3 | 74.0 | 75.9 |
| Wood and wood products — Bois et articles en bois | 1.5 | 100.0 | 95.0 | 96.0 | 97.6 | 101.2 | 102.6 | 101.6 |
| Paper, printing, publishing and recorded media / Papier, imprimerie, édition et supports enregistré | 7.6 | 100.0 | 96.2 | 95.1 | 94.1 | 95.6 | 96.3 | 96.9 |
| Chemicals and related products / Produits chimiques et alliés | 13.3 | 100.0 | 99.5 | 102.4 | 105.2 | 109.3 | 112.8 | 116.7 |
| Non-metallic mineral products / Produits minéraux non métalliques | 3.3 | 100.0 | 98.3 | 98.6 | 99.6 | 102.4 | 105.3 | 110.2 |
| Basic metals — Métallurgie de base | 4.0 | 100.0 | 97.0 | 98.7 | 102.0 | 107.9 | 108.5 | 114.5 |
| Fabricated metal products / Fabrications d'ouvrages en métaux | 11.2 | 100.0 | 96.1 | 94.5 | 95.0 | 100.1 | 102.7 | 108.8 |
| Office and related electrical products / Machines de bureau et autres appareils élect. | 12.6 | 100.0 | 93.9 | 92.9 | 99.3 | 108.5 | 116.2 | 133.2 |
| Transport equipment — Equipement de transports | 8.2 | 100.0 | 99.7 | 103.2 | 105.7 | 111.2 | 116.7 | 123.2 |
| Electricity, gas, water [E] — Électricité, gaz et eau [E] | 9.6 | 100.0 | 101.0 | 103.8 | 106.6 | 109.8 | 113.1 | 115.0 |
| **Developed regions[1] — Régions développées[1]** | | | | | | | | |
| Total industry [CDE] — Total, industrie [CDE] | 100.0 | 100.0 | 97.3 | 97.0 | 98.1 | 100.6 | 102.9 | 107.0 |
| Total mining [C] — Total, industries extractives [C] | 5.9 | 100.0 | 99.3 | 97.7 | 97.0 | 96.0 | 94.7 | 94.3 |
| Coal — Houille | 0.4 | 100.0 | 100.8 | 98.9 | 97.5 | 98.4 | 98.7 | 100.2 |
| Crude petroleum and natural gas / Pétrole brut et gaz naturel | 4.2 | 100.0 | 100.2 | 99.0 | 98.3 | 96.7 | 93.9 | 93.0 |
| Metal ores — Minerais métalliques | 0.8 | 100.0 | 93.5 | 88.5 | 84.6 | 83.8 | 88.1 | 88.4 |
| Total manufacturing [D] / Total, industries manufacturières [D] | 84.6 | 100.0 | 96.8 | 96.4 | 97.4 | 100.3 | 102.7 | 107.6 |
| Food, beverages, tobacco / Industries alimentaires, boissons, tabac | 8.5 | 100.0 | 100.5 | 101.3 | 102.3 | 102.8 | 104.5 | 106.1 |
| Textiles — Textiles | 1.6 | 100.0 | 93.5 | 89.9 | 85.8 | 83.0 | 80.4 | 78.0 |
| Wearing apparel, leather and footwear / Articles d'habillement, cuir et chaussures | 1.8 | 100.0 | 90.9 | 78.2 | 72.6 | 66.4 | 61.3 | 60.0 |
| Wood and wood products — Bois et articles en bois | 1.7 | 100.0 | 94.7 | 95.7 | 96.2 | 99.4 | 101.9 | 101.3 |
| Paper, printing, publishing and recorded media / Papier, imprimerie, édition et supports enregistré | 9.5 | 100.0 | 96.2 | 94.9 | 93.3 | 94.3 | 94.7 | 94.8 |
| Chemicals and related products / Produits chimiques et alliés | 13.0 | 100.0 | 99.2 | 102.8 | 104.2 | 106.7 | 108.4 | 110.3 |
| Non-metallic mineral products / Produits minéraux non métalliques | 3.0 | 100.0 | 97.4 | 95.4 | 95.4 | 97.0 | 98.0 | 100.3 |
| Basic metals — Métallurgie de base | 3.7 | 100.0 | 95.9 | 96.5 | 97.3 | 102.0 | 101.1 | 104.7 |
| Fabricated metal products / Fabrications d'ouvrages en métaux | 12.9 | 100.0 | 95.7 | 93.1 | 92.8 | 96.0 | 99.0 | 104.3 |
| Office and related electrical products / Machines de bureau et autres appareils élect. | 14.3 | 100.0 | 93.8 | 91.4 | 97.9 | 106.1 | 113.4 | 130.4 |

| Region and industry [ISIC Rev. 3] / Région et industrie [CITI Rév. 3] | Weight (%) / Pondération (%) | 2000 | 2001 | 2002 | 2003 | 2004 | 2005 | 2006 |
|---|---|---|---|---|---|---|---|---|
| Transport equipment — Equipement de transports | 9.5 | 100.0 | 99.1 | 101.9 | 103.1 | 106.2 | 109.1 | 113.7 |
| Electricity, gas, water [E] — Electricité, gaz et eau [E] | 9.5 | 100.0 | 100.4 | 102.5 | 104.7 | 106.6 | 109.1 | 109.8 |
| **Developing economies[2] — Economies en dévelopment[2]** | | | | | | | | |
| Total industry [CDE] — Total, industrie [CDE] | 100.0 | 100.0 | 99.1 | 100.3 | 106.3 | 114.5 | 119.9 | 127.6 |
| Total mining [C] — Total, industries extractives [C] | 21.6 | 100.0 | 99.5 | 95.7 | 105.5 | 112.0 | 114.3 | 118.3 |
| Coal — Houille | 1.6 | 100.0 | 105.5 | 106.0 | 112.0 | 118.4 | 133.6 | 141.3 |
| Crude petroleum and natural gas Pétrole brut et gaz naturel | 17.5 | 100.0 | 98.7 | 93.9 | 103.6 | 110.0 | 112.6 | 116.3 |
| Metal ores — Minerais métalliques | 1.4 | 100.0 | 103.9 | 107.1 | 125.1 | 131.1 | 125.0 | 128.9 |
| Total manufacturing [D] Total, industries manufacturières [D] | 68.6 | 100.0 | 98.5 | 100.8 | 105.8 | 114.8 | 121.2 | 130.6 |
| Food, beverages, tobacco Industries alimentaires, boissons, tabac | 11.8 | 100.0 | 99.8 | 102.2 | 106.6 | 112.1 | 118.4 | 126.1 |
| Textiles — Textiles | 4.2 | 100.0 | 94.9 | 94.2 | 94.5 | 98.4 | 98.7 | 102.4 |
| Wearing apparel, leather and footwear Articles d'habillement, cuir et chaussures | 3.2 | 100.0 | 96.6 | 93.0 | 91.5 | 95.7 | 92.5 | 99.2 |
| Wood and wood products — Bois et articles en bois | 1.1 | 100.0 | 96.3 | 97.0 | 102.8 | 108.3 | 105.6 | 102.8 |
| Paper, printing, publishing and recorded media Papier, imprimerie, édition et supports enregistré | 2.7 | 100.0 | 96.2 | 97.0 | 101.0 | 107.2 | 110.7 | 115.6 |
| Chemicals and related products Produits chimiques et alliés | 14.2 | 100.0 | 100.2 | 101.5 | 107.6 | 115.3 | 123.2 | 131.8 |
| Non-metallic mineral products Produits minéraux non métalliques | 4.0 | 100.0 | 100.0 | 104.5 | 107.6 | 112.6 | 119.2 | 129.1 |
| Basic metals — Métallurgie de base | 4.7 | 100.0 | 99.1 | 103.0 | 111.4 | 119.7 | 123.4 | 134.1 |
| Fabricated metal products Fabrications d'ouvrages en métaux | 7.1 | 100.0 | 97.5 | 100.9 | 105.4 | 118.9 | 119.9 | 129.7 |
| Office and related electrical products Machines de bureau et autres appareils élect. | 8.1 | 100.0 | 94.1 | 99.6 | 105.3 | 119.0 | 129.0 | 146.0 |
| Transport equipment — Equipement de transports | 4.9 | 100.0 | 102.5 | 109.2 | 118.3 | 135.7 | 153.8 | 169.4 |
| Electricity, gas, water [E] — Electricité, gaz et eau [E] | 9.8 | 100.0 | 102.6 | 107.0 | 111.3 | 117.6 | 122.9 | 127.7 |
| **Northern America[3] — Amérique septentrionale[3]** | | | | | | | | |
| Total industry [CDE] — Total, industrie [CDE] | 100.0 | 100.0 | 96.2 | 96.7 | 97.9 | 100.2 | 104.5 | 109.6 |
| Total mining [C] — Total, industries extractives [C] | 7.5 | 100.0 | 99.3 | 96.5 | 97.3 | 97.5 | 97.9 | 100.3 |
| Coal — Houille | 0.5 | 100.0 | 104.7 | 100.8 | 98.3 | 101.6 | 102.9 | 107.8 |
| Crude petroleum and natural gas Pétrole brut et gaz naturel | 5.4 | 100.0 | 100.6 | 98.9 | 100.3 | 100.0 | 99.0 | 101.8 |
| Metal ores — Minerais métalliques | 1.4 | 100.0 | 91.4 | 84.5 | 79.8 | 79.5 | 85.0 | 85.6 |
| Total manufacturing [D] Total, industries manufacturières [D] | 83.5 | 100.0 | 95.6 | 96.0 | 97.3 | 99.8 | 104.6 | 110.6 |
| Food, beverages, tobacco Industries alimentaires, boissons, tabac | 7.7 | 100.0 | 100.3 | 100.9 | 102.5 | 103.2 | 106.7 | 110.0 |
| Textiles — Textiles | 1.4 | 100.0 | 90.3 | 89.4 | 85.3 | 83.8 | 84.4 | 80.9 |
| Wearing apparel, leather and footwear Articles d'habillement, cuir et chaussures | 1.4 | 100.0 | 85.9 | 68.1 | 63.7 | 56.7 | 54.9 | 54.8 |
| Wood and wood products — Bois et articles en bois | 2.0 | 100.0 | 93.9 | 98.0 | 98.8 | 102.9 | 108.1 | 104.8 |
| Paper, printing, publishing and recorded media Papier, imprimerie, édition et supports enregistré | 11.9 | 100.0 | 94.4 | 92.1 | 89.3 | 89.8 | 90.9 | 90.9 |
| Chemicals and related products Produits chimiques et alliés | 13.1 | 100.0 | 97.1 | 103.3 | 104.4 | 107.8 | 110.3 | 111.9 |
| Non-metallic mineral products Produits minéraux non métalliques | 2.4 | 100.0 | 96.9 | 96.8 | 98.0 | 101.0 | 104.8 | 108.8 |
| Basic metals — Métallurgie de base | 2.8 | 100.0 | 91.6 | 92.4 | 91.1 | 99.3 | 98.0 | 102.0 |
| Fabricated metal products Fabrications d'ouvrages en métaux | 12.4 | 100.0 | 91.2 | 88.4 | 87.6 | 89.2 | 93.5 | 98.8 |
| Office and related electrical products Machines de bureau et autres appareils élect. | 12.3 | 100.0 | 98.2 | 95.8 | 105.3 | 113.8 | 129.2 | 154.3 |
| Transport equipment — Equipement de transports | 10.2 | 100.0 | 96.1 | 99.5 | 100.6 | 100.6 | 103.7 | 108.3 |
| Electricity, gas, water [E] — Electricité, gaz et eau [E] | 9.0 | 100.0 | 99.3 | 102.9 | 104.8 | 106.2 | 108.8 | 108.3 |

| Region and industry [ISIC Rev. 3]<br>Région et industrie [CITI Rév. 3] | Weight (%)<br>Pondération (%) | 2000 | 2001 | 2002 | 2003 | 2004 | 2005 | 2006 |
|---|---|---|---|---|---|---|---|---|
| **Latin America and the Caribbean — Amérique latine et Caraïbes** | | | | | | | | |
| Total industry [CDE] — Total, industrie [CDE] | 100.0 | 100.0 | 98.4 | 97.5 | 100.5 | 108.6 | 112.5 | 117.6 |
| Total mining [C] — Total, industries extractives [C] | 11.8 | 100.0 | 102.9 | 99.3 | 102.2 | 107.8 | 112.2 | 114.2 |
| Coal — Houille | 0.3 | 100.0 | 109.9 | 89.6 | 86.8 | 86.7 | 122.1 | 129.1 |
| Crude petroleum and natural gas<br>Pétrole brut et gaz naturel | 7.5 | 100.0 | 102.0 | 96.1 | 97.4 | 102.2 | 107.3 | 108.3 |
| Metal ores — Minerais métalliques | 2.3 | 100.0 | 100.2 | 102.9 | 110.9 | 118.5 | 118.0 | 119.7 |
| Total manufacturing [D]<br>Total, industries manufacturières [D] | 77.3 | 100.0 | 97.6 | 96.6 | 99.4 | 108.1 | 112.2 | 117.8 |
| Food, beverages, tobacco<br>Industries alimentaires, boissons, tabac | 17.8 | 100.0 | 99.6 | 101.3 | 105.2 | 112.3 | 117.8 | 124.9 |
| Textiles — Textiles | 2.9 | 100.0 | 91.2 | 83.8 | 88.2 | 97.9 | 99.6 | 100.7 |
| Wearing apparel, leather and footwear<br>Articles d'habillement, cuir et chaussures | 3.3 | 100.0 | 91.8 | 85.1 | 85.8 | 91.2 | 92.8 | 92.7 |
| Wood and wood products — Bois et articles en bois | 1.7 | 100.0 | 96.2 | 100.1 | 106.7 | 116.5 | 112.4 | 110.2 |
| Paper, printing, publishing and recorded media<br>Papier, imprimerie, édition et supports enregistré | 3.6 | 100.0 | 95.3 | 94.9 | 99.1 | 106.8 | 112.6 | 117.3 |
| Chemicals and related products<br>Produits chimiques et alliés | 18.3 | 100.0 | 97.7 | 95.7 | 98.1 | 105.2 | 108.3 | 111.8 |
| Non-metallic mineral products<br>Produits minéraux non métalliques | 3.8 | 100.0 | 98.1 | 97.7 | 98.7 | 105.5 | 111.2 | 119.4 |
| Basic metals — Métallurgie de base | 3.6 | 100.0 | 97.1 | 99.2 | 106.2 | 118.0 | 120.9 | 125.6 |
| Fabricated metal products<br>Fabrications d'ouvrages en métaux | 7.6 | 100.0 | 99.6 | 96.3 | 97.8 | 111.7 | 114.1 | 121.8 |
| Office and related electrical products<br>Machines de bureau et autres appareils élect. | 5.4 | 100.0 | 96.1 | 89.8 | 88.9 | 97.0 | 102.5 | 111.2 |
| Transport equipment — Equipement de transports | 6.2 | 100.0 | 99.1 | 102.1 | 103.5 | 116.6 | 122.9 | 131.9 |
| Electricity, gas, water [E] — Electricité, gaz et eau [E] | 11.0 | 100.0 | 98.6 | 101.7 | 106.3 | 112.3 | 115.6 | 119.6 |
| **Asia — Asie** | | | | | | | | |
| Total industry [CDE] — Total, industrie [CDE] | 100.0 | 100.0 | 96.2 | 96.8 | 101.0 | 106.8 | 110.0 | 116.1 |
| Total mining [C] — Total, industries extractives [C] | 11.9 | 100.0 | 98.7 | 93.8 | 102.2 | 106.9 | 107.8 | 109.9 |
| Coal — Houille | 1.3 | 100.0 | 105.6 | 109.2 | 116.9 | 124.7 | 135.8 | 143.8 |
| Crude petroleum and natural gas<br>Pétrole brut et gaz naturel | 9.6 | 100.0 | 98.3 | 92.4 | 101.2 | 105.8 | 106.6 | 108.5 |
| Metal ores — Minerais métalliques | 0.4 | 100.0 | 105.0 | 122.3 | 116.2 | 112.5 | 90.8 | 89.8 |
| Total manufacturing [D]<br>Total, industries manufacturières [D] | 78.0 | 100.0 | 95.0 | 96.1 | 99.9 | 106.0 | 109.3 | 116.3 |
| Food, beverages, tobacco<br>Industries alimentaires, boissons, tabac | 8.9 | 100.0 | 99.7 | 101.0 | 103.7 | 104.1 | 107.2 | 110.5 |
| Textiles — Textiles | 3.1 | 100.0 | 95.9 | 95.9 | 92.9 | 93.8 | 93.0 | 96.5 |
| Wearing apparel, leather and footwear<br>Articles d'habillement, cuir et chaussures | 2.7 | 100.0 | 93.2 | 86.1 | 81.1 | 78.9 | 71.7 | 75.3 |
| Wood and wood products — Bois et articles en bois | 0.9 | 100.0 | 92.2 | 86.2 | 87.0 | 86.9 | 85.5 | 83.1 |
| Paper, printing, publishing and recorded media<br>Papier, imprimerie, édition et supports enregistré | 4.8 | 100.0 | 97.7 | 97.0 | 96.7 | 97.2 | 97.6 | 97.7 |
| Chemicals and related products<br>Produits chimiques et alliés | 12.5 | 100.0 | 100.2 | 101.9 | 106.2 | 111.1 | 116.1 | 119.9 |
| Non-metallic mineral products<br>Produits minéraux non métalliques | 3.7 | 100.0 | 96.3 | 95.9 | 96.1 | 95.9 | 96.7 | 97.8 |
| Basic metals — Métallurgie de base | 5.6 | 100.0 | 98.1 | 100.6 | 105.2 | 109.4 | 111.1 | 117.2 |
| Fabricated metal products<br>Fabrications d'ouvrages en métaux | 8.2 | 100.0 | 92.4 | 90.6 | 94.2 | 103.3 | 104.9 | 110.4 |
| Office and related electrical products<br>Machines de bureau et autres appareils élect. | 16.6 | 100.0 | 86.6 | 89.9 | 98.9 | 111.4 | 115.5 | 131.9 |
| Transport equipment — Equipement de transports | 6.9 | 100.0 | 101.4 | 109.0 | 113.8 | 124.7 | 135.2 | 145.5 |
| Electricity, gas, water [E] — Electricité, gaz et eau [E] | 10.1 | 100.0 | 102.0 | 105.0 | 107.8 | 112.8 | 117.5 | 121.6 |

| Region and industry [ISIC Rev. 3]<br>Région et industrie [CITI Rév. 3] | Weight (%)<br>Pondération (%) | 2000 | 2001 | 2002 | 2003 | 2004 | 2005 | 2006 |
|---|---|---|---|---|---|---|---|---|
| **Asia excluding Israel and Japan — Asie à l'exception de l'Israël et du Japon** | | | | | | | | |
| Total industry [CDE] — Total, industrie [CDE] | 100.0 | 100.0 | 99.4 | 102.7 | 109.7 | 118.5 | 125.2 | 134.3 |
| Total mining [C] — Total, industries extractives [C] | 21.4 | 100.0 | 98.7 | 93.8 | 102.2 | 106.9 | 107.8 | 109.9 |
| Coal — Houille | 2.3 | 100.0 | 105.7 | 110.3 | 118.2 | 126.0 | 137.5 | 145.4 |
| Crude petroleum and natural gas<br>Pétrole brut et gaz naturel | 17.6 | 100.0 | 98.3 | 92.3 | 101.1 | 105.7 | 106.6 | 108.4 |
| Metal ores — Minerais métalliques | 0.7 | 100.0 | 105.2 | 122.7 | 116.6 | 112.9 | 90.7 | 89.5 |
| Total manufacturing [D]<br>Total, industries manufacturières [D] | 69.6 | 100.0 | 98.9 | 104.4 | 111.4 | 121.7 | 130.2 | 141.9 |
| Food, beverages, tobacco<br>Industries alimentaires, boissons, tabac | 9.6 | 100.0 | 100.4 | 104.9 | 111.2 | 114.6 | 122.9 | 131.9 |
| Textiles — Textiles | 5.0 | 100.0 | 96.9 | 99.8 | 97.7 | 99.8 | 100.0 | 105.4 |
| Wearing apparel, leather and footwear<br>Articles d'habillement, cuir et chaussures | 3.3 | 100.0 | 100.3 | 98.5 | 96.0 | 100.2 | 91.1 | 104.1 |
| Wood and wood products — Bois et articles en bois | 0.9 | 100.0 | 95.3 | 92.1 | 97.3 | 98.0 | 96.9 | 92.1 |
| Paper, printing, publishing and recorded media<br>Papier, imprimerie, édition et supports enregistré | 2.5 | 100.0 | 96.4 | 98.6 | 101.9 | 105.4 | 105.4 | 108.9 |
| Chemicals and related products<br>Produits chimiques et alliés | 13.5 | 100.0 | 101.4 | 105.5 | 113.5 | 123.1 | 134.3 | 143.4 |
| Non-metallic mineral products<br>Produits minéraux non métalliques | 4.2 | 100.0 | 101.3 | 109.2 | 114.0 | 117.8 | 122.3 | 129.1 |
| Basic metals — Métallurgie de base | 5.5 | 100.0 | 101.5 | 106.9 | 114.9 | 122.7 | 127.4 | 142.4 |
| Fabricated metal products<br>Fabrications d'ouvrages en métaux | 7.4 | 100.0 | 95.7 | 105.5 | 113.8 | 128.1 | 127.3 | 138.8 |
| Office and related electrical products<br>Machines de bureau et autres appareils élect. | 10.1 | 100.0 | 93.6 | 102.4 | 110.0 | 125.2 | 136.4 | 156.1 |
| Transport equipment — Equipement de transports | 4.9 | 100.0 | 106.5 | 117.2 | 135.4 | 158.1 | 189.2 | 212.1 |
| Electricity, gas, water [E] — Electricité, gaz et eau [E] | 9.0 | 100.0 | 104.4 | 110.1 | 114.5 | 121.6 | 127.9 | 133.7 |
| **Europe — Europe** | | | | | | | | |
| Total industry [CDE] — Total, industrie [CDE] | 100.0 | 100.0 | 100.4 | 99.9 | 100.7 | 103.5 | 104.5 | 108.2 |
| Total mining [C] — Total, industries extractives [C] | 6.9 | 100.0 | 99.5 | 100.1 | 99.0 | 98.1 | 94.6 | 91.4 |
| Coal — Houille | 0.7 | 100.0 | 97.1 | 94.1 | 93.3 | 92.6 | 90.0 | 89.0 |
| Crude petroleum and natural gas<br>Pétrole brut et gaz naturel | 5.3 | 100.0 | 100.1 | 100.8 | 99.2 | 97.9 | 93.5 | 89.0 |
| Metal ores — Minerais métalliques | 0.2 | 100.0 | 101.4 | 107.6 | 112.6 | 115.4 | 115.0 | 116.6 |
| Total manufacturing [D]<br>Total, industries manufacturières [D] | 83.9 | 100.0 | 100.3 | 99.6 | 100.3 | 103.6 | 104.8 | 109.4 |
| Food, beverages, tobacco<br>Industries alimentaires, boissons, tabac | 9.7 | 100.0 | 101.9 | 104.4 | 105.8 | 107.4 | 109.3 | 111.4 |
| Textiles — Textiles | 2.2 | 100.0 | 96.6 | 92.4 | 89.7 | 86.4 | 82.0 | 80.8 |
| Wearing apparel, leather and footwear<br>Articles d'habillement, cuir et chaussures | 2.3 | 100.0 | 97.1 | 87.8 | 82.5 | 77.2 | 70.0 | 69.2 |
| Wood and wood products — Bois et articles en bois | 1.8 | 100.0 | 97.0 | 96.8 | 98.5 | 103.0 | 104.4 | 108.0 |
| Paper, printing, publishing and recorded media<br>Papier, imprimerie, édition et supports enregistré | 7.6 | 100.0 | 98.3 | 98.9 | 99.2 | 101.9 | 101.3 | 102.4 |
| Chemicals and related products<br>Produits chimiques et alliés | 13.9 | 100.0 | 101.4 | 104.2 | 106.4 | 109.4 | 111.1 | 115.1 |
| Non-metallic mineral products<br>Produits minéraux non métalliques | 3.9 | 100.0 | 99.9 | 98.3 | 99.2 | 102.5 | 103.0 | 107.4 |
| Basic metals — Métallurgie de base | 3.8 | 100.0 | 99.1 | 98.9 | 99.9 | 104.2 | 102.9 | 107.9 |
| Fabricated metal products<br>Fabrications d'ouvrages en métaux | 15.4 | 100.0 | 101.5 | 100.3 | 100.4 | 104.8 | 107.5 | 114.5 |
| Office and related electrical products<br>Machines de bureau et autres appareils élect. | 10.7 | 100.0 | 98.8 | 93.0 | 93.5 | 98.9 | 102.2 | 111.4 |
| Transport equipment — Equipement de transports | 8.6 | 100.0 | 101.9 | 101.6 | 103.9 | 109.1 | 111.2 | 115.7 |
| Electricity, gas, water [E] — Electricité, gaz et eau [E] | 9.2 | 100.0 | 101.7 | 102.7 | 105.5 | 107.2 | 109.0 | 110.0 |

| Region and industry [ISIC Rev. 3]<br>Région et industrie [CITI Rév. 3] | Weight (%)<br>Pondération (%) | 2000 | 2001 | 2002 | 2003 | 2004 | 2005 | 2006 |
|---|---|---|---|---|---|---|---|---|
| **Oceania — Océanie** | | | | | | | | |
| Total industry [CDE] — Total, industrie [CDE] | 100.0 | 100.0 | 102.8 | 103.9 | 107.4 | 107.3 | 108.0 | 107.9 |
| Total mining [C] — Total, industries extractives [C] | 20.3 | 100.0 | 103.2 | 101.8 | 101.8 | 98.0 | 100.5 | 99.7 |
| Coal — Houille | 3.2 | 100.0 | 106.2 | 112.7 | 114.4 | 117.4 | 124.2 | 127.4 |
| Crude petroleum and natural gas<br>Pétrole brut et gaz naturel | 9.9 | 100.0 | 102.6 | 98.1 | 93.6 | 83.2 | 81.9 | 78.4 |
| Metal ores — Minerais métalliques | 6.7 | 100.0 | 103.8 | 101.8 | 107.1 | 110.1 | 114.8 | 116.9 |
| Total manufacturing [D]<br>Total, industries manufacturières [D] | 66.5 | 100.0 | 102.5 | 104.4 | 109.0 | 110.1 | 109.7 | 109.6 |
| Food, beverages, tobacco<br>Industries alimentaires, boissons, tabac | 14.9 | 100.0 | 104.0 | 104.1 | 108.9 | 108.7 | 109.7 | 109.9 |
| Textiles — Textiles | 1.5 | 100.0 | 92.8 | 82.4 | 77.5 | 72.1 | 61.1 | 56.1 |
| Wearing apparel, leather and footwear<br>Articles d'habillement, cuir et chaussures | 1.3 | 100.0 | 92.6 | 82.6 | 78.3 | 73.0 | 62.7 | 57.3 |
| Wood and wood products — Bois et articles en bois | 2.8 | 100.0 | 99.2 | 101.0 | 104.4 | 104.4 | 105.4 | 101.3 |
| Paper, printing, publishing and recorded media<br>Papier, imprimerie, édition et supports enregistré | 8.9 | 100.0 | 103.2 | 105.9 | 107.4 | 109.8 | 109.0 | 106.6 |
| Chemicals and related products<br>Produits chimiques et alliés | 9.0 | 100.0 | 102.8 | 103.2 | 109.3 | 104.0 | 104.7 | 100.2 |
| Non-metallic mineral products<br>Produits minéraux non métalliques | 3.5 | 100.0 | 101.8 | 107.8 | 116.7 | 120.9 | 127.2 | 141.0 |
| Basic metals — Métallurgie de base | 4.8 | 100.0 | 99.7 | 107.0 | 110.6 | 111.6 | 108.8 | 107.6 |
| Fabricated metal products<br>Fabrications d'ouvrages en métaux | 8.1 | 100.0 | 102.1 | 106.6 | 111.5 | 114.7 | 113.7 | 114.8 |
| Office and related electrical products<br>Machines de bureau et autres appareils élect. | 3.5 | 100.0 | 105.2 | 105.7 | 112.8 | 118.6 | 119.7 | 124.8 |
| Transport equipment — Equipement de transports | 5.7 | 100.0 | 104.8 | 105.2 | 112.5 | 118.2 | 119.2 | 125.0 |
| Electricity, gas, water [E] — Electricité, gaz et eau [E] | 13.2 | 100.0 | 103.4 | 104.8 | 108.1 | 107.6 | 111.0 | 111.7 |

Source

United Nations Statistics Division, New York, the index numbers of industrial production database, last accessed November 2007.

Notes

1  Northern America (Canada and the United States), Europe, Australia, Israel, Japan, New Zealand and South Africa.
2  Latin America and the Caribbean, Africa (excluding South Africa), Asia (excluding Israel and Japan), Oceania (excluding Australia and New Zealand).
3  Canada and the United States.

Source

Organisation des Nations Unies, Division de statistique, New York, la base de données pour les indices de la production industrielle, dernier accès novembre 2007.

Notes

1  Amérique septentrionale (le Canada et les Etats-Unis), Europe, l'Australie, l'Israël, la Nouvelle-Zélande et l'Afrique du Sud.
2  Amérique latine et Caraïbes, Afrique (non compris l'Afrique du Sud), Asie (non compris l'Israël et le Japon), Océanie (non compris l'Australie et la Nouvelle-Zélande).
3  Le Canada et les Etats-Unis.

# Production, trade and consumption of commercial energy
Thousand metric tons of oil equivalent and kilograms per capita

# Production, commerce et consommation d'énergie commerciale
Milliers de tonnes d'équivalent pétrole et kilogrammes par habitant

| Region | Year Année | Primary energy production – Production d'énergie primaire | | | | | Changes in stocks Variations des stocks | Imports Importations | Exports Exportations |
| | | Total Totale | Solids Solides | Liquids Liquides | Gas Gaz | Electricity Electricité | | | |
|---|---|---|---|---|---|---|---|---|---|
| World | 1999 | 8 373 797 | 2 138 516 | 3 518 387 | 2 266 119 | 450 776 | -59 045 | 3 469 486 | 3 464 034 |
| | 2000 | 8 583 368 | 2 155 479 | 3 669 420 | 2 296 400 | 462 069 | -73 029 | 3 708 974 | 3 672 610 |
| | 2001 | 8 771 064 | 2 263 455 | 3 692 984 | 2 354 070 | 460 555 | 61 063 | 3 774 166 | 3 727 313 |
| | 2002 | 8 823 516 | 2 287 920 | 3 664 952 | 2 400 256 | 470 388 | -1 966 | 3 825 266 | 3 744 159 |
| | 2003 | 9 212 188 | 2 445 137 | 3 810 222 | 2 486 698 | 470 130 | 5 401 | 3 998 129 | 3 944 290 |
| | 2004 | 9 655 102 | 2 645 425 | 3 947 932 | 2 566 635 | 495 109 | 11 830 | 4 278 007 | 4 227 782 |
| | 2005 | 9 980 024 | 2 813 819 | 4 015 831 | 2 641 355 | 509 019 | 4 368 | 4 388 723 | 4 348 144 |
| Africa | 1999 | 645 360 | 129 638 | 395 974 | 112 158 | 7 589 | 9 653 | 77 254 | 419 749 |
| | 2000 | 673 155 | 127 644 | 417 417 | 120 258 | 7 836 | -402 | 77 485 | 445 461 |
| | 2001 | 673 040 | 126 983 | 418 219 | 120 040 | 7 798 | 1 161 | 74 945 | 444 794 |
| | 2002 | 676 525 | 125 068 | 413 110 | 129 651 | 8 696 | 50 | 75 482 | 439 905 |
| | 2003 | 712 548 | 129 587 | 438 507 | 135 960 | 8 493 | 857 | 80 889 | 473 014 |
| | 2004 | 759 374 | 131 770 | 474 544 | 144 065 | 8 995 | -1 152 | 86 663 | 512 226 |
| | 2005 | 817 608 | 133 114 | 504 117 | 171 449 | 8 928 | -37 | 97 342 | 553 119 |
| America, North | 1999 | 1 999 831 | 510 235 | 635 096 | 718 566 | 135 935 | -8 867 | 776 677 | 387 676 |
| | 2000 | 2 010 200 | 494 073 | 660 162 | 718 717 | 137 248 | -57 151 | 840 869 | 428 493 |
| | 2001 | 2 048 815 | 519 145 | 665 029 | 735 682 | 128 959 | 66 318 | 872 324 | 430 184 |
| | 2002 | 2 032 417 | 498 017 | 674 399 | 721 715 | 138 286 | -19 850 | 852 792 | 439 201 |
| | 2003 | 2 038 831 | 481 383 | 687 171 | 733 557 | 136 721 | -6 860 | 900 212 | 458 718 |
| | 2004 | 2 054 949 | 506 542 | 684 834 | 722 798 | 140 775 | 854 | 957 615 | 478 030 |
| | 2005 | 2 039 123 | 515 421 | 665 336 | 715 424 | 142 942 | -3 572 | 988 518 | 478 481 |
| America, South | 1999 | 509 963 | 30 907 | 344 694 | 90 008 | 44 354 | -5 135 | 83 375 | 240 701 |
| | 2000 | 513 675 | 35 754 | 348 821 | 82 064 | 47 037 | -93 | 83 628 | 248 695 |
| | 2001 | 534 554 | 38 258 | 364 298 | 87 038 | 44 960 | 1 575 | 84 790 | 259 935 |
| | 2002 | 518 983 | 37 834 | 348 874 | 85 465 | 46 810 | 3 536 | 82 593 | 244 543 |
| | 2003 | 520 363 | 39 812 | 343 018 | 88 558 | 48 976 | 5 341 | 80 188 | 238 557 |
| | 2004 | 535 265 | 42 197 | 346 988 | 95 579 | 50 502 | -296 | 91 371 | 263 092 |
| | 2005 | 559 017 | 46 697 | 361 055 | 98 113 | 53 152 | 161 | 88 705 | 269 205 |
| Asia | 1999 | 3 006 915 | 953 561 | 1 474 757 | 485 295 | 93 302 | -35 863 | 1 164 766 | 1 308 165 |
| | 2000 | 3 138 734 | 981 171 | 1 548 129 | 513 779 | 95 654 | -17 392 | 1 264 422 | 1 373 822 |
| | 2001 | 3 228 621 | 1 048 267 | 1 534 345 | 546 226 | 99 783 | -9 795 | 1 264 254 | 1 386 443 |
| | 2002 | 3 266 209 | 1 096 659 | 1 491 524 | 577 658 | 100 368 | 2 703 | 1 314 648 | 1 346 075 |
| | 2003 | 3 552 928 | 1 254 772 | 1 580 053 | 617 210 | 100 893 | -1 831 | 1 380 594 | 1 453 752 |
| | 2004 | 3 866 407 | 1 422 563 | 1 658 037 | 672 690 | 113 116 | 977 | 1 526 502 | 1 570 300 |
| | 2005 | 4 121 928 | 1 566 332 | 1 710 101 | 723 896 | 121 599 | -6 065 | 1 553 669 | 1 622 939 |
| Europe | 1999 | 1 993 975 | 366 227 | 637 989 | 824 071 | 165 688 | -13 255 | 1 331 385 | 968 329 |
| | 2000 | 2 011 956 | 358 944 | 658 603 | 824 134 | 170 275 | 7 116 | 1 408 412 | 1 022 321 |
| | 2001 | 2 036 285 | 361 269 | 673 023 | 826 675 | 175 318 | -3 863 | 1 442 548 | 1 044 073 |
| | 2002 | 2 074 851 | 354 992 | 701 350 | 846 292 | 172 216 | 9 885 | 1 463 057 | 1 105 720 |
| | 2003 | 2 135 643 | 363 837 | 728 477 | 872 205 | 171 124 | 8 003 | 1 519 274 | 1 152 487 |
| | 2004 | 2 181 935 | 359 004 | 753 457 | 891 965 | 177 509 | 11 160 | 1 578 319 | 1 231 633 |
| | 2005 | 2 174 813 | 358 353 | 748 595 | 889 406 | 178 460 | 14 018 | 1 620 440 | 1 244 540 |
| Oceania | 1999 | 217 754 | 147 948 | 29 878 | 36 020 | 3 907 | -5 578 | 36 029 | 139 413 |
| | 2000 | 235 647 | 157 893 | 36 288 | 37 448 | 4 018 | -5 108 | 34 157 | 153 819 |
| | 2001 | 249 750 | 169 534 | 38 070 | 38 409 | 3 738 | 5 667 | 35 307 | 161 885 |
| | 2002 | 254 532 | 175 350 | 35 694 | 39 475 | 4 013 | 1 710 | 36 694 | 168 714 |
| | 2003 | 251 874 | 175 745 | 32 998 | 39 209 | 3 923 | -109 | 36 972 | 167 761 |
| | 2004 | 257 172 | 183 348 | 30 072 | 39 539 | 4 212 | 286 | 37 536 | 172 500 |
| | 2005 | 267 535 | 193 902 | 26 627 | 43 067 | 3 939 | -137 | 40 048 | 179 861 |

Source

United Nations Statistics Division, New York, the energy statistics database, last accessed January 2008.

**Production, trade and consumption of commercial energy**—Thousand metric tons of oil equivalent and kilograms per capita (*continued*)

**Production, commerce et consommation d'énergie commerciale**—Milliers de tonnes d'équivalent pétrole et kilogrammes par habitant (*suite*)

| Bunkers - Soutes | | | Consumption - Consommation | | | | | | | |
|---|---|---|---|---|---|---|---|---|---|---|
| Air | Sea | Unallocated | Per capita | Total | Solids | Liquids | Gas | Electricity | Year | |
| Avion | Maritime | Nondistribué | Par habitant | Totale | Solides | Liquides | Gaz | Electricité | Année | Région |
| 107 960 | 145 505 | 210 719 | 1 334 | 7 964 147 | 2 187 547 | 3 064 115 | 2 261 452 | 451 033 | 1999 | Monde |
| 112 059 | 148 223 | 283 881 | 1 346 | 8 140 675 | 2 261 938 | 3 100 240 | 2 316 400 | 462 097 | 2000 | |
| 109 494 | 140 657 | 279 293 | 1 342 | 8 219 178 | 2 276 062 | 3 142 956 | 2 338 661 | 461 499 | 2001 | |
| 110 033 | 144 886 | 268 118 | 1 351 | 8 374 684 | 2 330 120 | 3 165 954 | 2 406 827 | 471 783 | 2002 | |
| 111 066 | 144 944 | 325 681 | 1 383 | 8 667 837 | 2 512 166 | 3 196 297 | 2 488 910 | 470 465 | 2003 | |
| 119 587 | 157 762 | 314 596 | 1 433 | 9 090 710 | 2 719 323 | 3 322 169 | 2 554 101 | 495 118 | 2004 | |
| 127 039 | 166 210 | 315 282 | 1 462 | 9 395 473 | 2 854 392 | 3 370 983 | 2 661 733 | 508 364 | 2005 | |
| 4 446 | 8 137 | 8 176 | 356 | 272 078 | 95 827 | 112 275 | 56 107 | 7 868 | 1999 | Afrique |
| 5 150 | 7 538 | 15 003 | 353 | 277 154 | 95 336 | 117 663 | 56 295 | 7 860 | 2000 | |
| 4 702 | 7 400 | 8 465 | 350 | 280 784 | 96 046 | 117 913 | 58 616 | 8 209 | 2001 | |
| 4 603 | 6 487 | 6 464 | 359 | 293 908 | 93 033 | 124 249 | 67 634 | 8 992 | 2002 | |
| 4 469 | 7 449 | 10 410 | 354 | 296 808 | 96 737 | 123 114 | 68 419 | 8 538 | 2003 | |
| 4 423 | 6 487 | 8 199 | 364 | 315 556 | 104 011 | 130 351 | 72 145 | 9 049 | 2004 | |
| 4 939 | 6 893 | 16 255 | 374 | 333 496 | 103 469 | 134 691 | 86 403 | 8 934 | 2005 | |
| 23 541 | 31 390 | 5 265 | 4 941 | 2 337 890 | 469 072 | 1 014 406 | 718 420 | 135 992 | 1999 | Amérique du Nord |
| 23 616 | 33 591 | 22 292 | 5 014 | 2 400 627 | 491 580 | 1 022 683 | 749 185 | 137 179 | 2000 | |
| 21 657 | 24 640 | 29 904 | 4 774 | 2 348 814 | 479 367 | 1 031 026 | 709 543 | 128 877 | 2001 | |
| 21 105 | 28 089 | 21 084 | 4 806 | 2 395 939 | 484 785 | 1 033 623 | 738 988 | 138 544 | 2002 | |
| 20 580 | 23 830 | 35 901 | 4 779 | 2 407 225 | 488 664 | 1 050 322 | 731 623 | 136 616 | 2003 | |
| 20 965 | 29 324 | 34 078 | 4 808 | 2 449 688 | 499 953 | 1 085 323 | 723 649 | 140 764 | 2004 | |
| 21 606 | 30 401 | 22 202 | 4 846 | 2 478 887 | 504 696 | 1 106 908 | 724 366 | 142 916 | 2005 | |
| 2 216 | 4 487 | 28 261 | 948 | 322 649 | 23 566 | 165 769 | 88 976 | 44 338 | 1999 | Amérique du Sud |
| 1 967 | 5 129 | 26 170 | 913 | 315 275 | 23 625 | 162 802 | 81 925 | 46 923 | 2000 | |
| 1 929 | 5 733 | 28 853 | 911 | 321 161 | 22 394 | 167 488 | 86 398 | 44 880 | 2001 | |
| 1 912 | 5 823 | 29 222 | 884 | 316 472 | 21 177 | 163 535 | 85 084 | 46 677 | 2002 | |
| 2 131 | 5 599 | 30 579 | 877 | 318 273 | 20 623 | 160 349 | 88 474 | 48 827 | 2003 | |
| 2 778 | 5 942 | 16 566 | 920 | 338 403 | 21 542 | 170 458 | 95 892 | 50 511 | 2004 | |
| 2 718 | 7 099 | 17 404 | 939 | 351 017 | 22 177 | 177 565 | 97 949 | 53 326 | 2005 | |
| 26 167 | 57 036 | 136 188 | 734 | 2 670 204 | 1 098 284 | 981 942 | 496 158 | 93 820 | 1999 | Asie |
| 27 405 | 55 094 | 191 424 | 751 | 2 766 155 | 1 138 857 | 1 019 133 | 511 604 | 96 562 | 2000 | |
| 28 615 | 54 639 | 187 283 | 762 | 2 838 531 | 1 168 664 | 1 025 124 | 544 071 | 100 673 | 2001 | |
| 31 727 | 55 309 | 187 691 | 783 | 2 949 525 | 1 225 990 | 1 048 445 | 573 843 | 101 247 | 2002 | |
| 31 526 | 58 543 | 213 003 | 833 | 3 168 453 | 1 386 081 | 1 069 023 | 612 229 | 101 120 | 2003 | |
| 36 000 | 63 153 | 219 609 | 909 | 3 493 208 | 1 579 365 | 1 143 917 | 656 781 | 113 146 | 2004 | |
| 39 030 | 66 638 | 221 887 | 957 | 3 721 269 | 1 715 641 | 1 154 482 | 729 995 | 121 151 | 2005 | |
| 48 456 | 43 288 | 38 411 | 3 089 | 2 240 091 | 456 566 | 742 487 | 875 932 | 165 107 | 1999 | Europe |
| 50 797 | 45 653 | 35 120 | 3 107 | 2 258 567 | 468 224 | 730 552 | 890 235 | 169 556 | 2000 | |
| 49 225 | 47 128 | 32 148 | 3 184 | 2 309 486 | 466 919 | 756 037 | 911 407 | 175 123 | 2001 | |
| 47 900 | 48 037 | 26 414 | 3 177 | 2 299 201 | 461 903 | 753 308 | 911 677 | 172 312 | 2002 | |
| 49 272 | 48 453 | 37 897 | 3 258 | 2 357 928 | 477 212 | 750 151 | 959 124 | 171 441 | 2003 | |
| 52 224 | 51 700 | 39 217 | 3 271 | 2 373 205 | 470 663 | 748 753 | 976 353 | 177 436 | 2004 | |
| 55 198 | 54 001 | 40 610 | 3 281 | 2 384 584 | 460 909 | 751 877 | 993 700 | 178 099 | 2005 | |
| 3 136 | 1 168 | -5 581 | 4 051 | 121 235 | 44 232 | 47 236 | 25 860 | 3 907 | 1999 | Océanie |
| 3 125 | 1 218 | -6 127 | 4 056 | 122 896 | 44 317 | 47 407 | 27 155 | 4 018 | 2000 | |
| 3 366 | 1 117 | -7 360 | 3 915 | 120 403 | 42 672 | 45 368 | 28 625 | 3 738 | 2001 | |
| 2 786 | 1 141 | -2 758 | 3 839 | 119 640 | 43 232 | 42 794 | 29 601 | 4 013 | 2002 | |
| 3 088 | 1 071 | -2 107 | 3 743 | 119 150 | 42 850 | 43 337 | 29 040 | 3 923 | 2003 | |
| 3 197 | 1 157 | -3 072 | 3 740 | 120 649 | 43 789 | 43 367 | 29 280 | 4 212 | 2004 | |
| 3 547 | 1 177 | -3 076 | 3 860 | 126 219 | 47 501 | 45 459 | 29 320 | 3 939 | 2005 | |

Source

Organisation des Nations Unies, Division de statistique, New York, la base de données pour les statistiques énergétiques, dernier accès janvier 2008.

# Total imports and exports: index numbers
Volume and unit value indices and terms of trade (2000 = 100)

# Importations et exportations totales : indices
Indices du volume et de la valeur unitaire et termes de l'échange (2000 = 100)

| Region | 1998 | 1999 | 2001 | 2002 | 2003 | 2004 | 2005 | 2006 | Région |
|---|---|---|---|---|---|---|---|---|---|
| **Total** | | | | | | | | | **Total** |
| Imports : Volume[1] | 84 | 90 | 100 | 104 | 111 | 123 | 131 | 143 | Imp.: Volume[1] |
| Imports : Unit value indices US $[2] | 101 | 99 | 96 | 96 | 104 | 115 | 121 | 127 | Imp.: Indices de la val. unit. en $ E.-U.[2] |
| Exports : Volume[1] | 83 | 88 | 99 | 103 | 108 | 120 | 131 | 145 | Exp.: Volume[1] |
| Exports : Unit value indices US $[2] | 105 | 102 | 97 | 98 | 108 | 117 | 122 | 127 | Exp.: Indices de la val. unit. en $ E.-U.[2] |
| Developed economies[3] | | | | | | | | | Economies développées[3] |
| Imports : Volume[1] | 84 | 91 | 100 | 102 | 108 | 117 | 124 | 132 | Imp.: Volume[1] |
| Imports : Unit value indices US $[2] | 103 | 100 | 96 | 97 | 107 | 117 | 123 | 130 | Imp.: Indices de la val. unit. en $ E.-U.[2] |
| Exports : Volume[1] | 86 | 91 | 99 | 101 | 103 | 111 | 116 | 126 | Exp.: Volume[1] |
| Exports : Unit value indices US $[2] | 107 | 103 | 99 | 100 | 112 | 123 | 128 | 132 | Exp.: Indices de la val. unit. en $ E.-U.[2] |
| Terms of trade[4] | 104 | 104 | 102 | 103 | 105 | 105 | 104 | 102 | Termes de l'échange[4] |
| North America | | | | | | | | | Amérique du Nord |
| Imports : Volume[1] | 83 | 91 | 97 | 101 | 106 | 116 | 124 | 130 | Imp.: Volume[1] |
| Imports : Unit value indices US $[2] | 93 | 94 | 96 | 94 | 97 | 103 | 110 | 116 | Imp.: Indices de la val. unit. en $ E.-U.[2] |
| Exports : Volume[1] | 86 | 91 | 94 | 91 | 92 | 97 | 104 | 113 | Exp.: Volume[1] |
| Exports : Unit value indices US $[2] | 99 | 98 | 100 | 98 | 102 | 107 | 113 | 118 | Exp.: Indices de la val. unit. en $ E.-U.[2] |
| Terms of trade[4] | 107 | 105 | 103 | 104 | 105 | 104 | 103 | 101 | Termes de l'échange[4] |
| Europe | | | | | | | | | Europe |
| Imports : Volume[1] | 85 | 91 | 101 | 103 | 108 | 117 | 124 | 134 | Imp.: Volume[1] |
| Imports : Unit value indices US $[2] | 111 | 104 | 98 | 100 | 115 | 128 | 132 | 140 | Imp.: Indices de la val. unit. en $ E.-U.[2] |
| Exports : Volume[1] | 85 | 90 | 102 | 105 | 108 | 116 | 122 | 134 | Exp.: Volume[1] |
| Exports : Unit value indices US $[2] | 114 | 107 | 99 | 103 | 119 | 132 | 136 | 140 | Exp.: Indices de la val. unit. en $ E.-U.[2] |
| Terms of trade[4] | 103 | 103 | 101 | 103 | 103 | 103 | 103 | 100 | Termes de l'échange[4] |
| Asia and the Pacific | | | | | | | | | Asie et le Pacifique |
| Imports : Volume[1] | 83 | 91 | 103 | 102 | 109 | 117 | 119 | 120 | Imp.: Volume[1] |
| Imports : Unit value indices US $[2] | 92 | 93 | 88 | 88 | 94 | 104 | 113 | 120 | Imp.: Indices de la val. unit. en $ E.-U.[2] |
| Exports : Volume[1] | 89 | 91 | 91 | 96 | 99 | 108 | 106 | 110 | Exp.: Volume[1] |
| Exports : Unit value indices US $[2] | 92 | 96 | 94 | 91 | 98 | 108 | 115 | 117 | Exp.: Indices de la val. unit. en $ E.-U.[2] |
| Terms of trade[4] | 100 | 103 | 107 | 103 | 105 | 104 | 101 | 98 | Termes de l'échange[4] |
| Africa | | | | | | | | | Afrique |
| Imports : Volume[1] | 106 | 100 | 111 | 112 | 113 | 122 | 141 | ... | Imp.: Volume[1] |
| Imports : Unit value indices US $[2] | 98 | 100 | 94 | 94 | 113 | 131 | 137 | ... | Imp.: Indices de la val. unit. en $ E.-U.[2] |
| Exports : Volume[1] | 78 | 84 | 100 | 101 | 109 | 128 | 166 | 190 | Exp.: Volume[1] |
| Exports : Unit value indices US $[2] | 93 | 95 | 93 | 95 | 109 | 121 | 124 | 123 | Exp.: Indices de la val. unit. en $ E.-U.[2] |
| Terms of trade[4] | 95 | 96 | 99 | 101 | 97 | 93 | 90 | ... | Termes de l'échange[4] |
| Northern Africa | | | | | | | | | Afrique du Nord |
| Exports : Volume[1] | 85 | 82 | 102 | 98 | 122 | 152 | 204 | 239 | Exp.: Volume[1] |
| Exports : Unit value indices US $[2] | 74 | 87 | 90 | 93 | 95 | 98 | 100 | 102 | Exp.: Indices de la val. unit. en $ E.-U.[2] |
| Sub-Saharan Africa | | | | | | | | | Afrique subsaharienne |
| Exports : Volume[1] | 74 | 85 | 100 | 102 | 101 | 113 | 139 | 155 | Exp.: Volume[1] |
| Exports : Unit value indices US $[2] | 106 | 101 | 95 | 97 | 119 | 141 | 149 | 148 | Exp.: Indices de la val. unit. en $ E.-U.[2] |
| Latin America and the Caribbean | | | | | | | | | Amérique latine et Caraïbes |
| Imports : Volume[1] | 86 | 88 | 99 | 100 | 106 | 110 | 112 | 121 | Imp.: Volume[1] |
| Imports : Unit value indices US $[2] | 105 | 98 | 99 | 91 | 90 | 105 | 122 | 134 | Imp.: Indices de la val. unit. en $ E.-U.[2] |
| Exports : Volume[1] | 86 | 91 | 102 | 102 | 105 | 119 | 134 | 149 | Exp.: Volume[1] |
| Exports : Unit value indices US $[2] | 91 | 92 | 94 | 95 | 101 | 109 | 117 | 127 | Exp.: Indices de la val. unit. en $ E.-U.[2] |
| Terms of trade[4] | 87 | 94 | 95 | 104 | 113 | 104 | 96 | 95 | Termes de l'échange[4] |

**Total imports and exports: index numbers** — Volume and unit value indices and terms of trade (2000 = 100) *(continued)*

**Importations et exportations totales : indices** — Indices du volume et de la valeur unitaire et termes de l'échange (2000 = 100) *(suite)*

| Region | 1998 | 1999 | 2001 | 2002 | 2003 | 2004 | 2005 | 2006 | Région |
|---|---|---|---|---|---|---|---|---|---|
| **Latin America** | | | | | | | | | **Amérique latine** |
| Exports : Volume[1] | 86 | 91 | 102 | 102 | 104 | 119 | 134 | 148 | Exp.: Volume[1] |
| Exports : Unit value indices US $[2] | 91 | 92 | 94 | 95 | 101 | 109 | 117 | 127 | Exp.: Indices de la val. unit. en $ E.-U.[2] |
| **Western Asia** | | | | | | | | | **Asie occidentale** |
| Imports : Volume[1] | 85 | 89 | 97 | 106 | 116 | 141 | 150 | 167 | Imp.: Volume[1] |
| Imports : Unit value indices US $[2] | 101 | 96 | 99 | 99 | 106 | 118 | 127 | 137 | Imp.: Indices de la val. unit. en $ E.-U.[2] |
| Exports : Volume[1] | 61 | 76 | 96 | 101 | 117 | 140 | 171 | 193 | Exp.: Volume[1] |
| Exports : Unit value indices US $[2] | 106 | 102 | 97 | 96 | 103 | 115 | 124 | 129 | Exp.: Indices de la val. unit. en $ E.-U.[2] |
| Terms of trade[4] | 105 | 106 | 98 | 97 | 97 | 98 | 98 | 94 | Termes de l'échange[4] |
| **Other Asia** | | | | | | | | | **Autre Asie** |
| Imports : Volume[1] | 80 | 84 | 98 | 111 | 129 | 152 | 170 | 199 | Imp.: Volume[1] |
| Imports : Unit value indices US $[2] | 90 | 94 | 95 | 93 | 96 | 106 | 112 | 111 | Imp.: Indices de la val. unit. en $ E.-U.[2] |
| Exports : Volume[1] | 76 | 83 | 99 | 114 | 131 | 160 | 185 | 212 | Exp.: Volume[1] |
| Exports : Unit value indices US $[2] | 100 | 99 | 94 | 90 | 93 | 98 | 102 | 106 | Exp.: Indices de la val. unit. en $ E.-U.[2] |
| Terms of trade[4] | 111 | 105 | 98 | 97 | 97 | 93 | 91 | 96 | Termes de l'échange[4] |
| **Eastern Asia** | | | | | | | | | **Asie orientale** |
| Imports : Volume[1] | 72 | 82 | 99 | 115 | 140 | 169 | 184 | 207 | Imp.: Volume[1] |
| Imports : Unit value indices US $[2] | 93 | 92 | 94 | 91 | 95 | 104 | 109 | 115 | Imp.: Indices de la val. unit. en $ E.-U.[2] |
| Exports : Volume[1] | 78 | 84 | 101 | 118 | 145 | 179 | 213 | 258 | Exp.: Volume[1] |
| Exports : Unit value indices US $[2] | 98 | 97 | 93 | 90 | 92 | 97 | 100 | 100 | Exp.: Indices de la val. unit. en $ E.-U.[2] |
| Terms of trade[4] | 105 | 105 | 99 | 99 | 97 | 94 | 91 | 87 | Termes de l'échange[4] |
| **Southern Asia** | | | | | | | | | **Asie australe** |
| Imports : Volume[1] | 95 | 94 | 106 | 111 | 126 | 143 | 199 | 219 | Imp.: Volume[1] |
| Imports : Unit value indices US $[2] | 90 | 96 | 96 | 102 | 113 | 132 | 126 | 137 | Imp.: Indices de la val. unit. en $ E.-U.[2] |
| Exports : Volume[1] | 65 | 80 | 101 | 118 | 121 | 137 | 165 | 181 | Exp.: Volume[1] |
| Exports : Unit value indices US $[2] | 109 | 103 | 94 | 92 | 105 | 119 | 126 | 141 | Exp.: Indices de la val. unit. en $ E.-U.[2] |
| Terms of trade[4] | 121 | 107 | 98 | 90 | 94 | 90 | 100 | 103 | Termes de l'échange[4] |
| **South-eastern Asia** | | | | | | | | | **Asie du Sud-Est** |
| Imports : Volume[1] | 77 | 83 | 94 | 101 | 104 | 123 | 133 | 130 | Imp.: Volume[1] |
| Imports : Unit value indices US $[2] | 98 | 97 | 97 | 95 | 98 | 104 | 116 | 125 | Imp.: Indices de la val. unit. en $ E.-U.[2] |
| Exports : Volume[1] | 75 | 83 | 96 | 106 | 111 | 134 | 144 | 148 | Exp.: Volume[1] |
| Exports : Unit value indices US $[2] | 101 | 102 | 94 | 90 | 92 | 96 | 102 | 110 | Exp.: Indices de la val. unit. en $ E.-U.[2] |
| Terms of trade[4] | 103 | 104 | 96 | 94 | 94 | 92 | 88 | 88 | Termes de l'échange[4] |

Source

United Nations Statistics Division, New York, trade statistics database, last accessed March 2008.

Notes

1 Volume indices are derived from value data and unit value indices. They are base-period weighted.

2 Regional aggregates are current-period weighted.

3 This classification is intended for statistical convenience and does not, necessarily, express a judgement about the stage reached by a particular country in the development process.

4 Unit value index of exports divided by unit value index of imports.

Source

Organisation des Nations Unies, Division de statistique, New York, la base de données pour les statistiques du commerce extérieur, dernier accès mars 2008.

Notes

1 Les indices du volume sont calculés à partir des chiffres de la valeur et des indices de valeur unitaire. Ils sont à coéfficients de pondération correspondant à la périod en base.

2 Les totaux régionaux sont à coéfficients de pondération correspondant à la période en cours.

3 Cette classification est utilisée pour plus de commodité dans la presentation des statistique et n'implique pas nécessairement un jugement quant au stage de développement auquel est parvenu un pays donné.

4 Indices de la valeur unitaire des exportations divisé par l'indice de la valeur unitaire des importations.

*Table 1:* The series of world aggregates on population, output, production, external trade and finance have been compiled from statistical publications and databases of the United Nations and the specialized agencies and other institutions. The sources should be consulted for detailed information on compilation and coverage.

*Table 2* presents estimates of population size, rates of population increase, crude birth and death rates, surface area and population density for the world and regions. Unless otherwise specified, all figures are estimates of the order of magnitude and are subject to a substantial margin of error.

The population estimates and rates presented in this table were prepared by the Population Division of the United Nations Secretariat and published in *World Population Prospects: The 2006 Revision.*

The average annual percentage rates of population growth were calculated by the Population Division of the United Nations Secretariat, using an exponential rate of increase formula.

Crude birth and crude death rates are expressed in terms of the average annual number of births and deaths respectively, per 1 000 mid-year population. These rates are estimated.

Surface area totals were obtained by summing the figures for the individual countries or areas.

Density is the number of persons in the 2005 total population per square kilometre of total surface area.

The scheme of regionalization used for the purpose of making these estimates is presented in annex I. Although some continental totals are given, and all can be derived, the basic scheme presents macro regions that are so drawn as to obtain greater homogeneity in sizes of population, types of demographic circumstances and accuracy of demographic statistics.

*Tables 3-4:* The index numbers in table 3 refer to agricultural production, which is defined to include both crop and livestock products. Seeds and feed are excluded. The index numbers of food refer to commodities which are considered edible and contain nutrients. Coffee, tea and other inedible commodities are excluded.

The index numbers of total agricultural and food production in table 3 are calculated by the Laspeyres formula with the base year period 1999-2001. The latter is provided in order to diminish the impact of annual fluctuations in agricultural output during base years on the indices for the period. Production quantities of each commodity are weighted by 1999-2001 average national producer prices and summed for each year. The index numbers are based on production data for a calendar year.

Index numbers for the world and regions are computed in a similar way to the country index numbers except that in-

*Tableau 1:* Les séries d'agrégats mondiaux sur la population, la production, le commerce extérieur et les finances ont été établies à partir de publications statistiques et bases de données des Nations Unies et les institutions spécialisées et autres organismes. On doit se référer aux sources pour tous renseignements détaillés sur les méthodes de calcul et la portée des statistiques.

Le *Tableau 2* présente les estimations mondiales et régionales de la population, des taux d'accroissement de la population, des taux bruts de natalité et de mortalité, de la superficie et de la densité de population. Sauf indication contraire, tous les chiffres sont des estimations de l'ordre de grandeur et comportent une assez grande marge d'erreur.

Les estimations de la population et tous les taux présentés dans ce tableau ont été établis par la Division de la population du Secrétariat des Nations Unies et publiés dans "*World Population Prospects: The 2006 Revision*".

Les pourcentages annuels moyens de l'accroissement de la population ont été calculés par la Division de la population du Secrétariat des Nations Unies, sur la base d'une formule de taux d'accroissement exponentiel.

Les taux bruts de natalité et de mortalité sont exprimés, respectivement, sur la base du nombre annuel moyen de naissances et de décès par tranche de 1 000 habitants au milieu de l'année. Ces taux sont estimatifs.

On a déterminé les superficies totales en additionnant les chiffres correspondant aux différents pays ou régions.

La densité est le nombre de personnes de la population totale de 2005 par kilomètre carré de la superficie totale.

Le schéma de régionalisation utilisé aux fins de l'établissement de ces estimations est présenté dans l'annexe I. Bien que les totaux de certains continents soient donnés et que tous puissent être déterminés, le schéma de base présente les grandes régions qui sont établies de manière à obtenir une plus grande homogénéité en ce qui concerne l'ampleur des populations, les types de conditions démographiques et la précision des statistiques démographiques.

*Tableaux 3-4:* Les indices du tableau 3 se rapportent à la production agricole, qui est définie comme comprenant à la fois les produits de l'agriculture et de l'élevage. Les semences et les aliments pour les animaux sont exclus de cette définition. Les indices de la production alimentaire se rapportent aux produits considérés comme comestibles et contenant des éléments nutritifs. Le café, le thé et les produits non comestibles sont exclus.

Les indices de la production agricole et de la production alimentaire présentés au tableau 3 sont calculés selon la formule de Laspeyres avec les années 1999-2001 comme période de référence, cela afin de limiter l'incidence, sur les

stead of using different commodity prices for each country group, "international commodity prices" derived from the Gheary-Khamis formula are used for all country groupings. This method assigns a single "price" to each commodity.

The indexes in table 4 are calculated as a ratio between the index numbers of total agricultural and food production in table 3 described above and the corresponding index numbers of population.

For further information on the series presented in these tables, see the FAO *Statistical Yearbook* and http://faostat.fao.org.

*Table 5:* The index numbers of industrial production are classified according to tabulation categories, divisions and combinations of divisions of the International Standard Industrial Classification of All Economic Activities, Revision 3, (ISIC Rev. 3) for mining (category C), manufacturing (category D), and electricity, gas and water (category E).

The indices indicate trends in value added at constant prices. The measure of value added used is the national accounts concept, which is defined as gross output less the cost of materials, supplies, fuel and electricity consumed and services received.

Each series is compiled using the Laspeyres formula, that is, the indices are base-weighted arithmetic means. The weight base year is 2000 and value added, generally at factor cost, is used in weighting.

For most countries the estimates of value added used as weights are derived from the results of national industrial censuses or similar inquiries relating to 2000. These data, in national currency, are adjusted to the ISIC where necessary and are subsequently converted into US dollars.

Within each of the ISIC categories (tabulation categories, divisions and combinations of divisions) shown in the tables, the indices for the country aggregations (regions or economic groupings) are calculated directly from the country data. The indices for the World, however, are calculated from the aggregated indices for the groupings of developed and developing countries.

*Table 6:* For a description of the series in table 6, see the technical notes to chapter XII.

*Table 7:* For a description of the series in table 7, see the technical notes to chapter XV. The composition of the regions is presented in table 55.

indices correspondant à la période considérée, des fluctuations annuelles de la production agricole enregistrée pendant les années de référence. Les chiffres de production de chaque produit sont pondérés par les prix nationaux moyens à la production pour la période 1999-2001 et additionnés pour chaque année. Les indices sont fondés sur les données de production de l'année civile.

Les indices pour le monde et les régions sont calculés de la même façon que les indices par pays, mais au lieu d'appliquer des prix différents aux produits de base pour chaque groupe de pays, on a utilisé des "prix internationaux" établis d'après la formule de Gheary-Khamis pour tous les groupes de pays. Cette méthode attribue un seul "prix" à chaque produit de base.

Les indices du tableau 4 sont calculés comme ratio entre les indices de la production alimentaire et de la production agricole totale du tableau 3 décrits cidessus et les indices de population correspondants.

Pour tout renseignement complémentaire sur les séries présentées dans ces tableaux, voir l'*Annuaire Statistique de la FAO* et http://faostat.fao.org.

*Tableau 5:* Les indices de la production industrielle sont classés selon les catégories de classement, les divisions ou des combinaisons des divisions de la Classification Internationale type, par industrie, de toutes les branches d'activité économique, Révision 3 (CITI Rev. 3) qui concernent les industries extractives (la catégorie C) et les industries manufacturières (la catégorie D), ainsi que l'électricité, le gaz et l'eau (la catégorie E).

Ces indices représentent les tendances de la valeur ajoutée aux prix constants. La mesure utilisée pour la valeur ajoutée correspond à celle qui est appliquée aux fins de la comptabilité nationale, c'est-à-dire égale à la valeur de la production brute diminuée des coûts des matériaux, des fournitures, de la consommation de carburant et d'électricité ainsi que des services reçus.

Chaque série a été établie au moyen de la formule de Laspeyres, ce qui signifie que les indices sont des moyennes arithmétiques affectées de coefficients de pondération. L'année de base de pondération est l'année 2000 et on utilise généralement pour la pondération la valeur ajoutée au coût des facteurs.

Pour la plupart des pays, les estimations de la valeur ajoutée qui sont utilisées comme coefficients de pondération sont tirées des résultats des recensements industriels nationaux ou enquêtes analogues concernant l'année 2000. Ces données, en monnaie nationale, sont ajustées s'il y a lieu aux normes de la CITI et ultérieurement converties en dollars des Etats-Unis.

A l'intérieur de chacune des subdivisions de la CITI (catégories de classement, divisions et combinaisons des di-

visions) indiquées dans les tableaux, les indices relatifs aux assemblages de pays (régions géographiques ou groupements économiques) sont calculés directement à partir des données des pays. Toutefois, les indices concernant le *Monde* sont calculés à partir des indices agrégés applicables aux groupements de pays développés et de pays en développement.

*Tableau 6:* On trouvera une description de la série de statis-tiques du tableau 6 dans les notes techniques du chapitre XII.

*Tableau 7:* On trouvera une description de la série de statistiques du tableau 7 dans les notes techniques du chapitre XV. La composition des régions est présentée au tableau 55.

# Population and social statistics

# Population et statistiques sociales

Part Two of the *Yearbook* presents statistical series on a wide range of population and social topics for all countries or areas of the world for which data have been made available. The topics include population and population growth, surface area and density; gender; education; daily newspapers; telephones; cellular mobile phones and Internet users.

La deuxième partie de l'*Annuaire* présente, pour tous les pays ou zones du monde pour lesquels des données sont disponibles, des séries statistiques concernant une large gamme de questions démographiques et sociales: population et croissance démographique, superficie et densité; éducation; disponibilités alimentaires; téléphones et usagers d'Internet.

# 8 Population by sex, rate of population increase, surface area and density

## Population selon le sexe, taux d'accroissement de la population, superficie et densité

| Country or area[+]<br>Pays ou zone[+] | Date | Latest census<br>Dernier recensement<br>Both sexes<br>Les deux sexes | Men<br>Hommes | Women<br>Femmes | Mid-year estimates<br>(thousands)<br>Estimations au milieu<br>de l'année (milliers)<br>2000 | 2005 | Annual rate<br>of increase<br>Taux d'accroisse-<br>ment annuel %<br>2000 - 2005 | Surface area<br>Superficie<br>(km²)<br>2005 | Density<br>Densité<br>2005[&] |
|---|---|---|---|---|---|---|---|---|---|
| **Africa**<br>**Afrique** | | | | | | | | | |
| Algeria[1]<br>Algérie[1] | 25 VI 1998 | 29 100 867 | 14 698 589 | 14 402 278 | 30 416 | 32 906 | 1.6 | 2 381 741 | 14 |
| Angola[2]<br>Angola[2] | 15 XII 1970 | 5 646 166 | 2 943 974 | 2 702 192 | ... | ... | ... | 1 246 700 | ... |
| Benin<br>Bénin | 11 II 2002 | 6 769 914[1] | 3 284 119[1] | 3 485 795[1] | 6 169 | ... | ... | 112 622 | ... |
| Botswana<br>Botswana | 17 VIII 2001 | 1 680 863 | 813 488 | 867 375 | 1 653 | ... | ... | 581 730 | ... |
| Burkina Faso[3]<br>Burkina Faso[3] | 10 XII 1996 | 10 862 075 | 5 355 982 | 5 506 093 | 11 347[1] | 12 802[1] | 2.4 | 274 200 | 47 |
| Burundi<br>Burundi | 16 VIII 1990 | 5 139 073 | 2 473 599 | 2 665 474 | ... | ... | ... | 27 834 | ... |
| Cameroon[4]<br>Cameroun[4] | 10 IV 1987 | 10 493 655 | ... | ... | 15 292 | ... | ... | 475 442 | ... |
| Cape Verde<br>Cap-Vert | 16 VI 2000 | 436 863 | 211 479 | 225 384 | 435 | ... | ... | 4 033 | ... |
| Central African Rep.<br>Rép. centrafricaine | 8 XII 2003 | 3 151 072 | 1 569 446 | 1 581 626 | ... | ... | ... | 622 984 | ... |
| Chad[5]<br>Tchad[5] | 8 IV 1993 | 6 279 931 | ... | ... | ... | ... | ... | 1 284 000 | ... |
| Comoros[6]<br>Comores[6] | 1 IX 2003 | 575 660 | ... | ... | ... | ... | ... | 2 235 | ... |
| Congo<br>Congo | 6 VI 1996 | *2 600 000 | ... | ... | 2 893 | ... | ... | 342 000 | ... |
| Côte d'Ivoire<br>Côte d'Ivoire | 21 XI 1998 | 15 366 672 | 7 844 621 | 7 522 050 | 16 402 | 19 097 | 3.0 | 322 463 | 59 |
| Dem. Rep. of the Congo<br>Rép. dém. du Congo | 1 VII 1984 | 29 916 800 | 14 543 800 | 15 373 000 | ... | ... | ... | 2 344 858 | ... |
| Djibouti<br>Djibouti | 11 XII 1960 | 81 200 | ... | ... | ... | ... | ... | 23 200 | ... |
| Egypt[7]<br>Egypte[7] | 11 XI 2006 | *72 579 030 | *37 100 853 | *35 478 177 | 63 976 | 71 898 | 2.3 | 1 002 000 | 72 |
| Equatorial Guinea[8]<br>Guinée équatoriale[8] | 1 II 2002 | 1 014 999 | 501 387 | 513 612 | ... | ... | ... | 28 051 | ... |
| Eritrea<br>Erythrée | 9 V 1984 | 2 748 304 | 1 374 452 | 1 373 852 | ... | ... | ... | 117 600 | ... |
| Ethiopia<br>Ethiopie | 11 X 1994 | 53 477 265 | 26 910 698 | 26 566 567 | 63 495 | ... | ... | 1 104 300 | ... |
| Gabon<br>Gabon | 1 XII 2003 | *1 269 000 | ... | ... | 1 206 | ... | ... | 267 668 | ... |
| Gambia<br>Gambie | 15 IV 2003 | *1 364 507 | *676 726 | *687 781 | 1 393 | ... | ... | 11 295 | ... |
| Ghana<br>Ghana | 26 III 2000 | 18 912 079 | 9 357 382 | 9 554 697 | 18 412 | ... | ... | 238 533 | ... |
| Guinea<br>Guinée | 1 XII 1996 | 7 156 406 | 3 497 979 | 3 658 427 | ... | ... | ... | 245 857 | ... |
| Guinea-Bissau[4]<br>Guinée-Bissau[4] | 1 XII 1991 | 983 367 | 476 210 | 507 157 | ... | 1 326 | ... | 36 125 | 37 |
| Kenya<br>Kenya | 24 VIII 1999 | 28 686 607 | 14 205 589 | 14 481 018 | 30 150 | 35 267 | 3.1 | 580 367 | 61 |

| Country or area[+]<br>Pays ou zone[+] | Date | Latest census<br>Dernier recensement<br>Both sexes<br>Les deux sexes | Latest census<br>Men<br>Hommes | Latest census<br>Women<br>Femmes | Mid-year estimates (thousands)<br>Estimations au milieu de l'année (milliers)<br>2000 | Mid-year estimates<br>2005 | Annual rate of increase<br>Taux d'accroissement annuel %<br>2000 - 2005 | Surface area<br>Superficie (km²)<br>2005 | Density<br>Densité<br>2005[&] |
|---|---|---|---|---|---|---|---|---|---|
| Lesotho[9]<br>Lesotho[9] | 9 IV 2006 | *1 872 721[1] | *911 847[1] | *960 874[1] | 2 144 | ... | ... | 30 355 | ... |
| Liberia<br>Libéria | 1 II 1984 | 2 101 628 | 1 063 127 | 1 038 501 | ... | ... | ... | 111 369 | ... |
| Libyan Arab Jamah.[10]<br>Jamah. arabe libyenne[10] | 11 VIII 1995 | 4 404 986 | 2 236 943 | 2 168 043 | 5 125 | ... | ... | 1 759 540 | ... |
| Madagascar<br>Madagascar | 1 VIII 1993 | 12 238 914 | 6 088 116 | 6 150 798 | 15 085 | 17 730 | 3.2 | 587 041 | 30 |
| Malawi[4]<br>Malawi[4] | 1 IX 1998 | 9 933 868 | 4 867 563 | 5 066 305 | 10 475 | *12 341 | 3.3 | 118 484 | 104 |
| Mali[1]<br>Mali[1] | 1 IV 1998 | 9 790 492 | 4 847 436 | 4 943 056 | 10 243 | ... | ... | 1 240 192 | ... |
| Mauritania<br>Mauritanie | 1 XI 2000 | 2 548 157 | 1 240 414 | 1 307 743 | 2 645 | 2 906 | 1.9 | 1 025 520 | 3 |
| Mauritius[1]<br>Maurice[1] | 2 VII 2000 | 1 178 848 | 583 756 | 595 092 | 1 187 | 1 243 | 0.9 | 2 040 | 609 |
| Morocco<br>Maroc | 1 IX 2004 | 29 680 069 | 14 640 662 | 15 039 407 | 28 705 | *30 172 | 1.0 | 446 550 | 68 |
| Mozambique[11,12]<br>Mozambique[11,12] | 1 VIII 1997 | 16 099 246 | 7 714 306 | 8 384 940 | 17 691 | *19 420 | 1.9 | 801 590 | 24 |
| Namibia[13]<br>Namibie[13] | 27 VIII 2001 | 1 830 330 | 887 721 | 942 572 | *1 817 | ... | ... | 824 292 | ... |
| Niger<br>Niger | 20 V 2001 | *10 790 352 | *5 380 287 | *5 410 065 | 10 493[1] | 12 628[1] | 3.7 | 1 267 000 | 10 |
| Nigeria[4]<br>Nigéria[4] | 21 III 2006 | *140 003 542 | *71 709 859 | *68 293 683 | 115 224 | 133 767 | 3.0 | 923 768 | 145 |
| Réunion<br>Réunion | 8 III 1999 | 706 180[1] | 347 076[1] | 359 104[1] | 722 | 779 | 1.5 | 2 510 | 310 |
| Rwanda[1]<br>Rwanda[1] | 16 VIII 2002 | 8 128 553 | 3 879 448 | 4 249 105 | ... | ... | ... | 26 338 | ... |
| Saint Helena ex. dep.<br>Sainte-Hélène sans dép. | 8 III 1998 | 5 157 | 2 612 | 2 545 | ... | ... | ... | 122 | ... |
| Ascension[1]<br>Ascension[1] | 8 III 1998 | 712 | 458 | 254 | ... | ... | ... | 88 | ... |
| Tristan da Cunha<br>Tristan da Cunha | 31 XII 1988 | 296 | 139 | 157 | ... | ... | ... | 98 | ... |
| Sao Tome and Principe<br>Sao Tomé-et-Principe | 25 VIII 2001 | 137 599[1] | 68 236[1] | 69 363[1] | 135 | 149 | 1.9 | 964 | 155 |
| Senegal[1]<br>Sénégal[1] | 8 XII 2002 | *9 956 202 | *4 886 485 | *5 069 717 | 9 427 | 10 848 | 2.8 | 196 722 | 55 |
| Seychelles[14]<br>Seychelles[14] | 26 VIII 2002 | 81 755[1] | 40 751[1] | 41 004[1] | 81 | 83 | 0.4 | 455 | 182 |
| Sierra Leone<br>Sierra Leone | 4 XII 2004 | *4 963 298 | *2 412 860 | *2 550 438 | 4 944 | ... | ... | 71 740 | ... |
| Somalia<br>Somalie | 15 II 1987 | 7 114 431 | 3 741 664 | 3 372 767 | ... | ... | ... | 637 657 | ... |
| South Africa[12]<br>Afrique du Sud[12] | 10 X 2001 | *44 819 778 | *21 434 041 | *23 385 737 | 43 686 | 46 888 | 1.4 | 1 221 037 | 38 |
| Sudan<br>Soudan | 15 IV 1993 | 24 940 683 | 12 518 638 | 12 422 045 | 31 081 | 35 397 | 2.6 | 2 505 813 | 14 |
| Swaziland<br>Swaziland | 11 V 1997 | 929 718 | 440 154 | 489 564 | 1 003 | 1 126 | 2.3 | 17 364 | 65 |
| Togo<br>Togo | 22 XI 1981 | 2 719 567 | 1 325 641 | 1 393 926 | 4 629 | 5 337 | 2.8 | 56 785 | 94 |
| Tunisia<br>Tunisie | 28 IV 2004 | 9 932 400 | ... | ... | 9 564 | 10 029 | 1.0 | 163 610 | 61 |

| Country or area[+] / Pays ou zone[+] | Date | Latest census / Dernier recensement Both sexes / Les deux sexes | Men / Hommes | Women / Femmes | Mid-year estimates (thousands) Estimations au milieu de l'année (milliers) 2000 | 2005 | Annual rate of increase Taux d'accroissement annuel % 2000 - 2005 | Surface area Superficie (km²) 2005 | Density Densité 2005[&] |
|---|---|---|---|---|---|---|---|---|---|
| Uganda / Ouganda | 12 IX 2002 | 24 442 084 | 11 929 803 | 12 512 281 | 22 972 | ... | ... | 241 038 | ... |
| United Rep. of Tanzania / Rép.-Unie de Tanzanie | 24 VIII 2002 | *34 443 603 | *16 829 861 | *17 613 742 | ... | 37 379 | ... | 945 087 | 40 |
| Western Sahara[15] / Sahara occidental[15] | 31 XII 1970 | 76 425 | 43 981 | 32 444 | ... | ... | ... | 266 000 | ... |
| Zambia / Zambie | 25 X 2000 | 9 885 591 | 4 946 298 | 4 939 293 | 9 337 | ... | ... | 752 618 | ... |
| Zimbabwe / Zimbabwe | 17 VIII 2002 | 11 631 657 | 5 634 180 | 5 997 477 | | ... | ... | 390 757 | ... |
| **America, North** / **Amérique du Nord** | | | | | | | | | |
| Anguilla / Anguilla | 9 V 2001 | 11 430 | 5 628 | 5 802 | 11 | 14 | 3.8 | 91 | 150 |
| Antigua and Barbuda / Antigua-et-Barbuda | 28 V 2001 | 77 426 | 37 002 | 40 424 | 72 | 83 | 2.7 | 442 | 187 |
| Aruba[1] / Aruba[1] | 14 X 2000 | 90 508 | 43 435 | 47 073 | 91 | 101 | 2.1 | 180 | 559 |
| Bahamas / Bahamas | 1 V 2000 | 303 611 | 147 715 | 155 896 | 303 | ... | ... | 13 878 | ... |
| Barbados / Barbade | 1 V 2000 | 250 010 | 119 926 | 130 084 | 269 | 273 | 0.3 | 430 | 635 |
| Belize / Belize | 12 V 2000 | 240 204 | 121 278 | 118 926 | 250 | 292 | 3.1 | 22 966 | 13 |
| Bermuda[1,16] / Bermudes[1,16] | 20 V 2000 | 62 059 | 29 802 | 32 257 | 63 | 64 | 0.2 | 54 | 1 177 |
| British Virgin Islands / Iles Vierges britanniques | 21 V 2001 | 20 647 | 10 627 | 10 020 | 20 | ... | ... | 151 | ... |
| Canada[1,17] / Canada[1,17] | 15 V 2001 | 30 007 095 | 14 706 850 | 15 300 245 | 30 689 | 32 312 | 1.0 | 9 984 670 | 3 |
| Cayman Islands / Iles Caïmanes | 10 X 1999 | 39 020 | 19 033 | 19 987 | 40[1] | 48[1] | 3.7 | 264 | 183 |
| Costa Rica[1] / Costa Rica[1] | 26 VI 2000 | 3 810 179 | 1 902 614 | 1 907 565 | 3 810 | 4 266 | 2.3 | 51 100 | 83 |
| Cuba / Cuba | 6 IX 2002 | 11 177 743[1] | 5 597 233[1] | 5 580 510[1] | 11 130 | 11 243 | 0.2 | 109 886 | 102 |
| Dominica[9] / Dominique[9] | 12 V 2001 | 69 625 | 35 073 | 34 552 | 72 | ... | ... | 751 | ... |
| Dominican Republic / Rép. dominicaine | 20 X 2002 | 8 562 541[1] | 4 265 215[1] | 4 297 326[1] | 8 552 | 9 028 | 1.1 | 48 671 | 185 |
| El Salvador / El Salvador | 27 IX 1992 | 5 118 599 | 2 485 613 | 2 632 986 | 6 276 | 6 875 | 1.8 | 21 041 | 327 |
| Greenland[1,18] / Groenland[1,18] | 1 VII 2000 | 56 124 | 29 989 | 26 135 | 56 | ... | ... | 2 166 086 | ... |
| Grenada[19] / Grenade[19] | 25 V 2001 | 102 632 | 50 481 | 52 151 | 101 | ... | ... | 344 | ... |
| Guadeloupe[1,20] / Guadeloupe[1,20] | 8 III 1999 | 422 222 | 203 146 | 219 076 | 428 | *446 | 0.8 | 1 705 | 261 |
| Guatemala[12] / Guatemala[12] | 24 XI 2002 | 11 237 196[1] | ... | ... | 11 385 | 12 701 | 2.2 | 108 889 | 117 |
| Haiti[1] / Haïti[1] | 11 I 2003 | 8 373 750 | ... | ... | 7 959 | ... | ... | 27 750 | ... |
| Honduras / Honduras | 28 VII 2001 | 6 071 200 | 3 000 530 | 3 070 670 | 6 369 | ... | ... | 112 088 | ... |
| Jamaica[1] / Jamaïque[1] | 10 IX 2001 | 2 607 632 | 1 283 547 | 1 324 085 | 2 589 | 2 661 | 0.5 | 10 991 | 242 |

| Country or area[+] / Pays ou zone[+] | Latest census / Dernier recensement | | | | Mid-year estimates (thousands) / Estimations au milieu de l'année (milliers) | | Annual rate of increase / Taux d'accroissement annuel % | Surface area / Superficie (km²) | Density / Densité |
|---|---|---|---|---|---|---|---|---|---|
| | Date | Both sexes / Les deux sexes | Men / Hommes | Women / Femmes | 2000 | 2005 | 2000 - 2005 | 2005 | 2005[&] |
| Martinique[1] / Martinique[1] | 8 III 1999 | 381 325 | 180 910 | 200 415 | 385 | 398 | 0.7 | 1 102 | 361 |
| Mexico[1] / Mexique[1] | 14 II 2000 | 97 483 412 | 47 592 253 | 49 891 159 | 98 439 | 103 947 | 1.1 | 1 964 375 | 53 |
| Montserrat / Montserrat | 12 V 2001 | 4 491 | 2 418 | 2 073 | 5 | ... | ... | 102 | ... |
| Netherlands Antilles[1,21] / Antilles néerlandaises[1,21] | 29 I 2001 | 175 653 | 82 521 | 93 132 | 179 | ... | ... | 800 | ... |
| Nicaragua[1] / Nicaragua[1] | 4 VI 2005 | 5 144 553 | 2 535 461 | 2 609 092 | 5 106 | 5 457 | 1.3 | 120 340 | 45 |
| Panama / Panama | 14 V 2000 | 2 839 177 | 1 432 566 | 1 406 611 | 2 856 | 3 228 | 2.5 | 75 517 | 43 |
| Puerto Rico[1,22] / Porto Rico[1,22] | 1 IV 2000 | 3 808 610 | 1 833 577 | 1 975 033 | 3 816 | 3 912 | 0.5 | 8 870 | 441 |
| Saint Kitts and Nevis / Saint-Kitts-et-Nevis | 14 V 2001 | 45 841 | 22 784 | 23 057 | 40 | ... | ... | 261 | ... |
| Saint Lucia / Sainte-Lucie | 22 V 2001 | 157 164 | 76 741 | 80 423 | 156 | 165 | 1.1 | 539 | 306 |
| Saint Pierre and Miquelon / Saint-Pierre-et-Miquelon | 8 III 1999 | 6 316 | 3 147 | 3 169 | ... | ... | ... | 242 | ... |
| St. Vincent-Grenadines[23,24] / St. Vincent-Grenadines[23,24] | 14 V 2001 | 109 022 | 55 456 | 53 566 | 110 | 104 | -1.1 | 389 | 267 |
| Trinidad and Tobago / Trinité-et-Tobago | 15 V 2000 | 1 262 366 | 633 051 | 629 315 | 1 290 | ... | ... | 5 130 | |
| Turks and Caicos Islands / Iles Turques et Caïques | 20 VIII 2001 | 19 886 | 9 896 | 9 990 | 18[1] | 31[1] | 10.1 | 948 | 32 |
| United States[1,25] / Etats-Unis[1,25] | 1 IV 2000 | 281 421 906 | 138 053 563 | 143 368 343 | 282 193 | 296 410 | 1.0 | 9 629 091 | 31 |
| United States Virgin Is.[1,22] / Iles Vierges américaines[1,22] | 1 IV 2000 | 108 612 | 51 864 | 56 748 | 109 | ... | ... | 347 | ... |
| **America, South** **Amérique du Sud** | | | | | | | | | |
| Argentina / Argentine | 18 XI 2001 | 36 260 130 | 17 659 072 | 18 601 058 | 36 784 | 38 592 | 1.0 | 2 780 400 | 14 |
| Bolivia / Bolivie | 5 IX 2001 | 8 280 184 | 4 130 342 | 4 149 842 | 8 428 | 9 427 | 2.2 | 1 098 581 | 9 |
| Brazil[26] / Brésil[26] | 1 VIII 2000 | 169 799 170[1] | 83 576 015[1] | 86 223 155[1] | 171 280 | 184 184 | 1.5 | 8 514 877 | 22 |
| Chile / Chili | 24 IV 2002 | 15 116 435 | 7 447 695 | 7 668 740 | 15 398 | 16 267 | 1.1 | 756 102 | 22 |
| Colombia / Colombie | 22 V 2005 | 41 468 384 | 20 336 117 | 21 132 267 | 42 299 | 46 045 | 1.7 | 1 138 914 | 40 |
| Ecuador[27] / Equateur[27] | 25 XI 2001 | 12 156 608 | 6 018 353 | 6 138 255 | 12 299 | 13 215 | 1.4 | 283 561 | 47 |
| Falkland Is. (Malvinas)[28,29] / Iles Falkland (Malvinas)[28,29] | 8 X 2006 | 2 955 | 1 569 | 1 386 | ... | ... | ... | 12 173 | ... |
| French Guiana[1] / Guyane française[1] | 8 III 1999 | 156 790 | 78 963 | 77 827 | 164 | *200 | 4.0 | 90 000 | 2 |
| Guyana / Guyana | 15 IX 2002 | 751 223 | 376 034 | 375 189 | 742 | 758 | 0.4 | 214 969 | 4 |
| Paraguay / Paraguay | 28 VIII 2002 | 5 163 198 | 2 603 242 | 2 559 956 | 5 346 | 5 899 | 2.0 | 406 752 | 15 |
| Peru[12,30,31] / Pérou[12,30,31] | 18 VII 2005 | *26 152 265 | *13 061 026 | *13 091 239 | 25 939 | 27 947 | 1.5 | 1 285 216 | 22 |
| Suriname[32,33] / Suriname[32,33] | 2 VIII 2004 | 492 829 | 247 846 | 244 618 | 464[1] | 499[1] | 1.5 | 163 820 | 3 |

| Country or area[+] / Pays ou zone[+] | Latest census / Dernier recensement | | | | Mid-year estimates (thousands) / Estimations au milieu de l'année (milliers) | | Annual rate of increase / Taux d'accroisse-ment annuel % | Surface area / Superficie (km²) | Density / Densité |
|---|---|---|---|---|---|---|---|---|---|
| | Date | Both sexes / Les deux sexes | Men / Hommes | Women / Femmes | 2000 | 2005 | 2000 - 2005 | 2005 | 2005[6] |
| Uruguay[12,34] Uruguay[12,34] | 1 VI 2004 | 3 241 003 | 1 565 533 | 1 675 470 | 3 301 | 3 306 | 0.0 | 176 215 | 19 |
| Venezuela (Bolivarian Rep. of)[30] Venezuela (Rép. bolivar. du)[30] | 30 X 2001 | 23 054 210 | 11 402 869 | 11 651 341 | 24 311 | 26 577 | 1.8 | 912 050 | 29 |
| **Asia** **Asie** | | | | | | | | | |
| Afghanistan[35] Afghanistan[35] | 23 VI 1979 | 13 051 358 | 6 712 377 | 6 338 981 | 21 770 | ... | ... | 652 090 | ... |
| Armenia[36] Arménie[36] | 10 X 2001 | 3 002 594 | 1 407 220 | 1 595 374 | 3 221[1] | 3 218[1] | 0.0 | 29 800 | 108 |
| Azerbaijan Azerbaïdjan | 27 I 1999 | 7 953 438[1] | 3 883 155[1] | 4 070 283[1] | 8 049 | *8 392 | 0.8 | 86 600 | 97 |
| Bahrain Bahreïn | 7 IV 2001 | 650 604 | 373 649 | 276 955 | 638 | 725 | 2.6 | 694 | 1 044 |
| Bangladesh[37] Bangladesh[37] | 22 I 2001 | 130 522 598 | 67 731 320 | 62 791 278 | 129 300 | 138 600 | 1.4 | 143 998 | 963 |
| Bhutan Bhoutan | 30 V 2005 | 634 982 | 333 595 | 301 387 | 678 | ... | ... | 47 000 | ... |
| Brunei Darussalam Brunéi Darussalam | 21 VIII 2001 | *332 844 | *168 974 | *163 870 | 325 | 370 | 2.6 | 5 765 | 64 |
| Cambodia[38] Cambodge[38] | 3 III 1998 | 11 437 656 | 5 511 408 | 5 926 248 | 12 688 | *13 661 | 1.5 | 181 035 | 75 |
| China[39,40,41] Chine[39,40,41] | 1 XI 2000 | 1 242 612 226[1] | 640 275 969[1] | 602 336 257[1] | 1 262 645 | 1 303 720 | 0.6 | 9 596 961 | 136 |
| China, Hong Kong SAR[1] Chine, Hong Kong RAS[1] | 14 VII 2006 | 6 864 346 | 3 272 956 | 3 591 390 | 6 665 | 6 813 | 0.4 | 1 104 | 6 171 |
| China, Macao SAR[1,42] Chine, Macao RAS[1,42] | 19 VIII 2006 | 502 113 | 245 167 | 256 946 | 431 | 473 | 1.9 | 29 | 16 326 |
| Cyprus[1,43,44] Chypre[1,43,44] | 1 X 2001 | 689 565 | 338 497 | 351 068 | 694 | 758 | 1.8 | 9 251 | 82 |
| Georgia Géorgie | 17 I 2002 | 4 371 535[1] | 2 061 753[1] | 2 309 782[1] | 4 418 | 4 361 | -0.3 | 69 700 | 63 |
| India[45,46] Inde[45,46] | 1 III 2001 | 1 028 610 328 | 532 156 772 | 496 453 556 | 1 016 320 | *1 101 000 | 1.6 | 3 287 263 | 335 |
| Indonesia[47] Indonésie[47] | 30 VI 2000 | 206 264 595 | 103 417 180 | 102 847 415 | ... | *219 898[1] | ... | 1 904 569 | 115 |
| Iran (Islamic Rep. of)[1,43] Iran (Rép. islamique d')[1,48] | 23 X 1996 | 60 055 488 | 30 515 159 | 29 540 329 | 63 664 | 68 467 | 1.5 | 1 648 195 | 42 |
| Iraq[49] Iraq[49] | 16 X 1997 | 19 184 543 | 9 536 570 | 9 647 973 | 24 086 | 27 963 | 3.0 | 438 317 | 64 |
| Israel[1,50] Israël[1,50] | 4 XI 1995 | 5 548 523 | 2 738 175 | 2 810 348 | 6 289 | 6 930 | 1.9 | 22 072 | 314 |
| Japan[51] Japon[51] | 1 X 2005 | *127 756 815 | *62 340 864 | *65 415 951 | 126 843 | 127 773 | 0.1 | 377 873 | 338 |
| Jordan[52] Jordanie[52] | 1 X 2004 | 5 103 639 | 2 626 287 | 2 477 352 | 4 857 | *5 473 | 2.4 | 89 342 | 61 |
| Kazakhstan Kazakhstan | 26 II 1999 | 14 953 126[1] | 7 201 785[1] | 7 751 341[1] | 14 884 | 15 147 | 0.4 | 2 724 900 | 6 |
| Korea, Dem. P. R. Corée, R. p. dém. de | 31 XII 1993 | 21 213 378 | 10 329 699 | 10 883 679 | 22 963 | ... | ... | 120 538 | ... |
| Korea, Republic of[53,54] Corée, République de[53,54] | 1 XI 2000 | 46 136 101 | 23 158 582 | 22 977 519 | 47 008 | 48 294 | 0.5 | 99 538 | 485 |
| Kuwait Koweït | 20 IV 2005 | *2 213 403 | *1 310 067 | *903 336 | 2 138 | 2 457 | 2.8 | 17 818 | 138 |
| Kyrgyzstan Kirghizistan | 24 III 1999 | 4 822 938[1] | 2 380 465[1] | 2 442 473[1] | 4 915 | 5 144 | 0.9 | 199 951 | 26 |

| Country or area[+]<br>Pays ou zone[+] | Latest census<br>Dernier recensement | | | | Mid-year estimates<br>(thousands)<br>Estimations au milieu<br>de l'année (milliers) | | Annual rate<br>of increase<br>Taux d'accroisse-<br>ment annuel % | Surface area<br>Superficie<br>(km²) | Density<br>Densité |
|---|---|---|---|---|---|---|---|---|---|
| | Date | Both sexes<br>Les deux sexes | Men<br>Hommes | Women<br>Femmes | 2000 | 2005 | 2000 - 2005 | 2005 | 2005[&] |
| Lao People's Dem. Rep.[55]<br>Rép. dém. pop. lao[55] | 1 III 2005 | 5 621 982[1] | 2 800 551[1] | 2 821 431[1] | 5 218 | 5 679 | 1.7 | 236 800 | 24 |
| Lebanon[56,57]<br>Liban[56,57] | 15 X 1970 | 2 126 325 | 1 080 015 | 1 046 310 | ... | ... | ... | 10 400 | ... |
| Malaysia[58,59]<br>Malaisie[58,59] | 5 VII 2000 | 23 274 690[1] | 11 853 432[1] | 11 421 258[1] | 23 495 | 26 128 | 2.1 | 329 847 | 79 |
| Maldives<br>Maldives | 21 III 2006 | 298 968 | 151 459 | 147 509 | 271 | 294 | 1.6 | 298 | 986 |
| Mongolia<br>Mongolie | 5 I 2000 | 2 373 493 | 1 177 981 | 1 195 512 | 2 390 | 2 548 | 1.3 | 1 564 100 | 2 |
| Myanmar<br>Myanmar | 31 III 1983 | 35 307 913 | 17 518 255 | 17 789 658 | ... | ... | ... | 676 578 | ... |
| Nepal[1,60]<br>Népal[1,60] | 22 VI 2001 | 23 151 423 | 11 563 921 | 11 587 502 | *22 904 | 25 343 | 2.0 | 147 181 | 172 |
| Occupied Palestinian Terr.[61]<br>Terr. palestinien occupé[61] | 9 XII 1997 | 2 601 669 | 1 322 264 | 1 279 405 | 3 149 | 3 762 | 3.6 | 6 020 | 625 |
| Oman<br>Oman | 7 XII 2003 | 2 340 815 | 1 313 239 | 1 027 576 | 2 401 | 2 509 | 0.9 | 309 500 | 8 |
| Pakistan[62]<br>Pakistan[62] | 2 III 1998 | 130 579 571 | 67 840 137 | 62 739 434 | 138 945 | 153 455 | 2.0 | 796 095 | 193 |
| Philippines[1]<br>Philippines[1] | 1 V 2000 | 76 504 077 | 38 524 267 | 37 979 810 | 76 348 | *85 237 | 2.2 | 300 000 | 284 |
| Qatar<br>Qatar | 16 III 2004 | 744 029 | 496 382 | 247 647 | 617 | 796 | 5.1 | 11 493 | 69 |
| Saudi Arabia<br>Arabie saoudite | 15 IX 2004 | 22 678 262 | 12 557 240 | 10 121 022 | 20 476 | 23 119 | 2.4 | 2 149 690 | 11 |
| Singapore[63]<br>Singapour[63] | 1 VII 2000 | 4 017 700 | 2 061 800 | 1 955 900 | 4 028 | 4 342 | 1.5 | 699 | 6 208 |
| Sri Lanka[64]<br>Sri Lanka[64] | 17 VII 2001 | *16 864 544 | *8 343 964 | *8 520 580 | 19 359 | *19 668 | 0.3 | 65 610 | 300 |
| Syrian Arab Republic[65]<br>Rép. arabe syrienne[65] | 3 IX 1994 | 13 782 315 | 7 048 906 | 6 733 409 | 16 320 | 18 138 | 2.1 | 185 180 | 98 |
| Tajikistan<br>Tadjikistan | 20 I 2000 | *6 127 000 | *3 082 000 | *3 045 000 | 6 188 | 6 850 | 2.0 | 143 100 | 48 |
| Thailand[1]<br>Thaïlande[1] | 1 IV 2000 | 60 617 200 | 29 850 100 | 30 767 100 | 61 770 | 64 839 | 1.0 | 513 120 | 126 |
| Timor-Leste<br>Timor-Leste | 11 VII 2004 | *924 642 | *467 757 | *456 885 | ... | ... | ... | 14 874 | ... |
| Turkey<br>Turquie | 22 X 2000 | 67 803 927 | 34 346 735 | 33 457 192 | 67 420 | 72 065 | 1.3 | 783 562 | 92 |
| Turkmenistan<br>Turkménistan | 10 I 1995 | 4 483 251 | 2 225 331 | 2 257 920 | ... | ... | ... | 488 100 | ... |
| United Arab Emirates[66]<br>Emirats arabes unis[66] | 17 XII 1995 | 2 411 041 | 1 606 804 | 804 237 | ... | ... | ... | 83 600 | ... |
| Uzbekistan<br>Ouzbékistan | 12 I 1989 | 19 810 077[1] | 9 784 156[1] | 10 025 921[1] | 24 650 | ... | ... | 447 400 | ... |
| Viet Nam<br>Viet Nam | 1 IV 1999 | 76 323 173 | 37 469 117 | 38 854 056 | 77 635 | 83 106 | 1.4 | 331 689 | 251 |
| Yemen<br>Yémen | 16 XII 2004 | 19 685 161 | 10 036 953 | 9 648 208 | 18 261 | ... | ... | 527 968 | ... |
| **Europe**<br>**Europe** | | | | | | | | | |
| Albania<br>Albanie | 1 IV 2001 | 3 069 300 | 1 530 500 | 1 538 800 | 3 061 | 3 142 | 0.5 | 28 748 | 109 |
| Andorra[18]<br>Andorre[18] | 1 VII 2000 | 66 089 | 34 344 | 31 745 | 66[1] | 79[1] | 3.5 | 468 | 168 |

| Country or area[+] <br> Pays ou zone[+] | Date | Latest census <br> Dernier recensement | | | Mid-year estimates (thousands) <br> Estimations au milieu de l'année (milliers) | | Annual rate of increase <br> Taux d'accroisse-ment annuel % | Surface area <br> Superficie (km²) | Density <br> Densité |
| | | Both sexes <br> Les deux sexes | Men <br> Hommes | Women <br> Femmes | 2000 | 2005 | 2000 - 2005 | 2005 | 2005[&] |
|---|---|---|---|---|---|---|---|---|---|
| Austria[1] <br> Autriche[1] | 15 V 2001 | 8 032 926 | 3 889 189 | 4 143 737 | 8 012 | 8 233 | 0.5 | 83 858 | 98 |
| Belarus <br> Bélarus | 16 II 1999 | 10 045 237[1] | 4 717 621[1] | 5 327 616[1] | 10 005 | 9 775 | -0.5 | 207 600 | 47 |
| Belgium[1] <br> Belgique[1] | 1 X 2001 | 10 296 350 | 5 035 446 | 5 260 904 | 10 251 | 10 479 | 0.4 | 30 528 | 343 |
| Bosnia and Herzegovina <br> Bosnie-Herzégovine | 31 III 1991 | 4 377 033[1] | 2 183 795[1] | 2 193 238[1] | 3 781 | 3 843 | 0.3 | 51 197 | 75 |
| Bulgaria <br> Bulgarie | 1 III 2001 | 7 928 901 | 3 862 465 | 4 066 436 | 8 170 | 7 740 | -1.1 | 110 912 | 70 |
| Channel Is.: Guernsey <br> Iles Anglo-Norm.: Guernesey | 29 IV 2001 | 59 807[1] | 29 138[1] | 30 669[1] | 60 | ... | ... | 78 | ... |
| Channel Is.: Jersey <br> Iles Anglo-Norm.: Jersey | 11 III 2001 | 87 186[1] | 42 485[1] | 44 701[1] | ... | 88 | ... | 116 | 756 |
| Croatia[1] <br> Croatie[1] | 31 III 2001 | 4 437 460 | 2 135 900 | 2 301 560 | 4 381 | 4 442 | 0.3 | 56 538 | 79 |
| Czech Republic[1] <br> République tchèque[1] | 1 III 2001 | 10 230 060 | 4 982 071 | 5 247 989 | 10 273 | 10 234 | -0.1 | 78 866 | 130 |
| Denmark[1,18,67] <br> Danemark[1,18,67] | 1 I 2001 | 5 349 212 | 2 644 319 | 2 704 893 | 5 337 | 5 416 | 0.3 | 43 094 | 126 |
| Estonia <br> Estonie | 31 III 2000 | 1 370 052[1] | 631 851[1] | 738 201[1] | 1 370 | 1 346 | -0.3 | 45 228 | 30 |
| Faeroe Islands[1,18] <br> Iles Féroé[1,18] | 1 VII 2002 | 47 350 | ... | ... | 46 | 48 | 1.1 | 1 393 | 35 |
| Finland[1,18] <br> Finlande[1,18] | 31 XII 2000 | 5 181 115 | 2 529 341 | 2 651 774 | 5 176 | 5 246 | 0.3 | 338 145 | 16 |
| France[1,68,69] <br> France[1,68,69] | 8 III 1999 | 58 520 688 | 28 419 419 | 30 101 269 | 59 049 | *60 996 | 0.6 | 551 500 | 111 |
| Germany[70,71,72] <br> Allemagne[70,71,72] | 28 III 2004 | 82 491 000[73] | 40 330 000[73] | 42 161 000[73] | 82 188[1] | 82 464[1] | 0.1 | 357 022 | 231 |
| Gibraltar[74] <br> Gibraltar[74] | 12 XI 2001 | 27 495 | 13 644 | 13 851 | 27 | 29 | 1.2 | 6 | 4 804 |
| Greece[75,76] <br> Grèce[75,76] | 18 III 2001 | 10 964 020 | 5 431 816 | 5 532 204 | 10 917 | 11 104 | 0.3 | 131 957 | 84 |
| Holy See *[18,77] <br> Saint-Siège *[18,77] | 1 VII 2000 | 798 | 529 | 269 | ... | ... | ... | ... | ... |
| Hungary <br> Hongrie | 1 II 2001 | 10 198 315 | 4 850 650 | 5 347 665 | 10 024 | 10 087 | 0.1 | 93 032 | 108 |
| Iceland[1,18] <br> Islande[1,18] | 1 VII 2000 | 281 154 | 140 718 | 140 436 | 281 | 296 | 1.0 | 103 000 | 3 |
| Ireland[78] <br> Irlande[78] | 28 IV 2002 | 3 917 203 | 1 946 164 | 1 971 039 | 3 790 | 4 131 | 1.7 | 70 273 | 59 |
| Isle of Man[1] <br> Ile de Man[1] | 23 IV 2006 | 80 058 | 39 523 | 40 535 | 75 | 78 | 0.8 | 572 | 136 |
| Italy <br> Italie | 21 X 2001 | 57 110 144 | 27 617 335 | 29 492 809 | 56 942[1] | 58 607[1] | 0.6 | 301 318 | 195 |
| Latvia[1] <br> Lettonie[1] | 31 III 2000 | 2 377 383 | 1 094 964 | 1 282 419 | 2 373 | 2 301 | -0.6 | 64 600 | 36 |
| Liechtenstein <br> Liechtenstein | 5 XII 2000 | 33 307 | 16 420 | 16 887 | 33 | 35 | 1.2 | 160 | 217 |
| Lithuania[1] <br> Lituanie[1] | 6 IV 2001 | 3 483 972 | 1 629 148 | 1 854 824 | 3 500 | 3 414 | -0.5 | 65 300 | 52 |
| Luxembourg[1] <br> Luxembourg[1] | 15 II 2001 | 439 539 | 216 541 | 222 998 | 436 | 457 | 0.9 | 2 586 | 177 |
| Malta[1,79] <br> Malte[1,79] | 26 XI 1995 | 378 132 | 186 836 | 191 296 | 383 | 404 | 1.1 | 316 | 1 277 |

| Country or area[+]<br>Pays ou zone[+] | Date | Latest census<br>Dernier recensement<br>Both sexes<br>Les deux sexes | Men<br>Hommes | Women<br>Femmes | Mid-year estimates (thousands)<br>Estimations au milieu de l'année (milliers)<br>2000 | 2005 | Annual rate of increase<br>Taux d'accroissement annuel %<br>2000 - 2005 | Surface area<br>Superficie (km²)<br>2005 | Density<br>Densité<br>2005[&] |
|---|---|---|---|---|---|---|---|---|---|
| Moldova[80]<br>Moldova[80] | 5 X 2004 | *3 388 071 | *1 632 519 | *1 755 549 | 3 639[1] | 3 595[1] | -0.2 | 33 851 | 106 |
| Monaco[1]<br>Monaco[1] | 21 VI 2000 | 32 020 | 15 544 | 16 476 | ... | ... | ... | 2 | ... |
| Netherlands[1,81]<br>Pays-Bas[1,81] | 1 I 2002 | 16 105 285 | 7 971 967 | 8 133 318 | 15 926 | 16 320 | 0.5 | 41 528 | 393 |
| Norway[1,18,82,83]<br>Norvège[1,18,82,83] | 3 XI 2001 | 4 520 947 | 2 240 281 | 2 280 666 | 4 491 | 4 623 | 0.6 | 323 802 | 14 |
| Poland[84,85,86]<br>Pologne[84,85,86] | 20 V 2002 | 38 230 080 | 18 516 403 | 19 713 677 | 38 256 | 38 161 | 0.0 | 312 685 | 122 |
| Portugal[87]<br>Portugal[87] | 12 III 2001 | *10 148 259 | *4 862 699 | *5 285 560 | 10 226[1] | 10 549[1] | 0.6 | 92 090 | 115 |
| Romania[1]<br>Roumanie[1] | 18 III 2002 | 21 680 974 | 10 568 741 | 11 112 233 | 22 435 | 21 624 | -0.7 | 238 391 | 91 |
| Russian Federation[1,88]<br>Fédération de Russie[1,88] | 9 X 2002 | 145 166 731 | 67 605 133 | 77 561 598 | 146 597 | *143 150 | -0.5 | 17 098 242 | 8 |
| San Marino[18]<br>Saint-Marin[18] | 1 VII 2000 | 26 941 | 13 185 | 13 756 | 27 | 31 | 2.7 | 61 | 506 |
| Serbia and Montenegro[1,89]<br>Serbie-et-Monténégro[1,89] | 31 III 1991 | 10 394 026 | 5 157 120 | 5 236 906 | 10 634 | ... | ... | 102 173 | ... |
| Slovakia[1]<br>Slovaquie[1] | 25 V 2001 | 5 379 455 | 2 612 515 | 2 766 940 | 5 401 | 5 387 | 0.0 | 49 033 | 110 |
| Slovenia[1]<br>Slovénie[1] | 31 III 2002 | *1 964 036 | *958 576 | *1 005 460 | 1 990 | 2 001 | 0.1 | 20 256 | 99 |
| Spain[90]<br>Espagne[90] | 1 XI 2001 | 40 847 371 | 20 012 882 | 20 834 489 | 40 264[1] | 43 398[1] | 1.5 | 505 992 | 86 |
| Svalbard and Jan Mayen Is.[91]<br>Svalbard et îles Jan Mayen[91] | 1 XI 1960 | 3 431 | 2 545 | 886 | ... | ... | ... | 62 422 | ... |
| Sweden[1,18]<br>Suède[1,18] | 1 VII 2000 | 8 872 110 | 4 386 436 | 4 485 674 | 8 872 | 9 030 | 0.4 | 449 964 | 20 |
| Switzerland[1,92]<br>Suisse[1,92] | 5 XII 2000 | 7 204 055 | 3 519 698 | 3 684 357 | 7 204 | 7 459 | 0.7 | 41 277 | 181 |
| TFYR of Macedonia<br>L'ex-R.y. Macédoine | 1 XI 2002 | 2 022 547[1] | 1 015 377[1] | 1 007 170[1] | 2 024 | 2 037 | 0.1 | 25 713 | 79 |
| Ukraine<br>Ukraine | 5 XII 2001 | 48 240 902 | 22 316 317 | 25 924 585 | 49 176[1] | *47 075[1] | -0.9 | 603 700 | 78 |
| United Kingdom[93,94]<br>Royaume-Uni[93,94] | 29 IV 2001 | 58 789 187 | 28 579 867 | 30 209 320 | 58 886 | 60 209 | 0.4 | 242 900 | 248 |
| **Oceania**<br>**Océanie** | | | | | | | | | |
| American Samoa[1,22]<br>Samoa américaines[1,22] | 1 IV 2000 | 57 291 | 29 264 | 28 027 | 58 | 66 | 2.5 | 199 | 329 |
| Australia[12,95]<br>Australie[12,95] | 7 VIII 2001 | 18 769 249 | 9 270 466 | 9 498 783 | 19 153[1] | 20 409[1] | 1.3 | 7 692 024 | 3 |
| Cook Islands[96]<br>Iles Cook[96] | 1 XII 2001 | 18 027 | 9 303 | 8 724 | 18 | 20 | 2.3 | 236 | 86 |
| Fiji<br>Fidji | 25 VIII 1996 | 775 077 | 393 931 | 381 146 | 808 | *842 | 0.8 | 18 274 | 46 |
| French Polynesia[97]<br>Polynésie française[97] | 7 XI 2002 | 245 516 | ... | ... | 235 | 255 | 1.6 | 4 000 | 64 |
| Guam[1,22]<br>Guam[1,22] | 1 IV 2000 | 154 805 | 79 181 | 75 624 | ... | *169 | ... | 549 | 307 |
| Kiribati[98]<br>Kiribati[98] | 7 XII 2005 | *92 533 | *45 612 | *46 921 | ... | ... | ... | 726 | ... |
| Marshall Islands<br>Iles Marshall | 1 VI 1999 | 50 848 | 26 034 | 24 814 | 53 | ... | ... | 181 | ... |

## 8 Population by sex, rate of population increase, surface area and density (*continued*)
## 8 Population selon le sexe, taux d'accroissement de la population, superficie et densité (*suite*)

| Country or area[+]<br>Pays ou zone[+] ˑ | Date | Latest census<br>Dernier recensement | | | Mid-year estimates (thousands)<br>Estimations au milieu de l'année (milliers) | | Annual rate of increase<br>Taux d'accroisse-ment annuel % | Surface area<br>Superficie (km²) | Density<br>Densité |
|---|---|---|---|---|---|---|---|---|---|
| | | Both sexes<br>Les deux sexes | Men<br>Hommes | Women<br>Femmes | 2000 | 2005 | 2000 - 2005 | 2005 | 2005[&] |
| Micronesia (Fed. States of)[1]<br>Micronésie (Etats féd. de)[1] | 1 IV 2000 | 107 008 | 54 191 | 52 817 | 119 | ... | ... | 702 | ... |
| Nauru<br>Nauru | 17 IV 1992 | 9 919 | 5 079 | 4 840 | 12 | ... | ... | 21 | ... |
| New Caledonia[99]<br>Nouvelle-Calédonie[99] | 31 VIII 2004 | *230 789 | *116 485 | *114 304 | 213 | ... | ... | 18 575 | ... |
| New Zealand[1,100]<br>Nouvelle-Zélande[1,100] | 6 III 2001 | 3 820 749 | 1 863 309 | 1 957 440 | 3 858 | 4 099 | 1.2 | 270 534 | 15 |
| Niue<br>Nioué | 7 IX 2001 | 1 788 | 897 | 891 | ... | ... | ... | 260 | ... |
| Norfolk Island<br>Ile Norfolk | 8 VIII 2006 | 2 523 | 1 218 | 1 305 | ... | ... | ... | 36 | ... |
| Northern Mariana Islands<br>Iles Mariannes du Nord | 1 IV 2000 | 69 221 | 31 984 | 37 237 | 72 | ... | ... | 464 | ... |
| Palau<br>Palaos | 1 IV 2005 | 19 907 | 10 699 | 9 208 | 19 | ... | ... | 459 | ... |
| Papua New Guinea[101]<br>Papouasie-Nvl-Guinée[101] | 9 VII 2000 | 5 190 786 | 2 691 744 | 2 499 042 | 5 100 | ... | ... | 462 840 | ... |
| Pitcairn<br>Pitcairn | 31 XII 1991 | 66 | ... | ... | ... | ... | ... | 5 | ... |
| Samoa<br>Samoa | 5 XI 2001 | 176 710 | 92 050 | 84 660 | 171 | 183 | 1.4 | 2 831 | 65 |
| Solomon Islands[102]<br>Iles Salomon[102] | 21 XI 1999 | 409 042 | 211 381 | 197 661 | 415 | 471 | 2.5 | 28 896 | 16 |
| Tokelau<br>Tokélaou | 11 X 2001 | 1 537 | 761 | 776 | ... | ... | ... | 12 | ... |
| Tonga[103]<br>Tonga[103] | 30 XI 2006 | *101 134 | *51 197 | *49 937 | 100 | ... | ... | 747 | ... |
| Tuvalu<br>Tuvalu | 1 XI 2002 | 9 561 | 4 729 | 4 832 | 9 | ... | ... | 26 | ... |
| Vanuatu[1]<br>Vanuatu[1] | 16 XI 1999 | 186 678 | 95 682 | 90 996 | ... | ... | ... | 12 189 | ... |
| Wallis and Futuna Islands<br>Iles Wallis et Futuna | 22 VII 2003 | 14 944 | 7 494 | 7 450 | ... | ... | ... | 142 | ... |

Source

United Nations Statistics Division, New York, "Demographic Yearbook 2005".

Notes

[+]  Unless otherwise indicated, figures refer to de facto (present-in-area) population for the present territory.

[&]  Population per square kilometre of surface area in 2005. Figures are merely the quotients of population divided by surface area and are not to be considered either as reflecting density in the urban sense or as indicating the supporting power of a territory's land and resources.

1  De jure population.
2  Including the enclave of Cabinda.
3  Census result, including emigrants.
4  Data for estimates refer to national projections.
5  Census results have been adjusted for under-enumeration, estimated at 1.4 per cent.

Source

Organisation des Nations Unies, Division de statistique, New York, "Annuaire démographique 2005".

Notes

[+]  Sauf indication contraire, les chiffres se rapportent à la population effectivement présente sur le territoire (population de fait), tel qu'il est actuellement défini.

[&]  Nombre d'habitants au kilomètre carré en 2005. Il s'agit simplement du quotient du chiffre de la population divisé par celui de la superficie: il ne faut pas y voir d'indication de la densité au sens urbain du terme ni de l'effectif de population que les terres et les ressources du territoire sont capables de nourrir.

1  Population de droit.
2  Y compris l'enclave de Cabinda.
3  Les résultat du recensement, y compris les émigrants.
4  Les données se réfèrent aux projections nationales.
5  Les résultats du recensement ont été ajustées pour compenser les lacunes du dénombrement, estimées à 1,4 p. 100.

6 Census results, excluding Mayotte.

7 Census result, exclude border population.

8 Comprising Bioko (which includes Pagalu) and Rio Muni (which includes Corisco and Elobeys).

9 Census data excluding the institutional population.

10 For Libyan nationals only.

11 Census results have been adjusted for under-enumeration, estimated at 5.1 per cent.

12 Mid-year estimates have been adjusted for under-enumeration, at latest census.

13 The number of males and / or females excludes persons whose sex is not stated (18 urban, 19 rural).

14 Data exclude adjustment for under-enumeration, estimated at 2.4 per cent.

15 Comprising the Northern Region (former Saguia el Hamra) and Southern Region (former Rio de Oro).

16 Excluding the institutional population.

17 For 2000, final intercensal estimates. For 2005, updated postcensal estimates.

18 Population statistics are compiled from registers.

19 Including Carriacou and other dependencies in the Grenadines.

20 Including dependencies: Marie-Galante, la Désirade, les Saintes, Petite-Terre, St. Barthélemy and French part of St. Martin.

21 Comprising Bonaire, Curaçao, Saba, St. Eustatius and Dutch part of St. Martin.

22 Including armed forces stationed in the area.

23 Including Bequia and other islands in the Grenadines.

24 Census data exclude adjustment for under-enumeration. Excluding persons residing in institutions.

25 Excluding armed forces overseas and civilian citizens absent from country for an extended period of time.

26 Data include persons in remote areas, military personnel outside the country, merchant seamen at sea, civilian seasonal workers outside the country, and other civilians outside the country, and exclude nomads, foreign military, civilian aliens temporarily in the country, transients on ships and Indian jungle population.

27 Excluding nomadic Indian tribes.

28 A dispute exists between the governments of Argentina and the United Kingdom of Great Britain and Northern Ireland concerning sovereignty over the Falkland Islands (Malvinas).

29 Excluding dependencies, of which South Georgia (area 3 755 km2) had an estimated population of 499 in 1964 (494 males, 5 females). The other dependencies namely, the South Sandwich group (surface area 337 km2) and a number of smaller islands, are presumed to be uninhabited.

30 Excluding Indian jungle population.

31 The population for the year 2005 corresponds to the population enumerated in the census conducted between 18 July and 20 August 2005. The total population is 27 219 264 inhabitants.

32 The previous census was conducted only 16 months earlier (on 31 Mar 2003) but it was repeated because all of its data were destroyed in a fire before they could be fully processed, analyzed, and reported.

33 Figures for male and female population do not add up to the figure for total population, because they exclude 365 persons of unknown sex.

6 Les résultats du recensement, non compris Mayotte.

7 Les résultat du recensement, à l'exception de la population frontalière.

8 Comprend Bioko (qui comprend Pagalu) et Rio Muni (qui comprend Corisco et Elobeys).

9 Les données de recensement non compris la population dans les institutions.

10 Pour les nationaux libyens seulement.

11 Les résultats du recensement ont été ajustées pour compenser les lacunes du dénombrement, estimées à 5,1 p. 100.

12 Les estimations au milieu de l'année tiennent compte d'une ajustement destiné à compenser les lacunes du dénombrement lors du dernier recensement.

13 Il n'est pas tenu compte dans le nombre d'hommes et de femmes des personnes dont le sexe n'est pas indiqué (18 en zone urbaine et 19 en zone rurale).

14 Les données n'ont pas été ajustées pour compenser les lacunes du dénombrement, estimées à 2,4 p. 100.

15 Comprend la région septentrionale (ancien Saguia-el-Hamra) et la région méridionale (ancien Rio de Oro).

16 Non compris la population dans les institutions.

17 Pour 2000, estimations inter censitaires finales. Pour 2005, estimations post censitaires mises à jour.

18 Les statistiques de la population sont compilées à partir des registres.

19 Y compris Carriacou et les autres dépendances du groupe des îles Grenadines.

20 Y compris les dépendances: Marie-Galante, la Désirade, les Saintes, Petite-Terre, Saint-Barthélemy et la partie française de Saint-Martin.

21 Comprend Bonaire, Curaçao, Saba, Saint-Eustache et la partie néederlandaise de Saint-Martin.

22 Y compris les militaires en garnison sur le territoire.

23 Y compris Bequia et des autres îles dans les Grenadines.

24 Les données de recensement n'ont pas été ajustées pour compenser les lacunes du dénombrement. Non compris les personnes dans les institutions.

25 Non compris les militaires à l'étranger, et les civils hors du pays pendant une période prolongée.

26 Y compris les personnes dans des régions éloignées, le personnel militaire en dehors du pays, les marins marchands, les ouvriers saisonniers civils de couture en dehors du pays, et autres civils en dehors du pays, et non compris les nomades, les militaires étrangers, les étrangers civils temporairement dans le pays, les transiteurs sur des bateaux et les Indiens de la jungle.

27 Non compris les tribus d'Indiens nomades.

28 La sourveraineté sur les îles Falkland (Malvinas) fait l'objet d'un différend entre le Gouvernement argentin et le Gouvernement du Royaume-Uni de Grande-Bretagne et d'Irlande du Nord.

29 Non compris les dépendances, parmi lesquelles figure la Georgie du Sud (3 755 km2) avec une population estimée à 499 personnes en 1964 (494 du sexe masculin et 5 du sexe féminin). Les autres dépendances, c'est-à-dire le groupe des Sandwich de Sud (superficie: 337 km2) et certaines petites-îles, sont présumées inhabitées.

30 Non compris les Indiens de la jungle.

31 La population pour 2005 correspond à la population dénombrée lors du recensement réalisé entre le 18 juillet et le 20 août 2005. La population totale compte 27 219 264 habitants.

32 Le recensement précédent a eu lieu seulement 16 mois auparavant (le 31 mars 2003), mais a dû être refait parce que toutes les données ont été détruites dans un incendie avant que l'on n'ait pu les traiter et les analyser.

33 Les chiffres relatifs à la population masculine et féminine ne correspondent pas au chiffre de la population totale, parce que l'on en a exclu 365 personnes de sexe inconnu.

**Population by sex, rate of population increase, surface area and density** (*continued*)

**Population selon le sexe, taux d'accroissement de la population, superficie et densité** (*suite*)

34  Data refer to resident population in Uruguay according to Census Phase 1, carried out between the months of June and July 2004.

35  Census results, excluding nomad population.

36  The methodology used for calculating the number of the de facto and de jure population in the 2001 census data differs as follows from the methodology used in previous censuses: the duration that defines a person as being ' temporary present ' or ' temporary absent ' is now ' under one year '. The previously applied definition was for 6 months.

37  Census results have been adjusted for under-enumeration, estimated at 4.96 per cent.

38  Excluding foreign diplomatic personnel and their dependants. Data for estimates based on 1998 census result.

39  Estimates for 2000 have been adjusted on the basis of the Population Census of 2000. Data for 2005 are estimated from the National Sample Survey of 1 Per cent population.

40  For statistical purposes, the data for China do not include those for the Hong Kong Special Administrative Region (Hong Kong SAR), Macao Special Administrative Region (Macao SAR) and Taiwan Province of China.

41  For the civilian population of 31 provinces, municipalities and autonomous regions.

42  Data derived from the By-Census 2006 held during 19 to 31 of August 2006.

43  Data include all population irrespective of citizenship, who at the time of the census resided in the country or intended to reside for a period of at least one year. It does not distinguish between those present or absent at the time of census.

44  Data refer to government-controlled areas.

45  Census data exclude Mao-Maram, Paomata and Purul sub-divisions of Senapati district of Manipur. The population of Manipur including the estimated population of the three sub-divisions of Senapati district is 2,291,125 (Males 1,161,173 and females 1,129,952).

46  Including data for the Indian-held part of Jammu and Kashmir, the final status of which has not yet been determined.

47  Census data include an estimated population of 459 557 persons in urban and 1 857 659 persons in rural areas that were not directly enumerated, and a population of 566 403 persons in urban and 1 717 578 persons in rural areas that decline the participation. Also included are 421 399 non permanent residents (the homeless, the crew of ships carrying national flags, boat/floating house people, remote located tribesmen and refugees).

48  Estimates relate to the Iranian Year which begins on 21 March and ends on 20 March of the following year. For 2005, data relate to the population for the Iranian Year 1384 ( 21 March 2005-20 March 2006).

49  For the 1997 population census, data exclude population in three autonomous provinces in the north of the country.

50  Including data for East Jerusalem and Israeli residents in certain other territories under occupation by Israeli military forces since June 1967.

51  Excluding diplomatic personnel outside the country and foreign military and civilian personnel and their dependants stationed in the area.

52  Excluding data for Jordanian territory under occupation since June 1967 by Israeli military forces. Excluding foreigners, including registered Palestinian refugees.

34  Les données se rapportent à la population résidente en Uruguay d'après la phase 1 du recensement, qui a eu lieu entre juin et juillet 2004.

35  Les résultats du recensement, non compris les nomades.

36  La méthode utilisée pour dénombrer la population présente et la population légale dans le contexte du recensement de 2001 diffère de celle qui a été appliquée lors des recensements antérieurs en ce que la durée considérée pour définir la ' présence temporaire ' ou ' l'absence temporaire ' était dorénavant fixée à ' moins d'un an ' alors qu'elle était de 6 mois auparavant.

37  Les données ont été ajustées pour compenser les lacunes du dénombrement, estimées à 4,96 p.100.

38  Non compris le personnel diplomatique étranger et les membres de leur famille les accompagnant. Les estimations se réfèrent aux des résultats 1998 de recensement.

39  Les estimations pour 2000 ont été ajustées à partir des résultats du recensement de la population de 2000. Les données pour 2005 ont été estimées à partir de l'enquête nationale qui a porté sur un échantillon de 1 % de la population.

40  Pour la présentation des statistiques, les données pour la Chine ne comprennent pas la Région Administrative Spéciale de Hong Kong (Hong Kong RAS), la Région Administrative Spéciale de Macao (Macao RAS) et la province de Taiwan.

41  Pour la population civile seulement de 31 provinces, municipalités et régions autonomes.

42  Donnes dérivées du recensement partiel de 2006 organisé entre les 19 et 31 août 2006.

43  Les chiffres comprennent toute la population, quelle que soit la nationalité, qui à l'époque de recensement avait résidé dans le pays, ou avait l'intention de résider, pendant une période d'au moins un an. Il n'y a pas de distinction entre les personnes présentes ou absentes au moment du recensement.

44  Les données se rapportent aux zones contrôlées par le Gouvernement.

45  Les données de recensement non compris les subdivisions Mao-Maram Paomata et Purul du district de Senapati dans l'État du Manipur. Cet État compte 2 291 125 habitants (1 161 173 hommes et 1 129 952 femmes), y compris la population estimative des trois subdivisions du district de Senapati.

46  Y compris les données pour la partie du Jammu et du Cachemire occupée par l'Inde dont le statut définitif n'a pas encore été déterminé.

47  Les données du recensement, y compris l'estimation de 459 557 personnes dans les zones urbaines et de 1 857 659 personnes dans les zones rurales qui n'ont pas été énumérées directement, aussi que 566 403 personnes qui n'ont pas répondu dans les zones urbaines et de 1 717 578 personnes dans les zones rurales. Y compris 421 399 résidants non permanents (les sans abri, l'équipage des bateaux portant le drapeau national, les habitants des embarcations ou des maisons flottantes, les habitants des tribus isolées et les réfugiés).

48  Les estimations concernent l'année iranienne, qui commence le 21 mars et se termine le 20 mars de l'année suivante. Pour 2005, les données concernent la population pour l'année iranienne 1384 (21 mars 2005-20 mars 2006).

49  Pour le recensement de 1997, la population des trois provinces autonomes dans le nord du pays est exclue.

50  Y compris les données pour Jérusalem-Est et les résidents israéliens dans certains autres territoires occupés depuis 1967 par les forces armées israéliennes.

51  Non compris le personnel diplomatique hors du pays ni les militaires et agents civils étrangers en poste sur le territoire et les membres de leur famille les accompagnant.

52  Non compris les données pour le territoire jordanien occupé depuis juin 1967 par les forces armées israéliennes. Non compris les étrangers, mais y compris les réfugiés de Palestine enregistrés.

53 Including diplomats and their families abroad, but excluding foreign diplomats, foreign military personnel, and their families in the country.

54 Excluding foreigners.

55 For 2000, calculated base on Population census 1995 structure and growth rate at year 2000.

56 Sample survey, de facto.

57 Excluding Palestinian refugees in camps.

58 Census results have been adjusted for under-enumeration.

59 Excluding Malaysian citizens and permanent residents who were away or intended to be away from the country for more than six months Excluding Malaysian military, naval and diplomatic personnel and their families outside the country, and tourists, businessman who intended to be in Malaysia for less than six months.

60 Data including estimated population from household listing from Village Development Committees and Wards which could not be enumerated at the time of the census.

61 Total population does not include the Palestinian population living in those parts of Jerusalem governorate which were annexed by Israel in 1967, amounting to 210,209 persons. Likewise, the result does not include the estimates of not enumerated population based on the findings of the post enumeration study, i.e. 83,805 persons.

62 Excluding data for the Pakistan-held part of Jammu and Kashmir, the final status of which has not yet been determined.

63 Census results, excluding transients afloat and non-locally domiciled military and civilian services personnel and their dependants.

64 The Population and Housing Census 2001 did not cover the whole area of the country due to the security problems; the Census was complete in 18 districts only; in three districts it was not possible to conduct it; and in four districts it was partially conducted.

65 Including Palestinian refugees.

66 Comprising 7 sheikdoms of Abu Dhabi, Dubai, Sharjah, Ajaman, Umm al Qaiwain, Ras al Khaimah and Fujairah, and the area lying within the modified Riyadh line as announced in October 1955.

67 Excluding the Faeroe Islands and Greenland.

68 Excluding diplomatic personnel outside the country and including members of alien armed forces not living in military camps and foreign diplomatic personnel not living in embassies or consulates.

69 Excluding Overseas Departments, namely, French Guiana, Guadeloupe, Martinique and Reunion, shown separately.

70 Data of the microcensus - a 1% household sample survey - refer to a single reference week in spring (usually last week in April).

71 Excluding homeless persons.

72 Excluding foreign military personnel and foreign diplomatic and consular personnel and their family members in the country.

73 Sample survey, de jure.

74 Excluding families of military personnel, visitors and transients.

75 Mid-year population excludes armed forces stationed outside the country, but includes alien armed forces stationed in the area.

76 Census data including armed forces stationed outside the country, but excluding alien armed forces stationed in the area.

53 Y compris le personnel diplomatique et les membres de leurs familles à l'étranger, mais sans tenir compte du personnel diplomatique et militaire étranger et des membres de leurs familles.

54 Non compris étrangers.

55 Pour 2000, on a pris pour base la structure issue du recensement de population de 1995 et le taux de croissance de 2000.

56 Enquête par sondage, population de fait.

57 Non compris les réfugiés de Palestine dans les camps.

58 Les résultats du recensement ont été ajustées pour compenser les lacunes du dénombrement.

59 Non compris les citoyens malaisiens et les résidents permanents qui étaient ou qui ont prévu d'être hors du pays pour six mois ou plus. Non compris le personnel militaire Malaisien, le personnel naval ou diplomatique et leurs familles hors du pays, et les touristes et les hommes d'affaires qui avaient l'intention de rester en Malaisie moins de six mois.

60 Les données incluent la population estimée par les listes des ménages des comités de développement des villages et des circonscriptions qui n'ont pas pu être énumérée au moment du recensement.

61 Les données relatives à la population totale ne comprennent pas la population palestinienne -équivalent à 210 209 personnes - habitant dans les territoires du gouvernorat de Jérusalem qui ont été annexés par Israël en 1967 Egalement, les données ne tiennent pas compte des estimations de la population calculée sur la base des résultats de l'enquête postcensitaire, équivalent à 83 805 personnes.

62 Non compris les données pour le Jammu et Cachemire occupée par le Pakistan dont le statut définitif n'a pas encore été déterminé.

63 Les résultats du recensement, non compris les personnes de passage à bord de navires ni les militaires et agents civils non-résidents et les membres de leur famille les accompagnant et visiteurs.

64 Le recensement de la population et de l'habitat en 2001 n' pas couvert la totalité du pays pour des problèmes de sécurité ; le recensement à été complété seulement en 18 districts ; dans 3 districts ça n'a pas été possible de conduire le recensement et dans 4 districts il a été partialement conduit.

65 Y compris les réfugiés de Palestine.

66 Comprend les sept cheikhats de Abou Dhabi, Dabai, Ghârdja, Adjmân, Oumm-al-Quiwaïn, Ras al Khaîma et Foudjaïra, ainsi que la zone délimitée par la ligne de Riad modifiée comme il a été annoncé en octobre 1955.

67 Non compris les îles Féroé et Groenland.

68 Non compris le personnel diplomatique hors du pays et y compris les militaires étrangers ne vivant pas dans des camps militaires et le personnel diplomatique étranger ne vivant pas dans les ambassades ou les consulats.

69 Non compris les départements d'outre-mer, c'est-à-dire la Guyane française, la Guadeloupe, la Martinique et la Réunion, qui font l'objet de rubriques distinctes.

70 Les données du microrecensement (enquête sur les ménages, réalisée sur un échantillon de 1 %) concernent une seule semaine de référence au printemps (habituellement la dernière semaine d'avril).

71 Non compris les personnes sans domicile fixe.

72 Non compris le personnel militaire étranger, le personnel diplomatique et consulaire étranger et les membres de leur famille se trouvant dans le pays.

73 Enquête par sondage, Population de droit.

74 Non compris les familles des militaires, ni les visiteurs et transients.

75 Les estimations au milieu de l'année non compris les militaires en garnison hors du pays, mais y compris les militaires étrangers en garnison sur le territoire.

76 Les données de recensement y compris les militaires hors du pays, mais non compris les militaires étrangers en garnison sur le territoire.

77 Data refer to the Vatican City State.

78 Estimates refer to 15th of April.

79 Including foreigners residing in Malta for 12 months before the census date and excluding foreign diplomatic personnel.

80 Data do not include information for Transnistria and the municipality of Bender.

81 Census results, based on compilation of continuous accounting and sample surveys.

82 Including residents temporarily outside the country.

83 Excluding Svalbard and Jan Mayen Island shown separately.

84 Surface area includes inland waters as well as part of internal waters.

85 Average year data for 2000 contain revised data according to the final results of population census 2002.

86 Excluding civilian aliens within country, but including civilian nationals temporarily outside country.

87 Including the Azores and Madeira Islands.

88 Estimates were updated taking into account the results of the 2002 All-Russian population census.

89 For 2000, estimates of Kosovo and Metohia computed on the basis of natural increases from year 1997.

90 Including the Balearic and Canary Islands, and Alhucemas, Ceuta, Chafarinas, Melilla and Penon de Vélez de la Gomera.

91 Inhabited only during the winter season. Census data are for total population while estimates refer to Norwegian population only. Included also in the de jure population of Norway.

92 Surface area do not include state forests and communanzas (7.15 km2).

93 Excluding Channel Islands and Isle of Man, shown separately.

94 Population estimate for 2000 were revised in light of the local studies.

95 Census result, exclude visitors.

96 Excluding Niue, shown separately, which is part of Cook Islands, but because of remoteness is administered separately.

97 Comprising Austral, Gambier, Marquesas, Rapa, Society and Tuamotu Islands.

98 Including Christmas, Fanning, Ocean and Washington Islands.

99 Including the islands of Huon, Chesterfield, Loyalty, Walpole and Belep Archipelago.

100 Including Campbell and Kermadec Islands (population 20 in 1961, surface area 148 km2) as well as Antipodes, Auckland, Bounty, Snares, Solander and Three Kings Island, all of which are uninhabited.

101 Comprising eastern part of New Guinea, the Bismarck Archipelago, Bougainville and Buka of Solomon Islands group and about 600 smaller islands.

102 Comprising the Solomon Islands group (except Bougainville and Buka which are included with Papua New Guinea shown separately), Ontong, Java, Rennel and Santa Cruz Islands.

103 Data for estimates based on the results of the 1996 population census not necessarily mid-year estimated.

77 Les données se réfèrent à la Cité du Vatican.

78 Les estimations se rapportent au 15 avril.

79 Y compris les étrangers habitant à Malte pour 12 mois avant le recensement et le personnel diplomatique étrangers.

80 Les données ne tiennent pas compte de l'information sur la Transnistria et la municipalité de Bender.

81 Les résultats du recensement, d'après les résultats des dénombrements et enquêtes par sondage continue.

82 Y compris les nationaux se trouvant temporairement hors du pays.

83 Non compris Svalbard et Jan Mayen qui font l'objet de rubriques distinctes.

84 Superficie comprends les eaux intérieures et une partie des eaux situées en deçà de la ligne de base de la mer.

85 Les données annuelles moyennes pour 2000 comportent des données révisées en fonction des résultats du recensement de 2002.

86 Non compris les civils étrangers dans le pays, mais y compris les civils nationaux temporairement hors du pays.

87 Y compris les Açores et Madère.

88 Les estimations ont été calculés compte tenu des résultats du recensement de la population de la Fédération de Russie de 2002.

89 Pour 2000, les estimations pour le Kosovo et la Metohia ont été calculées sur la base des incréments naturelles depuis 1997.

90 Y compris les Baléares et les Canaries, Al Hoceima, Ceuta, les îles Zaffarines, Melilla et Penon de Vélez de la Gomera.

91 N'est habitée pendant la saison d'hiver. Les données de recensement se rapportent à la population totale, mais les estimations ne concernent que la population norvégienne, comprise également dans la population de droit de la Norvège.

92 Superficie ne comprend pas les forêts domaniales et communanzas (7,15 km2) non comprises.

93 Non compris les îles Anglo-Normandes et l'île de Man, qui font l'objet de rubriques distinctes.

94 Les estimations de la population pour l'année 2000 ont été révisées en fonction d'études locales.

95 Les résultat du recensement, non compris des visiteurs.

96 Non compris Nioué, qui fait l'objet d'une rubrique distincte et qui fait partie des îles Cook, mais qui, en raison de son éloignement, est administrée séparément.

97 Comprend les îles Australes, Gambier, Marquises, Rapa, de la Société et Tuamotou.

98 Y compris les îles Christmas, Fanning, Océan et Washington.

99 Y compris les îles Huon, Chesterfield, Loyauté et Walpole, et l'archipel Belep.

100 Y compris les îles Campbell et Kermadec (20 habitants en 1961, superficie: 148 km2) ainsi que les îles Antipodes, Auckland, Bounty, Snares, Solander et Three Kings, qui sont toutes inhabitées.

101 Comprend l'est de la Nouvelle-Guinée, l'archipel Bismarck, Bougainville et Buka (ces deux dernières du groupe des Salomon) et environ 600 îlots.

102 Comprend les îles Salomon (à l'exception de Bougainville et de Buka dont la population est comprise dans celle de Papouasie-Nouvelle Guinée qui font l'objet d'une rubrique distincte), ainsi que les îles Ontong, Java, Rennel et Santa Cruz.

103 Les estimations d'après les résultats du recensement de la population de 1996, pas nécessairement des estimations en milieu d'année.

# Selected indicators of life expectancy, childbearing and mortality

## Choix d'indicateurs de l'espérance de vie, de la maternité et de la mortalité

| Country or area<br>Pays ou zone | Year<br>Année | Life expectancy at birth (years)<br>Espérance de vie à la naissance (en années) | | Total fertility rate<br>Taux de fecondité | Mortality rates - Taux de mortalité | | | | Maternal<br>Maternale<br>p. 100 000 |
|---|---|---|---|---|---|---|---|---|---|
| | | Males<br>Hommes | Females<br>Femmes | | Infant - Infantile<br>p. 1000 | | Under 5 years<br>Moins de 5 ans<br>p. 1 000 | | |
| | | | | | Males<br>Hommes | Females<br>Femmes | Males<br>Hommes | Females<br>Femmes | 2005 |
| Afghanistan | 2000-2005 | 42.2 | 42.1 | 7.5 | 171.2 | 164.8 | 249.0 | 255.0 | ... |
| Afghanistan | 2005-2010 | 43.9 | 43.8 | 7.1 | 159.9 | 154.0 | 233.0 | 238.0 | 1 800 |
| Albania | 2000-2005 | 72.6 | 79.0 | 2.2 | 24.1 | 19.0 | 29.0 | 23.0 | ... |
| Albanie | 2005-2010 | 73.4 | 79.7 | 2.1 | 21.0 | 17.3 | 24.0 | 20.0 | 92 |
| Algeria | 2000-2005 | 69.7 | 72.2 | 2.5 | 38.4 | 36.3 | 42.0 | 40.0 | ... |
| Algérie | 2005-2010 | 70.9 | 73.7 | 2.4 | 32.7 | 29.3 | 35.0 | 31.0 | 180 |
| American Samoa | 2000-2005 | 69.5 | 76.4 | 3.7 | 27.6 | 13.3 | ... | ... | ... |
| Samoa américaines | 2005-2010 | 70.4 | 77.1 | 3.3 | 24.4 | 12.4 | ... | ... | ... |
| Andorra | 2000-2005 | 76.8 | 83.6 | 1.3 | 8.8 | 6.3 | ... | ... | ... |
| Andorre | 2005-2010 | 77.6 | 84.3 | 1.4 | 8.1 | 5.7 | ... | ... | ... |
| Angola | 2000-2005 | 39.3 | 42.7 | 6.8 | 152.2 | 128.9 | 260.0 | 232.0 | ... |
| Angola | 2005-2010 | 41.2 | 44.3 | 6.4 | 143.3 | 120.2 | 245.0 | 216.0 | 1 400 |
| Anguilla | 2000-2005 | 70.8 | 73.9 | 2.1 | 23.0 | 18.6 | ... | ... | ... |
| Anguilla | 2005-2010 | 71.6 | 74.6 | 2.1 | 20.4 | 16.4 | ... | ... | ... |
| Antigua and Barbuda | 2000-2005 | 69.0 | 73.9 | 2.3 | 21.9 | 23.6 | ... | ... | ... |
| Antigua-et-Barbuda | 2005-2010 | 69.8 | 74.7 | 2.2 | 20.1 | 21.8 | ... | ... | ... |
| Argentina | 2000-2005 | 70.6 | 78.1 | 2.4 | 17.0 | 13.0 | 20.0 | 15.0 | ... |
| Argentine | 2005-2010 | 71.6 | 79.1 | 2.3 | 15.0 | 11.8 | 17.0 | 14.0 | 77 |
| Armenia | 2000-2005 | 67.9 | 74.6 | 1.3 | 32.1 | 28.1 | 37.0 | 32.0 | ... |
| Arménie | 2005-2010 | 68.4 | 75.1 | 1.4 | 30.7 | 26.8 | 36.0 | 31.0 | 76 |
| Aruba | 2000-2005 | 70.5 | 76.4 | 2.1 | 24.2 | 13.2 | 28.0 | 15.0 | ... |
| Aruba | 2005-2010 | 71.3 | 77.1 | 2.0 | 21.4 | 12.3 | 25.0 | 14.0 | ... |
| Australia | 2000-2005 | 77.9[1] | 82.9[1] | 1.8[1] | 5.2[1] | 4.5[1] | 6.0 | 6.0 | ... |
| Australie | 2005-2010 | 78.9[1] | 83.6[1] | 1.8[1] | 4.6[1] | 4.3[1] | 6.0 | 5.0 | 4 |
| Austria | 2000-2005 | 75.9 | 81.7 | 1.4 | 4.9 | 4.3 | 6.0 | 5.0 | ... |
| Autriche | 2005-2010 | 76.9 | 82.6 | 1.4 | 4.6 | 4.2 | 6.0 | 5.0 | 4 |
| Azerbaijan | 2000-2005 | 63.2 | 70.5 | 1.7 | 78.2 | 72.5 | 94.0 | 86.0 | ... |
| Azerbaïdjan | 2005-2010 | 63.8 | 71.2 | 1.8 | 75.1 | 69.1 | 90.0 | 81.0 | 82 |
| Bahamas | 2000-2005 | 68.5 | 73.6 | 2.1 | 17.9 | 12.7 | 23.0 | 16.0 | ... |
| Bahamas | 2005-2010 | 70.6 | 76.3 | 2.0 | 15.7 | 11.8 | 20.0 | 14.0 | 16 |
| Bahrain | 2000-2005 | 73.5 | 76.5 | 2.5 | 12.7 | 12.7 | 16.0 | 16.0 | ... |
| Bahreïn | 2005-2010 | 74.3 | 77.5 | 2.3 | 11.2 | 11.2 | 14.0 | 14.0 | 32 |
| Bangladesh | 2000-2005 | 61.3 | 62.8 | 3.2 | 63.0 | 59.5 | 83.0 | 83.0 | ... |
| Bangladesh | 2005-2010 | 63.2 | 65.0 | 2.8 | 54.4 | 50.5 | 70.0 | 69.0 | 570 |
| Barbados | 2000-2005 | 72.8 | 78.8 | 1.5 | 14.3 | 10.2 | 16.0 | 11.0 | ... |
| Barbade | 2005-2010 | 74.4 | 79.8 | 1.5 | 10.9 | 9.2 | 12.0 | 10.0 | 16 |
| Belarus | 2000-2005 | 62.5 | 74.6 | 1.2 | 11.2 | 8.0 | 14.0 | 10.0 | ... |
| Bélarus | 2005-2010 | 63.1 | 75.2 | 1.2 | 11.0 | 7.8 | 14.0 | 10.0 | 18 |
| Belgium | 2000-2005 | 75.1 | 81.2 | 1.6 | 5.0 | 3.7 | 6.0 | 5.0 | ... |
| Belgique | 2005-2010 | 76.5 | 82.3 | 1.6 | 4.7 | 3.7 | 6.0 | 5.0 | 8 |
| Belize | 2000-2005 | 72.8 | 78.8 | 3.4 | 20.3 | 16.7 | 25.0 | 20.0 | ... |
| Belize | 2005-2010 | 73.3 | 79.2 | 2.9 | 18.1 | 14.8 | 22.0 | 18.0 | 52 |
| Benin | 2000-2005 | 53.0 | 55.7 | 5.9 | 109.7 | 102.1 | 164.0 | 159.0 | ... |
| Bénin | 2005-2010 | 55.6 | 57.8 | 5.4 | 101.1 | 94.7 | 148.0 | 144.0 | 840 |
| Bermuda | 2000-2005 | 73.2 | 79.6 | 1.9 | 15.4 | 9.5 | ... | ... | ... |
| Bermudes | 2005-2010 | 74.0 | 80.3 | 1.9 | 13.2 | 8.9 | ... | ... | ... |
| Bhutan | 2000-2005 | 61.8 | 65.2 | 2.9 | 57.2 | 48.1 | 83.0 | 74.0 | ... |
| Bhoutan | 2005-2010 | 64.0 | 67.5 | 2.2 | 49.0 | 40.8 | 69.0 | 60.0 | 440 |

Selected indicators of life expectancy, childbearing and mortality (*continued*)

Choix d'indicateurs de l'espérance de vie, de la maternité et de la mortalité (*suite*)

| | | Life expectancy at birth (years) Espérance de vie à la naissance (en années) | | Total fertility rate | Mortality rates - Taux de mortalité | | | | Maternal Maternale p. 100 000 |
|---|---|---|---|---|---|---|---|---|---|
| | | | | | Infant - Infantile p. 1000 | | Under 5 years Moins de 5 ans p. 1 000 | | |
| Country or area | Year | Males | Females | | Males | Females | Males | Females | |
| Pays ou zone | Année | Hommes | Femmes | Taux de fecondité | Hommes | Femmes | Hommes | Femmes | 2005 |
| Bolivia | 2000-2005 | 61.8 | 66.0 | 4.0 | 60.0 | 51.0 | 77.0 | 67.0 | ... |
| Bolivie | 2005-2010 | 63.4 | 67.7 | 3.5 | 50.0 | 41.0 | 65.0 | 56.0 | 290 |
| Bosnia and Herzegovina | 2000-2005 | 71.4 | 76.7 | 1.3 | 14.9 | 11.9 | 17.0 | 14.0 | ... |
| Bosnie-Herzégovine | 2005-2010 | 72.2 | 77.4 | 1.2 | 13.0 | 11.0 | 15.0 | 13.0 | 3 |
| Botswana | 2000-2005 | 45.7 | 47.4 | 3.2 | 64.3 | 53.3 | 95.0 | 83.0 | ... |
| Botswana | 2005-2010 | 50.5 | 50.7 | 2.9 | 52.0 | 40.8 | 74.0 | 61.0 | 380 |
| Brazil | 2000-2005 | 67.3 | 74.9 | 2.3 | 31.0 | 23.5 | 38.0 | 29.0 | ... |
| Brésil | 2005-2010 | 68.8 | 76.1 | 2.2 | 27.0 | 20.0 | 33.0 | 25.0 | 110 |
| British Virgin Islands | 2000-2005 | 74.6 | 82.6 | 2.3 | 10.4 | 8.5 | ... | ... | ... |
| les Vierges britanniques | 2005-2010 | 75.4 | 83.2 | 2.2 | 9.4 | 7.8 | ... | ... | ... |
| Brunei Darussalam | 2000-2005 | 74.2 | 78.9 | 2.5 | 7.2 | 4.9 | 8.0 | 6.0 | ... |
| Brunéi Darussalam | 2005-2010 | 75.0 | 79.7 | 2.3 | 6.2 | 4.8 | 7.0 | 6.0 | 13 |
| Bulgaria | 2000-2005 | 68.9 | 76.0 | 1.3 | 14.3 | 10.8 | 17.0 | 13.0 | ... |
| Bulgarie | 2005-2010 | 69.5 | 76.7 | 1.3 | 13.3 | 10.2 | 16.0 | 12.0 | 11 |
| Burkina Faso | 2000-2005 | 49.0 | 52.2 | 6.4 | 111.7 | 108.0 | 196.0 | 190.0 | ... |
| Burkina Faso | 2005-2010 | 50.7 | 53.8 | 6.0 | 106.4 | 102.4 | 184.0 | 177.0 | 700 |
| Burundi | 2000-2005 | 45.9 | 48.7 | 6.8 | 115.3 | 97.4 | 193.0 | 171.0 | ... |
| Burundi | 2005-2010 | 48.1 | 51.0 | 6.8 | 108.1 | 90.5 | 180.0 | 158.0 | 1 100 |
| Cambodia | 2000-2005 | 53.7 | 59.5 | 3.6 | 76.5 | 68.8 | 109.0 | 102.0 | ... |
| Cambodge | 2005-2010 | 57.3 | 61.9 | 3.2 | 66.9 | 58.2 | 93.0 | 85.0 | 540 |
| Cameroon | 2000-2005 | 49.3 | 50.3 | 4.9 | 95.8 | 84.0 | 156.0 | 143.0 | ... |
| Cameroun | 2005-2010 | 50.0 | 50.8 | 4.3 | 93.7 | 81.1 | 151.0 | 137.0 | 1 000 |
| Canada | 2000-2005 | 77.3 | 82.3 | 1.5 | 5.4 | 4.7 | 6.0 | 6.0 | ... |
| Canada | 2005-2010 | 78.3 | 82.9 | 1.5 | 5.1 | 4.6 | 6.0 | 6.0 | 7 |
| Cape Verde | 2000-2005 | 66.8 | 73.0 | 3.8 | 38.2 | 21.2 | 46.0 | 25.0 | ... |
| Cap-Vert | 2005-2010 | 68.3 | 74.5 | 3.4 | 32.1 | 16.8 | 39.0 | 20.0 | 210 |
| Cayman Islands | 2000-2005 | 74.5 | 79.5 | 1.6 | 12.0 | 9.7 | ... | ... | ... |
| Iles Caïmanes | 2005-2010 | 75.2 | 80.2 | 1.5 | 10.3 | 9.0 | ... | ... | ... |
| Central African Rep. | 2000-2005 | 41.7 | 44.8 | 5.0 | 113.4 | 90.4 | 188.0 | 155.0 | ... |
| Rép. centrafricaine | 2005-2010 | 43.3 | 46.1 | 4.6 | 108.0 | 85.2 | 179.0 | 146.0 | 980 |
| Chad | 2000-2005 | 49.1 | 52.0 | 6.5 | 131.0 | 117.3 | 206.0 | 191.0 | ... |
| Tchad | 2005-2010 | 49.3 | 52.0 | 6.2 | 125.8 | 112.4 | 197.0 | 181.0 | 1 500 |
| Channel Islands | 2000-2005 | 75.9 | 80.8 | 1.4 | 5.6 | 5.3 | 7.0 | 6.0 | ... |
| Iles Anglo-Normandes | 2005-2010 | 76.6 | 81.5 | 1.4 | 5.3 | 5.0 | 6.0 | 6.0 | ... |
| Chile | 2000-2005 | 74.8 | 80.8 | 2.0 | 9.0 | 7.0 | 11.0 | 9.0 | ... |
| Chili | 2005-2010 | 75.5 | 81.5 | 1.9 | 8.1 | 6.3 | 10.0 | 8.0 | 16 |
| China[2] | 2000-2005 | 70.5 | 73.7 | 1.7 | 20.4 | 31.9 | 27.0 | 38.0 | ... |
| Chine[2] | 2005-2010 | 71.3 | 74.8 | 1.7 | 18.4 | 28.2 | 25.0 | 35.0 | 45 |
| China, Hong Kong SAR | 2000-2005 | 78.6 | 84.5 | 0.9 | 3.9 | 3.7 | 5.0 | 5.0 | ... |
| Chine, Hong Kong RAS | 2005-2010 | 79.4 | 85.1 | 1.0 | 3.7 | 3.6 | 5.0 | 4.0 | ... |
| China, Macao SAR | 2000-2005 | 77.6 | 82.2 | 0.8 | 8.0 | 7.3 | 9.0 | 8.0 | ... |
| Chine, Macao RAS | 2005-2010 | 78.5 | 82.8 | 0.9 | 7.3 | 6.8 | 8.0 | 7.0 | ... |
| Colombia | 2000-2005 | 68.0 | 75.4 | 2.5 | 23.4 | 17.4 | 32.0 | 25.0 | ... |
| Colombie | 2005-2010 | 69.2 | 76.6 | 2.2 | 21.9 | 16.1 | 30.0 | 22.0 | 130 |
| Comoros | 2000-2005 | 60.9 | 65.1 | 4.9 | 64.8 | 50.2 | 86.0 | 68.0 | ... |
| Comores | 2005-2010 | 63.0 | 67.4 | 4.3 | 55.2 | 41.3 | 71.0 | 54.0 | 400 |
| Congo | 2000-2005 | 51.7 | 54.2 | 4.8 | 84.2 | 65.7 | 120.0 | 97.0 | ... |
| Congo | 2005-2010 | 54.0 | 56.6 | 4.5 | 79.5 | 61.0 | 113.0 | 90.0 | 740 |
| Cook Islands | 2000-2005 | 70.6 | 75.8 | 2.7 | 18.1 | 19.6 | ... | ... | ... |
| Iles Cook | 2005-2010 | 71.7 | 76.8 | 2.4 | 15.9 | 17.5 | ... | ... | ... |
| Costa Rica | 2000-2005 | 75.8 | 80.6 | 2.3 | 11.8 | 9.1 | 14.0 | 11.0 | ... |
| Costa Rica | 2005-2010 | 76.5 | 81.2 | 2.1 | 11.2 | 8.5 | 13.0 | 10.0 | 30 |

| Country or area<br>Pays ou zone | Year<br>Année | Life expectancy at birth (years)<br>Espérance de vie à la naissance (en années)<br>Males<br>Hommes | Females<br>Femmes | Total fertility rate<br>Taux de fecondité | Mortality rates - Taux de mortalité<br>Infant - Infantile<br>p. 1000<br>Males<br>Hommes | Females<br>Femmes | Under 5 years<br>Moins de 5 ans<br>p. 1 000<br>Males<br>Hommes | Females<br>Femmes | Maternal<br>Maternale<br>p. 100 000<br>2005 |
|---|---|---|---|---|---|---|---|---|---|
| Côte d'Ivoire | 2000-2005 | 45.9 | 48.0 | 5.1 | 129.1 | 114.2 | 200.0 | 181.0 | ... |
| Côte d'Ivoire | 2005-2010 | 47.5 | 49.3 | 4.5 | 124.2 | 109.4 | 193.0 | 174.0 | 810 |
| Croatia | 2000-2005 | 71.3 | 78.4 | 1.3 | 7.2 | 6.6 | 9.0 | 8.0 | ... |
| Croatie | 2005-2010 | 72.3 | 79.2 | 1.3 | 6.6 | 6.2 | 8.0 | 7.0 | 7 |
| Cuba | 2000-2005 | 75.3 | 79.1 | 1.6 | 6.7 | 5.5 | 8.0 | 7.0 | ... |
| Cuba | 2005-2010 | 76.2 | 80.4 | 1.5 | 5.6 | 4.6 | 7.0 | 6.0 | 45 |
| Cyprus | 2000-2005 | 76.6 | 81.3 | 1.6 | 6.4 | 5.4 | 8.0 | 6.0 | ... |
| Chypre | 2005-2010 | 76.5 | 81.6 | 1.6 | 6.5 | 5.2 | 8.0 | 6.0 | 10 |
| Czech Republic | 2000-2005 | 72.1 | 78.7 | 1.2 | 4.3 | 3.5 | 5.0 | 4.0 | ... |
| République tchèque | 2005-2010 | 73.4 | 79.5 | 1.2 | 4.0 | 3.5 | 5.0 | 4.0 | 4 |
| Dem. Rep. of the Congo | 2000-2005 | 43.5 | 46.4 | 6.7 | 128.6 | 110.4 | 222.0 | 200.0 | ... |
| Rép. dém. du Congo | 2005-2010 | 45.2 | 47.7 | 6.7 | 122.5 | 104.2 | 207.0 | 185.0 | 1 100 |
| Denmark | 2000-2005 | 75.0 | 79.6 | 1.8 | 4.8 | 4.4 | 6.0 | 6.0 | ... |
| Danemark | 2005-2010 | 76.0 | 80.6 | 1.8 | 4.4 | 4.3 | 6.0 | 6.0 | 3 |
| Djibouti | 2000-2005 | 51.9 | 54.9 | 4.5 | 103.1 | 86.5 | 150.0 | 132.0 | ... |
| Djibouti | 2005-2010 | 53.6 | 56.0 | 3.9 | 92.9 | 77.4 | 134.0 | 117.0 | 650 |
| Dominica | 2000-2005 | 73.3 | 80.1 | 2.0 | 12.7 | 11.8 | ... | ... | ... |
| Dominique | 2005-2010 | 73.4 | 80.0 | 1.9 | 12.6 | 11.9 | ... | ... | ... |
| Dominican Republic | 2000-2005 | 67.9 | 74.2 | 3.0 | 39.7 | 30.0 | 44.0 | 34.0 | ... |
| Rép. dominicaine | 2005-2010 | 69.3 | 75.5 | 2.8 | 33.7 | 25.3 | 37.0 | 29.0 | 150 |
| Ecuador | 2000-2005 | 71.3 | 77.2 | 2.8 | 28.8 | 20.8 | 34.0 | 25.0 | ... |
| Equateur | 2005-2010 | 72.1 | 78.0 | 2.6 | 24.0 | 18.0 | 29.0 | 22.0 | 210 |
| Egypt | 2000-2005 | 67.7 | 72.0 | 3.2 | 39.5 | 32.1 | 46.0 | 38.0 | ... |
| Egypte | 2005-2010 | 69.1 | 73.6 | 2.9 | 32.7 | 25.9 | 37.0 | 30.0 | 130 |
| El Salvador | 2000-2005 | 67.7 | 73.7 | 2.9 | 28.6 | 24.1 | 38.0 | 31.0 | ... |
| El Salvador | 2005-2010 | 68.8 | 74.9 | 2.7 | 23.2 | 19.8 | 32.0 | 26.0 | 170 |
| Equatorial Guinea | 2000-2005 | 48.0 | 50.7 | 5.6 | 108.5 | 93.0 | 181.0 | 163.0 | ... |
| Guinée équatoriale | 2005-2010 | 50.4 | 52.8 | 5.4 | 99.4 | 85.0 | 164.0 | 147.0 | 680 |
| Eritrea | 2000-2005 | 52.5 | 57.8 | 5.5 | 66.0 | 59.3 | 94.0 | 85.0 | ... |
| Erythrée | 2005-2010 | 55.6 | 60.3 | 5.0 | 57.8 | 52.8 | 80.0 | 73.0 | 450 |
| Estonia | 2000-2005 | 65.1 | 76.7 | 1.4 | 8.5 | 6.2 | 12.0 | 9.0 | ... |
| Estonie | 2005-2010 | 65.9 | 76.8 | 1.5 | 8.1 | 6.3 | 11.0 | 8.0 | 25 |
| Ethiopia | 2000-2005 | 49.4 | 52.1 | 5.8 | 102.3 | 88.3 | 169.0 | 153.0 | ... |
| Ethiopie | 2005-2010 | 51.7 | 54.3 | 5.3 | 93.4 | 80.2 | 153.0 | 138.0 | 720 |
| Faeroe Islands | 2000-2005 | 76.8 | 81.2 | 2.5 | 12.3 | 9.5 | ... | ... | ... |
| Iles Féroé | 2005-2010 | 77.6 | 81.7 | 2.4 | 10.8 | 9.0 | ... | ... | ... |
| Falkland Is. (Malvinas) | 2000-2005 | 74.6 | 82.6 | 2.3 | 10.4 | 8.5 | ... | ... | ... |
| Iles Falkland (Malvinas) | 2005-2010 | 75.4 | 83.2 | 2.2 | 9.4 | 7.8 | ... | ... | ... |
| Fiji | 2000-2005 | 65.7 | 70.1 | 3.0 | 22.9 | 20.2 | 28.0 | 26.0 | ... |
| Fidji | 2005-2010 | 66.6 | 71.1 | 2.8 | 20.5 | 18.6 | 25.0 | 24.0 | 210 |
| Finland | 2000-2005 | 74.9 | 81.7 | 1.8 | 4.1 | 3.7 | 5.0 | 4.0 | ... |
| Finlande | 2005-2010 | 76.1 | 82.4 | 1.8 | 3.8 | 3.6 | 5.0 | 4.0 | 7 |
| France | 2000-2005 | 76.0 | 83.2 | 1.9 | 4.8 | 4.0 | 6.0 | 5.0 | ... |
| France | 2005-2010 | 77.1 | 84.1 | 1.9 | 4.5 | 3.9 | 6.0 | 5.0 | 8 |
| French Guiana | 2000-2005 | 71.9 | 79.1 | 3.7 | 19.3 | 10.0 | 22.0 | 11.0 | ... |
| Guyane française | 2005-2010 | 72.6 | 79.9 | 3.3 | 17.3 | 9.2 | 20.0 | 10.0 | ... |
| French Polynesia | 2000-2005 | 70.6 | 75.8 | 2.4 | 9.2 | 8.3 | 11.0 | 11.0 | ... |
| Polynésie française | 2005-2010 | 71.7 | 76.8 | 2.3 | 8.3 | 7.8 | 11.0 | 11.0 | ... |
| Gabon | 2000-2005 | 55.7 | 57.8 | 3.4 | 66.0 | 57.4 | 102.0 | 92.0 | ... |
| Gabon | 2005-2010 | 56.4 | 57.1 | 3.1 | 57.6 | 49.9 | 90.0 | 81.0 | 520 |
| Gambia | 2000-2005 | 56.8 | 59.3 | 5.2 | 83.6 | 76.1 | 147.0 | 139.0 | ... |
| Gambie | 2005-2010 | 58.6 | 60.3 | 4.7 | 76.9 | 71.5 | 130.0 | 126.0 | 690 |

Selected indicators of life expectancy, childbearing and mortality (*continued*)
Choix d'indicateurs de l'espérance de vie, de la maternité et de la mortalité (*suite*)

| Country or area | Year | Life expectancy at birth (years) Espérance de vie à la naissance (en années) | | Total fertility rate | Mortality rates - Taux de mortalité | | | | |
| | | | | | Infant - Infantile p. 1000 | | Under 5 years Moins de 5 ans p. 1 000 | | Maternal Maternelle p. 100 000 |
| | | Males | Females | | Males | Females | Males | Females | |
| Pays ou zone | Année | Hommes | Femmes | Taux de fecondité | Hommes | Femmes | Hommes | Femmes | 2005 |
|---|---|---|---|---|---|---|---|---|---|
| Georgia | 2000-2005 | 66.5 | 74.3 | 1.5 | 44.5 | 36.0 | 47.0 | 39.0 | ... |
| Géorgie | 2005-2010 | 67.1 | 74.8 | 1.4 | 42.6 | 34.5 | 45.0 | 37.0 | 66 |
| Germany | 2000-2005 | 75.7 | 81.5 | 1.3 | 4.5 | 4.4 | 6.0 | 6.0 | ... |
| Allemagne | 2005-2010 | 76.5 | 82.1 | 1.4 | 4.4 | 4.3 | 5.0 | 5.0 | 4 |
| Ghana | 2000-2005 | 58.0 | 58.9 | 4.4 | 66.0 | 60.7 | 103.0 | 99.0 | ... |
| Ghana | 2005-2010 | 59.6 | 60.5 | 3.8 | 59.1 | 53.9 | 92.0 | 88.0 | 560 |
| Gibraltar | 2000-2005 | 75.9 | 80.6 | 1.7 | 13.8 | 10.2 | ... | ... | ... |
| Gibraltar | 2005-2010 | 76.7 | 81.2 | 1.7 | 12.5 | 9.5 | ... | ... | ... |
| Greece | 2000-2005 | 76.4 | 80.1 | 1.3 | 7.7 | 7.7 | 9.0 | 9.0 | ... |
| Grèce | 2005-2010 | 77.1 | 81.9 | 1.3 | 6.9 | 6.5 | 8.0 | 8.0 | 3 |
| Greenland | 2000-2005 | 63.7 | 69.4 | 2.4 | 22.4 | 22.4 | ... | ... | ... |
| Groenland | 2005-2010 | 64.8 | 70.5 | 2.3 | 20.7 | 20.7 | ... | ... | ... |
| Grenada | 2000-2005 | 66.1 | 69.3 | 2.4 | 41.3 | 34.0 | 51.0 | 43.0 | ... |
| Grenade | 2005-2010 | 67.0 | 70.4 | 2.3 | 37.4 | 30.0 | 45.0 | 37.0 | ... |
| Guadeloupe | 2000-2005 | 75.1 | 81.5 | 2.1 | 8.1 | 6.4 | 11.0 | 9.0 | ... |
| Guadeloupe | 2005-2010 | 76.0 | 82.2 | 2.1 | 7.5 | 6.0 | 10.0 | 8.0 | ... |
| Guam | 2000-2005 | 72.4 | 77.0 | 2.7 | 11.1 | 8.9 | 13.0 | 10.0 | ... |
| Guam | 2005-2010 | 73.3 | 77.9 | 2.5 | 9.8 | 8.3 | 11.0 | 10.0 | ... |
| Guatemala | 2000-2005 | 65.5 | 72.5 | 4.6 | 44.0 | 33.0 | 54.0 | 42.0 | ... |
| Guatemala | 2005-2010 | 66.7 | 73.8 | 4.2 | 35.0 | 25.0 | 45.0 | 34.0 | 290 |
| Guinea | 2000-2005 | 52.0 | 55.4 | 5.8 | 120.6 | 105.2 | 188.0 | 168.0 | ... |
| Guinée | 2005-2010 | 54.4 | 57.6 | 5.4 | 109.3 | 95.4 | 165.0 | 146.0 | 910 |
| Guinea-Bissau | 2000-2005 | 43.8 | 47.3 | 7.1 | 130.8 | 111.3 | 223.0 | 200.0 | ... |
| Guinée-Bissau | 2005-2010 | 44.9 | 47.9 | 7.1 | 121.9 | 103.2 | 206.0 | 183.0 | 1 100 |
| Guyana | 2000-2005 | 60.6 | 66.5 | 2.4 | 57.2 | 41.2 | 78.0 | 57.0 | ... |
| Guyana | 2005-2010 | 64.2 | 69.9 | 2.3 | 49.7 | 35.9 | 66.0 | 48.0 | 470 |
| Haiti | 2000-2005 | 56.4 | 59.9 | 4.0 | 61.0 | 51.4 | 93.0 | 71.0 | ... |
| Haïti | 2005-2010 | 59.1 | 62.8 | 3.5 | 52.6 | 44.8 | 84.0 | 60.0 | 670 |
| Holy See | 2000-2005 | 67.3 | 74.9 | 1.0 | 36.0 | 15.4 | ... | ... | ... |
| Saint-Siège | 2005-2010 | 68.9 | 76.1 | 1.0 | 30.0 | 13.6 | ... | ... | ... |
| Honduras | 2000-2005 | 64.8 | 72.6 | 3.7 | 35.9 | 27.1 | 51.0 | 41.0 | ... |
| Honduras | 2005-2010 | 66.9 | 73.7 | 3.3 | 32.2 | 24.0 | 46.0 | 37.0 | 280 |
| Hungary | 2000-2005 | 68.3 | 76.6 | 1.3 | 7.3 | 7.0 | 9.0 | 8.0 | ... |
| Hongrie | 2005-2010 | 69.2 | 77.4 | 1.3 | 6.9 | 6.7 | 9.0 | 8.0 | 6 |
| Iceland | 2000-2005 | 79.3 | 82.7 | 2.0 | 3.4 | 2.8 | 4.0 | 4.0 | ... |
| Islande | 2005-2010 | 80.2 | 83.3 | 2.1 | 3.1 | 2.8 | 4.0 | 4.0 | 4 |
| India | 2000-2005 | 61.7 | 64.2 | 3.1 | 60.9 | 64.2 | 84.0 | 96.0 | ... |
| Inde | 2005-2010 | 63.2 | 66.4 | 2.8 | 53.5 | 56.5 | 74.0 | 84.0 | 450 |
| Indonesia | 2000-2005 | 66.7 | 70.5 | 2.4 | 38.5 | 29.7 | 47.0 | 37.0 | ... |
| Indonésie | 2005-2010 | 68.7 | 72.7 | 2.2 | 30.7 | 22.3 | 37.0 | 27.0 | 420 |
| Iran (Islamic Rep. of) | 2000-2005 | 68.0 | 71.0 | 2.1 | 37.7 | 36.6 | 44.0 | 44.0 | ... |
| Iran (Rép. islamique d') | 2005-2010 | 69.4 | 72.6 | 2.0 | 31.5 | 29.7 | 36.0 | 35.0 | 140 |
| Iraq | 2000-2005 | 54.9 | 59.3 | 4.9 | 100.3 | 88.1 | 129.0 | 119.0 | ... |
| Iraq | 2005-2010 | 57.8 | 61.5 | 4.3 | 86.2 | 76.6 | 109.0 | 102.0 | 300 |
| Ireland | 2000-2005 | 75.3 | 80.3 | 2.0 | 5.4 | 5.4 | 7.0 | 7.0 | ... |
| Irlande | 2005-2010 | 76.5 | 81.4 | 2.0 | 4.9 | 4.9 | 6.0 | 6.0 | 1 |
| Isle of Man | 2000-2005 | 76.0 | 80.5 | 1.7 | 13.6 | 10.3 | ... | ... | ... |
| Ile de Man | 2005-2010 | 76.8 | 81.1 | 1.8 | 12.2 | 9.7 | ... | ... | ... |
| Israel | 2000-2005 | 77.6 | 81.7 | 2.9 | 5.3 | 4.8 | 6.0 | 6.0 | ... |
| Israël | 2005-2010 | 78.6 | 82.8 | 2.8 | 5.0 | 4.5 | 6.0 | 5.0 | 4 |
| Italy | 2000-2005 | 76.9 | 82.9 | 1.3 | 5.5 | 4.9 | 7.0 | 6.0 | ... |
| Italie | 2005-2010 | 77.5 | 83.5 | 1.4 | 5.2 | 4.7 | 6.0 | 6.0 | 3 |

| Country or area<br>Pays ou zone | Year<br>Année | Life expectancy at birth (years)<br>Espérance de vie à la naissance (en années) | | Total fertility rate<br>Taux de fecondité | Mortality rates - Taux de mortalité | | | | | | Maternal<br>Maternale<br>p. 100 000 |
|---|---|---|---|---|---|---|---|---|---|---|---|
| | | | | | Infant - Infantile<br>p. 1000 | | Under 5 years<br>Moins de 5 ans<br>p. 1 000 | | | | |
| | | Males<br>Hommes | Females<br>Femmes | | Males<br>Hommes | Females<br>Femmes | Males<br>Hommes | Females<br>Femmes | | | 2005 |
| Jamaica | 2000-2005 | 69.5 | 74.7 | 2.6 | 15.7 | 13.4 | 20.0 | 18.0 | | | ... |
| Jamaïque | 2005-2010 | 70.0 | 75.2 | 2.4 | 14.6 | 12.5 | 18.0 | 16.0 | | | 170 |
| Japan | 2000-2005 | 78.3 | 85.2 | 1.3 | 3.4 | 3.0 | 5.0 | 4.0 | | | ... |
| Japon | 2005-2010 | 79.0 | 86.1 | 1.3 | 3.3 | 3.0 | 5.0 | 4.0 | | | 6 |
| Jordan | 2000-2005 | 69.7 | 73.1 | 3.5 | 25.3 | 21.0 | 28.0 | 24.0 | | | ... |
| Jordanie | 2005-2010 | 70.8 | 74.5 | 3.1 | 21.7 | 17.0 | 24.0 | 19.0 | | | 62 |
| Kazakhstan | 2000-2005 | 59.5 | 70.6 | 2.0 | 36.5 | 27.3 | 43.0 | 33.0 | | | ... |
| Kazakhstan | 2005-2010 | 61.6 | 72.4 | 2.3 | 28.0 | 20.0 | 34.0 | 23.0 | | | 140 |
| Kenya | 2000-2005 | 49.9 | 52.1 | 5.0 | 75.9 | 63.9 | 120.0 | 105.0 | | | ... |
| Kenya | 2005-2010 | 53.0 | 55.2 | 5.0 | 70.5 | 58.2 | 112.0 | 96.0 | | | 560 |
| Kiribati | 2000-2005 | 62.7 | 68.4 | 3.6 | 56.6 | 37.5 | ... | ... | | | ... |
| Kiribati | 2005-2010 | 64.2 | 69.9 | 3.2 | 49.8 | 31.8 | ... | ... | | | ... |
| Korea, Dem. P. R. | 2000-2005 | 64.2 | 68.8 | 1.9 | 50.0 | 50.0 | 65.0 | 65.0 | | | ... |
| Corée, R. p. dém. de | 2005-2010 | 65.1 | 69.3 | 1.9 | 48.2 | 48.2 | 62.0 | 62.0 | | | 370 |
| Korea, Republic of | 2000-2005 | 73.5 | 80.6 | 1.2 | 5.0 | 4.4 | 6.0 | 5.0 | | | ... |
| Corée, République de | 2005-2010 | 75.0 | 82.2 | 1.2 | 4.2 | 4.1 | 5.0 | 5.0 | | | 14 |
| Kuwait | 2000-2005 | 75.3 | 79.2 | 2.3 | 9.7 | 7.5 | 12.0 | 9.0 | | | ... |
| Koweït | 2005-2010 | 76.0 | 79.9 | 2.2 | 9.1 | 7.1 | 11.0 | 9.0 | | | 4 |
| Kyrgyzstan | 2000-2005 | 61.4 | 69.4 | 2.5 | 59.8 | 50.0 | 72.0 | 60.0 | | | ... |
| Kirghizistan | 2005-2010 | 62.0 | 69.9 | 2.5 | 57.7 | 48.3 | 69.0 | 58.0 | | | 150 |
| Lao People's Dem. Rep. | 2000-2005 | 60.7 | 63.1 | 3.6 | 65.9 | 58.2 | 87.0 | 81.0 | | | ... |
| Rép. dém. pop. lao | 2005-2010 | 63.0 | 65.8 | 3.2 | 55.1 | 47.4 | 71.0 | 64.0 | | | 660 |
| Latvia | 2000-2005 | 65.7 | 76.8 | 1.2 | 13.3 | 9.8 | 18.0 | 12.0 | | | ... |
| Lettonie | 2005-2010 | 67.3 | 77.7 | 1.3 | 11.6 | 9.1 | 16.0 | 11.0 | | | 10 |
| Lebanon | 2000-2005 | 68.9 | 73.2 | 2.3 | 29.7 | 20.5 | 35.0 | 24.0 | | | ... |
| Liban | 2005-2010 | 69.9 | 74.2 | 2.2 | 26.2 | 17.6 | 31.0 | 21.0 | | | 150 |
| Lesotho | 2000-2005 | 43.2 | 45.7 | 3.8 | 80.3 | 68.0 | 119.0 | 105.0 | | | ... |
| Lesotho | 2005-2010 | 42.9 | 42.3 | 3.4 | 70.5 | 58.6 | 105.0 | 91.0 | | | 960 |
| Liberia | 2000-2005 | 42.8 | 44.8 | 6.8 | 152.4 | 132.9 | 231.0 | 213.0 | | | ... |
| Libéria | 2005-2010 | 44.8 | 46.6 | 6.8 | 142.0 | 122.8 | 214.0 | 196.0 | | | 1 200 |
| Libyan Arab Jamah. | 2000-2005 | 70.5 | 75.7 | 3.0 | 22.1 | 19.5 | 24.0 | 22.0 | | | ... |
| Jamah. arabe libyenne | 2005-2010 | 71.7 | 76.9 | 2.7 | 18.9 | 17.1 | 20.0 | 19.0 | | | 97 |
| Liechtenstein | 2000-2005 | 75.3 | 81.8 | 1.5 | 10.2 | 7.6 | ... | ... | | | ... |
| Liechtenstein | 2005-2010 | 76.1 | 82.4 | 1.5 | 9.5 | 7.0 | ... | ... | | | ... |
| Lithuania | 2000-2005 | 66.4 | 77.7 | 1.3 | 11.3 | 7.5 | 15.0 | 10.0 | | | ... |
| Lituanie | 2005-2010 | 67.5 | 78.3 | 1.3 | 9.8 | 7.2 | 13.0 | 9.0 | | | 11 |
| Luxembourg | 2000-2005 | 75.1 | 81.1 | 1.7 | 4.7 | 4.7 | 7.0 | 7.0 | | | ... |
| Luxembourg | 2005-2010 | 75.7 | 81.6 | 1.7 | 4.5 | 4.5 | 7.0 | 6.0 | | | 12 |
| Madagascar | 2000-2005 | 55.7 | 58.9 | 5.3 | 80.1 | 69.5 | 129.0 | 117.0 | | | ... |
| Madagascar | 2005-2010 | 57.7 | 61.3 | 4.8 | 70.4 | 60.5 | 112.0 | 100.0 | | | 510 |
| Malawi | 2000-2005 | 44.4 | 45.7 | 6.0 | 105.0 | 97.1 | 158.0 | 150.0 | | | ... |
| Malawi | 2005-2010 | 48.1 | 48.4 | 5.6 | 93.3 | 85.4 | 136.0 | 128.0 | | | 1 100 |
| Malaysia | 2000-2005 | 70.8 | 75.5 | 2.9 | 11.5 | 8.5 | 15.0 | 11.0 | | | ... |
| Malaisie | 2005-2010 | 72.0 | 76.7 | 2.6 | 9.9 | 7.9 | 12.0 | 10.0 | | | 62 |
| Maldives | 2000-2005 | 65.6 | 65.6 | 2.8 | 43.5 | 48.2 | 54.0 | 65.0 | | | ... |
| Maldives | 2005-2010 | 67.6 | 69.5 | 2.6 | 34.8 | 33.3 | 42.0 | 42.0 | | | 120 |
| Mali | 2000-2005 | 49.5 | 54.0 | 6.7 | 143.3 | 132.7 | 228.0 | 210.0 | | | ... |
| Mali | 2005-2010 | 52.1 | 56.6 | 6.5 | 133.6 | 123.3 | 208.0 | 191.0 | | | 970 |
| Malta | 2000-2005 | 76.2 | 80.8 | 1.5 | 6.9 | 6.9 | 8.0 | 8.0 | | | ... |
| Malte | 2005-2010 | 77.3 | 81.4 | 1.4 | 6.5 | 6.5 | 8.0 | 8.0 | | | 8 |
| Marshall Islands | 2000-2005 | 67.0 | 70.8 | 5.3 | 37.5 | 28.5 | ... | ... | | | ... |
| Iles Marshall | 2005-2010 | 68.7 | 72.8 | 4.7 | 30.5 | 21.9 | ... | ... | | | ... |

| Country or area / Pays ou zone | Year / Année | Life expectancy at birth (years) Espérance de vie à la naissance (en années) | | Total fertility rate / Taux de fecondité | Mortality rates - Taux de mortalité | | | | | |
|---|---|---|---|---|---|---|---|---|---|---|
| | | | | | Infant - Infantile p. 1000 | | Under 5 years Moins de 5 ans p. 1 000 | | Maternal Maternale p. 100 000 |
| | | Males Hommes | Females Femmes | | Males Hommes | Females Femmes | Males Hommes | Females Femmes | 2005 |
| Martinique | 2000-2005 | 75.7 | 81.6 | 2.0 | 7.6 | 6.4 | 9.0 | 9.0 | ... |
| Martinique | 2005-2010 | 76.5 | 82.3 | 1.9 | 7.1 | 6.1 | 8.0 | 8.0 | ... |
| Mauritania | 2000-2005 | 60.5 | 64.0 | 4.8 | 75.6 | 59.7 | 108.0 | 94.0 | ... |
| Mauritanie | 2005-2010 | 62.4 | 66.0 | 4.4 | 70.1 | 55.4 | 98.0 | 86.0 | 820 |
| Mauritius | 2000-2005 | 68.6[3] | 75.5[3] | 1.9[3] | 17.7[3] | 12.6[3] | 20.0 | 15.0 | ... |
| Maurice | 2005-2010 | 69.5[3] | 76.2[3] | 1.9[3] | 16.1[3] | 11.8[3] | 18.0 | 15.0 | 15 |
| Mexico | 2000-2005 | 72.4 | 77.4 | 2.4 | 22.9 | 18.0 | 27.0 | 22.0 | ... |
| Mexique | 2005-2010 | 73.7 | 78.6 | 2.2 | 18.7 | 14.6 | 22.0 | 18.0 | 60 |
| Micronesia (Fed. States of) | 2000-2005 | 66.9 | 68.2 | 4.2 | 37.7 | 38.2 | 46.0 | 49.0 | ... |
| Micronésie (Etats féd. de) | 2005-2010 | 67.7 | 69.3 | 3.7 | 34.3 | 33.8 | 41.0 | 43.0 | ... |
| Moldova | 2000-2005 | 64.3 | 71.5 | 1.5 | 19.0 | 14.4 | 23.0 | 18.0 | ... |
| Moldova | 2005-2010 | 65.1 | 72.5 | 1.4 | 17.6 | 13.9 | 21.0 | 18.0 | 22 |
| Monaco | 2000-2005 | 77.4 | 84.2 | 2.0 | 8.3 | 5.8 | ... | ... | ... |
| Monaco | 2005-2010 | 78.5 | 85.2 | 2.0 | 7.4 | 5.2 | ... | ... | ... |
| Mongolia | 2000-2005 | 61.9 | 68.4 | 2.1 | 48.0 | 41.2 | 67.0 | 56.0 | ... |
| Mongolie | 2005-2010 | 63.9 | 69.9 | 1.9 | 42.1 | 37.4 | 58.0 | 50.0 | 46 |
| Montenegro | 2000-2005 | 71.8 | 76.5 | 1.8 | 25.8 | 21.3 | 28.0 | 24.0 | ... |
| Monténégro | 2005-2010 | 72.4 | 76.8 | 1.8 | 23.6 | 20.8 | 25.0 | 23.0 | ... |
| Montserrat | 2000-2005 | 74.6 | 82.6 | 2.3 | 10.4 | 8.5 | ... | ... | ... |
| Montserrat | 2005-2010 | 75.4 | 83.2 | 2.2 | 9.4 | 7.8 | ... | ... | ... |
| Morocco | 2000-2005 | 67.5 | 71.8 | 2.5 | 42.6 | 32.1 | 53.0 | 38.0 | ... |
| Maroc | 2005-2010 | 69.0 | 73.4 | 2.4 | 35.7 | 25.3 | 43.0 | 29.0 | 240 |
| Mozambique | 2000-2005 | 42.8 | 45.3 | 5.5 | 115.1 | 100.0 | 195.0 | 177.0 | ... |
| Mozambique | 2005-2010 | 41.7 | 42.4 | 5.1 | 102.8 | 88.8 | 172.0 | 155.0 | 520 |
| Myanmar | 2000-2005 | 56.7 | 63.4 | 2.2 | 83.2 | 66.1 | 119.0 | 100.0 | ... |
| Myanmar | 2005-2010 | 59.1 | 65.3 | 2.1 | 73.3 | 58.3 | 106.0 | 88.0 | 380 |
| Namibia | 2000-2005 | 50.3 | 52.5 | 3.6 | 60.4 | 49.6 | 89.0 | 76.0 | ... |
| Namibie | 2005-2010 | 52.5 | 53.1 | 3.2 | 47.2 | 37.2 | 72.0 | 59.0 | 210 |
| Nauru | 2000-2005 | 74.6 | 82.6 | 2.2 | 10.4 | 8.5 | ... | ... | ... |
| Nauru | 2005-2010 | 75.4 | 83.2 | 2.2 | 9.4 | 7.8 | ... | ... | ... |
| Nepal | 2000-2005 | 61.0 | 61.6 | 3.7 | 64.5 | 64.4 | 85.0 | 91.0 | ... |
| Népal | 2005-2010 | 63.2 | 64.2 | 3.3 | 54.2 | 53.6 | 69.0 | 74.0 | 830 |
| Netherlands | 2000-2005 | 76.3 | 81.0 | 1.7 | 5.4 | 4.6 | 7.0 | 6.0 | ... |
| Pays-Bas | 2005-2010 | 77.5 | 81.9 | 1.7 | 5.0 | 4.4 | 6.0 | 6.0 | 6 |
| Netherlands Antilles | 2000-2005 | 71.2 | 78.7 | 2.1 | 17.4 | 12.4 | 21.0 | 13.0 | ... |
| Antilles néerlandaises | 2005-2010 | 71.3 | 78.8 | 1.9 | 17.2 | 12.4 | 20.0 | 13.0 | ... |
| New Caledonia | 2000-2005 | 71.9 | 78.7 | 2.2 | 6.9 | 6.4 | 10.0 | 9.0 | ... |
| Nouvelle-Calédonie | 2005-2010 | 72.8 | 79.7 | 2.1 | 6.3 | 6.0 | 9.0 | 8.0 | ... |
| New Zealand | 2000-2005 | 77.0 | 81.3 | 2.0 | 5.6 | 5.6 | 7.0 | 7.0 | ... |
| Nouvelle-Zélande | 2005-2010 | 78.2 | 82.2 | 2.0 | 5.0 | 5.0 | 6.0 | 6.0 | 9 |
| Nicaragua | 2000-2005 | 68.0 | 73.8 | 3.0 | 29.9 | 22.8 | 36.0 | 28.0 | ... |
| Nicaragua | 2005-2010 | 69.9 | 76.0 | 2.8 | 24.3 | 18.5 | 29.0 | 22.0 | 170 |
| Niger | 2000-2005 | 55.4 | 53.6 | 7.4 | 121.8 | 116.0 | 211.0 | 215.0 | ... |
| Niger | 2005-2010 | 57.8 | 56.0 | 7.2 | 113.2 | 108.4 | 186.0 | 190.0 | 1 800 |
| Nigeria | 2000-2005 | 45.9 | 47.3 | 5.8 | 120.9 | 110.1 | 202.0 | 194.0 | ... |
| Nigéria | 2005-2010 | 46.4 | 47.3 | 5.3 | 114.9 | 103.9 | 191.0 | 183.0 | 1 100 |
| Niue | 2000-2005 | 74.1 | 82.3 | 2.3 | 13.0 | 7.2 | ... | ... | ... |
| Nioué | 2005-2010 | 74.7 | 82.8 | 2.2 | 11.3 | 6.8 | ... | ... | ... |
| Northern Mariana Islands | 2000-2005 | 72.9 | 78.1 | 1.1 | 16.4 | 11.1 | ... | ... | ... |
| Iles Mariannes du Nord | 2005-2010 | 73.7 | 79.0 | 1.0 | 14.0 | 10.2 | ... | ... | ... |
| Norway | 2000-2005 | 76.7 | 81.8 | 1.8 | 4.3 | 3.3 | 5.0 | 4.0 | ... |
| Norvège | 2005-2010 | 77.8 | 82.5 | 1.8 | 3.5 | 3.1 | 4.0 | 4.0 | 7 |

| Country or area<br>Pays ou zone | Year<br>Année | Life expectancy at birth (years)<br>Espérance de vie à la naissance (en années) | | Total fertility rate | Mortality rates - Taux de mortalité | | | | Maternal Maternale p. 100 000 |
|---|---|---|---|---|---|---|---|---|---|
| | | | | | Infant - Infantile p. 1000 | | Under 5 years Moins de 5 ans p. 1 000 | | |
| | | Males<br>Hommes | Females<br>Femmes | Taux de fecondité | Males<br>Hommes | Females<br>Femmes | Males<br>Hommes | Females<br>Femmes | 2005 |
| Occupied Palestinian Terr. | 2000-2005 | 70.8 | 73.9 | 5.6 | 23.1 | 18.5 | 27.0 | 22.0 | ... |
| Terr. palestinien occupé | 2005-2010 | 71.8 | 75.0 | 5.1 | 19.7 | 15.2 | 23.0 | 18.0 | ... |
| Oman | 2000-2005 | 72.9 | 75.9 | 3.7 | 16.3 | 13.9 | 19.0 | 16.0 | ... |
| Oman | 2005-2010 | 74.2 | 77.5 | 3.0 | 12.7 | 11.9 | 14.0 | 13.0 | 64 |
| Pakistan | 2000-2005 | 63.3 | 63.9 | 4.0 | 73.4 | 77.5 | 104.0 | 113.0 | ... |
| Pakistan | 2005-2010 | 65.2 | 65.8 | 3.5 | 64.8 | 70.3 | 91.0 | 100.0 | 320 |
| Palau | 2000-2005 | 67.0 | 70.8 | 2.2 | 37.5 | 28.5 | ... | ... | ... |
| Palaos | 2005-2010 | 68.7 | 72.8 | 2.3 | 30.5 | 21.9 | ... | ... | ... |
| Panama | 2000-2005 | 72.3 | 77.4 | 2.7 | 24.1 | 17.0 | 31.0 | 23.0 | ... |
| Panama | 2005-2010 | 73.0 | 78.2 | 2.6 | 21.2 | 15.0 | 27.0 | 20.0 | 130 |
| Papua New Guinea | 2000-2005 | 54.1 | 59.9 | 4.3 | 70.3 | 59.8 | 98.0 | 83.0 | ... |
| Papouasie-Nvl-Guinée | 2005-2010 | 54.6 | 60.4 | 3.8 | 65.3 | 55.7 | 91.0 | 77.0 | 470 |
| Paraguay | 2000-2005 | 68.7 | 72.9 | 3.5 | 40.4 | 30.4 | 48.0 | 36.0 | ... |
| Paraguay | 2005-2010 | 69.7 | 73.9 | 3.1 | 36.7 | 27.2 | 44.0 | 32.0 | 150 |
| Peru | 2000-2005 | 67.5 | 72.5 | 2.7 | 33.8 | 26.7 | 44.0 | 37.0 | ... |
| Pérou | 2005-2010 | 68.9 | 74.0 | 2.5 | 23.9 | 18.3 | 31.0 | 26.0 | 240 |
| Philippines | 2000-2005 | 68.2 | 72.5 | 3.5 | 32.5 | 22.8 | 39.0 | 27.0 | ... |
| Philippines | 2005-2010 | 69.5 | 73.9 | 3.2 | 27.6 | 18.3 | 33.0 | 22.0 | 230 |
| Pitcairn | 2000-2005 | 67.3 | 74.9 | 2.1 | 31.0 | 23.5 | ... | ... | ... |
| Pitcairn | 2005-2010 | 68.9 | 76.1 | 2.0 | 27.0 | 20.0 | ... | ... | ... |
| Poland | 2000-2005 | 70.4 | 78.8 | 1.3 | 7.9 | 6.6 | 9.0 | 8.0 | ... |
| Pologne | 2005-2010 | 71.3 | 79.8 | 1.2 | 7.3 | 6.2 | 9.0 | 7.0 | 8 |
| Portugal | 2000-2005 | 73.9 | 80.5 | 1.5 | 5.6 | 5.4 | 7.0 | 7.0 | ... |
| Portugal | 2005-2010 | 75.0 | 81.2 | 1.5 | 5.0 | 5.0 | 7.0 | 7.0 | 11 |
| Puerto Rico | 2000-2005 | 73.7 | 82.0 | 1.8 | 8.5 | 7.7 | 11.0 | 9.0 | ... |
| Porto Rico | 2005-2010 | 74.7 | 82.7 | 1.8 | 7.4 | 7.1 | 9.0 | 8.0 | ... |
| Qatar | 2000-2005 | 73.7 | 75.3 | 2.9 | 9.7 | 9.7 | 11.0 | 13.0 | ... |
| Qatar | 2005-2010 | 75.2 | 76.4 | 2.7 | 8.2 | 8.2 | 9.0 | 12.0 | 12 |
| Réunion | 2000-2005 | 71.5 | 80.0 | 2.5 | 20.6 | 9.2 | 24.0 | 10.0 | ... |
| Réunion | 2005-2010 | 72.3 | 80.5 | 2.4 | 18.0 | 8.6 | 21.0 | 10.0 | ... |
| Romania | 2000-2005 | 67.8 | 75.0 | 1.3 | 18.9 | 14.5 | 23.0 | 17.0 | ... |
| Roumanie | 2005-2010 | 69.0 | 76.1 | 1.3 | 16.5 | 13.2 | 20.0 | 15.0 | 24 |
| Russian Federation | 2000-2005 | 58.5 | 71.8 | 1.3 | 19.5 | 14.8 | 25.0 | 19.0 | ... |
| Fédération de Russie | 2005-2010 | 59.0 | 72.6 | 1.3 | 18.9 | 14.2 | 24.0 | 18.0 | 28 |
| Rwanda | 2000-2005 | 41.7 | 45.0 | 6.0 | 124.9 | 110.5 | 203.0 | 180.0 | ... |
| Rwanda | 2005-2010 | 44.6 | 47.8 | 5.9 | 122.8 | 102.0 | 201.0 | 175.0 | 1 300 |
| Saint Helena | 2000-2005 | 74.6 | 82.6 | 2.3 | 10.4 | 8.5 | ... | ... | ... |
| Sainte-Hélène | 2005-2010 | 75.4 | 83.2 | 2.2 | 9.4 | 7.8 | ... | ... | ... |
| Saint Kitts and Nevis | 2000-2005 | 68.6 | 73.3 | 2.4 | 30.8 | 20.2 | ... | ... | ... |
| Saint-Kitts-et-Nevis | 2005-2010 | 69.9 | 74.7 | 2.2 | 26.1 | 16.1 | ... | ... | ... |
| Saint Lucia | 2000-2005 | 70.7 | 74.4 | 2.2 | 16.8 | 12.4 | 21.0 | 17.0 | ... |
| Sainte-Lucie | 2005-2010 | 71.9 | 75.6 | 2.2 | 14.3 | 10.7 | 18.0 | 14.0 | ... |
| Saint Pierre and Miquelon | 2000-2005 | 74.6 | 82.6 | 2.3 | 10.4 | 8.5 | ... | ... | ... |
| Saint-Pierre-et-Miquelon | 2005-2010 | 75.4 | 83.2 | 2.2 | 9.4 | 7.8 | ... | ... | ... |
| Saint Vincent-Grenadines | 2000-2005 | 68.5 | 72.8 | 2.3 | 31.5 | 21.8 | 38.0 | 26.0 | ... |
| Saint Vincent-Grenadines | 2005-2010 | 69.5 | 73.8 | 2.2 | 27.7 | 18.8 | 33.0 | 22.0 | ... |
| Samoa | 2000-2005 | 67.1 | 73.5 | 4.4 | 27.0 | 24.4 | 33.0 | 29.0 | ... |
| Samoa | 2005-2010 | 68.5 | 74.9 | 3.9 | 23.1 | 21.5 | 28.0 | 25.0 | ... |
| San Marino | 2000-2005 | 77.3 | 84.1 | 1.3 | 8.3 | 5.9 | ... | ... | ... |
| Sain-Marin | 2005-2010 | 77.8 | 84.5 | 1.3 | 7.9 | 5.6 | ... | ... | ... |
| Sao Tome and Principe | 2000-2005 | 62.5 | 66.1 | 4.3 | 80.7 | 72.9 | 106.0 | 98.0 | ... |
| Sao Tomé-et-Principe | 2005-2010 | 63.6 | 67.4 | 3.9 | 76.3 | 68.1 | 99.0 | 90.0 | ... |

Selected indicators of life expectancy, childbearing and mortality (*continued*)

Choix d'indicateurs de l'espérance de vie, de la maternité et de la mortalité (*suite*)

| Country or area<br>Pays ou zone | Year<br>Année | Life expectancy at birth (years)<br>Espérance de vie à la naissance (en années) | | Total fertility rate | Mortality rates - Taux de mortalité | | | | Maternal<br>Maternelle<br>p. 100 000 |
|---|---|---|---|---|---|---|---|---|---|
| | | | | | Infant - Infantile<br>p. 1000 | | Under 5 years<br>Moins de 5 ans<br>p. 1 000 | | |
| | | Males<br>Hommes | Females<br>Femmes | Taux de<br>fecondité | Males<br>Hommes | Females<br>Femmes | Males<br>Hommes | Females<br>Femmes | 2005 |
| Saudi Arabia | 2000-2005 | 69.8 | 74.0 | 3.8 | 26.5 | 18.2 | 31.0 | 21.0 | ... |
| Arabie saoudite | 2005-2010 | 70.9 | 75.3 | 3.4 | 22.7 | 14.8 | 26.0 | 17.0 | 18 |
| Senegal | 2000-2005 | 59.7 | 63.6 | 5.2 | 73.8 | 64.3 | 129.0 | 118.0 | ... |
| Sénégal | 2005-2010 | 61.1 | 65.1 | 4.7 | 70.4 | 60.8 | 121.0 | 109.0 | 980 |
| Serbia | 2000-2005 | 70.9 | 75.6 | 1.7 | 14.3 | 11.6 | 17.0 | 14.0 | ... |
| Serbie | 2005-2010 | 71.7 | 76.3 | 1.8 | 12.6 | 10.8 | 15.0 | 13.0 | ... |
| Seychelles | 2000-2005 | 67.0 | 77.0 | 2.0 | 27.3 | 17.1 | ... | ... | ... |
| Seychelles | 2005-2010 | 67.7 | 77.6 | 2.0 | 25.2 | 15.9 | ... | ... | ... |
| Sierra Leone | 2000-2005 | 39.3 | 42.8 | 6.5 | 176.3 | 154.5 | 303.0 | 277.0 | ... |
| Sierra Leone | 2005-2010 | 41.0 | 44.2 | 6.5 | 170.9 | 149.5 | 291.0 | 265.0 | 2 100 |
| Singapore | 2000-2005 | 76.8 | 80.8 | 1.4 | 3.0 | 2.9 | 4.0 | 4.0 | ... |
| Singapour | 2005-2010 | 78.0 | 81.9 | 1.3 | 3.0 | 3.0 | 4.0 | 4.0 | 14 |
| Slovakia | 2000-2005 | 69.8 | 77.8 | 1.2 | 8.0 | 6.8 | 9.0 | 8.0 | ... |
| Slovaquie | 2005-2010 | 70.7 | 78.5 | 1.3 | 7.4 | 6.5 | 9.0 | 8.0 | 6 |
| Slovenia | 2000-2005 | 72.9 | 80.4 | 1.2 | 5.4 | 5.2 | 7.0 | 7.0 | ... |
| Slovénie | 2005-2010 | 74.1 | 81.5 | 1.3 | 4.8 | 4.8 | 6.0 | 6.0 | 6 |
| Solomon Islands | 2000-2005 | 61.6 | 63.0 | 4.4 | 61.3 | 58.7 | 80.0 | 82.0 | ... |
| Iles Salomon | 2005-2010 | 62.7 | 64.5 | 3.9 | 56.3 | 52.7 | 73.0 | 72.0 | 220 |
| Somalia | 2000-2005 | 44.8 | 47.1 | 6.4 | 134.6 | 119.8 | 218.0 | 208.0 | ... |
| Somalie | 2005-2010 | 46.9 | 49.4 | 6.0 | 123.4 | 108.9 | 198.0 | 188.0 | 1 400 |
| South Africa | 2000-2005 | 51.2 | 55.6 | 2.8 | 56.1 | 47.5 | 82.0 | 70.0 | ... |
| Afrique du Sud | 2005-2010 | 48.8 | 49.7 | 2.6 | 48.3 | 41.2 | 71.0 | 61.0 | 400 |
| Spain | 2000-2005 | 76.6 | 83.4 | 1.3 | 4.8 | 4.1 | 6.0 | 5.0 | ... |
| Espagne | 2005-2010 | 77.7 | 84.2 | 1.4 | 4.5 | 3.9 | 6.0 | 5.0 | 4 |
| Sri Lanka | 2000-2005 | 67.0 | 75.0 | 2.0 | 13.5 | 11.2 | 15.0 | 13.0 | ... |
| Sri Lanka | 2005-2010 | 68.8 | 76.2 | 1.9 | 11.8 | 10.2 | 14.0 | 12.0 | 58 |
| Sudan | 2000-2005 | 55.0 | 57.8 | 4.8 | 78.1 | 66.7 | 125.0 | 111.0 | ... |
| Soudan | 2005-2010 | 57.1 | 60.1 | 4.2 | 70.2 | 59.3 | 111.0 | 98.0 | 450 |
| Suriname | 2000-2005 | 66.0 | 72.5 | 2.6 | 36.9 | 26.3 | 45.0 | 33.0 | ... |
| Suriname | 2005-2010 | 67.0 | 73.6 | 2.4 | 32.2 | 22.9 | 40.0 | 29.0 | 72 |
| Swaziland | 2000-2005 | 42.6 | 45.1 | 3.9 | 94.5 | 79.8 | 144.0 | 126.0 | ... |
| Swaziland | 2005-2010 | 39.8 | 39.4 | 3.4 | 78.0 | 63.9 | 122.0 | 105.0 | 390 |
| Sweden | 2000-2005 | 77.8 | 82.3 | 1.7 | 3.5 | 3.1 | 4.0 | 4.0 | ... |
| Suède | 2005-2010 | 78.7 | 83.0 | 1.8 | 3.3 | 3.1 | 4.0 | 4.0 | 3 |
| Switzerland | 2000-2005 | 77.9 | 83.2 | 1.4 | 4.7 | 4.0 | 6.0 | 5.0 | ... |
| Suisse | 2005-2010 | 79.0 | 84.2 | 1.4 | 4.4 | 3.8 | 6.0 | 5.0 | 5 |
| Syrian Arab Republic | 2000-2005 | 71.2 | 74.9 | 3.5 | 21.6 | 15.4 | 25.0 | 18.0 | ... |
| Rép. arabe syrienne | 2005-2010 | 72.3 | 76.1 | 3.1 | 18.2 | 13.7 | 21.0 | 16.0 | 130 |
| Tajikistan | 2000-2005 | 63.4 | 68.6 | 3.8 | 66.2 | 59.8 | 87.0 | 78.0 | ... |
| Tadjikistan | 2005-2010 | 64.1 | 69.4 | 3.3 | 63.2 | 57.1 | 83.0 | 74.0 | 170 |
| Thailand | 2000-2005 | 63.7 | 74.0 | 1.8 | 13.3 | 10.5 | 19.0 | 15.0 | ... |
| Thaïlande | 2005-2010 | 66.5 | 75.0 | 1.9 | 12.2 | 8.9 | 17.0 | 13.0 | 110 |
| TFYR of Macedonia | 2000-2005 | 71.1 | 75.9 | 1.6 | 17.5 | 15.4 | 20.0 | 18.0 | ... |
| L'ex-R.y. Macédoine | 2005-2010 | 71.8 | 76.6 | 1.4 | 15.4 | 14.3 | 17.0 | 16.0 | 10 |
| Timor-Leste | 2000-2005 | 57.5 | 59.1 | 7.0 | 81.3 | 75.6 | 111.0 | 109.0 | ... |
| Timor-Leste | 2005-2010 | 60.0 | 61.7 | 6.5 | 69.2 | 64.0 | 92.0 | 91.0 | 380 |
| Togo | 2000-2005 | 55.6 | 59.5 | 5.4 | 100.2 | 87.6 | 145.0 | 128.0 | ... |
| Togo | 2005-2010 | 56.7 | 60.1 | 4.8 | 95.1 | 81.9 | 135.0 | 118.0 | 510 |
| Tokelau | 2000-2005 | 74.5 | 82.4 | 3.5 | 10.6 | 8.7 | ... | ... | ... |
| Tokélaou | 2005-2010 | 75.3 | 83.0 | 3.2 | 9.5 | 8.0 | ... | ... | ... |
| Tonga | 2000-2005 | 71.3 | 73.3 | 3.7 | 16.8 | 24.9 | 20.0 | 30.0 | ... |
| Tonga | 2005-2010 | 72.3 | 74.3 | 3.8 | 14.7 | 22.8 | 17.0 | 27.0 | ... |

| Country or area<br>Pays ou zone | Year<br>Année | Life expectancy at birth (years)<br>Espérance de vie à la naissance (en années) | | Total fertility rate<br>Taux de fecondité | Mortality rates - Taux de mortalité | | | | Maternal<br>Maternale<br>p. 100 000 |
|---|---|---|---|---|---|---|---|---|---|
| | | | | | Infant - Infantile<br>p. 1000 | | Under 5 years<br>Moins de 5 ans<br>p. 1 000 | | |
| | | Males<br>Hommes | Females<br>Femmes | | Males<br>Hommes | Females<br>Femmes | Males<br>Hommes | Females<br>Femmes | 2005 |
| Trinidad and Tobago | 2000-2005 | 66.8 | 71.1 | 1.6 | 17.2 | 13.0 | 23.0 | 18.0 | ... |
| Trinité-et-Tobago | 2005-2010 | 67.8 | 71.8 | 1.6 | 14.2 | 10.5 | 20.0 | 15.0 | 45 |
| Tunisia | 2000-2005 | 71.1 | 75.1 | 2.0 | 24.3 | 20.5 | 27.0 | 23.0 | ... |
| Tunisie | 2005-2010 | 71.9 | 76.0 | 1.9 | 21.1 | 18.4 | 24.0 | 21.0 | 100 |
| Turkey | 2000-2005 | 68.5 | 73.3 | 2.2 | 35.5 | 27.1 | 41.0 | 32.0 | ... |
| Turquie | 2005-2010 | 69.4 | 74.3 | 2.1 | 31.4 | 23.5 | 36.0 | 27.0 | 44 |
| Turkmenistan | 2000-2005 | 58.2 | 66.7 | 2.8 | 86.6 | 69.6 | 109.0 | 89.0 | ... |
| Turkménistan | 2005-2010 | 59.0 | 67.5 | 2.5 | 82.5 | 66.5 | 104.0 | 85.0 | 130 |
| Turks and Caicos Islands | 2000-2005 | 68.6 | 73.3 | 2.3 | 30.8 | 20.2 | ... | ... | ... |
| Iles Turques et Caïques | 2005-2010 | 69.9 | 74.7 | 2.2 | 26.1 | 16.1 | ... | ... | ... |
| Tuvalu | 2000-2005 | 62.5 | 66.0 | 3.7 | 40.5 | 43.0 | ... | ... | ... |
| Tuvalu | 2005-2010 | 64.0 | 67.7 | 3.5 | 35.8 | 38.5 | ... | ... | ... |
| Uganda | 2000-2005 | 47.3 | 48.2 | 6.7 | 89.6 | 78.6 | 146.0 | 134.0 | ... |
| Ouganda | 2005-2010 | 50.8 | 52.2 | 6.5 | 82.4 | 71.3 | 134.0 | 121.0 | 550 |
| Ukraine | 2000-2005 | 62.0 | 73.4 | 1.2 | 15.5 | 11.3 | 19.0 | 14.0 | ... |
| Ukraine | 2005-2010 | 62.1 | 73.8 | 1.2 | 14.6 | 10.9 | 18.0 | 13.0 | 18 |
| United Arab Emirates | 2000-2005 | 76.3 | 80.5 | 2.5 | 9.3 | 8.7 | 10.0 | 10.0 | ... |
| Emirats arabes unis | 2005-2010 | 77.2 | 81.5 | 2.3 | 8.4 | 7.9 | 9.0 | 9.0 | 37 |
| United Kingdom | 2000-2005 | 76.1 | 80.7 | 1.7 | 5.5 | 5.0 | 7.0 | 6.0 | ... |
| Royaume-Uni | 2005-2010 | 77.2 | 81.6 | 1.8 | 4.9 | 4.7 | 6.0 | 6.0 | 8 |
| United Rep. of Tanzania | 2000-2005 | 48.7 | 50.6 | 5.7 | 83.4 | 72.8 | 138.0 | 125.0 | ... |
| Rép.-Unie de Tanzanie | 2005-2010 | 51.4 | 53.6 | 5.2 | 78.3 | 66.7 | 125.0 | 111.0 | 950 |
| United States | 2000-2005 | 74.7 | 80.0 | 2.0 | 6.8 | 6.8 | 8.0 | 8.0 | ... |
| Etats-Unis | 2005-2010 | 75.6 | 80.8 | 2.1 | 6.3 | 6.3 | 8.0 | 8.0 | 11 |
| United States Virgin Is. | 2000-2005 | 74.6 | 82.6 | 2.2 | 10.4 | 8.5 | 12.0 | 9.0 | ... |
| Iles Vierges américaines | 2005-2010 | 75.5 | 83.3 | 2.1 | 9.4 | 7.7 | 11.0 | 9.0 | ... |
| Uruguay | 2000-2005 | 71.6 | 78.9 | 2.2 | 16.0 | 12.6 | 20.0 | 15.0 | ... |
| Uruguay | 2005-2010 | 72.8 | 79.9 | 2.1 | 14.4 | 11.7 | 18.0 | 15.0 | 20 |
| Uzbekistan | 2000-2005 | 63.3 | 69.7 | 2.7 | 63.5 | 52.2 | 76.0 | 64.0 | ... |
| Ouzbékistan | 2005-2010 | 64.0 | 70.4 | 2.5 | 60.3 | 49.5 | 72.0 | 60.0 | 24 |
| Vanuatu | 2000-2005 | 66.8 | 70.4 | 4.2 | 38.4 | 30.0 | 47.0 | 37.0 | ... |
| Vanuatu | 2005-2010 | 68.3 | 72.1 | 3.7 | 32.3 | 24.1 | 39.0 | 29.0 | ... |
| Venezuela (Bolivarian Rep. of) | 2000-2005 | 69.9 | 75.8 | 2.7 | 21.2 | 16.4 | 27.0 | 21.0 | ... |
| Venezuela (Rép. bòlivar. du) | 2005-2010 | 70.9 | 76.8 | 2.5 | 19.1 | 14.8 | 24.0 | 19.0 | 57 |
| Viet Nam | 2000-2005 | 71.2 | 74.9 | 2.3 | 25.4 | 19.2 | 31.0 | 23.0 | ... |
| Viet Nam | 2005-2010 | 72.3 | 76.2 | 2.1 | 22.2 | 16.7 | 27.0 | 20.0 | 150 |
| Wallis and Futuna Islands | 2000-2005 | 67.1 | 73.5 | 2.7 | 27.0 | 24.4 | ... | ... | ... |
| Iles Wallis et Futuna | 2005-2010 | 68.5 | 74.9 | 2.4 | 23.1 | 21.5 | ... | ... | ... |
| Western Sahara | 2000-2005 | 62.3 | 65.8 | 3.0 | 58.5 | 47.4 | 76.0 | 64.0 | ... |
| Sahara occidental | 2005-2010 | 64.3 | 68.1 | 2.7 | 49.5 | 38.7 | 62.0 | 50.0 | ... |
| Yemen | 2000-2005 | 58.8 | 61.8 | 6.0 | 74.7 | 63.5 | 101.0 | 90.0 | ... |
| Yémen | 2005-2010 | 61.1 | 64.4 | 5.5 | 63.8 | 53.2 | 84.0 | 73.0 | 430 |
| Zambia | 2000-2005 | 38.9 | 39.4 | 5.6 | 108.1 | 94.9 | 180.0 | 164.0 | ... |
| Zambie | 2005-2010 | 42.1 | 42.5 | 5.2 | 99.2 | 86.0 | 165.0 | 149.0 | 830 |
| Zimbabwe | 2000-2005 | 40.2 | 39.7 | 3.6 | 69.3 | 59.4 | 110.0 | 98.0 | ... |
| Zimbabwe | 2005-2010 | 44.1 | 42.7 | 3.2 | 63.0 | 52.9 | 101.0 | 87.0 | 880 |

# 9

**Selected indicators of life expectancy, childbearing and mortality** (*continued*)
**Choix d'indicateurs de l'espérance de vie, de la maternité et de la mortalité** (*suite*)

Source

Life expectancy, total fertility, infant and under 5 years mortality rates: United Nations, "World Population Prospects: The 2006 Revision". Maternal mortality: World Health Organization, the United Nations Children's Fund and the United Nations Population Fund, "Maternal Mortality in 2005: Estimates developed by WHO, UNICEF, UNFPA and the World Bank".

Notes

1 Including Christmas Island, Cocos (Keeling) Islands and Norfolk Island.
2 For statistical purposes, the data for China do not include those for the Hong Kong Special Administrative Region (Hong Kong SAR) and Macao Special Administrative Region (Macao SAR).

3 Including Agalega, Rodrigues and Saint Brandon.

Source

Espérance de vie à la naissance, taux de fecondité, taux de mortalité infantile, et taux de mortalité des moins de 5 ans : Organisation des Nations Unies, "World Population Prospects: The 2006 Revision". Taux de mortalité maternal : Organisation mondiale de la la santé, Fonds des Nations Unies pour l'enfance et Fonds des Nations Unies pour la population, "Maternal Mortality in 2005 : Estimates developed by WHO, UNICEF, UNFPA and the World Bank".

Notes

1 Y compris les îles Christmas, Cocos (Keeling) et Norfolk.

2 Pour la présentation des statistiques, les données pour la Chine ne comprennent pas la Région Administrative Spéciale de Hong Kong (Hong Kong RAS) et la Région Administrative Spéciale de Macao (Macao RAS).

3 Y compris Agalega, Rodrigues et Saint Brandon.

*Table 8* is based on detailed data on population and its growth and distribution published in the United Nations Demographic Yearbook. Only official national population estimates reported to the United Nations Statistics Division are included in this table. For a comprehensive description of methods of evaluation and the limitations of the data, consult the *Demographic Yearbook*.

Unless otherwise indicated, figures refer to de facto (present-in-area) population for the present territory; surface area estimates include inland waters.

*Table 9*: "Life expectancy at birth", "Infant mortality rate" and "Total fertility rate" are taken from the estimates and projections prepared by the Population Division of the United Nations Secretariat, published in *World Population Prospects: The 2006 Revision.*

"Life expectancy at birth" is an overall estimate of the expected average number of years to be lived by a female or male newborn. Many developing countries lack complete and reliable statistics of births and deaths based on civil registration, so various estimation techniques are used to calculate life expectancy using other sources of data, mainly population censuses and demographic surveys. Life expectancy at birth by sex gives a statistical summary of current differences in male and female mortality across all ages. However, trends and differentials in infant and child mortality rates are the predominant influence on trends and differentials in life expectancy at birth in most developing countries. Thus, life expectancy at birth is of limited usefulness in these countries in assessing levels and differentials in male and female mortality at other ages.

"Total fertility rate" is the average number of children that would be born alive to a hypothetical cohort of women if, throughout their reproductive years, the age specific fertility rates for the specified year remained unchanged.

"Infant mortality rate" is the total number of deaths in a given year of children less than one year old divided by the total number of live births in the same year, multiplied by 1,000. It is an approximation of the number of deaths per 1,000 children born alive who die within one year of birth. In most developing countries where civil registration data are deficient, the most reliable sources are demographic surveys of households. Where these are not available, other sources and general estimates are made which are necessarily of limited reliability. Where countries lack comprehensive and accurate systems of civil registration, infant mortality statistics by sex are difficult to collect or to estimate with any degree of reliability because of reporting biases, and thus are not shown here.

Le *tableau 8* est fondé sur des données détaillées sur la population, sa croissance et sa distribution, publiées dans l'*Annuaire démographique* des Nations Unies. Le tableau inclut seulement des estimations officielles de la population qui ont été envoyées à la Division de Statistique des Nations Unies. Pour une description complète des méthodes d'évaluation et une indication des limites des données, voir l'*Annuaire démographique.*

Sauf indication contraire, les chiffres se rapportent à la population effectivement présente sur le territoire tel qu'il est actuellement défini; les estimations de superficie comprennent les étendues d'eau intérieures.

*Tableau 9* : "L'espérance de vie à la naissance", le "taux de mortalité infantile" et le "taux de fécondité" sont proviennent des estimations et projections de la Division de la population du Secrétariat de l'ONU, qui ont publiées dans *"World Population Prospects: The 2006 Revision".*

"L'espérance de vie à la naissance" est une estimation globale du nombre d'années qu'un nouveauné de sexe masculin ou féminin vivant, peut s'attendre à vivre. Comme dans beaucoup de pays en développement, les registres d'état civil ne permettent pas d'établir des statistiques fiables et complètes des naissances et des décès, diverses techniques d'estimation ont été utilisées pour calculer l'espérance de vie à partir d'autres sources et notamment des recensements et enquêtes démographiques. Sur la base des statistiques de l'espérance de vie par sexe, on peut calculer la différence entre la longévité des hommes et celle des femmes à tous les âges. Cependant, ce sont les tendances et les écarts des taux de mortalité infantile et juvénile qui influent de façon prépondérante sur les tendances et les écarts de l'espérance de vie à la naissance dans la plupart des pays en développement. Ainsi, l'espérance de vie à la naissance ne revêt qu'une utilité limitée dans ce pays pour évaluer les niveaux et les écarts de la mortalité des femmes et des hommes à des âges plus avancés.

Le "taux de fécondité" est le nombre moyen d'enfants que mettrait au monde une cohorte hypothétique de femmes si, pendant toutes leurs années d'âge reproductif, les taux de fécondité par âge de l'année en question restaient inchangés.

Le "taux de mortalité infantile" correspond au nombre total de décès au cours d'une année donnée des enfants de moins d'un an divisé par le nombre total de naissances vivantes au cours de la même année, multiplié par 1 000. Il s'agit d'une approximation du nombre de décès pour 1 000 enfants nés vivants qui meurent la première année. Dans la plupart des pays en développement, où les données d'état civil sont déficientes, les sources les plus fiables sont les enquêtes démographiques

The "under-five mortality rate" is the probability (expressed as a rate per 1,000 live births) of a child born in a specified year dying before reaching the age of five if subject to current age-specific mortality rates.

Data on maternal mortality are estimates developed by the World Health Organization, UNICEF and the United Nations Population Fund and published in *Maternal Mortality in 2005*.

The *maternal mortality ratio* is the number of women who die from any cause related to or aggravated by pregnancy or its management (excluding accidental or incidental causes) during pregnancy and childbirth or within 42 days of termination of pregnancy, irrespective of the duration and site of the pregnancy, per 100,000 live births. The 10th revision of the *International Classification of Diseases* makes provisions for including late maternal deaths occurring between six weeks and one year after childbirth.

auprès des ménages. Lorsque de telles enquêtes ne sont pas réalisées, d'autres sources sont utilisées et des estimations générales sont réalisées qui est nécessairement d'une fiabilité limitée. Lorsqu'il n'a pas dans les pays de systèmes complets et exacts d'enregistrement des faits d'état civil, les statistiques de la mortalité infantile par sexe sont difficiles à rassembler ou à estimer avec quelque fiabilité que ce soit en raison des distorsions de la notification; elles ne sont donc pas indiquées ici.

Le "taux de mortalité des enfants de moins de 5 ans" est la probabilité (exprimée en tant que taux par 1 000 naissances vivantes) qu'un enfant né une année donnée meure avant d'atteindre l'âge de 5 ans compte tenu des taux de mortalité actuels liés à l'âge.

Les données concernant la mortalité maternelle sont des estimations de l'Organisation mondiale de la santé, de l'UNICEF, et du Fonds des Nations Unies pour la Population publiées dans "*Maternal Mortality in 2005*".

Le *taux de mortalité maternelle* est le nombre de femmes qui meurent d'une cause quelconque liée à la grossesse ou à sa gestion (à l'exclusion des causes accidentelles ou secondaires) ou d'une aggravée par elle pendant la grossesse ou l'accouchement ou dans un délai de 42 jours après la fin de la grossesse, sans considération ede la durée et du lieu de la grossesse, par 100 000 naissances vivantes. La dixième révision de la *Classification internationale des maladies* prévoit l'inclusion des décès tardifs survenant entre six semaines et un an après l'accouchement.

# Proportion of seats held by women in national parliament
Percentage

# Proportion de sièges occupés par des femmes au parlement national
Pourcentage

| Country or area<br>Pays ou zone | 1990 | 2000 | 2001 | 2002 | 2003 | 2004 | 2005 | 2006 | 2007 | 2008 |
|---|---|---|---|---|---|---|---|---|---|---|
| Afghanistan<br>Afghanistan | 3.7 | ... | ... | ... | ... | ... | ... | 27.3 | 27.3 | 27.7 |
| Albania<br>Albanie | 28.8 | 5.2 | 5.2 | 5.7 | 5.7 | 5.7 | 6.4 | 7.1 | 7.1 | 7.1 |
| Algeria<br>Algérie | 2.4 | 3.2 | 3.4 | 3.4 | 6.2 | 6.2 | 6.2 | 6.2 | 6.2 | 7.7 |
| Andorra<br>Andorre | ... | 7.1 | 7.1 | 14.3 | 14.3 | 14.3 | 14.3 | 28.6 | 28.6 | 25.0 |
| Angola<br>Angola | 14.5 | 15.5 | 15.5 | 15.5 | 15.5 | 15.5 | 15.0 | 15.0 | 15.0 | 15.0 |
| Antigua and Barbuda<br>Antigua-et-Barbuda | 0.0 | ... | 5.3 | 5.3 | 5.3 | 5.3 | 10.5 | 10.5 | 10.5 | 10.5 |
| Argentina<br>Argentine | 6.3 | 28.0 | 26.5 | 30.7 | 30.7 | 30.7 | 33.7 | 35.0 | 35.0 | 40.0 |
| Armenia<br>Arménie | 35.6 | 3.1 | 3.1 | 3.1 | 3.1 | 4.6 | 5.3 | 5.3 | 5.3 | 9.2 |
| Australia<br>Australie | 6.1 | 22.4 | 23.0 | 25.3 | 25.3 | 25.3 | 24.7 | 24.7 | 24.7 | 26.7 |
| Austria<br>Autriche | 11.5 | 26.8 | 26.8 | 26.8 | 33.9 | 33.9 | 33.9 | 33.9 | 32.2 | 32.8 |
| Azerbaijan<br>Azerbaïdjan | ... | 12.0 | ... | 10.5 | 10.5 | 10.5 | 10.5 | 13.0 | 11.3 | 11.4 |
| Bahamas<br>Bahamas | 4.1 | 15.0 | 15.0 | 15.0 | 20.0 | 20.0 | 20.0 | 20.0 | 20.0 | 12.2 |
| Bahrain<br>Bahreïn | ... | ... | ... | ... | 0.0 | 0.0 | 0.0 | 0.0 | 2.5 | 2.5 |
| Bangladesh<br>Bangladesh | 10.3 | 9.1 | 9.1 | ... | 2.0 | 2.0 | 2.0 | 14.8[1,2] | ... | ... |
| Barbados<br>Barbade | 3.7 | 10.7 | 10.7 | 10.7 | 10.7 | 13.3 | 13.3 | 13.3 | 13.3 | 10.0 |
| Belarus<br>Bélarus | ... | 4.5 | ... | 10.3 | 10.3 | 10.3 | 29.4 | 29.1 | 29.1 | 29.1 |
| Belgium<br>Belgique | 8.5 | 23.3 | 23.3 | 23.3 | 23.3 | 35.3 | 34.7 | 34.7 | 34.7 | 35.3 |
| Belize<br>Belize | 0.0 | 6.9 | 6.9 | 6.9 | 6.9 | 3.3 | 6.7 | 6.7 | 6.7 | 3.3 |
| Benin<br>Bénin | 2.9 | 6.0 | 6.0 | 6.0 | 6.0 | 7.2 | 7.2 | 7.2 | 7.2 | 10.8 |
| Bhutan<br>Bhoutan | 2.0 | 2.0 | 9.3 | 9.3 | 9.3 | 9.3 | 9.2 | 9.3 | 2.7 | 2.7 |
| Bolivia<br>Bolivie | 9.2 | 11.5 | 11.5 | 11.5 | 18.5 | 18.5 | 19.2 | 16.9 | 16.9 | 16.9 |
| Bosnia and Herzegovina<br>Bosnie-Herzégovine | ... | 28.6 | ... | 7.1 | 16.7 | 16.7 | 16.7 | 16.7 | 14.3 | 11.9 |
| Botswana<br>Botswana | 5.0 | ... | 17.0 | 17.0 | 17.0 | 17.0 | 11.1 | 11.1 | 11.1 | 11.1 |
| Brazil<br>Brésil | 5.3 | 5.7 | 5.7 | 6.8 | 8.6 | 8.6 | 8.6 | 8.6 | 8.8 | 9.0 |
| Bulgaria<br>Bulgarie | 21.0 | 10.8 | 10.8 | 26.3 | 26.3 | 26.3 | 26.3 | 22.1 | 22.1 | 21.7 |

| Country or area<br>Pays ou zone | 1990 | 2000 | 2001 | 2002 | 2003 | 2004 | 2005 | 2006 | 2007 | 2008 |
|---|---|---|---|---|---|---|---|---|---|---|
| Burkina Faso<br>Burkina Faso | ... | 8.1 | 8.1 | 8.1 | 11.7 | 11.7 | 11.7 | 11.7 | 11.7 | 15.3 |
| Burundi<br>Burundi | ... | 6.0 | 14.4 | 19.5 | 18.4 | 18.4 | 18.4 | 30.5 | 30.5 | 30.5 |
| Cambodia<br>Cambodge | ... | 8.2 | 7.4 | 7.4 | 7.4 | 9.8 | 9.8 | 9.8 | 9.8 | 19.5 |
| Cameroon<br>Cameroun | 14.4 | 5.6 | 5.6 | 5.6 | 8.9 | 8.9 | 8.9 | 8.9 | 8.9 | 13.9 |
| Canada<br>Canada | 13.3 | 20.6 | 20.6 | 20.6 | 20.6 | 20.6 | 21.1 | 21.1 | 20.8 | 21.3 |
| Cape Verde<br>Cap-Vert | 12.0 | 11.1 | 11.1 | 11.1 | 11.1 | 11.1 | 11.1 | 11.1 | 15.3 | 18.1 |
| Central African Rep.<br>Rép. centrafricaine | 3.8 | 7.3 | 7.3 | 7.3 | 7.3 | ... | ... | 10.5 | 10.5 | 10.5 |
| Chad<br>Tchad | ... | 2.4 | 2.4 | 2.4 | 5.8 | 5.8 | 6.5 | 6.5 | 6.5 | 5.2 |
| Chile<br>Chili | ... | 10.8 | 10.8 | 12.5 | 12.5 | 12.5 | 12.5 | 15.0 | 15.0 | 15.0 |
| China<br>Chine | 21.3 | 21.8 | 21.8 | 21.8 | 21.8 | 20.2 | 20.2 | 20.3 | 20.3 | 20.6 |
| Colombia<br>Colombie | 4.5 | 11.8 | 11.8 | 11.8 | 12.0 | 12.0 | 12.0 | 12.1 | 8.4 | 8.4 |
| Comoros<br>Comores | 0.0 | ... | ... | ... | ... | ... | 3.0 | 3.0 | 3.0 | 3.0 |
| Congo<br>Congo | 14.3 | 12.0 | 12.0 | 12.0 | 9.3 | 8.5 | 8.5 | 8.5 | 8.5 | 7.3 |
| Costa Rica<br>Costa Rica | 10.5 | 19.3 | 19.3 | 19.3 | 35.1 | 35.1 | 35.1 | 35.1 | 38.6 | 36.8 |
| Côte d'Ivoire<br>Côte d'Ivoire | 5.7 | ... | ... | 8.5 | 8.5 | 8.5 | 8.5 | 8.5 | 8.5 | 8.9 |
| Croatia<br>Croatie | ... | ... | 20.5 | 20.5 | 20.5 | 17.8 | 21.7 | 21.7 | 21.7 | 20.9 |
| Cuba<br>Cuba | 33.9 | 27.6 | 27.6 | 27.6 | 36.0 | 36.0 | 36.0 | 36.0 | 36.0 | 43.2 |
| Cyprus<br>Chypre | 1.8 | 5.4 | 7.1 | 10.7 | 10.7 | 10.7 | 16.1 | 16.1 | 14.3 | 14.3 |
| Czech Republic<br>République tchèque | ... | 15.0 | 15.0 | 15.0 | 17.0 | 17.0 | 17.0 | 17.0 | 15.5 | 15.5 |
| Dem. Rep. of the Congo<br>Rép. dém. du Congo | 5.4 | ... | ... | ... | ... | 8.3 | 12.0 | 12.0 | 8.4 | 8.4 |
| Denmark<br>Danemark | 30.7 | 37.4 | 37.4 | 38.0 | 38.0 | 38.0 | 38.0 | 36.9 | 36.9 | 38.0 |
| Djibouti<br>Djibouti | 0.0 | 0.0 | 0.0 | 0.0 | 10.8 | 10.8 | 10.8 | 10.8 | 10.8 | 13.8 |
| Dominica<br>Dominique | 10.0 | 9.4 | ... | 18.8 | 18.8 | 18.8 | 19.4 | 12.9 | 12.9 | 16.1 |
| Dominican Republic<br>Rép. dominicaine | 7.5 | 16.1 | 16.1 | 16.1 | 17.3 | 17.3 | 17.3 | 17.3 | 19.7 | 19.7 |
| Ecuador<br>Equateur | 4.5 | 17.4 | 14.6 | 14.6 | 16.0 | 16.0 | 16.0 | 16.0 | 25.0 | 25.0 |
| Egypt<br>Egypte | 3.9 | 2.0 | ... | 2.4 | 2.4 | 2.4 | 2.9 | 2.0 | 2.0 | 1.8 |
| El Salvador<br>El Salvador | 11.7 | 16.7 | 9.5 | 9.5 | 9.5 | 10.7 | 10.7 | 10.7 | 16.7 | 16.7 |

**Proportion of seats held by women in national parliament**—Percentage (*continued*)
**Proportion de sièges occupés par des femmes au parlement national**—Pourcentage (*suite*)

| Country or area<br>Pays ou zone | 1990 | 2000 | 2001 | 2002 | 2003 | 2004 | 2005 | 2006 | 2007 | 2008 |
|---|---|---|---|---|---|---|---|---|---|---|
| Equatorial Guinea<br>Guinée équatoriale | 13.3 | 5.0 | 5.0 | 5.0 | 5.0 | 5.0 | 18.0 | 18.0 | 18.0 | 18.0 |
| Eritrea<br>Erythrée | ... | 14.7 | 14.7 | 14.7 | 22.0 | 22.0 | 22.0 | 22.0 | 22.0 | 22.0 |
| Estonia<br>Estonie | ... | 17.8 | 17.8 | 17.8 | 17.8 | 18.8 | 18.8 | 18.8 | 18.8 | 20.8 |
| Ethiopia<br>Ethiopie | ... | 2.0 | 7.7 | 7.7 | 7.7 | 7.7 | 7.7 | 21.4 | 21.9 | 21.9 |
| Fiji<br>Fidji | ... | 11.3 | ... | 5.7 | 5.7 | 5.7 | 8.5 | 8.5[3] | ... | ... |
| Finland<br>Finlande | 31.5 | 37.0 | 36.5 | 36.5 | 36.5 | 37.5 | 37.5 | 37.5 | 38.0 | 41.5 |
| France<br>France | 6.9 | 10.9 | 10.9 | 10.9 | 12.2 | 12.2 | 12.2 | 12.2 | 12.2 | 18.2 |
| Gabon<br>Gabon | 13.3 | 8.3 | 9.2 | ... | 9.2 | 9.2 | 9.2 | 9.2 | 12.5 | 16.7 |
| Gambia<br>Gambie | 7.8 | 2.0 | 2.0 | ... | 13.2 | 13.2 | 13.2 | 13.2 | 9.4 | 9.4 |
| Georgia<br>Géorgie | ... | 7.2 | 7.2 | 7.2 | 7.2 | 7.2 | 9.4 | 9.4 | 9.4 | 9.4 |
| Germany<br>Allemagne | ... | 30.9 | 30.9 | 31.7 | 32.2 | 32.2 | 32.8 | 31.8 | 31.6 | 31.6 |
| Ghana<br>Ghana | ... | 9.0 | ... | 9.0 | 9.0 | 9.0 | 10.9 | 10.9 | 10.9 | 10.9 |
| Greece<br>Grèce | 6.7 | 6.3 | 8.7 | 8.7 | 8.7 | 8.7 | 14.0 | 13.0 | 13.0 | 14.7 |
| Grenada<br>Grenade | ... | ... | 26.7 | 26.7 | 26.7 | 26.7 | 26.7 | 26.7 | 26.7 | 26.7 |
| Guatemala<br>Guatemala | 7.0 | 7.1 | 8.8 | 8.8 | 8.8 | 8.2 | 8.2 | 8.2 | 8.2 | 12.0 |
| Guinea<br>Guinée | ... | 8.8 | 8.8 | 8.8 | 19.3 | 19.3 | 19.3 | 19.3 | 19.3 | 19.3 |
| Guinea-Bissau<br>Guinée-Bissau | 20.0 | ... | 7.8 | 7.8 | 7.8 | ... | 14.0 | 14.0 | 14.0 | 14.0 |
| Guyana<br>Guyana | 36.9 | 18.5 | 18.5 | 20.0 | 20.0 | 20.0 | 30.8 | 30.8 | 29.0 | 29.0 |
| Haiti<br>Haïti | ... | 3.6 | ... | 3.6 | 3.6 | 3.6 | 3.6 | 3.6 | 4.1 | 4.1 |
| Honduras<br>Honduras | 10.2 | 9.4 | 9.4 | 9.4 | 5.5 | 5.5 | 5.5 | 23.4 | 23.4 | 23.4 |
| Hungary<br>Hongrie | 20.7 | 8.3 | 8.3 | 8.3 | 9.8 | 9.8 | 9.1 | 9.1 | 10.4 | 11.1 |
| Iceland<br>Islande | 20.6 | 34.9 | 34.9 | 34.9 | 34.9 | 30.2 | 30.2 | 33.3 | 33.3 | 33.3 |
| India<br>Inde | 5.0 | 9.0 | 9.0 | 8.8 | 8.8 | 8.8 | 8.3 | 8.3 | 8.3 | 9.1 |
| Indonesia<br>Indonésie | 12.4 | ... | 8.0 | 8.0 | 8.0 | 8.0 | 11.3 | 11.3 | 11.3 | 11.6 |
| Iran (Islamic Rep. of)<br>Iran (Rép. islamique d') | 1.5 | 4.9 | 3.4 | 3.4 | 4.1 | 4.1 | 4.1 | 4.1 | 4.1 | 4.1 |
| Iraq<br>Iraq | 10.8 | 6.4 | 7.6 | 7.6 | 7.6 | ... | ... | 25.5 | 25.5 | 25.5 |
| Ireland<br>Irlande | 7.8 | 12.0 | 12.0 | 12.0 | 13.3 | 13.3 | 13.3 | 13.3 | 13.3 | 13.3 |

| Country or area<br>Pays ou zone | 1990 | 2000 | 2001 | 2002 | 2003 | 2004 | 2005 | 2006 | 2007 | 2008 |
|---|---|---|---|---|---|---|---|---|---|---|
| Israel<br>Israël | 6.7 | 11.7 | 12.5 | 13.3 | 15.0 | 15.0 | 15.0 | 15.0 | 14.2 | 14.2 |
| Italy<br>Italie | 12.9 | 11.1 | 11.1 | 9.8 | 11.5 | 11.5 | 11.5 | 11.5 | 17.3 | 17.3 |
| Jamaica<br>Jamaïque | 5.0 | 13.3 | 13.3 | 13.3 | 11.7 | 11.7 | 11.7 | 11.7 | 11.7 | 13.3 |
| Japan<br>Japon | 1.4 | 4.6 | 7.3 | 7.3 | 7.3 | 7.1 | 7.1 | 9.0 | 9.4 | 9.4 |
| Jordan<br>Jordanie | 0.0 | 0.0 | 0.0 | 1.3 | 1.3 | 5.5 | 5.5 | 5.5 | 5.5 | 6.4 |
| Kazakhstan<br>Kazakhstan | ... | 10.4 | 10.4 | 10.4 | 10.4 | 10.4 | 10.4 | 10.4 | 10.4 | 15.9 |
| Kenya<br>Kenya | 1.1 | 3.6 | 3.6 | 3.6 | 7.1 | 7.1 | 7.1 | 7.1 | 7.3 | 7.2[4] |
| Kiribati<br>Kiribati | 0.0 | 4.9 | 4.9 | 4.8 | 4.8 | 4.8 | 4.8 | 4.8 | 7.1 | 4.3 |
| Korea, Dem. P. R.<br>Corée, R. p. dém. de | 21.1 | 20.1 | 20.1 | 20.1 | 20.1 | ... | 20.1 | 20.1 | 20.1 | 20.1 |
| Korea, Republic of<br>Corée, République de | 2.0 | 3.7 | 5.9 | 5.9 | 5.9 | 5.5 | 13.0 | 13.4 | 13.4 | 14.4 |
| Kuwait<br>Koweït | ... | 0.0 | 0.0 | 0.0 | 0.0 | 0.0 | 0.0 | 1.5 | 1.5[5] | 1.5 |
| Kyrgyzstan<br>Kirghizistan | ... | 1.4 | 2.3 | 10.0 | 10.0 | 10.0 | 10.0 | 0.0 | 0.0 | 25.6 |
| Lao People's Dem. Rep.<br>Rép. dém. pop. lao | 6.3 | 21.2 | 21.2 | 21.2 | 22.9 | 22.9 | 22.9 | 22.9 | 25.2 | 25.2 |
| Latvia<br>Lettonie | ... | 17.0 | 17.0 | 17.0 | 21.0 | 21.0 | 21.0 | 21.0 | 19.0 | 20.0 |
| Lebanon<br>Liban | 0.0 | 2.3 | 2.3 | 2.3 | 2.3 | 2.3 | 2.3 | 4.7 | 4.7 | 4.7 |
| Lesotho<br>Lesotho | ... | 3.8 | 3.8 | 3.8 | 11.7 | 11.7 | 11.7 | 11.7 | 11.7 | 25.0 |
| Liberia<br>Libéria | ... | ... | 7.8 | 7.8 | 7.8 | 7.8 | 5.3 | 12.5 | 12.5 | 12.5 |
| Libyan Arab Jamah.<br>Jamah. arabe libyenne | ... | ... | ... | ... | ... | ... | ... | 4.7 | 7.7 | 7.7 |
| Liechtenstein<br>Liechtenstein | 4.0 | 4.0 | 4.0 | 12.0 | 12.0 | 12.0 | 12.0 | 24.0 | 24.0 | 24.0 |
| Lithuania<br>Lituanie | ... | 17.5 | 10.6 | 10.6 | 10.6 | 10.6 | 22.0 | 22.0 | 24.8 | 22.7 |
| Luxembourg<br>Luxembourg | 13.3 | 16.7 | 16.7 | 16.7 | 16.7 | 16.7 | 23.3 | 23.3 | 23.3 | 23.3 |
| Madagascar<br>Madagascar | 6.5 | 8.0 | 8.0 | 8.0 | 3.8 | 3.8 | 6.9 | 6.9 | 6.9 | 7.9 |
| Malawi<br>Malawi | 9.8 | 8.3 | 9.3 | 9.3 | 9.3 | 9.3 | 14.0 | 13.6 | 13.6 | 13.0 |
| Malaysia<br>Malaisie | 5.1 | ... | 10.4 | 10.4 | 10.4 | 10.5 | 9.1 | 9.1 | 9.1 | 10.0 |
| Maldives<br>Maldives | 6.3 | ... | 6.0 | 6.0 | 6.0 | 6.0 | 6.0 | 12.0 | 12.0 | 12.0 |
| Mali<br>Mali | ... | 12.2 | 12.2 | 12.2 | 10.2 | 10.2 | 10.2 | 10.2 | 10.2 | 10.2 |
| Malta<br>Malte | 2.9 | 9.2 | 9.2 | 9.2 | 9.2 | 9.2 | 9.2 | 9.2 | 9.2 | 9.2 |

**Proportion of seats held by women in national parliament**—Percentage (*continued*)
**Proportion de sièges occupés par des femmes au parlement national**—Pourcentage (*suite*)

| Country or area<br>Pays ou zone | 1990 | 2000 | 2001 | 2002 | 2003 | 2004 | 2005 | 2006 | 2007 | 2008 |
|---|---|---|---|---|---|---|---|---|---|---|
| Marshall Islands<br>Iles Marshall | ... | ... | 3.0 | 3.0 | 3.0 | 3.0 | 3.0 | 3.0 | 3.0 | 3.0 |
| Mauritania<br>Mauritanie | ... | 3.8 | 3.8 | ... | ... | 3.7 | 3.7 | ... | 17.9 | 22.1 |
| Mauritius<br>Maurice | 7.1 | 7.6 | 5.7 | 5.7 | 5.7 | 5.7 | 5.7 | 17.1 | 17.1 | 17.1 |
| Mexico<br>Mexique | 12.0 | 18.2 | 16.0 | 16.0 | 16.0 | 22.6 | 22.6 | 25.8 | 22.6 | 23.2 |
| Micronesia (Fed. States of)<br>Micronésie (Etats féd. de) | ... | 0.0 | 0.0 | 0.0 | 0.0 | 0.0 | 0.0 | 0.0 | 0.0 | 0.0 |
| Moldova<br>Moldova | ... | 8.9 | 7.9 | 12.9 | 12.9 | 12.9 | 15.8 | 21.8 | 21.8 | 21.8 |
| Monaco<br>Monaco | 11.1 | 22.2 | 22.2 | 22.2 | 22.2 | 20.8 | 20.8 | 20.8 | 20.8 | 20.8 |
| Mongolia<br>Mongolie | 24.9 | 7.9 | 10.5 | 10.5 | 10.5 | 10.5 | 6.8 | 6.7 | 6.6 | 6.6 |
| Montenegro<br>Monténégro | ... | ... | ... | ... | ... | ... | ... | ... | 8.6 | 11.1 |
| Morocco<br>Maroc | 0.0 | 0.6 | 0.6 | 0.6 | 10.8 | 10.8 | 10.8 | 10.8 | 10.8 | 10.5 |
| Mozambique<br>Mozambique | 15.7 | ... | 30.0 | 30.0 | 30.0 | 30.0 | 34.8 | 34.8 | 34.8 | 34.8 |
| Namibia<br>Namibie | 6.9 | 22.2 | 25.0 | 25.0 | 26.4 | 26.4 | 25.0 | 26.9 | 26.9 | 26.9 |
| Nauru<br>Nauru | 5.6 | 0.0 | ... | 0.0 | 0.0 | 0.0 | 0.0 | 0.0 | 0.0 | 0.0 |
| Nepal<br>Népal | 6.1 | 5.9 | 5.9 | 5.9[6] | ... | ... | ... | ... | 17.3[7] | 17.3[7] |
| Netherlands<br>Pays-Bas | 21.3 | 36.0 | 36.0 | 36.0 | 36.7 | 36.7 | 36.7 | 36.7 | 36.7 | 39.3 |
| New Zealand<br>Nouvelle-Zélande | 14.4 | 29.2 | 30.8 | 30.8 | 29.2 | 28.3 | 28.3 | 32.2 | 32.2 | 33.1 |
| Nicaragua<br>Nicaragua | 14.8 | 9.7 | 9.7 | 20.7 | 20.7 | 20.7 | 20.7 | 20.7 | 18.5 | 18.5 |
| Niger<br>Niger | 5.4 | 1.2 | 1.2 | 1.2 | 1.2 | 1.2 | 12.4 | 12.4 | 12.4 | 12.4 |
| Nigeria<br>Nigéria | ... | ... | 3.4 | 3.4 | 3.4 | 6.7 | 4.7 | 6.4 | 6.1 | 7.0 |
| Norway<br>Norvège | 35.8 | 36.4 | 36.4 | 35.8 | 36.4 | 36.4 | 38.2 | 37.9 | 37.9 | 36.1 |
| Oman<br>Oman | ... | ... | ... | ... | ... | ... | 2.4 | 2.4 | 2.4 | 0.0 |
| Pakistan<br>Pakistan | 10.1 | ... | ... | ... | 21.6 | 21.6 | 21.3 | 21.3 | 21.3 | 21.1 |
| Palau<br>Palaos | ... | 0.0 | ... | 0.0 | 0.0 | 0.0 | 0.0 | 0.0 | 0.0 | 0.0 |
| Panama<br>Panama | 7.5 | ... | 9.9 | 9.9 | 9.9 | 9.9 | 16.7 | 16.7 | 16.7 | 16.7 |
| Papua New Guinea<br>Papouasie-Nvl-Guinée | 0.0 | 1.8 | 1.8 | 1.8 | 0.9 | 0.9 | 0.9 | 0.9 | 0.9 | 0.9 |
| Paraguay<br>Paraguay | 5.6 | 2.5 | 2.5 | 2.5 | 2.5 | 10.0 | 10.0 | 10.0 | 10.0 | 10.0 |
| Peru<br>Pérou | 5.6 | 10.8 | 20.0 | 18.3 | 18.3 | 18.3 | 18.3 | 18.3 | 29.2 | 29.2 |

| Country or area<br>Pays ou zone | 1990 | 2000 | 2001 | 2002 | 2003 | 2004 | 2005 | 2006 | 2007 | 2008 |
|---|---|---|---|---|---|---|---|---|---|---|
| Philippines<br>Philippines | 9.1 | 12.4 | 11.3 | 17.8 | 17.8 | 17.8 | 15.3 | 15.7 | 15.3 | 20.5 |
| Poland<br>Pologne | 13.5 | 13.0 | 13.0 | 20.2 | 20.2 | 20.2 | 20.2 | 20.4 | 20.4 | 20.4 |
| Portugal<br>Portugal | 7.6 | 18.7 | 17.4 | 18.7 | 19.1 | 19.1 | 19.1 | 21.3 | 21.3 | 28.3 |
| Qatar<br>Qatar | ... | ... | ... | ... | ... | ... | ... | 0.0 | 0.0 | 0.0 |
| Romania<br>Roumanie | 34.4 | 7.3 | 10.7 | 10.7 | 10.7 | 10.7 | 11.4 | 11.2 | 11.2 | 9.4 |
| Russian Federation<br>Fédération de Russie | ... | 7.7 | 7.7 | 7.6 | 7.6 | 9.8 | 9.8 | 9.8 | 9.8 | 14.0 |
| Rwanda<br>Rwanda | 17.1 | 17.1 | 25.7 | 25.7 | 25.7 | 48.8 | 48.8 | 48.8 | 48.8 | 48.8 |
| Saint Kitts and Nevis<br>Saint-Kitts-et-Nevis | 6.7 | 13.3 | 13.3 | 13.3 | 13.3 | 13.3 | 0.0 | 0.0 | 0.0 | 6.7 |
| Saint Lucia<br>Sainte-Lucie | 0.0 | 11.1 | 11.1 | ... | 11.1 | 11.1 | 11.1 | 11.1 | 5.6[8] | 11.1 |
| Saint Vincent-Grenadines<br>Saint Vincent-Grenadines | 9.5 | 4.8 | 4.8 | 22.7 | 22.7 | 22.7 | 22.7 | 18.2 | 18.2 | 18.2 |
| Samoa<br>Samoa | 0.0 | 8.2 | 8.2 | 6.1 | 6.1 | 6.1 | 6.1 | 6.1 | 6.1 | 8.2 |
| San Marino<br>Saint-Marin | 11.7 | 13.3 | 13.3 | 16.7 | 16.7 | 16.7 | 16.7 | 16.7 | 11.7 | 11.7 |
| Sao Tome and Principe<br>Sao Tomé-et-Principe | 11.8 | 9.1 | 9.1 | 9.1 | 9.1 | 9.1 | 9.1 | 9.1 | 7.3 | 1.8 |
| Saudi Arabia<br>Arabie saoudite | ... | ... | ... | ... | 0.0 | 0.0 | 0.0 | 0.0 | 0.0 | 0.0 |
| Senegal<br>Sénégal | 12.5 | 12.1 | 12.1 | 16.7 | 19.2 | 19.2 | 19.2 | 19.2 | 19.2 | 22.0 |
| Serbia<br>Serbie | ... | ... | ... | ... | ... | ... | ... | ... | 20.4 | 20.4 |
| Serbia and Montenegro<br>Serbie-et-Monténégro | ... | 5.1 | ... | 7.2 | 7.2 | 7.9 | 7.9 | 7.9 | ... | ... |
| Seychelles<br>Seychelles | 16.0 | 23.5 | 23.5 | 23.5 | 29.4 | 29.4 | 29.4 | 29.4 | 29.4 | 23.5 |
| Sierra Leone<br>Sierra Leone | ... | 8.8 | 8.8 | 8.8 | 14.5 | 14.5 | 14.5 | 14.5 | 14.5 | 13.2 |
| Singapore<br>Singapour | 4.9 | 4.3 | 6.5 | 11.8 | 11.8 | 16.0 | 16.0 | 16.0 | 24.5 | 24.5 |
| Slovakia<br>Slovaquie | ... | 12.7 | 14.0 | 14.0 | 19.3 | 19.3 | 16.7 | 16.7 | 20.0 | 19.3 |
| Slovenia<br>Slovénie | ... | 7.8 | 12.2 | 12.2 | 12.2 | 12.2 | 12.2 | 12.2 | 12.2 | 12.2 |
| Solomon Islands<br>Iles Salomon | 0.0 | 2.0 | 2.0 | 0.0 | 0.0 | 0.0 | 0.0 | 0.0 | 0.0 | 0.0 |
| Somalia<br>Somalie | 4.0 | ... | ... | ... | ... | ... | ... | 7.8 | 7.8 | 8.2 |
| South Africa<br>Afrique du Sud | 2.8 | 30.0 | 29.8 | 29.8 | 29.8 | 29.8 | 32.8 | 32.8 | 32.8 | 33.0 |
| Spain<br>Espagne | 14.6 | 21.6 | 28.3 | 28.3 | 28.3 | 28.3 | 36.0 | 36.0 | 36.0 | 36.6 |
| Sri Lanka<br>Sri Lanka | 4.9 | 4.9 | ... | ... | 4.4 | 4.4 | 4.9 | 4.9 | 4.9 | 5.8 |

**Proportion of seats held by women in national parliament**—Percentage (*continued*)
**Proportion de sièges occupés par des femmes au parlement national**—Pourcentage (*suite*)

| Country or area<br>Pays ou zone | 1990 | 2000 | 2001 | 2002 | 2003 | 2004 | 2005 | 2006 | 2007 | 2008 |
|---|---|---|---|---|---|---|---|---|---|---|
| Sudan<br>Soudan | ... | ... | ... | 9.7 | 9.7 | 9.7 | 9.7 | 14.7 | 17.8 | 18.1 |
| Suriname<br>Suriname | 7.8 | 15.7 | ... | 17.6 | 17.6 | 17.6 | 19.6 | 25.5 | 25.5 | 25.5 |
| Swaziland<br>Swaziland | 3.6 | 3.1 | 3.1 | 3.1 | 3.1 | 10.8 | 10.8 | 10.8 | 10.8 | 10.8 |
| Sweden<br>Suède | 38.4 | 42.7 | 42.7 | 42.7 | 45.3 | 45.3 | 45.3 | 45.3 | 47.3 | 47.0 |
| Switzerland<br>Suisse | 14.0 | 22.5 | 23.0 | 23.0 | 23.0 | 25.0 | 25.0 | 25.0 | 25.0 | 28.5 |
| Syrian Arab Republic<br>Rép. arabe syrienne | 9.2 | 10.4 | 10.4 | 10.4 | 10.4 | 12.0 | 12.0 | 12.0 | 12.0 | 12.0 |
| Tajikistan<br>Tadjikistan | ... | 2.8 | 15.0 | 12.7 | 12.7 | 12.7 | 12.7 | 17.5 | 17.5 | 17.5 |
| Thailand<br>Thaïlande | 2.8 | 5.6 | ... | 9.2 | 9.2 | 9.2 | 8.8 | 10.6 | 8.7 | 11.7 |
| TFYR of Macedonia<br>Ex-R.Y. Macédoine | ... | 7.5 | 6.7 | 6.7 | 18.3 | 18.3 | 19.2 | 19.2 | 28.3 | 29.2 |
| Timor-Leste<br>Timor-Leste | ... | ... | ... | ... | 26.1 | 26.1 | 25.3 | 25.3 | 25.3 | 29.2 |
| Togo<br>Togo | 5.2 | ... | 4.9 | 4.9 | 7.4 | 7.4 | 6.2 | 7.4 | 8.6 | 11.1 |
| Tonga<br>Tonga | 0.0 | ... | 0.0 | 0.0 | ... | 0.0 | 0.0 | 3.4 | 3.3 | 3.3 |
| Trinidad and Tobago<br>Trinité-et-Tobago | 16.7 | 11.1 | ... | 16.7 | 19.4 | 19.4 | 19.4 | 19.4 | 19.4 | 26.8 |
| Tunisia<br>Tunisie | 4.3 | 11.5 | 11.5 | 11.5 | 11.5 | 11.5 | 22.8 | 22.8 | 22.8 | 22.8 |
| Turkey<br>Turquie | 1.3 | 4.2 | 4.2 | 4.2 | 4.4 | 4.4 | 4.4 | 4.4 | 4.4 | 9.1 |
| Turkmenistan<br>Turkménistan | 26.0 | 26.0 | 26.0 | 26.0 | 26.0 | 26.0 | ... | 16.0 | 16.0 | 16.0 |
| Tuvalu<br>Tuvalu | 7.7 | 0.0 | 0.0 | 0.0 | 0.0 | 0.0 | 0.0 | 0.0 | 0.0 | 0.0 |
| Uganda<br>Ouganda | 12.2 | 17.9 | 17.8 | 24.7 | 24.7 | 24.7 | 23.9 | 23.9 | 29.8 | 30.7 |
| Ukraine<br>Ukraine | ... | 7.8 | 7.8 | 7.8 | 5.3 | 5.3 | 5.3 | 5.3 | 8.7 | 8.2 |
| United Arab Emirates<br>Emirats arabes unis | 0.0 | 0.0 | 0.0 | 0.0 | 0.0 | 0.0 | 0.0 | 0.0 | 22.5 | 22.5 |
| United Kingdom<br>Royaume-Uni | 6.3 | 18.4 | 18.4 | 17.9 | 17.9 | 17.9 | 18.1 | 19.7 | 19.7 | 19.5 |
| United Rep. of Tanzania<br>Rép.-Unie de Tanzanie | ... | 16.4 | ... | 22.3 | 22.3 | 21.4 | 21.4 | 30.4 | 30.4 | 30.4 |
| United States<br>Etats-Unis | 6.6 | 13.3 | 14.0 | 14.0 | 14.3 | 14.3 | 14.9 | 15.2 | 16.3 | 16.8 |
| Uruguay<br>Uruguay | 6.1 | 12.1 | 12.1 | 12.1 | 12.1 | 12.1 | 12.1 | 11.1 | 11.1 | 12.1 |
| Uzbekistan<br>Ouzbékistan | ... | 6.8 | 7.2 | 7.2 | 7.2 | 7.2 | 17.5 | 17.5 | 17.5 | 17.5 |
| Vanuatu<br>Vanuatu | 4.3 | 0.0 | 0.0 | 0.0 | 1.9 | 1.9 | 3.8 | 3.8 | 3.8 | 3.8 |

| Country or area<br>Pays ou zone | 1990 | 2000 | 2001 | 2002 | 2003 | 2004 | 2005 | 2006 | 2007 | 2008 |
|---|---|---|---|---|---|---|---|---|---|---|
| Venezuela (Bolivarian Rep. of)<br>Venezuela (Rép. bolivar. du) | 10.0 | 12.1 | 9.7 | 9.7 | 9.7 | 9.7 | 9.7 | 18.0 | 18.0 | 18.6 |
| Viet Nam<br>Viet Nam | 17.7 | 26.0 | 26.0 | 26.0 | 27.3 | 27.3 | 27.3 | 27.3 | 27.3 | 25.8 |
| Yemen<br>Yemen | 4.1 | 0.7 | 0.7 | 0.7 | 0.7 | 0.3 | 0.3 | 0.3 | 0.3 | 0.3 |
| Zambia<br>Zambie | 6.6 | 10.1 | 10.1 | 12.0 | 12.0 | 12.0 | 12.0 | 12.7 | 14.6 | 15.2 |
| Zimbabwe<br>Zimbabwe | 11.0 | 14.0 | 9.3 | 10.0 | 10.0 | 10.0 | 10.0 | 16.0 | 16.7 | 16.0 |

Source

Inter-parliamentary Union (IPU), Geneva, "Women in National Parliaments 2008".

Notes

1 In 2004, the number of seats in parliament was raised from 300 to 345, with the addition of 45 reserved seats for women. These reserved seats were filled in September and October 2005, being allocated to political parties in proportion to their share of the national vote received in the 2001 election.

2 The parliament was dissolved on 27 October 2006, in view of elections that are yet to take place. Women held 52 of the 345 seats (15%) in the outgoing parliament.

3 Parliament has been dissolved or suspended for an indefinite period.

4 Situation for 1 January 2008 for directly elected members endorsed by the electoral commission. The additional twelve appointed seats and two ex-officio seats had yet to be filled.

5 No woman candidate was elected in the 2006 elections. One woman was appointed to the 16-member cabinet. As cabinet ministers also sit in parliament, there is therefore one woman out of a total of 65 members.

6 The parliament (elected in the parliamentary elections in 1999) was dissolved on 22 May 2002. Women held 12 of the 205 (5.9%) seats in the outgoing parliament.

7 After the promulgation of the interim constitution in January 2007, the House of Representatives dissolved itself in favour of a 330-member interim legislature, called the Legislative Parliament. This interim legislature comprises all members of the previous parliament and other appointed members. It is due to be replaced by an elected unicameral 425-member Constituent Assembly in 2008.

8 No woman was elected in the 2006 elections. However one woman was appointed Speaker of the House and therefore became a member of the House.

Source

Union interparlementaire (UIP), Genève, "Les femmes dans les parlements nationaux 2008".

Notes

1 En 2004, le nombre de sièges parlementaires est passé de 300 à 345, les nouveaux sièges étant réservés aux femmes. Les sièges réservés ont été pourvus en septembre et en octobre 2005, au prorata des voix obtenues par les partis politiques lors des élections nationales de 2001.

2 Le parlement où les femmes occupaient 52 des 345 sièges (15%) a été dissous le 27 octobre 2006 en vue des élections à venir.

3 Le Parlement a été dissous ou suspendu pour une durée indéterminée.

4 Au 1er janvier 2008, la situation des membres directement élus et approuvés par la commission électorale est la suivante: les sièges des 12 membres nommés et 2 des membres de droits restent vacants.

5 Aucune femme n'a été élue en 2006. Une femme a été nommée parmi les 16 membres du cabinet. Les membres du cabinet siégeant au parlement, il y a donc une femme sur un total de 65 membres.

6 Le parlement élu aux élections de 1999 a été dissous le 22 may 2002. Les femmes y occupaient 12 des 205 sièges, soit 5.9%.

7 Après la promulgation de la constitution provisoire en janvier 2007, la Chambre des représentants a prononcé sa dissolution au profit d'une législature provisoire de 330 membres, baptisée Parlement législatif. Cet organe provisoire se compose de tous les membres du parlement précédent, ainsi que de membres nommés. Il doit être remplacé en 2008 par une Assemblée constituante monocamérale de 425 membres élus.

8 Aucune femme n'a été élue en 2006. Une femme a cependant été nommée à la présidence de la chambre des députés et est donc devenue membre de cette dernière.

# Share of women in wage employment in the non-agricultural sector
Percentage of total employment

# Proportion de femmes salariées dans le secteur non agricole
Pourcentage d'emploi total

| Country or area / Pays ou zone | Source[&] Source[&] | 1990 | 1999 | 2000 | 2001 | 2002 | 2003 | 2004 | 2005 | 2006 |
|---|---|---|---|---|---|---|---|---|---|---|
| Afghanistan[*1,2] Afghanistan[*1,2] | | 17.8 | ... | ... | ... | ... | ... | ... | ... | ... |
| Albania[3,4] Albanie[3,4] | | ... | 29.2 | 28.9 | 26.9 | 31.6 | 33.0 | ... | ... | ... |
| Algeria[5] Algérie[5] | BA | ... | ... | 13.0 | 15.7 | ... | 15.7 | 17.0 | ... | ... |
| American Samoa[6] Samoa américaines[6] | A | 41.3 | ... | ... | ... | ... | ... | ... | ... | ... |
| Andorra Andorre | FA | ... | ... | ... | ... | ... | 45.6 | 45.7 | 45.8 | 46.1 |
| Anguilla[5] Anguilla[5] | BA | ... | 47.0 | ... | ... | *45.5[7] | ... | ... | ... | ... |
| Antigua and Barbuda[5] Antigua-et-Barbuda[5] | A | ... | ... | ... | 50.6 | ... | ... | ... | ... | ... |
| Argentina Argentine | BA | 37.1 | 42.1 | 42.6 | 43.3 | 45.9 | 45.5 | 44.8 | 45.1 | 45.0 |
| Armenia[5] Arménie[5] | E | ... | *48.8[7] | *47.3[7] | *47.8[7] | 49.6 | 49.7 | 47.9 | 45.4 | 45.7 |
| Australia Australie | | 44.6[4] | *47.6[8] | *48.1[8] | *48.6[8] | *48.6[8] | *48.9[8] | *48.6[8] | *48.9[8] | *48.9[8] |
| Austria Autriche | | *41.0[9,10] | *43.3[9,10] | *43.7[9,10] | 44.2[8] | 44.9[8] | 45.5[8] | 46.2[8] | 46.6[8] | 46.6[8] |
| Azerbaijan[5] Azerbaïdjan[5] | E | ... | 43.3 | 43.6 | 45.4 | 48.4 | 48.5 | 48.8 | 49.1 | 50.2 |
| Bahamas[5] Bahamas[5] | BA | ... | 48.4 | ... | 49.8 | 49.7 | 50.1 | 50.4 | 50.0 | 50.1 |
| Bahrain Bahreïn | FA | 7.6 | 12.3 | 12.4 | 13.2 | 12.7 | 12.8 | 11.5 | 11.0 | 9.8 |
| Bangladesh[5] Bangladesh[5] | BA | ... | ... | 22.9 | ... | ... | ... | ... | ... | ... |
| Barbados[5] Barbade[5] | BA | 45.5 | 46.8 | 47.5 | 47.6 | 47.8 | 48.4 | 48.7 | ... | ... |
| Belarus[4] Bélarus[4] | | ... | 55.4 | 55.9 | 56.0 | ... | ... | ... | ... | ... |
| Belgium Belgique | | ... | *43.0[11] | 43.3[8] | 43.4[8] | 43.9[8] | 44.4[8] | 44.8[8] | 45.3[8] | 45.7[8] |
| Belize[5] Belize[5] | BA | ... | 40.0 | ... | *41.0[7] | *39.9[7] | ... | ... | *44.1[7] | ... |
| Benin[3] Bénin[3] | A | ... | ... | ... | ... | 24.3 | ... | ... | ... | ... |
| Bermuda[12] Bermudes[12] | | 48.7 | 49.9 | 49.8 | 49.3 | 49.4 | 48.9 | 48.7 | ... | ... |
| Bhutan Bhoutan | BA | ... | 19.0 | ... | ... | ... | ... | ... | ... | ... |
| Bolivia[*] Bolivie[*] | BA | ... | 35.7 | 35.9 | 37.4 | 36.4 | ... | ... | ... | ... |
| Bosnia and Herzegovina[6] Bosnie-Herzégovine[6] | BA | ... | ... | ... | ... | ... | ... | ... | ... | 34.9 |
| Botswana Botswana | | 33.5[4] | 40.5[4] | *39.4[7,8] | 41.1[4] | ... | *41.7[7,8] | ... | ... | *42.4[7,8] |

| Country or area<br>Pays ou zone | Source[&]<br>Source[&] | 1990 | 1999 | 2000 | 2001 | 2002 | 2003 | 2004 | 2005 | 2006 |
|---|---|---|---|---|---|---|---|---|---|---|
| Brazil<br>Brésil | FD | *35.1 | 40.3 | 40.3 | 40.7 | 41.0 | ... | ... | ... | ... |
| Brunei Darussalam[12]<br>Brunéi Darussalam[12] | | ... | 26.7 | 30.3 | 28.9 | 29.0 | 30.3 | ... | ... | ... |
| Bulgaria[4]<br>Bulgarie[4] | | ... | 52.4 | 52.8 | 53.1 | 53.1 | 53.1 | 52.7 | *52.3 | *52.5 |
| Burkina Faso[6]<br>Burkina Faso[6] | E | 12.5 | ... | ... | ... | ... | ... | ... | ... | ... |
| Burundi[3]<br>Burundi[3] | A | 14.3 | ... | ... | ... | ... | ... | ... | ... | ... |
| Cambodia[6]<br>Cambodge[6] | BA | ... | ... | 51.9 | 51.7 | ... | ... | 51.9 | ... | ... |
| Canada<br>Canada | BA | 46.9 | 48.2 | 48.3 | 48.8 | 48.8 | 49.2 | 49.4 | 49.4 | 49.5 |
| Cape Verde[3]<br>Cap-Vert[3] | E | ... | ... | 38.9 | | | | | | |
| Cayman Islands[5]<br>Iles Caïmanes[5] | BA | ... | ... | ... | ... | *50.2[7] | *52.5[7] | *50.6[7] | 48.0 | 48.1 |
| Central African Rep.[6]<br>Rép. centrafricaine[6] | A | ... | ... | ... | ... | ... | 46.8 | ... | ... | ... |
| Chad[4]<br>Tchad[4] | | 3.8 | ... | ... | ... | ... | ... | ... | ... | ... |
| Chile[5]<br>Chili[5] | BA | 36.2 | 37.1 | 36.9 | 36.6 | 36.5 | 37.3 | 38.1 | 37.9 | 38.5 |
| China[4,13]<br>Chine[4,13] | | 37.8 | 39.2 | ... | ... | ... | ... | ... | ... | ... |
| China, Hong Kong SAR[4]<br>Chine, Hong Kong RAS[4] | | 41.2 | 44.1 | 44.8 | 45.5 | 45.9 | 46.8 | 47.3 | 47.8 | 48.1 |
| China, Macao SAR<br>Chine, Macao RAS | BA | 42.7 | 48.7 | 48.9 | 48.8 | 50.0 | 49.0 | 49.4 | 49.5 | 48.0 |
| Colombia<br>Colombie | BA | *41.8 | 47.8 | 48.8 | 49.1 | *48.7 | 48.8 | 48.3 | *48.3 | *49.1 |
| Congo*[1,2]<br>Congo*[1,2] | | 26.1 | ... | ... | ... | ... | ... | ... | ... | ... |
| Cook Islands[4]<br>Iles Cook[4] | | 38.4 | ... | ... | ... | ... | ... | ... | ... | ... |
| Costa Rica<br>Costa Rica | BA | 37.2 | *39.5[7] | 39.3 | 40.1 | *39.9[7] | 39.5 | 38.5 | 39.6 | 40.7 |
| Croatia[4]<br>Croatie[4] | | 44.2 | 47.0 | 47.2 | 47.1 | 46.6 | 46.3 | 46.2 | 46.4 | 46.3 |
| Cuba<br>Cuba | BA | ... | 43.3 | 43.3 | 42.8 | 42.3 | 42.8 | 42.6 | 42.6 | 42.7 |
| Cyprus<br>Chypre | BA | ... | 43.2 | 44.4 | 47.4 | 48.2 | 49.3 | 48.2 | 47.7 | 48.1 |
| Czech Republic<br>République tchèque | BA | 51.0 | 46.5 | 46.5 | 46.6 | 46.7 | 46.8 | 47.1 | 46.6 | 46.4 |
| Dem. Rep. of the Congo*[1,2]<br>Rép. dém. du Congo*[1,2] | | 25.9 | ... | ... | ... | ... | ... | ... | ... | ... |
| Denmark<br>Danemark | BA | *48.1 | *48.9 | 48.5 | 48.9 | 49.0 | 48.3 | 48.8 | 48.8 | 48.8 |
| Djibouti[6,14]<br>Djibouti[6,14] | | ... | ... | ... | ... | 26.7 | ... | ... | ... | ... |
| Dominica[5]<br>Dominique[5] | A | ... | ... | ... | 45.9 | ... | ... | ... | ... | ... |

**Share of women in wage employment in the non-agricultural sector**—Percentage of total employment (*continued*)
**Proportion de femmes salariées dans le secteur non agricole**—Pourcentage d'emploi total (*suite*)

| Country or area<br>Pays ou zone | Source[&]<br>Source[&] | 1990 | 1999 | 2000 | 2001 | 2002 | 2003 | 2004 | 2005 | 2006 |
|---|---|---|---|---|---|---|---|---|---|---|
| Dominican Republic[5]<br>Rép. dominicaine[5] | BA | ... | 36.0 | 38.6 | 38.0 | 39.5 | *39.3 | *38.7 | *39.4 | ... |
| Ecuador[5]<br>Equateur[5] | BA | 37.3 | 40.7 | 40.2 | 41.4 | 40.0 | *41.0[7] | 42.7 | 42.0 | 41.8 |
| Egypt<br>Egypte | BA | 20.5 | 18.4 | 18.6 | 17.9 | 18.2 | 18.8 | 19.9 | *19.8[7] | 20.7 |
| El Salvador<br>El Salvador | BA | *45.6[15] | 48.9 | 49.1 | 48.3 | 49.5 | 47.9 | 47.8 | 48.5 | 48.6 |
| Equatorial Guinea[* 1,2]<br>Guinée équatoriale[* 1,2] | | 10.5 | ... | ... | ... | ... | ... | ... | ... | ... |
| Estonia<br>Estonie | BA | 52.3 | 51.6 | 51.7 | 51.7 | 51.5 | 51.5 | 52.2 | 52.6 | 52.5 |
| Ethiopia<br>Ethiopie | BA | ... | *40.9[7] | ... | ... | ... | ... | 40.6 | *43.8[7] | *47.3[7] |
| Faeroe Islands[5]<br>Iles Féroé[5] | BA | ... | ... | ... | ... | ... | ... | ... | 45.8 | ... |
| Fiji[12]<br>Fidji[12] | | 29.9 | 34.9 | 33.2 | ... | ... | 33.9 | ... | 30.6 | ... |
| Finland<br>Finlande | BA | 50.6 | 50.3 | 50.3 | 50.2 | 50.7 | 50.6 | 50.7 | 50.9 | 51.0 |
| France<br>France | E | 43.9 | 46.5 | 46.5 | 46.6 | 47.0 | 47.3 | 47.5 | 47.7 | ... |
| French Guiana<br>Guyane française | E | 36.1 | ... | ... | ... | ... | ... | ... | ... | ... |
| French Polynesia[6]<br>Polynésie française[6] | FA | ... | 41.7 | 42.4 | 41.8 | 42.5 | ... | ... | ... | ... |
| Gambia[* 1,2]<br>Gambie[* 1,2] | | 20.9 | ... | ... | ... | ... | ... | ... | ... | ... |
| Georgia<br>Géorgie | BA | ... | 49.2 | ... | ... | 49.6 | 48.9 | 50.4 | 48.6 | ... |
| Germany<br>Allemagne | BA | ... | 44.8 | 45.1 | 45.5 | 45.9 | 46.4 | 46.6 | 46.6 | 46.9 |
| Ghana[3]<br>Ghana[3] | A | ... | ... | 31.7 | ... | ... | ... | ... | ... | ... |
| Gibraltar[4]<br>Gibraltar[4] | | 34.5 | 46.5 | 39.7 | 39.9 | 40.2 | 41.6 | 41.5 | 41.9 | ... |
| Greece<br>Grèce | BA | *35.3[15] | 38.8 | 39.1 | 39.6 | 39.8 | 40.1 | 40.9 | 41.0 | 41.6 |
| Greenland[6]<br>Groenland[6] | E | ... | 49.4 | 48.8 | 49.6 | 49.1 | 49.4 | 49.5 | 49.3 | ... |
| Guadeloupe[6]<br>Guadeloupe[6] | BA | ... | ... | ... | ... | 45.7 | ... | ... | ... | ... |
| Guam[4]<br>Guam[4] | | ... | ... | ... | ... | 45.6 | 43.6 | ... | 44.6 | ... |
| Guatemala[5]<br>Guatemala[5] | BA | 36.8 | ... | 37.5 | ... | 39.2 | *40.8 | *38.3 | ... | ... |
| Guinea-Bissau[* 1,2]<br>Guinée-Bissau[* 1,2] | | 10.8 | ... | ... | ... | ... | ... | ... | ... | ... |
| Haiti[3]<br>Haïti[3] | E | 44.2 | ... | ... | ... | ... | ... | ... | ... | ... |
| Honduras[5]<br>Honduras[5] | BA | 48.1 | 50.5 | ... | ... | ... | ... | 46.8 | 45.3 | ... |
| Hungary<br>Hongrie | BA | ... | 48.7 | 48.6 | 48.5 | 48.4 | 49.1 | 48.9 | 48.7 | 48.3 |

| Country or area<br>Pays ou zone | Source[&]<br>Source[&] | 1990 | 1999 | 2000 | 2001 | 2002 | 2003 | 2004 | 2005 | 2006 |
|---|---|---|---|---|---|---|---|---|---|---|
| Iceland<br>Islande | BA | ... | 52.6 | 52.2 | 52.3 | 53.0 | 52.5 | 51.8 | 52.2 | 47.7 |
| India[4]<br>Inde[4] | | 12.7 | 16.3 | 16.6 | 16.8 | 17.3 | 17.6 | 17.9 | 18.1 | ... |
| Indonesia<br>Indonésie | BA | 29.2 | 31.1 | 31.7 | 30.7 | 29.7 | *27.9[15] | *29.0[15] | *29.6[15] | *29.3[15] |
| Iran (Islamic Rep. of)<br>Iran (Rép. islamique d') | A | ... | 14.1 | 13.6 | 13.1 | 11.6 | ... | ... | ... | ... |
| Iraq[6]<br>Iraq[6] | BA | ... | ... | ... | ... | ... | 21.3 | ... | ... | ... |
| Ireland<br>Irlande | BA | 41.7 | 46.1 | 46.3 | 46.5 | 47.6 | 47.4 | 47.6 | 47.9 | 47.7 |
| Isle of Man<br>Ile de Man | A | ... | ... | ... | 49.3 | ... | ... | ... | ... | ... |
| Israel<br>Israël | BA | 43.0 | 48.0 | 48.3 | 48.4 | 48.7 | 48.9 | 48.7 | 49.3 | 49.0 |
| Italy<br>Italie | BA | *35.9[15] | 39.1 | 39.8 | 40.6 | 40.9 | 41.2 | 42.7 | 42.6 | 42.8 |
| Jamaica[5]<br>Jamaïque[5] | BA | *49.6[7] | 47.1 | 46.9 | 46.7 | 47.2 | 47.8 | 47.0 | 47.3 | 47.6 |
| Japan<br>Japon | BA | 38.0 | 39.7 | 40.0 | 40.4 | 40.6 | 40.8 | 41.2 | 41.3 | 41.6 |
| Jordan[3]<br>Jordanie[3] | BA | ... | 24.3 | 23.4 | 23.4 | 24.6 | 24.2 | 24.3 | 25.9 | ... |
| Kazakhstan<br>Kazakhstan | BA | ... | ... | ... | 48.4 | 48.1 | 48.7 | 49.4 | ... | ... |
| Kenya[4]<br>Kenya[4] | | 21.4 | ... | ... | ... | ... | ... | ... | ... | ... |
| Kiribati[5]<br>Kiribati[5] | A | ... | ... | 37.5 | ... | ... | ... | ... | ... | ... |
| Korea, Dem. P. R.*[1,2]<br>Corée, R. p. dém. de*[1,2] | | 40.7 | ... | ... | ... | ... | ... | ... | ... | ... |
| Korea, Republic of<br>Corée, République de | BA | 38.1 | 39.3 | 40.1 | 40.8 | 41.1 | 41.2 | 41.6 | 41.8 | 42.0 |
| Kyrgyzstan<br>Kirghizistan | E | ... | 47.7 | 45.8 | 45.6 | 44.9 | 47.3 | 49.4 | 51.9 | 52.2 |
| Lao People's Dem. Rep.[6]<br>Rép. dém. pop. lao[6] | A | ... | ... | ... | ... | ... | ... | ... | 50.2 | ... |
| Latvia[4]<br>Lettonie[4] | | ... | 52.7 | 53.1 | 52.5 | 53.1 | 53.3 | 53.2 | 53.4 | 52.8 |
| Lesotho[3]<br>Lesotho[3] | B | ... | 51.0 | ... | ... | ... | ... | ... | ... | ... |
| Liberia<br>Libéria | E | ... | ... | ... | ... | 11.4 | ... | ... | ... | ... |
| Libyan Arab Jamah.<br>Jamah. arabe libyenne | E | ... | ... | ... | 15.8 | ... | ... | ... | ... | ... |
| Liechtenstein[5]<br>Liechtenstein[5] | E | ... | ... | 38.7 | 38.7 | 39.1 | 38.9 | 39.1 | 39.4 | ... |
| Lithuania[4]<br>Lituanie[4] | | *55.4 | 52.0 | 53.2 | 52.7 | 52.6 | 53.2 | 53.3 | 53.0 | *53.5 |
| Luxembourg<br>Luxembourg | BA | ... | ... | ... | ... | ... | 40.6 | 41.9 | 42.4 | ... |
| Madagascar<br>Madagascar | BA | ... | ... | *35.6[5,7] | *36.2[5,7] | ... | *36.1[5,7] | ... | 37.7 | ... |

**11**   **Share of women in wage employment in the non-agricultural sector**—Percentage of total employment (*continued*)
     **Proportion de femmes salariées dans le secteur non agricole**—Pourcentage d'emploi total (*suite*)

| Country or area / Pays ou zone | Source[&] / Source[&] | 1990 | 1999 | 2000 | 2001 | 2002 | 2003 | 2004 | 2005 | 2006 |
|---|---|---|---|---|---|---|---|---|---|---|
| Malawi[4] / Malawi[4] | | 10.5 | ... | ... | ... | ... | ... | ... | ... | ... |
| Malaysia / Malaisie | | 37.8[4] | *35.8[7,8] | *36.7[7,8] | *37.4[7,8] | *37.7[7,8] | *38.0[7,8] | *38.1[7,8] | ... | ... |
| Maldives[5] / Maldives[5] | A | ... | ... | 36.7 | ... | ... | ... | ... | ... | 38.6 |
| Mali[3] / Mali[3] | BA | ... | ... | | ... | | ... | 34.6 | | ... |
| Malta / Malte | | ... | *31.0[4] | 32.1[8] | 30.8[8] | 33.8[8] | 33.0[8] | 32.9[8] | 33.3[8] | 34.2[8] |
| Marshall Islands[6] / Iles Marshall[6] | BA | ... | ... | ... | ... | ... | ... | ... | 33.2 | ... |
| Martinique[6] / Martinique[6] | BA | ... | ... | ... | ... | 48.1 | ... | ... | ... | ... |
| Mauritania / Mauritanie | E | ... | ... | 35.8 | ... | ... | ... | ... | ... | ... |
| Mauritius / Maurice | | 36.7[4] | 38.4[4] | 38.6[4] | 39.0[4] | 38.1[4] | 38.4[4] | 37.5[4] | 36.9[4] | *37.5[7,8] |
| Mexico / Mexique | BA | ... | 36.4 | 37.3 | 37.2 | 37.5 | 36.8 | 37.5 | 39.1 | 39.3 |
| Moldova / Moldova | BA | ... | 52.9 | 52.8 | 52.6 | 53.6 | 54.6 | 54.6 | 54.9 | 53.5 |
| Monaco[6] / Monaco[6] | A | ... | ... | 39.2 | ... | ... | ... | ... | ... | ... |
| Mongolia[5] / Mongolie[5] | E | ... | 48.6 | 50.4 | 50.7 | 51.7 | 51.1 | 53.1 | 53.1 | ... |
| Montenegro[5] / Monténégro[5] | BA | ... | ... | ... | ... | ... | ... | ... | 40.8 | ... |
| Morocco / Maroc | BA | *28.7[7] | 25.6 | 26.2 | 26.6 | *26.3[7] | *27.4[7] | *28.3[7] | *28.1[7] | *28.2[7] |
| Mozambique[15] / Mozambique[15] | A | 11.4 | ... | ... | ... | ... | ... | ... | ... | ... |
| Myanmar[5] / Myanmar[5] | BA | 40.6 | ... | ... | ... | ... | ... | ... | ... | ... |
| Namibia[5] / Namibie[5] | BA | ... | ... | 48.8 | *46.4[7] | ... | ... | 46.8 | ... | ... |
| Nepal / Népal | BA | ... | 15.1 | ... | ... | ... | ... | ... | ... | ... |
| Netherlands / Pays-Bas | BA | 37.7 | *43.6[7] | 44.0 | 44.4 | 45.0 | 45.7 | 46.2 | 46.8 | ... |
| Netherlands Antilles[5] / Antilles néerlandaises[5] | | *41.4[7,11] | ... | 48.1[8] | ... | ... | ... | ... | ... | ... |
| New Zealand / Nouvelle-Zélande | BA | 44.9 | 46.4 | 46.3 | 46.7 | 46.5 | 46.9 | 47.4 | 47.1 | 47.0 |
| Nicaragua[6] / Nicaragua[6] | BA | ... | ... | 28.8 | ... | ... | ... | ... | ... | ... |
| Niger / Niger | FA | 11.0 | ... | ... | ... | ... | ... | ... | ... | ... |
| Nigeria[4,16] / Nigéria[4,16] | | ... | 19.0 | 18.6 | 19.3 | 20.1 | 20.8 | 21.0 | 21.1 | ... |
| Niue[5] / Nioué[5] | A | ... | ... | ... | 43.1 | ... | ... | ... | ... | ... |
| Northern Mariana Islands[6] / Iles Mariannes du Nord[6] | BA | ... | ... | ... | ... | ... | 59.2 | ... | ... | ... |

## 11

**Share of women in wage employment in the non-agricultural sector**—Percentage of total employment (*continued*)
**Proportion de femmes salariées dans le secteur non agricole**—Pourcentage d'emploi total (*suite*)

| Country or area / Pays ou zone | Source[&] | 1990 | 1999 | 2000 | 2001 | 2002 | 2003 | 2004 | 2005 | 2006 |
|---|---|---|---|---|---|---|---|---|---|---|
| Norway / Norvège | BA | *47.0[15] | 48.3 | 48.2 | 48.3 | 48.9 | 49.1 | 49.2 | 49.0 | 49.3 |
| Occupied Palestinian Terr. / Terr. palestinien occupé | BA | ... | 12.5 | 13.5 | 15.9 | 17.0 | 16.8 | 17.9 | 16.1 | 17.1 |
| Oman[4] / Oman[4] | | 18.7 | 23.4 | 24.5 | 25.3 | ... | ... | ... | ... | ... |
| Pakistan[5] / Pakistan[5] | BA | 6.6 | 8.1 | 7.4 | 7.4 | 8.9 | 8.9 | 9.7 | 9.7 | 10.7 |
| Panama / Panama | BA | ... | 42.2 | 43.0 | 43.0 | 43.5 | 44.0 | 43.6 | 43.4 | 42.5 |
| Papua New Guinea / Papouasie-Nvl-Guinée | A | *27.9[17] | ... | 32.1 | ... | ... | ... | ... | ... | ... |
| Paraguay / Paraguay | BA | 41.0 | ... | ... | ... | *42.0[7] | *42.6[7] | ... | ... | ... |
| Peru / Pérou | BA | ... | 35.5 | 33.3 | 34.6 | 35.8 | 37.2 | 34.6 | 37.5 | 36.4 |
| Philippines / Philippines | | *40.3[4] | 41.3[8] | 41.1[8] | 41.9[8] | 42.1[8] | 41.2[8] | 40.4[8] | 41.9[8] | 41.8[8] |
| Poland / Pologne | BA | ... | 47.1 | 46.9 | 47.0 | 47.5 | 47.7 | 47.2 | 46.7 | 46.6 |
| Portugal / Portugal | BA | *42.5 | 45.7 | 45.7 | 46.2 | 46.4 | 46.9 | 47.4 | 47.3 | 47.3 |
| Puerto Rico / Porto Rico | | 46.5[4] | 40.0[4] | 39.6[4] | 41.3[4] | 40.7[4] | 40.1[4] | *40.3[8,15] | *40.6[8,15] | *40.6[8,15] |
| Qatar / Qatar | | ... | ... | ... | 14.5[8] | ... | ... | *15.5[15,18] | ... | ... |
| Réunion / Réunion | FA | 30.7 | ... | ... | ... | ... | ... | ... | ... | ... |
| Romania / Roumanie | | *42.0[11,15] | 44.7[8] | 45.5[8] | 45.7[8] | 45.2[8] | 45.3[8] | 46.5[8] | 46.2[8] | 46.6[8] |
| Russian Federation / Fédération de Russie | BA | ... | 50.2 | 50.4 | 50.4 | 50.6 | 51.0 | 50.9 | 50.9 | 51.2 |
| Rwanda[14] / Rwanda[14] | | ... | ... | 33.0 | ... | ... | ... | ... | ... | ... |
| Saint Helena[* 5,7] / Sainte-Hélène[* 5,7] | A | ... | ... | 24.0 | ... | ... | ... | ... | ... | ... |
| Saint Lucia[5] / Sainte-Lucie[5] | BA | ... | 49.4 | 48.5 | | 46.9 | 45.1 | 46.6 | ... | ... |
| Samoa[6] / Samoa[6] | A | ... | ... | 30.2 | ... | ... | ... | ... | ... | ... |
| San Marino / Saint-Marin | E | 40.4 | 41.2 | *41.3[7] | 41.5 | 41.7 | 41.9 | 42.2 | 42.1 | 42.1 |
| Sao Tome and Principe[6] / Sao Tomé-et-Principe[6] | E | ... | ... | 34.8 | 35.3 | 38.8 | 37.9 | 36.8 | 37.2 | 37.7 |
| Saudi Arabia / Arabie saoudite | BA | ... | 14.9 | 14.0 | 14.2 | 12.1 | ... | ... | ... | *12.6[15] |
| Senegal / Sénégal | E | ... | ... | ... | 10.6 | ... | ... | ... | ... | ... |
| Serbia[5] / Serbie[5] | BA | ... | ... | ... | ... | ... | ... | 41.6 | 40.2 | 41.6 |
| Sierra Leone / Sierra Leone | A | ... | ... | ... | ... | ... | ... | 23.2 | ... | ... |
| Singapore / Singapour | BA | ... | 45.4 | ... | 46.9 | 46.7 | 47.8 | 48.1 | ... | *49.5[7] |

**Share of women in wage employment in the non-agricultural sector**—Percentage of total employment (*continued*)

**Proportion de femmes salariées dans le secteur non agricole**—Pourcentage d'emploi total (*suite*)

| Country or area / Pays ou zone | Source[&] / Source[&] | 1990 | 1999 | 2000 | 2001 | 2002 | 2003 | 2004 | 2005 | 2006 |
|---|---|---|---|---|---|---|---|---|---|---|
| Slovakia[4] / Slovaquie[4] | | 48.6 | 50.9 | 50.8 | 51.9 | 51.9 | 52.1 | 52.0 | 51.4 | 50.3 |
| Slovenia / Slovénie | | *47.8[4] | 47.9[8] | 48.0[8] | 47.7[8] | 47.9[8] | 47.4[8] | 47.6[8] | 47.4[8] | 47.9[8] |
| Solomon Islands[6] / Iles Salomon[6] | A | ... | 30.8 | ... | ... | ... | ... | ... | ... | ... |
| Somalia[* 1,2] / Somalie[* 1,2] | | 21.7 | ... | ... | ... | ... | ... | ... | ... | ... |
| South Africa[5] / Afrique du Sud[5] | BA | ... | ... | ... | 44.6 | 43.1 | 43.4 | 42.7 | 42.9 | 43.1 |
| Spain / Espagne | BA | 32.3 | 38.0 | 38.9 | 39.4 | 40.0 | 40.7 | 41.5 | 42.3 | 43.0 |
| Sri Lanka / Sri Lanka | | 39.1[4] | 41.2[4] | 46.0[4] | 45.4[4] | 37.3[4] | 44.9[4] | 40.3[4] | 39.8[4] | *44.5[7,8] |
| Sudan[4] / Soudan[4] | | 22.2 | ... | ... | ... | ... | ... | ... | ... | ... |
| Suriname[5] / Suriname[5] | BA | 39.1 | 36.0 | ... | ... | ... | ... | ... | ... | ... |
| Sweden / Suède | BA | 50.5 | 50.5 | 50.6 | 50.7 | 50.9 | 50.9 | 50.9 | 50.5 | 50.3 |
| Switzerland / Suisse | | *43.4[11,15] | 45.9[8] | 45.7[8] | 46.3[8] | 47.1[8] | 46.9[8] | 47.1[8] | 47.1[8] | 46.9[8] |
| Syrian Arab Republic[5] / Rép. arabe syrienne[5] | BA | ... | ... | ... | 11.2 | 11.1 | *10.3[7] | ... | ... | ... |
| Thailand[5] / Thaïlande[5] | BA | 45.3 | 46.2 | 46.1 | 46.8 | 46.7 | 46.9 | 46.4 | 47.9 | 47.3 |
| TFYR of Macedonia / Ex-R.Y. Macédoine | | 38.3[4] | 41.3[4] | 41.6[4] | 41.9[4] | *40.3[7,8] | *41.5[7,8] | *40.1[7,8] | *40.6[7,8] | *39.7[7,8] |
| Timor-Leste / Timor-Leste | E | ... | ... | ... | 35.0 | ... | ... | ... | ... | ... |
| Togo[* 1,2] / Togo[* 1,2] | | 41.0 | ... | ... | ... | ... | ... | ... | ... | ... |
| Tokelau / Tokélaou | A | ... | ... | ... | 37.0 | ... | ... | ... | ... | ... |
| Tonga / Tonga | BA | ... | ... | ... | ... | ... | 38.6 | ... | ... | ... |
| Trinidad and Tobago / Trinité-et-Tobago | BA | 35.6 | *40.0[15] | *40.0[15] | *39.8[15] | *40.6[15] | *41.1[15] | *41.7[15] | *42.6[15] | ... |
| Tunisia[6] / Tunisie[6] | BA | ... | 24.4 | 24.6 | 24.9 | 25.2 | 25.3 | ... | ... | ... |
| Turkey / Turquie | | *16.7[9] | 18.3[8] | 19.1[8] | 19.0[8] | 20.6[8] | 20.6[8] | 19.9[8] | 20.3[8] | 20.9[8] |
| Turkmenistan / Turkménistan | E | ... | ... | ... | ... | 42.1 | ... | ... | ... | ... |
| Turks and Caicos Islands[6] / Iles Turques et Caïques[6] | E | ... | ... | ... | 43.1 | 40.4 | 39.9 | 40.9 | 40.7 | ... |
| Tuvalu / Tuvalu | FA | ... | ... | ... | ... | 34.3 | 39.1 | 33.9 | ... | ... |
| Uganda[5] / Ouganda[5] | BA | ... | ... | ... | ... | ... | 39.0 | ... | ... | ... |
| Ukraine[4] / Ukraine[4] | | ... | 53.2 | 52.9 | ... | 54.4 | 54.4 | 55.1 | 54.9 | 54.6 |

| Country or area<br>Pays ou zone | Source[&]<br>Source[&] | 1990 | 1999 | 2000 | 2001 | 2002 | 2003 | 2004 | 2005 | 2006 |
|---|---|---|---|---|---|---|---|---|---|---|
| United Kingdom<br>Royaume-Uni | | 47.8[11] | 49.8[11] | 49.8[11] | 49.6[11] | 49.8[11] | 49.6[11] | 49.4[11] | *49.5[8,17] | ... |
| United Rep. of Tanzania[3]<br>Rép.-Unie de Tanzanie[3] | BA | ... | ... | ... | 29.3 | ... | ... | ... | ... | ... |
| United States<br>Etats-Unis | BA | 46.6 | 47.6 | 47.4 | 47.4 | 47.5 | 47.7 | 47.5 | 47.3 | 47.3 |
| Uruguay<br>Uruguay | BA | 42.3 | *46.3[7] | 46.4 | 46.5 | 45.8 | *46.3[7] | *46.1[7] | *48.0[7] | *45.2[7] |
| Vanuatu[6]<br>Vanuatu[6] | A | ... | 45.1 | ... | ... | ... | ... | ... | ... | ... |
| Venezuela (Bolivarian Rep. of)[5]<br>Venezuela (Rép. bolivar. du)[5] | BA | 35.2 | 39.3 | 39.8 | 41.1 | 41.8 | 42.4 | *41.8[7] | ... | 40.9 |
| Viet Nam[5]<br>Viet Nam[5] | BA | ... | 49.4 | 48.2 | 48.0 | 47.9 | 46.6 | 46.4 | ... | ... |
| Yemen<br>Yemen | BA | ... | 6.5 | 7.0 | ... | ... | ... | ... | ... | ... |
| Zambia[5]<br>Zambie[5] | A | ... | ... | 33.7 | ... | ... | ... | ... | ... | ... |
| Zimbabwe[4]<br>Zimbabwe[4] | | 15.4 | 18.9 | 20.4 | 21.5 | 21.9 | ... | ... | ... | ... |

Source

International Labour Organization (ILO), Gevena, the ILO labour statistics database, last accessed April 2008.

[&] Data sources:

A: Population census.
B: Household surveys.
BA: Labour force surveys.
E: Official estimates.
FA: Insurance records.
FD: Administration reports.

Notes

1 ILO Economically Active Population Estimates and Projections: 1980-2020.
2 Economically Active Population in non-agriculture.
3 Total employees.
4 Labour-related establishment survey.
5 Total employment in non-agriculture.
6 Total employment.
7 Estimated on basis of total employment.
8 Labour Force Survey.
9 Insurance Records.
10 Estimated on basis of paid employment.
11 Official Estimates.
12 Labour-related establishment census.
13 For statistical purposes, the data for China do not include those for the Hong Kong Special Administrative Region (Hong Kong SAR) and Macao Special Administrative Region (Macao SAR).
14 MDG report - national estimates.
15 Estimated on basis of total employment in non-agriculture.
16 Total paid employment.
17 Estimated on basis of total employees.
18 Population census.

Source

Bureau international du travail (BIT), Genève, la base de données du BIT, dernier accès avril 2008.

[&] Sources de données :

A: Recensement de la population.
B: Enquêtes auprès des ménages.
BA: Enquêtes par sondage sur la main-d'œuvre.
E: Evaluations officielles.
FA: Fichiers des assurances.
FD: Rapports administratifs.

Notes

1 BIT, estimations et projections de la population active : 1980-2020.
2 Population active dans le secteur non agricole.
3 Nombre total d'employés.
4 Enquête sur les employés menée auprès des entreprises.
5 Population active totale dans le secteur non agricole.
6 Emploi total.
7 Estimations fondées sur la population active totale.
8 Enquêtes par sondage sur la main-d'œuvre.
9 Fichiers des assurances.
10 Sur la base des emplois rémunérés.
11 Estimations officielles.
12 Recensement concernant les employés mené auprès des entreprises.
13 Pour la présentation des statistiques, les données pour la Chine ne comprennent pas la Région Administrative Spéciale de Hong Kong (Hong Kong RAS) et la Région Administrative Spéciale de Macao (Macao RAS).
14 Rapport sur les objectifs du Millénaire pour le développement – estimations nationales.
15 Estimations fondées sur la population active totale dans le secteur non agricole.
16 Emplois rémunérés (total).
17 Estimations fondées sur le nombre total d'employés.
18 Recensement de la population.

# Ratio of girls to boys in primary, secondary and tertiary education

## Rapport filles/garçons dans l'enseignement primaire, secondaire et supérieur

| Country or area | 1991 | 2000 | 2001 | 2002 | 2003 | 2004 | 2005 | 2006 | Pays ou zone |
|---|---|---|---|---|---|---|---|---|---|
| Afghanistan | | | | | | | | | Afghanistan |
| Primary education | 0.55 | ... | ... | 0.46 | 0.57 | 0.44 | 0.59 | ... | Enseignement primaire |
| Secondary education | 0.51 | ... | ... | ... | *0.35 | 0.21 | 0.33 | ... | Enseignement secondaire |
| Tertiary education | ... | ... | ... | ... | *0.28 | 0.28 | ... | ... | Enseignement supérieur |
| Albania | | | | | | | | | Albanie |
| Primary education | 1.00 | 0.99 | 1.00 | 0.97 | 0.98 | 0.99 | ... | ... | Enseignement primaire |
| Secondary education | 0.86 | 0.99 | 1.00 | *0.93 | 0.98 | 0.96 | ... | ... | Enseignement secondaire |
| Tertiary education | 1.13 | 1.43 | 1.52 | 1.57 | 1.60 | 1.60 | ... | ... | Enseignement supérieur |
| Algeria | | | | | | | | | Algérie |
| Primary education | 0.85 | 0.92 | 0.92 | 0.93 | 0.93 | 0.93 | 0.93 | 0.93 | Enseignement primaire |
| Secondary education | 0.80 | ... | ... | *1.05 | 1.07 | 1.07 | *1.08 | ... | Enseignement secondaire |
| Tertiary education | ... | ... | ... | ... | ... | 1.08 | 1.28 | 1.26 | Enseignement supérieur |
| Andorra[1] | | | | | | | | | Andorre[1] |
| Primary education | ... | ... | ... | 0.99 | 0.99 | *0.98 | 0.95 | 1.00 | Enseignement primaire |
| Secondary education | ... | ... | ... | 1.05 | 1.05 | *1.03 | 1.12 | 1.04 | Enseignement secondaire |
| Tertiary education | ... | ... | ... | 1.05 | 1.01 | *1.00 | 1.06 | 1.25 | Enseignement supérieur |
| Angola | | | | | | | | | Angola |
| Primary education | 0.92 | ... | ... | ... | ... | ... | ... | ... | Enseignement primaire |
| Secondary education | ... | 0.82 | 0.78 | 0.83 | ... | ... | ... | ... | Enseignement secondaire |
| Tertiary education | ... | ... | ... | 0.66 | ... | ... | ... | ... | Enseignement supérieur |
| Anguilla | | | | | | | | | Anguilla |
| Primary education[1] | ... | *1.04 | *0.98 | 0.98 | *1.01 | *1.03 | *1.06 | *0.99 | Enseignement primaire[1] |
| Secondary education*[1] | ... | 0.98 | 1.00 | 1.01 | 0.99 | 1.00 | 0.97 | 1.02 | Enseignement secondaire*[1] |
| Tertiary education* | ... | ... | ... | ... | ... | 4.23[1] | 3.11[1] | 4.86 | Enseignement supérieur* |
| Argentina | | | | | | | | | Argentine |
| Primary education | ... | 1.00 | 1.00 | 1.00 | 0.99 | 0.99 | 0.99 | ... | Enseignement primaire |
| Secondary education | ... | 1.07 | 1.06 | 1.06 | 1.07 | 1.10 | 1.11 | ... | Enseignement secondaire |
| Tertiary education | ... | *1.55 | 1.48 | 1.49 | 1.51 | 1.42 | 1.45 | ... | Enseignement supérieur |
| Armenia | | | | | | | | | Arménie |
| Primary education | ... | ... | *1.01 | 1.02 | 1.02 | 1.03 | 1.04 | 1.04 | Enseignement primaire |
| Secondary education | ... | ... | *1.06 | 1.06 | 1.04 | 1.03 | 1.03 | 1.04 | Enseignement secondaire |
| Tertiary education | ... | 1.09 | 1.14 | 1.11 | 1.12 | 1.21 | 1.22 | 1.18 | Enseignement supérieur |
| Aruba | | | | | | | | | Aruba |
| Primary education[1] | ... | 0.96 | 0.97 | 0.95 | 0.95 | 0.95 | 0.97 | 0.98 | Enseignement primaire[1] |
| Secondary education | ... | 1.02 | 1.05 | 1.07 | 1.06 | 1.02 | 1.03 | 1.04 | Enseignement secondaire |
| Tertiary education | ... | 1.50 | 1.50 | 1.50 | 1.45 | 1.51 | 1.49 | 1.56 | Enseignement supérieur |
| Australia | | | | | | | | | Australie |
| Primary education | 0.99 | 1.00 | 1.00 | 1.00 | 1.00 | 1.00 | 1.00 | 1.00 | Enseignement primaire |
| Secondary education | 1.03 | 1.00 | 0.98 | 0.97 | 0.97 | 0.96 | 0.96 | 0.95 | Enseignement secondaire |
| Tertiary education | 1.19 | 1.23 | 1.23 | 1.22 | 1.23 | 1.24 | 1.25 | 1.28 | Enseignement supérieur |
| Austria | | | | | | | | | Autriche |
| Primary education | 1.00 | 0.99 | 0.99 | 0.99 | 0.99 | 1.00 | 1.00 | 0.99 | Enseignement primaire |
| Secondary education | 0.93 | 0.96 | 0.96 | 0.95 | 0.95 | 0.95 | 0.95 | 0.96 | Enseignement secondaire |
| Tertiary education | 0.88 | 1.09 | 1.14 | 1.18 | 1.19 | 1.20 | 1.21 | 1.21 | Enseignement supérieur |
| Azerbaijan | | | | | | | | | Azerbaïdjan |
| Primary education | *0.99 | 1.01 | 0.98 | 0.98 | 0.97 | 0.98 | 0.98 | 0.97 | Enseignement primaire |
| Secondary education | 1.01 | 1.00 | 0.97 | 0.97 | 0.97 | 0.97 | 0.97 | 0.96 | Enseignement secondaire |
| Tertiary education | 0.67 | 0.67 | 0.71 | 0.79 | 0.82 | 0.87 | 0.90 | 0.94 | Enseignement supérieur |

| Country or area | 1991 | 2000 | 2001 | 2002 | 2003 | 2004 | 2005 | 2006 | Pays ou zone |
|---|---|---|---|---|---|---|---|---|---|
| Bahamas | | | | | | | | | Bahamas |
| Primary education | *1.03 | *0.98 | *1.00 | 1.01 | *1.01 | *1.00 | 1.00 | 1.00 | Enseignement primaire |
| Secondary education | ... | *0.95 | *0.95 | 1.05 | *1.02 | *1.00 | 1.00 | 1.01 | Enseignement secondaire |
| Bahrain | | | | | | | | | Bahreïn |
| Primary education | 1.00 | 1.01 | 1.01 | 1.00 | 1.01 | 1.00 | 0.99 | 1.00 | Enseignement primaire |
| Secondary education | 1.04 | 1.08 | 1.10 | 1.09 | 1.07 | 1.05 | 1.05 | 1.04 | Enseignement secondaire |
| Tertiary education | 1.36 | ... | ... | ... | 1.86 | *1.95 | 2.41 | 2.46 | Enseignement supérieur |
| Bangladesh | | | | | | | | | Bangladesh |
| Primary education | ... | 1.00 | 1.01 | 1.03 | 1.02 | 1.03 | ... | ... | Enseignement primaire |
| Secondary education | ... | 1.05 | 1.10 | 1.11 | 1.11 | 1.03 | ... | ... | Enseignement secondaire |
| Tertiary education | ... | 0.51 | 0.54 | 0.50 | 0.50 | 0.49 | 0.53 | ... | Enseignement supérieur |
| Barbados | | | | | | | | | Barbade |
| Primary education | *1.00 | 0.98 | 0.99 | 1.00 | 0.99 | 0.99 | 1.00 | 0.98 | Enseignement primaire |
| Secondary education | ... | 1.04 | 1.00 | 1.00 | 1.02 | 1.01 | 1.00 | 1.04 | Enseignement secondaire |
| Tertiary education | 1.24 | 2.66 | 2.46 | ... | ... | ... | ... | ... | Enseignement supérieur |
| Belarus | | | | | | | | | Bélarus |
| Primary education | *0.96 | 0.99 | 0.99 | 0.99 | 0.99 | 0.97 | 0.97 | 0.98 | Enseignement primaire |
| Secondary education | ... | 1.04 | 1.04 | 1.04 | 1.03 | 1.02 | 1.02 | 1.02 | Enseignement secondaire |
| Tertiary education | *1.11 | 1.32 | 1.32 | 1.36 | 1.37 | 1.38 | 1.36 | 1.37 | Enseignement supérieur |
| Belgium | | | | | | | | | Belgique |
| Primary education | 1.01 | 0.99 | 0.99 | 0.99 | 0.99 | 1.00 | 1.00 | 0.99 | Enseignement primaire |
| Secondary education | 1.01 | 1.10 | 1.11 | 1.12 | 1.10 | 0.97 | 0.97 | 0.97 | Enseignement secondaire |
| Tertiary education | 0.97 | 1.13 | 1.16 | 1.17 | 1.18 | 1.20 | 1.23 | 1.25 | Enseignement supérieur |
| Belize | | | | | | | | | Belize |
| Primary education | *0.98 | 0.96 | 0.97 | *0.96 | 0.98 | 0.97 | 0.96 | 0.97 | Enseignement primaire |
| Secondary education | 1.15 | 1.07 | 1.06 | *1.04 | *1.05 | 1.04 | *1.02 | 1.06 | Enseignement secondaire |
| Tertiary education | ... | ... | ... | ... | 1.91 | 2.43 | ... | ... | Enseignement supérieur |
| Benin | | | | | | | | | Bénin |
| Primary education | 0.51 | 0.69 | 0.71 | 0.73 | 0.74 | 0.77 | 0.80 | 0.83 | Enseignement primaire |
| Secondary education | *0.42 | 0.46 | *0.48 | *0.48 | 0.47 | 0.48 | *0.57 | ... | Enseignement secondaire |
| Tertiary education | 0.15 | *0.25 | *0.25 | ... | ... | ... | ... | ... | Enseignement supérieur |
| Bermuda | | | | | | | | | Bermudes |
| Primary education[1] | ... | ... | 0.99 | 1.02 | 1.00 | 1.06 | 1.03 | 0.85 | Enseignement primaire[1] |
| Secondary education | ... | ... | 1.05 | 1.06 | 1.10 | 1.11 | 1.09 | 1.06 | Enseignement secondaire |
| Tertiary education | ... | ... | 1.18 | *1.18 | ... | ... | 1.80 | ... | Enseignement supérieur |
| Bhutan | | | | | | | | | Bhoutan |
| Primary education | ... | 0.87 | 0.89 | *0.92 | ... | ... | 0.97 | 0.98 | Enseignement primaire |
| Secondary education | ... | 0.82 | 0.84 | *0.83 | ... | ... | 0.88 | 0.91 | Enseignement secondaire |
| Tertiary education | ... | *0.52 | *0.53 | ... | ... | ... | ... | 0.59 | Enseignement supérieur |
| Bolivia | | | | | | | | | Bolivie |
| Primary education | 0.92 | 0.99 | 0.99 | 0.99 | 0.99 | *1.00 | ... | 1.00 | Enseignement primaire |
| Secondary education | ... | *0.96 | 0.96 | *0.97 | 0.97 | ... | ... | 0.96 | Enseignement secondaire |
| Botswana | | | | | | | | | Botswana |
| Primary education | 1.07 | 1.00 | 1.00 | 0.99 | 0.99 | 0.98 | 0.99 | ... | Enseignement primaire |
| Secondary education | 1.18 | *1.05 | 1.05 | 1.06 | 1.07 | *1.05 | 1.05 | ... | Enseignement secondaire |
| Tertiary education | 0.73 | 0.74 | 0.90 | 0.82 | ... | 0.87 | 1.00 | ... | Enseignement supérieur |
| Brazil | | | | | | | | | Brésil |
| Primary education | ... | 0.94 | 0.95 | 0.95 | 0.95 | 0.93 | ... | ... | Enseignement primaire |
| Secondary education | ... | 1.10 | 1.10 | 1.10 | 1.11 | 1.10 | ... | ... | Enseignement secondaire |
| Tertiary education | *1.11 | 1.30 | 1.30 | 1.32 | 1.32 | 1.32 | ... | ... | Enseignement supérieur |
| British Virgin Islands[1] | | | | | | | | | Iles Vierges britanniques[1] |
| Primary education | ... | 1.00 | *1.00 | 0.98 | 0.94 | 0.96 | 0.96 | 0.97 | Enseignement primaire |
| Secondary education | ... | *1.04 | 1.06 | 1.02 | 1.16 | 1.06 | 1.18 | 1.13 | Enseignement secondaire |
| Tertiary education | ... | *2.68 | 1.80 | 2.34 | *2.65 | 2.33 | *2.28 | ... | Enseignement supérieur |

| Country or area | 1991 | 2000 | 2001 | 2002 | 2003 | 2004 | 2005 | 2006 | Pays ou zone |
|---|---|---|---|---|---|---|---|---|---|
| **Brunei Darussalam** | | | | | | | | | **Brunéi Darussalam** |
| Primary education | 0.94 | 0.99 | 0.99 | 1.00 | 1.01 | 1.00 | 1.00 | 0.99 | Enseignement primaire |
| Secondary education | 1.09 | 1.06 | 1.06 | 1.05 | 1.06 | 1.05 | 1.04 | 1.04 | Enseignement secondaire |
| Tertiary education | ... | 1.87 | 1.74 | 1.74 | 1.85 | 1.97 | 2.02 | 1.99 | Enseignement supérieur |
| **Bulgaria** | | | | | | | | | **Bulgarie** |
| Primary education | 0.98 | 0.98 | 0.97 | 0.98 | 0.98 | 0.98 | 0.99 | 0.99 | Enseignement primaire |
| Secondary education | 1.04 | 0.98 | 0.98 | 0.98 | 0.97 | 0.96 | 0.96 | 0.96 | Enseignement secondaire |
| Tertiary education | 1.10 | 1.41 | 1.36 | 1.24 | 1.18 | 1.17 | 1.15 | 1.21 | Enseignement supérieur |
| **Burkina Faso** | | | | | | | | | **Burkina Faso** |
| Primary education | 0.64 | 0.71 | 0.73 | *0.74 | 0.75 | 0.79 | 0.80 | 0.82 | Enseignement primaire |
| Secondary education | *0.54 | 0.66 | 0.66 | *0.66 | 0.68 | *0.70 | 0.71 | 0.72 | Enseignement secondaire |
| Tertiary education | 0.30 | *0.31 | *0.35 | 0.35 | 0.30 | *0.30 | 0.46 | 0.46 | Enseignement supérieur |
| **Burundi** | | | | | | | | | **Burundi** |
| Primary education | 0.84 | 0.80 | 0.80 | 0.79 | 0.81 | 0.83 | 0.86 | 0.91 | Enseignement primaire |
| Secondary education | 0.58 | ... | ... | ... | 0.77 | 0.75 | *0.74 | *0.74 | Enseignement secondaire |
| Tertiary education | 0.36 | 0.35 | 0.36 | 0.42 | *0.46 | 0.38 | *0.38 | 0.43 | Enseignement supérieur |
| **Cambodia** | | | | | | | | | **Cambodge** |
| Primary education | *0.81 | 0.87 | 0.89 | 0.90 | 0.91 | 0.92 | 0.93 | 0.93 | Enseignement primaire |
| Secondary education | *0.43 | 0.55 | 0.57 | 0.60 | 0.64 | *0.69 | ... | 0.79 | Enseignement secondaire |
| Tertiary education | ... | 0.33 | 0.38 | 0.41 | *0.41 | 0.46 | 0.47 | 0.50 | Enseignement supérieur |
| **Cameroon** | | | | | | | | | **Cameroun** |
| Primary education | 0.86 | 0.85 | 0.87 | 0.86 | 0.85 | 0.86 | *0.84 | 0.84 | Enseignement primaire |
| Secondary education | 0.71 | ... | 0.80 | ... | *0.84 | 0.79 | 0.79 | 0.79 | Enseignement secondaire |
| Tertiary education | ... | ... | ... | *0.64 | *0.64 | *0.64 | 0.66 | 0.72 | Enseignement supérieur |
| **Canada** | | | | | | | | | **Canada** |
| Primary education | 0.98 | 1.00 | ... | *1.00 | ... | *0.99 | ... | ... | Enseignement primaire |
| Secondary education | 1.00 | 1.00 | ... | *1.00 | ... | *0.97 | ... | ... | Enseignement secondaire |
| Tertiary education | 1.23 | 1.34 | ... | 1.36 | ... | *1.36 | ... | ... | Enseignement supérieur |
| **Cape Verde** | | | | | | | | | **Cap-Vert** |
| Primary education | *0.94 | 0.97 | 0.96 | 0.96 | 0.95 | 0.95 | 0.95 | 0.95 | Enseignement primaire |
| Secondary education | ... | ... | *1.04 | 1.05 | 1.09 | 1.10 | 1.07 | 1.15 | Enseignement secondaire |
| Tertiary education | ... | *1.00 | 1.01 | 1.01 | 1.10 | 1.10 | 1.04 | *1.04 | Enseignement supérieur |
| **Cayman Islands[1]** | | | | | | | | | **Iles Caïmanes[1]** |
| Primary education | ... | 0.97 | *0.97 | *0.98 | ... | *0.95 | *0.89 | *0.96 | Enseignement primaire |
| Secondary education | ... | 1.01 | *1.01 | *1.09 | ... | *1.10 | *0.92 | *1.06 | Enseignement secondaire |
| Tertiary education* | ... | 2.79 | 3.01 | ... | ... | ... | ... | 2.66 | Enseignement supérieur* |
| **Central African Rep.** | | | | | | | | | **Rép. centrafricaine** |
| Primary education | 0.64 | ... | 0.68 | 0.67 | 0.69 | 0.66 | 0.69 | 0.69 | Enseignement primaire |
| Secondary education | 0.40 | ... | ... | ... | ... | ... | ... | ... | Enseignement secondaire |
| Tertiary education | 0.15 | 0.19 | ... | ... | ... | ... | ... | 0.28 | Enseignement supérieur |
| **Chad** | | | | | | | | | **Tchad** |
| Primary education | 0.45 | 0.61 | 0.64 | 0.65 | 0.66 | 0.66 | 0.68 | *0.68 | Enseignement primaire |
| Secondary education | *0.20 | 0.28 | *0.28 | 0.33 | *0.32 | 0.33 | *0.33 | ... | Enseignement secondaire |
| Tertiary education | ... | 0.18 | *0.18 | ... | 0.11 | 0.14 | *0.14 | ... | Enseignement supérieur |
| **Chile** | | | | | | | | | **Chili** |
| Primary education | 0.98 | 0.98 | ... | 0.98 | 0.97 | 0.95 | 0.96 | 0.95 | Enseignement primaire |
| Secondary education | 1.07 | 1.02 | ... | 1.02 | 1.01 | 1.01 | 1.01 | 1.02 | Enseignement secondaire |
| Tertiary education | ... | 0.92 | ... | 0.93 | 0.94 | 0.95 | 0.96 | 1.00 | Enseignement supérieur |
| **China** | | | | | | | | | **Chine** |
| Primary education | 0.93 | ... | 1.01 | 1.00 | 1.00 | ... | ... | 0.99 | Enseignement primaire |
| Secondary education | 0.75 | ... | *0.97 | ... | 0.97 | ... | ... | 1.01 | Enseignement secondaire |
| Tertiary education | *0.53 | ... | ... | ... | 0.85 | ... | ... | 0.98 | Enseignement supérieur |

| Country or area | 1991 | 2000 | 2001 | 2002 | 2003 | 2004 | 2005 | 2006 | Pays ou zone |
|---|---|---|---|---|---|---|---|---|---|
| China, Hong Kong SAR | | | | | | | | | Chine, Hong Kong RAS |
| Primary education | *1.01 | 0.96 | 0.95 | 0.95 | 0.95 | 0.95 | 0.95 | 0.95 | Enseignement primaire |
| Secondary education | *1.05 | ... | 0.97 | 0.97 | 0.99 | 1.00 | 1.01 | 1.00 | Enseignement secondaire |
| Tertiary education | ... | ... | ... | ... | 0.96 | 1.02 | 1.04 | 1.03 | Enseignement supérieur |
| China, Macao SAR | | | | | | | | | Chine, Macao RAS |
| Primary education | 0.96 | 0.95 | 0.95 | 0.94 | 0.93 | 0.92 | 0.92 | 0.94 | Enseignement primaire |
| Secondary education | 1.11 | 1.05 | 1.04 | 1.04 | 1.04 | 1.02 | 1.01 | 1.01 | Enseignement secondaire |
| Tertiary education | 0.48 | 0.95 | 0.71 | 0.52 | 0.52 | 0.63 | 0.70 | 0.81 | Enseignement supérieur |
| Colombia | | | | | | | | | Colombie |
| Primary education | 1.02 | 1.00 | 0.99 | 0.99 | *0.99 | 0.99 | 0.98 | 0.99 | Enseignement primaire |
| Secondary education | 1.19 | 1.10 | 1.10 | 1.11 | *1.10 | 1.11 | 1.11 | 1.11 | Enseignement secondaire |
| Tertiary education | 1.07 | 1.09 | 1.10 | 1.08 | *1.09 | 1.08 | 1.08 | 1.09 | Enseignement supérieur |
| Comoros | | | | | | | | | Comores |
| Primary education | 0.73 | *0.85 | *0.83 | 0.82 | 0.82 | 0.88 | *0.88 | ... | Enseignement primaire |
| Secondary education | 0.65 | *0.82 | ... | 0.84 | 0.83 | 0.76 | *0.76 | ... | Enseignement secondaire |
| Tertiary education | ... | *0.73 | ... | ... | 0.77 | *0.77 | ... | ... | Enseignement supérieur |
| Congo | | | | | | | | | Congo |
| Primary education | 0.90 | 0.92 | 0.93 | 0.94 | 0.93 | 0.93 | 0.92 | 0.90 | Enseignement primaire |
| Secondary education | *0.72 | 0.69 | ... | *0.73 | 0.68 | *0.84 | ... | ... | Enseignement secondaire |
| Tertiary education | 0.21 | 0.31 | 0.13 | 0.19 | *0.19 | ... | ... | ... | Enseignement supérieur |
| Cook Islands[1] | | | | | | | | | Iles Cook[1] |
| Primary education | ... | 0.98 | *0.95 | *0.97 | *0.98 | *0.98 | ... | *1.02 | Enseignement primaire |
| Secondary education | ... | 1.10 | *1.09 | *1.03 | *1.02 | *1.02 | ... | *1.04 | Enseignement secondaire |
| Costa Rica | | | | | | | | | Costa Rica |
| Primary education | 0.99 | 0.98 | 1.00 | 0.98 | *0.98 | 0.99 | 0.99 | 0.99 | Enseignement primaire |
| Secondary education | 1.06 | 1.09 | 1.08 | 1.08 | *1.08 | 1.06 | 1.06 | 1.06 | Enseignement secondaire |
| Tertiary education | ... | 1.20 | 1.17 | 1.16 | *1.16 | 1.25 | *1.26 | ... | Enseignement supérieur |
| Côte d'Ivoire | | | | | | | | | Côte d'Ivoire |
| Primary education | 0.71 | 0.75 | 0.76 | 0.73 | 0.79 | | | 0.79 | Enseignement primaire |
| Secondary education* | 0.48 | 0.54 | 0.55 | 0.55 | ... | ... | ... | ... | Enseignement secondaire* |
| Croatia | | | | | | | | | Croatie |
| Primary education | 0.99 | 0.99 | 0.99 | 0.99 | 0.99 | ... | 1.00 | 1.00 | Enseignement primaire |
| Secondary education | 1.10 | 1.02 | 1.02 | 1.02 | 1.02 | ... | 1.03 | 1.03 | Enseignement secondaire |
| Tertiary education | ... | 1.16 | 1.15 | 1.15 | 1.19 | ... | 1.22 | 1.23 | Enseignement supérieur |
| Cuba | | | | | | | | | Cuba |
| Primary education | 0.97 | 0.96 | 0.96 | 0.96 | 0.96 | 0.96 | 0.97 | 0.97 | Enseignement primaire |
| Secondary education | 1.15 | 1.05 | 1.06 | 0.99 | 0.98 | 1.02 | 1.01 | 1.02 | Enseignement secondaire |
| Tertiary education | 1.40 | 1.21 | 1.16 | 1.27 | 1.37 | *1.76 | 1.74 | 1.65 | Enseignement supérieur |
| Cyprus | | | | | | | | | Chypre |
| Primary education | 1.00 | 1.00[1] | 1.00[1] | 1.00[1] | 1.00[1] | 1.00[1] | 1.00[1] | 1.00[1] | Enseignement primaire |
| Secondary education | 1.02 | 1.04[1] | 1.01[1] | 1.02[1] | 1.02[1] | 1.03[1] | 1.02[1] | 1.02[1] | Enseignement secondaire |
| Tertiary education | 1.11 | 1.31[1] | 1.37[1] | 1.26[1] | 1.03[1] | 0.98[1] | 1.13[1] | 1.05[1] | Enseignement supérieur |
| Czech Republic | | | | | | | | | République tchèque |
| Primary education | 1.00 | 0.99 | 0.99 | 0.99 | 0.98 | 0.99 | 0.99 | 0.99 | Enseignement primaire |
| Secondary education | 0.97 | 1.02 | 1.03 | 1.03 | 1.03 | 1.01 | 1.02 | 1.01 | Enseignement secondaire |
| Tertiary education | 0.81 | 1.03 | 1.05 | 1.10 | 1.07 | 1.10 | 1.16 | 1.22 | Enseignement supérieur |
| Dem. Rep. of the Congo | | | | | | | | | Rép. dém. du Congo |
| Primary education | 0.75 | ... | ... | 0.78 | *0.78 | ... | ... | ... | Enseignement primaire |
| Secondary education | ... | *0.52 | ... | 0.58 | *0.58 | ... | ... | ... | Enseignement secondaire |
| Denmark | | | | | | | | | Danemark |
| Primary education | 1.00 | 1.00 | 1.00 | 1.00 | *1.00 | 1.00 | 1.00 | ... | Enseignement primaire |
| Secondary education | 1.01 | 1.04 | 1.05 | 1.05 | 1.05 | 1.04 | 1.03 | ... | Enseignement secondaire |
| Tertiary education | 1.14 | 1.36 | 1.34 | 1.39 | 1.42 | 1.41 | 1.39 | ... | Enseignement supérieur |

| Country or area | 1991 | 2000 | 2001 | 2002 | 2003 | 2004 | 2005 | 2006 | Pays ou zone |
|---|---|---|---|---|---|---|---|---|---|
| Djibouti | | | | | | | | | Djibouti |
| Primary education | 0.72 | 0.73 | 0.76 | 0.76 | *0.78 | 0.79 | 0.82 | 0.81 | Enseignement primaire |
| Secondary education | *0.66 | 0.66 | 0.62 | 0.62 | *0.66 | 0.69 | 0.66 | 0.67 | Enseignement secondaire |
| Tertiary education | ... | 0.89 | 0.73 | 0.81 | 0.70 | 0.82 | 0.73 | 0.68 | Enseignement supérieur |
| Dominica[1] | | | | | | | | | Dominique[1] |
| Primary education | ... | 0.96 | 0.91 | 0.97 | 0.99 | 0.99 | 1.02 | 1.02 | Enseignement primaire |
| Secondary education | ... | 1.16 | 1.06 | 1.06 | 1.04 | 0.99 | 1.00 | 0.98 | Enseignement secondaire |
| Dominican Republic | | | | | | | | | Rép. dominicaine |
| Primary education | *1.00 | 0.97 | *1.01 | 1.01 | *1.01 | 0.95 | 0.95 | 0.95 | Enseignement primaire |
| Secondary education | | 1.23 | *1.21 | 1.21 | *1.21 | 1.21 | 1.19 | 1.20 | Enseignement secondaire |
| Tertiary education | ... | ... | ... | ... | 1.59 | *1.59 | ... | ... | Enseignement supérieur |
| Ecuador | | | | | | | | | Equateur |
| Primary education | *0.99 | 0.99 | 1.00 | 1.00 | 1.00 | 1.00 | 1.00 | 1.00 | Enseignement primaire |
| Secondary education | | 1.02 | 1.02 | 1.01 | 1.02 | 1.00 | 1.01 | 1.02 | Enseignement secondaire |
| Egypt | | | | | | | | | Egypte |
| Primary education | 0.83 | *0.92 | *0.93 | *0.94 | *0.95 | *0.96 | 0.94 | 0.94 | Enseignement primaire |
| Secondary education | 0.79 | *0.93 | *0.93 | *0.93 | *0.93 | *0.94 | ... | ... | Enseignement secondaire |
| Tertiary education* | 0.54 | ... | ... | ... | ... | ... | ... | ... | Enseignement supérieur* |
| El Salvador | | | | | | | | | El Salvador |
| Primary education | 1.01 | 0.95 | 0.96 | 0.95 | 0.96 | 0.97 | 0.96 | 0.96 | Enseignement primaire |
| Secondary education | 1.22 | 0.99 | 1.01 | 1.01 | 1.02 | 1.02 | 1.02 | 1.04 | Enseignement secondaire |
| Tertiary education | ... | 1.20 | 1.20 | 1.20 | 1.18 | 1.20 | 1.22 | 1.21 | Enseignement supérieur |
| Equatorial Guinea | | | | | | | | | Guinée équatoriale |
| Primary education | *0.96 | *0.95 | 0.96 | 0.91 | 0.97 | ... | 0.95 | *0.95 | Enseignement primaire |
| Secondary education* | ... | 0.60 | ... | 0.57 | ... | ... | ... | ... | Enseignement secondaire* |
| Tertiary education | 0.14 | 0.43 | ... | ... | ... | ... | ... | ... | Enseignement supérieur |
| Eritrea | | | | | | | | | Erythrée |
| Primary education | 0.95 | 0.82 | 0.82 | 0.80 | 0.80 | 0.80 | 0.81 | 0.81 | Enseignement primaire |
| Secondary education | ... | 0.69 | 0.70 | 0.64 | 0.64 | 0.56 | 0.59 | 0.60 | Enseignement secondaire |
| Tertiary education | ... | 0.17 | 0.16 | 0.15 | *0.15 | 0.15 | ... | ... | Enseignement supérieur |
| Estonia | | | | | | | | | Estonie |
| Primary education | 0.97 | 0.97 | 0.96 | 0.96 | 0.96 | 0.97 | 0.97 | 0.98 | Enseignement primaire |
| Secondary education | *1.08 | 1.04 | 1.03 | 1.02 | 1.04 | 1.02 | 1.01 | 1.02 | Enseignement secondaire |
| Tertiary education | *1.04 | 1.45 | 1.55 | 1.65 | 1.66 | 1.68 | 1.66 | 1.67 | Enseignement supérieur |
| Ethiopia | | | | | | | | | Ethiopie |
| Primary education | 0.66 | 0.65 | 0.69 | 0.71 | 0.73 | 0.77 | 0.83 | 0.86 | Enseignement primaire |
| Secondary education | 0.75 | 0.67 | 0.66 | 0.62 | 0.57 | 0.57 | 0.60 | 0.63 | Enseignement secondaire |
| Tertiary education | 0.22 | 0.28 | 0.27 | 0.36 | 0.34 | 0.34 | 0.32 | 0.32 | Enseignement supérieur |
| Fiji | | | | | | | | | Fidji |
| Primary education | 1.00 | 0.98 | 0.99 | 1.01 | 0.99 | 0.98 | *0.98 | 0.98 | Enseignement primaire |
| Secondary education | 0.95 | 1.09 | 1.08 | 1.08 | 1.08 | 1.07 | *1.07 | 1.10 | Enseignement secondaire |
| Tertiary education | ... | ... | ... | ... | *1.20 | 1.20 | *1.20 | ... | Enseignement supérieur |
| Finland | | | | | | | | | Finlande |
| Primary education | 0.99 | 0.99 | 0.99 | 0.99 | 0.99 | 0.99 | 0.99 | 1.00 | Enseignement primaire |
| Secondary education | 1.19 | 1.09 | 1.11 | 1.12 | 1.11 | 1.05 | 1.04 | 1.04 | Enseignement secondaire |
| Tertiary education | 1.13 | 1.21 | 1.22 | 1.23 | 1.20 | 1.20 | 1.21 | 1.22 | Enseignement supérieur |
| France | | | | | | | | | France |
| Primary education | 0.99 | 0.99 | 0.99 | 0.99 | 0.99 | 0.99 | 0.99 | 0.99 | Enseignement primaire |
| Secondary education | 1.05 | 1.00 | 1.01 | 1.01 | 1.01 | 1.01 | 1.01 | 1.00 | Enseignement secondaire |
| Tertiary education | 1.17 | 1.24 | 1.23 | 1.27 | 1.27 | 1.27 | 1.27 | 1.27 | Enseignement supérieur |
| Gabon | | | | | | | | | Gabon |
| Primary education | *0.98 | *1.00 | 1.00 | 0.99 | 0.99 | *0.99 | ... | ... | Enseignement primaire |
| Secondary education* | ... | 0.86 | ... | ... | ... | ... | ... | ... | Enseignement secondaire* |

| Country or area | 1991 | 2000 | 2001 | 2002 | 2003 | 2004 | 2005 | 2006 | Pays ou zone |
|---|---|---|---|---|---|---|---|---|---|
| **Gambia** | | | | | | | | | **Gambie** |
| Primary education | *0.70 | 0.87 | 0.93 | 1.01 | 1.00 | 1.07 | ... | 1.08 | Enseignement primaire |
| Secondary education | 0.50 | 0.69 | 0.72 | *0.76 | *0.84 | 0.83 | ... | 0.90 | Enseignement secondaire |
| Tertiary education | ... | ... | ... | ... | ... | 0.24 | ... | ... | Enseignement supérieur |
| **Georgia** | | | | | | | | | **Géorgie** |
| Primary education | 1.00 | 1.00 | 1.03 | 1.04 | 1.02 | 1.00 | 1.00 | 1.03 | Enseignement primaire |
| Secondary education | 0.97 | 0.99 | 1.00 | 0.99 | 0.99 | 1.00 | 0.99 | *1.04 | Enseignement secondaire |
| Tertiary education | *1.18 | 0.95 | 0.95 | 0.98 | 0.95 | 1.03 | 1.04 | 1.13 | Enseignement supérieur |
| **Germany** | | | | | | | | | **Allemagne** |
| Primary education | *1.01 | 0.99 | 0.99 | 0.99 | 1.00 | 1.00 | 1.00 | 1.00 | Enseignement primaire |
| Secondary education | *0.97 | 0.99 | 0.99 | 0.99 | 0.98 | 0.98 | 0.98 | 0.98 | Enseignement secondaire |
| Tertiary education | ... | ... | ... | ... | ... | ... | ... | 1.03 | Enseignement supérieur |
| **Ghana** | | | | | | | | | **Ghana** |
| Primary education | 0.85 | 0.93 | 0.94 | 0.94 | 0.98 | 0.94 | 0.96 | 0.99 | Enseignement primaire |
| Secondary education | *0.65 | 0.81 | 0.84 | *0.85 | *0.85 | 0.83 | *0.85 | 0.85 | Enseignement secondaire |
| Tertiary education | 0.30 | 0.34 | 0.41 | 0.40 | 0.48 | 0.48 | 0.56 | 0.53 | Enseignement supérieur |
| **Greece** | | | | | | | | | **Grèce** |
| Primary education | 0.99 | 1.00 | 1.00 | 0.99 | 0.99 | 0.99 | 0.99 | 1.00 | Enseignement primaire |
| Secondary education | 0.98 | 1.06 | 1.05 | ... | 1.02 | 1.01 | 0.98 | 0.97 | Enseignement secondaire |
| Tertiary education | 0.99 | 1.10 | 1.15 | 1.15 | 1.14 | 1.17 | 1.14 | 1.13 | Enseignement supérieur |
| **Grenada** | | | | | | | | | **Grenade** |
| Primary education | *0.85 | 0.96[1] | 0.93[1] | *0.89[1] | 0.99[1] | 0.96[1] | *0.96[1] | ... | Enseignement primaire |
| Secondary education | 1.16 | ... | ... | *1.05[1] | 0.99[1] | 1.09[1] | 1.03[1] | ... | Enseignement secondaire |
| **Guatemala** | | | | | | | | | **Guatemala** |
| Primary education | 0.87 | 0.89 | 0.90 | 0.91 | *0.91 | 0.92 | 0.92 | 0.93 | Enseignement primaire |
| Secondary education | ... | 0.88 | 0.89 | 0.89 | *0.89 | 0.90 | 0.91 | 0.92 | Enseignement secondaire |
| Tertiary education | ... | ... | ... | 0.72 | *0.72 | ... | ... | 0.82 | Enseignement supérieur |
| **Guinea** | | | | | | | | | **Guinée** |
| Primary education | 0.48 | 0.69 | 0.72 | 0.75 | 0.77 | 0.79 | 0.82 | 0.84 | Enseignement primaire |
| Secondary education | 0.34 | *0.38 | *0.41 | *0.43 | *0.47 | 0.46 | *0.51 | 0.53 | Enseignement secondaire |
| Tertiary education | 0.07 | ... | ... | ... | *0.19 | 0.19 | 0.24 | 0.28 | Enseignement supérieur |
| **Guinea-Bissau** | | | | | | | | | **Guinée-Bissau** |
| Primary education | *0.55 | 0.67 | *0.67 | ... | ... | ... | ... | ... | Enseignement primaire |
| Secondary education | ... | 0.54 | *0.54 | ... | ... | ... | ... | ... | Enseignement secondaire |
| Tertiary education | ... | 0.18 | *0.18 | ... | ... | ... | ... | ... | Enseignement supérieur |
| **Guyana** | | | | | | | | | **Guyana** |
| Primary education | 0.99 | 0.97 | 0.98 | *0.98 | 0.98 | *0.97 | 0.99 | ... | Enseignement primaire |
| Secondary education | 1.06 | *1.03 | 1.04 | *1.03 | ... | *1.03 | 0.99 | *0.98 | Enseignement secondaire |
| Tertiary education | ... | ... | ... | ... | ... | 1.89 | 2.09 | 2.17 | Enseignement supérieur |
| **Haiti** | | | | | | | | | **Haïti** |
| Primary education | 0.95 | ... | ... | ... | ... | ... | ... | ... | Enseignement primaire |
| Secondary education | 0.94 | ... | ... | ... | ... | ... | ... | ... | Enseignement secondaire |
| **Honduras** | | | | | | | | | **Honduras** |
| Primary education | 1.04 | 1.01 | *1.01 | ... | ... | 0.99 | 0.99 | 0.99 | Enseignement primaire |
| Secondary education | 1.23 | ... | ... | ... | ... | 1.22 | 1.30 | ... | Enseignement secondaire |
| Tertiary education | 0.79 | 1.26 | *1.26 | *1.39 | 1.40 | *1.41 | ... | ... | Enseignement supérieur |
| **Hungary** | | | | | | | | | **Hongrie** |
| Primary education | 1.00 | 0.98 | 0.98 | 0.99 | 0.99 | 0.99 | 0.98 | 0.98 | Enseignement primaire |
| Secondary education | 1.01 | 1.01 | 1.01 | 1.01 | 1.00 | 0.99 | 0.99 | 0.99 | Enseignement secondaire |
| Tertiary education | 1.06 | 1.22 | 1.27 | 1.29 | 1.37 | 1.40 | 1.46 | 1.47 | Enseignement supérieur |
| **Iceland** | | | | | | | | | **Islande** |
| Primary education | *0.99 | 0.98 | 0.99 | 0.99 | 0.98 | 0.98 | 0.97 | 0.99 | Enseignement primaire |
| Secondary education | 0.96 | 1.07 | 1.06 | 1.06 | 1.06 | 1.03 | 1.02 | 1.03 | Enseignement secondaire |
| Tertiary education | 1.39 | 1.67 | 1.72 | 1.76 | 1.80 | 1.87 | 1.91 | 1.87 | Enseignement supérieur |

Ratio of girls to boys in primary, secondary and tertiary education (*continued*)
Rapport filles/garçons dans l'enseignement primaire, secondaire et supérieur (*suite*)

| Country or area | 1991 | 2000 | 2001 | 2002 | 2003 | 2004 | 2005 | 2006 | Pays ou zone |
|---|---|---|---|---|---|---|---|---|---|
| India | | | | | | | | | Inde |
| Primary education | 0.77 | 0.85 | 0.85 | 0.87 | 0.97 | *0.97 | 0.98 | 0.96 | Enseignement primaire |
| Secondary education | *0.60 | 0.71 | 0.72 | 0.75 | 0.81 | 0.81 | 0.82 | ... | Enseignement secondaire |
| Tertiary education | 0.54 | 0.66 | 0.69 | 0.70 | 0.68 | 0.72 | 0.71 | 0.72 | Enseignement supérieur |
| Indonesia | | | | | | | | | Indonésie |
| Primary education | 0.98 | *0.97 | 0.98 | 0.98 | 0.98 | 0.98 | *0.97 | 0.96 | Enseignement primaire |
| Secondary education | 0.83 | *0.95 | 0.98 | 0.99 | 0.99 | 0.99 | *0.99 | 1.00 | Enseignement secondaire |
| Tertiary education | ... | ... | 0.76 | 0.87 | 0.80 | 0.79 | *0.79 | ... | Enseignement supérieur |
| Iran (Islamic Rep. of) | | | | | | | | | Iran (Rép. islamique d') |
| Primary education | 0.90 | 0.95 | 0.96 | 0.96 | 0.97 | 1.10 | 1.22 | 1.27 | Enseignement primaire |
| Secondary education | 0.75 | 0.94 | 0.94 | 0.95 | 0.94 | 0.94 | 0.94 | ... | Enseignement secondaire |
| Tertiary education | *0.48 | 0.87 | 0.94 | 1.01 | 1.08 | 1.11 | 1.09 | 1.11 | Enseignement supérieur |
| Iraq | | | | | | | | | Iraq |
| Primary education | 0.83 | 0.82 | *0.82 | *0.83 | 0.83 | 0.83 | *0.83 | ... | Enseignement primaire |
| Secondary education | *0.63 | 0.61 | 0.60 | *0.60 | 0.71 | 0.66 | *0.66 | ... | Enseignement secondaire |
| Tertiary education | ... | 0.54 | ... | *0.54 | ... | 0.59 | *0.59 | ... | Enseignement supérieur |
| Ireland | | | | | | | | | Irlande |
| Primary education | 1.00 | 0.99 | 0.99 | 1.00 | 0.99 | 0.99 | 1.00 | 0.99 | Enseignement primaire |
| Secondary education | 1.09 | 1.08 | 1.08 | 1.09 | 1.09 | 1.08 | 1.09 | 1.07 | Enseignement secondaire |
| Tertiary education | 0.90 | 1.23 | 1.26 | 1.28 | 1.31 | 1.28 | 1.26 | 1.27 | Enseignement supérieur |
| Israel | | | | | | | | | Israël |
| Primary education | 1.03 | 0.99 | 1.00 | 1.00 | 1.00 | 1.01 | 1.01 | 1.02 | Enseignement primaire |
| Secondary education | 1.08 | 1.00 | 0.99 | 0.99 | 0.98 | 1.00 | 0.99 | 0.99 | Enseignement secondaire |
| Tertiary education | 1.01 | 1.42 | 1.39 | 1.38 | 1.33 | 1.33 | 1.34 | 1.29 | Enseignement supérieur |
| Italy | | | | | | | | | Italie |
| Primary education | 1.00 | 1.00 | 0.99 | 0.98 | 0.99 | 1.00 | 0.99 | 0.99 | Enseignement primaire |
| Secondary education | 1.00 | ... | 0.97 | 0.96 | *0.99 | 0.99 | 0.99 | 0.99 | Enseignement secondaire |
| Tertiary education | 0.94 | 1.30 | 1.32 | 1.34 | 1.34 | 1.34 | 1.36 | 1.38 | Enseignement supérieur |
| Jamaica | | | | | | | | | Jamaïque |
| Primary education | *0.99 | 1.00 | 0.99 | 1.00 | 1.00 | 1.00 | 1.00 | ... | Enseignement primaire |
| Secondary education | *1.06 | 1.03 | *1.03 | 1.03 | 1.02 | 1.02 | 1.03 | ... | Enseignement secondaire |
| Tertiary education | *0.74 | 1.82 | *1.97 | 2.16 | *2.29 | ... | ... | ... | Enseignement supérieur |
| Japan | | | | | | | | | Japon |
| Primary education | 1.00 | 1.00 | 1.00 | 1.00 | 1.00 | 1.00 | 1.00 | 1.00 | Enseignement primaire |
| Secondary education | 1.02 | 1.01 | 1.01 | 1.01 | 1.00 | 1.00 | 1.00 | 1.00 | Enseignement secondaire |
| Tertiary education | 0.65 | 0.85 | 0.85 | 0.86 | 0.88 | 0.89 | 0.89 | 0.88 | Enseignement supérieur |
| Jordan | | | | | | | | | Jordanie |
| Primary education | 1.01 | 1.00 | ... | 1.00 | 1.00 | 1.00 | 1.00 | 1.02 | Enseignement primaire |
| Secondary education | 1.04 | *1.03 | ... | 1.02 | 1.02 | 1.01 | 1.02 | 1.03 | Enseignement secondaire |
| Tertiary education | 1.12 | 1.12 | ... | 1.00 | 1.09 | 1.09 | 1.05 | 1.11 | Enseignement supérieur |
| Kazakhstan | | | | | | | | | Kazakhstan |
| Primary education | *0.99 | 1.01 | 1.00 | 1.00 | 1.00 | 1.00 | 1.00 | 1.00 | Enseignement primaire |
| Secondary education | *1.03 | 1.02 | 0.98 | 0.99 | 1.01 | 0.99 | 0.98 | 0.98 | Enseignement secondaire |
| Tertiary education | ... | 1.18 | 1.20 | 1.25 | 1.33 | 1.38 | 1.43 | 1.43 | Enseignement supérieur |
| Kenya | | | | | | | | | Kenya |
| Primary education | 0.96 | 0.99 | ... | 0.95 | 0.95 | 0.94 | 0.96 | 0.97 | Enseignement primaire |
| Secondary education | *0.77 | 0.95 | ... | 0.96 | 1.02 | *0.94 | *0.95 | 0.93 | Enseignement secondaire |
| Tertiary education | ... | 0.54 | 0.54 | *0.54 | ... | 0.60 | ... | ... | Enseignement supérieur |
| Kiribati[1] | | | | | | | | | Kiribati[1] |
| Primary education | ... | 0.99 | *1.01 | *0.99 | *0.98 | *1.03 | 1.01 | ... | Enseignement primaire |
| Secondary education | ... | 1.61 | *1.39 | *1.17 | *1.19 | *1.18 | 1.14 | ... | Enseignement secondaire |
| Korea, Republic of | | | | | | | | | Corée, République de |
| Primary education | 1.01 | 0.95 | 0.94 | 0.93 | 0.93 | 0.94 | 0.95 | 0.96 | Enseignement primaire |
| Secondary education | 0.97 | 1.01 | 1.01 | 1.00 | 0.99 | 0.98 | 0.96 | 0.95 | Enseignement secondaire |
| Tertiary education | 0.49 | 0.57 | 0.59 | 0.60 | 0.61 | 0.62 | 0.63 | 0.64 | Enseignement supérieur |

| Country or area | 1991 | 2000 | 2001 | 2002 | 2003 | 2004 | 2005 | 2006 | Pays ou zone |
|---|---|---|---|---|---|---|---|---|---|
| Kuwait | | | | | | | | | Koweït |
| Primary education | 0.95 | 1.02 | 1.02 | 1.00 | 1.01 | 1.00 | 0.98 | 0.99 | Enseignement primaire |
| Secondary education | *0.98 | 1.03 | *1.05 | *1.05 | 1.04 | 1.06 | 1.05 | 1.05 | Enseignement secondaire |
| Tertiary education | ... | ... | *1.90 | 1.93 | 2.09 | *2.14 | 2.87 | 2.32 | Enseignement supérieur |
| Kyrgyzstan | | | | | | | | | Kirghizistan |
| Primary education | ... | 0.99 | 0.98 | 0.98 | 0.99 | 1.00 | 0.99 | 0.99 | Enseignement primaire |
| Secondary education | 1.02 | 1.03 | 1.00 | 1.00 | 1.01 | 1.01 | 1.01 | 1.01 | Enseignement secondaire |
| Tertiary education | ... | 1.01 | 1.04 | 1.14 | 1.19 | 1.19 | 1.25 | 1.27 | Enseignement supérieur |
| Lao People's Dem. Rep. | | | | | | | | | Rép. dém. pop. lao |
| Primary education | 0.79 | 0.85 | 0.86 | 0.86 | 0.87 | 0.88 | 0.88 | 0.89 | Enseignement primaire |
| Secondary education | 0.62 | 0.70 | 0.72 | 0.73 | 0.74 | 0.75 | 0.76 | 0.78 | Enseignement secondaire |
| Tertiary education | ... | 0.53 | 0.59 | 0.57 | 0.57 | 0.62 | 0.71 | 0.68 | Enseignement supérieur |
| Latvia | | | | | | | | | Lettonie |
| Primary education | 1.00 | 0.98 | 0.99 | 0.98 | 0.97 | 0.97 | 0.96 | 0.96 | Enseignement primaire |
| Secondary education | 1.02 | 1.03 | 1.02 | 1.01 | 1.00 | 0.99 | 1.00 | 1.00 | Enseignement secondaire |
| Tertiary education | 1.28 | 1.78 | 1.65 | 1.64 | 1.66 | 1.71 | 1.79 | 1.80 | Enseignement supérieur |
| Lebanon | | | | | | | | | Liban |
| Primary education | *0.97 | 0.95 | 0.96 | 0.96 | 0.96 | 0.96 | 0.97 | 0.97 | Enseignement primaire |
| Secondary education | ... | 1.08 | 1.09 | 1.09 | 1.08 | 1.09 | 1.10 | 1.10 | Enseignement secondaire |
| Tertiary education | ... | 1.05 | 1.05 | 1.10 | 1.16 | 1.09 | 1.13 | 1.16 | Enseignement supérieur |
| Lesotho | | | | | | | | | Lesotho |
| Primary education | 1.22 | 1.04 | 1.02 | 1.02 | 1.01 | 1.00 | 1.00 | 1.00 | Enseignement primaire |
| Secondary education | 1.42 | 1.31 | 1.27 | 1.28 | 1.27 | 1.27 | 1.26 | 1.27 | Enseignement secondaire |
| Tertiary education | 1.30 | *1.53 | 1.65 | 1.32 | 1.52 | ... | 1.27 | 1.19 | Enseignement supérieur |
| Liberia | | | | | | | | | Libéria |
| Primary education | ... | 0.73 | ... | ... | ... | ... | ... | 0.90 | Enseignement primaire |
| Secondary education | ... | 0.72 | ... | ... | ... | ... | ... | ... | Enseignement secondaire |
| Tertiary education | ... | 0.76 | ... | ... | ... | ... | ... | ... | Enseignement supérieur |
| Libyan Arab Jamah. | | | | | | | | | Jamah. arabe libyenne |
| Primary education | 0.94 | *0.98 | 1.01 | 1.00 | 0.96 | 0.96 | 0.98 | 0.95 | Enseignement primaire |
| Secondary education | ... | ... | ... | 1.06 | *1.06 | ... | *1.19 | 1.17 | Enseignement secondaire |
| Tertiary education | ... | 0.98 | *1.04 | 1.09 | *1.10 | ... | ... | ... | Enseignement supérieur |
| Liechtenstein[1] | | | | | | | | | Liechtenstein[1] |
| Primary education | ... | ... | ... | ... | 0.98 | 1.01 | ... | ... | Enseignement primaire |
| Secondary education | ... | ... | ... | ... | 0.88 | 0.87 | ... | ... | Enseignement secondaire |
| Tertiary education | ... | ... | ... | ... | 0.38 | 0.37 | ... | ... | Enseignement supérieur |
| Lithuania | | | | | | | | | Lituanie |
| Primary education | *0.95 | 0.99 | 0.99 | 0.99 | 0.99 | 0.99 | 0.99 | 0.99 | Enseignement primaire |
| Secondary education | ... | 0.99 | 0.99 | 0.99 | 0.98 | 0.99 | 1.00 | 1.00 | Enseignement secondaire |
| Tertiary education | *1.28 | 1.53 | 1.52 | 1.57 | 1.55 | 1.55 | 1.56 | 1.56 | Enseignement supérieur |
| Luxembourg | | | | | | | | | Luxembourg |
| Primary education | 1.08 | 1.02 | 1.00 | 1.00 | 1.00 | 1.00 | 1.01 | 1.01 | Enseignement primaire |
| Secondary education | ... | 1.05 | 1.06 | 1.06 | 1.05 | 1.05 | 1.06 | 1.04 | Enseignement secondaire |
| Tertiary education | ... | *1.10 | 1.17 | *1.16 | 1.19 | *1.17 | ... | 1.12 | Enseignement supérieur |
| Madagascar | | | | | | | | | Madagascar |
| Primary education | 0.98 | 0.96 | 0.96 | 0.96 | 0.96 | 0.96 | 0.96 | 0.96 | Enseignement primaire |
| Secondary education | *0.97 | ... | ... | ... | ... | ... | *0.96 | 0.95 | Enseignement secondaire |
| Tertiary education | 0.82 | *0.86 | *0.84 | *0.83 | *0.83 | 0.90 | 0.89 | 0.87 | Enseignement supérieur |
| Malawi | | | | | | | | | Malawi |
| Primary education | 0.84 | 0.96 | 0.97 | 0.97 | ... | 1.03 | 1.03 | 1.04 | Enseignement primaire |
| Secondary education | *0.46 | 0.75 | 0.77 | *0.78 | ... | 0.81 | 0.82 | 0.84 | Enseignement secondaire |
| Tertiary education | 0.34 | ... | ... | ... | 0.41 | 0.55 | ... | ... | Enseignement supérieur |

| Country or area | 1991 | 2000 | 2001 | 2002 | 2003 | 2004 | 2005 | 2006 | Pays ou zone |
|---|---|---|---|---|---|---|---|---|---|
| Malaysia | | | | | | | | | Malaisie |
| Primary education | 0.99 | 1.00 | 1.00 | 1.00 | 1.00 | 1.00 | 1.00 | ... | Enseignement primaire |
| Secondary education | 1.05 | 1.08 | 1.08 | 1.09 | 1.12 | 1.12 | 1.10 | ... | Enseignement secondaire |
| Tertiary education | ... | 1.06 | 1.21 | 1.25 | 1.36 | 1.26 | 1.29 | ... | Enseignement supérieur |
| Maldives | | | | | | | | | Maldives |
| Primary education | ... | 1.00 | 1.00 | 0.99 | 0.98 | 0.97 | 0.98 | 0.97 | Enseignement primaire |
| Secondary education | ... | 1.08 | 1.07 | 1.15 | 1.11 | *1.14 | ... | 1.11 | Enseignement secondaire |
| Tertiary education | ... | ... | ... | ... | 2.37 | *2.37 | ... | ... | Enseignement supérieur |
| Mali | | | | | | | | | Mali |
| Primary education | 0.59 | 0.73 | 0.72 | 0.74 | 0.75 | 0.76 | 0.77 | 0.79 | Enseignement primaire |
| Secondary education | 0.50 | *0.54 | ... | ... | 0.53 | 0.58 | *0.60 | 0.61 | Enseignement secondaire |
| Tertiary education | 0.15 | 0.46 | 0.49 | 0.49 | *0.45 | 0.52 | *0.45 | ... | Enseignement supérieur |
| Malta | | | | | | | | | Malte |
| Primary education | 0.96 | 1.01 | 1.00 | 0.99 | 0.99 | 0.99 | 0.98 | ... | Enseignement primaire |
| Secondary education | 0.94 | 1.00 | 0.97 | 0.99 | 0.99 | 0.93 | 1.00 | ... | Enseignement secondaire |
| Tertiary education | 0.83 | 1.22 | 1.29 | 1.40 | 1.40 | 1.33 | 1.35 | ... | Enseignement supérieur |
| Marshall Islands[*1] | | | | | | | | | Iles Marshall[*1] |
| Primary education | ... | 0.96 | 0.95 | 0.94 | 0.94 | 0.96 | 0.96 | ... | Enseignement primaire |
| Secondary education | ... | ... | ... | 1.04 | 1.04 | 1.05 | 1.05 | ... | Enseignement secondaire |
| Tertiary education | ... | ... | 1.29 | 1.30 | 1.30 | ... | ... | ... | Enseignement supérieur |
| Mauritania | | | | | | | | | Mauritanie |
| Primary education | 0.77 | 0.99 | 0.98 | 1.01 | 1.02 | 1.03 | 1.06 | 1.05 | Enseignement primaire |
| Secondary education | 0.49 | 0.75 | 0.79 | 0.80 | 0.84 | 0.88 | 0.90 | 0.86 | Enseignement secondaire |
| Tertiary education | 0.17 | ... | 0.21 | 0.29 | 0.29 | 0.33 | 0.34 | 0.36 | Enseignement supérieur |
| Mauritius | | | | | | | | | Maurice |
| Primary education | 1.00 | 1.00 | 1.00 | 1.01 | 1.01 | 1.00 | 1.00 | 1.00 | Enseignement primaire |
| Secondary education | *1.04 | *0.96 | 0.97 | 1.00 | 0.99 | 0.98 | *0.99 | ... | Enseignement secondaire |
| Tertiary education | 0.73 | 0.84 | 1.35 | 1.29 | 1.41 | 1.39 | 1.26 | 1.15 | Enseignement supérieur |
| Mexico | | | | | | | | | Mexique |
| Primary education | 0.97 | 0.98 | 0.98 | 0.98 | 0.98 | 0.98 | 0.97 | 0.97 | Enseignement primaire |
| Secondary education | 0.99 | 1.02 | 1.03 | 1.04 | 1.05 | 1.03 | 1.02 | 1.02 | Enseignement secondaire |
| Tertiary education | *0.74 | 0.93 | 0.94 | 0.94 | 0.94 | 0.94 | 0.94 | 0.93 | Enseignement supérieur |
| Micronesia (Fed. States of) | | | | | | | | | Micronésie (Etats féd. de) |
| Primary education | ... | ... | ... | ... | ... | 0.99 | 0.98 | ... | Enseignement primaire |
| Secondary education | ... | ... | ... | ... | ... | 1.05 | 1.07 | ... | Enseignement secondaire |
| Moldova | | | | | | | | | Moldova |
| Primary education | 1.01 | 0.99[1] | 1.00[1] | 0.99[1] | 0.99[1] | 0.99[1] | 0.99[1] | 0.99 | Enseignement primaire |
| Secondary education | 1.10 | 0.99[1] | 1.02[1] | 1.03[1] | 1.04[1] | 1.05[1] | 1.04[1] | 1.04 | Enseignement secondaire |
| Tertiary education[1] | ... | 1.31 | 1.29 | 1.34 | 1.32 | 1.35 | 1.45 | 1.38 | Enseignement supérieur[1] |
| Mongolia | | | | | | | | | Mongolie |
| Primary education | 1.02 | 1.04 | 1.04 | 1.03 | 1.02 | 1.01 | 1.02 | 1.02 | Enseignement primaire |
| Secondary education | 1.14 | 1.23 | 1.22 | 1.20 | 1.16 | 1.13 | 1.13 | 1.12 | Enseignement secondaire |
| Tertiary education | 1.89 | 1.79 | 1.74 | 1.75 | 1.69 | 1.64 | 1.62 | 1.57 | Enseignement supérieur |
| Montserrat[1] | | | | | | | | | Montserrat[1] |
| Primary education | ... | ... | ... | 0.96 | *0.98 | 0.97 | 1.04 | ... | Enseignement primaire |
| Secondary education | ... | ... | ... | 1.13 | *1.13 | 1.10 | 1.10 | ... | Enseignement secondaire |
| Morocco | | | | | | | | | Maroc |
| Primary education | 0.69 | 0.84 | 0.87 | 0.89 | 0.90 | 0.90 | 0.89 | 0.89 | Enseignement primaire |
| Secondary education | 0.72 | 0.79 | *0.80 | *0.81 | 0.82 | 0.83 | *0.84 | ... | Enseignement secondaire |
| Tertiary education | 0.58 | 0.72 | 0.77 | *0.76 | 0.80 | 0.83 | 0.81 | 0.81 | Enseignement supérieur |
| Mozambique | | | | | | | | | Mozambique |
| Primary education | 0.74 | 0.75 | 0.77 | 0.79 | ... | 0.83 | 0.84 | 0.86 | Enseignement primaire |
| Secondary education | 0.57 | 0.63 | 0.64 | 0.66 | ... | 0.70 | 0.69 | 0.72 | Enseignement secondaire |
| Tertiary education | ... | ... | ... | ... | 0.47 | 0.46 | 0.49 | ... | Enseignement supérieur |

| Country or area | 1991 | 2000 | 2001 | 2002 | 2003 | 2004 | 2005 | 2006 | Pays ou zone |
|---|---|---|---|---|---|---|---|---|---|
| Myanmar | | | | | | | | | Myanmar |
| Primary education | 0.97 | 1.00 | 1.00 | 1.01 | 1.01 | 1.02 | 1.02 | 1.01 | Enseignement primaire |
| Secondary education | 0.99 | 1.08 | 0.96 | 0.95 | 0.95 | 0.94 | 0.99 | 1.00 | Enseignement secondaire |
| Tertiary education* | ... | ... | 1.77 | ... | ... | ... | ... | ... | Enseignement supérieur* |
| Namibia | | | | | | | | | Namibie |
| Primary education | 1.03 | 1.01 | 1.01 | 1.01 | 1.00 | 1.01 | 1.00 | 1.00 | Enseignement primaire |
| Secondary education | 1.22 | 1.12 | 1.13 | 1.12 | 1.12 | 1.13 | 1.14 | 1.15 | Enseignement secondaire |
| Tertiary education | 1.75 | ... | 0.84 | 1.37 | 1.14 | 1.14 | 0.88 | 0.88 | Enseignement supérieur |
| Nauru[1] | | | | | | | | | Nauru[1] |
| Primary education | ... | 1.16 | 1.07 | 1.12 | *0.99 | 1.02 | 1.04 | 0.97 | Enseignement primaire |
| Secondary education | ... | 1.21 | 1.01 | 1.21 | *1.07 | 1.16 | 1.14 | 1.21 | Enseignement secondaire |
| Nepal | | | | | | | | | Népal |
| Primary education | 0.63 | 0.79 | 0.84 | 0.86 | 0.88 | 0.88 | 0.91 | 0.95 | Enseignement primaire |
| Secondary education | 0.46 | 0.71 | 0.72 | 0.74 | 0.77 | ... | *0.86 | *0.89 | Enseignement secondaire |
| Tertiary education | 0.33 | 0.40 | *0.27 | 0.27 | 0.34 | 0.40 | ... | ... | Enseignement supérieur |
| Netherlands | | | | | | | | | Pays-Bas |
| Primary education | 1.03 | 0.98 | 0.98 | 0.98 | 0.98 | 0.97 | 0.98 | 0.98 | Enseignement primaire |
| Secondary education | 0.92 | 0.96 | 0.97 | 0.97 | 0.98 | 0.98 | 0.98 | 0.98 | Enseignement secondaire |
| Tertiary education | 0.83 | 1.04 | 1.06 | 1.07 | 1.08 | 1.07 | 1.07 | 1.08 | Enseignement supérieur |
| Netherlands Antilles | | | | | | | | | Antilles néerlandaises |
| Primary education | ... | 0.96 | 0.87 | 0.99 | *0.99 | ... | ... | ... | Enseignement primaire |
| Secondary education | 1.19 | 1.11 | 1.11 | 1.10 | *1.09 | ... | ... | ... | Enseignement secondaire |
| Tertiary education | ... | 1.21 | 1.32 | 1.43 | ... | ... | ... | ... | Enseignement supérieur |
| New Zealand | | | | | | | | | Nouvelle-Zélande |
| Primary education | 0.99 | 1.00 | 0.99 | *1.00 | 1.00 | 1.00 | 1.00 | 1.00 | Enseignement primaire |
| Secondary education | 1.02 | 1.06 | ... | 1.11 | 1.11 | 1.07 | 1.07 | 1.05 | Enseignement secondaire |
| Tertiary education | 1.14 | 1.45 | 1.45 | 1.47 | 1.46 | 1.46 | 1.49 | 1.51 | Enseignement supérieur |
| Nicaragua | | | | | | | | | Nicaragua |
| Primary education | 1.06 | 1.01 | 1.01 | 0.99 | 0.99 | 0.98 | 0.97 | 0.98 | Enseignement primaire |
| Secondary education | *1.20 | 1.17 | 1.17 | 1.17 | *1.13 | 1.13 | 1.13 | 1.14 | Enseignement secondaire |
| Tertiary education | 0.96 | ... | *1.08 | 1.08 | *1.09 | ... | ... | ... | Enseignement supérieur |
| Niger | | | | | | | | | Niger |
| Primary education | 0.61 | 0.69 | 0.70 | 0.70 | 0.71 | 0.72 | 0.73 | 0.73 | Enseignement primaire |
| Secondary education | 0.37 | *0.61 | *0.61 | 0.60 | 0.62 | 0.61 | 0.64 | 0.63 | Enseignement secondaire |
| Tertiary education | ... | ... | ... | ... | *0.31 | 0.31 | 0.34 | 0.29 | Enseignement supérieur |
| Nigeria | | | | | | | | | Nigéria |
| Primary education | 0.79 | *0.79 | ... | ... | *0.82 | 0.83 | 0.83 | ... | Enseignement primaire |
| Secondary education | 0.72 | ... | ... | ... | ... | 0.79 | 0.82 | ... | Enseignement secondaire |
| Tertiary education | ... | ... | ... | ... | *0.53 | 0.53 | 0.69 | ... | Enseignement supérieur |
| Niue[1] | | | | | | | | | Nioué[1] |
| Primary education | ... | *0.97 | 0.94 | ... | ... | 1.19 | 0.95 | ... | Enseignement primaire |
| Secondary education | ... | *1.03 | 0.98 | ... | ... | 0.96 | 1.07 | ... | Enseignement secondaire |
| Norway | | | | | | | | | Norvège |
| Primary education | 1.00 | 1.00 | 1.00 | 1.00 | 1.00 | 1.00 | 1.00 | 1.01 | Enseignement primaire |
| Secondary education | 1.03 | 1.02 | 1.02 | 1.02 | 1.02 | 1.03 | 1.01 | 0.99 | Enseignement secondaire |
| Tertiary education | 1.19 | 1.46 | 1.51 | 1.54 | 1.54 | 1.53 | 1.53 | 1.54 | Enseignement supérieur |
| Occupied Palestinian Terr. | | | | | | | | | Terr. palestinien occupé |
| Primary education | ... | 1.00 | 1.01 | 1.00 | 1.00 | 1.00 | 0.99 | 1.00 | Enseignement primaire |
| Secondary education | ... | 1.06 | 1.08 | 1.06 | 1.06 | 1.05 | 1.05 | 1.06 | Enseignement secondaire |
| Tertiary education | ... | 0.92 | 0.96 | 0.98 | 1.04 | 1.04 | 1.03 | 1.22 | Enseignement supérieur |
| Oman | | | | | | | | | Oman |
| Primary education | 0.92 | 0.97 | 0.98 | 0.98 | 0.99 | 1.00 | 1.00 | 1.01 | Enseignement primaire |
| Secondary education | 0.81 | 1.00 | 0.99 | 0.98 | 0.96 | 0.96 | 0.96 | 0.96 | Enseignement secondaire |
| Tertiary education | 0.97 | ... | ... | *0.79 | 0.79 | 1.16 | 1.09 | 1.04 | Enseignement supérieur |

| Country or area | 1991 | 2000 | 2001 | 2002 | 2003 | 2004 | 2005 | 2006 | Pays ou zone |
|---|---|---|---|---|---|---|---|---|---|
| Pakistan | | | | | | | | | Pakistan |
| Primary education | ... | *0.68 | 0.68 | 0.68 | 0.72 | 0.73 | 0.76 | 0.78 | Enseignement primaire |
| Secondary education | 0.48 | ... | ... | ... | *0.79 | *0.78 | *0.78 | 0.78 | Enseignement secondaire |
| Tertiary education | *0.58 | ... | ... | *0.81 | 0.81 | 0.80 | 0.88 | 0.85 | Enseignement supérieur |
| Palau[1] | | | | | | | | | Palaos[1] |
| Primary education | ... | 0.97 | ... | ... | *0.78 | *0.93 | *0.94 | ... | Enseignement primaire |
| Secondary education | ... | 1.03 | *1.00 | ... | *1.18 | *1.10 | ... | ... | Enseignement secondaire |
| Tertiary education | ... | *2.35 | 2.16 | *2.15 | ... | ... | ... | ... | Enseignement supérieur |
| Panama | | | | | | | | | Panama |
| Primary education | ... | 0.97 | 0.97 | 0.97 | *0.97 | 0.97 | 0.97 | 0.97 | Enseignement primaire |
| Secondary education | ... | 1.06 | 1.07 | 1.07 | *1.07 | 1.07 | 1.07 | 1.09 | Enseignement secondaire |
| Tertiary education | ... | 1.69 | 1.72 | 1.70 | 1.59 | 1.66 | 1.63 | 1.61 | Enseignement supérieur |
| Papua New Guinea | | | | | | | | | Papouasie-Nvl-Guinée |
| Primary education | 0.85 | 0.86 | 0.85 | 0.84 | 0.85 | 0.86 | 0.84 | 0.84 | Enseignement primaire |
| Secondary education | 0.62 | ... | ... | ... | ... | ... | ... | ... | Enseignement secondaire |
| Paraguay | | | | | | | | | Paraguay |
| Primary education | 0.97 | *0.96 | *0.96 | 0.96 | 0.97 | 0.97 | 0.97 | ... | Enseignement primaire |
| Secondary education | 1.05 | 1.03 | 1.02 | *1.02 | 1.01 | 1.02 | 1.03 | ... | Enseignement secondaire |
| Tertiary education | ... | 1.36 | 1.38 | *1.40 | *1.38 | *1.34 | *1.13 | ... | Enseignement supérieur |
| Peru | | | | | | | | | Pérou |
| Primary education | 0.97 | 0.99 | 1.00 | 1.00 | 1.00 | 1.00 | 1.01 | 1.01 | Enseignement primaire |
| Secondary education | 0.94 | 0.93 | 0.93 | 0.93 | 1.00 | 1.01 | 1.02 | 1.03 | Enseignement secondaire |
| Tertiary education* | ... | ... | 0.97 | 1.07 | 1.07 | 1.02 | 1.02 | 1.06 | Enseignement supérieur* |
| Philippines | | | | | | | | | Philippines |
| Primary education | 0.99 | ... | 1.00 | 0.99 | 0.99 | 0.99 | 0.99 | 0.99 | Enseignement primaire |
| Secondary education | *1.04 | ... | 1.10 | 1.10 | 1.10 | 1.11 | 1.12 | 1.11 | Enseignement secondaire |
| Tertiary education | *1.42 | ... | ... | 1.30 | 1.28 | 1.28 | 1.23 | 1.24 | Enseignement supérieur |
| Poland | | | | | | | | | Pologne |
| Primary education | 0.99 | 0.99 | 0.99 | 0.99 | 1.00 | 1.00 | 1.00 | 1.00 | Enseignement primaire |
| Secondary education | 1.05 | 0.98 | 0.97 | 0.97 | 0.96 | 1.01 | 0.99 | 0.99 | Enseignement secondaire |
| Tertiary education | 1.34 | 1.40 | 1.43 | 1.42 | 1.42 | 1.40 | 1.40 | 1.40 | Enseignement supérieur |
| Portugal | | | | | | | | | Portugal |
| Primary education | 0.95 | 0.96 | 0.98 | 0.96 | 0.95 | 0.95 | 0.95 | 0.95 | Enseignement primaire |
| Secondary education | 1.16 | 1.07 | 1.06 | ... | 1.09 | 1.10 | 1.09 | 1.09 | Enseignement secondaire |
| Tertiary education | 1.29 | 1.34 | 1.37 | 1.37 | 1.35 | 1.32 | 1.30 | 1.28 | Enseignement supérieur |
| Qatar | | | | | | | | | Qatar |
| Primary education | 0.93 | 0.97 | 0.99 | 0.96 | 0.97 | 0.98 | 0.99 | 0.99 | Enseignement primaire |
| Secondary education | 1.06 | 1.07 | 1.12 | 1.09 | 1.05 | 1.00 | 1.00 | 0.97 | Enseignement secondaire |
| Tertiary education | 3.34 | ... | 3.65 | 3.60 | 3.87 | 3.86 | 3.45 | *3.41 | Enseignement supérieur |
| Romania | | | | | | | | | Roumanie |
| Primary education | 1.00 | 0.98 | 0.98 | 0.98 | 0.98 | 0.98 | 0.99 | 0.99 | Enseignement primaire |
| Secondary education | 0.99 | 1.02 | 1.01 | 1.02 | 1.02 | 1.01 | 1.01 | 1.00 | Enseignement secondaire |
| Tertiary education | 0.93 | 1.12 | 1.20 | 1.25 | 1.24 | 1.27 | 1.26 | 1.30 | Enseignement supérieur |
| Russian Federation | | | | | | | | | Fédération de Russie |
| Primary education | 1.00 | 0.99 | 0.99 | 0.99 | 1.00 | ... | 1.00 | 1.00 | Enseignement primaire |
| Secondary education | *1.06 | ... | ... | ... | 1.00 | 0.99 | 0.99 | 0.98 | Enseignement secondaire |
| Tertiary education | 1.27 | ... | ... | ... | 1.35 | 1.36 | 1.36 | 1.36 | Enseignement supérieur |
| Rwanda | | | | | | | | | Rwanda |
| Primary education | 0.93 | 0.97 | 0.98 | 0.99 | 1.00 | 1.02 | *1.04 | 1.04 | Enseignement primaire |
| Secondary education | 0.73 | 0.94 | 0.96 | ... | 0.89 | 0.89 | *0.89 | ... | Enseignement secondaire |
| Tertiary education | ... | *0.44 | 0.45 | 0.47 | 0.54 | 0.61 | *0.62 | ... | Enseignement supérieur |

| Country or area | 1991 | 2000 | 2001 | 2002 | 2003 | 2004 | 2005 | 2006 | Pays ou zone |
|---|---|---|---|---|---|---|---|---|---|
| Saint Kitts and Nevis[1] | | | | | | | | | Saint-Kitts-et-Nevis[1] |
| Primary education | *1.02 | 1.04 | 1.09 | 1.03 | 1.03 | 1.07 | 1.06 | ... | Enseignement primaire |
| Secondary education | *1.11 | *1.09 | *1.02 | 0.98 | 1.06 | *1.03 | *0.98 | ... | Enseignement secondaire |
| Saint Lucia | | | | | | | | | Sainte-Lucie |
| Primary education | *0.94 | 0.99 | 0.97 | 0.98 | 0.96 | 0.96 | 0.97 | 0.94 | Enseignement primaire |
| Secondary education | 1.45 | 1.33 | 1.29 | 1.32 | *1.14 | 1.12 | 1.21 | 1.19 | Enseignement secondaire |
| Tertiary education | *1.35 | ... | ... | ... | *2.05 | 3.45 | 2.79 | 5.46 | Enseignement supérieur |
| Saint Vincent-Grenadines | | | | | | | | | Saint Vincent-Grenadines |
| Primary education | 0.98 | 0.94 | 0.95 | 0.95 | 0.96 | 0.95 | 0.90 | ... | Enseignement primaire |
| Secondary education | 1.24 | *1.33 | *1.16 | 1.11 | 1.09 | *1.07 | 1.24 | ... | Enseignement secondaire |
| Samoa | | | | | | | | | Samoa |
| Primary education | 1.02 | 1.00 | 1.00 | 0.99 | 0.99 | 1.00 | *1.00 | ... | Enseignement primaire |
| Secondary education | 1.96 | 1.14 | 1.14 | 1.12 | 1.14 | 1.13 | *1.13 | ... | Enseignement secondaire |
| Tertiary education | ... | 0.93 | *0.93 | ... | ... | ... | ... | ... | Enseignement supérieur |
| Sao Tome and Principe | | | | | | | | | Sao Tomé-et-Principe |
| Primary education | ... | ... | *0.94 | *0.96 | 0.96 | 0.97 | 0.97 | *0.97 | Enseignement primaire |
| Secondary education | ... | ... | ... | *0.85 | 1.18 | 1.05 | 1.07 | *1.07 | Enseignement secondaire |
| Saudi Arabia | | | | | | | | | Arabie saoudite |
| Primary education | 0.85 | ... | ... | ... | ... | 0.98 | 0.97 | ... | Enseignement primaire |
| Secondary education | 0.80 | ... | ... | ... | ... | 0.93 | 0.92 | ... | Enseignement secondaire |
| Tertiary education | 0.88 | 1.45 | *1.39 | *1.62 | 1.56 | 1.57 | 1.50 | *1.50 | Enseignement supérieur |
| Senegal | | | | | | | | | Sénégal |
| Primary education | 0.73 | 0.86 | 0.88 | 0.90 | 0.92 | 0.95 | 0.96 | 0.98 | Enseignement primaire |
| Secondary education | *0.53 | 0.65 | 0.66 | 0.67 | 0.69 | 0.72 | 0.75 | *0.76 | Enseignement secondaire |
| Serbia | | | | | | | | | Serbie |
| Primary education | ... | *0.99 | *0.99 | *0.99 | *1.00 | *1.00 | 1.01 | 1.01 | Enseignement primaire |
| Secondary education | ... | *1.02 | *1.02 | *1.03 | *1.03 | *1.03 | 1.03 | 1.03 | Enseignement secondaire |
| Seychelles[1] | | | | | | | | | Seychelles[1] |
| Number (thousands) | ... | 1.00 | 0.99 | 0.99 | 1.01 | 1.01 | 1.01 | ... | Enseignement primaire |
| Per 100 inhabitants | ... | 1.03 | 1.05 | 1.00 | 1.04 | 1.08 | 0.99 | ... | Enseignement secondaire |
| Sierra Leone | | | | | | | | | Sierra Leone |
| Primary education | *0.70 | ... | 0.71 | ... | ... | ... | ... | ... | Enseignement primaire |
| Secondary education | 0.57 | ... | *0.71 | ... | ... | ... | ... | ... | Enseignement secondaire |
| Tertiary education | ... | ... | 0.40 | *0.40 | ... | ... | ... | ... | Enseignement supérieur |
| Singapore | | | | | | | | | Singapour |
| Primary education | 0.97 | ... | ... | ... | ... | ... | ... | ... | Enseignement primaire |
| Secondary education | 0.93 | ... | ... | ... | ... | ... | ... | ... | Enseignement secondaire |
| Tertiary education | 0.71 | ... | ... | ... | ... | ... | ... | ... | Enseignement supérieur |
| Slovakia | | | | | | | | | Slovaquie |
| Primary education | ... | 0.99 | 0.99 | 0.99 | 0.98 | 0.98 | 0.98 | 0.98 | Enseignement primaire |
| Secondary education | ... | 1.02 | 1.01 | 1.01 | 1.01 | 1.01 | 1.01 | 1.01 | Enseignement secondaire |
| Tertiary education | ... | 1.05 | 1.09 | 1.13 | 1.18 | 1.23 | 1.29 | 1.42 | Enseignement supérieur |
| Slovenia | | | | | | | | | Slovénie |
| Primary education | ... | 1.02 | 0.99 | 0.99 | 1.00 | 1.00 | 0.99 | 0.99 | Enseignement primaire |
| Secondary education | ... | 1.03 | 1.02 | 1.00 | 0.99 | 1.00 | 1.00 | 1.00 | Enseignement secondaire |
| Tertiary education | 1.32 | 1.36 | 1.36 | 1.44 | 1.36 | 1.38 | 1.43 | 1.46 | Enseignement supérieur |
| Solomon Islands | | | | | | | | | Iles Salomon |
| Primary education | 0.87 | 0.94 | *0.95 | 0.95 | *0.95 | *0.96 | 0.96 | ... | Enseignement primaire |
| Secondary education | 0.61 | 0.79 | 0.82 | 0.82 | *0.82 | *0.84 | 0.84 | ... | Enseignement secondaire |
| South Africa | | | | | | | | | Afrique du Sud |
| Primary education | 0.99 | 0.95 | 0.96 | 0.97 | 0.96 | 0.96 | ... | ... | Enseignement primaire |
| Secondary education | 1.18 | 1.11 | 1.10 | 1.08 | 1.07 | 1.07 | ... | ... | Enseignement secondaire |
| Tertiary education | 0.83 | 1.24 | 1.15 | 1.16 | 1.17 | 1.19 | 1.21 | 1.24 | Enseignement supérieur |

| Country or area | 1991 | 2000 | 2001 | 2002 | 2003 | 2004 | 2005 | 2006 | Pays ou zone |
|---|---|---|---|---|---|---|---|---|---|
| Spain | | | | | | | | | Espagne |
| Primary education | 0.99 | 0.99 | 0.99 | 0.99 | 0.99 | 0.99 | 0.99 | 0.98 | Enseignement primaire |
| Number (thousands) | 1.07 | 1.06 | 1.05 | 1.06 | 1.05 | 1.06 | 1.06 | 1.06 | Enseignement secondaire |
| Per 100 inhabitants | 1.09 | 1.18 | 1.16 | 1.19 | 1.19 | 1.22 | 1.22 | 1.23 | Enseignement supérieur |
| Sri Lanka | | | | | | | | | Sri Lanka |
| Primary education | 0.96 | ... | ... | *0.99 | *1.00 | ... | *1.00 | . ... | Enseignement primaire |
| Secondary education | 1.09 | ... | ... | *1.06 | *1.06 | *1.02 | ... | ... | Enseignement secondaire |
| Tertiary education* | 0.55 | ... | ... | ... | ... | ... | ... | ... | Enseignement supérieur* |
| Sudan | | | | | | | | | Soudan |
| Primary education | 0.77 | 0.85 | 0.85 | 0.85 | 0.86 | 0.87 | 0.87 | 0.87 | Enseignement primaire |
| Secondary education | 0.79 | ... | 0.96 | 0.94 | 0.92 | 0.92 | 0.94 | 0.96 | Enseignement secondaire |
| Tertiary education* | 0.88 | 0.92 | ... | ... | ... | ... | ... | ... | Enseignement supérieur* |
| Suriname | | | | | | | | | Suriname |
| Primary education | 1.03 | ... | 1.04 | 1.03 | *1.03 | ... | 1.01 | 1.00 | Enseignement primaire |
| Secondary education | 1.16 | ... | 1.16 | 1.38 | *1.34 | ... | 1.33 | 1.37 | Enseignement secondaire |
| Tertiary education | ... | ... | ... | 1.62 | ... | ... | ... | ... | Enseignement supérieur |
| Swaziland | | | | | | | | | Swaziland |
| Primary education | 0.99 | 0.94 | 0.95 | 0.93 | 0.95 | 0.93 | 0.93 | ... | Enseignement primaire |
| Secondary education | *0.96 | 1.00 | 1.03 | 1.02 | 1.01 | 0.96 | 1.00 | ... | Enseignement secondaire |
| Tertiary education | 0.76 | 0.89 | ... | 1.16 | *1.16 | 1.08 | 1.06 | 0.98 | Enseignement supérieur |
| Sweden | | | | | | | | | Suède |
| Primary education | 1.00 | 1.03 | 1.03 | 1.03 | 1.03 | 1.00 | 1.00 | 1.00 | Enseignement primaire |
| Secondary education | 1.05 | 1.27 | 1.26 | 1.21 | 1.18 | 1.03 | 0.99 | 0.99 | Enseignement secondaire |
| Tertiary education | 1.22 | 1.46 | 1.51 | 1.54 | 1.55 | 1.54 | 1.55 | 1.55 | Enseignement supérieur |
| Switzerland | | | | | | | | | Suisse |
| Primary education | 1.01 | 1.00 | 1.00 | 1.00 | 1.00 | 0.99 | 0.99 | 0.99 | Enseignement primaire |
| Secondary education | 0.95 | 0.93 | 0.94 | 0.94 | 0.94 | 0.94 | 0.95 | 0.95 | Enseignement secondaire |
| Tertiary education | 0.57 | 0.77 | 0.77 | 0.79 | 0.82 | 0.84 | 0.87 | 0.90 | Enseignement supérieur |
| Syrian Arab Republic | | | | | | | | | Rép. arabe syrienne |
| Primary education | 0.90 | 0.92 | 0.93 | 0.93 | 0.94 | 0.95 | 0.95 | 0.96 | Enseignement primaire |
| Secondary education | 0.73 | 0.92 | 0.90 | 0.91 | 0.93 | 0.93 | 0.94 | 0.95 | Enseignement secondaire |
| Tertiary education | 0.65 | ... | ... | ... | ... | ... | ... | ... | Enseignement supérieur |
| Tajikistan | | | | | | | | | Tadjikistan |
| Primary education | 0.98 | 0.93 | 0.93 | 0.96 | 0.95 | 0.95 | 0.96 | 0.95 | Enseignement primaire |
| Secondary education | ... | 0.86 | 0.83 | 0.82 | 0.83 | 0.84 | 0.83 | 0.83 | Enseignement secondaire |
| Tertiary education | *0.62 | 0.34 | 0.32 | 0.33 | 0.34 | 0.33 | 0.35 | 0.37 | Enseignement supérieur |
| Thailand | | | | | | | | | Thaïlande |
| Primary education | 0.98 | 0.99 | 1.00 | 1.00 | *1.00 | 1.00 | 0.99 | 1.00 | Enseignement primaire |
| Secondary education | 0.96 | ... | *0.98 | *1.01 | *1.01 | 1.09 | *1.07 | 1.09 | Enseignement secondaire |
| Tertiary education | ... | 1.20 | 1.13 | 1.11 | *1.14 | 1.18 | 1.13 | 1.07 | Enseignement supérieur |
| TFYR of Macedonia | | | | | | | | | L'ex-R.y. Macédoine |
| Primary education | 0.98 | 0.99 | 1.00 | 1.01 | 1.00 | 1.00 | 1.00 | ... | Enseignement primaire |
| Secondary education | *0.99 | 0.97 | 0.97 | 0.97 | 0.98 | 0.98 | 0.98 | ... | Enseignement secondaire |
| Tertiary education | 1.11 | 1.28 | 1.32 | 1.29 | 1.34 | 1.39 | 1.38 | ... | Enseignement supérieur |
| Timor-Leste | | | | | | | | | Timor-Leste |
| Primary education | ... | ... | ... | ... | ... | 0.93 | 0.92 | ... | Enseignement primaire |
| Secondary education | ... | ... | ... | ... | ... | 0.99 | 1.00 | ... | Enseignement secondaire |
| Tertiary education | ... | ... | ... | 1.26 | ... | ... | ... | ... | Enseignement supérieur |
| Togo | | | | | | | | | Togo |
| Primary education | 0.65 | 0.78 | 0.79 | 0.81 | 0.82 | 0.84 | 0.85 | 0.86 | Enseignement primaire |
| Secondary education | 0.34 | *0.44 | ... | ... | *0.47 | 0.50 | *0.51 | ... | Enseignement secondaire |
| Tertiary education | 0.16 | 0.20 | *0.20 | ... | ... | ... | ... | ... | Enseignement supérieur |

| Country or area | 1991 | 2000 | 2001 | 2002 | 2003 | 2004 | 2005 | 2006 | Pays ou zone |
|---|---|---|---|---|---|---|---|---|---|
| Tokelau[1] | | | | | | | | | Tokélaou[1] |
| Primary education | ... | *1.19 | 1.10 | *1.08 | *1.29 | *1.35 | ... | ... | Enseignement primaire |
| Secondary education | ... | *0.94 | 1.22 | *1.22 | *0.87 | *0.88 | ... | ... | Enseignement secondaire |
| Tonga | | | | | | | | | Tonga |
| Primary education | 0.98 | 0.97 | 0.98 | 0.97 | 0.96 | 0.95 | 0.96 | 0.95 | Enseignement primaire |
| Secondary education | 1.04 | 1.10 | 1.10 | 1.12 | ... | *1.09 | ... | 1.04 | Enseignement secondaire |
| Tertiary education | ... | *1.64 | *1.66 | *1.68 | 1.70 | *1.68 | ... | ... | Enseignement supérieur |
| Trinidad and Tobago | | | | | | | | | Trinité-et-Tobago |
| Primary education | 1.00 | 0.99 | 0.98 | 0.99 | 0.98 | 0.97 | 0.98 | ... | Enseignement primaire |
| Secondary education | 1.04 | *1.10 | *1.08 | *1.11 | *1.09 | 1.07 | 1.05 | ... | Enseignement secondaire |
| Tertiary education | 0.78 | 1.49 | 1.54 | 1.51 | 1.61 | 1.28 | *1.28 | ... | Enseignement supérieur |
| Tunisia | | | | | | | | | Tunisie |
| Primary education | 0.90 | 0.96 | 0.96 | 0.97 | 0.97 | 0.97 | 0.97 | 0.97 | Enseignement primaire |
| Secondary education | 0.79 | *1.06 | 1.06 | 1.05 | 1.09 | ... | 1.10 | *1.10 | Enseignement secondaire |
| Tertiary education | 0.66 | ... | *0.98 | 1.23 | 1.28 | 1.36 | 1.40 | 1.42 | Enseignement supérieur |
| Turkey | | | | | | | | | Turquie |
| Primary education | 0.92 | *0.91 | *0.92 | *0.93 | *0.94 | *0.94 | *0.95 | *0.95 | Enseignement primaire |
| Secondary education | 0.63 | ... | *0.75 | *0.76 | *0.75 | *0.75 | *0.82 | *0.83 | Enseignement secondaire |
| Tertiary education | 0.53 | *0.68 | 0.71 | 0.73 | 0.75 | 0.73 | 0.74 | 0.75 | Enseignement supérieur |
| Turks and Caicos Islands[1] | | | | | | | | | Iles Turques et Caïques[1] |
| Primary education | ... | ... | ... | 0.96 | 0.95 | *1.03 | *1.04 | ... | Enseignement primaire |
| Secondary education* | ... | ... | ... | 1.02 | 1.00 | 0.98 | 0.94 | ... | Enseignement secondaire* |
| Tuvalu[1] | | | | | | | | | Tuvalu[1] |
| Primary education | ... | 1.04 | 1.13 | 1.13 | *1.11 | 1.07 | 0.99 | 0.99 | Enseignement primaire |
| Secondary education | ... | ... | 0.93 | ... | ... | ... | ... | ... | Enseignement secondaire |
| Uganda | | | | | | | | | Ouganda |
| Primary education | *0.84 | 0.94 | 0.97 | 0.99 | 0.98 | 0.99 | 1.00 | 1.01 | Enseignement primaire |
| Secondary education | *0.59 | 0.77 | *0.77 | *0.81 | *0.81 | 0.81 | *0.81 | ... | Enseignement secondaire |
| Tertiary education | 0.38 | 0.51 | 0.53 | *0.53 | *0.53 | 0.62 | ... | ... | Enseignement supérieur |
| Ukraine | | | | | | | | | Ukraine |
| Primary education | 1.00 | 0.99 | 1.00 | 1.00 | 1.00 | 0.99 | 1.00 | 1.00 | Enseignement primaire |
| Secondary education | ... | 1.01 | 0.99 | 1.00 | 1.00 | 0.99 | ... | 0.98 | Enseignement secondaire |
| Tertiary education | *1.03 | 1.14 | 1.17 | 1.19 | 1.21 | 1.22 | 1.23 | 1.23 | Enseignement supérieur |
| United Arab Emirates | | | | | | | | | Emirats arabes unis |
| Primary education | 0.97 | 0.96 | 0.97 | 0.97 | 0.98 | 0.98 | 0.99 | 0.99 | Enseignement primaire |
| Secondary education | 1.16 | 1.06 | 1.04 | 1.05 | 1.03 | 1.02 | 1.01 | 1.02 | Enseignement secondaire |
| Tertiary education | 4.03 | *3.12 | *2.84 | *2.82 | *2.81 | ... | ... | ... | Enseignement supérieur |
| United Kingdom | | | | | | | | | Royaume-Uni |
| Primary education | 1.01 | 1.00 | 1.00 | 1.00 | 1.00 | 1.00 | 1.00 | ... | Enseignement primaire |
| Secondary education | *1.04 | 1.01 | 1.01 | 1.01 | 1.03 | 1.03 | 1.03 | ... | Enseignement secondaire |
| Tertiary education | 0.96 | 1.19 | 1.22 | 1.26 | 1.30 | 1.37 | 1.39 | ... | Enseignement supérieur |
| United Rep. of Tanzania | | | | | | | | | Rép.-Unie de Tanzanie |
| Primary education | 0.98 | 0.99 | 0.98 | 0.97 | 0.96 | 0.96 | 0.96 | 0.97 | Enseignement primaire |
| Secondary education | 0.77 | ... | ... | ... | ... | ... | ... | ... | Enseignement secondaire |
| Tertiary education | 0.19 | ... | 0.15 | *0.31 | 0.44 | 0.41 | *0.48 | ... | Enseignement supérieur |
| United States | | | | | | | | | Etats-Unis |
| Primary education | 0.98 | 0.98 | 1.00 | 1.01 | 1.00 | 0.97 | 0.99 | 1.01 | Enseignement primaire |
| Secondary education | 1.01 | 1.01 | 1.01 | 0.99 | 1.00 | 1.02 | 1.02 | 0.99 | Enseignement secondaire |
| Tertiary education | 1.25 | 1.32 | 1.33 | 1.35 | 1.37 | 1.39 | 1.40 | 1.41 | Enseignement supérieur |
| Uruguay | | | | | | | | | Uruguay |
| Primary education | 0.99 | 0.98 | 0.98 | 0.98 | 0.98 | 0.97 | 0.98 | 0.97 | Enseignement primaire |
| Secondary education | ... | 1.14 | 1.14 | 1.13 | 1.15 | 1.15 | 1.15 | 1.16 | Enseignement secondaire |
| Tertiary education | ... | *1.84 | *1.81 | *1.95 | *2.03 | *2.02 | 1.74 | 1.68 | Enseignement supérieur |
| Uzbekistan | | | | | | | | | Ouzbékistan |
| Primary education | 0.98 | 0.99 | 0.99 | 0.98 | 0.99 | 0.98 | 0.98 | 0.98 | Enseignement primaire |
| Secondary education | *0.91 | 0.97 | 0.97 | 0.97 | 0.96 | 0.96 | 0.97 | 0.97 | Enseignement secondaire |
| Tertiary education | ... | 0.83 | 0.81 | 0.80 | 0.77 | 0.79 | 0.70 | 0.71 | Enseignement supérieur |

| Country or area | 1991 | 2000 | 2001 | 2002 | 2003 | 2004 | 2005 | 2006 | Pays ou zone |
|---|---|---|---|---|---|---|---|---|---|
| Vanuatu | | | | | | | | | Vanuatu |
| Primary education | 0.96 | 0.98 | 0.99 | 0.99 | 0.99 | 0.98 | 0.97 | 0.98 | Enseignement primaire |
| Secondary education | 0.80 | 1.14 | 0.91 | 0.94 | 0.84 | 0.86 | ... | ... | Enseignement secondaire |
| Tertiary education | ... | ... | ... | *0.57 | 0.59 | *0.59 | ... | ... | Enseignement supérieur |
| Venezuela (Bolivarian Rep. of) | | | | | | | | | Venezuela (Rép. bolivar. du) |
| Primary education | 1.03 | 0.98 | 0.98 | 0.98 | 0.98 | 0.98 | 0.98 | 0.98 | Enseignement primaire |
| Secondary education | 1.38 | 1.20 | 1.17 | 1.16 | 1.15 | 1.14 | 1.13 | 1.12 | Enseignement secondaire |
| Tertiary education | ... | 1.46 | ... | *1.09 | *1.08 | ... | ... | ... | Enseignement supérieur |
| Viet Nam | | | | | | | | | Viet Nam |
| Primary education | *0.93 | 0.95 | 0.94 | 0.94 | 0.94 | 0.93 | 0.94 | 0.96 | Enseignement primaire |
| Secondary education | ... | 0.91 | 0.92 | 0.93 | 0.93 | 0.96 | 0.98 | 0.99 | Enseignement secondaire |
| Tertiary education | ... | 0.72 | 0.74 | 0.76 | 0.77 | *0.71 | 0.71 | ... | Enseignement supérieur |
| Yemen | | | | | | | | | Yémen |
| Primary education | *0.35 | *0.63 | 0.63 | 0.66 | 0.69 | 0.71 | 0.74 | *0.74 | Enseignement primaire |
| Secondary education | ... | *0.42 | *0.42 | ... | 0.45 | 0.48 | 0.49 | *0.49 | Enseignement secondaire |
| Tertiary education | ... | *0.28 | ... | ... | ... | 0.38 | 0.37 | ... | Enseignement supérieur |
| Zambia | | | | | | | | | Zambie |
| Primary education | ... | 0.93 | 0.94 | 0.93 | ... | 0.96 | 0.95 | 0.98 | Enseignement primaire |
| Secondary education | ... | 0.81 | 0.77 | 0.83 | ... | 0.79 | *0.82 | ... | Enseignement secondaire |
| Tertiary education* | ... | 0.46 | ... | ... | ... | ... | ... | ... | Enseignement supérieur* |
| Zimbabwe | | | | | | | | | Zimbabwe |
| Primary education | 0.97 | 0.97 | 0.97 | 0.98 | 0.98 | ... | ... | 0.99 | Enseignement primaire |
| Secondary education | 0.79 | 0.88 | 0.89 | .0.88 | 0.91 | ... | ... | 0.93 | Enseignement secondaire |
| Tertiary education* | 0.50 | 0.59 | 0.58 | 0.68 | 0.63 | ... | ... | ... | Enseignement supérieur* |

Source

United Nations Educational, Scientific and Cultural Organization (UNESCO) Institute for Statistics, Montreal, May 2008.

Notes

1 National population data were used to calculate enrollment ratios.

Source

L'Institut de statistique de l'Organisation des Nations Unies pour l'éducation, la science et la culture (UNESCO), Montréal, mai 2008.

Notes

1 Taux d'inscription calculés à partir des données sur la population nationale.

The three tables on gender presented in this chapter are all based on indicators for the Millennium Development Goals (MDGs). For more on MDGs, visit mdgs.un.org

*Table 10* shows the percentage of seats held by women members in single or lower chambers of national parliaments. National parliaments can be bicameral or unicameral. This table covers the single chamber in unicameral parliaments and the lower chamber in bicameral parliaments. It does not cover the upper chamber of bicameral parliaments. Seats are usually won by members in general parliamentary elections. Seats may also be filled by nomination, appointment, indirect election, rotation of members and by-election.

The proportion of seats held by women in national parliament is derived by dividing the total number of seats occupied by women by the total number of seats in parliament. There is no weighting or normalizing of statistics.

The source for this table is the Inter-Parliamentary Union (IPU). For more information visit www.ipu.org

*Table 11*: The share of women in wage employment in the non-agricultural sector is the share of female workers in wage employment in the non-agricultural sector expressed as a percentage of total wage employment in that same sector.

The non-agricultural sector includes industry and services. 'Industry' includes mining and quarrying (including oil production), manufacturing, construction, electricity, gas, and water, corresponding to divisions 2-5 in the *International Standard Industrial Classification of All Economic Activities* (ISIC-Rev.2) and to tabulation categories C-F in ISIC-Rev. 3. 'Services' include wholesale and retail trade and restaurants and hotels; transport, storage, and communications; financing, insurance, real estate, and business services; and community, social, and personal services, corresponding to divisions 6-9 in ISIC-Rev. 2, and to tabulation categories G-Q in ISIC-Rev. 3.

Employment refers to people above a certain age who worked or held a job during a specified reference period (according to the ILO Resolution concerning statistics of the economically active population, employment, unemployment and underemployment, adopted by the Thirteenth International Conference of Labour Statisticians (ICLS), October 1982).

Wage employment refers only to wage earners and salaried employees, or "persons in paid employment jobs". Employees are typically remunerated by wages and salaries, but may be paid by commission from sales, piece-rates, bonuses or payments in kind such as food, housing, training, etc. These persons are in wage employment as opposed to

Les trois tableaux sur la réparti-tion des sexes figurant dans le présent chapitre reposent tous sur des indicateurs liés aux objectifs du Millénaire pour le développement. Pour plus d'informations sur les objectifs du Millénaire pour le développement, veuillez consulter le site Web suivant : mdgs.un.org.

*Tableau 10* : ce tableau indique le pourcentage des sièges des chambres uniques ou basses des parlements nationaux occupés par des femmes. Les parlements nationaux peuvent être bicaméraux ou unicaméraux. Ce tableau porte sur la chambre unique des parlements unicaméraux et sur la chambre basse des parlements bicaméraux. Il ne porte pas sur la chambre haute des parlements bicaméraux. Les sièges sont habituellement attribués aux membres à l'issue d'élections parlementaires générales. Certains sièges peuvent aussi être pourvus à l'issue de nominations, d'élections indirectes, de roulement des membres et d'élections partielles.

La proportion d'élues est obtenue en divisant le nombre total de sièges occupés par des femmes par le nombre total de sièges que compte le parlement. Les statistiques ne sont ni pondérées ni normalisées.

La source de ce tableau est l'Union interparlementaire. Pour plus d'informations, veuillez consulter le site Web suivant : www.ipu.org.

*Tableau 11* : la proportion des femmes rémunérées dans le secteur non agricole correspond au pourcentage du nombre total de salariés employés dans le secteur agricole qui sont des femmes.

Le secteur non agricole comprend l'industrie et les services. L'industrie comporte les industries extractives (y compris la production pétrolière), le secteur manufacturier, le bâtiment, l'électricité, le gaz et l'eau, correspondant aux divisions 2 à 5 de la *Classification internationale type, par industrie, de toutes les branches d'activité économique* (CITI) et aux catégories C à F de la CITI-Rev.3. Les services comportent le commerce de gros et de détail, la restauration et l'hôtellerie; les transports, l'entreposage et les communications; les finances, les assurances, l'immobilier et les services commerciaux; et les services communautaires, sociaux et personnels, correspondant aux divisions 6 à 9 de la CITI-Rev.2 et aux catégories G à Q de la CITI-Rev.3.

L'emploi se rapporte aux personnes d'un âge minimum donné qui ont travaillé ou occupé un emploi pendant une période donnée de référence (conformément à la résolution de l'OIT sur les statistiques de la population économiquement active, l'emploi, le chômage et le sous-emploi, adoptée par la treizième Conférence internationale des statisticiens du travail (CIST), octobre 1982).

L'emploi salarié se réfère uniquement aux travailleurs salariés ou recevant un traitement et aux "personnes dans

self-employment that is employers, own-account workers, members of producers' cooperatives and contributing family workers. The different statuses in employment are defined according to the ILO Resolution concerning the *International Classification of Status in Employment* (ICSE), adopted by the 15th ICLS (1993).

The source for this table is the International Labour Organization (ILO). For more information visit http://laborsta.ilo.org.

*Table 12*: Ratio of girls to boys (gender parity index) in primary, secondary and tertiary education is the ratio of the number of female students enrolled at primary, secondary and tertiary levels of education to the number of male students in each level. To standardize the effects of the population structure of the appropriate age groups, the Gender Parity Index (GPI) of the Gross Enrolment Ratio (GER) for each level of education is used.

The source for this table is the UNESCO Institute for Statistics (UIS). For more information visit www.uis.unesco.org

des emplois rémunérés". Les employés sont généralement rémunérés par des salaires et des traitements, mais leur rémunération peut aussi provenir de commissions, de travaux à la pièce, de primes ou d'avantages en nature tels que repas, logement, formation, etc. Il s'agit de salariés par opposition aux travailleurs indépendants – employeurs, travailleurs à leur compte, membres de coopératives de producteurs et travailleurs familiaux. Les différentes situations d'après la profession sont dé-finies conformément à la résolution de l'OIT concernant *la Classification internationale d'après la situation dans la profession* (CISP), adoptée par la quinzième Conférence internationale des statisticiens du travail (CIST) (1993).

La source de ce tableau est l'Organisation internationale du Travail (OIT). Pour plus d'informations, veuillez consulter le site Web suivant : http://laborsta.ilo.org.

*Tableau 12* : ce tableau indique la proportion de filles par rapport aux garçons (indice de parité des sexes) dans l'enseignement primaire, secondaire et supérieur, à savoir le rapport entre le nombre de filles inscrites dans l'enseignement primaire, secondaire et supérieur et le nombre de garçons à chaque niveau. Pour normaliser les effets de la pyramide des âges, l'indice de parité des sexes du taux brut de scolarisation pour chaque niveau d'enseignement est utilisé.

La source de ce tableau est l'Institut de statistique de l'UNESCO. Pour plus d'informations, veuillez consulter le site Web suivant : www.uis.unesco.org.

# Education at the primary, secondary and tertiary levels
Number of students enrolled and percentage female

# Enseignement primaire, secondaire et supérieur
Nombre d'élèves inscrits et pourcentage de sexe féminin

| Country or area<br>Pays ou zone | Year[t]<br>Année[t] | Primary education<br>Enseignement primaire | | Secondary education<br>Enseignement secondaire | | Tertiary education<br>Enseignement supérieur | |
|---|---|---|---|---|---|---|---|
| | | Total | % F | Total | % F | Total | % F |
| Afghanistan | 2002 | 2 667 629 | 30.2 | ... | ... | ... | ... |
| Afghanistan | 2003 | 3 781 015 | 34.8 | 406 895[1] | 24.4[1] | 26 211[1] | 20.4[1] |
| | 2004 | 4 430 142 | 29.1 | 594 306 | 16.3 | 27 648 | 20.4 |
| | 2005 | 4 318 819 | 35.7 | 651 453 | 23.4 | ... | ... |
| Albania | 2002 | 263 603 | 47.8 | 382 779[1] | 47.2[1] | 42 160 | 62.0 |
| Albanie | 2003 | 252 829 | 48.1 | 396 139 | 48.3 | 43 600 | 62.3 |
| | 2004 | 250 487 | 48.2 | 397 056 | 47.9 | 53 014 | 62.1 |
| Algeria | 2002 | 4 691 870 | 47.0 | 3 424 208[1] | 50.1[1] | 624 788[1] | ... |
| Algérie | 2003 | 4 612 574 | 47.0 | 3 548 484 | 50.5 | 682 775[1] | ... |
| | 2004 | 4 507 703 | 47.0 | 3 677 107 | 50.7 | 716 452 | 51.0 |
| | 2005 | 4 361 744 | 47.0 | 3 755 821[1] | 50.7[1] | 792 121 | 55.2 |
| | 2006 | 4 196 580 | 47.0 | ... | ... | 817 968 | 54.8 |
| Andorra | 2002 | 4 108 | 47.4 | 3 132 | 50.3 | 267 | 49.8 |
| Andorre | 2003 | 4 142 | 47.2 | 3 194 | 50.2 | 306 | 48.7 |
| | 2004 | 4 264 | 47.1 | 3 250 | 49.9 | 331 | 48.6 |
| | 2005 | 4 085 | 46.9 | 3 737 | 50.3 | 342 | 50.9 |
| | 2006 | 4 332 | 47.4 | 3 843 | 49.9 | 401 | 53.1 |
| Angola | 2002 | ... | ... | 460 844 | 45.7 | 12 566 | 39.9[2] |
| Angola | 2003 | ... | ... | ... | ... | 48 184 | ... |
| | 2004 | | | | | 37 547 | ... |
| | 2005 | ... | ... | ... | ... | 48 184 | ... |
| Anguilla | 2002 | 1 427 | 49.0 | 1 073[1] | 51.4[1] | ... | ... |
| Anguilla | 2003 | 1 447 | 49.7 | 1 100[1] | 50.7[1] | 12 | 100.0 |
| | 2004 | 1 433 | 50.0 | 1 076 | 51.1 | 21 | 81.0 |
| | 2005 | 1 449 | 50.8 | 1 024 | 50.5 | 33 | 75.8 |
| | 2006 | 1 512 | 48.9 | 998 | 51.6 | 47 | 83.0 |
| Argentina | 2002 | 4 914 441 | 49.2 | 3 976 213 | 50.7 | 2 026 735 | 59.3 |
| Argentine | 2003 | 4 674 869 | 49.0 | 3 499 181 | 50.9 | 2 101 437 | 59.7 |
| | 2004 | 4 701 149 | 48.9 | 3 497 541 | 51.7 | 2 116 876 | 58.1 |
| | 2005 | 4 651 255 | 48.8 | 3 476 306 | 51.9 | 2 082 577 | 58.7 |
| Armenia | 2002 | 155 423 | 48.7 | 379 199 | 51.0 | 75 474 | 53.7 |
| Arménie | 2003 | 143 822 | 48.5 | 377 727 | 50.2 | 73 603 | 53.7 |
| | 2004 | 144 790 | 48.4 | 364 782 | 49.8 | 79 321 | 55.5 |
| | 2005 | 125 149 | 48.2 | 365 400 | 49.6 | 86 629 | 55.5 |
| | 2006 | 121 473 | 47.8 | 356 355 | 49.6 | 99 293 | 54.5 |
| Aruba | 2002 | 9 840 | 48.2 | 6 757 | 51.5 | 1 592 | 60.4 |
| Aruba | 2003 | 9 897 | 48.0 | 6 869 | 51.6 | 1 672 | 59.3 |
| | 2004 | 10 185 | 47.9 | 6 973 | 50.6 | 1 704 | 60.2 |
| | 2005 | 10 250 | 48.3 | 7 116 | 50.7 | 2 106 | 59.8 |
| | 2006 | 10 390 | 48.8 | 7 439 | 50.4 | 2 094 | 60.3 |
| Australia | 2002 | 1 933 765 | 48.6 | 2 513 670 | 48.0 | 1 012 210 | 54.0 |
| Australie | 2003 | 1 931 817 | 48.6 | 2 568 791 | 48.1 | 1 005 977 | 54.1 |
| | 2004 | 1 934 549 | 48.6 | 2 492 235 | 47.8 | 1 002 998 | 54.2 |
| | 2005 | 1 934 941 | 48.6 | 2 496 917 | 47.6 | 1 024 589 | 54.5 |
| | 2006 | 1 938 861 | 48.6 | 2 536 684 | 47.4 | 1 040 153 | 54.9 |
| Austria | 2002 | 386 484 | 48.5 | 755 581 | 47.5 | 223 735 | 52.7 |
| Autriche | 2003 | 379 920 | 48.6 | 764 426 | 47.5 | 229 802 | 53.0 |
| | 2004 | 372 963 | 48.7 | 770 391 | 47.4 | 238 522 | 53.3 |
| | 2005 | 362 822 | 48.7 | 781 292 | 47.5 | 244 410 | 53.7 |
| | 2006 | 355 293 | 48.5 | 782 981 | 47.7 | 253 139 | 53.8 |

| Country or area<br>Pays ou zone | Year[t]<br>Année[t] | Primary education<br>Enseignement primaire | | Secondary education<br>Enseignement secondaire | | Tertiary education<br>Enseignement supérieur | |
|---|---|---|---|---|---|---|---|
| | | Total | % F | Total | % F | Total | % F |
| Azerbaijan | 2002 | 668 902 | 48.1 | 1 040 175 | 48.1 | 121 475 | 44.2 |
| Azerbaïdjan | 2003 | 635 652 | 47.7 | 1 094 387 | 47.9 | 121 156 | 44.7 |
| | 2004 | 607 007 | 47.8 | 1 085 632 | 48.0 | 122 770 | 46.0 |
| | 2005 | 568 097 | 47.7 | 1 069 980 | 47.9 | 128 634 | 46.7 |
| | 2006 | 538 339 | 47.1 | 1 051 591 | 47.6 | 131 507 | 47.5 |
| Bahamas | 2002 | 34 153 | 49.5 | 31 713 | 51.0 | ... | ... |
| Bahamas | 2003[1] | 34 579 | 49.4 | 29 985 | 50.3 | ... | ... |
| | 2004[1] | 36 070 | 49.2 | 30 857 | 49.6 | ... | ... |
| | 2005 | 37 050 | 49.1 | 32 089 | 49.7 | ... | ... |
| | 2006 | 35 921 | 49.1 | 32 709 | 49.8 | ... | ... |
| Bahrain | 2002 | 81 057 | 48.7 | 64 439 | 50.7 | ... | ... |
| Bahreïn | 2003 | 81 887 | 48.9 | 67 160 | 50.2 | 19 079 | 61.9 |
| | 2004 | 82 708 | 48.9 | 69 638 | 49.9 | 18 524[1] | 63.1[1] |
| | 2005 | 83 299 | 48.7 | 71 645 | 50.0 | 18 841 | 67.8 |
| | 2006 | 89 721 | 48.8 | 73 767 | 49.7 | 18 403 | 68.3 |
| Bangladesh | 2002 | 17 561 828 | 49.7 | 11 024 326 | 51.3 | 855 339 | 32.0 |
| Bangladesh | 2003 | 17 462 973 | 49.3 | 11 051 234 | 51.3 | 877 335 | 32.0 |
| | 2004 | 17 953 300 | 49.6 | 10 354 760 | 49.6 | 821 364 | 31.6 |
| | 2005 | ... | ... | ... | ... | 911 600 | 33.5 |
| Barbados | 2002 | 23 394 | 49.2 | 20 872 | 49.4 | ... | ... |
| Barbade | 2003 | 23 074 | 48.9 | 20 947 | 49.7 | ... | ... |
| | 2004 | 22 327 | 48.9 | 21 300 | 49.7 | ... | ... |
| | 2005 | 22 249 | 49.2 | 21 418 | 49.4 | ... | ... |
| | 2006 | 22 461 | 48.7 | 20 855 | 50.2 | ... | ... |
| Belarus | 2002 | 511 863 | 48.3 | 982 230 | 49.7 | 463 544 | 56.8 |
| Bélarus | 2003 | 437 005 | 48.3 | 997 760 | 49.6 | 488 650 | 57.1 |
| | 2004 | 403 841 | 47.8 | 969 768 | 49.1 | 507 360 | 57.1 |
| | 2005 | 379 577 | 47.8 | 928 488 | 49.1 | 528 508 | 56.8 |
| | 2006 | 367 736 | 48.1 | 878 943 | 49.1 | 544 328 | 56.8 |
| Belgium | 2002 | 767 787 | 48.7 | 1 149 329 | 51.6 | 366 982 | 53.1 |
| Belgique | 2003 | 761 730 | 48.7 | 1 181 327 | 51.3 | 374 532 | 53.3 |
| | 2004 | 747 111 | 48.8 | 805 778 | 48.0 | 386 110 | 53.8 |
| | 2005 | 738 580 | 48.8 | 814 539 | 48.0 | 389 547 | 54.4 |
| | 2006 | 732 808 | 48.8 | 821 996 | 48.1 | 394 427 | 54.7 |
| Belize | 2002[1] | 46 999 | 48.3 | 25 604 | 50.3 | ... | ... |
| Belize | 2003 | 47 187 | 48.8 | 27 880[1] | 50.6[1] | 527 | 64.9[2] |
| | 2004 | 48 996 | 48.7 | 31 224 | 50.3 | 722 | 70.2 |
| | 2005 | 50 389 | 48.4 | 31 377[1] | 49.7[1] | ... | ... |
| | 2006 | 51 497 | 48.6 | 30 084 | 50.7 | ... | ... |
| Benin | 2002 | 1 152 798 | 41.3 | 287 292[1] | 31.8[1] | 34 336 | ... |
| Bénin | 2003 | 1 233 214 | 41.9 | 312 427[1] | 31.5[1] | 39 406 | ... |
| | 2004 | 1 319 648 | 42.8 | 344 890 | 31.7 | 41 282 | ... |
| | 2005 | 1 318 140 | 43.6 | 435 449[1] | 35.4[1] | 42 197 | ... |
| | 2006 | 1 356 818 | 44.4 | ... | ... | 42 603 | ... |
| Bermuda | 2002 | 4 910 | 50.3 | 4 565 | 51.5 | 1 960[1] | 55.1[1] |
| Bermudes | 2003 | 4 879 | 50.1 | 4 660 | 52.4 | ... | ... |
| | 2004 | 4 810 | 50.7 | 4 803 | 53.1 | ... | ... |
| | 2005 | 4 760 | 50.4 | 4 756 | 52.4 | 639 | 65.1 |
| | 2006 | 4 678 | 46.2 | 4 518 | 51.5 | ... | ... |
| | 2007 | ... | ... | ... | ... | 886 | 71.1 |
| Bhutan | 2002[1] | 91 390 | 47.4 | 29 194 | 45.4 | ... | ... |
| Bhoutan | 2005 | 99 458 | 48.7 | 42 144 | 47.1 | ... | ... |
| | 2006 | 102 225 | 48.9 | 45 035 | 47.8 | 4 141 | 32.7 |

| Country or area Pays ou zone | Year[t] Année[t] | Primary education Enseignement primaire | | Secondary education Enseignement secondaire | | Tertiary education Enseignement supérieur | |
|---|---|---|---|---|---|---|---|
| | | Total | % F | Total | % F | Total | % F |
| Bolivia Bolivie | 2002 | 1 544 430 | 48.8 | 996 577[1] | 48.3[1] | 311 015 | ... |
| | 2003 | 1 531 996 | 48.9 | 1 048 881 | 48.4 | 337 914 | ... |
| | 2004[1] | 1 541 559 | 49.0 | ... | ... | 346 056 | ... |
| | 2006 | 1 508 194 | 49.0 | 1 043 127 | 48.1 | ... | ... |
| Botswana Botswana | 2002 | 330 835 | 49.4 | 166 000 | 51.2 | 8 372 | 44.8 |
| | 2003 | 330 376 | 49.5 | 166 915 | 51.4 | ... | ... |
| | 2004 | 328 692 | 49.3 | 169 727[1] | 51.0[1] | 10 197 | 46.4 |
| | 2005 | 326 500 | 49.3 | 168 720 | 50.9 | 10 950 | 49.8 |
| Brazil Brésil | 2002 | 19 380 387 | 47.7 | 26 789 210 | 51.6 | 3 582 105 | 56.5 |
| | 2003 | 18 919 122 | 47.7 | 24 592 569 | 51.7 | 3 994 422 | 56.4 |
| | 2004 | 18 979 209 | 47.2 | 25 155 104 | 51.5 | 4 275 027 | 56.3 |
| | 2005 | 18 661 105 | 47.6 | 24 863 112 | 51.6 | 4 572 297 | 55.9 |
| British Virgin Islands Iles Vierges britanniques | 2002 | 2 811 | 49.0 | 1 593 | 50.5 | 758 | 69.0 |
| | 2003 | 2 780 | 47.9 | 1 633 | 53.7 | 1 025[1] | 71.7[1] |
| | 2004 | 2 824 | 48.2 | 1 707 | 52.1 | 1 136 | 69.5 |
| | 2005 | 2 898 | 48.2 | 1 882 | 54.2 | 1 200[1] | 68.8[1] |
| | 2006 | 2 923 | 48.3 | 1 959 | 53.0 | ... | ... |
| Brunei Darussalam Brunéi Darussalam | 2002 | 44 882 | 47.9 | 38 692 | 49.2 | 4 418 | 63.2 |
| | 2003 | 46 242 | 48.1 | 40 022 | 49.3 | 4 546 | 64.7 |
| | 2004 | 46 382 | 47.9 | 42 167 | 49.0 | 4 917 | 66.0 |
| | 2005 | 46 012 | 47.9 | 43 900 | 48.8 | 5 023 | 66.5 |
| | 2006 | 46 086 | 47.7 | 45 887 | 48.9 | 5 094 | 66.1 |
| Bulgaria Bulgarie | 2002 | 349 616 | 48.2 | 693 289 | 48.1 | 228 394 | 54.0 |
| | 2003 | 333 016 | 48.2 | 707 251 | 48.1 | 230 513 | 52.8 |
| | 2004 | 314 221 | 48.3 | 704 678 | 47.7 | 228 468 | 52.5 |
| | 2005 | 290 017 | 48.4 | 685 640 | 47.7 | 237 909 | 52.1 |
| | 2006 | 273 045 | 48.3 | 667 286 | 47.8 | 243 464 | 53.5 |
| Burkina Faso Burkina Faso | 2002 | 956 721[1] | 41.7[1] | 204 847[1] | 39.2[1] | 15 535 | 25.4 |
| | 2003 | 1 012 150 | 42.1 | 236 914 | 39.9 | 18 200 | 22.4 |
| | 2004 | 1 139 512 | 43.2 | 266 538[1] | 40.3[1] | 18 868[1] | 22.4[1] |
| | 2005 | 1 270 837 | 43.7 | 295 412 | 40.7 | 27 942 | 30.7 |
| | 2006 | 1 390 571 | 44.2 | 319 749 | 41.3 | 30 472 | 31.0 |
| Burundi Burundi | 2002 | 817 223 | 44.0 | ... | ... | 10 546 | 30.4 |
| | 2003 | 894 859 | 44.6 | 129 204 | 43.5 | 11 915[1] | 31.9[1] |
| | 2004 | 968 488 | 45.4 | 152 251 | 43.0 | 15 706 | 27.7 |
| | 2005 | 1 036 859 | 46.2 | 171 110[1] | 42.5[1] | 16 889[1] | 27.7[1] |
| | 2006 | 1 324 937 | 47.7 | 192 296[1] | 42.6[1] | 17 061 | 30.6 |
| Cambodia Cambodge | 2002 | 2 728 698 | 46.5 | 475 637 | 37.0 | 32 010 | 28.8 |
| | 2003 | 2 772 113 | 46.8 | 560 197 | 38.4 | 43 210 | 28.8[1] |
| | 2004 | 2 762 882 | 47.0 | 631 508[1] | 40.2[1] | 45 370 | 31.3 |
| | 2005 | 2 695 372 | 47.2 | ... | ... | 56 810 | 31.5 |
| | 2006 | 2 582 250 | 47.3 | 824 883 | 43.3 | 75 989 | 32.8 |
| Cameroon Cameroun | 2002 | 2 741 627[2] | 45.9[2] | ... | ... | 77 707 | 38.8[1] |
| | 2003 | 2 798 523 | 45.7 | 823 068[1] | 45.3[1] | 81 318 | 38.8[1] |
| | 2004 | 2 979 011 | 45.8 | 751 580 | 43.8 | 83 903[1] | 38.8[1] |
| | 2005 | 2 977 781 | 45.2[2] | 784 203 | 43.8 | 99 864[1] | 39.5[1] |
| | 2006 | 2 998 135 | 45.2 | 698 444 | 43.9 | 120 298 | 41.8 |
| Canada Canada | 2002 | 2 460 943[1] | 48.6[1] | 2 709 025[1] | 48.6[1] | 1 254 833 | 56.4 |
| | 2004[1] | 2 389 188 | 48.6 | 2 999 244 | 48.1 | 1 326 711 | 56.4 |
| Cape Verde Cap-Vert | 2002 | 89 809 | 48.9 | 48 055 | 50.9 | 1 810 | 51.0 |
| | 2003 | 87 841 | 48.7 | 49 522 | 52.0 | 2 215 | 52.9 |
| | 2004 | 85 138 | 48.6 | 49 790 | 52.2 | 3 036 | 52.6 |
| | 2005 | 82 952 | 48.5 | 51 672 | 51.7 | 3 910 | 51.0 |
| | 2006 | 81 434 | 48.6 | 61 465 | 53.5 | 4 567 | 52.1 |

| Country or area<br>Pays ou zone | Year[t]<br>Année[t] | Primary education<br>Enseignement primaire | | Secondary education<br>Enseignement secondaire | | Tertiary education<br>Enseignement supérieur | |
|---|---|---|---|---|---|---|---|
| | | Total | % F | Total | % F | Total | % F |
| Cayman Islands<br>Iles Caïmanes | 2002 | 3 579 | 49.4 | 2 341 | 50.4 | ... | ... |
| | 2004 | 3 361 | 48.5 | 2 701 | 50.8 | ... | ... |
| | 2005 | 3 240 | 48.4 | 2 824 | 47.8 | ... | ... |
| | 2006 | 3 461 | 48.0 | 2 899 | 49.0 | 567 | 71.6 |
| Central African Rep.<br>Rép. centrafricaine | 2002 | 410 562[2] | 40.4[2] | 71 893[1] | ... | ... | ... |
| | 2003 | 414 537 | 41.0 | ... | ... | ... | ... |
| | 2004 | 363 158 | 40.2 | ... | ... | 6 384 | ... |
| | 2005 | 412 381 | 41.1 | ... | ... | 6 270[1] | ... |
| | 2006 | 418 825 | 41.0 | ... | ... | 4 462 | 22.5 |
| Chad<br>Tchad | 2002 | 1 085 247 | 39.1 | 184 996 | 24.9 | ... | ... |
| | 2003 | 1 164 093 | 39.7 | 212 632[1] | 24.3[1] | 7 397 | 10.2 |
| | 2004 | 1 271 985 | 39.5 | 227 856 | 24.8 | 10 081 | 12.5 |
| | 2005 | 1 262 393 | 40.1 | 236 754[1] | 24.8[1] | 10 468[1] | 12.5[1] |
| Chile<br>Chili | 2002 | 1 753 952 | 48.5 | 1 496 937 | 49.6 | 521 609 | 47.5 |
| | 2003 | 1 713 538 | 48.5 | 1 557 120 | 49.5 | 567 114 | 47.8 |
| | 2004 | 1 755 997 | 47.9 | 1 594 966 | 49.5 | 580 815 | 48.0 |
| | 2005 | 1 720 951 | 48.0 | 1 630 099 | 49.5 | 663 694 | 48.1 |
| | 2006 | 1 694 765 | 48.0 | 1 633 868 | 49.6 | 661 142 | 49.2 |
| China[3]<br>Chine[3] | 2002 | 125 756 891 | 47.3 | 90 722 795 | ... | 12 143 723 | ... |
| | 2003 | 121 662 360 | 47.2 | 95 624 760 | 46.8 | 15 186 217 | 43.8 |
| | 2006 | 108 925 227 | 46.8 | 101 195 119 | 47.7 | 23 360 535 | 47.1 |
| China, Hong Kong SAR<br>Chine, Hong Kong RAS | 2002 | 497 376 | 48.1 | 488 537 | 48.5 | ... | ... |
| | 2003 | 487 465 | 48.1 | 487 218 | 48.8 | 146 039[2] | 50.3[2] |
| | 2004 | 472 863 | 48.1 | 492 779 | 48.9 | 147 724 | 51.2 |
| | 2005 | 451 171 | 48.0 | 498 354 | 48.9 | 152 294 | 51.0 |
| | 2006 | 429 892 | 48.0 | 500 708 | 48.8 | 155 324 | 50.5 |
| China, Macao SAR<br>Chine, Macao RAS | 2002 | 44 368 | 47.0 | 42 017 | 50.2 | 20 420 | 36.9 |
| | 2003 | 41 917 | 46.8 | 44 425 | 50.2 | 26 272 | 36.5 |
| | 2004 | 39 872 | 46.7 | 46 509 | 49.6 | 24 815 | 40.5 |
| | 2005 | 37 401 | 46.8 | 46 539 | 49.4 | 23 420 | 42.8 |
| | 2006 | 34 739 | 47.2 | 46 393 | 49.3 | 23 291 | 45.9 |
| Colombia<br>Colombie | 2002 | 5 193 055 | 48.8 | 3 723 348 | 51.6 | 989 745 | 51.5 |
| | 2003[1] | 5 207 149 | 48.7 | 3 788 991 | 51.6 | 986 680 | 51.5 |
| | 2004 | 5 259 033 | 48.7 | 4 050 525 | 51.6 | 1 112 574 | 51.3 |
| | 2005 | 5 298 257 | 48.5 | 4 297 228 | 51.6 | 1 223 594 | 51.3 |
| | 2006 | 5 296 190 | 48.6 | 4 484 496 | 51.6 | 1 314 972 | 51.5 |
| Comoros<br>Comores | 2002 | 104 274 | 44.3 | 33 874 | 45.3 | ... | ... |
| | 2003 | 104 274 | 44.3 | 38 272 | 44.9 | 1 707 | 43.2 |
| | 2004 | 103 809 | 46.2 | 42 919 | 42.5 | 1 779[1] | 43.2[1] |
| | 2005 | 106 700[1] | 46.2[1] | 43 349[1] | 42.5 | ... | ... |
| Congo<br>Congo | 2002 | 525 093 | 48.3 | 194 101[1] | 42.3[1] | 12 164 | 15.8 |
| | 2003 | 509 507 | 48.2 | 204 096 | 40.5 | 12 456[1] | 15.8[1] |
| | 2004 | 584 370 | 48.1 | 235 294[1] | 45.5[1] | ... | ... |
| | 2005 | 597 304 | 47.9 | ... | ... | ... | ... |
| | 2006 | 617 010 | 47.2 | ... | ... | ... | ... |
| Cook Islands<br>Iles Cook | 2002 | 2 388 | 46.9 | 1 881 | 49.0 | ... | ... |
| | 2003 | 2 254 | 47.2 | 1 891 | 48.7 | ... | ... |
| | 2004[1] | 2 265 | 47.2 | 1 901 | 48.6 | ... | ... |
| | 2005 | 2 201 | 48.1 | 1 899 | 49.2 | ... | ... |
| Costa Rica<br>Costa Rica | 2002 | 545 509 | 48.1 | 288 965 | 50.5 | 77 283 | 52.4 |
| | 2003 | 541 494[1] | 48.1[1] | 305 940 | 50.5[1] | 79 499[1] | 52.3[1] |
| | 2004 | 558 084 | 48.3 | 339 763 | 50.0 | 108 765 | 54.3 |
| | 2005 | 542 087 | 48.3 | 347 244 | 50.0 | 110 717[1] | 54.3[1] |
| | 2006 | 546 542 | 48.3 | 374 428 | 50.1 | ... | ... |

**Education at the primary, secondary and tertiary levels**—Number of students enrolled and percentage female (*continued*)

**Enseignement primaire, secondaire et supérieur**—Nombre d'élèves inscrits et pourcentage de sexe feminin (*suite*)

| Country or area<br>Pays ou zone | Year[t]<br>Année[t] | Primary education<br>Enseignement primaire | | Secondary education<br>Enseignement secondaire | | Tertiary education<br>Enseignement supérieur | |
|---|---|---|---|---|---|---|---|
| | | Total | % F | Total | % F | Total | % F |
| Côte d'Ivoire<br>Côte d'Ivoire | 2002 | 2 116 223 | 42.3 | 736 649[1] | 35.6[1] | ... | ... |
| | 2003[2] | 2 046 165 | 44.2 | ... | ... | ... | ... |
| | 2006 | 2 111 975 | 44.1 | ... | ... | ... | ... |
| Croatia<br>Croatie | 2002 | 193 179 | 48.6 | 401 921 | 49.4 | 112 537 | 52.5 |
| | 2003 | 192 004 | 48.6 | 399 845 | 49.3 | 121 722 | 53.2 |
| | 2005 | 196 253 | 48.7 | 400 123 | 49.7 | 134 658 | 53.8 |
| | 2006 | 194 748 | 48.6 | 395 836 | 49.7 | 136 646 | 54.1 |
| Cuba<br>Cuba | 2002 | 971 542 | 47.8 | 895 742 | 48.5 | 191 262 | 54.4 |
| | 2003 | 925 335 | 47.7 | 938 047 | 48.3 | 235 997 | 56.2 |
| | 2004 | 906 293 | 47.7 | 932 338 | 49.1 | 396 516 | 62.3[1] |
| | 2005 | 895 045 | 47.8 | 937 493 | 49.1 | 471 858 | 62.1[1] |
| | 2006 | 889 834 | 47.9 | 928 342 | 49.1 | 681 629 | 60.8 |
| Cyprus<br>Chypre | 2002 | 63 717 | 48.6 | 63 871 | 49.0 | 13 927 | 54.8 |
| | 2003 | 62 868 | 48.6 | 64 711 | 48.9 | 18 272 | 49.5 |
| | 2004 | 61 731 | 48.8 | 64 534 | 49.2 | 20 849 | 47.9 |
| | 2005 | 61 247 | 48.7 | 64 293 | 49.2 | 20 078 | 52.0 |
| | 2006 | 59 710 | 48.8 | 64 714 | 49.2 | 20 587 | 50.9 |
| Czech Republic<br>République tchèque | 2002 | 603 843 | 48.4 | 998 608 | 49.5 | 284 485 | 51.2 |
| | 2003 | 566 581 | 48.3 | 1 000 493 | 49.5 | 287 001 | 50.7 |
| | 2004 | 534 366 | 48.3 | 982 208 | 49.1 | 318 858 | 51.2 |
| | 2005 | 502 831 | 48.3 | 975 284 | 49.2 | 336 307 | 52.6 |
| | 2006 | 473 269 | 48.4 | 966 280 | 49.1 | 338 009 | 53.8 |
| Dem. Rep. of the Congo<br>Rép. dém. du Congo | 2002 | 5 455 391 | 43.9 | 1 612 840 | 36.7 | ... | ... |
| | 2003[1] | 5 589 634 | 43.9 | 1 655 023 | 36.7 | ... | ... |
| Denmark<br>Danemark | 2002 | 415 205 | 48.7 | 434 517 | 50.0 | 196 204 | 57.4 |
| | 2003 | 417 506[1] | 48.7[1] | 446 863 | 50.1 | 201 746 | 57.9 |
| | 2004 | 419 806 | 48.7 | 449 750 | 49.8 | 217 130 | 57.9 |
| | 2005 | 414 103 | 48.7 | 464 952 | 49.5 | 232 255 | 57.4 |
| | 2006 | 415 793 | 48.7 | 463 617 | 49.4 | 228 893 | 57.4 |
| Djibouti<br>Djibouti | 2002 | 44 321 | 42.9 | 20 516 | 37.9 | 728 | 44.5 |
| | 2003 | 46 564[1] | 43.3[1] | 23 496[1] | 39.3[1] | 906 | 40.9 |
| | 2004 | 48 713 | 43.8 | 26 549 | 40.4 | 1 134 | 44.8 |
| | 2005 | 50 651 | 44.6 | 30 142 | 39.5 | 1 696 | 41.7 |
| | 2006 | 53 745 | 44.4 | 30 265 | 39.8 | 1 928 | 40.0 |
| Dominica<br>Dominique | 2002 | 10 984 | 48.0 | 7 500 | 52.1 | ... | ... |
| | 2003 | 10 460 | 48.3 | 7 724 | 51.7 | ... | ... |
| | 2004 | 9 872 | 48.3 | 7 477 | 50.4 | ... | ... |
| | 2005 | 9 441 | 48.7 | 7 476 | 50.0 | ... | ... |
| | 2006 | 8 912 | 48.7 | 7 475 | 49.7 | ... | ... |
| Dominican Republic<br>Rép. dominicaine | 2002 | 1 399 844 | 49.4 | 757 790 | 54.3 | ... | ... |
| | 2003 | 1 374 624 | 49.4[1] | 752 096[1] | 54.4[1] | 286 954 | 61.3 |
| | 2004 | 1 281 885 | 47.8 | 782 690 | 54.3 | 293 565[1] | 61.3[1] |
| | 2005 | 1 289 745 | 47.9 | 808 352 | 53.9 | ... | ... |
| | 2006 | 1 234 450 | 47.9 | 794 000 | 54.1 | ... | ... |
| Ecuador<br>Equateur | 2002 | 1 982 636 | 49.1 | 966 362 | 49.4 | ... | ... |
| | 2003 | 1 987 465 | 49.1 | 972 777 | 49.6 | ... | ... |
| | 2004 | 1 989 665 | 49.0 | 996 535 | 49.3 | ... | ... |
| | 2005 | 1 997 624 | 49.0 | 1 053 175 | 49.4 | ... | ... |
| | 2006 | 2 006 430 | 48.9 | 1 103 258 | 49.5 | ... | ... |
| Egypt<br>Egypte | 2002[1] | 7 855 433 | 47.4 | 8 360 316 | 47.1 | ... | ... |
| | 2003 | 7 874 308[1] | 47.6[1] | 8 384 065[1] | 47.3[1] | 2 153 865 | ... |
| | 2004[1] | 7 928 380 | 47.9 | 8 329 822 | 47.4 | 2 512 399 | ... |
| | 2005 | 9 563 627 | 47.3 | ... | ... | 2 594 186[1] | ... |
| | 2006 | 9 794 591 | 47.4 | ... | ... | ... | ... |
| | 2007 | 9 988 181 | 47.6 | ... | ... | ... | ... |

| Country or area<br>Pays ou zone | Year[t]<br>Année[t] | Primary education<br>Enseignement primaire | | Secondary education<br>Enseignement secondaire | | Tertiary education<br>Enseignement supérieur | |
|---|---|---|---|---|---|---|---|
| | | Total | %F | Total | %F | Total | %F |
| El Salvador | 2002 | 987 676 | 47.8 | 461 215 | 49.6 | 113 366 | 54.2 |
| El Salvador | 2003 | 1 016 098 | 48.2 | 488 515 | 49.9 | 116 521 | 53.9 |
| | 2004 | 1 045 485 | 48.2 | 520 332 | 49.9 | 120 264 | 54.4 |
| | 2005 | 1 045 484 | 48.2 | 524 202 | 50.0 | 122 431 | 54.7 |
| | 2006 | 1 035 100 | 48.2 | 529 057 | 50.3 | 124 956 | 54.7 |
| Equatorial Guinea | 2002 | 78 390 | 47.6 | 21 173[1] | 36.4[1] | ... | ... |
| Guinée équatoriale | 2003 | 73 771 | 49.2 | ... | ... | ... | ... |
| | 2005 | 75 809 | 48.7 | ... | ... | ... | ... |
| Eritrea | 2002 | 330 278 | 44.3 | 152 723 | 39.3 | 5 507 | 13.4 |
| Erythrée | 2003 | 359 299 | 44.4 | 161 273 | 39.2 | 5 755[1] | 13.3[1] |
| | 2004 | 374 997 | 44.2 | 194 124 | 36.1 | 4 612 | 13.1 |
| | 2005 | 377 512 | 44.4 | 216 944 | 37.2 | ... | ... |
| | 2006 | 364 263 | 44.4 | 227 786 | 37.6 | ... | ... |
| Estonia | 2002 | 108 637 | 47.8 | 123 269 | 49.4 | 60 648 | 61.5 |
| Estonie | 2003 | 100 171 | 47.7 | 123 074 | 49.7 | 63 625 | 61.5 |
| | 2004 | 92 098 | 47.9 | 124 382 | 49.4 | 65 659 | 61.8 |
| | 2005 | 85 539 | 47.9 | 124 493 | 49.1 | 67 760 | 61.5 |
| | 2006 | 79 589 | 48.0 | 120 286 | 49.3 | 68 286 | 61.6 |
| Ethiopia | 2002 | 7 213 043 | 41.4 | 1 734 131 | 38.3 | 101 829 | 26.4 |
| Ethiopie | 2003 | 7 623 074 | 41.9 | 1 857 817 | 36.4 | 147 954 | 25.2 |
| | 2004 | 8 269 663 | 43.5 | 2 140 751 | 36.3 | 172 111 | 25.2 |
| | 2005 | 10 019 729 | 45.1 | 2 488 465 | 37.3 | 191 165 | 24.4 |
| | 2006 | 10 971 581 | 46.1 | 2 992 589 | 38.5 | 180 286 | 24.2 |
| | 2007 | 12 174 719 | 46.5 | 3 430 129 | 40.0 | 210 456 | 25.5 |
| Fiji | 2002 | 114 267 | 48.6 | 97 696 | 50.4 | ... | ... |
| Fidji | 2003 | 113 432 | 48.3 | 99 210 | 50.3 | 12 779[1] | 53.2[1] |
| | 2004 | 113 449 | 48.0 | 102 023 | 50.1 | 12 783 | 53.1 |
| | 2005[1] | 113 643 | 48.0 | 101 741 | 50.1 | 12 717 | 53.1 |
| | 2006 | 109 702 | 48.0 | 100 243 | 50.7 | ... | ... |
| Finland | 2002 | 393 267 | 48.9 | 492 757 | 51.6 | 283 805 | 54.1 |
| Finlande | 2003 | 392 741 | 48.8 | 496 834 | 51.4 | 291 664 | 53.5 |
| | 2004 | 387 934 | 48.8 | 425 966 | 50.0 | 299 888 | 53.4 |
| | 2005 | 381 785 | 48.9 | 430 596 | 50.0 | 305 996 | 53.6 |
| | 2006 | 372 128 | 48.9 | 432 565 | 50.0 | 308 966 | 53.9 |
| France | 2002 | 3 807 739 | 48.6 | 5 851 530 | 49.0 | 2 029 179 | 54.8 |
| France | 2003 | 3 791 555 | 48.6 | 5 859 127 | 49.1 | 2 119 149 | 55.0 |
| | 2004 | 3 783 197 | 48.6 | 5 826 848 | 49.0 | 2 160 300 | 55.0 |
| | 2005 | 4 015 490 | 48.5 | 6 036 192 | 49.0 | 2 187 383 | 55.2 |
| | 2006 | 4 051 861 | 48.5 | 5 993 897 | 48.9 | 2 201 201 | 55.3 |
| Gabon | 2002 | 281 871 | 49.5 | 105 191[1] | ... | ... | ... |
| Gabon | 2003 | 279 816 | 49.5 | ... | ... | ... | ... |
| | 2004[1] | 281 371 | 49.4 | ... | ... | ... | ... |
| Gambia | 2002 | 170 922 | 49.6 | 75 339[1] | 42.9[1] | ... | ... |
| Gambie | 2003 | 174 984 | 49.5 | 74 140[1] | 45.3[1] | ... | ... |
| | 2004 | 174 836 | 51.1 | 84 768 | 45.1 | 1 530 | 19.2 |
| | 2006 | 181 768 | 51.5 | 90 442 | 47.0 | ... | ... |
| Georgia | 2002 | 255 029 | 49.6 | 450 787 | 48.8 | 149 142 | 49.8 |
| Géorgie | 2003 | 239 298 | 48.9 | 452 685 | 48.7 | 155 453 | 48.8 |
| | 2004 | 363 951 | 48.2 | 312 333 | 49.1 | 155 058 | 50.5 |
| | 2005 | 338 222 | 48.3 | 316 430 | 48.8 | 174 255 | 50.4 |
| | 2006 | 326 597 | 48.8 | 314 427 | 49.8 | 144 991 | 52.4 |
| Germany | 2002 | 3 373 176 | 48.5 | 8 465 150 | 48.3 | ... | ... |
| Allemagne | 2003 | 3 303 737 | 48.6 | 8 446 559 | 48.3 | ... | ... |
| | 2004 | 3 305 386 | 48.6 | 8 381 930 | 48.2 | ... | ... |
| | 2005 | 3 306 136 | 48.7 | 8 267 636 | 48.2 | ... | ... |
| | 2006 | 3 329 349 | 48.7 | 8 184 604 | 48.1 | ... | ... |

| Country or area Pays ou zone | Year[t] Année[t] | Primary education Enseignement primaire | | Secondary education Enseignement secondaire | | Tertiary education Enseignement supérieur | |
|---|---|---|---|---|---|---|---|
| | | Total | % F | Total | % F | Total | % F |
| Ghana Ghana | 2002 | 2 586 434 | 47.5 | 1 107 247[1] | 44.9[1] | 68 389 | 27.8 |
| | 2003 | 2 519 272 | 48.4 | 1 170 764[1] | 45.0[1] | 70 293 | 31.8 |
| | 2004 | 2 678 912 | 47.4 | 1 276 670 | 44.5 | 69 968 | 31.5 |
| | 2005 | 2 929 536 | 47.9 | 1 350 410[1] | 45.0[1] | 119 559 | 34.9 |
| | 2006 | 3 130 575 | 48.5 | 1 454 097 | 44.9 | 110 184 | 33.7 |
| | 2007 | 3 365 762 | 48.5 | 1 580 917[1] | 45.8[1] | 140 017 | 34.2 |
| Greece Grèce | 2002 | 646 343 | 48.3 | ... | ... | 529 233 | 51.2 |
| | 2003 | 652 052 | 48.4 | 713 850 | 48.5 | 561 468 | 51.0 |
| | 2004 | 657 492 | 48.2 | 695 838 | 48.3 | 597 007 | 51.7 |
| | 2005 | 650 242 | 48.5 | 715 537 | 47.7 | 646 587 | 51.1 |
| | 2006 | 645 324 | 48.6 | 704 515 | 47.7 | 653 003 | 50.9 |
| Grenada Grenade | 2002 | 17 378 | 48.3 | 14 467 | 52.9 | ... | ... |
| | 2003 | 16 598 | 49.6 | 14 860 | 48.9 | ... | ... |
| | 2004 | 15 819 | 48.6 | 13 660 | 51.4 | ... | ... |
| | 2005 | 16 072[1] | 48.7[1] | 13 675[2] | 50.1[2] | ... | ... |
| Guatemala Guatemala | 2002 | 2 075 694 | 47.2 | 608 420 | 47.0 | 111 739 | 43.0 |
| | 2003[1] | 2 178 200 | 47.4 | 653 492 | 47.2 | 114 764 | 43.0 |
| | 2004 | 2 280 706 | 47.5 | 698 561 | 47.4 | ... | ... |
| | 2005 | 2 345 301 | 47.6 | 754 496 | 47.6 | ... | ... |
| | 2006 | 2 405 041 | 47.7 | 809 131 | 47.8 | 112 215[1] | 45.9[1] |
| Guinea Guinée | 2002 | 997 645 | 42.1 | 279 173[1] | 29.1[1] | ... | ... |
| | 2003 | 1 073 458 | 42.7 | 310 482[1] | 31.0[1] | 16 858[1] | 15.6[1] |
| | 2004 | 1 147 388 | 43.3 | 344 630 | 30.7 | 17 218 | 15.6 |
| | 2005 | 1 206 743 | 44.1 | 420 057[1] | 32.9[1] | 23 788 | 18.6 |
| | 2006 | 1 258 038 | 44.8 | 482 825 | 34.0 | 42 711 | 21.4 |
| Guyana Guyana | 2002[1] | 109 012 | 48.8 | 69 259 | 50.3 | ... | ... |
| | 2003 | 110 828 | 49.0 | 64 954 | ... | 4 848 | ... |
| | 2004 | 114 637[1] | 48.7[1] | 68 979[1] | 50.8[1] | 6 933 | 65.3 |
| | 2005 | 116 756 | 49.0 | 70 615 | 50.0 | 7 278 | 67.6 |
| | 2006 | ... | ... | 70 848[1] | 50.1[1] | 7 370 | 68.7 |
| Honduras Honduras | 2002[1] | ... | ... | ... | ... | 110 489 | 58.6 |
| | 2003 | ... | ... | ... | ... | 119 877 | 58.6 |
| | 2004 | 1 257 358 | 49.0 | 554 810 | 54.6 | 122 874[1] | 58.6[1] |
| | 2005 | 1 231 533 | 49.1 | 635 304 | 56.2 | ... | ... |
| | 2006 | 1 293 333 | 49.0 | ... | ... | ... | ... |
| Hungary Hongrie | 2002 | 477 865 | 48.4 | 1 013 471 | 49.1 | 354 386 | 55.3 |
| | 2003 | 464 013 | 48.5 | 1 029 979 | 49.0 | 390 453 | 56.7 |
| | 2004 | 446 610 | 48.4 | 963 242 | 48.7 | 422 177 | 57.3 |
| | 2005 | 430 561 | 48.3 | 960 215 | 48.7 | 436 012 | 58.4 |
| | 2006 | 415 858 | 48.3 | 948 856 | 48.7 | 438 702 | 58.5 |
| Iceland Islande | 2002 | 31 465 | 48.6 | 33 486 | 50.3 | 11 584 | 63.2 |
| | 2003 | 31 470 | 48.4 | 34 587 | 50.4 | 13 347 | 63.7 |
| | 2004 | 30 984 | 48.4 | 32 700 | 49.5 | 14 710 | 64.5 |
| | 2005 | 30 785 | 48.3 | 33 323 | 49.3 | 15 169 | 64.9 |
| | 2006 | 30 421 | 48.6 | 33 900 | 49.5 | 15 721 | 64.3 |
| India Inde | 2002 | 115 194 579 | 44.2 | 76 215 685 | 40.7 | 10 576 653 | 39.1 |
| | 2003 | 125 568 597 | 46.8 | 81 050 129 | 42.6 | 11 295 041 | 38.4 |
| | 2004 | 136 193 772[1] | 46.8[1] | 84 569 081 | 42.6 | 11 852 936 | 38.2 |
| | 2005 | 142 364 593 | 47.1 | 89 461 794 | 42.9 | 11 777 296 | 39.4 |
| | 2006 | 139 169 873 | 46.6 | ... | ... | 12 852 684 | 39.9 |

| Country or area<br>Pays ou zone | Year[t]<br>Année[t] | Primary education<br>Enseignement primaire | | Secondary education<br>Enseignement secondaire | | Tertiary education<br>Enseignement supérieur | |
|---|---|---|---|---|---|---|---|
| | | Total | % F | Total | % F | Total | % F |
| Indonesia | 2002 | 28 926 377 | 48.6 | 15 140 713 | 49.0 | 3 175 833 | 45.9 |
| Indonésie | 2003 | 29 050 834 | 48.7 | 15 872 535 | 49.0 | 3 441 429 | 43.9 |
| | 2004 | 29 142 093 | 48.7 | 16 353 933 | 49.1 | 3 551 092 | 43.8 |
| | 2005 | 29 149 746 | 48.3[1] | 15 993 187 | 49.0[1] | 3 660 270[1] | 43.7[1] |
| | 2006 | 28 982 708 | 48.2 | 16 423 911 | 49.2 | 3 657 429 | ... |
| Iran (Islamic Rep. of) | 2002 | 7 513 015 | 47.8 | 9 916 372 | 47.5 | 1 566 509 | 49.1 |
| Iran (Rép. islamique d') | 2003 | 7 028 924 | 47.9 | 10 024 105 | 47.2 | 1 714 433 | 50.7 |
| | 2004 | 7 306 634 | 51.1 | 10 312 561 | 47.1 | 1 954 920 | 51.4 |
| | 2005 | 7 307 056 | 53.7 | 9 942 201 | 47.2 | 2 126 274 | 51.0 |
| | 2006 | 7 273 911 | 54.7 | ... | ... | 2 398 811 | 51.6 |
| Iraq | 2002[1] | 4 135 761 | 44.5 | 1 294 395 | 36.6 | 317 993 | 34.0 |
| Iraq | 2003 | 4 280 602 | 44.5 | 1 477 616 | 40.5 | ... | ... |
| | 2004 | 4 334 609 | 44.3 | 1 706 234 | 38.9 | 412 545 | 36.2 |
| | 2005[1] | 4 430 267 | 44.3 | 1 751 164 | 38.9 | 424 908 | 36.2 |
| Ireland | 2002 | 445 947 | 48.5 | 323 043 | 51.0 | 176 296 | 55.1 |
| Irlande | 2003 | 447 618 | 48.5 | 320 620 | 50.9 | 181 557 | 55.7 |
| | 2004 | 450 413 | 48.5 | 320 560 | 50.7 | 188 315 | 55.2 |
| | 2005 | 454 060 | 48.5 | 317 337 | 51.0 | 186 561 | 54.9 |
| | 2006 | 461 588 | 48.5 | 313 479 | 50.6 | 186 044 | 55.1 |
| Israel | 2002 | 760 346 | 48.7 | 606 141 | 48.5 | 299 716 | 56.5 |
| Israël | 2003 | 769 856 | 48.6 | 603 321 | 48.3 | 301 326 | 55.7 |
| | 2004 | 775 021 | 48.8 | 607 224 | 48.8 | 301 227 | 55.8 |
| | 2005 | 784 663 | 48.9 | 610 341 | 48.7 | 310 937 | 56.0 |
| | 2006 | 802 555 | 49.0 | 613 366 | 48.6 | 310 014 | 55.1 |
| Italy | 2002 | 2 789 880 | 48.1 | 4 515 802 | 47.8 | 1 854 200 | 56.2 |
| Italie | 2003 | 2 778 877 | 48.4 | 4 528 300 | 48.5[1] | 1 913 352 | 56.2 |
| | 2004 | 2 768 386 | 48.4 | 4 505 699 | 48.5 | 1 986 497 | 56.2 |
| | 2005 | 2 771 247 | 48.3 | 4 507 408 | 48.4 | 2 014 998 | 56.6 |
| | 2006 | 2 790 254 | 48.3 | 4 531 571 | 48.4 | 2 029 023 | 56.9 |
| Jamaica | 2002 | 329 762 | 48.9 | 228 316 | 50.4 | 45 394 | 68.8 |
| Jamaïque | 2003 | 325 302 | 48.9 | 229 701 | 50.1 | 45 770[1] | 69.9[1] |
| | 2004 | 331 286 | 48.9 | 245 533 | 49.9 | ... | ... |
| | 2005 | 326 411 | 48.8 | 246 332 | 50.1 | ... | ... |
| Japan | 2002 | 7 325 866 | 48.8 | 8 394 050 | 49.0 | 3 966 667 | 45.1 |
| Japon | 2003 | 7 268 928 | 48.8 | 8 131 217 | 48.9 | 3 984 400 | 45.6 |
| | 2004 | 7 257 223 | 48.8 | 7 894 456 | 48.9 | 4 031 604 | 45.8 |
| | 2005 | 7 231 854 | 48.8 | 7 710 439 | 48.8 | 4 038 302 | 45.9 |
| | 2006 | 7 229 135 | 48.8 | 7 561 241 | 48.8 | 4 084 861 | 45.7 |
| Jordan | 2002 | 766 093 | 48.8 | 606 615 | 49.4 | 162 688 | 48.9 |
| Jordanie | 2003 | 786 154 | 48.9 | 613 120 | 49.3 | 186 189 | 51.1 |
| | 2004 | 799 888 | 48.9 | 615 731 | 49.2 | 214 106 | 51.2 |
| | 2005 | 804 904 | 48.9 | 625 682 | 49.2 | 217 823 | 50.3 |
| | 2006 | 805 457 | 49.3 | 649 242 | 49.5 | 220 103 | 51.6 |
| Kazakhstan | 2002 | 1 158 299 | 48.8 | 2 019 821 | 48.7 | 519 815 | 55.2 |
| Kazakhstan | 2003 | 1 120 005 | 48.9 | 2 067 168 | 49.2 | 603 072 | 56.6 |
| | 2004 | 1 079 598 | 48.8 | 2 090 152 | 48.6 | 664 449 | 57.4 |
| | 2005 | 1 023 974 | 48.8 | 2 039 911 | 48.5 | 753 181 | 58.1 |
| | 2006 | 972 931 | 48.8 | 1 982 190 | 48.4 | 780 783 | 58.0 |
| | 2007 | 947 807 | 48.8 | 1 874 213 | 48.6 | 772 600 | 58.2 |

| Country or area / Pays ou zone | Year[t] / Année[t] | Primary education Enseignement primaire Total | %F | Secondary education Enseignement secondaire Total | %F | Tertiary education Enseignement supérieur Total | %F |
|---|---|---|---|---|---|---|---|
| Kenya / Kenya | 2002 | 4 903 529 | 48.4 | 2 063 409 | 48.7 | 98 115[1] | 34.8[1] |
| | 2003 | 5 811 381 | 48.5 | 2 197 336 | 50.4 | ... | ... |
| | 2004 | 5 926 078 | 48.3 | 2 419 856[1] | 48.1[1] | 102 798 | 37.5 |
| | 2005 | 6 075 706 | 48.7 | 2 464 042[1] | 48.6[1] | ... | ... |
| | 2006 | 6 101 390 | 49.0 | 2 583 755 | 48.1 | ... | ... |
| Kiribati / Kiribati | 2002 | 14 809 | 48.7 | 10 334 | 52.5 | ... | ... |
| | 2003 | 15 798 | 48.3 | 11 372 | 52.9 | ... | ... |
| | 2004 | 15 611 | 49.6 | 11 581 | 52.8 | ... | ... |
| | 2005 | 16 132 | 49.4 | 11 331 | 51.7 | ... | ... |
| Korea, Republic of / Corée, République de | 2002 | 4 099 649 | 46.9 | 3 768 040 | 47.7 | 3 129 899 | 36.0 |
| | 2003 | 4 148 432 | 46.9 | 3 661 759 | 47.5 | 3 210 142 | 36.4 |
| | 2004 | 4 185 330 | 47.0 | 3 645 617 | 47.4 | 3 223 431 | 36.6 |
| | 2005 | 4 125 423 | 47.1 | 3 692 513 | 47.2 | 3 224 875 | 36.8 |
| | 2006 | 4 031 496 | 47.2 | 3 786 224 | 47.1 | 3 210 184 | 37.1 |
| | 2007 | 3 933 186 | 47.4 | 3 864 005 | 46.9 | 3 204 036 | 37.5 |
| Kuwait / Koweït | 2002 | 148 712 | 48.6 | 243 468[1] | 49.8[1] | 36 982 | 63.3 |
| | 2003 | 154 056 | 49.0 | 260 695 | 49.7 | 37 153 | 64.5 |
| | 2004 | 158 271 | 49.0 | 267 114 | 49.9 | 36 866[1] | 64.3[1] |
| | 2005 | 202 826 | 48.5 | 248 895 | 49.7 | 38 630 | 70.2 |
| | 2006 | 203 423 | 48.8 | 236 410 | 49.8 | 37 521 | 65.4 |
| Kyrgyzstan / Kirghizistan | 2002 | 453 357 | 48.7 | 689 036 | 49.6 | 209 245 | 53.0 |
| | 2003 | 449 399 | 48.9 | 739 259 | 49.7 | 201 128 | 54.1 |
| | 2004 | 444 417 | 49.0 | 732 618 | 49.6 | 205 224 | 54.0 |
| | 2005 | 434 155 | 48.7 | 721 205 | 49.5 | 220 460 | 55.3 |
| | 2006 | 423 930 | 48.8 | 718 585 | 49.5 | 233 463 | 55.6 |
| Lao People's Dem. Rep. / Rép. dém. pop. lao | 2002 | 852 857 | 45.5 | 320 275 | 41.4 | 23 018[2] | 35.6[2] |
| | 2003 | 875 300 | 45.6 | 353 362 | 41.9 | 28 117 | 35.8 |
| | 2004 | 884 629 | 45.9 | 379 579 | 42.2 | 33 760 | 38.0 |
| | 2005 | 890 821 | 46.0 | 393 856 | 42.5 | 47 424 | 41.2 |
| | 2006 | 891 881 | 46.1 | 395 382 | 43.0 | 56 716 | 40.0 |
| Latvia / Lettonie | 2002 | 113 923 | 48.4 | 278 230 | 49.1 | 110 500 | 61.5 |
| | 2003 | 103 359 | 48.2 | 276 072 | 48.8 | 118 944 | 61.7 |
| | 2004 | 92 453 | 48.1 | 275 586 | 48.8 | 127 656 | 62.3 |
| | 2005 | 84 369 | 47.9 | 271 631 | 49.0 | 130 706 | 63.2 |
| | 2006 | 78 796 | 47.9 | 258 432 | 49.1 | 131 125 | 63.3 |
| Lebanon / Liban | 2002 | 452 050 | 48.1 | 336 170 | 51.5 | 142 951 | 52.9 |
| | 2003 | 449 311 | 48.2 | 350 211 | 51.3 | 144 050 | 54.0 |
| | 2004 | 453 578 | 48.2 | 359 062 | 51.4 | 154 635 | 52.3 |
| | 2005 | 452 607 | 48.2 | 362 366 | 51.5 | 165 730 | 52.8 |
| | 2006 | 447 593 | 48.4 | 365 571 | 51.5 | 173 123 | 53.2 |
| Lesotho / Lesotho | 2002 | 418 668 | 50.1 | 82 258 | 56.1 | 5 005 | 58.0 |
| | 2003 | 429 522 | 50.0 | 84 318 | 56.0 | 6 108 | 61.3 |
| | 2004 | 427 009 | 49.7 | 89 468 | 55.9 | ... | ... |
| | 2005 | 422 278 | 49.6 | 94 460 | 55.8 | 7 918 | 56.9 |
| | 2006 | 424 855 | 49.6 | 93 996 | 56.0 | 8 500 | 55.2 |
| Liberia / Libéria | 2006 | 538 450 | 47.2 | ... | ... | ... | ... |
| Libyan Arab Jamah. / Jamah. arabe libyenne | 2002 | 750 204 | 48.8 | 824 538 | 50.5 | 359 146 | 51.4 |
| | 2003 | 739 028 | 48.0 | 797 992[1] | 50.5[1] | 375 028[1] | 51.4[1] |
| | 2004 | 745 428 | 48.0 | ... | ... | ... | ... |
| | 2005 | 713 902 | 48.4 | 701 536 | 53.3[1] | ... | ... |
| | 2006 | 755 338 | 47.7 | 732 614 | 52.9 | ... | ... |

| Country or area<br>Pays ou zone | Year[t]<br>Année[t] | Primary education<br>Enseignement primaire | | Secondary education<br>Enseignement secondaire | | Tertiary education<br>Enseignement supérieur | |
|---|---|---|---|---|---|---|---|
| | | Total | % F | Total | % F | Total | % F |
| Liechtenstein<br>Liechtenstein | 2003 | 2 218 | 49.8 | 3 255 | 45.0 | 440 | 27.0 |
| | 2004 | 2 266 | 49.8 | 3 273 | 45.2 | 532 | 26.7 |
| | 2005 | 2 242 | 50.0 | 3 142 | 45.6 | 527 | 28.8 |
| | 2006 | 2 247 | 50.7 | 3 190 | 45.5 | 636 | 30.3 |
| Lithuania<br>Lituanie | 2002 | 197 463 | 48.6 | 442 830 | 48.6 | 148 788 | 60.5 |
| | 2003 | 183 542 | 48.5 | 447 952 | 48.5 | 167 606 | 60.0 |
| | 2004 | 170 216 | 48.6 | 431 303 | 48.8 | 182 656 | 60.0 |
| | 2005 | 158 105 | 48.6 | 423 706 | 48.8 | 195 405 | 60.1 |
| | 2006 | 150 422 | 48.4 | 410 507 | 48.9 | 198 868 | 59.9 |
| Luxembourg<br>Luxembourg | 2002 | 33 966 | 48.6 | 34 038 | 50.4 | 2 965 | 52.8[1] |
| | 2003 | 34 081 | 48.7 | 34 716 | 50.2 | 3 077 | 53.3 |
| | 2004 | 34 603 | 48.7 | 35 208 | 50.2 | 3 042[1] | 52.9[1] |
| | 2005 | 35 016 | 48.8 | 35 946 | 50.4 | ... | ... |
| | 2006 | 35 431 | 48.9 | 37 009 | 50.0 | 2 692 | 51.6 |
| Madagascar<br>Madagascar | 2002 | 2 407 644 | 49.0 | ... | ... | 31 925 | 45.4[1] |
| | 2003 | 2 856 480 | 48.9 | ... | ... | 35 480 | 45.4[1] |
| | 2004 | 3 366 470 | 48.9 | ... | ... | 42 143 | 47.3 |
| | 2005 | 3 597 731 | 48.9 | 621 173[1] | 49.0 | 44 948 | 47.0 |
| | 2006 | 3 698 906 | 49.0 | 730 406 | 48.7 | 49 680 | 46.5 |
| Malawi<br>Malawi | 2002 | 2 846 589 | 48.9 | 517 690[1] | 43.6[1] | ... | ... |
| | 2003 | ... | ... | ... | ... | 4 565 | 29.2 |
| | 2004 | 2 841 640 | 50.3 | 505 303 | 44.6 | 5 089 | 35.3 |
| | 2005 | 2 867 993 | 50.2 | 515 462 | 44.8 | ... | ... |
| | 2006 | 2 933 695 | 50.5 | 565 491 | 45.5 | ... | ... |
| Malaysia<br>Malaisie | 2002 | 3 009 009 | 48.7 | 2 300 062 | 51.3 | 632 309 | 55.1 |
| | 2003 | 3 056 266 | 48.6 | 2 518 642 | 51.9 | 725 865 | 57.2 |
| | 2004 | 3 159 376 | 48.6 | 2 583 993 | 51.9 | 731 077 | 55.4 |
| | 2005 | 3 202 008 | 48.6 | 2 489 117 | 51.3 | 696 760 | 56.0 |
| Maldives<br>Maldives | 2002 | 68 242 | 48.1 | 25 365 | 52.6 | ... | ... |
| | 2003 | 66 169 | 47.8 | 28 612 | 51.6 | 73 | 69.9 |
| | 2004 | 63 300 | 47.6 | 28 878[1] | 51.9[1] | 73[1] | 69.9[1] |
| | 2005 | 57 873 | 47.8 | ... | ... | ... | ... |
| | 2006 | 54 770 | 47.7 | 32 645[1] | 50.3[1] | ... | ... |
| Mali<br>Mali | 2002 | 1 227 267 | 42.3 | ... | ... | 22 632 | 33.0 |
| | 2003 | 1 294 672 | 42.7 | 349 615 | 34.6 | 25 516[1] | 31.5[1] |
| | 2004 | 1 396 791 | 43.1 | 388 418 | 36.7 | 28 578 | 34.6 |
| | 2005 | 1 505 903 | 43.4 | 429 716 | 37.5[1] | 32 609 | 31.5[1] |
| | 2006 | 1 609 979 | 44.0 | 462 703 | 37.8 | ... | ... |
| Malta<br>Malte | 2002 | 32 717 | 48.2 | 36 478 | 48.4 | 7 259 | 56.9 |
| | 2003 | 31 710 | 48.1 | 37 556 | 48.4 | 8 946 | 57.0 |
| | 2004 | 31 064 | 48.2 | 41 723 | 46.8 | 7 867 | 55.9 |
| | 2005 | 29 596 | 48.0 | 38 479 | 48.6 | 9 441 | 56.3 |
| Marshall Islands<br>Iles Marshall | 2002 | 8 757 | 47.0 | 6 353 | 49.5 | 903 | 56.5 |
| | 2003[1] | 8 907 | 47.0 | 6 460 | 49.5 | 919 | 56.5 |
| | 2004 | 8 250 | 47.5 | 5 846 | 49.8 | ... | ... |
| | 2005[1] | 8 393 | 47.5 | 5 901 | 49.8 | ... | ... |
| | 2007 | 8 215 | 47.9 | 5 369 | 49.1 | ... | ... |
| Mauritania<br>Mauritanie | 2002 | 375 695 | 48.8 | 78 730 | 43.1 | 8 173 | 21.3 |
| | 2003 | 394 401 | 49.2 | 84 407 | 44.4 | 8 941 | 21.4[2] |
| | 2004 | 434 181 | 49.4 | 88 926 | 45.3 | 9 292 | 23.7 |
| | 2005 | 443 615 | 50.0 | 92 796 | 45.9 | 8 758 | 24.5 |
| | 2006 | 465 970 | 49.8 | 98 946[1] | 45.0[1] | 10 157 | 25.6 |

**Education at the primary, secondary and tertiary levels**—Number of students enrolled and percentage female (*continued*)

**Enseignement primaire, secondaire et supérieur**—Nombre d'élèves inscrits et pourcentage de sexe feminin (*suite*)

| Country or area<br>Pays ou zone | Year[t]<br>Année[t] | Primary education<br>Enseignement primaire | | Secondary education<br>Enseignement secondaire | | Tertiary education<br>Enseignement supérieur | |
|---|---|---|---|---|---|---|---|
| | | Total | % F | Total | % F | Total | % F |
| Mauritius | 2002 | 132 432 | 49.4 | 111 766 | 49.4 | 12 602 | 55.8 |
| Maurice | 2003 | 129 616 | 49.4 | 118 234 | 49.2 | 16 764 | 57.9 |
| | 2004 | 126 226 | 49.3 | 122 556 | 49.0 | 17 781 | 57.6 |
| | 2005 | 123 562 | 49.2 | 127 891[1] | 49.1[1] | 16 852 | 55.3 |
| | 2006 | 121 387 | 49.2 | ... | ... | 16 773 | 52.9 |
| Mexico | 2002 | 14 843 381 | 48.8 | 9 692 976 | 50.9 | 2 147 075 | 49.3 |
| Mexique | 2003 | 14 857 191 | 48.8 | 10 188 185 | 51.5 | 2 236 791 | 49.6 |
| | 2004 | 14 781 327 | 48.8 | 10 403 853 | 51.2 | 2 322 781 | 50.0 |
| | 2005 | 14 700 005 | 48.8 | 10 564 404 | 51.2 | 2 384 858 | 50.3 |
| | 2006 | 14 595 195 | 48.7 | 10 883 455 | 51.3 | 2 446 726 | 50.3 |
| Micronesia (Fed. States of) | 2004 | 19 105 | 48.3 | 13 506 | 48.8 | ... | ... |
| Micronésie (Etats féd. de) | 2005 | 18 793 | 48.1 | 13 634 | 49.3 | ... | ... |
| | 2007 | 18 512 | 49.0 | 14 742[1] | ... | ... | ... |
| Moldova | 2002 | 227 470 | 48.7 | 413 916 | 49.9 | 107 731 | 56.6 |
| Moldova | 2003 | 215 442 | 48.7 | 410 590 | 50.0 | 114 238 | 56.4 |
| | 2004 | 201 650 | 48.6 | 406 716 | 50.3 | 119 981 | 56.9 |
| | 2005 | 184 159 | 48.5 | 394 469 | 50.1 | 130 350 | 58.7 |
| | 2006 | 171 024 | 48.6 | 381 543 | 50.1 | 143 750 | 57.4 |
| Monaco<br>Monaco | 2004 | 1 831 | ... | 3 078 | ... | ... | ... |
| Mongolia | 2002 | 241 258 | 50.0 | 282 089 | 53.9 | 90 275 | 63.2 |
| Mongolie | 2003 | 238 676 | 49.6 | 312 774 | 53.1 | 98 031 | 62.4 |
| | 2004 | 235 730 | 49.4 | 333 193 | 52.5 | 108 738 | 61.8 |
| | 2005 | 251 205 | 49.5 | 339 249 | 52.4 | 123 824 | 61.4 |
| | 2006 | 249 622 | 49.5 | 329 269 | 52.1 | 138 019 | 60.7 |
| Montserrat | 2002 | 456 | 45.2 | 301 | 48.2 | ... | ... |
| Montserrat | 2003[1] | 465 | 45.2 | 285 | 49.5 | ... | ... |
| | 2004 | 468 | 44.7 | 284 | 48.9 | ... | ... |
| | 2005 | 509 | 46.2 | 298 | 49.3 | ... | ... |
| | 2006 | 508 | 45.9 | 328 | 46.3 | ... | ... |
| Morocco | 2002 | 4 029 112 | 46.2 | 1 685 063[1] | 44.0[1] | 315 343[1] | 43.7[1] |
| Maroc | 2003 | 4 101 157 | 46.4 | 1 758 057 | 44.5 | 335 755 | 44.9 |
| | 2004 | 4 070 182 | 46.5 | 1 879 483 | 44.8 | 343 599 | 45.7 |
| | 2005 | 4 022 600 | 46.4 | 1 952 456[1] | 45.1[1] | 366 879 | 45.1 |
| | 2006 | 3 943 831 | 46.3 | 2 061 046 | ... | 384 595 | 45.2 |
| Mozambique | 2002 | 3 023 321 | 44.1 | 180 531 | 39.6 | ... | ... |
| Mozambique | 2003 | ... | ... | ... | ... | 17 225 | 32.2 |
| | 2004 | 3 569 473 | 45.3 | 243 428 | 41.1 | 22 256 | 31.6 |
| | 2005 | 3 942 829 | 45.7 | 305 877 | 40.8 | 28 298 | 33.1 |
| | 2006 | 4 172 749 | 46.2 | 367 395 | 41.8 | ... | ... |
| Myanmar | 2002 | 4 778 851 | 49.6 | 2 372 593 | 48.1 | 555 060[1] | ... |
| Myanmar | 2003 | 4 889 325 | 49.7 | 2 382 608 | 48.1 | ... | ... |
| | 2004 | 4 932 646 | 49.7 | 2 544 437 | 48.0 | ... | ... |
| | 2005 | 4 948 198 | 49.9 | 2 589 312 | 49.1 | ... | ... |
| | 2006 | 4 969 445 | 49.6 | 2 696 307 | 49.3 | ... | ... |
| Namibia | 2002 | 404 783 | 50.1 | 138 099 | 52.7 | 11 030 | 57.9 |
| Namibie | 2003 | 408 912 | 49.9 | 140 976 | 52.9 | 11 788 | 53.2 |
| | 2004 | 403 412 | 50.0 | 144 289 | 53.0 | 12 197 | 53.2 |
| | 2005 | 404 198 | 49.8 | 148 104 | 53.1 | 13 566 | 46.7 |
| | 2006 | 402 529 | 49.8 | 152 637 | 53.4 | 13 185 | 46.7 |

13    Education at the primary, secondary and tertiary levels — Number of students enrolled and percentage female (*continued*)

Enseignement primaire, secondaire et supérieur — Nombre d'élèves inscrits et pourcentage de sexe feminin (*suite*)

| Country or area Pays ou zone | Year[t] Année[t] | Primary education Enseignement primaire | | Secondary education Enseignement secondaire | | Tertiary education Enseignement supérieur | |
|---|---|---|---|---|---|---|---|
| | | Total | % F | Total | % F | Total | % F |
| Nauru Nauru | 2002 | 1 324 | 49.8 | 573 | 53.6 | ... | ... |
| | 2003 | 1 375 | 46.8 | 645 | 50.4 | ... | ... |
| | 2004 | 1 529 | 47.4 | 508 | 52.4 | ... | ... |
| | 2005 | 1 812 | 48.2 | 600 | 50.7 | ... | ... |
| | 2006 | 1 393 | 47.1 | 815 | 51.7 | ... | ... |
| | 2007 | 1 235 | 48.6 | 689 | 51.4 | ... | ... |
| Nepal Népal | 2002 | 3 853 618 | 44.8 | 1 690 198 | 41.0 | 119 670 | 20.6 |
| | 2003 | 3 928 684 | 45.4 | 1 822 063 | 41.9 | 124 817 | 24.1 |
| | 2004 | 4 025 692 | 45.4 | ... | ... | 147 123 | 27.6 |
| | 2005 | 4 030 045 | 46.3 | 2 054 165 | 44.7[1] | ... | ... |
| | 2006 | 4 502 697 | 47.4 | 1 983 561[1] | 45.5[1] | ... | ... |
| Netherlands Pays-Bas | 2002 | 1 287 069 | 48.3 | 1 397 939 | 48.2 | 516 769 | 50.7 |
| | 2003 | 1 290 625 | 48.2 | 1 415 170 | 48.6 | 526 767 | 51.0 |
| | 2004 | 1 283 014 | 48.2 | 1 396 696 | 48.5 | 543 396 | 50.9 |
| | 2005 | 1 277 990 | 48.2 | 1 410 547 | 48.4 | 564 983 | 51.0 |
| | 2006 | 1 277 478 | 48.2 | 1 423 262 | 48.4 | 579 622 | 51.1 |
| Netherlands Antilles Antilles néerlandaises | 2002 | 22 924 | 49.2 | 15 093 | 52.2 | 2 285 | 59.7 |
| | 2003[1] | 22 667 | 49.2 | 15 268 | 52.1 | ... | ... |
| New Zealand Nouvelle-Zélande | 2002 | 361 866 | 48.4[1] | 482 959 | 51.6 | 185 099 | 58.8 |
| | 2003 | 356 442 | 48.5 | 503 706 | 51.3 | 195 511 | 58.6 |
| | 2004 | 353 062 | 48.5 | 503 241 | 50.3 | 243 425 | 58.4 |
| | 2005 | 352 845 | 48.5 | 526 152 | 50.2 | 239 983 | 58.7 |
| | 2006 | 350 810 | 48.6 | 522 325 | 49.8 | 237 784 | 59.0 |
| Nicaragua Nicaragua | 2002 | 923 391 | 48.9 | 382 951 | 53.3 | 100 363 | 52.2 |
| | 2003 | 927 217 | 48.7 | 412 343[1] | 52.7[1] | 103 577[1] | 52.1[1] |
| | 2004 | 941 957 | 48.6 | 416 405 | 52.7 | ... | ... |
| | 2005 | 945 089 | 48.4 | 437 853 | 52.7 | ... | ... |
| | 2006 | 966 206 | 48.4 | 448 258 | 52.6 | ... | ... |
| Niger Niger | 2002 | 760 987 | 39.8 | 112 033 | 38.5 | ... | ... |
| | 2003 | 857 592 | 40.1 | 126 137 | 38.9 | 8 596[1] | 27.4[1] |
| | 2004 | 980 033 | 40.3 | 158 343 | 38.5 | 8 774 | 27.4 |
| | 2005 | 1 064 056 | 40.8 | 181 641 | 39.1 | 10 799 | 29.6 |
| | 2006 | 1 127 156 | 41.0 | 216 961 | 38.8 | 11 208 | 26.6 |
| Nigeria Nigéria | 2003[1] | 20 936 749 | 44.4 | ... | ... | 1 234 219 | 34.6 |
| | 2004 | 21 110 003 | 44.7 | 6 316 302 | 43.7 | 1 289 656 | 34.6 |
| | 2005 | 22 267 407 | 44.9 | 6 397 581 | 44.6 | 1 391 527 | 40.7 |
| Niue Nioué | 2002 | 251 | ... | 240 | ... | ... | ... |
| | 2004 | 184 | 51.1 | 209 | 50.7 | ... | ... |
| | 2005 | 178 | 50.6 | 206 | 48.1 | ... | ... |
| Norway Norvège | 2002 | 429 445 | 48.7 | 373 015 | 49.3 | 197 064 | 59.6 |
| | 2003 | 432 618 | 48.6 | 385 009 | 49.3 | 212 395 | 59.7 |
| | 2004 | 432 345 | 48.7 | 400 159 | 49.5 | 213 845 | 59.6 |
| | 2005 | 429 652 | 48.7 | 403 026 | 48.9 | 213 940 | 59.6 |
| | 2006 | 429 680 | 48.8 | 412 311 | 48.5 | 214 711 | 59.7 |
| Occupied Palestinian Terr. Terr. palestinien occupé | 2002 | 402 370 | 49.0 | 544 935 | 50.3 | 88 930 | 47.9 |
| | 2003 | 401 372 | 49.0 | 582 736 | 50.2 | 104 567 | 49.5 |
| | 2004 | 388 948 | 48.9 | 628 495 | 50.1 | 121 928 | 49.5 |
| | 2005 | 387 138 | 48.8 | 656 797 | 50.1 | 138 139 | 49.5 |
| | 2006 | 381 904 | 49.0 | 685 585 | 50.3 | 169 375 | 53.6 |
| Oman Oman | 2002 | 316 633 | 48.3 | 266 923 | 48.6 | 36 204[1] | 41.0[1] |
| | 2003 | 314 064 | 48.5 | 279 302 | 48.1 | 36 826 | 41.5 |
| | 2004 | 306 210 | 48.6 | 286 413 | 47.9 | 41 578 | 51.8 |
| | 2005 | 297 120 | 48.8 | 292 783 | 47.7 | 48 483 | 50.8 |
| | 2006 | 287 938 | 48.9 | 299 484 | 47.8 | 68 154 | 49.9 |

| Country or area / Pays ou zone | Year[t] / Année[t] | Primary education / Enseignement primaire | | Secondary education / Enseignement secondaire | | Tertiary education / Enseignement supérieur | |
|---|---|---|---|---|---|---|---|
| | | Total | % F | Total | % F | Total | % F |
| Pakistan | 2002 | 14 489 107[2] | 39.1[1] | ... | ... | 385 506[1] | 43.2[1] |
| Pakistan | 2003 | 15 093 960 | 40.6 | 7 307 218[1] | 42.6 | 401 056 | 43.2 |
| | 2004 | 16 207 286 | 40.8 | 8 249 163[1] | 42.3 | 520 666 | 42.7 |
| | 2005 | 17 257 947 | 41.8 | 7 994 299[1] | 42.3 | 782 621 | 45.1 |
| | 2006 | 16 687 658 | 42.4 | 8 421 015 | 42.3 | 820 347 | 44.5 |
| Palau | 2002[1] | ... | ... | ... | ... | 484 | 63.4 |
| Palaos | 2003[1] | 1 809 | 43.6 | 2 465 | 52.2 | ... | ... |
| | 2004 | 1 855 | 48.0 | 2 273 | 50.4 | ... | ... |
| | 2005[1] | 1 913 | 48.1 | 2 282 | ... | ... | ... |
| Panama | 2002 | 419 904 | 48.2 | 251 228 | 50.7 | 117 601 | 62.1 |
| Panama | 2003 | 424 500[1] | 48.2[1] | 253 012[1] | 50.7[1] | 130 026 | 60.6 |
| | 2004 | 429 837 | 48.3 | 253 900 | 50.8 | 128 558 | 61.6 |
| | 2005 | 430 152 | 48.2 | 256 224 | 50.8 | 126 242 | 61.2 |
| | 2006 | 436 945 | 48.3 | 257 378 | 51.0 | 130 838 | 60.9 |
| Papua New Guinea | 2002 | 514 735 | 44.4 | ... | ... | ... | ... |
| Papouasie-Nvl-Guinée | 2003 | 496 616 | 44.6 | ... | ... | ... | ... |
| | 2004 | 508 333 | 44.9 | ... | ... | ... | ... |
| | 2005 | 531 759 | 44.4 | ... | ... | ... | ... |
| | 2006 | 532 250 | 44.3 | ... | ... | ... | ... |
| Paraguay | 2002 | 962 661 | 48.2 | 519 930 | 49.7[1] | 146 892[1] | 57.6[1] |
| Paraguay | 2003 | 935 722 | 48.3 | 510 881 | 49.6 | 143 913[1] | 57.2[1] |
| | 2004 | 930 918 | 48.4 | 526 001 | 49.7 | 149 120[1] | 56.6[1] |
| | 2005 | 933 995 | 48.4 | 529 309 | 49.9 | 156 167[1] | 52.3[1] |
| Peru | 2002 | 4 283 046 | 49.1 | 2 539 682 | 47.5 | 831 345[1] | 51.1[1] |
| Pérou | 2003 | 4 200 489 | 49.0 | 2 605 247 | 49.4 | 839 584[1] | 51.1[1] |
| | 2004 | 4 133 386 | 49.0 | 2 661 880 | 49.6 | 896 501[1] | 50.0[1] |
| | 2005 | 4 077 361 | 49.1 | 2 691 311 | 49.6 | 909 315[1] | 50.0[1] |
| | 2006 | 4 026 316 | 49.0 | 2 760 349 | 49.8 | 952 437[1] | 50.9[1] |
| Philippines | 2002 | 12 826 218 | 48.7 | 5 816 699 | 51.4 | 2 467 267 | 55.6 |
| Philippines | 2003 | 12 970 635 | 48.6 | 6 069 063 | 51.5 | 2 427 211 | 55.3 |
| | 2004 | 13 017 973 | 48.5 | 6 308 792 | 51.6 | 2 420 997 | 55.2 |
| | 2005 | 13 083 744 | 48.6 | 6 352 482 | 51.7 | 2 402 649 | 54.2 |
| | 2006 | 13 006 648 | 48.5 | 6 301 582 | 51.6 | 2 483 988 | 54.5 |
| Poland | 2002 | 3 105 262 | 48.5 | 3 949 993 | 48.1 | 1 906 268 | 57.9 |
| Pologne | 2003 | 2 983 070 | 48.6 | 3 895 167 | 47.8 | 1 983 360 | 57.8 |
| | 2004 | 2 855 692 | 48.6 | 3 480 054 | 49.1 | 2 044 298 | 57.6 |
| | 2005 | 2 723 661 | 48.6 | 3 444 903 | 48.6 | 2 118 081 | 57.5 |
| | 2006 | 2 602 020 | 48.6 | 3 316 939 | 48.4 | 2 145 687 | 57.4 |
| Portugal | 2002 | 769 910 | 47.8 | 797 065 | ... | 396 601 | 57.0 |
| Portugal | 2003 | 767 872 | 47.5 | 766 172 | 51.0 | 400 831 | 56.6 |
| | 2004 | 758 476 | 47.5 | 665 213 | 51.4 | 395 063 | 56.1 |
| | 2005 | 752 739 | 47.6 | 669 529 | 51.2 | 380 937 | 55.7 |
| | 2006 | 750 493 | 47.6 | 661 748 | 51.0 | 367 312 | 55.2 |
| Qatar | 2002 | 64 255 | 47.9 | 49 042 | 49.7 | 7 831 | 72.5 |
| Qatar | 2003 | 66 473 | 48.3 | 51 888 | 49.5 | 7 826 | 72.8 |
| | 2004 | 65 351 | 48.5 | 53 953 | 48.9 | 9 287 | 71.4 |
| | 2005 | 69 991 | 48.7 | 55 705 | 49.4 | 9 760 | 68.0 |
| | 2006 | 70 927 | 48.8 | 58 787 | 49.2 | 10 161[1] | 67.6[1] |
| Romania | 2002 | 1 028 697 | 48.3 | 2 254 849 | 49.4 | 582 221 | 54.4 |
| Roumanie | 2003 | 990 807 | 48.3 | 2 218 124 | 49.4 | 643 911 | 54.3 |
| | 2004 | 1 005 533 | 48.3 | 2 154 734 | 49.3 | 685 718 | 54.8 |
| | 2005 | 970 295 | 48.4 | 2 089 646 | 49.2 | 738 806 | 54.6 |
| | 2006 | 938 095 | 48.4 | 2 013 016 | 49.0 | 834 969 | 55.4 |

| Country or area | Year[t] | Primary education | | Secondary education | | Tertiary education | |
| Pays ou zone | Année[t] | Enseignement primaire | | Enseignement secondaire | | Enseignement supérieur | |
| | | Total | % F | Total | % F | Total | % F |
|---|---|---|---|---|---|---|---|
| Russian Federation | 2002 | 5 554 607 | 48.6 | ... | ... | ... | ... |
| Fédération de Russie | 2003 | 5 416 925 | 48.7 | 14 521 818 | 48.9 | 8 099 662 | 56.8 |
| | 2004 | ... | ... | 13 558 904 | 48.8 | 8 605 952 | 57.0 |
| | 2005 | 5 308 605 | 48.8 | 12 433 155 | 48.7 | 9 003 208 | 57.1 |
| | 2006 | 5 164 735 | 48.9 | 11 548 337 | 48.5 | 9 167 277 | 56.9 |
| Rwanda | 2002 | 1 534 510 | 50.3 | ... | ... | 15 940 | 34.1 |
| Rwanda | 2003 | 1 636 563 | 50.5 | 189 153 | 47.5 | 20 393 | 36.8 |
| | 2004 | 1 752 588 | 50.8 | 203 551 | 47.7 | 25 233 | 39.1 |
| | 2005[1] | 1 851 879 | 51.3 | 203 822 | 47.6 | 26 378 | 39.0 |
| | 2006 | 2 019 991 | 51.3 | ... | ... | ... | ... |
| Saint Kitts and Nevis | 2002 | 6 440 | 49.3 | 4 240 | 50.9 | ... | ... |
| Saint-Kitts-et-Nevis | 2003 | 6 401 | 49.0 | 4 098 | 52.6 | ... | ... |
| | 2004 | 6 394 | 50.2 | 3 903[1] | 52.0[1] | ... | ... |
| | 2005 | 6 350 | 49.8 | 3 939[1] | 50.7[1] | ... | ... |
| | 2007 | 6 196 | 53.6 | 4 521 | 49.5 | ... | ... |
| Saint Lucia | 2002 | 24 954 | 48.9 | 12 743 | 56.9 | ... | ... |
| Sainte-Lucie | 2003 | 24 573 | 48.4 | 14 110[1] | 53.1[1] | 2 051[1] | 67.7[1] |
| | 2004 | 23 821 | 48.3 | 14 209 | 52.6 | 2 285 | 77.8 |
| | 2005 | 23 573 | 48.6 | 13 786 | 54.3 | 2 197 | 73.8 |
| | 2006 | 24 046 | 47.8 | 14 377 | 53.9 | 1 628 | 84.6 |
| St. Vincent-Grenadines | 2002 | 18 130 | 48.4 | 9 920 | 52.4 | ... | ... |
| St. Vincent-Grenadines | 2003 | 18 629 | 48.7 | 9 624 | 52.0 | ... | ... |
| | 2004 | 17 536 | 48.4 | 10 398 | 51.5[1] | ... | ... |
| | 2005 | 17 858 | 47.0 | 9 780 | 55.2 | ... | ... |
| | 2007 | 15 058 | 51.1 | ... | ... | ... | ... |
| Samoa | 2002 | 30 164 | 47.9 | 22 941 | 50.3 | ... | ... |
| Samoa | 2003 | 31 059 | 47.8 | 23 427 | 50.7 | ... | ... |
| | 2004 | 31 175 | 48.0 | 23 764 | 50.6 | ... | ... |
| | 2005[1] | 31 596 | 47.9 | 24 242 | 50.7 | ... | ... |
| San Marino | | | | | | | |
| Saint-Marin | 2004 | 1 445 | ... | ... | ... | ... | ... |
| Sao Tome and Principe | 2002[1] | 28 780 | 48.3 | 7 367 | 45.4 | ... | ... |
| Sao Tomé-et-Principe | 2003 | 29 347 | 48.5 | 6 753 | 53.5 | ... | ... |
| | 2004 | 29 784 | 48.7 | 7 423 | 50.5 | ... | ... |
| | 2005 | 30 468 | 48.6 | 8 091 | 51.1 | ... | ... |
| | 2006[1] | 31 066 | 48.6 | 8 142 | 51.2 | ... | ... |
| | 2007 | 31 397 | 49.3 | ... | ... | ... | ... |
| Saudi Arabia | 2002[1] | ... | ... | ... | ... | 444 800 | 58.8 |
| Arabie saoudite | 2003 | ... | ... | ... | ... | 525 344 | 58.2 |
| | 2004 | ... | ... | ... | ... | 573 732 | 58.7 |
| | 2005 | ... | ... | ... | ... | 603 671 | 58.1 |
| | 2006[1] | ... | ... | ... | ... | 614 870 | 58.6 |
| Senegal | 2002 | 1 197 081 | 47.1 | 289 263 | 39.9 | ... | ... |
| Sénégal | 2003 | 1 287 093 | 47.5 | 309 959 | 40.6 | 50 375[1] | ... |
| | 2004 | 1 382 749 | 48.3 | 360 016 | 41.6 | 52 282 | ... |
| | 2005 | 1 444 163 | 48.6 | 405 899 | 42.5 | 59 127[1] | ... |
| | 2006 | 1 473 464 | 49.2 | 447 425[1] | 42.8 | ... | ... |
| Serbia | 2002 | 342 611[1] | 48.6 | 668 319[1] | 49.5 | ... | ... |
| Serbie | 2003 | 334 771[1] | 48.9 | 655 904[1] | 49.7 | ... | ... |
| | 2004 | 328 439[1] | 48.8 | 641 743[1] | 49.5 | ... | ... |
| | 2005 | 324 490 | 48.8 | 632 761 | 49.5 | ... | ... |
| | 2006 | 312 469 | 48.8 | 622 854 | 49.6 | ... | ... |
| | 2007 | 297 429 | 48.8 | 615 522 | 49.4 | ... | ... |

| Country or area<br>Pays ou zone | Year[t]<br>Année[t] | Primary education<br>Enseignement primaire | | Secondary education<br>Enseignement secondaire | | Tertiary education<br>Enseignement supérieur | |
|---|---|---|---|---|---|---|---|
| | | Total | % F | Total | % F | Total | % F |
| Seychelles<br>Seychelles | 2002 | 9 623 | 48.8 | 7 525 | 49.9 | ... | ... |
| | 2003 | 9 477 | 48.6 | 7 551 | 50.2 | ... | ... |
| | 2004 | 8 906 | 48.8 | 7 406 | 50.7 | ... | ... |
| | 2005 | 9 204 | 48.3 | 7 520 | 48.2 | ... | ... |
| | 2007 | 8 864 | 49.3 | 7 816 | 50.1 | ... | ... |
| Sierra Leone<br>Sierra Leone | 2002[1] | ... | ... | ... | ... | 9 041 | 28.8 |
| | 2007 | 1 322 205 | 47.5 | 239 579 | 41.0 | ... | ... |
| Singapore<br>Singapour | 2002 | 302 501 | 48.3 | ... | ... | ... | ... |
| | 2003 | 299 939 | 48.2 | ... | ... | ... | ... |
| | 2004 | 296 419 | 48.2 | 213 534 | 48.3 | ... | ... |
| | 2005 | 290 261 | 48.2 | 213 063 | 48.3 | ... | ... |
| | 2006 | 284 600 | 48.1 | 215 097 | 48.3 | ... | ... |
| Slovakia<br>Slovaquie | 2002 | 284 312 | 48.7 | 666 238 | 49.2 | 152 182 | 52.1 |
| | 2003 | 270 004 | 48.5 | 669 578 | 49.1 | 158 089 | 53.1 |
| | 2004 | 254 906 | 48.5 | 682 780 | 49.3 | 164 667 | 54.1 |
| | 2005 | 242 459 | 48.5 | 672 670 | 49.2 | 181 419 | 55.3 |
| | 2006 | 235 378 | 48.5 | 640 120 | 49.1 | 197 943 | 57.7 |
| Slovenia<br>Slovénie | 2002 | 86 021 | 48.5 | 220 804 | 48.9 | 99 214 | 57.5 |
| | 2003 | 87 085 | 48.5 | 217 587 | 48.6 | 101 458 | 56.2 |
| | 2004 | 93 371 | 48.6 | 187 817 | 48.8 | 104 396 | 56.9 |
| | 2005 | 93 156 | 48.4 | 181 299 | 48.7 | 112 228 | 57.8 |
| | 2006 | 93 274 | 48.4 | 174 330 | 48.7 | 114 794 | 58.4 |
| Solomon Islands<br>Iles Salomon | 2002 | 66 480 | 46.5 | 21 700 | 42.9 | ... | ... |
| | 2003[1] | 68 146 | 46.5 | 21 885 | 42.8 | ... | ... |
| | 2004[1] | 70 906 | 46.8 | 22 157 | 43.5 | ... | ... |
| | 2005 | 75 082 | 46.8 | 22 487 | 43.5 | ... | ... |
| South Africa<br>Afrique du Sud | 2002 | 7 465 728 | 48.9 | 4 353 817 | 51.7 | 675 160 | 53.7 |
| | 2003 | 7 470 476 | 48.8 | 4 446 841 | 51.5 | 717 793 | 53.8 |
| | 2004 | 7 444 142 | 48.7 | 4 593 492 | 51.5 | 744 489 | 54.2 |
| | 2005 | ... | ... | ... | ... | 735 073 | 54.6 |
| | 2006 | ... | ... | ... | ... | 741 380 | 55.1 |
| Spain<br>Espagne | 2002 | 2 490 744 | 48.3 | 3 106 777 | 50.2 | 1 832 760 | 53.1 |
| | 2003 | 2 488 319 | 48.3 | 3 052 662 | 50.0 | 1 840 607 | 53.1 |
| | 2004 | 2 497 513 | 48.4 | 3 048 188 | 50.2 | 1 839 903 | 53.8 |
| | 2005 | 2 484 903 | 48.3 | 3 107 816 | 50.1 | 1 809 353 | 53.7 |
| | 2006 | 2 501 205 | 48.3 | 3 091 036 | 50.1 | 1 789 254 | 53.9 |
| Sri Lanka[1]<br>Sri Lanka[1] | 2002 | 1 764 300 | 48.9 | 2 344 960 | 50.7 | ... | ... |
| | 2003 | 1 702 035 | 49.1 | 2 320 093 | 50.6 | ... | ... |
| | 2004 | 1 612 318 | ... | 2 332 326 | 49.4 | ... | ... |
| | 2005 | 1 635 308 | 49.1 | ... | ... | ... | ... |
| Sudan<br>Soudan | 2002 | 2 889 062 | 45.1 | 1 172 732 | 47.8 | ... | ... |
| | 2003 | 3 028 127 | 45.5 | 1 278 633 | 47.1 | ... | ... |
| | 2004 | 3 208 186 | 45.5 | 1 393 778 | 47.1 | ... | ... |
| | 2005 | 3 278 090 | 45.6 | 1 369 735 | 47.5 | ... | ... |
| | 2006 | 3 880 705 | 45.6 | 1 446 539 | 48.1 | ... | ... |
| Suriname<br>Suriname | 2002 | 64 023 | 48.7 | 42 253 | 57.2 | 5 186 | 62.0 |
| | 2003[1] | 64 659 | 48.7 | 41 000 | 56.3 | ... | ... |
| | 2005 | 65 527 | 48.3 | 45 818 | 55.8 | ... | ... |
| | 2006 | 66 121 | 48.3 | 46 725 | 56.3 | ... | ... |
| Swaziland<br>Swaziland | 2002 | 209 037 | 48.1 | 62 676 | 50.4 | 5 193 | 54.6 |
| | 2003 | 208 444 | 48.5 | 62 401 | 50.2 | 5 369[1] | 54.4[1] |
| | 2004 | 218 352 | 48.1 | 67 696 | 49.1 | 6 594 | 52.4 |
| | 2005 | 221 596 | 48.0 | 71 124 | 49.9 | 5 897 | 52.0 |
| | 2006 | ... | ... | ... | ... | 5 692 | 49.8 |

13 Education at the primary, secondary and tertiary levels—Number of students enrolled and percentage female (*continued*)

Enseignement primaire, secondaire et supérieur—Nombre d'élèves inscrits et pourcentage de sexe feminin (*suite*)

| Country or area Pays ou zone | Year[t] Année[t] | Primary education Enseignement primaire | | Secondary education Enseignement secondaire | | Tertiary education Enseignement supérieur | |
|---|---|---|---|---|---|---|---|
| | | Total | % F | Total | % F | Total | % F |
| Sweden | 2002 | 785 774 | 49.4 | 934 608 | 53.5 | 382 851 | 59.5 |
| Suède | 2003 | 774 888 | 49.4 | 917 978 | 52.9 | 414 657 | 59.6 |
| | 2004 | 690 758 | 48.6 | 711 798 | 49.5 | 429 623 | 59.6 |
| | 2005 | 658 461 | 48.7 | 735 494 | 48.6 | 426 723 | 59.6 |
| | 2006 | 626 847 | 48.7 | 750 567 | 48.5 | 422 614 | 59.6 |
| Switzerland | 2002 | 536 423 | 48.6 | 550 317 | 47.2 | 170 085 | 43.3 |
| Suisse | 2003 | 535 577 | 48.6 | 555 505 | 47.3 | 185 965 | 44.2 |
| | 2004 | 532 092 | 48.5 | 563 701 | 47.2 | 195 947 | 44.9 |
| | 2005 | 524 222 | 48.6 | 574 783 | 47.3 | 199 696 | 46.0 |
| | 2006 | 517 056 | 48.5 | 584 073 | 47.3 | 204 999 | 46.9 |
| Syrian Arab Republic | 2002 | 2 904 569 | 47.2 | 1 182 424 | 46.6 | ... | ... |
| Rép. arabe syrienne | 2003 | 2 149 493 | 47.5 | 2 119 690 | 47.1 | ... | ... |
| | 2004 | 2 192 764 | 47.6 | 2 249 116 | 47.2 | ... | ... |
| | 2005 | 2 252 145 | 47.8 | 2 389 383 | 47.4 | ... | ... |
| | 2006 | 2 279 545 | 47.8 | 2 464 688 | 47.7 | ... | ... |
| Tajikistan | 2002 | 684 542 | 48.1 | 899 236 | 44.5 | 85 171 | 24.5 |
| Tadjikistan | 2003 | 694 930 | 48.0 | 948 341 | 44.8 | 97 466 | 25.0 |
| | 2004 | 690 270 | 48.0 | 973 673 | 45.1 | 108 456 | 24.8 |
| | 2005 | 693 078 | 48.2 | 984 410 | 44.8 | 119 317 | 25.9 |
| | 2006 | 687 900 | 48.0 | 998 928 | 44.7 | 133 385 | 26.8 |
| Thailand | 2002 | 6 056 420 | 48.3 | 4 150 184[1] | 49.2[1] | 2 155 334 | 52.1 |
| Thaïlande | 2003[1] | 5 997 390 | 48.3 | 4 128 232 | 49.2 | 2 205 581 | 52.9 |
| | 2004 | 6 054 517 | 48.4 | 4 253 380 | 50.9 | 2 251 453 | 53.7 |
| | 2005 | 5 974 615 | 48.1 | 4 533 173 | 50.5[1] | 2 359 127 | 52.4 |
| | 2006 | 5 843 512 | 48.4 | 4 530 029 | 50.8 | 2 338 572 | 51.0 |
| TFYR of Macedonia | 2002 | 121 109 | 48.8 | 218 834 | 48.0 | 44 710 | 55.2 |
| L'ex-R.y. Macédoine | 2003 | 116 635 | 48.4 | 218 649 | 48.1 | 45 624 | 56.2 |
| | 2004 | 113 362 | 48.4 | 215 760 | 48.0 | 46 637 | 57.0 |
| | 2005 | 110 149 | 48.3 | 214 005 | 48.0 | 49 364 | 56.7 |
| Timor-Leste | 2002 | 183 626 | ... | 46 680 | ... | 6 349[2] | 52.9[2] |
| Timor-Leste | 2003 | 183 800 | ... | ... | ... | ... | ... |
| | 2004 | 183 483 | 47.1 | 73 005 | 48.1 | ... | ... |
| | 2005 | 177 970 | 46.9 | 74 822 | 48.7 | ... | ... |
| Togo | 2002 | 977 534 | 44.9 | ... | ... | ... | ... |
| Togo | 2003 | 975 063 | 45.2 | 353 781[1] | 32.3[1] | ... | ... |
| | 2004 | 984 846 | 45.6 | 375 385 | 33.2 | ... | ... |
| | 2005 | 996 707 | 45.9 | 399 038[1] | 33.7[1] | ... | ... |
| | 2006 | 1 051 872 | 46.3 | ... | ... | ... | ... |
| Tokelau | 2002 | 266 | 45.9 | 202 | 55.9 | ... | ... |
| Tokélaou | 2003 | 227 | 50.2 | 191 | 47.6 | ... | ... |
| | 2004[1] | 243 | 57.2 | 175 | 45.1 | ... | ... |
| Tonga | 2002 | 17 105 | 47.1 | 14 567 | 49.8 | 600 | 60.5[1] |
| Tonga | 2003 | 17 891 | 46.9 | 15 743 | ... | 668 | 60.5 |
| | 2004 | 17 113 | 46.9 | 14 032 | 49.2[1] | 657[1] | 59.8[1] |
| | 2005 | 17 857 | 47.1 | ... | ... | ... | ... |
| | 2006 | 16 941 | 47.1 | 13 938 | 48.4 | ... | ... |
| Trinidad and Tobago | 2002 | 141 427[2] | 49.1[2] | 108 778[1] | 51.8[1] | 12 036 | 59.5 |
| Trinité-et-Tobago | 2003 | 141 036 | 48.6 | 107 880[1] | 51.4[1] | 12 316 | 61.1 |
| | 2004 | 137 313[2] | 48.5[2] | 105 381[1] | 51.1[1] | 16 751 | 55.4 |
| | 2005 | 129 703[2] | 48.6[2] | 97 080[1] | 50.4[1] | 16 920[1] | 55.6[1] |

13  Education at the primary, secondary and tertiary levels—Number of students enrolled and percentage female (*continued*)

Enseignement primaire, secondaire et supérieur—Nombre d'élèves inscrits et pourcentage de sexe feminin (*suite*)

| Country or area<br>Pays ou zone | Year[t]<br>Année[t] | Primary education<br>Enseignement primaire | | Secondary education<br>Enseignement secondaire | | Tertiary education<br>Enseignement supérieur | |
|---|---|---|---|---|---|---|---|
| | | Total | % F | Total | % F | Total | % F |
| Tunisia<br>Tunisie | 2002 | 1 325 707 | 47.6 | 1 169 368 | 49.9 | 226 102 | 53.9 |
| | 2003 | 1 277 124 | 47.7 | 1 148 523 | 50.8 | 263 414 | 54.9 |
| | 2004 | 1 228 347 | 47.7 | 1 210 012 | ... | 291 842 | 56.5 |
| | 2005 | 1 184 301 | 47.7 | 1 239 468 | 51.1 | 311 569 | 57.2 |
| | 2006 | 1 134 414 | 47.7 | 1 247 046 | 51.0[1] | 325 325 | 57.5 |
| Turkey<br>Turquie | 2002 | 8 210 961[1] | 47.2[1] | 5 500 246[1] | 42.5[1] | 1 677 936 | 41.4 |
| | 2003 | 7 904 361[1] | 47.5[1] | 5 742 070[1] | 42.0[1] | 1 918 483 | 42.3 |
| | 2004 | 7 872 546[1] | 47.6[1] | 5 330 923[1] | 42.0[1] | 1 972 662 | 41.4 |
| | 2005 | 7 947 603[1] | 47.7[1] | 5 075 720[1] | 44.2[1] | 2 106 351 | 41.9 |
| | 2006 | 7 949 758[1] | 47.9[1] | 5 388 119[1] | 44.5[1] | 2 342 898 | 42.4 |
| Turks and Caicos Islands<br>Iles Turques et Caïques | 2002 | 2 137 | 48.9 | 1 411[1] | 49.8[1] | ... | ... |
| | 2003 | 1 810 | 48.8 | 1 395[1] | 49.2[1] | ... | ... |
| | 2004 | 2 117 | 50.9 | 1 516 | 48.9 | ... | ... |
| | 2005 | 2 220 | 51.1 | 1 686[1] | 47.8[1] | ... | ... |
| Tuvalu<br>Tuvalu | 2002 | 1 283 | 51.1 | ... | ... | ... | ... |
| | 2003 | 1 344 | 50.5 | ... | ... | ... | ... |
| | 2004 | 1 404 | 49.9 | ... | ... | ... | ... |
| | 2005 | 1 450 | 48.3 | ... | ... | ... | ... |
| | 2006 | 1 460 | 47.9 | ... | ... | ... | ... |
| Uganda<br>Ouganda | 2002 | 7 354 153 | 49.4 | 687 613[1] | 44.5[1] | 71 544[1] | 34.5[1] |
| | 2003 | 7 633 314 | 49.3 | 716 736[1] | 44.6[1] | 74 090[1] | 34.5[1] |
| | 2004 | 7 377 292 | 49.4 | 732 792 | 44.4 | 88 360 | 38.4 |
| | 2005 | 7 223 879 | 49.6 | 760 337[1] | 44.5[1] | ... | ... |
| | 2006 | 7 363 721 | 49.8 | ... | ... | ... | ... |
| Ukraine<br>Ukraine | 2002 | 2 047 085 | 48.7 | 4 982 947 | 48.9 | 2 134 676 | 53.4[2] |
| | 2003 | 1 960 512 | 48.7 | 4 824 077 | 48.7 | 2 296 221 | 53.8[2] |
| | 2004 | 1 850 734 | 48.6 | 4 445 974 | 48.5[2] | 2 465 074 | 53.9[2] |
| | 2005 | 1 945 715 | 48.6 | 4 042 827 | ... | 2 604 875 | 54.1 |
| | 2006 | 1 753 689 | 48.6 | 3 896 263 | 48.4[2] | 2 740 342 | 54.2[2] |
| United Arab Emirates<br>Emirats arabes unis | 2002 | 285 744 | 48.1 | 226 407 | 49.9 | 63 419[1] | 66.4[1] |
| | 2003 | 248 370 | 48.3 | 273 491 | 49.4 | 68 182[1] | 66.3[1] |
| | 2004 | 254 602 | 48.3 | 279 496 | 49.1 | ... | ... |
| | 2005 | 262 807 | 48.5 | 284 978 | 48.9 | ... | ... |
| | 2006 | 272 331 | 48.5 | 298 447 | 49.0 | ... | ... |
| United Kingdom<br>Royaume-Uni | 2002 | 4 536 143 | 48.8 | 5 507 398 | 49.1 | 2 240 680 | 55.2 |
| | 2003 | 4 488 162 | 48.8 | 5 530 597 | 49.6 | 2 287 833 | 55.9 |
| | 2004 | 4 685 733 | 48.8 | 5 699 526 | 49.4 | 2 247 441 | 57.0 |
| | 2005 | 4 634 991 | 48.7 | 5 747 422 | 49.3 | 2 287 541 | 57.2 |
| | 2006 | 4 517 618 | 48.9 | 5 357 793 | 49.3 | 2 336 111 | 57.3 |
| United Rep. of Tanzania<br>Rép.-Unie de Tanzanie | 2002 | 5 981 338 | 49.0 | ... | ... | 26 505[1] | 23.5[1] |
| | 2003 | 6 562 772 | 48.7 | ... | ... | 31 049 | 30.7 |
| | 2004 | 7 083 063 | 48.8 | ... | ... | 42 948 | 29.2 |
| | 2005 | 7 541 208 | 48.9 | ... | ... | 51 080[1] | 32.4[1] |
| | 2006 | 7 959 884 | 49.1 | ... | ... | ... | ... |
| | 2007 | 8 316 925 | 49.3 | ... | ... | 55 134 | 32.3 |
| United States<br>Etats-Unis | 2002 | 24 855 480 | 49.0 | 23 196 310 | 48.5 | 15 927 987 | 56.3 |
| | 2003 | 24 848 518 | 48.9 | 23 854 458 | 48.7 | 16 611 711 | 56.6 |
| | 2004 | 24 559 494 | 48.1 | 24 185 786 | 49.2 | 16 900 471 | 57.1 |
| | 2005 | 24 454 602 | 48.5 | 24 431 934 | 49.2 | 17 272 044 | 57.2 |
| | 2006 | 24 319 033 | 49.0 | 24 552 317 | 48.6 | 17 487 475 | 57.4 |

| Country or area | Year[t] | Primary education Enseignement primaire | | Secondary education Enseignement secondaire | | Tertiary education Enseignement supérieur | |
|---|---|---|---|---|---|---|---|
| Pays ou zone | Année[t] | Total | % F | Total | % F | Total | % F |
| Uruguay | 2002 | 364 858 | 48.4 | 332 175 | 52.0 | 98 520[1] | 65.3[1] |
| Uruguay | 2003 | 365 423 | 48.4 | 343 617 | 52.5 | 101 298[1] | 66.3[1] |
| | 2004 | 366 205 | 48.3 | 339 057 | 52.6 | 103 431[1] | 66.2[1] |
| | 2005 | 365 536 | 48.4 | 323 087 | 52.6 | 110 684 | 62.8 |
| | 2006 | 365 388 | 48.3 | 323 027 | 52.8 | 113 368 | 61.9 |
| Uzbekistan | 2002 | 2 567 685 | 48.7 | 3 884 736 | 48.5 | 344 604 | 44.1 |
| Ouzbékistan | 2003 | 2 513 342 | 49.0 | 4 258 787 | 48.3 | 359 708 | 43.2 |
| | 2004 | 2 451 125 | 48.7 | 4 338 358 | 48.1 | 376 904 | 43.6 |
| | 2005 | 2 383 326 | 48.6 | 4 515 852 | 48.4 | 265 957 | 40.7 |
| | 2006 | 2 277 191 | 48.6 | 4 542 174 | 48.5 | 280 837 | 40.9 |
| | 2007 | 2 164 897 | 48.5 | 4 598 037 | 48.7 | 288 550 | 41.0 |
| Vanuatu | 2002 | 37 470 | 48.0 | 12 313 | 47.0 | 895 | 35.4[1] |
| Vanuatu | 2003 | 39 388 | 48.1 | 12 800 | 44.0 | 914 | 36.2 |
| | 2004 | 38 960 | 47.8 | 13 837 | 44.7 | 955[1] | 36.1[1] |
| | 2005 | 38 530 | 47.7 | ... | ... | ... | ... |
| | 2006 | 37 060 | 47.8 | ... | ... | ... | ... |
| | 2007 | 37 518 | 47.6 | ... | ... | ... | ... |
| Venezuela (Bolivarian Republic of) | 2002 | 3 506 780 | 48.5 | 1 811 127 | 52.8 | 927 835 | 51.4[1] |
| Venezuela (République bolivarienne du) | 2003 | 3 449 984 | 48.4 | 1 866 114 | 52.5 | 983 217[1] | 51.0[1] |
| | 2004 | 3 453 379 | 48.4 | 1 953 506 | 52.3 | 1 049 780[1] | ... |
| | 2005 | 3 449 290 | 48.4 | 2 028 388 | 52.1 | ... | ... |
| | 2006 | 3 452 062 | 48.4 | 2 104 857 | 51.9 | 1 381 126[1] | ... |
| Viet Nam | 2002 | 9 336 913 | 47.5 | 8 783 340 | 47.4 | 784 675 | 42.8 |
| Viet Nam | 2003 | 8 841 004 | 47.5 | 9 265 801 | 47.4 | 829 459 | 43.0 |
| | 2004 | 8 350 191 | 47.3 | 9 588 698 | 48.0 | 1 328 485[1] | 40.9[1] |
| | 2005 | 7 773 484 | 47.5 | 9 939 319 | 48.6 | 1 354 543 | 40.9 |
| | 2006 | 7 317 813 | 47.9 | 9 975 113 | 48.8 | ... | ... |
| Yemen | 2002 | 2 783 371 | 38.8 | ... | ... | ... | ... |
| Yémen | 2003 | 2 950 403 | 39.8 | 1 373 362 | 30.1 | ... | ... |
| | 2004 | 3 107 801 | 40.5 | 1 446 369 | 31.2 | 192 071 | 26.2 |
| | 2005 | 3 219 564 | 41.6 | 1 455 206 | 32.1 | 201 043 | 26.1 |
| | 2006[1] | ... | ... | ... | ... | 209 386 | 26.1 |
| Zambia | 2002 | 1 731 579 | 48.1 | 351 442 | 45.2 | ... | ... |
| Zambie | 2004 | 2 251 357 | 48.7 | 363 613 | 44.1 | ... | ... |
| | 2005 | 2 565 419 | 48.4 | 408 971[1] | 44.8[1] | ... | ... |
| | 2006 | 2 678 610 | 49.3 | ... | ... | ... | ... |
| Zimbabwe | 2002 | 2 399 250 | 49.4 | 828 456 | 46.9 | 60 221[1] | 40.8[1] |
| Zimbabwe | 2003 | 2 361 588 | 49.5 | 758 229 | 47.5 | 55 689[1] | 38.8[1] |
| | 2006 | 2 445 520 | 49.6 | 831 488 | 48.1 | ... | ... |

**Source**

United Nations Educational, Scientific and Cultural Organization (UNESCO) Institute for Statistics, Montreal, the UNESCO Institute for Statistics (UIS) database, last accessed May 2008.

**Notes**

[t] Data relate to the calendar year in which the academic year ends.

[1] UIS estimation.

[2] National estimation.

[3] For statistical purposes, the data for China do not include those for the Hong Kong Special Administrative Region (Hong Kong SAR) and Macao Special Administrative Region (Macao SAR).

**Source**

L'Institut de statistique de l'Organisation des Nations Unies pour l'éducation, la science et la culture (UNESCO), Montréal, la base de données de l'institut de statistique de l'UNESCO (ISU), dernier accès mai 2008.

**Notes**

[t] Les données se réfèrent à l'année civile durant laquelle l'année scolaire se termine.

[1] Estimation de l'ISU.

[2] Estimation nationale.

[3] Pour la présentation des statistiques, les données pour la Chine ne comprennent pas la Région Administrative Spéciale de Hong Kong (Hong Kong RAS) et la Région Administrative Spéciale de Macao (Macao RAS).

# 14

## Public expenditure on education: percentage of GNI and government expenditure

## Dépenses publiques afférentes à l'éducation : pourcentage par rapport au RNB et aux dépenses du gouvernement

| Country or area / Pays ou zone | As % of Gross National Income (GNI) En % du Revenu National Brut (RNB) | | | | As % of total government expenditure En % des dépenses totales du gouvernement | | | |
|---|---|---|---|---|---|---|---|---|
| | 2003 | 2004 | 2005 | 2006 | 2003 | 2004 | 2005 | 2006 |
| Andorra Andorre | ... | ... | 1.7 | 2.3 | ... | ... | ... | ... |
| Angola Angola | ... | ... | 2.7 | ... | ... | ... | ... | ... |
| Anguilla Anguilla | ... | ... | 4.0 | ... | ... | ... | 14.0 | ... |
| Argentina Argentine | 3.8 | 4.0 | ... | ... | 12.0 | 13.1 | ... | ... |
| Aruba Aruba | ... | ... | 5.1 | ... | ... | 13.8 | 15.4 | ... |
| Australia Australie | 4.7 | 4.8 | 4.7 | ... | ... | ... | ... | ... |
| Austria Autriche | 5.5 | 5.5 | 5.5 | ... | 10.8 | 10.8 | 10.9 | ... |
| Azerbaijan Azerbaïdjan | 3.5 | 3.6[1] | 2.7 | 2.4 | 19.2 | ... | 19.6 | 17.4 |
| Bangladesh Bangladesh | 2.3 | 2.1 | 2.6 | ... | 15.5 | 14.8 | 14.2 | ... |
| Barbados Barbade | 8.2 | 7.5 | 7.2 | ... | 17.3 | 16.7 | 16.4 | ... |
| Belarus Bélarus | 5.8[1] | 5.7 | 6.0 | 6.2 | ... | 13.0 | 11.3 | 12.9 |
| Belgium Belgique | 6.0 | 6.0 | ... | ... | 11.8 | 12.2 | ... | ... |
| Belize Belize | 5.7 | 5.8 | ... | ... | 18.1 | ... | ... | ... |
| Benin Bénin | ... | 4.4 | ... | ... | ... | 17.1 | ... | ... |
| Bermuda Bermudes | ... | ... | 2.0 | 1.2 | ... | ... | ... | ... |
| Bhutan Bhoutan | ... | ... | 7.2 | ... | ... | ... | 17.2 | ... |
| Bolivia Bolivie | 6.6 | ... | ... | ... | 18.1 | ... | ... | ... |
| Botswana Botswana | ... | ... | 10.9 | ... | ... | ... | 21.5 | ... |
| Brazil Brésil | ... | 4.1 | ... | ... | ... | ... | ... | ... |
| British Virgin Islands Iles Vierges britanniques | ... | ... | 3.3 | 4.0 | ... | 17.8 | 12.5 | ... |
| Bulgaria Bulgarie | 4.2 | 2.4 | 4.5 | ... | ... | 6.2 | ... | ... |
| Burkina Faso Burkina Faso | ... | ... | 4.3 | 4.2 | ... | ... | 16.4 | 15.4 |
| Burundi Burundi | 4.9[1] | 5.3 | 5.2 | ... | ... | 17.3 | 17.7 | ... |
| Cambodia Cambodge | 1.9[1] | 1.8 | ... | ... | ... | ... | ... | ... |
| Cameroon Cameroun | 3.4 | 3.4 | 3.2 | 3.3 | 17.3 | 17.2 | 15.9 | 16.8 |
| Cape Verde Cap-Vert | 7.8[1] | 7.6 | 7.0 | 6.6 | ... | 20.7 | 25.4 | 15.6 |
| Cayman Islands Iles Caïmanes | ... | ... | ... | 2.9 | ... | ... | ... | ... |
| Central African Rep Rép. centrafricaine | ... | ... | ... | 1.4 | ... | ... | ... | ... |

| Country or area<br>Pays ou zone | As % of Gross National Income (GNI)<br>En % du Revenu National Brut (RNB) | | | | As % of total government expenditure<br>En % des dépenses totales du gouvernement | | | |
|---|---|---|---|---|---|---|---|---|
| | 2003 | 2004 | 2005 | 2006 | 2003 | 2004 | 2005 | 2006 |
| Chad<br>Tchad | 2.0 | 1.9 | 2.3 | ... | ... | 7.7 | 10.1 | ... |
| Chile<br>Chili | 4.3 | 3.9 | 3.6 | 3.6 | 17.4 | 16.8 | 16.0 | 16.0 |
| China, Hong Kong SAR<br>Chine, Hong Kong RAS | 4.3 | 4.5 | 4.1 | 3.9 | 23.3 | 23.3 | 23.0 | 23.9 |
| China, Macao SAR<br>Chine, Macao RAS | ... | ... | ... | ... | 15.2 | 14.0 | 14.1 | ... |
| Colombia<br>Colombie | 5.4[1] | 5.1 | 5.0 | 4.9 | ... | 11.7 | 11.1 | ... |
| Congo<br>Congo | 3.7 | 3.3 | 2.5 | ... | 9.9 | 9.0 | 8.1 | ... |
| Costa Rica<br>Costa Rica | 5.3[1] | 5.1 | ... | 4.9 | ... | 18.5 | ... | 20.6 |
| Croatia<br>Croatie | 4.7 | 4.6 | ... | ... | 10.0 | ... | ... | ... |
| Cuba<br>Cuba | ... | ... | ... | 9.3 | ... | 19.4 | 16.6 | 14.2 |
| Cyprus<br>Chypre | 7.6 | 6.5 | ... | ... | 16.2 | 14.4 | 14.5 | ... |
| Czech Republic<br>République tchèque | 4.7 | 4.7 | ... | ... | 9.5 | 10.0 | ... | ... |
| Denmark<br>Danemark | 8.3 | 8.5 | 8.3 | ... | 15.1 | 15.3 | 15.5 | ... |
| Djibouti<br>Djibouti | 8.1 | 8.4 | 7.6 | 7.6 | ... | ... | ... | 22.4 |
| Dominican Republic<br>Rép. dominicaine | 2.5[1] | ... | ... | 3.9 | ... | ... | ... | 16.8 |
| Egypt<br>Egypte | 4.9 | 4.7 | 4.8 | 4.2 | 16.2 | 15.5 | 16.0 | 12.5 |
| El Salvador<br>El Salvador | 2.8 | ... | 2.8 | 3.2 | ... | ... | ... | ... |
| Equatorial Guinea[1]<br>Guinée équatoriale[1] | 1.4 | ... | ... | ... | 4.0 | ... | ... | ... |
| Eritrea<br>Erythrée | 4.1[1] | 3.8 | 5.3 | 2.4 | ... | ... | ... | ... |
| Estonia<br>Estonie | 5.7 | 5.4 | ... | ... | 15.4 | 14.9 | ... | ... |
| Ethiopia<br>Ethiopie | ... | ... | ... | 6.0 | ... | ... | ... | 17.5 |
| Fiji<br>Fidji | 6.5[1] | 6.5 | ... | ... | ... | ... | ... | ... |
| Finland<br>Finlande | 6.6 | 6.6 | 6.4 | ... | 12.8 | 12.8 | 12.5 | ... |
| France<br>France | 5.8 | 5.8 | 5.7 | ... | 11.0 | 10.9 | 10.6 | ... |
| Gambia[1]<br>Gambie[1] | 2.4 | 2.1 | ... | ... | ... | ... | ... | ... |
| Georgia<br>Géorgie | 2.0 | 2.9 | 2.5 | 3.2 | 11.6 | 13.1 | 8.8 | 9.3 |
| Germany<br>Allemagne | 4.7 | 4.6 | ... | ... | 9.7 | 9.8 | ... | ... |
| Ghana<br>Ghana | ... | ... | 5.5 | ... | ... | ... | ... | ... |
| Greece<br>Grèce | 4.0 | 4.3 | 4.4 | ... | 8.0 | 8.5 | 9.2 | ... |
| Grenada<br>Grenade | 6.0 | ... | ... | ... | 12.9 | ... | ... | ... |
| Guatemala<br>Guatemala | ... | ... | ... | 2.6 | ... | ... | ... | ... |

Public expenditure on education: percentage of GNI and government expenditure (*continued*)

Dépenses publiques afférentes à l'èducation : pourcentage par rapport au RNB et aux dépenses du gouvernement (*suite*)

| Country or area | As % of Gross National Income (GNI) En % du Revenu National Brut (RNB) | | | | As % of total government expenditure En % des dépenses totales du gouvernement | | | |
|---|---|---|---|---|---|---|---|---|
| Pays ou zone | 2003 | 2004 | 2005 | 2006 | 2003 | 2004 | 2005 | 2006 |
| Guinea Guinée | ... | 2.0 | 1.7 | ... | ... | ... | ... | ... |
| Guyana Guyana | 7.5[1] | 6.4 | 9.0 | 8.6 | ... | 12.0 | 14.5 | 15.5 |
| Hungary Hongrie | 6.2 | 5.8 | 5.8 | ... | 11.9 | 11.1 | 10.9 | ... |
| Iceland Islande | 8.0 | 7.9 | ... | ... | 16.8 | 16.6 | ... | ... |
| India Inde | 3.7 | 3.8 | 3.3 | ... | 10.7 | ... | ... | ... |
| Indonesia[1] Indonésie[1] | 3.3 | 2.9 | 3.0 | 3.8 | 16.0 | 14.2 | 14.9 | 17.2 |
| Iran (Islamic Rep. of) Iran (Rép. islamique d') | 4.9 | 5.0 | 4.8 | 5.2 | 17.7 | 17.9 | 22.8 | 18.6 |
| Ireland Irlande | 5.2 | 5.6 | 5.6 | ... | 13.2 | 14.0 | 13.9 | ... |
| Israel Israël | 7.5 | 7.1 | ... | ... | 13.7 | ... | ... | ... |
| Italy Italie | 4.8 | 4.6 | 4.5 | ... | 9.8 | 9.6 | 9.2 | ... |
| Jamaica Jamaïque | 5.2 | 4.7 | 5.6 | ... | 9.5 | ... | 8.8 | ... |
| Japan Japon | 3.7 | 3.6 | 3.5 | ... | 9.7 | 9.8 | 9.2 | ... |
| Kazakhstan Kazakhstan | 3.2[1] | 2.4 | 2.5 | ... | ... | ... | ... | ... |
| Kenya Kenya | 6.7 | 7.0 | 7.4 | 6.9 | 22.1 | 29.2 | 17.9 | ... |
| Korea, Republic of Corée, République de | 4.6 | 4.6 | ... | ... | 15.0 | 16.5 | ... | ... |
| Kuwait Koweït | 6.0 | 5.2 | 4.3 | 3.4[1] | ... | 13.6 | 12.7 | 12.9[1] |
| Kyrgyzstan Kirghizistan | 4.6[1] | ... | 5.0 | | ... | ... | ... | ... |
| Lao People's Dem. Rep. Rép. dém. pop. lao | 2.4[1] | 2.4 | 2.5 | 3.4 | 11.0[1] | 10.8 | 11.7 | 14.0 |
| Latvia Lettonie | 5.3 | 5.2 | ... | ... | 15.4 | 14.2 | ... | ... |
| Lebanon Liban | 2.7[1] | 2.7 | 2.7 | 2.8 | ... | 12.7 | 11.0 | ... |
| Lesotho Lesotho | ... | ... | 11.3 | 10.8 | ... | ... | 29.8 | ... |
| Lithuania Lituanie | 5.6 | 5.6 | 5.3 | ... | 15.7 | 15.6 | 14.7 | ... |
| Madagascar Madagascar | ... | 3.4[1] | 3.2 | 3.1 | ... | 18.2[1] | 25.3 | |
| Malawi Malawi | 5.9 | ... | ... | ... | ... | ... | ... | ... |
| Malaysia Malaisie | 8.4 | 6.6 | ... | ... | 28.0 | 25.2 | ... | ... |
| Maldives Maldives | 8.6 | 7.7[1] | 8.0 | 8.3 | ... | ... | 15.0 | ... |
| Mali Mali | 4.3 | 4.5 | 4.3 | 4.4 | 16.8 | 16.9 | 14.8 | 16.8 |
| Malta Malte | ... | 5.2 | ... | ... | ... | 10.5 | ... | ... |
| Marshall Islands Iles Marshall | 9.2 | 9.5[1] | ... | ... | 15.8 | ... | ... | ... |
| Mauritania Mauritanie | 3.6 | 3.0[1] | 2.3 | 2.8 | ... | ... | 8.3 | 10.1 |

| Country or area<br>Pays ou zone | As % of Gross National Income (GNI)<br>En % du Revenu National Brut (RNB) | | | | As % of total government expenditure<br>En % des dépenses totales du gouvernement | | | |
|---|---|---|---|---|---|---|---|---|
| | 2003 | 2004 | 2005 | 2006 | 2003 | 2004 | 2005 | 2006 |
| Mauritius<br>Maurice | 4.7 | 4.7 | 4.5 | 3.9 | ... | 15.7 | 14.3 | 12.7 |
| Mexico<br>Mexique | 5.9 | 5.5 | 5.6 | ... | 23.8 | 25.6 | ... | ... |
| Moldova<br>Moldova | 4.9 | 6.0 | 6.3 | 6.6 | 24.3 | 19.3 | 19.4 | 20.2 |
| Mongolia<br>Mongolie | 7.3[1] | 5.3 | ... | ... | ... | ... | ... | ... |
| Morocco<br>Maroc | 6.5[1] | 6.4 | 6.8 | ... | ... | 27.8 | 27.2 | ... |
| Mozambique<br>Mozambique | ... | 4.6 | 5.3 | ... | ... | 22.6 | ... | ... |
| Namibia<br>Namibie | 6.8 | ... | ... | ... | ... | ... | ... | ... |
| Nepal<br>Népal | 3.2 | ... | ... | ... | 14.9 | ... | ... | ... |
| Netherlands<br>Pays-Bas | 5.1 | 5.2 | 5.2 | ... | 10.8 | 11.2 | 11.5 | ... |
| New Zealand<br>Nouvelle-Zélande | 7.0 | 7.1 | 7.0 | 6.1 | 20.9 | ... | 15.5 | ... |
| Nicaragua[1]<br>Nicaragua[1] | 3.3 | ... | ... | ... | ... | ... | ... | ... |
| Niger<br>Niger | 2.4 | ... | ... | 3.3 | 13.2 | ... | ... | 17.6 |
| Norway<br>Norvège | 7.6 | 7.5 | 7.1 | ... | 15.7 | 16.6 | 16.7 | ... |
| Oman<br>Oman | 4.1 | 4.3 | ... | 5.0 | 21.3 | 24.2 | 24.2 | 31.1 |
| Pakistan<br>Pakistan | 2.0[1] | 2.0 | 2.3 | 2.7 | ... | 6.4 | 10.9 | 12.2 |
| Panama[1]<br>Panama[1] | 4.7 | 4.1 | ... | ... | ... | 8.9 | ... | ... |
| Paraguay<br>Paraguay | 4.7 | 4.1 | ... | ... | 10.8 | 10.0 | ... | ... |
| Peru<br>Pérou | 2.9 | 3.0 | 2.9 | 2.7 | ... | 17.0 | ... | 15.4 |
| Philippines<br>Philippines | 3.0 | 2.5 | 2.3 | ... | 17.2 | 16.4 | 15.2 | ... |
| Poland<br>Pologne | 5.4 | 5.7 | 5.7 | ... | 12.0 | 12.7 | ... | ... |
| Portugal<br>Portugal | 5.7 | 5.4 | 5.5 | ... | 12.2 | 11.5 | 11.3 | ... |
| Qatar<br>Qatar | ... | ... | ... | ... | ... | ... | 19.6 | ... |
| Romania<br>Roumanie | 3.5 | 3.4 | 3.6 | ... | ... | 8.6 | ... | ... |
| Russian Federation<br>Fédération de Russie | 3.8 | 3.6 | 3.9 | ... | 12.3 | 12.9 | ... | ... |
| Rwanda<br>Rwanda | ... | ... | 3.8 | ... | ... | ... | 12.2 | ... |
| Saint Kitts and Nevis<br>Saint-Kitts-et-Nevis | 5.1 | 4.9[1] | 10.8 | ... | 12.7 | ... | ... | ... |
| Saint Lucia<br>Sainte-Lucie | 5.2[1] | 5.2 | 6.2 | 7.1 | ... | 15.6 | 16.9 | 19.1 |
| Saint Vincent-Grenadines<br>Saint Vincent-Grenadines | 11.7[1] | 11.6 | 8.8 | ... | ... | 20.5 | 16.1 | ... |
| Saudi Arabia<br>Arabie saoudite | 7.2 | 6.7 | ... | ... | 28.5 | 27.6 | ... | ... |
| Senegal<br>Sénégal | 3.8 | 4.1 | 5.5 | 5.0 | 20.1 | ... | 18.9 | 26.3 |

**Public expenditure on education: percentage of GNI and government expenditure** (*continued*)

**Dépenses publiques afférentes à l'èducation : pourcentage par rapport au RNB et aux dépenses du gouvernement** (*suite*)

| Country or area | As % of Gross National Income (GNI) En % du Revenu National Brut (RNB) | | | | As % of total government expenditure En % des dépenses totales du gouvernement | | | |
|---|---|---|---|---|---|---|---|---|
| Pays ou zone | 2003 | 2004 | 2005 | 2006 | 2003 | 2004 | 2005 | 2006 |
| Seychelles Seychelles | 5.7 | 5.7[1] | ... | 6.8 | ... | ... | ... | 12.6 |
| Sierra Leone[1] Sierra Leone[1] | 4.7 | 4.3 | 3.9 | ... | ... | ... | ... | ... |
| Slovakia Slovaquie | 4.4 | 4.3 | 4.1 | ... | 11.0 | 10.8 | ... | ... |
| Slovenia Slovénie | 6.1 | 6.0 | 6.0 | ... | 12.6 | 12.6 | 12.7 | ... |
| South Africa Afrique du Sud | 5.2 | 5.5 | 5.5 | 5.5 | 18.5 | 18.1 | 17.9 | 17.6 |
| Spain Espagne | 4.4 | 4.3 | 4.3 | ... | 11.2 | 11.0 | 11.0 | ... |
| Swaziland Swaziland | 7.0 | 6.2 | 6.9 | ... | ... | ... | ... | ... |
| Sweden Suède | 7.4 | 7.3 | 7.2 | ... | 12.8 | 12.9 | ... | ... |
| Switzerland Suisse | 5.6 | 5.5 | 5.3 | ... | 13.0 | ... | ... | ... |
| Tajikistan Tadjikistan | 2.6 | 2.9 | 3.6 | 3.5 | 16.3 | 16.9 | 18.0 | 19.0 |
| Thailand Thaïlande | ... | 4.3 | 4.3 | ... | ... | 26.8 | 25.0 | ... |
| Tokelau Tokélaou | ... | ... | ... | ... | 14.5 | ... | ... | ... |
| Tonga Tonga | 5.2 | 4.9 | ... | ... | 13.5 | ... | ... | ... |
| Tunisia Tunisie | 7.8 | 7.8 | 7.7 | ... | ... | ... | 20.8 | ... |
| Turkey Turquie | 3.8 | 4.1 | ... | ... | ... | ... | ... | ... |
| Turks and Caicos Islands Iles Turques et Caïques | ... | ... | ... | ... | ... | ... | 11.8 | ... |
| Uganda[1] Ouganda[1] | ... | 5.3 | ... | ... | ... | 18.3 | ... | ... |
| Ukraine Ukraine | 5.7 | 5.4 | 6.1 | 6.4 | 19.8 | 18.1 | 18.9 | 19.3 |
| United Arab Emirates Emirats arabes unis | 1.8[2] | 1.6[2] | ... | ... | 24.9[2] | 25.0[2] | 28.3[1] | ... |
| United Kingdom Royaume-Uni | 5.3 | 5.3 | 5.5 | ... | 12.0 | 11.7 | 12.5 | ... |
| United States Etats-Unis | 5.8 | 5.6 | 5.3 | ... | 15.2 | 14.4 | 13.7 | ... |
| Uruguay Uruguay | 2.3 | 2.7 | 2.9 | 3.0 | 7.9 | 11.1 | 12.7 | 11.6 |
| Vanuatu Vanuatu | 10.0 | ... | ... | ... | ... | ... | ... | ... |
| Venezuela (Bolivarian Rep. of) Venezuela (Rép. bolivarienne du) | ... | ... | ... | 3.7 | ... | ... | ... | ... |
| Zambia Zambie | ... | 3.1 | 2.1 | ... | ... | 14.8 | ... | ... |

Source

United Nations Educational, Scientific and Cultural Organization (UNESCO) Institute for Statistics, Montreal, the UNESCO Institute for Statistics (UIS) database, May 2008.

Notes

1  UIS estimation.
2  National estimation.

Source

L'Institut de statistique de l'Organisation des Nations Unies pour l'éducation, la science et la culture (UNESCO), Montréal, la base de données de l'institut de statistique de l'UNESCO (ISU), mai 2008.

Notes

1  Estimation de l'ISU.
2  Estimation nationale.

Detailed data and explanatory notes on education can be found on the UNESCO Institute for Statistics web site www.uis.unesco.org. Brief notes which pertain to the statistical information shown in tables 13 and 14 are given below.

*Table 13:* The definitions and classifications applied by UNESCO are those set out in the *Revised Recommendation concerning the International Standardization of Education Statistics* (1978) and the 1976 and 1997 versions of the *International Standard Classification of Education* (ISCED). Data are presented in table 13 according to the terminology of the ISCED-97.

According to the ISCED, these educational levels are defined as follows:

- Primary education (ISCED level 1): Programmes normally designed on a unit or project basis to give pupils a sound basic education in reading, writing and mathematics along with an elementary understanding of other subjects such as history, geography, natural science, social science, art and music. Religious instruction may also be featured. It is sometimes called elementary education.

- Secondary education (ISCED levels 2 and 3): Lower secondary education (ISCED 2) is generally designed to continue the basic programmes of the primary level but the teaching is typically more subject-focused, requiring more specialized teachers for each subject area. The end of this level often coincides with the end of compulsory education. In upper secondary education (ISCED 3), the final stage of secondary education in most countries, education is often organized even more along subject lines and teachers typically need a higher or more subject-specific qualification than at ISCED level 2.

- Tertiary education (ISCED levels 5 and 6): Programmes with an educational content more advanced than what is offered at ISCED levels 3 and 4. The first stage of tertiary education, ISCED level 5, covers level 5A, composed of largely theoretically based programmes intended to provide sufficient qualifications for gaining entry to advanced research programmes and professions with high skill requirements; and level 5B, where programmes are generally more practical, technical and/or occupationally specific. The second stage of tertiary education, ISCED level 6, comprises programmes devoted to advanced study and original research, and leading to the award of an advanced research qualification

The ISCED-97 also introduced a new category or level between upper secondary and tertiary education called post-secondary non-tertiary education (ISCED level 4). This level includes programmes that lie between the upper-secondary

On trouvera des données détaillées et des notes explicatives sur l'éducation sur le site Web de l'Institut de statistique de l'UNESCO www.uis.unesco.org. Ciaprès figurent des notes sommaires, relatives aux principaux éléments d'information statistique figurant dans les tableaux 13 et 14.

*Tableau 13:* Les définitions et classifications appliquées par l'UNESCO sont tirées de la *Recommandation révisée concernant la normalisation internationale des statistiques de l'éducation* (1978) et des versions de 1976 et de 1997 de la *Classification internationale type de l'éducation* (CITE). La terminologie utilisée dans le tableau 13 est celle de la CITE-1997.

Dans la CITE, les niveaux d'enseignement sont définis comme suit:

- Enseignement primaire (niveau 1 de la CITE): Programmes s'articulant normalement autour d'une unité ou d'un projet visant à donner aux élèves un solide enseignement de base en lecture, en écriture et en mathématiques et des connaissances élémentaires dans d'autres matières telles que l'histoire, la géographie, les sciences naturelles, les sciences sociales, le dessin et la musique. Dans certains cas, une instruction religieuse est aussi considérée. Appelé parfois enseignement élémentaire.

- Enseignement secondaire (niveaux 2 et 3 de la CITE): Le premier cycle de l'enseignement secondaire (CITE 2) est généralement destiné à compléter les programmes de base de l'enseignement primaire mais dont l'enseignementest généralement plus orienté vers les matières enseignées faisant appel à des enseignants plus spécialisés. La fin de ce niveau coïncide souvent avec celle de la scolarité obligatoire. Dans le deuxième cycle de l'enseignement secondaire (CITE 3), étape finale de l'enseignement secondaire dans plusieurs pays, l'enseignement est souvent organisé en une plus grande spécialisation et les enseignants doivent souvent être plus qualifiés ou spécialisés qu'au niveau 2 de la CITE.

- Enseignement supérieur (niveaux 5 et 6 de la CITE): Programmes dont le contenu est plus avancé que celui offert aux niveaux 3 et 4 de la CITE. Le premier cycle de l'enseignement supérieur, niveau 5 de la CITE, couvre le niveau 5A, composé de programmes fondés dans une large mesure sur la théorie et destinés à offrir des qualifications suffisantes pour être admis à suivre des programmes de recherche de pointe ou à exercer une profession exigeant de hautes compétences; et le niveau 5B, dont les programmes sont dans une large mesure d'ordre pratique, technique et/ou spécifiquement professionnel. Le deuxième cycle de l'enseignement supérieur, niveau 6 de la CITE, comprend des programmes consacrés à

and tertiary levels of education from an international point of view, even though they might clearly be considered as upper-secondary or tertiary programmes in a national context. They are often not significantly more advanced than programmes at ISCED 3 (upper secondary) but they serve to broaden the knowledge of participants who have already completed a programme at level 3. The students are usually older than those at level 3. ISCED 4 programmes typically last between six months and two years.

*Table 14:* Public expenditure on education consists of current and capital expenditures on education by local, regional and national governments, including municipalities. Household contributions are excluded. Current expenditure on education includes expenditure for goods and services consumed within the current year and which would need to be renewed if needed the following year. It includes expenditure on: staff salaries and benefits; contracted or purchased services; other resources including books and teaching materials; welfare services; and other current expenditure such as subsidies to students and households, furniture and equipment, minor repairs, fuel, telecommunications, travel, insurance and rents. Capital expenditure on education includes expenditure for assets that last longer than one year. It includes expenditure for construction, renovation and major repairs of buildings and the purchase of heavy equipment or vehicles.

des études approfondies et à des travaux de recherche originaux, et conduisant à l'obtention d'un titre de chercheur hautement qualifié.

La CITE de 1997 a également introduit une nouvelle catégorie (ou nouveau niveau) entre l'enseignement secondaire et l'enseignement supérieur, appelée enseignement postsecondaire non supérieur (niveau 4 de la CITE). À ce niveau se trouvent des programmes qui, du point de vue des établissements, sont intermédiaires entre le deuxième cycle du secondaire et le premier cycle du supérieur, encore qu'il serait tout à fait possible de les considérer, dans le contexte national, comme appartenant au deuxième cycle du secondaire ou au supérieur. Ils ne sont souvent pas beaucoup plus avancés que des programmes du niveau 3 de la CITE (deuxième cycle du secondaire) mais servent à élargir les connaissances de ceux qui les suivent et qui ont déjà achevé un programme de niveau 3. Les étudiants y sont généralement plus âgés que ceux du niveau 3. Pour la plupart, ces programmes du niveau 4 de la CITE ont une durée comprise entre six mois et deux ans.

*Tableau 14:* Les données relatives aux dépenses publiques afférentes à l'éducation se rapportent aux dépenses courantes et en capital de l'éducation engagées par l'administration au niveau local, régional, national/central, y inclus les municipalités. Les contributions des ménages sont exclues. Les dépenses ordinaires (ou courantes) en éducation se réfèrent aux dépenses couvrant les biens et les services consommés dans l'année en cours et qui doivent être renouvelées périodiquement. Elles comprennent les dépenses en: salaires et avantages du personnel, services achetés ou assurés sous contrat, l'achat d'autres ressources y compris les manuels scolaires et du matériel pour l'enseignement, les services sociaux et d'autres dépenses de fonctionnement telles que les subventions aux étudiants et aux ménages, les fournitures et l'équipement, les réparations légères, les combustibles, les télécommunications, les voyages, les assurances et les loyers. Dépenses en capital pour l'éducation se réfèrent aux dépenses qui couvrent l'achat de biens d'une durée supérieure à une année. Elles peuvent comprendre les dépenses de construction, de rénovation et de grosses réparations de bâtiments, ainsi que l'achat d'équipements ou véhicules.

# 15

## Daily newspapers
## Journaux quotidiens

| Country or area<br>Pays ou zone | Number of titles - Nombre de titres | | | | Total average daily circulation or copies printed (thousands)<br>Diffusion moyenne ou nombre imprimé (en milliers) | | | | Circulation or copies printed per 1000 inhabitants t<br>Diffusion ou nombre imprimé pour 1000 habitants t | | | |
|---|---|---|---|---|---|---|---|---|---|---|---|---|
| | 2001 | 2002 | 2003 | 2004 | 2001 | 2002 | 2003 | 2004 | 2001 | 2002 | 2003 | 2004 |
| Albania[1]<br>Albanie[1] | 16 | 18 | 19 | 21 | ... | ... | 76 | ... | ... | ... | 24.6 | ... |
| Algeria[1]<br>Algérie[1] | 14 | 15 | 16 | 17 | ... | ... | ... | ... | ... | ... | ... | ... |
| Angola<br>Angola | 1 | 1 | 1 | 1 | 35[2] | 35[2] | 35[2] | 35[2] | 2.5 | 2.4 | 2.3 | 2.3 |
| Antigua and Barbuda[1]<br>Antigua-et-Barbuda[1] | 2 | 2 | 2 | 2 | ... | ... | ... | ... | ... | ... | ... | ... |
| Argentina[1]<br>Argentine[1] | 114 | 123 | 182 | 184 | 1 954 | 1 572 | 1 579 | 1 363 | 52.4 | 41.8 | 41.6 | 35.5 |
| Armenia<br>Arménie | 6 | 6 | 7 | 5 | 17 | 26 | 26 | 23 | 5.6 | 8.5 | 8.6 | 7.6 |
| Aruba<br>Aruba | 8 | 8 | 8 | 9 | ... | ... | ... | ... | ... | ... | ... | ... |
| Australia[1]<br>Australie[1] | 51 | 50 | 49 | 49 | ... | ... | 3 150 | 3 114 | ... | ... | 159.7 | 156.2 |
| Austria<br>Autriche | 15 | 15 | 16 | 17 | 2 438 | 2 553 | 2 522 | 2 570 | 300.6 | 314.1 | 309.5 | 314.5 |
| Azerbaijan[1]<br>Azerbaïdjan[1] | 22 | 22 | 24 | ... | 132 | ... | ... | ... | 16.1 | ... | ... | ... |
| Bahamas[1]<br>Bahamas[1] | 4 | 4 | 4 | 4 | ... | ... | ... | ... | ... | ... | ... | ... |
| Bahrain[1]<br>Bahreïn[1] | 6 | 6 | 6 | 6 | ... | ... | ... | ... | ... | ... | ... | ... |
| Bangladesh[1]<br>Bangladesh[1] | 20 | 20 | 20 | 20 | ... | ... | ... | ... | ... | ... | ... | ... |
| Barbados[1]<br>Barbade[1] | 2 | 2 | 2 | 2 | ... | ... | ... | ... | ... | ... | ... | ... |
| Belarus<br>Bélarus | 14 | 15 | 21 | 13 | 1 697 | 1 401 | 814 | 800 | 170.1 | 141.3 | 82.5 | 81.6 |
| Belgium[1]<br>Belgique[1] | 28 | 29 | 29 | 29 | 1 851 | 1 651 | 1 678 | 1 706 | 179.2 | 159.4 | 161.7 | 164.0 |
| Benin<br>Bénin | 24[2] | 27[2] | 31 | 34 | 2[2] | 2[2] | 3 | 3 | 0.3 | 0.3 | 0.4 | 0.4 |
| Bermuda<br>Bermudes | 1 | 1 | 1 | 1 | ... | ... | ... | 17 | ... | ... | ... | 263.9 |
| Bolivia[1]<br>Bolivie[1] | 17 | 19 | 19 | 19 | ... | ... | ... | ... | ... | ... | ... | ... |
| Bosnia and Herzegovina[1]<br>Bosnie-Herzégovine[1] | 7 | 7 | 7 | 7 | ... | ... | ... | ... | ... | ... | ... | ... |
| Botswana<br>Botswana | 1 | 1 | 1 | 2 | 51 | 51 | 63 | 75 | 28.8 | 28.7 | 35.4 | 42.6 |
| Brazil<br>Brésil | 491 | 523 | 529 | 532 | 7 670 | 6 972 | 6 470 | 6 552 | 43.5 | 39.0 | 35.7 | 35.6 |
| British Virgin Islands[1]<br>Iles Vierges britanniques[1] | 1 | 1 | 1 | 1 | ... | ... | ... | ... | ... | ... | ... | ... |

| Country or area<br>Pays ou zone | Number of titles - Nombre de titres | | | | Total average daily circulation or copies printed (thousands)<br>Diffusion moyenne ou nombre imprimé (en milliers) | | | | Circulation or copies printed per 1000 inhabitants t<br>Diffusion ou nombre imprimé pour 1000 habitants t | | | |
|---|---|---|---|---|---|---|---|---|---|---|---|---|
| | 2001 | 2002 | 2003 | 2004 | 2001 | 2002 | 2003 | 2004 | 2001 | 2002 | 2003 | 2004 |
| Brunei Darussalam[1]<br>Brunéi Darussalam[1] | 2 | 2 | 2 | 2 | ... | 30 | 25 | 25 | ... | 85.9 | 69.9 | 68.4 |
| Bulgaria<br>Bulgarie | 60 | 59 | 62 | 58 | 1 009 | 853 | 667 | 616 | 127.1 | 108.1 | 85.2 | 79.1 |
| Burkina Faso[1]<br>Burkina Faso[1] | 5 | 5 | 5 | 5 | ... | ... | ... | ... | ... | ... | ... | ... |
| Burundi[1]<br>Burundi[1] | 1 | 1 | 1 | 1 | ... | ... | ... | ... | ... | ... | ... | ... |
| Cameroon[2,3]<br>Cameroun[2,3] | 12 | 10 | 10 | 10 | ... | ... | ... | ... | ... | ... | ... | ... |
| Canada[1]<br>Canada[1] | 107 | 104 | 105 | 103 | 5 566 | 5 461 | 5 590 | 5 578 | 179.6 | 174.4 | 176.7 | 174.5 |
| Cayman Islands<br>Iles Caïmanes | 2 | 2 | 2 | 2 | 15 | 12 | 12 | 15 | 353.2 | 281.4 | 274.1 | 348.1 |
| Chile[4]<br>Chili[4] | 51[5] | 47[5] | 54[5] | 59[1] | 1 326[6] | ... | 928[6] | 816 | 85.0 | ... | 58.2 | 50.6 |
| China[1,7]<br>Chine[1,7] | 975 | 1 007 | 1 035 | 963 | 82 047 | 85 470 | 88 657 | 96 704 | 63.9 | 66.2 | 68.2 | 73.9 |
| China, Hong Kong SAR<br>Chine, Hong Kong RAS | 52 | 52 | 52 | 46 | ... | ... | ... | ... | ... | ... | ... | ... |
| China, Macao SAR<br>Chine, Macao RAS | 11 | 11 | 11 | 12 | ... | ... | ... | ... | ... | ... | ... | ... |
| Colombia[8]<br>Colombie[8] | 23[5] | 23[5] | 23[5] | 23[5] | ... | ... | ... | 1 004[5] | ... | ... | ... | 22.4 |
| Comoros[1]<br>Comores[1] | 2 | 2 | 2 | 1 | ... | ... | ... | ... | ... | ... | ... | ... |
| Cook Islands[1]<br>Iles Cook[1] | 1 | 1 | 1 | 1 | ... | ... | ... | ... | ... | ... | ... | ... |
| Costa Rica[1]<br>Costa Rica[1] | 6 | 6 | 7 | 7 | 301 | 288 | 281 | 275 | 75.0 | 70.3 | 67.3 | 64.7 |
| Cote d'Ivoire[1]<br>Cote d'Ivoire[1] | 20 | 20 | 20 | 21 | ... | ... | ... | ... | ... | ... | ... | ... |
| Croatia<br>Croatie | 14 | 13 | 12 | 13 | ... | ... | ... | ... | ... | ... | ... | ... |
| Cuba<br>Cuba | 2 | 2 | 2 | 2 | 719 | 719 | 717 | 728 | 64.4 | 64.2 | 63.9 | 64.7 |
| Cyprus[5,9]<br>Chypre[5,9] | 8 | 7 | 7 | 8 | ... | ... | ... | ... | ... | ... | ... | ... |
| Czech Republic<br>République tchèque | 67 | 74 | 66 | 81 | 1 927 | 1 890 | 1 867 | 1 861 | 187.9 | 184.5 | 182.4 | 181.9 |
| Dem. Rep. of the Congo<br>Rép. dém. du Congo | 12 | 12 | 12 | 12 | ... | ... | ... | ... | ... | ... | ... | ... |
| Denmark[1]<br>Danemark[1] | 32 | 33 | 35 | 35 | 1 736 | 1 806 | 1 911 | 1 906 | 323.9 | 335.7 | 354.1 | 352.0 |
| Dominican Republic[1]<br>Rép. dominicaine[1] | 11 | 13 | 12 | 11 | 242 | 486 | 466 | 365 | 28.9 | 57.1 | 53.9 | 41.6 |
| El Salvador[1]<br>El Salvador[1] | 5 | 5 | 5 | 5 | ... | 250 | 250 | 250 | ... | 38.3 | 37.6 | 37.0 |
| Estonia<br>Estonie | 14 | 13 | 14 | 13 | 258 | 255 | 251 | 257 | 190.4 | 189.1 | 187.2 | 192.5 |

| Country or area<br>Pays ou zone | Number of titles - Nombre de titres | | | | Total average daily circulation or copies printed (thousands)<br>Diffusion moyenne ou nombre imprimé (en milliers) | | | | Circulation or copies printed per 1000 inhabitants t<br>Diffusion ou nombre imprimé pour 1000 habitants t | | | |
|---|---|---|---|---|---|---|---|---|---|---|---|---|
| | 2001 | 2002 | 2003 | 2004 | 2001 | 2002 | 2003 | 2004 | 2001 | 2002 | 2003 | 2004 |
| Ethiopia<br>Ethiopie | 3 | 3 | 3 | 3 | 342 | 350 | 354 | 358 | 4.9 | 4.9 | 4.8 | 4.7 |
| Fiji<br>Fidji | 3 | 3 | 3 | 3 | 48 | 44 | 50 | 44 | 58.6 | 53.3 | 60.0 | 52.3 |
| Finland[10]<br>Finlande[10] | 54 | 53 | 53 | 53 | 2 307 | 2 268 | 2 243 | 2 255 | 444.5 | 435.7 | 429.7 | 430.7 |
| France[11]<br>France[11] | 94[2] | 97[2] | 98[2] | 101[2] | 9 346[6] | 9 638[6] | 9 678[6] | 9 890[6] | 157.0 | 161.3 | 161.3 | 164.1 |
| Gabon[1]<br>Gabon[1] | 1 | 1 | 1 | 1 | ... | ... | ... | ... | ... | ... | ... | ... |
| Gambia[1]<br>Gambie[1] | 2 | 2 | 2 | 2 | ... | ... | ... | ... | ... | ... | ... | ... |
| Georgia[3]<br>Géorgie[3] | 17[5] | 19[5] | 15[5] | 9[5] | ... | 16[5] | 12[5] | 18[5] | ... | 3.5 | 2.6 | 3.9 |
| Germany<br>Allemagne | 356 | 349 | 349 | 347 | 23 800 | 23 200 | 22 600 | 22 100 | 288.7 | 281.2 | 273.7 | 267.4 |
| Gibraltar<br>Gibraltar | 2 | 2 | 2 | 2 | 6[2] | 6[2] | 6[2] | 6[2] | ... | ... | ... | ... |
| Guinea[1]<br>Guinée[1] | 2 | 2 | 2 | 2 | ... | ... | ... | ... | ... | ... | ... | ... |
| Guyana[1]<br>Guyana[1] | 2 | 2 | 3 | 3 | ... | ... | ... | ... | ... | ... | ... | ... |
| Haiti[1]<br>Haïti[1] | 2 | 2 | 2 | 2 | ... | ... | ... | ... | ... | ... | ... | ... |
| Hungary<br>Hongrie | 35 | 35 | 35 | 34 | 2 104 | 2 078 | 2 120 | 2 195 | 206.3 | 204.2 | 208.9 | 216.8 |
| Iceland<br>Islande | 4 | 3 | 3 | 3 | 149 | 162 | 168 | 162 | 524.1 | 564.7 | 581.7 | 553.4 |
| India[3]<br>Inde[3] | 1 329[5] | 1 931[5] | 1 749[5] | 1 874[5] | 58 360[5] | 73 486[5] | 74 714[5] | 79 243[5] | 56.2 | 69.7 | 69.8 | 72.9 |
| Indonesia<br>Indonésie | 566 | 680 | ... | ... | ... | ... | ... | ... | ... | ... | ... | ... |
| Iran (Islamic Rep. of)[1]<br>Iran (Rép. islamique d')[1] | 117 | 121 | 130 | 172 | ... | ... | ... | ... | ... | ... | ... | ... |
| Ireland[1]<br>Irlande[1] | 6 | 6 | 7 | 7 | 588 | 591 | 772 | 742 | 152.2 | 150.3 | 192.7 | 181.9 |
| Italy[1]<br>Italie[1] | 93 | 96 | 96 | 96 | 7 786 | 7 811 | 7 876 | 8 017 | 134.7 | 135.0 | 135.9 | 138.2 |
| Jamaica[1]<br>Jamaïque[1] | 3 | 3 | 3 | 3 | ... | ... | ... | ... | ... | ... | ... | ... |
| Japan<br>Japon | 111[10] | 107[10] | 106[10] | 108[10] | 71 694[1,6] | 70 892[1] | 70 419[1] | 70 446[1] | 563.2[1] | 555.9[1] | 551.3[1] | 550.7[1] |
| Jordan[1]<br>Jordanie[1] | 5 | 5 | 4 | 4 | ... | ... | ... | ... | ... | ... | ... | ... |
| Kenya<br>Kenya | 5 | 5 | 5 | 5 | ... | ... | ... | ... | ... | ... | ... | ... |
| Korea, Dem. P. R.[1]<br>Corée, R. p. dém. de[1] | ... | ... | ... | 15 | ... | ... | ... | ... | ... | ... | ... | ... |
| Korea, Republic of<br>Corée, République de | 123 | 125 | 134 | 139 | ... | ... | ... | ... | ... | ... | ... | ... |

| Country or area<br>Pays ou zone | Number of titles - Nombre de titres | | | | Total average daily circulation or copies printed (thousands)<br>Diffusion moyenne ou nombre imprimé (en milliers) | | | | Circulation or copies printed per 1000 inhabitants t<br>Diffusion ou nombre imprimé pour 1000 habitants t | | | |
|---|---|---|---|---|---|---|---|---|---|---|---|---|
| | 2001 | 2002 | 2003 | 2004 | 2001 | 2002 | 2003 | 2004 | 2001 | 2002 | 2003 | 2004 |
| Kuwait<br>Koweït | 8 | 8 | 8 | 8 | ... | ... | ... | ... | ... | ... | ... | ... |
| Kyrgyzstan<br>Kirghizistan | 2 | 1 | 2 | 2 | 8 | 9 | 13 | 5 | 1.6 | 1.8 | 2.6 | 1.0 |
| Lao People's Dem. Rep.<br>Rép. dém. pop. lao | 5 | 5 | 6 | 6 | 12 | 12 | 15 | 15 | 2.2 | 2.2 | 2.6 | 2.5 |
| Latvia<br>Lettonie | 27 | 24 | 24 | 23 | 412 | 373 | 343 | 357 | 174.8 | 159.2 | 147.2 | 153.9 |
| Lebanon[1]<br>Liban[1] | 13 | 13 | 14 | 15 | 215 | 215 | 215 | 215 | 62.6 | 62.0 | 61.4 | 60.7 |
| Liberia[1]<br>Libéria[1] | 2 | 3 | 3 | 3 | ... | ... | ... | ... | ... | ... | ... | ... |
| Libyan Arab Jamah[1]<br>Jamah. arabe libyenne[1] | 4 | 4 | 4 | 4 | ... | ... | ... | ... | ... | ... | ... | ... |
| Liechtenstein<br>Liechtenstein | 2 | 2 | 2 | 2 | 18 | 18 | 18 | 18 | ... | 521.9 | 513.6 | ... |
| Lithuania<br>Lituanie | 13 | 14 | 14 | 14 | 304 | 315 | 304 | 371 | 87.3 | 90.9 | 88.0 | 107.7 |
| Luxembourg[1]<br>Luxembourg[1] | 7 | 6 | 6 | 6 | 120 | 118 | 115 | 115 | 270.9 | 263.9 | 254.2 | 250.9 |
| Madagascar[1]<br>Madagascar[1] | ... | 4 | 6 | 9 | ... | ... | ... | ... | ... | ... | ... | ... |
| Malawi<br>Malawi | 2[1] | 2[1] | 2[1] | 2 | ... | ... | ... | ... | ... | ... | ... | ... |
| Malaysia[1]<br>Malaisie[1] | 34 | 33 | 33 | 35 | 2 399 | 2 474 | 2 572 | 2 753 | 102.1 | 103.2 | 105.3 | 110.6 |
| Maldives[1]<br>Maldives[1] | 3 | 3 | 3 | 3 | ... | ... | ... | ... | ... | ... | ... | ... |
| Mali[1]<br>Mali[1] | 8 | 8 | 9 | 9 | ... | ... | ... | ... | ... | ... | ... | ... |
| Malta<br>Malte | 4 | 4 | 4 | 4 | ... | ... | ... | ... | ... | ... | ... | ... |
| Mauritania[1]<br>Mauritanie[1] | 3 | 3 | 3 | 3 | ... | ... | ... | ... | ... | ... | ... | ... |
| Mauritius<br>Maurice | ... | ... | 9 | 10 | ... | ... | ... | 95 | ... | ... | ... | 77.0 |
| Mexico[1]<br>Mexique[1] | 341 | 300 | ... | ... | ... | ... | ... | ... | ... | ... | ... | ... |
| Monaco<br>Monaco | ... | ... | ... | 1 | ... | ... | ... | 8 | ... | ... | ... | ... |
| Mongolia[1]<br>Mongolie[1] | 5 | 5 | 6 | 6 | 39 | 42 | 38 | 50 | 15.5 | 16.5 | 14.7 | 19.1 |
| Morocco<br>Maroc | 23 | 23 | 23 | 24 | ... | ... | 350[1,6] | ... | ... | ... | 11.5[1] | ... |
| Mozambique<br>Mozambique | 11 | 13 | 14 | 19 | 51 | 52 | 53 | 55 | 2.8 | 2.8 | 2.8 | 2.8 |
| Namibia<br>Namibie | 3 | 3 | 3 | 4 | 37 | 40 | 44 | 56 | 19.1 | 20.3 | 22.3 | 27.8 |
| Netherlands[1]<br>Pays-Bas[1] | 38 | 38 | 37 | 37 | 5 115 | 5 062 | 5 007 | 5 001 | 320.0 | 315.1 | 310.1 | 308.2 |

| Country or area Pays ou zone | Number of titles - Nombre de titres | | | | Total average daily circulation or copies printed (thousands) Diffusion moyenne ou nombre imprimé (en milliers) | | | | Circulation or copies printed per 1000 inhabitants t Diffusion ou nombre imprimé pour 1000 habitants t | | | |
|---|---|---|---|---|---|---|---|---|---|---|---|---|
| | 2001 | 2002 | 2003 | 2004 | 2001 | 2002 | 2003 | 2004 | 2001 | 2002 | 2003 | 2004 |
| Netherlands Antilles[1] Antilles néerlandaises[1] | 5 | 5 | 5 | 5 | ... | ... | ... | ... | ... | ... | ... | ... |
| New Zealand Nouvelle-Zélande | 26[5,8] | 24[5,8] | 24[5,8] | 23[5,8] | 764[1,6] | 745[1,6] | 739[1,6] | 739[1,6] | 198.0[1] | 191.0[1] | 187.2[1] | 185.3[1] |
| Nicaragua[1] Nicaragua[1] | 6 | 6 | 6 | 6 | ... | ... | ... | ... | ... | ... | ... | ... |
| Niger Niger | 1 | 1 | 1 | 1 | 3 | 3 | 3 | 3 | 0.2 | 0.2 | 0.2 | 0.2 |
| Nigeria[1] Nigéria[1] | 34 | 35 | 36 | 38 | ... | ... | ... | ... | ... | ... | ... | ... |
| Niue Nioué | 1 | 1 | 1 | 1 | ... | ... | ... | ... | ... | ... | ... | ... |
| Norway Norvège | 78 | 76 | 74 | 74 | 2 507 | 2 475 | 2 421 | 2 378 | 553.7 | 543.7 | 529.1 | 517.2 |
| Occupied Palestinian Terr. Terr. palestinien occupé | 3 | 3 | 3 | 3 | ... | ... | 35[1,6] | 35[1,6] | ... | ... | 10.1[1] | 9.8[1] |
| Oman Oman | 5 | 5 | 5 | 6 | ... | ... | ... | ... | ... | ... | ... | ... |
| Pakistan Pakistan | 168 | 169 | 204 | 291 | 5 726 | 6 009 | 6 246 | 7 818 | 39.3 | 40.4 | 41.2 | 50.5 |
| Panama Panama | ... | ... | ... | 8 | ... | ... | ... | 207 | ... | ... | ... | 65.1 |
| Papua New Guinea[1] Papouasie-Nvl-Guinée[1] | 2 | 2 | 2 | 2 | ... | ... | ... | 51 | ... | ... | ... | 8.8 |
| Peru[1] Pérou[1] | 40 | 45 | 59 | 73 | ... | ... | ... | ... | ... | ... | ... | ... |
| Philippines Philippines | ... | 78 | ... | 82 | ... | 5 721 | ... | 6 514 | ... | 72.7 | ... | 79.8 |
| Poland Pologne | 43 | 43 | 42 | 42 | 3 836 | 3 463 | 3 992 | 4 345 | 99.3 | 89.7 | 103.5 | 112.7 |
| Portugal Portugal | 27 | 27 | 27 | 27 | ... | ... | ... | ... | ... | ... | ... | ... |
| Qatar Qatar | 5 | 5 | 5 | 5 | ... | ... | ... | ... | ... | ... | ... | ... |
| Romania Roumanie | 118 | 131 | 140 | 163 | 843 | 1 300 | 1 367 | 1 528 | 38.3 | 59.3 | 62.5 | 70.1 |
| Russian Federation Fédération de Russie | 236 | 136 | 249 | 250 | 9 261 | 11 168 | 13 900 | 13 280 | 63.4 | 76.9 | 96.1 | 92.3 |
| Saint Kitts and Nevis[1] Saint-Kitts-et-Nevis[1] | 1 | 1 | 1 | 1 | ... | ... | ... | ... | ... | ... | ... | ... |
| Samoa[1] Samoa[1] | 2 | 2 | 2 | 2 | ... | ... | ... | ... | ... | ... | ... | ... |
| San Marino[1] Saint-Marin[1] | 3 | 3 | 2 | 2 | ... | ... | ... | ... | ... | ... | ... | ... |
| Sao Tome and Principe[1] Sao Tomé-et-Principe[1] | 1 | 1 | 1 | 1 | ... | ... | ... | ... | ... | ... | ... | ... |
| Saudi Arabia[1] Arabie saoudite[1] | 10 | 10 | 11 | 12 | ... | ... | ... | ... | ... | ... | ... | ... |
| Senegal Sénégal | 9 | 10 | 11 | 13 | ... | ... | ... | 100 | ... | ... | ... | 8.8 |

| Country or area Pays ou zone | Number of titles - Nombre de titres | | | | Total average daily circulation or copies printed (thousands) Diffusion moyenne ou nombre imprimé (en milliers) | | | | Circulation or copies printed per 1000 inhabitants t Diffusion ou nombre imprimé pour 1000 habitants t | | | |
|---|---|---|---|---|---|---|---|---|---|---|---|---|
| | 2001 | 2002 | 2003 | 2004 | 2001 | 2002 | 2003 | 2004 | 2001 | 2002 | 2003 | 2004 |
| Serbia and Montenegro[1] Serbie-et-Monténégro[1] | ... | 29 | ... | ... | | | | | ... | ... | ... | ... |
| Seychelles[1] Seychelles[1] | 1 | 1 | 1 | 1 | ... | ... | ... | ... | ... | ... | ... | ... |
| Singapore[1] Singapour[1] | 10 | 10 | 11 | 11 | 1 300 | 1 325 | 1 496 | 1 542 | 317.3 | 318.3 | 354.5 | 360.9 |
| Slovakia Slovaquie | 16 | 16 | 21 | 13 | 623 | 653 | 756 | 677 | 115.2 | 120.9 | 139.9 | 125.4 |
| Slovenia Slovénie | 6 | 6 | 5 | 5 | ... | 344[1,6] | ... | ... | ... | 174.9[1] | ... | ... |
| Solomom Islands[1] Iles Salomon[1] | 1 | 1 | 1 | 1 | ... | 5 | 5 | 5 | ... | 11.3 | 11.0 | 10.7 |
| South Africa Afrique du Sud | 17 | 18 | 18 | 18 | 1 169 | 1 137 | 1 286 | 1 408 | 25.3 | 24.4 | 27.4 | 29.8 |
| Spain[1] Espagne[1] | 142 | 136 | 145 | 151 | 5 548 | 5 340 | 5 905 | 6 183 | 134.9 | 128.3 | 140.1 | 145.0 |
| Sri Lanka Sri Lanka | 13 | 13 | 13 | 12 | 497[1,6] | 493[1,6] | ... | ... | 24.8[1] | 24.4[1] | ... | ... |
| Sudan Soudan | 22 | 25 | 15 | 22 | ... | ... | ... | ... | ... | ... | ... | ... |
| Suriname[1] Suriname[1] | 3 | 3 | 3 | 3 | ... | ... | ... | ... | ... | ... | ... | ... |
| Swaziland Swaziland | 2 | 2 | 2 | 2 | 25 | 25 | 25 | 27 | 24.3 | 24.2 | 24.2 | 26.1 |
| Sweden[1] Suède[1] | 95 | 93 | 92 | 93 | 4 062 | 4 251 | 4 264 | 4 324 | 456.4 | 475.9 | 475.3 | 480.0 |
| Switzerland[1] Suisse[1] | 102 | 102 | 101 | 96 | 3 396 | 3 364 | 3 289 | 3 105 | 472.3 | 466.6 | 455.2 | 428.9 |
| Syrian Arab Republic[1] Rép. arabe syrienne[1] | 4 | 4 | 4 | 4 | ... | ... | ... | ... | ... | ... | ... | ... |
| TFYR of Macedonia L'ex-R.y. Macédoine | 8 | 9 | 9 | 10 | 104 | 151 | 142 | 180 | 51.7 | 74.9 | 69.8 | 88.7 |
| Timor-Leste[1] Timor-Leste[1] | 2 | 2 | 2 | 2 | ... | ... | ... | ... | ... | ... | ... | ... |
| Togo[1] Togo[1] | 1 | 1 | 1 | 1 | ... | ... | ... | ... | ... | ... | ... | ... |
| Trinidad and Tobago Trinité-et-Tobago | 3 | 3 | 3 | 3 | 191 | 187 | 196 | ... | 148.2 | 144.6 | 151.1 | ... |
| Tunisia Tunisie | 8 | 7[1] | 8[1] | 10[1] | 219 | ... | ... | ... | 22.7 | ... | ... | ... |
| Turkey Turquie | ... | ... | ... | 588 | ... | ... | ... | ... | ... | ... | ... | ... |
| Turkmenistan[1] Turkménistan[1] | 2 | 2 | 2 | 2 | ... | ... | 45 | 45 | ... | ... | 9.6 | 9.4 |
| Uganda Ouganda | 6 | 6 | 7 | 7 | ... | ... | ... | ... | ... | ... | ... | ... |
| Ukraine Ukraine | 97 | 66 | 58 | 55 | 8 459 | 9 614 | 10 803 | 6 192 | 174.1 | 200.2 | 227.4 | 131.8 |
| United Arab Emirates[1] Emirats arabes unis[1] | 8 | 9 | 9 | 9 | ... | ... | ... | ... | ... | ... | ... | ... |

| Country or area Pays ou zone | Number of titles - Nombre de titres | | | | Total average daily circulation or copies printed (thousands) Diffusion moyenne ou nombre imprimé (en milliers) | | | | Circulation or copies printed per 1000 inhabitants t Diffusion ou nombre imprimé pour 1000 habitants t | | | |
|---|---|---|---|---|---|---|---|---|---|---|---|---|
| | 2001 | 2002 | 2003 | 2004 | 2001 | 2002 | 2003 | 2004 | 2001 | 2002 | 2003 | 2004 |
| United Kingdom[1] Royaume-Uni[1] | 108 | 107 | 107 | 109 | 19 197 | 19 186 | 18 070 | 17 375 | 326.1 | 324.8 | 304.8 | 292.1 |
| United Rep. of Tanzania Rép.-Unie de Tanzanie | 11 | 12 | 13 | 14 | 30 | 40 | 50 | 60 | 0.9 | 1.1 | 1.4 | 1.6 |
| United States[1] Etats-Unis[1] | 1 487 | 1 477 | 1 484 | 1 486 | 57 031 | 56 712 | 57 497 | 57 347 | 198.7 | 195.7 | 196.5 | 194.1 |
| Uzbekistan[1] Ouzbékistan[1] | 3 | 3 | 4 | 5 | ... | ... | ... | ... | ... | ... | ... | ... |
| Vanuatu[1] Vanuatu[1] | 1 | 1 | 1 | 1 | ... | ... | 3 | 3 | ... | ... | 14.8 | 14.5 |
| Venezuela (Bolivarian Rep. of)[1] Venezuela (Rép. bolivarienne du)[1] | ... | ... | ... | 92 | ... | ... | ... | 2 450 | ... | ... | ... | 93.2 |
| Yemen Yémen | 4 | 4 | 6 | 6 | 72 | 72 | 101 | 83 | 3.9 | 3.8 | 5.1 | 4.1 |
| Zambia Zambie | 3 | 3 | 3 | 3 | ... | 56[1,6] | 55[1,6] | 55[1,6] | ... | 5.0[1] | 4.9[1] | 4.8[1] |
| Zimbabwe Zimbabwe | 3 | 3 | 3 | 3 | ... | ... | ... | ... | ... | ... | ... | ... |

Source

United Nations Educational, Scientific and Cultural Organization (UNESCO) Institute for Statistics, Montreal, the UNESCO Institute for Statistics database, last accessed November 2007.

t  Calculated using data from the United Nations Population Division, "World Population Prospects, The 2006 Revision".

Notes

1  Source: World Association of Newspapers.
2  National estimation.
3  Includes only newspapers which report to a governmental or national institution.
4  Does not include newspapers from remote areas.
5  Partial data.
6  UIS estimation.
7  For statistical purposes, the data for China do not include those for the Hong Kong Special Administrative Region (Hong Kong SAR) and Macao Special Administrative Region (Macao SAR).
8  Includes only newspapers affiliated to a national association.
9  Does not include newspapers published in the Turkish occupied area of Cyprus.
10  Does not include free newspapers.
11  Includes specialized daily newspapers for the general public and specialized technical and professional daily newspapers.

Source

L'Institut de statistique de l'Organisation des Nations Unies pour l'éducation, la science et la culture (UNESCO), Montréal, la base de données de l'Institut de statistique de l'UNESCO, dernier accès novembre 2007.

t  Calculé avec des données du "World Population Prospects, The 2006 Revision" de la Division de la population du Secrétariat des Nations Unies.

Notes

1  Source: Association Mondiale des Journaux.
2  Estimation nationale.
3  Inclut seulement les journaux se rapportant à une institution gouvernementale ou nationale.
4  N'inclut pas les journaux des régions éloignées.
5  Données partielles.
6  Estimation de l'ISU.
7  Pour la présentation des statistiques, les données pour la Chine ne comprennent pas la Région Administrative Spéciale de Hong Kong (Hong Kong RAS) et la Région Administrative Spéciale de Macao (Macao RAS).
8  Inclut seulement les journaux affiliés à une association nationale.
9  N'inclut pas les journaux publiés dans la zone occupée turque de Chypre.
10  N'inclut pas les journaux gratuits.
11  Inclut la presse quotidienne spécialisée grand public et la presse quotidienne spécialisée technique professionnelle.

## Telephones
Main telephone lines in operation (in thousands) and lines per 100 inhabitants

## Téléphones
Nombre de lignes téléphoniques en service (en milliers) et lignes pour 100 habitants

| Country or area | Fiscal year [&] Ex. budgét. [&] | 1999 | 2000 | 2001 | 2002 | 2003 | 2004 | 2005 | 2006 | Pays ou zone |
|---|---|---|---|---|---|---|---|---|---|---|
| Afghanistan | | | | | | | | | | Afghanistan |
| Number (thousands) | | *29 | *29 | 29 | *33 | *37 | *50 | *100 | *165 | Nombre (en milliers) |
| Per 100 inhabitants | | 0.1 | 0.1 | 0.1 | 0.1 | 0.1 | 0.2 | 0.3 | 0.5 | Pour 100 habitants |
| Albania | | | | | | | | | | Albanie |
| Number (thousands) | | 140 | 153 | 198 | 220 | 255 | 275 | 354 | ... | Nombre (en milliers) |
| Per 100 inhabitants | | 4.5 | 4.9 | 6.4 | 7.1 | 8.3 | 8.6 | 11.3 | ... | Pour 100 habitants |
| Algeria | | | | | | | | | | Algérie |
| Number (thousands) | | 1 600 | 1 761 | 1 880 | 1 950 | 2 147 | 2 487 | 2 572 | 2 841 | Nombre (en milliers) |
| Per 100 inhabitants | | 5.3 | 5.8 | 6.1 | 6.2 | 6.7 | 7.7 | 7.8 | 8.5 | Pour 100 habitants |
| American Samoa | | | | | | | | | | Samoa américaines |
| Number (thousands) | | 10 | *10 | *13 | 14 | 11 | 10 | ... | ... | Nombre (en milliers) |
| Per 100 inhabitants | | 18.2 | 17.9 | 21.5 | 23.6 | 17.6 | 16.7 | ... | ... | Pour 100 habitants |
| Andorra | | | | | | | | | | Andorre |
| Number (thousands) | | 34 | 34 | 35[1] | 35[1] | 35[1] | 35 | 35 | 37 | Nombre (en milliers) |
| Per 100 inhabitants | | 51.0 | 51.9 | 52.2 | 52.6 | 52.8 | 52.3 | 52.8 | ... | Pour 100 habitants |
| Angola | | | | | | | | | | Angola |
| Number (thousands) | | 67[2] | 65 | 77 | 80 | 85 | 94 | 97 | 98[3] | Nombre (en milliers) |
| Per 100 inhabitants | | 0.5 | 0.5 | 0.6 | 0.6 | 0.6 | 0.7 | 0.6 | 0.6 | Pour 100 habitants |
| Anguilla | | | | | | | | | | Anguilla |
| Number (thousands) | | 6[4] | 6 | 6 | ... | 5 | 6 | 6 | ... | Nombre (en milliers) |
| Per 100 inhabitants | | 52.8 | 54.9 | 54.3 | ... | 46.1 | 47.2 | 45.2 | ... | Pour 100 habitants |
| Antigua and Barbuda | (01/04) | | | | | | | | | Antigua-et-Barbuda |
| Number (thousands) | | 37 | 38 | 37[5] | 38 | 38 | 38 | 36 | 38 | Nombre (en milliers) |
| Per 100 inhabitants | | 48.5 | 50.1 | 48.0 | 48.4 | 47.7 | 47.2 | 44.8 | 45.5 | Pour 100 habitants |
| Argentina | (30/09) | | | | | | | | | Argentine |
| Number (thousands) | | 7 223[6] | 7 894[6] | 8 131[6] | 7 709[6] | 8 604 | 8 761 | 9 442 | 9 460 | Nombre (en milliers) |
| Per 100 inhabitants | | 19.8 | 21.5 | 21.9 | 20.5 | 22.7 | 22.9 | 24.5 | 24.2 | Pour 100 habitants |
| Armenia | | | | | | | | | | Arménie |
| Number (thousands) | | 544 | 533 | 531 | 543 | 564 | 579 | 594 | ... | Nombre (en milliers) |
| Per 100 inhabitants | | 17.6 | 17.3 | 17.3 | 17.8 | 18.6 | 19.1 | 19.7 | ... | Pour 100 habitants |
| Aruba | | | | | | | | | | Aruba |
| Number (thousands) | | 37 | *38 | 37 | 37 | 37[4] | 38[4] | 38 | 39 | Nombre (en milliers) |
| Per 100 inhabitants | | 40.3 | 41.4 | 39.7 | 39.0 | 38.7 | 38.7 | 38.5 | 38.4 | Pour 100 habitants |
| Ascension | | | | | | | | | | Ascension |
| Number (thousands) | | 1 | 1 | 1[5] | ... | 1 | 1 | ... | ... | Nombre (en milliers) |
| Per 100 inhabitants | | 45.2 | 46.1 | 49.0 | ... | 50.8 | 50.2 | ... | ... | Pour 100 habitants |
| Australia | (30/06) | | | | | | | | | Australie |
| Number (thousands) | | 9 760 | 10 050 | 10 060 | 10 400 | 10 460 | 10 370 | 10 120 | 9 940 | Nombre (en milliers) |
| Per 100 inhabitants | | 51.6 | 52.5 | 51.8 | 53.0 | 52.6 | 52.1 | 50.2 | 48.8 | Pour 100 habitants |
| Austria | | | | | | | | | | Autriche |
| Number (thousands)[7] | | 3 939 | 3 997 | 3 997 | 3 883 | 3 877 | 3 821 | 3 739 | 3 561 | Nombre (en milliers)[7] |
| Per 100 inhabitants | | 49.3 | 49.9 | 49.6 | 47.9 | 47.6 | 46.6 | 45.7 | 43.4 | Pour 100 habitants |
| Azerbaijan | | | | | | | | | | Azerbaïdjan |
| Number (thousands) | | 730 | 801 | 865 | 924 | 941 | 1 013 | 1 094 | 1 189 | Nombre (en milliers) |
| Per 100 inhabitants | | 9.0 | 9.8 | 10.5 | 11.2 | 11.3 | 12.1 | 13.0 | 14.0 | Pour 100 habitants |
| Bahamas | | | | | | | | | | Bahamas |
| Number (thousands) | | 111 | 114 | 123 | 127 | 132 | 140 | 133 | 132 | Nombre (en milliers) |
| Per 100 inhabitants | | 37.4 | 37.9 | 40.3 | 40.8 | 41.9 | 43.9 | 41.2 | 40.2 | Pour 100 habitants |
| Bahrain | | | | | | | | | | Bahreïn |
| Number (thousands) | | 165 | 171 | 174 | 175 | 186 | 192 | 194 | 194 | Nombre (en milliers) |
| Per 100 inhabitants | | 25.2 | 25.4 | 25.4 | 25.2 | 26.3 | 26.8 | 26.6 | 26.3 | Pour 100 habitants |

| Country or area | Fiscal year [&] Ex. budgét.[&] | 1999 | 2000 | 2001 | 2002 | 2003 | 2004 | 2005 | 2006 | Pays ou zone |
|---|---|---|---|---|---|---|---|---|---|---|
| Bangladesh | (30/06) | | | | | | | | | Bangladesh |
| Number (thousands) | | 433 | 491 | 565 | 606 | 742 | 831 | 1 070 | 1 134 | Nombre (en milliers) |
| Per 100 inhabitants | | 0.3 | 0.4 | 0.4 | 0.5 | 0.5 | 0.6 | 0.8 | 0.8 | Pour 100 habitants |
| Barbados | (01/04) | | | | | | | | | Barbade |
| Number (thousands) | | 115 | *124 | 129 | 133 | 134 | 136 | 135 | ... | Nombre (en milliers) |
| Per 100 inhabitants | | 43.0 | 46.3 | 48.1 | 49.4 | 49.7 | 50.1 | 50.1 | ... | Pour 100 habitants |
| Belarus | | | | | | | | | | Bélarus |
| Number (thousands) | | 2 638 | 2 752 | 2 862 | 2 967 | 3 071 | 3 176 | 3 284 | 3 368 | Nombre (en milliers) |
| Per 100 inhabitants | | 26.2 | 27.4 | 28.7 | 29.9 | 31.1 | 32.4 | 33.7 | 34.7 | Pour 100 habitants |
| Belgium | | | | | | | | | | Belgique |
| Number (thousands)[7] | | 5 009 | 5 036 | 5 132 | 4 932 | 4 875 | 4 801 | 4 767 | 4 719 | Nombre (en milliers)[7] |
| Per 100 inhabitants | | 48.9 | 49.1 | 49.8 | 47.6 | 46.9 | 46.0 | 45.4 | 45.2 | Pour 100 habitants |
| Belize | (01/04) | | | | | | | | | Belize |
| Number (thousands) | | 36 | 36 | 35 | 31 | 33 | 34 | 34 | 34 | Nombre (en milliers) |
| Per 100 inhabitants | | 15.4 | 14.9 | 13.7 | 12.1 | 12.8 | 12.9 | 12.7 | 12.3 | Pour 100 habitants |
| Benin | | | | | | | | | | Bénin |
| Number (thousands) | | 44 | 52 | 59 | 63 | 67 | 73 | 76 | 77 | Nombre (en milliers) |
| Per 100 inhabitants | | 0.7 | 0.8 | 0.9 | 0.9 | 0.9 | 1.0 | 1.0 | 0.9 | Pour 100 habitants |
| Bermuda | (01/04) | | | | | | | | | Bermudes |
| Number (thousands) | | 55 | 56 | 56 | *56 | ... | 54 | 52 | 58 | Nombre (en milliers) |
| Per 100 inhabitants | | 87.8 | 89.2 | 88.9 | 88.3 | ... | 84.2 | 81.8 | 89.5 | Pour 100 habitants |
| Bhutan | | | | | | | | | | Bhoutan |
| Number (thousands) | | 12 | 14 | 18 | 20 | 25 | 30 | 33 | 32 | Nombre (en milliers) |
| Per 100 inhabitants | | 1.8 | 2.2 | 2.6 | 2.8 | 3.4 | 3.9 | 4.0 | 3.8 | Pour 100 habitants |
| Bolivia | | | | | | | | | | Bolivie |
| Number (thousands) | | 503 | 511 | 524 | 591 | 610 | 625 | 646 | 667 | Nombre (en milliers) |
| Per 100 inhabitants | | 6.2 | 6.1 | 6.2 | 6.8 | 6.9 | 6.9 | 7.0 | 7.1 | Pour 100 habitants |
| Bosnia and Herzegovina | | | | | | | | | | Bosnie-Herzégovine |
| Number (thousands) | | 368 | 780[8] | 847[8] | 903[8] | 938[8] | 952[8] | 969[8] | 989[8] | Nombre (en milliers) |
| Per 100 inhabitants | | 9.6 | 20.6 | 22.3 | 23.7 | 24.5 | 24.6 | 24.8 | 25.3 | Pour 100 habitants |
| Botswana | (01/04) | | | | | | | | | Botswana |
| Number (thousands) | | 124 | 136 | 148 | 132 | 132 | 136 | 132 | 137 | Nombre (en milliers) |
| Per 100 inhabitants | | 7.7 | 8.3 | 8.8 | 7.7 | 7.4 | 7.7 | 7.5 | 7.8 | Pour 100 habitants |
| Brazil | | | | | | | | | | Brésil |
| Number (thousands)[9] | | 24 985 | 30 926 | 37 431 | 38 811 | 39 205 | 39 579 | 39 853 | 38 799 | Nombre (en milliers)[9] |
| Per 100 inhabitants | | 14.6 | 17.8 | 21.2 | 21.7 | 21.6 | 21.5 | 21.4 | 20.5 | Pour 100 habitants |
| British Virgin Islands | (01/04) | | | | | | | | | Iles Vierges britanniques |
| Number (thousands) | | *10 | *10 | *11 | 12[10] | ... | ... | ... | ... | Nombre (en milliers) |
| Per 100 inhabitants | | 50.6 | 50.7 | 50.3 | 55.3 | ... | ... | ... | ... | Pour 100 habitants |
| Brunei Darussalam | | | | | | | | | | Brunéi Darussalam |
| Number (thousands) | | 79 | *81 | *88 | 81 | 82 | 83 | 84 | 80 | Nombre (en milliers) |
| Per 100 inhabitants | | 24.6 | 24.2 | 25.9 | 23.6 | 23.4 | 23.2 | 22.4 | 21.0 | Pour 100 habitants |
| Bulgaria | | | | | | | | | | Bulgarie |
| Number (thousands) | | 2 833 | 2 882 | 2 887 | 2 872 | 2 818 | 2 727 | 2 490 | 2 399 | Nombre (en milliers) |
| Per 100 inhabitants | | 34.2 | 35.4 | 36.6 | 36.6 | 36.1 | 35.1 | 32.2 | 31.3 | Pour 100 habitants |
| Burkina Faso | | | | | | | | | | Burkina Faso |
| Number (thousands) | | 47 | 53 | 58 | 62 | 67 | 85 | 91 | 95 | Nombre (en milliers) |
| Per 100 inhabitants | | 0.4 | 0.5 | 0.5 | 0.5 | 0.5 | 0.6 | 0.7 | 0.7 | Pour 100 habitants |
| Burundi | | | | | | | | | | Burundi |
| Number (thousands) | | 19 | *20 | *21 | 22 | 24 | 28 | 31[4] | ... | Nombre (en milliers) |
| Per 100 inhabitants | | 0.3 | 0.3 | 0.3 | 0.3 | 0.3 | 0.4 | 0.4 | ... | Pour 100 habitants |
| Cambodia | | | | | | | | | | Cambodge |
| Number (thousands)[11] | | 28 | 31 | 33 | 35 | 31 | 32 | 33 | 33 | Nombre (en milliers)[11] |
| Per 100 inhabitants | | 0.2 | 0.2 | 0.2 | 0.3 | 0.2 | 0.2 | 0.2 | 0.2 | Pour 100 habitants |

| Country or area | Fiscal year[8] Ex. budgét.[8] | 1999 | 2000 | 2001 | 2002 | 2003 | 2004 | 2005 | 2006 | Pays ou zone |
|---|---|---|---|---|---|---|---|---|---|---|
| Cameroon | | | | | | | | | | Cameroun |
| Number (thousands) | | 95 | *95 | *106 | 111 | 97 | 99 | 100 | ... | Nombre (en milliers) |
| Per 100 inhabitants | | 0.6 | 0.6 | 0.7 | 0.7 | 0.6 | 0.6 | 0.6 | ... | Pour 100 habitants |
| Canada | | | | | | | | | | Canada |
| Number (thousands) | | 20 380 | 20 840 | 21 126 | 20 622 | 20 612 | 20 563 | 20 780 | 21 000 | Nombre (en milliers) |
| Per 100 inhabitants | | 66.8 | 67.7 | 67.9 | 65.5 | 64.9 | 64.1 | 64.1 | 64.5 | Pour 100 habitants |
| Cape Verde | | | | | | | | | | Cap-Vert |
| Number (thousands) | | 47 | 55 | 64 | 70 | 72 | 73 | 71 | 72 | Nombre (en milliers) |
| Per 100 inhabitants | | 10.9 | 12.6 | 14.5 | 15.6 | 15.6 | 15.7 | 15.0 | 13.8 | Pour 100 habitants |
| Cayman Islands | (01/04) | | | | | | | | | Iles Caïmanes |
| Number (thousands) | | 32 | 35 | 38 | ... | ... | ... | ... | ... | Nombre (en milliers) |
| Per 100 inhabitants | | 82.0 | 88.2 | 92.9 | ... | ... | ... | ... | ... | Pour 100 habitants |
| Central African Rep. | | | | | | | | | | Rép. centrafricaine |
| Number (thousands) | | 10 | 9 | 9 | 9 | 10 | 10 | 10 | 12 | Nombre (en milliers) |
| Per 100 inhabitants | | 0.3 | 0.3 | 0.2 | 0.2 | 0.2 | 0.3 | 0.2 | 0.3 | Pour 100 habitants |
| Chad | | | | | | | | | | Tchad |
| Number (thousands) | | 10 | 10[4] | 11[4] | 12 | 12 | 13 | 13 | 13 | Nombre (en milliers) |
| Per 100 inhabitants | | 0.1 | 0.1 | 0.1 | 0.2 | 0.2 | 0.1 | 0.1 | 0.1 | Pour 100 habitants |
| Chile | | | | | | | | | | Chili |
| Number (thousands) | | 3 109 | 3 303 | 3 478 | 3 467 | 3 251 | 3 318 | 3 436 | 3 326 | Nombre (en milliers) |
| Per 100 inhabitants | | 20.7 | 21.7 | 22.6 | 23.0 | 21.3 | 21.5 | 22.0 | 20.2 | Pour 100 habitants |
| China[12] | | | | | | | | | | Chine[12] |
| Number (thousands) | | 108 716 | 144 829 | 180 368 | 214 222 | 262 747 | 311 756 | 350 445 | 367 786 | Nombre (en milliers) |
| Per 100 inhabitants | | 8.6 | 11.4 | 14.1 | 16.6 | 20.2 | 23.8 | 26.6 | 27.8 | Pour 100 habitants |
| China, Hong Kong SAR | (01/04) | | | | | | | | | Chine, Hong Kong RAS |
| Number (thousands) | | 3 869 | 3 926 | 3 898 | 3 832 | 3 806 | 3 763 | 3 798 | 3 850 | Nombre (en milliers) |
| Per 100 inhabitants | | 58.6 | 58.9 | 58.0 | 56.5 | 55.9 | 54.4 | 53.9 | 54.1 | Pour 100 habitants |
| China, Macao SAR | | | | | | | | | | Chine, Macao RAS |
| Number (thousands) | | 178 | 177 | 176 | 176 | 175 | 174 | 174 | 177 | Nombre (en milliers) |
| Per 100 inhabitants | | 41.5 | 40.9 | 40.4 | 39.9 | 38.9 | 37.4 | 37.9 | 38.1 | Pour 100 habitants |
| Colombia | | | | | | | | | | Colombie |
| Number (thousands) | | 6 665 | 7 193 | 7 372[13] | 7 766 | 7 848 | 7 589 | 7 679 | 7 860 | Nombre (en milliers) |
| Per 100 inhabitants | | 16.0 | 17.0 | 17.2 | 17.9 | 17.9 | 16.7 | 16.8 | 17.0 | Pour 100 habitants |
| Comoros | | | | | | | | | | Comores |
| Number (thousands) | | 7 | 7 | 9 | 10 | 13 | 15 | 17 | 19 | Nombre (en milliers) |
| Per 100 inhabitants | | 1.0 | 1.0 | 1.2 | 1.3 | 1.7 | 1.9 | 2.1 | 2.3 | Pour 100 habitants |
| Congo | | | | | | | | | | Congo |
| Number (thousands) | | 22[4] | 22[4] | 22[4] | 22[4] | 7[4] | 14 | 16 | ... | Nombre (en milliers) |
| Per 100 inhabitants | | 0.8 | 0.7 | 0.7 | 0.7 | 0.2 | 0.4 | 0.4 | ... | Pour 100 habitants |
| Cook Islands | (01/04) | | | | | | | | | Iles Cook |
| Number (thousands) | | 5 | 6 | 6[14] | 6 | 7 | 6[4] | 7 | ... | Nombre (en milliers) |
| Per 100 inhabitants | | 29.4 | 31.0 | 32.8 | 33.5 | 35.7 | 33.0 | 36.5 | ... | Pour 100 habitants |
| Costa Rica | | | | | | | | | | Costa Rica |
| Number (thousands) | | 803 | 899 | 945 | 1 038 | 1 159 | 1 343 | 1 389 | 1 351 | Nombre (en milliers) |
| Per 100 inhabitants | | 22.4 | 23.5 | 23.7 | 25.8 | 27.8 | 31.6 | 32.1 | 30.7 | Pour 100 habitants |
| Côte d'Ivoire | | | | | | | | | | Côte d'Ivoire |
| Number (thousands) | | 219 | 264 | 294 | 325 | 238 | 258 | 259 | 261 | Nombre (en milliers) |
| Per 100 inhabitants | | 1.5 | 1.8 | 1.8 | 2.0 | 1.4 | 1.5 | 1.4 | 1.4 | Pour 100 habitants |
| Croatia | | | | | | | | | | Croatie |
| Number (thousands) | | 1 634 | 1 721 | *1 781 | 1 825 | 1 871 | 1 888 | 1 883 | 1 827 | Nombre (en milliers) |
| Per 100 inhabitants | | 36.5 | 38.5 | 40.7 | 41.7 | 42.8 | 42.7 | 41.4 | 40.1 | Pour 100 habitants |
| Cuba | | | | | | | | | | Cuba |
| Number (thousands) | | 434 | 489 | 574 | 666 | 724 | 768 | 856 | 973 | Nombre (en milliers) |
| Per 100 inhabitants | | 3.9 | 4.4 | 5.1 | 5.9 | 6.4 | 6.8 | 7.6 | 8.6 | Pour 100 habitants |

**Telephones**—Main telephone lines in operation (in thousands) and lines per 100 inhabitants (*continued*)
**Téléphones**—Nombre de lignes téléphoniques en service (en milliers) et lignes pour 100 habitants (*suite*)

| Country or area | Fiscal year [&] Ex. budgét.[&] | 1999 | 2000 | 2001 | 2002 | 2003 | 2004 | 2005 | 2006 | Pays ou zone |
|---|---|---|---|---|---|---|---|---|---|---|
| Cyprus | | | | | | | | | | Chypre |
| Number (thousands) | | 424 | 440 | 435 | 427 | 424[7] | 418 | 420 | 408 | Nombre (en milliers) |
| Per 100 inhabitants | | 63.4 | 64.8 | 63.1 | 59.8 | 59.0 | 51.8 | 50.3 | 48.3 | Pour 100 habitants |
| Czech Republic | | | | | | | | | | République tchèque |
| Number (thousands) | | 3 806 | 3 872 | 3 861 | 3 675 | 3 626 | 3 428 | 3 217 | 2 888 | Nombre (en milliers) |
| Per 100 inhabitants | | 37.0 | 37.7 | 37.8 | 36.0 | 35.5 | 33.6 | 31.5 | 28.3 | Pour 100 habitants |
| Dem. Rep. of the Congo | | | | | | | | | | Rép. dém. du Congo |
| Number (thousands) * | | 10 | 10 | 10 | 10 | 10 | 11 | 11 | 10 | Nombre (en milliers)* |
| Per 100 inhabitants^ | | 0.0 | 0.0 | 0.0 | 0.0 | 0.0 | 0.0 | 0.0 | 0.0 | Pour 100 habitants^ |
| Denmark | | | | | | | | | | Danemark |
| Number (thousands)[7] | | 3 638 | 3 835 | 3 865 | 3 701 | 3 614 | 3 491 | 3 348 | 3 099 | Nombre (en milliers)[7] |
| Per 100 inhabitants | | 68.5 | 72.0 | 72.2 | 68.9 | 67.0 | 64.5 | 61.7 | 56.9 | Pour 100 habitants |
| Djibouti | | | | | | | | | | Djibouti |
| Number (thousands) | | 9 | 10 | 10 | 10 | 10 | 11 | 11 | ... | Nombre (en milliers) |
| Per 100 inhabitants | | 1.4 | 1.5 | 1.5 | 1.5 | 1.5 | 1.6 | 1.6 | ... | Pour 100 habitants |
| Dominica | (01/04) | | | | | | | | | Dominique |
| Number (thousands) | | 21 | *23 | 23[15] | 24 | 22 | 21 | ... | ... | Nombre (en milliers) |
| Per 100 inhabitants | | 29.8 | 31.7 | 32.5 | 33.2 | 31.5 | 29.4 | ... | ... | Pour 100 habitants |
| Dominican Republic | | | | | | | | | | Rép. dominicaine |
| Number (thousands) | | 827 | 894 | 955 | 909 | 909 | 936 | 896 | 897 | Nombre (en milliers) |
| Per 100 inhabitants | | 10.5 | 11.2 | 11.8 | 10.6 | 10.5 | 10.6 | 10.1 | 9.9 | Pour 100 habitants |
| Ecuador | | | | | | | | | | Equateur |
| Number (thousands) | | 1 130 | 1 224 | 1 336 | 1 426 | 1 549 | 1 616 | 1 680 | 1 754 | Nombre (en milliers) |
| Per 100 inhabitants | | 9.1 | 9.7 | 10.4 | 11.0 | 11.8 | 12.2 | 12.7 | 13.1 | Pour 100 habitants |
| Egypt | (30/06) | | | | | | | | | Egypte |
| Number (thousands) | | 4 686[3] | 5 484[3] | 6 695 | 7 736 | 8 736 | 9 464 | 10 396 | 10 808 | Nombre (en milliers) |
| Per 100 inhabitants | | 7.5 | 8.6 | 10.4 | 11.5 | 12.7 | 13.5 | 14.6 | 14.3 | Pour 100 habitants |
| El Salvador | | | | | | | | | | El Salvador |
| Number (thousands) | | 495 | 625 | 650 | 668 | 753 | 888 | 971 | 1 037 | Nombre (en milliers) |
| Per 100 inhabitants | | 8.0 | 10.0 | 10.2 | 10.3 | 11.3 | 13.4 | 14.1 | 14.8 | Pour 100 habitants |
| Equatorial Guinea | | | | | | | | | | Guinée équatoriale |
| Number (thousands) * | | 6 | 6 | 7 | 9 | 10 | 11 | 10 | ... | Nombre (en milliers)* |
| Per 100 inhabitants | | 1.3 | 1.3 | 1.5 | 1.7 | 1.8 | 2.1 | 2.0 | ... | Pour 100 habitants |
| Eritrea | | | | | | | | | | Erythrée |
| Number (thousands) | | 27 | 31 | 31 | 36 | 38 | 39 | 38 | 38 | Nombre (en milliers) |
| Per 100 inhabitants | | 0.8 | 0.8 | 0.8 | 0.9 | 0.9 | 0.9 | 0.9 | 0.8 | Pour 100 habitants |
| Estonia | | | | | | | | | | Estonie |
| Number (thousands) | | 515 | 523 | 506 | 475 | 461 | 444 | 442 | 452 | Nombre (en milliers) |
| Per 100 inhabitants | | 35.7 | 36.3 | 35.4 | 35.1 | 34.1 | 33.3 | 33.3 | 34.1 | Pour 100 habitants |
| Ethiopia | (30/06) | | | | | | | | | Ethiopie |
| Number (thousands) | | 194 | 232 | 284 | 354 | 405 | 484 | 610 | 725 | Nombre (en milliers) |
| Per 100 inhabitants | | 0.3 | 0.4 | 0.4 | 0.5 | 0.6 | 0.7 | 0.8 | 0.9 | Pour 100 habitants |
| Faeroe Islands | | | | | | | | | | Iles Féroé |
| Number (thousands) | | 25 | 25 | 23 | 24 | 24 | 24 | 24 | 23 | Nombre (en milliers) |
| Per 100 inhabitants | | 55.1 | 54.7 | 50.4 | 52.8 | 52.3 | 51.3 | 50.7 | 48.7 | Pour 100 habitants |
| Falkland Is. (Malvinas) | | | | | | | | | | Iles Falkland (Malvinas) |
| Number (thousands) | | 2 | 2 | 2 | 2 | 3 | 3 | 3 | ... | Nombre (en milliers) |
| Per 100 inhabitants | | 74.6 | 76.6 | 77.7 | 78.9 | 85.1 | 84.4 | 83.4 | ... | Pour 100 habitants |
| Fiji | | | | | | | | | | Fidji |
| Number (thousands) | | 82 | 86[4] | 92 | 98 | 102 | 105 | 112 | ... | Nombre (en milliers) |
| Per 100 inhabitants | | 10.1 | 10.7 | 11.3 | 11.9 | 12.4 | 12.4 | 13.3 | ... | Pour 100 habitants |
| Finland | | | | | | | | | | Finlande |
| Number (thousands)[16] | | 2 850 | 2 849 | 2 806 | 2 726 | 2 568 | 2 368 | 2 120 | 1 920 | Nombre (en milliers)[16] |
| Per 100 inhabitants | | 55.2 | 55.0 | 54.0 | 52.3 | 49.2 | 45.4 | 40.4 | 36.5 | Pour 100 habitants |

| Country or area | Fiscal year[&] Ex. budgét.[&] | 1999 | 2000 | 2001 | 2002 | 2003 | 2004 | 2005 | 2006 | Pays ou zone |
|---|---|---|---|---|---|---|---|---|---|---|
| France | | | | | | | | | | France |
| Number (thousands)[7] | | 33 888 | 33 987 | 34 084 | 34 124 | 33 913 | 33 703 | 33 707 | 33 897 | Nombre (en milliers)[7] |
| Per 100 inhabitants | | 57.8 | 57.7 | 57.4 | 57.2 | 56.6 | 55.8 | 55.7 | 55.8 | Pour 100 habitants |
| French Guiana | | | | | | | | | | Guyane française |
| Number (thousands) | | 49 | 50[4] | 51[4] | ... | ... | ... | ... | ... | Nombre (en milliers) |
| Per 100 inhabitants | | 31.3 | 30.7 | 30.2 | ... | ... | ... | ... | ... | Pour 100 habitants |
| French Polynesia | | | | | | | | | | Polynésie française |
| Number (thousands) | | 52 | 54[4] | 53 | 53 | 54 | 53 | 53 | 54 | Nombre (en milliers) |
| Per 100 inhabitants | | 22.4 | 22.6 | 22.1 | 21.7 | 21.5 | 21.1 | 20.8 | 20.7 | Pour 100 habitants |
| Gabon | | | | | | | | | | Gabon |
| Number (thousands) | | 38 | 39 | 37 | 32 | 38 | 39 | 39 | 36 | Nombre (en milliers) |
| Per 100 inhabitants | | 3.2 | 3.2 | 3.0 | 2.5 | 2.9 | 2.9 | 2.8 | 2.6 | Pour 100 habitants |
| Gambia | (01/04) | | | | | | | | | Gambie |
| Number (thousands)[17] | | 29 | *33 | 35 | 38 | 42[4] | 43[4] | 44 | 46 | Nombre (en milliers)[17] |
| Per 100 inhabitants | | 2.4 | 2.6 | 2.7 | 2.9 | 3.1 | 2.9 | 2.9 | 3.0 | Pour 100 habitants |
| Georgia | | | | | | | | | | Géorgie |
| Number (thousands) | | 672 | 509[18] | 569[18] | 640[18] | 667 | 683 | 570 | 553 | Nombre (en milliers) |
| Per 100 inhabitants | | 14.1 | 10.8 | 12.2 | 13.9 | 14.6 | 15.1 | 12.7 | 12.5 | Pour 100 habitants |
| Germany | | | | | | | | | | Allemagne |
| Number (thousands)[19] | | 48 210 | 50 220 | 52 330 | 53 670 | 54 233 | 54 526 | 54 791 | 54 540 | Nombre (en milliers)[19] |
| Per 100 inhabitants | | 58.7 | 61.1 | 63.5 | 65.0 | 65.7 | 66.1 | 66.3 | 65.9 | Pour 100 habitants |
| Ghana | | | | | | | | | | Ghana |
| Number (thousands) | | 161 | 213 | 245 | 275 | 291 | 313 | 322 | 356 | Nombre (en milliers) |
| Per 100 inhabitants | | 0.8 | 1.1 | 1.2 | 1.3 | 1.4 | 1.5 | 1.5 | 1.6 | Pour 100 habitants |
| Gibraltar | | | | | | | | | | Gibraltar |
| Number (thousands) | | 22 | 24 | 25 | 25 | ... | 25 | ... | ... | Nombre (en milliers) |
| Per 100 inhabitants | | 80.2 | 85.9 | 89.2 | 87.7 | ... | 89.0 | ... | ... | Pour 100 habitants |
| Greece | | | | | | | | | | Grèce |
| Number (thousands)[7] | | 5 611 | 5 659 | 5 608 | 6 294 | 6 300 | 6 352 | 6 310 | *6 170 | Nombre (en milliers)[7] |
| Per 100 inhabitants | | 52.8 | 53.6 | 52.9 | 57.1 | 55.0 | 57.2 | 56.7 | 55.4 | Pour 100 habitants |
| Greenland | | | | | | | | | | Groenland |
| Number (thousands) | | 26 | 26 | 26 | 25 | ... | ... | ... | ... | Nombre (en milliers) |
| Per 100 inhabitants | | 45.7 | 46.8 | 46.7 | 44.7 | ... | ... | ... | ... | Pour 100 habitants |
| Grenada | | | | | | | | | | Grenade |
| Number (thousands) | | 29 | 31 | 33 | 34 | 33 | 33 | 27 | 28 | Nombre (en milliers) |
| Per 100 inhabitants | | 29.0 | 30.9 | 32.2 | 32.9 | 32.0 | 32.0 | 26.6 | 26.7 | Pour 100 habitants |
| Guadeloupe | | | | | | | | | | Guadeloupe |
| Number (thousands) | | 201 | 205 | 210[4] | ... | ... | ... | ... | ... | Nombre (en milliers) |
| Per 100 inhabitants | | 47.6 | 48.0 | 48.7 | ... | ... | ... | ... | ... | Pour 100 habitants |
| Guam | | | | | | | | | | Guam |
| Number (thousands) | | 78[20] | 74[20] | 80 | ... | ... | ... | ... | ... | Nombre (en milliers) |
| Per 100 inhabitants | | 50.9 | 48.0 | 50.9 | ... | ... | ... | ... | ... | Pour 100 habitants |
| Guatemala | | | | | | | | | | Guatemala |
| Number (thousands) | | 611 | 677 | 756 | 846 | 944 | 1 132 | 1 248 | 1 355 | Nombre (en milliers) |
| Per 100 inhabitants | | 5.5 | 5.9 | 6.5 | 7.1 | 7.7 | 8.9 | 9.9 | 10.5 | Pour 100 habitants |
| Guernsey | | | | | | | | | | Guernesey |
| Number (thousands)[7] | | 51 | 53 | 55 | 56 | 46 | 45 | ... | ... | Nombre (en milliers)[7] |
| Per 100 inhabitants | | 81.2 | 84.7 | 97.7 | 99.5 | 81.9 | 80.9 | ... | ... | Pour 100 habitants |
| Guinea | | | | | | | | | | Guinée |
| Number (thousands) | | 21 | 24 | 25 | 26 | 26 | 26 | 26[4] | ... | Nombre (en milliers) |
| Per 100 inhabitants | | 0.3 | 0.3 | 0.3 | 0.3 | 0.3 | 0.3 | 0.3 | ... | Pour 100 habitants |
| Guinea-Bissau | | | | | | | | | | Guinée-Bissau |
| Number (thousands) | | 6 | 11 | 10 | 11 | 11 | 10 | 10 | 7 | Nombre (en milliers) |
| Per 100 inhabitants | | 0.5 | 0.9 | 0.8 | 0.9 | 0.8 | 0.7 | 0.8 | 0.4 | Pour 100 habitants |

| Country or area | Fiscal year &<br>Ex. budgét.& | 1999 | 2000 | 2001 | 2002 | 2003 | 2004 | 2005 | 2006 | Pays ou zone |
|---|---|---|---|---|---|---|---|---|---|---|
| Guyana | | | | | | | | | | Guyana |
| Number (thousands) | | 64 | *68 | 80 | 80 | 92 | 103 | 110 | ... | Nombre (en milliers) |
| Per 100 inhabitants | | 8.6 | 9.2 | 10.7 | 10.8 | 12.3 | 13.7 | 14.7 | ... | Pour 100 habitants |
| Haiti | | | | | | | | | | Haïti |
| Number (thousands)[4] | | 70 | 73 | 80 | 130 | 140 | 140 | 145 | 150 | Nombre (en milliers)[4] |
| Per 100 inhabitants | | 0.9 | 0.9 | 1.0 | 1.6 | 1.8 | 1.7 | 1.7 | 1.7 | Pour 100 habitants |
| Honduras | | | | | | | | | | Honduras |
| Number (thousands) | | 279 | 299 | 310 | 323 | 334 | 387 | 494 | 714 | Nombre (en milliers) |
| Per 100 inhabitants | | 4.4 | 4.8 | 4.7 | 4.9 | 4.9 | 5.5 | 6.9 | 9.7 | Pour 100 habitants |
| Hungary | | | | | | | | | | Hongrie |
| Number (thousands) | | 3 726 | 3 798 | 3 742 | 3 669 | 3 603 | 3 564 | 3 416 | 3 360 | Nombre (en milliers) |
| Per 100 inhabitants | | 36.7 | 37.2 | 36.8 | 36.2 | 35.6 | 35.3 | 33.8 | 33.4 | Pour 100 habitants |
| Iceland | | | | | | | | | | Islande |
| Number (thousands)[7] | | 185 | 196 | 197 | 188 | 193 | 190 | 194 | 189 | Nombre (en milliers)[7] |
| Per 100 inhabitants | | 66.4 | 69.9 | 68.5 | 65.3 | 66.6 | 65.0 | 65.9 | 63.5 | Pour 100 habitants |
| India | (01/04) | | | | | | | | | Inde |
| Number (thousands) | | 26 511 | 32 436 | 38 536 | 41 420[21] | 42 000 | 46 198 | 50 177 | 40 770[22] | Nombre (en milliers) |
| Per 100 inhabitants | | 2.6 | 3.2 | 3.7 | 3.9 | 3.9 | 4.2 | 4.5 | 3.6 | Pour 100 habitants |
| Indonesia | | | | | | | | | | Indonésie |
| Number (thousands) | | 6 080 | 6 663 | 7 219 | 7 750[23] | 8 058 | 10 376 | 13 508 | 14 821 | Nombre (en milliers) |
| Per 100 inhabitants | | 3.0 | 3.2 | 3.5 | 3.7 | 3.7 | 4.7 | 6.1 | 6.6 | Pour 100 habitants |
| Iran (Islamic Rep. of) | (22/03) | | | | | | | | | Iran (Rép. islamique d') |
| Number (thousands) | | 8 371 | 9 486 | 10 897 | 12 888 | 15 341 | 16 342 | ... | 21 981 | Nombre (en milliers) |
| Per 100 inhabitants | | 13.3 | 14.9 | 16.9 | 19.7 | 23.1 | 23.4 | ... | 31.2 | Pour 100 habitants |
| Iraq | (30/06) | | | | | | | | | Iraq |
| Number (thousands) | | *675 | *675 | 675 | 1 128[24] | 1 183[24] | *1 034 | ... | ... | Nombre (en milliers) |
| Per 100 inhabitants | | 3.0 | 2.9 | 2.9 | 4.7 | 4.7 | 4.0 | ... | ... | Pour 100 habitants |
| Ireland | (01/04) | | | | | | | | | Irlande |
| Number (thousands)[7] | | 1 737 | 1 832 | 1 860 | 1 975 | 1 955 | 2 015 | 2 052 | 2 102 | Nombre (en milliers)[7] |
| Per 100 inhabitants | | 46.4 | 48.4 | 48.5 | 50.2 | 49.1 | 49.8 | 49.5 | 49.9 | Pour 100 habitants |
| Israel | | | | | | | | | | Israël |
| Number (thousands) | | 2 878 | 2 974 | 3 033 | 3 006 | 2 913 | 2 896 | 2 936 | 3 005 | Nombre (en milliers) |
| Per 100 inhabitants | | 47.1 | 47.4 | 46.6 | 45.3 | 43.1 | 42.2 | 42.6 | 43.9 | Pour 100 habitants |
| Italy | | | | | | | | | | Italie |
| Number (thousands)[7] | | 26 502 | 27 153 | 27 353[25] | 27 142 | 26 596[26] | 25 957[26] | 25 049 | ... | Nombre (en milliers)[7] |
| Per 100 inhabitants | | 46.2 | 47.4 | 47.1 | 48.1 | 45.9 | 44.8 | 43.1 | ... | Pour 100 habitants |
| Jamaica | (01/04) | | | | | | | | | Jamaïque |
| Number (thousands) | | 487 | 494 | *511 | 435 | 459 | 423 | 319 | 342 | Nombre (en milliers) |
| Per 100 inhabitants | | 18.9 | 19.0 | 19.6 | 16.6 | 17.4 | 15.8 | 12.0 | 12.8 | Pour 100 habitants |
| Japan | (01/04) | | | | | | | | | Japon |
| Number (thousands) | | 62 054 | 61 957 | 61 326 | 60 772 | 60 219 | 59 608 | 58 053[15] | 55 165 | Nombre (en milliers) |
| Per 100 inhabitants | | 49.0 | 48.8 | 48.2 | 47.7 | 47.2 | 46.6 | 45.3 | 43.0 | Pour 100 habitants |
| Jersey | | | | | | | | | | Jersey |
| Number (thousands) | | 70 | 73 | 74 | ... | ... | ... | ... | ... | Nombre (en milliers) |
| Per 100 inhabitants | | 81.5 | 84.1 | 84.8 | ... | ... | ... | ... | ... | Pour 100 habitants |
| Jordan | | | | | | | | | | Jordanie |
| Number (thousands) | | 565 | 620 | 660 | 675 | 623 | 638 | 628 | 614 | Nombre (en milliers) |
| Per 100 inhabitants | | 11.5 | 12.3 | 12.7 | 12.7 | 11.4 | 11.4 | 11.0 | 10.5 | Pour 100 habitants |
| Kazakhstan | | | | | | | | | | Kazakhstan |
| Number (thousands) | | 1 760 | 1 834 | 1 940 | 2 082 | 2 228 | 2 550 | 2 708 | 2 928 | Nombre (en milliers) |
| Per 100 inhabitants | | 11.6 | 12.2 | 13.0 | 14.0 | 15.0 | 17.2 | 18.3 | 19.8 | Pour 100 habitants |
| Kenya | (30/06) | | | | | | | | | Kenya |
| Number (thousands) | | *290 | 292 | 309 | 321 | 328 | 299 | 282 | 293 | Nombre (en milliers) |
| Per 100 inhabitants | | 1.0 | 1.0 | 1.0 | 1.0 | 1.0 | 0.9 | 0.8 | 0.8 | Pour 100 habitants |

| Country or area | Fiscal year &<br>Ex. budgét.& | 1999 | 2000 | 2001 | 2002 | 2003 | 2004 | 2005 | 2006 | Pays ou zone |
|---|---|---|---|---|---|---|---|---|---|---|
| Kiribati | | | | | | | | | | Kiribati |
| Number (thousands) | | 3 | 3[4] | 4 | 4 | ... | ... | ... | ... | Nombre (en milliers) |
| Per 100 inhabitants | | 3.7 | 4.0 | 4.2 | 5.1 | ... | ... | ... | ... | Pour 100 habitants |
| Korea, Dem. P. R. | | | | | | | | | | Corée, R. p. dém. de |
| Number (thousands)* | | 500 | 500 | 860 | 916 | 980 | ... | ... | ... | Nombre (en milliers)* |
| Per 100 inhabitants | | 2.3 | 2.3 | 3.9 | 4.1 | 4.4 | ... | ... | ... | Pour 100 habitants |
| Korea, Republic of | | | | | | | | | | Corée, République de |
| Number (thousands)[16] | | 25 619 | 25 863 | 25 775 | 25 735 | 25 128 | 23 568 | 23 905 | 23 905 | Nombre (en milliers)[16] |
| Per 100 inhabitants | | 56.1 | 56.2 | 54.4 | 54.0 | 52.5 | 49.0 | 49.5 | 49.8 | Pour 100 habitants |
| Kuwait | | | | | | | | | | Koweït |
| Number (thousands) | | 456 | 467 | 472 | 482 | 487 | 497 | 510 | 517 | Nombre (en milliers) |
| Per 100 inhabitants | | 21.6 | 21.3 | 20.8 | 20.4 | 19.6 | 19.5 | 19.0 | 18.7 | Pour 100 habitants |
| Kyrgyzstan | | | | | | | | | | Kirghizistan |
| Number (thousands) | | 371 | 376 | 388 | 395 | 396 | 416 | 440 | 459 | Nombre (en milliers) |
| Per 100 inhabitants | | 7.6 | 7.7 | 7.8 | 7.9 | 7.9 | 8.2 | 8.4 | 8.6 | Pour 100 habitants |
| Lao People's Dem. Rep. | | | | | | | | | | Rép. dém. pop. lao |
| Number (thousands) | | 35 | 41 | 53 | 62 | 70 | 75 | 75 | 92 | Nombre (en milliers) |
| Per 100 inhabitants | | 0.7 | 0.8 | 1.0 | 1.1 | 1.2 | 1.3 | 1.3 | 1.5 | Pour 100 habitants |
| Latvia | | | | | | | | | | Lettonie |
| Number (thousands) | | 732[27] | 735[27] | 722 | 701 | 654 | 650 | 731 | 657 | Nombre (en milliers) |
| Per 100 inhabitants | | 30.0 | 30.3 | 30.7 | 30.1 | 28.2 | 28.5 | 31.7 | 28.6 | Pour 100 habitants |
| Lebanon | | | | | | | | | | Liban |
| Number (thousands) | | 571[4] | 576 | 626 | 679 | 700 | 630 | 635 | 681 | Nombre (en milliers) |
| Per 100 inhabitants | | 17.6 | 17.5 | 18.7 | 19.9 | 20.0 | 17.7 | 17.7 | 18.9 | Pour 100 habitants |
| Lesotho | (01/04) | | | | | | | | | Lesotho |
| Number (thousands) | | *22 | *22 | 21[15] | 29[15] | 35[15] | 37[15] | 48[15] | 53 | Nombre (en milliers) |
| Per 100 inhabitants | | 1.2 | 1.2 | 1.2 | 1.6 | 2.0 | 2.1 | 2.7 | 3.0 | Pour 100 habitants |
| Liberia | | | | | | | | | | Libéria |
| Number (thousands)* | | 7 | 7 | 7 | 7 | ... | ... | ... | ... | Nombre (en milliers)* |
| Per 100 inhabitants | | 0.2 | 0.2 | 0.2 | 0.2 | ... | ... | ... | ... | Pour 100 habitants |
| Libyan Arab Jamah. | | | | | | | | | | Jamah. arabe libyenne |
| Number (thousands) | | 550[4] | 605[4] | 660[4] | 720[4] | 750[4] | ... | ... | 483 | Nombre (en milliers) |
| Per 100 inhabitants | | 10.1 | 10.8 | 11.8 | 13.0 | 13.6 | ... | ... | 8.1 | Pour 100 habitants |
| Liechtenstein | | | | | | | | | | Liechtenstein |
| Number (thousands) | | 20 | 20 | 20 | 20 | 20 | 20 | 20 | 20 | Nombre (en milliers) |
| Per 100 inhabitants | | 60.9 | 61.1 | 60.0 | 58.8 | 58.0 | 57.7 | 57.5 | 57.2 | Pour 100 habitants |
| Lithuania | | | | | | | | | | Lituanie |
| Number (thousands)[17,28] | | 1 153 | 1 188 | 1 152 | 936 | 824 | 820 | 801 | 792 | Nombre (en milliers)[17,28] |
| Per 100 inhabitants | | 31.2 | 32.2 | 33.0 | 26.9 | 23.9 | 23.8 | 23.4 | 23.2 | Pour 100 habitants |
| Luxembourg | | | | | | | | | | Luxembourg |
| Number (thousands)[28,29] | | 252 | 249 | 257 | 249 | 245 | 245 | 245 | 247 | Nombre (en milliers)[28,29] |
| Per 100 inhabitants | | 58.2 | 56.8 | 58.4 | 55.7 | 54.3 | 53.4 | 52.6 | 52.4 | Pour 100 habitants |
| Madagascar | | | | | | | | | | Madagascar |
| Number (thousands) | | 50 | 55 | 58 | 59 | 60 | 59 | 67 | 130 | Nombre (en milliers) |
| Per 100 inhabitants | | 0.3 | 0.3 | 0.4 | 0.3 | 0.3 | 0.3 | 0.4 | 0.7 | Pour 100 habitants |
| Malawi | | | | | | | | | | Malawi |
| Number (thousands) | | 42 | 46 | 55 | 73 | 85 | 93 | 103 | ... | Nombre (en milliers) |
| Per 100 inhabitants | | 0.4 | 0.4 | 0.5 | 0.7 | 0.8 | 0.8 | 0.8 | ... | Pour 100 habitants |
| Malaysia | | | | | | | | | | Malaisie |
| Number (thousands) | | 4 431 | 4 634 | 4 710 | 4 670 | 4 572 | 4 446 | 4 366 | 4 342 | Nombre (en milliers) |
| Per 100 inhabitants | | 20.3 | 19.9 | 19.7 | 19.0 | 18.2 | 17.4 | 16.8 | 16.8 | Pour 100 habitants |
| Maldives | | | | | | | | | | Maldives |
| Number (thousands) | | 22 | 24 | 27 | 29 | 30 | 32 | 32 | 33 | Nombre (en milliers) |
| Per 100 inhabitants | | 8.4 | 9.0 | 9.9 | 10.2 | 10.5 | 10.7 | 10.7 | 10.9 | Pour 100 habitants |

| Country or area | Fiscal year[&] Ex. budgét.[&] | 1999 | 2000 | 2001 | 2002 | 2003 | 2004 | 2005 | 2006 | Pays ou zone |
|---|---|---|---|---|---|---|---|---|---|---|
| Mali | | | | | | | | | | Mali |
| Number (thousands) | | 34 | 39 | 51 | 57 | 61 | 75 | 75 | 83 | Nombre (en milliers) |
| Per 100 inhabitants | | 0.3 | 0.4 | 0.5 | 0.5 | 0.6 | 0.7 | 0.7 | 0.6 | Pour 100 habitants |
| Malta | | | | | | | | | | Malte |
| Number (thousands) | | 198 | 204 | 208 | 207 | 208 | 207 | 203 | 202 | Nombre (en milliers) |
| Per 100 inhabitants | | 51.2 | 52.4 | 53.0 | 52.3 | 52.1 | 51.6 | 50.5 | 50.0 | Pour 100 habitants |
| Marshall Islands | | | | | | | | | | Iles Marshall |
| Number (thousands) | | 4 | 4 | 4 | 4 | 4 | ... | ... | ... | Nombre (en milliers) |
| Per 100 inhabitants | | 7.6 | 7.7 | 8.0 | 8.2 | 8.3 | ... | ... | ... | Pour 100 habitants |
| Martinique | | | | | | | | | | Martinique |
| Number (thousands) | | 172 | 172[4] | 172[4] | ... | ... | ... | ... | ... | Nombre (en milliers) |
| Per 100 inhabitants | | 45.1 | 44.7 | 44.5 | ... | ... | ... | ... | ... | Pour 100 habitants |
| Mauritania | | | | | | | | | | Mauritanie |
| Number (thousands) | | 17 | 19 | 25 | 32 | 38 | 39 | 41 | 35 | Nombre (en milliers) |
| Per 100 inhabitants | | 0.7 | 0.7 | 1.0 | 1.2 | 1.4 | 1.3 | 1.3 | 1.1 | Pour 100 habitants |
| Mauritius | | | | | | | | | | Maurice |
| Number (thousands) | | 257 | 281 | 307 | 327 | 348 | 354 | 357 | 357 | Nombre (en milliers) |
| Per 100 inhabitants | | 21.9 | 23.5 | 25.6 | 27.0 | 28.5 | 28.7 | 28.7 | 28.5 | Pour 100 habitants |
| Mayotte | | | | | | | | | | Mayotte |
| Number (thousands) | | 10 | 10 | *10 | *10 | ... | ... | ... | ... | Nombre (en milliers) |
| Per 100 inhabitants | | 6.8 | 6.8 | 6.5 | 6.2 | ... | ... | ... | ... | Pour 100 habitants |
| Mexico | | | | | | | | | | Mexique |
| Number (thousands)[30] | | 10 927 | 12 332 | 13 774 | 14 975 | 16 330 | 18 073[3] | 19 512 | 19 861 | Nombre (en milliers)[30] |
| Per 100 inhabitants | | 11.2 | 12.5 | 13.9 | 14.9 | 16.0 | 17.2 | 18.2 | 18.3 | Pour 100 habitants |
| Micronesia (Fed. States of) | | | | | | | | | | Micronésie (Etats féd. de) |
| Number (thousands) | | 10[4] | 10[4] | 10 | 10 | 11 | 12 | 12 | ... | Nombre (en milliers) |
| Per 100 inhabitants | | 9.2 | 9.0 | 9.4 | 9.4 | 10.3 | 10.8 | 11.2 | ... | Pour 100 habitants |
| Moldova | | | | | | | | | | Moldova |
| Number (thousands) | | 555 | 584 | 639 | 719 | 791 | 863 | 929 | 1 018 | Nombre (en milliers) |
| Per 100 inhabitants | | 12.9 | 13.7 | 15.0 | 16.9 | 18.7 | 20.3 | 22.1 | 24.3 | Pour 100 habitants |
| Monaco | | | | | | | | | | Monaco |
| Number (thousands) | | 30 | 30 | 30 | 34 | 34 | 34 | 34 | 34 | Nombre (en milliers) |
| Per 100 inhabitants | | 90.2 | 89.8 | 87.9 | 98.8 | 97.1 | 97.1 | 96.4 | 96.8 | Pour 100 habitants |
| Mongolia | | | | | | | | | | Mongolie |
| Number (thousands) | | 103 | 118 | 124 | 128 | 138 | 146 | 156 | 159 | Nombre (en milliers) |
| Per 100 inhabitants | | 4.4 | 5.0 | 5.2 | 5.3 | 5.6 | 5.6 | 5.9 | 5.9 | Pour 100 habitants |
| Montenegro | | | | | | | | | | Monténégro |
| Number (thousands) | | ... | ... | ... | ... | ... | ... | ... | 353 | Nombre (en milliers) |
| Per 100 inhabitants | | ... | ... | ... | ... | ... | ... | ... | 58.9 | Pour 100 habitants |
| Montserrat | | | | | | | | | | Montserrat |
| Number (thousands)[31] | | *3 | 3 | ... | ... | ... | ... | ... | ... | Nombre (en milliers)[31] |
| Per 100 inhabitants | | 74.3 | 70.3 | ... | ... | ... | ... | ... | ... | Pour 100 habitants |
| Morocco | | | | | | | | | | Maroc |
| Number (thousands) | | 1 471 | 1 425 | 1 191 | 1 127 | 1 219 | 1 309 | 1 341 | 1 266 | Nombre (en milliers) |
| Per 100 inhabitants | | 5.3 | 5.0 | 4.2 | 3.9 | 4.1 | 4.4 | 4.4 | 4.1 | Pour 100 habitants |
| Mozambique | | | | | | | | | | Mozambique |
| Number (thousands) | | 78 | 86 | 89 | 84 | 78 | 70 | 70 | 67 | Nombre (en milliers) |
| Per 100 inhabitants | | 0.5 | 0.5 | 0.5 | 0.5 | 0.4 | 0.4 | 0.4 | 0.3 | Pour 100 habitants |
| Myanmar | | | | | | | | | | Myanmar |
| Number (thousands) | | 249 | 271 | 295 | 342 | 363 | 425 | 504 | ... | Nombre (en milliers) |
| Per 100 inhabitants | | 0.6 | 0.5 | 0.6 | 0.7 | 0.7 | 0.8 | 0.9 | ... | Pour 100 habitants |
| Namibia | (30/09) | | | | | | | | | Namibie |
| Number (thousands) | | 108 | 110 | 117 | 121 | 127 | 128 | 139 | ... | Nombre (en milliers) |
| Per 100 inhabitants | | 6.2 | 6.2 | 6.4 | 6.5 | 6.6 | 6.4 | 6.8 | ... | Pour 100 habitants |

| Country or area | Fiscal year[&] Ex. budgét.[&] | 1999 | 2000 | 2001 | 2002 | 2003 | 2004 | 2005 | 2006 | Pays ou zone |
|---|---|---|---|---|---|---|---|---|---|---|
| Nauru | | | | | | | | | | Nauru |
| Number (thousands) | | 2[4] | 2[4] | 2 | ... | ... | ... | ... | ... | Nombre (en milliers) |
| Per 100 inhabitants | | 15.5 | 15.7 | 16.0 | ... | ... | ... | ... | ... | Pour 100 habitants |
| Nepal | (15/07) | | | | | | | | | Népal |
| Number (thousands) | | 253 | 267 | 298[5] | 328 | 372 | 418 | 485 | 612 | Nombre (en milliers) |
| Per 100 inhabitants | | 1.2 | 1.2 | 1.3 | 1.4 | 1.6 | 1.7 | 1.8 | 2.2 | Pour 100 habitants |
| Netherlands | | | | | | | | | | Pays-Bas |
| Number (thousands)[7] | | 9 613 | 9 889 | 8 158 | 8 026[4] | 7 846 | 7 861 | 7 600 | ... | Nombre (en milliers)[7] |
| Per 100 inhabitants | | 60.6 | 61.9 | 50.7 | 49.6 | 48.2 | 48.4 | 46.6 | ... | Pour 100 habitants |
| Netherlands Antilles | | | | | | | | | | Antilles néerlandaises |
| Number (thousands)* | | 79 | 80 | 81 | ... | ... | ... | ... | ... | Nombre (en milliers)* |
| Per 100 inhabitants | | 36.8 | 37.2 | 37.2 | ... | ... | ... | ... | ... | Pour 100 habitants |
| New Caledonia | | | | | | | | | | Nouvelle-Calédonie |
| Number (thousands) | | 51 | 51 | 51 | 52 | 52 | 53 | 55 | ... | Nombre (en milliers) |
| Per 100 inhabitants | | 24.1 | 23.8 | 23.1 | 23.2 | 22.7 | 23.0 | 23.3 | ... | Pour 100 habitants |
| New Zealand | (01/04) | | | | | | | | | Nouvelle-Zélande |
| Number (thousands) | | 1 833 | 1 831 | 1 823 | 1 765 | 1 798 | 1 801 | 1 729 | 1 790 | Nombre (en milliers) |
| Per 100 inhabitants | | 47.8 | 47.5 | 47.0 | 44.8 | 45.6 | 45.1 | 42.9 | 44.1 | Pour 100 habitants |
| Nicaragua | | | | | | | | | | Nicaragua |
| Number (thousands) | | 150 | 164 | 158 | 172 | 205 | 214 | 221 | 248 | Nombre (en milliers) |
| Per 100 inhabitants | | 3.0 | 3.2 | 3.0 | 3.3 | 3.7 | 3.8 | 3.8 | 4.4 | Pour 100 habitants |
| Niger | | | | | | | | | | Niger |
| Number (thousands) | | 19[4] | 20 | 22 | 22 | 23 | 24 | 24 | ... | Nombre (en milliers) |
| Per 100 inhabitants | | 0.2 | 0.2 | 0.2 | 0.2 | 0.2 | 0.2 | 0.2 | ... | Pour 100 habitants |
| Nigeria | | | | | | | | | | Nigéria |
| Number (thousands) | | 473 | 553 | 600 | 702 | 889 | 1 028 | 1 223 | 1 688 | Nombre (en milliers) |
| Per 100 inhabitants | | 0.4 | 0.5 | 0.5 | 0.6 | 0.7 | 0.8 | 0.9 | 1.3 | Pour 100 habitants |
| Niue | | | | | | | | | | Nioué |
| Number (thousands) | | 1[4] | 1[4] | 1 | 1 | 1 | 1 | 1 | ... | Nombre (en milliers) |
| Per 100 inhabitants | | 49.7 | 56.5 | 60.8 | 61.0 | 61.8 | 61.8 | 61.8 | ... | Pour 100 habitants |
| Northern Mariana Islands | | | | | | | | | | Iles Mariannes du Nord |
| Number (thousands) | | 21 | 21 | ... | ... | ... | ... | ... | ... | Nombre (en milliers) |
| Per 100 inhabitants | | 30.6 | 30.3 | ... | ... | ... | ... | ... | ... | Pour 100 habitants |
| Norway | | | | | | | | | | Norvège |
| Number (thousands) | | 2 446 | 2 401 | 2 338 | 2 317 | 2 236 | 2 180 | 2 129 | 2 055 | Nombre (en milliers) |
| Per 100 inhabitants | | 54.6 | 53.3 | 51.7 | 50.9 | 48.9 | 47.4 | 46.1 | 44.3 | Pour 100 habitants |
| Occupied Palestinian Terr. | | | | | | | | | | Terr. palestinien occupé |
| Number (thousands) | | 222 | 272 | 292 | 302 | 252 | 290 | 349 | 341 | Nombre (en milliers) |
| Per 100 inhabitants | | 7.4 | 8.6 | 8.9 | 8.7 | 7.0 | 7.9 | 9.4 | 9.2 | Pour 100 habitants |
| Oman | | | | | | | | | | Oman |
| Number (thousands) | | 220 | 222 | 231 | 228 | 236 | 243 | 258 | 270 | Nombre (en milliers) |
| Per 100 inhabitants | | 9.2 | 9.1 | 9.3 | 9.1 | 9.4 | 9.6 | 10.1 | 10.3 | Pour 100 habitants |
| Pakistan | (30/06) | | | | | | | | | Pakistan |
| Number (thousands) | | 2 874 | 3 053 | 3 252 | 3 655 | 4 047 | 4 502 | 5 228 | 5 240 | Nombre (en milliers) |
| Per 100 inhabitants | | 2.1 | 2.2 | 2.3 | 2.5 | 2.7 | 3.0 | 3.4 | 3.3 | Pour 100 habitants |
| Palau | | | | | | | | | | Palaos |
| Number (thousands) | | ... | ... | ... | 7 | 7 | 8 | 8 | 7 | Nombre (en milliers) |
| Panama | | | | | | | | | | Panama |
| Number (thousands) | | 462 | 429 | 382 | 387 | 381 | 410 | 469 | 433 | Nombre (en milliers) |
| Per 100 inhabitants | | 16.4 | 15.1 | 13.2 | 12.9 | 12.2 | 12.9 | 14.5 | 13.2 | Pour 100 habitants |
| Papua New Guinea | | | | | | | | | | Papouasie-Nvl-Guinée |
| Number (thousands) | | 60 | 65 | 62 | 62 | 63 | 63 | 64 | ... | Nombre (en milliers) |
| Per 100 inhabitants | | 1.2 | 1.3 | 1.2 | 1.1 | 1.1 | 1.1 | 1.1 | ... | Pour 100 habitants |

| Country or area | Fiscal year [&] Ex. budgét.[&] | 1999 | 2000 | 2001 | 2002 | 2003 | 2004 | 2005 | 2006 | Pays ou zone |
|---|---|---|---|---|---|---|---|---|---|---|
| Paraguay | | | | | | | | | | Paraguay |
| Number (thousands) | | 268 | 283 | 289[32] | 273 | 281 | 303 | 320 | 331 | Nombre (en milliers) |
| Per 100 inhabitants | | 5.0 | 5.1 | 5.1 | 4.7 | 4.7 | 5.0 | 5.2 | 5.3 | Pour 100 habitants |
| Peru | | | | | | | | | | Pérou |
| Number (thousands) | | 1 688 | 1 717 | 1 571 | 1 657 | 1 839 | 2 050 | 2 251 | 2 401 | Nombre (en milliers) |
| Per 100 inhabitants | | 6.7 | 6.7 | 6.0 | 6.2 | 6.7 | 7.4 | 8.0 | 8.5 | Pour 100 habitants |
| Philippines | | | | | | | | | | Philippines |
| Number (thousands) | | 2 892[16] | 3 061 | 3 315 | 3 311 | 3 340 | 3 437 | 3 367 | 3 633 | Nombre (en milliers) |
| Per 100 inhabitants | | 3.9 | 4.0 | 4.2 | 4.2 | 4.1 | 4.2 | 4.0 | 4.3 | Pour 100 habitants |
| Poland | | | | | | | | | | Pologne |
| Number (thousands)[7] | | 10 175 | 10 946 | 11 400 | 11 860 | *12 292 | 12 553 | 11 836 | 11 476 | Nombre (en milliers)[7] |
| Per 100 inhabitants | | 26.3 | 28.3 | 29.5 | 30.7 | 31.9 | 32.6 | 30.7 | 29.8 | Pour 100 habitants |
| Portugal | | | | | | | | | | Portugal |
| Number (thousands) | | 4 230 | 4 321 | 4 385 | 4 310 | 4 281 | 4 238 | 4 234 | 4 234 | Nombre (en milliers) |
| Per 100 inhabitants | | 42.3 | 43.1 | 42.4 | 41.4 | 40.9 | 40.3 | 40.3 | 40.2 | Pour 100 habitants |
| Puerto Rico | | | | | | | | | | Porto Rico |
| Number (thousands)[33] | | 1 295 | 1 299 | 1 288 | 1 276 | 1 213[3] | 1 112[3] | 1 038[4] | ... | Nombre (en milliers)[33] |
| Per 100 inhabitants | | 34.3 | 34.1 | 33.6 | 33.1 | 31.3 | 28.5 | 26.2 | ... | Pour 100 habitants |
| Qatar | | | | | | | | | | Qatar |
| Number (thousands) | | 155 | 160 | 167 | 177 | 185 | 191 | 205 | 228 | Nombre (en milliers) |
| Per 100 inhabitants | | 26.8 | 26.4 | 26.2 | 26.3 | 26.1 | 25.7 | 26.4 | 27.2 | Pour 100 habitants |
| Réunion | | | | | | | | | | Réunion |
| Number (thousands) | | 269 | 280[4] | 300[4] | ... | ... | ... | ... | ... | Nombre (en milliers) |
| Per 100 inhabitants | | 38.0 | 40.1 | 41.0 | ... | ... | ... | ... | ... | Pour 100 habitants |
| Romania | | | | | | | | | | Roumanie |
| Number (thousands) | | 3 740 | 3 899 | 4 116 | 4 215 | 4 332 | 4 388 | 4 383 | 4 197 | Nombre (en milliers) |
| Per 100 inhabitants | | 16.7 | 17.4 | 18.4 | 19.3 | 20.0 | 20.2 | 20.3 | 19.4 | Pour 100 habitants |
| Russian Federation | | | | | | | | | | Fédération de Russie |
| Number (thousands) | | 30 949 | 32 070 | 33 278 | 35 500 | 36 100 | 38 500[34] | 40 100[34] | 43 900 | Nombre (en milliers) |
| Per 100 inhabitants | | 21.0 | 21.9 | 22.8 | 24.4 | 25.0 | 26.8 | 27.9 | 30.8 | Pour 100 habitants |
| Rwanda | | | | | | | | | | Rwanda |
| Number (thousands) | | 13 | 18 | 22 | 25 | 26 | 23 | 24[4] | 17 | Nombre (en milliers) |
| Per 100 inhabitants | | 0.2 | 0.2 | 0.3 | 0.3 | 0.3 | 0.3 | 0.3 | 0.2 | Pour 100 habitants |
| Saint Helena | (01/04) | | | | | | | | | Sainte-Hélène |
| Number (thousands) | | 2 | 2 | 2[5] | 2 | 2 | 2 | 2 | ... | Nombre (en milliers) |
| Per 100 inhabitants | | 40.7 | 41.7 | 43.4 | 44.1 | 44.9 | 46.0 | 45.6 | ... | Pour 100 habitants |
| Saint Kitts and Nevis | (01/04) | | | | | | | | | Saint-Kitts-et-Nevis |
| Number (thousands) | | 20 | *22 | *23 | 24 | ... | 25 | ... | ... | Nombre (en milliers) |
| Per 100 inhabitants | | 49.8 | 54.2 | 55.2 | 57.1 | ... | 59.3 | ... | ... | Pour 100 habitants |
| Saint Lucia | (01/04) | | | | | | | | | Sainte-Lucie |
| Number (thousands) | | 44 | *49 | 50 | 51 | ... | ... | ... | ... | Nombre (en milliers) |
| Per 100 inhabitants | | 29.0 | 31.7 | 32.1 | 32.6 | ... | ... | ... | ... | Pour 100 habitants |
| Saint Pierre and Miquelon | | | | | | | | | | Saint-Pierre-et-Miquelon |
| Number (thousands) | | 5 | *5 | ... | ... | ... | ... | ... | ... | Nombre (en milliers) |
| Per 100 inhabitants | | 69.1 | 72.7 | ... | ... | ... | ... | ... | ... | Pour 100 habitants |
| Saint Vincent-Grenadines | (01/04) | | | | | | | | | Saint Vincent-Grenadines |
| Number (thousands) | | 24 | 25 | 26 | 27 | 21 | 19 | 23 | 23 | Nombre (en milliers) |
| Per 100 inhabitants | | 20.9 | 22.0 | 22.7 | 23.4 | 17.8 | 15.7 | 18.9 | 19.0 | Pour 100 habitants |
| Samoa | | | | | | | | | | Samoa |
| Number (thousands) | | 9[4] | 9[4] | 10 | 12 | 13 | 16[4] | 20 | ... | Nombre (en milliers) |
| Per 100 inhabitants | | 4.9 | 4.9 | 5.5 | 6.7 | 7.5 | 9.2 | 10.9 | ... | Pour 100 habitants |
| San Marino | | | | | | | | | | Saint-Marin |
| Number (thousands) | | 20 | 20 | 21 | 21 | 21 | 21 | 21 | 21 | Nombre (en milliers) |
| Per 100 inhabitants | | 76.0 | 75.2 | 75.9 | 76.3 | 76.6 | 76.9 | 77.2 | 77.8 | Pour 100 habitants |

| Country or area | Fiscal year & Ex. budgét.& | 1999 | 2000 | 2001 | 2002 | 2003 | 2004 | 2005 | 2006 | Pays ou zone |
|---|---|---|---|---|---|---|---|---|---|---|
| Sao Tome and Principe | | | | | | | | | | Sao Tomé-et-Principe |
| Number (thousands) | | 5 | 5 | 5 | 6 | 7 | 7 | 7[4] | 8 | Nombre (en milliers) |
| Per 100 inhabitants | | 3.3 | 3.3 | 3.8 | 4.4 | 4.7 | 4.6 | 4.5 | 4.7 | Pour 100 habitants |
| Saudi Arabia | | | | | | | | | | Arabie saoudite |
| Number (thousands) | | 2 706 | 2 965 | 3 233 | 3 417 | 3 503 | 3 695 | 3 844 | 3 951 | Nombre (en milliers) |
| Per 100 inhabitants | | 13.0 | 13.8 | 14.6 | 15.1 | 15.0 | 15.4 | 15.6 | 15.7 | Pour 100 habitants |
| Senegal | | | | | | | | | | Sénégal |
| Number (thousands) | | 166 | 206 | 237 | 225 | 229 | 245 | 267 | 283 | Nombre (en milliers) |
| Per 100 inhabitants | | 1.8 | 2.2 | 2.4 | 2.2 | 2.2 | 2.4 | 2.3 | 2.4 | Pour 100 habitants |
| Serbia | | | | | | | | | | Serbie |
| Number (thousands) | | ... | ... | ... | ... | ... | ... | ... | 2 719 | Nombre (en milliers) |
| Per 100 inhabitants | | ... | ... | ... | ... | ... | ... | ... | 25.9 | Pour 100 habitants |
| Serbia and Montenegro | | | | | | | | | | Serbie-et-Monténégro |
| Number (thousands) | | 2 281 | 2 406 | 2 444 | 2 493 | 2 612 | 2 685 | 2 698[4] | ... | Nombre (en milliers) |
| Per 100 inhabitants | | 21.4 | 22.6 | 22.9 | 30.7 | 32.1 | 32.9 | 33.0 | ... | Pour 100 habitants |
| Seychelles | (01/04) | | | | | | | | | Seychelles |
| Number (thousands) | | 20 | 21 | 21 | 21 | 21 | 21 | 21 | 21 | Nombre (en milliers) |
| Per 100 inhabitants | | 25.6 | 26.7 | 27.3 | 27.1 | 26.8 | 26.6 | 26.5 | 25.4 | Pour 100 habitants |
| Sierra Leone | | | | | | | | | | Sierra Leone |
| Number (thousands) | | 18 | 19 | 23 | 24 | ... | ... | ... | ... | Nombre (en milliers) |
| Per 100 inhabitants | | 0.4 | 0.4 | 0.5 | 0.5 | ... | ... | ... | ... | Pour 100 habitants |
| Singapore | (01/04) | | | | | | | | | Singapour |
| Number (thousands) | | 1 877 | 1 946 | 1 948 | 1 927 | 1 890 | 1 857 | 1 844 | 1 854 | Nombre (en milliers) |
| Per 100 inhabitants | | 47.5 | 48.4 | 47.1 | 46.3 | 45.3 | 44.4 | 42.4 | 42.3 | Pour 100 habitants |
| Slovakia | | | | | | | | | | Slovaquie |
| Number (thousands) | | 1 655 | 1 698 | 1 556 | 1 403 | 1 295 | 1 250 | 1 197 | 1 167 | Nombre (en milliers) |
| Per 100 inhabitants | | 30.7 | 31.4 | 28.9 | 26.1 | 24.1 | 23.2 | 22.2 | 21.6 | Pour 100 habitants |
| Slovenia | | | | | | | | | | Slovénie |
| Number (thousands)[35] | | 758 | 785 | 802 | 808 | 812 | 811 | 816 | 837 | Nombre (en milliers)[35] |
| Per 100 inhabitants | | 38.1 | 39.5 | 40.2 | 40.5 | 40.7 | 40.9 | 41.5 | 42.6 | Pour 100 habitants |
| Solomon Islands | (01/04) | | | | | | | | | Iles Salomon |
| Number (thousands)[36] | | 8 | 8[37] | 7[37] | 7[37] | 6[37] | 7 | 7 | ... | Nombre (en milliers)[36] |
| Per 100 inhabitants | | 2.0 | 1.8 | 1.7 | 1.5 | 1.3 | 1.4 | 1.5 | ... | Pour 100 habitants |
| Somalia | | | | | | | | | | Somalie |
| Number (thousands) | | *24 | *25 | *35 | *35 | *100 | *100 | *100 | 100 | Nombre (en milliers) |
| Per 100 inhabitants | | 0.4 | 0.4 | 0.5 | 0.5 | 1.3 | 1.3 | 1.2 | 1.2 | Pour 100 habitants |
| South Africa | (01/04) | | | | | | | | | Afrique du Sud |
| Number (thousands) | | 5 493 | 4 962 | 4 924 | 4 844 | 4 821 | 4 850 | 4 729 | ... | Nombre (en milliers) |
| Per 100 inhabitants | | 12.2 | 10.9 | 10.7 | 10.4 | 10.3 | 10.3 | 10.0 | ... | Pour 100 habitants |
| Spain | | | | | | | | | | Espagne |
| Number (thousands) | | 16 480 | 17 104 | 17 531 | 17 641 | 17 759 | 17 934 | 18 004 | 18 385 | Nombre (en milliers) |
| Per 100 inhabitants | | 41.0 | 42.2 | 42.6 | 42.9 | 41.6 | 41.5 | 42.2 | 42.4 | Pour 100 habitants |
| Sri Lanka | | | | | | | | | | Sri Lanka |
| Number (thousands) | | 669 | 767 | 827 | 883 | 939 | 991 | 1 244 | 1 884 | Nombre (en milliers) |
| Per 100 inhabitants | | 3.7 | 4.2 | 4.4 | 4.7 | 4.9 | 5.1 | 6.0 | 9.0 | Pour 100 habitants |
| Sudan | | | | | | | | | | Soudan |
| Number (thousands) | | 251 | 387 | 448 | 672 | 937 | 1 029 | 570 | 637 | Nombre (en milliers) |
| Per 100 inhabitants | | 0.8 | 1.2 | 1.4 | 2.0 | 2.8 | 3.0 | 1.6 | 1.7 | Pour 100 habitants |
| Suriname | | | | | | | | | | Suriname |
| Number (thousands) | | 71 | 75 | 77 | 79 | 80 | 82 | 81 | 82 | Nombre (en milliers) |
| Per 100 inhabitants | | 16.5 | 17.4 | 17.7 | 17.9 | 18.0 | 18.3 | 18.0 | 18.0 | Pour 100 habitants |
| Swaziland | (01/04) | | | | | | | | | Swaziland |
| Number (thousands) | | 31 | 32 | 34 | 35 | 46 | 45 | 35 | 44 | Nombre (en milliers) |
| Per 100 inhabitants | | 3.2 | 3.2 | 3.3 | 3.4 | 4.4 | 4.1 | 3.4 | 4.3 | Pour 100 habitants |

**Telephones**—Main telephone lines in operation (in thousands) and lines per 100 inhabitants (*continued*)

**Téléphones**—Nombre de lignes téléphoniques en service (en milliers) et lignes pour 100 habitants (*suite*)

| Country or area | Fiscal year & Ex. budgét.& | 1999 | 2000 | 2001 | 2002 | 2003 | 2004 | 2005 | 2006 | Pays ou zone |
|---|---|---|---|---|---|---|---|---|---|---|
| Sweden | | | | | | | | | | Suède |
| Number (thousands)[7] | | 5 890 | 5 751 | 5 667 | 5 585 | 5 535 | 5 688 | 5 635 | 5 399 | Nombre (en milliers)[7] |
| Per 100 inhabitants | | 66.5 | 64.8 | 63.6 | 62.4 | 61.7 | 63.1 | 62.3 | 59.5 | Pour 100 habitants |
| Switzerland | | | | | | | | | | Suisse |
| Number (thousands)[7] | | 5 066 | 5 236 | 5 383[38] | 5 388 | 5 323 | ... | 5 150 | 5 022 | Nombre (en milliers)[7] |
| Per 100 inhabitants | | 70.6 | 72.6 | 74.2 | 73.7 | 72.3 | ... | 69.0 | 66.9 | Pour 100 habitants |
| Syrian Arab Republic | | | | | | | | | | Rép. arabe syrienne |
| Number (thousands) | | 1 600 | 1 675 | 1 817 | 2 099 | 2 414 | 2 660 | 2 903 | 3 243 | Nombre (en milliers) |
| Per 100 inhabitants | | 9.9 | 10.3 | 10.9 | 12.3 | 13.8 | 14.6 | 15.2 | 16.6 | Pour 100 habitants |
| Tajikistan | | | | | | | | | | Tadjikistan |
| Number (thousands) | | 213 | 219 | 227 | 238 | 245 | 273 | 280 | ... | Nombre (en milliers) |
| Per 100 inhabitants | | 3.5 | 3.6 | 3.7 | 3.7 | 3.7 | 4.3 | 4.3 | ... | Pour 100 habitants |
| Thailand | (30/09) | | | | | | | | | Thaïlande |
| Number (thousands) | | 5 216 | 5 591 | 6 049 | 6 557 | 6 632 | 6 812 | 7 035 | 7 073 | Nombre (en milliers) |
| Per 100 inhabitants | | 8.6 | 9.1 | 9.8 | 10.5 | 10.5 | 10.7 | 11.0 | 10.9 | Pour 100 habitants |
| TFYR of Macedonia | | | | | | | | | | L'ex-R.y. Macédoine |
| Number (thousands) | | 471 | 507 | 539 | 560 | 525 | 537 | 534 | 491 | Nombre (en milliers) |
| Per 100 inhabitants | | 23.5 | 25.2 | 26.7 | 27.7 | 25.9 | 26.4 | 26.2 | 24.1 | Pour 100 habitants |
| Timor-Leste | | | | | | | | | | Timor-Leste |
| Number (thousands) | | ... | ... | ... | ... | 2 | 2 | 2 | 2 | Nombre (en milliers) |
| Per 100 inhabitants | | ... | ... | ... | ... | 0.2 | 0.2 | 0.2 | 0.2 | Pour 100 habitants |
| Togo | | | | | | | | | | Togo |
| Number (thousands) | | 38 | 43 | 48 | 51 | 61 | 66 | 63[39] | 82 | Nombre (en milliers) |
| Per 100 inhabitants | | 0.8 | 0.9 | 1.0 | 1.0 | 1.2 | 1.3 | 1.2 | 1.3 | Pour 100 habitants |
| Tokelau | | | | | | | | | | Tokélaou |
| Number (thousands) | | *0 | ^0 | ^0 | ^0 | ^0 | ^0 | ... | ... | Nombre (en milliers) |
| Per 100 inhabitants | | 12.3 | 11.5 | 15.0 | 14.0 | 13.0 | 13.5 | ... | ... | Pour 100 habitants |
| Tonga | | | | | | | | | | Tonga |
| Number (thousands) | | 9 | 10[4] | 11 | 11 | 12[4] | 13[4] | 14 | ... | Nombre (en milliers) |
| Per 100 inhabitants | | 9.3 | 9.8 | 10.9 | 11.3 | 12.1 | 13.0 | 13.7 | ... | Pour 100 habitants |
| Trinidad and Tobago | (01/04) | | | | | | | | | Trinité-et-Tobago |
| Number (thousands) | | 279 | 317 | 312 | 318 | 319 | 322 | 323 | 326 | Nombre (en milliers) |
| Per 100 inhabitants | | 21.6 | 24.5 | 24.0 | 24.4 | 24.5 | 24.7 | 24.8 | 24.9 | Pour 100 habitants |
| Tunisia | | | | | | | | | | Tunisie |
| Number (thousands) | | 850 | 955 | 1 056 | 1 149 | 1 164 | 1 204 | 1 257 | 1 268 | Nombre (en milliers) |
| Per 100 inhabitants | | 9.0 | 10.0 | 10.9 | 11.7 | 11.8 | 12.1 | 12.5 | 12.4 | Pour 100 habitants |
| Turkey | | | | | | | | | | Turquie |
| Number (thousands) | | 17 912 | 18 395 | 18 904 | 18 890 | 18 917 | 19 125 | 18 978 | 18 832 | Nombre (en milliers) |
| Per 100 inhabitants | | 26.7 | 27.0 | 27.3 | 26.9 | 26.5 | 26.5 | 25.9 | 25.4 | Pour 100 habitants |
| Turkmenistan | | | | | | | | | | Turkménistan |
| Number (thousands) | | 359 | 364 | 388 | 374 | 376 | 388 | 398 | ... | Nombre (en milliers) |
| Per 100 inhabitants | | 8.2 | 8.2 | 8.0 | 7.7 | 7.7 | 7.9 | 8.2 | ... | Pour 100 habitants |
| Turks and Caicos Islands | | | | | | | | | | Iles Turques et Caïques |
| Number (thousands) [40] | | 3[41] | 3[41] | 4[41] | 4[41] | 4[41] | 4 | ... | ... | Nombre (en milliers) [40] |
| Per 100 inhabitants | | 15.4 | 17.5 | 18.4 | 16.3 | 15.6 | 14.8 | ... | ... | Pour 100 habitants |
| Tuvalu | | | | | | | | | | Tuvalu |
| Number (thousands) | | 1 | *1 | 1 | 1 | 1 | 1 | 1 | 1 | Nombre (en milliers) |
| Per 100 inhabitants | | 6.7 | 7.0 | 6.8 | 6.9 | 7.0 | 7.3 | 8.5 | 10.3 | Pour 100 habitants |
| Uganda | (30/06) | | | | | | | | | Ouganda |
| Number (thousands) | | 57[42] | 62 | 56 | 55 | 61 | 72 | 88 | 108 | Nombre (en milliers) |
| Per 100 inhabitants | | 0.2 | 0.3 | 0.2 | 0.2 | 0.2 | 0.3 | 0.3 | 0.4 | Pour 100 habitants |
| Ukraine | | | | | | | | | | Ukraine |
| Number (thousands) | | 10 074 | 10 417 | 10 670 | 10 833 | 11 110 | 12 142 | 11 667 | 12 341 | Nombre (en milliers) |
| Per 100 inhabitants | | 20.3 | 21.2 | 22.0 | 22.6 | 23.4 | 25.8 | 25.1 | 26.8 | Pour 100 habitants |

| Country or area | Fiscal year [&] Ex. budgét. [&] | 1999 | 2000 | 2001 | 2002 | 2003 | 2004 | 2005 | 2006 | Pays ou zone |
|---|---|---|---|---|---|---|---|---|---|---|
| **United Arab Emirates** | | | | | | | | | | **Emirats arabes unis** |
| Number (thousands) | | 975 | 1 020 | 1 053 | 1 094 | 1 136 | 1 188 | 1 237 | 1 310 | Nombre (en milliers) |
| Per 100 inhabitants | | 32.2 | 31.4 | 30.2 | 29.1 | 28.1 | 27.7 | 27.5 | 28.1 | Pour 100 habitants |
| **United Kingdom** | (01/04) | | | | | | | | | **Royaume-Uni** |
| Number (thousands)[7] | | 34 021 | 35 228 | 34 579 | 34 738 | 34 550 | 34 576 | 34 068 | 33 603 | Nombre (en milliers)[7] |
| Per 100 inhabitants | | 57.2 | 58.9 | 57.6 | 58.8 | 58.1 | 57.8 | 57.1 | 56.1 | Pour 100 habitants |
| **United Rep. of Tanzania** | | | | | | | | | | **Rép.-Unie de Tanzanie** |
| Number (thousands) | | 150 | 174 | 178 | 162 | 147 | 148 | 154 | 157 | Nombre (en milliers) |
| Per 100 inhabitants | | 0.4 | 0.5 | 0.5 | 0.4 | 0.4 | 0.4 | 0.4 | 0.4 | Pour 100 habitants |
| **United States** | | | | | | | | | | **Etats-Unis** |
| Number (thousands)[43] | | 189 502 | 192 513 | 191 571 | 189 250 | 182 933 | 177 691 | 175 161 | 172 032 | Nombre (en milliers)[43] |
| Per 100 inhabitants | | 67.9 | 68.4 | 67.2 | 65.7 | 62.9 | 60.5 | 58.7 | 57.1 | Pour 100 habitants |
| **United States Virgin Is.** | | | | | | | | | | **Iles Vierges américaines** |
| Number (thousands) | | 67 | 68 | *69 | 69 | 70 | 71 | 72[4] | ... | Nombre (en milliers) |
| Per 100 inhabitants | | 62.3 | 62.9 | 63.5 | 63.1 | 63.0 | 63.9 | 64.0 | ... | Pour 100 habitants |
| **Uruguay** | | | | | | | | | | **Uruguay** |
| Number (thousands) | | 897 | 929 | 951 | 947 | 938 | 997 | 1 006 | 987 | Nombre (en milliers) |
| Per 100 inhabitants | | 28.1 | 29.0 | 29.6 | 29.4 | 29.0 | 30.8 | 31.0 | 28.3 | Pour 100 habitants |
| **Uzbekistan** | | | | | | | | | | **Ouzbékistan** |
| Number (thousands) | | 1 599 | 1 655 | 1 663 | 1 681 | 1 717 | 1 750 | 1 794 | ... | Nombre (en milliers) |
| Per 100 inhabitants | | 6.6 | 6.7 | 6.7 | 6.6 | 6.7 | 6.6 | 6.7 | ... | Pour 100 habitants |
| **Vanuatu** | | | | | | | | | | **Vanuatu** |
| Number (thousands) | | *6 | 7 | 7 | 7 | 7 | 7 | 7 | ... | Nombre (en milliers) |
| Per 100 inhabitants | | 2.9 | 3.5 | 3.4 | 3.3 | 3.1 | 3.1 | 3.2 | ... | Pour 100 habitants |
| **Venezuela (Bolivarian Rep. of)** | | | | | | | | | | **Venezuela (Rép. bolivar. du)** |
| Number (thousands) | | 2 551 | 2 536 | 2 705 | 2 842 | 2 956 | 3 346 | 3 651 | 4 217 | Nombre (en milliers) |
| Per 100 inhabitants | | 10.8 | 10.5 | 10.9 | 11.3 | 11.5 | 12.8 | 13.6 | 15.5 | Pour 100 habitants |
| **Viet Nam** | | | | | | | | | | **Viet Nam** |
| Number (thousands) | | 2 106 | 2 543 | 3 050 | 3 929 | 4 402 | 10 125 | 15 845 | ... | Nombre (en milliers) |
| Per 100 inhabitants | | 2.7 | 3.2 | 3.8 | 4.9 | 5.4 | 12.2 | 18.8 | ... | Pour 100 habitants |
| **Wallis and Futuna Islands** | | | | | | | | | | **Iles Wallis et Futuna** |
| Number (thousands) | | 2 | 2 | 2 | 2 | 2 | 2 | 2 | 2 | Nombre (en milliers) |
| Per 100 inhabitants | | 10.6 | 11.8 | 13.0 | 11.5 | 11.3 | 11.3 | 11.4 | 13.7 | Pour 100 habitants |
| **Yemen** | | | | | | | | | | **Yémen** |
| Number (thousands) | | 284 | 347 | 422 | 542 | 694 | 795 | 901[4] | 968 | Nombre (en milliers) |
| Per 100 inhabitants | | 1.6 | 1.9 | 2.2 | 2.8 | 3.4 | 3.8 | 4.3 | 4.5 | Pour 100 habitants |
| **Zambia** | (01/04) | | | | | | | | | **Zambie** |
| Number (thousands) | | 83 | 83 | 86 | 88 | 88 | 92 | 95 | 93 | Nombre (en milliers) |
| Per 100 inhabitants | | 0.8 | 0.8 | 0.8 | 0.8 | 0.8 | 0.8 | 0.8 | 0.8 | Pour 100 habitants |
| **Zimbabwe** | (30/06) | | | | | | | | | **Zimbabwe** |
| Number (thousands) | | 239 | 249 | 254 | 288 | 301 | 317 | 328 | 332 | Nombre (en milliers) |
| Per 100 inhabitants | | 2.1 | 2.2 | 2.2 | 2.5 | 2.6 | 2.7 | 2.8 | 2.5 | Pour 100 habitants |

**Source**

International Telecommunication Union (ITU), Geneva, the ITU database, last accessed March 2008.

[&] Fiscal year refers to the fiscal year used in each country or area. Countries or areas whose reference periods coincide with the calendar year ending 31 December are not footnoted. Those that have a fiscal year other than calendar year are denoted as follows:

22/03: Year beginning 22 March
01/04: Year beginning 1 April
30/06: Year ending 30 June
15/07: Year ending 15 July
30/09: Year ending 30 September

**Source**

Union internationale des télécommunications (UIT), Genève, la base de données de l'UIT, dernier accès mars 2008.

[&] Ex. budgét. fait référence à l'exercice budgétaire en vigueur dans chaque pays ou territoire. Les pays ou les territoires dont l'exercice budgétaire terminent le 31 décembre de l'année civile ne sont pas signalés. Dans le cas contraire, ils sont désignés de la manière suivante:

22/03 : Exercice commençant le 22 mars
01/04 : Exercice commençant le 1er avril
30/06 : Exercice se terminant le 30 juin
15/07 : Exercice se terminant le 15 juillet
30/09 : Exercice se terminant le 30 septembre

| Notes | Notes |
|---|---|
| 1 Analogic lines and XDSI lines. | 1 Lignes analogiques et "XDSI". |
| 2 Data refer to Angola Telecom. | 2 Les données se réfèrent à "Angola Telecom". |
| 3 June. | 3 Juin. |
| 4 ITU estimate. | 4 Estimation de l'UIT. |
| 5 As of 31 December. | 5 Dès le 31 décembre. |
| 6 1994-2002 only refers to "Telefónica de Argentina S.A. y Telecom Argentina S.A." From 2002 all licensees are included (352 in 2003). | 6 Les chiffres de 1994-2002 ne concernent que "Telefónica de Argentina S.A. y Telecom Argentina S.A." À partir de 2002 tous les détenteurs de licence sont compris (352 en 2003). |
| 7 Including ISDN channels. | 7 RNIS inclus. |
| 8 Including ISDN equivalents. | 8 Y compris les équivalents du RNIS. |
| 9 Conventional telephony terminals in service. | 9 Terminaux de téléphonie conventionnelle en service. |
| 10 Caribbean Telecommunications Union. | 10 "Caribbean Telecommunications Union". |
| 11 WLL lines included. | 11 Y compris les lignes "WLL". |
| 12 For statistical purposes, the data for China do not include those for the Hong Kong Special Administrative Region (Hong Kong SAR), Macao Special Administrative Region (Macao SAR) and Taiwan Province of China. | 12 Pour la présentation des statistiques, les données pour la Chine ne comprennent pas la Région Administrative Spéciale de Hong Kong (Hong Kong RAS), la Région Administrative Spéciale de Macao (Macao RAS) et la province de Taiwan. |
| 13 Ministry of Communication estimate. | 13 Estimation du ministère de communication. |
| 14 Data refer to 31 December. | 14 Les données se réfèrent au 31 décembre. |
| 15 December. | 15 Décembre. |
| 16 Telephone subscribers. | 16 Abonnés au téléphone. |
| 17 Excluding public call offices. | 17 Cabines publiques exclues. |
| 18 Data provided by the Commission based on counts made by technical experts. | 18 Données fournies par la Commission fondées sur un dénombrement effectué par des experts techniques. |
| 19 Telephone channels including ISDN and own consumption, excluding public payphones. | 19 Voies téléphoniques, y compris RNIS et consommation personnelle, excluant les téléphones publics payants. |
| 20 US Federal Communications Commission's Statistics of Communications Common Carriers. | 20 "US Federal Communications Commission's Statistics of Communications Common Carriers". |
| 21 Subscriber lines. | 21 Lignes d'abonnés au téléphone. |
| 22 Break in comparability. | 22 Discontinuité dans la comparabilité. |
| 23 September. Telkom. | 23 Septembre. Telkom. |
| 24 Central Organisation for Statistics & IT. | 24 "Central Organisation for Statistics & IT". |
| 25 September. | 25 Septembre. |
| 26 Data refer to Telecom Italia Wireline. | 26 Les données se réfèrent au "Telecom Italia Wireline". |
| 27 Lattelekom. | 27 Lattelekom. |
| 28 Without ISDN channels. | 28 Sans RNIS. |
| 29 Including digital lines. | 29 Y compris les lignes digitales. |
| 30 Lines in service. | 30 Lignes en service. |
| 31 Decrease due to the reduction of population since the volcanic crisis in 1995. | 31 Baisse due à la diminution de la population depuis l'éruption volcanique de 1995. |
| 32 Decrease in lines available in the public sector. | 32 Diminution des lignes disponibles dans le secteur publique. |
| 33 Switched access lines. | 33 Lignes d'accès déviées. |
| 34 October. | 34 Octobre. |
| 35 Including ISDN subscribers. | 35 Y compris les abonnés au ISDN. |
| 36 Billable lines. | 36 Lignes payables. |
| 37 The number of fixed lines declined due to civil war. | 37 Le nombre de lignes fixes a diminué en raison de la guerre civile. |
| 38 SWISSCOM at September 2001. | 38 SWISSCOM: Septembre 2001. |
| 39 Drop results from the termination of contract for clients that had not paid. | 39 2005 : la diminution est due à la résiliation des contrats de clients dont le compte était en souffrance. |
| 40 Residential Fixed lines. | 40 Lignes fixes de domicile. |
| 41 Cable and Wireless | 41 Câble et sans fil. |
| 42 Including data from MTN. | 42 Y compris les données du "MTN". |
| 43 Data up to 1980 refer to main stations reported by FCC. From 1981, data refer to "Local Loops". | 43 Les données pour 1980 se réfèrent aux stations principales. Dès 1981, les données se réfèrent aux "Local Loops". |

# 17

## Cellular mobile telephone subscribers
Number (thousands) and per 100 inhabitants

## Abonnés au téléphone mobile
Nombre (en milliers) et pour 100 habitants

| Country or area | Fiscal year&<br>Ex. budgét. & | 1999 | 2000 | 2001 | 2002 | 2003 | 2004 | 2005 | 2006 | Pays ou zone |
|---|---|---|---|---|---|---|---|---|---|---|
| Afghanistan | | | | | | | | | | Afghanistan |
| Number (thousands) | | 0 | 0 | 0 | 25 | 200 | 600 | 1 200 | 2 520 | Nombre (en milliers) |
| Per 100 inhabitants | | 0 | 0 | 0 | ^0 | 1 | 2 | 4 | 8 | Pour 100 habitants |
| Albania | | | | | | | | | | Albanie |
| Number (thousands) | | 11 | 30 | 393 | 851 | 1 100 | 1 260 | 1 530 | 1 900 | Nombre (en milliers) |
| Per 100 inhabitants | | ^0 | 1 | 13 | 28 | 36 | 39 | 49 | 60 | Pour 100 habitants |
| Algeria | | | | | | | | | | Algérie |
| Number (thousands) | | 72 | 86 | 100 | 450 | 1 447 | 4 882 | 13 661 | 20 998 | Nombre (en milliers) |
| Per 100 inhabitants | | ^0 | ^0 | ^0 | 1 | 5 | 15 | 42 | 63 | Pour 100 habitants |
| American Samoa | | | | | | | | | | Samoa américaines |
| Number (thousands) | | 2 | 2 | 2 | 2 | 2 | 2 | ... | ... | Nombre (en milliers) |
| Per 100 inhabitants | | 3 | 3 | 4 | 3 | 3 | 4 | ... | ... | Pour 100 habitants |
| Andorra | | | | | | | | | | Andorre |
| Number (thousands) | | 21 | 24 | 29 | 33 | 52 | 58 | 65 | 69 | Nombre (en milliers) |
| Per 100 inhabitants | | 31 | 36 | 45 | 49 | 78 | 87 | 96 | ... | Pour 100 habitants |
| Angola | | | | | | | | | | Angola |
| Number (thousands) | | 24 | 26 | 75 | 140 | 350 | 740 | 1 611 | 2 264 | Nombre (en milliers) |
| Per 100 inhabitants | | ^0 | ^0 | 1 | 1 | 2 | 5 | 10 | 14 | Pour 100 habitants |
| Anguilla | | | | | | | | | | Anguilla |
| Number (thousands) | | *1 | 2 | 2 | 3 | 9 | 7[1] | 13[1] | ... | Nombre (en milliers) |
| Per 100 inhabitants | | 13 | 19 | 16 | 26 | 75 | 60 | 107 | ... | Pour 100 habitants |
| Antigua and Barbuda | (01/04) | | | | | | | | | Antigua-et-Barbuda |
| Number (thousands) | | 9 | 22 | 25[2] | 38 | 46[3] | 54 | 86 | 110 | Nombre (en milliers) |
| Per 100 inhabitants | | 11 | 29 | 32 | 49 | 58 | 67 | 106 | ... | Pour 100 habitants |
| Argentina | (30/09) | | | | | | | | | Argentine |
| Number (thousands) | | 3 849 | 6 488 | 6 742 | 6 567 | 7 842 | 13 512 | 22 156 | 31 510 | Nombre (en milliers) |
| Per 100 inhabitants | | 11 | 18 | 18 | 18 | 21 | 35 | 57 | 81 | Pour 100 habitants |
| Armenia | | | | | | | | | | Arménie |
| Number (thousands) | | 8 | 17 | 26 | 71 | 114 | 203 | 318 | ... | Nombre (en milliers) |
| Per 100 inhabitants | | ^0 | 1 | 1 | 2 | 4 | 7 | 11 | ... | Pour 100 habitants |
| Aruba | | | | | | | | | | Aruba |
| Number (thousands) | | 12 | 15 | 53 | 62 | 70 | 98 | 108 | 106 | Nombre (en milliers) |
| Per 100 inhabitants | | 13 | 16 | 57 | 65 | 72 | 100 | 109 | ... | Pour 100 habitants |
| Australia | (30/06) | | | | | | | | | Australie |
| Number (thousands) | | 6 315 | 8 562 | 11 132 | 12 670 | 14 347 | 16 480 | 18 420 | 19 760 | Nombre (en milliers) |
| Per 100 inhabitants | | 33 | 45 | 57 | 65 | 72 | 83 | 91 | 97 | Pour 100 habitants |
| Austria | | | | | | | | | | Autriche |
| Number (thousands) | | 4 250 | 6 117 | 6 541 | 6 736 | 7 274[4] | 7 992 | 8 650 | 9 256 | Nombre (en milliers) |
| Per 100 inhabitants | | 53 | 76 | 81 | 83 | 89 | 97 | 106 | 113 | Pour 100 habitants |
| Azerbaijan | | | | | | | | | | Azerbaïdjan |
| Number (thousands) | | 370 | 420 | 730 | 794 | 1 057 | 1 457 | 2 242 | 3 324 | Nombre (en milliers) |
| Per 100 inhabitants | | 5 | 5 | 9 | 10 | 13 | 17 | 27 | 39 | Pour 100 habitants |
| Bahamas | | | | | | | | | | Bahamas |
| Number (thousands) | | 16 | 32 | 61 | 122 | 122 | 186 | 228 | 253 | Nombre (en milliers) |
| Per 100 inhabitants | | 5 | 10 | 20 | 39 | 39 | 58 | 71 | 77 | Pour 100 habitants |
| Bahrain | | | | | | | | | | Bahreïn |
| Number (thousands) | | 133 | 206 | 300 | 389 | 443 | 650 | 749 | 907 | Nombre (en milliers) |
| Per 100 inhabitants | | 20 | 31 | 44 | 56 | 63 | 91 | 103 | 123 | Pour 100 habitants |
| Bangladesh | (30/06) | | | | | | | | | Bangladesh |
| Number (thousands) | | 149 | 279 | 520[3] | 1 075 | 1 365 | 2 782 | 9 000 | 19 131 | Nombre (en milliers) |
| Per 100 inhabitants | | ^0 | ^0 | ^0 | 1 | 1 | 2 | 6 | 13 | Pour 100 habitants |

| Country or area | Fiscal year& Ex. budgét. & | 1999 | 2000 | 2001 | 2002 | 2003 | 2004 | 2005 | 2006 | Pays ou zone |
|---|---|---|---|---|---|---|---|---|---|---|
| Barbados | (01/04) | | | | | | | | | Barbade |
| Number (thousands) | | 20 | 28 | 53 | 97 | 140 | 200 | 206 | ... | Nombre (en milliers) |
| Per 100 inhabitants | | 8 | 11 | 20 | 36 | 52 | 74 | 77 | ... | Pour 100 habitants |
| Belarus | | | | | | | | | | Bélarus |
| Number (thousands) | | 23 | 49 | 138 | 463 | 1 118 | 2 239 | 4 100 | 5 960 | Nombre (en milliers) |
| Per 100 inhabitants | | ^0 | ^0 | 1 | 5 | 11 | 23 | 42 | 61 | Pour 100 habitants |
| Belgium | | | | | | | | | | Belgique |
| Number (thousands) | | 3 187 | 5 629 | 7 697 | 8 102[3] | 8 606 | 9 132 | 9 460 | 9 660 | Nombre (en milliers) |
| Per 100 inhabitants | | 31 | 55 | 75 | 78 | 83 | 87 | 90 | 93 | Pour 100 habitants |
| Belize | (01/04) | | | | | | | | | Belize |
| Number (thousands) | | 7 | 17 | 39 | 52 | 60 | 92 | 120 | 121 | Nombre (en milliers) |
| Per 100 inhabitants | | 3 | 7 | 15 | 20 | 23 | 35 | 44 | 44 | Pour 100 habitants |
| Benin | | | | | | | | | | Bénin |
| Number (thousands) | | 7 | 55 | ·125[3] | 219 | 236 | 459 | 596 | 1 056 | Nombre (en milliers) |
| Per 100 inhabitants | | ^0 | 1 | 2 | 3 | 3 | 6 | 8 | 12 | Pour 100 habitants |
| Bermuda | (01/04) | | | | | | | | | Bermudes |
| Number (thousands) | | 13 | 13 | 13 | 30[3] | 40 | 49[2] | 53 | 60 | Nombre (en milliers) |
| Per 100 inhabitants | | 20 | 21 | 21 | 47 | 63 | 77 | 82 | ... | Pour 100 habitants |
| Bhutan | | | | | | | | | | Bhoutan |
| Number (thousands) | | 0 | 0 | 0 | 0 | 8 | 19 | 38 | 82 | Nombre (en milliers) |
| Per 100 inhabitants | | 0 | 0 | 0 | 0 | 1 | 2 | 5 | ... | Pour 100 habitants |
| Bolivia | | | | | | | | | | Bolivie |
| Number (thousands) | | 420 | 583 | 780 | 1 023 | 1 279 | 1 801 | 2 421 | 2 876 | Nombre (en milliers) |
| Per 100 inhabitants | | 5 | 7 | 9 | 12 | 14 | 20 | 26 | 31 | Pour 100 habitants |
| Bosnia and Herzegovina | | | | | | | | | | Bosnie-Herzégovine |
| Number (thousands) | | 53 | 93 | 445 | 749 | 1 075 | 1 407 | 1 594 | 1 888 | Nombre (en milliers) |
| Per 100 inhabitants | | 1 | 2 | 12 | 20 | 28 | 36 | 41 | 48 | Pour 100 habitants |
| Botswana[5] | (01/04) | | | | | | | | | Botswana[5] |
| Number (thousands) | | 92 | 222 | 332 | 445 | 523 | 564 | 823 | 980 | Nombre (en milliers) |
| Per 100 inhabitants | | 6 | 14 | 20 | 26 | 30 | 32 | 47 | 56 | Pour 100 habitants |
| Brazil | | | | | | | | | | Brésil |
| Number (thousands) | | 15 033 | 23 188 | 28 746 | 34 881 | 46 373 | 65 605 | 86 210 | 99 919 | Nombre (en milliers) |
| Per 100 inhabitants | | 9 | 13 | 16 | 19 | 26 | 36 | 46 | 53 | Pour 100 habitants |
| British Virgin Islands | (01/04) | | | | | | | | | Iles Vierges britanniques |
| Number (thousands) | | ... | ... | ... | 8 | ... | ... | ... | ... | Nombre (en milliers) |
| Per 100 inhabitants | | ... | ... | ... | 38 | ... | ... | ... | ... | Pour 100 habitants |
| Brunei Darussalam | | | | | | | | | | Brunéi Darussalam |
| Number (thousands) | | 66 | 95 | 143 | 154 | 177 | 202 | 233 | 254 | Nombre (en milliers) |
| Per 100 inhabitants | | 21 | 29 | 42 | 45 | 51 | 57 | 62 | 67 | Pour 100 habitants |
| Bulgaria | | | | | | | | | | Bulgarie |
| Number (thousands) | | 350 | 738 | 1 550 | 2 598 | 3 501 | 4 730 | 6 245 | 8 253 | Nombre (en milliers) |
| Per 100 inhabitants | | 4 | 9 | 20 | 33 | 45 | 61 | 81 | 108 | Pour 100 habitants |
| Burkina Faso | | | | | | | | | | Burkina Faso |
| Number (thousands) | | 5 | 25 | ·76[6] | 111[6] | 238[6] | 396[6] | 634[6] | 1 017[6] | Nombre (en milliers) |
| Per 100 inhabitants | | ^0 | ^0 | 1 | 1 | 2 | 3 | 5 | 7 | Pour 100 habitants |
| Burundi | | | | | | | | | | Burundi |
| Number (thousands) | | 1 | 16 | 33[3] | 52 | 64 | 101 | 153 | ... | Nombre (en milliers) |
| Per 100 inhabitants | | ^0 | ^0 | ^0 | 1 | 1 | 1 | 2 | ... | Pour 100 habitants |
| Cambodia | | | | | | | | | | Cambodge |
| Number (thousands) | | 89 | 131 | 223 | 380 | 498 | 862 | 1 062 | 1 140 | Nombre (en milliers) |
| Per 100 inhabitants | | 1 | 1 | 2 | 3 | 4 | 6 | 8 | 8 | Pour 100 habitants |
| Cameroon | | | | | | | | | | Cameroun |
| Number (thousands) | | 6 | 103 | 417 | 702 | 1 077 | 1 537 | 2 253 | ... | Nombre (en milliers) |
| Per 100 inhabitants | | ^0 | 1 | 3 | 4 | 7 | 9 | 14 | ... | Pour 100 habitants |

| Country or area | Fiscal year[&] Ex. budgét. [&] | 1999 | 2000 | 2001 | 2002 | 2003 | 2004 | 2005 | 2006 | Pays ou zone |
|---|---|---|---|---|---|---|---|---|---|---|
| Canada | | | | | | | | | | Canada |
| Number (thousands) | | 6 911 | 8 727 | 10 649 | 11 872 | 13 291 | 15 020 | 17 017 | 18 749 | Nombre (en milliers) |
| Per 100 inhabitants | | 23 | 28 | 34 | 38 | 42 | 47 | 53 | 58 | Pour 100 habitants |
| Cape Verde | | | | | | | | | | Cap-Vert |
| Number (thousands) | | 8 | 20 | 32 | 43 | 53 | 66 | 82 | 109 | Nombre (en milliers) |
| Per 100 inhabitants | | 2 | 5 | 7 | 10 | 12 | 14 | 17 | 21 | Pour 100 habitants |
| Cayman Islands | (01/04) | | | | | | | | | Iles Caïmanes |
| Number (thousands) | | 8 | 11 | 17 | ... | 21 | 34 | ... | ... | Nombre (en milliers) |
| Per 100 inhabitants | | 22 | 27 | 42 | ... | 49 | 77 | ... | ... | Pour 100 habitants |
| Central African Rep. | | | | | | | | | | Rép. centrafricaine |
| Number (thousands) | | 4 | 5 | 11 | 13 | 40 | 60 | 100 | ... | Nombre (en milliers) |
| Per 100 inhabitants | | ^0 | ^0 | ^0 | ^0 | 1 | 2 | 2 | ... | Pour 100 habitants |
| Chad | | | | | | | | | | Tchad |
| Number (thousands) | | 0 | 6 | 22 | 34 | 65 | 123 | 210[4] | 466 | Nombre (en milliers) |
| Per 100 inhabitants | | 0 | ^0 | ^0 | ^0 | 1 | 1 | 2 | 5 | Pour 100 habitants |
| Chile | | | | | | | | | | Chili |
| Number (thousands) | | 2 261 | 3 402 | 5 101 | 6 244[3] | 7 520 | 9 567 | 10 570 | 12 451 | Nombre (en milliers) |
| Per 100 inhabitants | | 15 | 22 | 33 | 41 | 49 | 62 | 68 | 76 | Pour 100 habitants |
| China[7] | | | | | | | | | | Chine[7] |
| Number (thousands) | | 43 296 | 85 260 | 144 820 | 206 005 | 269 953 | 334 824 | 393 406 | 461 058 | Nombre (en milliers) |
| Per 100 inhabitants | | 3 | 7 | 11 | 16 | 21 | 26 | 30 | 35 | Pour 100 habitants |
| China, Hong Kong SAR | (01/04) | | | | | | | | | Chine, Hong Kong RAS |
| Number (thousands) | | 4 275 | 5 447 | 5 776 | 6 396 | 7 349 | 8 214 | 8 693 | 9 356 | Nombre (en milliers) |
| Per 100 inhabitants | | 65 | 82 | 86 | 94 | 108 | 119 | 123 | 131 | Pour 100 habitants |
| China, Macao SAR | | | | | | | | | | Chine, Macao RAS |
| Number (thousands) | | 118 | 141 | 194 | 276 | 364 | 432 | 533 | 636 | Nombre (en milliers) |
| Per 100 inhabitants | | 27 | 33 | 45 | 63 | 81 | 93 | 116 | 137 | Pour 100 habitants |
| Colombia | | | | | | | | | | Colombie |
| Number (thousands) | | 1 967 | 2 257 | 3 265 | 4 597 | 6 186 | 10 401 | 21 850 | 29 763 | Nombre (en milliers) |
| Per 100 inhabitants | | 5 | 5 | 8 | 11 | 14 | 23 | 48 | 64 | Pour 100 habitants |
| Comoros | | | | | | | | | | Comores |
| Number (thousands) | | 0 | 0 | 0 | 0 | 2 | 8 | 16 | 37 | Nombre (en milliers) |
| Per 100 inhabitants | | 0 | 0 | 0 | 0 | ^0 | 1 | 2 | 5 | Pour 100 habitants |
| Congo | | | | | | | | | | Congo |
| Number (thousands) | | 5 | 70 | 150 | 222[4] | 330 | 384 | 490 | ... | Nombre (en milliers) |
| Per 100 inhabitants | | ^0 | 2 | 5 | 7 | 9 | 10 | 12 | ... | Pour 100 habitants |
| Cook Islands | (01/04) | | | | | | | | | Iles Cook |
| Number (thousands) | | 1 | 1 | 1[2] | 1 | 3 | 4 | 4 | ... | Nombre (en milliers) |
| Per 100 inhabitants | | 3 | 3 | 5 | 8 | 18 | 20 | 22 | ... | Pour 100 habitants |
| Costa Rica | | | | | | | | | | Costa Rica |
| Number (thousands) | | 138 | 212 | 327 | 502 | 778 | 923 | 1 101 | 1 444 | Nombre (en milliers) |
| Per 100 inhabitants | | 4 | 6 | 8 | 12 | 19 | 22 | 25 | 33 | Pour 100 habitants |
| Côte d'Ivoire | | | | | | | | | | Côte d'Ivoire |
| Number (thousands) | | 257 | 473 | 729 | 1 027 | 1 281 | 1 674 | 2 349 | 4 065 | Nombre (en milliers) |
| Per 100 inhabitants | | 2 | 3 | 4 | 6 | 8 | 10 | 13 | 22 | Pour 100 habitants |
| Croatia | | | | | | | | | | Croatie |
| Number (thousands) | | 295 | 1 033 | *1755 | 2 340 | 2 537 | 2 836 | 3 650 | 4 395 | Nombre (en milliers) |
| Per 100 inhabitants | | 7 | 23 | 40 | 53 | 58 | 64 | 80 | 96 | Pour 100 habitants |
| Cuba | | | | | | | | | | Cuba |
| Number (thousands) | | 5 | 7 | 9 | 18 | 35 | 76 | 136 | 153 | Nombre (en milliers) |
| Per 100 inhabitants | | ^0 | ^0 | ^0 | ^0 | ^0 | 1 | 1 | 1 | Pour 100 habitants |
| Cyprus | | | | | | | | | | Chypre |
| Number (thousands) | | 152 | 218 | 314 | 418 | 552 | 658 | 783 | 868 | Nombre (en milliers) |
| Per 100 inhabitants | | 23 | 32 | 46 | 58 | 77 | 82 | 94 | 103 | Pour 100 habitants |

| Country or area | Fiscal year[&]<br>Ex. budgét. [&] | 1999 | 2000 | 2001 | 2002 | 2003 | 2004 | 2005 | 2006 | Pays ou zone |
|---|---|---|---|---|---|---|---|---|---|---|
| Czech Republic | | | | | | | | | | République tchèque |
| Number (thousands) | | 1 945 | 4 346 | 6 947 | 8 610 | 9 709 | 10 783 | 11 776 | 11 882 | Nombre (en milliers) |
| Per 100 inhabitants | | 19 | 42 | 68 | 84 | 95 | 106 | 115 | 116 | Pour 100 habitants |
| Dem. Rep. of the Congo[3] | | | | | | | | | | Rép. dém. du Congo[3] |
| Number (thousands) | | 12 | 15 | 150 | 560 | 1 246 | 1 991 | 2 746 | 4 415 | Nombre (en milliers) |
| Per 100 inhabitants | | ^0 | ^0 | ^0 | 1 | 2 | 4 | 5 | 7 | Pour 100 habitants |
| Denmark | | | | | | | | | | Danemark |
| Number (thousands) | | 2 629 | 3 364 | 3 960 | 4 478 | 4 767 | 5 167 | 5 449 | 5 828 | Nombre (en milliers) |
| Per 100 inhabitants | | 49 | 63 | 74 | 83 | 88 | 95 | 100 | 107 | Pour 100 habitants |
| Djibouti | | | | | | | | | | Djibouti |
| Number (thousands) | | ^0 | ^0 | 3 | 15 | 23 | 34 | 44 | ... | Nombre (en milliers) |
| Per 100 inhabitants | | ^0 | ^0 | ^0 | 2 | 3 | 5 | 6 | ... | Pour 100 habitants |
| Dominica | (01/04) | | | | | | | | | Dominique |
| Number (thousands) | | *1 | *1 | 8 | 12 | 24 | 42 | ... | ... | Nombre (en milliers) |
| Per 100 inhabitants | | 1 | 2 | 11 | 17 | 33 | 59 | ... | ... | Pour 100 habitants |
| Dominican Republic | | | | | | | | | | Rép. dominicaine |
| Number (thousands) | | 424 | 705 | 1 270 | 1 701 | 2 123 | 2 534 | 3 623 | 4 606 | Nombre (en milliers) |
| Per 100 inhabitants | | 5 | 9 | 16 | 20 | 24 | 29 | 41 | 51 | Pour 100 habitants |
| Ecuador | | | | | | | | | | Equateur |
| Number (thousands) | | 383 | 482 | 859 | 1 561 | 2 398 | 3 544 | 6 246 | 8 485 | Nombre (en milliers) |
| Per 100 inhabitants | | 3 | 4 | 7 | 12 | 18 | 27 | 47 | 63 | Pour 100 habitants |
| Egypt | (30/06) | | | | | | | | | Egypte |
| Number (thousands) | | 481[8] | 1 360[8] | 2 794 | 4 495 | 5 798 | 7 643 | 13 630 | 18 001 | Nombre (en milliers) |
| Per 100 inhabitants | | 1 | 2 | 4 | 7 | 8 | 11 | 19 | 24 | Pour 100 habitants |
| El Salvador | | | | | | | | | | El Salvador |
| Number (thousands) | | 511 | 744 | 858 | 889 | 1 150 | 1 833 | 2 412 | 3 852 | Nombre (en milliers) |
| Per 100 inhabitants | | 8 | 12 | 13 | 14 | 17 | 28 | 35 | 55 | Pour 100 habitants |
| Equatorial Guinea | | | | | | | | | | Guinée équatoriale |
| Number (thousands) | | 1 | 5 | 15 | 32 | 42 | 62 | 97 | ... | Nombre (en milliers) |
| Per 100 inhabitants | | ^0 | 1 | 3 | 6 | 8 | 12 | 19 | ... | Pour 100 habitants |
| Eritrea | | | | | | | | | | Erythrée |
| Number (thousands) | | 0 | 0 | 0 | 0 | 0 | 20 | 40 | 62 | Nombre (en milliers) |
| Per 100 inhabitants | | 0 | 0 | 0 | 0 | 0 | ^0 | 1 | 1 | Pour 100 habitants |
| Estonia | | | | | | | | | | Estonie |
| Number (thousands) | | 387 | 557 | 651 | 881 | 1 050 | 1 256 | 1 445 | 1 659 | Nombre (en milliers) |
| Per 100 inhabitants | | 27 | 39 | 46 | 65 | 78 | 94 | 109 | 125 | Pour 100 habitants |
| Ethiopia | (30/06) | | | | | | | | | Ethiopie |
| Number (thousands) | | 7 | 18 | 28 | 50 | 51 | 156 | 411 | 867 | Nombre (en milliers) |
| Per 100 inhabitants | | ^0 | ^0 | ^0 | ^0 | ^0 | ^0 | 1 | 1 | Pour 100 habitants |
| Faeroe Islands | | | | | | | | | | Iles Féroé |
| Number (thousands) | | 11 | 17 | 24 | 35 | 38 | 41 | 42 | 50 | Nombre (en milliers) |
| Per 100 inhabitants | | 24 | 37 | 53 | 75 | 82 | 88 | 89 | ... | Pour 100 habitants |
| Falkland Is. (Malvinas) | | | | | | | | | | Iles Falkland (Malvinas) |
| Number (thousands) | | 0 | 0 | 0 | 0 | 0 | 0 | 1[9] | 2 | Nombre (en milliers) |
| Per 100 inhabitants | | 0 | 0 | 0 | 0 | 0 | 0 | 25[9] | ... | Pour 100 habitants |
| Fiji | | | | | | | | | | Fidji |
| Number (thousands) | | 23 | 55 | 81 | 90 | 110 | 142 | 205 | ... | Nombre (en milliers) |
| Per 100 inhabitants | | 3 | 7 | 10 | 11 | 13 | 17 | 24 | ... | Pour 100 habitants |
| Finland | | | | | | | | | | Finlande |
| Number (thousands) | | 3 273 | 3 729 | 4 176 | 4 517 | 4 747 | 4 988 | 5 270 | 5 670 | Nombre (en milliers) |
| Per 100 inhabitants | | 63 | 72 | 80 | 87 | 91 | 96 | 100 | 108 | Pour 100 habitants |
| France | | | | | | | | | | France |
| Number (thousands) | | 21 434 | 29 052 | 36 997 | 38 585 | 41 702 | 44 544 | 48 088 | 51 662 | Nombre (en milliers) |
| Per 100 inhabitants | | 37 | 49 | 62 | 65 | 70 | 74 | 79 | 85 | Pour 100 habitants |

| Country or area | Fiscal year[&] Ex. budgét. [&] | 1999 | 2000 | 2001 | 2002 | 2003 | 2004 | 2005 | 2006 | Pays ou zone |
|---|---|---|---|---|---|---|---|---|---|---|
| French Guiana | | | | | | | | | | Guyane française |
| Number (thousands) | | 18 | 40 | 75 | 87 | 92 | 98 | ... | .... | Nombre (en milliers) |
| Per 100 inhabitants | | 11 | 24 | 45 | 50 | 51 | 54 | ... | ... | Pour 100 habitants |
| French Polynesia | | | | | | | | | | Polynésie française |
| Number (thousands) | | 22 | 40 | 67 | 52 | 60 | 96 | 120 | 152 | Nombre (en milliers) |
| Per 100 inhabitants | | 9 | 17 | 28 | 21 | 24 | 38 | 47 | 59 | Pour 100 habitants |
| Gabon | | | | | | | | | | Gabon |
| Number (thousands) | | 9 | 120 | 150 | 279 | 300 | 489 | 652 | 765 | Nombre (en milliers) |
| Per 100 inhabitants | | 1 | 10 | 12 | 21 | 22 | 36 | 47 | 54 | Pour 100 habitants |
| Gambia | (01/04) | | | | | | | | | Gambie |
| Number (thousands) | | 5 | *6 | 55 | 100 | 149 | 175 | 247 | 404 | Nombre (en milliers) |
| Per 100 inhabitants | | ^0 | ^0 | 4 | 8 | 11 | 12 | 16 | 26 | Pour 100 habitants |
| Georgia | | | | | | | | | | Géorgie |
| Number (thousands) | | 133 | 195 | 301 | 504 | 711 | 841 | 1 174 | 1 704 | Nombre (en milliers) |
| Per 100 inhabitants | | 3 | 4 | 6 | 11 | 16 | 19 | 26 | 38 | Pour 100 habitants |
| Germany | | | | | | | | | | Allemagne |
| Number (thousands) | | 23 446 | 48 202 | 56 126 | 59 128 | 64 800 | 71 322 | 79 271 | 85 652 | Nombre (en milliers) |
| Per 100 inhabitants | | 29 | 59 | 68 | 72 | 79 | 86 | 96 | 104 | Pour 100 habitants |
| Ghana | | | | | | | | | | Ghana |
| Number (thousands) | | 70 | 130 | 244 | 387 | 796 | 1 695 | 2 875 | 5 207 | Nombre (en milliers) |
| Per 100 inhabitants | | ^0 | 1 | 1 | 2 | 4 | 8 | 13 | 23 | Pour 100 habitants |
| Gibraltar | | | | | | | | | | Gibraltar |
| Number (thousands) | | 4 | 6 | 10 | 12 | 16[5] | 18 | ... | ... | Nombre (en milliers) |
| Per 100 inhabitants | | 13 | 20 | 36 | 43 | 56 | 65 | ... | ... | Pour 100 habitants |
| Greece | | | | | | | | | | Grèce |
| Number (thousands) | | 3 904 | 5 932 | 7 964 | 9 314[10] | 8 936 | 9 324 | 10 260 | 10 980 | Nombre (en milliers) |
| Per 100 inhabitants | | 37 | 56 | 75 | 85 | 78 | 84 | 92 | 99 | Pour 100 habitants |
| Greenland | | | | | | | | | | Groenland |
| Number (thousands) | | 14 | 16 | 17 | 20 | 27 | 32 | ... | ... | Nombre (en milliers) |
| Per 100 inhabitants | | 24 | 29 | 30 | 35 | 48 | ... | ... | ... | Pour 100 habitants |
| Grenada | | | | | | | | | | Grenade |
| Number (thousands) | | 2 | 4 | 6 | 8 | 42 | 43 | 47 | 46 | Nombre (en milliers) |
| Per 100 inhabitants | | 2 | 4 | 6 | 7 | *41 | 42 | 46 | ... | Pour 100 habitants |
| Guadeloupe[1] | | | | | | | | | | Guadeloupe[1] |
| Number (thousands) | | 88 | 170 | 293 | 299 | 289 | 315 | ... | ... | Nombre (en milliers) |
| Per 100 inhabitants | | 21 | 40 | 68 | 69 | 66 | 71 | ... | ... | Pour 100 habitants |
| Guam | | | | | | | | | | Guam |
| Number (thousands) | | 20 | 27 | 33 | 71 | 80 | 98 | ... | ... | Nombre (en milliers) |
| Per 100 inhabitants | | 13 | 18 | 21 | 44 | 49 | 59 | ... | ... | Pour 100 habitants |
| Guatemala | | | | | | | | | | Guatemala |
| Number (thousands) | | 338 | 857 | 1 146 | 1 577 | 2 035 | 3 168 | 4 510 | 7 179 | Nombre (en milliers) |
| Per 100 inhabitants | | 3 | 8 | 10 | 13 | 17 | 25 | 36 | 56 | Pour 100 habitants |
| Guernsey | | | | | | | | | | Guernesey |
| Number (thousands) | | 15 | 22 | 32 | 37 | 42 | 44 | ... | ... | Nombre (en milliers) |
| Per 100 inhabitants | | 25 | 35 | 56 | 65 | 74 | 79 | ... | ... | Pour 100 habitants |
| Guinea | | | | | | | | | | Guinée |
| Number (thousands) | | 25 | 42 | 56 | 91 | 112 | 155 | 189 | ... | Nombre (en milliers) |
| Per 100 inhabitants | | ^0 | 1 | 1 | 1 | 1 | 2 | 2 | ... | Pour 100 habitants |
| Guinea-Bissau | | | | | | | | | | Guinée-Bissau |
| Number (thousands) | | 0 | 0 | 0 | 0 | 1 | 42 | 95 | ... | Nombre (en milliers) |
| Per 100 inhabitants | | 0 | 0 | 0 | 0 | ^0 | 3 | 7 | ... | Pour 100 habitants |
| Guyana[1] | | | | | | | | | | Guyana[1] |
| Number (thousands) | | 3 | 40 | 75 | 79 | 138 | 172 | 281 | ... | Nombre (en milliers) |
| Per 100 inhabitants | | ^0 | 5 | 10 | 11 | 18 | 23 | 37 | ... | Pour 100 habitants |

| Country or area | Fiscal year[&] Ex. budgét. [&] | 1999 | 2000 | 2001 | 2002 | 2003 | 2004 | 2005 | 2006 | Pays ou zone |
|---|---|---|---|---|---|---|---|---|---|---|
| Haiti | | | | | | | | | | Haïti |
| Number (thousands) | | 25 | 55 | 92 | 140 | 320 | 400 | 500[3] | ... | Nombre (en milliers) |
| Per 100 inhabitants | | ^0 | 1 | 1 | 2 | 4 | 5 | 6 | ... | Pour 100 habitants |
| Honduras | | | | | | | | | | Honduras |
| Number (thousands) | | 79 | 155 | 238 | 327 | 379 | 707 | 1 281 | 2 241 | Nombre (en milliers) |
| Per 100 inhabitants | | 1 | 2 | 4 | 5 | 6 | 10 | 18 | 30 | Pour 100 habitants |
| Hungary | | | | | | | | | | Hongrie |
| Number (thousands) | | 1 628 | 3 076 | 4 967 | 6 886 | 7 945 | 8 727[11] | 9 320 | 9 966 | Nombre (en milliers) |
| Per 100 inhabitants | | 16 | 30 | 49 | 68 | 79 | 86 | 92 | 99 | Pour 100 habitants |
| Iceland | | | | | | | | | | Islande |
| Number (thousands) | | 173 | 215 | 248 | 260[3] | 280 | 290 | 304 | 323 | Nombre (en milliers) |
| Per 100 inhabitants | | 62 | 76 | 86 | 90 | 97 | 99 | 103 | 109 | Pour 100 habitants |
| India | (01/04) | | | | | | | | | Inde |
| Number (thousands) | | 1 884 | 3 577 | 6 540 | 13 000 | 33 690 | 52 220 | 90 140 | 166 050 | Nombre (en milliers) |
| Per 100 inhabitants | | ^0 | ^0 | 1 | 1 | 3 | 5 | 8 | 15 | Pour 100 habitants |
| Indonesia | | | | | | | | | | Indonésie |
| Number (thousands) | | 2 221 | 3 669 | 6 521 | 11 700 | 18 495 | 30 337 | 46 910 | 63 803 | Nombre (en milliers) |
| Per 100 inhabitants | | 1 | 2 | 3 | 6 | 9 | 14 | 21 | 28 | Pour 100 habitants |
| Iran (Islamic Rep. of) | (22/03) | | | | | | | | | Iran (Rép. islamique d') |
| Number (thousands) | | 490 | 963 | 2 087 | 2 279 | 3 450 | 5 076 | 8 511[12] | 15 385 | Nombre (en milliers) |
| Per 100 inhabitants | | 1 | 2 | 3 | 3 | 5 | 7 | 12 | 22 | Pour 100 habitants |
| Iraq | (30/06) | | | | | | | | | Iraq |
| Number (thousands) | | 0 | 0 | 0 | 20 | 80 | 574 | ... | ... | Nombre (en milliers) |
| Per 100 inhabitants | | 0 | 0 | 0 | ^0 | ^0 | 2 | ... | ... | Pour 100 habitants |
| Ireland | (01/04) | | | | | | | | | Irlande |
| Number (thousands) | | 1 677 | 2 461 | 2 970 | 3 000 | 3 500 | 3 860 | 4 270 | 4 740 | Nombre (en milliers) |
| Per 100 inhabitants | | 45 | 65 | 77 | 76 | 88 | 95 | 103 | 113 | Pour 100 habitants |
| Israel | | | | | | | | | | Israël |
| Number (thousands) | | 2 880 | 4 400 | 5 501 | 6 300 | 6 618 | 7 222 | 7 757 | 8 404 | Nombre (en milliers) |
| Per 100 inhabitants | | 47 | 70 | 85 | 95 | 98 | 105 | 112 | 123 | Pour 100 habitants |
| Italy | | | | | | | | | | Italie |
| Number (thousands) | | 30 296 | 42 246 | 51 246 | 54 200[4] | 56 770[8] | 62 750 | 71 500 | 78 571 | Nombre (en milliers) |
| Per 100 inhabitants | | 53 | 74 | 88 | 96 | 98 | 108 | 123 | 135 | Pour 100 habitants |
| Jamaica | (01/04) | | | | | | | | | Jamaïque |
| Number (thousands) | | 144 | 367 | *598 | 1 245 | 1 576 | 1 838 | 1 981 | 2 495 | Nombre (en milliers) |
| Per 100 inhabitants | | 6 | 14 | 23 | 47 | 60 | 69 | 75 | 94 | Pour 100 habitants |
| Japan[13] | (01/04) | | | | | | | | | Japon[13] |
| Number (thousands) | | 56 846 | 66 784 | 74 819 | 81 118 | 86 655 | 91 474 | 96 484[5] | 101 698 | Nombre (en milliers) |
| Per 100 inhabitants | | 45 | 53 | 59 | 64 | 68 | 72 | 75 | 79 | Pour 100 habitants |
| Jersey | | | | | | | | | | Jersey |
| Number (thousands) | | 25 | 45 | 61 | ... | 81 | 84 | ... | ... | Nombre (en milliers) |
| Per 100 inhabitants | | 29 | 52 | 70 | ... | 92 | 95 | ... | ... | Pour 100 habitants |
| Jordan | | | | | | | | | | Jordanie |
| Number (thousands) | | 118 | 389 | 866 | 1 220 | 1 325 | 1 624 | 3 138 | 4 343 | Nombre (en milliers) |
| Per 100 inhabitants | | 2 | 8 | 17 | 23 | 24 | 29 | 55 | 74 | Pour 100 habitants |
| Kazakhstan | | | | | | | | | | Kazakhstan |
| Number (thousands) | | 50 | 197 | 582 | 1 027 | 1 331 | 2 447 | 5 398 | 7 830 | Nombre (en milliers) |
| Per 100 inhabitants | | ^0 | 1 | 4 | 7 | 9 | 16 | 36 | 53 | Pour 100 habitants |
| Kenya | (30/06) | | | | | | | | | Kenya |
| Number (thousands) | | 24 | 127[5] | 600 | 1 187[5] | 1 591 | 2 546 | 4 612 | 7 340 | Nombre (en milliers) |
| Per 100 inhabitants | | ^0 | ^0 | 2 | 4 | 5 | 8 | 13 | 21 | Pour 100 habitants |
| Kiribati | | | | | | | | | | Kiribati |
| Number (thousands) | | ^0 | ^0 | ^0 | ^0 | 1 | 1 | ... | ... | Nombre (en milliers) |
| Per 100 inhabitants | | ^0 | ^0 | ^0 | 1 | 1 | 1 | ... | ... | Pour 100 habitants |

| Country or area | Fiscal year[&] Ex. budgét. [&] | 1999 | 2000 | 2001 | 2002 | 2003 | 2004 | 2005 | 2006 | Pays ou zone |
|---|---|---|---|---|---|---|---|---|---|---|
| Korea, Republic of | | | | | | | | | | Corée, République de |
| Number (thousands) | | 23 443 | 26 816 | 29 046 | 32 342 | 33 592 | 36 586 | 38 342 | 40 197 | Nombre (en milliers) |
| Per 100 inhabitants | | 51 | 58 | 61 | 68 | 70 | 76 | 79 | 84 | Pour 100 habitants |
| Kuwait | | | | | | | | | | Koweït |
| Number (thousands) | | 300 | 476 | 878 | 1 227 | 1 420 | 2 000 | 2 380 | ... | Nombre (en milliers) |
| Per 100 inhabitants | | 14 | 22 | 39 | 52 | 57 | 78 | 89 | ... | Pour 100 habitants |
| Kyrgyzstan | | | | | | | | | | Kirghizistan |
| Number (thousands) | | 3 | 9 | 27 | 53 | 138 | 263 | 542 | ... | Nombre (en milliers) |
| Per 100 inhabitants | | ^0 | ^0 | 1 | 1 | 3 | 5 | 10 | ... | Pour 100 habitants |
| Lao People's Dem. Rep. | | | | | | | | | | Rép. dém. pop. lao |
| Number (thousands) | | 12 | 13 | 30 | 55 | 112 | 204 | 638 | ... | Nombre (en milliers) |
| Per 100 inhabitants | | ^0 | ^0 | 1 | 1 | 2 | 4 | 11 | ... | Pour 100 habitants |
| Latvia | | | | | | | | | | Lettonie |
| Number (thousands) | | 274 | 401 | 657 | 917 | 1 220 | 1 537 | 1 872 | 2 184 | Nombre (en milliers) |
| Per 100 inhabitants | | 11 | 17 | 28 | 39 | 53 | 67 | 81 | 95 | Pour 100 habitants |
| Lebanon[3] | | | | | | | | | | Liban[3] |
| Number (thousands) | | 627 | 743 | 767 | 775 | 795 | 884 | 994 | 1 106 | Nombre (en milliers) |
| Per 100 inhabitants | | 19 | 23 | 23 | 23 | 23 | 25 | 28 | 31 | Pour 100 habitants |
| Lesotho | (01/04) | | | | | | | | | Lesotho |
| Number (thousands) | | 12 | 22 | 57 | 138 | 126 | 196 | 250 | ... | Nombre (en milliers) |
| Per 100 inhabitants | | 1 | 1 | 3 | 8 | 7 | 11 | 14 | ... | Pour 100 habitants |
| Liberia | | | | | | | | | | Libéria |
| Number (thousands) | | 0 | 2 | 2 | ... | 47[3] | 94 | 160 | ... | Nombre (en milliers) |
| Per 100 inhabitants | | 0 | ^0 | ^0 | ... | 1 | 3 | 5 | ... | Pour 100 habitants |
| Libyan Arab Jamah. | | | | | | | | | | Jamah. arabe libyenne |
| Number (thousands) | | 30 | 40 | 50 | 70 | 127 | ... | ... | 3 928[3] | Nombre (en milliers) |
| Per 100 inhabitants | | 1 | 1 | 1 | 1 | 2 | ... | ... | 66 | Pour 100 habitants |
| Liechtenstein[3] | | | | | | | | | | Liechtenstein[3] |
| Number (thousands) | | 9 | 10 | 11 | 11 | 25 | 26 | 28 | 29 | Nombre (en milliers) |
| Per 100 inhabitants | | 28 | 30 | 33 | 34 | 73 | 74 | 79 | ... | Pour 100 habitants |
| Lithuania | | | | | | | | | | Lituanie |
| Number (thousands)[1] | | 332 | 524 | 1 018 | 1 646 | 2 170 | 3 051 | 4 353 | 4 718 | Nombre (en milliers)[1] |
| Per 100 inhabitants | | 9 | 14 | 29 | 47 | 63 | 89 | 127 | 138 | Pour 100 habitants |
| Luxembourg | | | | | | | | | | Luxembourg |
| Number (thousands) | | 209 | 303 | 409 | 473[3] | 539 | 646 | 720 | 714 | Nombre (en milliers) |
| Per 100 inhabitants | | 48 | 69 | 93 | 106 | 119 | 141 | 155 | 152 | Pour 100 habitants |
| Madagascar | | | | | | | | | | Madagascar |
| Number (thousands) | | 36 | 63 | 148 | 163 | 284 | 334 | 510 | 1 046 | Nombre (en milliers) |
| Per 100 inhabitants | | ^0 | ^0 | 1 | 1 | 2 | 2 | 3 | 5 | Pour 100 habitants |
| Malawi | | | | | | | | | | Malawi |
| Number (thousands) | | 23 | 49 | 56 | 86 | 135 | 222 | 429 | ... | Nombre (en milliers) |
| Per 100 inhabitants | | ^0 | ^0 | 1 | 1 | 1 | 2 | 3 | ... | Pour 100 habitants |
| Malaysia | | | | | | | | | | Malaisie |
| Number (thousands) | | 2 990 | 5 122 | 7 385 | 9 053 | 11 124 | 14 611 | 19 545 | 19 464 | Nombre (en milliers) |
| Per 100 inhabitants | | 14 | 22 | 31 | 37 | 44 | 57 | 75 | 75 | Pour 100 habitants |
| Maldives | | | | | | | | | | Maldives |
| Number (thousands) | | 3 | 8 | 19 | 42 | 66 | 113 | 202 | 263 | Nombre (en milliers) |
| Per 100 inhabitants | | 1 | 3 | 7 | 15 | 23 | 38 | 67 | 88 | Pour 100 habitants |
| Mali | | | | | | | | | | Mali |
| Number (thousands) | | 6 | 10 | 45 | 52 | 244 | 1 494 | 869 | 1 512 | Nombre (en milliers) |
| Per 100 inhabitants | | ^0 | ^0 | ^0 | ^0 | 2 | 13 | 8 | 11 | Pour 100 habitants |
| Malta | | | | | | | | | | Malte |
| Number (thousands) | | 38 | 114 | 239 | 277 | 290 | 306 | 324 | 347 | Nombre (en milliers) |
| Per 100 inhabitants | | 10 | 29 | 61 | 70 | 72 | 77 | 81 | 86 | Pour 100 habitants |

**Cellular mobile telephone subscribers**— Number (thousands) and per 100 inhabitants (*continued*)

**Abonnés au téléphone mobile**— Nombre (en milliers) et pour 100 habitants (*suite*)

| Country or area | Fiscal year[&] Ex. budgét. [&] | 1999 | 2000 | 2001 | 2002 | 2003 | 2004 | 2005 | 2006 | Pays ou zone |
|---|---|---|---|---|---|---|---|---|---|---|
| Marshall Islands | | | | | | | | | | Iles Marshall |
| Number (thousands) | | ^0 | ^0 | ^0 | ^0 | 1 | 1 | ... | ... | Nombre (en milliers) |
| Per 100 inhabitants | | 1 | 1 | 1 | 1 | 1 | 1 | ... | ... | Pour 100 habitants |
| Martinique | | | | | | | | | | Martinique |
| Number (thousands)[1] | | 102 | 162 | 286 | 298 | 278 | 295 | ... | ... | Nombre (en milliers)[1] |
| Per 100 inhabitants | | 27 | 42 | 74 | 77 | 71 | 75 | ... | ... | Pour 100 habitants |
| Mauritania | | | | | | | | | | Mauritanie |
| Number (thousands) | | 0 | 15 | 110 | 247 | 351 | 522 | 746 | 1 060 | Nombre (en milliers) |
| Per 100 inhabitants | | 0 | 1 | 4 | 9 | 13 | 18 | 24 | 34 | Pour 100 habitants |
| Mauritius | | | | | | | | | | Maurice |
| Number (thousands) | | 102 | 180 | 272 | 348 | 462 | 548 | 657 | 772 | Nombre (en milliers) |
| Per 100 inhabitants | | 9 | 15 | 23 | 29 | 38 | 44 | 53 | 62 | Pour 100 habitants |
| Mayotte | | | | | | | | | | Mayotte |
| Number (thousands) | | 0 | 0 | 0 | 20 | 33 | 48 | ... | ... | Nombre (en milliers) |
| Per 100 inhabitants | | 0 | 0 | 0 | 13 | 20 | 29 | ... | ... | Pour 100 habitants |
| Mexico | | | | | | | | | | Mexique |
| Number (thousands) | | 7 732 | 14 078 | 21 758 | 25 928 | 30 098 | 38 451 | 47 129 | 57 016 | Nombre (en milliers) |
| Per 100 inhabitants | | 8 | 14 | 22 | 26 | 29 | 37 | 44 | 53 | Pour 100 habitants |
| Micronesia (Fed. States of) | | | | | | | | | | Micronésie (Etats féd. de) |
| Number (thousands) | | 0 | 0 | 0 | ^0 | 6 | 13 | 14 | ... | Nombre (en milliers) |
| Per 100 inhabitants | | 0 | 0 | 0 | ^0 | 5 | 12 | 13 | ... | Pour 100 habitants |
| Moldova | | | | | | | | | | Moldova |
| Number | | 18 | 139 | 225 | 338 | 476 | 787 | 1 090 | 1 358 | Nombre |
| Per 100 inhabitants | | ^0 | 3 | 5 | 8 | 11 | 18 | 26 | 32 | Pour 100 habitants |
| Monaco | | | | | | | | | | Monaco |
| Number | | 13 | 14 | 14 | 15 | 15 | 16 | 17 | 18 | Nombre |
| Per 100 inhabitants | | 40 | 42 | 42 | 44 | 44 | 45 | 49 | 52 | Pour 100 habitants |
| Mongolia | | | | | | | | | | Mongolie |
| Number (thousands) | | 35 | 155 | 195 | 216 | 319 | 429 | 557 | 775 | Nombre (en milliers) |
| Per 100 inhabitants | | 1 | 7 | 8 | 9 | 13 | 16 | 21 | 29 | Pour 100 habitants |
| Montenegro | | | | | | | | | | Monténégro |
| Number (thousands) | | ... | ... | ... | ... | ... | ... | ... | 822 | Nombre (en milliers) |
| Per 100 inhabitants | | ... | ... | ... | ... | ... | ... | ... | 8 | Pour 100 habitants |
| Montserrat | | | | | | | | | | Montserrat |
| Number (thousands) | | ^0 | 1 | 1 | 2 | 2 | 2 | ... | ... | Nombre (en milliers) |
| Per 100 inhabitants | | 8 | 12 | 30 | 38 | 45 | 55 | ... | ... | Pour 100 habitants |
| Morocco | | | | | | | | | | Maroc |
| Number (thousands) | | 369 | 2 342 | 4 772 | 6 199 | 7 360 | 9 337 | 12 393 | 16 005 | Nombre (en milliers) |
| Per 100 inhabitants | | 1 | 8 | 17 | 21 | 25 | 31 | 41 | 52 | Pour 100 habitants |
| Mozambique | | | | | | | | | | Mozambique |
| Number (thousands) | | 12 | 51 | 153 | 255 | 436 | 708 | 1 504 | 2 339 | Nombre (en milliers) |
| Per 100 inhabitants | | ^0 | ^0 | 1 | 1 | 2 | 4 | 8 | 12 | Pour 100 habitants |
| Myanmar | | | | | | | | | | Myanmar |
| Number (thousands) | | 11 | 13 | 23 | 48 | 67 | 92 | 129 | 214 | Nombre (en milliers) |
| Per 100 inhabitants^ | | 0 | 0 | 0 | 0 | 0 | 0 | 0 | 0 | Pour 100 habitants^ |
| Namibia | (30/09) | | | | | | | | | Namibie |
| Number (thousands)[3] | | 30 | 82 | 107 | 150[5] | 224 | 286 | 495 | ... | Nombre (en milliers) |
| Per 100 inhabitants | | 2 | 5 | 6 | 8 | 12 | 14 | 24 | ... | Pour 100 habitants |
| Nauru | | | | | | | | | | Nauru |
| Number (thousands) | | 1 | 1 | 2 | ... | ... | ... | ... | ... | Nombre (en milliers)[3] |
| Per 100 inhabitants | | 9 | 10 | 13 | ... | ... | ... | ... | ... | Pour 100 habitants |
| Nepal | (15/07) | | | | | | | | | Népal |
| Number (thousands) | | 6 | 10 | 17[2] | 22 | 82 | 117 | 227 | 11 571 | Nombre (en milliers) |
| Per 100 inhabitants | | ^0 | ^0 | ^0 | ^0 | ^0 | ^0 | 1 | 42 | Pour 100 habitants |

| Country or area | Fiscal year[&] Ex. budgét. [&] | 1999 | 2000 | 2001 | 2002 | 2003 | 2004 | 2005 | 2006 | Pays ou zone |
|---|---|---|---|---|---|---|---|---|---|---|
| Netherlands | | | | | | | | | | Pays-Bas |
| Number (thousands) | | 6 745 | 10 755 | 12 200 | 12 100 | 13 200 | 14 800 | 15 834 | 17 500[14] | Nombre (en milliers) |
| Per 100 inhabitants | | 43 | 67 | 76 | 75 | 81 | 91 | 97 | 107 | Pour 100 habitants |
| Netherlands Antilles | | | | | | | | | | Antilles néerlandaises |
| Number (thousands) | | 30 | ... | ... | ... | 200 | 200 | ... | ... | Nombre (en milliers) |
| Per 100 inhabitants | | 14 | ... | ... | ... | 90 | 90 | ... | ... | Pour 100 habitants |
| New Caledonia | | | | | | | | | | Nouvelle-Calédonie |
| Number (thousands) | | 25 | 50 | 68 | 80 | 97 | 116 | 134 | ... | Nombre (en milliers) |
| Per 100 inhabitants | | 12 | 23 | 31 | 36 | 42 | 50 | 57 | ... | Pour 100 habitants |
| New Zealand | (01/04) | | | | | | | | | Nouvelle-Zélande |
| Number (thousands) | | 1 395 | 1 542 | 2 288 | 2 449 | 2 599 | 3 027 | 3 530 | ... | Nombre (en milliers) |
| Per 100 inhabitants | | 36 | 40 | 59 | 62 | 66 | 76 | 88 | ... | Pour 100 habitants |
| Nicaragua | | | | | | | | | | Nicaragua |
| Number (thousands) | | 44 | 90 | 165 | 237 | 467 | 739 | 1 119 | 1 830 | Nombre (en milliers) |
| Per 100 inhabitants | | 1 | 2 | 3 | 5 | 8 | 13 | 19 | 33 | Pour 100 habitants |
| Niger | | | | | | | | | | Niger |
| Number (thousands) | | 2 | 2 | 2 | 58 | 82 | 172 | 324 | ... | Nombre (en milliers) |
| Per 100 inhabitants | | ^0 | ^0 | ^0 | ^0 | 1 | 1 | 2 | ... | Pour 100 habitants |
| Nigeria | | | | | | | | | | Nigéria |
| Number (thousands) | | 25 | 30 | *400 | 1 608 | 3 149 | 9 147 | 18 587[15] | 32 322 | Nombre (en milliers) |
| Per 100 inhabitants | | ^0 | ^0 | ^0 | 1 | 3 | 7 | 14 | 24 | Pour 100 habitants |
| Niue | | | | | | | | | | Nioué |
| Number (thousands) | | ^0 | ^0 | ^0 | ^0 | 1 | 1 | ... | ... | Nombre (en milliers) |
| Per 100 inhabitants | | 20 | 22 | 23 | 28 | 35 | 38 | ... | ... | Pour 100 habitants |
| Northern Mariana Islands | | | | | | | | | | Iles Marianes du Nord |
| Number (thousands) | | 3[16] | 3 | 13 | 17 | 19 | 20 | ... | ... | Nombre (en milliers) |
| Per 100 inhabitants | | 4 | 4 | 19 | 24 | 26 | 27 | ... | ... | Pour 100 habitants |
| Norway | | | | | | | | | | Norvège |
| Number (thousands) | | 2 664 | 3 224 | 3 593 | 3 790[3] | 4 061 | 4 525 | 4 754 | 5 041 | Nombre (en milliers) |
| Per 100 inhabitants | | 59 | 72 | 79 | 83 | 89 | 98 | 103 | 109 | Pour 100 habitants |
| Occupied Palestinian Terr [17]. | | | | | | | | | | Terr. palestinien occupé[17] |
| Number (thousands) | | 117 | 176 | 300 | 320 | 480 | 974 | 1 095 | 822 | Nombre (en milliers) |
| Per 100 inhabitants | | 4 | 6 | 9 | 9 | 13 | 26 | 30 | ... | Pour 100 habitants |
| Oman | | | | | | | | | | Oman |
| Number (thousands) | | 121 | 162 | 323 | 463 | 594 | 806 | 1 333 | 1 818 | Nombre (en milliers) |
| Per 100 inhabitants | | 5 | 7 | 13 | 19 | 24 | 32 | 52 | 70 | Pour 100 habitants |
| Pakistan | (30/06) | | | | | | | | | Pakistan |
| Number (thousands) | | 266 | 306 | 743 | 1 699 | 2 404 | 5 023 | 12 771 | 34 507 | Nombre (en milliers) |
| Per 100 inhabitants | | ^0 | ^0 | 1 | 1 | 2 | 3 | 8 | 22 | Pour 100 habitants |
| Palau | | | | | | | | | | Palos |
| Number (thousands) | | ... | ... | ... | 2 | 4 | 4 | 6 | 8 | Nombre (en milliers) |
| Per 100 inhabitants | | ... | ... | ... | ... | ... | ... | ... | ... | Pour 100 habitants |
| Panama | | | | | | | | | | Panama |
| Number (thousands) | | 233 | 410 | 475 | 526 | 692 | 1 260 | 1 693 | ... | Nombre (en milliers) |
| Per 100 inhabitants | | 8 | 14 | 16 | 17 | 22 | 40 | 52 | ... | Pour 100 habitants |
| Papua New Guinea | | | | | | | | | | Papouasie-Nvl-Guinée |
| Number (thousands) | | 7 | 9 | 11 | 15 | 18 | 48 | 75 | ... | Nombre (en milliers) |
| Per 100 inhabitants | | ^0 | ^0 | ^0 | ^0 | ^0 | 1 | 1 | ... | Pour 100 habitants |
| Paraguay | | | | | | | | | | Paraguay |
| Number (thousands) | | 436 | 821 | 1 150 | 1 667 | 1 770 | 1 749 | 1 887 | 3 233 | Nombre (en milliers) |
| Per 100 inhabitants | | 8 | 15 | 20 | 29 | 30 | 29 | 31 | 51 | Pour 100 habitants |
| Peru | | | | | | | | | | Pérou |
| Number (thousands) | | 1 013 | 1 274 | 1 793 | 2 307 | 2 930 | 4 093 | 5 583 | 8 772 | Nombre (en milliers) |
| Per 100 inhabitants | | 4 | 5 | 7 | 9 | 11 | 15 | 20 | 31 | Pour 100 habitants |

| Country or area | Fiscal year[&] Ex. budgét. [&] | 1999 | 2000 | 2001 | 2002 | 2003 | 2004 | 2005 | 2006 | Pays ou zone |
|---|---|---|---|---|---|---|---|---|---|---|
| Philippines | | | | | | | | | | Philippines |
| Number (thousands) | | 2 850 | 6 454 | 12 159 | 15 383 | 22 510 | 32 936 | 34 779 | 42 869 | Nombre (en milliers) |
| Per 100 inhabitants | | 4 | 8 | 16 | 19 | 28 | 40 | 41 | 51 | Pour 100 habitants |
| Poland | | | | | | | | | | Pologne |
| Number (thousands) | | 3 957 | 6 747 | 10 005 | *13 898 | *17 401 | 23 096 | 29 166 | 36 745 | Nombre (en milliers) |
| Per 100 inhabitants | | 10 | 17 | 26 | 36 | 45 | 60 | 76 | 95 | Pour 100 habitants |
| Portugal | | | | | | | | | | Portugal |
| Number (thousands) | | 4 671 | 6 665 | 7 978 | 8 670 | 10 030 | 10 362[18] | 11 447 | 12 226 | Nombre (en milliers) |
| Per 100 inhabitants | | 47 | 66 | 77 | 83 | 96 | 98 | 109 | 116 | Pour 100 habitants |
| Puerto Rico | | | | | | | | | | Porto Rico |
| Number (thousands) | | 814 | 926 | 1 129 | 1 800 | 1 860 | 2 682 | 3 354[3] | ... | Nombre (en milliers) |
| Per 100 inhabitants | | 22 | 24 | 29 | 47 | 48 | 69 | 85 | ... | Pour 100 habitants |
| Qatar | | | | | | | | | | Qatar |
| Number (thousands) | | 84 | 121 | 178 | 267 | 377 | 490 | 717 | 920 | Nombre (en milliers) |
| Per 100 inhabitants | | 15 | 20 | 28 | 40 | 53 | 66 | 92 | 110 | Pour 100 habitants |
| Réunion | | | | | | | | | | Réunion |
| Number (thousands)[1] | | 111 | 276 | 421 | 455 | 522 | 579 | ... | ... | Nombre (en milliers)[1] |
| Per 100 inhabitants | | 16 | 39 | 58 | 61 | 69 | 76 | ... | ... | Pour 100 habitants |
| Romania | | | | | | | | | | Roumanie |
| Number (thousands) | | 1 356 | 2 499 | 3 845 | 5 111 | 7 040 | 10 215 | 13 354 | 17 400 | Nombre (en milliers) |
| Per 100 inhabitants | | 6 | 11 | 17 | 23 | 32 | 47 | 62 | 80 | Pour 100 habitants |
| Russian Federation | | | | | | | | | | Fédération de Russie |
| Number (thousands) | | 1 371 | 3 263 | 7 750 | 17 609 | 36 135 | 73 722 | 120 000 | 150 000 | Nombre (en milliers) |
| Per 100 inhabitants | | 1 | 2 | 5 | 12 | 25 | 51 | 84 | 105 | Pour 100 habitants |
| Rwanda | | | | | | | | | | Rwanda |
| Number (thousands) | | 11 | 39 | 65 | 82[4] | 131 | 137 | 220 | 314 | Nombre (en milliers) |
| Per 100 inhabitants | | ^0 | 1 | 1 | 1 | 2 | 2 | 2 | 3 | Pour 100 habitants |
| Saint Kitts and Nevis | (01/04) | | | | | | | | | Saint-Kitts-et-Nevis |
| Number (thousands) | | 1 | 1 | *2 | 5 | ... | 10[5] | ... | ... | Nombre (en milliers) |
| Per 100 inhabitants | | 2 | 3 | 5 | 12 | ... | 24 | ... | ... | Pour 100 habitants |
| Saint Lucia* | (01/04) | | | | | | | | | Sainte-Lucie* |
| Number (thousands) | | 2 | 3 | 3 | 14 | ... | 93 | 106 | ... | Nombre (en milliers) |
| Per 100 inhabitants | | 2 | 2 | 2 | 9 | ... | 58 | 66 | ... | Pour 100 habitants |
| Saint Vincent-Grenadines | (01/04) | | | | | | | | | Saint Vincent-Grenadines |
| Number (thousands) | | 1 | 2 | 7 | 10 | 63 | 72 | 71 | 88 | Nombre (en milliers) |
| Per 100 inhabitants | | 1 | 2 | 7 | 9 | 53 | 60 | 59 | 74 | Pour 100 habitants |
| Samoa | | | | | | | | | | Samoa |
| Number (thousands) | | 2 | 3 | 3 | 3 | 11 | 16 | 24 | ... | Nombre (en milliers) |
| Per 100 inhabitants | | 1 | 1 | 1 | 2 | 6 | 9 | 13 | ... | Pour 100 habitants |
| San Marino | | | | | | | | | | Saint-Marin |
| Number (thousands) | | 10 | 15 | 16 | 17 | 17 | 17 | 17 | 17 | Nombre (en milliers) |
| Per 100 inhabitants | | 37 | 54 | 59 | 62 | 63 | 63 | 64 | ... | Pour 100 habitants |
| Sao Tome and Principe | | | | | | | | | | Sao Tomé-et-Principe |
| Number (thousands) | | 0 | 0 | 0 | 2 | 5 | 8 | 12 | 18 | Nombre (en milliers) |
| Per 100 inhabitants | | 0 | 0 | 0 | 1 | 3 | 5 | 8 | 12 | Pour 100 habitants |
| Saudi Arabia | | | | | | | | | | Arabie saoudite |
| Number (thousands) | | 837 | 1 376 | 2 529 | 5 008 | 7 238 | 9 176 | 14 164 | 19 663 | Nombre (en milliers) |
| Per 100 inhabitants | | 4 | 6 | 11 | 22 | 31 | 38 | 58 | 78 | Pour 100 habitants |
| Senegal | | | | | | | | | | Sénégal |
| Number (thousands) | | 88 | 250 | 302 | 553 | 782 | 1 121 | 1 730 | 2 983 | Nombre (en milliers) |
| Per 100 inhabitants | | 1 | 3 | 3 | 5 | 8 | 11 | 15 | 25 | Pour 100 habitants |
| Serbia | | | | | | | | | | Serbie |
| Number (thousands) | | ... | ... | ... | ... | ... | ... | ... | 6 644 | Nombre (en milliers) |
| Per 100 inhabitants | | ... | ... | ... | ... | ... | ... | ... | 63 | Pour 100 habitants |

| Country or area | Fiscal year[&] Ex. budgét. [&] | 1999 | 2000 | 2001 | 2002 | 2003 | 2004 | 2005 | 2006 | Pays ou zone |
|---|---|---|---|---|---|---|---|---|---|---|
| Serbia and Montenegro[*] | | | | | | | | | | Serbie-et-Monténégro[*] |
| Number (thousands) | | 606 | 1 304 | 1 998 | 2 750 | 3 635 | 4 730 | 5 229 | ... | Nombre (en milliers) |
| Per 100 inhabitants | | 6 | 12 | 19 | 34 | 45 | 58 | 64 | ... | Pour 100 habitants |
| Seychelles | (01/04) | | | | | | | | | Seychelles |
| Number (thousands) | | 16 | 26 | 37 | 45 | 49 | 54 | 59 | 70 | Nombre (en milliers) |
| Per 100 inhabitants | | 21 | 34 | 47 | 57 | 62 | 68 | 73 | 87 | Pour 100 habitants |
| Sierra Leone | | | | | | | | | | Sierra Leone |
| Number (thousands) | | 0 | 12 | 27 | 67 | 113[3] | ... | ... | ... | Nombre (en milliers) |
| Per 100 inhabitants | | 0 | ^0 | 1 | 1 | 2 | ... | ... | ... | Pour 100 habitants |
| Singapore | (01/04) | | | | | | | | | Singapour |
| Number (thousands) | | 1 631 | 2 747 | 2 992 | 3 313 | 3 577 | 3 991[5] | 4 385 | 4 789 | Nombre (en milliers) |
| Per 100 inhabitants | | 41 | 68 | 72 | 80 | 86 | 95 | 101 | 109 | Pour 100 habitants |
| Slovakia | | | | | | | | | | Slovaquie |
| Number (thousands) | | 664 | 1 244 | 2 147 | 2 923 | 3 679 | 4 275 | 4 540 | 4 893 | Nombre (en milliers) |
| Per 100 inhabitants | | 12 | 23 | 40 | 54 | 68 | 79 | 84 | 91 | Pour 100 habitants |
| Slovenia | | | | | | | | | | Slovénie |
| Number (thousands) | | 631 | 1 216 | 1 470 | 1 667 | 1 739 | 1 849 | 1 759[19] | 1 820 | Nombre (en milliers) |
| Per 100 inhabitants | | 32 | 61 | 74 | 84 | 87 | 93 | 89 | 93 | Pour 100 habitants |
| Solomon Islands | (01/04) | | | | | | | | | Iles Salomon |
| Number (thousands) | | 1 | 1 | 1 | 1 | 1 | 3 | 6 | ... | Nombre (en milliers) |
| Per 100 inhabitants | | ^0 | ^0 | ^0 | ^0 | ^0 | 1 | 1 | ... | Pour 100 habitants |
| Somalia | | | | | | | | | | Somalie |
| Number (thousands) | | 0 | 80 | 85 | 100 | 200 | 500 | 500 | ... | Nombre (en milliers) |
| Per 100 inhabitants | | 0 | 1 | 1 | 1 | 3 | 6 | 6 | ... | Pour 100 habitants |
| South Africa | (01/04) | | | | | | | | | Afrique du Sud |
| Number (thousands) | | 5 188 | 8 339 | 10 787 | 13 702 | 16 860 | 20 839 | 33 960 | 39 662 | Nombre (en milliers) |
| Per 100 inhabitants | | 12 | 18 | 23 | 29 | 36 | 44 | 72 | 83 | Pour 100 habitants |
| Spain | | | | | | | | | | Espagne |
| Number (thousands) | | 15 004 | 24 265 | 29 656 | 33 531 | 37 220 | 38 623 | 42 694 | 46 152 | Nombre (en milliers) |
| Per 100 inhabitants | | 37 | 60 | 72 | 82 | 87 | 89 | 100 | 106 | Pour 100 habitants |
| Sri Lanka | | | | | | | | | | Sri Lanka |
| Number (thousands) | | 257 | 430 | 668 | 931 | 1 393 | 2 211 | 3 362 | 5 412 | Nombre (en milliers) |
| Per 100 inhabitants | | 1 | 2 | 4 | 5 | 7 | 11 | 16 | 26 | Pour 100 habitants |
| Sudan | | | | | | | | | | Soudan |
| Number (thousands) | | 13 | 23 | 104 | 191 | 527 | 1 049 | 1 828 | 4 683 | Nombre (en milliers) |
| Per 100 inhabitants | | ^0 | ^0 | ^0 | 1 | 2 | 3 | 5 | 13 | Pour 100 habitants |
| Suriname | | | | | | | | | | Suriname |
| Number (thousands) | | 18 | 41 | 87 | 108 | 169 | 213 | 233 | 320 | Nombre (en milliers) |
| Per 100 inhabitants | | 4 | 9 | 20 | 25 | 38 | 48 | 52 | 71 | Pour 100 habitants |
| Swaziland | (01/04) | | | | | | | | | Swaziland |
| Number (thousands) | | 14 | 33 | 55 | 68 | 85[5] | 145 | 200 | 250 | Nombre (en milliers) |
| Per 100 inhabitants | | 1 | 3 | 5 | 7 | 8 | 13 | 19 | 24 | Pour 100 habitants |
| Sweden | | | | | | | | | | Suède |
| Number (thousands) | | 5 126 | 6 372 | 7 178 | 7 949 | 8 801 | 8 785[8] | 9 104 | 9 607 | Nombre (en milliers) |
| Per 100 inhabitants | | 58 | 72 | 81 | 89 | 98 | 97 | 101 | 106 | Pour 100 habitants |
| Switzerland | | | | | | | | | | Suisse |
| Number (thousands) | | 3 058 | 4 639 | 5 276 | 5 736 | 6 189 | 6 275 | 6 834 | 7 436 | Nombre (en milliers) |
| Per 100 inhabitants | | 43 | 64 | 73 | 78 | 84 | 85 | 92 | 99 | Pour 100 habitants |
| Syrian Arab Republic | | | | | | | | | | Rép. arabe syrienne |
| Number (thousands) | | 4 | 30 | 200 | 400 | 1 185 | 2 345 | 2 950 | 4 675 | Nombre (en milliers) |
| Per 100 inhabitants | | ^0 | ^0 | 1 | 2 | 7 | 13 | 15 | 24 | Pour 100 habitants |
| Tajikistan | | | | | | | | | | Tadjikistan |
| Number (thousands) | | 1 | 1 | 2 | 13 | 48 | 135 | 265 | ... | Nombre (en milliers) |
| Per 100 inhabitants | | ^0 | ^0 | ^0 | ^0 | 1 | 2 | 4 | ... | Pour 100 habitants |

| Country or area | Fiscal year[&] Ex. budgét.[&] | 1999 | 2000 | 2001 | 2002 | 2003 | 2004 | 2005 | 2006 | Pays ou zone |
|---|---|---|---|---|---|---|---|---|---|---|
| Thailand | (30/09) | | | | | | | | | Thaïlande |
| Number (thousands) | | 2 339 | 3 056 | 7 550 | 10 172 | 21 828 | 27 379 | 31 137 | 40 815 | Nombre (en milliers) |
| Per 100 inhabitants | | 4 | 5 | 12 | 16 | 35 | 43 | 48 | 63 | Pour 100 habitants |
| TFYR of Macedonia | | | | | | | | | | L'ex-R.y. Macédoine |
| Number (thousands) | | 49 | 116 | 223 | 365 | 776 | 986 | 1 261 | 1 417 | Nombre (en milliers) |
| Per 100 inhabitants | | 2 | 6 | 11 | 18 | 38 | 49 | 62 | 70 | Pour 100 habitants |
| Timor-Leste | | | | | | | | | | Timor-Leste |
| Number (thousands) | | ... | ... | ... | ... | 20 | 26 | 33 | 49 | Nombre (en milliers) |
| Per 100 inhabitants | | ... | ... | ... | ... | 2 | 3 | 3 | 5 | Pour 100 habitants |
| Togo | | | | | | | | | | Togo |
| Number (thousands) | | 17 | 50 | 95 | 170 | 244 | 333 | 434 | 708 | Nombre (en milliers) |
| Per 100 inhabitants | | ^0 | 1 | 2 | 3 | 5 | 7 | 9 | 11 | Pour 100 habitants |
| Tonga[3] | | | | | | | | | | Tonga[3] |
| Number (thousands) | | ^0 | ^0 | ^0 | 3 | 11 | 16 | 30 | ... | Nombre (en milliers) |
| Per 100 inhabitants | | ^0 | ^0 | ^0 | 3 | 11 | 16 | 30 | ... | Pour 100 habitants |
| Trinidad and Tobago | (01/04) | | | | | | | | | Trinité-et-Tobago |
| Number (thousands) | | 39 | 162 | 256 | 263 | 336 | 651 | 800 | 1 655 | Nombre (en milliers) |
| Per 100 inhabitants | | 3 | 13 | 20 | 20 | 26 | 50 | 61 | 126 | Pour 100 habitants |
| Tunisia | | | | | | | | | | Tunisie |
| Number (thousands) | | 55 | 119 | 389 | 574 | 1 918 | 3 736 | 5 681 | ... | Nombre (en milliers) |
| Per 100 inhabitants | | 1 | 1 | 4 | 6 | 19 | 37 | 56 | ... | Pour 100 habitants |
| Turkey | | | | | | | | | | Turquie |
| Number (thousands) | | 8 122 | 16 133 | 19 573 | 23 323 | 27 888 | 34 708 | 43 609 | 52 663 | Nombre (en milliers) |
| Per 100 inhabitants | | 12 | 24 | 28 | 33 | 39 | 48 | 60 | 71 | Pour 100 habitants |
| Turkmenistan | | | | | | | | | | Turkménistan |
| Number (thousands) | | 4 | 8 | 8 | 8 | 9 | 50 | 105[3] | ... | Nombre (en milliers) |
| Per 100 inhabitants | | ^0 | ^0 | ^0 | ^0 | ^0 | 1 | 2 | ... | Pour 100 habitants |
| Turks and Caicos Islands | | | | | | | | | | Iles Turques et Caïques |
| Number | | ... | ... | ... | 9 | 19 | 25 | ... | ... | Nombre (en milliers) |
| Per 100 inhabitants | | ... | ... | ... | 41 | 81 | 100 | ... | ... | Pour 100 habitants |
| Tuvalu | | | | | | | | | | Tuvalu |
| Number (thousands) | | 0 | 0 | 0 | 0 | 0 | 1 | 1 | 2 | Nombre (en milliers) |
| Per 100 inhabitants | | 0 | 0 | 0 | 0 | 0 | 5 | 12 | 15 | Pour 100 habitants |
| Uganda | (30/06) | | | | | | | | | Ouganda |
| Number (thousands) | | 56 | 127 | 284 | 393 | 776 | 1 165[11] | 1 315 | 2 009 | Nombre (en milliers) |
| Per 100 inhabitants | | ^0 | 1 | 1 | 2 | 3 | 4 | 5 | 7 | Pour 100 habitants |
| Ukraine | | | | | | | | | | Ukraine |
| Number (thousands) | | 217 | 819 | 2 225 | 3 693 | 6 498 | 13 735 | 30 000 | 49 076 | Nombre (en milliers) |
| Per 100 inhabitants | | ^0 | 2 | 5 | 8 | 14 | 29 | 65 | 107 | Pour 100 habitants |
| United Arab Emirates | | | | | | | | | | Emirats arabes unis |
| Number (thousands) | | 832 | 1 428 | 1 909 | 2 428 | 2 972 | 3 683 | 4 534 | 5 519 | Nombre (en milliers) |
| Per 100 inhabitants | | 27 | 44 | 55 | 65 | 74 | 86 | 101 | 119 | Pour 100 habitants |
| United Kingdom | (01/04) | | | | | | | | | Royaume-Uni |
| Number (thousands) | | 27 185 | 43 452 | 46 283 | 49 228 | 54 256 | 59 688 | 65 472 | 69 657 | Nombre (en milliers) |
| Per 100 inhabitants | | 46 | 73 | 77 | 83 | 91 | 100 | 110 | 116 | Pour 100 habitants |
| United Rep. of Tanzania | | | | | | | | | | Rép.-Unie de Tanzanie |
| Number (thousands) | | 51 | 111 | 276 | 607 | 1 942 | 1 942 | 3 390 | 5 767 | Nombre (en milliers) |
| Per 100 inhabitants | | ^0 | ^0 | 1 | 2 | 5 | 5 | 9 | 15 | Pour 100 habitants |
| United States | | | | | | | | | | Etats-Unis |
| Number (thousands) | | 86 047 | 109 478 | 128 500 | 141 800 | 160 637 | 184 819 | 213 212 | 233 000 | Nombre (en milliers) |
| Per 100 inhabitants | | 31 | 39 | 45 | 49 | 55 | 63 | 71 | 77 | Pour 100 habitants |
| United States Virgin Is.[3] | | | | | | | | | | Iles Vierges américaines[3] |
| Number (thousands) | | 30 | 35 | 41 | 45 | 49 | 64 | 80 | ... | Nombre (en milliers) |
| Per 100 inhabitants | | 28 | 32 | 38 | 41 | 45 | 58 | 72 | ... | Pour 100 habitants |

| Country or area | Fiscal year[&] Ex. budgét. [&] | 1999 | 2000 | 2001 | 2002 | 2003 | 2004 | 2005 | 2006 | Pays ou zone |
|---|---|---|---|---|---|---|---|---|---|---|
| Uruguay | | | | | | | | | | Uruguay |
| Number (thousands) | | 319 | 411 | 520 | 514 | 498 | 600 | 1 155 | 2 330 | Nombre (en milliers) |
| Per 100 inhabitants | | 10 | 13 | 16 | 16 | 15 | 19 | 36 | 67 | Pour 100 habitants |
| Uzbekistan | | | | | | | | | | Ouzbékistan |
| Number (thousands) | | 40 | 53 | 128 | 187 | 321 | 544 | 720 | ... | Nombre (en milliers) |
| Per 100 inhabitants | | ^0 | ^0 | 1 | 1 | 1 | 2 | 3 | ... | Pour 100 habitants |
| Vanuatu | | | | | | | | | | Vanuatu |
| Number (thousands) | | ^0 | ^0 | ^0 | 5 | 8 | 11 | 13 | ... | Nombre (en milliers) |
| Per 100 inhabitants | | ^0 | ^0 | ^0 | 2 | 4 | 5 | 6 | ... | Pour 100 habitants |
| Venezuela (Bolivarian Rep. of) | | | | | | | | | | Venezuela (Rép. bolivar. du) |
| Number (thousands) | | 3 785 | 5 447 | 6 473 | 6 542 | 7 015 | 8 421 | 12 496 | 18 789 | Nombre (en milliers) |
| Per 100 inhabitants | | 16 | 23 | 26 | 26 | 27 | 32 | 47 | 69 | Pour 100 habitants |
| Viet Nam | | | | | | | | | | Viet Nam |
| Number (thousands) | | 329 | 789 | 1 251 | 1 902 | 2 742 | 4 960 | 9 593 | 15 505 | Nombre (en milliers) |
| Per 100 inhabitants | | ^0 | 1 | 2 | 2 | 3 | 6 | 11 | 18 | Pour 100 habitants |
| Yemen | | | | | | | | | | Yémen |
| Number (thousands) | | 28 | 32 | 148 | 487 | 675 | 1 483 | 2 278 | 2 978 | Nombre (en milliers) |
| Per 100 inhabitants | | ^0 | ^0 | 1 | 2 | 3 | 7 | 11 | 14 | Pour 100 habitants |
| Zambia | (01/04) | | | | | | | | | Zambie |
| Number (thousands) | | 28 | 99 | 121 | 139 | 241 | 464 | 950 | 1 663 | Nombre (en milliers) |
| Per 100 inhabitants | | ^0 | 1 | 1 | 1 | 2 | 4 | 8 | 14 | Pour 100 habitants |
| Zimbabwe | (30/06) | | | | | | | | | Zimbabwe |
| Number (thousands) | | 174 | 266 | 314 | 339 | 364 | 424 | 668 | 832 | Nombre (en milliers) |
| Per 100 inhabitants | | 2 | 2 | 3 | 3 | 3 | 4 | 6 | 6 | Pour 100 habitants |

Source

International Telecommunication Union (ITU), Geneva, the ITU database, last accessed January 2008.

Notes

& Fiscal year refers to the fiscal year used in each country or area. Countries or areas whose reference periods coincide with the calendar year ending 31 December are not footnoted. Those that have a fiscal year other than calendar year are denoted as follows:

22/03: Year beginning 22 March
01/04: Year beginning 1 April
30/06: Year ending 30 June
15/07: Year ending 15 July
30/09: Year ending 30 September

1 Active mobile subscribers
2 Data refer to 31 December.
3 ITU estimate.
4 September.
5 December.
6 Including Celtel subscribers.
7 For statistical purposes, the data for China do not include those for the Hong Kong Special Administrative Region (Hong Kong SAR), Macao Special Administrative Region (Macao SAR) and Taiwan Province of China.
8 June.
9 GSM mobile was launched on 12 December 2005
10 Including inactive subscribers.
11 November.
12 October.
13 Including Personal Handyphone System.

Source

Union internationale des télécommunications (UIT), Genève, la base de données de l'UIT, dernier accès janvier 2008.

Notes

& Ex. budgét. fait référence à l'exercice budgétaire en vigueur dans chaque pays ou territoire. Les pays ou les territoires dont l'exercice budgétaire terminent le 31 décembre de l'année civile ne sont pas signalés. Dans le cas contraire, ils sont désignés de la manière suivante:

22/03 : Exercice commençant le 22 mars
01/04 : Exercice commençant le 1er avril
30/06 : Exercice se terminant le 30 juin
15/07 : Exercice se terminant le 15 juillet
30/09 : Exercice se terminant le 30 septembre

1 Nombre d'abonnés actifs de la téléphonie mobile.
2 Les données se réfèrent au 31 décembre.
3 Estimation de l'UIT.
4 Septembre.
5 Décembre.
6 Y compris les abonnés au Celtel.
7 Pour la présentation des statistiques, les données pour la Chine ne comprennent pas la Région Administrative Spéciale de Hong Kong (Hong Kong RAS), la Région Administrative Spéciale de Macao (Macao RAS) et la province de Taiwan.
8 Juin.
9 Le service de téléphonie mobile GSM a été lancé le 12 décembre 2005.
10 Y compris d'abonnés inactifs.
11 Novembre.
12 Octobre.
13 Y compris "Personal Handyphone System".

14  Third quarter.
15  July.
16  At 31 March 2000.
17  Users use Israel cellular network.
18  Includes 3G subscribers.
19  New methodology.

14  Troisième trimestre.
15  Juillet.
16  31 mars 2000.
17  Les abonnés utilisent le réseau israélien de téléphonie mobile.
18  Y compris d'abonnés 3G.
19  Nouvelle méthodologie.

# Internet users
Estimated number (thousands) and number per 100 inhabitants

# Usagers d'Internet
Nombre estimatif (en milliers) et nombre pour 100 habitants

| Country or area | Fiscal year[&] Ex. budgét.[&] | 1999 | 2000 | 2001 | 2002 | 2003 | 2004 | 2005 | 2006 | Pays ou zone |
|---|---|---|---|---|---|---|---|---|---|---|
| Afghanistan | | | | | | | | | | Afghanistan |
| Number (thousands) | | ... | ... | 1[1] | 1 | 20 | 25 | 300 | 535 | Nombre (en milliers) |
| Per 100 inhabitants | | ... | ... | ^0 | ^0 | ^0 | ^0 | 1 | 2 | Pour 100 habitants |
| Albania | | | | | | | | | | Albanie |
| Number (thousands) | | 3 | 4 | 10 | 12 | 30 | 75 | 188 | 471 | Nombre (en milliers) |
| Per 100 inhabitants | | ^0 | ^0 | ^0 | ^0 | 1 | 2 | 6 | 15 | Pour 100 habitants |
| Algeria | | | | | | | | | | Algérie |
| Number (thousands) | | 60 | 150 | 200 | 500 | 700 | 1 500 | 1 920 | 2 460 | Nombre (en milliers) |
| Per 100 inhabitants | | ^0 | ^0 | 1 | 2 | 2 | 5 | 6 | 7 | Pour 100 habitants |
| Andorra | | | | | | | | | | Andorre |
| Number (thousands) | | 5 | 7 | ... | ... | 10 | 21 | 22 | 23 | Nombre (en milliers) |
| Per 100 inhabitants | | 8 | 11 | ... | ... | 15 | 31 | 33 | 33 | Pour 100 habitants |
| Angola | | | | | | | | | | Angola |
| Number (thousands) | | 10 | 15 | 20 | 41 | ... | 75 | 85 | ... | Nombre (en milliers) |
| Per 100 inhabitants | | ^0 | ^0 | ^0 | ^0 | ... | 1 | 1 | ... | Pour 100 habitants |
| Anguilla | | | | | | | | | | Anguilla |
| Number (thousands) | | ... | 3 | 3 | ... | 4 | 3 | 4 | ... | Nombre (en milliers) |
| Per 100 inhabitants | | ... | 22 | 26 | ... | 31 | 27 | 31 | ... | Pour 100 habitants |
| Antigua and Barbuda | (01/04) | | | | | | | | | Antigua-et-Barbuda |
| Number (thousands) | | 4 | 5 | 7[1] | 10 | 14[1] | 20 | 29 | 53 | Nombre (en milliers) |
| Per 100 inhabitants | | 5 | 7 | 9 | 13 | 18 | 25 | 36 | 64 | Pour 100 habitants |
| Argentina | (30/09) | | | | | | | | | Argentine |
| Number (thousands) | | 1 200 | 2 600 | 3 650 | 4 100 | 4 530 | 6 154 | 6 863 | 8 184 | Nombre (en milliers) |
| Per 100 inhabitants | | 3 | 7 | 10 | 11 | 12 | 16 | 18 | 21 | Pour 100 habitants |
| Armenia | | | | | | | | | | Arménie |
| Number (thousands) | | 30 | 40 | 50 | 60 | 140 | 150 | 161 | 173 | Nombre (en milliers) |
| Per 100 inhabitants | | 1 | 1 | 2 | 2 | 5 | 5 | 5 | 6 | Pour 100 habitants |
| Aruba | | | | | | | | | | Aruba |
| Number (thousands) | | 4 | 14 | 24 | 24[1] | 24[1] | 24[1] | 24[1] | ... | Nombre (en milliers) |
| Per 100 inhabitants | | 4 | 15 | 26 | 25 | 25 | 24 | 24 | ... | Pour 100 habitants |
| Ascension | | | | | | | | | | Ascension |
| Number (thousands) | | ^0 | ^0 | 1[2] | ... | ^0 | ^0 | ^0 | ... | Nombre (en milliers) |
| Per 100 inhabitants | | 30 | 35 | 38 | ... | 26 | 20 | ... | ... | Pour 100 habitants |
| Australia | (30/06) | | | | | | | | | Australie |
| Number (thousands)[1] | | 5 600 | 6 600 | 7 700 | 9 000 | 9 500 | 9 500 | 10 000 | 10 600 | Nombre (en milliers)[1] |
| Per 100 inhabitants | | 30 | 34 | 40 | 46 | 48 | 48 | 50 | 52 | Pour 100 habitants |
| Austria | | | | | | | | | | Autriche |
| Number (thousands)[3] | | 1 840 | 2 700 | 3 150 | 3 340 | 3 730 | 3 900 | 4 000 | 4 210 | Nombre (en milliers)[3] |
| Per 100 inhabitants | | 23 | 34 | 39 | 41 | 46 | 48 | 49 | 51 | Pour 100 habitants |
| Azerbaijan | | | | | | | | | | Azerbaïdjan |
| Number (thousands) | | 8 | 12 | 25 | 300 | 350 | 408 | 679 | 829 | Nombre (en milliers) |
| Per 100 inhabitants | | ^0 | ^0 | ^0 | 4 | 4 | 5 | 8 | 10 | Pour 100 habitants |
| Bahamas | | | | | | | | | | Bahamas |
| Number (thousands) | | 11 | 13 | 17 | 60[4] | 84 | 93 | 103 | ... | Nombre (en milliers) |
| Per 100 inhabitants | | 4 | 4 | 6 | 19 | 27 | 29 | 32 | ... | Pour 100 habitants |
| Bahrain | | | | | | | | | | Bahreïn |
| Number (thousands) | | 30 | 40 | 100 | 123 | 150 | 153 | 155 | 210 | Nombre (en milliers) |
| Per 100 inhabitants | | 5 | 6 | 15 | 18 | 21 | 21 | 21 | 28 | Pour 100 habitants |
| Bangladesh | (30/06) | | | | | | | | | Bangladesh |
| Number (thousands) | | 50 | 100 | 186 | 204 | 243 | 300 | 370 | 450 | Nombre (en milliers) |
| Per 100 inhabitants^ | | 0 | 0 | 0 | 0 | 0 | 0 | 0 | 0 | Pour 100 habitants^ |

**Internet users**—Estimated number (thousands) and number per 100 inhabitants *(continued)*
**Usagers d'Internet**—Nombre estimatif (en milliers) et nombre pour 100 habitants *(suite)*

| Country or area | Fiscal year &<br>Ex. budgét.& | 1999 | 2000 | 2001 | 2002 | 2003 | 2004 | 2005 | 2006 | Pays ou zone |
|---|---|---|---|---|---|---|---|---|---|---|
| Barbados | (01/04) | | | | | | | | | Barbade |
| Number (thousands) | | 6 | 10 | 15 | 30¹ | 100 | 150 | 160 | ... | Nombre (en milliers) |
| Per 100 inhabitants | | 2 | 4 | 6 | 11 | 37 | 55 | 59 | ... | Pour 100 habitants |
| Belarus | | | | | | | | | | Bélarus |
| Number (thousands) | | 50 | 187 | 430 | 891 | 1 607 | 2 461 | 3 394 | 5 478 | Nombre (en milliers) |
| Per 100 inhabitants | | ^0 | 2 | 4 | 9 | 16 | 25 | 35 | 56 | Pour 100 habitants |
| Belgium | | | | | | | | | | Belgique |
| Number (thousands) | | 1 400 | 3 000 | 3 200 | 3 400 | 4 000 | 4 200 | 4 800 | 5 490 | Nombre (en milliers) |
| Per 100 inhabitants | | 14 | 29 | 31 | 33 | 38 | 40 | 46 | 53 | Pour 100 habitants |
| Belize | (01/04) | | | | | | | | | Belize |
| Number (thousands) | | 10 | 15 | ... | ... | ... | 16 | 26 | 34 | Nombre (en milliers) |
| Per 100 inhabitants | | 4 | 6 | ... | ... | ... | 6 | 10 | 12 | Pour 100 habitants |
| Benin | | | | | | | | | | Bénin |
| Number (thousands) | | 10 | 15 | 25 | 50 | 70 | 100 | 125 | 150 | Nombre (en milliers) |
| Per 100 inhabitants | | ^0 | ^0 | ^0 | 1 | 1 | 1 | 2 | 2 | Pour 100 habitants |
| Bermuda | (01/04) | | | | | | | | | Bermudes |
| Number (thousands) | | 25 | 27 | 30 | ... | 36 | 39 | 42 | ... | Nombre (en milliers) |
| Per 100 inhabitants | | 40 | 43 | 48 | ... | 57 | 61 | 65 | ... | Pour 100 habitants |
| Bhutan | | | | | | | | | | Bhoutan |
| Number (thousands) | | 1 | 2 | 5 | 10 | 15 | 20 | 25 | 30 | Nombre (en milliers) |
| Per 100 inhabitants | | ^0 | ^0 | 1 | 1 | 2 | 3 | 3 | 4 | Pour 100 habitants |
| Bolivia | | | | | | | | | | Bolivie |
| Number (thousands) | | 80¹ | 120¹ | 180¹ | 270¹ | 310 | 400 | 480 | 580 | Nombre (en milliers) |
| Per 100 inhabitants | | 1 | 1 | 2 | 3 | 4 | 4 | 5 | 6 | Pour 100 habitants |
| Bosnia and Herzegovina | | | | | | | | | | Bosnie-Herzégovine |
| Number (thousands) | | 7 | 40 | 45 | 100 | 150¹ | 585 | 806 | 950 | Nombre (en milliers) |
| Per 100 inhabitants | | ^0 | 1 | 1 | 3 | 4 | 15 | 21 | 24 | Pour 100 habitants |
| Botswana | (01/04) | | | | | | | | | Botswana |
| Number (thousands) | | 19 | 50 | 60 | 60 | 60 | 60 | 60¹ | 80 | Nombre (en milliers) |
| Per 100 inhabitants | | 1 | 3 | 4 | 3 | 3 | 3 | 3 | 5 | Pour 100 habitants |
| Brazil | | | | | | | | | | Brésil |
| Number (thousands)¹ | | 3 500 | 5 000 | 8 000 | 14 300 | 18 000 | 22 000 | 32 130⁵ | 42 600⁵ | Nombre (en milliers)¹ |
| Per 100 inhabitants | | 2 | 3 | 5 | 8 | 10 | 12 | 17⁶ | 23 | Pour 100 habitants |
| British Virgin Islands | (01/04) | | | | | | | | | Iles Vierges britanniques |
| Number (thousands) | | ... | ... | ... | 4 | ... | ... | ... | ... | Nombre (en milliers) |
| Per 100 inhabitants | | ... | ... | ... | 19 | ... | ... | ... | ... | Pour 100 habitants |
| Brunei Darussalam | | | | | | | | | | Brunéi Darussalam |
| Number (thousands) | | 25 | 30 | 44 | 53 | 70 | 108 | 135 | 166 | Nombre (en milliers) |
| Per 100 inhabitants | | 8 | 9 | 13 | 16 | 20 | 30 | 36 | 43 | Pour 100 habitants |
| Bulgaria | | | | | | | | | | Bulgarie |
| Number (thousands) | | 235 | 430 | 605 | 630 | 932¹ | *1 234 | 1 592 | 1 662 | Nombre (en milliers) |
| Per 100 inhabitants | | 3 | 5 | 8 | 8 | 12 | 16 | 21 | 22 | Pour 100 habitants |
| Burkina Faso | | | | | | | | | | Burkina Faso |
| Number (thousands) | | 7 | 9 | 19 | 25 | 48 | 53 | 65 | 80 | Nombre (en milliers) |
| Per 100 inhabitants | | ^0 | ^0 | ^0 | ^0 | ^0 | ^0 | ^0 | 1 | Pour 100 habitants |
| Burundi | | | | | | | | | | Burundi |
| Number (thousands) | | 3 | 5 | 7 | 8 | 14 | 25 | 40 | 60 | Nombre (en milliers) |
| Per 100 inhabitants | | ^0 | ^0 | ^0 | ^0 | ^0 | ^0 | 1 | 1 | Pour 100 habitants |
| Cambodia | | | | | | | | | | Cambodge |
| Number (thousands) | | 4 | 6 | 10 | 30 | 35 | 41 | 44¹ | ... | Nombre (en milliers) |
| Per 100 inhabitants^ | | 0 | 0 | 0 | 0 | 0 | 0 | 0 | ... | Pour 100 habitants^ |
| Cameroon | | | | | | | | | | Cameroun |
| Number (thousands) | | 20 | 40 | 45 | 60 | 100 | 170 | 250 | 370 | Nombre (en milliers) |
| Per 100 inhabitants | | ^0 | ^0 | ^0 | ^0 | 1 | 1 | 2 | 2 | Pour 100 habitants |

| Country or area | Fiscal year[8] Ex. budgét.[8] | 1999 | 2000 | 2001 | 2002 | 2003 | 2004 | 2005 | 2006 | Pays ou zone |
|---|---|---|---|---|---|---|---|---|---|---|
| Canada | | | | | | | | | | Canada |
| Number (thousands) | | 11 000 | 12 971[7] | 14 000[8] | 15 200[1] | 17 600 | 20 000 | 22 000[9] | ... | Nombre (en milliers) |
| Per 100 inhabitants | | 36 | 42 | 45 | 48 | 55 | 62 | 68 | ... | Pour 100 habitants |
| Cape Verde | | | | | | | | | | Cap-Vert |
| Number (thousands) | | 5 | 8 | 12 | 16[1] | 20 | 25 | 29 | 33 | Nombre (en milliers) |
| Per 100 inhabitants | | 1 | 2 | 3 | 4 | 4 | 5 | 6 | 6 | Pour 100 habitants |
| Cayman Islands | (01/04) | | | | | | | | | Iles Caïmanes |
| Number (thousands) | | ... | ... | ... | ... | ... | ... | 20 | 21 | Nombre (en milliers) |
| Per 100 inhabitants | | ... | ... | ... | ... | ... | ... | 44 | 46 | Pour 100 habitants |
| Central African Rep. | | | | | | | | | | Rép. centrafricaine |
| Number (thousands) | | 2 | 2 | 3 | 5 | 6 | 9 | 11 | 13 | Nombre (en milliers) |
| Per 100 inhabitants^ | | 0 | 0 | 0 | 0 | 0 | 0 | 0 | 0 | Pour 100 habitants^ |
| Chad | | | | | | | | | | Tchad |
| Number (thousands) | | 1 | 3 | 4 | 15 | 30 | 35 | 40 | 60 | Nombre (en milliers) |
| Per 100 inhabitants | | ^0 | ^0 | ^0 | ^0 | ^0 | ^0 | ^0 | 1 | Pour 100 habitants |
| Chile | | | | | | | | | | Chili |
| Number (thousands) | | 625 | 2 537 | 3 102 | 3 575 | 4 000 | 4 300 | 4 511 | 4 156 | Nombre (en milliers) |
| Per 100 inhabitants | | 4 | 17 | 20 | 24 | 26 | 28 | 29 | 25 | Pour 100 habitants |
| China[10] | | | | | | | | | | Chine[10] |
| Number (thousands) | | 8 900 | 22 500 | 33 700 | 59 100 | 79 500 | 94 000 | 111 000 | 137 000[11,12] | Nombre (en milliers) |
| Per 100 inhabitants | | 1 | 2 | 3 | 5 | 6 | 7 | 8 | 10 | Pour 100 habitants |
| China, Hong Kong SAR | (01/04) | | | | | | | | | Chine, Hong Kong RAS |
| Number (thousands) | | 1 400[1] | 1 855[13] | 2 601[13] | 2 919[13] | 3 213[13] | 3 480[13] | 3 526[13] | 3 770[13] | Nombre (en milliers) |
| Per 100 inhabitants | | 21 | 28 | 39 | 43 | 47 | 50 | 50 | 53 | Pour 100 habitants |
| China, Macao SAR | | | | | | | | | | Chine, Macao RAS |
| Number (thousands)* | | 40 | 60 | 101 | 115 | 120 | 150 | 170 | 217 | Nombre (en milliers)* |
| Per 100 inhabitants | | 9 | 14 | 23 | 26 | 27 | 32 | 37 | 47 | Pour 100 habitants |
| Colombia | | | | | | | | | | Colombie |
| Number (thousands) | | 664 | 878 | 1 154[14] | 2 000 | 3 084[15] | 3 866 | 4 739 | 6 705 | Nombre (en milliers) |
| Per 100 inhabitants | | 2 | 2 | 3 | 5 | 7 | 9 | 10 | 14 | Pour 100 habitants |
| Comoros | | | | | | | | | | Comores |
| Number (thousands) | | 1 | 2 | 3 | 3 | 5 | 8 | 20 | 21 | Nombre (en milliers) |
| Per 100 inhabitants | | ^0 | ^0 | ^0 | ^0 | 1 | 1 | 3 | 3 | Pour 100 habitants |
| Congo | | | | | | | | | | Congo |
| Number (thousands) | | 1 | 1 | 1 | 5 | 15 | 36 | 50 | 70 | Nombre (en milliers) |
| Per 100 inhabitants | | ^0 | ^0 | ^0 | ^0 | ^0 | 1 | 1 | 2 | Pour 100 habitants |
| Cook Islands | (01/04) | | | | | | | | | Iles Cook |
| Number (thousands)[1] | | 2 | 3 | 3 | 4 | 4 | 5 | 5 | 5 | Nombre (en milliers)[1] |
| Per 100 inhabitants | | 12 | 15 | 18 | 20 | 23 | 25 | 27 | ... | Pour 100 habitants |
| Costa Rica | | | | | | | | | | Costa Rica |
| Number (thousands) | | 150 | 228 | 384 | 816 | 850 | 885 | 923 | 1 214 | Nombre (en milliers) |
| Per 100 inhabitants | | 4 | 6 | 10 | 20 | 20 | 21 | 21 | 28 | Pour 100 habitants |
| Côte d'Ivoire | | | | | | | | | | Côte d'Ivoire |
| Number (thousands) | | 20 | 40 | 70 | 90 | 140 | 160 | 200 | 300 | Nombre (en milliers) |
| Per 100 inhabitants | | ^0 | ^0 | ^0 | 1 | 1 | 1 | 1 | 2 | Pour 100 habitants |
| Croatia | | | | | | | | | | Croatie |
| Number (thousands) | | 200 | 299 | 518 | 789 | 1 014 | 1 375 | 1 472 | 1 685 | Nombre (en milliers) |
| Per 100 inhabitants | | 4 | 7 | 12 | 18 | 23 | 31 | 32 | 37 | Pour 100 habitants |
| Cuba | | | | | | | | | | Cuba |
| Number (thousands) | | 35[16] | 60[16] | 120[16] | 160[16] | 98[17] | 150[17] | 190[17] | 240[17] | Nombre (en milliers) |
| Per 100 inhabitants | | ^0 | 1 | 1 | 1 | 1 | 1 | 2 | 2 | Pour 100 habitants |
| Cyprus | | | | | | | | | | Chypre |
| Number (thousands) | | 88 | 120 | 150 | 210 | 250 | 298 | 326 | 357 | Nombre (en milliers) |
| Per 100 inhabitants | | 13 | 18 | 22 | 29 | 35 | 37 | 39 | 42 | Pour 100 habitants |

| Country or area | Fiscal year [&] Ex. budgét.[&] | 1999 | 2000 | 2001 | 2002 | 2003 | 2004 | 2005 | 2006 | Pays ou zone |
|---|---|---|---|---|---|---|---|---|---|---|
| Czech Republic | | | | | | | | | | République tchèque |
| Number (thousands) | | 700 | 1 000 | 1 500 | 2 600 | 2 395[18] | 2 740[18] | 2 790[18] | 3 541[19] | Nombre (en milliers) |
| Per 100 inhabitants | | 7 | 10 | 15 | 25 | 23 | 27 | 27 | 35 | Pour 100 habitants |
| Dem. Rep. of the Congo | | | | | | | | | | Rép. dém. du Congo |
| Number (thousands) | | 1 | 3 | 6 | 50 | 75 | 113 | 141 | 180 | Nombre (en milliers) |
| Per 100 inhabitants[^] | | 0 | 0 | 0 | 0 | 0 | 0 | 0 | 0 | Pour 100 habitants[^] |
| Denmark | | | | | | | | | | Danemark |
| Number (thousands) | | 1 626[20] | 2 090[20] | 2 300[1] | 2 391[1] | 2 481[1,21] | 2 725[1,21] | 2 854[1,21] | 3 171[1,21] | Nombre (en milliers) |
| Per 100 inhabitants | | 31 | 39 | 43 | 44 | 46 | 50 | 53 | 58 | Pour 100 habitants |
| Djibouti | | | | | | | | | | Djibouti |
| Number (thousands) | | 1 | 1 | 3 | 5 | 7 | 9 | 10 | 11 | Nombre (en milliers) |
| Per 100 inhabitants | | [^]0 | [^]0 | 1 | 1 | 1 | 1 | 1 | 1 | Pour 100 habitants |
| Dominica | (01/04) | | | | | | | | | Dominique |
| Number (thousands) | | 2 | 6 | 9 | 13 | 16 | 21 | 26 | ... | Nombre (en milliers) |
| Per 100 inhabitants | | 3 | 8 | 13 | 17 | 22 | 29 | 37 | ... | Pour 100 habitants |
| Dominican Republic | | | | | | | | | | Rép. dominicaine |
| Number (thousands) | | 96 | 327 | 397[22] | 500 | 650 | 800 | 1 500 | 2 000 | Nombre (en milliers) |
| Per 100 inhabitants | | 1 | 4 | 5 | 6 | 7 | 9 | 17 | 22 | Pour 100 habitants |
| Ecuador | | | | | | | | | | Equateur |
| Number (thousands) | | 100 | 180 | 333 | 538 | 570 | 625 | 968 | 1 549 | Nombre (en milliers) |
| Per 100 inhabitants | | 1 | 1 | 3 | 4 | 4 | 5 | 7 | 12 | Pour 100 habitants |
| Egypt | (30/06) | | | | | | | | | Egypte |
| Number (thousands) | | 200[15] | 450 | 600 | 1 900 | 3 000 | 3 900 | 5 100 | 6 000 | Nombre (en milliers) |
| Per 100 inhabitants | | [^]0 | 1 | 1 | 3 | 4 | 6 | 7 | 8 | Pour 100 habitants |
| El Salvador | | | | | | | | | | El Salvador |
| Number (thousands) | | 50 | 70 | 150 | 300 | 550 | 588 | 637 | 700[1] | Nombre (en milliers) |
| Per 100 inhabitants | | 1 | 1 | 2 | 5 | 8 | 9 | 9 | 10 | Pour 100 habitants |
| Equatorial Guinea | | | | | | | | | | Guinée équatoriale |
| Number (thousands) | | 1 | 1 | 1 | 2 | 3 | 5 | 7 | 8 | Nombre (en milliers) |
| Per 100 inhabitants | | [^]0 | [^]0 | [^]0 | [^]0 | 1 | 1 | 1 | 2 | Pour 100 habitants |
| Eritrea | | | | | | | | | | Erythrée |
| Number (thousands) | | 1 | 5 | 6 | 9 | 30 | 50 | 80 | 100 | Nombre (en milliers) |
| Per 100 inhabitants | | [^]0 | [^]0 | [^]0 | [^]0 | 1 | 1 | 2 | 2 | Pour 100 habitants |
| Estonia | | | | | | | | | | Estonie |
| Number (thousands) | | 200 | 392 | 430 | 444 | 600 | 670 | 690[14] | 760 | Nombre (en milliers) |
| Per 100 inhabitants | | 14 | 27 | 30 | 33 | 44 | 50 | 52 | 57 | Pour 100 habitants |
| Ethiopia | (30/06) | | | | | | | | | Ethiopie |
| Number (thousands) | | 8 | 10 | 25 | 50 | 75 | 113 | 164 | ... | Nombre (en milliers) |
| Per 100 inhabitants[^] | | 0 | 0 | 0 | 0 | 0 | 0 | 0 | ... | Pour 100 habitants[^] |
| Faeroe Islands | | | | | | | | | | Iles Féroé |
| Number (thousands) | | 10 | 15 | 20 | 25 | 28 | 32 | 33 | 34 | Nombre (en milliers) |
| Per 100 inhabitants | | 22 | 33 | 44 | 54 | 60 | 68 | 70 | 72 | Pour 100 habitants |
| Falkland Is. (Malvinas) | | | | | | | | | | Iles Falkland (Malvinas) |
| Number (thousands) | | 2 | 2 | 2 | 2 | 2 | 2 | 3 | 3 | Nombre (en milliers) |
| Per 100 inhabitants | | 55 | 57 | 63 | 62 | 62 | 65 | 82 | ... | Pour 100 habitants |
| Fiji | | | | | | | | | | Fidji |
| Number (thousands) | | 8 | 12 | 15 | 50 | 55 | 61 | 70 | 80 | Nombre (en milliers) |
| Per 100 inhabitants | | 1 | 1 | 2 | 6 | 7 | 7 | 8 | 9 | Pour 100 habitants |
| Finland | | | | | | | | | | Finlande |
| Number (thousands)[23] | | 1 667 | 1 927 | 2 235 | 2 529 | 2 560 | 2 680 | 2 800[24] | 2 925 | Nombre (en milliers)[23] |
| Per 100 inhabitants | | 32 | 37 | 43 | 49 | 49 | 51 | 53 | 56 | Pour 100 habitants |
| France | | | | | | | | | | France |
| Number (thousands)[25] | | 5 370 | 8 460 | 15 653 | 18 057 | 21 765 | 23 732 | 26 154 | 30 100 | Nombre (en milliers)[25] |
| Per 100 inhabitants | | 9 | 14 | 26 | 30 | 36 | 39 | 43 | 50 | Pour 100 habitants |

| Country or area | Fiscal year[&] Ex. budgét.[&] | 1999 | 2000 | 2001 | 2002 | 2003 | 2004 | 2005 | 2006 | Pays ou zone |
|---|---|---|---|---|---|---|---|---|---|---|
| French Guiana | | | | | | | | | | Guyane française |
| Number (thousands) | | 2 | 16 | 20 | 25 | 31 | 38 | 42 | ... | Nombre (en milliers) |
| Per 100 inhabitants | | 1 | 10 | 12 | 14 | 17 | 21 | 22 | ... | Pour 100 habitants |
| French Polynesia | | | | | | | | | | Polynésie française |
| Number (thousands) | | 8 | 15 | 15 | 20 | 35 | 45 | 55 | 65 | Nombre (en milliers) |
| Per 100 inhabitants | | 3 | 6 | 6 | 8 | 14 | 18 | 21 | 25 | Pour 100 habitants |
| Gabon | | | | | | | | | | Gabon |
| Number (thousands) | | 3 | 15 | 17 | 25 | 35 | 40 | 67 | 81 | Nombre (en milliers) |
| Per 100 inhabitants | | ^0 | 1 | 1 | 2 | 3 | 3 | 5 | 6 | Pour 100 habitants |
| Gambia | (01/04) | | | | | | | | | Gambie |
| Number (thousands) | | 9 | 12 | 18 | 25 | 35 | 49 | 58[1] | 82 | Nombre (en milliers) |
| Per 100 inhabitants | | 1 | 1 | 1 | 2 | 3 | 3 | 4 | 5 | Pour 100 habitants |
| Georgia | | | | | | | | | | Géorgie |
| Number (thousands) | | 20 | 23 | 47 | 74 | 117 | 176 | 271[1] | 332 | Nombre (en milliers) |
| Per 100 inhabitants | | ^0 | ^0 | 1 | 2 | 3 | 4 | 6 | 7 | Pour 100 habitants |
| Germany | | | | | | | | | | Allemagne |
| Number (thousands) | | 17 100 | 24 800 | 26 000 | 28 000 | 33 000 | 35 700 | 35 700 | 38 600 | Nombre (en milliers) |
| Per 100 inhabitants | | 21 | 30 | 32 | 34 | 40 | 43 | 43 | 47 | Pour 100 habitants |
| Ghana | | | | | | | | | | Ghana |
| Number (thousands) | | 20 | 30 | *40 | 170 | 250 | 368 | 401 | 610 | Nombre (en milliers) |
| Per 100 inhabitants | | ^0 | ^0 | ^0 | 1 | 1 | 2 | 2 | 3 | Pour 100 habitants |
| Gibraltar | | | | | | | | | | Gibraltar |
| Number (thousands) | | 2 | 6 | 6 | ... | ... | 6 | ... | ... | Nombre (en milliers) |
| Per 100 inhabitants | | 6 | 20 | 22 | ... | ... | 22 | ... | ... | Pour 100 habitants |
| Greece | | | | | | | | | | Grèce |
| Number (thousands) | | 750 | 1 000 | 915 | 1 485 | 1 718 | 1 955 | 2 001 | 2 048 | Nombre (en milliers) |
| Per 100 inhabitants | | 7 | 9 | 9 | 13 | 15 | 18 | 18 | 18 | Pour 100 habitants |
| Greenland | | | | | | | | | | Groenland |
| Number (thousands) | | 12 | 18 | 20 | 25 | 31 | 38 | ... | ... | Nombre (en milliers) |
| Per 100 inhabitants | | 22 | 32 | 36 | 44 | 54 | 66 | ... | ... | Pour 100 habitants |
| Grenada | | | | | | | | | | Grenade |
| Number (thousands) | | 3 | 4 | 5 | 15 | 19 | ... | ... | ... | Nombre (en milliers) |
| Per 100 inhabitants | | 2 | 4 | 5 | 15 | 19 | ... | ... | ... | Pour 100 habitants |
| Guadeloupe | | | | | | | | | | Guadeloupe |
| Number (thousands) | | 7 | 25 | 40 | 50 | 63 | 79 | 85 | ... | Nombre (en milliers) |
| Per 100 inhabitants | | 2 | 6 | 9 | 11 | 14 | 18 | 19 | ... | Pour 100 habitants |
| Guam | | | | | | | | | | Guam |
| Number (thousands) | | 13 | 25 | 40 | 50 | 55 | 60 | 65 | ... | Nombre (en milliers) |
| Per 100 inhabitants | | 9 | 16 | 25 | 31 | 34 | 36 | 38 | ... | Pour 100 habitants |
| Guatemala | | | | | | | | | | Guatemala |
| Number (thousands) | | 65 | 80 | 200 | 400 | 550 | 760 | 1 000 | 1 320 | Nombre (en milliers) |
| Per 100 inhabitants | | 1 | 1 | 2 | 3 | 4 | 6 | 8 | 10 | Pour 100 habitants |
| Guernsey | | | | | | | | | | Guernesey |
| Number (thousands) | | 10 | 20 | 25 | 30 | 33 | *36 | ... | ... | Nombre (en milliers) |
| Per 100 inhabitants | | 15 | 32 | 44 | 54 | 59 | 65 | ... | ... | Pour 100 habitants |
| Guinea | | | | | | | | | | Guinée |
| Number (thousands) | | 5 | 8 | 15 | 35 | 40 | 46 | 50 | 50 | Nombre (en milliers) |
| Per 100 inhabitants | | ^0 | ^0 | ^0 | ^0 | 1 | 1 | 1 | 1 | Pour 100 habitants |
| Guinea-Bissau | | | | | | | | | | Guinée-Bissau |
| Number (thousands) | | 2 | 3 | 4 | 14 | 19 | 26 | 31 | 37 | Nombre (en milliers) |
| Per 100 inhabitants | | ^0 | ^0 | ^0 | 1 | 1 | 2 | 2 | 2 | Pour 100 habitants |
| Guyana | | | | | | | | | | Guyana |
| Number (thousands) | | 30 | 50 | 100 | 125 | 140 | 145 | 160 | ... | Nombre (en milliers) |
| Per 100 inhabitants | | 4 | 7 | 13 | 17 | 19 | 19 | 21 | ... | Pour 100 habitants |

| Country or area | Fiscal year [&] Ex. budgét. [&] | 1999 | 2000 | 2001 | 2002 | 2003 | 2004 | 2005 | 2006 | Pays ou zone |
|---|---|---|---|---|---|---|---|---|---|---|
| Haiti | | | | | | | | | | Haïti |
| Number (thousands) | | 6 | 20 | 30 | 80 | 150 | 500 | 600 | 650 | Nombre (en milliers) |
| Per 100 inhabitants | | ^0 | ^0 | ^0 | 1 | 2 | 6 | 7 | 8 | Pour 100 habitants |
| Honduras | | | | | | | | | | Honduras |
| Number (thousands) | | 35 | 75 | 90 | 169 | 186 | 222 | 258 | 344 | Nombre (en milliers) |
| Per 100 inhabitants | | 1 | 1 | 1 | 3 | 3 | 3 | 4 | 5 | Pour 100 habitants |
| Hungary | | | | | | | | | | Hongrie |
| Number (thousands) | | 600 | 715 | 1 480 | 1 600 | 2 400 | 2 700 | 3 000 | *3 500 | Nombre (en milliers) |
| Per 100 inhabitants | | 6 | 7 | 15 | 16 | 24 | 27 | 30 | 35 | Pour 100 habitants |
| Iceland | | | | | | | | | | Islande |
| Number (thousands)[26] | | 115 | 125 | 140 | 150 | 166 | 168 | 183 | 194 | Nombre (en milliers)[26] |
| Per 100 inhabitants | | 41 | 44 | 49 | 52 | 57 | 57 | 62 | 65 | Pour 100 habitants |
| India | (01/04) | | | | | | | | | Inde |
| Number (thousands) | | 2 800 | 5 500 | 7 000 | 16 580 | 18 480[27] | 35 000 | 60 000 | 120 000 | Nombre (en milliers) |
| Per 100 inhabitants | | ^0 | 1 | 1 | 2 | 2 | 3 | 5 | 11 | Pour 100 habitants |
| Indonesia | | | | | | | | | | Indonésie |
| Number (thousands) | | 900 | 1 900 | 4 200 | 4 500 | 8 081 | 5 628 | 7 896 | 10 576 | Nombre (en milliers) |
| Per 100 inhabitants | | ^0 | 1 | 2 | 2 | 4 | 3 | 4 | 5 | Pour 100 habitants |
| Iran (Islamic Rep. of) | (22/03) | | | | | | | | | Iran (Rép. islamique d') |
| Number (thousands) | | 250 | 625 | 1 005 | 3 168 | 4 800 | 10 600 | 12 300 | 18 000 | Nombre (en milliers) |
| Per 100 inhabitants | | ^0 | 1 | 2 | 5 | 7 | 15 | 18 | 26 | Pour 100 habitants |
| Iraq | (30/06) | | | | | | | | | Iraq |
| Number (thousands) | | ... | ... | 13 | 25 | 30 | 36 | ... | ... | Nombre (en milliers) |
| Per 100 inhabitants ^ | | ... | ... | 0 | 0 | 0 | 0 | ... | ... | Pour 100 habitants ^ |
| Ireland | (01/04) | | | | | | | | | Irlande |
| Number (thousands)[18] | | 410 | 679 | 895 | 1 102 | 1 260 | 1 198 | 1 400[28] | 1 441 | Nombre (en milliers)[18] |
| Per 100 inhabitants | | 11 | 18 | 23 | 28 | 32 | 30 | 34 | 34 | Pour 100 habitants |
| Israel | | | | | | | | | | Israël |
| Number (thousands) | | 800 | 1 270 | 1 079 | 1 125 | 1 265 | 1 497 | 1 686 | 1 899 | Nombre (en milliers) |
| Per 100 inhabitants | | 13 | 20 | 17 | 17 | 19 | 22 | 24 | 26 | Pour 100 habitants |
| Italy | | | | | | | | | | Italie |
| Number (thousands) | | 8 200 | 13 200 | 15 600 | 19 800 | 22 880 | 27 170 | 28 000[15] | 28 855 | Nombre (en milliers) |
| Per 100 inhabitants | | 14 | 23 | 27 | 35 | 40 | 47 | 48 | 50 | Pour 100 habitants |
| Jamaica | (01/04) | | | | | | | | | Jamaïque |
| Number (thousands) | | 60 | 80 | 100 | 600 | 800 | 1 067 | 1 232[1] | 783 | Nombre (en milliers) |
| Per 100 inhabitants | | 2 | 3 | 4 | 23 | 30 | 40 | 46 | 29 | Pour 100 habitants |
| Japan | (01/04) | | | | | | | | | Japon |
| Number (thousands) | | 27 060[29] | 38 000[29] | 48 900[29] | 59 220[29] | 61 640[29] | 79 480[30] | 85 290[30] | 87 540[30] | Nombre (en milliers) |
| Per 100 inhabitants | | 21 | 30 | 38 | 46 | 48 | 62 | 67 | 68 | Pour 100 habitants |
| Jersey | | | | | | | | | | Jersey |
| Number (thousands) | | 6 | 8 | ... | ... | 20 | 27 | ... | ... | Nombre (en milliers) |
| Per 100 inhabitants | | 7 | 9 | ... | ... | 23 | 31 | ... | ... | Pour 100 habitants |
| Jordan | | | | | | | | | | Jordanie |
| Number (thousands) | | 120 | 127 | 234 | 307 | 444 | 630 | 720 | 797 | Nombre (en milliers) |
| Per 100 inhabitants | | 2 | 3 | 5 | 6 | 8 | 11 | 13 | 14 | Pour 100 habitants |
| Kazakhstan | | | | | | | | | | Kazakhstan |
| Number (thousands) | | 70 | 100 | 150 | 250 | 300 | 400 | 609 | 1 247 | Nombre (en milliers) |
| Per 100 inhabitants | | ^0 | 1 | 1 | 2 | 2 | 3 | 4 | 8 | Pour 100 habitants |
| Kenya | (30/06) | | | | | | | | | Kenya |
| Number (thousands) | | 35 | 100 | 200 | 400 | 1 000 | 1 055 | 1 111 | 2 770 | Nombre (en milliers) |
| Per 100 inhabitants | | ^0 | ^0 | 1 | 1 | 3 | 3 | 3 | 8 | Pour 100 habitants |
| Kiribati | | | | | | | | | | Kiribati |
| Number (thousands) | | 1 | 2 | 2 | 2 | 2 | 2 | 2 | 2 | Nombre (en milliers) |
| Per 100 inhabitants | | 1 | 2 | 2 | 2 | 2 | 2 | 2 | 2 | Pour 100 habitants |

| Country or area | Fiscal year [&] Ex. budgét.[&] | 1999 | 2000 | 2001 | 2002 | 2003 | 2004 | 2005 | 2006 | Pays ou zone |
|---|---|---|---|---|---|---|---|---|---|---|
| **Korea, Republic of** | | | | | | | | | | **Corée, République de** |
| Number (thousands) | | 10 860 | 19 040 | 24 380 | 26 270 | 29 220 | 31 580 | 33 880 | 34 910 | Nombre (en milliers) |
| Per 100 inhabitants | | 24 | 41 | 51 | 55 | 61 | 66 | 70 | 73 | Pour 100 habitants |
| **Kuwait** | | | | | | | | | | **Koweït** |
| Number (thousands) | | 100 | 150 | 200 | 250 | 567 | 600 | 700 | 817 | Nombre (en milliers) |
| Per 100 inhabitants | | 5 | 7 | 9 | 11 | 23 | 24 | 26 | 30 | Pour 100 habitants |
| **Kyrgyzstan** | | | | | | | | | | **Kirghizistan** |
| Number (thousands) | | 10 | 52 | 151 | 152 | 200 | 263 | 280 | 298 | Nombre (en milliers) |
| Per 100 inhabitants | | ^0 | 1 | 3 | 3 | 4 | 5 | 5 | 6 | Pour 100 habitants |
| **Lao People's Dem. Rep.** | | | | | | | | | | **Rép. dém. pop. lao** |
| Number (thousands) | | 2 | 6 | 10 | 15 | 19 | 21 | 25 | 70 | Nombre (en milliers) |
| Per 100 inhabitants | | ^0 | ^0 | ^0 | ^0 | ^0 | ^0 | ^0 | 1 | Pour 100 habitants |
| **Latvia** | | | | | | | | | | **Lettonie** |
| Number (thousands) | | 105 | 150 | 170 | 310 | 560[1] | 810 | 1 030 | 1 071 | Nombre (en milliers) |
| Per 100 inhabitants | | 4 | 6 | 7 | 13 | 24 | 35 | 45 | 47 | Pour 100 habitants |
| **Lebanon** | | | | | | | | | | **Liban** |
| Number (thousands) | | 200 | 300 | 260 | 400 | 500 | 600 | 700 | 950 | Nombre (en milliers) |
| Per 100 inhabitants | | 6 | 9 | 8 | 12 | 14 | 17 | 20 | 26 | Pour 100 habitants |
| **Lesotho** | (01/04) | | | | | | | | | **Lesotho** |
| Number (thousands) | | 1 | 4 | 5 | 21 | 30 | 43 | 51[1] | ... | Nombre (en milliers) |
| Per 100 inhabitants | | ^0 | ^0 | ^0 | 1 | 2 | 2 | 3 | ... | Pour 100 habitants |
| **Liberia** | | | | | | | | | | **Libéria** |
| Number (thousands) | | 0 | 1 | 1 | ... | ... | ... | ... | ... | Nombre (en milliers) |
| Per 100 inhabitants^ | | 0 | 0 | 0 | ... | ... | ... | ... | ... | Pour 100 habitants^ |
| **Libyan Arab Jamah.** | | | | | | | | | | **Jamah. arabe libyenne** |
| Number (thousands) | | 7 | 10 | 20 | 125 | 160 | 205 | 232[1] | ... | Nombre (en milliers) |
| Per 100 inhabitants | | ^0 | ^0 | ^0 | 2 | 3 | 4 | 4 | ... | Pour 100 habitants |
| **Liechtenstein** | | | | | | | | | | **Liechtenstein** |
| Number (thousands) | | ... | 12 | 15 | 20 | 20 | 22 | 22 | 22 | Nombre (en milliers) |
| Per 100 inhabitants | | ... | 37 | 45 | 59 | 58 | 64 | 63 | 64 | Pour 100 habitants |
| **Lithuania** | | | | | | | | | | **Lituanie** |
| Number (thousands) | | 103 | 225 | 250 | 500 | 696 | 767 | 883 | 1 083 | Nombre (en milliers) |
| Per 100 inhabitants | | 3 | 6 | 7 | 14 | 20 | 22 | 26 | 32 | Pour 100 habitants |
| **Luxembourg** | | | | | | | | | | **Luxembourg** |
| Number (thousands) | | 75[1] | 100[1] | 160[31] | 165[18] | 170[1] | 271[1] | 315[1] | 339[1] | Nombre (en milliers) |
| Per 100 inhabitants | | 17 | 23 | 36 | 37 | 38 | 59 | 68 | 72 | Pour 100 habitants |
| **Madagascar** | | | | | | | | | | **Madagascar** |
| Number (thousands) | | 25 | 30 | 35 | 55 | 71 | 90 | 100 | 110 | Nombre (en milliers) |
| Per 100 inhabitants | | ^0 | ^0 | ^0 | ^0 | ^0 | ^0 | 1 | 1 | Pour 100 habitants |
| **Malawi** | | | | | | | | | | **Malawi** |
| Number (thousands) | | 10 | 15 | 20 | 27 | 36 | 46 | 53 | 60 | Nombre (en milliers) |
| Per 100 inhabitants^ | | 0 | 0 | 0 | 0 | 0 | 0 | 0 | 0 | Pour 100 habitants^ |
| **Malaysia** | | | | | | | | | | **Malaisie** |
| Number (thousands) | | 2 800 | 4 977 | 6 346 | 7 842 | 8 643 | 10 637 | 12 537 | 13 989 | Nombre (en milliers) |
| Per 100 inhabitants | | 13 | 21 | 27 | 32 | 35 | 42 | 48 | 54 | Pour 100 habitants |
| **Maldives** | | | | | | | | | | **Maldives** |
| Number (thousands) | | 3 | 6 | 10 | 15 | 17 | 19 | 20[1] | ... | Nombre (en milliers) |
| Per 100 inhabitants | | 1 | 2 | 4 | 5 | 6 | 6 | 7 | ... | Pour 100 habitants |
| **Mali** | | | | | | | | | | **Mali** |
| Number (thousands) | | 6 | 15 | 20 | 25 | 35 | 50 | 60 | 88 | Nombre (en milliers) |
| Per 100 inhabitants | | ^0 | ^0 | ^0 | ^0 | ^0 | ^0 | 1 | 1 | Pour 100 habitants |
| **Malta** | | | | | | | | | | **Malte** |
| Number (thousands) | | 30 | 51 | 70 | 80 | 96 | 112 | 127 | ... | Nombre (en milliers) |
| Per 100 inhabitants | | 8 | 13 | 18 | 20 | 24 | 28 | 32 | ... | Pour 100 habitants |

| Country or area | Fiscal year &<br>Ex. budgét.& | 1999 | 2000 | 2001 | 2002 | 2003 | 2004 | 2005 | 2006 | Pays ou zone |
|---|---|---|---|---|---|---|---|---|---|---|
| Marshall Islands | | | | | | | | | | Iles Marshall |
| Number (thousands) | | 1 | 1 | 1 | 1 | 1 | 2 | 2 | 2 | Nombre (en milliers) |
| Per 100 inhabitants | | 1 | 2 | 2 | 2 | 3 | 4 | ... | ... | Pour 100 habitants |
| Martinique | | | | | | | | | | Martinique |
| Number (thousands) | | 5 | 30 | 40 | 60 | 80 | 110 | 130 | ... | Nombre (en milliers) |
| Per 100 inhabitants | | 1 | 8 | 10 | 15 | 20 | 28 | 33 | ... | Pour 100 habitants |
| Mauritania | | | | | | | | | | Mauritanie |
| Number (thousands) | | 3 | 5 | 7 | 10 | 12 | 14 | 20 | 30 | Nombre (en milliers) |
| Per 100 inhabitants | | ^0 | ^0 | ^0 | ^0 | ^0 | ^0 | 1 | 1 | Pour 100 habitants |
| Mauritius | | | | | | | | | | Maurice |
| Number (thousands) | | 55 | 87 | 106 | 125[31] | 150 | 240 | 300 | ... | Nombre (en milliers) |
| Per 100 inhabitants | | 5 | 7 | 9 | 10 | 12 | 19 | 24 | ... | Pour 100 habitants |
| Mayotte | | | | | | | | | | Mayotte |
| Number (thousands) | | ... | 2 | ... | ... | ... | ... | ... | ... | Nombre (en milliers) |
| Per 100 inhabitants | | ... | 1 | ... | ... | ... | ... | ... | ... | Pour 100 habitants |
| Mexico | | | | | | | | | | Mexique |
| Number (thousands) | | 1 822 | 5 058 | 7 047 | 10 765 | 12 219 | 14 036 | 18 092 | 20 564 | Nombre (en milliers) |
| Per 100 inhabitants | | 2 | 5 | 7 | 11 | 12 | 13 | 17 | 19 | Pour 100 habitants |
| Micronesia (Fed. States of) | | | | | | | | | | Micronésie (Etats féd. de) |
| Number (thousands) | | 3 | 4 | 5 | 6 | 10 | 12 | 14 | 16 | Nombre (en milliers) |
| Per 100 inhabitants | | 3 | 4 | 5 | 6 | 9 | 11 | 13 | 14 | Pour 100 habitants |
| Moldova | | | | | | | | | | Moldova |
| Number (thousands) | | 25 | 53 | 60 | 150 | 288 | 406 | 550 | 728 | Nombre (en milliers) |
| Per 100 inhabitants | | 1 | 1 | 1 | 4 | 7 | 10 | 13 | 17 | Pour 100 habitants |
| Monaco | | | | | | | | | | Monaco |
| Number (thousands) | | ... | 14 | 15 | 16 | 16 | 17 | 18 | 20 | Nombre (en milliers) |
| Per 100 inhabitants | | ... | 40 | 44 | 45 | 46 | 49 | 51 | 56 | Pour 100 habitants |
| Mongolia | | | | | | | | | | Mongolie |
| Number (thousands) | | 12 | 30 | 40 | 50 | 143 | 200 | 268 | 310 | Nombre (en milliers) |
| Per 100 inhabitants | | 1 | 1 | 2 | 2 | 6 | 8 | 10 | 12 | Pour 100 habitants |
| Montenegro | | | | | | | | | | Monténégro |
| Number (thousands) | | ... | ... | ... | ... | ... | ... | 243 | 266 | Nombre (en milliers) |
| Per 100 inhabitants | | ... | ... | ... | ... | ... | ... | 40 | 44 | Pour 100 habitants |
| Morocco | | | | | | | | | | Maroc |
| Number (thousands) | | 50 | 200 | 400 | 700 | 1 000 | 3 500[32] | 4 600[32] | 6 100[32] | Nombre (en milliers) |
| Per 100 inhabitants | | ^0 | 1 | 1 | 2 | 3 | 12 | 15 | 20 | Pour 100 habitants |
| Mozambique | | | | | | | | | | Mozambique |
| Number (thousands) | | 10 | 20 | 30 | 50 | 83 | 138 | 178[1] | ... | Nombre (en milliers) |
| Per 100 inhabitants | | ^0 | ^0 | ^0 | ^0 | ^0 | 1 | 1 | ... | Pour 100 habitants |
| Myanmar | | | | | | | | | | Myanmar |
| Number (thousands) | | ^0 | ... | ^0 | ^0 | 11 | 12 | 32 | 94 | Nombre (en milliers) |
| Per 100 inhabitants^ | | 0 | ... | 0 | 0 | 0 | 0 | 0 | 0 | Pour 100 habitants^ |
| Namibia | (30/09) | | | | | | | | | Namibie |
| Number (thousands) | | 6 | 30 | 45 | 50 | 65 | 75 | 81[1] | ... | Nombre (en milliers) |
| Per 100 inhabitants | | ^0 | 2 | 2 | 3 | 3 | 4 | 4 | ... | Pour 100 habitants |
| Nauru | | | | | | | | | | Nauru |
| Number (thousands) | | ... | ... | ^0 | ... | ... | ... | ... | ... | Nombre (en milliers) |
| Per 100 inhabitants | | ... | ... | 3 | ... | ... | ... | ... | ... | Pour 100 habitants |
| Nepal | (15/07) | | | | | | | | | Népal |
| Number (thousands) | | 35 | 50 | 60[2] | 80 | 100 | 120 | 225 | 317 | Nombre (en milliers) |
| Per 100 inhabitants | | ^0 | ^0 | ^0 | ^0 | ^0 | ^0 | 1 | 1 | Pour 100 habitants |
| Netherlands | | | | | | | | | | Pays-Bas |
| Number (thousands) | | 6 200 | 7 000 | 7 900 | 8 200 | 8 500 | 10 000 | *12 060[26] | 14 544 | Nombre (en milliers) |
| Per 100 inhabitants | | 39 | 44 | 49 | 51 | 52 | 62 | 74 | 89 | Pour 100 habitants |

| Country or area | Fiscal year[&] Ex. budgét.[&] | 1999 | 2000 | 2001 | 2002 | 2003 | 2004 | 2005 | 2006 | Pays ou zone |
|---|---|---|---|---|---|---|---|---|---|---|
| Netherlands Antilles | | | | | | | | | | Antilles néerlandaises |
| Number (thousands) | | 2 | ... | ... | ... | ... | ... | ... | ... | Nombre (en milliers) |
| Per 100 inhabitants | | 1 | ... | ... | ... | ... | ... | ... | ... | Pour 100 habitants |
| New Caledonia | | | | | | | | | | Nouvelle-Calédonie |
| Number (thousands) | | 12 | 30 | 40 | 50 | 60 | 70 | 76 | 80 | Nombre (en milliers) |
| Per 100 inhabitants | | 6 | 14 | 18 | 22 | 26 | 30 | 32 | 33 | Pour 100 habitants |
| New Zealand | (01/04) | | | | | | | | | Nouvelle-Zélande |
| Number (thousands) | | 1 113 | 1 515 | 1 762 | 1 908 | 2 110 | 2 350[1] | 2 754 | 3 200 | Nombre (en milliers) |
| Per 100 inhabitants | | 29 | 39 | 45 | 48 | 53 | 59 | 68 | 79 | Pour 100 habitants |
| Nicaragua | | | | | | | | | | Nicaragua |
| Number (thousands) | | 25 | 50 | 75 | 90 | 100 | 125 | 140 | 155 | Nombre (en milliers) |
| Per 100 inhabitants | | 1 | 1 | 1 | 2 | 2 | 2 | 2 | 3 | Pour 100 habitants |
| Niger | | | | | | | | | | Niger |
| Number (thousands) | | 3 | 4 | 12 | 15 | 19 | 24 | 29 | 40 | Nombre (en milliers) |
| Per 100 inhabitants^ | | 0 | 0 | 0 | 0 | 0 | 0 | 0 | 0 | Pour 100 habitants^ |
| Nigeria | | | | | | | | | | Nigéria |
| Number (thousands) | | 50 | 80 | 115 | 420 | 750 | 1 770 | *5 000 | 8 000 | Nombre (en milliers) |
| Per 100 inhabitants | | ^0 | ^0 | ^0 | ^0 | 1 | 1 | 4 | 6 | Pour 100 habitants |
| Niue | | | | | | | | | | Nioué |
| Number (thousands) | | ^0 | 1 | 1 | 1 | 1 | 1 | 1 | ... | Nombre (en milliers) |
| Per 100 inhabitants | | 16 | 27 | 35 | 41 | 44 | 47 | 50 | ... | Pour 100 habitants |
| Norway | | | | | | | | | | Norvège |
| Number (thousands)[33] | | 1 100 | 1 200 | 1 319 | 1 399 | 1 583 | 1 792 | 2 702 | 3 792 | Nombre (en milliers) [33] |
| Per 100 inhabitants | | 25 | 27 | 29 | 31 | 35 | 39 | 58 | 82 | Pour 100 habitants |
| Occupied Palestinian Terr. | | | | | | | | | | Terr. palestinien occupé |
| Number (thousands) | | ... | 35 | 60 | 105 | 145 | 160 | 243 | 266 | Nombre (en milliers) |
| Per 100 inhabitants | | ... | 1 | 2 | 3 | 4 | 4 | 7 | 7 | Pour 100 habitants |
| Oman | | | | | | | | | | Oman |
| Number (thousands) | | 50 | 90 | 120 | 180 | 210 | 245 | 285 | 319 | Nombre (en milliers) |
| Per 100 inhabitants | | 2 | 4 | 5 | 7 | 8 | 10 | 11 | 12 | Pour 100 habitants |
| Pakistan | (30/06) | | | | | | | | | Pakistan |
| Number (thousands) | | 80 | 300 | 500 | 1 000 | 8 000 | 10 000 | 10 500 | 12 000 | Nombre (en milliers) |
| Per 100 inhabitants | | ^0 | ^0 | ^0 | 1 | 5 | 7 | 7 | 8 | Pour 100 habitants |
| Palau | | | | | | | | | | Palaos |
| Number (thousands) | | ... | ... | ... | 4 | 4 | 5 | ... | ... | Nombre (en milliers) |
| Panama | | | | | | | | | | Panama |
| Number (thousands) | | 62 | 107 | 121 | 145 | 173 | 197 | 206 | 220 | Nombre (en milliers) |
| Per 100 inhabitants | | 2 | 4 | 4 | 5 | 6 | 6 | 6 | 7 | Pour 100 habitants |
| Papua New Guinea | | | | | | | | | | Papouasie-Nvl-Guinée |
| Number (thousands) | | 35 | 45 | 50 | 75 | 80 | 90 | 105 | 110 | Nombre (en milliers) |
| Per 100 inhabitants | | 1 | 1 | 1 | 1 | 1 | 2 | 2 | 2 | Pour 100 habitants |
| Paraguay | | | | | | | | | | Paraguay |
| Number (thousands) | | 20 | 40 | 60 | 100 | 120 | 200 | 200 | 260 | Nombre (en milliers) |
| Per 100 inhabitants | | ^0 | 1 | 1 | 2 | 2 | 3 | 3 | 4 | Pour 100 habitants |
| Peru | | | | | | | | | | Pérou |
| Number (thousands)[1] | | 500 | 800 | *2 000 | *2 400 | *2 850 | 3 220 | 4 600 | 7 324 | Nombre (en milliers)[1] |
| Per 100 inhabitants | | 2 | 3 | 8 | 9 | 10 | 12 | 16 | 26 | Pour 100 habitants |
| Philippines | | | | | | | | | | Philippines |
| Number (thousands) | | 1 090 | 1 540 | 2 000 | 3 500 | 4 000 | 4 400 | 4 615[1] | ... | Nombre (en milliers) |
| Per 100 inhabitants | | 1 | 2 | 3 | 4 | 5 | 5 | 5 | ... | Pour 100 habitants |
| Poland | | | | | | | | | | Pologne |
| Number (thousands) | | 2 100 | 2 800 | 3 800 | 8 880 | *8 970 | 9 000 | 10 000 | 14 085 | Nombre (en milliers) |
| Per 100 inhabitants | | 5 | 7 | 10 | 23 | 23 | 23 | 26 | 37 | Pour 100 habitants |

| Country or area | Fiscal year &<br>Ex. budgét.& | 1999 | 2000 | 2001 | 2002 | 2003 | 2004 | 2005 | 2006 | Pays ou zone |
|---|---|---|---|---|---|---|---|---|---|---|
| Portugal | | | | | | | | | | Portugal |
| Number (thousands) | | 1 500 | 1 680[1] | 1 860[1] | 2 267[1] | 2 674 | 2 576[26] | 2 856[26] | 3 213[26] | Nombre (en milliers) |
| Per 100 inhabitants | | 15 | 17 | 18 | 22 | 26 | 24 | 27 | 30 | Pour 100 habitants |
| Puerto Rico | | | | | | | | | | Porto Rico |
| Number (thousands) | | 200 | 400 | 600 | 677 | 764 | 862 | 916[1] | ... | Nombre (en milliers) |
| Per 100 inhabitants | | 5 | 11 | 16 | 18 | 20 | 22 | 23 | ... | Pour 100 habitants |
| Qatar | | | | | | | | | | Qatar |
| Number (thousands) | | 24 | 30 | 40 | 70 | 141 | 165 | 219 | 290 | Nombre (en milliers) |
| Per 100 inhabitants | | 4 | 5 | 6 | 10 | 20 | 22 | 28 | 35 | Pour 100 habitants |
| Réunion | | | | | | | | | | Réunion |
| Number (thousands)[34] | | 10 | 100 | 120 | 150 | 180 | 200 | 220 | ... | Nombre (en milliers)[34] |
| Per 100 inhabitants | | 1 | 14 | 16 | 20 | 24 | 26 | 28 | ... | Pour 100 habitants |
| Romania | | | | | | | | | | Roumanie |
| Number (thousands) | | 600 | 800 | 1 000 | 2 200 | 4 000 | 4 500 | 4 773[1] | ... | Nombre (en milliers) |
| Per 100 inhabitants | | 3 | 4 | 4 | 10 | 18 | 21 | 22 | ... | Pour 100 habitants |
| Russian Federation | | | | | | | | | | Fédération de Russie |
| Number (thousands) | | 1 500 | 2 900 | 4 300 | 6 000 | 12 000 | 18 500 | 21 800 | 25 689 | Nombre (en milliers) |
| Per 100 inhabitants | | 1 | 2 | 3 | 4 | 8 | 13 | 15 | 18 | Pour 100 habitants |
| Rwanda | | | | | | | | | | Rwanda |
| Number (thousands) | | 5 | 5 | 20 | 25 | 31 | 38 | 50 | ... | Nombre (en milliers) |
| Per 100 inhabitants | | ^0 | ^0 | ^0 | ^0 | ^0 | ^0 | 1 | ... | Pour 100 habitants |
| Saint Helena | (01/04) | | | | | | | | | Sainte-Hélène |
| Number (thousands) | | ^0 | ^0 | ^0[2] | 1 | 1 | 1 | 1 | 1 | Nombre (en milliers) |
| Per 100 inhabitants | | 6 | 6 | 8 | 10 | 12 | 14 | 15 | ... | Pour 100 habitants |
| Saint Kitts and Nevis | (01/04) | | | | | | | | | Saint-Kitts-et-Nevis |
| Number (thousands) | | 2 | 3 | 4 | 10 | ... | ... | ... | ... | Nombre (en milliers) |
| Per 100 inhabitants | | 5 | 7 | 9 | 24 | ... | ... | ... | ... | Pour 100 habitants |
| Saint Lucia | (01/04) | | | | | | | | | Sainte-Lucie |
| Number (thousands) | | 3 | 8 | 13 | ... | 34 | 55 | ... | ... | Nombre (en milliers) |
| Per 100 inhabitants | | 2 | 5 | 8 | ... | 21 | 34 | ... | ... | Pour 100 habitants |
| Saint Vincent-Grenadines | (01/04) | | | | | | | | | Saint Vincent-Grenadines |
| Number (thousands) | | 3 | 4 | 6 | 6 | 7 | 8 | 10 | 15 | Nombre (en milliers) |
| Per 100 inhabitants | | 3 | 3 | 5 | 5 | 6 | 7 | 8 | 13 | Pour 100 habitants |
| Samoa | | | | | | | | | | Samoa |
| Number (thousands) | | 1 | 1 | 3 | 4 | 5 | 6 | 6 | 8 | Nombre (en milliers) |
| Per 100 inhabitants | | ^0 | 1 | 2 | 2 | 3 | 3 | 3 | 4 | Pour 100 habitants |
| San Marino | | | | | | | | | | Saint-Marin |
| Number (thousands) | | 11 | 13 | 14 | 14 | 14 | 15 | 15 | 15 | Nombre (en milliers) |
| Per 100 inhabitants | | 43 | 49 | 51 | 53 | 54 | 56 | 56 | 57 | Pour 100 habitants |
| Sao Tome and Principe | | | | | | | | | | Sao Tomé-et-Principe |
| Number (thousands) | | 1 | 7 | 9 | 11 | 15 | 20 | 23[1] | 29 | Nombre (en milliers) |
| Per 100 inhabitants | | ^0 | 5 | 6 | 8 | 10 | 13 | 15 | 18 | Pour 100 habitants |
| Saudi Arabia | | | | | | | | | | Arabie saoudite |
| Number (thousands) | | 100 | 460 | 1 000 | 1 400 | 1 800 | 2 360 | 3 000 | 4 700 | Nombre (en milliers) |
| Per 100 inhabitants | | ^0 | 2 | 5 | 6 | 8 | 10 | 12 | 19 | Pour 100 habitants |
| Senegal | | | | | | | | | | Sénégal |
| Number (thousands) | | 30 | 40 | 100 | 105 | 225 | 482 | 540 | 650 | Nombre (en milliers) |
| Per 100 inhabitants | | ^0 | ^0 | 1 | 1 | 2 | 5 | 5 | 5 | Pour 100 habitants |
| Serbia | | | | | | | | | | Serbie |
| Number (thousands) | | ... | ... | ... | ... | ... | ... | 777 | 1 400 | Nombre (en milliers) |
| Per 100 inhabitants | | ... | ... | ... | ... | ... | ... | ... | 13 | Pour 100 habitants |
| Serbia and Montenegro | | | | | | | | | | Serbie-et-Monténégro |
| Number (thousands) | | 80 | 400 | 600 | 640 | 847 | 1 517 | ... | ... | Nombre (en milliers) |
| Per 100 inhabitants | | 1 | 4 | 6 | 8 | 10 | 19 | ... | ... | Pour 100 habitants |

| Country or area | Fiscal year [&] Ex. budgét. [&] | 1999 | 2000 | 2001 | 2002 | 2003 | 2004 | 2005 | 2006 | Pays ou zone |
|---|---|---|---|---|---|---|---|---|---|---|
| Seychelles | (01/04) | | | | | | | | | Seychelles |
| Number (thousands) | | 5 | 6[1] | 9[2] | 12 | 12 | 20 | 21 | 29 | Nombre (en milliers) |
| Per 100 inhabitants | | 7 | 8 | 12 | 15 | 15 | 25 | 26 | 36 | Pour 100 habitants |
| Sierra Leone | | | | | | | | | | Sierra Leone |
| Number (thousands) | | 2 | 5 | 7 | 8 | 9 | 10 | ... | ... | Nombre (en milliers) |
| Per 100 inhabitants [^] | | 0 | 0 | 0 | 0 | 0 | 0 | ... | ... | Pour 100 habitants [^] |
| Singapore | (01/04) | | | | | | | | | Singapour |
| Number (thousands) [1] | | 950 | 1 300 | 1 700 | 2 100 | 2 135 | 2 422 | 1 732[18] | 1 910[18] | Nombre (en milliers) [1] |
| Per 100 inhabitants | | 24 | 32 | 41 | 50 | 51 | 58 | 40 | 44 | Pour 100 habitants |
| Slovakia | | | | | | | | | | Slovaquie |
| Number (thousands) | | 292 | 507 | 674 | 863 | 1 376 | 1 652 | 1 905 | 2 256 | Nombre (en milliers) |
| Per 100 inhabitants | | 5 | 9 | 13 | 16 | 26 | 31 | 35 | 42 | Pour 100 habitants |
| Slovenia | | | | | | | | | | Slovénie |
| Number (thousands) | | 250 | 300 | 600 | 750 | 800 | 950 | 1 090 | 1 251 | Nombre (en milliers) |
| Per 100 inhabitants | | 13 | 15 | 30 | 38 | 40 | 48 | 55 | 64 | Pour 100 habitants |
| Solomon Islands | (01/04) | | | | | | | | | Iles Salomon |
| Number (thousands) | | 2 | 2 | 2 | 2 | 3 | 3 | 4 | 8 | Nombre (en milliers) |
| Per 100 inhabitants | | ^0 | ^0 | ^0 | ^0 | 1 | 1 | 1 | 2 | Pour 100 habitants |
| Somalia | | | | | | | | | | Somalie |
| Number (thousands) | | 1 | 15 | 6[1] | 9[1] | 30[1] | 86 | 90 | 94 | Nombre (en milliers) |
| Per 100 inhabitants | | ^0 | ^0 | ^0 | ^0 | ^0 | 1 | 1 | 1 | Pour 100 habitants |
| South Africa | (01/04) | | | | | | | | | Afrique du Sud |
| Number (thousands) | | 1 820 | 2 400 | 2 890 | 3 100 | 3 325 | 3 566 | 5 100 | ... | Nombre (en milliers) |
| Per 100 inhabitants | | 4 | 5 | 6 | 7 | 7 | 8 | 11 | ... | Pour 100 habitants |
| Spain | | | | | | | | | | Espagne |
| Number (thousands) [35] | | 2 830 | 5 486 | 7 388 | 7 856 | 15 300 | 15 140 | 17 233 | 18 578 | Nombre (en milliers) [35] |
| Per 100 inhabitants | | 7 | 14 | 18 | 19 | 36 | 35 | 40 | 43 | Pour 100 habitants |
| Sri Lanka | | | | | | | | | | Sri Lanka |
| Number (thousands) | | 65 | 122 | 150 | 200 | 280 | 280 | 350[1] | ... | Nombre (en milliers) |
| Per 100 inhabitants | | ^0 | 1 | 1 | 1 | 1 | 1 | 2 | ... | Pour 100 habitants |
| Sudan | | | | | | | | | | Soudan |
| Number (thousands) | | 5 | 30 | 150 | 300 | 937 | 1 140 | 2 800 | 3 500 | Nombre (en milliers) |
| Per 100 inhabitants | | ^0 | ^0 | ^0 | 1 | 3 | 3 | 8 | 9 | Pour 100 habitants |
| Suriname | | | | | | | | | | Suriname |
| Number (thousands) | | 9 | 12 | 15 | 20 | 23 | 30 | 32 | ... | Nombre (en milliers) |
| Per 100 inhabitants | | 2 | 3 | 3 | 5 | 5 | 7 | 7 | ... | Pour 100 habitants |
| Swaziland | (01/04) | | | | | | | | | Swaziland |
| Number (thousands) | | 5 | 10 | 14 | 20 | 27 | 36 | 42[1] | 42 | Nombre (en milliers) |
| Per 100 inhabitants | | 1 | 1 | 1 | 2 | 3 | 3 | 4 | 4 | Pour 100 habitants |
| Sweden | | | | | | | | | | Suède |
| Number (thousands) | | 3 666 | 4 048 | 4 600 | 5 125 | 5 655 | 6 800[26] | 6 890[26] | 6 981 | Nombre (en milliers) |
| Per 100 inhabitants | | 41 | 46 | 52 | 57 | 63 | 75 | 76 | 77 | Pour 100 habitants |
| Switzerland | | | | | | | | | | Suisse |
| Number (thousands) | | 1 473 | 2 096 | 2 800 | 3 000 | 3 300 | 3 500 | 3 800 | 4 360 | Nombre (en milliers) |
| Per 100 inhabitants | | 21 | 29 | 39 | 41 | 45 | 47 | 51 | 58 | Pour 100 habitants |
| Syrian Arab Republic | | | | | | | | | | Rép. arabe syrienne |
| Number (thousands) | | 20 | 30 | 60 | 365 | 610 | 800 | 1 100 | 1 500 | Nombre (en milliers) |
| Per 100 inhabitants | | ^0 | ^0 | ^0 | 2 | 3 | 4 | 6 | 8 | Pour 100 habitants |
| Tajikistan | | | | | | | | | | Tadjikistan |
| Number (thousands) | | 2 | 3 | 3 | 4 | 4 | 5 | 20 | ... | Nombre (en milliers) |
| Per 100 inhabitants [^] | | 0 | 0 | 0 | 0 | 0 | 0 | 0 | ... | Pour 100 habitants [^] |
| Thailand | (30/09) | | | | | | | | | Thaïlande |
| Number (thousands) | | 1 300 | 2 300 | 3 536 | 4 800 | 6 030[11] | 6 972 | 7 284 | 8 466 | Nombre (en milliers) |
| Per 100 inhabitants | | 2 | 4 | 6 | 8 | 10 | 11 | 11 | 13 | Pour 100 habitants |

| Country or area | Fiscal year & Ex. budgét.& | 1999 | 2000 | 2001 | 2002 | 2003 | 2004 | 2005 | 2006 | Pays ou zone |
|---|---|---|---|---|---|---|---|---|---|---|
| TFYR of Macedonia | | | | | | | | | | L'ex-R.y. Macédoine |
| Number (thousands) | | 30 | 50 | 70 | 100 | 126 | 159 | 160 | 268 | Nombre (en milliers) |
| Per 100 inhabitants | | 1 | 2 | 3 | 5 | 6 | 8 | 8 | 13 | Pour 100 habitants |
| Timor-Leste | | | | | | | | | | Timor-Leste |
| Number (thousands) | | ... | ... | ... | ... | ... | ... | 1 | 1 | Nombre (en milliers) |
| Per 100 inhabitants^ | | ... | ... | ... | ... | ... | ... | 0 | 0 | Pour 100 habitants^ |
| Togo | | | | | | | | | | Togo |
| Number (thousands) | | 30 | 100 | 150 | 200 | 210 | 221 | 300 | 320 | Nombre (en milliers) |
| Per 100 inhabitants | | 1 | 2 | 3 | 4 | 4 | 4 | 6 | 5 | Pour 100 habitants |
| Tokelau | | | | | | | | | | Tokélaou |
| Number (thousands) | | ... | ... | ... | ... | ^0 | ^0 | ^0 | ... | Nombre (en milliers) |
| Per 100 inhabitants | | ... | ... | ... | ... | 1 | 8 | ... | ... | Pour 100 habitants |
| Tonga | | | | | | | | | | Tonga |
| Number (thousands) | | 1 | 2 | 3 | 3 | 3 | 3 | 3 | 3 | Nombre (en milliers) |
| Per 100 inhabitants | | 1 | 2 | 3 | 3 | 3 | 3 | 3 | 3 | Pour 100 habitants |
| Trinidad and Tobago | (01/04) | | | | | | | | | Trinité-et-Tobago |
| Number (thousands) | | 75 | 100 | 120[27] | 138[27] | 153 | 160 | 163[1] | ... | Nombre (en milliers) |
| Per 100 inhabitants | | 6 | 8 | 9 | 11 | 12 | 12 | 12 | ... | Pour 100 habitants |
| Tunisia | | | | | | | | | | Tunisie |
| Number (thousands) | | 150 | 260 | 410 | 506 | 630 | 835 | 954 | 1 295 | Nombre (en milliers) |
| Per 100 inhabitants | | 2 | 3 | 4 | 5 | 6 | 8 | 9 | 13 | Pour 100 habitants |
| Turkey | | | | | | | | | | Turquie |
| Number (thousands) | | 1 500 | 2 500 | 3 500 | 4 300 | 6 000 | 10 220 | 11 204[26] | 13 150 | Nombre (en milliers) |
| Per 100 inhabitants | | 2 | 4 | 5 | 6 | 8 | 14 | 15 | 18 | Pour 100 habitants |
| Turkmenistan | | | | | | | | | | Turkménistan |
| Number (thousands) | | 2 | 6 | 8 | 14[1] | 20[1] | 36 | 48[1] | 65 | Nombre (en milliers) |
| Per 100 inhabitants | | ^0 | ^0 | ^0 | ^0 | ^0 | 1 | 1 | 1 | Pour 100 habitants |
| Tuvalu | | | | | | | | | | Tuvalu |
| Number (thousands) | | ... | 1 | 1 | 1 | 2 | 2 | 3 | 5 | Nombre (en milliers) |
| Per 100 inhabitants | | ... | 5 | 11 | 13 | 15 | 19 | 29 | 47 | Pour 100 habitants |
| Uganda | (30/06) | | | | | | | | | Ouganda |
| Number (thousands) | | 25 | 40 | 60 | 100 | 125 | 200 | 500 | 750 | Nombre (en milliers) |
| Per 100 inhabitants | | ^0 | ^0 | ^0 | ^0 | ^0 | 1 | 2 | 3 | Pour 100 habitants |
| Ukraine | | | | | | | | | | Ukraine |
| Number (thousands) | | 200 | 350 | 600 | 900 | 2 500 | 3 750 | *4 560 | 5 545 | Nombre (en milliers) |
| Per 100 inhabitants | | ^0 | 1 | 1 | 2 | 5 | 8 | î0 | 12 | Pour 100 habitants |
| United Arab Emirates | | | | | | | | | | Emirats arabes unis |
| Number (thousands) | | 458 | 765 | 897 | 1 017 | 1 110 | 1 185 | 1 322 | 1 708 | Nombre (en milliers) |
| Per 100 inhabitants | | 15 | 24 | 26 | 27 | 27 | 28 | 29 | 37 | Pour 100 habitants |
| United Kingdom | (01/04) | | | | | | | | | Royaume-Uni |
| Number (thousands) | | 12 500[1] | 15 800[36] | 19 800[36] | 25 000[36] | 26 025[36] | 28 094[36] | 32 076[36] | 33 534[36] | Nombre (en milliers) |
| Per 100 inhabitants | | 21 | 26 | 33 | 42 | 44 | 47 | 54 | 56 | Pour 100 habitants |
| United Rep. of Tanzania | | | | | | | | | | Rép.-Unie de Tanzanie |
| Number (thousands) | | 25 | 40 | 60 | 80 | 250 | 333 | 384[1] | ... | Nombre (en milliers) |
| Per 100 inhabitants | | ^0 | ^0 | ^0 | ^0 | 1 | 1 | 1 | ... | Pour 100 habitants |
| United States | | | | | | | | | | Etats-Unis |
| Number (thousands)[1] | | 102 000 | 124 000 | 143 000 | 159 000 | 162 000 | 185 000 | 198 000 | 208 000 | Nombre (en milliers)[1] |
| Per 100 inhabitants | | 37 | 44 | 50 | 55 | 56 | 63 | 66 | 69 | Pour 100 habitants |
| United States Virgin Is. | | | | | | | | | | Iles Vierges américaines |
| Number (thousands) | | 12 | 15 | 20 | 30 | 30[1] | 30[1] | 30[1] | ... | Nombre (en milliers) |
| Per 100 inhabitants | | 11 | 14 | 18 | 27 | 27 | 27 | 27 | ... | Pour 100 habitants |
| Uruguay | | | | | | | | | | Uruguay |
| Number (thousands) | | 330 | 350 | 370 | 380 | 530 | 567 | 668 | ... | Nombre (en milliers) |
| Per 100 inhabitants | | 10 | 11 | 12 | 12 | 16 | 18 | 21 | ... | Pour 100 habitants |

| Country or area | Fiscal year [&] Ex. budgét.[&] | 1999 | 2000 | 2001 | 2002 | 2003 | 2004 | 2005 | 2006 | Pays ou zone |
|---|---|---|---|---|---|---|---|---|---|---|
| Uzbekistan | | | | | | | | | | Ouzbékistan |
| Number (thousands) | | 8 | 120 | 150 | 275 | 492 | 675 | 880 | 1 700 | Nombre (en milliers) |
| Per 100 inhabitants | | ^0 | ^0 | 1 | 1 | 2 | 3 | 3 | 6 | Pour 100 habitants |
| Vanuatu | | | | | | | | | | Vanuatu |
| Number (thousands) | | 1 | 4 | 6 | 7 | 8 | 8 | 8 | ... | Nombre (en milliers) |
| Per 100 inhabitants | | 1 | 2 | 3 | 3 | 4 | 3 | 3 | ... | Pour 100 habitants |
| Venezuela (Bolivarian Rep. of) | | | | | | | | | | Venezuela (Rép. bolivar. du) |
| Number (thousands) | | 680 | 820 | 1 153 | 1 244 | 1 935 | 2 207 | 3 355 | 4 140 | Nombre (en milliers) |
| Per 100 inhabitants | | 3 | 3 | 5 | 5 | 8 | 8 | 13 | 15 | Pour 100 habitants |
| Viet Nam | | | | | | | | | | Viet Nam |
| Number (thousands) | | 100 | 200 | 1 010 | 1 500 | 3 098 | 6 345 | 10 711 | 14 684 | Nombre (en milliers) |
| Per 100 inhabitants | | ^0 | ^0 | 1 | 2 | 4 | 8 | 13 | 17 | Pour 100 habitants |
| Wallis and Futuna Islands | | | | | | | | | | Iles Wallis et Futuna |
| Number (thousands) | | ^0 | 1 | 1 | ... | 1 | 1 | 1 | 1 | Nombre (en milliers) |
| Per 100 inhabitants | | 2 | 6 | 6 | ... | 7 | 8 | 8 | 8 | Pour 100 habitants |
| Yemen | | | | | | | | | | Yémen |
| Number (thousands) | | 10 | 15 | 17 | 100 | 120 | 180 | 220[1] | 270 | Nombre (en milliers) |
| Per 100 inhabitants | | ^0 | ^0 | ^0 | 1 | 1 | 1 | 1 | 1 | Pour 100 habitants |
| Zambia | (01/04) | | | | | | | | | Zambie |
| Number (thousands) | | 15 | 20 | 25 | 52[27] | 110 | 231 | 335[1] | 500 | Nombre (en milliers) |
| Per 100 inhabitants | | ^0 | ^0 | ^0 | ^0 | 1 | 2 | 3 | 4 | Pour 100 habitants |
| Zimbabwe | (30/06) | | | | | | | | | Zimbabwe |
| Number (thousands) | | 20 | 50 | 100 | 500 | 800 | 820 | 1 000 | 1 220 | Nombre (en milliers) |
| Per 100 inhabitants | | ^0 | ^0 | 1 | 4 | 7 | 7 | 8 | 9 | Pour 100 habitants |

Source

International Telecommunication Union (ITU), Geneva, the ITU database, last accessed March 2008.

[&] Fiscal year refers to the fiscal year used in each country or area. Countries or areas whose reference periods coincide with the calendar year ending 31 December are not footnoted. Those that have a fiscal year other than calendar year are denoted as follows:

22/03: Year ending 22 March
01/04: Year ending 1 April
30/06: Year ending 30 June
15/07: Year ending 15 July
30/09: Year ending 30 September

Notes

1 ITU estimate.
2 Data refer to 31 December.
3 Regular users of the Internet, age 14+.
4 ITU estimate based on 3 times the number of subscribers.
5 Refer to users aged 10+.
6 Users aged 10+ divided by total population. Internet penetration of users aged 10+ is 21%.
7 Population age 15+ using in last year.
8 Population age 18+ using in last week.

9 Persons aged 18 years and over.
10 For statistical purposes, the data for China do not include those for the Hong Kong Special Administrative Region (Hong Kong SAR), Macao Special Administrative Region (Macao SAR) and Taiwan Province of China.
11 Age 6+.
12 Online at least one hour per week.

Source

Union internationale des télécommunications (UIT), Genève, la base de données de l'UIT, dernier accès mars 2008.

[&] Ex. budgét. fait référence à l'exercice budgétaire en vigueur dans chaque pays ou territoire. Les pays ou les territoires dont l'exercice budgétaire terminent le 31 décembre de l'année civile ne sont pas signalés. Dans le cas contraire, ils sont désignés de la manière suivante:

22/03 : Exercice commençant le 22 mars
01/04 : Exercice commençant le 1er avril
30/06 : Exercice se terminant le 30 juin
15/07 : Exercice se terminant le 15 juillet
30/09 : Exercice se terminant le 30 septembre

Notes

1 Estimation de l'UIT.
2 Les données se réfèrent au 31 décembre.
3 Utilisateurs réguliers de l'Internet âgés de plus de 14 ans.
4 Estimation de l'UIT basée sur le nombre d'abonnés multiplié par 3.
5 Usagers âgés de plus de 10 ans.
6 Nombre d'usagers de plus de 10 ans, divisé par la population totale. La pénétration de l'Internet dans cette catégorie d'usagers est égale à 21%.
7 Population âgée de plus de 15 ans utilisant au cours de l'année écoulée.
8 Population âgée de plus de 18 ans utilisant au cours de la dernière semaine.
9 Personnes âgées de 18 ans et plus.
10 Pour la présentation des statistiques, les données pour la Chine ne comprennent pas la Région Administrative Spéciale de Hong Kong (Hong Kong RAS), la Région Administrative Spéciale de Macao (Macao RAS) et la province de Taiwan.
11 Population âgée de plus de 6 ans.
12 En ligne au moins une heure par semaine.

13 Population age 10+ who accessed Internet in previous year.

14 Ministry of Communication estimate.

15 June.

16 Including those who used only international email.

17 Only persons who use Internet (not just email).

18 Age 15+.

19 Age 16+.

20 e-Mail users.

21 Age 15-74 using at least once in the last week

22 As of 30 September.

23 Has used at least one other Internet application besides e-mail in last 3 months. Age 15+.

24 Persons aged 15 to 74 years.

25 1996-98, 18+; 1999-00, 15+ using in the last year; from 2001, 11+, using in the last month.

26 Persons aged 16 to 74 years.

27 December.

28 Those who used Internet in the last 3 months.

29 PC-based only.

30 Including users accessing internet through cell phones, PHS and game console.

31 Age 12+.

32 Including users who went on the internet at least once, no matter the location.

33 Norsk Gallup.

34 France Télécom only.

35 At November of year indicated. Age 14+.

36 Adult (age 16+) population using the internet in the last 3 months.

13 Population âgée de plus de 10 ans s'étant branchée sur l'Internet au cours de l'année écoulée.

14 Estimation du ministère de communication.

15 Juin.

16 Y compris ceux qui n'ont utilisé que des services internationaux de messagerie électronique.

17 Exclusivement les utilisateurs d'Internet (mais non seulement du courrier électronique).

18 Population âgée de plus de 15 ans.

19 Population âgée de plus de 16 ans

20 Utilisateurs de courrier électronique.

21 Personnes de 15 à 74 ans l'ayant utilisé au moins une fois au cours de la semaine précédente.

22 Au 30 septembre.

23 A utilisé au moins une application Internet autre que le courrier électronique au cours des trois derniers mois. Population âgée de plus de 15 ans.

24 Personnes âgées de 15 à 74 ans.

25 1996 à 1998, population âgée de plus de 18 ans; 1999 à 2000, 15+ ayant utilisé l'Internet au cours de la dernière année; à partir de 2001, population âgée de plus de 11 ans ayant utilisé l'Internet au cours du dernier mois.

26 Personnes âgées de 16 à 74 ans.

27 Décembre.

28 Personnes ayant utilisé Internet au cours des trois derniers mois.

29 Pour ordinateurs personnels seulement.

30 Comprend les utilisateurs qui naviguent sur Internet au moyen de téléphones mobiles, de téléphones PHS et de consoles de jeux.

31 Population âgée de plus de 12 ans.

32 Y compris les usagers ayant accédé à l'Internet une fois au moins quel que soit le lieu.

33 Norsk Gallup.

34 France Télécom seulement.

35 En novembre de l'année indiquée. Population âgée de plus de 14 ans.

36 Population âgée de plus de 16 ans utilisant au cours des trois derniers mois.

*Table 15:* The data on newspapers have been compiled from the UNESCO Institute for Statistics database (see www.uis.unesco.org).

Newspapers are periodic publications intended for the general public and mainly designed to be a primary source of written information on current events connected with public affairs, international questions, politics, etc. They may also include articles on literary or other subjects as well as illustrations and advertising.

Daily newspapers are newspapers mainly reporting events that have occurred in the 24-hour period before going to press.

Circulation figures show the average daily circulation. These figures include the number of copies sold directly, sold by subscription, or mainly distributed free of charge. Circulation figures refer to the number of copies distributed both inside the country and abroad. The figures for copies printed, unlike the circulation figures, also include the number of unsold copies (returns).

The statistics included in Tables 15-18 were obtained from the statistics database (see www.itu.int) and the *Yearbook of Statistics, Telecommunication Services* of the International Telecommunication Union.

*Table 16*: This table shows the number of main (fixed) lines in operation and the main lines in operation per 100 inhabitants for the years indicated. Main telephone lines refer to the telephone lines connecting a customer's equipment to the Public Switched Telephone Network (PSTN) and which have a dedicated port on a telephone exchange. Note that in most countries, main lines also include public telephones. The number of main telephone lines per 100 inhabitants is calculated by dividing the number of main lines by the population and multiplying by 100.

*Table 17:* The number of mobile cellular telephone subscribers (as well as the number of subscribers per 100 inhabitants) refers to users of portable telephones subscribing to an automatic public mobile telephone service using cellular technology, which provides access to the Public Switched Telephone Network (PSTN). Users of both post-paid subscriptions and pre-paid accounts are included. The number of subscribers per 100 inhabitants is calculated by dividing the number of subscribers by the population and multiplying by 100.

*Table 18:* Many Internet users obtain access without paying directly, either as the member of a household, or from work or school. Therefore the number of Internet users will always be much larger than the number of subscribers, typically by a factor of 2-3 in developed countries or more in developing ones. The estimated number of Internet users is

*Tableau 15 :* Les données concernant les journaux proviennent de la base de données de l'Institut de statistique de l'UNESCO (voir www.uis.unesco.org). Les journaux sont les publications périodiques destinées au grand public qui ont essentiellement pour objet de constituer une source primaire d'information écrite sur les événements d'actualité concernant les affaires publiques, les questions internationales, la politique, etc. Ils peuvent aussi contenir des articles portant sur des sujets littéraires ou autres, ainsi que sur des illustrations et de la publicité.

Les quotidiens sont les journaux rapportant principalement les événements survenus dans les vingt-quatre heures précédant leur mise sous presse.

Les chiffres concernant la diffusion sont ceux de la diffusion quotidienne moyenne. Ces chiffres comprennent le nombre d'exemplaires vendus directement, vendus par abonnement principalement distribués gratuitement. Les chiffres concernant la diffusion se réfèrent au nombre d'exemplaires distribuéssaussi bien à l'étranger que dans le pays. Contrairement aux chiffres concernant la diffusion, le nombre d'exemplaires imprimés incluent les exemplaires invendus (retours).

Les données présentées dans les Tableaux 16 à 18 proviennent de la base de données (voir www.itu.int) et l'*Annuaire statistique, Services de télécommunications* de l'Union internationale des télécommunications.

*Tableau 16:* Ce tableau indique le nombre de lignes principales (fixes) en service et les lignes principales en service pour 100 habitants pour les années indiquées. Les lignes principales sont des lignes téléphoniques qui relient l'équipement terminal de l'abonné au Réseau de téléphone public connecté (RTPC) et qui possèdent un accès individualisé aux équipements d'un central téléphonique. Pour la plupart des pays, le nombre de lignes principales en service indiqué comprend également les lignes publiques. Le nombre de lignes principales pour 100 habitants se calcule en divisant le nombre de lignes principales par la population et en multipliant par 100.

*Tableau 17:* Les abonnés mobiles (et les abonnés mobiles pour 100 habitants) désignent les utilisateurs de téléphones portatifs abonnés à un service automatique public de téléphones mobiles ayant accès au Réseau de téléphone public connecté (RTPC). Sont pris en compte aussi bien les abonnements post-payés que les cartes prépayées. Le nombre d'abonnés pour 100 habitants se calcule en divisant le nombre d'abonnés par la population et en multipliant par 100.

*Tableau 18*: Un certain nombre d'utilisateurs de l'Internet y accèdent sans payer directement, soit en tant que membres d'un ménage, soit parce qu'ils l'utilisent au travail ou à l'école. C'est pourquoi le nombre d'utilisateurs de l'Internet sera toujours bien supérieur au nombre d'abonnés, générale-

measured in a growing number of countries through regular surveys. In situations where surveys are not available, an estimate can be derived based on the number of subscribers. The number of users per 100 inhabitants is calculated by dividing the number of users by the population and multiplying by 100.

ment de deux à trois fois dans les pays développés et plus encore dans les pays en développement. Le nombre d'utilisateurs d'internet est recensé à l'aide d'enquêtes standards dans un nombre croissant de pays. Quand les enquêtes ne sont pas disponibles, il est estimé grâce au nombre d'abonnés. Le nombre d'utilisateurs pour 100 habitants est calculé en divisant le nombre d'utilisateurs par le nombre d'habitants, multiplié par 100.

## PART THREE
# Economic activity

## TROISIÈME PARTIE
# Activité économique

Part Three of the *Yearbook* presents statistical series on production and consumption for a wide range of economic activities, and other basic series on major economic topics, for all countries or areas of the world for which data are available. Included are basic tables on national accounts, finance, labour force, wages and prices, a wide range of agricultural, mined and manufactured commodities, energy, environment and research and development personnel and expenditure.

International economic topics such as external trade are covered in Part Four.

La troisième partie de l'*Annuaire* présente, pour une large gamme d'activités économiques, des séries statistiques sur la production et la consommation, et, pour tous les pays ou zones du monde pour lesquels des données sont disponibles, d'autres séries fondamentales ayant trait à des questions économiques importantes. Y figurent des tableaux de base consacrés à la comptabilité nationale, aux finances, à la main-d'œuvre, aux salaires et aux prix, à un large éventail de produits agricoles, miniers et manufacturés, à l'énergie, à l'environnement, au personnel employé à des travaux de recherche et développement et dépenses de recherche et développement.

Les questions économiques internationales comme le commerce extérieur sont traitées dans la quatrième partie.

# 19

## Gross domestic product and gross domestic product per capita
In millions of US dollars at current and constant 1990 prices; per capita US dollars; real rates of growth

## Produit intérieur brut et produit intérieur brut par habitant
En millions de dollars E.-U. aux prix courants et constants de 1990 ; par habitant en dollars E.-U. ; taux de croissance réels

| Country or area | 2000 | 2001 | 2002 | 2003 | 2004 | 2005 | 2006 | Pays ou zone |
|---|---|---|---|---|---|---|---|---|
| **World** | | | | | | | | **Monde** |
| GDP at current prices | 31 850 291 | 31 640 017 | 32 930 150 | 37 018 681 | 41 609 769 | 44 923 470 | 48 597 903 | PIB aux prix courants |
| GDP per capita | 5 201 | 5 101 | 5 243 | 5 822 | 6 465 | 6 896 | 7 372 | PIB par habitant |
| GDP at constant prices | 29 066 127 | 29 564 323 | 30 138 082 | 30 972 484 | 32 208 859 | 33 336 142 | 34 694 120 | PIB aux prix constants |
| Growth rates | 4.2 | 1.7 | 1.9 | 2.8 | 4.0 | 3.5 | 4.1 | Taux de croissance |
| **Afghanistan** | | | | | | | | **Afghanistan** |
| GDP at current prices | 2 963 | 2 221 | 4 741 | 4 786 | 5 700 | 6 840 | 8 309 | PIB aux prix courants |
| GDP per capita | 143 | 104 | 213 | 207 | 237 | 273 | 319 | PIB par habitant |
| GDP at constant prices | 2 539 | 2 300 | 3 207 | 3 666 | 4 012 | 4 595 | 5 105 | PIB aux prix constants |
| Growth rates | -33.6 | -9.4 | 39.5 | 14.3 | 9.4 | 14.5 | 11.1 | Taux de croissance |
| **Albania** | | | | | | | | **Albanie** |
| GDP at current prices | 3 709 | 4 114 | 4 505 | 5 859 | 7 549 | 8 488 | 9 290 | PIB aux prix courants |
| GDP per capita | 1 204 | 1 333 | 1 454 | 1 881 | 2 408 | 2 691 | 2 929 | PIB par habitant |
| GDP at constant prices | 2 444 | 2 618 | 2 731 | 2 886 | 3 079 | 3 252 | 3 595 | PIB aux prix constants |
| Growth rates | 6.6 | 7.1 | 4.3 | 5.7 | 6.7 | 5.6 | 10.5 | Taux de croissance |
| **Algeria** | | | | | | | | **Algérie** |
| GDP at current prices | 54 790 | 55 181 | 56 948 | 68 017 | 85 032 | 102 334 | 115 945 | PIB aux prix courants |
| GDP per capita | 1 796 | 1 783 | 1 813 | 2 133 | 2 627 | 3 115 | 3 476 | PIB par habitant |
| GDP at constant prices | 73 277 | 75 183 | 78 265 | 83 983 | 88 350 | 93 033 | 95 532 | PIB aux prix constants |
| Growth rates | 2.4 | 2.6 | 4.1 | 7.3 | 5.2 | 5.3 | 2.7 | Taux de croissance |
| **Andorra** | | | | | | | | **Andorre** |
| GDP at current prices | 1 360 | 1 538 | 1 809 | 2 378 | 2 786 | 3 050 | 3 337 | PIB aux prix courants |
| GDP per capita | 20 470 | 22 783 | 26 206 | 33 623 | 38 535 | 41 503 | 44 962 | PIB par habitant |
| GDP at constant prices | 1 618 | 1 833 | 1 982 | 2 112 | 2 176 | 2 304 | 2 423 | PIB aux prix constants |
| Growth rates | 5.0 | 13.3 | 8.1 | 6.6 | 3.0 | 5.9 | 5.2 | Taux de croissance |
| **Angola** | | | | | | | | **Angola** |
| GDP at current prices | 9 130 | 8 936 | 11 432 | 13 956 | 19 775 | 32 811 | 47 268 | PIB aux prix courants |
| GDP per capita | 655 | 624 | 776 | 919 | 1 265 | 2 039 | 2 855 | PIB par habitant |
| GDP at constant prices | 11 677 | 12 044 | 13 794 | 14 250 | 15 844 | 19 110 | 21 838 | PIB aux prix constants |
| Growth rates | 3.0 | 3.1 | 14.5 | 3.3 | 11.2 | 20.6 | 14.3 | Taux de croissance |
| **Anguilla** | | | | | | | | **Anguilla** |
| GDP at current prices | 108 | 110 | 113 | 118 | 149 | 168 | 201 | PIB aux prix courants |
| GDP per capita | 9 617 | 9 639 | 9 716 | 9 934 | 12 360 | 13 703 | 16 183 | PIB par habitant |
| GDP at constant prices | 85 | 88 | 86 | 89 | 108 | 117 | 117 | PIB aux prix constants |
| Growth rates | 1.3 | 2.6 | -1.4 | 2.6 | 21.6 | 8.8 | 0.1 | Taux de croissance |
| **Antigua and Barbuda** | | | | | | | | **Antigua-et-Barbuda** |
| GDP at current prices | 665 | 697 | 715 | 754 | 819 | 870 | 962 | PIB aux prix courants |
| GDP per capita | 8 665 | 8 909 | 8 977 | 9 334 | 9 988 | 10 481 | 11 437 | PIB par habitant |
| GDP at constant prices | 534 | 546 | 560 | 589 | 632 | 661 | 714 | PIB aux prix constants |
| Growth rates | 1.5 | 2.2 | 2.5 | 5.2 | 7.2 | 4.6 | 8.0 | Taux de croissance |
| **Argentina** | | | | | | | | **Argentine** |
| GDP at current prices | 284 346 | 268 831 | 102 042 | 129 596 | 153 129 | 183 196 | 216 324 | PIB aux prix courants |
| GDP per capita | 7 707 | 7 212 | 2 711 | 3 410 | 3 991 | 4 728 | 5 528 | PIB par habitant |
| GDP at constant prices | 213 758 | 204 333 | 182 072 | 198 162 | 216 055 | 235 887 | 254 707 | PIB aux prix constants |
| Growth rates | -0.8 | -4.4 | -10.9 | 8.8 | 9.0 | 9.2 | 8.0 | Taux de croissance |
| **Armenia** | | | | | | | | **Arménie** |
| GDP at current prices | 1 912 | 2 118 | 2 376 | 2 807 | 3 577 | 4 903 | 6 406 | PIB aux prix courants |
| GDP per capita | 620 | 691 | 779 | 924 | 1 182 | 1 625 | 2 128 | PIB par habitant |
| GDP at constant prices | 1 463 | 1 604 | 1 815 | 2 069 | 2 514 | 3 047 | 3 563 | PIB aux prix constants |
| Growth rates | 5.9 | 9.6 | 13.2 | 14.0 | 21.5 | 21.2 | 16.9 | Taux de croissance |
| **Aruba** | | | | | | | | **Aruba** |
| GDP at current prices | 1 859 | 1 899 | 1 911 | 2 011 | 2 134 | 2 258 | 2 380 | PIB aux prix courants |
| GDP per capita | 20 576 | 20 492 | 20 009 | 20 410 | 21 103 | 21 940 | 22 934 | PIB par habitant |
| GDP at constant prices | 1 408 | 1 397 | 1 362 | 1 383 | 1 432 | 1 465 | 1 500 | PIB aux prix constants |
| Growth rates | 3.7 | -0.7 | -2.6 | 1.5 | 3.5 | 2.3 | 2.4 | Taux de croissance |

**Gross domestic product and gross domestic product per capita**—In millions of US dollars at current and constant 1990 prices; per capita US dollars; real rates of growth (*continued*)

**Produit intérieur brut et produit intérieur brut par habitant**—En millions de dollars E.-U. aux prix courants et constants de 1990; par habitant en dollars E.-U. ; taux de croissance réels (*suite*)

| Country or area | 2000 | 2001 | 2002 | 2003 | 2004 | 2005 | 2006 | Pays ou zone |
|---|---|---|---|---|---|---|---|---|
| **Australia** | | | | | | | | **Australie** |
| GDP at current prices | 399 612 | 380 520 | 424 694 | 544 962 | 659 361 | 737 677 | 778 601 | PIB aux prix courants |
| GDP per capita | 20 880 | 19 648 | 21 664 | 27 462 | 32 835 | 36 321 | 37 924 | PIB par habitant |
| GDP at constant prices | 453 889 | 470 982 | 485 829 | 505 518 | 519 048 | 533 625 | 555 991 | PIB aux prix constants |
| Growth rates | 2.0 | 3.8 | 3.2 | 4.1 | 2.7 | 2.8 | 4.2 | Taux de croissance |
| **Austria** | | | | | | | | **Autriche** |
| GDP at current prices | 193 838 | 193 178 | 207 840 | 255 343 | 292 810 | 304 809 | 321 730 | PIB aux prix courants |
| GDP per capita | 23 897 | 23 740 | 25 434 | 31 094 | 35 478 | 36 759 | 38 635 | PIB par habitant |
| GDP at constant prices | 212 260 | 214 025 | 215 859 | 218 209 | 223 537 | 228 106 | 235 198 | PIB aux prix constants |
| Growth rates | 3.4 | 0.8 | 0.9 | 1.1 | 2.4 | 2.0 | 3.1 | Taux de croissance |
| **Azerbaijan** | | | | | | | | **Azerbaïdjan** |
| GDP at current prices | 5 273 | 5 708 | 6 236 | 7 276 | 8 680 | 13 245 | 19 851 | PIB aux prix courants |
| GDP per capita | 647 | 697 | 758 | 880 | 1 045 | 1 586 | 2 362 | PIB par habitant |
| GDP at constant prices | 3 835 | 4 214 | 4 660 | 5 179 | 5 705 | 7 214 | 9 701 | PIB aux prix constants |
| Growth rates | 11.1 | 9.9 | 10.6 | 11.2 | 10.2 | 26.5 | 34.5 | Taux de croissance |
| **Bahamas** | | | | | | | | **Bahamas** |
| GDP at current prices | 5 004 | 5 131 | 5 389 | 5 503 | 5 661 | 5 869 | 6 207 | PIB aux prix courants |
| GDP per capita | 16 506 | 16 697 | 17 307 | 17 448 | 17 728 | 18 155 | 18 965 | PIB par habitant |
| GDP at constant prices | 3 902 | 3 934 | 4 023 | 4 081 | 4 155 | 4 268 | 4 436 | PIB aux prix constants |
| Growth rates | 1.9 | 0.8 | 2.3 | 1.5 | 1.8 | 2.7 | 3.9 | Taux de croissance |
| **Bahrain** | | | | | | | | **Bahreïn** |
| GDP at current prices | 7 971 | 7 928 | 8 447 | 9 699 | 11 013 | 13 381 | 16 069 | PIB aux prix courants |
| GDP per capita | 12 261 | 11 924 | 12 422 | 13 952 | 15 507 | 18 462 | 21 747 | PIB par habitant |
| GDP at constant prices | 6 998 | 7 321 | 7 702 | 8 253 | 8 702 | 9 392 | 10 119 | PIB aux prix constants |
| Growth rates | 5.3 | 4.6 | 5.2 | 7.2 | 5.4 | 7.9 | 7.7 | Taux de croissance |
| **Bangladesh** | | | | | | | | **Bangladesh** |
| GDP at current prices | 48 626 | 48 955 | 51 924 | 57 261 | 61 916 | 64 693 | 68 220 | PIB aux prix courants |
| GDP per capita | 349 | 344 | 358 | 388 | 411 | 422 | 437 | PIB par habitant |
| GDP at constant prices | 51 416 | 53 687 | 56 508 | 60 052 | 63 280 | 67 519 | 71 908 | PIB aux prix constants |
| Growth rates | 5.3 | 4.4 | 5.3 | 6.3 | 5.4 | 6.7 | 6.5 | Taux de croissance |
| **Barbados** | | | | | | | | **Barbade** |
| GDP at current prices | 2 559 | 2 554 | 2 476 | 2 695 | 2 816 | 3 062 | 3 446 | PIB aux prix courants |
| GDP per capita | 8 933 | 8 881 | 8 576 | 9 298 | 9 681 | 10 488 | 11 765 | PIB par habitant |
| GDP at constant prices | 1 950 | 1 899 | 1 908 | 1 946 | 2 018 | 2 097 | 2 185 | PIB aux prix constants |
| Growth rates | 2.3 | -2.6 | 0.5 | 2.0 | 3.7 | 3.9 | 4.2 | Taux de croissance |
| **Belarus** | | | | | | | | **Bélarus** |
| GDP at current prices | 10 418 | 12 355 | 14 595 | 17 825 | 23 142 | 30 210 | 36 945 | PIB aux prix courants |
| GDP per capita | 1 036 | 1 235 | 1 467 | 1 801 | 2 350 | 3 084 | 3 792 | PIB par habitant |
| GDP at constant prices | 16 673 | 17 461 | 18 336 | 19 618 | 21 860 | 23 924 | 26 303 | PIB aux prix constants |
| Growth rates | 5.8 | 4.7 | 5.0 | 7.0 | 11.4 | 9.4 | 9.9 | Taux de croissance |
| **Belgium** | | | | | | | | **Belgique** |
| GDP at current prices | 231 934 | 231 661 | 251 826 | 309 900 | 357 712 | 370 815 | 392 706 | PIB aux prix courants |
| GDP per capita | 22 754 | 22 648 | 24 518 | 30 040 | 34 529 | 35 662 | 37 651 | PIB par habitant |
| GDP at constant prices | 250 202 | 252 824 | 256 624 | 258 971 | 265 678 | 268 992 | 276 284 | PIB aux prix constants |
| Growth rates | 3.9 | 1.1 | 1.5 | 0.9 | 2.6 | 1.3 | 2.7 | Taux de croissance |
| **Belize** | | | | | | | | **Belize** |
| GDP at current prices | 832 | 871 | 932 | 988 | 1 055 | 1 111 | 1 217 | PIB aux prix courants |
| GDP per capita | 3 400 | 3 473 | 3 626 | 3 752 | 3 917 | 4 032 | 4 320 | PIB par habitant |
| GDP at constant prices | 615 | 645 | 671 | 734 | 768 | 792 | 834 | PIB aux prix constants |
| Growth rates | 7.5 | 4.9 | 4.1 | 9.4 | 4.7 | 3.1 | 5.3 | Taux de croissance |
| **Benin** | | | | | | | | **Bénin** |
| GDP at current prices | 2 359 | 2 499 | 2 808 | 3 557 | 4 051 | 4 358 | 4 694 | PIB aux prix courants |
| GDP per capita | 326 | 335 | 364 | 447 | 493 | 513 | 536 | PIB par habitant |
| GDP at constant prices | 2 871 | 3 051 | 3 186 | 3 309 | 3 413 | 3 510 | 3 637 | PIB aux prix constants |
| Growth rates | 4.9 | 6.3 | 4.4 | 3.9 | 3.1 | 2.9 | 3.6 | Taux de croissance |
| **Bermuda** | | | | | | | | **Bermudes** |
| GDP at current prices | 3 476 | 3 622 | 3 924 | 4 176 | 4 450 | 4 857 | 5 194 | PIB aux prix courants |
| GDP per capita | 55 294 | 57 360 | 61 870 | 65 566 | 69 592 | 75 685 | 80 676 | PIB par habitant |
| GDP at constant prices | 2 615 | 2 617 | 2 783 | 2 865 | 2 966 | 3 102 | 3 210 | PIB aux prix constants |
| Growth rates | 3.1 | 0.1 | 6.4 | 2.9 | 3.5 | 4.6 | 3.5 | Taux de croissance |

**19** Gross domestic product and gross domestic product per capita—In millions of US dollars at current and constant 1990 prices; per capita US dollars; real rates of growth (*continued*)

Produit intérieur brut et produit intérieur brut par habitant—En millions de dollars E.-U. aux prix courants et constants de 1990 ; par habitant en dollars E.U. ; taux de croissance réels (*suite*)

| Country or area | 2000 | 2001 | 2002 | 2003 | 2004 | 2005 | 2006 | Pays ou zone |
|---|---|---|---|---|---|---|---|---|
| **Bhutan** | | | | | | | | **Bhoutan** |
| GDP at current prices | 446 | 484 | 540 | 628 | 710 | 837 | 922 | PIB aux prix courants |
| GDP per capita | 799 | 843 | 914 | 1 034 | 1 140 | 1 314 | 1 422 | PIB par habitant |
| GDP at constant prices | 466 | 500 | 550 | 591 | 631 | 672 | 729 | PIB aux prix constants |
| Growth rates | 7.6 | 7.2 | 10.0 | 7.6 | 6.8 | 6.5 | 8.5 | Taux de croissance |
| **Bolivia** | | | | | | | | **Bolivie** |
| GDP at current prices | 8 398 | 8 142 | 7 924 | 8 089 | 8 773 | 9 441 | 10 301 | PIB aux prix courants |
| GDP per capita | 1 010 | 959 | 915 | 916 | 974 | 1 028 | 1 101 | PIB par habitant |
| GDP at constant prices | 7 047 | 7 165 | 7 340 | 7 544 | 7 814 | 8 175 | 8 510 | PIB aux prix constants |
| Growth rates | 2.5 | 1.7 | 2.4 | 2.8 | 3.6 | 4.6 | 4.1 | Taux de croissance |
| **Bosnia and Herzegovina** | | | | | | | | **Bosnie-Herzégovine** |
| GDP at current prices | 5 047 | 5 307 | 6 173 | 7 757 | 9 318 | 10 040 | 11 326 | PIB aux prix courants |
| GDP per capita | 1 333 | 1 380 | 1 591 | 1 991 | 2 386 | 2 564 | 2 885 | PIB par habitant |
| GDP at constant prices | 20 457 | 18 870 | 17 327 | 15 829 | 14 623 | 15 398 | 16 245 | PIB aux prix constants |
| Growth rates | 5.4 | -7.8 | -8.2 | -8.7 | -7.6 | 5.3 | 5.5 | Taux de croissance |
| **Botswana** | | | | | | | | **Botswana** |
| GDP at current prices | 4 889 | 4 903 | 5 045 | 7 341 | 8 498 | 8 935 | 8 836 | PIB aux prix courants |
| GDP per capita | 2 828 | 2 796 | 2 842 | 4 089 | 4 682 | 4 867 | 4 755 | PIB par habitant |
| GDP at constant prices | 5 774 | 6 265 | 6 406 | 6 834 | 7 288 | 7 899 | 8 227 | PIB aux prix constants |
| Growth rates | 6.6 | 8.5 | 2.2 | 6.7 | 6.6 | 8.4 | 4.2 | Taux de croissance |
| **Brazil** | | | | | | | | **Brésil** |
| GDP at current prices | 601 732 | 508 433 | 460 838 | 505 732 | 603 948 | 795 925 | 1 067 803 | PIB aux prix courants |
| GDP per capita | 3 455 | 2 877 | 2 571 | 2 782 | 3 277 | 4 260 | 5 640 | PIB par habitant |
| GDP at constant prices | 568 704 | 576 169 | 587 271 | 590 471 | 619 618 | 633 727 | 657 192 | PIB aux prix constants |
| Growth rates | 4.4 | 1.3 | 1.9 | 0.5 | 4.9 | 2.3 | 3.7 | Taux de croissance |
| **British Virgin Islands** | | | | | | | | **Iles Vierges britanniques** |
| GDP at current prices[1] | 784 | 839 | 813 | 782 | 873 | 972 | 1 034 | PIB aux prix courants[1] |
| GDP per capita | 38 203 | 40 207 | 38 385 | 36 425 | 40 147 | 44 150 | 46 407 | PIB par habitant |
| GDP at constant prices | 819 | 850 | 820 | 762 | 842 | 919 | 957 | PIB aux prix constants |
| Growth rates | 13.7 | 3.8 | -3.5 | -7.2 | 10.5 | 9.2 | 4.2 | Taux de croissance |
| **Brunei Darussalam** | | | | | | | | **Brunéi Darussalam** |
| GDP at current prices | 6 001 | 5 601 | 5 843 | 6 557 | 7 872 | 9 531 | 11 481 | PIB aux prix courants |
| GDP per capita | 17 997 | 16 404 | 16 721 | 18 339 | 21 527 | 25 497 | 30 058 | PIB par habitant |
| GDP at constant prices | 4 241 | 4 357 | 4 526 | 4 658 | 4 681 | 4 699 | 4 875 | PIB aux prix constants |
| Growth rates | 2.9 | 2.8 | 3.9 | 2.9 | 0.5 | 0.4 | 3.7 | Taux de croissance |
| **Bulgaria** | | | | | | | | **Bulgarie** |
| GDP at current prices | 12 600 | 13 599 | 15 568 | 19 938 | 24 300 | 26 648 | 30 434 | PIB aux prix courants |
| GDP per capita | 1 574 | 1 711 | 1 972 | 2 542 | 3 117 | 3 441 | 3 956 | PIB par habitant |
| GDP at constant prices | 17 419 | 18 128 | 19 014 | 19 861 | 20 999 | 22 163 | 22 763 | PIB aux prix constants |
| Growth rates | 5.4 | 4.1 | 4.9 | 4.5 | 5.7 | 5.5 | 2.7 | Taux de croissance |
| **Burkina Faso** | | | | | | | | **Burkina Faso** |
| GDP at current prices | 2 415 | 2 635 | 3 006 | 4 028 | 4 945 | 5 397 | 5 976 | PIB aux prix courants |
| GDP per capita | 203 | 215 | 237 | 308 | 366 | 387 | 416 | PIB par habitant |
| GDP at constant prices | 4 932 | 5 232 | 5 473 | 5 905 | 6 295 | 6 665 | 7 057 | PIB aux prix constants |
| Growth rates | -4.9 | 6.1 | 4.6 | 7.9 | 6.6 | 5.9 | 5.9 | Taux de croissance |
| **Burundi** | | | | | | | | **Burundi** |
| GDP at current prices | 709 | 662 | 628 | 595 | 680 | 797 | 932 | PIB aux prix courants |
| GDP per capita | 106 | 97 | 89 | 82 | 90 | 101 | 114 | PIB par habitant |
| GDP at constant prices | 970 | 991 | 1 035 | 1 023 | 1 068 | 1 077 | 1 143 | PIB aux prix constants |
| Growth rates | -0.9 | 2.1 | 4.5 | -1.2 | 4.4 | 0.9 | 6.1 | Taux de croissance |
| **Cambodia** | | | | | | | | **Cambodge** |
| GDP at current prices | 3 668 | 3 794 | 4 088 | 4 357 | 5 264 | 6 194 | 6 431 | PIB aux prix courants |
| GDP per capita | 287 | 291 | 308 | 323 | 384 | 444 | 453 | PIB par habitant |
| GDP at constant prices | 3 285 | 3 466 | 3 647 | 3 905 | 4 485 | 5 086 | 5 452 | PIB aux prix constants |
| Growth rates | 8.4 | 5.5 | 5.3 | 7.1 | 14.9 | 13.4 | 7.2 | Taux de croissance |
| **Cameroon** | | | | | | | | **Cameroun** |
| GDP at current prices | 9 287 | 9 633 | 10 880 | 13 723 | 15 775 | 16 985 | 18 526 | PIB aux prix courants |
| GDP per capita | 586 | 593 | 654 | 806 | 906 | 954 | 1 019 | PIB par habitant |
| GDP at constant prices | 17 621 | 18 417 | 19 155 | 19 959 | 20 980 | 21 526 | 22 428 | PIB aux prix constants |
| Growth rates | 4.6 | 4.5 | 4.0 | 4.2 | 5.1 | 2.6 | 4.2 | Taux de croissance |

**19** Gross domestic product and gross domestic product per capita — In millions of US dollars at current and constant 1990 prices; per capita US dollars; real rates of growth *(continued)*

**Produit intérieur brut et produit intérieur brut par habitant** — En millions de dollars E.-U. aux prix courants et constants de 1990 ; par habitant en dollars E.-U. ; taux de croissance réels *(suite)*

| Country or area | 2000 | 2001 | 2002 | 2003 | 2004 | 2005 | 2006 | Pays ou zone |
|---|---|---|---|---|---|---|---|---|
| **Canada** | | | | | | | | **Canada** |
| GDP at current prices | 724 916 | 715 443 | 734 657 | 866 071 | 992 138 | 1 131 764 | 1 270 625 | PIB aux prix courants |
| GDP per capita | 23 621 | 23 085 | 23 465 | 27 379 | 31 048 | 35 071 | 39 004 | PIB par habitant |
| GDP at constant prices | 777 038 | 790 904 | 814 188 | 829 029 | 856 379 | 881 522 | 908 874 | PIB aux prix constants |
| Growth rates | 5.2 | 1.8 | 2.9 | 1.8 | 3.3 | 2.9 | 3.1 | Taux de croissance |
| **Cape Verde** | | | | | | | | **Cap-Vert** |
| GDP at current prices | 539 | 563 | 621 | 814 | 925 | 983 | 1 116 | PIB aux prix courants |
| GDP per capita | 1 197 | 1 220 | 1 315 | 1 683 | 1 867 | 1 940 | 2 153 | PIB par habitant |
| GDP at constant prices | 593 | 630 | 663 | 694 | 724 | 766 | 808 | PIB aux prix constants |
| Growth rates | 7.3 | 6.1 | 5.3 | 4.7 | 4.4 | 5.8 | 5.5 | Taux de croissance |
| **Cayman Islands** | | | | | | | | **Iles Caïmanes** |
| GDP at current prices | 1 734 | 1 779 | 1 855 | 1 924 | 2 027 | 2 309 | 2 447 | PIB aux prix courants |
| GDP per capita | 43 097 | 42 868 | 43 499 | 44 018 | 45 355 | 50 655 | 52 707 | PIB par habitant |
| GDP at constant prices | 1 289 | 1 296 | 1 318 | 1 344 | 1 356 | 1 445 | 1 505 | PIB aux prix constants |
| Growth rates | 1.0 | 0.6 | 1.7 | 2.0 | 0.9 | 6.5 | 4.2 | Taux de croissance |
| **Central African Rep.** | | | | | | | | **Rép. centrafricaine** |
| GDP at current prices | 906 | 928 | 984 | 1 126 | 1 239 | 1 320 | 1 418 | PIB aux prix courants |
| GDP per capita | 234 | 236 | 246 | 277 | 300 | 315 | 333 | PIB par habitant |
| GDP at constant prices | 1 453 | 1 457 | 1 448 | 1 338 | 1 355 | 1 385 | 1 430 | PIB aux prix constants |
| Growth rates | 1.8 | 0.3 | -0.6 | -7.6 | 1.3 | 2.2 | 3.2 | Taux de croissance |
| **Chad** | | | | | | | | **Tchad** |
| GDP at current prices | 1 385 | 1 710 | 1 987 | 2 723 | 4 415 | 5 885 | 6 637 | PIB aux prix courants |
| GDP per capita | 164 | 195 | 218 | 288 | 450 | 580 | 634 | PIB par habitant |
| GDP at constant prices | 2 172 | 2 422 | 2 629 | 3 004 | 4 016 | 4 360 | 4 485 | PIB aux prix constants |
| Growth rates | -0.5 | 11.5 | 8.5 | 14.3 | 33.7 | 8.6 | 2.9 | Taux de croissance |
| **Chile** | | | | | | | | **Chili** |
| GDP at current prices | 75 197 | 68 568 | 67 266 | 73 986 | 95 844 | 118 908 | 145 841 | PIB aux prix courants |
| GDP per capita | 4 879 | 4 396 | 4 264 | 4 638 | 5 944 | 7 297 | 8 857 | PIB par habitant |
| GDP at constant prices | 62 293 | 64 397 | 65 803 | 68 381 | 72 472 | 76 614 | 79 652 | PIB aux prix constants |
| Growth rates | 4.5 | 3.4 | 2.2 | 3.9 | 6.0 | 5.7 | 4.0 | Taux de croissance |
| **China[2]** | | | | | | | | **Chine[2]** |
| GDP at current prices | 1 192 836 | 1 316 558 | 1 454 040 | 1 647 918 | 1 936 502 | 2 278 419 | 2 666 772 | PIB aux prix courants |
| GDP per capita | 956 | 1 047 | 1 149 | 1 293 | 1 510 | 1 766 | 2 055 | PIB par habitant |
| GDP at constant prices | 1 090 368 | 1 180 869 | 1 288 328 | 1 417 161 | 1 560 294 | 1 719 444 | 1 903 424 | PIB aux prix constants |
| Growth rates | 8.4 | 8.3 | 9.1 | 10.0 | 10.1 | 10.2 | 10.7 | Taux de croissance |
| **China, Hong Kong SAR** | | | | | | | | **Chine, Hong Kong RAS** |
| GDP at current prices | 168 754 | 166 541 | 163 710 | 158 364 | 165 743 | 177 783 | 189 537 | PIB aux prix courants |
| GDP per capita | 25 330 | 24 689 | 23 982 | 22 935 | 23 740 | 25 191 | 26 575 | PIB par habitant |
| GDP at constant prices | 119 628 | 120 390 | 122 604 | 126 452 | 136 857 | 147 715 | 157 796 | PIB aux prix constants |
| Growth rates | 10.0 | 0.6 | 1.8 | 3.1 | 8.2 | 7.9 | 6.8 | Taux de croissance |
| **China, Macao SAR** | | | | | | | | **Chine, Macao RAS** |
| GDP at current prices | 6 102 | 6 187 | 6 824 | 7 925 | 10 359 | 11 603 | 14 293 | PIB aux prix courants |
| GDP per capita | 13 834 | 13 824 | 15 016 | 17 179 | 22 152 | 24 526 | 29 931 | PIB par habitant |
| GDP at constant prices | 3 893 | 4 005 | 4 410 | 5 035 | 6 475 | 6 910 | 8 057 | PIB aux prix constants |
| Growth rates | 5.8 | 2.9 | 10.1 | 14.2 | 28.6 | 6.7 | 16.6 | Taux de croissance |
| **Colombia** | | | | | | | | **Colombie** |
| GDP at current prices | 83 766 | 81 995 | 81 243 | 79 411 | 98 054 | 123 120 | 130 928 | PIB aux prix courants |
| GDP per capita | 2 010 | 1 936 | 1 889 | 1 818 | 2 213 | 2 739 | 2 874 | PIB par habitant |
| GDP at constant prices | 62 016 | 62 928 | 64 145 | 66 620 | 69 862 | 73 536 | 77 066 | PIB aux prix constants |
| Growth rates | 2.9 | 1.5 | 1.9 | 3.9 | 4.9 | 5.3 | 4.8 | Taux de croissance |
| **Comoros** | | | | | | | | **Comores** |
| GDP at current prices | 204 | 220 | 247 | 318 | 369 | 382 | 398 | PIB aux prix courants |
| GDP per capita | 292 | 306 | 334 | 419 | 475 | 479 | 486 | PIB par habitant |
| GDP at constant prices | 282 | 288 | 295 | 301 | 307 | 316 | 320 | PIB aux prix constants |
| Growth rates | 1.9 | 2.3 | 2.3 | 2.1 | 1.9 | 2.8 | 1.2 | Taux de croissance |
| **Congo** | | | | | | | | **Congo** |
| GDP at current prices | 3 220 | 2 794 | 3 018 | 3 564 | 4 384 | 5 794 | 7 178 | PIB aux prix courants |
| GDP per capita | 1 005 | 851 | 896 | 1 033 | 1 242 | 1 605 | 1 946 | PIB par habitant |
| GDP at constant prices | 3 255 | 3 379 | 3 534 | 3 562 | 3 704 | 4 036 | 4 336 | PIB aux prix constants |
| Growth rates | 7.6 | 3.8 | 4.6 | 0.8 | 4.0 | 9.0 | 7.4 | Taux de croissance |

**19**

Gross domestic product and gross domestic product per capita—In millions of US dollars at current and constant 1990 prices; per capita US dollars; real rates of growth (*continued*)

**Produit intérieur brut et produit intérieur brut par habitant**—En millions de dollars E.-U. aux prix courants et constants de 1990 ; par habitant en dollars E.-U. ; taux de croissance réels (*suite*)

| Country or area | 2000 | 2001 | 2002 | 2003 | 2004 | 2005 | 2006 | Pays ou zone |
|---|---|---|---|---|---|---|---|---|
| **Cook Islands** | | | | | | | | **Iles Cook** |
| GDP at current prices | 81 | 86 | 102 | 143 | 171 | 183 | 177 | PIB aux prix courants |
| GDP per capita | 5 055 | 5 565 | 6 748 | 9 705 | 11 940 | 13 098 | 13 005 | PIB par habitant |
| GDP at constant prices | 78 | 82 | 84 | 90 | 94 | 94 | 96 | PIB aux prix constants |
| Growth rates | 13.9 | 4.9 | 2.6 | 8.2 | 4.3 | 0.1 | 1.8 | Taux de croissance |
| **Costa Rica** | | | | | | | | **Costa Rica** |
| GDP at current prices | 15 946 | 16 403 | 16 844 | 17 514 | 18 593 | 19 973 | 22 145 | PIB aux prix courants |
| GDP per capita | 4 059 | 4 086 | 4 111 | 4 194 | 4 372 | 4 616 | 5 034 | PIB par habitant |
| GDP at constant prices | 12 041 | 12 171 | 12 523 | 13 324 | 13 897 | 14 718 | 15 878 | PIB aux prix constants |
| Growth rates | 1.8 | 1.1 | 2.9 | 6.4 | 4.3 | 5.9 | 7.9 | Taux de croissance |
| **Côte d'Ivoire** | | | | | | | | **Côte d'Ivoire** |
| GDP at current prices | 10 682 | 10 735 | 11 692 | 14 255 | 16 064 | 16 960 | 18 014 | PIB aux prix courants |
| GDP per capita | 627 | 618 | 661 | 793 | 879 | 913 | 952 | PIB par habitant |
| GDP at constant prices | 15 156 | 15 156 | 15 154 | 15 152 | 15 419 | 15 706 | 16 009 | PIB aux prix constants |
| Growth rates | -2.7 | 0.0 | 0.0 | 0.0 | 1.8 | 1.9 | 1.9 | Taux de croissance |
| **Croatia** | | | | | | | | **Croatie** |
| GDP at current prices | 18 425 | 19 857 | 23 023 | 29 593 | 35 269 | 38 498 | 42 240 | PIB aux prix courants |
| GDP per capita | 4 089 | 4 414 | 5 110 | 6 544 | 7 769 | 8 458 | 9 271 | PIB par habitant |
| GDP at constant prices | 21 232 | 22 176 | 23 332 | 24 329 | 25 253 | 26 339 | 27 519 | PIB aux prix constants |
| Growth rates | 2.9 | 4.4 | 5.2 | 4.3 | 3.8 | 4.3 | 4.5 | Taux de croissance |
| **Cuba** | | | | | | | | **Cuba** |
| GDP at current prices | 32 685 | 33 820 | 36 089 | 38 625 | 41 065 | 46 084 | 52 393 | PIB aux prix courants |
| GDP per capita | 2 933 | 3 027 | 3 221 | 3 440 | 3 651 | 4 093 | 4 650 | PIB par habitant |
| GDP at constant prices | 26 635 | 27 434 | 27 927 | 28 989 | 30 554 | 34 173 | 38 441 | PIB aux prix constants |
| Growth rates | 6.1 | 3.0 | 1.8 | 3.8 | 5.4 | 11.8 | 12.5 | Taux de croissance |
| **Cyprus** | | | | | | | | **Chypre** |
| GDP at current prices | *9 294 | *9 672 | 10 507 | 13 269 | 15 770 | *16 941 | 18 221 | PIB aux prix courants |
| GDP per capita | 13 399 | 13 792 | 14 808 | 18 414 | 21 395 | 22 349 | 23 774 | PIB par habitant |
| GDP at constant prices | *8 977 | *9 335 | 9 519 | 9 693 | 10 098 | *10 490 | 10 887 | PIB aux prix constants |
| Growth rates | 5.0 | 4.0 | 2.0 | 1.8 | 4.2 | 3.9 | 3.8 | Taux de croissance |
| **Czech Republic** | | | | | | | | **République tchèque** |
| GDP at current prices | 56 717 | 61 843 | 75 276 | 91 358 | 108 214 | 123 981 | 141 249 | PIB aux prix courants |
| GDP per capita | 5 549 | 6 058 | 7 379 | 8 959 | 10 615 | 12 165 | 13 863 | PIB par habitant |
| GDP at constant prices | 37 989 | 38 922 | 39 660 | 41 089 | 42 821 | 45 424 | 48 149 | PIB aux prix constants |
| Growth rates | 3.7 | 2.5 | 1.9 | 3.6 | 4.2 | 6.1 | 6.0 | Taux de croissance |
| **Dem. Rep. of the Congo** | | | | | | | | **Rép. dém. du Congo** |
| GDP at current prices | 5 256[3] | 5 270[3] | 5 548 | 5 636 | 6 591 | 7 102 | 8 261 | PIB aux prix courants |
| GDP per capita | 104[3] | 101[3] | 104 | 102 | 116 | 121 | 136 | PIB par habitant |
| GDP at constant prices | 4 696[3] | 4 598[3] | 4 757 | 5 032 | 5 367 | 5 713 | 6 085 | PIB aux prix constants |
| Growth rates | -6.9 | -2.1 | 3.5 | 5.8 | 6.6 | 6.5 | 6.5 | Taux de croissance |
| **Denmark** | | | | | | | | **Danemark** |
| GDP at current prices | 160 081 | 160 476 | 173 881 | 213 909 | 244 917 | 259 140 | 277 334 | PIB aux prix courants |
| GDP per capita | 30 004 | 29 971 | 32 369 | 39 702 | 45 331 | 47 839 | 51 074 | PIB par habitant |
| GDP at constant prices | 175 528 | 176 767 | 177 590 | 178 820 | 182 166 | 187 593 | 193 244 | PIB aux prix constants |
| Growth rates | 3.5 | 0.7 | 0.5 | 0.7 | 1.9 | 3.0 | 3.0 | Taux de croissance |
| **Djibouti** | | | | | | | | **Djibouti** |
| GDP at current prices | 553 | 573 | 591 | 622 | 660 | 705 | 757 | PIB aux prix courants |
| GDP per capita | 758 | 767 | 775 | 801 | 836 | 877 | 925 | PIB par habitant |
| GDP at constant prices | 516 | 526 | 540 | 559 | 575 | 594 | 619 | PIB aux prix constants |
| Growth rates | 0.7 | 1.9 | 2.6 | 3.5 | 3.0 | 3.2 | 4.2 | Taux de croissance |
| **Dominica** | | | | | | | | **Dominique** |
| GDP at current prices | 271 | 266 | 255 | 263 | 285 | 300 | 316 | PIB aux prix courants |
| GDP per capita | 3 961 | 3 894 | 3 734 | 3 857 | 4 194 | 4 427 | 4 667 | PIB par habitant |
| GDP at constant prices | 201 | 192 | 184 | 188 | 200 | 206 | 215 | PIB aux prix constants |
| Growth rates | 1.3 | -4.6 | -4.0 | 2.2 | 6.3 | 3.3 | 4.1 | Taux de croissance |
| **Dominican Republic** | | | | | | | | **Rép. dominicaine** |
| GDP at current prices | 19 772 | 21 605 | 21 625 | 16 325 | 18 452 | 29 101 | 31 593 | PIB aux prix courants |
| GDP per capita | 2 261 | 2 430 | 2 393 | 1 778 | 1 979 | 3 073 | 3 286 | PIB par habitant |
| GDP at constant prices | 13 266 | 13 748 | 14 356 | 14 088 | 14 363 | 15 696 | 17 381 | PIB aux prix constants |
| Growth rates | 8.1 | 3.6 | 4.4 | -1.9 | 2.0 | 9.3 | 10.7 | Taux de croissance |

19 **Gross domestic product and gross domestic product per capita**—In millions of US dollars at current and constant 1990 prices; per capita US dollars; real rates of growth (*continued*)

**Produit intérieur brut et produit intérieur brut par habitant**—En millions de dollars E.-U. aux prix courants et constants de 1990 ; par habitant en dollars E.-U. ; taux de croissance réels (*suite*)

| Country or area | 2000 | 2001 | 2002 | 2003 | 2004 | 2005 | 2006 | Pays ou zone |
|---|---|---|---|---|---|---|---|---|
| **Ecuador** | | | | | | | | **Equateur** |
| GDP at current prices | 15 934 | 21 250 | 24 899 | 28 636 | 32 636 | 36 489 | 40 892 | PIB aux prix courants |
| GDP per capita | 1 295 | 1 705 | 1 973 | 2 242 | 2 526 | 2 794 | 3 097 | PIB par habitant |
| GDP at constant prices | 13 937 | 14 681 | 15 304 | 15 852 | 17 108 | 17 919 | 18 689 | PIB aux prix constants |
| Growth rates | 2.8 | 5.3 | 4.3 | 3.6 | 7.9 | 4.7 | 4.3 | Taux de croissance |
| **Egypt** | | | | | | | | **Egypte** |
| GDP at current prices | 99 601 | 94 438 | 90 064 | 77 109 | 82 429 | 101 382 | 110 075 | PIB aux prix courants |
| GDP per capita | 1 497 | 1 394 | 1 305 | 1 097 | 1 152 | 1 392 | 1 484 | PIB par habitant |
| GDP at constant prices | 62 801 | 64 801 | 67 478 | 70 258 | 73 436 | 78 462 | 83 719 | PIB aux prix constants |
| Growth rates | 3.5 | 3.2 | 4.1 | 4.1 | 4.5 | 6.8 | 6.7 | Taux de croissance |
| **El Salvador** | | | | | | | | **El Salvador** |
| GDP at current prices | 13 134 | 13 813 | 14 312 | 15 047 | 15 822 | 16 974 | 18 353 | PIB aux prix courants |
| GDP per capita | 2 120 | 2 194 | 2 239 | 2 320 | 2 406 | 2 545 | 2 714 | PIB par habitant |
| GDP at constant prices | 7 531 | 7 660 | 7 839 | 8 019 | 8 166 | 8 391 | 8 681 | PIB aux prix constants |
| Growth rates | 2.2 | 1.7 | 2.3 | 2.3 | 1.8 | 2.8 | 3.5 | Taux de croissance |
| **Equatorial Guinea** | | | | | | | | **Guinée équatoriale** |
| GDP at current prices | 1 177 | 1 695 | 2 084 | 2 825 | 4 618 | 7 295 | 9 499 | PIB aux prix courants |
| GDP per capita | 2 734 | 3 845 | 4 617 | 6 116 | 9 765 | 15 069 | 19 166 | PIB par habitant |
| GDP at constant prices | 873 | 1 465 | 1 761 | 2 000 | 2 600 | 2 842 | 2 813 | PIB aux prix constants |
| Growth rates | 13.1 | 67.8 | 20.2 | 13.6 | 30.0 | 9.3 | -1.0 | Taux de croissance |
| **Eritrea** | | | | | | | | **Erythrée** |
| GDP at current prices | 637 | 675 | 635 | 754 | 944 | 969 | 1 169 | PIB aux prix courants |
| GDP per capita | 173 | 176 | 159 | 181 | 217 | 214 | 249 | PIB par habitant |
| GDP at constant prices | 1 369 | 1 495 | 1 505 | 1 563 | 1 594 | 1 671 | 1 704 | PIB aux prix constants |
| Growth rates | -13.1 | 9.2 | 0.6 | 3.9 | 2.0 | 4.8 | 2.0 | Taux de croissance |
| **Estonia** | | | | | | | | **Estonie** |
| GDP at current prices | 5 627 | 6 192 | 7 306 | 9 592 | 11 646 | 13 753 | 16 089 | PIB aux prix courants |
| GDP per capita | 4 108 | 4 544 | 5 385 | 7 093 | 8 638 | 10 230 | 12 007 | PIB par habitant |
| GDP at constant prices | 5 208 | 5 607 | 6 056 | 6 485 | 7 008 | 7 742 | 8 588 | PIB aux prix constants |
| Growth rates | 7.9 | 7.7 | 8.0 | 7.1 | 8.1 | 10.5 | 10.9 | Taux de croissance |
| **Ethiopia** | | | | | | | | **Ethiopie** |
| GDP at current prices | 7 837 | 7 767 | 7 407 | 8 012 | 9 467 | 11 354 | 13 288 | PIB aux prix courants |
| GDP per capita | 113 | 109 | 101 | 107 | 123 | 144 | 164 | PIB par habitant |
| GDP at constant prices | 14 446 | 15 559 | 15 751 | 15 199 | 17 195 | 18 967 | 20 985 | PIB aux prix constants |
| Growth rates | 5.9 | 7.7 | 1.2 | -3.5 | 13.1 | 10.3 | 10.6 | Taux de croissance |
| **Fiji** | | | | | | | | **Fidji** |
| GDP at current prices | 1 686 | 1 662 | 1 843 | 2 309 | 2 728 | 2 998 | 3 103 | PIB aux prix courants |
| GDP per capita | 2 103 | 2 059 | 2 268 | 2 824 | 3 315 | 3 620 | 3 724 | PIB par habitant |
| GDP at constant prices | 1 687 | 1 720 | 1 775 | 1 793 | 1 888 | 1 901 | 1 966 | PIB aux prix constants |
| Growth rates | -1.7 | 2.0 | 3.2 | 1.0 | 5.3 | 0.7 | 3.4 | Taux de croissance |
| **Finland** | | | | | | | | **Finlande** |
| GDP at current prices | 121 865 | 125 160 | 135 498 | 164 709 | 188 654 | 195 713 | 209 678 | PIB aux prix courants |
| GDP per capita | 23 545 | 24 121 | 26 045 | 31 574 | 36 063 | 37 307 | 39 853 | PIB par habitant |
| GDP at constant prices | 169 585 | 174 055 | 176 915 | 180 053 | 186 369 | 191 821 | 201 550 | PIB aux prix constants |
| Growth rates | 5.0 | 2.6 | 1.6 | 1.8 | 3.5 | 2.9 | 5.1 | **Taux** de croissance |
| **France**[4] | | | | | | | | **France**[4] |
| GDP at current prices | 1 327 961 | 1 339 737 | 1 457 397 | 1 799 942 | 2 059 960 | 2 126 573 | 2 234 388 | PIB aux prix courants |
| GDP per capita | 21 812 | 21 887 | 23 662 | 29 030 | 33 005 | 33 861 | 35 375 | PIB par habitant |
| GDP at constant prices | 1 512 195 | 1 540 239 | 1 556 060 | 1 572 982 | 1 609 461 | 1 628 534 | 1 663 699 | PIB aux prix constants |
| Growth rates | 4.0 | 1.9 | 1.0 | 1.1 | 2.3 | 1.2 | 2.2 | Taux de croissance |
| **French Polynesia** | | | | | | | | **Polynésie française** |
| GDP at current prices | 3 242 | 3 224 | 3 564 | 4 471 | 5 144 | 5 388 | 5 643 | PIB aux prix courants |
| GDP per capita | 13 732 | 13 424 | 14 598 | 18 026 | 20 423 | 21 077 | 21 766 | PIB par habitant |
| GDP at constant prices | 3 692 | 3 741 | 3 904 | 4 059 | 4 203 | 4 347 | 4 492 | PIB aux prix constants |
| Growth rates | 4.0 | 1.3 | 4.4 | 4.0 | 3.5 | 3.4 | 3.3 | Taux de croissance |
| **Gabon** | | | | | | | | **Gabon** |
| GDP at current prices | 5 019 | 4 617 | 4 830 | 5 969 | 7 099 | 8 711 | 9 497 | PIB aux prix courants |
| GDP per capita | 4 245 | 3 831 | 3 934 | 4 778 | 5 589 | 6 749 | 7 245 | PIB par habitant |
| GDP at constant prices | 6 471 | 6 633 | 6 613 | 6 759 | 6 853 | 7 059 | 7 212 | PIB aux prix constants |
| Growth rates | -1.9 | 2.5 | -0.3 | 2.2 | 1.4 | 3.0 | 2.2 | Taux de croissance |

**Gross domestic product and gross domestic product per capita**— In millions of US dollars at current and constant 1990 prices; per capita US dollars; real rates of growth *(continued)*

**Produit intérieur brut et produit intérieur brut par habitant**— En millions de dollars E.-U. aux prix courants et constants de 1990 ; par habitant en dollars E.-U. ; taux de croissance réels *(suite)*

| Country or area | 2000 | 2001 | 2002 | 2003 | 2004 | 2005 | 2006 | Pays ou zone |
|---|---|---|---|---|---|---|---|---|
| **Gambia** | | | | | | | | **Gambie** |
| GDP at current prices | 421 | 418 | 370 | 367 | 401 | 461 | 511 | PIB aux prix courants |
| GDP per capita | 304 | 292 | 250 | 241 | 255 | 285 | 307 | PIB par habitant |
| GDP at constant prices | 474 | 501 | 485 | 518 | 544 | 571 | 604 | PIB aux prix constants |
| Growth rates | 5.5 | 5.8 | -3.3 | 6.9 | 5.1 | 5.0 | 5.6 | Taux de croissance |
| **Georgia** | | | | | | | | **Géorgie** |
| GDP at current prices | 3 058 | 3 219 | 3 396 | 3 991 | 5 126 | 6 411 | 7 742 | PIB aux prix courants |
| GDP per capita | 648 | 690 | 736 | 875 | 1 135 | 1 433 | 1 746 | PIB par habitant |
| GDP at constant prices | 3 180 | 3 332 | 3 516 | 3 904 | 4 149 | 4 547 | 4 956 | PIB aux prix constants |
| Growth rates | 1.8 | 4.8 | 5.5 | 11.1 | 6.3 | 9.6 | 9.0 | Taux de croissance |
| **Germany** | | | | | | | | **Allemagne** |
| GDP at current prices | 1 900 220 | 1 890 954 | 2 017 013 | 2 439 522 | 2 740 621 | 2 786 897 | 2 888 699 | PIB aux prix courants |
| GDP per capita | 23 086 | 22 950 | 24 453 | 29 546 | 33 168 | 33 718 | 34 955 | PIB par habitant |
| GDP at constant prices | 2 111 079 | 2 137 262 | 2 137 262 | 2 133 249 | 2 159 841 | 2 179 483 | 2 233 311 | PIB aux prix constants |
| Growth rates | 3.2 | 1.2 | 0.0 | -0.2 | 1.3 | 0.9 | 2.5 | Taux de croissance |
| **Ghana** | | | | | | | | **Ghana** |
| GDP at current prices | 4 978 | 5 309 | 6 160 | 7 624 | 8 869 | 10 695 | 12 245 | PIB aux prix courants |
| GDP per capita | 247 | 258 | 292 | 353 | 402 | 475 | 532 | PIB par habitant |
| GDP at constant prices | 9 480 | 9 876 | 10 325 | 10 867 | 11 437 | 12 106 | 12 828 | PIB aux prix constants |
| Growth rates | 3.7 | 4.2 | 4.6 | 5.3 | 5.2 | 5.9 | 6.0 | Taux de croissance |
| **Greece** | | | | | | | | **Grèce** |
| GDP at current prices | 145 956 | 150 329 | 170 347 | 221 890 | 264 146 | 283 734 | 307 856 | PIB aux prix courants |
| GDP per capita | 13 299 | 13 653 | 15 432 | 20 063 | 23 842 | 25 562 | 27 679 | PIB par habitant |
| GDP at constant prices | 136 291 | 142 386 | 147 925 | 155 106 | 162 435 | 168 496 | 174 869 | PIB aux prix constants |
| Growth rates | 4.5 | 4.5 | 3.9 | 4.9 | 4.7 | 3.7 | 3.8 | Taux de croissance |
| **Greenland** | | | | | | | | **Groenland** |
| GDP at current prices | 1 068 | 1 086 | 1 169 | 1 426 | 1 645 | 1 703 | 1 657 | PIB aux prix courants |
| GDP per capita | 18 986 | 19 241 | 20 631 | 25 064 | 28 767 | 29 622 | 28 670 | PIB par habitant |
| GDP at constant prices | 1 215 | 1 230 | 1 218 | 1 214 | 1 246 | 1 271 | 1 323 | PIB aux prix constants |
| Growth rates | 7.1 | 1.3 | -1.0 | -0.4 | 2.7 | 2.0 | 4.1 | Taux de croissance |
| **Grenada** | | | | | | | | **Grenade** |
| GDP at current prices | 335 | 325 | 333 | 357 | 345 | 404 | 440 | PIB aux prix courants |
| GDP per capita | 3 336 | 3 211 | 3 253 | 3 448 | 3 301 | 3 835 | 4 167 | PIB par habitant |
| GDP at constant prices | 260 | 248 | 250 | 265 | 247 | 277 | 297 | PIB aux prix constants |
| Growth rates | 7.0 | -4.4 | 0.8 | 5.8 | -6.9 | 12.1 | 7.4 | Taux de croissance |
| **Guatemala** | | | | | | | | **Guatemala** |
| GDP at current prices | 17 196 | 18 703 | 20 777 | 21 918 | 23 965 | 27 285 | 30 426 | PIB aux prix courants |
| GDP per capita | 1 531 | 1 626 | 1 762 | 1 813 | 1 933 | 2 147 | 2 335 | PIB par habitant |
| GDP at constant prices | 10 208 | 10 446 | 10 850 | 11 125 | 11 475 | 11 872 | 12 415 | PIB aux prix constants |
| Growth rates | 3.6 | 2.3 | 3.9 | 2.5 | 3.2 | 3.5 | 4.6 | Taux de croissance |
| **Guinea** | | | | | | | | **Guinée** |
| GDP at current prices | 3 134 | 3 044 | 3 044 | 3 446 | 3 839 | 2 927 | 2 857 | PIB aux prix courants |
| GDP per capita | 382 | 364 | 358 | 397 | 435 | 325 | 311 | PIB par habitant |
| GDP at constant prices | 4 200 | 4 367 | 4 550 | 4 606 | 4 730 | 4 887 | 5 134 | PIB aux prix constants |
| Growth rates | 1.9 | 4.0 | 4.2 | 1.2 | 2.7 | 3.3 | 5.1 | Taux de croissance |
| **Guinea-Bissau** | | | | | | | | **Guinée-Bissau** |
| GDP at current prices | 215 | 199 | 204 | 239 | 270 | 301 | 322 | PIB aux prix courants |
| GDP per capita | 157 | 141 | 140 | 159 | 174 | 189 | 196 | PIB par habitant |
| GDP at constant prices | 265 | 265 | 246 | 248 | 253 | 262 | 274 | PIB aux prix constants |
| Growth rates | 7.5 | 0.2 | -7.1 | 0.6 | 2.2 | 3.5 | 4.6 | Taux de croissance |
| **Guyana** | | | | | | | | **Guyana** |
| GDP at current prices | 713 | 712 | 726 | 743 | 788 | 826 | 901 | PIB aux prix courants |
| GDP per capita | 970 | 969 | 986 | 1 007 | 1 067 | 1 117 | 1 219 | PIB par habitant |
| GDP at constant prices | 639 | 653 | 660 | 656 | 666 | 647 | 678 | PIB aux prix constants |
| Growth rates | -1.4 | 2.3 | 1.1 | -0.7 | 1.6 | -2.8 | 4.7 | Taux de croissance |
| **Haiti** | | | | | | | | **Haïti** |
| GDP at current prices | 3 515 | 3 365 | 3 083 | 2 711 | 3 511 | 3 985 | 4 619 | PIB aux prix courants |
| GDP per capita | 410 | 386 | 348 | 301 | 384 | 429 | 489 | PIB par habitant |
| GDP at constant prices | 2 359 | 2 334 | 2 328 | 2 336 | 2 254 | 2 295 | 2 348 | PIB aux prix constants |
| Growth rates | 1.1 | -1.0 | -0.3 | 0.4 | -3.5 | 1.8 | 2.3 | Taux de croissance |

19 Gross domestic product and gross domestic product per capita—In millions of US dollars at current and constant 1990 prices; per capita US dollars; real rates of growth (*continued*)

Produit intérieur brut et produit intérieur brut par habitant—En millions de dollars E.-U. aux prix courants et constants de 1990 ; par habitant en dollars E.-U. ; taux de croissance réels (*suite*)

| Country or area | 2000 | 2001 | 2002 | 2003 | 2004 | 2005 | 2006 | Pays ou zone |
|---|---|---|---|---|---|---|---|---|
| **Honduras** | | | | | | | | **Honduras** |
| GDP at current prices | 6 025 | 6 400 | 6 580 | 6 945 | 7 538 | 8 372 | 9 301 | PIB aux prix courants |
| GDP per capita | 972 | 1 013 | 1 021 | 1 057 | 1 125 | 1 225 | 1 335 | PIB par habitant |
| GDP at constant prices | 4 213 | 4 323 | 4 440 | 4 594 | 4 825 | 5 022 | 5 325 | PIB aux prix constants |
| Growth rates | 5.8 | 2.6 | 2.7 | 3.5 | 5.0 | 4.1 | 6.0 | Taux de croissance |
| **Hungary** | | | | | | | | **Hongrie** |
| GDP at current prices | 47 958 | 53 317 | 66 710 | 84 419 | 102 159 | 110 364 | 111 990 | PIB aux prix courants |
| GDP per capita | 4 695 | 5 233 | 6 563 | 8 326 | 10 101 | 10 942 | 11 134 | PIB par habitant |
| GDP at constant prices | 39 695 | 41 319 | 43 112 | 44 888 | 47 076 | 49 075 | 50 994 | PIB aux prix constants |
| Growth rates | 5.2 | 4.1 | 4.3 | 4.1 | 4.9 | 4.3 | 3.9 | Taux de croissance |
| **Iceland** | | | | | | | | **Islande** |
| GDP at current prices | 8 641 | 7 847 | 8 779 | 10 828 | 13 040 | 16 071 | 15 642 | PIB aux prix courants |
| GDP per capita | 30 742 | 27 629 | 30 592 | 37 342 | 44 519 | 54 344 | 52 413 | PIB par habitant |
| GDP at constant prices | 8 156 | 8 450 | 8 425 | 8 652 | 9 314 | 10 014 | 10 425 | PIB aux prix constants |
| Growth rates | 4.5 | 3.6 | -0.3 | 2.7 | 7.7 | 7.5 | 4.1 | Taux de croissance |
| **India** | | | | | | | | **Inde** |
| GDP at current prices | 468 978 | 483 466 | 503 954 | 592 535 | 688 803 | 808 884 | 903 226 | PIB aux prix courants |
| GDP per capita | 448 | 454 | 466 | 539 | 617 | 713 | 784 | PIB par habitant |
| GDP at constant prices | 558 420 | 587 895 | 609 233 | 659 677 | 715 927 | 779 245 | 850 962 | PIB aux prix constants |
| Growth rates | 4.0 | 5.3 | 3.6 | 8.3 | 8.5 | 8.8 | 9.2 | Taux de croissance |
| **Indonesia** | | | | | | | | **Indonésie** |
| GDP at current prices | 165 021 | 160 447 | 195 661 | 234 772 | 254 299 | 281 276 | 364 459 | PIB aux prix courants |
| GDP per capita | 780 | 748 | 900 | 1 065 | 1 139 | 1 244 | 1 592 | PIB par habitant |
| GDP at constant prices | 190 071 | 196 997 | 205 860 | 215 701 | 226 595 | 239 276 | 252 557 | PIB aux prix constants |
| Growth rates | 4.9 | 3.6 | 4.5 | 4.8 | 5.1 | 5.6 | 5.6 | Taux de croissance |
| **Iran (Islamic Rep. of)** | | | | | | | | **Iran (Rép. islamique d')** |
| GDP at current prices | 102 930 | 110 411 | 135 525 | 136 646 | 162 747 | 192 020 | 242 146 | PIB aux prix courants |
| GDP per capita | 1 557 | 1 654 | 2 011 | 2 009 | 2 370 | 2 766 | 3 446 | PIB par habitant |
| GDP at constant prices | 130 569 | 135 473 | 145 303 | 155 417 | 162 249 | 169 566 | 178 662 | PIB aux prix constants |
| Growth rates | 2.8 | 3.8 | 7.3 | 7.0 | 4.4 | 4.5 | 5.4 | Taux de croissance |
| **Iraq** | | | | | | | | **Iraq** |
| GDP at current prices | 20 969 | 17 682 | 17 437 | 10 621 | 25 491 | 33 961 | 46 952 | PIB aux prix courants |
| GDP per capita | 837 | 688 | 663 | 395 | 928 | 1 213 | 1 647 | PIB par habitant |
| GDP at constant prices | 15 002 | 15 348 | 14 289 | 9 559 | 11 753 | 12 136 | 12 622 | PIB aux prix constants |
| Growth rates | 1.4 | 2.3 | -6.9 | -33.1 | 23.0 | 3.3 | 4.0 | Taux de croissance |
| **Ireland** | | | | | | | | **Irlande** |
| GDP at current prices | 96 327 | 104 479 | 122 297 | 156 812 | 183 232 | 200 422 | 218 090 | PIB aux prix courants |
| GDP per capita | 25 324 | 27 056 | 31 154 | 39 255 | 45 045 | 48 373 | 51 665 | PIB par habitant |
| GDP at constant prices | 95 371 | 100 947 | 107 037 | 111 632 | 116 443 | 122 876 | 129 359 | PIB aux prix constants |
| Growth rates | 9.4 | 5.9 | 6.0 | 4.3 | 4.3 | 5.5 | 5.3 | Taux de croissance |
| **Israel** | | | | | | | | **Israël** |
| GDP at current prices | 120 989 | 118 628 | 109 328 | 115 101 | 122 476 | 129 753 | 140 294 | PIB aux prix courants |
| GDP per capita | 19 886 | 19 098 | 17 258 | 17 831 | 18 630 | 19 389 | 20 601 | PIB par habitant |
| GDP at constant prices | 99 592 | 98 979 | 98 039 | 99 515 | 104 288 | 109 761 | 115 207 | PIB aux prix constants |
| Growth rates | 8.7 | -0.6 | -1.0 | 1.5 | 4.8 | 5.3 | 5.0 | Taux de croissance |
| **Italy** | | | | | | | | **Italie** |
| GDP at current prices | 1 097 346 | 1 117 350 | 1 218 981 | 1 507 109 | 1 724 522 | 1 762 473 | 1 848 001 | PIB aux prix courants |
| GDP per capita | 19 021 | 19 313 | 20 997 | 25 864 | 29 492 | 30 053 | 31 440 | PIB par habitant |
| GDP at constant prices | 1 326 898 | 1 350 716 | 1 355 339 | 1 355 840 | 1 370 290 | 1 369 800 | 1 393 635 | PIB aux prix constants |
| Growth rates | 3.6 | 1.8 | 0.3 | 0.0 | 1.1 | 0.0 | 1.7 | Taux de croissance |
| **Jamaica** | | | | | | | | **Jamaïque** |
| GDP at current prices | 7 889 | 8 116 | 8 471 | 8 190 | 8 837 | 9 715 | 10 316 | PIB aux prix courants |
| GDP per capita | 3 047 | 3 111 | 3 223 | 3 094 | 3 316 | 3 622 | 3 823 | PIB par habitant |
| GDP at constant prices | 4 929 | 5 004 | 5 060 | 5 174 | 5 224 | 5 299 | 5 453 | PIB aux prix constants |
| Growth rates | 0.7 | 1.5 | 1.1 | 2.3 | 1.0 | 1.4 | 2.9 | Taux de croissance |
| **Japan** | | | | | | | | **Japon** |
| GDP at current prices | 4 649 614 | 4 087 726 | 3 904 823 | 4 231 255 | 4 584 890 | 4 559 020 | 4 434 993 | PIB aux prix courants |
| GDP per capita | 36 601 | 32 118 | 30 630 | 33 145 | 35 876 | 35 646 | 34 661 | PIB par habitant |
| GDP at constant prices | 3 413 333 | 3 426 468 | 3 431 044 | 3 492 002 | 3 572 388 | 3 666 229 | 3 764 172 | PIB aux prix constants |
| Growth rates | 2.9 | 0.4 | 0.1 | 1.8 | 2.3 | 2.6 | 2.7 | Taux de croissance |

**Gross domestic product and gross domestic product per capita**—In millions of US dollars at current and constant 1990 prices; per capita US dollars; real rates of growth (*continued*)

**Produit intérieur brut et produit intérieur brut par habitant**—En millions de dollars E.-U. aux prix courants et constants de 1990 ; par habitant en dollars E.-U. ; taux de croissance réels (*suite*)

| Country or area | 2000 | 2001 | 2002 | 2003 | 2004 | 2005 | 2006 | Pays ou zone |
|---|---|---|---|---|---|---|---|---|
| **Jordan** | | | | | | | | **Jordanie** |
| GDP at current prices | 8 461 | 8 976 | 9 582 | 10 196 | 11 398 | 12 711 | 14 336 | PIB aux prix courants |
| GDP per capita | 1 763 | 1 825 | 1 896 | 1 958 | 2 122 | 2 293 | 2 502 | PIB par habitant |
| GDP at constant prices | 6 371 | 6 707 | 7 095 | 7 391 | 8 014 | 8 593 | 9 134 | PIB aux prix constants |
| Growth rates | 4.3 | 5.3 | 5.8 | 4.2 | 8.4 | 7.2 | 6.3 | Taux de croissance |
| **Kazakhstan** | | | | | | | | **Kazakhstan** |
| GDP at current prices | 18 292 | 22 153 | 24 637 | 30 834 | 43 152 | 57 124 | 77 237 | PIB aux prix courants |
| GDP per capita | 1 223 | 1 486 | 1 650 | 2 055 | 2 856 | 3 756 | 5 043 | PIB par habitant |
| GDP at constant prices | 20 594 | 23 384 | 25 664 | 28 058 | 30 748 | 33 730 | 37 305 | PIB aux prix constants |
| Growth rates | 9.9 | 13.6 | 9.8 | 9.3 | 9.6 | 9.7 | 10.6 | Taux de croissance |
| **Kenya** | | | | | | | | **Kenya** |
| GDP at current prices | 12 604 | 12 983 | 13 151 | 14 986 | 16 199 | 18 730 | 23 753 | PIB aux prix courants |
| GDP per capita | 403 | 405 | 400 | 444 | 467 | 526 | 650 | PIB par habitant |
| GDP at constant prices | 13 225 | 13 815 | 13 894 | 14 309 | 15 003 | 15 875 | 16 735 | PIB aux prix constants |
| Growth rates | 0.5 | 4.5 | 0.6 | 3.0 | 4.9 | 5.8 | 5.4 | Taux de croissance |
| **Kiribati** | | | | | | | | **Kiribati** |
| GDP at current prices | 51 | 46 | 50 | 62 | 70 | 75 | 75 | PIB aux prix courants |
| GDP per capita | 606 | 537 | 572 | 704 | 776 | 811 | 801 | PIB par habitant |
| GDP at constant prices | 46 | 50 | 52 | 53 | 51 | 53 | 54 | PIB aux prix constants |
| Growth rates | -0.6 | 8.4 | 4.7 | 0.9 | -2.0 | 3.6 | 0.8 | Taux de croissance |
| **Korea, Dem. P. R.** | | | | | | | | **Corée, R. p. dém. de** |
| GDP at current prices | 10 608 | 11 022 | 10 910 | 11 051 | 11 168 | 12 260 | 12 127 | PIB aux prix courants |
| GDP per capita | 462 | 476 | 468 | 471 | 473 | 517 | 509 | PIB par habitant |
| GDP at constant prices | 11 538 | 11 960 | 12 105 | 12 320 | 12 320 | 12 430 | 12 485 | PIB aux prix constants |
| Growth rates | 1.3 | 3.7 | 1.2 | 1.8 | 0.0 | 0.9 | 0.4 | Taux de croissance |
| **Korea, Republic of** | | | | | | | | **Corée, République de** |
| GDP at current prices | 511 659 | 481 894 | 546 935 | 608 146 | 680 492 | 787 627 | 872 789 | PIB aux prix courants |
| GDP per capita | 10 938 | 10 243 | 11 568 | 12 806 | 14 271 | 16 454 | 18 164 | PIB par habitant |
| GDP at constant prices | 475 958 | 494 218 | 528 667 | 545 040 | 570 819 | 593 434 | 623 157 | PIB aux prix constants |
| Growth rates | 8.5 | 3.8 | 7.0 | 3.1 | 4.7 | 4.0 | 5.0 | Taux de croissance |
| **Kosovo** | | | | | | | | **Kosovo** |
| GDP at current prices | 1 845 | 2 171 | 2 438 | 2 827 | 3 070 | 3 244 | 3 391 | PIB aux prix courants |
| GDP per capita | 706 | 844 | 971 | 1 146 | 1 261 | 1 339 | 1 402 | PIB par habitant |
| GDP at constant prices | 1 034 | 1 160 | 1 113 | 1 066 | 1 053 | 1 127 | 1 161 | PIB aux prix constants |
| Growth rates | 5.2 | 12.2 | -4.1 | -4.3 | -1.2 | 7.0 | 3.0 | Taux de croissance |
| **Kuwait** | | | | | | | | **Koweït** |
| GDP at current prices | 37 718 | 34 890 | 38 136 | 47 827 | 59 267 | 80 781 | 101 131 | PIB aux prix courants |
| GDP per capita | 16 926 | 14 918 | 15 634 | 18 897 | 22 647 | 29 919 | 36 396 | PIB par habitant |
| GDP at constant prices | 29 663 | 29 727 | 30 624 | 35 683 | 39 426 | 43 353 | 46 057 | PIB aux prix constants |
| Growth rates | 4.7 | 0.2 | 3.0 | 16.5 | 10.5 | 10.0 | 6.2 | Taux de croissance |
| **Kyrgyzstan** | | | | | | | | **Kirghizistan** |
| GDP at current prices | 1 370 | 1 527 | 1 606 | 1 922 | 2 212 | 2 460 | 2 819 | PIB aux prix courants |
| GDP per capita | 277 | 305 | 317 | 376 | 429 | 473 | 536 | PIB par habitant |
| GDP at constant prices | 1 006 | 1 060 | 1 060 | 1 134 | 1 214 | 1 212 | 1 244 | PIB aux prix constants |
| Growth rates | -5.2 | 5.3 | 0.0 | 7.0 | 7.0 | -0.2 | 2.7 | Taux de croissance |
| **Lao People's Dem. Rep.** | | | | | | | | **Rép. dém. pop. lao** |
| GDP at current prices | 1 733 | 1 753 | 1 830 | 2 130 | 2 512 | 2 872 | 3 451 | PIB aux prix courants |
| GDP per capita | 332 | 330 | 339 | 388 | 451 | 507 | 599 | PIB par habitant |
| GDP at constant prices | 1 593 | 1 684 | 1 784 | 1 887 | 2 017 | 2 165 | 2 323 | PIB aux prix constants |
| Growth rates | 5.8 | 5.8 | 5.9 | 5.8 | 6.9 | 7.3 | 7.3 | Taux de croissance |
| **Latvia** | | | | | | | | **Lettonie** |
| GDP at current prices | 7 833 | 8 313 | 9 315 | 11 186 | 13 762 | 16 042 | 20 101 | PIB aux prix courants |
| GDP per capita | 3 293 | 3 520 | 3 972 | 4 802 | 5 944 | 6 969 | 8 781 | PIB par habitant |
| GDP at constant prices | 5 717 | 6 177 | 6 577 | 7 050 | 7 662 | 8 474 | 9 485 | PIB aux prix constants |
| Growth rates | 6.9 | 8.0 | 6.5 | 7.2 | 8.7 | 10.6 | 11.9 | Taux de croissance |
| **Lebanon** | | | | | | | | **Liban** |
| GDP at current prices | 16 679 | 17 065 | 18 712 | 19 802 | 21 464 | 21 802 | 22 064 | PIB aux prix courants |
| GDP per capita | 4 421 | 4 467 | 4 836 | 5 055 | 5 414 | 5 436 | 5 441 | PIB par habitant |
| GDP at constant prices | 5 627 | 5 831 | 5 754 | 5 927 | 6 223 | 6 285 | 6 087 | PIB aux prix constants |
| Growth rates | 0.0 | 3.6 | -1.3 | 3.0 | 5.0 | 1.0 | -3.2 | Taux de croissance |

**Gross domestic product and gross domestic product per capita**—In millions of US dollars at current and constant 1990 prices; per capita US dollars; real rates of growth (*continued*)

**Produit intérieur brut et produit intérieur brut par habitant**—En millions de dollars E.-U. aux prix courants et constants de 1990 ; par habitant en dollars E.-U. ; taux de croissance réels (*suite*)

| Country or area | 2000 | 2001 | 2002 | 2003 | 2004 | 2005 | 2006 | Pays ou zone |
|---|---|---|---|---|---|---|---|---|
| **Lesotho** | | | | | | | | **Lesotho** |
| GDP at current prices | 863 | 752 | 687 | 1 039 | 1 319 | 1 457 | 1 446 | PIB aux prix courants |
| GDP per capita | 457 | 394 | 356 | 533 | 671 | 735 | 725 | PIB par habitant |
| GDP at constant prices | 867 | 896 | 915 | 939 | 977 | 1 006 | 1 022 | PIB aux prix constants |
| Growth rates | 1.5 | 3.4 | 2.1 | 2.7 | 4.1 | 3.0 | 1.6 | Taux de croissance |
| **Liberia** | | | | | | | | **Libéria** |
| GDP at current prices | 561 | 543 | 559 | 435 | 497 | 548 | 687 | PIB aux prix courants |
| GDP per capita | 183 | 171 | 172 | 132 | 148 | 159 | 192 | PIB par habitant |
| GDP at constant prices | 481 | 495 | 513 | 352 | 361 | 380 | 407 | PIB aux prix constants |
| Growth rates | 22.6 | 2.9 | 3.7 | -31.3 | 2.6 | 5.3 | 7.0 | Taux de croissance |
| **Libyan Arab Jamah.** | | | | | | | | **Jamah. arabe libyenne** |
| GDP at current prices | 34 265 | 28 420 | 19 131 | 23 230 | 30 162 | 38 738 | 50 413 | PIB aux prix courants |
| GDP per capita | 6 410 | 5 209 | 3 436 | 4 088 | 5 201 | 6 546 | 8 348 | PIB par habitant |
| GDP at constant prices | 35 348 | 35 529 | 35 443 | 42 267 | 44 208 | 45 772 | 48 056 | PIB aux prix constants |
| Growth rates | 2.3 | 0.5 | -0.2 | 19.3 | 4.6 | 3.5 | 5.0 | Taux de croissance |
| **Lithuania** | | | | | | | | **Lituanie** |
| GDP at current prices | 11 418 | 12 146 | 14 134 | 18 558 | 22 508 | 25 667 | 29 283 | PIB aux prix courants |
| GDP per capita | 3 260 | 3 487 | 4 076 | 5 373 | 6 543 | 7 494 | 8 592 | PIB par habitant |
| GDP at constant prices | 7 227 | 7 707 | 8 240 | 9 090 | 9 755 | 10 493 | 11 315 | PIB aux prix constants |
| Growth rates | 4.1 | 6.7 | 6.9 | 10.3 | 7.3 | 7.6 | 7.8 | Taux de croissance |
| **Luxembourg** | | | | | | | | **Luxembourg** |
| GDP at current prices | 20 270 | 20 199 | 22 664 | 28 900 | 33 520 | 36 557 | 40 520 | PIB aux prix courants |
| GDP per capita | 46 405 | 45 780 | 50 921 | 64 413 | 74 091 | 80 062 | 87 829 | PIB par habitant |
| GDP at constant prices | 20 709 | 21 231 | 22 047 | 22 343 | 23 155 | 24 073 | 25 403 | PIB aux prix constants |
| Growth rates | 8.4 | 2.5 | 3.8 | 1.3 | 3.6 | 4.0 | 5.5 | Taux de croissance |
| **Madagascar** | | | | | | | | **Madagascar** |
| GDP at current prices | 3 878 | 4 530 | 4 397 | 5 474 | 4 364 | 5 276 | 5 506 | PIB aux prix courants |
| GDP per capita | 240 | 272 | 256 | 310 | 241 | 283 | 287 | PIB par habitant |
| GDP at constant prices | 3 657 | 3 877 | 3 386 | 3 717 | 3 913 | 4 092 | 4 286 | PIB aux prix constants |
| Growth rates | 4.7 | 6.0 | -12.7 | 9.8 | 5.3 | 4.6 | 4.7 | Taux de croissance |
| **Malawi** | | | | | | | | **Malawi** |
| GDP at current prices | 1 744 | 1 717 | 1 935 | 1 764 | 1 903 | 2 077 | 2 226 | PIB aux prix courants |
| GDP per capita | 150 | 144 | 158 | 140 | 148 | 157 | 164 | PIB par habitant |
| GDP at constant prices | 3 071 | 2 923 | 3 001 | 3 183 | 3 397 | 3 461 | 3 756 | PIB aux prix constants |
| Growth rates | 1.6 | -4.8 | 2.7 | 6.1 | 6.7 | 1.9 | 8.5 | Taux de croissance |
| **Malaysia** | | | | | | | | **Malaisie** |
| GDP at current prices | 90 320 | 88 001 | 95 266 | 103 952 | 118 461 | 130 770 | 148 941 | PIB aux prix courants |
| GDP per capita | 3 881 | 3 701 | 3 927 | 4 204 | 4 702 | 5 098 | 5 704 | PIB par habitant |
| GDP at constant prices | 87 469 | 87 747 | 91 567 | 96 526 | 103 569 | 108 912 | 115 350 | PIB aux prix constants |
| Growth rates | 8.9 | 0.3 | 4.4 | 5.4 | 7.3 | 5.2 | 5.9 | Taux de croissance |
| **Maldives** | | | | | | | | **Maldives** |
| GDP at current prices | 624 | 625 | 641 | 692 | 776 | 751 | 907 | PIB aux prix courants |
| GDP per capita | 2 287 | 2 253 | 2 274 | 2 420 | 2 672 | 2 542 | 3 020 | PIB par habitant |
| GDP at constant prices | 445 | 460 | 488 | 533 | 593 | 569 | 693 | PIB aux prix constants |
| Growth rates | 4.4 | 3.3 | 6.1 | 9.2 | 11.3 | -4.0 | 21.7 | Taux de croissance |
| **Mali** | | | | | | | | **Mali** |
| GDP at current prices | 2 655 | 3 018 | 3 189 | 4 222 | 4 982 | 5 487 | 5 965 | PIB aux prix courants |
| GDP per capita | 265 | 293 | 301 | 386 | 442 | 473 | 498 | PIB par habitant |
| GDP at constant prices | 3 742 | 4 186 | 4 367 | 4 699 | 4 805 | 5 100 | 5 335 | PIB aux prix constants |
| Growth rates | -3.3 | 11.9 | 4.3 | 7.6 | 2.3 | 6.1 | 4.6 | Taux de croissance |
| **Malta** | | | | | | | | **Malte** |
| GDP at current prices | 3 914 | 3 893 | 4 223 | 4 928 | 5 399 | 5 613 | 5 914 | PIB aux prix courants |
| GDP per capita | 10 065 | 9 943 | 10 707 | 12 403 | 13 494 | 13 942 | 14 612 | PIB par habitant |
| GDP at constant prices | 4 224 | 4 204 | 4 298 | 4 195 | 4 197 | 4 288 | 4 356 | PIB aux prix constants |
| Growth rates | 5.0 | -0.5 | 2.2 | -2.4 | 0.1 | 2.2 | 1.6 | Taux de croissance |
| **Marshall Islands** | | | | | | | | **Iles Marshall** |
| GDP at current prices | 99 | 99 | 106 | 109 | 115 | 123 | 128 | PIB aux prix courants |
| GDP per capita | 1 896 | 1 881 | 1 972 | 2 000 | 2 074 | 2 166 | 2 204 | PIB par habitant |
| GDP at constant prices | 59 | 58 | 61 | 62 | 62 | 64 | 67 | PIB aux prix constants |
| Growth rates | -2.0 | -1.5 | 4.0 | 2.0 | 0.4 | 3.5 | 4.0 | Taux de croissance |

**Gross domestic product and gross domestic product per capita**—In millions of US dollars at current and constant 1990 prices; per capita US dollars; real rates of growth (*continued*)

**Produit intérieur brut et produit intérieur brut par habitant**—En millions de dollars E.-U. aux prix courants et constants de 1990 ; par habitant en dollars E.-U. ; taux de croissance réels (*suite*)

| Country or area | 2000 | 2001 | 2002 | 2003 | 2004 | 2005 | 2006 | Pays ou zone |
|---|---|---|---|---|---|---|---|---|
| **Mauritania** | | | | | | | | **Mauritanie** |
| GDP at current prices | 1 075 | 1 115 | 1 145 | 1 281 | 1 537 | 1 872 | 2 737 | PIB aux prix courants |
| GDP per capita | 419 | 422 | 421 | 457 | 533 | 632 | 899 | PIB par habitant |
| GDP at constant prices | 1 410 | 1 452 | 1 467 | 1 549 | 1 630 | 1 718 | 1 961 | PIB aux prix constants |
| Growth rates | 1.8 | 2.9 | 1.1 | 5.6 | 5.2 | 5.4 | 14.1 | Taux de croissance |
| **Mauritius** | | | | | | | | **Maurice** |
| GDP at current prices | 4 583 | 4 537 | 4 755 | 5 641 | 6 386 | 6 288 | 6 413 | PIB aux prix courants |
| GDP per capita | 3 864 | 3 789 | 3 934 | 4 625 | 5 189 | 5 067 | 5 124 | PIB par habitant |
| GDP at constant prices | 4 336 | 4 462 | 4 535 | 4 732 | 4 989 | 5 059 | 5 269 | PIB aux prix constants |
| Growth rates | 9.4 | 2.9 | 1.6 | 4.4 | 5.4 | 1.4 | 4.2 | Taux de croissance |
| **Mexico** | | | | | | | | **Mexique** |
| GDP at current prices | 580 792 | 621 867 | 648 630 | 638 797 | 683 070 | 767 970 | 829 618 | PIB aux prix courants |
| GDP per capita | 5 823 | 6 167 | 6 376 | 6 231 | 6 610 | 7 365 | 7 875 | PIB par habitant |
| GDP at constant prices | 369 622 | 369 500 | 372 353 | 377 530 | 393 240 | 404 859 | 421 054 | PIB aux prix constants |
| Growth rates | 6.6 | 0.0 | 0.8 | 1.4 | 4.2 | 3.0 | 4.0 | Taux de croissance |
| **Micronesia (Fed. States of)** | | | | | | | | **Micronésie (Etats féd. de)** |
| GDP at current prices | 217 | 221 | 224 | 230 | 224 | 237 | 245 | PIB aux prix courants |
| GDP per capita | 2 027 | 2 057 | 2 073 | 2 121 | 2 051 | 2 154 | 2 212 | PIB par habitant |
| GDP at constant prices | 165 | 166 | 169 | 174 | 166 | 169 | 168 | PIB aux prix constants |
| Growth rates | 4.2 | 0.4 | 1.4 | 3.3 | -4.4 | 1.5 | -0.7 | Taux de croissance |
| **Moldova** | | | | | | | | **Moldova** |
| GDP at current prices | 1 288 | 1 481 | 1 662 | 1 981 | 2 598 | 2 988 | 3 356 | PIB aux prix courants |
| GDP per capita | 311 | 362 | 412 | 498 | 662 | 771 | 876 | PIB par habitant |
| GDP at constant prices | 1 380 | 1 465 | 1 579 | 1 684 | 1 808 | 1 944 | 2 021 | PIB aux prix constants |
| Growth rates | 2.1 | 6.1 | 7.8 | 6.6 | 7.4 | 7.5 | 4.0 | Taux de croissance |
| **Monaco** | | | | | | | | **Monaco** |
| GDP at current prices | 698 | 702 | 761 | 937 | 1 069 | 1 100 | 1 153 | PIB aux prix courants |
| GDP per capita | 21 812 | 21 887 | 23 662 | 29 030 | 33 005 | 33 861 | 35 375 | PIB par habitant |
| GDP at constant prices | 795 | 807 | 813 | 819 | 835 | 843 | 859 | PIB aux prix constants |
| Growth rates | 3.8 | 1.6 | 0.7 | 0.7 | 2.0 | 0.9 | 1.9 | Taux de croissance |
| **Mongolia** | | | | | | | | **Mongolie** |
| GDP at current prices | 947 | 1 018 | 1 121 | 1 285 | 1 625 | 2 065 | 2 802 | PIB aux prix courants |
| GDP per capita | 384 | 409 | 447 | 508 | 636 | 800 | 1 076 | PIB par habitant |
| GDP at constant prices | 1 251 | 1 265 | 1 317 | 1 398 | 1 548 | 1 657 | 1 658 | PIB aux prix constants |
| Growth rates | 1.1 | 1.1 | 4.2 | 6.1 | 10.8 | 7.0 | 0.1 | Taux de croissance |
| **Montenegro** | | | | | | | | **Monténégro** |
| GDP at current prices | 942 | 1 114 | 1 225 | 1 571 | 1 943 | 2 102 | 2 251 | PIB aux prix courants |
| GDP per capita | 1 405 | 1 678 | 1 881 | 2 473 | 3 136 | 3 457 | 3 745 | PIB par habitant |
| GDP at constant prices | 1 442 | 1 440 | 1 464 | 1 499 | 1 562 | 1 629 | 1 719 | PIB aux prix constants |
| Growth rates | 3.1 | -0.2 | 1.7 | 2.4 | 4.2 | 4.3 | 5.5 | Taux de croissance |
| **Montserrat** | | | | | | | | **Montserrat** |
| GDP at current prices | 35 | 35 | 38 | 38 | 41 | 44 | 46 | PIB aux prix courants |
| GDP per capita | 7 014 | 7 486 | 8 109 | 7 590 | 7 656 | 7 813 | 7 967 | PIB par habitant |
| GDP at constant prices | 25 | 24 | 25 | 24 | 26 | 27 | 27 | PIB aux prix constants |
| Growth rates | -3.6 | -6.9 | 6.6 | -3.1 | 6.8 | 2.0 | 1.1 | Taux de croissance |
| **Morocco** | | | | | | | | **Maroc** |
| GDP at current prices | 37 060 | 37 766 | 40 474 | 49 819 | 56 392 | 58 956 | 65 365 | PIB aux prix courants |
| GDP per capita | 1 272 | 1 280 | 1 356 | 1 649 | 1 845 | 1 906 | 2 087 | PIB par habitant |
| GDP at constant prices | 36 025 | 38 294 | 39 515 | 41 697 | 43 467 | 44 213 | 47 449 | PIB aux prix constants |
| Growth rates | 1.0 | 6.3 | 3.2 | 5.5 | 4.2 | 1.7 | 7.3 | Taux de croissance |
| **Mozambique** | | | | | | | | **Mozambique** |
| GDP at current prices | 3 832 | 3 697 | 4 092 | 4 789 | 5 912 | 6 636 | 7 311 | PIB aux prix courants |
| GDP per capita | 211 | 198 | 214 | 244 | 294 | 323 | 349 | PIB par habitant |
| GDP at constant prices | 4 511 | 5 102 | 5 518 | 5 955 | 6 401 | 6 798 | 7 378 | PIB aux prix constants |
| Growth rates | 1.9 | 13.1 | 8.2 | 7.9 | 7.5 | 6.2 | 8.5 | Taux de croissance |
| **Myanmar** | | | | | | | | **Myanmar** |
| GDP at current prices | 7 275 | 7 634 | 10 369 | 10 000 | 10 254 | 11 900 | 13 612 | PIB aux prix courants |
| GDP per capita | 159 | 165 | 222 | 212 | 216 | 248 | 281 | PIB par habitant |
| GDP at constant prices | 10 333 | 11 505 | 12 888 | 14 672 | 16 662 | 18 867 | 20 186 | PIB aux prix constants |
| Growth rates | 13.8 | 11.3 | 12.0 | 13.8 | 13.6 | 13.2 | 7.0 | Taux de croissance |

Gross domestic product and gross domestic product per capita—In millions of US dollars at current and constant 1990 prices; per capita US dollars; real rates of growth (*continued*)

Produit intérieur brut et produit intérieur brut par habitant—En millions de dollars E.-U. aux prix courants et constants de 1990 ; par habitant en dollars E.-U. ; taux de croissance réels (*suite*)

| Country or area | 2000 | 2001 | 2002 | 2003 | 2004 | 2005 | 2006 | Pays ou zone |
|---|---|---|---|---|---|---|---|---|
| **Namibia** | | | | | | | | **Namibie** |
| GDP at current prices | 3 414 | 3 216 | 3 122 | 4 473 | 5 713 | 6 130 | 6 312 | PIB aux prix courants |
| GDP per capita | 1 816 | 1 681 | 1 607 | 2 272 | 2 865 | 3 035 | 3 084 | PIB par habitant |
| GDP at constant prices | 3 540 | 3 625 | 3 867 | 4 001 | 4 239 | 4 389 | 4 585 | PIB aux prix constants |
| Growth rates | 3.5 | 2.4 | 6.7 | 3.5 | 6.0 | 3.5 | 4.5 | Taux de croissance |
| **Nauru** | | | | | | | | **Nauru** |
| GDP at current prices | 33 | 31 | 36 | 44 | 51 | 54 | 55 | PIB aux prix courants |
| GDP per capita | 3 283 | 3 134 | 3 546 | 4 326 | 5 023 | 5 351 | 5 474 | PIB par habitant |
| GDP at constant prices | 30 | 30 | 30 | 30 | 30 | 30 | 30 | PIB aux prix constants |
| Growth rates | -0.1 | 0.6 | 0.8 | 0.0 | 0.0 | 0.0 | 0.0 | Taux de croissance |
| **Nepal** | | | | | | | | **Népal** |
| GDP at current prices | 5 338 | 5 487 | 5 429 | 5 998 | 6 743 | 7 476 | 8 012 | PIB aux prix courants |
| GDP per capita | 219 | 220 | 213 | 230 | 254 | 276 | 290 | PIB par habitant |
| GDP at constant prices | 5 738 | 6 061 | 6 025 | 6 225 | 6 460 | 6 635 | 6 759 | PIB aux prix constants |
| Growth rates | 6.1 | 5.6 | -0.6 | 3.3 | 3.8 | 2.7 | 1.9 | Taux de croissance |
| **Netherlands** | | | | | | | | **Pays-Bas** |
| GDP at current prices | 385 074 | 400 651 | 437 827 | 538 292 | 608 239 | 628 819 | 663 929 | PIB aux prix courants |
| GDP per capita | 24 182 | 25 019 | 27 189 | 33 253 | 37 399 | 38 512 | 40 535 | PIB par habitant |
| GDP at constant prices | 402 461 | 410 212 | 410 525 | 411 903 | 419 947 | 426 371 | 438 958 | PIB aux prix constants |
| Growth rates | 3.9 | 1.9 | 0.1 | 0.3 | 2.0 | 1.5 | 3.0 | Taux de croissance |
| **Netherlands Antilles** | | | | | | | | **Antilles néerlandaises** |
| GDP at current prices | 2 860 | 2 910 | 2 935 | 3 031 | 3 115 | 3 204 | 3 352 | PIB aux prix courants |
| GDP per capita | 15 830 | 16 133 | 16 213 | 16 619 | 16 909 | 17 188 | 17 750 | PIB par habitant |
| GDP at constant prices | 2 221 | 2 249 | 2 256 | 2 288 | 2 313 | 2 334 | 2 355 | PIB aux prix constants |
| Growth rates | -2.7 | 1.3 | 0.3 | 1.4 | 1.1 | 0.9 | 0.9 | Taux de croissance |
| **New Caledonia** | | | | | | | | **Nouvelle-Calédonie** |
| GDP at current prices | 3 166 | 3 058 | 3 314 | 4 098 | 4 595 | 4 656 | 4 743 | PIB aux prix courants |
| GDP per capita | 14 722 | 13 961 | 14 863 | 18 075 | 19 940 | 19 883 | 19 935 | PIB par habitant |
| GDP at constant prices | 2 978 | 2 976 | 3 005 | 3 035 | 3 054 | 3 081 | 3 107 | PIB aux prix constants |
| Growth rates | 2.1 | -0.1 | 1.0 | 1.0 | 0.6 | 0.9 | 0.8 | Taux de croissance |
| **New Zealand** | | | | | | | | **Nouvelle-Zélande** |
| GDP at current prices | 52 673 | 52 397 | 60 442 | 80 681 | 98 420 | 109 757 | 105 986 | PIB aux prix courants |
| GDP per capita | 13 667 | 13 439 | 15 309 | 20 171 | 24 300 | 26 789 | 25 603 | PIB par habitant |
| GDP at constant prices | 58 053 | 60 342 | 63 156 | 65 404 | 67 818 | 69 108 | 70 032 | PIB aux prix constants |
| Growth rates | 2.1 | 3.9 | 4.7 | 3.6 | 3.7 | 1.9 | 1.3 | Taux de croissance |
| **Nicaragua** | | | | | | | | **Nicaragua** |
| GDP at current prices | 3 938 | 4 125 | 4 026 | 4 102 | 4 496 | 4 910 | 5 371 | PIB aux prix courants |
| GDP per capita | 771 | 796 | 766 | 770 | 834 | 899 | 971 | PIB par habitant |
| GDP at constant prices | 5 022 | 5 171 | 5 210 | 5 341 | 5 616 | 5 840 | 6 056 | PIB aux prix constants |
| Growth rates | 4.1 | 3.0 | 0.8 | 2.5 | 5.1 | 4.0 | 3.7 | Taux de croissance |
| **Niger** | | | | | | | | **Niger** |
| GDP at current prices | 1 666 | 1 814 | 2 065 | 2 523 | 2 792 | 3 245 | 3 388 | PIB aux prix courants |
| GDP per capita | 150 | 157 | 173 | 204 | 218 | 245 | 247 | PIB par habitant |
| GDP at constant prices | 3 126 | 3 358 | 3 538 | 3 671 | 3 649 | 3 909 | 4 047 | PIB aux prix constants |
| Growth rates | -2.6 | 7.4 | 5.3 | 3.8 | -0.6 | 7.1 | 3.6 | Taux de croissance |
| **Nigeria** | | | | | | | | **Nigéria** |
| GDP at current prices | 67 359 | 63 429 | 66 218 | 78 441 | 87 845 | 113 461 | 132 737 | PIB aux prix courants |
| GDP per capita | 540 | 495 | 504 | 583 | 637 | 803 | 917 | PIB par habitant |
| GDP at constant prices | 77 637 | 81 300 | 85 066 | 93 204 | 99 337 | 105 522 | 111 131 | PIB aux prix constants |
| Growth rates | 4.9 | 4.7 | 4.6 | 9.6 | 6.6 | 6.2 | 5.3 | Taux de croissance |
| **Norway** | | | | | | | | **Norvège** |
| GDP at current prices | 166 906 | 169 739 | 190 277 | 222 698 | 254 706 | 295 513 | 333 924 | PIB aux prix courants |
| GDP per capita | 37 183 | 37 573 | 41 843 | 48 646 | 55 268 | 63 704 | 71 525 | PIB par habitant |
| GDP at constant prices | 167 353 | 171 915 | 173 817 | 175 778 | 181 190 | 185 281 | 190 769 | PIB aux prix constants |
| Growth rates | 2.8 | 2.7 | 1.1 | 1.1 | 3.1 | 2.3 | 3.0 | Taux de croissance |
| **Occupied Palestinian Terr.** | | | | | | | | **Terr. palestinien occupé** |
| GDP at current prices | 4 116 | 3 816 | 3 484 | 3 921 | 4 068 | 4 179 | 4 241 | PIB aux prix courants |
| GDP per capita | 1 307 | 1 168 | 1 029 | 1 117 | 1 119 | 1 111 | 1 090 | PIB par habitant |
| GDP at constant prices | 3 263 | 3 054 | 2 940 | 3 189 | 3 253 | 3 412 | 3 549 | PIB aux prix constants |
| Growth rates | -5.6 | -6.4 | -3.8 | 8.5 | 2.0 | 4.9 | 4.0 | Taux de croissance |

**19**

**Gross domestic product and gross domestic product per capita**—In millions of US dollars at current and constant 1990 prices; per capita US dollars; real rates of growth (*continued*)

**Produit intérieur brut et produit intérieur brut par habitant**—En millions de dollars E.-U. aux prix courants et constants de 1990 ; par habitant en dollars E.-U. ; taux de croissance réels (*suite*)

| Country or area | 2000 | 2001 | 2002 | 2003 | 2004 | 2005 | 2006 | Pays ou zone |
|---|---|---|---|---|---|---|---|---|
| **Oman** | | | | | | | | **Oman** |
| GDP at current prices | 19 868 | 19 949 | 20 304 | 21 698 | 24 749 | 30 834 | 35 991 | PIB aux prix courants |
| GDP per capita | 8 271 | 8 221 | 8 307 | 8 823 | 9 985 | 12 299 | 14 135 | PIB par habitant |
| GDP at constant prices | 18 343 | 19 720 | 20 175 | 20 551 | 21 741 | 22 991 | 24 341 | PIB aux prix constants |
| Growth rates | 5.5 | 7.5 | 2.3 | 1.9 | 5.8 | 5.8 | 5.9 | Taux de croissance |
| **Pakistan** | | | | | | | | **Pakistan** |
| GDP at current prices | 78 472 | 71 901 | 81 637 | 97 669 | 112 965 | 129 600 | 146 888 | PIB aux prix courants |
| GDP per capita | 544 | 488 | 544 | 640 | 727 | 820 | 913 | PIB par habitant |
| GDP at constant prices | 81 353 | 83 976 | 88 046 | 94 533 | 101 426 | 107 744 | 115 277 | PIB aux prix constants |
| Growth rates | 2.0 | 3.2 | 4.9 | 7.4 | 7.3 | 6.2 | 7.0 | Taux de croissance |
| **Palau** | | | | | | | | **Palaos** |
| GDP at current prices | 117 | 121 | 115 | 117 | 134 | 145 | 156 | PIB aux prix courants |
| GDP per capita | 6 081 | 6 180 | 5 836 | 5 867 | 6 670 | 7 188 | 7 698 | PIB par habitant |
| GDP at constant prices | 79 | 80 | 77 | 76 | 80 | 84 | 89 | PIB aux prix constants |
| Growth rates | 0.3 | 1.3 | -3.5 | -1.3 | 4.9 | 5.5 | 5.0 | Taux de croissance |
| **Panama** | | | | | | | | **Panama** |
| GDP at current prices | 11 621 | 11 808 | 12 272 | 12 933 | 14 179 | 15 483 | 17 113 | PIB aux prix courants |
| GDP per capita | 3 939 | 3 927 | 4 007 | 4 146 | 4 465 | 4 791 | 5 205 | PIB par habitant |
| GDP at constant prices | 9 957 | 10 014 | 10 237 | 10 668 | 11 470 | 12 263 | 13 259 | PIB aux prix constants |
| Growth rates | 2.7 | 0.6 | 2.2 | 4.2 | 7.5 | 6.9 | 8.1 | Taux de croissance |
| **Papua New Guinea** | | | | | | | | **Papouasie-Nvl-Guinée** |
| GDP at current prices | 3 864 | 3 470 | 3 434 | 4 169 | 4 935 | 5 635 | 6 136 | PIB aux prix courants |
| GDP per capita | 718 | 629 | 607 | 719 | 832 | 928 | 989 | PIB par habitant |
| GDP at constant prices | 5 708 | 5 862 | 5 981 | 6 101 | 6 278 | 6 473 | 6 712 | PIB aux prix constants |
| Growth rates | 0.0 | 2.7 | 2.0 | 2.0 | 2.9 | 3.1 | 3.7 | Taux de croissance |
| **Paraguay** | | | | | | | | **Paraguay** |
| GDP at current prices | 7 095 | 6 446 | 5 092 | 5 552 | 6 950 | 7 473 | 9 110 | PIB aux prix courants |
| GDP per capita | 1 326 | 1 181 | 914 | 977 | 1 200 | 1 266 | 1 514 | PIB par habitant |
| GDP at constant prices | 5 853 | 5 973 | 5 970 | 6 200 | 6 456 | 6 641 | 6 906 | PIB aux prix constants |
| Growth rates | -3.4 | 2.1 | -0.1 | 3.8 | 4.1 | 2.9 | 4.0 | Taux de croissance |
| **Peru** | | | | | | | | **Pérou** |
| GDP at current prices | 53 336 | 53 954 | 57 059 | 61 504 | 69 662 | 79 382 | 90 048 | PIB aux prix courants |
| GDP per capita | 2 078 | 2 076 | 2 168 | 2 309 | 2 584 | 2 911 | 3 264 | PIB par habitant |
| GDP at constant prices | 43 493 | 43 586 | 45 833 | 47 621 | 50 106 | 53 338 | 56 538 | PIB aux prix constants |
| Growth rates | 3.0 | 0.2 | 5.2 | 3.9 | 5.2 | 6.5 | 6.0 | Taux de croissance |
| **Philippines** | | | | | | | | **Philippines** |
| GDP at current prices | 75 031 | 71 216 | 76 814 | 79 634 | 86 703 | 98 371 | 116 931 | PIB aux prix courants |
| GDP per capita | 984 | 915 | 966 | 981 | 1 046 | 1 163 | 1 356 | PIB par habitant |
| GDP at constant prices | 59 115 | 60 873 | 63 581 | 66 716 | 70 841 | 74 364 | 78 357 | PIB aux prix constants |
| Growth rates | 4.7 | 3.0 | 4.5 | 4.9 | 6.2 | 5.0 | 5.4 | Taux de croissance |
| **Poland** | | | | | | | | **Pologne** |
| GDP at current prices | 171 332 | 190 333 | 198 003 | 216 535 | 252 118 | 302 641 | 335 675 | PIB aux prix courants |
| GDP per capita | 4 458 | 4 959 | 5 165 | 5 655 | 6 592 | 7 923 | 8 801 | PIB par habitant |
| GDP at constant prices | 93 498 | 94 546 | 95 869 | 99 552 | 104 795 | 108 193 | 113 813 | PIB aux prix constants |
| Growth rates | 4.2 | 1.1 | 1.4 | 3.8 | 5.3 | 3.2 | 5.2 | Taux de croissance |
| **Portugal** | | | | | | | | **Portugal** |
| GDP at current prices | 112 650 | 115 711 | 127 461 | 155 212 | 178 153 | 183 787 | 191 777 | PIB aux prix courants |
| GDP per capita | 11 015 | 11 251 | 12 319 | 14 910 | 17 013 | 17 457 | 18 129 | PIB par habitant |
| GDP at constant prices | 100 075 | 102 093 | 102 872 | 101 720 | 102 929 | 103 337 | 104 612 | PIB aux prix constants |
| Growth rates | 3.9 | 2.0 | 0.8 | -1.1 | 1.2 | 0.4 | 1.2 | Taux de croissance |
| **Puerto Rico** | | | | | | | | **Porto Rico** |
| GDP at current prices | 69 208 | 71 624 | 74 827 | 79 209 | 82 650 | 86 464 | 90 734 | PIB aux prix courants |
| GDP per capita | 18 051 | 18 565 | 19 280 | 20 294 | 21 057 | 21 907 | 22 863 | PIB par habitant |
| GDP at constant prices | 50 424 | 50 887 | 50 910 | 52 456 | 52 789 | 53 114 | 53 873 | PIB aux prix constants |
| Growth rates | 6.3 | 0.9 | 0.1 | 3.0 | 0.6 | 0.6 | 1.4 | Taux de croissance |
| **Qatar** | | | | | | | | **Qatar** |
| GDP at current prices | 17 760 | 17 741 | 17 881 | 23 534 | 31 734 | 42 463 | 52 722 | PIB aux prix courants |
| GDP per capita | 28 797 | 27 327 | 26 028 | 32 378 | 41 521 | 53 333 | 64 193 | PIB par habitant |
| GDP at constant prices | 13 097 | 13 923 | 14 916 | 15 436 | 18 652 | 19 798 | 21 545 | PIB aux prix constants |
| Growth rates | 7.3 | 6.3 | 7.1 | 3.5 | 20.8 | 6.2 | 8.8 | Taux de croissance |

19 **Gross domestic product and gross domestic product per capita**—In millions of US dollars at current and constant 1990 prices; per capita US dollars; real rates of growth (*continued*)

**Produit intérieur brut et produit intérieur brut par habitant**—En millions de dollars E.-U. aux prix courants et constants de 1990 ; par habitant en dollars E.-U. ; taux de croissance réels (*suite*)

| Country or area | 2000 | 2001 | 2002 | 2003 | 2004 | 2005 | 2006 | Pays ou zone |
|---|---|---|---|---|---|---|---|---|
| **Romania** | | | | | | | | **Roumanie** |
| GDP at current prices | 37 025 | 40 181 | 45 825 | 59 507 | 75 489 | 98 566 | 121 581 | PIB aux prix courants |
| GDP per capita | 1 673 | 1 824 | 2 090 | 2 726 | 3 475 | 4 557 | 5 647 | PIB par habitant |
| GDP at constant prices | 32 464 | 34 329 | 36 087 | 37 972 | 41 181 | 42 856 | 45 938 | PIB aux prix constants |
| Growth rates | 2.2 | 5.8 | 5.1 | 5.2 | 8.5 | 4.1 | 7.2 | Taux de croissance |
| **Russian Federation** | | | | | | | | **Fédération de Russie** |
| GDP at current prices | 259 718 | 306 618 | 345 488 | 431 488 | 591 666 | 764 382 | 984 927 | PIB aux prix courants |
| GDP per capita | 1 762 | 2 088 | 2 364 | 2 967 | 4 089 | 5 310 | 6 877 | PIB par habitant |
| GDP at constant prices | 382 917 | 402 412 | 421 501 | 452 475 | 484 798 | 515 825 | 550 385 | PIB aux prix constants |
| Growth rates | 10.1 | 5.1 | 4.7 | 7.4 | 7.1 | 6.4 | 6.7 | Taux de croissance |
| **Rwanda** | | | | | | | | **Rwanda** |
| GDP at current prices | 1 749 | 1 653 | 1 672 | 1 684 | 1 826 | 2 085 | 2 290 | PIB aux prix courants |
| GDP per capita | 214 | 194 | 191 | 189 | 202 | 226 | 242 | PIB par habitant |
| GDP at constant prices | 2 646 | 2 822 | 3 086 | 3 107 | 3 227 | 3 420 | 3 523 | PIB aux prix constants |
| Growth rates | 6.3 | 6.7 | 9.3 | 0.7 | 3.9 | 6.0 | 3.0 | Taux de croissance |
| **Saint Kitts and Nevis** | | | | | | | | **Saint-Kitts-et-Nevis** |
| GDP at current prices | 329 | 342 | 362 | 362 | 396 | 429 | 487 | PIB aux prix courants |
| GDP per capita | 7 149 | 7 338 | 7 659 | 7 560 | 8 153 | 8 724 | 9 776 | PIB par habitant |
| GDP at constant prices | 206 | 209 | 208 | 206 | 221 | 230 | 240 | PIB aux prix constants |
| Growth rates | 6.5 | 1.7 | -0.3 | -1.3 | 7.3 | 4.1 | 4.4 | Taux de croissance |
| **Saint Lucia** | | | | | | | | **Sainte-Lucie** |
| GDP at current prices | 707 | 685 | 703 | 746 | 798 | 882 | 933 | PIB aux prix courants |
| GDP per capita | 4 627 | 4 444 | 4 512 | 4 734 | 5 004 | 5 473 | 5 723 | PIB par habitant |
| GDP at constant prices | 534 | 504 | 511 | 536 | 562 | 577 | 596 | PIB aux prix constants |
| Growth rates | -0.7 | -5.7 | 1.5 | 4.9 | 4.9 | 2.6 | 3.4 | Taux de croissance |
| **St. Vincent-Grenadines** | | | | | | | | **St. Vincent-Grenadines** |
| GDP at current prices | 335 | 346 | 365 | 382 | 415 | 432 | 449 | PIB aux prix courants |
| GDP per capita | 2 891 | 2 964 | 3 116 | 3 243 | 3 501 | 3 625 | 3 749 | PIB par habitant |
| GDP at constant prices | 270 | 272 | 282 | 291 | 309 | 315 | 326 | PIB aux prix constants |
| Growth rates | 1.8 | 1.0 | 3.7 | 3.3 | 6.1 | 1.9 | 3.4 | Taux de croissance |
| **Samoa** | | | | | | | | **Samoa** |
| GDP at current prices | 231 | 241 | 262 | 319 | 377 | 417 | 435 | PIB aux prix courants |
| GDP per capita | 1 301 | 1 344 | 1 455 | 1 759 | 2 064 | 2 267 | 2 348 | PIB par habitant |
| GDP at constant prices | 141 | 151 | 152 | 157 | 163 | 172 | 178 | PIB aux prix constants |
| Growth rates | 6.8 | 6.5 | 1.0 | 3.5 | 3.7 | 5.1 | 4.0 | Taux de croissance |
| **San Marino** | | | | | | | | **Saint-Marin** |
| GDP at current prices | 774 | 815 | 880 | 1 123 | 1 317 | 1 346 | 1 412 | PIB aux prix courants |
| GDP per capita | 28 720 | 29 634 | 31 204 | 38 796 | 44 443 | 44 562 | 46 083 | PIB par habitant |
| GDP at constant prices | 1 223 | 1 292 | 1 295 | 1 345 | 1 407 | 1 407 | 1 431 | PIB aux prix constants |
| Growth rates | 2.2 | 5.6 | 0.3 | 3.9 | 4.6 | 0.0 | 1.7 | Taux de croissance |
| **Sao Tome and Principe** | | | | | | | | **Sao Tomé-et-Principe** |
| GDP at current prices | 46 | 48 | 54 | 59 | 64 | 71 | 74 | PIB aux prix courants |
| GDP per capita | 331 | 335 | 369 | 400 | 423 | 465 | 480 | PIB par habitant |
| GDP at constant prices | 69 | 72 | 75 | 78 | 81 | 83 | 88 | PIB aux prix constants |
| Growth rates | 3.1 | 4.4 | 3.6 | 4.1 | 4.0 | 3.0 | 5.5 | Taux de croissance |
| **Saudi Arabia** | | | | | | | | **Arabie saoudite** |
| GDP at current prices | 188 442 | 183 012 | 188 551 | 214 573 | 250 339 | 309 772 | 363 707 | PIB aux prix courants |
| GDP per capita | 9 057 | 8 569 | 8 603 | 9 545 | 10 862 | 13 119 | 15 045 | PIB par habitant |
| GDP at constant prices | 152 479 | 153 314 | 153 510 | 165 268 | 173 973 | 185 376 | 196 047 | PIB aux prix constants |
| Growth rates | 4.9 | 0.6 | 0.1 | 7.7 | 5.3 | 6.6 | 5.8 | Taux de croissance |
| **Senegal** | | | | | | | | **Sénégal** |
| GDP at current prices | 4 680 | 4 878 | 5 334 | 6 815 | 7 947 | 8 594 | 9 274 | PIB aux prix courants |
| GDP per capita | 453 | 460 | 490 | 610 | 693 | 730 | 768 | PIB par habitant |
| GDP at constant prices | 8 414 | 8 799 | 8 857 | 9 447 | 9 973 | 10 519 | 10 941 | PIB aux prix constants |
| Growth rates | 3.2 | 4.6 | 0.7 | 6.7 | 5.6 | 5.5 | 4.0 | Taux de croissance |
| **Serbia** | | | | | | | | **Serbie** |
| GDP at current prices[5] | 9 034 | 11 715 | 16 906 | 21 070 | 24 437 | 24 159 | 35 880 | PIB aux prix courants[5] |
| GDP per capita | 1 202 | 1 561 | 2 254 | 2 817 | 3 274 | 3 247 | 4 828 | PIB par habitant |
| GDP at constant prices[5] | 16 079 | 16 897 | 17 661 | 18 091 | 19 780 | 23 133 | 24 462 | PIB aux prix constants[5] |
| Growth rates | 5.2 | 5.1 | 4.5 | 2.4 | 9.3 | 17.0 | 5.7 | Taux de croissance |

**Gross domestic product and gross domestic product per capita**—In millions of US dollars at current and constant 1990 prices; per capita US dollars; real rates of growth (*continued*)

**Produit intérieur brut et produit intérieur brut par habitant**—En millions de dollars E.-U. aux prix courants et constants de 1990 ; par habitant en dollars E.-U. ; taux de croissance réels (*suite*)

| Country or area | 2000 | 2001 | 2002 | 2003 | 2004 | 2005 | 2006 | Pays ou zone |
|---|---|---|---|---|---|---|---|---|
| **Seychelles** | | | | | | | | **Seychelles** |
| GDP at current prices | 618 | 618 | 699 | 706 | 700 | 723 | 707 | PIB aux prix courants |
| GDP per capita | 7 619 | 7 518 | 8 407 | 8 399 | 8 249 | 8 449 | 8 209 | PIB par habitant |
| GDP at constant prices | 564 | 552 | 559 | 523 | 513 | 501 | 494 | PIB aux prix constants |
| Growth rates | -0.1 | -2.2 | 1.3 | -6.3 | -2.0 | -2.3 | -1.4 | Taux de croissance |
| **Sierra Leone** | | | | | | | | **Sierra Leone** |
| GDP at current prices | 921 | 1 167 | 1 307 | 1 421 | 1 416 | 1 523 | 1 828 | PIB aux prix courants |
| GDP per capita | 204 | 248 | 265 | 275 | 263 | 273 | 318 | PIB par habitant |
| GDP at constant prices | 590 | 697 | 825 | 914 | 1 002 | 1 076 | 1 181 | PIB aux prix constants |
| Growth rates | 3.7 | 18.2 | 18.4 | 10.8 | 9.6 | 7.5 | 9.8 | Taux de croissance |
| **Singapore** | | | | | | | | **Singapour** |
| GDP at current prices | 92 717 | 85 485 | 88 068 | 92 350 | 107 405 | 116 704 | 132 155 | PIB aux prix courants |
| GDP per capita | 23 079 | 20 864 | 21 151 | 21 879 | 25 129 | 26 968 | 30 159 | PIB par habitant |
| GDP at constant prices | 77 374 | 75 518 | 78 658 | 81 106 | 88 247 | 94 090 | 101 500 | PIB aux prix constants |
| Growth rates | 10.0 | -2.4 | 4.2 | 3.1 | 8.8 | 6.6 | 7.9 | Taux de croissance |
| **Slovakia** | | | | | | | | **Slovaquie** |
| GDP at current prices | 20 448 | 21 106 | 24 522 | 32 977 | 42 015 | 47 428 | 55 072 | PIB aux prix courants |
| GDP per capita | 3 795 | 3 917 | 4 552 | 6 122 | 7 800 | 8 804 | 10 221 | PIB par habitant |
| GDP at constant prices | 18 154 | 18 740 | 19 511 | 20 323 | 21 424 | 22 735 | 24 237 | PIB aux prix constants |
| Growth rates | 2.0 | 3.2 | .4.1 | 4.2 | 5.4 | 6.1 | 6.6 | Taux de croissance |
| **Slovenia** | | | | | | | | **Slovénie** |
| GDP at current prices | 19 314 | 19 772 | 22 291 | 28 069 | 32 601 | 34 354 | 36 901 | PIB aux prix courants |
| GDP per capita | 9 737 | 9 950 | 11 197 | 14 075 | 16 323 | 17 182 | 18 443 | PIB par habitant |
| GDP at constant prices | 20 929 | 21 485 | 22 227 | 22 816 | 23 826 | 24 786 | 25 983 | PIB aux prix constants |
| Growth rates | 4.1 | 2.7 | 3.5 | 2.7 | 4.4 | 4.0 | 4.8 | Taux de croissance |
| **Solomon Islands** | | | | | | | | **Iles Salomon** |
| GDP at current prices | 338 | 335 | 274 | 289 | 334 | 374 | 416 | PIB aux prix courants |
| GDP per capita | 814 | 784 | 625 | 642 | 725 | 792 | 860 | PIB par habitant |
| GDP at constant prices | 234 | 214 | 209 | 222 | 240 | 252 | 264 | PIB aux prix constants |
| Growth rates | -14.2 | -8.2 | -2.7 | 6.5 | 8.0 | 5.0 | 5.0 | Taux de croissance |
| **Somalia** | | | | | | | | **Somalie** |
| GDP at current prices | 2 070 | 1 974 | 2 056 | 2 100 | 2 213 | 2 316 | 2 390 | PIB aux prix courants |
| GDP per capita | 293 | 271 | 274 | 272 | 278 | 283 | 283 | PIB par habitant |
| GDP at constant prices | 759 | 786 | 813 | 831 | 854 | 874 | 896 | PIB aux prix constants |
| Growth rates | 3.5 | 3.5 | 3.5 | 2.1 | 2.8 | 2.4 | 2.4 | Taux de croissance |
| **South Africa** | | | | | | | | **Afrique du Sud** |
| GDP at current prices | 132 878[6] | 118 479[6] | 110 874[6] | 166 654[6] | 216 443[6] | 242 046[6] | 247 814 | PIB aux prix courants |
| GDP per capita | 2 927 | 2 575 | 2 380 | 3 5396 | 4 553 | 5 049 | 5 133 | PIB par habitant |
| GDP at constant prices | 134 158[6] | 137 828[6] | 142 883[6] | 147 341[6] | 154 471[6] | 162 343[6] | 167 933 | PIB aux prix constants |
| Growth rates | 4.2 | 2.7 | 3.7 | 3.1 | 4.8 | 5.1 | 3.4 | Taux de croissance |
| Spain | | | | | | | | Espagne |
| GDP at current prices | 580 673 | 609 102 | 686 278 | 883 184 | 1 043 137 | 1 126 020 | 1 225 007 | PIB aux prix courants |
| GDP per capita | 14 434 | 14 950 | 16 581 | 20 977 | 24 375 | 25 947 | 27 913 | PIB par habitant |
| GDP at constant prices | 686 489 | 711 533 | 730 774 | 753 032 | 777 453 | 804 904 | 835 147 | PIB aux prix constants |
| Growth rates | 5.1 | 3.7 | 2.7 | 3.1 | 3.2 | 3.5 | 3.8 | Taux de croissance |
| **Sri Lanka** | | | | | | | | **Sri Lanka** |
| GDP at current prices | 16 717 | 16 046 | 16 861 | 18 600 | 20 355 | 23 958 | 27 373 | PIB aux prix courants |
| GDP per capita | 893 | 853 | 893 | 981 | 1 069 | 1 253 | 1 425 | PIB par habitant |
| GDP at constant prices | 13 696 | 13 497 | 14 035 | 14 860 | 15 667 | 16 645 | 17 893 | PIB aux prix constants |
| Growth rates | 6.1 | -1.5 | 4.0 | 5.9 | 5.4 | 6.2 | 7.5 | Taux de croissance |
| **Sudan** | | | | | | | | **Soudan** |
| GDP at current prices | 11 549 | 13 028 | 14 718 | 16 108 | 19 040 | 24 917 | 35 219 | PIB aux prix courants |
| GDP per capita | 346 | 382 | 424 | 455 | 527 | 675 | 934 | PIB par habitant |
| GDP at constant prices | 29 487 | 31 370 | 33 394 | 35 431 | 37 970 | 40 977 | 45 921 | PIB aux prix constants |
| Growth rates | 8.3 | 6.4 | 6.5 | 6.1 | 7.2 | 7.9 | 12.1 | Taux de croissance |
| **Suriname** | | | | | | | | **Suriname** |
| GDP at current prices[7] | 775 | 665 | 937 | 1 094 | 1 283 | 1 543 | 1 820 | PIB aux prix courants[7] |
| GDP per capita | 1 775 | 1 510 | 2 113 | 2 449 | 2 853 | 3 410 | 3 998 | PIB par habitant |
| GDP at constant prices | 504 | 533 | 547 | 585 | 629 | 665 | 705 | PIB aux prix constants |
| Growth rates | 4.0 | 5.9 | 2.6 | 6.9 | 7.5 | 5.8 | 5.9 | Taux de croissance |

19 Gross domestic product and gross domestic product per capita—In millions of US dollars at current and constant 1990 prices; per capita US dollars; real rates of growth (*continued*)

Produit intérieur brut et produit intérieur brut par habitant—En millions de dollars E.-U. aux prix courants et constants de 1990 ; par habitant en dollars E.-U. ; taux de croissance réels (*suite*)

| Country or area | 2000 | 2001 | 2002 | 2003 | 2004 | 2005 | 2006 | Pays ou zone |
|---|---|---|---|---|---|---|---|---|
| **Swaziland** | | | | | | | | **Swaziland** |
| GDP at current prices | 1 388 | 1 260 | 1 192 | 1 904 | 2 518 | 2 730 | 2 719 | PIB aux prix courants |
| GDP per capita | 1 311 | 1 172 | 1 094 | 1 727 | 2 260 | 2 428 | 2 399 | PIB par habitant |
| GDP at constant prices | 1 185 | 1 205 | 1 238 | 1 268 | 1 297 | 1 321 | 1 337 | PIB aux prix constants |
| Growth rates | 2.1 | 1.7 | 2.8 | 2.4 | 2.3 | 1.8 | 1.2 | Taux de croissance |
| **Sweden** | | | | | | | | **Suède** |
| GDP at current prices | 242 003 | 221 543 | 243 564 | 304 145 | 349 041 | 357 356 | 382 825 | PIB aux prix courants |
| GDP per capita | 27 290 | 24 922 | 27 305 | 33 955 | 38 792 | 39 539 | 42 170 | PIB par habitant |
| GDP at constant prices | 293 656 | 296 794 | 302 720 | 307 845 | 320 549 | 329 855 | 343 018 | PIB aux prix constants |
| Growth rates | 4.3 | 1.1 | 2.0 | 1.7 | 4.1 | 2.9 | 4.0 | Taux de croissance |
| **Switzerland** | | | | | | | | **Suisse** |
| GDP at current prices | 246 044 | 250 344 | 276 225 | 322 848 | 359 719 | 365 887 | 374 583 | PIB aux prix courants |
| GDP per capita | 33 875 | 34 332 | 37 716 | 43 877 | 48 663 | 49 282 | 50 247 | PIB par habitant |
| GDP at constant prices | 261 716 | 264 441 | 265 250 | 264 803 | 270 876 | 276 102 | 283 606 | PIB aux prix constants |
| Growth rates | 3.6 | 1.0 | 0.3 | -0.2 | 2.3 | 1.9 | 2.7 | Taux de croissance |
| **Syrian Arab Republic** | | | | | | | | **Rép. arabe syrienne** |
| GDP at current prices | 19 651 | 21 174 | 21 659 | 20 724 | 24 295 | 27 892 | 31 326 | PIB aux prix courants |
| GDP per capita | 1 190 | 1 249 | 1 244 | 1 158 | 1 321 | 1 476 | 1 614 | PIB par habitant |
| GDP at constant prices | 19 693 | 20 702 | 21 926 | 22 170 | 24 086 | 25 171 | 25 986 | PIB aux prix constants |
| Growth rates | 0.6 | 5.1 | 5.9 | 1.1 | 8.6 | 4.5 | 3.2 | Taux de croissance |
| **Tajikistan** | | | | | | | | **Tadjikistan** |
| GDP at current prices | 861 | 1 081 | 1 221 | 1 555 | 2 076 | 2 312 | 2 813 | PIB aux prix courants |
| GDP per capita | 139 | 173 | 193 | 243 | 321 | 353 | 424 | PIB par habitant |
| GDP at constant prices | 1 091 | 1 196 | 1 325 | 1 472 | 1 624 | 1 733 | 1 854 | PIB aux prix constants |
| Growth rates | 8.3 | 9.6 | 10.8 | 11.1 | 10.3 | 6.7 | 7.0 | Taux de croissance |
| **Thailand** | | | | | | | | **Thaïlande** |
| GDP at current prices | 122 725 | 115 536 | 126 877 | 142 640 | 161 349 | 176 222 | 206 247 | PIB aux prix courants |
| GDP per capita | 2 023 | 1 888 | 2 057 | 2 296 | 2 579 | 2 797 | 3 251 | PIB par habitant |
| GDP at constant prices | 132 031 | 134 892 | 142 065 | 152 209 | 161 766 | 169 023 | 177 461 | PIB aux prix constants |
| Growth rates | 4.8 | 2.2 | 5.3 | 7.1 | 6.3 | 4.5 | 5.0 | Taux de croissance |
| **TFYR of Macedonia** | | | | | | | | **L'ex-R.y. Macédoine** |
| GDP at current prices | 3 587 | 3 437 | 3 791 | 4 630 | 5 369 | 5 816 | 6 304 | PIB aux prix courants |
| GDP per capita | 1 785 | 1 705 | 1 875 | 2 285 | 2 644 | 2 860 | 3 096 | PIB par habitant |
| GDP at constant prices | 4 215 | 4 024 | 4 058 | 4 173 | 4 343 | 4 521 | 4 702 | PIB aux prix constants |
| Growth rates | 4.6 | -4.5 | 0.9 | 2.8 | 4.1 | 4.1 | 4.0 | Taux de croissance |
| **Timor-Leste** | | | | | | | | **Timor-Leste** |
| GDP at current prices | 316 | 368 | 343 | 336 | 339 | 350 | 356 | PIB aux prix courants |
| GDP per capita | 386 | 434 | 383 | 352 | 334 | 328 | 319 | PIB par habitant |
| GDP at constant prices | 184 | 215 | 200 | 188 | 189 | 193 | 190 | PIB aux prix constants |
| Growth rates | 13.7 | 16.5 | -6.7 | -6.2 | 0.4 | 2.2 | -1.6 | Taux de croissance |
| **Togo** | | | | | | | | **Togo** |
| GDP at current prices | 1 294 | 1 332 | 1 473 | 1 728 | 2 009 | 2 105 | 2 284 | PIB aux prix courants |
| GDP per capita | 240 | 239 | 256 | 292 | 331 | 337 | 356 | PIB par habitant |
| GDP at constant prices | 1 868 | 1 871 | 1 949 | 1 986 | 2 045 | 2 061 | 2 147 | PIB aux prix constants |
| Growth rates | 1.0 | 0.2 | 4.1 | 1.9 | 3.0 | 0.8 | 4.2 | Taux de croissance |
| **Tonga** | | | | | | | | **Tonga** |
| GDP at current prices | 148 | 130 | 142 | 163 | 189 | 215 | 232 | PIB aux prix courants |
| GDP per capita | 1 513 | 1 323 | 1 444 | 1 648 | 1 906 | 2 159 | 2 328 | PIB par habitant |
| GDP at constant prices | 161 | 164 | 169 | 174 | 176 | 180 | 184 | PIB aux prix constants |
| Growth rates | 5.3 | 1.8 | 3.2 | 2.8 | 1.3 | 2.3 | 1.9 | Taux de croissance |
| **Trinidad and Tobago** | | | | | | | | **Trinité-et-Tobago** |
| GDP at current prices | 8 154 | 8 825 | 9 008 | 11 236 | 12 673 | 15 089 | 18 147 | PIB aux prix courants |
| GDP per capita | 6 270 | 6 760 | 6 876 | 8 547 | 9 607 | 11 399 | 13 661 | PIB par habitant |
| GDP at constant prices | 7 815 | 8 141 | 8 787 | 10 056 | 10 941 | 11 811 | 13 227 | PIB aux prix constants |
| Growth rates | 6.9 | 4.2 | 7.9 | 14.4 | 8.8 | 8.0 | 12.0 | Taux de croissance |
| **Tunisia** | | | | | | | | **Tunisie** |
| GDP at current prices | 19 444 | 19 969 | 21 048 | 24 993 | 28 221 | 28 758 | 30 673 | PIB aux prix courants |
| GDP per capita | 2 033 | 2 064 | 2 152 | 2 528 | 2 823 | 2 846 | 3 003 | PIB par habitant |
| GDP at constant prices | 19 566 | 20 516 | 20 869 | 22 030 | 23 359 | 24 346 | 25 588 | PIB aux prix constants |
| Growth rates | 4.7 | 4.9 | 1.7 | 5.6 | 6.0 | 4.2 | 5.1 | Taux de croissance |

**Gross domestic product and gross domestic product per capita**—In millions of US dollars at current and constant 1990 prices; per capita US dollars; real rates of growth (*continued*)

**Produit intérieur brut et produit intérieur brut par habitant**—En millions de dollars E.-U. aux prix courants et constants de 1990 ; par habitant en dollars E.-U. ; taux de croissance réels (*suite*)

| Country or area | 2000 | 2001 | 2002 | 2003 | 2004 | 2005 | 2006 | Pays ou zone |
|---|---|---|---|---|---|---|---|---|
| **Turkey** | | | | | | | | **Turquie** |
| GDP at current prices | 199 263 | 145 573 | 184 162 | 239 701 | 301 999 | 362 614 | 392 336 | PIB aux prix courants |
| GDP per capita | 2 924 | 2 105 | 2 626 | 3 372 | 4 193 | 4 969 | 5 307 | PIB par habitant |
| GDP at constant prices | 214 154 | 198 103 | 213 835 | 226 226 | 246 431 | 264 618 | 280 608 | PIB aux prix constants |
| Growth rates | 7.4 | -7.5 | 7.9 | 5.8 | 8.9 | 7.4 | 6.0 | Taux de croissance |
| **Turkmenistan** | | | | | | | | **Turkménistan** |
| GDP at current prices[3] | 4 157 | 4 442 | 4 531 | 4 779 | 5 160 | 5 795 | 6 500 | PIB aux prix courants[3] |
| GDP per capita | 923 | 973 | 979 | 1 017 | 1 083 | 1 199 | 1 327 | PIB par habitant |
| GDP at constant prices[3] | 2 413 | 2 517 | 2 524 | 2 606 | 2 737 | 2 983 | 3 251 | PIB aux prix constants[3] |
| Growth rates | 5.5 | 4.3 | 0.3 | 3.3 | 5.0 | 9.0 | 9.0 | Taux de croissance |
| **Turks and Caicos Islands** | | | | | | | | **Iles Turques et Caïques** |
| GDP at current prices | 319 | 359 | 367 | 410 | 486 | 570 | 648 | PIB aux prix courants |
| GDP per capita | 16 931 | 17 991 | 17 331 | 18 283 | 20 621 | 23 316 | 25 811 | PIB par habitant |
| GDP at constant prices | 259 | 277 | 281 | 307 | 342 | 389 | 432 | PIB aux prix constants |
| Growth rates | 4.9 | 7.0 | 1.2 | 9.3 | 11.4 | 13.9 | 11.1 | Taux de croissance |
| **Tuvalu** | | | | | | | | **Tuvalu** |
| GDP at current prices | 12[8] | 13[8] | 15[8] | 19 | 23 | 25 | 26 | PIB aux prix courants |
| GDP per capita | 1 204 | 1 253 | 1 421 | 1 815 | 2 191 | 2 385 | 2 441 | PIB par habitant |
| GDP at constant prices | 12[9] | 14[9] | 15[9] | 15 | 16 | 16 | 16 | PIB aux prix constants |
| Growth rates | -12.8 | 13.2 | 5.5 | 4.0 | 4.0 | 2.0 | 1.0 | Taux de croissance |
| **Uganda** | | | | | | | | **Ouganda** |
| GDP at current prices | 5 734 | 5 788 | 6 031 | 6 498 | 7 793 | 9 190 | 10 340 | PIB aux prix courants |
| GDP per capita | 232 | 227 | 229 | 239 | 278 | 317 | 346 | PIB par habitant |
| GDP at constant prices | 7 152 | 7 605 | 7 961 | 8 479 | 8 950 | 9 531 | 10 124 | PIB aux prix constants |
| Growth rates | 4.4 | 6.3 | 4.7 | 6.5 | 5.6 | 6.5 | 6.2 | Taux de croissance |
| **Ukraine** | | | | | | | | **Ukraine** |
| GDP at current prices | 31 262 | 38 009 | 42 393 | 50 133 | 64 881 | 86 142 | 106 469 | PIB aux prix courants |
| GDP per capita | 640 | 785 | 883 | 1 052 | 1 372 | 1 836 | 2 287 | PIB par habitant |
| GDP at constant prices | 38 967 | 42 565 | 44 799 | 49 097 | 55 062 | 56 562 | 60 578 | PIB aux prix constants |
| Growth rates | 5.9 | 9.2 | 5.3 | 9.6 | 12.2 | 2.7 | 7.1 | Taux de croissance |
| **United Arab Emirates** | | | | | | | | **Emirats arabes unis** |
| GDP at current prices | 70 522 | 69 546 | 74 959 | 88 536 | 104 204 | 133 583 | 182 218 | PIB aux prix courants |
| GDP per capita | 21 718 | 20 309 | 20 805 | 23 429 | 26 400 | 32 547 | 42 890 | PIB par habitant |
| GDP at constant prices | 57 797 | 59 800 | 60 871 | 68 105 | 73 150 | 79 318 | 88 420 | PIB aux prix constants |
| Growth rates | 12.3 | 3.5 | 1.8 | 11.9 | 7.4 | 8.4 | 11.5 | Taux de croissance |
| **United Kingdom** | | | | | | | | **Royaume-Uni** |
| GDP at current prices | 1 442 249 | 1 435 226 | 1 571 843 | 1 812 816 | 2 154 107 | 2 226 298 | 2 372 504 | PIB aux prix courants |
| GDP per capita | 24 500 | 24 278 | 26 467 | 30 378 | 35 923 | 36 954 | 39 207 | PIB par habitant |
| GDP at constant prices | 1 259 058 | 1 288 671 | 1 315 207 | 1 350 268 | 1 394 316 | 1 420 146 | 1 460 101 | PIB aux prix constants |
| Growth rates | 3.8 | 2.4 | 2.1 | 2.7 | 3.3 | 1.9 | 2.8 | Taux de croissance |
| **United Rep. of Tanzania** | | | | | | | | **Rép.-Unie de Tanzanie** |
| GDP at current prices | 9 093 | 9 453 | 9 772 | 10 297 | 11 351 | 12 586 | 12 870 | PIB aux prix courants |
| GDP per capita | 276 | 280 | 282 | 290 | 311 | 336 | 335 | PIB par habitant |
| GDP at constant prices | 6 795 | 7 219 | 7 742 | 8 292 | 8 848 | 9 465 | 10 026 | PIB aux prix constants |
| Growth rates | 5.1 | 6.2 | 7.2 | 7.1 | 6.7 | 7.0 | 5.9 | Taux de croissance |
| **United States** | | | | | | | | **Etats-Unis** |
| GDP at current prices | 9 764 800 | 10 075 900 | 10 417 600 | 10 908 000 | 11 657 300 | 12 397 900 | 13 192 290 | PIB aux prix courants |
| GDP per capita | 34 280 | 35 006 | 35 820 | 37 123 | 39 271 | 41 347 | 43 562 | PIB par habitant |
| GDP at constant prices | 7 968 520 | 8 028 989 | 8 158 495 | 8 364 302 | 8 692 270 | 8 973 072 | 9 276 652 | PIB aux prix constants |
| Growth rates | 3.7 | 0.8 | 1.6 | 2.5 | 3.9 | 3.2 | 3.4 | Taux de croissance |
| **Uruguay** | | | | | | | | **Uruguay** |
| GDP at current prices | 20 086 | 18 561 | 12 277 | 11 191 | 13 216 | 16 615 | 19 308 | PIB aux prix courants |
| GDP per capita | 6 053 | 5 582 | 3 691 | 3 366 | 3 976 | 4 996 | 5 796 | PIB par habitant |
| GDP at constant prices | 11 341 | 10 961 | 9 735 | 9 972 | 11 159 | 11 871 | 12 702 | PIB aux prix constants |
| Growth rates | -1.4 | -3.4 | -11.2 | 2.4 | 11.9 | 6.4 | 7.0 | Taux de croissance |
| **Uzbekistan** | | | | | | | | **Ouzbékistan** |
| GDP at current prices | 13 759 | 9 312[3] | 9 877 | 10 155 | 12 016 | 13 751 | 16 137 | PIB aux prix courants |
| GDP per capita | 557 | 371[3] | 388 | 393 | 458 | 517 | 598 | PIB par habitant |
| GDP at constant prices | 14 469 | 15 087[3] | 15 726 | 16 426 | 17 698 | 18 955 | 20 660 | PIB aux prix constants |
| Growth rates | 4.0 | 4.3 | 4.2 | 4.5 | 7.7 | 7.1 | 9.0 | Taux de croissance |

**Gross domestic product and gross domestic product per capita**—In millions of US dollars at current and constant 1990 prices; per capita US dollars; real rates of growth (*continued*)

**Produit intérieur brut et produit intérieur brut par habitant**—En millions de dollars E.-U. aux prix courants et constants de 1990 ; par habitant en dollars E.-U. ; taux de croissance réels (*suite*)

| Country or area | 2000 | 2001 | 2002 | 2003 | 2004 | 2005 | 2006 | Pays ou zone |
|---|---|---|---|---|---|---|---|---|
| **Vanuatu** | | | | | | | | **Vanuatu** |
| GDP at current prices | 245 | 234 | 235 | 276 | 320 | 347 | 361 | PIB aux prix courants |
| GDP per capita | 1 289 | 1 206 | 1 181 | 1 351 | 1 526 | 1 610 | 1 635 | PIB par habitant |
| GDP at constant prices | 223 | 216 | 206 | 211 | 220 | 227 | 234 | PIB aux prix constants |
| Growth rates | 2.7 | -2.7[3] | -4.9 | 2.4 | 4.2 | 3.1 | 3.4 | Taux de croissance |
| **Venezuela (Bolivarian Rep. of)** | | | | | | | | **Venezuela (Rép. bolivar. du)** |
| GDP at current prices | 117 148 | 122 910 | 92 889 | 83 529 | 112 451 | 143 625 | 180 358 | PIB aux prix courants |
| GDP per capita | 4 801 | 4 943 | 3 667 | 3 238 | 4 282 | 5 374 | 6 633 | PIB par habitant |
| GDP at constant prices | 57 831 | 59 793 | 54 498 | 50 272 | 59 465 | 65 012 | 71 730 | PIB aux prix constants |
| Growth rates | 3.7 | 3.4 | -8.9 | -7.8 | 18.3 | 9.3 | 10.3 | Taux de croissance |
| **Viet Nam** | | | | | | | | **Viet Nam** |
| GDP at current prices | 31 173 | 32 685 | 35 064 | 39 553 | 45 724 | 52 832 | 57 983 | PIB aux prix courants |
| GDP per capita | 394 | 407 | 431 | 479 | 545 | 621 | 673 | PIB par habitant |
| GDP at constant prices | 13 433 | 14 359 | 15 376 | 16 505 | 17 791 | 19 290 | 20 795 | PIB aux prix constants |
| Growth rates | 6.8 | 6.9 | 7.1 | 7.3 | 7.8 | 8.4 | 7.8 | Taux de croissance |
| **Yemen** | | | | | | | | **Yémen** |
| GDP at current prices | 9 636 | 9 854 | 10 693 | 11 778 | 13 874 | 15 890 | 18 543 | PIB aux prix courants |
| GDP per capita | 530 | 526 | 554 | 593 | 677 | 753 | 853 | PIB par habitant |
| GDP at constant prices | 7 207 | 7 485 | 7 779 | 8 070 | 8 378 | 8 764 | 9 109 | PIB aux prix constants |
| Growth rates | 9.5 | 3.9 | 3.9 | 3.7 | 3.8 | 4.6 | 3.9 | Taux de croissance |
| **Zambia** | | | | | | | | **Zambie** |
| GDP at current prices | 3 239 | 3 637 | 3 697 | 4 305 | 5 440 | 7 315 | 10 974 | PIB aux prix courants |
| GDP per capita | 310 | 341 | 340 | 389 | 483 | 637 | 938 | PIB par habitant |
| GDP at constant prices | 4 002 | 4 198 | 4 336 | 4 523 | 4 803 | 5 050 | 5 354 | PIB aux prix constants |
| Growth rates | 3.6 | 4.9 | 3.3 | 4.3 | 6.2 | 5.1 | 6.0 | Taux de croissance |
| **Zanzibar** | | | | | | | | **Zanzibar** |
| GDP at current prices | 238 | 254 | 265 | 276 | 316 | 351 | 358 | PIB aux prix courants |
| GDP per capita | 260 | 269 | 270 | 273 | 304 | 327 | 329 | PIB par habitant |
| GDP at constant prices | 175 | 192 | 208 | 220 | 235 | 248 | 263 | PIB aux prix constants |
| Growth rates | 3.6 | 9.3 | 8.6 | 5.9 | 6.5 | 5.6 | 5.9 | Taux de croissance |
| **Zimbabwe** | | | | | | | | **Zimbabwe** |
| GDP at current prices | 5 628[3,9] | 5 609[3,9] | 5 427[3,9] | 5 004[3,9] | 3 071 | 2 227 | 1 765 | PIB aux prix courants |
| GDP per capita | 445[3] | 439[3] | 422[3] | 387[3] | 236 | 170 | 133 | PIB par habitant |
| GDP at constant prices | 9 267[3,9] | 9 018[3,9] | 8 576[3,9] | 7 743[3,9] | 7 796 | 7 243 | 6 895 | PIB aux prix constants |
| Growth rates | -7.7 | -2.7 | -4.9 | -9.7 | 0.7 | -7.1 | -4.8 | Taux de croissance |

Source

United Nations Statistics Division, New York, the national accounts database, last accessed December 2007.

Notes

1  At producers' prices.
2  For statistical purposes, the data for China do not include those for the Hong Kong Special Administrative Region (Hong Kong SAR), Macao Special Administrative Region (Macao SAR) and Taiwan Province of China.
3  Price-adjusted rates of exchange (PARE) are used for selected years for conversion to US dollars due to large distortions in the dollar levels of per capita GDP with the use of IMF market exchange rates.

4  Includes Guadeloupe, Martinique, Réunion and French Guiana.
5  Beginning 1999, data for Kosovo and Metohia are excluded.
6  Estimates are prepared by the South African Reserve Bank.
7  Excluding the informal sector.
8  GDP at market prices.
9  At factor cost.

Source

Organisation des Nations Unies, Division de statistique, New York, la base de données sur les comptes nationaux, dernier accès décembre 2007.

Notes

1  Aux prix à la production.
2  Pour la présentation des statistiques, les données pour la Chine ne comprennent pas la Région Administrative Spéciale de Hong Kong (Hong Kong RAS), la Région Administrative Spéciale de Macao (Macao RAS) et la province de Taiwan.
3  Pour certaines années, on utilise les Taux de change corrigés des prix (TCCP) pour effectuer la conversion en dollars des États-Unis, en raison des aberrations importantes relevées dans les niveaux du PNB exprimés en dollars après conversion à l'aide des taux de change du marché communiqués par le FMI.

4  Y compris Guadeloupe, Martinique, Réunion et Guyane française.
5  A compter de 1999, non compris les données de Kosovo et Metohia.
6  Chiffres établis par la South African Reserve Bank.
7  Non compris le secteur informel.
8  PIB aux prix du marché.
9  Au coût des facteurs.

# Implicit price deflators of gross domestic product
Index base: 1990 = 100

# Déflateurs implicites des prix de produit intérieur brut
Indice base : 1990 = 100

| Country or area<br>Pays ou zone | Year<br>Année | GDP at current price<br>PIB aux prix courants | | GDP at constant prices<br>PIB aux prix constants | GDP implicit price deflators<br>PIB déflateurs implicites des prix | | Exchange rates<br>Cours des changes |
|---|---|---|---|---|---|---|---|
| | | National currency<br>Monnaie nationale | US dollars<br>Dollars E.-U. | National currency<br>Monnaie nationale | National currency<br>Monnaie nationale | US dollars<br>Dollars E.-U. | |
| **Africa — Afrique** | | | | | | | |
| Algeria<br>Algérie | 2000 | 743.8 | 88.5 | 118.4 | 628.2 | 74.8 | 840.2 |
| | 2004 | 1 105.3 | 137.4 | 142.8 | 774.3 | 96.2 | 804.5 |
| | 2005 | 1 352.6 | 165.4 | 150.3 | 899.8 | 110.0 | 818.0 |
| | 2006 | 1 519.3 | 187.3 | 154.4 | 984.3 | 121.4 | 811.0 |
| Angola<br>Angola | 2000 | 29 761.7[1] | 88.7 | 113.4 | 26 238.9[1] | 78.2 | 33 562.2[1] |
| | 2004 | 536 379.7[1] | 192.1 | 153.9 | 348 516.8[1] | 124.8 | 279 237.8[1] |
| | 2005 | 928 489.8[1] | 318.7 | 185.6 | 500 188.2[1] | 171.7 | 291 332.2[1] |
| | 2006 | 1 233 390.1[1] | 459.1 | 212.1 | 581 442.6[1] | 216.5 | 268 626.7[1] |
| Benin<br>Bénin | 2000 | 334.4 | 127.9 | 155.6 | 214.9 | 82.2 | 261.5 |
| | 2004 | 426.0 | 219.6 | 185.0 | 230.3 | 118.7 | 194.0 |
| | 2005 | 457.6 | 236.2 | 190.3 | 240.5 | 124.2 | 193.7 |
| | 2006 | 488.6 | 254.4 | 197.1 | 247.8 | 129.1 | 192.0 |
| Botswana<br>Botswana | 2000 | 384.3 | 140.1 | 165.5 | 232.2 | 84.7 | 274.2 |
| | 2004 | 614.4 | 243.6 | 208.9 | 294.1 | 116.6 | 252.2 |
| | 2005 | 703.5 | 256.1 | 226.4 | 310.7 | 113.1 | 274.7 |
| | 2006 | 794.6 | 253.3 | 235.8 | 337.0 | 107.4 | 313.7 |
| Burkina Faso<br>Burkina Faso | 2000 | 202.4 | 77.4 | 158.1 | 128.0 | 49.0 | 261.5 |
| | 2004 | 307.5 | 158.5 | 201.7 | 152.4 | 78.6 | 194.0 |
| | 2005 | 335.1 | 173.0 | 213.6 | 156.9 | 81.0 | 193.7 |
| | 2006 | 367.9 | 191.5 | 226.2 | 162.6 | 84.7 | 192.1 |
| Burundi<br>Burundi | 2000 | 259.9 | 61.8 | 84.5 | 307.6 | 73.1 | 420.8 |
| | 2004 | 380.6 | 59.2 | 93.0 | 409.3 | 63.7 | 642.9 |
| | 2005 | 438.4 | 69.4 | 93.8 | 467.3 | 74.0 | 631.5 |
| | 2006 | 487.2 | 81.1 | 99.5 | 489.6 | 81.5 | 600.5 |
| Cameroon<br>Cameroun | 2000 | 169.7 | 64.9 | 123.1 | 137.8 | 52.7 | 261.5 |
| | 2004 | 213.9 | 110.2 | 146.6 | 145.9 | 75.2 | 194.0 |
| | 2005 | 230.0 | 118.7 | 150.4 | 152.9 | 78.9 | 193.7 |
| | 2006 | 248.6 | 129.5 | 156.7 | 158.6 | 82.6 | 192.1 |
| Cape Verde<br>Cap-Vert | 2000 | 299.2 | 175.1 | 192.6 | 155.4 | 90.9 | 170.9 |
| | 2004 | 380.6 | 300.2 | 235.1 | 161.9 | 127.7 | 126.8 |
| | 2005 | 404.1 | 319.1 | 248.7 | 162.5 | 128.3 | 126.6 |
| | 2006 | 454.9 | 362.4 | 262.3 | 173.4 | 138.2 | 125.5 |
| Central African Rep.<br>Rép. centrafricaine | 2000 | 182.7 | 69.9 | 112.1 | 163.0 | 62.3 | 261.5 |
| | 2004 | 185.4 | 95.5 | 104.5 | 177.3 | 91.4 | 194.0 |
| | 2005 | 197.3 | 101.9 | 106.8 | 184.7 | 95.3 | 193.7 |
| | 2006 | 210.1 | 109.4 | 110.3 | 190.6 | 99.2 | 192.1 |
| Chad<br>Tchad | 2000 | 235.0 | 89.9 | 140.9 | 166.8 | 63.8 | 261.5 |
| | 2004 | 555.6 | 286.4 | 260.5 | 213.3 | 109.9 | 194.0 |
| | 2005 | 739.5 | 381.7 | 282.8 | 261.5 | 135.0 | 193.7 |
| | 2006 | 826.7 | 430.5 | 290.9 | 284.2 | 148.0 | 192.1 |
| Comoros<br>Comores | 2000 | 164.0 | 83.6 | 115.6 | 141.9 | 72.4 | 196.1 |
| | 2004 | 220.5 | 151.5 | 125.9 | 175.1 | 120.3 | 145.5 |
| | 2005 | 227.6 | 156.7 | 129.5 | 175.8 | 121.0 | 145.3 |
| | 2006 | 235.1 | 163.2 | 131.1 | 179.3 | 124.5 | 144.0 |

| Country or area<br>Pays ou zone | Year<br>Année | GDP at current price<br>PIB aux prix courants | | GDP at constant prices<br>PIB aux prix constants | GDP implicit price deflators<br>PIB déflateurs implicites des prix | | Exchange rates<br>Cours des changes |
|---|---|---|---|---|---|---|---|
| | | National currency<br>Monnaie nationale | US dollars<br>Dollars E.-U. | National currency<br>Monnaie nationale | National currency<br>Monnaie nationale | US dollars<br>Dollars E.-U. | |
| Congo<br>Congo | 2000 | 300.8 | 115.0 | 116.3 | 258.7 | 98.9 | 261.5 |
| | 2004 | 303.9 | 156.6 | 132.3 | 229.7 | 118.4 | 194.0 |
| | 2005 | 401.0 | 207.0 | 144.2 | 278.1 | 143.6 | 193.7 |
| | 2006 | 492.5 | 256.4 | 154.9 | 317.9 | 165.6 | 192.1 |
| Côte d'Ivoire<br>Côte d'Ivoire | 2000 | 234.9 | 89.8 | 127.4 | 184.3 | 70.5 | 261.5 |
| | 2004 | 262.1 | 135.1 | 129.7 | 202.2 | 104.2 | 194.0 |
| | 2005 | 276.3 | 142.6 | 132.1 | 209.2 | 108.0 | 193.7 |
| | 2006 | 290.9 | 151.5 | 134.6 | 216.1 | 112.5 | 192.1 |
| Dem. Rep. of the Congo<br>Rép. dém. du Congo | 2000 | 1 485 325.0[1] | 62.9[2] | 56.2 | 2 641 502.9[1] | 111.9[2] | 2 359 959.7[1] |
| | 2004 | 13 047 750.0[1] | 78.9 | 64.3 | 20 305 054.9[1] | 122.8 | 16 533 714.6[1] |
| | 2005 | 16 828 000.0[1] | 85.0 | 68.4 | 24 598 056.4[1] | 124.3 | 19 789 265.0[1] |
| | 2006 | 19 342 264.2[1] | 98.9 | 72.9 | 26 549 044.8[1] | 135.8 | 19 554 426.4[1] |
| Djibouti<br>Djibouti | 2000 | 121.0 | 121.0 | 113.0 | 107.1 | 107.1 | 100.0 |
| | 2004 | 144.6 | 144.6 | 125.9 | 114.8 | 114.8 | 100.0 |
| | 2005 | 154.4 | 154.4 | 129.9 | 118.8 | 118.8 | 100.0 |
| | 2006 | 165.7 | 165.7 | 135.4 | 122.4 | 122.4 | 100.0 |
| Egypt<br>Egypte | 2000 | 319.7 | 252.7 | 159.3 | 200.7 | 158.6 | 126.5 |
| | 2004 | 472.2 | 209.2 | 186.3 | 253.4 | 112.3 | 225.8 |
| | 2005 | 541.7 | 257.2 | 199.1 | 272.1 | 129.2 | 210.6 |
| | 2006 | 583.5 | 279.3 | 212.4 | 274.7 | 131.5 | 208.9 |
| Equatorial Guinea<br>Guinée équatoriale | 2000 | 2 311.2 | 883.8 | 655.3 | 352.7 | 134.9 | 261.5 |
| | 2004 | 6 725.8 | 3 466.3 | 1 951.8 | 344.6 | 177.6 | 194.0 |
| | 2005 | 10 608.8 | 5 476.0 | 2 133.4 | 497.3 | 256.7 | 193.7 |
| | 2006 | 13 694.4 | 7 130.6 | 2 111.4 | 648.6 | 337.7 | 192.0 |
| Eritrea<br>Erythrée | 2000 | 391.5 | 84.3 | 181.2 | 216.0 | 46.5 | 464.5 |
| | 2004 | 831.4 | 125.0 | 211.0 | 394.1 | 59.2 | 665.4 |
| | 2005 | 951.8 | 128.3 | 221.1 | 430.4 | 58.0 | 741.7 |
| | 2006 | 1 148.7 | 154.8 | 225.6 | 509.3 | 68.6 | 742.0 |
| Ethiopia<br>Ethiopie | 2000 | 285.9 | 72.0 | 132.7 | 215.4 | 54.3 | 397.0 |
| | 2004 | 362.9 | 87.0 | 158.0 | 229.7 | 55.1 | 417.2 |
| | 2005 | 436.8 | 104.3 | 174.3 | 250.6 | 59.9 | 418.7 |
| | 2006 | 513.1 | 122.1 | 192.8 | 266.1 | 63.3 | 420.2 |
| Gabon<br>Gabon | 2000 | 239.1 | 91.4 | 117.9 | 202.8 | 77.6 | 261.5 |
| | 2004 | 251.0 | 129.3 | 124.9 | 201.0 | 103.6 | 194.0 |
| | 2005 | 307.5 | 158.7 | 128.6 | 239.1 | 123.4 | 193.7 |
| | 2006 | 332.3 | 173.0 | 131.4 | 252.9 | 131.7 | 192.0 |
| Gambia<br>Gambie | 2000 | 204.9 | 126.3 | 142.1 | 144.2 | 88.9 | 162.2 |
| | 2004 | 458.2 | 120.3 | 163.3 | 280.6 | 73.6 | 381.0 |
| | 2005 | 501.7 | 138.4 | 171.4 | 292.7 | 80.7 | 362.5 |
| | 2006 | 545.6 | 153.2 | 181.1 | 301.3 | 84.6 | 356.1 |
| Ghana<br>Ghana | 2000 | 1 336.5 | 80.0 | 152.3 | 877.7 | 52.5 | 1 671.5 |
| | 2004 | 3 930.9 | 142.5 | 183.7 | 2 139.9 | 77.6 | 2 759.4 |
| | 2005 | 4 776.1 | 171.8 | 194.4 | 2 456.3 | 88.4 | 2 780.1 |
| | 2006 | 5 529.4 | 196.7 | 206.0 | 2 683.6 | 95.5 | 2 811.5 |
| Guinea<br>Guinée | 2000 | 294.3 | 111.2 | 149.0 | 197.5 | 74.6 | 264.6 |
| | 2004 | 459.2 | 136.2 | 167.8 | 273.6 | 81.2 | 337.0 |
| | 2005 | 573.4 | 103.9 | 173.4 | 330.7 | 59.9 | 552.0 |
| | 2006 | 763.4 | 101.4 | 182.2 | 419.1 | 55.7 | 753.0 |

| Country or area<br>Pays ou zone | Year<br>Année | GDP at current price<br>PIB aux prix courants | | GDP at constant prices<br>PIB aux prix constants | GDP implicit price deflators<br>PIB déflateurs implicites des prix | | |
|---|---|---|---|---|---|---|---|
| | | National currency<br>Monnaie nationale | US dollars<br>Dollars E.-U. | National currency<br>Monnaie nationale | National currency<br>Monnaie nationale | US dollars<br>Dollars E.-U. | Exchange rates<br>Cours des changes |
| Guinea-Bissau | 2000 | 1 954.7 | 92.3 | 113.4 | 1 723.2 | 81.4 | 2 117.7 |
| Guinée-Bissau | 2004 | 1 817.1 | 115.7 | 108.6 | 1 673.7 | 106.5 | 1 571.3 |
| | 2005 | 2 023.6 | 129.0 | 112.4 | 1 800.8 | 114.8 | 1 568.8 |
| | 2006 | 2 143.7 | 137.8 | 117.6 | 1 823.3 | 117.2 | 1 555.2 |
| Kenya | 2000 | 379.7 | 114.2 | 119.8 | 316.8 | 95.3 | 332.4 |
| Kenya | 2004 | 507.2 | 146.8 | 136.0 | 373.0 | 108.0 | 345.5 |
| | 2005 | 559.6 | 169.7 | 143.9 | 389.0 | 118.0 | 329.7 |
| | 2006 | 677.3 | 215.2 | 151.7 | 446.6 | 141.9 | 314.7 |
| Lesotho | 2000 | 374.2 | 139.5 | 140.2 | 267.0 | 99.5 | 268.2 |
| Lesotho | 2004 | 532.5 | 213.3 | 158.0 | 336.9 | 135.0 | 249.7 |
| | 2005 | 579.1 | 235.6 | 162.7 | 355.9 | 144.8 | 245.8 |
| | 2006 | 612.3 | 234.0 | 165.3 | 370.5 | 141.6 | 261.7 |
| Liberia | 2000 | 145.9 | 145.9 | 125.1 | 116.7 | 116.7 | 100.0 |
| Libéria | 2004 | 129.2 | 129.2 | 94.0 | 137.5 | 137.5 | 100.0 |
| | 2005 | 142.7 | 142.7 | 98.9 | 144.2 | 144.2 | 100.0 |
| | 2006 | 178.7 | 178.7 | 105.9 | 168.8 | 168.8 | 100.0 |
| Libyan Arab Jamah. | 2000 | 214.4 | 118.5 | 122.3 | 175.3 | 96.9 | 180.9 |
| Jamah. arabe libyenne | 2004 | 480.9 | 104.4 | 152.9 | 314.4 | 68.2 | 460.8 |
| | 2005 | 619.2 | 134.0 | 158.4 | 391.0 | 84.6 | 462.0 |
| | 2006 | 809.0 | 174.4 | 166.3 | 486.6 | 104.9 | 463.9 |
| Madagascar | 2000 | 570.3 | 125.9 | 118.8 | 480.2 | 106.0 | 452.9 |
| Madagascar | 2004 | 886.2 | 141.7 | 127.0 | 697.5 | 111.5 | 625.4 |
| | 2005 | 1 148.3 | 171.3 | 132.9 | 864.2 | 128.9 | 670.3 |
| | 2006 | 1 281.7 | 178.8 | 139.2 | 921.0 | 128.5 | 716.9 |
| Malawi | 2000 | 2 171.0 | 99.5 | 175.2 | 1 239.0 | 56.8 | 2 182.1 |
| Malawi | 2004 | 4 333.2 | 108.6 | 193.9 | 2 235.4 | 56.0 | 3 990.3 |
| | 2005 | 5 144.5 | 118.6 | 197.5 | 2 604.4 | 60.0 | 4 339.2 |
| | 2006 | 6 332.9 | 127.1 | 214.4 | 2 954.3 | 59.3 | 4 984.5 |
| Mali | 2000 | 276.7 | 105.8 | 149.1 | 185.6 | 71.0 | 261.5 |
| Mali | 2004 | 385.2 | 198.5 | 191.5 | 201.2 | 103.7 | 194.0 |
| | 2005 | 423.5 | 218.6 | 203.2 | 208.4 | 107.6 | 193.7 |
| | 2006 | 456.5 | 237.7 | 212.6 | 214.8 | 111.8 | 192.1 |
| Mauritania | 2000 | 303.5 | 102.4 | 134.4 | 225.9 | 76.2 | 296.4 |
| Mauritanie | 2004 | 467.1 | 146.4 | 155.3 | 300.9 | 94.3 | 319.0 |
| | 2005 | 587.4 | 178.3 | 163.7 | 358.9 | 108.9 | 329.4 |
| | 2006 | 885.6 | 260.7 | 186.8 | 474.0 | 139.6 | 339.7 |
| Mauritius | 2000 | 312.8 | 177.1 | 167.6 | 186.7 | 105.7 | 176.6 |
| Maurice | 2004 | 456.5 | 246.8 | 192.8 | 236.8 | 128.0 | 185.0 |
| | 2005 | 482.3 | 243.0 | 195.5 | 246.7 | 124.3 | 198.4 |
| | 2006 | 528.7 | 247.8 | 203.6 | 259.6 | 121.7 | 213.3 |
| Morocco | 2000 | 165.5 | 128.4 | 124.8 | 132.6 | 102.9 | 128.9 |
| Maroc | 2004 | 210.2 | 195.4 | 150.6 | 139.6 | 129.7 | 107.6 |
| | 2005 | 219.7 | 204.3 | 153.2 | 143.4 | 133.4 | 107.6 |
| | 2006 | 241.7 | 226.5 | 164.4 | 147.0 | 137.8 | 106.7 |
| Mozambique | 2000 | 2 319.7 | 141.5 | 166.6 | 1 392.4 | 85.0 | 1 638.9 |
| Mozambique | 2004 | 5 307.3 | 218.4 | 236.4 | 2 245.0 | 92.4 | 2 430.4 |
| | 2005 | 6 083.7 | 245.1 | 251.1 | 2 423.1 | 97.6 | 2 482.2 |
| | 2006 | 7 381.8 | 270.0 | 272.5 | 2 708.9 | 99.1 | 2 733.8 |

| Country or area<br>Pays ou zone | Year<br>Année | GDP at current price<br>PIB aux prix courants | | GDP at constant prices<br>PIB aux prix constants | GDP implicit price deflators<br>PIB déflateurs implicites des prix | | |
|---|---|---|---|---|---|---|---|
| | | National currency<br>Monnaie nationale | US dollars<br>Dollars E.-U. | National currency<br>Monnaie nationale | National currency<br>Monnaie nationale | US dollars<br>Dollars E.-U. | Exchange rates<br>Cours des changes |
| Namibia<br>Namibie | 2000 | 391.3 | 145.9 | 151.3 | 258.7 | 96.4 | 268.2 |
| | 2004 | 609.5 | 244.1 | 181.2 | 336.4 | 134.8 | 249.7 |
| | 2005 | 644.0 | 262.0 | 187.6 | 343.3 | 139.7 | 245.8 |
| | 2006 | 706.1 | 269.8 | 196.0 | 360.3 | 137.7 | 261.7 |
| Niger<br>Niger | 2000 | 173.9 | 66.5 | 124.7 | 139.4 | 53.3 | 261.5 |
| | 2004 | 216.2 | 111.4 | 145.6 | 148.5 | 76.5 | 194.0 |
| | 2005 | 250.8 | 129.5 | 156.0 | 160.8 | 83.0 | 193.7 |
| | 2006 | 259.7 | 135.2 | 161.5 | 160.8 | 83.7 | 192.1 |
| Nigeria<br>Nigéria | 2000 | 1 377.3 | 108.9 | 125.5 | 1 097.7 | 86.8 | 1 265.2 |
| | 2004 | 2 347.2 | 142.0 | 160.6 | 1 462.0 | 88.4 | 1 653.2 |
| | 2005 | 2 994.8 | 183.4 | 170.6 | 1 756.0 | 107.5 | 1 633.2 |
| | 2006 | 3 400.8 | 214.5 | 179.6 | 1 893.4 | 119.4 | 1 585.2 |
| Rwanda<br>Rwanda | 2000 | 320.5 | 68.8 | 104.1 | 307.7 | 66.1 | 465.6 |
| | 2004 | 495.8 | 71.9 | 127.0 | 390.3 | 56.6 | 689.9 |
| | 2005 | 546.9 | 82.1 | 134.6 | 406.2 | 61.0 | 666.4 |
| | 2006 | 594.2 | 90.1 | 138.7 | 428.5 | 65.0 | 659.2 |
| Sao Tome and Principe<br>Sao Tomé-et-Principe | 2000 | 4 478.8 | 80.5 | 120.2 | 3 726.9 | 67.0 | 5 565.9 |
| | 2004 | 7 628.0 | 110.4 | 140.7 | 5 423.4 | 78.5 | 6 908.8 |
| | 2005 | 9 083.4 | 123.3 | 144.9 | 6 270.6 | 85.1 | 7 366.0 |
| | 2006 | 11 229.4 | 129.3 | 152.8 | 7 348.0 | 84.6 | 8 683.5 |
| Senegal<br>Sénégal | 2000 | 201.1 | 76.9 | 138.3 | 145.5 | 55.6 | 261.5 |
| | 2004 | 253.5 | 130.6 | 163.9 | 154.6 | 79.7 | 194.0 |
| | 2005 | 273.6 | 141.3 | 172.9 | 158.3 | 81.7 | 193.7 |
| | 2006 | 292.7 | 152.4 | 179.8 | 162.8 | 84.8 | 192.0 |
| Seychelles<br>Seychelles | 2000 | 179.5 | 167.7 | 153.1 | 117.3 | 109.6 | 107.1 |
| | 2004 | 195.7 | 189.9 | 139.1 | 140.7 | 136.5 | 103.1 |
| | 2005 | 202.0 | 196.1 | 135.9 | 148.7 | 144.3 | 103.1 |
| | 2006 | 198.4 | 191.8 | 133.9 | 148.1 | 143.2 | 103.4 |
| Sierra Leone<br>Sierra Leone | 2000 | 1 352.1 | 97.9 | 62.7 | 2 157.4 | 156.2 | 1 381.4 |
| | 2004 | 2 684.5 | 150.5 | 106.5 | 2 521.9 | 141.4 | 1 783.6 |
| | 2005 | 3 088.4 | 161.9 | 114.4 | 2 699.7 | 141.5 | 1 908.0 |
| | 2006 | 3 800.4 | 194.3 | 125.6 | 3 027.0 | 154.8 | 1 955.7 |
| Somalia<br>Somalie | 2000 | 1 139.7 | 208.3 | 76.4 | 1 491.9 | 272.6 | 547.2 |
| | 2004 | 1 895.0 | 222.7 | 85.9 | 2 206.2 | 259.2 | 851.0 |
| | 2005 | 2 031.0 | 232.9 | 88.0 | 2 309.2 | 264.8 | 871.9 |
| | 2006 | 1 936.9 | 240.4 | 90.1 | 2 149.9 | 266.9 | 805.6 |
| South Africa<br>Afrique du Sud | 2000 | 318.2 | 118.6 | 119.8 | 265.7 | 99.1 | 268.2 |
| | 2004 | 482.4 | 193.2 | 137.9 | 349.8 | 140.1 | 249.7 |
| | 2005 | 531.1 | 216.1 | 144.9 | 366.5 | 149.1 | 245.8 |
| | 2006 | 579.0 | 221.2 | 149.9 | 386.2 | 147.6 | 261.7 |
| Sudan<br>Soudan | 2000 | 19 615.1 | 72.4 | 184.8 | 10 614.0 | 39.2 | 27 097.1 |
| | 2004 | 32 436.9 | 119.3 | 238.0 | 13 630.4 | 50.1 | 27 184.8 |
| | 2005 | 40 096.3 | 156.2 | 256.8 | 15 612.7 | 60.8 | 25 674.5 |
| | 2006 | 50 519.3 | 220.7 | 287.8 | 17 553.1 | 76.7 | 22 888.4 |
| Swaziland<br>Swaziland | 2000 | 427.4 | 159.3 | 136.1 | 314.1 | 117.1 | 268.2 |
| | 2004 | 721.8 | 289.1 | 149.0 | 484.5 | 194.1 | 249.7 |
| | 2005 | 770.6 | 313.5 | 151.7 | 508.1 | 206.7 | 245.8 |
| | 2006 | 817.2 | 312.3 | 153.5 | 532.3 | 203.4 | 261.7 |

| Country or area<br>Pays ou zone | Year<br>Année | GDP at current price<br>PIB aux prix courants | | GDP at constant prices<br>PIB aux prix constants | GDP implicit price deflators<br>PIB déflateurs implicites des prix | | |
|---|---|---|---|---|---|---|---|
| | | National currency<br>Monnaie nationale | US dollars<br>Dollars E.-U. | National currency<br>Monnaie nationale | National currency<br>Monnaie nationale | US dollars<br>Dollars E.-U. | Exchange rates<br>Cours des changes |
| Togo<br>Togo | 2000 | 195.9 | 74.9 | 108.1 | 181.2 | 69.3 | 261.5 |
| | 2004 | 225.7 | 116.3 | 118.4 | 190.7 | 98.3 | 194.0 |
| | 2005 | 236.1 | 121.9 | 119.3 | 197.9 | 102.2 | 193.7 |
| | 2006 | 254.0 | 132.3 | 124.3 | 204.3 | 106.4 | 192.0 |
| Tunisia<br>Tunisie | 2000 | 246.4 | 157.9 | 158.9 | 155.1 | 99.4 | 156.0 |
| | 2004 | 325.0 | 229.2 | 189.7 | 171.3 | 120.8 | 141.8 |
| | 2005 | 345.0 | 233.5 | 197.7 | 174.5 | 118.1 | 147.7 |
| | 2006 | 377.5 | 249.1 | 207.8 | 181.7 | 119.9 | 151.5 |
| Uganda<br>Ouganda | 2000 | 602.0 | 157.0 | 195.8 | 307.4 | 80.2 | 383.5 |
| | 2004 | 900.8 | 213.4 | 245.1 | 367.6 | 87.1 | 422.1 |
| | 2005 | 1 044.9 | 251.6 | 261.0 | 400.4 | 96.4 | 415.2 |
| | 2006 | 1 209.0 | 283.1 | 277.2 | 436.2 | 102.1 | 427.1 |
| United Rep. of Tanzania<br>Rép.-Unie de Tanzanie | 2000 | 815.7 | 198.8 | 148.6 | 549.1 | 133.8 | 410.3 |
| | 2004 | 1 386.0 | 248.2 | 193.5 | 716.5 | 128.3 | 558.5 |
| | 2005 | 1 592.6 | 275.2 | 206.9 | 769.6 | 133.0 | 578.8 |
| | 2006 | 1 805.9 | 281.4 | 219.2 | 823.8 | 128.4 | 641.8 |
| Zambia<br>Zambie | 2000 | 8 888.8 | 86.6 | 106.9 | 8 311.8 | 80.9 | 10 270.3 |
| | 2004 | 22 937.5 | 145.4 | 128.4 | 17 871.6 | 113.3 | 15 777.9 |
| | 2005 | 28 805.9 | 195.5 | 135.0 | 21 345.7 | 144.9 | 14 736.4 |
| | 2006 | 34 885.7 | 293.3 | 143.1 | 24 380.7 | 205.0 | 11 895.4 |
| Zanzibar<br>Zanzibar | 2000 | 894.7 | 218.0 | 160.7 | 556.7 | 135.7 | 410.3 |
| | 2004 | 1 617.0 | 289.5 | 215.1 | 751.8 | 134.6 | 558.5 |
| | 2005 | 1 858.3 | 321.1 | 227.1 | 818.4 | 141.4 | 578.8 |
| | 2006 | 2 107.1 | 328.3 | 240.5 | 876.0 | 136.5 | 641.8 |
| Zimbabwe<br>Zimbabwe | 2000 | 1 681.3 | 64.2[2] | 105.7 | 1 590.6 | 60.7[2] | 2 619.1 |
| | 2004 | 72 410.5 | 35.0 | 88.9 | 81 426.8 | 39.4 | 206 719.5 |
| | 2005 | 231 739.6 | 25.4 | 82.6 | 280 511.2 | 30.8 | 912 231.5 |
| | 2006 | 2 463 138.1 | 20.1 | 78.7 | 3 131 855.7 | 25.6 | 12 233 811.4 |
| **America, North — Amérique du Nord** | | | | | | | |
| Anguilla<br>Anguilla | 2000 | 198.4 | 198.4 | 156.9 | 126.4 | 126.4 | 100.0 |
| | 2004 | 273.7 | 273.7 | 197.9 | 138.3 | 138.3 | 100.0 |
| | 2005 | 308.4 | 308.4 | 215.4 | 143.2 | 143.2 | 100.0 |
| | 2006 | 369.8 | 369.8 | 215.6 | 171.6 | 171.6 | 100.0 |
| Antigua and Barbuda<br>Antigua-et-Barbuda | 2000 | 169.9 | 169.9 | 136.5 | 124.5 | 124.5 | 100.0 |
| | 2004 | 209.0 | 209.0 | 161.4 | 129.5 | 129.5 | 100.0 |
| | 2005 | 222.3 | 222.3 | 168.8 | 131.7 | 131.7 | 100.0 |
| | 2006 | 245.6 | 245.6 | 182.3 | 134.8 | 134.8 | 100.0 |
| Aruba<br>Aruba | 2000 | 224.5 | 224.5 | 170.0 | 132.0 | 132.0 | 100.0 |
| | 2004 | 257.7 | 257.7 | 172.9 | 149.0 | 149.0 | 100.0 |
| | 2005 | 272.7 | 272.7 | 176.9 | 154.1 | 154.1 | 100.0 |
| | 2006 | 287.5 | 287.5 | 181.2 | 158.7 | 158.7 | 100.0 |
| Bahamas<br>Bahamas | 2000 | 158.1 | 158.1 | 123.3 | 128.2 | 128.2 | 100.0 |
| | 2004 | 178.8 | 178.8 | 131.3 | 136.2 | 136.2 | 100.0 |
| | 2005 | 185.4 | 185.4 | 134.8 | 137.5 | 137.5 | 100.0 |
| | 2006 | 196.1 | 196.1 | 140.1 | 139.9 | 139.9 | 100.0 |
| Barbados<br>Barbade | 2000 | 148.8 | 148.8 | 113.4 | 131.2 | 131.2 | 100.0 |
| | 2004 | 163.7 | 163.7 | 117.3 | 139.5 | 139.5 | 100.0 |
| | 2005 | 178.0 | 178.0 | 121.9 | 146.0 | 146.0 | 100.0 |
| | 2006 | 200.4 | 200.4 | 127.0 | 157.7 | 157.7 | 100.0 |

| Country or area / Pays ou zone | Year / Année | GDP at current price PIB aux prix courants | | GDP at constant prices PIB aux prix constants | GDP implicit price deflators PIB déflateurs implicites des prix | | Exchange rates Cours des changes |
|---|---|---|---|---|---|---|---|
| | | National currency Monnaie nationale | US dollars Dollars E.-U. | National currency Monnaie nationale | National currency Monnaie nationale | US dollars Dollars E.-U. | |
| Belize | 2000 | 205.1 | 205.1 | 151.6 | 135.4 | 135.4 | 100.0 |
| Belize | 2004 | 260.3 | 260.3 | 189.5 | 137.3 | 137.3 | 100.0 |
| | 2005 | 274.0 | 274.0 | 195.4 | 140.2 | 140.2 | 100.0 |
| | 2006 | 300.1 | 300.1 | 205.8 | 145.8 | 145.8 | 100.0 |
| Bermuda | 2000 | 171.9 | 171.9 | 129.3 | 132.9 | 132.9 | 100.0 |
| Bermudes | 2004 | 220.0 | 220.0 | 146.6 | 150.1 | 150.1 | 100.0 |
| | 2005 | 240.2 | 240.2 | 153.4 | 156.6 | 156.6 | 100.0 |
| | 2006 | 256.8 | 256.8 | 158.7 | 161.8 | 161.8 | 100.0 |
| British Virgin Islands | 2000 | 747.3 | 747.3 | 780.6 | 95.7 | 95.7 | 100.0 |
| Iles Vierges britanniques | 2004 | 832.2 | 832.2 | 802.5 | 103.7 | 103.7 | 100.0 |
| | 2005 | 926.5 | 926.5 | 876.0 | 105.8 | 105.8 | 100.0 |
| | 2006 | 985.7 | 985.7 | 912.6 | 108.0 | 108.0 | 100.0 |
| Canada | 2000 | 158.3 | 124.4 | 133.3 | 118.8 | 93.3 | 127.3 |
| Canada | 2004 | 189.8 | 170.3 | 147.0 | 129.2 | 115.9 | 111.5 |
| | 2005 | 201.7 | 194.2 | 151.3 | 133.3 | 128.4 | 103.9 |
| | 2006 | 212.0 | 218.1 | 156.0 | 135.9 | 139.8 | 97.2 |
| Cayman Islands | 2000 | 244.9 | 244.9 | 182.0 | 134.6 | 134.6 | 100.0 |
| Iles Caïmanes | 2004 | 286.2 | 286.2 | 191.6 | 149.4 | 149.4 | 100.0 |
| | 2005 | 326.2 | 326.2 | 204.0 | 159.9 | 159.9 | 100.0 |
| | 2006 | 345.7 | 345.7 | 212.6 | 162.6 | 162.6 | 100.0 |
| Costa Rica | 2000 | 739.8 | 219.8 | 166.0 | 445.7 | 132.4 | 336.5 |
| Costa Rica | 2004 | 1 225.7 | 256.3 | 191.6 | 639.8 | 133.8 | 478.2 |
| | 2005 | 1 436.5 | 275.3 | 202.9 | 708.0 | 135.7 | 521.7 |
| | 2006 | 1 704.4 | 305.3 | 218.9 | 778.7 | 139.5 | 558.3 |
| Cuba | 2000 | 141.7 | 106.5 | 86.8 | 163.2 | 122.7 | 133.0 |
| Cuba | 2004 | 178.0 | 133.8 | 99.6 | 178.7 | 134.4 | 133.0 |
| | 2005 | 199.7 | 150.2 | 111.4 | 179.3 | 134.9 | 133.0 |
| | 2006 | 227.1 | 170.8 | 125.3 | 181.2 | 136.3 | 133.0 |
| Dominica | 2000 | 162.1 | 162.1 | 120.0 | 135.1 | 135.1 | 100.0 |
| Dominique | 2004 | 170.6 | 170.6 | 119.4 | 142.8 | 142.8 | 100.0 |
| | 2005 | 179.5 | 179.5 | 123.4 | 145.5 | 145.5 | 100.0 |
| | 2006 | 188.7 | 188.7 | 128.5 | 146.9 | 146.9 | 100.0 |
| Dominican Republic | 2000 | 538.2 | 279.5 | 187.5 | 287.0 | 149.1 | 192.5 |
| Rép. dominicaine | 2004 | 1 288.8 | 260.9 | 203.1 | 634.7 | 128.5 | 494.1 |
| | 2005 | 1 467.4 | 411.4 | 221.9 | 661.3 | 185.4 | 356.7 |
| | 2006 | 1 747.9 | 446.6 | 245.7 | 711.4 | 181.8 | 391.4 |
| El Salvador | 2000 | 273.6 | 273.6 | 156.9 | 174.4 | 174.4 | 100.0 |
| El Salvador | 2004 | 329.6 | 329.6 | 170.1 | 193.7 | 193.7 | 100.0 |
| | 2005 | 353.6 | 353.6 | 174.8 | 202.3 | 202.3 | 100.0 |
| | 2006 | 382.3 | 382.3 | 180.8 | 211.4 | 211.4 | 100.0 |
| Greenland | 2000 | 136.9 | 104.8 | 119.2 | 114.8 | 87.9 | 130.6 |
| Groenland | 2004 | 156.3 | 161.4 | 122.3 | 127.8 | 132.0 | 96.8 |
| | 2005 | 161.9 | 167.1 | 124.7 | 129.8 | 134.0 | 96.9 |
| | 2006 | 156.3 | 162.6 | 129.8 | 120.4 | 125.3 | 96.1 |
| Grenada | 2000 | 189.3 | 189.3 | 146.8 | 129.0 | 129.0 | 100.0 |
| Grenade | 2004 | 195.0 | 195.0 | 139.4 | 139.9 | 139.9 | 100.0 |
| | 2005 | 228.1 | 228.1 | 156.3 | 145.9 | 145.9 | 100.0 |
| | 2006 | 248.7 | 248.7 | 167.8 | 148.2 | 148.2 | 100.0 |

| Country or area Pays ou zone | Year Année | GDP at current price PIB aux prix courants | | GDP at constant prices PIB aux prix constants | GDP implicit price deflators PIB déflateurs implicites des prix | | |
|---|---|---|---|---|---|---|---|
| | | National currency Monnaie nationale | US dollars Dollars E.-U. | National currency Monnaie nationale | National currency Monnaie nationale | US dollars Dollars E.-U. | Exchange rates Cours des changes |
| Guatemala Guatemala | 2000 | 436.4 | 252.1 | 149.7 | 291.5 | 168.5 | 173.1 |
| | 2004 | 622.5 | 351.4 | 168.3 | 370.0 | 208.8 | 177.1 |
| | 2005 | 680.9 | 400.1 | 174.1 | 391.1 | 229.8 | 170.2 |
| | 2006 | 756.1 | 446.1 | 182.0 | 415.4 | 245.1 | 169.5 |
| Haiti Haïti | 2000 | 569.4 | 134.5 | 90.2 | 631.0 | 149.0 | 423.4 |
| | 2004 | 1 030.4 | 134.3 | 86.3 | 1 194.7 | 155.8 | 767.0 |
| | 2005 | 1 233.3 | 152.5 | 87.8 | 1 404.7 | 173.6 | 808.9 |
| | 2006 | 1 428.3 | 176.7 | 89.9 | 1 589.7 | 196.7 | 808.2 |
| Honduras Honduras | 2000 | 713.1 | 197.6 | 138.2 | 516.1 | 143.0 | 360.9 |
| | 2004 | 1 094.7 | 247.2 | 158.3 | 691.7 | 156.2 | 442.8 |
| | 2005 | 1 257.6 | 274.6 | 164.7 | 763.5 | 166.7 | 458.0 |
| | 2006 | 1 401.8 | 305.1 | 174.6 | 802.7 | 174.7 | 459.5 |
| Jamaica Jamaïque | 2000 | 1 105.3 | 184.7 | 115.4 | 957.8 | 160.1 | 598.4 |
| | 2004 | 1 762.6 | 206.9 | 122.3 | 1 440.9 | 169.2 | 851.9 |
| | 2005 | 1 972.0 | 227.5 | 124.1 | 1 589.4 | 183.3 | 866.9 |
| | 2006 | 2 210.6 | 241.6 | 127.7 | 1 731.5 | 189.2 | 915.1 |
| Mexico Mexique | 2000 | 743.2 | 221.1 | 140.7 | 528.3 | 157.1 | 336.2 |
| | 2004 | 1 043.3 | 260.0 | 149.7 | 697.0 | 173.7 | 401.3 |
| | 2005 | 1 132.7 | 292.3 | 154.1 | 735.0 | 189.7 | 387.5 |
| | 2006 | 1 223.7 | 315.8 | 160.3 | 763.5 | 197.0 | 387.5 |
| Montserrat Montserrat | 2000 | 51.8 | 51.8 | 37.8 | 137.1 | 137.1 | 100.0 |
| | 2004 | 61.0 | 61.0 | 38.8 | 157.3 | 157.3 | 100.0 |
| | 2005 | 65.5 | 65.5 | 39.6 | 165.5 | 165.5 | 100.0 |
| | 2006 | 68.7 | 68.7 | 40.0 | 171.8 | 171.8 | 100.0 |
| Netherlands Antilles Antilles néerlandaises | 2000 | 144.4 | 144.4 | 112.1 | 128.8 | 128.8 | 100.0 |
| | 2004 | 157.3 | 157.3 | 116.8 | 134.7 | 134.7 | 100.0 |
| | 2005 | 161.8 | 161.8 | 117.9 | 137.3 | 137.3 | 100.0 |
| | 2006 | 169.3 | 169.3 | 118.9 | 142.4 | 142.4 | 100.0 |
| Nicaragua Nicaragua | 2000 | 9 850.5 | 109.4 | 139.6 | 7 058.0 | 78.4 | 9 001.4 |
| | 2004 | 14 131.5 | 125.0 | 156.1 | 9 055.0 | 80.1 | 11 308.8 |
| | 2005 | 16 202.3 | 136.5 | 162.3 | 9 984.2 | 84.1 | 11 874.6 |
| | 2006 | 18 607.9 | 149.3 | 168.3 | 11 056.2 | 88.7 | 12 467.5 |
| Panama Panama | 2000 | 191.2 | 191.2 | 163.9 | 116.7 | 116.7 | 100.0 |
| | 2004 | 233.4 | 233.4 | 188.8 | 123.6 | 123.6 | 100.0 |
| | 2005 | 254.8 | 254.8 | 201.8 | 126.3 | 126.3 | 100.0 |
| | 2006 | 281.6 | 281.6 | 218.2 | 129.1 | 129.1 | 100.0 |
| Puerto Rico Porto Rico | 2000 | 214.4 | 214.4 | 156.2 | 137.3 | 137.3 | 100.0 |
| | 2004 | 256.0 | 256.0 | 163.5 | 156.6 | 156.6 | 100.0 |
| | 2005 | 267.8 | 267.8 | 164.5 | 162.8 | 162.8 | 100.0 |
| | 2006 | 281.0 | 281.0 | 166.9 | 168.4 | 168.4 | 100.0 |
| Saint Kitts and Nevis Saint-Kitts-et-Nevis | 2000 | 206.8 | 206.8 | 129.1 | 160.2 | 160.2 | 100.0 |
| | 2004 | 248.4 | 248.4 | 138.7 | 179.1 | 179.1 | 100.0 |
| | 2005 | 269.3 | 269.3 | 144.4 | 186.5 | 186.5 | 100.0 |
| | 2006 | 305.6 | 305.6 | 150.7 | 202.8 | 202.8 | 100.0 |
| Saint Lucia Sainte-Lucie | 2000 | 169.8 | 169.8 | 128.3 | 132.3 | 132.3 | 100.0 |
| | 2004 | 191.7 | 191.7 | 135.1 | 141.9 | 141.9 | 100.0 |
| | 2005 | 212.1 | 212.1 | 138.6 | 153.0 | 153.0 | 100.0 |
| | 2006 | 224.3 | 224.3 | 143.2 | 156.6 | 156.6 | 100.0 |

| Country or area Pays ou zone | Year Année | GDP at current price PIB aux prix courants | | GDP at constant prices PIB aux prix constants | GDP implicit price deflators PIB déflateurs implicites des prix | | Exchange rates Cours des changes |
|---|---|---|---|---|---|---|---|
| | | National currency Monnaie nationale | US dollars Dollars E.-U. | National currency Monnaie nationale | National currency Monnaie nationale | US dollars Dollars E.-U. | |
| St. Vincent-Grenadines St. Vincent-Grenadines | 2000 | 169.2 | 169.2 | 136.0 | 124.4 | 124.4 | 100.0 |
| | 2004 | 209.4 | 209.4 | 156.0 | 134.2 | 134.2 | 100.0 |
| | 2005 | 217.9 | 217.9 | 158.9 | 137.1 | 137.1 | 100.0 |
| | 2006 | 226.6 | 226.6 | 164.3 | 137.9 | 137.9 | 100.0 |
| Trinidad and Tobago Trinité-et-Tobago | 2000 | 238.5 | 160.9 | 154.2 | 154.7 | 104.3 | 148.2 |
| | 2004 | 370.6 | 250.1 | 215.9 | 171.7 | 115.8 | 148.2 |
| | 2005 | 441.3 | 297.7 | 233.1 | 189.4 | 127.8 | 148.2 |
| | 2006 | 531.5 | 358.1 | 261.0 | 203.6 | 137.2 | 148.4 |
| Turks and Caicos Islands Iles Turques et Caïques | 2000 | 301.6 | 301.6 | 244.7 | 123.3 | 123.3 | 100.0 |
| | 2004 | 458.4 | 458.4 | 322.7 | 142.1 | 142.1 | 100.0 |
| | 2005 | 538.4 | 538.4 | 367.6 | 146.5 | 146.5 | 100.0 |
| | 2006 | 611.6 | 611.6 | 408.2 | 149.8 | 149.8 | 100.0 |
| United States Etats-Unis | 2000 | 169.6 | 169.6 | 138.4 | 122.5 | 122.5 | 100.0 |
| | 2004 | 202.5 | 202.5 | 151.0 | 134.1 | 134.1 | 100.0 |
| | 2005 | 215.4 | 215.4 | 155.9 | 138.2 | 138.2 | 100.0 |
| | 2006 | 229.1 | 229.1 | 161.1 | 142.2 | 142.2 | 100.0 |
| **America, South — Amérique du Sud** | | | | | | | |
| Argentina Argentine | 2000 | 412.4 | 201.2 | 151.2 | 272.7 | 133.0 | 205.0 |
| | 2004 | 649.5 | 108.3 | 152.9 | 424.9 | 70.9 | 599.5 |
| | 2005 | 771.8 | 129.6 | 166.9 | 462.5 | 77.7 | 595.5 |
| | 2006 | 958.7 | 153.0 | 180.2 | 532.0 | 84.9 | 626.4 |
| Bolivia Bolivie | 2000 | 336.3 | 172.5 | 144.8 | 232.3 | 119.2 | 194.9 |
| | 2004 | 450.9 | 180.2 | 160.5 | 280.8 | 112.3 | 250.1 |
| | 2005 | 493.1 | 194.0 | 168.0 | 293.6 | 115.5 | 254.2 |
| | 2006 | 534.4 | 211.6 | 174.8 | 305.7 | 121.1 | 252.5 |
| Brazil Brésil | 2000 | 10 117 462.2 | 137.3 | 129.8 | 7 796 737.5 | 105.8 | 7 368 620.7 |
| | 2004 | 16 230 320.1 | 137.8 | 141.4 | 11 479 701.2 | 97.5 | 11 777 676.4 |
| | 2005 | 17 801 124.6 | 181.6 | 144.6 | 12 310 414.7 | 125.6 | 9 802 066.0 |
| | 2006 | 21 340 237.7 | 243.7 | 150.0 | 14 230 970.6 | 162.5 | 8 758 598.4 |
| Chile Chili | 2000 | 397.2 | 224.4 | 185.9 | 213.6 | 120.7 | 177.0 |
| | 2004 | 571.7 | 286.0 | 216.3 | 264.3 | 132.3 | 199.9 |
| | 2005 | 651.9 | 354.9 | 228.7 | 285.1 | 155.2 | 183.7 |
| | 2006 | 757.0 | 435.3 | 237.7 | 318.4 | 183.1 | 173.9 |
| Colombia Colombie | 2000 | 729.4 | 175.5 | 129.9 | 561.5 | 135.1 | 415.7 |
| | 2004 | 1 074.9 | 205.4 | 146.3 | 734.6 | 140.4 | 523.4 |
| | 2005 | 1 191.6 | 257.9 | 154.0 | 773.7 | 167.4 | 462.1 |
| | 2006 | 1 289.2 | 274.2 | 161.4 | 798.7 | 169.9 | 470.1 |
| Ecuador Equateur | 2000 | 141.7 | 141.7 | 123.9 | 114.3 | 114.3 | 100.0 |
| | 2004 | 290.1 | 290.1 | 152.1 | 190.8 | 190.8 | 100.0 |
| | 2005 | 324.4 | 324.4 | 159.3 | 203.6 | 203.6 | 100.0 |
| | 2006 | 363.5 | 363.5 | 166.2 | 218.8 | 218.8 | 100.0 |
| Guyana Guyana | 2000 | 830.0 | 179.9 | 161.2 | 514.9 | 111.6 | 461.5 |
| | 2004 | 998.1 | 199.0 | 168.0 | 594.1 | 118.4 | 501.6 |
| | 2005 | 1 053.5 | 208.4 | 163.3 | 645.1 | 127.6 | 505.6 |
| | 2006 | 1 150.9 | 227.3 | 171.0 | 673.1 | 132.9 | 506.4 |
| Paraguay Paraguay | 2000 | 410.2 | 144.7 | 119.3 | 343.7 | 121.2 | 283.5 |
| | 2004 | 688.5 | 141.7 | 131.7 | 523.0 | 107.7 | 485.8 |
| | 2005 | 765.5 | 152.4 | 135.4 | 565.3 | 112.5 | 502.3 |
| | 2006 | 851.3 | 185.8 | 140.8 | 604.5 | 131.9 | 458.2 |

| Country or area<br>Pays ou zone | Year<br>Année | GDP at current price<br>PIB aux prix courants | | GDP at constant prices<br>PIB aux prix constants | GDP implicit price deflators<br>PIB déflateurs implicites des prix | | |
|---|---|---|---|---|---|---|---|
| | | National currency<br>Monnaie nationale | US dollars<br>Dollars E.-U. | National currency<br>Monnaie nationale | National currency<br>Monnaie nationale | US dollars<br>Dollars E.-U. | Exchange rates<br>Cours des changes |
| Peru | 2000 | 3 383.5 | 182.2 | 148.5 | 2 277.9 | 122.6 | 1 857.5 |
| Pérou | 2004 | 4 321.9 | 237.9 | 171.1 | 2 525.6 | 139.0 | 1 816.6 |
| | 2005 | 4 755.7 | 271.1 | 182.2 | 2 610.7 | 148.8 | 1 754.2 |
| | 2006 | 5 358.6 | 307.5 | 193.1 | 2 775.2 | 159.3 | 1 742.4 |
| Suriname | 2000 | 31 781.4 | 161.5 | 105.0 | 30 259.9 | 153.8 | 19 676.1 |
| Suriname | 2004 | 108 764.9 | 267.4 | 131.1 | 82 952.2 | 204.0 | 40 670.8 |
| | 2005 | 130 774.1 | 321.8 | 138.8 | 94 253.7 | 231.9 | 40 642.4 |
| | 2006 | 154 928.3 | 379.5 | 147.0 | 105 415.2 | 258.2 | 40 822.2 |
| Uruguay | 2000 | 2 483.9 | 240.1 | 135.6 | 1 832.3 | 177.1 | 1 034.6 |
| Uruguay | 2004 | 3 877.3 | 158.0 | 133.4 | 2 906.8 | 118.4 | 2 454.5 |
| | 2005 | 4 156.8 | 198.6 | 141.9 | 2 929.4 | 140.0 | 2 093.0 |
| | 2006 | 4 750.6 | 230.8 | 151.8 | 3 128.9 | 152.0 | 2 058.5 |
| Venezuela (Bolivar. Rep.of) | 2000 | 3 611.5 | 249.1 | 123.0 | 2 936.9 | 202.6 | 1 449.8 |
| Venezuela (Rép. Boliv. du) | 2004 | 9 642.8 | 239.1 | 126.5 | 7 626.0 | 189.1 | 4 032.6 |
| | 2005 | 13 608.0 | 305.4 | 138.2 | 9 843.5 | 220.9 | 4 455.7 |
| | 2006 | 17 556.5 | 383.5 | 152.5 | 11 510.4 | 251.4 | 4 577.8 |
| **Asia — Asie** | | | | | | | |
| Afghanistan | 2000 | 99 643.9 | 81.8 | 70.1 | 142 131.2 | 116.7 | 121 792.0 |
| Afghanistan | 2004 | 148 802.0 | 157.4 | 110.8 | 134 319.2 | 142.1 | 94 557.7 |
| | 2005 | 184 724.3 | 188.9 | 126.9 | 145 609.6 | 148.9 | 97 816.4 |
| | 2006 | 225 420.3 | 229.4 | 140.9 | 159 935.1 | 162.8 | 98 258.4 |
| Armenia | 2000 | 2 050 170.0 | 88.6 | 67.8 | 3 022 490.9 | 130.6 | 2 313 602.9 |
| Arménie | 2004 | 3 792 753.6 | 165.8 | 116.5 | 3 254 787.5 | 142.3 | 2 287 432.4 |
| | 2005 | 4 460 694.8 | 227.3 | 141.2 | 3 158 226.0 | 160.9 | 1 962 606.3 |
| | 2006 | 5 297 757.1 | 297.0 | 165.2 | 3 207 471.4 | 179.8 | 1 784 009.9 |
| Azerbaijan | 2000 | 1 609 174.6 | 80.9 | 58.9 | 2 733 940.9 | 137.5 | 1 988 320.6 |
| Azerbaïdjan | 2004 | 2 909 345.2 | 133.2 | 87.6 | 3 322 099.5 | 152.2 | 2 183 437.1 |
| | 2005 | 4 270 975.4 | 203.3 | 110.7 | 3 856 836.1 | 183.6 | 2 100 673.2 |
| | 2006 | 6 049 045.0 | 304.7 | 148.9 | 4 062 418.0 | 204.6 | 1 985 153.4 |
| Bahrain | 2000 | 185.7 | 185.7 | 163.0 | 113.9 | 113.9 | 100.0 |
| Bahreïn | 2004 | 256.5 | 256.5 | 202.7 | 126.6 | 126.6 | 100.0 |
| | 2005 | 311.7 | 311.7 | 218.8 | 142.5 | 142.5 | 100.0 |
| | 2006 | 374.3 | 374.3 | 235.7 | 158.8 | 158.8 | 100.0 |
| Bangladesh | 2000 | 230.4 | 152.8 | 161.5 | 142.7 | 94.6 | 150.8 |
| Bangladesh | 2004 | 334.9 | 194.5 | 198.8 | 168.5 | 97.8 | 172.2 |
| | 2005 | 378.2 | 203.2 | 212.1 | 178.3 | 95.8 | 186.1 |
| | 2006 | 427.4 | 214.3 | 225.9 | 189.2 | 94.9 | 199.4 |
| Bhutan | 2000 | 411.2 | 160.2 | 167.3 | 245.7 | 95.7 | 256.7 |
| Bhoutan | 2004 | 659.6 | 254.8 | 226.5 | 291.2 | 112.5 | 258.9 |
| | 2005 | 756.7 | 300.4 | 241.2 | 313.7 | 124.5 | 251.9 |
| | 2006 | 856.7 | 331.0 | 261.7 | 327.3 | 126.5 | 258.8 |
| Brunei Darussalam | 2000 | 165.9 | 174.4 | 123.2 | 134.6 | 141.5 | 95.1 |
| Brunéi Darussalam | 2004 | 213.3 | 228.8 | 136.0 | 156.8 | 168.2 | 93.3 |
| | 2005 | 254.3 | 277.0 | 136.6 | 186.3 | 202.8 | 91.8 |
| | 2006 | 292.5 | 333.6 | 141.7 | 206.5 | 235.5 | 87.7 |
| Cambodia | 2000 | 1 947.0 | 216.1 | 193.5 | 1 006.1 | 111.7 | 901.1 |
| Cambodge | 2004 | 2 921.4 | 310.1 | 264.2 | 1 105.8 | 117.4 | 942.3 |
| | 2005 | 3 503.1 | 364.9 | 299.6 | 1 169.3 | 121.8 | 960.1 |
| | 2006 | 3 646.8 | 378.8 | 321.1 | 1 135.6 | 118.0 | 962.6 |

| Country or area<br>Pays ou zone | Year<br>Année | GDP at current price<br>PIB aux prix courants | | GDP at constant prices<br>PIB aux prix constants | GDP implicit price deflators<br>PIB déflateurs implicites des prix | | |
|---|---|---|---|---|---|---|---|
| | | National currency<br>Monnaie nationale | US dollars<br>Dollars E.-U. | National currency<br>Monnaie nationale | National currency<br>Monnaie nationale | US dollars<br>Dollars E.-U. | Exchange rates<br>Cours des changes |
| China[3] | 2000 | 510.4 | 294.9 | 269.6 | 189.3 | 109.4 | 173.1 |
| Chine[3] | 2004 | 828.4 | 478.8 | 385.7 | 214.8 | 124.1 | 173.0 |
| | 2005 | 965.0 | 563.3 | 425.1 | 227.0 | 132.5 | 171.3 |
| | 2006 | 1 099.0 | 659.3 | 470.6 | 233.6 | 140.1 | 166.7 |
| China, Hong Kong SAR | 2000 | 222.3 | 222.2 | 157.5 | 141.1 | 141.1 | 100.0 |
| Chine, Hong Kong RAS | 2004 | 218.2 | 218.3 | 180.2 | 121.1 | 121.1 | 100.0 |
| | 2005 | 233.8 | 234.1 | 194.5 | 120.2 | 120.4 | 99.8 |
| | 2006 | 248.9 | 249.6 | 207.8 | 119.8 | 120.1 | 99.7 |
| China, Macao SAR | 2000 | 204.2 | 204.1 | 130.2 | 156.8 | 156.8 | 100.1 |
| Chine, Macao RAS | 2004 | 346.5 | 346.4 | 216.6 | 160.0 | 160.0 | 100.0 |
| | 2005 | 387.6 | 388.0 | 231.1 | 167.7 | 167.9 | 99.9 |
| | 2006 | 476.8 | 478.0 | 269.5 | 177.0 | 177.4 | 99.8 |
| Cyprus | 2000 | 218.6 | 160.9 | 155.4 | 140.7 | 103.5 | 135.9 |
| Chypre | 2004 | 279.3 | 273.0 | 174.8 | 159.8 | 156.2 | 102.3 |
| | 2005 | 297.1 | 293.3 | 181.6 | 163.6 | 161.5 | 101.3 |
| | 2006 | 316.0 | 315.4 | 188.5 | 167.7 | 167.4 | 100.2 |
| Georgia | 2000 | 40 287.0[4] | 35.8 | 37.3 | 108 085.8[4] | 96.2 | 112 402.0[4] |
| Géorgie | 2004 | 65 495.3[4] | 60.1 | 48.6 | 134 675.6[4] | 123.5 | 109 013.8[4] |
| | 2005 | 77 473.0[4] | 75.1 | 53.3 | 145 362.4[4] | 141.0 | 103 101.2[4] |
| | 2006 | 91 892.8[4] | 90.7 | 58.1 | 158 181.9[4] | 156.2 | 101 268.8[4] |
| India | 2000 | 367.2 | 143.0 | 170.3 | 215.6 | 84.0 | 256.8 |
| Inde | 2004 | 543.8 | 210.1 | 218.3 | 249.1 | 96.2 | 258.9 |
| | 2005 | 621.5 | 246.7 | 237.6 | 261.5 | 103.8 | 252.0 |
| | 2006 | 712.9 | 275.4 | 259.5 | 274.7 | 106.1 | 258.8 |
| Indonesia | 2000 | 599.9 | 131.3 | 151.2 | 396.8 | 86.8 | 457.0 |
| Indonésie | 2004 | 981.2 | 202.3 | 180.2 | 544.4 | 112.2 | 485.0 |
| | 2005 | 1 178.2 | 223.7 | 190.3 | 619.1 | 117.6 | 526.6 |
| | 2006 | 1 440.9 | 289.9 | 200.9 | 717.3 | 144.3 | 497.0 |
| Iran (Islamic Rep. of) | 2000 | 1 655.9 | 113.9 | 144.5 | 1 146.1 | 78.8 | 1 453.9 |
| Iran (Rép. islamique d') | 2004 | 3 935.4 | 180.1 | 179.5 | 2 191.9 | 100.3 | 2 185.1 |
| | 2005 | 4 831.9 | 212.5 | 187.6 | 2 575.1 | 113.2 | 2 274.0 |
| | 2006 | 6 233.9 | 268.0 | 197.7 | 3 153.1 | 135.5 | 2 326.5 |
| Iraq | 2000 | 57 935.8 | 122.1 | 87.4 | 66 304.8 | 139.8 | 47 435.1 |
| Iraq | 2004 | 53 037.5 | 148.5 | 68.5 | 77 477.0 | 216.9 | 35 721.8 |
| | 2005 | 71 563.7 | 197.8 | 70.7 | 101 239.1 | 279.8 | 36 178.8 |
| | 2006 | 99 258.7 | 273.5 | 73.5 | 135 017.8 | 372.0 | 36 296.1 |
| Israel | 2000 | 429.8 | 212.6 | 175.0 | 245.7 | 121.5 | 202.2 |
| Israël | 2004 | 478.3 | 215.2 | 183.2 | 261.1 | 117.4 | 222.3 |
| | 2005 | 507.4 | 227.9 | 192.8 | 263.1 | 118.2 | 222.6 |
| | 2006 | 544.7 | 246.5 | 202.4 | 269.1 | 121.8 | 221.0 |
| Japan | 2000 | 114.7 | 154.1 | 113.1 | 101.4 | 136.2 | 74.4 |
| Japon | 2004 | 113.5 | 151.9 | 118.4 | 95.9 | 128.3 | 74.7 |
| | 2005 | 115.0 | 151.1 | 121.5 | 94.7 | 124.4 | 76.1 |
| | 2006 | 118.0 | 147.0 | 124.7 | 94.6 | 117.8 | 80.3 |
| Jordan | 2000 | 224.8 | 210.5 | 158.5 | 141.9 | 132.8 | 106.8 |
| Jordanie | 2004 | 302.9 | 283.5 | 199.4 | 151.9 | 142.2 | 106.8 |
| | 2005 | 337.8 | 316.2 | 213.7 | 158.0 | 147.9 | 106.8 |
| | 2006 | 380.9 | 356.6 | 227.2 | 167.7 | 157.0 | 106.8 |
| Kazakhstan | 2000 | 2 715 557.2 | 61.7 | 69.4 | 3 910 934.5 | 88.8 | 4 403 213.8 |
| Kazakhstan | 2004 | 6 131 264.9 | 145.5 | 103.7 | 5 914 207.4 | 140.3 | 4 214 199.4 |
| | 2005 | 7 928 258.0 | 192.6 | 113.7 | 6 971 418.9 | 169.4 | 4 116 331.4 |
| | 2006 | 10 172 026.6 | 260.4 | 125.8 | 8 087 155.0 | 207.0 | 3 906 083.4 |

| Country or area<br>Pays ou zone | Year<br>Année | GDP at current price<br>PIB aux prix courants | | GDP at constant prices<br>PIB aux prix constants | GDP implicit price deflators<br>PIB déflateurs implicites des prix | | Exchange rates<br>Cours des changes |
|---|---|---|---|---|---|---|---|
| | | National currency<br>Monnaie nationale | US dollars<br>Dollars E.-U. | National currency<br>Monnaie nationale | National currency<br>Monnaie nationale | US dollars<br>Dollars E.-U. | |
| Korea, Dem. P. R.<br>Corée, R. p. dém. de | 2000 | 71.5 | 72.2 | 78.5 | 91.1 | 91.9 | 99.1 |
| | 2004 | 5 250.8 | 76.0 | 83.8 | 6 265.9 | 90.7 | 6 912.2 |
| | 2005 | 5 312.5 | 83.4 | 84.5 | 6 283.8 | 98.6 | 6 371.0 |
| | 2006 | 5 371.8 | 82.5 | 84.9 | 6 325.9 | 97.1 | 6 512.8 |
| Korea, Republic of<br>Corée, République de | 2000 | 310.0 | 194.0 | 180.4 | 171.8 | 107.5 | 159.8 |
| | 2004 | 417.5 | 258.0 | 216.4 | 192.9 | 119.2 | 161.8 |
| | 2005 | 432.1 | 298.6 | 225.0 | 192.1 | 132.7 | 144.7 |
| | 2006 | 446.4 | 330.9 | 236.3 | 188.9 | 140.1 | 134.9 |
| Kuwait<br>Koweït | 2000 | 217.2 | 204.2 | 160.6 | 135.2 | 127.2 | 106.3 |
| | 2004 | 327.8 | 320.9 | 213.5 | 153.6 | 150.3 | 102.2 |
| | 2005 | 442.7 | 437.3 | 234.7 | 188.6 | 186.3 | 101.2 |
| | 2006 | 550.8 | 547.5 | 249.4 | 220.9 | 219.6 | 100.6 |
| Kyrgyzstan<br>Kirghizistan | 2000 | 152 705.4 | 204.5 | 150.2 | 101 675.0 | 136.2 | 74 678.7 |
| | 2004 | 220 445.6 | 330.2 | 181.2 | 121 673.8 | 182.2 | 66 765.7 |
| | 2005 | 235 745.8 | 367.2 | 180.9 | 130 347.5 | 203.0 | 64 201.1 |
| | 2006 | 264 428.9 | 420.7 | 185.7 | 142 398.9 | 226.6 | 62 855.4 |
| Lao People's Dem. Rep.<br>Rép. dém. pop. lao | 2000 | 2 231.1 | 200.2 | 184.0 | 1 212.8 | 108.8 | 1 114.5 |
| | 2004 | 4 340.0 | 290.2 | 233.1 | 1 862.3 | 124.5 | 1 495.7 |
| | 2005 | 4 994.4 | 331.8 | 250.0 | 1 997.5 | 132.7 | 1 505.5 |
| | 2006 | 5 723.4 | 398.7 | 268.3 | 2 133.3 | 148.6 | 1 435.5 |
| Lebanon<br>Liban | 2000 | 1 286.6 | 593.2 | 200.1 | 642.9 | 296.4 | 216.9 |
| | 2004 | 1 655.7 | 763.4 | 221.3 | 748.1 | 344.9 | 216.9 |
| | 2005 | 1 681.8 | 775.4 | 223.6 | 752.3 | 346.9 | 216.9 |
| | 2006 | 1 702.0 | 784.8 | 216.5 | 786.2 | 362.5 | 216.9 |
| Malaysia<br>Malaisie | 2000 | 288.2 | 205.2 | 198.7 | 145.1 | 103.3 | 140.5 |
| | 2004 | 378.0 | 269.1 | 235.3 | 160.7 | 114.4 | 140.5 |
| | 2005 | 415.9 | 297.0 | 247.4 | 168.1 | 120.1 | 140.0 |
| | 2006 | 458.8 | 338.3 | 262.0 | 175.1 | 129.1 | 135.6 |
| Maldives<br>Maldives | 2000 | 357.7 | 290.3 | 207.0 | 172.9 | 140.3 | 123.2 |
| | 2004 | 483.9 | 361.1 | 275.7 | 175.5 | 131.0 | 134.0 |
| | 2005 | 467.7 | 349.0 | 264.6 | 176.8 | 131.9 | 134.0 |
| | 2006 | 565.1 | 421.7 | 322.1 | 175.5 | 130.9 | 134.0 |
| Mongolia<br>Mongolie | 2000 | 7 594.3 | 75.4 | 99.6 | 7 625.0 | 75.7 | 10 067.3 |
| | 2004 | 14 341.0 | 129.4 | 123.3 | 11 635.3 | 105.0 | 11 082.3 |
| | 2005 | 18 531.7 | 164.5 | 131.9 | 14 048.6 | 124.7 | 11 268.7 |
| | 2006 | 24 612.4 | 223.1 | 132.0 | 18 645.3 | 169.0 | 11 030.1 |
| Myanmar<br>Myanmar | 2000 | 1 680.1 | 140.5 | 199.5 | 842.1 | 70.4 | 1 196.0 |
| | 2004 | 5 975.3 | 198.0 | 321.7 | 1 857.2 | 61.5 | 3 017.9 |
| | 2005 | 8 065.3 | 229.8 | 364.3 | 2 214.0 | 63.1 | 3 510.3 |
| | 2006 | 10 899.5 | 262.8 | 389.8 | 2 796.5 | 67.4 | 4 147.2 |
| Nepal<br>Népal | 2000 | 367.0 | 151.6 | 163.0 | 225.2 | 93.0 | 242.1 |
| | 2004 | 480.3 | 191.5 | 183.5 | 261.8 | 104.4 | 250.9 |
| | 2005 | 515.9 | 212.3 | 188.4 | 273.8 | 112.7 | 243.0 |
| | 2006 | 563.7 | 227.5 | 192.0 | 293.7 | 118.5 | 247.7 |
| Occupied Palestinian Terr.<br>Terr. palestinien occupé | 2000 | 212.6 | 212.6 | 168.6 | 126.1 | 126.1 | 100.0 |
| | 2004 | 210.1 | 210.1 | 168.0 | 125.1 | 125.1 | 100.0 |
| | 2005 | 215.9 | 215.9 | 176.3 | 122.5 | 122.5 | 100.0 |
| | 2006 | 219.1 | 219.1 | 183.3 | 119.5 | 119.5 | 100.0 |

Implicit price deflators of gross domestic product—Index base: 1990 = 100 (*continued*)

Déflateurs implicites des prix de produit intérieur brut—Indice base : 1990 = 100 (*suite*)

| Country or area<br>Pays ou zone | Year<br>Année | GDP at current price<br>PIB aux prix courants | | GDP at constant prices<br>PIB aux prix constants | GDP implicit price deflators<br>PIB déflateurs implicites des prix | | Exchange rates<br>Cours des changes |
|---|---|---|---|---|---|---|---|
| | | National currency<br>Monnaie nationale | US dollars<br>Dollars E.-U. | National currency<br>Monnaie nationale | National currency<br>Monnaie nationale | US dollars<br>Dollars E.-U. | |
| Oman<br>Oman | 2000 | 170.0 | 170.0 | 157.0 | 108.3 | 108.3 | 100.0 |
| | 2004 | 211.8 | 211.8 | 186.1 | 113.8 | 113.8 | 100.0 |
| | 2005 | 263.9 | 263.9 | 196.8 | 134.1 | 134.1 | 100.0 |
| | 2006 | 308.0 | 308.0 | 208.3 | 147.9 | 147.9 | 100.0 |
| Pakistan<br>Pakistan | 2000 | 339.3 | 137.3 | 142.3 | 238.4 | 96.5 | 247.1 |
| | 2004 | 530.4 | 197.6 | 177.4 | 298.9 | 111.4 | 268.4 |
| | 2005 | 621.6 | 226.7 | 188.5 | 329.8 | 120.3 | 274.2 |
| | 2006 | 713.5 | 257.0 | 201.7 | 353.8 | 127.4 | 277.7 |
| Philippines<br>Philippines | 2000 | 307.8 | 169.3 | 133.4 | 230.7 | 126.9 | 181.8 |
| | 2004 | 451.1 | 195.7 | 159.9 | 282.1 | 122.4 | 230.5 |
| | 2005 | 503.0 | 222.0 | 167.8 | 299.7 | 132.3 | 226.6 |
| | 2006 | 557.0 | 263.9 | 176.8 | 315.0 | 149.2 | 211.1 |
| Qatar<br>Qatar | 2000 | 241.3 | 241.3 | 177.9 | 135.6 | 135.6 | 100.0 |
| | 2004 | 431.1 | 431.1 | 253.4 | 170.1 | 170.1 | 100.0 |
| | 2005 | 576.9 | 576.9 | 269.0 | 214.5 | 214.5 | 100.0 |
| | 2006 | 716.3 | 716.3 | 292.7 | 244.7 | 244.7 | 100.0 |
| Saudi Arabia<br>Arabie saoudite | 2000 | 161.6 | 161.6 | 130.8 | 123.6 | 123.6 | 100.0 |
| | 2004 | 214.7 | 214.7 | 149.2 | 143.9 | 143.9 | 100.0 |
| | 2005 | 265.4 | 265.6 | 159.0 | 167.0 | 167.1 | 99.9 |
| | 2006 | 311.5 | 311.9 | 168.1 | 185.3 | 185.5 | 99.9 |
| Singapore<br>Singapour | 2000 | 239.0 | 251.3 | 209.7 | 114.0 | 119.8 | 95.1 |
| | 2004 | 271.4 | 291.1 | 239.1 | 113.5 | 121.7 | 93.3 |
| | 2005 | 290.4 | 316.3 | 255.0 | 113.9 | 124.0 | 91.8 |
| | 2006 | 314.0 | 358.1 | 275.1 | 114.1 | 130.2 | 87.7 |
| Sri Lanka<br>Sri Lanka | 2000 | 391.6 | 203.8 | 166.9 | 234.6 | 122.1 | 192.2 |
| | 2004 | 626.7 | 248.1 | 191.0 | 328.2 | 129.9 | 252.6 |
| | 2005 | 732.5 | 292.0 | 202.9 | 361.1 | 143.9 | 250.9 |
| | 2006 | 865.4 | 333.6 | 218.1 | 396.8 | 153.0 | 259.4 |
| Syrian Arab Republic<br>Rép. arabe syrienne | 2000 | 336.9 | 176.2 | 176.6 | 190.8 | 99.8 | 191.2 |
| | 2004 | 467.3 | 217.9 | 216.0 | 216.4 | 100.9 | 214.5 |
| | 2005 | 551.4 | 250.1 | 225.7 | 244.3 | 110.8 | 220.5 |
| | 2006 | 608.7 | 280.9 | 233.0 | 261.2 | 120.6 | 216.7 |
| Tajikistan<br>Tadjikistan | 2000 | 2 447 671.2 | 30.0 | 38.0 | 6 433 712.8 | 78.9 | 8 159 432.8 |
| | 2004 | 8 448 219.2 | 72.4 | 56.6 | 14 927 827.7 | 127.9 | 11 674 222.1 |
| | 2005 | 9 872 054.8 | 80.6 | 60.4 | 16 345 399.8 | 133.5 | 12 248 332.6 |
| | 2006 | 12 711 271.8 | 98.1 | 64.6 | 19 669 495.4 | 151.7 | 12 962 630.4 |
| Thailand<br>Thaïlande | 2000 | 225.4 | 143.8 | 154.7 | 145.7 | 93.0 | 156.8 |
| | 2004 | 297.2 | 189.0 | 189.5 | 156.8 | 99.7 | 157.2 |
| | 2005 | 324.5 | 206.4 | 198.0 | 163.9 | 104.3 | 157.2 |
| | 2006 | 357.7 | 241.6 | 207.9 | 172.1 | 116.2 | 148.1 |
| Timor-Leste<br>Timor-Leste | 2000 | 176.8 | 176.8 | 103.1 | 171.6 | 171.6 | 100.0 |
| | 2004 | 189.3 | 189.3 | 105.6 | 179.3 | 179.3 | 100.0 |
| | 2005 | 195.6 | 195.6 | 107.9 | 181.3 | 181.3 | 100.0 |
| | 2006 | 198.9 | 198.9 | 106.2 | 187.3 | 187.3 | 100.0 |
| Turkey<br>Turquie | 2000 | 31 695.7 | 132.3 | 142.1 | 22 300.7 | 93.1 | 23 966.3 |
| | 2004 | 109 528.0 | 200.4 | 163.6 | 66 969.1 | 122.6 | 54 646.4 |
| | 2005 | 123 951.0 | 240.7 | 175.6 | 70 579.0 | 137.0 | 51 506.2 |
| | 2006 | 142 582.2 | 260.4 | 186.2 | 76 561.4 | 139.8 | 54 757.1 |

| Country or area / Pays ou zone | Year / Année | GDP at current price PIB aux prix courants | | GDP at constant prices PIB aux prix constants | GDP implicit price deflators PIB déflateurs implicites des prix | | Exchange rates Cours des changes |
|---|---|---|---|---|---|---|---|
| | | National currency Monnaie nationale | US dollars Dollars E.-U. | National currency Monnaie nationale | National currency Monnaie nationale | US dollars Dollars E.-U. | |
| Turkmenistan Turkménistan | 2000 | 168 736.8[4] | 135.4[2] | 78.6 | 214 651.6[4] | 172.3[2] | 124 587.4[4] |
| | 2004 | 423 318.5[4] | 168.1[2] | 89.2 | 474 732.4[4] | 188.6[2] | 251 767.3[4] |
| | 2005 | 512 149.0[4] | 188.8[2] | 97.2 | 526 928.3[4] | 194.3[2] | 271 249.0[4] |
| | 2006 | 651 453.6[4] | 211.8[2] | 105.9 | 614 962.1[4] | 199.9[2] | 307 573.3[4] |
| United Arab Emirates Emirats arabes unis | 2000 | 208.9 | 208.8 | 171.1 | 122.1 | 122.0 | 100.0 |
| | 2004 | 308.6 | 308.5 | 216.6 | 142.5 | 142.5 | 100.0 |
| | 2005 | 395.6 | 395.5 | 234.8 | 168.5 | 168.4 | 100.0 |
| | 2006 | 539.6 | 539.4 | 261.8 | 206.2 | 206.1 | 100.0 |
| Uzbekistan Ouzbékistan | 2000 | 10 048 148.2 | 93.5 | 98.4 | 10 215 552.9 | 95.1 | 10 743 036.0 |
| | 2004 | 37 621 774.7 | 81.7 | 120.3 | 31 271 044.1 | 67.9 | 46 054 556.8 |
| | 2005 | 46 945 680.6 | 93.5 | 128.9 | 36 434 202.9 | 72.6 | 50 219 438.8 |
| | 2006 | 60 543 209.9 | 109.7 | 140.5 | 43 107 474.2 | 78.1 | 55 188 163.1 |
| Viet Nam Viet Nam | 2000 | 1 052.7 | 481.7 | 207.6 | 507.1 | 232.1 | 218.5 |
| | 2004 | 1 704.9 | 706.5 | 274.9 | 620.2 | 257.0 | 241.3 |
| | 2005 | 1 997.0 | 816.4 | 298.1 | 670.0 | 273.9 | 244.6 |
| | 2006 | 2 210.5 | 895.9 | 321.3 | 687.9 | 278.8 | 246.7 |
| Yemen Yémen | 2000 | 1 199.1 | 250.5 | 187.3 | 640.1 | 133.7 | 478.7 |
| | 2004 | 1 972.5 | 360.6 | 217.8 | 905.7 | 165.6 | 547.0 |
| | 2005 | 2 334.1 | 413.0 | 227.8 | 1 024.6 | 181.3 | 565.1 |
| | 2006 | 2 811.6 | 482.0 | 236.8 | 1 187.5 | 203.6 | 583.3 |
| **Europe — Europe** | | | | | | | |
| Albania Albanie | 2000 | 3 170.0 | 169.8 | 111.9 | 2 832.2 | 151.7 | 1 866.5 |
| | 2004 | 4 614.7 | 345.7 | 141.0 | 3 272.7 | 245.2 | 1 334.9 |
| | 2005 | 5 042.0 | 388.7 | 149.0 | 3 385.1 | 261.0 | 1 297.1 |
| | 2006 | 5 420.7 | 425.4 | 164.6 | 3 292.5 | 258.4 | 1 274.1 |
| Andorra Andorre | 2000 | 177.7 | 100.3 | 119.3 | 149.0 | 84.1 | 177.2 |
| | 2004 | 270.0 | 205.4 | 160.4 | 168.3 | 128.1 | 131.5 |
| | 2005 | 295.1 | 224.9 | 169.9 | 173.7 | 132.4 | 131.3 |
| | 2006 | 320.1 | 246.0 | 178.6 | 179.2 | 137.7 | 130.1 |
| Austria Autriche | 2000 | 154.3 | 117.5 | 128.7 | 120.0 | 91.3 | 131.4 |
| | 2004 | 173.0 | 177.5 | 135.5 | 127.7 | 131.0 | 97.5 |
| | 2005 | 179.8 | 184.8 | 138.3 | 130.0 | 133.6 | 97.3 |
| | 2006 | 188.1 | 195.0 | 142.6 | 132.0 | 136.8 | 96.5 |
| Belarus Bélarus | 2000 | 210 942.3[4] | 55.3 | 88.5 | 238 267.2[4] | 62.5 | 381 349.5[4] |
| | 2004 | 1 154 545.0[4] | 122.9 | 116.1 | 994 678.4[4] | 105.9 | 939 616.8[4] |
| | 2005 | 1 502 704.4[4] | 160.4 | 127.0 | 1 182 943.3[4] | 126.3 | 936 762.2[4] |
| | 2006 | 1 829 824.5[4] | 196.2 | 139.7 | 1 310 171.2[4] | 140.5 | 932 771.8[4] |
| Belgium Belgique | 2000 | 149.9 | 114.4 | 123.4 | 121.5 | 92.7 | 131.0 |
| | 2004 | 171.6 | 176.5 | 131.1 | 130.9 | 134.6 | 97.2 |
| | 2005 | 177.6 | 183.0 | 132.7 | 133.8 | 137.9 | 97.1 |
| | 2006 | 186.4 | 193.8 | 136.3 | 136.8 | 142.1 | 96.2 |
| Bosnia and Herzegovina Bosnie-Herzégovine | 2000 | 1 381 539.3 | 74.8 | 303.3 | 455 469.0 | 24.7 | 1 846 246.5 |
| | 2004 | 1 892 784.4 | 138.2 | 216.8 | 872 972.6 | 63.7 | 1 370 013.4 |
| | 2005 | 2 036 258.4 | 148.9 | 228.3 | 891 875.0 | 65.2 | 1 367 906.4 |
| | 2006 | 2 277 147.7 | 167.9 | 240.9 | 945 387.5 | 69.7 | 1 355 977.4 |
| Bulgaria Bulgarie | 2000 | 58 939.9 | 60.8 | 84.1 | 70 128.5 | 72.3 | 96 956.3 |
| | 2004 | 84 325.5 | 117.2 | 101.3 | 83 228.0 | 115.7 | 71 921.8 |
| | 2005 | 92 417.1 | 128.6 | 106.9 | 86 426.8 | 120.2 | 71 878.6 |
| | 2006 | 104 547.7 | 146.8 | 109.8 | 95 190.8 | 133.7 | 71 197.3 |

| Country or area<br>Pays ou zone | Year<br>Année | GDP at current price<br>PIB aux prix courants | | GDP at constant prices<br>PIB aux prix constants | GDP implicit price deflators<br>PIB déflateurs implicites des prix | | Exchange rates<br>Cours des changes |
|---|---|---|---|---|---|---|---|
| | | National currency<br>Monnaie nationale | US dollars<br>Dollars E.-U. | National currency<br>Monnaie nationale | National currency<br>Monnaie nationale | US dollars<br>Dollars E.-U. | |
| Croatia | 2000 | 54 373.9 | 74.4 | 85.7 | 63 454.8 | 86.8 | 73 121.5 |
| Croatie | 2004 | 75 873.8 | 142.3 | 101.9 | 74 448.6 | 139.7 | 53 303.2 |
| | 2005 | 81 651.0 | 155.4 | 106.3 | 76 814.2 | 146.2 | 52 554.9 |
| | 2006 | 87 909.6 | 170.5 | 111.1 | 79 153.4 | 153.5 | 51 569.1 |
| Czech Republic | 2000 | 329.2 | 153.1 | 102.6 | 321.0 | 149.3 | 215.0 |
| République tchèque | 2004 | 418.2 | 292.2 | 115.6 | 361.8 | 252.7 | 143.1 |
| | 2005 | 446.7 | 334.8 | 122.6 | 364.2 | 272.9 | 133.4 |
| | 2006 | 480.0 | 381.4 | 130.0 | 369.2 | 293.4 | 125.9 |
| Denmark | 2000 | 153.9 | 117.9 | 129.2 | 119.1 | 91.2 | 130.6 |
| Danemark | 2004 | 174.6 | 180.3 | 134.1 | 130.2 | 134.5 | 96.8 |
| | 2005 | 184.9 | 190.8 | 138.1 | 133.9 | 138.1 | 96.9 |
| | 2006 | 196.2 | 204.2 | 142.3 | 137.9 | 143.5 | 96.1 |
| Estonia | 2000 | 11 970.8 | 99.1 | 91.7 | 13 058.6 | 108.1 | 12 084.6 |
| Estonie | 2004 | 18 389.6 | 205.0 | 123.4 | 14 906.6 | 166.2 | 8 970.2 |
| | 2005 | 21 695.2 | 242.1 | 136.3 | 15 918.7 | 177.6 | 8 961.7 |
| | 2006 | 25 142.6 | 283.2 | 151.2 | 16 632.3 | 187.4 | 8 877.2 |
| Finland | 2000 | 147.4 | 87.3 | 121.5 | 121.3 | 71.9 | 168.8 |
| Finlande | 2004 | 169.3 | 135.2 | 133.5 | 126.8 | 101.2 | 125.2 |
| | 2005 | 175.4 | 140.2 | 137.5 | 127.6 | 102.0 | 125.0 |
| | 2006 | 186.2 | 150.2 | 144.4 | 129.0 | 104.0 | 124.0 |
| France[5] | 2000 | 140.1 | 107.2 | 122.0 | 114.8 | 87.8 | 130.7 |
| France[5] | 2004 | 161.3 | 166.2 | 129.9 | 124.2 | 128.0 | 97.0 |
| | 2005 | 166.2 | 171.6 | 131.4 | 126.5 | 130.6 | 96.9 |
| | 2006 | 173.1 | 180.3 | 134.3 | 129.0 | 134.3 | 96.0 |
| Germany | 2000 | 145.6 | 110.8 | 123.1 | 118.3 | 90.0 | 131.4 |
| Allemagne | 2004 | 155.8 | 159.9 | 126.0 | 123.7 | 126.9 | 97.5 |
| | 2005 | 158.2 | 162.6 | 127.1 | 124.5 | 127.9 | 97.3 |
| | 2006 | 162.6 | 168.5 | 130.3 | 124.8 | 129.4 | 96.5 |
| Greece | 2000 | 311.2 | 135.0 | 126.1 | 246.9 | 107.1 | 230.5 |
| Grèce | 2004 | 422.9 | 244.3 | 150.2 | 281.5 | 162.6 | 173.1 |
| | 2005 | 453.6 | 262.4 | 155.8 | 291.1 | 168.4 | 172.9 |
| | 2006 | 487.9 | 284.7 | 161.7 | 301.7 | 176.1 | 171.4 |
| Hungary | 2000 | 582.5 | 130.5 | 108.0 | 539.4 | 120.8 | 446.4 |
| Hongrie | 2004 | 891.6 | 278.0 | 128.1 | 696.1 | 217.0 | 320.8 |
| | 2005 | 948.2 | 300.3 | 133.5 | 710.1 | 224.9 | 315.8 |
| | 2006 | 1 014.2 | 304.7 | 138.7 | 731.0 | 219.6 | 332.9 |
| Iceland | 2000 | 182.9 | 135.6 | 128.0 | 142.9 | 106.0 | 134.9 |
| Islande | 2004 | 246.5 | 204.7 | 146.2 | 168.6 | 140.0 | 120.4 |
| | 2005 | 272.6 | 252.3 | 157.2 | 173.4 | 160.5 | 108.1 |
| | 2006 | 295.7 | 245.5 | 163.6 | 180.7 | 150.0 | 120.4 |
| Ireland | 2000 | 284.6 | 201.3 | 199.3 | 142.8 | 101.0 | 141.4 |
| Irlande | 2004 | 401.7 | 382.9 | 243.3 | 165.1 | 157.4 | 104.9 |
| | 2005 | 438.7 | 418.8 | 256.8 | 170.9 | 163.1 | 104.7 |
| | 2006 | 473.2 | 455.7 | 270.8 | 175.1 | 168.6 | 103.8 |
| Italy | 2000 | 169.8 | 96.8 | 117.1 | 145.1 | 82.7 | 175.4 |
| Italie | 2004 | 198.0 | 152.2 | 120.9 | 163.8 | 125.9 | 130.2 |
| | 2005 | 202.1 | 155.5 | 120.9 | 167.2 | 128.7 | 130.0 |
| | 2006 | 210.0 | 163.0 | 123.0 | 170.8 | 132.6 | 128.8 |

| Country or area  Pays ou zone | Year  Année | GDP at current price  PIB aux prix courants | | GDP at constant prices  PIB aux prix constants | GDP implicit price deflators  PIB déflateurs implicites des prix | | |
|---|---|---|---|---|---|---|---|
| | | National currency  Monnaie nationale | US dollars  Dollars E.-U. | National currency  Monnaie nationale | National currency  Monnaie nationale | US dollars  Dollars E.-U. | Exchange rates  Cours des changes |
| Kosovo  Kosovo | 2000 | 115.7 | 88.1 | 49.4 | 234.3 | 178.3 | 131.4 |
| | 2004 | 142.9 | 146.6 | 50.3 | 284.2 | 291.5 | 97.5 |
| | 2005 | 150.8 | 154.9 | 53.8 | 280.2 | 287.9 | 97.3 |
| | 2006 | 156.3 | 161.9 | 55.4 | 281.9 | 292.2 | 96.5 |
| Latvia  Lettonie | 2000 | 7 608.5 | 88.5 | 64.6 | 11 785.0 | 137.0 | 8 602.2 |
| | 2004 | 11 906.6 | 155.4 | 86.5 | 13 761.4 | 179.6 | 7 662.2 |
| | 2005 | 14 508.5 | 181.1 | 95.7 | 15 162.0 | 189.3 | 8 009.5 |
| | 2006 | 18 040.8 | 227.0 | 107.1 | 16 844.4 | 211.9 | 7 948.4 |
| Liechtenstein  Liechtenstein | 2000 | 212.4 | 174.7 | 175.2 | 121.2 | 99.7 | 121.6 |
| | 2004 | 216.7 | 242.1 | 173.5 | 124.9 | 139.6 | 89.5 |
| | 2005 | 220.7 | 246.2 | 176.8 | 124.8 | 139.3 | 89.6 |
| | 2006 | 227.5 | 252.1 | 181.6 | 125.3 | 138.8 | 90.3 |
| Lithuania  Lituanie | 2000 | 33 549.7 | 112.1 | 71.0 | 47 276.2 | 158.0 | 29 919.7 |
| | 2004 | 45 973.0 | 221.0 | 95.8 | 47 989.9 | 230.7 | 20 799.1 |
| | 2005 | 52 300.0 | 252.1 | 103.0 | 50 758.5 | 244.6 | 20 749.9 |
| | 2006 | 59 200.2 | 287.6 | 111.1 | 53 278.6 | 258.8 | 20 586.8 |
| Luxembourg  Luxembourg | 2000 | 209.6 | 160.0 | 163.5 | 128.2 | 97.9 | 131.0 |
| | 2004 | 257.2 | 264.6 | 182.8 | 140.7 | 144.8 | 97.2 |
| | 2005 | 280.1 | 288.5 | 190.0 | 147.4 | 151.9 | 97.1 |
| | 2006 | 307.7 | 319.8 | 200.5 | 153.5 | 159.5 | 96.2 |
| Malta  Malte | 2000 | 210.7 | 152.8 | 164.9 | 127.8 | 92.7 | 137.9 |
| | 2004 | 228.7 | 210.8 | 163.9 | 139.5 | 128.7 | 108.5 |
| | 2005 | 238.5 | 219.2 | 167.4 | 142.4 | 130.9 | 108.8 |
| | 2006 | 247.7 | 230.9 | 170.1 | 145.7 | 135.8 | 107.3 |
| Moldova  Moldova | 2000 | 126 327.3 | 32.5 | 34.8 | 363 218.6 | 93.3 | 389 134.9 |
| | 2004 | 252 596.6 | 65.5 | 45.6 | 554 431.5 | 143.7 | 385 879.4 |
| | 2005 | 296 915.6 | 75.3 | 49.0 | 606 232.6 | 153.7 | 394 323.3 |
| | 2006 | 347 518.3 | 84.6 | 50.9 | 682 517.8 | 166.1 | 410 957.3 |
| Monaco  Monaco | 2000 | 142.3 | 108.8 | 123.9 | 114.8 | 87.8 | 130.7 |
| | 2004 | 161.7 | 166.7 | 130.2 | 124.2 | 128.0 | 97.0 |
| | 2005 | 166.2 | 171.6 | 131.4 | 126.5 | 130.6 | 96.9 |
| | 2006 | 172.7 | 179.8 | 133.9 | 129.0 | 134.3 | 96.0 |
| Montenegro  Monténégro | 2000 | 58.0 | 44.1 | 67.6 | 85.8 | 65.3 | 131.4 |
| | 2004 | 88.7 | 91.0 | 73.2 | 121.3 | 124.4 | 97.5 |
| | 2005 | 95.8 | 98.4 | 76.3 | 125.6 | 129.0 | 97.3 |
| | 2006 | 101.7 | 105.4 | 80.5 | 126.3 | 130.9 | 96.5 |
| Netherlands  Pays-Bas | 2000 | 169.9 | 129.3 | 135.2 | 125.7 | 95.7 | 131.4 |
| | 2004 | 199.1 | 204.3 | 141.1 | 141.2 | 144.8 | 97.5 |
| | 2005 | 205.6 | 211.2 | 143.2 | 143.5 | 147.5 | 97.3 |
| | 2006 | 215.1 | 223.0 | 147.4 | 145.9 | 151.3 | 96.5 |
| Norway  Norvège | 2000 | 202.1 | 143.8 | 144.1 | 140.2 | 99.7 | 140.6 |
| | 2004 | 236.2 | 219.4 | 156.1 | 151.4 | 140.6 | 107.7 |
| | 2005 | 262.0 | 254.5 | 159.6 | 164.2 | 159.5 | 102.9 |
| | 2006 | 294.7 | 287.6 | 164.3 | 179.3 | 175.0 | 102.5 |
| Poland  Pologne | 2000 | 1 214.3 | 265.4 | 144.9 | 838.3 | 183.3 | 457.5 |
| | 2004 | 1 503.8 | 390.6 | 162.4 | 926.3 | 240.6 | 385.0 |
| | 2005 | 1 596.8 | 468.9 | 167.6 | 952.7 | 279.7 | 340.6 |
| | 2006 | 1 698.7 | 520.0 | 176.3 | 963.4 | 294.9 | 326.7 |

| Country or area Pays ou zone | Year Année | GDP at current price PIB aux prix courants | | GDP at constant prices PIB aux prix constants | GDP implicit price deflators PIB déflateurs implicites des prix | | Exchange rates |
|---|---|---|---|---|---|---|---|
| | | National currency Monnaie nationale | US dollars Dollars E.-U. | National currency Monnaie nationale | National currency Monnaie nationale | US dollars Dollars E.-U. | Cours des changes |
| Portugal Portugal | 2000 | 228.4 | 149.6 | 132.9 | 171.8 | 112.6 | 152.7 |
| | 2004 | 268.1 | 236.7 | 136.7 | 196.0 | 173.1 | 113.3 |
| | 2005 | 276.1 | 244.1 | 137.3 | 201.1 | 177.9 | 113.1 |
| | 2006 | 285.6 | 254.8 | 139.0 | 205.5 | 183.3 | 112.1 |
| Romania Roumanie | 2000 | 93 043.3 | 96.1 | 84.3 | 110 371.6 | 114.1 | 96 774.8 |
| | 2004 | 285 195.3 | 196.0 | 106.9 | 266 703.9 | 183.3 | 145 493.4 |
| | 2005 | 332 441.5 | 256.0 | 111.3 | 298 734.6 | 230.0 | 129 890.3 |
| | 2006 | 395 337.3 | 315.7 | 119.3 | 331 417.0 | 264.7 | 125 223.7 |
| Russian Federation Fédération de Russie | 2000 | 1 134 064.9 | 45.6 | 67.2 | 1 687 277.6 | 67.8 | 2 487 509.3 |
| | 2004 | 2 646 402.0 | 103.9 | 85.1 | 3 109 911.3 | 122.0 | 2 548 272.1 |
| | 2005 | 3 356 117.9 | 134.2 | 90.5 | 3 706 702.8 | 148.2 | 2 501 317.8 |
| | 2006 | 4 157 265.3 | 172.9 | 96.6 | 4 303 223.3 | 179.0 | 2 404 707.1 |
| San Marino Saint-Marin | 2000 | 240.5 | 137.1 | 216.6 | 111.0 | 63.3 | 175.4 |
| | 2004 | 303.7 | 233.4 | 249.3 | 121.8 | 93.6 | 130.2 |
| | 2005 | 309.9 | 238.5 | 249.2 | 124.4 | 95.7 | 129.9 |
| | 2006 | 322.2 | 250.1 | 253.6 | 127.1 | 98.6 | 128.8 |
| Serbia Serbie | 2000 | 278 631.7[6] | 26.5 | 47.2 | 590 355.1[6] | 56.2 | 1 050 827.9[6] |
| | 2004 | 1 002 901.1[6] | 71.7 | 58.1 | 1 727 322.2[6] | 123.5 | 1 398 188.6[6] |
| | 2005 | 1 226 200.5[6] | 70.9 | 67.9 | 1 805 836.6[6] | 104.4 | 1 729 231.7[6] |
| | 2006 | 1 499 327.9[6] | 105.3 | 71.8 | 2 088 156.0[6] | 146.7 | 1 423 613.3[6] |
| Slovakia Slovaquie | 2000 | 316.4 | 123.4 | 109.6 | 288.8 | 112.6 | 256.4 |
| | 2004 | 455.5 | 253.5 | 129.3 | 352.4 | 196.1 | 179.7 |
| | 2005 | 494.5 | 286.2 | 137.2 | 360.4 | 208.6 | 172.8 |
| | 2006 | 549.7 | 332.3 | 146.3 | 375.9 | 227.2 | 165.4 |
| Slovenia Slovénie | 2000 | 2 185.5 | 111.1 | 120.4 | 1 815.1 | 92.3 | 1 967.0 |
| | 2004 | 3 187.4 | 187.6 | 137.1 | 2 325.4 | 136.8 | 1 699.5 |
| | 2005 | 3 364.4 | 197.6 | 142.6 | 2 359.5 | 138.6 | 1 702.4 |
| | 2006 | 3 582.4 | 212.3 | 149.5 | 2 396.6 | 142.0 | 1 687.5 |
| Spain Espagne | 2000 | 197.5 | 111.5 | 131.8 | 149.9 | 84.6 | 177.2 |
| | 2004 | 263.2 | 200.2 | 149.2 | 176.4 | 134.2 | 131.5 |
| | 2005 | 283.7 | 216.2 | 154.5 | 183.6 | 139.9 | 131.3 |
| | 2006 | 306.0 | 235.2 | 160.3 | 190.9 | 146.7 | 130.1 |
| Sweden Suède | 2000 | 154.7 | 99.9 | 121.3 | 127.6 | 82.4 | 154.8 |
| | 2004 | 179.0 | 144.1 | 132.4 | 135.2 | 108.9 | 124.2 |
| | 2005 | 186.3 | 147.6 | 136.2 | 136.8 | 108.3 | 126.3 |
| | 2006 | 197.1 | 158.1 | 141.6 | 139.1 | 111.6 | 124.6 |
| Switzerland Suisse | 2000 | 126.9 | 104.3 | 111.0 | 114.3 | 94.0 | 121.6 |
| | 2004 | 136.6 | 152.5 | 114.9 | 118.9 | 132.8 | 89.5 |
| | 2005 | 139.1 | 155.2 | 117.1 | 118.8 | 132.5 | 89.6 |
| | 2006 | 143.4 | 158.9 | 120.3 | 119.2 | 132.1 | 90.3 |
| TFYR of Macedonia L'ex-R.y. Macédoine | 2000 | 48 929.6 | 84.0 | 98.7 | 49 556.1 | 85.1 | 58 226.0 |
| | 2004 | 54 904.8 | 125.8 | 101.7 | 53 964.7 | 123.6 | 43 657.2 |
| | 2005 | 59 326.3 | 136.2 | 105.9 | 56 012.7 | 128.6 | 43 545.6 |
| | 2006 | 63 679.5 | 147.7 | 110.2 | 57 810.3 | 134.1 | 43 119.5 |
| Ukraine Ukraine | 2000 | 10 175 971.9 | 34.7 | 43.2 | 23 557 544.3 | 80.2 | 29 362 513.1 |
| | 2004 | 20 649 498.3 | 71.9 | 61.0 | 33 830 396.1 | 117.8 | 28 711 190.7 |
| | 2005 | 26 413 848.0 | 95.5 | 62.7 | 42 126 199.5 | 152.3 | 27 661 829.1 |
| | 2006 | 32 170 778.3 | 118.0 | 67.2 | 47 906 308.1 | 175.8 | 27 258 212.3 |

| Country or area | Year | GDP at current price PIB aux prix courants | | GDP at constant prices PIB aux prix constants | GDP implicit price deflators PIB déflateurs implicites des prix | | |
|---|---|---|---|---|---|---|---|
| | | National currency Monnaie nationale | US dollars Dollars E.-U. | National currency Monnaie nationale | National currency Monnaie nationale | US dollars Dollars E.-U. | Exchange rates Cours des changes |
| Pays ou zone | Année | | | | | | |
| United Kingdom | 2000 | 170.8 | 145.5 | 127.0 | 134.4 | 114.6 | 117.4 |
| Royaume-Uni | 2004 | 210.8 | 217.4 | 140.7 | 149.8 | 154.5 | 97.0 |
| | 2005 | 219.4 | 224.6 | 143.3 | 153.1 | 156.8 | 97.7 |
| | 2006 | 231.0 | 239.4 | 147.3 | 156.8 | 162.5 | 96.5 |
| **Oceania — Océanie** | | | | | | | |
| Australia | 2000 | 168.6 | 125.2 | 142.2 | 118.5 | 88.0 | 134.6 |
| Australie | 2004 | 219.3 | 206.6 | 162.6 | 134.8 | 127.0 | 106.1 |
| | 2005 | 236.3 | 231.2 | 167.2 | 141.3 | 138.2 | 102.2 |
| | 2006 | 252.9 | 244.0 | 174.2 | 145.2 | 140.0 | 103.7 |
| Cook Islands | 2000 | 181.3 | 138.1 | 132.8 | 136.5 | 104.0 | 131.3 |
| Iles Cook | 2004 | 263.4 | 292.7 | 161.2 | 163.4 | 181.6 | 90.0 |
| | 2005 | 265.2 | 313.0 | 161.3 | 164.4 | 194.0 | 84.7 |
| | 2006 | 278.9 | 303.1 | 164.2 | 169.8 | 184.6 | 92.0 |
| Fiji | 2000 | 181.3 | 126.1 | 126.2 | 143.7 | 100.0 | 143.7 |
| Fidji | 2004 | 238.8 | 204.0 | 141.2 | 169.1 | 144.5 | 117.0 |
| | 2005 | 256.0 | 224.2 | 142.2 | 180.0 | 157.7 | 114.2 |
| | 2006 | 271.4 | 232.1 | 147.1 | 184.5 | 157.9 | 116.9 |
| French Polynesia | 2000 | 144.8 | 110.7 | 126.0 | 114.9 | 87.8 | 130.8 |
| Polynésie française | 2004 | 170.5 | 175.6 | 143.5 | 118.8 | 122.4 | 97.1 |
| | 2005 | 178.2 | 183.9 | 148.4 | 120.1 | 123.9 | 96.9 |
| | 2006 | 185.8 | 192.6 | 153.3 | 121.2 | 125.6 | 96.5 |
| Kiribati | 2000 | 241.4 | 179.3 | 161.4 | 149.6 | 111.1 | 134.6 |
| Kiribati | 2004 | 262.0 | 246.8 | 181.1 | 144.7 | 136.3 | 106.1 |
| | 2005 | 268.4 | 262.6 | 187.5 | 143.2 | 140.1 | 102.2 |
| | 2006 | 273.3 | 263.6 | 189.0 | 144.6 | 139.5 | 103.7 |
| Marshall Islands | 2000 | 143.9 | 143.9 | 86.2 | 166.9 | 166.9 | 100.0 |
| Iles Marshall | 2004 | 167.8 | 167.8 | 90.4 | 185.5 | 185.5 | 100.0 |
| | 2005 | 178.8 | 178.8 | 93.6 | 191.1 | 191.1 | 100.0 |
| | 2006 | 186.0 | 186.0 | 97.4 | 191.1 | 191.1 | 100.0 |
| Micronesia (Fed. States of) | 2000 | 149.1 | 149.1 | 113.6 | 131.2 | 131.2 | 100.0 |
| Micronésie (Etats féd. de) | 2004 | 154.1 | 154.1 | 114.3 | 134.8 | 134.8 | 100.0 |
| | 2005 | 162.8 | 162.8 | 116.0 | 140.3 | 140.3 | 100.0 |
| | 2006 | 168.0 | 168.0 | 115.2 | 145.8 | 145.8 | 100.0 |
| Nauru | 2000 | 86.8 | 64.5 | 58.7 | 147.9 | 109.9 | 134.6 |
| Nauru | 2004 | 105.2 | 99.1 | 59.5 | 176.9 | 166.6 | 106.1 |
| | 2005 | 108.2 | 105.8 | 59.5 | 181.8 | 177.9 | 102.2 |
| | 2006 | 112.4 | 108.5 | 59.5 | 189.0 | 182.3 | 103.7 |
| New Caledonia | 2000 | 163.7 | 125.2 | 117.7 | 139.1 | 106.3 | 130.8 |
| Nouvelle-Calédonie | 2004 | 176.3 | 181.7 | 120.8 | 146.0 | 150.4 | 97.1 |
| | 2005 | 178.4 | 184.1 | 121.8 | 146.5 | 151.1 | 96.9 |
| | 2006 | 180.9 | 187.5 | 122.8 | 147.3 | 152.7 | 96.5 |
| New Zealand | 2000 | 157.6 | 120.0 | 132.2 | 119.2 | 90.7 | 131.3 |
| Nouvelle-Zélande | 2004 | 201.8 | 224.2 | 154.5 | 130.6 | 145.1 | 90.0 |
| | 2005 | 211.9 | 250.0 | 157.4 | 134.6 | 158.8 | 84.7 |
| | 2006 | 222.1 | 241.4 | 159.5 | 139.2 | 151.3 | 92.0 |
| Palau | 2000 | 152.5 | 152.5 | 102.7 | 148.4 | 148.4 | 100.0 |
| Palaos | 2004 | 173.7 | 173.7 | 104.0 | 167.1 | 167.1 | 100.0 |
| | 2005 | 188.2 | 188.2 | 109.7 | 171.6 | 171.6 | 100.0 |
| | 2006 | 202.5 | 202.5 | 115.2 | 175.8 | 175.8 | 100.0 |

| Country or area<br>Pays ou zone | Year<br>Année | GDP at current prices<br>PIB aux prix courants | | GDP at constant prices<br>PIB aux prix constants | GDP implicit price deflators<br>PIB déflateurs implicites des prix | | Exchange rates |
|---|---|---|---|---|---|---|---|
| | | National currency<br>Monnaie nationale | US dollars<br>Dollars E.-U. | National currency<br>Monnaie nationale | National currency<br>Monnaie nationale | US dollars<br>Dollars E.-U. | Cours des changes |
| Papua New Guinea | 2000 | 342.6 | 117.6 | 173.7 | 197.2 | 67.7 | 291.3 |
| Papouasie-Nvl-Guinée | 2004 | 506.9 | 150.2 | 191.1 | 265.3 | 78.6 | 337.5 |
| | 2005 | 557.1 | 171.5 | 197.0 | 282.8 | 87.1 | 324.8 |
| | 2006 | 597.7 | 186.7 | 204.3 | 292.6 | 91.4 | 320.1 |
| Samoa | 2000 | 293.1 | 206.0 | 126.2 | 232.2 | 163.2 | 142.3 |
| Samoa | 2004 | 404.8 | 336.2 | 145.7 | 277.9 | 230.9 | 120.4 |
| | 2005 | 436.5 | 372.0 | 153.1 | 285.0 | 242.9 | 117.3 |
| | 2006 | 467.5 | 388.5 | 159.3 | 293.5 | 244.0 | 120.3 |
| Solomon Islands | 2000 | 327.0 | 162.5 | 112.3 | 291.3 | 144.7 | 201.2 |
| Iles Salomon | 2004 | 475.3 | 160.6 | 115.3 | 412.3 | 139.3 | 296.0 |
| | 2005 | 535.4 | 179.8 | 121.0 | 442.4 | 148.6 | 297.8 |
| | 2006 | 601.6 | 199.9 | 127.1 | 473.4 | 157.3 | 300.9 |
| Tonga | 2000 | 164.8 | 119.9 | 130.3 | 126.5 | 92.1 | 137.4 |
| Tonga | 2004 | 234.9 | 152.5 | 142.5 | 164.8 | 107.0 | 154.0 |
| | 2005 | 263.2 | 173.4 | 145.8 | 180.4 | 118.9 | 151.8 |
| | 2006 | 287.3 | 187.8 | 148.6 | 193.4 | 126.4 | 153.0 |
| Tuvalu | 2000 | 173.1 | 128.6 | 127.6 | 135.7 | 100.8 | 134.6 |
| Tuvalu | 2004 | 253.5 | 238.8 | 164.9 | 153.7 | 144.8 | 106.1 |
| | 2005 | 266.9 | 261.1 | 168.2 | 158.7 | 155.3 | 102.2 |
| | 2006 | 278.2 | 268.4 | 169.9 | 163.8 | 158.0 | 103.7 |
| Vanuatu | 2000 | 188.1 | 159.9 | 145.5 | 129.2 | 109.9 | 117.6 |
| Vanuatu | 2004 | 200.0 | 209.5 | 143.7 | 139.2 | 145.8 | 95.5 |
| | 2005 | 211.6 | 226.8 | 148.2 | 142.8 | 153.0 | 93.3 |
| | 2006 | 224.3 | 236.0 | 153.2 | 146.4 | 154.1 | 95.0 |

Source

United Nations Statistics Division, New York, national accounts main aggregates database, last accessed January 2008.

Notes

1 Figures in millions.

2 Price-adjusted rates of exchange (PARE) are used for selected years for conversion to US dollars due to large distortions in the dollar levels of per capita GDP with the use of IMF market exchange rates.

3 For statistical purposes, the data for China do not include those for the Hong Kong Special Administrative Region (Hong Kong SAR), Macao Special Administrative Region (Macao SAR) and Taiwan Province of China.

4 Figures in thousands.

5 Includes Guadeloupe, Martinique, Réunion and French Guiana.

6 Figures in billions

Source

Organisation des Nations Unies, Division de statistique, New York, la base de données sur les principaux agrégats des comptes nationaux, dernier accès janvier 2008.

Notes

1 Chiffres en millions.

2 Pour certaines années, on utilise les Taux de change corrigés des prix (TCCP) pour effectuer la conversion en dollars des États-Unis, en raison des aberrations importantes relevées dans les niveaux du PNB exprimés en dollars après conversion à l'aide des taux de change du marché communiqués par le FMI.

3 Pour la présentation des statistiques, les données pour la Chine ne comprennent pas la Région Administrative Spéciale de Hong Kong (Hong Kong RAS), la Région Administrative Spéciale de Macao (Macao RAS) et la province de Taiwan.

4 Données en milliers.

5 Y compris Guadeloupe, Martinique, Réunion et Guyane française.

6 Chiffres en milliards.

# Gross domestic product by type of expenditure at current prices
Percentage distribution

# Dépenses imputées au produit intérieur brut aux prix courants
Répartition en pourcentage

| Country or area<br>Pays ou zone | Year<br>Année | GDP at<br>current prices<br>(mil. nat.cur.)<br><br>PIB aux prix<br>courants<br>(millions<br>monnaie nat.) | % of Gross domestic product – en % du Produit intérieur brut | | | | | |
|---|---|---|---|---|---|---|---|---|
| | | | Household final<br>consumption<br>expenditure<br><br>Consom. finale<br>des ménages | Govt. final<br>consumption<br>expenditure<br><br>Consom. finale<br>des admin.<br>publiques | Gross fixed<br>capital<br>formation<br><br>Formation<br>brute de<br>capital fixe | Changes in<br>inventories<br><br>Variation<br>des stocks | Exports<br>of goods<br>and services<br><br>Exportations<br>de biens<br>et services | Imports<br>of goods<br>and services<br><br>Importations<br>de biens<br>et services |
| Afghanistan+[1] | 2002 | 182 862 | 101.5 | 7.9 | 12.3 | ... | 58.4 | 80.0 |
| Afghanistan+[1] | 2003 | 217 898 | 96.4 | 8.0 | 12.7 | ... | 48.5 | 65.6 |
| Albania | 2003 | 694 098 | 75.2[2] | 10.9 | 40.5 | -1.8 | 20.4 | 45.1 |
| Albanie | 2004 | 751 024 | 78.2[2] | 11.0 | 37.2 | -4.0 | 22.0 | 44.4 |
| | 2005 | 817 374 | 76.2[2] | 10.8 | 36.3 | 1.2 | 22.8 | 47.3 |
| Algeria[1] | 2001 | 4 260 811 | 43.4 | 14.7 | 22.7 | 4.8 | 36.4 | 21.8 |
| Algérie[1] | 2002 | 4 537 691 | 43.8 | 15.4 | 24.5 | 6.4 | 35.4 | 25.5 |
| | 2003 | 5 264 187 | 40.4 | 14.8 | 24.0 | 6.3 | 38.2 | 23.8 |
| Angola[1] | 1988 | 239 640 | 45.5 | 32.9 | 14.6 | 0.0 | 32.8 | 25.8 |
| Angola[1] | 1989 | 278 866 | 48.2 | 28.9 | 11.2 | 0.9 | 33.8 | 23.1 |
| | 1990 | 308 062 | 44.7 | 28.5 | 11.1 | 0.6 | 38.9 | 23.8 |
| Anguilla[1] | 2004 | 402 | 84.1 | 16.4 | 34.4 | ... | 57.0 | 91.8 |
| Anguilla[1] | 2005 | 453 | 89.0 | 16.8 | 35.4 | ... | 57.6 | 98.9 |
| | 2006 | 544[3] | 96.9 | 15.7 | 33.7 | ... | 54.0 | 100.3 |
| Antigua and Barbuda[1] | 1984 | 468 | 69.8 | 18.5 | 23.6 | 0.0 | 73.7 | 85.6 |
| Antigua-et-Barbuda[1] | 1985 | 541 | 71.5 | 18.3 | 28.0 | 0.0 | 75.7 | 93.5 |
| | 1986 | 642 | 69.7 | 18.9 | 36.1 | 0.0 | 75.2 | 99.9 |
| Argentina | 2003 | 375 909 | 63.2 | 11.4 | 15.1[4] | ... | 25.0 | 14.2 |
| Argentine | 2004 | 447 643 | 62.8 | 11.1 | 19.2[4] | ... | 25.7 | 18.4 |
| | 2005 | 531 939 | 61.3 | 11.9 | 21.5[4] | ... | 25.1 | 19.2 |
| Armenia | #2004 | 1 907 945 | 82.5[2] | 10.2 | 23.9 | 1.0[5] | 27.4 | 42.1 |
| Arménie | 2005 | 2 243 953 | 76.2[2] | 10.6 | 29.3 | 0.4[5] | 26.9 | 39.9 |
| | 2006 | 2 665 037 | 72.2[2] | 11.4 | 32.7 | 0.2[5] | 21.6 | 34.4 |
| Aruba | 2000 | 3 327 | 50.0 | 22.0 | 23.7 | 0.9 | 74.4 | 71.0 |
| Aruba | 2001 | 3 399 | 50.4 | 23.7 | 21.9 | 0.6 | 72.6 | 69.1 |
| | 2002 | 3 421 | 52.6 | 26.3 | 22.4 | 0.9 | 69.3 | 71.5 |
| Australia+ | 2003 | 840 285 | 58.6 | 17.9 | 25.4 | 0.7 | 17.5 | 20.1 |
| Australie+ | 2004 | 896 568 | 58.1 | 18.2 | 25.8 | 0.5 | 18.7 | 21.2 |
| | 2005 | 965 969 | 56.6 | 18.2 | 26.5 | 0.2 | 20.3 | 21.8 |
| Austria | 2004 | 235 819 | 56.4[2] | 18.1 | 20.9 | 0.4[5] | 51.6 | 47.3 |
| Autriche | 2005 | 245 103 | 56.1[2] | 18.1 | 20.5 | 0.3[5] | 54.3 | 49.5 |
| | 2006 | 256 667 | 55.4[2] | 17.9 | 20.8 | 0.1[5] | 57.7 | 52.0 |
| Azerbaijan | 2004 | 8 530 | 55.8[2] | 12.9 | 57.7 | 0.3[5] | 48.8 | 72.7 |
| Azerbaïdjan | 2005 | 12 523 | 42.1[2] | 10.4 | 41.3 | 0.2[5] | 62.9 | 52.9 |
| | 2006 | 17 736 | 35.6[2] | 8.0 | 31.4 | 0.2[5] | 70.3 | 41.0 |
| Bahamas | 2003 | 5 503 | 68.5 | 14.3 | 29.3 | 2.7 | 44.0 | 55.4 |
| Bahamas | 2004 | 5 661[3] | 68.8 | 14.6 | 29.4 | 2.8 | 46.8 | 59.4 |
| | 2005 | 5 869[3] | 67.8 | 14.9 | 29.8 | 3.0 | 49.1 | 61.7 |
| Bahrain[1] | 2002 | 3 176 | 45.2 | 18.5 | 17.3 | 4.3 | 81.2 | 66.6 |
| Bahreïn[1] | 2003 | 3 647 | 43.0 | 18.4 | 19.7 | 1.8 | 81.1 | 64.0 |
| | 2004 | 4 141 | 42.0 | 17.0 | 21.6 | 1.1 | 82.4 | 64.2 |
| Bangladesh+ | 2003 | 3 329 731 | 74.9 | 5.5 | 24.0 | ... | 15.5 | 20.8 |
| Bangladesh+ | 2004 | 3 707 070 | 74.4 | 5.5 | 24.5 | ... | 16.6 | 23.0 |
| | 2005 | 4 161 546 | 74.2 | 5.6 | 25.0 | ... | 17.8 | 24.4 |
| Barbados[1] | 2002 | 4 952 | 64.1 | 24.6 | 16.9 | -0.3 | 50.1 | 55.3 |
| Barbade[1] | 2003 | 5 390 | 65.7 | 23.2 | 16.9 | -0.1 | 50.7 | 56.3 |
| | 2004 | 5 632 | 70.7 | 21.3 | 19.2 | 0.2 | 49.4 | 60.8 |
| Belarus | 2004 | 49 991 800 | 53.7[2] | 20.6 | 25.3 | 3.3 | 67.9 | 74.3 |
| Bélarus | 2005 | 65 067 100 | 52.0[2] | 20.8 | 26.5 | 1.9 | 59.8 | 59.1 |
| | 2006 | 79 231 400 | 52.4[2] | 19.9 | 28.3 | 2.1 | 59.9 | 64.2 |

| Country or area / Pays ou zone | Year / Année | GDP at current prices (mil. nat.cur.) / PIB aux prix courants (millions monnaie nat.) | % of Gross domestic product – en % du Produit intérieur brut | | | | | |
|---|---|---|---|---|---|---|---|---|
| | | | Household final consumption expenditure / Consom. finale des ménages | Govt. final consumption expenditure / Consom. finale des admin. publiques | Gross fixed capital formation / Formation brute de capital fixe | Changes in inventories / Variation des stocks | Exports of goods and services / Exportations de biens et services | Imports of goods and services / Importations de biens et services |
| Belgium Belgique | 2004 | 289 509 | 52.8[2] | 22.9 | 19.4 | 0.9 | 83.4 | 79.4 |
| | 2005 | 298 541 | 53.1[2] | 22.9 | 19.8 | 1.1 | 86.3 | 83.3 |
| | 2006 | 314 084 | 52.8[2] | 22.6 | 20.4 | 1.5 | 87.7 | 85.1 |
| Belize Belize | 1998 | 1 258 | 67.3 | 17.4 | 21.3 | 3.1 | 52.9 | 62.1 |
| | 1999 | 1 377 | 65.1 | 17.1 | 26.5 | 3.0 | 51.3 | 63.2 |
| | 2000 | 1 514 | 68.4 | 15.3 | 31.0 | 3.2 | 48.8 | 66.7 |
| Benin[1] Bénin[1] | 2004 | 2 140 013 | 75.8 | 12.1 | 19.4 | 1.3 | 20.0 | 28.6 |
| | 2005 | 2 298 714 | 76.8 | 12.0 | 19.4 | -1.2 | 21.6 | 28.5 |
| | 2006 | 2 454 202 | 76.2 | 12.1 | 19.6 | 1.4 | 18.5 | 27.8 |
| Bermuda+ Bermudes+ | 2000 | 6 756 | 51.5[2] | 10.9 | 19.5 | 0.6[5] | 47.3 | 34.4 |
| | 2001 | 3 539 | 50.2[2] | ... | ... | ... | 1.4[6] | 20.4[7] |
| | 2002 | 3 715 | 49.3[2] | ... | ... | ... | 1.5[6] | 20.1[7] |
| Bhutan+ Bhoutan+ | 2004 | 32 178 | 42.9 | 20.7 | 61.5 | -0.3 | 30.1 | 63.6 |
| | 2005 | 36 915 | 39.5 | 21.4 | 51.1 | 0.3 | 35.1 | 50.9 |
| | 2006 | 41 794[8] | 48.8 | 22.0 | 53.2 | 0.3 | 40.4 | 64.7 |
| Bolivia[1] Bolivie[1] | 2002 | 56 818 | 73.6 | 15.9 | 15.7 | 0.9 | 21.6 | 27.6 |
| | 2003 | 61 959 | 71.0 | 16.5 | 12.9 | 0.5 | 25.5 | 26.3 |
| | 2004 | 69 626 | 68.2 | 15.2 | 12.6 | -0.3 | 30.7 | 26.4 |
| Botswana+ Botswana+ | 2002 | 31 922 | 29.2[2] | 33.1 | 24.3 | 1.9 | 48.8 | 36.8 |
| | 2003 | 36 338 | 28.4[2] | 33.5 | 24.0 | 5.5 | 44.4 | 34.9 |
| | 2004 | 39 881 | 28.8[2] | 34.3 | 24.0 | 6.0 | 39.8 | 32.2 |
| Brazil Brésil | 2003 | 1 699 948 | 61.9[2] | 19.4 | 15.3 | 0.5 | 15.0 | 12.1 |
| | 2004 | 1 941 498 | 59.8[2] | 19.2 | 16.1 | 1.0 | 16.4 | 12.5 |
| | 2005 | 2 147 944 | 60.4 | 20.1 | 16.3 | -0.3 | 15.1 | 11.5 |
| British Virgin Islands Iles Vierges britanniques | 2003 | 782[3,9] | 38.2 | 9.6 | 24.0 | -1.4 | 107.5 | 78.0 |
| | 2004 | 873[3,9] | 37.7 | 9.4 | 24.1 | -1.5 | 108.2 | 77.9 |
| | 2005 | 972[3,9] | 37.1 | 9.3 | 24.0 | -1.5 | 108.8 | 77.7 |
| Brunei Darussalam Brunéi Darussalam | 2004 | 13 306 | 26.6 | 22.1 | 13.4 | 0.1 | 68.8 | 31.8 |
| | 2005 | 15 864 | 22.5 | 18.4 | 11.4 | 0.0 | 70.2 | 27.3 |
| | 2006 | 18 370 | 19.7 | 17.9 | 10.4 | 0.0 | 71.2 | 25.0 |
| Bulgaria Bulgarie | 2003 | 34 547 | 68.8[2] | 19.0 | 19.4 | 2.4[5] | 53.6 | 63.0 |
| | 2004 | 38 275 | 68.2[2] | 18.6 | 20.8 | 2.6[5] | 58.0 | 68.2 |
| | 2005 | 41 948 | 70.0[2] | 18.6 | 23.8 | 4.2[5] | 60.8 | 77.4 |
| Burkina Faso Burkina Faso | 2004 | 2 698 401 | 76.6 | 21.6 | 19.3 | -3.9 | 10.7 | 24.3 |
| | 2005 | 2 961 171 | 72.5 | 21.5 | 19.5 | 1.1 | 9.7 | 24.3 |
| | 2006 | 3 144 954 | 74.9 | 21.1 | 19.3 | -2.2 | 11.4 | 24.5 |
| Burundi[1] Burundi[1] | 1990 | 196 656 | 83.0 | 19.5 | 16.4 | -0.6 | 8.0 | 26.2 |
| | 1991 | 211 898 | 83.9 | 17.0 | 18.1 | -0.5 | 10.0 | 28.5 |
| | 1992 | 226 384 | 82.9 | 15.6 | 21.1 | 0.4 | 9.0 | 29.0 |
| Cambodia Cambodge | 2003 | 17 310 521 | 78.9[2] | 5.6 | 21.4 | 3.8 | 58.6 | 67.8 |
| | 2004 | 21 140 580 | 85.2[2] | 4.5 | 17.6 | -0.1 | 64.5 | 71.9 |
| | 2005 | 25 350 108 | 84.7[2] | 4.1 | 17.6 | 2.1 | 65.1 | 73.9 |
| Cameroon Cameroun | 2003 | 7 916 959 | 72.2[2] | 10.0 | 18.1 | -0.6 | 20.2 | 19.9 |
| | 2004 | 8 333 881 | 71.4[2] | 10.2 | 18.3 | 0.7 | 19.4 | 19.8 |
| | 2005 | 8 781 028 | 71.7[2] | 9.9 | 17.6 | 1.7 | 20.4 | 21.4 |
| Canada Canada | 2003 | 1 213 408 | 56.6[2] | 19.7 | 19.6 | 0.4 | 38.0 | 34.3 |
| | 2004 | 1 290 788 | 55.8[2] | 19.4 | 20.2 | 0.5 | 38.3 | 34.2 |
| | 2005 | 1 371 425 | 55.4[2] | 19.3 | 20.7 | 0.8 | 37.9 | 34.1 |
| Cape Verde[1] Cap-Vert[1] | 2002 | 72 758 | 88.5 | 18.4 | 35.9 | -0.1 | 20.9 | 63.7 |
| | 2003 | 79 527 | 86.5 | 20.1 | 31.1 | -0.1 | 14.6 | 52.1 |
| | 2004 | 82 086 | 83.7 | 21.3 | 38.9 | 0.5 | 13.8 | 58.3 |
| Cayman Islands[1] Iles Caïmanes[1] | 1989 | 474 | 65.0 | 14.1 | 23.2 | ... | 60.1 | 68.8 |
| | 1990 | 590 | 62.5 | 14.2 | 21.4 | ... | 64.1 | 58.5 |
| | 1991 | 616 | 62.5 | 15.1 | 21.8 | ... | 58.9 | 52.8 |

**Gross domestic product by type of expenditure at current prices** — Percentage distribution (*continued*)

**Dépenses imputées au produit intérieur brut aux prix courants** — Répartition en pourcentage (*suite*)

| Country or area<br>Pays ou zone | Year<br>Année | GDP at<br>current prices<br>(mil. nat.cur.)<br>PIB aux prix<br>courants<br>(millions<br>monnaie nat.) | % of Gross domestic product – en % du Produit intérieur brut | | | | | |
|---|---|---|---|---|---|---|---|---|
| | | | Household final<br>consumption<br>expenditure<br>Consom. finale<br>des ménages | Govt. final<br>consumption<br>expenditure<br>Consom. finale<br>des admin.<br>publiques | Gross fixed<br>capital<br>formation<br>Formation<br>brute de<br>capital fixe | Changes in<br>inventories<br>Variation<br>des stocks | Exports<br>of goods<br>and services<br>Exportations<br>de biens<br>et services | Imports<br>of goods<br>and services<br>Importations<br>de biens<br>et services |
| Central African Rep.[1]<br>Rép. centrafricaine[1] | 1986 | 388 647 | 82.1 | 15.6 | 12.9 | -0.1 | 18.2 | 28.6 |
| | 1987 | 360 942 | 80.6 | 17.5 | 12.9 | -0.2 | 17.8 | 28.6 |
| | 1988 | 376 748 | 80.7 | 16.1 | 9.8 | 0.7 | 17.7 | 25.1 |
| Chad<br>Tchad | 2004 | 2 332 367 | 30.9 | 23.4 | 25.8 | 1.4 | 50.5 | 31.9 |
| | 2005 | 3 104 242 | 24.7 | 20.8 | 21.6 | 5.1 | 54.4 | 26.6 |
| | 2006 | 3 470 374 | 24.0 | 24.0 | 23.2 | 0.4 | 55.7 | 27.4 |
| Chile<br>Chili | 2004 | 58 404 603 | 59.4[2] | 11.4 | 19.1 | 1.0 | 40.6 | 31.5 |
| | 2005 | 66 598 991 | 58.2[2] | 10.9 | 20.6 | 1.7 | 41.0 | 32.5 |
| | 2006 | 77 337 701 | ... | 10.1 | 19.3 | 1.1 | 45.4 | 30.9 |
| China[10]<br>Chine[10] | 2003 | 13 582 280 | 41.8 | 15.2 | 39.4 | 1.8 | 29.6 | 27.4 |
| | 2004 | 15 987 830 | 39.9 | 14.5 | 40.7 | 2.5 | 34.0 | 31.4 |
| | 2005 | 18 308 480 | 38.7 | 14.2 | 42.3 | 1.1 | 37.4 | 31.9 |
| China, Hong Kong SAR<br>Chine, Hong Kong RAS | 2002 | 1 276 757 | 58.6[2] | 10.3 | 22.4 | 0.4 | 149.6 | 141.3 |
| | 2003 | 1 233 143 | 58.3[2] | 10.6 | 21.2 | 0.7 | 171.2 | 162.0 |
| | 2004 | 1 290 808 | 59.1[2] | 9.9 | 21.6 | 0.4 | 189.7 | 180.8 |
| China, Macao SAR<br>Chine, Macao RAS | 2002 | 54 819 | 36.9[2] | 11.5 | 10.6 | 0.4 | 104.3 | 63.7 |
| | 2003 | 63 566 | 32.5[2] | 10.7 | 14.1 | 0.5 | 103.3 | 61.2 |
| | 2004 | 83 103 | 27.4[2] | 8.5 | 16.2 | 0.7 | 105.0 | 57.9 |
| Colombia<br>Colombie | 2002 | 203 451 400 | 66.5[2] | 19.6 | 14.5 | 0.7[5] | 19.4 | 20.7 |
| | 2003 | 228 516 603 | 64.7[2] | 18.6 | 16.5 | 0.7[5] | 21.2 | 21.7 |
| | 2004 | 257 746 373 | 63.9[2] | 17.5 | 18.4 | 0.8[5] | 21.5 | 22.1 |
| Comoros[1]<br>Comores[1] | 1989 | 63 397 | 77.8 | 27.6 | 14.4 | 4.6 | 14.9 | 39.3 |
| | 1990 | 66 370 | 79.7 | 25.7 | 12.2 | 8.0 | 11.7 | 37.3 |
| | 1991 | 69 248 | 80.9 | 25.3 | 12.3 | 4.0 | 15.5 | 38.0 |
| Congo[1]<br>Congo[1] | 1987 | 690 523 | 56.6[2] | 20.6 | 20.9 | -1.1 | 41.7 | 38.6 |
| | 1988 | 658 964 | 60.1[2] | 21.1 | 19.6 | -1.0 | 40.6 | 40.4 |
| | 1989 | 773 524 | 52.8 | 18.7 | 16.4 | -0.5 | 47.6 | 35.0 |
| Cook Islands[1]<br>Iles Cook[1] | 2003 | 246 | ... | ... | ... | ... | 76.1 | 65.7 |
| | 2004 | 258 | ... | ... | ... | ... | 68.0 | 61.3 |
| | 2005 | 260 | ... | ... | ... | ... | 76.8 | 62.2 |
| Costa Rica<br>Costa Rica | 2004 | 8 142 428 | 66.1 | 14.1 | 18.6 | 4.4 | 46.3 | 49.5 |
| | 2005 | 9 542 858 | 66.3 | 13.8 | 19.0 | 6.2 | 48.7 | 54.0 |
| | 2006 | 11 322 819 | 65.8 | 13.6 | 20.1 | 7.5 | 49.7 | 56.7 |
| Côte d'Ivoire[1]<br>Côte d'Ivoire[1] | 1998 | 7 457 508 | 65.1[2] | 13.7 | 14.3 | 0.6 | 41.3 | 34.9 |
| | 1999 | 7 734 000 | 63.2[2] | 14.6 | 14.5 | -1.3 | 39.7 | 30.8 |
| | 2000 | 7 605 000 | 67.2[2] | 15.5 | 12.3 | -1.0 | 39.8 | 33.8 |
| Croatia<br>Croatie | 2003 | 198 422 | 58.0 | 21.8 | 28.6 | 2.5 | 47.1 | 57.9 |
| | 2004 | 212 826 | 57.4 | 21.0 | 28.6 | 2.3 | 47.4 | 56.7 |
| | 2005 | 229 032 | 57.0 | 20.4 | 28.6 | 2.7 | 47.1 | 55.8 |
| Cuba<br>Cuba | 2003 | 38 625 | 54.3 | 38.4 | 7.6 | 0.3 | 12.0 | 12.7 |
| | 2004 | 41 065 | 51.2 | 40.0 | 7.9 | 0.3 | 14.9 | 14.2 |
| | 2005 | 46 084 | 49.0 | 38.8 | 8.3 | 1.7 | 19.2 | 16.9 |
| Cyprus<br>Chypre | 2004 | 7 390 | 64.4[2] | 17.9 | 18.8 | 1.5 | 47.9 | 50.3 |
| | 2005 | 7 862 | 65.1[2] | 18.1 | 18.9 | 0.5 | 48.4 | 51.0 |
| | 2006 | 8 362 | ... | 17.9 | 19.6 | 1.4 | ... | ... |
| Czech Republic<br>République tchèque | 2003 | 2 577 110 | 51.7[2] | 23.4 | 26.7 | 0.5[5] | 61.8 | 64.1 |
| | 2004 | 2 781 060 | 50.7[2] | 22.4 | 26.2 | 1.2[5] | 71.0 | 71.6 |
| | 2005 | 2 970 261 | 49.6[2] | 22.3 | 24.9 | 1.2[5] | 71.7 | 69.8 |
| Dem. Rep. of the Congo[1]<br>Rép. dém. du Congo[1] | 1987 | 326 946 | 77.1 | 22.4 | 20.3 | 5.3 | 63.2 | 88.2 |
| | 1988 | 622 822 | ... | 37.2 | 19.0 | 3.7 | 81.0 | ... |
| | 1989 | 2 146 811 | ... | 14.4 | 13.4 | 3.2 | 46.5 | ... |
| Denmark<br>Danemark | 2004 | 1 459 399 | 48.5[2] | 26.6 | 19.4 | 0.5[5] | 45.7 | 40.8 |
| | 2005 | 1 551 967 | 48.6[2] | 25.9 | 20.4 | 0.4[5] | 48.8 | 44.1 |
| | 2006 | 1 637 603 | 48.6[2] | 25.5 | 22.1 | 0.8[5] | 51.9 | 49.0 |

| Country or area<br>Pays ou zone | Year<br>Année | GDP at<br>current prices<br>(mil. nat.cur.)<br>PIB aux prix<br>courants<br>(millions<br>monnaie nat.) | % of Gross domestic product – en % du Produit intérieur brut | | | | | |
|---|---|---|---|---|---|---|---|---|
| | | | Household final<br>consumption<br>expenditure<br>Consom. finale<br>des ménages | Govt. final<br>consumption<br>expenditure<br>Consom. finale<br>des admin.<br>publiques | Gross fixed<br>capital<br>formation<br>Formation<br>brute de<br>capital fixe | Changes in<br>inventories<br>Variation<br>des stocks | Exports<br>of goods<br>and services<br>Exportations<br>de biens<br>et services | Imports<br>of goods<br>and services<br>Importations<br>de biens<br>et services |
| Djibouti[1]<br>Djibouti[1] | 1996 | 88 233 | 64.6 | 33.6 | 19.3 | -0.9 | 40.3 | 56.8 |
| | 1997 | 87 289 | 59.3 | 34.7 | 21.4 | 0.2 | 42.2 | 57.8 |
| | 1998 | 88 461 | 67.3 | 29.0 | 23.2 | 0.2 | 43.4 | 63.0 |
| Dominica[1]<br>Dominique[1] | 2003 | 710 | 67.4 | 19.0 | 25.0 | 0.0 | 45.0 | 56.5 |
| | 2004 | 770 | 70.0 | 18.1 | 27.3 | 0.0 | 45.6 | 61.0 |
| | 2005 | 811 | 77.0 | 18.1 | 28.5 | 0.0 | 42.2 | 65.8 |
| Dominican Republic<br>Rép. dominicaine | 1994 | 179 130 | 76.8 | 4.6 | 17.9 | 3.4 | 37.4 | 40.2 |
| | 1995 | 209 646 | 78.6 | 4.3 | 16.1 | 3.3 | 34.5 | 36.7 |
| | 1996 | 232 993 | 81.4 | 4.7 | 17.3 | 3.6 | 18.1 | 25.1 |
| Ecuador<br>Equateur | 2004 | 32 636 | 67.3 | 11.4 | 21.6 | 1.8 | 27.5 | 29.6 |
| | 2005 | 36 489 | 66.0 | 11.3 | 21.9 | 2.3 | 30.9 | 32.4 |
| | 2006 | 40 892[3] | 64.1 | 10.8 | 21.8 | 2.1 | 34.0 | 32.8 |
| Egypt+<br>Egypte+ | 2002 | 405 256 | 74.2[2] | 12.2 | 16.4 | 0.7 | 19.5 | 23.0 |
| | 2003 | 451 154 | 71.3[2] | 11.6 | 17.2 | 1.0 | 21.8 | 22.8 |
| | 2004 | 510 750 | 72.1[2] | 11.1 | 15.5 | 0.7 | 28.8 | 28.3 |
| El Salvador[1]<br>El Salvador[1] | 2004 | 15 822 | 91.6 | 9.7 | 15.6 | 0.4 | 27.9 | 45.2 |
| | 2005 | 16 974 | 93.1 | 9.6 | 15.4 | 0.0 | 26.9 | 45.1 |
| | 2006 | 18 353 | 94.0 | 10.1 | 15.7 | 0.0 | 26.5 | 46.2 |
| Equatorial Guinea[1]<br>Guinée équatoriale[1] | 1989 | 42 256 | 54.3 | 22.2 | 19.6 | 0.0 | 40.4 | 36.6 |
| | 1990 | 44 349 | 53.2 | 15.3 | 34.6 | -3.1 | 59.7 | 59.7 |
| | 1991 | 46 429 | 75.9 | 14.4 | 18.4 | -2.3 | 28.4 | 34.7 |
| Estonia<br>Estonie | 2003 | 132 904 | 55.7[2] | 18.7 | 29.3 | 3.7 | 71.0 | 78.8 |
| | 2004 | 146 694 | 55.0[2] | 18.5 | 31.5 | 4.7 | 75.8 | 84.0 |
| | 2005 | 173 062 | 51.8[2] | 17.4 | 31.1 | 4.2 | 80.0 | 86.1 |
| Ethiopia+<br>Ethiopie+ | 2004 | 81 755 | 78.0 | 14.7 | 21.4[4] | ... | 14.2 | 31.0 |
| | 2005 | 98 398 | 79.8 | 13.8 | 20.5[4] | ... | 15.8 | 34.3 |
| | 2006 | 115 589 | 80.0 | 12.4 | 19.8[4] | ... | 15.1 | 32.6 |
| Fiji<br>Fidji | 2003 | 4 378 | 51.2 | 16.7 | 21.5 | 0.6 | 60.0 | 68.4 |
| | 2004 | 4 728 | 49.0 | 15.6 | 18.5 | 0.7 | 53.8 | 70.4 |
| | 2005 | 5 069 | 47.3 | 15.2 | 18.3 | 0.7 | 55.0 | 72.6 |
| Finland<br>Finlande | 2004 | 152 345 | 51.3[2] | 21.9 | 18.2 | 0.6[5] | 39.9 | 31.9 |
| | 2005 | 157 162 | 51.7[2] | 22.1 | 18.9 | 1.6[5] | 41.8 | 36.2 |
| | 2006 | 167 911 | 50.8[2] | 21.4 | 19.2 | 1.5[5] | 44.4 | 37.9 |
| France<br>France | 2004 | 1 660 189 | 56.6[2] | 23.7 | 19.3 | 0.3[5] | 25.7 | 25.6 |
| | 2005 | 1 717 921 | 56.9[2] | 23.8 | 19.8 | 0.4[5] | 26.0 | 26.9 |
| | 2006 | 1 791 953 | 56.7[2] | 23.6 | 20.4 | 0.6[5] | 26.9 | 28.3 |
| French Guiana[1]<br>Guyane française[1] | 1990 | 6 526 | 64.4 | 35.0 | 47.8 | -0.2 | 67.3 | 114.3 |
| | 1991 | 7 404 | 60.1 | 34.4 | 40.5 | 1.5 | 81.1 | 117.6 |
| | 1992 | 7 976 | 58.9 | 34.2 | 30.8 | 1.5 | 65.4 | 90.8 |
| French Polynesia[1]<br>Polynésie française[1] | 2002 | 324 431 | 102.5 | 12.9 | 26.7[4] | 26.7[5] | 19.6 | 61.6 |
| | 2003 | 338 749 | 106.5 | 11.9 | 25.0[4] | 25.0[5] | 17.3 | 60.6 |
| | 2004 | 345 706 | 98.7 | 11.2 | 25.6[4] | 25.6[5] | 17.5 | 53.0 |
| Gabon[1]<br>Gabon[1] | 1999 | 2 855 800 | 39.2 | 16.9 | 25.1 | -0.4 | ... | ... |
| | 2000 | 3 631 400 | 32.7 | 12.8 | 21.9 | 0.3 | ... | ... |
| | 2001 | 3 412 700 | 35.3 | 14.1 | 29.1 | -2.3 | ... | ... |
| Gambia+[1]<br>Gambie+[1] | 1991 | 2 920 | 83.7 | 13.0 | 18.2[11] | ... | 45.3[12] | 60.1[13] |
| | 1992 | 3 078 | 81.2 | 13.2 | 22.4[11] | ... | 45.2[12] | 61.9[13] |
| | 1993 | 3 243 | 78.1 | 15.1 | 27.1[11] | ... | 36.6[12] | 56.9[13] |
| Georgia<br>Géorgie | 2004 | 9 824 | 73.2[2] | 14.0 | 27.5 | 0.8[5] | 31.6 | 48.2 |
| | 2005 | 11 621 | 68.0[2] | 12.5 | 28.1 | 0.5[5] | 33.7 | 51.6 |
| | 2006 | 13 784 | 74.3[2] | 16.4 | 26.9 | 1.1[5] | 32.9 | 56.9 |
| Germany<br>Allemagne | 2004 | 2 207 200 | 59.0[2] | 18.8 | 17.4 | -0.3[5] | 38.2 | 33.2 |
| | 2005 | 2 241 000 | 58.9[2] | 18.7 | 17.3 | -0.1[5] | 40.7 | 35.5 |
| | 2006 | 2 309 100 | 58.4[2] | 18.4 | 17.8 | -0.1[5] | 45.1 | 39.6 |

| Country or area<br>Pays ou zone | Year<br>Année | GDP at current prices (mil. nat.cur.)<br>PIB aux prix courants (millions monnaie nat.) | % of Gross domestic product – en % du Produit intérieur brut | | | | | |
|---|---|---|---|---|---|---|---|---|
| | | | Household final consumption expenditure<br>Consom. finale des ménages | Govt. final consumption expenditure<br>Consom. finale des admin. publiques | Gross fixed capital formation<br>Formation brute de capital fixe | Changes in inventories<br>Variation des stocks | Exports of goods and services<br>Exportations de biens et services | Imports of goods and services<br>Importations de biens et services |
| Ghana[1]<br>Ghana[1] | 1994 | 5 205 200 | 73.7 | 13.7 | 22.6 | 1.4[14] | 22.5 | 33.9 |
| | 1995 | 7 752 600 | 76.2 | 12.1 | 21.1 | -1.1[14] | 24.5 | 32.8 |
| | 1996 | 11 339 200 | 76.1 | 12.0 | 20.6 | 0.9[14] | 24.9 | 34.5 |
| Greece<br>Grèce | 2004 | 212 734 | 68.5[2] | 14.9 | 24.4 | 1.0 | 18.3 | 27.1 |
| | 2005 | 228 156 | 68.7[2] | 14.2 | 23.4 | 0.8 | 18.4 | 25.6 |
| | 2006 | 245 865 | 68.0[2] | 14.2 | 25.7 | 0.5 | 18.6 | 27.0 |
| Greenland[1]<br>Groenland[1] | 2003 | 9 397 | ... | 55.7 | ... | ... | 24.3[6] | 32.3[7] |
| | 2004 | 9 855 | ... | 54.0 | ... | ... | 23.2[6] | 33.2[7] |
| | 2005 | 10 210 | ... | 51.1 | ... | ... | 23.9[6] | 35.1[7] |
| Grenada[1]<br>Grenade[1] | 1990 | 541 | 64.9 | 20.5 | 38.9 | 3.1 | 44.4 | 71.8 |
| | 1991 | 567 | 69.2 | 18.8 | 40.0 | 3.7 | 45.4 | 77.1 |
| | 1992 | 578 | 66.5 | 19.9 | 32.4 | 2.1 | 38.6 | 59.4 |
| Guadeloupe[1]<br>Guadeloupe[1] | 1990 | 15 201 | 92.8 | 30.8 | 33.9 | 1.1 | 4.9 | 63.5 |
| | 1991 | 16 415 | 87.3 | 31.0 | 33.0 | 1.0 | 6.1 | 58.4 |
| | 1992 | 17 972 | 84.1 | 29.3 | 27.8 | 1.3 | 4.5 | 47.0 |
| Guatemala[1]<br>Guatemala[1] | 2003 | 197 599 | 86.6 | 7.3 | 14.3 | 4.5 | 16.7 | 29.4 |
| | 2004 | 216 749 | 88.1 | 6.4 | 14.5 | 5.3 | 16.8 | 31.1 |
| | 2005 | 243 699 | 89.2 | 5.9 | 15.0 | 4.2 | 15.6 | 29.9 |
| Guinea-Bissau[1]<br>Guinée-Bissau[1] | 1990 | 510 094 | 100.9 | 11.4 | 13.8 | 0.9 | 12.0 | 39.0 |
| | 1991 | 854 985 | 100.6 | 12.6 | 10.4 | 0.9 | 13.4 | 38.0 |
| | 1992 | 1 530 010 | 111.1 | 10.7 | 26.5[4] | ... | 8.2 | 56.5 |
| Guyana[1]<br>Guyana[1] | 2004 | 156 358 | 54.4 | 24.1 | 32.0[4] | ... | 95.8 | 109.2 |
| | 2005 | 165 028 | 73.3 | 26.9 | 32.3[4] | ... | 84.7 | 119.9 |
| | 2006 | 180 282 | 64.7 | 24.6 | 45.9[4] | ... | -28.5[15] | ... |
| Haiti+[1]<br>Haïti+[1] | 1997 | 51 578 | ... | ... | 12.5 | ... | 11.5 | 27.1 |
| | 1998 | 59 055 | ... | ... | 12.9 | ... | 13.2 | 28.6 |
| | 1999 | 66 425 | ... | ... | 13.1 | ... | 13.3 | 28.2 |
| Honduras[1]<br>Honduras[1] | 2004 | 137 242 | 75.7 | 13.2 | 26.5 | 3.9 | 41.2 | 60.4 |
| | 2005 | 157 668 | 76.9 | 13.7 | 23.2 | 6.9 | 41.7 | 62.4 |
| | 2006 | 175 740 | 78.8 | 14.0 | 24.9 | 8.1 | 40.8 | 66.5 |
| Hungary<br>Hongrie | 2004 | 20 717 110 | 54.7[2] | 22.4 | 22.4 | 3.6 | 63.6 | 66.7 |
| | 2005 | 22 055 093 | 55.3[2] | 22.5 | 22.7 | 1.0 | 66.4 | 67.8 |
| | 2006 | 23 752 721 | 53.8[2] | 22.3 | 21.8 | 1.2 | 77.3 | 76.5 |
| Iceland<br>Islande | 2004 | 926 459 | 57.3[2] | 24.9 | 23.6 | -0.1 | 34.2 | 39.9 |
| | 2005 | 1 021 510 | 59.7[2] | 24.6 | 28.2 | -0.1 | 31.8 | 44.2 |
| | 2006 | 1 141 747 | 60.1[2] | 24.6 | 32.0 | 1.2 | 32.6 | 50.5 |
| India+[1]<br>Inde+[1] | 2003 | 27 654 905 | 61.8 | 11.2 | 24.8 | 1.7[5] | 14.7 | 16.0 |
| | 2004 | 31 265 958 | 59.7 | 11.0 | 26.3 | 3.4[5] | 18.2 | 20.0 |
| | 2005 | 35 671 769 | 57.9 | 11.3 | 28.1 | 4.1[5] | 20.3 | 23.3 |
| Indonesia<br>Indonésie | 2003 | 2 013 674 600 | 68.1 | 8.1 | 19.5 | 6.1 | 30.5 | 23.1 |
| | 2004 | 2 273 141 500 | 67.4 | 8.4 | 21.7 | 1.5 | 32.1 | 27.4 |
| | 2005 | 2 729 708 200 | 65.4 | 8.2 | 22.0 | 0.3 | 33.5 | 29.2 |
| Iran (Islamic Rep. of)+<br>Iran (Rép. Islamique d')+ | 2003 | 1 119 661 000 | 45.2[2] | 12.6 | 28.5 | 6.2 | 27.0 | 25.5 |
| | 2004 | 1 401 899 100 | 45.7[2] | 12.0 | 28.7 | 6.0 | 29.1 | 26.0 |
| | 2005 | 1 721 260 900 | 44.5[2] | 12.7 | 27.1 | 2.5 | 33.2 | 24.7 |
| Iraq[1]<br>Iraq[1] | 2003 | 20 562 256 | 66.2 | 17.7 | 15.3[4] | ... | 111.4 | 110.6 |
| | 2004 | 37 049 252 | 48.2 | 36.7 | 7.7 | 17.5 | 80.0 | 90.2 |
| | 2005 | 49 990 680 | 43.5 | 29.4 | 20.4 | 5.8 | 79.3 | 78.3 |
| Ireland<br>Irlande | 2003 | 138 941 | 45.3[2] | 15.1 | 23.0 | 0.9[5] | 83.8 | 67.7 |
| | 2004 | 147 569 | 44.9[2] | 15.7 | 24.6 | 0.2[5] | 84.1 | 69.2 |
| | 2005 | 161 163 | 44.4[2] | 15.9 | 27.0 | 0.1[5] | 81.3 | 68.6 |
| Israel<br>Israël | 2003 | 524 187 | 55.2[2] | 28.9 | 17.1 | -0.5 | 37.7 | 38.4 |
| | 2004 | 548 936 | 55.6[2] | 27.5 | 16.9 | -0.4 | 43.1 | 42.7 |
| | 2005 | 582 291 | 55.1[2] | 26.9 | 16.8 | 0.9 | 44.6 | 44.3 |

| Country or area<br>Pays ou zone | Year<br>Année | GDP at<br>current prices<br>(mil. nat.cur.)<br>PIB aux prix<br>courants<br>(millions<br>monnaie nat.) | % of Gross domestic product – en % du Produit intérieur brut | | | | | |
|---|---|---|---|---|---|---|---|---|
| | | | Household final<br>consumption<br>expenditure<br>Consom. finale<br>des ménages | Govt. final<br>consumption<br>expenditure<br>Consom. finale<br>des admin.<br>publiques | Gross fixed<br>capital<br>formation<br>Formation<br>brute de<br>capital fixe | Changes in<br>inventories<br>Variation<br>des stocks | Exports<br>of goods<br>and services<br>Exportations<br>de biens<br>et services | Imports<br>of goods<br>and services<br>Importations<br>de biens<br>et services |
| Italy<br>Italie | 2004 | 1 390 539 | 58.6[2] | 19.9 | 20.5 | 0.3[5] | 25.4 | 24.7 |
| | 2005 | 1 423 048 | 59.0[2] | 20.4 | 20.6 | 0.1[5] | 26.1 | 26.1 |
| | 2006 | 1 475 401 | 59.3[2] | 20.3 | 20.8 | 0.4[5] | 27.8 | 28.7 |
| Jamaica[1]<br>Jamaïque[1] | 2003 | 472 918 | 72.6 | 15.4 | 29.7 | 0.2 | 40.6 | 58.5 |
| | 2004 | 540 809 | 72.4 | 14.3 | 30.6 | 0.1 | 42.8 | 60.2 |
| | 2005 | 605 030 | 72.8 | 15.2 | 31.7 | 0.0 | 41.1 | 60.9 |
| Japan<br>Japon | 2003 | 490 294 000 | 57.5[2] | 18.1 | 22.8 | 0.0 | 12.0 | 10.4 |
| | 2004 | 498 328 400 | 57.1[2] | 18.0 | 22.7 | 0.3 | 13.3 | 11.4 |
| | 2005 | 501 402 600 | 57.2[2] | 18.1 | 23.1 | 0.2 | 14.3 | 13.0 |
| Jordan[1]<br>Jordanie[1] | 2002 | 6 794 | 75.9[2] | 22.7 | 18.9 | 1.1 | 47.4 | 66.1 |
| | 2003 | 7 229 | 76.5[2] | 23.2 | 20.6 | 0.2 | 47.3 | 67.8 |
| | 2004 | 8 081 | 81.1[2] | 21.3 | 24.8 | 2.6 | 52.1 | 82.0 |
| Kazakhstan<br>Kazakhstan | 2003 | 4 611 975 | 54.5[2] | 11.3 | 23.0 | 2.7 | 48.4 | 43.0 |
| | 2004 | 5 870 134 | 53.5[2] | 11.6 | 25.1 | 1.2 | 52.5 | 43.9 |
| | 2005 | 7 590 594 | 49.9[2] | 11.2 | 28.0 | 3.0 | 53.5 | 44.7 |
| Kenya<br>Kenya | 2003 | 1 137 975 | 76.9[2] | 18.0 | 15.8 | 0.6[16] | 23.7 | 29.7 |
| | 2004 | 1 282 504 | 75.3[2] | 17.6 | 16.1 | 0.8[16] | 26.2 | 33.9 |
| | 2005 | 1 415 155 | 76.1[2] | 17.1 | 18.6 | -1.8[16] | 26.7 | 37.4 |
| Korea, Republic of<br>Corée, République de | 2004 | 779 380 500 | 51.5[2] | 13.5 | 29.5 | 0.8[5] | 44.0 | 39.7 |
| | 2005 | 810 515 900 | 52.6[2] | 14.2 | 29.3 | 0.8[5] | 42.3 | 39.9 |
| | 2006 | 847 876 400 | 53.5[2] | 14.8 | 29.0 | 0.7[5] | 43.2 | 42.1 |
| Kuwait[1]<br>Koweït[1] | 2003 | 14 253 | 42.8[2] | 23.0 | 16.0 | 0.6 | 52.1 | 34.5 |
| | 2004 | 17 466 | 37.6[2] | 19.9 | 14.9 | 2.9 | 57.1 | 32.5 |
| | 2005 | 23 588 | 31.4 | 15.4 | 16.9 | 2.8 | 63.8 | 30.4 |
| Kyrgyzstan<br>Kirghizistan | 2004 | 94 351 | 76.0[2] | 18.2 | 14.6 | -0.1[5] | 42.6 | 51.3 |
| | 2005 | 100 899 | 84.5[2] | 17.5 | 16.0 | 0.4[5] | 38.3 | 56.8 |
| | 2006 | 113 176 | 97.1[2] | 18.9 | 16.9 | 4.3[5] | 39.3 | 76.5 |
| Latvia<br>Lettonie | 2004 | 7 434 | 62.9[2] | 19.5 | 27.5 | 5.7[5] | 44.0 | 59.6 |
| | 2005 | 9 059 | 62.5[2] | 17.4 | 30.6 | 3.8[5] | 47.8 | 62.2 |
| | 2006 | 11 265 | 65.2[2] | 16.9 | 34.4 | 3.7[5] | 44.2 | 64.4 |
| Lebanon<br>Liban | 2002 | 28 209 000 | ... | ... | 19.4 | -1.3 | 16.3 | 35.6 |
| | 2003 | 29 851 000 | ... | ... | 19.6 | -0.4 | 16.7 | 37.7 |
| | 2004 | 32 357 000 | ... | ... | 20.6 | 1.2 | 19.9 | 42.1 |
| Lesotho<br>Lesotho | 2003 | 7 862 | 99.4[2] | 17.9 | 40.5 | 0.6 | 50.0 | 108.4 |
| | 2004 | 8 518 | 95.2[2] | 17.2 | 35.7 | 0.1 | 57.9 | 106.2 |
| | 2005 | 9 263 | 84.5[2] | 17.0 | 35.0 | 0.2 | 49.0 | 85.6 |
| Liberia[1]<br>Libéria[1] | 1987 | 1 090 | 65.5 | 13.2 | 11.1 | 0.6[17] | 40.2 | 32.7 |
| | 1988 | 1 158 | 63.3 | 11.8 | 10.0 | 0.3[17] | 39.0 | 27.8 |
| | 1989 | 1 194 | 55.0 | 11.9 | 8.1 | 0.3[17] | 43.7 | 23.1 |
| Libyan Arab Jamah.[1]<br>Jamah. arabe libyenne[1] | 1983 | 8 805 | 39.2 | 32.7 | 25.1 | -1.1 | 42.1 | 38.0 |
| | 1984 | 8 013 | 38.6 | 33.6 | 25.3 | 0.5 | 41.4 | 39.4 |
| | 1985 | 8 277 | 37.6 | 31.7 | 19.7 | 0.4 | 37.4 | 26.7 |
| Lithuania<br>Lituanie | 2003 | 56 804 | 64.2[2] | 18.4 | 21.2 | 2.1[5] | 51.3 | 57.1 |
| | 2004 | 62 587 | 65.2[2] | 17.9 | 22.3 | 1.6[5] | 52.1 | 59.2 |
| | 2005 | 71 200 | 65.3[2] | 16.7 | 22.4 | 2.7[5] | 58.3 | 65.3 |
| Luxembourg<br>Luxembourg | 2004 | 26 996 | 41.0[2] | 16.9 | 20.6 | 0.5[5] | 148.3 | 127.4 |
| | 2005 | 29 396 | 40.4[2] | 17.0 | 19.7 | 1.7[5] | 159.3 | 138.0 |
| | 2006 | 33 055 | 38.5[2] | 15.9 | 18.3 | -0.5[5] | 177.2 | 149.4 |
| Madagascar[1]<br>Madagascar[1] | 1990 | 4 601 600 | 86.0[18] | 8.0 | 17.0 | ... | 15.9 | 26.9 |
| | 1991 | 4 906 400 | 92.2[18] | 8.6 | 8.2 | ... | 17.3 | 26.2 |
| | 1992 | 5 584 500 | 90.0[18] | 8.2 | 11.6 | ... | 15.6 | 25.3 |
| Malawi<br>Malawi | 2002 | 204 382 | 88.6[2] | 8.6 | 13.5 | 2.6 | 20.8 | 34.2 |
| | 2003 | 236 240 | 88.1[2] | 8.7 | 14.1 | 3.0 | 26.7 | 40.6 |
| | 2004 | 285 870 | 89.6[2] | 10.4 | 16.2 | 2.0 | 25.0 | 43.2 |

| Country or area<br>Pays ou zone | Year<br>Année | GDP at current prices (mil. nat.cur.)<br>PIB aux prix courants (millions monnaie nat.) | % of Gross domestic product – en % du Produit intérieur brut | | | | | |
|---|---|---|---|---|---|---|---|---|
| | | | Household final consumption expenditure<br>Consom. finale des ménages | Govt. final consumption expenditure<br>Consom. finale des admin. publiques | Gross fixed capital formation<br>Formation brute de capital fixe | Changes in inventories<br>Variation des stocks | Exports of goods and services<br>Exportations de biens et services | Imports of goods and services<br>Importations de biens et services |
| Malaysia<br>Malaisie | 2004 | 474 048 | 44.0[2] | 12.6 | 21.0 | 2.1 | 115.4 | 95.0 |
| | 2005 | 519 451 | 44.9[2] | 12.4 | 20.6 | -0.4 | 117.6 | 95.2 |
| | 2006 | 572 555 | 45.0[2] | 12.0 | 20.9 | -0.2 | 117.0 | 94.7 |
| Maldives<br>Maldives | 2004 | 9 939 | 32.8 | 23.7 | 41.8 | 0.0 | 86.4 | 84.8 |
| | 2005 | 9 607 | 33.8 | 38.1 | 61.3 | 0.0 | 67.3 | 100.5 |
| | 2006 | 11 608 | 29.8 | 37.9 | 55.6 | 0.0 | 82.6 | 105.9 |
| Mali[1]<br>Mali[1] | 2004 | 2 632 057 | 68.3 | 18.0 | 17.0 | 5.0 | 24.4 | 32.6 |
| | 2005 | 2 893 858 | 68.9 | 16.9 | 15.4 | 6.6 | 25.0 | 32.9 |
| | 2006 | 3 201 472 | 65.3 | 17.3 | 16.5 | 3.9 | 29.9 | 32.9 |
| Malta<br>Malte | 2003 | 1 859 | 64.1[2] | 21.4 | 19.7 | -1.8[5,16] | 78.6 | 82.1 |
| | 2004 | 1 861 | 66.3[2] | 22.4 | 20.0 | -2.6[5,16] | 78.9 | 85.0 |
| | 2005 | 1 941 | 67.0[2] | 21.9 | 21.0 | 0.2[5,16] | 72.5 | 82.6 |
| Martinique[1]<br>Martinique[1] | 1990 | 19 320 | 83.6 | 29.7 | 26.7 | 1.9 | 8.4 | 50.3 |
| | 1991 | 20 787 | 84.0 | 28.8 | 25.6 | 1.4 | 7.4 | 47.1 |
| | 1992 | 22 093 | 84.3 | 28.7 | 23.6 | -0.9 | 6.8 | 42.5 |
| Mauritania[1]<br>Mauritanie[1] | 1987 | 67 216 | 82.6 | 13.6 | 20.8 | 1.7 | 48.3 | 67.0 |
| | 1988 | 72 635 | 79.6 | 14.2 | 17.0 | 1.4 | 49.1 | 61.3 |
| | 1989 | 83 520 | ... | ... | ... | ... | 47.9 | 54.9 |
| Mauritius<br>Maurice | 2004 | 175 592 | 63.7 | 14.3 | 21.6 | 2.8 | 54.0 | 56.4 |
| | 2005 | 185 487 | 69.5 | 14.8 | 21.3 | 0.4 | 59.9 | 65.9 |
| | 2006 | 203 337 | 72.4 | 14.3 | 23.8 | -0.4 | 61.8 | 71.9 |
| Mexico<br>Mexique | 2003 | 6 891 992 | 68.7[2] | 12.4 | 18.9 | 1.6 | 27.8 | 29.5 |
| | 2004 | 7 709 096 | 68.1[2] | 11.9 | 19.6 | 2.4 | 29.6 | 31.6 |
| | 2005 | 8 369 246 | 68.3[2] | 11.6 | 19.3 | 2.4 | 29.9 | 31.5 |
| Moldova<br>Moldova | 2004 | 32 032 | 89.0[2] | 14.9 | 21.2 | 5.2 | 51.2 | 81.5 |
| | 2005 | 37 652 | 93.4[2] | 16.4 | 24.6 | 6.2 | 51.2 | 91.9 |
| | 2006 | 44 069 | 95.1[2] | 18.3 | 27.9 | 6.3 | 46.7 | 94.4 |
| Mongolia<br>Mongolie | 2003 | 1 473 677 | 69.6 | ... | 41.8 | ... | ... | 84.3 |
| | 2004 | 1 926 322 | 61.6 | ... | 39.1 | ... | 74.5 | 86.5 |
| | 2005 | 2 489 218 | 56.6[2] | 13.8 | 39.7 | 2.5[5] | 71.8 | 76.2 |
| Montserrat[1]<br>Montserrat[1] | 1984 | 94 | 96.4 | 20.6 | 23.7 | 2.7 | 13.6 | 56.9 |
| | 1985 | 100 | 96.3 | 20.3 | 24.7 | 1.5 | 11.7 | 54.4 |
| | 1986 | 114 | 89.5 | 18.7 | 33.0 | 2.8 | 10.1 | 53.9 |
| Morocco<br>Maroc | 2003 | 476 987 | 57.5 | 18.0 | 25.2 | 2.2 | 28.3 | 31.3 |
| | 2004 | 500 081 | 57.6 | 18.8 | 26.7 | 2.1 | 29.2 | 34.4 |
| | 2005 | 522 649 | 56.6 | 19.2 | 28.5 | 1.7 | 31.6 | 37.8 |
| Mozambique<br>Mozambique | 2003 | 113 902 523 | 67.9[2] | 12.5 | 26.3 | 1.2 | 25.4 | 33.2 |
| | 2004 | 133 510 417 | 65.7[2] | 12.5 | 21.2 | 1.4 | 33.8 | 34.7 |
| | 2005 | 157 345 427 | 69.1[2] | 12.9 | 28.1 | 1.8 | 30.9 | 42.9 |
| Myanmar+[1]<br>Myanmar+[1] | 1996 | 791 980 | ... | ... | 14.9 | -2.7 | 0.7 | 1.5 |
| | 1997 | 1 109 554 | ... | ... | 13.5 | -0.9 | 0.6 | 1.3 |
| | 1998 | 1 559 996 | ... | ... | 11.8 | -0.7 | 0.5 | 1.0 |
| Namibia<br>Namibie | 2003 | 33 842 | 55.5[2] | 26.5 | 29.2 | 0.7 | 51.4 | 55.0 |
| | 2004 | 36 181 | 58.0[2] | 25.3 | 25.9 | 0.5 | 46.3 | 52.5 |
| | 2005 | 38 560 | 58.4[2] | 24.3 | 27.1 | 1.4 | 47.9 | 53.1 |
| Nepal+<br>Népal+ | 2004 | 589 412 | 82.6 | 8.9 | 19.9 | 6.5 | 14.6 | 29.5 |
| | 2005 | 646 471 | 86.4 | 8.8 | 20.9 | 5.0 | 13.6 | 31.7 |
| | 2006 | 719 477 | 84.9 | 8.7 | 20.3 | 5.0 | 12.5 | 28.5 |
| Netherlands<br>Pays-Bas | 2004 | 489 854 | 49.3[2] | 24.3 | 19.1 | 0.2[5] | 66.5 | 59.3 |
| | 2005 | 505 646 | 48.9[2] | 24.1 | 19.3 | 0.0[5] | 69.9 | 62.2 |
| | 2006 | 527 916 | 47.1[2] | 25.3 | 20.1 | ... | 74.2 | 66.5 |
| Netherlands Antilles<br>Antilles néerlandaises | 2002 | 5 254 | 54.2[2] | 20.3 | 29.5 | 2.4 | 75.1 | 81.4 |
| | 2003 | 5 425 | 54.3[2] | 21.2 | 28.2 | 0.7 | 77.6 | 81.9 |
| | 2004 | 5 576 | 55.0[2] | 20.3 | 28.1 | 2.4 | 82.7 | 88.5 |

| Country or area<br>Pays ou zone | Year<br>Année | GDP at current prices (mil. nat.cur.)<br>PIB aux prix courants (millions monnaie nat.) | % of Gross domestic product – en % du Produit intérieur brut | | | | | |
|---|---|---|---|---|---|---|---|---|
| | | | Household final consumption expenditure<br>Consom. finale des ménages | Govt. final consumption expenditure<br>Consom. finale des admin. publiques | Gross fixed capital formation<br>Formation brute de capital fixe | Changes in inventories<br>Variation des stocks | Exports of goods and services<br>Exportations de biens et services | Imports of goods and services<br>Importations de biens et services |
| New Caledonia<br>Nouvelle-Calédonie | 2001 | 439 383 | 69.6 | 28.3 | 23.1 | -0.2 | 18.7 | 39.5 |
| | 2002 | 471 996 | 67.1 | 28.4 | 24.7 | -0.2 | 18.1 | 38.1 |
| | 2003 | 518 545 | 64.0 | 27.2 | 28.9 | 0.6 | 20.6 | 41.3 |
| New Zealand+<br>Nouvelle-Zélande+ | 2003 | 138 941 | 59.0[2] | 17.4 | 22.8 | 0.9[5] | 29.0 | 29.0 |
| | 2004 | 148 484 | 59.0[2] | 17.7 | 23.5 | 1.1[5] | 28.9 | 30.0 |
| | 2005 | 155 885 | 59.8[2] | 18.3 | 23.9 | 0.8[5] | 27.8 | 30.5 |
| Nicaragua+<br>Nicaragua+ | 2004 | 71 661 | 81.7[2] | 17.8 | 26.5 | 0.6 | 27.2 | 53.8 |
| | 2005 | 82 162 | 82.4[2] | 17.8 | 27.9 | 1.5 | 28.0 | 57.6 |
| | 2006 | 94 361 | 80.2[2] | 19.6 | 28.0 | 1.1 | 30.1 | 59.1 |
| Niger[1]<br>Niger[1] | 2003 | 1 471 712 | 77.4 | 16.8 | 15.2 | 1.1 | 16.4 | 26.9 |
| | 2004 | 1 468 393 | 78.9 | 17.9 | 17.0 | -2.3 | 19.1 | 30.7 |
| | 2005 | 1 701 950 | 77.7 | 15.0 | 16.8 | 2.0 | 20.9 | 32.5 |
| Nigeria[1]<br>Nigéria[1] | 1999 | 3 320 311 | 59.3 | 7.6 | 5.3 | 0.0 | 49.7 | 21.9 |
| | 2000 | 4 980 943 | 49.1 | 5.2 | 5.4 | 0.0 | 58.9 | 18.6 |
| | 2001 | 5 639 863 | 60.3 | 4.9 | 7.0 | 0.0 | 55.4 | 27.5 |
| Norway<br>Norvège | 2004 | 1 743 041 | 45.1[2] | 21.4 | 18.0 | ... | 42.0 | 28.5 |
| | 2005 | 1 942 887 | 42.2[2] | 20.1 | 18.5 | ... | 44.5 | 28.1 |
| | 2006 | 2 147 986 | 40.7[2] | 19.3 | 18.8 | ... | 46.4 | 28.6 |
| Occupied Palestinian Terr.<br>Terr. palestinien occupé | 2001 | 3 816 | 94.6[2] | 32.8 | 24.9 | 0.6 | 12.1 | 64.9 |
| | 2002 | 3 484 | 96.7[2] | 34.7 | 17.9 | 0.6 | 11.0 | 60.8 |
| | 2003 | 3 921 | 102.1[2] | 27.2 | 23.5 | 0.2 | 9.6 | 62.6 |
| Oman<br>Oman | 2003 | 8 376 | 43.7 | 22.1 | 15.6[4] | ... | 56.5 | 37.9 |
| | 2004 | 9 516 | 44.0 | 21.4 | 20.6[4] | ... | 57.0 | 42.9 |
| | 2005 | 11 856[3] | 35.1 | 19.4 | 18.1[4] | ... | 63.3 | 35.9 |
| Pakistan+<br>Pakistan+ | 2004 | 5 640 580 | 74.2 | 8.2 | 15.0 | 1.6 | 15.7 | 14.6 |
| | 2005 | 6 581 103 | 78.0 | 7.7 | 16.5 | 1.6 | 15.5 | 19.3 |
| | 2006 | 7 713 064 | 81.4 | 7.6 | 18.4 | 1.6 | 15.5 | 24.4 |
| Panama<br>Panama | 2003 | 12 933 | 62.0 | 14.0 | 17.1 | 1.9 | 63.6 | 58.5 |
| | 2004 | 14 179 | 64.0 | 13.6 | 16.6 | 2.1 | 67.6 | 63.9 |
| | 2005 | 15 483 | 62.4 | 13.1 | 16.8 | 1.5 | 74.8 | 68.7 |
| Papua New Guinea<br>Papouasie-Nvl-Guinée | 2000 | 10 750 | 60.1 | 16.2 | 20.0 | 1.3 | 43.9 | 41.5 |
| | 2001 | 11 758 | 71.9 | 15.5 | 20.2 | 1.6 | 42.3 | 51.5 |
| | 2002 | 13 375 | 73.9 | 14.4 | 18.3 | 1.5 | 38.8 | 46.9 |
| Paraguay<br>Paraguay | 2003 | 35 665 000 | 73.4 | 10.5 | 19.0 | 1.0 | 47.5 | 51.3 |
| | 2004 | 41 521 000 | 73.4 | 9.9 | 18.7 | 2.1 | 46.0 | 50.0 |
| | 2005 | 46 169 000 | 75.1 | 10.2 | 19.3 | 0.3 | 49.9 | 54.8 |
| Peru<br>Pérou | 2003 | 213 938 | 70.7 | 10.2 | 17.8 | 0.9 | 17.7 | 17.3 |
| | 2004 | 237 769 | 68.4 | 10.0 | 17.9 | 0.9 | 20.7 | 17.9 |
| | 2005 | 261 632 | 66.1 | 10.1 | 18.8 | -0.3 | 24.5 | 19.1 |
| Philippines[1]<br>Philippines[1] | 2003 | 4 316 402 | 69.2 | 11.1 | 16.8 | 0.0 | 49.6 | 55.6 |
| | 2004 | 4 858 835 | 68.8 | 10.1 | 16.1 | 0.7 | 50.8 | 54.7 |
| | 2005 | 5 418 839 | 69.6 | 9.7 | 14.9 | 0.2 | 47.3 | 52.0 |
| Poland<br>Pologne | 2004 | 923 248 | 64.2[2] | 17.7 | 18.1 | 2.0[5] | 37.5 | 39.5 |
| | 2005 | 980 666 | 62.8[2] | 18.3 | 18.2 | 1.0[5] | 37.2 | 37.5 |
| | 2006 | 1 050 919 | 62.5[2] | 17.9 | 20.0 | 0.2[5] | 40.6 | 41.3 |
| Portugal<br>Portugal | 2004 | 144 223 | 64.1[2] | 20.6 | 22.7 | 0.3[5] | 28.4 | 36.2 |
| | 2005 | 148 928 | 65.0[2] | 21.2 | 21.9 | 0.6[5] | 28.5 | 37.1 |
| | 2006 | 155 216 | 65.2[2] | 20.6 | 21.2 | 0.9[5] | 31.1 | 38.9 |
| Puerto Rico+[1]<br>Porto Rico+[1] | 2003 | 79 209 | 54.8[2] | 11.5 | 15.1 | 0.4 | 81.5 | 63.3 |
| | 2004 | 82 650 | 56.0[2] | 12.2 | 14.4 | 0.4 | 79.3 | 62.3 |
| | 2005 | 86 464 | 57.3[2] | 12.0 | 14.1 | 0.4 | 79.4 | 63.3 |
| Qatar<br>Qatar | 2000 | 64 646 | 15.2 | 19.7 | 19.5 | 0.7 | 67.3 | 22.3 |
| | 2001 | 64 579 | 15.5 | 19.8 | 22.5 | 0.8 | 65.1 | 23.7 |
| | 2002 | 65 088 | 15.8 | 20.0 | 22.2 | 0.7 | 65.6 | 24.2 |

**Gross domestic product by type of expenditure at current prices** — Percentage distribution (*continued*)

**Dépenses imputées au produit intérieur brut aux prix courants** — Répartition en pourcentage (*suite*)

| Country or area<br>Pays ou zone | Year<br>Année | GDP at<br>current prices<br>(mil. nat.cur.)<br>PIB aux prix<br>courants<br>(millions<br>monnaie nat.) | % of Gross domestic product – en % du Produit intérieur brut | | | | | |
|---|---|---|---|---|---|---|---|---|
| | | | Household final<br>consumption<br>expenditure<br>Consom. finale<br>des ménages | Govt. final<br>consumption<br>expenditure<br>Consom. finale<br>des admin.<br>publiques | Gross fixed<br>capital<br>formation<br>Formation<br>brute de<br>capital fixe | Changes in<br>inventories<br>Variation<br>des stocks | Exports<br>of goods<br>and services<br>Exportations<br>de biens<br>et services | Imports<br>of goods<br>and services<br>Importations<br>de biens<br>et services |
| Réunion[1]<br>Réunion[1] | 1992 | 33 787 | 76.1 | 28.4 | 28.6 | 2.1 | 3.4 | 38.6 |
| | 1993 | 33 711 | 76.4 | 28.6 | 25.7 | -0.4 | 3.1 | 36.2 |
| | 1994 | 35 266 | 78.0 | 28.9 | 28.1 | 0.1 | 2.9 | 38.0 |
| Romania<br>Roumanie | 2004 | 2 464 687 900 | 69.1[2] | 16.1 | 21.8 | 1.9[5] | 35.9 | 45.0 |
| | #2005 | 288 048 | 69.4[2] | 18.2 | 23.1 | -0.8[5] | 32.9 | 43.3 |
| | 2006[19] | 342 418 | 69.9[2] | 18.0 | 24.6 | -0.4[5] | 32.4 | 44.5 |
| Russian Federation<br>Fédération de Russie | 2004 | 17 048 122 | 50.2[2] | 16.7 | 18.1 | 2.7[5] | 34.4 | 22.1 |
| | 2005 | 21 620 111 | 49.8[2] | 16.6 | 17.5 | 2.6[5] | 35.1 | 21.6 |
| | 2006 | 26 781 103 | 48.7[2] | 17.5 | 17.6 | 2.6[5] | 33.9 | 21.2 |
| Rwanda[1]<br>Rwanda[1] | 2000 | 681 455 | 90.2 | 8.9 | 18.0 | ... | 6.3 | 23.4 |
| | 2001 | 732 276 | 90.4 | 9.5 | 17.4 | ... | 8.7 | 26.1 |
| | 2002 | 784 000 | 91.5 | 9.5 | 17.9 | ... | 7.1 | 24.6 |
| Saint Kitts and Nevis[1]<br>Saint-Kitts-et-Nevis[1] | 2004 | 1 068 | 53.0 | 20.4 | 44.2 | ... | 48.7 | 66.2 |
| | 2005 | 1 157 | 51.6 | 18.5 | 45.5 | ... | 49.2 | 64.9 |
| | 2006 | 1 314 | 57.1 | 17.7 | 46.4 | ... | 45.4 | 66.6 |
| Saint Lucia[1]<br>Sainte-Lucie[11] | 2003 | 2 015 | 71.8 | 20.6 | 20.3 | ... | 51.3 | 64.0 |
| | 2004 | 2 154 | 67.5 | 19.1 | 21.0 | ... | 50.2 | 57.9 |
| | 2005 | 2 382 | 65.7 | 18.3 | 23.1 | ... | 47.0 | 54.2 |
| Saint Vincent-Grenadines[1]<br>Saint Vincent-Grenadines[1] | 2003 | 1 032 | 65.1 | 19.6 | 33.3 | ... | 45.3 | 63.2 |
| | 2004 | 1 120 | 69.4 | 19.7 | 32.1 | ... | 44.5[3] | 65.6[3] |
| | 2005 | 1 166 | 68.7 | 20.7 | 32.7 | ... | 46.9 | 68.9 |
| San Marino[1]<br>Saint-Marin[1] | 2002 | 935 | ... | ... | 60.2 | -1.3 | 177.5 | 187.8 |
| | 2003 | 995 | ... | ... | 57.3 | 1.4 | 177.2 | 185.6 |
| | 2004 | 1 061 | ... | ... | 53.6 | 2.2 | 186.1 | 190.3 |
| Sao Tome and Principe[1]<br>Sao Tomé-et-Principe[1] | 1986 | 2 478 | 76.1 | 30.3 | 13.6 | 0.9 | ... | 50.8 |
| | 1987 | 3 003 | 63.1 | 24.8 | 15.4 | 1.1 | ... | 43.1 |
| | 1988 | 4 221 | 71.8 | 21.2 | 15.7 | 0.0 | ... | 66.8 |
| Saudi Arabia+[1]<br>Arabie saoudite+[1] | 2003 | 804 648 | 33.6 | 24.6 | 18.4 | 1.4 | 46.1 | 24.1 |
| | 2004 | 938 771 | 30.4 | 23.6 | 16.7 | 1.5 | 52.7 | 24.9 |
| | 2005 | 1 160 742 | 26.3 | 23.1 | 15.0 | 1.2 | 60.7 | 26.4 |
| Senegal<br>Sénégal | 2002 | 3 717 639 | 80.2[2] | 13.0 | 24.8 | -7.6 | 28.5 | 39.0 |
| | 2003 | 3 960 841 | 78.0[2] | 13.2 | 21.3 | -0.3 | 26.8 | 39.0 |
| | 2004 | 4 198 473 | 78.4[2] | 13.6 | 22.9 | -1.8 | 26.7 | 39.8 |
| Serbia<br>Serbie | 2004 | 1 431 313[20] | 70.7[2] | 19.8 | 17.7 | 20.1 | 22.2[21] | 50.6[22] |
| | 2005 | *1 750 000[20] | 71.0[2] | 20.9 | 12.2 | 17.3 | 25.5[21] | 46.9[22] |
| | 2006 | *2 139 800[20] | 70.1[2] | 20.9 | 10.2 | 17.9 | 27.1[21] | 46.3[22] |
| Serbia and Montenegro<br>Serbie-et-Monténégro | 1998[1] | 148 370 | 70.7[2] | 28.2 | 11.6 | -1.1[5] | 23.4 | 32.8 |
| | 1999[20] | 191 099 | 68.0[2] | 28.9 | 12.6 | -0.5[5] | 11.2 | 20.3 |
| | 2000[20] | 381 661 | 70.5[2] | 28.3 | 15.4 | -6.6[5] | 9.2 | 16.8 |
| Seychelles[1]<br>Seychelles[1] | 1998 | 3 201 | 50.0 | 31.2 | 34.0 | 0.6 | -15.8[15] | ... |
| | 1999 | 3 330 | 45.3 | 27.8 | 41.5 | 1.8 | -16.4[15] | ... |
| | 2000 | 3 424 | 39.4 | 27.1 | 35.7 | 0.5 | -2.6[15] | ... |
| Sierra Leone<br>Sierra Leone | 2003 | 3 335 650 | 116.1[2] | 10.1 | 5.8 | 3.9[16] | 12.4 | 48.2 |
| | 2004 | 3 825 518 | 102.2[2] | 11.7 | 5.8 | 8.7[16] | 14.2 | 42.5 |
| | 2005 | 4 400 978 | 91.2[2] | 14.8 | 5.2 | 13.4[16] | 14.4 | 39.1 |
| Singapore<br>Singapour | 2004 | 181 540 | 43.2 | 10.7 | 23.8 | -4.2 | 230.6 | 203.3 |
| | 2005 | 194 242 | 41.9 | 10.8 | 22.3 | -3.3 | 244.3 | 214.8 |
| | 2006 | 209 991 | 40.2 | 11.3 | 23.1 | -4.2 | 252.6 | 220.9 |
| Slovakia<br>Slovaquie | 2004 | 1 355 262 | 56.7[2] | 20.0 | 24.1 | 1.9[5] | 75.2 | 77.9 |
| | 2005 | 1 471 131 | 57.4[2] | 18.5 | 26.8 | 2.4[5] | 77.3 | 82.4 |
| | 2006 | 1 636 263 | 57.6[2] | 18.2 | 26.4 | 2.6[5] | 85.7 | 90.3 |
| Slovenia<br>Slovénie | 2004 | 6 271 795 | 54.8[2] | 19.6 | 24.5 | 2.3[5] | 60.0 | 61.2 |
| | 2005 | 6 620 145 | 54.9[2] | 19.6 | 24.4 | 1.6[5] | 64.6 | 65.1 |
| | 2006 | 7 126 012 | 54.0[2] | 19.3 | 25.8 | 1.6[5] | 69.2 | 69.9 |

| Country or area<br>Pays ou zone | Year<br>Année | GDP at current prices (mil. nat.cur.)<br>PIB aux prix courants (millions monnaie nat.) | % of Gross domestic product – en % du Produit intérieur brut | | | | | |
| --- | --- | --- | --- | --- | --- | --- | --- | --- |
| | | | Household final consumption expenditure<br>Consom. finale des ménages | Govt. final consumption expenditure<br>Consom. finale des admin. publiques | Gross fixed capital formation<br>Formation brute de capital fixe | Changes in inventories<br>Variation des stocks | Exports of goods and services<br>Exportations de biens et services | Imports of goods and services<br>Importations de biens et services |
| Solomon Islands[1]<br>Iles Salomon[1] | 1986 | 253 | 63.1 | 33.3 | 25.2 | 1.0 | 52.6 | 75.2[23] |
| | 1987 | 293 | 63.1 | 36.3 | 20.4 | 2.7 | 55.9 | 78.4[23] |
| | 1988 | 367 | 68.6 | 31.4 | 30.0 | 2.7 | 52.4 | 85.0[23] |
| Somalia[1]<br>Somalie[1] | 1985 | 87 290 | 90.5[18] | 10.6[24] | 8.9[24] | 2.9[25] | 4.2[6] | 17.0[26] |
| | 1986 | 118 781 | 89.1[18] | 9.7[24] | 16.8[24] | 1.0[25] | 5.8[6] | 22.4[26] |
| | 1987 | 169 608 | 88.8[18] | 11.1[24] | 16.8[24] | 4.8[25] | 5.9[6] | 27.2[26] |
| South Africa<br>Afrique du Sud | 2003 | 1 260 693 | 62.3 | 19.3 | 15.9 | 1.0 | 28.1 | 25.8 |
| | 2004 | 1 398 157 | 62.3 | 19.6 | 16.2 | 1.5 | 26.7 | 27.0 |
| | 2005 | 1 539 253 | 62.6 | 19.6 | 17.0 | 1.2 | 27.5 | 28.4 |
| Spain<br>Espagne | 2004 | 840 106 | 57.9[2] | 17.8 | 28.1 | 0.2 | 26.0 | 30.0 |
| | 2005 | 905 455 | 57.9[2] | 18.0 | 29.3 | 0.2 | 25.5 | 30.9 |
| | 2006 | 976 189 | 57.7[2] | 17.9 | 30.3 | 0.3 | 26.1 | 32.3 |
| Sri Lanka<br>Sri Lanka | 2003 | 1 795 259 | 71.8 | 12.3 | 20.3 | 1.3 | 35.2 | 41.3 |
| | 2004 | 2 059 832 | 71.0 | 12.8 | 23.0 | 1.7 | 35.9 | 44.8 |
| | 2005 | 2 407 775 | 69.5 | 12.8 | 23.7 | 2.4 | 32.9 | 42.0 |
| Sudan[1]<br>Soudan[1] | 1994 | 5 522 838 | 84.1 | 4.6 | 9.4 | 6.8 | 4.6 | 9.5 |
| | #1996 | 10 330 678 | 81.9 | 7.5 | 12.3 | 9.6 | 8.0 | 19.2 |
| | 1997 | 16 769 372 | 85.6 | 5.4 | 12.2 | 5.7 | 10.2 | 19.2 |
| Suriname[1]<br>Suriname[1] | 2002 | 2 240 127[27] | ... | 27.0 | 81.8[4] | ... | 42.0 | 50.8 |
| | 2003 | 2 918 132[27] | ... | 31.8 | 77.7[4] | ... | 49.3 | 58.8 |
| | 2004 | 3 513 565[27] | ... | 14.6 | 92.3[4] | ... | 60.7 | 67.7 |
| Swaziland+<br>Swaziland+ | 2003 | 14 401 | 76.2 | 14.8 | 18.0 | ... | 77.8 | 86.9 |
| | 2004 | 15 585 | 63.7 | 15.2 | 22.3 | ... | 91.3 | 92.5 |
| | 2005 | 16 260 | 65.4 | 15.4 | 23.4 | ... | 82.5 | 86.7 |
| Sweden<br>Suède | 2004 | 2 565 056 | 48.3[2] | 27.4 | 16.3 | 0.0[5] | 46.2 | 38.2 |
| | 2005 | 2 670 547 | 48.1[2] | 27.1 | 17.2 | -0.1[5] | 48.7 | 41.1 |
| | 2006 | 2 831 746 | 47.3[2] | 26.8 | 17.9 | 0.0[5] | 51.3 | 43.2 |
| Switzerland<br>Suisse | 2003 | 434 764 | 60.4[2] | 12.0 | 20.7 | 0.3[5] | 43.4 | 36.7 |
| | 2004 | 447 309 | 60.1[2] | 11.7 | 21.0 | -0.1[5] | 45.9 | 38.6 |
| | 2005 | 455 594 | 60.3[2] | 11.4 | 21.4 | 0.1[5] | 47.9 | 41.1 |
| Syrian Arab Republic[1]<br>Rép. arabe syrienne[1] | 2003 | 1 067 265 | 60.3 | 13.5 | 23.3 | ... | 32.4 | 29.5 |
| | 2004 | 1 253 944 | 64.6 | 13.9 | 24.0 | -5.3 | 40.9 | 38.1 |
| | 2005 | 1 479 667 | 68.0 | 12.6 | 23.7 | -6.3 | 41.8 | 39.8 |
| Tajikistan<br>Tadjikistan | 2003 | 4 761 | 78.5[2] | 12.2 | 8.0 | 2.0 | 58.3 | 65.9 |
| | 2004 | 6 167 | 74.0[2] | 11.8 | 10.4 | 1.8 | 52.8 | 59.4 |
| | 2005 | 7 207 | 81.1[2] | 14.6 | 11.1 | 0.5 | 47.9 | 61.9 |
| Thailand[1]<br>Thaïlande[1] | 2003 | 5 917 368 | 57.2 | 10.7 | 24.1 | 0.9 | 65.7 | 58.9 |
| | 2004 | 6 489 847 | 57.2 | 11.1 | 25.9 | 0.9 | 70.7 | 65.8 |
| | 2005 | 7 087 660 | 57.1 | 11.9 | 29.0 | 2.5 | 73.8 | 75.1 |
| TFYR of Macedonia<br>L'ex-R.y. Macédoine | 2003 | 251 486 | 76.3[2] | 20.7 | 16.7 | 3.2 | 37.9 | 54.8 |
| | 2004 | 265 257 | 78.8[2] | 20.0 | 17.8 | 3.6 | 40.2 | 60.5 |
| | 2005 | 286 619 | 77.7[2] | 18.8 | 17.0 | 3.7 | 44.7 | 62.0 |
| Timor-Leste[1]<br>Timor-Leste[1] | 2000 | 393[28] | 52.1 | 43.3 | 31.7 | 3.2 | 21.2 | 51.6 |
| Togo[1]<br>Togo[1] | 1984 | 304 800 | 66.0 | 14.0 | 21.2 | -1.5 | 51.9 | 51.6 |
| | 1985 | 332 500 | 66.0 | 14.2 | 22.9 | 5.2 | 48.3 | 56.7 |
| | 1986 | 363 600 | 69.0 | 14.4 | 23.8 | 5.3 | 35.6 | 48.2 |
| Tonga+[1]<br>Tonga+[1] | 2002 | 312 | 110.9[2] | 15.7 | 19.2 | 1.0 | 18.9 | 66.3 |
| | 2003 | 349 | 111.7[2] | 14.3 | 18.1 | 0.9 | 20.3 | 65.0 |
| | 2004 | 372 | 109.9[2] | 14.0 | 16.7 | 0.8 | 21.2 | 62.6 |
| Trinidad and Tobago<br>Trinité-et-Tobago | 2003 | 70 732 | 54.5 | 12.8 | 18.0 | 0.5 | 52.1 | 37.9 |
| | 2004 | 79 826 | 55.0 | 12.0 | 17.0 | 0.4 | 57.0 | 41.4 |
| | 2005 | 95 057 | 50.9 | 12.5 | 15.2 | 0.3 | 64.5 | 43.5 |

**Gross domestic product by type of expenditure at current prices** — Percentage distribution (*continued*)

**Dépenses imputées au produit intérieur brut aux prix courants** — Répartition en pourcentage (*suite*)

| Country or area<br>Pays ou zone | Year<br>Année | GDP at current prices (mil. nat.cur.)<br>PIB aux prix courants (millions monnaie nat.) | % of Gross domestic product – en % du Produit intérieur brut | | | | | |
|---|---|---|---|---|---|---|---|---|
| | | | Household final consumption expenditure<br>Consom. finale des ménages | Govt. final consumption expenditure<br>Consom. finale des admin. publiques | Gross fixed capital formation<br>Formation brute de capital fixe | Changes in inventories<br>Variation des stocks | Exports of goods and services<br>Exportations de biens et services | Imports of goods and services<br>Importations de biens et services |
| Tunisia | 2003 | 32 202 | 63.1 | 15.7 | 23.4 | 1.7 | 43.8 | 47.7 |
| Tunisie | 2004 | 35 148 | 63.1 | 15.4 | 22.7 | 1.7 | 46.8 | 49.7 |
| | 2005 | 37 311 | 63.6 | 15.5 | 22.5 | -0.3 | 48.8 | 50.1 |
| Turkey[1] | 2004 | 430 511 | 66.1 | 13.2 | 17.8 | 7.9 | 28.9 | 34.7 |
| Turquie[1] | 2005 | 487 202 | 67.4 | 13.1 | 19.6 | 5.2 | 27.4 | 34.0 |
| | 2006 | 576 322 | 66.4 | 13.1 | 21.0 | 2.9 | 28.2 | 35.9 |
| Turkmenistan | 2000 | 25 648 000 | 70.8[2] | ... | ... | ... | ... | ... |
| Turkménistan | 2001 | 35 118 973 | 70.8[2] | ... | ... | ... | ... | ... |
| | 2002 | 45 239 913 | 70.8[2] | ... | ... | ... | ... | ... |
| Turks and Caicos Islands | 2004 | 486 | 31.1 | 20.5 | 31.0[4] | ... | 68.0 | 50.6 |
| Iles Turques et Caïques | 2005 | 570 | 38.2 | 17.1 | 39.0[4] | ... | 64.8 | 59.2 |
| | 2006 | 648 | 33.0 | 17.0 | 39.2[4] | ... | 67.2 | 56.5 |
| Tuvalu[1] | 1996 | 16[29] | ... | ... | 67.6[4] | ... | ... | ... |
| Tuvalu[1] | 1997 | 18[29] | ... | ... | 51.2[4] | ... | ... | ... |
| | 1998 | 21[29] | ... | ... | 54.9[4] | ... | ... | ... |
| Uganda[1] | 2003 | 12 760 199 | 78.2 | 14.4 | 21.5 | 0.4 | 12.7 | 27.0 |
| Ouganda[1] | 2004 | 14 108 038 | 77.6 | 14.6 | 22.9 | 0.1 | 13.4 | 29.0 |
| | 2005 | 16 365 055 | 77.2 | 14.1 | 23.5 | 0.3 | 14.1 | 30.1 |
| Ukraine | 2004 | 345 113 | 53.6[2] | 17.6 | 22.5 | -1.4[5] | 63.6 | 56.0 |
| Ukraine | 2005 | 441 452 | 58.3[2] | 18.2 | 22.0 | 0.7[5] | 51.5 | 50.6 |
| | 2006 | 537 667 | 59.7[2] | 18.9 | 24.0 | 0.3[5] | 47.2 | 50.1 |
| United Arab Emirates[1] | 1990 | 124 008 | 38.6 | 16.3 | 19.4 | 1.0 | 65.4 | 40.8 |
| Emirats arabes unis[1] | 1991 | 124 500 | 41.4 | 16.9 | 20.7 | 1.1 | 67.6 | 47.7 |
| | 1992 | 128 400 | 45.5 | 17.8 | 23.2 | 1.2 | 69.1 | 56.8 |
| United Kingdom | 2004 | 1 176 527 | 64.7[2] | 21.3 | 16.5 | 0.4[5] | 25.4 | 28.4 |
| Royaume-Uni | 2005 | 1 225 978 | 64.6[2] | 22.0 | 16.8 | 0.3[5] | 26.6 | 30.2 |
| | 2006 | 1 289 989 | 64.1[2] | 22.3 | 17.3 | 0.4[5] | 28.7 | 32.9 |
| United Rep. of Tanzania | 2001 | 8 284 690 | 83.5 | 6.2 | 16.8 | 0.2 | 15.5 | 23.7 |
| Rép.-Unie de Tanzanie | 2002 | 9 445 482 | 79.4 | 6.3 | 18.9 | 0.2 | 16.1 | 22.3 |
| | 2003 | 10 692 420 | 82.0 | 6.5 | 18.5 | 0.2 | 17.8 | 26.7 |
| United States | 2003 | 10 908 000 | 70.6[2] | 15.9 | 17.9 | 0.1 | 9.5 | 14.1 |
| Etats-Unis | 2004 | 11 657 300 | 70.4[2] | 15.9 | 18.4 | 0.5 | 10.1 | 15.4 |
| | 2005 | 12 397 900 | 70.5[2] | 16.0 | 19.1 | 0.2 | 10.5 | 16.3 |
| Uruguay[1] | 2004 | 379 353 | 73.0[2] | 10.8 | 11.3 | 1.8[30] | 31.8 | 28.7 |
| Uruguay[1] | 2005 | 406 705 | 73.2[2] | 11.0 | 13.1 | 0.0[30] | 31.1 | 28.5 |
| | 2006 | 464 802 | 73.1[2] | 11.0 | 16.0 | 0.4[30] | 29.9 | 30.3 |
| Uzbekistan | 1999 | 2 128 660 | 62.1[2] | 20.6 | 27.2 | -10.1 | 0.1[15] | ... |
| Ouzbékistan | 2000 | 3 255 600 | 61.9[2] | 18.7 | 24.0 | -4.4 | -0.2[15] | ... |
| | 2001 | 4 868 400 | 61.6[2] | 18.4 | 25.7 | -5.5 | -0.3[15] | ... |
| Vanuatu[1] | 1993 | 23 779 | 49.2 | 28.4 | 25.5 | 2.3 | 45.3 | 53.8 |
| Vanuatu[1] | 1994 | 24 961 | 49.2 | 27.7 | 26.5 | 2.3 | 47.3 | 57.2 |
| | 1995 | 27 255 | 46.9 | 25.4 | 29.8 | 2.1 | 44.2 | 53.6 |
| Venezuela (Bolivarian Rep. of) | 2002 | 107 840 166 | 53.5[2] | 13.0 | 21.9 | -0.8[5] | 30.4 | 18.1 |
| Venezuela (Rép. bolivarienne du) | 2003 | 134 227 833 | 54.8[2] | 12.9 | 15.5 | -0.3[5] | 33.9 | 16.7 |
| | 2004 | 212 683 082 | 49.2[2] | 12.0 | 18.3 | 3.5[5] | 36.2 | 19.2 |
| Viet Nam | 2003 | 613 443 000 | 66.3 | 6.3 | 33.4 | 2.1 | -8.4[15] | ... |
| Viet Nam | 2004 | 715 307 000 | 65.1 | 6.4 | 33.3 | 2.2 | -7.5[15] | ... |
| | 2005 | 837 858 000 | 63.6 | 6.2 | 33.1 | 2.3 | -4.6[15] | ... |
| Yemen | 2002 | 1 878 007 | 67.4 | 14.9 | 19.8 | -1.3 | 37.0 | 37.8 |
| Yémen | 2003 | 2 160 608 | 67.1 | 13.7 | 22.5 | -1.8 | 36.4 | 37.9 |
| | 2004 | 2 563 490 | 66.2 | 12.6 | 21.0 | -0.7 | 36.4 | 35.4 |

| Country or area<br>Pays ou zone | Year<br>Année | GDP at current prices (mil. nat.cur.)<br>PIB aux prix courants (millions monnaie nat.) | Household final consumption expenditure<br>Consom. finale des ménages | Govt. final consumption expenditure<br>Consom. finale des admin. publiques | Gross fixed capital formation<br>Formation brute de capital fixe | Changes in inventories<br>Variation des stocks | Exports of goods and services<br>Exportations de biens et services | Imports of goods and services<br>Importations de biens et services |
|---|---|---|---|---|---|---|---|---|
| | | | | % of Gross domestic product – en % du Produit intérieur brut | | | | |
| Zambia[1]<br>Zambie[1] | 2003 | 20 377 051 | 66.6 | 14.6 | 24.8 | 1.3 | 20.6 | 28.0 |
| | 2004 | 25 997 450 | 64.6 | 18.7 | 28.3 | 1.3 | 26.9 | 40.0 |
| | 2005 | 32 456 520 | 63.3 | 20.2 | 27.2 | 1.1 | 23.4 | 35.3 |
| Zimbabwe[1]<br>Zimbabwe[1] | 2002 | 1 698 180 | 107.4[2] | 9.5 | 5.5 | -14.3 | 5.5 | 9.2 |
| | 2003 | 5 518 757 | 112.6[2] | 11.0 | 3.2 | -16.2 | 1.5 | 3.3 |
| | 2004 | 15 563 920 | 114.6[2] | 32.8 | 2.7 | 1.8 | 61.4 | 84.1 |

Source

United Nations Statistics Division, New York, national accounts database, last accessed January 2008.

Data for most countries have been compiled in accordance with the concepts and definitions of the System of National Accounts 1993 (1993 SNA). Countries that follow the 1968 SNA are footnoted accordingly.

+ Note: The national accounts data generally relate to the fiscal year used in each country, unless indicated otherwise. Countries or areas whose reference periods coincide with the calendar year ending 31 December are not listed below.

Year beginning 21 March: Afghanistan, Iran (Islamic Republic).
Year beginning 1 April: Bermuda, India, Myanmar, New Zealand.

Year beginning 1 July: Australia, Bhutan, Gambia, Nicaragua, Pakistan, Puerto Rico, Saudi Arabia.
Year ending 30 June: Bangladesh, Botswana, Egypt, Swaziland, Tonga.

Year ending 7 July: Ethiopia.
Year ending 15 July: Nepal.
Year ending 30 September: Haiti.

Source

Organisation des Nations Unies, Division de statistique, New York, la base de données sur les comptes nationaux, dernier accès janvier 2008.

Les données pour la majorité des pays sont compilées selon les concepts et définitions du Système de comptabilité nationale, 1993 (SCN93). Seuls les pays qui suivent toujours le SCN68 seront donc signalés par une note.

+ Note : Sauf indication contraire, les données sur les comptes nationaux concernent généralement l'exercice budgétaire utilisé dans chaque pays. Les pays ou territoires dont la période de référence coïncide avec l'année civile se terminant le 31 décembre ne sont pas répertoriés ci-dessous.

Exercice commençant le 21 mars: Afghanistan, Iran (République islamique d'). Exercice commençant le 1er avril: Bermudes, Inde, Myanmar, Nouvelle-Zélande.
Exercice commençant le 1er juillet: Arabie saoudite, Australie, Bhoutan, Gambie, Nicaragua, Pakistan, Porto Rico.
Exercice se terminant le 30 juin: Bangladesh, Botswana, Égypte, Swaziland, Tonga.
Exercice se terminant le 7 juillet: Éthiopie.
Exercice se terminant le 15 juillet: Népal.
Exercice se terminant le 30 septembre: Haïti.

Notes

1 Data compiled in accordance with the System of National Accounts 1968 (1968 SNA).
2 Including "Non-profit institutions serving households" (NPISHs) final consumption expenditure.
3 Preliminary data.
4 Gross capital formation.
5 Including acquisitions less disposals of valuables.
6 Exports of goods only.
7 Imports of goods only.
8 Forecast.
9 At producers' prices.
10 For statistical purposes, the data for China do not include those for the Hong Kong Special Administrative Region (Hong Kong SAR), Macao Special Administrative Region (Macao SAR) and Taiwan Province of China.
11 The estimates refer to central government capital formation only.
12 Including net travel and tourism income.
13 Including net freight and insurance.
14 Cocoa is valued at cost to the Ghana Cocoa Marketing Board. Stocks of other export commodities, including minerals, are valued at export prices.
15 Net exports.

Notes

1 Données compilées selon le Système de comptabilité nationale de 1968 (SCN 1968).
2 Y compris la consommation finale des institutions sans but lucratif au service des ménages.
3 Données préliminaires.
4 Formation brute de capital.
5 Y compris les acquisitions moins cessions d'objets de valeur.
6 Exportations de biens uniquement.
7 Importations de biens uniquement.
8 Prévision.
9 Aux prix à la production.
10 Pour la présentation des statistiques, les données pour la Chine ne comprennent pas la Région Administrative Spéciale de Hong Kong (Hong Kong RAS), la Région Administrative Spéciale de Macao (Macao RAS) et la province de Taiwan.
11 Les chiffres ne concernent que la formation de capital des administrations centrales.
12 Comprend les recettes nettes des voyages et du tourisme.
13 Comprend les montants nets du fret et de l'assurance.
14 Le cacao est valorisé au prix coûtant du "Ghana Cocoa Marketing Board". Les stocks des autres produits d'exportation, minéraux compris, sont valorisés au prix à l'exportation.
15 Exportations nettes.

16  Including statistical discrepancy.
17  Does not include direct purchases in the domestic market by non-resident households.
18  Obtained as a residual.
19  Semi-final data.
20  Beginning 1999, data for Kosovo and Metohia are excluded.
21  Includes exports of goods and services to Montenegro.
22  Includes imports of goods and services from Montenegro.
23  Valued f.o.b.
24  Including the value of technical assistance from abroad.
25  Including livestock only.
26  Refers to imports of goods and non-factor services.

27  Excluding the informal sector.
28  Data in US dollars.
29  GDP at market prices.
30  Refers to increase in stocks of wool and livestock in the private sector, and to stocks held by the public sector.

16  Y compris une divergence statistique.
17  Non compris les achats directs effectués sur le marché intérieur par les ménages non résidents.
18  Obtenu comme valeur résiduelle.
19  Données demi-finales.
20  A compter de 1999, non compris les données de Kosovo et Metohia.
21  Y compris exportations de biens et services à Monténégro.
22  Y compris importations de biens et services de Monténégro.
23  Valeur f.o.b.
24  Compris la valeur de l'assistance technique étrangère.
25  Ne comprend que le bétail.
26  Concerne les importations de biens et de services autres que les services des facteurs.

27  Non compris le secteur informel.
28  Les données sont exprimées en dollars des États-Unis.
29  PIB aux prix du marché.
30  Concerne les accroissements de stocks de laine et de bétail dans le secteur privé, et les stocks dans le secteur public.

# Value added by industries at current prices
Percentage distribution

# Valeur ajoutée par branche d'activité aux prix courants
Répartition en pourcentage

| Country or area<br>Pays ou zone | Year<br>Année | Value added, gross (mil. nat.cur)<br>Valeur ajoutée, brute (mil. mon. nat.) | % of Value added – % de la valeur ajoutée | | | | | | | |
|---|---|---|---|---|---|---|---|---|---|---|
| | | | Agriculture, hunting, forestry and fishing<br>Agriculture, chasse, sylviculture et pêche | Mining and quarrying<br>Activités extractives | Manufac-turing<br>Activités de fabri-cation | Electric-ity, gas and water supply<br>Electricité, gaz et eau | Construc-tion<br>Construc-tion | Wholesale, retail trade, restaurants and hotels<br>Commerce, restaurants, hôtels | Transport, storage & communi-cation<br>Transports, entrepôts, communi-cations | Other activities<br>Autres activités |
| Afghanistan+[1] | 2002 | 180 292 | 49.8 | 0.1 | 15.1 | 0.0 | 4.8 | 10.1 | 9.6 | 10.4 |
| Afghanistan+[1] | 2003 | 220 393 | 48.5 | 0.2 | 15.1 | 0.4 | 5.5 | 9.2 | 11.3 | 9.7 |
| Albania | 2003 | 633 247 | 23.5 | 0.6 | 5.2 | 2.9 | 13.7 | 22.1 | 8.7 | 23.3 |
| Albanie | 2004 | 679 636 | 22.3 | 0.8 | 5.8 | 3.4 | 13.9 | 21.6 | 9.0 | 23.2 |
| | 2005 | 740 213 | 20.7 | 0.8 | 5.4 | 3.5 | 14.3 | 22.4 | 8.9 | 24.0 |
| Algeria[1] | 2001 | 4 075 738 | 10.1 | 36.5 | 6.3 | 1.3 | 7.9 | 12.9 | 8.3 | 16.8 |
| Algérie[1] | 2002 | 4 284 371 | 9.7 | 35.5 | 6.2 | 1.3 | 8.6 | 13.2 | 8.5 | 16.9 |
| | 2003 | 4 991 489 | 10.2 | 38.5 | 5.6 | 1.2 | 8.0 | 12.3 | 8.3 | 15.9 |
| Andorra[1] | 2004 | 1 964 | 0.4 | ... | 2.0 | 0.9 | 12.8 | 37.7 | 3.3 | 42.9 |
| Andorre[1] | 2005 | 2 188 | 0.3 | ... | 2.1 | 0.8 | 13.1 | 35.8 | 3.2 | 44.7 |
| | 2006 | 2 381 | 0.3 | ... | 2.1 | 0.8 | 13.2 | 34.4 | 3.1 | 46.0 |
| Angola[1] | 1988 | 236 682 | 16.0 | 27.1 | 8.3 | 0.2 | 4.1 | 11.7[2] | 3.5 | 29.1[2] |
| Angola[1] | 1989 | 276 075 | 19.3 | 29.7 | 6.2 | 0.2 | 3.3 | 11.4[2] | 3.0 | 27.1[2] |
| | 1990 | 305 831 | 18.0 | 32.9 | 5.0 | 0.1 | 2.9 | 10.7[2] | 3.2 | 27.0[2] |
| Anguilla[1] | 2004 | 340[3] | 2.3 | 1.4 | 0.9 | 4.5 | 12.7 | 31.3 | 14.4 | 32.5 |
| Anguilla[1] | 2005 | 388[3] | 2.1 | 1.4 | 2.0 | 4.7 | 12.9 | 32.3 | 14.7 | 30.0 |
| | 2006 | 451[3] | 1.8 | 1.3 | 2.0 | 4.9 | 12.9 | 34.7 | 14.3 | 28.2 |
| Antigua and Barbuda[1] | 1986 | 567[3] | 4.3 | 1.7 | 3.8 | 3.5 | 8.9 | 23.6 | 15.6 | 38.5 |
| Antigua-et-Barbuda[1] | 1987 | 649[3] | 4.5 | 2.2 | 3.5 | 3.5 | 11.3 | 24.1 | 15.6 | 35.3 |
| | 1988 | 776[3] | 4.1 | 2.2 | 3.1 | 4.0 | 12.7 | 23.7 | 14.3 | 35.9 |
| Argentina | 2003 | 353 374[4] | 11.0 | 5.8 | 23.9 | 1.7 | 3.3 | 14.0 | 8.5 | 31.8 |
| Argentine | 2004 | 414 039[4] | 10.4 | 5.7 | 24.1 | 1.7 | 4.2 | 14.1 | 9.0 | 30.9 |
| | 2005 | 492 825[4] | 9.4 | 5.8 | 23.2 | 1.7 | 4.9 | 14.3 | 9.0 | 31.7 |
| Armenia | #2004 | 1 772 230[5] | 24.4 | 3.5 | 14.6 | 5.7 | 16.7 | 12.9 | 6.4 | 15.8 |
| Arménie | 2005 | 2 081 444[5] | 20.3 | 3.5 | 14.2 | 5.4 | 23.4 | 12.0 | 6.0 | 15.2 |
| | 2006 | 2 479 477[5] | 19.2 | 2.9 | 11.3 | 4.5 | 28.7 | 11.7 | 6.8 | 15.0 |
| Aruba | 2000 | 3 231 | 0.4[6] | ... | 3.8[7] | 6.2[7] | 6.0 | 24.4 | 9.0 | 50.3 |
| Aruba | 2001 | 3 308 | 0.4[6] | ... | 3.3[7] | 7.0[7] | 5.4 | 23.6 | 9.3 | 51.0 |
| | 2002 | 3 333 | 0.4[6] | ... | 3.3[7] | 6.9[7] | 4.7 | 22.4 | 9.2 | 53.1 |
| Australia+ | 2003 | 764 791 | 3.5 | 4.3 | 12.4 | 2.5 | 6.8 | 14.4 | 7.9 | 48.2 |
| Australie+ | 2004 | 820 621 | 3.3 | 5.6 | 11.7 | 2.5 | 6.9 | 14.1 | 7.9 | 47.9 |
| | 2005 | 885 647 | 3.1 | 7.5 | 11.0 | 2.5 | 7.0 | 13.5 | 7.5 | 47.9 |
| Austria | 2003 | 203 566 | 1.9 | 0.4 | 19.5 | 2.4 | 7.8 | 17.5 | 7.4 | 43.1 |
| Autriche | 2004 | 211 498 | 1.9 | 0.5 | 19.4 | 2.3 | 7.6 | 17.6 | 7.1 | 43.7 |
| | 2005 | 219 439 | 1.6 | 0.4 | 19.4 | 2.3 | 7.6 | 17.4 | 7.0 | 44.2 |
| Azerbaijan | 2004 | 7 914[8] | 11.8 | 31.3 | 8.9 | 1.1 | 13.4 | 8.3 | 10.3 | 15.7 |
| Azerbaïdjan | 2005 | 11 576[8] | 9.9 | 45.6 | 7.0 | 0.8 | 10.1 | 7.2 | 8.1 | 11.9 |
| | 2006 | 16 586[8] | 7.6 | 55.2 | 5.7 | 0.6 | 8.0 | 6.3 | 8.0 | 9.1 |
| Bahamas | 2002 | 5 388[4] | 2.7 | 1.0 | 4.6 | 3.2 | 7.4 | 22.2 | 9.2 | 49.6 |
| Bahamas | 2003 | 5 624[4] | 2.7 | 1.0 | 4.4 | 3.3 | 7.2 | 22.0 | 9.3 | 50.0 |
| | 2004 | 5 799[4] | 2.1 | 1.0 | 4.5 | 3.3 | 6.8 | 22.3 | 8.8 | 51.3 |
| Bahrain[1] | 2002 | 3 459 | 0.6 | 22.7 | 10.8 | 1.3 | 3.9 | 10.3 | 7.2 | 43.3 |
| Bahreïn[1] | 2003 | 3 972 | 0.6 | 22.9 | 10.2 | 1.2 | 3.5 | 9.7 | 6.6 | 45.2 |
| | 2004 | 4 583 | 0.4 | 21.3 | 9.6 | 1.1 | 3.3 | 11.0 | 6.6 | 46.7 |

| Country or area / Pays ou zone | Year / Année | Value added, gross (mil. nat.cur.) / Valeur ajoutée, brute (mil. mon. nat.) | Agriculture, hunting, forestry and fishing / Agriculture, chasse, sylviculture et pêche | Mining and quarrying / Activités extractives | Manufacturing / Activités de fabrication | Electricity, gas and water supply / Electricité, gaz et eau | Construction / Construction | Wholesale, retail trade, restaurants and hotels / Commerce, restaurants, hôtels | Transport, storage & communication / Transports, entrepôts, communications | Other activities / Autres activités |
|---|---|---|---|---|---|---|---|---|---|---|
| Bangladesh+ Bangladesh+ | 2003 | 3 194 631 | 21.0 | 1.1 | 16.1 | 1.4 | 7.9 | 14.5 | 10.8 | 27.1 |
| | 2004 | 3 555 937 | 20.1 | 1.1 | 16.5 | 1.4 | 8.2 | 14.8 | 10.8 | 27.0 |
| | 2005 | 3 999 078 | 19.5 | 1.1 | 17.2 | 1.3 | 8.4 | 15.0 | 10.8 | 26.7 |
| Barbados[1] Barbade[1] | 2002 | 4 066[3] | 3.8 | 0.7 | 6.5 | 3.4 | 5.6 | 28.4 | 7.3 | 44.4 |
| | 2003 | 4 335[3] | 4.5 | 0.7 | 6.8 | 3.3 | 5.4 | 28.9 | 6.7 | 43.9 |
| | 2004 | 4 600[3] | 3.6 | 0.8 | 6.9 | 3.1 | 5.6 | 28.9 | 6.9 | 44.2 |
| Belarus Bélarus | 2004 | 43 455 600 | 10.2 | ... | 33.0 | ... | 7.4 | 11.8 | 11.1 | 26.5 |
| | 2005 | 56 678 200 | 9.6 | ... | 33.4 | ... | 7.9 | 11.4 | 10.9 | 26.8 |
| | 2006 | 68 912 200 | 9.2 | ... | 32.4 | ... | 9.1 | 12.3 | 10.6 | 26.4 |
| Belgium Belgique | 2003 | 245 687 | 1.1 | 0.1 | 17.4 | 2.4 | 4.9 | 14.5 | 8.1 | 51.5 |
| | 2004 | 257 583 | 1.1 | 0.1 | 17.4 | 2.2 | 4.9 | 14.7 | 8.2 | 51.5 |
| | 2005 | 265 552 | 1.1 | 0.1 | 17.1 | 2.0 | 4.9 | 14.6 | 8.4 | 51.7 |
| Belize Belize | 1998 | 1 051[8] | 19.1 | 0.6 | 13.2 | 3.4 | 5.7 | 18.9 | 10.4 | 37.9 |
| | 1999 | 1 154[8] | 19.7 | 0.6 | 13.0 | 3.4 | 6.5 | 20.8 | 11.0 | 36.1 |
| | 2000 | 1 311[8] | 17.2 | 0.7 | 13.1 | 3.3 | 7.1 | 21.6 | 9.9 | 29.8 |
| Benin[1] Bénin[1] | 2004 | 1 920 988 | 36.0 | 0.3 | 8.7 | 1.3 | 4.5 | 18.4 | 8.5 | 22.3 |
| | 2005 | 2 067 145 | 35.9 | 0.3 | 8.1 | 1.3 | 4.5 | 18.7 | 8.5 | 22.1 |
| | 2006 | 2 208 239 | 37.3 | 0.3 | 8.3 | 1.3 | 4.5 | 18.0 | 8.3 | 22.0 |
| Bermuda+ Bermudes+ | 2003 | 4 188 | 0.8 | ... | 1.7 | 2.0 | 5.9[6] | 14.1 | 6.3 | 69.2 |
| | 2004 | 4 492 | 0.8 | ... | 1.7 | 1.8 | 6.1[6] | 13.5 | 6.3 | 69.8 |
| | 2005 | 4 996 | 0.8 | ... | 1.6 | 1.6 | 6.6[6] | 13.0 | 6.0 | 70.3 |
| Bhutan+ Bhoutan+ | 2004 | 30 786[3] | 25.5 | 1.4 | 7.7 | 10.0 | 18.3 | 6.2 | 10.7 | 19.7 |
| | 2005 | 35 247[3] | 23.4 | 1.5 | 7.6 | 10.4 | 18.0 | 6.5 | 10.9 | 21.1 |
| | 2006 | 39 946[3] | 22.1 | 1.5 | 7.5 | 14.4 | 15.7 | 6.8 | 11.2 | 20.5 |
| Bolivia[1] Bolivie[1] | 2001 | 48 407 | 14.7 | 7.0 | 14.8 | 3.3 | 3.1 | 11.5 | 12.8 | 34.1 |
| | 2002 | 50 805 | 14.5 | 7.2 | 14.7 | 3.2 | 3.5 | 11.5 | 13.3 | 33.4 |
| | 2003 | 54 742 | 15.2 | 8.5 | 14.6 | 3.3 | 2.6 | 11.4 | 13.7 | 32.7 |
| Bosnia and Herzegovina Bosnie-Herzégovine | 2003 | 11 103 | 9.6 | 2.2 | 11.4 | 6.4 | 4.3 | 14.9 | 10.1 | 41.2[9] |
| | 2004 | 12 240 | 10.4 | 2.3 | 11.1 | 6.6 | 4.3 | 15.6 | 9.9 | 39.7[9] |
| | 2005 | 13 207 | 10.1 | 2.5 | 11.1 | 6.5 | 4.2 | 16.2 | 9.5 | 39.9[9] |
| Botswana+ Botswana+ | 2002 | 30 881 | 2.6 | 36.4 | 4.5 | 2.4 | 5.6 | 11.8 | 3.7 | 32.9 |
| | 2003 | 34 733 | 2.5 | 36.4 | 4.5 | 2.7 | 5.7 | 12.0 | 3.7 | 32.6 |
| | 2004 | 37 517 | 2.5 | 36.1 | 4.3 | 2.8 | 5.6 | 12.0 | 3.7 | 33.0 |
| Brazil Brésil | 2003 | 1 470 614 | 7.4 | 1.7 | 18.0 | 3.4 | 4.7 | 17.7 | 8.3 | 38.8 |
| | 2004 | 1 666 258 | 6.9 | 1.9 | 19.2 | 3.9 | 5.1 | 18.1 | 8.6 | 36.3 |
| | 2005 | 1 842 253 | 5.7 | 2.5 | 18.1 | 3.8 | 4.9 | 18.4 | 8.9 | 37.7 |
| British Virgin Islands Iles Vierges britanniques | 2003 | 805 | 1.1 | 0.0 | 3.4 | 2.0 | 6.1 | 26.7 | 11.1 | 49.6 |
| | 2004 | 896 | 1.0 | 0.0 | 3.0 | 2.0 | 4.9 | 27.6 | 11.4 | 50.0 |
| | 2005 | 1 002 | 0.9 | 0.0 | 2.7 | 2.0 | 6.0 | 27.1 | 11.2 | 49.9 |
| Brunei Darussalam[1] Brunéi Darussalam[1] | 1995 | 7 583 | 2.5 | 36.5[10] | ... | 1.0 | 5.3 | 11.2 | 4.7 | 38.8 |
| | 1996 | 7 886 | 2.5 | 34.7[10] | ... | 1.0 | 5.8 | 11.9 | 4.8 | 39.3 |
| | 1997 | 8 268 | 2.6 | 33.6[10] | ... | 1.0 | 6.2 | 12.1 | 4.9 | 39.6 |
| Bulgaria Bulgarie | 2003 | 30 227 | 11.6 | 1.5 | 18.2 | 5.5 | 4.5 | 9.3 | 13.8 | 35.7 |
| | 2004 | 33 169 | 10.8 | 1.6 | 18.1 | 5.2 | 5.0 | 9.7 | 13.8 | 35.8 |
| | 2005 | 36 023 | 9.3 | 1.6 | 18.7 | 4.5 | 5.6 | 10.7 | 13.7 | 35.8 |
| Burkina Faso Burkina Faso | 2004 | 2 515 766 | 32.9 | 0.4 | 15.1 | 1.1 | 6.5 | 11.9 | 4.4 | 27.7 |
| | 2005 | 2 771 713 | 34.1 | 0.5 | 14.6 | 1.2 | 6.5 | 11.7 | 4.4 | 26.9 |
| | 2006 | 2 902 383 | 34.9 | 0.7 | 13.9 | 1.3 | 6.8 | 11.2 | 4.5 | 26.6 |

| Country or area<br>Pays ou zone | Year<br>Année | Value added, gross (mil. nat.cur)<br>Valeur ajoutée, brute (mil. mon. nat.) | % of Value added – % de la valeur ajoutée | | | | | | | |
|---|---|---|---|---|---|---|---|---|---|---|
| | | | Agriculture, hunting, forestry and fishing<br>Agriculture, chasse, sylviculture et pêche | Mining and quarrying<br>Activités extractives | Manufacturing<br>Activités de fabrication | Electricity, gas and water supply<br>Electricité, gaz et eau | Construction<br>Construction | Wholesale, retail trade, restaurants and hotels<br>Commerce, restaurants, hôtels | Transport, storage & communication<br>Transports, entrepôts, communications | Other activities<br>Autres activités |
| Burundi[1]<br>Burundi[1] | 1988 | 149 067 | 48.9 | 1.0[11] | 16.5 | ... | 2.9 | 12.9 | 2.6 | 15.2 |
| | 1989 | 175 627 | 47.0 | 1.2[11] | 18.5 | ... | 3.3 | 10.8 | 3.3 | 16.0 |
| | 1990 | 192 050 | 52.4 | 0.8[11] | 16,8 | ... | 3.4 | 4.9 | 3.1 | 18.5 |
| Cambodia<br>Cambodge | 2003 | 16 399 945 | 35.1 | 0.3 | 20.5 | 0.6 | 6.4 | 14.5 | 7.1 | 15.5 |
| | 2004 | 19 994 798 | 32.7 | 0.4 | 20.3 | 0.6 | 6.4 | 14.1 | 6.8 | 18.7 |
| | 2005 | 24 005 503 | 34.2 | 0.4 | 19.1 | 0.5 | 6.7 | 13.9 | 7.0 | 18.2 |
| Cameroon<br>Cameroun | 2003 | 7 381 215[5] | 21.6 | 6.8 | 20.1 | 0.7 | 2.9 | 22.3 | 6.8 | 18.8 |
| | 2004 | 7 798 957[5] | 20.3 | 7.1 | 19.1 | 1.0 | 3.2 | 23.9 | 6.4 | 19.0 |
| | 2005 | 8 177 418[5] | 20.4 | 8.9 | 18.7 | 1.0 | 3.3 | 22.9 | 5.9 | 18.9 |
| Canada<br>Canada | 2001 | 1 032 173 | 2.2 | 5.8 | 17.9 | 2.9 | 5.3 | 13.6 | 7.2 | 45.1 |
| | 2002 | 1 068 762 | 2.2 | 5.0 | 17.6 | 2.9 | 5.4 | 13.8 | 7.3 | 45.8 |
| | 2003 | 1 129 008 | 2.1 | 6.3 | 16.5 | 2.9 | 5.4 | 13.8 | 7.2 | 45.7 |
| Cape Verde[1]<br>Cap-Vert[1] | 2002 | 67 055 | 11.3 | 1.8 | 4.8 | 0.6 | 8.8 | 23.8 | 22.5 | 26.4 |
| | 2003 | 73 361 | 11.0 | 1.8 | 4.5 | 1.4 | 8.3 | 23.8 | 23.5 | 25.8 |
| | 2004 | 76 331 | 10.6 | 2.4 | 4.0 | 1.5 | 8.3 | 23.9 | 22.7 | 26.5 |
| Cayman Islands[1]<br>Iles Caïmanes[1] | 1989 | 473 | 0.4 | 0.6 | 1.9 | 3.2 | 11.0 | 24.5 | 11.0 | 47.6 |
| | 1990 | 580 | 0.3 | 0.3 | 1.6 | 3.1 | 9.7 | 24.5 | 10.9 | 49.8 |
| | 1991 | 605 | 0.3 | 0.3 | 1.5 | 3.1 | 9.1 | 22.8 | 10.7 | 52.1 |
| Central African Rep.[1]<br>Rép. centrafricaine[1] | 1983 | 243 350 | 40.8 | 2.5 | 7.8[12] | 0.5 | 2.1 | 21.2[2] | 4.2 | 20.8[2] |
| | 1984 | 268 725 | 40.7 | 2.8 | 8.1[12] | 0.9 | 2.7 | 21.7[2] | 4.3 | 18.8[2] |
| | 1985 | 308 549 | 42.4 | 2.5 | 7.5[12] | 0.8 | 2.6 | 22.0[2] | 4.2 | 17.9[2] |
| Chad<br>Tchad | 2004 | 2 275 463 | 23.5 | 39.1 | 6.4 | 0.3 | 1.2 | 13.6 | 1.9 | 13.8 |
| | 2005 | 3 039 272 | 21.4 | 46.6 | 5.8 | 0.3 | 1.0 | 11.1 | 1.8 | 12.0 |
| | 2006 | 3 398 804 | 21.3 | 45.9 | 6.7 | 0.3 | 1.0 | 10.9 | 1.7 | 12.2 |
| Chile<br>Chili | 2004 | 55 341 067 | 4.5 | 13.5 | 16.8 | 2.9 | 6.6 | 9.6 | 9.7 | 36.3 |
| | 2005 | 62 871 862 | 4.4 | 16.8 | 15.7 | 3.0 | 6.9 | 9.3 | 8.9 | 35.0 |
| | 2006 | 73 065 553 | 4.1 | 24.4 | 13.5 | 3.0 | 6.8 | 8.3 | 7.9 | 32.0 |
| China[13]<br>Chine[13] | 2004 | 15 987 830[14] | 13.4 | 4.8 | 32.4 | 3.6 | 5.4 | 9.5 | 5.8 | 25.2 |
| | 2005 | 18 386 790[14] | 12.5 | 5.6 | 32.7 | 3.7 | 5.5 | 7.4 | 5.9 | 9.5 |
| | 2006 | 21 087 100[14] | 11.7 | 43.3[10,11] | ... | ... | 5.6 | ... | 5.7 | ... |
| China, Hong Kong SAR<br>Chine, Hong Kong RAS | 2002 | 1 234 949 | 0.1[15] | 0.0 | 4.2 | 3.2 | 4.2 | 25.1[16] | 9.9 | 53.4[16] |
| | 2003 | 1 202 908 | 0.1[15] | 0.0 | 3.7 | 3.2 | 3.7 | 25.7[16] | 9.8 | 53.8[16] |
| | 2004 | 1 245 621 | 0.1[15] | 0.0 | 3.6 | 3.2 | 3.2 | 27.0[16] | 10.1 | 52.8[16] |
| China, Macao SAR<br>Chine, Macao RAS | 2001 | 42 509 | ... | 0.0 | 7.9 | 3.0 | 2.2 | 11.2 | 6.5 | 69.3 |
| | 2002 | 45 989 | ... | 0.0 | 6.9 | 2.6 | 2.6 | 12.0 | 6.5 | 69.4 |
| | 2003 | 51 064 | ... | 0.0 | 6.1 | 2.6 | 3.9 | 11.5 | 5.3 | 70.6 |
| Colombia<br>Colombie | 2002 | 194 052 700 | 12.7 | 5.2 | 15.1 | 4.4 | 4.1 | 11.0 | 8.1 | 39.3 |
| | 2003 | 217 878 298 | 12.3 | 6.2 | 15.5 | 4.6 | 4.6 | 10.8 | 7.9 | 38.2 |
| | 2004 | 245 368 414 | 11.7 | 6.4 | 15.9 | 4.5 | 5.5 | 10.7 | 8.1 | 37.2 |
| Comoros[1]<br>Comores[1] | 1989 | 64 731 | 40.0 | ... | 3.9 | 0.8 | 3.4 | 25.1 | 3.9 | 22.8 |
| | 1990 | 67 992 | 40.4 | ... | 4.1 | 0.9 | 3.1 | 25.1 | 4.1 | 22.3 |
| | 1991 | 71 113 | 40.8 | ... | 4.2 | 0.9 | 2.7 | 25.1 | 4.2 | 22.1 |
| Congo[1]<br>Congo[1] | 1987 | 678 106 | 12.2 | 22.9 | 8.8 | 1.6 | 3.2 | 15.1 | 10.5 | 25.8 |
| | 1988 | 643 830 | 14.2 | 17.1 | 8.8 | 2.0 | 2.7 | 16.7 | 11.3 | 27.2 |
| | 1989 | 757 088 | 13.3 | 28.6 | 7.2 | 1.9 | 1.8 | 14.7 | 9.3 | 23.3 |
| Cook Islands[1]<br>Iles Cook[1] | 2003 | 252 | 14.9 | ... | 3.4 | 1.5 | 3.5 | 36.7 | 13.1 | 26.8 |
| | 2004 | 264 | 13.3 | ... | 3.5 | 1.6 | 4.4 | 37.7 | 13.2 | 26.8 |
| | 2005 | 266 | 12.5 | ... | 3.6 | 1.8 | 2.9 | 39.6 | 13.4 | 26.2 |

| Country or area<br>Pays ou zone | Year<br>Année | Value<br>added, gross<br>(mil. nat.cur)<br>Valeur<br>ajoutée, brute<br>(mil. mon. nat.) | Agriculture,<br>hunting,<br>forestry<br>and fishing<br>Agriculture,<br>chasse,<br>sylviculture<br>et pêche | Mining and<br>quarrying<br>Activités<br>extractives | Manufac-<br>turing<br>Activités<br>de fabri-<br>cation | Electric-<br>ity, gas<br>and water<br>supply<br>Electricité,<br>gaz et eau | Construc-<br>tion<br>Construc-<br>tion | Wholesale,<br>retail trade,<br>restaurants<br>and hotels<br>Commerce,<br>restaurants,<br>hôtels | Transport,<br>storage &<br>communi-<br>cation<br>Transports,<br>entrepôts,<br>communi-<br>cations | Other<br>activities<br>Autres<br>activités |
|---|---|---|---|---|---|---|---|---|---|---|
| Costa Rica | 2004 | 7 698 497[5] | 8.3 | 0.1 | 20.8 | 2.8 | 4.5 | 18.6 | 9.2 | 35.6 |
| Costa Rica | 2005 | 9 028 446[5] | 8.3 | 0.2 | 20.8 | 2.6 | 4.3 | 18.9 | 9.3 | 35.6 |
| | 2006 | 10 710 435[5] | 8.3 | 0.2 | 21.1 | 2.6 | 4.7 | 18.8 | 9.1 | 35.2 |
| Côte d'Ivoire[1] | 1998 | 6 984 000 | 25.6 | 0.6 | 21.9 | 1.6 | 2.3 | 20.4 | 6.0 | 21.3 |
| Côte d'Ivoire[1] | 1999 | 7 449 000 | 23.2 | 0.3 | 22.2 | 2.0 | 3.5 | 21.9 | 5.7 | 21.1 |
| | 2000 | 7 323 000 | 24.8 | 0.3 | 22.4 | 1.6 | 2.9 | 19.0 | 5.5 | 23.2 |
| Croatia | 2002 | 153 277 | 8.7 | 0.7 | 19.2 | 3.0 | 5.3 | 16.5 | 9.8 | 36.8 |
| Croatie | 2003 | 169 338 | 7.0 | 0.7 | 19.2 | 2.9 | 6.3 | 17.5 | 9.6 | 36.8 |
| | 2004 | 185 805 | 7.5 | 0.8 | 19.3 | 3.2 | 6.6 | 16.1 | 10.0 | 36.4 |
| Cuba | 2003 | 32 162[17] | 6.9 | 1.8 | 10.4 | 1.7 | 5.5 | 14.1 | 9.8 | 48.7 |
| Cuba | 2004 | 34 559[17] | 6.5 | 1.6 | 10.1 | 1.5 | 5.8 | 13.5 | 9.6 | 50.3 |
| | 2005 | 38 936[17] | 5.2 | 1.4 | 8.9 | 1.4 | 6.1 | 12.2 | 9.3 | 54.3 |
| Cyprus | 2004 | 6 664 | 3.0 | 0.4 | 9.2 | 2.2 | 8.0 | 20.1 | 8.2 | 49.0 |
| Chypre | 2005 | 7 068 | 2.9 | 0.4 | 9.0 | 2.2 | 8.3 | 19.6 | 8.2 | 49.5 |
| | 2006 | 7 475 | 2.8 | 0.3 | 8.6 | 2.3 | 8.4 | 19.7 | 7.9 | 50.0 |
| Czech Republic | 2003 | 2 343 055 | 3.1 | 1.1 | 24.7 | 3.7 | 6.4 | 15.1 | 11.7 | 34.3 |
| République tchèque | 2004 | 2 495 976 | 3.3 | 1.4 | 25.6 | 3.8 | 6.5 | 14.4 | 10.8 | 34.0 |
| | 2005 | 2 662 204 | 2.9 | 1.5 | 25.9 | 4.2 | 6.6 | 14.4 | 10.3 | 34.1 |
| Denmark | 2003 | 1 201 067 | 2.0 | 2.5 | 15.0 | 2.1 | 5.3 | 13.6 | 8.4 | 51.1 |
| Danemark | 2004 | 1 246 521 | 1.9 | 3.0 | 14.5 | 2.0 | 5.5 | 13.3 | 8.5 | 51.5 |
| | 2005 | 1 315 362 | 1.5 | 3.9 | 14.2 | 1.9 | 5.6 | 12.8 | 9.2 | 51.0 |
| Djibouti[1] | 1996 | 76 435 | 3.5[18] | 0.2 | 2.8 | 6.8[19] | 5.7 | 15.9 | 21.7 | 43.4 |
| Djibouti[1] | 1997 | 75 964 | 3.6[18] | 0.2 | 2.8 | 6.6[19] | 6.0 | 16.1 | 23.1 | 41.6 |
| | 1998 | 78 263 | 3.6[18] | 0.2 | 2.7 | 5.3[19] | 6.4 | 16.4 | 26.0 | 39.4 |
| Dominica[1] | 2003 | 581[3,8] | 18.3 | 0.8 | 8.0 | 6.3 | 7.9 | 15.2 | 12.9 | 38.8 |
| Dominique[1] | 2004 | 611[3,8] | 18.7 | 0.9 | 8.3 | 6.4 | 8.3 | 15.6 | 13.4 | 37.0 |
| | 2005 | 644[3,8] | 18.5 | 0.9 | 8.1 | 6.4 | 8.4 | 16.4 | 12.9 | 36.8 |
| Dominican Republic | 1994 | 165 808 | 10.8 | 1.1 | 20.2 | 1.4 | 7.7 | 16.4 | 9.8 | 32.6 |
| Rép. dominicaine | 1995 | 193 436 | 10.1 | 1.3 | 19.6 | 1.7 | 7.7 | 17.3 | 9.0 | 33.3 |
| | 1996 | 228 022 | 8.9 | 1.0 | 19.3 | 1.8 | 7.3 | 20.4 | 8.8 | 32.5 |
| Ecuador | 2004 | 30 296[4] | 7.3 | 17.7[20] | 5.0 | 2.0 | 8.9 | 14.9 | 12.0 | 32.2 |
| Equateur | 2005 | 34 217[4] | 6.9 | 22.0[20] | 2.5 | 1.5 | 8.7 | 14.3 | 12.0 | 32.1 |
| | 2006 | 38 477[4] | 6.5 | 25.9[20] | 1.9 | 1.4 | 8.4 | ... | ... | 5.5 |
| Egypt+ | 2002 | 428 151 | 13.1 | 9.5 | 16.6 | 1.8 | 4.2 | 17.3 | 8.0 | 29.5 |
| Egypte+ | 2003 | 475 035 | 13.7 | 10.1 | 16.1 | 2.0 | 4.4 | 16.5 | 8.5 | 28.6 |
| | 2004 | 534 427 | 14.6 | 11.9 | 17.6 | 1.8 | 3.6 | 13.6 | 8.8 | 28.2 |
| El Salvador[1] | 2004 | 15 305[4,5] | 9.2 | 0.4 | 22.8 | 1.8 | 4.3 | 20.5 | 9.5 | 31.6[9] |
| El Salvador[1] | 2005 | 16 341[4,5] | 9.9 | 0.4 | 22.2 | 1.9 | 4.3 | 20.2 | 9.6 | 31.5[9] |
| | 2006 | 17 617[4,5] | 9.7 | 0.4 | 21.6 | 2.0 | 4.4 | 20.4 | 10.0 | 31.6[9] |
| Equatorial Guinea[1] | 1989 | 40 948 | 56.1 | ... | 1.3 | 3.1 | 3.7 | 8.8 | 2.0 | 25.0 |
| Guinée équatoriale[1] | 1990 | 42 765 | 53.6 | ... | 1.3 | 3.4 | 3.8 | 7.6 | 2.2 | 28.0 |
| | 1991 | 43 932 | 53.1 | ... | 1.4 | 3.1 | 3.0 | 7.6 | 1.9 | 30.0 |
| Estonia | 2003 | 118 339 | 3.7 | 1.1 | 17.7 | 3.6 | 6.2 | 15.7 | 12.8 | 39.3 |
| Estonie | 2004 | 130 602 | 3.8 | 1.1 | 17.1 | 3.5 | 6.5 | 16.0 | 12.3 | 39.7 |
| | 2005 | 152 153 | 3.7 | 1.0 | 16.8 | 3.4 | 7.3 | 16.9 | 12.1 | 38.8 |
| Ethiopia+ | 2004 | 74 949[5] | 43.0 | 0.7 | 5.6 | 2.3 | 5.5 | 14.5 | 5.9 | 22.3 |
| Ethiopie+ | 2005 | 90 813[5] | 46.5 | 0.6 | 5.1 | 2.0 | 5.4 | 13.7 | 5.9 | 20.7 |
| | 2006 | 107 202[5] | 47.5 | 0.5 | 4.6 | 1.8 | 5.5 | 14.0 | 5.9 | 20.2 |

**Value added by industries at current prices**— Percentage distribution (*continued*)

**Valeur ajoutée par branche d'activité aux prix courants**— Répartition en pourcentage (*suite*)

| Country or area<br>Pays ou zone | Year<br>Année | Value added, gross (mil. nat.cur)<br>Valeur ajoutée, brute (mil. mon. nat.) | % of Value added – % de la valeur ajoutée | | | | | | | |
|---|---|---|---|---|---|---|---|---|---|---|
| | | | Agriculture, hunting, forestry and fishing<br>Agriculture, chasse, sylviculture et pêche | Mining and quarrying<br>Activités extractives | Manufac-turing<br>Activités de fabri-cation | Electric-ity, gas and water supply<br>Electricité, gaz et eau | Construc-tion<br>Construc-tion | Wholesale, retail trade, restaurants and hotels<br>Commerce, restaurants, hôtels | Transport, storage & communi-cation<br>Transports, entrepôts, communi-cations | Other activities<br>Autres activités |
| Fiji<br>Fidji | 2003 | 3 684 | 14.8 | ... | ... | ... | 4.3 | 17.0 | 17.4 | ... |
| | 2004 | 3 991 | ... | ... | ... | ... | ... | 19.8 | 15.7 | ... |
| | 2005 | 4 297 | 14.3 | 0.8 | 13.1 | 2.6 | 5.3 | 20.0 | 17.3 | 18.8 |
| Finland<br>Finlande | 2003 | 126 585 | 3.2 | 0.3 | 24.1 | 2.3 | 5.3 | 11.8 | 11.0 | 42.0 |
| | 2004 | 132 621 | 3.0 | 0.3 | 23.5 | 2.3 | 5.4 | 12.0 | 10.8 | 42.6 |
| | 2005 | 136 381 | 2.9 | 0.3 | 23.1 | 2.1 | 5.9 | 12.2 | 10.4 | 43.1 |
| France<br>France | 2004 | 1 490 230 | 2.5 | 0.1 | 13.6 | 1.7 | 5.5 | 13.1 | 6.5 | 57.1 |
| | 2005 | 1 539 607 | 2.3 | 0.1 | 13.0 | 1.8 | 5.8 | 12.8 | 6.4 | 57.8 |
| | 2006 | 1 600 030 | 2.0 | 0.1 | 12.4 | 1.9 | 6.3 | 12.3 | 6.3 | 58.6 |
| French Guiana[1]<br>Guyane française[1] | 1990 | 6 454 | 10.1 | 7.6 | ... | 0.7 | 12.8 | 13.5 | 7.7 | 47.5 |
| | 1991 | 7 385 | 7.4 | 7.6 | ... | 0.5 | 12.1 | 13.1 | 12.3 | 47.0 |
| | 1992 | 8 052 | 7.2 | 9.0 | ... | 0.6 | 10.8 | 11.9 | 11.4 | 49.1 |
| French Polynesia[1]<br>Polynésie française[1] | 1991 | 305 211 | 4.1 | ... | 7.5[21] | 1.8[21] | 5.7 | ... | ... | 29.3 |
| | 1992 | 314 265 | 3.8 | ... | 7.5[21] | 2.1[21] | 5.9 | ... | ... | 29.5 |
| | 1993 | 329 266 | 3.9 | ... | 6.7[21] | 2.1[21] | 5.7 | ... | ... | 29.0 |
| Gabon[1]<br>Gabon[1] | 1987 | 986 000 | 10.9 | 28.4 | 7.1[22] | 2.7 | 7.2 | 9.2 | 8.1 | 26.5 |
| | 1988 | 965 700 | 11.2 | 22.6 | 7.3[22] | 3.0 | 5.2 | 14.4 | 9.1 | 27.3 |
| | 1989 | 1 128 400 | 10.4 | 32.3 | 5.7[22] | 2.5 | 5.5 | 12.4 | 8.2 | 23.1 |
| Gambia+[1]<br>Gambie+[1] | 1991 | 2 962 | 22.3 | 0.0 | 5.5 | 0.9 | 4.4 | 39.1 | 10.9 | 17.0 |
| | 1992 | 3 100 | 18.4 | 0.0 | 5.7 | 1.0 | 4.7 | 41.7 | 11.2 | 17.4 |
| | 1993 | 3 296 | 20.2 | 0.0 | 5.1 | 1.0 | 4.5 | 38.3 | 12.5 | 18.4 |
| Georgia<br>Géorgie | 2004 | 9 064 | 17.8 | 0.8 | 13.2 | 3.4 | 8.8 | 16.7 | 14.5 | 24.8 |
| | 2005 | 10 414 | 16.5 | 0.9 | 13.5 | 3.1 | 9.0 | 16.5 | 13.9 | 26.6 |
| | 2006 | 12 167 | 12.8 | 1.2 | 12.6 | 3.1 | 7.8 | 17.9 | 13.0 | 31.6 |
| Germany<br>Allemagne | 2003 | 1 947 110 | 1.1 | 0.2 | 22.3 | 1.9 | 4.4 | 12.0 | 5.7 | 52.4 |
| | 2004 | 1 994 210 | 1.2 | 0.2 | 22.6 | 2.0 | 4.1 | 12.1 | 5.8 | 52.0 |
| | 2005 | 2 022 470 | 1.0 | 0.2 | 23.2 | 2.0 | 3.9 | 12.2 | 5.9 | 51.6 |
| Ghana[1]<br>Ghana[1] | 1994 | 4 686 000 | 42.0 | 6.3 | 10.1 | 3.0 | 8.3 | 6.4 | 4.8 | 18.2 |
| | 1995 | 7 040 200 | 42.7 | 5.3 | 10.3 | 2.9 | 8.3 | 6.5 | 4.3 | 18.8 |
| | 1996 | 10 067 000 | 43.9 | 5.3 | 9.7 | 3.0 | 8.5 | 6.5 | 4.2 | 17.9 |
| Greece<br>Grèce | 2003 | 177 949 | 5.1 | 0.5 | 9.7 | 2.4 | 9.1 | 22.3 | 7.6 | 43.4 |
| | 2004 | 193 286 | 4.4 | 0.4 | 9.0 | 2.3 | 8.7 | 22.9 | 8.8 | 43.6 |
| | 2005 | 207 751 | 4.0 | 0.3 | 9.5 | 2.2 | 7.3 | 23.8 | 8.3 | 44.4 |
| Grenada[1]<br>Grenade[1] | 2004 | 1 029[4] | 7.9 | 0.6 | 5.2 | 5.7 | 10.2 | 16.0 | 19.7 | 34.8 |
| | 2005 | 1 193[4] | 4.8 | 0.6 | 5.5 | 5.2 | 19.6 | 13.6 | 21.1 | 29.6 |
| | 2006 | 1 299[4] | 4.9 | 0.5 | 5.4 | 5.3 | 19.8 | 14.1 | 21.4 | 28.5 |
| Guadeloupe[1]<br>Guadeloupe[1] | 1990 | 15 036 | 6.7 | 5.4[10] | ... | 1.0 | 7.4 | 18.3 | 5.9 | 55.2 |
| | 1991 | 16 278 | 7.3 | 6.1[10] | ... | 1.4 | 7.0 | 16.5 | 6.0 | 55.5 |
| | 1992 | 17 968 | 6.7 | 6.9[10] | ... | 1.7 | 6.5 | 16.2 | 7.9 | 54.1 |
| Guinea-Bissau[1]<br>Guinée-Bissau[1] | 1989 | 358 875 | 44.6 | 7.9[10,11] | ... | ... | 9.7 | 25.7 | 3.6 | 8.5 |
| | 1990 | 510 094 | 44.6 | 8.2[10,11] | ... | ... | 10.0 | 25.7 | 3.7 | 7.8 |
| | 1991 | 854 985 | 44.7 | 8.5[10,11] | ... | ... | 8.4 | 25.8 | 3.9 | 8.7 |
| Guyana[1]<br>Guyana[1] | 2004 | 130 533[3] | 37.8 | 12.1 | 3.1[11] | ... | 5.2[25] | 4.1[2] | 9.7 | 27.9[2] |
| | 2005 | 137 788[3] | 34.7 | 10.2 | 3.7[11] | ... | 6.1[25] | 5.1[2] | 11.0 | 29.2[2] |
| | 2006 | 151 198[3] | 34.9 | 9.3 | 3.6[11] | ... | 6.4[25] | 5.3[2] | 11.4 | 29.0[2] |
| Honduras[1]<br>Honduras[1] | 2004 | 121 249[3] | 13.4 | 1.7 | 20.4 | 4.8 | 4.5 | 12.5 | 6.0 | 36.6 |
| | 2005 | 140 241[3] | 13.9 | 1.7 | 20.1 | 5.1 | 4.4 | 12.3 | 6.0 | 36.4 |
| | 2006 | 157 961[3] | 13.8 | 1.8 | 19.7 | 5.2 | 4.4 | 12.2 | 6.1 | 36.7 |

**Value added by industries at current prices** — Percentage distribution (*continued*)
**Valeur ajoutée par branche d'activité aux prix courants** — Répartition en pourcentage (*suite*)

| Country or area / Pays ou zone | Year / Année | Value added, gross (mil. nat.cur) / Valeur ajoutée, brute (mil. mon. nat.) | Agriculture, hunting, forestry and fishing / Agriculture, chasse, sylviculture et pêche | Mining and quarrying / Activités extractives | Manufacturing / Activités de fabrication | Electricity, gas and water supply / Electricité, gaz et eau | Construction / Construction | Wholesale, retail trade, restaurants and hotels / Commerce, restaurants, hôtels | Transport, storage & communication / Transports, entrepôts, communications | Other activities / Autres activités |
|---|---|---|---|---|---|---|---|---|---|---|
| Hungary | 2003 | 16 235 556 | 4.3 | 0.2 | 22.0 | 2.9 | 4.8 | 13.1 | 7.8 | 44.9 |
| Hongrie | 2004 | 17 654 438 | 4.8 | 0.2 | 22.1 | 3.1 | 4.9 | 12.8 | 7.9 | 44.2 |
|  | 2005 | 18 891 603 | 4.3 | 0.2 | 22.2 | 2.9 | 4.9 | 12.7 | 7.7 | 45.1 |
| Iceland | 2003 | 716 948[3] | 7.5 | 0.1 | 13.3 | 3.5 | 7.6 | 11.4 | 8.0 | 49.2 |
| Islande | 2004 | 781 200[3] | 6.5 | 0.1 | 12.7 | 3.6 | 8.5 | 12.2 | 7.6 | 49.3 |
|  | 2005 | 852 669[3] | 5.8 | 0.1 | 10.1 | 4.0 | 9.5 | 12.3 | 6.2 | 52.7 |
| India+[1] | 2003 | 25 494 175[3] | 20.9 | 2.5 | 15.2 | 2.2 | 6.2 | 15.7 | 8.3 | 29.0 |
| Inde+[1] | 2004 | 28 559 328[3] | 18.8 | 3.0 | 15.9 | 2.1 | 6.5 | 16.3 | 8.8 | 28.7 |
|  | 2005 | 32 509 319[3] | 18.3 | 2.8 | 16.0 | 2.0 | 6.8 | 16.6 | 8.8 | 28.7 |
| Indonesia | 2003 | 2 013 674 600[14] | 15.2 | 8.3 | 28.3 | 1.0 | 6.2 | 16.6[2] | 5.9 | 23.6[2] |
| Indonésie | 2004 | 2 273 141 500[14] | 14.6 | 8.6 | 28.1 | 1.0 | 6.3 | 16.2[2] | 6.3 | 24.2[2] |
|  | 2005 | 2 729 708 200[14] | 13.4 | 10.4 | 28.1 | 0.9 | 6.4 | 15.8[2] | 6.6 | 23.4[2] |
| Iran (Islamic Rep.of)+ | 2003 | 1 103 857 800 | 11.7 | 23.1[26] | 11.2 | 1.4 | 4.2 | 11.8 | 7.5 | 28.9 |
| Iran (République | 2004 | 1 387 903 500 | 11.0 | 25.3[26] | 11.2 | 1.4 | 4.0 | 11.5 | 7.0 | 28.7 |
| islamique d')+ | 2005 | 1 718 477 700 | 9.9 | 27.7[26] | 10.5 | 1.2 | 3.6 | 10.8 | 6.7 | 29.5 |
| Iraq[1] | 2003 | 29 894 476[3,5] | 8.3 | 68.1 | 1.0 | 0.2 | 0.7 | 6.5 | 7.6 | 7.4 |
| Iraq[1] | 2004 | 48 206 525[3,5] | 7.3 | 63.4 | 1.6 | 0.5 | 1.0 | 6.7 | 7.6 | 11.9 |
|  | 2005 | 64 227 556[3,5] | 6.6 | 61.3 | 1.9 | 0.6 | 4.6 | 6.6 | 7.6 | 10.7 |
| Ireland | 2003 | 124 287 | 2.5 | 0.5 | 28.5 | 1.1 | 8.4 | 12.2 | 5.7 | 41.0 |
| Irlande | 2004 | 131 045 | 2.5 | 0.4 | 26.5 | 1.1 | 8.9 | 12.4 | 5.6 | 42.7 |
|  | 2005 | 142 229 | 2.1 | 0.3 | 24.5 | 1.2 | 10.0 | 11.9 | 5.3 | 44.7 |
| Israel | 2003 | 469 332 | 1.8 | ... | 15.0[6] | 2.2 | 5.3 | 9.8 | 7.4 | 58.4 |
| Israël | 2004 | 497 266 | 1.9 | ... | 15.1[6] | 2.2 | 4.9 | 10.3 | 7.1 | 58.5 |
|  | 2005 | 525 341 | 1.9 | ... | 14.6[6] | 2.4 | 4.9 | 10.6 | 7.2 | 58.4 |
| Italy | 2004 | 1 251 033 | 2.5 | 0.4 | 18.8 | 2.0 | 5.8 | 15.7 | 7.7 | 47.1 |
| Italie | 2005 | 1 277 992 | 2.2 | 0.4 | 18.2 | 2.0 | 6.0 | 15.6 | 7.7 | 47.9 |
|  | 2006 | 1 316 584 | 2.1 | 0.4 | 18.1 | 2.0 | 6.1 | 15.4 | 7.7 | 48.3 |
| Jamaica[1] | 2003 | 462 941[4] | 5.2 | 4.4 | 12.8 | 3.4 | 9.5 | 24.3[27] | 12.2 | 28.2 |
| Jamaïque[1] | 2004 | 523 844[4] | 5.3 | 4.3 | 13.1 | 3.5 | 10.2 | 24.9[27] | 11.8 | 26.8 |
|  | 2005 | 586 379[4] | 5.4 | 4.1 | 13.0 | 4.1 | 10.4 | 25.3[27] | 11.6 | 26.1 |
| Japan | 2003 | 511 935 300[28] | 1.6 | 0.1 | 20.1 | 2.5 | 6.3 | 12.9[2] | 6.7 | 49.7[2] |
| Japon | 2004 | 516 981 300[28] | 1.6 | 0.1 | 20.4 | 2.5 | 6.4 | 13.1[2] | 6.6 | 49.4[2] |
|  | 2005 | 520 829 800[28] | 1.4 | 0.1 | 20.2 | 2.3 | 6.1 | 13.3[2] | 6.6 | 50.0[2] |
| Jordan[1] | 2002 | 6 049[5] | 2.5 | 3.1 | 15.7 | 2.6 | 4.2 | 11.1 | 15.5 | 45.4 |
| Jordanie[1] | 2003 | 6 507[5] | 2.7 | 3.0 | 16.0 | 2.5 | 4.1 | 10.6 | 15.6 | 45.4 |
|  | 2004 | 7 405[5] | 2.7 | 3.1 | 17.0 | 2.6 | 4.4 | 10.8 | 15.9 | 43.5 |
| Kazakhstan | 2003 | 4 370 285 | 8.3 | 12.8 | 15.0 | 2.9 | 6.3 | 13.2 | 13.1 | 28.4 |
| Kazakhstan | 2004 | 5 626 811 | 7.4 | 14.2 | 13.9 | 2.5 | 6.3 | 13.9 | 12.3 | 29.5 |
|  | 2005 | 7 288 444 | 6.6 | 16.4 | 12.5 | 2.0 | 8.2 | 13.3 | 12.3 | 28.6 |
| Kenya | 2003 | 1 022 737[5] | 28.7 | 0.6 | 10.8 | 2.3 | 3.7 | 11.2 | 10.2 | 32.6 |
| Kenya | 2004 | 1 151 851[5] | 27.6 | 0.6 | 11.1 | 2.2 | 4.0 | 12.4 | 11.0 | 31.1 |
|  | 2005 | 1 302 639[5] | 26.8 | 0.6 | 11.4 | 2.1 | 4.3 | 13.3 | 11.9 | 29.7 |
| Kiribati[1] | 2004 | 76 | 10.6 | ... | 0.8 | 1.5 | 4.4 | 9.5 | 11.7 | 61.4 |
| Kiribati[1] | 2005 | 76 | 6.8 | ... | 0.8 | 0.4 | 5.3 | 9.5 | 11.7 | 65.4 |
|  | 2006 | 77 | 7.0 | ... | 0.8 | 0.5 | 5.2 | 9.3 | 11.4 | 65.9 |
| Korea, Republic of | 2004 | 694 317 500 | 3.8 | 0.3 | 28.6 | 2.4 | 9.3 | 9.8 | 7.3 | 38.4 |
| Corée, République de | 2005 | 721 474 200 | 3.4 | 0.4 | 28.4 | 2.3 | 9.2 | 9.8 | 7.3 | 39.3 |
|  | 2006 | 753 801 800 | 3.2 | 0.4 | 27.8 | 2.3 | 9.1 | 9.8 | 7.2 | 40.2 |

| Country or area<br>Pays ou zone | Year<br>Année | Value added, gross (mil. nat.cur)<br>Valeur ajoutée, brute (mil. mon. nat.) | % of Value added – % de la valeur ajoutée | | | | | | | |
|---|---|---|---|---|---|---|---|---|---|---|
| | | | Agriculture, hunting, forestry and fishing<br>Agriculture, chasse, sylviculture et pêche | Mining and quarrying<br>Activités extractives | Manufac-turing<br>Activités de fabri-cation | Electric-ity, gas and water supply<br>Electricité, gaz et eau | Construc-tion<br>Construc-tion | Wholesale, retail trade, restaurants and hotels<br>Commerce, restaurants, hôtels | Transport, storage & communi-cation<br>Transports, entrepôts, communi-cations | Other activities<br>Autres activités |
| Kosovo<br>Kosovo | 2002 | 2 193 | 8.6 | 16.4[10,11] | ... | ... | 9.5 | 12.1 | 4.1 | 49.4 |
| | 2003 | 2 067 | 9.0 | 15.6[10,11] | ... | ... | 10.7 | 12.6 | 4.2 | 47.9 |
| | 2004 | 2 076 | 8.6 | 15.1[10,11] | ... | ... | 12.0 | 13.5 | 4.8 | 46.1 |
| Kuwait[1]<br>Koweït[1] | 2003 | 14 731[4,5] | 0.4 | 39.5 | 7.7 | 2.0 | 2.4 | 7.2 | 5.4 | 35.4 |
| | 2004 | 18 028[4,5] | 0.4 | 43.5 | 8.1 | 1.7 | 2.2 | 6.1 | 5.8 | 32.2 |
| | 2005 | 24 251[4,5] | 0.3 | 53.0 | 7.2 | 1.3 | 1.9 | 4.8 | 5.3 | 26.2 |
| Kyrgyzstan<br>Kirghizistan | 2004 | 86 043 | 32.8 | 0.7 | 16.8 | 3.6 | 2.7 | 19.2 | 7.0 | 17.2 |
| | 2005 | 91 698 | 31.3 | 0.6 | 14.1 | 4.2 | 3.0 | 21.1 | 7.2 | 18.4 |
| | 2006 | 99 313 | 33.0 | 0.6 | 12.9 | 3.5 | 3.1 | 23.7 | 7.1 | 16.1 |
| Lao People's Dem. Republic[1]<br>Rép. dém. pop. lao[1] | 1999 | 10 253 626 | 53.7 | 0.5 | 17.0 | 2.4 | 2.7 | 11.8 | 5.8 | 6.1 |
| | 2000 | 13 565 564 | 52.5 | 0.5 | 17.0 | 3.1 | 2.3 | 11.7 | 5.9 | 7.0 |
| | 2001 | 15 563 971 | 51.2 | 0.5 | 17.9 | 2.9 | 2.4 | 11.8 | 6.0 | 7.3 |
| Latvia<br>Lettonie | 2004 | 6 662 | 4.4 | 0.3 | 13.2 | 3.0 | 5.8 | 20.5 | 14.8 | 38.0 |
| | 2005 | 8 029 | 4.0 | 0.3 | 12.6 | 2.5 | 6.1 | 21.6 | 13.9 | 38.9 |
| | 2006 | 9 931 | 3.7 | 0.3 | 11.8 | 2.5 | 6.8 | 22.4 | 13.0 | 39.4 |
| Lebanon<br>Liban | 2002 | 28 209 000[14] | 5.8 | ... | 11.5 | 0.9 | 7.6 | 21.6[29,30] | 7.0 | 45.6[29] |
| | 2003 | 29 851 000[14] | 5.5 | ... | 11.8 | 0.6 | 7.4 | 22.4[29,30] | 7.0 | 45.3[29] |
| | 2004 | 32 357 000[14] | 5.2 | ... | 11.7 | 0.3 | 7.4 | 24.0[29,30] | 7.4 | 44.0[29] |
| Lesotho<br>Lesotho | 2003 | 7 413[3,5] | 16.4 | 0.2 | 19.2 | 4.7 | 15.0 | 12.4 | 4.6 | 27.5 |
| | 2004 | 7 770[3,5] | 16.4 | 2.2 | 17.8 | 4.8 | 14.2 | 12.5 | 4.5 | 27.5 |
| | 2005 | 8 551[3,5] | 15.8 | 5.0 | 15.3 | 6.5 | 13.9 | 11.5 | 4.8 | 27.2 |
| Liberia[1]<br>Libéria[1] | 1987 | 1 009 | 37.8 | 10.4 | 7.2 | 1.9 | 3.2 | 6.0 | 7.5 | 26.0 |
| | 1988 | 1 080 | 38.2 | 10.7 | 7.4 | 1.7 | 2.7 | 5.9 | 7.3 | 26.1 |
| | 1989 | 1 119 | 36.7 | 10.9 | 7.3 | 1.7 | 2.4 | 5.7 | 7.1 | 28.3 |
| Libyan Arab Jamah.[1]<br>Jamah. arabe libyenne[1] | 1983 | 8 482 | 3.0 | 48.8 | 3.2 | 0.9 | 10.4 | 6.1 | 4.6 | 23.0 |
| | 1984 | 7 681 | 3.4 | 40.9 | 3.9 | 1.2 | 11.1 | 7.9 | 5.3 | 26.4 |
| | 1985 | 8 050 | 3.5 | 41.6 | 4.5 | 1.3 | 11.4 | 7.0 | 5.0 | 25.8 |
| Lithuania<br>Lituanie | 2003 | 50 826 | 6.4 | 0.6 | 19.3 | 4.7 | 7.1 | 19.0 | 13.4 | 29.5 |
| | 2004 | 56 571 | 5.8 | 0.5 | 20.9 | 4.4 | 7.3 | 19.0 | 12.7 | 29.3 |
| | 2005 | 64 312 | 5.7 | 0.5 | 22.1 | 4.1 | 7.6 | 19.0 | 12.5 | 28.5 |
| Luxembourg<br>Luxembourg | 2003 | 23 001 | 0.6 | 0.1 | 9.7 | 1.4 | 6.5 | 11.9 | 9.9 | 59.9 |
| | 2004 | 24 036 | 0.5 | 0.1 | 9.4 | 1.4 | 6.3 | 11.8 | 10.6 | 59.9 |
| | 2005 | 26 321 | 0.4 | 0.1 | 8.8 | 1.4 | 5.8 | 11.4 | 10.3 | 61.6 |
| Madagascar[1]<br>Madagascar[1] | 1983 | 1 187 400 | 44.2 | 15.6 | ... | ... | ... | 30.4 | ... | 9.7 |
| | 1984 | 1 323 100 | 43.9 | 16.2 | ... | ... | ... | 30.3 | ... | 9.7 |
| | 1985 | 1 500 600 | 43.5 | 16.9 | ... | ... | ... | 30.1 | ... | 9.5 |
| Malawi<br>Malawi | 2002 | 203 101[5] | 35.1 | 0.8 | 10.0 | 1.7 | 4.3 | 15.6 | 6.0 | 26.4 |
| | 2003 | 232 520[5] | 33.9 | 1.2 | 11.1 | 1.6 | 4.3 | 14.3 | 6.1 | 27.4 |
| | 2004 | 273 761[5] | 33.5 | 1.2 | 9.6 | 1.8 | 4.1 | 16.0 | 5.7 | 28.1 |
| Malaysia[1]<br>Malaisie[1] | 1997 | 292 837 | 10.7 | 6.6 | 27.3 | 2.6 | 6.3 | 14.2 | 6.4 | 25.8 |
| | 1998 | 300 687 | 12.5 | 6.3 | 27.1 | 3.1 | 4.8 | 14.4 | 6.5 | 25.3 |
| | 1999 | 316 357 | 10.3 | 7.3 | 29.4 | 3.0 | 4.4 | 14.0 | 6.4 | 25.1 |
| Mali[1]<br>Mali[1] | 2004 | 2 384 823 | 37.8 | 6.8 | 10.4 | 1.8 | 4.9 | 13.6 | 4.8 | 20.0 |
| | 2005 | 2 673 523 | 37.5 | 7.7 | 9.8 | 1.9 | 4.7 | 13.6 | 4.9 | 20.0 |
| | 2006 | 2 912 731 | 36.5 | 8.3 | 8.9 | 2.1 | 5.0 | 14.4 | 5.3 | 19.5 |
| Malta<br>Malte | 2003 | 1 635 | 2.6 | 0.3 | 19.2 | 1.5 | 4.5 | 19.3 | 9.5 | 43.1 |
| | 2004 | 1 611 | 2.5 | 0.3 | 17.5 | 1.2 | 4.6 | 19.5 | 10.0 | 44.3 |
| | 2005 | 1 666 | 2.5 | 0.4 | 17.2 | 0.7 | 4.9 | 18.9 | 10.2 | 45.4 |

| Country or area<br>Pays ou zone | Year<br>Année | Value added, gross<br>(mil. nat.cur)<br>Valeur ajoutée, brute<br>(mil. mon. nat.) | Agriculture, hunting, forestry and fishing<br>Agriculture, chasse, sylviculture et pêche | Mining and quarrying<br>Activités extractives | Manufac-turing<br>Activités de fabri-cation | Electric-ity, gas and water supply<br>Electricité, gaz et eau | Construc-tion<br>Construc-tion | Wholesale, retail trade, restaurants and hotels<br>Commerce, restaurants, hôtels | Transport, storage & communi-cation<br>Transports, entrepôts, communi-cations | Other activities<br>Autres activités |
|---|---|---|---|---|---|---|---|---|---|---|
| Marshall Islands[1]<br>Iles Marshall[1] | 1995 | 105 | 14.9 | 0.3 | 2.6 | 2.0 | 10.2 | 17.0 | 6.2 | 46.8 |
| | 1996 | 95 | 14.3 | 0.3 | 1.6 | 2.7 | 7.0 | 18.7 | 7.3 | 48.2 |
| | 1997 | 90 | 14.3 | 0.4 | 1.7 | 3.1 | 7.0 | 17.9 | 7.9 | 47.7 |
| Martinique[1]<br>Martinique[1] | 1990 | 18 835 | 5.7 | 7.9[10] | ... | 2.5 | 4.9 | 18.9 | 6.2 | 53.9 |
| | 1991 | 20 377 | 5.7 | 7.8[10] | ... | 2.4 | 5.3 | 18.9 | 6.3 | 53.6 |
| | 1992 | 21 869 | 5.1 | 8.1[10] | ... | 2.2 | 5.2 | 18.4 | 6.5 | 54.5 |
| Mauritania[1]<br>Mauritanie[1] | 1987 | 60 302[3] | 32.3 | 8.3 | 12.1 | ... | 6.3 | 13.0 | 5.1 | 22.8 |
| | 1988 | 65 069[3] | 32.4 | 7.7 | 13.0 | ... | 6.3 | 13.2 | 5.1 | 22.3 |
| | 1989 | 75 486[3] | 34.2 | 10.4 | 10.3 | ... | 6.4 | ... | 4.9 | 14.5 |
| Mauritius<br>Maurice | 2004 | 160 238[5] | 6.0 | 0.1 | 19.8 | 2.2 | 5.5 | 17.9 | 12.5 | 36.0 |
| | 2005 | 171 176[5] | 5.6 | 0.1 | 18.7 | 2.0 | 5.3 | 18.6 | 12.2 | 37.5 |
| | 2006 | 188 409[5] | 5.1 | 0.0 | 18.5 | 2.0 | 5.3 | 19.1 | 12.1 | 37.9 |
| Mexico<br>Mexique | 2002 | 5 819 424[5] | 3.8 | 1.3[31] | 18.4[31] | 1.4 | 5.0 | 19.7 | 10.5 | 39.8 |
| | 2003 | 6 320 583[5] | 3.8 | 1.3[31] | 17.8[31] | 1.3 | 5.2 | 20.1 | 10.2 | 40.4 |
| | 2004 | 7 042 434[5] | 3.8 | 1.4[31] | 17.8[31] | 1.3 | 5.4 | 20.6 | 10.3 | 39.3 |
| Moldova<br>Moldova | 2004 | 28 247 | 19.9 | 0.4 | 16.5 | 2.5 | 3.9 | 13.1 | 13.4 | 30.3 |
| | 2005 | 32 373 | 19.1 | 0.4 | 15.5 | 2.4 | 3.9 | 13.4 | 14.2 | 31.1 |
| | 2006 | 37 662 | 17.6 | 0.6 | 14.1 | 2.1 | 4.6 | 13.4 | 14.2 | 33.4 |
| Mongolia<br>Mongolie | 2003 | 1 316 697 | 22.3 | ... | ... | ... | 3.8 | ... | ... | 14.0 |
| | 2004 | 1 722 034 | 23.2 | ... | ... | ... | 3.0 | ... | ... | 12.7 |
| | 2005 | 2 257 339 | 21.7 | 27.3 | 4.5 | 3.6 | 2.7 | 12.2 | 13.4 | 14.6 |
| Montserrat[1]<br>Montserrat[1] | 1985 | 90[3] | 4.8 | 1.3 | 5.7 | 3.7 | 7.9 | 18.0 | 11.5 | 47.2 |
| | 1986 | 103[3] | 4.3 | 1.4 | 5.6 | 3.7 | 11.3 | 18.7 | 11.6 | 43.4 |
| | 1987 | 118[3] | 4.1 | 1.3 | 5.7 | 3.2 | 11.5 | 22.1 | 11.1 | 41.0 |
| Morocco<br>Maroc | 2003 | 447 235[5] | 16.5 | 1.7 | 16.4 | 3.1 | 5.5 | 14.0 | 7.0 | 35.8 |
| | 2004 | 470 429[5] | 15.7 | 1.6 | 15.8 | 3.0 | 6.1 | 13.9 | 7.3 | 36.6 |
| | 2005 | 492 905[5] | 12.7 | 1.8 | 16.4 | 3.3 | 6.2 | 14.1 | 7.4 | 38.1 |
| Mozambique<br>Mozambique | 2003 | 114 031 683 | 22.1 | 0.3 | 12.6 | 4.4 | 8.1 | 23.8 | 12.5 | 16.2 |
| | 2004 | 133 244 995 | 21.2 | 0.9 | 13.5 | 5.3 | 7.0 | 23.3 | 13.9 | 14.9 |
| | 2005 | 157 099 999 | 19.8 | 0.9 | 12.8 | 6.0 | 6.4 | 23.1 | 16.4 | 14.6 |
| Myanmar+[1]<br>Myanmar+[1] | 1996 | 791 980 | 60.1 | 0.6 | 7.1 | 0.3[32] | 2.4 | 22.6[2] | 3.5 | 3.4[2,33] |
| | 1997 | 1 109 554 | 59.4 | 0.6 | 7.1 | 0.1[32] | 2.4 | 23.2[2] | 3.9 | 3.1[2,33] |
| | 1998 | 1 559 996 | 59.1 | 0.5 | 7.2 | 0.1[32] | 2.4 | 23.9[2] | 4.0 | 2.7[2,33] |
| Namibia<br>Namibie | 2003 | 31 619 | 11.3 | 9.4 | 12.2 | 3.2 | 3.3 | 14.7 | 7.5 | 38.4 |
| | 2004 | 33 344 | 10.3 | 10.5 | 12.0 | 3.6 | 3.4 | 13.9 | 7.9 | 38.5 |
| | 2005 | 35 398 | 12.2 | 9.4 | 11.6 | 3.8 | 3.5 | 13.3 | 8.0 | 38.2 |
| Nepal+<br>Népal+ | 2004 | 548 485[8] | 36.3 | 0.5 | 8.2 | 2.3 | 6.7 | 16.2 | 9.4 | 23.7 |
| | 2005 | 603 673[8] | 35.0 | 0.5 | 7.9 | 2.2 | 6.8 | 16.5 | 10.7 | 23.7 |
| | 2006 | 670 589[8] | 34.1 | 0.5 | 7.7 | 2.0 | 6.6 | 15.8 | 12.1 | 24.2 |
| Netherlands<br>Pays-Bas | 2003 | 425 256 | 2.3 | 2.5 | 14.1 | 1.7 | 5.5 | 15.2 | 7.4 | 51.2 |
| | 2004 | 435 837 | 2.2 | 2.6 | 14.3 | 1.6 | 5.5 | 15.0 | 7.3 | 51.6 |
| | 2005 | 449 041 | 2.2 | 3.1 | 14.1 | 1.5 | 5.5 | 14.5 | 7.1 | 52.1 |
| Netherlands Antilles<br>Antilles néerlandaises | 2002 | 4 840 | 0.8 | ... | 6.2 | 4.3 | 5.4 | 17.2 | 10.6 | 55.6 |
| | 2003 | 5 018 | 0.7 | ... | 5.8 | 4.9 | 5.5 | 16.7 | 10.7 | 55.7 |
| | 2004 | 5 146 | 0.6 | ... | 5.8 | 5.0 | 5.3 | 16.8 | 10.3 | 56.1 |
| New Caledonia<br>Nouvelle-Calédonie | 2001 | 407 816[5] | 2.5 | ... | 10.9[6] | 2.0 | 9.3 | 13.2[2] | 7.2 | 54.7[2] |
| | 2002 | 435 713[5] | 2.0 | ... | 12.1[6] | 1.9 | 9.3 | 13.4[2] | 7.3 | 54.0[2] |
| | 2003 | 477 656[5] | 1.9 | ... | 14.3[6] | 1.7 | 9.3 | 13.0[2] | 7.4 | 52.3[2] |

| Country or area / Pays ou zone | Year / Année | Value added, gross (mil. nat.cur) / Valeur ajoutée, brute (mil. mon. nat.) | % of Value added – % de la valeur ajoutée | | | | | | | |
|---|---|---|---|---|---|---|---|---|---|---|
| | | | Agriculture, hunting, forestry and fishing / Agriculture, chasse, sylviculture et pêche | Mining and quarrying / Activités extractives | Manufac-turing / Activités de fabri-cation | Electric-ity, gas and water supply / Electricité, gaz et eau | Construc-tion / Construc-tion | Wholesale, retail-trade, restaurants and hotels / Commerce, restaurants, hôtels | Transport, storage & communi-cation / Transports, entrepôts, communi-cations | Other activities / Autres activités |
| New Zealand+ Nouvelle-Zélande+ | 2000 | 111 314[4,5] | 8.6 | 1.2 | 16.3 | 2.5 | 4.3 | 14.7 | 7.4 | 44.8 |
| | 2001 | 119 889[4,5] | 8.9 | 1.2 | 15.8 | 2.4 | 4.4 | 15.5 | 7.2 | 44.5 |
| | 2002 | 125 944[4,5] | 7.0 | 1.2 | 15.6 | 2.6 | 4.6 | 15.6 | 7.5 | 46.0 |
| Nicaragua+ Nicaragua+ | 2004 | 66 858[5] | 17.7 | 1.3 | 18.4 | 2.6 | 6.3 | 14.0 | 6.5 | 33.2 |
| | 2005 | 76 059[5] | 18.6 | 1.2 | 17.9 | 2.5 | 6.4 | 14.1 | 6.5 | 32.8 |
| | 2006 | 86 907[5] | 18.9 | 1.2 | 17.6 | 2.5 | 6.5 | 13.6 | 6.4 | 33.2 |
| Niger[1] Niger[1] | 2003 | 1 384 493[5] | 44.4 | 2.1 | 6.6 | 1.4 | 2.6 | 14.0 | 6.8 | 22.1 |
| | 2004 | 1 365 354[5] | 40.6 | 2.3 | 6.9 | 1.3 | 2.8 | 15.0 | 7.8 | 23.3 |
| | 2005 | 1 581 666[5] | 45.4 | 1.9 | 6.2 | 1.2 | 2.6 | 14.2 | 7.2 | 21.2 |
| Nigeria[1] Nigéria[1] | 2003 | 9 913 518 | 32.6 | 41.6 | 4.7 | 0.2 | 1.2 | 11.3 | 2.5 | 5.9 |
| | 2004 | 11 411 067 | 34.2 | 37.3 | 3.1 | 0.2 | 1.5 | 13.3 | 3.4 | 7.0 |
| | 2005 | 14 610 881 | 32.5 | 38.9 | 2.8 | 0.2 | 1.5 | 13.5 | 2.9 | 7.7 |
| Norway Norvège | 2004 | 1 542 833 | 1.6 | 22.6 | 10.3 | 2.4 | 4.6 | 9.9 | 8.1 | 40.6 |
| | 2005 | 1 729 417 | 1.6 | 26.3 | 9.6 | 2.5 | 4.5 | 9.4 | 7.5 | 38.5 |
| | 2006 | 1 915 238 | 1.6 | 28.1 | 9.4 | 2.8 | 4.6 | 9.0 | 7.2 | 37.4 |
| Occupied Palestinian Terr. Terr. palestinien occupé | 2001 | 3 464 | 9.8 | 0.6 | 13.5 | 2.0 | 4.5 | 10.6 | 7.4 | 46.4 |
| | 2002 | 3 192 | 10.7 | 0.6 | 12.8 | 1.8 | 3.7 | 11.8 | 7.9 | 46.8 |
| | 2003 | 3 565 | 10.6 | 0.3 | 11.4 | 2.0 | 5.5 | 12.5 | 6.9 | 48.8 |
| Oman Oman | 2003 | 8 311[4,8] | 2.0 | 41.4 | 8.7 | 1.3 | 2.3 | 12.7 | 7.0 | 27.4 |
| | 2004 | 9 445[4,8] | 1.8 | 42.8 | 8.5 | 1.3 | 2.9 | 12.9 | 7.0 | 25.2 |
| | 2005 | 11 767[4,8] | 1.4 | 49.4 | 8.4 | 1.2 | 2.5 | 11.3 | 5.8 | 22.2 |
| Pakistan+ Pakistan+ | 2004 | 5 250 527 | 22.2 | 4.0 | 17.2 | 3.6 | 2.2 | 17.1 | 12.9 | 20.9 |
| | 2005 | 6 203 889 | 22.2 | 2.9 | 17.8 | 3.3 | 2.5 | 17.7 | 12.8 | 20.8 |
| | 2006 | 7 295 210 | 20.5 | 2.9 | 18.3 | 3.0 | 2.5 | 18.6 | 13.5 | 20.8 |
| Palau Palaos | 1999 | 111 | 4.1 | 0.2 | 1.5 | 3.1 | 7.4 | 31.7 | 8.9 | 43.3 |
| | 2000 | 115 | 4.1 | 0.2 | 1.5 | 3.1 | 7.6 | 31.3 | 9.0 | 43.3 |
| | 2001 | 118 | 4.0 | 0.2 | 1.5 | 3.2 | 7.8 | 31.1 | 9.2 | 43.1 |
| Panama Panama | 2003 | 12 492[5] | 7.7 | 1.0 | 7.8 | 2.9 | 4.8 | 15.5 | 14.9 | 45.6 |
| | 2004 | 13 680[5] | 7.2 | 1.0 | 7.5 | 3.1 | 4.9 | 16.3 | 15.8 | 44.0 |
| | 2005 | 14 848[5] | 7.1 | 1.0 | 7.1 | 3.4 | 4.7 | 17.2 | 16.2 | 43.3 |
| Papua New Guinea Papouasie-Nvl-Guinée | 2000 | 10 258[8] | 32.2 | 24.0 | 10.0 | 1.4 | 4.4 | 8.8 | 4.3 | 16.5 |
| | 2001 | 11 226[8] | 31.9 | 21.4 | 11.4 | 1.5 | 6.1 | 9.6 | 5.0 | 14.7 |
| | 2002 | 12 803[8] | 34.6 | 16.8 | 11.1 | 1.5 | 7.6 | 11.3 | 4.9 | 13.7 |
| Paraguay Paraguay | 2003 | 32 727 000 | 22.0 | 0.1 | 16.3 | 2.7 | 5.4 | 21.3 | 7.7 | 24.4 |
| | 2004 | 37 730 000 | 23.9 | 0.1 | 15.6 | 2.4 | 5.1 | 23.1 | 7.5 | 22.2 |
| | 2005 | 42 086 000 | 23.2 | 0.1 | 15.2 | 2.2 | 5.1 | 22.8 | 8.4 | 22.9 |
| Peru Pérou | 2003 | 195 304 | 7.6 | 6.9 | 15.7 | 2.4 | 5.9 | 18.7 | 8.6 | 34.3 |
| | 2004 | 216 418 | 7.5 | 8.7 | 16.4 | 2.3 | 5.8 | 18.3 | 8.4 | 32.8 |
| | 2005 | 238 331 | 7.2 | 10.3 | 16.3 | 2.4 | 5.8 | 17.7 | 8.4 | 32.0 |
| Philippines[1] Philippines[1] | 2003 | 4 316 402 | 14.6 | 1.0 | 23.3 | 3.2 | 4.5 | 15.8 | 7.3 | 30.4 |
| | 2004 | 4 858 835 | 15.1 | 1.1 | 22.9 | 3.2 | 4.4 | 15.9 | 7.6 | 29.9 |
| | 2005 | 5 418 841 | 14.3 | 1.2 | 23.3 | 3.6 | 4.2 | 16.1 | 7.6 | 29.7 |
| Poland Pologne | 2004 | 820 375 | 5.1 | 2.5 | 19.1 | 3.6 | 5.5 | 20.1 | 7.4 | 36.6 |
| | 2005 | 863 684 | 4.6 | 2.5 | 18.5 | 3.7 | 6.1 | 20.2 | 7.2 | 37.1 |
| | 2006 | 924 753 | 4.5 | 2.9 | 18.3 | 3.7 | 6.6 | 20.7 | 7.1 | 36.2 |
| Portugal Portugal | 2001 | 112 817 | 3.6 | 0.4 | 16.7 | 2.4 | 7.8 | 17.6 | 6.8 | 44.7 |
| | 2002 | 117 751 | 3.3 | 0.4 | 16.4 | 2.5 | 7.6 | 17.6 | 6.8 | 45.4 |
| | 2003 | 120 465 | 3.2 | 0.3 | 15.7 | 2.7 | 7.1 | 17.4 | 6.8 | 46.7 |

| | | | % of Value added – % de la valeur ajoutée | | | | | | | |
|---|---|---|---|---|---|---|---|---|---|---|
| Country or area<br><br>Pays ou zone | Year<br><br>Année | Value<br>added, gross<br>(mil. nat.cur)<br>Valeur<br>ajoutée, brute<br>(mil. mon. nat.) | Agriculture,<br>hunting,<br>forestry<br>and fishing<br>Agriculture,<br>chasse,<br>sylviculture<br>et pêche | Mining and<br>quarrying<br><br>Activités<br>extractives | Manufac-<br>turing<br>Activités<br>de fabri-<br>cation | Electric-<br>ity, gas<br>and water<br>supply<br>Electricité,<br>gaz et eau | Construc-<br>tion<br>Construc-<br>tion | Wholesale,<br>retail trade,<br>restaurants<br>and hotels<br>Commerce,<br>restaurants,<br>hôtels | Transport,<br>storage &<br>communi-<br>cation<br>Transports,<br>entrepôts,<br>communi-<br>cations | Other<br>activities<br><br>Autres<br>activités |
| Puerto Rico+[1]<br>Porto Rico+[1] | 2003 | 78 795 | 0.5 | 0.1 | 42.2 | 2.2 | 2.3[34] | 13.3 | 4.6 | 34.8 |
| | 2004 | 82 400 | 0.4 | 0.1 | 41.7 | 2.0 | 2.2[34] | 13.3 | 4.5 | 35.8 |
| | 2005 | 86 257 | 0.4 | 0.1 | 42.4 | 2.0 | 2.0[34] | 13.3 | 4.4 | 35.4 |
| Qatar<br>Qatar | 2000 | 65 707 | 0.4 | 59.5 | 5.3 | 1.2 | 3.5 | 5.7 | 3.1 | 21.3 |
| | 2001 | 65 776 | 0.4 | 56.0 | 5.9 | 1.5 | 4.5 | 6.0 | 3.4 | 22.4 |
| | 2002 | 66 410 | 0.4 | 56.5 | 5.9 | 1.5 | 4.1 | 5.9 | 3.4 | 22.3 |
| Réunion[1]<br>Réunion[1] | 1990 | 27 417 | 4.0 | 9.1[10] | ... | 4.7 | 5.9 | 20.5 | 4.0 | 51.7 |
| | 1991 | 30 371 | 3.7 | 9.1[10] | ... | 4.1 | 7.1 | 19.9 | 4.6 | 51.5 |
| | 1992 | 32 832 | 3.5 | 9.0[10] | ... | 4.1 | 6.8 | 20.0 | 4.5 | 50.1 |
| Romania<br>Roumanie | 2003 | 1 754 018 400 | 13.0 | 1.6 | 23.4 | 3.2 | 6.5 | 11.7 | 11.0 | 29.5 |
| | #2005 | 254 503 | 9.5 | 1.5 | 23.8 | 2.6 | 7.3 | 13.4 | 11.0 | 30.8 |
| | 2006[35] | 304 155 | 8.8 | 27.5[10,11] | ... | ... | 8.4 | 14.4 | 11.0 | 29.8 |
| Russian Federation<br>Fédération de Russie | 2004 | 15 186 845 | 6.0 | 9.4 | 17.7 | 3.7 | 5.7 | 21.0 | 10.9 | 25.6 |
| | 2005 | 18 970 876 | 5.4 | 10.9 | 18.8 | 3.3 | 5.4 | 20.0 | 10.0 | 26.1 |
| | 2006 | 23 419 068 | 4.8 | 10.4 | 18.9 | 3.3 | 5.8 | 20.1 | 9.6 | 27.0 |
| Rwanda[1]<br>Rwanda[1] | 2000 | 680 822 | 40.7 | 0.3 | 10.0 | 0.6 | 8.9 | 10.4 | 7.3 | 22.0 |
| | 2001 | 731 919 | 41.4 | 0.5 | 9.9 | 0.5 | 8.5 | 10.2 | 7.5 | 21.5 |
| | 2002 | 794 978 | 43.1 | 0.5 | 9.5 | 0.4 | 8.1 | 10.0 | 7.5 | 20.9 |
| Saint Kitts and Nevis[1]<br>Saint-Kitts-et-Nevis[1] | 2004 | 981 | 2.9 | 0.3 | 9.1 | 2.5 | 13.4 | 18.4 | 14.0 | 39.4 |
| | 2005 | 1 058 | 2.7 | 0.3 | 8.7 | 2.5 | 13.3 | 18.9 | 14.1 | 39.5 |
| | 2006 | 1 175 | 2.2 | 0.4 | 8.7 | 2.4 | 14.6 | 19.5 | 13.5 | 38.7 |
| Saint Lucia[1]<br>Sainte-Lucie[1] | 2003 | 1 811 | 4.7 | 0.3 | 4.6 | 4.9 | 6.3 | 23.8 | 18.9 | 36.5 |
| | 2004 | 1 923 | 4.8 | 0.3 | 4.6 | 5.2 | 6.2 | 24.3 | 18.7 | 36.0 |
| | 2005 | 2 092 | 3.6 | 0.3 | 5.1 | 4.8 | 7.2 | 25.2 | 18.8 | 35.1 |
| St. Vincent-Grenadines[1]<br>St. Vincent-Grenadines[1] | 2003 | 907 | 8.3 | 0.2 | 5.5 | 6.2 | 11.1 | 19.4 | 18.4 | 31.0 |
| | 2004 | 995 | 7.6 | 0.2 | 5.4 | 5.9 | 11.8 | 19.9 | 19.1 | 30.0 |
| | 2005 | 1 037 | 7.6 | 0.2 | 5.3 | 6.1 | 11.5 | 20.4 | 17.7 | 31.2 |
| Samoa[1]<br>Samoa[1] | 2001 | 846 | 14.7 | ... | 15.8 | 4.6 | 6.4 | 20.8 | 11.6 | 26.0 |
| | 2002 | 898 | 14.5 | ... | 15.1 | 4.7 | 6.0 | 21.9 | 11.7 | 26.1 |
| | 2003 | 953 | 12.9 | ... | 16.3 | 4.5 | 5.9 | 21.6 | 12.1 | 26.7 |
| Sao Tome and Principe[1]<br>Sao Tomé-et-Principe[1] | 1986 | 2 259 | 29.2 | ... | 2.3 | 0.3 | 3.4 | 19.4 | 5.3 | 40.1 |
| | 1987 | 2 797 | 31.5 | ... | 1.3 | 1.4 | 3.8 | 17.1 | 5.6 | 39.2 |
| | 1988 | 3 800 | 32.1 | ... | 1.7 | 1.0 | 4.2 | 18.8 | 4.1 | 38.1 |
| Saudi Arabia+[1]<br>Arabie saoudite+[1] | 2003 | 811 805[4,5] | 4.5 | 36.2 | 10.6 | 1.2 | 5.8 | 6.6 | 4.1 | 30.9 |
| | 2004 | 945 896[4,5] | 3.9 | 40.6 | 10.1 | 1.1 | 5.4 | 6.1 | 3.8 | 28.9 |
| | 2005 | 1 167 365[4,5] | 3.3 | 47.8 | 9.5 | 0.9 | 4.7 | 5.4 | 3.3 | 25.1 |
| Senegal<br>Sénégal | 2002 | 3 260 778 | 15.5 | 1.4 | 17.2 | 2.5 | 4.4 | 21.5 | 8.5 | 31.3 |
| | 2003 | 3 474 661 | 17.7 | 1.4 | 16.4 | 2.5 | 4.1 | 20.4 | 9.1 | 30.5 |
| | 2004 | 3 673 574 | 16.0 | 1.3 | 16.5 | 2.5 | 4.9 | 20.4 | 9.9 | 30.7 |
| Serbia<br>Serbie | 2004 | 1 201 150 | 13.7 | 1.9 | 17.2 | 4.4 | 4.7 | 10.8 | 7.9 | 39.4 |
| | 2005 | 1 449 238 | 13.4 | 1.8 | 16.9 | 4.2 | 4.5 | 10.4 | 8.0 | 40.8 |
| | 2006 | 1 808 807 | 13.6 | 1.9 | 17.0 | 4.3 | 4.6 | 10.6 | 7.9 | 40.1 |
| Serbia and<br>Montenegro[36]<br>Serbie-et-Monténégro[36] | 2000 | 358 753 | 21.1 | 3.6 | 22.1 | 2.5 | 3.9 | 11.9 | 7.1 | 27.8 |
| | 2001 | 702 402 | 20.9 | 4.0 | 21.8 | 2.6 | 3.7 | 11.1 | 7.8 | 28.0 |
| | 2002 | 857 966 | 16.3 | 4.3 | 19.5 | 4.2 | 3.8 | 9.5 | 9.1 | 33.3 |
| Seychelles[1]<br>Seychelles[1] | 1999 | 3 179 | 3.2 | ... | 15.8[6,37] | 2.4 | 10.2 | 8.3 | 32.8 | 21.7 |
| | 2000 | 3 274 | 3.0 | ... | 20.6[6,37] | 1.5 | 9.1 | 9.9 | 33.8 | 22.6 |
| | 2001 | 3 278 | 3.1 | ... | 20.0[6,37] | 1.9 | 9.4 | 10.7 | 33.0 | 23.3 |

| Country or area<br>Pays ou zone | Year<br>Année | Value added, gross (mil. nat.cur)<br>Valeur ajoutée, brute (mil. mon. nat.) | % of Value added – % de la valeur ajoutée | | | | | | | |
|---|---|---|---|---|---|---|---|---|---|---|
| | | | Agriculture, hunting, forestry and fishing<br>Agriculture, chasse, sylviculture et pêche | Mining and quarrying<br>Activités extractives | Manufac-turing<br>Activités de fabri-cation | Electric-ity, gas and water supply<br>Electricité, gaz et eau | Construc-tion<br>Construc-tion | Wholesale, retail trade, restaurants and hotels<br>Commerce, restaurants, hôtels | Transport, storage & communi-cation<br>Transports, entrepôts, communi-cations | Other activities<br>Autres activités |
| Sierra Leone | 2003 | 3 188 590[4,5] | 44.4 | 6.9 | 2.5 | 0.7 | 1.6 | 14.2 | 6.8 | 22.9 |
| Sierra Leone | 2004 | 3 642 113[4,5] | 47.7 | 7.0 | 2.3 | 0.5 | 1.6 | 11.4 | 7.2 | 22.2 |
| | 2005 | 4 252 341[4,5] | 49.4 | 7.3 | 2.7 | 0.5 | 2.3 | 9.7 | 7.0 | 21.1 |
| Singapore | 2004 | 178 743 | 0.1 | ... | 26.9 | 1.9 | 3.8 | 16.4 | 13.9 | 36.9 |
| Singapour | 2005 | 192 018 | 0.1 | ... | 26.8 | 1.7 | 3.8 | 16.9 | 14.1 | 36.7 |
| | 2006 | 208 999 | 0.1 | ... | 27.7 | 1.7 | 3.6 | 17.1 | 13.5 | 36.4 |
| Slovakia | 2004 | 1 210 674 | 4.5 | 0.6 | 23.6 | 4.8 | 6.3 | 15.1 | 10.0 | 35.1 |
| Slovaquie | 2005 | 1 304 080 | 4.3 | 0.6 | 23.4 | 4.9 | 6.8 | 15.7 | 10.4 | 33.8 |
| | 2006 | 1 479 732 | 4.0 | 0.5 | 21.9 | 5.6 | 6.9 | 16.9 | 9.9 | 34.3 |
| Slovenia | 2003 | 5 048 599 | 2.6 | 0.5 | 26.4 | 2.9 | 5.8 | 14.0 | 7.1 | 40.7 |
| Slovénie | 2004 | 5 459 552 | 2.7 | 0.6 | 25.7 | 3.0 | 5.7 | 13.8 | 7.6 | 41.0 |
| | 2005 | 5 769 285 | 2.5 | 0.5 | 24.6 | 3.1 | 5.9 | 14.0 | 8.1 | 41.2 |
| Solomon Islands[1] | 1984 | 199 | 53.5 | -0.2 | 3.6 | 0.9 | 3.8 | 10.6 | 5.2 | 22.6 |
| Iles Salomon[1] | 1985 | 213 | 50.4 | -0.7 | 3.8 | 1.0 | 4.2 | 10.4 | 5.1 | 25.8 |
| | 1986 | 224 | 48.3 | -1.2 | 4.5 | 1.2 | 5.1 | 8.4 | 5.8 | 27.9 |
| Somalia[1] | 1985 | 84 050[3] | 66.1 | 0.3 | 4.9 | 0.1 | 2.2 | 10.1 | 6.7 | 9.5 |
| Somalie[1] | 1986 | 112 584[3] | 62.5 | 0.4 | 5.5 | 0.2 | 2.7 | 10.3 | 7.3 | 11.1 |
| | 1987 | 163 175[3] | 64.9 | 0.3 | 5.1 | -0.5 | 2.9 | 10.7 | 6.8 | 9.8 |
| South Africa | 2003 | 1 143 679 | 3.6 | 7.4 | 19.4 | 2.5 | 2.4 | 13.8 | 9.7 | 41.4 |
| Afrique du Sud | 2004 | 1 253 852 | 3.1 | 7.1 | 18.9 | 2.4 | 2.4 | 14.0 | 9.7 | 42.3 |
| | 2005 | 1 368 522 | 2.7 | 7.3 | 18.6 | 2.3 | 2.4 | 14.0 | 9.6 | 42.9 |
| Spain | 2003 | 706 534 | 4.0 | 0.3 | 16.6 | 1.9 | 10.0 | 18.4 | 7.3 | 41.4 |
| Espagne | 2004 | 755 733 | 3.8 | 0.3 | 16.1 | 1.9 | 10.7 | 18.5 | 7.2 | 41.5 |
| | 2005 | 810 822 | 3.3 | 0.3 | 15.5 | 1.9 | 11.6 | 18.4 | 7.1 | 42.0 |
| Sri Lanka | 2003 | 1 615 228[3] | 15.1 | 1.6 | 20.0 | 2.6 | 6.6 | 19.3 | 12.6 | 22.3 |
| Sri Lanka | 2004 | 1 841 245 | 14.6 | 1.6 | 19.9 | 2.6 | 6.6 | 19.5 | 13.2 | 22.1 |
| | 2005 | 2 136 930 | 14.1 | 1.7 | 20.8 | 2.6 | 7.5 | 17.1 | 13.6 | 22.6 |
| Sudan[1] | 1994 | 4 440 648 | 40.5 | 6.5[10] | ... | 0.7 | 3.8 | 46.6[38] | ... | 1.9 |
| Soudan[1] | #1996 | 9 015 824 | 37.1 | 9.6[10] | ... | 0.9 | 5.0 | 44.4[38] | ... | 3.0 |
| | 1997 | 15 865 432 | 40.5 | 9.1[10] | ... | 0.8 | 6.9 | 39.8[38] | ... | 2.8 |
| Suriname[1] | 2003 | 2 993 102 | 7.2 | 7.6 | 14.1 | 6.3 | 2.9 | 11.5 | 7.6 | 27.5 |
| Suriname[1] | 2004 | 3 758 544 | 5.8 | 9.1 | 16.5 | 6.2 | 3.2 | 10.6 | 7.6 | 25.7 |
| | 2005 | 4 568 607 | 5.5 | 9.9 | 19.1 | 6.0 | 3.4 | 10.3 | 7.0 | 24.9 |
| Swaziland+ | 2003 | 8 703[5] | 12.1 | 0.6 | 37.6 | 1.5 | 6.2 | 9.9 | 5.3 | 26.9 |
| Swaziland+ | 2004 | 9 340[5] | 11.3 | 0.6 | 36.9 | 1.4 | 6.3 | 10.1 | 5.4 | 28.0 |
| | 2005 | 9 979[5] | 10.8 | 0.4 | 36.1 | 1.3 | 6.8 | 10.4 | 5.3 | 28.8 |
| Sweden | 2002 | 2 074 721 | 1.8 | 0.2 | 20.2 | 2.6 | 4.4 | 12.0 | 8.2 | 50.5 |
| Suède | 2003 | 2 151 248 | 1.8 | 0.3 | 19.7 | 2.8 | 4.3 | 12.1 | 8.2 | 50.9 |
| | 2004 | 2 247 304 | 1.8 | 0.3 | 19.7 | 3.0 | 4.5 | 12.2 | 8.0 | 50.5 |
| Switzerland | 2002 | 435 734 | 1.3 | 0.2 | 18.8 | 2.4 | 5.4 | 15.4 | 6.2 | 50.3 |
| Suisse | 2003 | 438 698 | 1.2 | 0.2 | 18.5 | 2.3 | 5.5 | 15.4 | 6.3 | 50.7 |
| | 2004 | 447 976 | 1.3 | 0.2 | 18.6 | 2.1 | 5.4 | 15.3 | 6.4 | 50.6 |
| Syrian Arab Republic[1] | 2003 | 1 067 265[14] | 24.8 | 19.1 | 4.0 | 1.2 | 3.7 | 16.7 | 14.1 | 16.4 |
| Rép. arabe syrienne[1] | 2004 | 1 253 358[14] | 23.8 | 21.2 | 3.9 | 1.2 | 2.9 | 17.0 | 12.5 | 17.4 |
| | 2005 | 1 479 120[14] | 22.0 | 25.1 | 3.5 | 0.4 | 2.8 | 16.5 | 12.4 | 17.3 |
| Tajikistan | 2003 | 4 265 | 27.0[5] | ... | 33.8[6,11] | ... | 3.2 | 12.7 | 6.1 | 17.2 |
| Tadjikistan | 2004 | 5 518 | 21.5[5] | ... | 29.8[6,11] | ... | 4.8 | 18.4 | 7.4 | 18.1 |
| | 2005 | 6 428 | 23.8[5] | ... | 25.6[6,11] | ... | 5.1 | 18.5 | 8.3 | 18.7 |

| Country or area<br>Pays ou zone | Year<br>Année | Value<br>added, gross<br>(mil. nat.cur.)<br>Valeur<br>ajoutée, brute<br>(mil. mon. nat.) | % of Value added – % de la valeur ajoutée | | | | | | | |
|---|---|---|---|---|---|---|---|---|---|---|
| | | | Agriculture,<br>hunting,<br>forestry<br>and fishing<br>Agriculture,<br>chasse,<br>sylviculture<br>et pêche | Mining and<br>quarrying<br>Activités<br>extractives | Manufac-<br>turing<br>Activités<br>de fabri-<br>cation | Electric-<br>ity, gas<br>and water<br>supply<br>Electricité,<br>gaz et eau | Construc-<br>tion<br>Construc-<br>tion | Wholesale,<br>retail trade,<br>restaurants<br>and hotels<br>Commerce,<br>restaurants,<br>hôtels | Transport,<br>storage &<br>communi-<br>cation<br>Transports,<br>entrepôts,<br>communi-<br>cations | Other<br>activities<br>Autres<br>activités |
| Thailand[1,14]<br>Thaïlande[1,14] | 2003 | 5 917 368 | 10.4 | 2.6 | 34.8 | 3.2 | 3.0 | 20.1 | 7.7 | 18.2 |
| | 2004 | 6 489 847 | 10.3 | 2.7 | 34.5 | 3.2 | 3.0 | 20.1 | 7.6 | 18.6 |
| | 2005 | 7 087 660 | 10.2 | 3.1 | 34.8 | 3.1 | 3.1 | 19.5 | 7.4 | 18.8 |
| TFYR of Macedonia<br>L'ex-R.y. Macédoine | 2003 | 218 766 | 13.1 | 0.5 | 18.1 | 5.4 | 6.2 | 15.1 | 9.6 | 32.1 |
| | 2004 | 232 877 | 12.9 | 0.4 | 17.0 | 4.8 | 6.3 | 17.3 | 8.9 | 32.4 |
| | 2005 | 248 952 | 12.5 | 0.6 | 17.9 | 4.1 | 6.4 | 17.4 | 9.5 | 31.6 |
| Timor-Leste[1]<br>Timor-Leste[1] | 1996 | 368 | 30.4 | 1.0[39] | 3.0 | 0.7[19] | 19.9 | 9.7 | 9.9 | 25.4 |
| | 1997 | 342 | 33.7 | 1.0[39] | 3.1 | 0.7[19] | 18.1 | 9.1 | 9.7 | 24.6 |
| | 1998 | 127 | 41.1 | 0.6[39] | 2.8 | 0.8[19] | 10.6 | 7.2 | 12.0 | 24.9 |
| Togo[1]<br>Togo[1] | 1980 | 223 479 | 28.5 | 9.8 | 7.4 | 1.8 | 6.2 | 20.6 | 6.9 | 5.7 |
| | 1981 | 242 311 | 28.6 | 9.3 | 6.7 | 1.7 | 4.5 | 21.8 | 7.1 | 6.2 |
| Tonga+[1]<br>Tonga+[1] | 2002 | 265 | 27.5 | 0.4 | 4.5 | 1.9 | 9.1 | 15.1 | 7.5 | 34.0 |
| | 2003 | 293 | 29.0 | 0.3 | 4.4 | 1.7 | 8.5 | 15.7 | 7.5 | 32.8 |
| | 2004 | 315 | 27.3 | 0.3 | 4.4 | 1.9 | 7.9 | 17.5 | 6.7 | 34.0 |
| Trinidad and Tobago<br>Trinité-et-Tobago | 2002 | 58 477[4,5] | 1.1 | 15.6 | 15.2 | 1.4 | 6.9 | 18.2 | 9.4 | 28.1 |
| | 2003 | 73 225[4,5] | 0.8 | 22.5 | 17.0 | 1.2 | 7.0 | 15.7 | 7.5 | 25.0 |
| | 2004 | 82 715[4,5] | 0.6 | 24.3 | 16.5 | 1.1 | 7.4 | 15.2 | 6.7 | 24.2 |
| Tunisia<br>Tunisie | 2003 | 28 254[3] | 13.8 | 3.2 | 20.4 | 1.6[19] | 6.1 | 17.2 | 10.0 | 19.3 |
| | 2004 | 30 889[3] | 14.4 | 3.8 | 20.1 | 1.7[19] | 6.0 | 17.0 | 10.4 | 18.7 |
| | 2005 | 33 180[3] | 13.1 | ... | 19.7 | 1.5[19] | 5.9 | 17.3 | 11.2 | 3.3 |
| Turkey[1]<br>Turquie[1] | 2004 | 422 530 | 11.5 | 1.2 | 20.7 | 3.4 | 3.6 | 21.0 | 14.7 | 23.9 |
| | 2005 | 477 842 | 10.5 | 1.5 | 21.2 | 3.2 | 4.5 | 20.9 | 15.0 | 23.3 |
| | 2006 | 563 472 | 9.4 | 1.5 | 21.6 | 3.1 | 5.4 | 20.9 | 14.4 | 23.8 |
| Turkmenistan<br>Turkménistan | 1999 | 20 056 000 | 24.8 | ... | 31.4[6,11] | ... | 12.2 | 4.1 | 6.7 | 20.8 |
| | 2000 | 25 648 000 | 22.9 | ... | 35.0[6,11] | ... | 6.8 | 3.5 | 6.6 | 25.1 |
| | 2001 | 33 863 000 | 24.7 | ... | 36.6[6,11] | ... | 5.7 | 4.2 | 5.4 | 23.5 |
| Turks and Caicos Islands<br>Iles Turques et Caïques | 2004 | 448 | 1.4 | 0.8 | 2.5 | 4.5 | 10.3 | 34.3 | 10.5 | 35.7 |
| | 2005 | 521 | 1.3 | 1.0 | 2.4 | 4.1 | 12.3 | 33.9 | 9.9 | 35.1 |
| | 2006 | 591 | 1.2 | 1.0 | 2.3 | 3.9 | 12.4 | 35.5 | 9.3 | 34.3 |
| Tuvalu[1]<br>Tuvalu[1] | 2000 | 25 | 17.3 | 0.8 | 3.2 | 4.5 | 4.6 | 12.6 | 10.0 | 47.0 |
| | 2001 | 27 | 17.4 | 0.7 | 3.3 | 4.9 | 4.4 | 12.3 | 10.5 | 46.4 |
| | 2002 | 29 | 15.9 | 0.8 | 3.5 | 5.0 | 4.8 | 12.9 | 11.9 | 45.3 |
| Uganda[1]<br>Ouganda[1] | 2003 | 11 687 518 | 33.3 | 0.7 | 8.8 | 1.3 | 10.0 | 14.2 | 6.8 | 24.9 |
| | 2004 | 12 899 457 | 31.4 | 0.8 | 9.3 | 1.3 | 10.5 | 14.2 | 7.8 | 24.7 |
| | 2005 | 14 994 530 | 32.0 | 0.7 | 9.0 | 1.3 | 10.5 | 14.8 | 8.6 | 23.1 |
| Ukraine<br>Ukraine | 2004 | 318 321 | 11.7 | 3.9 | 20.1 | 3.9 | 4.5 | 13.6 | 13.4 | 28.7 |
| | 2005 | 396 003 | 10.3 | 4.5 | 21.9 | 3.8 | 4.1 | 14.8 | 12.0 | 28.6 |
| | 2006 | 481 077 | 8.4 | 4.3 | 20.0 | 4.2 | 4.9 | 14.6 | 12.4 | 9.2 |
| United Arab Emirates[1]<br>Emirats arabes unis[1] | 1988 | 90 137[3] | 1.8 | 33.2 | 9.1 | 2.3 | 9.8 | 11.3 | 5.6 | 26.8 |
| | 1989 | 104 730[3] | 1.8 | 37.3 | 8.3 | 2.1 | 9.1 | 10.2 | 5.4 | 25.7 |
| | 1990 | 127 737[3] | 1.6 | 45.4 | 7.2 | 1.8 | 7.8 | 8.8 | 4.6 | 22.7 |
| United Kingdom<br>Royaume-Uni | 2003 | 1 030 927[5] | 1.0 | 2.1 | 14.0 | 1.6 | 5.8 | 14.7 | 7.4 | 53.4 |
| | 2004 | 1 094 329[5] | 0.9 | 2.0 | 13.5 | 1.6 | 5.9 | 14.7 | 7.2 | 54.2 |
| | 2005 | 1 138 578[5] | 0.9 | 2.2 | 13.0 | 2.2 | 5.8 | 14.5 | 7.1 | 54.3 |
| United Rep. of Tanzania<br>Rép.-Unie de Tanzanie | 2001 | 7 792 480[3] | 43.7 | 1.5 | 7.2[37] | 1.6 | 5.2 | 11.9 | 4.6 | 24.0 |
| | 2002 | 8 868 717[3] | 43.8 | 1.7 | 7.2[37] | 1.6 | 5.3 | 11.7 | 4.6 | 24.1 |
| | 2003 | 9 993 889[3] | 44.2 | 1.9 | 7.1[37] | 1.6 | 5.5 | 11.5 | 4.5 | 23.6 |

| Country or area<br>Pays ou zone | Year<br>Année | Value added, gross (mil. nat.cur)<br>Valeur ajoutée, brute (mil. mon. nat.) | Agriculture, hunting, forestry and fishing<br>Agriculture, chasse, sylviculture et pêche | Mining and quarrying<br>Activités extractives | Manufacturing<br>Activités de fabrication | Electricity, gas and water supply<br>Electricité, gaz et eau | Construction<br>Construction | Wholesale, retail trade, restaurants and hotels<br>Commerce, restaurants, hôtels | Transport, storage & communication<br>Transports, entrepôts, communications | Other activities<br>Autres activités |
|---|---|---|---|---|---|---|---|---|---|---|
| United States<br>Etats-Unis | 2003 | 10 148 700[3,40] | 1.1[41] | 1.4 | 14.6 | 2.2 | 4.9 | 16.6 | 6.5 | 60.2 |
| | 2004 | 10 838 000[3,40] | 1.3[41] | 1.6 | 14.5 | 2.2 | 5.0 | 16.4 | 6.4 | 60.1 |
| | 2005 | 11 532 800[3,40] | 1.1[41] | 2.0 | 14.4 | 2.2 | 5.3 | 16.5 | 6.2 | 59.9 |
| Uruguay[1]<br>Uruguay[1] | 2004 | 390 482[4] | 11.6 | 0.2 | 20.7 | 4.5 | 3.4 | 12.6 | 9.3 | 37.7 |
| | 2005 | 412 521[4] | 9.1 | 0.2 | 22.2 | 4.9 | 3.8 | 12.8 | 9.5 | 37.4 |
| | 2006 | 470 541[4] | 9.1 | 0.3 | 22.9 | 4.6 | 4.2 | 13.0 | 9.6 | 36.4 |
| Uzbekistan<br>Ouzbékistan | 2000 | 2 788 137 | 34.9 | ... | 15.8[6,11] | ... | 7.0 | 10.9 | 9.3 | 22.2 |
| | 2002 | 6 565 515 | 34.2 | ... | 16.7[6,11] | ... | 5.6 | 11.3 | ... | 22.9 |
| | 2003 | 8 369 111 | 33.3 | ... | 17.6[6,11] | ... | 5.2 | 10.9 | ... | 23.3 |
| Vanuatu[1]<br>Vanuatu[1] | 1999 | 34 016[4] | 15.5 | ... | 4.4 | 1.9 | 2.9 | 38.3 | 11.0 | 26.1 |
| | 2000 | 35 284[4] | 14.9 | ... | 4.2 | 1.7 | 3.0 | 38.0 | 11.6 | 26.7 |
| | 2001 | 35 712[4] | 14.3 | ... | 3.8 | 1.9 | 3.0 | 37.8 | 12.6 | 26.5 |
| Venezuela (Bol. Rep. of)<br>Venezuela (Rép. bolivarienne du) | 2002 | 103 987 703[5] | 4.0 | 19.5 | 17.0 | 2.4 | 9.5 | 9.4 | 6.5 | 31.7 |
| | 2003 | 130 552 420[5] | 4.4 | 24.1 | 17.6 | 2.1 | 6.4 | 10.1 | 6.4 | 28.9 |
| | 2004 | 200 008 986[5] | 4.0 | 28.3 | 17.5 | 1.7 | 6.9 | 10.5 | 6.0 | 25.1 |
| Viet Nam<br>Viet Nam | 2003 | 613 442 800[14] | 22.5 | 9.3 | 20.5 | 3.6 | 6.0 | 16.6 | 4.0 | 17.4 |
| | 2004 | 715 307 000[14] | 21.8 | 10.1 | 20.3 | 3.5 | 6.2 | 16.7 | 4.3 | 13.3 |
| | 2005 | 837 858 267[14] | 20.9 | 10.5 | 20.7 | 3.5 | 6.4 | 17.1 | 4.4 | 13.2 |
| Yemen<br>Yémen | 2002 | 1 890 242 | 13.3 | 29.8 | 6.4 | 0.8 | 4.8 | 13.0 | 12.3 | 19.5 |
| | 2003 | 2 169 681 | 12.8 | 30.2 | 6.4 | 0.9 | 5.3 | 13.4 | 11.9 | 19.0 |
| | 2004 | 2 574 135 | 11.7 | 30.9 | 7.3 | 0.8 | 5.9 | 13.9 | 11.3 | 18.1 |
| Yugoslavia, SFR[1]<br>Yougoslavie, Rfs[1] | 1988 | 14 645 | 11.2 | 2.7 | 40.3 | 2.2 | 6.2 | 7.6 | 11.1 | 18.6 |
| | 1989 | 224 684 | 11.3 | 2.4 | 41.4 | 1.7 | 6.4 | 6.6 | 10.5 | 19.7 |
| | 1990 | 966 420 | 12.9 | 2.5 | 31.2 | 1.7 | 7.9 | 8.5 | 12.3 | 23.1 |
| Zambia[1]<br>Zambie[1] | 2004 | 25 090 145 | 22.2 | 3.2 | 11.3 | 2.8 | 9.6 | 22.0 | 5.0 | 24.0 |
| | 2005 | 31 454 842 | 21.4 | 3.3 | 10.9 | 2.9 | 11.9 | 21.5 | 4.4 | 23.7 |
| | 2006 | 37 732 202 | 20.7 | 5.3 | 10.4 | 3.1 | 13.2 | 20.3 | 4.3 | 22.7 |
| Zanzibar<br>Zanzibar | 2004 | 300 024 | 26.8 | 0.8 | 5.7 | 1.9 | 6.8 | 16.8 | 9.0 | 32.1 |
| | 2005 | 345 283 | 26.8 | 0.9 | 5.6 | 1.9 | 7.1 | 20.0 | 9.1 | 28.5 |
| | 2006 | 447 968 | 33.6 | 0.9 | 5.2 | 2.2 | 8.5 | 18.8 | 7.7 | 23.1 |
| Zimbabwe[1]<br>Zimbabwe[1] | 2002 | 1 652 756 | 18.1 | 0.7 | 7.4 | 1.5[19] | 0.8 | 8.2 | 10.4 | 53.0 |
| | 2003 | 5 129 106 | 15.7 | 0.6 | 11.6 | 1.4[19] | 0.8 | 9.0 | 8.1 | 52.9 |
| | 2004 | 12 879 575 | 13.1 | 7.0 | ... | 2.9[19] | 0.9 | 15.0 | 8.0 | 32.2 |

Source

United Nations Statistics Division, New York, national accounts database, last accessed January 2008.

Notes

Data for most countries have been compiled in accordance with the concepts and definitions of the System of National Accounts 1993 (1993 SNA). Countries that follow the 1968 SNA are footnoted accordingly.

+ Note: The national accounts data generally relate to the fiscal year used in each country, unless indicated otherwise. Countries or areas whose reference periods coincide with the calendar year ending 31 December are not listed below.

Year beginning 21 March: Afghanistan, Iran (Islamic Republic).

Source

Organisation des Nations Unies, Division de statistique, New York, la base de données sur les comptes nationaux, dernier accès janvier 2008.

Notes

Les données pour la majorité des pays sont compilées selon les concepts et définitions du Système de comptabilité nationale, 1993 (SCN93). Seuls les pays qui suivent toujours le SCN68 seront donc signalés par une note.

+ Note : Sauf indication contraire, les données sur les comptes nationaux concernent généralement l'exercice budgétaire utilisé dans chaque pays. Les pays ou territoires dont la période de référence coïncide avec l'année civile se terminant le 31 décembre ne sont pas répertoriés ci-dessous.

Exercice commençant le 21 mars: Afghanistan, Iran (République

Year beginning 1 April: Bermuda, India, Myanmar, New Zealand.

Year beginning 1 July: Australia, Bhutan, Gambia, Nicaragua, Pakistan, Puerto Rico, Saudi Arabia.
Year ending 30 June:  Bangladesh, Botswana, Egypt, Swaziland, Tonga.
Year ending 7 July: Ethiopia.
Year ending 15 July: Nepal.
Year ending 30 September: Haiti.

1  Data compiled in accordance with the System of National Accounts 1968 (1968 SNA).
2  Restaurants and hotels are included in "Other activities".
3  Value added at factor cost.
4  Value added at producers' prices.
5  Including Financial intermediation services indirectly measured (FISIM).
6  Including mining and quarrying.
7  Oil refining included in "Electricity, gas and water".
8  Excluding Financial intermediation services indirectly measured (FISIM).
9  Includes imputed rentals of owner-occupied dwellings.
10  Including "Manufacturing".
11  Including "Electricity, gas and water".
12  Including diamond cutting.
13  For statistical purposes, the data for China do not include those for the Hong Kong Special Administrative Region (Hong Kong SAR) and Macao Special Administrative Region (Macao SAR).

14  Refers to gross domestic product.
15  Agriculture and fishing only.
16  Repair of motor vehicles, motorcycles and personal and households goods are included in "Other Activities".
17  Including import duties.
18  Excluding hunting.
19  Excluding gas.
20  Including petroleum refining.
21  Including manufacturing of energy-generating products.
22  Including repair services.
23  Quarrying is included in manufacturing.
24  Structural steel erection is included in Manufacturing.

25  Including engineering and sewage services.
26  Including oil production.
27  Excluding repair of motor vehicles, motorcycles and personal and household goods.
28  Gross value added approximately at market prices.
29  Vehicle repairs, hotels and restaurants are included in "Other activities".
30  Wholesale and retail trade only.
31  Basic petroleum manufacturing is included in mining and quarrying.

32  Electricity only. Gas and water are included in "Other activities".
33  Including gas and water supply.
34  Contract construction only.
35  Semi-final data.
36  As from 1999: excluding Kosovo and Metohia.
37  Including handicrafts.
38  Including Transport, storage and communications; Financial intermediation, real estate, renting and business activities; and Education, health and social work; other community, social and personal services, and Private households with employed persons.

Islamique d').
Exercice commençant le 1er avril: Bermudes, Inde, Myanmar, Nouvelle-Zélande.
Exercice commençant le 1er juillet: Arabie saoudite, Australie, Bangladesh, Cameroun, Gambie, Pakistan, Porto Rico.
Exercice se terminant le 30 juin: Botswana, Égypte, Swaziland, Tonga.
Exercice se terminant le 7 juillet: Éthiopie.
Exercice se terminant le 15 juillet: Népal.
Exercice se terminant le 30 septembre: Haïti.

1  Données compilées selon le Système de comptabilité nationale de 1968 (SCN 1968).
2  Restaurants et hôtels sont inclus dans "autres activités".
3  Valeur ajoutée au coût des facteurs.
4  Valeur ajoutée aux prix à la production.
5  Y compris les Services d'intermédiation financière mesurés indirectement (SIFMI).
6  Y compris les industries extractives.
7  Le raffinage du pétrole y compris dans "l'électricité, le gaz et l'eau".
8  Non compris les Services d'intermédiation financière mesurés indirectement (SIFMI).
9  Y compris les loyers fictifs des logements occupés par leur propriétaire.
10  Y compris "les industries manufacturières".
11  Y compris "l'électricité, le gaz et l'eau".
12  Y compris la taille de diamant.
13  Pour la présentation des statistiques, les données pour la Chine ne comprennent pas la Région Administrative Spéciale de Hong Kong (Hong Kong RAS) et la Région Administrative Spéciale de Macao (Macao RAS).

14  Concerné le produit intérieur brut.
15  Agriculture et la pêche seulement.
16  Les réparations de véhicules à moteur, de motocycles et d'articles personnels et ménagers sont incluses dans "autres activités".
17  Droits d'importation compris.
18  Non compris la chasse.
19  Non compris le gaz.
20  Y compris le raffinage du pétrole.
21  Y compris la fabrication de produits producteurs d'énergie.
22  Y compris les services de réparation.
23  Industries extractives sont incluses dans les industries manufacturières.
24  La construction de charpentes métalliques est comptabilisée dans la colonne Activités de fabrication.

25  Y compris génie civil et services d'égouts.
26  Y compris la production de pétrole.
27  Non compris les réparations de véhicules à moteur, de motocycles et d'articles personnels et ménagers.
28  Valeur brute ajoutée à environ aux prix du marché.
29  Restaurants et hôtels, et les réparations de véhicules à moteur, sont inclus dans "autres activités".
30  Commerce de gros et de détail seulement.
31  Les industries extractives y compris la fabrication de produits pétroliers de base.

32  Seulement électricité. Le gaz et l'eau sont inclus dans les "autres activités".
33  Y compris le gaz et l'eau.
34  Construction sous contrat seulement.
35  Données demi-finales.
36  A partir de 1999: non compris Kosovo et Metohia.
37  Y compris l'artisanat.
38  Comprend Transports, entreposage et communications ; Intermédiation financière, activités immobilières, de location et commerciales ; Éducation, santé et action sociale ; Autres services communautaires, sociaux et individuels, et Ménages privés comptant des salariés.

| | |
|---|---|
| 39 Refers to non-oil and gas mining only, excluding Quarrying. | 39 Activités extractives hormis pétrole et gaz, non compris les carrières. |
| 40 Discrepancy between components and total as data for individual industries include all taxes less all subsidies. | 40 Les écarts entre le total et la somme de ses composantes tiennent au fait que les données de chaque industrie comprennent la totalité des taxes, moins la totalité des subventions. |
| 41 Excluding fishing. | 41 Non compris la pêche. |
| 42 Including crude petroleum production. | 42 Y compris la production de pétrole brut. |

# 23 Relationships among the principal national accounting aggregates
As a percentage of GDP

## Relations entre les principaux agrégats de la comptabilité nationale
En pourcentage du PIB

| Country or area<br>Pays ou zone | Year<br>Année | GDP at current prices (mil.nat.cur.)<br>PIB aux prix courants (millions monnaie nat.) | As a percentage of GDP — En pourcentage du PIB | | | | | |
|---|---|---|---|---|---|---|---|---|
| | | | Plus: Compensation of employees and property income from/to the rest of the world, net<br>Plus : Rémunération des salariés et revenus de la propriété du/au reste du monde, net | Equals: Gross national income<br>Égale : Revenu national brut | Plus: Net current transfers from/to the rest of the world<br>Plus : Transfers courants du/au reste du monde, net | Equals: Gross national disposable income<br>Égale : Revenu national disponible brut | Less: Final consumption expenditure<br>Moins : Dépense de consommation finale | Equals: Gross savings<br>Égale : Épargne brut |
| Algeria[1]<br>Algérie[1] | 2001 | 4 260 811 | -2.9[2] | 97.1 | 2.5 | 99.6 | 58.0 | 41.6 |
| | 2002 | 4 537 691 | -3.8[2] | 96.2 | 3.0 | 99.2 | 59.2 | 39.9 |
| | 2003 | 5 264 187 | -3.6[2] | 96.4 | 3.5 | 99.9 | 55.1 | 44.8 |
| Angola[1]<br>Angola[1] | 1988 | 239 640 | -11.1 | 88.9 | -1.9 | 87.0 | 78.4 | 8.6 |
| | 1989 | 278 866 | -10.5 | 89.5 | -1.6 | 87.9 | 77.1 | 10.8 |
| | 1990 | 308 062 | -12.4 | 87.6 | -4.2 | 83.4 | 73.2 | 10.2 |
| Anguilla[1]<br>Anguilla[1] | 2004 | 402 | 0.5 | 100.5 | 3.1 | 103.6 | 100.4 | 3.2 |
| | 2005 | 453 | 0.7 | 100.7 | 0.7 | 101.4 | 105.8 | -4.4 |
| | 2006 | 544[3] | -1.6 | 98.4 | 0.1 | 98.5 | 112.6 | -14.1 |
| Argentina<br>Argentine | 2003 | 375 909 | -6.0 | 94.0 | 0.4 | 94.4 | 74.6 | 19.7[4] |
| | 2004 | 447 643 | -5.8 | 94.2 | 0.4 | 94.6 | 73.9 | 20.6[4] |
| | 2005 | 531 939 | -3.4 | 96.6 | 0.3 | 96.9 | 73.2 | 23.7[4] |
| Armenia<br>Arménie | 2002 | 1 362 472 | -0.5 | 99.5 | 7.5 | 107.1 | 99.1 | 8.0 |
| | 2003 | 1 624 643 | -1.1 | 98.9 | 8.0 | 106.9 | 93.5 | 13.4 |
| | #2004 | 1 907 900 | -4.0 | 96.0 | 11.6 | 107.6 | 92.7 | 15.0 |
| Aruba<br>Aruba | 2000 | 3 327 | -4.7 | 95.3 | -1.7 | 93.5 | 72.0 | 21.5 |
| | 2001 | 3 399 | -6.6 | 93.4 | 2.7 | 96.1 | 74.1 | 22.1 |
| | 2002 | 3 421 | ... | ... | ... | ... | 78.9 | ... |
| Australia+<br>Australie+ | 2003 | 840 285 | -2.8 | 97.2 | 0.0 | 97.2 | 76.5 | 20.7 |
| | 2004 | 896 568 | -3.6 | 96.4 | 0.0 | 96.3 | 76.3 | 20.1 |
| | 2005 | 965 969 | -3.9 | 96.0 | 0.0 | 95.9 | 74.9 | 21.0 |
| Austria<br>Autriche | 2004 | 235 819 | -1.2 | 98.8 | -1.0 | 97.8 | 74.5 | 23.3 |
| | 2005 | 245 103 | -1.0 | 99.0 | -0.8 | 98.1 | 74.3 | 23.9 |
| | 2006 | 256 667 | 0.0 | 100.0 | -0.8 | 99.2 | 73.4 | 25.8 |
| Azerbaijan<br>Azerbaïdjan | 2003 | 7 147 | -3.5 | 96.5 | 9.1 | 105.7 | 72.4 | 33.3 |
| | 2004 | 8 530 | -5.9 | 94.1 | 8.3 | 102.4 | 68.7 | 33.7 |
| | 2005 | 12 523 | ... | ... | ... | ... | 47.3 | ... |
| Bahamas<br>Bahamas | 2003 | 5 503 | -3.0 | 97.0 | 0.9 | 97.8 | 82.8[5] | 16.1 |
| | 2004 | 5 661[3] | -2.7 | 97.3 | 4.4 | 101.7 | 83.4[5] | 19.5 |
| | 2005 | 5 869[3] | -2.1 | 97.9 | 1.5 | 99.4 | 82.7[5] | 17.9 |
| Bahrain[1]<br>Bahreïn[1] | 2002 | 3 176 | -5.2[2] | 93.8 | -10.1 | 83.5 | 63.7 | ... |
| | 2003 | 3 647 | -5.1[2] | 93.7 | -11.2 | 83.8 | 61.4 | ... |
| | 2004 | 4 141 | -5.2[2] | 94.8 | -10.2 | 84.6 | 59.0 | ... |
| Bangladesh+<br>Bangladesh+ | 2003 | 3 329 731 | 5.3 | 105.3 | 0.6 | 105.9 | 80.5 | 25.4 |
| | 2004 | 3 707 070 | 5.1 | 105.1 | 0.7 | 105.8 | 80.0 | 25.8 |
| | 2005 | 4 161 546 | 6.5 | 105.6 | 0.7 | 106.4 | 79.7 | 26.6 |
| Barbados[1]<br>Barbade[1] | 2002 | 4 952 | -4.3 | 95.7 | 3.5 | 99.1 | 88.7 | 10.5 |
| | 2003 | 5 390 | -4.0 | 96.0 | 3.4 | 99.5 | 88.8 | 10.6 |
| | 2004 | 5 632 | -3.8 | 96.2 | 3.5 | 99.7 | 92.0 | 7.7 |
| Belarus<br>Bélarus | 2004 | 49 991 800[6] | -0.1 | 99.9 | 1.2 | 101.2 | 74.3 | 26.8 |
| | 2005 | 65 067 100[6] | 0.2 | 100.2 | 0.6 | 100.7 | 72.8 | 28.0 |
| | 2006 | 79 231 400[6] | -0.3 | 99.7 | 0.5 | 100.2 | 72.3 | 27.9 |
| Belgium<br>Belgique | 2004 | 289 509 | 0.9 | 100.9 | -1.4 | 99.6 | 75.6 | 23.9 |
| | 2005 | 298 541 | 0.9 | 100.9 | -1.3 | 99.5 | 76.1 | 23.4 |
| | 2006 | 314 084 | 1.0 | 101.0 | -1.4 | 99.6 | 75.4 | 24.2 |
| Belize<br>Belize | 1998 | 1 258 | ... | 94.9 | ... | 100.2 | 84.8 | ... |
| | 1999 | 1 377 | ... | 95.1 | ... | ... | 82.3 | ... |
| | 2000 | 1 514 | ... | ... | ... | ... | 83.7 | ... |

| Country or area<br>Pays ou zone | Year<br>Année | GDP at current prices (mil.nat.cur.)<br>PIB aux prix courants (millions monnaie nat.) | Plus: Compensation of employees and property income from/to the rest of the world, net<br>Plus: Rémuneration des salariés et revenus de la propriété du/au reste du monde, net | Equals: Gross national income<br>Égale: Revenu national brut | Plus: Net current transfers from/to the rest of the world<br>Plus: Transfers courants du/au reste du monde, net | Equals: Gross national disposable income<br>Égale: Revenu national disponible brut | Less: Final consumption expenditure<br>Moins: Dépense de consommation finale | Equals: Gross savings<br>Égale: Épargne brut |
|---|---|---|---|---|---|---|---|---|
| Benin[1]<br>Bénin[1] | 1989 | 479 200 | ... | 99.2 | 11.1 | 110.2 | 94.4 | 12.6 |
| | 1990 | 502 300 | ... | ... | ... | ... | 93.6 | ... |
| | 1991 | 535 500 | ... | ... | ... | ... | 94.6 | ... |
| Bermuda+<br>Bermudes+ | 2000 | 3 378 | 4.9 | 104.9 | ... | ... | 72.4 | ... |
| | 2001 | 3 539 | 7.0 | 107.0 | ... | ... | ... | ... |
| | 2002 | 3 715 | 2.8 | 102.8 | ... | ... | ... | ... |
| Bhutan+<br>Bhoutan+ | 2004 | 32 178 | -2.3[8] | 97.7 | 9.6 | ... | ... | ... |
| | 2005 | 36 915 | -1.6[8] | 98.4 | 8.3 | ... | ... | ... |
| | 2006 | 41 794[7] | -0.2[8] | 99.8 | 10.9 | ... | ... | ... |
| Bolivia[1]<br>Bolivie[1] | 2000 | 51 884 | -2.7 | 97.3 | 2.4 | 99.7 | 91.2 | 8.5 |
| | 2001 | 53 010 | -2.6 | 97.4 | 4.1 | 101.5 | 91.6 | 9.9 |
| | 2002 | 55 933 | -2.6 | 97.4 | 3.7 | 101.1 | 90.2 | 10.8 |
| Botswana+<br>Botswana+ | 2000 | 24 943 | -6.0 | 94.0 | 0.0 | 94.0 | 61.6 | 32.4 |
| | 2001 | 28 671 | -5.0 | 95.0 | -0.2 | 94.9 | 59.9 | 34.9 |
| | 2002 | 32 000 | -4.2 | 95.8 | -0.1 | 95.7 | 62.1 | 33.6 |
| Brazil<br>Brésil | 2003 | 1 699 948 | -3.2 | 96.8 | 0.5 | 97.3 | 81.3 | 16.0 |
| | 2004 | 1 941 498 | -3.0 | 97.0 | 0.5 | 97.5 | 79.0 | 18.5 |
| | 2005 | 2 147 944 | -2.9 | 97.1 | 0.4 | 97.5 | 80.4 | 17.1 |
| British Virgin Islands<br>Iles Vierges britanniques | 2003 | 782[3,9] | -6.9 | 93.1 | 5.1 | 98.2 | 47.8 | 50.4 |
| | 2004 | 873[3,9] | -6.4 | 93.7 | 5.0 | 98.7 | 47.1 | 51.8 |
| | 2005 | 972[3,9] | -5.9 | 94.1 | 5.2 | 99.4 | 46.3 | 53.1 |
| Bulgaria<br>Bulgarie | 2003 | 34 547 | -3.2 | 96.8 | 3.5 | 100.3 | 87.7 | 12.5 |
| | 2004 | 38 275 | 1.2 | 101.2 | 4.6 | 105.8 | 86.8 | 19.0 |
| | 2005 | 41 948 | 1.1 | 101.1 | 4.6 | 105.8 | 88.6 | 17.2 |
| Burkina Faso<br>Burkina Faso | 1999 | 1 836 037 | -0.6 | 99.4 | 4.8 | 104.2 | 96.3 | 7.9 |
| | 2000 | 1 863 300 | -0.8 | 99.2 | 4.7 | 103.9 | 97.7 | 6.2 |
| | 2001 | 2 046 308 | -0.9 | 99.1 | 4.4 | 103.5 | 99.8 | 3.7 |
| Burundi[1]<br>Burundi[1] | 1990 | 196 656 | ... | 98.0 | ... | ... | 102.5 | ... |
| | 1991 | 211 898 | ... | 99.0 | ... | ... | 100.9 | ... |
| | 1992 | 226 384 | ... | 98.7 | ... | ... | 98.5 | ... |
| Cambodia[1]<br>Cambodge[1] | 1994 | 6 201 001 | | 92.1 | ... | ... | 104.7 | ... |
| | 1995 | 7 542 711 | ... | 95.1 | ... | ... | 95.6 | ... |
| | 1996 | 8 324 792 | ... | 93.6 | ... | ... | 95.5 | ... |
| Cameroon<br>Cameroun | 2000 | 6 612 385 | -4.4 | 95.6 | 1.7 | 97.3 | 79.7 | 17.6 |
| | 2001 | 7 061 440 | -3.4 | 96.6 | 0.5 | 97.1 | 81.0 | 16.1 |
| | 2002 | 7 583 077 | -3.6 | 96.4 | 0.3 | 96.6 | 81.0 | 15.6 |
| Canada<br>Canada | 2003 | 1 213 408 | -2.3 | 97.7 | 0.0 | 97.6 | 76.3 | 21.3 |
| | 2004 | 1 290 788 | -2.0 | 98.0 | 0.0 | 97.9 | 75.1 | 22.8 |
| | 2005 | 1 371 425 | -1.7 | 98.3 | 0.0 | 98.3 | 74.7 | 23.6 |
| Cape Verde[1]<br>Cap-Vert[1] | 1993 | 29 078 | ... | ... | ... | ... | 106.8 | ... |
| | 1994 | 33 497 | ... | ... | ... | ... | 104.5 | ... |
| | 1995 | 37 705 | ... | ... | ... | ... | 109.1 | ... |
| Cayman Islands[1]<br>Iles Caïmanes[1] | 1989 | 474 | -10.8 | 89.2 | ... | 92.0 | 79.3 | 12.7 |
| | 1990 | 590 | -10.3 | 89.7 | ... | 92.2 | 76.8 | 15.4 |
| | 1991 | 616 | -9.4 | 90.6 | ... | 93.0 | 77.6 | 15.4 |
| Chad<br>Tchad | 2004 | 2 332 367 | ... | 62.9 | ... | ... | ... | ... |
| | 2005 | 3 104 242 | ... | 56.2 | ... | ... | ... | ... |
| | 2006 | 3 470 374 | ... | 52.9 | ... | ... | ... | ... |
| Chile<br>Chili | 2004 | 58 404 603 | -8.2 | 91.8 | 1.2 | 93.0 | 70.8 | 22.2 |
| | 2005 | 66 598 991 | -8.9 | 91.1 | 1.5 | 92.6 | 69.1 | 23.5 |
| | 2006 | 77 337 701 | -13.3 | 86.7 | 2.3 | 89.0 | 65.1 | 24.0 |

| Country or area / Pays ou zone | Year / Année | GDP at current prices (mil.nat.cur.) / PIB aux prix courants (millions monnaie nat.) | Plus: Compensation of employees and property income from/to the rest of the world, net / Plus : Rémuneration des salariés et revenus de la propriété du/au reste du monde, net | Equals: Gross national income / Égale : Revenu national brut | Plus: Net current transfers from/to the rest of the world / Plus : Transferts courants du/au reste du monde, net | Equals: Gross national disposable income / Égale : Revenu national disponible brut | Less: Final consumption expenditure / Moins : Dépense de consommation finale | Equals: Gross savings / Égale : Épargne brut |
|---|---|---|---|---|---|---|---|---|
| China[10] | 2003 | 13 582 280 | -0.5 | 99.5 | ... | ... | ... | ... |
| Chine[10] | 2004 | 15 987 830 | -0.2 | 99.8 | ... | ... | ... | ... |
| | 2005 | 18 308 480 | 0.5 | 100.5 | ... | ... | ... | ... |
| China, Hong Kong SAR | 2002 | 1 276 757 | 0.4 | 100.4 | -1.2 | 99.3 | 68.9 | 30.4 |
| Chine, Hong Kong RAS | 2003 | 1 233 143 | 2.3 | 102.3 | -1.2 | 101.2 | 68.8 | 32.3 |
| | 2004 | 1 290 808 | 2.1 | 102.1 | -1.2 | 100.9 | 69.0 | 31.9 |
| Colombia | 2002 | 203 451 400 | -3.5 | 96.5 | 3.7 | 100.2 | 86.1 | 14.1 |
| Colombie | 2003 | 228 516 603 | -4.3 | 95.7 | 4.2 | 99.9 | 83.3 | 16.6 |
| | 2004 | 257 746 373 | -4.4 | 95.6 | 4.8 | 100.4 | 81.4 | 18.9 |
| Comoros[1] | 1989 | 63 397 | ... | 100.7 | | | | |
| Comores[1] | 1990 | 66 370 | ... | 99.8 | 12.3 | 112.1 | 105.5 | 6.7 |
| | 1991 | 69 248 | ... | 99.6 | ... | ... | ... | ... |
| Congo[1] | 1986 | 640 407 | -6.5 | 93.5 | -1.3 | 92.2 | 84.4 | 7.8 |
| Congo[1] | 1987 | 690 523 | -11.1 | 88.9 | -1.6 | 87.3 | 77.2 | 10.2 |
| | 1988 | 658 964 | -13.7 | 86.3 | -1.8 | 84.5 | 81.2 | 3.3 |
| Costa Rica | 2004 | 8 142 428 | -4.2 | 95.8 | 1.1 | 97.0 | 80.2 | 16.8 |
| Costa Rica | 2005 | 9 542 858 | -3.9 | 96.1 | 1.4 | 97.4 | 80.0 | 17.4 |
| | 2006 | 11 322 819 | -3.5 | 96.5 | 1.5 | 98.0 | 79.4 | 18.6 |
| Côte d'Ivoire[1] | 1998 | 7 457 508 | -5.7 | 94.3 | -3.1 | 91.2 | 78.7 | 12.4 |
| Côte d'Ivoire[1] | 1999 | 7 734 000 | -6.9 | 92.1 | -2.7 | 89.1 | 77.8 | 11.3 |
| | 2000 | 7 605 000 | -5.7 | 94.3 | -3.5 | 90.8 | 82.7 | 8.1 |
| Cuba | 2001 | 33 820 | 4.0[5] | ... | ... | ... | ... | ... |
| Cuba | 2002 | 36 089 | 1.5[5] | ... | ... | ... | ... | ... |
| | 2003 | 38 625 | -0.8[5] | ... | ... | ... | ... | ... |
| Cyprus | 2003 | 6 866 | ... | 96.9 | ... | ... | ... | ... |
| Chypre | 2004 | 7 390 | ... | 94.2 | ... | ... | ... | ... |
| | 2005 | 7 862 | ... | 99.8 | ... | ... | ... | ... |
| Czech Republic | 2003 | 2 577 110 | -4.2 | 95.7 | 0.1 | 95.8 | 75.1 | 20.7 |
| République tchèque | 2004 | 2 781 060 | -5.6 | 94.3 | 0.0 | 94.3 | 73.1 | 21.2 |
| | 2005 | 2 970 261 | -4.6 | 95.6 | -0.2 | 95.4 | 71.9 | 23.4 |
| Dem. Rep. of the Congo[1] | 1983 | 59 134 | ... | 95.7 | ... | ... | 76.9 | ... |
| Rép. dém. du Congo[1] | 1984 | 99 723 | ... | 88.5 | ... | ... | 49.5 | ... |
| | 1985 | 147 263 | ... | 97.2 | ... | ... | 59.4 | ... |
| Denmark | 2004 | 1 459 399 | 0.5 | 100.5 | -2.3 | 98.1 | 75.2 | 23.0 |
| Danemark | 2005 | 1 551 967 | 0.8 | 100.8 | -2.0 | 98.9 | 74.5 | 24.4 |
| | 2006 | 1 637 603 | 1.4 | 101.4 | -1.9 | 99.5 | 74.2 | 25.3 |
| Djibouti[1] | 1996 | 88 233 | 1.0[2] | 100.0 | 9.4 | 109.4 | 97.3 | 12.1 |
| Djibouti[1] | 1997 | 87 289 | 1.2[2] | 99.9 | 8.3 | 108.2 | 94.2 | 14.0 |
| | 1998 | 88 461 | 1.2[2] | 99.9 | 8.3 | 108.3 | 96.4 | 11.8 |
| Dominica[1] | 1989 | 423 | ... | 101.0 | ... | ... | 92.0 | ... |
| Dominique[1] | 1990 | 452 | ... | 101.1 | ... | ... | 84.4 | ... |
| | 1991 | 479 | ... | 101.0 | ... | ... | 91.4 | ... |
| Dominican Republic | 1994 | 179 130 | -2.2 | 97.8 | 6.7 | 104.5 | 81.4 | 23.1 |
| Rép. dominicaine | 1995 | 209 646 | -2.3 | 97.7 | 6.2 | 103.9 | 82.9 | 21.0 |
| | 1996 | 243 973 | -5.4 | 94.6 | 6.1 | 100.7 | 82.2 | 18.5 |
| Ecuador | 2004 | 32 636 | ... | ... | ... | ... | 78.7 | ... |
| Equateur | 2005 | 36 489 | ... | ... | ... | ... | 77.3 | ... |
| | 2006 | 40 892 | ... | ... | ... | ... | 74.9 | ... |
| Egypt+ | 2001 | 375 203 | -0.2 | 102.3 | 3.5 | 105.8 | 86.9 | 18.8 |
| Egypte+ | 2002 | 405 256 | -0.9 | 101.3 | 4.1 | 105.5 | 86.4 | 19.1 |
| | 2003 | 451 154 | -0.7 | 101.6 | 3.9 | 105.5 | 82.9 | 22.6 |

| Country or area / Pays ou zone | Year / Année | GDP at current prices (mil.nat.cur.) / PIB aux prix courants (millions monnaie nat.) | Plus: Compensation of employees and property income from/to the rest of the world, net / Plus : Rémunération des salariés et revenus de la propriété du/au reste du monde, net | Equals: Gross national income / Égale : Revenu national brut | Plus: Net current transfers from/to the rest of the world / Plus : Transfers courants du/au reste du monde, net | Equals: Gross national disposable income / Égale : Revenu national disponible brut | Less: Final consumption expenditure / Moins : Dépense de consommation finale | Equals: Gross savings / Égale : Épargne brut |
|---|---|---|---|---|---|---|---|---|
| El Salvador[1] El Salvador[1] | 2003 | 15 047 | -2.8 | 97.2 | 14.1 | 111.2 | 98.9 | 12.3 |
| | 2004 | 15 822 | -2.9 | 97.1 | 16.2 | 113.3 | 101.3 | 12.0 |
| | 2005 | 16 974 | -3.4 | 96.6 | 16.9 | 113.5 | 102.7 | 10.8 |
| Estonia Estonie | 2003 | 132 904 | -5.4 | 94.6 | 1.7 | 96.3 | 74.5 | 21.8 |
| | 2004 | 146 694 | -5.4 | 95.0 | 0.7 | 95.7 | 73.4 | 22.3 |
| | 2005 | 173 062 | -5.1 | 95.2 | -0.1 | 95.0 | 69.2 | 25.8 |
| Ethiopia+ Ethiopie+ | 2004 | 74 279[11] | -0.4[2] | 109.6 | 12.7 | 122.3 | 102.0 | 20.3 |
| | 2005 | 89 930[11] | -0.1[2] | 109.3 | 9.8 | 119.0 | 102.4 | 16.7 |
| | 2006 | 105 891[11] | -0.1[2] | 109.1 | 12.8 | 121.9 | 100.8 | 21.0 |
| Fiji Fidji | 2003 | 4 378 | 0.0 | 100.0 | 4.2 | 104.2 | 67.9 | 54.7 |
| | 2004 | 4 728 | 0.0 | 100.0 | 2.9 | 102.9 | 64.7 | 71.0 |
| | 2005 | 5 069 | 1.4 | 101.4 | 4.9 | 106.3 | 62.5 | 79.9 |
| Finland Finlande | 2004 | 152 345 | 0.6 | 100.6 | -1.0 | 99.6 | 73.2 | 26.5 |
| | 2005 | 157 162 | 0.4 | 100.4 | -1.1 | 99.3 | 73.8 | 25.5 |
| | 2006 | 167 911 | 0.4 | 100.4 | -1.0 | 99.4 | 72.2 | 27.2 |
| France France | 2004 | 1 660 189 | 0.4 | 100.8 | -1.5 | 99.3 | 80.3 | 19.0 |
| | 2005 | 1 717 921 | 0.5 | 100.8 | -1.6 | 99.2 | 80.7 | 18.6 |
| | 2006 | 1 791 953 | 0.5 | 100.8 | -1.5 | 99.3 | 80.4 | 18.9 |
| French Guiana[1] Guyane française[1] | 1990 | 6 526 | -1.9[2] | 98.1 | 36.3 | 134.4 | 99.4 | 35.0 |
| | 1991 | 7 404 | -5.8[2] | 94.2 | 35.9 | 130.1 | 94.5 | 35.6 |
| | 1992 | 7 976 | -6.9[2] | 93.1 | 36.4 | 129.6 | 93.1 | 36.4 |
| Gabon[1] Gabon[1] | 1987 | 1 020 600 | -6.2[2] | 93.8 | -4.2 | 89.7 | 72.4 | 17.3 |
| | 1988 | 1 013 600 | -7.4[2] | 92.6 | -7.6 | 85.0 | 69.9 | 15.1 |
| | 1989 | 1 168 066 | -8.6[2] | 91.4 | -6.1 | 85.3 | 66.8 | 18.5 |
| Gambia+[1] Gambie+[1] | 1991 | 2 920 | ... | 98.3 | ... | 115.7 | 96.7 | 19.0 |
| | 1992 | 3 078 | ... | 98.7 | ... | 114.1 | 94.4 | 19.7 |
| | 1993 | 3 243 | ... | 98.5 | ... | 114.4 | 93.3 | 21.1 |
| Georgia Géorgie | 2004 | 9 824 | 1.9 | 106.2 | 8.0 | 114.2 | 87.3 | 26.9 |
| | 2005 | 11 621 | 1.4 | 105.5 | 5.6 | 111.1 | 80.5 | 30.5 |
| | 2006 | 13 784 | 2.3 | 107.2 | 6.4 | 113.6 | 90.7 | 22.9 |
| Germany Allemagne | 2004 | 2 207 200 | 0.1 | 100.1 | -1.3 | 98.8 | 77.8 | 21.0 |
| | 2005 | 2 241 000 | 0.3 | 100.3 | -1.3 | 99.1 | 77.7 | 21.4 |
| | 2006 | 2 309 100 | 1.1 | 101.1 | -1.2 | 100.0 | 76.8 | 23.1 |
| Ghana[1] Ghana[1] | 1994 | 5 205 200 | ... | 98.0 | ... | ... | ... | ... |
| | 1995 | 7 752 600 | ... | 98.0 | ... | ... | ... | ... |
| | 1996 | 11 339 200 | ... | 98.1 | ... | ... | ... | ... |
| Greece Grèce | 2004 | 212 734 | -1.0 | 99.0 | 0.2 | 99.2 | 83.4 | 15.7 |
| | 2005 | 228 156 | -1.7 | 98.3 | -0.1 | 98.2 | 83.0 | 15.2 |
| | 2006 | 245 865 | -1.6 | 98.4 | 0.0 | 98.4 | 82.2 | 16.1 |
| Greenland[1] Groenland[1] | 2003 | 9 397 | -2.6[12] | 97.4 | 38.7 | 136.1 | ... | ... |
| | 2004 | 9 827 | -2.5[12] | 97.5 | 36.7 | 134.2 | ... | ... |
| | 2005 | 10 210 | -2.4[12] | 97.6 | 35.9 | 133.5 | ... | ... |
| Grenada[1] Grenade[1] | 1984 | 275 | ... | 98.9 | ... | ... | 99.1 | ... |
| | 1985 | 311 | ... | 98.9 | ... | ... | 99.0 | ... |
| | 1986 | 350 | ... | 99.2 | ... | ... | 97.7 | ... |
| Guadeloupe[1] Guadeloupe[1] | 1990 | 15 201 | -2.5[2] | 97.5 | 37.3 | 134.8 | 123.6 | 11.2 |
| | 1991 | 16 415 | -3.4[2] | 96.6 | 35.4 | 132.0 | 118.3 | 13.7 |
| | 1992 | 17 972 | -3.0[2] | 97.0 | 36.6 | 133.6 | 113.4 | 20.2 |
| Guatemala[1] Guatemala[1] | 2003 | 197 599 | -1.4[2] | 98.6 | 9.9 | 108.5 | 93.8 | 14.6 |
| | 2004 | 216 749 | -1.3[2] | 98.7 | 11.0 | 109.7 | 94.5 | 15.2 |
| | 2005 | 243 699 | -1.2[2] | 98.8 | 10.9 | 109.8 | 95.1 | 14.7 |

| Country or area<br>Pays ou zone | Year<br>Année | GDP at current prices (mil.nat.cur.)<br>PIB aux prix courants (millions monnaie nat.) | Plus: Compensation of employees and property income from/to the rest of the world, net<br>Plus : Rémuneration des salariés et revenus de la propriété du/au reste du monde, net | Equals: Gross national income<br>Égale : Revenu national brut | Plus: Net current transfers from/ to the rest of the world<br>Plus : Transferts courants du/au reste du monde, net | Equals: Gross national disposable income<br>Égale : Revenu national disponible brut | Less: Final consumption expenditure<br>Moins : Dépense de consommation finale | Equals: Gross savings<br>Égale : Épargne brut |
|---|---|---|---|---|---|---|---|---|
| Guinea-Bissau[1]<br>Guinée-Bissau[1] | 1986 | 46 973 | -1.7 | 98.3 | 2.9 | 101.3 | 102.8 | -1.5 |
| | 1987 | 92 375 | -0.5 | 99.5 | 4.1 | 103.6 | 100.8 | 2.8 |
| | 1988 | 171 949 | ... | ... | ... | ... | ... | ... |
| Guyana[1]<br>Guyana[1] | 2004 | 156 358 | ... | 96.0 | ... | ... | 78.6 | ... |
| | 2005 | 165 028 | ... | 97.5 | ... | ... | 100.2 | ... |
| | 2006 | 180 282 | ... | 95.1 | ... | ... | 89.3 | ... |
| Haiti+[1]<br>Haïti+[1] | 1995 | 35 207 | ... | 98.7 | 22.8 | 121.5 | 108.1 | 13.4 |
| | 1996 | 43 234 | ... | 99.6 | 17.1 | 116.7 | 104.9 | 11.8 |
| | 1997 | 51 789 | ... | 99.6 | 14.1 | 113.7 | 103.7 | 10.0 |
| Honduras[1]<br>Honduras[1] | 2004 | 137 242 | ... | 95.0 | 18.2 | 113.2 | 88.9 | 24.3 |
| | 2005 | 157 668 | ... | 95.7 | 23.6 | 119.3 | 90.6 | 28.7 |
| | 2006 | 175 740 | ... | 96.6 | 27.1 | 123.7 | 92.7 | 31.0 |
| Hungary<br>Hongrie | 2004 | 20 717 110 | -5.9 | 94.1 | ... | ... | 77.1 | ... |
| | 2005 | 22 055 093 | -5.9 | 94.1 | ... | ... | 77.8 | ... |
| | 2006 | 23 752 721 | ... | ... | ... | ... | 76.1 | ... |
| Iceland<br>Islande | 2004 | 926 459 | -4.1 | 95.9 | -0.1 | 95.8 | 82.2 | 13.6 |
| | 2005 | 1 021 510 | -3.5 | 96.5 | -0.2 | 96.3 | 84.3 | 12.0 |
| | 2006 | 1 141 747 | -8.6 | 91.4 | -0.2 | 91.2 | 84.7 | 6.4 |
| India+[1]<br>Inde+[1] | 2003 | 27 654 905 | -0.7 | 99.3 | 3.8 | 103.1 | 73.0 | 29.7 |
| | 2004 | 31 265 958 | -0.7 | 99.3 | 2.9 | 102.2 | 70.6 | 31.1 |
| | 2005 | 35 671 769 | -0.7 | 99.3 | 3.0 | 102.3 | 69.2 | 32.4 |
| Indonesia[1]<br>Indonésie[1] | 2001 | 1 467 660 000 | ... | 95.8 | ... | ... | 74.0 | ... |
| | 2002 | 1 610 570 000 | ... | 96.6 | ... | ... | 77.8 | ... |
| | 2003 | 1 786 690 000 | ... | 95.5 | ... | ... | 78.5 | ... |
| Iran (Islamic Rep. of)+<br>Iran (Rép. islamique d')+ | 2003 | 1 119 661 000 | -1.9 | 98.1 | 0.0 | 98.1 | 57.7 | 40.3 |
| | 2004 | 1 401 899 100 | -1.8 | 98.2 | 0.0 | 98.2 | 57.7 | 40.5 |
| | 2005 | 1 721 260 900 | -1.8 | 98.2 | 0.0 | 98.2 | 57.1 | 41.0 |
| Iraq[1]<br>Iraq[1] | 2003 | 20 562 256 | 0.2 | 100.2 | 9.3 | 109.5 | 83.9 | 25.6 |
| | 2004 | 37 049 252 | 0.2 | 100.2 | 7.5 | 107.7 | 85.0 | 22.8 |
| | 2005 | 49 990 680 | 2.2 | 102.2 | 9.7 | 111.9 | 72.9 | 39.0 |
| Ireland<br>Irlande | 2003 | 138 941 | -14.7 | 85.3 | -0.6 | 84.7 | 60.4 | 24.2 |
| | 2004 | 147 569 | -14.7 | 85.3 | -0.7 | 84.5 | 60.7 | 23.9 |
| | 2005 | 161 163 | -14.5 | 85.5 | -0.7 | 84.7 | 60.2 | 24.5 |
| Israel<br>Israël | 2003 | 524 187 | -3.4 | 96.6 | 5.6 | 102.2 | 84.1 | 18.1 |
| | 2004 | 548 936 | -2.9 | 97.1 | 5.1 | 102.2 | 83.1 | 19.1 |
| | 2005 | 582 291 | -2.0 | 98.0 | 4.7 | 102.6 | 82.0 | 20.6 |
| Italy<br>Italie | 2004 | 1 390 539 | -0.6 | 99.4 | -0.6 | 98.8 | 78.5 | 20.3 |
| | 2005 | 1 423 048 | -0.4 | 99.6 | -0.7 | 98.9 | 79.4 | 19.4 |
| | 2006 | 1 475 401 | -0.3 | 99.7 | -0.9 | 98.8 | 79.6 | 19.2 |
| Jamaica[1]<br>Jamaïque[1] | 2003 | 472 918 | -6.0 | 94.0 | 13.0 | 107.0 | 88.0 | 19.0 |
| | 2004 | 540 809 | -4.6 | 95.4 | 14.3 | 109.7 | 86.8 | 22.9 |
| | 2005 | 605 030 | -8.4 | 91.6 | 14.7 | 106.3 | 88.0 | 18.3 |
| Japan<br>Japon | 2003 | 490 294 000 | 1.7 | 101.7 | -0.1 | 101.6 | 75.5 | 25.4 |
| | 2004 | 498 328 400 | 1.9 | 101.9 | -0.1 | 101.8 | 75.0 | 25.8 |
| | 2005 | 501 402 600 | 2.4 | 102.4 | -0.1 | 102.3 | 75.2 | 26.4 |
| Jordan[1]<br>Jordanie[1] | 2002 | 6 794 | 1.2 | 101.2 | 23.6 | 124.8 | 98.6 | 26.2 |
| | 2003 | 7 229 | 1.2 | 101.2 | 31.4 | 132.6 | 99.7 | 32.9 |
| | 2004 | 8 081 | 1.7 | 101.7 | 28.6 | 130.3 | 102.5 | 27.8 |
| Kazakhstan<br>Kazakhstan | 2003 | 4 611 975 | -5.7 | 94.3 | -0.5 | 93.8 | 65.7 | 28.1 |
| | 2004 | 5 870 134 | -6.6 | 93.4 | -1.1 | 92.3 | 65.1 | 27.1 |
| | 2005 | 7 590 594 | -9.4 | 90.6 | -0.7 | 89.9 | 61.1 | 28.8 |

| | | | As a percentage of GDP — En pourcentage du PIB | | | | | |
|---|---|---|---|---|---|---|---|---|
| Country or area<br><br>Pays ou zone | Year<br><br>Année | GDP at current prices (mil.nat.cur.)<br><br>PIB aux prix courants (millions monnaie nat.) | Plus: Compensation of employees and property income from/to the rest of the world, net<br><br>Plus : Rémuneration des salariés et revenus de la propriété du/au reste du monde, net | Equals: Gross national income<br><br>Égale : Revenu national brut | Plus: Net current transfers from/ to the rest of the world<br><br>Plus : Transfers courants du/au reste du monde, net | Equals: Gross national disposable income<br><br>Égale : Revenu national disponible brut | Less: Final consumption expenditure<br><br>Moins : Dépense de consommation finale | Equals: Gross savings<br><br>Égale : Épargne brut |
| Kenya<br>Kenya | 2003 | 1 137 975 | -0.6[2] | 99.4 | 5.8 | 105.2 | 94.9 | 10.3 |
| | 2004 | 1 282 504 | -0.8[2] | 99.2 | 4.1 | 103.3 | 92.9 | 10.4 |
| | 2005 | 1 415 155 | -0.6[2] | 99.4 | 5.5 | 104.9 | 93.2 | 11.7 |
| Korea, Republic of<br>Corée, République de | 2004 | 779 380 500 | 0.2 | 100.2 | -0.4 | 99.9 | 65.0 | 34.8 |
| | 2005 | 810 515 900 | -0.2 | 99.9 | -0.3 | 99.5 | 66.8 | 32.7 |
| | 2006 | 847 876 400 | 0.0 | 100.0 | -0.4 | 99.6 | 68.3 | 31.2 |
| Kuwait[1]<br>Koweït[1] | 1999 | 9 170 | 17.0[12] | 117.0 | -6.7 | 110.3 | 78.9 | 31.4 |
| | 2000 | 11 510 | 17.9[12] | 118.4 | -5.2 | 113.2 | 63.3 | 49.8 |
| | 2001 | 10 700 | 14.0[12] | 114.0 | -6.0 | 108.1 | 69.9 | 38.2 |
| Kyrgyzstan<br>Kirghizistan | 2003 | 83 872 | -3.1 | 96.9 | 5.5 | 102.4 | 94.7 | 7.6 |
| | 2004 | 94 351 | -4.5 | 95.5 | 9.1 | 104.6 | 94.2 | 10.4 |
| | 2005 | 100 899 | -3.3 | 96.7 | 13.5 | 110.2 | 102.1 | 8.2 |
| Latvia<br>Lettonie | 2004 | 7 434 | -2.3 | 97.8 | 4.9 | 102.7 | 82.4 | 20.3 |
| | 2005 | 9 059 | -1.9 | 98.7 | 3.2 | 101.8 | 80.0 | 21.8 |
| | 2006 | 11 265 | -3.3 | 97.2 | 1.9 | 99.1 | 82.1 | 17.0 |
| Lebanon<br>Liban | 2002 | 28 209 000 | -1.1 | 98.9 | 10.5 | 109.5 | 101.2 | 8.2 |
| | 2003 | 29 851 000 | -1.2 | 98.8 | 17.0 | 115.8 | 101.8 | 14.0 |
| | 2004 | 32 357 000 | -3.8 | 96.2 | 15.7 | 111.9 | 100.4 | 11.4 |
| Lesotho<br>Lesotho | 2003 | 7 862 | 23.8[8] | 123.8 | 18.7 | 142.5 | 117.3 | 25.3 |
| | 2004 | 8 518 | 22.9[8] | 122.9 | 21.1 | 144.0 | 112.4 | 31.5 |
| | 2005 | 9 263 | 20.9[8] | 120.9 | 21.4 | 142.3 | 101.5 | 40.8 |
| Liberia[1]<br>Libéria[1] | 1987 | 1 090 | ... | 83.2 | ... | ... | ... | ... |
| | 1988 | 1 158 | ... | 84.2 | ... | ... | ... | ... |
| | 1989 | 1 194 | ... | 84.9 | ... | ... | ... | ... |
| Libyan Arab Jamah.[1]<br>Jamah. arabe libyenne[1] | 1983 | 8 805 | -6.9[12] | 91.0 | -0.2 | 90.9 | 72.0 | 18.9 |
| | 1984 | 8 013 | -4.6[12] | 92.7 | -0.3 | 92.4 | 72.2 | 20.2 |
| | 1985 | 8 277 | -2.9[12] | 96.7 | -0.2 | 96.5 | 69.2 | 27.3 |
| Liechtenstein<br>Liechtenstein | 2003 | 4 135 | ... | 85.6 | ... | ... | ... | ... |
| | 2004 | 4 296 | ... | 82.7 | ... | ... | ... | ... |
| | 2005 | 4 555 | ... | 85.4 | ... | ... | ... | ... |
| Lithuania<br>Lituanie | 2003 | 56 804 | -2.5 | 97.5 | 1.6 | 99.1 | 82.6 | 16.5 |
| | 2004 | 62 587 | -2.6 | 97.9 | 1.7 | 99.6 | 83.1 | 16.4 |
| | 2005 | 71 200 | -2.4 | 98.4 | 1.7 | 100.1 | 82.0 | 18.2 |
| Luxembourg<br>Luxembourg | 2003 | 25 607 | -19.1 | 80.9 | ... | ... | 57.5 | ... |
| | 2004 | 26 996 | -17.8 | 82.2 | ... | ... | 57.9 | ... |
| | 2005 | 29 396 | -18.3 | 81.7 | ... | ... | 57.4 | ... |
| Madagascar[1] — Madagascar[1] | 1980 | 689 800 | ... | 99.9 | ... | ... | ... | ... |
| Malawi[1]<br>Malawi[1] | 1994 | 11 209 | -3.6 | 96.4 | 9.2 | 105.6 | ... | ... |
| | 1995 | 20 246 | -3.1 | 96.9 | 9.6 | 105.0 | ... | ... |
| | 1996 | 23 993 | -1.8 | 98.2 | 3.4 | 101.6 | ... | ... |
| Malaysia<br>Malaisie | 2004 | 474 048 | -5.1[2] | 94.9 | -3.1 | 91.8 | 56.6 | 35.2 |
| | 2005 | 519 451 | -4.6[2] | 95.4 | -3.3 | 92.1 | 57.3 | 34.8 |
| | 2006 | 572 555 | -3.0[2] | 97.0 | -2.9 | 94.1 | 57.0 | 37.1 |
| Maldives<br>Maldives | 2004 | 9 939 | -5.5[2] | 94.5 | -7.0 | 87.5 | 56.5 | 31.0 |
| | 2005 | 9 607 | -4.9[2] | 95.1 | 4.9 | 100.0 | 71.9 | 28.1 |
| | 2006 | 11 608 | -4.1[2] | 95.9 | 5.7 | 101.6 | 67.7 | 33.9 |
| Mali[1]<br>Mali[1] | 1990 | 683 300 | -1.2[2] | 98.8 | 11.5 | 110.3 | 94.3 | 16.1 |
| | 1991 | 691 400 | -1.3[2] | 98.7 | 13.0 | 111.9 | 100.4 | 11.5 |
| | 1992 | 737 400 | -1.2[2] | 98.8 | 11.4 | 110.2 | 96.4 | 13.8 |

| Country or area<br>Pays ou zone | Year<br>Année | GDP at current prices (mil.nat.cur.)<br>PIB aux prix courants (millions monnaie nat.) | Plus: Compensation of employees and property income from/to the rest of the world, net<br>Plus : Rémunération des salariés et revenus de la propriété du/au reste du monde, net | Equals: Gross national income<br>Égale : Revenu national brut | Plus: Net current transfers from/ to the rest of the world<br>Plus : Transfers courants du/au reste du monde, net | Equals: Gross national disposable income<br>Égale : Revenu national disponible brut | Less: Final consumption expenditure<br>Moins : Dépense de consommation finale | Equals: Gross savings<br>Égale : Épargne brut |
|---|---|---|---|---|---|---|---|---|
| Malta | 2003 | 1 859 | -0.3 | 99.7 | ... | ... | ... | ... |
| Malte | 2004 | 1 861 | -0.8 | 99.0 | ... | ... | ... | ... |
| | 2005 | 1 941 | -1.1 | 98.5 | ... | ... | ... | ... |
| Martinique[1] | 1990 | 19 320 | -4.2[2] | 95.8 | 33.7 | ... | 113.3 | ... |
| Martinique[1] | 1991 | 20 787 | -4.4[2] | 95.6 | 30.7 | ... | 112.8 | ... |
| | 1992 | 22 093 | -3.9[2] | 96.1 | 33.4 | ... | 113.1 | ... |
| Mauritania[1] | 1987 | 67 216 | -5.1 | 94.9 | 8.1 | 103.0 | 96.2 | 6.7 |
| Mauritanie[1] | 1988 | 72 635 | -5.6 | 94.4 | 7.9 | 102.3 | 93.7 | 8.5 |
| | 1989 | 83 520 | -3.6 | 96.4 | 9.0 | 105.4 | | |
| Mauritius | 2004 | 175 592 | -0.2 | 99.8 | 0.8 | 100.6 | 77.9 | 22.6 |
| Maurice | 2005 | 185 487 | -0.1 | 99.9 | 1.0 | 100.8 | 84.3 | 16.6 |
| | 2006 | 203 337 | ... | 100.7 | 1.0 | 101.8 | 86.6 | 15.1 |
| Mexico | 2002 | 6 263 137 | -1.8 | 98.2 | 1.6 | 99.8 | 81.2 | 18.6 |
| Mexique | 2003 | 6 891 992 | -1.8 | 98.2 | 2.2 | 100.3 | 81.1 | 19.2 |
| | 2004 | 7 709 096 | -1.5 | 98.5 | 2.5 | 101.0 | 80.0 | 21.0 |
| Moldova | 2004 | 32 032 | 13.7 | 113.7 | 14.0 | 127.7 | 104.0 | 23.8 |
| Moldova | 2005 | 37 652 | 13.5 | 113.5 | 19.1 | 132.6 | 109.9 | 22.7 |
| | 2006 | 44 069 | ... | 100.0 | ... | ... | ... | ... |
| Mongolia | 2003 | 1 473 677 | 4.9 | 104.9 | ... | ... | ... | ... |
| Mongolie | 2004 | 1 926 322 | 8.3 | 108.3 | ... | ... | ... | ... |
| | 2005 | 2 489 218 | 4.0 | 104.0 | ... | ... | ... | ... |
| Morocco | 2003 | 476 987 | -2.1[2] | 97.9 | 8.3 | 106.2 | 75.5 | 30.7 |
| Maroc | 2004 | 500 081 | -1.8[2] | 98.2 | 8.7 | 106.9 | 76.5 | 30.5 |
| | 2005 | 522 649 | -1.1[2] | 98.9 | 9.2 | 108.1 | 75.9 | 32.2 |
| Mozambique | 2003 | 113 902 523 | -3.4 | 96.6 | 4.6 | 101.2 | 80.4 | 20.8 |
| Mozambique | 2004 | 133 510 417 | -4.9 | 95.1 | 5.2 | 100.3 | 78.2 | 22.0 |
| | 2005 | 157 345 427 | -5.6 | 94.4 | 5.9 | 100.3 | 82.0 | 18.3 |
| Myanmar+[1] | 1996 | 791 980 | 0.0[2] | 100.0 | ... | 100.0 | 88.5 | 11.4 |
| Myanmar+[1] | 1997 | 1 109 554 | 0.0[2] | 100.0 | ... | 100.0 | 88.1 | 11.9 |
| | 1998 | 1 559 996 | 0.0[2] | 100.0 | ... | 100.0 | 89.4 | 10.6 |
| Namibia | 2003 | 33 842 | 5.1 | 105.1 | 10.2 | 115.4 | 82.0 | 33.3 |
| Namibie | 2004 | 36 181 | 1.5 | 101.5 | 11.9 | 115.2 | 83.3 | 37.0 |
| | 2005 | 38 560 | -0.5 | 99.5 | ... | ... | 82.7 | ... |
| Nepal+ | 2004 | 589 412 | 0.3[13] | 100.3 | 16.6[14] | 116.9 | 88.4 | 28.4 |
| Népal+ | 2005 | 646 471 | 0.8[13] | 100.8 | 19.5[14] | 120.3 | 92.1 | 28.2 |
| | 2006 | 719 477 | ... | 100.6 | 18.6[14] | 119.2 | 90.6 | 28.6 |
| Netherlands | 2004 | 489 854 | 2.8 | 102.8 | -1.5 | 101.4 | 73.5 | 27.9 |
| Pays-Bas | 2005 | 505 646 | 0.9 | 100.9 | -1.5 | 99.4 | 73.0 | 26.5 |
| | 2006 | 527 916 | 3.8 | 103.8 | -1.6 | 102.2 | 72.4 | 29.8 |
| Netherlands Antilles | 2002 | 5 254 | 0.0 | 100.0 | 4.3 | 104.4 | 74.5 | 29.9 |
| Antilles néerlandaises | 2003 | 5 425 | -0.2 | 99.8 | 4.6 | 104.4 | 75.5 | 28.9 |
| | 2004 | 5 576 | -0.3 | 99.7 | 2.5 | 102.2 | 75.2 | 26.9 |
| New Zealand+ | 2003 | 138 941 | -5.2 | 94.8 | 0.2 | 95.0 | 76.4 | 18.6 |
| Nouvelle-Zélande+ | 2004 | 148 484 | -6.6 | 93.4 | 0.3 | 93.7 | 76.7 | 17.0 |
| | 2005 | 155 885 | -7.2 | 92.8 | 0.3 | 93.1 | 78.1 | 15.0 |
| Nicaragua+ | 2004 | 71 661 | -4.3[2] | 95.7 | 15.0 | 110.7 | 99.5 | 11.2 |
| Nicaragua+ | 2005 | 82 162 | -2.4[2] | 97.6 | 15.3 | 112.9 | 100.3 | 12.6 |
| | 2006 | 94 361 | -2.6[2] | 97.4 | 15.3 | 112.7 | 99.8 | 12.9 |
| Niger[1] | 2003 | 1 471 712 | -1.0 | 99.0 | 3.7 | 102.6 | 94.2 | 8.4 |
| Niger[1] | 2004 | 1 468 393 | -0.5 | 99.5 | 3.7 | 103.3 | 96.8 | 6.4 |
| | 2005 | 1 701 950 | 0.0 | 100.0 | 4.8 | 104.7 | 92.7 | 12.0 |

| | | GDP at current prices (mil.nat.cur.) PIB aux prix courants (millions monnaie nat.) | As a percentage of GDP — En pourcentage du PIB | | | | | |
|---|---|---|---|---|---|---|---|---|
| Country or area Pays ou zone | Year Année | | Plus: Compensation of employees and property income from/to the rest of the world, net Plus : Rémuneration des salariés et revenus de la propriété du/au reste du monde, net | Equals: Gross national income Égale : Revenu national brut | Plus: Net current transfers from/ to the rest of the world Plus : Transfers courants du/au reste du monde, net | Equals: Gross national disposable income Égale : Revenu national disponible brut | Less: Final consumption expenditure Moins : Dépense de consommation finale | Equals: Gross savings Égale : Épargne brut |
| Nigeria[1] Nigéria[1] | 1992 | 549 809 | -11.7 | 88.3 | 2.3 | 90.6 | 77.2 | 13.4 |
| | 1993 | 701 473 | -10.5 | 89.5 | 2.5 | 92.0 | 80.6 | 11.5 |
| | 1994 | 914 334 | -7.2 | 92.8 | 1.2 | 94.0 | 85.5 | 8.5 |
| Norway Norvège | 2004 | 1 743 041 | 0.2 | 100.2 | -1.0 | 99.2 | 66.5 | 32.7 |
| | 2005 | 1 942 887 | 0.0 | 100.0 | -0.9 | 99.1 | 62.3 | 36.8 |
| | 2006 | 2 147 986 | ... | 100.0 | ... | 99.2 | 60.0 | 39.2 |
| Occupied Palestinian Terr. Terr. palestinien occupé | 2001 | 3 816 | 8.6 | 108.6 | 24.6 | 133.2 | 127.4 | 5.8 |
| | 2002 | 3 484 | 6.4 | 106.4 | 30.6 | 137.0 | 131.4 | 5.5 |
| | 2003 | 3 921 | 7.2 | 107.2 | 36.2 | 143.5 | 129.3 | 14.1 |
| Oman Oman | 2003 | 8 376 | -4.3 | 95.7 | -7.5 | 88.2 | 65.8 | 22.4 |
| | 2004 | 9 516 | -4.5 | 95.5 | -7.2 | 88.3 | 65.4 | 22.9 |
| | 2005 | 11 856 | -4.9 | 95.1 | -7.2 | 87.9 | 54.5 | 33.4 |
| Pakistan+ Pakistan+ | 2004 | 5 640 580 | ... | 102.2 | ... | ... | 82.4 | ... |
| | 2005 | 6 581 103 | ... | 102.0 | ... | ... | 85.7 | ... |
| | 2006 | 7 713 064 | ... | 102.0 | ... | ... | 88.9 | ... |
| Panama Panama | 2003 | 12 933 | -7.5 | 92.5 | 1.4 | 93.9 | 75.9 | 17.9 |
| | 2004 | 14 179 | -8.9 | 91.1 | 1.1 | 92.1 | 77.6 | 14.5 |
| | 2005 | 15 483 | -9.2 | 90.8 | 1.1 | 91.8 | 75.5 | 16.3 |
| Papua New Guinea Papouasie-Nvl-Guinée | 2000 | 10 750 | -3.6 | 90.5[15] | 2.3 | 92.8 | 76.3 | 16.5 |
| | 2001 | 11 758 | -3.5 | 89.7[15] | 0.4 | 90.1 | 87.4 | 2.7 |
| | 2002 | 13 375 | -3.0 | 90.2[15] | 0.7 | 90.8 | 88.3 | 2.5 |
| Paraguay[1] Paraguay[1] | 1993 | 11 991 719 | ... | 100.4 | ... | 100.4 | 88.0 | 12.4 |
| | 1994 | 14 960 131 | ... | 100.5 | ... | 100.5 | 95.2 | 5.3 |
| | 1995 | 17 699 000 | ... | 100.9 | ... | 100.9 | 92.5 | 8.4 |
| Peru[1] Pérou[1] | 1996 | 148 278 | ... | 97.3 | ... | ... | 80.6 | ... |
| | 1997 | 172 389 | ... | 97.5 | ... | ... | 78.7 | ... |
| | 1998 | 183 179 | ... | 97.7 | ... | ... | 80.9 | ... |
| Philippines[1] Philippines[1] | 2003 | 4 316 402 | 7.3 | 107.3 | 1.0 | 108.3 | 80.3 | 28.1 |
| | 2004 | 4 858 835 | 7.7 | 107.7 | 0.8 | 108.5 | 79.0 | 29.6 |
| | 2005 | 5 418 839 | 8.4 | 108.4 | 0.8 | 109.3 | 79.3 | 30.0 |
| Poland Pologne | 2003 | 842 120 | -1.5 | 98.5 | 2.0 | 100.4 | 83.8 | 16.6 |
| | 2004 | 923 248 | -4.1 | 95.9 | 1.7 | 97.6 | 81.9 | 15.7 |
| | 2005 | 980 666 | -3.4 | 96.6 | 2.1 | 98.7 | 81.1 | 17.5 |
| Portugal Portugal | 2004 | 144 223 | -2.0 | 98.0 | 1.7 | 99.7 | 84.7 | 15.0 |
| | 2005 | 148 928 | -2.7 | 97.3 | 1.6 | 99.0 | 86.2 | 12.8 |
| | 2006 | 155 216 | -4.0 | 96.0 | 1.9 | 97.9 | 85.8 | 12.2 |
| Puerto Rico+[1] Porto Rico+[1] | 2003 | 79 209 | -36.5 | 63.5 | 11.7 | 75.2 | 66.3 | 4.6 |
| | 2004 | 82 650 | -35.6 | 64.4 | 11.3 | 75.7 | 68.2 | 6.0 |
| | 2005 | 86 464 | -34.8 | 65.2 | 11.4 | 76.6 | 69.3 | 6.1 |
| Réunion[1] Réunion[1] | 1990 | 28 374 | -2.5[2] | 97.5 | 44.3 | 141.7 | 108.1 | 33.6 |
| | 1991 | 31 339 | 0.1[2] | 100.7 | 42.7 | 143.4 | 103.5 | 39.9 |
| | 1992 | 33 787 | -1.5[2] | 98.4 | 43.6 | 142.1 | 104.5 | 37.6 |
| Romania Roumanie | 2004 | 2 464 687 900 | -4.2 | 95.8 | 8.2 | 104.1 | 85.3 | 18.8 |
| | #2005 | 288 048 | -2.9 | 97.1 | ... | ... | 87.6 | ... |
| | 2006[16] | 342 418 | -3.1 | 96.9 | ... | ... | 87.9 | ... |
| Russian Federation Fédération de Russie | 2004 | 17 048 122[17] | -2.2 | 97.8 | -0.1 | 97.7 | 66.9 | 30.8 |
| | 2005 | 21 620 111[17] | -2.5 | 97.5 | -0.1 | 97.4 | 66.4 | 30.9 |
| | 2006 | 26 781 103[17] | -2.9 | 97.1 | -0.1 | 97.0 | 66.3 | 30.7 |
| Rwanda[1] Rwanda[1] | 1987 | 171 430 | -1.6 | 98.4 | 2.5 | 100.9 | 93.5 | 7.4 |
| | 1988 | 177 920 | -2.0 | 98.0 | 2.9 | 100.9 | 93.6 | 7.3 |
| | 1989 | 190 220 | -1.2 | 98.8 | 2.4 | 101.3 | 95.4 | 5.9 |

| Country or area<br>Pays ou zone | Year<br>Année | GDP at current prices (mil.nat.cur.)<br>PIB aux prix courants (millions monnaie nat.) | Plus: Compensation of employees and property income from/to the rest of the world, net<br>Plus : Rémuneration des salariés et revenus de la propriété du/au reste du monde, net | Equals: Gross national income<br>Égale : Revenu national brut | Plus: Net current transfers from/ to the rest of the world<br>Plus : Transfers courants du/au reste du monde, net | Equals: Gross national disposable income<br>Égale : Revenu national disponible brut | Less: Final consumption expenditure<br>Moins : Dépense de consommation finale | Equals: Gross savings<br>Égale : Épargne brut |
|---|---|---|---|---|---|---|---|---|
| Saint Kitts and Nevis[1]<br>Saint-Kitts-et-Nevis[1] | 2004 | 1 078 | -9.7 | 90.3 | 4.6 | 94.8 | 72.7 | 22.2 |
| | 2005 | 1 158 | -7.8 | 92.2 | 4.8 | 97.0 | 70.2 | 26.8 |
| | 2006 | 1 314 | -6.9 | 93.1 | 4.1 | 97.3 | 74.8 | 22.5 |
| Saint Lucia[1]<br>Sainte-Lucie[1] | 2003 | 2 015 | -6.4 | 93.6 | 1.8 | 95.3 | 92.4 | 2.9 |
| | 2004 | 2 154 | -6.7 | 93.3 | 1.7 | 95.0 | 86.7 | 8.3 |
| | 2005 | 2 383 | -6.5 | 93.5 | 1.6 | 95.0 | 84.1 | 11.0 |
| Saint Vincent-Grenadines[1]<br>Saint Vincent-Grenadines[1] | 2003 | 1 032 | -6.2 | 93.8 | 3.4 | 97.2 | 84.7 | 12.5 |
| | 2004 | 1 121 | -7.0 | 93.0 | 3.4 | 96.4 | 89.0 | 7.4 |
| | 2005 | 1 166 | -5.7 | 94.3 | 4.2 | 98.5 | 89.4 | 9.2 |
| San Marino[1]<br>Saint-Marin[1] | 2002 | 935 | ... | 88.7 | ... | 74.7 | ... | ... |
| | 2003 | 995 | ... | 89.5 | ... | 76.7 | ... | ... |
| | 2004 | 1 061 | ... | 88.8 | ... | 76.1 | ... | ... |
| Saudi Arabia+[1]<br>Arabie saoudite+[1] | 2002 | 707 067 | 0.7 | 100.7 | -11.8 | 88.9 | 62.9 | 26.0 |
| | 2003 | 804 648 | 0.3 | 100.3 | -9.3 | 91.1 | 58.2 | 32.9 |
| | 2004 | 938 771 | 0.9 | 100.9 | -7.9 | 92.9 | 54.1 | 38.9 |
| Senegal<br>Sénégal | 2002 | 3 717 639 | -7.5 | 101.9 | 6.9 | 108.8 | 93.2 | 15.6 |
| | 2003 | 3 960 841 | -9.3 | 99.7 | 7.0 | 106.7 | 91.2 | 15.5 |
| | 2004 | 4 198 473 | -10.2 | 99.7 | 6.5 | 106.2 | 92.0 | 14.2 |
| Seychelles[1]<br>Seychelles[1] | 1998 | 3 201 | ... | 97.2 | ... | ... | 81.2 | ... |
| | 1999 | 3 330 | ... | 97.3 | ... | ... | 73.1 | ... |
| | 2000 | 3 424 | ... | 96.3 | ... | ... | 66.4 | ... |
| Sierra Leone<br>Sierra Leone | 2003 | 3 335 650 | ... | 98.9 | 11.3 | 111.7 | 126.1 | -14.4 |
| | 2004 | 3 825 095 | ... | 95.3 | 8.4 | 105.3 | 113.9 | -8.6 |
| | 2005 | 4 402 185 | ... | 96.7 | 9.0 | 107.9 | 106.0 | 1.9 |
| Singapore<br>Singapour | 2004 | 181 540 | -6.2 | 93.8 | -1.1 | 92.7 | 54.0 | 39.7 |
| | 2005 | 194 242 | -3.9 | 96.1 | -1.0 | 95.0 | 52.7 | 43.5 |
| | 2006 | 209 991 | -3.2 | 96.8 | -1.0 | 95.8 | 51.5 | 46.3 |
| Slovakia<br>Slovaquie | 2004 | 1 355 262 | 0.4 | 100.4 | -0.2 | 100.2 | 76.7 | 23.5 |
| | 2005 | 1 471 131 | -2.6 | 97.4 | -0.3 | 97.2 | 75.9 | 21.3 |
| | 2006 | 1 636 263 | -3.0 | 97.0 | 0.0 | 96.9 | 75.7 | 21.2 |
| Slovenia<br>Slovénie | 2004 | 6 271 795 | -1.2 | 98.8 | -0.2 | 98.6 | 74.4 | 24.2 |
| | 2005 | 6 620 145 | -1.1 | 99.1 | -0.5 | 98.6 | 74.5 | 24.1 |
| | 2006 | 7 126 012 | ... | 98.8 | -0.8 | 98.0 | 73.3 | 24.8 |
| Solomon Islands[1]<br>Iles Salomon[1] | 1984 | 222 | -3.2[2] | 94.2 | ... | 100.8 | 78.2 | 22.6 |
| | 1985 | 237 | -2.3[2] | 95.0 | ... | 101.0 | 91.6 | 9.4 |
| | 1986 | 253 | -2.0[2] | 92.6 | ... | 115.7 | 94.8 | 20.9 |
| Somalia[1]<br>Somalie[1] | 1985 | 87 290 | ... | 97.8 | 10.1 | 107.9 | 101.1 | 6.8 |
| | 1986 | 118 781 | ... | 96.3 | 14.2 | 110.5 | 98.8 | 11.7 |
| | 1987 | 169 608 | ... | 96.8 | 21.3 | 118.0 | 99.9 | 18.2 |
| South Africa<br>Afrique du Sud | 2003 | 1 260 693 | -2.8 | 97.2 | -0.6 | 96.6 | 81.6 | 15.8 |
| | 2004 | 1 398 157 | -2.0 | 98.0 | -0.8 | 97.2 | 81.9 | 14.5 |
| | 2005 | 1 539 253 | -2.0 | 98.0 | -0.8 | 97.1 | 82.2 | 14.5 |
| Spain<br>Espagne | 2004 | 840 106 | -1.3 | 98.7 | -0.6 | 98.1 | 75.7 | 22.4 |
| | 2005 | 905 455 | -1.4 | 98.6 | -0.7 | 97.9 | 75.8 | 22.1 |
| | 2006 | 976 189 | -1.6 | 98.4 | -0.8 | 97.7 | 75.6 | 22.1 |
| Sri Lanka<br>Sri Lanka | 2003 | 1 795 259 | -0.9 | 99.1 | 6.5 | 105.6 | 84.2 | 21.1 |
| | 2004 | 2 059 831 | -1.0 | 99.0 | 6.6 | 105.6 | 83.8 | 21.4 |
| | 2005 | 2 407 775 | -1.2 | 98.8 | 7.2 | 106.0 | 82.3 | 23.1 |
| Sudan[1]<br>Soudan[1] | 1991 | 421 819 | ... | 85.5 | ... | 104.0 | 86.0 | 18.0 |
| | 1992 | 948 448 | ... | 99.7 | ... | 102.2 | 88.2 | 14.0 |
| | 1993 | 1 881 289 | ... | 99.8 | ... | 100.6 | 88.3 | 12.3 |

| | | | As a percentage of GDP — En pourcentage du PIB | | | | | |
|---|---|---|---|---|---|---|---|---|
| Country or area<br><br>Pays ou zone | Year<br><br>Année | GDP at<br>current prices<br>(mil.nat.cur.)<br><br>PIB aux prix<br>courants<br>(millions<br>monnaie<br>nat.) | Plus: Compensation<br>of employees and<br>property income<br>from/to the rest of<br>the world, net<br><br>Plus : Rémuneration<br>des salariés et<br>revenus de la<br>propriété du/au<br>reste du monde, net | Equals:<br>Gross<br>national<br>income<br><br>Égale :<br>Revenu<br>national<br>brut | Plus: Net<br>current<br>transfers from/<br>to the rest<br>of the world<br><br>Plus : Transfers<br>courants<br>du/au reste du<br>monde, net | Equals: Gross<br>national<br>disposable<br>income<br><br>Égale : Revenu<br>national<br>disponible<br>brut | Less: Final<br>consumption<br>expenditure<br><br>Moins :<br>Dépense de<br>consommation<br>finale | Equals:<br>Gross<br>savings<br><br>Égale :<br>Épargne<br>brut |
| Suriname[1]<br>Suriname[1] | 2002 | 2 240 127 | -4.5 | 95.5 | -0.9 | 94.5 | ... | ... |
| | 2003 | 2 918 132 | -4.4 | 95.6 | -0.5 | 95.1 | ... | ... |
| | 2004 | 3 513 565 | -4.9 | 95.1 | 1.0 | 96.1 | ... | ... |
| Swaziland+<br>Swaziland+ | 2003 | 14 401 | 3.5[8] | 103.5 | 0.6 | 104.1 | 91.0 | 13.0 |
| | 2004 | 15 585 | 0.8[8] | 100.8 | 5.2 | 106.0 | 78.9 | 27.1 |
| | 2005 | 16 260 | 0.8[8] | 100.8 | 5.0 | 105.8 | 80.7 | 25.1 |
| Sweden<br>Suède | 2004 | 2 565 056 | -0.2 | 99.8 | -1.3 | 98.5 | 75.8 | 22.8 |
| | 2005 | 2 670 547 | -0.3 | 99.7 | -1.5 | 98.2 | 75.2 | 23.0 |
| | 2006 | 2 831 746 | 0.4 | 100.4 | -1.4 | 98.9 | 74.1 | 24.9 |
| Switzerland<br>Suisse | 2003 | 434 764 | 8.0 | 108.1 | -2.3 | 105.7 | 72.4 | 33.2 |
| | 2004 | 447 309 | 8.3 | 108.3 | -2.6 | 105.7 | 71.8 | 33.8 |
| | 2005 | 455 594 | 10.0 | 110.0 | -1.9 | 108.0 | 71.7 | 36.1 |
| Syrian Arab Republic[1]<br>Rép. arabe syrienne[1] | 2003 | 1 067 265 | ... | 91.9 | 1.1 | 93.0 | 73.8 | 19.2 |
| | 2004 | 1 253 944 | ... | 93.1 | 0.9 | 93.9 | 78.5 | 20.7 |
| | 2005 | 1 479 667 | ... | 89.9 | 0.8 | 90.7 | 80.6 | 16.4 |
| Tajikistan<br>Tadjikistan | 2003 | 4 762 | 21.8 | 121.8 | 3.7 | 125.5 | 90.7 | 34.8 |
| | 2004 | 6 167 | 29.3 | 129.3 | 2.3 | 131.5 | 85.8 | 45.7 |
| | 2005 | 7 207 | 27.8 | 127.8 | 3.1 | 130.9 | 95.7 | 35.2 |
| Thailand[1]<br>Thaïlande[1] | 2003 | 5 917 368 | -1.9 | 98.1 | 0.6 | 98.7 | 68.0 | 30.5 |
| | 2004 | 6 489 847 | -1.9 | 98.1 | 1.3 | 99.3 | 68.3 | 31.0 |
| | 2005 | 7 087 660 | -2.4 | 97.6 | 1.6 | 99.2 | 69.0 | 29.5 |
| TFYR of Macedonia<br>L'ex-R.y. Macédoine | 2003 | 251 486 | ... | 99.3 | ... | 113.8 | 97.0 | 16.9 |
| | 2004 | 265 257 | ... | 99.3 | ... | 112.5 | 98.9 | 13.7 |
| | 2005 | 286 619 | ... | 99.1 | ... | 115.9 | 96.5 | 19.3 |
| Togo[1]<br>Togo[1] | 1984 | 304 800 | ... | ... | ... | ... | 80.0 | ... |
| | 1985 | 332 500 | ... | ... | ... | ... | 80.2 | ... |
| | 1986 | 363 600 | ... | ... | ... | ... | 83.4 | ... |
| Tonga+[1]<br>Tonga+[1] | 2002 | 312 | 2.9 | 102.9 | 40.1 | 142.9 | 126.6 | 16.3 |
| | 2003 | 349 | 2.3 | 102.3 | 35.0 | 137.2 | 126.1 | 11.2 |
| | 2004 | 372 | 1.1 | 101.1 | 36.6 | 137.6 | 123.9 | 13.7 |
| Trinidad and Tobago<br>Trinité-et-Tobago | 2003 | 70 732 | -6.0[2] | 94.0 | 0.5 | 94.5 | 67.3 | 27.2 |
| | 2004 | 79 826 | -3.1[2] | 96.9 | 0.4 | 97.3 | 67.0 | 30.4 |
| | 2005 | 95 057 | -3.7[2] | 96.3 | 0.3 | 96.7 | 63.5 | 33.2 |
| Tunisia<br>Tunisie | 2002 | 29 924 | -4.5 | 95.5 | 5.3 | 100.7 | 78.6 | 22.1 |
| | 2003 | 32 202 | -4.1 | 95.9 | 5.1 | 101.0 | 78.8 | 22.2 |
| | 2004 | 35 148 | -4.4 | 95.6 | 5.3 | 101.0 | 78.5 | 22.4 |
| Turkey[1]<br>Turquie[1] | 2004 | 430 511 | -0.4 | 99.6 | 0.0 | 99.6 | 79.3 | 20.3 |
| | 2005 | 487 202 | -0.2 | 99.8 | 0.0 | 99.8 | 80.5 | 19.3 |
| | 2006 | 576 322 | -0.1 | 99.9 | ... | ... | 79.5 | ... |
| Ukraine<br>Ukraine | 2003 | 267 344 | -1.2 | 98.8 | 4.4 | 103.2 | 75.4 | 27.8 |
| | 2004 | 345 113 | -1.0 | 99.0 | 4.0 | 103.0 | 71.2 | 31.8 |
| | 2005 | 441 452 | -1.1 | 98.9 | 3.4 | 102.2 | 76.5 | 25.7 |
| United Arab Emirates[1]<br>Emirats arabes unis[1] | 1988 | 87 106 | 0.3 | 100.3 | -1.2 | 99.1 | 65.8 | 33.3 |
| | 1989 | 100 976 | 0.4 | 100.4 | -0.7 | 99.7 | 61.7 | 38.0 |
| | 1990 | 124 008 | -1.0 | 99.0 | -8.9 | 90.1 | 54.9 | 35.1 |
| United Kingdom<br>Royaume-Uni | 2004 | 1 176 527 | 2.2 | 102.2 | -0.8 | 101.3 | 86.0 | 15.3 |
| | 2005 | 1 225 978 | 2.2 | 102.2 | -0.9 | 101.2 | 86.6 | 14.7 |
| | 2006 | 1 289 989 | 1.7 | 101.7 | -0.9 | 100.8 | 86.4 | 14.5 |
| United Rep. of Tanzania<br>Rép.-Unie de Tanzanie | 2000 | 7 277 800 | -0.9[2] | 99.0 | 4.6 | 101.1 | 90.0 | 11.0 |
| | 2001 | 8 284 690 | -0.9[2] | 99.0 | 4.2 | 100.9 | 89.7 | 11.2 |
| | 2002 | 9 374 560 | -0.9[2] | 98.9 | 4.3 | 100.3 | 86.4 | 13.9 |

| Country or area<br><br>Pays ou zone | Year<br><br>Année | GDP at current prices (mil.nat.cur.)<br><br>PIB aux prix courants (millions monnaie nat.) | As a percentage of GDP — En pourcentage du PIB | | | | | |
|---|---|---|---|---|---|---|---|---|
| | | | Plus: Compensation of employees and property income from/to the rest of the world, net<br><br>Plus : Rémuneration des salariés et revenus de la propriété du/au reste du monde, net | Equals: Gross national income<br><br>Égale : Revenu national brut | Plus: Net current transfers from/ to the rest of the world<br><br>Plus : Transfers courants du/au reste du monde, net | Equals: Gross national disposable income<br><br>Égale : Revenu national disponible brut | Less: Final consumption expenditure<br><br>Moins : Dépense de consommation finale | Equals: Gross savings<br><br>Égale : Épargne brut |
| United States | 2003 | 10 908 000 | 0.5 | 100.1 | -0.6 | 99.4 | 86.5 | 12.9 |
| Etats-Unis | 2004 | 11 657 300 | 0.4 | 99.8 | -0.7 | 99.1 | 86.4 | 12.8 |
| | 2005 | 12 397 900 | 0.3 | 99.7 | -0.7 | 99.0 | 86.5 | 12.5 |
| Uruguay[1] | 2004 | 379 353 | -4.6[2] | 95.4 | 0.9 | 96.4 | 83.8 | 12.6 |
| Uruguay[1] | 2005 | 406 705 | -3.3[2] | 96.7 | 1.0 | 97.7 | 84.3 | 13.4 |
| | 2006 | 464 802 | -2.6[2] | 97.4 | 0.7 | 98.1 | 84.1 | 14.0 |
| Vanuatu[1] | 1996 | 28 227 | ... | 91.1 | ... | ... | ... | ... |
| Vanuatu[1] | 1997 | 29 477 | ... | 91.7 | ... | ... | ... | ... |
| | 1998 | 29 545 | ... | 93.5 | ... | ... | ... | ... |
| Venezuela (Bolivarian Rep. of) | 2002 | 107 840 166 | -3.0 | 97.0 | -0.2 | 96.9 | 66.5 | 30.3 |
| Venezuela (Rép. bolivarienne du) | 2003 | 134 227 833 | -2.6 | 97.4 | 0.0 | 97.4 | 67.7 | 29.8 |
| | 2004 | 212 683 082 | -3.1 | 96.9 | -0.1 | 96.8 | 61.2 | 35.7 |
| Yemen | 2002 | 1 878 007 | -7.0 | 93.0 | 11.9 | 104.9 | 82.3 | 22.6 |
| Yémen | 2003 | 2 160 608 | -8.1 | 91.9 | 11.1 | 103.0 | 80.8 | 22.2 |
| | 2004 | 2 563 490 | -9.2 | 90.8 | 9.9 | 100.7 | 78.8 | 21.9 |
| Zambia[1] | 1986 | 12 963 | -18.1 | 81.9 | -1.2 | 80.7 | 77.4 | 3.3 |
| Zambie[1] | 1987 | 19 778 | -11.4[2] | 88.6 | 0.5 | 89.1 | 82.0 | 7.1 |
| | 1988 | 27 725 | -14.2[2] | 85.8 | 1.0 | 86.9 | 79.8 | 7.1 |
| Zimbabwe[1] | 2001 | 709 214 | ... | 98.3 | ... | ... | ... | ... |
| Zimbabwe[1] | 2002 | 1 698 180 | ... | 99.5 | ... | ... | ... | ... |
| | 2003 | 5 518 757 | ... | 99.9 | ... | ... | ... | ... |

Source

United Nations Statistics Division, New York, national accounts database, last accessed January 2008.

Data for most countries have been compiled in accordance with the concepts and definitions of the System of National Accounts 1993 (1993 SNA). Countries that follow the 1968 SNA are footnoted accordingly.

[+] The national accounts data generally relate to the fiscal year used in each country, unless indicated otherwise. Countries whose reference periods coincide with the calendar year ending 31 December are not listed below.

Year beginning 21 March: Afghanistan, Iran (Islamic Republic).

Year beginning 1 April: Bermuda, India, Myanmar, New Zealand, Nigeria.
Year beginning 1 July: Australia, Bangladesh, Cameroon, Gambia, Pakistan, Puerto Rico, Saudi Arabia, Sierra Leone, Sudan.

Year ending 30 June: Botswana, Egypt, Swaziland, Tonga.
Year ending 7 July: Ethiopia.
Year ending 15 July: Nepal.
Year ending 30 September: Haiti.

Notes

1   Data compiled in accordance with the System of National Accounts 1968 (1968 SNA).
2   Property income - from and to the rest of the world, net.

Source

Organisation des Nations Unies, Division de statistique, New York, la base de données sur les comptes nationaux, dernier accès janvier 2008.

Les données pour la majorité des pays sont compilées selon les concepts et définitions du Système de comptabilité nationale, 1993 (SCN93). Seuls les pays qui suivent toujours le SCN68 seront donc signalés par une note.

[+] Sauf indication contraire, les données sur les comptes nationaux concernent généralement l'exercice budgétaire utilisé dans chaque pays. Les pays où territoires dont la période de référence coïncide avec l'année civile se terminant le 31 décembre ne sont pas répertoriés ci-dessous.

Exercice commençant le 21 mars: Afghanistan, Iran (République islamique d').
Exercice commençant le 1er avril: Bermudes, Inde, Myanmar, Nigéria Nouvelle-Zélande.
Exercice commençant le 1er juillet: Arabie saoudite, Australie, Bangladesh, Cameroun, Gambie, Pakistan, Porto Rico, Sierra Leone, Soudan.
Exercice se terminant le 30 juin: Botswana, Égypte, Swaziland, Tonga.
Exercice se terminant le 7 juillet: Éthiopie.
Exercice se terminant le 15 juillet: Népal.
Exercice se terminant le 30 septembre: Haïti.

Notes

1   Données compilées selon le Système de comptabilité nationale de 1968 (SCN 1968).
2   Revenus de la propriété - du et au reste du monde, net.

3 Preliminary data.
4 Including acquisitions less disposals of valuables.
5 Derived from available data.
6 Beginning 2000, re-denomination of Belarusian roubles at 1 to 1000.

7 Forecast.
8 Refers to Net Primary Income.
9 At producers' prices.
10 For statistical purposes, the data for China do not include those for the Hong Kong Special Administrative Region (Hong Kong SAR), Macao Special Administrative Region (Macao SAR) and Taiwan Province of China.
11 Refers to gross value added at basic prices.
12 Compensation of employees - from and to the rest of the world, net.
13 Includes taxes less subsidies on production.
14 Excluding official grants.
15 Net national income.
16 Semi-final data.
17 Re-denomination of Russian rubles at 1 to 1000.

3 Données préliminaires.
4 Y compris les acquisitions moins cessions d'objets de valeur.
5 Calculés à partir des données disponibles.
6 A partir de 2000, instauration du nouveau rouble bélarussien par division par 1000 du rouble bélarussien ancien.

7 Prévision.
8 Revenu primaire net.
9 Aux prix à la production.
10 Pour la présentation des statistiques, les données pour la Chine ne comprennent pas la Région Administrative Spéciale de Hong Kong (Hong Kong RAS), la Région Administrative Spéciale de Macao (Macao RAS) et la province de Taiwan.
11 Valeur ajoutée brute aux prix de base.
12 Rémunération des salariés - du et au reste du monde, net.
13 Y compris les impôts, moins les subventions dans les production.
14 Non compris les dons officiels.
15 Revenu national net.
16 Données demi-finales.
17 Instauration du nouveau rouble russe par division par 1000 du rouble russe ancien .

# 24

## Government final consumption expenditure by function at current prices
Percentage distribution by divisions of Classification of the Functions of Government (COFOG)

## Dépenses de consommation finale des administrations publiques par fonction aux prix courants
Répartition en pourcentage par divisions de la Classification des fonctions des administrations publiques (COFOG)

| Country or area &<br>Pays ou zone & | Year<br>Année | Total<br>(mil. nat. curr.)<br>Totale<br>(millions<br>monnaie nat.) | Divisions of the Classification of the Functions of Government (COFOG) t<br>Divisions de la Classification des fonctions des administrations publiques (COFOG) t ||||||||||
|---|---|---|---|---|---|---|---|---|---|---|---|---|
| | | | Div. 01<br>(%) | Div. 02<br>(%) | Div. 03<br>(%) | Div. 04<br>(%) | Div. 05<br>(%) | Div. 06<br>(%) | Div. 07<br>(%) | Div. 08<br>(%) | Div. 09<br>(%) | Div. 10<br>(%) |
| Anguilla[1]<br>Anguilla[1] | 1999 | 64 | 42.2 | ... | 9.4 | 7.8 | ... | 3.1 | 15.6 | ... | 17.2 | 1.6 |
| | 2000 | 58 | 41.4 | ... | 10.3 | 8.6 | ... | 1.7 | 15.5 | ... | 19.0 | 3.4 |
| | 2001 | 62 | 38.7 | ... | 11.3 | 8.1 | ... | 1.6 | 16.1 | ... | 19.4 | 3.2 |
| Antigua and Barbuda[1]<br>Antigua-et-Barbuda[1] | 1984 | 67[2] | 22.8 | 2.2 | 11.4 | 22.5 | ... | 6.7 | 9.7 | 0.5 | 15.8 | 8.4 |
| | 1985 | 81[2] | 25.1 | 2.2 | 11.4 | 20.9 | ... | 7.7 | 11.5 | 0.6 | 14.0 | 6.6 |
| | 1986 | 108[2] | 26.1 | 2.3 | 11.6 | 21.2 | ... | 6.4 | 10.0 | 0.5 | 14.7 | 7.2 |
| Argentina[1]<br>Argentine[1] | 1996 | 43 617 | 10.8 | 4.5 | 3.2 | 6.0 | 0.2 | 2.1 | 8.4 | ... | 5.9[3] | 43.2 |
| | 1997 | 45 156 | 9.4 | 4.4 | 3.1 | 5.9 | 0.2 | 2.1 | 7.1 | ... | 6.0[3] | 42.0 |
| | 1998 | 46 463 | 9.5 | 4.2 | 3.0 | 5.8 | 0.2 | 2.0 | 6.6 | ... | 6.0[3] | 41.0 |
| Armenia<br>Arménie | 2002 | 84 958[4] | 82.8[5] | ... | ... | 3.5 | ... | 3.6 | ... | 3.2 | ... | 1.0 |
| | 2003 | 101 859[4] | 85.3[5] | ... | ... | 3.7 | ... | 4.2 | ... | 3.2 | ... | 1.1 |
| | 2004 | 118 788[4] | 84.8[5] | ... | ... | 3.3 | ... | 4.7 | ... | 3.0 | ... | 1.1 |
| Australia<br>Australie | 2000 | 125 184 | 9.1 | 8.3 | 7.0 | 7.1 | ^0.0 | 1.2 | 26.0 | 3.0 | 17.4 | 8.8 |
| | 2001 | 132 230 | 7.3 | 8.4 | 7.0 | 8.3 | 0.1 | 1.2 | 26.8 | 2.7 | 17.6 | 8.6 |
| | 2002 | 141 088 | 6.1 | 8.8 | 7.3 | 8.2 | 0.3 | 1.3 | 27.1 | 2.6 | 17.9 | 9.3 |
| Austria<br>Autriche | 2003 | 41 492 | 13.7 | 4.8 | 7.5 | 9.7 | 1.1 | 0.5 | 28.2 | 2.5 | 28.3 | 3.7 |
| | 2004 | 42 737 | 13.1 | 4.8 | 7.5 | 9.7 | 1.1 | 0.5 | 28.9 | 2.7 | 27.8 | 4.0 |
| | 2005 | 44 420 | 13.2 | 4.8 | 7.6 | 9.6 | 1.1 | 0.5 | 28.5 | 2.7 | 27.7 | 4.3 |
| Azerbaijan<br>Azerbaïdjan | 2003 | 885 | 29.1 | 15.4 | 2.0 | 2.3 | ... | -0.1 | 17.6 | 3.5 | 28.2 | 2.0 |
| | 2004 | 1 100 | 29.7 | 15.8 | 1.7 | 0.5 | ... | ^0.0 | 17.7 | 3.4 | 28.9 | 2.2 |
| | 2005 | 1 305 | 29.8 | 15.8 | 1.8 | 0.5 | ... | 0.2 | 18.7 | 4.0 | 27.4 | 1.7 |
| Bahamas<br>Bahamas | 1993 | 408 | 17.4 | 4.2 | 14.5 | 15.9 | ... | ... | 18.6 | 1.5[6] | 24.0 | 4.2 |
| | 1994 | 511 | 20.2 | 3.7 | 13.3 | 17.2 | ... | ... | 18.0 | 1.6[6] | 23.1 | 3.5 |
| | 1995 | 484 | 18.4 | 3.9 | 14.5 | 17.6 | ... | ... | 18.0 | 1.9[6] | 22.1 | 3.9 |
| Bangladesh<br>Bangladesh | 2004 | 156 232 | 13.1 | 18.8 | 11.1 | 12.8 | ... | 3.2 | 9.8 | 0.6 | 12.8 | 1.8 |
| | 2005 | 148 507 | 15.1 | 20.8 | 12.9 | 1.4 | ... | 3.6 | 11.2 | 0.9 | 14.3 | 1.8 |
| | 2006 | 169 764 | 13.6 | 19.6 | 13.8 | 1.3 | ... | 3.3 | 11.6 | 0.8 | 13.7 | 1.8 |
| Belarus<br>Bélarus | 2002 | 1 948 700 | 72.3 | ... | ... | 22.3 | ... | ... | ... | ... | ... | 0.6 |
| | 2003 | 2 918 400 | 74.1 | ... | ... | 20.5 | ... | ... | ... | ... | ... | 0.6 |
| | 2004 | 4 203 500 | 69.9 | ... | ... | 25.1 | ... | ... | ... | ... | ... | 0.5 |
| Belgium<br>Belgique | 2003 | 63 163 | 13.5 | 5.0 | 7.0 | 10.1 | 0.9 | 0.2 | 28.7 | 2.6 | 25.3 | 6.7 |
| | 2004 | 66 177 | 13.7 | 4.8 | 6.8 | 9.4 | 0.9 | 0.3 | 30.0 | 2.6 | 24.8 | 6.7 |
| | 2005 | 68 496 | 14.0 | 4.6 | 6.8 | 9.2 | 0.7 | 0.3 | 29.8 | 2.5 | 25.3 | 6.9 |
| Belize[1]<br>Belize[1] | 1989 | 229 | 12.7 | 4.3 | 5.3 | 40.3 | ... | 6.3 | 7.9 | 1.4 | 16.5 | 0.7 |
| | 1990 | 279 | 12.7 | 3.4 | 7.9 | 37.5 | ... | 6.7 | 6.8 | 2.6 | 15.3 | 3.3 |
| | 1991 | 321 | 16.6 | 3.4 | 7.0 | 32.6 | ... | 6.1 | 6.6 | 2.4 | 16.8 | 4.0 |
| Bermuda[1]<br>Bermudes[1] | 1985 | 138 | 36.9 | 2.0 | ... | 27.1 | ... | 6.0 | 3.7 | 2.9 | 21.3 | 3.6 |
| | 1986 | 141 | 34.4 | 2.1 | ... | 28.3 | ... | 6.4 | 3.9 | 2.9 | 22.2 | 3.8 |
| | 1987 | 157 | 34.0 | 2.3 | ... | 30.1 | ... | 6.2 | 3.8 | 2.9 | 21.5 | 3.8 |
| Bolivia[1]<br>Bolivie[1] | 1991 | 2 310 | 74.7 | ^0.0 | ... | 4.2 | ... | 0.1 | ^0.0 | 0.1 | 7.7 | 1.9 |
| | 1992 | 2 833 | 76.2 | ... | ... | 3.0 | ... | 0.1 | ^0.0 | 0.2 | 8.1 | 1.9 |
| | 1993 | 3 270 | 75.9 | ... | ... | 2.5 | ... | 0.2 | ^0.0 | 0.2 | 9.0 | 2.4 |
| Botswana<br>Botswana | 2000 | 7 525 | 44.0[7] | ... | ... | 11.2 | ... | 6.2 | 6.5 | 2.4 | 26.4 | 3.4 |
| | 2001 | 8 742 | 43.7[7] | ... | ... | 11.0 | ... | 5.2 | 6.8 | 2.4 | 27.4 | 3.5 |
| | 2002 | 10 553 | 45.3[7] | ... | ... | 10.8 | ... | 4.3 | 6.3 | 2.5 | 27.4 | 3.4 |
| Brazil<br>Brésil | 2003 | 329 596 | 63.2 | ... | ... | ... | ... | ... | 13.3 | ... | 20.0 | ... |
| | 2004 | 373 284 | 64.4 | ... | ... | ... | ... | ... | 14.2 | ... | 18.4 | ... |
| | 2005 | 427 553 | 65.7 | ... | ... | ... | ... | ... | 13.2 | ... | 18.4 | ... |

**Government final consumption expenditure by function at current prices**—Percentage distribution by divisions of Classification of the Functions of Government (COFOG) *(continued)*

**Dépenses de consommation administrations publiques par fonction aux prix courants**—Répartition en pourcentage par divisions de la Classification des fonctions des administrations publiques (COFOG) *(suite)*

| Country or area &<br>Pays ou zone & | Year<br>Année | Total<br>(mil. nat. curr.)<br>Totale<br>(millions<br>monnaie nat.) | Div. 01<br>(%) | Div. 02<br>(%) | Div. 03<br>(%) | Div. 04<br>(%) | Div. 05<br>(%) | Div. 06<br>(%) | Div. 07<br>(%) | Div. 08<br>(%) | Div. 09<br>(%) | Div. 10<br>(%) |
|---|---|---|---|---|---|---|---|---|---|---|---|---|
| British Virgin Islands[1]<br>Iles Vierges britanniques[1] | 1985 | 17[2] | 23.3 | ... | 10.8 | 20.7 | ... | 4.1 | 14.9 | 0.8 | 23.6 | 1.8 |
| | 1986 | 19[2] | 21.8 | ... | 11.4 | 22.1 | ... | 4.4 | 14.5 | 0.7 | 22.7 | 2.4 |
| | 1987 | 21[2] | 23.3 | ... | 11.0 | 20.2 | ... | 5.5 | 15.8 | 0.5 | 21.1 | 2.6 |
| Brunei Darussalam[1]<br>Brunéi Darussalam[1] | 1982 | 914 | 22.9 | 41.4 | 5.5 | 5.0 | ... | 0.7 | 5.0 | 4.8 | 14.2 | 0.2 |
| | 1983 | 922 | 24.6 | 35.3 | 6.0 | 5.5 | ... | 0.7 | 5.7 | 5.7 | 15.2 | 0.2 |
| | 1984 | 2 512 | 69.3 | 12.8 | 2.7 | 2.5 | ... | 0.4 | 2.6 | 2.3 | 6.5 | 0.1 |
| Burkina Faso[1]<br>Burkina Faso[1] | 1982 | 38 198[2] | 8.2 | 28.3 | 8.7 | 9.9 | ... | 0.3 | 10.0 | 2.4 | 16.6 | ... |
| | 1983 | 38 864[2] | 8.1 | 28.7 | 9.1 | 10.5 | ... | 0.4 | 10.5 | 2.5 | 18.3 | ... |
| | 1984 | 38 760[2] | 7.3 | 30.4 | 8.7 | 10.8 | ... | 0.2 | 10.3 | 2.5 | 19.0 | ... |
| Cameroon[1]<br>Cameroun[1] | 1986 | 476 700 | 30.6 | 12.0 | ... | 10.6 | ... | 6.0 | 5.7 | 2.1 | 19.1 | 0.7 |
| | 1987 | 391 000 | 28.3 | 14.7 | ... | 7.3 | ... | 5.0 | 6.1 | 2.3 | 21.6 | 0.8 |
| | 1988 | 378 400 | 35.5 | 12.4 | ... | 6.2 | ... | 4.9 | 6.0 | 2.2 | 21.5 | 0.9 |
| Cayman Islands[1]<br>Iles Caïmanes[1] | 1989 | 74[8] | 31.1 | ... | 14.9 | 20.3 | ... | 1.4 | 13.5 | ... | 13.5 | 4.1 |
| | 1990 | 94[8] | 26.6 | ... | 14.9 | 19.1 | ... | 1.1 | 16.0 | ... | 14.9 | 4.3 |
| | 1991 | 103[8] | 27.2 | ... | 14.6 | 20.4 | ... | .9 | 14.6 | ... | 14.6 | 5.8 |
| Chad[1]<br>Tchad[1] | 1997 | 40 078[9] | 1.0[10] | 26.6 | 9.5[11] | 6.6[12] | 5.2[13] | 1.1[14] | 6.9[15] | ... | 23.6 | 20.7[16] |
| | 2001 | 60 157[9] | ... | 20.2 | 8.4[11] | 5.9[12] | 5.2[13] | 1.0[14] | 6.3[15] | ... | 25.0 | 28.0[16] |
| | 2003 | 74 579[9] | ... | 24.7 | 10.0[11] | 5.8[12] | ... | ... | 7.2[15] | ... | 26.9 | ... |
| China, Macao SAR<br>Chine, Macao RAS | 2002 | 6 323 | 18.7 | ... | 28.8 | 11.4 | 0.1 | 0.7 | 15.6 | 4.1 | 11.9 | 8.7 |
| | 2003 | 6 830 | 19.6 | ... | 27.7 | 12.0 | 0.2 | 0.7 | 15.7 | 3.9 | 11.4 | 9.0 |
| | 2004 | 7 093 | 19.8 | ... | 27.9 | 11.7 | 0.2 | 0.6 | 15.2 | 3.7 | 11.6 | 9.3 |
| Colombia[1]<br>Colombie[1] | 1992 | 3 965 104 | 29.5 | 10.8 | ... | 16.6 | ... | 0.6 | 7.7 | 0.8 | 24.8 | 8.9 |
| | 1993 | 5 108 076 | 28.5 | 10.2 | ... | 16.2 | ... | 0.6 | 11.0 | 0.9 | 24.0 | 8.2 |
| | 1994 | 7 652 736 | 36.2 | 9.8 | ... | 8.5 | ... | 0.4 | 14.3 | 0.9 | 21.0 | 8.6 |
| Cook Islands[1]<br>Iles Cook[1] | 2003 | 81 | 19.3 | ... | 5.2 | 39.3 | ... | 9.2 | 11.7 | 0.9 | 14.4 | ... |
| | 2004 | 84 | 17.8 | ... | 4.7 | 41.2 | ... | 9.7 | 11.2 | 0.8 | 14.6 | ... |
| | 2005 | 86 | 23.3 | ... | 4.8 | 31.4 | ... | 10.6 | 13.2 | 1.0 | 15.8 | ... |
| Costa Rica<br>Costa Rica | 2003 | 1 011 041 | 32.1 | ... | ... | ... | ... | ... | 34.1 | ... | 33.9 | ... |
| | 2004 | 1 150 404 | 32.0 | ... | ... | ... | ... | ... | 34.4 | ... | 33.7 | ... |
| | 2005 | 1 316 343 | 32.3 | ... | ... | ... | ... | ... | 34.5 | ... | 33.2 | ... |
| Côte d'Ivoire[1]<br>Côte d'Ivoire[1] | 1996 | 983 370 | 73.5 | ... | ... | ... | ... | ... | 6.2 | ... | 20.3 | ... |
| | 1997 | 1 029 358 | 69.3 | ... | ... | ... | ... | ... | 19.7 | ... | 11.0 | ... |
| | 1998 | 1 018 653 | 68.3 | ... | ... | ... | ... | ... | 19.9 | ... | 11.8 | ... |
| Croatia<br>Croatie | 1996 | 30 973 | 6.2 | 25.1 | 12.0 | 15.0 | ... | 8.4 | 0.5 | 1.3 | 11.6 | 14.2 |
| | 1997 | 34 395 | 6.3 | 20.3 | 12.1 | 15.7 | ... | 6.0 | 0.5 | 1.6 | 11.8 | 18.8 |
| | 1998 | 41 390 | 8.2 | 17.8 | 10.3 | 15.6 | ... | 6.3 | 2.0 | 1.4 | 11.3 | 19.4 |
| Cuba<br>Cuba | 2003 | 14 834 | 14.5 | ... | ... | ... | ... | 5.5 | 30.0 | 6.7 | 40.8 | 1.4 |
| | 2004 | 16 416 | 16.2 | ... | ... | ... | ... | 5.9 | 23.9 | 7.3 | 42.2 | 3.6 |
| | 2005 | 17 867 | 16.3 | ... | ... | ... | ... | 5.7 | 25.9 | 8.0 | 39.7 | 3.5 |
| Cyprus<br>Chypre | 2002 | 1 169 | 21.5 | 18.7 | 8.5 | 10.6 | 0.0 | 6.2 | 11.0 | 0.9 | 20.9 | 1.7 |
| | 2003 | 1 359 | 22.4 | 14.2 | 8.8 | 10.4 | 0.0 | 6.5 | 12.0 | 0.9 | 21.8 | 2.9 |
| | 2004 | 1 320 | 23.6 | 10.5 | 9.7 | 7.5 | 0.1 | 8.3 | 12.9 | 1.7 | 24.8 | 2.3 |
| Czech Republic<br>République tchèque | 2003 | 603 175 | 12.9 | 9.0 | 10.8 | 10.6 | 2.6 | 1.1 | 26.1 | 2.8 | 20.3 | 3.8 |
| | 2004 | 624 182 | 12.6 | 7.3 | 10.8 | 11.0 | 2.7 | 1.1 | 26.9 | 2.7 | 20.7 | 4.3 |
| | 2005 | 663 097 | 11.8 | 8.8 | 10.8 | 10.9 | 2.9 | 1.1 | 26.7 | 2.7 | 20.3 | 4.0 |
| Denmark<br>Danemark | 2004 | 388 453 | 6.7 | 5.9 | 3.4 | 7.3 | 1.4 | 0.5 | 24.4 | 4.4 | 23.6 | 22.4 |
| | 2005 | 401 433 | 6.7 | 5.7 | 3.5 | 7.3 | 1.4 | 0.5 | 24.6 | 4.4 | 23.5 | 22.5 |
| | 2006 | 419 643 | 6.6 | 5.9 | 3.5 | 6.8 | 1.3 | 0.5 | 24.6 | 4.2 | 23.2 | 23.3 |
| Dominican Republic<br>Rép. dominicaine | 1994 | 8 265 | 66.3 | ... | 2.7 | ... | ... | ... | 12.8 | ... | 18.1 | ... |
| | 1995 | 9 115 | 61.2 | ... | 2.7 | ... | ... | ... | 12.6 | ... | 23.4 | ... |
| | 1996 | 10 843 | 61.1 | ... | 2.3 | ... | ... | ... | 12.5 | ... | 24.1 | ... |

**Government final consumption expenditure by function at current prices**— Percentage distribution by divisions of Classification of the Functions of Government (COFOG) (*continued*)

**Dépenses de consommation administrations publiques par fonction aux prix courants**— Répartition en pourcentage par divisions de la Classification des fonctions des administrations publiques (COFOG) (*suite*)

| Country or area &<br>Pays ou zone & | Year<br>Année | Total<br>(mil. nat. curr.)<br>Totale<br>(millions<br>monnaie nat.) | Div. 01<br>(%) | Div. 02<br>(%) | Div. 03<br>(%) | Div. 04<br>(%) | Div. 05<br>(%) | Div. 06<br>(%) | Div. 07<br>(%) | Div. 08<br>(%) | Div. 09<br>(%) | Div. 10<br>(%) |
|---|---|---|---|---|---|---|---|---|---|---|---|---|
| Ecuador[1]<br>Equateur[1] | 1990 | 777 131[17] | 13.0 | 14.5 | 7.0 | 13.9 | ... | 4.4 | 4.8 | 0.2 | 27.5 | 6.1 |
| | 1991 | 1 009 000[17] | 13.0 | 15.0 | 7.1 | 14.9 | ... | 5.0 | 4.6 | 0.3 | 27.8 | 6.2 |
| | 1992 | 1 498 000[17] | 12.8 | 15.9 | 7.3 | 16.1 | ... | 4.3 | 3.9 | 0.2 | 26.8 | 7.8 |
| Estonia<br>Estonie | 1996 | 12 632 | 11.0 | 4.6 | 11.7 | 11.0 | ... | 4.2 | 17.3 | 5.6 | 27.8 | 4.1 |
| | #2003 | 24 898 | 11.6 | 7.3 | 11.5 | 8.9 | 2.7 | 0.7 | 18.4 | 6.0 | 27.5 | 5.5 |
| | 2004 | 27 097 | 11.4 | 6.7 | 11.3 | 9.1 | 2.8 | 0.6 | 19.9 | 5.7 | 26.9 | 5.6 |
| Fiji[1]<br>Fidji[1] | 2000 | 561 | 18.9 | 12.2 | 9.3 | 16.4 | ... | 1.0 | 14.7 | ... | 27.1 | 0.4 |
| | 2001 | 566 | 20.4 | 12.0 | 10.0 | 19.4 | ... | 1.0 | 12.8 | ... | 23.9 | 0.5 |
| | 2002 | 572 | 16.1 | 9.8 | 10.0 | 18.3 | ... | 1.3 | 14.3 | ... | 29.4 | 0.6 |
| Finland<br>Finlande | 2003 | 31 673 | 10.8 | 6.1 | 5.4 | 9.7 | 0.8 | 1.0 | 25.5 | 3.1 | 20.7 | 16.8 |
| | 2004 | 33 314 | 10.9 | 6.1 | 5.1 | 10.0 | 0.8 | 0.8 | 25.7 | 3.0 | 20.5 | 17.2 |
| | 2005 | 34 809 | 10.4 | 6.4 | 5.2 | 9.7 | 0.8 | 0.7 | 26.1 | 3.0 | 20.2 | 17.4 |
| France<br>France | 2003 | 378 397 | 11.5 | 7.9 | 5.4 | 3.6 | 0.9 | 4.1 | 27.8 | 3.7 | 21.7 | 13.3 |
| | 2004 | 393 629 | 11.5 | 8.0 | 5.4 | 3.9 | 0.9 | 4.1 | 26.8 | 3.8 | 20.7 | 14.9 |
| | 2005 | 405 600 | 11.2 | 7.7 | 5.6 | 3.8 | 0.9 | 4.2 | 26.7 | 3.9 | 20.6 | 15.5 |
| Gambia[1]<br>Gambie[1] | 1989 | 659[2] | 23.3 | ... | ... | 25.2 | ... | 3.6 | 6.3 | ... | 10.3[18] | 0.1 |
| | 1990 | 819[2] | 22.0 | ... | ... | 18.6 | ... | 3.0 | 6.4 | ... | 12.9[18] | 0.1 |
| | 1991 | 804[2] | 22.2 | ... | ... | 24.1 | ... | 3.8 | 5.7 | ... | 12.6[18] | 0.1 |
| Georgia<br>Géorgie | #1993 | 1 213 | ... | 1.9 | 8.2 | 30.3 | ... | ... | 0.6 | 0.2 | 5.7 | 0.5 |
| | 1994 | 119 012 | ... | 5.4 | 10.1 | 63.6 | ... | ... | 3.2 | 1.2 | 4.8 | 9.0 |
| | #1995 | 295 | ... | 12.9 | 45.8 | 5.8 | ... | ... | 6.1 | 6.4 | 10.2 | 12.5 |
| Germany<br>Allemagne | 2003 | 417 230 | 12.2 | 6.2 | 8.4 | 2.0 | 0.4 | 1.3 | 32.7 | 2.1 | 18.6 | 16.1 |
| | 2004 | 415 060 | 12.4 | 6.1 | 8.6 | 2.1 | 0.4 | 1.3 | 31.8 | 2.1 | 18.7 | 16.4 |
| | 2005 | 419 640 | 12.8 | 6.1 | 8.5 | 1.4 | 0.4 | 1.3 | 32.4 | 2.1 | 18.5 | 16.4 |
| Greece<br>Grèce | 2003 | 29 534 | 25.1 | 19.1 | 7.8 | 3.8 | 0.0 | 0.7 | 17.1 | 1.4 | 20.6 | 4.4 |
| | 2004 | 31 709 | 28.5 | 15.5 | 9.7 | 3.9 | 0.0 | 0.7 | 16.0 | 1.5 | 20.3 | 3.9 |
| | 2005 | 32 492 | 25.7 | 17.5 | 8.8 | 3.9 | 0.0 | 0.7 | 17.0 | 1.5 | 21.0 | 3.8 |
| Greenland[1]<br>Groenland[1] | 2003 | 5 238 | 15.4 | 5.0 | 3.9 | 8.3 | ... | 3.2 | 16.0 | 3.1 | 20.8 | 17.6 |
| | 2004 | 5 319 | 16.0 | 4.1 | 4.4 | 7.7 | ... | 2.8 | 15.9 | 3.3 | 21.1 | 17.9 |
| | 2005 | 5 221 | 16.3 | 4.4 | 4.3 | 7.0 | ... | 1.6 | 16.6 | 3.2 | 21.5 | 18.4 |
| Guinea-Bissau[1]<br>Guinée-Bissau[1] | 1986 | 6 423 | 44.0 | ... | ... | 22.7 | ... | ... | 11.8 | ... | 18.4 | 0.9 |
| | 1987 | 10 776 | 44.0 | ... | ... | 22.7 | ... | ... | 11.8 | ... | 18.4 | 1.2 |
| Honduras<br>Honduras | 1995 | 3 495 | 27.8 | 9.5 | ... | ... | ... | ... | 20.5 | ... | 39.1 | ... |
| | 1996 | 4 556 | 26.0 | 8.2 | ... | ... | ... | ... | 27.6 | ... | 36.7 | ... |
| | 1997 | 5 377 | 31.0 | 7.3 | ... | ... | ... | ... | 24.9 | ... | 35.2 | ... |
| Hungary<br>Hongrie | 1994 | 1 145 444 | 17.1 | 6.2 | 8.0 | 9.4 | ... | 6.3 | 15.7 | 3.6 | 21.4 | 9.3 |
| | #2004 | 4 633 647 | 20.3 | 7.5 | 8.8 | 4.2 | 0.7 | 2.0 | 22.9 | 4.1 | 21.6 | 7.9 |
| | 2005 | 4 953 437 | 21.9 | 6.3 | 8.5 | 4.4 | 0.4 | 2.0 | 22.9 | 4.1 | 21.1 | 8.5 |
| Iceland<br>Islande | 2002 | 204 921 | 7.3 | ... | 5.2 | 8.2 | ... | 3.3 | 29.8 | 5.1 | 20.3 | 8.1 |
| | 2003 | 217 425 | 7.4 | ... | 5.3 | 8.3 | ... | 3.3 | 30.2 | 5.2 | 20.6 | 8.2 |
| | 2004 | 230 858 | 7.5 | ... | 5.4 | 8.5 | ... | 3.4 | 30.7 | 5.3 | 20.9 | 8.3 |
| India[1]<br>Inde[1] | 2002 | 2 183 290 | 29.5 | 32.2 | ... | 9.1 | ... | 2.3 | 6.1 | 0.7 | 16.4 | 3.2 |
| | 2003 | 2 305 000 | 26.6 | 33.2 | ... | 9.9 | ... | 2.5 | 6.2 | 0.8 | 16.3 | 4.2 |
| | 2004 | 2 510 090 | 24.8 | 34.9 | ... | 8.7 | ... | 2.5 | 6.7 | 0.8 | 17.2 | 4.2 |
| Iran (Islamic Rep. of)<br>Iran (Rép. islamique d') | 2003 | 140 795 300 | 13.0 | 20.7 | 7.9 | 12.7 | 0.1 | 1.1 | 7.9 | 2.9 | 7.6 | 16.9 |
| | 2004 | 168 704 700 | 12.7 | 18.6 | 6.8 | 16.4 | 0.1 | 1.2 | 7.1 | 3.1 | 7.7 | 18.0 |
| | 2005 | 217 918 500 | 11.5 | 19.5 | 6.4 | 17.9 | 0.4 | 1.9 | 6.7 | 2.8 | 7.0 | 17.3 |
| Ireland<br>Irlande | 2003 | 20 998 | 9.2 | 3.5 | 8.0 | 11.2 | ... | 2.3 | 40.1 | 1.8 | 17.4 | 6.4 |
| | 2004 | 23 216 | 9.3 | 3.4 | 8.6 | 10.1 | ... | 2.5 | 40.5 | 1.7 | 17.5 | 6.3 |
| | 2005 | 25 556 | 9.3 | 3.4 | 8.6 | 10.1 | ... | 2.5 | 40.5 | 1.7 | 17.5 | 6.3 |

24 Government final consumption expenditure by function at current prices — Percentage distribution by divisions of Classification of the Functions of Government (COFOG) *(continued)*

Dépenses de consommation administrations publiques par fonction aux prix courants — Répartition en pourcentage par divisions de la Classification des fonctions des administrations publiques (COFOG) *(suite)*

| Country or area &<br>Pays ou zone & | Year<br>Année | Total<br>(mil. nat. curr.)<br>Totale<br>(millions<br>monnaie nat.) | Divisions of the Classification of the Functions of Government (COFOG) t<br>Divisions de la Classification des fonctions des administrations publiques (COFOG) t | | | | | | | | | |
|---|---|---|---|---|---|---|---|---|---|---|---|---|
| | | | Div. 01<br>(%) | Div. 02<br>(%) | Div. 03<br>(%) | Div. 04<br>(%) | Div. 05<br>(%) | Div. 06<br>(%) | Div. 07<br>(%) | Div. 08<br>(%) | Div. 09<br>(%) | Div. 10<br>(%) |
| Israel<br>Israël | 2003 | 151 489 | 7.3 | 31.2 | 5.8 | 3.4 | 2.9 | 1.2 | 17.3 | 2.0 | 23.7 | 5.2 |
| | 2004 | 151 161 | 7.5 | 29.7 | 6.1 | 3.5 | 3.2 | 1.3 | 17.3 | 2.1 | 24.0 | 5.3 |
| | 2005 | 156 746 | 7.6 | 30.1 | 6.1 | 3.5 | 3.1 | 1.3 | 17.5 | 2.1 | 23.4 | 5.3 |
| Italy<br>Italie | 2003 | 262 942 | 15.0 | 6.9 | 9.5 | 6.4 | 1.3 | 2.1 | 30.8 | 2.0 | 21.7 | 4.4 |
| | 2004 | 275 482 | 14.8 | 7.1 | 9.5 | 6.3 | 1.3 | 2.1 | 32.3 | 2.0 | 20.3 | 4.3 |
| | 2005 | 287 558 | 14.4 | 7.4 | 9.4 | 6.3 | 1.3 | 2.1 | 32.4 | 1.9 | 20.8 | 4.1 |
| Japan<br>Japon | 2003 | 88 613 300 | 9.3 | 4.7 | 6.4 | 13.1 | 6.3 | 1.4 | 35.5 | 0.4 | 19.3 | 3.7 |
| | 2004 | 89 789 900 | 8.6 | 4.6 | 6.3 | 13.5 | 6.5 | 1.4 | 36.2 | 0.4 | 18.8 | 3.6 |
| | 2005 | 90 678 000 | 8.5 | 4.5 | 6.3 | 13.7 | 6.5 | 1.4 | 36.6 | 0.4 | 18.5 | 3.5 |
| Jordan[1]<br>Jordanie[1] | 1993 | 939 | 53.6[7] | ... | ... | ... | ... | ... | 10.2 | 6.4 | 21.9 | 1.0 |
| | 1994 | 986 | 59.3[7] | ... | ... | ... | ... | ... | 8.2 | 6.0 | 20.4 | 1.0 |
| | 1995 | 1 111 | 60.0[7] | ... | ... | ... | ... | ... | 8.3 | 5.6 | 21.3 | 0.9 |
| Kazakhstan<br>Kazakhstan | 2003 | 519 195 | 11.8 | 7.8 | 17.6 | 12.6 | ... | 2.3 | 15.7 | 4.3 | 24.6 | 3.4 |
| | 2004 | 681 787 | 13.0 | 7.5 | 17.4 | 12.2 | ... | 2.3 | 16.2 | 4.3 | 23.7 | 3.5 |
| | 2005 | 853 830 | 12.1 | 7.9 | 18.1 | 11.5 | ... | 2.3 | 16.5 | 4.3 | 23.9 | 3.4 |
| Kenya<br>Kenya | 2003 | 205 140 | ... | ... | ... | ... | ... | ... | 7.8 | ... | 43.3 | ... |
| | 2004 | 226 016 | ... | ... | ... | ... | ... | ... | 8.1 | ... | 43.7 | ... |
| | 2005 | 242 409 | ... | ... | ... | ... | ... | ... | 8.6 | ... | 42.6 | ... |
| Korea, Republic of<br>Corée, République de | 2002 | 88 512 200 | 13.9 | 17.4 | 9.6 | 12.7 | 1.5 | 0.7 | 17.1 | 1.3 | 21.6 | 4.2 |
| | 2003 | 96 203 200 | 13.8 | 17.3 | 9.4 | 11.8 | 1.5 | 0.6 | 16.8 | 1.3 | 22.7 | 4.7 |
| | 2004 | 105 516 900 | 13.8 | 17.5 | 9.1 | 12.4 | 1.5 | 0.6 | 16.7 | 1.3 | 22.5 | 4.8 |
| Kuwait[1]<br>Koweït[1] | 2003 | 3 281 | ... | 56.2 | ... | 4.5 | ... | 2.6 | 9.7 | 4.4 | 19.0 | 3.6 |
| | 2004 | 3 478 | ... | 55.7 | ... | 4.6 | ... | 2.4 | 9.9 | 4.5 | 19.2 | 3.6 |
| | 2005 | 3 637 | ... | 54.6 | ... | 4.8 | ... | 2.5 | 10.2 | 4.4 | 19.7 | 3.7 |
| Kyrgyzstan<br>Kirghizistan | 2003 | 14 116 | 29.4 | 10.8 | 4.4 | 7.0 | 0.4 | 2.2 | 12.5 | 3.0 | 25.1 | 4.9 |
| | 2004 | 17 146 | 31.3 | 9.8 | 3.3 | 6.5 | 0.9 | 1.2 | 13.9 | 3.3 | 23.3 | 5.1 |
| | 2005 | 17 677 | 28.8 | 9.2 | 3.7 | 5.1 | 0.6 | 1.2 | 14.7 | 2.7 | 21.1 | 11.5 |
| Latvia<br>Lettonie | 2003 | 1 371 | ... | 3.3 | ... | ... | ... | ... | 15.7 | 5.2 | 24.1 | 2.9 |
| | 2004 | 1 451 | ... | 3.8 | ... | ... | ... | ... | 16.7 | 5.4 | 24.5 | 3.0 |
| | 2005 | 1 581 | ... | 4.4 | ... | ... | ... | ... | 16.6 | 4.9 | 23.6 | 3.3 |
| Lesotho<br>Lesotho | 1999 | 1 188 | 25.6 | ... | 19.1 | 4.7 | ... | 10.7 | 13.1 | ... | 6.1 | ... |
| | 2000 | 1 144 | 27.7 | ... | 20.2 | 5.5 | ... | 11.6 | 13.2 | ... | 8.1 | ... |
| | 2001 | 1 176 | 27.4 | ... | 20.6 | 6.7 | ... | 11.8 | 14.0 | ... | 7.7 | ... |
| Libyan Arab Jamah.[1]<br>Jamah. arabe libyenne[1] | 1980 | 2 351 | 68.8 | ... | ... | 7.7 | ... | 1.2 | 7.4 | 0.9 | 11.5 | 2.3 |
| Lithuania<br>Lituanie | 2003 | 10 433 | 7.5 | 7.0 | 9.9 | 11.9 | 2.0 | 2.6 | 21.8 | 3.9 | 27.1 | 6.5 |
| | 2004 | 11 207 | 10.5 | 6.8 | 9.6 | 10.4 | 1.9 | 1.6 | 20.3 | 3.5 | 27.6 | 7.9 |
| | 2005 | 11 921 | 8.7 | 7.3 | 9.7 | 9.8 | 2.1 | 1.5 | 20.2 | 4.0 | 28.6 | 8.1 |
| Luxembourg<br>Luxembourg | 2004 | 4 622 | 15.6 | 1.4 | 5.4 | 10.4 | 3.2 | 1.5 | 25.3 | 4.0 | 23.9 | 9.4 |
| | 2005 | 4 986 | 16.1 | 1.3 | 5.4 | 9.7 | 3.2 | 1.5 | 25.6 | 4.0 | 23.6 | 9.5 |
| | 2006 | 5 245 | 15.3 | 1.4 | 5.6 | 9.6 | 3.0 | 1.4 | 25.6 | 4.2 | 24.2 | 9.6 |
| Malaysia<br>Malaisie | 2004 | 59 635 | 6.3 | 4.6 | 5.3 | 5.5 | ... | ... | 6.3 | ... | 23.0 | 1.7 |
| | 2005 | 64 278 | 6.4 | 4.6 | 5.0 | 5.0 | ... | ... | 6.4 | ... | 23.3 | 2.2 |
| | 2006 | 68 525 | 6.4 | 5.1 | 5.4 | 4.9 | ... | ... | 6.5 | ... | 24.5 | 2.0 |
| Maldives[1]<br>Maldives[1] | 1984 | 103 | 30.4 | 15.6 | ... | 13.9 | ... | 5.8 | 7.9 | ... | 14.6 | 6.8 |
| | 1985 | 121 | 29.9 | 15.0 | ... | 11.8 | ... | 8.0 | 7.9 | ... | 14.5 | 5.6 |
| | 1986 | 139 | 32.3 | 16.3 | ... | 5.6 | ... | 7.8 | 8.3 | ... | 16.2 | 5.3 |
| Malta<br>Malte | 2003 | 398 | 11.8 | 4.0 | 8.3 | 16.8 | 3.5 | 0.5 | 23.4 | 1.5 | 23.6 | 6.8 |
| | 2004 | 416 | 12.5 | 3.6 | 7.9 | 15.4 | 3.4 | 0.5 | 24.8 | 1.4 | 23.6 | 6.5 |
| | 2005 | 425 | 12.2 | 3.8 | 8.0 | 15.8 | 3.3 | 0.5 | 24.7 | 1.4 | 23.5 | 6.6 |

**Government final consumption expenditure by function at current prices**— Percentage distribution by divisions
of Classification of the Functions of Government (COFOG) (*continued*)

**Dépenses de consommation administrations publiques par fonction aux prix courants**— Répartition en pourcentage
par divisions de la Classification des fonctions des administrations publiques (COFOG) (*suite*)

| Country or area &<br>Pays ou zone & | Year<br>Année | Total<br>(mil. nat. curr.)<br>Totale<br>(millions<br>monnaie nat.) | Div. 01<br>(%) | Div. 02<br>(%) | Div. 03<br>(%) | Div. 04<br>(%) | Div. 05<br>(%) | Div. 06<br>(%) | Div. 07<br>(%) | Div. 08<br>(%) | Div. 09<br>(%) | Div. 10<br>(%) |
|---|---|---|---|---|---|---|---|---|---|---|---|---|
| Mauritius<br>Maurice | 2002 | 19 854 | 22.6 | 1.4 | 13.5 | 11.7 | ... | 6.0 | 15.8 | 1.9 | 24.8 | 2.2 |
| | 2003 | 22 271 | 22.1 | 1.3 | 13.3 | 11.4 | ... | 5.9 | 15.6 | 2.3 | 25.9 | 2.3 |
| | 2004 | 25 042 | 22.8 | 1.2 | 13.3 | 10.6 | ... | 6.0 | 16.7 | 1.9 | 25.3 | 2.3 |
| Mexico<br>Mexique | 2002 | 759 866 | 11.4 | ... | 16.3 | 7.5 | ... | ... | 21.2 | 5.2 | 36.8 | 1.6 |
| | 2003 | 855 747 | 12.0 | ... | 16.0 | 7.7 | ... | ... | 20.7 | 5.4 | 36.6 | 1.6 |
| | 2004 | 913 971 | 12.0 | ... | 16.2 | 7.6 | ... | ... | 21.1 | 5.2 | 36.4 | 1.6 |
| Moldova<br>Moldova | 2004 | 4 774 | 35.9[5] | ... | ... | 11.9[19] | ... | 1.6 | 3.8 | ... | 37.8 | 2.0 |
| | 2005 | 6 189 | 34.6[5] | ... | ... | 13.1[19] | ... | 2.0 | 4.8 | ... | 37.9 | 2.0 |
| | 2006 | 8 044 | 40.1[5] | ... | ... | 10.7[19] | ... | 2.1 | 4.5 | ... | 35.8 | 2.0 |
| Mongolia<br>Mongolie | 2004 | 312 843 | 14.1 | 9.1 | 11.0 | 6.6 | ... | 0.9 | 20.4 | 4.0 | 32.0 | 2.0 |
| | 2005 | 344 488 | 14.6 | 9.3 | 10.8 | 6.4 | ... | 0.8 | 20.4 | 3.9 | 31.9 | 1.9 |
| | 2006 | 425 279 | 14.5 | 8.3 | 10.2 | 8.3 | ... | 0.8 | 18.7 | 4.7 | 32.6 | 1.9 |
| Montserrat[1]<br>Montserrat[1] | 1983 | 18 | 15.1 | 0.4 | 10.9 | 27.0 | ... | 0.8 | 17.4 | 1.4 | 17.7 | 9.2 |
| | 1984 | 19 | 19.6 | 0.3 | 10.5 | 27.2 | ... | -0.2 | 15.9 | 0.6 | 19.3 | 6.6 |
| | 1985 | 20 | 18.7 | 0.3 | 11.3 | 24.5 | ... | 0.9 | 15.3 | 1.7 | 22.4 | 4.8 |
| Nepal[1]<br>Népal[1] | 1986 | 5 065 | 14.7 | 11.7 | 9.7 | 23.1 | ... | 2.5 | 8.0 | 6.0 | 23.9 | 0.7 |
| | 1987 | 5 797 | 16.9 | 13.1 | 8.1 | 34.6 | ... | 3.2 | 8.7 | 0.8 | 27.5 | 0.5 |
| | 1988 | 6 895 | 15.2 | 7.5 | 11.0 | 37.0 | ... | 3.9 | 3.8 | 1.6 | 24.0 | 1.7 |
| Netherlands<br>Pays-Bas | 2002 | 110 246 | 9.3 | 6.4 | 6.4 | 12.1 | 1.6 | 2.2 | 17.2 | 4.2 | 18.3 | 22.2 |
| | 2003 | 116 793 | 9.3 | 6.1 | 6.5 | 12.0 | 1.7 | 2.0 | 17.4 | 4.1 | 18.1 | 22.1 |
| | 2004 | 118 821 | 9.2 | 5.9 | 6.9 | 11.4 | 1.6 | 1.9 | 18.2 | 4.0 | 18.6 | 22.0 |
| Netherlands Antilles<br>Antilles néerlandaises | 2002 | 1 068 | 13.6 | 1.5 | 14.0 | 2.1 | 1.4 | ... | 7.5 | 1.0 | 17.4 | 7.9 |
| | 2003 | 1 150 | 13.5 | 1.5 | 14.1 | 2.2 | 1.3 | ... | 7.4 | 1.0 | 18.4 | 7.8 |
| | 2004 | 1 130 | 14.5 | 1.6 | 15.1 | 2.2 | 1.6 | ... | 7.7 | 1.0 | 19.8 | 8.4 |
| New Zealand<br>Nouvelle-Zélande | #2003 | 24 386 | 9.2 | 6.0 | 7.4 | 8.2 | 3.2 | 2.0 | 30.9 | 2.9 | 22.2 | 8.0 |
| | 2004 | 26 238 | 9.6 | 5.4 | 7.2 | 7.7 | 3.2 | 2.0 | 31.1 | 2.9 | 22.5 | 8.5 |
| | 2005 | 28 659 | 10.2 | 4.5 | 7.6 | 6.4 | 3.8 | 2.3 | 31.6 | 2.8 | 22.2 | 8.6 |
| Nicaragua<br>Nicaragua | 2001 | 9 702 | 23.8 | 3.5 | 8.9 | 21.7 | 2.4 | 0.5 | 13.2 | 0.4 | 18.7 | 4.8 |
| | 2002 | 9 872 | 20.7 | 4.2 | 10.1 | 19.3 | 1.6 | 0.5 | 15.3 | 0.4 | 21.7 | 3.7 |
| | 2003 | 11 130 | 19.8 | 4.2 | 10.3 | 22.0 | 1.9 | 0.5 | 13.9 | 0.4 | 21.8 | 3.0 |
| Norway<br>Norvège | 2002 | 338 429 | 9.6 | 8.9 | 4.6 | 8.1 | 0.7 | 0.4 | 29.5 | 2.8 | 22.1 | 13.4 |
| | 2003 | 354 305 | 8.9 | 8.5 | 4.4 | 7.6 | 0.7 | 0.4 | 30.3 | 2.7 | 22.8 | 13.7 |
| | 2004 | 370 769 | 8.6 | 8.2 | 4.3 | 7.5 | 0.8 | 0.3 | 30.2 | 2.7 | 22.6 | 14.8 |
| Oman<br>Oman | 2000 | 1 580 | 10.5 | 29.3[20] | 11.6 | 7.7 | ... | 5.4 | 10.1 | 2.8 | 21.4 | 1.2 |
| | 2001 | 1 712 | 10.7 | 33.2[20] | 11.3 | 6.8 | ... | 4.6 | 9.4 | 2.5 | 20.5 | 1.1 |
| | 2002 | 1 800 | 10.8 | 32.6[20] | 12.0 | 5.9 | ... | 4.7 | 9.5 | 2.5 | 20.8 | 1.0 |
| Pakistan<br>Pakistan | 2004 | 468 701 | 47.3 | ... | 10.3 | 7.1 | 0.6 | 1.0 | 4.3 | 0.3 | 11.7 | 16.7 |
| | 2005 | 517 516 | 43.8 | ... | 9.8 | 12.6 | 0.6 | 1.2 | 4.8 | 0.5 | 10.2 | 16.0 |
| | 2006 | 591 370 | 43.8 | ... | 9.8 | 12.6 | 0.6 | 1.2 | 4.8 | 0.5 | 10.2 | 16.0 |
| Panama<br>Panama | 2003 | 1 807 | 17.7 | ... | 18.5 | 6.1 | 0.2 | 0.4 | 7.3 | 0.9 | 25.1 | 23.6 |
| | 2004 | 1 930 | 22.1 | ... | 14.6 | 8.0 | 0.2 | 0.4 | 6.4 | 0.9 | 24.2 | 23.1 |
| | 2005 | 2 034 | 20.0 | ... | 10.8 | 7.8 | 0.2 | 0.7 | 7.0 | 0.8 | 23.7 | 29.1 |
| Peru[1]<br>Pérou[1] | 1986 | 43[21] | 56.6 | ... | ... | 5.7 | ... | 0.2 | 9.2 | 1.3 | 25.0 | 2.1 |
| | 1987 | 94[21] | 55.5 | ... | ... | 5.3 | ... | 0.2 | 7.1 | 1.8 | 27.3 | 2.9 |
| | 1988 | 475[21] | 54.1 | ... | ... | 6.7 | ... | 0.2 | 7.6 | 2.5 | 26.1 | 2.7 |
| Portugal<br>Portugal | 2003 | 28 129 | 9.2 | 6.3 | 9.4 | 7.7 | 1.7 | 0.9 | 28.3 | 2.1 | 29.8 | 4.6 |
| | 2004 | 29 744 | 10.7 | 6.3 | 9.1 | 7.4 | 1.2 | 0.9 | 28.6 | 1.8 | 29.4 | 4.7 |
| | 2005 | 31 423 | 12.5 | 6.1 | 9.0 | 7.6 | 1.1 | 0.8 | 28.8 | 1.8 | 29.2 | 3.2 |

**Government final consumption expenditure by function at current prices**—Percentage distribution by divisions of Classification of the Functions of Government (COFOG) (*continued*)

**Dépenses de consommation administrations publiques par fonction aux prix courants**—Répartition en pourcentage par divisions de la Classification des fonctions des administrations publiques (COFOG) (*suite*)

| Country or area [&] / Pays ou zone [&] | Year / Année | Total (mil. nat. curr.) Totale (millions monnaie nat.) | Div. 01 (%) | Div. 02 (%) | Div. 03 (%) | Div. 04 (%) | Div. 05 (%) | Div. 06 (%) | Div. 07 (%) | Div. 08 (%) | Div. 09 (%) | Div. 10 (%) |
|---|---|---|---|---|---|---|---|---|---|---|---|---|
| Romania[1] Roumanie[1] | 1993 | 2 473 200 | 36.5[7] | ... | ... | 11.7 | ... | ... | 22.3 | 4.7 | 22.6 | 2.1 |
| | 1994 | 6 851 800 | 39.0[7] | ... | ... | 8.4 | ... | ... | 28.6 | 4.6 | 19.4 | 2.2 |
| | 1995 | 9 877 000 | 37.3[7] | ... | ... | 14.5 | ... | ... | 19.0 | 5.5 | 21.4 | 2.3 |
| Russian Federation Fédération de Russie | 2003 | 2 330 573 | 53.2[5] | ... | ... | 1.7[22] | ... | 2.9 | 22.7 | 2.9 | 15.1 | ... |
| | 2004 | 2 847 486 | 52.7[5] | ... | ... | 1.6[22] | ... | 3.0 | 23.0 | 2.9 | 15.4 | ... |
| | 2005 | 3 598 306 | 8.1[5] | ... | 29.5 | 7.9[22] | 0.2 | 2.6 | 17.1 | 2.7 | 19.2 | 12.6 |
| Saint Vincent-Grenadines[1] Saint Vincent-Grenadines[1] | 2003 | 202 | 10.9 | ... | 11.9 | 21.8 | ... | 1.5 | 18.3 | ... | 25.2 | 7.9 |
| | 2004 | 217[23] | 11.1 | ... | 12.0 | 24.9 | ... | 1.4 | 17.5 | ... | 25.3 | 8.3 |
| | 2005 | 241 | 12.9 | ... | 11.6 | 23.7 | ... | 1.2 | 16.6 | ... | 24.1 | 7.9 |
| San Marino[1] Saint-Marin[1] | 1999 | 423 728 | 17.0 | 0.3 | 5.0 | 8.9 | ... | 7.4 | 20.7 | 6.5 | 16.8 | 17.4 |
| | #2003 | 271 | 26.5 | 4.6 | ... | ... | 1.9 | 3.3 | 22.7 | 4.1 | 14.8 | 11.5 |
| | 2004 | 314 | 21.2 | 4.1 | ... | ... | 2.7 | 4.4 | 21.0 | 4.2 | 12.4 | 20.3 |
| Saudi Arabia[1] Arabie saoudite[1] | 1999 | 154 094 | 19.8 | 27.4 | ... | 3.4 | ... | 4.7 | 11.0 | 2.9[24] | 29.4 | 0.4 |
| | 2000 | 183 804 | 18.0 | 27.9 | ... | 4.7 | ... | 5.3 | 11.7 | 3.0[24] | 27.0 | 0.5 |
| | 2001 | 188 695 | 18.4 | 27.4 | ... | 4.9 | ... | 5.5 | 11.8 | 3.0[24] | 26.4 | 0.5 |
| Senegal Sénégal | 2002 | 484 692 | 68.0 | ... | ... | ... | ... | ... | 6.5 | 1.5 | 24.0 | ... |
| | 2003 | 522 522 | 68.7 | ... | ... | ... | ... | ... | 6.5 | 1.6 | 23.2 | ... |
| | 2004 | 572 821 | 69.0 | ... | ... | ... | ... | ... | 6.5 | 1.5 | 23.0 | ... |
| Seychelles[1] Seychelles[1] | 1989 | 475 | 9.4 | 11.5 | 4.9 | 17.1 | ... | 2.1 | 11.8 | 3.1 | 29.7 | 2.6 |
| | 1990 | 544 | 9.5 | 10.2 | 5.1 | 18.3 | ... | 2.6 | 12.8 | 5.9 | 29.2 | 3.5 |
| | 1991 | 558 | 10.3 | 11.0 | 5.7 | 17.0 | ... | 2.4 | 13.7 | 5.7 | 26.4 | 5.2 |
| Sierra Leone[1] Sierra Leone[1] | 1988 | 3 883[25] | 18.5 | 7.2 | ... | 28.0 | ... | 0.8 | 5.9 | 0.0 | 13.2 | 1.0 |
| | 1989 | 7 620[25] | 14.4 | 7.3 | ... | 45.9 | ... | 1.4 | 5.0 | 0.0 | 10.2 | 1.4 |
| | 1990 | 32 337[25] | 11.9 | 5.6 | ... | 27.9 | ... | 1.0 | 2.1 | ^0.0 | 6.2 | 0.6 |
| Slovenia Slovénie | 2003 | 1 139 127 | 14.7 | 5.0 | 8.9 | 8.5 | 0.9 | 1.0 | 29.6 | 3.2 | 24.8 | 3.6 |
| | 2004 | 1 227 520 | 15.6 | 5.1 | 8.8 | 7.6 | 1.0 | 0.9 | 29.6 | 3.1 | 24.8 | 3.4 |
| | 2005 | 1 295 422 | 15.7 | 6.6 | 8.0 | 7.7 | 1.0 | 0.9 | 29.1 | 3.0 | 24.8 | 3.3 |
| Spain[1] Espagne[1] | 1994 | 10 963 200[26] | 8.0 | 8.7 | 11.9 | 7.4 | ... | 3.5 | 25.8 | 3.2 | 22.3 | 4.9 |
| | 1995 | 11 647 100[26] | 8.3 | 9.0 | 12.5 | 7.4 | ... | 3.7 | 24.1 | 3.2 | 22.9 | 4.8 |
| Sri Lanka Sri Lanka | 2003 | 221 620 | 16.4 | 22.0 | 8.4 | 9.2 | ... | 0.1 | 12.7 | 0.6 | 13.1 | 17.4 |
| | 2004 | 264 069 | 14.4 | 21.3 | 7.2 | 7.5 | ... | 0.1 | 12.8 | 1.9 | 14.7 | 20.1 |
| | 2005 | 307 866 | 12.3 | 19.9 | 6.2 | 8.7 | ... | 0.2 | 11.6 | 0.4 | 16.6 | 24.0 |
| Sudan[1] Soudan[1] | 1981 | 720 | 25.2[27] | 18.6 | ... | 12.4[28] | ... | 0.1 | 9.7 | 3.2 | 30.9 | ... |
| | 1982 | 854 | 27.7[27] | 19.0 | ... | 14.4[28] | ... | 0.0 | 8.6 | 2.6 | 27.7 | ... |
| | 1983 | 1 113 | 32.4[27] | 22.5 | ... | 14.4[28] | ... | -0.2 | 5.1 | 2.2 | 23.7 | ... |
| Sweden Suède | 2003 | 691 124 | 9.2 | 6.5 | 4.9 | 6.3 | 0.2 | 0.6 | 24.4 | 2.7 | 23.5 | 21.8 |
| | 2004 | 703 219 | 9.7 | 6.2 | 4.8 | 6.1 | 0.2 | 0.6 | 24.4 | 2.7 | 23.6 | 21.8 |
| | 2005 | 724 161 | 8.7 | 5.7 | 4.8 | 6.2 | 0.4 | 0.6 | 24.6 | 2.8 | 24.6 | 21.8 |
| Thailand[1] Thaïlande[1] | 2003 | 636 002 | 24.1 | 26.1[29] | ... | 1.5 | ... | 2.1[18] | 10.0 | ... | 35.4 | 0.9 |
| | 2004 | 720 515 | 25.6 | 25.2[29] | ... | 1.8 | ... | 2.1[18] | 9.7 | ... | 34.6 | 1.0 |
| | 2005 | 842 268 | 25.7 | 23.7[29] | ... | 2.6 | ... | 2.3[18] | 11.4 | ... | 33.3 | 0.9 |
| TFYR of Macedonia L'ex-R.y. Macédoine | 1991 | 199 | 37.6 | ... | ... | ... | ... | 2.5 | 21.8 | 3.8 | 27.1 | 6.7 |
| | 1992 | 2 302 | 38.3 | ... | ... | ... | ... | 1.2 | 28.9 | 3.0 | 23.4 | 4.7 |
| | 1993 | 12 472 | 42.6 | ... | ... | ... | ... | 0.4 | 24.3 | 3.4 | 23.5 | 5.5 |
| Tonga[1] Tonga[1] | 1985 | 21 | 20.7 | 4.2 | 7.0 | 31.9 | ... | ... | 12.2 | ... | 13.6 | 1.9 |
| | 1986 | 27 | 22.7 | 3.7 | 7.1 | 29.0 | ... | ... | 11.9 | ... | 13.8 | 1.9 |
| | 1987 | 32 | 26.9 | 3.4 | 6.9 | 26.3 | ... | ... | 10.3 | ... | 13.1 | 1.9 |
| Trinidad and Tobago Trinité-et-Tobago | 2003 | 9 042 | 20.1 | ... | 22.8 | 16.1 | ... | 6.5 | 9.8 | ... | 24.2 | 0.6 |
| | 2004 | 9 585 | 20.1 | ... | 22.2 | 18.0 | ... | 6.5 | 9.5 | ... | 23.2 | 0.6 |
| | 2005 | 11 885 | 20.9 | ... | 21.8 | 16.7 | ... | 6.6 | 8.9 | ... | 24.6 | 0.6 |

24 **Government final consumption expenditure by function at current prices**— Percentage distribution by divisions of Classification of the Functions of Government (COFOG) (*continued*)

**Dépenses de consommation administrations publiques par fonction aux prix courants**— Répartition en pourcentage par divisions de la Classification des fonctions des administrations publiques (COFOG) (*suite*)

| Country or area [&]<br>Pays ou zone [&] | Year<br>Année | Total<br>(mil. nat. curr.)<br>Totale<br>(millions<br>monnaie nat.) | Div. 01<br>(%) | Div. 02<br>(%) | Div. 03<br>(%) | Div. 04<br>(%) | Div. 05<br>(%) | Div. 06<br>(%) | Div. 07<br>(%) | Div. 08<br>(%) | Div. 09<br>(%) | Div. 10<br>(%) |
|---|---|---|---|---|---|---|---|---|---|---|---|---|
| Ukraine<br>Ukraine | 2003 | 50 830 | 11.4 | 7.9 | 10.4 | 8.3 | 0.9 | 1.7 | 18.2 | 2.9 | 26.0 | 12.3 |
| | 2004 | 60 610 | 11.3 | 8.0 | 11.0 | 6.0 | 0.7 | 1.7 | 19.0 | 2.7 | 26.7 | 12.8 |
| | 2005 | 80 528 | 13.8 | 5.8 | 10.8 | 5.2 | 0.5 | 2.3 | 19.6 | 2.8 | 29.5 | 9.7 |
| United Kingdom<br>Royaume-Uni | 2002 | 212 464 | 5.3 | 12.3 | 10.7 | 6.4 | 2.6 | 2.0 | 29.8 | 2.0 | 17.7 | 10.6 |
| | 2003 | 232 699 | 5.9 | 12.4 | 10.6 | 6.5 | 2.5 | 1.8 | 30.0 | 1.9 | 17.1 | 11.0 |
| | 2004 | 250 708 | 5.9 | 11.7 | 10.3 | 5.8 | 2.4 | 2.1 | 31.0 | 1.7 | 16.8 | 10.9 |
| United Rep. of Tanzania[1,30]<br>Rép.-Unie de Tanzanie[1,30] | 1992 | 225 639[2] | 17.5 | 8.5 | 8.5 | 16.5 | ... | 0.4 | 5.9 | 2.5 | 7.7 | 0.7 |
| | 1993 | 336 855[2] | 21.5 | 6.8 | 6.8 | 22.6 | ... | 0.5 | 5.7 | 2.0 | 7.5 | 0.2 |
| | 1994 | 408 440[2] | 21.1 | 4.9 | 7.5 | 22.9 | ... | 0.6 | 7.2 | 2.1 | 7.6 | 0,2 |
| United States<br>Etats-Unis | 2003 | 1 731 898 | 9.3 | 25.0 | 12.6 | 11.6 | 0.0 | 0.5 | 4.8 | 1.4 | 30.3 | 4.4 |
| | 2004 | 1 855 019 | 9.4 | 26.1 | 12.5 | 11.3 | 0.0 | 0.5 | 4.8 | 1.4 | 29.9 | 4.3 |
| | 2005 | 1 977 901 | 9.4 | 26.2 | 12.6 | 11.1 | 0.0 | 0.5 | 4.9 | 1.4 | 29.4 | 4.4 |
| Vanuatu[1]<br>Vanuatu[1] | 1991 | 4 693 | 20.5 | 8.4 | ... | 22.6 | ... | 18.5[31] | 10.3 | ... | 19.8 | ... |
| | 1992 | 5 112 | 22.6 | 8.7 | ... | 21.2 | ... | 16.1[31] | 10.1 | ... | 21.2 | ... |
| | 1993 | 5 194 | 27.1 | 9.2 | ... | 20.1 | ... | 13.9[31] | 9.7 | ... | 20.0 | ... |
| Venezuela (Bolivarian Rep. of)<br>Venezuela (Rép. bolivarienne du) | 2003 | 17 276 165 | 13.7 | 6.5 | 5.8 | 5.2 | 0.4 | 3.4 | 14.6 | 1.3 | 41.9 | 7.2 |
| | 2004 | 25 428 211 | 14.0 | 9.2 | 6.7 | 4.9 | 0.9 | 2.5 | 17.0 | 1.3 | 37.7 | 5.8 |
| | 2005 | 33 619 547 | 12.8 | 8.9 | 6.4 | 6.1 | 0.8 | 0.2 | 17.5 | 1.3 | 37.9 | 5.9 |
| Zimbabwe[1]<br>Zimbabwe[1] | 1989 | 5 568[32] | 6.2 | 15.7 | 5.9 | 14.1 | ... | 1.2 | 8.1 | 1.4 | 28.1 | 2.6 |
| | 1990 | 7 425[32] | 28.1 | 13.1 | 4.9 | 20.8 | ... | 1.6 | 6.5 | 2.0 | 19.9 | 3.1 |
| | 1991 | 7 788[32] | 16.7 | 14.3 | 6.1 | 23.0 | ... | 1.7 | 7.4 | 2.8 | 26.7 | 4.1 |

Table header: **Divisions of the Classification of the Functions of Government (COFOG) [t]** / **Divisions de la Classification des fonctions des administrations publiques (COFOG) [t]**

Source

United Nations Statistics Division, New York, national accounts database, last accessed January 2008.

Data for most countries have been compiled in accordance with the concepts and definitions of the System of National Accounts 1993 (1993 SNA). Countries that follow the 1968 SNA are footnoted accordingly.

[t] COFOG Divisions:
   Div. 01: General public services
   Div. 02: Defence
   Div. 03: Public order and safety
   Div. 04: Economic affairs
   Div. 05: Environmental protection
   Div. 06: Housing and community amenities
   Div. 07: Health
   Div. 08: Recreation, culture and religion
   Div. 09: Education
   Div. 10: Social protection

[&] Data for most countries or areas refers to the western calendar year ending 31 December. The following countries are exceptions, with fiscal years as follows:

Year beginning 21 March: Afghanistan, Iran (Islamic Republic).

Year beginning 1 April: Bermuda, India, Myanmar, New Zealand, Nigeria.
Year beginning 1 July: Australia, Bhutan, Gambia, Nicaragua, Pakistan, Puerto Rico, Saudi Arabia.

Source

Organisation des Nations Unies, Division de statistique, New York, la base de données sur les comptes nationaux, dernier accès janvier 2008.

Les données pour la majorité des pays sont compilées selon les concepts et définitions du Système de comptabilité nationale, 1993 (SCN93). Seuls les pays qui suivent toujours le SCN68 seront donc signalés par une note.

[t] Divisions de la COFOG:
   Div. 01: Services généraux des administrations publiques
   Div. 02: Défense
   Div. 03: Ordre et sécurité publics
   Div. 04: Affaires économiques
   Div. 05: Protection de l'environnement
   Div. 06: Logements et équipements collectifs
   Div. 07: Santé
   Div. 08: Loisirs, culture et culte
   Div. 09: Enseignement
   Div. 10: Protection sociale

[&] Les données pour la plupart des pays ou territoires concernent l'année civile se terminant le 31 décembre, sauf les pays ci-dessous dont les exercices budgétaires sont les suivants :

Exercice commençant le 21 mars: Afghanistan, Iran (République islamique d').

Exercice commençant le 1er avril: Bermudes, Inde, Myanmar, Nigéria, Nouvelle-Zélande.
Exercice commençant le 1er juillet: Arabie saoudite, Australie, Bhoutan, Gambie, Nicaragua, Pakistan, Porto Rico.

# 24

**Government final consumption expenditure by function at current prices**—Percentage distribution by divisions of Classification of the Functions of Government (COFOG) *(continued)*

**Dépenses de consommation administrations publiques par fonction aux prix courants**—Répartition en pourcentage par divisions de la Classification des fonctions des administrations publiques (COFOG) *(suite)*

Year ending 30 June:  Bangladesh, Botswana, Egypt, Swaziland, Tonga.

Year ending 7 July: Ethiopia.
Year ending 15 July: Nepal.
Year ending 30 September: Haiti.

Exercice se terminant le 30 juin: Bangladesh, Botswana, Égypte, Swaziland, Tonga.
Exercice se terminant le 7 juillet: Éthiopie.
Exercice se terminant le 15 juillet: Népal.
Exercice se terminant le 30 septembre: Haïti.

## Notes

1 Data compiled in accordance with the System of National Accounts 1968 (1968 SNA).
2 Central government estimates only.
3 Including expenditure on culture.
4 Data refer only to collective government consumption expenditure (excluding individual consumption).

5 Including "Defence".
6 Including housing and community amenities.
7 Including defence and public order and safety.
8 Total government current expenditure only.
9 Excluding Office of the President, Ministries of Justice, Foreign Affairs, Information, among others.
10 Refers to inter-ministerial expenses only.
11 Refers to the Ministry of the Interior.
12 Refers to the Ministry of Finance and Planning.
13 Refers to the Ministry of Agriculture, Livestock Development and Environmental Protection.
14 Refers to the Ministry of Equipment, Transport and Telecommunication.
15 Refers to the Ministry of Health, Public Services and Social Affairs.

16 Twinning projects in the health sector.
17 Including compensation of employees and intermediate consumption of the following departmental enterprises: electricity, gas and steam, water works and supply and medical and other health services.

18 Including Recreation, culture and religion.
19 Including agriculture, transport, and other branches of the economy.
20 Data refer to defence affairs and services.
21 Figures in thousands.
22 Data refer to agriculture, geology, exploration, hydrometerorology, transport, and communication.
23 Preliminary data.
24 Data refer to other community and social services.
25 Central government estimates only; including development expenditure.
26 Data in pesetas.
27 Including "Public order and safety".
28 Including other functions.
29 Including justice and police.
30 Tanganyika only.
31 Including "Social protection".
32 Central and local government estimates only.

## Notes

1 Données compilées selon le Système de comptabilité nationale de 1968 (SCN 1968).
2 Administration centrale seulement.
3 Y compris dépenses de culture.
4 Les données ne concernent que les dépenses de consommation collective des administrations publiques (à l'exclusion de la consommation individuelle).
5 Y compris "Défense".
6 Y compris logement et équipements collectifs.
7 Y compris défense et sureté publique.
8 Dépenses publiques courants seulement.
9 Non compris notamment le Cabinet du Président, et les Ministères de la justice, des affaires étrangères et de l'information.
10 Ne concerne que les dépenses interministérielles.
11 Concerne le Ministère de l'intérieur.
12 Concerne le Ministère des finances et de la planification.
13 Concerne le Ministère de l'agriculture, du développement de l'élevage et de la protection de l'environnement.
14 Concerne le Ministère de l'équipement, des transports et des télécommunications.
15 Concerne le Ministère de la santé, des services publics et des affaires sociales.
16 Projets jumelés dans le secteur de la santé.
17 Y compris la rémunération des employés et la consommation intermédiaire des entreprises suivantes : électricité, gaz et vapeur, approvisionnement en eau, services médicaux et autres services sanitaires.
18 Y compris Loisirs, culture et culte.
19 Y compris l'agriculture, les transports, et d'autres branches d'activité.
20 Les données se réfèrent aux affaires et services de la défense.
21 Données en milliers.
22 Les données concernent l'agriculture, la géologie, l'exploration, l'hydrométéorologie, les transports et les communications.
23 Données préliminaires.
24 Les données concernent les autres services collectifs et sociaux.
25 Administration centrale seulement; y compris les dépenses de développement.
26 Les données sont exprimées en pesetas.
27 Y compris "Ordre et sécurité publics".
28 Y compris les autres fonctions.
29 Y compris justice et police.
30 Tanganyika seulement.
31 Y compris "protection sociale".
32 Administration centrale et locale seulement.

# Household consumption expenditure by purpose at current prices
Percentage distribution by divisions of the Classification of Individual Consumption according to Purpose (COICOP)

# Dépenses de consommation des ménages par fonction aux prix courants
Répartition en pourcentage par divisions de la Nomenclature des fonctions de la consommation individuelle (COICOP)

| Country or area &<br>Pays ou zone & | Year<br>Année | Total (mil.<br>nat. curr.)<br>Totale<br>(millions<br>monn. nat.) | Divisions of the Classification of Individual Consumption according to Purpose (COICOP) t<br>Divisions de la Nomenclature des fonctions de la consommation individuelle (COICOP) t | | | | | | | | | |
|---|---|---|---|---|---|---|---|---|---|---|---|---|
| | | | Div. 01 + 02<br>(%) | Div. 03<br>(%) | Div. 04<br>(%) | Div. 05<br>(%) | Div. 06<br>(%) | Div. 07 + 08<br>(%) | Div. 09<br>(%) | Div. 10<br>(%) | Div. 11<br>(%) | Div. 12<br>(%) |
| Andorra[1]<br>Andorre[1] | 2001 | 797 | 20.2[2] | 7.6 | 14.7 | 4.0 | 3.2 | 19.5[3] | 3.9 | 0.9 | 7.2 | 7.8 |
| | 2002 | 870 | 19.1[2] | 7.6 | 14.9 | 4.1 | 3.4 | 19.6[3] | 4.3 | 0.9 | 6.3 | 7.9 |
| | 2003 | 921 | 18.4[2] | 6.3 | 15.0 | 4.1 | 3.6 | 21.2[3] | 4.2 | 1.0 | 5.8 | 8.0 |
| Australia<br>Australie | 2003 | 492 315 | 14.9 | 3.7 | 19.4 | 5.7 | 5.0 | 14.7 | 12.2 | 3.2 | 7.7 | 13.5 |
| | 2004 | 520 982 | 14.9 | 3.8 | 19.3 | 5.6 | 5.0 | 14.9 | 12.2 | 3.3 | 7.5 | 13.4 |
| | 2005 | 547 138 | 14.9 | 3.7 | 19.5 | 5.5 | 5.1 | 14.8 | 12.2 | 3.4 | 7.6 | 13.4 |
| Austria<br>Autriche | 2003 | 123 936 | 14.5 | 7.1 | 20.2 | 8.0 | 3.4 | 15.5 | 12.4 | 0.7 | 12.8 | 9.7 |
| | 2004 | 128 554 | 14.2 | 7.0 | 20.4 | 7.9 | 3.4 | 16.0 | 12.5 | 0.7 | 12.9 | 9.8 |
| | 2005 | 133 001 | 13.9 | 7.0 | 21.8 | 7.7 | 3.4 | 15.8 | 12.4 | 0.7 | 13.0 | 9.6 |
| Azerbaijan<br>Azerbaïdjan | 2004 | 4 698[4] | 78.6 | 5.8 | 1.3 | 1.7 | 1.8 | 6.2 | 0.3 | 3.3 | 0.4 | 0.6 |
| | 2005 | 5 211[4] | 78.6 | 5.8 | 1.3 | 1.7 | 1.8 | 6.2 | 0.3 | 3.3 | 0.4 | 0.6 |
| | 2006 | 6 245[4] | 78.6 | 5.8 | 1.3 | 1.7 | 1.8 | 6.2 | 0.3 | 3.3 | 0.4 | 0.6 |
| Belarus<br>Bélarus | 2003 | 20 331 800 | 52.7 | 8.3 | 11.7 | 4.2 | 2.2 | 11.0 | 2.9 | 1.3 | 2.1 | 3.6 |
| | 2004 | 26 130 200 | 51.5 | 7.9 | 12.3 | 4.4 | 2.2 | 11.0 | 3.4 | 1.3 | 2.5 | 3.5 |
| | 2005 | 32 954 600 | 49.9 | 7.6 | 11.9 | 4.7 | 2.1 | 12.2 | 3.8 | 1.5 | 2.7 | 3.6 |
| Belgium<br>Belgique | 2003 | 144 329 | 17.3 | 5.3 | 22.6 | 5.3 | 4.2 | 16.1 | 9.1 | 0.5 | 5.3 | 12.3 |
| | 2004 | 150 049 | 17.3 | 5.2 | 22.4 | 5.3 | 4.1 | 16.6 | 9.1 | 0.5 | 5.1 | 12.2 |
| | 2005 | 155 774 | 16.9 | 5.3 | 22.6 | 5.3 | 4.2 | 16.9 | 9.2 | 0.5 | 5.0 | 12.2 |
| Bolivia[1]<br>Bolivie[1] | 1994 | 21 444 | 34.7[5] | 6.7 | ... | ... | ... | ... | ... | ... | 9.2 | ... |
| | 1995 | 24 440 | 34.4[5] | 6.5 | ... | ... | ... | ... | ... | ... | 9.5 | ... |
| | 1996 | 28 200 | 35.7[5] | 6.5 | ... | ... | ... | ... | ... | ... | 9.8 | ... |
| Botswana<br>Botswana | 1999 | 6 619 | 43.3 | 5.4 | 12.2 | 4.1 | 2.3 | 7.9 | ... | 6.8 | 1.1 | ... |
| | 2000 | 7 469 | 42.7 | 5.1 | 13.4 | 3.7 | 2.4 | 7.2 | ... | 7.0 | 1.0 | ... |
| | 2001 | 8 281 | 41.1 | 3.8 | 14.0 | ... | 2.6 | 7.4 | ... | 8.2 | 1.0 | ... |
| British Virgin Islands<br>Iles Vierges britanniques | 1997 | 231 | 16.5 | 10.4 | 19.5 | 6.9 | 1.7 | 13.0 | 2.2 | 1.3 | 7.8 | 21.2 |
| | 1998 | 253 | 16.2 | 9.5 | 20.6 | 6.7 | 2.0 | 12.6 | 1.6 | 1.2 | 7.5 | 22.1 |
| | 1999 | 280 | 15.7 | 10.0 | 20.7 | 6.4 | 2.5 | 11.8 | 2.9 | 1.1 | 6.1 | 22.9 |
| Bulgaria<br>Bulgarie | 2003 | 23 590 | 29.4 | 3.7 | 23.9 | 3.6 | 4.3 | 23.6 | 5.0 | 1.1 | 9.3 | 3.0 |
| | 2004 | 25 915 | 29.5 | 3.5 | 22.6 | 4.0 | 4.3 | 24.0 | 5.6 | 1.0 | 9.7 | 3.2 |
| | 2005 | 29 199 | 29.5 | 3.5 | 21.8 | 4.0 | 4.3 | 24.6 | 5.4 | 1.0 | 9.9 | 3.2 |
| Cameroon<br>Cameroun | 2002 | 5 342 410 | 49.5 | 12.2 | 6.9 | 3.0 | 0.3 | 7.6 | ... | 0.9 | 8.4 | 11.2 |
| | 2003 | 5 690 774 | 49.5 | 12.2 | 6.9 | 3.0 | 0.3 | 7.6 | ... | 0.9 | 8.4 | 11.1 |
| | 2004 | 5 919 214 | 47.9 | 13.1 | 7.0 | 3.0 | 0.3 | 8.2 | ... | 0.9 | 8.6 | 10.9 |
| Canada<br>Canada | 2003 | 670 472 | 13.8 | 5.0 | 23.1 | 6.5 | 4.0 | 16.6 | 10.3 | 1.3 | 7.1 | 12.2 |
| | 2004 | 702 754 | 13.7 | 4.9 | 23.0 | 6.5 | 4.1 | 16.3 | 10.3 | 1.3 | 7.1 | 12.4 |
| | 2005 | 742 158 | 13.5 | 4.8 | 22.9 | 6.5 | 4.2 | 16.6 | 10.2 | 1.4 | 7.0 | 12.4 |
| Cape Verde[1]<br>Cap-Vert[1] | 1986 | 13 406 | 61.2 | 2.7 | 14.1 | 7.2 | 0.5 | ... | ... | ... | ... | ... |
| | 1987 | 15 134 | 60.4 | 2.9 | 13.6 | 7.2 | 0.6 | ... | ... | ... | ... | ... |
| | 1988 | 17 848 | 62.6 | 2.5 | 13.5 | 6.9 | 0.5 | ... | ... | ... | ... | ... |
| China, Hong Kong SAR<br>Chine, Hong Kong RAS | 2002 | 687 054 | 13.8 | 12.8[6] | 21.9[7] | 11.8 | 4.6 | 10.2 | 6.6[8] | 2.6 | ... | 12.8[9] |
| | 2003 | 659 083 | 14.0 | 12.5[6] | 22.7[7] | 12.5 | 4.8 | 9.8 | 6.1[8] | 2.7 | ... | 12.8[9] |
| | 2004 | 706 010 | 13.6 | 13.7[6] | 20.8[7] | 12.7 | 5.0 | 10.1 | 6.6[8] | 2.6 | ... | 13.2[9] |
| China, Macao SAR<br>Chine, Macao RAS | 2002 | 19 285 | 12.1 | 4.4 | 17.6 | 2.5 | 3.1 | 12.5 | 11.8 | 3.9 | 13.7 | 5.6 |
| | 2003 | 19 779 | 12.6 | 4.0 | 17.3 | 2.6 | 3.2 | 13.9 | 11.7 | 3.9 | 13.8 | 5.6 |
| | 2004 | 21 791 | 12.5 | 4.1 | 16.3 | 2.6 | 3.0 | 14.7 | 11.7 | 3.9 | 14.5 | 5.2 |
| Colombia<br>Colombie | 2002 | 135 035 600 | 34.0 | 4.7 | 16.2 | 5.2 | 4.7 | 14.1 | 4.5 | 5.0 | 6.0 | 5.4 |
| | 2003 | 147 626 161 | 33.3 | 4.6 | 15.9 | 5.3 | 4.9 | 14.4 | 4.8 | 4.8 | 6.3 | 5.6 |
| | 2004 | 164 474 505 | 33.0 | 4.6 | 15.4 | 5.4 | 5.2 | 15.1 | 4.6 | 4.6 | 6.5 | 5.7 |

## 25

**Household consumption expenditure by purpose in current prices**—Percentage distribution by divisions of the Classification of Individual Consumption according to Purpose (COICOP) (*continued*)

**Dépenses de consommation des ménages par fonction aux prix courants**—Répartition en pourcentage par divisions de la Nomenclature des fonctions de la consommation individuelle (COICOP) (*suite*)

| Country or area & / Pays ou zone & | Year / Année | Total (mil. nat. curr.) / Totale (millions monn. nat.) | Div. 01 + 02 (%) | Div. 03 (%) | Div. 04 (%) | Div. 05 (%) | Div. 06 (%) | Div. 07 + 08 (%) | Div. 09 (%) | Div. 10 (%) | Div. 11 (%) | Div. 12 (%) |
|---|---|---|---|---|---|---|---|---|---|---|---|---|
| Côte d'Ivoire[1] | 1996 | 4 046 064 | 51.1 | 5.3 | 7.2 | 3.8 | 0.4 | 9.9 | 1.8 | 0.2 | 2.7 | 16.8 |
| Côte d'Ivoire[1] | 1997 | 4 329 400 | 49.8 | 5.3 | 7.2 | 4.0 | 0.5 | 10.0 | 1.8 | 0.2 | 2.5 | 17.4 |
| | 1998 | 4 836 550 | 49.9 | 5.4 | 7.2 | 4.0 | 0.5 | 9.3 | 1.7 | 0.3 | 1.9 | 18.3 |
| Croatia | 2003 | 115 081 | 35.2 | 7.7 | 21.0 | 11.0 | 3.4 | 19.1 | 7.7 | 3.0 | 12.3 | 6.5 |
| Croatie | 2004 | 123 123 | 35.2 | 5.8 | 20.5 | 11.5 | 3.3 | 18.5 | 8.1 | 2.9 | 12.0 | 6.6 |
| | 2005 | 131 673 | 35.2 | 5.8 | 20.5 | 11.5 | 3.3 | 18.5 | 8.1 | 2.9 | 12.0 | 6.6 |
| Cyprus | 2003 | 4 324 | 25.4 | 8.4 | 15.5 | 8.0 | 4.6 | 21.1 | 9.7 | 3.4 | 15.3 | 11.6 |
| Chypre | 2004 | 4 687 | 24.8 | 7.5 | 14.3 | 8.2 | 4.5 | 21.2 | 9.6 | 3.4 | 14.1 | 11.4 |
| | 2005 | 5 040 | 25.3 | 7.3 | 15.1 | 8.0 | 4.6 | 19.3 | 9.5 | 3.5 | 14.7 | 11.7 |
| Czech Republic | 2003 | 1 317 440 | 26.0 | 5.2 | 22.6 | 5.6 | 1.7 | 14.3 | 12.1 | 0.6 | 6.6 | 8.9 |
| République tchèque | 2004 | 1 391 123 | 25.8 | 5.1 | 22.6 | 5.4 | 1.9 | 14.7 | 12.0 | 0.8 | 6.7 | 8.7 |
| | 2005 | 1 454 357 | 25.1 | 5.1 | 23.2 | 5.9 | 2.1 | 15.4 | 12.2 | 0.6 | 6.9 | 8.6 |
| Denmark | 2003 | 656 340 | 16.2 | 5.0 | 27.4 | 5.8 | 2.6 | 13.1 | 11.3 | 0.8 | 4.9 | 12.9 |
| Danemark | 2004 | 697 478 | 15.3 | 4.9 | 26.9 | 5.7 | 2.6 | 14.7 | 11.4 | 0.8 | 4.9 | 12.7 |
| | 2005 | 742 330 | 14.9 | 4.8 | 26.5 | 5.8 | 2.6 | 15.8 | 11.2 | 0.7 | 5.0 | 12.9 |
| Dominican Republic | 1994 | 137 616 | 33.3 | 4.1 | 20.6 | 6.4 | 5.2 | 14.2 | 2.1 | 2.5 | 5.6 | 5.9 |
| Rép. dominicaine | 1995 | 164 689 | 34.1 | 4.0 | 20.3 | 6.2 | 5.2 | 13.5 | 2.0 | 2.2 | 6.9 | 5.6 |
| | 1996 | 189 675 | 32.0 | 3.4 | 20.1 | 6.5 | 5.0 | 14.1 | 3.1 | 2.2 | 8.8 | 4.8 |
| Ecuador[1] | 1991 | 8 432 000 | 38.9 | 9.9 | 5.3[10] | 7.4 | 4.2 | ... | ... | ... | 4.2 | 17.5 |
| Equateur[1] | 1992 | 13 147 000 | 38.7 | 9.5 | 5.1[10] | 7.2 | 4.5 | ... | ... | ... | 4.4 | 18.3 |
| | 1993 | 19 374 000 | 37.8 | 9.2 | 5.2[10] | 6.6 | 4.6 | ... | ... | ... | 4.4 | 18.6 |
| Estonia | 2003 | 72 176 | 28.2 | 7.1 | 22.0 | 5.7 | 3.5 | 15.7 | 9.0 | 1.2 | 6.7 | 8.0 |
| Estonie | 2004 | 78 581 | 28.9 | 7.3 | 21.4 | 5.9 | 3.4 | 16.1 | 9.2 | 1.2 | 7.2 | 7.8 |
| | 2005 | 87 224 | 28.3 | 7.8 | 20.6 | 6.1 | 3.0 | 16.1 | 8.6 | 1.2 | 8.3 | 7.8 |
| Fiji[1] | 1989 | 1 197 | 30.9 | 8.6 | 12.4 | 8.6 | 2.0 | ... | ... | ... | ... | ... |
| Fidji[1] | 1990 | 1 277 | 31.6 | 8.2 | 13.1 | 7.8 | 2.0 | ... | ... | ... | ... | ... |
| | 1991 | 1 405 | 31.2 | 7.9 | 13.2 | 7.9 | 2.0 | ... | ... | ... | ... | ... |
| Finland | 2003 | 71 989 | 18.5 | 4.7 | 25.5 | 5.0 | 4.0 | 16.3 | 11.1 | 0.4 | 6.3 | 8.5 |
| Finlande | 2004 | 74 765 | 17.8 | 4.8 | 25.4 | 5.3 | 4.1 | 16.1 | 11.3 | 0.5 | 6.4 | 8.7 |
| | 2005 | 77 707 | 17.5 | 4.9 | 25.3 | 5.5 | 4.2 | 15.8 | 11.4 | 0.4 | 6.5 | 8.7 |
| France | 2004 | 917 719 | 17.5 | 5.0 | 24.0 | 6.1 | 3.4 | 17.4 | 9.5 | 0.7 | 6.3 | 11.2 |
| France | 2005 | 954 969 | 17.0 | 4.9 | 24.6 | 6.0 | 3.4 | 17.7 | 9.4 | 0.7 | 6.2 | 11.0 |
| | 2006 | 993 226 | 16.8 | 4.7 | 25.2 | 5.9 | 3.4 | 17.5 | 9.3 | 0.7 | 6.2 | 11.2 |
| Germany | 2003 | 1 244 430 | 14.5 | 5.3 | 23.0 | 6.9 | 4.3 | 16.1 | 9.3 | 0.7 | 5.2 | 11.7 |
| Allemagne | 2004 | 1 265 310 | 14.5 | 5.3 | 23.3 | 6.9 | 4.4 | 16.2 | 9.3 | 0.7 | 5.2 | 11.8 |
| | 2005 | 1 285 290 | 14.7 | 5.2 | 23.7 | 6.8 | 4.4 | 16.0 | 9.3 | 0.7 | 5.2 | 11.7 |
| Greece | 2003 | 130 610 | 20.0 | 5.8 | 16.0 | 5.6 | 7.4 | 12.6 | 7.3 | 3.3 | 17.6 | 10.2 |
| Grèce | 2004 | 140 028 | 19.6 | 5.8 | 15.7 | 5.5 | 7.4 | 12.5 | 7.8 | 3.2 | 18.3 | 10.1 |
| | 2005 | 150 581 | 19.2 | 5.6 | 15.9 | 5.3 | 8.0 | 12.0 | 8.2 | 3.0 | 18.4 | 10.3 |
| Honduras[1] | 1984 | 4 742 | 44.6[5] | 9.1 | 22.5 | 8.3 | 7.0 | ... | ... | ... | ... | ... |
| Honduras[1] | 1985 | 5 033 | 44.6[5] | 9.1 | 22.5 | 8.3 | 7.0 | ... | ... | ... | ... | ... |
| | 1986 | 5 421 | 44.5[5] | 9.1 | 22.5 | 8.3 | 7.0 | ... | ... | ... | ... | ... |
| Hungary | 2004 | 11 006 489 | 26.6 | 3.9 | 18.8 | 7.3 | 3.7 | 19.8 | 7.8 | 1.2 | 5.0 | 7.9 |
| Hongrie | 2005 | 11 835 646 | 25.6 | 3.7 | 18.9 | 6.8 | 3.8 | 20.8 | 8.1 | #1.2 | 5.1 | 8.2 |
| | 2006 | 12 394 866 | 26.0 | 3.5 | 18.8 | 7.0 | 3.6 | 21.2 | 8.2 | 1.2 | 5.2 | 8.1 |
| Iceland | 2004 | 511 378 | 17.0 | 4.6 | 18.6 | 6.2 | 3.1 | 18.4 | 11.8 | 1.3 | 7.8 | 6.5 |
| Islande | 2005 | 589 412 | 15.1 | 4.4 | 19.3 | 6.2 | 2.9 | 19.5 | 11.2 | 1.3 | 7.5 | 6.5 |
| | 2006 | 662 875 | 14.9 | 4.3 | 19.6 | 5.9 | 2.7 | 18.6 | 10.8 | 1.2 | 7.7 | 6.9 |

# 25

**Household consumption expenditure by purpose in current prices** — Percentage distribution by divisions of the Classification of Individual Consumption according to Purpose (COICOP) (*continued*)

**Dépenses de consommation des ménages par fonction aux prix courants** — Répartition en pourcentage par divisions de la Nomenclature des fonctions de la consommation individuelle (COICOP) (*suite*)

| Country or area &<br>Pays ou zone & | Year<br>Année | Total (mil.<br>nat. curr.)<br>Totale<br>(millions<br>monn. nat.) | Div. 01 + 02<br>(%) | Div. 03<br>(%) | Div. 04<br>(%) | Div. 05<br>(%) | Div. 06<br>(%) | Div. 07 + 08<br>(%) | Div. 09<br>(%) | Div. 10<br>(%) | Div. 11<br>(%) | Div. 12<br>(%) |
|---|---|---|---|---|---|---|---|---|---|---|---|---|
| India[1]<br>Inde[1] | 2003 | 17 093 890 | 40.1 | 5.1 | 12.5 | 3.4 | 6.0 | 16.9 | 1.6 | 2.2 | 2.0 | 10.4 |
| | 2004 | 18 656 450 | 37.6 | 5.4 | 12.3 | 3.5 | 6.3 | 18.5 | 1.8 | 2.3 | 2.2 | 10.6 |
| | 2005 | 20 646 380 | 37.3 | 5.1 | 11.8 | 3.6 | 6.6 | 19.2 | 1.8 | 2.3 | 2.3 | 10.3 |
| Iran (Islamic Rep. of)<br>Iran (Rép. Islamique d') | 2003 | 503 164 600 | 31.0[5] | 7.2 | 30.0 | 6.3 | 5.8 | 11.8[11] | 3.3 | ... | ... | 4.6 |
| | 2004 | 636 564 800 | 30.8[5] | 7.5 | 30.1 | 6.6 | 6.1 | 11.0[11] | 3.3 | ... | ... | 4.6 |
| | 2005 | 761 075 900 | 30.8[5] | 7.4 | 30.2 | 6.5 | 6.1 | 11.2[11] | 3.3 | ... | ... | 4.5 |
| Ireland<br>Irlande | 2003 | 60 250 | 15.2 | 5.3 | 20.6 | 7.2 | 3.5 | 13.1 | 6.9 | 1.3 | 14.3 | 11.9 |
| | 2004 | 63 288 | 14.5 | 4.9 | 20.5 | 7.1 | 3.7 | 13.9 | 7.4 | 1.2 | 14.1 | 12.2 |
| | 2005 | 68 364 | 13.9 | 4.9 | 20.3 | 7.0 | 3.7 | 14.5 | 7.4 | 1.3 | 13.7 | 12.3 |
| Israel<br>Israël | 2003 | 281 790 | 19.8 | 3.6 | 28.8 | 9.3 | 4.4 | 13.3 | 5.7 | 3.3 | 4.4 | 7.4 |
| | 2004 | 297 337 | 19.2 | 3.5 | 27.9 | 9.6 | 4.6 | 14.1 | 5.8 | 3.3 | 4.6 | 7.5 |
| | 2005 | 312 731 | 19.0 | 3.5 | 27.4 | 9.3 | 4.6 | 14.6 | 6.0 | 3.3 | 5.1 | 7.8 |
| Italy<br>Italie | 2004 | 810 148 | 17.9 | 8.4 | 20.5 | 7.9 | 3.3 | 16.5 | 7.3 | 0.9 | 10.0 | 9.3 |
| | 2005 | 834 264 | 17.8 | 8.1 | 21.0 | 7.8 | 3.2 | 16.4 | 7.0 | 0.9 | 10.0 | 9.5 |
| | 2006 | 869 209 | 17.8 | 7.9 | 20.9 | 7.7 | 3.2 | 16.5 | 7.0 | 0.9 | 10.1 | 9.9 |
| Jamaica[1]<br>Jamaïque[1] | 1986 | 8 497 | 52.6 | 5.4 | 15.2 | 6.8 | 3.2 | ... | 2.8 | 0.2 | 16.1 | 10.0 |
| | 1987 | 9 849 | 52.1 | 6.0 | 14.5 | 6.9 | 3.4 | ... | 2.7 | 0.2 | 16.2 | 10.7 |
| | 1988 | 11 388 | 49.6 | 5.8 | 13.1 | 6.8 | 3.5 | ... | 2.5 | 0.2 | 13.6 | 10.6 |
| Japan<br>Japon | 2003 | 275 914 500 | 18.7 | 3.7 | 24.1 | 3.8 | 4.2 | 13.4 | 11.0 | 2.2 | 7.5 | 10.6 |
| | 2004 | 278 310 400 | 18.5 | 3.6 | 24.1 | 3.7 | 4.1 | 13.6 | 11.1 | 2.2 | 7.5 | 10.7 |
| | 2005 | 280 193 000 | 17.7 | 3.5 | 24.3 | 3.7 | 4.3 | 13.9 | 10.9 | 2.3 | 7.6 | 10.9 |
| Jordan[1]<br>Jordanie[1] | 1984 | 1 375 | 39.6[5] | 6.1 | 6.7 | 5.1 | 4.2[12] | ... | 2.9 | 3.4 | ... | ... |
| | 1985 | 1 415 | 38.5[5] | 5.7 | 6.5 | 4.8 | 4.1[12] | ... | 2.9 | 3.4 | ... | ... |
| | 1986 | 1 238 | 38.8[5] | 5.6 | 6.5 | 4.9 | 4.1[12] | ... | 3.0 | 3.4 | ... | ... |
| Kenya<br>Kenya | 2003 | 875 154[13] | 47.7[14] | 4.3 | 7.6 | ... | 2.8 | 11.5 | ... | 2.6 | 4.0 | ... |
| | 2004 | 965 528[13] | 46.9[14] | 3.4 | 7.7 | ... | 2.8 | 12.7 | ... | 2.7 | 5.4 | ... |
| | 2005 | 1 077 071[13] | 47.4[14] | 3.3 | 8.0 | ... | 2.7 | 12.9 | ... | 2.6 | 5.8 | ... |
| Korea, Republic of<br>Corée, République de | 2004 | 392 865 800 | 17.7 | 4.2 | 17.0 | 4.0 | 4.7 | 16.3 | 7.2 | 6.0 | 7.5 | 13.8 |
| | 2005 | 417 425 100 | 17.6 | 4.2 | 16.9 | 4.0 | 4.9 | 16.3 | 7.2 | 6.0 | 7.2 | 13.6 |
| | 2006 | 443 886 900 | 17.0 | 4.4 | 16.8 | 4.0 | 5.1 | 16.2 | 7.0 | 6.1 | 7.2 | 13.8 |
| Kyrgyzstan<br>Kirghizistan | 2003 | 63 352 | 54.0 | 12.9 | 11.2 | 3.1 | 1.7 | 9.6 | 1.7 | 2.1 | 1.0 | 2.6 |
| | 2004 | 69 983 | 55.3 | 9.3 | 7.8 | 3.3 | 1.5 | 13.6 | 2.4 | 2.5 | 3.3 | 2.4 |
| | 2005 | 83 471 | 55.9 | 9.0 | 8.0 | 3.4 | 1.5 | 13.4 | 2.2 | 2.3 | 3.1 | 2.2 |
| Latvia<br>Lettonie | 2003 | 3 973 | 30.5 | 7.0 | 21.0 | 3.3 | 4.5 | 13.6 | 7.6 | 2.7 | 4.0 | 4.0 |
| | 2004 | 4 593 | 29.1 | 7.1 | 21.1 | 3.4 | 4.4 | 15.0 | 8.2 | 2.3 | 4.1 | 4.0 |
| | 2005 | 5 578 | 28.7 | 6.9 | 20.6 | 3.6 | 4.0 | 15.1 | 7.5 | 2.5 | 5.3 | 3.8 |
| Lebanon — Liban | 1997 | 20 158 200 | 27.1 | 6.0 | 15.1 | 6.4 | 7.8 | 13.4[11] | 1.2 | 10.8 | 2.8 | 0.7 |
| Lithuania<br>Lituanie | 2003 | 36 333 | 36.3 | 6.0 | 15.3 | 5.2 | 4.5 | 18.5 | 6.8 | 0.7 | 3.2 | 5.7 |
| | 2004 | 40 649 | 35.9 | 6.6 | 14.6 | 5.3 | 4.2 | 18.4 | 6.8 | 0.7 | 3.1 | 6.0 |
| | 2005 | 46 319 | 33.2 | 6.6 | 14.0 | 5.4 | 5.1 | 19.1 | 7.5 | 0.7 | 3.1 | 6.9 |
| Luxembourg<br>Luxembourg | 2003 | 10 103 | 24.3 | 4.9 | 25.1 | 9.3 | 1.7 | 21.6 | 9.3 | 0.4 | 8.4 | 11.2 |
| | 2004 | 10 629 | 24.9 | 4.6 | 24.8 | 9.4 | 1.7 | 23.4 | 9.4 | 0.4 | 8.5 | 10.4 |
| | 2005 | 11 373 | 23.1 | 4.3 | 24.4 | 9.4 | 1.7 | 23.7 | 9.1 | 0.3 | 8.6 | 11.3 |
| Malaysia<br>Malaisie | 2004 | 208 454 | 27.1 | 3.0 | 20.3 | 5.4 | 2.1 | 22.0 | 5.0 | 1.6 | 8.1 | 15.0 |
| | 2005 | 233 183 | 26.3 | 3.0 | 19.4 | 5.3 | 2.1 | 22.1 | 5.0 | 1.5 | 8.9 | 14.8 |
| | 2006 | 257 740 | 26.0 | 3.2 | 19.4 | 5.6 | 2.2 | 22.1 | 5.3 | 1.5 | 9.1 | 14.0 |
| Malta<br>Malte | 2003 | 1 160 | 24.8 | 7.2 | 10.3 | 10.9 | 3.1 | 21.7 | 12.7 | 1.5 | 17.7 | 9.7 |
| | 2004 | 1 202 | 24.3 | 7.2 | 10.1 | 10.6 | 3.1 | 21.7 | 13.0 | 1.4 | 17.0 | 9.9 |
| | 2005 | 1 268 | 23.4 | 7.2 | 9.9 | 10.6 | 2.8 | 22.1 | 12.6 | 1.3 | 16.2 | 10.5 |

25 Household consumption expenditure by purpose in current prices— Percentage distribution by divisions of the Classification of Individual Consumption according to Purpose (COICOP) (*continued*)

Dépenses de consommation des ménages par fonction aux prix courants— Répartition en pourcentage par divisions de la Nomenclature des fonctions de la consommation individuelle (COICOP) (*suite*)

| Country or area &<br>Pays ou zone & | Year<br>Année | Total (mil. nat. curr.)<br>Totale (millions monn. nat.) | Divisions of the Classification of Individual Consumption according to Purpose (COICOP) ŧ<br>Divisions de la Nomenclature des functions de la consommation individuelle (COICOP) ŧ | | | | | | | | | |
|---|---|---|---|---|---|---|---|---|---|---|---|---|
| | | | Div. 01 + 02 (%) | Div. 03 (%) | Div. 04 (%) | Div. 05 (%) | Div. 06 (%) | Div. 07 + 08 (%) | Div. 09 (%) | Div. 10 (%) | Div. 11 (%) | Div. 12 (%) |
| Mexico<br>Mexique | 2002 | 4 286 979 | 27.1[13] | 3.4[13] | 13.4[13] | 8.5[13] | 4.7[13] | 18.8[13] | 2.8[13] | 3.8[13] | 7.8[13] | 11.3[13] |
| | 2003 | 4 690 918 | 27.3[13] | 3.2[13] | 13.6[13] | 8.2[13] | 4.9[13] | 18.8[13] | 2.7[13] | 4.0[13] | 7.5[13] | 11.5[13] |
| | 2004 | 5 208 861 | 27.3[13] | 3.1[13] | 13.6[13] | 8.0[13] | 4.7[13] | 19.3[13] | 2.9[13] | 3.9[13] | 7.4[13] | 11.4[13] |
| Moldova<br>Moldova | 1993 | 728 | ... | 6.5 | 6.0 | 5.7 | 8.6 | 4.2 | 1.7 | 12.5 | 3.5 | 1.9 |
| | 1996 | 5 243 | 42.9 | 6.6 | 5.0 | 2.9 | 9.9 | 9.3 | 1.4 | 12.6 | 2.2 | 7.2 |
| | 2000 | 14 031 | 48.7 | 7.8 | 13.0 | 3.4 | 3.3 | 12.9 | 3.6 | 1.4 | 1.3 | 1.8 |
| Mongolia<br>Mongolie | 2003 | 1 024 971 | 54.2 | 11.5 | 6.7 | 1.9 | 1.9 | 8.6 | 4.0 | 8.1 | 0.7 | 2.3 |
| | 2004 | 1 187 277 | 57.3 | 10.6 | 5.9 | 1.1 | 1.4 | 9.3 | 3.5 | 8.6 | 0.7 | 1.5 |
| | 2005 | 1 398 469 | 63.5 | 8.5 | 7.4 | 2.5 | 1.0 | 7.7 | 1.7 | 4.1 | 0.8 | 2.7 |
| Namibia<br>Namibie | 2003 | 17 753 | 42.8[5] | 7.5 | 15.7 | ... | ... | ... | ... | ... | ... | ... |
| | 2004 | 19 865 | 44.9[5] | 6.7 | 15.4 | ... | ... | ... | ... | ... | ... | ... |
| | 2005 | 21 353 | 44.9[5] | 4.7 | 15.2 | ... | ... | ... | ... | ... | ... | ... |
| Netherlands<br>Pays-Bas | 2003 | 233 912 | 14.1 | 5.5 | 21.1 | 6.8 | 5.0 | 15.8 | 10.4 | 0.6 | 5.2 | 14.9 |
| | 2004 | 237 193 | 13.9 | 5.3 | 21.5 | 6.4 | 5.3 | 15.9 | 10.2 | 0.6 | 5.1 | 15.1 |
| | 2005 | 242 694 | 13.6 | 5.4 | 22.1 | 6.2 | 5.3 | 15.8 | 10.0 | 0.5 | 5.1 | 15.5 |
| New Zealand<br>Nouvelle-Zélande | 2003 | 80 153 | 18.0 | 4.8 | 19.7 | 11.1 | ... | 14.7[11] | ... | ... | 7.7 | 11.3[15] |
| | 2004 | 85 704 | 17.7 | 4.8 | 19.3 | 11.3 | ... | 14.9[11] | ... | ... | 7.8 | 11.1[15] |
| | 2005 | 91 235 | 17.7 | 4.8 | 18.8 | 11.2 | ... | 14.9[11] | ... | ... | 7.8 | 10.8[15] |
| Nicaragua<br>Nicaragua | 2001 | 43 174 | 42.2 | 4.4 | 14.6 | 6.5 | 8.0 | 14.3 | 2.9 | 1.8 | 6.4 | 1.6 |
| | 2002 | 46 546 | 41.3 | 4.4 | 14.7 | 6.5 | 8.3 | 14.8 | 2.6 | 1.8 | 6.5 | 1.8 |
| | 2003 | 50 245 | 40.1 | 4.2 | 15.2 | 6.3 | 8.5 | 15.9 | 2.7 | 1.8 | 6.7 | 1.9 |
| Norway<br>Norvège | 2002 | 669 722 | 18.3 | 5.5 | 20.9 | 6.2 | 2.8 | 16.9 | 12.7 | 0.6 | 6.0 | 8.7 |
| | 2003 | 709 583 | 17.9 | 5.4 | 21.2 | 6.0 | 2.9 | 16.5 | 12.7 | 0.5 | 5.8 | 9.2 |
| | 2004 | 754 220 | 17.4 | 5.4 | 20.2 | 5.9 | 2.9 | 17.5 | 12.6 | 0.5 | 5.5 | 9.5 |
| Panama — Panama | 1996 | 5 456 | 26.3 | 6.1 | 25.8 | 5.2 | 4.5 | 15.5 | 5.4 | 1.7 | 4.3 | 11.9 |
| Peru[1]<br>Pérou[1] | 1986 | 255[16] | ... | 9.3 | 1.8 | 12.4 | 3.9 | ... | ... | ... | ... | ... |
| | 1987 | 498[16] | ... | 10.1 | 1.4 | 12.5 | 4.4 | ... | ... | ... | ... | ... |
| | 1988 | 3 214[16] | ... | 11.6 | 0.8 | 13.6 | 4.6 | ... | ... | ... | ... | ... |
| Philippines[1]<br>Philippines[1] | 2003 | 2 988 240 | 48.8[17] | 2.6 | 4.9[18] | 13.4 | ... | 7.1 | ... | ... | ... | 23.2 |
| | 2004 | 3 344 220 | 48.6[17] | 2.5 | 4.7[18] | 12.7 | ... | 8.3 | ... | ... | ... | 23.2 |
| | 2005 | 3 773 142 | 48.2[17] | 2.3 | 4.9[18] | 12.1 | ... | 9.9 | ... | ... | ... | 22.7 |
| Poland<br>Pologne | 2003 | 543 203 | 25.4 | 4.4 | 24.4 | 4.4 | 4.6 | 13.5 | 7.1 | 1.7 | 2.9 | 11.5 |
| | 2004 | 583 691 | 25.7 | 4.5 | 24.0 | 4.4 | 4.9 | 13.3 | 7.3 | 1.8 | 2.8 | 11.1 |
| | 2005 | 607 270 | 25.4 | 4.2 | 26.4 | 4.3 | 4.7 | 13.4 | 6.5 | 1.5 | 2.9 | 10.7 |
| Portugal<br>Portugal | 2001 | 79 266 | 21.6 | 8.1 | 13.6 | 7.6 | 5.0 | 18.7 | 6.6 | 1.2 | 11.0 | 11.2 |
| | 2002 | 82 730 | 21.5 | 8.2 | 13.9 | 7.6 | 5.1 | 18.1 | 6.8 | 1.2 | 11.1 | 11.0 |
| | 2003 | 85 075 | 21.8 | 7.9 | 14.5 | 7.4 | 5.6 | 17.2 | 6.7 | 1.2 | 10.8 | 11.3 |
| Puerto Rico[1]<br>Porto Rico[1] | 2003 | 41 629 | 18.3 | 6.9 | 18.8 | 5.2 | 13.3 | 15.5 | 4.0 | 3.8 | 6.6 | 11.7 |
| | 2004 | 44 439 | 18.0 | 6.7 | 19.1 | 5.4 | 13.1 | 16.5 | 3.8 | 3.7 | 6.4 | 11.3 |
| | 2005 | 47 699 | 18.4 | 6.5 | 19.5 | 5.6 | 13.0 | 16.0 | 3.9 | 3.5 | 6.2 | 11.2 |
| Saudi Arabia[1]<br>Arabie saoudite[1] | 1996 | 206 336 | 17.3[5] | 3.9 | 7.4 | 4.6 | 0.5 | 8.9[11] | 1.0 | ... | ... | 3.6 |
| | 1997 | 206 185 | 17.4[5] | 3.9 | 7.3 | 4.5 | 0.5 | 8.9[11] | 1.0 | ... | ... | 3.5 |
| | 1998 | 198 574 | 18.6[5] | 4.1 | 7.8 | 4.9 | 0.5 | 9.4[11] | 1.1 | ... | ... | 3.6 |
| Sierra Leone<br>Sierra Leone | 2003 | 3 794 745 | 49.1 | 7.2 | 6.0 | 2.3 | 13.0 | 6.2 | 2.9 | 1.7 | 1.1 | 9.4 |
| | 2004 | 3 856 375 | 49.1 | 7.2 | 6.0 | 2.3 | 13.0 | 6.2 | 2.9 | 1.7 | 1.1 | 9.4 |
| | 2005 | 3 983 914 | 49.1 | 7.2 | 6.0 | 2.3 | 13.0 | 6.2 | 2.9 | 1.7 | 1.1 | 9.4 |
| Singapore<br>Singapour | 2004 | 78 458 | 10.1 | 3.5 | 15.4 | 6.2 | 6.5 | 20.4 | 11.2 | 2.6 | 7.6 | 12.0 |
| | 2005 | 81 466 | 10.3 | 3.5 | 15.2 | 6.5 | 6.7 | 19.6 | 11.3 | 2.6 | 8.0 | 12.3 |
| | 2006 | 84 325 | 10.2 | 3.6 | 15.5 | 6.6 | 7.1 | 19.7 | 11.4 | 2.8 | 8.4 | 12.5 |

**25**

Household consumption expenditure by purpose in current prices — Percentage distribution by divisions of the Classification of Individual Consumption according to Purpose (COICOP) (*continued*)

**Dépenses de consommation des ménages par fonction aux prix courants** — Répartition en pourcentage par divisions de la Nomenclature des fonctions de la consommation individuelle (COICOP) (*suite*)

| Country or area [&] <br> Pays ou zone [&] | Year <br> Année | Total (mil. nat. curr.) <br> Totale (millions monn. nat.) | Divisions of the Classification of Individual Consumption according to Purpose (COICOP) [t] <br> Divisions de la Nomenclature des functions de la consommation individuelle (COICOP) [t] | | | | | | | | | |
|---|---|---|---|---|---|---|---|---|---|---|---|---|
| | | | Div. 01 + 02 <br> (%) | Div. 03 <br> (%) | Div. 04 <br> (%) | Div. 05 <br> (%) | Div. 06 <br> (%) | Div. 07 + 08 <br> (%) | Div. 09 <br> (%) | Div. 10 <br> (%) | Div. 11 <br> (%) | Div. 12 <br> (%) |
| Slovakia <br> Slovaquie | 2004 | 754 351 | 24.9 | 3.4 | 26.1 | 4.8 | 2.7 | 12.9 | 8.4 | 1.1 | 7.1 | 8.9 |
| | 2005 | 829 771 | 23.7 | 3.6 | 26.2 | 5.1 | 2.9 | 13.0 | 8.8 | 1.4 | 7.3 | 9.5 |
| | 2006 | 927 159 | 23.1 | 3.5 | 26.8 | 5.3 | 2.9 | 12.6 | 8.7 | 1.4 | 7.9 | 9.6 |
| Slovenia <br> Slovénie | 2003 | 3 167 528 | 22.4 | 6.6 | 20.3 | 6.4 | 3.4 | 18.3 | 10.0 | 1.0 | 7.2 | 9.6 |
| | 2004 | 3 363 221 | 21.3 | 6.5 | 20.5 | 6.4 | 3.4 | 19.3 | 10.3 | 1.1 | 7.2 | 9.6 |
| | 2005 | 3 559 682 | 20.5 | 6.2 | 20.7 | 6.4 | 3.4 | 20.3 | 10.2 | 1.1 | 7.2 | 9.6 |
| South Africa <br> Afrique du Sud | 2003 | 785 632 | 26.9[5] | 5.4 | 12.7 | 7.9 | 9.0 | 16.4[11] | 4.3 | 3.1 | 3.1 | 11.3 |
| | 2004 | 870 806 | 26.7[5] | 5.7 | 12.7 | 7.8 | 9.0 | 16.8[11] | 4.2 | 3.1 | 3.1 | 10.9 |
| | 2005 | 963 291 | 26.3[5] | 5.8 | 12.9 | 7.7 | 8.6 | 17.5[11] | 4.2 | 3.2 | 2.6 | 11.2 |
| Spain <br> Espagne | 2003 | 443 932 | 19.0 | 6.0 | 17.0 | 5.8 | 3.7 | 14.6 | 9.8 | 1.6 | 19.8 | 9.1 |
| | 2004 | 478 928 | 18.4 | 5.8 | 16.9 | 5.6 | 3.7 | 15.0 | 9.7 | 1.6 | 19.9 | 9.5 |
| | 2005 | 515 851 | 17.9 | 5.8 | 17.1 | 5.5 | 3.7 | 15.0 | 9.6 | 1.6 | 19.9 | 9.4 |
| Sri Lanka <br> Sri Lanka | 2003 | 1 289 411 | 46.3 | 10.2 | 7.9 | 4.1 | 1.3 | 16.4 | 2.8 | 0.1 | 2.0 | 2.8 |
| | 2004 | 1 462 192 | 39.9 | 10.1 | 7.8 | 7.1 | 1.6 | 19.7 | 2.7 | 0.1 | 1.8 | 2.5 |
| | 2005 | 1 674 210 | 38.9 | 8.5 | 8.2 | 6.8 | 1.5 | 21.4 | 3.2 | 0.1 | 1.8 | 3.5 |
| Sudan[1] <br> Soudan[1] | 1981 | 5 386 | 62.8 | 5.6 | 15.8 | 4.6 | 5.2 | ... | ... | ... | ... | ... |
| | 1982 | 7 897 | 60.4 | 7.5 | 15.3 | 5.6 | 5.3 | ... | ... | ... | ... | ... |
| | 1983 | 9 385 | 64.7 | 5.3 | 15.2 | 5.5 | 4.1 | ... | ... | ... | ... | ... |
| Sweden <br> Suède | 2003 | 1 161 793 | 16.3 | 5.1 | 28.8 | 4.9 | 2.7 | 16.2 | 11.9 | 0.2 | 5.0 | 8.8 |
| | 2004 | 1 196 849 | 16.0 | 5.2 | 28.6 | 5.0 | 2.7 | 16.1 | 11.8 | 0.3 | 5.0 | 9.1 |
| | 2005 | 1 240 860 | 15.7 | 5.3 | 28.2 | 5.2 | 2.7 | 16.3 | 11.8 | 0.3 | 5.1 | 9.3 |
| Switzerland <br> Suisse | 2003 | 254 100 | 14.8 | 4.0 | 23.6 | 4.6 | 14.7 | 10.2 | 8.6 | 0.5 | 7.4 | 11.6 |
| | 2004 | 260 013 | 14.4 | 3.9 | 23.6 | 4.6 | 15.1 | 10.4 | 8.4 | 0.5 | 7.6 | 11.4 |
| | 2005 | 265 597 | 14.1 | 4.0 | 24.1 | 4.6 | 15.4 | 10.4 | 8.3 | 0.5 | 7.5 | 11.0 |
| Thailand[1] <br> Thaïlande[1] | 2003 | 3 385 602 | 32.4 | 9.9 | 8.5 | 6.9 | 6.9 | 17.8 | 6.8 | 1.1 | 8.8 | 6.7 |
| | 2004 | 3 709 059 | 32.6 | 9.0 | 8.3 | 6.9 | 6.8 | 18.3 | 7.1 | 1.0 | 9.1 | 6.7 |
| | 2005 | 4 048 654 | 33.1 | 8.5 | 8.0 | 6.8 | 6.8 | 18.4 | 6.9 | 1.0 | 9.0 | 6.6 |
| Ukraine <br> Ukraine | 1997 | 50 617 | ... | ... | 7.4[19] | ... | 1.1[20] | 4.9 | 0.2[21] | 0.8 | ... | ... |
| | 1998 | 58 323 | ... | ... | 8.0[19] | ... | 0.9[20] | 5.2 | 0.2[21] | 1.3 | ... | ... |
| | 1999 | 71 310 | ... | ... | 7.2[19] | ... | 0.8[20] | 5.9 | 0.2[21] | 1.3 | ... | ... |
| United Kingdom <br> Royaume-Uni | 2003 | 697 160 | 13.0 | 5.9 | 18.5 | 6.1 | 1.6 | 17.2 | 12.1 | 1.4 | 11.3 | 11.1 |
| | 2004 | 732 531 | 12.7 | 5.8 | 18.8 | 6.0 | 1.6 | 17.2 | 12.4 | 1.4 | 11.4 | 10.9 |
| | 2005 | 760 032 | 12.5 | 5.8 | 19.5 | 5.8 | 1.6 | 17.1 | 12.4 | 1.4 | 11.7 | 10.9 |
| United States <br> Etats-Unis | 2003 | 7 703 600 | 9.1 | 4.7 | 17.5 | 4.8 | 18.7 | 13.3 | 9.1 | 2.6 | 6.1 | 14.1 |
| | 2004 | 8 211 500 | 9.0 | 4.6 | 17.4 | 4.8 | 18.8 | 13.2 | 9.1 | 2.6 | 6.1 | 14.4 |
| | 2005 | 8 742 400 | 9.1 | 4.6 | 17.4 | 4.8 | 18.8 | 13.3 | 9.1 | 2.6 | 6.1 | 14.3 |
| Vanuatu[1] <br> Vanuatu[1] | 1987 | 8 198 | 47.6[5] | 5.2 | 7.5 | 2.7 | ... | ... | ... | ... | ... | ... |
| | 1988 | 9 562 | 46.6[5] | 5.5 | 7.4 | 2.7 | ... | ... | ... | ... | ... | ... |
| | 1989 | 10 545 | 46.0[5] | 4.9 | 7.9 | 2.8 | ... | ... | ... | ... | ... | ... |
| Venezuela (Bolivarian Rep. of) <br> Venezuela (Rép. bolivar. du) | 2002 | 56 775 684 | 30.0 | 4.7 | 13.4 | 7.4 | 6.0 | 15.3 | 4.4 | 4.4 | 8.9 | 4.4 |
| | 2003 | 72 324 512 | 32.4 | 4.4 | 12.0 | 7.4 | 6.2 | 15.1 | 4.3 | 4.0 | 9.2 | 4.2 |
| | 2004 | 103 147 547 | 31.2 | 4.9 | 9.7 | 8.0 | 6.1 | 17.1 | 4.6 | 3.3 | 10.2 | 4.2 |
| Zimbabwe[1] <br> Zimbabwe[1] | 1985 | 3 842 | 25.4[5] | 11.6 | 17.1 | 7.8 | 4.2 | ... | 1.4 | 5.2 | 9.0 | 7.1[15] |
| | 1986 | 4 464 | 23.3[5] | 10.7 | 15.7 | 11.8 | 5.3 | ... | 0.6 | 5.3 | 9.0 | 7.4[15] |
| | 1987 | 4 324 | 20.4[5] | 10.3 | 15.4 | 12.9 | 7.1 | ... | 0.6 | 6.0 | 8.7 | 7.9[15] |

Source

United Nations Statistics Division, New York, national accounts database, last accessed January 2008.

Source

Organisation des Nations Unies, Division de statistique, New York, base de données sur les comptes nationaux, dernier accès janvier 2008.

**25** Household consumption expenditure by purpose in current prices — Percentage distribution by divisions of the Classification of Individual Consumption according to Purpose (COICOP) (*continued*)

**Dépenses de consommation des ménages par fonction aux prix courants** — Répartition en pourcentage par divisions de la Nomenclature des fonctions de la consommation individuelle (COICOP) (*suite*)

Notes

Data for most countries have been compiled in accordance with the concepts and definitions of the System of National Accounts 1993 (1993 SNA). Countries that follow the 1968 SNA are footnoted accordingly.

† COICOP Divisions:

Div. 01+ 02: Food, beverages, tobacco and narcotics
Div. 03: Clothing and footwear
Div. 04: Housing, water, electricity, gas and other fuels
Div. 05: Furnishings, household equipment and routine household maintenance
Div. 06: Health
Div. 07 + 08: Transport and communication
Div. 09: Recreation and culture
Div. 10: Education
Div. 11: Restaurants and hotels
Div. 12: Miscellaneous goods and services

& Data for most countries or areas refers to the western calendar year ending 31 December. The following countries are exceptions, with fiscal years as follows:

Year beginning 21 March: Afghanistan, Iran (Islamic Republic).

Year beginning 1 April: Bermuda, India, Myanmar, New Zealand.

Year beginning 1 July: Australia, Bhutan, Gambia, Nicaragua, Pakistan, Puerto Rico, Saudi Arabia.
Year ending 30 June: Bangladesh, Botswana, Egypt, Swaziland, Tonga.
Year ending 7 July: Ethiopia.
Year ending 15 July: Nepal.
Year ending 30 September: Haiti.

1 Data compiled in accordance with the System of National Accounts 1968 (1968 SNA).
2 Alcoholic beverages, tobacco and narcotics only.
3 Communications only.
4 Excluding direct purchases abroad by resident households and direct purchases in the domestic market by non-resident households.
5 Food and non-alcoholic beverages only.
6 Including personal effects.
7 Including housing maintenance charges.
8 Including hotel expenditures.
9 Including restaurant expenditure.
10 Including transport and communication.
11 Transport only.
12 Including personal care.
13 Including "Non-profit institutions serving households" (NPISHs) final consumption expenditure.
14 Excluding narcotics.
15 Including communication.
16 Thousands.
17 Excluding alcoholic beverages and narcotics.
18 Refers to water, electricity, gas and other fuels only.
19 Data refers to housing and communal services only.
20 Including recreational, cultural and sporting activities, and social security.
21 Refers to culture, art, and mass media.

Notes

Les données pour la majorité des pays sont compilées selon les concepts et définitions du Système de comptabilité nationale, 1993 (SCN93). Seuls les pays qui suivent toujours le SCN68 seront donc signalés par une note.

† Divisions de la COICOP:

Div. 01+ 02 : Alimentation, boissons, tabac et stupéfiants
Div. 03 : Articles d'habillement et chaussures
Div. 04 : Logement, eau, gaz, électricité et autres combustibles
Div. 05: Meubles, articles de ménage et entretien courant de l'habitation
Div. 06 : Santé
Div. 07 + 08 : Transports et communication
Div. 09 : Loisirs et culture
Div. 10 : Enseignement
Div. 11 : Restaurants et hôtels
Div. 12 : Biens et services divers

& Les données pour la plupart des pays ou territoires concernent l'année civile se terminant le 31 décembre, sauf les pays ci-dessous dont les exercices budgétaires sont les suivants:

Exercice commençant le 21 mars: Afghanistan, Iran (République islamique d').
Exercice commençant le 1er avril: Bermudes, Inde, Myanmar, Nouvelle-Zélande.
Exercice commençant le 1er juillet: Arabie saoudite, Australie, Bhoutan, Gambie, Nicaragua, Pakistan, Porto Rico.
Exercice se terminant le 30 juin: Bangladesh, Botswana, Égypte, Swaziland, Tonga.
Exercice se terminant le 7 juillet: Éthiopie.
Exercice se terminant le 15 juillet: Népal.
Exercice se terminant le 30 septembre: Haïti.

1 Données compilées selon le Système de comptabilité nationale de 1968 (SCN 1968).
2 Boissons alcoolisées, tabac et stupéfiants seulement.
3 Les communications seulement.
4 À l'exclusion des achats directs à l'étranger des ménages résidents et des achats directs des ménages non résidents sur le marché intérieur.
5 Alimentation et boissons non alcoolisées seulement.
6 Y compris les effets personnels.
7 Y compris coût d'entretien du logement.
8 Y compris les dépenses d'hôtel.
9 Y compris les dépenses de restauration.
10 Y compris transports et communications.
11 Transports seulement.
12 Y compris les soins personnels.
13 Y compris la consommation finale des institutions sans but lucratif au service des ménages.
14 À l'exclusion des stupéfiants.
15 Y compris communications.
16 En milliers.
17 Non compris boissons alcoolisées et stupéfiants.
18 Données provenant exclusivement l'eau, l'électricité, le gaz et les autres combustibles seulement.
19 Les données concernent le logement et les services collectifs.
20 Y compris les loisirs, les affaires culturelles et sportives et la sécurité sociale.
21 Concerne la culture, les arts et les médias.

# Index numbers of industrial production
2000 = 100

# Indices de la production industrielle
2000 = 100

| Country or area and industry [ISIC Rev. 3] Pays ou zone et industrie [CITI Rév. 3] | 1999 | 2000 | 2001 | 2002 | 2003 | 2004 | 2005 | 2006 |
|---|---|---|---|---|---|---|---|---|
| **Africa — Afrique** | | | | | | | | |
| **Algeria — Algérie** | | | | | | | | |
| Total industry [CDE] Total, industrie [CDE] | 98.7 | 100.0 | 99.8 | 100.8 | 102.1 | 102.5 | 104.1 | 103.8 |
| Total mining [C] Total, industries extractives [C] | 94.7 | 100.0 | 97.1 | 104.3 | 104.9 | 103.9 | 114.3 | 131.7 |
| Total manufacturing [D] Total, industries manufacturières [D] | 101.8 | 100.0 | 99.1 | 97.5 | 94.2 | 91.9 | 89.8 | 87.9 |
| Food, beverages and tobacco — Aliments, boissons et tabac | 109.8 | 100.0 | 87.5 | 70.8 | 56.1 | 47.4 | 40.5 | 37.3 |
| Textiles, wearing apparel, leather, footwear Textiles, habillement, cuir et chaussures | 113.2 | 100.0 | 90.8 | 94.8 | 93.2 | 86.0 | 83.8 | 68.4 |
| Chemicals, petroleum, rubber and plastic products Prod. chimiques, pétroliers, caoutch. et plast. | 99.2 | 100.0 | 104.0 | 101.4 | 99.9 | 89.5 | 89.8 | 90.0 |
| Basic metals — Métaux de base | 104.1 | 100.0 | 107.9 | 118.9 | 145.6 | 145.4 | 152.2 | 171.3 |
| Metal products — Produits métalliques | 99.8 | 100.0 | 119.1 | 115.1 | 106.8 | 121.6 | 115.3 | 103.6 |
| Electricity [E] Electricité [E] | 97.7 | 100.0 | 105.0 | 109.6 | 116.8 | 123.5 | 135.3 | 139.9 |
| **Burkina Faso — Burkina Faso** | | | | | | | | |
| Total industry [CDE] Total, industrie [CDE] | 91.9 | 100.0 | 101.1 | 106.3 | 109.5 | ... | ... | ... |
| **Cameroon[1] — Cameroun[1]** | | | | | | | | |
| Total industry [DE] Total, industrie [DE] | 98.7 | 100.0 | 99.6 | 102.5 | 105.3 | 111.5 | 110.7 | 114.3 |
| Total manufacturing [D] Total, industries manufacturières [D] | 106.4 | 100.0 | 116.4 | 116.3 | 120.7 | 127.8 | 125.6 | 130.7 |
| Electricity, gas and water [E] Electricité, gaz et eau [E] | 99.0 | 100.0 | 92.0 | 103.8 | 109.0 | 114.7 | 117.2 | 120.7 |
| **Côte d'Ivoire — Côte d'Ivoire** | | | | | | | | |
| Total industry [CDE] Total, industrie [CDE] | 108.5 | 100.0 | 95.9 | 91.7 | 87.0 | 89.7 | 96.3 | ... |
| Total mining [C] Total, industries extractives [C] | 115.8 | 100.0 | 67.6 | 121.4 | 211.3 | 218.7 | 242.2 | ... |
| Total manufacturing [D] Total, industries manufacturières [D] | 110.0 | 100.0 | 95.8 | 84.3 | 73.3 | 75.2 | 80.6 | ... |
| Food, beverages and tobacco — Aliments, boissons et tabac | 104.9 | 100.0 | 97.9 | 81.9 | ... | ... | ... | ... |
| Textiles and wearing apparel — Textiles et habillement | 148.1 | 100.0 | 87.2 | 66.0 | ... | ... | ... | ... |
| Chemicals, petroleum, rubber and plastic products Prod. chimiques, pétroliers, caoutch. et plast. | 106.5 | 100.0 | 99.0 | 126.5 | ... | ... | ... | ... |
| Metal products — Produits métalliques | 129.3 | 100.0 | 80.6 | 83.4 | ... | ... | ... | ... |
| Electricity and water [E] Electricité et eau [E] | 100.3 | 100.0 | 102.1 | 110.2 | 105.5 | 110.4 | 117.1 | ... |
| **Egypt[2] — Egypte[2]** | | | | | | | | |
| Total industry [CDE] Total, industrie [CDE] | 101.4 | 100.0 | 104.1 | 110.5 | 136.1 | 149.3 | ... | ... |
| Total mining [C] Total, industries extractives [C] | 96.7 | 100.0 | 113.1 | 124.8 | 201.6 | 244.2 | ... | ... |
| Total manufacturing [D][3] Total, industries manufacturières [D][3] | 105.1 | 100.0 | 98.3 | 104.3 | 98.6 | 104.8 | 115.1 | 132.9 |
| Food, beverages and tobacco — Aliments, boissons et tabac | 90.0 | 100.0 | 75.2 | 70.0 | 60.7 | 61.4 | 64.3 | 68.4 |
| Textiles and wearing apparel — Textiles et habillement | 112.3 | 100.0 | 91.0 | 95.5 | 103.5 | 90.6 | 92.4 | 108.3 |
| Chemicals, petroleum, rubber and plastic products Prod. chimiques, pétroliers, caoutch. et plast. | 121.8 | 100.0 | 114.9 | 112.1 | 146.6 | 133.7 | 159.8 | 247.6 |
| Basic metals — Métaux de base | 95.2 | 100.0 | 89.2 | 92.3 | 129.2 | 103.3 | 93.5 | 119.1 |
| Metal products — Produits métalliques | 104.5 | 100.0 | 86.9 | 90.2 | 79.5 | 76.3 | 83.0 | 97.9 |
| Electricity, gas and water [E] Electricité, gaz et eau [E] | 92.5 | 100.0 | 110.3 | 132.4 | 143.4 | 154.4 | ... | ... |

| Country or area and industry [ISIC Rev. 3]<br>Pays ou zone et industrie [CITI Rév. 3] | 1999 | 2000 | 2001 | 2002 | 2003 | 2004 | 2005 | 2006 |
|---|---|---|---|---|---|---|---|---|
| Ethiopia[2] — Ethiopie[2] | | | | | | | | |
| Total industry [CDE]<br>Total, industrie [CDE] | 93.7 | 100.0 | 103.6 | 107.7 | 109.9 | 117.2 | 126.6 | 137.8 |
| Total mining [C]<br>Total, industries extractives [C] | 89.9 | 100.0 | 105.2 | 116.1 | 121.0 | 128.7 | 138.8 | 150.3 |
| Total manufacturing [D]<br>Total, industries manufacturières [D] | 93.0 | 100.0 | 103.6 | 104.9 | 105.7 | 112.6 | 121.7 | 131.5 |
| Electricity [E]<br>Electricité [E] | 96.2 | 100.0 | 103.3 | 113.3 | 118.1 | 126.5 | 136.7 | 151.5 |
| Gabon — Gabon | | | | | | | | |
| Total industry [DE]<br>Total, industrie [DE] | 106.8 | 100.0 | 111.8 | 116.7 | 114.8 | 117.6 | 124.2 | 131.6 |
| Total manufacturing [D]<br>Total, industries manufacturières [D] | 110.2 | 100.0 | 113.4 | 116.9 | 109.3 | 111.4 | 120.3 | 124.9 |
| Food, beverages and tobacco — Aliments, boissons et tabac | 93.5 | 100.0 | 113.3 | 109.9 | 106.0 | 105.1 | 115.9 | 123.3 |
| Chemicals and petroleum products<br>Produits chimiques et pétroliers | 130.5 | 100.0 | 109.3 | 139.0 | 124.3 | 120.2 | 126.9 | 128.7 |
| Electricity and water [E]<br>Electricité et eau [E] | 102.7 | 100.0 | 110.0 | 116.7 | 121.4 | 125.0 | 128.9 | 139.5 |
| Ghana — Ghana | | | | | | | | |
| Total industry [CDE][3]<br>Total, industrie [CDE][3] | 99.4 | 100.0 | 120.2 | 119.1 | 126.8 | 138.6 | ... | ... |
| Total mining [C]<br>Total, industries extractives [C] | 103.3 | 100.0 | 100.8 | 96.1 | 100.7 | 95.4 | 101.7 | 111.8 |
| Total manufacturing [D]<br>Total, industries manufacturières [D] | 96.7 | 100.0 | 134.3 | 137.2 | 154.7 | 179.0 | ... | ... |
| Food, beverages and tobacco — Aliments, boissons et tabac | 99.5 | 100.0 | 148.2 | 182.4 | 184.3 | 222.0 | ... | ... |
| Textiles, wearing apparel, leather, footwear<br>Textiles, habillement, cuir et chaussures | 99.6 | 100.0 | 102.8 | 106.8 | 119.9 | 121.0 | ... | ... |
| Chemicals, petroleum, rubber and plastic products<br>Prod. chimiques, pétroliers, caoutch. et plast. | 91.1 | 100.0 | 93.8 | 100.2 | 128.5 | 121.9 | ... | ... |
| Basic metals — Métaux de base | 99.9 | 100.0 | 70.8 | 58.8 | 16.6 | 12.0 | ... | ... |
| Metal products — Produits métalliques | 100.0 | 100.0 | 102.6 | 83.2 | 88.4 | 94.3 | ... | ... |
| Electricity [E]<br>Electricité [E] | 101.5 | 100.0 | 108.8 | 101.0 | 81.7 | 83.6 | 94.0 | 116.7 |
| Kenya — Kenya | | | | | | | | |
| Total industry [CD][4]<br>Total, industrie [CD][4] | 101.9 | 100.0 | 101.6 | 101.9 | 103.5 | 111.3 | 120.2 | 128.7 |
| Total mining [C]<br>Total, industries extractives [C] | 110.5 | 100.0 | 124.9 | 103.3 | 109.4 | 137.7 | 156.0 | 169.8 |
| Total manufacturing [D]<br>Total, industries manufacturières [D] | 101.5 | 100.0 | 100.6 | 101.8 | 103.3 | 110.2 | 118.7 | 127.0 |
| Food, beverages and tobacco — Aliments, boissons et tabac | 101.0 | 100.0 | 99.2 | 103.3 | 105.1 | 117.1 | 123.5 | 130.8 |
| Textiles, wearing apparel, leather, footwear<br>Textiles, habillement, cuir et chaussures | 95.9 | 100.0 | 103.3 | 118.5 | 114.0 | 104.8 | 143.7 | 168.7 |
| Chemicals, petroleum, rubber and plastic products<br>Prod. chimiques, pétroliers, caoutch. et plast. | 95.5 | 100.0 | 110.4 | 104.8 | 127.8 | 141.6 | 139.7 | 150.1 |
| Metal products — Produits métalliques | 118.3 | 100.0 | 98.4 | 127.1 | 128.1 | 198.9 | 188.5 | 196.7 |
| Madagascar — Madagascar | | | | | | | | |
| Total industry [CDE]<br>Total, industrie [CDE] | 88.2 | 100.0 | 107.9 | 105.8 | 112.3 | 116.5 | 130.7 | 140.1 |
| Total mining [C]<br>Total, industries extractives [C] | 68.8 | 100.0 | 99.4 | 67.7 | 80.2 | 83.6 | 96.2 | 104.1 |
| Total manufacturing [D]<br>Total, industries manufacturières [D] | 88.3 | 100.0 | 108.5 | 84.2 | 112.4 | 116.7 | 129.8 | 149.2 |
| Food, beverages and tobacco — Aliments, boissons et tabac | 94.8 | 100.0 | 108.5 | 95.1 | 115.6 | 118.3 | 137.6 | 154.0 |
| Textiles, wearing apparel, leather, footwear<br>Textiles, habillement, cuir et chaussures | 111.2 | 100.0 | 126.4 | 72.3 | 93.1 | 95.4 | 119.9 | 131.4 |
| Chemicals, petroleum, rubber and plastic products<br>Prod. chimiques, pétroliers, caoutch. et plast. | 89.3 | 100.0 | 112.8 | 70.6 | 119.3 | 124.2 | 108.5 | 109.3 |

| Country or area and industry [ISIC Rev. 3] Pays ou zone et industrie [CITI Rév. 3] | 1999 | 2000 | 2001 | 2002 | 2003 | 2004 | 2005 | 2006 |
|---|---|---|---|---|---|---|---|---|
| Metal products — Produits métalliques | 120.2 | 100.0 | 110.2 | 92.1 | 108.2 | 106.0 | 149.2 | 133.6 |
| Electricity, gas and water [E] Électricité, gaz et eau [E] | 85.1 | 100.0 | 104.3 | 103.7 | 116.1 | 119.8 | 142.9 | 151.0 |
| **Malawi — Malawi** | | | | | | | | |
| Total industry [DE] Total, industrie [DE] | 99.2 | 100.0 | 89.8 | 89.9 | 87.4 | 94.3 | 154.3 | ... |
| Total manufacturing [D] Total, industries manufacturières [D] | 101.3 | 100.0 | 85.0 | 85.1 | 82.5 | 89.7 | 100.3 | ... |
| Food, beverages and tobacco — Aliments, boissons et tabac | 103.2 | 100.0 | 89.4 | 85.4 | 70.7 | 98.3 | 89.2 | ... |
| Textiles, wearing apparel, leather, footwear Textiles, habillement, cuir et chaussures | 162.0 | 100.0 | 81.4 | 44.2 | 44.3 | 67.1 | 74.4 | ... |
| Electricity and water [E] Électricité et eau [E] | 92.6 | 100.0 | 102.7 | 107.5 | 105.1 | 111.4 | 121.2 | ... |
| **Mali — Mali** | | | | | | | | |
| Total industry [DE] Total, industrie [DE] | 91.7 | 100.0 | 110.0 | 129.5 | 139.2 | 150.3 | 163.7 | ... |
| Food, beverages and tobacco — Aliments, boissons et tabac | 93.1 | 100.0 | 100.6 | 103.8 | 104.3 | 95.3 | 122.4 | ... |
| Wearing apparel — Habillement | 114.7 | 100.0 | 86.3 | 163.3 | 119.7 | 151.6 | 142.2 | ... |
| Chemicals and chemical products — Produits chimiques | 109.0 | 100.0 | 83.8 | 85.2 | 81.7 | 78.3 | 70.2 | ... |
| **Mauritius — Maurice** | | | | | | | | |
| Total industry [CDE] Total, industrie [CDE] | 91.6 | 100.0 | 105.2 | 102.9 | 103.2 | 103.4 | 97.0 | 100.9 |
| Total mining [C] Total, industries extractives [C] | 97.1 | 100.0 | 94.2 | 48.0 | 48.5 | 48.7 | 46.9 | 51.2 |
| Total manufacturing [D] Total, industries manufacturières [D] | 92.1 | 100.0 | 104.7 | 102.4 | 101.8 | 101.3 | 93.8 | 97.5 |
| Food, beverages and tobacco — Aliments, boissons et tabac | 82.7 | 100.0 | 108.6 | 109.0 | 116.2 | 119.9 | 121.0 | 130.2 |
| Textiles, wearing apparel, leather, footwear Textiles, habillement, cuir et chaussures | 94.4 | 100.0 | 103.7 | 95.9 | 88.6 | 80.1 | 68.8 | 69.7 |
| Chemicals, petroleum, rubber and plastic products Prod. chimiques, pétroliers, caoutch. et plast. | 92.8 | 100.0 | 100.5 | 102.2 | 120.9 | 98.2 | 77.4 | 75.9 |
| Basic metals — Métaux de base | 95.2 | 100.0 | 105.6 | 124.2 | 112.6 | 137.6 | 101.5 | 136.6 |
| Metal products — Produits métalliques | 96.7 | 100.0 | 101.6 | 100.3 | 110.3 | 181.0 | 233.9 | 327.1 |
| Electricity, gas and water [E] Électricité, gaz et eau [E] | 81.2 | 100.0 | 110.7 | 112.4 | 121.6 | 126.6 | 131.4 | 137.1 |
| **Morocco — Maroc** | | | | | | | | |
| Total industry [CDE][4] Total, industrie [CDE][4] | 97.9 | 100.0 | 105.7 | 109.9 | 114.3 | 119.3 | 127.7 | 132.0 |
| Total mining [C][5] Total, industries extractives [C][5] | 103.6 | 100.0 | 102.4 | 105.0 | 100.5 | 108.6 | 115.7 | 117.8 |
| Total manufacturing [D][3] Total, industries manufacturières [D][3] | 96.6 | 100.0 | 103.3 | 106.3 | 110.0 | 113.4 | 116.3 | 120.6 |
| Food, beverages and tobacco — Aliments, boissons et tabac | 95.2 | 100.0 | 107.1 | 108.8 | 112.9 | 120.7 | 123.4 | 126.3 |
| Textiles, wearing apparel, leather, footwear Textiles, habillement, cuir et chaussures | 98.8 | 100.0 | 98.8 | 98.6 | 95.9 | 95.2 | 93.5 | 94.9 |
| Chemicals, petroleum, rubber and plastic products Prod. chimiques, pétroliers, caoutch. et plast. | 98.8 | 100.0 | 104.4 | 108.0 | 106.2 | 112.4 | 115.5 | 114.8 |
| Basic metals — Métaux de base | 99.8 | 100.0 | 107.0 | 124.5 | 139.5 | 137.8 | 157.5 | 167.8 |
| Metal products — Produits métalliques | 95.5 | 100.0 | 104.9 | 107.9 | 114.4 | 117.0 | 118.7 | 127.5 |
| Electricity [E] Électricité [E] | 98.8 | 100.0 | 114.0 | 122.3 | 132.9 | 141.0 | 165.4 | 171.2 |
| **Namibia—Namibie** | | | | | | | | |
| Total industry [CDE] Total, industrie [CDE] | 97.8 | 100.0 | 98.1 | 109.3 | 111.6 | 130.9 | 127.1 | 129.5 |
| Total mining [C] Total, industries extractives [C] | 101.7 | 100.0 | 93.9 | 108.9 | 103.9 | 141.8 | 139.9 | 161.5 |
| Total manufacturing [D] Total, industries manufacturières [D] | 96.5 | 100.0 | 105.5 | 115.7 | 121.7 | 129.9 | 128.0 | 117.3 |
| Electricity, gas and water [E] Électricité, gaz et eau [E] | 89.6 | 100.0 | 76.3 | 76.9 | 89.0 | 93.1 | 105.4 | 100.0 |

| Country or area and industry [ISIC Rev. 3]<br>Pays ou zone et industrie [CITI Rév. 3] | 1999 | 2000 | 2001 | 2002 | 2003 | 2004 | 2005 | 2006 |
|---|---|---|---|---|---|---|---|---|
| **Senegal — Sénégal** | | | | | | | | |
| Total industry [CDE]<br>Total, industrie [CDE] | 104.7 | 100.0 | 100.8 | 125.3 | 131.1 | 146.3 | 148.9 | 140.5 |
| Total mining [C]<br>Total, industries extractives [C] | 98.9 | 100.0 | 87.1 | 96.9 | 124.9 | 113.4 | 96.6 | 65.7 |
| Total manufacturing [D]4<br>Total, industries manufacturières [D]4 | 106.9 | 100.0 | 99.2 | 131.2 | 131.7 | 151.5 | 153.4 | 144.6 |
| Food, beverages and tobacco — Aliments, boissons et tabac | 103.3 | 100.0 | 95.4 | 101.1 | 109.3 | 139.0 | 149.1 | 173.0 |
| Textiles — Textiles | 103.8 | 100.0 | 124.9 | 63.3 | 89.5 | 71.9 | 66.5 | 74.9 |
| Chemicals, petroleum, rubber and plastic products<br>Prod. chimiques, pétroliers, caoutch. et plast. | 78.5 | 100.0 | 83.5 | 122.4 | 114.4 | 115.6 | 104.7 | 56.2 |
| Metal products — Produits métalliques | 98.2 | 100.0 | 47.6 | 82.0 | 83.6 | 83.5 | 75.5 | 75.9 |
| Electricity and water [E]<br>Electricité et eau [E] | 95.8 | 100.0 | 113.1 | 110.0 | 130.0 | 131.4 | 144.1 | 144.9 |
| **South Africa — Afrique du Sud** | | | | | | | | |
| Total industry [CDE]4<br>Total, industrie [CDE]4 | 97.7 | 100.0 | 102.2 | 105.8 | 106.1 | 111.2 | 113.5 | 117.1 |
| Total mining [C]<br>Total, industries extractives [C] | 101.5 | 100.0 | 101.4 | 102.2 | 106.4 | 112.5 | 111.7 | 110.5 |
| Total manufacturing [D]<br>Total, industries manufacturières [D] | 96.4 | 100.0 | 102.8 | 107.4 | 105.4 | 110.0 | 113.8 | 119.3 |
| Food and beverages — Aliments et boissons | 102.8 | 100.0 | 105.0 | 102.0 | 103.9 | 111.8 | 118.7 | 119.7 |
| Textiles, wearing apparel, leather, footwear<br>Textiles, habillement, cuir et chaussures | 102.9 | 100.0 | 96.4 | 102.7 | 95.4 | 99.5 | 97.2 | 99.3 |
| Chemicals, petroleum, rubber and plastic products<br>Prod. chimiques, pétroliers, caoutch. et plast. | 99.0 | 100.0 | 103.9 | 112.6 | 107.0 | 111.5 | 115.0 | 119.6 |
| Basic metals — Métaux de base | 84.6 | 100.0 | 99.3 | 104.4 | 106.8 | 110.7 | 105.7 | 114.1 |
| Metal products — Produits métalliques | 93.1 | 100.0 | 106.4 | 113.6 | 110.3 | 113.4 | 117.9 | 127.7 |
| Electricity [E]<br>Electricité [E] | 96.4 | 100.0 | 99.7 | 104.7 | 111.1 | 116.1 | 116.2 | 120.4 |
| **Swaziland — Swaziland** | | | | | | | | |
| Total industry [CDE]4<br>Total, industrie [CDE]4 | 100.3 | 100.0 | 100.8 | 111.3 | 120.7 | 126.6 | 127.6 | ... |
| Total mining [C]<br>Total, industries extractives [C] | 129.8 | 100.0 | 80.1 | 89.5 | 71.0 | 78.0 | 60.8 | ... |
| Total manufacturing [D]<br>Total, industries manufacturières [D] | 99.1 | 100.0 | 100.9 | 111.1 | 121.7 | 128.2 | 129.4 | ... |
| Electricity, gas and water [E]<br>Electricité, gaz et eau [E] | 107.2 | 100.0 | 105.4 | 120.4 | 123.3 | 120.3 | 124.9 | ... |
| **Tunisia — Tunisie** | | | | | | | | |
| Total industry [CDE]<br>Total, industrie [CDE] | 94.0 | 100.0 | 105.4 | 106.0 | 105.7 | 110.0 | 110.9 | 114.3 |
| Total mining [C]<br>Total, industries extractives [C] | 103.0 | 100.0 | 98.1 | 97.5 | 94.1 | 98.4 | 99.7 | 94.1 |
| Total manufacturing [D]<br>Total, industries manufacturières [D] | 91.9 | 100.0 | 106.7 | 107.3 | 107.1 | 111.3 | 111.8 | 116.8 |
| Food, beverages and tobacco — Aliments, boissons et tabac | 92.8 | 100.0 | 99.6 | 102.9 | 104.7 | 112.7 | 111.5 | 117.0 |
| Textiles, wearing apparel, leather, footwear<br>Textiles, habillement, cuir et chaussures | 88.6 | 100.0 | 111.0 | 108.5 | 102.4 | 101.5 | 95.9 | 94.4 |
| Chemicals, petroleum, rubber and plastic products<br>Prod. chimiques, pétroliers, caoutch. et plast. | 96.9 | 100.0 | 100.2 | 102.1 | 102.9 | 100.4 | 98.1 | 95.5 |
| Basic metals — Métaux de base | 96.1 | 100.0 | 96.4 | 86.0 | 71.3 | 69.5 | 84.7 | 94.7 |
| Metal products — Produits métalliques | 93.2 | 100.0 | 111.0 | 114.8 | 119.9 | 125.0 | 136.3 | 162.2 |
| Electricity and water [E]<br>Electricité et eau [E] | 94.6 | 100.0 | 107.3 | 110.5 | 117.1 | 121.7 | 127.2 | 132.1 |
| **Uganda — Ouganda** | | | | | | | | |
| Total manufacturing [D]<br>Total, industries manufacturières [D] | 100.4 | 100.0 | 118.6 | 122.1 | 126.8 | 141.4 | 146.1 | 150.3 |
| Food, beverages and tobacco — Aliments, boissons et tabac | 312.7 | 100.0 | 320.1 | 335.4 | 364.0 | 381.7 | 347.7 | 395.7 |

| Country or area and industry [ISIC Rev. 3] / Pays ou zone et industrie [CITI Rév. 3] | 1999 | 2000 | 2001 | 2002 | 2003 | 2004 | 2005 | 2006 |
|---|---|---|---|---|---|---|---|---|
| Textiles, wearing apparel, leather, footwear / Textiles, habillement, cuir et chaussures | 128.5 | 100.0 | 74.0 | 93.1 | 98.9 | 102.7 | 82.9 | 72.5 |
| Chemicals, rubber and plastic prod. / Prod. chimiques, caoutchouc et plastiques | 101.4 | 100.0 | 128.5 | 120.1 | 130.0 | 142.6 | 158.3 | 150.6 |
| Basic metals — Métaux de base | 111.3 | 100.0 | 107.1 | 182.6 | 159.3 | 200.2 | 246.6 | 272.5 |
| Metal products — Produits métalliques | 107.2 | 100.0 | 103.2 | 116.7 | 95.9 | 116.1 | 87.4 | 80.8 |
| **United Rep. of Tanzania — Rép.-Unie de Tanzanie** | | | | | | | | |
| Total manufacturing [D] / Total, industries manufacturières [D] | 87.0 | 100.0 | 104.1 | 119.6 | 135.4 | 146.0 | 156.7 | ... |
| Food, beverages and tobacco — Aliments, boissons et tabac | 84.8 | 100.0 | 106.3 | 119.3 | 151.5 | 146.2 | 172.9 | ... |
| Textiles, leather and footwear — Textiles, cuir et chaussures | 67.5 | 100.0 | 116.4 | 144.1 | 174.8 | 181.1 | 170.3 | ... |
| Chemicals, rubber and plastic prod. / Prod. chimiques, caoutchouc et plastiques | 70.7 | 100.0 | 101.2 | 90.7 | 142.9 | 149.7 | 175.0 | ... |
| Basic metals — Métaux de base | 93.8 | 100.0 | 106.2 | 140.9 | 165.1 | 162.9 | 166.0 | ... |
| Metal products — Produits métalliques | 120.3 | 100.0 | 106.2 | 83.4 | 92.6 | 80.5 | 75.2 | ... |
| **Zambia — Zambie** | | | | | | | | |
| Total industry [CDE] / Total, industrie [CDE] | 97.5 | 100.0 | 105.1 | 103.6 | 113.1 | 122.9 | 133.3 | 145.1 |
| Total mining [C] / Total, industries extractives [C] | 96.6 | 100.0 | 113.9 | 111.4 | 126.7 | 147.6 | 168.3 | 186.7 |
| Total manufacturing [D] / Total, industries manufacturières [D] | 91.7 | 100.0 | 96.3 | 97.4 | 105.5 | 111.3 | 115.8 | 122.4 |
| Food, beverages and tobacco — Aliments, boissons et tabac | 99.3 | 100.0 | 112.6 | 122.1 | 129.4 | 137.0 | 141.9 | 154.9 |
| Textiles and wearing apparel — Textiles et habillement | 97.8 | 100.0 | 68.0 | 72.2 | 74.5 | 73.1 | 71.0 | 65.4 |
| Chemicals, petroleum, rubber and plastic products / Prod. chimiques, pétroliers, caoutch. et plast. | 70.8 | 100.0 | 67.9 | 73.8 | 79.6 | 85.0 | 87.7 | 91.2 |
| Basic metals — Métaux de base | 95.9 | 100.0 | 56.6 | 59.0 | 67.9 | 70.0 | 68.6 | 68.4 |
| Metal products — Produits métalliques | 89.9 | 100.0 | 95.4 | 71.0 | 84.2 | 88.2 | 94.8 | 99.9 |
| Electricity and water [E] / Electricité et eau [E] | 98.3 | 100.0 | 115.4 | 106.9 | 106.8 | 103.5 | 109.9 | 124.4 |
| **Zimbabwe — Zimbabwe** | | | | | | | | |
| Total industry [CDE][4] / Total, industrie [CDE][4] | 106.2 | 100.0 | 92.8 | 83.7 | 77.5 | 74.6 | ... | ... |
| Total mining [C] / Total, industries extractives [C] | 108.8 | 100.0 | 86.0 | 87.9 | 76.8 | 106.7 | ... | ... |
| Total manufacturing [D] / Total, industries manufacturières [D] | 106.5 | 100.0 | 90.9 | 78.1 | 71.2 | 62.6 | 64.1 | ... |
| Food, beverages and tobacco — Aliments, boissons et tabac | 97.0 | 100.0 | 85.6 | 69.6 | 59.5 | 54.6 | 53.9 | ... |
| Textiles, wearing apparel, leather, footwear / Textiles, habillement, cuir et chaussures | 112.6 | 100.0 | 98.1 | 77.4 | 53.6 | 63.3 | 69.6 | ... |
| Chemicals, petroleum, rubber and plastic products / Prod. chimiques, pétroliers, caoutch. et plast. | 141.7 | 100.0 | 99.9 | 104.2 | 89.5 | 88.0 | 86.6 | ... |
| Basic metals and metal products / Métaux de base et produits métalliques | 103.8 | 100.0 | 88.9 | 77.6 | 81.0 | 63.5 | 68.8 | ... |
| Electricity [E] / Electricité [E] | 101.5 | 100.0 | 112.2 | 120.9 | 124.0 | 136.4 | 147.0 | ... |
| **America, North — Amérique du Nord** | | | | | | | | |
| **Barbados — Barbade** | | | | | | | | |
| Total industry [CDE] / Total, industrie [CDE] | 101.7 | 100.0 | 93.9 | 94.3 | 93.6 | 95.4 | 97.1 | 98.4 |
| Total mining [C] / Total, industries extractives [C] | 126.8 | 100.0 | 83.8 | 70.8 | 66.7 | 64.1 | 69.3 | 67.1 |
| Total manufacturing [D] / Total, industries manufacturières [D] | 100.6 | 100.0 | 92.3 | 92.8 | 91.8 | 93.2 | 95.0 | 94.2 |
| Food, beverages and tobacco — Aliments, boissons et tabac | 102.7 | 100.0 | 97.2 | 99.2 | 99.0 | 99.3 | 99.1 | 93.9 |
| Wearing apparel — Habillement | 93.0 | 100.0 | 63.0 | 47.0 | 44.0 | 46.0 | 45.1 | 39.7 |
| Chemicals and petroleum products / Produits chimiques et pétroliers | 124.9 | 100.0 | 93.9 | 90.0 | 86.8 | 109.6 | 115.6 | 112.1 |

| Country or area and industry [ISIC Rev. 3] Pays ou zone et industrie [CITI Rév. 3] | 1999 | 2000 | 2001 | 2002 | 2003 | 2004 | 2005 | 2006 |
|---|---|---|---|---|---|---|---|---|
| Metal products — Produits métalliques | 102.5 | 100.0 | 69.6 | 68.1 | 59.6 | 65.8 | 51.3 | 55.4 |
| Electricity and gas [E] Electricité et gaz [E] | 100.0 | 100.0 | 103.6 | 105.4 | 108.2 | 110.8 | 110.1 | 119.2 |
| **Belize — Belize** | | | | | | | | |
| Total industry [DE] Total, industrie [DE] | 87.5 | 100.0 | 100.1 | 96.4 | ... | ... | ... | ... |
| Total manufacturing [D] Total, industries manufacturières [D] | 85.5 | 100.0 | 99.9 | 95.4 | ... | ... | ... | ... |
| Food, beverages and tobacco — Aliments, boissons et tabac | 86.6 | 100.0 | 100.6 | 96.0 | ... | ... | ... | ... |
| Wearing apparel — Habillement | 121.7 | 100.0 | 85.7 | 67.3 | ... | ... | ... | ... |
| Chemicals and chemical products — Produits chimiques | 108.4 | 100.0 | 102.0 | 116.8 | ... | ... | ... | ... |
| Metal products — Produits métalliques | 118.9 | 100.0 | 78.6 | 76.3 | ... | ... | ... | ... |
| Electricity and water [E] Electricité et eau [E] | 102.6 | 100.0 | 102.3 | 103.7 | ... | ... | ... | ... |
| **Canada — Canada** | | | | | | | | |
| Total industry [CDE] Total, industrie [CDE] | 92.2 | 100.0 | 96.2 | 97.9 | 98.5 | 100.4 | 101.7 | 101.1 |
| Total mining [C] Total, industries extractives [C] | 97.0 | 100.0 | 100.1 | 102.5 | 108.0 | 111.3 | 112.1 | 113.3 |
| Total manufacturing [D] Total, industries manufacturières [D] | 90.2 | 100.0 | 95.3 | 96.1 | 95.6 | 97.3 | 98.2 | 97.3 |
| Food, beverages and tobacco — Aliments, boissons et tabac | 96.2 | 100.0 | 104.9 | 104.5 | 102.9 | 104.9 | 106.6 | 105.0 |
| Textiles, wearing apparel, leather, footwear Textiles, habillement, cuir et chaussures | 86.6 | 100.0 | 95.5 | 91.9 | 85.0 | 79.6 | 72.0 | 65.9 |
| Chemicals, petroleum, rubber and plastic products Prod. chimiques, pétroliers, caoutch. et plast. | 91.0 | 100.0 | 102.1 | 107.0 | 108.9 | 111.6 | 110.9 | 109.7 |
| Basic metals — Métaux de base | 92.4 | 100.0 | 98.0 | 102.5 | 99.3 | 100.8 | 103.6 | 104.2 |
| Metal products — Produits métalliques | 88.6 | 100.0 | 89.1 | 86.4 | 86.8 | 89.1 | 91.0 | 91.4 |
| Electricity, gas and water [E] Electricité, gaz et eau [E] | 99.5 | 100.0 | 97.7 | 104.3 | 106.1 | 106.9 | 111.6 | 110.5 |
| **Costa Rica — Costa Rica** | | | | | | | | |
| Total industry [DE][4] Total, industrie [DE][4] | 101.0 | 100.0 | 93.8 | 97.4 | 105.0 | 109.1 | 119.4 | 130.6 |
| Total manufacturing [D] Total, industries manufacturières [D] | 103.0 | 100.0 | 90.9 | 94.0 | 101.9 | 106.0 | 117.4 | 129.7 |
| Food, beverages and tobacco — Aliments, boissons et tabac | 102.1 | 100.0 | 94.1 | 92.1 | 94.0 | 93.6 | 98.7 | ... |
| Textiles, wearing apparel, leather, footwear Textiles, habillement, cuir et chaussures | 112.3 | 100.0 | 90.3 | 88.4 | 85.7 | 88.8 | 90.7 | ... |
| Chemicals, petroleum, rubber and plastic products Prod. chimiques, pétroliers, caoutch. et plast. | 96.3 | 100.0 | 108.8 | 127.8 | 132.8 | 134.0 | 136.9 | ... |
| Metal products — Produits métalliques | 103.0 | 100.0 | 92.1 | 99.0 | 99.3 | 102.0 | 108.2 | ... |
| Electricity and water [E] Electricité et eau [E] | 93.9 | 100.0 | 104.1 | 109.6 | 116.1 | 120.7 | 126.5 | 134.2 |
| **Cuba — Cuba** | | | | | | | | |
| Total industry [CDE] Total, industrie [CDE] | 95.0 | 100.0 | 100.6 | 96.9 | 93.8 | 94.8 | 91.7 | 94.8 |
| Total mining [C] Total, industries extractives [C] | 85.3 | 100.0 | 101.5 | 118.8 | 122.8 | 113.7 | 107.3 | 120.3 |
| Total manufacturing [D] Total, industries manufacturières [D] | 95.1 | 100.0 | 102.2 | 95.5 | 98.4 | 99.3 | 103.1 | 106.0 |
| Food, beverages and tobacco — Aliments, boissons et tabac | 100.2 | 100.0 | 107.6 | 102.3 | 96.5 | 100.7 | 104.4 | 107.3 |
| Textiles, wearing apparel, leather, footwear Textiles, habillement, cuir et chaussures | 118.3 | 100.0 | 100.9 | 72.9 | 69.9 | 64.2 | 58.4 | 55.7 |
| Chemicals, petroleum, rubber and plastic products Prod. chimiques, pétroliers, caoutch. et plast. | 83.7 | 100.0 | 98.5 | 78.7 | 83.2 | 81.7 | 83.3 | 91.5 |
| Basic metals — Métaux de base | 94.8 | 100.0 | 102.9 | 99.8 | 93.5 | 98.4 | 100.1 | 95.9 |
| Metal products — Produits métalliques | 139.6 | 100.0 | 104.9 | 92.4 | 84.6 | 80.4 | 34.5 | 37.5 |
| Electricity and water [E] Electricité et eau [E] | 96.5 | 100.0 | 101.8 | 104.5 | 105.2 | 104.1 | 102.1 | 109.6 |

| Country or area and industry [ISIC Rev. 3]<br>Pays ou zone et industrie [CITI Rév. 3] | 1999 | 2000 | 2001 | 2002 | 2003 | 2004 | 2005 | 2006 |
|---|---|---|---|---|---|---|---|---|
| **Dominican Republic — Rép. dominicaine** | | | | | | | | |
| Total industry [CDE]<br>Total, industrie [CDE] | 91.6 | 100.0 | 98.0 | 102.4 | 99.5 | 98.3 | 102.6 | 109.0 |
| Total mining [C]<br>Total, industries extractives [C] | 88.3 | 100.0 | 84.4 | 82.1 | 89.2 | 92.6 | 91.1 | 100.6 |
| Total manufacturing [D]<br>Total, industries manufacturières [D] | 91.7 | 100.0 | 96.9 | 101.6 | 98.4 | 99.1 | 104.5 | 110.4 |
| Electricity and water [E]<br>Electricité et eau [E] | 95.4 | 100.0 | 118.4 | 127.6 | 116.8 | 94.0 | 98.3 | 105.4 |
| **El Salvador — El Salvador** | | | | | | | | |
| Total industry [CDE]<br>Total, industrie [CDE] | 96.3 | 100.0 | 104.2 | 107.3 | 109.8 | 110.5 | 112.3 | 115.9 |
| Total mining [C]<br>Total, industries extractives [C] | 104.7 | 100.0 | 111.4 | 117.8 | 121.9 | 102.4 | 105.1 | 110.1 |
| Total manufacturing [D]<br>Total, industries manufacturières [D] | 96.0 | 100.0 | 104.0 | 107.1 | 109.5 | 110.5 | 112.2 | 115.7 |
| Food and beverages — Aliments et boissons | 95.7 | 100.0 | 105.1 | 106.7 | 108.9 | 112.1 | 115.1 | 119.3 |
| Textiles, wearing apparel, leather, footwear<br>Textiles, habillement, cuir et chaussures | 98.4 | 100.0 | 93.2 | 93.1 | 92.4 | 95.0 | 99.6 | 103.1 |
| Chemicals, petroleum, rubber and plastic products<br>Prod. chimiques, pétroliers, caoutch. et plast. | 102.8 | 100.0 | 104.5 | 107.2 | 108.6 | 107.3 | 111.0 | 116.3 |
| Basic metals and metal products<br>Métaux de base et produits métalliques | 97.2 | 100.0 | 102.6 | 106.1 | 108.7 | 110.9 | 114.2 | 117.8 |
| Electricity [E]<br>Electricité [E] | 109.4 | 100.0 | 106.6 | 114.2 | 119.8 | 121.2 | 130.7 | 141.0 |
| **Guatemala — Guatemala** | | | | | | | | |
| Total industry [CDE]<br>Total, industrie [CDE] | 95.5 | 100.0 | 100.1 | 103.1 | 105.1 | 108.1 | 110.6 | ... |
| Total mining [C]<br>Total, industries extractives [C] | 109.1 | 100.0 | 100.8 | 110.6 | 115.2 | 106.4 | 104.2 | ... |
| Total manufacturing [D]<br>Total, industries manufacturières [D] | 98.2 | 100.0 | 101.1 | 101.9 | 103.0 | 105.4 | 108.2 | ... |
| Electricity [E]<br>Electricité [E] | 85.2 | 100.0 | 97.0 | 105.8 | 110.5 | 117.1 | 119.2 | ... |
| **Haiti[6] — Haïti[6]** | | | | | | | | |
| Total industry [DE][4]<br>Total, industrie [DE][4] | 94.5 | 100.0 | 91.4 | 101.0 | 105.7 | 107.3 | 115.4 | ... |
| Total manufacturing [D]<br>Total, industries manufacturières [D] | 93.8 | 100.0 | 102.4 | 104.0 | 108.4 | 110.1 | 116.6 | ... |
| Food, beverages and tobacco — Aliments, boissons et tabac | 86.4 | 100.0 | 103.7 | 105.2 | 105.7 | 107.9 | 118.5 | ... |
| Chemicals and chemical products — Produits chimiques | 97.2 | 100.0 | 103.4 | 105.8 | 121.1 | 119.7 | 126.1 | ... |
| Electricity [E]<br>Electricité [E] | 100.9 | 100.0 | 69.5 | 70.4 | 77.4 | 78.6 | 103.1 | ... |
| **Honduras — Honduras** | | | | | | | | |
| Total industry [CDE]<br>Total, industrie [CDE] | 94.4 | 100.0 | 103.5 | 107.8 | 112.8 | 117.2 | 124.5 | 131.5 |
| Total mining [C]<br>Total, industries extractives [C] | 98.3 | 100.0 | 99.2 | 103.3 | 106.7 | 104.2 | 108.3 | 116.7 |
| Total manufacturing [D]<br>Total, industries manufacturières [D] | 94.7 | 100.0 | 105.2 | 109.2 | 113.2 | 117.8 | 123.8 | 129.9 |
| Food, beverages and tobacco — Aliments, boissons et tabac | 91.9 | 100.0 | 109.0 | 116.9 | 124.6 | 132.5 | 142.1 | 147.9 |
| Textiles, wearing apparel, leather, footwear<br>Textiles, habillement, cuir et chaussures | 89.9 | 100.0 | 110.3 | 117.5 | 124.6 | 133.2 | 141.6 | 146.3 |
| Chemicals, petroleum, rubber and plastic products<br>Prod. chimiques, pétroliers, caoutch. et plast. | 91.1 | 100.0 | 107.1 | 114.4 | 122.6 | 132.8 | 141.9 | 150.2 |
| Basic metals — Métaux de base | 89.2 | 100.0 | 111.0 | 119.2 | 128.5 | 139.2 | 150.9 | 160.2 |
| Metal products — Produits métalliques | 90.3 | 100.0 | 109.7 | 117.7 | 126.8 | 137.1 | 147.1 | 155.7 |
| Electricity, gas and water [E]<br>Electricité, gaz et eau [E] | 90.4 | 100.0 | 98.2 | 103.7 | 114.2 | 121.5 | 137.0 | 147.0 |

| Country or area and industry [ISIC Rev. 3]<br>Pays ou zone et industrie [CITI Rév. 3] | 1999 | 2000 | 2001 | 2002 | 2003 | 2004 | 2005 | 2006 |
|---|---|---|---|---|---|---|---|---|
| **Mexico — Mexique** | | | | | | | | |
| Total industry [CDE][7]<br>Total, industrie [CDE][7] | 94.2 | 100.0 | 96.6 | 96.4 | 96.3 | 100.3 | 102.0 | 107.1 |
| Total mining [C]<br>Total, industries extractives [C] | 96.3 | 100.0 | 101.4 | 101.9 | 105.6 | 109.3 | 111.5 | 114.0 |
| Total manufacturing [D]<br>Total, industries manufacturières [D] | 93.6 | 100.0 | 96.2 | 95.6 | 94.3 | 98.1 | 99.4 | 104.1 |
| Food, beverages and tobacco — Aliments, boissons et tabac | 96.2 | 100.0 | 102.6 | 104.3 | 106.1 | 109.6 | 112.4 | 115.3 |
| Textiles and wearing apparel — Textiles et habillement | 94.9 | 100.0 | 91.9 | 86.1 | 80.2 | 82.6 | 80.1 | 79.3 |
| Chemicals, petroleum, rubber and plastic products<br>Prod. chimiques, pétroliers, caoutch. et plast. | 96.8 | 100.0 | 96.2 | 95.9 | 97.4 | 100.4 | 101.0 | 103.4 |
| Basic metals — Métaux de base | 97.1 | 100.0 | 92.9 | 94.1 | 98.0 | 104.7 | 106.8 | 109.8 |
| Metal products — Produits métalliques | 88.0 | 100.0 | 93.1 | 91.2 | 86.8 | 91.3 | 92.6 | 101.9 |
| Electricity [E]<br>Electricité [E] | 97.1 | 100.0 | 102.2 | 103.3 | 104.9 | 107.8 | 109.6 | 115.1 |
| **Panama — Panama** | | | | | | | | |
| Total industry [CDE][4]<br>Total, industrie [CDE][4] | 102.6 | 100.0 | 94.0 | 97.2 | 100.0 | 102.8 | 106.2 | 113.0 |
| Total mining [C]<br>Total, industries extractives [C] | 112.6 | 100.0 | 96.9 | 113.3 | 141.5 | 158.8 | 159.7 | 188.7 |
| Total manufacturing [D]<br>Total, industries manufacturières [D] | 105.3 | 100.0 | 93.4 | 94.7 | 96.0 | 96.6 | 99.4 | 104.7 |
| Food, beverages and tobacco — Aliments, boissons et tabac | 103.2 | 100.0 | 98.7 | 98.7 | 100.1 | 101.2 | 104.5 | 109.2 |
| Textiles, wearing apparel, leather, footwear<br>Textiles, habillement, cuir et chaussures | 113.4 | 100.0 | 87.3 | 74.3 | 55.2 | 44.8 | 38.7 | 38.3 |
| Chemicals, petroleum, rubber and plastic products<br>Prod. chimiques, pétroliers, caoutch. et plast. | 104.7 | 100.0 | 87.3 | 89.2 | 89.0 | 81.7 | 84.3 | 87.6 |
| Basic metals — Métaux de base | 130.6 | 100.0 | 40.6 | 51.6 | 52.1 | 56.8 | 54.1 | 53.8 |
| Metal products — Produits métalliques | 93.3 | 100.0 | 90.6 | 60.9 | 56.0 | 64.0 | 69.3 | 68.8 |
| Electricity and water [E]<br>Electricité et eau [E] | 91.5 | 100.0 | 95.3 | 101.7 | 103.3 | 109.7 | 116.0 | 122.2 |
| **Trinidad and Tobago — Trinité-et-Tobago** | | | | | | | | |
| Total industry [DE]<br>Total, industrie [DE] | 94.9 | 100.0 | 107.7 | 128.2 | 140.4 | 148.9 | 164.1 | ... |
| Total manufacturing [D][4]<br>Total, industries manufacturières [D][4] | 94.1 | 100.0 | 109.3 | 130.3 | 144.2 | 153.1 | 169.2 | ... |
| Food, beverages and tobacco — Aliments, boissons et tabac | 70.4 | 100.0 | 119.1 | 87.5 | 85.9 | 103.1 | 123.2 | ... |
| Textiles, leather and footwear — Textiles, cuir et chaussures | 85.7 | 100.0 | 90.3 | 85.2 | 133.4 | 154.8 | 181.6 | ... |
| Chemicals and petroleum products<br>Produits chimiques et pétroliers | 88.3 | 100.0 | 100.4 | 122.1 | 150.7 | 172.7 | 235.4 | ... |
| Metal products — Produits métalliques | 97.2 | 100.0 | 116.3 | 130.6 | 171.5 | 313.6 | 398.4 | ... |
| Electricity [E]<br>Electricité [E] | 104.6 | 100.0 | 87.6 | 103.6 | 94.2 | 98.4 | 103.1 | ... |
| **United States — Etats-Unis** | | | | | | | | |
| Total industry [CDE]<br>Total, industrie [CDE] | 95.7 | 100.0 | 96.5 | 96.5 | 97.6 | 100.0 | 103.2 | 107.2 |
| Total mining [C]<br>Total, industries extractives [C] | 97.8 | 100.0 | 101.0 | 96.6 | 96.5 | 95.8 | 94.3 | 96.8 |
| Total manufacturing [D]<br>Total, industries manufacturières [D] | 95.4 | 100.0 | 95.9 | 95.9 | 96.9 | 99.7 | 103.5 | 108.3 |
| Food, beverages and tobacco — Aliments, boissons et tabac | 98.6 | 100.0 | 99.8 | 100.5 | 102.4 | 103.1 | 106.7 | 110.5 |
| Textiles, wearing apparel, leather, footwear<br>Textiles, habillement, cuir et chaussures | 103.4 | 100.0 | 87.3 | 77.6 | 73.6 | 69.4 | 69.6 | 68.2 |
| Chemicals, petroleum, rubber and plastic products<br>Prod. chimiques, pétroliers, caoutch. et plast. | 99.0 | 100.0 | 96.8 | 103.1 | 104.1 | 107.5 | 110.3 | 112.1 |
| Basic metals — Métaux de base | 103.4 | 100.0 | 90.5 | 90.7 | 89.7 | 99.1 | 97.1 | 101.6 |
| Metal products — Produits métalliques | 93.2 | 100.0 | 95.6 | 94.9 | 98.5 | 102.2 | 110.5 | 123.5 |
| Electricity and gas [E]<br>Electricité et gaz [E] | 97.2 | 100.0 | 99.6 | 102.7 | 104.6 | 106.1 | 108.3 | 107.9 |

| Country or area and industry [ISIC Rev. 3]<br>Pays ou zone et industrie [CITI Rév. 3] | 1999 | 2000 | 2001 | 2002 | 2003 | 2004 | 2005 | 2006 |
|---|---|---|---|---|---|---|---|---|
| **America, South — Amérique du Sud** | | | | | | | | |
| **Argentina — Argentine** | | | | | | | | |
| Total manufacturing [D]<br>Total, industries manufacturières [D] | 101.9 | 100.0 | 88.8 | 80.2 | 94.2 | 107.4 | 117.3 | 127.9 |
| Food, beverages and tobacco — Aliments, boissons et tabac | 103.6 | 100.0 | 91.4 | 87.0 | 98.0 | 108.7 | 116.9 | 123.1 |
| Textiles, wearing apparel, leather, footwear<br>Textiles, habillement, cuir et chaussures | 100.9 | 100.0 | 85.7 | 67.8 | 94.6 | 104.9 | 116.6 | 122.1 |
| Chemicals, petroleum, rubber and plastic products<br>Prod. chimiques, pétroliers, caoutch. et plast. | 99.3 | 100.0 | 91.6 | 87.5 | 97.6 | 104.6 | 111.2 | 121.1 |
| Basic metals — Métaux de base | 96.4 | 100.0 | 94.2 | 99.8 | 111.0 | 122.1 | 130.9 | 143.2 |
| Metal products — Produits métalliques | 103.9 | 100.0 | 83.7 | 68.3 | 88.2 | 111.4 | 124.7 | 142.8 |
| **Bolivia — Bolivie** | | | | | | | | |
| Total industry [CDE][4]<br>Total, industrie [CDE][4] | 100.1 | 100.0 | 98.5 | 99.1 | 101.5 | 101.6 | 108.1 | 116.5 |
| Total mining [C]<br>Total, industries extractives [C] | 101.6 | 100.0 | 96.7 | 96.9 | 97.6 | 91.3 | 102.7 | 109.1 |
| Total manufacturing [D]<br>Total, industries manufacturières [D] | 99.6 | 100.0 | 99.2 | 99.9 | 103.4 | 106.9 | 110.4 | 120.2 |
| Food, beverages and tobacco — Aliments, boissons et tabac | 96.0 | 100.0 | 102.4 | 105.4 | 108.4 | 108.2 | 108.5 | 119.9 |
| Textiles, wearing apparel, leather, footwear<br>Textiles, habillement, cuir et chaussures | 96.1 | 100.0 | 84.1 | 79.9 | 95.6 | 95.3 | 107.9 | 114.5 |
| Chemicals, petroleum, rubber and plastic products<br>Prod. chimiques, pétroliers, caoutch. et plast. | 107.7 | 100.0 | 97.3 | 98.5 | 104.5 | 123.3 | 122.5 | 127.1 |
| Basic metals — Métaux de base | 96.2 | 100.0 | 87.4 | 91.1 | 98.5 | 99.4 | 98.4 | 99.1 |
| Metal products — Produits métalliques | 116.8 | 100.0 | 92.3 | 79.9 | 64.7 | 67.9 | 53.7 | 64.4 |
| Electricity, gas and water [E]<br>Electricité, gaz et eau [E] | 97.0 | 100.0 | 100.7 | 104.5 | 106.0 | 109.2 | 115.6 | 123.0 |
| **Brazil — Brésil** | | | | | | | | |
| Total industry [CD]<br>Total, industrie [CD] | 93.8 | 100.0 | 101.6 | 104.4 | 104.4 | 113.2 | 116.6 | 119.9 |
| Total mining [C]<br>Total, industries extractives [C] | 89.4 | 100.0 | 103.4 | 123.0 | 128.8 | 134.3 | 148.0 | 158.9 |
| Total manufacturing [D]<br>Total, industries manufacturières [D] | 94.2 | 100.0 | 101.3 | 101.8 | 101.6 | 110.3 | 113.3 | 116.2 |
| Food, beverages and tobacco — Aliments, boissons et tabac | 102.0 | 100.0 | 103.8 | 101.7 | 99.4 | 104.5 | 106.4 | 109.8 |
| Textiles, wearing apparel, leather, footwear<br>Textiles, habillement, cuir et chaussures | 94.4 | 100.0 | 93.5 | 95.0 | 87.4 | 92.6 | 89.6 | 88.5 |
| Chemicals, petroleum, rubber and plastic products<br>Prod. chimiques, pétroliers, caoutch. et plast. | 98.6 | 100.0 | 98.6 | 97.2 | 95.9 | 100.5 | 101.9 | 103.2 |
| Basic metals and metal products<br>Métaux de base et produits métalliques | 91.5 | 100.0 | 100.2 | 103.8 | 110.1 | 113.7 | 111.5 | 114.6 |
| Metal products — Produits métalliques | 87.3 | 100.0 | 107.0 | 112.0 | 115.4 | 132.1 | 136.1 | 139.0 |
| **Chile — Chili** | | | | | | | | |
| Total industry [CDE][4]<br>Total, industrie [CDE][4] | 96.1 | 100.0 | 101.6 | 102.5 | 108.3 | 117.6 | 122.2 | 125.6 |
| Total mining [C]<br>Total, industries extractives [C] | 94.8 | 100.0 | 101.6 | 98.0 | 104.4 | 114.9 | 114.0 | 114.8 |
| Total manufacturing [D]<br>Total, industries manufacturières [D] | 96.7 | 100.0 | 101.2 | 103.7 | 109.1 | 117.8 | 124.4 | 128.5 |
| Food, beverages and tobacco — Aliments, boissons et tabac | 97.3 | 100.0 | 103.9 | 107.0 | 110.5 | 118.7 | 125.1 | 138.5 |
| Textiles, wearing apparel, leather, footwear<br>Textiles, habillement, cuir et chaussures | 102.6 | 100.0 | 87.3 | 82.9 | 90.1 | 100.1 | 97.9 | 85.6 |
| Chemicals, petroleum, rubber and plastic products<br>Prod. chimiques, pétroliers, caoutch. et plast. | 91.0 | 100.0 | 106.1 | 110.7 | 114.4 | 119.3 | 135.9 | 130.7 |
| Basic metals — Métaux de base | 134.6 | 100.0 | 104.7 | 103.6 | 120.7 | 153.4 | 164.1 | 153.7 |
| Metal products — Produits métalliques | 95.0 | 100.0 | 101.7 | 95.6 | 96.5 | 102.8 | 112.6 | 111.0 |
| Electricity [E]<br>Electricité [E] | 96.0 | 100.0 | 104.3 | 107.0 | 114.3 | 123.5 | 130.3 | 137.4 |

| Country or area and industry [ISIC Rev. 3]<br>Pays ou zone et industrie [CITI Rév. 3] | 1999 | 2000 | 2001 | 2002 | 2003 | 2004 | 2005 | 2006 |
|---|---|---|---|---|---|---|---|---|
| Colombia — Colombie | | | | | | | | |
| Total industry [CDE][4]<br>Total, industrie [CDE][4] | 91.4 | 100.0 | 104.3 | 100.5 | 114.5 | 123.4 | 130.2 | 143.2 |
| Total mining [C]<br>Total, industries extractives [C] | 89.3 | 100.0 | 113.3 | 95.0 | 145.2 | 163.6 | 177.8 | 196.8 |
| Total manufacturing [D]<br>Total, industries manufacturières [D] | 90.4 | 100.0 | 100.7 | 100.8 | 103.5 | 110.1 | 114.3 | 127.1 |
| Food, beverages and tobacco — Aliments, boissons et tabac | 100.6 | 100.0 | 101.6 | 102.8 | 102.3 | 102.5 | 101.2 | 108.5 |
| Textiles, wearing apparel, leather, footwear<br>Textiles, habillement, cuir et chaussures | 84.8 | 100.0 | 99.3 | 88.7 | 92.4 | 99.7 | 98.5 | 105.7 |
| Chemicals, petroleum, rubber and plastic products<br>Prod. chimiques, pétroliers, caoutch. et plast. | 91.8 | 100.0 | 95.8 | 97.3 | 102.5 | 110.2 | 113.2 | 119.7 |
| Basic metals — Métaux de base | 76.4 | 100.0 | 96.1 | 103.8 | 135.1 | 156.2 | 174.5 | 211.6 |
| Metal products — Produits métalliques | 87.8 | 100.0 | 112.1 | 112.8 | 112.1 | 134.9 | 153.9 | 183.4 |
| Electricity [E]<br>Electricité [E] | 98.8 | 100.0 | 105.3 | 107.6 | 113.1 | 116.8 | 122.8 | 127.5 |
| Ecuador — Equateur | | | | | | | | |
| Total industry [CDE]<br>Total, industrie [CDE] | 98.3 | 100.0 | 102.5 | 102.2 | 107.6 | 124.5 | 129.4 | 134.3 |
| Total mining [C]<br>Total, industries extractives [C] | 92.6 | 100.0 | 101.1 | 98.5 | 104.5 | 130.9 | 132.4 | 133.7 |
| Total manufacturing [D][3]<br>Total, industries manufacturières [D][3] | 107.4 | 100.0 | 104.9 | 107.5 | 112.5 | 116.1 | 126.8 | 137.7 |
| Food, beverages and tobacco — Aliments, boissons et tabac | 121.3 | 100.0 | 107.1 | 109.4 | 118.5 | 123.5 | 139.9 | 156.2 |
| Textiles, wearing apparel, leather, footwear<br>Textiles, habillement, cuir et chaussures | 93.8 | 100.0 | 100.7 | 101.4 | 101.0 | 102.6 | 104.5 | 106.5 |
| Chemicals and chemical products<br>Produits chimiques | 96.2 | 100.0 | 106.2 | 111.1 | 120.4 | 124.7 | 126.1 | 133.9 |
| Basic metals and metal products<br>Métaux de base et prod. métalliques | 91.9 | 100.0 | 112.8 | 116.9 | 125.3 | 129.1 | 148.7 | 167.4 |
| Electricity [E]<br>Electricité [E] | 97.5 | 100.0 | 104.2 | 112.0 | 110.2 | 110.3 | 113.1 | 113.5 |
| Paraguay — Paraguay | | | | | | | | |
| Total manufacturing [D]<br>Total, industries manufacturières [D] | 98.9 | 100.0 | 101.4 | 100.5 | 100.7 | 105.0 | 109.6 | ... |
| Food, beverages and tobacco — Aliments, boissons et tabac | 98.7 | 100.0 | 102.0 | 102.4 | 102.7 | 110.0 | 118.3 | ... |
| Textiles, wearing apparel, leather, footwear<br>Textiles, habillement, cuir et chaussures | 98.8 | 100.0 | 101.0 | 102.0 | 115.5 | 121.3 | 111.7 | ... |
| Chemicals, petroleum, rubber and plastic products<br>Prod. chimiques, pétroliers, caoutch. et plast. | 107.2 | 100.0 | 105.0 | 97.6 | 93.5 | 83.1 | 70.9 | ... |
| Basic metals — Métaux de base | 91.0 | 100.0 | 97.4 | 87.2 | 94.0 | 101.6 | 105.8 | ... |
| All machinery and transport equipment<br>Fabrication de machines et de matériel de transport | 89.7 | 100.0 | 107.4 | 107.2 | 95.0 | 90.9 | 109.0 | ... |
| Peru — Pérou | | | | | | | | |
| Total industry [CDE]<br>Total, industrie [CDE] | 97.2 | 100.0 | 100.3 | 105.5 | 109.6 | 115.1 | 122.5 | 132.0 |
| Total mining [C]<br>Total, industries extractives [C] | 97.6 | 100.0 | 109.9 | 123.1 | 129.8 | 136.7 | 148.1 | 150.2 |
| Total manufacturing [D]<br>Total, industries manufacturières [D] | 94.5 | 100.0 | 100.6 | 106.4 | 110.1 | 118.6 | 127.2 | 136.7 |
| Food, beverages and tobacco — Aliments, boissons et tabac | 92.1 | 100.0 | 97.4 | 100.8 | 101.4 | 107.7 | 114.0 | 124.0 |
| Textiles, wearing apparel, leather, footwear<br>Textiles, habillement, cuir et chaussures | 88.2 | 100.0 | 95.9 | 108.0 | 117.8 | 132.4 | 136.9 | 133.7 |
| Chemicals, petroleum, rubber and plastic products<br>Prod. chimiques, pétroliers, caoutch. et plast. | 96.6 | 100.0 | 103.3 | 107.3 | 108.7 | 115.0 | 127.8 | 138.9 |
| Basic metals — Métaux de base | 95.2 | 100.0 | 103.6 | 100.8 | 103.8 | 105.6 | 105.6 | 109.9 |
| Metal products — Produits métalliques | 91.3 | 100.0 | 98.6 | 94.8 | 96.4 | 97.4 | 107.2 | 128.4 |
| Electricity [E]<br>Electricité [E] | 97.0 | 100.0 | 101.7 | 107.2 | 111.1 | 116.1 | 122.6 | 131.1 |

| Country or area and industry [ISIC Rev. 3]<br>Pays ou zone et industrie [CITI Rév. 3] | 1999 | 2000 | 2001 | 2002 | 2003 | 2004 | 2005 | 2006 |
|---|---|---|---|---|---|---|---|---|
| **Uruguay — Uruguay** | | | | | | | | |
| Total manufacturing [D]<br>Total, industries manufacturières [D] | 96.2 | 100.0 | 101.7 | 107.2 | 115.5 | 140.1 | 156.1 | 169.9 |
| Food, beverages and tobacco — Aliments, boissons et tabac | 105.5 | 100.0 | 93.2 | 93.3 | 95.8 | 114.6 | 133.4 | 148.0 |
| Textiles, wearing apparel, leather, footwear<br>Textiles, habillement, cuir et chaussures | 99.5 | 100.0 | 81.0 | 61.9 | 72.7 | 88.7 | 98.0 | 97.0 |
| Chemicals, petroleum, rubber and plastic products<br>Prod. chimiques, pétroliers, caoutch. et plast. | 95.9 | 100.0 | 91.8 | 86.7 | 99.7 | 122.3 | 124.9 | 128.3 |
| Basic metals — Métaux de base | 104.2 | 100.0 | 98.7 | 98.7 | 119.1 | 151.2 | 168.9 | 182.2 |
| Metal products — Produits métalliques | 94.1 | 100.0 | 81.5 | 47.7 | 46.3 | 64.0 | 82.8 | 107.0 |
| **Venezuela (Bolivarian Republic of) — Venezuela (République bolivarienne du)** | | | | | | | | |
| Total industry [CDE]<br>Total, industrie [CDE] | 94.9 | 100.0 | 103.8 | 92.5 | 87.1 | 104.0 | 113.3 | 124.3 |
| Total mining [C]<br>Total, industries extractives [C] | 86.8 | 100.0 | 102.8 | 107.2 | 102.4 | 117.0 | 115.0 | 119.5 |
| Total manufacturing [D]<br>Total, industries manufacturières [D] | 94.0 | 100.0 | 103.9 | 86.4 | 78.8 | 101.5 | 113.0 | 124.4 |
| Food, beverages and tobacco — Aliments, boissons et tabac | 94.8 | 100.0 | 105.7 | 98.6 | 86.7 | 93.9 | 100.8 | 112.9 |
| Textiles, wearing apparel, leather, footwear<br>Textiles, habillement, cuir et chaussures | 96.5 | 100.0 | 98.5 | 59.1 | 57.9 | 90.4 | 102.5 | 106.1 |
| Chemicals, petroleum, rubber and plastic products<br>Prod. chimiques, pétroliers, caoutch. et plast. | 104.9 | 100.0 | 101.0 | 88.4 | 91.5 | 116.0 | 114.4 | 112.9 |
| Basic metals — Métaux de base | 90.1 | 100.0 | 95.1 | 94.9 | 93.1 | 113.7 | 114.1 | 120.4 |
| Metal products — Produits métalliques | 90.5 | 100.0 | 102.0 | 68.3 | 56.5 | 83.4 | 101.4 | 124.1 |
| Electricity [E]<br>Electricité [E] | 95.7 | 100.0 | 105.2 | 107.8 | 108.6 | 116.7 | 125.9 | 134.3 |
| **Asia — Asie** | | | | | | | | |
| **Armenia — Arménie** | | | | | | | | |
| Total industry [CDE]<br>Total, industrie [CDE] | 93.9 | 100.0 | 105.3 | 120.7 | 139.0 | 142.3 | 153.1 | 151.7 |
| Total mining [C]<br>Total, industries extractives [C] | 80.2 | 100.0 | 119.7 | 143.2 | 160.2 | 177.0 | 168.9 | 179.4 |
| Total manufacturing [D]<br>Total, industries manufacturières [D] | 93.5 | 100.0 | 109.6 | 137.3 | 163.6 | 162.7 | 178.8 | 175.2 |
| Food, beverages and tobacco — Aliments, boissons et tabac | 95.7 | 100.0 | 106.8 | 118.6 | 136.5 | 141.9 | 150.8 | 154.9 |
| Textiles, wearing apparel, leather, footwear<br>Textiles, habillement, cuir et chaussures | 103.9 | 100.0 | 114.8 | 115.2 | 141.2 | 176.3 | 132.4 | 136.9 |
| Chemicals, petroleum, rubber and plastic products<br>Prod. chimiques, pétroliers, caoutch. et plast. | 93.9 | 100.0 | 86.6 | 80.2 | 94.8 | 136.9 | 199.6 | 205.4 |
| Basic metals — Métaux de base | 47.6 | 100.0 | 144.7 | 178.3 | 192.3 | 188.5 | 250.9 | 262.7 |
| Metal products — Produits métalliques | 84.9 | 100.0 | 137.6 | 159.7 | 205.4 | 261.9 | 226.1 | 243.7 |
| Electricity and gas [E]<br>Electricité et gaz [E] | 97.5 | 100.0 | 92.7 | 79.3 | 81.3 | 92.7 | 105.5 | 104.9 |
| **Azerbaijan — Azerbaïdjan** | | | | | | | | |
| Total industry [CDE]<br>Total, industrie [CDE] | 93.5 | 100.0 | 105.1 | 108.9 | 115.5 | 122.1 | 163.1 | 222.7 |
| Total mining [C]<br>Total, industries extractives [C] | 98.9 | 100.0 | 105.9 | 108.5 | 110.0 | 112.5 | 159.3 | 230.5 |
| Total manufacturing [D]<br>Total, industries manufacturières [D] | 86.7 | 100.0 | 102.8 | 108.5 | 127.7 | 140.6 | 163.2 | 174.5 |
| Food, beverages and tobacco — Aliments, boissons et tabac | ... | 100.0 | 113.6 | 112.8 | 118.7 | 118.8 | 126.2 | 131.8 |
| Textiles, wearing apparel, leather, footwear<br>Textiles, habillement, cuir et chaussures | ... | 100.0 | 86.2 | 95.8 | 104.9 | 109.2 | 160.3 | 140.1 |
| Chemicals, petroleum, rubber and plastic products<br>Prod. chimiques, pétroliers, caoutch. et plast. | ... | 100.0 | 76.9 | 83.2 | 87.6 | 99.1 | 109.8 | 115.5 |
| Basic metals — Métaux de base | ... | 100.0 | 121.4 | 133.5 | 286.3 | 457.1 | 595.2 | 665.7 |
| Electricity, gas and water [E]<br>Electricité, gaz et eau [E] | 98.8 | 100.0 | 98.0 | 91.4 | 96.0 | 97.0 | 131.4 | 143.0 |

| Country or area and industry [ISIC Rev. 3]<br>Pays ou zone et industrie [CITI Rév. 3] | 1999 | 2000 | 2001 | 2002 | 2003 | 2004 | 2005 | 2006 |
|---|---|---|---|---|---|---|---|---|
| **Bangladesh[2] — Bangladesh[2]** | | | | | | | | |
| Total industry [CDE]<br>Total, industrie [CDE] | 92.3 | 100.0 | 107.1 | 112.2 | 119.5 | 128.0 | 138.3 | 152.9 |
| Total mining [C]<br>Total, industries extractives [C] | 85.3 | 100.0 | 112.2 | 117.8 | 126.5 | 136.0 | 144.2 | 157.8 |
| Total manufacturing [D]<br>Total, industries manufacturières [D] | 93.2 | 100.0 | 105.4 | 110.1 | 117.3 | 127.2 | 135.9 | 150.9 |
| Food, beverages and tobacco — Aliments, boissons et tabac | 92.6 | 100.0 | 102.8 | 119.2 | 121.1 | 124.3 | 134.7 | 144.4 |
| Textiles, wearing apparel, leather, footwear<br>Textiles, habillement, cuir et chaussures | 97.5 | 100.0 | 107.5 | 115.8 | 121.5 | 128.7 | 150.0 | 176.0 |
| Chemicals, petroleum, rubber and plastic products<br>Prod. chimiques, pétroliers, caoutch. et plast. | 94.7 | 100.0 | 108.8 | 106.4 | 127.4 | 127.7 | 133.1 | 133.3 |
| Basic metals — Métaux de base | 96.0 | 100.0 | 110.8 | 116.0 | 120.1 | 122.8 | 139.0 | 148.4 |
| Metal products — Produits métalliques | 99.5 | 100.0 | 95.0 | 100.3 | 94.0 | 97.9 | 118.3 | 128.3 |
| Electricity [E]<br>Electricité [E] | 93.8 | 100.0 | 110.3 | 118.2 | 125.3 | 136.2 | 143.7 | 153.1 |
| **Brunei Darussalam — Brunéi Darussalam** | | | | | | | | |
| Total industry [CDE]<br>Total, industrie [CDE] | ... | 100.0 | 100.0 | 104.2 | 107.9 | 107.0 | 104.4 | ... |
| Total mining [C]<br>Total, industries extractives [C] | ... | 100.0 | 99.9 | 103.2 | 107.0 | 106.2 | 103.3 | ... |
| Total manufacturing [D]<br>Total, industries manufacturières [D] | ... | 100.0 | 100.1 | 107.0 | 110.2 | 108.9 | 106.8 | ... |
| Electricity and gas [E]<br>Electricité et gaz [E] | ... | 100.0 | 102.9 | 108.5 | 112.6 | 113.0 | 117.7 | ... |
| **China, Hong Kong SAR — Chine, Hong Kong RAS** | | | | | | | | |
| Total industry [DE][4]<br>Total, industrie [DE][4] | 98.3 | 100.0 | 98.3 | 94.0 | 90.1 | 93.1 | 95.7 | 96.9 |
| Total manufacturing [D]<br>Total, industries manufacturières [D] | 100.6 | 100.0 | 95.6 | 86.2 | 78.3 | 80.6 | 82.6 | 84.4 |
| Food, beverages and tobacco — Aliments, boissons et tabac | 103.3 | 100.0 | 98.3 | 106.4 | 94.1 | 99.4 | 100.6 | 110.3 |
| Textiles and wearing apparel — Textiles et habillement | 96.8 | 100.0 | 99.8 | 92.9 | 89.4 | 87.6 | 83.4 | 82.2 |
| Chemicals and other non-metallic mineral products<br>Produits chimiques et minéraux non-métalliques | 116.8 | 100.0 | 92.2 | 76.3 | 77.3 | 76.0 | 77.3 | 82.9 |
| Basic metals and metal products<br>Métaux de base et produits métalliques | 102.4 | 100.0 | 91.3 | 70.3 | 56.0 | 62.1 | 68.4 | 66.4 |
| Electricity and gas [E]<br>Electricité et gaz [E] | 94.3 | 100.0 | 103.2 | 108.2 | 111.5 | 115.8 | 119.4 | 119.6 |
| **China, Macao SAR — Chine, Macao RAS** | | | | | | | | |
| Total industry [DE]<br>Total, industrie [DE] | 89.9 | 100.0 | 106.2 | 119.0 | 132.6 | 131.6 | 116.8 | 108.5 |
| Total manufacturing [D]<br>Total, industries manufacturières [D] | 87.3 | 100.0 | 105.6 | 122.6 | 143.9 | 135.4 | 105.9 | 104.9 |
| Textiles and wearing apparel — Textiles et habillement | 91.6 | 100.0 | 105.2 | 123.7 | 144.1 | 138.0 | 102.9 | 98.7 |
| Basic metals and other non-metallic products<br>Métaux de base et autre produits non-métalliques | 167.1 | 100.0 | 99.8 | 69.6 | 153.4 | 163.3 | 381.3 | 532.1 |
| Electricity and gas [E]<br>Electricité et gaz [E] | 96.9 | 100.0 | 108.6 | 115.1 | 116.3 | 128.1 | 137.1 | 112.9 |
| **Cyprus — Chypre** | | | | | | | | |
| Total industry [CDE]<br>Total, industrie [CDE] | 95.7 | 100.0 | 99.7 | 99.8 | 107.8 | 109.8 | 110.7 | 111.6 |
| Total mining [C]<br>Total, industries extractives [C] | 96.2 | 100.0 | 95.3 | 106.1 | 110.1 | 115.3 | 115.9 | 116.2 |
| Total manufacturing [D]<br>Total, industries manufacturières [D] | 96.2 | 100.0 | 98.1 | 95.7 | 103.7 | 105.4 | 104.8 | 104.2 |
| Food, beverages and tobacco — Aliments, boissons et tabac | 96.3 | 100.0 | 100.4 | 98.1 | 99.7 | 97.4 | 97.8 | 91.9 |
| Textiles, wearing apparel, leather, footwear<br>Textiles, habillement, cuir et chaussures | 108.9 | 100.0 | 95.7 | 79.1 | 56.3 | 48.1 | 41.6 | 34.2 |
| Chemicals, petroleum, rubber and plastic products<br>Prod. chimiques, pétroliers, caoutch. et plast. | 98.8 | 100.0 | 105.1 | 106.4 | 101.3 | 99.7 | 95.8 | 101.0 |
| Metal products — Produits métalliques | 93.0 | 100.0 | 102.5 | 112.0 | 102.9 | 107.9 | 107.7 | 115.4 |

| Country or area and industry [ISIC Rev. 3]<br>Pays ou zone et industrie [CITI Rév. 3] | 1999 | 2000 | 2001 | 2002 | 2003 | 2004 | 2005 | 2006 |
|---|---|---|---|---|---|---|---|---|
| Electricity, gas and water [E]<br>Electricité, gaz et eau [E] | 93.8 | 100.0 | 107.5 | 116.6 | 125.7 | 129.7 | 136.8 | 143.8 |
| **Georgia — Géorgie** | | | | | | | | |
| Total industry [CDE]<br>Total, industrie [CDE] | ... | 100.0 | 95.0 | 115.2 | 137.9 | 144.6 | 194.5 | 263.2 |
| Total mining [C]<br>Total, industries extractives [C] | ... | 100.0 | 106.9 | 135.8 | 172.7 | 139.7 | 139.8 | 146.4 |
| Total manufacturing [D]<br>Total, industries manufacturières [D] | ... | 100.0 | 97.8 | 131.6 | 162.8 | 177.7 | 249.8 | 349.3 |
| Electricity, gas and water [E]<br>Electricité, gaz et eau [E] | ... | 100.0 | 89.4 | 76.9 | 78.5 | 71.4 | 77.0 | 83.3 |
| **India[8] — Inde[8]** | | | | | | | | |
| Total industry [CDE]<br>Total, industrie [CDE] | 95.3 | 100.0 | 102.7 | 108.7 | 116.2 | 126.0 | 136.2 | 151.7 |
| Total mining [C]<br>Total, industries extractives [C] | 97.2 | 100.0 | 101.2 | 107.1 | 112.8 | 117.7 | 118.9 | 124.9 |
| Total manufacturing [D]<br>Total, industries manufacturières [D] | 94.9 | 100.0 | 102.9 | 109.1 | 117.2 | 127.8 | 139.5 | 156.7 |
| Food, beverages and tobacco — Aliments, boissons et tabac | 95.0 | 100.0 | 98.4 | 110.6 | 111.7 | 116.1 | 127.8 | 140.6 |
| Textiles, wearing apparel, leather, footwear<br>Textiles, habillement, cuir et chaussures | 93.9 | 100.0 | 99.2 | 100.3 | 102.2 | 110.8 | 114.5 | 126.6 |
| Chemicals, petroleum, rubber and plastic products<br>Prod. chimiques, pétroliers, caoutch. et plast. | 92.1 | 100.0 | 105.9 | 110.4 | 118.6 | 132.2 | 141.7 | 156.2 |
| Basic metals — Métaux de base | 98.2 | 100.0 | 104.3 | 113.9 | 124.3 | 131.1 | 151.7 | 186.4 |
| Metal products — Produits métalliques | 96.5 | 100.0 | 99.2 | 109.1 | 125.5 | 141.4 | 155.4 | 177.4 |
| Electricity [E]<br>Electricité [E] | 96.1 | 100.0 | 103.0 | 106.3 | 111.7 | 117.5 | 123.6 | 132.6 |
| **Indonesia — Indonésie** | | | | | | | | |
| Total industry [CDE]<br>Total, industrie [CDE] | 88.7 | 100.0 | 110.5 | 106.6 | 111.1 | 98.9 | 116.4 | 98.3 |
| Total mining [C]<br>Total, industries extractives [C] | 82.3 | 100.0 | 120.3 | 118.9 | 109.6 | 84.0 | 115.2 | 83.4 |
| Total manufacturing [D]<br>Total, industries manufacturières [D] | 96.5 | 100.0 | 98.9 | 91.8 | 113.6 | 117.3 | 118.9 | 116.6 |
| Food, beverages and tobacco — Aliments, boissons et tabac | 100.9 | 100.0 | 99.6 | 97.4 | 110.6 | 118.8 | 142.5 | 157.0 |
| Textiles, wearing apparel, leather, footwear<br>Textiles, habillement, cuir et chaussures | 98.4 | 100.0 | 93.2 | 92.5 | 94.1 | 104.3 | 91.9 | 127.1 |
| Chemicals, petroleum, rubber and plastic products<br>Prod. chimiques, pétroliers, caoutch. et plast. | 97.2 | 100.0 | 102.5 | 102.2 | 111.7 | 126.8 | 166.6 | 187.4 |
| Basic metals — Métaux de base | 81.7 | 100.0 | 102.1 | 89.8 | 70.6 | 75.2 | 73.2 | 89.4 |
| Metal products — Produits métalliques | 70.6 | 100.0 | 123.1 | 141.8 | 175.5 | 210.7 | 220.7 | 237.9 |
| Electricity [E]<br>Electricité [E] | 90.4 | 100.0 | 101.1 | 99.2 | 99.5 | 100.5 | 101.6 | 102.7 |
| **Iran (Islamic Rep. of) — Iran (Rép. islamique d')** | | | | | | | | |
| Total manufacturing [D]<br>Total, industries manufacturières [D] | 96.2 | 100.0 | 103.8 | 107.7 | 111.5 | 115.4 | 119.2 | 123.1 |
| Food and beverages — Aliments et boissons | 94.4 | 100.0 | 96.4 | 114.5 | 126.1 | 130.8 | 144.9 | 156.9 |
| Textiles, wearing apparel, leather, footwear<br>Textiles, habillement, cuir et chaussures | 113.3 | 100.0 | 119.3 | 119.2 | 97.4 | 93.9 | 88.5 | 81.9 |
| Chemicals, rubber and plastic products<br>Produits chimiques, caoutchouc et plastiques | 96.0 | 100.0 | 106.2 | 113.8 | 127.7 | 140.8 | 154.7 | 171.4 |
| Metal products — Produits métalliques | 92.8 | 100.0 | 114.2 | 179.4 | 257.7 | 311.6 | 450.7 | 629.6 |
| **Israel — Israël** | | | | | | | | |
| Total industry [CD]<br>Total, industrie [CD] | 91.0 | 100.0 | 95.1 | 93.2 | 93.0 | 99.4 | 103.1 | 113.9 |
| Total mining [C]<br>Total, industries extractives [C] | 102.4 | 100.0 | 102.0 | 110.0 | 106.7 | 103.7 | 105.9 | 105.6 |
| Total manufacturing [D]<br>Total, industries manufacturières [D] | 90.7 | 100.0 | 94.9 | 92.9 | 92.7 | 99.3 | 103.0 | 114.1 |
| Food, beverages and tobacco — Aliments, boissons et tabac | 99.9 | 100.0 | 98.9 | 97.5 | 95.3 | 96.9 | 97.4 | 99.4 |
| Textiles — Textiles | 105.8 | 100.0 | 91.4 | 87.5 | 84.3 | 84.7 | 85.0 | 88.6 |

| Country or area and industry [ISIC Rev. 3]<br>Pays ou zone et industrie [CITI Rév. 3] | 1999 | 2000 | 2001 | 2002 | 2003 | 2004 | 2005 | 2006 |
|---|---|---|---|---|---|---|---|---|
| Chemicals, petroleum, rubber and plastic products<br>Prod. chimiques, pétroliers, caoutch. et plast. | 96.7 | 100.0 | 104.9 | 119.0 | 125.8 | 138.8 | 147.2 | 178.7 |
| Basic metals — Métaux de base | 98.1 | 100.0 | 92.9 | 84.5 | 75.1 | 80.9 | 82.7 | 82.8 |
| Metal products — Produits métalliques | 90.9 | 100.0 | 94.7 | 91.9 | 90.2 | 92.8 | 96.0 | 106.3 |
| **Japan — Japon** | | | | | | | | |
| Total industry [CDE]<br>Total, industrie [CDE] | 94.7 | 100.0 | 93.6 | 92.5 | 95.4 | 100.5 | 101.7 | 106.5 |
| Total mining [C]<br>Total, industries extractives [C] | 99.2 | 100.0 | 99.6 | 93.6 | 95.5 | 95.4 | 98.6 | 102.9 |
| Total manufacturing [D]<br>Total, industries manufacturières [D] | 94.6 | 100.0 | 93.2 | 92.0 | 95.0 | 100.2 | 101.3 | 106.2 |
| Food, beverages and tobacco — Aliments, boissons et tabac | 99.6 | 100.0 | 99.2 | 98.1 | 98.3 | 96.4 | 95.5 | 94.6 |
| Textiles, wearing apparel, leather, footwear<br>Textiles, habillement, cuir et chaussures | 109.1 | 100.0 | 89.8 | 79.6 | 73.0 | 67.6 | 62.5 | 59.6 |
| Chemicals, petroleum, rubber and plastic products<br>Prod. chimiques, pétroliers, caoutch. et plast. | 98.9 | 100.0 | 99.1 | 98.6 | 100.1 | 101.0 | 101.0 | 99.9 |
| Basic metals — Métaux de base | 91.4 | 100.0 | 96.9 | 98.4 | 101.9 | 104.7 | 105.4 | 108.3 |
| Metal products — Produits métalliques | 90.6 | 100.0 | 89.8 | 90.5 | 96.0 | 105.5 | 108.0 | 118.1 |
| Electricity and gas [E]<br>Electricité et gaz [E] | 96.8 | 100.0 | 100.2 | 101.0 | 102.4 | 105.9 | 109.3 | 111.9 |
| **Jordan — Jordanie** | | | | | | | | |
| Total industry [CDE]<br>Total, industrie [CDE] | 107.9 | 100.0 | 111.8 | 136.7 | 125.0 | 140.0 | 154.3 | 163.3 |
| Total mining [C]<br>.Total, industries extractives [C] | 98.3 | 100.0 | 102.3 | 109.7 | 107.5 | 103.3 | 102.1 | 93.6 |
| Total manufacturing [D]<br>Total, industries manufacturières [D] | 92.8 | 100.0 | 113.6 | 120.3 | 108.6 | 123.7 | 138.0 | 146.8 |
| Food, beverages and tobacco — Aliments, boissons et tabac | 97.3 | 100.0 | 105.7 | 120.1 | 105.2 | 120.4 | 142.2 | 151.7 |
| Textiles, wearing apparel, leather, footwear<br>Textiles, habillement, cuir et chaussures | 111.5 | 100.0 | 77.9 | 78.3 | 72.9 | 86.2 | 82.1 | 88.6 |
| Chemicals, petroleum, rubber and plastic products<br>Prod. chimiques, pétroliers, caoutch. et plast. | 97.8 | 100.0 | 112.3 | 111.9 | 104.9 | 117.5 | 127.6 | 131.4 |
| Basic metals — Métaux de base | 106.4 | 100.0 | 124.6 | 119.0 | 130.1 | 143.0 | 166.3 | 138.6 |
| Electricity [E]<br>Electricité [E] | 95.7 | 100.0 | 102.9 | 108.7 | 107.7 | 121.8 | 131.0 | 153.2 |
| **Kazakhstan** | | | | | | | | |
| Total industry [CDE]<br>Total, industrie [CDE] | ... | 100.0 | 114.0 | 126.0 | 137.0 | 151.0 | 159.0 | 170.0 |
| Total mining [C]<br>Total, industries extractives [C] | ... | 100.0 | 114.0 | 132.0 | 146.0 | 165.0 | 170.0 | 181.0 |
| Total manufacturing [D]<br>Total, industries manufacturières [D] | ... | 100.0 | 115.0 | 124.0 | 134.0 | 146.0 | 158.0 | 169.0 |
| Food, beverages and tobacco — Aliments, boissons et tabac | ... | 100.0 | 108.0 | 118.0 | 130.0 | 142.0 | 165.0 | 174.0 |
| Textiles and wearing apparel — Textiles et habillement | ... | 100.0 | 126.0 | 145.0 | 139.0 | 143.0 | 163.0 | 163.0 |
| Chemicals and chemical products — Produits chimiques | ... | 100.0 | 125.8 | 138.6 | 158.0 | 167.1 | 186.3 | 193.3 |
| Metal and Metal Products, except machinery and equipment<br>Metallurgie et travail des métaux à l'exclusion de la fabrication de machines et d'équipements | ... | 100.0 | 107.0 | 114.0 | 115.0 | 120.0 | 113.0 | 120.0 |
| All machinery and transport equipment<br>Fabrication de machines et de matériel de transport | ... | 100.0 | 122.0 | 140.0 | 159.0 | 219.0 | 233.0 | 223.0 |
| Electricity and gas [E]<br>Electricité et gaz [E] | ... | 100.0 | 109.0 | 111.0 | 122.0 | 125.0 | 130.0 | 135.0 |
| **Korea, Republic of — Corée, République de** | | | | | | | | |
| Total industry [CDE]<br>Total, industrie [CDE] | 85.6 | 100.0 | 100.6 | 108.8 | 114.5 | 126.2 | 134.1 | 147.6 |
| Total mining [C]<br>Total, industries extractives [C] | 101.5 | 100.0 | 99.9 | 103.8 | 103.1 | 100.0 | 93.8 | 92.5 |
| Total manufacturing [D]<br>Total, industries manufacturières [D] | 85.4 | 100.0 | 100.2 | 108.4 | 114.2 | 126.2 | 134.0 | 148.1 |
| Food, beverages and tobacco — Aliments, boissons et tabac | 97.2 | 100.0 | 105.3 | 108.0 | 108.4 | 111.1 | 108.7 | 110.1 |

| Country or area and industry [ISIC Rev. 3] Pays ou zone et industrie [CITI Rév. 3] | 1999 | 2000 | 2001 | 2002 | 2003 | 2004 | 2005 | 2006 |
|---|---|---|---|---|---|---|---|---|
| Textiles, wearing apparel, leather, footwear Textiles, habillement, cuir et chaussures | 99.1 | 100.0 | 91.0 | 87.2 | 77.3 | 71.9 | 66.7 | 64.0 |
| Chemicals, petroleum, rubber and plastic products Prod. chimiques, pétroliers, caoutch. et plast. | 95.1 | 100.0 | 101.2 | 104.3 | 107.9 | 112.4 | 115.6 | 119.7 |
| Basic metals — Métaux de base | 92.2 | 100.0 | 101.4 | 106.4 | 111.9 | 117.6 | 118.0 | 121.3 |
| Metal products — Produits métalliques | 84.9 | 100.0 | 99.0 | 107.4 | 112.6 | 124.6 | 131.7 | 144.7 |
| Electricity and gas [E] Electricité et gaz [E] | 89.2 | 100.0 | 106.9 | 115.0 | 121.3 | 128.4 | 137.5 | 143.5 |
| **Kyrgyzstan — Kirghizistan** | | | | | | | | |
| Total industry [CDE] Total, industrie [CDE] | ... | 100.0 | 105.4 | 93.9 | 122.4 | 136.8 | 124.8 | 104.8 |
| Total mining [C] Total, industries extractives [C] | ... | 100.0 | 100.2 | 101.8 | 100.2 | 147.9 | 143.6 | 131.4 |
| Total manufacturing [D] Total, industries manufacturières [D] | ... | 100.0 | 109.3 | 97.1 | 130.8 | 145.6 | 129.3 | 101.8 |
| Food, beverages and tobacco — Aliments, boissons et tabac | ... | 100.0 | 94.0 | 102.0 | 110.0 | 115.0 | 114.3 | 123.7 |
| Textiles and wearing apparel — Textiles et habillement | ... | 100.0 | 116.0 | 135.0 | 132.0 | 184.0 | 208.6 | 248.4 |
| Chemicals and chemical products — Produits chimiques | ... | 100.0 | 107.0 | 179.0 | 191.0 | 272.9 | 236.9 | 211.7 |
| Metal and Metal Products, except machinery and equipment Metallurgie et travail des métaux à l'exclusion de la fabrication de machines et d'équipements | ... | 100.0 | 114.0 | 79.0 | 99.0 | 94.3 | 71.8 | 46.1 |
| All machinery and transport equipment Fabrication de machines et de matériel de transport | ... | 100.0 | 120.6 | 126.9 | 141.8 | 139.6 | 110.7 | 110.6 |
| Electricity, gas and water [E] Electricité, gaz et eau [E] | ... | 100.0 | 92.2 | 81.6 | 98.6 | 108.1 | 109.4 | 113.2 |
| **Malaysia — Malaisie** | | | | | | | | |
| Total industry [CDE] Total, industrie [CDE] | 84.0 | 100.0 | 95.9 | 100.2 | 109.6 | 122.5 | 127.5 | 133.9 |
| Total mining [C] Total, industries extractives [C] | 100.3 | 100.0 | 102.8 | 104.6 | 110.2 | 117.0 | 117.6 | 114.3 |
| Total manufacturing [D] Total, industries manufacturières [D] | 80.0 | 100.0 | 93.4 | 97.6 | 107.8 | 123.0 | 129.3 | 138.9 |
| Food, beverages and tobacco — Aliments, boissons et tabac | 87.0 | 100.0 | 106.4 | 112.6 | 125.4 | 130.0 | 139.5 | 146.8 |
| Textiles, wearing apparel, leather, footwear Textiles, habillement, cuir et chaussures | 90.7 | 100.0 | 93.6 | 88.5 | 84.9 | 78.3 | 82.1 | 86.3 |
| Chemicals, petroleum, rubber and plastic products Prod. chimiques, pétroliers, caoutch. et plast. | 87.0 | 100.0 | 105.0 | 104.2 | 116.5 | 126.2 | 138.2 | 150.8 |
| Basic metals — Métaux de base | 95.0 | 100.0 | 99.4 | 101.7 | 112.8 | 117.7 | 111.5 | 114.9 |
| Metal products — Produits métalliques | 73.2 | 100.0 | 87.8 | 91.7 | 97.8 | 113.4 | 116.2 | 125.9 |
| Electricity [E] Electricité [E] | 94.2 | 100.0 | 108.6 | 118.7 | 126.7 | 137.2 | 145.0 | 152.4 |
| **Mongolia — Mongolie** | | | | | | | | |
| Total industry [CDE] Total, industrie [CDE] | 96.7 | 100.0 | 108.2 | 127.8 | 134.2 | 151.7 | 144.8 | 151.1 |
| Total mining [C] Total, industries extractives [C] | 94.4 | 100.0 | 103.7 | 104.2 | 103.2 | 123.4 | 137.2 | 132.4 |
| Total manufacturing [D] Total, industries manufacturières [D] | 105.1 | 100.0 | 122.5 | 197.5 | 223.0 | 240.6 | 181.7 | 215.0 |
| Food and beverages — Aliments et boissons | 102.0 | 100.0 | 120.0 | 123.2 | 139.9 | 143.3 | 140.1 | 158.5 |
| Textiles, wearing apparel, leather, footwear Textiles, habillement, cuir et chaussures | 106.5 | 100.0 | 157.3 | 402.0 | 542.7 | 525.8 | 214.6 | 252.9 |
| Chemicals and chemical products — Produits chimiques | 99.6 | 100.0 | 132.3 | 127.5 | 113.9 | 129.8 | 80.1 | 177.0 |
| Basic metals — Métaux de base | 108.8 | 100.0 | 78.0 | 151.6 | 197.4 | 316.8 | 434.7 | 561.0 |
| Electricity and gas [E] Electricité et gaz [E] | 97.6 | 100.0 | 101.6 | 103.3 | 105.1 | 113.6 | 118.4 | 120.7 |
| **Oman** | | | | | | | | |
| Total industry [CDE] Total, industrie [CDE] | 91.4 | 100.0 | 104.0 | 103.6 | 98.9 | 99.2 | 102.9 | ... |
| Total mining [C] Total, industries extractives [C] | 94.7 | 100.0 | 99.7 | 96.2 | 88.3 | 87.0 | 88.6 | ... |

| Country or area and industry [ISIC Rev. 3]<br>Pays ou zone et industrie [CITI Rév. 3] | 1999 | 2000 | 2001 | 2002 | 2003 | 2004 | 2005 | 2006 |
|---|---|---|---|---|---|---|---|---|
| Total manufacturing [D]<br>Total, industries manufacturières [D] | 71.3 | 100.0 | 130.1 | 146.0 | 155.6 | 161.7 | 178.1 | ... |
| Electricity [E]<br>Electricité [E] | 89.3 | 100.0 | 106.8 | 115.2 | 128.6 | 143.9 | 148.8 | ... |
| **Pakistan[1] — Pakistan[1]** | | | | | | | | |
| Total industry [CDE][4]<br>Total, industrie [CDE][4] | 94.3 | 100.0 | 107.5 | 117.6 | 132.7 | 152.6 | 168.3 | 173.2 |
| Total mining [C]<br>Total, industries extractives [C] | 92.1 | 100.0 | 99.2 | 109.8 | 114.1 | 118.1 | 132.8 | 145.7 |
| Total manufacturing [D]<br>Total, industries manufacturières [D] | 89.8 | 100.0 | 103.8 | 111.5 | 132.4 | 156.8 | 173.5 | 177.1 |
| Electricity [E]<br>Electricité [E] | 105.8 | 100.0 | 119.6 | 135.5 | 139.6 | 152.0 | 167.7 | 173.2 |
| **Philippines** | | | | | | | | |
| Total industry [CDE][4]<br>Total, industrie [CDE][4] | 88.1 | 100.0 | 99.4 | 94.6 | 95.3 | 97.1 | 99.3 | 91.2 |
| Total mining [C]<br>Total, industries extractives [C] | 88.6 | 100.0 | 95.8 | 141.1 | 167.2 | 175.5 | 189.4 | 184.2 |
| Total manufacturing [D]<br>Total, industries manufacturières [D] | 87.7 | 100.0 | 98.2 | 92.3 | 92.2 | 93.2 | 95.2 | 85.8 |
| Food, beverages and tobacco — Aliments, boissons et tabac | ... | 100.0 | 96.5 | 94.9 | 87.4 | 85.9 | 92.3 | 92.6 |
| Textiles and wearing apparel<br>Textiles et habillement | ... | 100.0 | 92.4 | 110.9 | 130.4 | 127.2 | 144.5 | 129.3 |
| Chemicals, petroleum, rubber and plastic products<br>Prod. chimiques, pétroliers, caoutch. et plast | ... | 100.0 | 85.7 | 75.2 | 70.7 | 77.3 | 82.8 | 78.4 |
| Basic metals — Métaux de base | ... | 100.0 | 91.3 | 82.5 | 106.8 | 135.4 | 106.8 | 145.7 |
| Metal products — Produits métalliques | ... | 100.0 | 102.2 | 103.0 | 98.9 | 104.3 | 99.7 | 79.3 |
| Electricity and water [E]<br>Electricité et eau [E] | 91.0 | 100.0 | 107.9 | 105.7 | 109.0 | 116.7 | 118.7 | 119.5 |
| **Saudi Arabia** | | | | | | | | |
| Total industry [CDE]<br>Total, industrie [CDE] | 93.9 | 100.0 | 98.3 | 93.7 | 107.3 | 114.4 | 121.6 | ... |
| Total mining [C]<br>Total, industries extractives [C] | 93.3 | 100.0 | 95.6 | 87.6 | 103.6 | 110.4 | 117.0 | ... |
| Total manufacturing [D]<br>Total, industries manufacturières [D] | 95.4 | 100.0 | 104.4 | 108.0 | 115.7 | 123.6 | 132.4 | ... |
| Electricity and water [E]<br>Electricité et eau [E] | 95.5 | 100.0 | 111.1 | 116.3 | 123.5 | 131.5 | 138.6 | ... |
| **Singapore — Singapour** | | | | | | | | |
| Total industry [DE][4]<br>Total, industrie [DE][4] | 87.8 | 100.0 | 90.9 | 98.0 | 100.7 | 112.8 | 123.0 | 135.6 |
| Total manufacturing [D]<br>Total, industries manufacturières [D] | 86.8 | 100.0 | 88.4 | 95.9 | 98.7 | 112.4 | 123.1 | 137.7 |
| Food, beverages and tobacco — Aliments, boissons et tabac | 98.5 | 100.0 | 104.2 | 101.3 | 101.0 | 102.7 | 110.0 | 114.2 |
| Textiles, wearing apparel, leather, footwear<br>Textiles, habillement, cuir et chaussures | 87.0 | 100.0 | 85.5 | 71.5 | 70.0 | 68.0 | 58.0 | 53.0 |
| Chemicals, petroleum, rubber and plastic products<br>Prod. chimiques, pétroliers, caoutch. et plast. | 95.7 | 100.0 | 102.2 | 130.4 | 141.2 | 165.6 | 178.7 | 206.2 |
| Basic metals — Métaux de base | 94.2 | 100.0 | 100.6 | 103.2 | 88.7 | 105.4 | 123.1 | 145.3 |
| Metal products — Produits métalliques | 83.2 | 100.0 | 84.6 | 88.4 | 90.2 | 103.1 | 114.7 | 126.3 |
| Electricity and water [E]<br>Electricité et eau [E] | 93.2 | 100.0 | 104.5 | 109.5 | 111.6 | 115.0 | 122.7 | 124.3 |
| **Sri Lanka — Sri Lanka** | | | | | | | | |
| Total manufacturing [D]<br>Total, industries manufacturières [D] | 98.4 | 100.0 | 103.6 | 108.1 | 108.9 | 112.2 | 116.2 | 120.4 |
| Food, beverages and tobacco — Aliments, boissons et tabac | 95.4 | 100.0 | 102.8 | 107.1 | 113.0 | 117.1 | 123.0 | 130.2 |
| Textiles, wearing apparel, leather, footwear<br>Textiles, habillement, cuir et chaussures | 86.3 | 100.0 | 98.0 | 95.7 | 93.3 | 100.9 | 105.4 | 109.3 |
| Chemicals, petroleum, rubber and plastic products<br>Prod. chimiques, pétroliers, caoutch. et plast. | 91.5 | 100.0 | 103.1 | 104.8 | 109.1 | 114.6 | 130.5 | 140.6 |
| Basic metals — Métaux de base | 97.2 | 100.0 | 101.5 | 105.8 | 109.7 | 119.0 | 126.4 | 134.1 |
| Metal products — Produits métalliques | 93.9 | 100.0 | 102.5 | 105.8 | 108.3 | 111.2 | 114.3 | 118.6 |

| Country or area and industry [ISIC Rev. 3]<br>Pays ou zone et industrie [CITI Rév. 3] | 1999 | 2000 | 2001 | 2002 | 2003 | 2004 | 2005 | 2006 |
|---|---|---|---|---|---|---|---|---|
| **Syrian Arab Republic — Rép. arabe syrienne** | | | | | | | | |
| Total industry [CDE]<br>Total, industrie [CDE] | 100.0 | 100.0 | 103.0 | 109.0 | 102.0 | 92.0 | 89.0 | 89.0 |
| Total mining [C]<br>Total, industries extractives [C] | 104.1 | 100.0 | 96.0 | 98.0 | 100.0 | 102.0 | 104.0 | 106.0 |
| Total manufacturing [D]<br>Total, industries manufacturières [D] | 100.9 | 100.0 | 97.0 | 101.0 | 88.0 | 99.0 | 100.0 | 105.0 |
| Food, beverages and tobacco — Aliments, boissons et tabac | 100.8 | 100.0 | 104.3 | 115.0 | 110.4 | 119.0 | 128.0 | 140.3 |
| Textiles, wearing apparel, leather, footwear<br>Textiles, habillement, cuir et chaussures | 90.6 | 100.0 | 106.4 | 111.6 | 103.9 | 114.2 | 114.6 | 112.2 |
| Chemicals, petroleum, rubber and plastic products<br>Prod. chimiques, pétroliers, caoutch. et plast. | 99.5 | 100.0 | 122.1 | 114.7 | 102.9 | 119.4 | 104.0 | 94.0 |
| Basic metals — Métaux de base | 106.5 | 100.0 | 109.0 | 95.0 | 92.0 | 84.0 | 94.0 | 90.0 |
| Metal products — Produits métalliques | 168.5 | 100.0 | 182.4 | 148.0 | 118.0 | 150.9 | 143.1 | 146.9 |
| Electricity and water [E]<br>Electricité et eau [E] | 92.0 | 100.0 | 106.0 | 111.0 | 117.0 | 127.0 | 143.0 | 148.0 |
| **Tajikistan — Tadjikistan** | | | | | | | | |
| Total industry [CDE]<br>Total, industrie [CDE] | 90.2 | 100.0 | 114.6 | 124.4 | 139.0 | 156.1 | 173.2 | 182.9 |
| Total mining [C]<br>Total, industries extractives [C] | 105.0 | 100.0 | 103.8 | 110.0 | 123.7 | 122.5 | 123.7 | 132.1 |
| Total manufacturing [D]<br>Total, industries manufacturières [D] | 86.1 | 100.0 | 116.7 | 127.8 | 138.9 | 163.9 | 183.3 | 191.7 |
| Electricity, gas and water [E]<br>Electricité, gaz et eau [E] | 112.1 | 100.0 | 103.7 | 112.1 | 119.6 | 116.8 | 122.4 | 129.0 |
| **Thailand — Thaïlande** | | | | | | | | |
| Total manufacturing [D]<br>Total, industries manufacturières [D] | 97.1 | 100.0 | 101.4 | 110.2 | 123.7 | 133.9 | 139.0 | 149.2 |
| **Turkey — Turquie** | | | | | | | | |
| Total industry [CDE]<br>Total, industrie [CDE] | 94.3 | 100.0 | 91.3 | 99.9 | 108.7 | 119.2 | 125.7 | 133.1 |
| Total mining [C]<br>Total, industries extractives [C] | 102.9 | 100.0 | 91.9 | 84.4 | 81.5 | 84.8 | 96.5 | 100.7 |
| Total manufacturing [D]<br>Total, industries manufacturières [D] | 93.9 | 100.0 | 90.5 | 100.4 | 109.7 | 121.1 | 126.9 | 134.0 |
| Food, beverages and tobacco — Aliments, boissons et tabac | 95.7 | 100.0 | 98.6 | 101.9 | 107.3 | 103.3 | 110.3 | 119.6 |
| Textiles, wearing apparel, leather, footwear<br>Textiles, habillement, cuir et chaussures | 91.9 | 100.0 | 94.9 | 104.3 | 106.2 | 106.7 | 93.5 | 92.0 |
| Chemicals, petroleum, rubber and plastic products<br>Prod. chimiques, pétroliers, caoutch. et plast. | 101.1 | 100.0 | 97.5 | 108.6 | 116.1 | 122.5 | 129.2 | 131.2 |
| Basic metals — Métaux de base | 96.4 | 100.0 | 95.0 | 104.6 | 117.0 | 130.6 | 135.0 | 149.3 |
| Metal products — Produits métalliques | 86.8 | 100.0 | 76.7 | 92.4 | 109.3 | 142.7 | 156.5 | 175.8 |
| Electricity, gas and water [E]<br>Electricité, gaz et eau [E] | 93.2 | 100.0 | 98.3 | 103.6 | 112.3 | 120.0 | 129.1 | 140.8 |
| **Turkmenistan — Turkménistan** | | | | | | | | |
| Total industry [CDE]   Total, industrie [CDE | 77.8 | 100.0 | 130.0 | 157.0 | 187.0 | ... | ... | ... |
| **Uzbekistan — Ouzbékistan** | | | | | | | | |
| Total industry [CDE]   Total, industrie [CDE] | 94.0 | 100.0 | 108.1 | 116.7 | 124.0 | 135.7 | 146.0 | ... |
| **Europe — Europe** | | | | | | | | |
| **Albania — Albanie** | | | | | | | | |
| Total industry [CDE]<br>Total, industrie [CDE] | 49.2 | 100.0 | 75.3 | 88.9 | 101.1 | 103.6 | 119.6 | ... |
| Total mining [C]<br>Total, industries extractives [C] | 113.7 | 100.0 | 88.3 | 91.8 | 164.8 | 143.3 | 159.2 | ... |
| Total manufacturing [D]<br>Total, industries manufacturières [D] | 67.0 | 100.0 | 66.9 | 75.9 | 82.1 | 92.3 | 126.0 | ... |
| Electricity, gas and water [E]<br>Electricité, gaz et eau [E] | 116.2 | 100.0 | 77.9 | 102.8 | 116.4 | 102.3 | 86.8 | ... |

| Country or area and industry [ISIC Rev. 3]<br>Pays ou zone et industrie [CITI Rév. 3] | 1999 | 2000 | 2001 | 2002 | 2003 | 2004 | 2005 | 2006 |
|---|---|---|---|---|---|---|---|---|
| **Austria — Autriche** | | | | | | | | |
| Total industry [CDE]<br>Total, industrie [CDE] | 91.9 | 100.0 | 103.0 | 103.8 | 105.9 | 112.6 | 117.3 | 126.9 |
| Total mining [C]<br>Total, industries extractives [C] | 95.6 | 100.0 | 97.6 | 100.7 | 100.2 | 94.6 | 93.0 | 102.3 |
| Total manufacturing [D]<br>Total, industries manufacturières [D] | 91.0 | 100.0 | 101.9 | 101.9 | 104.3 | 111.9 | 116.6 | 126.4 |
| Food, beverages and tobacco — Aliments, boissons et tabac | 96.6 | 100.0 | 101.5 | 104.8 | 104.9 | 106.2 | 108.6 | 113.4 |
| Textiles, wearing apparel, leather, footwear<br>Textiles, habillement, cuir et chaussures | 102.5 | 100.0 | 97.4 | 96.4 | 94.7 | 86.8 | 82.5 | 80.1 |
| Chemicals, petroleum, rubber and plastic products<br>Prod. chimiques, pétroliers, caoutch. et plast. | 92.1 | 100.0 | 103.9 | 97.9 | 101.0 | 107.0 | 114.4 | 126.9 |
| Basic metals — Métaux de base | 90.0 | 100.0 | 106.2 | 107.2 | 107.8 | 117.2 | 122.2 | 131.5 |
| Metal products — Produits métalliques | 89.0 | 100.0 | 102.1 | 102.9 | 105.6 | 118.4 | 125.5 | 137.6 |
| Electricity, gas and water [E]<br>Electricité, gaz et eau [E] | 98.5 | 100.0 | 112.5 | 119.7 | 120.5 | 120.9 | 127.1 | 134.6 |
| **Belarus — Bélarus** | | | | | | | | |
| Total industry [CDE]<br>Total, industrie [CDE] | 92.9 | 100.0 | 106.1 | 111.0 | 118.9 | 137.9 | 152.5 | 169.4 |
| Total mining [C]<br>Total, industries extractives [C] | 105.4 | 100.0 | 111.2 | 114.7 | 125.5 | 136.9 | 147.7 | 151.6 |
| Total manufacturing [D]<br>Total, industries manufacturières [D] | 92.3 | 100.0 | 105.6 | 110.4 | 118.1 | 137.3 | 151.7 | 169.3 |
| Electricity [E]<br>Electricité [E] | 102.7 | 100.0 | 98.9 | 101.9 | 102.8 | 115.8 | 115.0 | 118.5 |
| **Belgium — Belgique** | | | | | | | | |
| Total industry [CDE]<br>Total, industrie [CDE] | 95.3 | 100.0 | 99.6 | 101.0 | 101.7 | 105.2 | 104.8 | 110.0 |
| Total mining [C]<br>Total, industries extractives [C] | 90.7 | 100.0 | 101.0 | 131.9 | 125.9 | 127.4 | 135.2 | 141.6 |
| Total manufacturing [D]<br>Total, industries manufacturières [D] | 94.4 | 100.0 | 99.9 | 100.8 | 101.3 | 105.6 | 103.5 | 108.5 |
| Food, beverages and tobacco — Aliments, boissons et tabac | 96.2 | 100.0 | 103.6 | 108.6 | 112.2 | 117.8 | 119.8 | 124.5 |
| Textiles, wearing apparel, leather, footwear<br>Textiles, habillement, cuir et chaussures | 103.3 | 100.0 | 94.7 | 89.8 | 85.5 | 87.1 | 82.5 | 88.5 |
| Chemicals, petroleum, rubber and plastic products<br>Prod. chimiques, pétroliers, caoutch. et plast. | 90.9 | 100.0 | 97.9 | 104.9 | 110.7 | 116.7 | 111.7 | 114.9 |
| Basic metals — Métaux de base | 94.9 | 100.0 | 88.6 | 89.3 | 91.6 | 83.8 | 69.6 | 72.1 |
| Metal products — Produits métalliques | 96.9 | 100.0 | 104.0 | 100.5 | 97.3 | 104.9 | 106.5 | 114.1 |
| Electricity, gas and water [E]<br>Electricité, gaz et eau [E] | 102.7 | 100.0 | 97.4 | 99.8 | 102.4 | 100.3 | 110.9 | 118.0 |
| **Bulgaria — Bulgarie** | | | | | | | | |
| Total industry [CDE]<br>Total, industrie [CDE] | 92.3 | 100.0 | 102.2 | 106.9 | 122.0 | 142.8 | 152.3 | 161.3 |
| Total mining [C]<br>Total, industries extractives [C] | 97.4 | 100.0 | 91.3 | 90.8 | 97.1 | 117.4 | 117.8 | 119.8 |
| Total manufacturing [D]<br>Total, industries manufacturières [D] | 93.3 | 100.0 | 101.4 | 108.9 | 129.3 | 156.7 | 169.4 | 181.8 |
| Food, beverages and tobacco — Aliments, boissons et tabac | 100.7 | 100.0 | 96.6 | 97.2 | 115.1 | 133.3 | 139.8 | 139.6 |
| Textiles, wearing apparel, leather, footwear<br>Textiles, habillement, cuir et chaussures | 87.7 | 100.0 | 110.5 | 135.6 | 174.5 | 199.7 | 196.6 | 217.5 |
| Chemicals, petroleum, rubber and plastic products<br>Prod. chimiques, pétroliers, caoutch. et plast. | 88.3 | 100.0 | 101.2 | 96.7 | 112.6 | 117.2 | 129.0 | 129.1 |
| Basic metals — Métaux de base | 86.0 | 100.0 | 83.7 | 90.1 | 112.8 | 191.5 | 205.9 | 219.7 |
| Metal products — Produits métalliques | 97.8 | 100.0 | 107.6 | 126.4 | 141.3 | 170.9 | 198.7 | 217.7 |
| Electricity, gas and water [E]<br>Electricité, gaz et eau [E] | 84.6 | 100.0 | 108.4 | 106.9 | 109.9 | 113.1 | 117.2 | 118.8 |
| **Croatia — Croatie** | | | | | | | | |
| Total industry [CDE]<br>Total, industrie [CDE] | 98.3 | 100.0 | 106.0 | 111.8 | 116.3 | 120.6 | 126.7 | 138.9 |

| Country or area and industry [ISIC Rev. 3]<br>Pays ou zone et industrie [CITI Rév. 3] | 1999 | 2000 | 2001 | 2002 | 2003 | 2004 | 2005 | 2006 |
|---|---|---|---|---|---|---|---|---|
| Total mining [C]<br>Total, industries extractives [C] | 98.2 | 100.0 | 102.0 | 119.4 | 122.1 | 118.1 | 114.6 | 125.5 |
| Total manufacturing [D]<br>Total, industries manufacturières [D] | 97.2 | 100.0 | 106.4 | 111.1 | 116.8 | 121.5 | 129.5 | 139.2 |
| Food, beverages and tobacco — Aliments, boissons et tabac | 99.8 | 100.0 | 106.6 | 112.5 | 118.2 | 121.6 | 128.3 | 132.8 |
| Textiles, wearing apparel, leather, footwear<br>Textiles, habillement, cuir et chaussures | 101.4 | 100.0 | 104.4 | 93.9 | 89.1 | 75.3 | 70.2 | 69.1 |
| Chemicals, petroleum, rubber and plastic products<br>Prod. chimiques, pétroliers, caoutch. et plast. | 94.6 | 100.0 | 95.3 | 99.3 | 98.8 | 102.0 | 100.0 | 91.1 |
| Basic metals — Métaux de base | 95.8 | 100.0 | 104.2 | 93.9 | 98.7 | 123.9 | 129.7 | 134.4 |
| Metal products — Produits métalliques | 100.5 | 100.0 | 115.3 | 120.0 | 125.4 | 134.2 | 150.0 | 157.8 |
| Electricity, gas and water [E]<br>Electricité, gaz et eau [E] | 105.0 | 100.0 | 104.8 | 106.6 | 110.1 | 114.7 | 113.5 | 154.9 |
| **Czech Republic — République tchèque** | | | | | | | | |
| Total industry [CDE]<br>Total, industrie [CDE] | 99.1 | 100.0 | 106.7 | 108.7 | 114.7 | 125.7 | 134.0 | 149.0 |
| Total mining [C]<br>Total, industries extractives [C] | 92.5 | 100.0 | 100.8 | 101.7 | 102.0 | 101.4 | 101.9 | 104.5 |
| Total manufacturing [D]<br>Total, industries manufacturières [D] | 99.7 | 100.0 | 107.4 | 109.6 | 115.5 | 127.9 | 137.6 | 154.2 |
| Food, beverages and tobacco — Aliments, boissons et tabac | 104.1 | 100.0 | 102.0 | 103.6 | 103.8 | 102.4 | 98.7 | 99.3 |
| Textiles, wearing apparel, leather, footwear<br>Textiles, habillement, cuir et chaussures | 95.8 | 100.0 | 101.2 | 93.6 | 91.6 | 90.6 | 90.4 | 84.6 |
| Chemicals, petroleum, rubber and plastic products<br>Prod. chimiques, pétroliers, caoutch. et plast. | 102.8 | 100.0 | 107.5 | 110.9 | 118.6 | 131.3 | 143.6 | 155.4 |
| Basic metals — Métaux de base | 117.5 | 100.0 | 101.7 | 98.3 | 110.7 | 120.6 | 112.6 | 123.6 |
| Metal products — Produits métalliques | 93.0 | 100.0 | 110.6 | 117.0 | 124.4 | 145.8 | 164.4 | 196.0 |
| Electricity, gas and water [E]<br>Electricité, gaz et eau [E] | 94.0 | 100.0 | 101.7 | 101.8 | 110.8 | 111.9 | 110.5 | 113.4 |
| **Denmark — Danemark** | | | | | | | | |
| Total industry [CDE]<br>Total, industrie [CDE] | ... | 100.0 | 101.6 | 103.0 | 103.2 | 103.2 | 104.9 | 108.6 |
| Total mining [C]<br>Total, industries extractives [C] | 99.7 | 100.0 | 98.4 | 104.0 | 102.1 | 107.3 | 111.9 | 105.8 |
| Total manufacturing [D]<br>Total, industries manufacturières [D] | 94.9 | 100.0 | 102.0 | 103.0 | 102.3 | 102.0 | 103.8 | 108.1 |
| Food, beverages and tobacco — Aliments, boissons et tabac | 98.3 | 100.0 | 100.0 | 107.5 | 114.2 | 110.8 | 109.7 | 111.0 |
| Textiles, wearing apparel, leather, footwear<br>Textiles, habillement, cuir et chaussures | 97.8 | 100.0 | 90.3 | 85.3 | 81.3 | 67.5 | 65.5 | 67.0 |
| Chemicals, petroleum, rubber and plastic products<br>Prod. chimiques, pétroliers, caoutch. et plast. | 92.5 | 100.0 | 106.9 | 108.7 | 105.9 | 98.6 | 108.9 | 107.6 |
| Basic metals — Métaux de base | 81.4 | 100.0 | 90.7 | 68.6 | 73.4 | 67.8 | 66.4 | 65.6 |
| Metal products — Produits métalliques | 93.9 | 100.0 | 104.7 | 105.9 | 104.2 | 106.7 | 106.9 | 115.8 |
| Electricity and gas [E]<br>Electricité et gaz [E] | ... | 100.0 | 103.7 | 101.9 | 120.5 | 112.3 | 105.6 | 123.2 |
| **Estonia — Estonie** | | | | | | | | |
| Total industry [CDE]<br>Total, industrie [CDE] | 87.3 | 100.0 | 108.9 | 117.8 | 130.7 | 144.4 | 160.3 | 172.0 |
| Total mining [C]<br>Total, industries extractives [C] | 94.8 | 100.0 | 103.6 | 119.6 | 125.8 | 114.7 | 127.7 | 136.7 |
| Total manufacturing [D]<br>Total, industries manufacturières [D] | 85.8 | 100.0 | 110.2 | 119.8 | 132.7 | 148.8 | 166.4 | 180.7 |
| Food, beverages and tobacco — Aliments, boissons et tabac | 93.4 | 100.0 | 109.8 | 112.0 | 114.8 | 120.7 | 127.2 | 135.2 |
| Textiles, wearing apparel, leather, footwear<br>Textiles, habillement, cuir et chaussures | 85.1 | 100.0 | 110.8 | 117.9 | 124.0 | 119.7 | 111.0 | 112.2 |
| Chemicals, rubber and plastic prod.<br>Prod. chimiques, caoutchouc et plastiques | 92.6 | 100.0 | 112.3 | 123.8 | 148.9 | 173.3 | 199.1 | 228.7 |
| Basic metals — Métaux de base | 89.7 | 100.0 | 153.3 | 199.1 | 343.1 | 268.3 | 243.4 | 216.3 |
| Metal products — Produits métalliques | 81.5 | 100.0 | 116.2 | 136.2 | 156.3 | 191.9 | 224.2 | 239.9 |

| Country or area and industry [ISIC Rev. 3]<br>Pays ou zone et industrie [CITI Rév. 3] | 1999 | 2000 | 2001 | 2002 | 2003 | 2004 | 2005 | 2006 |
|---|---|---|---|---|---|---|---|---|
| Electricity and gas [E]<br>Electricité et gaz [E] | 99.5 | 100.0 | 101.2 | 101.8 | 116.3 | 118.7 | 117.5 | 112.8 |
| **Finland — Finlande** | | | | | | | | |
| Total industry [CDE]<br>Total, industrie [CDE] | 89.5 | 100.0 | 100.1 | 102.2 | 103.4 | 109.0 | 109.1 | 117.6 |
| Total mining [C]<br>Total, industries extractives [C] | 128.9 | 100.0 | 120.7 | 131.9 | 132.5 | 116.2 | 152.0 | 188.7 |
| Total manufacturing [D]<br>Total, industries manufacturières [D] | 88.5 | 100.0 | 99.5 | 101.5 | 101.9 | 108.1 | 109.3 | 116.8 |
| Food, beverages and tobacco — Aliments, boissons et tabac | 101.3 | 100.0 | 103.8 | 106.5 | 108.6 | 109.7 | 107.6 | 106.2 |
| Textiles, wearing apparel, leather, footwear<br>Textiles, habillement, cuir et chaussures | 102.2 | 100.0 | 101.9 | 99.8 | 91.5 | 89.6 | 89.3 | 87.5 |
| Chemicals, petroleum, rubber and plastic products<br>Prod. chimiques, pétroliers, caoutch. et plast. | 92.5 | 100.0 | 99.0 | 98.7 | 98.6 | 102.6 | 102.1 | 105.1 |
| Basic metals — Métaux de base | 94.7 | 100.0 | 99.7 | 100.5 | 103.1 | 107.5 | 99.6 | 109.0 |
| Metal products — Produits métalliques | 81.1 | 100.0 | 101.7 | 103.6 | 103.0 | 113.4 | 120.9 | 130.3 |
| Electricity, gas and water [E]<br>Electricité, gaz et eau [E] | 99.1 | 100.0 | 105.6 | 107.0 | 118.8 | 120.3 | 101.0 | 116.1 |
| **France — France** | | | | | | | | |
| Total industry [CDE]<br>Total, industrie [CDE] | 96.1 | 100.0 | 101.3 | 100.0 | 99.6 | 102.1 | 102.3 | 102.8 |
| Total mining [C]<br>Total, industries extractives [C] | 98.2 | 100.0 | 98.9 | 93.9 | 92.7 | 91.9 | 89.5 | 91.9 |
| Total manufacturing [D]<br>Total, industries manufacturières [D] | 95.9 | 100.0 | 101.1 | 99.6 | 98.8 | 101.4 | 101.6 | 102.3 |
| Food, beverages and tobacco — Aliments, boissons et tabac | 102.1 | 100.0 | 100.7 | 103.4 | 102.2 | 102.8 | 102.6 | 102.7 |
| Textiles, wearing apparel, leather, footwear<br>Textiles, habillement, cuir et chaussures | 111.7 | 100.0 | 93.2 | 81.4 | 71.8 | 65.7 | 57.4 | 54.2 |
| Chemicals, petroleum, rubber and plastic products<br>Prod. chimiques, pétroliers, caoutch. et plast. | 95.0 | 100.0 | 102.2 | 102.3 | 105.2 | 108.5 | 110.4 | 112.2 |
| Basic metals — Métaux de base | 93.4 | 100.0 | 97.8 | 95.7 | 92.7 | 95.0 | 91.1 | 93.5 |
| Metal products — Produits métalliques | 93.3 | 100.0 | 102.4 | 100.8 | 99.8 | 103.5 | 104.4 | 105.4 |
| Electricity, gas and water [E]<br>Electricité, gaz et eau [E] | 97.3 | 100.0 | 103.2 | 103.2 | 106.1 | 108.1 | 108.3 | 107.1 |
| **Germany — Allemagne** | | | | | | | | |
| Total industry [CDE]<br>Total, industrie [CDE] | 94.7 | 100.0 | 100.1 | 99.1 | 99.5 | 102.5 | 106.0 | 112.2 |
| Total mining [C]<br>Total, industries extractives [C] | 107.5 | 100.0 | 93.4 | 92.0 | 91.2 | 88.3 | 87.0 | 84.2 |
| Total manufacturing [D]<br>Total, industries manufacturières [D] | 94.1 | 100.0 | 100.4 | 99.3 | 99.5 | 102.7 | 106.5 | 113.3 |
| Food, beverages and tobacco — Aliments, boissons et tabac | 97.8 | 100.0 | 99.3 | 99.9 | 99.7 | 100.5 | 104.7 | 106.6 |
| Textiles, wearing apparel, leather, footwear<br>Textiles, habillement, cuir et chaussures | 102.8 | 100.0 | 95.7 | 87.9 | 81.7 | 79.1 | 75.0 | 71.8 |
| Chemicals, petroleum, rubber and plastic products<br>Prod. chimiques, pétroliers, caoutch. et plast. | 96.9 | 100.0 | 98.4 | 100.9 | 101.4 | 104.5 | 108.6 | 112.8 |
| Basic metals — Métaux de base | 92.4 | 100.0 | 101.1 | 101.9 | 99.9 | 103.7 | 104.6 | 111.7 |
| Metal products — Produits métalliques | 91.2 | 100.0 | 102.6 | 101.2 | 102.3 | 106.7 | 112.0 | 121.7 |
| Electricity and gas [E]<br>Electricité et gaz [E] | 98.8 | 100.0 | 98.2 | 98.5 | 102.1 | 104.7 | 104.7 | 105.9 |
| **Greece — Grèce** | | | | | | | | |
| Total industry [CDE]<br>Total, industrie [CDE] | 93.2 | 100.0 | 98.2 | 99.0 | 99.3 | 100.5 | 99.4 | 100.1 |
| Total mining [C]<br>Total, industries extractives [C] | 88.2 | 100.0 | 102.4 | 112.3 | 106.5 | 106.6 | 100.9 | 98.0 |
| Total manufacturing [D]<br>Total, industries manufacturières [D] | 95.1 | 100.0 | 97.5 | 97.4 | 97.0 | 98.1 | 97.4 | 98.2 |
| Food, beverages and tobacco — Aliments, boissons et tabac | 98.4 | 100.0 | 101.7 | 102.9 | 100.8 | 106.8 | 105.2 | 106.7 |
| Textiles, wearing apparel, leather, footwear<br>Textiles, habillement, cuir et chaussures | 99.9 | 100.0 | 93.3 | 88.8 | 86.5 | 80.0 | 67.7 | 59.6 |

| Country or area and industry [ISIC Rev. 3] Pays ou zone et industrie [CITI Rév. 3] | 1999 | 2000 | 2001 | 2002 | 2003 | 2004 | 2005 | 2006 |
|---|---|---|---|---|---|---|---|---|
| Chemicals, petroleum, rubber and plastic products Prod. chimiques, pétroliers, caoutch. et plast. | 95.3 | 100.0 | 101.0 | 104.2 | 105.2 | 107.1 | 108.2 | 106.9 |
| Basic metals — Métaux de base | 87.0 | 100.0 | 103.8 | 110.9 | 109.2 | 114.8 | 116.8 | 120.2 |
| Metal products — Produits métalliques | 94.0 | 100.0 | 91.0 | 87.2 | 88.9 | 89.7 | 90.1 | 94.4 |
| Electricity and gas [E] Electricité et gaz [E] | 89.5 | 100.0 | 99.2 | 100.8 | 108.1 | 109.6 | 110.6 | 109.9 |
| **Hungary — Hongrie** | | | | | | | | |
| Total industry [CDE] Total, industrie [CDE] | 84.6 | 100.0 | 103.9 | 107.3 | 114.4 | 122.9 | 131.6 | 145.1 |
| Total mining [C] Total, industries extractives [C] | 110.2 | 100.0 | 116.4 | 105.4 | 101.8 | 111.9 | 108.2 | 125.6 |
| Total manufacturing [D] Total, industries manufacturières [D] | 82.9 | 100.0 | 104.2 | 107.9 | 115.5 | 125.3 | 134.8 | 149.5 |
| Food, beverages and tobacco — Aliments, boissons et tabac | 94.3 | 100.0 | 99.7 | 101.1 | 99.9 | 95.9 | 90.9 | 92.0 |
| Textiles, wearing apparel, leather, footwear Textiles, habillement, cuir et chaussures | 91.5 | 100.0 | 102.9 | 97.8 | 88.8 | 83.5 | 75.4 | 76.9 |
| Chemicals, petroleum, rubber and plastic products Prod. chimiques, pétroliers, caoutch. et plast. | 93.1 | 100.0 | 101.0 | 104.7 | 107.0 | 114.1 | 122.1 | 127.3 |
| Basic metals — Métaux de base | 85.8 | 100.0 | 96.6 | 100.7 | 108.9 | 116.6 | 111.3 | 127.7 |
| Metal products — Produits métalliques | 76.6 | 100.0 | 114.7 | 121.6 | 129.1 | 145.8 | 160.7 | 185.9 |
| Electricity and gas [E] Electricité et gaz [E] | 102.7 | 100.0 | 100.4 | 104.3 | 108.6 | 107.7 | 108.3 | 109.3 |
| **Ireland — Irlande** | | | | | | | | |
| Total industry [CDE] Total, industrie [CDE] | 86.6 | 100.0 | 110.1 | 118.0 | 123.5 | 123.9 | 127.6 | 134.1 |
| Total mining [C] Total, industries extractives [C] | 81.0 | 100.0 | 99.9 | 95.0 | 115.7 | 113.2 | 112.8 | 123.0 |
| Total manufacturing [D] Total, industries manufacturières [D] | 86.4 | 100.0 | 110.4 | 118.7 | 124.1 | 124.3 | 128.2 | 135.0 |
| Food, beverages and tobacco — Aliments, boissons et tabac | 94.9 | 100.0 | 106.5 | 110.7 | 114.8 | 120.6 | 122.1 | 123.0 |
| Textiles, wearing apparel, leather, footwear Textiles, habillement, cuir et chaussures | 124.6 | 100.0 | 104.9 | 73.4 | 65.1 | 63.6 | 54.0 | 44.5 |
| Chemicals, rubber and plastic prod. Prod. chimiques, caoutchouc et plastiques | 88.2 | 100.0 | 121.4 | 149.7 | 156.0 | 141.9 | 142.5 | 147.7 |
| Basic metals — Métaux de base | 97.2 | 100.0 | 89.5 | 88.1 | 84.3 | 80.0 | 91.2 | 95.3 |
| Metal products — Produits métalliques | 78.6 | 100.0 | 106.3 | 100.7 | 106.2 | 111.9 | 118.4 | 127.0 |
| Electricity, gas and water [E] Electricité, gaz et eau [E] | 95.0 | 100.0 | 106.5 | 110.0 | 113.2 | 117.8 | 119.8 | 120.6 |
| **Italy — Italie** | | | | | | | | |
| Total industry [CDE] Total, industrie [CDE] | 96.9 | 100.0 | 99.2 | 97.9 | 96.9 | 97.8 | 96.0 | 98.1 |
| Total mining [C] Total, industries extractives [C] | 109.6 | 100.0 | 92.3 | 107.9 | 110.0 | 107.7 | 116.0 | 112.5 |
| Total manufacturing [D] Total, industries manufacturières [D] | 97.1 | 100.0 | 99.2 | 97.3 | 95.6 | 96.3 | 93.9 | 96.1 |
| Food, beverages and tobacco — Aliments, boissons et tabac | 97.9 | 100.0 | 103.7 | 104.9 | 107.0 | 106.6 | 107.5 | 107.9 |
| Textiles, wearing apparel, leather, footwear Textiles, habillement, cuir et chaussures | 99.6 | 100.0 | 99.6 | 92.3 | 88.9 | 85.3 | 78.3 | 77.8 |
| Chemicals, petroleum, rubber and plastic products Prod. chimiques, pétroliers, caoutch. et plast. | 97.9 | 100.0 | 98.1 | 98.9 | 97.9 | 99.3 | 97.7 | 100.0 |
| Basic metals — Métaux de base | 93.4 | 100.0 | 96.0 | 94.9 | 96.2 | 100.6 | 101.1 | 107.3 |
| Metal products — Produits métalliques | 96.3 | 100.0 | 98.4 | 95.6 | 92.8 | 93.6 | 90.9 | 95.4 |
| Electricity and gas [E] Electricité et gaz [E] | 94.2 | 100.0 | 100.6 | 102.0 | 107.2 | 111.2 | 113.8 | 115.7 |
| **Latvia — Lettonie** | | | | | | | | |
| Total industry [CDE] Total, industrie [CDE] | 96.9 | 100.0 | 106.9 | 113.1 | 120.5 | 127.7 | 134.9 | 141.4 |
| Total mining [C] Total, industries extractives [C] | 91.8 | 100.0 | 104.8 | 114.3 | 120.4 | 133.6 | 167.7 | 183.3 |
| Total manufacturing [D] Total, industries manufacturières [D] | 95.6 | 100.0 | 107.5 | 114.2 | 123.2 | 130.8 | 139.3 | 146.0 |

| Country or area and industry [ISIC Rev. 3]<br>Pays ou zone et industrie [CITI Rév. 3] | 1999 | 2000 | 2001 | 2002 | 2003 | 2004 | 2005 | 2006 |
|---|---|---|---|---|---|---|---|---|
| Food, beverages and tobacco — Aliments, boissons et tabac | 102.1 | 100.0 | 105.2 | 111.3 | 118.1 | 125.7 | 132.0 | 138.3 |
| Textiles, wearing apparel, leather, footwear<br>Textiles, habillement, cuir et chaussures | 91.1 | 100.0 | 103.8 | 103.5 | 99.9 | 99.0 | 107.4 | 117.9 |
| Chemicals, rubber and plastic prod.<br>Prod. chimiques, caoutchouc et plastiques | 116.6 | 100.0 | 112.2 | 129.6 | 123.2 | 145.8 | 168.6 | 203.0 |
| Basic metals — Métaux de base | 100.0 | 100.0 | 116.6 | 114.6 | 140.1 | 151.5 | 143.9 | 148.0 |
| Metal products — Produits métalliques | 81.8 | 100.0 | 108.2 | 116.5 | 136.7 | 147.1 | 157.4 | 165.5 |
| Electricity, gas and water [E]<br>Electricité, gaz et eau [E] | 103.0 | 100.0 | 105.4 | 110.0 | 113.1 | 118.8 | 122.3 | 127.1 |
| **Lithuania — Lituanie** | | | | | | | | |
| Total industry [CDE]<br>Total, industrie [CDE] | 95.0 | 100.0 | 116.0 | 119.5 | 138.8 | 153.9 | 164.8 | 176.9 |
| Total mining [C]<br>Total, industries extractives [C] | 89.4 | 100.0 | 132.8 | 126.6 | 137.2 | 126.8 | 116.8 | 115.5 |
| Total manufacturing [D]<br>Total, industries manufacturières [D] | 91.9 | 100.0 | 115.8 | 119.1 | 135.9 | 152.0 | 165.1 | 168.7 |
| Food, beverages and tobacco — Aliments, boissons et tabac | 93.7 | 100.0 | 102.3 | 100.4 | 109.8 | 114.2 | 124.9 | 140.9 |
| Textiles, wearing apparel, leather, footwear<br>Textiles, habillement, cuir et chaussures | 92.0 | 100.0 | 109.6 | 109.0 | 105.7 | 104.6 | 100.2 | 107.7 |
| Chemicals, petroleum, rubber and plastic products<br>Prod. chimiques, pétroliers, caouth. et plast. | 99.4 | 100.0 | 126.9 | 132.3 | 152.0 | 175.0 | 194.7 | 209.7 |
| Basic metals — Métaux de base | 67.3 | 100.0 | 103.7 | 82.5 | 60.8 | 47.3 | 58.9 | 50.1 |
| Metal products — Produits métalliques | 101.0 | 100.0 | 115.2 | 123.2 | 145.5 | 179.1 | 207.1 | 256.8 |
| Electricity, gas and water [E]<br>Electricité, gaz et eau [E] | 117.5 | 100.0 | 115.1 | 121.3 | 157.3 | 168.8 | 168.7 | 179.4 |
| **Luxembourg — Luxembourg** | | | | | | | | |
| Total industry [CDE]<br>Total, industrie [CDE] | 95.2 | 100.0 | 103.5 | 106.0 | 109.8 | 114.1 | 114.8 | 117.3 |
| Total mining [C]<br>Total, industries extractives [C] | 99.1 | 100.0 | 101.0 | 91.9 | 81.5 | 80.0 | 78.7 | 61.7 |
| Total manufacturing [D]<br>Total, industries manufacturières [D] | 95.2 | 100.0 | 102.5 | 104.3 | 108.6 | 113.5 | 115.5 | 118.2 |
| Food and beverages — Aliments et boissons | 99.1 | 100.0 | 114.1 | 116.3 | 113.6 | 118.4 | 126.4 | 117.0 |
| Textiles, wearing apparel, leather, footwear<br>Textiles, habillement, cuir et chaussures | 93.1 | 100.0 | 102.1 | 104.2 | 108.5 | 108.7 | 114.4 | 116.8 |
| Chemicals, rubber and plastic products<br>Produits chimiques, caoutchouc et plastiques | 93.0 | 100.0 | 107.6 | 116.6 | 124.4 | 130.8 | 134.7 | 135.1 |
| Basic metals — Métaux de base | 94.7 | 100.0 | 99.0 | 95.9 | 98.1 | 102.2 | 91.8 | 107.2 |
| Metal products — Produits métalliques | 99.7 | 100.0 | 96.1 | 95.2 | 97.9 | 101.9 | 108.6 | 111.0 |
| Electricity and gas [E]<br>Electricité et gaz [E] | 93.4 | 100.0 | 108.8 | 115.8 | 119.9 | 121.4 | 120.4 | 118.4 |
| **Malta — Malte** | | | | | | | | |
| Total industry [CDE]<br>Total, industrie [CDE] | 88.1 | 100.0 | 91.9 | ... | ... | ... | ... | ... |
| Total mining [C]<br>Total, industries extractives [C] | 74.6 | 100.0 | 101.9 | ... | ... | ... | ... | ... |
| Total manufacturing [D]<br>Total, industries manufacturières [D] | 87.4 | 100.0 | 90.8 | ... | ... | ... | ... | ... |
| Food, beverages and tobacco — Aliments, boissons et tabac | 97.1 | 100.0 | 98.5 | ... | ... | ... | ... | ... |
| Textiles, wearing apparel, leather, footwear<br>Textiles, habillement, cuir et chaussures | 100.7 | 100.0 | 103.7 | ... | ... | ... | ... | ... |
| Chemicals, petroleum, rubber and plastic products<br>Prod. chimiques, pétroliers, caouth. et plast. | 115.4 | 100.0 | 89.5 | ... | ... | ... | ... | ... |
| Metal products — Produits métalliques | 91.1 | 100.0 | 94.9 | ... | ... | ... | ... | ... |
| Electricity and water [E]<br>Electricité et eau [E] | 96.5 | 100.0 | 103.2 | ... | ... | ... | ... | ... |
| **Moldova** | | | | | | | | |
| Total industry [CDE]<br>Total, industrie [CDE] | 92.9 | 100.0 | 113.7 | 126.0 | 145.7 | 157.6 | 168.7 | 157.1 |
| Total mining [C]<br>Total, industries extractives [C] | 102.3 | 100.0 | 109.0 | 135.3 | 170.7 | 211.0 | 220.0 | 269.5 |

| Country or area and industry [ISIC Rev. 3]<br>Pays ou zone et industrie [CITI Rév. 3] | 1999 | 2000 | 2001 | 2002 | 2003 | 2004 | 2005 | 2006 |
|---|---|---|---|---|---|---|---|---|
| Total manufacturing [D]<br>Total, industries manufacturières [D] | 84.9 | 100.0 | 115.1 | 130.4 | 153.9 | 168.2 | 179.3 | 164.1 |
| Food, beverages and tobacco — Aliments, boissons et tabac | 96.5 | 100.0 | 108.6 | 105.1 | 119.3 | 122.9 | 126.5 | 101.3 |
| Textiles, wearing apparel, leather, footwear<br>Textiles, habillement, cuir et chaussures | 77.5 | 100.0 | 119.6 | 136.8 | 150.1 | 174.5 | 178.8 | 200.0 |
| Chemicals, petroleum, rubber and plastic products<br>Prod. chimiques, pétroliers, caoutchouc. et plastiques. | 77.1 | 100.0 | 119.6 | 164.5 | 196.5 | 222.1 | 268.0 | 268.5 |
| Basic metals — Métaux de base | 99.0 | 100.0 | 131.2 | 102.1 | 119.0 | 132.0 | 196.4 | 222.9 |
| Metal products — Produits métalliques | 97.5 | 100.0 | 103.6 | 128.9 | 166.4 | 192.7 | 155.5 | 170.4 |
| Electricity and gas [E]<br>Electricité et gaz [E] | 140.8 | 100.0 | 109.0 | 107.0 | 109.8 | 109.9 | 121.8 | 128.5 |
| **Netherlands — Pays-Bas** | | | | | | | | |
| Total industry [CDE]<br>Total, industrie [CDE] | 94.9 | 100.0 | 101.0 | 101.9 | 100.5 | 104.6 | 103.5 | 104.7 |
| Total mining [C]<br>Total, industries extractives [C] | 104.8 | 100.0 | 107.1 | 107.5 | 104.2 | 115.5 | 105.4 | 101.5 |
| Total manufacturing [D]<br>Total, industries manufacturières [D] | 93.7 | 100.0 | 99.8 | 99.9 | 98.8 | 102.2 | 102.2 | 104.5 |
| Food, beverages and tobacco — Aliments, boissons et tabac | 97.7 | 100.0 | 100.1 | 102.0 | 101.6 | 102.9 | 104.0 | 106.4 |
| Textiles, wearing apparel, leather, footwear<br>Textiles, habillement, cuir et chaussures | 95.7 | 100.0 | 98.3 | 94.0 | 91.9 | 80.2 | 77.4 | 80.1 |
| Chemicals, petroleum, rubber and plastic products<br>Prod. chimiques, pétroliers, caoutch. et plast. | 94.4 | 100.0 | 104.1 | 114.8 | 114.8 | 121.1 | 120.6 | 124.0 |
| Basic metals — Métaux de base | 95.2 | 100.0 | 98.8 | 101.4 | 105.0 | 118.7 | 118.7 | 117.2 |
| Metal products — Produits métalliques | 86.8 | 100.0 | 96.3 | 90.0 | 88.8 | 93.2 | 92.4 | 95.8 |
| Electricity, gas and water [E]<br>Electricité, gaz et eau [E] | 96.7 | 100.0 | 104.0 | 115.7 | 113.9 | 114.4 | 115.4 | 115.5 |
| **Norway — Norvège** | | | | | | | | |
| Total industry [CDE]<br>Total, industrie [CDE] | 96.8 | 100.0 | 98.6 | 99.3 | 95.3 | 97.5 | 96.7 | 94.4 |
| Total mining [C][9]<br>Total, industries extractives [C][9] | 94.7 | 100.0 | 103.0 | 101.3 | 99.7 | 98.4 | 95.3 | 90.6 |
| Total manufacturing [D]<br>Total, industries manufacturières [D] | 102.8 | 100.0 | 98.7 | 97.9 | 93.7 | 95.4 | 97.9 | 102.3 |
| Food, beverages and tobacco — Aliments, boissons et tabac | 101.7 | 100.0 | 98.8 | 97.1 | 93.2 | 93.6 | 90.6 | 91.6 |
| Textiles, wearing apparel, leather, footwear<br>Textiles, habillement, cuir et chaussures | 109.0 | 100.0 | 94.7 | 86.8 | 74.6 | 71.9 | 72.2 | 79.5 |
| Chemicals, petroleum, rubber and plastic products<br>Prod. chimiques, pétroliers, caoutch. et plast. | 101.6 | 100.0 | 99.7 | 98.7 | 98.0 | 100.8 | 103.8 | 104.9 |
| Basic metals — Métaux de base | 98.8 | 100.0 | 95.5 | 93.6 | 93.9 | 103.7 | 102.5 | 104.1 |
| Metal products — Produits métalliques | 105.2 | 100.0 | 100.0 | 101.8 | 95.0 | 95.4 | 100.8 | 111.7 |
| Electricity and gas [E]<br>Electricité et gaz [E] | 85.8 | 100.0 | 85.1 | 90.7 | 75.0 | 76.2 | 95.0 | 83.9 |
| **Poland — Pologne** | | | | | | | | |
| Total industry [CDE]<br>Total, industrie [CDE] | 93.0 | 100.0 | 100.4 | 101.8 | 110.7 | 124.8 | 129.9 | 145.5 |
| Total mining [C]<br>Total, industries extractives [C] | 101.3 | 100.0 | 94.9 | 92.0 | 90.3 | 93.0 | 90.4 | 91.7 |
| Total manufacturing [D]<br>Total, industries manufacturières [D] | 92.6 | 100.0 | 99.9 | 101.7 | 112.4 | 128.8 | 134.7 | 153.1 |
| Food, beverages and tobacco — Aliments, boissons et tabac | 100.0 | 100.0 | 102.5 | 106.1 | 111.6 | 118.3 | 123.7 | 132.1 |
| Textiles, wearing apparel, leather, footwear<br>Textiles, habillement, cuir et chaussures | 101.0 | 100.0 | 96.3 | 95.6 | 95.0 | 95.4 | 88.1 | 92.3 |
| Chemicals, petroleum, rubber and plastic products<br>Prod. chimiques, pétroliers, caoutch. et plast. | 89.6 | 100.0 | 103.8 | 108.1 | 122.2 | 135.4 | 140.4 | 157.8 |
| Basic metals — Métaux de base | 91.2 | 100.0 | 84.1 | 80.5 | 83.8 | 100.7 | 94.0 | 107.8 |
| Metal products — Produits métalliques | 92.0 | 100.0 | 101.0 | 103.7 | 119.1 | 144.9 | 161.2 | 190.6 |
| Electricity, gas and water [E]<br>Electricité, gaz et eau [E] | 91.6 | 100.0 | 108.1 | 107.9 | 108.4 | 109.6 | 112.9 | 113.1 |

| Country or area and industry [ISIC Rev. 3]<br>Pays ou zone et industrie [CITI Rév. 3] | 1999 | 2000 | 2001 | 2002 | 2003 | 2004 | 2005 | 2006 |
|---|---|---|---|---|---|---|---|---|
| **Portugal — Portugal** | | | | | | | | |
| Total industry [CDE]<br>Total, industrie [CDE] | 99.6 | 100.0 | 103.1 | 102.6 | 102.7 | 100.0 | 100.3 | 103.1 |
| Total mining [C]<br>Total, industries extractives [C] | 98.5 | 100.0 | 101.9 | 96.5 | 87.4 | 91.1 | 89.1 | 80.3 |
| Total manufacturing [D]<br>Total, industries manufacturières [D] | 99.7 | 100.0 | 102.3 | 102.7 | 102.2 | 101.4 | 99.8 | 102.1 |
| Food, beverages and tobacco — Aliments, boissons et tabac | 97.3 | 100.0 | 102.0 | 104.9 | 104.4 | 107.0 | 106.8 | 110.7 |
| Textiles, wearing apparel, leather, footwear<br>Textiles, habillement, cuir et chaussures | 107.6 | 100.0 | 100.8 | 95.6 | 88.1 | 81.8 | 74.2 | 70.1 |
| Chemicals, petroleum, rubber and plastic products<br>Prod. chimiques, pétroliers, caoutch. et plast. | 101.8 | 100.0 | 98.6 | 103.9 | 106.9 | 106.9 | 110.2 | 111.6 |
| Basic metals — Métaux de base | 101.8 | 100.0 | 92.4 | 93.1 | 91.9 | 94.5 | 90.7 | 99.0 |
| Metal products — Produits métalliques | 102.2 | 100.0 | 105.2 | 104.3 | 101.6 | 99.8 | 98.7 | 104.8 |
| Electricity and gas [E]<br>Electricité et gaz [E] | 99.1 | 100.0 | 109.0 | 103.3 | 108.9 | 91.2 | 104.1 | 113.8 |
| **Romania — Roumanie** | | | | | | | | |
| Total industry [CDE]<br>Total, industrie [CDE] | 93.3 | 100.0 | 108.5 | 113.4 | 117.2 | 122.5 | 125.4 | 135.0 |
| Total mining [C]<br>Total, industries extractives [C] | 95.4 | 100.0 | 105.8 | 100.2 | 99.5 | 101.7 | 101.0 | 103.7 |
| Total manufacturing [D]<br>Total, industries manufacturières [D] | 92.4 | 100.0 | 110.1 | 117.1 | 121.8 | 128.5 | 132.3 | 143.7 |
| Food, beverages and tobacco — Aliments, boissons et tabac | 89.8 | 100.0 | 120.8 | 134.6 | 141.5 | 134.4 | 139.6 | 161.8 |
| Textiles, wearing apparel, leather, footwear<br>Textiles, habillement, cuir et chaussures | 89.3 | 100.0 | 110.8 | 115.6 | 130.3 | 127.0 | 110.7 | 101.7 |
| Chemicals, petroleum, rubber and plastic products<br>Prod. chimiques, pétroliers, caoutch. et plast. | 90.1 | 100.0 | 102.8 | 111.8 | 116.5 | 136.6 | 142.3 | 149.6 |
| Basic metals — Métaux de base | 78.4 | 100.0 | 113.0 | 137.5 | 111.2 | 126.6 | 128.9 | 130.1 |
| Metal products — Produits métalliques | 109.7 | 100.0 | 107.0 | 108.4 | 114.1 | 121.8 | 127.1 | 141:0 |
| Electricity, gas and water [E]<br>Electricité, gaz et eau [E] | 100.3 | 100.0 | 96.9 | 94.2 | 95.7 | 92.5 | 91.4 | 94.9 |
| **Russian Federation — Fédération de Russie** | | | | | | | | |
| Total industry [CDE]<br>Total, industrie [CDE] | 91.9 | 100.0 | 102.9 | 106.2 | 115.6 | 125.2 | 130.2 | 135.3 |
| Total mining [C]<br>Total, industries extractives [C] | 94.0 | 100.0 | 106.0 | 113.1 | 123.0 | 131.3 | 133.0 | 136.0 |
| Total manufacturing [D]<br>Total, industries manufacturières [D] | 90.1 | 100.0 | 102.0 | 103.1 | 113.7 | 125.6 | 132.7 | 138.6 |
| Food, beverages and tobacco — Aliments, boissons et tabac | 96.6 | 100.0 | 108.3 | 116.3 | 125.5 | 131.6 | 137.2 | 144.7 |
| Textiles, wearing apparel, leather, footwear<br>Textiles, habillement, cuir et chaussures | 82.4 | 100.0 | 108.9 | 109.2 | 112.8 | 109.7 | 108.1 | 117.7 |
| Chemicals, petroleum, rubber and plastic products<br>Prod. chimiques, pétroliers, caoutch. et plast. | 89.9 | 100.0 | 101.3 | 103.1 | 107.5 | 113.8 | 118.2 | 123.6 |
| Basic metals — Métaux de base | 86.7 | 100.0 | 101.8 | 106.8 | 114.5 | 118.3 | 120.9 | 130.0 |
| Metal products — Produits métalliques | 89.1 | 100.0 | 101.3 | 96.5 | 113.8 | 132.8 | 141.0 | 147.7 |
| Electricity and gas [E]<br>Electricité et gaz [E] | 96.1 | 100.0 | 101.4 | 106.3 | 109.8 | 111.3 | 112.5 | 117.3 |
| **Serbia and Montenegro — Serbie-et-Monténégro** | | | | | | | | |
| Total industry [CDE]<br>Total, industrie [CDE] | 89.8 | 100.0 | 100.1 | 102.0 | 99.2 | 106.8 | 107.3 | 112.4 |
| Total mining [C]<br>Total, industries extractives [C] | 91.7 | 100.0 | 87.3 | 89.1 | 90.2 | 89.1 | 90.9 | 94.1 |
| Total manufacturing [D]<br>Total, industries manufacturières [D] | 87.3 | 100.0 | 100.8 | 103.8 | 99.2 | 109.1 | 108.2 | 114.0 |
| Food, beverages and tobacco — Aliments, boissons et tabac | 99.2 | 100.0 | 97.3 | 105.2 | 103.0 | 106.7 | 112.8 | 120.3 |
| Textiles, wearing apparel, leather, footwear<br>Textiles, habillement, cuir et chaussures | 85.1 | 100.0 | 101.5 | 81.3 | 57.8 | 54.7 | 50.3 | 48.7 |
| Chemicals, petroleum, rubber and plastic products<br>Prod. chimiques, pétroliers, caoutch. et plast. | 88.3 | 100.0 | 117.0 | 122.0 | 132.2 | 153.0 | 159.5 | 167.9 |

| Country or area and industry [ISIC Rev. 3]<br>Pays ou zone et industrie [CITI Rév. 3] | 1999 | 2000 | 2001 | 2002 | 2003 | 2004 | 2005 | 2006 |
|---|---|---|---|---|---|---|---|---|
| Basic metals — Métaux de base | 74.0 | 100.0 | 97.3 | 103.3 | 105.3 | 137.8 | 168.8 | 208.5 |
| Metal products — Produits métalliques | 84.9 | 100.0 | 89.0 | 94.6 | 84.3 | 95.8 | 88.1 | 83.9 |
| Electricity, gas and water [E]<br>Electricité, gaz et eau [E] | 98.5 | 100.0 | 100.7 | 98.6 | 101.8 | 103.5 | 108.7 | 111.1 |
| **Slovakia — Slovaquie** | | | | | | | | |
| Total industry [CDE]<br>Total, industrie [CDE] | 92.2 | 100.0 | 106.9 | 113.6 | 119.2 | 124.2 | 128.9 | 141.7 |
| Total mining [C]<br>Total, industries extractives [C] | 101.9 | 100.0 | 86.8 | 111.7 | 105.4 | 94.0 | 90.6 | 81.9 |
| Total manufacturing [D]<br>Total, industries manufacturières [D] | 91.4 | 100.0 | 110.0 | 119.0 | 127.7 | 133.8 | 140.8 | 158.3 |
| Food, beverages and tobacco — Aliments, boissons et tabac | 100.5 | 100.0 | 101.4 | 106.2 | 103.6 | 103.0 | 103.2 | 103.0 |
| Textiles, wearing apparel, leather, footwear<br>Textiles, habillement, cuir et chaussures | 93.9 | 100.0 | 109.2 | 116.8 | 112.4 | 106.8 | 104.6 | 118.6 |
| Chemicals, petroleum, rubber and plastic products<br>Prod. chimiques, pétroliers, caoutch. et plast. | 89.6 | 100.0 | 104.1 | 113.3 | 114.6 | 118.8 | 120.7 | 126.8 |
| Basic metals — Métaux de base | 92.3 | 100.0 | 103.9 | 114.5 | 120.9 | 117.4 | 115.3 | 120.8 |
| Metal products — Produits métalliques | 88.8 | 100.0 | 117.2 | 131.4 | 152.9 | 167.7 | 186.3 | 226.3 |
| Electricity, gas and water [E]<br>Electricité, gaz et eau [E] | 93.6 | 100.0 | 98.2 | 92.3 | 87.8 | 91.0 | 88.4 | 86.3 |
| **Slovenia — Slovénie** | | | | | | | | |
| Total industry [CDE]<br>Total, industrie [CDE] | 94.1 | 100.0 | 102.9 | 105.4 | 106.9 | 112.8 | 116.5 | 123.7 |
| Total mining [C]<br>Total, industries extractives [C] | 102.7 | 100.0 | 92.1 | 99.2 | 104.9 | 97.6 | 104.2 | 115.0 |
| Total manufacturing [D]<br>Total, industries manufacturières [D] | 93.4 | 100.0 | 102.8 | 104.8 | 106.5 | 111.6 | 115.7 | 123.2 |
| Food, beverages and tobacco — Aliments, boissons et tabac | 94.2 | 100.0 | 102.4 | 100.9 | 102.0 | 91.1 | 89.7 | 89.6 |
| Textiles, wearing apparel, leather, footwear<br>Textiles, habillement, cuir et chaussures | 96.8 | 100.0 | 94.1 | 79.7 | 70.3 | 61.9 | 56.9 | 56.4 |
| Chemicals, petroleum, rubber and plastic products<br>Prod. chimiques, pétroliers, caoutch. et plast. | 90.7 | 100.0 | 105.8 | 109.7 | 119.9 | 137.3 | 146.7 | 163.1 |
| Basic metals — Métaux de base | 89.3 | 100.0 | 104.5 | 107.5 | 114.8 | 105.9 | 109.2 | 130.5 |
| Metal products — Produits métalliques | 93.4 | 100.0 | 107.6 | 114.0 | 117.2 | 134.9 | 143.9 | 155.6 |
| Electricity [E]<br>Electricité [E] | 98.4 | 100.0 | 109.3 | 115.3 | 111.3 | 132.9 | 130.9 | 129.6 |
| **Spain — Espagne** | | | | | | | | |
| Total industry [CDE]<br>Total, industrie [CDE] | 96.2 | 100.0 | 98.8 | 98.9 | 100.5 | 102.3 | 102.4 | 106.2 |
| Total mining [C]<br>Total, industries extractives [C] | 98.9 | 100.0 | 96.8 | 96.3 | 96.3 | 91.7 | 88.0 | 90.1 |
| Total manufacturing [D]<br>Total, industries manufacturières [D] | 96.8 | 100.0 | 98.0 | 98.4 | 99.9 | 101.1 | 100.8 | 104.9 |
| Food, beverages and tobacco — Aliments, boissons et tabac | 100.9 | 100.0 | 101.1 | 105.0 | 107.4 | 109.0 | 110.7 | 110.5 |
| Textiles, wearing apparel, leather, footwear<br>Textiles, habillement, cuir et chaussures | 101.9 | 100.0 | 96.6 | 86.8 | 80.7 | 75.4 | 66.8 | 64.9 |
| Chemicals, petroleum, rubber and plastic products<br>Prod. chimiques, pétroliers, caoutch. et plast. | 99.4 | 100.0 | 99.8 | 104.1 | 108.8 | 108.6 | 108.5 | 111.6 |
| Basic metals — Métaux de base | 87.9 | 100.0 | 96.4 | 102.6 | 103.8 | 110.2 | 107.8 | 113.7 |
| Metal products — Produits métalliques | 95.4 | 100.0 | 96.0 | 92.6 | 93.7 | 95.7 | 95.0 | 102.5 |
| Electricity and gas [E]<br>Electricité et gaz [E] | 92.1 | 100.0 | 104.3 | 104.3 | 107.3 | 114.8 | 119.5 | 120.8 |
| **Sweden — Suède** | | | | | | | | |
| Total industry [CDE]<br>Total, industrie [CDE] | 94.6 | 100.0 | 98.9 | 98.9 | 100.2 | 105.5 | 108.3 | 111.5 |
| Total mining [C]<br>Total, industries extractives [C] | 98.5 | 100.0 | 98.3 | 101.6 | 98.3 | 108.0 | 114.9 | 115.8 |
| Total manufacturing [D]<br>Total, industries manufacturières [D] | 94.1 | 100.0 | 98.9 | 99.9 | 102.3 | 106.9 | 109.5 | 114.5 |
| Food, beverages and tobacco — Aliments, boissons et tabac | 101.5 | 100.0 | 103.1 | 100.4 | 96.0 | 97.0 | 97.2 | 97.0 |

| Country or area and industry [ISIC Rev. 3]<br>Pays ou zone et industrie [CITI Rév. 3] | 1999 | 2000 | 2001 | 2002 | 2003 | 2004 | 2005 | 2006 |
|---|---|---|---|---|---|---|---|---|
| Chemicals, petroleum, rubber and plastic products<br>Prod. chimiques, pétroliers, caoutch. et plast. | 93.5 | 100.0 | 105.8 | 110.8 | 118.7 | 125.7 | 125.9 | 135.8 |
| Basic metals — Métaux de base | 95.0 | 100.0 | 109.2 | 114.1 | 112.5 | 119.4 | 115.3 | 110.7 |
| Metal products — Produits métalliques | 91.8 | 100.0 | 96.4 | 94.9 | 98.7 | 106.4 | 111.1 | 117.6 |
| Electricity, gas and water [E]<br>Electricité, gaz et eau [E] | 99.2 | 100.0 | 98.5 | 89.4 | 82.7 | 92.2 | 96.0 | 87.4 |
| **Switzerland — Suisse** | | | | | | | | |
| Total industry [CDE]<br>Total, industrie [CDE] | 92.2 | 100.0 | 99.3 | 94.2 | 94.2 | 98.4 | 101.0 | 108.9 |
| Total mining [C]<br>Total, industries extractives [C] | 99.3 | 100.0 | 100.5 | 99.0 | 98.3 | 102.4 | 97.1 | 106.6 |
| Total manufacturing [D]<br>Total, industries manufacturières [D] | 91.6 | 100.0 | 98.9 | 93.7 | 93.6 | 98.1 | 101.2 | 109.7 |
| Food, beverages and tobacco — Aliments, boissons et tabac | 101.3 | 100.0 | 95.8 | 95.8 | 95.0 | 96.3 | 97.2 | 101.0 |
| Textiles and wearing apparel — Textiles et habillement | 102.8 | 100.0 | 87.2 | 80.3 | 76.6 | 81.9 | 83.1 | 87.1 |
| Chemicals and chemical products — Produits chimiques | 93.3 | 100.0 | 105.5 | 111.5 | 121.0 | 126.6 | 137.4 | 151.0 |
| Basic metals and metal products<br>Métaux de base et produits métalliques | 88.3 | 100.0 | 98.0 | 87.8 | 84.5 | 88.0 | 89.3 | 96.8 |
| Electricity, gas and water [E]<br>Electricité, gaz et eau [E] | 100.5 | 100.0 | 104.3 | 100.0 | 102.0 | 101.6 | 99.2 | 101.1 |
| **TFYR of Macedonia — L'ex-R.y. Macédoine** | | | | | | | | |
| Total industry [CDE]<br>Total, industrie [CDE] | 96.6 | 100.0 | 89.9 | 85.1 | 89.1 | 87.2 | 93.3 | 96.7 |
| Total mining [C]<br>Total, industries extractives [C] | ... | 100.0 | 98.2 | 74.1 | 45.2 | 42.9 | 56.5 | 63.0 |
| Total manufacturing [D]<br>Total, industries manufacturières [D] | ... | 100.0 | 96.6 | 92.1 | 97.5 | 95.4 | 102.5 | 106.2 |
| Food, beverages and tobacco — Aliments, boissons et tabac | ... | 100.0 | 97.6 | 90.9 | 108.1 | 101.0 | 104.6 | 105.4 |
| Textiles, wearing apparel, leather, footwear<br>Textiles, habillement, cuir et chaussures | ... | 100.0 | 96.3 | 85.5 | 66.4 | 65.9 | 67.7 | 70.9 |
| Chemicals, petroleum, rubber and plastic products<br>Prod. chimiques, pétroliers, caoutch. et plast. | ... | 100.0 | 98.4 | 97.6 | 88.9 | 89.9 | 94.6 | 96.4 |
| Basic metals — Métaux de base | ... | 100.0 | 94.8 | 77.2 | 91.7 | 104.6 | 139.5 | 152.0 |
| Metal products — Produits métalliques | ... | 100.0 | 98.3 | 106.1 | 72.6 | 61.0 | 63.3 | 64.1 |
| Electricity, gas and water [E]<br>Electricité, gaz et eau [E] | 100.8 | 100.0 | 100.1 | 96.2 | 105.7 | 102.9 | 105.6 | 106.4 |
| **Ukraine — Ukraine** | | | | | | | | |
| Total industry [CDE]<br>Total, industrie [CDE] | 88.0 | 100.0 | 112.9 | 120.4 | 139.6 | 156.1 | 160.5 | 169.7 |
| Total mining [C]<br>Total, industries extractives [C] | 94.0 | 100.0 | 103.3 | 105.7 | 111.6 | 116.2 | 121.2 | 128.3 |
| Total manufacturing [D]<br>Total, industries manufacturières [D] | 85.8 | 100.0 | 117.2 | 127.7 | 150.9 | 172.9 | 178.1 | 189.3 |
| Food, beverages and tobacco — Aliments, boissons et tabac | ... | 100.0 | 118.6 | 128.3 | 154.5 | 174.1 | 197.8 | 216.8 |
| Textiles, wearing apparel, leather, footwear<br>Textiles, habillement, cuir et chaussures | ... | 100.0 | 115.4 | 116.2 | 120.1 | 137.3 | 139.5 | 135.2 |
| Chemicals, petroleum, rubber and plastic products<br>Prod. chimiques, pétroliers, caoutch. et plast. | ... | 100.0 | 114.3 | 124.8 | 144.6 | 163.4 | 175.0 | 178.1 |
| Metal and Metal Products, except machinery and equipment<br>Metallurgie et travail des métaux à l'exclusion de la fabrication de machines et d'équipements | ... | 100.0 | 105.9 | 110.1 | 125.9 | 141.4 | 139.4 | 151.9 |
| All machinery and transport equipment<br>Fabrication de machines et de matériel de transport | ... | 100.0 | 120.3 | 132.8 | 178.1 | 225.0 | 250.7 | 275.3 |
| Electricity, gas and water [E]<br>Electricité, gaz et eau [E] | 99.0 | 100.0 | 102.2 | 103.7 | 106.4 | 105.3 | 107.7 | 114.7 |
| **United Kingdom — Royaume-Uni** | | | | | | | | |
| Total industry [CDE]<br>Total, industrie [CDE] | 98.2 | 100.0 | 98.6 | 96.6 | 96.3 | 97.1 | 95.4 | 95.5 |
| Total mining [C]<br>Total, industries extractives [C] | 103.3 | 100.0 | 94.5 | 94.9 | 90.0 | 82.9 | 75.7 | 69.6 |

| Country or area and industry [ISIC Rev. 3]<br>Pays ou zone et industrie [CITI Rév. 3] | 1999 | 2000 | 2001 | 2002 | 2003 | 2004 | 2005 | 2006 |
|---|---|---|---|---|---|---|---|---|
| Total manufacturing [D]<br>Total, industries manufacturières [D] | 97.7 | 100.0 | 98.7 | 96.1 | 96.3 | 98.3 | 97.2 | 98.7 |
| Food, beverages and tobacco — Aliments, boissons et tabac | 101.0 | 100.0 | 101.4 | 103.4 | 103.4 | 105.0 | 105.5 | 105.2 |
| Textiles, wearing apparel, leather, footwear<br>Textiles, habillement, cuir et chaussures | 103.7 | 100.0 | 89.3 | 82.3 | 80.3 | 72.0 | 70.2 | 68.4 |
| Chemicals, petroleum, rubber and plastic products<br>Prod. chimiques, pétroliers, caoutch. et plast. | 96.5 | 100.0 | 102.0 | 100.9 | 100.9 | 103.2 | 103.2 | 106.0 |
| Basic metals — Métaux de base | 103.5 | 100.0 | 97.7 | 87.5 | 87.9 | 90.2 | 88.0 | 88.5 |
| Metal products — Produits métalliques | 96.5 | 100.0 | 97.6 | 92.4 | 92.7 | 95.6 | 95.0 | 97.3 |
| Electricity, gas and water [E]<br>Electricité, gaz et eau [E] | 97.0 | 100.0 | 103.3 | 103.7 | 105.4 | 106.5 | 106.5 | 103.7 |
| **Oceania · Océanie** | | | | | | | | |
| **Australia[2] — Australie[2]** | | | | | | | | |
| Total industry [CDE]<br>Total, industrie [CDE] | 96.2 | 100.0 | 105.0 | 106.3 | 108.7 | 108.5 | 109.1 | 108.4 |
| Total mining [C]<br>Total, industries extractives [C] | 93.4 | 100.0 | 106.7 | 106.4 | 105.4 | 101.8 | 105.2 | 103.4 |
| Total manufacturing [D]<br>Total, industries manufacturières [D] | 99.1 | 100.0 | 102.2 | 104.4 | 108.2 | 109.2 | 108.0 | 107.6 |
| Food, beverages and tobacco — Aliments, boissons et tabac | 98.5 | 100.0 | 104.3 | 103.9 | 104.9 | 104.7 | 105.9 | 105.4 |
| Textiles, wearing apparel, leather, footwear<br>Textiles, habillement, cuir et chaussures | 103.8 | 100.0 | 93.0 | 81.5 | 75.0 | 69.4 | 56.5 | 52.8 |
| Chemicals, petroleum, rubber and plastic products<br>Prod. chimiques, pétroliers, caoutch. et plast. | 96.8 | 100.0 | 102.3 | 103.3 | 109.3 | 104.4 | 104.4 | 100.3 |
| Basic metals and metal products<br>Métaux de base et produits métalliques | 102.2 | 100.0 | 102.3 | 105.7 | 111.5 | 114.9 | 114.0 | 117.1 |
| Electricity, gas and water [E]<br>Electricité, gaz et eau [E] | 98.0 | 100.0 | 101.6 | 101.1 | 101.6 | 102.4 | 103.1 | 104.0 |
| **Fiji — Fidji** | | | | | | | | |
| Total industry [CDE]<br>Total, industrie [CDE] | 105.6 | 100.0 | 107.0 | 108.8 | 109.2 | 122.1 | 106.7 | 107.3 |
| Total mining [C]<br>Total, industries extractives [C] | 115.6 | 100.0 | 100.7 | 97.7 | 91.9 | 105.5 | 76.7 | 42.9 |
| Total manufacturing [D]<br>Total, industries manufacturières [D] | 106.1 | 100.0 | 113.1 | 112.8 | 110.6 | 124.8 | 104.3 | 105.9 |
| Food, beverages and tobacco — Aliments, boissons et tabac | 119.6 | 100.0 | 110.1 | 118.9 | 126.3 | 136.3 | 151.6 | 164.8 |
| Textiles and wearing apparel — Textiles et habillement | 105.9 | 100.0 | 130.9 | 115.0 | 103.2 | 127.7 | 57.6 | 41.7 |
| Chemicals and chemical products — Produits chimiques | 115.4 | 100.0 | 96.0 | 111.0 | 95.2 | 111.0 | 129.8 | 144.4 |
| Electricity and water [E]<br>Electricité et eau [E] | 101.6 | 100.0 | 92.5 | 99.4 | 109.8 | 119.0 | 120.9 | 128.7 |
| **New Zealand[10] — Nouvelle-Zélande[10]** | | | | | | | | |
| Total industry [CDE][11]<br>Total, industrie [CDE][11] | 96.3 | 100.0 | 102.3 | 102.6 | 111.2 | 110.7 | 112.8 | 110.3 |
| Total mining [C]<br>Total, industries extractives [C] | 95.9 | 100.0 | 101.6 | 102.6 | 104.4 | 95.2 | 93.9 | 92.0 |
| Total manufacturing [D]<br>Total, industries manufacturières [D] | 95.3 | 100.0 | 102.6 | 103.3 | 113.2 | 114.1 | 116.2 | 113.0 |
| Food, beverages and tobacco — Aliments, boissons et tabac | 98.2 | 100.0 | 102.3 | 104.2 | 124.7 | 124.1 | 123.2 | 125.6 |
| Textiles, wearing apparel, leather, footwear<br>Textiles, habillement, cuir et chaussures | 96.2 | 100.0 | 88.4 | 84.2 | 88.5 | 82.4 | 86.4 | 75.4 |
| Chemicals, petroleum, rubber and plastic products<br>Prod. chimiques, pétroliers, caoutch. et plast. | 97.0 | 100.0 | 106.4 | 102.6 | 109.3 | 101.5 | 106.4 | 99.2 |
| Basic metals and metal products<br>Métaux de base et produits métalliques | 94.0 | 100.0 | 106.4 | 109.7 | 113.5 | 120.6 | 122.5 | 120.0 |
| Electricity, gas and water [E]<br>Electricité, gaz et eau [E] | 104.6 | 100.0 | 101.0 | 97.4 | 105.8 | 106.5 | 112.3 | 106.0 |

Source

United Nations Statistics Division, New York, the index numbers of industrial production database, last accessed January 2008.

Source

Organisation des Nations Unies, Division de statistique, New York, la base de données pour les indices de la production industrielle, dernier accès janvier 2008.

Notes

1 Twelve months beginning 1 July of the year stated.
2 Twelve months ending 30 June of the year stated.
3 Excluding petroleum refineries.
4 Calculated by the Statistics Division of the United Nations from component national indices.
5 Excluding coal mining and crude petroleum.
6 Twelve months ending 30 September of the year stated.
7 Including construction.
8 Twelve months beginning 1 April of the year stated.
9 Excluding gas and oil extraction.
10 Twelve months ending 31 March of the year stated.
11 Including forestry and fishing.

Notes

1 Période de 12 mois commençant le 1er juillet de l'année indiquée.
2 Période de 12 mois finissant le 30 juin de l'année indiquée.
3 Non compris les raffineries de pétrole.
4 Calculé par la Division de Statistiques de l'Organisation des Nations Unies à partir d'indices nationaux plus détaillés.
5 Non compris l'extraction du charbon et de pétrole brut.
6 Période de 12 mois finissant le 30 septembre de l'année indiquée.
7 Y compris la construction.
8 Période de 12 mois commençant le 1er avril de l'année indiquée.
9 Non compris l'extraction de gaz et de pétrole brut.
10 Période de 12 mois finissant le 31 mars de l'année indiquée.
11 Y compris l'exploitation forestière et la pêche.

Detailed internationally comparable data on national accounts are compiled and published annually by the Statistics Division, Department of Economic and Social Affairs of the United Nations Secretariat. Data for national accounts aggregates for countries or areas are based on the concepts and definitions contained in *A System of National Accounts* (1968 SNA) and in *System of National Accounts* 1993 (1993 SNA). A summary of the conceptual framework, classifications and definitions of transactions is found in the annual United Nations publication, *National Accounts Statistics: Main Aggregates and Detailed Tables*, which presents, in the form of analytical tables, a summary of selected principal national accounts aggregates based on official detailed national accounts data of over 200 countries and areas. Every effort has been made to present the estimates of the various countries or areas in a form designed to facilitate international comparability. The data for some countries or areas has been compiled according to the 1993 SNA. Data for those countries or areas which still follow the concepts and definitions of the 1968 SNA is indicated with a footnote. To the extent possible, any other differences in concept, scope, coverage and classification are footnoted as well. Detailed footnotes identifying these differences are also available in the annual national accounts publication mentioned above. Such differences should be taken into account in order to avoid misleading comparisons among countries or areas.

*Table 19* shows gross domestic product (GDP) and GDP per capita in US dollars at current prices, GDP at constant 1990 prices and the corresponding real rates of growth. The table is designed to facilitate international comparisons of levels of income generated in production. In order to present comparable coverage for as many countries as possible, the official GDP national currency data are supplemented by estimates prepared by the Statistics Division, based on a variety of data derived from national and international sources. The conversion rates used to translate national currency data into US dollars are the period averages of market exchange rates (MERs) for members of the International Monetary Fund (IMF). These rates, which are published in the *International Financial Statistics*, are communicated to the IMF by national central banks and consist of three types: (a) market rates, determined largely by market forces; (b) official rates, determined by government authorities; and (c) principal rates for countries maintaining multiple exchange rate arrangements. Market rates always take priority and official rates are used only when a free market rate is not available.

For non-members of the IMF, averages of the United Nations operational rates, used for accounting purposes in United Nations transactions with member countries, are

La Division de statistique du Département des affaires économiques et sociales du Secrétariat de l'Organisation des Nations Unies établit et publie chaque année des données détaillées, comparables au plan international, sur les comptes nationaux. Les données relatives aux agrégats des différents pays et territoires sont établies en fonction des concepts et des définitions du *Système de comptabilité nationale* (SCN de 1968) et du *Système de comptabilité nationale* 1993 (SCN de 1993). On trouvera un résumé de l'appareil conceptuel, des classifications et des définitions des opérations dans "*National Accounts Statistics: Main Aggregates and Detailed Tables*", publication annuelle des Nations Unies, qui présente, sous forme de tableaux analytiques, un choix d'agrégats essentiels de comptabilité nationale, issus des comptes nationaux détaillés de plus que 200 pays et territoires. On n'a rien négligé pour présenter les chiffres des différents pays et territoires sous une forme facilitant les comparaisons internationales. Pour plusiers pays, les chiffres ont été établis selon le SCN de 1993. Les données des pays et territoires qui encore appliques les concepts et les définitions du SCN de 1968 sont signalés par une note. Dans la mesure du possible, on signale également au moyen de notes les cas où les concepts, la portée, la couverture et la classification ne seraient pas les mêmes. Il y a en outre des notes détaillées explicitant ces différences dans la publication annuelle mentionnée plus haut. Il y a lieu de tenir compte de ces différences pour éviter de tenter des comparaisons qui donneraient matière à confusion.

Le *tableau 19* fait apparaître le produit intérieur brut (PIB) total et par habitant, exprimé en dollars des États-Unis aux prix courants et à prix constants (base 1990), ainsi que les taux de croissance correspondants. Le tableau est conçu pour faciliter les comparaisons internationales du revenu issu de la production. Afin que la couverture soit comparable pour le plus grand nombre possible de pays, la Division de statistique s'appuie non seulement sur les chiffres officiels du PIB exprimé dans la monnaie nationale, mais aussi sur diverses données provenant de sources nationales et internationales. Les taux de conversion utilisés pour exprimer les données nationales en dollars des États-Unis sont, pour les membres du Fonds monétaire international (FMI), les moyennes pour la période considérée des taux de change du marché. Ces derniers, publiés dans Statistiques financières internationales, sont communiqués au FMI par les banques centrales des pays et reposent sur trois types de taux : a) taux du marché, déterminés dans une large mesure par les facteurs du marché; b) taux officiels, déterminés par les pouvoirs publics; c) taux principaux, pour les pays pratiqua différents arrangements en matière de taux de change. On donne toujours la

applied. These are based on official, commercial and/or tourist rates of exchange.

It should be noted that there are practical constraints in the use of MERs for conversion purposes. Their use may result in excessive fluctuations or distortions in the dollar income levels of a number of countries, particularly in those with multiple exchange rates, those coping with inordinate levels of inflation or countries experiencing misalignments caused by market fluctuations. Caution is therefore urged when making inter-country comparisons of incomes as expressed in US dollars.

Alternative methods of making international comparisons have been developed in recent years. One is the Purchasing Power Parities (PPPs) which have been developed as part of the International Comparison Programme; another is the World Bank Atlas method of conversion based on the average of the exchange rates of the current year and the two immediately preceding years that have been adjusted for differences in inflation rates between individual countries and the average of G-5 countries (Germany, France, Japan, the United Kingdom, and the United States). The Statistics Division of the United Nations has developed the Price-Adjusted Rates of Exchange method (PARE) which, like the Atlas method, is designed to adjust exchange rates that do not adequately reflect relative movements of domestic and international inflation. PARE is mainly applied to countries with fixed exchange rate regimes and countries going through a period of high inflation (e.g. transition countries from 1990-1995).

The GDP at constant price series, based primarily on data officially provided by countries or areas and partly on estimates made by the Statistics Division, is transformed into index numbers and rebased to 1990=100. The resulting data are then converted into US dollars at the rate prevailing in the base year 1990. The growth rates are based on the estimates of GDP at constant 1990 prices. The growth rate of the year in question is obtained by dividing the GDP of that year by the GDP of the preceding year.

*Table 20* presents a desegregation of economic development by analyzing the movement of prices and exchange rates in relation to overall economic growth.

GDP indices based on current prices expressed in US dollars and national currencies are shown in columns 1 and 2. The annual changes of GDP in volume terms are reflected in column 3, where the indices are based on the movement of GDP at constant prices.

Column 4 presents indices of price changes of GDP expressed in national currency and column 5 includes indices of price changes of GDP in US dollars. The price indices in columns 4 and 5 are obtain by dividing, respectively, the indices of GDP at current prices in national currencies and

priorité aux taux du marché, n'utilisant les taux officiels que lorsqu'on n'a pas de taux du marché libre.

Pour les pays qui ne sont pas membres du FMI, on utilise les moyennes des taux de change opérationnels de l'ONU (qui servent à des fins comptables pour les opérations de l'ONU avec les pays qui en sont membres). Ces taux reposent sur les taux de change officiels, les taux du commerce et/ou les taux touristiques.

Il faut noter que l'utilisation des taux de change du marché pour la conversion des données se heurte à des obstacles pratiques. On risque, ce faisant, d'aboutir à des fluctuations excessives ou à des distorsions du revenu en dollars de certains pays, surtout dans le cas des pays qui pratiquent plusieurs taux de change et de ceux qui connaissent des taux d'inflation exceptionnels ou des décalages provenant des fluctuations du marché. Les comparaisons de revenu entre pays sont donc sujettes à caution lorsqu'on se fonde sur le revenu exprimé en dollars des États-Unis.

D'autres méthodes ont été élaborées ces dernières années pour les comparaisons internationales. L'une, celle de la parité de pouvoir d'achat (PPA), procède du Programme de comparaison internationale ; une autre méthode de conversion, celle de l'Atlas de la Banque mondiale, est basée sur la moyenne des taux de change de l'année en cours et des deux années immédiatement précédentes, ajustés en fonction des différences d'inflation entre les pays considérés et la moyenne des pays du G-5 (Allemagne, États-Unis, France, Japon, et Royaume-Uni). La Division de statistique de l'ONU a mis au point la méthode des Taux de Change Corrigés des Prix (TCCP) qui, comme celle de l'Atlas, est conçue pour corriger les taux de change qui ne rendent pas convenablement compte de l'évolution relative de l'inflation dans un pays par rapport à l'inflation à l'échelon international. Le TCCP sert surtout pour les pays à taux de change fixe et ceux qui connaissent une période de forte inflation (par ex. les pays en transition entre 1990 et 1995).

La série de statistiques du PIB à prix constants est fondée principalement sur des données officiellement communiquées par les pays, et en partie sur des estimations de la Division de statistique; les données permettent de calculer des indices, la base 100 correspondant à 1990. Les chiffres ainsi obtenus sont alors convertis en dollars des États-Unis au taux de change de l'année de base (1990). Les taux de croissance sont calculés à partir des estimations du PIB aux prix constants de 1990. Le taux de croissance de l'année considérée est obtenu en divisant le PIB de l'année par celui de l'année précédente.

Le *tableau 20* envisage le développement économique sous l'angle d'une analyse de l'évolution des prix et des taux de change par rapport à la croissance économique mondiale.

Les indices du PIB fondés sur les prix courants exprimés en monnaies nationales et en dollars des États-Unis sont indiqués

in US dollars shown in columns 1 and 2, by the volume indices presented in column 3.

Column 6 provides an implied development in exchange rates derived either by dividing the GDP deflators in national currency (column 4) by the GDP deflators converted in US dollars (column 5), or by dividing the GDP indices expressed in national currencies by the US dollar indices listed in column 1 and 2, respectively.

*Table 21* features the percentage distribution of GDP at current prices by expenditure breakdown. It shows the portions of GDP spent on consumption by the household sector (including the non-profit institutions serving households) and the government, the portions spent on gross fixed capital formation, on changes in inventories, and on exports of goods and services, deducting imports of goods and services. The percentages are derived from official data reported to the United Nations by the countries and published in the annual national accounts publication.

*Table 22* shows the percentage distribution of value added originating from the various industry components of the *International Standard Industrial Classification of All Economic Activities, Revision 3* (ISIC Rev. 3). This table reflects the economic structure of production in the different countries or areas. The percentages are based on official gross value added at basic current prices broken down by the kind of economic activity: agriculture, hunting, forestry and fishing (categories A+B); mining and quarrying (C); manufacturing (D); electricity, gas and water supply (E); construction (F); wholesale and retail trade, repair of motor vehicles, motorcycles and personal and household goods, restaurants and hotels (G+H); transport, storage and communication (I) and "other activities", comprised of financial intermediation (J), real estate, renting and business activities (K), public administration and defence, compulsory social security (L), education (M), health and social work (N), other community, social and personal service activities (O) and private households with employed persons (P).

*Table 23* presents the relationships among the principal national accounting aggregates, namely: gross domestic product (GDP), gross national income (GNI), gross national disposable income (GNDI) and gross savings. GNI is the term used in the 1993 SNA instead of the term Gross National Product (GNP) which was used in the 1968 SNA. The ratio of each aggregate to GDP is derived cumulatively by adding net primary income (or net factor income) from the rest of the world (GNI), adding net current transfers from the rest of the world (GNDI), and deducting final consumption to arrive at gross saving.

*Table 24* presents the distribution of government final consumption expenditure by function at current prices.

dans les colonnes 1 et 2. L'évolution annuelle du PIB en volume apparaît dans la colonne 3, les indices étant fondés sur l'évolution du PIB à prix constants.

La colonne 4 présente l'évolution des indices des prix exprimés en monnaie nationale et la colonne 5 celle des indices des prix exprimés en dollars des États-Unis. Les indices de prix dans les colonnes 4 et 5 sont obtenus en divisant, respectivement, les indices du PIB fondés sur les prix courants exprimés en monnaies nationales et en dollars des États-Unis, qui sont indiqués dans les colonnes 1 et 2, par les indices de volume présentés dans la colonne 3.

La colonne 6 montre l'évolution implicite des taux de change obtenue soit en divisant les déflateurs du PIB en monnaie nationale (colonne 4) par les déflateurs du PIB convertis en dollars (colonne 5), soit en divisant les indices du PIB exprimés en monnaies nationales (colonne 1) par les indices exprimés en dollars des États-Unis (colonne 2).

Le *tableau 21* montre la répartition (en pourcentage) du PIB aux prix courants par catégorie de dépense. Il indique la part du PIB consacrée aux dépenses de consommation du secteur des ménages (y compris les institutions sans but lucratif au service des ménages) et des administrations publiques et celle qui est consacrée à l'investissement fixe brut, celle qui correspond aux variations de stocks et celle qui correspond aux exportations de biens et services, déduction faite des importations de biens et services. Ces pourcentages sont calculés à partir des chiffres officiels communiqués à l'ONU par les pays, publiés dans l'ouvrage annuel.

Le *tableau 22* montre la répartition (en pourcentage) de la valeur ajoutée par branche d'activité, selon le classement retenu dans la *Classification internationale type, par industrie, de toutes les branches d'activité économique, Révision 3* (CITI Révision 3). Il rend donc compte de la structure économique de la production dans chaque pays. Les pourcentages sont établis à partir des chiffres officiels de valeur ajoutée brute aux prix de base courants, répartis selon les différentes catégories d'activité économique: agriculture, chasse, sylviculture et pêche (catégories A + B); activités extractives (C); activités de fabrication (D); production et distribution d'électricité, de gaz et d'eau (E); construction (F); commerce de gros et de détail, réparation de véhicules automobiles, de motocycles et de biens personnels et domestiques, hôtels et restaurants (G + H); transports, entreposage et communications (I) et autres activités, y compris intermédiation financière (J), immobilier, locations et activités de services aux entreprises (K), administration publique et défense, sécurité sociale obligatoire (L), éducation (M), santé et action sociale (N), autres activités de services collectifs, sociaux et personnels (O), et ménages privés employant du personnel domestique (P).

The breakdown by function includes: general public services; defence; public order and safety; economic affairs; environmental protection; housing and community amenities; health; recreation, culture and religion; education; and social protection. The government expenditure is equal to the service produced by general government for its own use. These services are not sold; they are valued in the GDP at their cost to the government.

*Table 25* shows the distribution of household final consumption expenditure in the domestic market by purpose at current prices. The percentage shares include: food, beverages, tobacco and narcotics; clothing and footwear; housing, water, electricity, gas and other fuels; furnishings, household equipment and routine maintenance of the house; health; transport and communication; recreation and culture; education; restaurants and hotels; and miscellaneous goods and services.

*Table 26*: The national indices in this table are shown for the categories "Mining and Quarrying", "Manufacturing" and "Electricity, gas and water". These categories are classified according to Tabulation Categories C, D and E of the ISIC Revision 3 at the 2-digit level. Major deviations from ISIC in the scope of the indices for the above categories are indicated by footnotes to the table.

The category "Total industry" covers Mining, Manufacturing and Electricity, gas and water. The indices for "Total industry", however, are the combination of the components shown and share all deviations from ISIC as footnoted for the component series.

The weights used in the calculation of the indices for a particular country are the value added contribution to the gross domestic product (GDP) of the given industry during the base year (value added = output - intermediate consumption). These value added contributions are measured at factor cost. Ideally, every five years the base year is changed, the corresponding base weights are updated and the indices of subsequent years are rebased.

Currently, the national indices have been rebased to 2000=100.

Le *tableau 23* montre les rapports entre les principaux agrégats de la comptabilité nationale, à savoir le produit intérieur brut (PIB), le revenu national brut (RNB), le revenu national brut disponible et l'épargne brute. Le revenu national brut est l'agrégat qui remplace dans le SCN de 1993 le produit national brut, utilisé dans le SCN de 1968. Chacun d'entre eux est obtenu par rapport au PIB, en ajoutant les revenus primaires nets (ou revenus nets de facteurs) engendrés dans le reste du monde, pour obtenir le revenu national brut; en ajoutant les transferts courants nets reçus de non-résidents, pour obtenir le revenu national disponible; en soustrayant la consommation finale pour obtenir l'épargne brute.

Le *tableau 24* donne la répartition des dépenses de consommation finale des administrations publiques, par fonction, aux prix courants. La répartition par fonction est la suivante: services généraux des administrations publiques; défense; ordre et sécurité publiques; affaires économiques; protection de l'environnement; logements et équipements collectifs; santé; loisirs, culture et culte; enseignement ; protection sociale. Les dépenses des administrations sont considérées comme égales aux services produits par l'administration pour son propre usage. Ces services ne sont pas vendus et ils sont évalués, dans le PIB, à leur coût pour l'administration.

Le *tableau 25* donne la répartition des dépenses de consommation finale des ménages sur le marché intérieur par fonction aux prix courants. La répartition en pourcentage distingue les rubriques suivantes: alimentation, boissons, tabac et stupéfiants; articles d'habillement et chaussures; logement, eau, gaz, électricité et autres combustibles; meubles, articles de ménage et entretien courant de l'habitation; santé; transports et communication; loisirs et culture; enseignement; restaurants et hôtels; et autres fonctions, y compris les biens et services divers.

*Tableau 26*: Les indices nationaux de ce tableau sont donnés pour les catégories "Industries extractives et carrières", "Industries manufacturières" et "Électricité, gaz et eau". Les catégories correspondent à celles des catégories C, D et E de la *Classification internationale type, par industrie, de toutes les branches d'activité économique* (CITI Révision 3) au niveau des classes à deux chiffres. Tous les indices pour lesquels les catégories s'écartent sensiblement de celles de la CITI sont signalés en note au tableau.

La catégorie "Ensemble de l'industrie" comprend les Industries extractives et carrières, les Industries manufacturières et l'Électricité, gaz et eau. Les indices pour « Ensemble de l'industrie », toutefois, combinent les composantes indiquées et présentent tous les écarts par rapport à la CITI que signalent les notes concernant les séries des composantes.

Les coefficients de pondération utilisés pour le calcul des indices d'un pays donné correspondent à la part de la valeur

ajoutée de la branche considérée dans le produit intérieur brut (PIB) pendant l'année de référence (valeur ajoutée = production - consommation intermédiaire). Cette part de la valeur ajoutée est mesurée au coût des facteurs. En principe, l'année de référence change tous les cinq ans, les coefficients de pondération correspondants sont actualisés et les indices des années suivantes sont calculés sur une nouvelle base. À l'heure actuelle, la nouvelle base des indices est 2000=100.

# 27

## Rates of discount of central banks
Per cent per annum, end of period

## Taux d'escompte des banques centrales
Pour cent par année, fin de la période

| Country or area — Pays ou zone | 1998 | 1999 | 2000 | 2001 | 2002 | 2003 | 2004 | 2005 | 2006 | 2007 |
|---|---|---|---|---|---|---|---|---|---|---|
| Albania[1] — Albanie[1] | 23.44 | 18.00 | 10.82 | 7.00 | 8.50 | 6.50 | 5.25 | 5.00 | 5.50 | 6.25 |
| Algeria — Algérie | 9.50 | 8.50 | 6.00 | 6.00 | 5.50 | 4.50 | 4.00 | 4.00 | 4.00 | 4.00 |
| Angola — Angola | 58.00 | 120.00 | 150.00 | 150.00 | 150.00 | 150.00 | 95.00 | 95.00 | 14.00 | 19.57 |
| Anguilla — Anguilla | 8.00 | 8.00 | 8.00 | 7.00 | 7.00 | 6.50 | 6.50 | 6.50 | 6.50 | 6.50 |
| Antigua and Barbuda — Antigua-et-Barbuda | 8.00 | 8.00 | 8.00 | 7.00 | 7.00 | 6.50 | 6.50 | 6.50 | 6.50 | 6.50 |
| Aruba[1] — Aruba[1] | 9.50 | 6.50 | 6.50 | 6.50 | 6.50 | 5.00 | 5.00 | 5.00 | 5.00 | 5.00 |
| Austria[2] — Autriche[2] | 2.50 | ... | ... | ... | ... | ... | ... | ... | ... | ... |
| Azerbaijan[3] — Azerbaïdjan[3] | 14.00 | 10.00 | 10.00 | 10.00 | 7.00 | 7.00 | 7.00 | 9.00 | 9.50 | 13.00 |
| Bahamas[1] — Bahamas[1] | 6.50 | 5.75 | 5.75 | 5.75 | 5.75 | 5.75 | 5.75 | 5.25 | 5.25 | 5.25 |
| Bangladesh — Bangladesh | 8.00 | 7.00 | 7.00 | 6.00 | 6.00 | 5.00 | 5.00 | 5.00 | 5.00 | 5.00 |
| Barbados[1] — Barbade[1] | 9.00 | 10.00 | 10.00 | 7.50 | 7.50 | 7.50 | 7.50 | 10.00 | 12.00 | ... |
| Belarus[3] — Bélarus[3] | 9.60 | 23.40 | #80.00 | 48.00 | 38.00 | 28.00 | 17.00 | 11.00 | 10.00 | 10.00 |
| Belgium[2] — Belgique[2] | 2.75 | ... | ... | ... | ... | ... | ... | ... | ... | ... |
| Belize[4] — Belize[4] | 12.00 | 12.00 | 12.00 | 12.00 | 12.00 | 12.00 | 12.00 | 12.00 | 12.00 | 12.00 |
| Benin — Bénin | 6.00 | 6.00 | 6.00 | 6.00 | 6.00 | 4.50 | 4.00 | 4.00 | 4.25 | 4.25 |
| Bolivia — Bolivie | 14.10 | 12.50 | 10.00 | 8.50 | 12.50 | 7.50 | 6.00 | 5.25 | 5.25 | 6.50 |
| Botswana[4] — Botswana[4] | 12.75 | 13.75 | 14.25 | 14.25 | 15.25 | 14.25 | 14.25 | 14.50 | 15.00 | 14.50 |
| Brazil — Brésil | 39.41 | 21.37 | #18.52 | 21.43 | 30.42 | 23.92 | 24.55 | 25.34 | 19.98 | 17.85 |
| Bulgaria[1] — Bulgarie[1] | 5.08 | 4.46 | 4.63 | 4.65 | 3.31 | 2.83 | 2.37 | #2.05 | 3.26 | 4.58 |
| Burkina Faso — Burkina Faso | 6.00 | 6.00 | 6.00 | 6.00 | 6.00 | 4.50 | 4.00 | 4.00 | 4.25 | 4.25 |
| Burundi[5] — Burundi[5] | 12.00 | 12.00 | 14.00 | 14.00 | 15.50 | 14.50 | 14.50 | 14.50 | 11.07 | ... |
| Cameroon — Cameroun | 7.00 | 7.30 | 7.00 | 6.50 | 6.30 | 6.00 | 6.00 | 5.50 | 5.25 | 5.25 |
| Canada[1] — Canada[1] | 5.25 | 5.00 | 6.00 | 2.50 | 3.00 | 3.00 | 2.75 | 3.50 | 4.50 | 4.50 |
| Cape Verde — Cap-Vert | ... | ... | ... | 11.50 | 10.00 | 8.50 | 8.50 | 8.50 | 8.50 | ... |
| Central African Rep. — Rép. centrafricaine | 7.00 | 7.60 | 7.00 | 6.50 | 6.30 | 6.00 | 6.00 | 5.50 | 5.25 | 5.25 |
| Chad — Tchad | 7.00 | 7.60 | 7.00 | 6.50 | 6.30 | 6.00 | 6.00 | 5.50 | 5.25 | 5.25 |
| Chile — Chili | 9.12 | 7.44 | 8.73 | 6.50 | 3.00 | 2.45 | 2.25 | 4.50 | 5.25 | 6.00 |
| China[1] — Chine[1] | 4.59 | 3.24 | 3.24 | 3.24 | 2.70 | 2.70 | 3.33 | 3.33 | 3.33 | 3.33 |
| China, Hong Kong SAR — Chine, Hong Kong RAS | 6.25 | 7.00 | 8.00 | 3.25 | 2.75 | 2.50 | 3.75 | 5.75 | 6.75 | 5.75 |
| Colombia — Colombie | 42.28 | 23.05 | 18.28 | 13.25 | 10.00 | 12.00 | 11.25 | 10.75 | 9.50 | 11.50 |
| Comoros — Comores | ... | #6.36 | 5.63 | 5.89 | 4.79 | 3.83 | 3.55 | 3.59 | 4.34 | ... |
| Congo — Congo | 7.00 | 7.60 | 7.00 | 6.50 | 6.30 | 6.00 | 6.00 | 5.50 | 5.25 | 5.25 |
| Costa Rica[6] — Costa Rica[6] | 37.00 | 34.00 | 31.50 | 28.75 | 31.25 | 26.00 | 26.00 | 27.00 | 24.75 | 17.00 |
| Côte d'Ivoire — Côte d'Ivoire | 6.00 | 6.00 | 6.00 | 6.00 | 6.00 | 4.50 | 4.00 | 4.00 | 4.25 | 4.25 |
| Croatia — Croatie | 5.90 | 7.90 | 5.90 | 5.90 | 4.50 | 4.50 | 4.50 | 4.50 | 4.50 | 9.00 |
| Cyprus — Chypre | 7.00 | 7.00 | 7.00 | 5.50 | 5.00 | 4.50 | 5.50 | 4.25 | 4.50 | 5.00 |
| Czech Republic[1] — République tchèque[1] | 9.50 | 5.25 | 5.25 | 4.50 | 2.75 | 2.00 | 2.50 | 2.00 | 2.50 | 3.50 |
| Dem. Rep. of the Congo — Rép. dém. du Congo | 22.00 | 120.00 | 120.00 | 140.00 | 24.00 | 8.00 | ... | ... | ... | ... |
| Denmark — Danemark | 3.50 | 3.00 | 4.75 | 3.25 | 2.86 | 2.00 | 2.00 | 2.25 | 3.50 | 4.00 |
| Dominica — Dominique | 8.00 | 8.00 | 8.00 | 7.00 | 7.00 | 6.50 | 6.50 | 6.50 | 6.50 | 6.50 |
| Ecuador — Equateur | 61.84 | 64.40 | #13.16 | 16.44 | 14.55 | 11.19 | 9.86 | 9.61 | 9.22 | 10.72 |
| Egypt — Egypte | 12.00 | 12.00 | 12.00 | 11.00 | 10.00 | 10.00 | 10.00 | 10.00 | 9.00 | 9.00 |
| Equatorial Guinea — Guinée équatoriale | 7.00 | 7.60 | 7.00 | 6.50 | 6.30 | 6.00 | 6.00 | 5.50 | 5.25 | 5.25 |
| Euro Area[7,8] — Zone euro[7,8] | ... | 4.00 | 5.75 | 4.25 | 3.75 | 3.00 | 3.00 | 3.25 | 4.50 | 5.00 |
| Fiji[1] — Fidji[1] | 2.50 | 2.50 | 8.00 | 1.75 | 1.75 | 1.75 | 2.25 | 2.75 | 5.25 | 9.25 |
| Finland[1,2] — Finlande[1,2] | 3.50 | ... | ... | ... | ... | ... | ... | ... | ... | ... |
| Gabon — Gabon | 7.00 | 7.60 | 7.00 | 6.50 | 6.30 | 6.00 | 6.00 | 5.50 | 5.25 | 5.25 |
| Gambia — Gambie | 12.00 | 10.50 | 10.00 | 13.00 | 18.00 | 29.00 | 28.00 | 14.00 | 9.00 | 10.00 |
| Germany[2] — Allemagne[2] | 2.50 | ... | ... | ... | ... | ... | ... | ... | ... | ... |

| Country or area — Pays ou zone | 1998 | 1999 | 2000 | 2001 | 2002 | 2003 | 2004 | 2005 | 2006 | 2007 |
|---|---|---|---|---|---|---|---|---|---|---|
| Ghana — Ghana | 37.00 | 27.00 | 27.00 | 27.00 | 24.50 | 21.50 | 18.50 | 15.50 | 12.50 | ... |
| Greece[1,2] — Grèce[1,2] | ... | #11.81 | 8.10 | ... | ... | ... | ... | ... | ... | ... |
| Grenada — Grenade | 8.00 | 8.00 | 8.00 | 7.00 | 7.00 | 6.50 | 6.50 | 6.50 | 6.50 | 6.50 |
| Guinea[3] — Guinée[3] | ... | ... | 11.50 | 16.25 | 16.25 | 16.25 | 16.25 | 22.25 | ... | ... |
| Guinea-Bissau — Guinée-Bissau | 6.00 | 6.00 | 6.00 | 6.00 | 6.00 | 4.50 | 4.00 | 4.00 | 4.25 | 4.25 |
| Guyana — Guyana | 11.25 | 13.25 | 11.75 | 8.75 | 6.25 | 5.50 | 6.00 | 6.00 | 6.75 | 6.50 |
| Hungary — Hongrie | 17.00 | 14.50 | 11.00 | 9.75 | 8.50 | 12.50 | 9.50 | 6.00 | 8.00 | 7.50 |
| Iceland — Islande | #8.50 | 10.00 | 12.40 | 12.00 | 8.20 | 7.70 | 10.25 | 12.00 | 15.25 | 15.25 |
| India[1] — Inde[1] | 9.00 | 8.00 | 8.00 | 6.50 | 6.25 | 6.00 | 6.00 | 6.00 | 6.00 | 6.00 |
| Indonesia — Indonésie | 38.44 | 12.51 | 14.53 | 17.62 | 12.93 | 8.31 | 7.43 | 12.75 | 9.75 | 8.00 |
| Iran (Islamic Rep. of) — Iran (Rép. islamique d') | ... | ... | ... | ... | ... | 11.68 | ... | ... | ... | ... |
| Iraq — Iraq | ... | ... | ... | ... | ... | ... | 6.00 | 6.33 | 10.42 | 20.00 |
| Ireland[2,9] — Irlande[2,9] | 4.06 | ... | ... | ... | ... | ... | ... | ... | ... | ... |
| Israel — Israël | 13.47 | 11.20 | 8.21 | 5.67 | 9.18 | 5.20 | 3.90 | 4.44 | 5.00 | ... |
| Italy[2] — Italie[2] | 3.00 | ... | ... | ... | ... | ... | ... | ... | ... | ... |
| Japan — Japon | 0.50 | 0.50 | 0.50 | 0.10 | 0.10 | 0.10 | 0.10 | 0.10 | 0.40 | 0.75 |
| Jordan — Jordanie | 9.00 | 8.00 | 6.50 | 5.00 | 4.50 | 2.50 | 3.75 | 6.50 | 7.50 | 7.00 |
| Kazakhstan[3] — Kazakhstan[3] | 25.00 | 18.00 | 14.00 | 9.00 | 7.50 | 7.00 | 7.00 | 8.00 | 9.00 | 11.00 |
| Kenya — Kenya | 17.07 | 26.46 | ... | ... | ... | ... | ... | ... | ... | ... |
| Korea, Republic of — Corée, République de | 3.00 | 3.00 | 3.00 | 2.50 | 2.50 | 2.50 | 2.00 | 2.00 | 2.75 | 3.25 |
| Kuwait — Koweït | 7.00 | 6.75 | 7.25 | 4.25 | 3.25 | 3.25 | 4.75 | 6.00 | 6.25 | 6.25 |
| Kyrgyzstan — Kirghizistan | 53.95 | 51.65 | 32.77 | 10.73 | 6.77 | 3.99 | 4.62 | 4.30 | 3.94 | 5.63 |
| Lao People's Dem. Rep.[1] — Rép. dém. pop. lao[1] | 35.00 | 34.89 | 35.17 | 35.00 | 20.00 | 20.00 | 20.00 | 20.00 | 20.00 | ... |
| Latvia — Lettonie | 4.00 | 4.00 | 3.50 | 3.50 | 3.00 | 3.00 | 4.00 | 4.00 | 5.00 | 6.00 |
| Lebanon — Liban | 30.00 | 25.00 | 20.00 | 20.00 | 20.00 | 20.00 | 20.00 | 12.00 | 12.00 | 12.00 |
| Lesotho — Lesotho | 19.50 | 19.00 | 15.00 | 13.00 | 16.19 | 15.00 | 13.00 | 13.00 | 10.76 | 12.82 |
| Libyan Arab Jamah. — Jamah. arabe libyenne | 3.00 | 5.00 | 5.00 | 5.00 | 5.00 | 5.00 | 4.00 | 4.00 | 4.00 | 4.00 |
| Lithuania — Lituanie | ... | ... | ... | ... | ... | ... | ... | 3.02 | 3.79 | 4.85 |
| Madagascar — Madagascar | ... | 15.00 | ... | ... | ... | ... | ... | ... | ... | ... |
| Malawi — Malawi | 43.00 | 47.00 | 50.23 | 46.80 | 40.00 | 35.00 | 25.00 | 25.00 | 20.00 | ... |
| Maldives — Maldives | ... | ... | 18.00 | 18.54 | 19.00 | 18.25 | 18.00 | #12.00 | 12.50 | |
| Mali[1] — Mali[1] | 6.00 | 6.00 | 6.00 | 6.00 | 6.00 | 4.50 | 4.00 | 4.00 | 4.25 | 4.25 |
| Malta — Malte | 5.50 | 4.75 | 4.75 | 4.25 | 3.75 | #3.00 | 3.00 | 3.25 | 3.75 | ... |
| Mauritania — Mauritanie | 18.00 | 18.00 | 13.00 | 11.00 | 11.00 | 11.00 | 11.00 | 14.00 | 14.00 | 12.00 |
| Mauritius — Maurice | 17.19 | ... | ... | ... | ... | ... | ... | ... | ... | ... |
| Mongolia[1] — Mongolie[1] | 23.30 | 11.40 | 8.65 | 8.60 | 9.90 | 11.50 | 15.75 | 4.40 | 6.42 | 9.87 |
| Montserrat — Montserrat | 8.00 | 8.00 | 8.00 | 7.00 | 7.00 | 6.50 | 6.50 | 6.50 | 6.50 | 6.50 |
| Morocco — Maroc | 6.04 | 5.42 | 5.00 | 4.71 | 3.79 | 3.25 | 3.25 | 3.25 | 3.25 | 3.25 |
| Mozambique — Mozambique | 9.95 | 9.95 | 9.95 | 9.95 | 9.95 | 9.95 | 9.95 | 9.95 | 9.95 | 9.95 |
| Myanmar[1] — Myanmar[1] | 15.00 | 12.00 | 10.00 | 10.00 | 10.00 | 10.00 | 10.00 | 10.00 | ... | ... |
| Namibia[10] — Namibie[10] | 18.75 | 11.50 | 11.25 | 9.25 | 12.75 | 7.75 | 7.50 | 7.00 | 9.00 | 10.50 |
| Nepal[1] — Népal[1] | 9.00 | 9.00 | 7.50 | 6.50 | 5.50 | 5.50 | 5.50 | 6.00 | 6.25 | ... |
| Netherlands Antilles — Antilles néerlandaises | 6.00 | 6.00 | 6.00 | 6.00 | 6.00 | ... | ... | ... | ... | ... |
| New Zealand — Nouvelle-Zélande | 5.60 | 5.00 | 6.50 | 4.75 | 5.75 | 5.00 | 6.50 | 7.25 | 7.25 | 8.25 |
| Niger — Niger | 6.00 | 6.00 | 6.00 | 6.00 | 6.00 | 4.50 | 4.00 | 4.00 | 4.25 | 4.25 |
| Nigeria — Nigéria | 13.50 | 18.00 | 14.00 | 20.50 | 16.50 | 15.00 | 15.00 | 13.00 | 10.00 | ... |
| Norway — Norvège | 10.00 | 7.50 | 9.00 | 8.50 | 8.50 | 4.25 | 3.75 | 4.25 | 5.50 | 6.25 |
| Oman — Oman | 7.30 | 7.30 | 7.30 | 7.50 | 7.50 | 7.50 | #0.69 | 3.12 | 3.63 | ... |
| Pakistan — Pakistan | 16.50 | 13.00 | 13.00 | 10.00 | 7.50 | 7.50 | 7.50 | 9.00 | 9.50 | 10.00 |
| Papua New Guinea — Papouasie-Nvl-Guinée | 17.07 | 16.66 | 9.79 | 11.73 | 11.71 | #15.50 | 12.67 | 9.67 | 8.13 | 7.38 |
| Paraguay — Paraguay | 20.00 | 20.00 | 20.00 | 20.00 | 20.00 | 20.00 | 20.00 | 20.00 | 20.00 | 20.00 |
| Peru — Pérou | 18.72 | 17.80 | 14.00 | 5.00 | 4.50 | 3.25 | 3.75 | 4.00 | 5.25 | 5.75 |
| Philippines — Philippines | 12.40 | 7.89 | 13.81 | 8.30 | 4.19 | 5.53 | 8.36 | 5.70 | 5.04 | 4.28 |

| Country or area — Pays ou zone | 1998 | 1999 | 2000 | 2001 | 2002 | 2003 | 2004 | 2005 | 2006 | 2007 |
|---|---|---|---|---|---|---|---|---|---|---|
| Poland — Pologne | 15.50 | 16.50 | 19.00 | 11.50 | 6.75 | 5.25 | 6.50 | 4.50 | 4.00 | 5.00 |
| Portugal[2] — Portugal[2] | 3.00 | ... | ... | ... | ... | ... | ... | ... | ... | ... |
| Qatar — Qatar | ... | ... | ... | ... | 1.70 | 1.33 | 2.60 | 4.50 | 5.50 | 5.50 |
| Russian Federation[3] — Fédération de Russie[3] | 60.00 | 55.00 | 25.00 | 25.00 | 21.00 | 16.00 | 13.00 | 12.00 | 11.00 | 10.00 |
| Rwanda — Rwanda | 11.38 | 11.19 | 11.69 | 13.00 | 13.00 | 14.50 | 14.50 | 12.50 | 12.50 | 12.50 |
| Saint Kitts and Nevis — Saint-Kitts-et-Nevis | 8.00 | 8.00 | 8.00 | 7.00 | 7.00 | 6.50 | 6.50 | 6.50 | 6.50 | 6.50 |
| Saint Lucia — Sainte-Lucie | 8.00 | 8.00 | 8.00 | 7.00 | 7.00 | 6.50 | 6.50 | 6.50 | 6.50 | 6.50 |
| St. Vincent-Grenadines — St. Vincent-Grenadines | 8.00 | 8.00 | 8.00 | 7.00 | 7.00 | 6.50 | 6.50 | 6.50 | 6.50 | 6.50 |
| Sao Tome and Principe — Sao Tomé-et-Principe | 29.50 | 17.00 | 17.00 | 15.50 | 15.50 | 14.50 | 14.50 | 18.20 | 28.00 | 28.00 |
| Senegal — Sénégal | 6.00 | 6.00 | 6.00 | 6.00 | 6.00 | 4.50 | 4.00 | 4.00 | 4.25 | 4.25 |
| Serbia[1] — Serbie[1] | ... | ... | ... | 18.67 | 9.72 | 10.63 | #17.21 | 19.16 | 15.35 | 9.57 |
| Seychelles — Seychelles | 5.50 | 5.50 | 5.50 | 5.50 | 5.50 | 4.67 | 3.51 | 3.87 | 4.44 | ... |
| Slovakia — Slovaquie | 8.80 | 8.80 | 8.80 | #7.75 | 6.50 | 6.00 | 4.00 | 3.00 | 4.75 | 4.25 |
| Slovenia[1] — Slovénie[1] | 11.00 | 9.00 | 11.00 | 12.00 | 10.50 | 7.25 | 5.00 | 5.00 | 4.50 | ... |
| South Africa — Afrique du Sud | #19.32 | 12.00 | 12.00 | 9.50 | 13.50 | 8.00 | 7.50 | 7.00 | 9.00 | 11.00 |
| Spain[1,2] — Espagne[1,2] | 3.00 | ... | ... | ... | ... | ... | ... | ... | ... | ... |
| Sri Lanka[5] — Sri Lanka[5] | 17.00 | 16.00 | 25.00 | ... | 18.00 | 15.00 | 15.00 | 15.00 | ... | ... |
| Swaziland — Swaziland | 18.00 | 12.00 | 11.00 | 9.50 | 13.50 | 8.00 | 7.50 | 7.00 | 9.00 | 11.00 |
| Sweden[1] — Suède[1] | 2.00 | 1.50 | 2.00 | 2.00 | #4.50 | 3.00 | 2.00 | 1.50 | 2.50 | 3.50 |
| Switzerland — Suisse | 1.00 | 0.50 | #3.20 | 1.59 | 0.50 | 0.11 | 0.54 | 0.73 | 1.90 | 2.05 |
| Syrian Arab Republic — Rép. arabe syrienne | 5.00 | 5.00 | 5.00 | 5.00 | 5.00 | ... | ... | ... | ... | ... |
| Tajikistan[3] — Tadjikistan[3] | 36.40 | 20.10 | 20.60 | 20.00 | #24.75 | #15.00 | 10.00 | 9.00 | 12.00 | ... |
| Thailand — Thaïlande | 12.50 | 4.00 | 4.00 | 3.75 | 3.25 | 2.75 | 3.50 | 5.50 | 6.50 | 3.75 |
| TFYR of Macedonia[1] — L'ex-R.y. Macédoine[1] | 8.90 | 8.90 | 7.90 | 10.70 | 10.70 | 6.50 | 6.50 | 6.50 | 6.50 | 6.50 |
| Togo — Togo | 6.00 | 6.00 | 6.00 | 6.00 | 6.00 | 4.50 | 4.00 | 4.00 | 4.25 | 4.25 |
| Trinidad and Tobago[1] — Trinité-et-Tobago[1] | 13.00 | 13.00 | 13.00 | 13.00 | 7.25 | 7.00 | 7.00 | 8.00 | 10.00 | ... |
| Turkey — Turquie | 67.00 | 60.00 | 60.00 | 60.00 | 55.00 | 43.00 | 38.00 | 23.00 | 27.00 | 25.00 |
| Uganda[1] — Ouganda[1] | 9.10 | 15.75 | 18.86 | 8.88 | 13.08 | 25.62 | 16.15 | 14.36 | 16.30 | ... |
| Ukraine[3] — Ukraine[3] | 60.00 | 45.00 | 27.00 | 12.50 | 7.00 | 7.00 | 9.00 | 9.50 | 8.50 | 8.00 |
| United Rep. of Tanzania — Rép.-Unie de Tanzanie | 17.60 | 20.20 | 10.70 | 8.70 | 9.18 | 12.34 | 14.42 | 19.33 | 20.07 | 16.40 |
| United States — Etats-Unis | 4.50 | 5.00 | 6.00 | 1.33 | 0.75 | #2.00 | 3.15 | 5.16 | 6.25 | 4.83 |
| Uruguay[11] — Uruguay[11] | 73.70 | 66.39 | 57.26 | 71.66 | 316.01 | 46.27 | 10.00 | 10.00 | 10.00 | ... |
| Vanuatu — Vanuatu | 7.00 | 7.00 | 7.00 | 6.50 | 6.50 | 6.50 | 6.50 | 6.25 | 6.00 | 6.00 |
| Venezuela (Boliv. Rep. of) — Venezuela (Rép. bolivar. du) | 60.00 | 38.00 | 38.00 | 37.00 | 40.00 | 28.50 | 28.50 | 28.50 | 28.50 | 28.50 |
| Viet Nam[3] — Viet Nam[3] | 12.00 | 6.00 | 6.00 | 4.80 | 4.80 | 5.00 | 5.00 | 5.00 | 5.00 | ... |
| Yemen — Yémen | 19.95 | 18.53 | 15.89 | 15.16 | 13.13 | ... | ... | ... | ... | ... |
| Zambia — Zambie | ... | 32.93 | 25.67 | 40.10 | 27.87 | 14.35 | 16.68 | 14.81 | 8.79 | 11.73 |
| Zimbabwe[1] — Zimbabwe[1] | #39.50 | 74.41 | 57.84 | 57.20 | 29.65 | 300.00 | 110.00 | 540.00 | 500.00 | ... |

**Source**

International Monetary Fund (IMF), Washington, D.C., "International Financial Statistics" database, last accessed April 2008.

**Notes**

1  Central Bank rate.
2  Beginning 1999, see Euro Area. For Greece, beginning 2001, see Euro Area.
3  Refinance rate.
4  Lending rate.
5  Advance rate.
6  Discount rate: commercial.
7  Marginal lending facility rate.

**Source**

Fonds monétaire international (FMI), Washington, D.C.,"Statistiques Financières Internationales", dernier accès avril 2008.

**Notes**

1  Taux de la Banque centrale.
2  À compter de 1999, voir zone euro. Pour la Grèce, à compter de 2001, voir zone euro.
3  Taux de refinancement.
4  Taux prêteur.
5  Avances ordinaires à l'état.
6  Taux de l'escompte : effet de commerce.
7  Taux de facilité de prêt marginal.

8 "Euro Area" is an official descriptor for the European Economic and Monetary Union (EMU). The participating member states of the EMU are Austria, Belgium, Finland, France, Germany, Greece (beginning 2001), Ireland, Italy, Luxembourg, Netherlands, Portugal, and Spain.

9 Short-term facility rate.

10 Bank of Namibia overdraft rate.

11 Domestic currency.

8 L'expression "zone euro" est un intitulé officiel pour l'Union économique et monétaire (UEM) européenne. L'UEM est composée des pays membres suivants : Allemagne, Autriche, Belgique, Espagne, Finlande, France, Grèce (à partir de 2001), Irlande, Italie, Luxembourg, Pays-Bas et Portugal.

9 Taux de facilité à court terme.

10 Taux de découvert à la "Bank of Namibia".

11 Monnaie locale.

# Short-term interest rates
Treasury bill and money market rates: per cent per annum

# Taux d'intérêt à court terme
Taux des bons du Trésor et du marché monétaire : pour cent par année

| Country or area — Pays ou zone | 1998 | 1999 | 2000 | 2001 | 2002 | 2003 | 2004 | 2005 | 2006 | 2007 |
|---|---|---|---|---|---|---|---|---|---|---|
| Afghanistan — Afghanistan | | | | | | | | | | |
| Money market — Marché monétaire | ... | ... | ... | ... | ... | ... | ... | ... | 2.50 | 5.65 |
| Money market B[1] — Marché monétaire B[1] | ... | ... | ... | ... | ... | ... | ... | ... | 5.23 | 4.53 |
| Albania — Albanie | | | | | | | | | | |
| Treasury bill — Bons du trésor | 27.49 | 17.54 | 10.80 | 7.72 | 9.49 | 8.81 | 6.79 | 5.52 | 5.49 | 5.93 |
| Algeria — Algérie | | | | | | | | | | |
| Money market — Marché monétaire | 10.13 | 9.99 | 9.49 | 5.37 | 2.80 | 2.73 | 1.65 | 1.43 | 2.05 | 3.13 |
| Treasury bill — Bons du trésor | #9.96 | 10.04 | 9.54 | 5.85 | 2.86 | 1.67 | 0.87 | 0.75 | 2.14 | 0.96 |
| Anguilla — Anguilla | | | | | | | | | | |
| Money market — Marché monétaire | 5.25 | 5.25 | 5.25 | #5.64 | 6.32 | 6.07 | 4.67 | 4.01 | 4.76 | 5.19 |
| Antigua and Barbuda — Antigua-et-Barbuda | | | | | | | | | | |
| Money market — Marché monétaire | 5.25 | 5.25 | 5.25 | #5.64 | 6.32 | 6.07 | 4.67 | 4.01 | 4.76 | 5.19 |
| Treasury bill — Bons du trésor | 7.00 | 7.00 | 7.00 | 7.00 | 7.00 | 7.00 | 7.00 | 7.00 | 6.52 | 6.33 |
| Argentina — Argentine | | | | | | | | | | |
| Money market — Marché monétaire | 6.81 | 6.99 | 8.15 | 24.90 | 41.35 | 3.74 | 1.96 | 4.11 | 7.20 | 8.67 |
| Money market B[1] — Marché monétaire B[1] | 6.55 | 6.07 | 7.53 | 12.76 | 13.01 | 1.64 | 2.03 | 2.86 | 3.32 | 4.55 |
| Armenia — Arménie | | | | | | | | | | |
| Money market — Marché monétaire | 27.84 | 23.65 | 18.63 | 19.40 | 12.29 | 7.51 | 4.18 | 3.17 | 4.34 | 4.47 |
| Treasury bill — Bons du trésor | 46.99 | 55.10 | 24.40 | #20.59 | 14.75 | 11.91 | 5.27 | 4.05 | 4.87 | 6.09 |
| Aruba — Aruba | | | | | | | | | | |
| Money market — Marché monétaire | 2.80 | 2.62 | 3.37 | 2.19 | 0.45 | 0.18 | 0.11 | 0.51 | 2.27 | 2.53 |
| Australia — Australie | | | | | | | | | | |
| Money market — Marché monétaire | 4.99 | #4.78 | 5.90 | 5.06 | 4.55 | 4.81 | 5.25 | 5.46 | 5.81 | 6.39 |
| Treasury bill A[2] — Bons du trésor A[2] | 4.84 | 4.76 | 5.98 | 4.80 | ... | ... | ... | ... | ... | ... |
| Austria[3] — Autriche[3] | | | | | | | | | | |
| Money market — Marché monétaire | 3.36 | ... | ... | ... | ... | ... | ... | ... | ... | ... |
| Azerbaijan — Azerbaïdjan | | | | | | | | | | |
| Treasury bill — Bons du trésor | 14.10 | 18.31 | 16.73 | 16.51 | 14.12 | 8.00 | 4.62 | 7.52 | 10.04 | 10.64 |
| Bahamas — Bahamas | | | | | | | | | | |
| Treasury bill — Bons du trésor | 3.84 | 1.97 | 1.03 | 1.94 | 2.50 | 1.78 | 0.56 | 0.14 | 0.87 | 2.63 |
| Bahrain — Bahreïn | | | | | | | | | | |
| Money market B[4] — Marché monétaire B[4] | 5.69 | 5.58 | 6.89 | 3.85 | 2.02 | 1.24 | 1.74 | 3.64 | 5.33 | ... |
| Treasury bill — Bons du trésor | 5.53 | 5.46 | 6.56 | 3.78 | 1.75 | 1.13 | 1.56 | 3.57 | 5.04 | 4.86 |
| Barbados — Barbade | | | | | | | | | | |
| Treasury bill — Bons du trésor | 5.61 | 5.83 | 5.29 | 3.14 | 2.10 | 1.41 | 1.20 | 4.62 | 5.96 | ... |
| Belgium — Belgique | | | | | | | | | | |
| Money market B[3,5] — Marché monétaire B[3,5] | 3.58 | ... | ... | ... | ... | ... | ... | ... | ... | ... |
| Treasury bill — Bons du trésor | 3.51 | 2.72 | 4.02 | 4.16 | 3.17 | 2.23 | 1.97 | 2.02 | 2.73 | 3.80 |
| Belize[6] — Belize[6] | | | | | | | | | | |
| Treasury bill B — Bons du trésor B | 3.83 | 5.91 | 5.91 | 5.91 | 4.59 | 3.22 | 3.22 | 3.22 | 3.22 | 3.22 |
| Benin[7] — Bénin[7] | | | | | | | | | | |
| Money market A — Marché monétaire A | 4.95 | 4.95 | 4.95 | 4.95 | 4.95 | 4.95 | 4.95 | 4.95 | 4.95 | 3.93 |
| Bolivia — Bolivie | | | | | | | | | | |
| Money market — Marché monétaire | 12.57 | 13.49 | 7.40 | 6.99 | 8.41 | 4.07 | 4.05 | 3.53 | 3.80 | 4.27 |
| Money market B[1] — Marché monétaire B[1] | 9.26 | 8.29 | 5.68 | 3.57 | 2.96 | 2.12 | 3.02 | 3.37 | 4.62 | 4.59 |
| Treasury bill — Bons du trésor | 12.33 | 14.07 | 10.99 | 11.48 | 12.41 | 9.92 | 7.41 | 4.96 | 4.56 | 6.04 |
| Treasury bill B[1] — Bons du trésor B[1] | 7.48 | 7.84 | 7.02 | 4.19 | 3.56 | 2.53 | 3.34 | 2.85 | 3.68 | 4.31 |

| Country or area — Pays ou zone | 1998 | 1999 | 2000 | 2001 | 2002 | 2003 | 2004 | 2005 | 2006 | 2007 |
|---|---|---|---|---|---|---|---|---|---|---|
| Brazil — Brésil | | | | | | | | | | |
| Money market — Marché monétaire | 29.50 | 26.26 | 17.59 | 17.47 | 19.11 | 23.37 | 16.24 | 19.12 | 15.28 | 11.98 |
| Treasury bill — Bons du trésor | 28.57 | 26.39 | 18.51 | 20.06 | 19.43 | 22.11 | 17.14 | 18.76 | 14.38 | 11.50 |
| Treasury bill B[1] — Bons du trésor B[1] | 15.04 | ... | ... | 11.46 | ... | ... | ... | ... | ... | ... |
| Bulgaria — Bulgarie | | | | | | | | | | |
| Money market B[4] — Marché monétaire B[4] | 2.48 | 2.93 | 3.02 | 3.74 | 2.47 | 1.95 | 1.95 | #2.02 | 2.79 | 4.03 |
| Treasury bill — Bons du trésor | 6.02 | 5.43 | 4.21 | 4.57 | 4.29 | 2.81 | 2.64 | 2.23 | #2.58 | 3.79 |
| Burkina Faso[7] — Burkina Faso[7] | | | | | | | | | | |
| Money market A — Marché monétaire A | 4.95 | 4.95 | 4.95 | 4.95 | 4.95 | 4.95 | 4.95 | 4.95 | 4.95 | 3.93 |
| Canada — Canada | | | | | | | | | | |
| Money market A[8] — Marché monétaire A[8] | 4.87 | 4.74 | 5.52 | 4.11 | 2.45 | 2.93 | 2.25 | 2.66 | 4.02 | 4.34 |
| Treasury bill — Bons du trésor | 4.73 | 4.72 | 5.49 | 3.77 | 2.59 | 2.87 | 2.22 | 2.73 | 4.03 | 4.15 |
| Cape Verde — Cap-Vert | | | | | | | | | | |
| Treasury bill — Bons du trésor | ... | 7.19 | 8.53 | 10.33 | 8.04 | 5.81 | 6.42 | 4.07 | 2.70 | ... |
| Chile — Chili | | | | | | | | | | |
| Money market — Marché monétaire | ... | ... | 10.09 | 6.81 | 4.08 | 2.72 | 1.88 | 3.48 | 5.02 | 5.36 |
| China, Hong Kong SAR — Chine, Hong Kong RAS | | | | | | | | | | |
| Money market — Marché monétaire | 5.50 | 5.75 | 7.13 | 2.69 | 1.50 | 0.07 | 0.13 | 4.25 | 3.94 | 1.88 |
| Treasury bill — Bons du trésor | 5.04 | 4.94 | 5.69 | 1.69 | 1.35 | -0.08 | 0.07 | 3.65 | 3.29 | 1.96 |
| China, Macao SAR[4] — Chine, Macao RAS[4] | | | | | | | | | | |
| Money market B — Marché monétaire B | 5.41 | 5.70 | 6.29 | 2.11 | 1.48 | 0.11 | 0.27 | 4.09 | 3.91 | 3.27 |
| Colombia[4] — Colombie[4] | | | | | | | | | | |
| Money market B — Marché monétaire B | 35.00 | 18.81 | 10.87 | 10.43 | 6.06 | 6.95 | 7.01 | 6.18 | 6.49 | 8.66 |
| Côte d'Ivoire[7] — Côte d'Ivoire[7] | | | | | | | | | | |
| Money market A — Marché monétaire A | 4.95 | 4.95 | 4.95 | 4.95 | 4.95 | 4.95 | 4.95 | 4.95 | 4.95 | 3.93 |
| Croatia — Croatie | | | | | | | | | | |
| Money market — Marché monétaire | 11.16 | 10.21 | 6.78 | 3.42 | 1.75 | 3.31 | 5.11 | 3.10 | 2.06 | 4.27 |
| Cyprus — Chypre | | | | | | | | | | |
| Money market — Marché monétaire | 4.80 | 5.15 | 5.96 | 4.93 | 3.42 | 3.35 | 4.01 | 3.27 | 2.90 | 4.01 |
| Treasury bill — Bons du trésor | 5.59 | 5.59 | 6.02 | ... | ... | 3.56 | ... | ... | ... | ... |
| Czech Republic — République tchèque | | | | | | | | | | |
| Money market — Marché monétaire | 10.08 | 5.58 | 5.42 | 4.69 | 2.63 | 2.08 | 2.56 | 2.17 | 2.55 | 4.11 |
| Treasury bill — Bons du trésor | 10.51 | 5.71 | 5.37 | 5.06 | 2.72 | 2.04 | 2.57 | 1.96 | 2.51 | 3.55 |
| Denmark[5] — Danemark[5] | | | | | | | | | | |
| Money market B — Marché monétaire B | 4.27 | 3.37 | 4.98 | ... | 3.56 | 2.38 | 2.16 | 2.20 | 3.18 | #4.33 |
| Dominica — Dominique | | | | | | | | | | |
| Money market — Marché monétaire | 5.25 | 5.25 | 5.25 | #5.64 | 6.32 | 6.07 | 4.67 | 4.01 | 4.76 | 5.19 |
| Treasury bill — Bons du trésor | 6.40 | 6.40 | 6.40 | 6.40 | 6.40 | 6.40 | 6.40 | 6.40 | 6.40 | 6.40 |
| Dominican Republic — Rép. dominicaine | | | | | | | | | | |
| Money market — Marché monétaire | 16.68 | 15.30 | 18.28 | 13.47 | 14.50 | 24.24 | 36.76 | 12.57 | 10.60 | 8.24 |
| Egypt — Egypte | | | | | | | | | | |
| Treasury bill — Bons du trésor | 8.80 | 9.00 | 9.10 | 7.20 | 5.50 | 6.90 | 9.90 | 8.57 | 9.53 | 6.85 |
| El Salvador — El Salvador | | | | | | | | | | |
| Money market — Marché monétaire | 9.43 | 10.68 | 6.93 | 5.28 | 4.40 | 3.86 | 4.36 | 5.18 | 6.00 | 5.25 |
| Estonia — Estonie | | | | | | | | | | |
| Money market — Marché monétaire | 11.66 | 5.39 | #5.68 | 5.31 | 3.88 | 2.92 | 2.50 | 2.38 | 3.16 | 4.87 |
| Ethiopia — Ethiopie | | | | | | | | | | |
| Treasury bill — Bons du trésor | 3.48 | 3.65 | 2.74 | 3.06 | 1.30 | #1.31 | 0.56 | 0.25 | 0.08 | ... |

| Country or area — Pays ou zone | 1998 | 1999 | 2000 | 2001 | 2002 | 2003 | 2004 | 2005 | 2006 | 2007 |
|---|---|---|---|---|---|---|---|---|---|---|
| **Euro Area[9] — Zone euro[9]** | | | | | | | | | | |
| Money market A — Marché monétaire A | 3.96 | 2.96 | 4.39 | 4.26 | 3.32 | 2.33 | 2.11 | 2.18 | 3.08 | 4.28 |
| **Fiji — Fidji** | | | | | | | | | | |
| Money market A[10] — Marché monétaire A[10] | 1.27 | 1.27 | 2.58 | 0.79 | 0.92 | 0.86 | 0.90 | 1.28 | 4.78 | 4.74 |
| Treasury bill — Bons du trésor | 2.00 | 2.00 | 3.63 | 1.51 | 1.66 | 1.06 | 1.56 | 1.94 | 7.45 | 4.48 |
| **Finland[11] — Finlande[11]** | | | | | | | | | | |
| Money market B — Marché monétaire B | 3.57 | 2.96 | 4.39 | 4.26 | 3.32 | 2.33 | 2.11 | 2.18 | 3.08 | 4.28 |
| **France — France** | | | | | | | | | | |
| Money market B[3,5] — Marché monétaire B[3,5] | 3.39 | ... | ... | ... | ... | ... | ... | ... | ... | ... |
| Treasury bill A[12] — Bons du trésor A[12] | 3.45 | 2.72 | 4.23 | 4.26 | 3.28 | 2.27 | ... | ... | ... | ... |
| **Georgia — Géorgie** | | | | | | | | | | |
| Money market — Marché monétaire | 42.62 | 31.26 | 16.77 | 17.54 | 27.69 | 16.88 | 11.87 | 7.71 | 9.46 | 7.42 |
| Treasury bill — Bons du trésor | ... | ... | ... | 29.93 | 43.42 | 44.26 | 19.16 | ... | ... | ... |
| **Germany — Allemagne** | | | | | | | | | | |
| Money market B[5] — Marché monétaire B[5] | 3.41 | 2.73 | 4.11 | 4.37 | 3.28 | 2.32 | 2.05 | 2.09 | 2.84 | 3.86 |
| Treasury bill — Bons du trésor | 3.42 | 2.88 | 4.32 | 3.66 | 2.97 | 1.98 | 2.00 | 2.03 | 3.08 | ... |
| **Ghana — Ghana** | | | | | | | | | | |
| Money market — Marché monétaire | ... | ... | ... | ... | ... | 24.71 | 15.73 | 14.70 | 10.57 | ... |
| Treasury bill B[13] — Bons du trésor B[13] | 34.33 | 26.37 | 36.28 | 40.96 | 25.11 | 27.25 | 16.57 | 14.89 | 9.95 | |
| **Greece — Grèce** | | | | | | | | | | |
| Money market A[3,9] — Marché monétaire A[3,9] | 13.99 | ... | ... | ... | ... | ... | ... | ... | ... | ... |
| Treasury bill A[14] — Bons du trésor A[14] | 10.30 | 8.30 | #6.22 | 4.08 | 3.50 | 2.34 | 2.27 | 2.33 | 3.44 | 4.45 |
| **Grenada — Grenade** | | | | | | | | | | |
| Money market — Marché monétaire | 5.25 | 5.25 | 5.25 | #5.64 | 6.32 | 6.07 | 4.67 | 4.01 | 4.76 | 5.06 |
| Treasury bill — Bons du trésor | 6.50 | 6.50 | 6.50 | #7.00 | 7.00 | 6.50 | 5.50 | 5.50 | 6.25 | 6.38 |
| **Guatemala — Guatemala** | | | | | | | | | | |
| Money market — Marché monétaire | 6.62 | 9.23 | 9.33 | 10.58 | 9.11 | 6.65 | 6.16 | 6.54 | 6.56 | ... |
| **Guinea-Bissau — Guinée-Bissau** | | | | | | | | | | |
| Money market — Marché monétaire | 4.95 | 4.95 | 4.95 | 4.95 | 4.95 | 4.95 | 4.95 | 4.95 | 4.95 | 3.93 |
| **Guyana — Guyana** | | | | | | | | | | |
| Treasury bill — Bons du trésor | 8.33 | 11.31 | 9.88 | 7.78 | 4.94 | 3.04 | 3.62 | 3.79 | 3.95 | 3.94 |
| **Hungary — Hongrie** | | | | | | | | | | |
| Treasury bill — Bons du trésor | 17.83 | 14.68 | 11.03 | 10.79 | 8.91 | 8.22 | 11.32 | 6.95 | 6.87 | 7.67 |
| **Iceland — Islande** | | | | | | | | | | |
| Money market — Marché monétaire | 8.12 | 9.24 | 11.61 | 14.51 | 11.21 | 5.14 | 6.22 | 9.05 | 12.41 | 13.96 |
| Treasury bill B[15] — Bons du trésor B[15] | 7.40 | 8.61 | 11.12 | 11.03 | 8.01 | 4.93 | 6.04 | 8.80 | 13.41 | 15.13 |
| **India[5] — Inde[5]** | | | | | | | | | | |
| Money market B — Marché monétaire B | ... | ... | ... | ... | ... | ... | ... | ... | ... | 15.29 |
| **Indonesia[5] — Indonésie[5]** | | | | | | | | | | |
| Money market B — Marché monétaire B | 62.79 | 23.58 | 10.32 | 15.03 | 13.54 | 7.76 | 5.38 | 6.78 | 9.18 | 6.02 |
| **Iraq[16] — Iraq[16]** | | | | | | | | | | |
| Money market B — Marché monétaire B | ... | ... | ... | ... | ... | ... | ... | 8.90 | 9.49 | 21.00 |
| **Ireland — Irlande** | | | | | | | | | | |
| Money market A[17] — Marché monétaire A[17] | 3.23 | 3.14 | 4.84 | 3.31 | 2.88 | 2.08 | 2.13 | 2.40 | 3.64 | 4.71 |
| Treasury bill B[18] — Bons du trésor B[18] | 5.37 | ... | ... | ... | ... | ... | ... | ... | ... | ... |
| **Israel — Israël** | | | | | | | | | | |
| Treasury bill — Bons du trésor | 11.33 | 11.41 | 8.81 | 6.50 | 7.38 | 7.00 | 4.78 | 4.34 | ... | ... |

| Country or area — Pays ou zone | 1998 | 1999 | 2000 | 2001 | 2002 | 2003 | 2004 | 2005 | 2006 | 2007 |
|---|---|---|---|---|---|---|---|---|---|---|
| Italy — Italie | | | | | | | | | | |
| Money market — Marché monétaire | 4.99 | 2.95 | 4.39 | 4.26 | 3.32 | 2.33 | 2.10 | 2.18 | 3.09 | 4.29 |
| Treasury bill — Bons du trésor | 4.59 | 3.01 | 4.53 | 4.05 | 3.26 | 2.19 | 2.08 | 2.17 | 3.18 | 4.04 |
| Jamaica — Jamaïque | | | | | | | | | | |
| Money market — Marché monétaire | 24.44 | 21.50 | 19.90 | 19.10 | 15.09 | 25.53 | 12.79 | 10.96 | 9.37 | 9.04 |
| Treasury bill — Bons du trésor | 25.65 | 20.75 | 18.24 | 16.71 | 15.54 | 25.94 | 15.47 | 13.39 | 12.79 | 12.56 |
| Japan[5] — Japon[5] | | | | | | | | | | |
| Money market B — Marché monétaire B | 0.37 | 0.06 | 0.11 | 0.06 | 0.01 | ^0.00 | ^0.00 | ^0.00 | 0.12 | 0.47 |
| Jordan — Jordanie | | | | | | | | | | |
| Money market — Marché monétaire | ... | 5.19 | 5.28 | 4.63 | 3.49 | 2.58 | 2.18 | 3.59 | 5.55 | 5.70 |
| Kazakhstan — Kazakhstan | | | | | | | | | | |
| Treasury bill — Bons du trésor | 23.59 | 15.63 | 6.59 | 5.28 | 5.20 | 5.86 | 3.28 | 3.28 | 3.28 | 7.01 |
| Kenya — Kenya | | | | | | | | | | |
| Treasury bill — Bons du trésor | 22.83 | 13.87 | 12.05 | 12.60 | 8.95 | 3.51 | 3.17 | 8.43 | 6.73 | 6.49 |
| Korea, Republic of — Corée, République de | | | | | | | | | | |
| Money market — Marché monétaire | 14.98 | 5.01 | 5.16 | 4.69 | 4.21 | 4.00 | 3.65 | 3.33 | 4.19 | 4.77 |
| Money market B[19] — Marché monétaire B[19] | 15.10 | 8.86 | 9.35 | 7.05 | 6.56 | 5.43 | 4.73 | 4.68 | 5.17 | 5.70 |
| Kuwait — Koweït | | | | | | | | | | |
| Money market A[20] — Marché monétaire A[20] | 7.24 | 6.32 | 6.82 | 4.62 | 2.99 | 2.47 | 2.14 | 2.83 | 5.62 | 4.88 |
| Treasury bill A[12,21] — Bons du trésor A[12,21] | 6.95 | 6.08 | 6.83 | 4.23 | 2.82 | 2.33 | 1.75 | 1.99 | ... | ... |
| Kyrgyzstan — Kirghizistan | | | | | | | | | | |
| Money market — Marché monétaire | 43.98 | 43.71 | 24.26 | 11.92 | 6.30 | 4.65 | 4.78 | 3.24 | 2.83 | 3.18 |
| Treasury bill — Bons du trésor | 43.67 | 47.19 | 32.26 | 19.08 | 10.15 | 7.21 | 4.94 | 4.40 | 4.75 | 4.90 |
| Lao People's Dem. Rep. — Rép. dém. pop. lao | | | | | | | | | | |
| Treasury bill — Bons du trésor | 23.66 | 30.00 | 29.94 | 22.70 | 21.41 | 24.87 | 20.37 | 18.61 | 18.34 | ... |
| Latvia — Lettonie | | | | | | | | | | |
| Money market — Marché monétaire | 4.42 | 4.72 | 2.97 | 5.23 | 3.01 | 2.86 | 3.25 | 2.49 | 3.24 | 5.07 |
| Treasury bill — Bons du trésor | 5.27 | 6.23 | #4.85 | 5.63 | 3.52 | 3.24 | 3.43 | 2.56 | 4.13 | ... |
| Lebanon — Liban | | | | | | | | | | |
| Treasury bill — Bons du trésor | 12.70 | 11.57 | 11.18 | 11.18 | 10.90 | 6.46 | 5.25 | 5.22 | 5.22 | 5.22 |
| Lesotho — Lesotho | | | | | | | | | | |
| Treasury bill — Bons du trésor | 15.47 | 12.45 | 9.06 | 9.49 | 11.34 | 11.96 | 8.52 | 7.23 | 6.87 | 7.81 |
| Libyan Arab Jamah.[22] — Jamah. arabe libyenne[22] | | | | | | | | | | |
| Money market B — Marché monétaire B | 4.00 | 4.00 | 4.00 | 4.00 | 4.00 | 4.00 | 4.00 | ... | ... | ... |
| Lithuania — Lituanie | | | | | | | | | | |
| Money market — Marché monétaire | #6.12 | 6.26 | 3.60 | 3.37 | 2.21 | 1.79 | 1.53 | 1.97 | 2.76 | 4.18 |
| Money market B[1] — Marché monétaire B[1] | 5.52 | 5.05 | 6.10 | 4.03 | 1.92 | 1.72 | 1.73 | 2.59 | 3.06 | 4.25 |
| Treasury bill — Bons du trésor | 10.69 | 11.14 | #9.27 | 5.68 | 3.72 | 2.61 | 2.23 | 2.36 | 2.95 | ... |
| Luxembourg[3,4] — Luxembourg[3,4] | | | | | | | | | | |
| Money market B — Marché monétaire B | 3.48 | ... | ... | ... | ... | ... | ... | ... | ... | ... |
| Madagascar — Madagascar | | | | | | | | | | |
| Money market — Marché monétaire | 12.00 | 17.25 | 16.00 | 9.00 | 9.00 | 10.50 | 16.50 | 16.50 | 14.50 | 11.00 |
| Treasury bill — Bons du trésor | ... | ... | ... | 10.28 | ... | 11.94 | 12.95 | 18.84 | 21.16 | 11.84 |
| Malawi — Malawi | | | | | | | | | | |
| Treasury bill — Bons du trésor | 32.98 | 42.85 | 39.52 | 42.41 | 41.75 | 39.32 | 28.58 | 24.36 | 19.27 | ... |
| Malaysia — Malaisie | | | | | | | | | | |
| Money market A[23] — Marché monétaire A[23] | 8.46 | 3.38 | 2.66 | 2.79 | 2.73 | 2.74 | 2.70 | 2.72 | 3.38 | 3.50 |
| Treasury bill A[12] — Bons du trésor A[12] | 6.86 | 3.53 | 2.86 | 2.79 | 2.73 | 2.79 | 2.40 | 2.48 | 3.23 | 3.43 |

| Country or area — Pays ou zone | 1998 | 1999 | 2000 | 2001 | 2002 | 2003 | 2004 | 2005 | 2006 | 2007 |
|---|---|---|---|---|---|---|---|---|---|---|
| Maldives — Maldives | | | | | | | | | | |
| Money market B[5] — Marché monétaire B[5] | 6.80 | 6.80 | 6.80 | ... | ... | ... | ... | ... | ... | ... |
| Treasury bill — Bons du trésor | ... | ... | ... | ... | ... | ... | ... | ... | 5.00 | 5.50 |
| Mali[7] — Mali[7] | | | | | | | | | | |
| Money market A — Marché monétaire A | 4.95 | 4.95 | 4.95 | 4.95 | 4.95 | 4.95 | 4.95 | 4.95 | 4.95 | 3.93 |
| Malta[12] — Malte[12] | | | | | | | | | | |
| Treasury bill A — Bons du trésor A | 5.41 | 5.15 | 4.89 | 4.93 | 4.03 | 3.29 | 2.94 | 3.18 | 3.49 | ... |
| Mauritania — Mauritanie | | | | | | | | | | |
| Treasury bill — Bons du trésor | 16.16 | 14.16 | 10.93 | 3.14 | 6.01 | 7.65 | 7.22 | 11.84 | 11.50 | 10.43 |
| Mauritius — Maurice | | | | | | | | | | |
| Money market — Marché monétaire | 8.99 | 10.01 | 7.66 | 7.25 | 6.20 | 3.22 | 1.33 | 2.45 | 5.59 | 8.52 |
| Mexico — Mexique | | | | | | | | | | |
| Money market B[24] — Marché monétaire B[24] | 26.89 | 24.10 | 16.96 | 12.89 | 8.17 | 6.83 | 7.15 | 9.59 | 7.51 | 7.66 |
| Treasury bill — Bons du trésor | 24.76 | 21.41 | 15.24 | 11.31 | 7.09 | 6.23 | 6.82 | 9.20 | 7.19 | 7.19 |
| Moldova — Moldova | | | | | | | | | | |
| Money market — Marché monétaire | 30.91 | 32.60 | 20.77 | 11.04 | 5.13 | 11.51 | 13.19 | 5.87 | 9.50 | 12.19 |
| Money market B[1] — Marché monétaire B[1] | ... | 11.88 | 6.86 | 9.06 | 4.80 | 2.51 | 0.78 | 2.49 | 4.13 | 4.21 |
| Treasury bill — Bons du trésor | 30.54 | 28.49 | 22.20 | 14.24 | 5.89 | 15.08 | 11.89 | 3.70 | 7.30 | 13.10 |
| Montenegro — Monténégro | | | | | | | | | | |
| Treasury bill — Bons du trésor | ... | ... | ... | ... | ... | ... | 9.00 | 1.01 | 0.49 | ... |
| Montserrat — Montserrat | | | | | | | | | | |
| Money market — Marché monétaire | 5.25 | 5.25 | 5.25 | #5.64 | 6.32 | 6.07 | 4.67 | 4.01 | 4.76 | 5.19 |
| Morocco — Maroc | | | | | | | | | | |
| Money market — Marché monétaire | 6.30 | 5.64 | 5.41 | 4.44 | 2.99 | 3.22 | 2.39 | 2.78 | 2.58 | 3.31 |
| Mozambique — Mozambique | | | | | | | | | | |
| Money market — Marché monétaire | ... | 9.92 | 16.12 | #25.00 | 20.40 | 13.34 | 9.87 | 6.35 | 15.25 | 15.15 |
| Treasury bill — Bons du trésor | ... | ... | 16.97 | 24.77 | 29.55 | 15.31 | 12.37 | 9.10 | 15.05 | 15.16 |
| Namibia — Namibie | | | | | | | | | | |
| Money market — Marché monétaire | 17.14 | 13.17 | 9.19 | 9.53 | 10.46 | 10.03 | 6.93 | 6.93 | 7.12 | 8.61 |
| Treasury bill — Bons du trésor | 17.24 | 13.28 | 10.26 | 9.29 | 11.00 | 10.51 | 7.78 | 7.09 | 7.26 | 8.59 |
| Nepal — Népal | | | | | | | | | | |
| Treasury bill — Bons du trésor | 3.70 | 4.30 | 5.30 | 5.00 | 3.80 | 3.85 | 2.40 | 2.20 | 1.98 | ... |
| Netherlands[3,5] — Pays-Bas[3,5] | | | | | | | | | | |
| Money market B — Marché monétaire B | 3.21 | ... | ... | ... | ... | ... | ... | ... | ... | ... |
| Netherlands Antilles[12] — Antilles néerlandaises[12] | | | | | | | | | | |
| Treasury bill A — Bons du trésor A | 5.82 | 6.15 | 6.15 | 6.15 | 5.15 | 2.80 | 3.86 | 3.52 | 5.39 | ... |
| New Zealand — Nouvelle-Zélande | | | | | | | | | | |
| Money market — Marché monétaire | 6.86 | 4.33 | 6.12 | 5.76 | 5.40 | 5.33 | 5.77 | 6.76 | 7.30 | 7.93 |
| Treasury bill A[25] — Bons du trésor A[25] | 7.10 | 4.58 | 6.39 | 5.56 | 5.52 | 5.21 | 5.85 | 6.52 | 7.05 | 7.55 |
| Niger[7] — Niger[7] | | | | | | | | | | |
| Money market A — Marché monétaire A | 4.95 | 4.95 | 4.95 | 4.95 | 4.95 | 4.95 | 4.95 | 4.95 | 4.95 | 3.93 |
| Nigeria — Nigéria | | | | | | | | | | |
| Treasury bill — Bons du trésor | 12.26 | 17.82 | 15.50 | 17.50 | 19.03 | 14.79 | 14.34 | 7.63 | 9.99 | ... |
| Norway[5] — Norvège[5] | | | | | | | | | | |
| Money market B — Marché monétaire B | 6.03 | 6.87 | 6.72 | 7.38 | 7.05 | 4.45 | 2.17 | 2.26 | 3.12 | ... |
| Oman[23] — Oman[23] | | | | | | | | | | |
| Money market A — Marché monétaire A | ... | ... | ... | ... | ... | ... | 0.66 | 2.25 | 3.40 | ... |

| Country or area — Pays ou zone | 1998 | 1999 | 2000 | 2001 | 2002 | 2003 | 2004 | 2005 | 2006 | 2007 |
|---|---|---|---|---|---|---|---|---|---|---|
| Pakistan — Pakistan | | | | | | | | | | |
| Money market B[5] — Marché monétaire B[5] | 10.76 | 9.04 | 8.57 | 8.49 | 5.53 | 2.14 | 2.70 | 6.83 | 8.89 | 9.30 |
| Treasury bill A[26] — Bons du trésor A[26] | ... | ... | 8.38 | 10.71 | 6.08 | 1.87 | 2.49 | 7.18 | 8.54 | 8.99 |
| Panama — Panama | | | | | | | | | | |
| Money market — Marché monétaire | ... | ... | ... | ... | 2.22 | 1.50 | 1.90 | 3.13 | 5.06 | 5.05 |
| Papua New Guinea — Papouasie-Nvl-Guinée | | | | | | | | | | |
| Money market B[4] — Marché monétaire B[4] | ... | ... | 9.54 | 11.05 | 9.11 | 13.58 | 7.79 | 4.36 | 3.29 | 3.00 |
| Treasury bill A[27] — Bons du trésor A[27] | 21.18 | 22.70 | 17.00 | 12.36 | 10.93 | 18.69 | 8.85 | 3.81 | 4.01 | 4.67 |
| Paraguay — Paraguay | | | | | | | | | | |
| Money market — Marché monétaire | 20.74 | 17.26 | 10.70 | 13.45 | 13.19 | 13.02 | 1.33 | 2.29 | 8.33 | 3.93 |
| Peru[4] — Pérou[4] | | | | | | | | | | |
| Money market — Marché monétaire | 12.94 | 16.91 | 11.41 | 3.15 | 3.80 | 2.51 | 3.00 | 3.34 | 4.51 | 4.99 |
| Money market B[1] — Marché monétaire B[1] | 11.20 | 6.60 | 8.40 | 2.07 | 2.22 | 1.09 | 2.19 | 4.19 | 5.37 | 5.92 |
| Philippines — Philippines | | | | | | | | | | |
| Money market — Marché monétaire | 13.90 | 10.16 | 10.84 | 9.75 | 7.15 | 6.97 | 7.05 | 7.31 | 7.84 | 7.02 |
| Treasury bill A[16] — Bons du trésor A[16] | 15.00 | 10.00 | 9.91 | 9.73 | 5.49 | 5.87 | 7.32 | 6.13 | 5.29 | 3.38 |
| Poland — Pologne | | | | | | | | | | |
| Money market — Marché monétaire | 21.11 | 13.89 | 17.55 | 17.14 | 9.49 | 5.69 | 5.67 | 5.34 | 4.10 | 4.42 |
| Treasury bill — Bons du trésor | 18.90 | 12.99 | 17.42 | 14.73 | 8.22 | 5.38 | 6.60 | 4.90 | 4.19 | 4.70 |
| Portugal — Portugal | | | | | | | | | | |
| Money market A[3,28] — Marché monétaire A[3,28] | 4.34 | 2.71 | ... | ... | ... | ... | ... | ... | ... | ... |
| Qatar — Qatar | | | | | | | | | | |
| Money market — Marché monétaire | ... | ... | ... | ... | ... | ... | 2.09 | 3.13 | 4.77 | 4.38 |
| Romania — Roumanie | | | | | | | | | | |
| Money market — Marché monétaire | 80.88 | 80.76 | 44.78 | 40.97 | 29.05 | 18.95 | 20.01 | 8.99 | 8.34 | 7.55 |
| Treasury bill A[16] — Bons du trésor A[16] | 63.99 | 74.21 | 51.86 | 42.18 | 27.03 | 15.07 | ... | ... | ... | 5.80 |
| Russian Federation — Fédération de Russie | | | | | | | | | | |
| Money market — Marché monétaire | 50.56 | 14.79 | 7.14 | 10.10 | 8.19 | 3.77 | 3.33 | 2.68 | 3.43 | 4.43 |
| Treasury bill — Bons du trésor | ... | ... | 12.12 | 12.45 | 12.72 | 5.35 | ... | ... | ... | ... |
| Rwanda — Rwanda | | | | | | | | | | |
| Money market B[4] — Marché monétaire B[4] | 8.10 | ... | ... | 10.29 | 10.09 | 10.13 | 11.02 | 8.28 | 8.26 | ... |
| Treasury bill — Bons du trésor | ... | ... | ... | ... | 9.36 | 11.32 | 12.55 | 8.70 | 9.90 | #7.24 |
| Saint Kitts and Nevis — Saint-Kitts-et-Nevis | | | | | | | | | | |
| Money market — Marché monétaire | 5.25 | 5.25 | 5.25 | #5.64 | 6.32 | 6.07 | 4.67 | 4.01 | 4.76 | 5.19 |
| Treasury bill — Bons du trésor | 6.50 | 6.50 | 6.50 | 7.50 | 7.50 | 7.17 | 7.00 | 7.00 | 7.00 | 7.00 |
| Saint Lucia — Sainte-Lucie | | | | | | | | | | |
| Money market — Marché monétaire | 5.25 | 5.25 | 5.25 | #5.64 | 6.32 | 6.07 | 4.67 | 4.01 | 4.76 | 5.19 |
| Treasury bill — Bons du trésor | 6.02 | 6.02 | 6.02 | 5.84 | 5.84 | 5.44 | #5.50 | 4.48 | 5.17 | 5.83 |
| St. Vincent-Grenadines — St. Vincent-Grenadines | | | | | | | | | | |
| Money market — Marché monétaire | 5.25 | 5.25 | 5.25 | #5.64 | 6.32 | 6.07 | 4.67 | 4.01 | 4.76 | 5.19 |
| Treasury bill — Bons du trésor | 6.50 | 6.50 | 6.50 | 7.00 | 7.00 | 5.73 | 4.60 | 4.85 | 5.62 | 5.75 |
| Senegal — Sénégal | | | | | | | | | | |
| Money market — Marché monétaire | 4.95 | 4.95 | 4.95 | 4.95 | 4.95 | 4.95 | 4.95 | 4.95 | 4.95 | 3.93 |
| Serbia — Serbie | | | | | | | | | | |
| Money market — Marché monétaire | ... | ... | ... | 31.91 | 15.48 | 12.69 | 12.86 | 20.51 | 16.51 | 10.31 |
| Treasury bill — Bons du trésor | ... | ... | ... | ... | ... | 20.02 | 21.17 | 14.58 | 10.24 | 4.42 |
| Seychelles — Seychelles | | | | | | | | | | |
| Treasury bill — Bons du trésor | 8.13 | 5.00 | 5.00 | 5.00 | 5.00 | 4.61 | 3.17 | 3.34 | 3.70 | ... |

| Country or area — Pays ou zone | 1998 | 1999 | 2000 | 2001 | 2002 | 2003 | 2004 | 2005 | 2006 | 2007 |
|---|---|---|---|---|---|---|---|---|---|---|
| Sierra Leone — Sierra Leone | | | | | | | | | | |
| Treasury bill — Bons du trésor | 22.10 | 32.42 | 26.22 | 13.74 | 15.15 | 15.68 | 26.14 | 22.98 | 17.71 | 18.41 |
| Singapore — Singapour | | | | | | | | | | |
| Money market A[9] — Marché monétaire A[9] | 5.00 | 2.04 | 2.57 | 1.99 | 0.96 | 0.74 | 1.04 | 2.28 | 3.46 | 2.72 |
| Treasury bill — Bons du trésor | 2.12 | 1.12 | 2.18 | 1.69 | 0.81 | 0.64 | 0.96 | 2.04 | 2.95 | 2.34 |
| Slovakia — Slovaquie | | | | | | | | | | |
| Money market — Marché monétaire | ... | ... | 8.08 | 7.76 | 6.33 | 6.08 | 3.82 | 3.02 | 4.83 | 4.25 |
| Slovenia — Slovénie | | | | | | | | | | |
| Money market — Marché monétaire | 7.45 | 6.87 | 6.95 | 6.90 | 4.93 | 5.59 | 4.40 | 3.73 | 3.38 | 4.08 |
| Treasury bill — Bons du trésor | ... | 8.63 | 10.94 | 10.88 | 8.73 | 6.53 | 4.17 | 3.66 | 3.30 | 3.90 |
| Solomon Islands[12] — Iles Salomon[12] | | | | | | | | | | |
| Treasury bill A — Bons du trésor A | 6.00 | 6.00 | 7.05 | 8.23 | 6.87 | 5.85 | 6.00 | 4.53 | 3.41 | 3.17 |
| South Africa — Afrique du Sud | | | | | | | | | | |
| Money market — Marché monétaire | 17.11 | 13.06 | 9.54 | #8.49 | 11.11 | 10.93 | 7.15 | 6.62 | 7.19 | #9.22 |
| Treasury bill — Bons du trésor | 16.53 | 12.85 | 10.11 | 9.68 | 11.16 | 10.67 | 7.53 | 6.91 | 7.34 | 9.12 |
| Spain — Espagne | | | | | | | | | | |
| Money market B[5] — Marché monétaire B[5] | 4.34 | 2.72 | 4.11 | 4.36 | 3.28 | 2.31 | 2.04 | 2.09 | 2.83 | 3.85 |
| Treasury bill — Bons du trésor | 3.79 | 3.01 | 4.61 | 3.92 | 3.34 | 2.21 | 2.17 | 2.19 | 3.26 | 4.07 |
| Sri Lanka — Sri Lanka | | | | | | | | | | |
| Money market B[29] — Marché monétaire B[29] | 15.74 | 16.69 | 17.30 | 21.24 | 12.33 | 9.68 | 8.87 | 10.15 | ... | ... |
| Treasury bill — Bons du trésor | 12.59 | 12.51 | 14.02 | 17.57 | 12.47 | 8.09 | 7.71 | 9.03 | ... | ... |
| Swaziland — Swaziland | | | | | | | | | | |
| Money market — Marché monétaire | 10.63 | 8.86 | 5.54 | 5.06 | 7.31 | 6.98 | 4.12 | 3.47 | 4.40 | 6.67 |
| Treasury bill — Bons du trésor | 13.09 | 11.19 | 8.30 | 7.16 | 8.59 | 10.61 | 7.94 | 7.08 | 7.54 | 9.09 |
| Sweden — Suède | | | | | | | | | | |
| Money market B[5] — Marché monétaire B[5] | 4.24 | 3.14 | 3.81 | 4.09 | 4.19 | 3.29 | ... | ... | ... | ... |
| Treasury bill A[30] — Bons du trésor A[30] | 4.19 | 3.12 | 3.95 | 4.00 | 4.07 | 3.03 | 2.11 | 1.72 | ... | ... |
| Switzerland — Suisse | | | | | | | | | | |
| Money market — Marché monétaire | 1.22 | 0.93 | #3.50 | 1.65 | 0.44 | 0.09 | 0.55 | 0.63 | 1.94 | 2.00 |
| Treasury bill — Bons du trésor | 1.32 | 1.17 | 2.93 | 2.68 | 0.94 | 0.16 | 0.37 | 0.71 | 1.36 | 2.16 |
| Thailand — Thaïlande | | | | | | | | | | |
| Money market — Marché monétaire | 13.02 | 1.77 | 1.95 | 2.00 | 1.76 | 1.31 | 1.23 | 2.62 | 4.64 | 3.75 |
| Togo[7] — Togo[7] | | | | | | | | | | |
| Money market A — Marché monétaire A | 4.95 | 4.95 | 4.95 | 4.95 | 4.95 | 4.95 | 4.95 | 4.95 | 4.95 | 3.93 |
| Trinidad and Tobago — Trinité-et-Tobago | | | | | | | | | | |
| Treasury bill — Bons du trésor | 11.93 | 10.40 | 10.56 | 8.55 | 4.83 | 4.71 | 4.77 | 4.86 | 6.07 | ... |
| Tunisia — Tunisie | | | | | | | | | | |
| Money market — Marché monétaire | 6.89 | 5.99 | 5.88 | 6.04 | 5.93 | 5.14 | 5.00 | 5.00 | 5.07 | 5.24 |
| Turkey — Turquie | | | | | | | | | | |
| Money market B[4] — Marché monétaire B[4] | 74.60 | 73.53 | 56.72 | 91.95 | 49.51 | 36.16 | 21.42 | 14.73 | 15.59 | 17.24 |
| Treasury bill — Bons du trésor | ... | ... | 25.18 | 93.24 | 59.50 | 34.90 | 22.08 | 15.49 | 18.37 | ... |
| Uganda[16] — Ouganda[16] | | | | | | | | | | |
| Treasury bill A — Bons du trésor A | 7.77 | 7.43 | 13.19 | 11.00 | 5.85 | 16.87 | 9.02 | 8.50 | 8.12 | ... |
| Ukraine — Ukraine | | | | | | | | | | |
| Money market — Marché monétaire | 40.41 | 44.98 | 18.34 | 16.57 | 5.50 | 7.90 | 6.34 | 4.16 | 3.58 | 2.27 |
| Money market B[1] — Marché monétaire B[1] | 10.61 | 5.44 | 6.27 | 5.87 | 3.14 | 3.61 | 2.15 | 2.85 | 4.13 | 4.82 |

| Country or area — Pays ou zone | 1998 | 1999 | 2000 | 2001 | 2002 | 2003 | 2004 | 2005 | 2006 | 2007 |
|---|---|---|---|---|---|---|---|---|---|---|
| United Kingdom — Royaume-Uni | | | | | | | | | | |
| Money market A[31] — Marché monétaire A[31] | 7.21 | 5.20 | 5.77 | 5.08 | 3.89 | 3.59 | 4.29 | 4.70 | 4.77 | 5.67 |
| Treasury bill — Bons du trésor | 6.82 | 5.04 | 5.80 | 4.77 | 3.86 | 3.55 | 4.43 | 4.55 | 4.65 | 5.52 |
| Treasury bill B[32] — Bons du trésor B[32] | 7.23 | 5.14 | 5.83 | 4.79 | 3.96 | 3.55 | 4.44 | 4.59 | 4.67 | 5.60 |
| United Rep. of Tanzania — Rép.-Unie de Tanzanie | | | | | | | | | | |
| Treasury bill — Bons du trésor | 11.83 | 10.05 | 9.78 | 4.14 | 3.55 | 6.26 | 8.35 | 10.67 | 11.64 | 13.38 |
| United States — Etats-Unis | | | | | | | | | | |
| Money market A[33] — Marché monétaire A[33] | 5.34 | 5.18 | 6.31 | 3.61 | 1.69 | 1.11 | 1.49 | 3.38 | 5.03 | 4.99 |
| Money market B[34] — Marché monétaire B[34] | 5.35 | 4.97 | 6.24 | 3.89 | 1.67 | 1.13 | 1.35 | 3.21 | 4.96 | 5.02 |
| Treasury bill — Bons du trésor | 4.82 | 4.66 | 5.84 | 3.45 | 1.61 | 1.01 | 1.37 | 3.15 | 4.72 | 4.41 |
| Treasury bill A[12] — Bons du trésor A[12] | 4.90 | 4.77 | 6.00 | 3.48 | 1.63 | 1.02 | 1.39 | 3.21 | 4.85 | 4.45 |
| Uruguay — Uruguay | | | | | | | | | | |
| Money market — Marché monétaire | 20.48 | 13.96 | 14.82 | 22.10 | 86.10 | 20.76 | 3.57 | 1.25 | 1.60 | #4.11 |
| Treasury bill — Bons du trésor | ... | ... | ... | ... | ... | 32.53 | 14.75 | 4.14 | 4.54 | ... |
| Vanuatu[35] — Vanuatu[35] | | | | | | | | | | |
| Money market B — Marché monétaire B | 8.65 | 6.99 | 5.58 | 5.50 | 5.50 | 5.50 | 5.50 | 5.50 | 5.50 | 5.50 |
| Venezuela (Bolivarian Republic of) — Venezuela (République bolivarienne du) | | | | | | | | | | |
| Money market — Marché monétaire | 18.58 | 7.48 | 8.14 | 13.33 | 28.87 | 13.23 | 4.38 | 2.62 | 5.26 | 8.72 |
| Viet Nam — Viet Nam | | | | | | | | | | |
| Treasury bill — Bons du trésor | ... | ... | 5.42 | 5.49 | 5.92 | 5.83 | ... | 6.13 | 4.73 | ... |
| Yemen — Yémen | | | | | | | | | | |
| Treasury bill — Bons du trésor | 12.53 | 20.57 | 14.16 | 13.25 | 11.55 | 12.92 | 13.84 | 14.89 | 15.65 | 15.86 |
| Zambia — Zambie | | | | | | | | | | |
| Treasury bill — Bons du trésor | 24.94 | 36.19 | 31.37 | 44.28 | 34.54 | 29.97 | 12.60 | 16.32 | 10.37 | 11.95 |
| Zimbabwe — Zimbabwe | | | | | | | | | | |
| Money market A[9] — Marché monétaire A[9] | 37.22 | 53.13 | 64.98 | 21.52 | 32.35 | 110.05 | 129.58 | ... | ... | ... |
| Treasury bill — Bons du trésor | 32.78 | 50.48 | 64.78 | 17.60 | 28.51 | 52.72 | 125.68 | 185.11 | 322.36 | ... |

Source

International Monetary Fund (IMF), Washington, D.C., "International Financial Statistics", May 2008 and the IMF database.

Notes

+ The naming conventions for money market rates and treasury bill yields sometimes vary among countries. In this table, three money market and treasury bill descriptions are used: (i) "Money market"/"Treasury bill", (ii) "Money market A"/"Treasury bill A" and (iii) "Money market B"/"Treasury bill B". These distinctions are shown for those countries for which more than one type of money market rate or treasury bill yield is differentiated by the International Monetary Fund in "International Financial Statistics". In general, "Money market A" and "Treasury bill A" refer to those interest rates or yields whose durations have been specified (e.g. overnight, one month, 91 days, etc.) and "Money market B" and "Treasury bill B" refer to all others containing specific descriptors such as "call money rate", "foreign currency", "interbank", "discounted rate", etc.

1 Foreign currency.
2 13 weeks.
3 Beginning 1999, see Euro Area. For Greece, beginning 2001, see Euro Area.
4 Interbank.

Source

Fonds monétaire international (FMI), Washington, D.C.,"Statistiques Financières Internationales", mai 2008 et la base de données du FMI.

Notes

+ La manière dont par convention on dénomme les taux du marché monétaire et le rendement des bons du Trésor peut varier selon les pays. Dans le tableau, on utilise trois termes pour le marché monétaire et les bons du Trésor : i) « Marché monétaire »/ « Bons du Trésor », ii) « Marché monétaire A »/ « Bons du Trésor A », iii) « Marché monétaire B »/ « Bons du Trésor B ». Ces distinctions apparaissent pour les pays où le Fonds monétaire international (FMI) distingue dans Statistiques financières internationales plus d'un type de taux du marché monétaire ou de rendement de bons du Trésor. En général, « Marché monétaire A » et « Bons du Trésor A » désignent les taux d'intérêt ou les rendements dont la durée a été précisée (au jour le jour, à un mois, à 91 jours, etc.), « Marché monétaire B » et « Bons du Trésor B » désignant tous les autres assortis de descripteurs précis tels que taux de l'argent au jour le jour, en devises, interbancaire, taux escompté, etc.

1 Devises.
2 Treize semaines.
3 À compter de 1999, voir zone euro. Pour la Grèce, à compter de 2001, voir zone euro.
4 Interbancaire.

| | | | |
|---|---|---|---|
| 5 | Call money rate. | 5 | Taux de l'argent au jour le jour. |
| 6 | Discount rate. | 6 | Taux de l'escompte. |
| 7 | Overnight advances. | 7 | Taux des avances à un jour. |
| 8 | Overnight rate. | 8 | Taux à un jour. |
| 9 | 3-month interbank rate. | 9 | Taux interbancaire à trois mois. |
| 10 | Overnight interbank. | 10 | Taux interbancaire à un jour. |
| 11 | Average cost of Central Bank debt. | 11 | Coût moyen de la dette à la Banque centrale. |
| 12 | 3 months. | 12 | Trois mois. |
| 13 | Discounted. | 13 | Taux actualisé. |
| 14 | 12 months. | 14 | Douze mois. |
| 15 | Yield. | 15 | Rendement. |
| 16 | 91 days. | 16 | Quatre-vingt-onze jours. |
| 17 | 1-month fixed rate. | 17 | Taux forfaitaire à un mois. |
| 18 | Exchequer bills. | 18 | Bon du Trésor. |
| 19 | Corporate bond rate. | 19 | Taux des obligations de société. |
| 20 | Interbank deposit rate (3 months). | 20 | Taux des dépôts interbancaires (à trois mois). |
| 21 | Central Bank bill rate. | 21 | Taux d'escompte de la Banque Centrale (a trois mois). |
| 22 | Interbank call loans (maximum rate). | 22 | Prêts interbancaires remboursables sur demande (taux maximum). |
| 23 | Interbank overnight. | 23 | Taux interbancaire au jour le jour. |
| 24 | Bankers' acceptances. | 24 | Traite bancaire. |
| 25 | New issue rate: 3-month treasury bills. | 25 | Taux des émissions nouvelles : bons du Trésor à trois mois. |
| 26 | 6 months. | 26 | Six mois. |
| 27 | 182 days. | 27 | 182 jours. |
| 28 | Up-to-5-days interbank deposit. | 28 | Dépôts interbancaires jusqu'à cinq jours. |
| 29 | Interbank call loans. | 29 | Prêts interbancaires remboursables sur demande. |
| 30 | 3-month discount notes. | 30 | Billets à escompte à trois mois. |
| 31 | Overnight interbank minimum. | 31 | Taux minimum des prêts interbancaires à un jour. |
| 32 | Bond equivalent. | 32 | Équivalant à obligation. |
| 33 | Commercial paper (3 months). | 33 | Effet de commerce (à trois mois). |
| 34 | Federal funds rate. | 34 | Taux des fonds fédéraux. |
| 35 | Interbank borrowing rate. | 35 | Taux des prêts interbancaires. |

Detailed information and current figures relating to tables 27 and 28 are contained in *International Financial Statistics*, published by the International Monetary Fund (see also www.imf.org) and in the United Nations *Monthly Bulletin of Statistics*.

*Table 27*: The discount rates shown represent the rates at which the central bank lends or discounts eligible paper for deposit money banks, typically shown on an end-of-period basis.

*Table 28:* The rates shown represent short-term treasury bill rates and money market rates. The treasury bill rate is the rate at which short-term securities are issued or traded in the market. The money market rate is the rate on short-term lending between financial institutions.

The naming conventions for money market rates and treasury bill yields sometimes vary among countries. In table 28, three money market and treasury bill descriptions are used: (i) "Money market"/"Treasury bill", (ii) "Money market A"/"Treasury bill A" and (iii) "Money market B"/"Treasury bill B". These distinctions are shown for those countries for which more than one type of money market rate or treasury bill yield is differentiated by the International Monetary Fund in *International Financial Statistics*. In this table, "Money market A" and "Treasury bill A" generally refer to those interest rates or yields whose durations have been specified (e.g. overnight, one month, 91 days, etc.) and "Money market B" and "Treasury bill B" refer to all others containing specific descriptors such as "call money rate", "foreign currency", "interbank", "discounted rate", etc.

Les informations détaillées et les chiffres courants concernant les tableaux 27 et 28 figurent dans les *Statistiques financières internationales* publiées par le Fonds monétaire international (voir aussi www.imf.org) et dans le *Bulletin mensuel de statistique* des Nations Unies.

*Tableau 27*: Les taux d'escomptes indiqués représentent les taux que la banque centrale applique à ses prêts ou auquel elle réescompte les effets escomptables des banques créatrices de monnaie (généralement, taux de fin de période).

*Tableau 28:* Les taux indiqués représentent le taux des bons du Trésor et le taux du marché monétaire à court terme. Le taux des bons du Trésor est le taux auquel les effets à court terme sont émis ou négociés sur le marché. Le taux du marché monétaire est le taux prêteur à court terme entre institutions financières.

La manière dont par convention on dénomme les taux du marché monétaire et le rendement des bons du Trésor peut varier selon les pays. Dans le tableau 28, on utilise trois termes pour le marché monétaire et les bons du Trésor : i) "Marché monétaire"/"Bons du Trésor", ii) "Marché monétaire A"/ "Bons du Trésor A" et iii) "Marché monétaire B"/"Bons du Trésor B". Ces distinctions apparaissent pour les pays où le Fonds monétaire international distingue dans *Statistiques financières internationales* plus d'un type de taux du marché monétaire ou de rendement de bons du Trésor. En général, dans ce tableau, "Marché monétaire A" et "Bons du Trésor A" désignent les taux d'intérêt ou les rendements dont la durée a été précisée (au jour le jour, à un mois, à 91 jours, etc.), "Marché monétaire B" et "Bons du Trésor B" désignant tous les autres assortis de descripteurs précis tels que taux de l'argent au jour le jour, en devises, interbancaire, taux escompté, etc.

# Unemployment
Number (thousands) and percentage unemployed, by sex

# Chômage
Nombre (milliers) et pourcentage des chômeurs, par sexe

| Country or area, source§ — Pays ou zone, source§ | 1999 | 2000 | 2001 | 2002 | 2003 | 2004 | 2005 | 2006 |
|---|---|---|---|---|---|---|---|---|
| **Afghanistan[1] — Afghanistan[1]** | | | | | | | | |
| MF [BA] | ... | ... | ... | ... | ... | ... | 363.8 | ... |
| M [BA] | ... | ... | ... | ... | ... | ... | 172.7 | ... |
| F [BA] | ... | ... | ... | ... | ... | ... | 191.1 | ... |
| %MF [BA] | ... | ... | ... | ... | ... | ... | 8.5 | ... |
| %M [BA] | ... | ... | ... | ... | ... | ... | 7.6 | ... |
| %F [BA] | ... | ... | ... | ... | ... | ... | 9.5 | ... |
| **Albania[1] — Albanie[1]** | | | | | | | | |
| MF [A][2] | ... | ... | 305.5 | ... | ... | ... | ... | ... |
| M [A][2] | ... | ... | 150.1 | ... | ... | ... | ... | ... |
| F [A][2] | ... | ... | 155.4 | ... | ... | ... | ... | ... |
| MF [FB][3] | 239.8 | 215.1 | 180.5 | 172.4 | 163.0 | 157.0 | 153.0 | 150.0 |
| M [FB][3] | 130.0 | 113.0 | 96.0 | 91.0 | 86.0 | 82.0 | 79.0 | 77.0 |
| F [FB][3] | 110.0 | 102.1 | 85.0 | 81.4 | 77.0 | 75.0 | 74.0 | 73.0 |
| %MF [FB][3] | 18.4 | 16.8 | 16.4 | 15.8 | 15.0 | 14.4 | 14.1 | 13.8 |
| %M [FB][3] | 16.4 | 14.9 | 14.2 | 13.6 | 12.9 | 12.4 | 12.1 | 11.8 |
| %F [FB][3] | 21.4 | 19.3 | 19.9 | 19.1 | 18.2 | 17.5 | 17.2 | 16.8 |
| **Algeria[1] — Algérie[1]** | | | | | | | | |
| MF [BA] | ... | 2 427.7 | 2 339.4 | 2 247.3 | 2 078.0 | 1 671.5 | 1 474.5 | 1 240.8 |
| M [BA] | ... | 2 132.7 | 1 934.9 | ... | 1 759.9 | 1 370.4 | 1 221.0 | 988.3 |
| F [BA] | ... | 295.0 | 404.5 | ... | 318.3 | 301.1 | 253.5 | 252.6 |
| %MF [BA] | ... | ... | 27.3 | 25.9 | 23.7 | 17.7 | 15.3 | 12.3 |
| %M [BA] | ... | ... | 26.6 | ... | 23.4 | 17.5 | ... | ... |
| %F [BA] | ... | ... | 31.4 | ... | 25.4 | 18.1 | ... | ... |
| **Anguilla[1] — Anguilla[1]** | | | | | | | | |
| MF [A][4] | ... | ... | 0.4 | ... | ... | ... | ... | ... |
| M [A][4] | ... | ... | 0.2 | ... | ... | ... | ... | ... |
| F [A][4] | ... | ... | 0.2 | ... | ... | ... | ... | ... |
| %MF [A][4] | ... | ... | 6.7 | ... | ... | ... | ... | ... |
| %M [A][4] | ... | ... | 6.5 | ... | ... | ... | ... | ... |
| %F [A][4] | ... | ... | 7.0 | ... | ... | ... | ... | ... |
| MF [BA] | 0.6[5] | ... | ... | 0.5[6] | ... | ... | ... | ... |
| M [BA] | 0.2[5] | ... | ... | 0.2[6] | ... | ... | ... | ... |
| F [BA] | 0.4[5] | ... | ... | 0.3[6] | ... | ... | ... | ... |
| %MF [BA] | 8.3[5] | ... | ... | 7.8[6] | ... | ... | ... | ... |
| %M [BA] | 4.6[5] | ... | ... | 6.3[6] | ... | ... | ... | ... |
| %F [BA] | 12.1[5] | ... | ... | 9.5[6] | ... | ... | ... | ... |
| **Argentina[7] — Argentine[7]** | | | | | | | | |
| MF [BA] | 1 359.6[8,9] | 1 460.9[8,9] | 1 709.8[8,9] | 1 955.8[8,9] | 1 633.0[8,10,11] | 1 361.6[8,10,11] | 1 141.5[8,10,11] | 1 049.2[11,12] |
| M [BA] | 764.9[8,9] | 809.9[8,9] | 1 021.9[8,9] | 1 175.2[8,9] | 824.8[8,10,11] | 687.6[8,10,11] | 561.7[8,10,11] | 488.9[11,12] |
| F [BA] | 594.7[8,9] | 651.0[8,9] | 688.4[8,9] | 780.6[8,9] | 808.2[8,10,11] | 673.9[8,10,11] | 579.8[8,10,11] | 560.3[11,12] |
| %MF [BA] | 14.1[8,9] | 15.0[8,9] | 17.4[8,9] | 19.6[8,9] | 15.4[8,10,11] | 12.6[8,10,11] | 10.6[8,10,11] | 9.5[11,12] |
| %M [BA] | 13.3[8,9] | 14.1[8,9] | 17.4[8,9] | 20.2[8,9] | 13.8[8,10,11] | 11.2[8,10,11] | 9.2[8,10,11] | 7.8[11,12] |
| %F [BA] | 15.2[8,9] | 16.4[8,9] | 17.2[8,9] | 18.8[8,9] | 17.5[8,10,11] | 14.5[8,10,11] | 12.4[8,10,11] | 11.7[11,12] |
| **Armenia — Arménie** | | | | | | | | |
| MF [A][1,13] | ... | ... | 570.5 | ... | ... | ... | ... | ... |
| M [A][1,13] | ... | ... | 268.8 | ... | ... | ... | ... | ... |
| F [A][1,13] | ... | ... | 301.7 | ... | ... | ... | ... | ... |
| MF [E][1] | 164.2 | 169.5 | 146.8 | 133.7 | 124.8 | 114.8 | 98.0 | 88.9 |
| M [E][1] | 56.4 | 61.0 | 50.9 | 44.9 | 40.1 | 35.0 | 29.0 | 25.5 |
| F [E][1] | 107.8 | 108.5 | 95.9 | 88.8 | 84.7 | 79.8 | 69.0 | 63.4 |
| %MF [E][1] | 11.2 | 11.7 | 10.4 | 10.8 | 10.1 | 9.6 | 8.2 | 7.4 |
| %M [E][1] | 7.6 | 8.0 | 6.9 | 7.2 | 5.9 | 5.2 | 4.6 | 4.0 |

| Country or area, source§ — Pays ou zone, source§ | 1999 | 2000 | 2001 | 2002 | 2003 | 2004 | 2005 | 2006 |
|---|---|---|---|---|---|---|---|---|
| %F [E][1] | 15.0 | 15.7 | 14.1 | 14.5 | 14.4 | 14.3 | 12.1 | 11.1 |
| MF [FB][3,14] | 175.0 | 153.9 | 138.4 | 127.3 | 118.6 | 108.6 | 89.0 | 84.6 |
| M [FB][3,14] | 62.3 | 54.4 | 47.1 | 85.7 | 37.0 | 32.3 | 26.0 | 23.9 |
| F [FB][3,14] | 112.7 | 99.5 | 91.3 | 41.6 | 81.6 | 76.3 | 63.0 | 60.7 |
| **Australia[1,15,16] — Australie[1,15,16]** | | | | | | | | |
| MF [BA] | 654.9 | 607.5 | 667.1 | 636.9 | 607.4 | 570.6 | 535.0 | 525.6 |
| M [BA] | 379.5 | 347.7 | 383.8 | 363.5 | 330.0 | 308.8 | 286.8 | 283.7 |
| F [BA] | 275.4 | 259.8 | 283.3 | 273.4 | 277.3 | 261.7 | 248.2 | 241.9 |
| %MF [BA] | 7.0 | 6.4 | 6.9 | 6.4 | 6.0 | 5.6 | 5.1 | 5.0 |
| %M [BA] | 7.2 | 6.5 | 7.1 | 6.6 | 5.9 | 5.5 | 5.0 | 4.2 |
| %F [BA] | 6.8 | 6.2 | 6.6 | 6.2 | 6.2 | 5.7 | 5.3 | 6.0 |
| **Austria[1] — Autriche[1]** | | | | | | | | |
| MF [BA] | 146.7[17] | 138.8[17] | 142.5[17] | 161.0[17] | 168.8 | 194.6[10] | 207.7 | 195.6 |
| M [BA] | 81.7[17] | 73.8[17] | 77.0[17] | 91.7[17] | 94.7 | 98.0[10] | 107.8 | 97.1 |
| F [BA] | 65.0[17] | 65.0[17] | 65.5[17] | 69.3[17] | 74.3 | 96.6[10] | 100.0 | 98.5 |
| %MF [BA] | 3.8[17] | 3.6[17] | 3.6[17] | 4.0[17] | 4.3 | 4.9[10] | 5.2 | 4.7 |
| %M [BA] | 3.7[17] | 3.3[17] | 3.5[17] | 4.1[17] | 4.3 | 4.5[10] | 4.9 | 4.3 |
| %F [BA] | 3.9[17] | 3.8[17] | 3.8[17] | 3.9[17] | 4.2 | 5.4[10] | 5.5 | 5.2 |
| MF [FB] | 221.7 | 194.3 | 203.9 | 232.4 | 240.1 | 243.9 | 252.7 | 239.2 |
| M [FB] | 121.5 | 107.5 | 115.3 | 134.4 | 139.7 | 140.2 | 144.2 | 135.8 |
| F [FB] | 100.2 | 86.8 | 88.6 | 98.0 | 100.4 | 103.6 | 108.4 | 103.4 |
| %MF [FB] | 6.7 | 5.8 | 6.1 | 6.9 | 7.0 | 7.1 | 7.3 | 6.8 |
| %M [FB] | 6.5 | 5.8 | 6.2 | 7.2 | 7.5 | 7.5 | 7.7 | 7.1 |
| %F [FB] | 6.9 | 5.9 | 5.9 | 6.4 | 6.5 | 6.6 | 6.8 | 6.4 |
| **Azerbaijan — Azerbaïdjan** | | | | | | | | |
| MF [BA][1] | ... | ... | ... | ... | ... | ... | 368.8 | ... |
| M [BA][1] | ... | ... | ... | ... | ... | ... | 172.7 | ... |
| F [BA][1] | ... | ... | ... | ... | ... | ... | 196.1 | ... |
| %MF [BA][1] | ... | ... | ... | ... | ... | ... | 8.5 | ... |
| %M [BA][1] | ... | ... | ... | ... | ... | ... | 7.6 | ... |
| %F [BA][1] | ... | ... | ... | ... | ... | ... | 9.5 | ... |
| MF [FB][3] | 45.2 | 43.7 | 48.4 | 51.0 | 54.4 | 55.9 | 56.3 | 53.9 |
| M [FB][3] | 19.6 | 19.3 | 21.8 | 23.1 | 25.3 | 26.7 | 27.3 | 26.3 |
| F [FB][3] | 25.6 | 24.5 | 26.6 | 27.9 | 29.1 | 29.3 | 29.1 | 27.5 |
| %MF [FB][3] | 1.2 | 1.2 | 1.3 | 1.3 | 1.4 | 1.4 | 1.4 | 1.3 |
| %M [FB][3] | 1.0 | 1.0 | 1.1 | 1.2 | 1.3 | 1.3 | 1.3 | 1.2 |
| %F [FB][3] | 1.4 | 1.4 | 1.5 | 1.5 | 1.6 | 1.6 | 1.6 | 1.3 |
| **Bahamas[1] — Bahamas[1]** | | | | | | | | |
| MF [BA] | 12.3[18] | ... | 11.3[18] | 15.3[18] | 18.8[18] | 18.0[18] | 18.2[18] | 13.8[4] |
| M [BA] | 5.0[18] | ... | 5.7[18] | 7.6[18] | 8.8[18] | 8.5[18] | 8.4[18] | 6.4[4] |
| F [BA] | 7.3[18] | ... | 5.6[18] | 7.7[18] | 10.1[18] | 9.5[18] | 9.8[18] | 7.5[4] |
| %MF [BA] | 7.8[18] | ... | 6.9[18] | 9.1[18] | 10.8[18] | 10.2[18] | 10.2[18] | 7.6[4] |
| %M [BA] | 6.0[18] | ... | 7.1[18] | 9.1[18] | 10.8[18] | 9.4[18] | 9.2[18] | 8.4[4] |
| %F [BA] | 9.7[18] | ... | 6.8[18] | 8.8[18] | 10.0[18] | 11.0[18] | 11.2[18] | 6.9[4] |
| **Bahrain[1] — Bahreïn[1]** | | | | | | | | |
| MF [A][2] | ... | ... | 17.0 | ... | ... | ... | ... | ... |
| M [A][2] | ... | ... | 10.0 | ... | ... | ... | ... | ... |
| F [A][2] | ... | ... | 7.0 | ... | ... | ... | ... | ... |
| MF [FB][19] | 3.8 | 6.2 | ... | 8.7 | 11.8 | 6.3 | 6.4 | 6.8 |
| M [FB][19] | 2.6 | 4.2 | ... | 4.4 | 6.0 | 3.1 | 2.9 | 1.5 |
| F [FB][19] | 1.1 | 2.0 | ... | 4.4 | 5.7 | 3.2 | 3.5 | 5.3 |
| **Bangladesh[1,20] — Bangladesh[1,20]** | | | | | | | | |
| MF [BA] | ... | 1 750.0 | ... | ... | 2 002.0 | ... | ... | ... |
| M [BA] | ... | 1 083.0 | ... | ... | 1 500.0 | ... | ... | ... |
| F [BA] | ... | 666.0 | ... | ... | 502.0 | ... | ... | ... |
| %MF [BA] | ... | 3.3 | ... | ... | 4.3 | ... | ... | ... |
| %M [BA] | ... | 3.2 | ... | ... | 4.2 | ... | ... | ... |
| %F [BA] | ... | 3.3 | ... | ... | 4.9 | ... | ... | ... |

| Country or area, source§ — Pays ou zone, source§ | 1999 | 2000 | 2001 | 2002 | 2003 | 2004 | 2005 | 2006 |
|---|---|---|---|---|---|---|---|---|
| **Barbados[1] — Barbade[1]** | | | | | | | | |
| MF [BA] | 14.4 | 13.3 | 14.3 | 14.8 | 16.0 | 14.3 | ... | ... |
| M [BA] | 5.6 | 5.5 | 6.0 | 6.4 | 7.1 | 6.7 | ... | ... |
| F [BA] | 8.8 | 7.9 | 8.3 | 8.4 | 8.9 | 7.5 | ... | ... |
| %MF [BA] | 10.5 | 9.4 | 9.9 | 10.3 | 11.0 | 9.8 | ... | ... |
| %M [BA] | 7.7 | 7.5 | 8.0 | 8.2 | 9.6 | 9.0 | ... | ... |
| %F [BA] | 13.3 | 11.5 | 11.9 | 12.4 | 12.6 | 10.6 | ... | ... |
| **Belarus[3,21] — Bélarus[3,21]** | | | | | | | | |
| MF [FB] | 95.4 | 95.8 | 102.9 | 130.5 | 136.1 | 83.0 | 67.9 | 52.0 |
| M [FB] | 34.2 | 37.6 | 40.9 | 47.8 | 46.1 | 25.5 | 21.1 | 17.7 |
| F [FB] | 61.2 | 58.2 | 62.0 | 82.7 | 90.0 | 57.5 | 46.8 | 34.3 |
| %MF [FB] | 2.1 | 2.1 | 2.3 | 3.0 | 3.1 | 1.9 | 1.5 | 1.2 |
| %M [FB] | 1.6 | 1.7 | 1.9 | 2.3 | 1.2 | 1.2 | 1.0 | 0.8 |
| %F [FB] | 2.6 | 2.4 | 2.6 | 3.5 | 3.9 | 2.4 | 2.0 | 1.5 |
| **Belgium — Belgique** | | | | | | | | |
| MF [BA][1] | 375.2 | 308.5 | 286.4 | 332.1 | 364.3 | 380.3 | 390.3 | 383.2 |
| M [BA][1] | 179.4 | 144.6 | 147.9 | 168.1 | 193.0 | 191.4 | 196.0 | 191.0 |
| F [BA][1] | 195.8 | 163.9 | 138.4 | 164.0 | 171.3 | 188.9 | 194.3 | 192.2 |
| %MF [BA][1] | 8.6 | 7.0 | 6.6 | 7.5 | 8.2 | 8.5 | 8.4 | 8.2 |
| %M [BA][1] | 7.2 | 5.8 | 6.0 | 6.7 | 7.7 | 7.6 | 7.6 | 7.4 |
| %F [BA][1] | 10.4 | 8.7 | 7.5 | 8.7 | 8.9 | 9.6 | 9.5 | 9.3 |
| MF [FB][22] | 507.5 | 474.4 | 469.7 | 491.5 | 538.1 | ... | ... | ... |
| M [FB][22] | 224.7 | 208.7 | 210.8 | 228.1 | 253.1 | ... | ... | ... |
| F [FB][22] | 282.9 | 265.8 | 258.9 | 263.4 | 285.1 | ... | ... | ... |
| %MF [FB][22] | 11.6 | 10.9 | 10.8 | 11.2 | 12.3 | ... | ... | ... |
| %M [FB][22] | 9.2 | 8.6 | 8.7 | 9.4 | 10.4 | ... | ... | ... |
| %F [FB][22] | 14.7 | 13.8 | 13.4 | 13.6 | 14.7 | ... | ... | ... |
| **Belize[18,23] — Belize[18,23]** | | | | | | | | |
| MF [BA] | 11.5 | ... | 8.6 | 9.5 | ... | ... | 12.2 | ... |
| M [BA] | 5.3 | ... | 3.6 | 4.7 | ... | ... | 5.2 | ... |
| F [BA] | 6.1 | ... | 5.0 | 4.7 | ... | ... | 7.0 | ... |
| %MF [BA] | 12.8 | ... | 9.1 | 10.0 | ... | ... | 11.0 | ... |
| %M [BA] | 9.0 | ... | 5.8 | 7.5 | ... | ... | 7.4 | ... |
| %F [BA] | 20.3 | ... | 15.4 | 15.3 | ... | ... | 17.2 | ... |
| **Bolivia[7,24] — Bolivie[7,24]** | | | | | | | | |
| MF [BA] | 164.5 | 183.2 | 214.9 | 221.6 | ... | ... | ... | ... |
| M [BA] | 76.9 | 83.3 | 99.4 | 97.4 | ... | ... | ... | ... |
| F [BA] | 87.6 | 99.9 | 115.5 | 124.2 | ... | ... | ... | ... |
| %MF [BA] | 4.3 | 4.8 | 5.2 | 5.5 | ... | ... | ... | ... |
| %M [BA] | 3.7 | 3.9 | 4.5 | 4.3 | ... | ... | ... | ... |
| %F [BA] | 5.1 | 5.9 | 6.2 | 6.9 | ... | ... | ... | ... |
| **Bosnia and Herzegovina[1] — Bosnie-Herzégovine[1]** | | | | | | | | |
| MF [BA] | ... | ... | ... | ... | ... | ... | ... | 366.0 |
| M [BA] | ... | ... | ... | ... | ... | ... | ... | 215.0 |
| F [BA] | ... | ... | ... | ... | ... | ... | ... | 151.0 |
| %MF [BA] | ... | ... | ... | ... | ... | ... | ... | 31.1 |
| %M [BA] | ... | ... | ... | ... | ... | ... | ... | 28.9 |
| %F [BA] | ... | ... | ... | ... | ... | ... | ... | 34.9 |
| **Botswana[25] — Botswana[25]** | | | | | | | | |
| MF [A][26] | ... | ... | 109.5 | ... | ... | ... | ... | ... |
| M [A][26] | ... | ... | 51.9 | ... | ... | ... | ... | ... |
| F [A][26] | ... | ... | 57.6 | ... | ... | ... | ... | ... |
| %MF [A][26] | ... | ... | 19.6 | ... | ... | ... | ... | ... |
| %M [A][26] | ... | ... | 16.4 | ... | ... | ... | ... | ... |
| %F [A][26] | ... | ... | 23.9 | ... | ... | ... | ... | ... |
| MF [BA] | ... | 90.7 | ... | ... | 144.5 | ... | ... | 114.4 |
| M [BA] | ... | 46.3 | ... | ... | 66.9 | ... | ... | 50.9 |
| F [BA] | ... | 44.5 | ... | ... | 77.6 | ... | ... | 63.5 |

| Country or area, source[§] — Pays ou zone, source[§] | 1999 | 2000 | 2001 | 2002 | 2003 | 2004 | 2005 | 2006 |
|---|---|---|---|---|---|---|---|---|
| %MF [BA] | ... | 15.8 | ... | ... | 23.8 | ... | ... | 17.6 |
| %M [BA] | ... | 14.7 | ... | ... | 21.4 | ... | ... | 15.3 |
| %F [BA] | ... | 17.2 | ... | ... | 26.3 | ... | ... | 19.9 |
| **Brazil[7,27,28] — Brésil[7,27,28]** | | | | | | | | |
| MF [BA] | 7 639.1 | ... | 7 853.4 | 7 958.5 | 8 640.0 | 8 263.8 | ... | ... |
| M [BA] | 3 667.9 | ... | 3 674.9 | 3 685.1 | 3 972.8 | 3 590.7 | ... | ... |
| F [BA] | 3 971.2 | ... | 4 178.5 | 4 273.3 | 4 667.1 | 4 673.1 | ... | ... |
| %MF [BA] | 9.6 | ... | 9.4 | 9.2 | 9.7 | 8.9 | ... | ... |
| %M [BA] | 7.9 | ... | 7.5 | 7.4 | 7.8 | 6.8 | ... | ... |
| %F [BA] | 12.1 | ... | 11.9 | 11.6 | 12.3 | 11.7 | ... | ... |
| **Brunei Darussalam[29] — Brunéi Darussalam[29]** | | | | | | | | |
| MF [FB] | 5.2 | 7.0 | 8.6 | 5.6 | 7.1 | ... | ... | ... |
| M [FB] | 2.1 | 2.7 | 3.3 | 2.1 | 3.1 | ... | ... | ... |
| F [FB] | 3.1 | 4.3 | 5.3 | 3.4 | 4.0 | ... | ... | ... |
| **Bulgaria — Bulgarie** | | | | | | | | |
| MF [BA][1] | 486.7[31] | 559.0[31] | 661.1[31] | 599.2[31] | 449.1 | 399.8 | 334.2 | 305.7 |
| M [BA][1] | 258.6[31] | 306.3[31] | 363.2[31] | 328.7[31] | 246.1 | 221.6 | 182.5 | 156.4 |
| F [BA][1] | 228.1[31] | 252.6[31] | 297.8[31] | 270.4[31] | 203.0 | 178.2 | 151.6 | 149.3 |
| %MF [BA][1] | 14.1[31] | 16.3[31] | 19.4[31] | 17.6[31] | 13.7 | 12.0 | 10.1 | 9.0 |
| %M [BA][1] | 14.0[31] | 16.7[31] | 20.2[31] | 18.3[31] | 14.1 | 12.5 | 10.3 | 8.6 |
| %F [BA][1] | 14.1[31] | 15.9[31] | 18.4[31] | 16.9[31] | 13.2 | 11.5 | 9.8 | 9.3 |
| MF [FB][3,30] | 610.6 | 682.8 | 662.3 | 602.5 | 500.7 | 450.6 | 397.3 | 337.8 |
| M [FB][3,30] | 284.5 | 323.4 | 321.1 | 281.1 | 227.1 | 201.6 | 171.8 | 140.0 |
| F [FB][3,30] | 326.1 | 359.4 | 341.2 | 321.5 | 273.6 | 249.0 | 225.5 | 197.8 |
| %MF [FB][3,30] | 16.0 | 17.9 | 17.3 | 16.3 | 13.5 | 12.2 | 10.7 | 9.1 |
| **Burkina Faso[29,32] — Burkina Faso[29,32]** | | | | | | | | |
| MF [FB] | 7.5 | 6.6 | ... | ... | ... | ... | ... | ... |
| M [FB] | 6.2 | 5.4 | ... | ... | ... | ... | ... | ... |
| F [FB] | 1.4 | 1.2 | ... | ... | ... | ... | ... | ... |
| **Burundi[29,33] — Burundi[29,33]** | | | | | | | | |
| MF [FB] | 0.7 | ... | ... | ... | ... | ... | ... | ... |
| %MF [FB] | 14.0 | ... | ... | ... | ... | ... | ... | ... |
| %M [FB] | 15.0 | ... | ... | ... | ... | ... | ... | ... |
| %F [FB] | 13.2 | ... | ... | ... | ... | ... | ... | ... |
| **Cambodia[34] — Cambodge[34]** | | | | | | | | |
| MF [BA] | ... | 133.6[7] | 115.8[35] | ... | ... | 503.4 | ... | ... |
| M [BA] | ... | 55.0[7] | 44.9[35] | ... | ... | 259.5 | ... | ... |
| F [BA] | ... | 78.6[7] | 71.0[35] | ... | ... | 243.9 | ... | ... |
| %MF [BA] | ... | 2.5[7] | 1.8[35] | ... | ... | ... | ... | ... |
| %M [BA] | ... | 2.1[7] | 1.5[35] | ... | ... | ... | ... | ... |
| %F [BA] | ... | 2.8[7] | 2.2[35] | ... | ... | ... | ... | ... |
| **Cameroon[1] — Cameroun[1]** | | | | | | | | |
| MF [B] | ... | ... | 468.0 | ... | ... | ... | ... | ... |
| M [B] | ... | ... | 263.0 | ... | ... | ... | ... | ... |
| F [B] | ... | ... | 205.0 | ... | ... | ... | ... | ... |
| %MF [B] | ... | ... | 7.5 | ... | ... | ... | ... | ... |
| %M [B] | ... | ... | 8.2 | ... | ... | ... | ... | ... |
| %F [B] | ... | ... | 6.7 | ... | ... | ... | ... | ... |
| **Canada[1,36] — Canada[1,36]** | | | | | | | | |
| MF [BA] | 1 181.6 | 1 082.8 | 1 163.6 | 1 268.9 | 1 286.2 | 1 235.3 | 1 172.8 | 1 108.4 |
| M [BA] | 660.4 | 595.3 | 655.1 | 721.7 | 719.6 | 685.4 | 649.0 | 608.3 |
| F [BA] | 521.2 | 487.5 | 508.5 | 547.2 | 566.6 | 549.9 | 523.8 | 500.1 |
| %MF [BA] | 7.6 | 6.8 | 7.2 | 7.7 | 7.6 | 7.2 | 6.8 | 6.3 |
| %M [BA] | 7.8 | 6.9 | 7.5 | 8.1 | 7.9 | 7.5 | 7.0 | 6.5 |
| %F [BA] | 7.3 | 6.7 | 6.9 | 7.1 | 7.2 | 6.9 | 6.5 | 6.1 |
| **Cayman Islands[1] — Îles Caïmanes[1]** | | | | | | | | |
| MF [BA] | ... | ... | 2.1[13] | 1.6[13] | 1.1[13] | 1.3[37] | 1.3[13] | 0.9[2] |

**29** **Unemployment**—Number (thousands) and percentage unemployed, by sex (*continued*)
**Chômage**—Nombre (milliers) et pourcentage des chômeurs, par sexe (*suite*)

| Country or area, source[§] — Pays ou zone, source[§] | 1999 | 2000 | 2001 | 2002 | 2003 | 2004 | 2005 | 2006 |
|---|---|---|---|---|---|---|---|---|
| M [BA][2] | ... | ... | ... | ... | ... | ... | ... | 0.5 |
| F [BA][2] | ... | ... | ... | ... | ... | ... | ... | 0.5 |
| %MF [BA] | ... | ... | 7.5[13] | 5.4[13] | 3.6[13] | 4.3[37] | 3.5[13] | 2.6[2] |
| **Chile[1,38] — Chili[1,38]** | | | | | | | | |
| MF [BA] | 529.1 | 489.4 | 469.4 | 468.7 | 453.1 | 494.7 | 440.4 | 409.9[10] |
| M [BA] | 322.9 | 312.5 | 302.6 | 298.5 | 279.2 | 280.8 | 248.2 | 239.3[10] |
| F [BA] | 206.2 | 176.9 | 166.9 | 170.2 | 173.9 | 213.9 | 192.2 | 170.6[10] |
| %MF [BA] | 8.9 | 8.3 | 7.9 | 7.8 | 7.4 | 7.8 | 6.9 | 6.0[10] |
| %M [BA] | 8.2 | 8.0 | 7.6 | 7.5 | 6.9 | 6.9 | 6.1 | 5.5[10] |
| %F [BA] | 10.3 | 9.0 | 8.4 | 8.5 | 8.3 | 9.5 | 8.5 | 7.0[10] |
| **China[1,3,39,40] — Chine[1,3,39,40]** | | | | | | | | |
| MF [E] | 5 750.0 | 5 950.0 | 6 810.0 | 7 700.0 | 8 000.0 | 8 270.0 | 8 390.0 | ... |
| %MF [E] | 3.1 | 3.1 | 3.6 | 4.0 | 4.3 | 4.2 | 4.2 | ... |
| **China, Hong Kong SAR[1,41,42] — Chine, Hong Kong RAS[1,41,42]** | | | | | | | | |
| MF [BA] | 207.5 | 166.9 | 174.6 | 253.8 | 275.1 | 239.4 | 197.3 | 170.9 |
| M [BA] | 140.6 | 109.6 | 118.2 | 163.7 | 179.9 | 151.6 | 127.1 | 110.2 |
| F [BA] | 66.9 | 57.3 | 56.4 | 90.0 | 95.2 | 87.8 | 70.2 | 60.7 |
| %MF [BA] | 6.2 | 4.9 | 5.1 | 7.3 | 7.9 | 6.8 | 5.6 | 4.8 |
| %M [BA] | 7.2 | 5.6 | 6.0 | 8.4 | 9.2 | 7.8 | 6.5 | 5.6 |
| %F [BA] | 4.9 | 4.1 | 3.9 | 5.9 | 6.2 | 5.6 | 4.4 | 3.7 |
| **China, Macao SAR[23] — Chine, Macao RAS[23]** | | | | | | | | |
| MF [BA] | 13.2 | 14.2 | 14.0 | 13.7 | 13.1 | 11.2 | 10.3 | 10.4 |
| M [BA] | 9.1 | 9.8 | 9.5 | 9.1 | 8.3 | 6.8 | 5.8 | 5.6 |
| F [BA] | 4.2 | 4.4 | 4.5 | 4.6 | 4.8 | 4.4 | 4.5 | 4.8 |
| %MF [BA] | 6.3 | 6.8 | 6.4 | 6.3 | 6.0 | 4.9 | 4.1 | 3.8 |
| %M [BA] | 8.0 | 8.6 | 8.1 | 7.9 | 7.1 | 5.6 | 4.4 | 3.8 |
| %F [BA] | 4.4 | 4.6 | 4.4 | 4.5 | 4.7 | 4.0 | 3.8 | 3.8 |
| **Colombia[43,44] — Colombie[43,44]** | | | | | | | | |
| MF [BA] | 1 415.4[45] | 1 526.0[45] | 2 846.0[7] | 3 084.4[7] | 2 878.1[7] | 2 766.7[7] | 2 406.0[7] | 2 568.0[7] |
| M [BA] | 649.8[45] | 660.2[45] | 1 303.5[7] | 1 440.7[7] | 1 274.0[7] | 1 243.1[7] | 1 066.0[7] | 1 112.6[7] |
| F [BA] | 765.6[45] | 865.8[45] | 1 542.5[7] | 1 643.8[7] | 1 604.1[7] | 1 523.6[7] | 1 340.0[7] | 1 455.4[7] |
| %MF [BA] | 20.1[45] | 20.5[45] | 14.7[7] | 15.7[7] | 14.2[7] | 13.6[7] | 11.8[7] | 12.7[7] |
| %M [BA] | 17.2[45] | 16.9[45] | 11.6[7] | 12.7[7] | 11.0[7] | 10.6[7] | 9.0[7] | 9.7[7] |
| %F [BA] | 23.3[45] | 24.5[45] | 19.1[7] | 19.7[7] | 18.5[7] | 17.7[7] | 15.6[7] | 16.8[7] |
| **Costa Rica[25,46] — Costa Rica[25,46]** | | | | | | | | |
| MF [BA] | 83.3 | 71.9 | 100.4 | 108.5 | 117.2 | 114.9 | 126.2 | 116.0 |
| M [BA] | 45.6 | 41.2 | 55.8 | 61.6 | 66.0 | 62.5 | 60.2 | 53.8 |
| F [BA] | 37.7 | 30.8 | 44.6 | 46.9 | 51.2 | 52.4 | 66.0 | 62.3 |
| %MF [BA] | 6.0 | 5.2 | 6.1 | 6.4 | 6.7 | 6.5 | 6.6 | 6.0 |
| %M [BA] | 4.9 | 4.4 | 5.2 | 5.6 | 5.8 | 5.4 | 5.0 | 4.4 |
| %F [BA] | 8.2 | 6.9 | 7.6 | 7.9 | 8.2 | 8.5 | 9.6 | 8.7 |
| **Croatia — Croatie** | | | | | | | | |
| MF [BA][1] | 234.0 | 297.2 | 276.2 | 265.8 | 255.7 | 249.7 | 229.1 | 198.7 |
| M [BA][1] | 117.4 | 149.8 | 134.8 | 129.7 | 127.7 | 120.0 | 114.4 | 94.4 |
| F [BA][1] | 116.6 | 147.4 | 141.4 | 136.0 | 128.1 | 129.7 | 114.7 | 104.2 |
| %MF [BA][1] | 13.5 | 16.1 | 15.8 | 14.8 | 14.3 | 13.8 | 12.7 | 11.1 |
| %M [BA][1] | 12.8 | 15.0 | 14.2 | 13.4 | 13.1 | 12.0 | 11.7 | 9.8 |
| %F [BA][1] | 14.5 | 17.3 | 17.9 | 16.6 | 15.7 | 15.7 | 14.0 | 12.7 |
| MF [FB][47] | 322.0 | 358.0 | 380.0 | 390.0 | 330.0 | 310.0 | 309.0 | 292.0 |
| M [FB][47] | 153.0 | 169.0 | 177.0 | 177.0 | 140.0 | 129.0 | 128.0 | 117.0 |
| F [FB][47] | 169.0 | 189.0 | 203.0 | 213.0 | 190.0 | 181.0 | 181.0 | 175.0 |
| %MF [FB][47] | 19.1 | 21.1 | 22.0 | 22.3 | 19.2 | ... | ... | ... |
| %M [FB][47] | 17.2 | 19.0 | 19.5 | 19.3 | 15.5 | ... | ... | ... |
| %F [FB][47] | 21.2 | 23.4 | 24.7 | 25.6 | 23.2 | ... | ... | ... |
| **Cuba[48,49] — Cuba[48,49]** | | | | | | | | |
| MF [BA] | 290.9 | 252.3 | 191.6 | 156.1 | 109.7 | 87.7 | 93.9 | 92.7 |
| M [BA] | 126.1 | 111.8 | 93.8 | 76.9 | 51.3 | 49.7 | 55.0 | 52.6 |

| Country or area, source[§] — Pays ou zone, source[§] | 1999 | 2000 | 2001 | 2002 | 2003 | 2004 | 2005 | 2006 |
|---|---|---|---|---|---|---|---|---|
| F [BA] | 164.8 | 140.5 | 97.8 | 79.2 | 58.4 | 38.0 | 38.9 | 40.1 |
| %MF [BA] | 6.3 | 5.4 | 4.1 | 3.3 | 2.3 | 1.9 | 1.9 | 1.9 |
| %M [BA] | 4.3 | 3.8 | 3.1 | 2.6 | 1.7 | 1.7 | 1.8 | 1.7 |
| %F [BA] | 9.6 | 8.3 | 5.8 | 4.6 | 3.4 | 2.2 | 2.2 | 2.2 |
| **Cyprus[1,50] — Chypre[1,50]** | | | | | | | | |
| MF [BA] | 16.9 | 14.5 | 12.8 | 10.8 | 14.1 | 16.7 | 19.5 | 17.0 |
| M [BA] | 7.7 | 5.5 | 4.8 | 4.7 | 7.1 | 7.0 | 9.0 | 8.0 |
| F [BA] | 9.1 | 8.9 | 8.1 | 6.0 | 7.0 | 9.7 | 10.4 | 9.0 |
| %MF [BA] | 5.7 | 4.9 | 4.0 | 3.3 | 4.1 | 4.7 | 5.3 | 4.5 |
| %M [BA] | 4.3 | 3.2 | 2.6 | 2.6 | 3.8 | 3.5 | 4.4 | 3.9 |
| %F [BA] | 7.9 | 7.4 | 5.7 | 4.2 | 4.6 | 6.2 | 6.5 | 5.4 |
| MF [FB] | 11.4 | 10.9 | 9.5 | 10.6 | 12.0 | 12.7 | 13.2 | 12.8 |
| M [FB] | 5.6 | 5.3 | 4.5 | 4.7 | 5.1 | 5.4 | 5.8 | 5.7 |
| F [FB] | 5.8 | 5.7 | 5.0 | 5.9 | 6.8 | 7.2 | 7.3 | 7.1 |
| %MF [FB] | 3.6 | 3.4 | 2.9 | 3.2 | 3.5 | 3.6 | 3.7 | ... |
| %M [FB] | 2.9 | 2.7 | 2.3 | 2.3 | 2.5 | 2.6 | 2.9 | ... |
| %F [FB] | 4.8 | 4.4 | 3.8 | 4.3 | 5.0 | 5.1 | 4.7 | ... |
| **Czech Republic — République tchèque** | | | | | | | | |
| MF [BA][1] | 454.0 | 455.0 | 418.0 | 374.0 | 399.0 | 426.0 | 410.0 | 371.0 |
| M [BA][1] | 211.0 | 212.0 | 193.0 | 169.0 | 175.0 | 201.0 | 187.0 | 169.0 |
| F [BA][1] | 243.0 | 243.0 | 225.0 | 205.0 | 224.0 | 225.0 | 223.0 | 202.0 |
| %MF [BA][1] | 8.7 | 8.8 | 8.1 | 7.3 | 7.8 | 8.3 | 7.9 | 7.1 |
| %M [BA][1] | 7.3 | 7.3 | 6.8 | 5.9 | 6.1 | 7.0 | 6.5 | 5.8 |
| %F [BA][1] | 10.5 | 10.6 | 9.9 | 9.0 | 9.9 | 9.9 | 9.8 | 8.8 |
| MF [FB][3] | 488.0 | 457.0 | 462.0 | 514.0 | 542.0 | 542.0 | 510.0 | 449.0 |
| M [FB][3] | 240.0 | 227.0 | 230.0 | 257.0 | 270.0 | 266.0 | 244.0 | 210.0 |
| F [FB][3] | 248.0 | 230.0 | 232.0 | 257.0 | 272.0 | 276.0 | 266.0 | 239.0 |
| %MF [FB][3] | 9.4 | 8.8 | 8.9 | 9.8 | 10.3 | 9.5 | 8.9 | 7.7 |
| %M [FB][3] | 8.2 | 7.8 | 7.9 | 8.7 | 9.2 | 8.3 | 7.6 | 6.4 |
| %F [FB][3] | 10.8 | 10.0 | 10.1 | 11.2 | 11.8 | 10.9 | 10.5 | 9.3 |
| **Denmark — Danemark** | | | | | | | | |
| MF [BA][51] | 158.0 | 131.1 | 137.0 | 134.0 | 157.6 | 162.6 | 143.3 | 117.9 |
| M [BA][51] | 71.0 | 61.2 | 66.0 | 66.0 | 75.7 | 79.9 | 69.4 | 53.4 |
| F [BA][51] | 87.0 | 69.8 | 71.0 | 68.0 | 81.8 | 82.7 | 73.9 | 64.5 |
| %MF [BA][51] | 5.5 | 4.6 | 4.8 | 4.7 | 5.5 | 5.6 | 5.0 | 4.1 |
| %M [BA][51] | 4.8 | 4.0 | 4.4 | 4.4 | 5.0 | 5.2 | 4.6 | 3.5 |
| %F [BA][51] | 6.5 | 5.2 | 5.3 | 5.1 | 6.2 | 6.1 | 5.5 | 4.7 |
| MF [FB][52] | 158.2 | 150.5 | 145.1 | 144.7 | 170.6 | 176.4 | 157.4 | 124.4 |
| M [FB][52] | 72.8 | 68.5 | 66.5 | 68.8 | 83.3 | 84.6 | 72.9 | 54.7 |
| F [FB][52] | 85.4 | 82.0 | 78.6 | 75.9 | 87.3 | 91.8 | 84.5 | 69.6 |
| %MF [FB][52] | 5.7 | 5.4 | 5.2 | 5.2 | 6.2 | 6.4 | 5.7 | 4.5 |
| %M [FB][52] | 4.9 | 4.6 | 4.5 | 4.7 | 5.7 | 5.8 | 5.0 | 3.8 |
| %F [FB][52] | 6.5 | 6.0 | 5.9 | 5.8 | 6.6 | 7.0 | 6.4 | 5.3 |
| **Dominica[1] — Dominique[1]** | | | | | | | | |
| MF [A][4] | ... | ... | 3.1 | ... | ... | ... | ... | ... |
| M [A][4] | ... | ... | 2.0 | ... | ... | ... | ... | ... |
| F [A][4] | ... | ... | 1.0 | ... | ... | ... | ... | ... |
| %MF [A][4] | ... | ... | 11.0 | ... | ... | ... | ... | ... |
| %M [A][4] | ... | ... | 11.9 | ... | ... | ... | ... | ... |
| %F [A][4] | ... | ... | 9.5 | ... | ... | ... | ... | ... |
| MF [BA] | 5.2 | ... | ... | ... | ... | ... | ... | ... |
| M [BA] | 2.6 | ... | ... | ... | ... | ... | ... | ... |
| F [BA] | 2.6 | ... | ... | ... | ... | ... | ... | ... |
| %MF [BA] | 15.7 | ... | ... | ... | ... | ... | ... | ... |
| %M [BA] | 13.1 | ... | ... | ... | ... | ... | ... | ... |
| %F [BA] | 19.4 | ... | ... | ... | ... | ... | ... | ... |
| **Dominican Republic[7] — Rép. dominicaine[7]** | | | | | | | | |
| MF [BA] | 477.9 | 491.4 | 556.3 | 596.3 | 619.7 | 723.7 | 715.8 | ... |

| Country or area, source[§] — Pays ou zone, source[§] | 1999 | 2000 | 2001 | 2002 | 2003 | 2004 | 2005 | 2006 |
|---|---|---|---|---|---|---|---|---|
| M [BA] | 175.8 | 174.7 | 208.0 | 215.5 | 243.0 | 252.5 | 269.6 | ... |
| F [BA] | 302.1 | 316.8 | 348.2 | 380.8 | 376.8 | 471.2 | 446.3 | ... |
| %MF [BA] | 13.8 | 13.9 | 15.6 | 16.1 | 16.7 | 18.4 | 17.9 | ... |
| %M [BA] | 7.8 | 7.9 | 9.3 | 9.4 | 10.6 | 10.5 | 11.3 | ... |
| %F [BA] | 24.9 | 23.8 | 26.0 | 26.6 | 26.6 | 30.7 | 28.8 | ... |
| **Ecuador[7,39] — Equateur[7,39]** | | | | | | | | |
| MF [BA] | 543.5[34] | 333.1[34] | 450.9[6] | 352.9[34] | 461.1[34] | 362.1[34] | 333.6[34] | 341.8[34] |
| M [BA] | 239.5[34] | 138.3[34] | 169.0[6] | 136.2[34] | 215.0[34] | 160.7[34] | 143.3[34] | 143.4[34] |
| F [BA] | 304.0[34] | 194.8[34] | 282.0[6] | 216.7[34] | 246.1[34] | 201.4[34] | 190.3[34] | 198.4[34] |
| %MF [BA] | 14.0[34] | 9.0[34] | 11.0[6] | 9.3[34] | 11.5[34] | 8.6[34] | 7.9[34] | ... |
| %M [BA] | 10.8[34] | 6.2[34] | 7.1[6] | 6.0[34] | 9.1[34] | 6.6[34] | 5.8[34] | ... |
| %F [BA] | 19.6[34] | 13.1[34] | 16.2[6] | 14.0[34] | 15.0[34] | 11.4[34] | 10.8[34] | ... |
| **Egypt[53,54] — Egypte[53,54]** | | | | | | | | |
| MF [BA] | 1 480.5 | 1 698.0 | 1 783.0 | 2 020.6 | 2 240.7 | 2 153.9 | 2 450.0 | ... |
| M [BA] | 726.2 | 743.5 | 851.8 | 983.2 | 1 186.7 | 942.6 | 1 194.5 | ... |
| F [BA] | 754.3 | 954.5 | 931.2 | 1 037.4 | 1 054.0 | 1 211.3 | 1 255.5 | ... |
| %MF [BA] | 8.1 | 9.0 | 9.2 | 10.2 | 11.0 | 10.3 | 11.2 | ... |
| %M [BA] | 5.1 | 5.1 | 5.6 | 6.3 | 7.5 | 5.9 | 7.1 | ... |
| %F [BA] | 19.4 | 22.7 | 22.6 | 23.9 | 23.3 | 25.1 | 24.3 | ... |
| **El Salvador[7,49] — El Salvador[7,49]** | | | | | | | | |
| MF [BA] | 170.2 | 173.7 | 183.5 | 160.2 | 187.2 | 183.9 | 201.6 | 188.7 |
| M [BA] | 125.2 | 136.8 | 128.8 | 123.6 | 148.6 | 142.7 | 147.0 | 142.4 |
| F [BA] | 45.0 | 36.9 | 54.7 | 36.6 | 38.6 | 41.1 | 54.5 | 46.4 |
| %MF [BA] | 7.0 | 7.0 | 7.0 | 6.2 | 6.9 | 6.8 | ... | 6.6 |
| %M [BA] | 8.5 | 9.1 | 8.1 | 8.1 | 9.2 | 8.7 | ... | 8.5 |
| %F [BA] | 4.6 | 3.6 | 5.2 | 3.5 | 3.7 | 3.8 | ... | 3.9 |
| **Estonia — Estonie** | | | | | | | | |
| MF [BA][55] | 80.5[57] | 89.9 | 83.1 | 67.2 | 66.2 | 63.6 | 52.2 | 40.5 |
| M [BA][55] | 45.7[57] | 49.5 | 43.7 | 36.1 | 34.2 | 34.7 | 28.9 | 21.3 |
| F [BA][55] | 34.8[57] | 40.5 | 39.3 | 31.0 | 32.0 | 28.9 | 23.3 | 19.2 |
| %MF [BA][55] | 12.2[57] | 13.6 | 12.6 | 10.3 | 10.0 | 9.7 | 7.9 | 5.9 |
| %M [BA][55] | 13.4[57] | 14.5 | 12.9 | 10.8 | 10.2 | 10.4 | 8.8 | 6.2 |
| %F [BA][55] | 10.9[57] | 12.6 | 12.2 | 9.7 | 9.9 | 8.9 | 7.1 | 5.6 |
| MF [FB][56] | 44.0 | 46.3 | 46.7[10] | 41.5 | 38.2 | 32.3 | 26.0 | 15.4 |
| %MF [FB][56] | 5.1 | 5.3 | 7.1[10] | 6.4 | 5.8 | 4.9 | 3.9 | 2.2 |
| **Ethiopia[7] — Ethiopie[7]** | | | | | | | | |
| MF [BA] | ... | ... | ... | ... | ... | 845.9[2,39] | 1 653.7[37] | 767.1[6,39] |
| M [BA] | ... | ... | ... | ... | ... | 304.5[2,39] | 427.9[37] | 273.1[6,39] |
| F [BA] | ... | ... | ... | ... | ... | 541.4[2,39] | 1 225.8[37] | 493.9[6,39] |
| %MF [BA] | ... | ... | ... | ... | ... | 22.9[2,39] | 5.0[37] | 16.7[6,39] |
| %M [BA] | ... | ... | ... | ... | ... | 15.8[2,39] | 2.5[37] | 11.5[6,39] |
| %F [BA] | ... | ... | ... | ... | ... | 30.6[2,39] | 7.8[37] | 22.1[6,39] |
| **Faeroe Islands [5,56] — Iles Féroé[5,56]** | | | | | | | | |
| MF [BA] | ... | 1.0 | 1.0 | 0.0 | 1.0 | 1.0 | 0.9 | ... |
| M [BA] | ... | ... | ... | ... | ... | ... | 0.4 | ... |
| F [BA] | ... | ... | ... | ... | ... | ... | 0.5 | ... |
| **Fiji [58] — Fidji[58]** | | | | | | | | |
| MF [BA] | ... | ... | ... | ... | ... | ... | 15.5 | ... |
| M [BA] | ... | ... | ... | ... | ... | ... | 9.4 | ... |
| F [BA] | ... | ... | ... | ... | ... | ... | 6.1 | ... |
| %MF [BA] | ... | ... | ... | ... | ... | ... | 4.6 | ... |
| %M [BA] | ... | ... | ... | ... | ... | ... | 4.1 | ... |
| %F [BA] | ... | ... | ... | ... | ... | ... | 5.9 | ... |
| **Finland[59] — Finlande[59]** | | | | | | | | |
| MF [BA][55] | 261.0 | 253.0 | 238.0 | 237.0 | 235.0 | 229.0 | 220.0 | 204.0 |
| M [BA][55] | 130.0 | 122.0 | 117.0 | 123.0 | 124.0 | 118.0 | 111.0 | 101.0 |
| F [BA][55] | 131.0 | 131.0 | 121.0 | 114.0 | 111.0 | 111.0 | 109.0 | 103.0 |
| %MF [BA][55] | 10.1 | 9.7 | 9.1 | 9.1 | 9.0 | 8.8 | 8.3 | 7.7 |

| Country or area, source§ — Pays ou zone, source§ | 1999 | 2000 | 2001 | 2002 | 2003 | 2004 | 2005 | 2006 |
|---|---|---|---|---|---|---|---|---|
| %M [BA][55] | 9.6 | 8.9 | 8.6 | 9.1 | 9.2 | 8.7 | 8.1 | 7.4 |
| %F [BA][55] | 10.7 | 10.6 | 9.7 | 9.1 | 8.9 | 8.9 | 8.6 | 8.1 |
| MF [FB][1,60] | 337.0 | 321.0 | 302.0 | 294.0 | 288.0 | 288.0 | 275.0 | 250.0 |
| M [FB][1,60] | 169.0 | 162.0 | 153.0 | 154.0 | 153.0 | 152.0 | 144.0 | 129.0 |
| F [FB][1,60] | 168.0 | 159.0 | 149.0 | 140.0 | 135.0 | 136.0 | 131.0 | 120.0 |
| **France — France** | | | | | | | | |
| MF [BA][1] | 3 014.3[19] | 2 604.0[63] | 2 305.0[63] | 2 407.0[63] | 2 682.0 | 2 734.0 | 2 717.0 | ... |
| M [BA][1] | 1 424.6[19] | 1 191.0[63] | 1 016.0[63] | 1 161.0[63] | 1 300.0 | 1 330.0 | 1 328.0 | ... |
| F [BA][1] | 1 589.7[19] | 1 413.0[63] | 1 290.0[63] | 1 246.0[63] | 1 383.0 | 1 404.0 | 1 389.0 | ... |
| %MF [BA][1] | 11.7[19] | 10.0[63] | 8.8[63] | 8.9[63] | 9.8 | 9.9 | 9.8 | ... |
| %M [BA][1] | 10.2[19] | 8.4[63] | 7.1[63] | 7.9[63] | 8.8 | 9.0 | 9.0 | ... |
| %F [BA][1] | 13.6[19] | 11.8[63] | 10.7[63] | 10.1[63] | 11.0 | 11.0 | 10.8 | ... |
| MF [E][1] | 2 844.3 | 2 516.6 | 2 328.5 | 2 445.1 | 2 682.5 | 2 733.9 | 2 716.6 | ... |
| M [E][1] | 1 329.2 | 1 140.7 | 1 050.9 | 1 171.2 | 1 299.7 | 1 329.6 | 1 327.6 | ... |
| F [E][1] | 1 515.8 | 1 375.9 | 1 277.5 | 1 273.9 | 1 382.7 | 1 404.3 | 1 389.0 | ... |
| %MF [E][1] | 10.8 | 9.5 | 8.7 | 9.0 | 9.8 | 9.9 | 9.8 | ... |
| %M [E][1] | 9.3 | 7.9 | 7.2 | 8.0 | 8.8 | 9.0 | 9.0 | ... |
| %F [E][1] | 12.7 | 11.4 | 10.4 | 10.2 | 11.0 | 11.0 | 10.8 | ... |
| MF [FB][56,61,62] | 2 786.7 | 2 356.1 | 2 122.9 | 2 254.4 | 2 389.9 | 2 439.5 | 2 425.1 | ... |
| M [FB][56,61,62] | 1 365.2 | 1 138.5 | 1 039.4 | 1 154.1 | 1 246.6 | 1 265.8 | 1 252.5 | ... |
| F [FB][56,61,62] | 1 421.5 | 1 217.5 | 1 083.5 | 1 100.3 | 1 143.3 | 1 173.7 | 1 172.5 | ... |
| **French Guiana[1,64] — Guyane française[1,64]** | | | | | | | | |
| MF [BA] | 15.5 | 15.2 | 15.0 | 13.5 | 14.1 | 15.2 | 15.9 | 18.4 |
| M [BA] | 7.8 | 7.3 | 7.4 | 6.4 | 6.6 | 7.3 | 7.9 | 8.2 |
| F [BA] | 7.7 | 7.9 | 7.6 | 7.1 | 7.5 | 8.0 | 8.0 | 10.3 |
| %MF [BA] | 26.6 | 25.8 | 26.3 | 23.4 | 24.5 | 26.3 | 26.5 | 29.1 |
| %M [BA] | 22.8 | 21.2 | 23.0 | 19.8 | 20.5 | 22.6 | 23.8 | 23.9 |
| %F [BA] | 32.1 | 32.2 | 30.5 | 27.8 | 29.6 | 30.8 | 29.7 | 35.3 |
| **Georgia — Géorgie** | | | | | | | | |
| MF [BA][1] | 277.5 | 212.2 | 235.6 | 265.0 | 235.9 | 257.6 | 279.3 | ... |
| M [BA][1] | 160.1 | 116.7 | 126.9 | 155.5 | 124.2 | 143.2 | 159.2 | ... |
| F [BA][1] | 117.4 | 95.5 | 108.7 | 109.5 | 111.7 | 114.4 | 120.1 | ... |
| %MF [BA][1] | 13.8 | 10.8 | 11.0 | 12.3 | 11.5 | 12.6 | 13.8 | ... |
| %M [BA][1] | 15.3 | 11.1 | 11.6 | 13.7 | 11.5 | 13.4 | 14.8 | ... |
| %F [BA][1] | 12.2 | 10.5 | 10.7 | 10.7 | 11.5 | 11.8 | 12.6 | ... |
| MF [FB][3] | 92.2 | 101.0 | 97.8 | 21.9[10] | 42.9 | 46.6 | 34.2 | ... |
| M [FB][3] | 38.9 | 46.5 | 40.1 | 12.1[10] | 23.2 | 24.1 | 17.1 | ... |
| F [FB][3] | 53.3 | 54.1 | 57.7 | 9.8[10] | 19.7 | 22.5 | 17.1 | ... |
| %MF [FB][3] | 5.0 | 3.5 | 5.5 | 1.2[10] | ... | ... | ... | ... |
| **Germany — Allemagne** | | | | | | | | |
| MF [BA][1] | 3 503.0[18] | 3 127.0[4] | 3 150.0[18] | 3 486.0[37] | 4 023.0[4] | 4 388.0[37] | 4 583.0[10,37] | 4 279.0[37] |
| M [BA][1] | 1 905.0[18] | 1 691.0[4] | 1 754.0[18] | 1 982.0[37] | 2 316.0[4] | 2 551.0[37] | 2 574.0[10,37] | 2 358.0[37] |
| F [BA][1] | 1 598.0[18] | 1 436.0[4] | 1 396.0[18] | 1 504.0[37] | 1 707.0[4] | 1 836.0[37] | 2 009.0[10,37] | 1 921.0[37] |
| %MF [BA][1] | 8.8[18] | 7.9[4] | 7.9[18] | 8.7[37] | 10.0[4] | 11.0[37] | 11.1[10,37] | 10.3[37] |
| %M [BA][1] | 8.4[18] | 7.6[4] | 7.8[18] | 8.9[37] | 10.4[4] | 11.5[37] | 11.3[10,37] | 10.3[37] |
| %F [BA][1] | 9.2[18] | 8.3[4] | 7.9[18] | 8.5[37] | 9.5[4] | 10.3[37] | 10.9[10,37] | 10.2[37] |
| MF [FB][54,65] | 4 100.5 | 3 889.7 | 3 852.6 | 4 061.3 | 4 376.8 | 4 381.0[10] | 4 861.0 | 4 487.0 |
| M [FB][54,65] | 2 160.5 | 2 053.4 | 2 063.9 | 2 239.9 | 2 446.2 | 2 449.0[10] | 2 606.0 | 2 338.0 |
| F [FB][54,65] | 1 940.0 | 1 836.3 | 1 788.7 | 1 821.4 | 1 930.6 | 1 932.0[10] | 2 255.0 | 2 149.0 |
| %MF [FB][54,65] | 11.7 | 10.7 | 10.4 | 10.8 | 11.6 | 11.7[10] | 13.0 | 12.0 |
| %M [FB][54,65] | 11.3 | 10.5 | 10.4 | 11.3 | 12.4 | 12.5[10] | 13.4 | 12.0 |
| %F [FB][54,65] | 12.2 | 10.9 | 10.2 | 10.3 | 10.8 | 10.8[10] | 12.7 | 12.0 |
| **Gibraltar[66] — Gibraltar[66]** | | | | | | | | |
| MF [FB] | 0.4 | 0.4 | 0.4 | 0.5 | 0.5 | 0.4 | 0.5 | ... |
| M [FB] | 0.3 | 0.3 | 0.2 | 0.3 | 0.3 | 0.3 | 0.3 | ... |
| F [FB] | 0.1 | 0.1 | 0.2 | 0.2 | 0.2 | 0.2 | 0.2 | ... |
| **Greece[1,57] — Grèce[1,57]** | | | | | | | | |
| MF [BA] | 543.3 | 519.3 | 478.4 | 462.1 | 441.8 | 492.7 | 466.7 | 427.4 |

| Country or area, source[§] — Pays ou zone, source[§] | 1999 | 2000 | 2001 | 2002 | 2003 | 2004 | 2005 | 2006 |
|---|---|---|---|---|---|---|---|---|
| M [BA] | 212.8 | 207.2 | 191.4 | 180.5 | 170.8 | 181.7 | 166.8 | 160.9 |
| F [BA] | 330.5 | 312.1 | 287.0 | 281.6 | 271.0 | 311.0 | 299.9 | 266.5 |
| %MF [BA] | 11.9 | 11.2 | 10.4 | 9.9 | 9.3 | 10.2 | 9.6 | 8.8 |
| %M [BA] | 7.7 | 7.4 | 6.9 | 6.4 | 6.0 | 6.3 | 5.8 | 5.6 |
| %F [BA] | 18.2 | 17.0 | 15.9 | 15.2 | 14.3 | 15.9 | 15.2 | 13.4 |
| **Greenland[1,67] — Groenland[1,67]** | | | | | | | | |
| MF [E] | 2.3 | 2.8 | 2.5 | 2.3 | 2.7 | 2.8 | 2.5 | 2.3 |
| M [E] | 1.4 | 1.6 | 1.5 | 1.3 | 1.6 | 1.7 | 1.5 | 1.4 |
| F [E] | 0.9 | 1.3 | 1.0 | 1.0 | 1.1 | 1.2 | 1.1 | 0.9 |
| %MF [E] | 9.0 | 11.0 | 9.5 | 8.8 | 10.3 | 10.4 | 9.3 | ... |
| %M [E] | 10.6 | 12.0 | 11.3 | 9.8 | 11.9 | 12.0 | 10.4 | ... |
| %F [E] | 7.4 | 10.0 | 7.7 | 7.8 | 8.6 | 8.8 | 8.0 | ... |
| **Guadeloupe[1,64] — Guadeloupe[1,64]** | | | | | | | | |
| MF [BA] | 55.0 | 49.4 | 43.7 | 41.5 | 44.0 | 40.3 | 42.0 | 46.2 |
| M [BA] | 22.3 | 21.7 | 19.1 | 19.0 | 20.9 | 17.5 | 18.1 | 20.8 |
| F [BA] | 32.7 | 27.7 | 24.6 | 22.5 | 23.1 | 22.8 | 23.9 | 25.4 |
| %MF [BA] | 29.8 | 25.7 | 27.6 | 25.7 | 26.9 | 24.7 | 26.0 | 27.3 |
| %M [BA] | 23.2 | 21.2 | 23.4 | 22.6 | 24.6 | 21.0 | 22.0 | 24.2 |
| %F [BA] | 37.1 | 30.8 | 32.0 | 29.1 | 29.4 | 28.5 | 30.1 | 30.5 |
| **Guatemala[7] — Guatemala[7]** | | | | | | | | |
| MF [BA] | 79.8 | 64.9 | 62.2 | 154.3 | 172.2 | 156.2 | ... | ... |
| M [BA] | 59.2 | 40.3 | 34.4 | 77.1 | 79.4 | 91.7 | ... | ... |
| F [BA] | 20.6 | 24.6 | 27.8 | 77.2 | 92.8 | 64.5 | ... | ... |
| %MF [BA] | 1.9 | 1.4 | 1.3 | 3.1 | 3.4 | 3.1 | ... | ... |
| %M [BA] | 2.2 | 1.4 | 1.3 | 2.5 | 2.5 | 2.8 | ... | ... |
| %F [BA] | 1.4 | 1.5 | 1.4 | 4.3 | 4.9 | 3.7 | ... | ... |
| **Honduras[7] — Honduras[7]** | | | | | | | | |
| MF [BA] | 89.3[63] | ... | 103.4[5] | 93.7[5] | 130.3[5] | 153.2[4] | 107.8[63] | 87.4[63] |
| M [BA] | 56.7[63] | ... | 62.0[5] | ... | ... | 81.0[4] | 55.2[63] | 46.8[63] |
| F [BA] | 32.6[63] | ... | 41.4[5] | ... | ... | 72.2[4] | 52.6[63] | 40.7[63] |
| %MF [BA] | 3.7[63] | ... | 4.2[5] | 3.8[5] | 5.1[5] | 5.9[4] | 4.1[63] | ... |
| %M [BA] | 3.7[63] | ... | 4.0[5] | ... | ... | 4.7[4] | 3.1[63] | ... |
| %F [BA] | 3.8[63] | ... | 4.8[5] | ... | ... | 8.3[4] | 6.1[63] | ... |
| **Hungary — Hongrie** | | | | | | | | |
| MF [BA][55] | 284.7 | 262.5 | 232.9 | 238.8[68] | 244.5 | 252.9 | 303.9 | 316.8 |
| M [BA][55] | 170.7 | 159.5 | 142.7 | 138.0[68] | 138.5 | 136.8 | 159.1 | 164.6 |
| F [BA][55] | 114.0 | 103.0 | 90.2 | 100.8[68] | 106.0 | 116.1 | 144.8 | 152.2 |
| %MF [BA][55] | 7.0 | 6.4 | 5.7 | 5.8[68] | 5.7 | 6.1 | 7.2 | 7.5 |
| %M [BA][55] | 7.5 | 7.0 | 6.3 | 6.1[68] | 6.1 | 6.1 | 7.0 | 7.2 |
| %F [BA][55] | 6.3 | 5.6 | 5.0 | 5.4[68] | 5.3 | 6.1 | 7.5 | 7.8 |
| MF [FB][3] | 404.5 | 372.4 | 342.8 | 344.9 | 359.9 | 400.6 | 410.6 | 403.4 |
| M [FB][3] | 220.1 | 202.2 | 188.7 | 186.8 | 189.4 | 209.6 | 213.7 | 210.1 |
| F [FB][3] | 184.4 | 170.2 | 154.1 | 158.1 | 170.5 | 191.0 | 197.0 | 193.3 |
| %MF [FB][3] | 9.6 | ... | ... | ... | 8.4 | ... | ... | ... |
| %M [FB][3] | ... | ... | ... | ... | 7.9 | ... | ... | ... |
| %F [FB][3] | ... | ... | ... | ... | 8.9 | ... | ... | ... |
| **Iceland — Islande** | | | | | | | | |
| MF [BA][69,70] | 3.1 | 3.7 | 3.7 | 5.3 | 5.4 | 4.9 | 4.3 | 5.0 |
| M [BA][69,70] | 1.2 | 1.5 | 1.8 | 3.1 | 3.1 | 2.7 | 2.3 | 2.6 |
| F [BA][69,70] | 1.9 | 2.2 | 1.9 | 2.2 | 2.4 | 2.2 | 2.0 | 2.4 |
| %MF [BA][69,70] | 2.0 | 2.3 | 2.3 | 3.3 | 3.4 | 3.1 | 2.6 | 2.9 |
| %M [BA][69,70] | 1.5 | 1.8 | 2.0 | 3.6 | 3.6 | 2.9 | 2.6 | 2.7 |
| %F [BA][69,70] | 2.6 | 2.9 | 2.5 | 2.9 | 3.1 | 2.9 | 2.6 | 3.1 |
| MF [FB][56] | 2.6 | 1.9 | 2.0 | 3.6 | 4.9 | ... | ... | ... |
| M [FB][56] | 1.0 | 0.7 | 0.8 | 1.8 | 2.5 | ... | ... | ... |
| F [FB][56] | 1.6 | 1.1 | 1.2 | 1.8 | 2.4 | ... | ... | ... |
| %MF [FB][56] | 1.9 | 1.3 | 1.4 | 2.5 | 3.4 | ... | ... | ... |
| %M [FB][56] | 1.2 | 0.9 | 1.0 | 2.1 | 3.0 | ... | ... | ... |

| Country or area, source§ — Pays ou zone, source§ | 1999 | 2000 | 2001 | 2002 | 2003 | 2004 | 2005 | 2006 |
|---|---|---|---|---|---|---|---|---|
| %F [FB][56] | 2.7 | 1.9 | 1.9 | 3.0 | 3.9 | ... | ... | ... |
| **India — Inde** | | | | | | | | |
| MF [BA][19] | ... | 16 634.0 | ... | ... | ... | ... | ... | ... |
| M [BA][19] | ... | 11 837.5 | ... | ... | ... | ... | ... | ... |
| F [BA][19] | ... | 4 796.5 | ... | ... | ... | ... | ... | ... |
| %MF [BA][19] | ... | 4.3 | ... | ... | ... | ... | ... | ... |
| %M [BA][19] | ... | 4.3 | ... | ... | ... | ... | ... | ... |
| %F [BA][19] | ... | 4.3 | ... | ... | ... | ... | ... | ... |
| MF [FB][3,23,29] | 40 371.0 | 41 344.0 | 41 996.0 | 41 171.0 | 41 389.0 | 40 458.0 | 39 348.0 | 41 466.0 |
| M [FB][3,23,29] | 30 438.0 | 30 887.0 | 31 111.0 | 30 521.0 | 30 636.0 | 29 746.0 | 28 742.0 | 29 685.0 |
| F [FB][3,23,29] | 9 933.0 | 10 457.0 | 10 885.0 | 10 650.0 | 10 752.0 | 10 712.0 | 10 606.0 | 11 781.0 |
| **Indonesia[1] — Indonésie[1]** | | | | | | | | |
| MF [BA] | 6 030.3[71] | 5 813.2[71] | 8 005.0[71] | 9 132.1[71] | 9 531.1[71] | 10 251.4[71] | 10 854.3[71] | 11 104.7[72] |
| M [BA] | ... | ... | 4 032.4[71] | 4 727.8[71] | 4 928.3[71] | 5 345.7[71] | 5 483.3[71] | 5 808.2[72] |
| F [BA] | ... | ... | 3 972.6[71] | 4 404.3[71] | 4 602.8[71] | 4 905.7[71] | 5 371.0[71] | 5 296.5[72] |
| %MF [BA] | 6.4[71] | 6.1[71] | 8.1[71] | 9.1[71] | 9.5[71] | 9.9[71] | 10.3[71] | 10.5[72] |
| %M [BA] | ... | ... | ... | ... | 7.6[71] | 8.1[71] | 8.3[71] | 8.6[72] |
| %F [BA] | ... | ... | ... | ... | 13.0[71] | 12.9[71] | 13.5[71] | 13.7[72] |
| MF [FB] | 1 191.8 | ... | ... | ... | ... | ... | ... | ... |
| **Iran (Islamic Rep. of)[7] — Iran (Rép. islamique d')[7]** | | | | | | | | |
| MF [BA] | ... | ... | ... | ... | ... | ... | 2 556.0 | ... |
| M [BA] | ... | ... | ... | ... | ... | ... | 1 780.0 | ... |
| F [BA] | ... | ... | ... | ... | ... | ... | 776.0 | ... |
| %MF [BA] | ... | ... | ... | 12.8 | ... | 10.3 | 11.5 | ... |
| %M [BA] | ... | ... | ... | 11.2 | ... | 9.8 | 10.0 | ... |
| %F [BA] | ... | ... | ... | 22.4 | ... | 17.8 | 17.0 | ... |
| **Iraq[1] — Iraq[1]** | | | | | | | | |
| %MF [BA] | ... | ... | ... | ... | 28.1 | 26.8 | ... | ... |
| %M [BA] | ... | ... | ... | ... | 30.2 | 29.4 | ... | ... |
| %F [BA] | ... | ... | ... | ... | 16.0 | 15.0 | ... | ... |
| **Ireland — Irlande** | | | | | | | | |
| MF [BA][1,57] | 96.9 | 74.9 | 65.4 | 77.2 | 82.1 | 84.2 | 85.6 | 91.4 |
| M [BA][1,57] | 59.4 | 44.9 | 39.8 | 48.8 | 51.7 | 54.4 | 53.2 | 55.2 |
| F [BA][1,57] | 37.5 | 30.0 | 25.6 | 28.3 | 30.4 | 29.8 | 32.4 | 36.1 |
| %MF [BA][1,57] | 5.7 | 4.3 | 3.7 | 4.2 | 4.4 | 4.4 | 4.2 | 4.3 |
| %M [BA][1,57] | 5.9 | 4.3 | 3.8 | 4.6 | 4.7 | 4.9 | 4.6 | 4.5 |
| %F [BA][1,57] | 5.5 | 4.2 | 3.5 | 3.7 | 3.9 | 3.7 | 3.8 | 4.1 |
| MF [FB][56] | 193.2 | 155.4 | 142.3 | 162.5 | 172.4 | 166.0 | 153.3 | ... |
| M [FB][56] | 111.6 | 88.7 | 83.0 | 96.3 | 100.2 | 96.1 | 91.0 | ... |
| F [FB][56] | 81.6 | 66.7 | 59.3 | 66.2 | 72.2 | 70.0 | 62.3 | ... |
| %MF [FB][56] | 5.5 | 4.1 | 3.9 | 4.4 | 4.6 | 4.4 | 4.2 | ... |
| **Isle of Man — Ile de Man** | | | | | | | | |
| MF [A][1] | ... | ... | 0.6 | ... | ... | ... | ... | 1.0[2] |
| M [A][1] | ... | ... | 0.4 | ... | ... | ... | ... | 0.6[2] |
| F [A][1] | ... | ... | 0.3 | ... | ... | ... | ... | 0.4[2] |
| %MF [A][1] | ... | ... | 1.6 | ... | ... | ... | ... | 2.4[2] |
| %M [A][1] | ... | ... | 1.7 | ... | ... | ... | ... | 2.8[2] |
| %F [A][1] | ... | ... | 1.5 | ... | ... | ... | ... | 2.0[2] |
| MF [FB] | 0.3 | 0.2 | 0.2 | 0.2 | 0.3 | 0.4 | 0.6 | ... |
| M [FB] | 0.2 | 0.2 | 0.1 | 0.1 | 0.2 | 0.3 | 0.4 | ... |
| F [FB] | 0.1 | 0.1 | 0.1 | 0.1 | 0.1 | 0.1 | 0.2 | ... |
| %MF [FB][73] | 0.8 | 0.6 | 0.5 | 0.5 | 0.8 | 1.0 | 1.4 | ... |
| %M [FB][73] | 1.0 | 0.8 | 0.6 | 0.7 | 1.0 | 1.3 | 1.8 | ... |
| %F [FB][73] | 0.5 | 0.4 | 0.3 | 0.4 | 0.5 | 0.6 | 0.9 | ... |
| **Israel[1] — Israël[1]** | | | | | | | | |
| MF [BA] | 208.5 | 213.8 | 233.9 | 262.4 | 279.9 | 277.7 | 246.4 | 236.1 |
| M [BA] | 108.8 | 111.7 | 120.9 | 138.4 | 142.8 | 136.5 | 124.9 | 118.5 |

| Country or area, source§ — Pays ou zone, source§ | 1999 | 2000 | 2001 | 2002 | 2003 | 2004 | 2005 | 2006 |
|---|---|---|---|---|---|---|---|---|
| F [BA] | 99.7 | 102.1 | 113.0 | 124.0 | 137.1 | 141.2 | 121.5 | 117.6 |
| %MF [BA] | 8.9 | 8.8 | 9.4 | 10.3 | 10.7 | 10.4 | 9.0 | 8.4 |
| %M [BA] | 8.5 | 8.4 | 8.9 | 10.1 | 10.2 | 9.5 | 8.5 | 7.9 |
| %F [BA] | 9.4 | 9.2 | 9.9 | 10.6 | 11.3 | 11.4 | 9.5 | 9.0 |
| Italy[1] — Italie[1] | | | | | | | | |
| MF [BA] | 2 669.0 | 2 495.0 | 2 267.0 | 2 163.0 | 2 096.0 | 1 960.0[10] | 1 889.0 | 1 673.0 |
| M [BA] | 1 266.0 | 1 179.0 | 1 066.0 | 1 016.0 | 996.0 | 925.0[10] | 902.0 | 801.0 |
| F [BA] | 1 404.0 | 1 316.0 | 1 201.0 | 1 147.0 | 1 100.0 | 1 036.0[10] | 986.0 | 873.0 |
| %MF [BA] | 11.4 | 10.5 | 9.5 | 9.0 | 8.7 | 8.0[10] | 7.7 | 6.8 |
| %M [BA] | 8.8 | 8.1 | 7.3 | 6.9 | 6.7 | 6.4[10] | 6.2 | 5.4 |
| %F [BA] | 15.7 | 14.5 | 13.0 | 12.2 | 11.6 | 10.5[10] | 10.1 | 8.8 |
| Jamaica[23] — Jamaïque[23] | | | | | | | | |
| MF [BA] | 175.2 | 171.8 | 165.4[74] | 171.8 | 128.9 | 136.8 | 133.3 | 119.6 |
| M [BA] | 61.4 | 62.5 | 63.4[74] | 65.7 | 47.6 | 54.0 | 50.0 | 48.0 |
| F [BA] | 113.8 | 109.2 | 102.1[74] | 106.1 | 81.3 | 82.8 | 83.3 | 71.6 |
| %MF [BA] | 15.7 | 15.5 | 15.0[74] | 14.3 | 10.9 | 11.4 | 10.9 | 9.6 |
| %M [BA] | 10.0 | 10.2 | 10.3[74] | 9.9 | 7.2 | 8.1 | 7.4 | 6.9 |
| %F [BA] | 22.4 | 22.3 | 21.0[74] | 19.8 | 15.6 | 15.7 | 15.3 | 13.0 |
| Japan[1] — Japon[1] | | | | | | | | |
| MF [BA] | 3 170.0[75] | 3 190.0[75] | 3 400.0[75] | 3 590.0 | 3 500.0 | 3 130.0 | 2 940.0 | 2 750.0 |
| M [BA] | 1 940.0[75] | 1 960.0[75] | 2 090.0[75] | 2 190.0 | 2 150.0 | 1 920.0 | 1 780.0 | 1 680.0 |
| F [BA] | 1 230.0[75] | 1 230.0[75] | 1 310.0[75] | 1 400.0 | 1 350.0 | 1 210.0 | 1 160.0 | 1 070.0 |
| %MF [BA] | 4.7[75] | 4.7[75] | 5.0[75] | 5.4 | 5.3 | 4.7 | 4.4 | 4.1 |
| %M [BA] | 4.8[75] | 4.9[75] | 5.2[75] | 5.5 | 5.5 | 4.9 | 4.6 | 4.3 |
| %F [BA] | 4.5[75] | 4.5[75] | 4.7[75] | 5.1 | 4.9 | 4.4 | 4.2 | 3.9 |
| Jersey — Jersey | | | | | | | | |
| MF [A][56] | ... | ... | 1.0 | ... | ... | ... | ... | ... |
| M [A][56] | ... | ... | 0.6 | ... | ... | ... | ... | ... |
| F [A][56] | ... | ... | 0.4 | ... | ... | ... | ... | ... |
| MF [FB][49] | 169.0 | 209.0 | 189.0 | 193.0 | 667.0 | 477.0 | 366.0 | ... |
| Kazakhstan — Kazakhstan | | | | | | | | |
| MF [BA][1] | ... | ... | 780.3 | 690.7 | 672.1 | 658.8 | ... | ... |
| M [BA][1] | ... | ... | 338.0 | 283.8 | 281.4 | 281.1 | ... | ... |
| F [BA][1] | ... | ... | 442.3 | 406.9 | 390.7 | 377.7 | ... | ... |
| %MF [BA][1] | ... | ... | 10.4 | 9.3 | 8.8 | 8.4 | ... | ... |
| %M [BA][1] | ... | ... | 8.9 | 7.5 | 7.2 | 7.0 | ... | ... |
| %F [BA][1] | ... | ... | 12.0 | 11.2 | 10.4 | 9.8 | ... | ... |
| MF [E] | 950.0 | 906.4 | ... | ... | ... | ... | ... | ... |
| %MF [E] | 13.5 | 12.8 | ... | ... | ... | ... | ... | ... |
| MF [FB][47] | 251.4 | 231.4 | 216.1 | 193.7 | 142.8 | 117.7 | ... | ... |
| M [FB][47] | 102.0 | ... | ... | ... | ... | ... | ... | ... |
| F [FB][47] | 149.4 | ... | ... | ... | ... | ... | ... | ... |
| %MF [FB][47] | 3.9 | 3.7 | 2.9 | 2.6 | 1.8 | 1.5 | ... | ... |
| Kenya[1,26] — Kenya[1,26] | | | | | | | | |
| MF [A] | 1 275.8 | ... | ... | ... | ... | ... | ... | ... |
| Korea, Republic of[1] — Corée, République de[1] | | | | | | | | |
| MF [BA] | 1 353.0 | 979.0[76] | 899.0 | 752.0 | 818.0 | 860.0 | 887.0 | 827.0 |
| M [BA] | 911.0 | 647.0[76] | 591.0 | 491.0 | 508.0 | 534.0 | 553.0 | 533.0 |
| F [BA] | 442.0 | 332.0[76] | 308.0 | 261.0 | 309.7 | 325.9 | 334.0 | 294.0 |
| %MF [BA] | 6.3 | 4.4[76] | 4.0 | 3.3 | 3.6 | 3.7 | 3.7 | 3.5 |
| %M [BA] | 7.1 | 5.0[76] | 4.5 | 3.7 | 3.8 | 3.9 | 4.0 | 3.8 |
| %F [BA] | 5.1 | 3.6[76] | 3.3 | 2.8 | 3.3 | 3.4 | 3.4 | 2.9 |
| Kosovo — Kosovo | | | | | | | | |
| %MF [BA] | ... | ... | ... | ... | ... | ... | 39.6 | 41.3 |
| %M [BA] | ... | ... | ... | ... | ... | ... | 31.4 | 32.7 |

| Country or area, source[§] — Pays ou zone, source[§] | 1999 | 2000 | 2001 | 2002 | 2003 | 2004 | 2005 | 2006 |
|---|---|---|---|---|---|---|---|---|
| %F [BA] | ... | ... | ... | ... | ... | ... | 60.9 | 60.2 |
| **Kuwait[64] — Koweït[64]** | | | | | | | | |
| MF [FD] | 8.9 | 9.3 | 9.5 | 15.1 | 18.1 | 23.2 | 25.7 | 24.9 |
| M [FD] | 7.3 | 7.5 | 7.6 | 9.4 | 10.1 | 11.6 | 12.8 | 11.9 |
| F [FD] | 1.7 | 1.8 | 1.9 | 5.6 | 7.9 | 11.6 | 12.9 | 13.0 |
| %MF [FD] | 0.7 | 0.8 | 0.8 | 1.1 | 1.3 | 1.4 | 1.5 | 1.3 |
| %M [FD] | 0.8 | 0.8 | 0.8 | 1.0 | 1.0 | 0.9 | 1.0 | 0.8 |
| %F [FD] | 0.6 | 0.7 | 0.6 | 1.7 | 2.2 | 2.9 | 3.1 | 2.9 |
| **Kyrgyzstan — Kirghizistan** | | | | | | | | |
| MF [BA][1,34] | ... | ... | ... | 265.5 | 212.3 | 185.7 | 183.5 | |
| M [BA][1,34] | ... | ... | ... | 132.6 | 113.1 | 98.8 | 95.7 | ... |
| F [BA][1,34] | ... | ... | ... | 132.9 | 99.2 | 86.9 | 87.8 | |
| %MF [BA][1,34] | ... | ... | ... | 12.5 | 9.9 | 8.5 | 8.1 | |
| %M [BA][1,34] | ... | ... | ... | 11.2 | 9.4 | 8.0 | 7.4 | |
| %F [BA][1,34] | ... | ... | ... | 14.3 | 10.5 | 9.3 | 9.1 | ... |
| MF [FB] | 54.7 | 58.3 | 60.5 | 60.2 | 57.4 | 58.2 | 68.0 | 73.4 |
| M [FB] | 24.2 | 27.1 | 28.0 | 27.6 | 26.5 | 26.8 | 32.2 | 37.9 |
| F [FB] | 30.6 | 31.2 | 32.5 | 32.6 | 30.9 | 31.4 | 35.8 | 35.5 |
| **Lao People's Dem. Rep.[1,19] — Rép. dém. pop. lao[1,19]** | | | | | | | | |
| MF [A] | ... | ... | ... | ... | ... | ... | 37.5 | |
| M [A] | ... | ... | ... | ... | ... | ... | 18.6 | ... |
| F [A] | ... | ... | ... | ... | ... | ... | 18.9 | ... |
| **Latvia — Lettonie** | | | | | | | | |
| MF [BA] | 161.4[1] | 158.7[1] | 144.7[1] | 134.5[55] | 119.2[55] | 118.6[55] | 99.1[55] | 79.9[55] |
| M [BA] | 88.7[1] | 87.0[1] | 81.9[1] | 74.9[55] | 61.7[55] | 61.7[55] | 52.8[55] | 43.7[55] |
| F [BA] | 72.7[1] | 71.7[1] | 62.7[1] | 59.6[55] | 57.5[55] | 56.9[55] | 46.2[55] | 36.2[55] |
| %MF [BA] | 14.3[1] | 14.4[1] | 13.1[1] | 12.0[55] | 10.6[55] | 10.4[55] | 8.7[55] | 6.8[55] |
| %M [BA] | 15.0[1] | 15.4[1] | 14.4[1] | 12.9[55] | 10.7[55] | 10.6[55] | 9.0[55] | 7.2[55] |
| %F [BA] | 13.5[1] | 13.5[1] | 11.7[1] | 11.0[55] | 10.5[55] | 10.3[55] | 8.4[55] | 6.4[55] |
| MF [FB][47,77] | 109.5 | 93.3 | 91.6 | 89.7 | 90.6 | 90.8 | 78.5 | 68.9 |
| M [FB][47,77] | 46.7 | 39.5 | 39.1 | 37.0 | 37.6 | 37.3 | 31.5 | 27.0 |
| F [FB][47,77] | 62.8 | 53.8 | 52.6 | 52.7 | 53.0 | 53.5 | 47.0 | 42.0 |
| %MF [FB][47,77] | 9.1 | 7.8 | 7.7 | 8.5 | 8.6 | 8.5 | 7.4 | 6.5 |
| %M [FB][47,77] | 7.6 | 6.5 | 6.4 | 6.7 | 6.8 | ... | ... | ... |
| %F [FB][47,77] | 10.7 | 9.2 | 9.0 | 10.5 | 10.6 | ... | ... | ... |
| **Lesotho[7] — Lesotho[7]** | | | | | | | | |
| MF [B] | 231.7 | ... | ... | ... | ... | ... | ... | ... |
| M [B] | 91.0 | ... | ... | ... | ... | ... | ... | ... |
| F [B] | 140.8 | ... | ... | ... | ... | ... | ... | ... |
| %MF [B] | 27.3 | ... | ... | ... | ... | ... | ... | ... |
| %M [B] | 20.8 | ... | ... | ... | ... | ... | ... | ... |
| %F [B] | 34.2 | ... | ... | ... | ... | ... | ... | ... |
| **Liechtenstein — Liechtenstein** | | | | | | | | |
| MF [E] | 0.3 | 0.3 | 0.4 | 0.4 | 0.7 | 0.7 | ... | ... |
| **Lithuania — Lituanie** | | | | | | | | |
| MF [BA][1] | 249.0 | 273.7 | 284.0 | 224.4 | 203.9 | 184.4 | 132.9 | 89.3 |
| M [BA][1] | 140.5 | 158.5 | 165.6 | 121.1 | 105.4 | 90.6 | 67.1 | 46.7 |
| F [BA][1] | 108.5 | 115.2 | 118.4 | 103.3 | 98.4 | 93.8 | 65.8 | 42.6 |
| %MF [BA][1] | 14.6 | 16.4 | 17.4 | 13.8 | 12.4 | 11.4 | 8.3 | 5.6 |
| %M [BA][1] | 16.2 | 18.8 | 19.9 | 14.6 | 12.7 | 11.0 | 8.2 | 5.8 |
| %F [BA][1] | 13.0 | 13.9 | 14.7 | 12.9 | 12.2 | 11.8 | 8.3 | 5.4 |
| MF [FB][47,78] | 177.4 | 225.9 | 224.0 | 191.2 | 158.8 | 126.4 | 87.2 | 79.3 |
| M [FB][47,78] | 94.6 | 123.1 | 117.7 | 95.1 | 73.7 | 53.8 | 33.9 | 29.9 |
| F [FB][47,78] | 82.8 | 102.8 | 106.3 | 96.1 | 85.1 | 72.6 | 53.3 | 49.4 |
| %MF [FB][47,78] | 10.0 | 12.6 | 12.9 | 10.9 | 9.8 | 7.8 | 5.4 | ... |
| %M [FB][47,78] | 10.6 | 13.5 | 13.5 | 10.8 | 9.0 | 6.5 | 4.1 | ... |

| Country or area, source[§] — Pays ou zone, source[§] | 1999 | 2000 | 2001 | 2002 | 2003 | 2004 | 2005 | 2006 |
|---|---|---|---|---|---|---|---|---|
| %F [FB][47,78] | 9.3 | 11.6 | 12.2 | 11.0 | 10.5 | 9.1 | 6.8 | ... |
| **Luxembourg[79] — Luxembourg[79]** | | | | | | | | |
| MF [FB] | 5.4 | 5.0 | 4.9 | 5.8 | 7.6 | 8.7 | 9.8 | 9.5 |
| M [FB] | 2.8 | 2.6 | 2.6 | 3.2 | 4.1 | 4.7 | 5.4 | 5.0 |
| F [FB] | 2.5 | 2.3 | 2.3 | 2.7 | 3.5 | 4.0 | 4.4 | 4.5 |
| %MF [FB] | 2.9 | 2.7 | 2.7 | 3.0 | 3.8 | 4.2 | 4.7 | 4.6 |
| %M [FB] | ... | ... | ... | ... | ... | ... | ... | 4.3 |
| %F [FB] | ... | ... | ... | ... | ... | ... | ... | 5.0 |
| **Madagascar — Madagascar** | | | | | | | | |
| MF [B][80] | ... | ... | ... | ... | 383.0[82] | ... | 274.3 | ... |
| M [B][80] | ... | ... | ... | ... | 149.8[82] | ... | 100.4 | ... |
| F [B][80] | ... | ... | ... | ... | 233.2[82] | ... | 173.8 | ... |
| %MF [B][80] | ... | ... | ... | ... | 4.5 | ... | 2.8 | ... |
| %M [B][80] | ... | ... | ... | ... | 3.5 | ... | 2.0 | ... |
| %F [B][80] | ... | ... | ... | ... | 5.6 | ... | 3.6 | ... |
| MF [BA][7,71,81] | ... | 50.1 | 47.4 | ... | ... | ... | ... | ... |
| M [BA][7,71,81] | ... | 26.4 | 24.7 | ... | ... | ... | ... | ... |
| F [BA][7,71,81] | ... | 23.7 | 22.7 | ... | ... | ... | ... | ... |
| %MF [BA][7,71,81] | ... | 5.8 | 5.3 | ... | ... | ... | ... | ... |
| %M [BA][7,71,81] | ... | 6.0 | 5.3 | ... | ... | ... | ... | ... |
| %F [BA][7,71,81] | ... | 5.7 | 5.4 | ... | ... | ... | ... | ... |
| **Malaysia — Malaisie** | | | | | | | | |
| MF [BA][54] | 313.7 | 286.9 | 342.4 | 343.6 | 369.8 | ... | ... | ... |
| M [BA][54] | 212.3 | 182.7 | 212.3 | 210.5 | 235.8 | ... | ... | ... |
| F [BA][54] | 101.4 | 104.2 | 130.1 | 133.1 | 134.0 | ... | ... | ... |
| %MF [BA][54] | 3.4 | 3.0 | 3.5 | 3.5 | 3.6 | ... | ... | ... |
| %M [BA][54] | 3.5 | 3.0 | 3.4 | 3.3 | 3.6 | ... | ... | ... |
| %F [BA][54] | 3.3 | 3.1 | 3.8 | 3.8 | 3.6 | ... | ... | ... |
| MF [FB][1,29] | 31.8 | 34.3 | 33.5 | 37.2 | 34.8 | ... | ... | ... |
| **Maldives — Maldives** | | | | | | | | |
| MF [A] | ... | 1.7[25] | ... | ... | ... | ... | ... | 18.6[1] |
| M [A] | ... | 0.9[25] | ... | ... | ... | ... | ... | 5.9[1] |
| F [A] | ... | 0.8[25] | ... | ... | ... | ... | ... | 12.6[1] |
| **Mali[1] — Mali[1]** | | | | | | | | |
| MF [BA] | ... | ... | ... | ... | ... | 227.5 | ... | ... |
| M [BA] | ... | ... | ... | ... | ... | 107.0 | ... | ... |
| F [BA] | ... | ... | ... | ... | ... | 120.5 | ... | ... |
| %MF [BA] | ... | ... | ... | ... | ... | 8.8 | ... | ... |
| %M [BA] | ... | ... | ... | ... | ... | 7.2 | ... | ... |
| %F [BA] | ... | ... | ... | ... | ... | 10.9 | ... | ... |
| **Malta — Malte** | | | | | | | | |
| MF [BA][1] | ... | 10.3 | 10.1 | 11.0 | 12.1 | 11.5 | 11.7 | 11.9 |
| M [BA][1] | ... | 7.3 | 6.8 | 7.2 | 7.8 | 7.1 | 7.3 | 7.2 |
| F [BA][1] | ... | 3.0 | 3.2 | 3.8 | 4.3 | 4.4 | 4.5 | 4.7 |
| %MF [BA][1] | ... | 6.7 | 6.4 | 7.0 | 7.6 | 7.2 | 7.3 | 7.3 |
| %M [BA][1] | ... | 6.8 | 6.2 | 6.6 | 7.1 | 6.4 | 6.6 | 6.5 |
| %F [BA][1] | ... | 6.4 | 7.0 | 7.7 | 8.7 | 9.0 | 8.9 | 8.9 |
| MF [FB][3,83] | 7.7 | 6.6 | 6.8 | 6.8 | 8.2[10] | 8.1 | 7.4 | 7.2 |
| M [FB][3,83] | 6.6 | 5.7 | 5.6 | 5.6 | 6.6[10] | 6.5 | 5.7 | 5.5 |
| F [FB][3,83] | 1.1 | 0.9 | 1.1 | 1.2 | 1.6[10] | 1.6 | 1.7 | 1.6 |
| %MF [FB][3,83] | 5.3 | 4.5 | 4.7 | 4.7 | 5.7[10] | 5.4 | 5.1 | 5.0 |
| %M [FB][3,83] | 6.3 | 5.4 | 5.4 | 5.4 | 6.4[10] | 6.1 | 5.6 | 5.5 |
| %F [FB][3,83] | 2.6 | 2.2 | 2.7 | 2.9 | 3.8[10] | 3.8 | 3.9 | 3.9 |
| **Marshall Islands[1] — Iles Marshall[1]** | | | | | | | | |
| MF [A] | 4.5 | ... | ... | ... | ... | ... | ... | ... |
| M [A] | 2.7 | ... | ... | ... | ... | ... | ... | ... |
| F [A] | 1.9 | ... | ... | ... | ... | ... | ... | ... |

| Country or area, source§ — Pays ou zone, source§ | 1999 | 2000 | 2001 | 2002 | 2003 | 2004 | 2005 | 2006 |
|---|---|---|---|---|---|---|---|---|
| %MF [A] | 30.9 | ... | ... | ... | ... | ... | ... | ... |
| %M [A] | 27.6 | ... | ... | ... | ... | ... | ... | ... |
| %F [A] | 37.3 | ... | ... | ... | ... | ... | ... | ... |
| **Martinique[1,64] — Martinique[1,64]** | | | | | | | | |
| MF [BA] | 46.9 | 44.1 | 39.8 | 35.8[10] | 36.1 | 35.9 | 34.8 | 42.2 |
| M [BA] | 20.9 | 18.9 | 16.3 | 15.4[10] | 16.1 | 15.9 | 16.2 | 19.1 |
| F [BA] | 26.0 | 25.2 | 23.6 | 20.4[10] | 20.1 | 20.0 | 18.6 | 23.1 |
| %MF [BA] | 28.1 | 26.3 | 24.7 | 22.3[10] | 22.3 | 22.4 | 21.7 | 25.2 |
| %M [BA] | 24.5 | 22.1 | 20.1 | 19.2[10] | 19.9 | 19.9 | 20.1 | 23.1 |
| %F [BA] | 32.0 | 30.8 | 29.3 | 25.4[10] | 24.6 | 24.7 | 20.1 | 27.3 |
| **Mauritania[7] — Mauritanie[7]** | | | | | | | | |
| MF [E] | ... | 158.2 | ... | ... | ... | ... | ... | ... |
| M [E] | ... | 43.2 | ... | ... | ... | ... | ... | ... |
| F [E] | ... | 115.0 | ... | ... | ... | ... | ... | ... |
| **Mauritius — Maurice** | | | | | | | | |
| MF [BA] | ... | ... | ... | ... | ... | 45.1 | 52.1 | 50.1 |
| M [BA] | ... | ... | ... | ... | ... | 20.3 | 20.3 | 19.5 |
| F [BA] | ... | ... | ... | ... | ... | 24.8 | 31.8 | 30.6 |
| %MF [BA][1] | ... | ... | ... | ... | ... | 8.5 | 9.6 | 9.1 |
| %M [BA][1] | ... | ... | ... | ... | ... | 5.8 | 5.8 | 5.5 |
| %F [BA][1] | ... | ... | ... | ... | ... | 13.5 | 16.5 | 15.5 |
| MF [E] | 39.0 | 45.0 | 47.7 | 50.8 | 54.4 | ... | ... | ... |
| M [E] | 23.8 | 28.5 | 30.5 | 29.6 | 31.7 | ... | ... | ... |
| F [E] | 15.2 | 16.5 | 17.2 | 21.2 | 22.7 | ... | ... | ... |
| %MF [E] | 7.7 | 8.8 | 9.1 | 9.7 | 10.2 | ... | ... | ... |
| %M [E] | 7.0 | 8.3 | 8.8 | 8.5 | 9.0 | ... | ... | ... |
| %F [E] | 9.0 | 9.6 | 9.8 | 12.0 | 12.6 | ... | ... | ... |
| MF [FB][1,84] | 12.1 | 18.0 | 21.6 | 22.0 | 23.4 | 22.0 | 33.6 | ... |
| M [FB][1,84] | 5.3 | 8.6 | 10.5 | 10.1 | 10.1 | 10.5 | 15.4 | ... |
| F [FB][1,84] | 6.8 | 9.5 | 11.1 | 11.9 | 13.3 | 11.4 | 18.2 | ... |
| **Mexico[23,57] — Mexique[23,57]** | | | | | | | | |
| MF [BA] | 962.9 | 1 003.0 | 1 001.0 | 1 152.4 | 1 204.1 | 1 555.5 | 1 482.5[10] | 1 377.7 |
| M [BA] | 497.3 | 561.9 | 553.4 | 660.6 | 692.5 | 837.6 | 917.8[10] | 811.7 |
| F [BA] | 465.6 | 441.1 | 447.6 | 491.8 | 511.5 | 717.9 | 564.7[10] | 566.3 |
| %MF [BA] | 2.5 | 2.6 | 2.5 | 2.9 | 3.0 | 3.7 | 3.5[10] | 3.2 |
| %M [BA] | 2.0 | 2.2 | 2.2 | 2.5 | 2.6 | 3.1 | 3.4[10] | 3.0 |
| %F [BA] | 3.5 | 3.3 | 3.3 | 3.5 | 3.6 | 4.7 | 3.6[10] | 3.5 |
| **Moldova — Moldova** | | | | | | | | |
| MF [BA][1] | 187.2 | 140.1 | 117.7 | 110.0 | 117.1 | 116.5 | 103.7 | 99.9 |
| M [BA][1] | 113.6 | 80.6 | 70.1 | 64.4 | 69.9 | 70.1 | 59.8 | 61.7 |
| F [BA][1] | 73.6 | 59.5 | 47.6 | 45.4 | 47.2 | 46.4 | 43.9 | 38.2 |
| %MF [BA][1] | 11.1 | 8.5 | 7.3 | 6.8 | 7.9 | 8.1 | 7.3 | 7.4 |
| %M [BA][1] | 13.3 | 9.7 | 8.7 | 8.1 | 9.6 | 10.0 | 8.7 | 8.9 |
| %F [BA][1] | 8.9 | 7.2 | 5.9 | 5.5 | 6.4 | 6.3 | 6.0 | 5.7 |
| MF [FB][3] | 34.9 | 28.9 | 27.6 | 24.0 | 19.7 | 21.0 | 21.7 | 20.4 |
| M [FB][3] | 13.3 | 11.9 | 13.6 | 11.7 | 10.3 | 11.7 | 11.3 | 9.6 |
| F [FB][3] | 21.6 | 17.0 | 14.0 | 12.3 | 9.4 | 9.3 | 10.4 | 10.8 |
| %MF [FB][3] | 2.1 | 2.3 | 2.2 | 2.1 | 2.0 | 2.0 | 2.0 | 1.9 |
| **Mongolia[3,56] — Mongolie[3,56]** | | | | | | | | |
| MF [E] | 39.8 | 38.6 | 40.3 | 30.9 | 33.3 | 35.6 | 32.9 | ... |
| M [E] | 18.1 | 17.8 | 18.5 | 14.1 | 15.3 | 15.9 | 14.6 | ... |
| F [E] | 21.6 | 20.7 | 21.9 | 16.8 | 18.1 | 19.6 | 18.3 | ... |
| %MF [E] | 4.7 | 4.6 | 4.6 | 3.5 | 3.5 | 3.6 | 3.3 | ... |
| %M [E] | 4.1 | 4.1 | 4.2 | 3.4 | 3.2 | 3.3 | 3.0 | ... |
| %F [E] | 5.3 | 5.0 | 5.1 | 3.8 | 3.8 | 3.9 | 3.6 | ... |
| **Montenegro[54,85] — Monténégro[54,85]** | | | | | | | | |
| MF [BA] | ... | ... | ... | ... | ... | ... | 77.8 | ... |

| Country or area, source[§] — Pays ou zone, source[§] | 1999 | 2000 | 2001 | 2002 | 2003 | 2004 | 2005 | 2006 |
|---|---|---|---|---|---|---|---|---|
| M [BA] | ... | ... | ... | ... | ... | ... | 37.4 | ... |
| F [BA] | ... | ... | ... | ... | ... | ... | 40.3 | ... |
| %MF [BA] | ... | ... | ... | ... | ... | ... | 30.3 | ... |
| %M [BA] | ... | ... | ... | ... | ... | ... | 26.2 | ... |
| %F [BA] | ... | ... | ... | ... | ... | ... | 35.5 | ... |
| **Morocco[1] — Maroc[1]** | | | | | | | | |
| MF [BA] | 1 432.2 | 1 394.3 | 1 275.0 | 1 202.7 | 1 299.0 | 1 192.5 | 1 226.4 | 1 062.5 |
| M [BA] | 1 044.8 | 1 035.5 | 952.0 | 878.4 | 922.4 | 851.2 | 877.6 | 774.1 |
| F [BA] | 387.9 | 358.7 | 323.0 | 324.3 | 376.6 | 341.4 | 348.8 | 288.4 |
| %MF [BA] | 13.9 | 13.6 | 12.5 | 11.6 | 11.9 | 10.8 | 11.0 | 9.7 |
| %M [BA] | 14.2 | 13.8 | 12.5 | 11.6 | 11.5 | 10.6 | 10.8 | 9.7 |
| %F [BA] | 13.3 | 13.0 | 12.5 | 12.5 | 13.0 | 11.4 | 11.5 | 9.7 |
| **Myanmar[86] — Myanmar[86]** | | | | | | | | |
| MF [FB] | 425.3 | 382.1 | 398.4 | 435.7 | 326.5 | 291.3 | 189.7 | |
| **Namibia[87] — Namibie[87]** | | | | | | | | |
| MF [BA] | ... | 220.6 | ... | ... | ... | ... | ... | ... |
| M [BA] | ... | 89.4 | ... | ... | ... | ... | ... | ... |
| F [BA] | ... | 131.3 | ... | ... | ... | ... | ... | ... |
| %MF [BA] | ... | 33.8 | ... | ... | ... | ... | ... | ... |
| %M [BA] | ... | 28.3 | ... | ... | ... | ... | ... | ... |
| %F [BA] | ... | 39.0 | ... | ... | ... | ... | ... | ... |
| **Nepal[1] — Népal[1]** | | | | | | | | |
| MF [BA] | 178.0 | ... | ... | ... | ... | ... | ... | ... |
| M [BA] | 98.0 | ... | ... | ... | ... | ... | ... | ... |
| F [BA] | 80.0 | ... | ... | ... | ... | ... | ... | ... |
| %MF [BA] | 1.8 | ... | ... | ... | ... | ... | ... | ... |
| %M [BA] | 2.0 | ... | ... | ... | ... | ... | ... | ... |
| %F [BA] | 1.7 | ... | ... | ... | ... | ... | ... | ... |
| **Netherlands — Pays-Bas** | | | | | | | | |
| MF [BA][54] | 277.0 | 231.0[10] | 221.0 | 259.0 | 357.0 | 419.0 | 430.0 | ... |
| M [BA][54] | 124.0 | 105.0[10] | 102.0 | 130.0 | 193.0 | 228.0 | 221.0 | ... |
| F [BA][54] | 153.0 | 126.0[10] | 120.0 | 129.0 | 164.0 | 191.0 | 209.0 | ... |
| %MF [BA][54] | 3.5 | 2.9[10] | 2.8 | 3.2 | 4.4 | 5.1 | 5.2 | ... |
| %M [BA][54] | 2.8 | 2.3[10] | 3.2 | 2.9 | 4.2 | 5.0 | 4.9 | ... |
| %F [BA][54] | 4.5 | 3.6[10] | 3.4 | 3.6 | 4.5 | 5.2 | 5.6 | ... |
| MF [FB][79,88] | 221.5 | 187.0 | 146.0 | 170.0 | 255.0 | ... | ... | ... |
| M [FB][79,88] | 115.0 | 98.0 | 77.0 | 91.0 | 144.0 | ... | ... | ... |
| F [FB][79,88] | 106.0 | 90.0 | 69.0 | 79.0 | 111.0 | ... | ... | ... |
| %MF [FB][79] | 3.2 | 2.6 | 2.0 | 2.3 | 3.4 | ... | ... | ... |
| %M [FB][79] | 2.7 | 2.3 | 1.8 | 2.1 | 3.3 | ... | ... | ... |
| %F [FB][79] | 3.7 | 3.1 | 2.4 | 2.6 | 3.5 | ... | ... | ... |
| **Netherlands Antilles[1,85,89] — Antilles néerlandaises[1,85,89]** | | | | | | | | |
| MF [BA] | ... | 8.5 | ... | 9.1 | 9.3 | ... | ... | ... |
| M [BA] | ... | 3.7 | ... | 4.1 | 4.0 | ... | ... | ... |
| F [BA] | ... | 4.8 | ... | 4.9 | 5.3 | ... | ... | ... |
| %MF [BA] | ... | 14.2 | 15.8 | 15.6 | 15.1 | ... | ... | ... |
| %M [BA] | ... | 12.0 | ... | ... | ... | ... | ... | ... |
| %F [BA] | ... | 16.2 | ... | ... | ... | ... | ... | ... |
| **New Caledonia[56] — Nouvelle-Calédonie[56]** | | | | | | | | |
| MF [FB] | 8.8 | 9.4 | 9.9 | 10.5 | 10.2 | ... | ... | ... |
| M [FB] | 3.9 | 4.2 | 4.4 | 4.8 | 4.6 | ... | ... | ... |
| F [FB] | 4.9 | 5.2 | 5.4 | 5.7 | 5.6 | ... | ... | ... |
| **New Zealand — Nouvelle-Zélande** | | | | | | | | |
| MF [BA][1] | 127.8 | 113.4 | 102.3 | 102.5 | 93.9 | 82.0 | 79.3 | 82.6 |
| M [BA][1] | 72.4 | 63.4 | 56.2 | 54.6 | 48.0 | 39.5 | 39.5 | 41.2 |
| F [BA][1] | 55.4 | 50.0 | 46.1 | 47.9 | 45.9 | 42.4 | 39.8 | 41.4 |
| %MF [BA][1] | 6.8 | 6.0 | 5.3 | 5.2 | 4.7 | 3.9 | 3.7 | 3.8 |
| %M [BA][1] | 7.0 | 6.1 | 5.4 | 5.1 | 4.4 | 3.5 | 3.4 | 3.5 |

| Country or area, source§ — Pays ou zone, source§ | 1999 | 2000 | 2001 | 2002 | 2003 | 2004 | 2005 | 2006 |
|---|---|---|---|---|---|---|---|---|
| %F [BA][1] | 6.5 | 5.8 | 5.3 | 5.3 | 5.0 | 4.4 | 4.0 | 4.1 |
| MF [FB][90,91] | 221.4 | 226.9 | 192.2 | 168.3 | ... | ... | ... | ... |
| M [FB][90,91] | 127.2 | 120.3 | 103.5 | 89.1 | ... | ... | ... | ... |
| F [FB][90,91] | 94.1 | 106.6 | 88.7 | 79.2 | ... | ... | ... | ... |
| **Nicaragua[7] — Nicaragua[7]** | | | | | | | | |
| MF [E] | 185.1 | 178.0 | 122.5 | 135.3 | ... | ... | ... | ... |
| M [E] | 122.8 | 118.0 | 77.3 | 84.0 | ... | ... | ... | ... |
| F [E] | 62.3 | 60.0 | 45.2 | 51.3 | ... | ... | ... | ... |
| %MF [E] | 10.9 | 9.8 | 11.3 | 12.2 | ... | ... | ... | ... |
| **Northern Mariana Islands[56] — Îles Mariannes du Nord [56]** | | | | | | | | |
| MF [BA] | ... | ... | ... | ... | 1.8 | ... | ... | ... |
| M [BA] | ... | ... | ... | ... | 0.8 | ... | ... | ... |
| F [BA] | ... | ... | ... | ... | 1.0 | ... | ... | ... |
| %MF [BA] | ... | ... | ... | ... | 4.6 | ... | ... | ... |
| %M [BA] | ... | ... | ... | ... | 5.0 | ... | ... | ... |
| %F [BA] | ... | ... | ... | ... | 4.3 | ... | ... | ... |
| **Norway — Norvège** | | | | | | | | |
| MF [BA] | 75.0[69] | 81.0[69] | 84.0[69] | 92.0[69] | 107.0[69] | 106.0[69] | 111.0[69] | 84.0[55] |
| M [BA] | 42.0[69] | 46.0[69] | 46.0[69] | 52.0[69] | 62.0[69] | 62.0[69] | 61.0[69] | 45.0[55] |
| F [BA] | 33.0[69] | 35.0[69] | 38.0[69] | 40.0[69] | 45.0[69] | 45.0[69] | 49.0[69] | 39.0[55] |
| %MF [BA] | 3.2[69] | 3.4[69] | 3.6[69] | 3.9[69] | 4.5[69] | 4.5[69] | 4.6[69] | 3.4[55] |
| %M [BA] | 3.4[69] | 3.6[69] | 3.7[69] | 4.1[69] | 4.9[69] | 4.9[69] | 4.8[69] | 3.5[55] |
| %F [BA] | 3.0[69] | 3.2[69] | 3.4[69] | 3.6[69] | 4.0[69] | 4.0[69] | 4.4[69] | 3.4[55] |
| MF [FB] | 59.6[10,69] | 62.6[69] | 62.7[69] | 75.2[69] | 92.6[69] | 91.6[69] | 83.5[69] | 63.0[55] |
| M [FB] | 33.5[10,69] | 36.3[69] | 35.7[69] | 42.6[69] | 54.0[69] | 52.2[69] | 45.7[69] | 33.0[55] |
| F [FB][55] | 26.0[10,69] | 26.4[69] | 27.0[69] | 32.6[69] | 38.6[69] | 39.4[69] | 37.8[69] | 30.0[55] |
| %MF [FB] | 2.6[10,69] | 2.7[69] | 2.7[69] | 3.2[69] | 3.9[69] | 3.9[69] | 3.5[69] | 2.6[55] |
| %M [FB] | ... | ... | ... | ... | 4.3[69] | 4.1[69] | 3.6[69] | 2.6[55] |
| %F [FB] | ... | ... | ... | ... | 3.5[69] | 3.5[69] | 3.4[69] | 2.7[55] |
| **Occupied Palestinian Terr.[92] — Terr. palestinien occupé[92]** | | | | | | | | |
| MF [BA] | 79.0[1] | 98.8[1] | 170.5[7] | 217.5[7] | 194.3[7] | 212.2[7] | 194.5[7] | 206.2[7] |
| M [BA] | 66.1[1] | 85.4[1] | 158.0[7] | 201.5[7] | 172.2[7] | 185.8[7] | 164.6[7] | 175.2[7] |
| F [BA] | 12.9[1] | 13.4[1] | 12.5[7] | 16.0[7] | 22.1[7] | 26.4[7] | 30.1[7] | 31.0[7] |
| %MF [BA] | 11.8[1] | 14.1[1] | 25.2[7] | 31.2[7] | 25.4[7] | 26.7[7] | 23.3[7] | 23.2[7] |
| %M [BA] | 11.6[1] | 14.4[1] | 26.9[7] | 33.5[7] | 26.7[7] | 28.0[7] | 23.6[7] | 23.9[7] |
| %F [BA] | 13.0[1] | 12.3[1] | 14.0[7] | 17.0[7] | 18.4[7] | 20.0[7] | 22.1[7] | 20.1[7] |
| **Pakistan — Pakistan** | | | | | | | | |
| MF [BA][6,7] | 2 334.0 | 3 127.0 | 3 181.0 | 3 506.0 | 3 594.0 | 3 499.0 | 3 566.0 | 3 103.0 |
| M [BA][6,7] | 1 419.0 | 2 046.0 | 2 082.0 | 2 381.0 | 2 441.0 | 2 461.0 | 2 508.0 | 2 166.0 |
| F [BA][6,7] | 915.0 | 1 081.0 | 1 099.0 | 1 125.0 | 1 153.0 | 1 038.0 | 1 058.0 | 937.0 |
| %MF [BA][6,7] | 5.9 | 7.8 | 7.8 | 8.3 | 8.3 | 7.7 | 7.7 | 6.2 |
| %M [BA][6,7] | 4.2 | 6.1 | 6.1 | 6.7 | 6.7 | 6.6 | 6.6 | 5.4 |
| %F [BA][6,7] | 15.0 | 17.3 | 17.3 | 16.5 | 16.5 | 12.8 | 12.8 | 6.2 |
| MF [FB][29,93] | 217.0 | 469.0 | 477.0 | 493.0 | 505.0 | 576.0 | 587.0 | 420.0 |
| M [FB][29,93] | 190.0 | 421.0 | 428.0 | 442.0 | 453.0 | 477.0 | 486.0 | 360.0 |
| F [FB][29,93] | 27.0 | 48.0 | 49.0 | 51.0 | 52.0 | 99.0 | 101.0 | 60.0 |
| **Panama[1,94] — Panama[1,94]** | | | | | | | | |
| MF [BA] | 128.0 | 147.0 | 169.7 | 172.4 | 170.4 | 159.9 | 136.8 | 121.4 |
| M [BA] | 62.1 | 77.7 | 92.0 | 86.5 | 82.9 | 76.3 | 66.7 | 60.2 |
| F [BA] | 65.9 | 69.3 | 77.8 | 85.9 | 87.3 | 83.6 | 70.2 | 61.1 |
| %MF [BA] | 11.8 | 13.5 | 14.7 | 14.1 | 13.6 | 12.4 | 10.3 | 9.1 |
| %M [BA] | 8.9 | 11.1 | 12.2 | 11.2 | 10.5 | 9.4 | 8.1 | 7.2 |
| %F [BA] | 16.9 | ... | 19.3 | 19.2 | 18.8 | 17.3 | 14.0 | 12.4 |
| **Papua New Guinea[6,7] — Papouasie-Nvl-Guinée[6,7]** | | | | | | | | |
| MF [A] | ... | 68.6 | ... | ... | ... | ... | ... | ... |
| M [A] | ... | 53.7 | ... | ... | ... | ... | ... | ... |
| F [A] | ... | 15.0 | ... | ... | ... | ... | ... | ... |

**29**

**Unemployment**—Number (thousands) and percentage unemployed, by sex (*continued*)
**Chômage**—Nombre (milliers) et pourcentage des chômeurs, par sexe (*suite*)

| Country or area, source[§] — Pays ou zone, source[§] | 1999 | 2000 | 2001 | 2002 | 2003 | 2004 | 2005 | 2006 |
|---|---|---|---|---|---|---|---|---|
| %MF [A] | ... | 2.8 | ... | ... | ... | ... | ... | ... |
| %M [A] | ... | 4.3 | ... | ... | ... | ... | ... | ... |
| %F [A] | ... | 1.3 | ... | ... | ... | ... | ... | ... |
| **Paraguay[7] — Paraguay[7]** | | | | | | | | |
| MF [BA] | ... | 198.7[95] | ... | 272.6 | 206.0 | ... | ... | ... |
| M [BA] | ... | 108.5[95] | ... | 141.9 | 105.6 | ... | ... | ... |
| F [BA] | ... | 89.9[95] | ... | 130.9 | 100.4 | ... | ... | ... |
| %MF [BA] | 6.8 | 7.6[95] | ... | 10.8 | 8.1 | ... | ... | ... |
| %M [BA] | ... | 6.8[95] | ... | 9.0 | 6.7 | ... | ... | ... |
| %F [BA] | ... | 8.9[95] | ... | 13.6 | 10.1 | ... | ... | ... |
| **Peru[23] — Pérou[23]** | | | | | | | | |
| MF [B][43,96] | 624.9 | 566.5 | 651.5 | ... | ... | ... | ... | ... |
| M [B][43,96] | 322.8 | 318.8 | 327.5 | ... | ... | ... | ... | ... |
| F [B][43,96] | 302.2 | 247.7 | 324.0 | ... | ... | ... | ... | ... |
| %MF [B][43,96] | 8.0 | 7.4 | 7.9 | ... | ... | ... | ... | ... |
| %M [B][43,96] | 7.5 | 7.3 | 7.2 | ... | ... | ... | ... | ... |
| %F [B][43,96] | 8.6 | 7.5 | 8.7 | ... | ... | ... | ... | ... |
| MF [BA][97] | ... | ... | ... | 359.0[13] | 386.0[6] | 394.4[26] | 437.1[5] | 350.9[13] |
| M [BA][97] | ... | ... | ... | 173.4[13] | 187.9[6] | 207.0[26] | 209.9[5] | 155.7[13] |
| F [BA][97] | ... | ... | ... | 185.7[13] | 198.1[6] | 187.4[26] | 227.2[5] | 195.2[13] |
| %MF [BA][97] | ... | ... | ... | 9.7[13] | 10.3[6] | 10.5[26] | 11.4[5] | 8.8[13] |
| %M [BA][97] | ... | ... | ... | 8.3[13] | 9.0[6] | 9.4[26] | 9.6[5] | 6.8[13] |
| %F [BA][97] | ... | ... | ... | 11.6[13] | 11.9[6] | 12.0[26] | 13.7[5] | 11.3[13] |
| **Philippines[1,85] — Philippines[1,85]** | | | | | | | | |
| MF [BA] | 2 931.0 | 3 133.0 | 3 269.0 | 3 423.0 | 3 567.0 | 3 888.0 | 2 619.0[10] | 2 620.0 |
| M [BA] | 1 835.0 | 1 978.0 | 1 912.0 | 2 076.0 | 2 183.0 | 2 312.0 | 1 617.0[10] | 1 684.0 |
| F [BA] | 1 096.0 | 1 156.0 | 1 356.0 | 1 346.0 | 1 384.0 | 1 576.0 | 1 002.0[10] | 936.0 |
| %MF [BA] | 9.6 | 10.1 | 9.8 | 10.2 | 10.2 | 10.9 | 7.4[10] | 7.3 |
| %M [BA] | 9.7 | 10.3 | 9.4 | 10.1 | 10.1 | 10.4 | 7.4[10] | 7.6 |
| %F [BA] | 9.3 | 9.9 | 10.3 | 10.2 | 10.3 | 11.7 | 7.3[10] | 6.8 |
| **Poland — Pologne** | | | | | | | | |
| MF [BA] | 2 391.0[1,99] | 2 785.0[1] | 3 170.0[55] | 3 431.0[55] | 3 329.0[55] | 3 230.0[55] | 3 045.0[55] | 2 344.0[55] |
| M [BA] | 1 147.0[1,99] | 1 344.0[1] | 1 583.0[55] | 1 779.0[55] | 1 741.0[55] | 1 681.0[55] | 1 553.0[55] | 1 202.0[55] |
| F [BA] | 1 244.0[1,99] | 1 440.0[1] | 1 587.0[55] | 1 652.0[55] | 1 588.0[55] | 1 550.0[55] | 1 493.0[55] | 1 140.0[55] |
| %MF [BA] | 13.9[1,99] | 16.1[1] | 18.2[55] | 19.9[55] | 19.6[55] | 19.0[55] | 17.7[55] | 13.8[55] |
| %M [BA] | 12.4[1,99] | 14.4[1] | 16.9[55] | 19.1[55] | 19.0[55] | 18.2[55] | 16.6[55] | 13.0[55] |
| %F [BA] | 15.8[1,99] | 18.1[1] | 19.8[55] | 20.9[55] | 20.4[55] | 19.9[55] | 19.1[55] | 14.9[55] |
| MF [FB][47,98] | 2 349.8 | 2 702.6 | 3 115.1 | 3 217.0[10] | 3 175.7 | 2 999.6 | 2 773.0 | 2 309.4 |
| M [FB][47,98] | 1 042.5 | 1 211.0 | 1 473.0 | 1 571.2[10] | 1 541.0 | 1 431.1 | 1 286.6 | 1 003.7 |
| F [FB][47,98] | 1 307.3 | 1 491.6 | 1 642.1 | 1 645.8[10] | 1 634.7 | 1 568.5 | 1 486.4 | 1 305.7 |
| %MF [FB][47,98] | 13.1 | 15.1 | 17.5 | 20.0[10] | 20.0 | 19.1 | 17.6 | 14.9 |
| **Portugal — Portugal** | | | | | | | | |
| MF [BA][1] | 225.8 | 205.5 | 213.5 | 270.5 | 342.3 | 365.0 | 422.3 | 427.8 |
| M [BA][1] | 108.9 | 89.3 | 91.6 | 121.4 | 160.9 | 172.9 | 198.1 | 194.8 |
| F [BA][1] | 116.9 | 116.2 | 122.0 | 149.1 | 181.4 | 192.2 | 224.1 | 233.1 |
| %MF [BA][1] | 4.4 | 3.9 | 4.0 | 5.0 | 6.3 | 6.7 | 7.6 | 7.7 |
| %M [BA][1] | 3.9 | 3.1 | 3.2 | 4.1 | 5.5 | 5.8 | 6.7 | 6.5 |
| %F [BA][1] | 5.0 | 4.9 | 5.0 | 6.0 | 7.2 | 7.6 | 8.7 | 9.0 |
| MF [FB] | 356.8 | 327.4 | 324.7 | 344.6 | 427.3 | ... | ... | ... |
| M [FB] | 144.9 | 128.7 | 127.0 | 139.6 | 182.3 | ... | ... | ... |
| F [FB] | 211.9 | 198.8 | 197.7 | 205.3 | 245.0 | ... | ... | ... |
| **Puerto Rico[56,60] — Porto Rico[56,60]** | | | | | | | | |
| MF [BA] | 152.0 | 131.0 | 145.0 | 163.0 | 164.0 | 145.0 | 160.0 | 156.0 |
| M [BA] | 101.0 | 90.0 | 97.0 | 101.0 | 99.0 | 92.0 | 97.0 | 90.0 |
| F [BA] | 51.0 | 42.0 | 48.0 | 62.0 | 65.0 | 53.0 | 63.0 | 66.0 |
| %MF [BA] | 11.8 | 10.1 | 11.4 | 12.3 | 12.0 | 10.6 | 11.3 | 11.1 |
| %M [BA] | 13.2 | 11.8 | 13.0 | 13.2 | 12.8 | 11.8 | 12.2 | 11.5 |

| Country or area, source[§] — Pays ou zone, source[§] | 1999 | 2000 | 2001 | 2002 | 2003 | 2004 | 2005 | 2006 |
|---|---|---|---|---|---|---|---|---|
| %F [BA] | 9.6 | 7.7 | 9.1 | 10.9 | 10.9 | 9.0 | 10.2 | 10.5 |
| **Qatar[1,37] — Qatar[1,37]** | | | | | | | | |
| MF [BA] | ... | ... | 12.6 | ... | ... | ... | ... | ... |
| M [BA] | ... | ... | 6.1 | ... | ... | ... | ... | ... |
| F [BA] | ... | ... | 6.5 | ... | ... | ... | ... | ... |
| %MF [BA] | ... | ... | 3.9 | ... | ... | ... | ... | ... |
| %M [BA] | ... | ... | 2.3 | ... | ... | ... | ... | ... |
| %F [BA] | ... | ... | 12.6 | ... | ... | ... | ... | ... |
| **Réunion[1] — Réunion[1]** | | | | | | | | |
| MF [A][37] | 124.2 | ... | ... | ... | ... | ... | ... | ... |
| M [A][37] | 63.5 | ... | ... | ... | ... | ... | ... | ... |
| F [A][37] | 60.7 | ... | ... | ... | ... | ... | ... | ... |
| MF [BA][57] | 101.6 | 103.8 | 98.4 | 92.8 | 99.5 | 102.5 | 97.4 | 93.9 |
| M [BA][57] | 54.7 | 54.4 | 51.3 | 47.5 | 53.4 | 55.3 | 49.5 | 50.7 |
| F [BA][57] | 46.9 | 49.4 | 47.1 | 45.2 | 46.1 | 47.2 | 47.9 | 43.3 |
| %MF [BA][57] | 37.7 | 36.5 | 33.3 | 31.0 | 32.9 | 33.5 | 31.3 | 29.1 |
| %M [BA][57] | 36.3 | 34.4 | 30.9 | 28.5 | 31.4 | 31.8 | 28.1 | 28.0 |
| %F [BA][57] | 39.5 | 39.1 | 36.4 | 34.2 | 34.8 | 35.8 | 35.3 | 30.4 |
| **Romania — Roumanie** | | | | | | | | |
| MF [BA][1] | 789.9 | 821.2 | 750.0 | 845.3[100] | 691.8 | 799.5 | 704.5 | 728.4 |
| M [BA][1] | 462.5 | 481.6 | 436.1 | 494.1[100] | 408.0 | 490.8 | 420.3 | 452.4 |
| F [BA][1] | 327.4 | 339.6 | 313.9 | 351.2[100] | 283.7 | 308.7 | 284.1 | 276.0 |
| %MF [BA][1] | 6.8 | 7.1 | 6.6 | 8.4[100] | 7.0 | 8.0 | 7.2 | 7.3 |
| %M [BA][1] | 7.4 | 7.7 | 7.1 | 8.9[100] | 7.5 | 9.0 | 7.7 | 8.2 |
| %F [BA][1] | 6.2 | 6.4 | 5.9 | 7.7[100] | 6.4 | 6.9 | 6.4 | 6.1 |
| MF [FB][3] | 1 130.3 | 1 007.1 | 826.9 | 760.6 | 658.9 | 557.9 | 523.0 | 460.5 |
| M [FB][3] | 600.2 | 535.5 | 445.8 | 421.1 | 372.6 | 323.3 | 303.8 | 269.0 |
| F [FB][3] | 530.1 | 471.6 | 381.1 | 339.5 | 286.3 | 234.6 | 219.2 | 191.5 |
| %MF [FB][3] | 11.8 | 10.5 | 8.8 | 8.4 | 7.4 | 6.2 | 5.9 | 5.2 |
| %M [FB][3] | 12.1 | 10.8 | 9.2 | 8.9 | 7.8 | 6.8 | 6.4 | 5.7 |
| %F [FB][3] | 11.6 | 10.1 | 8.4 | 7.8 | 6.6 | 5.6 | 5.2 | 4.6 |
| **Russian Federation — Fédération de Russie** | | | | | | | | |
| MF [BA][101] | 9 436.0 | 7 700.0 | 6 424.0 | 5 698.0 | 5 959.0 | 5 675.0 | 5 263.0 | 5 312.0 |
| M [BA][101] | 4 939.0 | 4 057.0 | 3 450.0 | 3 014.0 | 3 121.0 | 2 975.0 | 2 725.0 | 2 811.0 |
| F [BA][101] | 4 497.0 | 3 643.0 | 2 974.0 | 2 685.0 | 2 838.0 | 2 699.0 | 2 538.0 | 2 501.0 |
| %MF [BA][101] | 12.6 | 9.8 | 8.9 | 7.9 | 8.0 | 7.8 | 7.2 | 7.2 |
| %M [BA][101] | 12.8 | 10.2 | 9.3 | 7.9 | 8.3 | 7.6 | 7.3 | 7.5 |
| %F [BA][101] | 12.3 | 9.4 | 8.5 | 7.9 | 7.8 | 8.0 | 7.0 | 6.8 |
| MF [FB][3] | 1 263.4 | 1 037.0 | 1 122.7 | 1 499.7 | 1 638.9 | 1 920.3 | 1 830.1 | ... |
| M [FB][3] | 383.0 | 322.2 | 359.5 | ... | ... | ... | ... | ... |
| F [FB][3] | 880.0 | 714.8 | 763.2 | ... | ... | ... | ... | ... |
| **Rwanda[26] — Rwanda[26]** | | | | | | | | |
| MF [A] | ... | ... | ... | 30.6 | ... | ... | ... | ... |
| M [A] | ... | ... | ... | 17.7 | ... | ... | ... | ... |
| F [A] | ... | ... | ... | 12.9 | ... | ... | ... | ... |
| **Saint Helena — Sainte-Hélène** | | | | | | | | |
| MF [FB] | 0.4 | 0.3 | 0.3 | ... | 0.2 | 0.2 | 0.1 | 0.1 |
| M [FB] | 0.3 | 0.2 | 0.2 | ... | 0.2 | 0.1 | 0.1 | 0.1 |
| F [FB] | 0.1 | 0.1 | 0.1 | ... | 0.1 | 0.1 | 0.0 | 0.0 |
| **Saint Lucia[1] — Sainte-Lucie[1]** | | | | | | | | |
| MF [BA] | 13.2 | 12.5 | ... | 15.0 | 18.2 | 16.5 | ... | ... |
| M [BA] | 6.1 | 5.1 | ... | 6.7 | 7.6 | 7.4 | ... | ... |
| F [BA] | 7.2 | 7.5 | ... | 8.3 | 10.6 | 9.1 | ... | ... |
| %MF [BA] | 18.1 | 16.4 | ... | 20.4 | 22.3 | 21.0 | ... | ... |
| %M [BA] | 16.0 | 12.6 | ... | 17.3 | 17.3 | 17.5 | ... | ... |

| Country or area, source§ — Pays ou zone, source§ | 1999 | 2000 | 2001 | 2002 | 2003 | 2004 | 2005 | 2006 |
|---|---|---|---|---|---|---|---|---|
| %F [BA] | 20.3 | 20.7 | ... | 23.8 | 28.0 | 25.0 | ... | ... |
| San Marino[1,49] — Saint-Marin[1,49] | | | | | | | | |
| MF [E] | 0.4 | 0.4 | 0.5 | 0.7 | 0.6 | 0.6 | 0.7 | 0.6 |
| M [E] | 0.1 | 0.1 | 0.2 | 0.2 | 0.2 | 0.1 | 0.2 | 0.1 |
| F [E] | 0.3 | 0.3 | 0.4 | 0.5 | 0.5 | 0.4 | 0.5 | 0.5 |
| %MF [E] | 3.0 | 2.8 | 2.6 | 3.6 | 3.1 | 2.8 | 2.1 | 1.6 |
| %M [E] | 1.6 | 1.7 | 1.4 | 1.6 | 1.5 | 1.1 | 1.7 | 1.2 |
| %F [E] | 4.6 | 4.1 | 4.3 | 6.3 | 5.5 | 5.2 | 2.6 | 2.0 |
| Sao Tome and Principe — Sao Tomé-et-Principe | | | | | | | | |
| MF [E] | ... | 6.3 | 8.2 | 9.5 | 9.0 | 8.3 | 8.7 | 8.9 |
| M [E] | ... | 3.5 | 3.1 | 3.7 | 3.3 | 3.4 | 3.4 | 3.4 |
| F [E] | ... | 2.8 | 5.2 | 5.8 | 5.7 | 4.9 | 5.4 | 5.4 |
| Saudi Arabia[1] — Arabie saoudite[1] | | | | | | | | |
| MF [BA] | 254.1 | 273.6 | 281.2 | 326.6 | ... | ... | ... | 501.9[2] |
| M [BA] | 183.8 | 194.3 | 202.6 | 225.0 | ... | ... | ... | 319.1[2] |
| F [BA] | 70.3 | 79.3 | 78.6 | 103.7 | ... | ... | ... | 182.8[2] |
| %MF [BA] | 4.3 | 4.6 | 4.6 | 5.2 | ... | ... | ... | 6.3[2] |
| %M [BA] | 3.7 | 3.8 | 3.9 | 4.2 | ... | ... | ... | 4.7[2] |
| %F [BA] | 8.1 | 9.3 | 9.1 | 11.5 | ... | ... | ... | 14.7[2] |
| Seychelles[1,26] — Seychelles[1,26] | | | | | | | | |
| MF [A] | ... | ... | ... | 4.3 | ... | ... | ... | ... |
| Sierra Leone[7,49,102] — Sierra Leone[7,49,102] | | | | | | | | |
| MF [A] | ... | ... | ... | ... | ... | 68.3 | ... | ... |
| M [A] | ... | ... | ... | ... | ... | 45.9 | ... | ... |
| F [A] | ... | ... | ... | ... | ... | 22.3 | ... | ... |
| %MF [A] | ... | ... | ... | ... | ... | 2.8 | ... | ... |
| %M [A] | ... | ... | ... | ... | ... | 3.1 | ... | ... |
| %F [A] | ... | ... | ... | ... | ... | 2.5 | ... | ... |
| Singapore — Singapour | | | | | | | | |
| MF [A][1,31] | ... | 94.0 | ... | ... | ... | ... | ... | ... |
| M [A][1,31] | ... | 52.3 | ... | ... | ... | ... | ... | ... |
| F [A][1,31] | ... | 41.7 | ... | ... | ... | ... | ... | ... |
| MF [BA][31,103] | 77.5 | ... | 61.9 | 94.2 | 101.0 | 101.3 | ... | 84.2 |
| M [BA][31,103] | 44.3 | ... | 35.7 | 55.3 | 57.6 | 56.8 | ... | 44.7 |
| F [BA][31,103] | 33.3 | ... | 26.2 | 39.0 | 43.4 | 44.5 | ... | 39.5 |
| %MF [BA][31,103] | 4.9 | ... | 3.8 | 5.6 | 5.9 | 5.8 | ... | 4.5 |
| %M [BA][31,103] | 4.6 | ... | 3.7 | 5.6 | 5.7 | 5.6 | ... | 4.1 |
| %F [BA][31,103] | 5.2 | ... | 3.9 | 5.8 | 6.2 | 6.2 | ... | 4.9 |
| MF [FB][23] | 5.9 | 4.2 | 6.4 | 11.6 | 13.9 | 49.6[10] | 43.8 | 22.2[10] |
| M [FB][23] | 3.2 | 2.3 | 3.2 | 5.6 | 6.8 | 25.3[10] | 22.0 | 11.2[10] |
| F [FB][23] | 2.7 | 1.8 | 3.2 | 6.0 | 7.1 | 24.3[10] | 21.8 | 11.0[10] |
| Slovakia — Slovaquie | | | | | | | | |
| MF [BA][1,104] | 416.8 | 485.2 | 508.0 | 486.9 | 459.2 | 481.0 | 427.5 | 353.4 |
| M [BA][1,104] | 226.6 | 265.5 | 282.5 | 263.9 | 246.5 | 250.0 | 223.6 | 179.5 |
| F [BA][1,104] | 190.2 | 219.7 | 225.5 | 223.0 | 212.7 | 231.0 | 203.8 | 173.9 |
| %MF [BA][1,104] | 16.2 | 18.6 | 19.2 | 18.5 | 17.4 | 18.1 | 16.2 | 13.3 |
| %M [BA][1,104] | 16.0 | 18.6 | 19.5 | 18.4 | 17.2 | 17.3 | 15.3 | 12.0 |
| %F [BA][1,104] | 16.4 | 18.6 | 18.8 | 18.7 | 17.7 | 19.1 | 17.2 | 14.7 |
| MF [FB] | 485.2 | 517.9 | 520.6 | 513.2 | 443.4 | 409.0 | 340.4 | 299.2 |
| M [FB] | 265.8 | 283.7 | 284.7 | 280.8 | 240.0 | 211.0 | 167.9 | 143.6 |
| F [FB] | 219.4 | 234.2 | 235.9 | 232.4 | 203.4 | 198.0 | 172.5 | 155.6 |
| %MF [FB] | 17.3 | 18.2 | 18.3 | 17.8 | 15.2 | 14.3 | 11.6 | 10.4 |
| %M [FB] | 17.9 | 18.8 | 18.9 | 19.0 | 15.3 | 13.7 | 10.8 | 9.2 |
| %F [FB] | 16.6 | 17.6 | 17.5 | 16.5 | 15.0 | 14.9 | 12.7 | 11.8 |
| Slovenia[1] — Slovénie[1] | | | | | | | | |
| MF [BA][57] | 71.0 | 69.0 | 57.0 | 58.0 | 63.0 | 61.0 | 58.0 | 61.0 |
| M [BA][57] | 37.0 | 36.0 | 29.0 | 30.0 | 32.0 | 31.0 | 30.0 | 28.0 |
| F [BA][57] | 34.0 | 33.0 | 28.0 | 28.0 | 31.0 | 30.0 | 28.0 | 33.0 |

| Country or area, source§ — Pays ou zone, source§ | 1999 | 2000 | 2001 | 2002 | 2003 | 2004 | 2005 | 2006 |
|---|---|---|---|---|---|---|---|---|
| %MF [BA][57] | 7.4 | 7.2 | 5.9 | 5.9 | 6.6 | 6.1 | 5.8 | 5.9 |
| %M [BA][57] | 7.2 | 7.0 | 5.6 | 5.7 | 6.1 | 5.7 | 5.5 | 5.1 |
| %F [BA][57] | 7.6 | 7.4 | 6.3 | 6.3 | 7.1 | 6.4 | 6.1 | 6.8 |
| MF [FB] | 119.0 | 106.6 | 101.9 | 102.6 | 97.7 | 93.1 | ... | ... |
| M [FB] | 58.8 | 52.5 | 50.2 | 50.1 | 46.1 | 43.8 | ... | ... |
| F [FB] | 60.2 | 54.1 | 51.7 | 52.1 | 51.6 | 49.3 | ... | ... |
| %MF [FB] | 13.6 | 12.2 | 11.6 | 11.6 | 11.2 | 10.6 | ... | ... |
| %M [FB] | 12.4 | 11.1 | 10.4 | 10.4 | 9.7 | 9.1 | ... | ... |
| %F [FB] | 15.0 | 13.5 | 12.9 | 13.1 | 13.0 | 12.4 | ... | ... |
| **South Africa[27,66] — Afrique du Sud[27,66]** | | | | | | | | |
| MF [BA] | ... | 4 162.0 | 4 655.0 | 4 936.0 | 4 434.0 | 4 135.0 | 4 487.0 | 4 391.0 |
| M [BA] | ... | 1 983.0 | 2 236.0 | 2 316.0 | 2 166.0 | 2 029.0 | 2 057.0 | 1 967.0 |
| F [BA] | ... | 2 179.0 | 2 420.0 | 2 619.0 | 2 268.0 | 2 103.0 | 2 428.0 | 2 424.0 |
| %MF [BA] | ... | 25.4 | 29.4 | 30.4 | 28.0 | 26.2 | 26.7 | 25.5 |
| %M [BA] | ... | 22.2 | 25.8 | 25.9 | 24.7 | 23.1 | 22.6 | 21.2 |
| %F [BA] | ... | 29.2 | 33.8 | 35.9 | 32.0 | 30.2 | 31.7 | 30.7 |
| **Spain — Espagne** | | | | | | | | |
| MF [BA][56] | 2 722.2 | 2 496.4 | 1 904.4[10] | 2 155.3 | 2 242.2 | 2 213.6 | 1 912.5[10] | 1 837.1 |
| M [BA][56] | 1 158.3 | 1 037.4 | 828.1[10] | 929.3 | 976.4 | 970.8 | 862.9[10] | 791.5 |
| F [BA][56] | 1 563.9 | 1 458.9 | 1 076.3[10] | 1 226.0 | 1 265.8 | 1 242.8 | 1 049.6[10] | 1 045.6 |
| %MF [BA][56] | 15.6 | 13.9 | 10.6[10] | 11.5 | 11.5 | 11.0 | 9.2[10] | 8.5 |
| %M [BA][56] | 10.9 | 9.6 | 7.5[10] | 8.2 | 8.4 | 8.2 | 7.0[10] | 6.3 |
| %F [BA][56] | 22.9 | 20.4 | 15.2[10] | 16.4 | 16.0 | 15.0 | 12.2[10] | 11.6 |
| MF [FB][79] | 2 085.2 | 1 963.5 | 1 930.2[10] | 2 049.6 | 2 096.9 | 2 113.7 | 2 069.9[10] | 2 039.4 |
| M [FB][79] | 871.3 | 789.7 | 771.5[10] | 836.7 | 851.1 | 854.3 | 818.0[10] | 788.2 |
| F [FB][79] | 1 213.9 | 1 173.8 | 1 158.7[10] | 1 212.9 | 1 245.8 | 1 259.4 | 1 251.8[10] | 1 251.2 |
| %MF [FB][79] | 12.0 | 10.9 | 10.7[10] | 10.9 | 10.7 | 10.5 | 9.9[10] | 9.4 |
| %M [FB][79] | 8.2 | 7.3 | 7.0[10] | 7.4 | 7.3 | 7.2 | 6.7[10] | 6.3 |
| %F [FB][79] | 17.8 | 16.4 | 16.4[10] | 16.2 | 15.8 | 15.2 | 14.5[10] | 13.8 |
| **Sri Lanka[1] — Sri Lanka[1]** | | | | | | | | |
| MF [BA] | 612.7[43,105] | 546.1[105] | 565.9[105] | 632.8[105] | 700.4[105,106] | 679.1[43,105] | 523.7[107] | 498.2[107,108] |
| M [BA] | 330.7[43,105] | 290.2[105] | 309.5[105] | 305.8[105] | 323.8[105,106] | 318.5[43,105] | 256.1[107] | 233.7[107,108] |
| F [BA] | 282.0[43,105] | 255.9[105] | 256.4[105] | 327.0[105] | 376.6[105,106] | 360.6[43,105] | 267.6[107] | 264.5[107,108] |
| %MF [BA] | 9.1[43,105] | 8.0[105] | 7.7[105] | 8.7[105] | 9.2[105,106] | 8.5[43,105] | 7.2[107] | 6.6[107,108] |
| %M [BA] | 7.4[43,105] | 6.4[105] | 5.8[105] | 6.5[105] | 6.4[105,106] | 6.0[43,105] | 5.3[107] | 4.8[107,108] |
| %F [BA] | 12.6[43,105] | 11.1[105] | 11.7[105] | 12.8[105] | 14.6[105,106] | 13.5[43,105] | 10.7[107] | 9.6[107,108] |
| **Suriname[1] — Suriname[1]** | | | | | | | | |
| MF [A][26] | ... | ... | ... | ... | ... | 16.4 | ... | ... |
| M [A][26] | ... | ... | ... | ... | ... | 7.7 | ... | ... |
| F [A][26] | ... | ... | ... | ... | ... | 8.7 | ... | ... |
| MF [BA][109] | 11.8 | ... | ... | ... | ... | ... | ... | ... |
| M [BA][109] | 5.4 | ... | ... | ... | ... | ... | ... | ... |
| F [BA][109] | 6.5 | ... | ... | ... | ... | ... | ... | ... |
| %MF [BA][109] | 14.0 | ... | ... | ... | ... | ... | ... | ... |
| %M [BA][109] | 10.0 | ... | ... | ... | ... | ... | ... | ... |
| %F [BA][109] | 20.0 | ... | ... | ... | ... | ... | ... | ... |
| **Sweden — Suède** | | | | | | | | |
| MF [BA][79] | 241.0 | 203.0 | 175.0 | 176.0 | 217.0 | 246.0 | 270.0[10] | 246.0 |
| M [BA][79] | 133.0 | 114.0 | 99.0 | 101.0 | 123.0 | 137.0 | 148.0[10] | 131.0 |
| F [BA][79] | 107.0 | 89.0 | 76.0 | 76.0 | 94.0 | 109.0 | 123.0[10] | 114.0 |
| %MF [BA][79] | 5.6 | 4.7 | 4.0 | 4.0 | 4.9 | 5.5 | 6.0[10] | 5.4 |
| %M [BA][79] | 5.9 | 5.0 | 4.3 | 4.4 | 5.3 | 5.9 | 6.2[10] | 5.5 |
| %F [BA][79] | 5.2 | 4.3 | 3.6 | 3.6 | 4.4 | 5.1 | 5.7[10] | 5.2 |
| MF [FB][1] | 276.7 | 231.2 | 193.0 | 185.8 | 223.0 | 239.2 | 241.4 | 210.9 |
| M [FB][1] | 151.7 | 126.9 | 107.2 | 105.4 | 127.4 | 135.1 | 132.0 | 114.2 |
| F [FB][1] | 125.0 | 104.3 | 85.8 | 80.4 | 95.6 | 104.1 | 109.4 | 96.7 |

**Unemployment**—Number (thousands) and percentage unemployed, by sex (*continued*)
**Chômage**—Nombre (milliers) et pourcentage des chômeurs, par sexe (*suite*)

| Country or area, source[§] — Pays ou zone, source[§] | 1999 | 2000 | 2001 | 2002 | 2003 | 2004 | 2005 | 2006 |
|---|---|---|---|---|---|---|---|---|
| %MF [FB][1] | 6.4 | 5.3 | 4.4 | 4.2 | 4.9 | 5.5 | 5.3 | 4.6 |
| %M [FB][1] | 6.7 | 5.6 | 4.7 | 4.6 | 5.3 | 5.9 | ... | 4.7 |
| %F [FB][1] | 6.1 | 5.0 | 4.1 | 3.8 | 4.4 | 5.1 | ... | 4.4 |
| **Switzerland[1] — Suisse[1]** | | | | | | | | |
| MF [BA][57] | 121.6 | 105.9 | 100.6 | 119.0 | 170.0 | 179.0 | 185.0 | 169.0 |
| M [BA][57] | 59.2 | 51.0 | 37.9 | 62.0 | 86.0 | 89.0 | 88.0 | 78.0 |
| F [BA][57] | 62.4 | 54.9 | 62.6 | 57.0 | 84.0 | 89.0 | 97.0 | 91.0 |
| %MF [BA][57] | 3.1 | 2.7 | 2.5 | 2.9 | 4.1 | 4.3 | 4.4 | 4.0 |
| %M [BA][57] | 2.7 | 2.3 | 1.7 | 2.8 | 3.8 | 3.9 | 3.9 | 3.4 |
| %F [BA][57] | 3.5 | 3.1 | 3.5 | 3.1 | 4.5 | 4.8 | 5.1 | 4.7 |
| MF [FB] | 98.6 | 72.0 | 67.2 | 100.5 | 145.7 | 153.1 | 148.5 | ... |
| M [FB] | 52.6 | 37.8 | 35.4 | 55.9 | 81.7 | 83.6 | 78.8 | ... |
| F [FB] | 46.0 | 34.2 | 31.8 | 44.6 | 64.0 | 69.5 | 69.7 | ... |
| %MF [FB] | 2.7 | 1.8 | 1.7 | 2.5 | 3.7[110] | 3.9[110] | 3.8[110] | ... |
| %M [FB] | 2.4 | 1.7 | 1.6 | 2.5 | 3.7[110] | 3.8[110] | 3.6[110] | ... |
| %F [FB] | 3.3 | 2.0 | 1.8 | 2.6 | 3.7[110] | 4.0[110] | 4.0[110] | ... |
| **Syrian Arab Republic[1,27] — Rép. arabe syrienne[1,27]** | | | | | | | | |
| MF [BA] | ... | ... | 613.4 | 637.8 | 512.9[10] | ... | ... | ... |
| M [BA] | ... | ... | 348.4 | 355.8 | 311.6[10] | ... | ... | ... |
| F [BA] | ... | ... | 265.0 | 282.0 | 201.3[10] | ... | ... | ... |
| %MF [BA] | ... | ... | 11.2 | 11.7 | 10.3[10] | ... | ... | ... |
| %M [BA] | ... | ... | 8.0 | 8.3 | 7.6[10] | ... | ... | ... |
| %F [BA] | ... | ... | 23.9 | 24.1 | 20.9[10] | ... | ... | ... |
| **Tajikistan — Tadjikistan** | | | | | | | | |
| MF [FB] | ... | 43.2 | 42.9 | 46.7 | 42.9 | 38.8 | 44.5 | ... |
| **Thailand[43] — Thaïlande[43]** | | | | | | | | |
| MF [BA] | 985.7[111] | 812.6[111] | 896.3[1] | 616.3[1] | 543.7[1] | 548.9[1] | 495.8[1] | 449.9[1] |
| M [BA] | 546.4[111] | 454.5[111] | 511.2[1] | 372.1[1] | 314.7[1] | 324.2[1] | 289.9[1] | 259.7[1] |
| F [BA] | 439.3[111] | 358.0[111] | 385.1[1] | 244.2[1] | 229.0[1] | 224.7[1] | 206.0[1] | 190.2[1] |
| %MF [BA] | 3.0[111] | 2.4[111] | 2.6[1] | 1.8[1] | 1.5[1] | 1.5[1] | 1.4[1] | 1.2[1] |
| %M [BA] | 3.0[111] | 2.4[111] | 2.7[1] | 2.0[1] | 1.6[1] | 1.6[1] | 1.5[1] | 1.3[1] |
| %F [BA] | 3.0[111] | 2.3[111] | 2.5[1] | 1.6[1] | 1.4[1] | 1.4[1] | 1.2[1] | 1.1[1] |
| **TFYR of Macedonia — L'ex-R.y. Macédoine** | | | | | | | | |
| MF [BA][1] | ... | ... | 263.2[18] | 263.5[18] | 315.9[18] | 309.3 | 323.9 | 321.3 |
| M [BA][1] | ... | ... | 149.4[18] | 159.1[18] | 191.9[18] | 186.2 | 191.1 | 191.9 |
| F [BA][1] | ... | ... | 113.8[18] | 104.3[18] | 124.0[18] | 123.1 | 132.8 | 129.4 |
| %MF [BA][1] | ... | ... | 30.5[18] | 31.9[18] | 36.7[18] | 37.2 | 37.3 | 36.0 |
| %M [BA][1] | ... | ... | 29.5[18] | 31.7[18] | 37.0[18] | 36.7 | 36.5 | 35.3 |
| %F [BA][1] | ... | ... | 32.0[18] | 32.3[18] | 36.3[18] | 37.8 | 38.4 | 37.2 |
| MF [FB][29] | ... | 366.2 | 360.3 | 374.1 | 390.4 | 391.1 | 360.0 | 366.6 |
| M [FB][29] | ... | ... | ... | ... | 222.4 | 224.6 | 208.4 | 213.9 |
| F [FB][29] | ... | ... | ... | ... | 167.9 | 166.5 | 151.6 | 152.6 |
| %MF [FB][29] | 51.5 | 53.7 | ... | ... | ... | ... | ... | ... |
| **Tonga[1] — Tonga[1]** | | | | | | | | |
| MF [BA] | ... | ... | ... | ... | 1.9 | ... | ... | ... |
| M [BA] | ... | ... | ... | ... | 0.8 | ... | ... | ... |
| F [BA] | ... | ... | ... | ... | 1.1 | ... | ... | ... |
| %MF [BA] | ... | ... | ... | ... | 5.2 | ... | ... | ... |
| %M [BA] | ... | ... | ... | ... | 3.6 | ... | ... | ... |
| %M [BA] | ... | ... | ... | ... | 7.4 | ... | ... | ... |
| **Trinidad and Tobago[1,112] — Trinité-et-Tobago[1,112]** | | | | | | | | |
| MF [BA] | 74.0 | 69.6 | 62.4 | 61.1 | 62.4 | 51.1 | 49.7 | ... |
| M [BA] | 37.9 | 36.1 | 30.7 | 27.9 | 29.8 | 23.4 | 21.3 | ... |
| F [BA] | 36.1 | 33.5 | 31.7 | 33.2 | 32.6 | 27.7 | 28.4 | ... |
| %MF [BA] | 13.1 | 12.2 | 10.8 | 10.4 | 10.5 | 8.3 | 8.0 | ... |
| %M [BA] | 10.9 | 10.2 | 8.6 | 7.8 | 8.3 | 6.4 | 5.8 | ... |

| Country or area, source[§] — Pays ou zone, source[§] | 1999 | 2000 | 2001 | 2002 | 2003 | 2004 | 2005 | 2006 |
|---|---|---|---|---|---|---|---|---|
| %F [BA] | 16.8 | 15.2 | 14.4 | 14.5 | 13.8 | 11.2 | 11.0 | ... |
| **Tunisia — Tunisie** | | | | | | | | |
| MF [BA][1] | 472.5[113] | 475.1[113] | 469.2[113] | 485.5[113] | 473.4[113] | 473.9 | 486.4 | ... |
| M [BA][1] | 345.1[113] | 347.4[113] | 341.4[113] | 351.6[113] | 334.7[113] | 322.7 | 328.8 | ... |
| F [BA][1] | 127.5[113] | 127.7[113] | 127.8[113] | 133.9[113] | 138.6[113] | 151.2 | 157.6 | ... |
| %MF [BA][1] | 16.0[113] | 15.7[113] | 15.1[113] | 15.3[113] | 14.5[113] | 14.2 | 14.2 | ... |
| %M [BA][1] | 15.6[113] | 15.3[113] | 14.5[113] | 14.9[113] | 13.9[113] | 13.2 | 13.1 | ... |
| %F [BA][1] | 17.2[113] | 16.9[113] | 16.2[113] | 16.3[113] | 16.2[113] | 17.1 | 17.3 | ... |
| MF [FB][29,86,113] | ... | 77.0 | 71.9 | 73.5 | 77.9 | ... | ... | ... |
| M [FB][29,86,113] | ... | 42.7 | 40.5 | 40.5 | 41.7 | ... | ... | ... |
| F [FB][29,86,113] | ... | 34.3 | 31.5 | 33.1 | 36.2 | ... | ... | ... |
| **Turkey — Turquie** | | | | | | | | |
| MF [BA] | 1 774.0[25] | 1 497.0[1,76] | 1 967.0[1] | 2 464.0[1] | 2 493.0[1] | 2 498.0[1] | 2 519.0[1] | 2 446.0[1] |
| M [BA] | 1 275.0[25] | 1 111.0[1,76] | 1 485.0[1] | 1 826.0[1] | 1 830.0[1] | 1 878.0[1] | 1 867.0[1] | 1 777.0[1] |
| F [BA] | 499.0[25] | 387.0[1,76] | 482.0[1] | 638.0[1] | 663.0[1] | 620.0[1] | 652.0[1] | 670.0[1] |
| %MF [BA] | 7.7[25] | 6.5[1,76] | 8.4[1] | 10.3[1] | 10.5[1] | 10.3[1] | 10.3[1] | 9.9[1] |
| %M [BA] | 7.7[25] | 6.6[1,76] | 8.7[1] | 10.7[1] | 10.7[1] | 10.5[1] | 10.3[1] | 9.7[1] |
| %F [BA] | 7.5[25] | 6.3[1,76] | 7.5[1] | 9.4[1] | 10.1[1] | 9.7[1] | 10.3[1] | 10.3[1] |
| MF [FB][3,23] | 487.5 | 730.5 | 718.7 | 464.3 | 587.4 | 811.9 | 881.3 | 1 061.9 |
| M [FB][3,23] | 413.8 | 591.9 | 582.9 | 379.8 | 469.4 | 611.3 | 656.2 | 782.7 |
| F [FB][3,23] | 73.7 | 138.6 | 135.8 | 84.5 | 118.0 | 200.6 | 225.0 | 279.2 |
| **Turks and Caicos Islands[1] — Iles Turques et Caïques[1]** | | | | | | | | |
| MF [E] | ... | ... | 1.1 | 0.8 | 1.2 | 1.7 | 1.5 | ... |
| **Uganda[7] — Ouganda[7]** | | | | | | | | |
| MF [BA] | ... | ... | ... | ... | 346.0 | ... | ... | ... |
| M [BA] | ... | ... | ... | ... | 128.0 | ... | ... | ... |
| F [BA] | ... | ... | ... | ... | 218.0 | ... | ... | ... |
| %MF [BA] | ... | ... | ... | ... | 3.2 | ... | ... | ... |
| %M [BA] | ... | ... | ... | ... | 2.5 | ... | ... | ... |
| %F [BA] | ... | ... | ... | ... | 3.9 | ... | ... | ... |
| **Ukraine — Ukraine** | | | | | | | | |
| MF [BA][114] | 2 614.3[68] | 2 655.8 | 2 455.0 | 2 140.7 | 2 008.0 | 1 906.7 | 1 600.8 | 1 515.0 |
| M [BA][114] | 1 346.5[68] | 1 357.4 | 1 263.0 | 1 106.5 | 1 055.7 | 1 001.6 | 862.5 | 804.1 |
| F [BA][114] | 1 267.8[68] | 1 298.4 | 1 192.0 | 1 034.2 | 952.3 | 905.1 | 738.3 | 710.9 |
| %MF [BA][114] | 11.6[68] | 11.6 | 10.9 | 9.6 | 9.1 | 8.6 | 7.2 | 6.8 |
| %M [BA][114] | 11.8[68] | 11.6 | 11.0 | 9.8 | 9.4 | 8.9 | 7.5 | 7.0 |
| %F [BA][114] | 11.3[68] | 11.6 | 10.8 | 9.5 | 8.7 | 8.3 | 6.8 | 6.6 |
| MF [FB][21,47] | 1 174.5 | 1 155.2 | 1 008.1 | 1 034.2 | 988.9 | 981.8 | 881.5 | 759.5 |
| M [FB][21,47] | 444.9 | 424.8 | 362.5 | 369.2 | 361.3 | 361.9 | 345.9 | 300.4 |
| F [FB][21,47] | 729.6 | 730.4 | 645.6 | 665.0 | 627.6 | 619.9 | 535.6 | 459.1 |
| %MF [FB][21,47] | 5.5 | 5.5 | 4.8 | 5.0 | 4.8 | 4.8 | 4.3 | 3.7 |
| %M [FB][21,47] | 4.0 | 3.8 | 3.3 | 3.4 | 3.4 | 3.4 | 3.2 | 2.7 |
| %F [FB][21,47] | 7.3 | 7.2 | 6.4 | 6.7 | 6.3 | 6.3 | 5.6 | 4.8 |
| **United Arab Emirates — Emirats arabes unis** | | | | | | | | |
| MF [E] | ... | 41.0 | ... | ... | ... | ... | ... | ... |
| M [E] | ... | 34.7 | ... | ... | ... | ... | ... | ... |
| F [E] | ... | 6.3 | ... | ... | ... | ... | ... | ... |
| %MF [E] | ... | 2.3 | ... | ... | ... | ... | ... | ... |
| %M [E] | ... | 2.2 | ... | ... | ... | ... | ... | ... |
| %F [E] | ... | 2.6 | ... | ... | ... | ... | ... | ... |
| **United Kingdom — Royaume-Uni** | | | | | | | | |
| MF [BA][56,115] | 1 751.7 | 1 619.1 | 1 412.9 | 1 519.4 | 1 414.0 | 1 361.0 | 1 351.6 | ... |
| M [BA][56,115] | 1 095.2 | 991.5 | 864.1 | 933.5 | 866.2 | 788.1 | 793.3 | ... |
| F [BA][56,115] | 656.5 | 627.6 | 548.8 | 585.9 | 547.8 | 572.9 | 558.3 | ... |
| %MF [BA][56,115] | 6.0 | 5.5 | 4.8 | 5.1 | 4.8 | 4.6 | 5.0 | ... |
| %M [BA][56,115] | 6.7 | 6.1 | 5.3 | 5.6 | 5.5 | 5.0 | 5.0 | ... |

| Country or area, source§ — Pays ou zone, source§ | 1999 | 2000 | 2001 | 2002 | 2003 | 2004 | 2005 | 2006 |
|---|---|---|---|---|---|---|---|---|
| %F [BA][56,115] | 5.1 | 4.8 | 4.2 | 4.4 | 4.1 | 4.2 | 4.0 | ... |
| MF [FA][60,116,117,118,119,120] | 1 263.1 | 1 102.3 | 983.0 | 958.8 | 945.9 | ... | ... | ... |
| M [FA][60,116,117,118,119,120] | 963.5 | 839.6 | 746.8 | 723.8 | 707.6 | ... | ... | ... |
| F [FA][60,116,119,120] | 299.5 | 262.6 | 236.2 | 235.0 | 238.5 | ... | ... | ... |
| %MF [FA][60,116,117,118,119,120] | 4.3 | 3.8 | 3.3 | 3.2 | 3.1 | ... | ... | ... |
| %M [FA][60,116,117,118,119,120] | 6.0 | 5.2 | 4.6 | 4.4 | 4.3 | ... | ... | ... |
| %F [FA][60,116,119,120] | 2.3 | 2.0 | 1.7 | 1.7 | 1.7 | ... | ... | ... |
| **United Rep. of Tanzania[7,37,121] — Rép.-Unie de Tanzanie[7,37,121]** | | | | | | | | |
| MF [BA] | ... | ... | 912.8 | ... | ... | ... | ... | ... |
| M [BA] | ... | ... | 388.4 | ... | ... | ... | ... | ... |
| F [BA] | ... | ... | 524.4 | ... | ... | ... | ... | ... |
| %MF [BA] | ... | ... | 5.1 | ... | ... | ... | ... | ... |
| %M [BA] | ... | ... | 4.4 | ... | ... | ... | ... | ... |
| %F [BA] | ... | ... | 5.8 | ... | ... | ... | ... | ... |
| **United States[56,122] — Etats-Unis[56,122]** | | | | | | | | |
| MF [BA] | 5 880.0 | 5 655.0 | 6 742.0 | 8 378.0 | 8 774.0 | 8 149.0 | 7 591.0 | 7 001.0 |
| M [BA] | 3 066.0 | 2 954.0 | 3 663.0 | 4 597.0 | 4 906.0 | 4 456.0 | 4 059.0 | 3 753.0 |
| F [BA] | 2 814.0 | 2 701.0 | 3 079.0 | 3 781.0 | 3 868.0 | 3 694.0 | 3 531.0 | 3 247.0 |
| %MF [BA] | 4.2 | 4.0 | 4.8 | 5.8 | 6.0 | 5.5 | 5.1 | 4.6 |
| %M [BA] | 4.1 | 3.9 | 4.8 | 5.9 | 6.3 | 5.6 | 5.1 | 4.6 |
| %F [BA] | 4.3 | 4.1 | 4.7 | 5.6 | 5.7 | 5.4 | 5.1 | 4.6 |
| **Uruguay[23] — Uruguay[23]** | | | | | | | | |
| MF [BA] | 137.7[39] | 167.7[39] | 193.2[39] | 211.3[39] | 208.5[39] | ... | 154.9[39] | 167.0 |
| M [BA] | 59.4[39] | 74.7[39] | 80.4[39] | 93.3[39] | 92.2[39] | ... | 65.4[39] | 70.0 |
| F [BA] | 78.3[39] | 93.0[39] | 112.8[39] | 118.0[39] | 116.2[39] | ... | 89.5[39] | 96.9 |
| %MF [BA] | 11.3[39] | 13.6[39] | 15.3[39] | 17.0[39] | 16.9[39] | ... | 12.2[39] | 10.6 |
| %M [BA] | 8.7[39] | 10.9[39] | 11.5[39] | 13.5[39] | 13.5[39] | ... | 9.5[39] | 7.8 |
| %F [BA] | 14.6[39] | 17.0[39] | 19.7[39] | 21.2[39] | 20.8[39] | ... | 15.3[39] | 14.1 |
| **Uzbekistan [29] — Ouzbékistan [29]** | | | | | | | | |
| MF [BA] | ... | ... | 35.4 | 37.5 | 45.6[5] | ... | ... | ... |
| **Venezuela (Bolivarian Republic of) — Venezuela (République bolivarienne du)** | | | | | | | | |
| MF [BA] | 1 525.5[1] | 1 423.5[1] | 1 435.8[1] | 1 822.6[1] | ... | ... | ... | 1 154.9[7] |
| M [BA] | 877.8[1] | 867.7[1] | 827.1[1] | 998.6[1] | ... | ... | ... | 626.0[7] |
| F [BA] | 647.8[1] | 555.8[1] | 608.7[1] | 824.0[1] | ... | ... | ... | 529.0[7] |
| %MF [BA][1] | 14.9 | 13.9 | 13.2 | 15.8 | ... | ... | ... | ... |
| %M [BA][1] | 13.6 | 13.4 | 12.4 | 14.3 | ... | ... | ... | ... |
| %F [BA][1] | 17.1 | 14.8 | 14.6 | 18.1 | ... | ... | ... | ... |
| **Viet Nam[1,46] — Viet Nam[1,46]** | | | | | | | | |
| MF [BA] | 908.9 | 885.7 | 1 107.4 | 871.0 | 949.0 | 926.4 | ... | ... |
| M [BA] | 438.6 | 468.0 | 457.9 | 398.0 | 402.4 | 409.8 | ... | ... |
| F [BA] | 470.3 | 417.7 | 649.6 | 473.0 | 546.6 | 516.6 | ... | ... |
| %MF [BA] | 2.3 | 2.3 | 2.8 | 2.1 | 2.3 | 2.1 | ... | ... |
| %M [BA] | 2.3 | 2.4 | 2.3 | 1.9 | 1.9 | 1.9 | ... | ... |
| %F [BA] | 2.4 | 2.1 | 3.3 | 2.3 | 2.6 | 2.4 | ... | ... |
| **Yemen[1] — Yémen[1]** | | | | | | | | |
| MF [BA] | 469.0 | ... | ... | ... | ... | ... | ... | ... |
| M [BA] | 389.6 | ... | ... | ... | ... | ... | ... | ... |
| F [BA] | 79.4 | ... | ... | ... | ... | ... | ... | ... |
| %MF [BA] | 11.5 | ... | ... | ... | ... | ... | ... | ... |
| %M [BA] | 12.5 | ... | ... | ... | ... | ... | ... | ... |
| %F [BA] | 8.2 | ... | ... | ... | ... | ... | ... | ... |
| **Zambia[13,25] — Zambie[13,25]** | | | | | | | | |
| MF [B] | ... | 409.8 | ... | ... | ... | ... | ... | ... |
| M [B] | ... | 262.0 | ... | ... | ... | ... | ... | ... |
| F [B] | ... | 147.7 | ... | ... | ... | ... | ... | ... |
| %MF [B] | ... | 12.9 | ... | ... | ... | ... | ... | ... |
| %M [B] | ... | 14.1 | ... | ... | ... | ... | ... | ... |

| Country or area, source§ — Pays ou zone, source§ | 1999 | 2000 | 2001 | 2002 | 2003 | 2004 | 2005 | 2006 |
|---|---|---|---|---|---|---|---|---|
| %F [B] | ... | 11.3 | ... | ... | ... | ... | ... | ... |
| Zimbabwe[25] — Zimbabwe[25] | | | | | | | | |
| MF [BA] | 297.8 | ... | ... | ... | ... | ... | ... | ... |
| M [BA] | 187.1 | ... | ... | ... | ... | ... | ... | ... |
| F [BA] | 110.7 | ... | ... | ... | ... | ... | ... | ... |
| %MF [BA] | 6.0 | ... | ... | ... | ... | ... | ... | ... |
| %M [BA] | 7.3 | ... | ... | ... | ... | ... | ... | ... |
| %F [BA] | 4.6 | ... | ... | ... | ... | ... | ... | ... |

Source

International Labour Office (ILO), Geneva, the ILO labour statistics database, last accessed December 2007.

Notes

§ Data sources:
  A: Population census.
  B: Household surveys.
  BA: Labour force sample surveys.
  E: Official estimates.
  FA: Insurance records.
  FB: Employment office records.
  FD: Administration reports.

1 Persons aged 15 years and over.
2 April.
3 December of each year.
4 May.
5 September.
6 July.
7 Persons aged 10 years and over.
8 28 urban agglomerations.
9 May and October.
10 Methodology revised; data not strictly comparable.
11 Second semester.
12 31 urban agglomerations.
13 October.
14 Persons aged 16 to 63 years.
15 Estimates based on 1996 census of population benchmarks.

16 February, May, August and November.
17 May and November of each year.
18 April of each year.
19 January.
20 Year ending in June of the year indicated.
21 Men aged 16 to 59 years; women aged 16 to 54 years.
22 Excluding some elderly unemployed no longer applicants for work.

23 Persons aged 14 years and over.
24 November.
25 Persons aged 12 years and over.
26 August.
27 September of each year.
28 Excluding rural population of Rondônia, Acre, Amazonas, Roraima, Pará and Amapá.
29 Work applicants.
30 Men aged 16 to 60 years; women aged 16 to 55 years. After 1999, age limits vary according to the year.
31 June.
32 Four employment offices.

Source

Bureau international du travail (BIT), Genève, la base de données du BIT, dernier accès Décembre 2007.

Notes

§ Sources de données :
  A : Recensement de la population.
  B : Enquêtes auprès des ménages.
  BA : Enquêtes par sondage sur la main-d'œuvre.
  E : Evaluations officielles.
  FA : Fichiers des assurances.
  FB : Fichiers des bureaux de placement.
  FD : Rapports administratifs.

1 Personnes âgées de 15 ans et plus.
2 Avril.
3 Décembre de chaque année.
4 Mai.
5 Septembre.
6 Juillet.
7 Personnes âgées de 10 ans et plus.
8 28 agglomérations urbaines.
9 Mai et octobre.
10 Méthodologie révisée; les données ne sont pas strictement comparables.
11 Second semestre.
12 31 agglomérations urbaines.
13 Octobre.
14 Personnes âgées de 16 à 63 ans.
15 Estimations basées sur les données de calage du recensement de population de 1996.
16 Février, mai, août et novembre.
17 Mai et novembre de chaque année.
18 Avril de chaque année.
19 Janvier.
20 Année se terminant en juin de l'année indiquée.
21 Hommes âgés de 16 à 59 ans; femmes âgées de 16 à 54 ans.
22 Non compris certains chômeurs âgés devenus non demandeurs d'emploi.
23 Personnes âgées de 14 ans et plus.
24 Novembre.
25 Personnes âgées de 12 ans et plus.
26 Août.
27 Septembre de chaque année.
28 Non compris la population rurale de Rondônia, Acre, Amazonas, Roraima, Pará et Amapá.
29 Demandeurs d'emploi.
30 Hommes âgés de 16 à 60 ans; femmes âgées de 16 à 55 ans. Après 1999, les limites d'âge varient selon l'année.
31 Juin.
32 Quatre bureaux de placement.

33 Bujumbura.

34 November of each year.

35 Persons aged 7 years and over.

36 Excluding residents of the Territories and indigenous persons living on reserves.

37 March.

38 Fourth quarter of each year.

39 Urban areas.

40 For statistical purposes, the data for China do not include those for the Hong Kong Special Administrative Region (Hong Kong SAR), Macao Special Administrative Region (Macao SAR) and Taiwan Province of China.

41 Excluding marine, military and institutional populations.

42 Excluding unpaid family workers who worked for one hour or more.

43 Third quarter.

44 Estimates based on the 1993 Population Census results.

45 7 main cities; September of each year; persons aged 12 years and over.

46 July of each year.

47 31 December of each year.

48 Men aged 17 to 60 years; women aged 17 to 55 years.

49 December.

50 Government-controlled area.

51 Persons aged 15 to 66 years.

52 Persons aged 16 to 66 years.

53 May and November.

54 Persons aged 15 to 64 years.

55 Persons aged 15 to 74 years.

56 Persons aged 16 years and over.

57 Second quarter of each year.

58 Persons aged 15 to 55 years.

59 Excluding elderly unemployment pensioners no longer seeking work.

60 Excluding persons temporarily laid off.

61 Excluding registered applicants for work who worked more than 78 hours during the month.

62 Series revised on the basis of new administrative procedures adopted in 1986.

63 March of each year.

64 June of each year.

65 Due to methodology revised, total may not equal sum of components.

66 Persons aged 15 to 65 years.

67 January of each year.

68 Estimates based on the 2001 Population Census results.

69 Persons aged 16 to 74 years.

70 April and November of each year.

71 May of each year.

72 February of each year.

73 Rates calculated on basis of 1991 Census.

74 First and second quarters.

75 As from the Special Survey of the Labour Force Survey; february of each year.

76 Estimates based on the 2000 Population Census results.

77 Age limits vary according to the year.

78 Men aged 16 to 61 years; women aged 16-57 years.

79 Persons aged 16 to 64 years.

33 Bujumbura.

34 Novembre de chaque année.

35 Personnes âgées de 7 ans et plus.

36 Non compris les habitants des Territoires et les populations indigènes vivant dans les réserves.

37 Mars.

38 Quatrième trimestre de chaque année.

39 Régions urbaines.

40 Pour la présentation des statistiques, les données pour la Chine ne comprennent pas la Région Administrative Spéciale de Hong Kong (Hong Kong RAS), la Région Administrative Spéciale de Macao (Macao RAS) et la province de Taiwan.

41 A l'exclusion des populations marines, militaires et institutionnelles.

42 Non compris les travailleurs familiaux non rémunérés ayant travaillé une heure ou plus.

43 Troisième trimestre.

44 Estimations basées sur les résultats du recensement de la population de 1993.

45 7 villes principales; septembre de chaque année;personnes âgées de 12 ans et plus.

46 Juillet de chaque année.

47 31 décembre de chaque année.

48 Hommes âgés de 17 à 60 ans; femmes âgées de 17 à 55 ans.

49 Décembre.

50 Région sous contrôle gouvernemental.

51 Personnes âgées de 15 à 66 ans.

52 Personnes âgées de 16 à 66 ans.

53 Mai et novembre.

54 Personnes âgées de 15 à 64 ans.

55 Personnes âgées de 15 à 74 ans.

56 Personnes âgées de 16 ans et plus.

57 Deuxième trimestre de chaque année.

58 Personnes âgées de 15 à 55 ans.

59 Non compris chômeurs âgés devenus non demandeurs d'emploi.

60 Non compris les personnes temporairement mises à pied.

61 Non compris les demandeurs d'emploi inscrits ayant travaillé plus de 78 heures dans le mois.

62 Série révisée sur la base de nouvelles procédures administratives adoptées en 1986.

63 Mars de chaque année.

64 Juin de chaque année.

65 En raison des changements méthodologiques, le total peut différer de la somme des composantes.

66 Personnes âgées de 15 à 65 ans.

67 Janvier de chaque année.

68 Estimations basées sur les résultats du Recensement de la population de 2001.

69 Personnes âgées de 16 à 74 ans.

70 Avril et novembre de chaque année.

71 Mai de chaque année.

72 Février de chaque année.

73 Taux calculés sur la base du recensement de 1991.

74 Premier et deuxième trimestres.

75 Enquête spéciale sur la main-d'oeuvre; février de chaque année.

76 Estimations basées sur les résultats du recensement de la population de 2000.

77 Les limites d'âge varient selon l'année.

78 Hommes âgés de 16 à 61 ans; femmes âgées de 16 à 57 ans.

79 Personnes âgées de 16 à 64 ans.

80 Persons aged 6 years and over.

81 Seven main cities.

82 Totals include persons still attending school (incl. full-time tertiary students).

83 Persons aged 16 to 61 years.

84 Excluding Rodrigues.

85 October of each year.

86 Persons aged 18 years and over.

87 Persons aged 15 to 69 years.

88 Persons seeking work for 20 hours or more a week.

89 Curaçao.

90 Persons aged 15 to 60 years.

91 Including students seeking vacation work.

92 West Bank and Gaza.

93 Persons aged 18 to 60 years.

94 August of each year.

95 Year beginning in September of year indicated.

96 Metropolitan area.

97 Metropolitan Lima.

98 Men aged 18 to 64 years; women aged 18 to 59 years (with the exception of juvenile graduates).

99 First and fourth quarters.

100 Estimates based on the 2002 Population Census results.

101 Persons aged 15 to 72 years.

102 The data refer to the usually active population.

103 Permanent residents aged 15 years and over.

104 Excluding persons on child-care leave.

105 Excluding Northern province.

106 First quarter of each year.

107 Excluding Northern and Eastern provinces.

108 First and third quarters.

109 First semester.

110 Rates calculated on basis of 2000 Census.

111 Persons aged 13 years and over.

112 Excluding the unemployed not previously employed.

113 Figures revised on the basis of the 2004 census results.

114 Persons aged 15-70 years.

115 March-May.

116 Excluding most under 18-years-old.

117 Excluding some men formerly employed in the coal mining industry.

118 Excluding some categories of men aged 60 and over.

119 Data not strictly comparable as a result of changes in compilation date.

120 Claimants at unemployment benefits offices.

121 Tanganyika only.

122 Estimates based on 1990 census benchmarks.

80 Personnes âgées de 6 ans et plus.

81 Sept villes principales.

82 Les totaux incluent les personnes encore en cours d'études (y compris les étudiants à plein temps de l'enseignement supérieur).

83 Personnes âgées de 16 à 61 ans.

84 Non compris Rodrigues.

85 Octobre de chaque année.

86 Personnes âgées de 18 ans et plus.

87 Personnes âgées de 15 à 69 ans.

88 personnes en quête de travail pour 20 heures ou plus par semaine.

89 Curaçao.

90 Personnes âgées de 15 à 60 ans.

91 Y compris les étudiants qui cherchent un emploi pendant les vacances.

92 Cisjordanie et Gaza.

93 Personnes âgées de 18 à 60 ans.

94 Août de chaque année.

95 Année commençant en septembre de l'année indiquée.

96 Région métropolitaine.

97 Lima métropolitaine.

98 Hommes âgés de 18 à 64 ans; femmes âgées de 18 à 59 ans (à l'exception des jeunes diplômés).

99 Premier et quatrième trimestres.

100 Estimations basées sur les résultats du Recensement de la population de 2002.

101 Personnes âgées de 15 à 72 ans.

102 Les données se réfèrent à la population habituellement active.

103 Résidents permanents âgés de 15 ans et plus.

104 Non compris les personnes en congé parental.

105 Non compris la province du Nord.

106 Le premier trimestre de chaque année.

107 Non compris les provinces du Nord et de l'Est.

108 Premier et troisième trimestres.

109 Premier trimestre.

110 Taux calculés sur la base du Recensement de 2000.

111 Personnes âgées de 13 ans et plus.

112 Non compris les chômeurs n'ayant jamais travaillé.

113 Données révisées sur la base des résultats du Recensement de 2004.

114 Personnes âgées de 15 à 70 ans.

115 Mars à mai.

116 Non compris la plupart des moins de 18 ans.

117 Non compris hommes ayant précédemment travaillé dans l'industrie charbonnière.

118 Non compris certaines catégories d'hommes âgés de 60 ans et plus.

119 Les données non strictement comparables en raison d'un changement de date de traitement.

120 Demandeurs auprès des bureaux de prestations de chômage.

121 Tanganyika seulement.

122 Estimations basées sur les données de calage du recensement de 1990.

# Employment by economic activity
Total employment and persons employed by ISIC Rev. 3 categories (thousands)

# Emploi par activité économique
Emploi total et personnes employées par branches de CITI Rév. 3 (milliers)

| Country or area [&]<br>Pays ou zone [&] | Year<br>Année | Sex<br>Sexe | Total employment<br>Emploi total | ISIC Rev. 3 Tabulation categories +<br>CITI Rév. 3 Catégories de classement + | | | | | | |
|---|---|---|---|---|---|---|---|---|---|---|
| | | | | Categ. A<br>Catég. A | Categ. B<br>Catég. B | Categ. C<br>Catég. C | Categ. D<br>Catég. D | Categ. E<br>Catég. E | Categ. F<br>Catég. F | Categ. G<br>Catég. G |
| Albania<br>Albanie | 2004 | MF | 931.0 | 545.0[1] | ... | 6.0 | 56.0 | 13.0 | 52.0 | 64.0 |
| | 2005 | MF | 932.1 | 545.0[1] | ... | 6.0 | 56.0 | 12.0 | 52.0 | 64.0 |
| | 2006 | MF | 935.0 | 542.0[1] | ... | 5.0 | 58.0 | 10.0 | 53.0 | 68.0 |
| Algeria[3,4]<br>Algérie[3,4] | 2001 | M | 5 345.2 | 1 132.4 | 69.4 | 111.0 | 406.8 | 99.1 | 643.8 | 761.6 |
| | 2001 | F | 883.6 | 109.1 | 1.2 | 8.5 | 225.0 | 10.8 | 6.2 | 27.3 |
| | 2003 | M | 5 751.0 | 1 303.1 | 5.8 | 78.7 | 406.3 | 93.4 | 790.4 | 853.7 |
| | 2003 | F | 933.0 | 101.5 | 1.3 | 4.2 | 210.3 | 11.1 | 9.5 | 27.2 |
| | 2004 | M | 6 439.2 | 1 289.3 | 24.1 | 125.9 | 489.0 | 74.6 | 956.6 | 1 129.0 |
| | 2004 | F | 1 356.1 | 295.9 | 6.9 | 9.2 | 357.7 | 4.5 | 11.0 | 45.4 |
| Anguilla[3,5,6]<br>Anguilla[3,5,6] | 2001 | M | 3.0 | ^0.0 | 0.1 | ^0.0 | 0.1 | 0.1 | 0.8 | 0.3 |
| | 2001 | F | 2.6 | ^0.0 | ^0.0 | ^0.0 | 0.1 | ^0.0 | ^0.0 | 0.3 |
| Antigua and Barbuda[3,5]<br>Antigua-et-Barbuda[3,5] | 2001 | M | 18.2 | 0.5 | 0.3 | 0.1 | 0.9 | 0.4 | 3.0 | 2.3 |
| | 2001 | F | 18.0 | 0.2 | ^0.0 | ^0.0 | 0.6 | 0.1 | 0.1 | 2.6 |
| Argentina[7,8]<br>Argentine[7,8] | 2004[9] | M | 5 446.9 | 65.7 | 8.4 | 30.6 | 925.4 | 33.8 | 717.8 | 1 230.0 |
| | 2004[9] | F | 3 968.0 | 32.0 | 2.9 | 2.6 | 435.0 | 10.2 | 14.0 | 715.7 |
| | 2005[9] | M | 5 557.3 | 74.5 | 6.4 | 23.2 | 947.2 | 44.0 | 801.1 | 1 227.0 |
| | 2005[9] | F | 4 081.4 | 25.3 | 1.0 | 7.7 | 412.5 | 5.0 | 21.9 | 724.8 |
| | 2006[10] | M | 5 786.7 | 59.2 | 8.2 | 34.1 | 988.3 | 38.1 | 854.8 | 1 263.5 |
| | 2006[10] | F | 4 253.8 | 13.6 | 0.8 | 5.7 | 422.3 | 6.0 | 29.9 | 755.2 |
| Armenia[6]<br>Arménie[6] | 2004 | M | 584.2 | 284.9 | 0.1 | 5.5 | 69.1 | 17.4 | 29.2 | 53.7 |
| | 2004 | F | 497.5 | 222.1 | ... | 1.4 | 42.4 | 3.8 | 4.1 | 49.5 |
| | 2005 | M | 597.1 | 275.1 | 0.1 | 6.0 | 73.8 | 16.0 | 30.0 | 67.5 |
| | 2005 | F | 500.7 | 232.4 | ... | 1.0 | 40.5 | 2.9 | 4.6 | 41.4 |
| | 2006 | M | 593.0 | 274.2 | 0.2 | 6.3 | 71.3 | 18.7 | 27.1 | 68.0 |
| | 2006 | F | 499.4 | 230.1 | ... | 1.3 | 39.2 | 4.1 | 2.6 | 37.9 |
| Aruba[3]<br>Aruba[3] | 1994 | M | 21.0 | ^0.0 | ^0.0 | ^0.0 | 1.8 | 0.5 | 3.6 | 3.0 |
| | 1994 | F | 14.9 | ^0.0 | ... | ... | 0.4 | 0.1 | 0.3 | 3.2 |
| | 1997 | M | 23.5 | 0.1 | ... | ... | 2.1 | 0.7 | 3.2 | 3.6 |
| | 1997 | F | 18.0 | ^0.0 | ... | ... | 0.5 | 0.1 | 0.2 | 3.7 |
| Australia[3,6,11]<br>Australie[3,6,11] | 2004 | M | 5 338.0 | 235.5 | 11.2 | 70.0 | 798.9 | 61.3 | 706.7 | 1 010.1 |
| | 2004 | F | 4 298.3 | 113.4 | 2.8 | 9.0 | 289.6 | 12.8 | 95.8 | 881.3 |
| | 2005 | M | 5 486.4 | 240.8 | 10.6 | 82.2 | 786.2 | 65.2 | 746.3 | 1 023.1 |
| | 2005 | F | 4 471.3 | 108.8 | 2.6 | 9.8 | 283.5 | 16.7 | 110.4 | 930.1 |
| | 2006 | M | 5 581.6 | 237.4 | 7.8 | 89.7 | 780.2 | 66.8 | 799.9 | 1 021.2 |
| | 2006 | F | 4 572.1 | 108.3 | 2.3 | 12.9 | 277.7 | 18.9 | 108.9 | 930.2 |
| Austria[3,12]<br>Autriche[3,12] | 2004 | M | 2 061.5 | 98.9 | ... | 7.6 | 513.3 | 23.8 | 268.9 | 276.4 |
| | 2004 | F | 1 682.5 | 88.5 | ... | 1.0 | 182.3 | 4.3 | 35.1 | 316.4 |
| | 2005 | M | 2 095.2 | 114.2 | 0.1 | 7.4 | 520.2 | 25.5 | 277.0 | 267.7 |
| | 2005 | F | 1 728.1 | 96.1 | 0.0 | 1.2 | 179.8 | 5.8 | 36.6 | 325.9 |
| | 2006 | M | 2 147.5 | 116.1 | 0.2 | 8.4 | 546.5 | 25.6 | 287.1 | 273.3 |
| | 2006 | F | 1 780.7 | 100.5 | 0.0 | 1.4 | 195.0 | 5.7 | 36.6 | 337.5 |
| Azerbaijan[13]<br>Azerbaïdjan[13] | 2004 | M | 1 995.8 | 814.3 | 2.0 | 33.9 | 75.8 | 29.9 | 163.7 | 237.5 |
| | 2004 | F | 1 813.3 | 688.4 | 1.3 | 8.0 | 105.4 | 9.9 | 26.9 | 393.2 |
| | 2005 | M | 2 017.4 | 827.0 | 2.1 | 34.2 | 76.3 | 30.1 | 165.4 | 238.4 |
| | 2005 | F | 1 832.8 | 683.0 | 1.7 | 8.0 | 112.4 | 9.6 | 29.0 | 400.4 |
| | 2006 | M | 2 054.1 | 845.5 | 2.4 | 35.1 | 77.6 | 26.7 | 192.0 | 237.7 |
| | 2006 | F | 1 918.9 | 702.5 | 1.9 | 9.9 | 117.4 | 13.5 | 30.8 | 412.7 |

30 **Employment by economic activity**—Total employment and persons employed by ISIC Rev. 3 categories (thousands) (*continued*)

**Emploi par activité économique**—Emploi total et personnes employées par branches de CITI Rév. 3 (milliers) (*suite*)

| ISIC Rev. 3 Tabulation categories + | | | | | | | | | | |
| --- | --- | --- | --- | --- | --- | --- | --- | --- | --- | --- |
| CITI Rév. 3 Catégories de classement + | | | | | | | | | | |
| Categ. H / Catég. H | Categ. I / Catég. I | Categ. J / Catég. J | Categ. K / Catég. K | Categ. L / Catég.L | Categ. M / Catég. M | Categ. N / Catég. N | Categ. O / Catég. O | Categ. P / Catég. P | Categ. Q / Catég. Q | Country or area [&] / Pays ou zone [&] |
| 17.0 | 20.0 | 81.0[2] | ... | ... | 48.0 | 27.0 | ... | ... | ... | Albania |
| 15.0 | 19.0 | 90.0[2] | ... | ... | 47.0 | 24.0 | ... | ... | ... | Albanie |
| 16.0 | 19.0 | 90.0[2] | ... | ... | 48.0 | 25.0 | ... | ... | ... | |
| 78.4 | 322.5 | 55.0 | 50.5 | 926.3 | 403.4 | 128.6 | 126.7 | 23.4 | 6.3 | Algeria[3,4] |
| 4.2 | 17.4 | 13.1 | 9.5 | 81.9 | 206.9 | 88.5 | 60.0 | 12.2 | 1.9 | Algérie[3,4] |
| 97.6 | 384.5 | 49.5 | 53.6 | 958.6 | 400.3 | 143.2 | 124.0 | 4.6 | 2.4 | |
| 4.9 | 20.9 | 18.1 | 14.4 | 112.6 | 227.5 | 101.9 | 59.4 | 7.6 | 0.5 | |
| 154.6 | 419.8 | 46.1 | 56.0 | 990.1 | 372.4 | 135.2 | 141.8 | 19.2 | 2.8 | |
| 10.2 | 16.2 | 22.8 | 16.4 | 114.2 | 261.6 | 100.3 | 67.1 | 15.7 | 1.1 | |
| 0.6 | 0.3 | 0.1 | 0.2 | 0.3 | 0.1 | ^0.0 | 0.1 | ^0.0 | ... | Anguilla[3,5,6] |
| 1.0 | 0.1 | 0.1 | 0.1 | 0.4 | 0.2 | 0.1 | 0.1 | 0.1 | ... | Anguilla[3,5,6] |
| 2.0 | 1.8 | 0.3 | 0.8 | 2.1 | 0.4 | 0.3 | 1.2 | 0.2 | 0.3 | Antigua and Barbuda[3,5] |
| 3.0 | 1.0 | 0.7 | 0.7 | 2.3 | 1.3 | 1.4 | 1.5 | 1.1 | 0.2 | Antigua-et-Barbuda[3,5] |
| 167.6 | 561.5 | 92.0 | 436.2 | 466.2 | 154.9 | 196.6 | 287.6 | 53.1 | ... | Argentina[7,8] |
| 153.5 | 86.4 | 51.8 | 240.2 | 306.7 | 557.4 | 455.9 | 242.3 | 649.3 | ... | Argentine[7,8] |
| 171.2 | 548.3 | 93.0 | 459.4 | 429.7 | 174.6 | 173.8 | 311.2 | 56.4 | 2.1 | |
| 144.3 | 100.6 | 69.8 | 283.3 | 299.0 | 561.8 | 454.5 | 269.7 | 684.6 | 1.4 | |
| 213.9 | 557.4 | 95.9 | 528.3 | 444.4 | 185.9 | 163.5 | 317.1 | 18.2 | 2.0 | |
| 167.0 | 86.6 | 93.5 | 281.5 | 324.3 | 620.9 | 426.7 | 229.6 | 778.8 | 0.2 | |
| 1.9 | 34.1 | 2.6 | 13.0 | 18.4 | 22.2 | 11.3 | 20.8 | ... | ... | Armenia[6] |
| 2.0 | 12.4 | 3.0 | 5.3 | 10.7 | 78.3 | 38.5 | 24.0 | ... | ... | Arménie[6] |
| 2.8 | 36.1 | 2.8 | 13.0 | 16.2 | 23.7 | 11.6 | 22.4 | ... | ... | |
| 2.9 | 13.6 | 3.3 | 6.1 | 12.0 | 75.0 | 39.0 | 26.0 | ... | ... | |
| 3.8 | 33.4 | 3.1 | 13.8 | 19.5 | 23.9 | 11.4 | 18.3 | ... | ... | |
| 3.9 | 15.2 | 3.5 | 9.5 | 15.4 | 76.9 | 37.4 | 22.5 | ... | ... | |
| 3.2 | 2.3 | 0.4 | 1.1 | 2.6 | 0.5 | 0.4 | 1.6 | 0.1 | ^0.0 | Aruba[3] |
| 3.1 | 0.8 | 1.0 | 0.9 | 1.3 | 0.8 | 1.2 | 0.8 | 1.2 | ^0.0 | Aruba[3] |
| 3.7 | 2.3 | 0.5 | 1.9 | 2.7 | 0.5 | 0.4 | 1.7 | ^0.0 | ... | |
| 3.4 | 1.0 | 1.0 | 1.4 | 1.6 | 0.8 | 1.6 | 1.4 | 1.3 | ^0.0 | |
| 213.8 | 450.1 | 159.6 | 633.4 | 312.4 | 223.8 | 213.6 | 224.2 | 0.4 | 0.3 | Australia[3,6,11] |
| 271.9 | 167.0 | 187.5 | 501.9 | 254.5 | 468.8 | 767.6 | 264.1 | 2.2 | 0.6 | Australie[3,6,11] |
| 216.5 | 469.3 | 167.1 | 662.2 | 325.7 | 222.2 | 220.7 | 231.3 | 0.2 | 0.5 | |
| 283.1 | 171.2 | 205.1 | 537.1 | 257.6 | 472.1 | 792.1 | 282.8 | 0.3 | 0.5 | |
| 200.4 | 474.1 | 179.2 | 683.3 | 332.5 | 220.3 | 233.7 | 235.5 | 0.1 | 0.7 | |
| 277.0 | 172.3 | 202.5 | 564.5 | 273.4 | 494.1 | 836.8 | 282.9 | 0.4 | 0.4 | |
| 83.4 | 181.0 | 68.1 | 162.7 | 146.6 | 64.5 | 76.1 | 84.7 | 1.0 | 4.5 | Austria[3,12] |
| 143.6 | 57.3 | 72.1 | 164.5 | 107.5 | 145.7 | 249.7 | 102.6 | 8.2 | 3.6 | Autriche[3,12] |
| 90.8 | 179.3 | 71.1 | 167.4 | 136.8 | 67.7 | 88.4 | 77.1 | 0.4 | 4.2 | |
| 153.4 | 62.0 | 72.4 | 166.7 | 101.9 | 154.3 | 261.3 | 98.4 | 9.2 | 4.0 | |
| 85.8 | 182.4 | 67.5 | 178.9 | 144.4 | 66.8 | 80.2 | 80.6 | 0.4 | 3.4 | |
| 156.8 | 59.4 | 65.6 | 171.8 | 108.6 | 155.4 | 267.6 | 106.3 | 9.6 | 2.7 | |
| 8.0 | 131.7 | 8.0 | 59.9 | 173.6 | 103.8 | 71.4 | 81.8 | ... | 0.5 | Azerbaijan[13] |
| 4.4 | 58.8 | 5.1 | 40.1 | 96.1 | 227.0 | 103.2 | 45.5 | ... | 0.0 | Azerbaïdjan[13] |
| 8.1 | 132.2 | 8.1 | 60.5 | 175.5 | 104.0 | 72.3 | 82.7 | ... | 0.5 | |
| 6.1 | 59.3 | 5.1 | 40.1 | 95.0 | 231.3 | 104.9 | 46.8 | ... | 0.1 | |
| 11.1 | 141.6 | 5.9 | 64.1 | 175.7 | 90.5 | 63.8 | 83.9 | ... | 0.5 | |
| 10.9 | 60.2 | 7.5 | 42.6 | 95.5 | 248.9 | 116.7 | 47.8 | ... | 0.1 | |

**30**

**Employment by economic activity**—Total employment and persons employed by ISIC Rev. 3 categories (thousands) (*continued*)

**Emploi par activité économique**—Emploi total et personnes employées par branches de CITI Rév. 3 (milliers) (*suite*)

| Country or area [&]<br>Pays ou zone [&] | Year<br>Année | Sex<br>Sexe | Total employment<br>Emploi total | Categ. A<br>Catég. A | Categ. B<br>Catég. B | Categ. C<br>Catég. C | Categ. D<br>Catég. D | Categ. E<br>Catég. E | Categ. F<br>Catég. F | Categ. G<br>Catég. G |
|---|---|---|---|---|---|---|---|---|---|---|
| Bahamas[3,6,14]<br>Bahamas[3,6,14] | 2004 | M | 81.7 | 6.7[1] | ... | 1.9[15] | 3.8 | ... | 15.8 | 13.0 |
| | 2004 | F | 76.6 | 0.3[1] | ... | 0.7[15] | 2.4 | ... | 0.9 | 13.9 |
| | 2005 | M | 82.8 | 5.3[1] | ... | 1.6[15] | 4.8 | ... | 18.1 | 11.2 |
| | 2005 | F | 77.7 | 0.3[1] | ... | 0.4[15] | 2.8 | ... | 0.8 | 12.7 |
| | 2006[5] | M | 86.6 | 5.7[1] | ... | 2.0[15] | 5.0 | ... | 19.4 | 12.1 |
| | 2006[5] | F | 81.5 | 0.4[1] | ... | 0.5[15] | 2.5 | ... | 1.2 | 12.6 |
| Bangladesh[3,18]<br>Bangladesh[3,18] | 2003 | M | 34 478.0 | 16 132.0 | 1 027.0 | 80.0 | 2 637.0 | 90.0 | 1 445.0 | 5 894.0 |
| | 2003 | F | 9 844.0 | 5 754.0 | 17.0 | 1.0 | 1 706.0 | 8.0 | 97.0 | 214.0 |
| Belgium [3,19]<br>Belgique [3,19] | 2004 | M | 2 354.3 | 57.3 | 0.6 | 6.1 | 545.7 | 26.3 | 252.8 | 301.5 |
| | 2004 | F | 1 784.9 | 24.2 | ... | 0.7 | 172.8 | 6.0 | 19.8 | 263.8 |
| | 2005 | M | 2 386.8 | 57.8 | ... | 7.8 | 548.5 | 25.8 | 253.8 | 295.8 |
| | 2005 | F | 1 848.5 | 27.0 | ... | 1.5 | 178.5 | 6.8 | 23.0 | 272.3 |
| | 2006 | M | 2 391.0 | 59.0 | 0.4 | 8.0 | 543.5 | 28.1 | 271.5 | 293.6 |
| | 2006 | F | 1 871.5 | 24.0 | ... | 1.4 | 171.7 | 7.0 | 21.4 | 265.9 |
| Belize[14,20,21]<br>Belize[14,20,21] | 1998 | M | 50.1 | 17.1[1] | ... | 0.3 | 5.3 | 1.0 | 4.2 | 7.8 |
| | 1998 | F | 23.3 | 1.2[1] | ... | ... | 2.3 | 0.2 | 0.1 | 5.1 |
| | 1999 | M | 53.7 | 19.8[1] | ... | 0.3 | 4.7 | 0.9 | 4.4 | 7.4 |
| | 1999 | F | 24.1 | 1.5[1] | ... | ^0.0 | 2.6 | 0.1 | 0.1 | 4.9 |
| | 2005 | M | 64.9 | #16.7 | 1.5 | 0.2 | 6.4 | 0.8 | 6.7 | 10.3 |
| | 2005 | F | 33.7 | #0.8 | 0.3 | ^0.0 | 3.2 | 0.2 | 0.2 | 6.6 |
| Bolivia[7,24,25]<br>Bolivie[7,24,25] | 1997 | M | 1 065.6 | 74.0 | 0.1 | 43.9 | 214.8 | 9.7 | 153.8 | 179.7 |
| | 1997 | F | 812.0 | 32.9 | ... | 4.9 | 124.0 | 1.3 | 4.9 | 271.4 |
| | 1999 | M | 1 130.2 | 55.6 | 1.0 | 16.3 | 224.9 | 4.8 | 174.9 | 206.0 |
| | 1999 | F | 886.8 | 20.9 | ... | ^0.0 | 145.6 | 0.8 | 1.7 | 336.5 |
| | 2000 | M | 1 167.7 | 71.7 | ... | 30.1 | 203.9 | 14.5 | 210.5 | 209.0 |
| | 2000 | F | 923.5 | 31.0 | ... | 5.3 | 116.2 | 1.4 | 8.4 | 327.1 |
| Botswana[6,26]<br>Botswana[6,26] | 1998 | M | 248.9 | 65.1[1] | ... | 11.6 | 22.5 | 2.7 | 29.6 | 21.2 |
| | 1998 | F | 192.2 | 24.8[1] | ... | 1.4 | 24.6 | 0.3 | 3.8 | 27.5 |
| | 2000 | M | 269.4 | 58.9[1] | ... | 10.0 | 19.8 | 2.0 | 39.0 | 25.3 |
| | 2000 | F | 214.0 | 36.4[1] | ... | 1.2 | 22.8 | 0.2 | 5.9 | 38.3 |
| | 2003 | M | 245.4 | 70.1[1] | ... | 11.3 | 18.3 | 3.5 | 35.7 | 20.9 |
| | 2003 | F | 217.0 | 28.0[1] | ... | 2.5 | 26.2 | 0.9 | 6.2 | 40.7 |
| Brazil[4,7,27]<br>Brésil[4,7,27] | 2002 | M | 46 334.2 | 10 601.2 | 291.0 | 235.6 | 6 763.9 | 259.3 | 5 468.3 | 8 533.2 |
| | 2002 | F | 32 624.6 | 5 351.3 | 33.0 | 18.9 | 3 914.2 | 54.4 | 147.8 | 5 019.9 |
| | 2003 | M | 46 935.1 | 10 928.6 | 298.9 | 284.8 | 6 839.5 | 273.1 | 5 097.7 | 8 923.8 |
| | 2003 | F | 33 228.4 | 5 296.6 | 44.0 | 28.2 | 4 037.9 | 59.3 | 122.1 | 5 291.9 |
| | 2004 | M | 49 242.0 | 11 714.7 | 348.3 | 303.1 | 7 370.0 | 299.6 | 5 220.1 | 9 043.9 |
| | 2004 | F | 35 354.3 | 5 615.3 | 55.6 | 22.4 | 4 353.6 | 54.0 | 134.2 | 5 609.3 |
| Brunei Darussalam[3,28]<br>Brunéi Darussalam[3,28] | 2001 | M | 85.8 | 1.3 | 0.5 | 3.2 | 7.8 | 2.2 | 11.4 | 8.5 |
| | 2001 | F | 60.4 | 0.2 | ^0.0 | 0.8 | 4.7 | 0.4 | 0.9 | 4.4 |
| Bulgaria[3,25]<br>Bulgarie[3,25] | 2004 | M | 1 550.7 | 181.1[1] | ... | 32.1 | 343.9 | 47.8 | 153.7 | 216.3 |
| | 2004 | F | 1 371.5 | 101.0[1] | ... | 6.8 | 353.3 | 14.7 | 16.0 | 219.3 |
| | 2005 | M | 1 591.4 | 170.6[1] | ... | 31.2 | 364.8 | 47.9 | 175.3 | 219.7 |
| | 2005 | F | 1 388.7 | 94.8[1] | ... | 5.6 | 363.9 | 16.1 | 15.2 | 227.4 |
| | 2006 | M | 1 652.8 | 162.7[1] | ... | 31.2 | 375.6 | 44.2 | 212.2 | 239.3 |
| | 2006 | F | 1 457.2 | 89.4[1] | ... | 7.0 | 369.4 | 14.7 | 17.8 | 254.7 |
| Cambodia[7,30]<br>Cambodge[7,30] | 2004 | MF | 6 560.6 | 2 577.6 | 31.5 | 3.9 | 218.3 | 0.2 | 8.9 | 404.8 |

| Categ. H Catég. H | Categ. I Catég. I | Categ. J Catég. J | Categ. K Catég. K | Categ. L Catég. L | Categ. M Catég. M | Categ. N Catég. N | Categ. O Catég. O | Categ. P Catég. P | Categ. Q Catég. Q | Country or area [&] Pays ou zone [&] |
|---|---|---|---|---|---|---|---|---|---|---|
| 9.2 | 6.8 | 6.9[16] | ... | 17.6[17] | ... | ... | ... | ... | ... | Bahamas[3,6,14] |
| 14.6 | 3.6 | 10.7[16] | ... | 29.5[17] | ... | ... | ... | ... | ... | Bahamas[3,6,14] |
| 11.4 | 7.2 | 6.3[16] | ... | 16.4[17] | ... | ... | ... | ... | ... | |
| 17.7 | 3.5 | 9.9[16] | ... | 29.6[17] | ... | ... | ... | ... | ... | |
| 11.0 | 7.3 | 8.0[16] | ... | 15.9[17] | ... | ... | ... | ... | ... | |
| 15.9 | 3.9 | 10.8[16] | ... | 33.5[17] | ... | ... | ... | ... | ... | |
| 530.0 | 2 989.0 | 204.0 | 186.0 | 903.0 | 867.0 | 357.0 | 1 136.0 | ... | ... | Bangladesh[3,18] |
| 33.0 | 25.0 | 19.0 | 7.0 | 85.0 | 318.0 | 146.0 | 1 413.0 | ... | ... | Bangladesh[3,18] |
| 66.9 | 245.7 | 80.2 | 217.2 | 230.2 | 121.1 | 116.5 | 76.9 | 2.1 | 7.3 | Belgium [3,19] |
| 65.2 | 67.6 | 72.1 | 161.5 | 189.2 | 250.2 | 392.1 | 82.6 | 11.2 | 6.0 | Belgique [3,19] |
| 74.0 | 236.8 | 88.3 | 214.8 | 236.5 | 128.3 | 120.0 | 79.0 | 4.0 | 16.5 | |
| 70.0 | 76.5 | 73.5 | 154.0 | 183.0 | 261.0 | 397.0 | 91.0 | 18.0 | 15.0 | |
| 71.7 | 243.0 | 82.4 | 227.5 | 225.0 | 120.1 | 122.4 | 78.1 | 2.8 | 14.0 | |
| 68.3 | 76.9 | 73.2 | 176.9 | 197.1 | 255.4 | 406.5 | 94.0 | 20.9 | 10.8 | |
| 2.3 | 3.3 | 0.6 | 1.0 | 3.4 | 1.9[22] | ... | 1.3 | 0.4 | 0.2[23] | Belize[14,20,21] |
| 3.0 | 0.5 | 0.6 | 0.4 | 1.5 | 4.6[22] | ... | 1.4 | 2.3 | 0.1[23] | Belize[14,20,21] |
| 2.5 | 3.7 | 0.8 | 1.2 | 3.4 | 2.3[22] | ... | 1.7 | 0.5 | 0.1[23] | |
| 3.3 | 0.5 | 0.7 | 0.3 | 1.6 | 4.7[22] | ... | 1.5 | 2.4 | 0.1[23] | |
| 3.2 | 5.4 | 0.6 | 1.5 | 4.6 | #2.1 | 0.7 | 2.2 | 1.5 | #0.3 | |
| 5.5 | 0.9 | 1.0 | 0.6 | 2.2 | #4.1 | 2.0 | 1.7 | 4.3 | #0.3 | |
| 21.8 | 141.4 | 12.2 | 36.5 | 58.9 | 46.5 | 22.3 | 37.4 | 11.0 | 1.6 | Bolivia[7,24,25] |
| 88.9 | 10.2 | 7.3 | 20.7 | 14.8 | 74.1 | 35.6 | 28.3 | 91.4 | 0.4 | Bolivie[7,24,25] |
| 34.6 | 164.0 | 9.1 | 43.7 | 59.9 | 69.3 | 20.1 | 41.8 | 3.1 | 1.2 | |
| 92.2 | 9.0 | 8.5 | 28.0 | 18.8 | 66.3 | 43.1 | 34.9 | 80.0 | ... | |
| 29.9 | 131.0 | 13.5 | 71.4 | 54.6 | 56.6 | 21.1 | 47.2 | 5.2 | 1.0 | |
| 94.5 | 13.4 | 6.4 | 24.5 | 18.1 | 76.2 | 27.7 | 51.6 | 121.6 | 1.8 | |
| 3.0 | 8.4 | 1.9 | 7.9 | 43.5 | 16.4 | 4.3 | 1.8 | 4.9 | 0.3 | Botswana[6,26] |
| 8.2 | 2.3 | 2.3 | 3.2 | 26.3 | 28.8 | 9.1 | 1.7 | 24.2 | 0.2 | Botswana[6,26] |
| 2.4 | 10.8 | 2.0 | 11.7 | 47.6 | 18.3 | 4.4 | 11.0 | 2.8 | 0.2 | |
| 7.4 | 3.0 | 2.3 | 6.1 | 25.7 | 24.3 | 7.8 | 11.0 | 18.4 | 0.1 | |
| 3.8 | 9.4 | 1.5 | 9.2 | 36.2 | 14.2 | 4.5 | 4.0 | 2.4 | 0.2 | |
| 10.9 | 3.2 | 3.4 | 5.1 | 31.0 | 24.5 | 9.5 | 5.5 | 19.2 | ... | |
| 1 500.9 | 3 290.9 | 523.2 | 2 831.5 | 2 503.8 | 921.6 | 652.2 | 1 342.0 | 433.3 | 3.0 | Brazil[4,7,27] |
| 1 430.8 | 401.3 | 459.4 | 1 430.0 | 1 366.9 | 3 382.3 | 2 106.6 | 1 806.5 | 5 676.8 | 2.1 | Brésil[4,7,27] |
| 1 458.7 | 3 301.2 | 540.5 | 2 986.3 | 2 518.8 | 932.7 | 688.5 | 1 282.2 | 402.7 | 1.7 | |
| 1 434.1 | 423.4 | 484.7 | 1 507.8 | 1 471.2 | 3 421.1 | 2 129.1 | 1 699.8 | 5 751.9 | 2.3 | |
| 1 518.4 | 3 428.3 | 523.7 | 3 066.8 | 2 636.9 | 990.4 | 686.4 | 1 449.6 | 432.4 | 2.0 | |
| 1 504.6 | 465.9 | 476.0 | 1 652.9 | 1 566.9 | 3 578.8 | 2 153.8 | 2 048.7 | 6 040.1 | 2.1 | |
| 3.8 | 3.4 | 5.1[16] | ... | 38.7[17] | ... | ... | ... | ... | ... | Brunei Darussalam[3,28] |
| 3.3 | 1.4 | 3.1[16] | ... | 41.1[17] | ... | ... | ... | ... | ... | Brunéi Darussalam[3,28] |
| 55.6 | 155.5 | 11.0 | 74.9 | 135.5 | 46.5 | 36.2 | 59.3[29] | ... | ... | Bulgaria[3,25] |
| 85.0 | 56.1 | 23.4 | 57.4 | 85.3 | 163.9 | 120.8 | 67.9[29] | ... | ... | Bulgarie[3,25] |
| 59.1 | 157.8 | 14.3 | 80.2 | 130.8 | 43.2 | 36.2 | 58.9[29] | ... | ... | |
| 91.1 | 56.1 | 23.5 | 61.4 | 83.3 | 164.0 | 123.4 | 61.9[29] | ... | ... | |
| 58.6 | 163.6 | 12.7 | 83.7 | 131.4 | 44.8 | 36.0 | 56.7[29] | ... | ... | |
| 97.8 | 56.7 | 26.4 | 63.4 | 93.7 | 170.1 | 127.7 | 68.4[29] | ... | ... | |
| 25.1 | 5.2 | 3.0 | 4.8 | 17.5 | 33.1 | 11.9 | 42.7 | 14.5 | 3.0 | Cambodia[7,30] Cambodge[7,30] |

**30**

**Employment by economic activity**—Total employment and persons employed by ISIC Rev. 3 categories (thousands) (*continued*)

**Emploi par activité économique**—Emploi total et personnes employées par branches de CITI Rév. 3 (milliers) (*suite*)

| Country or area &  Pays ou zone & | Year  Année | Sex  Sexe | Total employment  Emploi total | Categ. A  Catég. A | Categ. B  Catég. B | Categ. C  Catég. C | Categ. D  Catég. D | Categ. E  Catég. E | Categ. F  Catég. F | Categ. G  Catég. G |
|---|---|---|---|---|---|---|---|---|---|---|
| Canada[3,31,32]  Canada[3,31,22] | 2004 | M | 8 480.6 | 288.5 | 25.1 | 155.7 | 1 641.8 | 97.7 | 835.9 | 1 515.6 |
| | 2004 | F | 7 466.4 | 106.4 | 5.0 | 32.0 | 650.4 | 35.6 | 107.3 | 1 256.2 |
| | 2005 | M | 8 594.7 | 295.7 | 26.1 | 175.5 | 1 581.2 | 93.2 | 905.4 | 1 533.4 |
| | 2005 | F | 7 575.0 | 112.9 | 4.8 | 35.2 | 626.2 | 32.1 | 107.0 | 1 306.4 |
| | 2006 | M | 8 727.1 | 290.3 | 25.9 | 192.3 | 1 552.5 | 92.5 | 946.8 | 1 555.6 |
| | 2006 | F | 7 757.2 | 115.0 | 4.6 | 48.3 | 640.6 | 29.5 | 122.9 | 1 336.2 |
| Cayman Islands[3,33]  Iles Caïmanes[3,33] | 2005[34] | M | 18.6 | 0.5[1] | ... | 0.4[15] | 0.2 | ... | 6.7 | 2.8 |
| | 2005[34] | F | 16.8 | 0.1[1] | ... | 0.1[15] | 0.2 | ... | 0.3 | 2.4 |
| | 2006[35] | M | 18.4 | 0.6[1] | ... | 0.6[15] | 0.2 | ... | 6.0 | 2.3 |
| | 2006[35] | F | 16.6 | 0.2[1] | ... | 0.1[15] | 0.2 | ... | 0.4 | 2.0 |
| China, Macao SAR[21,33]  Chine, Macao RAS[21,33] | 2004 | M | 115.2 | 0.1 | 0.3 | ... | 11.4 | 0.9 | 16.1 | 18.6 |
| | 2004 | F | 103.9 | 0.1 | 0.1 | 0.0 | 24.7 | 0.2 | 2.0 | 16.7 |
| | 2005 | M | 124.3 | ... | 0.2 | ... | 11.8 | 1.0 | 20.5 | 18.5 |
| | 2005 | F | 113.2 | 0.1 | 0.1 | 0.0 | 23.5 | 0.2 | 2.5 | 16.8 |
| | 2006 | M | 141.6 | 0.1 | 0.2 | ... | 10.5 | 0.8 | 27.8 | 17.8 |
| | 2006 | F | 123.5 | 0.2 | 0.1 | 0.0 | 19.1 | 0.1 | 3.2 | 18.6 |
| Colombia[6,7,36]  Colombie[6,7,36] | 2004 | M | 10 547.1 | 3 096.2 | ... | 176.0 | 1 239.2 | 57.8 | 750.8 | 2 354.2[37] |
| | 2004 | F | 7 106.4 | 481.5 | ... | 21.4 | 1 182.2 | 13.6 | 28.3 | 2 020.9[37] |
| | 2005 | M | 10 877.6 | 3 459.4 | ... | 109.4 | 1 239.0 | 62.3 | 833.4 | 2 282.1[37] |
| | 2005 | F | 7 339.0 | 614.9 | ... | 21.6 | 1 112.1 | 21.7 | 25.5 | 2 149.4[37] |
| | 2006 | M | 10 381.8 | 2 932.4 | ... | 99.9 | 1 256.5 | 49.7 | 852.2 | 2 283.0[37] |
| | 2006 | F | 7 227.2 | 481.4 | ... | 16.4 | 1 055.7 | 22.0 | 44.5 | 2 137.5[37] |
| Costa Rica[6,26,39]  Costa Rica[6,26,39] | 2004 | M | 1 093.6 | 215.6 | 7.2 | 2.9 | 162.1 | 19.8 | 105.0 | 218.7 |
| | 2004 | F | 560.3 | 21.7 | 0.8 | 0.7 | 66.8 | 3.8 | 2.3 | 111.3 |
| | 2005 | M | 1 153.9 | 231.3 | 8.9 | 3.2 | 170.4 | 17.8 | 113.0 | 215.2 |
| | 2005 | F | 623.0 | 29.2 | 0.6 | 0.8 | 72.3 | 2.7 | 2.8 | 117.0 |
| | 2006 | M | 1 172.6 | 218.6 | 8.7 | 4.1 | 166.9 | 17.5 | 124.7 | 227.5 |
| | 2006 | F | 657.3 | 28.4 | 0.5 | 0.6 | 77.0 | 4.6 | 2.0 | 124.7 |
| Croatia[3,25]  Croatie[3,25] | 2004 | M | 866.4 | 130.4 | 4.1 | 8.3 | 189.3 | 21.9 | 116.9 | 101.4 |
| | 2004 | F | 696.4 | 121.1 | 0.9 | 0.5 | 111.5 | 6.9 | 10.5 | 114.4 |
| | 2005 | M | 867.0 | 134.7 | 3.9 | 8.3 | 174.6 | 22.2 | 117.2 | 105.4 |
| | 2005 | F | 705.9 | 132.7 | 0.7 | 0.8 | 109.4 | 6.6 | 11.0 | 114.1 |
| | 2006 | M | 868.1 | 115.5 | 3.0 | 5.9 | 192.7 | 16.6 | 121.9 | 107.9 |
| | 2006 | F | 718.3 | 106.7 | 0.6 | 1.4 | 109.3 | 6.1 | 11.2 | 126.0 |
| Cyprus[3,25,40]  Chypre[3,25,40] | 2004 | M | 190.8 | 10.5 | 0.4 | 0.5 | 24.4 | 3.0 | 37.3 | 34.5 |
| | 2004 | F | 147.2 | 5.4 | ... | ... | 13.2 | 0.6 | 2.0 | 26.6 |
| | 2005 | M | 197.3 | 10.8 | 0.5 | 0.7 | 27.2 | 2.2 | 37.7 | 34.2 |
| | 2005 | F | 150.7 | 5.3 | ... | 0.1 | 12.8 | 0.5 | 2.5 | 26.0 |
| | 2006 | M | 200.4 | 10.1 | 0.6 | 0.7 | 25.1 | 2.5 | 36.6 | 37.4 |
| | 2006 | F | 156.9 | 4.6 | ^0.0 | ^0.0 | 12.2 | 0.4 | 3.4 | 25.8 |
| Czech Republic[3]  République tchèque[3] | 2004 | M | 2 663.0 | 140.0[1] | ... | 52.0 | 786.0 | 61.0 | 402.0 | 308.0 |
| | 2004 | F | 2 044.0 | 62.0[1] | ... | 7.0 | 488.0 | 15.0 | 34.0 | 323.0 |
| | 2005 | M | 2 706.0 | 131.0[1] | ... | 44.0 | 813.0 | 60.0 | 420.0 | 292.0 |
| | 2005 | F | 2 059.0 | 58.0[1] | ... | 6.0 | 484.0 | 17.0 | 39.0 | 323.0 |
| | 2006 | M | 2 742.0 | 123.0[1] | ... | 48.0 | 856.0 | 60.0 | 403.0 | 286.0 |
| | 2006 | F | 2 086.0 | 58.0[1] | ... | 7.0 | 506.0 | 17.0 | 33.0 | 327.0 |

30 **Employment by economic activity**—Total employment and persons employed by ISIC Rev. 3 categories (thousands) (*continued*)

**Emploi par activité économique**—Emploi total et personnes employées par branches de CITI Rév. 3 (milliers) (*suite*)

| ISIC Rev. 3 Tabulation categories + CITI Rév. 3 Catégories de classement + | | | | | | | | | | Country or area [&] |
|---|---|---|---|---|---|---|---|---|---|---|
| Categ. H / Catég. H | Categ. I / Catég. I | Categ. J / Catég. J | Categ. K / Catég. K | Categ. L / Catég.L | Categ. M / Catég. M | Categ. N / Catég. N | Categ. O / Catég. O | Categ. P / Catég. P | Categ. Q / Catég. Q | Pays ou zone [&] |
| 402.2 | 788.6 | 246.3 | 1 064.7 | 424.6 | 354.4 | 317.5 | 317.5 | 3.7 | 0.0 | Canada[3,31,32] |
| 610.1 | 367.7 | 436.6 | 863.3 | 399.6 | 681.3 | 1 415.9 | 437.2 | 61.5 | 0.0 | Canada[3,31,22] |
| 402.4 | 792.2 | 254.4 | 1 100.3 | 425.8 | 379.4 | 310.1 | 313.9 | 4.7 | 0.8 | |
| 602.1 | 361.6 | 452.6 | 891.5 | 404.8 | 726.7 | 1 424.5 | 427.8 | 57.2 | 1.7 | |
| 402.2 | 779.8 | 275.8 | 1 145.6 | 426.1 | 410.4 | 312.8 | 344.7 | 4.2 | 2.3 | |
| 612.8 | 317.3 | 469.1 | 925.5 | 408.0 | 748.0 | 1 472.7 | 472.5 | 55.0 | 1.0 | |
| 1.2 | 0.9 | 1.0 | 2.0 | 1.0 | 0.7 | ... | 0.8 | 0.2 | ... | Cayman Islands[3,33] |
| 1.7 | 0.7 | 2.1 | 2.3 | 0.9 | 2.1[22] | ... | 0.9 | 2.9 | ... | Iles Caïmanes[3,33] |
| 1.6 | 0.9 | 1.0 | 2.1 | 1.2 | 0.6 | ... | 1.1 | 0.3 | ... | |
| 2.2 | 0.6 | 2.2 | 2.3 | 1.2 | 1.9[22] | ... | 0.7 | 2.7 | ... | |
| 11.9 | 11.2 | 2.6 | 8.1 | 12.6 | 3.3 | 1.5 | 16.3 | 0.4 | ... | China, Macao SAR[21,33] |
| 12.2 | 3.8 | 3.6 | 4.5 | 5.5 | 7.2 | 3.6 | 15.0 | 4.6 | ... | Chine, Macao RAS[21,33] |
| 11.5 | 11.0 | 2.8 | 9.0 | 12.6 | 3.0 | 1.4 | 20.5 | 0.3 | 0.1 | |
| 13.4 | 3.8 | 3.8 | 5.3 | 6.2 | 7.4 | 3.9 | 20.2 | 5.9 | 0.1 | |
| 14.6 | 12.0 | 2.9 | 9.9 | 14.0 | 3.7 | 1.4 | 25.6 | 0.3 | ... | |
| 15.4 | 4.8 | 4.0 | 6.4 | 6.4 | 7.7 | 4.1 | 26.9 | 6.6 | 0.1 | |
| ... | 1 117.6 | 111.7 | 480.6 | 1 160.3[38] | ... | ... | ... | ... | ... | Colombia[6,7,36] |
| ... | 175.7 | 115.9 | 297.8 | 2 767.2[38] | ... | ... | ... | ... | ... | Colombie[6,7,36] |
| ... | 1 012.8 | 113.0 | 530.9 | 1 234.6[38] | ... | ... | ... | ... | ... | |
| ... | 188.3 | 126.5 | 304.1 | 2 774.7[38] | ... | ... | ... | ... | ... | |
| ... | 1 038.2 | 116.3 | 535.3 | 1 182.3[38] | ... | ... | ... | ... | ... | |
| ... | 228.2 | 104.1 | 354.5 | 2 766.4[38] | ... | ... | ... | ... | ... | |
| 41.6 | 84.9 | 24.2 | 70.6 | 47.6 | 27.4 | 20.0 | 29.8 | 9.3 | 2.2 | Costa Rica[6,26,39] |
| 49.8 | 11.3 | 12.5 | 31.4 | 30.9 | 68.6 | 31.3 | 33.1 | 81.5 | 1.7 | Costa Rica[6,26,39] |
| 41.9 | 97.8 | 22.7 | 73.0 | 53.2 | 29.7 | 25.9 | 33.9 | 10.1 | 0.6 | |
| 56.2 | 14.1 | 13.5 | 30.0 | 28.2 | 74.4 | 36.8 | 31.0 | 111.1 | 1.5 | |
| 41.8 | 104.0 | 23.3 | 73.4 | 55.8 | 30.6 | 23.8 | 34.1 | 14.2 | 0.9 | |
| 56.0 | 14.5 | 14.9 | 34.8 | 30.7 | 77.8 | 38.7 | 31.7 | 116.9 | 1.7 | |
| 39.5 | 82.5 | 9.2 | 36.7 | 57.3 | 23.1 | 18.6 | 25.7 | 0.2 | ... | Croatia[3,25] |
| 46.7 | 20.8 | 21.3 | 26.5 | 44.6 | 67.5 | 68.7 | 31.4 | 3.1 | ... | Croatie[3,25] |
| 38.1 | 81.9 | 9.8 | 41.7 | 58.1 | 20.5 | 19.7 | 30.0 | 0.3 | ... | |
| 45.4 | 21.2 | 18.6 | 33.9 | 42.3 | 67.0 | 64.9 | 32.4 | 4.3 | ... | |
| 39.7 | 81.9 | 11.1 | 44.7 | 53.8 | 21.4 | 18.7 | 31.6 | 0.5 | ... | |
| 50.1 | 22.3 | 27.7 | 36.4 | 44.9 | 70.7 | 66.1 | 33.9 | 3.7 | ... | |
| 13.3 | 12.4 | 6.8 | 11.6 | 15.9 | 6.4 | 4.2 | 7.9 | 0.3 | 1.5 | Cyprus[3,25,40] |
| 16.7 | 5.8 | 9.0 | 10.9 | 7.6 | 15.1 | 10.9 | 9.0 | 13.4 | 0.7 | Chypre[3,25,40] |
| 12.3 | 12.6 | 9.2 | 11.6 | 17.9 | 5.6 | 4.2 | 8.5 | 0.4 | 1.9 | |
| 14.9 | 5.9 | 9.0 | 13.0 | 8.4 | 17.1 | 10.7 | 9.7 | 13.8 | 1.1 | |
| 11.0 | 13.2 | 9.3 | 11.9 | 20.1 | 6.1 | 4.0 | 9.6 | 0.4 | 2.0 | |
| 12.9 | 7.0 | 9.6 | 14.8 | 9.8 | 18.7 | 10.2 | 12.0 | 14.4 | 1.0 | |
| 82.0 | 246.0 | 33.0 | 159.0 | 180.0 | 64.0 | 62.0 | 88.0 | ... | ... | Czech Republic[3] |
| 93.0 | 118.0 | 61.0 | 122.0 | 143.0 | 215.0 | 262.0 | 97.0 | 3.0 | 1.0 | République tchèque[3] |
| 84.0 | 250.0 | 38.0 | 163.0 | 179.0 | 71.0 | 68.0 | 93.0 | 1.0 | 0.0 | |
| 97.0 | 110.0 | 59.0 | 126.0 | 155.0 | 226.0 | 260.0 | 97.0 | 3.0 | 1.0 | |
| 85.0 | 259.0 | 34.0 | 185.0 | 170.0 | 73.0 | 65.0 | 93.0 | 1.0 | 1.0 | |
| 102.0 | 102.0 | 58.0 | 136.0 | 155.0 | 215.0 | 265.0 | 100.0 | 3.0 | 1.0 | |

| Country or area [&]<br>Pays ou zone [&] | Year<br>Année | Sex<br>Sexe | Total<br>employment<br>Emploi<br>total | Categ. A<br>Catég. A | Categ. B<br>Catég. B | Categ. C<br>Catég. C | Categ. D<br>Catég. D | Categ. E<br>Catég. E | Categ. F<br>Catég. F | Categ. G<br>Catég. G |
|---|---|---|---|---|---|---|---|---|---|---|
| Denmark[41,42]<br>Danemark[41,42] | 2004 | M | 1 451.6 | 61.8 | 3.3 | 4.0 | 302.7 | 12.8 | 168.7 | 233.5 |
| | 2004 | F | 1 268.5 | 19.3 | 0.2 | 0.3 | 131.8 | 3.2 | 15.8 | 172.8 |
| | 2005 | M | 1 456.1 | 60.3 | ... | ... | 305.6 | 11.5 | 174.3 | 230.0 |
| | 2005 | F | 1 276.6 | 20.2 | 0.0 | ... | 136.8 | 3.7 | 18.2 | 170.8 |
| | 2006 | M | 1 482.3 | 60.9 | ... | 4.8 | 296.1 | 12.6 | 185.3 | 230.1 |
| | 2006 | F | 1 304.3 | 18.5 | ... | 0.8 | 131.5 | 3.9 | 15.9 | 179.0 |
| Dominican Republic[7]<br>Rép. dominicaine[7] | 2003 | M | 2 069.5 | 408.2[1] | ... | 7.3 | 310.9 | 21.2 | 213.7 | 425.0 |
| | 2003 | F | 1 029.0 | 17.8[1] | ... | ... | 145.1 | 5.2 | 6.5 | 216.2 |
| | 2004 | M | 2 146.4 | 455.7[1] | ... | 4.8 | 345.5 | 20.1 | 205.4 | 431.8 |
| | 2004 | F | 1 063.5 | 20.6[1] | ... | 0.1 | 148.6 | 6.6 | 7.8 | 220.7 |
| | 2005 | M | 2 173.4 | 446.9[1] | ... | 5.8 | 335.5 | 17.2 | 206.9 | 460.0 |
| | 2005 | F | 1 103.0 | 30.9[1] | ... | 0.1 | 151.2 | 9.0 | 6.4 | 247.5 |
| Ecuador[7,30,44]<br>Equateur[7,30,44] | 2004 | M | 2 288.5 | 247.5 | 34.2 | 14.6 | 335.6 | 17.3 | 239.9 | 589.5 |
| | 2004 | F | 1 570.1 | 73.3 | 3.3 | 1.5 | 203.4 | 5.6 | 8.8 | 506.7 |
| | 2005 | M | 2 327.8 | 218.7 | 38.4 | 10.6 | 361.4 | 15.4 | 249.4 | 597.3 |
| | 2005 | F | 1 564.0 | 54.8 | 12.7 | 0.1 | 175.7 | 3.4 | 9.4 | 501.6 |
| | 2006 | M | 2 416.5 | 222.8 | 42.2 | 14.2 | 368.3 | 15.7 | 278.2 | 623.0 |
| | 2006 | F | 1 615.1 | 62.2 | 6.8 | 1.6 | 187.2 | 3.6 | 11.9 | 528.8 |
| Egypt[6,45,46]<br>Egypte[6,45,46] | 2003 | M | 14 651.7 | 3 898.4 | 159.3 | 30.0 | 1 810.7 | 208.6 | 1 313.1 | 1 941.4 |
| | 2003 | F | 3 466.9 | 1 351.7 | 1.9 | 2.0 | 166.2 | 20.1 | 27.9 | 219.7 |
| | 2004 | M | 14 936.4 | 4 061.8 | 136.5 | 31.3 | 1 898.7 | 203.1 | 1 377.3 | 2 032.8 |
| | 2004 | F | 3 781.0 | 1 758.7 | 1.2 | 0.7 | 186.4 | 15.4 | 22.2 | 219.2 |
| | 2005 | M | 15 592.7 | 4 071.2 | 156.7 | 27.3 | 2 077.7 | 227.1 | 1 634.7 | 1 951.8 |
| | 2005 | F | 3 749.0 | 1 743.4 | 0.9 | 1.7 | 152.0 | 18.2 | 15.1 | 189.4 |
| El Salvador[7,47]<br>El Salvador[7,47] | 2004 | M | 1 494.0 | 433.0 | 15.4 | 1.7 | 206.2 | 9.0 | 157.8 | 302.9[37] |
| | 2004 | F | 1 032.4 | 32.7 | 2.0 | 0.1 | 217.2 | 1.3 | 4.9 | 436.6[37] |
| | 2005 | M | 1 509.8 | 453.1 | 12.8 | 2.5 | 205.4 | 6.3 | 144.2 | 314.4[37] |
| | 2005 | F | 1 081.2 | 51.2 | 0.9 | ^0.0 | 213.4 | 1.1 | 2.7 | 450.5[37] |
| | 2006 | M | 1 542.3 | 438.7 | 13.3 | 2.2 | 213.0 | 9.0 | 175.5 | 313.7[37] |
| | 2006 | F | 1 143.6 | 53.0 | 1.6 | 0.0 | 210.4 | 1.4 | 5.8 | 489.3[37] |
| Estonia[25,49]<br>Estonie[25,49] | 2004 | M | 299.1 | 21.1 | 3.1 | 6.5 | 75.1 | 8.5 | 42.1 | 33.4 |
| | 2004 | F | 296.4 | 10.3 | 0.5 | 1.5 | 65.8 | 3.5 | 4.7 | 46.7 |
| | 2005 | M | 300.5 | 19.0 | 2.5 | 5.4 | 73.2 | 9.4 | 44.2 | 33.0 |
| | 2005 | F | 306.9 | 10.4 | 0.3 | 0.5 | 66.2 | 3.1 | 4.5 | 47.7 |
| | 2006 | M | 322.9 | 19.7 | 2.0 | 4.7 | 74.2 | 10.2 | 58.1 | 35.5 |
| | 2006 | F | 323.3 | 10.2 | 0.2 | 0.3 | 62.2 | 2.2 | 4.7 | 53.1 |
| Ethiopia[6,7,50]<br>Ethiopie[6,7,50] | 2004[51] | M | 1 625.6 | 168.3[1] | ... | 9.2 | 236.9 | 21.6 | 141.2 | 325.4 |
| | 2004[51] | F | 1 228.8 | 56.8[1] | ... | 0.8 | 207.6 | 7.3 | 17.6 | 297.6 |
| | 2005 | M | 16 860.3 | 14 209.4[1] | ... | 51.4 | 444.0 | 25.2 | 349.9 | 652.2 |
| | 2005 | F | 14 574.8 | 10 998.8[1] | ... | 30.6 | 1 085.3 | 7.7 | 95.7 | 984.9 |
| | 2006[52] | M | 1 913.2 | 224.8[1] | ... | 11.9 | 290.7 | 30.0 | 179.9 | 450.6 |
| | 2006[52] | F | 1 923.6 | 106.2[1] | ... | 1.4 | 294.9 | 8.6 | 29.0 | 422.0 |
| Finland[42,49]<br>Finlande[42,49] | 2004 | M | 1 250.0 | 81.0 | 1.0 | 5.0 | 309.0 | 15.0 | 138.0 | 150.0 |
| | 2004 | F | 1 137.0 | 33.0 | 1.0 | ... | 126.0 | 4.0 | 11.0 | 143.0 |
| | 2005 | M | 1 263.0 | 81.0 | 1.0 | 5.0 | 310.0 | 14.0 | 147.0 | 153.0 |
| | 2005 | F | 1 158.0 | 33.0 | 1.0 | 1.0 | 127.0 | 5.0 | 11.0 | 147.0 |
| | 2006 | M | 1 288.0 | 80.0 | 1.0 | 5.0 | 317.0 | 13.0 | 152.0 | 155.0 |
| | 2006 | F | 1 178.0 | 33.0 | ... | ... | 125.0 | 4.0 | 10.0 | 149.0 |

**30** Employment by economic activity—Total employment and persons employed by ISIC Rev. 3 categories (thousands) (*continued*)

**Emploi par activité économique**—Emploi total et personnes employées par branches de CITI Rév. 3 (milliers) (*suite*)

| | | | | ISIC Rev. 3 Tabulation categories + | | | | | | |
| | | | | CITI Rév. 3 Catégories de classement + | | | | | | |
| Categ. H | Categ. I | Categ. J | Categ. K | Categ. L | Categ. M | Categ. N | Categ. O | Categ. P | Categ. Q | Country or area [&] |
| Catég. H | Catég. I | Catég. J | Catég. K | Catég.L | Catég. M | Catég. N | Catég. O | Catég. P | Catég. Q | Pays ou zone [&] |
|---|---|---|---|---|---|---|---|---|---|---|
| 28.7 | 127.7 | 42.1 | 146.5 | 83.4 | 85.1 | 80.6 | 68.4 | 0.1 | 0.5 | Denmark[41,42] |
| 40.2 | 57.8 | 39.2 | 101.6 | 80.3 | 127.9 | 399.9 | 72.0 | 3.1 | 1.1 | Danemark[41,42] |
| 29.8 | 125.6 | 41.6 | 148.0 | 81.8 | 89.5 | 81.2 | 68.2 | ... | ... | |
| 39.9 | 49.8 | 47.3 | 105.4 | 85.0 | 126.7 | 393.6 | 73.4 | ... | ... | |
| 33.4 | 124.1 | 44.9 | 159.3 | 86.4 | 87.7 | 75.1 | 77.1 | ... | ... | |
| 43.3 | 52.0 | 48.1 | 116.6 | 81.8 | 123.3 | 411.9 | 73.6 | ... | ... | |
| 86.1 | 217.9 | 31.4 | 250.6[43] | 97.3 | ... | ... | ... | ... | ... | Dominican Republic[7] |
| 83.8 | 21.5 | 32.3 | 460.1[43] | 40.5 | ... | ... | ... | ... | ... | Rép. dominicaine[7] |
| 90.2 | 205.8 | 28.9 | 263.4[43] | 94.8 | ... | ... | ... | ... | ... | |
| 89.6 | 27.0 | 26.8 | 469.8[43] | 45.9 | ... | ... | ... | ... | ... | |
| 88.4 | 215.5 | 34.5 | 258.9[43] | 103.6 | ... | ... | ... | ... | ... | |
| 103.2 | 23.0 | 27.8 | 460.1[43] | 43.9 | ... | ... | ... | ... | ... | |
| 62.2 | 233.9 | 26.3 | 138.0 | 124.9 | 100.6 | 47.4 | 68.5 | 7.0 | 1.2 | Ecuador[7,30,44] |
| 108.9 | 30.9 | 22.8 | 51.8 | 49.0 | 162.4 | 90.4 | 107.6 | 143.4 | 0.2 | Equateur[7,30,44] |
| 71.0 | 244.6 | 26.2 | 144.1 | 125.6 | 91.7 | 46.9 | 65.0 | 20.9 | 0.4 | |
| 119.8 | 35.5 | 25.7 | 55.6 | 42.6 | 167.2 | 85.1 | 93.7 | 180.8 | 0.3 | |
| 85.3 | 251.7 | 25.2 | 146.7 | 126.4 | 100.2 | 42.3 | 64.6 | 9.7 | ... | |
| 140.1 | 40.7 | 22.7 | 54.0 | 43.9 | 180.7 | 73.7 | 98.2 | 158.0 | 0.9 | |
| 276.5 | 1 093.5 | 152.0 | 298.2 | 1 579.7 | 1 190.4 | 293.6 | 376.7 | 28.4 | ... | Egypt[6,45,46] |
| 14.8 | 51.8 | 47.9 | 49.0 | 445.4 | 778.7 | 252.0 | 32.1 | 5.4 | ... | Egypte[6,45,46] |
| 320.2 | 1 114.9 | 148.5 | 307.0 | 1 520.0 | 1 118.8 | 258.3 | 376.1 | 29.7 | ... | |
| 14.2 | 56.5 | 47.3 | 48.1 | 406.2 | 726.7 | 245.0 | 28.4 | 4.7 | ... | |
| 357.4 | 1 276.4 | 129.0 | 347.0 | 1 446.7 | 1 133.6 | 244.4 | 434.6 | 43.6 | 1.9 | |
| 9.0 | 46.3 | 40.2 | 53.5 | 402.8 | 774.6 | 259.1 | 30.2 | 9.0 | 0.8 | |
| ... | 112.6 | 75.2[16] | ... | 73.3 | 30.2 | 65.5[48] | ... | 10.5 | ... | El Salvador[7,47] |
| ... | 13.2 | 27.9[16] | ... | 25.1 | 56.8 | 106.2[48] | ... | 108.2 | ... | El Salvador[7,47] |
| ... | 108.6 | 83.6[16] | ... | 70.8 | 31.0 | 66.2[48] | ... | 11.0 | ... | |
| ... | 12.3 | 39.2[16] | ... | 29.5 | 66.3 | 113.8[48] | ... | 100.5 | ... | |
| ... | 111.0 | 73.5[16] | ... | 76.9 | 33.2 | 69.2[48] | ... | 12.9 | ... | |
| ... | 9.4 | 41.4[16] | ... | 28.9 | 60.7 | 120.2[48] | ... | 121.5 | ... | |
| 4.3 | 35.3 | 2.2 | 22.6 | 18.4 | 10.4 | 5.6 | 10.7 | ... | ... | Estonia[25,49] |
| 11.9 | 16.2 | 5.7 | 16.9 | 18.5 | 44.1 | 32.0 | 18.2 | ... | ... | Estonie[25,49] |
| 4.7 | 38.7 | 1.2 | 27.3 | 17.5 | 9.1 | 4.9 | 10.3 | ... | ... | |
| 17.3 | 15.8 | 5.7 | 19.2 | 19.6 | 45.8 | 30.2 | 20.7 | ... | ... | |
| 4.2 | 42.1 | 1.7 | 26.4 | 18.8 | 9.8 | 4.8 | 10.8 | ... | ... | |
| 18.2 | 19.5 | 5.6 | 21.7 | 20.2 | 48.6 | 32.7 | 23.5 | ... | ... | |
| 53.4 | 108.7 | 16.4 | 34.4 | 139.3 | 137.7[22] | ... | 197.9 | 22.4 | 12.4 | Ethiopia[6,7,50] |
| 202.2 | 10.7 | 5.2 | 11.5 | 61.6 | 95.5[22] | ... | 57.9 | 192.2 | 3.4 | Ethiopie[6,7,50] |
| 96.8 | 132.0 | 21.6 | 36.1 | 242.0 | 178.2[51] | 45.6 | 303.5 | 23.1 | 42.7 | |
| 672.3 | 14.5 | 16.3 | 16.2 | 125.9 | 104.5[51] | 32.5[51] | 135.2 | 225.5 | 25.1 | |
| 73.8 | 143.7 | 31.2 | 38.6 | 184.2 | 175.0[22] | ... | 48.7 | 13.4 | 15.6 | |
| 296.2 | 10.9 | 13.2 | 17.8 | 84.4 | 139.4[22] | ... | 300.8 | 188.2 | 9.5 | |
| 20.0 | 127.0 | 15.0 | 151.0 | 76.0 | 56.0 | 44.0 | 55.0 | 2.0 | 1.0 | Finland[42,49] |
| 54.0 | 45.0 | 35.0 | 115.0 | 62.0 | 115.0 | 308.0 | 79.0 | 3.0 | ... | Finlande[42,49] |
| 22.0 | 127.0 | 15.0 | 151.0 | 72.0 | 58.0 | 44.0 | 58.0 | 4.0 | 1.0 | |
| 55.0 | 45.0 | 32.0 | 124.0 | 59.0 | 111.0 | 322.0 | 78.0 | 4.0 | ... | |
| 21.0 | 131.0 | 16.0 | 161.0 | 76.0 | 56.0 | 44.0 | 55.0 | 3.0 | ... | |
| 57.0 | 50.0 | 31.0 | 127.0 | 61.0 | 114.0 | 328.0 | 82.0 | 4.0 | 1.0 | |

**30** **Employment by economic activity**—Total employment and persons employed by ISIC Rev. 3 categories (thousands) (*continued*)

**Emploi par activité économique**—Emploi total et personnes employées par branches de CITI Rév. 3 (milliers) (*suite*)

| Country or area [&]<br>Pays ou zone [&] | Year<br>Année | Sex<br>Sexe | Total employment<br>Emploi total | ISIC Rev. 3 Tabulation categories +<br>CITI Rév. 3 Catégories de classement + | | | | | | |
|---|---|---|---|---|---|---|---|---|---|---|
| | | | | Categ. A<br>Catég. A | Categ. B<br>Catég. B | Categ. C<br>Catég. C | Categ. D<br>Catég. D | Categ. E<br>Catég. E | Categ. F<br>Catég. F | Categ. G<br>Catég. G |
| France[3]<br>France[3] | 2003 | M | 13 508.6 | 727.9 | 15.5 | 27.4 | 3 028.8 | 176.9 | 1 509.2 | 1 763.2 |
| | 2003 | F | 11 182.2 | 324.1 | 2.8 | 8.2 | 1 203.9 | 48.3 | 154.7 | 1 530.8 |
| | 2004 | M | 13 479.6 | 665.5 | 12.1 | 31.9 | 2 957.8 | 182.9 | 1 515.1 | 1 794.4 |
| | 2004 | F | 11 304.4 | 317.0 | 1.9 | 4.4 | 1 222.2 | 37.6 | 142.8 | 1 567.3 |
| | 2005 | M | 13 495.6 | 659.9 | 16.3 | 35.7 | 2 933.3 | 163.8 | 1 539.8 | 1 776.3 |
| | 2005 | F | 11 423.7 | 275.8 | 1.0 | 6.0 | 1 196.5 | 41.2 | 148.3 | 1 564.3 |
| Georgia[3]<br>Géorgie[3] | 2003 | M | 957.5 | 508.3 | 0.5 | 2.3 | 57.8 | 15.7 | 39.7 | 112.4 |
| | 2003 | F | 857.0 | 486.6 | 0.2 | 0.5 | 31.0 | 4.1 | 0.4 | 86.1 |
| | 2004 | M | 926.5 | 478.2 | 0.4 | 3.7 | 60.6 | 17.1 | 41.3 | 108.7 |
| | 2004 | F | 856.8 | 483.7 | ... | 0.2 | 30.1 | 3.6 | 0.7 | 88.2 |
| | 2005 | M | 915.2 | 473.5 | 0.0 | 5.2 | 60.1 | 18.1 | 42.4 | 107.9 |
| | 2005 | F | 829.4 | 474.3 | 0.0 | 0.6 | 29.7 | 5.3 | 0.7 | 80.3 |
| Germany[3,50]<br>Allemagne[3,50] | 2004 | M | 19 681.0 | 554.0 | 3.0 | 109.0 | 5 851.0 | 233.0 | 2 119.0 | 2 338.0 |
| | 2004 | F | 15 978.0 | 272.0 | 2.0 | 11.0 | 2 284.0 | 63.0 | 316.0 | 2 673.0 |
| | 2005[53] | M | 20 135.0 | 578.0 | 5.0 | 111.0 | 5 785.0 | 246.0 | 2 090.0 | 2 528.0 |
| | 2005[53] | F | 16 432.0 | 283.0 | 2.0 | 12.0 | 2 247.0 | 69.0 | 310.0 | 2 729.0 |
| | 2006 | M | 20 462.0 | 567.0 | 5.0 | 106.0 | 5 843.0 | 242.0 | 2 138.0 | 2 531.0 |
| | 2006 | F | 16 860.0 | 270.0 | 1.0 | 11.0 | 2 314.0 | 74.0 | 308.0 | 2 750.0 |
| Greece[3,25,54]<br>Grèce[3,25,54] | 2004 | M | 2 680.2 | 302.0 | 10.5 | 14.0 | 412.1 | 30.6 | 343.2 | 447.8 |
| | 2004 | F | 1 650.3 | 231.5 | 1.6 | 0.7 | 157.6 | 8.5 | 6.9 | 300.7 |
| | 2005 | M | 2 705.8 | 299.1 | 12.6 | 16.7 | 407.6 | 30.9 | 360.7 | 466.1 |
| | 2005 | F | 1 676.2 | 231.3 | 1.6 | 1.1 | 152.7 | 6.8 | 6.6 | 316.0 |
| | 2006 | M | 2 725.7 | 295.6 | 11.6 | 16.9 | 411.1 | 33.8 | 350.7 | 460.4 |
| | 2006 | F | 1 727.1 | 227.4 | 1.4 | 1.3 | 152.1 | 7.0 | 7.9 | 328.2 |
| Guyana[3]<br>Guyana[3] | 2002 | M | 169.2 | 40.8 | 5.3 | 8.8 | 23.5 | 1.8 | 15.9 | 22.3 |
| | 2002 | F | 70.4 | 4.8 | 0.3 | 0.7 | 7.1 | 0.5 | 0.3 | 15.6 |
| Hungary[25,49]<br>Hongrie[25,49] | 2004 | M | 2 117.3 | 158.0[1] | ... | 11.3 | 536.1 | 46.2 | 284.3 | 266.2 |
| | 2004 | F | 1 783.1 | 46.9[1] | ... | 2.9 | 357.8 | 17.5 | 24.4 | 279.5 |
| | 2005 | M | 2 116.1 | 145.4[1] | ... | 12.6 | 530.7 | 47.9 | 293.9 | 267.2 |
| | 2005 | F | 1 785.4 | 48.6[1] | ... | 2.3 | 338.7 | 16.7 | 21.2 | 318.7 |
| | 2006 | M | 2 137.4 | 142.2[1] | ... | 13.0 | 530.7 | 48.7 | 300.0 | 269.6 |
| | 2006 | F | 1 792.7 | 48.6[1] | ... | 2.0 | 334.5 | 18.9 | 21.6 | 312.4 |
| Iceland[33,55]<br>Islande[33,55] | 2004 | M | 82.5 | 3.5 | 4.2 | 0.2 | 14.6 | 1.4 | 11.0 | 11.4 |
| | 2004 | F | 73.6 | 1.8 | 0.4 | ... | 7.1 | 0.2 | 0.6 | 8.5 |
| | 2005 | M | 85.7 | 3.6 | 4.6 | 0.1 | 14.1 | 1.2 | 11.5 | 13.1 |
| | 2005 | F | 75.6 | 1.9 | 0.4 | ... | 6.9 | 0.3 | 0.8 | 9.4 |
| | 2006 | M | 92.0 | 4.5 | 4.0 | 0.1 | 14.0 | 1.1 | 13.9 | 13.6 |
| | 2006 | F | 77.5 | 1.8 | 0.3 | ... | 6.1 | 0.3 | 0.8 | 10.0 |
| Iran (Islamic Rep. of)[7]<br>Iran (Rép. islamique d')[7] | 2005 | M | 15 959.0 | 3 565.0 | 66.0 | 115.0 | 2 586.0 | 181.0 | 2 043.0 | 2 647.0 |
| | 2005 | F | 3 801.0 | 1 298.0 | 1.0 | 7.0 | 1 046.0 | 8.0 | 17.0 | 169.0 |
| Ireland[3,54]<br>Irlande[3,54] | 2004 | M | 1 065.0 | 103.0 | 2.6 | 6.3 | 192.0 | 10.7 | 196.0 | 131.0 |
| | 2004 | F | 771.0 | 11.0 | 0.2 | 0.6 | 88.3 | 2.8 | 10.3 | 129.0 |
| | 2005 | M | 1 110.1 | 100.7 | 2.0 | 8.0 | 187.8 | 10.1 | 230.2 | 133.2 |
| | 2005 | F | 819.1 | 11.0 | 0.1 | 0.9 | 84.4 | 3.0 | 12.2 | 133.7 |
| | 2006 | M | 1 162.0 | 101.5 | 2.3 | 9.9 | 185.7 | 9.0 | 249.4 | 143.7 |
| | 2006 | F | 855.0 | 10.5 | 0.2 | 0.9 | 80.8 | 2.2 | 13.3 | 140.7 |

30    **Employment by economic activity**—Total employment and persons employed by ISIC Rev. 3 categories (thousands) (*continued*)

    **Emploi par activité économique**—Emploi total et personnes employées par branches de CITI Rév. 3 (milliers) (*suite*)

| | | ISIC Rev. 3 Tabulation categories + | | | | | | | | |
|---|---|---|---|---|---|---|---|---|---|---|
| | | CITI Rév. 3 Catégories de classement + | | | | | | | | Country or area [&] |
| Categ. H | Categ. I | Categ. J | Categ. K | Categ. L | Categ. M | Categ. N | Categ. O | Categ. P | Categ. Q | |
| Catég. H | Catég. I | Catég. J | Catég. K | Catég.L | Catég. M | Catég. N | Catég. O | Catég. P | Catég. Q | Pays ou zone [&] |
| 420.2 | 1 104.6 | 326.1 | 1 359.0 | 1 158.0 | 584.0 | 643.6 | 454.2 | 136.3 | 6.8 | France[3] |
| 383.5 | 475.5 | 386.5 | 1 079.3 | 1 141.6 | 1 129.4 | 2 171.8 | 567.7 | 510.2 | 7.2 | France[3] |
| 436.6 | 1 113.0 | 299.1 | 1 400.2 | 1 201.8 | 582.2 | 660.0 | 451.9 | 123.1 | 6.1 | |
| 389.6 | 484.9 | 379.0 | 1 085.4 | 1 103.0 | 1 126.6 | 2 266.5 | 606.0 | 522.5 | 8.8 | |
| 438.4 | 1 098.9 | 328.8 | 1 424.2 | 1 218.1 | 586.1 | 645.1 | 475.6 | 104.9 | 6.2 | |
| 397.2 | 500.4 | 412.9 | 1 090.5 | 1 140.7 | 1 143.7 | 2 344.0 | 609.3 | 510.5 | 8.2 | |
| 6.8 | 65.4 | 4.8 | 19.0 | 63.5 | 27.5 | 8.0 | 22.2 | 1.0 | 2.4 | Georgia[3] |
| 9.8 | 11.5 | 5.0 | 13.3 | 27.9 | 108.1 | 41.0 | 23.0 | 6.8 | 1.1 | Géorgie[3] |
| 7.6 | 61.6 | 5.0 | 15.8 | 60.6 | 26.6 | 12.6 | 22.0 | 0.7 | 3.1 | |
| 11.1 | 12.7 | 7.8 | 12.6 | 26.1 | 107.4 | 42.1 | 20.7 | 7.7 | 1.3 | |
| 7.6 | 57.9 | 7.2 | 15.8 | 56.1 | 29.6 | 12.0 | 18.1 | 0.6 | 2.9 | |
| 8.7 | 11.3 | 6.1 | 10.1 | 25.7 | 101.2 | 46.0 | 20.1 | 8.6 | 0.4 | |
| 518.0 | 1 411.0 | 643.0 | 1 730.0 | 1 642.0 | 675.0 | 1 009.0 | 820.0 | 8.0 | 18.0 | Germany[3,50] |
| 688.0 | 560.0 | 654.0 | 1 546.0 | 1 254.0 | 1 358.0 | 3 055.0 | 1 091.0 | 144.0 | 8.0 | Allemagne[3,50] |
| 554.0 | 1 405.0 | 657.0 | 1 869.0 | 1 622.0 | 688.0 | 1 015.0 | 947.0 | 13.0 | 21.0 | |
| 742.0 | 544.0 | 649.0 | 1 653.0 | 1 257.0 | 1 412.0 | 3 135.0 | 1 206.0 | 166.0 | 13.0 | |
| 584.0 | 1 469.0 | 657.0 | 1 975.0 | 1 627.0 | 706.0 | 1 052.0 | 933.0 | 11.0 | 16.0 | |
| 796.0 | 591.0 | 650.0 | 1 760.0 | 1 274.0 | 1 468.0 | 3 213.0 | 1 192.0 | 176.0 | 13.0 | |
| 149.3 | 220.2 | 56.7 | 155.5 | 244.3 | 124.9 | 82.4 | 82.0 | 4.4 | 0.4 | Greece[3,25,54] |
| 130.3 | 52.2 | 55.7 | 127.5 | 111.7 | 193.3 | 136.6 | 73.1 | 61.4 | 1.0 | Grèce[3,25,54] |
| 167.6 | 219.5 | 56.9 | 153.3 | 232.3 | 122.5 | 78.5 | 78.5 | 2.6 | 0.6 | |
| 136.6 | 48.3 | 56.1 | 136.1 | 111.4 | 189.8 | 141.7 | 75.1 | 65.0 | 0.0 | |
| 168.8 | 227.2 | 61.2 | 147.3 | 251.6 | 126.7 | 79.8 | 79.6 | 3.3 | 0.1 | |
| 132.1 | 54.5 | 54.5 | 136.8 | 129.3 | 204.4 | 148.0 | 70.9 | 70.1 | 0.5 | |
| 2.0 | 15.0 | 1.4 | 4.6 | 8.7 | 3.1 | 1.3 | 6.5 | 1.3 | 0.2 | Guyana[3] |
| 3.6 | 1.9 | 1.7 | 2.9 | 6.4 | 10.0 | 4.3 | 3.2 | 4.9 | 0.3 | Guyana[3] |
| 62.6 | 215.5 | 25.7 | 149.2 | 151.0 | 72.0 | 61.3 | 77.2 | 0.2 | 0.5 | Hungary[25,49] |
| 86.2 | 80.6 | 54.5 | 123.3 | 147.8 | 261.0 | 208.1 | 91.2 | 1.3 | 0.2 | Hongrie[25,49] |
| 70.8 | 212.5 | 26.6 | 152.8 | 146.3 | 72.7 | 58.4 | 76.9 | 0.3 | 1.1 | |
| 83.5 | 72.9 | 53.7 | 123.0 | 151.6 | 250.7 | 204.3 | 97.5 | 1.8 | 0.2 | |
| 69.3 | 218.9 | 27.8 | 157.7 | 151.0 | 72.2 | 60.0 | 75.5 | 0.2 | 0.6 | |
| 87.9 | 82.4 | 52.5 | 125.1 | 148.2 | 250.7 | 209.5 | 96.9 | 1.5 | ... | |
| 2.2 | 7.1 | 2.1 | 8.4 | 3.4 | 4.0 | 3.6 | 4.9 | ... | 0.3 | Iceland[33,55] |
| 3.1 | 3.7 | 4.8 | 6.0 | 4.2 | 8.1 | 19.3 | 5.5 | ... | 0.1 | Islande[33,55] |
| 2.5 | 7.6 | 2.1 | 9.0 | 3.6 | 3.6 | 3.6 | 5.0 | ... | 0.2 | |
| 2.9 | 4.1 | 4.6 | 6.0 | 3.8 | 8.3 | 20.9 | 5.1 | ... | 0.2 | |
| 3.1 | 7.8 | 2.7 | 9.6 | 4.8 | 4.0 | 3.2 | 5.2 | ... | 0.3 | |
| 2.9 | 4.1 | 4.7 | 5.4 | 5.2 | 8.5 | 21.4 | 5.7 | ... | 0.1 | |
| 163.0 | 1 703.0 | 214.0 | 336.0 | 1 156.0 | 658.0 | 242.0 | 267.0 | 7.0 | 7.0 | Iran (Islamic Rep. of)[7] |
| 11.0 | 37.0 | 34.0 | 61.0 | 103.0 | 643.0 | 200.0 | 144.0 | 20.0 | 1.0 | Iran (Rép. islamique d')[7] |
| 49.4 | 87.2 | 35.1 | 85.8 | 48.8 | 33.2 | 33.8 | 43.5 | 0.9 | ... | Ireland[3,54] |
| 58.4 | 26.0 | 47.6 | 68.5 | 40.7 | 84.7 | 143.0 | 50.2 | 5.5 | ... | Irlande[3,54] |
| 45.7 | 91.1 | 36.3 | 93.2 | 48.8 | 35.8 | 33.5 | 43.8 | 0.8 | 0.3 | |
| 65.3 | 27.1 | 48.6 | 79.0 | 49.4 | 87.3 | 154.5 | 51.3 | 6.4 | 0.4 | |
| 49.7 | 91.8 | 36.1 | 100.1 | 51.5 | 38.9 | 34.9 | 48.6 | 0.6 | ... | |
| 66.6 | 28.9 | 49.6 | 81.5 | 53.6 | 96.7 | 166.4 | 51.7 | 7.0 | ... | |

30   **Employment by economic activity**—Total employment and persons employed by ISIC Rev. 3 categories (thousands) (*continued*)

**Emploi par activité économique**—Emploi total et personnes employées par branches de CITI Rév. 3 (milliers) (*suite*)

| Country or area [&]<br>Pays ou zone [&] | Year<br>Année | Sex<br>Sexe | Total employment<br>Emploi total | ISIC Rev. 3 Tabulation categories +<br>CITI Rév. 3 Catégories de classement + | | | | | | |
|---|---|---|---|---|---|---|---|---|---|---|
| | | | | Categ. A<br>Catég. A | Categ. B<br>Catég. B | Categ. C<br>Catég. C | Categ. D<br>Catég. D | Categ. E<br>Catég. E | Categ. F<br>Catég. F | Categ. G<br>Catég. G |
| Isle of Man[3]<br>Ile de Man[3] | 2001 | M | 21.3 | 0.4 | ^0.0 | 0.1 | 2.4 | 0.4 | 2.4 | 2.4 |
| | 2001 | F | 17.8 | 0.1 | ^0.0 | ^0.0 | 0.7 | 0.1 | 0.2 | 2.3 |
| | 2006[35] | M | 22.0 | 0.6 | 0.1 | 0.1 | 1.6 | 0.5 | 3.1 | 2.8 |
| | 2006[35] | F | 18.8 | 0.1 | ^0.0 | ^0.0 | 0.5 | 0.1 | 0.2 | 2.3 |
| Israel[3,6]<br>Israël[3,6] | 2004 | M | 1 300.3 | 39.8[1] | ... | 277.9[56] | ... | 15.4 | 117.9 | 195.6 |
| | 2004 | F | 1 100.5 | 9.2[1] | ... | 108.6[56] | ... | 3.9 | 10.8 | 129.1 |
| | 2005 | M | 1 339.9 | 40.9[1] | ... | 282.6[56] | ... | 16.8 | 117.3 | 197.0 |
| | 2005 | F | 1 153.7 | 9.1[1] | ... | 109.0[56] | ... | 4.5 | 9.8 | 140.2 |
| | 2006 | M | 1 383.6 | 37.9[1] | ... | 292.3[56] | ... | 15.2 | 125.7 | 194.9 |
| | 2006 | F | 1 190.0 | 7.2[1] | ... | 109.6[56] | ... | 3.0 | 8.7 | 141.8 |
| Italy[3]<br>Italie[3] | 2004[53] | M | 13 622.0 | 652.0 | 31.0 | 34.0 | 3 408.0 | 129.0 | 1 726.0 | 2 031.0 |
| | 2004[53] | F | 8 783.0 | 304.0 | 4.0 | 4.0 | 1 437.0 | 22.0 | 107.0 | 1 402.0 |
| | 2005 | M | 13 738.0 | 628.0 | 31.0 | 36.0 | 3 418.0 | 141.0 | 1 806.0 | 2 061.0 |
| | 2005 | F | 8 825.0 | 286.0 | 2.0 | 4.0 | 1 407.0 | 22.0 | 107.0 | 1 355.0 |
| | 2006 | M | 13 939.0 | 649.0 | 31.0 | 36.0 | 3 438.0 | 134.0 | 1 803.0 | 2 117.0 |
| | 2006 | F | 9 049.0 | 299.0 | 3.0 | 6.0 | 1 387.0 | 24.0 | 98.0 | 1 405.0 |
| Japan[3]<br>Japon[3] | 2004 | M | 37 130.0 | 1 480.0 | 160.0 | 30.0 | 7 900.0 | 270.0 | 4 980.0 | 6 150.0 |
| | 2004 | F | 26 160.0 | 1 170.0 | 50.0 | 10.0 | 3 870.0 | 40.0 | 860.0 | 5 750.0 |
| | 2005 | M | 37 230.0 | 1 460.0 | 170.0 | 30.0 | 7 920.0 | 310.0 | 4 870.0 | 6 090.0 |
| | 2005 | F | 26 330.0 | 1 130.0 | 60.0 | 10.0 | 3 770.0 | 40.0 | 810.0 | 5 770.0 |
| | 2006 | M | 37 300.0 | 1 420.0 | 160.0 | 30.0 | 8 070.0 | 320.0 | 4 780.0 | 6 040.0 |
| | 2006 | F | 26 520.0 | 1 080.0 | 60.0 | 10.0 | 3 830.0 | 40.0 | 820.0 | 5 760.0 |
| Jersey[47]<br>Jersey[47] | 2003 | MF | 41.6 | 1.5[1] | ... | 4.2[57] | 1.9 | 0.5 | ... | 7.8 |
| | 2004 | MF | 41.3 | 1.4[1] | ... | 4.3[57] | 1.7 | 0.5 | ... | 8.2 |
| | 2005 | MF | 41.9 | 1.4[1] | ... | 4.5[57] | 1.6 | 0.5 | ... | 8.3 |
| Kazakhstan[3]<br>Kazakhstan[3] | 2002 | M | 3 486.4 | 1 250.9 | 12.1 | 131.0 | 322.9 | 107.3 | 218.4 | 415.4 |
| | 2002 | F | 3 222.5 | 1 115.8 | 1.4 | 36.3 | 180.8 | 45.7 | 50.0 | 591.8 |
| | 2003 | M | 3 618.3 | 1 302.9 | 14.6 | 141.4 | 316.3 | 121.8 | 262.5 | 409.9 |
| | 2003 | F | 3 366.9 | 1 144.0 | 1.2 | 40.3 | 190.0 | 45.3 | 66.9 | 605.2 |
| | 2004 | M | 3 718.5 | 1 283.1 | 15.8 | 146.1 | 330.8 | 110.1 | 302.7 | 422.4 |
| | 2004 | F | 3 463.3 | 1 104.8 | 2.3 | 39.9 | 189.0 | 53.7 | 78.0 | 636.3 |
| Korea, Republic of[3,6]<br>Corée, République de[3,6] | 2004 | M | 13 193.0 | 911.0 | 48.0 | 15.0 | 2 797.0 | 59.0 | 1 658.0 | 2 010.0 |
| | 2004 | F | 9 364.0 | 838.0 | 28.0 | 1.0 | 1 493.0 | 13.0 | 162.0 | 1 795.0 |
| | 2005 | M | 13 330.1 | 920.3 | 45.1 | 15.9 | 2 820.7 | 58.3 | 1 656.4 | 1 993.8 |
| | 2005 | F | 9 526.0 | 826.7 | 23.4 | 1.2 | 1 413.4 | 12.8 | 158.0 | 1 754.5 |
| | 2006 | M | 13 444.0 | 905.0 | 42.0 | 16.0 | 2 795.0 | 60.0 | 1 668.0 | 1 992.0 |
| | 2006 | F | 9 706.0 | 816.0 | 22.0 | 2.0 | 1 372.0 | 16.0 | 167.0 | 1 721.0 |
| Kyrgyzstan[3,30]<br>Kirghizistan[3,30] | 2003 | M | 1 083.8 | 470.0 | 0.3 | 11.1 | 72.9 | 27.3 | 94.5 | 132.1 |
| | 2003 | F | 846.7 | 364.1 | 0.3 | 1.4 | 67.2 | 7.7 | 7.7 | 125.7 |
| | 2004 | M | 1 140.7 | 445.4 | 0.2 | 12.1 | 79.0 | 30.0 | 136.1 | 144.1 |
| | 2004 | F | 850.5 | 328.5 | 0.5 | 1.4 | 74.4 | 9.1 | 7.9 | 137.5 |
| | 2005 | M | 1 195.9 | 470.2 | 0.2 | 11.3 | 90.5 | 27.4 | 145.4 | 154.1 |
| | 2005 | F | 881.2 | 328.9 | 0.4 | 1.1 | 73.4 | 7.8 | 8.3 | 147.4 |
| Latvia[25,49]<br>Lettonie[25,49] | 2004 | M | 521.8 | 83.3 | ... | ... | 89.9 | 18.3 | 77.2 | 56.6 |
| | 2004 | F | 495.9 | 49.2 | ... | ... | 73.6 | 7.2 | 9.6 | 94.7 |
| | 2005 | M | 534.1 | 81.5 | ... | ... | 88.0 | 16.4 | 82.2 | 59.8 |
| | 2005 | F | 501.8 | 40.8 | ... | ... | 66.1 | 6.7 | 8.3 | 97.9 |
| | 2006 | M | 559.2 | 76.1 | ... | ... | 94.5 | 16.8 | 97.8 | 64.0 |
| | 2006 | F | 528.5 | 41.7 | ... | ... | 75.0 | 5.5 | 6.1 | 106.2 |
| Lesotho[7]<br>Lesotho[7] | 1999 | M | 346.6 | 270.9 | 0.1 | 2.4 | 8.0 | 1.7 | 18.9 | 11.1 |
| | 1999 | F | 271.0 | 175.8 | 0.0 | 0.6 | 13.8 | 1.5 | 10.5 | 17.9 |

**30**

**Employment by economic activity**—Total employment and persons employed by ISIC Rev. 3 categories (thousands) *(continued)*

**Emploi par activité économique**—Emploi total et personnes employées par branches de CITI Rév. 3 (milliers) *(suite)*

| | | | | ISIC Rev. 3 Tabulation categories +<br>CITI Rév. 3 Catégories de classement + | | | | | | Country or area [&] |
|---|---|---|---|---|---|---|---|---|---|---|
| Categ. H<br>Catég. H | Categ. I<br>Catég. I | Categ. J<br>Catég. J | Categ. K<br>Catég. K | Categ. L<br>Catég.L | Categ. M<br>Catég. M | Categ. N<br>Catég. N | Categ. O<br>Catég. O | Categ. P<br>Catég. P | Categ. Q<br>Catég. Q | Pays ou zone [&] |
| 1.0 | 2.0 | 3.3 | 1.6 | 1.7 | 0.9 | 0.7 | 2.0 | ^0.0 | ... | Isle of Man[3] |
| 1.0 | 0.9 | 4.1 | 1.4 | 1.1 | 1.8 | 2.5 | 1.5 | 0.1 | ... | Ile de Man[3] |
| 0.8 | 2.3 | 3.0 | 2.7 | 1.6 | 0.7 | 0.9 | 1.3 | ^0.0 | ... | |
| 0.8 | 0.9 | 3.9 | 2.1 | 1.1 | 2.1 | 3.3 | 1.4 | 0.1 | ... | |
| 59.1 | 109.0 | 30.4 | 190.4 | 62.6 | 70.9 | 60.5 | 55.5 | 2.7 | 1.3 | Israel[3,6] |
| 44.3 | 45.1 | 48.7 | 129.7 | 48.9 | 232.5 | 194.7 | 54.0 | 35.7 | 0.7 | Israël[3,6] |
| 69.5 | 115.9 | 34.3 | 196.4 | 64.6 | 70.1 | 59.1 | 60.9 | 2.4 | 1.3 | |
| 45.6 | 46.7 | 47.8 | 138.9 | 51.3 | 244.0 | 206.5 | 55.9 | 38.0 | 0.7 | |
| 72.3 | 121.8 | 35.1 | 208.3 | 63.9 | 74.4 | 60.5 | 63.4 | 4.3 | ... | |
| 49.8 | 49.7 | 52.3 | 146.1 | 51.8 | 251.5 | 203.2 | 64.8 | 41.5 | ... | |
| 521.0 | 972.0 | 379.0 | 1 275.0 | 989.0 | 421.0 | 515.0 | 492.0 | 34.0 | 12.0 | Italy[3] |
| 514.0 | 269.0 | 261.0 | 1 051.0 | 463.0 | 1 181.0 | 990.0 | 549.0 | 216.0 | 8.0 | Italie[3] |
| 533.0 | 960.0 | 379.0 | 1 299.0 | 967.0 | 394.0 | 529.0 | 504.0 | 41.0 | 11.0 | |
| 526.0 | 279.0 | 261.0 | 1 077.0 | 472.0 | 1 147.0 | 1 021.0 | 589.0 | 263.0 | 6.0 | |
| 567.0 | 939.0 | 404.0 | 1 331.0 | 971.0 | 400.0 | 528.0 | 544.0 | 41.0 | 7.0 | |
| 547.0 | 286.0 | 271.0 | 1 103.0 | 472.0 | 1 197.0 | 1 042.0 | 620.0 | 283.0 | 5.0 | |
| 1 400.0 | 3 200.0 | 780.0 | 4 210.0 | 1 850.0 | 1 330.0 | 1 230.0 | 1 760.0 | ... | ... | Japan[3] |
| 2 070.0 | 740.0 | 810.0 | 2 670.0 | 480.0 | 1 510.0 | 4 080.0 | 1 780.0 | ... | ... | Japon[3] |
| 1 410.0 | 3 080.0 | 790.0 | 4 490.0 | 1 800.0 | 1 290.0 | 1 300.0 | 1 770.0 | ... | ... | |
| 2 020.0 | 750.0 | 790.0 | 2 800.0 | 490.0 | 1 570.0 | 4 240.0 | 1 780.0 | ... | ... | |
| 1 360.0 | 3 180.0 | 770.0 | 4 560.0 | 1 750.0 | 1 300.0 | 1 350.0 | 1 800.0 | ... | ... | |
| 2 010.0 | 780.0 | 770.0 | 2 870.0 | 470.0 | 1 570.0 | 4 360.0 | 1 800.0 | ... | ... | |
| 4.4 | 2.4 | 11.7 | 3.0 | 4.2[58] | ... | ... | ... | ... | ... | Jersey[47] |
| 4.2 | 2.4 | 11.6 | 2.9 | 4.2[58] | ... | ... | ... | ... | ... | Jersey[47] |
| 4.3 | 2.4 | 11.7 | 3.0 | 4.2[58] | ... | ... | ... | ... | ... | |
| 15.9 | 364.2 | 19.5 | 131.4 | 158.7 | 160.1 | 61.8 | 90.0 | 26.5 | 0.3 | Kazakhstan[3] |
| 40.6 | 139.5 | 30.6 | 72.0 | 121.7 | 428.9 | 230.8 | 96.3 | 40.3 | ... | Kazakhstan[3] |
| 18.4 | 384.2 | 18.9 | 113.9 | 189.0 | 163.2 | 59.9 | 89.5 | 11.8 | 0.1 | |
| 51.7 | 119.7 | 34.6 | 93.2 | 129.2 | 467.9 | 239.9 | 106.9 | 30.7 | 0.2 | |
| 22.2 | 389.9 | 24.0 | 120.4 | 192.2 | 179.1 | 65.1 | 94.4 | 20.4 | ... | |
| 59.8 | 129.8 | 36.7 | 113.2 | 142.5 | 487.1 | 253.6 | 106.9 | 29.0 | 0.5 | |
| 636.0 | 1 193.0 | 364.0 | 1 324.0 | 554.0 | 515.0 | 174.0 | 914.0 | 4.0 | 18.0 | Korea, Republic of[3,6] |
| 1 421.0 | 183.0 | 374.0 | 590.0 | 213.0 | 991.0 | 419.0 | 713.0 | 121.0 | 7.0 | Corée, République de[3,6] |
| 638.6 | 1 227.8 | 369.5 | 1 360.5 | 552.2 | 522.1 | 171.1 | 956.0 | 4.1 | 17.7 | |
| 1 419.3 | 200.8 | 376.2 | 676.9 | 238.8 | 1 045.9 | 475.9 | 770.6 | 125.7 | 6.4 | |
| 635.0 | 1 272.0 | 382.0 | 1 423.0 | 542.0 | 532.0 | 181.0 | 981.0 | 4.0 | 15.0 | |
| 1 415.0 | 198.0 | 404.0 | 745.0 | 260.0 | 1 125.0 | 505.0 | 800.0 | 135.0 | 5.0 | |
| 11.3 | 82.2 | 4.7 | 17.6 | 70.4 | 46.1 | 18.3 | 18.4 | 6.2 | 0.3 | Kyrgyzstan[3,30] |
| 22.8 | 15.3 | 5.3 | 10.8 | 20.8 | 110.3 | 62.6 | 20.1 | 4.0 | 0.5 | Kirghizistan[3,30] |
| 14.2 | 95.8 | 3.7 | 25.1 | 64.2 | 44.2 | 19.9 | 20.4 | 6.2 | 0.1 | |
| 30.2 | 17.1 | 4.8 | 13.4 | 27.6 | 117.6 | 54.0 | 21.2 | 4.8 | 0.3 | |
| 17.1 | 96.5 | 3.7 | 18.6 | 67.4 | 44.6 | 20.3 | 23.7 | 4.9 | ... | |
| 31.9 | 19.2 | 4.5 | 15.5 | 34.9 | 117.2 | 65.1 | 21.2 | 3.9 | 0.5 | |
| 7.5 | 68.7 | 8.4 | 21.3 | 39.8 | 14.2 | 7.3 | 25.0 | ... | ... | Latvia[25,49] |
| 18.1 | 27.2 | 10.0 | 18.9 | 33.3 | 68.7 | 47.1 | 34.8 | ... | ... | Lettonie[25,49] |
| 7.3 | 66.0 | 7.6 | 24.9 | 44.7 | 17.3 | 8.8 | 25.3 | ... | ... | |
| 20.4 | 28.5 | 12.5 | 24.3 | 37.1 | 73.2 | 49.1 | 32.3 | ... | ... | |
| 4.9 | 70.2 | 7.2 | 31.4 | 46.0 | 15.9 | 7.1 | 20.3 | ... | ... | |
| 24.3 | 30.6 | 17.9 | 29.3 | 42.2 | 71.9 | 43.8 | 29.2 | ... | ... | |
| 0.9 | 9.3 | 1.0 | 3.4 | 5.2 | 5.1 | 2.1 | 1.8 | 4.5 | 0.1 | Lesotho[7] |
| 3.5 | 1.4 | 0.8 | 2.0 | 2.4 | 8.1 | 2.9 | 7.7 | 22.0 | 0.0 | Lesotho[7] |

| Country or area [&]<br>Pays ou zone [&] | Year<br>Année | Sex<br>Sexe | Total employment<br>Emploi total | Categ. A<br>Catég. A | Categ. B<br>Catég. B | Categ. C<br>Catég. C | Categ. D<br>Catég. D | Categ. E<br>Catég. E | Categ. F<br>Catég. F | Categ. G<br>Catég. G |
|---|---|---|---|---|---|---|---|---|---|---|
| Lithuania[3,25]<br>Lituanie[3,25] | 2004 | M | 733.8 | 131.6 | 1.8 | 3.2 | 129.7 | 23.1 | 106.2 | 112.1 |
| | 2004 | F | 702.5 | 94.0 | 0.2 | 1.2 | 125.2 | 6.4 | 9.9 | 116.0 |
| | 2005 | M | 750.9 | 122.6 | 2.2 | 2.3 | 134.6 | 20.8 | 120.5 | 111.1 |
| | 2005 | F | 723.0 | 81.6 | 0.6 | 0.9 | 131.8 | 5.7 | 12.0 | 122.2 |
| | 2006 | M | 755.8 | 108.1 | 2.5 | 3.9 | 137.9 | 19.1 | 139.0 | 115.9 |
| | 2006 | F | 743.2 | 75.7 | 0.2 | 0.4 | 126.7 | 7.9 | 9.7 | 138.7 |
| Luxembourg[59]<br>Luxembourg[59] | 2004 | MF | 298.5 | 3.9[1] | ... | 0.3 | 32.5 | 1.7 | 29.2 | 41.7 |
| | 2005 | MF | 307.3 | 3.9[1] | ... | 0.3 | 32.6 | 1.8 | 30.3 | 42.8 |
| | 2006 | MF | 318.7 | 4.0[1] | ... | ... | 34.8[60] | ... | 31.6 | ... |
| Madagascar[33,61]<br>Madagascar[33,61] | 2003 | M | 4 135.7 | 3 110.1 | 61.8 | 4.5 | 227.0 | 18.1 | 54.6 | 167.7 |
| | 2003 | F | 3 962.8 | 3 118.4 | 25.8 | 9.7 | 222.3 | 0.5 | 6.0 | 252.9 |
| | 2005 | M | 4 841.8 | 3 875.7 | 68.1 | 10.4 | 205.3 | 21.4 | 12.0 | 173.9 |
| | 2005 | F | 4 728.6 | 3 869.6 | 30.9 | 8.5 | 62.2 | 6.1 | 0.9 | 296.6 |
| Malaysia[6,45]<br>Malaisie[6,45] | 2004 | M | 6 390.4 | 952.3 | 123.2 | 32.4 | 1 205.7 | 50.7 | 824.8 | 1 054.8 |
| | 2004 | F | 3 589.1 | 374.3 | 2.9 | 2.3 | 817.3 | 7.2 | 65.9 | 552.4 |
| | 2005 | M | 6 470.5 | 996.6 | 110.3 | 31.5 | 1 201.5 | 49.0 | 832.1 | 1 063.5 |
| | 2005 | F | 3 574.8 | 358.6 | 4.9 | 4.5 | 787.8 | 7.6 | 72.3 | 556.8 |
| | 2006 | M | 6 618.6 | 1 013.9 | 123.2 | 35.9 | 1 270.4 | 63.4 | 834.4 | 1 081.0 |
| | 2006 | F | 3 656.8 | 361.4 | 5.0 | 6.1 | 812.4 | 12.0 | 74.5 | 569.6 |
| Maldives[3,25]<br>Maldives[3,25] | 1995[26] | M | 48.9 | 0.9 | 12.3 | 0.4 | 4.5 | 0.7 | 2.8 | 4.5 |
| | 1995[26] | F | 18.1 | 1.4 | 0.2 | ^0.0 | 7.6 | 0.1 | ^0.0 | 0.8 |
| | 2000[26] | M | 57.4 | 1.1 | 9.2 | 0.4 | 4.3 | 1.0 | 3.6 | 4.8 |
| | 2000[26] | F | 28.9 | 1.4 | 0.1 | ^0.0 | 6.8 | 0.1 | 0.1 | 1.0 |
| | 2006 | M | 69.7 | 1.5 | 8.2 | 0.3 | 6.8 | 1.1 | 5.7 | 7.4 |
| | 2006 | F | 40.5 | 2.7 | 0.2 | ^0.0 | 12.5 | 0.2 | 0.2 | 4.3 |
| Mali[3]<br>Mali[3] | 2004 | M | 1 388.3 | 657.7 | 33.3 | 8.4 | 136.1 | 5.1 | 97.5 | 266.1 |
| | 2004 | F | 982.5 | 291.7 | 2.0 | 3.0 | 136.4 | 0.0 | 4.7 | 402.1 |
| Malta[3]<br>Malte[3] | 2004 | M | 103.8 | 2.4 | ... | 0.7 | 21.7 | 2.9 | 10.4 | 16.5 |
| | 2004 | F | 44.8 | 0.3 | ... | ^0.0 | 7.4 | 0.3 | 0.3 | 5.7 |
| | 2005 | M | 102.8 | 2.3 | 0.5 | ... | 21.3 | 2.5 | 12.0 | 14.3 |
| | 2005 | F | 46.0 | ... | 0.3 | ... | 7.3 | 0.3 | 0.3 | 6.5 |
| | 2006 | M | 104.4 | 2.1 | ... | 0.7 | 19.8 | 3.1 | 12.0 | 16.2 |
| | 2006 | F | 48.1 | 0.1 | ... | ^0.0 | 6.7 | 0.2 | 0.2 | 7.7 |
| Mauritius[3,6]<br>Maurice[3,6] | 2004 | M | 327.9 | 30.4 | 5.4 | 0.1 | 60.8 | 3.2 | 49.4 | 48.6 |
| | 2004 | F | 159.1 | 12.3 | 0.7 | 0.1 | 48.3 | 0.3 | 1.1 | 24.7 |
| | 2005 | M | 329.1 | 29.5 | 5.2 | 0.3 | 58.4 | 3.7 | 50.1 | 44.6 |
| | 2005 | F | 161.3 | 13.5 | 0.8 | 0.0 | 45.3 | 0.1 | 1.0 | 24.0 |
| | 2006 | M | 332.5 | 28.5 | 6.1 | 0.3 | 60.9 | 3.3 | 50.3 | 43.2 |
| | 2006 | F | 166.6 | 12.9 | 0.6 | 0.1 | 44.4 | 0.2 | 0.8 | 26.4 |
| Mexico[21,54]<br>Mexique[21,54] | 2004 | M | 26 418.3 | 5 628.0 | 145.3 | 149.5 | 4 504.1 | 199.0 | 2 503.2 | 5 800.7 |
| | 2004 | F | 14 557.2 | 823.9 | 9.0 | 16.8 | 2 681.6 | 39.9 | 85.5 | 3 987.8 |
| | 2005[53] | M | 25 853.1 | 5 187.2 | 145.3 | 168.7 | 4 244.1 | 158.1 | 3 076.8 | 5 269.7 |
| | 2005[53] | F | 14 938.7 | 710.9 | 16.5 | 24.7 | 2 666.6 | 28.0 | 104.3 | 4 063.1 |
| | 2006 | M | 26 597.9 | 5 141.3 | 157.2 | 147.9 | 4 357.5 | 150.2 | 3 352.0 | 5 380.2 |
| | 2006 | F | 15 599.9 | 724.4 | 10.1 | 16.2 | 2 721.2 | 36.1 | 100.5 | 4 214.7 |
| Moldova[3]<br>Moldova[3] | 2004 | M | 631.5 | 257.6 | 1.0 | 0.7 | 68.4 | 19.1 | 46.1 | 66.3 |
| | 2004 | F | 684.6 | 274.3 | ... | 0.1 | 67.0 | 6.5 | 5.9 | 93.3 |
| | 2005 | M | 629.7 | 257.6 | 1.4 | 1.5 | 65.3 | 19.5 | 45.4 | 69.0 |
| | 2005 | F | 689.0 | 277.3 | 0.1 | 0.3 | 66.5 | 6.3 | 6.2 | 90.9 |
| | 2006 | M | 628.6 | 220.8 | 0.8 | 3.2 | 69.1 | 17.5 | 60.9 | 77.2 |
| | 2006 | F | 628.7 | 200.8 | 0.0 | 0.2 | 65.3 | 6.0 | 6.4 | 96.9 |

**Employment by economic activity**— Total employment and persons employed by ISIC Rev. 3 categories (thousands) (*continued*)

**Emploi par activité économique**— Emploi total et personnes employées par branches de CITI Rév. 3 (milliers) (*suite*)

| ISIC Rev. 3 Tabulation categories + / CITI Rév. 3 Catégories de classement + | | | | | | | | | | Country or area [&] |
|---|---|---|---|---|---|---|---|---|---|---|
| Categ. H / Catég. H | Categ. I / Catég. I | Categ. J / Catég. J | Categ. K / Catég. K | Categ. L / Catég.L | Categ. M / Catég. M | Categ. N / Catég. N | Categ. O / Catég. O | Categ. P / Catég. P | Categ. Q / Catég. Q | Pays ou zone [&] |
| 6.4 | 70.2 | 4.6 | 30.5 | 45.3 | 30.7 | 15.9 | 19.5 | 3.0 | 0.1 | Lithuania[3,25] |
| 26.3 | 23.7 | 10.4 | 25.4 | 32.6 | 110.3 | 82.5 | 36.3 | 2.1 | 0.1 | Lituanie[3,25] |
| 7.1 | 68.5 | 4.4 | 34.2 | 45.1 | 35.3 | 17.2 | 21.6 | 3.0 | 0.2 | |
| 26.0 | 25.4 | 11.9 | 28.1 | 36.6 | 112.7 | 81.3 | 42.1 | 4.1 | ... | |
| 7.6 | 69.6 | 5.5 | 43.2 | 38.4 | 25.6 | 16.6 | 21.7 | 1.1 | 0.1 | |
| 31.5 | 29.3 | 11.1 | 35.1 | 37.2 | 106.0 | 89.1 | 42.1 | 2.4 | ... | |
| 13.9 | 22.5 | 32.9 | 50.5 | 16.2 | 13.9 | 21.6 | 10.2 | 7.5 | ... | Luxembourg[59] |
| 14.2 | 22.9 | 34.1 | 52.0 | 16.7 | 14.4 | 22.8 | 10.6 | 8.2 | ... | Luxembourg[59] |
| ... | ... | 92.8[16] | ... | 74.0[17] | ... | ... | ... | ... | ... | Madagascar[33,61] |
| 21.0 | 108.1 | 4.4[16] | ... | 144.3 | 33.1 | 8.8 | 172.3 | ... | ... | Madagascar[33,61] |
| 26.7 | 9.1 | 1.3[16] | ... | 61.3 | 33.1 | 5.6 | 190.2 | ... | ... | |
| 30.5 | 80.8 | 2.7 | ... | 133.6 | 18.5 | 5.1 | 203.8 | ... | ... | |
| 33.5 | 5.4 | 1.4 | ... | 68.8 | 26.0 | 4.8 | 313.9 | ... | ... | |
| 354.6 | 452.2 | 118.1 | 281.2 | 501.6 | 224.6 | 63.1 | 135.6 | 13.8 | 1.8 | Malaysia[6,45] |
| 343.6 | 80.7 | 118.1 | 177.3 | 182.8 | 386.1 | 135.1 | 95.6 | 247.1 | 0.4 | Malaisie[6,45] |
| 349.3 | 464.9 | 120.3 | 284.8 | 525.8 | 219.6 | 69.8 | 134.0 | 16.1 | 1.3 | |
| 322.5 | 79.7 | 127.0 | 174.2 | 202.8 | 387.4 | 142.8 | 100.9 | 244.5 | 0.4 | |
| 385.5 | 449.9 | 120.5 | 317.8 | 486.5 | 209.7 | 70.6 | 135.2 | 19.6 | 1.0 | |
| 335.8 | 89.8 | 121.8 | 190.6 | 187.6 | 390.4 | 152.6 | 111.9 | 235.0 | 0.2 | |
| 6.9 | 5.8 | 1.4[16] | ... | 7.2[38] | ... | ... | ... | ... | ... | Maldives[3,25] |
| 0.3 | 0.6 | 0.7[16] | ... | 5.7[38] | ... | ... | ... | ... | ... | Maldives[3,25] |
| 9.2 | 7.2 | 1.1[16] | ... | 9.7[38] | ... | ... | ... | ... | ... | |
| 0.5 | 0.7 | 0.6[16] | ... | 8.4[38] | ... | ... | ... | ... | ... | |
| 10.6 | 6.2 | 0.3 | 0.9 | 11.7 | 2.7 | 1.3 | 2.1 | ... | 0.1 | |
| 1.5 | 0.9 | 0.3 | 0.3 | 4.3 | 7.1 | 2.8 | 1.1 | ... | 0.1 | |
| 1.4 | 51.8 | 4.4 | 3.5 | 33.3 | 35.6 | 11.4 | 23.8 | 18.8 | ... | Mali[3] |
| 6.3 | 3.5 | 0.0 | 0.6 | 6.6 | 18.3 | 9.5 | 11.5 | 85.1 | 0.9 | Mali[3] |
| 7.8 | 8.8 | 2.6 | 5.5 | 10.5 | 4.5 | 5.5 | 3.4 | ... | ... | Malta[3] |
| 4.5 | 2.4 | 1.8 | 2.4 | 3.6 | 8.0 | 5.6 | 2.1 | ... | ... | Malte[3] |
| 7.8 | 9.0 | 3.0 | 5.5 | 10.0 | 4.3 | 5.0 | 3.3 | ... | ... | |
| 4.5 | 2.5 | 3.0 | 2.0 | 2.8 | 7.0 | 6.3 | 3.3 | ... | ... | |
| 8.0 | 8.9 | 3.5 | 6.2 | 10.1 | 4.4 | 5.3 | 3.5 | ... | ... | |
| 3.5 | 2.6 | 3.0 | 2.9 | 4.3 | 7.9 | 6.2 | 2.5 | ... | ... | |
| 19.8 | 29.0 | 5.9 | 13.2 | 28.1 | 11.7 | 7.9 | 10.5 | 2.6 | 0.2 | Mauritius[3,6] |
| 7.5 | 4.2 | 4.0 | 4.7 | 7.9 | 16.2 | 7.4 | 4.4 | 15.2 | ... | Maurice[3,6] |
| 23.2 | 30.2 | 6.0 | 15.6 | 28.1 | 12.5 | 7.3 | 11.1 | 2.7 | 0.1 | |
| 11.1 | 4.3 | 4.0 | 5.3 | 8.3 | 15.8 | 8.9 | 4.7 | 14.0 | 0.1 | |
| 23.4 | 30.0 | 5.5 | 15.2 | 29.7 | 13.0 | 7.6 | 11.7 | 2.6 | 0.2 | |
| 11.7 | 4.9 | 4.4 | 6.5 | 8.2 | 15.4 | 8.2 | 5.5 | 16.0 | 0.1 | |
| 1 001.4 | 1 682.1 | 163.1 | 974.9 | 1 206.5 | 896.3 | 402.9 | 828.3 | 206.5 | 0.8 | Mexico[21,54] |
| 1 292.0 | 165.8 | 122.2 | 474.2 | 601.5 | 1 285.7 | 814.9 | 552.0 | 1 568.8 | 2.0 | Mexique[21,54] |
| 1 041.3 | 1 680.2 | 159.1 | 1 180.4 | 1 246.7 | 845.5 | 380.7 | 741.3 | 154.5 | 2.3 | |
| 1 397.0 | 166.3 | 148.2 | 648.2 | 670.2 | 1 335.6 | 755.6 | 586.4 | 1 539.0 | 1.3 | |
| 1 041.9 | 1 802.8 | 190.8 | 1 245.0 | 1 329.6 | 846.2 | 366.4 | 736.9 | 142.9 | 0.9 | |
| 1 473.1 | 198.6 | 171.7 | 680.2 | 702.5 | 1 406.2 | 794.9 | 632.5 | 1 613.5 | 1.9 | |
| 4.0 | 56.9 | 4.5 | 16.0 | 40.2 | 22.7 | 14.9 | 12.1 | 0.9 | 0.1 | Moldova[3] |
| 15.1 | 16.5 | 9.1 | 12.9 | 23.9 | 85.2 | 53.8 | 18.2 | 2.4 | 0.3 | Moldova[3] |
| 4.9 | 52.4 | 4.3 | 16.4 | 39.0 | 22.7 | 14.2 | 14.7 | 0.8 | 0.4 | |
| 18.1 | 18.6 | 9.1 | 12.2 | 22.6 | 85.6 | 55.2 | 17.4 | 2.5 | 0.1 | |
| 6.0 | 47.0 | 5.2 | 19.8 | 43.3 | 26.3 | 13.3 | 17.0 | 0.7 | 0.4 | |
| 15.9 | 18.2 | 9.9 | 11.2 | 28.6 | 94.1 | 51.0 | 19.5 | 4.0 | 0.7 | |

**30** Employment by economic activity—Total employment and persons employed by ISIC Rev. 3 categories (thousands) (*continued*)

**Emploi par activité économique**—Emploi total et personnes employées par branches de CITI Rév. 3 (milliers) (*suite*)

| Country or area [&] / Pays ou zone [&] | Year Année | Sex Sexe | Total employment Emploi total | ISIC Rev. 3 Tabulation categories + / CITI Rév. 3 Catégories de classement + | | | | | | |
|---|---|---|---|---|---|---|---|---|---|---|
| | | | | Categ. A Catég. A | Categ. B Catég. B | Categ. C Catég. C | Categ. D Catég. D | Categ. E Catég. E | Categ. F Catég. F | Categ. G Catég. G |
| Mongolia[62,63] Mongolie[62,63] | 2003 | M | 468.8 | 205.3[1] | ... | 21.9 | 24.7 | 14.3 | 20.2 | 60.0 |
| | 2003 | F | 457.7 | 182.2[1] | ... | 10.0 | 30.2 | 8.4 | 14.9 | 69.7 |
| | 2004 | M | 467.1 | 200.2[1] | ... | 23.3 | 26.6 | 14.6 | 22.3 | 53.7 |
| | 2004 | F | 483.4 | 181.6[1] | ... | 10.2 | 30.7 | 8.8 | 16.9 | 80.0 |
| | 2005 | M | 479.4 | 206.3[1] | ... | 26.1 | 21.9 | 15.9 | 26.5 | 59.3 |
| | 2005 | F | 488.9 | 179.9[1] | ... | 13.7 | 23.7 | 12.6 | 22.4 | 82.5 |
| Montenegro[45,64] Monténégro[45,64] | 2005 | M | 105.6 | 8.8 | 0.2 | 0.8 | 17.0 | 4.6 | 5.2 | 13.7 |
| | 2005 | F | 73.2 | 6.5 | 0.0 | 0.9 | 4.8 | 1.0 | 0.0 | 16.2 |
| Morocco[3] Maroc[3] | 2004 | M | 7 155.0 | 2 887.3[1] | ... | 39.4 | 740.5 | 27.9 | 656.8 | 1 476.7[37] |
| | 2004 | F | 2 666.9 | 1 610.3[1] | ... | 1.2 | 437.5 | 3.3 | 5.2 | 137.4[37] |
| | 2005 | M | 7 240.7 | 2 864.4[1] | ... | 41.1 | 739.5 | 29.0 | 699.4 | 1 519.5[37] |
| | 2005 | F | 2 672.6 | 1 640.8[1] | ... | 0.7 | 414.4 | 2.8 | 6.0 | 136.3[37] |
| | 2006 | M | 7 233.3 | 2 651.8[1] | ... | 39.3 | 760.8 | 39.2 | 783.1 | 1 461.6[37] |
| | 2006 | F | 2 694.4 | 1 651.6[1] | ... | 0.6 | 381.2 | 3.6 | 6.5 | 140.8[37] |
| Namibia[65] Namibie[65] | 2000 | M | 226.8 | 69.8 | 4.7 | 3.2 | 11.4 | 3.7 | 20.7 | 17.2 |
| | 2000 | F | 205.0 | 56.7 | 3.1 | 0.7 | 11.5 | 0.5 | 1.0 | 21.7 |
| | 2004 | M | 216.7 | 65.0 | 7.9 | 5.9 | 12.1 | 5.0 | 18.3 | 27.0 |
| | 2004 | F | 168.7 | 37.6 | 4.8 | 1.7 | 11.7 | 1.1 | 1.3 | 26.9 |
| Nepal[3] Népal[3] | 1999 | M | 4 736.0 | 3 164.0 | 12.0 | 6.0 | 366.0 | 24.0 | 292.0 | 283.0 |
| | 1999 | F | 4 727.0 | 4 026.0 | 1.0 | 2.0 | 186.0 | 2.0 | 52.0 | 125.0 |
| Netherlands[3] Pays-Bas[3] | 2003 | M | 4 370.0 | 152.0[1] | ... | 7.0 | 792.0 | 28.0 | 424.0 | 666.0 |
| | 2003 | F | 3 460.0 | 61.0[1] | ... | 1.0 | 243.0 | 4.0 | 36.0 | 566.0 |
| | 2004 | M | 4 305.0 | 166.0[1] | ... | 7.0 | 810.0 | 33.0 | 423.0 | 571.0 |
| | 2004 | F | 3 477.0 | 69.0[1] | ... | 1.0 | 241.0 | 9.0 | 39.0 | 537.0 |
| | 2005 | M | 4 342.0 | 165.0[1] | ... | 6.0 | 787.0 | 32.0 | 439.0 | 590.0 |
| | 2005 | F | 3 536.0 | 69.0[1] | ... | 2.0 | 235.0 | 12.0 | 44.0 | 544.0 |
| Netherlands Antilles[3,64] Antilles néerlandaises[3,64] | 1997 | M | 30.5 | 0.5[1] | ... | ^0.0 | 4.3 | 0.8 | 4.3 | 5.3 |
| | 1997 | F | 25.8 | 0.1[1] | ... | ^0.0 | 1.0 | 0.1 | 0.3 | 5.4 |
| | 1998 | M | 29.5 | 0.5[1] | ... | ^0.0 | 4.0 | 0.8 | 3.9 | 5.1 |
| | 1998 | F | 24.7 | ^0.0[1] | ... | ^0.0 | 0.9 | 0.1 | 0.3 | 5.1 |
| | 2000[66] | M | 27.3 | 0.5[1] | ... | 0.1 | 3.6 | 0.8 | 3.4 | 4.7 |
| | 2000[66] | F | 24.9 | ^0.0[1] | ... | ^0.0 | 1.0 | 0.1 | 0.3 | 5.2 |
| New Caledonia[21] Nouvelle-Calédonie[21] | 1996 | M | 39.6 | 3.6[1] | ... | 1.8 | 4.1 | 0.6 | 6.4 | 5.0 |
| | 1996 | F | 24.8 | 1.0[1] | ... | 0.1 | 1.4 | 0.1 | 0.5 | 3.4 |
| New Zealand[3,6] Nouvelle-Zélande[3,6] | 2004 | M | 1 094.8 | 100.9 | 2.7 | 3.6 | 207.2 | 7.3 | 135.7 | 196.8 |
| | 2004 | F | 922.3 | 47.6 | 0.5 | 0.3 | 84.9 | 2.2 | 16.6 | 162.4 |
| | 2005 | M | 1 118.4 | 97.9 | 2.1 | 3.5 | 203.8 | 5.7 | 143.4 | 195.6 |
| | 2005 | F | 954.5 | 47.3 | 0.6 | 0.5 | 78.7 | 2.4 | 18.2 | 167.6 |
| | 2006 | M | 1 142.8 | 99.4 | 1.2 | 4.0 | 200.3 | 5.9 | 161.5 | 197.5 |
| | 2006 | F | 974.4 | 49.8 | 0.5 | 0.8 | 75.5 | 2.3 | 22.6 | 170.9 |
| Norway Norvège | 2004[55] | M | 1 201.0 | 46.0 | 15.0 | 27.0 | 195.0 | 12.0 | 149.0 | 181.0 |
| | 2004[55] | F | 1 074.0 | 17.0 | 1.0 | 6.0 | 68.0 | 4.0 | 11.0 | 164.0 |
| | 2005[55] | M | 1 211.0 | 45.0 | 13.0 | 29.0 | 198.0 | 13.0 | 149.0 | 184.0 |
| | 2005[55] | F | 1 078.0 | 16.0 | 1.0 | 7.0 | 67.0 | 3.0 | 10.0 | 166.0 |
| | 2006[49] | M | 1 251.0 | 48.0 | 12.0 | 28.0 | 205.0 | 13.0 | 156.0 | 184.0 |
| | 2006[49] | F | 1 111.0 | 15.0 | 1.0 | 6.0 | 67.0 | 3.0 | 12.0 | 169.0 |

30  **Employment by economic activity**—Total employment and persons employed by ISIC Rev. 3 categories (thousands) (*continued*)

**Emploi par activité économique**—Emploi total et personnes employées par branches de CITI Rév. 3 (milliers) (*suite*)

| | | | | ISIC Rev. 3 Tabulation categories + CITI Rév. 3 Catégories de classement + | | | | | | |
|---|---|---|---|---|---|---|---|---|---|---|
| Categ. H Catég. H | Categ. I Catég. I | Categ. J Catég. J | Categ. K Catég. K | Categ. L Catég.L | Categ. M Catég. M | Categ. N Catég. N | Categ. O Catég. O | Categ. P Catég. P | Categ. Q Catég. Q | Country or area [&] Pays ou zone [&] |
| 8.1 | 22.6 | 5.4 | 5.3 | 27.0 | 20.3 | 12.0 | 18.5 | 3.2 | ... | Mongolia[62,63] |
| 15.2 | 16.9 | 7.2 | 4.0 | 17.8 | 35.0 | 24.8 | 18.5 | 2.9 | ... | Mongolie[62,63] |
| 10.0 | 24.8 | 6.2 | 5.4 | 26.1 | 20.3 | 13.6 | 16.9 | 3.1 | ... | |
| 18.4 | 17.6 | 9.7 | 5.8 | 20.1 | 37.5 | 25.8 | 17.6 | 2.9 | ... | |
| 10.3 | 26.0 | 6.3 | 4.3 | 26.1 | 20.4 | 12.6 | 13.7 | 3.7 | ... | |
| 19.2 | 16.4 | 9.8 | 4.7 | 20.6 | 38.4 | 26.9 | 13.0 | 5.0 | ... | |
| 7.0 | 11.4 | 1.0 | 2.9 | 14.4 | 4.4 | 4.0 | 9.8 | ... | 0.4 | Montenegro[45,64] |
| 4.0 | 3.2 | 1.2 | 1.6 | 8.4 | 9.1 | 8.3 | 8.0 | ... | 0.0 | Monténégro[45,64] |
| ... | 323.9 | 77.5[16] | ... | 919.1[38] | ... | ... | ... | ... | ... | Morocco[3] |
| ... | 23.5 | 38.5[16] | ... | 409.8[38] | ... | ... | ... | ... | ... | Maroc[3] |
| ... | 350.1 | 91.2[16] | ... | 902.1[38] | ... | ... | ... | ... | ... | |
| ... | 30.2 | 39.1[16] | ... | 399.3[38] | ... | ... | ... | ... | ... | |
| ... | 367.7 | 105.0[16] | ... | 1 016.2[38] | ... | ... | ... | ... | ... | |
| ... | 27.1 | 47.4[16] | ... | 433.3[38] | ... | ... | ... | ... | ... | |
| 3.0 | 12.2 | 2.5 | 17.9 | 15.4 | 11.7 | 3.0 | 24.3 | 4.8 | 0.2 | Namibia[65] |
| 4.7 | 2.1 | 2.4 | 21.4 | 9.0 | 18.8 | 10.1 | 22.0 | 17.5 | 0.2 | Namibie[65] |
| 5.9 | 12.7 | 3.5 | 5.3 | 20.2 | 12.3 | 3.5 | 7.5 | 4.1 | 0.1 | |
| 7.2 | 3.1 | 4.1 | 4.1 | 10.5 | 18.9 | 10.5 | 5.2 | 20.0 | 0.0 | |
| 63.0 | 130.0 | 17.0 | 25.0 | 64.0 | 126.0 | 26.0 | 51.0 | 80.0 | 6.0 | Nepal[3] |
| 52.0 | 6.0 | 2.0 | 6.0 | 6.0 | 37.0 | 7.0 | 6.0 | 209.0 | 1.0 | Népal[3] |
| 140.0 | 336.0 | 152.0 | 595.0 | 339.0 | 214.0 | 222.0 | 160.0 | ... | ... | Netherlands[3] |
| 157.0 | 128.0 | 121.0 | 401.0 | 197.0 | 296.0 | 952.0 | 197.0 | 3.0 | ... | Pays-Bas[3] |
| 146.0 | 363.0 | 145.0 | 531.0 | 341.0 | 201.0 | 211.0 | 137.0 | ... | ... | |
| 165.0 | 123.0 | 112.0 | 364.0 | 205.0 | 311.0 | 939.0 | 169.0 | 3.0 | ... | |
| 150.0 | 350.0 | 140.0 | 545.0 | 330.0 | 203.0 | 227.0 | 128.0 | ... | ... | |
| 157.0 | 135.0 | 120.0 | 367.0 | 208.0 | 315.0 | 980.0 | 179.0 | 3.0 | ... | |
| 1.6 | 2.9 | 1.4 | 2.4 | 3.6 | 0.9 | 0.9 | 1.3 | 0.1 | 0.1 | Netherlands Antilles[3,64] |
| 2.4 | 1.3 | 2.3 | 1.4 | 2.2 | 1.9 | 3.4 | 2.0 | 2.0 | 0.1 | Antilles néerlandaises[3,64] |
| 1.7 | 2.7 | 1.4 | 2.5 | 3.4 | 1.0 | 0.9 | 1.4 | 0.1 | 0.1 | |
| 2.1 | 1.4 | 2.3 | 1.5 | 2.0 | 1.9 | 3.4 | 1.9 | 1.7 | 0.1 | |
| 1.7 | 2.5 | 1.3 | 2.4 | 3.0 | 1.0 | 0.8 | 1.3 | 0.1 | 0.1 | |
| 1.9 | 1.5 | 2.2 | 1.6 | 1.9 | 1.9 | 3.5 | 2.0 | 1.7 | 0.1 | |
| 1.2 | 2.7 | 0.6 | 2.1 | 6.3 | 2.8 | 1.1 | 0.5 | 0.3 | 0.5 | New Caledonia[21] |
| 1.7 | 1.0 | 0.9 | 1.2 | 3.3 | 3.8 | 2.3 | 0.4 | 3.1 | 0.4 | Nouvelle-Calédonie[21] |
| 33.6 | 82.6 | 25.4 | 122.3 | 55.6 | 45.5 | 32.8 | 40.6 | 0.2 | ... | New Zealand[3,6] |
| 60.7 | 35.9 | 35.2 | 95.8 | 58.6 | 115.5 | 147.5 | 54.3 | 2.4 | ... | Nouvelle-Zélande[3,6] |
| 36.5 | 82.6 | 28.6 | 130.7 | 63.3 | 47.5 | 31.1 | 42.9 | 0.2 | ... | |
| 63.1 | 36.2 | 37.2 | 104.2 | 63.5 | 115.6 | 156.0 | 58.8 | 2.3 | ... | |
| 33.5 | 79.7 | 33.2 | 135.0 | 63.2 | 49.1 | 33.8 | 40.8 | 0.4 | ... | |
| 63.1 | 37.0 | 37.5 | 111.9 | 71.3 | 114.0 | 159.5 | 51.2 | 2.8 | ... | |
| 28.0 | 109.0 | 25.0 | 140.0 | 80.0 | 68.0 | 80.0 | 43.0 | ... | ... | Norway |
| 42.0 | 40.0 | 23.0 | 83.0 | 64.0 | 127.0 | 369.0 | 53.0 | 2.0 | ... | Norvège |
| 27.0 | 113.0 | 26.0 | 146.0 | 77.0 | 65.0 | 83.0 | 41.0 | 0.0 | ... | |
| 44.0 | 39.0 | 24.0 | 84.0 | 62.0 | 125.0 | 375.0 | 54.0 | 2.0 | ... | |
| 25.0 | 117.0 | 28.0 | 157.0 | 79.0 | 67.0 | 86.0 | 44.0 | 1.0 | ... | |
| 43.0 | 40.0 | 26.0 | 95.0 | 65.0 | 127.0 | 385.0 | 54.0 | 3.0 | ... | |

**30**

**Employment by economic activity**—Total employment and persons employed by ISIC Rev. 3 categories (thousands) *(continued)*
**Emploi par activité économique**—Emploi total et personnes employées par branches de CITI Rév. 3 (milliers) *(suite)*

| Country or area [&] / Pays ou zone [&] | Year / Année | Sex / Sexe | Total employment / Emploi total | ISIC Rev. 3 Tabulation categories + / CITI Rév. 3 Catégories de classement + | | | | | | |
|---|---|---|---|---|---|---|---|---|---|---|
| | | | | Categ. A / Catég. A | Categ. B / Catég. B | Categ. C / Catég. C | Categ. D / Catég. D | Categ. E / Catég. E | Categ. F / Catég. F | Categ. G / Catég. G |
| Occupied Palestinian Terr.[3] Terr. palestinien occupé[3] | 2004 | M | 473.8 | 56.4 | 0.3 | 1.7 | 63.1 | 2.0 | 67.3 | 94.9 |
| | 2004 | F | 104.7 | 35.3 | ... | ... | 8.4 | ^0.0 | 0.2 | 7.4 |
| | 2005 | M | 527.8 | 57.6 | 0.5 | 1.4 | 72.4 | 2.3 | 81.4 | 101.6 |
| | 2005 | F | 105.1 | 34.2 | ... | ... | 8.5 | 0.1 | 0.3 | 8.5 |
| | 2006 | M | 546.0 | 64.9 | 0.9 | 2.2 | 70.3 | 2.4 | 73.7 | 106.2 |
| | 2006 | F | 120.4 | 41.2 | ... | ... | 10.2 | 0.1 | 0.2 | 8.5 |
| Oman[6,26,67] Oman[6,26,67] | 1996 | M | 226.8 | 9.3 | 7.8 | 7.4 | 3.5 | 0.3 | 6.3 | 13.5 |
| | 1996 | F | 25.4 | 1.2 | 0.1 | 0.2 | 1.3 | ^0.0 | 0.2 | 1.7 |
| | 2000 | M | 243.1 | 8.9 | 7.2 | 7.8 | 9.4 | 1.1 | 7.8 | 14.2 |
| | 2000 | F | 38.6 | 2.0 | ^0.0 | 0.7 | 4.5 | ^0.0 | 0.2 | 2.4 |
| Panama[3,68] Panama[3,68] | 2004 | M | 734.3 | 161.0 | 8.8 | 0.7 | 67.7 | 7.5 | 88.8 | 130.2 |
| | 2004 | F | 400.4 | 11.3 | 0.7 | ... | 32.7 | 0.9 | 1.8 | 77.1 |
| | 2005 | M | 755.7 | 158.5 | 9.1 | 1.0 | 69.4 | 6.5 | 87.8 | 138.3 |
| | 2005 | F | 432.6 | 18.3 | 0.5 | ^0.0 | 34.9 | 1.3 | 3.3 | 88.6 |
| | 2006 | M | 777.5 | 164.1 | 9.5 | 2.0 | 72.8 | 6.7 | 99.2 | 143.5 |
| | 2006 | F | 433.2 | 19.0 | 0.4 | 0.3 | 32.4 | 1.8 | 3.6 | 86.0 |
| Papua New Guinea[7,69] Papouaise-Nvl-Guinée[7,69] | 2000 | MF | 2 344.7 | 1 666.2 | 30.0 | 9.3 | 25.6 | 2.2 | 48.3 | 353.2 |
| Peru[21,25,70] Pérou[21,25,70] | 2004[28] | M | 1 997.5 | 17.2 | 4.7 | 4.7 | 379.3 | 9.0 | 196.0 | 486.4 |
| | 2004[28] | F | 1 369.4 | 5.1 | ... | 0.9 | 150.4 | 0.4 | 2.0 | 490.6 |
| | 2005[71] | M | 1 965.9 | 18.4 | 3.7 | 8.7 | 430.5 | 3.4 | 173.5 | 462.8 |
| | 2005[71] | F | 1 434.4 | 2.4 | ... | ... | 188.7 | 0.2 | 3.7 | 476.5 |
| | 2006[34] | M | 2 123.5 | 12.7 | 8.3 | 11.5 | 411.7 | 9.0 | 203.8 | 488.7 |
| | 2006[34] | F | 1 533.2 | 5.9 | 0.5 | 4.8 | 201.1 | ... | 5.7 | 547.0 |
| Philippines[3,64,72] Philippines[3,64,72] | 2004 | M | 19 836.0 | 7 572.0 | 1 279.0 | 87.0 | 1 684.0 | 96.0 | 1 616.0 | 2 319.0 |
| | 2004 | F | 11 905.0 | 2 849.0 | 86.0 | 9.0 | 1 335.0 | 25.0 | 27.0 | 3 469.0 |
| | 2005 | M | 20 205.0 | 7 720.0 | 1 304.0 | 100.0 | 1 640.0 | 87.0 | 1 581.0 | 2 507.0 |
| | 2005 | F | 12 670.0 | 3 044.0 | 103.0 | 17.0 | 1 403.0 | 22.0 | 35.0 | 3 708.0 |
| | 2006 | M | 20 422.0 | 7 725.0 | 1 318.0 | 124.0 | 1 650.0 | 101.0 | 1 601.0 | 2 502.0 |
| | 2006 | F | 12 766.0 | 3 029.0 | 94.0 | 11.0 | 1 361.0 | 22.0 | 26.0 | 3 725.0 |
| Poland[3,73] Pologne[3,73] | 2004 | M | 7 566.0 | 1 400.0 | 10.0 | 199.0 | 1 795.0 | 179.0 | 735.0 | 950.0 |
| | 2004 | F | 6 230.0 | 1 072.0 | 2.0 | 28.0 | 945.0 | 43.0 | 54.0 | 1 047.0 |
| | 2005 | M | 7 809.0 | 1 391.0 | 11.0 | 201.0 | 1 882.0 | 181.0 | 784.0 | 961.0 |
| | 2005 | F | 6 307.0 | 1 048.0 | 2.0 | 25.0 | 949.0 | 47.0 | 59.0 | 1 059.0 |
| | 2006 | M | 8 081.0 | 1 316.0 | 9.0 | 212.0 | 1 989.0 | 172.0 | 864.0 | 963.0 |
| | 2006 | F | 6 513.0 | 977.0 | 1.0 | 26.0 | 1 000.0 | 51.0 | 61.0 | 1 097.0 |
| Portugal[3] Portugal[3] | 2004 | M | 2 788.8 | 302.1 | 18.8 | 13.3 | 574.7 | 26.3 | 521.9 | 437.6 |
| | 2004 | F | 2 338.6 | 294.6 | 2.6[74] | 1.3[74] | 427.5 | 4.9 | 26.2 | 344.4 |
| | 2005 | M | 2 765.4 | 285.4 | 16.5 | 17.9 | 561.5 | 20.4 | 528.7 | 435.0 |
| | 2005 | F | 2 357.2 | 302.2 | 2.2[74] | 1.2[74] | 407.1 | 4.4 | 25.3 | 337.9 |
| | 2006 | M | 2 789.7 | 295.5 | 14.9 | 16.2 | 565.5 | 21.0 | 527.9 | 419.7 |
| | 2006 | F | 2 369.8 | 292.2 | 1.3[74] | 1.4[74] | 414.9 | 5.1 | 25.1 | 331.6 |
| Qatar[3,75] Qatar[3,75] | 1997 | M | 242.4 | 9.0 | 1.3 | 9.0 | 24.0 | 3.2 | 55.9 | 30.1 |
| | 1997 | F | 37.7 | ^0.0 | ... | 0.4 | 0.1 | ^0.0 | 0.2 | 0.6 |
| | 2004 | M | 373.1 | 10.2 | 1.8 | 16.9 | 39.7 | 4.2 | 116.6 | 52.3 |
| | 2004 | F | 64.5 | ^0.0 | ^0.0 | 1.1 | 0.4 | 0.1 | 0.4 | 2.1 |

30

**Employment by economic activity**— Total employment and persons employed by ISIC Rev. 3 categories (thousands) (*continued*)

**Emploi par activité économique**— Emploi total et personnes employées par branches de CITI Rév. 3 (milliers) (*suite*)

| Categ. H / Catég. H | Categ. I / Catég. I | Categ. J / Catég. J | Categ. K / Catég. K | Categ. L / Catég. L | Categ. M / Catég. M | Categ. N / Catég. N | Categ. O / Catég. O | Categ. P / Catég. P | Categ. Q / Catég. Q | Country or area [&] / Pays ou zone [&] |
|---|---|---|---|---|---|---|---|---|---|---|
| 10.4 | 30.6 | 3.4 | 7.3 | 72.0 | 31.6 | 15.2 | 12.0 | 0.1 | 5.5 | Occupied Palestinian Terr.[3] |
| 0.2 | 0.7 | 1.1 | 2.1 | 6.1 | 29.3 | 8.6 | 3.4 | 0.2 | 1.8 | Terr. palestinien occupé[3] |
| 12.6 | 35.5 | 2.7 | 8.7 | 87.6 | 30.9 | 13.7 | 13.8 | ^0.0 | 5.2 | |
| 0.2 | 0.6 | 0.8 | 1.8 | 5.4 | 29.9 | 9.1 | 3.7 | 0.1 | 2.0 | |
| 13.1 | 37.2 | 3.3 | 8.9 | 92.7 | 34.2 | 15.1 | 15.6 | 0.2 | 5.3 | |
| 0.4 | 1.1 | 1.2 | 2.3 | 6.2 | 33.5 | 9.3 | 3.8 | 0.2 | 2.0 | |
| 0.6 | 14.6 | 4.9 | 2.7 | 141.3 | 9.6 | 3.3 | 0.9 | ^0.0 | 0.1 | Oman[6,26,67] |
| 0.2 | 0.3 | 1.9 | 0.7 | 6.6 | 8.3 | 2.4 | 0.1 | ... | ^0.0 | Oman[6,26,67] |
| 2.3 | 19.5 | 4.7 | 1.9 | 133.6 | 17.8 | 5.2 | 1.2 | ^0.0 | ^0.0 | |
| 0.2 | 0.8 | 1.4 | 1.1 | 3.3 | 16.0 | 5.4 | 0.2 | ... | 0.1 | |
| 26.7 | 76.4 | 9.1 | 32.1 | 42.8 | 21.9 | 14.9 | 37.1 | 8.0 | 0.7 | Panama[3,68] |
| 34.5 | 13.0 | 15.9 | 22.0 | 30.9 | 44.8 | 28.3 | 25.1 | 61.3 | 0.1 | Panama[3,68] |
| 28.5 | 79.5 | 9.5 | 39.0 | 40.3 | 21.8 | 15.2 | 42.1 | 9.0 | 0.1 | |
| 41.1 | 11.7 | 14.8 | 22.7 | 29.0 | 43.1 | 32.4 | 29.5 | 61.0 | 0.4 | |
| 25.0 | 77.9 | 11.2 | 40.3 | 41.8 | 20.3 | 15.9 | 39.2 | 7.6 | 0.6 | |
| 39.5 | 12.9 | 15.2 | 22.4 | 28.5 | 42.4 | 32.4 | 28.9 | 67.3 | 0.2 | |
| | | | | | | | | | | Papua New Guinea[7,69] |
| 4.4 | 24.5 | 3.7 | 27.5 | 32.0 | 27.1 | 12.3 | 31.4 | 15.5 | 0.2 | Papouaise-Nvl-Guinée[7,69] |
| 77.6 | 321.1 | 17.9 | 127.6 | 127.2 | 86.7 | 25.4 | 109.2 | 7.1 | ... | Peru[21,25,70] |
| 135.4 | 23.2 | 15.3 | 52.5 | 43.8 | 117.1 | 60.5 | 95.3 | 177.0 | ... | Pérou[21,25,70] |
| 68.1 | 303.2 | 21.9 | 167.3 | 106.8 | 83.8 | 33.1 | 73.9 | 6.7 | ... | |
| 150.0 | 33.7 | 20.1 | 75.8 | 48.8 | 139.5 | 62.8 | 83.1 | 149.0 | ... | |
| 74.0 | 323.6 | 27.0 | 195.8 | 121.6 | 87.8 | 40.8 | 97.2 | 9.8 | ... | |
| 115.4 | 36.4 | 22.1 | 76.9 | 55.5 | 143.8 | 61.4 | 84.2 | 172.4 | ... | |
| 361.0 | 2 319.0 | 132.0 | 481.0 | 907.0 | 241.0 | 99.0 | 423.0 | 220.0 | 1.0 | Philippines[3,64,72] |
| 437.0 | 126.0 | 166.0 | 221.0 | 543.0 | 717.0 | 262.0 | 386.0 | 1 245.0 | ... | Philippines[3,64,72] |
| 396.0 | 2 334.0 | 140.0 | 495.0 | 933.0 | 251.0 | 102.0 | 384.0 | 230.0 | 2.0 | |
| 475.0 | 136.0 | 197.0 | 241.0 | 562.0 | 739.0 | 260.0 | 397.0 | 1 332.0 | 1.0 | |
| 423.0 | 2 327.0 | 152.0 | 534.0 | 960.0 | 258.0 | 108.0 | 392.0 | 245.0 | 1.0 | |
| 492.0 | 142.0 | 220.0 | 279.0 | 580.0 | 751.0 | 268.0 | 382.0 | 1 383.0 | 1.0 | |
| 81.0 | 621.0 | 84.0 | 468.0 | 436.0 | 238.0 | 160.0 | 205.0 | ... | ... | Poland[3,73] |
| 155.0 | 211.0 | 187.0 | 331.0 | 429.0 | 822.0 | 664.0 | 231.0 | 15.0 | ... | Pologne[3,73] |
| 87.0 | 658.0 | 94.0 | 485.0 | 451.0 | 251.0 | 158.0 | 213.0 | 1.0 | ... | |
| 161.0 | 205.0 | 200.0 | 337.0 | 442.0 | 852.0 | 662.0 | 246.0 | 11.0 | ... | |
| 87.0 | 735.0 | 96.0 | 472.0 | 457.0 | 260.0 | 171.0 | 274.0 | 2.0 | ... | |
| 185.0 | 207.0 | 232.0 | 365.0 | 460.0 | 880.0 | 700.0 | 260.0 | 9.0 | ... | |
| 106.3 | 164.8 | 60.8 | 153.0 | 207.1 | 75.2 | 52.7 | 71.2 | 2.1 | 1.2[74] | Portugal[3] |
| 159.2 | 49.7 | 35.9 | 139.2 | 129.3 | 231.4 | 260.3 | 86.0 | 145.2 | 1.0[74] | Portugal[3] |
| 108.7 | 163.9 | 55.3 | 150.5 | 214.9 | 75.4 | 60.0 | 68.2 | 1.7 | 1.3[74] | |
| 167.1 | 56.8 | 39.9 | 133.2 | 132.6 | 239.5 | 266.9 | 90.3 | 149.2 | 1.3[74] | |
| 108.1 | 178.8 | 52.4 | 159.6 | 219.2 | 77.4 | 59.7 | 70.1 | 2.2 | 1.5[74] | |
| 171.9 | 60.8 | 37.7 | 134.9 | 135.1 | 241.3 | 270.1 | 94.8 | 150.2 | 1.4[74] | |
| 5.8 | 9.1 | 2.7 | 4.3 | 47.7 | 5.7 | 2.6 | 7.3 | 24.0 | 0.5 | Qatar[3,75] |
| 0.2 | 0.5 | 0.4 | 0.3 | 2.2 | 8.2 | 2.9 | 0.3 | 21.1 | 0.1 | Qatar[3,75] |
| 9.7 | 13.1 | 3.5 | 11.2 | 47.3 | 7.5 | 5.4 | 9.0 | 23.9 | 1.0 | |
| 0.6 | 2.2 | 1.3 | 0.7 | 6.2 | 12.4 | 6.2 | 1.2 | 29.4 | 0.2 | |

| Country or area [&]<br>Pays ou zone [&] | Year<br>Année | Sex<br>Sexe | Total employment<br>Emploi total | ISIC Rev. 3 Tabulation categories +<br>CITI Rév. 3 Catégories de classement + | | | | | | |
|---|---|---|---|---|---|---|---|---|---|---|
| | | | | Categ. A<br>Catég. A | Categ. B<br>Catég. B | Categ. C<br>Catég. C | Categ. D<br>Catég. D | Categ. E<br>Catég. E | Categ. F<br>Catég. F | Categ. G<br>Catég. G |
| Romania[3]<br>Roumanie[3] | 2004 | M | 4 980.0 | 1 543.1 | 2.3 | 115.0 | 1 072.4 | 147.7 | 430.9 | 430.1 |
| | 2004 | F | 4 177.6 | 1 349.7 | 1.0 | 19.5 | 978.9 | 44.1 | 47.6 | 513.3 |
| | 2005 | M | 5 011.2 | 1 572.9 | ... | 101.3 | 1 044.6 | 145.9 | 459.5 | 444.3 |
| | 2005 | F | 4 135.4 | 1 366.5 | ... | 17.9 | 915.1 | 44.4 | 47.1 | 523.4 |
| | 2006 | M | 5 074.0 | 1 508.7 | ... | 101.2 | 1 028.8 | 148.6 | 501.6 | 483.1 |
| | 2006 | F | 4 239.3 | 1 331.7 | ... | 18.5 | 949.4 | 49.0 | 56.0 | 566.3 |
| Russian Federation[76]<br>Fédération de Russie[76] | 2004 | M | 34 181.0 | 4 056.0 | 168.0 | 938.0 | 7 165.0 | 1 401.0 | 3 335.0 | 4 049.0 |
| | 2004 | F | 33 094.0 | 2 572.0 | 37.0 | 274.0 | 5 510.0 | 599.0 | 792.0 | 6 082.0 |
| | 2005 | M | 34 549.0 | 4 106.0 | 138.0 | 966.0 | 7 129.0 | 1 361.0 | 3 708.0 | 4 057.0 |
| | 2005 | F | 33 620.0 | 2 664.0 | 28.0 | 270.0 | 5 406.0 | 599.0 | 867.0 | 6 326.0 |
| | 2006 | M | 34 685.0 | 4 066.0 | 144.0 | 925.0 | 7 162.0 | 1 441.0 | 3 605.0 | 4 088.0 |
| | 2006 | F | 34 149.0 | 2 620.0 | 31.0 | 272.0 | 5 308.0 | 622.0 | 855.0 | 6 506.0 |
| Saint Helena[50,65]<br>Sainte-Hélène[50,65] | 1998 | M | 1.1 | 0.2 | ^0.0 | ... | 0.1 | ^0.0 | 0.3 | 0.1 |
| | 1998 | F | 0.9 | ^0.0 | ... | ... | ^0.0 | ^0.0 | ^0.0 | 0.2 |
| Saint Lucia[3]<br>Sainte-Lucie[3] | 2002 | M | 32.1 | 4.4 | 0.4 | ... | 2.0 | 0.5 | 4.6 | 3.4 |
| | 2002 | F | 26.4 | 2.3 | ^0.0 | ... | 2.5 | 0.1 | 0.3 | 5.2 |
| | 2003 | M | 36.5 | 5.4 | 0.6 | ... | 2.3 | 0.5 | 4.7 | 4.7 |
| | 2003 | F | 27.4 | 2.3 | ^0.0 | ... | 2.3 | 0.1 | 0.2 | 5.7 |
| | 2004 | M | 34.8 | 5.9 | 0.7 | ... | 2.3 | 0.4 | 4.8 | 4.4 |
| | 2004 | F | 27.4 | 2.6 | 0.1 | ... | 2.4 | 0.1 | 0.2 | 5.4 |
| San Marino[3,47]<br>Saint-Marin[3,47] | 2004 | M | 11.8 | 0.1 | ... | ... | 4.6 | ... | 1.6 | 1.5 |
| | 2004 | F | 8.1 | ^0.0 | ... | ... | 1.8 | ... | 0.1 | 1.7 |
| | 2005 | M | 11.9 | 0.1 | ... | ... | 4.4 | ... | 1.6 | 1.6 |
| | 2005 | F | 8.2 | ^0.0 | ... | ... | 1.8 | ... | 0.1 | 1.4 |
| | 2006 | M | 12.2 | 0.1 | ... | ... | 4.4 | ... | 1.6 | 1.7 |
| | 2006 | F | 8.5 | ^0.0 | ... | ... | 1.8 | ... | 0.1 | 1.5 |
| Saudi Arabia[3]<br>Arabie saoudite[3] | 2001 | M | 5 027.7 | 334.2 | 9.1 | 87.1 | 460.3 | 77.3 | 585.0 | 832.6 |
| | 2001 | F | 780.9 | 6.1 | ... | 0.8 | 7.5 | ... | 0.3 | 4.6 |
| | 2002 | M | 5 115.8 | 258.6 | 12.2 | 94.6 | 439.4 | 65.6 | 629.3 | 856.4 |
| | 2002 | F | 797.2 | 4.9 | ... | 0.8 | 8.9 | ... | 0.2 | 5.3 |
| | 2006[35] | M | 6 461.5 | 295.2 | ... | 102.1 | 495.7 | 79.5 | 835.4 | 1 200.3 |
| | 2006[35] | F | 1 061.5 | 4.3 | ... | 0.1 | 9.4 | ... | 1.5 | 9.8 |
| Serbia[3,34]<br>Serbie[3,34] | 2004 | M | 1 708.9 | 406.1 | 3.0 | 34.5 | 357.5 | 37.6 | 133.1 | 218.3 |
| | 2004 | F | 1 222.0 | 294.6 | 0.4 | 3.2 | 193.9 | 9.9 | 19.3 | 223.5 |
| | 2005 | M | 1 635.0 | 379.7 | 1.6 | 29.8 | 332.9 | 46.4 | 152.6 | 208.7 |
| | 2005 | F | 1 098.4 | 255.7 | 0.5 | 3.1 | 164.6 | 10.6 | 13.9 | 198.0 |
| | 2006 | M | 1 554.7 | 332.0 | 1.7 | 30.7 | 343.1 | 51.0 | 145.3 | 209.7 |
| | 2006 | F | 1 076.0 | 206.7 | ... | 0.4 | 175.5 | 10.9 | 13.9 | 197.2 |
| Sierra Leone[7,47]<br>Sierra Leone[7,47] | 2004 | M | 987.2 | 617.9 | 33.3 | 59.3 | 7.4 | 7.1 | 28.2 | 102.2 |
| | 2004 | F | 945.8 | 654.3 | 17.8 | 9.7 | 2.0 | 1.2 | 10.8 | 167.3 |
| Singapore[77,78]<br>Singapour[77,78] | 2003 | M | 948.7 | 10.4[79] | ... | ... | 188.6 | ... | 80.1 | 142.6 |
| | 2003 | F | 656.6 | 3.4[79] | ... | ... | 115.0 | ... | 17.6 | 111.1 |
| | 2004 | M | 960.8 | 10.9[79] | ... | ... | 183.9 | ... | 77.6 | 155.3 |
| | 2004 | F | 671.3 | 2.8[79] | ... | ... | 114.0 | ... | 15.0 | 120.1 |
| | 2006[53] | M | 1 036.5 | 16.5[79] | ... | ... | 191.3 | ... | 77.8 | 161.1 |
| | 2006[53] | F | 760.2 | 6.0[79] | ... | ... | 110.4 | ... | 17.2 | 140.0 |

30 **Employment by economic activity**—Total employment and persons employed by ISIC Rev. 3 categories (thousands) *(continued)*

**Emploi par activité économique**—Emploi total et personnes employées par branches de CITI Rév. 3 (milliers) *(suite)*

| ISIC Rev. 3 Tabulation categories +<br>CITI Rév. 3 Catégories de classement + | | | | | | | | | | Country or area [&] |
|---|---|---|---|---|---|---|---|---|---|---|
| Categ. H<br>Catég. H | Categ. I<br>Catég. I | Categ. J<br>Catég. J | Categ. K<br>Catég. K | Categ. L<br>Catég.L | Categ. M<br>Catég. M | Categ. N<br>Catég. N | Categ. O<br>Catég. O | Categ. P<br>Catég. P | Categ. Q<br>Catég. Q | Pays ou zone [&] |
| 49.4 | 339.5 | 29.1 | 140.7 | 370.1 | 107.5 | 77.6 | 124.8 | ... | ... | Romania[3] |
| 98.5 | 114.6 | 57.1 | 90.9 | 168.1 | 295.3 | 284.1 | 114.9 | ... | ... | Roumanie[3] |
| 52.2 | 341.9 | 30.2 | 139.2 | 349.9 | 110.4 | 80.8 | 135.0 | ... | ... | |
| 98.6 | 108.0 | 55.3 | 92.5 | 170.2 | 302.4 | 272.8 | 120.5 | ... | ... | |
| 52.6 | 376.6 | 29.2 | 172.3 | 335.5 | 107.0 | 86.7 | 139.6 | ... | ... | |
| 90.4 | 115.2 | 62.8 | 109.2 | 172.0 | 303.6 | 291.6 | 123.0 | ... | ... | |
| 270.0 | 4 412.0 | 290.0 | 2 343.0 | 2 967.0 | 1 215.0 | 893.0 | 679.0 | ... | ... | Russian Federation[76] |
| 953.0 | 1 849.0 | 628.0 | 1 776.0 | 1 734.0 | 4 926.0 | 3 941.0 | 1 421.0 | ... | 1.0 | Fédération de Russie[76] |
| 293.0 | 4 321.0 | 347.0 | 2 265.0 | 3 023.0 | 1 243.0 | 845.0 | 739.0 | 4.0 | 3.0 | |
| 1 004.0 | 1 928.0 | 615.0 | 1 774.0 | 1 792.0 | 4 960.0 | 3 856.0 | 1 507.0 | 22.0 | 1.0 | |
| 292.0 | 4 345.0 | 359.0 | 2 327.0 | 3 005.0 | 1 198.0 | 943.0 | 780.0 | 4.0 | 2.0 | |
| 1 100.0 | 1 867.0 | 701.0 | 1 819.0 | 1 871.0 | 4 998.0 | 3 951.0 | 1 610.0 | 17.0 | 1.0 | |
| ^0.0 | 0.1 | ^0.0 | ^0.0 | 0.1 | ^0.0 | ^0.0 | ^0.0 | ^0.0 | ^0.0 | Saint Helena[50,65] |
| ^0.0 | 0.1 | ^0.0 | ^0.0 | 0.2 | 0.1 | 0.1 | 0.1 | ^0.0 | ^0.0 | Sainte-Hélène[50,65] |
| 2.9 | 2.4 | 0.3 | 0.9 | 3.2 | 0.5 | 0.1 | 0.9 | 0.5 | ... | Saint Lucia[3] |
| 3.3 | 0.8 | 0.6 | 0.7 | 3.7 | 1.4 | 0.2 | 0.5 | 1.5 | ... | Sainte-Lucie[3] |
| 3.3 | 3.1 | 0.6 | 1.1 | 3.6 | 0.6 | 0.1 | 0.8 | 0.5 | ... | |
| 3.4 | 1.1 | 0.6 | 1.0 | 3.7 | 1.5 | 0.5 | 0.8 | 1.6 | ... | |
| 3.0 | 2.5 | 0.4 | 1.5 | 3.7 | 0.2 | 0.1 | 1.1 | 0.2 | ... | |
| 3.7 | 0.8 | 0.7 | 1.1 | 4.5 | 0.9 | 0.3 | 0.9 | 1.7 | ... | |
| ... | 0.3 | 0.4 | ... | 0.7 | ^0.0 | 0.3 | 2.2 | ... | ... | San Marino[3,47] |
| ... | 0.2 | 0.3 | ... | 1.4 | ^0.0 | 0.7 | 1.7 | ... | ... | Saint-Marin[3,47] |
| ^0.0 | 0.3 | 0.4 | 1.5 | 1.3 | 0.1 | 0.4 | 0.2 | ... | ... | |
| 0.1 | 0.2 | 0.4 | 1.1 | 1.1 | 0.5 | 0.8 | 0.7 | ... | ... | |
| 0.1 | 0.3 | 0.5 | 1.5 | 1.3 | 0.1 | 0.4 | 0.3 | ... | ... | |
| 0.1 | 0.2 | 0.4 | 1.2 | 1.1 | 0.5 | 0.8 | 0.7 | ... | ... | |
| 154.2 | 242.1 | 56.8 | 144.3 | 1 139.0 | 411.1 | 187.9 | 100.2 | 191.7 | 5.8 | Saudi Arabia[3] |
| 0.4 | 5.8 | 1.7 | ... | 18.6 | 308.9 | 90.2 | 1.7 | 329.6 | 1.0 | Arabie saoudite[3] |
| 166.8 | 258.9 | 48.5 | 142.4 | 1 195.2 | 419.2 | 172.6 | 112.5 | 235.6 | 8.0 | |
| 3.5 | 6.4 | 1.3 | 0.9 | 17.6 | 332.3 | 51.4 | 3.0 | 360.3 | 0.4 | |
| 239.8 | 289.5 | 81.5 | 245.3 | 1 394.8 | 490.2 | 235.2 | 162.3 | 307.0 | 7.9 | |
| 1.5 | 1.8 | 5.1 | 7.3 | 31.2 | 417.0 | 90.3 | 6.9 | 474.6 | 0.7 | |
| 41.2 | 132.6 | 19.1 | 40.9 | 111.0 | 51.1 | 41.7 | 73.9 | 2.1 | 2.7 | Serbia[3,34] |
| 39.5 | 31.1 | 26.0 | 41.5 | 59.8 | 97.9 | 124.9 | 48.3 | 6.1 | 1.2 | Serbie[3,34] |
| 36.4 | 125.6 | 16.5 | 38.9 | 108.9 | 47.4 | 37.8 | 71.2 | 0.4 | 0.4 | |
| 43.6 | 27.2 | 27.0 | 31.0 | 50.5 | 96.1 | 120.8 | 49.5 | 5.0 | 1.2 | |
| 43.4 | 119.2 | 17.0 | 32.9 | 91.0 | 33.7 | 37.9 | 64.3 | 1.5 | 0.4 | |
| 41.1 | 32.2 | 26.0 | 37.3 | 52.0 | 95.8 | 135.8 | 45.7 | 5.4 | ... | |
| 2.6 | 14.4 | 4.0 | 5.5 | 21.1 | 23.3 | 9.9 | 44.4 | 4.0 | 2.5 | Sierra Leone[7,47] |
| 2.3 | 1.3 | 2.9 | 5.3 | 4.9 | 11.3 | 10.0 | 39.1 | 4.3 | 1.3 | Sierra Leone[7,47] |
| 53.0 | 136.6 | 35.4 | 116.6 | 130.1[80] | ... | 13.6 | 41.6[29] | ... | ... | Singapore[77,78] |
| 54.8 | 46.9 | 53.2 | 90.1 | 86.3[80] | ... | 42.1 | 36.1[29] | ... | ... | Singapour[77,78] |
| 52.3 | 135.2 | 37.9 | 123.4 | 129.4[80] | ... | 14.1 | 40.7[29] | ... | ... | |
| 55.6 | 48.1 | 53.9 | 92.8 | 82.8[80] | ... | 47.8 | 38.0[29] | ... | ... | |
| 61.9 | 179.7 | 45.4 | 115.8 | 129.6[80] | ... | 16.6 | 40.9[29] | ... | ... | |
| 66.9 | 69.1 | 61.0 | 101.5 | 93.8[80] | ... | 54.2 | 40.1[29] | ... | ... | |

| Country or area [&]<br>Pays ou zone [&] | Year<br>Année | Sex<br>Sexe | Total<br>employment<br>Emploi<br>total | Categ. A<br>Catég. A | Categ. B<br>Catég. B | Categ. C<br>Catég. C | Categ. D<br>Catég. D | Categ. E<br>Catég. E | Categ. F<br>Catég. F | Categ. G<br>Catég. G |
|---|---|---|---|---|---|---|---|---|---|---|
| Slovakia[3,25,81]<br>Slovaquie[3,25,81] | 2004 | M | 1 193.7 | 82.4[1] | ... | 13.3 | 352.1 | 34.8 | 191.4 | 112.3 |
| | 2004 | F | 976.7 | 27.5[1] | ... | 1.1 | 230.5 | 9.6 | 14.0 | 147.9 |
| | 2005 | M | 1 233.0 | 79.2[1] | ... | 13.4 | 366.2 | 34.6 | 196.9 | 119.7 |
| | 2005 | F | 983.1 | 25.9[1] | ... | 1.4 | 225.7 | 8.1 | 12.9 | 149.8 |
| | 2006 | M | 1 291.1 | 76.7[1] | ... | 15.3 | 380.5 | 33.9 | 213.1 | 129.4 |
| | 2006 | F | 1 010.3 | 24.2[1] | ... | 0.8 | 228.2 | 8.0 | 13.0 | 161.2 |
| Slovenia[3,54]<br>Slovénie[3,54] | 2004 | M | 511.0 | 49.0 | ... | 5.0 | 168.0 | 9.0 | 50.0 | 56.0 |
| | 2004 | F | 434.0 | 42.0 | ... | 1.0 | 103.0 | 1.0 | 5.0 | 64.0 |
| | 2005 | M | 512.0 | 44.0 | ... | 5.0 | 174.0 | 8.0 | 55.0 | 51.0 |
| | 2005 | F | 435.0 | 39.0 | ... | ... | 104.0 | 2.0 | 4.0 | 60.0 |
| | 2006 | M | 521.0 | 51.0 | ... | 5.0 | 168.0 | 8.0 | 53.0 | 58.0 |
| | 2006 | F | 448.0 | 41.0 | ... | 1.0 | 97.0 | 2.0 | 5.0 | 63.0 |
| South Africa[3,4]<br>Afrique du Sud[3,4] | 2004 | M | 6 772.0 | 703.0[1] | ... | 394.0 | 1 117.0 | 74.0 | 747.0 | 1 347.0[37] |
| | 2004 | F | 4 866.0 | 359.0[1] | ... | 11.0 | 597.0 | 25.0 | 77.0 | 1 195.0[37] |
| | 2005 | M | 7 055.0 | 608.0[1] | ... | 388.0 | 1 113.0 | 77.0 | 858.0 | 1 543.0[37] |
| | 2005 | F | 5 242.0 | 317.0[1] | ... | 23.0 | 593.0 | 23.0 | 77.0 | 1 479.0[37] |
| | 2006 | M | 7 320.0 | 662.0[1] | ... | 375.0 | 1 146.0 | 95.0 | 911.0 | 1 581.0[37] |
| | 2006 | F | 5 480.0 | 426.0[1] | ... | 23.0 | 591.0 | 24.0 | 113.0 | 1 474.0[37] |
| Spain[62,82]<br>Espagne[62,82] | 2004 | M | 10 934.3 | 684.9 | 43.7 | 53.4 | 2 282.8 | 84.2 | 2 134.3 | 1 493.0 |
| | 2004 | F | 7 036.5 | 252.7 | 7.6 | 6.2 | 764.8 | 19.5 | 118.9 | 1 324.5 |
| | 2005[53] | M | 11 388.8 | 686.3 | 44.9 | 53.4 | 2 327.8 | 85.7 | 2 230.1 | 1 523.4 |
| | 2005[53] | F | 7 584.4 | 254.3 | 15.2 | 6.9 | 785.2 | 20.9 | 127.1 | 1 363.5 |
| | 2006 | M | 11 742.6 | 638.8 | 42.5 | 60.6 | 2 343.2 | 97.2 | 2 408.5 | 1 538.6 |
| | 2006 | F | 8 005.1 | 254.2 | 8.8 | 5.8 | 763.7 | 21.6 | 134.4 | 1 444.9 |
| Sri Lanka[3,83]<br>Sri Lanka[3,83] | 2005 | M | 4 548.0 | 1 270.6[1] | ... | 1 093.8[85] | ... | ... | ... | 629.2 |
| | 2005 | F | 2 240.1 | 788.7[1] | ... | 616.3[85] | ... | ... | ... | 187.9 |
| | 2006[84] | M | 4 608.8 | 1 326.3[1] | ... | 1 197.6[85] | ... | ... | ... | 716.7 |
| | 2006[84] | F | 2 481.7 | 937.0[1] | ... | 691.4[85] | ... | ... | ... | 245.3 |
| Suriname[3,28]<br>Suriname[3,28] | 2004 | M | 101.9 | 10.1[1] | ... | 8.4 | 8.1 | 1.4 | 13.5 | 15.7 |
| | 2004 | F | 54.8 | 2.5[1] | ... | 0.9 | 2.9 | 0.2 | 0.5 | 9.3 |
| Sweden[86]<br>Suède[86] | 2004 | M | 2 186.0 | 70.0 | 1.0 | 5.0 | 506.0 | 19.0 | 224.0 | 304.0 |
| | 2004 | F | 2 027.0 | 19.0 | ... | 1.0 | 173.0 | 7.0 | 18.0 | 225.0 |
| | 2005[53] | M | 2 225.0 | 65.0 | 2.0 | 6.0 | 489.0 | 19.0 | 236.0 | 306.0 |
| | 2005[53] | F | 2 038.0 | 19.0 | ... | 1.0 | 163.0 | 8.0 | 17.0 | 229.0 |
| | 2006 | M | 2 273.0 | 66.0 | 2.0 | 7.0 | 488.0 | 18.0 | 251.0 | 306.0 |
| | 2006 | F | 2 067.0 | 18.0 | ... | 1.0 | 165.0 | 7.0 | 19.0 | 230.0 |
| Switzerland[3,54,89]<br>Suisse[3,54,89] | 2004 | M | 2 173.0 | 102.0[1] | ... | 463.0[60] | ... | ... | 225.0 | 287.0 |
| | 2004 | F | 1 786.0 | 51.0[1] | ... | 179.0[60] | ... | ... | 28.0 | 290.0 |
| | 2005 | M | 2 172.0 | 103.0[1] | ... | 467.0[60] | ... | ... | 234.0 | 269.0 |
| | 2005 | F | 1 802.0 | 51.0[1] | ... | 176.0[60] | ... | ... | 27.0 | 297.0 |
| | 2006 | M | 2 214.0 | 104.0[1] | ... | 473.0[60] | ... | ... | 246.0 | 273.0 |
| | 2006 | F | 1 837.0 | 50.0[1] | ... | 180.0[60] | ... | ... | 30.0 | 287.0 |
| Tajikistan<br>Tadjikistan | 1995 | MF | 1 853.0 | 1 095.0 | ... | ... | 183.0 | 24.0 | 81.0 | 87.0 |
| | 1996 | MF | 1 731.0 | 1 026.0 | ... | ... | 181.0 | 21.0 | 68.0 | 69.0 |
| | 1997 | MF | 1 143.4 | 527.6 | ... | ... | 136.5 | 18.0 | 44.3 | 40.2 |
| Thailand[3,6,36]<br>Thaïlande[3,6,36] | 2004 | M | 19 698.8 | 8 341.0 | 313.9 | 26.1 | 2 550.2 | 87.2 | 1 594.8 | 2 868.9 |
| | 2004 | F | 16 012.8 | 6 378.4 | 82.1 | 9.1 | 2 763.1 | 11.5 | 283.3 | 2 582.7 |
| | 2005 | M | 19 470.3 | 8 250.9 | 348.7 | 30.2 | 2 507.3 | 88.9 | 1 578.3 | 2 759.0 |
| | 2005 | F | 16 832.1 | 6 756.9 | 92.2 | 9.9 | 2 842.9 | 18.0 | 274.8 | 2 538.0 |
| | 2006 | M | 19 638.4 | 8 117.9 | 337.7 | 42.6 | 2 479.6 | 85.0 | 1 716.4 | 2 817.0 |
| | 2006 | F | 16 706.2 | 6 669.2 | 90.5 | 12.0 | 2 827.0 | 14.3 | 322.5 | 2 584.9 |

**30** Employment by economic activity—Total employment and persons employed by ISIC Rev. 3 categories (thousands) *(continued)*

**Emploi par activité économique**—Emploi total et personnes employées par branches de CITI Rév. 3 (milliers) *(suite)*

| ISIC Rev. 3 Tabulation categories + CITI Rév. 3 Catégories de classement + | | | | | | | | | | Country or area [&] |
|---|---|---|---|---|---|---|---|---|---|---|
| Categ. H Catég. H | Categ. I Catég. I | Categ. J Catég. J | Categ. K Catég. K | Categ. L Catég.L | Categ. M Catég. M | Categ. N Catég. N | Categ. O Catég. O | Categ. P Catég. P | Categ. Q Catég. Q | Pays ou zone [&] |
| 31.6 | 103.1 | 15.1 | 70.4 | 78.9 | 34.9 | 28.3 | 41.7 | 0.8 | 0.2 | Slovakia[3,25,81] |
| 52.7 | 37.5 | 30.8 | 50.0 | 72.8 | 126.1 | 126.1 | 42.2 | 6.5 | 0.2 | Slovaquie[3,25,81] |
| 32.0 | 106.1 | 16.6 | 78.7 | 77.6 | 38.6 | 27.7 | 43.4 | 0.5 | 0.2 | |
| 58.3 | 41.2 | 31.5 | 50.6 | 77.0 | 125.1 | 122.4 | 44.9 | 7.0 | 0.1 | |
| 35.5 | 116.9 | 19.4 | 75.7 | 82.5 | 40.7 | 29.9 | 41.0 | 0.2 | 0.1 | |
| 66.3 | 39.3 | 32.5 | 55.9 | 79.3 | 126.1 | 124.6 | 44.4 | 5.6 | 0.1 | |
| 15.0 | 44.0 | 7.0 | 31.0 | 27.0 | 16.0 | 8.0 | 21.0 | ... | ... | Slovenia[3,54] |
| 23.0 | 13.0 | 15.0 | 27.0 | 29.0 | 49.0 | 40.0 | 19.0 | ... | ... | Slovénie[3,54] |
| 16.0 | 40.0 | 9.0 | 34.0 | 30.0 | 16.0 | 8.0 | 18.0 | ... | ... | |
| 25.0 | 13.0 | 14.0 | 28.0 | 29.0 | 53.0 | 43.0 | 19.0 | ... | ... | |
| 12.0 | 39.0 | 8.0 | 38.0 | 29.0 | 18.0 | 12.0 | 19.0 | ... | ... | |
| 26.0 | 15.0 | 13.0 | 28.0 | 30.0 | 57.0 | 48.0 | 20.0 | 1.0 | ... | |
| ... | 441.0 | 697.0[16] | ... | 1 006.0[58] | ... | ... | ... | 229.0 | ... | South Africa[3,4] |
| ... | 121.0 | 450.0[16] | ... | 1 175.0[58] | ... | ... | ... | 845.0 | ... | Afrique du Sud[3,4] |
| ... | 491.0 | 739.0[16] | ... | 1 000.0[58] | ... | ... | ... | 217.0 | ... | |
| ... | 125.0 | 556.0[16] | ... | 1 192.0[58] | ... | ... | ... | 850.0 | ... | |
| ... | 487.0 | 760.0[16] | ... | 1 055.0[58] | ... | ... | ... | 223.0 | ... | |
| ... | 123.0 | 550.0[16] | ... | 1 264.0[58] | ... | ... | ... | 884.0 | ... | |
| 591.0 | 834.5 | 244.4 | 776.8 | 685.6 | 350.7 | 263.8 | 352.7 | 54.6 | 0.7 | Spain[62,82] |
| 609.5 | 229.7 | 156.6 | 768.7 | 439.9 | 659.2 | 765.6 | 375.4 | 536.8 | 1.0 | Espagne[62,82] |
| 605.2 | 864.6 | 249.9 | 847.4 | 736.7 | 384.1 | 297.1 | 387.1 | 61.9 | 3.1 | |
| 685.9 | 252.6 | 207.4 | 831.0 | 460.1 | 706.4 | 837.5 | 406.6 | 620.9 | 3.0 | |
| 639.6 | 892.1 | 254.0 | 936.9 | 730.9 | 387.6 | 298.2 | 401.1 | 69.5 | 3.2 | |
| 763.1 | 266.0 | 218.5 | 920.5 | 490.7 | 721.2 | 882.6 | 414.3 | 691.1 | 3.8 | |
| 81.4 | 426.4 | 163.7[16] | ... | 340.7 | 67.4 | 52.3 | 81.4[29] | 6.5 | ... | Sri Lanka[3,83] |
| 33.6 | 22.0 | 62.4[16] | ... | 124.7 | 187.0 | 68.6 | 31.6[29] | 41.8 | ... | Sri Lanka[3,83] |
| 97.1 | 405.5 | 160.5[16] | ... | 304.2 | 85.5 | 43.7 | 82.0[29] | 16.5 | ... | |
| 38.5 | 21.8 | 69.1[16] | ... | 104.1 | 188.6 | 57.9 | 34.2[29] | 69.2 | ... | |
| 1.9 | 7.6 | 1.4 | 4.5 | 16.3 | 1.8 | 1.6 | 5.0 | ... | ... | Suriname[3,28] |
| 2.9 | 1.1 | 1.3 | 1.9 | 11.7 | 6.6 | 5.2 | 4.9 | ... | ... | Suriname[3,28] |
| 56.0 | 191.0 | 38.0 | 327.0 | 115.0[87] | 119.0 | 110.0 | 98.0[88] | ... | ... | Sweden[86] |
| 69.0 | 75.0 | 49.0 | 218.0 | 131.0[87] | 353.0 | 572.0 | 116.0[88] | ... | ... | Suède[86] |
| 54.0 | 199.0 | 35.0 | 357.0 | 110.0[87] | 119.0 | 119.0 | 105.0[88] | ... | ... | |
| 63.0 | 70.0 | 46.0 | 225.0 | 128.0[87] | 353.0 | 588.0 | 123.0[88] | ... | ... | |
| 58.0 | 203.0 | 37.0 | 370.0 | 113.0[87] | 122.0 | 122.0 | 105.0[88] | ... | ... | |
| 69.0 | 71.0 | 47.0 | 233.0 | 136.0[87] | 359.0 | 579.0 | 128.0[88] | ... | ... | |
| 63.0 | 159.0 | 132.0 | 286.0 | 127.0[87] | 111.0 | 113.0 | 102.0[88] | ... | ... | Switzerland[3,54,89] |
| 88.0 | 67.0 | 91.0 | 174.0 | 88.0[87] | 190.0 | 363.0 | 173.0[88] | ... | ... | Suisse[3,54,89] |
| 61.0 | 157.0 | 129.0 | 287.0 | 127.0[87] | 117.0 | 112.0 | 106.0[88] | ... | ... | |
| 87.0 | 70.0 | 90.0 | 166.0 | 94.0[87] | 196.0 | 370.0 | 176.0[88] | ... | ... | |
| 65.0 | 149.0 | 137.0 | 291.0 | 131.0[87] | 121.0 | 108.0 | 112.0[88] | ... | ... | |
| 95.0 | 68.0 | 94.0 | 175.0 | 93.0[87] | 204.0 | 377.0 | 182.0[88] | ... | ... | |
| ... | 58.0 | ... | ... | ... | 168.0 | 88.0 | ... | ... | ... | Tajikistan |
| ... | 58.0 | ... | ... | ... | 161.0 | 84.0 | ... | ... | ... | Tadjikistan |
| ... | 50.9 | ... | ... | ... | 160.0 | 82.3 | | | | |
| 781.7 | 914.7 | 145.7 | 385.9 | 679.4 | 469.0 | 159.8 | 334.7 | 31.0 | 0.3 | Thailand[3,6,36] |
| 1 424.7 | 152.8 | 157.7 | 247.8 | 335.6 | 613.5 | 375.2 | 378.0 | 208.0 | 0.6 | Thaïlande[3,6,36] |
| 759.8 | 900.8 | 162.1 | 377.5 | 726.3 | 469.2 | 155.9 | 298.5 | 29.8 | 0.3 | |
| 1 540.3 | 175.0 | 177.6 | 274.2 | 369.4 | 653.2 | 455.2 | 420.3 | 211.7 | 1.9 | |
| 777.2 | 887.4 | 147.8 | 371.7 | 784.0 | 454.4 | 143.7 | 307.9 | 34.0 | ... | |
| 1 437.7 | 165.5 | 201.9 | 287.6 | 386.1 | 625.5 | 459.1 | 402.4 | 187.9 | 0.4 | |

# 30

**Employment by economic activity**—Total employment and persons employed by ISIC Rev. 3 categories (thousands) (*continued*)
**Emploi par activité économique**—Emploi total et personnes employées par branches de CITI Rév. 3 (milliers) (*suite*)

| Country or area &<br>Pays ou zone & | Year<br>Année | Sex<br>Sexe | Total<br>employment<br>Emploi<br>total | Categ. A<br>Catég. A | Categ. B<br>Catég. B | Categ. C<br>Catég. C | Categ. D<br>Catég. D | Categ. E<br>Catég. E | Categ. F<br>Catég. F | Categ. G<br>Catég. G |
|---|---|---|---|---|---|---|---|---|---|---|
| TFYR of Macedonia[3]<br>L'ex-R.y. Macédoine[3] | 2004 | M | 320.6 | 57.4 | 0.4 | 2.5 | 62.2 | 13.6 | 32.5 | 43.1 |
| | 2004 | F | 202.4 | 30.3 | 0.1 | 0.3 | 54.1 | 2.1 | 4.0 | 31.1 |
| | 2005 | M | 332.2 | 65.4 | 0.3 | 3.3 | 62.2 | 14.6 | 32.1 | 43.6 |
| | 2005 | F | 213.1 | 40.8 | 0.1 | 0.2 | 57.8 | 2.4 | 3.2 | 31.1 |
| | 2006 | M | 352.0 | 70.1 | 0.3 | 3.6 | 64.7 | 13.7 | 40.3 | 45.0 |
| | 2006 | F | 218.4 | 44.4 | ^0.0 | 0.3 | 58.4 | 2.3 | 2.9 | 28.0 |
| Tonga[3]<br>Tonga[3] | 2003 | M | 20.4 | 9.5 | 0.9 | 0.1 | 0.9 | 0.4 | 1.4 | 1.3 |
| | 2003 | F | 14.1 | 0.5 | 0.2 | 0.0 | 7.6 | 0.2 | ^0.0 | 1.6 |
| Tunisia[3]<br>Tunisie[3] | 1989 | M | 1 592.8 | 422.2[1] | ... | 33.5[15] | 217.0 | ... | 244.8 | 201.0 |
| | 1989 | F | 386.0 | 87.5[1] | ... | 1.7[15] | 165.7 | ... | 2.8 | 12.8 |
| Turkey[3,6]<br>Turquie[3,6] | 2004 | M | 16 023.0 | 4 075.0 | 26.0 | 103.0 | 3 022.0 | 77.0 | 1 004.0 | 2 895.0 |
| | 2004 | F | 5 768.0 | 3 298.0 | 1.0 | 2.0 | 779.0 | 5.0 | 25.0 | 413.0 |
| | 2005 | M | 16 346.0 | 3 550.0[1] | ... | 117.0 | 3 262.0 | 74.0 | 1 145.0 | 3 130.0 |
| | 2005 | F | 5 700.0 | #2 943.0[1] | ... | 3.0 | 822.0 | 5.0 | 28.0 | 481.0 |
| | 2006 | M | 16 520.0 | 3 272.0[1] | ... | 126.0 | 3 358.0 | 87.0 | 1 231.0 | 3 167.0 |
| | 2006 | F | 5 810.0 | 2 816.0[1] | ... | 2.0 | 828.0 | 6.0 | 36.0 | 563.0 |
| Turks and Caicos Islands[3]<br>Iles Turques et Caïques[3] | 2003 | MF | 14.1 | 0.1 | 0.1 | 0.1 | 0.2 | 0.2 | 1.9 | 1.0 |
| | 2004 | MF | 15.2 | 0.1 | 0.2 | 0.1 | 0.2 | 0.2 | 2.1 | 1.3 |
| | 2005 | MF | 17.4 | 0.1 | 0.2 | 0.1 | 0.2 | 0.3 | 2.4 | 1.3 |
| Uganda[7]<br>Ouganda[7] | 2003 | M | 4 618.0 | 2 775.4 | 78.5 | 18.5 | 337.1 | 4.6 | 115.8 | 637.3 |
| | 2003 | F | 4 642.0 | 3 507.1 | 4.6 | 9.3 | 227.5 | 4.7 | 4.9 | 436.3 |
| Ukraine<br>Ukraine | 2004 | MF | 20 295.7 | 3 998.3[1] | ... | 4 077.1[60] | ... | ... | 907.5 | 3 971.2[37] |
| | 2005 | MF | 20 680.0 | 4 005.5[1] | ... | 4 072.4[60] | ... | ... | 941.5 | 4 175.2[37] |
| | 2006 | MF | 20 730.4 | 3 649.1[1] | ... | 4 036.9[60] | ... | ... | 987.1 | 4 406.9[37] |
| United Arab Emirates<br>Emirats arabes unis | 2000 | M | 1 553.0 | 129.5 | 10.8 | 39.4 | 167.7 | 17.4 | 337.8 | 231.9 |
| | 2000 | F | 226.0 | 0.1 | ^0.0 | 1.3 | 27.3 | 0.1 | 2.3 | 14.8 |
| United Kingdom[62,90]<br>Royaume-Uni[62,90] | 2003 | M | 14 973.4 | 258.8 | 13.5 | 93.5 | 3 042.4 | 132.5 | 1 882.9 | 2 128.4 |
| | 2003 | F | 12 847.4 | 74.5 | 0.8 | 9.9 | 1 056.8 | 50.3 | 198.8 | 2 207.2 |
| | 2004 | M | 15 037.7 | 266.6 | 12.2 | 75.8 | 2 816.5 | 128.6 | 1 948.8 | 2 167.6 |
| | 2004 | F | 12 970.7 | 76.5 | 0.9 | 10.2 | 959.1 | 50.9 | 218.1 | 2 170.8 |
| | 2005 | M | 15 061.4 | 276.8 | 10.1 | 89.0 | 2 777.7 | 128.0 | 1 971.2 | 2 144.2 |
| | 2005 | F | 13 104.2 | 95.0 | 1.7 | 13.8 | 945.3 | 48.3 | 230.5 | 2 156.8 |
| United States[6,62]<br>Etats-Unis[6,62] | 2004 | M | 74 524.0 | 1 687.0[1] | ... | 483.0 | 11 485.0 | 892.0 | 9 727.0 | 11 580.0 |
| | 2004 | F | 64 728.0 | 546.0[1] | ... | 55.0 | 4 998.0 | 276.0 | 1 041.0 | 9 289.0 |
| | 2005 | M | 75 973.0 | 1 654.0[1] | ... | 545.0 | 11 370.0 | 926.0 | 10 118.0 | 11 896.0 |
| | 2005 | F | 65 757.0 | 544.0[1] | ... | 80.0 | 4 882.0 | 250.0 | 1 079.0 | 9 508.0 |
| | 2006 | M | 77 502.0 | 1 663.0[1] | ... | 598.0 | 11 543.0 | 926.0 | 10 618.0 | 11 802.0 |
| | 2006 | F | 66 925.0 | 543.0[1] | ... | 89.0 | 4 834.0 | 259.0 | 1 131.0 | 9 526.0 |
| Uruguay[21,25]<br>Uruguay[21,25] | 2004[44] | M | 617.3 | 45.8[92] | ... | ... | 103.9[93] | ... | 69.9 | 148.3[37] |
| | 2004[44] | F | 460.6 | 8.5[92] | ... | ... | 56.3[93] | ... | 1.7 | 90.9[37] |
| | 2005[44] | M | 620.1 | 44.3[92] | ... | ... | 107.2[93] | ... | 73.2 | 152.2[37] |
| | 2005[44] | F | 494.4 | 7.4[92] | ... | ... | 62.0[93] | ... | 1.5 | 103.0[37] |
| | 2006 | M | 822.4 | 126.7[92] | ... | ... | 138.0[93] | ... | 88.5 | 184.3[37] |
| | 2006 | F | 591.0 | 30.5[92] | ... | ... | 71.6[93] | ... | 2.1 | 123.9[37] |
| Viet Nam[3,39]<br>Viet Nam[3,39] | 2002 | M | 20 355.6 | 11 460.7 | 948.6 | 156.5 | 1 972.1 | 97.8 | 1 357.3 | 1 521.5 |
| | 2002 | F | 19 806.7 | 12 184.7 | 323.3 | 87.8 | 2 078.8 | 20.3 | 133.6 | 2 785.0 |
| | 2003 | M | 20 959.2 | 11 072.5 | 1 023.1 | 194.7 | 2 203.6 | 103.9 | 1 631.8 | 1 673.1 |
| | 2003 | F | 20 216.5 | 12 164.2 | 311.3 | 127.4 | 2 308.0 | 24.3 | 164.7 | 2 834.2 |
| | 2004 | M | 21 649.3 | 11 041.3 | 1 059.3 | 182.7 | 2 429.1 | 117.6 | 1 774.1 | 1 778.0 |
| | 2004 | F | 20 666.3 | 12 027.3 | 369.9 | 112.2 | 2 520.8 | 24.1 | 182.5 | 2 918.0 |

| | | | | | ISIC Rev. 3 Tabulation categories + | | | | | |
| | | | | | CITI Rév. 3 Catégories de classement + | | | | | |
| Categ. H | Categ. I | Categ. J | Categ. K | Categ. L | Categ. M | Categ. N | Categ. O | Categ. P | Categ. Q | Country or area [&] |
| Catég. H | Catég. I | Catég. J | Catég. K | Catég.L | Catég. M | Catég. N | Catég. O | Catég. P | Catég. Q | Pays ou zone [&] |
|---|---|---|---|---|---|---|---|---|---|---|
| 8.8 | 26.0 | 2.9 | 7.7 | 28.0 | 13.7 | 7.9 | 13.0 | ... | 0.7 | TFYR of Macedonia[3] |
| 3.9 | 4.8 | 4.8 | 5.8 | 11.7 | 19.9 | 22.0 | 6.6 | 0.2 | 0.9 | L'ex-R.y. Macédoine[3] |
| 9.1 | 28.2 | 2.2 | 9.0 | 27.4 | 13.6 | 8.5 | 12.2 | ^0.0 | 0.4 | |
| 4.5 | 4.5 | 4.1 | 5.8 | 10.9 | 18.0 | 22.8 | 6.0 | 0.4 | 0.6 | |
| 12.9 | 25.6 | 3.3 | 7.5 | 27.6 | 14.7 | 9.8 | 12.7 | 0.1 | 0.3 | |
| 6.1 | 4.4 | 3.8 | 7.9 | 11.7 | 18.7 | 22.8 | 5.6 | 0.3 | 0.7 | |
| 0.2 | 1.2 | 0.2 | 0.2 | 1.9 | 0.7 | 0.3 | 1.0 | 0.3 | 0.1 | Tonga[3] |
| 0.4 | 0.4 | 0.3 | 0.1 | 0.7 | 1.1 | 0.4 | 0.3 | 0.4 | ^0.0 | Tonga[3] |
| 44.5 | 90.5 | 10.8 | 30.0 | 162.7 | 70.1 | 23.8 | 15.7 | ... | ... | Tunisia[3] |
| 4.6 | 5.3 | 4.6 | 21.7 | 15.2 | 34.7 | 18.4 | 6.5 | ... | ... | Tunisie[3] |
| 782.0 | 1 038.0 | 153.0 | 416.0 | 1 122.0 | 512.0 | 237.0 | 496.0 | 62.0 | 3.0 | Turkey[3,6] |
| 90.0 | 62.0 | 84.0 | 132.0 | 129.0 | 306.0 | 232.0 | 87.0 | 120.0 | 2.0 | Turquie[3,6] |
| 847.0 | 1 062.0 | 157.0 | 485.0 | 1 084.0 | 557.0 | 256.0 | 621.0[29] | ... | ... | |
| 102.0 | 71.0 | 82.0 | 154.0 | 132.0 | 350.0 | 275.0 | #253.0[29] | ... | ... | |
| 885.0 | 1 086.0 | 154.0 | 581.0 | 1 077.0 | 537.0 | 287.0 | 673.0[29] | ... | ... | |
| 115.0 | 77.0 | 84.0 | 192.0 | 148.0 | 370.0 | 304.0 | 269.0[29] | ... | ... | |
| 2.5 | 0.6 | 0.4 | 1.3 | 2.0 | 0.4[22] | ... | 1.0 | 0.9 | ... | Turks and Caicos Islands[3] |
| 2.6 | 0.6 | 0.5 | 1.3 | 2.3 | 0.5[22] | ... | 0.9 | 1.4 | ... | Iles Turques et Caïques[3] |
| 2.9 | 0.7 | 0.5 | 1.6 | 2.3 | 0.5[22] | ... | 1.0 | 1.6 | ... | |
| 64.7 | 175.5 | 0.0 | 23.1 | 64.7 | 152.4 | 32.3 | 97.0 | 27.7 | ... | Uganda[7] |
| 176.4 | 4.6 | 0.0 | 9.3 | 9.3 | 83.6 | 37.1 | 55.7 | 78.9 | ... | Ouganda[7] |
| ... | 1 374.9 | 216.1 | 919.9 | 1 050.2 | 1 648.7 | 1 348.9 | 782.9[29] | ... | ... | Ukraine |
| ... | 1 400.5 | 247.9 | 966.6 | 1 028.9 | 1 668.2 | 1 356.6 | 816.7[29] | ... | ... | Ukraine |
| ... | 1 428.8 | 286.0 | 1 041.9 | 1 033.7 | 1 690.5 | 1 356.7 | 812.8[29] | ... | ... | |
| 56.5 | 119.9 | 18.4 | 40.9 | 225.4 | 32.4 | 17.0 | 51.1 | 54.5 | 1.3 | United Arab Emirates |
| 5.4 | 6.3 | 4.4 | 4.4 | 10.0 | 37.2 | 16.2 | 2.7 | 92.8 | 0.4 | Emirats arabes unis |
| 508.3 | 1 458.8 | 593.9 | 1 782.0 | 973.3 | 652.4 | 627.5 | 739.2 | 45.1 | 9.2 | United Kingdom[62,90] |
| 683.3 | 477.4 | 637.4 | 1 302.0 | 931.2 | 1 726.2 | 2 575.8 | 797.5 | 95.2 | 5.6 | Royaume-Uni[62,90] |
| 537.9 | 1 450.8 | 576.0 | 1 848.4 | 978.5 | 714.4 | 660.8 | 738.5 | 58.2 | 9.0 | |
| 694.8 | 452.8 | 605.0 | 1 309.4 | 940.9 | 1 838.9 | 2 693.9 | 821.1 | 98.0 | 4.5 | |
| 534.9 | 1 465.8 | 576.1 | 1 852.2 | 980.8 | 686.4 | 727.6 | 749.0 | 45.8 | 4.9 | |
| 671.8 | 466.4 | 602.6 | 1 365.1 | 1 007.6 | 1 863.0 | 2 727.9 | 804.7 | 72.1 | 3.1 | |
| 4 323.0 | 4 449.0 | 2 791.0 | 9 673.0 | 3 458.0 | 3 752.0 | 3 470.0 | 6 752.0[91] | ... | ... | United States[6,62] |
| 4 807.0 | 1 395.0 | 4 149.0 | 7 463.0 | 2 908.0 | 8 306.0 | 13 191.0 | 6 304.0[91] | ... | ... | Etats-Unis[6,62] |
| 4 348.0 | 4 707.0 | 2 920.0 | 9 804.0 | 3 558.0 | 3 804.0 | 3 500.0 | 6 823.0[91] | ... | ... | |
| 4 958.0 | 1 477.0 | 4 115.0 | 7 657.0 | 2 971.0 | 8 459.0 | 13 410.0 | 6 365.0[91] | ... | ... | |
| 4 452.0 | 4 722.0 | 3 035.0 | 10 184.0 | 3 563.0 | 3 892.0 | 3 632.0 | 6 873.0[91] | ... | ... | |
| 5 023.0 | 1 547.0 | 4 219.0 | 7 920.0 | 2 961.0 | 8 630.0 | 13 784.0 | 6 459.0[91] | ... | ... | |
| ... | 51.6 | 56.8[16] | ... | 62.5 | 15.6 | 22.0 | 34.0 | 6.9 | ... | Uruguay[21,25] |
| ... | 11.0 | 35.9[16] | ... | 29.2 | 50.1 | 59.2 | 28.8 | 89.0 | ... | Uruguay[21,25] |
| ... | 49.1 | 64.0[16] | ... | 56.4 | 14.4 | 19.6 | 32.3 | 7.4 | ... | |
| ... | 12.4 | 40.0[16] | ... | 29.7 | 53.3 | 61.5 | 32.0 | 91.6 | ... | |
| ... | 61.5 | 61.1[16] | ... | 70.9 | 18.9 | 24.8 | 35.5 | 11.2 | ... | |
| ... | 14.3 | 40.6[16] | ... | 33.6 | 59.5 | 68.9 | 33.7 | 111.6 | ... | |
| 145.3 | 1 117.4 | 59.0 | 113.8 | 432.4 | 318.7 | 115.6 | 468.7 | 69.2 | 0.9 | Viet Nam[3,39] |
| 375.7 | 149.9 | 71.0 | 70.6 | 157.6 | 739.9 | 163.3 | 343.3 | 121.0 | 1.1 | Viet Nam[3,39] |
| 195.3 | 1 150.5 | 74.0 | 144.4 | 457.5 | 335.1 | 135.1 | 480.2 | 84.1 | 0.4 | |
| 447.9 | 146.8 | 74.5 | 74.2 | 162.6 | 762.9 | 171.0 | 308.6 | 132.9 | 1.0 | |
| 176.1 | 1 128.2 | 80.8 | 142.6 | 516.0 | 359.6 | 140.1 | 624.6 | 97.4 | 1.8 | |
| 418.9 | 164.7 | 78.2 | 76.6 | 182.8 | 825.4 | 187.9 | 431.8 | 143.7 | 1.4 | |

**30** **Employment by economic activity**—Total employment and persons employed by ISIC Rev. 3 categories (thousands) *(continued)*

**Emploi par activité économique**—Emploi total et personnes employées par branches de CITI Rév. 3 (milliers) *(suite)*

| Country or area &<br>Pays ou zone & | Year<br>Année | Sex<br>Sexe | Total<br>employment<br>Emploi<br>total | ISIC Rev. 3 Tabulation categories +<br>CITI Rév. 3 Catégories de classement + | | | | | | |
|---|---|---|---|---|---|---|---|---|---|---|
| | | | | Categ. A<br>Catég. A | Categ. B<br>Catég. B | Categ. C<br>Catég. C | Categ. D<br>Catég. D | Categ. E<br>Catég. E | Categ. F<br>Catég. F | Categ. G<br>Catég. G |
| Yemen[3]<br>Yémen[3] | 1999 | M | 2 731.6 | 1 146.4 | 31.4 | 16.7 | 112.5 | 11.0 | 236.9 | 382.3 |
| | 1999 | F | 890.1 | 781.3 | ... | 1.0 | 23.0 | 0.8 | 1.3 | 11.9 |

Source

International Labour Office (ILO), Geneva, the ILO labour statistics database and the "Yearbook of Labour Statistics 2007".

Notes

+ Tabulation categories of ISIC Rev. 3 :
A Agriculture, hunting and forestry.
B Fishing.
C Mining and quarrying.
D Manufacturing.
E Electricity, gas and water supply.
F Construction.
G Wholesale and retail trade, repair of motor vehicles, motor cycles and personal and household goods.
H Hotels and restaurants.
I Transport, storage and communications.
J Financial intermediation.
K Real estate, renting and business activities.
L Public administration and defence ; compulsory social security.
M Education.
N Health and social work.
O Other community, social and personal service activities.
P Private households with employed persons.
Q Extra-territorial organizations and bodies.

& Data for most countries are collected from labour force surveys. The following countries are exceptions, with sources as follows:

Administrative reports:
Jersey

Household surveys:
Lesotho

Official estimates:
Albania
Armenia
Azerbaijan
Luxembourg
Mongolia
San Marino
Tajikistan
Turks and Caicos Islands
United Arab Emirates

Population census:
Antigua and Barbuda
Brunei Darussalam
Guyana
Isle of Man
Maldives

Source

Bureau international du travail (BIT), Genève, la base de données du BIT et "l'Annuaire des statistiques du travail 2007".

Notes

+ Catégories de classement de la CITI Rév. 3 :
A Agriculture, chasse et sylviculture.
B Pêche.
C Activitiés extractives.
D Activitiés du fabrication.
E Production et distribution d'électricité, de gaz etd'eau.
F Construction.
G Commerce de gros et de détail; réparation de véhicules automobiles, de motorcycles et de biens personneles et domestiques.
H Hôtels et restaurants.
I Transports, entreposage et communications.
J Intermédiation financière.
K Immobilier, locations et activitiés de services aux enterprises.
L Administration publique et défense; sécurité sociale obligatoire.
M Education.
N Santé et action sociale.
O Autres activités de services collectifs, sociaux et personnels.
P Ménages privés employant du personnel domestique.
Q Organisations et organismes extraterritoriaux.

& Les données pour la plupart des pays sont extraites d'enquêtes par sondage sur la main-d'œuvre, sauf les pays ci-dessous dont les sources sont les suivantes :

Rapports administratifs:
Jersey

Enquêtes auprès des ménages:
Lesotho

Evaluations officielles:
Albanie
Arménie
Azerbaïdjan
Luxembourg
Mongolie
Saint-Marin
Tadjikistan
Îles Turques et Caïques
Emirats arabes unis

Recensement de la population:
Antigua-et-Barbuda
Brunei Darussalam
Guyane
Ile de Man
Maldives

30 Employment by economic activity—Total employment and persons employed by ISIC Rev. 3 categories (thousands) (*continued*)

Emploi par activité économique—Emploi total et personnes employées par branches de CITI Rév. 3 (milliers) (*suite*)

| ISIC Rev. 3 Tabulation categories +<br>CITI Rév. 3 Catégories de classement + | | | | | | | | | | |
| Categ. H<br>Catég. H | Categ. I<br>Catég. I | Categ. J<br>Catég. J | Categ. K<br>Catég. K | Categ. L<br>Catég.L | Categ. M<br>Catég. M | Categ. N<br>Catég. N | Categ. O<br>Catég. O | Categ. P<br>Catég. P | Categ. Q<br>Catég. Q | Country or area [&]<br>Pays ou zone [&] |
|---|---|---|---|---|---|---|---|---|---|---|
| 42.0 | 121.0 | 9.3 | 18.0 | 347.7 | 171.0 | 31.8 | 49.1 | 3.4 | 0.3 | Yemen[3] |
| 0.9 | 1.5 | 1.7 | 0.9 | 10.3 | 38.2 | 10.6 | 4.0 | 2.2 | 0.3 | Yémen[3] |

New Caledonia
Papua New Guinea
Qatar
Saint Helena
Sierra Leone
Suriname

Nouvelle-Calédonie
Papouasie-Nouvelle-Guinée
Qatar
Sainte Hélène
Sierra-Leone
Suriname

1 Tabulation categories A-B.
2 Tabulation categories J-L and O-Q.
3 Persons aged 15 years and over.
4 September of each year.
5 May.
6 Excluding armed forces.
7 Persons aged 10 years and over.
8 Second semester.
9 28 urban agglomerations.
10 31 urban agglomerations.
11 February, May, August and November.
12 Excl. conscripts on compulsory military service.
13 Men aged 15 to 61 years; women aged 15 to 56 years.
14 April of each year.
15 Tabulation categories C and E.
16 Tabulation categories J-K.
17 Tabulation categories L-P.
18 Year ending in June of the year indicated.
19 Including professional army.
20 Prior to 2003: Excluding armed forces.
21 Persons aged 14 years and over.
22 Tabulation categories M-N.
23 Tabulation categories Q and X. (Additional category X, not shown separately in the table, comprises activities which are not classifiable by economic activity).
24 Urban areas, Nov.
25 Excluding conscripts.
26 Persons aged 12 years and over.
27 Excluding rural population of Rondônia, Acre, Amazonas, Roraima, Pará and Amapá.
28 August.
29 Tabulation categories O-Q.
30 November of each year.
31 Excluding full-time members of the armed forces.
32 Excluding residents of the Territories and indigenous persons living on reserves.
33 Excl. armed forces and conscripts.
34 October.
35 April.
36 Third quarter.
37 Tabulation categories G-H.
38 Tabulation categories L-Q.
39 July of each year.
40 Government-controlled area.
41 Persons aged 15 to 66 years.

1 Catégories de classement A à B.
2 Catégories de classement J à L et O à Q.
3 Personnes âgées de 15 ans et plus.
4 Septembre de chaque année.
5 Mai.
6 Non compris les militaires.
7 Personnes âgées de 10 ans et plus.
8 Second semestre.
9 28 agglomérations urbaines.
10 31 agglomérations urbaines.
11 Février, mai, août et novembre.
12 Non compris conscrits ceux du contingent.
13 Hommes âgés de 15 à 61 ans; femmes âgées de 15 à 56 ans.
14 Avril de chaque année.
15 Catégories de classement C et E.
16 Catégories de classement J à K.
17 Catégories de classement L à P.
18 Année se terminant en juin de l'année indiquée.
19 Y compris les militaires de carrière.
20 Avant 2003: non compris les forces armées.
21 Personnes âgées de 14 ans et plus.
22 Catégories de classement M à N.
23 Catégories de classement Q et X. (la catégorie supplémentaire X, qui ne figure pas dans le tableau, comprend les activités qui ne peuvent être classées dans une activité économique).
24 Régions urbaines, nov.
25 Non compris les conscrits.
26 Personnes âgées de 12 ans et plus.
27 Non compris la population rurale de Rondônia, Acre, Amazonas, Roraima, Pará et Amapá.
28 Août.
29 Catégories de classement O à Q.
30 Novembre de chaque année.
31 Non compris les membres à temps complet des forces armées.
32 Non compris les habitants des Territoires et les populations indigènes vivant dans les réserves.
33 Excl. armed forces and conscripts.
34 Octobre.
35 Avril.
36 Troisième trimestre.
37 Catégories de classement G à H.
38 Catégories de classement L à Q.
39 Juillet de chaque année.
40 Région sous contrôle gouvernemental.
41 Personnes âgées de 15 à 66 ans.

30    **Employment by economic activity**—Total employment and persons employed by ISIC Rev. 3 categories (thousands) (*continued*)

**Emploi par activité économique**—Emploi total et personnes employées par branches de CITI Rév. 3 (milliers) (*suite*)

| | | | |
|---|---|---|---|
| 42 | Included armed forces and conscripts. | 42 | Y compris les forces armées et les conscrits. |
| 43 | Tabulation categories K, M and N. | 43 | Catégories de classement K, M et N. |
| 44 | Urban areas. | 44 | Régions urbaines. |
| 45 | Persons aged 15 to 64 years. | 45 | Personnes âgées de 15 à 64 ans. |
| 46 | May and November. | 46 | Mai et novembre. |
| 47 | December. | 47 | Décembre. |
| 48 | Tabulation categories N and O. | 48 | Catégories de classement N et O. |
| 49 | Persons aged 15 to 74 years. | 49 | Personnes âgées de 15 à 74 ans. |
| 50 | March. | 50 | Mars. |
| 51 | Urban areas, April. | 51 | Régions urbaines, avril. |
| 52 | Urban areas, July. | 52 | Régions urbaines, juillet. |
| 53 | Methodology revised; data not strictly comparable. | 53 | Méthodologie révisée; les données ne sont pas strictement comparables. |
| 54 | Second quarter of each year. | 54 | Deuxième trimestre de chaque année. |
| 55 | Persons aged 16 to 74 years. | 55 | Personnes âgées de 16 à 74 ans. |
| 56 | Tabulation categories C-D. | 56 | Catégories de classement C à D. |
| 57 | Tabulation categories C and F. | 57 | Catégories de classement C et F. |
| 58 | Tabulation categories L-O. | 58 | Catégories de classement L à O. |
| 59 | Including the armed forces. | 59 | Y compris les forces armées. |
| 60 | Tabulation categories C-E. | 60 | Catégories de classement C à E. |
| 61 | Persons aged 6 years and over. | 61 | Personnes âgées de 6 ans et plus. |
| 62 | Persons aged 16 years and over. | 62 | Personnes âgées de 16 ans et plus. |
| 63 | December of each year. | 63 | Décembre de chaque année. |
| 64 | October of each year. | 64 | Octobre de chaque année. |
| 65 | Persons aged 15 to 69 years. | 65 | Personnes âgées de 15 à 69 ans. |
| 66 | Curaçao. | 66 | Curaçao. |
| 67 | Omanis. | 67 | Omanais. |
| 68 | August of each year. | 68 | Août de chaque année. |
| 69 | July. | 69 | Juillet. |
| 70 | Metropolitan Lima. | 70 | Lima métropolitaine. |
| 71 | September. | 71 | Septembre. |
| 72 | Excluding regular military living in barracks. | 72 | Non compris les militaires de carrière vivant dans des casernes. |
| 73 | Excluding regular military living in barracks and conscripts. | 73 | Non compris les militaires de carrière vivant dans des casernes et les conscrits. |
| 74 | Data not reliable; coefficient of variation greater than 20%. | 74 | Données non fiables; coefficient de variation supérieur à 20%. |
| 75 | March of each year. | 75 | Mars de chaque année. |
| 76 | Persons aged 15 to 72 years. | 76 | Personnes âgées de 15 à 72 ans. |
| 77 | June. | 77 | Juin. |
| 78 | Permanent residents aged 15 years and over. | 78 | Résidents permanents âgés de 15 ans et plus. |
| 79 | Tabulation categories A-C, E and X (additional category X, not shown separately in the table, comprises activities which are not classifiable by economic activity). | 79 | Catégories de classement A à C, E et X. (la catégorie supplémentaire X, qui ne figure pas dans le tableau, comprend les activités qui ne peuvent être classées dans une activité économique). |
| 80 | Tabulation categories L and M. | 80 | Catégories de classement L et M. |
| 81 | Excluding persons on child-care leave. | 81 | Non compris les personnes en congé parental. |
| 82 | Excluding compulsory military service. | 82 | Non compris les militaires du contingent. |
| 83 | Excluding Northern and Eastern provinces. | 83 | Non compris les provinces du Nord et de l'Est. |
| 84 | First and third quarters. | 84 | Premier et troisième trimestres. |
| 85 | Tabulation categories C-F. | 85 | Catégories de classement C à F. |
| 86 | Persons aged 16 to 64 years. | 86 | Personnes âgées de 16 à 64 ans. |
| 87 | Tabulation categories L and Q. | 87 | Catégories de classement L et Q. |
| 88 | Tabulation categories O-P. | 88 | Catégories de classement O à P. |
| 89 | Excluding armed forces and seasonal / border workers. | 89 | Non compris les forces armées et les travailleurs saisonniers et frontaliers. |
| 90 | March - May. | 90 | Mars - mai. |
| 91 | Tabulation categories O-X. (Additional category X, not shown separately in the table, comprises activities which are not classifiable by economic activity). | 91 | Catégories de classement O à X. (la catégorie supplémentaire X, qui ne figure pas dans le tableau, comprend les activités qui ne peuvent être classées dans une activité économique). |
| 92 | Tabulation categories A-C. | 92 | Catégories de classement A à C. |
| 93 | Tabulation categories D-E. | 93 | Catégories de classement D à E. |

Detailed data on labour force and related topics are published in the ILO *Yearbook of Labour Statistics* and on the ILO web site http://laborsta.ilo.org. The series shown in the *Statistical Yearbook* give an overall picture of the availability and disposition of labour resources and, in conjunction with other macroeconomic indicators, can be useful for an overall assessment of economic performance. The ILO *Yearbook of Labour Statistics* provides a comprehensive description of the methodology underlying the labour series. Brief definitions of the major categories of labour statistics are given below.

"Employment" is defined to include persons above a specified age who, during a specified period of time, were in one of the following categories:

(a) "Paid employment", comprising persons who perform some work for pay or profit during the reference period or persons with a job but not at work due to temporary absence, such as vacation, strike, education leave;

(b) "Self-employment", comprising employers, own account workers, members of producers' cooperatives, persons engaged in production of goods and services for own consumption and unpaid family workers;

(c) Members of the armed forces, students, homemakers and others mainly engaged in non-economic activities during the reference period who, at the same time, were in paid employment or self-employment are considered as employed on the same basis as other categories.

"Unemployment" is defined to include persons above a certain age and who, during a specified period of time were:

(a) "Without work", i.e. were not in paid employment or self-employment;

(b) "Currently available for work", i.e. were available for paid employment or self employment during the reference period; and

(c) "Seeking work", i.e. had taken specific steps in a specified period to find paid employment or self-employment.

Persons not considered to be unemployed include:

(a) Persons intending to establish their own business or farm, but who had not yet arranged to do so and who were not seeking work for pay or profit;

(b) Former unpaid family workers not at work and not seeking work for pay or profit.

Des données détaillées sur la main-d'œuvre et des sujets connexes sont publiées dans l'*Annuaire des Statistiques du Travail* du BIT et sur le site Web du BIT http://laborsta.ilo.org. Les séries indiquées dans l'*Annuaire des Statistiques* donnent un tableau d'ensemble des disponibilités de main-d'œuvre et de l'emploi de ces ressources et, combinées à d'autres indicateurs économiques, elles peuvent être utiles pour une évaluation générale de la performance économique. L'*Annuaire des statistiques du Travail* du BIT donne une description complète de la méthodologie employée pour établir les séries sur la main-d'œuvre. On trouvera cidessous quelques brèves définitions des grandes catégories de statistiques du travail.

Le terme "Emploi" désigne les personnes dépassant un âge déterminé qui, au cours d'une période donnée, se trouvaient dans l'une des catégories suivantes:

(a) La catégorie "emploi rémunéré", composée des personnes faisant un certain travail en échange d'une rémunération ou d'un profit pendant la période de référence, ou les personnes ayant un emploi, mais qui ne travaillaient pas en raison d'une absence temporaire (vacances, grève, congé d'études);

(b) La catégorie "emploi indépendant" regroupe les employeurs, les travailleurs indépendants, les membres decoopératives de producteurs et les personnes s'adonnant à la production de biens et de services pour leur propre consommâtion et la main -d'œuvre familiale non rémunérée;

(c) Les membres des forces armées, les étudiants, les aides familiales et autres personnes qui s'adonnaient essentiellement à des activités non économiques pendant la période de référence et qui, en même temps, avaient un emploi rémunéré ou indépendant, sont considérés comme employés au même titre que les personnes des autres catégories.

Par "chômeurs", on entend les personnes dépassant un âge déterminé et qui, pendant une période donnée, étaient:

(a) "sans emploi", c'est-à-dire sans emploi rémunéré ou indépendant;

(b) "disponibles", c'est-à-dire qui pouvaient être engagées pour un emploi rémunéré ou pouvaient s'adonner à un emploi indépendant au cours de la période de référence; et

(c) "à la recherche d'un emploi", c'est-à-dire qui avaient pris des mesures précises à un certain moment pour trouver un emploi rémunéré ou un emploi indépendant.

Ne sont pas considérés comme chômeurs:

For various reasons, national definitions of employment and unemployment often differ from the recommended international standard definitions and thereby limit international comparability. Inter-country comparisons are also complicated by a variety of types of data collection systems used to obtain information on employed and unemployed persons.

*Table 29* presents absolute figures on the distribution of employed persons by economic activity, according to ISIC 3. The column for total employment includes economic activities not adequately defined and that are not accounted for in the other categories. Data are arranged as far as possible according to the major divisions of economic activity of the *International Standard Industrial Classification of All Economic Activities*.

*Table 30:* Figures are presented in absolute numbers and in percentages. Data are normally annual averages of monthly, quarterly or semi annual data.

The series generally represent the total number of persons wholly unemployed or temporarily laid-off. Percentage figures, where given, are calculated by comparing the number of unemployed to the total members of that group of the labour force on which the unemployment data are based.

(a) Les personnes qui, pendant la période de référence, avaient l'intention de créer leur propre entreprise ou exploitation agricole, mais n'avaient pas encore pris les dispositions nécessaires à cet effet et qui n'étaient pas à la recherche d'un emploi en vue d'une rémunération ou d'un profit;

(b) Les anciens travailleurs familiaux non rémunérés qui n'avaient pas d'emploi et n'étaient pas à la recherche d'un emploi en vue d'une rémunération ou d'un profit.

Pour diverses raisons, les définitions nationales de l'emploi et du chômage diffèrent souvent des définitions internationales types recommandées, limitant ainsi les possibilités de comparaison entre pays. Ces comparaisons se trouvent en outre compliquées par la diversité des systèmes de collecte de données utilisés pour recueillir des informations sur les personnes employées et les chômeurs.

Le *tableau 29* présente les effectifs de personnes employées par activité économique, classés en fonction de la Révision 3. L'emploi total inclut les personnes employées à des activités économiques mal définies et qui ne sont pas classées ailleurs. Les données sont ventilées autant que possible selon les branches d'activité économique de la *Classification internationale type, par industrie, de toutes les activités économiques*.

*Tableau 30*: Les chiffres sont présentés en valeur absolue et en pourcentage. Les données sont normalement des moyennes annuelles des données mensuelles, trimestrielles ou semestrielles.

Les séries représentent généralement le nombre total des chômeurs complets ou des personnes temporairement mises à pied. Les données en pourcentage, lorsqu'elles figurent dans le tableau, sont calculées en comparant le nombre de chômeurs au nombre total des personnes du groupe de main-d'œuvre sur lequel sont basées les données relatives au chômage.

# 31

## Wages in manufacturing
By hour, day, week or month, and by gender

## Salaires dans les industries manufacturières
Par heure, jour, semaine ou mois, et par sexe

| Country or area § / Pays ou zone § | 1999 | 2000 | 2001 | 2002 | 2003 | 2004 | 2005 | 2006 |
|---|---|---|---|---|---|---|---|---|
| **Albania[1,2] (lek) — Albanie[1,2] (lek)** | | | | | | | | |
| MF(I) - month mois | 10 734.0 | 11 708.0 | 14 056.0 | 14 334.0 | 16 572.0 | 17 559.0 | 18 333.0 | ... |
| **Anguilla (EC dollar) — Anguilla (dollar des Carraïbes orientales)** | | | | | | | | |
| MF(I) - month mois | ... | 1 494.7 | ... | ... | ... | ... | ... | ... |
| **Argentina[3,4] (Argentine peso) — Argentine[3,4] (peso argentin)** | | | | | | | | |
| MF(II) - hour heure | 4.2 | 4.3 | 4.3 | 4.5 | 5.1 | 6.3 | 7.6 | 9.7 |
| **Armenia (dram) — Arménie (dram)** | | | | | | | | |
| MF(I) - month mois | 24 515.0 | 29 307.0 | 35 848.0 | 30 061.0 | 41 881.0 | 48 191.0 | 54 536.0 | 61 490.0 |
| M(I) - month mois | ... | 29 208.0 | 33 921.0 | 41 452.0 | 49 831.0 | 57 043.0 | 67 067.0 | 74 735.0 |
| F(I) - month mois | ... | 15 160.0 | 15 528.0 | 16 865.0 | 20 990.0 | 30 485.0 | 37 382.0 | 48 319.0 |
| **Australia[5,6] (Australian dollar) — Australie[5,6] (dollar australien)** | | | | | | | | |
| MF(I) - hour heure | ... | 18.2 | ... | 20.5 | ... | 22.8 | ... | 25.4 |
| M(I) - hour heure | ... | 19.1 | ... | 20.8 | ... | 23.4 | ... | 26.1 |
| F(I)- hour heure | ... | 16.8 | ... | 18.5 | ... | 19.9 | ... | 23.6 |
| **Austria (Austrian schilling, euro) — Autriche (schilling autrichien, euro)** | | | | | | | | |
| MF(I) - hour heure[1,7] | #12.4 | 12.7 | 13.0 | 13.4 | 13.8 | 14.0 | 14.4 | *14.8 |
| MF(I) - month mois | 29 136.0[8] | 29 741.0[8] | 30 650.0[8] | #2 543.0 | 2 611.0 | ... | ... | ... |
| M(I) - month mois | 32 195.0[8] | 32 898.0[8] | 33 904.0[8] | #2 868.0 | 2 938.0 | ... | ... | ... |
| F(I) - month mois | 22 009.0[8] | 22 477.0[8] | 23 189.0[8] | #1 755.0 | 1 795.0 | ... | ... | ... |
| MF(II) - month mois | 26 104.0[8] | 26 685.0[8] | 27 488.0[8] | #2 047.0 | 2 093.0 | ... | ... | ... |
| M(II) - month mois | 28 646.0[8] | 29 324.0[8] | 30 197.0[8] | #2 257.0 | 2 303.0 | ... | ... | ... |
| F(II) - month mois | 18 702.0[8] | 19 142.0[8] | 19 698.0[8] | #1 412.0 | 1 444.0 | ... | ... | ... |
| MF(V) - month mois | 34 547.0[8] | 35 169.0[8] | #3 273.0 | 3 358.0 | 3 436.0 | ... | ... | ... |
| M(V) - month mois | 39 793.0[8] | 40 490.0[8] | #3 979.0 | 4 054.0 | 4 132.0 | ... | ... | ... |
| F(V) - month mois | 25 981.0[8] | 26 509.0[8] | #2 090.0 | 2 141.0 | 2 198.0 | ... | ... | ... |
| **Azerbaijan (manat) — Azerbaïdjan (manat)** | | | | | | | | |
| MF(I) - month mois | 244 087.1 | 284 272.3 | 303 163.6 | 348 815.6 | 445 436.5 | 491 330.2 | 115.0[9] | 141.0 |
| **Bahrain[10,11,12] (Bahrain dinar) — Bahreïn[10,11,12] (dinar de Bahreïn)** | | | | | | | | |
| MF(I) - month mois | 227.0 | 231.0 | 215.0 | 228.0 | 230.0 | 234.0 | 228.0 | 225.0 |
| M(I) - month mois | 250.0 | 255.0 | 241.0 | 252.0 | 250.0 | 249.0 | 239.0 | 230.0 |
| F(I) - month mois | 109.0 | 107.0 | 100.0 | 111.0 | 125.0 | 138.0 | 145.0 | 177.0 |
| **Belarus[13] (Belarussian rouble) — Bélarus[13] (rouble bélarussien)** | | | | | | | | |
| MF(I) - month mois | 34 587.5 | 87.4[14] | 165.0 | 220.3 | 297.0 | 430.0 | 556.0 | 659.0 |
| M(I) - month mois | 38 540.7 | 97.2[14] | 181.9 | 245.8 | 334.2 | 478.0 | 626.0 | 738.0 |
| F(I) - month mois | 31 051.0 | 78.7[14] | 150.4 | 198.8 | 265.5 | 388.0 | 495.0 | 589.0 |
| **Belgium (euro)[15,16] — Belgique (euro)[15,16]** | | | | | | | | |
| MF(I) - hour heure | #13.1 | 13.5 | 14.0 | 14.4 | 15.1 | 15.7 | 16.0 | ... |
| M(I) - hour heure | #13.6 | 14.0 | 14.5 | 14.9 | 15.5 | 16.2 | 17.0 | ... |
| F(I)- hour heure | #10.9 | 11.4 | 12.1 | 12.3 | 12.8 | 13.7 | 14.0 | ... |
| MF(I) - month mois | #2 189.0 | 2 261.0 | 2 350.0 | 2 391.0 | 2 520.0 | 2 609.0 | ... | ... |
| M(I) - month mois | #2 312.0 | 2 378.0 | 2 464.0 | 2 513.0 | 2 653.0 | 2 737.0 | ... | ... |
| F(I) - month mois | #1 739.0 | 1 830.0 | 1 945.0 | 1 944.0 | 2 051.0 | 2 160.0 | ... | ... |
| MF(II) - hour heure | #11.5 | 11.9 | 12.3 | 12.6 | 13.1 | 13.5 | ... | ... |
| M(II) - hour heure | #12.0 | 12.3 | 12.7 | 13.0 | 13.6 | 14.0 | ... | ... |
| F(II) - hour heure | #9.5 | 9.8 | 10.4 | 10.4 | 10.8 | 11.3 | ... | ... |
| MF(II) - month mois | #1 929.0 | 1 993.0 | 2 060.0 | 2 090.0 | 2 203.0 | 2 266.0 | ... | ... |
| M(II) - month mois | #2 023.0 | 2 081.0 | 2 147.0 | 2 179.0 | 2 306.0 | 2 366.0 | ... | ... |
| F(II) - month mois | #1 496.0 | 1 568.0 | 1 647.0 | 1 643.0 | 1 712.0 | 1 771.0 | ... | ... |
| MF(V) - hour heure | #16.5 | 16.7 | 17.5 | 17.9 | 18.5 | 19.4 | ... | ... |
| M(V) - hour heure | #18.0 | 18.2 | 19.1 | 19.5 | 20.2 | 21.1 | | |

| Country or area §<br>Pays ou zone § | 1999 | 2000 | 2001 | 2002 | 2003 | 2004 | 2005 | 2006 |
|---|---|---|---|---|---|---|---|---|
| F(V) - hour heure | #12.8 | 13.2 | 14.3 | 14.3 | 14.9 | 15.8 | ... | ... |
| MF(V) - month mois | #2 770.0 | 2 834.0 | 2 962.0 | 2 989.0 | 2 520.0 | 2 609.0 | ... | ... |
| M(V) - month mois | #3 067.0 | 3 135.0 | 3 275.0 | 3 316.0 | 3 496.0 | 3 590.0 | ... | ... |
| F(V) - month mois | #2 066.0 | 2 145.0 | 2 292.0 | 2 266.0 | 2 422.0 | 2 541.0 | ... | ... |
| **Bermuda[17,18] (Bermuda dollar) — Bermudes[17,18] (dollar des Bermudes)** | | | | | | | | |
| MF(I) - month mois | ... | ... | ... | ... | ... | 4 167.0 | 3 561.0 | ... |
| M(I) - month mois | ... | ... | ... | ... | ... | 4 333.0 | 3 691.0 | ... |
| F(I) - month mois | ... | ... | ... | ... | ... | 2 375.0 | 3 347.0 | ... |
| **Bolivia[19] (boliviano) — Bolivie[19] (boliviano)** | | | | | | | | |
| MF(I) - month mois | 1 055.0 | 1 120.0[20] | ... | ... | ... | ... | ... | ... |
| **Bosnia and Herzegovina[21] (convertible marka) Bosnie-Herzégovine[21] (marka convertible)** | | | | | | | | |
| MF(I) - month mois | 550.8 | 606.9 | 651.9 | 709.9 | 770.9 | 784.6 | 819.9 | 887.1 |
| **Botswana[22,23] (pula) — Botswana[22,23] (pula)** | | | | | | | | |
| MF(I) - month mois | 785.0 | 783.0 | 891.0 | 889.0 | 944.0[24] | 1 173.0 | 1 219.0[24] | 1 314.0 |
| M(I) - month mois | 1 004.0 | 1 067.0 | ... | 1 200.0 | 1 296.0[24] | 1 490.0 | 1 608.0[24] | 1 597.0 |
| F(I) - month mois | 588.0 | 555.0 | 681.0 | 651.0 | 671.0[24] | 876.0 | 720.0[24] | 1 059.0 |
| **Brazil[13] (real) — Brésil[13] (real)** | | | | | | | | |
| MF(I) - month mois | 752.2 | 763.1 | 844.6 | 901.9 | ... | ... | ... | ... |
| M(I) - month mois | 844.5 | 854.2 | 946.9 | 1 009.8 | ... | ... | ... | ... |
| F(I) - month mois | 505.5 | 524.0 | 576.5 | 618.6 | ... | ... | ... | ... |
| **Bulgaria[25] (lev) — Bulgarie[25] (lev)** | | | | | | | | |
| MF(I) - month mois | 203.0[26] | 219.0 | 227.0 | 236.0 | 246.0 | 262.0 | 289.0 | 321.0 |
| M(I) - month mois | 232.0[26] | 257.0 | 271.0 | 284.0 | 293.0 | 311.0 | 343.0 | ... |
| F(I) - month mois | 172.0[26] | 181.0 | 185.0 | 192.0 | 203.0 | 216.0 | 237.0 | ... |
| **Cambodia[11] (riel) — Cambodge[11] (riel)** | | | | | | | | |
| MF(I) - month mois | ... | ... | 243 000.0 | ... | ... | ... | ... | ... |
| **Canada[27] (Canadian dollar) — Canada[27] (dollar canadien)** | | | | | | | | |
| MF(I) - week semaine | 780.9 | 795.4 | 808.0 | 831.6 | 842.6 | 858.9 | 883.5 | 903.9 |
| MF(II) - hour heure[28] | 17.8 | 18.3 | 18.6 | 19.2 | 19.7 | 20.3 | 20.6 | 20.7 |
| **Chile[29,30] (Chilean peso) — Chili[29,30] (peso chilien)** | | | | | | | | |
| MF(I) - month mois | 203 540.0[10] | 208 257.0[10] | 213 394.0[10] | 218 740.0[10] | 221 860.0[10] | 229 575.0[10] | 242 160.0[10] | 300 948.0 |
| **China[31] (yuan) — Chine[31] (yuan)** | | | | | | | | |
| MF(I) - month mois | 649.5 | 729.2 | 814.5 | 916.8 | 1 041.3 | 1 169.4 | 1 313.1 | 1 497.2 |
| **China, Hong Kong SAR[10] (Hong Kong dollar) — Chine, Hong Kong RAS[10] (dollar de Hong Kong)** | | | | | | | | |
| MF(I) - month mois[18,32] | ... | ... | ... | ... | 10 000.0 | 9 500.0 | 9 800.0 | ... |
| M(I) - month mois[18,32] | ... | ... | ... | ... | ... | ... | 11 000.0 | ... |
| F(I) - month mois[18,32] | ... | ... | ... | ... | ... | ... | 7 000.0 | ... |
| MF(II) - day jour | 334.7 | 335.4 | 342.6 | 326.1 | 322.2 | 324.3 | 279.0 | 321.7 |
| M(II) - day jour | 422.6 | 428.8 | 428.5 | 419.2 | 406.1 | 380.4 | 282.4 | 420.8 |
| F(II) - day jour | 268.9 | 278.1 | 280.6 | 268.2 | 262.7 | 280.0 | 273.8 | 256.9 |
| MF(V) - month mois | 11 853.0 | 11 869.7 | 12 133.1 | 11 950.7 | 11 508.8 | 11 498.1 | 11 622.0 | 11 972.4 |
| M(V) - month mois | 12 893.2 | 12 697.1 | 12 929.7 | 12 810.2 | 12 082.7 | 11 880.7 | 12 248.6 | 12 483.3 |
| F(V) - month mois | 10 846.7 | 11 101.4 | 11 395.0 | 11 123.2 | 11 021.1 | 11 139.3 | 11 015.0 | 11 552.3 |
| **China, Macao SAR (Macao pataca) — Chine, Macao RAS (pataca de Macao)** | | | | | | | | |
| MF(I) - month mois[33] | ... | 4 044.0 | 4 102.0 | 3 970.0 | 4 010.0 | 4 178.0 | 4 390.0 | 4 652.0 |
| M(I) - month mois[33] | ... | 5 411.0 | 5 382.0 | 5 250.0 | 5 335.0 | 5 750.0 | 5 961.0 | 6 193.0 |
| F(I) - month mois[33] | ... | 3 606.0 | 3 683.0 | 3 575.0 | 3 584.0 | 3 689.0 | 3 860.0 | 4 074.0 |
| MF(VI) - month mois[18] | 2 921.0 | 2 960.0 | 2 758.0 | 2 758.0 | 2 834.0 | 2 983.0 | 3 101.0 | 3 140.0 |
| M(VI) - month mois[18] | 4 738.0 | 4 690.0 | 4 527.0 | 4 469.0 | 4 363.0 | 4 829.0 | 4 765.0 | 5 462.0 |
| F(VI) - month mois[18] | 2 510.0 | 2 613.0 | 2 429.0 | 2 430.0 | 2 542.0 | 2 652.0 | 2 795.0 | 2 698.0 |
| **Colombia (Colombian peso) — Colombie (peso colombien)** | | | | | | | | |
| MF(I) - month mois[34,35,36] | ... | ... | ... | #353 590.0 | 442 510.0 | 468 406.0 | 506 020.0 | 608 137.0 |
| M(I) - month mois[34,35,36] | ... | ... | ... | #457 189.0 | 531 791.0 | 557 571.0 | 605 537.0 | 707 408.0 |
| F(I) - month mois[34,35,36] | ... | ... | ... | #258 415.0 | 347 588.0 | 365 782.0 | 394 964.0 | 473 334.0 |
| MF(VI) - month mois[10,23,27] | 427 313.0 | 420 734.0 | ... | ... | ... | ... | ... | ... |

| Country or area §<br>Pays ou zone § | 1999 | 2000 | 2001 | 2002 | 2003 | 2004 | 2005 | 2006 |
|---|---|---|---|---|---|---|---|---|
| **Costa Rica[38] (Costa Rican colón) — Costa Rica[38] (colón costa-ricien)** | | | | | | | | |
| MF(I) - hour heure | ... | ... | 617.2 | 700.8 | 758.8 | 768.5 | 953.0 | 993.3 |
| M(I) - hour heure | ... | ... | 626.8 | 742.3 | 780.2 | 795.8 | 1 006.1 | 1 028.5 |
| F(I)- hour heure | ... | ... | 597.3 | 594.4 | 703.6 | 688.6 | 793.6 | 890.3 |
| MF(I) - month mois | 97 774.5 | 108 777.0 | 128 207.0 | ... | ... | ... | 393 518.0 | ... |
| M(I) - month mois | 106 594.0 | 115 642.0 | 135 707.0 | ... | ... | ... | 410 986.0 | ... |
| F(I) - month mois | 77 969.3 | 93 773.0 | 112 596.0 | ... | ... | ... | 335 824.0 | ... |
| **Croatia[39] (kuna) — Croatie[39] (kuna)** | | | | | | | | |
| MF(I) - month mois | 3 869.0 | 4 100.0 | 4 465.0 | 4 794.0 | 4 952.0 | 5 189.0 | 5 452.0 | ... |
| M(I) - month mois | ... | ... | ... | ... | 5 412.0 | 5 680.0 | 5 969.0 | ... |
| F(I) - month mois | ... | ... | ... | ... | 4 196.0 | 4 359.0 | 4 560.0 | ... |
| **Cuba[10,40] (Cuban peso) — Cuba[10,40] (peso cubain)** | | | | | | | | |
| MF(I) - month mois | 225.0 | 242.0[41] | 255.0 | 263.0 | 275.0 | 290.0 | 338.0 | 404.0 |
| **Cyprus[15,29,42] (Cyprus pound) — Chypre[15,29,42] (livre chypriote)** | | | | | | | | |
| MF(I) - hour heure | 3.9 | 4.0 | 4.3 | 4.5 | 4.6 | 4.8 | 4.9 | 5.0 |
| M(I) - hour heure | 4.7 | 4.8 | 4.9 | 5.2 | 5.4 | 5.7 | 5.8 | 5.7 |
| F(I)- hour heure | 2.8 | 2.9 | 3.2 | 3.2 | 3.4 | 3.5 | 3.6 | 3.7 |
| MF(II) - hour heure | 3.4 | 3.5 | 3.7 | 3.9 | 4.1 | 4.2 | 4.3 | 4.9 |
| M(II) - hour heure | 4.1 | 4.2 | 4.3 | 4.6 | 4.8 | 5.0 | 5.1 | 5.3 |
| F(II) - hour heure | 2.6 | 2.7 | 2.8 | 2.7 | 2.9 | 2.9 | 3.0 | 3.2 |
| MF(II) - week semaine | 139.2 | 141.9 | 152.4 | 157.3 | 165.7 | 169.4 | 171.8 | 200.6 |
| M(II) - week semaine | 185.9 | 172.5 | 176.6 | 186.3 | 194.9 | 203.3 | 202.9 | 223.1 |
| F(II) - week semaine | 100.2 | 107.2 | 109.0 | 105.5 | 113.5 | 108.8 | 115.6 | 125.1 |
| MF(V) - month mois | 776.0 | 806.0 | 814.5 | 842.0 | 876.6 | 928.4 | 936.8 | 887.2 |
| M(V) - month mois | 919.0 | 954.0 | 967.2 | 1 005.7 | 1 038.9 | 1 108.2 | 1 105.0 | 1 035.1 |
| F(V) - month mois | 545.0 | 556.0 | 593.2 | 604.3 | 641.1 | 667.5 | 692.9 | 654.8 |
| **Czech Republic[43] (Czech koruna) — République tchèque[43] (couronne tchèque)** | | | | | | | | |
| MF(I) - month mois | 12 797.0 | 13 614.0 | 14 793.0 | 15 866.0 | 16 917.0 | 18 035.0[44] | ... | ... |
| MF(II) - month mois | 10 294.0 | 11 005.0 | 11 769.0 | 12 324.0 | 13 049.0 | 14 095.0 | 14 662.0 | ... |
| M(II) - month mois | 11 666.0 | 12 792.0 | 13 629.0 | 14 272.0 | 15 112.0 | 16 323.0 | 16 980.0 | ... |
| F(II) - month mois | 7 973.0 | 8 308.0 | 8 912.0 | 9 332.0 | 9 881.0 | 10 674.0 | 11 103.0 | ... |
| **Denmark[11,45] (Danish krone) — Danemark[11,45] (couronne danoise)** | | | | | | | | |
| MF(I) - hour heure | 182.3 | 188.6 | 199.1 | 207.0 | 215.3 | 217.2 | 226.6 | ... |
| M(I) - hour heure | 192.2 | 197.6 | 207.7 | 215.3 | 223.8 | 226.1 | 235.5 | ... |
| F(I)- hour heure | 160.3 | 166.7 | 178.8 | 186.8 | 194.5 | 196.8 | 204.7 | ... |
| **Dominican Republic (Dominican peso) — Rép. dominicaine (peso dominicain)** | | | | | | | | |
| MF(I) - hour heure | 27.1 | 24.1 | 28.2 | 29.4 | 32.7 | 50.8 | ... | ... |
| **Ecuador (sucre, US dollar) — Equateur (sucre, dollar des Etats-Unis)** | | | | | | | | |
| MF(I) - month mois | 4 158.3[46] | 159.6[47] | 257.2 | 294.3 | 338.2 | 370.6 | ... | ... |
| MF(II) - hour heure | 8 556.2 | 0.8[47] | 1.3 | ... | ... | ... | ... | ... |
| **Egypt[12,15] (Egyptian pound) — Egypte[12,15] (livre égyptienne)** | | | | | | | | |
| MF(II) - week semaine | 121.0 | 125.0 | 136.0 | 147.0 | 150.0 | 162.0 | ... | ... |
| M(II) - week semaine | 125.0 | 131.0 | 142.0 | 154.0 | 157.0 | 168.0 | ... | ... |
| F(II) - week semaine | 94.0 | 87.0 | 97.0 | 104.0 | 104.0 | 126.0 | ... | ... |
| **El Salvador (El Salvadoran colón, US dollar) — El Salvador (cólon salvadorien, dollar des Etats-Unis)** | | | | | | | | |
| MF(I) - month mois | 1 746.6 | 1 790.0 | 1 750.4 | 208.7[49] | 209.6 | 211.3 | ... | ... |
| M(I) - month mois | 2 157.8 | 2 241.1 | 2 117.4 | 253.8[49] | 249.6 | 261.8 | ... | ... |
| F(I) - month mois | 1 337.1 | 1 370.4 | 1 370.5 | 167.7[49] | 171.2 | 162.5 | ... | ... |
| MF(II) - hour heure[48] | 10.7[10] | 10.1[10] | ... | 1.2[49] | 1.3 | 1.4 | 1.5 | ... |
| M(II) - hour heure[48] | 12.1[10] | 11.4[10] | 10.3 | 1.3[49] | 1.5 | 1.7 | 1.5 | ... |
| F(II) - hour heure[48] | 9.2[10] | 9.0[10] | 9.5[49] | ... | 1.2 | 1.2 | 1.2 | ... |
| **Estonia (Estonian kroon) — Estonie (couronne estonienne)** | | | | | | | | |
| MF(I) - month mois | 4 374.0[50] | 4 844.0[50] | 5 337.0[50] | 5 884.0[50] | 6 403.0 | 7 012.0 | 7 760.0 | ... |

| Country or area §<br>Pays ou zone § | 1999 | 2000 | 2001 | 2002 | 2003 | 2004 | 2005 | 2006 |
|---|---|---|---|---|---|---|---|---|
| Fiji[10,51] (Fiji dollar) — Fidji[10,51] (dollar des Fidji) | | | | | | | | |
| MF(II) - day jour | 15.2 | ... | ... | ... | 17.7 | ... | ... | ... |
| Finland[52] (Finnish markka, euro) — Finlande[52] (markka finlandais, euro) | | | | | | | | |
| MF(I) - month mois[53] | 12 510.0[54] | 13 124.0[54] | #2 275.0 | 2 357.0 | 2 463.0[55] | 2 564.0 | 2 641.0 | ... |
| M(I) - month mois[53] | 13 305.0[54] | 13 939.0[54] | #2 402.0 | 2 475.0 | 2 581.0[55] | 2 685.0 | 2 772.0 | ... |
| F(I) - month mois[53] | 10 683.0[54] | 11 239.0[54] | #1 969.0 | 2 063.0 | 2 160.0[55] | 2 252.0 | 2 315.0 | ... |
| MF(II) - hour heure[11] | ... | ... | ... | ... | ... | ... | 13.9 | ... |
| M(II) - hour heure[11] | ... | ... | ... | ... | ... | ... | 14.4 | ... |
| F(II) - hour heure[11] | ... | ... | ... | ... | ... | ... | 12.2 | ... |
| France (euro) — France (euro) | | | | | | | | |
| MF(I) - hour heure[56] | #13.4 | 14.1 | 14.7 | 15.3 | 15.9 | 16.4 | 16.8 | ... |
| M(I) - hour heure[56] | #14.3 | 15.0 | 15.6 | 16.2 | 16.8 | 17.3 | 17.7 | ... |
| F(I)- hour heure[56] | #11.2 | 11.8 | 12.4 | 13.0 | 13.5 | 14.0 | 14.5 | ... |
| MF(I) - month mois[57] | #1 459.4 | 1 477.0 | 1 506.9 | 1 562.7 | ... | ... | ... | ... |
| M(I) - month mois[57] | #1 573.8 | 1 591.0 | 1 618.5 | 1 668.8 | ... | ... | ... | ... |
| F(I) - month mois[57] | #1 191.8 | 1 205.9 | 1 241.7 | 1 307.9 | ... | ... | ... | ... |
| MF(II) - hour heure | #9.7 | 10.2 | 10.6 | 11.5 | 12.0 | 12.3 | 12.6 | ... |
| M(II) - hour heure | #10.1 | 10.6 | 11.1 | 12.0 | 12.4 | 12.8 | 13.0 | ... |
| F(II) - hour heure | #8.3 | 8.7 | 9.1 | 10.0 | 10.3 | 10.7 | 11.0 | ... |
| French Guiana (French franc, euro) — Guyane française (franc français, euro) | | | | | | | | |
| MF(I) - hour heure | 70.7 | 11.2[58] | 11.8 | ... | ... | ... | ... | ... |
| M(I) - hour heure | 74.5 | 11.9[58] | 12.5 | ... | ... | ... | ... | ... |
| French Polynesia (CFP franc) — Polynésie française (franc CFP) | | | | | | | | |
| M(I) - month mois | 187 996.0 | 196 279.0 | 202 046.0 | 205 866.0 | 213 876.0 | ... | ... | ... |
| F(I) - month mois | 160 946.0 | 165 206.0 | 176 580.0 | 177 719.0 | 186 653.0 | ... | ... | ... |
| Georgia (lari) — Géorgie (lari) | | | | | | | | |
| MF(I) - month mois | 87.4 | 99.3 | 120.8 | 143.4 | 152.5 | 183.9 | 212.1 | ... |
| M(I) - month mois | 101.1 | 111.2 | 141.5 | 165.1 | 174.9 | 210.2 | 243.5 | ... |
| F(I) - month mois | 63.3 | 69.3 | 82.7 | 101.6 | 108.4 | 132.2 | 147.7 | ... |
| Germany (deutsche mark, euro) — Allemagne (deutsche mark, euro) | | | | | | | | |
| MF(II) - hour heure | 27.5[59] | 27.8[59] | #14.4 | 14.7 | 15.1 | 15.4 | 15.6 | 15.7 |
| M(II) - hour heure | 28.8[59] | 29.1[59] | #15.1 | 15.4 | 15.7 | 16.0 | 16.2 | 16.4 |
| F(II) - hour heure | 21.4[59] | 21.4[59] | #11.1 | 11.4 | 11.6 | 11.9 | 12.0 | 12.1 |
| Gibraltar[15,60] (Gibraltar pound) — Gibraltar[15,60] (livre de Gibraltar) | | | | | | | | |
| MF(II) - hour heure | 6.8 | 6.4 | 6.6 | 7.0 | 7.2 | 8.0 | 8.4 | ... |
| M(II) - hour heure | 7.0 | 6.6 | 6.7 | 7.2 | 7.2 | 8.1 | 8.6 | ... |
| F(II) - hour heure | 5.3 | 5.3 | 5.7 | 5.7 | 5.9 | 6.0 | 6.9 | ... |
| MF(II) - week semaine[10] | 320.0 | 291.6 | 299.5 | 311.3 | 323.8 | 400.6 | 419.1 | ... |
| M(II) - week semaine[10] | 332.6 | 299.8 | 306.4 | 339.5 | 333.2 | 414.3 | 433.3 | ... |
| F(II) - week semaine[10] | 210.4 | 213.8 | 233.9 | 237.1 | 235.5 | 249.7 | 260.0 | ... |
| Greece[12] (euro) — Grèce[12] (euro) | | | | | | | | |
| MF(II) - hour heure | ... | 1 020.0 | ... | 1 140.0 | ... | ... | ... | ... |
| Guadeloupe (French franc, euro) — Guadeloupe (franc français, euro) | | | | | | | | |
| MF(I) - hour heure | 62.7 | 9.8[58] | 10.3 | ... | ... | ... | ... | ... |
| M(I) - hour heure | 66.0 | 10.4[58] | 10.8 | ... | ... | ... | ... | ... |
| F(I)- hour heure | 58.7 | 9.2[58] | 9.7 | ... | ... | ... | ... | ... |
| Guam[10,11,13] (US dollar) — Guam[10,11,13] (dollar des Etats-Unis) | | | | | | | | |
| MF(II) - hour heure | ... | 14.0 | 11.6 | 13.1 | 12.2 | 12.5 | 12.3 | 14.9 |
| Guatemala[10] (quetzal) — Guatemala[10] (quetzal) | | | | | | | | |
| MF(I) - month mois | 1 602.3 | 1 655.3 | 1 732.3 | 1 837.3 | ... | ... | ... | ... |
| Honduras[11] (lempira) — Honduras[11] (lempira) | | | | | | | | |
| MF(I) - day jour | ... | ... | ... | ... | ... | ... | ... | 21.7 |

| Country or area §<br>Pays ou zone § | 1999 | 2000 | 2001 | 2002 | 2003 | 2004 | 2005 | 2006 |
|---|---|---|---|---|---|---|---|---|
| Hungary[53,61] (forint) — Hongrie[53,61] (forint) | | | | | | | | |
| MF(I) - month mois | 76 099.0[62] | 88 551.0 | 101 700.0 | 114 297.0 | 124 770.0 | 136 992.0 | 147 234.0 | 158 662.0 |
| M(I) - month mois | 86 866.0[62] | 100 351.0 | 115 830.0 | 127 916.0 | 140 244.0 | 153 396.0 | 164 230.0 | ... |
| F(I) - month mois | 61 898.0[62] | 72 962.0 | 82 761.0 | 94 882.0 | 102 585.0 | 112 946.0 | 121 082.0 | ... |
| Iceland (Icelandic króna) — Islande (couronne islandaise) | | | | | | | | |
| MF(I) - hour heure[63] | 864.0 | 945.0 | 1 049.0 | 1 108.0 | 1 173.0 | 1 234.0 | ... | ... |
| M(I) - hour heure[63] | 957.0 | 1 044.0 | 1 153.0 | 1 216.0 | 1 295.0 | 1 353.0 | ... | ... |
| F(I)- hour heure[63] | 760.0 | 814.0 | 905.0 | 968.0 | 1 003.0 | 1 079.0 | ... | ... |
| MF(I) - month mois[64] | 136 200.0 | 149 200.0 | 166 400.0 | 176 800.0 | 186 100.0 | 194 900.0 | ... | ... |
| M(I) - month mois[64] | 150 800.0 | 164 600.0 | 182 600.0 | 194 000.0 | 206 000.0 | 214 000.0 | ... | ... |
| F(I) - month mois[64] | 121 300.0 | 129 900.0 | 145 700.0 | 156 600.0 | 161 200.0 | 173 200.0 | ... | ... |
| India[10,65] (Indian rupee) — Inde[10,65] (roupie indienne) | | | | | | | | |
| MF(II) - month mois | 1 548.5 | 1 280.8 | 1 893.2 | 1 158.6 | 1 078.9 | 1 731.8 | ... | ... |
| Indonesia[10,13,46,66] (Indonesian rupiah) — Indonésie[10,13,46,66] (roupie indonésien) | | | | | | | | |
| MF(II) - week semaine | 75.3 | 98.0 | 129.2 | ... | ... | ... | ... | ... |
| Iran (Islamic Rep. of) (Iranian rial) — Iran (Rép. islamique d') (rial iranien) | | | | | | | | |
| MF(I) - month mois | 698 899.0 | 867 526.0 | 1 014 285.0 | 1 189 654.0 | ... | ... | ... | ... |
| M(I) - month mois | 709 212.0 | 880 779.0 | 1 029 232.0 | 1 198 461.0 | ... | ... | ... | ... |
| F(I) - month mois | 554 231.0 | 685 514.0 | 828 265.0 | 1 078 610.0 | ... | ... | ... | ... |
| Ireland (euro) — Irlande (euro) | | | | | | | | |
| MF(I) - week semaine[12,67] | #462.3 | 498.2 | 543.9 | 569.8 | 603.5 | 632.8 | 659.4 | 678.3 |
| MF(II) - hour heure[12,68] | #9.8 | 10.5 | 11.6 | 12.5 | 12.9 | 13.6 | 14.0 | 14.5 |
| M(II) - hour heure[12,69] | #10.7 | 11.4 | 12.4 | 13.3 | 13.8 | 14.4 | 14.8 | 15.3 |
| F(II) - hour heure[12,69] | #8.0 | 8.6 | 9.4 | 10.1 | 10.7 | 11.1 | 11.6 | 12.3 |
| MF(II) - week semaine[12,68] | #396.6 | 423.2 | 457.0 | 483.0 | 511.8 | 534.2 | 557.6 | 575.2 |
| M(II) - week semaine[12,69] | #453.0 | 477.7 | 512.4 | 538.4 | 564.9 | 588.9 | 609.9 | 624.5 |
| F(II) - week semaine[12,69] | #298.2 | 324.7 | 347.3 | 365.2 | 393.8 | 406.8 | 430.2 | 451.1 |
| Isle of Man[51] (pound sterling) — Ile de Man[51] (livre sterling) | | | | | | | | |
| MF(I) - hour heure | 9.1 | 8.5 | 9.0 | 10.3 | 9.7 | 10.4 | 10.6 | 11.0 |
| M(I) - hour heure | 9.5 | 9.2 | 9.2 | 10.9 | 11.0 | 10.3 | 10.9 | 11.1 |
| F(I)- hour heure | 7.5 | 6.8 | 8.5 | 7.7 | 7.5 | 10.7 | 9.2 | 10.7 |
| MF(I) - week semaine | 377.1 | 366.9 | 361.4 | 392.0 | 409.6 | 412.4 | 441.0 | 445.8 |
| M(I) - week semaine | 408.9 | 407.3 | 381.5 | 417.3 | 504.5 | 455.4 | 468.0 | 463.2 |
| F(I) - week semaine | 241.1 | 258.2 | 278.3 | 292.8 | 253.9 | 265.2 | 325.0 | 401.1 |
| Israel (new sheqel) — Israël (nouveau sheqel) | | | | | | | | |
| MF(I) - hour heure | 42.0 | 44.0 | ... | ... | ... | ... | ... | ... |
| MF(I) - month mois[70] | 8 227.0[71] | 8 665.0[71] | 9 088.0[72] | 9 179.0[72] | 9 218.0[72] | 9 477.0[72,73] | 9 848.0[72] | 10 297.0[72] |
| Jamaica[10] (Jamaican dollar) — Jamaïque[10] (dollar jamaïcain) | | | | | | | | |
| MF(I) - week semaine | 5 549.4 | 5 208.8 | 5 725.2 | 6 092.9 | | | | |
| Japan[74,75] (yen) — Japon[74,75] (yen) | | | | | | | | |
| MF(I) - month mois | 291 100.0[10] | 293 100.0[10] | 297 500.0[10] | 296 400.0[10] | 296 500.0[10] | 293 100.0 | 292 100.0 | 299 600.0 |
| M(I) - month mois | 327 700.0[10] | 328 100.0[10] | 331 400.0[10] | 328 300.0[10] | 327 800.0[10] | 323 100.0 | 323 800.0 | 332 300.0 |
| F(I) - month mois | 189 000.0[10] | 190 700.0[10] | 195 000.0[10] | 195 600.0[10] | 195 800.0[10] | 194 100.0 | 190 900.0 | 194 600.0 |
| Jersey[51,76,77] (pound) — Jersey[51,76,77] (livre) | | | | | | | | |
| MF(I) - week semaine | 400.0 | 420.0 | 450.0 | 460.0 | 480.0 | 500.0 | 530.0 | 530.0 |
| Jordan[15] (Jordan dinar) — Jordanie[15] (dinar jordanien) | | | | | | | | |
| MF(I) - day jour[10,78] | 5.5 | ... | ... | ... | ... | ... | ... | ... |
| M(I) - day jour[10,78] | 5.8 | ... | ... | ... | ... | ... | ... | ... |
| F(I) - day jour[10,78] | 4.0 | ... | ... | ... | ... | ... | ... | ... |
| MF(I) - month mois | 172.0 | 189.0 | 185.0 | 186.7 | 198.0 | 186.0 | 203.0 | ... |
| M(I) - month mois | 180.0 | 198.0 | 195.0 | 196.0 | 208.0 | 201.0 | 222.0 | ... |
| F(I) - month mois | 123.0 | 131.0 | 126.0 | 129.3 | 136.0 | 130.0 | 136.0 | ... |

| Country or area §<br>Pays ou zone § | 1999 | 2000 | 2001 | 2002 | 2003 | 2004 | 2005 | 2006 |
|---|---|---|---|---|---|---|---|---|
| **Kazakhstan (tenge) — Kazakhstan (tenge)** | | | | | | | | |
| MF(I) - month mois | 13 821.0 | 17 717.0 | 19 982.0 | 22 130.0 | 24 823.0 | 30 234.0 | ... | ... |
| M(I) - month mois | 14 991.0 | 19 510.0 | 22 184.0 | 24 479.0 | 27 515.0 | 33 542.0 | ... | ... |
| F(I) - month mois | 11 433.0 | 13 981.0 | 15 597.0 | 17 433.0 | 19 382.0 | 23 433.0 | ... | ... |
| **Korea, Republic of[29,46,79] (Korean won) — Corée, République de[29,46,79] (won coréen)** | | | | | | | | |
| MF(I) - month mois | 1 475.5 | 1 601.5 | 1 702.4 | 1 907.0 | 2 074.0 | 2 279.7 | 2 458.0 | 2 594.8 |
| M(I) - month mois | 1 686.3 | 1 826.0 | 1 936.0 | 2 177.0 | 2 369.7 | 2 599.8 | 2 798.6 | 2 931.9 |
| F(I) - month mois | 933.1 | 1 055.8 | 1 121.3 | 1 211.0 | 1 320.0 | 1 419.7 | 1 556.1 | 1 675.6 |
| **Kuwait[10] (Kuwaiti dinar) — Koweït[10] (dinar koweïtien)** | | | | | | | | |
| MF(I) - hour heure | 1.2 | 1.4 | ... | ... | ... | ... | ... | ... |
| **Kyrgyzstan (Kyrgyz som) — Kirghizistan (som kirghize)** | | | | | | | | |
| MF(I) - month mois | 1 962.3 | 2 020.1 | 2 390.6 | 2 834.0 | 3 182.6 | 3 758.6 | 4 229.6 | ... |
| **Latvia[80] (lats) — Lettonie[80] (lats)** | | | | | | | | |
| MF(I) - month mois | 129.0 | 135.1 | 140.3 | 145.5 | 159.3 | 176.4 | 200.3 | 239.6 |
| M(I) - month mois | 137.5 | 146.0 | 150.9 | 157.3 | 172.8 | 192.1 | 217.9 | 263.1 |
| F(I) - month mois | 118.5 | 122.9 | 127.1 | 131.1 | 142.0 | 155.9 | 177.3 | 209.0 |
| **Lithuania[81,82] (litas) — Lituanie[81,82] (litas)** | | | | | | | | |
| MF(I) - hour heure | 6.2[83,84] | 6.2 | 6.3 | 6.5 | 6.6 | 6.9 | 7.6 | 8.9 |
| M(I) - hour heure | 6.9[83,84] | 6.9 | 7.1 | 7.2 | 7.5 | 7.7 | 8.6 | 10.2 |
| F(I)- hour heure | 5.4[83,84] | 5.5 | 5.5 | 5.7 | 5.8 | 5.9 | 6.5 | 7.5 |
| MF(I) - month mois | 963.0 | 955.0 | 963.0 | 982.0 | ·1 016.0 | 1 085.0 | 1 184.0 | 1 386.0 |
| **Luxembourg[15] (euro) — Luxembourg[15] (euro)** | | | | | | | | |
| MF(II) - hour heure | #12.2 | 12.5 | 12.6 | 13.1 | 13.5 | 14.2 | 14.7 | 14.7 |
| M(II) - hour heure | #12.7 | 13.1 | 13.1 | 13.6 | 14.0 | 14.7 | 15.2 | 15.2 |
| F(II) - hour heure | #8.7 | 9.4 | 9.5 | 9.8 | 10.2 | 10.6 | 11.1 | 11.0 |
| MF(V) - month mois | #3 680.0 | 3 727.0 | 3 816.0 | 3 941.0 | 4 090.0 | 4 189.0 | 4 334.0 | 4 374.0 |
| M(V) - month mois | #3 944.0 | 3 995.0 | 4 104.0 | 4 251.0 | 4 412.0 | 4 510.0 | 4 663.0 | 4 710.0 |
| F(V) - month mois | #2 535.0 | 2 621.0 | 2 710.0 | 2 782.0 | 2 911.0 | 3 030.0 | 3 185.0 | 3 229.0 |
| **Madagascar (Malagasy ariary) Madagascar (ariary malgache)** | | | | | | | | |
| MF(I) - hour heure | ... | ... | ... | ... | ... | ... | 2 033.0 | ... |
| M(I) - hour heure | ... | ... | ... | ... | ... | ... | 2 106.0 | ... |
| F(I)- hour heure | ... | ... | ... | ... | ... | ... | 1 794.0 | ... |
| **Malaysia[10] (ringgit) — Malaisie[10] (ringgit)** | | | | | | | | |
| MF(I) - month mois | ... | 1 387.8 | 1 530.7 | ... | ... | ... | ... | ... |
| **Malta[13,85] (Maltese lira) — Malte[13,85] (lire maltaise)** | | | | | | | | |
| MF(VI) - hour heure | ... | 2.1 | 2.2 | 2.3 | 2.3 | 2.3 | 2.4 | 2.6 |
| M(VI)- hour heure | ... | 2.2 | 2.3 | 2.4 | 2.4 | 2.4 | 2.5 | 2.6 |
| F(VI) - hour heure | ... | 1.8 | 1.9 | 2.1 | 2.2 | 2.2 | 2.2 | 2.3 |
| **Martinique (French franc, euro) Martinique (franc français, euro)** | | | | | | | | |
| MF(I) - hour heure | 63.5 | 10.0[58] | 10.4 | ... | ... | ... | ... | ... |
| M(I) - hour heure | 66.4 | 10.4[58] | 10.8 | ... | ... | ... | ... | ... |
| F(I)- hour heure | 60.1 | 9.5[58] | 9.9 | ... | ... | ... | ... | ... |
| **Mauritius[86] (Mauritian rupee) — Maurice[86] (roupie mauricienne)** | | | | | | | | |
| MF(I) - month mois[12] | 5 142.0 | 5 544.0 | 5 856.0 | 6 155.0 | 6 668.0 | 7 299.0 | 7 798.0 | 8 209.0 |
| MF(II) - day jour[87] | 166.0 | 174.3 | ... | ... | ... | ... | ... | ... |
| MF(V) - month mois[10,12] | 7 034.0 | 7 638.0 | ... | ... | ... | ... | ... | ... |
| **Mexico (Mexican peso) — Mexique (peso mexicain)** | | | | | | | | |
| MF(I) - day jour[10] | 108.7 | 125.6 | 143.6 | ... | ... | ... | ... | ... |
| MF(I) - hour heure | 12.3 | 15.3 | 17.8 | 18.0 | 19.4 | ... | ... | ... |
| M(I) - hour heure | 13.5 | 16.7 | 19.3 | 19.8 | 21.2 | ... | ... | ... |

| Country or area §<br>Pays ou zone § | 1999 | 2000 | 2001 | 2002 | 2003 | 2004 | 2005 | 2006 |
|---|---|---|---|---|---|---|---|---|
| F(I)- hour heure | 9.9 | 12.3 | 14.7 | 14.4 | 15.7 | ... | ... | ... |
| MF(I) - month mois[88,89] | 2 406.2 | 2 952.4 | 3 403.0 | 3 558.8 | 3 756.6 | 3 885.3 | 4 158.6[90] | 4 428.9 |
| M(I) - month mois[88,89] | 2 664.1 | 3 298.6 | 3 790.6 | 3 993.2 | 4 174.3 | 4 272.0 | 4 656.0[90] | 4 862.6 |
| F(I) - month mois[88,89] | 1 862.1 | 2 277.0 | 2 654.1 | 2 718.1 | 2 917.4 | 3 113.7 | 3 231.6[90] | 3 611.4 |
| MF(II) - hour heure | 17.8 | 20.8 | 23.5 | 25.2 | 26.9 | ... | ... | ... |
| Moldova[43] (Moldovan leu)    Moldova[43] (leu moldove) | | | | | | | | |
| MF(I) - month mois | 492.6 | 677.7 | 813.1 | 971.8 | 1 216.1 | 1 417.8 | 1 651.6 | 1 914.5 |
| Mongolia[46] (togrog) — Mongolie[46] (togrog) | | | | | | | | |
| MF(I) - month mois | ... | 66.0[36] | ... | 68.7 | 82.7 | 92.8 | 100.5 | ... |
| M(I) - month mois | ... | 60.0[36] | 65.9 | 69.3 | 86.9 | 98.1 | 114.9 | ... |
| F(I) - month mois | ... | 70.0[36] | 64.8 | 68.2 | 75.6 | 89.1 | 88.9 | ... |
| Myanmar[10,91] (kyat) — Myanmar[10,91] (kyat) | | | | | | | | |
| M(I) - hour heure[92] | ... | 13.5 | 19.0 | 20.8 | 22.8 | 29.9 | 31.9 | ... |
| F(I)- hour heure[92] | ... | 20.8 | 17.5 | 19.6 | 20.3 | 27.2 | 28.4 | ... |
| M(I) - month mois[93] | 1 066.0 | ... | ... | ... | ... | ... | ... | ... |
| F(I) - month mois[93] | 1 190.9 | ... | ... | ... | ... | ... | ... | ... |
| Nepal[85,94,95] (Nepalese rupee) — Népal[85,94,95] (roupie népalaise) | | | | | | | | |
| MF(I) - month mois | 2 567.0 | ... | ... | ... | ... | ... | ... | ... |
| M(I) - month mois | 2 867.0 | ... | ... | ... | ... | ... | ... | ... |
| F(I) - month mois | 1 292.0 | ... | ... | ... | ... | ... | ... | ... |
| Netherlands[13,96] (Netherlands guilder, euro) — Pays-Bas[13,96] (florin néerlandais, euro) | | | | | | | | |
| MF(I) - hour heure | 33.3[97] | 34.4[97] | #16.5 | 17.1 | 17.8 | 18.2 | 18.5 | ... |
| M(I) - hour heure | 34.7[97] | 35.8[97] | #17.2 | 17.8 | 18.5 | 18.9 | 19.1 | ... |
| F(I)- hour heure | 26.9[97] | 28.0[97] | #13.5 | 14.1 | 14.7 | 15.4 | 15.6 | ... |
| MF(I) - month mois[16] | 4 797.0[97] | 4 958.0[97] | #2 392.0 | 2 487.0 | 2 572.0 | 2 637.0 | 2 689.0 | ... |
| M(I) - month mois [16] | 4 932.0[97] | 5 099.0[97] | #2 458.0 | 2 549.0 | 2 634.0 | 2 692.0 | 2 740.0 | ... |
| F(I) - month mois [16] | 3 870.0[97] | 4 001.0[97] | #1 944.0 | 2 039.0 | 2 123.0 | 2 221.0 | 2 282.0 | ... |
| Netherlands Antilles[98] (Netherlands Antillean guilder) — Antilles néerlandaises[98] (florin des Antilles néerlandaises) | | | | | | | | |
| MF(I) - month mois | ... | 2 565.0 | ... | ... | ... | ... | ... | ... |
| New Zealand[76,99,100] (New Zealand dollar) — Nouvelle-Zélande[76,99,100] (dollar néo-zélandais) | | | | | | | | |
| MF(I) - hour heure | ... | 17.0 | 17.4 | 18.0 | 18.8 | 19.3 | 19.6 | ... |
| M(I) - hour heure | ... | 17.9 | 18.3 | 18.9 | 19.8 | 20.2 | 20.5 | ... |
| F(I)- hour heure | ... | 14.5 | 14.8 | 15.3 | 15.9 | 16.6 | 16.8 | ... |
| Nicaragua[10] (córdoba) — Nicaragua[10] (córdoba) | | | | | | | | |
| MF(I) - hour heure | 12.0 | 13.2 | 13.5 | 13.5 | 13.5 | 13.5 | ... | ... |
| MF(I) - month mois | 3 097.7 | 3 221.9 | 3 272.9 | 3 276.0 | 3 279.0 | 3 283.0 | ... | ... |
| Norway[15,53,101] (Norwegian krone) — Norvège[15,53,101] (couronne norvégienne) | | | | | | | | |
| MF(I) - month mois | 22 441.0 | 23 388.0 | 24 426.0 | 25 991.0 | 26 944.0 | 27 920.0 | 28 908.0 | 30 162.0 |
| M(I) - month mois | 23 039.0 | 23 964.0 | 25 006.0 | 26 623.0 | 27 625.0 | 28 588.0 | 29 513.0 | 30 767.0 |
| F(I) - month mois | 20 017.0 | 21 091.0 | 22 051.0 | 23 483.0 | 24 260.0 | 25 290.0 | 26 432.0 | 27 649.0 |
| Pakistan[10] (Pakistan rupee) — Pakistan[10] (roupie pakistanaise) | | | | | | | | |
| MF(I) - month mois | 2 865.8 | 2 981.0 | 3 002.2 | 4 113.7 | ... | ... | ... | ... |
| Panama[18] (balboa) — Panama[18] (balboa) | | | | | | | | |
| MF(I) - month mois[86] | 250.9 | ... | ... | ... | ... | ... | ... | ... |
| M(I) - month mois[86] | 259.0 | ... | ... | ... | ... | ... | ... | ... |
| F(I) - month mois[86] | 241.3 | ... | ... | ... | ... | ... | ... | ... |
| MF(VI) - hour heure[85,102] | ... | ... | ... | 1.8 | 1.7 | 1.9 | 2.2 | 2.2 |
| M(VI)- hour heure [85,102] | ... | ... | ... | 1.8 | 1.7 | 1.9 | 2.1 | 2.1 |
| F(VI) - hour heure [85,102] | ... | ... | ... | 1.9 | 1.8 | 2.1 | 2.7 | 2.7 |

| Country or area §<br>Pays ou zone § | 1999 | 2000 | 2001 | 2002 | 2003 | 2004 | 2005 | 2006 |
|---|---|---|---|---|---|---|---|---|
| Paraguay[10] (guaraní) — Paraguay[10] (guaraní) | | | | | | | | |
| MF(I) - month mois | ... | 813 765.0 | 639 988.0 | 739 738.0 | 816 428.0 | ... | ... | ... |
| M(I) - month mois | ... | 995 539.0 | 746 213.0 | 880 891.0 | 966 821.0 | ... | ... | ... |
| F(I) - month mois | ... | 402 798.0 | 408 608.0 | 453 064.0 | 514 766.0 | ... | ... | ... |
| Peru[103] (new sol) — Pérou[103] (nouveau sol) | | | | | | | | |
| MF(II) - day jour | 25.6 | 27.2 | 27.1[104] | 28.1[105] | 27.2[106] | 28.0[106] | 29.8[106] | 28.8[106] |
| MF(V) - month mois[48] | 2 155.6 | 2 315.7 | 2 286.8[104] | 2 430.2[105] | 2 356.1[106] | 2 460.0[106] | 2 418.2[106] | 2 362.9[106] |
| Philippines (Philippine peso) — Philippines (peso philippin) | | | | | | | | |
| MF(I) - day jour[15] | ... | ... | 230.7 | 234.3 | 237.7 | 236.7 | 252.8 | 275.3 |
| M(I) - day jour[15] | ... | ... | 241.1 | 244.4 | 249.3 | 239.8 | 258.8 | 277.6 |
| F(I) - day jour[15] | ... | ... | 216.6 | 220.3 | 221.2 | 232.1 | 244.6 | 272.2 |
| MF(I) - month mois[107,108] | 8 347.0[109] | ... | 9 936.0 | ... | 11 166.0 | ... | ... | ... |
| M(I) - month mois[107,108,109] | 9 453.0 | ... | ... | ... | ... | ... | ... | ... |
| F(I) - month mois[107,108,109] | 7 168.0 | ... | ... | ... | ... | ... | ... | ... |
| Poland[110] (zloty) — Pologne[110] (zloty) | | | | | | | | |
| MF(I) - month mois | 1 598.9 | 1 756.4 | 1 866.5 | 1 911.5 | 1 980.7 | 2 053.7 | 2 123.6 | 2 246.0 |
| Portugal (Portuguese escudo, euro) — Portugal (escudo portugais, euro) | | | | | | | | |
| MF(I) - month mois | 122 327.0[111] | 126 923.0[111] | 133 939.0[111] | #705.0 | 775.0 | 806.0 | 837.0 | ... |
| M(I) - month mois | 146 138.0[111] | 151 422.0[111] | 159 822.0[111] | #840.0 | 905.0 | 934.0 | 966.0 | ... |
| F(I) - month mois | 94 057.0[111] | 98 574.0[111] | 103 835.0[111] | #547.0 | 596.0 | 622.0 | 649.0 | ... |
| MF(II) - hour heure | 718.0[111] | 620.0[111] | 673.0[111] | #3.8 | 3.7 | 3.8 | 3.9 | ... |
| M(II) - hour heure | 856.0[111] | 731.0[111] | 784.0[111] | #4.3 | 4.2 | 4.4 | 4.5 | ... |
| F(II) - hour heure | 554.0[111] | 500.0[111] | 536.0[111] | #2.9 | 2.9 | 3.0 | 3.0 | ... |
| Puerto Rico[10] (US dollar) — Porto Rico[10] (dollar des Etats-Unis) | | | | | | | | |
| MF(II) - hour heure | 8.9 | 9.4 | 9.8 | 10.3 | 10.5 | 10.8 | 11.1 | 11.5 |
| Qatar (Qatar riyal) — Qatar (riyal qatarien) | | | | | | | | |
| MF(I) - month mois | ... | ... | ... | ... | ... | ... | 3 394.0 | ... |
| M(I) - month mois | ... | ... | ... | ... | ... | ... | 3 343.0 | ... |
| F(I) - month mois | ... | ... | ... | ... | ... | ... | 5 384.0 | ... |
| MF(VI) - month mois[30,112] | ... | ... | 1 546.0 | ... | ... | ... | ... | ... |
| M(VI) - month mois[30,112] | ... | ... | 1 543.0 | ... | ... | ... | ... | ... |
| F(VI) - month mois[30,112] | ... | ... | 2 987.0 | ... | ... | ... | ... | ... |
| Romania (Romanian leu) — Roumanie (leu roumain) | | | | | | | | |
| MF(I) - month mois | 1 712 748.0 | 2 535 223.0 | 3 734 701.0 | 4 632 583.0 | 5 804 147.0 | 7 196 971.0 | 829.0[113] | ... |
| M(I) - month mois | ... | ... | ... | ... | 6 662 800.0 | 8 167 249.0 | 945.0[113] | ... |
| F(I) - month mois | ... | ... | ... | ... | 4 915 058.0 | 6 203 325.0 | 710.0[113] | ... |
| Russian Federation (ruble) — Fédération de Russie (ruble) | | | | | | | | |
| MF(I) - month mois | 1 579.0 | 2 365.0 | 3 447.0 | 4 439.0 | 5 603.0 | 6 849.0 | 8 421.0 | 10 199.0 |
| Saint Helena[114] (pound sterling) — Sainte-Hélène[114] (livre sterling) | | | | | | | | |
| MF(I) - month mois | 237.5 | 263.1 | 263.4 | 296.8 | ... | ... | ... | ... |
| M(I) - month mois | 251.8 | 272.5 | 272.9 | 317.1 | ... | ... | ... | ... |
| F(I) - month mois | 195.3 | 222.4 | 229.0 | 229.5 | ... | ... | ... | ... |
| Saint Lucia[115] (EC dollar) — Sainte-Lucie[115] (dollar des Caraïbes orientales) | | | | | | | | |
| M(II) - hour heure | ... | 5.3 | 6.3 | 5.3 | 7.0[116] | ... | ... | ... |
| F(II) - hour heure | ... | 4.4 | 4.1 | 4.5 | 5.0[116] | ... | ... | ... |
| M(V) - hour heure | ... | 10.8 | 10.0 | ... | 14.5 | ... | ... | ... |
| F(V) - hour heure | ... | 8.2 | 10.2 | 14.9 | 11.7 | ... | ... | ... |
| M(V) - month mois | ... | 1 919.8 | 1 656.3 | 2 901.7 | ... | ... | ... | ... |
| F(V) - month mois | ... | 1 477.3 | 1 588.0 | 2 435.1 | ... | ... | ... | ... |
| Saint Vincent-Grenadines (EC dollar) — Saint Vincent-Grenadines (dollar des Caraïbes orientales) | | | | | | | | |
| MF(I) - day jour | 25.8 | 25.8 | 26.5 | 26.5 | ... | ... | ... | ... |

| Country or area §<br>Pays ou zone § | 1999 | 2000 | 2001 | 2002 | 2003 | 2004 | 2005 | 2006 |
|---|---|---|---|---|---|---|---|---|
| San Marino (Italian lira, euro) — Saint-Marin (lire italienne, euro) | | | | | | | | |
| MF(I) - day jour[10,117] | 157 158.0 | ... | ... | ... | ... | ... | ... | ... |
| MF(I) - month mois | ... | ... | 3 289 004.2[117] | #1 868.2 | 1 922.1 | 1 900.0 | ... | ... |
| Serbia[118] (new dinar) — Serbie[118] (nouveau dinar) | | | | | | | | |
| MF(I) - month mois | ... | ... | ... | ... | ... | ... | ... | 25 830.0 |
| Serbia and Montenegro (new dinar) — Serbie-et-Monténégro (nouveau dinar) | | | | | | | | |
| MF(I) - month mois | 1 053.0[119] | 2 230.0 | 4 786.0 | 11 065.0[120] | 12 996.0[121] | 16 065.0[121] | 20 366.0[121] | ... |
| Seychelles (Seychelles rupee) — Seychelles (roupie seychelloises) | | | | | | | | |
| MF(I) - month mois | 2 962.0 | 3 067.0 | 3 235.0 | 3 300.0 | 2 986.0 | 3 042.0 | 3 314.0 | 3 350.0 |
| Singapore (Singapore dollar) — Singapour (dollar singapourien) | | | | | | | | |
| MF(I) - month mois | 2 803.0 | 3 036.0 | 3 117.0 | 3 154.0 | 3 265.0 | 3 350.0 | 3 495.0 | 3 618.0[122] |
| M(I) - month mois | 3 384.0 | 3 653.0 | 3 752.0 | 3 762.0 | 3 881.0 | 3 969.0 | 4 111.0 | 4 218.0[122] |
| F(I) - month mois | 2 007.0 | 2 181.0 | 2 226.0 | 2 283.0 | 2 374.0 | 2 442.0 | 2 563.0 | 2 682.0[122] |
| Slovakia[123] (Slovak koruna) — Slovaquie[123] (couronne slovaque) | | | | | | | | |
| MF(I) - month mois | 10 758.0 | 11 722.0 | 12 908.0 | 13 837.0 | 14 873.0 | 16 378.0 | 17 604.0 | 18 817.0 |
| Slovenia (tolar) — Slovénie (tolar) | | | | | | | | |
| MF(I) - month mois | 144 110.0 | 161 296.0 | 178 596.0 | 196 220.0 | 211 060.0 | 226 029.0 | 238 985.0[124] | 252 162.0 |
| South Africa[10] (rand) — Afrique du Sud[10] (rand) | | | | | | | | |
| MF(I) - month mois | 4 018.0 | 4 323.0 | 4 701.0 | 5 197.0[44] | ... | ... | 6 546.5 | 6 911.8 |
| Spain[125] (euro) — Espagne[125] (euro) | | | | | | | | |
| MF(I) - hour heure | #9.8 | 9.8 | 10.4 | 10.7 | 11.4 | 11.4 | 11.8 | 12.3 |
| Sri Lanka[10,91] (Sri Lanka rupee) — Sri Lanka[10,91] (roupie sri-lankaise) | | | | | | | | |
| MF(II) - day jour | 199.2 | 222.5 | 230.7 | 273.1 | 306.3 | 309.0 | 336.5 | ... |
| M(II) - day jour | 203.9 | 222.6 | 233.1 | 278.1 | 311.2 | 312.1 | 338.1 | ... |
| F(II) - day jour | 165.8 | 185.6 | 201.3 | 235.1 | 253.0 | 270.0 | 327.9 | ... |
| MF(II) - hour heure | 22.0 | 24.9 | 27.1 | 31.9 | 33.2 | 35.5 | 36.9 | ... |
| M(II) - hour heure | 22.3 | 25.3 | 27.5 | 32.1 | 33.6 | 35.8 | 37.1 | ... |
| F(II) - hour heure | 18.1 | 20.4 | 22.6 | 28.0 | 28.9 | 31.2 | 35.1 | ... |
| Sweden[11,126,127] (Swedish krona) — Suède[11,126,127] (couronne suédoise) | | | | | | | | |
| MF(II) - hour heure | 106.9 | 111.3 | 114.9 | 118.2 | 122.0 | 126.1 | 129.9 | 133.8 |
| M(II) - hour heure | 108.7 | 113.3 | 116.9 | 120.2 | 124.1 | 128.4 | 132.2 | 136.1 |
| F(II) - hour heure | 99.6 | 103.4 | 106.6 | 109.4 | 112.9 | 116.8 | 119.9 | 124.1 |
| Switzerland[128] (Swiss franc) — Suisse[128] (franc suisse) | | | | | | | | |
| MF(I) - month mois | ... | 5 862.0 | ... | 6 155.0 | ... | 6 349.0 | ... | ... |
| M(I) - month mois | ... | 6 296.0 | ... | 6 552.0 | ... | 6 726.0 | ... | ... |
| F(I) - month mois | ... | 4 550.0 | ... | 4 926.0 | ... | 5 162.0 | ... | ... |
| Thailand (baht) — Thaïlande (baht) | | | | | | | | |
| MF(II) - month mois | 5 907.0[10,129,130] | 5 839.0[10,130] | 6 064.6 | 6 795.3 | 6 432.2 | 6 129.0 | 6 407.4 | 6 941.6 |
| M(II) - month mois | ... | 6 612.0[10] | 7 112.7 | 7 449.2 | 7 344.8 | ... | ... | 7 973.4 |
| F(II) - month mois | ... | 5 052.0[10] | 5 122.4 | 6 143.7 | 5 538.8 | ... | ... | 5 996.6 |
| TFYR of Macedonia[131] (TFYR Macedonian denar) — L'ex-R.y. Macédoine[131] (denar de l'ex-R.Y. Macédoine) | | | | | | | | |
| MF(I) - month mois | ... | ... | 9 577.0 | 9 944.0 | 10 028.0 | 10 486.0 | 10 298.0 | 10 624.0 |
| Trinidad and Tobago (Trinidad and Tobago dollar) — Trinité-et-Tobago (dollar de la Trinité-et-Tobago) | | | | | | | | |
| MF(I) - week semaine | 938.8 | 1 170.1 | 1 161.2 | 1 161.6 | ... | ... | ... | ... |
| Turkey[12] (new Turkish Lira) — Turquie[12] (nouveau livre turque) | | | | | | | | |
| MF(I) - day jour[46] | 10 477.2 | 16 225.0 | 21 882.0 | ... | ... | ... | ... | ... |
| MF(I) - hour heure[132,133] | 1 397.0 | 2 163.3 | 2 917.6 | ... | ... | ... | ... | ... |
| MF(I) - month mois[133,134] | 251 453.0 | 389 395.8 | 525 175.7 | ... | ... | ... | ... | ... |
| Ukraine (hryvnia) — Ukraine (hryvnia) | | | | | | | | |
| MF(I) - month mois | 188.0[10] | 289.0[10] | 395.3[10] | 441.3 | 552.9 | 700.0 | 905.1 | 1 137.3 |
| M(I) - month mois | 205.7[10] | 269.2[10] | 367.5[10] | 509.0 | 640.8 | 809.0 | 1 042.3 | 1 302.1 |
| F(I) - month mois | 148.9[10] | 190.9[10] | 256.2[10] | 358.9 | 443.5 | 562.9 | 727.0 | 920.0 |

| Country or area §<br>Pays ou zone § | 1999 | 2000 | 2001 | 2002 | 2003 | 2004 | 2005 | 2006 |
|---|---|---|---|---|---|---|---|---|
| **United Kingdom[135,136,137] (pound sterling) — Royaume-Uni[135,136,137] (livre sterling)** | | | | | | | | |
| MF(I) - hour heure | 9.8 | 10.1 | 10.7 | 11.1 | 11.7 | 12.0 | 12.5 | 13.0 |
| M(I) - hour heure | 10.3 | 10.6 | 11.2 | 11.6 | 12.1 | 12.5 | 13.0 | 13.4 |
| F(I)- hour heure | 7.7 | 8.0 | 8.5 | 9.0 | 9.6 | 10.0 | 10.5 | 10.9 |
| MF(I) - week semaine | 402.7 | 417.2 | 439.9 | 455.6 | 476.5 | 493.1 | 508.0 | 528.4 |
| M(I) - week semaine | 431.7 | 445.6 | 464.9 | 482.9 | 503.0 | 519.4 | 533.8 | 554.9 |
| F(I) - week semaine | 299.3 | 312.1 | 332.2 | 350.8 | 372.8 | 388.1 | 404.3 | 422.6 |
| **United States (US dollar) — Etats-Unis (dollar des Etats-Unis)** | | | | | | | | |
| MF(II) - hour heure[138,139] | 13.9 | 14.3 | 14.8 | 15.3 | 15.7 | 16.2 | 16.6 | 16.8 |
| MF(II) - week semaine [10] | 579.6 | 567.8 | 603.6 | 625.8[44] | ... | ... | ... | ... |
| **United States Virgin Is. (US dollar)    Iles Vierges américaines (dollar des Etats-Unis)** | | | | | | | | |
| MF(II) - hour heure | ... | ... | 22.6 | 23.0 | 23.4 | 23.4 | 23.5 | 26.5 |
| **Uruguay[140] (Uruguayan peso) — Uruguay[140] (peso uruguayen)** | | | | | | | | |
| MF(I) - month mois | ... | 6 855.0 | 6 856.0 | ... | ... | ... | ... | ... |
| **Zimbabwe (Zimbabwe dollar) — Zimbabwe (dollar zimbabwéen)** | | | | | | | | |
| MF(I) - hour heure | 29.4 | 45.9 | 80.2 | 144.0 | ... | ... | ... | ... |
| MF(I) - month mois | 4 700.4 | 7 351.1 | 12 823.7 | ... | ... | ... | ... | ... |

Source

International Labour Office (ILO), Geneva, the ILO labour statistics database, last accessed May 2008.

Notes

§ I.  Employees.
II.  Wage earners.
III. Skilled wage earners.
IV. Unskilled wage earners.
V.  Salaried employees.
VI. Total employment.

Data are classified according to ISIC Rev. 3 unless indicated otherwise.

1  Including mining and quarrying.
2  State sector.
3  Local units with 10 or more workers.
4  Production and related workers.
5  Full-time adult non-managerial employees.
6  May of each year.
7  Per hour paid.
8  ATS;1 Euro = 13.7603 ATS.
9  New denomination of AZM; 1 AZN=5000 AZM.
10 Data classified according to ISIC Rev. 2.
11 Private sector.
12 Establishments with 10 or more persons employed.
13 December of each year.
14 New denomination of the rouble: 1 new rouble = 1000 old roubles.

15 October of each year.
16 Full-time employees only.
17 August of each year.
18 Median.
19 Main cities, except Pando.
20 September.
21 Data refer to the Federation of Bosnia and Herzegovina.

Source

Bureau international du travail (BIT), Genève, la base de données du BIT, dernier accès mai 2008.

Notes

§ I.  Salariés.
II.  Ouvriers.
III. Ouvriers qualifiés.
IV. Ouvriers non qualifiés.
V.  Employés.
VI. Emploi total.

Sauf indication contraire, les données sont classifiées selon la CITI, Rév. 3.

1  Y compris les industries extractives.
2  Secteur d'Etat.
3  Unités locales occupant 10 ouvriers et plus.
4  Ouvriers à la production et assimilés.
5  Salariés adultes à plein temps, non compris les cadres dirigeants.
6  Mai de chaque année.
7  Salaire horaire.
8  ATS; 1 Euro = 13,7603 ATS.
9  Nouvelle dénomination de l'AZM; 1 AZN = 5000 AZM.
10 Données classifiées selon la CITI, Rév. 2.
11 Secteur privé.
12 Etablissements occupant 10 personnes et plus.
13 Décembre de chaque année.
14 Nouvelle dénomination du rouble: 1 nouveau rouble = 1000 anciens roubles.

15 Octobre de chaque année.
16 Salariés à plein temps seulement.
17 Août de chaque année.
18 Médiane.
19 Villes principales, sauf Pando.
20 Septembre.
21 Les données se réfèrent à la Fédération de Bosnie et Herzégovine.

| | |
|---|---|
| 22 Citizens only. | 22 Nationaux seulement. |
| 23 September of each year. | 23 Septembre de chaque année. |
| 24 March. | 24 Mars. |
| 25 Employees under labour contract. | 25 Salariés sous contrat de travail. |
| 26 New denomination: 1 new lev = 1,000 old leva. | 26 Nouvelle dénomination: 1 nouveau lev = 1,000 anciens leva. |
| 27 Including overtime. | 27 Y compris les heures supplémentaires. |
| 28 Employees paid by the hour. | 28 Salariés rémunérés à l'heure. |
| 29 Including family allowances and the value of payments in kind. | 29 Y compris les allocations familiales et la valeur des paiements en nature. |
| 30 April of each year. | 30 Avril de chaque année. |
| 31 State-owned units, urban collective-owned units and other ownership units. | 31 Unités d'Etat, unités collectives urbaines et autres. |
| 32 Including outworkers. | 32 Y compris les travailleurs externes. |
| 33 Third quarter of each year. | 33 Troisième trimestre de chaque année. |
| 34 Excluding armed forces. | 34 Non compris les militaires. |
| 35 Persons aged 10 years and over. | 35 Personnes âgées de 10 ans et plus. |
| 36 Fourth quarter. | 36 Quatrième trimestre. |
| 37 Seven main cities. | 37 Sept villes principales. |
| 38 Main occupation; July of each year. | 38 Occupation principale; juillet de chaque année. |
| 39 Excluding employees in craft and trade. | 39 Non compris les salariés dans l'artisanat et dans le commerce. |
| 40 State sector (civilian). | 40 Secteur d'Etat (civils). |
| 41 Including employment-related allowances received from the State. | 41 Y compris les allocations en espèces liées à l'emploi et reçues de l'Etat. |
| 42 Adults. | 42 Adultes. |
| 43 Enterprises with 20 or more employees. | 43 Entreprises occupant 20 salariés et plus. |
| 44 Series discontinued. | 44 Série arrêtée. |
| 45 Excluding young people aged less than 18 years and trainees. | 45 Non compris les jeunes gens âgés de moins de 18 ans et les apprentis. |
| 46 Figures in thousands. | 46 Données en milliers. |
| 47 Prior to March 2000: sucres; 25,000 sucres =1 US dollar. | 47 Avant mars 2000: sucres; 25 000 sucres = 1 dollar EU. |
| 48 Urban areas. | 48 Régions urbaines. |
| 49 Prior to 2002: colones; 8.75 colones=1 US dollar. | 49 Avant 2002: colones; 8.75 colones=1 dollar EU. |
| 50 Enterprises with 50 or more employees, state-owned and municipal enterprises, institutions and organisations. | 50 Entreprises occupant 50 salariés et plus, entreprises d'Etat et municipales, institutions et organisations. |
| 51 June of each year. | 51 Juin de chaque année. |
| 52 Fourth quarter of each year. | 52 Quatrième trimestre de chaque année. |
| 53 Full-time employees. | 53 Salariés à plein temps. |
| 54 Prior to 2001: FIM; 1 Euro = 5.94573 FIM. | 54 Avant 2001: FIM; 1 Euro = 5.94573 FIM. |
| 55 From 2003: excl. seasonal and end-of-year bonuses. | 55 A partir de 2003: non compris les primes saisonnières et de fin d'année. |
| 56 Including managerial staff and intermediary occupations. | 56 Y compris les cadres et les professions intermédiaires. |
| 57 Euros; 1 Euro=6.55957 FRF; net earnings. | 57 Euros; 1 euro=6,55957 FRF; salaires nets. |
| 58 As from 2000: Euros; 1 Euro=6.55957 FRF. Including the overseas departments of France (DOM). | 58 A partir de 2000: Euros; 1 Euro=6,55957 FRF.Y compris les départements d'outre-mer (DOM). |
| 59 Prior to 2001: DEM; 1 Euro = 1.95583 DEM. | 59 Avant 2001: DEM; 1 Euro = 1.95583 DEM. |
| 60 Excluding part-time workers and juveniles. | 60 Non compris les travailleurs à temps partiel et les jeunes. |
| 61 Enterprises with 5 or more employees. | 61 Entreprises occupant 5 salariés et plus. |
| 62 Prior to 1999: enterprises with more than 20 employees. | 62 Avant 1999: entreprises occupant moins de 20 salariés. |
| 63 Adult employees; excluding irregular bonuses and the value of payments in kind. | 63 Salariés adultes; non compris les prestations versées irrégulièrement et la valeur des paiements en nature. |
| 64 Adult employees; excluding overtime payments and payments in kind. | 64 Salariés adultes; non compris la rémunération des heures supplémentaires et la valeur des paiements en nature. |
| 65 Fluctuations due to various changes in workers' coverage. | 65 Fluctuations dues à divers changements dans la couverture des travailleurs. |
| 66 Production workers. | 66 Travailleurs à la production. |
| 67 Adult and non-adult rates of pay. | 67 Taux de rémunération des adultes et des mineurs. |
| 68 Including juveniles. | 68 Y compris les jeunes gens. |
| 69 Wage-earners on adult rates of pay. | 69 Salariés rémunérés sur la base du taux de rémunération des adultes. |
| 70 Incl. payments subject to income tax. | 70 Y compris les versements soumis à l'impôt sur le revenu. |
| 71 Including workers from the Judea, Samaria and Gaza areas. | 71 Y compris les travailleurs des régions de Judée, Samarie et Gaza. |
| 72 Israeli workers only. | 72 Travailleurs israéliens seulement. |
| 73 From 2004: new sample; data not strictly comparable. | 73 A partir de 2004: nouvel échantillon; données non strictement comparables. |

74 Private sector; establishments with 10 or more regular employees; June of each year.

75 Regular scheduled cash earnings.

76 Full-time equivalent employees.

77 Approximate levels since survey aims at measuring changes; excl. bonuses.

78 Prior to 1999: establishments with 5 or more persons employed.

79 Establishments with 10 or more regular employees.

80 First quarter of each year.

81 All employees converted into full-time units.

82 Excluding individual unincorporated enterprises.

83 April.

84 Prior to 2000: full-time employees only.

85 Persons aged 15 years and over.

86 March of each year.

87 Wage-earners on daily rates of pay.

88 Second quarter of each year.

89 Persons aged 14 years and over.

90 Revised averages based on 2005 Population and Housing Census results; data not comparable.

91 March and Sep. of each year

92 Temporary workers.

93 Regular employees.

94 12 months ending in May of year indicated; main occupation.

95 Fluctuations in wages due to small sample size.

96 Excluding overtime payments.

97 Prior to 2001: NLG; 1 Euro = 2.20371 NLG.

98 Curaçao.

99 Establishments with the equivalent of more than 0.5 full-time paid employees.

100 February of each year.

101 Only remuneration in cash; excl. overtime payments.

102 August.

103 Figures at the disaggregated level are not representative because of the small sample size.

104 Average of the first three quarters.

105 Metropolitan Lima.

106 Second quarter.

107 Computed on the basis of annual wages.

108 Establishments with 20 or more persons employed.

109 Before 1999: establishments with 10 or more persons employed.

110 Including the value of payments in kind.

111 Prior to 2002: PTE; 1 Euro= 200.482 PTE.

112 Per month.

113 New denomination: 1 leu = 10 000 old lei.

114 Year ending in March of the year indicated.

115 Unweighted survey results.

116 Minimum rates.

117 Prior to 2002: ITL; 1 Euro=1936.27 ITL.

118 Excluding Kosovo.

119 As from 1999: excluding Kosovo and Metohia.

120 Prior to 2002: excl. private sector; net earnings.

121 Excluding Montenegro.

122 Methodology revised; data not strictly comparable.

123 Excluding enterprises with less than 20 employees.

124 Beginning 2005, methodology revised: excl. family allowances and the value of payments in kind.

74 Secteur privé; établissements occupant 10 salariés stables ou plus; juin de chaque années.

75 Gains en espèce tarifés réguliers.

76 Salariés en équivalents à plein temps.

77 Niveaux approximatifs étant donné que l'enquête vise à mesurer l'évolution; non compris les primes.

78 Avant 1999: établissements occupant 5 personnes et plus.

79 Etablissements occupant 10 salariés stables ou plus.

80 Le premier trimestre de chaque année.

81 Ensemble des salariés convertis en unités à plein temps.

82 Non compris les entreprises individuelles non constituées en société.

83 Avril.

84 Avant 2000 : employés à plein temps seulement.

85 Personnes âgées de 15 ans et plus.

86 Mars de chaque année.

87 Ouvriers rémunérés sur la base de taux de salaire journaliers.

88 Deuxième trimestre de chaque année.

89 Personnes âgées de 14 ans et plus.

90 Moyennes révisées sur la base des résultats du recensement de la population et du logement effectué en 2005; données non comparables.

91 Mars et sept. de chaque année.

92 Personnel temporairement.

93 Salariés stables.

94 12 mois se terminant en mai de l'année indiquée; occupation principale.

95 Fluctuations des salaires dues à la faible taille de l'échantillon.

96 Non compris la rémunération des heures supplémentaires.

97 Avant 2001: NGL; 1 Euro = 2.20371 NLG.

98 Curaçao.

99 Etablissements occupant plus de l'équivalent de 0.5 salarié à plein temps.

100 Février de chaque année.

101 Seulement rémunération en espèces; non compris les paiements pour heures supplémentaires.

102 Août.

103 Chiffres non représentatifs au niveau desagrégé en raison de la faible taille de l'échantillonage.

104 Moyenne des trois premiers trimestres.

105 Lima métropolitaine.

106 Deuxième trimestre.

107 Calculés sur la base de salaires annuèls.

108 Entreprises occupant 20 salariés et plus.

109 Avant 1999: établissements occupant 10 personnes et plus.

110 Y compris la valeur des paiements en nature.

111 Avant 2002: PTE: 1 Euro= 200,482 PTE.

112 Par mois.

113 Nouvelle dénomination: 1 leu = 1,000 anciens lei.

114 Année se terminant en mars de l'année indiquée.

115 Résultats d'enquête non pondérés.

116 Taux minima.

117 Avant 2002: ITL; 1 Euro=1936,27 ITL.

118 Non compris Kosovo.

119 A partir de 1999: non compris Kosovo et Metohia.

120 Avant 2002: non compris le secteur privé; gains nets.

121 Non compris Monténégro.

122 Méthodologie révisée; les données ne sont pas strictement comparables.

123 Non compris les entreprises occupant moins de 20 salariés.

124 A partir de 2005, méthodologie révisée: non compris les allocations familiales et la valeur des paiements en nature.

125   Including overtime payments and irregular gratuities.

126   Adults; prior to 1998: 2nd quarter of each year; 1998-2000: Sept-Oct. of each year.

127   Excl. holidays, sick-leave and overtime payments.

128   Standardised monthly earnings (40 hours x 4 1/3 weeks).

129   Excl. public enterprises.

130   March of each year. Average wage rates for normal/usual hours of work.

131   Net earnings.

132   Excluding overtime payments and irregular bonuses and allowances.

133   Figures in thousands; Jan - June.

134   Including overtime payments and irregular bonuses and allowances.

135   Including overtime payments.

136   Results with imputation and weighting.

137   April; full-time employees on adult rates.

138   National classification not strictly compatible with ISIC.

139   Private sector; production workers.

140   Establishments with 5 or more persons employed.

125   Y compris la rémunération des heures supplémentaires et les prestations versées irrégulièrement.

126   Adultes; avant 1998: 2ème trimestre de chaque année; 1998-2000: sept.-oct. de chaque année.

127   Non compris les versements pour les vacances, congés maladie ainsi que la rémunération des heures supplémentaires.

128   Gains mensuels standardisés (40 heures x 4 1/3 semaines).

129   Non compris les entreprises publiques.

130   Mars de chaque année. Taux de salaire moyens pour la durée normale/usuelle du travail.

131   Gains nets.

132   Non compris la rémunération des heures supplémentaires et les prestations versées irrégulièrement.

133   Chiffres en milliers; jan - juin.

134   Y compris la rémunération des heures supplémentaires et les prestations versées irrégulièrement.

135   Y compris la rémunération des heures supplémentaires.

136   Résultats après imputation et pondération.

137   Avril; salariés à plein temps rémunérés sur la base de taux de salaires pour adultes.

138   Classification nationale non strictement compatible avec la CITI.

139   Secteur privé. Travailleurs à la production.

140   Entreprises occupant 5 salariés et plus.

# Producer price indices
Index base: 2000 = 100

# Indices des prix à la production
Indices base: 2000 = 100

| Country or area | 2000 | 2001 | 2002 | 2003 | 2004 | 2005 | 2006 | Pays ou zone |
|---|---|---|---|---|---|---|---|---|
| **Argentina** | | | | | | | | **Argentine** |
| Domestic supply[1,2] | 100 | 98 | 173 | 204 | 219 | 234 | 260 | Offre intérieure[1,2] |
| Domestic production | 100 | 98 | 168 | 200 | 216 | 232 | 258 | Production intérieure |
| Agricultural products[2] | 100 | 98 | 242 | 251 | 267 | 239 | 281 | Produits agricoles[2] |
| Industrial products[2,3] | 100 | 98 | 160 | 190 | 205 | 217 | 237 | Produits industriels[2,3] |
| Imported goods[3] | 100 | 97 | 253 | 258 | 266 | 268 | 289 | Produits importés[3] |
| **Australia[4,5]** | | | | | | | | **Australie[4,5]** |
| Domestic supply | 100 | 102 | 103 | 105 | 107 | 110 | 115 | Offre intérieure |
| Domestic production | 100 | 102 | 104 | 106 | 113 | 118 | 123 | Production intérieure |
| Agricultural products | 100 | 118 | 123 | 124 | ... | 130 | 128 | Produits agricoles |
| Industrial products[2,3,6] | 100 | 103 | ... | 104 | 108 | 114 | 123 | Produits industriels[2,3,6] |
| Imported goods | 100 | ... | 101 | 93 | 88 | 89 | 92 | Produits importés |
| Raw materials | 100 | 102 | 101 | 102 | 104 | 110 | 119 | Matières premières |
| Intermediate goods | 100 | 102 | 102 | 102 | 104 | 109 | 117 | Produits intermédiaires |
| Consumer goods | 100 | 102 | 105 | 104 | 104 | 106 | 111 | Biens de consommation |
| Capital goods | 100 | 102 | 105 | 106 | 109 | 114 | 118 | Biens d'équipement |
| **Austria** | | | | | | | | **Autriche** |
| Domestic supply[2,7] | 100 | 102 | 101 | 103 | 108 | 110 | 113 | Offre intérieure[2,7] |
| Agricultural products | 100 | 104 | 102 | 108 | 109 | 102 | 104 | Produits agricoles |
| Intermediate goods | 100 | 101 | 100 | 102 | 113 | 116 | 123 | Produits intermédiaires |
| Consumer goods[2] | 100 | 102 | 103 | 105 | 106 | 109 | 110 | Biens de consommation[2] |
| Capital goods[2] | 100 | 100 | 100 | 100 | 100 | 99 | 98 | Biens d'équipement[2] |
| **Bangladesh[5]** | | | | | | | | **Bangladesh[5]** |
| Domestic supply[2,7] | 100 | 100 | 102 | 108 | 112 | ... | ... | Offre intérieure[2,7] |
| Agricultural products[2,8] | 100 | 99 | 102 | 108 | 112 | ... | ... | Produits agricoles[2,8] |
| Industrial products[2,3,8] | 100 | 101 | 105 | 107 | 110 | ... | ... | Produits industriels[2,3,8] |
| Raw materials | 100 | 101 | 103 | 113 | 107 | ... | ... | Matières premières |
| **Belarus** | | | | | | | | **Bélarus** |
| Domestic supply | 100 | 172 | 241 | 332 | 412 | 461 | 500 | Offre intérieure |
| Intermediate goods | 100 | 177 | 259 | 389 | 489 | 551 | 601 | Produits intermédiaires |
| Consumer goods | 100 | 166 | 223 | 273 | 332 | 366 | 390 | Biens de consommation |
| Capital goods | 100 | 172 | 224 | 272 | 337 | 384 | 419 | Biens d'équipement |
| **Belgium** | | | | | | | | **Belgique** |
| Domestic production[9] | 100 | ... | 102 | 103 | 107 | 110 | ... | Production intérieure[9] |
| Agricultural products[2] | 100 | 104 | ... | ... | ... | ... | ... | Produits agricoles[2] |
| Industrial products | 100 | 100 | 101 | 100 | 107 | 107 | ... | Produits industriels |
| Intermediate goods | 100 | 101 | 101 | 102 | 108 | 112 | ... | Produits intermédiaires |
| Consumer goods | 100 | 98 | 98 | 95 | 94 | 96 | ... | Biens de consommation |
| Capital goods | 100 | 100 | 100 | 100 | 102 | 104 | ... | Biens d'équipement |
| **Bolivia** | | | | | | | | **Bolivie** |
| Industrial products | 100 | 102 | 104 | 107 | ... | ... | ... | Produits industriels |
| Raw materials | 100 | 107 | 108 | 117 | ... | ... | ... | Matières premières |
| Consumer goods | 100 | 101 | 103 | 106 | ... | ... | ... | Biens de consommation |
| Capital goods | 100 | 103 | 109 | 111 | ... | ... | ... | Biens d'équipement |
| **Botswana** | | | | | | | | **Botswana** |
| Domestic supply | 100 | 105 | 112 | 123 | 133 | ... | ... | Offre intérieure |
| **Brazil** | | | | | | | | **Brésil** |
| Domestic supply[10] | 100 | 113 | 130 | 164 | 185 | 195 | 197 | Offre intérieure[10] |
| Agricultural products[10] | 100 | 117 | 142 | 186 | 197 | 192 | 185 | Produits agricoles[10] |
| Industrial products[10] | 100 | 111 | 127 | 161 | 180 | 196 | 200 | Produits industriels[10] |
| Raw materials[10] | 100 | 113 | 133 | 169 | 191 | 192 | 187 | Matières premières[10] |
| Consumer goods[10] | 100 | 109 | 130 | 165 | 176 | 184 | 186 | Biens de consommation[10] |
| Capital goods | 100 | 109 | 121 | 147 | 172 | 190 | 194 | Biens d'équipement |

| Country or area | 2000 | 2001 | 2002 | 2003 | 2004 | 2005 | 2006 | Pays ou zone |
|---|---|---|---|---|---|---|---|---|
| Bulgaria | | | | | | | | Bulgarie |
| Domestic supply | 100 | 104 | 105 | 110 | 117 | ... | ... | Offre intérieure |
| Canada | | | | | | | | Canada |
| Agricultural products[2] | 100 | 107 | 111 | 107 | 104 | 102 | 101 | Produits agricoles[2] |
| Industrial products[2,3,11] | 127 | 128 | 128 | 126 | 130 | 132 | 135 | Produits industriels[2,3,11] |
| Raw materials[12] | 100 | 99 | 98 | 100 | 112 | 127 | 141 | Matières premières[12] |
| Intermediate goods[11] | 124 | 123 | 122 | 122 | 129 | 133 | 138 | Produits intermédiaires[11] |
| Chile | | | | | | | | Chili |
| Domestic supply | 100 | 108 | 115 | 123 | 126 | 133 | 142 | Offre intérieure |
| Domestic production | 100 | 106 | 112 | 120 | 126 | 135 | 146 | Production intérieure |
| Agricultural products | 100 | 99 | 113 | 113 | 120 | 129 | 141 | Produits agricoles |
| Industrial products[7] | 100 | 107 | 112 | 121 | 125 | 133 | 140 | Produits industriels[7] |
| Imported goods | 100 | 114 | 124 | 131 | 125 | 126 | 132 | Produits importés |
| China, Hong Kong SAR | | | | | | | | Chine, Hong Kong RAS |
| Industrial products | 100 | 93 | 94 | 95 | 98 | 98 | 101 | Produits industriels |
| Colombia[13] | | | | | | | | Colombie[13] |
| Domestic supply[2] | 100 | 107 | 117 | 124 | 129 | 132 | ... | Offre intérieure[2] |
| Domestic production | 100 | 108 | 115 | 123 | 131 | 135 | ... | Production intérieure |
| Agricultural products | 100 | 108 | 117 | 120 | 128 | 135 | ... | Produits agricoles |
| Industrial products | 100 | 107 | 116 | 124 | 129 | 130 | ... | Produits industriels |
| Imported goods | 100 | 105 | 121 | 127 | 124 | 122 | ... | Produits importés |
| Raw materials | 100 | 107 | 116 | 127 | 139 | 139 | ... | Matières premières |
| Intermediate goods | 100 | 106 | 116 | 124 | 131 | 135 | ... | Produits intermédiaires |
| Capital goods | 100 | 106 | 122 | 126 | 122 | 121 | ... | Biens d'équipement |
| Croatia | | | | | | | | Croatie |
| Agricultural products[14] | 100 | 108 | 92 | 91 | 95 | 95 | 94 | Produits agricoles[14] |
| Industrial products | 100 | 104 | 95 | 95 | 98 | 101 | 103 | Produits industriels |
| Consumer goods | 100 | 100 | 102 | 104 | 102 | 106 | 107 | Biens de consommation |
| Capital goods | 100 | 98 | 96 | 93 | 92 | 93 | 95 | Biens d'équipement |
| Cyprus[15] | | | | | | | | Chypre[15] |
| Industrial products | 100 | 102 | 105 | 108 | 117 | 121 | 125 | Produits industriels |
| Czech Republic | | | | | | | | République tchèque |
| Agricultural products | 100 | 108 | 103 | 102 | 108 | 111 | 113 | Produits agricoles |
| Industrial products | 100 | 103 | ... | ... | ... | ... | ... | Produits industriels |
| Denmark | | | | | | | | Danemark |
| Domestic supply[2,10] | 100 | 102 | 102 | 102 | 105 | 109 | 113 | Offre intérieure[2,10] |
| Domestic production[2,10] | 100 | 103 | 104 | 105 | 109 | 113 | 119 | Production intérieure[2,10] |
| Imported goods[10] | 100 | 101 | 100 | 99 | 100 | 104 | 107 | Produits importés[10] |
| Raw materials | 100 | 99 | 94 | 94 | 106 | 128 | ... | Matières premières |
| Consumer goods | 100 | 103 | 104 | 105 | 107 | 109 | ... | Biens de consommation |
| Ecuador | | | | | | | | Equateur |
| Domestic supply | 100 | 100 | 103 | 113 | 125 | 143 | 160 | Offre intérieure |
| Domestic production | 100 | 117 | 110 | 127 | 134 | 140 | 146 | Production intérieure |
| Agricultural products | 100 | 117 | 121 | 100 | 120 | 121 | 123 | Produits agricoles |
| Egypt | | | | | | | | Egypte |
| Domestic supply[5,7] | 100 | 98 | 103 | 119 | 139 | 168 | 180 | Offre intérieure[5,7] |
| Agricultural products | 100 | ... | ... | ... | ... | 148 | 210 | Produits agricoles |
| Raw materials[5] | 100 | 98 | 108 | 135 | 162 | ... | 176 | Matières premières[5] |
| Intermediate goods[5] | 100 | 98 | 103 | 118 | 143 | ... | 190 | Produits intermédiaires[5] |
| Consumer goods | 100 | 107 | ... | ... | 132 | ... | 126 | Biens de consommation |
| Capital goods[5] | 100 | 99 | 103 | 110 | 146 | ... | 208 | Biens d'équipement[5] |

| Country or area | 2000 | 2001 | 2002 | 2003 | 2004 | 2005 | 2006 | Pays ou zone |
|---|---|---|---|---|---|---|---|---|
| Finland | | | | | | | | Finlande |
| Domestic supply | 100 | 100 | 99 | 96 | 100 | 104 | 110 | Offre intérieure |
| Domestic production | 100 | 102 | 101 | 101 | 101 | 104 | 109 | Production intérieure |
| Industrial products | 100 | 99 | 96 | 95 | 96 | 98 | 102 | Produits industriels |
| Imported goods | 100 | 97 | 94 | 94 | 97 | 103 | 111 | Produits importés |
| Raw materials | 100 | 101 | 99 | 96 | 99 | 102 | 111 | Matières premières |
| Consumer goods[17] | 100 | 100 | 99 | 98 | 96 | 94 | 94 | Biens de consommation[17] |
| Capital goods | 100 | 101 | 94 | 90 | 89 | 89 | 90 | Biens d'équipement |
| France | | | | | | | | France |
| Agricultural products | 100 | 103 | ... | ... | ... | ... | ... | Produits agricoles |
| Intermediate goods | 100 | 102 | 102 | 101 | 104 | 107 | 111 | Produits intermédiaires |
| Consumer goods | 100 | ... | ... | 101 | 101 | 101 | 101 | Biens de consommation |
| Capital goods | 100 | ... | ... | 101 | 101 | 102 | 103 | Biens d'équipement |
| Georgia | | | | | | | | Géorgie |
| Industrial products | 100 | 104 | 110 | 114 | 119 | 128 | 142 | Produits industriels |
| Germany | | | | | | | | Allemagne |
| Domestic supply | 100 | 104 | 104 | 103 | 104 | ... | 112 | Offre intérieure |
| Agricultural products | 100 | 104 | 98 | 98 | 99 | 102 | 110 | Produits agricoles |
| Industrial products | 100 | 106 | 107 | 104 | 106 | ... | 117 | Produits industriels |
| Imported goods | 100 | 101 | 98 | 96 | 97 | ... | 107 | Produits importés |
| Intermediate goods | 100 | 111 | 111 | 100 | 102 | ... | 106 | Produits intermédiaires |
| Consumer goods | 100 | 106 | 106 | 104 | 104 | ... | 107 | Biens de consommation |
| Capital goods | 100 | 92 | 93 | 102 | 102 | ... | 103 | Biens d'équipement |
| Greece | | | | | | | | Grèce |
| Domestic supply[18,19] | 100 | 103 | 105 | 107 | 111 | 116 | 124 | Offre intérieure[18,19] |
| Domestic production[18,19] | 100 | 104 | 106 | 109 | 112 | 119 | 127 | Production intérieure[18,19] |
| Agricultural products[18,20] | 100 | 110 | 122 | 133 | ... | ... | ... | Produits agricoles[18,20] |
| Industrial products[18,19] | 100 | 103 | 105 | 108 | 112 | 115 | 121 | Produits industriels[18,19] |
| Imported goods[18,19] | 100 | 101 | 102 | 102 | 107 | 111 | 115 | Produits importés[18,19] |
| Intermediate goods | 100 | 105 | 105 | 106 | 109 | 112 | 124 | Produits intermédiaires |
| Consumer goods | 100 | 105 | 108 | 111 | 116 | 118 | 123 | Biens de consommation |
| Capital goods | 100 | 101 | 102 | 103 | 107 | 109 | 111 | Biens d'équipement |
| Guatemala | | | | | | | | Guatemala |
| Domestic supply | 100 | 105 | 109 | 114 | 120 | 125 | ... | Offre intérieure |
| Domestic production | 100 | 107 | 112 | 115 | 121 | 125 | ... | Production intérieure |
| Agricultural products | 100 | 108 | 109 | 112 | 112 | 113 | ... | Produits agricoles |
| Industrial products | 100 | 106 | ... | 117 | 127 | 136 | ... | Produits industriels |
| Imported goods | 100 | 103 | 106 | 112 | 118 | 124 | ... | Produits importés |
| India[21] | | | | | | | | Inde[21] |
| Domestic supply | 100 | 105 | 107 | 113 | 121 | ... | 132 | Offre intérieure |
| Agricultural products | 100 | 97 | 102 | 108 | 99 | ... | 118 | Produits agricoles |
| Industrial products[3] | 100 | 102 | 111 | 109 | 117 | ... | 125 | Produits industriels[3] |
| Raw materials[22] | 100 | 100 | 97 | 110 | 119 | ... | 123 | Matières premières[22] |
| Indonesia | | | | | | | | Indonésie |
| Domestic supply[19] | 100 | 114 | 117 | 120 | 130 | 151 | 172 | Offre intérieure[19] |
| Domestic production | 100 | 116 | 126 | 130 | 135 | 151 | 186 | Production intérieure |
| Agricultural products | 100 | 124 | 134 | 134 | 138 | 148 | 172 | Produits agricoles |
| Industrial products[3] | 100 | 111 | 122 | 127 | 133 | 152 | 195 | Produits industriels[3] |
| Imported goods[19] | 100 | 112 | 111 | 110 | 120 | 137 | 162 | Produits importés[19] |
| Raw materials | 100 | 110 | 110 | 116 | 137 | 176 | 179 | Matières premières |
| Intermediate goods | 100 | 114 | 119 | 119 | 130 | 151 | 176 | Produits intermédiaires |
| Consumer goods | 100 | 119 | 126 | 126 | 129 | 140 | 162 | Biens de consommation |
| Capital goods | 100 | 108 | 107 | 107 | 112 | 121 | 128 | Biens d'équipement |

| Country or area | 2000 | 2001 | 2002 | 2003 | 2004 | 2005 | 2006 | Pays ou zone |
|---|---|---|---|---|---|---|---|---|
| **Iran (Islamic Rep. of)[2,8]** | | | | | | | | **Iran (Rép. islamique d')[2,8]** |
| Domestic supply | 100 | 110 | 119 | 128 | 149 | 166 | 182 | Offre intérieure |
| Agricultural products | 100 | 108 | 122 | 135 | 158 | 176 | 191 | Produits agricoles |
| Industrial products | 100 | 93 | 97 | 100 | 119 | 127 | 136 | Produits industriels |
| Imported goods | 100 | 149 | ... | ... | ... | ... | ... | Produits importés |
| Raw materials | 100 | 112 | 118 | 128 | 164 | 183 | 206 | Matières premières |
| **Ireland** | | | | | | | | **Irlande** |
| Domestic supply[2,23] | 100 | 100 | 103 | 98 | 98 | ... | ... | Offre intérieure[2,23] |
| Agricultural products[2,23] | 100 | 105 | 100 | 91 | 102 | 103 | 107 | Produits agricoles[2,23] |
| Industrial products[2,3,23] | 100 | 102 | 101 | 92 | ... | ... | ... | Produits industriels[2,3,23] |
| Capital goods[8] | 100 | 98 | 92 | 80 | ... | ... | ... | Biens d'équipement[8] |
| **Israel[19]** | | | | | | | | **Israël[19]** |
| Industrial products | 100 | 101 | 105 | 108 | 113 | 118 | 123 | Produits industriels |
| **Italy** | | | | | | | | **Italie** |
| Domestic supply[2,19] | 100 | 102 | 102 | 105 | 107 | 111 | ... | Offre intérieure[2,19] |
| Intermediate goods | 100 | 102 | 100 | 103 | 108 | 111 | ... | Produits intermédiaires |
| Consumer goods | 100 | 102 | 104 | 107 | 108 | 108 | 109 | Biens de consommation |
| Capital goods | 100 | 101 | 102 | 103 | 105 | 107 | ... | Biens d'équipement |
| **Japan** | | | | | | | | **Japon** |
| Domestic supply[2] | 100 | 100 | 99 | 96 | 97 | 100 | 106 | Offre intérieure[2] |
| Domestic production | 100 | 98 | 96 | 95 | 96 | 98 | 101 | Production intérieure |
| Agricultural products[8] | 100 | 99 | 97 | 98 | 103 | 100 | 98 | Produits agricoles[8] |
| Industrial products[8] | 100 | 98 | 96 | 95 | 96 | 98 | 101 | Produits industriels[8] |
| Imported goods | 100 | 94 | 90 | 93 | 102 | 114 | 127 | Produits importés |
| Raw materials | 100 | 104 | 104 | 108 | 119 | 144 | 173 | Matières premières |
| Intermediate goods | 100 | 99 | 97 | 97 | 99 | 103 | 110 | Produits intermédiaires |
| Consumer goods | 100 | 99 | 97 | 95 | 95 | 95 | 95 | Biens de consommation |
| Capital goods | 100 | 96 | 92 | 89 | 87 | 85 | 85 | Biens d'équipement |
| **Jordan** | | | | | | | | **Jordanie** |
| Domestic supply[2] | 100 | 99 | 97 | 98 | 106 | 114 | 121 | Offre intérieure[2] |
| Agricultural products | 100 | 100 | 98 | 99 | 112 | 124 | 133 | Produits agricoles |
| Intermediate goods | 100 | 94 | 92 | 92 | 98 | 103 | 112 | Produits intermédiaires |
| Consumer goods | 100 | 97 | 97 | 98 | 98 | 100 | ... | Biens de consommation |
| **Korea, Republic of** | | | | | | | | **Corée, République de** |
| Domestic supply | 100 | 100 | 99 | 101 | 108 | 110 | 112 | Offre intérieure |
| Agricultural products[8,24] | 100 | 104 | 106 | 113 | 127 | 122 | 115 | Produits agricoles[8,24] |
| Industrial products | 100 | 98 | 96 | 98 | 106 | 109 | 112 | Produits industriels |
| Raw materials | 100 | 102 | 104 | 110 | 132 | 156 | 176 | Matières premières |
| Intermediate goods | 100 | 100 | 96 | 98 | 107 | 108 | 112 | Produits intermédiaires |
| Consumer goods | 100 | 101 | 100 | 102 | 105 | 106 | 106 | Biens de consommation |
| Capital goods | 100 | 99 | 95 | 94 | 96 | 94 | 95 | Biens d'équipement |
| **Kuwait** | | | | | | | | **Koweït** |
| Domestic supply | 100 | 102 | 105 | 107 | 108 | ... | ... | Offre intérieure |
| Domestic production | 100 | 100 | 102 | 102 | 102 | ... | ... | Production intérieure |
| Agricultural products | 100 | 96 | 102 | 106 | 116 | ... | ... | Produits agricoles |
| Industrial products | 100 | 102 | 105 | 107 | 107 | ... | ... | Produits industriels |
| Imported goods | 100 | 102 | 106 | 109 | 109 | ... | ... | Produits importés |
| Raw materials | 100 | 105 | 108 | ... | ... | ... | ... | Matières premières |
| Intermediate goods | 100 | 100 | 104 | ... | ... | ... | ... | Produits intermédiaires |
| Consumer goods | 100 | 100 | 103 | ... | ... | ... | ... | Biens de consommation |
| Capital goods | 100 | 106 | 115 | ... | ... | ... | ... | Biens d'équipement |
| **Latvia** | | | | | | | | **Lettonie** |
| Domestic supply | 100 | 102 | 103 | 106 | 115 | 124 | 137 | Offre intérieure |
| **Lithuania** | | | | | | | | **Lituanie** |
| Domestic supply | 100 | 98 | 93 | 93 | 100 | 113 | 121 | Offre intérieure |

| Country or area | 2000 | 2001 | 2002 | 2003 | 2004 | 2005 | 2006 | Pays ou zone |
|---|---|---|---|---|---|---|---|---|
| Luxembourg | | | | | | | | Luxembourg |
| Industrial products | 100 | 101 | 100 | 100 | 109 | 117 | ... | Produits industriels |
| Imported goods | 100 | 103 | 104 | 107 | 116 | 120 | ... | Produits importés |
| Intermediate goods | 100 | 99 | 97 | 98 | 111 | 122 | ... | Produits intermédiaires |
| Consumer goods[17] | 100 | 109 | 111 | 105 | 105 | 106 | ... | Biens de consommation[17] |
| Capital goods | 100 | 102 | 104 | 105 | 109 | 109 | ... | Biens d'équipement |
| Malaysia | | | | | | | | Malaisie |
| Domestic supply | 100 | 95 | 99 | 105 | 114 | 122 | 127 | Offre intérieure |
| Domestic production | 100 | 94 | 99 | 106 | 117 | 126 | 131 | Production intérieure |
| Imported goods | 100 | 100 | 99 | 100 | 102 | 103 | 104 | Produits importés |
| Mexico | | | | | | | | Mexique |
| Domestic supply[7,25] | 100 | 106 | 110 | 116 | 126 | 132 | 140 | Offre intérieure[7,25] |
| Agricultural products | 100 | 110 | 115 | 121 | 136 | 149 | 157 | Produits agricoles |
| Industrial products | 100 | 104 | 107 | 116 | 120 | 124 | 129 | Produits industriels |
| Raw materials | 100 | ... | 103 | 116 | ... | ... | ... | Matières premières |
| Consumer goods[8,25] | 100 | 106 | 110 | 116 | 126 | 132 | 136 | Biens de consommation[8,25] |
| Capital goods[7,8,25] | 100 | 105 | 108 | 118 | 130 | 133 | 145 | Biens d'équipement[7,8,25] |
| Morocco | | | | | | | | Maroc |
| Agricultural products | 100 | 99 | 102 | 97 | 97 | 98 | 103 | Produits agricoles |
| Industrial products | 100 | 98 | 97 | 98 | 103 | 113 | 119 | Produits industriels |
| Netherlands | | | | | | | | Pays-Bas |
| Agricultural products[26,27] | 100 | 105 | 103 | 105 | ... | ... | ... | Produits agricoles[26,27] |
| Industrial products | 100 | 101 | 102 | 101 | 105 | 104 | 105 | Produits industriels |
| Imported goods | 100 | 95 | 90 | 86 | 87 | 88 | ... | Produits importés |
| Raw materials | 100 | 100 | 97 | 98 | 105 | ... | ... | Matières premières |
| Intermediate goods | 100 | 91 | 92 | 92 | 96 | ... | ... | Produits intermédiaires |
| Consumer goods | 100 | 90 | 90 | 92 | 94 | ... | ... | Biens de consommation |
| Capital goods | 100 | 95 | 97 | 99 | 100 | ... | ... | Biens d'équipement |
| New Zealand | | | | | | | | Nouvelle-Zélande |
| Agricultural products | 100 | 124 | 123 | 112 | 113 | 114 | 116 | Produits agricoles |
| Industrial products[2,28] | 100 | 105 | 105 | 104 | 106 | 110 | 114 | Produits industriels[2,28] |
| Intermediate goods[29] | 100 | 107 | 107 | 106 | 108 | 114 | 121 | Produits intermédiaires[29] |
| Norway | | | | | | | | Norvège |
| Domestic supply | 100 | 105 | 105 | 106 | 107 | 107 | 111 | Offre intérieure |
| Domestic production | 100 | 105 | 106 | 106 | 107 | 107 | 110 | Production intérieure |
| Industrial products | 100 | 102 | 101 | 102 | 105 | 109 | 112 | Produits industriels |
| Imported goods | 100 | 107 | ... | ... | ... | ... | ... | Produits importés |
| Raw materials | 100 | 99 | 88 | 89 | 98 | 99 | 106 | Matières premières |
| Intermediate goods | 100 | 101 | 99 | 99 | 104 | 106 | 110 | Produits intermédiaires |
| Consumer goods | 100 | 104 | 104 | 104 | 106 | 108 | 112 | Biens de consommation |
| Capital goods | 100 | 102 | 105 | 97 | 108 | 110 | 111 | Biens d'équipement |
| Occupied Palestinian Terr. | | | | | | | | Terr. palestinien occupé |
| Domestic supply[30] | ... | ... | 129 | 131 | 135 | 139 | ... | Offre intérieure[30] |
| Domestic production[31] | ... | 4 236 | 4 169 | 4 019 | ... | ... | ... | Production intérieure[31] |
| Agricultural products[30] | ... | ... | 138 | 137 | 137 | ... | ... | Produits agricoles[30] |
| Imported goods[30] | ... | ... | 129 | 136 | 143 | 149 | 157 | Produits importés[30] |
| Oman[32] | | | | | | | | Oman[32] |
| Domestic supply | 100 | 104 | 103 | 104 | 107 | ... | ... | Offre intérieure |
| Pakistan[5] | | | | | | | | Pakistan[5] |
| Domestic supply[2,7] | 100 | 102 | 108 | 113 | 120 | 131 | 142 | Offre intérieure[2,7] |
| Agricultural products | 100 | 102 | 106 | 108 | 119 | 130 | 139 | Produits agricoles |
| Industrial products | 100 | 102 | 104 | 109 | 113 | 115 | 119 | Produits industriels |
| Raw materials | 100 | 101 | 116 | 125 | 122 | 115 | 130 | Matières premières |
| Panama | | | | | | | | Panama |
| Domestic supply | 100 | 97 | 94 | 95 | 100 | 105 | ... | Offre intérieure |

| Country or area | 2000 | 2001 | 2002 | 2003 | 2004 | 2005 | 2006 | Pays ou zone |
|---|---|---|---|---|---|---|---|---|
| Peru | | | | | | | | Pérou |
| Domestic supply | 100 | 101 | 100 | 102 | 109 | 110 | 113 | Offre intérieure |
| Domestic production | 100 | 102 | 100 | 102 | 107 | 110 | 113 | Production intérieure |
| Agricultural products[33] | 100 | 104 | 97 | 97 | 107 | 109 | 114 | Produits agricoles[33] |
| Industrial products[3,8] | 100 | 102 | 101 | 103 | 108 | 111 | 114 | Produits industriels[3,8] |
| Imported goods | 100 | 101 | 100 | 103 | 108 | 109 | 113 | Produits importés |
| Philippines[34] | | | | | | | | Philippines[34] |
| Domestic supply | 100 | 102 | 106 | 109 | 138 | 149 | 161 | Offre intérieure |
| Portugal | | | | | | | | Portugal |
| Domestic supply | 100 | 101 | 92 | 104 | 107 | ... | 116 | Offre intérieure |
| Intermediate goods | 100 | 101 | 98 | 101 | 103 | ... | 108 | Produits intermédiaires |
| Consumer goods | 100 | 104 | 102 | 106 | 107 | ... | 110 | Biens de consommation |
| Capital goods | 100 | 102 | 102 | 103 | 105 | ... | 109 | Biens d'équipement |
| Romania | | | | | | | | Roumanie |
| Industrial products | 100 | 141 | 176 | 213 | 242 | 267 | 298 | Produits industriels |
| Russian Federation | | | | | | | | Fédération de Russie |
| Agricultural products | ... | ... | 100 | 107 | 126 | 128 | 134 | Produits agricoles |
| Industrial products | ... | ... | 100 | 107 | 137 | 151 | 170 | Produits industriels |
| Serbia and Montenegro | | | | | | | | Serbie-et-Monténégro |
| Domestic supply[35] | ... | ... | 109 | 105 | 124 | ... | ... | Offre intérieure[35] |
| Agricultural products | 100 | 170 | ... | ... | ... | ... | ... | Produits agricoles |
| Industrial products | 100 | 185 | ... | ... | ... | ... | ... | Produits industriels |
| Consumer goods | 100 | 201 | ... | ... | ... | ... | ... | Biens de consommation |
| Capital goods | 100 | 143 | ... | ... | ... | ... | ... | Biens d'équipement |
| Singapore | | | | | | | | Singapour |
| Domestic supply[7] | 100 | 98 | 97 | 99 | 102 | 112 | 118 | Offre intérieure[7] |
| Domestic production[2,3] | 100 | 98 | 101 | 97 | 96 | 101 | 103 | Production intérieure[2,3] |
| Imported goods | 100 | 100 | 100 | 100 | 99 | 104 | 107 | Produits importés |
| Slovakia[36] | | | | | | | | Slovaquie[36] |
| Agricultural products | 100 | ... | ... | 95 | 103 | 102 | 101 | Produits agricoles |
| Industrial products | 100 | ... | ... | ... | 110 | 115 | 121 | Produits industriels |
| Slovenia | | | | | | | | Slovénie |
| Industrial products | 100 | 109 | 115 | 118 | 123 | 126 | 129 | Produits industriels |
| Intermediate goods | 100 | 110 | 114 | 116 | 123 | 127 | 131 | Produits intermédiaires |
| Consumer goods | 100 | 110 | 118 | 123 | 126 | 129 | 131 | Biens de consommation |
| Capital goods | 100 | 104 | 107 | 106 | 108 | 112 | 113 | Biens d'équipement |
| South Africa | | | | | | | | Afrique du Sud |
| Domestic supply[37] | 100 | 108 | 124 | 126 | 127 | 131 | 141 | Offre intérieure[37] |
| Domestic production[37] | 100 | 108 | 122 | 127 | 130 | 134 | 144 | Production intérieure[37] |
| Agricultural products | 100 | 113 | 140 | 132 | 131 | 124 | 145 | Produits agricoles |
| Industrial products[3] | 100 | 108 | 122 | 125 | 128 | 132 | 143 | Produits industriels[3] |
| Imported goods | 100 | 110 | 127 | 122 | 117 | 121 | 131 | Produits importés |
| Spain | | | | | | | | Espagne |
| Domestic supply[19] | 100 | 102 | 102 | 104 | 107 | 113 | ... | Offre intérieure[19] |
| Intermediate goods | 100 | 101 | 102 | 102 | 107 | 111 | ... | Produits intermédiaires |
| Consumer goods | 100 | 104 | 106 | 108 | 111 | 114 | ... | Biens de consommation |
| Capital goods | 100 | 101 | 103 | 104 | 106 | 108 | ... | Biens d'équipement |
| Sweden[19,38] | | | | | | | | Suède[19,38] |
| Domestic supply[2] | 100 | 103 | 104 | 103 | 105 | 111 | 117 | Offre intérieure[2] |
| Domestic production[2] | 100 | 103 | 103 | 103 | 106 | 109 | 114 | Production intérieure[2] |
| Imported goods | 100 | 105 | 105 | 102 | 105 | 113 | 119 | Produits importés |

| Country or area | 2000 | 2001 | 2002 | 2003 | 2004 | 2005 | 2006 | Pays ou zone |
|---|---|---|---|---|---|---|---|---|
| **Switzerland** | | | | | | | | **Suisse** |
| Domestic supply[2,7] | 100 | 100 | 99 | 102 | 104 | ... | ... | Offre intérieure[2,7] |
| Domestic production[2,7] | 100 | 101 | 100 | 104 | 107 | ... | ... | Production intérieure[2,7] |
| Agricultural products[2] | 100 | 110 | 92 | 122 | 119 | ... | ... | Produits agricoles[2] |
| Industrial products | 100 | 99 | 100 | 103 | 105 | ... | ... | Produits industriels |
| Imported goods[7] | 100 | 99 | 96 | 98 | 100 | ... | ... | Produits importés[7] |
| Raw materials | 100 | 89 | ... | ... | ... | ... | ... | Matières premières |
| Intermediate goods | 100 | 101 | 99 | 105 | 109 | ... | ... | Produits intermédiaires |
| Consumer goods | 100 | 102 | ... | ... | ... | ... | ... | Biens de consommation |
| Capital goods | 100 | 101 | 102 | 102 | 102 | ... | ... | Biens d'équipement |
| **Syrian Arab Republic** | | | | | | | | **Rép. arabe syrienne** |
| Domestic supply | 100 | 96 | 101 | ... | ... | ... | ... | Offre intérieure |
| Raw materials | 100 | 99 | 100 | ... | ... | 104 | 104 | Matières premières |
| Intermediate goods | 100 | ... | ... | ... | ... | 85 | 87 | Produits intermédiaires |
| Consumer goods[11] | 100 | ... | ... | ... | ... | 102 | 109 | Biens de consommation[11] |
| **Thailand** | | | | | | | | **Thaïlande** |
| Domestic supply[2,10] | 100 | 93 | 94 | 108 | 116 | 126 | 135 | Offre intérieure[2,10] |
| Agricultural products | 100 | 105 | 116 | 128 | 147 | 176 | 211 | Produits agricoles |
| Industrial products[3] | 100 | 102 | 103 | 106 | 111 | 119 | 125 | Produits industriels[3] |
| Raw materials | 100 | 108 | 112 | 120 | 133 | 154 | 174 | Matières premières |
| Intermediate goods | 100 | 101 | 101 | 108 | 119 | 128 | 138 | Produits intermédiaires |
| Consumer goods | 100 | 105 | 110 | 116 | 125 | 143 | 158 | Biens de consommation |
| Capital goods | 100 | 103 | 106 | 106 | 108 | 117 | 117 | Biens d'équipement |
| **TFYR of Macedonia** | | | | | | | | **Ex-R.Y. Macédoine** |
| Industrial products | 100 | 102 | 101 | 101 | 102 | 105 | ... | Produits industriels |
| **Trinidad and Tobago** | | | | | | | | **Trinité-et-Tobago** |
| Domestic supply[11] | 126 | 128 | 129 | 130 | 135 | ... | ... | Offre intérieure[11] |
| Industrial products | 100 | 101 | 102 | 103 | ... | ... | ... | Produits industriels |
| **Tunisia** | | | | | | | | **Tunisie** |
| Agricultural products | 100 | 102 | 107 | 111 | 116 | ... | ... | Produits agricoles |
| Industrial products | 100 | 103 | 105 | 108 | 111 | 114 | ... | Produits industriels |
| **Turkey** | | | | | | | | **Turquie** |
| Domestic supply[2,19,39] | 100 | 162 | 243 | 305 | 349 | 370 | 403 | Offre intérieure[2,19,39] |
| Agricultural products | 100 | 142 | 223 | 298 | 369 | 375 | 403 | Produits agricoles |
| Industrial products | 100 | 167 | 247 | 306 | 340 | 368 | 374 | Produits industriels |
| **United Kingdom** | | | | | | | | **Royaume-Uni** |
| Domestic supply | 100 | 100 | 101 | 101 | 104 | 107 | 109 | Offre intérieure |
| Domestic production | 100 | 100 | 101 | 102 | 104 | 107 | 109 | Production intérieure |
| Agricultural products | 100 | 108 | 103 | 110 | 113 | 110 | 115 | Produits agricoles |
| Industrial products[3] | 100 | 100 | 101 | 102 | 103 | 105 | 107 | Produits industriels[3] |
| Imported goods | 100 | 98 | 95 | 96 | 95 | 102 | 108 | Produits importés |
| Raw materials | 100 | 100 | 97 | 96 | 99 | 111 | 122 | Matières premières |
| Intermediate goods | 100 | 100 | 97 | 100 | 107 | 124 | 142 | Produits intermédiaires |
| Consumer goods | 100 | 102 | 103 | 104 | 106 | 108 | 109 | Biens de consommation |
| Capital goods | 100 | 99 | 99 | 96 | 94 | 100 | 101 | Biens d'équipement |
| **United States** | | | | | | | | **Etats-Unis** |
| Domestic supply[2] | 100 | 101 | 99 | 104 | 111 | 119 | 124 | Offre intérieure[2] |
| Agricultural products[2] | 100 | 104 | 100 | 112 | 125 | 119 | 118 | Produits agricoles[2] |
| Industrial products[2,40] | 100 | 101 | 98 | 103 | 110 | 119 | 125 | Produits industriels[2,40] |
| Raw materials | 100 | 99 | 90 | 113 | 132 | 152 | 154 | Matières premières |
| Intermediate goods | 100 | 101 | 99 | 104 | 110 | 119 | 127 | Produits intermédiaires |
| Consumer goods | 100 | 102 | 101 | 105 | 110 | 116 | 120 | Biens de consommation |
| Capital goods | 100 | 101 | 100 | 101 | 102 | 104 | 106 | Biens d'équipement |
| **Uruguay[41]** | | | | | | | | **Uruguay[41]** |
| Domestic production | 100 | 107 | 141 | 195 | ... | ... | 231 | Production intérieure |
| Agricultural products | 100 | 110 | 166 | 250 | ... | ... | ... | Produits agricoles |
| Industrial products[7] | 100 | 106 | 132 | 177 | ... | ... | ... | Produits industriels[7] |

| Country or area | 2000 | 2001 | 2002 | 2003 | 2004 | 2005 | 2006 | Pays ou zone |
|---|---|---|---|---|---|---|---|---|
| Venezuela (Bolivarian Rep. of) | | | | | | | | Venezuela (Rép. bolivar. du) |
| Domestic supply[7] | 100 | 115 | ... | 253 | ... | ... | 435 | Offre intérieure[7] |
| Domestic production[7] | 100 | 115 | ... | 237 | ... | ... | 421 | Production intérieure[7] |
| Agricultural products[7] | 100 | 141 | ... | 159 | ... | ... | ... | Produits agricoles[7] |
| Industrial products[7] | 100 | 112 | ... | 191 | ... | ... | 322 | Produits industriels[7] |
| Imported goods[7] | 100 | 108 | ... | 294 | ... | ... | 450 | Produits importés[7] |
| Raw materials | 100 | 123 | ... | ... | ... | ... | ... | Matières premières |

Source

United Nations Statistics Division, New York, price statistics database, last accessed June 2008.

Notes

1 Domestic agricultural products only.
2 Including exported products.
3 Manufacturing industry only.
4 Including service industries.
5 Annual average refers to average of 12 months ending June.
6 Prices relate only to products for sale or transfer to other sectors or for use as capital equipment.
7 Excluding mining and quarrying.
8 Including imported products.
9 Excluding construction.
10 Agricultural products and products of manufacturing industry.
11 Index base: 1990=100.
12 Valued at purchasers' values.
13 Annual average refers to average of 12 months ending May.
14 Forestry and fishing.
15 For government-controlled areas.
16 San Salvador.
17 Durable goods only.
18 Finished products only.
19 Excluding electricity, gas and water.
20 Including mining and quarrying.
21 Annual average refers to average of 12 months ending March.
22 Primary articles include food, non-food articles and minerals.

23 Excluding Value Added Tax.
24 Including marine foods.
25 Mexico City.
26 Excluding forestry, fishing and hunting.
27 Crop growing production only, excluding livestock production.
28 Including all outputs of manufacturing.
29 Including all industrial inputs.
30 Index base: 1996=100.
31 Index base: 1997=100.
32 Muscat.
33 Excluding fishing.
34 Metro Manila.
35 Index base: 1998=100.
36 Prices of producers are surveyed without value added tax and without excise taxes.
37 Excluding gold mining.
38 Excluding agriculture.
39 Excluding industrial finished goods.
40 Excluding foods and feeds production.
41 Montevideo.

Source

Organisation des Nations Unies, Division de statistique, New York, la base de données pour les statistiques des prix, dernier accès juin 2008.

Notes

1 Produits agricoles intérieurs seulement.
2 Y compris les produits exportés.
3 Industries manufacturières seulement.
4 Y compris industries de service.
5 La moyenne annuelle est la moyenne de douze mois finissant en juin.
6 Uniquement les prix des produits destinés à être vendus ou transférés à d'autres secteurs ou à être utilisés comme biens d'équipement.
7 Non compris les industries extractives.
8 Y compris les produits importés.
9 Non compris construction.
10 Produits agricoles et produits des industries manufacturières.
11 Indice base: 1990=100.
12 A la valeur d'acquisition.
13 La moyenne annuelle est la moyenne de 12 mois finissant en mai.
14 Exploitation forestière et pêche.
15 Pour les zones contrôlées par le Gouvernement.
16 San Salvador.
17 Biens durables seulement.
18 Produits finis uniquement.
19 Non compris l'électricité, le gaz et l'eau.
20 Y compris les industries extractives.
21 La moyenne annuelle est la moyenne de douze mois finissant en mars.
22 Les articles primaires comprennent des articles des produits alimentaires, non- alimentaires et des minéraux.
23 Non compris taxe sur la valeur ajoutée.
24 Y compris l'alimentation marine.
25 Mexico.
26 Non compris sylviculture, pêche et chasse.
27 Cultures uniquement, non compris les produits de l'élevage.
28 Y compris toute la production du secteur manufacturière.
29 Tous les intrants industriels.
30 Indices base: 1996=100.
31 Indice base: 1997=100.
32 Muscat.
33 Non compris la pêche.
34 L'agglomération de Manille.
35 Indice base : 1998=100.
36 Les enquêtes sur le prix à la production ne prennent pas en considération les taxes à la valeur ajoutée et excise.
37 Non compris l'extraction de l'or.
38 Non compris l'agriculture.
39 Non compris les produits finis industriels.
40 Non compris les produits alimentaires et d'affouragement.
41 Montevideo.

| Country or area | 1999 | 2000 | 2001 | 2002 | 2003 | 2004 | 2005 | 2006 | Pays ou zone |
|---|---|---|---|---|---|---|---|---|---|
| Albania | | | | | | | | | Albanie |
| General | 100.0 | 100.0[1] | 103.1 | 108.4 | 110.8 | 114.0 | 116.7 | 119.5 | Généraux |
| Food | ... | 100.0 | 103.7 | 110.2 | 115.0 | 114.9 | 114.3 | 115.6 | Alimentation |
| Algeria | | | | | | | | | Algérie |
| General | 100.6 | 100.0 | 103.5 | 105.8 | 109.5 | 114.5 | 116.7 | 118.8 | Généraux |
| Food | 102.2 | 100.0 | 104.4 | 106.2 | 111.0 | 116.4 | 116.6 | 119.3 | Alimentation |
| American Samoa | | | | | | | | | Samoa américaines |
| General[2] | 98.1 | 100.0 | 101.2 | 103.4 | 108.4 | 116.1 | 122.1 | 125.7 | Généraux[2] |
| Food | 100.5 | 100.0 | 101.6 | 103.1 | 109.7 | 123.5 | 130.4 | 132.2 | Alimentation |
| Andorra | | | | | | | | | Andorre |
| General (2001 = 100) | ... | ... | 100.0 | 104.5 | 107.5 | 111.1 | 118.2 | 116.2 | Généraux (2001 = 100) |
| Food (2001 = 100)[3] | ... | ... | 100.0 | 106.2 | 109.9 | 111.9 | 113.1 | 116.2 | Alimentation (2001 = 100)[3] |
| Angola | | | | | | | | | Angola |
| General | 23.5 | 100.0 | 252.6 | 527.6[1] | 1 045.8 | 1 501.2 | 1 846.0 | 2 091.6 | Généraux |
| Food | 25.7 | 100.0 | 251.1 | 508.6[1] | ... | ... | ... | ... | Alimentation |
| Anguilla | | | | | | | | | Anguilla |
| General (2001 = 100) | 92.5 | 100.0 | 100.0[4] | 100.5 | 103.8 | 108.3 | 113.5 | 122.7 | Généraux (2001 = 100) |
| Food (2001 = 100) | 98.9 | 100.0 | 100.0[4] | 100.5 | 98.0 | 102.1 | 105.4 | 112.4 | Alimentation (2001 = 100) |
| Antigua and Barbuda | | | | | | | | | Antigua-et-Barbuda |
| General | 99.3 | 100.0 | 101.5 | ... | ... | ... | ... | ... | Généraux |
| Food | 98.2 | 100.0 | 103.6 | ... | ... | ... | ... | ... | Alimentation |
| Argentina[5] | | | | | | | | | Argentine[5] |
| General | 100.9 | 100.0[1] | 98.9 | 124.5 | 141.3 | 147.5 | 161.7 | 179.4 | Généraux |
| Food | 102.7 | 100.0[1] | 98.1 | 132.0 | 157.3 | 165.1 | 183.3 | 205.5 | Alimentation |
| Armenia | | | | | | | | | Arménie |
| General | 100.8 | 100.0 | 103.1 | 104.2[1] | 109.2 | 116.3 | 117.0 | ... | Généraux |
| Food | 106.3 | 100.0 | 104.7 | 107.0[1] | 114.4 | 125.8 | 126.8 | ... | Alimentation |
| Aruba | | | | | | | | | Aruba |
| General | 96.1 | 100.0 | 102.9[1] | 106.3 | 110.2 | 113.0 | 116.8 | 121.0 | Généraux |
| Food | 98.2 | 100.0 | 103.3[1] | 106.7 | 110.1 | 114.4 | ... | ... | Alimentation |
| Australia | | | | | | | | | Australie |
| General | 95.7 | 100.0 | 104.4 | 107.6 | 110.5 | 113.1 | 116.1 | 120.2 | Généraux |
| Food | 97.6 | 100.0 | 106.5 | 110.4 | 114.4 | 117.1 | 120.0 | 129.2 | Alimentation |
| Austria | | | | | | | | | Autriche |
| General | 97.7 | 100.0[1] | 102.7 | 104.5 | 105.9 | 108.1 | 110.6 | 112.2[1] | Généraux |
| Food | 98.9 | 100.0[1] | 103.3 | 105.2 | 107.3 | 109.5 | 111.0 | 112.5[6] | Alimentation |
| Azerbaijan | | | | | | | | | Azerbaïdjan |
| General | 98.2 | 100.0 | 101.5 | 104.4 | 106.7 | 113.9 | 124.7 | 134.9 | Généraux |
| Food[7] | 97.7 | 100.0 | 102.7 | 106.5 | 109.9 | 120.9 | 134.1 | 150.2 | Alimentation[7] |
| Bahamas | | | | | | | | | Bahamas |
| General | 98.4 | 100.0 | 102.1 | 104.2 | 107.4 | 108.6 | 110.8 | 112.8 | Généraux |
| Food | 98.4 | 100.0 | 102.1 | 104.1 | 104.7 | 107.8 | 111.2 | 116.4 | Alimentation |
| Bahrain | | | | | | | | | Bahreïn |
| General | 100.7 | 100.0 | 98.8 | 98.3 | 100.0 | 102.3 | 104.9 | 107.1 | Généraux |
| Food | 101.3 | 100.0 | 98.6 | 97.6 | 96.2 | 98.3 | 101.3 | 103.3 | Alimentation |
| Bangladesh[8] | | | | | | | | | Bangladesh[8] |
| General | 97.9 | 100.0 | 101.5 | 105.4 | 111.5[1] | 118.4 | 126.7 | 135.3 | Généraux |
| Food | 98.0 | 100.0 | 100.8 | 103.4 | 110.1[1] | 118.3 | 127.8 | 137.5 | Alimentation |
| Barbados | | | | | | | | | Barbade |
| General | 97.6 | 100.0 | 102.6[1] | 103.0 | 104.6 | 106.1 | 112.5 | 120.8 | Généraux |
| Food | 97.5 | 100.0 | 105.2[1] | 107.1 | 110.1 | 115.0 | 123.1 | 132.8 | Alimentation |

| Country or area | 1999 | 2000 | 2001 | 2002 | 2003 | 2004 | 2005 | 2006 | Pays ou zone |
|---|---|---|---|---|---|---|---|---|---|
| Belarus | | | | | | | | | Bélarus |
| General | 37.2 | 100.0 | 161.1 | 229.8 | 295.0 | 348.3 | 384.3 | ... | Généraux |
| Food | 37.7 | 100.0 | 156.8 | 217.9 | 267.6 | 320.1 | 358.2 | ... | Alimentation |
| Belgium | | | | | | | | | Belgique |
| General | 97.5 | 100.0 | 102.5 | 104.2 | 105.8 | 108.0[1] | 111.0 | 113.0 | Généraux |
| Food | 99.1 | 100.0 | 104.2 | 106.5 | 108.7 | 110.4[1] | 112.5 | 115.0 | Alimentation |
| Belize | | | | | | | | | Belize |
| General | 99.4 | 100.0 | 101.2 | 103.4 | 106.1 | 109.3 | 113.1 | 118.2 | Généraux |
| Food[7] | 99.4 | 100.0 | 100.5 | 101.6 | 104.2 | 106.9 | 111.9 | 116.7 | Alimentation[7] |
| Benin | | | | | | | | | Bénin |
| General | 95.9 | 100.0 | 103.9 | 106.5 | 108.1 | 109.0 | 114.9 | 119.2 | Généraux |
| Food[9] | 98.8 | 100.0 | 102.3 | 108.0 | 105.5 | 104.7 | 114.4 | 113.8 | Alimentation[9] |
| Bermuda | | | | | | | | | Bermudes |
| General | 97.4 | 100.0 | 102.9 | 105.3 | 108.6 | 112.5 | 116.0 | 119.5[1] | Généraux |
| Food | 97.8 | 100.0 | 102.0 | 103.5 | 105.6 | 108.2 | 111.4 | 113.6[1] | Alimentation |
| Bhutan | | | | | | | | | Bhoutan |
| General | 96.1 | 100.0 | 103.4 | 106.0 | 107.6 | 110.9[1] | 116.8 | ... | Généraux |
| Food[7] | 99.1 | 100.0 | 101.5 | 103.6 | 104.5 | 102.9[1] | 108.8 | ... | Alimentation[7] |
| Bolivia[10] | | | | | | | | | Bolivie[10] |
| General | 95.6 | 100.0 | 101.6 | 102.5 | 105.9 | 110.6 | 116.6 | ... | Généraux |
| Food | 97.9 | 100.0 | 100.6 | 99.7 | 103.2 | 109.3 | 115.7 | ... | Alimentation |
| Botswana | | | | | | | | | Botswana |
| General | 92.2 | 100.0 | 106.6 | 115.1 | 125.8 | 134.4 | 146.1 | 163.0 | Généraux |
| Food | 95.5 | 100.0 | 102.6 | 112.2 | 125.0 | 130.9 | 137.9 | 155.2[1] | Alimentation |
| Brazil | | | | | | | | | Brésil |
| General | 93.4 | 100.0 | 106.8 | 115.9 | 132.9 | 141.7 | 151.4 | 157.8 | Généraux |
| Food[11] | 95.1 | 100.0 | 106.7 | 117.0 | 140.8 | 146.5 | 151.0 | 151.0 | Alimentation[11] |
| British Virgin Islands | | | | | | | | | Iles Vierges britanniques |
| General | 97.3 | 100.0 | 103.1 | 103.5 | 107.2 | 108.3 | 110.4 | ... | Généraux |
| Food | 99.7 | 100.0 | 104.3 | 105.3 | 107.1 | 108.4 | 112.1 | ... | Alimentation |
| Brunei Darussalam | | | | | | | | | Brunéi Darussalam |
| General | 98.8 | 100.0 | 100.6 | 98.3[1] | 98.6 | 99.5 | 100.5 | ... | Généraux |
| Food | 100.0 | 100.0 | 100.5 | 100.8[1] | 100.0 | 101.7 | 102.2 | ... | Alimentation |
| Bulgaria | | | | | | | | | Bulgarie |
| General | 90.6 | 100.0 | 107.4 | 113.6 | 116.3 | 123.4 | 129.6 | 139.0 | Généraux |
| Food | 90.7 | 100.0 | 106.5 | 106.5 | 105.4 | 112.5 | 117.0 | 123.4 | Alimentation |
| Burkina Faso | | | | | | | | | Burkina Faso |
| General | 100.3 | 100.0 | 104.9 | 107.3 | 109.5 | 109.0 | 116.0 | 118.8 | Généraux |
| Food | 106.1 | 100.0 | 108.8 | 112.2 | 110.3 | 104.9 | 120.2 | 120.0 | Alimentation |
| Burundi | | | | | | | | | Burundi |
| General | 79.6 | 100.0 | 108.1 | 106.7 | 118.1 | ... | ... | ... | Généraux |
| Food | 77.2 | 100.0 | 100.6 | 95.5 | 107.5 | ... | ... | ... | Alimentation |
| Cambodia | | | | | | | | | Cambodge |
| General | 100.8 | 100.0 | 99.4[1] | 102.7 | 103.9 | 107.9 | 114.1 | 119.5 | Généraux |
| Food[12] | 103.5 | 100.0 | 98.0[1] | 99.7 | 101.2 | 107.6 | 116.6 | 124.2 | Alimentation[12] |
| Cameroon | | | | | | | | | Cameroun |
| General | 98.8 | 100.0 | 104.4 | 107.4 | 108.1[13] | 108.4 | 110.5 | 116.2 | Généraux |
| Food | 97.8 | 100.0 | 107.0 | 112.1 | 111.4[13] | 109.2 | 110.3 | 117.9 | Alimentation |
| Canada | | | | | | | | | Canada |
| General | 97.4 | 100.0 | 102.6 | 104.8 | 107.8 | 109.8 | 112.2 | 114.4 | Généraux |
| Food | 98.7 | 100.0 | 104.5 | 107.2 | 109.1 | 111.3 | 114.1 | 116.8 | Alimentation |
| Cape Verde | | | | | | | | | Cap-Vert |
| General | 102.5 | 100.0 | 99.6 | 105.4 | 106.5 | 104.5 | 104.9 | 110.6 | Généraux |
| Food | 101.8 | 100.0 | 105.3 | ... | ... | ... | ... | ... | Alimentation |
| Cayman Islands | | | | | | | | | Iles Caïmanes |
| General | 97.4 | 100.0 | 101.1 | 103.6 | 104.2 | 108.8 | 116.4 | 117.3 | Généraux |
| Food | 98.3 | 100.0 | 103.5 | 105.7 | 109.1 | 113.9 | 117.0 | 120.1 | Alimentation |

| Country or area | 1999 | 2000 | 2001 | 2002 | 2003 | 2004 | 2005 | 2006 | Pays ou zone |
|---|---|---|---|---|---|---|---|---|---|
| Central African Rep. | | | | | | | | | Rép. centrafricaine |
| General[2] | 97.1 | 100.0 | 103.7 | 105.2 | 110.9 | 108.6 | 111.7 | 119.1 | Généraux[2] |
| Food | 96.3 | 100.0 | 104.7 | 106.8 | 112.4 | 107.2 | 110.9 | ... | Alimentation |
| Chad | | | | | | | | | Tchad |
| General | 96.7 | 100.0 | 112.4 | 117.5 | 116.4[14] | 116.6[1] | 125.7 | 136.1 | Généraux |
| Food | 92.9 | 100.0 | 119.3 | 125.8[1] | 122.6 | 116.0 | 129.2 | 144.0 | Alimentation |
| Chile | | | | | | | | | Chili |
| General | 96.3 | 100.0 | 103.6 | 106.1 | 109.1 | 110.3 | 113.6 | 117.5 | Généraux |
| Food | 98.6 | 100.0 | 100.8 | 102.9 | 105.8 | 104.4 | 107.4 | 110.6 | Alimentation |
| China | | | | | | | | | Chine |
| General | 99.9 | 100.0 | 100.7 | 99.9 | 101.1 | 105.0 | 106.9 | 108.5 | Généraux |
| Food | 102.7 | 100.0 | 100.0 | 99.4 | 102.8 | 113.0 | 116.2 | 118.9 | Alimentation |
| China, Hong Kong SAR | | | | | | | | | Chine, Hong Kong RAS |
| General | ... | 100.0 | 98.4 | 95.4 | 93.0 | 92.6 | 93.6[1] | 95.5 | Généraux |
| Food | ... | 100.0 | 99.2 | 97.1 | 95.7 | 96.7 | 98.4[1] | 100.1 | Alimentation |
| China, Macao SAR | | | | | | | | | Chine, Macao RAS |
| General | 101.6 | 100.0[1] | 98.0 | 95.4 | 93.9 | 94.9 | 99.0[1] | 104.1 | Généraux |
| Food | 101.5 | 100.0[1] | 98.6 | 96.5 | 95.2 | 97.4 | 101.3[1] | 105.0 | Alimentation |
| Colombia[15] | | | | | | | | | Colombie[15] |
| General | 91.3 | 100.0 | 108.6 | 116.5 | 125.0 | 132.5 | 139.6 | 145.2 | Généraux |
| Food | 91.7 | 100.0 | 108.7 | 118.4 | 127.2 | 134.6 | 143.1 | 150.5 | Alimentation |
| Congo | | | | | | | | | Congo |
| General | 100.9 | 100.0 | 100.1 | 104.4 | 103.8 | 106.4 | 109.6 | 116.8 | Généraux |
| Food | 105.5 | 100.0 | 98.3 | 102.9 | 96.9 | 90.8 | 95.6 | 105.3 | Alimentation |
| Cook Islands | | | | | | | | | Iles Cook |
| General | 96.9 | 100.0 | 108.7 | 112.3 | 114.6 | 115.6 | 118.4 | 122.4 | Généraux |
| Food[16] | 96.8 | 100.0 | 109.3 | 116.9 | 119.9 | 120.9 | 122.3 | 125.2 | Alimentation[16] |
| Costa Rica[17] | | | | | | | | | Costa Rica[17] |
| General | 90.1 | 100.0 | 111.3 | 121.5 | 132.9 | 149.3 | 169.9 | 189.4[1] | Généraux |
| Food[7] | 91.1 | 100.0 | 110.8 | 121.8 | 133.3 | 151.6 | 176.5 | ... | Alimentation[7] |
| Côte d'Ivoire | | | | | | | | | Côte d'Ivoire |
| General | 97.5 | 100.0 | 104.4 | 107.6 | 111.1 | 112.7 | 117.1 | 119.9 | Généraux |
| Food[9] | 100.0 | 100.0 | 105.7 | 111.6 | 116.1 | 111.6 | 114.3 | 117.5 | Alimentation[9] |
| Croatia | | | | | | | | | Croatie |
| General | 95.0 | 100.0 | 104.5[1] | 106.3 | 108.2 | 110.4 | 114.0[1] | 117.7 | Généraux |
| Food | 99.6 | 100.0 | 102.1[1] | 102.3 | 104.0 | 105.5 | 110.4[1] | 113.1 | Alimentation |
| Cyprus | | | | | | | | | Chypre |
| General | 96.0 | 100.0 | 102.0 | 104.8 | 109.2 | 111.7 | 114.5 | 117.4[1] | Généraux |
| Food | 94.8 | 100.0 | 104.1 | 108.9 | 114.4 | 119.0 | 120.9 | 126.7[1] | Alimentation |
| Czech Republic | | | | | | | | | République tchèque |
| General | 96.2 | 100.0[1] | 104.7 | 106.6 | 106.6 | 109.7 | 111.7 | 114.6 | Généraux |
| Food[18] | 98.2 | 100.0[1] | 104.3 | 104.3 | 104.0 | 109.0 | 110.3 | 111.5 | Alimentation[18] |
| Denmark | | | | | | | | | Danemark |
| General | 97.1 | 100.0[1] | 102.4 | 104.8 | 107.0 | 108.3 | 110.2 | 112.3 | Généraux |
| Food | 97.7 | 100.0[1] | 103.9 | 106.1 | 107.7 | 106.6 | 107.3 | 110.2 | Alimentation |
| Dominica | | | | | | | | | Dominique |
| General (2001 = 100) | 99.1 | 100.0 | 100.0[4] | 100.2 | 101.6 | 104.1 | 105.8 | ... | Généraux (2001 = 100) |
| Food (2001 = 100) | 100.3 | 100.0 | 100.0[4] | 101.5 | 101.9 | 104.8 | 107.4 | ... | Alimentation (2001 = 100) |
| Dominican Republic | | | | | | | | | Rép. dominicaine |
| General | 92.8 | 100.0 | 108.9 | 114.6 | 146.0 | 221.2 | 230.4 | 247.9 | Généraux |
| Food[9] | 99.6 | 100.0 | 106.1 | 110.7 | 140.1 | 237.0 | 233.2 | 242.8 | Alimentation[9] |
| Ecuador | | | | | | | | | Equateur |
| General | 51.0 | 100.0 | 137.7 | 154.9 | 167.1 | 171.7 | 175.5[1] | 181.2 | Généraux |
| Food | 45.3 | 100.0 | 131.2 | 141.7 | 145.8 | 146.9 | 100.0[19] | 106.0 | Alimentation |
| Egypt | | | | | | | | | Egypte |
| General | 97.4[1] | 100.0 | 102.2 | 105.0 | 109.5 | 127.4[1] | 133.7 | 143.9 | Généraux |
| Food | 97.6[1] | 100.0 | 101.1 | 105.3 | 112.3 | 100.0[20] | 105.0 | 115.7 | Alimentation |

| Country or area | 1999 | 2000 | 2001 | 2002 | 2003 | 2004 | 2005 | 2006 | Pays ou zone |
|---|---|---|---|---|---|---|---|---|---|
| El Salvador[10] | | | | | | | | | El Salvador[10] |
| General | 97.8 | 100.0 | 103.7 | 105.7 | 107.9 | 112.7 | 118.0 | 122.8 | Généraux |
| Food | 99.7 | 100.0 | 104.6 | 106.6 | 108.6 | 115.5 | 122.6 | 126.3 | Alimentation |
| Equatorial Guinea | | | | | | | | | Guinée équatoriale |
| General | ... | 100.0 | 108.8 | 117.0 | 125.5 | 130.9 | ... | 144.5 | Généraux |
| Food | ... | 100.0 | 111.5 | 122.2 | 130.0 | 135.7 | ... | 153.6 | Alimentation |
| Estonia | | | | | | | | | Estonie |
| General | 96.2 | 100.0 | 105.8 | 109.5 | 111.0 | 114.4 | 119.0 | 124.3 | Généraux |
| Food | 97.6 | 100.0 | 108.3 | 111.6 | 109.6 | 114.2 | 118.3 | 124.2 | Alimentation |
| Ethiopia | | | | | | | | | Ethiopie |
| General | 98.1 | 100.0 | 94.5[1] | 93.7 | 100.7 | 105.8 | 113.7 | 129.6 | Généraux |
| Food | 101.1 | 100.0 | 87.6[1] | 85.7 | 98.8 | 102.4 | 111.2 | 132.9 | Alimentation |
| Faeroe Islands | | | | | | | | | Iles Féroé |
| General | 96.1 | 100.0 | 104.9 | 105.2[1] | 106.5 | 107.2 | 109.3 | 111.0 | Généraux |
| Food | 97.5 | 100.0 | 106.2 | 108.9[1] | 109.4 | 109.9 | 111.1 | 114.1 | Alimentation |
| Falkland Is. (Malvinas) | | | | | | | | | Iles Falkland (Malvinas) |
| General | 96.0 | 100.0 | 101.3 | 102.0 | 103.2 | ... | ... | ... | Généraux |
| Fiji | | | | | | | | | Fidji |
| General | 98.9 | 100.0 | 104.3 | 105.0 | 109.4 | 112.5 | 115.1 | 118.1 | Généraux |
| Food | 103.3 | 100.0 | 104.1 | 104.6 | 111.0 | 115.2 | 117.1 | 119.2 | Alimentation |
| Finland | | | | | | | | | Finlande |
| General | 96.7 | 100.0[1] | 102.6 | 104.2 | 105.1 | 105.3 | 106.2 | 107.9[1] | Généraux |
| Food | 99.0 | 100.0[1] | 104.4 | 107.4 | 108.1 | 108.9 | 109.2 | 110.7[1] | Alimentation |
| France | | | | | | | | | France |
| General | 98.3 | 100.0 | 101.7 | 103.6 | 105.8 | 108.0 | 109.9 | 111.8 | Généraux |
| Food | 98.0 | 100.0 | 105.1 | 107.8 | 110.2 | 110.9 | 111.0 | 112.7 | Alimentation |
| French Guiana | | | | | | | | | Guyane française |
| General | 98.6 | 100.0 | 101.6 | 103.1 | 105.2 | 106.4 | 108.2 | 110.4 | Généraux |
| Food | 98.5 | 100.0 | 102.7 | 105.3 | 109.3 | 109.8 | 110.5 | 111.4 | Alimentation |
| French Polynesia | | | | | | | | | Polynésie française |
| General | 99.0 | 100.0 | 101.0 | 103.9 | 104.3[1] | 104.8 | 105.8 | 108.7 | Généraux |
| Food | 99.2 | 100.0 | 102.2 | 107.4 | 108.2[1] | 110.6 | 113.2 | 117.5 | Alimentation |
| Gabon | | | | | | | | | Gabon |
| General | 99.5 | 100.0 | 102.1 | 102.3 | 104.4 | 104.9 | 104.9 | 109.1 | Généraux |
| Food | 99.5 | 100.0 | 105.0 | 105.2 | 107.1 | 105.1 | 105.5 | 112.2 | Alimentation |
| Gambia | | | | | | | | | Gambie |
| General | 99.2 | 100.0 | 104.5 | 113.5 | 132.8 | 151.7 | 156.5 | ... | Généraux |
| Food | 99.8 | 100.0 | 99.3 | 117.2 | 141.2 | 164.0 | 169.2 | ... | Alimentation |
| Georgia[21] | | | | | | | | | Géorgie[21] |
| General | 96.1 | 100.0 | 104.7 | 110.5 | 115.8 | 122.4 | 132.5 | ... | Généraux |
| Food[7] | 98.7 | 100.0 | 106.6 | 114.6 | 122.7 | 132.2 | 149.6 | ... | Alimentation[7] |
| Germany | | | | | | | | | Allemagne |
| General | 98.1 | 100.0[1] | 102.0 | 103.4 | 104.5 | 106.2 | 108.3 | 110.1 | Généraux |
| Food | 100.5 | 100.0[1] | 104.5 | 105.3 | 105.2 | 104.8 | 105.3 | 107.3 | Alimentation |
| Ghana | | | | | | | | | Ghana |
| General | 79.9 | 100.0 | 132.9 | 151.8 | 193.3 | 217.7 | 250.7 | 278.0 | Généraux |
| Food | 89.4 | 100.0 | 123.2 | 145.6 | 181.6 | 211.8 | 244.7 | 267.2 | Alimentation |
| Gibraltar | | | | | | | | | Gibraltar |
| General | 98.9[1] | 100.0 | 101.8 | 102.5 | 105.2 | 107.6 | 110.9 | 113.8 | Généraux |
| Food | 99.2[1] | 100.0 | 103.5 | 107.1 | 111.3 | 115.1 | 117.4 | 120.4 | Alimentation |
| Greece | | | | | | | | | Grèce |
| General | 96.9[1] | 100.0 | 103.4 | 107.1 | 110.9 | 114.1 | 118.2[1] | 122.0 | Généraux |
| Food | 98.1[1] | 100.0 | 105.1 | 110.7 | 116.2 | 116.8 | 117.5[1] | 121.9 | Alimentation |
| Greenland | | | | | | | | | Groenland |
| General | 98.3 | 100.0 | 103.0 | 107.2 | 109.0 | 112.0 | 113.3 | 116.2 | Généraux |
| Food | 97.3 | 100.0 | 103.4 | 107.6 | 109.8 | 111.4 | 114.5 | 117.4 | Alimentation |
| Grenada | | | | | | | | | Grenade |
| General | 97.9 | 100.0 | 103.2[1] | 104.3 | 106.6 | 109.0 | ... | ... | Généraux |
| Food | 99.2 | 100.0 | 101.8[22] | 101.4 | 102.1 | 105.3 | ... | ... | Alimentation |

| Country or area | 1999 | 2000 | 2001 | 2002 | 2003 | 2004 | 2005 | 2006 | Pays ou zone |
|---|---|---|---|---|---|---|---|---|---|
| Guadeloupe | | | | | | | | | Guadeloupe |
| General | 100.0 | 100.0 | 102.6 | 105.0 | 107.1 | 108.6 | 112.1 | 114.3 | Généraux |
| Food | 101.2 | 100.0 | 105.3 | 108.0 | 111.7 | 113.1 | 116.1 | 115.7 | Alimentation |
| Guam | | | | | | | | | Guam |
| General | 98.0 | 100.0 | 98.7 | 99.4 | 102.0 | 108.1 | 116.3 | 129.8 | Généraux |
| Food | 98.3 | 100.0 | 106.0 | 112.6 | 118.9 | 130.1 | 140.8 | 150.0 | Alimentation |
| Guatemala | | | | | | | | | Guatemala |
| General | 94.4 | 100.0 | 107.3[1] | 116.0 | 122.5 | 131.8 | 143.8 | 153.2 | Généraux |
| Food | 95.8 | 100.0 | 110.0[1] | 121.5 | 128.5 | 141.7 | 160.5 | 171.9 | Alimentation |
| Guinea | | | | | | | | | Guinée |
| General | 93.5 | 100.0 | 105.4 | 108.4 | 122.4 | 141.1[1] | 185.3 | 249.6 | Généraux |
| Food | 96.2 | 100.0 | ... | 114.4[23] | 138.8 | 168.3 | 230.6 | 328.6 | Alimentation |
| Guinea-Bissau | | | | | | | | | Guinée-Bissau |
| General (2003 = 100) | ... | ... | ... | ... | 100.0 | 100.9 | 104.3 | 106.4 | Généraux (2003 = 100) |
| Food (2003 = 100)[9] | 93.2 | 100.0 | ... | ... | 100.0[24] | 101.1 | 104.7 | 105.2 | Alimentation (2003 = 100)[9] |
| Guyana | | | | | | | | | Guyana |
| General | 94.3 | 100.0 | 102.7 | 108.2 | 114.6 | 120.0 | 128.3 | 136.7 | Généraux |
| Food[7] | 96.0 | 100.0 | 100.6 | 104.4 | 108.5 | 113.3 | 121.7 | 129.7 | Alimentation[7] |
| Haiti[5] | | | | | | | | | Haïti[5] |
| General | 87.8 | 100.0 | 114.0 | 125.3 | 174.5 | 214.3 | 255.4[1] | 286.9 | Généraux |
| Food[9] | 91.1 | 100.0 | 115.5 | 127.4 | 174.2 | 223.2 | 263.2[1] | ... | Alimentation[9] |
| Honduras | | | | | | | | | Honduras |
| General | 94.3 | 100.0[1] | 109.6 | 118.0 | 127.1 | 137.5 | 149.5 | 157.9 | Généraux |
| Food | 95.2 | 100.0[1] | 108.7 | 112.8 | 117.0 | 124.9 | 137.5 | 143.7 | Alimentation |
| Hungary | | | | | | | | | Hongrie |
| General | 91.1 | 100.0 | 109.2 | 115.0 | 120.3 | 128.5 | 133.1 | 138.3 | Généraux |
| Food | 91.6 | 100.0 | 113.8 | 119.9 | 123.2 | 131.2 | 134.5 | 144.8 | Alimentation |
| Iceland[25] | | | | | | | | | Islande[25] |
| General | 95.2 | 100.0 | 106.7 | 111.8 | 114.2 | 117.8 | 122.6 | 130.9 | Généraux |
| Food | 96.2 | 100.0 | 107.4 | 111.1 | 108.4 | 109.7 | 106.7 | 115.7 | Alimentation |
| India | | | | | | | | | Inde |
| General | 96.1 | 100.0 | 103.9 | 108.2 | 112.5 | 116.6 | 121.5 | 127.7[1] | Généraux |
| Food | 98.2 | 100.0 | 102.2 | 104.9 | 108.4 | 111.5 | 115.0 | 124.7[1] | Alimentation |
| Indonesia | | | | | | | | | Indonésie |
| General | 96.4[26] | 100.0 | 111.5 | 124.7 | 133.0 | 141.3[1] | 156.0 | 176.5 | Généraux |
| Food | 105.0[26] | 100.0 | 108.5 | 120.2 | 121.2 | 128.3[1] | 140.3 | 161.9 | Alimentation |
| Iran (Islamic Rep. of) | | | | | | | | | Iran (Rép. islamique d') |
| General | 87.4[1] | 100.0 | 111.3 | 127.3 | 148.2 | 170.1 | 192.9 | 215.9 | Généraux |
| Food[7] | 89.3[1] | 100.0 | 106.6 | 124.0 | 145.9 | 164.8 | 186.3 | 205.5 | Alimentation[7] |
| Ireland | | | | | | | | | Irlande |
| General | 94.7 | 100.0 | 104.8[1] | 109.7 | 113.5 | 116.0 | 118.8 | 123.5 | Généraux |
| Food | 96.4 | 100.0 | 107.0[1] | 110.7 | 112.3 | 111.9 | 111.2 | 112.7 | Alimentation |
| Isle of Man | | | | | | | | | Ile de Man |
| General | 97.3 | 100.0[1] | 101.7 | 104.1 | 107.3 | 112.8 | 117.5 | 121.0 | Généraux |
| Food | 97.0 | 100.0[1] | 104.9 | 113.0 | 119.6 | 126.3 | 131.0 | 135.1 | Alimentation |
| Israel | | | | | | | | | Israël |
| General | 98.9 | 100.0[1] | 101.1 | 106.9[1] | 107.6 | 107.2 | 108.6 | 111.0 | Généraux |
| Food | 97.7 | 100.0[1] | 102.5 | 105.4[1] | 108.4 | 108.0 | 109.9 | 115.1 | Alimentation |
| Italy | | | | | | | | | Italie |
| General[27] | 97.5 | 100.0 | 102.8 | 105.4 | 108.2 | 110.5 | 112.4 | 114.7 | Généraux[27] |
| Food | 98.4 | 100.0 | 104.1 | 107.9 | 111.3 | 113.7 | 113.7 | 115.6 | Alimentation |
| Jamaica | | | | | | | | | Jamaïque |
| General | 92.4 | 100.0 | 107.0 | 114.6 | 126.4 | 143.6 | 165.5 | 179.8 | Généraux |
| Food | 93.4 | 100.0 | 103.4 | 109.7 | 120.2 | 136.5 | 161.4 | 172.0 | Alimentation |
| Japan | | | | | | | | | Japon |
| General | 100.7 | 100.0[1] | 99.3 | 98.4 | 98.1 | 98.1 | 97.8 | 98.1 | Généraux |
| Food | 102.0 | 100.0[1] | 99.4 | 98.6 | 98.4 | 99.3 | 98.4 | 98.9 | Alimentation |

| Country or area | 1999 | 2000 | 2001 | 2002 | 2003 | 2004 | 2005 | 2006 | Pays ou zone |
|---|---|---|---|---|---|---|---|---|---|
| Jersey[28] | | | | | | | | | Jersey[28] |
| General | 95.7 | 100.0[29] | 103.9 | 108.3 | 112.9 | 118.3 | 122.6 | 126.2 | Généraux |
| Food | 100.3 | 100.0[29] | 105.1 | 107.3 | 109.6 | 114.0 | 114.4 | 118.6 | Alimentation |
| Jordan | | | | | | | | | Jordanie |
| General | 99.3 | 100.0 | 101.8 | 103.6[1] | 105.3 | 108.9 | 112.7 | 119.7 | Généraux |
| Food[7] | 100.7 | 100.0 | 100.3 | 100.5[1] | 103.1 | 107.8 | 113.4 | 121.8 | Alimentation[7] |
| Kazakhstan | | | | | | | | | Kazakhstan |
| General | 88.4 | 100.0 | 108.4 | 114.7 | 122.1 | 130.5 | 140.3 | ... | Généraux |
| Food[9] | 86.2 | 100.0 | 111.5 | 119.0 | 127.3 | 137.1 | 148.2 | ... | Alimentation[9] |
| Kenya[15] | | | | | | | | | Kenya[15] |
| General | 94.5 | 100.0[1] | 103.6 | 105.3 | 116.7 | 133.5 | 149.1 | 178.3 | Généraux |
| Food | 96.8 | 100.0[1] | 102.4 | 103.9 | 120.9 | 143.8 | 164.8 | 210.8 | Alimentation |
| Kiribati | | | | | | | | | Kiribati |
| General | 99.6 | 100.0 | 106.0 | 109.4 | 111.4 | 110.3 | 110.0 | 108.3 | Généraux |
| Food | ... | 100.0[1] | 106.1 | 109.7 | 112.8 | 112.8 | 112.7 | 108.3 | Alimentation |
| Korea, Republic of | | | | | | | | | Corée, République de |
| General | 97.8 | 100.0[1] | 104.1 | 106.9 | 110.7 | 114.7 | 117.8[1] | 120.4 | Généraux |
| Food | 99.2 | 100.0[1] | 103.5 | 107.7 | 112.4 | 119.5 | 122.8[1] | 123.4 | Alimentation |
| Kosovo | | | | | | | | | Kosovo |
| General (2003 = 100) | ... | ... | ... | 98.8[30] | 100.0 | 98.9 | 97.6 | 98.2 | Généraux (2003 = 100) |
| Food (2003 = 100) | ... | ... | ... | 97.6[30] | 100.0 | 98.9 | 96.5 | 99.7 | Alimentation (2003 = 100) |
| Kuwait | | | | | | | | | Koweït |
| General | 98.2 | 100.0[1] | 101.8 | 102.3 | 103.2 | 104.5 | 108.8 | ... | Généraux |
| Food | 99.0 | 99.8[1] | 100.4 | 101.1 | 106.6 | 110.0 | 119.4 | ... | Alimentation |
| Kyrgyzstan | | | | | | | | | Kirghizistan |
| General | 84.2 | 100.0 | 106.9 | 109.1 | 112.5 | 117.1 | 122.2 | 129.0 | Généraux |
| Food | 84.4 | 100.0 | 105.7 | 105.9 | 108.9 | 112.4 | 118.3 | 128.7 | Alimentation |
| Lao People's Dem. Rep. | | | | | | | | | Rép. dém. pop. lao |
| General | 81.2 | 100.0[1] | 107.7 | 119.3 | 137.7 | 152.1 | 163.0 | ... | Généraux |
| Food | 84.7 | 100.0[1] | 106.6 | 117.0 | 134.8 | 148.8 | 160.2 | ... | Alimentation |
| Latvia | | | | | | | | | Lettonie |
| General | 97.4 | 100.0[1] | 102.5 | 104.5 | 107.5 | 114.2 | 121.9 | 129.9 | Généraux |
| Food | 99.4 | 100.0[1] | 104.8 | 108.4 | 111.2 | 119.5 | 130.5[31] | 141.1 | Alimentation |
| Lebanon | | | | | | | | | Liban |
| General | ... | 100.0 | 97.0 | 95.3 | ... | ... | ... | ... | Généraux |
| Lesotho | | | | | | | | | Lesotho |
| General[2] | 94.2 | 100.0 | 106.9 | 120.1 | 129.0 | 135.5 | 140.1 | 148.4 | Généraux[2] |
| Food | 95.6 | 100.0 | 106.5 | 134.8 | 142.4 | 148.1 | 152.0 | 165.9 | Alimentation |
| Lithuania | | | | | | | | | Lituanie |
| General | 99.1 | 100.0[1] | 101.3 | 101.6 | 100.4 | 101.6 | 104.3[1] | 108.2 | Généraux |
| Food | 102.5 | 100.0[1] | 103.5 | 102.8 | 99.0 | 101.2 | 105.3[1] | 111.7 | Alimentation |
| Luxembourg | | | | | | | | | Luxembourg |
| General | 96.9 | 100.0 | 102.7 | 104.8 | 106.9 | 109.3 | 112.0[1] | 115.0 | Généraux |
| Food | 98.0 | 100.0 | 104.8 | 108.9 | 111.0 | 113.0 | 114.8[1] | 117.6 | Alimentation |
| Madagascar | | | | | | | | | Madagascar |
| General[2] | ... | 100.0 | 107.4 | 125.1 | 123.0 | 140.0 | 152.6 | 183.7 | Généraux[2] |
| Food[3] | ... | 100.0 | 101.9 | 117.2 | 112.9 | 135.1 | 170.1 | 177.6 | Alimentation[3] |
| Malawi | | | | | | | | | Malawi |
| General | 77.2 | 100.0[1] | 122.7 | 140.8 | 154.3 | 172.0 | 198.5 | 226.1 | Généraux |
| Food | 83.5 | 100.0[1] | 117.6 | 136.4 | 143.6 | 154.4 | 181.0 | 209.1 | Alimentation |
| Malaysia | | | | | | | | | Malaisie |
| General | 98.5 | 100.0[1] | 101.4 | 103.2 | 104.4 | 105.9 | 109.1[1] | 113.0 | Généraux |
| Food | 98.1 | 100.0[1] | 100.7 | 101.4 | 102.7 | 105.0 | 108.8[1] | 112.5 | Alimentation |
| Maldives | | | | | | | | | Maldives |
| General | 101.2 | 100.0 | 100.7 | 101.6 | 98.7 | 105.0 | 108.5 | 112.4 | Généraux |
| Food[9] | 105.0 | 100.0 | 102.1 | 105.7 | 99.3 | 115.2 | 117.6 | 122.1 | Alimentation[9] |

| Country or area | 1999 | 2000 | 2001 | 2002 | 2003 | 2004 | 2005 | 2006 | Pays ou zone |
|---|---|---|---|---|---|---|---|---|---|
| Mali | | | | | | | | | Mali |
| General | 100.7 | 100.0 | 105.1 | 110.4 | 109.1 | 105.6 | 112.3 | 114.1 | Généraux |
| Food[32] | 104.7 | 100.0 | 108.0 | 115.8 | 111.1 | 103.3 | 115.1 | 114.6 | Alimentation[32] |
| Malta | | | | | | | | | Malte |
| General | 97.6 | 100.0 | 102.9 | 105.1 | 105.7[1] | 108.7 | 111.9 | 115.0 | Généraux |
| Food | 98.5 | 100.0 | 106.0 | 107.4 | 109.2[1] | 109.5 | 111.4 | 113.6 | Alimentation |
| Marshall Islands | | | | | | | | | Iles Marshall |
| General | 98.4 | 100.0 | 101.8 | 103.0 | 100.1 | 102.3 | 106.9 | ... | Généraux |
| Food | 100.2 | 100.0 | 100.3 | 102.7 | 102.5 | 106.0 | 106.3 | ... | Alimentation |
| Martinique | | | | | | | | | Martinique |
| General | 99.0 | 100.0 | 102.1 | 104.2 | 106.4 | 108.6 | 111.2 | 113.9 | Généraux |
| Food | 100.2 | 100.0 | 103.8 | 108.8 | 112.5 | 114.6 | 118.3 | 120.5 | Alimentation |
| Mauritania | | | | | | | | | Mauritanie |
| General | 96.8 | 100.0 | 104.7 | 108.9 | 114.4 | 124.2[1] | 139.3 | 147.9 | Généraux |
| Food | 96.3 | 100.0 | 106.5 | 111.3 | 117.9[33] | 131.2[1] | 149.3 | 157.3 | Alimentation |
| Mauritius | | | | | | | | | Maurice |
| General | 96.0 | 100.0 | 105.4 | 112.2[1] | 116.5 | 122.1 | 128.1 | 139.5 | Généraux |
| Food | 98.7 | 100.0 | 104.0 | 112.2[1] | 115.4 | 122.3 | 129.5 | 142.4 | Alimentation |
| Mexico | | | | | | | | | Mexique |
| General | 91.3 | 100.0 | 106.4 | 111.7[1] | 116.8 | 122.3 | 127.2 | 131.8 | Généraux |
| Food[9] | 94.1 | 100.0 | 105.4 | 109.6[1] | 115.1 | 122.9 | 129.4 | 134.1 | Alimentation[9] |
| Moldova | | | | | | | | | Moldova |
| General | 76.2 | 100.0 | 109.8 | 115.6 | 129.2 | 145.3 | 162.7 | 183.5 | Généraux |
| Food | 73.3 | 100.0 | 110.7 | 115.5 | 131.2 | 147.9 | 168.0 | 183.4 | Alimentation |
| Mongolia | | | | | | | | | Mongolie |
| General | 89.6 | 100.0 | 106.3[1] | 107.3 | 112.8 | 122.1 | 137.6 | ... | Généraux |
| Food[9] | 87.0 | 100.0 | 101.5 | 98.5 | 105.5 | 118.5 | 139.4 | ... | Alimentation[9] |
| Morocco | | | | | | | | | Maroc |
| General | 98.2 | 100.0 | 100.6 | 103.4 | 104.6 | 106.2 | 107.2 | 110.8 | Généraux |
| Food[7] | 98.5 | 100.0 | 99.0 | 103.2 | 104.6 | 106.2 | 106.5 | 110.7 | Alimentation[7] |
| Mozambique | | | | | | | | | Mozambique |
| General | 88.7 | 100.0 | 109.1 | 127.4 | 144.5 | 162.7 | 173.2[1] | 196.1 | Généraux |
| Food | 89.4 | 100.0 | 107.9 | 126.4 | 147.9 | ... | ... | ... | Alimentation |
| Myanmar | | | | | | | | | Myanmar |
| General | 100.1 | 100.0 | 121.1 | 190.2 | 259.8 | 271.6 | 297.1 | ... | Généraux |
| Food | 102.6 | 100.0 | 119.5 | 201.2 | 274.3 | 277.5 | 303.2 | ... | Alimentation |
| Namibia | | | | | | | | | Namibie |
| General | 91.5 | 100.0 | ... | ... | ... | ... | ... | ... | Généraux |
| General (2002 = 100) | ... | ... | ... | 100.0 | 107.1 | 111.6 | 114.1 | 119.9 | Généraux (2002 = 100) |
| Food | 93.5 | 100.0 | 111.5 | 133.2 | 144.1 | 147.1 | ... | ... | Alimentation |
| Food (2002 = 100) | ... | ... | ... | 100.0 | 109.5 | 110.4 | 112.0 | 119.3 | Alimentation (2002 = 100) |
| Nepal | | | | | | | | | Népal |
| General | 97.7 | 100.0 | 102.7 | 105.9 | 112.0 | 115.2 | 123.2 | 132.6 | Généraux |
| Food | 102.8 | 100.0 | 101.3 | 104.4 | 110.1 | 112.9 | 120.3 | 129.1 | Alimentation |
| Netherlands | | | | | | | | | Pays-Bas |
| General | 97.5 | 100.0[1] | 104.2 | 107.6 | 109.9 | 111.2 | 113.1 | 114.4 | Généraux |
| Food | 99.2 | 100.0[1] | 107.0 | 110.9 | 111.7 | 107.8 | 106.5 | 108.3 | Alimentation |
| Netherlands Antilles | | | | | | | | | Antilles néerlandaises |
| General | 94.5 | 100.0 | 101.8 | 102.1 | 103.8 | 105.2 | 109.4 | 113.0 | Généraux |
| Food | 94.1 | 100.0 | 103.4 | 107.3 | 109.5 | 114.7 | 123.3 | 133.0 | Alimentation |
| New Caledonia | | | | | | | | | Nouvelle-Calédonie |
| General | 98.5 | 100.0 | 102.3 | 104.1 | 105.4 | 106.2 | 107.6 | 110.7 | Généraux |
| Food | 99.4 | 100.0 | 102.6 | 105.0 | 107.0 | 108.2 | 109.7 | 113.0 | Alimentation |
| New Zealand | | | | | | | | | Nouvelle-Zélande |
| General | 97.5 | 100.0 | 102.6 | 105.4 | 107.2 | 109.7 | 113.0 | 116.8[1] | Généraux |
| Food | 98.7 | 100.0 | 106.0 | 109.4 | 109.4 | 110.3 | 113.1 | 116.2[1] | Alimentation |

| Country or area | 1999 | 2000 | 2001 | 2002 | 2003 | 2004 | 2005 | 2006 | Pays ou zone |
|---|---|---|---|---|---|---|---|---|---|
| Nicaragua | | | | | | | | | Nicaragua |
| General | 89.6 | 100.0 | 107.4[1] | 111.6 | 117.4 | 127.3 | ... | ... | Généraux |
| General (1999 = 100) | 100.0 | ... | 113.5 | 117.7 | 124.0 | 134.5 | 147.4 | 160.9 | Généraux (1999 = 100) |
| Food | 95.2 | 100.0 | 108.6[1] | 111.8 | 115.9 | 127.6 | ... | ... | Alimentation |
| Food (1999 = 100) | 100.0 | ... | 112.1 | 115.7 | 120.7 | 133.6 | 149.0 | 162.5 | Alimentation (1999 = 100) |
| Niger | | | | | | | | | Niger |
| General[2] | 97.2 | 100.0 | 104.0 | 106.7 | 105.1 | 105.2 | 113.5 | 113.6 | Généraux[2] |
| Food[7] | 97.0 | 100.0 | 107.1 | 111.9 | 106.7 | 105.1 | 120.7 | 118.4 | Alimentation[7] |
| Nigeria | | | | | | | | | Nigéria |
| General | 93.5 | 100.0 | 118.9 | 134.2 | 153.1[1] | 176.0 | 207.4 | 224.5 | **Généraux** |
| Food | 97.6 | 100.0 | 128.0 | 144.8 | 153.8[1] | 175.8 | 216.3 | 228.3 | Alimentation |
| Niue | | | | | | | | | Nioué |
| General | 96.6 | 100.0 | 106.8 | 109.7 | 112.3[1] | 116.6[34] | 117.0 | 119.7 | Généraux |
| Food | 94.9 | 100.0 | 111.2 | 115.1 | 118.3[1] | 121.2[34] | 122.0 | 127.2 | Alimentation |
| Norfolk Island | | | | | | | | | Ile Norfolk |
| General | 96.4 | 100.0 | 103.1 | 105.9 | 109.1 | 118.6 | 125.2 | 134.4 | Généraux |
| Food | 97.2 | 100.0 | 104.5 | 112.4 | 118.4 | 123.4 | 129.9 | 137.3 | Alimentation |
| Northern Mariana Islands | | | | | | | | | Iles Mariannes du Nord |
| General | 98.0 | 100.0 | 99.2 | 99.4 | 98.4[1] | 99.3 | ... | 104.7 | Généraux |
| Food | 100.6 | 100.0 | 96.6 | 93.0 | 90.7[1] | 94.9 | ... | 91.4 | Alimentation |
| Norway | | | | | | | | | Norvège |
| General | 97.0 | 100.0 | 103.0 | 104.4 | 106.9 | 107.4 | 109.1 | 111.6 | Généraux |
| Food | 98.2 | 100.0 | 98.1 | 96.5 | 99.7 | 101.5 | 103.1 | 104.6 | Alimentation |
| Occupied Palestinian Terr. | | | | | | | | | Terr. palestinien occupé |
| General | 97.3 | 100.0 | 101.2 | 107.0 | 111.7 | 115.1 | 119.1 | 123.5 | Généraux |
| Food | 98.4 | 100.0 | 99.5 | 102.1 | 106.8 | 109.1 | 113.3 | 118.8 | Alimentation |
| Oman | | | | | | | | | Oman |
| General | 101.2 | 100.0 | 99.0 | 98.3 | 97.9 | 98.3 | 100.2[1] | 103.3 | Généraux |
| Food[7] | 101.3 | 100.0 | 99.4 | 98.3 | 98.2 | 98.5 | 102.7[1] | 108.3 | Alimentation[7] |
| Pakistan | | | | | | | | | Pakistan |
| General | 95.8 | 100.0 | 103.2 | 107.4[1] | 110.5 | 118.7 | 129.5 | 139.7 | Généraux |
| Food | 96.9 | 100.0 | 101.8 | 105.9[1] | 108.6 | 120.2 | 132.1 | 143.3 | Alimentation |
| Panama | | | | | | | | | Panama |
| General | 98.5 | 100.0 | 100.3 | 101.3 | 102.7 | ... | ... | ... | Généraux |
| General (2003 = 100)[10] | ... | ... | ... | ... | 100.0 | 100.4 | 103.3 | 105.9 | Généraux (2003 = 100)[10] |
| Food | 99.3 | 100.0 | 99.6 | 98.9 | 100.2 | ... | ... | ... | Alimentation |
| Food (2003 = 100)[10] | ... | ... | ... | ... | 100.0 | 101.3 | 105.6 | 107.0 | Alimentation (2003 = 100)[10] |
| Papua New Guinea | | | | | | | | | Papouasie-Nvl-Guinée |
| General | 86.5 | 100.0 | 109.3 | 122.2 | 140.2 | 143.2 | 145.6 | 149.8 | Généraux |
| Food | 88.0 | 100.0 | 109.6 | 128.3 | 145.3 | 146.1 | 151.2 | 157.7 | Alimentation |
| Paraguay | | | | | | | | | Paraguay |
| General | 91.8 | 100.0 | 107.3 | 118.5 | 135.4 | 141.3 | 149.5 | 165.4 | Généraux |
| Food | 92.3 | 100.0 | 103.8 | 114.4 | 139.3 | 149.7 | 156.2 | 182.5 | Alimentation |
| Peru[5] | | | | | | | | | Pérou[5] |
| General | 96.4 | 100.0 | 102.0 | 102.2[1] | 104.5 | 108.3 | 110.1 | 112.3 | Généraux |
| Food | 99.3 | 100.0 | 100.5 | 100.2[1] | 101.0 | 106.6 | 107.6 | 110.2 | Alimentation |
| Philippines | | | | | | | | | Philippines |
| General | 95.9 | 100.0[1] | 106.8 | 110.1 | 113.9 | 120.6 | 129.8 | 137.9 | Généraux |
| Food[9] | 98.0 | 100.0[1] | 104.7 | 107.1 | 109.4 | 116.3 | 123.8 | 130.6 | Alimentation[9] |
| Poland | | | | | | | | | Pologne |
| General | 90.9 | 100.0 | 105.5 | 107.5 | 108.4 | 112.2 | 114.6 | 115.8 | Généraux |
| Food[11] | 91.2 | 100.0 | 105.1 | 104.6 | 103.0 | 108.6 | 110.6 | 110.6 | Alimentation[11] |
| Portugal | | | | | | | | | Portugal |
| General[2] | 97.2 | 100.0 | 104.3 | 108.0[1] | 111.6 | 114.2 | 116.7 | 120.4 | Généraux[2] |
| Food | 97.9 | 100.0 | 106.5 | 108.1[1] | 110.9 | 112.1 | 111.3 | 114.2 | Alimentation |
| Puerto Rico | | | | | | | | | Porto Rico |
| General | 94.0 | 100.0 | 107.0 | 113.6 | 122.5 | 137.1 | 156.1 | 178.9 | Généraux |
| Food | 91.7 | 100.0 | 114.1 | 127.8 | 145.8 | 176.3 | 212.1 | 257.1 | Alimentation |

| Country or area | 1999 | 2000 | 2001 | 2002 | 2003 | 2004 | 2005 | 2006 | Pays ou zone |
|---|---|---|---|---|---|---|---|---|---|
| Qatar | | | | | | | | | Qatar |
| General | 98.4 | 100.0[1] | 101.5 | 101.6 | 104.0 | 111.0 | 120.9 | 135.2 | Généraux |
| Food[7] | 99.6 | 100.0[1] | 99.8 | 101.1 | 100.7 | 104.4 | 107.3 | 115.1 | Alimentation[7] |
| Réunion | | | | | | | | | Réunion |
| General | 98.2 | 100.0 | 102.3 | 105.1 | 106.3 | 108.1 | 110.4 | 113.2 | Généraux |
| Food | 99.3 | 100.0 | 101.5 | 108.3 | 107.5 | 107.5 | 108.8 | 111.2 | Alimentation |
| Romania | | | | | | | | | Roumanie |
| General | 68.6 | 100.0 | 134.5 | 164.8 | 189.9 | 212.5 | 231.7 | 246.9 | Généraux |
| Food | 69.6 | 100.0 | 135.7 | 160.5 | 184.1 | 201.5 | 213.8 | 222.0 | Alimentation |
| Russian Federation | | | | | | | | | Fédération de Russie |
| General | 82.8 | 100.0 | 121.5[1] | 140.6 | 159.9 | 177.3 | 199.7 | 219.1 | Généraux |
| Food | 85.1 | 100.0 | 121.7[1] | 136.5 | 151.8 | 167.4 | 190.3 | 208.4 | Alimentation |
| Rwanda | | | | | | | | | Rwanda |
| General | 96.2 | 100.0 | 103.4 | 105.4 | 113.2[1] | 126.7 | 138.3 | 150.6 | Généraux |
| Food | 99.1 | 100.0 | 106.0 | 104.7 | 119.2[1] | 141.7 | ... | ... | Alimentation |
| Saint Helena | | | | | | | | | Sainte-Hélène |
| General (2002 = 100) | 98.6 | 100.0 | 103.5 | 100.0 | 100.0 | 108.8 | 112.9 | 116.5 | Généraux (2002 = 100) |
| Food (2002 = 100) | 99.4 | 100.0 | 102.6 | 100.0[35] | 103.8 | 112.9 | 116.1 | 117.4 | Alimentation (2002 = 100) |
| Saint Kitts and Nevis | | | | | | | | | Saint-Kitts-et-Nevis |
| General | 97.9 | 100.0 | ... | ... | ... | ... | ... | ... | Généraux |
| Food | 97.7 | 100.0 | ... | ... | ... | ... | ... | ... | Alimentation |
| Saint Lucia | | | | | | | | | Sainte-Lucie |
| General | 96.4 | 100.0 | 105.2 | 105.0 | 106.0 | 107.6 | 111.8 | 114.4 | Généraux |
| Food | 98.8 | 100.0 | 103.2 | 101.9 | 104.1 | 104.9 | 112.3 | 116.0 | Alimentation |
| Saint Pierre and Miquelon | | | | | | | | | Saint-Pierre-et-Miquelon |
| General | 92.2 | 100.0 | 102.3 | 102.5 | 104.8 | 106.9 | 114.0 | ... | Généraux |
| Food | 94.5 | 100.0 | 103.5 | 106.1 | 106.7 | 104.9 | 109.7 | ... | Alimentation |
| Saint Vincent-Grenadines | | | | | | | | | Saint Vincent-Grenadines |
| General | 99.8 | 100.0 | 100.8[1] | 101.5 | 101.8 | 104.8 | 108.7 | 112.0 | Généraux |
| Food | 101.1 | 100.0 | 101.0[1] | 101.6 | 100.9 | 105.6 | 111.3 | 115.3 | Alimentation |
| Samoa | | | | | | | | | Samoa |
| General[2] | 98.9 | 100.0 | 103.7 | 112.2 | 112.3 | 130.5[1] | 133.0 | 138.1 | Généraux[2] |
| Food | 100.1 | 100.0 | 105.1 | 117.3 | 115.1 | 146.2[1] | 146.7 | 152.5 | Alimentation |
| San Marino | | | | | | | | | Saint-Marin |
| General (2003 = 100) | 96.8 | 100.0 | ... | ... | 100.0 | 101.4 | 103.1 | 105.3 | Généraux (2003 = 100) |
| Food (2003 = 100) | 98.9 | 100.0 | ... | ... | 100.0 | 103.3 | 108.9 | 115.0 | Alimentation (2003 = 100) |
| Saudi Arabia[36] | | | | | | | | | Arabie saoudite[36] |
| General | 100.6[37] | 100.0[37] | 99.2[37] | 98.6[37] | 97.2 | 99.5[1] | 100.2 | 102.4 | Généraux |
| Food[7] | 100.9[37] | 100.0[37] | 100.6[37] | 100.0[37] | 96.9 | 104.4[1] | 107.5 | 113.3 | Alimentation[7] |
| Senegal | | | | | | | | | Sénégal |
| General | 99.3 | 100.0 | 103.0 | 105.4 | 105.3 | 105.9 | 107.7 | 110.0 | Généraux |
| Food[7] | 101.1 | 100.0 | 104.9 | 110.1 | 109.4 | 110.3 | 114.5 | 116.0 | Alimentation[7] |
| Seychelles | | | | | | | | | Seychelles |
| General | 94.2 | 100.0 | 106.0[1] | 106.2 | 109.7 | 114.0 | 115.0 | 114.6 | Généraux |
| Food | 98.6 | 100.0 | 104.9[1] | 105.6 | 108.2 | 109.2 | 110.3 | 114.3 | Alimentation |
| Sierra Leone | | | | | | | | | Sierra Leone |
| General | 100.9 | 100.0 | 102.2 | 98.8 | 106.3[1] | 122.1 | 140.1 | 151.4 | Généraux |
| Food | 100.4 | 100.0 | 105.2 | 104.4 | 112.2[1] | 134.7 | 154.5 | 158.2 | Alimentation |
| Singapore | | | | | | | | | Singapour |
| General | 98.7 | 100.0 | 101.0 | 100.6 | 101.1 | 102.8[1] | 103.2 | 104.2 | Généraux |
| Food | 99.4 | 100.0 | 100.5 | 100.5 | 101.1 | 103.2[1] | 104.6 | 106.2 | Alimentation |
| Slovakia | | | | | | | | | Slovaquie |
| General | 89.3 | 100.0 | 107.1[1] | 110.7 | 120.2 | 129.2 | 132.8 | 138.7 | Généraux |
| Food | 94.9 | 100.0 | 105.8[1] | 107.3 | 111.0 | 116.4 | 114.7 | 116.4 | Alimentation |
| Slovenia[10] | | | | | | | | | Slovénie[10] |
| General | 91.8 | 100.0 | 108.4 | 116.5 | 123.0 | 127.4 | 130.6 | 133.8 | Généraux |
| Food | 94.8 | 100.0 | 109.0 | 117.5 | 123.1 | 124.2 | 124.3 | 127.2 | Alimentation |

| Country or area | 1999 | 2000 | 2001 | 2002 | 2003 | 2004 | 2005 | 2006 | Pays ou zone |
|---|---|---|---|---|---|---|---|---|---|
| Solomon Islands | | | | | | | | | Iles Salomon |
| General | 93.6 | 100.0 | 107.8 | 119.5 | 129.4 | 138.7 | 149.3 | 161.2 | Généraux |
| Food | 93.1 | 100.0 | 108.9 | 122.1 | 125.0 | 136.8 | 145.1 | 156.7 | Alimentation |
| South Africa | | | | | | | | | Afrique du Sud |
| General | 95.0 | 100.0[1] | 105.7 | 115.4 | 122.1 | 123.8 | 128.0 | 134.0 | Généraux |
| Food | 92.8 | 100.0[1] | 105.4 | 122.0 | 131.9 | 134.9 | 137.9 | 147.8 | Alimentation |
| Spain | | | | | | | | | Espagne |
| General (2001 = 100) | 96.7 | 100.0 | 100.0 | 103.5 | 106.7 | 109.9 | 113.6 | 117.6 | Généraux (2001 = 100) |
| Food (2001 = 100) | 98.0 | 100.0 | 100.0 | 104.7 | 109.0 | 113.2 | 116.3 | 121.5 | Alimentation (2001 = 100) |
| Sri Lanka | | | | | | | | | Sri Lanka |
| General | 94.2 | 100.0 | 114.2 | 125.1 | 133.0 | 143.0 | 159.7 | 181.5 | Généraux |
| Food | 95.7 | 100.0 | 115.2 | 127.5 | 134.9 | 145.5 | 163.0 | 184.6 | Alimentation |
| Suriname | | | | | | | | | Suriname |
| General (2001 = 100) | 45.3 | 77.4[38] | 100.0[1] | 115.9 | ... | 156.9[39] | 171.4 | ... | Généraux (2001 = 100) |
| Food (2001 = 100) | 48.6 | 80.5[38] | 100.0[1] | 118.1 | ... | 157.8[39] | 174.2 | ... | Alimentation (2001 = 100) |
| Swaziland | | | | | | | | | Swaziland |
| General | 91.0 | 100.0 | 107.7 | 120.2 | 129.0 | 133.5 | 139.9 | ... | Généraux |
| Food | 93.7 | 100.0 | 106.5 | 129.8 | 145.7 | 155.7 | 169.2 | ... | Alimentation |
| Sweden | | | | | | | | | Suède |
| General | 99.1 | 100.0 | 102.4 | 104.6 | 106.6 | 107.0 | 107.5 | 109.0 | Généraux |
| Food | 100.0 | 100.0 | 102.9 | 106.2 | 106.6 | 106.1 | 105.4 | 106.2 | Alimentation |
| Switzerland | | | | | | | | | Suisse |
| General | 98.5 | 100.0[1] | 101.0 | 101.7 | 102.3 | 103.1 | 104.4 | 105.4[1] | Généraux |
| Food | 98.5 | 100.0[40] | 102.1 | 104.4 | 105.7 | 106.3 | 105.5 | 105.4 | Alimentation |
| Syrian Arab Republic | | | | | | | | | Rép. arabe syrienne |
| General | 100.8 | 100.0 | 100.4 | 101.4 | 108.8[1] | 113.5 | 121.9 | 134.1[1] | Généraux |
| Food | 102.1 | 100.0 | 100.2 | 99.6 | 107.2[1] | 112.8 | 122.5 | 138.0[1] | Alimentation |
| Tajikistan | | | | | | | | | Tadjikistan |
| General | 80.6 | 100.0 | ... | ... | ... | ... | ... | ... | Généraux |
| Thailand | | | | | | | | | Thaïlande |
| General | 98.5 | 100.0[1] | 101.6 | 102.3 | 104.1 | 107.0[1] | 111.8 | 117.0 | Généraux |
| Food | 101.1 | 100.0[1] | 100.7 | 101.0 | 104.7 | 109.4[1] | 114.9 | 120.1 | Alimentation |
| TFYR of Macedonia | | | | | | | | | Ex-R.Y. Macédoine |
| General | 94.5 | 100.0 | 105.5 | 107.4 | 108.7 | 108.2 | 108.8 | 112.3 | Généraux |
| Food | 100.4 | 100.0 | 106.9 | 108.8 | 107.3 | 104.0 | 102.7 | 105.0 | Alimentation |
| Togo | | | | | | | | | Togo |
| General | 98.2 | 100.0 | 103.9 | 107.1 | 106.0 | 106.5 | 113.7 | 116.3 | Généraux |
| Food[9] | 103.5 | 100.0 | 105.2 | 109.3 | 103.1 | 101.9 | 113.0 | 111.7 | Alimentation[9] |
| Tonga | | | | | | | | | Tonga |
| General[2] | 93.7 | 100.0 | 108.3 | 119.5[1] | 133.5 | 148.1 | 160.4 | 172.0 | Généraux[2] |
| Food | 99.7 | 100.0 | 111.8 | 130.6[1] | 143.1 | 156.1 | 165.5 | 170.4 | Alimentation |
| Trinidad and Tobago | | | | | | | | | Trinité-et-Tobago |
| General | 96.6 | 100.0 | 105.6 | 109.9 | 114.2[1] | 118.3 | 126.5 | 137.0 | Généraux |
| Food | 92.3 | 100.0 | 114.0 | 125.6 | 142.9[1] | 161.1 | 198.1 | 244.1 | Alimentation |
| Tunisia | | | | | | | | | Tunisie |
| General | 97.1 | 100.0[1] | 102.0 | 104.8 | 107.6 | 111.5 | 113.8 | 118.9 | Généraux |
| Food | 95.6 | 100.0[1] | 102.0 | 106.1 | 109.7 | 115.1 | 115.2 | 121.4 | Alimentation |
| Turkey | | | | | | | | | Turquie |
| General | 64.5 | 100.0 | 154.4 | 223.8 | 280.4 | 310.1 | 329.5[1] | 361.1 | Généraux |
| Food | 66.8 | 100.0 | 150.3 | 225.3 | 290.0 | 316.1 | 112.1[41] | 123.0 | Alimentation |
| Tuvalu | | | | | | | | | Tuvalu |
| General | 96.2 | 100.0 | 101.5 | 106.7[1] | 110.2 | 113.3 | 117.0 | ... | Généraux |
| Food | 99.0 | 100.0 | 105.3 | 109.4[1] | 117.4 | 120.8 | 127.4 | ... | Alimentation |
| Uganda | | | | | | | | | Ouganda |
| General | 96.8 | 100.0 | 101.9 | 101.6 | 110.5 | 114.5 | 124.1 | 133.3 | Généraux |
| Food | 99.0 | 100.0 | 96.6 | 92.5 | 106.7 | 111.4 | 126.1 | 139.1 | Alimentation |

| Country or area | 1999 | 2000 | 2001 | 2002 | 2003 | 2004 | 2005 | 2006 | Pays ou zone |
|---|---|---|---|---|---|---|---|---|---|
| Ukraine | | | | | | | | | Ukraine |
| General | 78.0 | 100.0 | 112.0 | 112.8 | 118.7 | 129.4 | 146.9 | 160.2 | Généraux |
| Food[9] | 74.3 | 100.0 | 114.4 | 114.4 | 121.5 | 135.1 | 157.5 | 166.5 | Alimentation[9] |
| United Arab Emirates | | | | | | | | | Emirats arabes unis |
| General | 98.6 | 100.0[1] | 102.8 | 105.8 | 109.1 | 114.6 | 121.7 | ... | Généraux |
| Food[3] | 99.5 | 100.0[1] | 101.0 | 102.4 | 104.7 | 112.0 | 117.0 | ... | Alimentation[3] |
| United Kingdom | | | | | | | | | Royaume-Uni |
| General | 97.1 | 100.0 | 101.8 | 103.5 | 106.5 | 109.6 | 112.7 | 116.3 | Généraux |
| Food | 100.3 | 100.0 | 103.3 | 104.0 | 105.4 | 106.0 | 107.3 | 109.6 | Alimentation |
| United Rep. of Tanzania | | | | | | | | | Rép.-Unie de Tanzanie |
| General (2001 = 100) | 94.4[42] | 100.0[43] | 105.1[1] | 106.2 | 109.8 | 114.5 | 119.4 | 130.3 | Généraux (2001 = 100) |
| Food (2001 = 100) | 93.6[42] | 100.0[43] | 106.1[1] | 107.1 | 112.0 | 118.6 | 125.6 | 140.5 | Alimentation (2001 = 100) |
| United States[44] | | | | | | | | | Etats-Unis[44] |
| General | 96.7 | 100.0 | 102.8 | 104.5 | 106.9 | 109.7 | 113.4 | 117.1 | Généraux |
| Food | 97.8 | 100.0 | 103.2 | 105.0 | 107.3 | 111.0 | 113.6 | 116.3 | Alimentation |
| Uruguay | | | | | | | | | Uruguay |
| General | 95.5 | 100.0 | 104.4 | 118.9 | 142.0 | 155.0 | 162.3 | 172.7 | Généraux |
| Food | 94.6 | 100.0 | 103.1 | 117.2 | 142.5 | 159.2 | 165.7 | 176.0 | Alimentation |
| Vanuatu | | | | | | | | | Vanuatu |
| General | 97.5 | 100.0 | 103.6 | 105.7 | 108.8 | 110.4 | 111.7 | 113.8 | Généraux |
| Food | 98.0 | 100.0 | 102.2 | 102.7 | 105.0 | 108.5 | 108.0 | 111.4 | Alimentation |
| Venezuela (Bolivarian Rep. of) | | | | | | | | | Venezuela (Rép. bolivarienne du) |
| General | 86.0 | 100.0[1] | 112.5 | 137.8 | 180.6 | 219.9 | 255.0 | 289.8 | Généraux |
| Food | 93.3 | 100.0[1] | 116.1 | 149.0 | 205.2 | 274.6 | 332.5 | 399.3 | Alimentation |
| Viet Nam | | | | | | | | | Viet Nam |
| General | 101.6 | 100.0 | 99.7 | 103.7 | 107.0 | 115.0 | ... | ... | Généraux |
| Food[9] | 104.0 | 100.0 | 98.6 | 106.1 | 108.7 | 119.8 | ... | ... | Alimentation[9] |
| Yemen | | | | | | | | | Yémen |
| General | 95.6 | 100.0 | 111.9 | 125.6 | 139.2 | 156.6 | 174.5 | 211.6 | Généraux |
| Food | 95.0 | 100.0 | 115.7 | 121.2 | 141.4 | 168.3 | 199.9 | 269.5 | Alimentation |
| Zambia | | | | | | | | | Zambie |
| General | 79.3 | 100.0 | 121.4 | 148.4 | 180.1 | 212.5 | 251.4 | 274.1 | Généraux |
| Food[9] | 81.6 | 100.0 | 118.9 | 151.1 | 184.5 | 214.7 | 254.5 | 267.1 | Alimentation[9] |
| Zimbabwe | | | | | | | | | Zimbabwe |
| General | 64.2 | 100.0 | 176.7 | 424.3 | 2 255.8 | 8 625.7 | 34 688.3[1] | 415 106.7 | Généraux |
| Food | 67.1 | 100.0 | 164.1 | 407.7 | 2 238.4 | 8 792.0 | 42 868.1[1] | ... | Alimentation |

Source

International Labour Office (ILO), Geneva, the ILO labour statistics database, last accessed December 2007.

Notes

1 Series linked to former series.
2 Excluding rent.
3 Including beverages and tobacco.
4 Series (base 2001 = 100) replacing former series.
5 Metropolitan area.
6 Series replacing former series; prior to 2006: incl. alcoholic beverages.

7 Including tobacco.
8 Government officials.
9 Including alcoholic beverages and tobacco.
10 Urban areas.
11 Including alcoholic beverages.
12 Beginning 1997, including tobacco.
13 Prior to December 2003: Douala and Yaoundé only.
14 January-October.
15 Low-income group.

Source

Bureau international du travail (BIT), Genève, la base de données du BIT, dernier accès décembre 2007.

Notes

1 Série enchaînée à la précédente.
2 Non compris le groupe "Loyer".
3 Y compris les boissons et le tabac.
4 Série (base 2001 = 100) remplaçant la précédente.
5 Région métropolitaine.
6 Série remplaçant la précédente; avant 2006: y compris les boissons alcoolisées.
7 Y compris le tabac.
8 Fonctionnaires.
9 Y compris les boissons alcoolisées et le tabac.
10 Régions urbaines.
11 Y compris les boissons alcoolisées.
12 A partir 1997, y compris le tabac.
13 Avant déc. 2003: Douala et Yaoundé seulement.
14 Janvier-octobre.
15 Familles à revenu modique.

| | |
|---|---|
| 16 Excluding beverages. | 16 Non compris les boissons. |
| 17 Central area. | 17 Région centrale. |
| 18 Including tobacco, beverages and public catering. | 18 Y compris le tabac, les boissons et la restauration. |
| 19 Series (base 2005=100) replacing former series; prior to 2005 incl. alcoholic beverages and tobacco. | 19 Série (base 2005=100) remplaçant la précédente; avant 2005 y compris les boissons alcoolisées et le tabac. |
| 20 Series (base 2004=100) replacing former series; prior to 2004: incl. tobacco. | 20 Série (base 2004=100) remplaçant la précédente; avant 2004: y compris le tabac. |
| 21 Five cities. | 21 Cinq villes. |
| 22 Series (base 2000=100) replacing former series; prior to 2001: incl. alcoholic beverages and tobacco. | 22 Série (base 2000=100) remplaçant la précédente; avant 2001 : y compris les boissons alcoolisées et le tabac. |
| 23 Series linked to former series; average July-December. | 23 Série enchaînée à la précédente; moyenne de juillet à décembre. |
| 24 Series (base 2003=100) replacing former series. | 24 Série (base 2003=100) remplaçant la précédente. |
| 25 Annual averages are based on the months Feb.-Dec. and the mean of January both years. | 25 Les moyennes annuelles sont basées sur les mois de fév.-déc. et la moyenne de janvier des deux années. |
| 26 Since November 1999: excluding Dili. | 26 A partir de novembre 1999: non compris Dili. |
| 27 Excluding tobacco. | 27 Non compris le tabac. |
| 28 June of each year. | 28 Juin de chaque année. |
| 33 Series linked to former series; June of each year. | 33 Série enchaînée à la précédente; juin de chaque année. |
| 30 May-December. | 30 Mai-décembre. |
| 31 Series replacing former series; prior to 2005: including alcoholic beverages and tobacco. | 31 Série remplaçant la précédente; avant 2005: y compris les boissons alcoolisées et le tabac. |
| 32 Beginning January 1998, including alcoholic beverages and tobacco. | 32 A partir de janvier, y compris les boissons alcoolisées et le tabac. |
| 33 January-November. | 33 Janvier-novembre. |
| 34 Average of the last three quarters. | 34 Moyenne des trois derniers trimestres. |
| 35 Series (base 2002=100) replacing former series. | 35 Série (base 2002=100) remplaçant la précédente. |
| 36 All cities. | 36 Ensemble des villes. |
| 37 Middle-income group. | 37 Familles à revenus moyens. |
| 38 April-December. | 38 Avril-décembre. |
| 39 March-December. | 39 Mars-décembre. |
| 40 Series (base 2000=100) replacing former series; prior to 2000: food only. | 40 Series (base 2000=100) replacing former series; prior to 2000: food only. |
| 41 Series (base 2003 = 100) replacing former series; prior to 2005 incl. alcoholic beverages and tobacco. | 41 Série (base 2003=100) remplaçant la précédente; avant 2005 y compris les boissons alcoolisées et le tabac. |
| 42 Half-year average. | 42 Moyenne de six mois. |
| 43 Average of 10 months. | 43 Moyenne de 10 mois. |
| 44 All urban consumers. | 44 Tous les consommateurs urbains. |

*Table 31*: The series generally relate to the average earnings per worker in manufacturing industries, according to the *International Standard Industrial Classification of All Economic Activities* (ISIC) Revision 2 or Revision 3. The data are published in the ILO *Yearbook of Labour Statistics* and on the ILO web site http://laborsta.ilo.org and generally cover all employees (i.e. wage earners and salaried employees) of both sexes, irrespective of age. Data which refer exclusively to wage earners (i.e. manual or production workers), salaried employees (i.e. non-manual workers), or to total employment are also shown when available. Earnings generally include bonuses, cost of living allowances, taxes, social insurance contributions payable by the employed person and, in some cases, payments in kind, and normally exclude social insurance contributions payable by the employers, family allowances and other social security benefits. The time of year to which the figures refer is not the same for all countries. In some cases, the series may show wage rates instead of earnings; this is indicated in footnotes.

*Table 32*: The producer price index (PPI) can be generally described as an index for measuring the average change in the prices of goods and services either as they leave the place of production or as they enter the production process. As such, producer price indices can represent input prices (at purchasers' prices) and output prices (at basic or producer prices) with different levels of aggregation.

The industrial coverage of the PPI can vary across countries. Normally, the PPIs refer to indices related to the agricultural, mining, manufacturing, transport and telecommunications, and public utilities sectors. Many countries are progressively developing service industry PPIs for incorporation within their larger PPI frameworks. PPI prices should be actual transaction prices recorded at the time the transaction occurs (i.e. when ownership changes).

PPIs can be calculated in a number of different combinations. In this publication, the PPIs are classified according to the following scheme:

(a)   Components of supply
     Domestic supply
     Domestic production for domestic market
     Agricultural products
     Industrial products
     Imported goods
(b)   Stage of processing
     Raw materials
     Intermediate goods
(c)   End-use
     Consumer goods
     Capital goods

*Tableau 31*: Les séries se rapportent généralement aux gains moyens des salariés des industries manufacturières (activités de fabrication), suivant la *Classification internationale type, par industrie, de toutes les branches d'activité économique* (CITI, Rev. 2 ou Rev.3). Les données sont publiées dans l'*Annuaire des statistiques du travail* du BIT et sur le site Web du BIT http://laborsta.ilo.org et généralement portent sur l'ensemble des salariés (qu'ils perçoivent un salaire ou un traitement au mois) des deux sexes, indépendamment de leur âge. Les données qui portent exclusivement sur les salariés horaires (ouvriers, travailleurs manuels), sur les employés percevant un traitement (travailleurs autres que manuels, cadres), ou sur l'emploi total sont aussi présentées si elles sont disponibles. Les gains comprennent en général les primes, les indemnités pour coût de la vie, les impôts, les cotisations de sécurité sociale à la charge de l'employé, et dans certains cas des paiements en nature, mais ne comprennent pas en règle générale la part patronale des cotisations d'assurance sociale, les allocations familiales et les autres prestations de sécurité sociale. La période de l'année visée par les données n'est pas la même pour tous les pays. Dans certains cas, les séries présentent les taux horaires et non pas les gains, ce présente qui est alors signalé en note.

*Tableau 32*: L'indice des prix à la production peut être caractérisé de manière générale comme un indice permettant de mesurer le changement moyen des prix des biens et des services soit au moment où ils quittent le lieu de production soit au moment où ils arrivent au processus de production. Les indices des prix à la production peuvent donc représenter les prix des intrants (aux prix d'acquisition) et les prix à la sortie de fabrique (aux prix de base, ou prix à la production), les agrégats étant de différents niveaux.

Les branches d'activité couvertes par l'indice des prix à la production peuvent n'être pas les mêmes d'un pays à l'autre. Normalement, l'indice concerne l'agriculture, les industries extractives, les industries manufacturières, les transports et télécommunications et les services publics de distribution. Nombre de pays mettent peu à peu au point des indices des prix à la production pour les services, de manière à pouvoir les intégrer à leurs indices des prix à la production plus généraux. Les prix servant pour ces indices doivent être des prix effectifs de transaction enregistrés au moment où s'effectue la transaction (au moment où le propriétaire change).

Les indices des prix à la production peuvent se calculer selon plusieurs combinaisons différentes. Dans la présente publication, on les classe de la manière ci-après:

(a)   Eléments de l'offre
     Offre intérieure
     Production nationale pour le marché intérieur

Though a few countries are still compiling the wholesale price index (WPI), which is the precedent of the PPI, the WPI has been replaced in most countries by the PPI because of the broader coverage provided by the PPI in terms of products and industries and the conceptual concordance between the PPI and the System of National Accounts. The WPI would normally cover the price of products as they flow from the wholesaler to the retailer and is an index for measuring the price level changes in markets other than retail.

For a more detailed explanation about the PPI, please refer to the *Producer Price Index Manual: Theory and Practice* published by the International Monetary Fund in 2004.

*Table 33*: Unless otherwise stated, the consumer price index covers all the main classes of expenditure on all items and on food. Monthly data for many of these series may be found in the United Nations *Monthly Bulletin of Statistics*.

       Produits agricoles
       Produits industriels
       Produits importés
(b)     Stade de la transformation
       Matières premières
       Produits intermédiaires
(c)     Utilisation finale
       Biens de consommation
       Biens d'équipement

Même s'il y a encore quelques pays qui compilent l'indice des prix de gros, qui est l'ancêtre de l'indice des prix à la production, la plupart l'ont remplacé par ce dernier, qui offre une couverture plus large de produits et de branches d'activité, et coïncide dans ses concepts avec le Système de comptabilité nationale. L'indice des prix de gros suivait normalement le prix des produits à mesure qu'ils passaient du grossiste au détaillant il permet de mesurer les changements du niveau des prix sur les marchés autres que le marché de détail.

Pour un complément de détails sur l'indice des prix à la production, on se reportera au "*Producer Price Index Manual, Theory and Practice*" publié par le Fonds monétaire international en 2004.

*Tableau 33*: Sauf indication contraire, les indices des prix à la consommation donnés englobent tous les groupes principaux de dépenses pour l'ensemble des prix et alimentation. Les données mensuelles pour plusieurs de ces séries figurent dans le *Bulletin mensuel de statistique*.

# 34

## Agricultural production
Index base: 1999-01 = 100

## Production agricole
Indices base : 1999-01 = 100

| Region, country or area — Région, pays ou zone | Agriculture — Agriculture | | | | | Food — Produits alimentaires | | | | |
|---|---|---|---|---|---|---|---|---|---|---|
| | 2002 | 2003 | 2004 | 2005 | 2006 | 2002 | 2003 | 2004 | 2005 | 2006 |
| World — Monde | 102.9 | 105.8 | 111.1 | 113.0 | 114.1 | 103.0 | 105.9 | 110.8 | 112.8 | 113.8 |
| Africa — Afrique | 104.5 | 109.4 | 112.3 | 116.4 | 118.8 | 104.8 | 110.3 | 113.1 | 117.3 | 119.9 |
| Algeria — Algérie | 105.6 | 124.9 | 137.5 | 137.3 | 142.9 | 105.7 | 125.2 | 137.7 | 137.5 | 143.1 |
| Angola — Angola | 123.2 | 129.9 | 139.1 | 147.8 | 151.1 | 124.1 | 130.9 | 140.2 | 149.0 | 152.5 |
| Benin — Bénin | 111.3 | 113.7 | 119.4 | 114.7 | 103.4 | 108.5 | 115.0 | 121.5 | 119.7 | 112.4 |
| Botswana — Botswana | 102.7 | 95.0 | 102.4 | 103.2 | 103.2 | 102.7 | 95.0 | 102.5 | 103.3 | 103.3 |
| Burkina Faso — Burkina Faso | 116.9 | 128.3 | 120.5 | 138.9 | 146.2 | 113.4 | 126.1 | 111.0 | 126.9 | 130.0 |
| Burundi — Burundi | 108.5 | 103.7 | 103.4 | 99.6 | 102.6 | 107.1 | 105.8 | 101.3 | 101.1 | 101.2 |
| Cameroon — Cameroun | 103.0 | 106.0 | 107.9 | 112.7 | 107.2 | 106.7 | 108.9 | 112.3 | 115.2 | 112.2 |
| Central African Rep. — Rép. centrafricaine | 103.7 | 101.4 | 106.4 | 107.5 | 104.0 | 105.1 | 104.9 | 110.4 | 111.7 | 108.1 |
| Chad — Tchad | 106.9 | 109.8 | 109.7 | 119.9 | 122.6 | 107.1 | 114.1 | 108.4 | 120.6 | 122.1 |
| Comoros — Comores | 101.5 | 105.2 | 105.8 | 100.3 | 98.7 | 101.5 | 105.2 | 105.8 | 100.3 | 98.7 |
| Congo — Congo | 103.2 | 105.4 | 110.2 | 109.1 | 112.5 | 103.1 | 105.2 | 110.0 | 108.9 | 112.4 |
| Côte d'Ivoire — Côte d'Ivoire | 99.1 | 100.1 | 101.9 | 106.6 | 100.9 | 101.1 | 102.9 | 106.0 | 109.2 | 105.3 |
| Dem. Rep. of the Congo — Rép. dém. du Congo | 96.1 | 96.7 | 96.5 | 96.6 | 95.4 | 96.4 | 96.9 | 96.7 | 96.9 | 95.6 |
| Djibouti — Djibouti | 105.2 | 104.8 | 104.9 | 105.3 | 105.3 | 105.2 | 104.8 | 104.9 | 105.3 | 105.3 |
| Egypt — Egypte | 104.4 | 109.0 | 112.8 | 113.8 | 114.5 | 104.2 | 110.0 | 112.8 | 114.2 | 114.8 |
| Ethiopia — Ethiopie | 110.4 | 112.7 | 119.8 | 132.3 | 133.5 | 110.8 | 113.2 | 120.3 | 134.8 | 134.5 |
| Gabon — Gabon | 100.7 | 101.3 | 101.7 | 103.2 | 103.2 | 100.7 | 101.3 | 101.7 | 103.3 | 103.3 |
| Gambia — Gambie | 68.1 | 85.1 | 106.5 | 91.9 | 96.0 | 68.1 | 85.0 | 106.4 | 91.8 | 95.9 |
| Ghana — Ghana | 112.8 | 117.6 | 123.6 | 132.0 | 131.1 | 113.3 | 118.1 | 124.1 | 132.5 | 131.5 |
| Guinea — Guinée | 103.7 | 107.9 | 112.4 | 113.7 | 122.0 | 105.1 | 109.3 | 114.1 | 115.4 | 124.4 |
| Guinea-Bissau — Guinée-Bissau | 101.4 | 100.2 | 109.9 | 117.4 | 114.6 | 101.3 | 100.0 | 109.8 | 117.4 | 114.6 |
| Kenya — Kenya | 109.1 | 112.3 | 113.1 | 115.4 | 126.6 | 109.7 | 112.9 | 113.0 | 115.5 | 128.5 |
| Liberia — Libéria | 98.3 | 98.4 | 101.6 | 101.0 | 103.9 | 96.0 | 96.3 | 98.4 | 98.4 | 101.8 |
| Libyan Arab Jamah. — Jamah. arabe libyenne | 98.7 | 99.6 | 101.2 | 105.2 | 104.8 | 98.7 | 99.6 | 101.1 | 105.1 | 104.7 |
| Madagascar — Madagascar | 96.7 | 99.5 | 106.6 | 111.3 | 114.3 | 97.4 | 99.8 | 107.1 | 112.5 | 114.7 |
| Malawi — Malawi | 80.5 | 86.5 | 99.2 | 86.8 | 91.4 | 79.3 | 86.3 | 100.0 | 86.4 | 91.8 |
| Mauritius — Maurice | 103.1 | 108.5 | 112.4 | 107.0 | 106.6 | 103.3 | 108.8 | 112.8 | 107.5 | 107.0 |
| Morocco — Maroc | 111.5 | 128.3 | 131.2 | 121.6 | 141.2 | 111.6 | 128.8 | 131.8 | 122.1 | 142.1 |
| Mozambique — Mozambique | 103.5 | 108.0 | 113.4 | 144.4 | 143.6 | 101.8 | 107.8 | 112.4 | 144.9 | 144.3 |
| Namibia — Namibie | 102.1 | 99.0 | 98.9 | 94.4 | 93.5 | 101.6 | 98.5 | 98.5 | 93.8 | 92.9 |
| Niger — Niger | 118.6 | 133.6 | 107.0 | 126.9 | 136.7 | 119.5 | 134.3 | 107.6 | 127.7 | 137.7 |
| Nigeria — Nigéria | 104.4 | 109.4 | 115.5 | 122.3 | 129.6 | 104.4 | 109.5 | 115.7 | 122.7 | 130.0 |
| Rwanda — Rwanda | 124.4 | 113.9 | 113.3 | 120.5 | 121.8 | 125.1 | 114.6 | 113.6 | 121.0 | 122.3 |
| Sao Tome and Principe — Sao Tomé-et-Principe | 104.5 | 108.7 | 109.9 | 110.3 | 110.3 | 104.6 | 108.8 | 110.0 | 110.3 | 110.3 |
| Senegal — Sénégal | 63.5 | 86.3 | 88.2 | 102.4 | 85.4 | 62.3 | 84.3 | 86.4 | 101.3 | 83.9 |
| Seychelles — Seychelles | 98.3 | 100.7 | 102.4 | 103.9 | 103.3 | 98.5 | 100.3 | 103.0 | 104.4 | 104.4 |
| Sierra Leone — Sierra Leone | 123.7 | 133.5 | 143.9 | 162.2 | 190.4 | 124.6 | 134.5 | 145.9 | 165.4 | 195.0 |
| South Africa — Afrique du Sud | 105.0 | 103.6 | 105.4 | 110.9 | 106.1 | 105.5 | 104.1 | 106.1 | 111.8 | 107.2 |
| Sudan — Soudan | 107.7 | 117.0 | 112.5 | 115.3 | 117.0 | 107.9 | 117.3 | 112.2 | 114.4 | 116.1 |
| Swaziland — Swaziland | 99.9 | 99.3 | 100.7 | 105.1 | 99.0 | 102.1 | 101.5 | 103.0 | 107.5 | 101.0 |
| Togo — Togo | 109.5 | 111.4 | 112.4 | 116.8 | 117.9 | 104.7 | 107.5 | 108.8 | 115.9 | 122.7 |
| Tunisia — Tunisie | 89.4 | 126.8 | 112.3 | 110.1 | 115.8 | 89.3 | 127.2 | 112.5 | 110.2 | 115.9 |
| Uganda — Ouganda | 109.1 | 107.3 | 107.6 | 106.6 | 105.2 | 108.3 | 107.8 | 107.4 | 106.2 | 105.5 |
| United Rep. of Tanzania — Rép.-Unie de Tanzanie | 104.4 | 98.5 | 106.0 | 113.8 | 109.9 | 104.7 | 98.4 | 103.5 | 110.0 | 107.4 |
| Zambia — Zambie | 96.6 | 106.4 | 110.5 | 108.7 | 110.0 | 97.4 | 107.8 | 111.5 | 105.5 | 107.0 |
| Zimbabwe — Zimbabwe | 80.7 | 78.0 | 72.8 | 73.7 | 73.3 | 81.2 | 87.9 | 84.9 | 89.3 | 89.1 |
| Nothern America — Amérique septentrionale | 96.9 | 100.5 | 107.4 | 107.0 | 105.6 | 97.1 | 100.7 | 106.9 | 106.5 | 105.4 |
| Canada — Canada | 87.5 | 100.3 | 108.9 | 113.1 | 109.7 | 87.5 | 100.5 | 109.1 | 113.4 | 109.9 |
| United States — Etats-Unis | 98.0 | 100.5 | 107.3 | 106.3 | 105.1 | 98.2 | 100.7 | 106.7 | 105.7 | 104.8 |

| Region, country or area — Région, pays ou zone | Agriculture — Agriculture | | | | | Food — Produits alimentaires | | | | |
|---|---|---|---|---|---|---|---|---|---|---|
| | 2002 | 2003 | 2004 | 2005 | 2006 | 2002 | 2003 | 2004 | 2005 | 2006 |
| **Latin Amer. and the Carib. — Amér. latine et Caraïb.** | **106.1** | **111.9** | **116.3** | **118.4** | **120.5** | **106.0** | **112.4** | **115.9** | **118.1** | **120.1** |
| Argentina — Argentine | 97.7 | 103.2 | 105.2 | 114.0 | 114.9 | 98.1 | 103.7 | 105.6 | 114.0 | 114.9 |
| Aruba — Aruba | 102.0 | 102.9 | 103.5 | 103.8 | ... | 102.0 | 102.9 | 103.4 | 103.8 | ... |
| Barbados — Barbade | 92.5 | 90.4 | 95.6 | 100.6 | 104.0 | 92.5 | 90.4 | 95.6 | 100.6 | 104.0 |
| Belize — Belize | 102.5 | 103.1 | 117.1 | 118.4 | 118.4 | 102.5 | 103.0 | 117.1 | 118.3 | 118.3 |
| Bolivia — Bolivie | 108.9 | 113.9 | 114.0 | 119.3 | 117.7 | 108.6 | 113.8 | 113.9 | 119.4 | 117.7 |
| Brazil — Brésil | 111.2 | 119.5 | 126.1 | 125.8 | 129.3 | 110.3 | 120.0 | 124.4 | 124.6 | 127.7 |
| Chile — Chili | 106.5 | 108.7 | 113.0 | 119.4 | 122.8 | 106.7 | 108.9 | 113.3 | 119.7 | 123.2 |
| Colombia — Colombie | 105.1 | 105.3 | 110.1 | 113.8 | 112.4 | 104.8 | 104.7 | 109.7 | 113.5 | 111.9 |
| Costa Rica — Costa Rica | 98.2 | 99.5 | 101.1 | 111.9 | 107.6 | 98.7 | 100.6 | 102.8 | 114.1 | 109.5 |
| Cuba — Cuba | 106.1 | 108.2 | 111.7 | 85.8 | 78.9 | 106.2 | 109.0 | 112.1 | 86.0 | 78.5 |
| Dominica — Dominique | 95.0 | 92.9 | 91.7 | 90.2 | 90.2 | 94.9 | 92.8 | 91.4 | 89.8 | 89.8 |
| Dominican Republic — Rép. dominicaine | 110.9 | 117.9 | 118.8 | 123.6 | 125.5 | 112.0 | 119.5 | 120.6 | 125.0 | 127.1 |
| Ecuador — Equateur | 100.8 | 106.7 | 111.4 | 111.4 | 110.5 | 102.4 | 108.4 | 113.2 | 112.7 | 111.7 |
| El Salvador — El Salvador | 97.7 | 94.5 | 98.7 | 101.7 | 110.3 | 102.0 | 99.6 | 103.8 | 106.8 | 117.1 |
| French Guyana — Guyane française | 97.5 | 98.8 | 103.1 | 94.7 | 94.7 | 97.5 | 98.8 | 103.1 | 94.7 | 94.7 |
| Grenada — Grenade | 99.9 | 102.3 | 100.0 | 99.4 | 99.0 | 99.9 | 102.3 | 100.0 | 99.4 | 99.0 |
| Guatemala — Guatemala | 102.8 | 103.4 | 105.7 | 109.8 | 111.2 | 106.3 | 105.9 | 110.0 | 112.9 | 114.5 |
| Guyana — Guyana | 95.2 | 104.1 | 87.1 | 82.7 | 82.7 | 95.2 | 104.1 | 87.1 | 82.7 | 82.7 |
| Haiti — Haïti | 101.4 | 102.6 | 101.5 | 101.0 | 100.8 | 102.0 | 103.5 | 102.4 | 102.0 | 101.8 |
| Honduras — Honduras | 129.9 | 144.5 | 151.2 | 159.4 | 158.6 | 136.1 | 153.1 | 160.1 | 169.2 | 168.3 |
| Jamaica — Jamaïque | 98.9 | 97.9 | 104.3 | 105.9 | 105.9 | 98.8 | 97.8 | 104.3 | 105.9 | 105.9 |
| Mexico — Mexique | 103.5 | 108.0 | 111.1 | 110.3 | 114.7 | 104.3 | 108.6 | 111.4 | 110.7 | 115.2 |
| Nicaragua — Nicaragua | 107.0 | 121.3 | 116.2 | 129.2 | 128.8 | 110.1 | 123.0 | 120.4 | 130.0 | 134.5 |
| Panama — Panama | 102.7 | 101.1 | 99.2 | 99.5 | 100.7 | 102.8 | 101.2 | 99.0 | 99.2 | 100.4 |
| Paraguay — Paraguay | 101.9 | 114.8 | 121.8 | 116.8 | 117.2 | 104.8 | 117.2 | 120.8 | 118.2 | 118.7 |
| Peru — Pérou | 108.8 | 115.6 | 115.5 | 125.8 | 125.2 | 109.3 | 116.2 | 115.3 | 126.7 | 126.1 |
| Puerto Rico — Porto Rico | 98.8 | 95.9 | 101.1 | 91.6 | 91.3 | 98.8 | 95.4 | 100.4 | 91.4 | 91.1 |
| St. Vincent-Grenadines — St. Vincent-Grenadines | 107.1 | 107.8 | 105.4 | 109.1 | 108.6 | 107.3 | 107.9 | 105.5 | 109.3 | 108.8 |
| Suriname — Suriname | 88.5 | 96.7 | 90.1 | 86.4 | 94.6 | 88.5 | 96.7 | 90.1 | 86.4 | 94.6 |
| Trinidad and Tobago — Trinité-et-Tobago | 128.2 | 114.4 | 109.1 | 105.7 | 105.7 | 128.4 | 114.3 | 109.2 | 105.6 | 105.6 |
| Uruguay — Uruguay | 93.3 | 97.5 | 114.7 | 116.7 | 118.6 | 94.5 | 99.3 | 117.1 | 119.2 | 121.2 |
| Venezuela (Boli. Rep. of) — Venezuela (Rép. boliv. du) | 102.0 | 96.8 | 96.5 | 105.0 | 104.1 | 102.2 | 97.2 | 96.7 | 105.4 | 104.5 |
| **Asia — Asie** | **104.8** | **108.8** | **113.6** | **117.9** | **120.9** | **105.0** | **108.8** | **113.1** | **117.7** | **120.5** |
| Armenia — Arménie | 105.2 | 112.2 | 129.7 | 147.2 | 144.9 | 105.4 | 113.0 | 130.8 | 148.8 | 146.4 |
| Azerbaijan — Azerbaïdjan | 115.8 | 121.8 | 124.0 | 139.0 | 138.6 | 119.1 | 124.0 | 124.3 | 137.4 | 140.5 |
| Bangladesh — Bangladesh | 103.0 | 105.0 | 102.8 | 111.8 | 118.0 | 103.0 | 105.1 | 102.8 | 112.1 | 118.5 |
| Brunei Darussalam — Brunéi Darussalam | 106.6 | 112.8 | 115.9 | 119.0 | 119.0 | 106.6 | 112.8 | 115.9 | 119.0 | 119.0 |
| Cambodia — Cambodge | 97.5 | 114.8 | 106.2 | 138.4 | 143.6 | 97.9 | 115.4 | 107.5 | 139.2 | 144.4 |
| China[1] — Chine[1] | 108.4 | 111.1 | 118.3 | 122.6 | 127.4 | 108.5 | 111.0 | 117.6 | 122.6 | 127.0 |
| Cyprus — Chypre | 101.1 | 98.9 | 102.2 | 91.6 | 87.6 | 101.1 | 98.9 | 102.2 | 91.6 | 87.5 |
| Georgia — Géorgie | 94.4 | 107.1 | 97.2 | 110.9 | 97.0 | 95.6 | 109.0 | 99.1 | 113.4 | 97.9 |
| India — Inde | 95.7 | 103.6 | 105.2 | 109.7 | 110.3 | 95.9 | 103.2 | 104.3 | 108.3 | 108.7 |
| Indonesia — Indonésie | 109.1 | 115.5 | 121.3 | 122.6 | 125.9 | 107.9 | 114.7 | 121.6 | 122.9 | 126.0 |
| Iran (Islamic Rep. of) — Iran (Rép. islamique d') | 112.9 | 118.3 | 118.3 | 125.2 | 126.4 | 113.5 | 119.1 | 119.0 | 126.2 | 127.5 |
| Israel — Israël | 111.5 | 107.5 | 115.1 | 115.5 | 115.3 | 111.8 | 107.9 | 115.1 | 116.0 | 115.5 |
| Japan — Japon | 99.0 | 95.1 | 96.5 | 103.7 | 101.0 | 99.0 | 95.2 | 96.5 | 103.9 | 101.1 |
| Jordan — Jordanie | 125.9 | 119.3 | 132.4 | 138.3 | 135.9 | 125.4 | 119.2 | 132.7 | 138.7 | 136.1 |
| Kazakhstan — Kazakhstan | 112.1 | 113.2 | 110.9 | 118.0 | 127.1 | 112.4 | 112.3 | 109.6 | 117.0 | 126.4 |
| Korea, Dem. P. R. — Corée, R. p. dém. de | 109.5 | 111.9 | 113.3 | 117.6 | 115.4 | 109.8 | 112.3 | 113.8 | 118.2 | 116.0 |
| Korea, Republic of — Corée, République de | 96.4 | 93.3 | 95.9 | 96.7 | 94.4 | 96.6 | 93.8 | 96.4 | 97.3 | 94.9 |
| Kuwait — Koweït | 103.5 | 102.5 | 106.0 | 108.9 | 108.9 | 103.5 | 102.6 | 106.0 | 108.9 | 108.9 |
| Kyrgyzstan — Kirghizistan | 98.5 | 101.5 | 104.5 | 99.8 | 103.2 | 100.9 | 103.9 | 106.0 | 101.1 | 104.6 |
| Lebanon — Liban | 103.6 | 100.5 | 102.9 | 103.6 | 103.6 | 104.2 | 100.8 | 103.1 | 104.2 | 104.2 |
| Malaysia — Malaisie | 104.8 | 113.1 | 119.4 | 125.1 | 130.3 | 104.8 | 112.9 | 118.1 | 124.7 | 128.9 |
| Maldives — Maldives | 111.8 | 128.3 | 105.6 | 95.8 | 94.0 | 111.8 | 128.3 | 105.6 | 95.8 | 94.0 |
| Mongolia — Mongolie | 76.2 | 65.8 | 77.2 | 73.4 | 79.4 | 75.9 | 65.4 | 77.4 | 73.5 | 79.8 |

| Region, country or area — Région, pays ou zone | Agriculture — Agriculture | | | | | Food — Produits alimentaires | | | | |
|---|---|---|---|---|---|---|---|---|---|---|
| | 2002 | 2003 | 2004 | 2005 | 2006 | 2002 | 2003 | 2004 | 2005 | 2006 |
| Myanmar — Myanmar | 111.8 | 120.5 | 128.7 | 133.8 | 133.7 | 112.0 | 121.3 | 129.7 | 134.9 | 134.8 |
| Nepal — Népal | 106.3 | 110.8 | 114.9 | 117.4 | 119.6 | 106.3 | 110.8 | 114.8 | 117.3 | 119.4 |
| Pakistan — Pakistan | 100.4 | 104.1 | 111.9 | 114.5 | 117.1 | 101.1 | 105.6 | 109.9 | 114.0 | 117.1 |
| Philippines — Philippines | 109.1 | 110.2 | 117.7 | 119.1 | 122.5 | 109.2 | 110.3 | 117.0 | 118.4 | 121.8 |
| Saudi Arabia — Arabie saoudite | 107.2 | 109.6 | 116.2 | 117.4 | 116.4 | 107.2 | 109.7 | 116.3 | 117.5 | 116.4 |
| Sri Lanka — Sri Lanka | 100.6 | 102.9 | 93.5 | 102.7 | 102.1 | 99.9 | 103.2 | 91.0 | 101.6 | 101.2 |
| Syrian Arab Republic — Rép. arabe syrienne | 115.3 | 113.3 | 117.3 | 116.4 | 117.3 | 121.2 | 117.2 | 119.8 | 118.4 | 119.5 |
| Thailand — Thaïlande | 103.9 | 109.2 | 109.1 | 108.4 | 112.1 | 103.5 | 108.7 | 108.0 | 107.2 | 110.8 |
| Turkey — Turquie | 102.2 | 103.5 | 104.9 | 110.3 | 110.7 | 102.0 | 104.3 | 105.1 | 111.3 | 111.6 |
| Turkmenistan — Turkménistan | 116.0 | 124.5 | 135.8 | 133.1 | 130.0 | 127.9 | 139.1 | 142.8 | 139.1 | 147.3 |
| Uzbekistan — Ouzbékistan | 106.7 | 111.1 | 121.3 | 130.1 | 138.1 | 109.3 | 117.8 | 124.6 | 133.2 | 146.8 |
| Viet Nam — Viet Nam | 112.6 | 116.9 | 123.0 | 127.4 | 128.9 | 113.0 | 117.1 | 123.1 | 127.9 | 128.3 |
| Yemen — Yémen | 106.1 | 114.2 | 115.2 | 118.0 | 127.8 | 106.1 | 114.6 | 115.2 | 117.9 | 127.1 |
| **Europe — Europe** | **101.2** | **97.6** | **105.1** | **101.5** | **100.2** | **101.3** | **97.7** | **105.2** | **101.6** | **100.3** |
| Albania — Albanie | 103.8 | 102.6 | 106.3 | 106.9 | 110.9 | 104.6 | 103.7 | 107.3 | 108.0 | 111.0 |
| Austria — Autriche | 99.7 | 93.2 | 98.6 | 95.7 | 95.1 | 99.7 | 93.2 | 98.6 | 95.7 | 95.1 |
| Belarus — Bélarus | 103.3 | 105.4 | 120.6 | 119.5 | 125.8 | 103.4 | 105.3 | 120.4 | 119.3 | 125.9 |
| Belgium — Belgique | 101.6 | 99.2 | 104.0 | 98.8 | 94.4 | 101.5 | 99.1 | 103.9 | 98.8 | 94.4 |
| Bosnia and Herzegovina — Bosnie-Herzégovine | 103.9 | 95.2 | 121.6 | 121.1 | 123.9 | 103.6 | 95.3 | 121.6 | 121.0 | 123.9 |
| Bulgaria — Bulgarie | 102.1 | 80.4 | 99.3 | 83.3 | 84.8 | 100.9 | 78.5 | 97.5 | 81.8 | 84.4 |
| Croatia — Croatie | 112.4 | 88.8 | 100.1 | 91.3 | 95.2 | 112.5 | 88.7 | 100.0 | 91.2 | 95.2 |
| Czech Republic — République tchèque | 95.0 | 84.7 | 101.8 | 94.6 | 89.0 | 95.0 | 84.7 | 101.8 | 94.7 | 89.1 |
| Denmark — Danemark | 99.8 | 101.0 | 102.4 | 101.2 | 98.0 | 99.8 | 101.0 | 102.4 | 101.2 | 98.0 |
| Estonia — Estonie | 95.2 | 94.0 | 97.0 | 104.7 | 98.4 | 95.2 | 94.0 | 97.0 | 104.7 | 98.4 |
| Finland — Finlande | 105.0 | 102.8 | 102.4 | 106.3 | 103.8 | 105.0 | 102.8 | 102.4 | 106.3 | 103.8 |
| France — France | 101.7 | 93.2 | 101.4 | 95.6 | 92.0 | 101.7 | 93.2 | 101.3 | 95.6 | 91.9 |
| Germany — Allemagne | 96.7 | 92.0 | 101.7 | 98.2 | 96.0 | 96.7 | 92.0 | 101.7 | 98.2 | 96.0 |
| Greece — Grèce | 93.3 | 85.5 | 92.8 | 95.7 | 92.0 | 93.8 | 85.8 | 92.8 | 96.1 | 91.9 |
| Hungary — Hongrie | 96.6 | 87.4 | 114.2 | 103.9 | 98.8 | 96.6 | 87.4 | 114.3 | 103.9 | 98.8 |
| Iceland — Islande | 103.5 | 104.4 | 105.3 | 104.7 | 104.7 | 104.6 | 105.6 | 106.1 | 105.7 | 105.7 |
| Ireland — Irlande | 96.2 | 97.2 | 100.8 | 97.3 | 98.9 | 96.2 | 97.2 | 100.8 | 97.3 | 98.9 |
| Italy — Italie | 95.1 | 91.6 | 101.6 | 99.3 | 96.1 | 95.1 | 91.6 | 101.7 | 99.4 | 96.2 |
| Latvia — Lettonie | 108.0 | 106.8 | 107.8 | 119.9 | 114.3 | 108.0 | 106.8 | 107.8 | 119.9 | 114.3 |
| Lithuania — Lituanie | 101.6 | 104.5 | 103.7 | 105.5 | 89.2 | 101.5 | 104.4 | 103.7 | 105.6 | 89.3 |
| Luxembourg — Luxembourg | 109.6 | 104.3 | 97.6 | 95.7 | 94.9 | 109.6 | 104.3 | 97.6 | 95.7 | 94.9 |
| Malta — Malte | 95.4 | 95.2 | 95.0 | 92.8 | 93.5 | 95.4 | 95.2 | 94.9 | 92.8 | 93.5 |
| Moldova — Moldova | 109.5 | 103.2 | 113.8 | 109.5 | 103.0 | 111.2 | 105.5 | 116.3 | 112.0 | 105.6 |
| Netherlands — Pays-Bas | 94.3 | 89.1 | 94.8 | 92.0 | 90.1 | 94.3 | 89.1 | 94.8 | 92.0 | 90.1 |
| Norway — Norvège | 97.4 | 96.9 | 101.1 | 98.7 | 99.2 | 97.3 | 96.9 | 101.1 | 98.7 | 99.3 |
| Poland — Pologne | 97.0 | 95.6 | 102.5 | 96.5 | 93.4 | 97.1 | 95.7 | 102.6 | 96.5 | 93.3 |
| Portugal — Portugal | 100.6 | 92.1 | 97.5 | 93.6 | 92.7 | 100.6 | 92.1 | 97.6 | 93.6 | 92.7 |
| Romania — Roumanie | 98.9 | 106.6 | 127.9 | 113.4 | 111.2 | 110.1 | 106.7 | 128.2 | 113.7 | 111.6 |
| Russian Federation — Fédération de Russie | 110.1 | 106.8 | 111.5 | 112.5 | 115.1 | 110.1 | 106.8 | 111.5 | 112.5 | 115.1 |
| Slovakia — Slovaquie | 100.5 | 91.1 | 96.0 | 92.5 | 85.1 | 100.5 | 91.1 | 96.0 | 92.6 | 85.2 |
| Slovenia — Slovénie | 104.8 | 95.1 | 105.4 | 103.3 | 99.9 | 104.8 | 95.1 | 105.4 | 103.2 | 99.9 |
| Spain — Espagne | 104.0 | 112.8 | 107.7 | 97.6 | 101.9 | 104.1 | 113.1 | 107.9 | 97.7 | 102.4 |
| Sweden — Suède | 99.6 | 98.0 | 101.3 | 97.7 | 92.9 | 99.6 | 98.0 | 101.3 | 97.7 | 92.9 |
| Switzerland — Suisse | 101.2 | 97.1 | 101.5 | 99.4 | 99.1 | 101.2 | 97.1 | 101.5 | 99.4 | 99.1 |
| TFYR of Macedonia — L'ex-R.y. Macédoine | 86.7 | 93.7 | 105.0 | 105.6 | 104.7 | 86.4 | 94.3 | 106.3 | 105.2 | 104.3 |
| Ukraine — Ukraine | 111.4 | 100.1 | 119.6 | 119.8 | 117.1 | 111.4 | 100.2 | 119.6 | 119.8 | 117.1 |
| United Kingdom — Royaume-Uni | 100.6 | 98.2 | 98.7 | 99.2 | 98.1 | 100.6 | 98.2 | 98.8 | 99.2 | 98.1 |
| **Oceania — Océanie** | **89.8** | **100.9** | **98.2** | **103.5** | **89.8** | **89.8** | **104.0** | **101.6** | **105.8** | **90.9** |
| American Samoa — Samoa américaines | 100.0 | 100.0 | 99.2 | 98.8 | 98.8 | 100.0 | 100.0 | 99.2 | 98.8 | 98.8 |
| Australia — Australie | 84.3 | 97.4 | 92.1 | 100.4 | 81.9 | 83.5 | 101.2 | 95.9 | 102.8 | 82.4 |
| Fiji — Fidji | 99.1 | 92.9 | 96.6 | 96.9 | 97.5 | 99.2 | 92.8 | 96.8 | 96.8 | 97.4 |
| Kiribati — Kiribati | 100.6 | 101.0 | 107.9 | 111.5 | 111.5 | 100.6 | 101.0 | 107.9 | 111.5 | 111.5 |

| Region, country or area — Région, pays ou zone | Agriculture — Agriculture | | | | | Food — Produits alimentaires | | | | |
|---|---|---|---|---|---|---|---|---|---|---|
| | 2002 | 2003 | 2004 | 2005 | 2006 | 2002 | 2003 | 2004 | 2005 | 2006 |
| Nauru — Nauru | 101.4 | 96.6 | 101.9 | 101.6 | 96.9 | 101.4 | 96.6 | 101.9 | 101.6 | 96.9 |
| New Zealand — Nouvelle-Zélande | 106.2 | 111.4 | 116.2 | 112.7 | 112.8 | 107.1 | 112.6 | 118.0 | 114.6 | 114.6 |
| Samoa — Samoa | 103.5 | 103.3 | 106.3 | 108.1 | 108.1 | 103.6 | 103.3 | 106.4 | 108.2 | 108.2 |
| Solomon Islands — Iles Salomon | 99.1 | 101.7 | 110.7 | 115.6 | 115.6 | 99.1 | 101.7 | 110.7 | 115.6 | 115.6 |
| Vanuatu — Vanuatu | 90.0 | 94.2 | 108.0 | 108.9 | 108.8 | 90.0 | 94.2 | 108.0 | 108.9 | 108.8 |

Source

Food and Agriculture Organization of the United Nations (FAO), Rome, FAOSTAT data, last accessed January 2008.

Notes

1 For statistical purposes, the data for China do not include those for the Hong Kong Special Administrative Region (Hong Kong SAR) and Macao Special Administrative Region (Macao SAR).

Source

Organisation des Nations Unies pour l'alimentation et l'agriculture (FAO), Rome, données FAOSTAT, dernier accès janvier 2008.

Notes

1 Pour la présentation des statistiques, les données pour la Chine ne comprennent pas la Région Administrative Spéciale de Hong Kong (Hong Kong RAS) et la Région Administrative Spéciale de Macao (Macao RAS).

# 35

## Cereals
Production: thousand metric tons

## Céréales
Production : milliers de tonnes

| Region, country or area<br>Région, pays ou zone | 1997 | 1998 | 1999 | 2000 | 2001 | 2002 | 2003 | 2004 | 2005 | 2006 |
|---|---|---|---|---|---|---|---|---|---|---|
| **World**<br>**Monde** | 2 095 763 | 2 083 691 | 2 085 927 | 2 061 054 | 2 108 528 | 2 029 285 | 2 085 084 | 2 279 812 | 2 268 250 | 2 221 119 |
| **Africa**<br>**Afrique** | 110 550 | 115 150 | 114 187 | 112 608 | 116 685 | 118 220 | 132 572 | 131 070 | 141 212 | 145 892 |
| Algeria<br>Algérie | 870 | 3 026 | 2 021 | 935 | 2 659 | 1 953 | 4 266 | 4 033 | 3 527 | 4 016 |
| Angola<br>Angola | 448 | 610 | 541 | 510 | 586 | 717 | 717 | 668 | 871 | 717 |
| Benin<br>Bénin | 877 | 867 | 974 | 993 | 943 | 926 | 1 043 | 1 109 | 1 152 | 934 |
| Botswana<br>Botswana | 45 | 16 | 21 | 25 | 24 | 35 | 37 | 29 | 26 | 26 |
| Burkina Faso<br>Burkina Faso | 2 014 | 2 657 | 2 700 | 2 286 | 3 109 | 3 119 | 3 564 | 2 902 | 3 650 | 3 858 |
| Burundi<br>Burundi | 305 | 261 | 265 | 245 | 273 | 282 | 279 | 280 | 274 | 278 |
| Cameroon<br>Cameroun | 1 267 | 1 412 | 1 185 | 1 275 | 1 356 | 1 499 | 1 584 | 1 684 | 1 652 | 1 507 |
| Cape Verde<br>Cap-Vert | 5 | 5 | 36 | 24 | 20 | 5 | 12 | 10 | 4 | 12 |
| Central African Rep.<br>Rép. centrafricaine | 138 | 148 | 161 | 166 | 183 | 193 | 201 | 195 | 179 | 174 |
| Chad<br>Tchad | 986 | 1 312 | 1 231 | 930 | 1 321 | 1 212 | 1 618 | 1 213 | 1 853 | 1 913 |
| Comoros<br>Comores | 21 | 21 | 21 | 21 | 21 | 21 | 21 | 21 | 21 | 21 |
| Congo<br>Congo | 10 | 11 | 7 | 8 | 16 | 8 | 10 | 10 | 9 | 9 |
| Côte d'Ivoire<br>Côte d'Ivoire | 1 405 | 1 377 | 1 278 | 1 314 | 1 332 | 1 346 | 1 363 | 1 425 | 1 483 | 1 399 |
| Dem. Rep. of the Congo<br>Rép. dém. du Congo | 1 532 | 1 621 | 1 593 | 1 572 | 1 546 | 1 520 | 1 521 | 1 522 | 1 526 | 1 525 |
| Egypt<br>Egypte | 18 071 | 17 964 | 19 401 | 20 106 | 18 561 | 20 194 | 20 682 | 20 825 | 22 405 | 22 736 |
| Eritrea<br>Erythrée | 95 | 458 | 319 | 121 | 183 | 52 | 99 | 80 | 152 | 152 |
| Ethiopia<br>Ethiopie | 9 488 | 7 213 | 8 394 | 8 020 | 9 586 | 9 004 | 9 536 | 10 700 | 13 369 | 13 394 |
| Gabon<br>Gabon | 25 | 27 | 28 | 27 | 26 | 25 | 32 | 32 | 31 | 31 |
| Gambia<br>Gambie | 101 | 107 | 151 | 176 | 200 | 139 | 205 | 224 | 206 | 256 |
| Ghana<br>Ghana | 1 669 | 1 788 | 1 686 | 1 711 | 1 627 | 2 155 | 2 041 | 1 830 | 1 948 | 1 919 |
| Guinea<br>Guinée | 1 494 | 1 572 | 1 656 | 1 801 | 1 721 | 1 846 | 1 984 | 2 136 | 2 039 | 2 445 |
| Guinea-Bissau<br>Guinée-Bissau | 140 | 139 | 145 | 178 | 162 | 151 | 121 | 171 | 213 | 225 |
| Kenya<br>Kenya | 2 700 | 2 927 | 2 802 | 2 591 | 3 369 | 3 046 | 3 351 | 3 199 | 3 585 | 3 955 |
| Lesotho<br>Lesotho | 210 | 176 | 174 | 179 | 400 | 299 | 110 | 103 | 94 | 120 |
| Liberia<br>Libéria | 169 | 210 | 197 | 184 | 145 | 110 | 100 | 110 | 96 | 66 |

| Region, country or area<br>Région, pays ou zone | 1997 | 1998 | 1999 | 2000 | 2001 | 2002 | 2003 | 2004 | 2005 | 2006 |
|---|---|---|---|---|---|---|---|---|---|---|
| Libyan Arab Jamah.<br>Jamah. arabe libyenne | 206 | 213 | 213 | 222 | 218 | 217 | 217 | 218 | 234 | 209 |
| Madagascar<br>Madagascar | 2 742 | 2 610 | 2 756 | 2 660 | 2 853 | 2 787 | 3 129 | 3 391 | 3 705 | 3 790 |
| Malawi<br>Malawi | 1 349 | 1 904 | 2 636 | 2 631 | 1 742 | 1 711 | 2 142 | 1 843 | 1 363 | 1 710 |
| Mali<br>Mali | 2 138 | 2 548 | 2 894 | 2 310 | 2 584 | 2 532 | 3 402 | 2 845 | 3 399 | 3 428 |
| Mauritania<br>Mauritanie | 154 | 189 | 194 | 180 | 124 | 113 | 155 | 120 | 177 | 175 |
| Mauritius<br>Maurice | ^0 | ^0 | ^0 | 1 | ^0 | ^0 | ^0 | ^0 | ^0 | ^0 |
| Morocco<br>Maroc | 4 098 | 6 632 | 3 846 | 2 002 | 4 607 | 5 293 | 7 973 | 8 604 | 4 284 | 9 091 |
| Mozambique<br>Mozambique | 1 531 | 1 688 | 1 912 | 1 587 | 1 585 | 1 662 | 1 813 | 2 006 | 1 921 | 1 831 |
| Namibia<br>Namibie | 185 | 70 | 74 | 121 | 107 | 100 | 97 | 117 | 105 | 129 |
| Niger<br>Niger | 1 719 | 2 973 | 2 853 | 2 127 | 3 162 | 3 235 | 3 580 | 2 732 | 3 669 | 4 077 |
| Nigeria<br>Nigéria | 21 853 | 22 040 | 22 405 | 21 370 | 20 090 | 21 373 | 22 736 | 24 321 | 26 031 | 28 070 |
| Réunion<br>Réunion | 12 | 12 | 12 | 12 | 12 | 12 | 12 | 12 | 12 | 12 |
| Rwanda<br>Rwanda | 223 | 194 | 179 | 240 | 285 | 308 | 298 | 319 | 413 | 366 |
| Sao Tome and Principe<br>Sao Tomé-et-Principe | 4 | 1 | 1 | 2 | 3 | 3 | 3 | 3 | 3 | 3 |
| Senegal<br>Sénégal | 781 | 717 | 1 131 | 1 026 | 1 023 | 785 | 1 452 | 1 054 | 1 433 | 988 |
| Sierra Leone<br>Sierra Leone | 467 | 373 | 280 | 222 | 391 | 466 | 496 | 608 | 815 | 1 154 |
| Somalia<br>Somalie | 305 | 201 | 298 | 392 | 429 | 442 | 403 | 366 | 407 | 402 |
| South Africa<br>Afrique du Sud | 13 246 | 10 221 | 10 065 | 14 528 | 10 706 | 13 046 | 11 821 | 12 028 | 14 176 | 9 453 |
| Sudan<br>Soudan | 4 209 | 5 583 | 3 066 | 3 259 | 5 339 | 3 714 | 6 373 | 3 502 | 5 515 | 6 717 |
| Swaziland<br>Swaziland | 139 | 119 | 125 | 114 | 84 | 69 | 70 | 69 | 75 | 27 |
| Togo<br>Togo | 748 | 624 | 759 | 741 | 715 | 801 | 815 | 799 | 833 | 889 |
| Tunisia<br>Tunisie | 1 081 | 1 697 | 1 837 | 1 118 | 1 391 | 550 | 2 318 | 2 161 | 2 133 | 1 646 |
| Uganda<br>Ouganda | 1 625 | 2 085 | 2 178 | 2 112 | 2 309 | 2 368 | 2 508 | 2 274 | 2 459 | 2 557 |
| United Rep. of Tanzania<br>Rép.-Unie de Tanzanie | 3 727 | 3 854 | 4 485 | 4 646 | 4 912 | 5 271 | 3 757 | 4 947 | 5 424 | 5 221 |
| Zambia<br>Zambie | 1 137 | 798 | 1 003 | 1 050 | 750 | 745 | 1 244 | 1 377 | 1 067 | 1 072 |
| Zimbabwe<br>Zimbabwe | 2 785 | 1 879 | 1 997 | 2 538 | 1 897 | 756 | 1 259 | 837 | 1 192 | 1 182 |
| **Northern America**<br>**Amérique septentrionale** | **386 094** | **400 437** | **389 630** | **393 846** | **368 473** | **333 424** | **398 479** | **441 785** | **422 565** | **397 456** |
| Canada<br>Canada | 49 557 | 50 993 | 54 078 | 51 038 | 43 391 | 36 303 | 50 174 | 52 684 | 53 086 | 50 895 |
| United States<br>Etats-Unis | 336 536 | 349 445 | 335 553 | 342 809 | 325 082 | 297 121 | 348 304 | 389 101 | 369 479 | 346 562 |

**Cereals** — Production: thousand metric tons (*continued*)
**Céréales** — Production : milliers de tonnes (*suite*)

| Region, country or area / Région, pays ou zone | 1997 | 1998 | 1999 | 2000 | 2001 | 2002 | 2003 | 2004 | 2005 | 2006 |
|---|---|---|---|---|---|---|---|---|---|---|
| **Latin Amer. and the Carib.** **Amér. latine et Caraïb.** | 132 785 | 130 407 | 133 805 | 137 988 | 150 718 | 138 054 | 162 346 | 163 018 | 152 297 | 154 677 |
| Argentina Argentine | 35 907 | 37 808 | 35 036 | 38 751 | 35 936 | 31 770 | 33 982 | 35 750 | 38 239 | 33 556 |
| Aruba Aruba | 1 | 1 | 1 | 1 | 1 | 1 | 1 | 1 | 1 | ... |
| Barbados Barbade | 1 | 1 | ^0 | ^0 | ^0 | ^0 | ^0 | ^0 | ^0 | ^0 |
| Belize Belize | 60 | 52 | 62 | 48 | 57 | 57 | 56 | 49 | 55 | 54 |
| Bolivia Bolivia | 920 | 1 146 | 1 128 | 1 256 | 1 280 | 1 257 | 1 460 | 1 296 | 1 622 | 1 839 |
| Brazil Brésil | 44 876 | 40 743 | 47 431 | 45 897 | 57 117 | 50 879 | 67 453 | 63 951 | 55 669 | 59 017 |
| Chile Chili | 3 077 | 3 098 | 2 168 | 2 590 | 3 116 | 3 380 | 3 693 | 3 999 | 3 989 | 3 566 |
| Colombia Colombie | 3 210 | 2 896 | 3 411 | 3 765 | 3 827 | 3 794 | 4 729 | 5 085 | 4 688 | 3 789 |
| Costa Rica Costa Rica | 282 | 263 | 292 | 285 | 229 | 201 | 198 | 210 | 196 | 173 |
| Cuba Cuba | 818 | 619 | 797 | 826 | 900 | 1 001 | 1 076 | 889 | 732 | 744 |
| Dominican Republic Rép. dominicaine | 564 | 530 | 605 | 610 | 771 | 766 | 656 | 620 | 634 | 734 |
| Ecuador Equateur | 1 815 | 1 485 | 1 847 | 1 909 | 1 644 | 1 940 | 2 113 | 2 704 | 2 410 | 2 233 |
| El Salvador El Salvador | 773 | 783 | 857 | 779 | 760 | 814 | 791 | 822 | 895 | 937 |
| French Guyana Guyane française | 31 | 25 | 20 | 20 | 32 | 22 | 23 | 26 | 18 | 18 |
| Guatemala Guatemala | 954 | 1 164 | 1 134 | 1 161 | 1 199 | 1 155 | 1 147 | 1 172 | 1 168 | 1 275 |
| Guyana Guyana | 576 | 526 | 566 | 453 | 498 | 446 | 506 | 329 | 277 | 276 |
| Haiti Haïti | 490 | 403 | 475 | 431 | 363 | 379 | 393 | 399 | 392 | 383 |
| Honduras Honduras | 757 | 590 | 562 | 607 | 603 | 579 | 594 | 502 | 531 | 529 |
| Jamaica Jamaïque | 3 | 2 | 2 | 2 | 2 | 2 | 1 | 1 | 1 | 2 |
| Mexico Mexique | 28 062 | 29 123 | 27 419 | 27 991 | 31 057 | 28 770 | 31 387 | 32 312 | 27 733 | 31 959 |
| Nicaragua Nicaragua | 608 | 618 | 559 | 765 | 755 | 911 | 972 | 773 | 964 | 888 |
| Panama Panama | 269 | 233 | 265 | 303 | 342 | 371 | 409 | 341 | 334 | 360 |
| Paraguay Paraguay | 1 450 | 1 156 | 1 156 | 1 003 | 1 455 | 1 371 | 1 643 | 1 979 | 1 579 | 1 871 |
| Peru Pérou | 2 584 | 2 840 | 3 397 | 3 556 | 3 741 | 3 845 | 3 920 | 3 438 | 4 132 | 3 873 |
| Puerto Rico Porto Ricco | 1 | 1 | 1 | ^0 | ^0 | ^0 | ^0 | 1 | 1 | 1 |
| St. Vincent-Grenadines St. Vincent-Grenadines | 1 | 2 | 1 | 1 | 1 | 1 | 1 | 1 | ^0 | ^0 |
| Suriname Suriname | 213 | 189 | 180 | 164 | 191 | 157 | 194 | 173 | 167 | 195 |
| Trinidad and Tobago Trinité-et-Tobago | 12 | 12 | 4 | 7 | 5 | 7 | 5 | 5 | 5 | 5 |

| Region, country or area<br>Région, pays ou zone | 1997 | 1998 | 1999 | 2000 | 2001 | 2002 | 2003 | 2004 | 2005 | 2006 |
|---|---|---|---|---|---|---|---|---|---|---|
| Uruguay<br>Uruguay | 2 057 | 1 961 | 2 194 | 1 860 | 1 718 | 1 606 | 1 827 | 2 523 | 2 187 | 2 319 |
| Venezuela (Bolivarian Rep. of)<br>Venezuela (Rép. Bolivar. du) | 2 413 | 2 134 | 2 234 | 2 948 | 3 117 | 2 569 | 3 116 | 3 664 | 3 676 | 4 078 |
| **Asia**<br>**Asie** | **992 883** | **1 016 772** | **1 036 047** | **996 292** | **1 001 400** | **983 002** | **993 548** | **1 038 427** | **1 083 544** | **1 102 274** |
| Afghanistan<br>Afghanistan | 3 683 | 3 876 | 3 257 | 1 940 | 2 108 | 3 737 | 4 207 | 3 232 | 5 407 | 4 220 |
| Armenia<br>Arménie | 254 | 323 | 297 | 221 | 364 | 412 | 310 | 452 | 392 | 212 |
| Azerbaijan<br>Azerbaïdjan | 1 119 | 918 | 1 069 | 1 496 | 1 956 | 2 133 | 1 993 | 2 087 | 2 056 | 2 012 |
| Bangladesh<br>Bangladesh | 29 674 | 31 577 | 36 403 | 39 503 | 38 029 | 39 341 | 40 018 | 37 759 | 41 156 | 45 010 |
| Bhutan<br>Bhoutan | 173 | 173 | 157 | 107 | 115 | 93 | 108 | 158 | 138 | 139 |
| Brunei Darussalam<br>Brunéi Darussalam | ^0 | ^0 | ^0 | ^0 | ^0 | ·^0 | 1 | 1 | 1 | 1 |
| Cambodia<br>Cambodge | 3 457 | 3 558 | 4 136 | 4 183 | 4 285 | 3 971 | 5 026 | 4 427 | 6 234 | 6 641 |
| China[1]<br>Chine[1] | 445 953 | 458 418 | 455 218 | 407 361 | 398 421 | 400 026 | 376 150 | 413 193 | 429 341 | 445 355 |
| Cyprus<br>Chypre | 48 | 66 | 127 | 48 | 127 | 142 | 165 | 111 | 70 | 66 |
| Georgia<br>Géorgie | 892 | 589 | 771 | 418 | 704 | 662 | 742 | 663 | 680 | 428 |
| India<br>Inde | 223 232 | 226 877 | 236 206 | 234 866 | 242 964 | 206 635 | 232 760 | 230 658 | 239 380 | 239 130 |
| Indonesia<br>Indonésie | 58 148 | 59 406 | 60 070 | 61 575 | 59 808 | 61 144 | 63 024 | 65 314 | 66 508 | 66 011 |
| Iran (Islamic Rep. of)<br>Iran (Rép. islamique d') | 15 823 | 18 979 | 14 186 | 12 874 | 14 945 | 19 861 | 20 942 | 21 987 | 21 907 | 22 810 |
| Iraq<br>Iraq | 2 216 | 2 432 | 1 605 | 904 | 1 819 | 4 125 | 3 516 | 3 308 | 3 701 | 3 468 |
| Israel<br>Israël | 187 | 249 | 123 | 183 | 242 | 271 | 306 | 273 | 307 | 237 |
| Japan<br>Japon | 13 320 | 11 934 | 12 283 | 12 796 | 12 255 | 12 184 | 10 824 | 11 994 | 12 433 | 11 741 |
| Jordan<br>Jordanie | 96 | 76 | 27 | 57 | 48 | 115 | 80 | 53 | 102 | 62 |
| Kazakhstan<br>Kazakhstan | 12 359 | 6 380 | 14 248 | 11 539 | 15 866 | 15 929 | 14 739 | 12 334 | 13 737 | 16 462 |
| Korea, Dem. P. R.<br>Corée, R. p. dém. de | 2 867 | 4 420 | 3 837 | 2 945 | 3 880 | 4 211 | 4 393 | 4 485 | 5 116 | 4 969 |
| Korea, Republic of<br>Corée, République de | 7 676 | 7 132 | 7 458 | 7 501 | 7 860 | 7 083 | 6 355 | 7 115 | 6 816 | 6 653 |
| Kuwait<br>Koweït | 2 | 3 | 3 | 3 | 3 | 5 | 3 | 3 | 4 | 4 |
| Kyrgyzstan<br>Kirghizistan | 1 611 | 1 608 | 1 618 | 1 550 | 1 795 | 1 712 | 1 634 | 1 709 | 1 622 | 1 606 |
| Lao People's Dem. Rep.<br>Rép. dém. pop. lao | 1 738 | 1 784 | 2 199 | 2 319 | 2 447 | 2 541 | 2 518 | 2 733 | 2 941 | 3 033 |
| Lebanon<br>Liban | 90 | 103 | 93 | 123 | 153 | 140 | 146 | 165 | 177 | 177 |
| Malaysia<br>Malaisie | 2 168 | 1 994 | 2 094 | 2 206 | 2 162 | 2 267 | 2 329 | 2 336 | 2 315 | 2 234 |
| Mongolia<br>Mongolie | 240 | 195 | 170 | 142 | 142 | 126 | 165 | 139 | 75 | 139 |

| Region, country or area / Région, pays ou zone | 1997 | 1998 | 1999 | 2000 | 2001 | 2002 | 2003 | 2004 | 2005 | 2006 |
|---|---|---|---|---|---|---|---|---|---|---|
| Myanmar / Myanmar | 17 217 | 17 636 | 20 774 | 21 964 | 22 717 | 22 695 | 24 165 | 25 791 | 26 501 | 26 474 |
| Nepal / Népal | 6 350 | 6 390 | 6 930 | 7 116 | 7 120 | 7 215 | 7 360 | 7 747 | 7 767 | 7 657 |
| Occupied Palestinian Terr. / Terr. palestinien occupé | 43 | 52 | 14 | 68 | 40 | 77 | 68 | 62 | 68 | 68 |
| Oman / Oman | 9 | 9 | 9 | 9 | 9 | 9 | 9 | 8 | 15 | 14 |
| Pakistan / Pakistan | 25 260 | 27 985 | 27 756 | 30 461 | 27 048 | 27 173 | 28 964 | 30 311 | 33 508 | 32 839 |
| Philippines / Philippines | 15 600 | 12 377 | 16 371 | 16 901 | 17 480 | 17 590 | 18 116 | 19 910 | 19 856 | 21 409 |
| Qatar / Qatar | 6 | 6 | 7 | 7 | 7 | 7 | 7 | 5 | 7 | 7 |
| Saudi Arabia / Arabie saoudite | 2 339 | 2 202 | 2 454 | 2 167 | 2 592 | 2 853 | 2 949 | 3 189 | 2 999 | 2 881 |
| Sri Lanka / Sri Lanka | 2 269 | 2 731 | 2 894 | 2 896 | 2 728 | 2 890 | 3 106 | 2 668 | 3 295 | 3 396 |
| Syrian Arab Republic / Rép. arabe syrienne | 4 322 | 5 271 | 3 301 | 3 511 | 6 919 | 5 930 | 6 224 | 5 279 | 5 631 | 5 592 |
| Tajikistan / Tadjikistan | 559 | 491 | 465 | 545 | 478 | 688 | 866 | 860 | 895 | 844 |
| Thailand / Thaïlande | 27 635 | 28 266 | 28 661 | 30 523 | 31 211 | 30 512 | 31 420 | 32 958 | 34 371 | 33 146 |
| Timor-Leste / Timor-Leste | 137 | 96 | 149 | 139 | 123 | 147 | 136 | 156 | 145 | 155 |
| Turkey / Turquie | 29 761 | 33 187 | 28 886 | 32 249 | 29 571 | 30 831 | 30 807 | 34 075 | 36 386 | 34 598 |
| Turkmenistan / Turkménistan | 759 | 1 278 | 1 567 | 1 751 | 1 832 | 2 461 | 2 667 | 2 785 | 3 035 | 3 489 |
| Uzbekistan / Ouzbékistan | 3 769 | 4 133 | 4 312 | 3 915 | 4 057 | 5 536 | 6 107 | 5 861 | 6 403 | 6 511 |
| Viet Nam / Viet Nam | 29 177 | 30 760 | 33 149 | 34 537 | 34 272 | 36 960 | 37 707 | 39 581 | 39 549 | 39 648 |
| Yemen / Yémen | 646 | 833 | 694 | 672 | 700 | 560 | 418 | 490 | 496 | 727 |
| **Europe / Europe** | **441 199** | **386 693** | **375 978** | **384 981** | **431 396** | **436 581** | **355 531** | **470 079** | **427 994** | **403 644** |
| Albania / Albanie | 602 | 606 | 498 | 566 | 503 | 519 | 489 | 499 | 511 | 508 |
| Austria / Autriche | 5 009 | 4 776 | 4 809 | 4 494 | 4 830 | 4 461 | 4 268 | 5 320 | 4 903 | 4 460 |
| Belarus / Bélarus | 5 924 | 4 497 | 3 413 | 4 565 | 4 871 | 5 710 | 5 117 | 6 590 | 6 089 | 5 686 |
| Belgium / Belgique | ... | ... | ... | 2 513 | 2 359 | 2 639 | 2 561 | 2 932 | 2 787 | 2 606 |
| Belgium-Luxembourg / Belgique-Luxembourg | 2 393 | 2 601 | 2 449 | ... | ... | ... | ... | ... | ... | ... |
| Bosnia and Herzegovina / Bosnie-Herzégovine | 1 242 | 1 327 | 1 369 | 930 | 1 138 | 1 308 | 793 | 1 439 | 1 350 | 1 341 |
| Bulgaria / Bulgarie | 6 188 | 5 378 | 5 221 | 4 389 | 6 076 | 6 770 | 3 814 | 7 463 | 5 839 | 5 532 |
| Croatia / Croatie | 3 179 | 3 210 | 2 883 | 2 770 | 3 396 | 3 722 | 2 355 | 3 248 | 3 027 | 3 028 |
| Czech Republic / République tchèque | 6 995 | 6 676 | 6 935 | 6 460 | 7 347 | 6 780 | 5 770 | 8 792 | 7 668 | 6 394 |
| Denmark / Danemark | 9 529 | 9 334 | 8 774 | 9 413 | 9 423 | 8 804 | 9 051 | 8 963 | 9 283 | 8 632 |

| Region, country or area<br>Région, pays ou zone | 1997 | 1998 | 1999 | 2000 | 2001 | 2002 | 2003 | 2004 | 2005 | 2006 |
|---|---|---|---|---|---|---|---|---|---|---|
| Estonia<br>Estonie | 651 | 576 | 402 | 697 | 558 | 525 | 506 | 608 | 760 | 619 |
| Finland<br>Finlande | 3 812 | 2 780 | 2 882 | 4 103 | 3 671 | 3 938 | 3 791 | 3 619 | 4 059 | 3 790 |
| France<br>France | 63 432 | 68 664 | 64 342 | 65 698 | 60 237 | 69 657 | 54 940 | 70 523 | 64 232 | 61 813 |
| Germany<br>Allemagne | 45 486 | 44 575 | 44 461 | 45 271 | 49 686 | 43 391 | 39 426 | 51 097 | 45 980 | 43 475 |
| Greece<br>Grèce | 4 970 | 4 611 | 4 576 | 4 968 | 4 939 | 4 827 | 4 710 | 5 088 | 5 084 | 3 592 |
| Hungary<br>Hongrie | 14 139 | 13 038 | 11 392 | 10 036 | 15 046 | 11 703 | 8 770 | 16 779 | 16 212 | 14 673 |
| Ireland<br>Irlande | 1 944 | 1 866 | 2 011 | 2 174 | 2 166 | 1 964 | 2 147 | 2 501 | 1 940 | 2 018 |
| Italy<br>Italie | 19 917 | 20 731 | 21 068 | 20 661 | 19 933 | 21 248 | 17 864 | 23 283 | 21 423 | 20 145 |
| Latvia<br>Lettonie | 1 040 | 964 | 783 | 924 | 928 | 1 029 | 932 | 1 060 | 1 323 | 1 168 |
| Lithuania<br>Lituanie | 2 945 | 2 717 | 2 048 | 2 657 | 2 344 | 2 531 | 2 632 | 2 859 | 2 811 | 1 858 |
| Luxembourg<br>Luxembourg | ... | ... | ... | 153 | 144 | 169 | 164 | 179 | 161 | 161 |
| Malta<br>Malte | 11 | 11 | 11 | 12 | 12 | 12 | 12 | 12 | 11 | 11 |
| Moldova<br>Moldova | 3 487 | 2 428 | 2 142 | 1 905 | 2 550 | 2 539 | 1 583 | 2 943 | 2 772 | 2 222 |
| Montenegro<br>Monténégro | ... | ... | ... | ... | ... | ... | ... | ... | ... | 13 |
| Netherlands<br>Pays-Bas | 1 450 | 1 497 | 1 368 | 1 732 | 1 672 | 1 740 | 1 820 | 1 822 | 1 775 | 1 755 |
| Norway<br>Norvège | 1 288 | 1 358 | 1 218 | 1 300 | 1 220 | 1 143 | 1 287 | 1 445 | 1 298 | 1 229 |
| Poland<br>Pologne | 25 402 | 27 162 | 25 754 | 22 345 | 26 965 | 26 882 | 23 391 | 29 635 | 26 928 | 21 776 |
| Portugal<br>Portugal | 1 559 | 1 622 | 1 678 | 1 608 | 1 298 | 1 497 | 1 186 | 1 363 | 785 | 1 167 |
| Romania<br>Roumanie | 22 107 | 15 453 | 17 037 | 10 499 | 18 900 | 14 357 | 12 966 | 24 402 | 19 350 | 15 759 |
| Russian Federation<br>Fédération de Russie | 86 801 | 46 937 | 53 845 | 64 326 | 83 398 | 84 859 | 65 562 | 76 231 | 76 564 | 76 866 |
| Serbia<br>Serbie | ... | ... | ... | ... | ... | ... | ... | ... | ... | 8 277 |
| Serbia and Montenegro<br>Serbie-et-Monténégro | 10 355 | 8 667 | 8 615 | 5 391 | 9 040 | 8 327 | 5 541 | 9 893 | 9 534 | ... |
| Slovakia<br>Slovaquie | 3 741 | 3 485 | 2 829 | 2 202 | 3 413 | 3 194 | 2 490 | 3 798 | 3 585 | 2 929 |
| Slovenia<br>Slovénie | 544 | 557 | 479 | 494 | 496 | 611 | 399 | 583 | 576 | 494 |
| Spain<br>Espagne | 19 324 | 22 557 | 17 988 | 24 556 | 18 050 | 21 710 | 21 412 | 24 809 | 14 364 | 19 353 |
| Sweden<br>Suède | 5 986 | 5 618 | 4 931 | 5 604 | 5 382 | 5 398 | 5 290 | 5 508 | 5 051 | 4 174 |
| Switzerland<br>Suisse | 1 223 | 1 263 | 1 055 | 1 206 | 1 094 | 1 101 | 847 | 1 089 | 1 057 | 1 008 |
| TFYR of Macedonia<br>L'ex-R.y. Macédoine | 610 | 660 | 638 | 563 | 475 | 556 | 472 | 682 | 645 | 595 |
| Ukraine<br>Ukraine | 34 393 | 25 724 | 23 950 | 23 807 | 38 879 | 37 994 | 19 662 | 40 997 | 37 258 | 33 698 |
| United Kingdom<br>Royaume-Uni | 23 523 | 22 768 | 22 125 | 23 989 | 18 959 | 22 966 | 21 511 | 22 028 | 20 998 | 20 820 |

**Cereals**—Production: thousand metric tons (*continued*)

**Céréales**—Production : milliers de tonnes (*suite*)

| Region, country or area / Région, pays ou zone | 1997 | 1998 | 1999 | 2000 | 2001 | 2002 | 2003 | 2004 | 2005 | 2006 |
|---|---|---|---|---|---|---|---|---|---|---|
| **Oceania** **Océanie** | **32 251** | **34 232** | **36 280** | **35 340** | **39 856** | **20 004** | **42 608** | **35 433** | **40 639** | **17 176** |
| Australia Australie | 31 237 | 33 339 | 35 369 | 34 447 | 38 877 | 19 029 | 41 631 | 34 564 | 39 870 | 16 332 |
| Fiji Fidji | 19 | 6 | 18 | 14 | 16 | 14 | 17 | 16 | 16 | 16 |
| Guam Guam | 3 | 2 | 2 | 2 | 2 | 3 | 2 | 2 | 2 | ^0 |
| New Caledonia Nouvelle-Calédonie | 2 | 2 | 2 | 5 | 5 | 4 | 6 | 6 | 6 | 6 |
| New Zealand Nouvelle-Zélande | 980 | 869 | 873 | 854 | 938 | 936 | 936 | 829 | 726 | 803 |
| Papua New Guinea Papouasie-Nvl-Guinée | 10 | 10 | 11 | 11 | 13 | 13 | 10 | 11 | 13 | 13 |
| Solomon Islands Iles Salomon | ^0 | 1 | 5 | 5 | 5 | 5 | 5 | 6 | 6 | 6 |
| Vanuatu Vanuatu | 1 | 1 | 1 | 1 | 1 | 1 | 1 | 1 | 1 | 1 |

Source

Food and Agriculture Organization of the United Nations (FAO), Rome, FAOSTAT data, last accessed January 2008.

Source

Organisation des Nations Unies pour l'alimentation et l'agriculture (FAO), Rome, données FAOSTAT, dernier accès janvier 2008.

Notes

1 For statistical purposes, the data for China do not include those for the Hong Kong Special Administrative Region (Hong Kong SAR) and Macao Special Administrative Region (Macao SAR).

Notes

1 Pour la présentation des statistiques, les données pour la Chine ne comprennent pas la Région Administrative Spéciale de Hong Kong (Hong Kong RAS) et la Région Administrative Spéciale de Macao (Macao RAS).

# Oil crops
Production: thousand metric tons

# Culture oléagineuses
Production: milliers de tonnes

| Region, country or area Région, pays ou zone | 1997 | 1998 | 1999 | 2000 | 2001 | 2002 | 2003 | 2004 | 2005 | 2006 |
|---|---|---|---|---|---|---|---|---|---|---|
| World Monde | 509 055 | 525 574 | 549 882 | 560 756 | 588 770 | 589 110 | 628 179 | 692 816 | 735 778 | 743 459 |
| Africa Afrique | 37 772 | 37 878 | 40 574 | 38 862 | 40 579 | 40 392 | 43 148 | 44 757 | 46 349 | 45 987 |
| Algeria Algérie | 352 | 158 | 399 | 250 | 234 | 224 | 200 | 502 | 349 | 397 |
| Angola Angola | 331 | 339 | 328 | 341 | 352 | 356 | 390 | 377 | 404 | 395 |
| Benin Bénin | 961 | 951 | 980 | 937 | 1 030 | 1 198 | 1 103 | 1 136 | 1 018 | 766 |
| Botswana Botswana | 10 | 10 | 11 | 11 | 13 | 12 | 12 | 13 | 14 | 14 |
| Burkina Faso Burkina Faso | 772 | 811 | 763 | 565 | 1 016 | 1 090 | 1 174 | 1 180 | 1 408 | 1 424 |
| Burundi Burundi | 32 | 30 | 30 | 27 | 24 | 26 | 29 | 26 | 25 | 25 |
| Cameroon Cameroun | 1 536 | 1 584 | 1 692 | 1 743 | 1 798 | 1 790 | 1 912 | 1 880 | 2 103 | 1 967 |
| Cape Verde Cap-Vert | 5 | 5 | 5 | 6 | 6 | 6 | 6 | 6 | 6 | 6 |
| Central African Rep. Rép. centrafricaine | 273 | 252 | 258 | 250 | 280 | 259 | 249 | 252 | 248 | 262 |
| Chad Tchad | 808 | 768 | 698 | 687 | 821 | 818 | 725 | 866 | 858 | 896 |
| Comoros Comores | 81 | 80 | 82 | 83 | 84 | 86 | 86 | 88 | 90 | 86 |
| Congo Congo | 118 | 117 | 123 | 124 | 124 | 124 | 124 | 123 | 123 | 125 |
| Côte d'Ivoire Côte d'Ivoire | 2 079 | 2 310 | 2 327 | 2 903 | 2 209 | 2 116 | 2 340 | 2 453 | 2 783 | 2 808 |
| Dem. Rep. of the Congo Rép. dém. du Congo | 1 679 | 1 717 | 1 659 | 1 659 | 1 611 | 1 562 | 1 579 | 1 596 | 1 615 | 1 633 |
| Egypt Egypte | 1 923 | 1 480 | 1 580 | 1 475 | 1 950 | 1 777 | 1 393 | 1 897 | 1 710 | 1 714 |
| Equatorial Guinea Guinée équatoriale | 44 | 42 | 44 | 44 | 44 | 44 | 44 | 42 | 41 | 41 |
| Eritrea Erythrée | 20 | 23 | 23 | 21 | 22 | 21 | 26 | 24 | 39 | 39 |
| Ethiopia Ethiopie | 289 | 283 | 275 | 298 | 351 | 350 | 431 | 645 | 612 | 632 |
| Gabon Gabon | 55 | 51 | 52 | 55 | 55 | 50 | 55 | 55 | 55 | 55 |
| Gambia Gambie | 118 | 112 | 163 | 178 | 190 | 111 | 133 | 176 | 147 | 140 |
| Ghana Ghana | 1 569 | 1 717 | 1 691 | 1 748 | 1 812 | 2 069 | 2 409 | 2 801 | 2 908 | 3 080 |
| Guinea Guinée | 1 099 | 1 132 | 1 168 | 1 198 | 1 193 | 1 188 | 1 209 | 1 273 | 1 317 | 1 324 |
| Guinea-Bissau Guinée-Bissau | 164 | 164 | 166 | 168 | 169 | 169 | 170 | 172 | 174 | 170 |
| Kenya Kenya | 189 | 188 | 207 | 197 | 201 | 184 | 184 | 184 | 190 | 192 |
| Liberia Libéria | 198 | 198 | 199 | 200 | 200 | 200 | 200 | 200 | 210 | 209 |
| Libyan Arab Jamah. Jamah. arabe libyenne | 206 | 218 | 293 | 185 | 170 | 172 | 174 | 213 | 235 | 235 |

**Oil crops**—Production: thousand metric tons (*continued*)
**Culture oléagineuses**—Production: milliers de tonnes (*suite*)

| Region, country or area<br>Région, pays ou zone | 1997 | 1998 | 1999 | 2000 | 2001 | 2002 | 2003 | 2004 | 2005 | 2006 |
|---|---|---|---|---|---|---|---|---|---|---|
| Madagascar<br>Madagascar | 215 | 217 | 214 | 200 | 189 | 173 | 177 | 179 | 174 | 180 |
| Malawi<br>Malawi | 150 | 162 | 217 | 182 | 215 | 231 | 263 | 255 | 175 | 228 |
| Mali<br>Mali | 996 | 991 | 1 026 | 629 | 1 035 | 962 | 1 244 | 1 160 | 1 239 | 1 046 |
| Mauritania<br>Mauritanie | 5 | 5 | 5 | 5 | 4 | 4 | 4 | 3 | 4 | 4 |
| Mauritius<br>Maurice | 3 | 2 | 2 | 2 | 2 | 2 | 3 | 3 | 2 | 2 |
| Morocco<br>Maroc | 643 | 822 | 557 | 462 | 495 | 533 | 946 | 605 | 819 | 807 |
| Mozambique<br>Mozambique | 834 | 884 | 872 | 552 | 588 | 545 | 573 | 579 | 565 | 569 |
| Namibia<br>Namibie | 4 | 6 | 9 | 9 | 9 | 10 | 9 | 9 | 10 | 10 |
| Niger<br>Niger | 103 | 125 | 124 | 141 | 116 | 190 | 430 | 209 | 194 | 199 |
| Nigeria<br>Nigéria | 12 671 | 12 779 | 13 515 | 13 822 | 14 207 | 14 551 | 15 028 | 15 521 | 16 392 | 16 230 |
| Réunion<br>Réunion | 1 | 1 | 1 | 1 | 1 | 1 | 1 | 1 | 1 | 1 |
| Rwanda<br>Rwanda | 12 | 15 | 14 | 21 | 26 | 28 | 30 | 29 | 34 | 36 |
| Sao Tome and Principe<br>Sao Tomé-et-Principe | 49 | 46 | 49 | 70 | 71 | 71 | 73 | 74 | 75 | 75 |
| Senegal<br>Sénégal | 683 | 674 | 1 116 | 1 170 | 1 020 | 398 | 624 | 781 | 897 | 653 |
| Seychelles<br>Seychelles | 4 | 3 | 4 | 4 | 4 | 3 | 3 | 3 | 3 | 3 |
| Sierra Leone<br>Sierra Leone | 320 | 267 | 230 | 216 | 238 | 266 | 293 | 295 | 300 | 309 |
| Somalia<br>Somalie | 45 | 39 | 41 | 45 | 52 | 53 | 56 | 56 | 48 | 48 |
| South Africa<br>Afrique du Sud | 878 | 1 083 | 1 784 | 983 | 1 300 | 1 456 | 1 016 | 1 155 | 1 112 | 1 136 |
| Sudan<br>Soudan | 1 919 | 1 532 | 1 706 | 1 556 | 1 761 | 1 789 | 1 632 | 1 686 | 1 419 | 1 364 |
| Swaziland<br>Swaziland | 49 | 46 | 42 | 24 | 20 | 15 | 15 | 14 | 14 | 14 |
| Togo<br>Togo | 455 | 458 | 390 | 370 | 419 | 457 | 460 | 456 | 452 | 400 |
| Tunisia<br>Tunisie | 521 | 971 | 1 147 | 573 | 172 | 372 | 1 422 | 673 | 624 | 1 024 |
| Uganda<br>Ouganda | 425 | 467 | 533 | 581 | 597 | 676 | 751 | 819 | 948 | 918 |
| United Rep. of Tanzania<br>Rép.-Unie de Tanzanie | 966 | 748 | 795 | 828 | 1 024 | 912 | 962 | 1 162 | 1 206 | 1 121 |
| Zambia<br>Zambie | 165 | 151 | 240 | 177 | 133 | 146 | 153 | 170 | 226 | 226 |
| Zimbabwe<br>Zimbabwe | 745 | 644 | 727 | 887 | 920 | 548 | 624 | 681 | 738 | 750 |
| **Northern America**<br>**Amérique septentrionale** | **104 252** | **104 551** | **105 237** | **105 892** | **109 132** | **101 631** | **97 323** | **120 641** | **125 279** | **124 374** |
| Canada<br>Canada | 10 336 | 11 813 | 12 946 | 10 930 | 7 579 | 7 736 | 10 173 | 11 656 | 14 197 | 13 951 |
| United States<br>Etats-Unis | 93 916 | 92 738 | 92 291 | 94 962 | 101 553 | 93 896 | 87 150 | 108 985 | 111 082 | 110 423 |

| Region, country or area<br>Région, pays ou zone | 1997 | 1998 | 1999 | 2000 | 2001 | 2002 | 2003 | 2004 | 2005 | 2006 |
|---|---|---|---|---|---|---|---|---|---|---|
| **Latin Amer. and the Carib.**<br>**Amér. latine et Caraïb.** | **63 900** | **78 436** | **80 413** | **82 705** | **94 860** | **102 055** | **117 716** | **115 408** | **124 600** | **126 373** |
| Argentina<br>Argentine | 18 666 | 26 978 | 28 784 | 27 736 | 31 434 | 35 029 | 39 311 | 35 757 | 43 410 | 45 594 |
| Aruba<br>Aruba | 1 | 1 | 1 | 1 | 1 | 1 | 1 | 1 | 1 | ... |
| Barbados<br>Barbade | 2 | 2 | 2 | 2 | 2 | 2 | 2 | 2 | 2 | 2 |
| Belize<br>Belize | 3 | 2 | 2 | 2 | 2 | 2 | 3 | 1 | 1 | 1 |
| Bolivia<br>Bolivie | 1 241 | 1 288 | 1 162 | 1 428 | 1 126 | 1 614 | 1 952 | 1 835 | 1 922 | 1 641 |
| Brazil<br>Brésil | 29 985 | 35 564 | 35 987 | 39 045 | 46 616 | 50 370 | 59 670 | 60 278 | 61 147 | 61 083 |
| Chile<br>Chili | 47 | 64 | 90 | 74 | 87 | 25 | 47 | 50 | 76 | 92 |
| Colombia<br>Colombie | 2 491 | 2 448 | 2 838 | 2 905 | 3 066 | 3 029 | 3 043 | 3 663 | 3 788 | 3 818 |
| Costa Rica<br>Costa Rica | 532 | 486 | 534 | 652 | 712 | 614 | 625 | 714 | 824 | 825 |
| Cuba<br>Cuba | 38 | 52 | 56 | 90 | 99 | 119 | 121 | 129 | 123 | 113 |
| Dominica<br>Dominique | 14 | 13 | 13 | 13 | 13 | 13 | 13 | 13 | 13 | 13 |
| Dominican Republic<br>Rép. dominicaine | 308 | 319 | 343 | 313 | 342 | 348 | 359 | 357 | 295 | 295 |
| Ecuador<br>Equateur | 1 483 | 1 607 | 1 118 | 1 521 | 1 630 | 1 837 | 1 715 | 2 087 | 2 127 | 2 133 |
| El Salvador<br>El Salvador | 94 | 97 | 113 | 99 | 111 | 37 | 66 | 70 | 71 | 73 |
| Grenada<br>Grenade | 7 | 7 | 7 | 7 | 7 | 7 | 7 | 7 | 7 | 7 |
| Guatemala<br>Guatemala | 422 | 436 | 500 | 572 | 623 | 744 | 737 | 756 | 770 | 768 |
| Guyana<br>Guyana | 122 | 64 | 79 | 86 | 46 | 49 | 50 | 65 | 71 | 71 |
| Haiti<br>Haïti | 62 | 57 | 59 | 56 | 52 | 54 | 55 | 51 | 49 | 49 |
| Honduras<br>Honduras | 613 | 714 | 663 | 674 | 731 | 801 | 1 118 | 1 203 | 1 306 | 1 309 |
| Jamaica<br>Jamaïque | 188 | 178 | 181 | 180 | 182 | 181 | 181 | 200 | 210 | 210 |
| Martinique<br>Martinique | 1 | 1 | 1 | 1 | 1 | 1 | 1 | 1 | 1 | 1 |
| Mexico<br>Mexique | 2 980 | 3 214 | 2 667 | 2 220 | 2 337 | 1 921 | 2 147 | 1 680 | 1 554 | 1 551 |
| Nicaragua<br>Nicaragua | 142 | 132 | 156 | 143 | 153 | 131 | 173 | 190 | 204 | 186 |
| Panama<br>Panama | 43 | 69 | 75 | 76 | 75 | 73 | 75 | 79 | 86 | 86 |
| Paraguay<br>Paraguay | 3 150 | 3 509 | 3 676 | 3 675 | 4 265 | 3 779 | 4 754 | 4 464 | 4 713 | 4 534 |
| Peru<br>Pérou | 440 | 370 | 468 | 455 | 459 | 422 | 470 | 548 | 572 | 584 |
| Puerto Rico<br>Porto Rico | 7 | 3 | 5 | 6 | 6 | 6 | 7 | 8 | 5 | 5 |
| Saint Kitts and Nevis<br>Saint-Kitts-et-Nevis | 2 | 2 | 1 | 1 | 1 | 1 | 1 | 1 | 1 | 1 |

| Region, country or area<br>Région, pays ou zone | 1997 | 1998 | 1999 | 2000 | 2001 | 2002 | 2003 | 2004 | 2005 | 2006 |
|---|---|---|---|---|---|---|---|---|---|---|
| Saint Lucia<br>Sainte-Lucie | 26 | 13 | 25 | 16 | 15 | 15 | 16 | 13 | 11 | 11 |
| Saint Vincent-Grenadines<br>Saint Vincent-Grenadines | 9 | 7 | 4 | 3 | 4 | 5 | 3 | 3 | 3 | 3 |
| Suriname<br>Suriname | 11 | 11 | 11 | 11 | 11 | 13 | 13 | 11 | 10 | 10 |
| Trinidad and Tobago<br>Trinité-et-Tobago | 21 | 25 | 22 | 25 | 28 | 24 | 17 | 15 | 12 | 12 |
| Uruguay<br>Uruguay | 135 | 104 | 187 | 47 | 93 | 225 | 425 | 561 | 635 | 720 |
| Venezuela (Boliv. Rep. of)<br>Venezuela (Rép. boliv. du) | 613 | 600 | 584 | 571 | 531 | 561 | 540 | 595 | 580 | 573 |
| **Asia**<br>**Asie** | **256 644** | **257 418** | **269 508** | **283 611** | **295 202** | **296 948** | **317 173** | **355 296** | **379 956** | **385 484** |
| Afghanistan<br>Afghanistan | 160 | 163 | 163 | 146 | 146 | 146 | 146 | 148 | 148 | 148 |
| Azerbaijan<br>Azerbaïdjan | 201 | 183 | 159 | 160 | 158 | 155 | 191 | 249 | 349 | 243 |
| Bangladesh<br>Bangladesh | 561 | 563 | 565 | 550 | 544 | 529 | 530 | 519 | 504 | 543 |
| Bhutan<br>Bhoutan | 3 | 3 | 3 | 2 | 3 | 3 | 4 | 3 | 2 | 2 |
| Cambodia<br>Cambodge | 149 | 107 | 125 | 121 | 118 | 146 | 181 | 201 | 300 | 220 |
| China[1]<br>Chine[1] | 62 439 | 63 776 | 62 478 | 70 014 | 73 797 | 73 280 | 70 816 | 82 847 | 79 325 | 83 328 |
| Cyprus<br>Chypre | 10 | 13 | 16 | 22 | 19 | 29 | 19 | 24 | 18 | 25 |
| Georgia<br>Géorgie | 33 | 24 | 42 | 6 | 44 | 24 | 30 | 25 | 34 | 15 |
| India<br>Inde | 43 103 | 44 131 | 40 118 | 38 620 | 38 674 | 33 002 | 41 347 | 47 729 | 52 927 | 53 971 |
| Indonesia<br>Indonésie | 45 664 | 48 688 | 53 155 | 57 217 | 61 464 | 68 037 | 74 847 | 83 438 | 103 137 | 101 562 |
| Iran (Islamic Rep. of)<br>Iran (Rép. islamique d') | 941 | 957 | 886 | 1 035 | 898 | 904 | 894 | 1 028 | 952 | 909 |
| Iraq<br>Iraq | 143 | 144 | 137 | 131 | 123 | 129 | 81 | 79 | 86 | 85 |
| Israel<br>Israël | 289 | 284 | 161 | 171 | 153 | 172 | 137 | 206 | 149 | 177 |
| Japan<br>Japon | 176 | 184 | 214 | 262 | 315 | 295 | 255 | 186 | 247 | 250 |
| Jordan<br>Jordanie | 57 | 138 | 38 | 135 | 66 | 181 | 118 | 161 | 113 | 147 |
| Kazakhstan<br>Kazakhstan | 415 | 395 | 572 | 635 | 877 | 873 | 1 115 | 1 149 | 1 162 | 1 145 |
| Korea, Dem. P. R.<br>Corée, R. p. dém. de | 415 | 396 | 396 | 408 | 406 | 410 | 412 | 411 | 401 | 406 |
| Korea, Republic of<br>Corée, République de | 227 | 210 | 177 | 180 | 183 | 172 | 146 | 187 | 233 | 203 |
| Kyrgyzstan<br>Kirghizistan | 135 | 167 | 197 | 196 | 221 | 241 | 247 | 288 | 276 | 281 |
| Lao People's Dem. Rep.<br>Rép. dém. pop. lao | 55 | 61 | 45 | 46 | 40 | 38 | 36 | 34 | 46 | 48 |
| Lebanon<br>Liban | 102 | 108 | 74 | 197 | 93 | 192 | 90 | 90 | 97 | 97 |
| Malaysia<br>Malaisie | 51 391 | 47 197 | 58 942 | 60 667 | 63 200 | 63 698 | 71 172 | 74 357 | 80 357 | 80 521 |

| Region, country or area<br>Région, pays ou zone | 1997 | 1998 | 1999 | 2000 | 2001 | 2002 | 2003 | 2004 | 2005 | 2006 |
|---|---|---|---|---|---|---|---|---|---|---|
| Maldives<br>Maldives | 16 | 14 | 12 | 18 | 26 | 42 | 72 | 16 | 15 | 5 |
| Myanmar<br>Myanmar | 1 583 | 1 529 | 1 574 | 1 728 | 2 110 | 2 182 | 2 565 | 2 704 | 2 669 | 2 682 |
| Nepal<br>Népal | 145 | 134 | 146 | 146 | 157 | 160 | 152 | 291 | 308 | 304 |
| Occupied Palestinian Terr.<br>Terr. palestinien occupé | 99 | 36 | 158 | 39 | 145 | 86 | 144 | 144 | 88 | 88 |
| Pakistan<br>Pakistan | 8 455 | 8 125 | 10 248 | 9 751 | 9 621 | 9 276 | 9 211 | 13 042 | 11 283 | 11 148 |
| Philippines<br>Philippines | 16 198 | 15 420 | 13 575 | 15 393 | 16 149 | 16 350 | 16 977 | 17 159 | 17 476 | 17 595 |
| Saudi Arabia<br>Arabie saoudite | 6 | 6 | 6 | 7 | 6 | 7 | 6 | 9 | 9 | 9 |
| Sri Lanka<br>Sri Lanka | 2 079 | 1 999 | 2 226 | 2 448 | 2 229 | 1 899 | 2 012 | 955 | 977 | 999 |
| Syrian Arab Republic<br>Rép. arabe syrienne | 2 144 | 2 488 | 1 982 | 2 696 | 2 224 | 2 366 | 1 813 | 2 594 | 2 239 | 2 239 |
| Tajikistan<br>Tadjikistan | 558 | 592 | 486 | 529 | 715 | 815 | 868 | 893 | 744 | 737 |
| Thailand<br>Thaïlande | 4 978 | 4 738 | 5 813 | 5 574 | 6 359 | 6 234 | 7 152 | 8 108 | 7 692 | 9 218 |
| Timor-Leste<br>Timor-Leste | 14 | 17 | 19 | 20 | 21 | 21 | 21 | 21 | 21 | 21 |
| Turkey<br>Turquie | 4 870 | 6 281 | 4 935 | 6 314 | 5 129 | 6 857 | 5 555 | 6 381 | 5 527 | 6 852 |
| Turkmenistan<br>Turkménistan | 1 014 | 1 131 | 2 080 | 1 495 | 1 830 | 1 150 | 1 184 | 1 660 | 1 660 | 1 160 |
| Uzbekistan<br>Ouzbékistan | 5 897 | 5 175 | 5 668 | 4 795 | 5 128 | 4 941 | 4 729 | 5 920 | 6 239 | 6 021 |
| Viet Nam<br>Viet Nam | 1 868 | 1 782 | 1 857 | 1 670 | 1 742 | 1 840 | 1 831 | 1 988 | 2 091 | 2 019 |
| Yemen<br>Yémen | 49 | 57 | 59 | 64 | 68 | 66 | 67 | 52 | 54 | 59 |
| **Europe**<br>**Europe** | **39 115** | **38 849** | **44 556** | **40 649** | **40 466** | **40 676** | **46 019** | **49 793** | **51 479** | **54 409** |
| Albania<br>Albanie | 37 | 51 | 47 | 41 | 45 | 32 | 31 | 62 | 34 | 44 |
| Austria<br>Autriche | 218 | 289 | 347 | 256 | 271 | 268 | 205 | 257 | 263 | 307 |
| Belarus<br>Bélarus | 53 | 79 | 88 | 110 | 130 | 92 | 92 | 185 | 184 | 146 |
| Belgium<br>Belgique | ... | ... | ... | 29 | 30 | 32 | 30 | 35 | 34 | 45 |
| Belgium-Luxembourg<br>Belgique-Luxembourg | 38 | 39 | 51 | ... | ... | ... | ... | ... | ... | ... |
| Bosnia and Herzegovina<br>Bosnie-Herzégovine | 9 | 9 | 10 | 6 | 7 | 10 | 5 | 9 | 14 | 15 |
| Bulgaria<br>Bulgarie | 481 | 565 | 653 | 472 | 454 | 692 | 823 | 1 122 | 977 | 1 241 |
| Croatia<br>Croatie | 97 | 182 | 256 | 165 | 177 | 251 | 190 | 209 | 276 | 303 |
| Czech Republic<br>République tchèque | 621 | 777 | 1 076 | 948 | 1 083 | 826 | 599 | 1 105 | 955 | 1 056 |
| Denmark<br>Danemark | 294 | 360 | 416 | 297 | 212 | 218 | 354 | 469 | 344 | 436 |
| Estonia<br>Estonie | 10 | 18 | 30 | 39 | 41 | 64 | 69 | 69 | 83 | 85 |

**Oil crops**—Production: thousand metric tons (*continued*)
**Culture oléagineuses**—Production: milliers de tonnes (*suite*)

| Region, country or area<br>Région, pays ou zone | 1997 | 1998 | 1999 | 2000 | 2001 | 2002 | 2003 | 2004 | 2005 | 2006 |
|---|---|---|---|---|---|---|---|---|---|---|
| Finland<br>Finlande | 93 | 64 | 88 | 71 | 101 | 103 | 94 | 75 | 106 | 148 |
| France<br>France | 5 843 | 5 805 | 6 655 | 5 590 | 4 837 | 5 115 | 5 115 | 5 683 | 6 277 | 5 779 |
| Germany<br>Allemagne | 3 079 | 3 676 | 4 536 | 3 746 | 4 254 | 3 918 | 3 729 | 5 377 | 5 154 | 5 423 |
| Greece<br>Grèce | 3 851 | 3 971 | 4 504 | 4 562 | 4 495 | 4 636 | 3 780 | 4 110 | 4 609 | 4 457 |
| Hungary<br>Hongrie | 737 | 875 | 1 231 | 710 | 895 | 1 067 | 1 174 | 1 576 | 1 490 | 1 602 |
| Ireland<br>Irlande | 12 | 17 | 5 | 9 | 7 | 7 | 7 | 7 | 14 | 17 |
| Italy<br>Italie | 5 357 | 4 380 | 5 247 | 4 332 | 4 466 | 4 297 | 4 287 | 5 431 | 4 723 | 4 388 |
| Latvia<br>Lettonie | 2 | 4 | 10 | 12 | 15 | 35 | 39 | 105 | 147 | 122 |
| Lithuania<br>Lituanie | 41 | 76 | 121 | 86 | 68 | 110 | 124 | 207 | 204 | 171 |
| Luxembourg<br>Luxembourg | ... | ... | ... | 8 | 9 | 13 | 13 | 17 | 15 | 16 |
| Moldova<br>Moldova | 204 | 205 | 299 | 280 | 264 | 330 | 409 | 376 | 400 | 467 |
| Montenegro<br>Monténégro | ... | ... | ... | ... | ... | ... | ... | ... | ... | 2 |
| Netherlands<br>Pays-Bas | 7 | 8 | 11 | 8 | 8 | 7 | 10 | 14 | 13 | 18 |
| Norway<br>Norvège | 14 | 13 | 10 | 9 | 19 | 18 | 11 | 12 | 11 | 11 |
| Poland<br>Pologne | 613 | 1 121 | 1 157 | 971 | 1 082 | 969 | 826 | 1 666 | 1 474 | 1 682 |
| Portugal<br>Portugal | 325 | 334 | 371 | 309 | 335 | 281 | 286 | 350 | 238 | 303 |
| Romania<br>Roumanie | 1 002 | 1 318 | 1 607 | 869 | 1 006 | 1 194 | 1 762 | 1 996 | 1 804 | 2 052 |
| Russian Federation<br>Fédération de Russie | 3 306 | 3 532 | 4 691 | 4 508 | 3 238 | 4 299 | 5 621 | 5 753 | 7 559 | 8 192 |
| Serbia<br>Serbie | ... | ... | ... | ... | ... | ... | ... | ... | ... | 823 |
| Serbia and Montenegro<br>Serbie-et-Monténégro | 423 | 447 | 572 | 501 | 533 | 532 | 585 | 763 | 724 | ... |
| Slovakia<br>Slovaquie | 271 | 234 | 378 | 260 | 373 | 395 | 326 | 478 | 453 | 515 |
| Slovenia<br>Slovénie | 1 | 1 | 2 | 1 | 1 | 3 | 1 | 8 | 8 | 7 |
| Spain<br>Espagne | 7 821 | 6 074 | 4 763 | 6 358 | 8 151 | 5 620 | 8 742 | 6 535 | 4 911 | 5 873 |
| Sweden<br>Suède | 133 | 130 | 195 | 129 | 109 | 164 | 136 | 239 | 214 | 233 |
| Switzerland<br>Suisse | 59 | 59 | 51 | 55 | 54 | 70 | 69 | 80 | 78 | 73 |
| TFYR of Macedonia<br>L'ex-R.y. Macédoine | 40 | 36 | 38 | 28 | 21 | 25 | 24 | 23 | 19 | 26 |
| Ukraine<br>Ukraine | 2 389 | 2 390 | 3 004 | 3 675 | 2 481 | 3 498 | 4 619 | 3 727 | 5 679 | 6 411 |
| United Kingdom<br>Royaume-Uni | 1 633 | 1 710 | 2 035 | 1 200 | 1 196 | 1 486 | 1 830 | 1 661 | 1 991 | 1 919 |

| Region, country or area<br>Région, pays ou zone | 1997 | 1998 | 1999 | 2000 | 2001 | 2002 | 2003 | 2004 | 2005 | 2006 |
|---|---|---|---|---|---|---|---|---|---|---|
| **Oceania**<br>**Océanie** | **7 373** | **8 443** | **9 594** | **9 038** | **8 532** | **7 408** | **6 801** | **6 920** | **8 114** | **6 832** |
| American Samoa<br>Samoa américaines | 5 | 5 | 5 | 5 | 5 | 5 | 5 | 5 | 5 | 5 |
| Australia<br>Australie | 3 457 | 4 456 | 5 601 | 4 937 | 5 031 | 3 879 | 3 298 | 3 070 | 4 109 | 2 967 |
| Cocos (Keeling) Islands<br>Iles des Cocos (Keeling) | 9 | 9 | 9 | 9 | 9 | 9 | 9 | 9 | 9 | 9 |
| Cook Islands<br>Iles Cook | 5 | 5 | 5 | 5 | 5 | 5 | 2 | 2 | 2 | 2 |
| Fiji<br>Fidji | 230 | 223 | 187 | 184 | 187 | 185 | 140 | 154 | 152 | 152 |
| French Polynesia<br>Polynésie française | 97 | 69 | 76 | 90 | 84 | 97 | 96 | 88 | 84 | 84 |
| Guam<br>Guam | 54 | 54 | 54 | 54 | 54 | 54 | 54 | 57 | 59 | 59 |
| Kiribati<br>Kiribati | 105 | 118 | 118 | 102 | 103 | 102 | 104 | 113 | 118 | 118 |
| Marshall Islands<br>Iles Marshall | 38 | 27 | 22 | 7 | 5 | 17 | 40 | 25 | 23 | 23 |
| Micronesia (Fed. States of)<br>Micronésie (Etats féd. de) | 45 | 45 | 45 | 45 | 45 | 45 | 45 | 45 | 45 | 45 |
| Nauru<br>Nauru | 2 | 2 | 2 | 2 | 2 | 2 | 2 | 2 | 2 | 2 |
| New Caledonia<br>Nouvelle-Calédonie | 17 | 15 | 15 | 15 | 16 | 16 | 16 | 16 | 17 | 16 |
| New Zealand<br>Nouvelle-Zélande | 6 | 5 | 5 | 5 | 5 | 5 | 6 | 6 | 6 | 6 |
| Niue<br>Nioué | 3 | 3 | 3 | 3 | 3 | 3 | 3 | 3 | 3 | 3 |
| Palau<br>Palaos | 140 | 140 | 140 | 140 | 140 | 140 | 140 | 140 | 140 | ... |
| Papua New Guinea<br>Papouasie-Nvl-Guinée | 2 049 | 2 116 | 2 343 | 2 515 | 1 950 | 2 011 | 1 999 | 2 174 | 2 279 | 2 279 |
| Samoa<br>Samoa | 181 | 174 | 146 | 154 | 151 | 151 | 151 | 160 | 164 | 164 |
| Solomon Islands<br>Iles Salomon | 470 | 479 | 439 | 423 | 368 | 360 | 365 | 429 | 469 | 469 |
| Tokelau<br>Tokélaou | 3 | 3 | 3 | 3 | 3 | 3 | 3 | 3 | 3 | 3 |
| Tonga<br>Tonga | 51 | 59 | 62 | 59 | 60 | 60 | 60 | 67 | 72 | 72 |
| Tuvalu<br>Tuvalu | 2 | 2 | 2 | 2 | 2 | 2 | 2 | 1 | 1 | 1 |
| Vanuatu<br>Vanuatu | 404 | 434 | 313 | 277 | 305 | 257 | 259 | 350 | 352 | 352 |
| Wallis and Futuna Islands<br>Iles Wallis et Futuna | 3 | 3 | 3 | 3 | 3 | 3 | 3 | 3 | 3 | 3 |

Source

Food and Agriculture Organization of the United Nations (FAO), Rome, FAOSTAT data, last accessed January 2008.

Notes

1 For statistical purposes, the data for China do not include those for the Hong Kong Special Administrative Region (Hong Kong SAR), Macao Special Administrative Region (Macao SAR) and Taiwan Province of China.

Source

Organisation de Nations Unies pour l'alimentation et l'agriculture (FAO), Rome, données FAOSTAT, dernier accès janvier 2008.

Notes

1 Pour la présentation des statistiques, les données pour la Chine ne comprennent pas la Région Administrative Spéciale de Hong Kong (Hong Kong RAS), la Région Administrative Spéciale de Macao (Macao RAS) et la province de Taiwan.

## 37

### Roundwood
Production (solid volume of roundwood without bark): million cubic metres

### Bois rond
Production (volume solide de bois rond sans écorce) : millions de mètres cubes

| Region, country or area — Région, pays ou zone | 1997 | 1998 | 1999 | 2000 | 2001 | 2002 | 2003 | 2004 | 2005 | 2006 |
|---|---|---|---|---|---|---|---|---|---|---|
| **World — Monde** | 3 305.8 | 3 225.0 | 3 334.2 | 3 395.1 | 3 302.7 | 3 332.0 | 3 383.7 | 3 446.5 | 3 550.9 | 3 535.6 |
| **Africa — Afrique** | 582.8 | 585.0 | 588.8 | 593.9 | 590.0 | 598.1 | 608.7 | 616.6 | 628.1 | 654.9 |
| Algeria — Algérie | 7.2 | 7.3 | 7.4 | 7.2 | 7.4 | 7.5 | 7.5 | 7.7 | 7.7 | 7.8 |
| Angola — Angola | 3.9 | 4.0 | 4.2 | 4.3 | 4.3 | 4.4 | 4.5 | 4.6 | 4.7 | 4.8 |
| Benin — Bénin | 6.2 | 6.2 | 6.2 | 6.2 | 0.5 | 0.5 | 0.5 | 0.5 | 6.4 | 6.4 |
| Botswana — Botswana | 0.7 | 0.7 | 0.7 | 0.7 | 0.7 | 0.7 | 0.8 | 0.8 | 0.8 | 0.8 |
| Burkina Faso — Burkina Faso | 11.1 | 11.3 | 7.8 | 8.0 | 8.0 | 7.2 | 7.3 | 9.2 | 11.7 | 13.2 |
| Burundi — Burundi | 7.4 | 7.7 | 5.6 | 5.8 | 8.3 | 8.4 | 8.6 | 8.7 | 8.9 | 9.0 |
| Cameroon — Cameroun | 12.2 | 11.1 | 10.9 | 11.0 | 10.5 | 10.6 | 11.0 | 11.2 | 11.3 | 11.4 |
| Central African Rep. — Rép. centrafricaine | 3.4 | 3.5 | 2.9 | 3.0 | 3.0 | 2.9 | 2.8 | 2.8 | 2.8 | 2.8 |
| Chad — Tchad | 6.2 | 6.3 | 6.5 | 6.6 | 6.8 | 6.9 | 7.0 | 7.1 | 7.2 | 7.4 |
| Congo — Congo | 2.7 | 2.7 | 2.4 | 2.4 | 2.4 | 2.4 | 2.1 | 2.3 | 2.3 | 2.2 |
| Côte d'Ivoire — Côte d'Ivoire | 11.6 | 11.8 | 11.7 | 11.9 | 11.2 | 10.7 | 10.2 | 10.3 | 10.1 | 10.1 |
| Dem. Rep. of the Congo — Rép. dém. du Congo | 64.9 | 66.0 | 67.3 | 68.6 | 69.7 | 70.9 | 72.2 | 73.4 | 74.7 | 75.8 |
| Egypt — Egypte | 16.0 | 16.1 | 16.3 | 16.4 | 16.6 | 16.8 | 16.9 | 17.1 | 17.2 | 17.3 |
| Equatorial Guinea — Guinée équatoriale | 1.2 | 0.9 | 1.2 | 1.1 | 1.1 | 1.0 | 0.9 | 0.9 | 0.9 | 0.9 |
| Eritrea — Erythrée | 2.0 | 2.1 | 2.2 | 2.2 | 2.3 | 1.3 | 1.3 | 2.4 | 2.4 | 2.5 |
| Ethiopia — Ethiopie | 85.5 | 86.5 | 88.2 | 89.9 | 91.3 | 92.7 | 94.5 | 96.0 | 97.4 | 98.6 |
| Gabon — Gabon | 3.3 | 3.3 | 2.8 | 3.1 | 3.1 | 2.2 | 4.6 | 4.6 | 3.7 | 4.0 |
| Gambia — Gambie | 0.6 | 0.6 | 0.6 | 0.7 | 0.7 | 0.7 | 0.7 | 0.8 | 0.8 | 0.8 |
| Ghana — Ghana | 22.0 | 21.9 | 21.8 | 21.7 | 21.9 | 21.8 | 22.1 | 22.0 | 21.9 | 34.3 |
| Guinea — Guinée | 8.7 | 8.7 | 12.2 | 12.1 | 12.1 | 12.2 | 12.2 | 12.3 | 12.3 | 12.4 |
| Guinea-Bissau — Guinée-Bissau | 0.6 | 0.6 | 0.6 | 0.6 | 0.6 | 0.6 | 0.6 | 0.6 | 0.6 | 0.6 |
| Kenya — Kenya | 21.3 | 21.3 | 21.5 | 21.6 | 21.7 | 21.8 | 21.9 | 22.2 | 22.4 | 22.5 |
| Lesotho — Lesotho | 1.6 | 1.6 | 2.0 | 2.0 | 2.0 | 2.0 | 2.0 | 2.0 | 2.1 | 2.1 |
| Liberia — Libéria | 3.5 | 4.1 | 4.5 | 5.8 | 6.1 | 6.7 | 6.3 | 5.9 | 6.1 | 6.3 |
| Libyan Arab Jamah. — Jamah. arabe libyenne | 0.7 | 0.7 | 0.7 | 0.7 | 0.7 | 0.7 | 0.7 | 0.7 | 0.7 | 1.0 |
| Madagascar — Madagascar | 9.2 | 9.2 | 9.5 | 9.8 | 10.0 | 10.3 | 10.7 | 11.0 | 11.2 | 11.5 |
| Malawi — Malawi | 5.3 | 5.4 | 5.4 | 5.5 | 5.5 | 5.5 | 5.6 | 5.6 | 5.7 | 5.7 |
| Mali — Mali | 5.0 | 5.0 | 5.1 | 5.1 | 5.2 | 5.3 | 5.3 | 5.4 | 5.4 | 5.5 |
| Mauritania — Mauritanie | 1.3 | 1.4 | 1.4 | 1.4 | 1.5 | 1.5 | 1.5 | 1.6 | 1.6 | 1.7 |
| Morocco — Maroc | 0.8 | 1.7 | 1.1 | 1.1 | 1.0 | 0.9 | 0.9 | 0.9 | 1.0 | 0.9 |
| Mozambique — Mozambique | 18.0 | 18.0 | 18.0 | 18.0 | 18.0 | 18.0 | 18.0 | 18.0 | 18.0 | 18.0 |
| Niger — Niger | 7.6 | 7.8 | 8.0 | 8.2 | 3.3 | 8.6 | 8.8 | 9.0 | 9.2 | 9.4 |
| Nigeria — Nigéria | 67.7 | 67.8 | 68.3 | 68.8 | 69.1 | 69.5 | 69.9 | 70.3 | 70.7 | 71.0 |
| Rwanda — Rwanda | 7.4 | 7.5 | 7.8 | 5.4 | 5.5 | 5.5 | 5.5 | 5.5 | 5.5 | 9.9 |
| Senegal — Sénégal | 5.8 | 5.8 | 5.9 | 5.9 | 5.9 | 6.0 | 6.0 | 6.0 | 6.1 | 6.1 |
| Sierra Leone — Sierra Leone | 5.1 | 5.2 | 5.3 | 5.5 | 5.5 | 5.5 | 5.5 | 5.5 | 5.5 | 5.6 |
| Somalia — Somalie | 8.3 | 8.6 | 9.0 | 9.3 | 9.6 | 9.9 | 10.3 | 10.6 | 10.9 | 11.2 |
| South Africa[1] — Afrique du Sud[1] | 33.2 | 30.6 | 30.6 | 30.6 | 30.6 | 30.6 | 33.2 | 33.3 | 30.2 | 30.1 |
| Sudan — Soudan | 18.4 | 18.6 | 18.7 | 18.9 | 19.0 | 19.2 | 19.4 | 19.7 | 19.9 | 20.1 |
| Swaziland — Swaziland | 1.5 | 0.9 | 0.9 | 0.9 | 0.9 | 0.9 | 0.9 | 0.9 | 0.9 | 1.3 |
| Togo — Togo | 5.6 | 5.7 | 5.7 | 5.8 | 5.8 | 5.8 | 5.9 | 4.7 | 5.9 | 6.0 |
| Tunisia — Tunisie | 2.3 | 2.3 | 2.3 | 2.3 | 2.3 | 2.3 | 2.3 | 2.3 | 2.4 | 2.4 |
| Uganda — Ouganda | 36.0 | 36.4 | 36.9 | 37.3 | 37.8 | 38.3 | 38.9 | 39.4 | 40.0 | 40.5 |
| United Rep. of Tanzania — Rép.-Unie de Tanzanie | 22.9 | 23.0 | 23.1 | 23.1 | 23.3 | 23.4 | 23.6 | 23.8 | 24.0 | 24.2 |
| Zambia — Zambie | 8.0 | 8.0 | 8.1 | 8.1 | 8.1 | 8.1 | 8.1 | 8.1 | 8.1 | 9.4 |
| Zimbabwe — Zimbabwe | 8.9 | 9.0 | 9.3 | 9.1 | 9.1 | 9.1 | 9.1 | 9.1 | 8.9 | 9.2 |
| **Northern America — Amérique septentrionale** | 677.1 | 671.0 | 663.2 | 668.4 | 635.0 | 646.1 | 628.2 | 670.1 | 678.8 | 678.5 |
| Canada — Canada | 191.2 | 176.9 | 193.9 | 201.8 | 185.9 | 198.1 | 179.6 | 208.4 | 211.5 | 205.9 |
| United States — Etats-Unis | 485.9 | 494.0 | 469.3 | 466.5 | 449.1 | 448.0 | 448.5 | 461.7 | 467.3 | 472.6 |
| **Latin Amer. and the Carib. — Amér. latine et Caraïb.** | 396.9 | 399.2 | 418.4 | 425.0 | 412.7 | 421.0 | 450.0 | 446.3 | 463.8 | 450.5 |
| Argentina — Argentine | 6.9 | 5.7 | 10.6 | 10.0 | 9.3 | 9.3 | 13.7 | 14.9 | 14.2 | 14.2 |
| Bahamas — Bahamas | 0.1 | ^0.0 | ^0.0 | ^0.0 | ^0.0 | ^0.0 | ^0.0 | ^0.0 | ^0.0 | ^0.0 |

| Region, country or area — Région, pays ou zone | 1997 | 1998 | 1999 | 2000 | 2001 | 2002 | 2003 | 2004 | 2005 | 2006 |
|---|---|---|---|---|---|---|---|---|---|---|
| Belize — Belize | 0.2 | 0.2 | 0.2 | 0.2 | 0.2 | 0.2 | 0.2 | 0.2 | 0.2 | 0.2 |
| Bolivia — Bolivie | 3.0 | 2.9 | 2.6 | 2.6 | 2.7 | 2.7 | 2.9 | 3.0 | 3.1 | 3.1 |
| Brazil — Brésil | 213.5 | 213.7 | 231.6 | 235.4 | 223.6 | 231.0 | 256.1 | 243.4 | 255.9 | 239.5 |
| Chile — Chili | 30.0 | 31.7 | 34.0 | 36.6 | 37.8 | 37.8 | 37.0 | 42.6 | 45.6 | 47.1 |
| Colombia — Colombie | 9.6 | 10.1 | 10.6 | 13.1 | 12.5 | 11.6 | 12.0 | 10.5 | 11.9 | 12.0 |
| Costa Rica — Costa Rica | 5.2 | 5.2 | 5.2 | 5.2 | 5.2 | 5.2 | 5.1 | 4.5 | 4.6 | 4.6 |
| Cuba — Cuba | 3.5 | 3.5 | 1.6 | 1.8 | 1.7 | 2.8 | 2.6 | 2.5 | 2.6 | 2.3 |
| Dominican Republic — Rép. dominicaine | 0.6 | 0.6 | 0.6 | 0.6 | 0.6 | 0.6 | 0.6 | 0.6 | 0.6 | 0.9 |
| Ecuador — Equateur | 12.1 | 11.5 | 5.5 | 5.7 | 6.1 | 6.2 | 6.3 | 6.6 | 6.7 | 6.8 |
| El Salvador — El Salvador | 5.2 | 5.1 | 5.2 | 5.2 | 5.2 | 5.2 | 4.8 | 4.9 | 4.9 | 4.9 |
| French Guiana — Guyane française | 0.1 | 0.1 | 0.1 | 0.1 | 0.1 | 0.2 | 0.2 | 0.2 | 0.2 | 0.2 |
| Guatemala — Guatemala | 13.8 | 14.1 | 14.7 | 15.0 | 15.3 | 15.7 | 15.9 | 16.3 | 16.7 | 17.1 |
| Guyana — Guyana | 1.5 | 1.3 | 1.3 | 1.2 | 1.2 | 1.2 | 1.2 | 1.3 | 1.4 | 1.4 |
| Haiti — Haïti | 2.2 | 2.2 | 2.2 | 2.2 | 2.2 | 2.2 | 2.2 | 2.2 | 2.2 | 2.2 |
| Honduras — Honduras | 9.4 | 9.5 | 9.6 | 9.5 | 9.6 | 9.7 | 9.5 | 9.6 | 9.6 | 9.5 |
| Jamaica — Jamaïque | 0.8 | 0.8 | 0.9 | 0.9 | 0.9 | 0.9 | 0.9 | 0.9 | 0.8 | 0.8 |
| Mexico — Mexique | 44.3 | 45.0 | 45.4 | 45.7 | 45.2 | 44.0 | 44.4 | 45.2 | 44.6 | 44.7 |
| Nicaragua — Nicaragua | 5.8 | 5.9 | 5.9 | 6.0 | 5.9 | 6.0 | 6.0 | 6.0 | 6.0 | 6.1 |
| Panama — Panama | 1.4 | 1.3 | 1.3 | 1.3 | 1.3 | 1.3 | 1.3 | 1.3 | 1.4 | 1.3 |
| Paraguay — Paraguay | 9.4 | 9.5 | 9.6 | 9.6 | 9.7 | 9.8 | 9.9 | 10.0 | 10.1 | 10.2 |
| Peru — Pérou | 8.4 | 9.2 | 9.2 | 9.3 | 8.6 | 8.8 | 8.4 | 8.9 | 9.1 | 9.3 |
| Suriname — Suriname | 0.2 | 0.2 | 0.1 | 0.2 | 0.2 | 0.2 | 0.2 | 0.2 | 0.2 | 0.2 |
| Trinidad and Tobago — Trinité-et-Tobago | 0.1 | 0.1 | 0.1 | 0.1 | 0.1 | 0.1 | 0.1 | 0.1 | 0.1 | 0.1 |
| Uruguay — Uruguay | 5.0 | 5.2 | 5.1 | 2.9 | 3.0 | 3.4 | 3.7 | 5.1 | 5.7 | 6.0 |
| Venezuela (Boliv. Rep. of) — Venezuela (Rép. boliv. du) | 4.7 | 4.6 | 5.3 | 4.7 | 4.6 | 5.1 | 4.8 | 5.3 | 5.3 | 5.6 |
| **Asia — Asie** | **1 071.2** | **1 043.9** | **1 076.6** | **1 055.8** | **1 039.9** | **1 027.7** | **1 027.1** | **1 030.6** | **1 030.3** | **1 020.0** |
| Afghanistan — Afghanistan | 2.8 | 2.9 | 3.0 | 3.0 | 3.1 | 3.1 | 3.1 | 3.2 | 3.2 | 3.3 |
| Armenia — Arménie | 0.1 | 0.0 | 0.0 | 0.1 | ^0.0 | 0.1 | 0.1 | 0.1 | ^0.0 | 0.1 |
| Azerbaijan — Azerbaïdjan | ... | ^0.0 | ^0.0 | ^0.0 | ^0.0 | 0.1 | ^0.0 | ^0.0 | ^0.0 | ^0.0 |
| Bangladesh — Bangladesh | 28.5 | 28.5 | 28.5 | 28.5 | 28.4 | 28.0 | 28.0 | 28.0 | 27.9 | 27.9 |
| Bhutan — Bhoutan | 4.0 | 4.1 | 4.3 | 4.4 | 4.4 | 4.5 | 4.5 | 4.6 | 4.7 | 4.7 |
| Brunei Darussalam — Brunéi Darussalam | 0.2 | 0.2 | 0.1 | 0.1 | 0.1 | 0.1 | 0.1 | 0.1 | 0.1 | 0.1 |
| Cambodia — Cambodge | 11.8 | 11.6 | 11.2 | 10.3 | 10.0 | 9.9 | 9.7 | 9.5 | 9.3 | 9.3 |
| China[2,3] — Chine[2,3] | 310.7 | 298.0 | 331.8 | 323.6 | 316.9 | 312.0 | 309.9 | 305.9 | 302.0 | 298.2 |
| Georgia — Géorgie | ... | 0.0 | 0.0 | 0.0 | 0.3 | 0.4 | 0.4 | 0.5 | 0.6 | 0.6 |
| India — Inde | 296.5 | 296.3 | 296.6 | 296.1 | 296.7 | 319.4 | 321.0 | 326.6 | 328.7 | 329.4 |
| Indonesia — Indonésie | 139.1 | 135.6 | 130.2 | 122.5 | 112.2 | 115.6 | 112.0 | 109.1 | 104.4 | 98.8 |
| Iran (Islamic Rep. of) — Iran (Rép. islamique d') | 1.5 | 1.3 | 1.1 | 1.1 | 1.3 | 0.7 | 0.9 | 0.8 | 0.8 | 0.8 |
| Iraq — Iraq | 0.2 | 0.2 | 0.1 | 0.1 | 0.1 | 0.1 | 0.1 | 0.1 | 0.1 | 0.1 |
| Israel — Israël | 0.1 | 0.1 | 0.1 | 0.1 | ^0.0 | ^0.0 | ^0.0 | ^0.0 | ^0.0 | ^0.0 |
| Japan — Japon | 22.3 | 19.6 | 19.0 | 18.1 | 15.9 | 15.2 | 15.3 | 15.7 | 16.3 | 16.7 |
| Jordan — Jordanie | 0.1 | 0.2 | 0.2 | 0.2 | 0.2 | 0.2 | 0.2 | 0.3 | 0.3 | 0.3 |
| Kazakhstan — Kazakhstan | 0.3 | 0.0 | 0.5 | 0.6 | 0.7 | 0.5 | 0.3 | 0.5 | 0.9 | 0.9 |
| Korea, Dem. P. R. — Corée, R. p. dém. de | 6.5 | 6.9 | 6.9 | 7.0 | 7.1 | 7.1 | 7.2 | 7.2 | 7.3 | 7.3 |
| Korea, Republic of — Corée, République de | 3.5 | 3.9 | 4.1 | 4.0 | 4.0 | 4.1 | 4.1 | 4.7 | 4.8 | 4.9 |
| Lao People's Dem. Rep. — Rép. dém. pop. lao | 6.5 | 6.4 | 6.7 | 6.4 | 6.5 | 6.3 | 6.3 | 6.2 | 6.1 | 6.1 |
| Lebanon — Liban | 0.1 | 0.1 | ^0.0 | ^0.0 | 0.1 | 0.1 | 0.1 | 0.1 | 0.1 | 0.1 |
| Malaysia — Malaisie | 36.0 | 26.4 | 26.6 | 18.4 | 19.4 | 21.1 | 24.7 | 27.5 | 27.6 | 25.5 |
| Mongolia — Mongolie | 0.6 | 0.6 | 0.6 | 0.6 | 0.7 | 0.7 | 0.7 | 0.7 | 0.7 | 0.7 |
| Myanmar — Myanmar | 34.8 | 34.3 | 37.6 | 38.1 | 39.4 | 38.9 | 42.2 | 41.8 | 42.5 | 42.5 |
| Nepal — Népal | 13.2 | 13.9 | 13.9 | 14.0 | 14.0 | 14.0 | 14.0 | 14.0 | 14.0 | 13.9 |
| Pakistan — Pakistan | 30.9 | 31.8 | 33.1 | 33.6 | 33.2 | 27.7 | 28.0 | 28.7 | 29.3 | 29.0 |
| Philippines — Philippines | 41.0 | 42.0 | 43.0 | 44.0 | 44.4 | 16.0 | 16.0 | 16.1 | 16.1 | 15.7 |
| Sri Lanka — Sri Lanka | 6.8 | 6.6 | 6.6 | 6.6 | 6.5 | 6.5 | 6.4 | 6.3 | 6.3 | 6.3 |
| Syrian Arab Republic — Rép. arabe syrienne | 0.1 | 0.1 | 0.1 | 0.1 | 0.1 | 0.1 | 0.1 | 0.1 | 0.1 | 0.1 |
| Thailand — Thaïlande | 23.4 | 23.4 | 23.4 | 26.8 | 27.5 | 28.1 | 28.8 | 28.7 | 28.6 | 28.4 |
| Turkey — Turquie | 18.1 | 17.7 | 16.6 | 15.9 | 15.3 | 16.1 | 15.8 | 16.5 | 16.2 | 16.8 |
| Viet Nam — Viet Nam | 31.3 | 31.0 | 30.2 | 30.9 | 30.8 | 30.7 | 26.4 | 26.5 | 30.8 | 30.8 |

**Roundwood** — Production (solid volume of roundwood without bark): million cubic metres (*continued*)

**Bois rond** — Production (volume solide de bois rond sans écorce) : millions de mètres cubes (*suite*)

| Region, country or area — Région, pays ou zone | 1997 | 1998 | 1999 | 2000 | 2001 | 2002 | 2003 | 2004 | 2005 | 2006 |
|---|---|---|---|---|---|---|---|---|---|---|
| Yemen — Yémen | 0.3 | 0.3 | 0.3 | 0.3 | 0.3 | 0.3 | 0.3 | 0.4 | 0.4 | 0.4 |
| **Europe — Europe** | **523.6** | **472.4** | **531.7** | **592.2** | **564.6** | **578.8** | **608.2** | **622.0** | **689.6** | **669.4** |
| Albania — Albanie | 0.4 | ^0.0 | 0.2 | 0.4 | 0.3 | 0.3 | 0.3 | 0.3 | 0.3 | 0.3 |
| Austria — Autriche | 15.3 | 14.0 | 14.1 | 13.3 | 13.5 | 14.8 | 17.1 | 16.5 | 16.5 | 19.1 |
| Belarus — Bélarus | 17.6 | 5.9 | 6.6 | 6.1 | 6.5 | 6.9 | 7.5 | 8.6 | 8.7 | 8.7 |
| Belgium — Belgique | ... | ... | 4.8 | 4.5 | 4.2 | 4.5 | 4.8 | 4.9 | 5.0 | 5.1 |
| Bosnia and Herzegovina — Bosnie-Herzégovine | 4.0 | 4.1 | 4.1 | 4.3 | 3.8 | 4.2 | 4.1 | 4.0 | 3.8 | 3.8 |
| Bulgaria — Bulgarie | 3.0 | 3.2 | 4.4 | 4.8 | 4.0 | 4.8 | 4.8 | 6.0 | 5.9 | 6.0 |
| Croatia — Croatie | 3.1 | 3.4 | 3.5 | 3.7 | 3.5 | 3.6 | 3.8 | 3.8 | 4.0 | 4.5 |
| Czech Republic — République tchèque | 13.5 | 14.0 | 14.2 | 14.4 | 14.4 | 14.5 | 15.1 | 15.6 | 15.5 | 17.7 |
| Denmark — Danemark | 2.1 | 1.6 | 1.6 | 3.0 | 1.6 | 1.4 | 1.6 | 1.5 | 3.0 | 2.4 |
| Estonia — Estonie | 5.4 | 6.1 | 6.7 | 8.9 | 10.2 | 10.5 | 10.5 | 6.8 | 5.5 | 5.8 |
| Finland — Finlande | 51.3 | 53.7 | 53.6 | 54.3 | 52.2 | 53.4 | 54.2 | 54.4 | 52.3 | 50.8 |
| France — France | 41.1 | 35.5 | 36.0 | 45.8 | 39.8 | 35.4 | 32.8 | 33.6 | 63.2 | 65.6 |
| Germany — Allemagne | 38.2 | 39.1 | 37.6 | 53.7 | 39.5 | 42.4 | 51.2 | 54.5 | 56.9 | 62.3 |
| Greece — Grèce | 1.7 | 1.7 | 2.2 | 2.2 | 1.9 | 1.6 | 1.7 | 1.7 | 1.5 | 1.5 |
| Hungary — Hongrie | 4.2 | 4.2 | 5.2 | 5.9 | 5.8 | 5.8 | 5.8 | 5.7 | 5.9 | 5.9 |
| Ireland — Irlande | 2.2 | 2.3 | 2.6 | 2.7 | 2.5 | 2.6 | 2.7 | 2.6 | 2.6 | 2.7 |
| Italy — Italie | 9.1 | 9.6 | 11.1 | 9.3 | 8.1 | 7.5 | 8.2 | 8.7 | 8.7 | 8.6 |
| Latvia — Lettonie | 8.7 | 10.0 | 14.0 | 14.3 | 12.8 | 13.5 | 12.9 | 12.8 | 12.8 | 12.8 |
| Lithuania — Lituanie | 5.1 | 4.9 | 4.9 | 5.5 | 5.7 | 6.1 | 6.3 | 6.1 | 6.0 | 5.9 |
| Luxembourg — Luxembourg | ... | ... | 0.3 | 0.3 | 0.3 | 0.3 | 0.3 | 0.3 | 0.2 | 0.3 |
| Moldova — Moldova | 0.4 | 0.4 | ^0.0 | 0.1 | 0.1 | 0.1 | 0.1 | 0.1 | 0.1 | 0.1 |
| Netherlands — Pays-Bas | 1.1 | 1.0 | 1.0 | 1.0 | 0.9 | 0.8 | 1.0 | 1.0 | 1.1 | 1.1 |
| Norway — Norvège | 8.3 | 8.2 | 8.4 | 8.2 | 9.0 | 8.7 | 8.3 | 8.8 | 9.7 | 8.6 |
| Poland — Pologne | 21.7 | 23.1 | 24.3 | 26.0 | 25.0 | 27.1 | 30.8 | 32.7 | 31.9 | 32.4 |
| Portugal — Portugal | 9.0 | 8.5 | 9.0 | 10.8 | 8.9 | 8.7 | 9.7 | 10.9 | 10.7 | 10.8 |
| Romania — Roumanie | 13.5 | 11.6 | 12.7 | 13.1 | 12.4 | 15.2 | 15.4 | 15.8 | 14.5 | 13.8 |
| Russian Federation — Fédération de Russie | 134.7 | 95.0 | 143.6 | 158.1 | 164.7 | 165.0 | 174.0 | 178.4 | 185.0 | 190.6 |
| Serbia and Montenegro — Serbie-et-Monténégro | 2.8 | 2.7 | 2.5 | 3.4 | 2.5 | 2.9 | 3.2 | 3.5 | 3.2 | 3.2 |
| Slovakia — Slovaquie | 4.9 | 5.5 | 5.8 | 6.2 | 5.8 | 5.8 | 6.4 | 7.2 | 9.3 | 7.9 |
| Slovenia — Slovénie | 2.2 | 2.1 | 2.1 | 2.3 | 2.3 | 2.3 | 2.6 | 2.6 | 2.7 | 3.2 |
| Spain — Espagne | 15.6 | 14.9 | 14.8 | 14.3 | 15.1 | 15.8 | 16.1 | 16.3 | 15.5 | 15.7 |
| Sweden — Suède | 60.2 | 60.6 | 58.7 | 63.3 | 63.2 | 66.6 | 67.1 | 67.3 | 98.2 | 62.0 |
| Switzerland — Suisse | 4.5 | 4.3 | 4.7 | 9.2 | 5.7 | 4.6 | 5.1 | 5.1 | 5.3 | 5.7 |
| TFYR of Macedonia — L'ex-R.y. Macédoine | 0.8 | 0.7 | 0.8 | 1.1 | 0.7 | 0.7 | 0.8 | 0.8 | 0.8 | 0.9 |
| Ukraine — Ukraine | 6.1 | 8.5 | 7.9 | 9.9 | 9.9 | 12.3 | 13.8 | 14.9 | 14.6 | 15.2 |
| United Kingdom — Royaume-Uni | 7.5 | 7.3 | 7.5 | 7.8 | 7.9 | 7.8 | 8.0 | 8.3 | 8.5 | 8.4 |
| **Oceania — Océanie** | **54.2** | **53.5** | **55.6** | **59.8** | **60.5** | **60.4** | **61.6** | **60.9** | **60.2** | **62.4** |
| Australia — Australie | 26.7 | 28.1 | 27.7 | 31.2 | 31.1 | 29.7 | 31.6 | 31.9 | 31.9 | 33.9 |
| Fiji — Fidji | 0.5 | 0.5 | 0.5 | 0.5 | 0.5 | 0.4 | 0.4 | 0.5 | 0.5 | 0.5 |
| New Zealand — Nouvelle-Zélande | 17.1 | 15.3 | 17.7 | 19.3 | 20.7 | 22.1 | 21.2 | 19.8 | 19.0 | 19.3 |
| Papua New Guinea — Papouasie-Nvl-Guinée | 8.8 | 8.6 | 8.6 | 7.7 | 7.2 | 7.2 | 7.2 | 7.2 | 7.2 | 7.2 |
| Samoa — Samoa | 0.1 | 0.1 | 0.1 | 0.1 | 0.1 | 0.1 | 0.1 | 0.1 | 0.1 | 0.1 |
| Solomon Islands — Iles Salomon | 0.9 | 0.9 | 0.9 | 0.9 | 0.7 | 0.7 | 0.9 | 1.2 | 1.3 | 1.3 |
| Vanuatu — Vanuatu | 0.1 | 0.1 | 0.1 | 0.1 | 0.1 | 0.1 | 0.1 | 0.1 | 0.1 | 0.1 |

Source

Food and Agriculture Organization of the United Nations (FAO), Rome, FAOSTAT database, last accessed February 2008.

Source

Organisation des Nations Unies pour l'alimentation et l'agriculture (FAO), Rome, la base de données de la FAOSTAT, dernier accès février 2008.

Notes

1 Data include those for Namibia.

2 For statistical purposes, the data for China do not include those for the Hong Kong Special Administrative Region (Hong Kong SAR) and Macao Special Administrative Region (Macao SAR).

3 Data include those for Taiwan Province of China.

Notes

1 Les données comprennent les chiffres pour la Namibie.

2 Pour la présentation des statistiques, les données pour la Chine ne comprennent pas la Région Administrative Spéciale de Hong Kong (Hong Kong RAS) et la Région Administrative Spéciale de Macao (Macao RAS).

3 Les données comprennent les chiffres pour la province de Taiwan.

| Country or area — Pays ou zone | Capture production — Captures | | | | | Aquaculture production — Production de l'aquaculture | | | | |
|---|---|---|---|---|---|---|---|---|---|---|
| | 2002 | 2003 | 2004 | 2005 | 2006 | 2002 | 2003 | 2004 | 2005 | 2006 |
| Afghanistan[1] Afghanistan[1] | 900 | 900 | 1 000 | 1 000 | 1 000 | ... | ... | ... | ... | ... |
| Albania Albanie | 3 655 | 2 800[1] | 4 549 | 5 000 | 5 729 | 860 | 1 473 | 1 569 | 1 473 | 1 970 |
| Algeria Algérie | 134 320 | 141 528 | 113 462 | 126 839 | 145 762 | 476 | 417[1] | 586[1] | 368 | 288 |
| American Samoa Samoa américaines | 6 971 | 4 984 | 4 043 | 3 950 | 5 421 | ... | ... | ... | ... | ... |
| Angola Angola | 254 973 | 211 539 | 240 005 | 227 000[1] | 213 948 | ... | ... | ... | ... | ... |
| Anguilla Anguilla | 250[1] | 250[1] | 250 | 250 | 250 | ... | ... | ... | ... | ... |
| Antigua and Barbuda Antigua-et-Barbuda | 2 374 | 2 587 | 2 527 | 2 999 | 3 092 | ... | ... | ... | ... | ... |
| Argentina Argentine | 958 644 | 915 994 | 945 943 | 931 333 | 1 182 185 | 1 457 | 1 647 | 1 848 | 2 430 | 2 528 |
| Armenia Arménie | 465 | 569 | 218 | 250[1] | 350 | 1 020 | 1 064 | 813 | 739[1] | 1 056 |
| Aruba Aruba | 163[1] | 160[1] | 162 | 162[1] | 145 | ... | ... | ... | ... | ... |
| Australia Australie | 197 184 | 215 259 | 230 679 | 237 042 | 192 574 | 38 566 | 38 793 | 44 142 | 41 389 | 48 882 |
| Austria Autriche | 350 | 372 | 400 | 370 | 360 | 2 333 | 2 233 | 2 267 | 2 420 | 2 503 |
| Azerbaijan Azerbaïdjan | 11 188 | 6 435 | 9 258 | 9 001 | 3 983 | 78 | 122 | 184 | 114 | 110 |
| Bahamas Bahamas | 12 192 | 12 611 | 11 347 | 11 064 | 10 598 | 25[1] | 42 | 10 | 10 | 22 |
| Bahrain Bahreïn | 11 204 | 13 638 | 14 334 | 11 854 | 15 594 | 3 | 4 | 8 | 3 | 2 |
| Bangladesh Bangladesh | 1 103 855 | 1 141 241 | 1 187 274 | 1 333 866 | 1 436 496 | 786 604 | 856 956 | 914 752 | 882 091 | 892 049 |
| Barbados Barbade | 2 520 | 2 838 | 2 148 | 2 182 | 1 974 | ... | ... | ... | ... | ... |
| Belarus Bélarus | 5 877 | 6 925 | 890 | 900[1] | 900[1] | 6 523 | 5 393 | 4 150 | 4 150[1] | 4 150[1] |
| Belgium Belgique | 29 028 | 26 831 | 26 735 | 24 567 | 23 019 | 1 600 | 1 010[1] | 1 200[1] | 1 200[1] | 1 200[1] |
| Belize Belize | 54 655 | 6 620 | 4 152 | 4 206 | 4 164 | 4 400 | 10 160 | 11 428 | 10 858 | 7 624 |
| Benin Bénin | 40 663 | 41 648 | 39 988 | 38 035 | 38 021 | 7 | 7[1] | 7 | 350 | 415 |
| Bermuda Bermudes | 394 | 352 | 379 | 406 | 380 | ... | ... | ... | ... | ... |
| Bhutan Bhoutan | 300[1] | 300[1] | 300[1] | 300[1] | 300[1] | ... | ... | ... | ... | ... |
| Bolivia Bolivie | 6 300[1] | 6 599 | 6 746 | 6 660 | 6 700[1] | 418 | 375 | 450 | 430 | 430[1] |
| Bosnia and Herzegovina Bosnie-Herzégovine | 2 005[1] | 2 005[1] | 2 005[1] | 2 005[1] | 2 005[1] | 4 685 | 6 635 | 6 394 | 7 070 | 7 621 |
| Botswana Botswana | 139 | 122 | 161 | 132 | 81 | ... | ... | ... | ... | ... |
| Brazil Brésil | 755 582 | 712 144 | 746 217 | 750 261 | 779 113 | 247 678 | 273 268 | 269 699 | 257 783 | 271 696 |
| British Indian Ocean Terr. Terr. brit. de l'océan Indien | 28 | ^0 | ^0 | ^0 | ^0 | ... | ... | ... | ... | ... |

| Country or area—Pays ou zone | Capture production — Captures | | | | | Aquaculture production — Production de l'aquaculture | | | | |
|---|---|---|---|---|---|---|---|---|---|---|
| | 2002 | 2003 | 2004 | 2005 | 2006 | 2002 | 2003 | 2004 | 2005 | 2006 |
| British Virgin Islands<br>Iles Vierges britanniques | 1 062 | 2 771 | 1 262 | 1 300[1] | 1 300[1] | ... | ... | ... | ... | ... |
| Brunei Darussalam<br>Brunéi Darussalam | 2 058 | 2 226 | 2 428 | 2 400[1] | 2 400[1] | 157 | 160 | 708 | 708[1] | 700[1] |
| Bulgaria<br>Bulgarie | 15 008 | 12 035 | 8 252 | 5 434 | 7 544 | 2 308 | 4 465 | 2 489 | 3 145 | 3 257 |
| Burkina Faso<br>Burkina Faso | 8 500 | 9 000 | 9 000[1] | 9 000 | 9 500 | 5 | 5 | 5[1] | 55[1] | 200 |
| Burundi<br>Burundi | 11 000[1] | 14 697 | 13 855 | 14 000[1] | 14 000[1] | 150[1] | 200 | 200 | 200[1] | 200[1] |
| Cambodia<br>Cambodge | 406 182 | 364 357 | 305 817 | 384 000 | 482 500 | 14 600 | 18 500 | 20 675 | 26 000 | 34 200 |
| Cameroon<br>Cameroun | 130 135 | 117 801 | 129 000[1] | 142 345 | 137 232 | 330 | 320 | 330[1] | 337 | 340[1] |
| Canada<br>Canada | 1 062 866 | 1 110 547 | 1 176 212 | 1 103 189 | 1 063 033 | 170 746 | 150 713 | 145 018 | 154 563 | 170 938 |
| Cape Verde<br>Cap-Vert | 8 145 | 8 169 | 8 510 | 8 794 | 9 673 | ... | ... | ... | ... | ... |
| Cayman Islands<br>Iles Caïmanes | 125 | 125 | 125 | 125 | 125 | ... | ... | ... | ... | ... |
| Central African Rep.[1]<br>Rép. centrafricaine[1] | 15 000 | 15 000 | 15 000 | 15 000 | 15 000 | ... | ... | ... | ... | ... |
| Chad[1]<br>Tchad[1] | 75 000 | 70 000 | 70 000 | 70 000 | 70 000 | ... | ... | ... | ... | ... |
| Channel Islands<br>Iles Anglo-Normandes | 3 449 | 3 526 | 3 201 | 3 505 | 3 468 | 580 | 684 | 775 | 650 | 660[1] |
| Chile<br>Chili | 4 276 065 | 3 613 525 | 4 921 425 | 4 328 646 | 4 168 461 | 545 655 | 563 435 | 665 421 | 698 214 | 802 410 |
| China[2]<br>Chine[2] | 16 553 144 | 16 755 653 | 16 892 793 | 17 053 191 | 17 092 146 | 27 767 251 | 28 886 199 | 30 614 968 | 32 415 523 | 34 429 122 |
| China, Hong Kong SAR<br>Chine, Hong Kong RAS | 169 790 | 157 444 | 167 544 | 161 964 | 154 536 | 4 302 | 4 857 | 4 615 | 4 130 | 4 125 |
| China, Macao SAR[1]<br>Chine, Macao RAS[1] | 1 500 | 1 500 | 1 500 | 1 500 | 1 500 | ... | ... | ... | ... | ... |
| Colombia<br>Colombie | 124 722 | 129 792 | 124 951 | 94 806 | 95 000[1] | 57 160 | 60 895 | 60 072 | 60 072 | 60 100[1] |
| Comoros<br>Comores | 13 102 | 14 115 | 14 935 | 15 070 | 15 070[1] | ... | ... | ... | ... | ... |
| Congo<br>Congo | 51 927 | 54 659 | 54 234 | 58 368 | 59 485 | 68 | 69 | 72 | 80 | 21 |
| Cook Islands<br>Iles Cook | 1 260[1] | 2 543[1] | 3 666 | 3 782 | 3 773 | ^0 | ^0 | ^0 | ^0 | ^0 |
| Costa Rica<br>Costa Rica | 33 020 | 29 397 | 20 850 | 22 340 | 22 340[1] | 17 892 | 20 546 | 24 708 | 24 038 | 19 962 |
| Côte d'Ivoire<br>Côte d'Ivoire | 70 156 | 69 539 | 54 401 | 31 565 | 32 644 | 806 | 866 | 866 | 866[1] | 817 |
| Croatia<br>Croatie | 21 230 | 19 946 | 30 164 | 34 665 | 37 853 | 9 786[1] | 9 465[1] | 11 637[1] | 12 137[1] | 14 897[1] |
| Cuba<br>Cuba | 32 538 | 40 353 | 36 090 | 28 664 | 27 567 | 27 044 | 26 897 | 27 842 | 22 635 | 27 186 |
| Cyprus<br>Chypre | 1 968 | 1 791 | 1 567 | 1 916 | 2 155 | 1 862 | 1 821 | 2 175 | 2 540[1] | 2 667[1] |
| Czech Republic<br>République tchèque | 4 983 | 5 127 | 4 528 | 4 242 | 4 646 | 19 210 | 19 670 | 19 384 | 20 455 | 20 431 |
| Dem. Rep. of the Congo<br>Rép. dém. du Congo | 239 000 | 235 765 | 237 372 | 236 640 | 236 588 | 2 965 | 2 965[1] | 2 965[1] | 2 965[1] | 2 970[1] |
| Denmark<br>Danemark | 1 442 348 | 1 036 154 | 1 090 596 | 910 599 | 867 706 | 32 026 | 37 772 | 42 814 | 39 012 | 37 188 |
| Djibouti<br>Djibouti | 260 | 260[1] | 260[1] | 260[1] | 260[1] | ... | ... | ... | ... | ... |

| Country or area — Pays ou zone | Capture production — Captures | | | | | Aquaculture production — Production de l'aquaculture | | | | |
|---|---|---|---|---|---|---|---|---|---|---|
| | 2002 | 2003 | 2004 | 2005 | 2006 | 2002 | 2003 | 2004 | 2005 | 2006 |
| Dominica<br>Dominique | 1 270 | 950[1] | 700[1] | 579 | 694 | 3 | 3[1] | 3[1] | ... | ... |
| Dominican Republic<br>Rép. dominicaine | 17 261 | 18 097 | 14 223 | 11 106 | 12 914 | 3 554 | 1 944[1] | 2 000[1] | 980 | 980[1] |
| Ecuador<br>Equateur | 318 542 | 397 764 | 338 910 | 407 376 | 448 828 | 62 735[1] | 74 500[1] | 77 300[1] | 78 300[1] | 78 300[1] |
| Egypt<br>Egypte | 425 170 | 430 809 | 393 494 | 349 553 | 375 894 | 376 296 | 445 181 | 471 535 | 539 748 | 595 030 |
| El Salvador<br>El Salvador | 34 455 | 35 410 | 42 415 | 41 114 | 43 218 | 781 | 1 131 | 2 219 | 2 203 | 3 078 |
| Equatorial Guinea[1]<br>Guinée équatoriale[1] | 3 400 | 3 200 | 3 000 | 2 750 | 2 500 | ... | ... | ... | ... | ... |
| Eritrea<br>Erythrée | 7 832 | 6 689 | 7 404 | 4 027 | 8 813 | ... | ... | ... | ... | ... |
| Estonia<br>Estonie | 101 453 | 79 082 | 87 906 | 98 772 | 86 490 | 257 | 372 | 252 | 555 | 703 |
| Ethiopia<br>Ethiopie | 12 300 | 9 213 | 10 005 | 9 450 | 9 890 | 0 | 0 | 0 | 0 | 0 |
| Faeroe Islands<br>Iles Féroé | 525 991 | 620 991 | 599 386 | 565 260 | 623 122 | 56 102 | 62 746 | 46 077 | 23 455 | 18 574 |
| Falkland Is. (Malvinas)<br>Iles Falkland (Malvinas) | 53 261 | 74 898 | 55 369 | 84 546 | 75 288 | 0 | 0 | 21 | 2 | 2 |
| Fiji<br>Fidji | 38 800 | 34 689 | 46 656 | 42 500[1] | 46 891 | 401 | 144 | 99 | 99[1] | 428 |
| Finland<br>Finlande | 142 301 | 121 954 | 135 427 | 131 741 | 149 450 | 15 132 | 12 558 | 12 821 | 14 355 | 12 891 |
| France<br>France | 631 621 | 638 393 | 599 542 | 574 552 | 573 375 | 251 990[1] | 239 844[1] | 261 470[1] | 258 810[1] | 238 860[1] |
| French Guiana<br>Guyane française | 4 782[1] | 5 565[1] | 5 514[1] | 6 474 | 5 170 | 38 | 37 | 37 | 37 | 37 |
| French Polynesia<br>Polynésie française | 15 543 | 14 099[1] | 12 198[1] | 12 152 | 13 409 | 65 | 60 | 65 | 75 | 64 |
| Gabon<br>Gabon | 41 570 | 45 481 | 46 072 | 43 863 | 41 521 | 83 | 80 | 80 | 78 | 126 |
| Gambia<br>Gambie | 45 769 | 36 864 | 31 423 | 33 086[1] | 34 912[1] | ... | ... | ... | ... | ... |
| Georgia<br>Géorgie | 1 811 | 3 306 | 2 951 | 3 000[1] | 3 000[1] | 52 | 56 | 72 | 72[1] | 75[1] |
| Germany<br>Allemagne | 224 452 | 260 867 | 262 103 | 285 668 | 297 837 | 49 852 | 74 280 | 57 233 | 44 685 | 35 379 |
| Ghana<br>Ghana | 371 178 | 390 755 | 399 371 | 391 867 | 366 919 | 6 000[1] | 938 | 950 | 1 154 | 1 150[1] |
| Greece<br>Grèce | 96 343 | 93 383 | 93 886 | 92 423 | 98 238 | 87 928 | 101 434 | 97 143 | 106 308[1] | 113 384[1] |
| Greenland<br>Groenland | 195 624 | 175 321 | 216 302 | 216 302[1] | 216 302[1] | ... | ... | ... | ... | ... |
| Grenada<br>Grenade | 2 171 | 2 544 | 2 039 | 2 053 | 2 169 | ... | ... | ... | ... | ... |
| Guadeloupe<br>Guadeloupe | 10 100 | 10 100 | 10 100 | 10 100 | 10 100 | 23 | 31 | 31 | 31 | 31 |
| Guam<br>Guam | 231 | 162 | 180 | 162 | 729 | 233[1] | ... | ... | | 162 |
| Guatemala<br>Guatemala | 23 427 | 23 696 | 10 012[1] | 18 366 | 18 667 | 7 978[1] | 6 346[1] | 4 908[1] | 9 008[1] | 16 293 |
| Guinea<br>Guinée | 92 755 | 120 242 | 93 947 | 96 571[1] | 94 000[1] | ... | ... | ... | ... | ... |
| Guinea-Bissau[1]<br>Guinée-Bissau[1] | 7 324 | 6 153 | 6 200 | 6 200 | 6 200 | ... | ... | ... | ... | ... |
| Guyana<br>Guyana | 48 017 | 59 695 | 56 719 | 53 370 | 54 000[1] | 608 | 608[1] | 608[1] | 608 | 660[1] |

**Fish production**—Capture and aquaculture: metric tons (*continued*)
**Production halieutique**—Pêche de capture et aquaculture : tonnes (*suite*)

| Country or area—Pays ou zone | Capture production — Captures | | | | | Aquaculture production — Production de l'aquaculture | | | | |
|---|---|---|---|---|---|---|---|---|---|---|
| | 2002 | 2003 | 2004 | 2005 | 2006 | 2002 | 2003 | 2004 | 2005 | 2006 |
| Haiti<br>Haïti | 7 400[1] | 8 000[1] | 8 300 | 9 000[1] | 10 000[1] | ... | ... | ... | ... | ... |
| Honduras<br>Honduras | 7 150[1] | 7 667[1] | 12 105[1] | 16 558[1] | 16 894[1] | 14 557 | 20 035 | 22 520 | 29 380 | 29 400[1] |
| Hungary<br>Hongrie | 6 750 | 6 536 | 7 242 | 7 609 | 7 543 | 11 574 | 11 870 | 12 744 | 13 661 | 14 686 |
| Iceland<br>Islande | 2 134 546 | 1 986 539 | 1 733 702 | 1 664 657 | 1 327 063 | 3 585 | 6 214 | 8 868 | 8 256 | 8 241 |
| India<br>Inde | 3 736 603 | 3 712 149 | 3 391 009 | 3 691 362 | 3 855 467 | 2 187 189 | 2 312 971 | 2 794 636 | 2 961 978 | 3 123 135 |
| Indonesia<br>Indonésie | 4 322 764 | 4 627 149 | 4 643 943 | 4 695 977 | 4 759 080 | 914 071 | 996 659 | 1 045 051 | 1 197 109 | 1 292 899[1] |
| Iran (Islamic Rep. of)<br>Iran (Rép. islamique d') | 324 853 | 350 122 | 369 990 | 410 558 | 445 852 | 76 817 | 91 714 | 104 330 | 112 001 | 129 708 |
| Iraq<br>Iraq | 26 000 | 17 200 | 12 936 | 29 929 | 59 259 | 2 000[1] | 2 000[1] | 13 947 | 17 941 | 14 867 |
| Ireland<br>Irlande | 282 857 | 266 218 | 280 620 | 262 548 | 211 110 | 62 568 | 62 516 | 58 359 | 60 050 | 53 122 |
| Isle of Man<br>Ile de Man | 3 127 | 2 984 | 2 627 | 2 764 | 1 209 | ... | ... | ... | ... | ... |
| Israel<br>Israël | 5 043 | 4 055 | 3 340 | 4 151 | 3 820 | 22 256 | 20 776 | 22 303 | 22 404 | 22 216 |
| Italy<br>Italie | 269 846 | 295 694 | 287 084 | 296 889 | 315 436 | 184 482 | 192 022 | 118 486 | 181 383 | 173 083 |
| Jamaica<br>Jamaïque | 7 797 | 8 702 | 13 471 | 13 096 | 13 000[1] | 6 150 | 2 969 | 4 495 | 5 670 | 5 700[1] |
| Japan<br>Japon | 4 360 664[1] | 4 670 452 | 4 311 819 | 4 089 821[1] | 4 186 980[1] | 826 715 | 823 873 | 776 421 | 746 221 | 733 891 |
| Jordan<br>Jordanie | 526 | 481 | 494 | 510 | 485 | 515 | 650 | 487 | 561 | 560 |
| Kazakhstan<br>Kazakhstan | 24 910 | 25 371 | 33 896 | 34 888 | 35 148 | 778 | 820 | 589 | 1 102 | 528 |
| Kenya<br>Kenya | 144 512 | 120 051 | 126 867 | 147 304 | 158 684 | 798 | 1 012 | 1 035 | 1 047 | 1 012 |
| Kiribati<br>Kiribati | 31 601 | 31 535 | 31 600[1] | 34 000[1] | 31 000[1] | 14 | 9 | 9[1] | 12 | 10[1] |
| Korea, Dem. P. R.[1]<br>Corée, R. p. dém. de[1] | 205 000 | 205 000 | 205 000 | 205 000 | 205 000 | 63 700 | 63 700 | 63 700 | 63 700 | 63 700 |
| Korea, Republic of<br>Corée, République de | 1 671 630 | 1 643 148 | 1 575 473 | 1 639 069 | 1 749 929 | 296 783 | 387 791 | 405 748 | 436 571 | 513 568 |
| Kuwait<br>Koweït | 5 360 | 4 059 | 4 833 | 4 895 | 5 635 | 195[1] | 366 | 375 | 327 | 568 |
| Kyrgyzstan<br>Kirghizistan | 48 | 14 | 7 | 7[1] | 7[1] | 94 | 12 | 20 | 20[1] | 20[1] |
| Lao People's Dem. Rep.<br>Rép. dém. pop. lao | 33 440 | 29 800 | 29 800[1] | 29 800[1] | 29 800[1] | 59 716 | 64 900 | 64 900 | 78 000 | 78 000 |
| Latvia<br>Lettonie | 113 677 | 114 543 | 125 391 | 150 618 | 140 389 | 430 | 637 | 545 | 542 | 565 |
| Lebanon<br>Liban | 3 970 | 3 898 | 3 866 | 3 798 | 3 811 | 790 | 790 | 790 | 803 | 803 |
| Lesotho<br>Lesotho | 40 | 42 | 45 | 45 | 45 | 8[1] | 4 | 2 | 1 | 2 |
| Liberia<br>Libéria | 11 042 | 10 864 | 14 525 | 13 347 | 10 424 | 14[1] | 14[1] | ... | ... | ... |
| Libyan Arab Jamah.<br>Jamah. arabe libyenne | 44 308[1] | 42 428[1] | 39 971 | 40 164[1] | 40 347[1] | 0 | 0 | 316[1] | 481[1] | 480[1] |
| Lithuania<br>Lituanie | 150 146 | 157 205 | 161 988 | 139 785 | 154 548 | 1 750 | 2 356 | 2 697 | 2 013 | 2 224 |
| Madagascar<br>Madagascar | 141 299 | 140 838 | 146 521 | 134 859 | 134 417 | 9 713 | 9 457 | 8 793 | 9 376 | 11 213 |

| Country or area — Pays ou zone | Capture production — Captures | | | | | Aquaculture production — Production de l'aquaculture | | | | |
|---|---|---|---|---|---|---|---|---|---|---|
| | 2002 | 2003 | 2004 | 2005 | 2006 | 2002 | 2003 | 2004 | 2005 | 2006 |
| Malawi<br>Malawi | 41 329 | 53 543 | 56 463 | 58 783 | 71 287 | 642 | 666 | 733 | 812 | 1 500 |
| Malaysia<br>Malaisie | 1 275 555 | 1 287 084 | 1 335 764 | 1 214 183 | 1 296 335 | 165 119 | 167 160 | 171 270 | 175 834 | 168 317 |
| Maldives<br>Maldives | 163 388 | 155 415 | 158 583 | 185 980 | 184 158 | ... | ... | ... | ... | ... |
| Mali<br>Mali | 100 000[1] | 100 000[1] | 100 000[1] | 100 000[1] | 100 000[1] | 1 008 | 1 008[1] | 1 008[1] | 1 008[1] | 1 000[1] |
| Malta<br>Malte | 1 084 | 1 138 | 1 138 | 1 406 | 2 411 | 1 116 | 887 | 868 | 736 | 1 126[1] |
| Marshall Islands<br>Iles Marshall | 39 752 | 38 775 | 47 576 | 57 164 | 42 019 | ... | ... | ... | ... | ... |
| Martinique<br>Martinique | 6 200[1] | 6 200 | 6 200 | 5 500 | 6 300 | 80 | 100 | 92 | 92 | 92 |
| Mauritania<br>Mauritanie | 156 131[1] | 199 650[1] | 270 733 | 304 877 | 193 230[1] | ... | ... | ... | ... | ... |
| Mauritius<br>Maurice | 10 706 | 10 968 | 9 971 | 9 855 | 8 341 | 56 | 33 | 350 | 400 | 443 |
| Mayotte<br>Mayotte | 4 754 | 3 464 | 2 306 | 2 214 | 5 772 | ... | 213 | 170 | 164 | 140 |
| Mexico<br>Mexique | 1 450 719 | 1 357 191 | 1 258 973 | 1 304 830 | 1 300 000[1] | 73 675 | 84 475 | 104 354 | 133 104 | 158 642 |
| Micronesia (Fed. States of)<br>Micronésie (Etats féd. de) | 22 157[1] | 32 378[1] | 29 235 | 29 336 | 11 630 | ^0 | ^0 | ^0 | ^0 | ^0 |
| Moldova<br>Moldova | 565 | 343 | 487 | 531 | 612 | 1 765 | 2 638 | 4 470 | 4 470[1] | 4 470[1] |
| Monaco[1]<br>Monaco[1] | 3 | 3 | 3 | 2 | 1 | ... | ... | ... | ... | ... |
| Mongolia<br>Mongolie | 263 | 382 | 305 | 366 | 289 | ... | ... | ... | ... | ... |
| Montenegro[1]<br>Monténégro[1] | ... | ... | ... | ... | 900 | ... | ... | ... | ... | 11 |
| Montserrat<br>Montserrat | 46 | 50[1] | 50[1] | 50[1] | 50[1] | ... | ... | ... | ... | ... |
| Morocco<br>Maroc | 894 977 | 885 131 | 940 932 | 1 024 484 | 864 922 | 1 670 | 1 538 | 1 718 | 2 257 | 1 161 |
| Mozambique<br>Mozambique | 36 462 | 43 933[1] | 44 683[1] | 42 514 | 42 536 | 677 | 409 | 446 | 1 222 | 1 174 |
| Myanmar<br>Myanmar | 1 284 340 | 1 343 860 | 1 586 600 | 1 732 250 | 2 006 790 | 190 120 | 252 010 | 400 360 | 485 220 | 574 990 |
| Namibia<br>Namibie | 625 099 | 637 227 | 571 708 | 553 995 | 509 395 | 50 | 50[1] | 50[1] | 50[1] | 50[1] |
| Nauru<br>Nauru | 22 | 44 | 18 | 39 | 39[1] | ... | ... | ... | ... | ... |
| Nepal<br>Népal | 17 900 | 18 888 | 19 947 | 19 983 | 20 016 | 17 100 | 17 680 | 20 000 | 22 480 | 25 409 |
| Netherlands<br>Pays-Bas | 464 036 | 526 281 | 521 636 | 549 208 | 435 335 | 54 429 | 66 540 | 78 598 | 71 370 | 43 945[1] |
| Netherlands Antilles[1]<br>Antilles néerlandaises[1] | 12 901 | 20 149 | 17 286 | 650 | 6 247 | ... | ... | ... | ... | ... |
| New Caledonia<br>Nouvelle-Calédonie | 3 417[1] | 3 513 | 3 768 | 3 315 | 3 091 | 1 918 | 1 784 | 2 290 | 2 533 | 2 365 |
| New Zealand<br>Nouvelle-Zélande | 588 691 | 550 943 | 545 950 | 545 118 | 470 708 | 86 583 | 84 641 | 92 220 | 105 301 | 107 522 |
| Nicaragua<br>Nicaragua | 16 421 | 15 326 | 19 297 | 30 920 | 33 285 | 6 089 | 7 005 | 7 880 | 9 983 | 11 220 |
| Niger<br>Niger | 23 560 | 55 860 | 51 466 | 50 018 | 29 835 | 40 | 40 | 40 | 40 | 40 |
| Nigeria<br>Nigéria | 481 056 | 475 162 | 465 251 | 523 182 | 552 323 | 30 663 | 30 677 | 43 950 | 56 355 | 84 578 |

| Country or area — Pays ou zone | Capture production — Captures | | | | | Aquaculture production — Production de l'aquaculture | | | | |
|---|---|---|---|---|---|---|---|---|---|---|
| | 2002 | 2003 | 2004 | 2005 | 2006 | 2002 | 2003 | 2004 | 2005 | 2006 |
| Niue[1] <br> Nioué[1] | 200 | 200 | 200 | 203 | 203 | ... | ... | ... | ... | ... |
| Northern Mariana Islands <br> Iles Mariannes du Nord | 198 | 173 | 170 | 196 | 183 | ... | ... | ... | ... | ... |
| Norway <br> Norvège | 2 740 344 | 2 548 975 | 2 524 464 | 2 392 988 | 2 255 513 | 551 297 | 584 423 | 636 802 | 661 811 | 708 780 |
| Occupied Palestinian Terr. <br> Terr. palestinien occupé | 2 379 | 1 508 | 2 951 | 1 805 | 1 000[1] | ... | ... | ... | ... | ... |
| Oman <br> Oman | 142 670 | 138 481 | 165 082 | 150 571 | 153 989 | ^0 | 352 | 503 | 173 | 89[1] |
| Pakistan <br> Pakistan | 532 134 | 491 834 | 479 785 | 434 473 | 489 421 | 66 970 | 73 047 | 76 653 | 80 622 | 121 825 |
| Palau <br> Palaos | 1 027 | 1 047 | 1 079 | 932 | 967 | 4 | 4 | 5 | 5 | 5[1] |
| Panama <br> Panama | 235 863 | 219 299 | 208 840 | 220 333 | 226 825 | 3 638 | 6 228 | 7 048 | 7 778 | 8 744 |
| Papua New Guinea <br> Papouasie-Nvl-Guinée | 176 146[1] | 218 363[1] | 253 198[1] | 287 160[1] | 274 680 | 15[1] | 15[1] | ... | ... | ... |
| Paraguay[1] <br> Paraguay[1] | 24 000 | 23 000 | 22 000 | 21 000 | 20 000 | 1 000 | 1 300 | 2 100 | 2 100 | 2 100 |
| Peru <br> Pérou | 8 765 183 | 6 086 059 | 9 604 528 | 9 388 662 | 7 017 491 | 11 532 | 13 621 | 22 114 | 26 156 | 28 393 |
| Philippines <br> Philippines | 2 030 031 | 2 165 812 | 2 211 147 | 2 245 934 | 2 318 984 | 443 537 | 459 615 | 512 220 | 557 251 | 623 369 |
| Pitcairn[1] <br> Pitcairn[1] | 5 | 5 | 3 | 3 | 3 | ... | ... | ... | ... | ... |
| Poland <br> Pologne | 223 440 | 180 399 | 192 108 | 155 247 | 144 398 | 32 709 | 35 436 | 35 131 | 37 920 | 35 867 |
| Portugal <br> Portugal | 202 853 | 212 073 | 221 316 | 211 756 | 229 075 | 8 288 | 8 033 | 6 700 | 6 696 | 6 778 |
| Puerto Rico <br> Porto Rico | 2 529 | 2 919 | 2 428 | 2 551 | 2 042 | 442 | 269 | 417 | 311 | 266 |
| Qatar <br> Qatar | 7 155 | 11 295 | 11 134 | 13 935 | 16 376 | ^0 | ^0 | ^0 | 11 | 36 |
| Réunion <br> Réunion | 2 872 | 2 904 | 3 373 | 4 282 | 3 587 | 110 | 121 | 107 | 161 | 161 |
| Romania <br> Roumanie | 6 989 | 9 890 | 5 095 | 6 068 | 6 664 | 9 248 | 9 042 | 8 137 | 7 284 | 8 088 |
| Russian Federation <br> Fédération de Russie | 3 232 282 | 3 281 448 | 2 941 533 | 3 197 565 | 3 284 126 | 101 330 | 108 684 | 109 802 | 114 752 | 105 525 |
| Rwanda <br> Rwanda | 7 000[1] | 7 400 | 7 826 | 7 800[1] | 7 800[1] | 612[1] | 1 027 | 386 | 386[1] | 400[1] |
| Saint Helena <br> Sainte-Hélène | 598 | 985 | 1 061 | 1 130 | 1 120 | ... | ... | ... | ... | ... |
| Saint Kitts and Nevis <br> Saint-Kitts-et-Nevis | 355 | 400[1] | 484 | 450[1] | 450[1] | ... | ... | ... | ... | ... |
| Saint Lucia <br> Sainte-Lucie | 1 637 | 1 462 | 1 508 | 1 409 | 1 496 | 2 | 2[1] | 1 | 1 | ^0 |
| Saint Pierre and Miquelon <br> Saint-Pierre-et-Miquelon | 3 889 | 3 894 | 4 399 | 4 694 | 2 855 | ... | ... | ... | ... | ... |
| Saint Vincent-Grenadines <br> Saint Vincent-Grenadines | 44 531 | 4 784 | 8 627 | 3 345 | 4 739 | | | | | |
| Samoa <br> Samoa | 7 700[1] | 6 600[1] | 4 720 | 3 200[1] | 3 340 | ^0 | ^0 | ... | ... | ... |
| Sao Tome and Principe <br> Sao Tomé-et-Principe | 4 177[1] | 3 927 | 4 232 | 4 100[1] | 4 000[1] | ... | ... | ... | ... | ... |
| Saudi Arabia <br> Arabie saoudite | 57 211 | 55 440 | 55 418 | 60 407 | 65 471 | 6 744 | 11 824 | 11 172 | 14 375 | 15 586 |

| Country or area — Pays ou zone | Capture production — Captures | | | | | Aquaculture production — Production de l'aquaculture | | | | |
|---|---|---|---|---|---|---|---|---|---|---|
| | 2002 | 2003 | 2004 | 2005 | 2006 | 2002 | 2003 | 2004 | 2005 | 2006 |
| Senegal Sénégal | 401 435 | 478 284 | 445 338 | 412 070 | 377 685 | 109 | 98 | 204 | 193[1] | 200[1] |
| Serbia Serbie | ... | ... | ... | ... | 2 628 | ... | ... | ... | ... | 4 835 |
| Serbia and Montenegro Serbie-et-Monténégro | 1 585 | 1 798 | 2 388 | 2 468[1] | ... | 3 326 | 3 194 | 4 616 | 4 554[1] | ... |
| Seychelles Seychelles | 63 375 | 85 990 | 100 671 | 106 928 | 92 623 | 234 | 1 084 | 1 175 | 772 | 704 |
| Sierra Leone Sierra Leone | 82 990 | 96 926 | 134 440 | 145 993 | 148 146 | ... | ... | ... | ... | ... |
| Singapore Singapour | 2 769 | 2 085 | 2 173 | 1 920 | 3 103 | 5 027 | 5 024 | 5 406 | 5 917 | 8 573 |
| Slovakia Slovaquie | 1 746 | 1 646 | 1 603 | 1 693 | 1 718 | 829 | 881 | 1 180 | 955 | 1 263 |
| Slovenia Slovénie | 1 686 | 1 281 | 1 022 | 1 223 | 1 131 | 1 289 | 1 353 | 1 571 | 1 346 | 1 369 |
| Solomon Islands[1] Iles Salomon[1] | 25 886 | 36 873 | 34 191 | 27 336 | 39 336 | ... | ... | ... | ... | ... |
| Somalia[1] Somalie[1] | 29 000 | 30 000 | 30 000 | 30 000 | 30 000 | ... | ... | ... | ... | ... |
| South Africa Afrique du Sud | 766 941 | 822 938 | 888 075 | 817 160 | 617 388 | 4 505[1] | 4 896 | 3 167 | 3 142 | 3 352[1] |
| Spain Espagne | 890 439 | 894 657 | 807 574 | 846 099 | 949 515 | 255 189 | 268 609 | 293 779 | 219 800 | 293 287 |
| Sri Lanka Sri Lanka | 298 225 | 309 099 | 309 200 | 167 678 | 230 564 | 2 651 | 3 462 | 2 513 | 1 724 | 3 782 |
| Sudan Soudan | 57 000 | 59 000 | 57 000 | 62 000 | 63 000 | 1 600 | 1 600[1] | 1 600[1] | 1 600[1] | 1 600[1] |
| Suriname Suriname | 25 242[1] | 28 180 | 31 344 | 28 266 | 30 621 | 422[1] | 260 | 288 | 242 | 180 |
| Swaziland[1] Swaziland[1] | 70 | 70 | 70 | 70 | 70 | ... | ... | ... | ... | ... |
| Sweden Suède | 294 964 | 286 875 | 269 922 | 256 359 | 269 251 | 5 618 | 6 334 | 5 989 | 5 880 | 7 549 |
| Switzerland Suisse | 1 544 | 1 815 | 1 602 | 1 475 | 1 422 | 1 135 | 1 100 | 1 205 | 1 214 | 1 214 |
| Syrian Arab Republic Rép. arabe syrienne | 9 178 | 8 911 | 8 528 | 8 447 | 8 264 | 5 988 | 7 217 | 8 682 | 8 533 | 8 902 |
| Tajikistan Tadjikistan | 181 | 158 | 184 | 184[1] | 184[1] | 143 | 167 | 26 | 26[1] | 26[1] |
| Thailand Thaïlande | 2 842 428 | 2 849 724 | 2 839 612 | 2 814 270 | 2 776 295 | 954 696 | 1 064 409 | 1 259 983 | 1 304 213 | 1 385 801 |
| TFYR of Macedonia L'ex-R.y. Macédoine | 148 | 162 | 213 | 246 | 89 | 883 | 910 | 959 | 868 | 646 |
| Timor-Leste[1] Timor-Leste[1] | 350 | 350 | 350 | 350 | 350 | ... | ... | ... | ... | ... |
| Togo Togo | 20 946 | 27 485 | 28 013 | 27 732 | 24 879 | 1 025 | 1 221 | 1 525[1] | 1 535 | 3 020 |
| Tokelau[1] Tokélaou[1] | 200 | 200 | 200 | 200 | 200 | ... | ... | ... | ... | ... |
| Tonga Tonga | 4 791 | 4 435 | 1 645 | 2 000[1] | 2 500[1] | 17 | 22 | 3 | 1 | 5 |
| Trinidad and Tobago Trinité-et-Tobago | 14 088 | 9 915 | 10 034 | 13 414 | 8 444 | 7[1] | 7[1] | ... | ... | ... |
| Tunisia Tunisie | 96 685 | 90 226 | 111 531 | 109 117 | 111 288 | 1 985[1] | 2 174[1] | 2 334[1] | 2 730[1] | 2 775 |
| Turkey Turquie | 566 682 | 507 772 | 550 482 | 426 496 | 533 048 | 61 165 | 79 943 | 94 720[1] | 119 807[1] | 129 073[1] |
| Turkmenistan Turkménistan | 12 812 | 14 543 | 14 992 | 15 000[1] | 15 000[1] | 38 | 24 | 16 | 16[1] | 16[1] |

**Fish production**—Capture and aquaculture: metric tons (*continued*)
**Production halieutique**—Pêche de capture et aquaculture : tonnes (*suite*)

| Country or area — Pays ou zone | Capture production — Captures | | | | | Aquaculture production — Production de l'aquaculture | | | | |
|---|---|---|---|---|---|---|---|---|---|---|
| | 2002 | 2003 | 2004 | 2005 | 2006 | 2002 | 2003 | 2004 | 2005 | 2006 |
| Turks and Caicos Islands Iles Turques et Caïques | 5 767 | 5 100 | 5 677 | 5 491 | 6 018 | 30 | 25 | 4 | 4 | 4 |
| Tuvalu Tuvalu | 600[1] | 1 500 | 2 400 | 2 560 | 2 200[1] | ... | 5 | 1 | 1 | 1[1] |
| Uganda Ouganda | 221 898 | 241 810 | 371 789 | 416 758 | 367 099 | 4 915 | 5 500 | 5 539 | 10 817 | 32 392 |
| Ukraine Ukraine | 265 599 | 222 349 | 202 674 | 244 943 | 238 734 | 30 819 | 25 616 | 26 223 | 28 745 | 4 030 |
| United Arab Emirates Emirats arabes unis | 97 574 | 95 150 | 90 000[1] | 86 734 | 87 000[1] | ^0 | 2 300 | 570[1] | 570[1] | 570[1] |
| United Kingdom Royaume-Uni | 689 891 | 635 486 | 653 408 | 669 907 | 623 823 | 179 036[1] | 181 838[1] | 207 203 | 172 813 | 171 848 |
| United Rep. of Tanzania Rép.-Unie de Tanzanie | 323 531 | 351 125 | 362 510 | 375 535 | 341 110 | 630 | 2 | 11 | 10[1] | 10 |
| United States Etats-Unis | 4 937 305 | 4 938 956 | 4 959 826 | 4 892 967 | 4 859 872 | 497 346 | 544 329 | 606 549 | 492 351 | 465 061[1] |
| United States Virgin Is. Iles Vierges américaines | 1 296[1] | 1 486 | 1 511 | 1 261 | 1 614 | ^0 | ^0 | ^0 | ^0 | 10 |
| Uruguay Uruguay | 108 765 | 117 269 | 122 989 | 125 907 | 134 103 | 17 | 24 | 21 | 47 | 37 |
| Uzbekistan Ouzbékistan | 1 564 | 1 349 | 1 230 | 2 000[1] | 3 400 | 3 824 | 3 118 | 3 093 | 3 800[1] | 3 800 |
| Vanuatu Vanuatu | 44 289[1] | 57 758 | 111 477 | 146 991 | 88 075 | 0 | 0 | 1 | 1 | 114 |
| Venezuela (Bolivarian Rep. of) Venezuela (Rép. bolivar. du) | 509 663 | 520 773 | 487 000[1] | 470 000[1] | 460 000[1] | 17 860 | 19 821 | 22 210 | 22 210[1] | 22 210[1] |
| Viet Nam Viet Nam | 1 802 598 | 1 856 105 | 1 879 488 | 1 929 900 | 1 959 900 | 703 041 | 937 502 | 1 198 617 | 1 437 300 | 1 657 727 |
| Wallis and Futuna Islands Iles Wallis et Futuna | 300[1] | 300 | 300[1] | 300[1] | 600 | ... | ... | ... | ... | ... |
| Yemen Yémen | 179 584 | 228 116 | 256 300 | 263 000 | 250 000[1] | ... | ... | ... | ... | ... |
| Zambia Zambie | 65 000[1] | 65 000[1] | 65 000[1] | 65 000[1] | 65 000[1] | 4 630[1] | 4 501 | 5 125 | 5 125[1] | 5 125[1] |
| Zimbabwe Zimbabwe | 13 000[1] | 13 000[1] | 13 000[1] | 13 000[1] | 13 000[1] | 2 213 | 2 600 | 2 955 | 2 452 | 2 450[1] |

Source

Food and Agriculture Organization of the United Nations (FAO), Rome, FISHSTAT database, last accessed April 2008.

Notes

1 FAO estimate.
2 For statistical purposes, the data for China do not include those for the Hong Kong Special Administrative Region (Hong Kong SAR), Macao Special Administrative Region (Macao SAR) and Taiwan Province of China.

Source

Organisation des Nations Unies pour l'alimentation et l'agriculture (FAO), Rome, les données des pêches de FISHSTAT, dernier accès avril 2008.

Notes

1 Estimation de la FAO.
2 Pour la présentation des statistiques, les données pour la Chine ne comprennent pas la Région Administrative Spéciale de Hong Kong (Hong Kong RAS), la Région Administrative Spéciale de Macao (Macao RAS) et la province de Taiwan.

The series shown on agriculture and fishing have been furnished by the Food and Agriculture Organization of the United Nations (FAO). They refer mainly to the long-term trends in the growth of agricultural output and the food supply, the output of principal agricultural commodities and fish production.

Agricultural production is defined to include all crops and livestock products except those used for seed and fodder and other intermediate uses in agriculture; for example deductions are made for eggs used for hatching. Intermediate input of seeds and fodder and similar items refer to both domestically produced and imported commodities. For further details, reference may be made to FAO *Statistical Yearbook*. FAO data are also available through the Internet at http://faostat.fao.org.

*Table 34*: "Agriculture" relates to the production of all crops and livestock products. The "Food Index" includes those commodities which are considered edible and contain nutrients.

The index numbers of agricultural output and food production are calculated by the Laspeyres formula with the base year period 1999 - 2001. The latter is provided in order to diminish the impact of annual fluctuations in agricultural output during base years on the indices for the period. Production quantities of each commodity are weighted by 1999 - 2001 average national producer prices and summed for each year. The index numbers are based on production data for a calendar year. These may differ in some instances from those actually produced and published by the individual countries themselves due to variations in concepts, coverage, weights and methods of calculation. Efforts have been made to estimate these methodological differences to achieve a better international comparability of data.

Detailed data on agricultural production are published by FAO in its *Statistical Yearbook*.

*Table 35*: The data on the production of cereals relate to crops harvested for dry grain only. Cereals harvested for hay, green feed or used for grazing are excluded.

*Table 36*: Oil crops, or oil bearing crops, are those crops yielding seeds, nuts or fruits which are used mainly for the extraction of culinary or industrial oils, excluding essential oils. In this table, data for oil crops represent the total production of oil seeds, oil nuts and oil fruits harvested in the year indicated. Naturally, the total production of oil crops is never processed into oil in its entirety, since depending on the crop, important quantities are also used for seed, feed and food. However, although oil extraction rates vary from country to country, in this table the same extraction rate for each crop has been applied for all countries. Moreover, it should be borne in mind that the crops harvested during the latter months of the year are generally processed into oil during the following year.

In spite of these deficiencies in coverage, extraction rates and time reference, the data reported here are useful as they pro-

Les séries présentées sur l'agriculture et la pêche ont été fournies par l'Organisation des Nations Unies pour l'alimentation et l'agriculture (FAO) et portent principalement sur les tendances à long terme de la croissance de la production agricole et des approvisionnements alimentaires, et sur la production des principales denrées agricoles et la production halieutique.

La production agricole se définit comme comprenant l'ensemble des produits agricoles et des produits de l'élevage à l'exception de ceux utilisés comme semences et comme aliments pour les animaux, et pour les autres utilisations intermédiaires en agriculture; par exemple, on déduit les œufs utilisés pour la reproduction. L'apport intermédiaire de semences et d'aliments pour les animaux et d'autres éléments similaires se rapportent à la fois à des produits locaux et importés. Pour tous détails complémentaires, on se reportera à l'*Annuaire statistique* de la FAO. Des statistiques peuvent également être consultées sur le site Web de la FAO http://faostat.fao.org.

*Tableau 34* : "L'agriculture" se rapporte à la production de tous les produits de l'agriculture et de l'élevage. "L'indice des produits alimentaires" comprend les produits considérés comme comestibles et qui contiennent des éléments nutritifs.

Les indices de la production agricole et de la production alimentaire sont calculés selon la formule de Laspeyres avec les années 1999 - 2001 pour période de base. Le choix d'une période de plusieurs années permet de diminuer l'incidence des fluctuations annuelles de la production agricole pendant les années de base sur les indices pour cette période. Les quantités produites de chaque denrée sont pondérées par les prix nationaux moyens à la production de 1999 - 2001, et additionnées pour chaque année. Les indices sont fondés sur les données de production d'une année civile. Ils peuvent différer dans certains cas des indices effectivement établis et publiés par les pays eux-mêmes par suite de différences dans les concepts, la couverture, les pondérations et les méthodes de calcul. On s'est efforcé d'estimer ces différences méthodologiques afin de rendre les données plus facilement comparables à l'échelle internationale.

Des chiffres détaillés de production sont publiés dans l'*Annuaire statistique* de la FAO.

*Tableau 35* : Les données sur la production de céréales se rapportent uniquement aux céréales récoltées pour le grain sec; celles cultivées pour le foin, le fourrage vert ou le pâturage en sont exclues.

*Tableau 36* : On désigne sous le nom de cultures oléagineuses l'ensemble des cultures produisant des graines, des noix ou des fruits, essentiellement destinées à l'extraction

vide a valid indication of year to year changes in the size of total oil crop production. The actual production of vegetable oils in the world is about 80 percent of the production reported here. In addition, about two million tonnes of vegetable oils are produced every year from crops which are not included among those defined above. The most important of these oils are maize germ oil and rice bran oil. The actual world production of cake/meal derived from oil crops is also about 80 percent of the production reported.

*Table 37*: The data on roundwood refer to wood in the rough, wood in its natural state as felled or otherwise harvested, with or without bark, round, split, roughly squared or in other form (i.e. roots, stumps, burls, etc.). It may also be impregnated (e.g. telegraph poles) or roughly shaped or pointed. It comprises all wood obtained from removals, i.e. the quantities removed from forests and from trees outside the forest, including wood recovered from natural, felling and logging losses during the period—calendar year or forest year.

*Table 38*: The data cover (i) capture production from marine and inland fisheries and (ii) aquaculture, and are expressed in terms of live weight. They include fish, crustaceans and molluscs but exclude sponges, corals, pearls, seaweed, crocodiles, and aquatic mammals (such as whales and dolphins).

The flag of the vessel is considered as the paramount indication of the nationality of the catch. Marine fisheries data include landings by domestic craft in foreign ports and exclude landings by foreign craft in domestic ports.

To separate aquaculture from capture fisheries production, at least two criteria must apply i.e., the human intervention in one or more of the phases of the growth cycle, and individual, corporate or state ownership of the organism reared and harvested.

Data on aquaculture production are published in the FAO *Yearbook of Fishery Statistics, Aquaculture Production*; capture production statistics are published in the FAO *Yearbook of Fishery Statistics, Capture Production*.

d'huiles alimentaires ou industrielles, à l'exclusion des huiles essentielles. Dans ce tableau, les chiffres se rapportent à la production totale de graines, noix et fruits oléagineux récoltés au cours de l'année de référence. Bien entendu, la production totale d'oléagineux n'est jamais transformée intégralement en huile, car des quantités importantes qui varient suivant les cultures sont également utilisées pour les semailles, l'alimentation animale et l'alimentation humaine. Toutefois, bien que les taux d'extraction d'huile varient selon les pays, on a appliqué dans ce tableau le même taux à tous les pays pour chaque oléagineux. En outre, il ne faut pas oublier que les produits récoltés au cours des derniers mois de l'année sont généralement transformés en huile dans le courant de l'année suivante.

En dépit de ces imperfections qui concernent le champ d'application, les taux d'extraction et les périodes de référence, les chiffres présentés ici sont utiles, car ils donnent une indication valable des variations de volume que la production totale d'oléagineux enregistre d'une année à l'autre. La production mondiale effective d'huiles végétales atteint 80 pour cent environ de la production indiquée ici. En outre, environ 2 millions de tonnes d'huiles végétales sont produites chaque année à partir de cultures non comprises dans les catégories définies ci dessus. Les principales sont l'huile de germes de maïs et l'huile de son de riz. La production mondiale effective tourteau/farine d'oléagineux représente environ 80 pour cent de la production indiquée.

*Tableau 37* : Les données sur le bois rond se réfèrent au bois brut, bois à l'état naturel, tel qu'il a été abattu ou récolté autrement, avec ou sans écorce, fendu, grossièrement équarri ou sous une autre forme (par exemple, racines, souches, loupes, etc.). Il peut être également imprégné (par exemple, dans le cas des poteaux télégraphiques) et dégrossi ou taillé en pointe. Cette catégorie comprend tous les bois provenant des quantités enlevées en forêt ou provenant des arbres poussant hors forêt, y compris le volume récupéré sur les déchets naturels et les déchets d'abattage et de transport pendant la période envisagée (année civile ou forestière).

*Tableau 38* : Les données ont trait (i) à la pêche maritime et intérieure et (ii) à l'aquaculture, et sont exprimées en poids vif. Elles comprennent poissons, crustacés et mollusques, mais excluent éponges, coraux, perles, algues, crocodiles et les mammifères aquatiques (baleines, dauphins, etc.).
Le pavillon du navire est considéré comme la principale indication de la nationalité de la prise. Les données de pêche maritime comprennent les quantités débarquées par des bateaux nationaux dans des ports étrangers et excluent les quantités débarquées par des bateaux étrangers dans des ports nationaux.

Pour séparer la production d'aquaculture de la pêche de capture, au moins deux critères doivent se vérifier, c'est-à-dire l'intervention humaine dans une ou plusieurs des phases du cycle de croissance, et l'appartenance de l'organisme élevé et récolté à une personne physique, à une personne morale ou à l'état.

Les données sur la production de l'aquaculture sont publiées dans l'*Annuaire statistique des pêches, production de l'aquaculture*; celles sur les captures sont publiées dans l'*Annuaire statistique des pêches, captures*.

# 39

## Sugar
Production and consumption: thousand metric tons; consumption per capita: kilograms

## Sucre
Production et consommation : milliers de tonnes ; consommation par habitant : kilogrammes

| Country or area | 2000 | 2001 | 2002 | 2003 | 2004 | 2005 | 2006 | Pays ou zone |
|---|---|---|---|---|---|---|---|---|
| **World** | | | | | | | | **Monde** |
| **Production** | 130 022 | 130 650 | 142 088 | 148 129 | 147 266 | 141 364 | 152 175 | **Production** |
| **Consumption** | 127 312 | 131 654 | 137 645 | 141 344 | 146 703 | 147 345 | 151 723 | **Consommation** |
| **Consumption per capita** | **21** | **22** | **22** | **23** | **23** | **23** | **23** | **Consommation par habitant** |
| Afghanistan | | | | | | | | Afghanistan |
| Consumption* | 60 | 60 | 70 | 90 | 120 | 140 | 150 | Consommation* |
| Consumption per capita | 3 | 3 | 3 | 4 | 5 | 5 | 6 | Consommation par habitant |
| Albania | | | | | | | | Albanie |
| Production* | 3 | 3 | 3 | 3 | 3 | 3 | 5 | Production* |
| Consumption* | 68 | 68 | 75 | 85 | 88 | 90 | 90 | Consommation* |
| Consumption per capita | 19 | 22 | 24 | 27 | 28 | 29 | 29 | Consommation par habitant |
| Algeria | | | | | | | | Algérie |
| Consumption* | 935 | 965 | 1 040 | 1 100 | 1 135 | 1 185 | 1 215 | Consommation* |
| Consumption per capita | 31 | 31 | 33 | 35 | 35 | 36 | 36 | Consommation par habitant |
| Angola | | | | | | | | Angola |
| Consumption* | 130 | 155 | 185 | 195 | 205 | 225 | 245 | Consommation* |
| Consumption per capita | 10 | 11 | 13 | 13 | 13 | 14 | 15 | Consommation par habitant |
| Argentina | | | | | | | | Argentine |
| Production | *1 580 | *1 630 | *1 680 | 1 952 | 1 857 | 2 165 | 2 470 | Production |
| Consumption | *1 485 | *1 520 | *1 515 | 1 515 | 1 574 | 1 654 | 1 866 | Consommation |
| Consumption per capita | 41 | 41 | 40 | 39 | 41 | 42 | 47 | Consommation par habitant |
| Armenia | | | | | | | | Arménie |
| Production | ... | ... | ... | ... | ... | 2 | 2 | Production |
| Consumption | *72 | *73 | *74 | 87 | *87 | *87 | *87 | Consommation |
| Consumption per capita | 19 | 19 | 23 | 27 | 27 | 27 | 27 | Consommation par habitant |
| Australia | | | | | | | | Australie |
| Production | 4 417 | 4 768 | 5 614 | 5 315 | 5 530 | 5 393 | 4 729 | Production |
| Consumption | 1 049 | 1 068 | 1 100 | 1 089 | 1 043 | 1 034 | *1 035 | Consommation |
| Consumption per capita | 55 | 55 | 56 | 54 | 51 | 50 | 50 | Consommation par habitant |
| Azerbaijan | | | | | | | | Azerbaïdjan |
| Production | ... | ... | ... | ... | ... | 2 | *60 | Production |
| Consumption* | 160 | 160 | 165 | 175 | 180 | 185 | 185 | Consommation* |
| Consumption per capita | 20 | 20 | 20 | 21 | 21 | 22 | 22 | Consommation par habitant |
| Bahamas | | | | | | | | Bahamas |
| Consumption | 11 | 8 | 9 | 11 | 12 | 13 | 14 | Consommation |
| Consumption per capita | 35 | 27 | 32 | 35 | 38 | 41 | 44 | Consommation par habitant |
| Bangladesh | | | | | | | | Bangladesh |
| Production | *110 | 109 | 229 | *166 | *125 | *120 | *145 | Production |
| Consumption* | 500 | 550 | 635 | 695 | 790 | 880 | 995 | Consommation* |
| Consumption per capita | 4 | 4 | 5 | 5 | 6 | 6 | 6 | Consommation par habitant |
| Barbados | | | | | | | | Barbade |
| Production | 58 | *50 | *45 | *36 | *35 | *40 | *35 | Production |
| Consumption* | 15 | 15 | 15 | 15 | 15 | 15 | 15 | Consommation* |
| Consumption per capita | 56 | 56 | 56 | 55 | 55 | 55 | 55 | Consommation par habitant |
| Belarus | | | | | | | | Bélarus |
| Production | 186 | 196 | 162 | *255 | *340 | *435 | *480 | Production |
| Consumption | 380 | 422 | 410 | *410 | *415 | *420 | *425 | Consommation |
| Consumption per capita | 38 | 42 | 41 | 42 | 42 | 43 | 43 | Consommation par habitant |
| Belize | | | | | | | | Belize |
| Production | 128 | 114 | 119 | 111 | 125 | 102 | 120 | Production |
| Consumption | 15 | 12[1] | 12 | 12 | 12 | 12 | 13 | Consommation |
| Consumption per capita | 58 | 46 | 44 | 44 | 42 | 42 | 44 | Consommation par habitant |

| Country or area | 2000 | 2001 | 2002 | 2003 | 2004 | 2005 | 2006 | Pays ou zone |
|---|---|---|---|---|---|---|---|---|
| Benin | | | | | | | | Bénin |
| Production* | 5 | 5 | 5 | 4 | 4 | 5 | 10 | Production* |
| Consumption | *46 | 22 | *28 | *35 | *36 | *37 | *38 | Consommation |
| Consumption per capita | 7 | 3 | 4 | 5 | 5 | 5 | 5 | Consommation par habitant |
| Bermuda | | | | | | | | Bermudes |
| Consumption | 2 | 2 | 2 | 2 | 2 | 2 | 2 | Consommation |
| Consumption per capita | 25 | 25 | 25 | 25 | 25 | 25 | 25 | Consommation par habitant |
| Bolivia | | | | | | | | Bolivie |
| Production | 311 | 390 | 426 | 387 | 464 | *400 | *370 | Production |
| Consumption* | 293 | 295 | 300 | 305 | 310 | 320 | 325 | Consommation* |
| Consumption per capita | 35 | 34 | 34 | 33 | 33 | 33 | 33 | Consommation par habitant |
| Bosnia and Herzegovina | | | | | | | | Bosnie-Herzégovine |
| Consumption* | 90 | 110 | 120 | 130 | 130 | 135 | 135 | Consommation* |
| Consumption per capita | 24 | 29 | 31 | 34 | 34 | 35 | 35 | Consommation par habitant |
| Botswana | | | | | | | | Botswana |
| Consumption | 46 | 46 | 47 | 48 | 48 | 50 | 51 | Consommation |
| Consumption per capita | 28 | 27 | 27 | 27 | 27 | 28 | 29 | Consommation par habitant |
| Brazil | | | | | | | | Brésil |
| Production | 16 464 | 20 336 | 23 567 | 25 730 | 27 290 | 28 135 | 31 622 | Production |
| Consumption | *9 725 | *9 800 | 10 520 | 10 217 | 10 857 | 10 950 | 11 261 | Consommation |
| Consumption per capita | 58 | 57 | 60 | 58 | 59 | 59 | 60 | Consommation par habitant |
| Brunei Darussalam | | | | | | | | Brunéi Darussalam |
| Consumption | 6 | 10 | 10 | 11 | 11 | 11 | 11 | Consommation |
| Consumption per capita | 19 | 30 | 29 | 31 | 31 | 30 | 29 | Consommation par habitant |
| Bulgaria | | | | | | | | Bulgarie |
| Production* | 2 | 3 | 3 | 3 | 3 | 5 | 4 | Production* |
| Consumption* | 230 | 240 | 255 | 265 | 270 | 275 | 280 | Consommation* |
| Consumption per capita | 28 | 30 | 33 | 34 | 35 | 36 | 37 | Consommation par habitant |
| Burkina Faso | | | | | | | | Burkina Faso |
| Production* | 30 | 35 | 40 | 40 | 40 | 40 | 40 | Production* |
| Consumption* | 50 | 55 | 60 | 65 | 65 | 75 | 80 | Consommation* |
| Consumption per capita | 4 | 5 | 6 | 5 | 5 | 6 | 6 | Consommation par habitant |
| Burundi | | | | | | | | Burundi |
| Production | 24 | 20 | 20 | 22 | 22 | 23 | 25 | Production |
| Consumption | 24 | 23 | 25 | 26 | 27 | 29 | 29 | Consommation |
| Consumption per capita | 4 | 4 | 3 | 3 | 4 | 7 | 12 | Consommation par habitant |
| Cambodia | | | | | | | | Cambodge |
| Consumption* | 85 | 90 | 115 | 120 | 130 | 170 | 185 | Consommation* |
| Consumption per capita | 7 | 7 | 9 | 9 | 10 | 12 | 12 | Consommation par habitant |
| Cameroon | | | | | | | | Cameroun |
| Production | 41 | 94 | 104 | 120 | *125 | 119 | 126 | Production |
| Consumption | *95 | 112 | 145 | 145 | *150 | 92 | 112 | Consommation |
| Consumption per capita | 6 | 7 | 10 | 10 | 9 | 5 | 5 | Consommation par habitant |
| Canada | | | | | | | | Canada |
| Production* | 123 | 95 | 64 | 85 | 115 | 105 | 135 | Production* |
| Consumption* | 1 235 | 1 240 | 1 255 | 1 400 | 1 425 | 1 425 | 1 430 | Consommation* |
| Consumption per capita | 40 | 40 | 40 | 44 | 45 | 44 | 44 | Consommation par habitant |
| Cape Verde | | | | | | | | Cap-Vert |
| Consumption* | 13 | 15 | 16 | 17 | 17 | 17 | 17 | Consommation* |
| Consumption per capita | 31 | 34 | 36 | 37 | 36 | 35 | 35 | Consommation par habitant |
| Central African Rep. | | | | | | | | Rép. centrafricaine |
| Consumption* | 4 | 4 | 5 | 6 | 9 | 11 | 11 | Consommation* |
| Consumption per capita | 1 | 1 | 1 | 2 | 2 | 3 | 2 | Consommation par habitant |
| Chad | | | | | | | | Tchad |
| Production* | 32 | 32 | 32 | 33 | 30 | 35 | 35 | Production* |
| Consumption* | 57 | 57 | 65 | 75 | 80 | 85 | 90 | Consommation* |
| Consumption per capita | 7 | 7 | 15 | 8 | 8 | 8 | 8 | Consommation par habitant |

**Sugar**—Production and consumption: thousand metric tons; consumption per capita: kilograms (*continued*)

**Sucre**—Production et consommation : milliers de tonnes ; consommation par habitant : kilogrammes (*suite*)

| Country or area | 2000 | 2001 | 2002 | 2003 | 2004 | 2005 | 2006 | Pays ou zone |
|---|---|---|---|---|---|---|---|---|
| Chile | | | | | | | | Chili |
| Production | 457 | *430 | 576 | 374 | 401 | 386 | *400 | Production |
| Consumption | 683 | *685 | *685 | *685 | 673 | *682 | *695 | Consommation |
| Consumption per capita | 45 | 44 | 46 | 43 | 41 | 41 | 42 | Consommation par habitant |
| China [2] | | | | | | | | Chine [2] |
| Production | 7 616 | 7 161 | 9 805 | 11 433 | 10 912 | *9 785 | *10 682 | Production |
| Consumption | *8 500 | *8 900 | *9 975 | 11 065 | 11 613 | *11 785 | *11 975 | Consommation |
| Consumption per capita | 7 | 7 | 8 | 9 | 9 | 9 | 9 | Consommation par habitant |
| China, Hong Kong SAR | | | | | | | | Chine, Hong Kong RAS |
| Consumption* | 181 | 181 | 181 | 185 | 185 | 185 | 185 | Consommation* |
| Consumption per capita | 27 | 27 | 27 | 27 | 27 | 26 | 26 | Consommation par habitant |
| China, Macao SAR | | | | | | | | Chine, Macao RAS |
| Consumption | 7 | 7 | 8 | 8 | 8 | 8 | 8 | Consommation |
| Consumption per capita | 16 | 17 | 17 | 19 | 21 | 17 | 15 | Consommation par habitant |
| Colombia | | | | | | | | Colombie |
| Production | 2 391 | 2 260 | 2 523 | 2 646 | 2 740 | 2 683 | 2 415 | Production |
| Consumption | 1 343[3] | 1 309[3] | 1 356[3] | 1 348 | 1 521 | 1 512 | 1 460 | Consommation |
| Consumption per capita | 32 | 30 | 31 | 30 | 34 | 33 | 34 | Consommation par habitant |
| Comoros | | | | | | | | Comores |
| Consumption | 6 | 8 | 9 | 9 | 9 | 9 | 9 | Consommation |
| Consumption per capita | 8 | 11 | 11 | 11 | 11 | 12 | 12 | Consommation par habitant |
| Congo | | | | | | | | Congo |
| Production | *40 | *45 | 33 | *45 | *55 | 63 | *65 | Production |
| Consumption | *35 | *45 | 32 | *50 | *55 | 76 | *80 | Consommation |
| Consumption per capita | 12 | 15 | 10 | 17 | 18 | 24 | 25 | Consommation par habitant |
| Costa Rica | | | | | | | | Costa Rica |
| Production | 338 | 358 | *360 | *358 | *405 | 398 | 348 | Production |
| Consumption | 208 | *210 | *225 | *230 | *230 | 225 | *230 | Consommation |
| Consumption per capita | 60 | 54 | 56 | 56 | 54 | 53 | 56 | Consommation par habitant |
| Côte d'Ivoire | | | | | | | | Côte d'Ivoire |
| Production | 189 | *155 | *170 | *145 | *120 | *145 | *145 | Production |
| Consumption* | 180 | 190 | 200 | 205 | 210 | 215 | 220 | Consommation* |
| Consumption per capita | 11 | 11 | 11 | 11 | 11 | 12 | 12 | Consommation par habitant |
| Croatia | | | | | | | | Croatie |
| Production | 57 | 131 | 160 | 116 | 173 | 204 | *250 | Production |
| Consumption* | 175 | 175 | 180 | 185 | 190 | 200 | 200 | Consommation* |
| Consumption per capita | 40 | 40 | 41 | 42 | 43 | 45 | 45 | Consommation par habitant |
| Cuba | | | | | | | | Cuba |
| Production | 4 057 | 3 748 | 3 522 | 2 278 | *2 600 | *1 300 | *1 275 | Production |
| Consumption | 705 | 698 | 698 | 682 | *700 | *700 | *700 | Consommation |
| Consumption per capita | 63 | 62 | 62 | 60 | 62 | 62 | 62 | Consommation par habitant |
| Cyprus [4] | | | | | | | | Chypre [4] |
| Consumption | *31 | 32 | *33 | *36 | ... | ... | ... | Consommation |
| Consumption per capita | 41 | 42 | 46 | 47 | ... | ... | ... | Consommation par habitant |
| Czech Republic [4] | | | | | | | | République tchèque [4] |
| Production | 434 | 484 | 523 | 522 | ... | ... | ... | Production |
| Consumption | 440 | *450 | *475 | 399 | ... | ... | ... | Consommation |
| Consumption per capita | 43 | 44 | 47 | 39 | ... | ... | ... | Consommation par habitant |
| Dem. Rep. of the Congo | | | | | | | | Rép. dém. du Congo |
| Production* | 75 | 60 | 65 | 65 | 60 | 60 | 65 | Production* |
| Consumption* | 75 | 75 | 85 | 85 | 90 | 95 | 105 | Consommation* |
| Consumption per capita | 1 | 1 | 2 | 2 | 2 | 2 | 2 | Consommation par habitant |
| Djibouti | | | | | | | | Djibouti |
| Consumption | 13 | 13 | 13 | 14 | 15 | 16 | 16 | Consommation |
| Consumption per capita | 15 | 15 | 15 | 16 | 17 | 18 | 18 | Consommation par habitant |

| Country or area | 2000 | 2001 | 2002 | 2003 | 2004 | 2005 | 2006 | Pays ou zone |
|---|---|---|---|---|---|---|---|---|
| Dominican Republic | | | | | | | | Rép. dominicaine |
| Production | 438 | 491 | 516 | 525 | *530 | *475 | 487 | Production |
| Consumption | 298 | 352 | 366 | 322 | *360 | *370 | 338 | Consommation |
| Consumption per capita | 35 | 41 | 44 | 36 | 39 | 38 | 36 | Consommation par habitant |
| Ecuador | | | | | | | | Equateur |
| Production | *500 | *495 | *475 | *505 | *490 | *470 | 520 | Production |
| Consumption* | 440 | 465 | 480 | 485 | 485 | 488 | 490 | Consommation* |
| Consumption per capita | 36 | 37 | 38 | 38 | 37 | 37 | 36 | Consommation par habitant |
| Egypt | | | | | | | | Egypte |
| Production | *1 450 | *1 585 | *1 490 | *1 425 | 1 489 | *1 625 | *1 725 | Production |
| Consumption* | 2 250 | 2 325 | 2 400 | 2 500 | 2 600 | 2 675 | 2 700 | Consommation* |
| Consumption per capita | 35 | 36 | 36 | 35 | 35 | 35 | 34 | Consommation par habitant |
| El Salvador | | | | | | | | El Salvador |
| Production | 562 | 527 | 476 | 530 | 555 | 633 | 542 | Production |
| Consumption | 236 | 244 | 217 | 209 | 212 | 225 | 240 | Consommation |
| Consumption per capita | 38 | 38 | 33 | 33 | 33 | 35 | 35 | Consommation par habitant |
| Eritrea | | | | | | | | Erythrée |
| Consumption | 8 | 8 | 9 | 15 | 16 | 20 | 20 | Consommation |
| Consumption per capita | 2 | 2 | 2 | 3 | 4 | 4 | 4 | Consommation par habitant |
| Estonia[4] | | | | | | | | Estonie[4] |
| Consumption* | 70 | 73 | 73 | 80 | ... | ... | ... | Consommation* |
| Consumption per capita | 49 | 53 | 49 | 60 | ... | ... | ... | Consommation par habitant |
| Ethiopia | | | | | | | | Ethiopie |
| Production | 251 | *305 | 287 | *295 | *325 | *345 | *360 | Production |
| Consumption | 246 | *240 | 211 | *260 | *295 | *320 | *350 | Consommation |
| Consumption per capita | 4 | 4 | 3 | 4 | 4 | 4 | 5 | Consommation par habitant |
| European Union[4] | | | | | | | | Union européenne[4] |
| Production | 17 854 | 15 500 | 18 268 | 16 578 | #21 843 | 21 698 | 18 098 | Production |
| Consumption | 14 112 | 13 588 | 14 370 | 14 137 | #17 691 | 16 765 | 17 527 | Consommation |
| Consumption per capita | 37 | 36 | 38 | 37 | #39 | 36 | 38 | Consommation par habitant |
| Fiji | | | | | | | | Fidji |
| Production | 353 | 327 | 334 | 330 | 330 | 306 | 324 | Production |
| Consumption | 41 | 45[5] | 53 | 55 | 58[5] | 55 | 61 | Consommation |
| Consumption per capita | 51 | 55 | 64 | 66 | 69 | 66 | 71 | Consommation par habitant |
| Gabon | | | | | | | | Gabon |
| Production | *17 | *18 | *18 | 25 | *19 | *21 | 21 | Production |
| Consumption | *19 | *19 | *20 | *21 | *21 | *21 | 21 | Consommation |
| Consumption per capita | 15 | 15 | 16 | 16 | 15 | 14 | 13 | Consommation par habitant |
| Gambia | | | | | | | | Gambie |
| Consumption* | 58 | 60 | 65 | 70 | 70 | 70 | 75 | Consommation* |
| Consumption per capita | 41 | 42 | 41 | 45 | 44 | 43 | 44 | Consommation par habitant |
| Georgia | | | | | | | | Géorgie |
| Consumption* | 108 | 110 | 120 | 125 | 135 | 135 | 135 | Consommation* |
| Consumption per capita | 24 | 25 | 28 | 29 | 31 | 31 | 31 | Consommation par habitant |
| Ghana | | | | | | | | Ghana |
| Consumption* | 150 | 155 | 170 | 185 | 200 | 205 | 215 | Consommation* |
| Consumption per capita | 8 | 8 | 9 | 9 | 10 | 10 | 10 | Consommation par habitant |
| Gibraltar | | | | | | | | Gibraltar |
| Consumption | 3 | 2 | 2 | 2 | 2 | 2 | 1 | Consommation |
| Consumption per capita | 83 | 73 | 55 | 60 | 67 | 53 | 37 | Consommation par habitant |
| Guatemala | | | | | | | | Guatemala |
| Production | 1 675 | 1 661 | 1 910 | 1 801 | 2 092 | 2 015 | 1 961 | Production |
| Consumption | 468 | 496 | 534 | 585 | 585 | 657 | 637 | Consommation |
| Consumption per capita | 41 | 42 | 45 | 48 | 47 | 52 | 49 | Consommation par habitant |

| Country or area | 2000 | 2001 | 2002 | 2003 | 2004 | 2005 | 2006 | Pays ou zone |
|---|---|---|---|---|---|---|---|---|
| Guinea | | | | | | | | Guinée |
| Production* | 25 | 25 | 25 | 26 | 26 | 25 | 25 | Production* |
| Consumption* | 90 | 95 | 100 | 110 | 110 | 120 | 125 | Consommation* |
| Consumption per capita | 11 | 11 | 12 | 13 | 12 | 13 | 13 | Consommation par habitant |
| Guinea-Bissau | | | | | | | | Guinée-Bissau |
| Consumption | 7 | 7 | 7 | 8 | 9 | 14 | 14 | Consommation |
| Consumption per capita | 6 | 6 | 6 | 6 | 7 | 11 | 11 | Consommation par habitant |
| Guyana | | | | | | | | Guyana |
| Production | 273 | 284 | 331 | *302 | *320 | 246 | *255 | Production |
| Consumption | 24 | 24 | 24 | *25 | *26 | 22 | *25 | Consommation |
| Consumption per capita | 31 | 35 | 31 | 33 | 35 | 29 | 33 | Consommation par habitant |
| Haiti | | | | | | | | Haïti |
| Production* | 5 | 5 | 5 | ... | ... | ... | ... | Production* |
| Consumption* | 165 | 165 | 170 | 175 | 175 | 185 | 185 | Consommation* |
| Consumption per capita | 21 | 20 | 21 | 22 | 22 | 23 | 23 | Consommation par habitant |
| Honduras | | | | | | | | Honduras |
| Production | *320 | 316 | *320 | 300 | 357 | *360 | *385 | Production |
| Consumption | 236 | 237 | *240 | 249 | 250 | *250 | *250 | Consommation |
| Consumption per capita | 37 | 39 | 33 | 36 | 35 | 36 | 36 | Consommation par habitant |
| Hungary[4] | | | | | | | | Hongrie[4] |
| Production | 309 | 434 | 347 | 257 | ... | ... | ... | Production |
| Consumption | 367 | 317 | 313 | 282 | ... | ... | ... | Consommation |
| Consumption per capita | 37 | 31 | 31 | 28 | ... | ... | ... | Consommation par habitant |
| Iceland | | | | | | | | Islande |
| Consumption* | 13 | 12 | 12 | 12 | 12 | 11 | 10 | Consommation* |
| Consumption per capita | 46 | 41 | 41 | 41 | 41 | 37 | 32 | Consommation par habitant |
| India | | | | | | | | Inde |
| Production | 20 247 | 19 906 | 19 525 | 21 702 | 14 432 | 15 216 | 22 347 | Production |
| Consumption | 16 546 | 17 274 | 17 857 | 18 625 | 19 858 | 20 110 | 20 110 | Consommation |
| Consumption per capita | 17 | 17 | 17 | 18 | 19 | 20 | 18 | Consommation par habitant |
| Indonesia | | | | | | | | Indonésie |
| Production | *1 685 | *1 850 | *2 150 | *1 780 | *2 225 | *2 435 | 2 510 | Production |
| Consumption* | 3 375 | 3 500 | 3 675 | 3 800 | 3 915 | 4 052 | 4 195 | Consommation* |
| Consumption per capita | 16 | 17 | 17 | 18 | 18 | 18 | 19 | Consommation par habitant |
| Iran (Islamic Rep. of) | | | | | | | | Iran (Rép. islamique d') |
| Production* | 920 | 900 | 995 | 1 270 | 1 310 | 1 300 | 1 425 | Production* |
| Consumption* | 1 960 | 1 965 | 1 975 | 2 025 | 2 060 | 2 110 | 2 160 | Consommation* |
| Consumption per capita | 31 | 30 | 30 | 30 | 30 | 30 | 31 | Consommation par habitant |
| Iraq | | | | | | | | Iraq |
| Consumption* | 405 | 425 | 500 | 650 | 675 | 675 | 685 | Consommation* |
| Consumption per capita | 17 | 18 | 20 | 26 | 26 | 25 | 25 | Consommation par habitant |
| Israel | | | | | | | | Israël |
| Consumption* | 380 | 400 | 410 | 425 | 440 | 455 | 460 | Consommation* |
| Consumption per capita | 60 | 62 | 62 | 62 | 63 | 65 | 64 | Consommation par habitant |
| Jamaica | | | | | | | | Jamaïque |
| Production | 210 | 205 | 175 | 154 | 181 | 126 | 144 | Production |
| Consumption | 129 | 136 | 126 | 129 | 111 | 123 | 98 | Consommation |
| Consumption per capita | 50 | 52 | 48 | 49 | 42 | 46 | 36 | Consommation par habitant |
| Japan | | | | | | | | Japon |
| Production | 842 | 823 | 901 | 934 | 976 | 965 | 909 | Production |
| Consumption | 2 413 | 2 339 | 2 433 | 2 415 | 2 403 | 2 397 | 2 229 | Consommation |
| Consumption per capita | 19 | 18 | 19 | 19 | 19 | 19 | 17 | Consommation par habitant |
| Jordan | | | | | | | | Jordanie |
| Consumption | *185 | *190 | *200 | 216 | *235 | *255 | *270 | Consommation |
| Consumption per capita | 37 | 36 | 37 | 40 | 44 | 46 | 47 | Consommation par habitant |

| Country or area | 2000 | 2001 | 2002 | 2003 | 2004 | 2005 | 2006 | Pays ou zone |
|---|---|---|---|---|---|---|---|---|
| Kazakhstan | | | | | | | | Kazakhstan |
| Production | *30 | *25 | 46 | 62 | 40 | *22 | *26 | Production |
| Consumption* | 312 | 365 | 438 | 442 | 450 | 455 | 460 | Consommation* |
| Consumption per capita | 21 | 25 | 29 | 29 | 30 | 30 | 30 | Consommation par habitant |
| Kenya | | | | | | | | Kenya |
| Production | 437 | 377 | 537 | 448 | 562 | 532 | 517 | Production |
| Consumption | 663 | *625 | 652 | 692 | 728 | 756 | 781 | Consommation |
| Consumption per capita | 22 | 20 | 21 | 21 | 22 | 23 | 23 | Consommation par habitant |
| Korea, Dem. P. R. | | | | | | | | Corée, R. p. dém. de |
| Consumption* | 65 | 70 | 70 | 75 | 85 | 90 | 90 | Consommation* |
| Consumption per capita | 3 | 3 | 3 | 3 | 4 | 4 | 4 | Consommation par habitant |
| Korea, Republic of | | | | | | | | Corée, République de |
| Consumption[6] | 1 012 | 1 086 | 1 129 | 1 134 | 1 171 | 1 198 | 1 156 | Consommation[6] |
| Consumption per capita | 21 | 23 | 24 | 24 | 24 | 25 | 24 | Consommation par habitant |
| Kuwait | | | | | | | | Koweït |
| Consumption* | 73 | 75 | 80 | 80 | 85 | 90 | 90 | Consommation* |
| Consumption per capita | 33 | 33 | 35 | 34 | 36 | 37 | 36 | Consommation par habitant |
| Kyrgyzstan | | | | | | | | Kirghizistan |
| Production | 57 | 29 | 41 | 75 | 88 | 45 | *40 | Production |
| Consumption* | 110 | 110 | 115 | 120 | 120 | 120 | 125 | Consommation* |
| Consumption per capita | 22 | 22 | 23 | 24 | 24 | 23 | 24 | Consommation par habitant |
| Lao People's Dem. Rep. | | | | | | | | Rép. dém. pop. lao |
| Consumption | 21 | 25 | 30 | 30 | 35 | 45 | 50 | Consommation |
| Consumption per capita | 4 | 5 | 5 | 5 | 6 | 8 | 9 | Consommation par habitant |
| Latvia[4] | | | | | | | | Lettonie[4] |
| Production | 68 | 56 | 77 | 75 | ... | ... | ... | Production |
| Consumption | 78 | *78 | *78 | 73 | ... | ... | ... | Consommation |
| Consumption per capita | 32 | 33 | 33 | 31 | ... | ... | ... | Consommation par habitant |
| Lebanon | | | | | | | | Liban |
| Production | 34 | ... | ... | ... | ... | 4 | *5 | Production |
| Consumption | 122 | *135 | *140 | *145 | *150 | 151 | *145 | Consommation |
| Consumption per capita | 35 | 38 | 36 | 39 | 43 | 42 | 40 | Consommation par habitant |
| Liberia | | | | | | | | Libéria |
| Consumption | 10 | 9 | 10 | 10 | 10 | 15 | 15 | Consommation |
| Consumption per capita | 3 | 3 | 3 | 3 | 3 | 4 | 4 | Consommation par habitant |
| Libyan Arab Jamah. | | | | | | | | Jamah. arabe libyenne |
| Consumption | 225 | 230 | 240 | 250 | 255 | 265 | 270 | Consommation |
| Consumption per capita | 44 | 43 | 45 | 46 | 46 | 47 | 47 | Consommation par habitant |
| Lithuania[4] | | | | | | | | Lituanie[4] |
| Production | 137 | 118 | 150 | 143 | ... | ... | ... | Production |
| Consumption | 95 | 111 | 89 | 89 | ... | ... | ... | Consommation |
| Consumption per capita | 26 | 32 | 26 | 26 | ... | ... | ... | Consommation par habitant |
| Madagascar | | | | | | | | Madagascar |
| Production | *70 | *50 | 32 | 27 | 26 | 27 | *20 | Production |
| Consumption | *98 | *98 | 104 | 117 | 129 | 132 | *135 | Consommation |
| Consumption per capita | 6 | 6 | 7 | 7 | 8 | 7 | 7 | Consommation par habitant |
| Malawi | | | | | | | | Malawi |
| Production | 209 | *205 | 261 | *257 | *255 | *265 | *230 | Production |
| Consumption | 127 | *140 | *145 | *150 | *155 | *160 | *165 | Consommation |
| Consumption per capita | 12 | 13 | 13 | 13 | 13 | 13 | 13 | Consommation par habitant |
| Malaysia | | | | | | | | Malaisie |
| Production* | 108 | 105 | 110 | 80 | 80 | 80 | 55 | Production* |
| Consumption* | 1 045 | 1 050 | 1 090 | 1 175 | 1 215 | 1 225 | 1 250 | Consommation* |
| Consumption per capita | 44 | 44 | 43 | 46 | 47 | 46 | 46 | Consommation par habitant |
| Maldives | | | | | | | | Maldives |
| Consumption | 6 | 5 | 5 | 5 | 5 | 6 | 6 | Consommation |
| Consumption per capita | 22 | 16 | 18 | 17 | 17 | 19 | 21 | Consommation par habitant |

| Country or area | 2000 | 2001 | 2002 | 2003 | 2004 | 2005 | 2006 | Pays ou zone |
|---|---|---|---|---|---|---|---|---|
| Mali | | | | | | | | Mali |
| Production* | 32 | 32 | 32 | 34 | 35 | 35 | 34 | Production* |
| Consumption* | 80 | 80 | 90 | 95 | 95 | 100 | 105 | Consommation* |
| Consumption per capita | 8 | 8 | 8 | 9 | 8 | 9 | 9 | Consommation par habitant |
| Malta⁴ | | | | | | | | Malte⁴ |
| Consumption* | 23 | 23 | 23 | 25 | ... | ... | ... | Consommation* |
| Consumption per capita | 58 | 59 | 59 | 63 | ... | ... | ... | Consommation par habitant |
| Mauritania | | | | | | | | Mauritanie |
| Consumption* | 130 | 135 | 135 | 140 | 140 | 145 | 155 | Consommation* |
| Consumption per capita | 49 | 50 | 48 | 48 | 45 | 44 | 45 | Consommation par habitant |
| Mauritius | | | | | | | | Maurice |
| Production | 604 | 685 | 553 | 538 | 606 | 524 | 505 | Production |
| Consumption | 42 | 44 | 43 | 41 | 42 | 39 | 39 | Consommation |
| Consumption per capita | 35 | 36 | 35 | 34 | 34 | 32 | 31 | Consommation par habitant |
| Mexico | | | | | | | | Mexique |
| Production | 4 816 | 5 614 | 5 073 | 5 442 | 5 672 | 5 619 | 5 412 | Production |
| Consumption | 4 619 | 4 857 | 5 069 | 5 328 | 5 300 | 4 877 | 4 979 | Consommation |
| Consumption per capita | 46 | 48 | 49 | 52 | 50 | 47 | 47 | Consommation par habitant |
| Moldova | | | | | | | | Moldova |
| Production | 102 | 130 | *125 | 107 | 111 | 133 | 161 | Production |
| Consumption | *105 | *105 | *110 | *115 | 106 | *125 | *130 | Consommation |
| Consumption per capita | 29 | 29 | 26 | 32 | 29 | 35 | 36 | Consommation par habitant |
| Mongolia | | | | | | | | Mongolie |
| Consumption | 20 | 20 | 21 | 22 | 23 | 25 | 25 | Consommation |
| Consumption per capita | 8 | 8 | 8 | 9 | 9 | 10 | 9 | Consommation par habitant |
| Morocco | | | | | | | | Maroc |
| Production | 556 | *530 | *505 | *505 | *540 | 513 | *450 | Production |
| Consumption | 1 034 | *1 050 | *1 100 | 1 057 | *1 150 | 1 163 | *1 170 | Consommation |
| Consumption per capita | 36 | 36 | 37 | 35 | 38 | 38 | 38 | Consommation par habitant |
| Mozambique | | | | | | | | Mozambique |
| Production | *45 | *60 | *170 | *225 | 205 | 265 | 243 | Production |
| Consumption | *90 | *95 | *110 | *120 | 134 | 135 | 144 | Consommation |
| Consumption per capita | 5 | 5 | 5 | 7 | 7 | 7 | 7 | Consommation par habitant |
| Myanmar | | | | | | | | Myanmar |
| Production | 75 | *125 | *125 | *135 | *150 | *150 | *155 | Production |
| Consumption* | 85 | 90 | 120 | 135 | 150 | 155 | 165 | Consommation* |
| Consumption per capita | 2 | 2 | 2 | 3 | 3 | 3 | 3 | Consommation par habitant |
| Namibia | | | | | | | | Namibie |
| Consumption* | 46 | 47 | 48 | 50 | 55 | 55 | 60 | Consommation* |
| Consumption per capita | 25 | 26 | 26 | 27 | 30 | 30 | 33 | Consommation par habitant |
| Nepal | | | | | | | | Népal |
| Production* | 110 | 65 | 110 | 125 | 140 | 130 | 135 | Production* |
| Consumption* | 115 | 120 | 125 | 125 | 130 | 135 | 135 | Consommation* |
| Consumption per capita | 5 | 5 | 5 | 5 | 5 | 5 | 5 | Consommation par habitant |
| Netherlands Antilles | | | | | | | | Antilles néerlandaises |
| Consumption* | 21 | 22 | 25 | 25 | 25 | 26 | 26 | Consommation* |
| Consumption per capita | 117 | 129 | 147 | 139 | 137 | 142 | 142 | Consommation par habitant |
| New Zealand | | | | | | | | Nouvelle-Zélande |
| Consumption | 212 | *215 | *220 | *225 | *230 | *235 | *235 | Consommation |
| Consumption per capita | 55 | 55 | 56 | 56 | 57 | 57 | 56 | Consommation par habitant |
| Nicaragua | | | | | | | | Nicaragua |
| Production | 398 | *390 | *370 | 333 | *440 | *470 | *435 | Production |
| Consumption | 157 | *160 | *175 | *190 | *200 | *205 | *210 | Consommation |
| Consumption per capita | 31 | 31 | 31 | 36 | 37 | 40 | 40 | Consommation par habitant |
| Niger | | | | | | | | Niger |
| Production* | 10 | 10 | 10 | 15 | 10 | 10 | 10 | Production* |
| Consumption* | 55 | 55 | 65 | 70 | 70 | 75 | 75 | Consommation* |
| Consumption per capita | 5 | 5 | 5 | 6 | 6 | 6 | 5 | Consommation par habitant |

| Country or area | 2000 | 2001 | 2002 | 2003 | 2004 | 2005 | 2006 | Pays ou zone |
|---|---|---|---|---|---|---|---|---|
| Nigeria | | | | | | | | Nigéria |
| Production | 36 | 7 | 7 | ... | ... | ... | *30 | Production |
| Consumption | *760 | 975 | 1 317 | 1 046 | 1 222 | 1 236 | *1 265 | Consommation |
| Consumption per capita | 7 | 8 | 11 | 8 | 9 | 9 | 8 | Consommation par habitant |
| Norway | | | | | | | | Norvège |
| Consumption* | 180 | 180 | 180 | 175 | 175 | 175 | 175 | Consommation* |
| Consumption per capita | 40 | 40 | 40 | 38 | 38 | 38 | 37 | Consommation par habitant |
| Pakistan | | | | | | | | Pakistan |
| Production | 2 053 | 2 720 | 3 334 | 4 063 | 4 481 | 2 839 | 3 263 | Production |
| Consumption | *3 295 | *3 390 | *3 490 | 3 875 | 4 004 | 4 075 | 3 951 | Consommation |
| Consumption per capita | 24 | 24 | 24 | 26 | 27 | 27 | 25 | Consommation par habitant |
| Panama | | | | | | | | Panama |
| Production | 161 | 146 | 152 | 147 | 157 | 157 | *170 | Production |
| Consumption* | 95 | 105 | 110 | 113 | 115 | 117 | 120 | Consommation* |
| Consumption per capita | 33 | 36 | 36 | 38 | 36 | 37 | 38 | Consommation par habitant |
| Papua New Guinea | | | | | | | | Papouasie-Nvl-Guinée |
| Production | 41 | 45 | 53 | 50 | 46 | 44 | *35 | Production |
| Consumption | 35 | 35 | 37 | 35 | 35 | 35 | *35 | Consommation |
| Consumption per capita | 7 | 7 | 8 | 7 | 6 | 6 | 6 | Consommation par habitant |
| Paraguay | | | | | | | | Paraguay |
| Production* | 90 | 95 | 115 | 116 | 115 | 117 | 120 | Production* |
| Consumption* | 108 | 110 | 110 | 115 | 115 | 120 | 120 | Consommation* |
| Consumption per capita | 20 | 20 | 19 | 21 | 19 | 19 | 17 | Consommation par habitant |
| Peru | | | | | | | | Pérou |
| Production | *725 | *755 | *850 | *970 | 813 | 695 | 805 | Production |
| Consumption | *925 | *950 | *975 | *995 | 967 | 896 | *960 | Consommation |
| Consumption per capita | 36 | 36 | 36 | 36 | 35 | 32 | 33 | Consommation par habitant |
| Philippines | | | | | | | | Philippines |
| Production | 1 826 | 1 895 | 1 988 | 2 245 | 2 423 | 2 184 | 2 413 | Production |
| Consumption | 2 052 | 1 974 | 2 059 | 2 117 | 2 102 | 2 037 | 2 021 | Consommation |
| Consumption per capita | 28 | 26 | 26 | 26 | 25 | 24 | 23 | Consommation par habitant |
| Poland[4] | | | | | | | | Pologne[4] |
| Production | 2 104 | 1 626 | 2 038 | 1 912 | ... | ... | ... | Production |
| Consumption* | 1 730 | 1 740 | 1 745 | 1 760 | ... | ... | ... | Consommation* |
| Consumption per capita | 45 | 45 | 45 | 46 | ... | ... | ... | Consommation par habitant |
| Romania | | | | | | | | Roumanie |
| Production | 54 | 71 | 75 | 57 | *55 | 67 | *125 | Production |
| Consumption | *550 | *565 | *570 | *590 | 584 | *595 | *600 | Consommation |
| Consumption per capita | 24 | 25 | 26 | 27 | 27 | 28 | 28 | Consommation par habitant |
| Russian Federation | | | | | | | | Fédération de Russie |
| Production | 1 705 | 1 757 | 1 757 | 1 892 | 2 496 | 2 719 | 3 459 | Production |
| Consumption | 5 707 | 5 848 | 6 673 | *6 850 | *6 700 | *6 600 | *6 500 | Consommation |
| Consumption per capita | 39 | 41 | 47 | 47 | 46 | 46 | 46 | Consommation par habitant |
| Rwanda | | | | | | | | Rwanda |
| Consumption* | 3 | 10 | 11 | 11 | 11 | 14 | 15 | Consommation* |
| Consumption per capita | ^0 | 1 | 1 | 1 | 1 | 2 | 2 | Consommation par habitant |
| Saint Kitts and Nevis | | | | | | | | Saint-Kitts-et-Nevis |
| Production* | 20 | 20 | 20 | 22 | 20 | 20 | ... | Production* |
| Consommation* | 3 | 3 | 3 | 4 | 5 | 6 | 7 | Consommation* |
| Consumption per capita | 63 | 50 | 50 | 51 | 64 | 77 | 90 | Consommation par habitant |
| Samoa | | | | | | | | Samoa |
| Production | 2 | 2 | 2 | 2 | 2 | 2 | 3 | Production |
| Consumption | 2 | 2 | 3 | 4 | 4 | 4 | 4 | Consommation |
| Consumption per capita | 8 | 8 | 12 | 15 | 15 | 15 | 15 | Consommation par habitant |
| Saudi Arabia | | | | | | | | Arabie saoudite |
| Consumption* | 595 | 620 | 650 | 690 | 720 | 760 | 780 | Consommation* |
| Consumption per capita | 29 | 30 | 30 | 31 | 31 | 32 | 32 | Consommation par habitant |

| Country or area | 2000 | 2001 | 2002 | 2003 | 2004 | 2005 | 2006 | Pays ou zone |
|---|---|---|---|---|---|---|---|---|
| Senegal | | | | | | | | Sénégal |
| Production* | 90 | 95 | 95 | 90 | 90 | 90 | 95 | Production* |
| Consumption* | 165 | 170 | 175 | 175 | 180 | 185 | 190 | Consommation* |
| Consumption per capita | 17 | 18 | 18 | 17 | 17 | 17 | 17 | Consommation par habitant |
| Serbia and Montenegro | | | | | | | | Serbie-et-Monténégro |
| Production | *170 | 209 | *230 | *270 | *335 | *415 | *505 | Production |
| Consumption* | 275 | 300 | 300 | 310 | 315 | 320 | 325 | Consommation* |
| Consumption per capita | 26 | 28 | 37 | 38 | 42 | 47 | 52 | Consommation par habitant |
| Sierra Leone | | | | | | | | Sierra Leone |
| Production* | 7 | 7 | 7 | 5 | 6 | 6 | 6 | Production* |
| Consumption* | 20 | 20 | 21 | 22 | 25 | 26 | 27 | Consommation* |
| Consumption per capita | 4 | 4 | 4 | 4 | 5 | 5 | 5 | Consommation par habitant |
| Singapore | | | | | | | | Singapour |
| Consumption* | 285 | 300 | 305 | 310 | 310 | 315 | 315 | Consommation* |
| Consumption per capita | 71 | 73 | 73 | 73 | 71 | 71 | 69 | Consommation par habitant |
| Slovakia [4] | | | | | | | | Slovaquie [4] |
| Production | 140 | 173 | 197 | 171 | ... | ... | ... | Production |
| Consumption | *230 | *235 | *240 | 206 | ... | ... | ... | Consommation |
| Consumption per capita | 43 | 44 | 45 | 38 | ... | ... | ... | Consommation par habitant |
| Slovenia [4] | | | | | | | | Slovénie [4] |
| Production | 44 | *50 | 44 | 55 | ... | ... | ... | Production |
| Consumption* | 105 | 90 | 90 | 100 | ... | ... | ... | Consommation* |
| Consumption per capita | 53 | 45 | 45 | 50 | ... | ... | ... | Consommation par habitant |
| Somalia | | | | | | | | Somalie |
| Production* | 15 | 20 | 20 | 20 | 20 | 15 | 20 | Production* |
| Consumption* | 180 | 185 | 190 | 200 | 200 | 205 | 205 | Consommation* |
| Consumption per capita | 21 | 20 | 19 | 25 | 23 | 22 | 21 | Consommation par habitant |
| South Africa | | | | | | | | Afrique du Sud |
| Production | 2 691 | 2 311 | 2 767 | 2 418 | 2 234 | 2 507 | 2 234 | Production |
| Consumption | 1 453 | 1 341 | 1 478 | 1 436 | 1 484 | 1 565 | *1 612 | Consommation |
| Consumption per capita | 33 | 30 | 33 | 31 | 32 | 33 | 33 | Consommation par habitant |
| Sri Lanka | | | | | | | | Sri Lanka |
| Production* | 15 | 20 | 20 | 21 | 60 | 60 | 70 | Production* |
| Consumption* | 560 | 575 | 600 | 620 | 640 | 655 | 670 | Consommation* |
| Consumption per capita | 29 | 31 | 32 | 32 | 33 | 33 | 33 | Consommation par habitant |
| Sudan | | | | | | | | Soudan |
| Production | 680 | 719 | 744 | 686 | 789 | 728 | 767 | Production |
| Consumption | 430 | 523 | 568 | 568 | 624 | 877 | 910 | Consommation |
| Consumption per capita | 14 | 17 | 17 | 16 | 18 | 25 | 26 | Consommation par habitant |
| Suriname | | | | | | | | Suriname |
| Production* | 10 | 10 | 10 | 5 | 5 | 5 | 7 | Production* |
| Consumption* | 19 | 19 | 20 | 20 | 20 | 21 | 21 | Consommation* |
| Consumption per capita | 45 | 46 | 39 | 41 | 40 | 41 | 40 | Consommation par habitant |
| Swaziland | | | | | | | | Swaziland |
| Production | 553 | 567 | 675 | 616 | 594 | 653 | 623 | Production |
| Consumption | 105 | 107 | 107 | 109 | 112 | *114 | *117 | Consommation |
| Consumption per capita | 113 | 107 | 112 | 99 | 98 | 97 | 102 | Consommation par habitant |
| Switzerland | | | | | | | | Suisse |
| Production | *231 | *187 | 222 | 185 | *225 | 221 | 198 | Production |
| Consumption | *375 | *385 | 393 | 463 | *475 | 526 | 558 | Consommation |
| Consumption per capita | 52 | 53 | 54 | 63 | 64 | 70 | 73 | Consommation par habitant |
| Syrian Arab Republic | | | | | | | | Rép. arabe syrienne |
| Production | 118 | 121 | *120 | *120 | *105 | *110 | 148 | Production |
| Consumption* | 730 | 745 | 760 | 775 | 790 | 800 | 825 | Consommation* |
| Consumption per capita | 45 | 45 | 44 | 44 | 44 | 44 | 44 | Consommation par habitant |

| Country or area | 2000 | 2001 | 2002 | 2003 | 2004 | 2005 | 2006 | Pays ou zone |
|---|---|---|---|---|---|---|---|---|
| Tajikistan | | | | | | | | Tadjikistan |
| Consumption* | 60 | 60 | 70 | 80 | 85 | 105 | 110 | Consommation* |
| Consumption per capita | 10 | 10 | 11 | 12 | 12 | 15 | 15 | Consommation par habitant |
| Thailand | | | | | | | | Thaïlande |
| Production | 6 157 | 5 370 | 6 438 | 7 737 | 7 462 | 4 589 | 5 646 | Production |
| Consumption | 1 816 | 1 955 | 1 978 | 2 073 | 2 303 | 2 352 | 2 464 | Consommation |
| Consumption per capita | 29 | 31 | 31 | 33 | 36 | 36 | 38 | Consommation par habitant |
| TFYR of Macedonia | | | | | | | | Ex-R.Y. Macédoine |
| Production | 13 | 6 | *10 | 16 | 16 | 16 | 19 | Production |
| Consumption* | 60 | 60 | 65 | 65 | 70 | 70 | 75 | Consommation* |
| Consumption per capita | 30 | 30 | 32 | 32 | 34 | 34 | 37 | Consommation par habitant |
| Togo | | | | | | | | Togo |
| Consumption | 45 | 45 | 45 | 48 | 50 | 60 | 65 | Consommation |
| Consumption per capita | 10 | 9 | 9 | 9 | 9 | 11 | 11 | Consommation par habitant |
| Trinidad and Tobago | | | | | | | | Trinité-et-Tobago |
| Production | 115 | 89 | 104 | 67 | 43 | 33 | *25 | Production |
| Consumption | 78 | 79 | 70 | 70 | *75 | *75 | *75 | Consommation |
| Consumption per capita | 60 | 62 | 54 | 55 | 59 | 59 | 59 | Consommation par habitant |
| Tunisia | | | | | | | | Tunisie |
| Production | 2 | ... | ... | ... | ... | ... | ... | Production |
| Consumption | 294 | 309 | 319 | *330 | 335 | 332 | 362 | Consommation |
| Consumption per capita | 31 | 32 | 33 | 33 | 34 | 33 | 36 | Consommation par habitant |
| Turkey | | | | | | | | Turquie |
| Production | 2 273 | 2 360 | 2 128 | 2 136 | 2 053 | 2 171 | 2 091 | Production |
| Consumption | *1 925 | 1 973 | 1 782 | 1 725 | 1 894 | 1 978 | 2 208 | Consommation |
| Consumption per capita | 29 | 29 | 26 | 24 | 27 | 27 | 30 | Consommation par habitant |
| Turkmenistan | | | | | | | | Turkménistan |
| Production | ... | ... | ... | 1 | *2 | *3 | *3 | Production |
| Consumption* | 70 | 70 | 70 | 75 | 75 | 80 | 85 | Consommation* |
| Consumption per capita | 15 | 14 | 15 | 15 | 14 | 14 | 13 | Consommation par habitant |
| Uganda | | | | | | | | Ouganda |
| Production | 149 | 146 | 180 | 192 | 213 | 211 | 208 | Production |
| Consumption | *155 | *160 | *180 | 225 | 257 | 263 | 260 | Consommation |
| Consumption per capita | 7 | 7 | 8 | 9 | 10 | 10 | 9 | Consommation par habitant |
| Ukraine | | | | | | | | Ukraine |
| Production | 1 686 | 1 802 | *1 545 | 1 690 | *1 945 | *2 060 | *2 800 | Production |
| Consumption* | 1 875 | 2 005 | 2 100 | 2 300 | 2 300 | 2 350 | 2 350 | Consommation* |
| Consumption per capita | 38 | 41 | 43 | 48 | 49 | 50 | 51 | Consommation par habitant |
| United Arab Emirates | | | | | | | | Emirats arabes unis |
| Consumption* | 102 | 105 | 113 | 119 | 127 | 140 | 151 | Consommation* |
| Consumption per capita | 33 | 32 | 30 | 30 | 29 | 30 | 30 | Consommation par habitant |
| United Rep. of Tanzania | | | | | | | | Rép.-Unie de Tanzanie |
| Production | *130 | *115 | 187 | 218 | 211 | 278 | 257 | Production |
| Consumption | *208 | *200 | 165 | 218 | 221 | 268 | 300 | Consommation |
| Consumption per capita | 6 | 6 | 5 | 6 | 6 | 7 | 8 | Consommation par habitant |
| United States | | | | | | | | Etats-Unis |
| Production | 8 080 | 7 774 | 6 805 | 7 964 | 7 647 | 6 784 | 7 034 | Production |
| Consumption | 9 051 | 9 139[7] | 9 079 | 8 844 | 8 994 | 9 248 | 9 228 | Consommation |
| Consumption per capita | 32 | 32 | 32 | 30 | 31 | 31 | 31 | Consommation par habitant |
| Uruguay | | | | | | | | Uruguay |
| Production* | 8 | 7 | 7 | 6 | 7 | 6 | 6 | Production* |
| Consumption* | 102 | 105 | 110 | 115 | 120 | 125 | 130 | Consommation* |
| Consumption per capita | 31 | 32 | 33 | 35 | 36 | 38 | 39 | Consommation par habitant |

| Country or area | 2000 | 2001 | 2002 | 2003 | 2004 | 2005 | 2006 | Pays ou zone |
|---|---|---|---|---|---|---|---|---|
| Uzbekistan | | | | | | | | Ouzbékistan |
| Production | 11 | *7 | *7 | ... | ... | ... | ... | Production |
| Consumption* | 450 | 475 | 490 | 495 | 495 | 505 | 510 | Consommation* |
| Consumption per capita | 18 | 19 | 19 | 19 | 19 | 20 | 20 | Consommation par habitant |
| Venezuela (Bolivarian Rep. of) | | | | | | | | Venezuela (Rép. bolivarienne du) |
| Production | *645 | *585 | *550 | *510 | 694 | *690 | *700 | Production |
| Consumption | *893 | *910 | *925 | *930 | 1 020 | *1 050 | *1 070 | Consommation |
| Consumption per capita | 37 | 37 | 37 | 36 | 38 | 39 | 39 | Consommation par habitant |
| Viet Nam | | | | | | | | Viet Nam |
| Production | 1 155 | *850 | *890 | *975 | *1 070 | 875 | *995 | Production |
| Consumption | *810 | *875 | *950 | *1 005 | *1 035 | 906 | *1 100 | Consommation |
| Consumption per capita | 10 | 11 | 12 | 12 | 13 | 11 | 12 | Consommation par habitant |
| Yemen | | | | | | | | Yémen |
| Consumption* | 410 | 425 | 445 | 470 | 480 | 495 | 510 | Consommation* |
| Consumption per capita | 22 | 23 | 23 | 23 | 23 | 23 | 24 | Consommation par habitant |
| Zambia | | | | | | | | Zambie |
| Production | *190 | 199 | 233 | 230 | 245 | 248 | *250 | Production |
| Consumption | *145 | 102 | 116 | 104 | 115 | 95 | *115 | Consommation |
| Consumption per capita | 14 | 11 | 11 | 9 | 10 | 8 | 10 | Consommation par habitant |
| Zimbabwe | | | | | | | | Zimbabwe |
| Production | 571 | 548 | 565 | 482 | 456 | 430 | 446 | Production |
| Consumption | 374 | 305 | 335 | 315 | 311 | 295 | 263 | Consommation |
| Consumption per capita | 30 | 24 | 27 | 25 | 27 | 25 | 23 | Consommation par habitant |

Source

International Sugar Organization (ISO), London, the "Sugar Yearbook 2007".

Notes

1 Including store losses of 1 159 tons and accidental losses of 129 tons.

2 For statistical purposes, the data for China do not include those for the Hong Kong Special Administrative Region (Hong Kong SAR), Macao Special Administrative Region (Macao SAR) and Taiwan Province of China.

3 Including non-human consumption: 1983 - 6 710 tons; 1984 - 19 797 tons; 1985 - 79 908 tons; 1986 - 98 608 tons; 1987 - 147 262 tons; 1988 - 122 058 tons; 1989 - 52 230 tons; 1991 - 13 541 tons; 1994 - 12 178 tons; 1995 - 10 211 tons; 1996 - 14 648 tons; 1997 - 13 893 tons; 1998 - 17 082 tons; 1999 - 42 635 tons; 2000 - 31 836 tons; 2001 - 13 534 tons; 2002 - 16 750 tons.

4 Beginning 2004, data for Cyprus, Czech Republic, Estonia, Hungary, Latvia, Lithuania, Malta, Poland, Slovakia, Slovenia are incorporated in the European Union data.

5 Including 11 572 tons sold to other Pacific Island nations in 1994; 12 520 tons in 1995; 14 154 tons in 1996; 13 109 tons in 1997; 6 444 tons in 2001; 10 686 tons in 2004 and 15 515 tons in 2006.

6 Including sugar used for the production of mono-sodium glutamate and llysin: 1987 - 44 600 tons; 1988 - 92 200 tons; 1989 - 94 500 tons; 1990 - 89 400 tons; 1991 - 77 300 tons; 1992 - 75 800 tons; 1993 - 89 800 tons; 1994 - 170 384 tons; 1995 - 200 863 tons; 1996 - 257 700 tons; 1997 - 257 310 tons; 1998 - 258 247 tons; 1999 - 152 739 tons; 2000 - 159 027 tons; 2001 - 210 498 tons; 2002 - 197 939 tons; 2003 - 226 191 tons; 2004 - 235 773 tons; 2005 - 241 101 tons; 2006 - 232 665 tons.

7 Including 19 780 tons used for livestock feed.

Source

Organisation internationale du sucre (OIS), Londres, "l'Annuaire du sucre 2007".

Notes

1 Y compris des pertes de 1 159 tonnes au cours du stockage et des pertes accidentelles de 129 tonnes.

2 Pour la présentation des statistiques, les données pour la Chine ne comprennent pas la Région Administrative Spéciale de Hong Kong (Hong Kong RAS), la Région Administrative Spéciale de Macao (Macao RAS) et la province de Taiwan.

3 Dont consommation non humaine : 1983 - 6 701 tonnes; 1984 - 19 797 tonnes; 1985 - 79 908 tonnes; 1986 - 98 608 tonnes; 1987 - 147 262 tonnes; 1988 - 122 058 tonnes; 1989 - 52 230 tonnes; 1991 - 13 541 tonnes; 1994 - 12 178 tonnes; 1995 - 10 211 tonnes; 1996 - 14 648 tonnes; 1997 -13 893 tonnes; 1998 - 17 082 tonnes; 1999 - 42 635 tonnes; 2000-31 836 tonnes; 2001 - 13 534 tonnes; 2002 - 16 750 tonnes.

4 À partir de 2004,  les données pour Chypre, République tchèque, Estonie, Hongrie, Lettonie, Lituanie, Malta, Pologne, Slovaquie, Slovénie sont inclues dans les données de l'Union européene.

5 Y compris 11 572 tonnes vendues aux autres iles pacifiques en 1994; 12 520 tonnes en 1995; 14 154 tonnes en 1996; 13 109 tonnes en 1997; 6 444 tonnes en 2001; 10 686 tonnes in 2004 et 15 515 tonnes en 2006.

6 Y compris la sucre utilisée pour la production du glutamate monosodium et lysine: 1987 - 44 600 tonnes ; 1988 - 92 200 tonnes; 1989 - 94 500 tonnes;  1990 - 89 400 tonnes; 1991 - 77 300 tonnes ; 1992 - 75 800 tonnes;  1993 - 89 800 tonnes; 1994 - 170 384 tonnes; 1995 - 200 863 tonnes;  1996 - 257 700 tonnes; 1997 - 257 310 tonnes; 1998 - 258 247 tonnes; 1999 - 152 739 tonnes; 2000 - 159 027 tonnes; 2001 - 210 498 tonnes; 2002 - 197 939 tonnes; 2003 - 226 191 tonnes; 2004 - 235 773 tonnes; 2005 - 241 101 tonnes; 2006 - 232 665 tonnes.

7 Y compris 19 780 tonnes utilisées pour les aliments du bétail.

# 40

## Meat
Production: thousand metric tons

## Viande
Production : milliers de tonnes

| Region, country or area | 1999 | 2000 | 2001 | 2002 | 2003 | 2004 | 2005 | 2006 | Région, pays ou zone |
|---|---|---|---|---|---|---|---|---|---|
| **World** | | | | | | | | | **Monde** |
| **Buffalo** | 2 965 | 2 993 | 2 953 | 3 018 | 2 990 | 3 104 | 3 154 | 3 183 | **Buffle** |
| Cattle | 56 345 | 56 918 | 56 069 | 57 698 | 58 286 | 59 532 | 59 928 | 61 033 | Bovine |
| Chicken | 56 367 | 59 479 | 62 114 | 64 555 | 66 403 | 69 144 | 71 940 | 73 057 | Poulet |
| Goat | 3 586 | 3 734 | 3 846 | 4 029 | 4 276 | 4 409 | 4 660 | 4 945 | Chèvre |
| Pig | 89 309 | 90 117 | 92 103 | 95 303 | 98 128 | 100 155 | 103 497 | 105 604 | Porc |
| Sheep | 7 383 | 7 591 | 7 608 | 7 664 | 7 847 | 8 188 | 8 462 | 8 633 | Mouton |
| **Africa** | | | | | | | | | **Afrique** |
| **Buffalo** | 277 | 288 | 189 | 203 | 229 | 269 | 270 | 270 | **Buffle** |
| Cattle | 3 796 | 3 990 | 3 910 | 4 128 | 4 221 | 4 320 | 4 455 | 4 565 | Bovine |
| Chicken | 2 799 | 2 909 | 3 107 | 3 222 | 3 245 | 3 284 | 3 435 | 3 472 | Poulet |
| Goat | 775 | 783 | 797 | 827 | 849 | 872 | 928 | 932 | Chèvre |
| Pig | 697 | 703 | 759 | 771 | 780 | 811 | 831 | 838 | Porc |
| Sheep | 1 050 | 1 066 | 1 100 | 1 092 | 1 114 | 1 128 | 1 150 | 1 167 | Mouton |
| **Algeria** | | | | | | | | | **Algérie** |
| Cattle | 117 | 133 | 105 | 116[1] | 121 | 125[2] | 120[1] | 122[1] | Bovine |
| Chicken[1] | 232 | 240 | 236 | 243 | 250 | 254 | 259 | 253 | Poulet[1] |
| Goat[1] | 12 | 12 | 12 | 12 | 12 | 13 | 13 | 14 | Chèvre[1] |
| Sheep | 163 | 164 | 165[1] | 165[1] | 165[1] | 172[1] | 178[1] | 185[1] | Mouton |
| **Angola[1]** | | | | | | | | | **Angola[1]** |
| Cattle | 85 | 85 | 85 | 85 | 85 | 76 | ... | 85 | Bovine |
| Chicken | 8 | 9 | 9 | 9 | 9 | 9 | 9 | 9 | Poulet |
| Goat | 9 | 10 | 10 | 9 | 9 | 9 | 9 | 9 | Chèvre |
| Pig | 29 | 29 | 29 | 28 | 28 | 28 | 30 | 30 | Porc |
| Sheep | 1 | 1 | 1 | 1 | 1 | 1 | 1 | 1 | Mouton |
| **Benin[1]** | | | | | | | | | **Bénin[1]** |
| Cattle | 19 | 18 | 19 | 20 | 20 | 21 | 22 | 22 | Bovine |
| Chicken | 12 | 12 | 12 | 12 | 12 | 12 | 12 | 16 | Poulet |
| Goat | 4 | 4 | 4 | 4 | 4 | 5 | 5 | 5 | Chèvre |
| Pig | 2 | 4 | 3 | 4 | 4 | 4 | 4 | 4 | Porc |
| Sheep | 2 | 3 | 3 | 3 | 3 | 3 | 3 | 3 | Mouton |
| **Botswana** | | | | | | | | | **Botswana** |
| Cattle | 27[1] | 29[1] | 34[1] | 31[1] | 27 | 31[1] | 31[1] | 31[1] | Bovine |
| Chicken[1] | 7 | 9 | 9 | 8 | 5 | 8 | 9 | 9 | Poulet[1] |
| Goat[1] | 6 | 5 | 5 | 5 | 5 | 5 | 5 | 5 | Chèvre[1] |
| Pig[1] | ^0 | 1 | ^0 | ^0 | ^0 | ^0 | ^0 | ^0 | Porc[1] |
| Sheep[1] | 2 | 2 | 2 | 2 | 2 | 2 | 2 | 2 | Mouton[1] |
| **Burkina Faso[1]** | | | | | | | | | **Burkina Faso[1]** |
| Cattle | 80 | 84 | 88 | 92 | 96 | 101 | 106 | 106 | Bovine |
| Chicken | 26 | 27 | 28 | 28 | 29 | 30 | 31 | 31 | Poulet |
| Goat | 23 | 24 | 24 | 25 | 26 | 27 | 28 | 28 | Chèvre |
| Pig | 18 | 20 | 22 | 25 | 27 | 30 | 33 | 33 | Porc |
| Sheep | 14 | 15 | 15 | 15 | 16 | 16 | 16 | 16 | Mouton |
| **Burundi** | | | | | | | | | **Burundi** |
| Cattle | 9 | 9 | 9[1] | 9[1] | 6 | 5 | 6 | 6[1] | Bovine |
| Chicken | 6 | 6[1] | 6[1] | 6[1] | 6[1] | 6[1] | 6[1] | 6[1] | Poulet |
| Goat | 3 | 3 | 3[1] | 3[1] | 3[1] | 3[1] | 3[1] | 3[1] | Chèvre |
| Pig[1] | 4 | 4 | 4 | 4 | 4 | 4 | 4 | 4 | Porc[1] |
| Sheep[1] | 1 | 1 | 1 | 1 | 1 | 1 | 1 | 1 | Mouton[1] |
| **Cameroon** | | | | | | | | | **Cameroun** |
| Cattle | 91[2] | 93[2] | 95[2] | 90[1] | 90[1] | 93[1] | 94[1] | 94[1] | Bovine |
| Chicken[1] | 29 | 21 | 30 | 30 | 30 | 32 | 33 | 30 | Poulet[1] |
| Goat[1] | 14 | 16 | 16 | 16 | 16 | 16 | 16 | 16 | Chèvre[1] |
| Pig[1] | 12 | 16 | 16 | 16 | 16 | 16 | 16 | 16 | Porc[1] |
| Sheep[1] | 16 | 16 | 16 | 16 | 16 | 16 | 16 | 16 | Mouton[1] |

| Region, country or area | 1999 | 2000 | 2001 | 2002 | 2003 | 2004 | 2005 | 2006 | Région, pays ou zone |
|---|---|---|---|---|---|---|---|---|---|
| Cape Verde | | | | | | | | | Cap-Vert |
| Cattle | ^0 | ^0 | 1[1] | ^0[1] | ^0[1] | ^0[1] | ^0[1] | ^0[1] | Bovine |
| Chicken | 1 | ^0 | ^0[1] | ^0[1] | ^0[1] | ^0[1] | ^0[1] | ^0[1] | Poulet |
| Pig | 7[1] | 7 | 7[1] | 7[1] | 7[1] | 7[1] | 7[1] | 7[1] | Porc |
| Central African Rep. | | | | | | | | | Rép. centrafricaine |
| Cattle | 51[2] | 67 | 67 | 69 | 71[1] | 74[2] | 74[1] | 74[1] | Bovine |
| Chicken | 3 | 3 | 3[1] | 4 | 4[1] | 4[1] | 4[1] | 4[1] | Poulet |
| Goat | 8[1] | 10[2] | 10[1] | 11 | 12[1] | 12[1] | 12[1] | 12[1] | Chèvre |
| Pig | 12[1] | 12[2] | 13[1] | 13 | 13 | 14[2] | 14[1] | 14[1] | Porc |
| Sheep[1] | 1 | 1 | 1 | 1 | 2 | 2 | 2 | 2 | Mouton[1] |
| Chad[1] | | | | | | | | | Tchad[1] |
| Cattle | 78 | 74 | 77 | 76 | 78 | 80 | 82 | 84 | Bovine |
| Chicken | 5 | 5 | 5 | 5 | 5 | 5 | 5 | 5 | Poulet |
| Goat | 18 | 19 | 20 | 20 | 21 | 21 | 22 | 22 | Chèvre |
| Pig | ^0 | ^0 | ^0 | ^0 | ^0 | ^0 | ^0 | 1 | Porc |
| Sheep | 11 | 12 | 12 | 13 | 13 | 13 | 14 | 14 | Mouton |
| Comoros[1] | | | | | | | | | Comores[1] |
| Cattle | 1 | 1 | 1 | 1 | 1 | 1 | 1 | 1 | Bovine |
| Chicken | 1 | 1 | 1 | 1 | 1 | 1 | 1 | 1 | Poulet |
| Goat | 1 | ^0 | ^0 | ^0 | ^0 | ^0 | ^0 | ^0 | Chèvre |
| Congo[1] | | | | | | | | | Congo[1] |
| Cattle | 2 | 2 | 2 | 2 | 2 | 2 | 2 | 2 | Bovine |
| Chicken | 6 | 6 | 6 | 5 | 5 | 5 | 6 | 6 | Poulet |
| Goat | 1 | 1 | 1 | 1 | 1 | 1 | 1 | 1 | Chèvre |
| Pig | 2 | 2 | 2 | 2 | 2 | 2 | 2 | 2 | Porc |
| Côte d'Ivoire | | | | | | | | | Côte d'Ivoire |
| Cattle | 47 | 48 | 46 | 53 | 51 | 52 | 52[1] | 52[1] | Bovine |
| Chicken[1] | 65 | 63 | 65 | 69 | 69 | 71 | 73 | 73 | Poulet[1] |
| Goat | 5[2] | 5[2] | 5[1] | 4[1] | 4[1] | 4[1] | 4[1] | 4[1] | Chèvre |
| Pig | 13[1] | 13[2] | 14[1] | 14[1] | 12[1] | 12[1] | 12[1] | 12[1] | Porc |
| Sheep | 6[2] | 5 | 5 | 5 | 5[1] | 5[1] | 5[1] | 5[1] | Mouton |
| Dem. Rep. of the Congo | | | | | | | | | Rép. dém. du Congo |
| Cattle | 14 | 14 | 13 | 12 | 12 | 12 | 12 | 13[1] | Bovine |
| Chicken | 12 | 12 | 11 | 11 | 11 | 11 | 11 | 11[1] | Poulet |
| Goat | 19 | 19 | 19 | 18 | 18 | 18 | 18 | 19[1] | Chèvre |
| Pig | 27 | 26 | 25 | 24 | 24 | 24 | 24 | 24[1] | Porc |
| Sheep | 3 | 3 | 3 | 3 | 3 | 3 | 3 | 3[1] | Mouton |
| Djibouti[1] | | | | | | | | | Djibouti[1] |
| Cattle | 4 | 6 | 6 | 6 | 6 | 6 | 6 | 6 | Bovine |
| Goat | 2 | 2 | 2 | 2 | 2 | 2 | 2 | 2 | Chèvre |
| Sheep | 2 | 2 | 2 | 2 | 2 | 2 | 2 | 2 | Mouton |
| Egypt | | | | | | | | | Egypte |
| Buffalo | 277 | 288 | 189 | 203 | 229 | 269 | 270[1] | 270[1] | Buffle |
| Cattle | 233 | 256[2] | 247[2] | 252 | 287 | 325 | 320[1] | 320[1] | Bovine |
| Chicken | 485 | 513 | 539 | 548[1] | 562[1] | 611[1] | 647[1] | 647[1] | Poulet |
| Goat | 30 | 25[1] | 25[1] | 26 | 21 | 17 | 18[1] | 18[1] | Chèvre |
| Pig | 3 | 3[2] | 3[2] | 3[1] | 2 | 2 | 2[1] | 2[1] | Porc |
| Sheep | 50[1] | 50 | 53 | 52 | 50 | 40 | 43[1] | 43[1] | Mouton |
| Eritrea[1] | | | | | | | | | Erythrée[1] |
| Cattle | 16 | 16 | 15 | 14 | 17 | 17 | 17 | ... | Bovine |
| Chicken | 2 | 2 | 2 | 2 | 2 | 2 | 2 | ... | Poulet |
| Goat | 6 | 6 | 6 | 6 | 6 | 6 | 6 | ... | Chèvre |
| Sheep | 6 | 6 | 6 | 6 | 7 | 7 | 6 | ... | Mouton |
| Ethiopia | | | | | | | | | Ethiopie |
| Cattle | 290 | 294[1] | 304[1] | 353[1] | 338[1] | ... | ... | 350[1] | Bovine |
| Chicken[1] | 37 | 38 | 50 | 54 | 50 | 47 | 53 | 53 | Poulet[1] |
| Goat[1] | 27 | 26 | 29 | ... | ... | ... | ... | 49 | Chèvre[1] |
| Pig[1] | 1 | 1 | 1 | 1 | 2 | 2 | 2 | 2 | Porc[1] |
| Sheep[1] | 36 | 36 | 38 | 48 | ... | ... | ... | 69 | Mouton[1] |

| Region, country or area | 1999 | 2000 | 2001 | 2002 | 2003 | 2004 | 2005 | 2006 | Région, pays ou zone |
|---|---|---|---|---|---|---|---|---|---|
| Gabon[1] | | | | | | | | | Gabon[1] |
| Cattle | 1 | 1 | 1 | 1 | 1 | 1 | 1 | 1 | Bovine |
| Chicken | 4 | 4 | 4 | 4 | 4 | 4 | 4 | 4 | Poulet |
| Pig | 3 | 3 | 3 | 3 | 3 | 3 | 3 | 3 | Porc |
| Sheep | 1 | 1 | 1 | 1 | 1 | 1 | 1 | 1 | Mouton |
| Gambia[1] | | | | | | | | | Gambie[1] |
| Cattle | 3 | 3 | 3 | 3 | 3 | 3 | 3 | 3 | Bovine |
| Chicken | 1 | 1 | 1 | 1 | 1 | 1 | 1 | 1 | Poulet |
| Goat | ^0 | ^0 | 1 | 1 | 1 | 1 | 1 | 1 | Chèvre |
| Pig | ^0 | ^0 | ^0 | ^0 | ^0 | ^0 | ^0 | 1 | Porc |
| Ghana | | | | | | | | | Ghana |
| Cattle | 21[1] | 24[1] | 24[1] | 24[1] | 24[1] | 23 | 25 | 24[1] | Bovine |
| Chicken[1] | 17 | 20 | 21 | 23 | 26 | 28 | 29 | 30 | Poulet[1] |
| Goat | 7[1] | 10[1] | 11[1] | 11[1] | 12[1] | 12 | 12 | 11[1] | Chèvre |
| Pig | 10[1] | 11[1] | 11[1] | 10[1] | 10[1] | 5 | 5 | 4[1] | Porc |
| Sheep | 7[1] | 9[1] | 10[1] | 10[1] | 10[1] | 10 | 10 | 10[1] | Mouton |
| Guinea[1] | | | | | | | | | Guinée[1] |
| Cattle | 30 | 32 | 33 | 34 | 34 | 35 | 37 | 39 | Bovine |
| Chicken | 4 | 4 | 4 | 4 | 5 | 5 | 5 | 5 | Poulet |
| Goat | 4 | 4 | 5 | 5 | 5 | 6 | 6 | 6 | Chèvre |
| Pig | 2 | 2 | 2 | 2 | 2 | 2 | 2 | 2 | Porc |
| Sheep | 3 | 3 | 4 | 4 | 4 | 4 | 5 | 5 | Mouton |
| Guinea-Bissau[1] | | | | | | | | | Guinée-Bissau[1] |
| Cattle | 4 | 5 | 5 | 5 | 5 | 5 | 5 | 5 | Bovine |
| Chicken | 1 | 1 | 1 | 1 | 1 | 1 | 1 | 2 | Poulet |
| Goat | 1 | 1 | 1 | 1 | 1 | 1 | 1 | 1 | Chèvre |
| Pig | 11 | 11 | 11 | 11 | 11 | 11 | 12 | 12 | Porc |
| Sheep | 1 | 1 | 1 | 1 | 1 | 1 | 1 | 1 | Mouton |
| Kenya | | | | | | | | | Kenya |
| Cattle | 279 | 257 | 282 | 319 | 343 | 350 | 396 | 396[1] | Bovine |
| Chicken | 55[1] | 13 | 19 | 20 | 21 | 19 | 18 | 18[1] | Poulet |
| Goat | 34[1] | 31[1] | 31 | 43 | 39 | 39 | 39 | 38 | Chèvre |
| Pig | 11 | 11 | 15[1] | 11 | 15 | 15 | 13 | 11 | Porc |
| Sheep | 28[1] | 27 | 34 | 39 | 36 | 36 | 37 | 37[1] | Mouton |
| Lesotho[1] | | | | | | | | | Lesotho[1] |
| Cattle | 9 | ... | ... | ... | ... | ... | ... | ... | Bovine |
| Goat | 2 | 2 | 2 | 2 | 2 | 2 | 2 | ... | Chèvre |
| Pig | 3 | 3 | 3 | 3 | 3 | 3 | 3 | ... | Porc |
| Sheep | 3 | ... | ... | ... | ... | ... | ... | ... | Mouton |
| Liberia[1] | | | | | | | | | Libéria[1] |
| Cattle | 1 | 1 | 1 | 1 | 1 | 1 | 1 | 1 | Bovine |
| Chicken | 6 | 6 | 7 | 7 | 8 | 8 | 8 | 9 | Poulet |
| Goat | 1 | 1 | 1 | 1 | 1 | 1 | 1 | 1 | Chèvre |
| Pig | 4 | 4 | 4 | 4 | 4 | 4 | 4 | 5 | Porc |
| Sheep | 1 | 1 | 1 | 1 | 1 | 1 | 1 | 1 | Mouton |
| Libyan Arab Jamah. | | | | | | | | | Jamah. arabe libyenne |
| Cattle[1] | 16 | 8 | 6 | 6 | 6 | 6 | 6 | 6 | Bovine[1] |
| Chicken[1] | 98 | 99 | 99 | 99 | 99 | 108 | 113 | 113 | Poulet[1] |
| Goat | 6[1] | 6[1] | 6[1] | 6[1] | 6[1] | 6[1] | 6 | 6[1] | Chèvre |
| Sheep | 34[1] | 27[1] | 32[1] | 27[1] | 27[1] | 27[1] | 27 | 27[1] | Mouton |
| Madagascar[1] | | | | | | | | | Madagascar[1] |
| Cattle | 148 | 148 | 119 | 112 | 115 | 147 | 147 | 147 | Bovine |
| Chicken | 32 | 36 | 40 | 40 | 40 | 42 | 43 | 43 | Poulet |
| Goat | 6 | 5 | 6 | 6 | 6 | 6 | 6 | 6 | Chèvre |
| Pig | 65 | 63 | 70 | 70 | 70 | 73 | 74 | 74 | Porc |
| Sheep | 2 | 2 | 2 | 2 | 3 | 2 | 2 | 2 | Mouton |

**Meat**—Production: thousand metric tons (*continued*)
**Viande**—Production : milliers de tonnes (*suite*)

| Region, country or area | 1999 | 2000 | 2001 | 2002 | 2003 | 2004 | 2005 | 2006 | Région, pays ou zone |
|---|---|---|---|---|---|---|---|---|---|
| Malawi[1] | | | | | | | | | Malawi[1] |
| Cattle | 15 | 16 | 16 | 16 | 16 | 16 | 16 | 16 | Bovine |
| Chicken | 15 | 15 | 15 | 15 | 15 | 16 | 16 | 16 | Poulet |
| Goat | 5 | 6 | 6 | 6 | 6 | 7 | 7 | 7 | Chèvre |
| Pig | 20 | 22 | 20 | 21 | 21 | 23 | 24 | 24 | Porc |
| Mali[1] | | | | | | | | | Mali[1] |
| Cattle | 89 | 76 | 85 | 103 | 113 | 98 | 98 | 101 | Bovine |
| Chicken | 29 | 29 | 27 | 33 | 34 | 35 | 36 | 37 | Poulet |
| Goat | 35 | 36 | 39 | 42 | 46 | 48 | 49 | 51 | Chèvre |
| Pig | 2 | 2 | 2 | 2 | 2 | 2 | 2 | 2 | Porc |
| Sheep | 25 | 26 | 29 | 31 | 34 | 36 | 36 | 36 | Mouton |
| Mauritania[1] | | | | | | | | | Mauritanie[1] |
| Cattle | 14 | 21 | 22 | 22 | 23 | 23 | 23 | ... | Bovine |
| Chicken | 4 | 4 | 5 | 4 | 4 | 4 | 5 | ... | Poulet |
| Goat | 12 | 12 | 13 | 14 | 14 | 14 | 14 | ... | Chèvre |
| Sheep | 21 | 22 | 23 | 24 | 24 | 25 | 25 | ... | Mouton |
| Mauritius | | | | | | | | | Maurice |
| Cattle | 3 | 3 | 2 | 3 | 3 | 2 | 2 | 2 | Bovine |
| Chicken | 21 | 21 | 27 | 29 | 30 | 33 | 33 | 36 | Poulet |
| Pig | 1 | 1 | 1 | 1 | 1 | 1 | 1 | 1 | Porc |
| Morocco | | | | | | | | | Maroc |
| Cattle | 135 | 140 | 145 | 170 | 150 | 140 | 150 | 150 | Bovine |
| Chicken | 260 | 250 | 255 | 280 | 320 | 325 | 350 | 340 | Poulet |
| Goat | 20 | 22 | 21 | 15 | 13 | 18 | 16 | 17 | Chèvre |
| Pig | 1 | 1[2] | 1[1] | 1[1] | 1[1] | 1[1] | 1[1] | 1[1] | Porc |
| Sheep | 126 | 125 | 125 | 110 | 105 | 105 | 108 | 112 | Mouton |
| Mozambique[1] | | | | | | | | | Mozambique[1] |
| Cattle | 38 | 38 | 38 | 38 | 38 | 38 | 38 | 38 | Bovine |
| Chicken | 38 | 40 | 40 | 44 | 40 | 43 | 44 | 44 | Poulet |
| Goat | 2 | 2 | 2 | 2 | 2 | 2 | 2 | 2 | Chèvre |
| Pig | 13 | 13 | 13 | 13 | 13 | 13 | 13 | 13 | Porc |
| Sheep | 1 | 1 | 1 | 1 | 1 | 1 | 1 | 1 | Mouton |
| Namibia | | | | | | | | | Namibie |
| Cattle | 45[1] | 64[1] | 58[1] | 50[1] | 45[1] | 43 | 39 | 36 | Bovine |
| Chicken[1] | 5 | 5 | 5 | 5 | 5 | 6 | 6 | 6 | Poulet[1] |
| Goat[1] | 5 | 5 | ... | ... | ... | ... | ... | 5 | Chèvre[1] |
| Pig[1] | 1 | 1 | 1 | 1 | 1 | ^0 | ^0 | ^0 | Porc[1] |
| Sheep[1] | 4[1] | ... | 6[1] | 6[1] | 6[1] | 7 | 7[1] | 7[1] | Mouton[1] |
| Niger | | | | | | | | | Niger |
| Cattle | 40[1] | 41[2] | 42[2] | ... | ... | ... | ... | 47[1] | Bovine |
| Chicken[1] | 27 | 27 | 28 | 28 | 29 | 30 | 30 | 30 | Poulet[1] |
| Goat[1] | 25 | 25 | 25 | ... | ... | ... | ... | 29 | Chèvre[1] |
| Pig[1] | 1 | 1 | 1 | 1 | 1 | 1 | 1 | 1 | Porc[1] |
| Sheep[1] | 15 | 15 | 16 | ... | ... | ... | ... | 17 | Mouton[1] |
| Nigeria | | | | | | | | | Nigéria |
| Cattle | 298 | 279[1] | 279[1] | 280[1] | 280[1] | 280[1] | 280[1] | 284[1] | Bovine |
| Chicken[1] | 172 | 160 | 184 | 190 | 201 | 192 | 190 | 222 | Poulet[1] |
| Goat[1] | 137 | 139 | 140 | 142 | 142 | 147 | 147 | 147 | Chèvre[1] |
| Pig[1] | 153 | 158 | 185 | 193 | 200 | 201 | 206 | 210 | Porc[1] |
| Sheep[1] | 91 | 95 | 94 | 97 | 99 | 101 | 101 | 103 | Mouton[1] |
| Réunion | | | | | | | | | Réunion |
| Cattle | 2 | 2 | 2 | 2 | 2 | 2 | 2 | 2[1] | Bovine |
| Chicken | 14 | 13[1] | 13 | 14 | 14 | 14 | 14 | 14[1] | Poulet |
| Pig | 12 | 12 | 12 | 12 | 10 | 11 | 12 | 12[1] | Porc |

| Region, country or area | 1999 | 2000 | 2001 | 2002 | 2003 | 2004 | 2005 | 2006 | Région, pays ou zone |
|---|---|---|---|---|---|---|---|---|---|
| Rwanda[1] | | | | | | | | | Rwanda[1] |
| Cattle | 18 | 17 | 19 | 20 | 24 | 23 | 23 | 23 | Bovine |
| Chicken | 2 | 1 | 2 | 2 | 2 | 2 | 2 | 2 | Poulet |
| Goat | 2 | 3 | 3 | 3 | 3 | 4 | 5 | 5 | Chèvre |
| Pig | 3 | 3 | 3 | 4 | 4 | 6 | 6 | 6 | Porc |
| Sheep | 1 | 1 | 1 | 1 | 1 | 1 | 1 | 1 | Mouton |
| Sao Tome and Principe[1] | | | | | | | | | Sao Tomé-et-Principe[1] |
| Chicken | ^0 | 1 | 1 | 1 | 1 | 1 | 1 | 1 | Poulet |
| Senegal | | | | | | | | | Sénégal |
| Cattle | 45 | 46 | 48 | 45 | 43 | 43 | 47 | 48[1] | Bovine |
| Chicken | 22 | 23 | 24 | 24 | 25 | 26 | 29 | 29[1] | Poulet |
| Goat | 9 | 10 | 9 | 9 | 9 | 10 | 11 | 12[1] | Chèvre |
| Pig | 7 | 9 | 9 | 11 | 10 | 9 | 10 | 10[1] | Porc |
| Sheep | 14 | 13 | 16 | 15 | 15 | 15 | 17 | 17[1] | Mouton |
| Seychelles[1] | | | | | | | | | Seychelles[1] |
| Chicken | 1 | 1 | 1 | 1 | 1 | 1 | 1 | 1 | Poulet |
| Pig | 1 | 1 | 1 | 1 | 1 | 1 | 1 | 1 | Porc |
| Sierra Leone[1] | | | | | | | | | Sierra Leone[1] |
| Cattle | ... | ... | ... | ... | ... | ... | ... | 4 | Bovine |
| Pig | 9 | 9 | 11 | 10 | 11 | 11 | 11 | 11 | Porc |
| Chicken | ^0 | ... | ... | ... | ... | ... | ... | 1 | Poulet |
| Goat | 2 | 2 | 2 | 2 | 2 | 2 | 2 | 2 | Chèvre |
| Sheep | ... | ... | ... | ... | ... | ... | ... | 1 | Mouton |
| Somalia[1] | | | | | | | | | Somalie[1] |
| Cattle | 58 | 62 | 63 | 62 | 66 | 66 | 66 | ... | Bovine |
| Chicken | 3 | 3 | 4 | 4 | 4 | 4 | 4 | ... | Poulet |
| Goat | 38 | 33 | 33 | 39 | 42 | 42 | 42 | ... | Chèvre |
| Sheep | 30 | 35 | 47 | 40 | 48 | 48 | 48 | ... | Mouton |
| South Africa | | | | | | | | | Afrique du Sud |
| Cattle | 512 | 625 | 525 | 574 | 610 | 655 | 705 | 804 | Bovine |
| Chicken | 756[2] | 869 | 950 | 986 | 959 | 906 | 949 | 971 | Poulet |
| Goat[1] | 36 | 36 | 36 | 36 | 36 | 36 | 37 | 37 | Chèvre[1] |
| Pig | 123 | 104 | 111 | 111 | 134 | 145 | 147 | 151 | Porc |
| Sheep | 112 | 118 | 104 | 105 | 120 | 120 | 115 | 117 | Mouton |
| Sudan | | | | | | | | | Soudan |
| Cattle[1] | 276 | 296 | 320 | 325 | ... | ... | ... | 340 | Bovine[1] |
| Chicken[1] | 26 | 26 | 27 | 27 | 30 | 29 | 29 | 29 | Poulet[1] |
| Goat | 114 | 118 | 122[1] | 126[1] | 138 | 139 | 186 | 186[1] | Chèvre |
| Sheep[1] | 142 | 143 | 150 | 144 | 144 | ... | ... | 148 | Mouton[1] |
| Swaziland | | | | | | | | | Swaziland |
| Cattle | 14[1] | 18 | 8 | 13 | 13[1] | 13[1] | 13[1] | 13[1] | Bovine |
| Chicken[1] | 6 | 7 | 6 | 5 | 5 | 6 | 7 | 5 | Poulet[1] |
| Goat[1] | 2 | 3 | 3 | 2 | 2 | 2 | 2 | 2 | Chèvre[1] |
| Pig[1] | 1 | 1 | 1 | 1 | 1 | 1 | 1 | 1 | Porc[1] |
| Sheep[1] | 1 | ^0 | ^0 | ^0 | ^0 | ^0 | ^0 | ^0 | Mouton[1] |
| Togo[1] | | | | | | | | | Togo[1] |
| Cattle | 5 | 5 | 6 | 6 | 6 | 6 | 6 | 6 | Bovine |
| Chicken | 10 | 10 | 10 | 10 | 10 | 11 | 11 | 12 | Poulet |
| Goat | 3 | 4 | 4 | 4 | 4 | 4 | 4 | 4 | Chèvre |
| Pig | 4 | 4 | 5 | 5 | 5 | 4 | 4 | 5 | Porc |
| Sheep | 3 | 3 | 4 | 4 | 4 | 4 | 4 | 4 | Mouton |
| Tunisia | | | | | | | | | Tunisie |
| Cattle | 58 | 60 | 60 | 64 | 58 | 53 | 55[1] | 55[1] | Bovine |
| Chicken | 83 | 87 | 91 | 94 | 90 | 96 | 101[1] | 101[1] | Poulet |
| Goat | 10 | 9 | 9 | 10 | 9 | 9 | 10[1] | 10[1] | Chèvre |
| Sheep | 53 | 54 | 56 | 58 | 51 | 52 | 55[1] | 55[1] | Mouton |

**Meat** — Production: thousand metric tons (*continued*)
**Viande** — Production : milliers de tonnes (*suite*)

| Region, country or area | 1999 | 2000 | 2001 | 2002 | 2003 | 2004 | 2005 | 2006 | Région, pays ou zone |
|---|---|---|---|---|---|---|---|---|---|
| Uganda | | | | | | | | | Ouganda |
| Cattle | 96[1] | 97[1] | 101[1] | 106 | 110[1] | 106[1] | 106[1] | 106[1] | Bovine |
| Chicken[1] | 37 | 44 | 49 | 54 | 38 | 38 | 44 | 44 | Poulet[1] |
| Goat[1] | 24 | 25 | 25 | 25 | 29 | 29 | 29 | 29 | Chèvre[1] |
| Pig[1] | 75 | 77 | 81 | 84 | 60 | 76 | 79 | 79 | Porc[1] |
| Sheep[1] | 5 | 5 | 6 | 6 | 8 | 8 | 6 | 6 | Mouton[1] |
| United Rep. of Tanzania | | | | | | | | | Rép.-Unie de Tanzanie |
| Cattle[1] | 215 | 225 | 230 | 246 | 246 | 246 | 246 | 246 | Bovine[1] |
| Chicken | 42[1] | 42[1] | 44 | 44[1] | 46[1] | 47[1] | 49[1] | 49[1] | Poulet |
| Goat[1] | 29 | 29 | 30 | 31 | 31 | 31 | 31 | 31 | Chèvre[1] |
| Pig[1] | 12 | 13 | 13 | 13 | 13 | 14 | 14 | 14 | Porc[1] |
| Sheep[1] | 11 | 10 | 10 | 10 | 10 | 10 | 10 | 10 | Mouton[1] |
| Zambia[1] | | | | | | | | | Zambie[1] |
| Cattle | 47 | 41 | 41 | 41 | 41 | 41 | 41 | 41 | Bovine |
| Chicken | 34 | 35 | 37 | 37 | 37 | 39 | 41 | 41 | Poulet |
| Goat | 4 | 5 | 5 | 5 | 5 | 5 | 5 | 5 | Chèvre |
| Pig | 11 | 10 | 11 | 11 | 11 | 11 | 11 | 11 | Porc |
| Sheep | ^0 | 1 | 1 | 1 | 1 | 1 | 1 | 1 | Mouton |
| Zimbabwe | | | | | | | | | Zimbabwe |
| Cattle | 95 | 101 | 101[1] | 99[1] | 97[1] | 97[1] | 97[1] | 97[1] | Bovine |
| Chicken[1] | 31 | 33 | 44 | 46 | 41 | 45 | 46 | 40 | Poulet[1] |
| Goat[1] | 13 | 13 | 13 | 13 | 13 | 13 | 13 | 13 | Chèvre[1] |
| Pig | 13 | 20[1] | 27[1] | 27[1] | 28[1] | 27[1] | 27[1] | 28[1] | Porc |
| Sheep[1] | 1 | 1 | 1 | 1 | 1 | 1 | 1 | 1 | Mouton[1] |
| **Northern America** | | | | | | | | | **Amérique septentrionale** |
| **Cattle** | **13 387** | **13 561** | **13 244** | **13 721** | **13 229** | **12 677** | **12 766** | **13 301** | **Bovine** |
| **Chicken** | **14 484** | **14 848** | **15 220** | **15 423** | **15 650** | **16 317** | **16 945** | **16 941** | **Poulet** |
| **Goat** | **...** | **...** | **...** | **...** | **...** | **...** | **...** | **21** | **Chèvre** |
| **Pig** | **10 324** | **10 237** | **10 422** | **10 787** | **10 938** | **11 233** | **11 296** | **11 448** | **Porc** |
| **Sheep** | **123** | **119** | **116** | **116** | **108** | **108** | **103** | **101** | **Mouton** |
| Canada | | | | | | | | | Canada |
| Cattle | 1 264 | 1 263 | 1 262 | 1 294 | 1 190 | 1 496 | 1 523 | 1 391 | Bovine |
| Chicken | 866 | 904 | 953 | 956 | 954 | 970 | 1 000 | 997 | Poulet |
| Pig | 1 566 | 1 640 | 1 731 | 1 858 | 1 882 | 1 920 | 1 914 | 1 898 | Porc |
| Sheep | 11 | 13 | 14 | 15 | 16 | 18 | 18 | 17 | Mouton |
| United States | | | | | | | | | Etats-Unis |
| Cattle | 12 123 | 12 298 | 11 982 | 12 427 | 12 039 | 11 181 | 11 243 | 11 910 | Bovine |
| Chicken | 13 618 | 13 944 | 14 267 | 14 467 | 14 696 | 15 347[1] | 15 945[1] | 15 945[1] | Poulet |
| Goat | ... | ... | ... | ... | ... | ... | ... | 21 | Chèvre |
| Pig | 8 758 | 8 597 | 8 691 | 8 929 | 9 056 | 9 313 | 9 383 | 9 550 | Porc |
| Sheep | 113 | 106 | 101 | 101[2] | 92[2] | 90 | 85 | 84 | Mouton |
| **Latin America and the Caribbean** | | | | | | | | | **Amérique latine et Caraïbes** |
| **Cattle** | **13 597** | **13 853** | **13 646** | **14 085** | **14 372** | **15 443** | **15 598** | **15 672** | **Bovine** |
| **Chicken** | **11 457** | **12 311** | **12 973** | **13 825** | **14 474** | **15 884** | **16 368** | **16 567** | **Poulet** |
| **Goat** | **127** | **133** | **130** | **135** | **137** | **137** | **139** | **138** | **Chèvre** |
| **Pig** | **4 801** | **5 049** | **5 167** | **5 355** | **5 634** | **5 807** | **5 947** | **6 011** | **Porc** |
| **Sheep** | **287** | **297** | **300** | **279** | **282** | **292** | **290** | **293** | **Mouton** |
| Antigua and Barbuda[1] | | | | | | | | | Antigua-et-Barbuda[1] |
| Cattle | ^0 | ^0 | 1 | 1 | 1 | 1 | 1 | ... | Bovine |
| Argentina | | | | | | | | | Argentina |
| Cattle | 2 720 | 2 718 | 2 461 | 2 493 | 2 658 | 3 024 | 2 980 | 2 980[1] | Bovine |
| Chicken | 940 | 958 | 951 | 699 | 738 | 866 | 1 010 | 1 156 | Poule |
| Goat[1] | 9 | 9 | 9 | 9 | 10 | 10 | 10 | 10 | Chèvre[1] |
| Pig | 215 | 214 | 198 | 165 | 150 | 178[1] | 188[1] | 188[1] | Porc |
| Sheep | 45[2] | 50[1] | 50[1] | 50[1] | 52[1] | 52[1] | 52[1] | 52[1] | Mouton |
| Bahamas | | | | | | | | | Bahamas |
| Chicken | 9 | 7 | 7 | 7[1] | 8[1] | 9[1] | 9[1] | ... | Poulet |

| Region, country or area | 1999 | 2000 | 2001 | 2002 | 2003 | 2004 | 2005 | 2006 | Région, pays ou zone |
|---|---|---|---|---|---|---|---|---|---|
| Barbados | | | | | | | | | Barbade |
| Cattle | 1 | 1 | ^0 | ^0 | ^0 | ^0 | ^0[1] | ^0[1] | Bovine |
| Chicken | 12 | 12[1] | 12[1] | 12[1] | 11 | 13 | 14[1] | 14[1] | Poulet |
| Pig | 2 | 2 | 2 | 1 | 2 | 2 | 2[1] | 2[1] | Porc |
| Belize | | | | | | | * | | Belize |
| Cattle | 1 | 1 | 1 | 2 | 2 | 3 | 2[1] | 2[1] | Bovine |
| Chicken | 8 | 9 | 10 | 14 | 14 | 14 | 14[1] | 14[1] | Poulet |
| Pig | 1 | 1 | 1 | 1 | 1 | 1 | 1[1] | 1[1] | Porc |
| Bolivia | | | | | | | | | Bolivie |
| Cattle | 155 | 160 | 161 | 165 | 168 | 172 | 172[1] | 172[1] | Bovine |
| Chicken | 138 | 134 | 128 | 135 | 135 | 155[1] | 168[1] | 168[1] | Poulet |
| Goat[1] | 6 | 6 | 6 | 6 | 6 | 6 | 6 | 6 | Chèvre[1] |
| Pig[1] | 74 | 76 | 97 | 101 | 104 | 101 | 101 | 101 | Porc[1] |
| Sheep | 15 | 16 | 16 | 17 | 18 | 18 | 18[1] | 18[1] | Mouton |
| Brazil | | | | | | | | | Brésil |
| Cattle | 6 413 | 6 579 | 6 824 | 7 139 | 7 230 | 7 774 | 7 774[1] | 7 774[1] | Bovine |
| Chicken | 5 526 | 5 981 | 6 208 | 7 050 | 7 760 | 8 668 | 8 507[1] | 8 507[1] | Poule |
| Goat[1] | 38 | 39 | 39 | 40 | 41 | 41 | 41 | 41 | Chèvre[1] |
| Pig | 2 400[1] | 2 600[1] | 2 637 | 2 798 | 3 059 | 3 110 | 3 140[1] | 3 140[1] | Porc |
| Sheep[1] | 71 | 72 | 72 | 69 | 68 | 76 | 76 | 76 | Mouton[1] |
| Chile | | | | | | | | | Chili |
| Cattle | 226 | 226 | 218 | 200 | 192 | 208 | 216 | 238 | Bovine |
| Chicken | 344 | 378 | 408 | 379 | 389 | 446 | 457 | 517 | Poulet |
| Goat[1] | 5 | 5 | 5 | 5 | 5 | 5 | 5 | 5 | Chèvre[1] |
| Pig | 244 | 261 | 303 | 351 | 365 | 373 | 411 | 468 | Porc |
| Sheep | 13 | 11 | 11 | 10 | 10 | 10 | 9 | 11 | Mouton |
| Colombia | | | | | | | | | Colombie |
| Cattle | 716 | 745 | 700[1] | 675[1] | 642 | 717 | 792 | 792[1] | Bovine |
| Chicken | 496 | 504 | 596 | 649 | 678 | 709 | 763 | 763[1] | Poulet |
| Goat | 6 | 7[1] | 6[1] | 6[1] | 7[1] | 7[1] | 7[1] | 7[1] | Chèvre |
| Pig | 107 | 105 | 98 | 109 | 124 | 130 | 128 | 128[1] | Porc |
| Sheep | 6 | 7[2] | 7[1] | 6[1] | 7[1] | 7[1] | 7[1] | 7[1] | Mouton |
| Costa Rica | | | | | | | | | Costa Rica |
| Cattle | 84 | 82 | 74 | 68 | 74 | 70 | 81 | 81[1] | Bovine |
| Chicken | 74 | 73 | 77 | 77 | 72 | 84 | 91 | 91[1] | Poulet |
| Pig | 29 | 31 | 36 | 36 | 36 | 38 | 39 | 39 | Porc |
| Cuba | | | | | | | | | Cuba |
| Cattle | 76 | 76 | 75 | 66 | 56 | 55 | 60 | 56 | Bovine |
| Goat | 74 | 73 | 70 | 35 | 34 | 36 | 29 | 31 | Chèvre |
| Chicken | 1 | 2 | 2 | 2 | 3 | 3 | 3 | 3 | Poulet |
| Pig | 99 | 94 | 76 | 90 | 94 | 98 | 97 | 100 | Porc |
| Sheep | 5 | 6[1] | 6 | 7 | 7 | 7 | 7 | 7 | Mouton |
| Dominica[1] | | | | | | | | | Dominique[1] |
| Cattle | 1 | 1 | 1 | 1 | 1 | 1 | ... | 1 | Bovine |
| Dominican Republic | | | | | | | | | Rép. dominicaine |
| Cattle | 66 | 69 | 71 | 72 | 69 | 71 | 73 | 73[1] | Bovine |
| Chicken | 183 | 211 | 203 | 185 | 157 | 238 | 297 | 297[1] | Poulet |
| Goat | 1[1] | 1[1] | 1[1] | 1[1] | 1 | 1 | 1 | 1[1] | Chèvre |
| Pig | 58 | 61 | 63 | 64 | 64 | 52 | 78 | 78[1] | Porc |
| Sheep | ^0[1] | ^0[1] | ^0[1] | ^0[1] | 1 | 1 | 1 | 1[1] | Mouton |
| Ecuador | | | | | | | | | Equateur |
| Cattle | 164 | 174 | 189 | 188 | 203 | 206 | 207 | 207[1] | Bovine |
| Chicken | 146 | 195 | 195 | 209 | 207 | 208 | 209 | 209[1] | Poulet |
| Goat | 1[1] | 1[1] | 1 | 1 | 1 | 1 | 1 | 1[1] | Chèvre |
| Pig | 110 | 108 | 128 | 140 | 148 | 157 | 165 | 165[1] | Porc |
| Sheep | 10[1] | 10[1] | 10[1] | 10 | 10 | 11 | 11 | 11[1] | Mouton |
| El Salvador | | | | | | | | | El Salvador |
| Cattle | 34 | 35 | 35 | 40 | 29 | 26 | 27 | 31 | Bovine |
| Chicken | 46 | 76 | 74 | 79 | 79 | 92 | 99 | 101 | Poulet |
| Pig | 14[1] | 11[1] | 9[1] | 9[1] | 8 | 8 | 11 | 14 | Porc |

**Meat**—Production: thousand metric tons (*continued*)
**Viande**—Production : milliers de tonnes (*suite*)

| Region, country or area | 1999 | 2000 | 2001 | 2002 | 2003 | 2004 | 2005 | 2006 | Région, pays ou zone |
|---|---|---|---|---|---|---|---|---|---|
| Falkland Is. (Malvinas)[1] | | | | | | | | | Iles Falkland (Malvinas)[1] |
| Sheep | 1 | 1 | 1 | 1 | 1 | 1 | 1 | 1 | Mouton |
| French Guiana | | | | | | | | · | Guyane française |
| Chicken | 1[1] | ^0 | ^0 | ^0 | ^0[1] | ^0[1] | ^0[1] | ^0[1] | Poulet |
| Pig | 1 | 1 | 1 | 1 | 1[1] | 1[1] | 1[1] | 1[1] | Porc |
| Grenada[1] | | | | | | | | | Grenade[1] |
| Chicken | 1 | 1 | 1 | 1 | 1 | 1 | 1 | 1 | Poulet |
| Guadeloupe | | | | | | | | | Guadeloupe |
| Cattle | 3 | 3[1] | 3[1] | 3[1] | 3[1] | 3[1] | 3[1] | 3[1] | Bovine |
| Chicken | 1 | 1[1] | 1[1] | 1[1] | 1[1] | 1[1] | 1[1] | 1[1] | Poulet |
| Pig | 1[1] | 1[1] | 1[1] | 1 | 1[1] | 1[1] | 1[1] | 1[1] | Porc |
| Guatemala | | | | | | | | | Guatemala |
| Cattle | 62 | 62[1] | 62[1] | 63[1] | 63[1] | 63[1] | ... | 63[1] | Bovine |
| Chicken | 137 | 140 | 144[2] | 155[2] | 155[1] | 168[1] | 176[1] | 176[1] | Poulet |
| Pig | 24 | 25[1] | 25[1] | 26[1] | 27[1] | 29[1] | 31[1] | 31[1] | Porc |
| Sheep[1] | 2 | 1 | 1 | 1 | 1 | 1 | ... | 1 | Mouton[1] |
| Guyana | | | | | | | | | Guyana |
| Cattle | 2 | 2 | 2[2] | 2[1] | 2[1] | 2[1] | 2[1] | 2[1] | Bovine |
| Chicken | 12 | 12 | 12 | 17 | 24 | 21[1] | 22[1] | 22[1] | Poulet |
| Pig[1] | 1 | 1 | 1 | 1 | 1 | 1 | 1 | 1 | Porc[1] |
| Sheep[1] | 1 | 1 | 1 | 1 | 1 | 1 | 1 | 1 | Mouton[1] |
| Haïti | | | | | | | | | Haïti |
| Cattle | 31[1] | 40 | 41[1] | 42[1] | 43[1] | 43[1] | 43[1] | 43[1] | Bovine |
| Chicken[1] | 7 | 8 | 8 | 8 | 8 | 8 | 8 | 8 | Poulet[1] |
| Goat | 5[1] | 6 | 7[1] | 7[1] | 7[1] | 6[1] | 6[1] | 6[1] | Chèvre |
| Pig | 27[1] | 28 | 31[1] | 33[1] | 33[1] | 35[1] | 37[1] | 37[1] | Porc |
| Sheep | 1[1] | 1 | 1[1] | 1[1] | 1[1] | 1[1] | 1[1] | 1[1] | Mouton |
| Honduras | | | | | | | | | Honduras |
| Cattle | 55 | 55 | 55 | 54 | 61 | 64 | 73 | 73[1] | Bovine |
| Chicken | 69 | 76 | 66 | 105 | 117 | 129 | 141 | 141[1] | Poulet |
| Pig | 9 | 10 | 10 | 9 | 8 | 9 | 9 | 9[1] | Porc |
| Jamaica | | | | | | | | | Jamaïque |
| Cattle | 15 | 14 | 13 | 14 | 15[1] | 15[1] | ... | 15[1] | Bovine |
| Chicken | 73 | 77 | 83[2] | 84 | 81 | 86[1] | 88[1] | 88[1] | Poulet |
| Goat[1] | 2 | 2 | 2 | 2 | 2 | 2 | ... | 2 | Chèvre[1] |
| Pig | 7 | 7 | 6 | 5 | 5[1] | 6[1] | 6[1] | 6[1] | Porc |
| Martinique | | | | | | | | | Martinique |
| Cattle | 2 | 2 | 2 | 2 | 2[1] | 2[1] | 2[1] | 2[1] | Bovine |
| Chicken | 1 | 1[1] | 1[1] | 1[1] | 1[1] | 1[1] | 1[1] | 1[1] | Poulet |
| Pig | 2 | 2 | 2 | 2 | 2[1] | 2[1] | 1[1] | 1[1] | Porc |
| Mexico | | | | | | | | | Mexique |
| Cattle | 1 400 | 1 409 | 1 445 | 1 468 | 1 504 | 1 543 | 1 557 | 1 602 | Bovine |
| Chicken | 1 732 | 1 825 | 1 928 | 2 076 | 2 116 | 2 225 | 2 437 | 2 411 | Poulet |
| Goat | 37 | 39 | 39 | 42 | 42 | 42 | 42 | 42 | Chèvre |
| Pig | 994 | 1 030 | 1 058 | 1 070 | 1 035 | 1 058 | 1 103 | 1 103 | Porc |
| Sheep | 31 | 33 | 36 | 38 | 42 | 42 | 46 | 48 | Mouton |
| Montserrat[1] | | | | | | | | | Montserrat[1] |
| Cattle | 1 | 1 | 1 | 1 | 1 | 1 | 1 | 1 | Bovine |
| Netherland Antilles[1] | | | | | | | | | Antilles néerlandaises[1] |
| Chicken | 1 | 1 | 1 | 1 | ^0 | 1 | 1 | ... | Poulet |
| Nicaragua | | | | | | | | | Nicaragua |
| Cattle | 46[1] | 53[1] | 54 | 60 | 66 | 75 | 76 | 84 | Bovine |
| Chicken | 37 | 47 | 55 | 56 | 62 | 67 | 71 | 84 | Poulet |
| Pig | 6 | 6 | 6 | 6 | 6 | 7 | 7 | 7 | Porc |
| Panama | | | | | | | | | Panama |
| Cattle | 71 | 70 | 67 | 65 | 61 | 54 | 56 | 56[1] | Bovine |
| Chicken | 72 | 81 | 88 | 89 | 83 | 87 | 85[1] | 85[1] | Poulet |
| Pig | 21 | 22 | 18 | 18 | 20 | 21 | 21[1] | 21[1] | Porc |

| Region, country or area | 1999 | 2000 | 2001 | 2002 | 2003 | 2004 | 2005 | 2006 | Région, pays ou zone |
|---|---|---|---|---|---|---|---|---|---|
| Paraguay | | | | | | | | | Paraguay |
| Cattle | 246[2] | 239 | 200 | 205 | 215 | 215 | 215[1] | 215[1] | Bovine |
| Chicken[1] | 40 | 33 | 36 | 35 | 37 | 40 | 43 | 43 | Poulet[1] |
| Goat[1] | 1 | 1 | 1 | 1 | 1 | 1 | 1 | 1 | Chèvre[1] |
| Pig[1] | 120 | 114 | 117 | 78 | 93 | 156 | 105 | 105 | Porc[1] |
| Sheep[1] | 3 | 2 | 2 | 3 | 3 | 3 | 3 | 3 | Mouton[1] |
| Peru | | | | | | | | | Pérou |
| Cattle | 134 | 136 | 138 | 142 | 138 | 146 | 153 | 153[1] | Bovine |
| Chicken | 495 | 542 | 571 | 609 | 690 | 669 | 733 | 733[1] | Poulet |
| Goat | 7 | 7 | 6 | 6 | 6 | 7 | 7 | 7[1] | Chèvre |
| Pig | 66 | 72 | 85 | 85 | 93 | 98 | 103 | 103[1] | Porc |
| Sheep | 30 | 31 | 32 | 32 | 32 | 34 | 34 | 34[1] | Mouton |
| Puerto Rico | | | | | | | | | Porto Rico |
| Cattle | 18 | 15 | 13 | 11 | 10 | 13 | 10 | 10[1] | Bovine |
| Chicken | 53 | 60 | 52 | 54 | 47 | 50 | 50 | 50[1] | Poulet |
| Pig | 9 | 9 | 10 | 9 | 9 | 12 | 11 | 11[1] | Porc |
| Saint Lucia | | | | | | | | | Sainte-Lucie |
| Cattle[1] | 1 | 1 | 1 | 1 | 1 | 1 | 1 | ... | Bovine[1] |
| Chicken | 1[1] | 1[1] | 1[1] | 1[1] | 1[1] | 1[1] | 1 | ... | Poulet |
| Pig[1] | 1 | 1 | 1 | 1 | 1 | 1 | 1 | ... | Porc[1] |
| Saint Vincent-Grenadines[1] | | | | | | | | | Saint Vincent-Grenadines[1] |
| Pig | 1 | 1 | 1 | 1 | 1 | 1 | 1 | 1 | Porc |
| Suriname | | | | | | | | | Suriname |
| Cattle | 2 | 2 | 2 | 2 | 2[1] | 2[1] | 2[1] | 2[1] | Bovine |
| Chicken | 4 | 4 | 5 | 6 | 6 | 3[1] | 2[1] | 2[1] | Poulet |
| Pig | 1 | 1 | 1 | 1 | 1[1] | 1[1] | 1[1] | 1[1] | Porc |
| Trinidad and Tobago | | | | | | | | | Trinité-et-Tobago |
| Cattle | 1 | 1 | 1 | 1 | 1 | 1[1] | 1[1] | 1[1] | Bovine |
| Chicken | 29[1] | 39 | 47 | 58 | 57 | 58 | 57[1] | 57[1] | Poulet |
| Pig | 2 | 2 | 2 | 3 | 3 | 2[1] | 2[1] | 2[1] | Porc |
| United States Virgin Is.[1] | | | | | | | | | Iles Vierges américaines[1] |
| Cattle | 1 | 1 | 1 | 1 | 1 | 1 | 1 | 1 | Bovine |
| Uruguay | | | | | | | | | Uruguay |
| Cattle | 458 | 453 | 317[2] | 412 | 424 | 496 | 516[2] | 516[1] | Bovine |
| Chicken[1] | 60 | 56 | 55 | 45 | 31 | 43 | 45 | 45 | Poulet[1] |
| Pig | 27 | 26 | 23 | 20 | 17 | 15 | 19 | 19[1] | Porc |
| Sheep | 51[2] | 51[2] | 51[1] | 31 | 27 | 27 | ... | 19[1] | Mouton |
| Venezuela (Bolivarian Rep. of) | | | | | | | | | Venezuela (Rép. bolivarienne du) |
| Cattle | 391 | 429 | 418 | 429 | 435 | 376 | 425 | 425[1] | Bovine |
| Chicken | 635[1] | 693 | 877 | 893 | 676 | 686 | 739 | 739[1] | Poulet |
| Goat | 5 | 7 | 4 | 5 | 5 | 5 | 6 | 6[1] | Chèvre |
| Pig | 128 | 126 | 119 | 119 | 120 | 101 | 126 | 126[1] | Porc |
| Sheep | 3 | 2 | 2 | 2 | 2 | 2 | 3 | 3[1] | Mouton |
| **Asia** | | | | | | | | | **Asie** |
| **Buffalo** | **2 687** | **2 704** | **2 763** | **2 813** | **2 759** | **2 832** | **2 877** | **2 911** | **Buffle** |
| **Cattle** | **10 847** | **11 161** | **11 081** | **11 497** | **12 057** | **12 797** | **13 116** | **13 664** | **Bovine** |
| **Chicken** | **17 501** | **19 204** | **20 061** | **20 898** | **21 902** | **22 202** | **23 354** | **24 226** | **Poulet** |
| **Goat** | **2 540** | **2 681** | **2 785** | **2 928** | **3 149** | **3 246** | **3 441** | **3 706** | **Chèvre** |
| **Pig** | **46 814** | **48 257** | **50 290** | **52 321** | **54 615** | **56 667** | **60 099** | **62 013** | **Porc** |
| **Sheep** | **3 337** | **3 482** | **3 540** | **3 716** | **3 937** | **4 296** | **4 494** | **4 653** | **Mouton** |
| Afghanistan | | | | | | | | | Afghanistan |
| Cattle | 149[2] | 126[2] | 108[2] | 150[2] | 144[1] | 144[1] | 144[1] | ... | Bovine |
| Chicken[1] | 14 | 13 | 12 | 16 | 16 | 16 | 16 | ... | Poulet[1] |
| Goat[1] | 34 | 33 | 27 | 39 | 33 | 33 | 33 | ... | Chèvre[1] |
| Sheep[1] | 141 | 120 | 104 | 88 | 72 | 72 | 72 | ... | Mouton[1] |
| Armenia | | | | | | | | | Arménie |
| Cattle | 32 | 31 | 29 | 30 | 30 | 33 | 34 | 35[1] | Bovine |
| Chicken | 4 | 1 | 4 | 4 | 5 | 4 | 5 | 5[1] | Poulet |
| Pig | 8 | 9 | 9 | 10 | 12 | 9 | 9 | 10[1] | Porc |
| Sheep | 5 | 8 | 7 | 6 | 6 | 7 | 8 | 8[1] | Mouton |

**Meat**—Production: thousand metric tons (*continued*)
**Viande**—Production : milliers de tonnes (*suite*)

| Region, country or area | 1999 | 2000 | 2001 | 2002 | 2003 | 2004 | 2005 | 2006 | Région, pays ou zone |
|---|---|---|---|---|---|---|---|---|---|
| **Azerbaijan** | | | | | | | | | **Azerbaïdjan** |
| Cattle | 52 | 56 | 57 | 63 | 67 | 69 | 71 | 76 | Bovine |
| Chicken | 16 | 17 | 19 | 23 | 27 | 32 | 35 | 35 | Poulet |
| Pig | 2 | 1 | 1 | 1 | 1 | 2 | 2 | 2 | Porc |
| Sheep | 35 | 35 | 37 | 38 | 39 | 41 | 42 | 44 | Mouton |
| **Bahrain** | | | | | | | | | **Bahreïn** |
| Cattle | 1[1] | 1[1] | 1[1] | 1[1] | 1[1] | 1 | 1[1] | ... | Bovine |
| Chicken | 5 | 6 | 6 | 5 | 5 | 5 | 5[1] | ... | Poulet |
| Goat[1] | 1 | ^0 | 5 | 6 | 5 | 6 | 6 | ... | Chèvre[1] |
| Sheep[1] | 8 | 7 | 3 | 1 | 2 | 2 | 2 | ... | Mouton[1] |
| **Bangladesh** | | | | | | | | | **Bangladesh** |
| Buffalo | 4[2] | 4[2] | 4[2] | 4[2] | 4[1] | 4[1] | 4[1] | 4[1] | Buffle |
| Cattle | 171[2] | 173[2] | 174[2] | 178[2] | 180[1] | 180[1] | ... | 180[1] | Bovine |
| Chicken | 99[2] | 99[2] | 99[2] | 101[2] | 102[1] | 110[1] | 114[1] | 114[1] | Poulet |
| Goat | 127[2] | 129[2] | 129[2] | 137[2] | 137[1] | 137[1] | 137[1] | 137[1] | Chèvre |
| Sheep | 3[2] | 3[2] | 3[2] | 3[2] | 3[1] | 3[1] | 3[1] | 3[1] | Mouton |
| **Bhutan[1]** | | | | | | | | | **Bhoutan[1]** |
| Cattle | 6 | 5 | 5 | 5 | 5 | 5 | 5 | ... | Bovine |
| Pig | 1 | 1 | 1 | 1 | 1 | 1 | 1 | ... | Porc |
| **Brunei Darussalam[1]** | | | | | | | | | **Brunéi Darussalam[1]** |
| Buffalo | ^0 | ^0 | ^0 | 1 | 1 | ^0 | ^0 | ^0 | Buffle |
| Cattle | 5 | 3 | 3 | 3 | 3 | 3 | 3 | 3 | Bovine |
| Chicken | 9 | 11 | 14 | 12 | 14 | 16 | 16 | 16 | Poulet |
| **Cambodia[1]** | | | | | | | | | **Cambodge[1]** |
| Buffalo | 9 | 10 | 9 | 9 | 10 | 9 | 9 | 10 | Buffle |
| Cattle | 42 | 57 | 58 | 53 | 54 | 55 | 57 | 60 | Bovine |
| Chicken | 19 | 20 | 20 | 19 | 18 | 16 | 17 | 17 | Poulet |
| Pig | 103 | 105 | 108 | 114 | 118 | 123 | 127 | 127 | Porc |
| **China[3]** | | | | | | | | | **Chine[3]** |
| Buffalo | 367 | 361 | 379 | 387 | 305 | 330 | 346 | 351 | Buffle |
| Cattle | 4 711 | 4 991 | 5 131 | 5 480 | 6 020 | 6 449 | 6 791 | 7 173 | Bovine |
| Chicken | 8 215 | 9 072 | 9 115 | 9 320 | 9 655 | 9 944 | 10 377 | 10 701 | Poulet |
| Goat[2] | 1 182 | 1 304 | 1 390 | 1 490 | 1 683 | 1 756 | 1 927 | 2 161 | Chèvre[2] |
| Pig | 39 900 | 41 406 | 42 982 | 44 358 | 46 233 | 48 118 | 51 202 | 52 927 | Porc |
| Sheep | 1 335 | 1 440 | 1 540 | 1 680 | 1 892 | 2 240 | 2 431 | 2 540 | Mouton |
| **Cyprus** | | | | | | | | | **Chypre** |
| Cattle | 4 | 4 | 4 | 4 | 4 | 4 | 4 | 4 | Bovine |
| Chicken | 33 | 32 | 34 | 35 | 33 | 32 | 33 | 27 | Poulet |
| Goat | 6 | 6 | 7 | 8 | 5 | 4 | 4 | 4 | Chèvre |
| Pig | 49 | 52 | 51 | 52 | 54 | 55 | 55 | 53 | Porc |
| Sheep | 4 | 4 | 4 | 5 | 3 | 3 | 3 | 3 | Mouton |
| **Georgia** | | | | | | | | | **Géorgie** |
| Cattle | 41 | 48 | 47 | 49 | 50 | 50 | 49 | 47[1] | Bovine |
| Chicken | 11 | 14 | 13 | 13 | 13 | 15 | 17 | 17[1] | Poulet |
| Pig | 41 | 37 | 35 | 36 | 37 | 35 | 33 | 32[1] | Porc |
| Sheep | 7 | 9 | 8 | 8 | 8 | 9 | 10 | 9[1] | Mouton |
| **India** | | | | | | | | | **Inde** |
| Buffalo[1] | 1 399 | 1 416 | 1 433 | 1 450 | 1 467 | 1 483 | 1 488 | 1 488 | Buffle[1] |
| Cattle[1] | 1 421 | 1 442 | 1 452 | ... | ... | ... | ... | 1 334 | Bovine[1] |
| Chicken[2] | 820 | 1 080 | 1 250 | 1 400 | 1 600 | 1 650 | 1 900 | 2 000 | Poulet[2] |
| Goat[1] | 466 | 467 | ... | ... | ... | ... | ... | 475 | Chèvre[1] |
| Pig[1] | 473 | 476 | 483 | 487 | 490 | 498 | 503 | 503 | Porc[1] |
| Sheep[1] | 228 | 229 | 230 | 233 | 236 | 239 | 239 | 239 | Mouton[1] |
| **Indonesia** | | | | | | | | | **Indonésie** |
| Buffalo | 48 | 46 | 44 | 42 | 41 | 40 | 38 | 40 | Buffle |
| Cattle | 309 | 340 | 339 | 330 | 370 | 448 | 359 | 389 | Bovine |
| Chicken | 680 | 904 | 1 013 | 1 083 | 1 118 | 1 191 | 1 126 | 1 333 | Poulet |
| Goat | 45 | 45 | 49 | 58 | 64 | 57 | 51 | 53 | Chèvre |

| Region, country or area | 1999 | 2000 | 2001 | 2002 | 2003 | 2004 | 2005 | 2006 | Région, pays ou zone |
|---|---|---|---|---|---|---|---|---|---|
| Pig[1] | 558 | 421 | 473 | 520 | 543 | 580 | 595 | 595 | Porc[1] |
| Sheep | 32 | 33 | 45 | 69 | 81 | 66 | 47 | 52 | Mouton |
| **Iran (Islamic Rep. of)** | | | | | | | | | **Iran (Rép. islamique d')** |
| Buffalo[1] | 11 | 12 | 12 | 13 | 13 | 13 | ... | 14 | Buffle[1] |
| Cattle | 286 | 269 | 274 | 284 | 314 | 337 | ... | 342[1] | Bovine |
| Chicken | 725 | 803 | 885 | 942 | 1 104 | 1 171 | 1 153[1] | 1 153[1] | Poulet |
| Goat | 104 | 110 | 111 | 105 | 105[1] | 105[1] | 105[1] | 105[1] | Chèvre |
| Sheep | 293 | 326 | 333 | 345 | 346[1] | 348[1] | 389[1] | 389[1] | Mouton |
| **Iraq** | | | | | | | | | **Iraq** |
| Buffalo[1] | 3 | 4 | 4 | 4 | 4 | 4 | 4 | ... | Buffle[1] |
| Cattle[1] | 45 | 46 | 49 | 50 | 50 | 50 | 50 | ... | Bovine[1] |
| Chicken | 49[2] | 74 | 83 | 95 | 97[1] | 97[1] | 97[1] | ... | Poulet |
| Goat[1] | 8 | 7 | 4 | 8 | 8 | 8 | 8 | ... | Chèvre[1] |
| Sheep[1] | 20 | 24 | 21 | 20 | 20 | 20 | 20 | ... | Mouton[1] |
| **Israel** | | | | | | | | | **Israël** |
| Cattle | 46 | 64 | 62 | 80 | 91 | 83 | 90 | 108 | Bovine |
| Chicken | 207[2] | 295 | 345 | 353 | 334 | 350 | 370 | 390 | Poulet |
| Goat | 2 | 2 | 2 | 2 | 2 | 3 | 3 | 4 | Chèvre |
| Pig | 9 | 15 | 16 | 16 | 17 | 18 | 19 | 18 | Porc |
| Sheep | 5[2] | 5[2] | 5[2] | 5[1] | 5[1] | 5[1] | 5[1] | 5[1] | Mouton |
| **Japan** | | | | | | | | | **Japon** |
| Cattle | 540 | 530 | 459 | 537 | 496 | 514 | 499 | 497 | Bovine |
| Chicken | 1 274 | 1 255 | 1 277 | 1 229 | 1 240 | 1 242 | 1 273 | 1 337 | Poulet |
| Pig | 1 277 | 1 256 | 1 232 | 1 246 | 1 274 | 1 263 | 1 245 | 1 247 | Porc |
| **Jordan** | | | | | | | | | **Jordanie** |
| Cattle | 4 | 3 | 4 | 3 | 4 | 4 | 4 | 4 | Bovine |
| Chicken | 111 | 119 | 117 | 110 | 123 | 127 | 133 | 116 | Poulet |
| Goat | 3 | 2 | 2 | 1 | 2[1] | 2[1] | 2[1] | 2 | Chèvre |
| Sheep | 4 | 5 | 5 | 4 | 4[1] | 4[1] | 4[1] | 4[1] | Mouton |
| **Kazakhstan** | | | | | | | | | **Kazakhstan** |
| Cattle | 344 | 306 | 288 | 296 | 312 | 330 | 345[1] | 366[1] | Bovine |
| Chicken | 29 | 33 | 34 | 36 | 38 | 41 | 43[1] | 50[1] | Poulet |
| Goat | 4[2] | 4[2] | 5[2] | 7 | 7[2] | 8[2] | 8[1] | 10[1] | Chèvre |
| Pig | 98 | 133 | 181 | 187 | 185 | 199 | 200[1] | 210[1] | Porc |
| Sheep | 95[2] | 91 | 92 | 94 | 96 | 102 | 110[1] | 106[1] | Mouton |
| **Korea, Dem. P. R.[1]** | | | | | | | | | **Corée, R. p. dém. de[1]** |
| Cattle | 20 | 20 | 21 | 22 | 22 | 21 | 21 | 21 | Bovine |
| Chicken | 23 | 27 | 31 | 34 | 36 | 37 | 37 | 37 | Poulet |
| Goat | 9 | 10 | 11 | 11 | 11 | 11 | 11 | 11 | Chèvre |
| Pig | 134 | 140 | 145 | 163 | 163 | 165 | 168 | 168 | Porc |
| Sheep | 1 | 1 | 1 | 1 | 1 | 1 | 1 | 1 | Mouton |
| **Korea, Republic of** | | | | | | | | | **Corée, République de** |
| Cattle | 342 | 306 | 233 | 211 | 188 | 207 | 218 | 224[1] | Bovine |
| Chicken | 390[2] | 374 | 377 | 381 | 383[2] | 386[2] | 536[2] | 496[2] | Poulet |
| Goat | 3[1] | 3[1] | 3[1] | 3[1] | 3[1] | 3[1] | 3 | 3[1] | Chèvre |
| Pig | 996 | 916 | 928 | 1 005 | 1 149[2] | 960 | 899 | 860[2] | Porc |
| **Kuwait** | | | | | | | | | **Koweït** |
| Cattle[1] | 2 | 2 | 2 | 2 | 2 | 2 | 2 | 2 | Bovine[1] |
| Chicken | 39 | 33 | 42 | 37 | 37 | 43[1] | 47[1] | 47[1] | Poulet |
| Goat[1] | 1 | 1 | ^0 | 1 | 1 | 1 | 1 | 1 | Chèvre[1] |
| Sheep[1] | 34 | 34 | 31 | 37 | 31 | 30 | 30 | 30 | Mouton[1] |
| **Kyrgyzstan** | | | | | | | | | **Kirghizistan** |
| Cattle | 95 | 101 | 100 | 105 | 94 | 95 | 91 | 91[1] | Bovine |
| Chicken | 5 | 5 | 5 | 6 | 6 | 5 | 5 | 5[1] | Poulet |
| Goat | 3 | 4 | 7 | 7 | 7 | 7 | 7 | 7[1] | Chèvre |
| Pig | 29 | 24 | 26 | 23 | 22 | 25 | 19 | 19[1] | Porc |
| Sheep | 43 | 39 | 37 | 37 | 37 | 38 | 39 | 39[1] | Mouton |

| Region, country or area | 1999 | 2000 | 2001 | 2002 | 2003 | 2004 | 2005 | 2006 | Région, pays ou zone |
|---|---|---|---|---|---|---|---|---|---|
| Lao People's Dem. Rep. | | | | | | | | | Rép. dém. pop. lao |
| Buffalo | 19 | 17 | 17 | 17 | 18 | 19[1] | 19[1] | ... | Buffle |
| Cattle | 19 | 16 | 17 | 20 | 22 | 22[1] | 23[1] | ... | Bovine |
| Chicken | 9[1] | 10 | 11 | 11 | 14 | 15[1] | 16[1] | ... | Poulet |
| Goat[1] | ^0 | ^0 | ^0 | ^0 | 1 | ^0 | 1 | ... | Chèvre[1] |
| Pig | 32 | 28 | 32 | 32 | 36 | 35[1] | 36[1] | ... | Porc |
| Lebanon | | | | | | | | | Liban |
| Cattle[1] | 51 | 58 | 43 | 55 | 53 | 53 | 53 | 53 | Bovine[1] |
| Chicken | 90 | 113 | 117 | 125 | 127 | 131[1] | 136[1] | 136[1] | Poulet |
| Goat | 3 | 3 | 3 | 3 | 3 | 3 | 3 | 3 | Chèvre |
| Pig[1] | 2 | 2 | 2 | 2 | 1 | 1 | 1 | 1 | Porc[1] |
| Sheep[1] | 6 | 6 | 17 | 14 | 14 | 15 | 15 | 15 | Mouton[1] |
| Malaysia | | | | | | | | | Malaisie |
| Buffalo[1] | 3 | 3 | 3 | 4 | 4 | 5 | 5 | 5 | Buffle[1] |
| Cattle[1] | 18 | 15 | 16 | 18 | 20 | 21 | 21 | 21 | Bovine[1] |
| Chicken | 798[1] | 691 | 726 | 809 | 813 | 877 | 914[2] | 914[1] | Poulet |
| Goat[1] | 1 | 1 | 1 | 1 | 1 | 1 | 1 | 1 | Chèvre[1] |
| Pig | 159 | 160 | 185 | 193 | 198 | 203 | 206[1] | 206[1] | Porc |
| Mongolia | | | | | | | | | Mongolie |
| Cattle | 105 | 113 | 67 | 61 | 44 | 52 | 47[1] | 50[1] | Bovine |
| Goat | 32 | 30 | 28 | 20[2] | 19[2] | 33[2] | 35[1] | 37[1] | Chèvre |
| Pig | ^0 | 1 | 1 | ^0 | ^0 | ^0 | ^0[1] | ^0[1] | Porc |
| Sheep | 97 | 90 | 77 | 75[2] | 62[2] | 65[2] | 67[1] | 70[1] | Mouton |
| Myanmar | | | | | | | | | Myanmar |
| Buffalo | 20[1] | 20[1] | 21[1] | 22[1] | 18 | 21 | 24 | 24[1] | Buffle |
| Cattle | 101[1] | 102[1] | 104[1] | 108[1] | 97 | 94 | 106 | 106[1] | Bovine |
| Chicken | 154 | 217 | 258 | 301 | 380 | 457 | 561 | 561[1] | Poulet |
| Goat | 8 | 9 | 10 | 10 | 12 | 15 | 17 | 17[1] | Chèvre |
| Pig | 126 | 123 | 132 | 193 | 221 | 261 | 328 | 328[1] | Porc |
| Sheep | 2 | 3 | 3 | 3 | 3 | 4 | 5 | 5[1] | Mouton |
| Nepal | | | | | | | | | Népal |
| Buffalo | 120 | 122 | 125 | 128 | 131 | 134 | 139 | 142 | Buffle |
| Cattle[1] | 48 | 48 | 47 | 47 | 48 | 48 | 49 | 49 | Bovine[1] |
| Chicken | 12 | 13 | 13 | 14 | 15 | 16 | 15 | 16 | Poulet |
| Goat | 36 | 37 | 38 | 39 | 40 | 41 | 42 | 43 | Chèvre |
| Pig | 14 | 15 | 15 | 16 | 16 | 15 | 16 | 16 | Porc |
| Sheep | 3 | 3 | 3 | 3 | 3 | 3 | 3 | 3 | Mouton |
| Occupied Palestinian Terr. | | | | | | | | | Terr. palestinien occupé |
| Cattle[1] | 12 | 14 | 11 | 8 | 7 | 6 | 7 | ... | Bovine[1] |
| Chicken | 77[1] | 70[1] | 75[1] | 80[1] | 63 | 57 | 69 | ... | Poulet |
| Goat[1] | 3 | 4 | 3 | 4 | 5 | 4 | 4 | ... | Chèvre[1] |
| Sheep[1] | 7 | 7 | 5 | 10 | 13 | 12 | 10 | ... | Mouton[1] |
| Oman | | | | | | | | | Oman |
| Cattle[1] | 5 | 4 | 4 | 4 | 4 | 4 | 4 | ... | Bovine[1] |
| Chicken[1] | 4 | 4 | 5 | 6 | 6 | 6 | 6 | ... | Poulet[1] |
| Goat | 4[1] | 5[1] | 6[1] | 8[1] | 23 | 15 | 23 | ... | Chèvre |
| Sheep[1] | 13 | 13 | 13 | 13 | 12 | 11 | 11 | ... | Mouton[1] |
| Pakistan | | | | | | | | | Pakistan |
| Buffalo | 454 | 466 | 480 | 494 | 508 | 524 | 540 | 571 | Buffle |
| Cattle | 413 | 420 | 423 | 431 | 445 | 455 | 465 | 486 | Bovine |
| Chicken | 310 | 322 | 339 | 355 | 372 | 378 | 384 | 463 | Poulet |
| Goat | 300 | 310 | 321 | 333 | 345 | 357 | 370 | 392 | Chèvre |
| Sheep | 156 | 157 | 159 | 159 | 161 | 161 | 162 | 172 | Mouton |

| Region, country or area | 1999 | 2000 | 2001 | 2002 | 2003 | 2004 | 2005 | 2006 | Région, pays ou zone |
|---|---|---|---|---|---|---|---|---|---|
| **Philippines** | | | | | | | | | **Philippines** |
| Buffalo | 69 | 72 | 72 | 76 | 76 | 80 | 77 | 70[1] | Buffle |
| Cattle | 190 | 190 | 183 | 183 | 181 | 179 | 173 | 167 | Bovine |
| Chicken | 496 | 533 | 587 | 627 | 635 | 658 | 650 | 643 | Poulet |
| Goat | 33 | 34 | 33 | 34 | 33 | 34 | 35 | 35[1] | Chèvre |
| Pig | 973 | 1 008 | 1 064 | 1 332 | 1 346 | 1 366 | 1 415 | 1 467 | Porc |
| **Qatar** | | | | | | | | | **Qatar** |
| Cattle[1] | ^0 | 1 | ^0 | ^0 | ^0 | ^0 | ^0 | ... | Bovine[1] |
| Chicken | 3 | 4 | 4 | 6 | 5 | 5[1] | 5[1] | ... | Poulet |
| Goat[1] | 1 | 1 | 1 | 1 | 1 | 1 | ... | ... | Chèvre[1] |
| Sheep[1] | 5 | 6 | 8 | 8 | 7 | 6 | ... | ... | Mouton[1] |
| **Saudi Arabia** | | | | | | | | | **Arabie saoudite** |
| Cattle | 21[2] | 22[2] | 22[2] | 22[2] | 22[2] | 22 | 22 | 22[1] | Bovine |
| Chicken | 460 | 531 | 556 | 514 | 515[2] | 528[2] | 545[2] | 545[1] | Poulet |
| Goat | 21 | 22[2] | 22[2] | 22[2] | 23[1] | 23[1] | 23[1] | 23[1] | Chèvre |
| Sheep | 77[2] | 76[2] | 76[2] | 76[2] | 76[1] | 76[1] | 76[1] | 76[1] | Mouton |
| **Singapore** | | | | | | | | | **Singapour** |
| Chicken[1] | 90 | 85 | 87 | 90 | 86 | 69 | 76 | 76 | Poulet[1] |
| Pig | 31[1] | 21[1] | 23 | 21 | 19 | 20 | 20 | 16 | Porc |
| **Sri Lanka** | | | | | | | | | **Sri Lanka** |
| Buffalo[1] | 4 | 4 | 3 | 3 | 3 | 4 | 4 | 4 | Buffle[1] |
| Cattle | 24 | 29 | 27 | 28 | 29 | 28 | 29 | 26 | Bovine |
| Chicken | 62 | 69 | 88 | 92 | 88 | 95 | 97 | 79 | Poulet |
| Goat | 2 | 2 | 2 | 2 | 1 | 1 | 1 | 1 | Chèvre |
| Pig | 2 | 2 | 2 | 2 | 2 | 2 | 2 | 2 | Porc |
| **Syrian Arab Republic** | | | | | | | | | **Rép. arabe syrienne** |
| Cattle | 47 | 47 | 42 | 47 | 47 | 47[1] | 55 | 55[1] | Bovine |
| Chicken | 104 | 107 | 114 | 123 | 123[1] | 128[1] | 132[1] | 132[1] | Poulet |
| Goat | 5 | 5 | 5 | 5 | 5[1] | 5[1] | 5[1] | 5[1] | Chèvre |
| Sheep | 177 | 184 | 169 | 184[1] | 207[1] | 207[1] | 180 | 200 | Mouton |
| **Tajikistan** | | | | | | | | | **Tadjikistan** |
| Cattle | 15[2] | 12[2] | 15[2] | 19[2] | 23[2] | 22 | 24 | 25 | Bovine |
| Chicken | 2[2] | 2[2] | 2[2] | 2[2] | 3[2] | 2[1] | 3[1] | 3[1] | Poulet |
| Sheep | 13[2] | 16[2] | 13[2] | 14[2] | 19[2] | 24 | 27 | 28 | Mouton |
| **Thailand** | | | | | | | | | **Thaïlande** |
| Buffalo[1] | 60 | 52 | 58 | 58 | 59 | 60 | ... | 63 | Buffle[1] |
| Cattle | 170[1] | 171[1] | 176[1] | ... | ... | 158 | 168 | 176 | Bovine |
| Chicken | 1 078[2] | 1 091[2] | 1 230[2] | 1 320[2] | 1 227 | 878 | 950[2] | 1 100[2] | Poulet |
| Goat[1] | 1 | 1 | 1 | 1 | 1 | 1 | 1 | 1 | Chèvre[1] |
| Pig | 454[1] | 475[1] | 632[1] | 645[1] | 661[1] | 680[1] | 687[1] | 700 | Porc |
| **Timor-Leste[1]** | | | | | | | | | **Timor-Leste[1]** |
| Buffalo | 1 | 1 | 1 | 1 | 1 | 1 | 1 | ... | Buffle |
| Cattle | 1 | 1 | 1 | 1 | 1 | 1 | 1 | ... | Bovine |
| Chicken | 1 | 1 | 1 | 1 | 1 | 1 | 1 | ... | Poulet |
| Goat | 1 | ^0 | ^0 | ^0 | ^0 | ^0 | ^0 | ... | Chèvre |
| Pig | 6 | 6 | 8 | 8 | 8 | 8 | 7 | ... | Porc |
| **Turkey** | | | | | | | | | **Turquie** |
| Buffalo | 5 | 4 | 2 | 2 | 2 | 2 | 2 | 2[1] | Buffle |
| Cattle | 350 | 355 | 332 | 328 | 290 | 365 | 322 | 322[1] | Bovine |
| Chicken | 597 | 643 | 615 | 696 | 872 | 877 | 937 | 937[1] | Poulet |
| Goat | 55[2] | 53[1] | 48[1] | 47[1] | 45[1] | 45[1] | 45[1] | 45[1] | Chèvre |
| Sheep | 313[2] | 321[1] | 303[1] | 286[1] | 267[1] | 273[1] | 272[1] | 272[1] | Mouton |
| **Turkmenistan** | | | | | | | | | **Turkménistan** |
| Cattle | 63 | 72[2] | 84[1] | 92[2] | 101[2] | 106[1] | 100[1] | 102[1] | Bovine |
| Chicken | 5 | 6[2] | 9[1] | 11[2] | 12[2] | 14[1] | 12[1] | 14[1] | Poulet |
| Goat | 3[2] | 5[2] | 5[1] | 6[2] | 6[2] | 7[1] | 7[1] | 7[1] | Chèvre |
| Pig | 1 | 1[2] | ^0[2] | ^0[2] | ^0[2] | ^0[1] | ^0[1] | ^0[1] | Porc |
| Sheep | 60[2] | 66[2] | 75[1] | 83[2] | 90[2] | 95[1] | 90[1] | 93[1] | Mouton |

| Region, country or area | 1999 | 2000 | 2001 | 2002 | 2003 | 2004 | 2005 | 2006 | Région, pays ou zone |
|---|---|---|---|---|---|---|---|---|---|
| United Arab Emirates[1] | | | | | | | | | Emirats arabes unis[1] |
| Cattle | 21 | 15 | 8 | 9 | 10 | 10 | 10 | ... | Bovine |
| Chicken | 29 | 27 | 28 | 29 | 41 | 35 | 36 | ... | Poulet |
| Goat | 8 | 8 | 9 | 11 | 10 | 14 | 15 | ... | Chèvre |
| Sheep | 18 | 16 | 14 | 17 | 14 | 14 | 14 | ... | Mouton |
| Uzbekistan | | | | | | | | | Ouzbékistan |
| Cattle | 371[2] | 390[2] | 404[2] | 425 | 456 | 494 | 518 | 552 | Bovine |
| Chicken | 16[2] | 16[2] | 15[2] | 10 | 16 | 17 | 21 | 23 | Poulet |
| Pig | 20[2] | 15[2] | 11[2] | 4 | 11 | 14 | 16 | 18 | Porc |
| Sheep | 73[2] | 79[2] | 75[2] | 71 | 74 | 70 | 74 | 84 | Mouton |
| Viet Nam | | | | | | | | | Viet Nam |
| Buffalo[1] | 90 | 92 | 97 | 99 | 97 | 101 | 103 | 103 | Buffle[1] |
| Cattle | 89 | 92 | 98 | 102 | 108 | 120 | 153 | 181[1] | Bovine |
| Chicken | 262 | 296 | 308 | 338 | 373 | 316 | 322 | 322[1] | Poulet |
| Goat[1] | 5 | 5 | 5 | 5 | 6 | 8 | 9 | 11 | Chèvre[1] |
| Pig | 1 318 | 1 409 | 1 515 | 1 654 | 1 795 | 2 012[2] | 2 288 | 2 446[1] | Porc |
| Yemen | | | | | | | | | Yémen |
| Cattle | 47 | 52 | 56 | 59 | 70 | 71 | 73 | 73 | Bovine |
| Chicken | 63 | 67 | 78 | 83 | 109 | 111 | 113 | 118 | Poulet |
| Goat[1] | 22 | 23 | 24 | ... | ... | ... | ... | 26 | Chèvre[1] |
| Sheep[1] | 24 | 24 | 25 | ... | ... | ... | ... | 32 | Mouton[1] |
| **Europe** | | | | | | | | | **Europe** |
| **Buffalo** | **1** | **2** | **1** | **2** | **2** | **3** | **6** | **1** | **Buffle** |
| **Cattle** | **12 124** | **11 772** | **11 458** | **11 642** | **11 654** | **11 533** | **11 159** | **11 033** | **Bovine** |
| **Chicken** | **9 430** | **9 469** | **9 996** | **10 365** | **10 277** | **10 585** | **10 892** | **10 908** | **Poulet** |
| **Goat** | **132** | **125** | **121** | **122** | **125** | **134** | **133** | **128** | **Chèvre** |
| **Pig** | **26 184** | **25 381** | **24 969** | **25 538** | **25 606** | **25 094** | **24 797** | **24 767** | **Porc** |
| **Sheep** | **1 439** | **1 415** | **1 275** | **1 296** | **1 262** | **1 286** | **1 288** | **1 294** | **Mouton** |
| Albania | | | | | | | | | Albanie |
| Cattle | 34[2] | 36[2] | 35[2] | 38[2] | 40 | 40[2] | 41 | 41 | Bovine |
| Chicken | 5 | 4 | 4 | 6 | 8 | 9 | 9 | 10 | Poulet |
| Goat | 6[2] | 7 | 7 | 7 | 7 | 8[2] | 7[1] | 7 | Chèvre |
| Pig | 6[2] | 8[2] | 8[2] | 9[2] | 9[2] | 10[2] | 11 | 11 | Porc |
| Sheep | 12[2] | 12[2] | 11[1] | 12 | 12 | 14[2] | 13 | 14 | Mouton |
| Austria | | | | | | | | | Autriche |
| Cattle | 203 | 203 | 215 | 212 | 208 | 206 | 204 | 216 | Bovine |
| Chicken | 86 | 87 | 88 | 88 | 88 | 89 | 89 | 88[1] | Poulet |
| Goat | 1 | 1 | 1 | 1 | 1 | 1 | 1 | 1 | Chèvre |
| Pig | 684[2] | 620[2] | 614[2] | 653[2] | 518 | 515 | 510 | 514 | Porc |
| Sheep | 6 | 7 | 7 | 7 | 7 | 7 | 7 | 7 | Mouton |
| Belarus | | | | | | | | | Bélarus |
| Cattle | 262 | 213 | 231 | 227 | 211 | 224 | 256 | 272 | Bovine |
| Chicken | 70 | 76 | 85 | 85 | 87 | 101 | 115 | 145 | Poulet |
| Pig | 311 | 302 | 303 | 301 | 301 | 299 | 321 | 346 | Porc |
| Sheep | 3 | 3 | 3 | 2 | 2 | 2 | 1 | 1 | Mouton |
| Belgium | | | | | | | | | Belgique |
| Cattle | ... | 275 | 285 | 305 | 275 | 281 | 271 | 265[1] | Bovine |
| Chicken | ... | 400 | 406 | 459 | 424 | 468 | 470[1] | 484[1] | Poulet |
| Pig | ... | 1 042 | 1 062 | 1 041 | 1 026 | 1 054 | 1 015 | 1 008[1] | Porc |
| Sheep | ... | 4 | 5 | 3 | 3 | 4 | 2 | 2[1] | Mouton |
| Belgium-Luxembourg | | | | | | | | | Belgique-Luxembourg |
| Cattle | 281 | ... | ... | ... | ... | ... | ... | ... | Bovine |
| Chicken | 359 | ... | ... | ... | ... | ... | ... | ... | Poulet |
| Pig | 1 005 | ... | ... | ... | ... | ... | ... | ... | Porc |
| Sheep | 5 | ... | ... | ... | ... | ... | ... | ... | Mouton |

| Region, country or area | 1999 | 2000 | 2001 | 2002 | 2003 | 2004 | 2005 | 2006 | Région, pays ou zone |
|---|---|---|---|---|---|---|---|---|---|
| **Bosnia and Herzegovina** | | | | | | | | | **Bosnie-Herzégovine** |
| Cattle | 12[1] | 13[2] | 13[2] | 14[1] | 15[1] | 19 | 24 | 22 | Bovine |
| Chicken | 6[1] | 5[2] | 5[1] | 5[1] | 5[1] | 16 | 12 | 14 | Poulet |
| Pig | 12[1] | 11[1] | 11[1] | 10[1] | 8[1] | 8 | 9 | 10 | Porc |
| Sheep | 3[1] | 3 | 3[1] | 2[1] | 2[1] | 1 | 2 | 2 | Mouton |
| **Bulgaria** | | | | | | | | | **Bulgarie** |
| Cattle | 61[2] | 60[2] | 69[2] | 24 | 29 | 31 | 30 | 23 | Bovine |
| Chicken | 106 | 105 | 110 | 120 | 60 | 71 | 80 | 73 | Poulet |
| Goat | 8[2] | 8[2] | 7[2] | 5 | 7 | 6 | 7 | 6 | Chèvre |
| Pig | 267 | 243 | 237 | 245[1] | 71 | 78 | 75 | 77 | Porc |
| Sheep | 50[2] | 51[2] | 44[2] | 47[2] | 13 | 14 | 18 | 18 | Mouton |
| **Croatia** | | | | | | | | | **Croatie** |
| Cattle | 28 | 28 | 26 | 27 | 28 | 32 | 25[2] | 25[1] | Bovine |
| Chicken | 24 | 25[2] | 26[2] | 35 | 41[2] | 39[2] | 31[1] | 31[1] | Poulet |
| Pig | 64 | 64[2] | 64[2] | 65[2] | 62[2] | 61[2] | 49[1] | 49[1] | Porc |
| Sheep | 4 | 2 | 2 | 2 | 3 | 2 | 3[2] | 3[1] | Mouton |
| **Czech Republic** | | | | | | | | | **République tchèque** |
| Cattle | 121 | 108 | 109 | 106 | 104 | 97 | 81 | 80 | Bovine |
| Chicken | 184 | 199 | 219 | 207 | 198 | 201 | 213 | 207 | Poulet |
| Pig | 452 | 417 | 415 | 416 | 411 | 426 | 380 | 359 | Porc |
| Sheep | 3 | 1 | 1 | 1 | 1 | 1 | 1 | 2 | Mouton |
| **Denmark** | | | | | | | | | **Danemark** |
| Cattle | 157 | 154 | 153 | 154 | 147 | 150 | 136 | 129 | Bovine |
| Chicken | 186 | 187 | 199 | 201 | 188 | 187 | 183 | 166 | Poulet |
| Pig | 1 642 | 1 625 | 1 716 | 1 759 | 1 762 | 1 810 | 1 793 | 1 749 | Porc |
| Sheep | 1 | 1 | 2 | 1 | 2 | 2 | 2 | 2 | Mouton |
| **Estonia** | | | | | | | | | **Estonie** |
| Cattle | 22 | 15 | 14 | 17 | 13 | 15 | 13 | 14 | Bovine |
| Chicken | 8 | 8 | 10 | 12 | 15 | 15 | 14 | 13 | Poulet |
| Pig | 31 | 30 | 34 | 40 | 40 | 38 | 38 | 35 | Porc |
| **Faeroe Islands[1]** | | | | | | | | | **Iles Féroé[1]** |
| Sheep | 1 | 1 | 1 | 1 | 1 | 1 | 1 | 1 | Mouton |
| **Finland** | | | | | | | | | **Finlande** |
| Cattle | 90 | 91 | 90 | 91 | 96 | 93 | 87 | 87 | Bovine |
| Chicken | 66 | 64 | 76 | 83 | 84 | 87 | 87 | 98 | Poulet |
| Pig | 182 | 173 | 174 | 184 | 193 | 198 | 204 | 208 | Porc |
| Sheep | 1 | 1 | 1 | 1 | 1 | 1 | 1 | 1 | Mouton |
| **France** | | | | | | | | | **France** |
| Cattle | 1 609 | 1 528 | 1 566 | 1 640 | 1 632 | 1 565 | 1 517 | 1 473 | Bovine |
| Chicken | 1 275 | 1 242 | 1 230 | 1 148 | 1 133 | 1 106[2] | 921 | 819 | Poulet |
| Goat | 6 | 7 | 7 | 7 | 7 | 7 | 7 | 7 | Chèvre |
| Pig | 2 353 | 2 312 | 2 315 | 2 346 | 2 339 | 2 293 | 2 018 | 2 011 | Porc |
| Sheep | 132 | 133 | 134 | 128 | 129 | 102 | 99 | 99 | Mouton |
| **Germany** | | | | | | | | | **Allemagne** |
| Cattle | 1 374 | 1 304 | 1 362 | 1 316 | 1 226 | 1 258 | 1 167 | 1 167[1] | Bovine |
| Chicken | 435 | 462 | 476 | 477 | 549 | 609 | 605 | 608 | Poulet |
| Pig | 4 103 | 3 982 | 4 074 | 4 110 | 4 239 | 4 323 | 4 500 | 4 500[1] | Porc |
| Sheep | 44 | 48 | 46 | 44 | 46 | 48 | 49 | 49[1] | Mouton |
| **Greece** | | | | | | | | | **Grèce** |
| Cattle | 67 | 63 | 60 | 62 | 62 | 77 | 72 | 72[1] | Bovine |
| Chicken | 151[2] | 152[2] | 152[1] | 155[1] | 132[1] | 143[1] | 144[1] | 144[1] | Poulet |
| Goat | 56 | 44 | 43 | 45 | 47 | 58 | 57 | 57[1] | Chèvre |
| Pig | 138 | 141 | 137 | 110 | 111 | 108 | 109 | 109[1] | Porc |
| Sheep | 90 | 81 | 79 | 82 | 80[1] | 94 | 93 | 93[1] | Mouton |

**Meat**—Production: thousand metric tons (*continued*)
**Viande**—Production : milliers de tonnes (*suite*)

| Region, country or area | 1999 | 2000 | 2001 | 2002 | 2003 | 2004 | 2005 | 2006 | Région, pays ou zone |
|---|---|---|---|---|---|---|---|---|---|
| Hungary | | | | | | | | | Hongrie |
| Cattle | 51 | 67 | 52 | 48 | 61 | 46 | 41 | 42 | Bovine |
| Chicken | 242 | 281 | 279 | 278 | 267 | 253 | 246 | 241 | Poulet |
| Pig | 626 | 613 | 556 | 580 | 510 | 540 | 508 | 518 | Porc |
| Sheep | 4 | 4 | 3 | 3[1] | 1 | 2 | 2 | 3 | Mouton |
| Iceland | | | | | | | | | Islande |
| Cattle | 4 | 4 | 4 | 4 | 4 | 4 | 4 | 4[1] | Bovine |
| Chicken | 3 | 3 | 4 | 5 | 6 | 5 | 6 | 6[1] | Poulet |
| Pig | 5 | 5 | 5 | 6 | 6 | 6 | 5 | 5[1] | Porc |
| Sheep | 9 | 10 | 9 | 9 | 9 | 9 | 9 | 9[1] | Mouton |
| Ireland | | | | | | | | | Irlande |
| Cattle | 644 | 577 | 579 | 540 | 568 | 564 | 546 | 572 | Bovine |
| Chicken | 91[2] | 86[2] | 90[2] | 89[2] | 90[1] | 95[1] | 98[1] | 98[1] | Poulet |
| Pig | 250 | 230 | 241 | 231 | 217 | 204 | 205 | 209 | Porc |
| Sheep | 90 | 83 | 78 | 67 | 63[2] | 72 | 73 | 70 | Mouton |
| Italy | | | | | | | | | Italie |
| Buffalo | 1 | 1 | 1 | 2 | 1 | 3 | 6 | 1 | Buffle |
| Cattle | 1 164 | 1 152 | 1 133 | 1 134 | 1 127 | 1 145 | 1 102 | 1 109 | Bovine |
| Chicken | 790[2] | 762[2] | 794[2] | 729 | 683 | 704 | 695 | 628 | Poulet |
| Goat | 4 | 4 | 4 | 4 | 3 | 3 | 3 | 3 | Chèvre |
| Pig | 1 472 | 1 479 | 1 510 | 1 536 | 1 590 | 1 590 | 1 515 | 1 559 | Porc |
| Sheep | 70 | 65 | 62 | 58 | 58 | 59 | 59 | 59 | Mouton |
| Latvia | | | | | | | | | Lettonie |
| Cattle | 23 | 22 | 19 | 16 | 21 | 22 | 20 | 21 | Bovine |
| Chicken | 6 | 7 | 9 | 11 | 12 | 14 | 17 | 21 | Poulet |
| Pig | 35 | 32 | 32 | 36 | 37 | 37 | 38 | 38 | Porc |
| Lithuania | | | | | | | | | Lituanie |
| Cattle | 77 | 75 | 47 | 45 | 43 | 48 | 53 | 47 | Bovine |
| Chicken | 24 | 26 | 31 | 35 | 39 | 49 | 57 | 57[1] | Poulet |
| Goat | ^0 | 1 | 1 | 1 | 1 | ^0 | 1 | ^0 | Chèvre |
| Pig | 91 | 85 | 72 | 95 | 91 | 97 | 106 | 106 | Porc |
| Sheep | 1 | 1 | 1 | 1 | ^0 | ^0 | ^0 | ^0 | Mouton |
| Luxembourg | | | | | | | | | Luxembourg |
| Cattle | ... | 17 | 11 | 19 | 17 | 16 | 17 | 17[1] | Bovine |
| Chicken | ... | 15[1] | 15[1] | 16[1] | 16[1] | ^0 | ^0 | ^0[1] | Poulet |
| Pig | ... | 13 | 11 | 11 | 12 | 11 | 13 | 13[1] | Porc |
| Malta | | | | | | | | | Malte |
| Cattle | 2 | 2 | 2 | 2 | 1 | 1 | 1 | 1 | Bovine |
| Chicken | 5 | 6 | 6 | 7 | 7 | 6 | 5 | 4 | Poulet |
| Pig | 10 | 9 | 10 | 10 | 10 | 8 | 9 | 8 | Porc |
| Moldova | | | | | | | | | Moldova |
| Cattle | 21 | 18 | 16 | 16 | 16 | 16 | 16 | 15 | Bovine |
| Chicken | 16 | 16 | 20 | 21 | 22 | 24 | 28 | 31 | Poulet |
| Pig | 61 | 50 | 44 | 45 | 43 | 41 | 40 | 48 | Porc |
| Sheep | 4 | 3 | 3 | 3 | 3 | 3 | 2 | 2 | Mouton |
| Netherlands | | | | | | | | | Pays-Bas |
| Cattle | 508 | 471 | 372 | 384 | 365 | 386 | 396 | 355 | Bovine |
| Chicken | 729 | 713 | 720 | 692[2] | 544 | 615 | 628 | 635[1] | Poulet |
| Goat | 1[2] | ^0[2] | ^0[1] | ^0[1] | ^0[1] | ^0[1] | ^0 | ^0[1] | Chèvre |
| Pig | 1 711 | 1 623 | 1 432 | 1 377 | 1 253 | 1 289 | 1 297 | 1 230 | Porc |
| Sheep | 18 | 18 | 18 | 17 | 15 | 16 | 13 | 14[1] | Mouton |
| Norway | | | | | | | | | Norvège |
| Cattle | 96 | 91 | 86 | 85 | 85 | 87 | 87 | 88 | Bovine |
| Chicken | 37 | 43 | 42 | 46 | 43 | 47 | 50 | 55 | Poulet |
| Pig | 109 | 103 | 109 | 104 | 106 | 114 | 113 | 116 | Porc |
| Sheep | 23 | 23 | 24 | 25 | 24 | 26 | 26 | 25 | Mouton |

| Region, country or area | 1999 | 2000 | 2001 | 2002 | 2003 | 2004 | 2005 | 2006 | Région, pays ou zone |
|---|---|---|---|---|---|---|---|---|---|
| **Poland** | | | | | | | | | **Pologne** |
| Cattle | 385 | 349 | 316 | 281 | 317 | 311 | 310 | 368 | Bovine |
| Chicken | 567[2] | 560[1] | 668[1] | 761[1] | 822[1] | 876[1] | 980[1] | 960[1] | Poulet |
| Pig | 2 043 | 1 923 | 1 849 | 2 023 | 2 190 | 1 956 | 1 956 | 2 092 | Porc |
| Sheep | 2 | 1 | 1 | 1 | 1 | 2 | 1 | 1 | Mouton |
| **Portugal** | | | | | | | | | **Portugal** |
| Cattle | 97 | 100 | 95 | 106 | 105 | 118 | 118 | 105 | Bovine |
| Chicken | 222 | 224 | 239 | 206 | 182 | 196 | 198 | 193 | Poulet |
| Goat | 3 | 2 | 2 | 2 | 2 | 2 | 1[2] | 1 | Chèvre |
| Pig | 346 | 329 | 317 | 330 | 329 | 315 | 327 | 339 | Porc |
| Sheep | 22 | 24 | 22 | 24 | 22 | 22 | 22[2] | 22[1] | Mouton |
| **Romania** | | | | | | | | | **Roumanie** |
| Cattle | 153 | 162 | 145 | 156 | 185 | 162 | 189 | 194 | Bovine |
| Chicken | 269 | 259 | 284 | 340 | 344 | 303 | 315 | 266 | Poulet |
| Goat | 4 | 4 | 4 | 3 | 5 | 6 | 3 | 5 | Chèvre |
| Pig | 595 | 502 | 460 | 476 | 533 | 374 | 454 | 468 | Porc |
| Sheep | 54 | 49 | 48 | 51 | 62 | 67 | 50 | 54 | Mouton |
| **Russian Federation** | | | | | | | | | **Fédération de Russie** |
| Cattle | 1 868 | 1 894 | 1 873 | 1 957 | 1 990 | 1 951 | 1 793 | 1 755 | Bovine |
| Chicken | 748 | 755 | 862 | 938 | 1 030 | 1 152 | 1 346 | 1 534 | Poulet |
| Goat | 20 | 20 | 20 | 20 | 19 | 18 | 18 | 18 | Chèvre |
| Pig | 1 485 | 1 569 | 1 498 | 1 583 | 1 706 | 1 643 | 1 520 | 1 602 | Porc |
| Sheep | 124 | 119 | 114 | 115 | 114 | 125 | 134 | 136 | Mouton |
| **Serbia** | | | | | | | | | **Serbie** |
| Cattle | ... | ... | ... | ... | ... | ... | ... | 83 | Bovine |
| Chicken | ... | ... | ... | ... | ... | ... | ... | 75 | Poulet |
| Pig | ... | ... | ... | ... | ... | ... | ... | 255 | Porc |
| Sheep | ... | ... | ... | ... | ... | ... | ... | 20 | Mouton |
| **Serbia and Montenegro** | | | | | | | | | **Serbie-et-Monténégro** |
| Cattle | 185[2] | 194[2] | 165[2] | 166[2] | 164[2] | 161[2] | 156 | ... | Bovine |
| Chicken | 73 | 68 | 64 | 67 | 59 | 65 | 67 | ... | Poulet |
| Goat[1] | 1 | 1 | 1 | 1 | 1 | 1 | 1 | ... | Chèvre[1] |
| Pig | 653[2] | 635[2] | 565[2] | 617[2] | 574[2] | 539[2] | 562 | ... | Porc |
| Sheep | 22 | 23 | 22 | 19 | 21 | 20 | 21 | ... | Mouton |
| **Slovakia** | | | | | | | | | **Slovaquie** |
| Cattle | 50 | 48 | 38 | 42 | 33 | 26 | 26 | 21 | Bovine |
| Chicken | 53[1] | 61[1] | 68[1] | 75[1] | 85 | 84 | 87 | 86 | Poulet |
| Pig | 220 | 164 | 153 | 154 | 183 | 165 | 140 | 122 | Porc |
| Sheep | 1 | 2 | 2 | 2 | 2 | 1 | 1 | 1 | Mouton |
| **Slovenia** | | | | | | | | | **Slovénie** |
| Cattle | 48 | 43 | 49 | 43 | 52 | 47 | 46[2] | 46[1] | Bovine |
| Chicken | 55 | 54 | 59 | 53 | 54 | 47[2] | 51[2] | 51[1] | Poulet |
| Pig | 71 | 60 | 66 | 62 | 64 | 71 | 70[2] | 70[1] | Porc |
| Sheep | 1 | 1 | 1 | 1 | 1 | 1[1] | 1[1] | 1[1] | Mouton |
| **Spain** | | | | | | | | | **Espagne** |
| Cattle | 661 | 651 | 651 | 679 | 706 | 714 | 715 | 671 | Bovine |
| Chicken | 980[2] | 965[2] | 1 009[2] | 1 191 | 1 185 | 1 083 | 1 048 | 1 048[1] | Poulet |
| Goat | 17 | 16 | 15 | 15 | 14 | 13 | 17 | 12 | Chèvre |
| Pig | 2 893 | 2 905 | 2 989 | 3 070 | 3 190 | 3 076 | 3 168 | 3 230 | Porc |
| Sheep | 221 | 232 | 236 | 237 | 236 | 231 | 224 | 227 | Mouton |
| **Sweden** | | | | | | | | | **Suède** |
| Cattle | 145 | 150 | 143 | 147 | 140 | 143 | 135 | 135[1] | Bovine |
| Chicken | 94 | 90 | 96 | 101 | 98 | 91 | 108[1] | 108[1] | Poulet |
| Pig | 325 | 277 | 276 | 284 | 288 | 295 | 275 | 275[1] | Porc |
| Sheep | 4 | 4 | 4 | 4 | 4 | 4 | 4 | 4[1] | Mouton |

**Meat**— Production: thousand metric tons (*continued*)
**Viande**— Production : milliers de tonnes (*suite*)

| Region, country or area | 1999 | 2000 | 2001 | 2002 | 2003 | 2004 | 2005 | 2006 | Région, pays ou zone |
|---|---|---|---|---|---|---|---|---|---|
| Switzerland | | | | | | | | | Suisse |
| Cattle | 146 | 128 | 138 | 140 | 137 | 134 | 132 | 135 | Bovine |
| Chicken | 42 | 46 | 47 | 51 | 53 | 60 | 58 | 52 | Poulet |
| Goat | 1 | 1 | ^0 | ^0 | ^0 | ^0 | 1 | 1 | Chèvre |
| Pig | 226 | 225 | 234 | 236 | 230 | 227 | 236 | 244 | Porc |
| Sheep | 6 | 6 | 6 | 6 | 6 | 7 | 6 | 6 | Mouton |
| TFYR of Macedonia | | | | | | | | | L'ex-R.y. Macédoine |
| Cattle | 7 | 6 | 7[2] | 7 | 9 | 9 | 8 | 8[1] | Bovine |
| Chicken | 5[1] | 5 | 5 | 4 | 4 | 3 | 4 | 4[1] | Poulet |
| Pig | 9 | 9 | 8 | 11 | 10 | 9 | 9 | 9[1] | Porc |
| Sheep | 4 | 5[1] | 6[1] | 5 | 6 | 7 | 7 | 7[1] | Mouton |
| Ukraine | | | | | | | | | Ukraine |
| Cattle | 791 | 754 | 646 | 704 | 723 | 618 | 562 | 592[1] | Bovine |
| Chicken | 204 | 193 | 239 | 300 | 324 | 375 | 497 | 523[1] | Poulet |
| Goat | 4 | 8 | 7 | 9 | 9 | 8 | 8 | 9[1] | Chèvre |
| Pig | 656 | 676 | 591 | 599 | 631 | 559 | 494 | 520[1] | Porc |
| Sheep | 15 | 9 | 8 | 8 | 8 | 8[2] | 8 | 9[1] | Mouton |
| United Kingdom | | | | | | | | | Royaume-Uni |
| Cattle | 679 | 705 | 645 | 694 | 699 | 719 | 762 | 762[1] | Bovine |
| Chicken | 1 214 | 1 215 | 1 263 | 1 272 | 1 295 | 1 295 | 1 331 | 1 331[1] | Poulet |
| Pig | 1 042 | 899 | 777 | 774 | 716 | 708 | 706 | 706[1] | Porc |
| Sheep | 392 | 383 | 267 | 307 | 303 | 312 | 331 | 331[1] | Mouton |
| **Oceania** | | | | | | | | | **Océanie** |
| **Cattle** | **2 593** | **2 581** | **2 731** | **2 625** | **2 754** | **2 763** | **2 834** | **2 797** | **Bovine** |
| **Chicken** | **696** | **739** | **758** | **822** | **856** | **872** | **947** | **944** | **Poulet** |
| **Goat** | **11** | **13** | **13** | **16** | **17** | **19** | **20** | **20** | **Chèvre** |
| **Pig** | **488** | **489** | **496** | **530** | **555** | **542** | **526** | **526** | **Porc** |
| **Sheep** | **1 145** | **1 213** | **1 277** | **1 165** | **1 143** | **1 079** | **1 138** | **1 126** | **Mouton** |
| Australia | | | | | | | | | Australie |
| Cattle | 2 011 | 1 988 | 2 119 | 2 028 | 2 073 | 2 033 | 2 162 | 2 077 | Bovine |
| Chicken | 575 | 610 | 619 | 667 | 690 | 694 | 760 | 773 | Poulet |
| Goat[1] | 8 | 11 | 11 | 14 | 14 | 17 | 17 | 17 | Chèvre[1] |
| Pig | 362 | 364 | 365 | 396 | 420 | 406 | 388 | 389 | Porc |
| Sheep | 628 | 680 | 715 | 644 | 597 | 561 | 595 | 626 | Mouton |
| Cook Islands[1] | | | | | | | | | Iles Cook[1] |
| Pig | 1 | 1 | 1 | 1 | 1 | 1 | 1 | ... | Porc |
| Fiji | | | | | | | | | Fidji |
| Cattle[1] | 9 | 9 | 9 | 9 | 8 | 8 | 8 | 8 | Bovine[1] |
| Chicken | 8 | 8 | 8 | 11 | 12 | 13 | 12 | 12[1] | Poulet |
| Goat | 1[1] | 1 | 1 | 1 | 1 | 1 | 1 | 1[1] | Chèvre |
| Pig[1] | 4 | 4 | 4 | 4 | 4 | 4 | 4 | 4 | Porc[1] |
| French Polynesia | | | | | | | | | Polynésie française |
| Chicken[1] | 1 | 1 | 1 | 1 | 1 | 1 | 1 | ... | Poulet[1] |
| Pig | 1 | 1 | 1 | 1 | 1 | 1 | 1[1] | ... | Porc |
| Kiribati[1] | | | | | | | | | Kiribati[1] |
| Pig | 1 | 1 | 1 | 1 | 1 | 1 | 1 | 1 | Porc |
| Micronesia (Fed. States of)[1] | | | | | | | | | Micronésie (Etats féd. de)[1] |
| Pig | 1 | 1 | 1 | 1 | 1 | 1 | 1 | 1 | Porc |
| New Caledonia | | | | | | | | | Nouvelle-Calédonie |
| Cattle | 4 | 4 | 4 | 4 | 4 | 4 | 4 | 3 | Bovine |
| Chicken | 1 | 1 | 1 | 1 | 1 | 1[1] | 1[1] | ... | Poulet |
| Pig | 1 | 1 | 1[1] | 1[1] | 1[1] | 2 | 2 | 2 | Porc |

| Region, country or area | 1999 | 2000 | 2001 | 2002 | 2003 | 2004 | 2005 | 2006 | Région, pays ou zone |
|---|---|---|---|---|---|---|---|---|---|
| New Zealand | | | | | | | | | Nouvelle-Zélande |
| Cattle | 561 | 572 | 590 | 576 | 660 | 709 | 652 | 700 | Bovine |
| Chicken | 104 | 112 | 121 | 135 | 144 | 156 | 165 | 149 | Poulet |
| Goat | 2 | 1 | 2 | 1 | 1 | 2 | 1 | 1[1] | Chèvre |
| Pig | 49 | 47 | 47 | 47 | 47 | 52 | 50 | 50[1] | Porc |
| Sheep | 517 | 533 | 562 | 521 | 546 | 518 | 543 | 500 | Mouton |
| Papua New Guinea[1] | | | | | | | | | Papouasie-Nvl-Guinée[1] |
| Cattle | 3 | 3 | 3 | 3 | 3 | 3 | 3 | ... | Bovine |
| Chicken | 5 | 5 | 5 | 6 | 6 | 6 | 6 | ... | Poulet |
| Pig | 58 | 58 | 64 | 68 | 68 | 64 | 66 | ... | Porc |
| Samoa | | | | | | | | | Samoa |
| Cattle[1] | 1 | 1 | 1 | 1 | 1 | 1 | 1 | 1 | Bovine[1] |
| Pig | 3[1] | 4[1] | 4 | 4[1] | 4[1] | 4[1] | 4[1] | 4[1] | Porc |
| Solomon Islands[1] | | | | | | | | | Iles Salomon[1] |
| Cattle | 1 | 1 | 1 | 1 | 1 | 1 | 1 | 1 | Bovine |
| Pig | 2 | 2 | 2 | 2 | 2 | 2 | 2 | 2 | Porc |
| Tonga[1] | | | | | | | | | Tonga[1] |
| Pig | 1 | 1 | 1 | 1 | 1 | 1 | 1 | ... | Porc |
| Vanuatu | | | | | | | | | Vanuatu |
| Cattle | 4 | 4 | 3 | 3 | 3 | 3 | ... | 3[1] | Bovine |
| Chicken[1] | 1 | 1 | 1 | 1 | 1 | 1 | 1 | 1 | Poulet[1] |
| Pig[1] | 3 | 3 | 3 | 3 | 3 | 3 | 3 | 3 | Porc[1] |

Source

Food and Agriculture Organization of the United Nations (FAO), Rome, FAOSTAT data, last accessed January 2008.

Notes

[1] FAO estimate.
[2] International source.
[3] For statistical purposes, the data for China do not include those for the Hong Kong Special Administrative Region (Hong Kong SAR) and Macao Special Administrative Region (Macao SAR).

Source

Organisation des Nations Unies pour l'alimentation et l'agriculture (FAO), Rome, données FAOSTAT, dernier accès janvier 2008.

Notes

[1] Estimation de la FAO.
[2] Source internationale.
[3] Pour la présentation des statistiques, les données pour la Chine ne comprennent pas la Région Administrative Spéciale de Hong Kong (Hong Kong RAS) et la Région Administrative Spéciale de Macao (Macao RAS).

# 41

## Beer
Production: thousand hectoliters

## Bière
Production : milliers d'hectolitres

| Country or area<br>Pays ou zone | 1996 | 1997 | 1998 | 1999 | 2000 | 2001 | 2002 | 2003 | 2004 | 2005 |
|---|---|---|---|---|---|---|---|---|---|---|
| Albania<br>Albanie | 9 | 151 | 93 | 87 | 86 | 117 | 150 | 144 | 296 | 285 |
| Algeria<br>Algérie | 377 | 370 | 382 | 383 | 453 | 435 | 283 | 186 | ... | ... |
| Angola[1]<br>Angola[1] | 797 | 1 150 | 1 288 | 1 609 | ... | ... | ... | ... | ... | ... |
| Argentina<br>Argentine | 11 615 | 12 687 | 12 395 | 12 448 | 12 685 | 12 390 | 11 990 | 12 950 | ... | ... |
| Armenia<br>Arménie | 29 | 50 | 133 | 84 | 79 | 100 | 71 | 73 | 88 | 108 |
| Australia[2,3]<br>Australie[2,3] | 17 430 | 17 350 | 17 570 | 17 380 | 17 680 | 17 450 | 17 440 | 17 270 | 17 360 | 16 850 |
| Austria<br>Autriche | 9 445 | 9 303 | 8 837 | 8 884 | 8 725 | 8 528 | 8 745 | 8 980 | ... | ... |
| Azerbaijan<br>Azerbaïdjan | 13 | 16 | 12 | 69 | 71 | 117 | 125 | 133 | 180 | 249 |
| Barbados<br>Barbade | 76 | 75 | 87 | 76 | 69 | 67 | 68 | 69 | 80 | 87 |
| Belarus<br>Bélarus | 2 013 | 2 413 | 2 604 | 2 728 | 2 371 | 2 174 | 2 026 | 2 056 | 2 272 | 2 715 |
| Belgium<br>Belgique | 14 648 | 14 758 | 14 763 | 15 094[4] | 15 509[4] | 15 068[4] | 15 063[4] | 15 924[4] | ... | ... |
| Belize<br>Belize | 41 | 37 | 42 | 66 | 92 | ... | ... | ... | ... | ... |
| Benin[5]<br>Bénin[5] | 349 | 364 | 329 | 347 | ... | ... | ... | ... | ... | ... |
| Bolivia<br>Bolivie | 160 | 187 | 186 | 166 | ... | ... | ... | ... | ... | ... |
| Bosnia and Herzegovina<br>Bosnie-Herzégovine | 537 | 745 | 844 | 975 | 676[6] | 480[6] | 652[6] | #1 316 | ... | ... |
| Botswana<br>Botswana | 1 351 | 1 005 | 1 019 | 1 591 | 1 976 | 1 692 | 1 396 | 1 198 | ... | ... |
| Brazil<br>Brésil | 63 559 | 66 582 | 66 453 | 62 491 | 87 882 | 91 372 | 79 883 | 76 921 | 86 633 | ... |
| Bulgaria<br>Bulgarie | 4 402 | 3 031 | 3 765 | 3 890 | 3 977 | 4 097 | 3 888 | 4 355 | 3 997 | 4 287 |
| Burkina Faso[5]<br>Burkina Faso[5] | 435 | 460 | 501 | 516 | ... | ... | ... | ... | ... | ... |
| Burundi<br>Burundi | 1 228 | 1 161 | 1 036 | 1 084 | 892 | 702 | 752 | 876 | 973 | 1 013 |
| Cameroon<br>Cameroun | 3 124[5] | 3 124 | 3 370 | 3 373 | 3 340 | 3 740 | 4 196 | 4 597 | 4 287 | 4 439 |
| Canada<br>Canada | 21 303 | 21 816 | 24 352 | 24 605 | 24 515 | 25 551 | 25 368 | 19 299 | ... | ... |
| Central African Rep.[5]<br>Rép. centrafricaine[5] | 175 | 209 | 219 | 243 | ... | ... | ... | ... | ... | ... |
| Chad[5]<br>Tchad[5] | 134 | 123 | ... | ... | ... | ... | ... | ... | ... | ... |
| Chile<br>Chili | 3 459 | 3 640 | 3 666 | 3 343 | 3 221 | 3 374 | 3 401 | 3 490 | ... | ... |

| Country or area Pays ou zone | 1996 | 1997 | 1998 | 1999 | 2000 | 2001 | 2002 | 2003 | 2004 | 2005 |
|---|---|---|---|---|---|---|---|---|---|---|
| China[7,8] Chine[7,8] | 137 664 | 154 610 | 162 693 | ... | ... | ... | ... | ... | ... | ... |
| China, Hong Kong SAR Chine, Hong Kong RAS | 897 | 894 | ... | ... | ... | ... | ... | ... | ... | ... |
| Colombia Colombie | ... | 18 290 | 16 461 | 14 213 | ... | ... | ... | ... | ... | ... |
| Congo Congo | 510 | 342 | 494 | 480 | 526 | 623 | 661 | 658 | 674 | ... |
| Croatia Croatie | 3 292 | 3 607 | 3 759 | 3 663 | 3 847 | 3 799 | 3 624 | 3 679 | 3 606 | 3 496 |
| Cuba Cuba | 1 504 | 1 639 | 1 759 | 2 009 | 2 136 | 2 197 | 2 331 | 2 313 | 2 221 | 2 255 |
| Cyprus Chypre | 331 | 333 | 365 | 405 | 409 | 404 | 383 | 367 | 371 | 377 |
| Czech Republic République tchèque | 18 057 | 18 558 | 18 290 | 17 945 | 17 796 | 17 734 | 17 987 | 18 216 | 18 596 | 18 885 |
| Denmark Danemark | 9 591 | 9 181 | 8 044 | 8 205 | 7 455 | 7 233 | 8 202 | 8 352 | 8 550 | 8 493 |
| Dominica Dominique | 14 | 11 | 11 | 8 | 11 | 9 | 10 | ... | ... | ... |
| Dominican Republic Rép. dominicaine | ... | 2 593 | 2 993 | 3 484 | 3 666 | 3 176 | 3 554 | 3 553 | 3 546 | 4 541 |
| Ecuador Equateur | 2 163 | 238 | 633 | 555 | 353 | ... | ... | ... | ... | ... |
| Egypt Egypte | 380 | ... | ... | 352 | 261 | 122 | ... | ... | ... | ... |
| Estonia Estonie | 459 | 543 | 744 | 957 | 950 | 1 015 | 1 044 | 1 040 | 1 189 | 1 346 |
| Ethiopia Ethiopie | 876[9] | 843[9] | 831[9] | 921[9] | 1 111[9] | 1 605[9] | 1 812 | 2 123 | ... | ... |
| Fiji Fidji | 170 | 170 | 170 | 185 | 179 | 180 | 200 | 150 | 200 | 220 |
| Finland Finlande | 4 980 | 4 840 | 4 341 | 4 733 | 4 574 | 4 650 | 4 777 | 4 606 | 4 948 | 4 527 |
| France France | 17 140 | 17 010 | 16 551 | 16 623 | 18 353 | 18 539 | 17 899 | 17 989 | 17 477 | 17 199 |
| Gabon Gabon | ... | 801 | 847 | 778 | 812 | 867 | 792 | 754 | ... | ... |
| Georgia Géorgie | 48 | 79 | 97 | 126 | 234 | 257 | 273 | 284 | 476 | ... |
| Germany Allemagne | 108 938 | 108 729 | 106 993 | 107 479 | 106 877 | 106 372 | 102 133 | 98 933 | 97 748 | 94 806 |
| Greece Grèce | 3 769 | 3 797 | 4 139 | 4 342 | 4 423 | 4 494 | 4 548 | 4 090 | 3 890 | ... |
| Guatemala Guatemala | 1 655 | 1 303 | 1 363 | 1 443 | 1 406 | ... | ... | ... | ... | ... |
| Guyana Guyana | 112 | 136 | 137 | 136 | 130 | 120 | 131 | 105 | 110 | 119 |
| Hungary Hongrie | 7 270 | 6 973 | 7 163 | 6 996 | 7 194 | 7 142 | 7 237 | 7 255 | 6 467 | 6 770 |
| Iceland Islande | 63 | 64 | 71 | 77 | 88 | 123 | 103 | 108 | ... | ... |
| India Inde | 4 255[10] | 4 331[10] | 4 332[10] | 3 632[10] | 3 025 | 2 352 | 2 696 | 7 101 | 7 365 | 8 996 |

**Beer**—Production: thousand hectolitres (*continued*)
**Bière**—Production : milliers d'hectolitres (*suite*)

| Country or area<br>Pays ou zone | 1996 | 1997 | 1998 | 1999 | 2000 | 2001 | 2002 | 2003 | 2004 | 2005 |
|---|---|---|---|---|---|---|---|---|---|---|
| Indonesia<br>Indonésie | ... | 531 | 502 | 401 | ... | 437 | 237 | ... | ... | ... |
| Iran (Islamic Rep. of)[11]<br>Iran (Rép. islamique d')[11] | ... | 130 | 155 | 127 | 145 | ... | ... | ... | ... | ... |
| Ireland<br>Irlande | 10 765 | 12 095 | 12 584 | ... | ... | ... | ... | ... | ... | ... |
| Italy<br>Italie | 9 559 | 10 379 | 11 073 | 11 123 | 11 173 | 11 375 | 11 208 | 13 994 | 13 692 | ... |
| Jamaica<br>Jamaïque | 690 | 674 | 670 | 656 | 697 | 784 | 774 | 585 | ... | ... |
| Japan[12]<br>Japon[12] | 67 439 | 66 971 | 63 297 | 58 573 | 55 081 | 51 855 | 46 215 | 41 323 | 37 833 | 36 169 |
| Kazakhstan<br>Kazakhstan | 636 | 693 | 850 | 824 | 1 357 | 1 732 | 2 020 | 2 348 | 2 780 | ... |
| Kenya<br>Kenya | 2 759 | 2 704 | 2 630 | 1 885 | 2 029 | 1 843 | 1 919 | 2 223 | 2 447 | 2 663 |
| Korea, Republic of<br>Corée, République de | 17 210 | 16 907 | 14 080 | 14 866 | 16 544 | 17 765 | 18 224 | 17 863 | 18 033 | 17 489 |
| Kyrgyzstan<br>Kirghizistan | 143 | 145 | 129 | 122 | 124 | 87 | 71 | 77 | 116 | 123 |
| Lao People's Dem. Rep.<br>Rép. dém. pop. lao | ... | ... | ... | ... | ... | 576 | 652 | 702 | 827 | 927 |
| Latvia<br>Lettonie | 645 | 715 | 721 | 946 | 931 | 989 | 1 199 | 1 364 | 1 313 | 1 285 |
| Lithuania<br>Lituanie | 1 139 | 1 406 | 1 557 | 1 852 | 2 065 | 2 174 | 2 683 | 2 520 | 2 782 | 2 916 |
| Luxembourg<br>Luxembourg | 483 | 481 | 469 | 450 | 438 | 397 | 386 | 391 | ... | ... |
| Madagascar<br>Madagascar | 347 | 234 | 297 | 446 | 467 | 502 | 439 | ... | 92 | 93 |
| Malawi<br>Malawi | 277 | 780 | 678 | 684 | 739 | 1 033 | ... | ... | ... | ... |
| Mali<br>Mali | 60 | 65 | 66 | 62 | 74 | 71 | 75 | 78 | 78 | 149 |
| Mauritius<br>Maurice | 312 | 340 | 376 | 358 | 375 | 386 | 376 | 401 | 364 | 339 |
| Mexico<br>Mexique | 48 111 | 51 315 | 54 569 | 57 905 | 59 851 | 61 632 | 63 530 | 65 462 | 67 575 | 72 030 |
| Moldova<br>Moldova | 226 | 238 | 278 | 202 | 249 | 318 | 438 | 566 | 653 | 724 |
| Mozambique<br>Mozambique | 374 | 631 | 75 | 95 | 989 | 982 | 779 | 1 044 | 1 025 | 1 412 |
| Nepal[13]<br>Népal[13] | 183 | 215 | 139 | 188 | 217 | 233 | 228 | 242 | 250 | 260 |
| Netherlands<br>Pays-Bas | 22 670[14,15] | 23 780[14,15] | 23 040[14,15] | 23 799[14,15] | 24 956[14,15] | 24 605[15] | 24 774[15] | 25 699 | 24 546[14,15] | 23 851[14,15] |
| New Zealand<br>Nouvelle-Zélande | 3 435 | 3 214 | 3 206 | 3 146 | 2 980 | 3 070 | 3 093 | 3 127 | 3 060 | 3 036 |
| Niger<br>Niger | 78 | 72 | 70 | 69 | 72 | 68 | 65 | ... | ... | ... |
| Norway<br>Norvège | ... | 2 396 | 1 833 | 2 651 | ... | 2 462 | 2 377 | ... | 2 352 | 2 442 |
| Panama<br>Panama | 1 229 | 1 335 | 1 448 | 1 461 | 1 399 | ... | ... | ... | ... | ... |

| Country or area<br>Pays ou zone | 1996 | 1997 | 1998 | 1999 | 2000 | 2001 | 2002 | 2003 | 2004 | 2005 |
|---|---|---|---|---|---|---|---|---|---|---|
| Peru<br>Pérou | 7 473 | 7 650 | 6 557 | 6 168 | 5 706 | 5 296 | 6 170 | 6 483 | 6 733 | 7 970 |
| Poland<br>Pologne | 16 667 | 19 281 | 21 017 | 23 360 | #24 739 | 15 069 | 26 715 | 28 412 | 29 794 | 31 343 |
| Portugal<br>Portugal | 6 619 | 6 494 | 6 617 | 6 641 | 6 718 | 6 509 | 6 689 | 7 110 | 7 712 | ... |
| Puerto Rico<br>Porto Rico | 360 | 317 | 263 | 259 | ... | ... | ... | ... | ... | ... |
| Romania<br>Roumanie | 8 118 | 7 651 | 9 989 | 11 133 | 12 664 | 12 087 | 11 513 | 13 087 | 14 159 | 14 713 |
| Russian Federation<br>Fédération de Russie | 20 832 | 26 103 | 33 631 | 44 484 | 51 563 | 63 780 | 70 266 | 75 540 | 83 787 | 90 986 |
| Saint Kitts and Nevis<br>Saint-Kitts-et-Nevis | 20 | 19 | 20 | 20 | 20 | 20 | 20 | ... | ... | ... |
| Serbia<br>Serbie | ... | ... | ... | ... | ... | ... | ... | ... | ... | 6 569 |
| Serbia and Montenegro<br>Serbie-et-Monténégro | 5 987 | 6 106 | 6 630 | #6 786 | 6 734 | 6 063 | 5 764 | 6 049 | | |
| Seychelles<br>Seychelles | 63 | 71 | 72 | 68 | 70 | 72 | 76 | 65 | 63 | 63 |
| Sierra Leone<br>Sierra Leone | 5 623 | 187 | 489 | ... | 3 818 | 9 838 | 1 116 | 9 247 | 9 420 | 10 124 |
| Slovakia<br>Slovaquie | 4 666 | 5 577 | 4 478 | 4 473 | 4 491 | 4 216 | 4 747 | 4 684 | 3 877 | 3 810 |
| Slovenia<br>Slovénie | 2 133 | ... | 1 976 | 2 084 | 2 463 | 2 449 | ... | ... | ... | ... |
| Spain<br>Espagne | 24 520 | 24 786 | 22 428 | 26 007 | 26 388 | 26 802 | 28 631 | 31 028 | 31 467 | 31 156 |
| Suriname<br>Suriname | 72 | ... | ... | ... | ... | ... | ... | ... | ... | |
| Sweden<br>Suède | 5 320 | 5 129 | 4 763 | 4 718 | 4 686 | 4 522 | 4 527 | 4 255 | 3 870 | 3 952 |
| Syrian Arab Republic<br>Rép. arabe syrienne | 102 | 97 | 97 | 121 | 91 | 100 | 104 | 100 | 109 | ... |
| Tajikistan<br>Tadjikistan | 6 | 6 | 9 | 7 | 4 | 8 | 9 | 9 | 11 | 16 |
| Thailand<br>Thaïlande | 7 590 | 8 740 | 9 770 | 10 420 | 11 650 | 12 380 | 12 750 | 16 020 | 16 320 | 16 950 |
| TFYR of Macedonia<br>L'ex-R.y. Macédoine | 622 | 600 | 578 | 652 | 661 | 618 | 657 | 680 | 716 | 695 |
| Trinidad and Tobago<br>Trinité-et-Tobago | 419 | 407 | 517 | 522 | 625 | ... | ... | ... | ... | ... |
| Tunisia<br>Tunisie | 662 | 780 | 813 | 912 | 1 066 | 1 087 | 1 100 | 997 | ... | ... |
| Turkey<br>Turquie | 7 381 | 7 656 | 7 130 | 7 188 | 7 649 | 7 441 | 7 845 | 8 363 | 8 812 | 8 936 |
| Turkmenistan<br>Turkménistan | 17 | 44 | 29 | 37 | 52 | 79 | 84 | ... | ... | ... |
| Uganda<br>Ouganda | 642 | 896 | 1 105 | 1 178 | 1 261 | 1 079 | 989 | ... | ... | ... |
| Ukraine<br>Ukraine | 6 025 | 6 125 | 6 842 | 8 407 | 10 765 | 13 059 | 15 000 | 17 012 | 19 373 | 23 805 |
| United Kingdom<br>Royaume-Uni | 63 124 | 64 816 | 60 915 | 62 510 | 54 206 | 57 032 | 60 646 | 64 253 | 73 622 | ... |

| Country or area<br>Pays ou zone | 1996 | 1997 | 1998 | 1999 | 2000 | 2001 | 2002 | 2003 | 2004 | 2005 |
|---|---|---|---|---|---|---|---|---|---|---|
| United Rep. of Tanzania<br>Rép.-Unie de Tanzanie | 1 251 | 1 483 | 1 707 | 1 674 | 1 830 | 1 756 | 1 759 | 1 941 | 2 026 | 2 166 |
| United States[16]<br>Etats-Unis[16] | 233 485 | ... | ... | ... | ... | ... | ... | ... | ... | ... |
| Uruguay<br>Uruguay | 913 | 939 | 860 | 741 | 706 | 629 | 507 | 415 | ... | ... |
| Uzbekistan<br>Ouzbékistan | 677 | 619 | 569[17] | 422[17] | 609[17] | ... | ... | ... | ... | ... |
| Viet Nam<br>Viet Nam | 5 334 | 5 811 | 6 700 | 6 898 | 7 791 | 8 712 | 9 398 | 11 189 | 13 428 | 14 270 |
| Zimbabwe<br>Zimbabwe | ... | ... | ... | ... | ... | 4 747 | 2 957 | ... | ... | ... |

Source

United Nations Statistics Division, New York, the "Industrial Commodity Statistics Yearbook 2005" and the industrial statistics database, last accessed June 2008.

Notes

1  Source: Economist Intelligence Unit (London).
2  Twelve months ending 30 June of the year stated.
3  Excluding light beer containing less than 1.15% by volume of alcohol.
4  Incomplete coverage.
5  Source: Afristat: Sub-Saharan African Observatory of Economics and Statistics (Bamako, Mali).
6  Excluding the Federation of Bosnia and Herzegovina.
7  For statistical purposes, the data for China do not include those for the Hong Kong Special Administrative Region (Hong Kong SAR), Macao Special Administrative Region (Macao SAR) and Taiwan Province of China.
8  Original data in metric tons.
9  Twelve months ending 7 July of the year stated.
10 Production by large- and medium-scale establishments only.
11 Production by establishments employing 10 or more persons.
12 Twelve months beginning 1 April of the year stated.
13 Twelve months beginning 16 July of the year stated.
14 Production by establishments employing 20 or more persons.
15 Sales.
16 Twelve months ending 30 September of the year stated.
17 Source: "Statistical Yearbook for Asia and the Pacific", United Nations Economic and Social Commission for Asia and the Pacific (Bangkok).

Source

Organisation des Nations Unies, Division de statistique, New York, "l'Annuaire de statistiques industrielles par produit 2005", et la base de données sur les statistiques industrielles, dernier accès juin 2008.

Notes

1  Source: "Economist Intelligence Unit (London)".
2  Période de 12 mois finissant le 30 juin de l'année indiquée.
3  Non compris la bière légère contenant moins de 1.15 p. 100 en volume d'alcool.
4  Couverture incomplète.
5  Source : Afristat : Observatoire Economique et Statistique d'Afrique Subsaharienne (Bamako, Mali).
6  Non compris la Fédération de Bosnie et Herzégovine.
7  Pour la présentation des statistiques, les données pour la Chine ne comprennent pas la Région Administrative Spéciale de Hong Kong (Hong Kong RAS), la Région Administrative Spéciale de Macao (Macao RAS) et la province de Taiwan.
8  Données d'origine exprimées en tonnes.
9  Période de 12 mois finissant le 7 juillet de l'année indiquée.
10 Production des grandes et moyennes entreprises seulement.
11 Production des établissements employant 10 personnes ou plus.
12 Période de 12 mois commençant le 1er avril de l'année indiquée.
13 Période de 12 mois commençant le 16 juillet de l'année indiquée.
14 Production des établissements employant 20 personnes ou plus.
15 Ventes.
16 Période de 12 mois finissant le 30 septembre de l'année indiquée.
17 Source : "Annuaire des Statistiques de l'Asie et Pacifique", Commission économique et sociale des Nations Unies pour l'Asie et le Pacifique (Bangkok).

| Country or area<br>Pays ou zone | 1996 | 1997 | 1998 | 1999 | 2000 | 2001 | 2002 | 2003 | 2004 | 2005 |
|---|---|---|---|---|---|---|---|---|---|---|
| Albania<br>Albanie | 483[1] | 414[1] | 764[1] | 647[1] | 372[1] | 126[1] | 50 | 15 | ... | ... |
| Andorra<br>Andorre | ... | ... | 1 | 1 | 1 | 1 | 1 | 2 | 2 | 3 |
| Argentina<br>Argentine | 1 971 | 1 940 | 1 967 | 1 996 | 1 843 | 1 739 | 1 812 | 1 990 | 1 890 | ... |
| Armenia<br>Arménie | 152 | 815 | 2 489 | 3 132 | 2 109 | 1 623 | 2 815 | 3 222 | 2 720 | 3 020 |
| Azerbaijan<br>Azerbaïdjan | 766 | 827 | 241 | 416 | 2 363 | 6 808 | 6 296 | 6 611 | 3 671 | 5 008 |
| Bangladesh[2]<br>Bangladesh[2] | 16 222 | 18 601 | 19 889 | 19 558 | 19 732 | 20 120 | 20 384 | 22 499 | ... | ... |
| Belarus<br>Bélarus | 6 267 | 6 787 | 7 296 | 9 259 | 10 356 | 11 182 | 10 524 | 10 442 | 12 627 | 12 008 |
| Belgium<br>Belgique | 17 471 | 18 061 | 17 519 | 14 713[3] | ... | ... | ... | ... | ... | ... |
| Belize<br>Belize | 79 | 88 | 94 | 91 | 84 | ... | ... | ... | ... | ... |
| Bolivia<br>Bolivie | 1 490 | 1 484 | 1 538 | 1 404 | ... | ... | ... | ... | ... | ... |
| Bosnia and Herzegovina<br>Bosnie-Herzégovine | 3 198 | 3 886 | 4 830 | 5 974 | ... | ... | ... | 5 062 | ... | ... |
| Brazil<br>Brésil | ... | ... | ... | ... | 17 860 | 15 820 | 100 193 | 21 099 | 96 828 | ... |
| Bulgaria<br>Bulgarie | 57 238 | 43 315 | 33 181 | 25 715 | 26 681 | 26 659 | 23 227 | 25 914 | 24 462 | 23 318 |
| Burundi<br>Burundi | 450 | 377 | 317 | 353 | 286 | 293 | 312 | 354 | 376 | 419 |
| Cameroon<br>Cameroun | ... | 2 704 | 3 084 | 3 249 | 2 984 | 2 814 | 2 785 | 1 903 | 1 966 | 1 755 |
| Canada<br>Canada | 49 362 | 47 263 | 48 854 | 47 224 | 46 068 | 44 403 | 37 127 | ... | ... | ... |
| Chad[4]<br>Tchad[4] | 714 | 786 | ... | ... | ... | ... | ... | ... | ... | ... |
| Chile<br>Chili | 11 569 | 12 522 | 12 904 | 13 271 | 13 796 | 13 305 | 13 839 | 13 776 | ... | ... |
| China[5]<br>Chine[5] | 34 | 34 | 34 | 33 | 34 | 34 | 35 | 36 | ... | ... |
| China, Hong Kong SAR<br>Chine, Hong Kong RAS | 21 386 | 20 929 | 13 470 | ... | ... | ... | ... | ... | ... | ... |
| China, Macao SAR[1,6]<br>Chine, Macao RAS[1,6] | 450 | ... | ... | ... | ... | ... | ... | ... | ... | ... |
| Colombia<br>Colombie | ... | 11 662 | 12 472 | 15 182 | ... | ... | ... | ... | ... | ... |
| Congo<br>Congo | 776 | 380 | ... | ... | ... | 102 | 662 | 748 | 750 | ... |
| Costa Rica[1,6]<br>Costa Rica[1,6] | 16 | ... | ... | ... | ... | ... | ... | ... | ... | ... |

| Country or area<br>Pays ou zone | 1996 | 1997 | 1998 | 1999 | 2000 | 2001 | 2002 | 2003 | 2004 | 2005 |
|---|---|---|---|---|---|---|---|---|---|---|
| Croatia<br>Croatie | 11 548 | 11 416 | 11 987 | 12 785 | 13 692 | 14 738 | 15 047 | 15 613 | 14 256 | 14 578 |
| Cuba<br>Cuba | 10 700 | 10 700 | 11 655 | 13 432 | 12 086 | 11 769 | 12 519 | 14 300 | 12 800 | 14 000 |
| Cyprus<br>Chypre | 2 728 | 3 662 | 4 362 | 4 783 | 4 980 | 3 803 | 2 534 | 2 661 | 3 845 | ... |
| Denmark<br>Danemark | 11 804 | 12 262 | 12 392 | 11 749 | 11 413 | 11 089 | 12 039 | 12 898 | 13 458 | 14 867 |
| Dominican Republic<br>Rép. dominicaine | 4 192 | 3 972 | 4 098 | 4 005 | 3 898 | 3 338 | 3 509 | 3 469 | 3 446 | 3 300 |
| Ecuador<br>Equateur | 1 745 | 1 678 | 1 997 | 2 178 | 2 773 | ... | ... | 2 975 | ... | ... |
| Egypt<br>Egypte | 46 000 | 50 000 | 52 000 | 52 336 | 56 614 | 61 000 | 62 018 | 63 396 | ... | ... |
| El Salvador<br>El Salvador | 1 756 | ... | ... | ... | ... | ... | ... | ... | ... | ... |
| Estonia<br>Estonie | 954 | ... | ... | ... | ... | ... | ... | ... | ... | ... |
| Ethiopia<br>Ethiopie | 1 862[7] | 2 024[7] | 2 029[7] | 1 829[7] | 1 931 | 1 904 | 1 511 | 1 511 | ... | ... |
| Fiji<br>Fidji | 439 | 450 | 410 | 446 | 396 | 389 | 422 | 416 | 454 | 420 |
| Finland<br>Finlande | 5 910 | 6 790 | 4 062 | 4 877 | 3 981 | 3 999 | 4 130 | 3 946 | 868 | 0 |
| France<br>France | 46 931 | 44 646 | 43 304 | 42 405 | 42 058 | 42 980 | 42 500 | 42 700 | 48 163 | 46 500 |
| Gabon<br>Gabon | ... | 331 | 463 | 670 | 859 | 880 | 860 | ... | ... | ... |
| Georgia<br>Géorgie | 1 183 | 917 | 601 | 132 | 296 | 1 615 | 1 894 | 2 972 | 2 808 | ... |
| Germany<br>Allemagne | 193 279 | 181 747 | 181 904 | 204 631 | 206 770 | 213 793 | 212 500 | 205 237 | 208 347 | 212 428 |
| Ghana<br>Ghana | ... | 1 747 | 1 399 | 1 158 | 1 166 | 1 481 | 1 800 | ... | ... | ... |
| Greece<br>Grèce | 36 478 | 29 529 | 31 705 | 31 535 | 34 256 | 25 516 | 28 091 | 26 249 | 28 048 | ... |
| Guatemala<br>Guatemala | 1 725 | 2 198 | 4 184 | 4 376 | 4 262 | ... | ... | ... | ... | ... |
| Guyana<br>Guyana | 400 | 221 | ... | ... | ... | ... | ... | ... | ... | ... |
| Honduras<br>Honduras | ... | ... | 3 814 | 4 586 | 5 655 | 5 984 | 6 010 | ... | ... | ... |
| Hungary<br>Hongrie | 27 594 | 26 057 | 26 849 | 22 985 | 21 608 | 20 787 | 21 748 | 20 181 | 12 119 | ... |
| India<br>Inde | 73 841[8] | 83 162[8] | 79 313[8] | 82 504[8] | 82 504[8] | 60 577[9] | 54 991[9] | 75 675 | ... | 81 598 |
| Iran (Islamic Rep. of)<br>Iran (Rép. islamique d') | 11 860[10] | 10 304[10] | 14 335 | 20 081 | 13 800 | 13 363 | 12 700 | 12 200 | 18 700 | ... |
| Iraq<br>Iraq | ... | ... | ... | ... | ... | ... | ... | ... | 812 | ... |
| Ireland<br>Irlande | 4 976 | 4 605 | 6 452 | 6 176 | 6 461 | 6 807 | 6 599 | ... | ... | ... |

| Country or area<br>Pays ou zone | 1996 | 1997 | 1998 | 1999 | 2000 | 2001 | 2002 | 2003 | 2004 | 2005 |
|---|---|---|---|---|---|---|---|---|---|---|
| Israel<br>Israël | 4 793 | ... | ... | ... | ... | ... | ... | ... | ... | ... |
| Italy<br>Italie | 51 489[1] | 51 894[1] | 50 785 | 45 159 | 43 694[1] | 45 368[1] | 37 342 | 40 350 | ... | ... |
| Jamaica<br>Jamaïque | 1 219 | 1 175 | 1 160 | 1 073 | 995 | 1 027 | 1 049 | 889 | ... | ... |
| Japan[11]<br>Japon[11] | 348 300 | 328 000 | 336 600 | 332 200 | 324 500 | 313 900 | ... | ... | ... | ... |
| Jordan<br>Jordanie | 4 738 | 1 853[12] | 1 144[12] | *1 602[12] | *1 300[12] | ... | ... | ... | ... | ... |
| Kazakhstan<br>Kazakhstan | 19 121 | 24 109 | 21 747 | 18 773 | 19 293 | 21 395 | 23 453 | 25 715 | 28 038 | ... |
| Kenya<br>Kenya | 8 436 | 8 898 | 7 599 | 7 231 | 6 009 | 5 850 | 4 631 | 4 753 | 5 351 | 7 324 |
| Korea, Republic of<br>Corée, République de | 94 709 | 96 725 | 101 011 | 95 995 | 94 531 | 94 116 | 94 433 | 123 166 | 133 206 | 107 247 |
| Kyrgyzstan<br>Kirghizistan | 975 | 716 | 862 | 2 103 | 3 169 | 3 013 | 2 927 | 3 102 | 3 170 | 3 179 |
| Lao People's Dem. Rep.<br>Rép. dém. pop. lao | ... | 856[11] | 1 104[11] | ... | ... | 41 | 55 | 68 | 84 | 105 |
| Latvia<br>Lettonie | 1 876 | 1 775 | 2 018 | 1 909 | ... | ... | ... | ... | ... | ... |
| Lebanon[1]<br>Liban[1] | 539 | 793 | 672 | 945 | 1 009 | ... | ... | ... | ... | ... |
| Lithuania<br>Lituanie | 4 538 | 5 755 | 7 427 | 8 217 | 7 207 | ... | ... | ... | ... | ... |
| Madagascar<br>Madagascar | 2 957[1] | 2 826[1] | 3 303[1] | ... | ... | ... | ... | ... | 8 | 8 |
| Malawi<br>Malawi | 975 | 731 | 501 | ... | ... | ... | ... | ... | ... | ... |
| Mali<br>Mali | 631 | 655 | 473 | 350 | 231 | 106 | 90 | 198 | 328 | 330 |
| Mauritius<br>Maurice | 1 193 | 1 144 | 1 034 | 979 | 1 049 | 861 | 928 | 938 | 918 | 900 |
| Mexico<br>Mexique | 38 331 | 38 786 | 44 917 | 45 373 | 44 400 | 44 904 | 43 834 | 41 856 | 40 752 | 41 439 |
| Moldova[13]<br>Moldova[13] | 9 657 | 9 539 | 7 512 | 8 731 | 9 262 | 9 421 | 6 310 | 7 126 | 7 050 | 6 195 |
| Mozambique<br>Mozambique | 250 | 250 | 950 | 1 084 | 1 417 | 1 359 | 1 255 | 1 390 | ... | ... |
| Myanmar[14]<br>Myanmar[14] | 1 727 | 1 991 | 2 040 | 2 270 | 2 559 | 2 650 | 2 657 | 2 806 | 3 183 | ... |
| Nepal[15]<br>Népal[15] | 8 067 | 7 944 | 8 127 | 7 315 | 6 584 | 6 979 | 6 900 | 6 812 | 7 268 | ... |
| New Zealand<br>Nouvelle-Zélande | 3 660 | 3 234 | 3 086 | 2 949 | 2 916 | 2 396 | 2 509 | 2 176 | 2 122 | 2 211 |
| Nicaragua<br>Nicaragua | ... | 1 580 | 1 789 | 780[16] | ... | ... | ... | ... | ... | ... |
| Pakistan[2]<br>Pakistan[2] | 45 506 | 46 101 | 48 215 | 51 579 | 46 976 | 58 259 | 55 318 | 49 365 | 55 399 | 61 100 |
| Panama<br>Panama | 663 | 752 | ... | ... | ... | ... | ... | ... | ... | ... |

**Cigarettes** — Production: millions (*continued*)
**Cigarettes** — Production : millions (*suite*)

| Country or area<br>Pays ou zone | 1996 | 1997 | 1998 | 1999 | 2000 | 2001 | 2002 | 2003 | 2004 | 2005 |
|---|---|---|---|---|---|---|---|---|---|---|
| Peru<br>Pérou | 3 358 | 3 029 | 3 115 | 3 581 | 3 605 | 3 310 | 3 766 | 2 707 | 2 168 | 1 460 |
| Philippines[1,6]<br>Philippines[1,6] | 7 440 | ... | ... | ... | ... | ... | ... | ... | ... | ... |
| Poland<br>Pologne | 95 293 | 95 798 | 96 741 | 95 056 | #78 792 | 82 421 | 78 746 | 78 792 | 83 376 | 95 531 |
| Portugal<br>Portugal | 12 743 | 14 606 | 15 889 | 18 189 | 20 561 | 23 376 | 25 581 | 24 950 | 26 415 | ... |
| Romania<br>Roumanie | 16 536 | 25 943 | ... | ... | ... | ... | 38 033 | 37 808 | 28 677 | 34 541 |
| Russian Federation<br>Fédération de Russie | 112 000 | 140 000 | 196 000 | 266 000 | 334 000 | 356 000 | 383 000 | 376 000 | 377 000 | 402 000 |
| Serbia<br>Serbie | ... | ... | ... | ... | ... | ... | ... | ... | ... | 18 127 |
| Serbia and Montenegro<br>Serbie-et-Monténégro | 13 176 | 10 988 | 14 597 | #13 126 | 14 451 | 13 968 | 15 388 | ... | ... | ... |
| Seychelles<br>Seychelles | 62 | 70 | 61 | 60 | 40 | 36 | 24 | 50 | 22 | 30 |
| Spain<br>Espagne | 77 675 | 77 315 | 81 940 | 74 873 | 74 799 | ... | ... | ... | 48 651 | 47 506 |
| Sri Lanka<br>Sri Lanka | 6 160 | 5 712 | 5 797 | 5 333 | 4 889 | *4 973 | 5 015[17] | 4 765[17] | 5 003[17] | ... |
| Suriname<br>Suriname | 483 | ... | ... | ... | ... | ... | ... | ... | ... | ... |
| Sweden<br>Suède | 7 251 | 6 291 | 5 692 | 6 060 | 5 958 | 5 959 | ... | ... | ... | ... |
| Switzerland<br>Suisse | 42 955 | 37 638 | 34 453 | 32 139 | 34 299 | 33 565 | 37 160 | 38 140 | 39 059 | 42 190 |
| Syrian Arab Republic[1]<br>Rép. arabe syrienne[1] | 8 528 | 10 137 | 10 398 | 10 991 | 11 097 | 12 007 | 12 863 | 13 412 | ... | ... |
| Tajikistan<br>Tadjikistan | 604 | 153 | 191 | 209 | 667 | 1 155 | 585 | 468 | 508 | 714 |
| Thailand<br>Thaïlande | 48 173 | 43 387 | 34 585 | 31 146 | 30 732 | 29 807 | 30 772 | 31 908 | 34 761 | 32 978 |
| TFYR of Macedonia<br>L'ex-R.y. Macédoine | ... | ... | ... | ... | ... | 7 766 | 6 567 | 5 120 | 5 654 | 5 763 |
| Trinidad and Tobago<br>Trinité-et-Tobago | 1 102 | 1 386 | 1 680 | 1 945 | 2 050 | ... | ... | ... | ... | ... |
| Tunisia<br>Tunisie | 7 159 | 7 735 | 9 813 | 11 066 | 12 231 | 12 354 | 13 230 | 13 227 | ... | ... |
| Turkey<br>Turquie | 73 787[1] | 74 984[1] | 81 616[1] | 75 135[1] | 76 613[1] | 77 160 | 131 561 | 111 881 | 103 371 | 104 170 |
| Uganda<br>Ouganda | 1 702 | 1 846 | 1 866 | 1 602 | 1 344 | 1 220 | 1 092 | ... | ... | ... |
| Ukraine<br>Ukraine | 44 900 | 54 488 | 59 275 | 54 052 | 58 774 | 69 731 | 81 088 | 96 776 | 108 946 | 120 218 |
| United Kingdom<br>Royaume-Uni | 168 514 | 167 670 | 152 998 | 143 794 | 139 125 | 109 025 | 124 896 | 89 639 | 85 691 | ... |
| United Rep. of Tanzania<br>Rép.-Unie de Tanzanie | 3 733 | 4 710 | 4 012 | 3 371 | 3 745 | 3 491 | 3 778 | 3 920 | 4 308 | 4 445 |
| United States<br>Etats-Unis | 754 500 | 719 600 | 679 700 | 611 929 | ... | ... | ... | ... | ... | ... |

| Country or area / Pays ou zone | 1996 | 1997 | 1998 | 1999 | 2000 | 2001 | 2002 | 2003 | 2004 | 2005 |
|---|---|---|---|---|---|---|---|---|---|---|
| Uruguay / Uruguay | 6 018 | 6 872 | 10 187 | 11 161 | 10 894 | 9 616 | 8 449 | 5 718 | ... | ... |
| Uzbekistan / Ouzbékistan | 5 172 | 8 521 | 7 582[11] | 10 668[11] | 7 766[11] | ... | ... | ... | ... | ... |
| Viet Nam / Viet Nam | 2 160 | 2 123 | 2 196 | 2 147 | 2 836 | 3 075 | 3 375 | 3 871 | 4 192 | 4 429 |
| Yemen / Yémen | 6 740 | 6 800 | 5 980 | 5 760 | 4 780 | 6 020 | 5 780 | 5 960 | ... | ... |

Source

United Nations Statistics Division, New York, the "Industrial Commodity Statistics Yearbook 2005" and the industrial statistics database, last accessed June 2008.

Notes

1  Original data in units of weight. Computed on the basis of one million cigarettes per ton.
2  Twelve months ending 30 June of the year stated.
3  Incomplete coverage.
4  Source: Afristat: Sub-Saharan African Observatory of Economics and Statistics (Bamako, Mali).
5  For statistical purposes, the data for China do not include those for the Hong Kong Special Administrative Region (Hong Kong SAR), Macao Special Administrative Region (Macao SAR) and Taiwan Province of China.
6  Source: Food and Agriculture Organization of the United Nations (Rome).
7  Twelve months ending 7 July of the year stated.
8  Production by large- and medium-scale establishments only.
9  Production by establishments employing 50 or more persons.
10  Production by establishments employing 10 or more persons.
11  Source: "Statistical Yearbook for Asia and the Pacific", United Nations Economic and Social Commission for Asia and the Pacific (Bangkok).
12  Source: "Bulletin of Industrial Statistics for the Arab Countries", United Nations Economic and Social Commission for Western Asia (Beirut).
13  Excluding the Transnistria region.
14  Government production only.
15  Twelve months beginning 16 July of the year stated.
16  Beginning August 1999, national production discontinued.
17  Source: "Country Economic Review", Asian Development Bank (Manila).

Source

Organisation des Nations Unies, Division de statistique, New York, "l'Annuaire de statistiques industrielles par produit 2005", et la base de données sur les statistiques industrielles, dernier accès juin 2008.

Notes

1  Données d'origine exprimées en poids. Calcul sur la base d'un million de cigarettes par tonne.
2  Période de 12 mois finissant le 30 juin de l'année indiquée.
3  Couverture incomplète.
4  Source : Afristat : Observatoire Economique et Statistique d'Afrique Subsaharienne (Bamako, Mali).
5  Pour la présentation des statistiques, les données pour la Chine ne comprennent pas la Région Administrative Spéciale de Hong Kong (Hong Kong RAS), la Région Administrative Spéciale de Macao (Macao RAS) et la province de Taiwan.
6  Source: Organisation des Nations Unies pour l'alimentation et l'agriculture (Rome).
7  Période de 12 mois finissant le 7 juillet de l'année indiquée.
8  Production des grandes et moyennes entreprises seulement.
9  Production des établissements occupant 50 personnes ou plus.
10  Production des établissements employant 10 personnes ou plus.
11  Source : "Annuaire des Statistiques de l'Asie et Pacifique", Commission économique et sociale des Nations Unies pour l'Asie et le Pacifique (Bangkok).
12  Source: "Bulletin of Industrial Statistics for the Arab Countries", Commission économique et sociale pour l'Asie occidentale (Beyrouth).
13  Non compris la région de Transnistria.
14  Production de l'état seulement.
15  Période de 12 mois commençant le 16 juillet de l'année indiquée.
16  A partir d'août 1999, la production nationale a été discontinuée.
17  Source: "La Revue Economique du Pays", La Banque de Développement Asiatique (Manila).

# 43

## Sawnwood
Production (sawn): thousand cubic metres

## Sciages
Production (sciés) : milliers de mètres cubes

| Region, country or area — Région, pays ou zone | 1997 | 1998 | 1999 | 2000 | 2001 | 2002 | 2003 | 2004 | 2005 | 2006 |
|---|---|---|---|---|---|---|---|---|---|---|
| **World**<br>**Monde** | 393 846 | 378 716 | 389 088 | 386 090 | 379 906 | 394 274 | 400 916 | 424 999 | 420 603 | 424 814 |
| **Africa**<br>**Afrique** | 7 505 | 7 423 | 7 415 | 8 320 | 7 921 | 7 490 | 8 474 | 9 516 | 8 986 | 8 893 |
| Algeria — Algérie | 13 | 13 | 13 | 13 | 13 | 13 | 13 | 13 | 13 | 13 |
| Angola — Angola | 5 | 5 | 5 | 5 | 5 | 5 | 5 | 5 | 5 | 5 |
| Benin — Bénin | 12 | 13 | 13 | 13 | 32 | 46 | 31 | 31 | 31 | 31 |
| Burkina Faso — Burkina Faso | 2 | 1 | 1 | 1 | 1 | 2 | 2 | 1 | 1 | 1 |
| Burundi — Burundi | 33 | 33 | 80 | 83 | 83 | 83 | 83 | 83 | 83 | 83 |
| Cameroon — Cameroun | 560 | 588 | 600 | 1 154 | 800 | 652 | 658 | 702 | 702 | 702 |
| Central African Rep. — Rép. centrafricaine | 72 | 91 | 79 | 102 | 150 | 97 | 69 | 69 | 69 | 69 |
| Chad — Tchad | 2 | 2 | 2 | 2 | 2 | 2 | 2 | 2 | 2 | 2 |
| Congo — Congo | 64 | 73 | 74 | 93 | 126 | 170 | 168 | 200 | 209 | 268 |
| Côte d'Ivoire — Côte d'Ivoire | 613 | 623 | 611 | 603 | 630 | 620 | 503 | 503 | 363 | 363 |
| Dem. Rep. of the Congo — Rép. dém. du Congo | 90 | 80 | 70 | 40 | 10 | 35 | 15 | 15 | 15 | 15 |
| Egypt — Egypte | ... | 3 | 4 | 4 | 2 | 3 | 3 | 2 | 2 | 2 |
| Equatorial Guinea — Guinée équatoriale | 4 | 4 | 4 | 4 | 4 | 4 | 4 | 4 | 4 | 4 |
| Ethiopia — Ethiopie | 60 | 60 | 60 | 60 | 60 | 14 | 18 | 18 | 18 | 18 |
| Gabon — Gabon | 30 | 60 | 98 | 88 | 112 | 176 | 231 | 133 | 230 | 235 |
| Gambia — Gambie | 1 | 1 | 1 | 1 | 1 | 1 | 1 | 1 | 1 | 1 |
| Ghana — Ghana | 575 | 590 | 454 | 475 | 480 | 461 | 496 | 480 | 520 | 527 |
| Guinea — Guinée | 25 | 26 | 26 | 26 | 26 | 26 | 26 | 26 | 3 | 2 |
| Guinea-Bissau — Guinée-Bissau | 16 | 16 | 16 | 16 | 16 | 16 | 16 | 16 | 16 | 16 |
| Kenya — Kenya | 185 | 185 | 185 | 185 | 84 | 78 | 78 | 78 | 78 | 78 |
| Liberia — Libéria | 90 | 6 | 4 | 10 | 20 | 30 | 25 | 50 | 50 | 60 |
| Libyan Arab Jamah. — Jamah. arabe libyenne | 31 | 31 | 31 | 31 | 31 | 31 | 31 | 31 | 31 | 31 |
| Madagascar — Madagascar | 84 | 84 | 102 | 485 | 400 | 95 | 493 | 893 | 893 | 893 |
| Malawi — Malawi | 45 | 45 | 45 | 45 | 45 | 45 | 45 | 45 | 45 | 45 |
| Mali — Mali | 13 | 13 | 13 | 13 | 13 | 13 | 13 | 13 | 13 | 13 |
| Mauritania — Mauritanie | ... | ... | ... | ... | ... | ... | ... | ... | 7 | 14 |
| Mauritius — Maurice | 3 | 5 | 5 | 3 | 3 | 3 | 3 | 3 | 3 | 4 |
| Morocco — Maroc | 83 | 83 | 83 | 83 | 83 | 83 | 83 | 83 | 83 | 83 |
| Mozambique — Mozambique | 33 | 28 | 28 | 28 | 28 | 28 | 28 | 32 | 38 | 43 |
| Niger — Niger | 4 | 4 | 4 | 4 | 4 | 4 | 4 | 4 | 4 | 4 |
| Nigeria — Nigéria | 2 000 | 2 000 | 2 000 | 2 000 | 2 000 | 2 000 | 2 000 | 2 000 | 2 000 | 2 000 |
| Réunion — Réunion | 2 | 2 | 2 | 2 | 2 | 2 | 2 | 2 | 2 | 2 |
| Rwanda — Rwanda | 74 | 76 | 79 | 79 | 79 | 79 | 79 | 79 | 79 | 79 |
| Sao Tome and Principe — Sao Tomé-et-Principe | 5 | 5 | 5 | 5 | 5 | 5 | 5 | 5 | 5 | 5 |
| Senegal — Sénégal | 23 | 23 | 23 | 23 | 23 | 23 | 23 | 23 | 23 | 23 |
| Sierra Leone — Sierra Leone | 5 | 5 | 5 | 5 | 5 | 5 | 5 | 5 | 5 | 5 |
| Somalia — Somalie | 14 | 14 | 14 | 14 | 14 | 14 | 14 | 14 | 14 | 14 |
| South Africa[1] — Afrique du Sud[1] | 1 574 | 1 498 | 1 498 | 1 498 | 1 498 | 1 498 | 2 171 | 2 824 | 2 217 | 2 091 |
| Sudan — Soudan | 45 | 51 | 51 | 51 | 51 | 51 | 51 | 51 | 51 | 51 |
| Swaziland — Swaziland | 102 | 102 | 102 | 102 | 102 | 102 | 102 | 102 | 102 | 102 |
| Togo — Togo | 17 | 18 | 21 | 19 | 15 | 13 | 13 | 13 | 14 | 14 |

| Region, country or area — Région, pays ou zone | 1997 | 1998 | 1999 | 2000 | 2001 | 2002 | 2003 | 2004 | 2005 | 2006 |
|---|---|---|---|---|---|---|---|---|---|---|
| Tunisia — Tunisie | 20 | 20 | 20 | 20 | 20 | 20 | 20 | 20 | 20 | 20 |
| Uganda — Ouganda | 229 | 245 | 264 | 264 | 264 | 264 | 264 | 264 | 125 | 117 |
| United Rep. of Tanzania — Rép.-Unie de Tanzanie | 24 | 24 | 24 | 24 | 24 | 24 | 24 | 24 | 24 | 24 |
| Zambia — Zambie | 157 | 157 | 157 | 157 | 157 | 157 | 157 | 157 | 157 | 157 |
| Zimbabwe — Zimbabwe | 465 | 416 | 438 | 386 | 397 | 397 | 397 | 397 | 617 | 565 |
| **Northern America**<br>**Amérique septentrionale** | **136 570** | **136 176** | **143 026** | **141 541** | **139 723** | **147 124** | **143 051** | **154 019** | **157 206** | **151 725** |
| Canada — Canada | 47 665 | 47 185 | 50 412 | 50 465 | 53 708 | 58 481 | 56 892 | 60 952 | 60 187 | 58 709 |
| United States — Etats-Unis | 88 906 | 88 991 | 92 615 | 91 076 | 86 015 | 88 643 | 86 159 | 93 067 | 97 020 | 93 016 |
| **Latin America and the Caribbean**<br>**Amér. latine et Caraïbes** | **35 129** | **35 935** | **36 621** | **36 653** | **38 169** | **39 249** | **39 961** | **41 623** | **41 914** | **42 894** |
| Argentina — Argentine | 1 170 | 1 377 | 1 408 | 821 | 2 130 | 2 130 | 1 388 | 1 562 | 1 739 | 1 739 |
| Bahamas — Bahamas | 1 | 1 | 1 | 1 | 1 | 1 | 1 | 1 | 1 | 1 |
| Belize — Belize | 35 | 35 | 35 | 35 | 35 | 35 | 35 | 35 | 35 | 35 |
| Bolivia — Bolivie | 180 | 515 | 244 | 239 | 308 | 299 | 347 | 402 | 408 | 408 |
| Brazil — Brésil | 19 310 | 19 520 | 20 530 | 21 600 | 21 950 | 22 488 | 23 090 | 23 480 | 23 557 | 23 557 |
| Chile — Chili | 4 661 | 4 551 | 5 254 | 5 698 | 5 872 | 6 439 | 7 004 | 8 015 | 8 298 | 8 718 |
| Colombia — Colombie | 1 085 | 910 | 730 | 587 | 539 | 527 | 599 | 622 | 407 | 389 |
| Costa Rica — Costa Rica | 780 | 780 | 780 | 812 | 812 | 812 | 812 | 426 | 488 | 488 |
| Cuba — Cuba | 130 | 130 | 146 | 179 | 190 | 147 | 181 | 189 | 220 | 243 |
| Dominica — Dominique | ... | ... | ... | ... | ... | ... | 47 | 66 | 66 | 66 |
| Dominican Republic — Rep. Dominicaine | 0 | 0 | 0 | 0 | 0 | 0 | 0 | 0 | 15 | 12 |
| Ecuador — Equateur | 2 075 | 2 079 | 1 455 | 715 | 794 | 750 | 750 | 755 | 755 | 755 |
| El Salvador — El Salvador | 58 | 58 | 58 | 58 | 58 | 68 | 68 | 16 | 16 | 16 |
| French Guiana — Guyane française | 15 | 15 | 15 | 15 | 15 | 15 | 15 | 15 | 15 | 15 |
| Guadeloupe — Guadeloupe | 1 | 1 | 1 | 1 | 1 | 1 | 1 | 1 | 1 | 1 |
| Guatemala — Guatemala | 355 | 308 | 235 | 340 | 340 | 340 | 366 | 366 | 366 | 366 |
| Guyana — Guyana | 57 | 50 | 50 | 29 | 30 | 31 | 38 | 36 | 58 | 68 |
| Haiti — Haïti | 14 | 14 | 14 | 14 | 14 | 14 | 14 | 14 | 14 | 14 |
| Honduras — Honduras | 379 | 369 | 419 | 442 | 419 | 470 | 421 | 454 | 400 | 400 |
| Jamaica — Jamaïque | 65 | 66 | 66 | 66 | 66 | 66 | 66 | 66 | 66 | 66 |
| Martinique — Martinique | 1 | 1 | 1 | 1 | 1 | 1 | 1 | 1 | 1 | 1 |
| Mexico — Mexique | 2 961 | 3 260 | 3 110 | 3 110 | 2 829 | 2 691 | 2 740 | 2 962 | 2 674 | 2 829 |
| Nicaragua — Nicaragua | 148 | 148 | 148 | 148 | 65 | 45 | 45 | 67 | 54 | 54 |
| Panama — Panama | 17 | 8 | 46 | 48 | 42 | 24 | 27 | 30 | 30 | 30 |
| Paraguay — Paraguay | 550 | 550 | 550 | 550 | 550 | 550 | 550 | 550 | 550 | 550 |
| Peru — Pérou | 482 | 590 | 835 | 646 | 506 | 626 | 528 | 671 | 743 | 856 |
| Suriname — Suriname | 41 | 41 | 28 | 60 | 56 | 47 | 56 | 58 | 65 | 69 |
| Trinidad and Tobago — Trinité-et-Tobago | 38 | 27 | 18 | 32 | 41 | 43 | 39 | 32 | 41 | 41 |
| Uruguay — Uruguay | 269 | 269 | 269 | 203 | 203 | 224 | 230 | 252 | 268 | 268 |
| Venezuela (Boliv. Rep. of) — Venezuela (Rép. boliv. du) | 250 | 261 | 174 | 202 | 301 | 364 | 501 | 479 | 562 | 838 |
| **Asia**<br>**Asie** | **90 189** | **72 096** | **71 648** | **61 905** | **59 616** | **63 742** | **68 334** | **71 814** | **61 649** | **65 267** |
| Afghanistan — Afghanistan | 400 | 400 | 400 | 400 | 400 | 400 | 400 | 400 | 400 | 400 |
| Armenia — Arménie | ... | ... | ... | 4 | 4 | 4 | 3 | 2 | 2 | 5 |
| Azerbaijan — Azerbaïdjan | ... | ... | ... | 1 | ^0 | ^0 | ^0 | ^0 | ^0 | ^0 |
| Bangladesh — Bangladesh | 70 | 70 | 70 | 70 | 70 | 255 | 388 | 388 | 388 | 388 |
| Bhutan — Bhoutan | 18 | 18 | 22 | 31 | 31 | 31 | 31 | 31 | 31 | 31 |
| Brunei Darussalam — Brunéi Darussalam | 90 | 90 | 67 | 56 | 51 | 54 | 51 | 51 | 51 | 51 |

| Region, country or area — Région, pays ou zone | 1997 | 1998 | 1999 | 2000 | 2001 | 2002 | 2003 | 2004 | 2005 | 2006 |
|---|---|---|---|---|---|---|---|---|---|---|
| Cambodia — Cambodge | 71 | 40 | 26 | 20 | 5 | 10 | 4 | 4 | 4 | 4 |
| China[2,3] — Chine[2,3] | 20 982 | 18 716 | 16 700 | 7 345 | 8 549 | 9 431 | 12 211 | 16 236 | 7 324 | 10 245 |
| Cyprus — Chypre | 14 | 11 | 12 | 9 | 9 | 7 | 6 | 5 | 4 | 4 |
| Georgia — Géorgie | 5 | 5 | 10 | 10 | 44 | 59 | 71 | 69 | 69 | 69 |
| India — Inde | 18 520 | 8 400 | 8 400 | 7 900 | 7 900 | 10 990 | 11 880 | 13 661 | 14 789 | 14 789 |
| Indonesia — Indonésie | 7 238 | 7 125 | 6 625 | 6 500 | 6 750 | 6 230 | 7 620 | 4 330 | 1 472 | 1 472 |
| Iran (Islamic Rep. of) — Iran (Rép. islamique d') | 141 | 129 | 96 | 106 | 106 | 170 | 79 | 68 | 62 | 50 |
| Iraq — Iraq | 8 | 12 | 12 | 12 | 12 | 12 | 12 | 12 | 12 | 12 |
| Japan — Japon | 21 709 | 18 625 | 17 952 | 17 094 | 15 485 | 14 402 | 13 929 | 13 603 | 12 825 | 12 554 |
| Kazakhstan — Kazakhstan | ... | 182 | 183 | 244 | 224 | 232 | 265 | 134 | 139 | 139 |
| Korea, Dem. P. R. — Corée, R. p. dém. de | 280 | 280 | 280 | 280 | 280 | 280 | 280 | 280 | 280 | 280 |
| Korea, Republic of — Corée, République de | 4 759 | 2 240 | 4 300 | 4 544 | 4 420 | 4 410 | 4 380 | 4 366 | 4 366 | 4 366 |
| Kyrgyzstan — Kirghizistan | 2 | 23 | 23 | 6 | 6 | 6 | 15 | 22 | 22 | 22 |
| Lao People's Dem. Rep. — Rép. dém. pop. lao | 498 | 389 | 439 | 200 | 185 | 192 | 125 | 125 | 130 | 130 |
| Lebanon — Liban | 9 | 9 | 9 | 9 | 9 | 9 | 9 | 9 | 9 | 9 |
| Malaysia — Malaisie | 7 326 | 5 091 | 5 237 | 5 590 | 4 696 | 4 643 | 4 769 | 4 934 | 5 173 | 5 129 |
| Mongolia — Mongolie | 200 | 300 | 300 | 300 | 300 | 300 | 300 | 300 | 300 | 300 |
| Myanmar — Myanmar | 372 | 299 | 298 | 545 | 671 | 1 012 | 1 001 | 1 056 | 1 530 | 1 530 |
| Nepal — Népal | 620 | 630 | 630 | 630 | 630 | 630 | 630 | 630 | 630 | 630 |
| Pakistan — Pakistan | 1 024 | 1 051 | 1 075 | 1 087 | 1 180 | 1 180 | 1 180 | 1 260 | 1 288 | 1 313 |
| Philippines — Philippines | 351 | 222 | 288 | 151 | 199 | 163 | 246 | 339 | 288 | 468 |
| Singapore — Singapour | 25 | 25 | 25 | 25 | 25 | 25 | 25 | 25 | 25 | 25 |
| Sri Lanka — Sri Lanka | 5 | 5 | 5 | 29 | 61 | 61 | 61 | 61 | 61 | 61 |
| Syrian Arab Republic — Rép. arabe syrienne | 9 | 9 | 9 | 9 | 9 | 9 | 9 | 9 | 9 | 9 |
| Thailand — Thaïlande | 426 | 103 | 178 | 220 | 233 | 288 | 288 | 288 | 288 | 288 |
| Turkey — Turquie | 3 833 | 4 891 | 5 039 | 5 528 | 5 036 | 5 579 | 5 615 | 6 215 | 6 445 | 7 079 |
| Viet Nam — Viet Nam | 1 184 | 2 705 | 2 937 | 2 950 | 2 036 | 2 667 | 2 450 | 2 900 | 3 232 | 3 414 |
| **Europe**<br>**Europe** | **117 378** | **119 718** | **122 822** | **129 501** | **126 558** | **127 933** | **132 187** | **138 702** | **141 661** | **146 731** |
| Albania — Albanie | 5 | 28 | 35 | 90 | 197 | 97 | 97 | 97 | 97 | 97 |
| Austria — Autriche | 8 450 | 8 737 | 9 628 | 10 390 | 10 227 | 10 415 | 10 473 | 11 133 | 11 074 | 10 507 |
| Belarus — Bélarus | 1 545 | 2 131 | 2 175 | 1 808 | 2 058 | 2 182 | 2 304 | 2 727 | 2 667 | 2 667 |
| Belgium — Belgique | ... | ... | 1 056 | 1 150 | 1 275 | 1 175 | 1 215 | 1 235 | 1 285 | 1 520 |
| Bosnia and Herzegovina — Bosnie-Herzégovine | 320 | 330 | 330 | 320 | 310 | 738 | 888 | 1 319 | 1 319 | 1 319 |
| Bulgaria — Bulgarie | 253 | 253 | 325 | 312 | 332 | 332 | 332 | 569 | 569 | 569 |
| Croatia — Croatie | 644 | 676 | 685 | 642 | 574 | 640 | 585 | 582 | 624 | 669 |
| Czech Republic — République tchèque | 3 393 | 3 427 | 3 584 | 4 106 | 3 889 | 3 800 | 3 805 | 3 940 | 4 003 | 5 080 |
| Denmark — Danemark | 583 | 238 | 344 | 364 | 283 | 244 | 248 | 196 | 196 | 196 |
| Estonia — Estonie | 729 | 850 | 1 200 | 1 436 | 1 623 | 1 825 | 1 954 | 2 029 | 2 063 | 2 030 |
| Finland — Finlande | 11 430 | 12 300 | 12 768 | 13 420 | 12 770 | 13 390 | 13 745 | 13 544 | 12 269 | 12 227 |
| France — France | 9 607 | 10 220 | 10 236 | 10 536 | 10 518 | 9 815 | 9 539 | 9 774 | 9 715 | 9 950 |
| Germany — Allemagne | 14 730 | 14 972 | 16 096 | 16 340 | 16 131 | 17 119 | 17 596 | 19 538 | 21 931 | 24 420 |
| Greece — Grèce | 130 | 137 | 140 | 123 | 123 | 196 | 191 | 191 | 191 | 191 |
| Hungary — Hongrie | 317 | 298 | 308 | 291 | 264 | 293 | 299 | 205 | 215 | 186 |
| Ireland — Irlande | 642 | 675 | 811 | 888 | 925 | 818 | 1 005 | 939 | 1 015 | 1 094 |
| Italy — Italie | 1 751 | 1 600 | 1 630 | 1 630 | 1 600 | 1 605 | 1 590 | 1 580 | 1 590 | 1 748 |
| Latvia — Lettonie | 2 700 | 3 200 | 3 640 | 3 900 | 3 840 | 3 947 | 3 951 | 3 988 | 4 227 | 4 320 |
| Lithuania — Lituanie | 1 250 | 1 150 | 1 150 | 1 300 | 1 200 | 1 300 | 1 400 | 1 450 | 1 445 | 1 466 |

| Region, country or area — Région, pays ou zone | 1997 | 1998 | 1999 | 2000 | 2001 | 2002 | 2003 | 2004 | 2005 | 2006 |
|---|---|---|---|---|---|---|---|---|---|---|
| Luxembourg — Luxembourg | ... | ... | 133 | 133 | 133 | 133 | 133 | 133 | 133 | 133 |
| Moldova — Moldova | 30 | 30 | 6 | 5 | 5 | 5 | 5 | 5 | 5 | 5 |
| Netherlands — Pays-Bas | 401 | 349 | 362 | 390 | 268 | 258 | 269 | 273 | 279 | 265 |
| Norway — Norvège | 2 520 | 2 525 | 2 336 | 2 280 | 2 253 | 2 225 | 2 186 | 2 230 | 2 326 | 2 389 |
| Poland — Pologne | 4 214 | 4 320 | 4 137 | 4 262 | 3 083 | 3 180 | 3 360 | 3 743 | 3 360 | 3 607 |
| Portugal — Portugal | 1 731 | 1 490 | 1 430 | 1 427 | 1 492 | 1 298 | 1 383 | 1 060 | 1 010 | 1 010 |
| Romania — Roumanie | 1 861 | 2 200 | 2 818 | 3 396 | 3 059 | 3 696 | 4 246 | 4 588 | 4 321 | 4 470 |
| Russian Federation — Fédération de Russie | 20 600 | 19 580 | 19 100 | 20 000 | 19 600 | 19 240 | 20 155 | 21 380 | 22 033 | 22 500 |
| Serbia and Montenegro — Serbie-et-Monténégro | 391 | 438 | 364 | 504 | 391 | 432 | 514 | 575 | 497 | 497 |
| Slovakia — Slovaquie | 767 | 1 265 | 1 265 | 1 265 | 1 265 | 1 265 | 1 651 | 1 837 | 2 621 | 2 440 |
| Slovenia — Slovénie | 510 | 664 | 455 | 439 | 460 | 506 | 511 | 514 | 527 | 580 |
| Spain — Espagne | 3 080 | 3 178 | 3 178 | 3 760 | 4 275 | 3 524 | 3 630 | 3 730 | 3 660 | 3 806 |
| Sweden — Suède | 15 669 | 15 124 | 14 858 | 16 176 | 15 988 | 16 172 | 16 800 | 16 900 | 17 600 | 18 000 |
| Switzerland — Suisse | 1 280 | 1 400 | 1 525 | 1 625 | 1 400 | 1 392 | 1 345 | 1 505 | 1 591 | 1 668 |
| TFYR of Macedonia — L'ex-R.y. Macédoine | 34 | 27 | 37 | 36 | 23 | 20 | 21 | 28 | 18 | 17 |
| Ukraine — Ukraine | 2 306 | 2 258 | 2 141 | 2 127 | 1 995 | 1 950 | 2 019 | 2 392 | 2 416 | 2 192 |
| United Kingdom — Royaume-Uni | 2 356 | 2 382 | 2 537 | 2 630 | 2 728 | 2 705 | 2 742 | 2 772 | 2 770 | 2 895 |
| **Oceania** **Océanie** | **7 076** | **7 369** | **7 556** | **8 171** | **7 920** | **8 736** | **8 910** | **9 325** | **9 187** | **9 304** |
| Australia — Australie | 3 544 | 3 789 | 3 743 | 4 093 | 3 921 | 4 215 | 4 411 | 4 668 | 4 687 | 4 784 |
| Fiji — Fidji | 133 | 131 | 64 | 72 | 72 | 84 | 84 | 112 | 125 | 125 |
| New Caledonia — Nouvelle-Calédonie | 3 | 3 | 3 | 3 | 3 | 3 | 3 | 3 | 3 | 3 |
| New Zealand — Nouvelle-Zélande | 3 136 | 3 178 | 3 653 | 3 910 | 3 821 | 4 301 | 4 289 | 4 419 | 4 249 | 4 269 |
| Papua New Guinea — Papouasie-Nvl-Guinée | 218 | 218 | 40 | 40 | 40 | 70 | 60 | 60 | 60 | 60 |
| Samoa — Samoa | 21 | 21 | 21 | 21 | 21 | 21 | 21 | 21 | 21 | 21 |
| Solomon Islands — Iles Salomon | 12 | 12 | 12 | 12 | 12 | 12 | 12 | 12 | 12 | 12 |
| Tonga — Tonga | 1 | 2 | 2 | 2 | 2 | 2 | 2 | 2 | 2 | 2 |
| Vanuatu — Vanuatu | 7 | 15 | 18 | 18 | 28 | 28 | 28 | 28 | 28 | 28 |

### Source

Food and Agriculture Organization of the United Nations (FAO), Rome, FAOSTAT database, last accessed February 2008.

### Notes

1 Data include those for Namibia.
2 For statistical purposes, the data for China do not include those for the Hong Kong Special Administrative Region (Hong Kong SAR) and Macao Special Administrative Region (Macao SAR).

3 Data include those for Taiwan Province of China.

### Source

Organisation des Nations Unies pour l'alimentation et l'agriculture (FAO), Rome, la base de données de la FAOSTAT, dernier accès février 2008.

### Notes

1 Les données comprennent les chiffres pour la Namibie.
2 Pour la présentation des statistiques, les données pour la Chine ne comprennent pas la Région Administrative Spéciale de Hong Kong (Hong Kong RAS) et la Région Administrative Spéciale de Macao (Macao RAS).

3 Les données comprennent les chiffres pour la province de Taiwan.

# Paper and paperboard
Production: thousand metric tons

# Papiers et cartons
Production : milliers de tonnes

| Region, country or area — Région, pays ou zone | 1997 | 1998 | 1999 | 2000 | 2001 | 2002 | 2003 | 2004 | 2005 | 2006 |
|---|---|---|---|---|---|---|---|---|---|---|
| **World**<br>**Monde** | 301 149 | 301 690 | 315 866 | 324 061 | 320 483 | 330 766 | 339 915 | 353 775 | 357 398 | 365 139 |
| **Africa**<br>**Afrique** | 2 924 | 3 046 | 3 799 | 3 979 | 4 491 | 4 557 | 4 685 | 4 894 | 4 894 | 4 028 |
| Algeria — Algérie | 104 | 113 | 65 | 59 | 53 | 52 | 39 | 35 | 35 | 35 |
| Dem. Rep. of the Congo — Rép. dém. du Congo | 3 | 3 | 3 | 3 | 3 | 3 | 3 | 3 | 3 | 3 |
| Egypt — Egypte | 282 | 343 | 343 | 440 | 460 | 460 | 460 | 460 | 460 | 460 |
| Ethiopia — Ethiopie | 10 | 6 | 10 | 12 | 12 | 11 | 14 | 16 | 16 | 16 |
| Kenya — Kenya | 129 | 129 | 129 | 129 | 67 | 80 | 100 | 165 | 165 | 165 |
| Libyan Arab Jamah. — Jamah. arabe libyenne | 6 | 6 | 6 | 6 | 6 | 6 | 6 | 6 | 6 | 6 |
| Madagascar — Madagascar | 4 | 13 | 7 | 11 | 10 | 9 | 10 | 10 | 10 | 10 |
| Morocco — Maroc | 107 | 110 | 109 | 109 | 129 | 129 | 129 | 129 | 129 | 129 |
| Nigeria — Nigéria | 19 | 19 | 19 | 19 | 19 | 19 | 19 | 19 | 19 | 19 |
| South Africa — Afrique du Sud | 2 047 | 2 105 | 2 900 | 2 982 | 3 523 | 3 579 | 3 645 | 3 774 | 3 774 | 2 915 |
| Sudan — Soudan | 3 | 3 | 3 | 3 | 3 | 3 | 3 | 3 | 3 | 3 |
| Tunisia — Tunisie | 97 | 88 | 94 | 94 | 94 | 94 | 109 | 121 | 121 | 121 |
| Uganda — Ouganda | 3 | 3 | 3 | 3 | 3 | 3 | 3 | 3 | 3 | 3 |
| United Rep. of Tanzania — Rép.-Unie de Tanzanie | 25 | 25 | 25 | 25 | 25 | 25 | 25 | 25 | 25 | 25 |
| Zambia — Zambie | 4 | 4 | 4 | 4 | 4 | 4 | 4 | 4 | 4 | 4 |
| Zimbabwe — Zimbabwe | 81 | 76 | 80 | 80 | 80 | 80 | 117 | 121 | 121 | 115 |
| **Northern America**<br>**Amérique septentrionale** | 107 630 | 105 326 | 108 950 | 107 211 | 101 083 | 101 952 | 100 676 | 102 546 | 103 195 | 102 493 |
| Canada — Canada | 19 119 | 18 875 | 20 280 | 20 959 | 19 834 | 20 073 | 19 964 | 20 462 | 19 498 | 18 176 |
| United States — Etats-Unis | 88 511 | 86 451 | 88 670 | 86 252 | 81 249 | 81 879 | 80 712 | 82 084 | 83 697 | 84 317 |
| **Latin America and the Caribbean**<br>**Amérique latine et Caraïbes** | 13 762 | 13 624 | 13 837 | 14 498 | 15 507 | 15 772 | 16 601 | 17 949 | 18 388 | 18 623 |
| Argentina — Argentine | 1 133 | 978 | 1 012 | 1 270 | 1 141 | 1 417 | 1 444 | 1 586 | 1 656 | 1 673 |
| Barbados — Barbade | ... | ... | ... | ... | ... | ... | ... | ... | 2 | 2 |
| Bolivia — Bolivie | 2 | 2 | 0 | 0 | 0 | 0 | 0 | 0 | 0 | 0 |
| Brazil — Brésil | 6 475 | 6 524 | 6 255 | 6 473 | 7 354 | 7 354 | 7 811 | 8 221 | 8 411 | 8 518 |
| Chile — Chili | 614 | 598 | 824 | 861 | 877 | 1 016 | 1 098 | 1 168 | 1 215 | 1 231 |
| Colombia — Colombie | 704 | 712 | 733 | 771 | 771 | 847 | 864 | 899 | 919 | 990 |
| Costa Rica — Costa Rica | 20 | 20 | 20 | 20 | 20 | 20 | 20 | 20 | 20 | 20 |
| Cuba — Cuba | 57 | 57 | 57 | 57 | 57 | 25 | 33 | 27 | 30 | 27 |
| Dominican Republic — Rép. dominicaine | 21 | 130 | 130 | 130 | 130 | 130 | 130 | 130 | 130 | 130 |
| Ecuador — Equateur | 91 | 91 | 91 | 91 | 91 | 94 | 101 | 100 | 100 | 100 |
| El Salvador — El Salvador | 56 | 56 | 56 | 56 | 56 | 56 | 56 | 56 | 56 | 56 |
| Guatemala — Guatemala | 31 | 31 | 31 | 31 | 31 | 31 | 31 | 31 | 31 | 31 |
| Honduras — Honduras | 88 | 95 | 95 | 95 | 95 | 95 | 95 | 95 | 95 | 95 |
| Mexico — Mexique | 3 491 | 3 673 | 3 784 | 3 865 | 4 056 | 3 987 | 4 149 | 4 689 | 4 841 | 4 844 |
| Panama — Panama | 28 | 0 | 0 | 0 | 0 | 0 | 0 | 0 | 0 | 0 |
| Paraguay — Paraguay | 13 | 13 | 13 | 13 | 13 | 13 | 13 | 13 | 13 | 13 |
| Peru — Pérou | 140 | 63 | 63 | 83 | 86 | 88 | 91 | 91 | 91 | 102 |
| Uruguay — Uruguay | 90 | 88 | 92 | 88 | 88 | 89 | 89 | 100 | 98 | 98 |

| Region, country or area — Région, pays ou zone | 1997 | 1998 | 1999 | 2000 | 2001 | 2002 | 2003 | 2004 | 2005 | 2006 |
|---|---|---|---|---|---|---|---|---|---|---|
| Venezuela (Boliv. Rep. of) — Venezuela (Rép. boliv. du) | 708 | 493 | 581 | 594 | 641 | 510 | 576 | 723 | 680 | 693 |
| **Asia**<br>**Asie** | **85 108** | **85 484** | **91 224** | **94 516** | **96 642** | **102 800** | **109 098** | **114 278** | **115 854** | **120 770** |
| Armenia — Arménie | ... | ... | ... | 20 | 1 | 2 | 2 | 2 | 4 | 4 |
| Azerbaijan — Azerbaïdjan | ... | ... | ... | 28 | 146 | 144 | 148 | 8 | 5 | 5 |
| Bahrain — Bahreïn | ... | ... | ... | ... | ... | ... | 15 | 15 | 15 | 15 |
| Bangladesh — Bangladesh | 70 | 46 | 46 | 46 | 46 | 46 | 83 | 58 | 58 | 58 |
| China[1] — Chine[1] | 31 663 | 32 203 | 33 627 | 34 894 | 36 578 | 41 703 | 46 451 | 52 086 | 54 083 | 57 983 |
| India — Inde | 2 922 | 3 320 | 3 845 | 3 794 | 4 094 | 4 105 | 4 075 | 4 434 | 4 183 | 4 183 |
| Indonesia — Indonésie | 4 822 | 5 487 | 6 978 | 6 977 | 6 995 | 6 995 | 7 040 | 7 223 | 7 223 | 7 223 |
| Iran (Islamic Rep. of) — Iran (Rép. islamique d') | 205 | 20 | 25 | 46 | 46 | 415 | 411 | 411 | 411 | 411 |
| Iraq — Iraq | 18 | 20 | 20 | 30 | 33 | 33 | 27 | 33 | 33 | 33 |
| Israel — Israël | 275 | 242 | 275 | 275 | 275 | 275 | 275 | 275 | 275 | 275 |
| Japan — Japon | 31 014 | 29 886 | 30 631 | 31 828 | 30 717 | 30 686 | 30 457 | 29 253 | 29 295 | 29 473 |
| Jordan — Jordanie | 32 | 32 | 32 | 19 | 27 | 25 | 54 | 54 | 54 | 54 |
| Kazakhstan — Kazakhstan | ... | ... | 3 | 24 | 47 | 64 | 58 | 69 | 81 | 81 |
| Korea, Dem. P. R. — Corée, R. p. dém. de | 80 | 80 | 80 | 80 | 80 | 80 | 80 | 80 | 80 | 80 |
| Korea, Republic of — Corée, République de | 8 334 | 7 750 | 8 875 | 9 308 | 9 332 | 9 812 | 10 148 | 10 511 | 10 254 | 11 040 |
| Kuwait — Koweït | ... | ... | ... | 42 | 42 | 42 | 56 | 56 | 56 | 56 |
| Kyrgyzstan — Kirghizistan | ... | ... | ... | 2 | 7 | 16 | 3 | 2 | 2 | 2 |
| Lebanon — Liban | 42 | 42 | 42 | 64 | 66 | 66 | 100 | 103 | 103 | 103 |
| Malaysia — Malaisie | 711 | 761 | 859 | 791 | 851 | 851 | 983 | 946 | 954 | 941 |
| Myanmar — Myanmar | 39 | 41 | 37 | 39 | 42 | 49 | 45 | 43 | 45 | 45 |
| Nepal — Népal | 13 | 13 | 13 | 13 | 13 | 13 | 13 | 13 | 13 | 13 |
| Pakistan — Pakistan | 500 | 527 | 574 | 592 | 1 165 | 1 165 | 1 165 | 986 | 1 010 | 1 010 |
| Philippines — Philippines | 613 | 987 | 1 010 | 1 107 | 1 056 | 1 056 | 1 091 | 1 097 | 1 097 | 1 097 |
| Saudi Arabia — Arabie saoudite | ... | ... | ... | 50 | 70 | 70 | 214 | 279 | 279 | 279 |
| Singapore — Singapour | 87 | 87 | 87 | 87 | 87 | 87 | 87 | 87 | 87 | 87 |
| Sri Lanka — Sri Lanka | 25 | 25 | 25 | 24 | 25 | 25 | 25 | 25 | 25 | 25 |
| Syrian Arab Republic — Rép. arabe syrienne | 1 | 1 | 1 | 11 | 15 | 15 | 62 | 75 | 75 | 75 |
| Thailand — Thaïlande | 2 271 | 2 367 | 2 434 | 2 312 | 2 445 | 2 444 | 3 420 | 3 431 | 3 431 | 3 495 |
| Turkey — Turquie | 1 246 | 1 357 | 1 349 | 1 567 | 1 513 | 1 643 | 1 643 | 1 643 | 1 643 | 1 643 |
| United Arab Emirates — Emirats arabes unis | ... | ... | ... | 55 | 58 | 58 | 78 | 81 | 81 | 81 |
| Uzbekistan — Ouzbékistan | ... | ... | ... | 8 | 8 | 9 | 11 | 11 | 11 | 11 |
| Viet Nam — Viet Nam | 125 | 190 | 356 | 384 | 762 | 807 | 779 | 888 | 888 | 888 |
| **Europe**<br>**Europe** | **88 418** | **90 825** | **94 675** | **100 144** | **99 245** | **102 166** | **104 951** | **110 090** | **110 869** | **114 391** |
| Albania — Albanie | 44 | 44 | 1 | 3 | 3 | 3 | 3 | 3 | 3 | 3 |
| Austria — Autriche | 3 816 | 4 009 | 4 142 | 4 386 | 4 250 | 4 419 | 4 565 | 4 852 | 4 950 | 5 213 |
| Belarus — Bélarus | 131 | 195 | 208 | 236 | 224 | 216 | 279 | 257 | 284 | 284 |
| Belgium — Belgique | ... | ... | 1 727 | 1 727 | 1 662 | 1 704 | 1 919 | 1 957 | 1 897 | 1 897 |
| Bosnia and Herzegovina — Bosnie-Herzégovine | ... | ... | ... | ... | ... | ... | 60 | 81 | 81 | 81 |
| Bulgaria — Bulgarie | 150 | 153 | 126 | 136 | 171 | 171 | 171 | 326 | 326 | 326 |
| Croatia — Croatie | 393 | 403 | 417 | 406 | 451 | 467 | 463 | 464 | 592 | 564 |
| Czech Republic — République tchèque | 772 | 768 | 770 | 804 | 864 | 870 | 950 | 934 | 969 | 1 042 |
| Denmark — Danemark | 391 | 393 | 397 | 263 | 389 | 384 | 388 | 402 | 423 | 423 |
| Estonia — Estonie | 35 | 43 | 48 | 54 | 70 | 75 | 64 | 66 | 64 | 73 |

| Region, country or area — Région, pays ou zone | 1997 | 1998 | 1999 | 2000 | 2001 | 2002 | 2003 | 2004 | 2005 | 2006 |
|---|---|---|---|---|---|---|---|---|---|---|
| Finland—Finlande | 12 149 | 12 703 | 12 947 | 13 509 | 12 502 | 12 789 | 13 058 | 14 036 | 12 391 | 14 149 |
| France—France | 9 143 | 9 161 | 9 603 | 10 006 | 9 625 | 9 809 | 9 939 | 10 255 | 10 332 | 10 006 |
| Germany—Allemagne | 15 930 | 16 311 | 16 742 | 18 182 | 17 879 | 18 526 | 19 310 | 20 391 | 21 679 | 22 655 |
| Greece—Grèce | 478 | 622 | 545 | 496 | 495 | 493 | 493 | 510 | 510 | 510 |
| Hungary—Hongrie | 820 | 434 | 473 | 506 | 495 | 517 | 546 | 579 | 571 | 553 |
| Ireland—Irlande | 0 | 42 | 42 | 43 | 43 | 44 | 45 | 45 | 45 | 45 |
| Italy—Italie | 8 032 | 8 254 | 8 568 | 9 129 | 8 926 | 9 317 | 9 491 | 9 667 | 9 999 | 10 008 |
| Latvia—Lettonie | 16 | 18 | 19 | 16 | 24 | 33 | 38 | 38 | 39 | 57 |
| Lithuania—Lituanie | 25 | 37 | 37 | 53 | 68 | 78 | 92 | 99 | 113 | 119 |
| Netherlands—Pays-Bas | 3 159 | 3 180 | 3 256 | 3 332 | 3 174 | 3 346 | 3 339 | 3 459 | 3 471 | 3 367 |
| Norway—Norvège | 2 129 | 2 260 | 2 241 | 2 300 | 2 220 | 2 114 | 2 186 | 2 294 | 2 223 | 2 109 |
| Poland—Pologne | 1 486 | 1 718 | 1 839 | 1 934 | 2 086 | 2 342 | 2 461 | 2 635 | 2 732 | 2 857 |
| Portugal—Portugal | 1 080 | 1 136 | 1 163 | 1 290 | 1 419 | 1 537 | 1 530 | 1 664 | 1 570 | 1 644 |
| Romania—Roumanie | 324 | 301 | 289 | 340 | 395 | 370 | 443 | 454 | 371 | 392 |
| Russian Federation—Fédération de Russie | 3 339 | 3 595 | 4 535 | 5 310 | 5 625 | 5 978 | 6 377 | 6 830 | 7 126 | 7 451 |
| Serbia and Montenegro—Serbie-et-Monténégro | 117 | 326 | 230 | 180 | 241 | 254 | 148 | 159 | 229 | 229 |
| Slovakia—Slovaquie | 526 | 597 | 738 | 925 | 988 | 710 | 674 | 798 | 858 | 888 |
| Slovenia—Slovénie | 430 | 491 | 417 | 411 | 633 | 704 | 511 | 763 | 768 | 740 |
| Spain—Espagne | 3 968 | 3 545 | 4 435 | 4 765 | 5 131 | 5 365 | 5 437 | 5 526 | 5 697 | 6 354 |
| Sweden—Suède | 9 756 | 9 879 | 10 071 | 10 782 | 10 534 | 10 724 | 11 062 | 11 589 | 11 775 | 12 066 |
| Switzerland—Suisse | 1 583 | 1 592 | 1 748 | 1 589 | 1 729 | 1 805 | 1 818 | 1 777 | 1 751 | 1 685 |
| TFYR of Macedonia—L'ex-R.y. Macédoine | 21 | 15 | 14 | 17 | 16 | 19 | 18 | 16 | 20 | 20 |
| Ukraine—Ukraine | 264 | 293 | 311 | 411 | 480 | 532 | 618 | 723 | 768 | 791 |
| United Kingdom—Royaume-Uni | 6 480 | 6 477 | 6 576 | 6 605 | 6 434 | 6 452 | 6 455 | 6 442 | 6 241 | 5 791 |
| **Oceania** **Océanie** | **3 308** | **3 385** | **3 381** | **3 713** | **3 515** | **3 519** | **3 904** | **4 018** | **4 199** | **4 834** |
| Australia—Australie | 2 418 | 2 541 | 2 564 | 2 836 | 2 672 | 2 645 | 3 090 | 3 097 | 3 244 | 3 890 |
| New Zealand—Nouvelle-Zélande | 890 | 844 | 817 | 877 | 843 | 874 | 814 | 921 | 955 | 944 |

Source

Food and Agriculture Organization of the United Nations (FAO), Rome, FAOSTAT database, last accessed February 2008.

Source

Organisation des Nations Unies pour l'alimentation et l'agriculture (FAO), Rome, la base de données de la FAOSTAT, dernier accès février 2008.

Notes

1 For statistical purposes, the data for China do not include those for the Hong Kong Special Administrative Region (Hong Kong SAR) and Macao Special Administrative Region (Macao SAR).

Notes

1 Pour la présentation des statistiques, les données pour la Chine ne comprennent pas la Région Administrative Spéciale de Hong Kong (Hong Kong RAS) et la Région Administrative Spéciale de Macao (Macao RAS).

# 45

## Cement
Production: thousand metric tons

## Ciment
Production : milliers de tonnes

| Country or area — Pays ou zone | 1996 | 1997 | 1998 | 1999 | 2000 | 2001 | 2002 | 2003 | 2004 | 2005 |
|---|---|---|---|---|---|---|---|---|---|---|
| Afghanistan — Afghanistan | 116[1] | 116[1] | 116[1] | 116[1] | 25[1] | 16[1] | 27[1] | 24 | 70[2] | ... |
| Albania — Albanie | 150[1] | 100[1] | 84[1] | 107[1] | 180[1] | 30[1] | 50[1] | 578 | 530 | 473 |
| Algeria — Algérie | 7 470[1] | 7 146[1] | 7 836[1] | 7 685[1] | 8 700[1] | 8 710[1] | 9 277[1] | 8 192 | 9 000[2] | ... |
| Angola[2] — Angola[2] | *270 | 301 | *350 | 207 | 201 | *200 | *250 | 250 | 250 | ... |
| Argentina — Argentine | 5 117 | 6 769 | 7 092 | 7 187 | 6 121 | 5 545 | 3 910 | 5 218 | 6 254 | 7 595[3] |
| Armenia — Arménie | 281 | 293 | 314 | 287 | 219 | 275 | 355 | 384 | 501 | 605 |
| Australia[4] — Australie[4] | 6 397 | 6 701 | 7 236 | 7 704 | 7 937 | 6 821 | 7 236 | 7 731 | 8 460 | 8 925 |
| Austria — Autriche | 3 900 | 3 852 | ... | ... | 3 776[2] | 3 863[2] | 3 800[2] | 3 800[2] | 3 800[2] | ... |
| Azerbaijan — Azerbaïdjan | 223[1] | 303[1] | 201[1] | 171[1] | 251[1] | 523[1] | 848[1] | 1 008[1] | 1 428[1] | 1 538 |
| Bahrain — Bahreïn | 192[1] | 172[1] | 230[1] | 156[1] | 89[1] | 89[1] | 67[1] | 70[1] | 75[2] | ... |
| Bangladesh[1] — Bangladesh[1] | 420 | 610 | 468 | 1 514 | 1 868 | 2 340 | 2 514 | 1 776 | 1 872 | ... |
| Barbados — Barbade | 108 | 176 | 257 | 257 | 268 | 250 | 298 | 325 | 322 | 342 |
| Belarus — Bélarus | 1 467 | 1 876 | 2 035 | 1 998 | 1 847 | 1 803 | 2 171 | 2 472 | 2 731 | 3 131 |
| Belgium — Belgique | 6 996 | 6 996 | 6 852 | 7 463 | 7 150[2] | *7 500[2] | *8 000[2] | 8 000[2] | 8 000[2] | ... |
| Benin — Bénin | 411[1] | 442[1] | 520[1] | 520[1] | 250[1] | 250[1] | 250[1] | *250[2] | 250[2] | ... |
| Bhutan*[2] — Bhoutan*[2] | 160 | 160 | 150 | 150 | 150 | 160 | 160 | 160 | 170 | ... |
| Bolivia — Bolivie | 709 | 762 | 938 | 1 234 | 1 072 | 983 | 1 011[3] | 1 138[3] | 1 276[3] | 1 440 |
| Bosnia and Herzegovina — Bosnie-Herzégovine | 200 | 414 | 563 | 683 | 164[5] | 145[5] | 213[5] | 891[6] | 1 045[2] | ... |
| Brazil — Brésil | 34 559 | 37 995 | 39 942 | 40 248 | 37 562 | 38 302 | 37 462 | 34 653 | 34 159 | ... |
| Brunei Darussalam — Brunéi Darussalam | ... | ... | ... | 222 | 241[1] | 234[1] | 220[1] | 235[2] | 240[2] | 234 |
| Bulgaria — Bulgarie | 2 137 | 1 654 | 1 723 | 2 047 | 2 207 | 2 061 | 2 141 | 2 398 | 2 943 | 3 600 |
| Burkina Faso — Burkina Faso | ... | 50[2] | 50[2] | 50[2] | 50[1] | 50[1] | 50[1] | *30[2] | 30[2] | ... |
| Cambodia[2] — Cambodge[2] | ... | ... | 150 | ... | ... | ... | ... | ... | ... | ... |
| Cameroon — Cameroun | 600[1] | 633[1] | 740[1] | 852[1] | 1 570[1] | 980[1] | 950[1] | 949 | 930[2] | 1 026 |
| Canada — Canada | 11 587 | 11 736[7] | 12 168 | 12 643 | 12 753 | 12 793 | 13 081 | 13 424[2] | 14 017[2] | ... |
| Chile — Chili | 3 627 | 3 718 | 3 890 | 2 508 | 2 686 | 3 145 | 3 462[2] | 3 622[2] | 3 798[2] | ... |
| China[8] — Chine[8] | 491 189 | 511 738 | 536 000 | 573 000 | 597 000 | 661 040 | 725 000 | 862 081 | 966 820 | 1 068 848 |
| China, Hong Kong SAR — Chine, Hong Kong RAS | 2 027 | 1 925 | 1 539 | 1 387 | 1 284 | 1 279 | 1 206 | 1 189 | 1 039 | 1 005 |
| Colombia — Colombie | ... | 10 878 | 8 673 | 6 677 | 7 131 | 6 776 | 6 633 | 7 337[3] | 7 822[3] | 9 959[3] |
| Congo — Congo | 43 | 20 | 0 | 0 | 0 | ... | ... | ... | ... | ... |
| Costa Rica[2] — Costa Rica[2] | 830 | 940 | 1 085 | 1 100 | 1 050 | 1 200 | 1 200 | 1 320 | 1 300 | ... |
| Côte d'Ivoire — Côte d'Ivoire | 1 000[1] | 1 100[1] | 650[1] | 650[1] | 650[1] | 650[1] | 650[1] | 650[2] | 650[2] | ... |
| Croatia — Croatie | 1 842 | 2 134 | 3 873 | 2 712 | 2 852 | 3 246 | 3 378 | 3 571 | 3 514 | 3 481 |
| Cuba — Cuba | 1 438 | 1 701 | 1 724 | 1 797 | 1 643 | 1 335 | 1 336 | 1 357 | 1 409 | 1 714 |
| Cyprus — Chypre | 1 021 | 910 | 1 207 | 1 157 | 1 398 | 1 367 | 1 445 | 1 638 | 1 688 | 1 800 |
| Czech Republic — République tchèque | 5 016 | 4 874 | 4 599 | 4 241 | 4 093 | 3 591 | 3 249 | 3 502 | 3 829 | 3 978 |
| Dem. Rep. of the Congo[2] — Rép. dém. du Congo[2] | 241 | 125 | 134 | 159 | 161 | 192 | *190 | 190 | ... | ... |
| Denmark — Danemark | 2 628 | 2 544 | 2 548 | 2 422 | 2 536 | 2 576 | 2 545 | 2 580 | 2 892 | 2 881 |
| Dominican Republic — Rép. dominicaine | 1 642 | 1 822 | 1 872 | 2 295 | 2 505 | 2 746 | 3 050 | 2 783 | 2 654 | 2 779 |
| Ecuador — Equateur | 2 601 | 2 900[2] | 2 539 | 2 262 | 2 800[2] | 2 947 | 3 113 | 3 100[2] | 3 100[2] | ... |
| Egypt — Egypte | 15 569[1] | 15 569[1] | 15 569[1] | 11 933[1] | 25 101[1] | 26 811[1] | 23 000[1] | 16 281 | 28 000[2] | ... |
| El Salvador — El Salvador | 996 | 1 667 | 1 073 | 1 031[2] | 1 064[2] | 1 174[2] | 1 318[2] | 1 390[2] | 1 400[2] | ... |
| Eritrea[2] — Erythrée[2] | ... | 60 | 50 | *45 | *45 | *45 | *45 | *45 | *45 | ... |
| Estonia — Estonie | 388 | 422 | 321 | 358 | 329 | 405 | 466 | 506 | 614 | 733 |

| Country or area — Pays ou zone | 1996 | 1997 | 1998 | 1999 | 2000 | 2001 | 2002 | 2003 | 2004 | 2005 |
|---|---|---|---|---|---|---|---|---|---|---|
| Ethiopia — Ethiopie | 672[9] | 775[9] | 783[9] | 767[9] | 816[9] | 819 | 919 | 890 | 1 300[2] | ... |
| Fiji — Fidji | 84 | 96 | 89 | 99 | 87 | 98 | 102 | 100 | 111 | 143 |
| Finland — Finlande | 975 | 1 152 | 1 232 | 1 310 | 1 422 | 1 325 | 1 198 | 1 493 | 1 691 | 1 321 |
| France — France | 18 337 | 18 309 | 19 434 | 20 302 | 20 000[2] | 20 652 | 20 244 | 20 544 | ... | ... |
| French Guiana[2] — Guyane française[2] | ... | 51 | 88 | *88 | *88 | *58 | *62 | *62 | 62 | |
| Gabon — Gabon | 180[1] | 200[1] | 198[1] | 162[1] | 166[1] | 240[1] | 257[1] | 261 | 350[2] | |
| Georgia — Géorgie | 85 | 94 | 199 | 341 | 348 | 335 | 347 | 345 | 442 | ... |
| Germany — Allemagne | 37 006 | 37 210 | 38 464 | 39 970 | 38 088 | 33 689 | 32 012 | 32 349[2] | 31 954[2] | ... |
| Ghana — Ghana | *1 500[2] | 1 446 | 1 573 | 1 851 | 1 673 | 1 490 | 1 414 | 1 900[2] | 2 000[2] | |
| Greece — Grèce | 13 391 | 13 660 | 14 207 | 13 624 | 14 147 | 15 563 | 15 500[2] | 18 742[10] | 15 000[2] | |
| Guadeloupe*[2] — Guadeloupe *[2] | 230 | 230 | 230 | 230 | 230 | 230 | 230 | 230 | 230 | ... |
| Guatemala — Guatemala | 1 173 | 1 480 | 1 496 | 2 120 | 2 039 | 1 976 | 2 068 | 1 900[2] | 1 900[2] | |
| Guinea — Guinée | ... | 260[1] | 277[1] | 297[1] | 300[1] | 300[1] | 300[1] | 360[2] | 360[2] | |
| Haiti[2] — Haïti[2] | ... | ... | ... | ... | ... | 204 | 290 | 200 | 300 | |
| Honduras[2] — Honduras[2] | 952 | *1 041 | 896 | 980 | 1 284 | *1 321 | *1 360 | 1 400 | 1 400 | ... |
| Hungary — Hongrie | 2 747 | 2 811 | 2 999 | 2 980 | 3 326 | 3 452 | 3 510 | 3 575 | 3 363 | 3 235 |
| Iceland — Islande | 90 | 110 | 118 | 131 | 144 | 125 | 83 | 85 | ... | ... |
| India — Inde | 73 261 | 82 873 | 87 646 | 100 230 | 99 227 | 106 491 | 111 778 | 117 035 | 125 000[2] | |
| Indonesia[1] — Indonésie[1] | 24 648 | 20 702 | 22 344 | 22 806 | 27 789 | 18 629 | 33 000 | 40 476 | 32 448 | ... |
| Iran (Islamic Rep. of) — Iran (Rép. islamique d') | 17 703[1] | 18 349[1] | 20 049[1] | 22 219[1] | 23 276[1] | 24 755[1] | 30 000[1] | 30 000[2] | 30 000[2] | |
| Iraq — Iraq | 2 100[1] | 2 500[1] | 2 000[1] | 2 000[1] | 2 000[1] | 2 000[1] | 2 000[1] | *1 000[2] | *3 000[2] | ... |
| Ireland — Irlande | 2 042 | 2 247 | 2 395 | 2 616 | 2 784 | 2 779 | 2 693 | 3 065 | 3 348 | ... |
| Israel — Israël | 6 723 | 5 916 | 6 476[2] | 6 354[2] | *5 703[2] | *4 700[2] | *4 584[2] | *4 632[2] | *4 494[2] | |
| Italy — Italie | 33 327 | 33 718 | 35 512 | 36 827 | 39 588 | 40 494 | 42 050 | 37 021[11] | 37 843[11] | |
| Jamaica — Jamaïque | 559 | 588 | 558 | 504[3] | 521[3] | 596 | 622 | 608 | 808 | 848[3] |
| Japan — Japon | 94 492 | 91 938 | 81 328 | 80 120 | 81 097 | 76 550 | ... | ... | ... | ... |
| Jordan — Jordanie | 3 512[1] | 3 250[1] | 2 650[1] | 2 688[1] | 2 640[1] | 3 149[1] | 3 558 | 3 515 | 3 908 | 4 046 |
| Kazakhstan — Kazakhstan | 1 115[1] | 657[1] | 622 | 838 | 1 175 | 2 029 | 2 128[1] | 2 580[1] | 3 660[1] | |
| Kenya — Kenya | 1 570 | 1 580 | 1 453 | 1 389 | 1 348 | 1 319 | 1 537 | 1 659 | 1 873 | 2 095 |
| Korea, Dem. P. R.[2] — Corée, R. p. dém. de[2] | *17 000 | 7 000 | 7 000 | *4 000 | *4 600 | *5 160 | *5 320 | *5 540 | 5 500 | |
| Korea, Republic of — Corée, République de | 58 434 | 60 317 | 46 791 | 48 579 | 51 417 | 53 062 | 56 823 | 60 725 | 56 955 | 51 391 |
| Kuwait — Koweït | 1 070[1] | 1 370[1] | 2 310[1] | 947[1] | 1 187[1] | 921[1] | 1 584[1] | 1 863[1] | 2 635 | 2 690 |
| Kyrgyzstan — Kirghizistan | 546[1] | 658[1] | 709[1] | 386[1] | 453[1] | 469[1] | 533[1] | 757 | 870 | 973 |
| Lao People's Dem. Rep.[2] — Rép. dém. pop. lao[2] | 78 | 84 | 80 | *80 | *92 | *92 | *240 | *250 | *250 | ... |
| Latvia — Lettonie | 325 | 246 | 366 | ... | ... | ... | ... | ... | ... | ... |
| Lebanon — Liban | 3 430[1] | 3 126[1] | 3 316[1] | 2 714[1] | 2 808[1] | 2 890[1] | 2 852[1] | 2 900[2] | 2 900[2] | |
| Liberia*[2] — Libéria*[2] | 15 | 7 | 10 | 15 | 71 | 63 | 54 | 30 | 30 | ... |
| Libyan Arab Jamah.[2] — Jamah. arabe libyenne[2] | 3 000 | 3 000 | 3 000 | 3 000 | 3 000 | 3 000 | 3 300 | 3 500 | 3 600 | ... |
| Lithuania — Lituanie | 656 | 710 | 781 | 668 | 559 | 541 | 601 | 599 | 753 | 840 |
| Luxembourg — Luxembourg | 667 | 683 | 699 | 742 | 749 | 725 | 729 | 709 | 750[2] | ... |
| Madagascar — Madagascar | 44 | 36 | 44 | 46[2] | 48[2] | 51 | 34 | 33[2] | 23 | 29 |
| Malawi — Malawi | 88 | 70 | 83 | 104 | 156[2] | 111 | 174[2] | 190[2] | 190[2] | ... |
| Malaysia — Malaisie | 12 349[1] | 12 668[1] | 10 379[1] | 10 104[1] | 11 445[1] | 13 820[1] | 14 336[1] | 17 244[1] | 17 328[1] | 16 659 |
| Mali — Mali | 21[1] | 10[1] | 10[1] | 10[1] | 10[1] | 18[12] | ... | ... | ... | ... |
| Martinique*[2] — Martinique*[2] | 220 | 220 | 220 | 220 | 255 | 255 | 221 | 225 | 225 | ... |
| Mauritania — Mauritanie | 120[1] | 125[1] | 50[1] | 50[1] | 156[1] | 181[1] | 174[1] | *200[2] | *200[2] | ... |
| Mexico — Mexique | 28 047 | 29 526 | 30 728 | 31 802 | 33 228 | 32 134 | 33 372 | 33 594 | 34 992 | 37 452 |
| Moldova — Moldova | 40 | 122 | 74 | 50 | 222 | 158 | 279 | 255 | 440 | 641 |

| Country or area — Pays ou zone | 1996 | 1997 | 1998 | 1999 | 2000 | 2001 | 2002 | 2003 | 2004 | 2005 |
|---|---|---|---|---|---|---|---|---|---|---|
| Mongolia — Mongolie | 106 | *112[2] | 109 | 104 | 92 | 68 | 148 | 162 | 62 | 112[13] |
| Morocco — Maroc | 6 588[1] | 7 236[1] | 7 155[1] | 7 194[1] | 7 497[1] | 8 058[1] | 8 486 | 9 277 | 9 796 | 10 289 |
| Mozambique — Mozambique | 179[1] | 217[1] | 264[1] | 266[1] | 348[1] | 421[1] | 274[1] | 582 | 552 | 564 |
| Myanmar[14] — Myanmar[14] | 513 | 524 | 371 | 343 | 400 | 384 | 462 | 581 | 527 | ... |
| Nepal[15] — Népal[15] | 309 | 227 | 139 | 191 | 206 | 215 | 233 | 255 | 279 | 278 |
| Netherlands — Pays-Bas | 3 140[2] | 3 230 | 3 200 | 3 200 | 3 200 | *3 450[2] | *3 400[2] | *3 400[2] | *3 400[2] | ... |
| New Caledonia — Nouvelle-Calédonie | 89 | 84 | 89 | 93 | 91 | 100 | 100 | 100[2] | 114[2] | 119 |
| New Zealand[2] — Nouvelle-Zélande[2] | 974 | 976 | 950 | *1 030 | 1 070 | 1 080 | 1 090 | 1 100 | 1 110 | ... |
| Nicaragua — Nicaragua | 360[2] | 361 | 412 | 536 | 568 | 588 | 549[2] | 590[2] | 590[2] | ... |
| Niger — Niger | 30[1] | 30[1] | 30[1] | 30[1] | 40[1] | 40[1] | 55[1] | 40[2] | 40[2] | ... |
| Nigeria — Nigéria | 2 545[1] | 2 520[1] | 2 700[1] | 2 500[1] | 2 500[1] | 3 000[1] | 3 000[1] | *2 100[2] | 2 300[2] | ... |
| Norway — Norvège | 1 690 | 1 724[2] | 1 676[2] | 1 827[2] | 1 851[2] | *1 870[2] | ... | ... | ... | ... |
| Occupied Palestinian Terr.[1] — Terr. palestinien occupé[1] | ... | ... | ... | ... | ... | 40 | 29 | ... | ... | ... |
| Oman — Oman | 1 206[1] | 1 233[1] | 1 217[1] | 1 990[1] | 1 815[1] | 1 370[1] | 1 523[16] | 1 593[16] | 1 648[16] | ... |
| Pakistan — Pakistan | 9 567 | 9 536 | 9 364 | 9 635 | 9 314[1] | 9 674[1] | 9 935[1] | 11 316[1] | 14 712[1] | ... |
| Panama — Panama | 651 | 752 | 814 | 976 | 849[3] | *760[2] | *760[2] | *770[2] | *770[2] | ... |
| Paraguay — Paraguay | 627 | 603 | 586 | 556 | 516 | 505 | 447 | 505 | 660[2] | ... |
| Peru — Pérou | 3 678 | 4 092 | 4 069 | 3 327 | 3 658 | 3 589 | 4 115 | 4 203 | 4 602 | 5 108 |
| Philippines — Philippines | 12 429[2] | 14 681 | 12 888 | 12 557 | 11 959 | 11 378 | 11 396 | 10 000[2] | ... | ... |
| Poland — Pologne | 13 959 | 15 003 | 14 970 | 15 555 | #14 943 | 12 090 | 11 213 | 11 624 | 12 148 | 12 190 |
| Portugal — Portugal | 8 536 | 9 445 | 9 845 | 10 057 | 10 293 | 10 168 | 9 728 | 8 598 | 8 839 | ... |
| Puerto Rico — Porto Rico | 1 508 | 1 586 | 1 646 | 1 757 | ... | ... | ... | ... | ... | ... |
| Qatar — Qatar | 486[1] | 584[1] | 857[1] | 959[1] | 1 029[1] | 1 209[1] | 1 346[16] | 1 340[16] | 1 200[16] | ... |
| Réunion — Réunion | 229 | 200 | 342 | 263 | 258 | *380[2] | *380[2] | *380[2] | *380[2] | ... |
| Romania — Roumanie | 6 956 | 6 553 | 7 300 | 6 252 | 8 411 | 5 668 | 5 767 | 5 879 | 6 211 | 7 023 |
| Russian Federation — Fédération de Russie | 27 791 | 26 688 | 25 974 | 28 529 | 32 389 | 35 271 | 37 705 | 40 998 | 45 615 | 48 534 |
| Rwanda — Rwanda | 42 | 61 | 60 | 66 | 71[2] | 91[2] | 101[2] | 105[2] | 104[2] | ... |
| Saudi Arabia — Arabie saoudite | 16 437[1] | 15 448[1] | 15 776[1] | 16 381[1] | 18 296[1] | 20 976 | 23 452 | 24 200 | 25 470 | 26 064 |
| Senegal — Sénégal | 810[1] | 854[1] | 847[1] | 1 030[1] | 1 000[1] | 1 000[1] | 1 000[1] | 1 694[12] | 2 150[2] | ... |
| Serbia — Serbie | ... | ... | ... | ... | ... | ... | ... | ... | ... | 2 565 |
| Serbia and Montenegro — Serbie-et-Monténégro | 2 212 | 2 011 | 2 253 | #1 575 | 2 117 | 2 418 | 2 396 | 2 075 | 2 240[2] | ... |
| Sierra Leone — Sierra Leone | 78 | 40 | 41 | 45 | 73 | 113 | 144 | 170 | 181 | 172 |
| Singapore[2] — Singapour[2] | *3 300 | *3 300 | 2 340 | 1 660 | 1 150 | *600 | *200 | 150 | 150 | ... |
| Slovakia — Slovaquie | 4 234 | 5 856 | 3 066 | 3 084 | 3 045 | 3 011 | 3 121 | 3 115 | 3 031 | 3 282 |
| Slovenia — Slovénie | ... | ... | ... | ... | ... | 1 186 | ... | ... | ... | ... |
| South Africa — Afrique du Sud | 7 664 | 7 891 | 7 676 | 8 211 | 8 715 | 8 036[2] | 8 525[2] | 8 883[2] | 12 348[2] | ... |
| Spain — Espagne | 26 339 | 27 860 | 27 943[2] | ... | ... | ... | ... | ... | ... | ... |
| Sri Lanka — Sri Lanka | 670 | 966 | 2 151 | 2 354 | 2 432 | 2 123 | 973 | 1 163 | 1 400[2] | ... |
| Sudan — Soudan | 380[17] | 276[17] | 198[17] | 231[17] | 146[17] | 190[17] | 220[17] | 320[17] | 244 | 244 |
| Suriname — Suriname | 50[1] | 65[1] | 65[1] | 65[1] | 60[1] | 65[1] | 65[1] | *65[2] | *65[2] | ... |
| Sweden — Suède | 2 503 | 2 320 | 2 373 | 2 293 | 2 613 | 2 644 | 2 765 | 2 841 | 2 731 | 2 791 |
| Switzerland — Suisse | 3 638[2] | 3 568[2] | *3 600[2] | 3 548[2] | 3 771[2] | 3 950[2] | *4 000[2] | 3 800[2] | 3 955 | ... |
| Syrian Arab Republic — Rép. arabe syrienne | 4 817[1] | 4 838[1] | 5 016[1] | 5 134[1] | 4 631[1] | 5 428[1] | 5 399[1] | 5 220[1] | 5 098 | ... |
| Tajikistan — Tadjikistan | 57[1] | 36[1] | 18[1] | 33[1] | 55[1] | 69[1] | 89[1] | 168[1] | 192[1] | 253 |
| Thailand — Thaïlande | 38 874 | 37 115 | 22 722 | 25 354 | 25 499 | 27 913 | 31 679 | 32 530 | 35 626 | 37 872 |
| TFYR of Macedonia — L'ex-R.y. Macédoine | 490 | 610 | 461 | 563 | 801 | 630 | 778 | 832 | 812 | 887 |
| Togo — Togo | 413[1] | 421[1] | 500[1] | 600[1] | 700[1] | 800[1] | 800[1] | *800[2] | ... | ... |

**Cement** — Production: thousand metric tons (*continued*)

**Ciment** — Production : milliers de tonnes (*suite*)

| Country or area — Pays ou zone | 1996 | 1997 | 1998 | 1999 | 2000 | 2001 | 2002 | 2003 | 2004 | 2005 |
|---|---|---|---|---|---|---|---|---|---|---|
| Trinidad and Tobago — Trinité-et-Tobago | 617 | 677 | 700 | 740 | 743 | 697 | 744 | 766 | 768 | 686 |
| Tunisia[1] — Tunisie[1] | 4 566 | 4 378 | 4 588 | 4 860 | 5 647 | 5 721 | 6 020 | 6 480 | 6 192 | ... |
| Turkey — Turquie | 35 090[1] | 36 035 | 38 175 | 34 215 | 36 238 | 30 111 | 32 546 | 35 264 | 38 594 | 41 100 |
| Turkmenistan — Turkménistan | 438[1] | 601[1] | 750[1] | 780[1] | 420[1] | 448[1] | 486[1] | 200 | 450[2] | ... |
| Uganda — Ouganda | 195[1] | 290[1] | 321[1] | 347[1] | 367[1] | 431[1] | 506[1] | 507[2] | 520[2] | ... |
| Ukraine — Ukraine | 3 339 | 3 535 | 3 358 | 3 387 | 3 631 | 4 367 | 4 456 | 8 923 | 10 648 | 12 161 |
| United Arab Emirates — Emirats arabes unis | 6 000[1] | 6 330[1] | 7 066[1] | 7 069[1] | 6 100[1] | 6 100[1] | 6 500[1] | *8 000[2] | *8 000[2] | ... |
| United Kingdom — Royaume-Uni | 13 530[11] | 14 307[11] | 14 764[11] | 14 544[11] | 12 452[2] | 11 854[2] | *11 089[2] | 11 215[2] | 11 250[2] | ... |
| United Rep. of Tanzania — Rép.-Unie de Tanzanie | 726 | 621 | 778[2] | 833 | 833 | 901[18] | 1 026 | 1 187[18] | 1 281[18] | 1 367[18] |
| United States[19] — Etats-Unis[19] | 79 266 | 82 582 | 83 931 | 85 952 | 87 546 | 88 900 | 89 732 | 92 843 | 97 434 | 99 319 |
| Uruguay — Uruguay | 631 | 818 | 940 | 839 | 688 | 1 015[2] | 442[20] | 489[20] | 658[20] | 691[20] |
| Uzbekistan — Ouzbékistan | 3 277[1] | 3 286[1] | 3 400[1] | 3 300[1] | 3 284[1] | 3 722[13] | 3 927[13] | 4 062[13] | 4 805[13] | 5 068[13] |
| Venezuela (Boliv. Rep. of)[2] — Venezuela (Rép. bolivar. du)[2] | 7 556 | 8 145 | 8 202 | *8 500 | *8 600 | *8 700 | *7 000 | *7 700 | *9 000 | ... |
| Viet Nam — Viet Nam | 6 585 | 8 019 | 9 738 | 10 489 | 13 298 | 16 073 | 21 121 | 24 127 | 26 153 | 28 050 |
| Yemen — Yémen | 1 028[1] | 1 038[1] | 1 195[1] | 1 454[1] | 1 406[1] | 1 449[1] | 1 582[1] | 1 541 | 1 546[2] | ... |
| Zambia — Zambie | 348[2] | 384[2] | 351[2] | 300[2] | 335 | 309 | 343 | 424 | 480[2] | ... |
| Zimbabwe — Zimbabwe | 996 | 954 | 1 066 | 1 105 | 1 000 | 549 | *600[2] | *400[2] | *400[2] | ... |

Source

United Nations Statistics Division, New York, the "Industrial Commodity Statistics Yearbook 2005" and the industrial statistics database, last accessed June 2008.

Notes

1 Source: Organisation of the Islamic Conference (Jeddah, Saudi Arabia).

2 Source: U. S. Geological Survey (Washington, D. C.).

3 Source: United Nations Economic Commission for Latin America and the Caribbean (Santiago).

4 Twelve months ending 30 September of the year stated.

5 Excluding the Federation of Bosnia and Herzegovina.

6 Break in series; data prior to the sign not comparable to following years.

7 Shipments.

8 For statistical purposes, the data for China do not include those for the Hong Kong Special Administrative Region (Hong Kong SAR), Macao Special Administrative Region (Macao SAR) and Taiwan Province of China.

9 Twelve months ending 7 July of the year stated.

10 Incomplete coverage.

11 Excluding Prodcom code 26.51.12.50.

12 Source: Afristat: Sub-Saharan African Observatory of Economics and Statistics (Bamako, Mali).

13 Source: "Country Economic Review", Asian Development Bank (Manila).

14 Government production only.

15 Twelve months beginning 16 July of the year stated.

16 Source: Arab Gulf Cooperation Council (Riyadh).

17 Source: "African Statistical Yearbook", Economic Commission for Africa (Addis Ababa).

18 Tanganyika only.

19 Excluding Puerto Rico.

20 Portland cement only.

Source

Organisation des Nations Unies, Division de statistique, New York, "l'Annuaire de statistiques industrielles par produit 2005", et la base de données sur les statistiques industrielles, dernier accès juin 2008.

Notes

1 Source: Organisation de la Conférence islamique (Jeddah, Arabie saoudite).

2 Source: "U. S. Geological Survey" (Washington, D. C.).

3 Source: Commission économique des Nations Unies pour l'Amérique Latine et des Caraïbes (Santiago).

4 Période de 12 mois finissant le 30 septembre de l'année indiquée.

5 Non compris la Fédération de Bosnie et Herzégovine.

6 Marque une interruption dans la série et la non-comparabilité des données précédant le symbole.

7 Expéditions.

8 Pour la présentation des statistiques, les données pour la Chine ne comprennent pas la Région Administrative Spéciale de Hong Kong (Hong Kong RAS), la Région Administrative Spéciale de Macao (Macao RAS) et la province de Taiwan.

9 Période de 12 mois finissant le 7 juillet de l'année indiquée.

10 Couverture incomplète.

11 Code Prodcom 26.51.12.50 non compris.

12 Source : Afristat : Observatoire Economique et Statistique d'Afrique Subsaharienne (Bamako, Mali).

13 Source: "La Revue Economique du Pays", La Banque de Développement Asiatique (Manila).

14 Production de l'état seulement.

15 Période de 12 mois commençant le 16 juillet de l'année indiquée.

16 Source: "Arab Gulf Cooperation Council (Riyadh)".

17 Source : "Annuaire des Statistiques de l'Afrique", Conseil Economique pour l'Afrique (Addis Ababa).

18 Tanganyika seulement.

19 Non compris Porto Rico.

20 Ciment Portland uniquement.

# Aluminium, unwrought
Total production: thousand metric tons

# Aluminium non travaillé
Production totale : milliers de tonnes

| Country or area — Pays ou zone | 1996 | 1997 | 1998 | 1999 | 2000 | 2001 | 2002 | 2003 | 2004 | 2005 |
|---|---|---|---|---|---|---|---|---|---|---|
| Argentina — Argentine | 185 | 187 | 187 | 206 | 261 | 248 | 269 | 272 | 272 | ... |
| Australia[1] — Australie[1] | 1 331 | 1 395 | 1 589 | 1 686 | ... | ... | ... | ... | ... | ... |
| Austria — Autriche | 98 | 119[2] | 126 | 143[2] | 158[2] | 158[2] | ... | ... | ... | ... |
| Azerbaijan — Azerbaïdjan | ... | ... | ... | ... | ... | ... | ... | 19[3] | 30[3] | 0 |
| Bahrain — Bahreïn | 456 | 490[3] | 501[3] | 502 | 512 | 523[3] | 519[3] | 532[3] | 530[3] | ... |
| Bosnia and Herzegovina — Bosnie-Herzégovine | ... | ... | 32 | 57 | 95[3] | 96[3] | 103[3] | 113 | 115[3] | ... |
| Brazil — Brésil | 1 343[2] | 1 369[2] | 1 388[2] | 1 440[3] | 1 035 | 951 | 1 449 | 1 195 | 1 275 | ... |
| Bulgaria — Bulgarie | ... | ... | ... | ... | 1 | ... | ... | 0 | 0 | 0 |
| Cameroon — Cameroun | 82[4] | 98 | 89 | 94 | 100 | 85 | 72 | 79 | 86 | 86 |
| Canada — Canada | 2 384[2] | 2 433[2] | 2 485[2] | 2 502 | 2 373[3] | 2 583[3] | 2 709[3] | 808 | 2 592[3] | ... |
| China[5] — Chine[5] | 1 896 | 2 180 | 2 362 | 2 809 | 2 989 | 3 576 | 4 511 | 5 866 | 6 690 | 7 787 |
| Croatia — Croatie | 33 | 18 | 16 | 14 | 14 | 15 | 15 | ... | ^0 | ^0 |
| Czech Republic — République tchèque | 45[3] | 45[3] | 45[3] | 40[3] | 40[3] | ... | ... | ... | ... | 0 |
| Denmark — Danemark | 0 | 0 | 0 | 0 | 0 | 0 | 0 | 0 | 0 | 3 |
| Egypt — Egypte | 150[6] | 119[6] | 187[6] | 193[3] | 189[3] | 191[3] | 195[3] | 195[3] | 215[3] | ... |
| Finland — Finlande | 5 | 2 | 2 | ... | ... | ... | ... | ... | ... | 0 |
| France* — France* | 380 | 635 | 663 | 694 | 701 | 713 | 713 | 685 | ... | ... |
| Germany — Allemagne | 358 | 349 | 375 | 395 | 404 | 404 | 410 | 438 | ... | 329 |
| Ghana — Ghana | 137[2] | 152 | 56 | 114 | 156 | 162 | 133 | ... | ... | ... |
| Greece — Grèce | 141 | 132 | 161 | 161 | 168[3] | 166[3] | 165[3] | 166[7] | 165[3] | ... |
| Hungary — Hongrie | 94 | 98 | 92 | 89 | 89[3] | 110[3] | ... | ... | 2 | ... |
| Iceland — Islande | 102 | 123 | 160 | 161 | 167 | 169 | 194 | 286 | 192 | 180 |
| India — Inde | 516 | 539 | 542[3] | 614[3] | 644[3] | 624[3] | 671[3] | ... | 124 | 209 |
| Indonesia — Indonésie | 223[2] | 219[2] | 133[2] | *223[2] | 160[3] | 180[3] | *320[3] | 200[3] | 230[3] | ... |
| Iran (Islamic Rep. of) — Iran (Rép. islamique d') | 104[2] | 125[2] | 137[2] | 164[2] | 146[3] | 160[3] | 169[3] | 170[3] | 170[3] | ... |
| Italy — Italie | 561 | 631 | 690 | 689 | 757 | 766 | 782 | #74 | 76 | ... |
| Japan — Japon | 1 238[8] | 1 330[8] | 1 207[8] | 1 158[8] | 1 214[8] | 1 171 | ... | ... | ... | 21 |
| Korea, Republic of — Corée, République de | ... | ... | ... | ... | 312 | 325 | 357 | 356 | 454 | 463 |
| Kuwait — Koweït | 6 | 6 | 4 | 7 | 7 | 7 | 6 | 6 | 6 | 7 |
| Mozambique — Mozambique | ... | ... | ... | ... | 54[3] | 266[3] | 273[3] | 409 | 548 | 539 |
| Netherlands — Pays-Bas | 377[3] | 382 | 366 | 391 | 405 | 294[3] | 284[3] | 278[3] | 326[3] | ... |
| New Zealand — Nouvelle-Zélande | 293[2] | 318[2] | 389[2] | 348[3] | 328[3] | 322[3] | 335[3] | 340[3] | 350[3] | ... |
| Norway — Norvège | *923 | 977[2] | 1 058[2] | 1 199[3] | 1 280[3] | 1 291[3] | ... | ... | ... | ... |
| Poland — Pologne | 52 | 54 | 54 | 51 | #12 | 12 | 14 | 15 | 14 | 19 |
| Romania[8,9] — Roumanie[8,9] | 145 | 164 | 175 | 174 | 181 | 183 | 190 | 205 | ... | ... |
| Russian Federation[3] — Fédération de Russie[3] | 2 874 | 2 906 | 3 005 | 3 146 | 3 245 | 3 300 | 3 347 | 3 478 | 3 593 | ... |
| Serbia and Montenegro — Serbie-et-Monténégro | 37 | 67 | 61 | #73 | 88 | 100 | 112 | 117 | 115[3] | ... |
| Slovakia — Slovaquie | 311 | 110[2] | 121 | 109 | 110 | ... | ... | ... | ... | ... |
| South Africa[3] — Afrique du Sud[3] | 570 | 673 | 677 | 689 | 673 | 662 | 707 | 738 | 863 | ... |
| Spain — Espagne | 515[2] | 533[2] | 570[2] | 588[2] | 366[3] | 376[3] | 380[3] | 389[3] | ... | ... |
| Suriname — Suriname | 29 | 29 | 28 | 7 | ... | ... | 2 | ... | ... | ... |
| Sweden — Suède | 28 | 34 | 31 | 36 | 35 | 35 | 29 | 28 | 0 | 0 |
| Switzerland — Suisse | 33[2] | 35[2] | 47[2] | 41[2] | 36[3] | 36[3] | 40[3] | 44[3] | 45[3] | ... |
| Tajikistan — Tadjikistan | 198 | 189 | 196 | 229 | 269[3] | 289[3] | 306[3] | 319[3] | 358[3] | ... |

| Country or area — Pays ou zone | 1996 | 1997 | 1998 | 1999 | 2000 | 2001 | 2002 | 2003 | 2004 | 2005 |
|---|---|---|---|---|---|---|---|---|---|---|
| TFYR of Macedonia — L'ex-R.y. Macédoine | 5 | 5 | 7 | 6 | 4 | 3 | 5 | 5 | ... | ... |
| Turkey — Turquie | 62 | 62 | 62 | 62 | 62 | 62 | 63 | 63 | 60[3] | 27 |
| Ukraine[3] — Ukraine[3] | *130 | 101 | 178 | 226 | 104 | 106 | 112 | ... | ... | ... |
| United Arab Emirates[3] — Emirats arabes unis[3] | ... | ... | ... | ... | ^0 | 1 | 1 | 1 | 1 | ... |
| United Kingdom — Royaume-Uni | 501[8] | 114 | 494[3] | 547[3] | 305[3] | 341[3] | 344[3] | 343[3] | 360[3] | ... |
| United States — Etats-Unis | 3 577 | 3 603 | 3 713 | 3 779 | 3 668 | 2 637 | 2 707 | 2 703 | 2 516 | 2 481 |
| Venezuela (Bolivarian Rep. of) Venezuela (Rép. bolivarienne du) | 656[2] | 668[2] | 617[2] | 595[2] | 571[3] | 571[3] | 605[3] | 601[3] | 624[3] | ... |

Source

United Nations Statistics Division, New York, the "Industrial Commodity Statistics Yearbook 2005" and the industrial statistics database, last accessed June 2008.

Notes

1  Twelve months ending 30 June of the year stated.
2  Source: World Metal Statistics (London).
3  Source: U. S. Geological Survey (Washington, D. C.).
4  Source: "African Statistical Yearbook", Economic Commission for Africa (Addis Ababa).
5  For statistical purposes, the data for China do not include those for the Hong Kong Special Administrative Region (Hong Kong SAR), Macao Special Administrative Region (Macao SAR) and Taiwan Province of China.
6  Including aluminium plates, shapes and bars.
7  Incomplete coverage.
8  Including alloys.
9  Including pure content of virgin alloys.

Source

Organisation des Nations Unies, Division de statistique, New York, "l'Annuaire de statistiques industrielles par produit 2005", et la base de données sur les statistiques industrielles, dernier accès juin 2008.

Notes

1  Période de 12 mois finissant le 30 juin de l'année indiquée.
2  Source: "World Metal Statistics" (Londres).
3  Source: "U. S. Geological Survey" (Washington, D. C.).
4  Source : "Annuaire des Statistiques de l'Afrique", Conseil Economique pour l'Afrique (Addis Ababa).
5  Pour la présentation des statistiques, les données pour la Chine ne comprennent pas la Région Administrative Spéciale de Hong Kong (Hong Kong RAS), la Région Administrative Spéciale de Macao (Macao RAS) et la province de Taiwan.
6  Y compris les tôles, les profilés et les barres d'aluminium.
7  Couverture incomplète.
8  Y compris les alliages.
9  Y compris la teneur pure des alliages de première fusion.

# Radio receivers
Production: thousands

# Récepteurs de radio
Production : milliers

| Country or area — Pays ou zone | 1996 | 1997 | 1998 | 1999 | 2000 | 2001 | 2002 | 2003 | 2004 | 2005 |
|---|---|---|---|---|---|---|---|---|---|---|
| Bangladesh — Bangladesh | 11 | 20 | 10 | 13 | 13 | 14 | 10 | 13 | ... | ... |
| Belarus — Bélarus | 138 | 170 | 114 | 195 | 101 | 56 | 47 | 31 | 22 | 13 |
| Brazil — Brésil | 2 941 | 4 211 | 2 753 | 2 039 | 2 958 | 3 456 | 1 364 | 2 481 | 6 335 | ... |
| Cuba — Cuba | 14 | 30 | 17 | 12 | 11 | 11 | 10 | 6 | 66 | 214 |
| Denmark — Danemark | 99 | 91 | 91 | 90 | 86 | 100 | 84 | 68 | 64 | 49 |
| France — France | ... | 3 853 | 4 586 | 2 961 | 3 195 | 3 508 | 3 357 | 3 498 | ... | ... |
| Germany — Allemagne | 3 342 | 3 632 | 3 884 | 4 021 | 4 025 | 4 746 | ... | ... | ... | ... |
| Hungary — Hongrie | 310 | 528 | 2 328 | 2 412 | 2 320 | 3 459 | 2 917 | 2 991 | 2 840 | 2 248 |
| India — Inde | 47 | 33 | 2 | 0 | 0 | 0 | 0 | 0 | ... | ... |
| Indonesia[1] — Indonésie[1] | ... | 4 177 | ... | 4 937 | ... | ... | ... | ... | ... | ... |
| Iran (Islamic Rep. of)[2] — Iran (Rép. islamique d')[2] | 56 | 76 | 127 | 114 | 139 | 129 | 275 | ... | ... | ... |
| Ireland — Irlande | 0 | 0 | 0 | 2 | 77 | 105 | 134 | 174 | 1 490 | ... |
| Japan — Japon | 2 638 | 2 434 | 2 623 | 2 678 | 2 384 | 1 972 | 2 496 | 2 892 | 2 324 | 1 769 |
| Kazakhstan — Kazakhstan | 3 | 3 | 3 | ^0 | ^0 | ^0 | ^0[3] | ... | ... | ... |
| Korea, Republic of — Corée, République de | 1 088 | 855 | 556 | 801 | 1 420 | 1 692 | 1 234 | 318 | 31 | 1 |
| Kyrgyzstan — Kirghizistan | 864 | ... | ... | ... | ... | ... | ... | ... | ... | ... |
| Latvia — Lettonie | 10 | 10 | 2 | 2 | ... | ... | ... | ... | ... | ... |
| Malaysia — Malaisie | 29 431 | 33 491 | 30 265 | 32 957 | 36 348 | 28 839 | 21 735 | 27 634 | 28 587 | 21 326 |
| Mexico — Mexique | 379 | 537 | 731 | 913 | 1 087 | 946 | 1 544 | 1 580 | 1 310 | 903 |
| Moldova — Moldova | 67 | 94 | 51 | 10 | 18 | 3 | 5 | 3 | 6 | 3 |
| Poland — Pologne | 206 | 143 | 154 | 132 | ... | ... | ... | ... | ... | 15 |
| Portugal — Portugal | 4 372 | 4 552 | 6 102 | 6 965 | 8 046 | 8 652 | 8 470 | 7 310 | 7 805 | ... |
| Romania — Roumanie | 76[1] | 28[1] | 10[1] | 0[1] | 0 | 0 | 4 | 0 | ... | 0 |
| Russian Federation — Fédération de Russie | 477 | 342 | 235 | 332 | 390 | 281 | 253 | 278 | 194 | 313 |
| Serbia and Montenegro — Serbie-et-Monténégro | 1 | ^0 | 0 | ^#0 | ^0 | ^0 | ... | ... | ... | ... |
| Spain — Espagne | 82 | 313 | 508 | 357 | 57 | 85 | 52 | 47 | 71 | 110 |
| Sweden — Suède | ... | 2 | 3 | 3 | 3 | 2 | ... | ... | ... | 275 |
| Ukraine — Ukraine | 47 | 25 | 10 | 27 | 36 | 26 | 33 | 21 | 106 | 18 |
| United Kingdom — Royaume-Uni | 1 531 | 2 062 | ... | ... | 505 | ... | ... | ... | ... | ... |
| United Rep. of Tanzania — Rép.-Unie de Tanzanie | 54 | 56 | 15[4] | ... | ... | ... | ... | ... | ... | ... |
| Viet Nam — Viet Nam | 94 | 145 | 205 | 140 | 145 | 71 | 67 | 24 | 24 | 25 |

Source

United Nations Statistics Division, New York, the "Industrial Commodity Statistics Yearbook 2005" and the industrial statistics database, last accessed June 2008

Notes

1 Including radios with tape recording units.

2 Production by establishments employing 10 or more persons.

3 Incomplete coverage.

4 Tanganyika only.

Source

Organisation des Nations Unies, Division de statistique, New York, "l'Annuaire de statistiques industrielles par produit 2005", et la base de données sur les statistiques industrielles, dernier accès juin 2008.

Notes

1 Y compris les récepteurs de radio avec appareil enregistreur à bande magnétique incorporés.

2 Production des établissements employant 10 personnes ou plus.

3 Couverture incomplète.

4 Tanganyika seulement.

# 48

## Refrigerators for household use
Production: thousands

## Réfrigérateurs à usage domestique
Production : milliers

| Country or area — Pays ou zone | 1996 | 1997 | 1998 | 1999 | 2000 | 2001 | 2002 | 2003 | 2004 | 2005 |
|---|---|---|---|---|---|---|---|---|---|---|
| Algeria — Algérie | 137 | 175 | 215 | 181 | 117 | 64 | 153 | 150 | ... | ... |
| Argentina — Argentine | 45 | 401 | 424 | 354 | 325 | 246 | 162 | ... | ... | ... |
| Australia — Australie | 403 | 398 | 441 | 427 | ... | ... | ... | ... | ... | ... |
| Azerbaijan — Azerbaïdjan | 7 | 0 | 3 | 1 | 1 | 2 | 4 | 5 | 10 | 13 |
| Belarus — Bélarus | 754 | 795 | 802 | 802 | 812 | 830 | 856 | 886 | 953 | 995 |
| Brazil — Brésil | 3 776 | 3 592 | 3 034 | 2 796 | ... | ... | ... | ... | ... | ... |
| Bulgaria — Bulgarie | 36 | 21 | ... | ... | ... | ... | ... | ... | ... | ... |
| Chile — Chili | 213 | 268 | 229 | 242 | 271 | 280 | 230 | 232 | ... | 0 |
| China[1] — Chine[1] | 9 797 | 10 444 | 10 600 | 12 100 | 12 790 | 13 513 | 15 989 | 22 426 | 30 076 | 29 871 |
| Cuba — Cuba | ... | ... | 6 | 10 | 9 | 9 | 10 | 8 | 7 | 0 |
| Denmark — Danemark | 941 | 1 091 | 1 046 | 1 061 | 1 008 | 863 | 805 | 798 | 667 | 511 |
| Ecuador — Equateur | 17 | 133 | 88 | 38 | 55 | ... | ... | 142 | ... | ... |
| Egypt — Egypte | 250 | ... | ... | 527 | 191 | 451 | 640 | 808 | ... | ... |
| Finland — Finlande | 68 | 102 | 107 | ... | ... | ... | 0 | ... | ... | ... |
| France — France | ... | 490 | 640 | 509 | 555 | 542 | 528 | 544 | ... | ... |
| Germany — Allemagne | ... | ... | ... | ... | ... | ... | 2 354 | 2 107 | 2 061 | 2 152 |
| Greece[2,3] — Grèce[2,3] | ... | ... | ... | ... | ... | ... | ... | 381 | ... | ... |
| Hungary — Hongrie | 736 | 835 | 708 | 849 | 995 | 1 058 | 1 866 | 1 883 | 1 625 | 1 535 |
| India — Inde | 1 705 | 1 600 | 1 902 | 2 012 | 2 009 | 2 469 | 2 735 | 3 715 | ... | ... |
| Indonesia — Indonésie | ... | 573 | 417 | 240 | 774 | ... | ... | ... | ... | ... |
| Iran (Islamic Rep. of) — Iran (Rép. islamique d') | 756[4] | 786[4] | 1 200 | 1 236 | 973 | 917 | 978 | 946 | 799 | ... |
| Ireland — Irlande | 24 | 160 | 0 | 15 | 0 | 10 | 10 | 11 | 12 | ... |
| Italy — Italie | 5 402 | 5 562 | 6 280 | 6 582 | 6 987 | 6 936 | 7 088 | 7 197 | 7 201 | ... |
| Japan — Japon | 5 163 | 5 369 | 4 851 | 4 543 | 4 224 | 3 875 | 3 317 | 2 859 | ... | ... |
| Kazakhstan — Kazakhstan | ... | ... | ... | ... | 2 | ... | ... | ... | ... | ... |
| Korea, Republic of — Corée, République de | 4 292 | 4 257 | 3 790 | 4 735 | 6 304 | 6 448 | 8 254 | 7 267 | 7 122 | 6 955 |
| Lithuania — Lituanie | 138 | 88 | 116 | 118 | 101 | 94 | 111 | 98 | 107 | 89 |
| Malaysia — Malaisie | 257 | 249 | 206 | 194 | 215 | 186 | 172 | 187 | ... | ... |
| Mexico — Mexique | 1 448 | 1 943 | 1 986 | 2 083 | 2 049 | 2 071 | 2 222 | 2 162 | 2 291 | 2 844 |
| Moldova — Moldova | 1 | 2 | 0 | ... | ... | ... | ... | ... | ... | ... |
| Peru — Pérou | 81 | 101 | 118 | 42 | 51 | *68 | 64 | *46 | 69 | 76 |
| Poland — Pologne | 584 | 705 | 714 | 726 | #172 | 152 | 101 | 215 | 273 | 329 |
| Portugal — Portugal | 265 | 333 | 403 | 430 | 424 | 417 | 440 | 452 | 399 | ... |
| Romania — Roumanie | 446[3] | 429[3] | 366[3] | 323[3] | 341[3] | 313[3] | 212 | 319 | 260 | 251 |
| Russian Federation — Fédération de Russie | 1 064 | 1 186 | 1 043 | 1 173 | 1 327 | 1 719 | 1 938 | 2 218 | 2 589 | 2 777 |
| Serbia and Monteneg. — Serbie-et-Monténég. | 51 | 81 | 48 | #5 | 20 | 0 | 10 | ... | ... | ... |
| Slovakia — Slovaquie | 393 | 258 | 228 | 206 | 177 | 53 | ... | ... | ... | ... |
| South Africa — Afrique du Sud | 411[5] | 388 | 399 | 440 | 508 | 662 | 702 | 711 | ... | ... |
| Spain — Espagne | 1 260 | 1 960 | 2 415 | 2 107 | 2 153 | ... | ... | ... | ... | ... |
| Soudan — Soudan | ... | ... | ... | ... | ... | ... | ... | ... | 47 | 47 |
| Sweden — Suède | 377 | 428 | 368 | 549 | 575 | 593 | 627 | 655 | 639 | 625 |
| Syrian Arab Republic — Rép. arabe syrienne | 155 | 138 | 137 | 120 | 96 | 110 | 113 | ... | ... | ... |
| Tajikistan — Tadjikistan | 1 | 2 | 1 | 2 | 2 | 2 | 1 | 1 | 2 | 1 |

| Country or area — Pays ou zone | 1996 | 1997 | 1998 | 1999 | 2000 | 2001 | 2002 | 2003 | 2004 | 2005 |
|---|---|---|---|---|---|---|---|---|---|---|
| Thailand — Thaïlande | 2 246 | 2 384 | 1 631[6] | ... | ... | ... | ... | ... | ... | ... |
| TFYR of Macedonia — L'ex-R.y. Macédoine | 20 | 12 | 4 | 0 | 0 | 9 | 1 | 0 | 0 | 0 |
| Turkey — Turquie | 1 612 | 1 945 | 1 993 | 2 083 | 2 405 | 2 245 | 3 017 | 4 011 | 4 867 | 4 269 |
| Ukraine — Ukraine | 431 | 382 | 390 | 409 | 451 | 509 | 583 | 340 | 313 | 313 |
| United Kingdom[7] — Royaume-Uni[7] | 749 | 746 | 662 | 620 | 581 | 565 | 476 | 745 | 317 | ... |
| United States[8,9] — Etats-Unis[8,9] | 11 132 | 12 092 | 11 279 | 11 716 | 12 355 | 11 776 | 11 145 | 11 639 | ... | ... |
| Uzbekistan — Ouzbékistan | 13 | 13 | 16[10] | 2[10] | 1[10] | ... | ... | ... | ... | ... |
| Viet Nam — Viet Nam | ... | ... | ... | ... | 174 | 223 | 342 | 479 | 621 | 627 |

Source

United Nations Statistics Division, New York, the "Industrial Commodity Statistics Yearbook 2005" and the industrial statistics database, last accessed June 2008.

Source

Organisation des Nations Unies, Division de statistique, New York, "l'Annuaire de statistiques industrielles par produit 2005", et la base de données sur les statistiques industrielles, dernier accès juin 2008.

Notes

1  For statistical purposes, the data for China do not include those for the Hong Kong Special Administrative Region (Hong Kong SAR), Macao Special Administrative Region (Macao SAR) and Taiwan Province of China.

2  Incomplete coverage.

3  Including freezers.

4  Production by establishments employing 10 or more persons.

5  Including deep freezers and deep freeze-refrigerator combinations.

6  Beginning 1999, series discontinued.

7  Excluding chest freezers of a capacity <= 800 litres.

8  Shipments.

9  Electric domestic refrigerators only.

10  Source: "Statistical Yearbook for Asia and the Pacific", United Nations Economic and Social Commission for Asia and the Pacific (Bangkok).

Notes

1  Pour la présentation des statistiques, les données pour la Chine ne comprennent pas la Région Administrative Spéciale de Hong Kong (Hong Kong RAS), la Région Administrative Spéciale de Macao (Macao RAS) et la province de Taiwan.

2  Couverture incomplète.

3  Y compris les congélateurs.

4  Production des établissements occupant 10 personnes ou plus.

5  Y compris congélateurs-conservateurs et congélateurs combinés avec un réfrigérateur.

6  A partir de 1999, les séries ont été discontinuées.

7  Non compris congélateurs-conservateurs de type coffre, à capacité <= 800 litres.

8  Expéditions.

9  Réfrigérateurs électriques de ménage seulement.

10  Source : "Annuaire des Statistiques de l'Asie et Pacifique", Commission économique et sociale des Nations Unies pour l'Asie et le Pacifique (Bangkok).

Industrial activity includes mining and quarrying, manufacturing and the production of electricity, gas and water. These activities correspond to the major divisions 2, 3 and 4 respectively of the *International Standard Industrial Classification of All Economic Activities*.

Many of the tables are based primarily on data compiled for the United Nations *Industrial Commodity Statistics Yearbook*. Data taken from alternate sources are footnoted.

The methods used by countries for the computation of industrial output are, as a rule, consistent with those described in the United Nations *International Recommendations for Industrial Statistics* and provide a satisfactory basis for comparative analysis. In some cases, however, the definitions and procedures underlying computations of output differ from approved guidelines. The differences, where known, are indicated in the footnotes to each table.

*Table 39*: The statistics on sugar were obtained from the database and the *Sugar Yearbook* of the International Sugar Organization. The data shown cover the production and consumption of centrifugal sugar from both beet and cane, and refer to calendar years.

The consumption data relate to the apparent consumption of centrifugal sugar in the country concerned, including sugar used for the manufacture of sugar-containing products whether exported or not and sugar used for purposes other than human consumption as food. Unless otherwise specified, the statistics are expressed in terms of raw value (i.e. sugar polarizing at 96 degrees). The world total also includes data for countries not shown separately whose sugar consumption was less than 10,000 metric tons.

*Table 40*: The data refer to meat from animals slaughtered within the national boundaries irrespective of the origin of the animals. Production figures of cattle, chicken, buffalo, pig (including bacon and ham), sheep and goat meat are in terms of carcass weight, excluding edible offal, tallow and lard. All data refer to total meat production, i.e. from both commercial and farm slaughter.

*Table 41*: The data refer to beer made from malt, including ale, stout, and porter.

*Table 42* presents data on cigarettes only, unless otherwise indicated.

*Table 43*: The data refer to the aggregate of sawnwood and sleepers, coniferous or non coniferous. The data cover wood planed, unplaned, grooved, tongued and the like, sawn lengthwise or produced by a profile chipping process, and planed wood which may also be finger jointed, tongued or grooved, chamfered, rabbeted, V jointed, beaded and so on. Wood flooring is excluded. Sleepers may be sawn or hewn.

L'activité industrielle comprend les industries extractives (mines et carrières), les industries manufacturières et la production d'électricité, de gaz et d'eau. Ces activités correspondent aux grandes divisions 2, 3 et 4, respectivement, de la *Classification internationale type par industrie de toutes les branches d'activité économique.*

Un grand nombre de ces tableaux sont établis principalement sur la base de données compilée pour l'*Annuaire de statistiques industrielles par produit* des Nations Unies. Les données tirées d'autres sources sont signalées par une note.

En règle générale, les méthodes employées par les pays pour le calcul de leur production industrielle sont conformes à celles dans *Recommandations internationales concernant les statistiques industrielles* des Nations Unies et offrent une base satisfaisante pour une analyse comparative. Toutefois, dans certains cas, les définitions des méthodes sur lesquelles reposent les calculs de la production diffèrent des directives approuvées. Lorsqu'elles sont connues, les différences sont indiquées par une note.

*Tableau 39*: Les données sur le sucre proviennent de la base de données et de l'*Annuaire du sucre* de l'Organisation internationale du sucre. Les données présentées portent sur la production et la consommation de sucre centrifugé à partir de la betterave et de la canne à sucre, et se rapportent à des années civiles.

Les données de la consommation se rapportent à la consommation apparente de sucre centrifugé dans le pays en question, y compris le sucre utilisé pour la fabrication de produits à base de sucre, exportés ou non, et le sucre utilisé à d'autres fins que pour la consommation alimentaire humaine. Sauf indication contraire, les statistiques sont exprimées en valeur brute (sucre polarisant à 96 degrés). Le total mondial compris également les données relatives aux pays où la consommation de sucre est inférieure à 10 000 tonnes.

Le *tableau 40* indique la production de viande provenant des animaux abattus à l'intérieur des frontières nationales, quelle que soient leurs origines. Les chiffres de production de viande bovine, de buffle, de poulet, de porc (y compris le bacon et le jambon), de mouton et de chèvre se rapportent à la production en poids de carcasses et ne comprennent pas le saindoux, le suif et les abats comestibles. Toutes les données se rapportent à la production totale de viande, c'est-à-dire à la fois aux animaux abattus à des fins commerciales et des animaux sacrifiés à la ferme.

*Tableau 41*: Les données se rapportent à la bière produite à partir du malte, y compris ale, stout et porter (bière anglaise, blonde et brune).

Le *tableau 42* se rapporte seulement aux cigarettes, sauf indication contraire.

*Table 44* presents statistics on the production of all paper and paper board. The data cover newsprint, printing and writing paper, construction paper and paperboard, household and sanitary paper, special thin paper, wrapping and packaging paper and paperboard.

*Table 45*: Statistics on all hydraulic cements used for construction (Portland, aluminous, slag, and so on) are shown, except in the form of clinkers.

*Table 46*: The data refer to unwrought aluminium obtained by electrolytic reduction of alumina (primary) and re-melting metal waste or scrap (secondary).

*Table 47*: The data on radio receivers include radio-broadcast receivers capable of operating without an external source of power, including apparatus capable of receiving also radio-telephony or radio-telegraphy, whether combined with sound recording or reproducing apparatus or not; radio-broadcast receivers not capable of operating without an external source of power, of a kind used in motor vehicles, including apparatus capable of receiving also radio-telephony or radio-telegraphy, whether combined with sound recording or reproducing apparatus or not; other radio-broadcast receivers, including apparatus capable of receiving also radio-telephony or radio-telegraphy, whether combined with sound recording or reproducing apparatus or not.

*Table 48*: The data refer to refrigerators of household type such as compression-type, absorption-type, electrical, and other household type refrigerators; freezers of the chest type, not exceeding 800 litres capacity; freezers of the upright type, not exceeding 900 litres capacity.

*Tableau 43*: Les données font référence à un agrégat des sciages de bois de conifères et de non-conifères et des traverses de chemins de fer. Elles comprennent les bois rabotés, non rabotés, rainés, languetés, etc. sciés en long ou obtenus à l'aide d'un procédé de profilage par enlèvement de copeaux et les bois rabotés qui peuvent être également à joints digitiformes languetés ou rainés, chanfreinés, à feuillures, à joints en V, à rebords, etc. Cette rubrique ne comprend pas les éléments de parquet en bois. Les traverses de chemin de fer comprennent les traverses sciées ou équarries à la hache.

Le *tableau 44* présente les statistiques sur la production de tout papier et carton. Les données comprennent le papier journal, les papiers d'impression et d'écriture, les papiers et cartons de construction, les papiers de ménage et les papiers hygiéniques, les papiers minces spéciaux, les papiers d'empaquetage et d'emballage et carton.

*Tableau 45*: Les données sur tous les ciments hydrauliques utilisés dans la construction (portland, alumineux, de laitier, etc.) sont présentées, autres que sous forme de "clinkers".

*Tableau 46*: Les données se rapportent à la production d'aluminium non travaillé obtenue par réduction électrolytique de l'alumine (formes primaires) et par refonte de déchets et débris de métal (formes secondaires).

*Tableau 47*: Les données sur les récepteurs de radio comprennent les appareils récepteurs de radiodiffusion pouvant fonctionner sans source d'énergie extérieure, y compris les appareils pouvant recevoir également la radiotéléphonie ou la radiotélégraphie, même combinés à un appareil d'enregistrement ou de reproduction du son; appareils récepteurs de radiodiffusion ne pouvant fonctionner qu'avec une source d'énergie extérieure, du type utilisé dans les véhicules automobiles, y compris les appareils pouvant recevoir également la radiotéléphonie ou la radiotélégraphie, même combinés à un appareil d'enregistrement ou de reproduction du son; autres appareils récepteurs de radiodiffusion, y compris les appareils pouvant recevoir également la radiotéléphonie ou la radiotélégraphie, même combinés à un appareil d'enregistrement ou de reproduction du son.

*Tableau 48*: Les données se rapportent aux réfrigérateurs de type ménager comme les réfrigérateurs à compression, à absorption, électriques, et autres réfrigérateurs de type ménager; meubles congélateurs conservateurs du type coffre, d'une capacité n'excédant pas 800 litres; meubles congélateurs conservateurs du type armoire, d'une capacité n'excédant pas 900 litres.

# 49

## Production, trade and consumption of commercial energy
Thousand metric tons of oil equivalent and kilograms per capita

## Production, commerce et consommation d'énergie commerciale
Milliers de tonnes d'équivalent pétrole et kilogrammes par habitant

| Region, country or area | Year Année | Primary energy production – Production d'énergie primaire | | | | | Changes in stocks Variations des stocks | Imports Importations | Export Exportation |
|---|---|---|---|---|---|---|---|---|---|
| | | Total Totale | Solids Solides | Liquids Liquides | Gas Gaz | Electricity Electricité | | | |
| World | 2002 | 8 823 516 | 2 287 920 | 3 664 952 | 2 400 256 | 470 388 | -1 966 | 3 825 266 | 3 744 159 |
| | 2003 | 9 212 188 | 2 445 137 | 3 810 222 | 2 486 698 | 470 130 | 5 401 | 3 998 129 | 3 944 290 |
| | 2004 | 9 655 102 | 2 645 425 | 3 947 932 | 2 566 635 | 495 109 | 11 830 | 4 278 007 | 4 227 78 |
| | 2005 | 9 980 024 | 2 813 819 | 4 015 831 | 2 641 355 | 509 019 | 4 368 | 4 388 723 | 4 348 14 |
| Africa | 2002 | 676 525 | 125 068 | 413 110 | 129 651 | 8 696 | 50 | 75 482 | 439 905 |
| | 2003 | 712 548 | 129 587 | 438 507 | 135 960 | 8 493 | 857 | 80 889 | 473 014 |
| | 2004 | 759 374 | 131 770 | 474 544 | 144 065 | 8 995 | -1 152 | 86 663 | 512 220 |
| | 2005 | 817 608 | 133 114 | 504 117 | 171 449 | 8 928 | -37 | 97 342 | 553 11 |
| Algeria | 2002 | 176 262 | ... | 99 499 | 76 759 | 5 | 68 | 1 062 | 129 014 |
| | 2003 | 183 893 | ... | 106 283 | 77 587 | 23 | -42 | 972 | 136 335 |
| | 2004 | 187 780 | ... | 110 940 | 76 819 | 22 | *102 | 1 235 | 141 768 |
| | 2005 | 199 780 | ... | 114 076 | 85 657 | 48 | -148 | 1 118 | 144 513 |
| Angola | 2002 | 44 706 | ... | 44 045 | 563 | 98 | -80 | 423 | 42 522 |
| | 2003 | 43 843 | ... | 43 083 | *653 | 107 | -166 | 588 | 41 676 |
| | 2004 | 50 274 | ... | 49 443 | 681 | 151 | 780 | 856 | 47 554 |
| | 2005 | 63 145 | ... | 62 314 | 681 | 150 | 390 | *1 073 | 60 627 |
| Benin | 2002 | 40 | ... | 40 | ... | 0 | 19 | 998 | 299 |
| | 2003 | 20 | ... | 20 | ... | 0 | 11 | 1 133 | 344 |
| | 2004 | *20 | ... | *20 | ... | 0 | 21 | 1 296 | 456 |
| | 2005 | *20 | ... | *20 | ... | 0 | -15 | 1 195 | 331 |
| Burkina Faso | 2002 | *6 | ... | ... | ... | *6 | ... | *233 | 0 |
| | 2003 | *8 | ... | ... | ... | *8 | ... | *237 | 0 |
| | 2004 | *9 | ... | ... | ... | *9 | ... | *237 | 0 |
| | 2005 | *9 | ... | ... | ... | *9 | ... | *243 | 0 |
| Burundi | 2002 | 13 | 2 | ... | ... | 11 | 0 | *93 | |
| | 2003 | *13 | 2 | ... | ... | *11 | 0 | *86 | |
| | 2004 | *13 | 2 | ... | ... | *11 | 0 | *84 | |
| | 2005 | 10 | 2 | ... | ... | 9 | 0 | *87 | |
| Cameroon | 2002 | 6 713 | ... | 6 439 | ... | 274 | -64 | 98 | 5 516 |
| | 2003 | 7 038 | ... | 6 735 | ... | 303 | -156 | 89 | 5 517 |
| | 2004 | 6 974 | ... | 6 637 | ... | 337 | 3 | 33 | 5 479 |
| | 2005 | 6 371 | ... | 6 035 | ... | 336 | -110 | 9 | 5 012 |
| Cape Verde | 2002 | 0 | ... | ... | ... | 0 | ... | *83 | ... |
| | 2003 | 0 | ... | ... | ... | 0 | ... | *90 | ... |
| | 2004 | 1 | ... | ... | ... | 1 | ... | *95 | ... |
| | 2005 | 1 | ... | ... | ... | 1 | ... | *105 | ... |
| Central African Rep.* | 2002 | 7 | ... | ... | ... | 7 | ... | 111 | ... |
| | 2003 | 7 | ... | ... | ... | 7 | ... | 105 | ... |
| | 2004 | 7 | ... | ... | ... | 7 | ... | 105 | ... |
| | 2005 | 7 | ... | ... | ... | 7 | ... | 105 | ... |
| Chad* | 2002 | ... | ... | ... | ... | ... | ... | 59 | ... |
| | 2003 | ... | ... | ... | ... | ... | ... | 58 | ... |
| | 2004 | ... | ... | ... | ... | ... | ... | 61 | ... |
| | 2005 | ... | ... | ... | ... | ... | ... | 66 | ... |
| Comoros* | 2002 | 0 | ... | ... | ... | 0 | ... | 27 | ... |
| | 2003 | 0 | ... | ... | ... | 0 | ... | 30 | ... |
| | 2004 | 0 | ... | ... | ... | 0 | ... | 30 | ... |
| | 2005 | 0 | ... | ... | ... | 0 | ... | 30 | ... |
| Congo | 2002 | 12 404 | ... | 12 251 | 118 | 34 | ... | 31 | 12 051 |
| | 2003 | 11 322 | ... | 11 177 | *116 | 29 | ... | 31 | 10 875 |
| | 2004 | 11 776 | ... | 11 626 | *116 | 34 | ... | 81 | 11 124 |
| | 2005 | 12 810 | ... | 12 665 | *114 | 31 | ... | 116 | 12 314 |

**Production, trade and consumption of commercial energy** — Thousand metric tons of oil equivalent and kilograms per capita (*continued*)

**Production, commerce et consommation d'énergie commerciale** — Milliers de tonnes d'équivalent pétrole et kilogrammes par habitant (*suite*)

| Bunkers - Soutes | | | Consumption - Consommation | | | | | | | |
|---|---|---|---|---|---|---|---|---|---|---|
| Air Avion | Sea Maritime | Unallocated Nondistribué | Per capita Par habitant | Total Totale | Solids Solides | Liquids Liquides | Gas Gaz | Electricity Electricité | Year Année | Région, pays ou zone |
| 110 033 | 144 886 | 268 118 | 1 351 | 8 374 684 | 2 330 120 | 3 165 954 | 2 406 827 | 471 783 | 2002 | Monde |
| 111 066 | 144 944 | 325 681 | 1 383 | 8 667 837 | 2 512 166 | 3 196 297 | 2 488 910 | 470 465 | 2003 | |
| 119 587 | 157 762 | 314 596 | 1 433 | 9 090 710 | 2 719 323 | 3 322 169 | 2 554 101 | 495 118 | 2004 | |
| 127 039 | 166 210 | 315 282 | 1 462 | 9 395 473 | 2 854 392 | 3 370 983 | 2 661 733 | 508 364 | 2005 | |
| 4 603 | 6 487 | 6 464 | 359 | 293 908 | 93 033 | 124 249 | 67 634 | 8 992 | 2002 | Afrique |
| 4 469 | 7 449 | 10 410 | 354 | 296 808 | 96 737 | 123 114 | 68 419 | 8 538 | 2003 | |
| 4 423 | 6 487 | 8 199 | 364 | 315 556 | 104 011 | 130 351 | 72 145 | 9 049 | 2004 | |
| 4 939 | 6 893 | 16 255 | 374 | 333 496 | 103 469 | 134 691 | 86 403 | 8 934 | 2005 | |
| *319 | 243 | 4 470 | 1 370 | 42 954 | 714 | 20 557 | 21 680 | 3 | 2002 | Algérie |
| *273 | 217 | 5 140 | 1 341 | 42 705 | 761 | 20 543 | 21 377 | 24 | 2003 | |
| 219 | 332 | 2 727 | 1 360 | 43 626 | 524 | 23 071 | 20 008 | 23 | 2004 | |
| 318 | 331 | 3 025 | 1 599 | 52 630 | 644 | 22 221 | 29 720 | 45 | 2005 | |
| 431 | 0 | 210 | 188 | 2 045 | ... | 1 384 | 563 | 98 | 2002 | Angola |
| 301 | 0 | 213 | 215 | 2 407 | ... | 1 647 | *653 | 107 | 2003 | |
| 343 | 0 | -258 | 238 | 2 711 | ... | 1 880 | 681 | 151 | 2004 | |
| 286 | 1 | 206 | 233 | 2 708 | ... | 1 877 | 681 | 150 | 2005 | |
| 24 | ... | 0 | 99 | 696 | ... | 650 | ... | 46 | 2002 | Bénin |
| 26 | ... | 0 | 107 | 772 | ... | 728 | ... | 44 | 2003 | |
| 25 | ... | *0 | 100 | 814 | ... | 764 | ... | 50 | 2004 | |
| 24 | ... | *0 | 104 | 875 | ... | 824 | ... | 51 | 2005 | |
| ... | ... | ... | *19 | *239 | 0 | *233 | ... | *6 | 2002 | Burkina Faso |
| ... | ... | ... | *19 | *245 | 0 | *237 | ... | *8 | 2003 | |
| ... | ... | ... | *19 | *246 | 0 | *237 | ... | *9 | 2004 | |
| ... | ... | ... | *20 | *252 | 0 | *243 | ... | *9 | 2005 | |
| *9 | ... | ... | *14 | *97 | 2 | *80 | ... | 14 | 2002 | Burundi |
| *9 | ... | ... | *12 | *90 | 2 | *74 | ... | *14 | 2003 | |
| *9 | ... | ... | *12 | *88 | 2 | *72 | ... | *14 | 2004 | |
| *9 | ... | ... | *11 | *88 | 2 | *72 | ... | 15 | 2005 | |
| 71 | 18 | 64 | 78 | 1 205 | ... | 931 | ... | 274 | 2002 | Cameroun |
| 71 | 14 | 433 | 79 | 1 249 | ... | 945 | ... | 303 | 2003 | |
| 71 | 15 | 158 | 80 | 1 281 | ... | 944 | ... | 337 | 2004 | |
| 64 | 12 | 107 | 79 | 1 295 | ... | 959 | ... | 336 | 2005 | |
| ... | *6 | ... | *170 | *77 | ... | *76 | ... | 0 | 2002 | Cap-Vert |
| ... | *6 | ... | *184 | *85 | ... | *84 | ... | 0 | 2003 | |
| ... | *7 | ... | *190 | *89 | ... | *88 | ... | 1 | 2004 | |
| ... | *10 | ... | *199 | *95 | ... | *95 | ... | 1 | 2005 | |
| 20 | ... | ... | 25 | 99 | ... | 91 | ... | 7 | 2002 | Rép. centrafricaine* |
| 21 | ... | ... | 23 | 92 | ... | 84 | ... | 7 | 2003 | |
| 21 | ... | ... | 23 | 92 | ... | 84 | ... | 7 | 2004 | |
| 21 | ... | ... | 23 | 92 | ... | 84 | ... | 7 | 2005 | |
| 19 | ... | ... | 5 | 40 | ... | 40 | ... | ... | 2002 | Tchad* |
| 19 | ... | ... | 4 | 39 | ... | 39 | ... | ... | 2003 | |
| 19 | ... | ... | 4 | 42 | ... | 42 | ... | ... | 2004 | |
| 20 | ... | ... | 5 | 46 | ... | 46 | ... | ... | 2005 | |
| ... | ... | ... | 44 | 27 | ... | 27 | ... | 0 | 2002 | Comores* |
| ... | ... | ... | 47 | 30 | ... | 30 | ... | 0 | 2003 | |
| ... | ... | ... | 46 | 30 | ... | 30 | ... | 0 | 2004 | |
| ... | ... | ... | 45 | 30 | ... | 30 | ... | 0 | 2005 | |
| ... | ... | 13 | 101 | 371 | ... | 187 | 118 | 65 | 2002 | Congo |
| ... | ... | 46 | 115 | 432 | ... | 256 | *116 | 60 | 2003 | |
| ... | ... | 253 | 124 | 480 | ... | 295 | *116 | 69 | 2004 | |
| ... | ... | 118 | 124 | 494 | ... | 314 | *114 | 66 | 2005 | |

49 **Production, trade and consumption of commercial energy**— Thousand metric tons of oil equivalent and kilograms per capita (*continued*)

**Production, commerce et consommation d'énergie commerciale**— Milliers de tonnes d'équivalent pétrole et kilogrammes par habitant (*suite*)

| Region, country or area | Year Année | Primary energy production – Production d'énergie primaire | | | | | Changes in stocks Variations des stocks | Imports Importations | Exports Exportations |
|---|---|---|---|---|---|---|---|---|---|
| | | Total Totale | Solids Solides | Liquids Liquides | Gas Gaz | Electricity Electricité | | | |
| Côte d'Ivoire | 2002 | 2 196 | ... | 749 | 1 298 | 149 | ... | 3 209 | 2 348 |
| | 2003 | 2 353 | ... | 1 055 | 1 141 | 158 | ... | 2 989 | 2 816 |
| | 2004 | 2 292 | ... | 1 302 | 840 | 150 | ... | 3 872 | 3 897 |
| | 2005 | 3 744 | ... | 2 072 | 1 548 | 124 | ... | 4 196 | 4 313 |
| Dem. Rep. of the Congo | 2002 | 1 743 | 71 | 1 151 | ... | 521 | ... | 505 | 1 267 |
| | 2003 | 1 693 | 73 | 1 083 | ... | 536 | ... | 513 | 1 202 |
| | 2004 | 1 696 | 76 | 1 033 | ... | 587 | ... | 689 | 1 163 |
| | 2005 | 1 704 | 84 | 984 | ... | 636 | ... | 689 | 1 144 |
| Djibouti | 2002 | ... | ... | ... | ... | ... | ... | *549 | ... |
| | 2003 | ... | ... | ... | ... | ... | ... | *560 | ... |
| | 2004 | ... | ... | ... | ... | ... | ... | *576 | ... |
| | 2005 | ... | ... | ... | ... | ... | ... | *585 | ... |
| Egypt | 2002 | 71 043 | 26 | 43 979 | 25 719 | 1 319 | 187 | 2 873 | 10 087 |
| | 2003 | 71 703 | 26 | 41 598 | 28 996 | 1 082 | *454 | 2 623 | 11 683 |
| | 2004 | 70 426 | 23 | 37 948 | 31 323 | 1 132 | *-398 | 3 901 | 10 848 |
| | 2005 | 83 283 | 20 | 37 220 | 44 908 | 1 135 | 0 | 6 959 | 18 484 |
| Equatorial Guinea | 2002 | 12 040 | ... | 11 597 | *443 | *0 | ... | *56 | 11 597 |
| | 2003 | 10 748 | ... | 10 299 | 448 | *0 | ... | *55 | 10 299 |
| | 2004 | 18 858 | ... | 18 410 | *447 | *0 | ... | *48 | 18 410 |
| | 2005 | 20 255 | ... | 19 807 | *447 | *0 | ... | *48 | 19 807 |
| Eritrea | 2002 | 0 | ... | ... | ... | 0 | -22 | 191 | 0 |
| | 2003 | 0 | ... | ... | ... | 0 | 21 | 258 | 0 |
| | 2004 | 0 | ... | ... | ... | 0 | -22 | 234 | 3 |
| | 2005 | 0 | ... | ... | ... | 0 | -41 | 212 | 0 |
| Ethiopia | 2002 | 175 | ... | ... | ... | 175 | -241 | 1 959 | ... |
| | 2003 | 197 | ... | ... | ... | 197 | -272 | 2 046 | ... |
| | 2004 | 217 | ... | ... | ... | 217 | -397 | 2 127 | ... |
| | 2005 | 245 | ... | ... | ... | 245 | -209 | 2 285 | ... |
| Gabon | 2002 | 11 511 | ... | 11 330 | 102 | 79 | -240 | 67 | 10 943 |
| | 2003 | 11 239 | ... | 11 056 | 106 | 77 | -224 | 116 | 10 703 |
| | 2004 | 10 930 | ... | 10 736 | 117 | 77 | -190 | 88 | 10 351 |
| | 2005 | 10 923 | ... | 10 736 | 117 | 70 | -195 | 90 | 10 345 |
| Gambia* | 2002 | ... | ... | ... | ... | ... | ... | 97 | 2 |
| | 2003 | ... | ... | ... | ... | ... | ... | 97 | 2 |
| | 2004 | ... | ... | ... | ... | ... | ... | 98 | 2 |
| | 2005 | ... | ... | ... | ... | ... | ... | 98 | 2 |
| Ghana | 2002 | 433 | ... | ... | ... | 433 | -6 | 2 608 | 345 |
| | 2003 | 334 | ... | ... | ... | 334 | -6 | 2 638 | 333 |
| | 2004 | 454 | ... | ... | ... | 454 | 0 | 2 418 | 432 |
| | 2005 | 458 | ... | ... | ... | 458 | -6 | 2 676 | 458 |
| Guinea* | 2002 | 38 | ... | ... | ... | 38 | ... | 400 | ... |
| | 2003 | 38 | ... | ... | ... | 38 | ... | 405 | ... |
| | 2004 | 38 | ... | ... | ... | 38 | ... | 405 | ... |
| | 2005 | 38 | ... | ... | ... | 38 | ... | 412 | ... |
| Guinea-Bissau* | 2002 | ... | ... | ... | ... | ... | ... | 100 | ... |
| | 2003 | ... | ... | ... | ... | ... | ... | 100 | ... |
| | 2004 | ... | ... | ... | ... | ... | ... | 100 | ... |
| | 2005 | ... | ... | ... | ... | ... | ... | 100 | ... |
| Kenya | 2002 | 301 | ... | ... | ... | 301 | ... | 2 901 | 404 |
| | 2003 | 348 | ... | ... | ... | 348 | ... | 2 992 | 322 |
| | 2004 | 336 | ... | ... | ... | 336 | ... | 3 667 | 424 |
| | 2005 | 336 | ... | ... | ... | 336 | ... | 3 599 | 241 |

**Production, trade and consumption of commercial energy**—Thousand metric tons of oil equivalent and kilograms per capita (*continued*)

**Production, commerce et consommation d'énergie commerciale**—Milliers de tonnes d'équivalent pétrole et kilogrammes par habitant (*suite*)

| Bunkers - Soutes | | | Consumption - Consommation | | | | | | | |
|---|---|---|---|---|---|---|---|---|---|---|
| Air Avion | Sea Maritime | Unallocated Nondistribué | Per capita Par habitant | Total Totale | Solids Solides | Liquids Liquides | Gas Gaz | Electricity Electricité | Year Année | Région, pays ou zone |
| *96 | 91 | 207 | 154 | 2 663 | ... | 1 350 | 1 298 | 14 | 2002 | Côte d'Ivoire |
| *108 | 91 | 281 | 116 | 2 046 | ... | 862 | 1 141 | 43 | 2003 | |
| 92 | 91 | 287 | 97 | 1 797 | ... | 928 | 840 | 29 | 2004 | |
| 92 | 75 | 906 | 134 | 2 552 | ... | 1 001 | 1 548 | 3 | 2005 | |
| *96 | 2 | 0 | 17 | 883 | 225 | 247 | ... | 410 | 2002 | Rép. dém. du Congo |
| *97 | 2 | 0 | 17 | 904 | 232 | 249 | ... | 422 | 2003 | |
| 121 | 2 | 0 | 20 | 1 099 | 251 | 385 | ... | 463 | 2004 | |
| 120 | 2 | 0 | 20 | 1 128 | 264 | 382 | ... | 482 | 2005 | |
| 89 | *348 | ... | *156 | *113 | ... | *113 | ... | ... | 2002 | Djibouti |
| 99 | *348 | ... | *152 | *114 | ... | *114 | ... | ... | 2003 | |
| 99 | *351 | ... | *164 | *126 | ... | *126 | ... | ... | 2004 | |
| 104 | *355 | ... | *160 | *126 | ... | *126 | ... | ... | 2005 | |
| 480 | 1 963 | 4 918 | 848 | 55 948 | 647 | 28 306 | 25 719 | 1 276 | 2002 | Egypte |
| 490 | 2 737 | 3 347 | 823 | 55 421 | 395 | 25 755 | 28 264 | 1 007 | 2003 | |
| 712 | 1 843 | 2 900 | 819 | 58 366 | 893 | 28 423 | 27 978 | 1 072 | 2004 | |
| 761 | 1 973 | 5 834 | 853 | 63 134 | 893 | 30 315 | 30 859 | 1 068 | 2005 | |
| ... | ... | 0 | *1 007 | *499 | ... | *56 | *443 | *0 | 2002 | Guinée équatoriale |
| ... | ... | 0 | 994 | 504 | ... | *55 | 448 | *0 | 2003 | |
| ... | ... | 0 | *957 | *496 | ... | *48 | *447 | *0 | 2004 | |
| ... | ... | 0 | *937 | *496 | ... | *48 | *447 | *0 | 2005 | |
| 8 | 0 | ... | 53 | 205 | ... | 205 | ... | 0 | 2002 | Erythrée |
| 11 | 1 | ... | 55 | 224 | ... | 224 | ... | 0 | 2003 | |
| 11 | 0 | ... | 57 | 242 | ... | 242 | ... | 0 | 2004 | |
| 9 | 0 | ... | 55 | 243 | ... | 243 | ... | 0 | 2005 | |
| 92 | ... | 756 | 23 | 1 527 | ... | 1 353 | ... | 175 | 2002 | Ethiopie |
| 89 | ... | *760 | 24 | 1 666 | ... | 1 469 | ... | 197 | 2003 | |
| 100 | ... | *764 | 27 | 1 877 | ... | 1 659 | ... | 217 | 2004 | |
| 151 | ... | *767 | 26 | 1 822 | ... | 1 577 | ... | 245 | 2005 | |
| *83 | 144 | 52 | 459 | 597 | ... | 415 | 102 | 79 | 2002 | Gabon |
| *72 | 145 | 49 | 458 | 609 | ... | 426 | 106 | 77 | 2003 | |
| *59 | 149 | 35 | 451 | 614 | ... | 420 | 117 | 77 | 2004 | |
| *60 | 153 | 25 | 449 | 626 | ... | 438 | 117 | 70 | 2005 | |
| ... | ... | ... | 65 | 95 | ... | 95 | ... | ... | 2002 | Gambie* |
| ... | ... | ... | 63 | 95 | ... | 95 | ... | ... | 2003 | |
| ... | ... | ... | 62 | 96 | ... | 96 | ... | ... | 2004 | |
| ... | ... | ... | 60 | 96 | ... | 96 | ... | ... | 2005 | |
| 94 | ... | 496 | 103 | 2 112 | ... | 1 633 | ... | 479 | 2002 | Ghana |
| 140 | ... | 512 | 95 | 1 993 | ... | 1 651 | ... | 341 | 2003 | |
| 115 | ... | 91 | 103 | 2 233 | ... | 1 761 | ... | 472 | 2004 | |
| 128 | ... | -119 | 121 | 2 672 | ... | 2 199 | ... | 473 | 2005 | |
| 22 | ... | ... | 47 | 415 | ... | 378 | ... | 38 | 2002 | Guinée* |
| 22 | ... | ... | 47 | 421 | ... | 383 | ... | 38 | 2003 | |
| 22 | ... | ... | 46 | 421 | ... | 383 | ... | 38 | 2004 | |
| 23 | ... | ... | 45 | 427 | ... | 389 | ... | 38 | 2005 | |
| 10 | ... | ... | 72 | 90 | ... | 90 | ... | ... | 2002 | Guinée-Bissau* |
| 10 | ... | ... | 71 | 90 | ... | 90 | ... | ... | 2003 | |
| 10 | ... | ... | 69 | 90 | ... | 90 | ... | ... | 2004 | |
| 10 | ... | ... | 67 | 90 | ... | 90 | ... | ... | 2005 | |
| ... | 84 | -81 | 89 | 2 795 | 70 | 2 405 | ... | 320 | 2002 | Kenya |
| ... | 13 | 48 | 90 | 2 957 | 65 | 2 529 | ... | 363 | 2003 | |
| ... | 37 | 361 | 93 | 3 181 | 76 | 2 762 | ... | 343 | 2004 | |
| ... | 42 | 162 | 99 | 3 490 | 76 | 3 079 | ... | 336 | 2005 | |

49 **Production, trade and consumption of commercial energy**—Thousand metric tons of oil equivalent and kilograms per capita (*continued*)

**Production, commerce et consommation d'énergie commerciale**—Milliers de tonnes d'équivalent pétrole et kilogrammes par habitant (*suite*)

| Region, country or area | Year Année | Primary energy production – Production d'énergie primaire | | | | | Changes in stocks Variations des stocks | Imports Importations | Exports Exportations |
|---|---|---|---|---|---|---|---|---|---|
| | | Total Totale | Solids Solides | Liquids Liquides | Gas Gaz | Electricity Electricité | | | |
| Liberia* | 2002 | ... | ... | ... | ... | ... | ... | 163 | 1 |
| | 2003 | ... | ... | ... | ... | ... | ... | 166 | 1 |
| | 2004 | ... | ... | ... | ... | ... | ... | 166 | 1 |
| | 2005 | ... | ... | ... | ... | ... | ... | 168 | 1 |
| Libyan Arab Jamah. | 2002 | 68 579 | ... | 62 791 | 5 788 | ... | ... | ... | 49 427 |
| | 2003 | 76 908 | ... | 70 943 | 5 965 | ... | ... | ... | 57 362 |
| | 2004 | 85 102 | ... | 77 590 | 7 512 | ... | ... | ... | 64 365 |
| | 2005 | 94 140 | ... | 83 236 | 10 904 | ... | ... | ... | 73 362 |
| Madagascar | 2002 | 46 | ... | ... | ... | 46 | ... | 802 | *20 |
| | 2003 | 52 | ... | ... | ... | 52 | ... | *860 | *20 |
| | 2004 | 55 | ... | ... | ... | 55 | ... | *924 | *20 |
| | *2005 | 57 | ... | ... | ... | 57 | ... | 943 | 20 |
| Malawi | 2002 | *139 | 42 | ... | ... | *97 | 0 | 272 | 12 |
| | 2003 | *148 | 46 | ... | ... | *101 | 0 | 271 | 11 |
| | 2004 | *158 | *49 | ... | ... | *109 | 0 | *284 | *11 |
| | 2005 | *155 | *45 | ... | ... | *109 | 0 | *270 | *11 |
| Mali | *2002 | 20 | ... | ... | ... | 20 | ... | 203 | ... |
| | 2003 | *20 | ... | ... | ... | *20 | ... | 201 | ... |
| | 2004 | *21 | ... | ... | ... | *21 | ... | *210 | ... |
| | 2005 | *21 | ... | ... | ... | *21 | ... | *210 | ... |
| Mauritania | 2002 | *3 | ... | ... | ... | *3 | ... | 437 | ... |
| | 2003 | *4 | ... | ... | ... | *4 | ... | 452 | ... |
| | 2004 | *4 | ... | ... | ... | *4 | ... | 485 | ... |
| | 2005 | *4 | ... | ... | ... | *4 | ... | 501 | ... |
| Mauritius | 2002 | *7 | ... | ... | ... | *7 | *-44 | 1 154 | ... |
| | 2003 | 10 | ... | ... | ... | 10 | -30 | 1 185 | ... |
| | 2004 | 10 | ... | ... | ... | 10 | 14 | 1 260 | ... |
| | 2005 | 10 | ... | ... | ... | 10 | -15 | 1 343 | ... |
| Morocco | 2002 | 143 | ... | 13 | 40 | 89 | -84 | 11 899 | 724 |
| | 2003 | 190 | ... | 10 | 39 | 141 | 93 | 11 406 | 296 |
| | 2004 | 213 | ... | 11 | 47 | 155 | -194 | 12 709 | 778 |
| | 2005 | 575 | ... | 7 | 429 | 139 | 38 | 14 637 | 576 |
| Mozambique | 2002 | 1 123 | 31 | ... | 2 | 1 090 | 10 | 930 | 945 |
| | 2003 | 937 | 26 | ... | 2 | 909 | 30 | 1 006 | 752 |
| | 2004 | 2 282 | 28 | ... | 1 249 | 1 004 | 47 | 1 377 | 2 076 |
| | 2005 | 3 270 | 28 | ... | 2 103 | 1 139 | *-49 | 1 270 | 2 981 |
| Niger | 2002 | 128 | 128 | ... | ... | ... | ... | 197 | ... |
| | 2003 | 132 | 132 | ... | ... | ... | ... | 214 | ... |
| | 2004 | 140 | 140 | ... | ... | ... | ... | 218 | ... |
| | 2005 | 127 | 127 | ... | ... | ... | ... | 219 | ... |
| Nigeria | 2002 | 118 155 | 30 | 102 525 | 14 881 | 718 | -159 | 4 756 | 101 056 |
| | 2003 | 136 383 | 16 | 117 964 | 17 729 | 674 | -396 | 7 501 | 124 399 |
| | 2004 | 150 196 | 2 | 128 734 | 20 866 | 594 | 224 | 7 680 | 136 250 |
| | 2005 | 154 656 | 6 | 133 807 | 20 318 | 526 | -1 | 7 959 | 136 520 |
| Réunion | 2002 | *49 | ... | ... | ... | *49 | ... | 768 | ... |
| | 2003 | *50 | ... | ... | ... | *50 | ... | *774 | ... |
| | 2004 | *50 | ... | ... | ... | *50 | ... | *783 | ... |
| | 2005 | *50 | ... | ... | ... | *50 | ... | *783 | ... |
| Rwanda | 2002 | *15 | ... | ... | *0 | *14 | ... | *207 | 1 |
| | 2003 | *15 | ... | ... | *0 | *14 | ... | *207 | 1 |
| | 2004 | *15 | ... | ... | *0 | *14 | ... | *195 | 1 |
| | *2005 | 15 | ... | ... | 0 | 15 | ... | 207 | 1 |

**Production, trade and consumption of commercial energy**—Thousand metric tons of oil equivalent and kilograms per capita (*continued*)

**Production, commerce et consommation d'énergie commerciale**—Milliers de tonnes d'équivalent pétrole et kilogrammes par habitant (*suite*)

| Bunkers - Soutes | | | Consumption - Consommation | | | | | | | |
|---|---|---|---|---|---|---|---|---|---|---|
| Air Avion | Sea Maritime | Unallocated Nondistribué | Per capita Par habitant | Total Totale | Solids Solides | Liquids Liquides | Gas Gaz | Electricity Electricité | Year Année | Région, pays ou zone |
| 3 | 13 | ... | 52 | 146 | ... | 146 | ... | ... | 2002 | Libéria* |
| 3 | 13 | ... | 53 | 149 | ... | 149 | ... | ... | 2003 | |
| 3 | 13 | ... | 53 | 149 | ... | 149 | ... | ... | 2004 | |
| 3 | 13 | ... | 46 | 151 | ... | 151 | ... | ... | 2005 | |
| 218 | 89 | 2 496 | 2 715 | 16 349 | ... | 11 133 | 5 216 | ... | 2002 | Jamah. arabe libyenne |
| 213 | 89 | 2 451 | 2 699 | 16 793 | ... | 11 509 | 5 284 | ... | 2003 | |
| 215 | 89 | 2 481 | 2 796 | 17 953 | ... | 11 439 | 6 514 | ... | 2004 | |
| 218 | 89 | 2 531 | 2 706 | 17 941 | ... | 11 937 | 6 003 | ... | 2005 | |
| 2 | *17 | 143 | *39 | *667 | *7 | *614 | ... | 46 | 2002 | Madagascar |
| *2 | *17 | *142 | *42 | *731 | *7 | *672 | ... | 52 | 2003 | |
| *2 | *17 | *145 | *44 | *795 | *7 | *733 | ... | 55 | 2004 | |
| 2 | 17 | 144 | 44 | 817 | 7 | 753 | ... | 57 | *2005 | |
| ... | ... | ... | 36 | 399 | 51 | 251 | ... | *96 | 2002 | Malawi |
| ... | ... | ... | 35 | 407 | 37 | 270 | ... | *101 | 2003 | |
| ... | ... | ... | *36 | *431 | *40 | *283 | ... | *109 | 2004 | |
| ... | ... | ... | *34 | *414 | *36 | *268 | ... | *109 | 2005 | |
| 18 | ... | ... | 19 | 206 | ... | 185 | ... | 20 | *2002 | Mali |
| 20 | ... | ... | *19 | 201 | ... | 181 | ... | *20 | 2003 | |
| 21 | ... | ... | *19 | *210 | ... | *189 | ... | *21 | 2004 | |
| 21 | ... | ... | *18 | *210 | ... | *189 | ... | *21 | 2005 | |
| 0 | *5 | ... | 154 | 435 | 0 | 427 | ... | *8 | 2002 | Mauritanie |
| 0 | *5 | ... | 155 | 450 | 0 | 443 | ... | *7 | 2003 | |
| 0 | *5 | ... | 161 | 484 | 0 | 478 | ... | *6 | 2004 | |
| 0 | *5 | ... | 162 | 500 | 0 | 492 | ... | *8 | 2005 | |
| 96 | *169 | ... | 783 | 940 | *219 | 714 | ... | *7 | 2002 | Maurice |
| 92 | 135 | ... | 825 | 998 | 221 | 766 | ... | 10 | 2003 | |
| 91 | 146 | ... | 835 | 1 019 | 202 | 806 | ... | 10 | 2004 | |
| 100 | 192 | ... | 863 | 1 077 | 255 | 812 | ... | 10 | 2005 | |
| 291 | 13 | 1 011 | 354 | 10 088 | 3 682 | 6 156 | 40 | 209 | 2002 | Maroc |
| 301 | 13 | 669 | 355 | 10 223 | 3 423 | 6 496 | 39 | 265 | 2003 | |
| 331 | *13 | 1 006 | 368 | 10 987 | 3 830 | 6 823 | 47 | 287 | 2004 | |
| 380 | 13 | 1 152 | 433 | 13 053 | 4 725 | 7 690 | 429 | 209 | 2005 | |
| 32 | 5 | ... | 57 | 1 061 | 6 | 416 | 2 | 637 | 2002 | Mozambique |
| 22 | 38 | ... | 59 | 1 101 | 15 | 441 | 2 | 642 | 2003 | |
| 36 | *73 | ... | 73 | 1 427 | 18 | 500 | 3 | 906 | 2004 | |
| 40 | *61 | ... | 78 | 1 507 | 18 | 490 | 68 | 931 | 2005 | |
| 12 | ... | ... | 28 | 313 | 128 | 166 | ... | *18 | 2002 | Niger |
| 13 | ... | ... | 29 | 333 | 132 | 182 | ... | *18 | 2003 | |
| 15 | ... | ... | 29 | 343 | 140 | 184 | ... | *19 | 2004 | |
| 16 | ... | ... | 26 | 330 | 127 | 184 | ... | *19 | 2005 | |
| 388 | 427 | 1 004 | 167 | 20 194 | 33 | 11 864 | 7 578 | 718 | 2002 | Nigéria |
| 400 | 574 | 700 | 146 | 18 206 | 18 | 10 767 | 6 747 | 674 | 2003 | |
| 197 | 523 | 719 | 155 | 19 963 | 4 | 10 354 | 9 011 | 594 | 2004 | |
| 497 | 476 | 5 100 | 150 | 20 022 | 7 | 10 509 | 8 980 | 526 | 2005 | |
| ... | 80 | ... | 992 | 738 | ... | 689 | ... | *49 | 2002 | Réunion |
| ... | 81 | ... | *985 | *743 | ... | *694 | ... | *50 | 2003 | |
| ... | 83 | ... | *980 | *751 | ... | *701 | ... | *50 | 2004 | |
| ... | 83 | ... | *966 | *751 | ... | *701 | ... | *50 | 2005 | |
| *12 | ... | ... | *24 | *208 | ... | *180 | *0 | 28 | 2002 | Rwanda |
| *12 | ... | ... | *23 | *209 | ... | *182 | *0 | *27 | 2003 | |
| *12 | ... | ... | *22 | *197 | ... | *173 | *0 | *24 | 2004 | |
| 12 | ... | ... | 22 | 208 | ... | 184 | 0 | 24 | *2005 | |

**49** Production, trade and consumption of commercial energy—Thousand metric tons of oil equivalent and kilograms per capita (*continued*)

Production, commerce et consommation d'énergie commerciale—Milliers de tonnes d'équivalent pétrole et kilogrammes par habitant (*suite*)

| Region, country or area | Year Année | Primary energy production – Production d'énergie primaire | | | | | Changes in stocks Variations des stocks | Imports Importations | Exports Exportations |
|---|---|---|---|---|---|---|---|---|---|
| | | Total Totale | Solids Solides | Liquids Liquides | Gas Gaz | Electricity Electricité | | | |
| Saint Helena | 2002 | ... | ... | ... | ... | ... | ... | 4 | ... |
| | 2003 | ... | ... | ... | ... | ... | ... | *4 | ... |
| | 2004 | ... | ... | ... | ... | ... | ... | 3 | ... |
| | 2005 | ... | ... | ... | ... | ... | ... | *3 | ... |
| Sao Tome and Principe* | 2002 | 1 | ... | ... | ... | 1 | ... | 31 | ... |
| | 2003 | 1 | ... | ... | ... | 1 | ... | 31 | ... |
| | 2004 | 1 | ... | ... | ... | 1 | ... | 31 | ... |
| | 2005 | 1 | ... | ... | ... | 1 | ... | 34 | ... |
| Senegal | 2002 | 20 | ... | ... | 3 | 17 | 0 | 1 608 | 70 |
| | 2003 | 39 | ... | ... | 10 | 29 | 70 | 1 779 | 190 |
| | 2004 | 38 | ... | ... | 12 | 25 | -94 | 1 774 | 187 |
| | 2005 | 38 | ... | ... | 15 | 23 | 72 | 2 081 | 273 |
| Seychelles | 2002 | ... | ... | ... | ... | ... | ... | 282 | ... |
| | *2003 | ... | ... | ... | ... | ... | ... | 287 | ... |
| | *2004 | ... | ... | ... | ... | ... | ... | 287 | ... |
| | *2005 | ... | ... | ... | ... | ... | ... | 301 | ... |
| Sierra Leone | 2002 | ... | ... | ... | ... | ... | ... | *340 | *6 |
| | 2003 | ... | ... | ... | ... | ... | ... | *343 | 17 |
| | 2004 | ... | ... | ... | ... | ... | ... | *454 | 20 |
| | 2005 | ... | ... | ... | ... | ... | ... | *460 | *22 |
| Somalia | 2002 | ... | ... | ... | ... | ... | ... | 254 | ... |
| | 2003 | ... | ... | ... | ... | ... | ... | 254 | ... |
| | 2004 | ... | ... | ... | ... | ... | ... | 263 | ... |
| | 2005 | ... | ... | ... | ... | ... | ... | 268 | ... |
| South Africa[1] | 2002 | 126 497 | 121 896 | 1 045 | 2 001 | 1 556 | 528 | 22 822 | 47 490 |
| | 2003 | 130 131 | 126 682 | 693 | 1 199 | 1 557 | 1 178 | 25 156 | 43 495 |
| | 2004 | 134 117 | 128 889 | 1 680 | 1 843 | 1 706 | -1 286 | 25 347 | 40 598 |
| | 2005 | 135 101 | 130 069 | 1 555 | 1 982 | 1 496 | 0 | 29 227 | 44 803 |
| Sudan | 2002 | 12 146 | ... | 12 035 | ... | 111 | 131 | 309 | 9 483 |
| | 2003 | 13 350 | ... | 13 250 | ... | 100 | 135 | 350 | 10 460 |
| | 2004 | 15 091 | ... | 15 000 | ... | 91 | 116 | 385 | 11 820 |
| | 2005 | 16 207 | ... | 16 100 | ... | 107 | 286 | 425 | 12 710 |
| Togo | 2002 | 15 | ... | ... | ... | 15 | 3 | 421 | 71 |
| | 2003 | 21 | ... | ... | ... | 21 | 2 | 650 | 159 |
| | 2004 | 7 | ... | ... | ... | 7 | 18 | 525 | 113 |
| | 2005 | 6 | ... | ... | ... | 6 | 18 | 525 | 113 |
| Tunisia | 2002 | 5 563 | ... | 3 621 | 1 934 | 8 | 116 | 5 435 | 3 969 |
| | 2003 | 5 242 | ... | 3 259 | 1 966 | 17 | 222 | 5 583 | 3 532 |
| | 2004 | 5 526 | ... | 3 436 | 2 074 | 17 | 39 | 5 677 | 3 884 |
| | 2005 | 5 598 | ... | 3 484 | 2 098 | 16 | -113 | 5 720 | 3 953 |
| Uganda | 2002 | 144 | ... | ... | ... | 144 | ... | 483 | *14 |
| | *2003 | 144 | ... | ... | ... | 144 | ... | 488 | 14 |
| | 2004 | *163 | ... | ... | ... | *163 | ... | 518 | *15 |
| | 2005 | 158 | ... | ... | ... | 158 | ... | 663 | *14 |
| United Rep. of Tanzania | 2002 | 289 | 55 | ... | 0 | 234 | ... | 1 053 | ... |
| | 2003 | 258 | 38 | ... | 0 | 219 | ... | 1 126 | ... |
| | 2004 | 367 | 45 | ... | 119 | 203 | ... | 1 209 | ... |
| | 2005 | 333 | 52 | ... | 127 | 153 | ... | 1 293 | ... |
| Western Sahara* | 2002 | ... | ... | ... | ... | ... | ... | 85 | ... |
| | 2003 | ... | ... | ... | ... | ... | ... | 85 | ... |
| | 2004 | ... | ... | ... | ... | ... | ... | 85 | ... |
| | 2005 | ... | ... | ... | ... | ... | ... | 85 | ... |

49  **Production, trade and consumption of commercial energy**—Thousand metric tons of oil equivalent and kilograms per capita (*continued*)

**Production, commerce et consommation d'énergie commerciale**—Milliers de tonnes d'équivalent pétrole et kilogrammes par habitant (*suite*)

| Bunkers - Soutes | | | Consumption - Consommation | | | | | | | |
| Air Avion | Sea Maritime | Unallocated Nondistribué | Per capita Par habitant | Total Totale | Solids Solides | Liquids Liquides | Gas Gaz | Electricity Electricité | Year Année | Région, pays ou zone |
|---|---|---|---|---|---|---|---|---|---|---|
| ... | ... | ... | 562 | 4 | 0 | 4 | ... | ... | 2002 | Sainte-Hélène |
| ... | ... | ... | *558 | *4 | 0 | *4 | ... | ... | 2003 | |
| ... | ... | ... | 415 | 3 | 0 | 3 | ... | ... | 2004 | |
| ... | ... | ... | *413 | *3 | 0 | *3 | ... | ... | 2005 | |
| ... | ... | ... | 186 | 32 | ... | 31 | ... | 1 | 2002 | Sao Tomé-et-Principe* |
| ... | ... | ... | 179 | 32 | ... | 31 | ... | 1 | 2003 | |
| ... | ... | ... | 174 | 32 | ... | 31 | ... | 1 | 2004 | |
| ... | ... | ... | 186 | 35 | ... | 34 | ... | 1 | 2005 | |
| 186 | 75 | 3 | 119 | 1 294 | *80 | 1 194 | 3 | 17 | 2002 | Sénégal |
| *193 | 85 | 5 | 114 | 1 275 | *84 | 1 152 | 10 | 29 | 2003 | |
| 261 | 83 | 26 | 118 | 1 349 | 89 | 1 223 | 12 | 25 | 2004 | |
| 263 | 115 | 10 | 118 | 1 386 | 106 | 1 241 | 15 | 23 | 2005 | |
| *24 | *78 | ... | 2 222 | 180 | ... | 180 | ... | ... | 2002 | Seychelles |
| 26 | 80 | ... | 2 230 | 181 | ... | 181 | ... | ... | *2003 | |
| 26 | 80 | ... | 2 230 | 181 | ... | 181 | ... | ... | *2004 | |
| 27 | 82 | ... | 2 368 | 192 | ... | 192 | ... | ... | *2005 | |
| *27 | *88 | *67 | *28 | *152 | 0 | *152 | ... | ... | 2002 | Sierra Leone |
| *27 | *88 | *69 | *26 | *143 | 0 | *143 | ... | ... | 2003 | |
| 27 | *91 | *84 | *40 | *232 | 0 | *232 | ... | ... | 2004 | |
| *27 | *92 | *87 | *40 | *233 | 0 | *233 | ... | ... | 2005 | |
| *52 | *22 | *14 | 22 | 167 | ... | 167 | ... | ... | 2002 | Somalie |
| *52 | *20 | *14 | 22 | 169 | ... | 169 | ... | ... | 2003 | |
| *52 | *20 | *23 | 21 | 169 | ... | 169 | ... | ... | 2004 | |
| *52 | *21 | *23 | 21 | 173 | ... | 173 | ... | ... | 2005 | |
| 894 | 2 470 | -9 644 | 2 113 | 107 582 | 84 464 | 19 117 | 2 001 | 2 001 | 2002 | Afrique du Sud[1] |
| 878 | 2 601 | -4 709 | 2 192 | 111 844 | 88 925 | 20 059 | 1 199 | 1 660 | 2003 | |
| 772 | 2 390 | -3 922 | 2 272 | 120 912 | 95 549 | 20 576 | 3 090 | 1 698 | 2004 | |
| 755 | 2 647 | -4 117 | 2 241 | 120 239 | 93 715 | 20 914 | 4 037 | 1 573 | 2005 | |
| 130 | 8 | 153 | 79 | 2 551 | ... | 2 440 | ... | 111 | 2002 | Soudan |
| 136 | 8 | 93 | 87 | 2 868 | ... | 2 768 | ... | 100 | 2003 | |
| 142 | 8 | 212 | 95 | 3 178 | ... | 3 087 | ... | 91 | 2004 | |
| 149 | 8 | 114 | 93 | 3 366 | ... | 3 259 | ... | 107 | 2005 | |
| 73 | 5 | ... | 58 | 283 | ... | 240 | ... | 43 | 2002 | Togo |
| 55 | 7 | ... | 90 | 448 | ... | 398 | ... | 50 | 2003 | |
| 30 | 3 | ... | 72 | 369 | ... | 320 | ... | 49 | 2004 | |
| 33 | 3 | ... | 68 | 365 | ... | 317 | ... | 48 | 2005 | |
| ... | ... | 76 | 699 | 6 837 | 57 | 3 905 | 2 871 | 3 | 2002 | Tunisie |
| ... | ... | 106 | 705 | 6 965 | 16 | 3 902 | 3 032 | 15 | 2003 | |
| ... | ... | 63 | 727 | 7 217 | 0 | 4 040 | 3 162 | 15 | 2004 | |
| ... | ... | 135 | 732 | 7 344 | 0 | 4 074 | 3 257 | 13 | 2005 | |
| ... | ... | ... | 25 | 612 | ... | 483 | ... | 129 | 2002 | Ouganda |
| ... | ... | ... | 24 | 617 | ... | 488 | ... | 129 | *2003 | |
| ... | ... | ... | 24 | 666 | ... | 518 | ... | *148 | 2004 | |
| ... | ... | ... | 29 | 806 | ... | 663 | ... | 144 | 2005 | |
| 69 | 23 | 0 | 35 | 1 250 | 55 | 954 | 0 | 241 | 2002 | Rép.-Unie de Tanzanie |
| 74 | 23 | 0 | 36 | 1 287 | 38 | 1 021 | 0 | 227 | 2003 | |
| 79 | 23 | 0 | 40 | 1 473 | 45 | 1 097 | 119 | 212 | 2004 | |
| 86 | 23 | 0 | 40 | 1 518 | 52 | 1 173 | 127 | 165 | 2005 | |
| 6 | ... | ... | 308 | 79 | ... | 79 | ... | ... | 2002 | Sahara occidental* |
| 6 | ... | ... | 301 | 79 | ... | 79 | ... | ... | 2003 | |
| 6 | ... | ... | 294 | 79 | ... | 79 | ... | ... | 2004 | |
| 6 | ... | ... | 290 | 79 | ... | 79 | ... | ... | 2005 | |

**49**

**Production, trade and consumption of commercial energy**— Thousand metric tons of oil equivalent and kilograms per capita (*continued*)

**Production, commerce et consommation d'énergie commerciale**— Milliers de tonnes d'équivalent pétrole et kilogrammes par habitant (*suite*)

| Region, country or area | Year Année | Primary energy production – Production d'énergie primaire | | | | | Changes in stocks Variations des stocks | Imports Importations | Exports Exportations |
| | | Total Totale | Solids Solides | Liquids Liquides | Gas Gaz | Electricity Electricité | | | |
|---|---|---|---|---|---|---|---|---|---|
| Zambia | 2002 | 821 | 124 | ... | ... | 697 | 52 | 597 | 78 |
| | 2003 | 840 | 130 | ... | ... | 710 | 56 | 627 | 54 |
| | 2004 | 865 | 137 | ... | ... | 727 | 56 | 657 | 35 |
| | 2005 | 908 | 144 | ... | ... | 764 | 60 | 691 | 37 |
| Zimbabwe | 2002 | 2 992 | 2 663 | ... | ... | 329 | -124 | 1 240 | 144 |
| | 2003 | 2 876 | 2 415 | ... | ... | 461 | -125 | 1 074 | 144 |
| | 2004 | 2 853 | 2 379 | ... | ... | 475 | 11 | 822 | 144 |
| | 2005 | 3 037 | 2 535 | ... | ... | 502 | 1 | 960 | 128 |
| America, North | 2002 | 2 032 417 | 498 017 | 674 399 | 721 715 | 138 286 | -19 850 | 852 792 | 439 201 |
| | 2003 | 2 038 831 | 481 383 | 687 171 | 733 557 | 136 721 | -6 860 | 900 212 | 458 718 |
| | 2004 | 2 054 949 | 506 542 | 684 834 | 722 798 | 140 775 | 854 | 957 615 | 478 030 |
| | 2005 | 2 039 123 | 515 421 | 665 336 | 715 424 | 142 942 | -3 572 | 988 518 | 478 481 |
| Anguilla | 2002 | ... | ... | ... | ... | ... | ... | 13 | ... |
| | 2003 | ... | ... | ... | ... | ... | ... | 13 | ... |
| | 2004 | ... | ... | ... | ... | ... | ... | 14 | ... |
| | 2005 | ... | ... | ... | ... | ... | ... | 17 | ... |
| Antigua and Barbuda* | 2002 | ... | ... | ... | ... | ... | ... | 180 | 6 |
| | 2003 | ... | ... | ... | ... | ... | ... | 190 | 8 |
| | 2004 | ... | ... | ... | ... | ... | ... | 196 | 8 |
| | 2005 | ... | ... | ... | ... | ... | ... | 199 | 9 |
| Aruba | 2002 | *120 | ... | *120 | ... | ... | ... | *10 702 | 10 495 |
| | 2003 | *120 | ... | *120 | ... | ... | ... | *10 706 | 10 495 |
| | 2004 | *120 | ... | *120 | ... | ... | ... | *10 706 | 10 495 |
| | 2005 | *120 | ... | *120 | ... | ... | ... | 10 713 | 10 495 |
| Bahamas | *2002 | ... | ... | ... | ... | ... | 3 | 3 062 | 2 104 |
| | *2003 | ... | ... | ... | ... | ... | 50 | 3 163 | 2 206 |
| | 2004 | ... | ... | ... | ... | ... | 0 | *3 209 | *2 247 |
| | 2005 | ... | ... | ... | ... | ... | 0 | *3 265 | *2 257 |
| Barbados | 2002 | 108 | ... | 81 | 27 | ... | ... | 337 | 80 |
| | 2003 | 99 | ... | 75 | 24 | ... | ... | 324 | 74 |
| | 2004 | 108 | ... | 85 | 23 | ... | ... | 351 | 84 |
| | 2005 | 113 | ... | 88 | 25 | ... | ... | 364 | 87 |
| Belize* | 2002 | 8 | ... | ... | ... | 8 | ... | 286 | ... |
| | 2003 | 9 | ... | ... | ... | 9 | ... | 300 | ... |
| | 2004 | 9 | ... | ... | ... | 9 | ... | 305 | ... |
| | 2005 | 9 | ... | ... | ... | 9 | ... | 316 | ... |
| Bermuda* | 2002 | ... | ... | ... | ... | ... | ... | 198 | ... |
| | 2003 | ... | ... | ... | ... | ... | ... | 196 | ... |
| | 2004 | ... | ... | ... | ... | ... | ... | 203 | ... |
| | 2005 | ... | ... | ... | ... | ... | ... | 211 | ... |
| British Virgin Islands* | 2002 | ... | ... | ... | ... | ... | ... | 23 | ... |
| | 2003 | ... | ... | ... | ... | ... | ... | 26 | ... |
| | 2004 | ... | ... | ... | ... | ... | ... | 29 | ... |
| | 2005 | ... | ... | ... | ... | ... | ... | 30 | ... |
| Canada | 2002 | 374 976 | 32 919 | 134 992 | 170 380 | 36 686 | -3 403 | 69 278 | 217 760 |
| | 2003 | 376 493 | 30 390 | 142 603 | 167 960 | 35 540 | -4 339 | 76 138 | 214 676 |
| | 2004 | 385 115 | 32 622 | 147 681 | 167 591 | 37 221 | -7 315 | 78 304 | 223 268 |
| | 2005 | 388 279 | 31 907 | 145 830 | 171 231 | 39 311 | -5 933 | 78 503 | 223 133 |
| Cayman Islands* | 2002 | ... | ... | ... | ... | ... | ... | 117 | ... |
| | 2003 | ... | ... | ... | ... | ... | ... | 123 | ... |
| | 2004 | ... | ... | ... | ... | ... | ... | 126 | ... |
| | 2005 | ... | ... | ... | ... | ... | ... | 128 | ... |

**Production, trade and consumption of commercial energy**—Thousand metric tons of oil equivalent and kilograms per capita (*continued*)

**Production, commerce et consommation d'énergie commerciale**—Milliers de tonnes d'équivalent pétrole et kilogrammes par habitant (*suite*)

| Bunkers - Soutes | | | Consumption - Consommation | | | | | | | |
|---|---|---|---|---|---|---|---|---|---|---|
| Air<br>Avion | Sea<br>Maritime | Unallocated<br>Nondistribué | Per capita<br>Par habitant | Total<br>Totale | Solids<br>Solides | Liquids<br>Liquides | Gas<br>Gaz | Electricity<br>Electricité | Year<br>Année | Région, pays ou zone |
| 46 | ... | 38 | 112 | 1 203 | 80 | 493 | ... | 630 | 2002 | Zambie |
| 49 | ... | 41 | 118 | 1 267 | 85 | 516 | ... | 667 | 2003 | |
| 51 | ... | 43 | 121 | 1 338 | 90 | 540 | ... | 708 | 2004 | |
| 53 | ... | 46 | 122 | 1 404 | 95 | 566 | ... | 743 | 2005 | |
| 62 | ... | ... | 348 | 4 149 | 2 511 | 964 | ... | 674 | 2002 | Zimbabwe |
| 35 | ... | ... | 324 | 3 895 | 2 280 | 881 | ... | 735 | 2003 | |
| 7 | ... | ... | 272 | 3 513 | 2 251 | 612 | ... | 650 | 2004 | |
| 0 | ... | ... | 298 | 3 868 | 2 446 | 665 | ... | 758 | 2005 | |
| 21 105 | 28 089 | 21 084 | 4 806 | 2 395 939 | 484 785 | 1 033 623 | 738 988 | 138 544 | 2002 | Amérique du Nord |
| 20 580 | 23 830 | 35 901 | 4 779 | 2 407 225 | 488 664 | 1 050 322 | 731 623 | 136 616 | 2003 | |
| 20 965 | 29 324 | 34 078 | 4 808 | 2 449 688 | 499 953 | 1 085 323 | 723 649 | 140 764 | 2004 | |
| 21 606 | 30 401 | 22 202 | 4 846 | 2 478 887 | 504 696 | 1 106 908 | 724 366 | 142 916 | 2005 | |
| ... | ... | ... | 1 011 | 13 | ... | 13 | ... | ... | 2002 | Anguilla |
| ... | ... | ... | 1 052 | 13 | ... | 13 | ... | ... | 2003 | |
| ... | ... | ... | 1 092 | 14 | ... | 14 | ... | ... | 2004 | |
| ... | ... | ... | 1 250 | 17 | ... | 17 | ... | ... | 2005 | |
| 50 | ... | ... | 1 570 | 124 | ... | 124 | ... | ... | 2002 | Antigua-et-Barbuda* |
| 48 | ... | ... | 1 665 | 133 | ... | 133 | ... | ... | 2003 | |
| 50 | ... | ... | 1 708 | 138 | ... | 138 | ... | ... | 2004 | |
| 50 | ... | ... | 1 732 | 140 | ... | 140 | ... | ... | 2005 | |
| *73 | ... | *5 | 2 663 | 248 | ... | 248 | ... | ... | 2002 | Aruba |
| *75 | ... | *5 | 2 636 | 251 | ... | 251 | ... | ... | 2003 | |
| *75 | ... | *5 | 2 566 | 251 | ... | 251 | ... | ... | 2004 | |
| *77 | ... | 5 | 2 544 | 256 | ... | 256 | ... | ... | 2005 | |
| 38 | 229 | ... | 2 332 | 688 | 1 | 686 | ... | ... | *2002 | Bahamas |
| 43 | 244 | ... | 2 084 | 619 | 2 | 617 | ... | ... | *2003 | |
| *44 | *254 | ... | *2 217 | *664 | *2 | *662 | ... | ... | 2004 | |
| *46 | *266 | ... | *2 298 | *696 | *2 | *694 | ... | ... | 2005 | |
| ... | ... | 0 | 1 348 | 365 | ... | 338 | 27 | ... | 2002 | Barbade |
| ... | ... | 0 | 1 285 | 349 | ... | 325 | 24 | ... | 2003 | |
| ... | ... | 0 | 1 376 | 375 | ... | 352 | 23 | ... | 2004 | |
| ... | ... | 0 | 1 428 | 390 | ... | 365 | 25 | ... | 2005 | |
| 19 | 12 | ... | 994 | 263 | ... | 253 | ... | 11 | 2002 | Belize* |
| 22 | 12 | ... | 1 006 | 275 | ... | 264 | ... | 11 | 2003 | |
| 23 | 12 | ... | 989 | 279 | ... | 268 | ... | 11 | 2004 | |
| 24 | 13 | ... | 988 | 288 | ... | 277 | ... | 12 | 2005 | |
| 19 | 3 | ... | 2 842 | 176 | ... | 176 | ... | ... | 2002 | Bermudes* |
| 17 | 3 | ... | 2 842 | 176 | ... | 176 | ... | ... | 2003 | |
| 18 | 3 | ... | 2 811 | 183 | ... | 183 | ... | ... | 2004 | |
| 18 | 3 | ... | 2 887 | 191 | ... | 191 | ... | ... | 2005 | |
| ... | ... | ... | 1 080 | 23 | ... | 23 | ... | ... | 2002 | Iles Vierges britanniques* |
| ... | ... | ... | 1 208 | 26 | ... | 26 | ... | ... | 2003 | |
| ... | ... | ... | 1 330 | 29 | ... | 29 | ... | ... | 2004 | |
| ... | ... | ... | 1 357 | 30 | ... | 30 | ... | ... | 2005 | |
| 907 | 882 | 1 808 | 7 213 | 226 301 | 26 127 | 83 712 | 81 498 | 34 963 | 2002 | Canada |
| 699 | 507 | 2 456 | 7 534 | 238 633 | 26 284 | 88 806 | 88 587 | 34 956 | 2003 | |
| 885 | 617 | 5 419 | 7 520 | 240 545 | 25 689 | 91 840 | 86 695 | 36 321 | 2004 | |
| 835 | 604 | 5 308 | 7 518 | 242 835 | 25 413 | 90 544 | 89 617 | 37 260 | 2005 | |
| 21 | ... | ... | 2 244 | 97 | ... | 97 | ... | ... | 2002 | Iles Caïmanes* |
| 22 | ... | ... | 2 312 | 102 | ... | 102 | ... | ... | 2003 | |
| 23 | ... | ... | 2 882 | 104 | ... | 104 | ... | ... | 2004 | |
| 23 | ... | ... | 2 034 | 106 | ... | 106 | ... | ... | 2005 | |

49 **Production, trade and consumption of commercial energy**—Thousand metric tons of oil equivalent and kilograms per capita (*continued*)

**Production, commerce et consommation d'énergie commerciale**—Milliers de tonnes d'équivalent pétrole et kilogrammes par habitant (*suite*)

| Region, country or area | Year Année | Primary energy production – Production d'énergie primaire | | | | | Changes in stocks Variations des stocks | Imports Importations | Exports Exportations |
|---|---|---|---|---|---|---|---|---|---|
| | | Total Totale | Solids Solides | Liquids Liquides | Gas Gaz | Electricity Electricité | | | |
| Costa Rica | 2002 | 629 | ... | ... | ... | 629 | 71 | 2 033 | 162 |
| | 2003 | 615 | ... | ... | ... | 615 | -16 | 2 093 | 47 |
| | 2004 | 668 | ... | ... | ... | 668 | -8 | 2 074 | 88 |
| | 2005 | 662 | ... | ... | ... | 662 | -15 | 2 114 | 9 |
| Cuba | 2002 | 4 213 | ... | 3 659 | 545 | 9 | *-294 | 4 376 | ... |
| | 2003 | 4 335 | ... | 3 711 | 613 | 11 | 32 | 4 413 | ... |
| | 2004 | 3 948 | ... | 3 284 | 656 | 8 | *21 | 4 422 | ... |
| | 2005 | 3 607 | ... | 2 916 | 684 | 7 | 401 | 5 306 | ... |
| Dominica | 2002 | 3 | ... | ... | ... | 3 | ... | 35 | ... |
| | 2003 | 2 | ... | ... | ... | 2 | ... | 38 | ... |
| | 2004 | 3 | ... | ... | ... | 3 | ... | 36 | ... |
| | 2005 | 2 | ... | ... | ... | 2 | ... | *38 | ... |
| Dominican Republic | 2002 | 75 | ... | ... | ... | 75 | 0 | 6 641 | ... |
| | 2003 | 103 | ... | ... | ... | 103 | 0 | 6 479 | ... |
| | 2004 | 136 | ... | ... | ... | 136 | 36 | 6 098 | ... |
| | 2005 | 163 | ... | ... | ... | 163 | -3 | 5 809 | ... |
| El Salvador | 2002 | 183 | ... | ... | ... | 183 | 15 | 2 235 | 318 |
| | 2003 | 209 | ... | ... | ... | 209 | 44 | 2 240 | 188 |
| | 2004 | 206 | ... | ... | ... | 206 | 38 | 2 284 | 274 |
| | 2005 | 234 | ... | ... | ... | 234 | 39 | 2 335 | 277 |
| Greenland* | 2002 | ... | ... | ... | ... | ... | ... | 195 | 7 |
| | 2003 | ... | ... | ... | ... | ... | ... | 196 | 7 |
| | 2004 | ... | ... | ... | ... | ... | ... | 197 | 7 |
| | 2005 | ... | ... | ... | ... | ... | ... | 200 | 7 |
| Grenada | 2002 | ... | ... | ... | ... | ... | ... | 81 | ... |
| | 2003 | ... | ... | ... | ... | ... | ... | 83 | ... |
| | 2004 | ... | ... | ... | ... | ... | ... | 82 | ... |
| | 2005 | ... | ... | ... | ... | ... | ... | 86 | ... |
| Guadeloupe* | 2002 | ... | ... | ... | ... | ... | ... | 624 | ... |
| | 2003 | ... | ... | ... | ... | ... | ... | 635 | ... |
| | 2004 | ... | ... | ... | ... | ... | ... | 642 | ... |
| | 2005 | ... | ... | ... | ... | ... | ... | 658 | ... |
| Guatemala | 2002 | 1 364 | ... | 1 218 | ... | 146 | 0 | 3 349 | 1 180 |
| | 2003 | 1 434 | ... | 1 221 | ... | 213 | 0 | 3 352 | 1 152 |
| | 2004 | 1 208 | ... | 999 | ... | 209 | 25 | 3 519 | 955 |
| | 2005 | 1 225 | ... | 910 | ... | 315 | 169 | 3 715 | 843 |
| Haiti | 2002 | 22 | ... | ... | ... | 22 | ... | 549 | ... |
| | 2003 | 22 | ... | ... | ... | 22 | ... | 538 | ... |
| | 2004 | 22 | ... | ... | ... | 22 | ... | 561 | ... |
| | 2005 | 23 | ... | ... | ... | 23 | ... | 565 | ... |
| Honduras | 2002 | 211 | ... | ... | ... | 211 | 242 | 2 052 | 0 |
| | 2003 | 187 | ... | ... | ... | 187 | 243 | 2 204 | 18 |
| | 2004 | 202 | ... | ... | ... | 202 | 5 | 2 278 | 27 |
| | 2005 | 148 | ... | ... | ... | 148 | 21 | 2 270 | 25 |
| Jamaica | 2002 | 8 | ... | ... | ... | 8 | -116 | 3 486 | 107 |
| | 2003 | 13 | ... | ... | ... | 13 | 35 | 3 802 | 129 |
| | 2004 | 14 | ... | ... | ... | 14 | 12 | 3 738 | 124 |
| | 2005 | 13 | ... | ... | ... | 13 | 26 | 3 431 | 0 |
| Martinique* | 2002 | ... | ... | ... | ... | ... | ... | 942 | 225 |
| | 2003 | ... | ... | ... | ... | ... | ... | 647 | 225 |
| | 2004 | ... | ... | ... | ... | ... | ... | 655 | 225 |
| | 2005 | ... | ... | ... | ... | ... | ... | 661 | 225 |

**Production, trade and consumption of commercial energy**—Thousand metric tons of oil equivalent and kilograms per capita (*continued*)

**Production, commerce et consommation d'énergie commerciale**—Milliers de tonnes d'équivalent pétrole et kilogrammes par habitant (*suite*)

| Bunkers - Soutes | | | Consumption - Consommation | | | | | | | |
|---|---|---|---|---|---|---|---|---|---|---|
| Air Avion | Sea Maritime | Unallocated Nondistribué | Per capita Par habitant | Total Totale | Solids Solides | Liquids Liquides | Gas Gaz | Electricity Electricité | Year Année | Région, pays ou zone |
| ... | ... | 76 | 575 | 2 352 | 53 | 1 706 | ... | 593 | 2002 | Costa Rica |
| ... | ... | 152 | 605 | 2 524 | 100 | 1 817 | ... | 608 | 2003 | |
| ... | ... | 116 | 599 | 2 545 | 82 | 1 815 | ... | 648 | 2004 | |
| ... | ... | 55 | 630 | 2 727 | 62 | 2 002 | ... | 663 | 2005 | |
| 202 | 68 | 325 | 735 | 8 288 | 18 | 7 715 | 545 | 9 | 2002 | Cuba |
| 221 | 67 | 820 | 673 | 7 608 | 18 | 6 966 | 613 | 11 | 2003 | |
| 223 | 72 | 351 | 679 | 7 703 | 19 | 7 020 | 656 | 8 | 2004 | |
| 225 | 73 | 150 | 717 | 8 064 | 24 | 7 350 | 684 | 7 | 2005 | |
| ... | ... | ... | 545 | 38 | ... | 35 | ... | 3 | 2002 | Dominique |
| ... | ... | ... | 582 | 41 | ... | 38 | ... | 2 | 2003 | |
| ... | ... | ... | 558 | 39 | ... | 36 | ... | 3 | 2004 | |
| ... | ... | ... | *589 | *41 | ... | *38 | ... | 2 | 2005 | |
| 80 | ... | 487 | 718 | 6 149 | 163 | 5 911 | 0 | 75 | 2002 | Rép. dominicaine |
| 92 | ... | 630 | 664 | 5 860 | 740 | 5 012 | 4 | 103 | 2003 | |
| 101 | ... | 188 | 666 | 5 909 | 544 | 5 224 | 5 | 136 | 2004 | |
| 100 | ... | 156 | 618 | 5 719 | 333 | 5 214 | 9 | 163 | 2005 | |
| 66 | ... | 44 | 303 | 1 975 | 1 | 1 758 | ... | 216 | 2002 | El Salvador |
| 70 | ... | 32 | 319 | 2 115 | 1 | 1 878 | ... | 236 | 2003 | |
| 75 | ... | -28 | 315 | 2 131 | 1 | 1 891 | ... | 239 | 2004 | |
| 78 | ... | -28 | 320 | 2 202 | 1 | 1 943 | ... | 258 | 2005 | |
| 8 | ... | ... | 3 178 | 179 | ... | 179 | ... | ... | 2002 | Groenland* |
| 8 | ... | ... | 3 196 | 180 | ... | 180 | ... | ... | 2003 | |
| 8 | ... | ... | 3 214 | 181 | ... | 181 | ... | ... | 2004 | |
| 8 | ... | ... | 3 270 | 184 | ... | 184 | ... | ... | 2005 | |
| *7 | ... | ... | 710 | 73 | ... | 73 | ... | ... | 2002 | Grenade |
| *8 | ... | ... | 715 | 75 | ... | 75 | ... | ... | 2003 | |
| *8 | ... | ... | 702 | 74 | ... | 74 | ... | ... | 2004 | |
| *7 | ... | ... | 739 | 79 | ... | 79 | ... | ... | 2005 | |
| 102 | ... | ... | 1 195 | 522 | ... | 522 | ... | ... | 2002 | Guadeloupe* |
| 103 | ... | ... | 1 210 | 531 | ... | 531 | ... | ... | 2003 | |
| 103 | ... | ... | 1 211 | 538 | ... | 538 | ... | ... | 2004 | |
| 108 | ... | ... | 1 207 | 551 | ... | 551 | ... | ... | 2005 | |
| 37 | 122 | 44 | 278 | 3 331 | 273 | 2 945 | ... | 113 | 2002 | Guatemala |
| 41 | 122 | 106 | 279 | 3 365 | 258 | 2 928 | ... | 179 | 2003 | |
| 44 | 122 | 83 | 282 | 3 497 | 291 | 3 033 | ... | 173 | 2004 | |
| 38 | 122 | 76 | 291 | 3 693 | 285 | 3 119 | ... | 288 | 2005 | |
| 35 | ... | ... | 62 | 537 | ... | 514 | ... | 22 | 2002 | Haïti |
| 27 | ... | ... | 60 | 533 | ... | 511 | ... | 22 | 2003 | |
| 24 | ... | ... | 62 | 559 | ... | 537 | ... | 22 | 2004 | |
| 24 | ... | ... | 66 | 564 | ... | 541 | ... | 23 | 2005 | |
| 24 | ... | ... | 293 | 1 998 | 99 | 1 652 | ... | 247 | 2002 | Honduras |
| 26 | ... | ... | 301 | 2 104 | 118 | 1 770 | ... | 215 | 2003 | |
| *29 | ... | ... | 337 | 2 419 | 122 | 2 064 | ... | 233 | 2004 | |
| *22 | ... | ... | 326 | 2 350 | 22 | 2 175 | ... | 153 | 2005 | |
| 195 | 30 | 35 | 1 237 | 3 243 | 62 | 3 173 | ... | 8 | 2002 | Jamaïque |
| 195 | 30 | 24 | 1 279 | 3 400 | 59 | 3 328 | ... | 13 | 2003 | |
| *186 | *25 | 57 | 1 252 | 3 350 | 46 | 3 290 | ... | 14 | 2004 | |
| 183 | 30 | 7 | 1 207 | 3 199 | 42 | 3 144 | ... | 13 | 2005 | |
| 3 | 44 | 74 | 1 529 | 596 | ... | 596 | ... | ... | 2002 | Martinique* |
| 3 | 44 | -224 | 1 533 | 599 | ... | 599 | ... | ... | 2003 | |
| 4 | 45 | -235 | 1 564 | 616 | ... | 616 | ... | ... | 2004 | |
| 4 | 45 | -233 | 1 562 | 620 | ... | 620 | ... | ... | 2005 | |

**49** **Production, trade and consumption of commercial energy**—Thousand metric tons of oil equivalent and kilograms per capita (*continued*)

**Production, commerce et consommation d'énergie commerciale**—Milliers de tonnes d'équivalent pétrole et kilogrammes par habitant (*suite*)

| Region, country or area | Year Année | Primary energy production – Production d'énergie primaire | | | | | Changes in stocks Variations des stocks | Imports Importations | Export Exportation |
|---|---|---|---|---|---|---|---|---|---|
| | | Total Totale | Solids Solides | Liquids Liquides | Gas Gaz | Electricity Electricité | | | |
| Mexico | 2002 | 221 836 | 3 343 | 179 047 | 35 994 | 3 452 | 376 | 22 659 | 101 94‹ |
| | 2003 | 233 827 | 2 944 | 190 001 | 37 726 | 3 157 | -1 055 | 22 525 | 109 39( |
| | 2004 | 237 911 | 3 044 | 191 899 | 39 440 | 3 528 | 1 643 | 24 544 | 109 241 |
| | 2005 | 236 591 | 3 474 | 188 168 | 41 004 | 3 945 | 602 | 26 866 | 104 304 |
| Montserrat* | 2002 | ... | ... | ... | ... | ... | ... | 20 | |
| | 2003 | ... | ... | ... | ... | ... | ... | 22 | .. |
| | 2004 | ... | ... | ... | ... | ... | ... | 22 | .. |
| | 2005 | ... | ... | ... | ... | ... | ... | 22 | |
| Netherlands Antilles | 2002 | ... | ... | ... | ... | ... | ... | 13 679 | 8 368 |
| | 2003 | ... | ... | ... | ... | ... | ... | 13 252 | 8 028 |
| | 2004 | ... | ... | ... | ... | ... | ... | 13 811 | 8 093 |
| | 2005 | ... | ... | ... | ... | ... | ... | 14 279 | 8 486 |
| Nicaragua | 2002 | 44 | ... | ... | ... | 44 | -33 | 1 217 | 12 |
| | 2003 | 49 | ... | ... | ... | 49 | 41 | 1 321 | 5 |
| | 2004 | 50 | ... | ... | ... | 50 | -42 | 1 286 | 5 |
| | 2005 | 61 | ... | ... | ... | 61 | 31 | 1 317 | 6 |
| Panama | 2002 | 292 | ... | ... | ... | 292 | -155 | 2 143 | 482 |
| | 2003 | 243 | ... | ... | ... | 243 | -20 | 2 054 | 209 |
| | 2004 | 325 | ... | ... | ... | 325 | -186 | 1 770 | 220 |
| | 2005 | 320 | ... | ... | ... | 320 | 0 | 2 037 | 226 |
| Puerto Rico | 2002 | 19 | ... | ... | ... | 19 | ... | 587 | ... |
| | 2003 | 22 | ... | ... | ... | 22 | ... | 689 | ... |
| | 2004 | 12 | ... | ... | ... | 12 | ... | 634 | .. |
| | *2005 | 12 | ... | ... | ... | 12 | ... | 647 | |
| Saint Kitts and Nevis* | 2002 | ... | ... | ... | ... | ... | ... | 38 | .. |
| | 2003 | ... | ... | ... | ... | ... | ... | 42 | .. |
| | 2004 | ... | ... | ... | ... | ... | ... | 42 | |
| | 2005 | ... | ... | ... | ... | ... | ... | 45 | |
| Saint Lucia | *2002 | ... | ... | ... | ... | ... | ... | 97 | .. |
| | 2003 | ... | ... | ... | ... | ... | ... | 118 | |
| | *2004 | ... | ... | ... | ... | ... | ... | 123 | |
| | *2005 | ... | ... | ... | ... | ... | ... | 125 | |
| Saint Pierre and Miquelon* | 2002 | ... | ... | ... | ... | ... | ... | 24 | |
| | 2003 | ... | ... | ... | ... | ... | ... | 28 | |
| | 2004 | ... | ... | ... | ... | ... | ... | 27 | |
| | 2005 | ... | ... | ... | ... | ... | ... | 28 | |
| Saint Vincent-Grenadines | 2002 | 2 | ... | ... | ... | 2 | ... | 62 | |
| | 2003 | 2 | ... | ... | ... | 2 | ... | *64 | .. |
| | 2004 | 2 | ... | ... | ... | 2 | ... | *64 | .. |
| | *2005 | 2 | ... | ... | ... | 2 | ... | 64 | |
| Trinidad and Tobago | 2002 | 23 440 | ... | 8 186 | 15 254 | ... | 290 | 4 728 | 14 771 |
| | 2003 | 31 831 | ... | 8 620 | 23 210 | ... | 324 | 4 702 | 22 437 |
| | 2004 | 32 476 | ... | 8 013 | 24 462 | ... | 290 | 3 449 | 21 477 |
| | 2005 | 34 608 | ... | 9 118 | 25 490 | ... | 105 | 4 544 | 24 033 |
| United States | 2002 | 1 404 861 | 461 755 | 347 095 | 499 516 | 96 495 | -16 845 | 696 746 | 81 181 |
| | 2003 | 1 389 216 | 448 050 | 340 819 | 504 022 | 96 325 | -2 200 | 737 498 | 89 422 |
| | 2004 | 1 392 414 | 470 876 | 332 753 | 490 625 | 98 160 | 6 335 | 791 813 | 101 193 |
| | 2005 | 1 372 931 | 480 041 | 318 187 | 476 990 | 97 713 | 986 | 817 610 | 104 059 |
| **America, South** | **2002** | **518 983** | **37 834** | **348 874** | **85 465** | **46 810** | **3 536** | **82 593** | **244 543** |
| | **2003** | **520 363** | **39 812** | **343 018** | **88 558** | **48 976** | **5 341** | **80 188** | **238 557** |
| | **2004** | **535 265** | **42 197** | **346 988** | **95 579** | **50 502** | **-296** | **91 371** | **263 092** |
| | **2005** | **559 017** | **46 697** | **361 055** | **98 113** | **53 152** | **161** | **88 705** | **269 205** |

**19** Production, trade and consumption of commercial energy — Thousand metric tons of oil equivalent and kilograms per capita (*continued*)

Production, commerce et consommation d'énergie commerciale — Milliers de tonnes d'équivalent pétrole et kilogrammes par habitant (*suite*)

| Bunkers - Soutes | | | Consumption - Consommation | | | | | | | |
|---|---|---|---|---|---|---|---|---|---|---|
| Air Avion | Sea Maritime | Unallocated Nondistribué | Per capita Par habitant | Total Totale | Solids Solides | Liquids Liquides | Gas Gaz | Electricity Electricité | Year Année | Région, pays ou zone |
| 2 571 | 796 | 6 105 | 1 303 | 132 702 | 5 158 | 81 478 | 42 597 | 3 469 | 2002 | Mexique |
| 2 593 | 815 | 7 001 | 1 332 | 137 609 | 5 638 | 82 246 | 46 643 | 3 082 | 2003 | |
| 2 491 | 773 | 5 315 | 1 365 | 142 992 | 5 070 | 85 907 | 48 570 | 3 445 | 2004 | |
| 2 581 | 877 | 7 033 | 1 434 | 148 059 | 6 056 | 89 044 | 49 117 | 3 842 | 2005 | |
| ... | 1 | ... | 2 214 | 19 | ... | 19 | ... | ... | 2002 | Montserrat* |
| ... | 1 | ... | 2 296 | 21 | ... | 21 | ... | ... | 2003 | |
| ... | 1 | ... | 2 235 | 21 | ... | 21 | ... | ... | 2004 | |
| ... | 1 | ... | 2 212 | 21 | ... | 21 | ... | ... | 2005 | |
| 71 | 1 704 | 1 690 | 8 611 | 1 846 | ... | 1 846 | ... | ... | 2002 | Antilles néerlandaises |
| 73 | 1 707 | 1 933 | 6 983 | 1 511 | ... | 1 511 | ... | ... | 2003 | |
| 75 | 1 710 | 1 754 | 9 982 | 2 179 | ... | 2 179 | ... | ... | 2004 | |
| 76 | 1 713 | 1 891 | 9 594 | 2 112 | ... | 2 112 | ... | ... | 2005 | |
| ... | ... | 24 | 235 | 1 258 | ... | 1 213 | ... | 45 | 2002 | Nicaragua |
| ... | ... | 35 | 245 | 1 289 | ... | 1 241 | ... | 48 | 2003 | |
| ... | ... | 30 | 249 | 1 342 | ... | 1 293 | ... | 50 | 2004 | |
| ... | ... | 35 | 239 | 1 306 | ... | 1 244 | ... | 62 | 2005 | |
| 2 | ... | 113 | 651 | 1 993 | 31 | 1 671 | ... | 291 | 2002 | Panama |
| 2 | ... | 0 | 676 | 2 105 | 0 | 1 878 | ... | 227 | 2003 | |
| 0 | ... | 0 | 650 | 2 061 | 1 | 1 746 | ... | 314 | 2004 | |
| 0 | ... | 0 | 662 | 2 132 | 0 | 1 816 | ... | 316 | 2005 | |
| ... | ... | ... | 157 | 606 | ... | ... | 587 | 19 | 2002 | Porto Rico |
| ... | ... | ... | 183 | 712 | ... | ... | 689 | 22 | 2003 | |
| ... | ... | ... | 166 | 646 | ... | ... | 634 | 12 | 2004 | |
| ... | ... | ... | 169 | 660 | ... | ... | 647 | 12 | *2005 | |
| ... | ... | ... | 974 | 38 | ... | 38 | ... | ... | 2002 | Saint-Kitts-et-Nevis* |
| ... | ... | ... | 1 080 | 42 | ... | 42 | ... | ... | 2003 | |
| ... | ... | ... | 1 080 | 42 | ... | 42 | ... | ... | 2004 | |
| ... | ... | ... | 1 159 | 45 | ... | 45 | ... | ... | 2005 | |
| ... | ... | ... | 608 | 97 | ... | 97 | ... | ... | *2002 | Sainte-Lucie |
| ... | ... | ... | 732 | 118 | ... | 118 | ... | ... | 2003 | |
| ... | ... | ... | 757 | 123 | ... | 123 | ... | ... | *2004 | |
| ... | ... | ... | 757 | 125 | ... | 125 | ... | ... | *2005 | |
| ... | 5 | ... | 2 770 | 19 | ... | 19 | ... | ... | 2002 | Saint-Pierre-et-Miquelon* |
| ... | 6 | ... | 3 065 | 21 | ... | 21 | ... | ... | 2003 | |
| ... | -6 | ... | 2 920 | 20 | ... | 20 | ... | ... | 2004 | |
| ... | 6 | ... | 3 060 | 21 | ... | 21 | ... | ... | 2005 | |
| ... | ... | ... | 591 | 64 | ... | 62 | ... | 2 | 2002 | Saint Vincent-Grenadines |
| ... | ... | ... | *626 | *66 | ... | *64 | ... | 2 | 2003 | |
| ... | ... | ... | *634 | *66 | ... | *64 | ... | 2 | 2004 | |
| ... | ... | ... | 639 | 66 | ... | 64 | ... | 2 | *2005 | |
| 8 | 668 | 680 | 9 001 | 11 755 | ... | 1 257 | 10 498 | ... | 2002 | Trinité-et-Tobago |
| 8 | 744 | 548 | 9 581 | 12 476 | ... | 1 380 | 11 096 | ... | 2003 | |
| 6 | 898 | 286 | 9 929 | 12 973 | ... | 1 322 | 11 651 | ... | 2004 | |
| 60 | 264 | 942 | 10 537 | 13 754 | ... | 1 584 | 12 170 | ... | 2005 | |
| 16 566 | 23 525 | 9 573 | 6 894 | 1 987 964 | 452 799 | 833 474 | 603 235 | 98 457 | 2002 | Etats-Unis |
| 16 183 | 19 528 | 22 383 | 6 815 | 1 981 743 | 455 445 | 845 455 | 583 966 | 96 877 | 2003 | |
| 16 469 | 24 786 | 20 737 | 6 863 | 2 015 080 | 468 085 | 872 447 | 575 415 | 99 132 | 2004 | |
| 17 020 | 26 383 | 6 805 | 6 868 | 2 035 646 | 472 455 | 891 254 | 572 098 | 99 839 | 2005 | |
| 1 912 | 5 823 | 29 222 | 884 | 316 472 | 21 177 | 163 535 | 85 084 | 46 677 | 2002 | Amérique du Sud |
| 2 131 | 5 599 | 30 579 | 877 | 318 273 | 20 623 | 160 349 | 88 474 | 48 827 | 2003 | |
| 2 778 | 5 942 | 16 566 | 920 | 338 403 | 21 542 | 170 458 | 95 892 | 50 511 | 2004 | |
| 2 718 | 7 099 | 17 404 | 939 | 351 017 | 22 177 | 177 565 | 97 949 | 53 326 | 2005 | |

**Production, trade and consumption of commercial energy** — Thousand metric tons of oil equivalent and kilograms per capita (*continued*)

**Production, commerce et consommation d'énergie commerciale** — Milliers de tonnes d'équivalent pétrole et kilogrammes pa habitant (*suite*)

| Region, country or area | Year Année | Primary energy production – Production d'énergie primaire | | | | | Changes in stocks Variations des stocks | Imports Importations | Export Exportation |
| | | Total Totale | Solids Solides | Liquids Liquides | Gas Gaz | Electricity Electricité | | | |
|---|---|---|---|---|---|---|---|---|---|
| Argentina | 2002 | 83 956 | 57 | 44 560 | 35 747 | 3 593 | 179 | 2 142 | 26 17. |
| | 2003 | 88 284 | 53 | 44 918 | 39 747 | 3 567 | 57 | 1 707 | 25 27 |
| | 2004 | 87 591 | 25 | 43 338 | 40 921 | 3 307 | -115 | 3 009 | 22 20 |
| | 2005 | 85 423 | 15 | 41 612 | 40 253 | 3 544 | 147 | 4 397 | 20 08. |
| Bolivia | 2002 | 7 232 | ... | 1 819 | 5 223 | 189 | -268 | 300 | 4 94 |
| | 2003 | 8 279 | ... | 1 978 | 6 108 | 193 | *-64 | 329 | 4 29 |
| | 2004 | 10 946 | ... | 2 267 | 8 494 | 185 | -510 | 193 | 7 90. |
| | 2005 | 13 220 | ... | 2 441 | 10 568 | 211 | -472 | 255 | 10 29 |
| Brazil | 2002 | 121 521 | 3 798 | 83 147 | 8 787 | 25 789 | -2 126 | 49 382 | 19 90. |
| | 2003 | 125 927 | 2 064 | 86 941 | 9 495 | 27 427 | 654 | 44 579 | 20 78. |
| | 2004 | 127 868 | 2 402 | 86 852 | 10 032 | 28 582 | -775 | 51 604 | 22 41 |
| | 2005 | 139 024 | 2 779 | 96 133 | 10 249 | 29 863 | -226 | 46 181 | 23 30. |
| Chile | 2002 | 4 774 | 303 | 476 | 2 001 | 1 994 | 384 | 19 021 | 78 |
| | 2003 | 4 540 | 403 | 433 | 1 760 | 1 944 | 388 | 20 351 | 1 21 |
| | 2004 | 4 143 | 132 | 432 | *1 750 | 1 829 | 964 | 22 528 | 99 |
| | 2005 | 5 061 | 446 | 403 | 1 965 | 2 248 | 662 | 23 005 | 1 03 |
| Colombia | 2002 | 67 826 | 28 502 | 29 971 | 6 432 | 2 921 | 3 065 | 479 | 41 41 |
| | 2003 | 70 010 | 32 517 | 28 223 | 6 157 | 3 114 | 616 | 334 | 45 39 |
| | 2004 | 71 707 | 34 900 | 26 877 | 6 481 | 3 449 | 8 | 319 | 48 34 |
| | 2005 | 75 043 | 38 391 | 26 420 | 6 800 | 3 430 | 357 | 947 | 50 66 |
| Ecuador | 2002 | 21 426 | ... | 20 543 | 236 | 647 | 718 | 1 695 | 14 06 |
| | 2003 | 22 504 | ... | 21 499 | 388 | 617 | 1 133 | 2 117 | 15 22 |
| | 2004 | 28 566 | ... | 27 466 | 463 | 637 | 305 | 2 108 | 20 33 |
| | 2005 | 28 023 | ... | 26 557 | 875 | 592 | 98 | 2 562 | 19 80 |
| Falkland Is. (Malvinas) | *2002 | 3 | 3 | ... | ... | ... | ... | 10 | |
| | *2003 | 3 | 3 | ... | ... | ... | ... | 11 | |
| | 2004 | 3 | 3 | ... | ... | ... | ... | *11 | |
| | *2005 | 3 | 3 | ... | ... | ... | ... | 11 | |
| French Guiana | 2002 | ... | ... | ... | ... | ... | ... | 286 | |
| | *2003 | ... | ... | ... | ... | ... | ... | 287 | |
| | *2004 | ... | ... | ... | ... | ... | ... | 287 | |
| | *2005 | ... | ... | ... | ... | ... | ... | 287 | |
| Guyana | 2002 | ... | ... | ... | ... | ... | -1 | 524 | |
| | 2003 | ... | ... | ... | ... | ... | 0 | 508 | |
| | 2004 | ... | ... | ... | ... | ... | 0 | 492 | |
| | 2005 | ... | ... | ... | ... | ... | 0 | 508 | |
| Paraguay | 2002 | 4 145 | ... | 0 | ... | 4 145 | 11 | 1 261 | 3 596 |
| | 2003 | 4 451 | ... | 0 | ... | 4 451 | -71 | 1 226 | 3 884 |
| | 2004 | 4 464 | ... | 0 | ... | 4 464 | -12 | 1 292 | 3 869 |
| | 2005 | 4 403 | ... | 5 | ... | 4 399 | -26 | 1 179 | 3 765 |
| Peru | 2002 | 7 079 | 15 | 4 955 | 557 | 1 551 | 24 | 5 644 | 2 870 |
| | 2003 | 7 307 | 11 | 5 086 | 616 | 1 594 | 883 | 6 438 | 3 393 |
| | 2004 | 7 632 | 15 | 5 147 | 963 | 1 507 | 36 | 6 542 | 2 924 |
| | 2005 | 8 746 | 29 | 5 376 | 1 624 | 1 717 | -63 | 6 550 | 3 452 |
| Suriname | 2002 | 731 | ... | 615 | ... | 116 | ... | 248 | 132 |
| | 2003 | 705 | ... | 588 | ... | 117 | ... | 268 | 129 |
| | 2004 | 730 | ... | 612 | ... | 118 | ... | 272 | 142 |
| | 2005 | 760 | ... | 637 | ... | 123 | ... | 284 | 148 |
| Uruguay | 2002 | 820 | ... | ... | ... | 820 | -241 | 1 600 | 251 |
| | 2003 | 734 | ... | ... | ... | 734 | 130 | 2 033 | 248 |
| | 2004 | 411 | ... | ... | ... | 411 | 76 | 2 714 | 390 |
| | 2005 | 575 | ... | ... | ... | 575 | -105 | 2 539 | 430 |

**Production, trade and consumption of commercial energy**—Thousand metric tons of oil equivalent and kilograms per capita (*continued*)

**Production, commerce et consommation d'énergie commerciale**—Milliers de tonnes d'équivalent pétrole et kilogrammes par habitant (*suite*)

| Bunkers - Soutes | | | Consumption - Consommation | | | | | | | |
|---|---|---|---|---|---|---|---|---|---|---|
| Air<br>Avion | Sea<br>Maritime | Unallocated<br>Nondistribué | Per capita<br>Par habitant | Total<br>Totale | Solids<br>Solides | Liquids<br>Liquides | Gas<br>Gaz | Electricity<br>Electricité | Year<br>Année | Région, pays ou zone |
| ... | 502 | 4 421 | 1 445 | 54 844 | 290 | 20 049 | 30 404 | 4 102 | 2002 | Argentine |
| ... | 588 | 4 875 | 1 564 | 59 224 | 429 | 21 259 | 33 536 | 4 000 | 2003 | |
| ... | 542 | 5 047 | 1 647 | 62 950 | 490 | 23 972 | 34 882 | 3 606 | 2004 | |
| ... | 695 | 3 968 | 1 683 | 64 956 | 708 | 24 688 | 35 683 | 3 877 | 2005 | |
| ... | ... | 353 | 287 | 2 502 | ... | 1 603 | 708 | 190 | 2002 | Bolivie |
| ... | ... | 411 | 439 | 3 964 | ... | 1 670 | 2 101 | 194 | 2003 | |
| ... | ... | 463 | 356 | 3 285 | ... | 1 559 | 1 541 | 185 | 2004 | |
| ... | ... | 639 | 320 | 3 019 | ... | 1 920 | 887 | 212 | 2005 | |
| 722 | 3 661 | 8 659 | 794 | 140 023 | 14 776 | 82 560 | 13 753 | 28 934 | 2002 | Brésil |
| 1 100 | 3 219 | 6 886 | 770 | 137 786 | 13 809 | 79 185 | 14 171 | 30 621 | 2003 | |
| 1 090 | 3 348 | 6 479 | 808 | 146 750 | 14 363 | 83 079 | 17 512 | 31 796 | 2004 | |
| 1 100 | 3 497 | 6 442 | 820 | 150 968 | 13 923 | 85 252 | 18 572 | 33 220 | 2005 | |
| 2 | 194 | 897 | 1 381 | 21 534 | 2 907 | 10 144 | 6 490 | 1 994 | 2002 | Chili |
| 6 | 372 | 586 | 1 401 | 22 321 | 2 864 | 10 186 | 7 159 | 2 111 | 2003 | |
| 4 | 479 | -94 | 1 511 | 24 322 | 3 888 | 10 968 | 7 474 | 1 992 | 2004 | |
| 0 | 586 | 394 | 1 558 | 25 391 | 3 934 | 11 394 | 7 630 | 2 433 | 2005 | |
| 629 | 232 | 1 708 | 485 | 21 253 | 2 445 | 9 508 | 6 432 | 2 868 | 2002 | Colombie |
| 589 | 249 | 2 309 | 475 | 21 188 | 2 746 | 9 268 | 6 157 | 3 018 | 2003 | |
| 587 | 303 | 1 485 | 470 | 21 295 | 1 941 | 9 565 | 6 481 | 3 308 | 2004 | |
| 616 | *396 | 1 360 | 491 | 22 598 | 2 700 | 9 817 | 6 800 | 3 281 | 2005 | |
| ... | 266 | 751 | 558 | 7 321 | ... | 6 434 | 236 | 652 | 2002 | Equateur |
| ... | 258 | 650 | 572 | 7 351 | ... | 6 250 | 388 | 714 | 2003 | |
| ... | 226 | 2 557 | 557 | 7 252 | ... | 6 010 | 463 | 779 | 2004 | |
| ... | 672 | 957 | 658 | 9 054 | ... | 7 439 | 875 | 740 | 2005 | |
| ... | ... | ... | 4 700 | 13 | 3 | 10 | ... | ... | *2002 | Iles Falkland (Malvinas) |
| ... | ... | ... | 5 250 | 14 | 3 | 11 | ... | ... | *2003 | |
| ... | ... | ... | *5 452 | *14 | 3 | *11 | ... | ... | 2004 | |
| ... | ... | ... | 5 670 | 14 | 3 | 11 | ... | ... | *2005 | |
| *18 | ... | ... | 1 537 | 269 | ... | 269 | ... | ... | 2002 | Guyane française |
| 18 | ... | ... | 1 488 | 269 | ... | 269 | ... | ... | *2003 | |
| 18 | ... | ... | 1 408 | 269 | ... | 269 | ... | ... | *2004 | |
| 18 | ... | ... | 1 378 | 269 | ... | 269 | ... | ... | *2005 | |
| 12 | ... | ... | 682 | 512 | ... | 512 | ... | ... | 2002 | Guyana |
| 12 | ... | ... | 658 | 496 | ... | 496 | ... | ... | 2003 | |
| 12 | ... | ... | 634 | 479 | ... | 479 | ... | ... | 2004 | |
| 13 | ... | ... | 652 | 495 | ... | 495 | ... | ... | 2005 | |
| 20 | ... | 1 | 308 | 1 778 | ... | 1 224 | ... | 554 | 2002 | Paraguay |
| 26 | ... | 1 | 312 | 1 836 | ... | 1 270 | ... | 567 | 2003 | |
| 19 | ... | 2 | 311 | 1 878 | ... | 1 282 | ... | 595 | 2004 | |
| 19 | ... | 1 | 295 | 1 823 | ... | 1 189 | ... | 634 | 2005 | |
| 201 | 49 | -337 | 370 | 9 903 | 737 | 7 057 | 557 | 1 551 | 2002 | Pérou |
| 139 | 44 | -500 | 360 | 9 770 | 730 | 6 831 | 616 | 1 594 | 2003 | |
| 443 | 57 | -586 | 409 | 11 278 | 857 | 7 951 | 963 | 1 507 | 2004 | |
| 313 | 228 | 258 | 396 | 11 076 | 871 | 6 864 | 1 624 | 1 717 | 2005 | |
| ... | ... | 161 | 1 441 | 686 | ... | 570 | ... | 116 | 2002 | Suriname |
| ... | ... | 137 | 1 469 | 707 | ... | 590 | ... | 117 | 2003 | |
| ... | ... | 144 | 1 453 | 716 | ... | 598 | ... | 118 | 2004 | |
| ... | ... | 149 | 1 497 | 747 | ... | 624 | ... | 123 | 2005 | |
| ... | 351 | 67 | 588 | 1 992 | 1 | 1 298 | 21 | 671 | 2002 | Uruguay |
| ... | 354 | 47 | 583 | 1 988 | 1 | 1 255 | 59 | 673 | 2003 | |
| ... | 340 | 45 | 689 | 2 274 | 1 | 1 558 | 103 | 611 | 2004 | |
| ... | 407 | 88 | 694 | 2 294 | 2 | 1 555 | 98 | 639 | 2005 | |

**49** Production, trade and consumption of commercial energy—Thousand metric tons of oil equivalent and kilograms per capita (*continued*)

Production, commerce et consommation d'énergie commerciale—Milliers de tonnes d'équivalent pétrole et kilogrammes pa habitant (*suite*)

| Region, country or area | Year Année | Primary energy production – Production d'énergie primaire | | | | | Changes in stocks Variations des stocks | Imports Importations | Exports Exportations |
|---|---|---|---|---|---|---|---|---|---|
| | | Total Totale | Solids Solides | Liquids Liquides | Gas Gaz | Electricity Electricité | | | |
| Venezuela (Bolivarian Rep. of) | 2002 | 199 470 | 5 155 | 162 787 | 26 483 | 5 045 | 1 791 | ... | 130 406 |
| | 2003 | 187 620 | 4 762 | 153 351 | 24 288 | 5 219 | 1 614 | ... | 118 706 |
| | 2004 | 191 204 | 4 721 | 153 997 | 26 473 | 6 013 | -271 | ... | 133 560 |
| | 2005 | 198 736 | 5 034 | 161 473 | 25 779 | 6 451 | -211 | ... | 136 234 |
| **Asia** | **2002** | **3 266 209** | **1 096 659** | **1 491 524** | **577 658** | **100 368** | **2 703** | **1 314 648** | **1 346 075** |
| | **2003** | **3 552 928** | **1 254 772** | **1 580 053** | **617 210** | **100 893** | **-1 831** | **1 380 594** | **1 453 752** |
| | **2004** | **3 866 407** | **1 422 563** | **1 658 037** | **672 690** | **113 116** | **977** | **1 526 502** | **1 570 300** |
| | **2005** | **4 121 928** | **1 566 332** | **1 710 101** | **723 896** | **121 599** | **-6 065** | **1 553 669** | **1 622 939** |
| Afghanistan | 2002 | 71 | 15 | ... | 7 | 49 | 0 | *98 | ... |
| | 2003 | 86 | 24 | ... | 6 | 56 | 0 | *100 | ... |
| | 2004 | 76 | 24 | ... | 3 | 50 | 0 | 197 | ... |
| | 2005 | *77 | *23 | ... | *2 | *51 | 0 | *210 | ... |
| Armenia | 2002 | 339 | ... | ... | ... | 339 | ... | 1 321 | 57 |
| | 2003 | 342 | ... | ... | ... | 342 | ... | 1 508 | 50 |
| | 2004 | 380 | ... | ... | ... | 380 | ... | 1 630 | 99 |
| | 2005 | 386 | ... | ... | ... | 386 | ... | 1 915 | 117 |
| Azerbaijan | 2002 | 20 149 | ... | 15 343 | 4 632 | 174 | -105 | 3 773 | 11 721 |
| | 2003 | 20 221 | ... | 15 391 | 4 618 | 212 | -3 | 3 886 | 10 978 |
| | 2004 | 20 457 | ... | 15 565 | 4 655 | 237 | 42 | 4 861 | 11 405 |
| | 2005 | 27 770 | ... | 22 453 | 5 058 | 259 | 781 | 4 751 | 16 169 |
| Bahrain | 2002 | 16 116 | ... | 10 007 | 6 108 | ... | -549 | 3 174 | 9 987 |
| | 2003 | 16 488 | ... | 10 187 | 6 300 | ... | -603 | 3 283 | 10 344 |
| | 2004 | 16 720 | ... | 10 168 | 6 552 | ... | -315 | 3 326 | 9 927 |
| | 2005 | 17 083 | ... | 10 143 | 6 941 | ... | -250 | 3 980 | 10 082 |
| Bangladesh | 2002 | 9 840 | ... | 93 | 9 655 | 92 | 21 | 4 208 | ... |
| | 2003 | 10 591 | ... | 108 | 10 386 | 97 | -133 | 4 227 | ... |
| | 2004 | 11 374 | ... | 97 | 11 171 | 105 | -56 | 4 269 | ... |
| | 2005 | 12 225 | ... | 104 | 12 010 | 111 | -326 | 4 495 | ... |
| Bhutan* | 2002 | 200 | 36 | ... | ... | 163 | ... | 85 | 147 |
| | 2003 | 198 | 35 | ... | ... | 163 | ... | 85 | 149 |
| | 2004 | 204 | 36 | ... | ... | 168 | ... | 89 | 152 |
| | 2005 | 212 | 36 | ... | ... | 176 | ... | 89 | 159 |
| Brunei Darussalam | 2002 | 20 994 | ... | 10 306 | 10 688 | ... | *-52 | 9 | 18 817 |
| | 2003 | 22 016 | ... | 10 492 | 11 524 | ... | *-96 | 0 | 19 924 |
| | 2004 | 21 739 | ... | 10 338 | 11 401 | ... | 55 | 0 | 19 378 |
| | 2005 | 21 309 | ... | 10 116 | 11 193 | ... | *-83 | 26 | 19 143 |
| Cambodia | *2002 | 3 | ... | ... | ... | 3 | ... | 182 | ... |
| | 2003 | 3 | ... | ... | ... | 3 | ... | *178 | ... |
| | 2004 | 2 | ... | ... | ... | 2 | ... | *183 | ... |
| | 2005 | 4 | ... | ... | ... | 4 | ... | *187 | ... |
| China[2] | 2002 | 958 234 | 726 772 | 167 000 | 37 540 | 26 922 | 5 104 | 104 577 | 72 812 |
| | 2003 | 1 098 103 | 860 139 | 169 600 | 40 246 | 28 119 | -278 | 128 182 | 80 862 |
| | 2004 | 1 242 421 | 995 163 | 175 873 | 36 897 | 34 488 | -124 | 179 041 | 72 578 |
| | 2005 | 1 366 651 | 1 101 259 | 181 353 | 45 337 | 38 702 | -4 162 | 182 116 | 68 796 |
| China, Hong Kong SAR | 2002 | ... | ... | ... | ... | ... | -45 | 22 101 | 1 342 |
| | 2003 | ... | ... | ... | ... | ... | -114 | 22 620 | 1 481 |
| | 2004 | ... | ... | ... | ... | ... | -2 | 24 563 | 1 635 |
| | 2005 | ... | ... | ... | ... | ... | -546 | 23 998 | 2 686 |
| China, Macao SAR | 2002 | ... | ... | ... | ... | ... | -8 | 613 | 0 |
| | 2003 | ... | ... | ... | ... | ... | -3 | 626 | 0 |
| | 2004 | ... | ... | ... | ... | ... | 18 | 760 | 0 |
| | 2005 | ... | ... | ... | ... | ... | 16 | 785 | 0 |

**Production, trade and consumption of commercial energy**—Thousand metric tons of oil equivalent and kilograms per capita (*continued*)

**Production, commerce et consommation d'énergie commerciale**—Milliers de tonnes d'équivalent pétrole et kilogrammes par habitant (*suite*)

| Bunkers - Soutes | | | Consumption - Consommation | | | | | | | |
|---|---|---|---|---|---|---|---|---|---|---|
| Air / Avion | Sea / Maritime | Unallocated / Nondistribué | Per capita / Par habitant | Total / Totale | Solids / Solides | Liquids / Liquides | Gas / Gaz | Electricity / Electricité | Year / Année | Région, pays ou zone |
| 307 | 569 | 12 540 | 2 134 | 53 841 | 17 | 22 296 | 26 483 | 5 045 | 2002 | Venezuela (Rép. Bolivar. du) |
| 241 | 517 | 15 177 | 1 998 | 51 357 | 41 | 21 809 | 24 288 | 5 219 | 2003 | |
| 606 | 649 | 1 023 | 2 130 | 55 642 | 0 | 23 156 | 26 473 | 6 013 | 2004 | |
| 640 | 618 | 3 147 | 2 194 | 58 313 | 36 | 26 047 | 25 779 | 6 451 | 2005 | |
| 31 727 | 55 309 | 187 691 | 783 | 2 949 525 | 1 225 990 | 1 048 445 | 573 843 | 101 247 | 2002 | Asie |
| 31 526 | 58 543 | 213 003 | 833 | 3 168 453 | 1 386 081 | 1 069 023 | 612 229 | 101 120 | 2003 | |
| 36 000 | 63 153 | 219 609 | 909 | 3 493 208 | 1 579 365 | 1 143 917 | 656 781 | 113 146 | 2004 | |
| 39 030 | 66 638 | 221 887 | 957 | 3 721 269 | 1 715 641 | 1 154 482 | 729 995 | 121 151 | 2005 | |
| *5 | … | … | *8 | *164 | 15 | *84 | 7 | 58 | 2002 | Afghanistan |
| *8 | … | … | 8 | 178 | 24 | *83 | 6 | 64 | 2003 | |
| 0 | … | … | 12 | 273 | 24 | 188 | 3 | 58 | 2004 | |
| *10 | … | … | *12 | *276 | *23 | *191 | *2 | *60 | 2005 | |
| 53 | … | 0 | 466 | 1 550 | 13 | 276 | 953 | 308 | 2002 | Arménie |
| 27 | … | 0 | 467 | 1 773 | 19 | 316 | 1 119 | 318 | 2003 | |
| 39 | … | 0 | 583 | 1 872 | 0 | 311 | 1 246 | 315 | 2004 | |
| 45 | … | 0 | 665 | 2 139 | 0 | 333 | 1 488 | 319 | 2005 | |
| 103 | … | 627 | 1 422 | 11 575 | … | 3 207 | 8 070 | 298 | 2002 | Azerbaïdjan |
| 201 | … | 492 | 1 516 | 12 438 | … | 3 812 | 8 280 | 347 | 2003 | |
| 228 | … | 77 | 1 641 | 13 567 | … | 4 170 | 9 042 | 354 | 2004 | |
| 428 | … | 575 | 1 745 | 14 568 | … | 5 177 | 9 029 | 362 | 2005 | |
| 426 | … | 1 810 | 11 029 | 7 413 | … | 1 305 | 6 108 | … | 2002 | Bahreïn |
| 477 | … | 1 683 | 11 114 | 7 662 | … | 1 362 | 6 300 | … | 2003 | |
| 521 | … | 1 719 | 11 297 | 7 989 | … | 1 437 | 6 552 | … | 2004 | |
| 563 | … | 1 854 | 11 852 | 8 589 | … | 1 648 | 6 941 | … | 2005 | |
| 209 | 36 | 403 | 93 | 13 379 | 350 | 3 282 | 9 655 | 92 | 2002 | Bangladesh |
| 234 | 36 | 474 | 105 | 14 207 | 350 | 3 374 | 10 386 | 97 | 2003 | |
| 242 | 36 | 426 | 110 | 14 994 | 350 | 3 367 | 11 171 | 105 | 2004 | |
| 279 | 36 | 472 | 117 | 16 260 | 350 | 3 788 | 12 010 | 111 | 2005 | |
| … | … | … | 66 | 138 | 43 | 52 | … | 42 | 2002 | Bhoutan* |
| … | … | … | ·63 | 134 | 42 | 49 | … | 42 | 2003 | |
| … | … | … | 65 | 141 | 45 | 53 | … | 43 | 2004 | |
| … | … | … | 63 | 142 | 45 | 53 | … | 44 | 2005 | |
| … | … | -293 | 7 405 | 2 525 | … | 1 142 | 1 383 | … | 2002 | Brunéi Darussalam |
| … | … | -358 | 7 318 | 2 539 | … | 1 131 | 1 409 | … | 2003 | |
| … | … | -519 | 7 831 | 2 817 | … | 1 243 | 1 574 | … | 2004 | |
| … | … | -511 | 7 512 | 2 780 | … | 1 186 | 1 594 | … | 2005 | |
| … | … | … | 14 | 185 | … | 182 | … | 3 | *2002 | Cambodge |
| … | … | … | *14 | *182 | … | *178 | … | 4 | 2003 | |
| … | … | … | *14 | *185 | … | *178 | … | 8 | 2004 | |
| … | … | … | *14 | *190 | … | *180 | … | 11 | 2005 | |
| 390 | 3 935 | 57 858 | 718 | 922 713 | 677 435 | 183 591 | 35 402 | 26 285 | 2002 | Chine[2] |
| 339 | 2 503 | 64 698 | 835 | 1 078 160 | 810 955 | 200 849 | 38 871 | 27 486 | 2003 | |
| 129 | 289 | 80 617 | 976 | 1 267 972 | 957 800 | 241 481 | 34 725 | 33 966 | 2004 | |
| 321 | 927 | 78 315 | 1 075 | 1 404 569 | 1 078 356 | 245 348 | 42 695 | 38 170 | 2005 | |
| 3 923 | 4 997 | … | 1 758 | 11 884 | 4 479 | 4 497 | 2 220 | 688 | 2002 | Chine, Hong Kong RAS |
| 3 547 | 5 411 | … | 1 805 | 12 295 | 5 743 | 4 498 | 1 418 | 635 | 2003 | |
| 3 243 | 7 724 | … | 1 764 | 11 963 | 5 244 | 4 089 | 2 049 | 580 | 2004 | |
| 3 763 | 5 717 | … | 1 817 | 12 378 | 5 839 | 3 931 | 2 048 | 559 | 2005 | |
| … | … | … | 1 406 | 621 | … | 604 | … | 17 | 2002 | Chine, Macao RAS |
| … | … | … | 1 404 | 630 | … | 614 | … | 15 | 2003 | |
| … | … | … | 1 594 | 742 | … | 729 | … | 13 | 2004 | |
| … | … | … | 1 574 | 768 | … | 739 | … | 29 | 2005 | |

49    Production, trade and consumption of commercial energy— Thousand metric tons of oil equivalent and kilograms per capita (*continued*)

Production, commerce et consommation d'énergie commerciale— Milliers de tonnes d'équivalent pétrole et kilogrammes par habitant (*suite*)

| Region, country or area | Year Année | Primary energy production – Production d'énergie primaire | | | | | Changes in stocks Variations des stocks | Imports Importations | Exports Exportations |
|---|---|---|---|---|---|---|---|---|---|
| | | Total Totale | Solids Solides | Liquids Liquides | Gas Gaz | Electricity Electricité | | | |
| Cyprus | 2002 | 0 | ... | ... | ... | 0 | 65 | 2 570 | ... |
| | 2003 | 0 | ... | ... | ... | 0 | -67 | 2 654 | ... |
| | 2004 | 0 | ... | ... | ... | 0 | -62 | 2 401 | ... |
| | 2005 | 0 | ... | ... | ... | 0 | 71 | 2 802 | ... |
| Georgia | 2002 | 675 | 4 | 74 | 16 | 582 | -43 | 1 363 | 112 |
| | 2003 | 723 | 5 | 140 | 17 | 561 | -23 | 1 514 | 124 |
| | 2004 | 634 | 5 | 98 | 11 | 520 | 0 | 1 699 | 106 |
| | 2005 | 618 | 3 | 67 | 12 | 536 | 0 | 2 067 | 90 |
| India | 2002 | 271 233 | 203 722 | 37 456 | 22 884 | 7 171 | 734 | 102 843 | 8 124 |
| | 2003 | 285 806 | 215 981 | 37 557 | 24 270 | 7 998 | 978 | 110 674 | 12 850 |
| | 2004 | 299 690 | 228 921 | 37 958 | 24 075 | 8 738 | 1 532 | 120 102 | 15 877 |
| | 2005 | 314 231 | 243 013 | 36 651 | 24 490 | 10 077 | 6 082 | 127 989 | 16 629 |
| Indonesia | 2002 | 201 842 | 72 360 | 62 524 | 65 566 | 1 391 | -1 302 | 31 187 | 123 580 |
| | 2003 | 212 945 | 80 695 | 63 077 | 67 850 | 1 324 | 310 | 32 969 | 128 988 |
| | 2004 | 224 971 | 92 646 | 60 648 | 70 273 | 1 404 | 0 | 40 593 | 135 174 |
| | 2005 | 237 529 | 106 543 | 58 661 | 70 832 | 1 493 | 2 | 42 482 | 138 511 |
| Iran (Islamic Rep. of) | 2002 | 243 393 | 877 | 176 827 | 64 995 | 695 | -138 | 8 687 | 111 727 |
| | 2003 | 271 356 | 862 | 195 996 | 73 544 | 954 | -132 | 10 575 | 131 710 |
| | 2004 | 286 969 | 872 | 203 407 | 81 776 | 914 | 0 | 12 821 | 136 955 |
| | 2005 | 313 208 | 931 | 220 109 | 90 784 | 1 384 | 0 | 12 822 | 150 777 |
| Iraq | 2002 | 102 720 | ... | 100 577 | 2 088 | 56 | 0 | 0 | 72 069 |
| | 2003 | 67 456 | ... | 66 003 | 1 416 | 37 | 0 | 393 | 41 737 |
| | 2004 | 101 482 | ... | 99 016 | 2 423 | 42 | 459 | 4 473 | 76 100 |
| | 2005 | 94 215 | ... | 91 766 | 2 405 | 45 | 448 | 5 133 | 68 533 |
| Israel | 2002 | 117 | 101 | 5 | 8 | 3 | 195 | 23 229 | 2 788 |
| | 2003 | 111 | 96 | 3 | 8 | 4 | -103 | 23 863 | 3 092 |
| | 2004 | 1 143 | 97 | 2 | 1 041 | 3 | -201 | 23 248 | 3 590 |
| | 2005 | 1 529 | 91 | 2 | 1 433 | 3 | 548 | 22 888 | 3 926 |
| Japan | 2002 | 36 984 | ... | 608 | 2 796 | 33 580 | -1 400 | 419 787 | 4 886 |
| | 2003 | 33 497 | ... | 670 | 2 884 | 29 943 | -383 | 430 314 | 4 843 |
| | 2004 | 37 223 | ... | 692 | 2 994 | 33 537 | -1 135 | 437 431 | 5 090 |
| | 2005 | 37 952 | ... | 733 | 3 179 | 34 040 | 2 443 | 439 811 | 8 984 |
| Jordan | 2002 | 216 | ... | 2 | 209 | 5 | 7 | 5 056 | 0 |
| | 2003 | 243 | ... | 2 | 237 | *5 | -47 | 5 241 | 0 |
| | 2004 | 247 | ... | 1 | 241 | 5 | 117 | 6 393 | 0 |
| | 2005 | 205 | ... | 1 | 199 | 5 | 163 | 7 117 | 0 |
| Kazakhstan | 2002 | 89 680 | 35 625 | 47 682 | 5 609 | 764 | 41 | 12 518 | 62 009 |
| | 2003 | 98 890 | 39 172 | 51 933 | 7 043 | 742 | 39 | 12 578 | 68 999 |
| | 2004 | 121 413 | 39 936 | 60 185 | 20 599 | 693 | 17 | 17 004 | 82 047 |
| | 2005 | 126 295 | 40 015 | 62 329 | 23 275 | 675 | 712 | 16 744 | 85 643 |
| Korea, Dem. P. R. | 2002 | 19 204 | 18 291 | ... | ... | 913 | 106 | 1 487 | 210 |
| | 2003 | 19 633 | 18 625 | ... | ... | 1 008 | 0 | 1 371 | 210 |
| | 2004 | 20 118 | 19 043 | ... | ... | 1 075 | 0 | 1 368 | 210 |
| | 2005 | 21 224 | 20 095 | ... | ... | 1 129 | 0 | 1 202 | 210 |
| Korea, Republic of | 2002 | 12 193 | 1 493 | 1 | 0 | 10 700 | -1 127 | 190 099 | 24 648 |
| | 2003 | 13 232 | 1 484 | 2 | 0 | 11 746 | 2 482 | 191 379 | 22 427 |
| | 2004 | 13 190 | 1 436 | 4 | 0 | 11 750 | 959 | 201 224 | 25 402 |
| | 2005 | 14 908 | 1 274 | 65 | 490 | 13 079 | -4 504 | 199 350 | 29 636 |
| Kuwait | 2002 | 104 190 | ... | 95 377 | 8 813 | ... | ... | 484 | 70 821 |
| | 2003 | 124 723 | ... | 114 453 | 10 269 | ... | ... | 589 | 85 707 |
| | 2004 | 135 274 | ... | 124 221 | 11 053 | ... | ... | 113 | 93 408 |
| | 2005 | 150 065 | ... | 137 670 | 12 394 | ... | ... | 1 | 105 226 |

# 49

**Production, trade and consumption of commercial energy**—Thousand metric tons of oil equivalent and kilograms per capita (*continued*)

**Production, commerce et consommation d'énergie commerciale**—Milliers de tonnes d'équivalent pétrole et kilogrammes par habitant (*suite*)

| Bunkers - Soutes | | | Consumption - Consommation | | | | | | | |
|---|---|---|---|---|---|---|---|---|---|---|
| Air / Avion | Sea / Maritime | Unallocated / Nondistribué | Per capita / Par habitant | Total / Totale | Solids / Solides | Liquids / Liquides | Gas / Gaz | Electricity / Electricité | Year / Année | Région, pays ou zone |
| 304 | 138 | 44 | 2 861 | 2 020 | 41 | 1 979 | ... | 0 | 2002 | Chypre |
| 330 | 124 | 36 | 3 054 | 2 231 | 40 | 2 191 | ... | 0 | 2003 | |
| 304 | 55 | 6 | 2 800 | 2 097 | 42 | 2 055 | ... | 0 | 2004 | |
| 300 | 291 | 0 | 2 792 | 2 140 | 39 | 2 100 | ... | 0 | 2005 | |
| 24 | ... | 14 | 443 | 1 931 | 14 | 535 | 755 | 627 | 2002 | Géorgie |
| 27 | ... | 54 | 475 | 2 055 | 30 | 528 | 857 | 640 | 2003 | |
| 38 | ... | 21 | 502 | 2 168 | 7 | 527 | 1 004 | 630 | 2004 | |
| 38 | ... | 15 | 583 | 2 542 | 19 | 676 | 1 195 | 652 | 2005 | |
| 2 329 | 39 | 30 488 | 316 | 332 383 | 219 802 | 82 409 | 22 884 | 7 287 | 2002 | Inde |
| 2 470 | 31 | 33 221 | 325 | 346 950 | 230 306 | 84 230 | 24 270 | 8 144 | 2003 | |
| 2 900 | 7 | 31 354 | 341 | 368 142 | 246 275 | 88 909 | 24 075 | 8 884 | 2004 | |
| 3 400 | 8 | 32 325 | 351 | 383 795 | 259 095 | 89 987 | 24 490 | 10 223 | 2005 | |
| 539 | 190 | 1 101 | 514 | 108 923 | 20 493 | 58 021 | 29 017 | 1 391 | 2002 | Indonésie |
| 811 | 490 | 4 682 | 515 | 110 635 | 21 481 | 57 178 | 30 652 | 1 324 | 2003 | |
| 794 | 358 | 7 005 | 562 | 122 235 | 25 372 | 62 064 | 33 396 | 1 404 | 2004 | |
| 729 | 374 | 12 258 | 583 | 128 139 | 28 957 | 62 524 | 35 165 | 1 493 | 2005 | |
| *818 | 606 | 2 143 | 2 088 | 136 869 | 1 330 | 66 070 | 68 758 | 711 | 2002 | Iran (Rép. islamique d') |
| 800 | 585 | 626 | 2 231 | 148 288 | 1 287 | 70 276 | 75 723 | 1 003 | 2003 | |
| 812 | 619 | 155 | 2 389 | 161 195 | 1 117 | 75 154 | 83 982 | 942 | 2004 | |
| 882 | 654 | -3 107 | 2 582 | 176 769 | 1 267 | 82 979 | 91 198 | 1 325 | 2005 | |
| 516 | ... | 4 437 | 1 006 | 25 709 | ... | 23 566 | 2 088 | 56 | 2002 | Iraq |
| 418 | ... | 3 648 | 837 | 22 052 | ... | 20 599 | 1 416 | 37 | 2003 | |
| 1 200 | ... | 1 382 | 988 | 26 821 | ... | 24 242 | 2 423 | 156 | 2004 | |
| 774 | ... | 1 637 | 1 017 | 27 962 | ... | 25 394 | 2 405 | 164 | 2005 | |
| 4 | 269 | -13 | 3 031 | 20 102 | 8 828 | 11 382 | 8 | -117 | 2002 | Israël |
| *4 | 272 | 400 | 3 009 | 20 309 | 8 963 | 11 461 | 8 | -123 | 2003 | |
| *4 | 229 | -240 | 3 058 | 21 009 | 9 110 | 10 980 | 1 041 | -122 | 2004 | |
| *4 | 259 | -1 272 | 2 998 | 20 952 | 8 578 | 11 080 | 1 433 | -140 | 2005 | |
| 6 938 | 4 659 | 13 114 | 3 362 | 428 574 | 111 962 | 209 104 | 73 928 | 33 580 | 2002 | Japon |
| 6 720 | 5 120 | 19 512 | 3 352 | 427 998 | 115 430 | 203 378 | 79 247 | 29 943 | 2003 | |
| 6 951 | 5 360 | 18 671 | 3 441 | 439 718 | 126 226 | 201 528 | 78 427 | 33 537 | 2004 | |
| 7 042 | 6 024 | 18 706 | 3 401 | 434 563 | 121 641 | 200 484 | 78 398 | 34 040 | 2005 | |
| 229 | 1 | 121 | 964 | 4 913 | ... | 4 672 | 209 | 32 | 2002 | Jordanie |
| 190 | 8 | 157 | 989 | 5 175 | ... | 4 906 | 237 | 32 | 2003 | |
| 307 | 48 | 188 | 1 172 | 5 980 | ... | 4 575 | 1 329 | 76 | 2004 | |
| 328 | 79 | 317 | 1 176 | 6 434 | ... | 4 828 | 1 538 | 69 | 2005 | |
| ... | ... | 1 116 | 2 627 | 39 032 | 26 577 | 8 054 | 3 503 | 898 | 2002 | Kazakhstan |
| ... | ... | 237 | 2 830 | 42 194 | 28 944 | 7 747 | 4 888 | 615 | 2003 | |
| ... | ... | 1 428 | 3 663 | 54 925 | 29 060 | 10 008 | 15 351 | 506 | 2004 | |
| ... | ... | 569 | 3 705 | 56 116 | 29 562 | 6 918 | 19 359 | 276 | 2005 | |
| ... | ... | 16 | 903 | 20 359 | 18 323 | 1 122 | | 913 | 2002 | Corée, R. p. dém. de |
| ... | ... | 15 | 917 | 20 779 | 18 662 | 1 109 | ... | 1 008 | 2003 | |
| ... | ... | 13 | 933 | 21 263 | 19 086 | 1 102 | ... | 1 075 | 2004 | |
| ... | ... | 10 | 987 | 22 207 | 20 152 | 925 | ... | 1 129 | 2005 | |
| 904 | 5 805 | 17 810 | 3 238 | 154 253 | 47 789 | 72 199 | 23 566 | 10 700 | 2002 | Corée, République de |
| 1 176 | 6 480 | 16 542 | 3 238 | 155 504 | 49 565 | 69 741 | 24 453 | 11 746 | 2003 | |
| 1 286 | 7 135 | 22 762 | 3 263 | 156 870 | 51 967 | 65 055 | 28 097 | 11 750 | 2004 | |
| 2 373 | 10 169 | 19 036 | 3 262 | 157 547 | 52 231 | 61 807 | 30 429 | 13 079 | 2005 | |
| 471 | 538 | 7 597 | 10 684 | 24 167 | ... | 15 353 | 8 813 | ... | 2002 | Koweït |
| 739 | 556 | 8 886 | 12 118 | 28 180 | ... | 17 910 | 10 269 | ... | 2003 | |
| 552 | 567 | 8 779 | 12 920 | 30 887 | ... | 19 834 | 11 053 | ... | 2004 | |
| 595 | 528 | 8 638 | 13 815 | 33 947 | ... | 21 553 | 12 394 | ... | 2005 | |

49 Production, trade and consumption of commercial energy—Thousand metric tons of oil equivalent and kilograms per capita *(continued)*

Production, commerce et consommation d'énergie commerciale—Milliers de tonnes d'équivalent pétrole et kilogrammes par habitant *(suite)*

| Region, country or area | Year Année | Primary energy production – Production d'énergie primaire | | | | | Changes in stocks Variations des stocks | Imports Importations | Exports Exportations |
|---|---|---|---|---|---|---|---|---|---|
| | | Total Totale | Solids Solides | Liquids Liquides | Gas Gaz | Electricity Electricité | | | |
| Kyrgyzstan | 2002 | 1 174 | 143 | 76 | 28 | 928 | -28 | 1 590 | 236 |
| | 2003 | 1 380 | 123 | 69 | 25 | 1 162 | -23 | 1 646 | 303 |
| | 2004 | 1 448 | 135 | 74 | 27 | 1 212 | -10 | 1 791 | 464 |
| | 2005 | 1 422 | 99 | 74 | 23 | 1 226 | 0 | 1 715 | 357 |
| Lao People's Dem. Rep.* | 2002 | 307 | 199 | ... | ... | 107 | ... | 144 | 64 |
| | 2003 | 307 | 199 | ... | ... | 107 | ... | 144 | 64 |
| | 2004 | 310 | 203 | ... | ... | 107 | ... | 149 | 64 |
| | 2005 | 318 | 210 | ... | ... | 108 | ... | 149 | 65 |
| Lebanon | 2002 | 106 | ... | ... | ... | 106 | -15 | 4 987 | ... |
| | 2003 | 69 | ... | ... | ... | 69 | 0 | 5 749 | ... |
| | 2004 | 97 | ... | ... | ... | 97 | 0 | 5 003 | ... |
| | 2005 | 90 | ... | ... | ... | 90 | -418 | 4 812 | ... |
| Malaysia | 2002 | *80 916 | 223 | 37 546 | *42 691 | 456 | 733 | 19 946 | 43 568 |
| | 2003 | *84 384 | 107 | 39 102 | *44 681 | 494 | -587 | 23 028 | 45 829 |
| | 2004 | 90 405 | 268 | 37 548 | 52 089 | 501 | 397 | 28 806 | 49 128 |
| | 2005 | 95 925 | 477 | 37 627 | 57 375 | 446 | 110 | 27 722 | 25 664 |
| Maldives | 2002 | ... | ... | ... | ... | ... | ... | 307 | *80 |
| | 2003 | ... | ... | ... | ... | ... | ... | 273 | *78 |
| | 2004 | ... | ... | ... | ... | ... | ... | 313 | *72 |
| | *2005 | ... | ... | ... | ... | ... | ... | 315 | 77 |
| Mongolia | 2002 | 1 742 | 1 742 | ... | ... | ... | ... | 496 | 1 |
| | 2003 | 1 742 | 1 742 | ... | ... | ... | ... | 542 | 101 |
| | 2004 | 2 111 | 2 111 | ... | ... | ... | ... | 595 | 361 |
| | 2005 | 2 311 | 2 311 | ... | ... | ... | ... | 577 | 490 |
| Myanmar | 2002 | 7 450 | 344 | 872 | 6 042 | 192 | -272 | 982 | 5 494 |
| | 2003 | 9 109 | 609 | 977 | 7 330 | 193 | -88 | 976 | 6 389 |
| | 2004 | 11 906 | 645 | 1 026 | 10 028 | 207 | -18 | 1 139 | 8 906 |
| | 2005 | 13 091 | 794 | 1 114 | 10 925 | 258 | 0 | 1 269 | 9 654 |
| Nepal | 2002 | 191 | 8 | ... | ... | 182 | ... | 866 | 16 |
| | 2003 | 202 | 8 | ... | ... | 195 | ... | 932 | 18 |
| | 2004 | 209 | 8 | ... | ... | 201 | ... | 965 | 18 |
| | 2005 | 215 | 8 | ... | ... | 207 | ... | 991 | 19 |
| Occupied Palestinian Terr. | 2002 | ... | ... | ... | ... | ... | 0 | 388 | ... |
| | 2003 | ... | ... | ... | ... | ... | 0 | 379 | ... |
| | 2004 | ... | ... | ... | ... | ... | *-1 | 390 | ... |
| | 2005 | ... | ... | ... | ... | ... | 0 | *394 | ... |
| Oman | 2002 | 60 002 | ... | 44 940 | 15 062 | ... | -1 286 | 385 | 50 153 |
| | 2003 | 57 595 | ... | 41 078 | 16 517 | ... | -1 562 | 299 | 47 510 |
| | 2004 | 56 115 | ... | 39 249 | 16 866 | ... | -1 016 | 422 | 46 370 |
| | 2005 | 56 577 | ... | 38 899 | 17 678 | ... | -1 485 | 701 | 46 644 |
| Pakistan | 2002 | 26 491 | 1 574 | 3 274 | 19 818 | 1 826 | -41 | 16 609 | 244 |
| | 2003 | 31 409 | 1 566 | 3 314 | 24 457 | 2 071 | -225 | 13 100 | 503 |
| | 2004 | 34 686 | 2 169 | 3 415 | 26 653 | 2 448 | -68 | 16 338 | 301 |
| | 2005 | 36 761 | 2 304 | 3 490 | 28 100 | 2 867 | *-28 | 16 652 | 411 |
| Philippines | 2002 | 4 135 | 786 | 277 | 1 585 | 1 487 | *-411 | 22 055 | 963 |
| | 2003 | 6 107 | 2 149 | 20 | 2 416 | 1 523 | 116 | 19 242 | 881 |
| | 2004 | 5 227 | 1 273 | 19 | 2 311 | 1 624 | -253 | 20 370 | 613 |
| | 2005 | 6 126 | 1 477 | 29 | 3 047 | 1 573 | -900 | 19 068 | 1 164 |
| Qatar | 2002 | 69 057 | ... | 40 215 | 28 842 | ... | 1 866 | ... | 48 199 |
| | 2003 | 71 131 | ... | 40 987 | 30 144 | ... | 2 598 | ... | 49 483 |
| | 2004 | 82 182 | ... | 43 494 | 38 688 | ... | -768 | ... | 62 622 |
| | 2005 | 82 030 | ... | 39 378 | 42 652 | ... | -1 307 | ... | 64 517 |

**Production, trade and consumption of commercial energy**—Thousand metric tons of oil equivalent and kilograms per capita (*continued*)

**Production, commerce et consommation d'énergie commerciale**—Milliers de tonnes d'équivalent pétrole et kilogrammes par habitant (*suite*)

| Bunkers - Soutes | | | Consumption - Consommation | | | | | | | |
|---|---|---|---|---|---|---|---|---|---|---|
| Air Avion | Sea Maritime | Unallocated Nondistribué | Per capita Par habitant | Total Totale | Solids Solides | Liquids Liquides | Gas Gaz | Electricity Electricité | Year Année | Région, pays ou zone |
| ... | ... | 2 | 511 | 2 554 | 491 | 368 | 826 | 869 | 2002 | Kirghizistan |
| ... | ... | 5 | 544 | 2 741 | 588 | 448 | 681 | 1 024 | 2003 | |
| ... | ... | 2 | 546 | 2 783 | 555 | 559 | 744 | 926 | 2004 | |
| ... | ... | 2 | 540 | 2 778 | 516 | 580 | 686 | 995 | 2005 | |
| ... | ... | ... | 70 | 386 | 199 | 126 | ... | 60 | 2002 | Rép. dém. pop. lao* |
| ... | ... | ... | 68 | 387 | 199 | 125 | ... | 62 | 2003 | |
| ... | ... | ... | 68 | 395 | 203 | 131 | ... | 62 | 2004 | |
| ... | ... | ... | 72 | 402 | 210 | 131 | ... | 62 | 2005 | |
| 129 | 15 | ... | 1 381 | 4 965 | 141 | 4 672 | ... | 152 | 2002 | Liban |
| *129 | 0 | ... | 1 526 | 5 688 | 141 | 5 479 | ... | 69 | 2003 | |
| 131 | 15 | ... | 1 312 | 4 954 | 140 | 4 699 | ... | 115 | 2004 | |
| 152 | 15 | ... | 1 347 | 5 154 | 140 | 4 885 | ... | 129 | 2005 | |
| 1 786 | 90 | 6 485 | 1 973 | 48 211 | 3 676 | 20 277 | *23 803 | 456 | 2002 | Malaisie |
| 1 853 | 71 | 10 501 | 1 988 | 49 750 | 5 336 | 19 592 | *24 328 | 494 | 2003 | |
| 2 074 | 85 | 8 607 | 2 304 | 58 927 | 9 293 | 21 176 | 28 002 | 456 | 2004 | |
| 1 954 | 59 | 8 626 | 3 327 | 86 943 | 7 966 | 21 143 | 57 580 | 254 | 2005 | |
| ... | ... | ... | 806 | 226 | ... | 226 | ... | ... | 2002 | Maldives |
| ... | ... | ... | 682 | 195 | ... | 195 | ... | ... | 2003 | |
| ... | ... | ... | 830 | 240 | ... | 240 | ... | ... | 2004 | |
| ... | ... | ... | 808 | 237 | ... | 237 | ... | ... | *2005 | |
| ... | ... | ... | 904 | 2 236 | 1 742 | 482 | ... | 13 | 2002 | Mongolie |
| ... | ... | ... | 841 | 2 183 | 1 642 | 527 | ... | 14 | 2003 | |
| ... | ... | ... | 902 | 2 345 | 1 751 | 580 | ... | 14 | 2004 | |
| ... | ... | ... | 936 | 2 398 | 1 822 | 562 | ... | 13 | 2005 | |
| 60 | 2 | 310 | 58 | 2 838 | 52 | 1 477 | 1 117 | 192 | 2002 | Myanmar |
| 69 | 3 | 216 | 71 | 3 496 | 97 | 1 722 | 1 484 | 193 | 2003 | |
| 66 | 3 | 60 | 81 | 4 028 | 102 | 1 800 | 1 919 | 207 | 2004 | |
| 51 | 3 | 56 | 82 | 4 596 | 106 | 1 878 | 2 354 | 258 | 2005 | |
| 43 | ... | ... | 42 | 997 | 160 | 659 | ... | 179 | 2002 | Népal |
| 40 | ... | ... | 44 | 1 077 | 204 | 683 | ... | 190 | 2003 | |
| 41 | ... | ... | 45 | 1 114 | 211 | 707 | ... | 196 | 2004 | |
| 42 | ... | ... | 45 | 1 145 | 216 | 727 | ... | 202 | 2005 | |
| ... | ... | ... | 114 | 388 | 3 | 187 | ... | 198 | 2002 | Terr. palestinien occupé |
| ... | ... | ... | 108 | 379 | 0 | 180 | ... | 199 | 2003 | |
| ... | ... | ... | 107 | 391 | *1 | 224 | ... | 166 | 2004 | |
| ... | ... | ... | *105 | *394 | 0 | *229 | ... | *166 | 2005 | |
| 369 | 34 | 57 | 4 358 | 11 060 | ... | 3 616 | 7 445 | ... | 2002 | Oman |
| 369 | 1 | 220 | 4 852 | 11 357 | ... | 3 313 | 8 044 | ... | 2003 | |
| *200 | 1 | 150 | 4 485 | 10 833 | ... | 3 358 | 7 474 | ... | 2004 | |
| 281 | 1 | 415 | 4 555 | 11 424 | ... | 3 625 | 7 799 | ... | 2005 | |
| 285 | 42 | 1 075 | 290 | 41 496 | 2 323 | 17 521 | 19 827 | 1 826 | 2002 | Pakistan |
| 142 | 15 | 1 165 | 294 | 42 910 | 2 659 | 13 716 | 24 463 | 2 071 | 2003 | |
| 168 | 63 | 1 292 | 331 | 49 268 | 4 460 | 15 700 | 26 660 | 2 448 | 2004 | |
| 214 | 72 | 1 727 | 337 | 51 020 | 4 272 | 15 778 | 28 103 | 2 867 | 2005 | |
| 610 | 226 | 463 | 306 | 24 340 | 5 698 | 15 570 | 1 585 | 1 487 | 2002 | Philippines |
| 588 | 185 | 984 | 279 | 22 595 | 4 304 | 14 353 | 2 416 | 1 523 | 2003 | |
| *619 | 139 | 867 | 286 | 23 612 | 4 947 | 14 730 | 2 311 | 1 624 | 2004 | |
| *722 | 120 | 785 | 277 | 23 302 | 4 767 | 13 915 | 3 047 | 1 573 | 2005 | |
| ... | ... | -90 | 27 716 | 19 021 | ... | 6 887 | 12 134 | ... | 2002 | Qatar |
| ... | ... | -127 | 26 051 | 19 101 | ... | 6 635 | 12 467 | ... | 2003 | |
| ... | ... | 1 139 | 24 602 | 19 114 | ... | 5 003 | 14 112 | ... | 2004 | |
| ... | ... | 1 173 | 21 713 | 17 649 | ... | 2 668 | 14 981 | ... | 2005 | |

**Production, trade and consumption of commercial energy** — Thousand metric tons of oil equivalent and kilograms per capita (*continued*)

**Production, commerce et consommation d'énergie commerciale** — Milliers de tonnes d'équivalent pétrole et kilogrammes par habitant (*suite*)

| Region, country or area | Year Année | Primary energy production – Production d'énergie primaire | | | | | Changes in stocks Variations des stocks | Imports Importations | Exports Exportations |
| | | Total Totale | Solids Solides | Liquids Liquides | Gas Gaz | Electricity Electricité | | | |
|---|---|---|---|---|---|---|---|---|---|
| Saudi Arabia | 2002 | 477 658 | ... | 424 237 | 53 421 | ... | 1 635 | 1 783 | 332 246 |
| | 2003 | 536 982 | ... | 481 008 | 55 975 | ... | 40 | 1 275 | 387 877 |
| | 2004 | 556 630 | ... | 495 418 | 61 212 | ... | -46 | 1 524 | 395 666 |
| | 2005 | 584 863 | ... | 518 469 | 66 394 | ... | 25 | 1 875 | 415 401 |
| Singapore | 2002 | ... | ... | ... | ... | ... | 85 | 86 039 | 38 475 |
| | 2003 | ... | ... | ... | ... | ... | -3 077 | 84 525 | 41 820 |
| | 2004 | ... | ... | ... | ... | ... | -1 256 | 96 971 | 46 290 |
| | 2005 | ... | ... | ... | ... | ... | -3 518 | 105 453 | 50 704 |
| Sri Lanka | 2002 | 232 | ... | ... | ... | 232 | 76 | 3 895 | 0 |
| | 2003 | 285 | ... | ... | ... | 285 | -114 | 3 496 | 0 |
| | 2004 | 255 | ... | ... | ... | 255 | -2 | 4 086 | 38 |
| | 2005 | 297 | ... | ... | ... | 297 | 41 | 4 013 | 0 |
| Syrian Arab Republic | 2002 | 37 574 | ... | 31 150 | 6 123 | 301 | 0 | 1 464 | 20 065 |
| | 2003 | 34 409 | ... | 28 000 | 6 168 | 241 | *11 | 1 100 | 16 983 |
| | 2004 | 30 058 | ... | 23 300 | 6 393 | 365 | -20 | 1 410 | 12 043 |
| | 2005 | 29 697 | ... | 22 828 | 6 573 | 296 | 18 | 1 288 | 11 292 |
| Tajikistan | 2002 | 1 355 | 27 | 16 | 27 | 1 285 | ... | 2 214 | 337 |
| | 2003 | 1 460 | 26 | 18 | 30 | 1 386 | ... | 2 111 | 398 |
| | 2004 | 1 460 | 29 | 18 | 30 | 1 383 | ... | 2 236 | 386 |
| | 2005 | 1 525 | 42 | 22 | 27 | 1 435 | ... | 2 324 | 371 |
| Thailand | 2002 | 34 946 | 8 623 | 8 574 | 17 106 | 643 | -1 363 | 48 059 | 8 089 |
| | 2003 | 35 923 | 8 289 | 10 113 | 16 893 | 628 | -936 | 52 192 | 7 870 |
| | 2004 | 36 439 | 8 824 | 10 348 | 16 747 | 520 | -981 | 58 712 | 8 564 |
| | 2005 | 39 556 | 9 184 | 11 871 | 18 002 | 499 | -1 286 | 57 150 | 8 938 |
| Timor-Leste* | 2002 | 7 317 | ... | 7 317 | ... | ... | ... | 53 | 7 242 |
| | 2003 | 7 317 | ... | 7 317 | ... | ... | ... | 53 | 7 242 |
| | 2004 | 7 367 | ... | 7 367 | ... | ... | ... | 58 | 7 291 |
| | 2005 | 7 394 | ... | 7 394 | ... | ... | ... | 58 | 7 318 |
| Turkey | 2002 | 17 502 | 11 827 | 2 420 | 346 | 2 909 | -222 | 55 546 | 2 251 |
| | 2003 | 16 544 | 10 630 | 2 351 | 512 | 3 051 | 437 | 62 760 | 3 729 |
| | 2004 | 17 000 | 10 144 | 2 251 | 629 | 3 975 | -453 | 65 413 | 4 515 |
| | 2005 | 19 151 | 12 657 | 2 258 | 821 | 3 415 | -644 | 70 292 | 4 939 |
| Turkmenistan | 2002 | 58 590 | ... | 10 174 | 48 416 | 0 | ... | 87 | 41 280 |
| | 2003 | 63 928 | ... | 10 390 | 53 538 | 0 | ... | 87 | 45 344 |
| | 2004 | 63 513 | ... | 10 120 | 53 393 | 0 | ... | 87 | 46 760 |
| | 2005 | 66 862 | ... | 9 849 | 57 013 | 0 | ... | 87 | 49 207 |
| United Arab Emirates | 2002 | 150 640 | ... | 110 200 | 40 440 | ... | ... | 9 180 | 101 617 |
| | 2003 | 174 931 | ... | 133 177 | 41 754 | ... | ... | 12 212 | 111 360 |
| | 2004 | 180 791 | ... | 137 649 | 43 142 | ... | ... | 13 659 | 125 971 |
| | 2005 | 182 461 | ... | 139 030 | 43 431 | ... | ... | 12 920 | 126 850 |
| Uzbekistan | 2002 | 61 543 | 738 | 7 524 | 52 737 | 545 | 18 | 1 839 | 5 441 |
| | 2003 | 61 512 | 516 | 8 046 | 52 405 | 546 | 12 | 2 296 | 8 059 |
| | 2004 | 62 239 | 727 | 7 533 | 53 415 | 564 | 17 | 2 174 | 10 300 |
| | 2005 | 61 964 | 809 | 6 203 | 54 425 | 527 | 19 | 1 952 | 12 405 |
| Viet Nam | 2002 | 32 490 | 11 130 | 17 167 | 2 571 | 1 622 | 0 | 10 111 | 21 487 |
| | 2003 | 33 521 | 11 690 | 17 131 | 3 009 | 1 690 | 0 | 10 437 | 21 571 |
| | 2004 | 45 408 | 17 850 | 20 844 | 5 127 | 1 587 | 700 | 11 526 | 27 018 |
| | 2005 | 51 111 | 22 677 | 19 462 | 6 890 | 2 082 | 633 | 12 347 | 32 271 |
| Yemen | 2002 | 21 618 | ... | 21 618 | ... | ... | 420 | 2 007 | 17 440 |
| | 2003 | 21 300 | ... | 21 300 | ... | ... | 567 | 2 425 | 17 065 |
| | 2004 | 20 050 | ... | 20 050 | ... | ... | 908 | 2 738 | 15 348 |
| | 2005 | 19 852 | ... | 19 852 | ... | ... | 920 | 2 829 | 14 911 |

**Production, trade and consumption of commercial energy**—Thousand metric tons of oil equivalent and kilograms per capita (*continued*)

**Production, commerce et consommation d'énergie commerciale**—Milliers de tonnes d'équivalent pétrole et kilogrammes par habitant (*suite*)

| Bunkers - Soutes | | | Consumption - Consommation | | | | | | | |
|---|---|---|---|---|---|---|---|---|---|---|
| Air Avion | Sea Maritime | Unallocated Nondistribué | Per capita Par habitant | Total Totale | Solids Solides | Liquids Liquides | Gas Gaz | Electricity Electricité | Year Année | Région, pays ou zone |
| 2 545 | 2 200 | 13 679 | 5 617 | 120 718 | ... | 67 297 | 53 421 | ... | 2002 | Arabie saoudite |
| 2 593 | 2 211 | 9 333 | 5 801 | 127 733 | ... | 71 759 | 55 975 | ... | 2003 | |
| 2 648 | 2 249 | 7 265 | 6 305 | 142 276 | ... | 81 064 | 61 212 | ... | 2004 | |
| 2 726 | 2 282 | 8 207 | 6 485 | 149 930 | ... | 83 536 | 66 394 | ... | 2005 | |
| 2 846 | 19 965 | 11 960 | 3 043 | 12 708 | 0 | 9 487 | 3 221 | ... | 2002 | Singapour |
| 2 420 | 20 662 | 9 188 | 3 228 | 13 512 | 0 | 8 529 | 4 983 | ... | 2003 | |
| 2 980 | 23 395 | 12 490 | 3 084 | 13 072 | 6 | 7 191 | 5 875 | ... | 2004 | |
| 3 184 | 25 292 | 15 015 | 3 403 | 14 776 | 2 | 8 179 | 6 595 | ... | 2005 | |
| 100 | 145 | 124 | 194 | 3 683 | 1 | 3 450 | | 232 | 2002 | Sri Lanka |
| 115 | 114 | 131 | 184 | 3 536 | 68 | 3 183 | ... | 285 | 2003 | |
| 132 | 119 | 118 | 202 | 3 937 | 67 | 3 615 | ... | 255 | 2004 | |
| 134 | 169 | 139 | 195 | 3 828 | 67 | 3 464 | ... | 297 | 2005 | |
| *109 | ... | 1 570 | 1 008 | 17 293 | 2 | 10 867 | 6 123 | 301 | 2002 | Rép. arabe syrienne |
| *100 | ... | 1 793 | 945 | 16 621 | 6 | 10 206 | 6 168 | 241 | 2003 | |
| 120 | ... | 1 653 | 983 | 17 671 | 3 | 10 910 | 6 393 | 365 | 2004 | |
| 108 | ... | 1 558 | 993 | 18 010 | 3 | 11 138 | 6 573 | 296 | 2005 | |
| 4 | ... | 12 | 494 | 3 216 | 30 | 1 135 | 698 | 1 352 | 2002 | Tadjikistan |
| 4 | ... | 15 | 475 | 3 154 | 30 | 1 226 | 511 | 1 387 | 2003 | |
| 4 | ... | 15 | 485 | 3 291 | 33 | 1 319 | 525 | 1 414 | 2004 | |
| 4 | ... | 17 | 499 | 3 457 | 47 | 1 417 | 537 | 1 456 | 2005 | |
| ... | ... | 5 191 | 1 131 | 71 053 | 12 768 | 33 852 | 23 571 | 862 | 2002 | Thaïlande |
| ... | ... | 7 343 | 1 170 | 73 796 | 13 281 | 35 800 | 23 899 | 815 | 2003 | |
| ... | ... | 6 707 | 1 268 | 80 809 | 14 859 | 40 882 | 24 289 | 779 | 2004 | |
| ... | ... | 7 252 | 1 262 | 81 760 | 14 367 | 40 331 | 26 238 | 823 | 2005 | |
| ... | ... | 0 | 56 | 53 | ... | 53 | ... | ... | 2002 | Timor-Leste* |
| ... | ... | 0 | 54 | 53 | ... | 53 | ... | ... | 2003 | |
| ... | ... | 0 | 57 | 58 | ... | 58 | ... | ... | 2004 | |
| ... | ... | 0 | 56 | 58 | ... | 58 | ... | ... | 2005 | |
| 867 | 537 | 3 301 | 952 | 66 315 | 20 518 | 26 245 | 16 373 | 3 180 | 2002 | Turquie |
| 904 | 626 | 3 063 | 1 005 | 70 545 | 22 127 | 25 629 | 19 690 | 3 100 | 2003 | |
| 974 | 1 008 | 3 462 | 1 025 | 72 907 | 22 646 | 25 556 | 20 788 | 3 917 | 2004 | |
| 1 090 | 1 072 | 3 720 | 1 086 | 79 266 | 25 530 | 25 097 | 25 324 | 3 315 | 2005 | |
| ... | ... | 512 | 3 647 | 16 885 | ... | 4 125 | 12 850 | -91 | 2002 | Turkménistan |
| ... | ... | 167 | 3 939 | 18 503 | ... | 4 333 | 14 262 | -92 | 2003 | |
| ... | ... | 25 | 3 528 | 16 814 | ... | 4 235 | 12 760 | -181 | 2004 | |
| ... | ... | 25 | 3 666 | 17 717 | ... | 4 343 | 13 625 | -251 | 2005 | |
| 1 271 | 8 253 | -1 091 | 13 273 | 49 826 | ... | 16 015 | 33 811 | ... | 2002 | Emirats arabes unis |
| 1 302 | 9 876 | 9 000 | 13 792 | 55 663 | ... | 20 607 | 35 055 | ... | 2003 | |
| 3 524 | 11 072 | -5 211 | 13 543 | 59 156 | ... | 22 581 | 36 574 | ... | 2004 | |
| 3 632 | 9 883 | -4 772 | 13 300 | 59 850 | ... | 22 773 | 37 077 | ... | 2005 | |
| ... | ... | -1 793 | 2 354 | 59 717 | 719 | 9 041 | 49 420 | 537 | 2002 | Ouzbékistan |
| ... | ... | -2 064 | 2 215 | 57 801 | 503 | 9 793 | 46 967 | 538 | 2003 | |
| ... | ... | -1 924 | 2 137 | 56 021 | 710 | 9 159 | 45 597 | 556 | 2004 | |
| ... | ... | -1 586 | 2 019 | 53 079 | 790 | 7 544 | 44 226 | 520 | 2005 | |
| 172 | ... | 0 | 263 | 20 945 | 6 896 | 9 856 | 2 571 | 1 622 | 2002 | Viet Nam |
| 159 | ... | 0 | 273 | 22 231 | 7 280 | 10 251 | 3 009 | 1 690 | 2003 | |
| 266 | ... | 0 | 352 | 28 952 | 10 430 | 11 808 | 5 127 | 1 587 | 2004 | |
| 265 | ... | 0 | 364 | 30 291 | 10 157 | 12 592 | 5 461 | 2 082 | 2005 | |
| 105 | 117 | 790 | 254 | 4 753 | ... | 4 753 | ... | ... | 2002 | Yémen |
| 94 | 126 | 678 | 268 | 5 194 | ... | 5 194 | ... | ... | 2003 | |
| 105 | 126 | 869 | 261 | 5 431 | ... | 5 431 | ... | ... | 2004 | |
| 105 | 126 | 865 | 274 | 5 754 | ... | 5 754 | ... | ... | 2005 | |

**Production, trade and consumption of commercial energy**—Thousand metric tons of oil equivalent and kilograms per capita (*continued*)

**Production, commerce et consommation d'énergie commerciale**—Milliers de tonnes d'équivalent pétrole et kilogrammes par habitant (*suite*)

| Region, country or area | Year Année | Primary energy production – Production d'énergie primaire | | | | | Changes in stocks Variations des stocks | Imports Importations | Exports Exportations |
|---|---|---|---|---|---|---|---|---|---|
| | | Total Totale | Solids Solides | Liquids Liquides | Gas Gaz | Electricity Electricité | | | |
| Europe | 2002 | 2 074 851 | 354 992 | 701 350 | 846 292 | 172 216 | 9 885 | 1 463 057 | 1 105 720 |
| | 2003 | 2 135 643 | 363 837 | 728 477 | 872 205 | 171 124 | 8 003 | 1 519 274 | 1 152 487 |
| | 2004 | 2 181 935 | 359 004 | 753 457 | 891 965 | 177 509 | 11 160 | 1 578 319 | 1 231 633 |
| | 2005 | 2 174 813 | 358 353 | 748 595 | 889 406 | 178 460 | 14 018 | 1 620 440 | 1 244 540 |
| Albania | 2002 | 726 | 18 | 393 | 13 | 302 | ... | 988 | 109 |
| | 2003 | 851 | 19 | 375 | 13 | 444 | ... | 935 | 64 |
| | 2004 | 931 | 26 | 420 | 15 | 470 | ... | 1 029 | 28 |
| | 2005 | 949 | 22 | 447 | 18 | 462 | ... | 955 | 0 |
| Austria | 2002 | 6 844 | 368 | 1 062 | 1 784 | 3 630 | -105 | 24 458 | 2 975 |
| | 2003 | 6 386 | 300 | 1 033 | 1 985 | 3 067 | -68 | 26 829 | 3 265 |
| | 2004 | 6 456 | 61 | 1 099 | 1 865 | 3 431 | 235 | 27 612 | 3 766 |
| | 2005 | 5 951 | 0 | 1 018 | 1 498 | 3 436 | 177 | 29 746 | 4 329 |
| Belarus | 2002 | 2 576 | 501 | 1 846 | 227 | 2 | 155 | 31 962 | 8 887 |
| | 2003 | 2 467 | 410 | 1 820 | 234 | 2 | -190 | 33 858 | 9 878 |
| | 2004 | 2 498 | 453 | 1 804 | 237 | 3 | 203 | 37 874 | 12 693 |
| | 2005 | 2 524 | 525 | 1 785 | 210 | 3 | -105 | 39 379 | 14 898 |
| Belgium | 2002 | 4 252 | 47 | ... | ... | 4 205 | -745 | 73 157 | 23 344 |
| | 2003 | 4 229 | 35 | ... | ... | 4 195 | 51 | 77 240 | 23 220 |
| | 2004 | 4 267 | 49 | ... | ... | 4 219 | 115 | 79 216 | 25 017 |
| | 2005 | 4 292 | 29 | 13 | ... | 4 250 | 391 | 78 139 | 25 703 |
| Bosnia and Herzegovina | 2002 | 5 518 | 5 065 | ... | ... | 453 | 133 | 1 303 | 183 |
| | 2003 | 5 327 | 4 862 | ... | ... | 465 | -126 | 1 437 | 272 |
| | 2004 | 5 555 | 5 047 | ... | ... | 507 | -117 | 1 499 | 265 |
| | 2005 | 5 866 | 5 397 | ... | ... | 469 | -112 | 1 786 | 308 |
| Bulgaria | 2002 | 6 369 | 4 326 | 37 | 34 | 1 971 | 479 | 11 441 | 2 357 |
| | 2003 | 6 343 | 4 513 | 30 | 31 | 1 770 | -332 | 11 508 | 2 089 |
| | 2004 | 6 421 | 4 345 | 30 | 311 | 1 735 | 461 | 12 340 | 2 899 |
| | 2005 | 6 555 | 4 040 | 30 | 474 | 2 011 | -24 | 13 092 | 3 306 |
| Croatia | 2002 | 3 773 | ... | 1 382 | 1 924 | 467 | 377 | 7 023 | 1 672 |
| | 2003 | 3 729 | ... | 1 317 | 1 987 | 424 | -142 | 7 171 | 1 842 |
| | 2004 | 3 876 | ... | 1 274 | 1 995 | 606 | -6 | 7 676 | 2 216 |
| | 2005 | 3 833 | ... | 1 206 | 2 072 | 554 | 4 | 7 859 | 2 326 |
| Czech Republic | 2002 | 25 566 | 23 090 | 492 | 127 | 1 856 | 29 | 19 708 | 7 685 |
| | 2003 | 26 102 | 23 019 | 558 | 146 | 2 379 | 107 | 19 978 | 7 801 |
| | 2004 | 26 955 | 23 624 | 640 | 206 | 2 485 | 462 | 19 739 | 7 349 |
| | 2005 | 25 612 | 22 345 | 681 | 197 | 2 388 | 381 | 21 130 | 7 443 |
| Denmark | 2002 | 27 051 | 0 | 18 178 | 8 451 | 422 | -651 | 12 198 | 21 969 |
| | 2003 | 26 669 | 0 | 18 183 | 8 006 | 480 | -130 | 14 442 | 21 755 |
| | 2004 | 29 331 | ... | 19 324 | 9 438 | 569 | 129 | 13 772 | 24 399 |
| | 2005 | 29 580 | ... | 18 580 | 10 429 | 571 | 323 | 13 163 | 24 561 |
| Estonia | 2002 | 2 951 | 2 950 | ... | ... | 1 | 27 | 1 826 | 177 |
| | 2003 | 3 441 | 3 439 | ... | ... | 2 | 40 | 1 975 | 253 |
| | 2004 | 3 220 | 3 217 | ... | ... | 3 | -112 | 2 238 | 250 |
| | 2005 | 3 381 | 3 375 | ... | ... | 7 | 1 | 2 030 | 210 |
| Faeroe Islands | 2002 | 8 | ... | ... | ... | 8 | ... | *217 | ... |
| | 2003 | 8 | ... | ... | ... | 8 | ... | *219 | ... |
| | 2004 | 8 | ... | ... | ... | 8 | ... | *219 | ... |
| | *2005 | 8 | ... | ... | ... | 8 | ... | 220 | ... |
| Finland | 2002 | 5 060 | 2 211 | ... | ... | 2 849 | -1 035 | 24 146 | 5 218 |
| | 2003 | 4 637 | 1 850 | ... | ... | 2 787 | 476 | 28 305 | 5 682 |
| | 2004 | 4 179 | 920 | ... | ... | 3 260 | -1 455 | 26 656 | 5 745 |
| | 2005 | 5 413 | 2 212 | ... | ... | 3 201 | 581 | 23 672 | 4 685 |

49 **Production, trade and consumption of commercial energy**—Thousand metric tons of oil equivalent and kilograms per capita
(*continued*)

**Production, commerce et consommation d'énergie commerciale**—Milliers de tonnes d'équivalent pétrole et kilogrammes par
habitant (*suite*)

| Bunkers - Soutes | | | Consumption - Consommation | | | | | | | |
|---|---|---|---|---|---|---|---|---|---|---|
| Air | Sea | Unallocated | Per capita | Total | Solids | Liquids | Gas | Electricity | Year | |
| Avion | Maritime | Nondistribué | Par habitant | Totale | Solides | Liquides | Gaz | Electricité | Année | Région, pays ou zone |
| 47 900 | 48 037 | 26 414 | 3 177 | 2 299 201 | 461 903 | 753 308 | 911 677 | 172 312 | 2002 | Europe |
| 49 272 | 48 453 | 37 897 | 3 258 | 2 357 928 | 477 212 | 750 151 | 959 124 | 171 441 | 2003 | |
| 52 224 | 51 700 | 39 217 | 3 271 | 2 373 205 | 470 663 | 748 753 | 976 353 | 177 436 | 2004 | |
| 55 198 | 54 001 | 40 610 | 3 281 | 2 384 584 | 460 909 | 751 877 | 993 700 | 178 099 | 2005 | |
| 44 | ... | 131 | 407 | 1 429 | 22 | 912 | 13 | 483 | 2002 | Albanie |
| 48 | ... | 155 | 431 | 1 519 | 21 | 961 | 13 | 523 | 2003 | |
| 59 | ... | 155 | 551 | 1 718 | 28 | 1 187 | 15 | 487 | 2004 | |
| 71 | ... | 232 | 509 | 1 601 | 25 | 1 066 | 16 | 494 | 2005 | |
| 499 | ... | 982 | 3 352 | 26 950 | 3 806 | 11 690 | 7 763 | 3 690 | 2002 | Autriche |
| 428 | ... | 1 093 | 3 533 | 28 497 | 4 141 | 12 412 | 8 394 | 3 550 | 2003 | |
| 502 | ... | 1 110 | 3 496 | 28 455 | 3 910 | 12 383 | 8 467 | 3 696 | 2004 | |
| 566 | ... | 853 | 3 628 | 29 772 | 4 162 | 12 836 | 9 109 | 3 665 | 2005 | |
| ... | ... | 2 833 | 2 283 | 22 663 | 673 | 5 074 | 16 350 | 566 | 2002 | Bélarus |
| ... | ... | 3 444 | 2 349 | 23 193 | 647 | 4 938 | 17 018 | 590 | 2003 | |
| ... | ... | 3 040 | 2 487 | 24 436 | 553 | 5 130 | 18 469 | 283 | 2004 | |
| ... | ... | 2 444 | 2 511 | 24 665 | 547 | 4 943 | 18 825 | 350 | 2005 | |
| 1 241 | 7 035 | 3 352 | 4 188 | 43 181 | 6 669 | 16 790 | 14 864 | 4 858 | 2002 | Belgique |
| 1 478 | 7 098 | 4 369 | 4 370 | 45 253 | 6 221 | 18 285 | 16 002 | 4 746 | 2003 | |
| 1 360 | 7 978 | 3 846 | 4 345 | 45 167 | 6 128 | 17 963 | 16 189 | 4 887 | 2004 | |
| 1 287 | 7 895 | 3 689 | 4 161 | 43 466 | 5 494 | 17 430 | 15 750 | 4 792 | 2005 | |
| ... | ... | ... | 1 699 | 6 506 | 4 933 | 936 | 280 | 357 | 2002 | Bosnie-Herzégovine |
| ... | ... | ... | 1 727 | 6 617 | 4 988 | 972 | 292 | 366 | 2003 | |
| ... | ... | ... | 1 797 | 6 905 | 5 164 | 1 072 | 341 | 328 | 2004 | |
| ... | ... | ... | 1 940 | 7 456 | 5 508 | 1 192 | 407 | 348 | 2005 | |
| 125 | 107 | 777 | 1 775 | 13 966 | 6 413 | 3 451 | 2 671 | 1 430 | 2002 | Bulgarie |
| 160 | 139 | 1 065 | 1 883 | 14 730 | 7 209 | 3 445 | 2 778 | 1 298 | 2003 | |
| 154 | 117 | 527 | 1 872 | 14 603 | 6 976 | 3 628 | 2 770 | 1 230 | 2004 | |
| 189 | 112 | 861 | 1 964 | 15 204 | 6 857 | 3 873 | 3 116 | 1 359 | 2005 | |
| 20 | 24 | 112 | 1 927 | 8 560 | 654 | 4 502 | 2 634 | 770 | 2002 | Croatie |
| 24 | 22 | -144 | 2 086 | 9 264 | 764 | 5 123 | 2 618 | 759 | 2003 | |
| 29 | 24 | 239 | 2 030 | 9 013 | 816 | 4 545 | 2 731 | 922 | 2004 | |
| 40 | 25 | 121 | 2 058 | 9 140 | 783 | 4 721 | 2 641 | 994 | 2005 | |
| 168 | ... | 1 782 | 3 491 | 35 609 | 19 807 | 6 301 | 8 624 | 877 | 2002 | République tchèque |
| 203 | ... | 1 787 | 3 547 | 36 182 | 20 070 | 6 413 | 8 714 | 985 | 2003 | |
| 291 | ... | 2 057 | 3 579 | 36 534 | 19 964 | 6 784 | 8 653 | 1 133 | 2004 | |
| 318 | ... | 2 315 | 3 546 | 36 285 | 19 430 | 6 988 | 8 565 | 1 302 | 2005 | |
| 692 | 941 | -308 | 3 094 | 16 607 | 4 080 | 7 142 | 5 141 | 244 | 2002 | Danemark |
| 720 | 991 | -107 | 3 384 | 17 883 | 5 702 | 7 257 | 5 179 | -255 | 2003 | |
| 821 | 806 | -88 | 3 154 | 17 037 | 4 398 | 7 169 | 5 149 | 322 | 2004 | |
| 864 | 833 | 71 | 2 971 | 16 091 | 3 738 | 6 776 | 4 888 | 689 | 2005 | |
| 20 | 120 | ... | 3 263 | 4 434 | 3 010 | 821 | 662 | -59 | 2002 | Estonie |
| 19 | 114 | ... | 3 687 | 4 990 | 3 537 | 859 | 756 | -161 | 2003 | |
| 28 | 153 | ... | 3 809 | 5 139 | 3 545 | 885 | 861 | -152 | 2004 | |
| 42 | 122 | ... | 3 741 | 5 035 | 3 388 | 891 | 889 | -132 | 2005 | |
| *2 | ... | ... | *4 835 | *222 | ... | *215 | ... | 8 | 2002 | Iles Féroé |
| *2 | ... | ... | *4 879 | *224 | ... | *217 | ... | 8 | 2003 | |
| *2 | ... | ... | *4 810 | *224 | ... | *217 | ... | 8 | 2004 | |
| 2 | ... | ... | 4 746 | 225 | ... | 218 | ... | 8 | *2005 | |
| 351 | 655 | -1 440 | 4 890 | 25 457 | 6 706 | 10 784 | 4 093 | 3 875 | 2002 | Finlande |
| 362 | 650 | -1 291 | 5 184 | 27 061 | 8 398 | 10 921 | 4 538 | 3 205 | 2003 | |
| 418 | 524 | -1 929 | 5 266 | 27 533 | 7 680 | 11 742 | 4 432 | 3 678 | 2004 | |
| 420 | 515 | -2 330 | 4 806 | 25 214 | 4 970 | 11 545 | 4 037 | 4 662 | 2005 | |

49 Production, trade and consumption of commercial energy—Thousand metric tons of oil equivalent and kilograms per capita (*continued*)

Production, commerce et consommation d'énergie commerciale—Milliers de tonnes d'équivalent pétrole et kilogrammes par habitant (*suite*)

| Region, country or area | Year Année | Primary energy production – Production d'énergie primaire | | | | | Changes in stocks Variations des stocks | Imports Importations | Exports Exportations |
|---|---|---|---|---|---|---|---|---|---|
| | | Total Totale | Solids Solides | Liquids Liquides | Gas Gaz | Electricity Electricité | | | |
| France[3] | 2002 | 48 094 | 1 307 | 1 884 | 1 611 | 43 292 | 2 193 | 163 122 | 22 724 |
| | 2003 | 48 217 | 1 454 | 1 802 | 1 424 | 43 538 | -481 | 167 394 | 26 300 |
| | 2004 | 47 823 | 566 | 1 809 | 1 231 | 44 217 | -579 | 172 295 | 27 915 |
| | 2005 | 46 835 | 416 | 1 695 | 920 | 43 804 | 1 350 | 178 603 | 30 321 |
| Germany | 2002 | 96 603 | 56 891 | 3 999 | 17 764 | 17 949 | -3 196 | 235 564 | 27 834 |
| | 2003 | 96 089 | 56 034 | 4 412 | 17 699 | 17 944 | -1 512 | 240 740 | 28 312 |
| | 2004 | 96 712 | 56 882 | 4 448 | 16 379 | 19 003 | 1 329 | 249 098 | 34 693 |
| | 2005 | 95 478 | 55 309 | 5 585 | 15 816 | 18 769 | 1 596 | 251 332 | 38 721 |
| Gibraltar | 2002 | ... | ... | ... | ... | ... | ... | 1 208 | ... |
| | 2003 | ... | ... | ... | ... | ... | ... | 1 239 | ... |
| | 2004 | ... | ... | ... | ... | ... | ... | 1 278 | ... |
| | 2005 | ... | ... | ... | ... | ... | ... | 1 308 | ... |
| Greece | 2002 | 9 029 | 8 432 | 191 | 47 | 359 | 990 | 27 733 | 3 710 |
| | 2003 | 8 900 | 8 176 | 138 | 34 | 551 | -863 | 28 920 | 5 299 |
| | 2004 | 9 261 | 8 545 | 134 | 32 | 549 | 1 017 | 30 704 | 5 044 |
| | 2005 | 9 249 | 8 536 | 101 | 20 | 591 | -498 | 29 682 | 5 664 |
| Hungary | 2002 | 8 165 | 2 686 | 1 624 | 2 638 | 1 217 | 126 | 18 536 | 2 991 |
| | 2003 | 7 900 | 2 743 | 1 634 | 2 561 | 962 | 466 | 20 117 | 2 800 |
| | 2004 | 7 581 | 2 182 | 1 706 | 2 650 | 1 043 | 13 | 19 660 | 2 606 |
| | 2005 | 7 357 | 1 748 | 1 790 | 2 611 | 1 208 | 134 | 22 471 | 3 486 |
| Iceland | 2002 | 959 | ... | ... | 236 | 723 | -24 | 947 | ... |
| | 2003 | 946 | ... | ... | 215 | 730 | -52 | 921 | ... |
| | 2004 | 963 | ... | ... | 222 | 741 | 31 | 1 047 | ... |
| | 2005 | 953 | ... | ... | 207 | 746 | 20 | 1 032 | ... |
| Ireland | 2002 | 1 535 | 636 | 0 | 753 | 146 | -165 | 15 521 | 1 481 |
| | 2003 | 1 950 | 1 220 | 0 | 604 | 126 | 271 | 15 346 | 1 599 |
| | 2004 | 1 885 | 974 | 0 | 765 | 146 | 446 | 15 225 | 1 242 |
| | 2005 | 1 574 | 877 | 1 | 512 | 184 | 53 | 15 256 | 1 394 |
| Italy[4] | 2002 | 23 532 | 103 | 5 535 | 13 307 | 4 587 | 3 314 | 178 139 | 19 247 |
| | 2003 | 22 757 | 157 | 5 570 | 12 635 | 4 394 | -1 699 | 184 480 | 21 546 |
| | 2004 | 22 474 | 62 | 5 698 | 11 795 | 4 920 | -191 | 188 826 | 22 767 |
| | 2005 | 21 685 | 60 | 6 288 | 10 985 | 4 353 | -1 621 | 194 455 | 26 805 |
| Latvia | 2002 | 245 | 32 | 0 | ... | 213 | -176 | 2 811 | 44 |
| | 2003 | 201 | 2 | 0 | ... | 199 | 78 | 3 222 | 9 |
| | 2004 | 274 | 3 | 0 | ... | 272 | 445 | 3 862 | 392 |
| | 2005 | 294 | 3 | 2 | ... | 290 | 117 | 3 768 | 557 |
| Lithuania | 2002 | 1 788 | 11 | 434 | 60 | 1 283 | -148 | 9 446 | 5 457 |
| | 2003 | 1 862 | 10 | 382 | 53 | 1 416 | 129 | 10 566 | 6 248 |
| | 2004 | 1 745 | 11 | 305 | 49 | 1 380 | 163 | 12 402 | 7 749 |
| | 2005 | 1 250 | 16 | 227 | 48 | 960 | 60 | 12 933 | 7 598 |
| Luxembourg | 2002 | 88 | ... | 0 | ... | 88 | 16 | 4 323 | 269 |
| | 2003 | 81 | ... | 0 | ... | 81 | 6 | 4 509 | 253 |
| | 2004 | 79 | ... | 1 | ... | 78 | -13 | 4 936 | 284 |
| | 2005 | 83 | ... | 1 | ... | 82 | -19 | 5 013 | 284 |
| Malta | 2002 | ... | ... | ... | ... | ... | ... | 801 | ... |
| | 2003 | ... | ... | ... | ... | ... | ... | 909 | ... |
| | 2004 | ... | ... | ... | ... | ... | ... | 925 | ... |
| | 2005 | ... | ... | ... | ... | ... | ... | 945 | ... |
| Moldova | 2002 | 10 | ... | 0 | ... | 10 | -15 | 3 143 | 1 |
| | 2003 | 6 | ... | 0 | ... | 6 | 54 | 3 492 | 12 |
| | 2004 | 13 | ... | 8 | ... | 5 | -6 | 3 562 | 43 |
| | 2005 | 10 | ... | 5 | ... | 5 | 1 | 3 743 | 21 |

**Production, trade and consumption of commercial energy**—Thousand metric tons of oil equivalent and kilograms per capita (*continued*)

**Production, commerce et consommation d'énergie commerciale**—Milliers de tonnes d'équivalent pétrole et kilogrammes par habitant (*suite*)

| Bunkers - Soutes | | | Consumption - Consommation | | | | | | | |
|---|---|---|---|---|---|---|---|---|---|---|
| Air<br>Avion | Sea<br>Maritime | Unallocated<br>Nondistribué | Per capita<br>Par habitant | Total<br>Totale | Solids<br>Solides | Liquids<br>Liquides | Gas<br>Gaz | Electricity<br>Electricité | Year<br>Année | Région, pays ou zone |
| 4 805 | 2 646 | 8 272 | 2 845 | 170 578 | 13 912 | 78 348 | 41 649 | 36 669 | 2002 | France[3] |
| 5 079 | 2 852 | 9 855 | 2 858 | 172 008 | 14 805 | 75 618 | 43 758 | 37 827 | 2003 | |
| 5 427 | 3 211 | 9 666 | 2 881 | 174 478 | 14 837 | 76 149 | 44 609 | 38 883 | 2004 | |
| 5 490 | 2 935 | 10 855 | 2 865 | 174 486 | 15 320 | 74 995 | 45 551 | 38 620 | 2005 | |
| 5 603 | 2 396 | 6 616 | 3 549 | 292 914 | 82 804 | 107 334 | 83 967 | 18 809 | 2002 | Allemagne |
| 5 737 | 2 641 | 6 453 | 3 577 | 295 198 | 83 442 | 105 926 | 87 923 | 17 907 | 2003 | |
| 6 201 | 2 704 | 6 292 | 3 571 | 294 592 | 84 125 | 104 211 | 87 479 | 18 778 | 2004 | |
| 6 674 | 2 532 | 6 410 | 3 528 | 290 877 | 80 236 | 102 424 | 89 840 | 18 376 | 2005 | |
| 4 | 1 088 | ... | 4 132 | 116 | ... | 116 | ... | ... | 2002 | Gibraltar |
| 4 | 1 115 | ... | 4 277 | 120 | ... | 120 | ... | ... | 2003 | |
| 4 | 1 150 | ... | 4 422 | 124 | ... | 124 | ... | ... | 2004 | |
| 4 | 1 176 | ... | 4 568 | 128 | ... | 128 | ... | ... | 2005 | |
| 760 | 3 158 | -1 462 | 2 694 | 29 605 | 8 833 | 18 164 | 2 001 | 608 | 2002 | Grèce |
| 785 | 3 237 | -1 263 | 2 780 | 30 626 | 8 909 | 18 734 | 2 251 | 731 | 2003 | |
| 809 | 3 263 | -699 | 2 765 | 30 531 | 9 124 | 18 138 | 2 476 | 792 | 2004 | |
| 781 | 2 909 | -1 365 | 2 831 | 31 439 | 8 970 | 18 937 | 2 615 | 916 | 2005 | |
| 208 | ... | 144 | 2 283 | 23 233 | 3 429 | 6 211 | 12 012 | 1 582 | 2002 | Hongrie |
| 204 | ... | 587 | 2 363 | 23 962 | 3 470 | 5 727 | 13 207 | 1 559 | 2003 | |
| 220 | ... | 740 | 2 339 | 23 666 | 3 132 | 5 835 | 13 014 | 1 685 | 2004 | |
| 218 | ... | 1 131 | 2 465 | 24 862 | 2 977 | 6 704 | 13 438 | 1 743 | 2005 | |
| 101 | 67 | 356 | 4 900 | 1 406 | 96 | 587 | ... | 723 | 2002 | Islande |
| 103 | 68 | 335 | 4 887 | 1 412 | 91 | 591 | ... | 730 | 2003 | |
| 119 | 71 | 348 | 4 918 | 1 441 | 103 | 597 | ... | 741 | 2004 | |
| 134 | 65 | 335 | 4 838 | 1 431 | 99 | 586 | ... | 746 | 2005 | |
| 746 | 150 | 3 | 3 789 | 14 841 | 2 937 | 7 627 | 4 087 | 189 | 2002 | Irlande |
| 731 | 172 | 62 | 3 634 | 14 461 | 2 802 | 7 375 | 4 058 | 226 | 2003 | |
| 691 | 151 | 6 | 3 604 | 14 573 | 2 501 | 7 741 | 4 050 | 280 | 2004 | |
| 798 | 105 | 136 | 3 473 | 14 345 | 2 917 | 7 213 | 3 855 | 360 | 2005 | |
| 3 199 | 3 002 | -2 967 | 3 036 | 175 876 | 14 008 | 88 813 | 64 118 | 8 938 | 2002 | Italie[4] |
| 3 598 | 3 234 | -1 070 | 3 132 | 181 627 | 15 272 | 86 888 | 70 690 | 8 776 | 2003 | |
| 3 568 | 3 381 | 1 611 | 3 097 | 180 163 | 17 190 | 80 775 | 73 354 | 8 844 | 2004 | |
| 3 718 | 3 411 | 1 110 | 3 118 | 182 718 | 16 978 | 78 659 | 78 501 | 8 580 | 2005 | |
| 28 | 194 | 14 | 1 262 | 2 952 | 75 | 1 028 | 1 435 | 415 | 2002 | Lettonie |
| 40 | 190 | 8 | 1 332 | 3 098 | 63 | 1 112 | 1 497 | 426 | 2003 | |
| 48 | 205 | 3 | 1 315 | 3 042 | 51 | 1 059 | 1 480 | 452 | 2004 | |
| 59 | 264 | 4 | 1 331 | 3 062 | 61 | 1 018 | 1 509 | 475 | 2005 | |
| 12 | 112 | 101 | 1 640 | 5 701 | 165 | 2 359 | 2 452 | 725 | 2002 | Lituanie |
| 22 | 111 | 140 | 1 669 | 5 779 | 211 | 2 138 | 2 661 | 769 | 2003 | |
| 34 | 112 | 207 | 1 707 | 5 881 | 206 | 2 263 | 2 651 | 761 | 2004 | |
| 46 | 146 | 206 | 1 795 | 6 126 | 226 | 2 398 | 2 797 | 704 | 2005 | |
| 377 | ... | ... | 8 443 | 3 749 | 93 | 2 103 | 1 170 | 383 | 2002 | Luxembourg |
| 392 | ... | ... | 8 793 | 3 939 | 78 | 2 279 | 1 182 | 400 | 2003 | |
| 427 | ... | ... | 9 524 | 4 317 | 94 | 2 522 | 1 333 | 368 | 2004 | |
| 433 | ... | ... | 9 616 | 4 397 | 82 | 2 644 | 1 310 | 362 | 2005 | |
| 90 | 23 | ... | 1 742 | 688 | ... | 688 | ... | ... | 2002 | Malte |
| 79 | 23 | ... | 2 017 | 806 | ... | 806 | ... | ... | 2003 | |
| 101 | 23 | ... | 1 990 | 801 | ... | 801 | ... | ... | 2004 | |
| 91 | *20 | ... | 2 059 | 834 | ... | 834 | ... | ... | 2005 | |
| 19 | ... | 0 | 869 | 3 149 | 73 | 549 | 2 293 | 234 | 2002 | Moldova |
| 12 | ... | 0 | 947 | 3 420 | 89 | 597 | 2 431 | 302 | 2003 | |
| 11 | ... | 0 | 979 | 3 527 | 84 | 640 | 2 545 | 258 | 2004 | |
| 12 | ... | 0 | 1 034 | 3 718 | 76 | 642 | 2 726 | 275 | 2005 | |

**Production, trade and consumption of commercial energy**—Thousand metric tons of oil equivalent and kilograms per capita (*continued*)

**Production, commerce et consommation d'énergie commerciale**—Milliers de tonnes d'équivalent pétrole et kilogrammes pa habitant (*suite*)

| Region, country or area | Year | Primary energy production – Production d'énergie primaire | | | | | Changes in stocks | Imports | Export |
| | Année | Total | Solids | Liquids | Gas | Electricity | Variations | Imports | Export |
| | | Totale | Solides | Liquides | Gaz | Electricité | des stocks | Importations | Exportatio |
|---|---|---|---|---|---|---|---|---|---|
| Netherlands | 2002 | 63 908 | ... | 3 173 | 60 305 | 429 | -900 | 132 510 | 102 28 |
| | 2003 | 61 676 | ... | 3 195 | 58 013 | 468 | -235 | 129 157 | 98 28 |
| | 2004 | 71 903 | ... | 2 975 | 68 428 | 500 | 432 | 130 747 | 107 46 |
| | 2005 | 65 701 | ... | 2 652 | 62 517 | 532 | 1 179 | 144 202 | 112 60 |
| Norway[5] | 2002 | 236 493 | 1 431 | 158 176 | 65 716 | 11 170 | 303 | 5 086 | 215 31 |
| | 2003 | 238 872 | 1 976 | 154 140 | 73 604 | 9 152 | 1 071 | 5 871 | 214 94 |
| | 2004 | 241 930 | 1 949 | 152 347 | 78 215 | 9 419 | -396 | 6 087 | 219 39 |
| | 2005 | 238 298 | 987 | 140 801 | 84 723 | 11 787 | 419 | 5 166 | 208 82 |
| Poland | 2002 | 76 084 | 71 049 | 728 | 3 966 | 341 | 1 091 | 31 781 | 19 38 |
| | 2003 | 76 233 | 71 132 | 794 | 4 013 | 294 | 260 | 32 287 | 18 15 |
| | 2004 | 75 844 | 70 253 | 900 | 4 362 | 330 | 341 | 34 388 | 18 26 |
| | 2005 | 74 058 | 68 448 | 958 | 4 316 | 336 | 1 933 | 36 689 | 18 30 |
| Portugal | 2002 | 750 | ... | ... | ... | 750 | -501 | 23 281 | 1 21 |
| | 2003 | 1 431 | ... | ... | ... | 1 431 | 449 | 23 415 | 1 57 |
| | 2004 | 950 | ... | ... | ... | 950 | -413 | 23 948 | 1 70 |
| | 2005 | 599 | ... | ... | ... | 599 | 370 | 26 361 | 2 148 |
| Romania | 2002 | 24 993 | 5 268 | 6 093 | 11 779 | 1 854 | 259 | 14 085 | 4 56 |
| | 2003 | 24 783 | 5 724 | 5 909 | 11 587 | 1 562 | -249 | 14 001 | 3 83 |
| | 2004 | 24 654 | 5 502 | 5 724 | 11 531 | 1 897 | 1 010 | 16 383 | 4 63 |
| | 2005 | 24 129 | 5 383 | 5 751 | 10 780 | 2 215 | -308 | 16 852 | 6 25 |
| Russian Federation | 2002 | 1 032 739 | 98 969 | 374 270 | 533 190 | 26 310 | 8 008 | 22 428 | 445 85 |
| | 2003 | 1 104 050 | 106 842 | 414 957 | 555 733 | 26 517 | 12 165 | 25 533 | 493 928 |
| | 2004 | 1 153 860 | 108 768 | 451 058 | 566 269 | 27 764 | 6 775 | 22 063 | 544 71 |
| | 2005 | 1 185 396 | 116 212 | 467 819 | 573 466 | 27 899 | 6 859 | 20 337 | 562 923 |
| Serbia and Montenegro | 2002 | 10 407 | 8 180 | 812 | 405 | 1 010 | ... | 4 985 | 553 |
| | 2003 | 10 522 | 8 574 | 773 | 328 | 847 | ... | 5 433 | 400 |
| | 2004 | 10 661 | 8 767 | 652 | 285 | 956 | ... | 6 920 | 756 |
| | 2005 | 10 524 | 8 626 | 609 | 254 | 1 035 | ... | 6 710 | 1 041 |
| Slovakia | 2002 | 3 333 | 997 | 110 | 211 | 2 015 | 114 | 16 477 | 4 122 |
| | 2003 | 3 081 | 907 | 86 | 236 | 1 852 | -137 | 16 472 | 4 185 |
| | 2004 | 2 959 | 864 | 53 | 215 | 1 826 | 474 | 17 314 | 4 697 |
| | 2005 | 2 930 | 735 | 65 | 197 | 1 932 | 93 | 17 366 | 4 860 |
| Slovenia | 2002 | 1 793 | 1 019 | 1 | 5 | 768 | -58 | 3 964 | 538 |
| | 2003 | 1 774 | 1 050 | 0 | 5 | 719 | 40 | 4 259 | 588 |
| | 2004 | 1 872 | 1 045 | 0 | 5 | 821 | 40 | 4 402 | 737 |
| | 2005 | 1 794 | 987 | 0 | 4 | 804 | 9 | 4 654 | 862 |
| Spain | 2002 | 16 647 | 7 189 | 456 | 519 | 8 483 | 2 061 | 114 467 | 4 928 |
| | 2003 | 17 680 | 6 811 | 515 | 219 | 10 137 | -82 | 116 795 | 5 569 |
| | 2004 | 17 245 | 6 632 | 484 | 344 | 9 785 | -782 | 125 425 | 7 026 |
| | 2005 | 15 668 | 6 331 | 426 | 151 | 8 760 | 1 777 | 134 433 | 7 229 |
| Sweden | 2002 | 11 982 | 332 | 33 | ... | 11 618 | -1 675 | 29 682 | 9 989 |
| | 2003 | 10 877 | 345 | 68 | ... | 10 464 | 1 037 | 32 829 | 10 490 |
| | 2004 | 12 423 | 369 | 144 | ... | 11 910 | -426 | 31 970 | 12 102 |
| | 2005 | 13 070 | 292 | 208 | ... | 12 570 | 767 | 31 640 | 11 786 |
| Switzerland[6] | 2002 | 5 544 | ... | 0 | 26 | 5 518 | 39 | 18 281 | 3 369 |
| | 2003 | 5 562 | ... | 0 | 27 | 5 535 | -160 | 18 126 | 3 463 |
| | 2004 | 5 400 | ... | 3 | 28 | 5 370 | 15 | 17 976 | 2 963 |
| | 2005 | 4 887 | ... | 7 | 26 | 4 854 | 138 | 19 249 | 3 230 |
| TFYR of Macedonia | 2002 | 2 108 | 2 043 | ... | ... | 65 | 163 | 1 332 | 160 |
| | 2003 | 2 108 | 1 989 | ... | ... | 118 | -37 | 1 331 | 336 |
| | 2004 | 2 080 | 1 953 | ... | ... | 127 | 4 | 1 314 | 210 |
| | 2005 | 1 983 | 1 854 | ... | ... | 128 | -60 | 1 517 | 330 |

**Production, trade and consumption of commercial energy**—Thousand metric tons of oil equivalent and kilograms per capita (*continued*)

**Production, commerce et consommation d'énergie commerciale**—Milliers de tonnes d'équivalent pétrole et kilogrammes par habitant (*suite*)

| Bunkers - Soutes | | | Consumption - Consommation | | | | | | | |
|---|---|---|---|---|---|---|---|---|---|---|
| Air<br>Avion | Sea<br>Maritime | Unallocated<br>Nondistribué | Per capita<br>Par habitant | Total<br>Totale | Solids<br>Solides | Liquids<br>Liquides | Gas<br>Gaz | Electricity<br>Electricité | Year<br>Année | Région, pays ou zone |
| 3 342 | 14 709 | -16 800 | 5 821 | 93 751 | 8 305 | 43 784 | 39 824 | 1 837 | 2002 | Pays-Bas |
| 3 288 | 13 774 | -16 387 | 5 684 | 92 047 | 8 535 | 41 585 | 39 998 | 1 929 | 2003 | |
| 3 518 | 14 965 | -14 635 | 5 590 | 90 881 | 8 333 | 39 826 | 40 828 | 1 895 | 2004 | |
| 3 616 | 17 178 | -13 689 | 5 451 | 88 965 | 7 992 | 39 338 | 39 531 | 2 105 | 2005 | |
| 399 | 670 | 513 | 5 232 | 23 670 | 813 | 7 964 | 4 558 | 10 335 | 2002 | Norvège[5] |
| 210 | 567 | 413 | 5 837 | 26 731 | 789 | 10 220 | 5 894 | 9 829 | 2003 | |
| 242 | 520 | 991 | 5 681 | 26 180 | 921 | 9 929 | 4 929 | 10 402 | 2004 | |
| 272 | 701 | 3 412 | 5 944 | 27 594 | 776 | 10 319 | 5 748 | 10 751 | 2005 | |
| 270 | 275 | 2 550 | 2 205 | 84 296 | 56 480 | 16 845 | 11 237 | -267 | 2002 | Pologne |
| 292 | 290 | 1 742 | 2 298 | 87 779 | 57 998 | 17 849 | 12 512 | -580 | 2003 | |
| 286 | 258 | 1 921 | 2 335 | 89 162 | 57 023 | 19 409 | 13 199 | -469 | 2004 | |
| 324 | 328 | 2 123 | 2 299 | 87 733 | 55 376 | 19 389 | 13 594 | -625 | 2005 | |
| 598 | 491 | 1 035 | 2 052 | 21 191 | 3 585 | 13 661 | 3 033 | 913 | 2002 | Portugal |
| 635 | 589 | 1 247 | 1 955 | 20 351 | 3 381 | 12 370 | 2 929 | 1 671 | 2003 | |
| 695 | 670 | 1 102 | 2 018 | 21 140 | 3 420 | 12 542 | 3 670 | 1 507 | 2004 | |
| 721 | 589 | 1 227 | 2 076 | 21 904 | 3 822 | 12 729 | 4 167 | 1 186 | 2005 | |
| 97 | ... | 616 | 1 547 | 33 543 | 7 800 | 8 992 | 15 143 | 1 608 | 2002 | Roumanie |
| 118 | ... | 401 | 1 596 | 34 681 | 8 111 | 8 821 | 16 366 | 1 383 | 2003 | |
| 137 | ... | 1 535 | 1 556 | 33 722 | 8 125 | 8 316 | 15 486 | 1 795 | 2004 | |
| 111 | ... | 1 088 | 1 565 | 33 831 | 7 915 | 8 459 | 15 491 | 1 966 | 2005 | |
| 9 599 | ... | 7 840 | 4 056 | 583 867 | 89 749 | 107 080 | 361 841 | 25 197 | 2002 | Fédération de Russie |
| 9 754 | ... | 10 042 | 4 214 | 603 695 | 90 429 | 107 232 | 380 667 | 25 367 | 2003 | |
| 9 897 | ... | 7 368 | 4 221 | 607 167 | 87 514 | 107 365 | 385 179 | 27 109 | 2004 | |
| 10 355 | ... | 9 604 | 4 303 | 615 992 | 86 988 | 113 648 | 388 521 | 26 835 | 2005 | |
| 59 | ... | 463 | 1 764 | 14 317 | 8 370 | 2 617 | 1 934 | 1 396 | 2002 | Serbie-et-Monténégro |
| 64 | ... | 593 | 1 839 | 14 897 | 8 921 | 2 867 | 2 022 | 1 087 | 2003 | |
| 47 | ... | 752 | 1 982 | 16 025 | 9 296 | 3 227 | 2 569 | 933 | 2004 | |
| 48 | ... | 772 | 1 906 | 15 372 | 9 032 | 3 322 | 2 151 | 867 | 2005 | |
| 48 | ... | 507 | 2 792 | 15 019 | 3 882 | 2 959 | 6 519 | 1 658 | 2002 | Slovaquie |
| 34 | ... | 457 | 2 791 | 15 015 | 4 201 | 2 858 | 6 299 | 1 658 | 2003 | |
| 27 | ... | 124 | 2 779 | 14 951 | 4 113 | 3 063 | 6 109 | 1 666 | 2004 | |
| 39 | ... | 162 | 2 810 | 15 141 | 3 826 | 3 126 | 6 537 | 1 652 | 2005 | |
| 28 | ... | 0 | 2 632 | 5 248 | 1 371 | 2 296 | 911 | 671 | 2002 | Slovénie |
| 26 | ... | 0 | 2 696 | 5 379 | 1 324 | 2 314 | 1 007 | 733 | 2003 | |
| 20 | ... | 52 | 2 717 | 5 425 | 1 340 | 2 331 | 999 | 754 | 2004 | |
| 23 | ... | 55 | 2 748 | 5 499 | 1 293 | 2 398 | 1 032 | 776 | 2005 | |
| 2 667 | 7 020 | 6 500 | 2 613 | 107 938 | 22 161 | 56 001 | 20 835 | 8 941 | 2002 | Espagne |
| 2 798 | 7 150 | 7 699 | 2 651 | 111 341 | 20 379 | 56 991 | 23 726 | 10 245 | 2003 | |
| 3 103 | 7 376 | 7 884 | 2 766 | 118 065 | 21 887 | 58 685 | 27 969 | 9 525 | 2004 | |
| 3 113 | 8 094 | 5 893 | 2 857 | 123 995 | 21 296 | 60 904 | 33 151 | 8 644 | 2005 | |
| 527 | 1 225 | 2 293 | 3 278 | 29 306 | 2 799 | 13 438 | 990 | 12 078 | 2002 | Suède |
| 513 | 1 645 | 2 291 | 3 089 | 27 729 | 2 645 | 12 530 | 987 | 11 567 | 2003 | |
| 628 | 1 937 | 2 027 | 3 121 | 28 126 | 2 908 | 12 506 | 983 | 11 729 | 2004 | |
| 634 | 1 978 | 2 099 | 3 033 | 27 446 | 2 580 | 11 995 | 936 | 11 934 | 2005 | |
| 1 330 | 8 | 5 | 2 604 | 19 074 | 137 | 11 044 | 2 762 | 5 131 | 2002 | Suisse[6] |
| 1 210 | 10 | 27 | 2 607 | 19 138 | 143 | 10 808 | 2 920 | 5 268 | 2003 | |
| 1 155 | 9 | 7 | 2 581 | 19 227 | 134 | 10 772 | 3 012 | 5 309 | 2004 | |
| 1 180 | 12 | 6 | 2 624 | 19 570 | 157 | 10 920 | 3 092 | 5 400 | 2005 | |
| 39 | ... | 8 | 1 511 | 3 070 | 2 000 | 854 | 83 | 133 | 2002 | L'ex-R.y. Macédoine |
| 7 | ... | 6 | 1 542 | 3 126 | 2 043 | 809 | 74 | 200 | 2003 | |
| 6 | ... | 12 | 1 558 | 3 162 | 2 046 | 823 | 65 | 229 | 2004 | |
| 6 | ... | 11 | 1 579 | 3 212 | 2 026 | 849 | 71 | 266 | 2005 | |

# 49

Production, trade and consumption of commercial energy — Thousand metric tons of oil equivalent and kilograms per capita (continued)

Production, commerce et consommation d'énergie commerciale — Milliers de tonnes d'équivalent pétrole et kilogrammes pa habitant (suite)

| Region, country or area | Year Année | Total Totale | Solids Solides | Liquids Liquides | Gas Gaz | Electricity Electricité | Changes in stocks Variations des stocks | Imports Importations | Expor Exportation |
|---|---|---|---|---|---|---|---|---|---|
| Ukraine | 2002 | 60 547 | 31 768 | 3 820 | 17 409 | 7 550 | 0 | 77 280 | 13 58 |
| | 2003 | 62 954 | 33 201 | 4 059 | 17 885 | 7 809 | 0 | 87 422 | 17 09 |
| | 2004 | 62 820 | 30 809 | 4 418 | 19 087 | 8 507 | 308 | 87 354 | 18 15 |
| | 2005 | 63 828 | 31 229 | 4 514 | 19 374 | 8 710 | -2 690 | 77 322 | 12 79 |
| United Kingdom | 2002 | 246 781 | 18 073 | 116 620 | 103 787 | 8 301 | -598 | 97 697 | 121 52 |
| | 2003 | 234 945 | 17 043 | 106 727 | 102 926 | 8 249 | -2 203 | 100 592 | 111 13 |
| | 2004 | 214 827 | 15 125 | 95 998 | 96 006 | 7 697 | 1 209 | 118 337 | 101 44 |
| | 2005 | 193 217 | 12 357 | 85 332 | 87 581 | 7 947 | 722 | 126 231 | 88 72 |
| **Oceania** | **2002** | **254 532** | **175 350** | **35 694** | **39 475** | **4 013** | **1 710** | **36 694** | **168 71** |
| | **2003** | **251 874** | **175 745** | **32 998** | **39 209** | **3 923** | **-109** | **36 972** | **167 76** |
| | **2004** | **257 172** | **183 348** | **30 072** | **39 539** | **4 212** | **286** | **37 536** | **172 50** |
| | **2005** | **267 535** | **193 902** | **26 627** | **43 067** | **3 939** | **-137** | **40 048** | **179 86** |
| Australia | 2002 | 240 018 | 173 380 | 31 516 | 33 711 | 1 410 | 1 674 | 27 597 | 163 66 |
| | 2003 | 239 092 | 173 536 | 29 308 | 34 790 | 1 458 | 115 | 27 344 | 162 99 |
| | 2004 | 244 532 | 181 098 | 26 451 | 35 557 | 1 426 | -58 | 27 428 | 168 01 |
| | 2005 | 255 513 | 191 613 | 23 085 | 39 372 | 1 443 | -172 | 30 001 | 175 14 |
| Cook Islands | 2002 | ... | ... | ... | ... | ... | ... | 12 | |
| | 2003 | ... | ... | ... | ... | ... | ... | 13 | |
| | 2004 | ... | ... | ... | ... | ... | ... | 18 | |
| | 2005 | ... | ... | ... | ... | ... | ... | 20 | |
| Fiji* | 2002 | 54 | ... | ... | ... | 54 | ... | 528 | 11 |
| | 2003 | 57 | ... | ... | ... | 57 | ... | 516 | 10 |
| | 2004 | 58 | ... | ... | ... | 58 | ... | 502 | 11 |
| | 2005 | 58 | ... | ... | ... | 58 | ... | 496 | 11 |
| French Polynesia | 2002 | 8 | ... | ... | ... | 8 | ... | 276 | |
| | 2003 | 8 | ... | ... | ... | 8 | ... | *272 | |
| | *2004 | 8 | ... | ... | ... | 8 | ... | 274 | |
| | *2005 | 8 | ... | ... | ... | 8 | ... | 280 | |
| Kiribati* | 2002 | ... | ... | ... | ... | ... | ... | 10 | |
| | 2003 | ... | ... | ... | ... | ... | ... | 10 | |
| | 2004 | ... | ... | ... | ... | ... | ... | 10 | |
| | 2005 | ... | ... | ... | ... | ... | ... | 10 | |
| Nauru* | 2002 | ... | ... | ... | ... | ... | ... | 52 | |
| | 2003 | ... | ... | ... | ... | ... | ... | 53 | |
| | 2004 | ... | ... | ... | ... | ... | ... | 53 | |
| | 2005 | ... | ... | ... | ... | ... | ... | 53 | |
| New Caledonia | 2002 | 28 | ... | ... | ... | 28 | ... | 755 | 2 |
| | 2003 | 28 | ... | ... | ... | 28 | ... | 868 | 3 |
| | 2004 | 29 | ... | ... | ... | 29 | ... | 808 | 3 |
| | *2005 | 29 | ... | ... | ... | 29 | ... | 829 | 3 |
| New Zealand | 2002 | 11 645 | 1 970 | 1 626 | 5 620 | 2 429 | 36 | 6 323 | 2 42 |
| | 2003 | 10 046 | 2 209 | 1 262 | 4 287 | 2 289 | -224 | 6 686 | 2 26 |
| | 2004 | 9 815 | 2 250 | 1 121 | 3 837 | 2 606 | 344 | 7 168 | 1 908 |
| | 2005 | 9 196 | 2 289 | 1 042 | 3 549 | 2 316 | 34 | 7 089 | 2 142 |
| Niue* | 2002 | ... | ... | ... | ... | ... | ... | 1 | |
| | 2003 | ... | ... | ... | ... | ... | ... | 1 | |
| | 2004 | ... | ... | ... | ... | ... | ... | 1 | |
| | 2005 | ... | ... | ... | ... | ... | ... | 1 | |
| Palau* | 2002 | 2 | ... | ... | ... | 2 | ... | 51 | |
| | 2003 | 2 | ... | ... | ... | 2 | ... | 54 | |
| | 2004 | 2 | ... | ... | ... | 2 | ... | 54 | |
| | 2005 | 2 | ... | ... | ... | 2 | ... | 54 | |

**Production, trade and consumption of commercial energy**—Thousand metric tons of oil equivalent and kilograms per capita (*continued*)

**Production, commerce et consommation d'énergie commerciale**—Milliers de tonnes d'équivalent pétrole et kilogrammes par habitant (*suite*)

| Bunkers - Soutes | | | Consumption - Consommation | | | | | | | |
|---|---|---|---|---|---|---|---|---|---|---|
| Air Avion | Sea Maritime | Unallocated Nondistribué | Per capita Par habitant | Total Totale | Solids Solides | Liquids Liquides | Gas Gaz | Electricity Electricité | Year Année | Région, pays ou zone |
| 302 | ... | 1 718 | 2 525 | 122 223 | 33 615 | 12 994 | 68 332 | 7 282 | 2002 | Ukraine |
| 372 | ... | 3 433 | 2 718 | 129 475 | 37 115 | 12 636 | 72 340 | 7 385 | 2003 | |
| 378 | ... | 3 772 | 2 698 | 127 558 | 33 042 | 13 275 | 73 192 | 8 049 | 2004 | |
| 376 | ... | 225 | 2 771 | 130 442 | 33 817 | 13 673 | 74 960 | 7 992 | 2005 | |
| 9 479 | 1 923 | -130 | 3 590 | 212 295 | 37 639 | 70 237 | 95 395 | 9 025 | 2002 | Royaume-Uni |
| 9 720 | 1 770 | 454 | 3 618 | 214 674 | 40 268 | 70 547 | 95 424 | 8 435 | 2003 | |
| 10 759 | 2 092 | -827 | 3 660 | 218 512 | 39 952 | 73 122 | 97 097 | 8 341 | 2004 | |
| 12 122 | 2 056 | 543 | 3 576 | 215 309 | 41 167 | 71 148 | 94 332 | 8 663 | 2005 | |
| **2 786** | **1 141** | **-2 758** | **3 839** | **119 640** | **43 232** | **42 794** | **29 601** | **4 013** | **2002** | **Océanie** |
| **3 088** | **1 071** | **-2 107** | **3 743** | **119 150** | **42 850** | **43 337** | **29 040** | **3 923** | **2003** | |
| **3 197** | **1 157** | **-3 072** | **3 740** | **120 649** | **43 789** | **43 367** | **29 280** | **4 212** | **2004** | |
| **3 547** | **1 177** | **-3 076** | **3 860** | **126 219** | **47 501** | **45 459** | **29 320** | **3 939** | **2005** | |
| 2 061 | 733 | -2 478 | 5 191 | 101 966 | 42 229 | 34 490 | 23 837 | 1 410 | 2002 | Australie |
| 2 246 | 733 | -1 960 | 5 148 | 102 314 | 41 460 | 34 775 | 24 621 | 1 458 | 2003 | |
| 2 266 | 842 | -2 803 | 5 161 | 103 702 | 42 418 | 34 583 | 25 274 | 1 426 | 2004 | |
| 2 654 | 857 | -2 633 | 5 395 | 109 665 | 46 006 | 36 605 | 25 612 | 1 443 | 2005 | |
| *2 | ... | ... | 561 | 10 | ... | 10 | ... | ... | 2002 | Iles Cook |
| *2 | ... | ... | 616 | 11 | ... | 11 | ... | ... | 2003 | |
| 0 | ... | ... | 909 | 18 | ... | 18 | ... | ... | 2004 | |
| 0 | ... | ... | 1 014 | 20 | ... | 20 | ... | ... | 2005 | |
| 25 | 41 | ... | 493 | 407 | 10 | 343 | ... | 54 | 2002 | Fidji* |
| 21 | 36 | ... | 492 | 409 | 9 | 342 | ... | 57 | 2003 | |
| 19 | 36 | ... | 472 | 395 | 9 | 329 | ... | 58 | 2004 | |
| 19 | 36 | ... | 461 | 390 | 8 | 324 | ... | 58 | 2005 | |
| *6 | *38 | ... | 992 | 239 | ... | 231 | ... | 8 | 2002 | Polynésie française |
| *6 | *36 | ... | *971 | *237 | ... | *229 | ... | 8 | 2003 | |
| 6 | 46 | ... | 864 | 230 | ... | 222 | ... | 8 | *2004 | |
| 6 | 47 | ... | 856 | 235 | ... | 227 | ... | 8 | *2005 | |
| 2 | ... | ... | 95 | 8 | ... | 8 | ... | ... | 2002 | Kiribati* |
| 2 | ... | ... | 88 | 8 | ... | 8 | ... | ... | 2003 | |
| 2 | ... | ... | 82 | 8 | ... | 8 | ... | ... | 2004 | |
| 2 | ... | ... | 81 | 8 | ... | 8 | ... | ... | 2005 | |
| 7 | ... | ... | 3 649 | 45 | ... | 45 | ... | ... | 2002 | Nauru* |
| 7 | ... | ... | 3 658 | 46 | ... | 46 | ... | ... | 2003 | |
| 7 | ... | ... | 3 590 | 46 | ... | 46 | ... | ... | 2004 | |
| 7 | ... | ... | 3 524 | 46 | ... | 46 | ... | ... | 2005 | |
| ... | ... | ... | 3 493 | 758 | 193 | 537 | ... | 28 | 2002 | Nouvelle-Calédonie |
| ... | ... | ... | 3 800 | 866 | 219 | 619 | ... | 28 | 2003 | |
| ... | ... | ... | 3 500 | 808 | 197 | 582 | ... | 29 | 2004 | |
| ... | ... | ... | 3 537 | 828 | 203 | 595 | ... | 29 | *2005 | |
| 634 | 326 | -289 | 3 794 | 14 843 | 800 | 5 994 | 5 620 | 2 429 | 2002 | Nouvelle-Zélande |
| 753 | 262 | -162 | 3 426 | 13 837 | 1 162 | 6 099 | 4 287 | 2 289 | 2003 | |
| 846 | 231 | -287 | 3 433 | 13 943 | 1 165 | 6 311 | 3 860 | 2 606 | 2004 | |
| 807 | 235 | -465 | 3 302 | 13 533 | 1 284 | 6 371 | 3 562 | 2 316 | 2005 | |
| ... | ... | ... | 507 | 1 | ... | 1 | ... | ... | 2002 | Nioué* |
| ... | ... | ... | 507 | 1 | ... | 1 | ... | ... | 2003 | |
| ... | ... | ... | 507 | 1 | ... | 1 | ... | ... | 2004 | |
| ... | ... | ... | 507 | 1 | ... | 1 | ... | ... | 2005 | |
| 14 | ... | ... | 1 954 | 38 | ... | 36 | ... | 2 | 2002 | Palaos* |
| 15 | ... | ... | 2 029 | 40 | ... | 38 | ... | 2 | 2003 | |
| 15 | ... | ... | 1 997 | 40 | ... | 38 | ... | 2 | 2004 | |
| 15 | ... | ... | 1 969 | 40 | ... | 38 | ... | 2 | 2005 | |

## 49 Production, trade and consumption of commercial energy—Thousand metric tons of oil equivalent and kilograms per capita (continued)

### Production, commerce et consommation d'énergie commerciale—Milliers de tonnes d'équivalent pétrole et kilogrammes par habitant (suite)

| Region, country or area | Year Année | Primary energy production – Production d'énergie primaire | | | | | Changes in stocks Variations des stocks | Imports Importations | Export Exportation |
|---|---|---|---|---|---|---|---|---|---|
| | | Total Totale | Solids Solides | Liquids Liquides | Gas Gaz | Electricity Electricité | | | |
| Papua New Guinea | 2002 | 2 775 | ... | 2 552 | 144 | 79 | ... | *914 | 2 49. |
| | 2003 | 2 638 | ... | 2 427 | 132 | 79 | ... | *974 | 2 36. |
| | *2004 | 2 726 | ... | 2 500 | 146 | 80 | ... | 1 037 | 2 43. |
| | *2005 | 2 726 | ... | 2 500 | 146 | 80 | ... | 1 032 | 2 43( |
| Samoa* | 2002 | 3 | ... | ... | ... | 3 | ... | 48 | .. |
| | 2003 | 3 | ... | ... | ... | 3 | ... | 50 | |
| | 2004 | 3 | ... | ... | ... | 3 | ... | 51 | |
| | 2005 | 3 | ... | ... | ... | 3 | ... | 51 | |
| Solomon Islands* | 2002 | ... | ... | ... | ... | ... | ... | 59 | |
| | 2003 | ... | ... | ... | ... | ... | ... | 61 | |
| | 2004 | ... | ... | ... | ... | ... | ... | 61 | |
| | 2005 | ... | ... | ... | ... | ... | ... | 61 | |
| Tonga | 2002 | ... | ... | ... | ... | ... | ... | *37 | |
| | 2003 | ... | ... | ... | ... | ... | ... | *39 | |
| | 2004 | ... | ... | ... | ... | ... | ... | *40 | |
| | 2005 | ... | ... | ... | ... | ... | ... | *40 | |
| Vanuatu* | 2002 | ... | ... | ... | ... | ... | ... | 29 | |
| | 2003 | ... | ... | ... | ... | ... | ... | 30 | |
| | 2004 | ... | ... | ... | ... | ... | ... | 30 | |
| | 2005 | ... | ... | ... | ... | ... | ... | 30 | |

Source

United Nations Statistics Division, New York, the energy statistics database, last accessed January 2008.

Notes

1 Refers to the Southern African Customs Union.
2 For statistical purposes, the data for China do not include those for the Hong Kong Special Administrative Region (Hong Kong SAR), Macao Special Administrative Region (Macao SAR) and Taiwan Province of China.
3 Including Monaco.
4 Including San Marino.
5 Including Svalbard and Jan Mayen Islands.
6 Including Liechtenstein.

Source

Organisation des Nations Unies, Division de statistique, New York, la base de données pour les statistiques énergétiques, dernier accès janvier 2008.

Notes

1 Se réfèrent à l'Union douanière d'afrique australe.
2 Pour la présentation des statistiques, les données pour la Chine ne comprennent pas la Région Administrative Spéciale de Hong Kong (Hong Kong RAS), la Région Administrative Spéciale de Macao (Macao RAS) et la province de Taiwan.
3 Y compris Monaco.
4 Y compris Saint-Marin.
5 Y compris îles Svalbard et Jan Mayen.
6 Y compris Liechtenstein.

**19** Production, trade and consumption of commercial energy — Thousand metric tons of oil equivalent and kilograms per capita (*continued*)

Production, commerce et consommation d'énergie commerciale — Milliers de tonnes d'équivalent pétrole et kilogrammes par habitant (*suite*)

| Bunkers - Soutes | | | Consumption - Consommation | | | | | | | |
|---|---|---|---|---|---|---|---|---|---|---|
| Air Avion | Sea Maritime | Unallocated Nondistribué | Per capita Par habitant | Total Totale | Solids Solides | Liquids Liquides | Gas Gaz | Electricity Electricité | Year Année | Région, pays ou zone |
| *31 | *3 | 10 | *229 | *1 153 | ... | *929 | 144 | 79 | 2002 | Papouasie-Nvl-Guinée |
| *31 | *3 | 15 | *227 | *1 201 | ... | *990 | 132 | 79 | 2003 | |
| 31 | 3 | 18 | 235 | 1 276 | ... | 1 050 | 146 | 80 | *2004 | |
| 32 | 3 | 22 | 229 | 1 271 | ... | 1 045 | 146 | 80 | *2005 | |
| ... | ... | ... | 287 | 51 | ... | 48 | ... | 3 | 2002 | Samoa* |
| ... | ... | ... | 300 | 54 | ... | 50 | ... | 3 | 2003 | |
| ... | ... | ... | 304 | 54 | ... | 51 | ... | 3 | 2004 | |
| ... | ... | ... | 304 | 54 | ... | 51 | ... | 3 | 2005 | |
| 3 | ... | ... | 128 | 56 | ... | 56 | ... | ... | 2002 | Iles Salomon* |
| 3 | ... | ... | 130 | 58 | ... | 58 | ... | ... | 2003 | |
| 3 | ... | ... | 127 | 58 | ... | 58 | ... | ... | 2004 | |
| 3 | ... | ... | 124 | 58 | ... | 58 | ... | ... | 2005 | |
| *1 | ... | ... | *357 | *36 | 0 | *36 | ... | ... | 2002 | Tonga |
| *1 | ... | ... | *377 | *38 | 0 | *38 | ... | ... | 2003 | |
| *1 | ... | ... | *384 | *39 | 0 | *39 | ... | ... | 2004 | |
| *1 | ... | ... | *383 | *39 | 0 | *39 | ... | ... | 2005 | |
| ... | ... | ... | 138 | 29 | ... | 29 | ... | ... | 2002 | Vanuatu* |
| ... | ... | ... | 140 | 30 | ... | 30 | ... | ... | 2003 | |
| ... | ... | ... | 139 | 30 | ... | 30 | ... | ... | 2004 | |
| ... | ... | ... | 137 | 30 | ... | 30 | ... | ... | 2005 | |

# Energy production

# Production d'énergie

| Region, country or area / Région, pays ou zone | Year / Année | Hard coal and lignite / Houille et lignite | Crude petroleum and NGL / Pétrole brut et LGN | Motor gasoline / Essence auto | Jet fuel / Carbu-réacteurs | Gas-diesel oil / Gazole/ carburant diesel | Residual fuel oil / Mazout résiduel | Liquefied petroleum gas / Gaz de pétrole liquéfiés | Natural gas (terajoules) / Gaz naturel (térajoules) | Electricity (million kWh) / Électricité (millions de kWh) |
|---|---|---|---|---|---|---|---|---|---|---|
| | | Thousand metric tons — Milliers de tonnes | | | | | | | | |
| World | 2002 | 4 856 084 | 3 628 602 | 867 055 | 206 078 | 1 039 797 | 595 550 | 221 074 | 100 782 625 | 16 171 336 |
| Monde | 2003 | 5 187 004 | 3 770 635 | 872 465 | 205 758 | 1 078 302 | 595 681 | 223 510 | 104 438 647 | 16 773 078 |
| | 2004 | 5 571 616 | 3 899 818 | 894 268 | 218 507 | 1 123 154 | 600 723 | 235 521 | 107 453 052 | 17 555 859 |
| | 2005 | 5 897 297 | 3 967 372 | 895 788 | 225 964 | 1 161 537 | 598 882 | 238 380 | 110 554 879 | 18 335 030 |
| Africa | 2002 | 226 093[1] | 407 899 | 24 232 | 7 933 | 36 962 | 39 426 | 13 196 | 5 434 041 | 480 385 |
| Afrique | 2003 | 244 117[1] | 433 729 | 23 030 | 7 897 | 35 866 | 35 107 | 12 807 | 5 697 615 | 505 636 |
| | 2004 | 248 243[1] | 469 758 | 21 979 | 7 954 | 36 163 | 33 895 | 12 356 | 6 054 552 | 536 300 |
| | 2005 | 250 703[1] | 499 116 | 19 487 | 8 517 | 37 657 | 35 143 | 12 586 | 7 178 251 | 557 676 |
| Algeria | 2002 | ... | 95 534 | 1 939 | 1 393 | 6 044 | 5 833 | 9 956 | 3 213 741 | 27 647 |
| Algérie | 2003 | ... | 102 501 | 1 893 | 1 315 | 6 186 | 6 093 | 9 756 | 3 248 416 | 29 571 |
| | 2004 | ... | 107 144 | 1 925 | 986 | 6 340 | 5 560 | 9 223 | 3 216 262 | 31 250 |
| | 2005 | ... | 110 285 | 2 059 | 1 069 | 5 946 | 5 055 | 9 337 | 3 586 296 | 32 873 |
| Angola | 2002 | ... | 44 045[2] | 105 | 350 | 669 | 591 | 39 | 23 560 | 1 765 |
| Angola | 2003 | ... | 43 083[2] | 108 | 352 | 683 | 609 | 40 | *27 360 | 1 995 |
| | 2004 | ... | 49 443[2] | 96 | 302 | 669 | 604 | 28 | 28 500 | 2 339 |
| | 2005 | ... | 62 314[2] | 134 | 290 | 461 | 609 | 24 | 28 500 | 2 653 |
| Benin | 2002 | ... | 40[2] | ... | ... | ... | ... | ... | ... | 63 |
| Bénin | 2003 | ... | 20[2] | ... | ... | ... | ... | ... | ... | 80 |
| | 2004 | ... | *20[2] | ... | ... | ... | ... | ... | ... | 81 |
| | 2005 | ... | *20[2] | ... | ... | ... | ... | ... | ... | 107 |
| Burkina Faso* | 2002 | ... | ... | ... | ... | ... | ... | ... | ... | 340 |
| Burkina Faso* | 2003 | ... | ... | ... | ... | ... | ... | ... | ... | 360 |
| | 2004 | ... | ... | ... | ... | ... | ... | ... | ... | 400 |
| | 2005 | ... | ... | ... | ... | ... | ... | ... | ... | 417 |
| Burundi | 2002 | ... | ... | ... | ... | ... | ... | ... | ... | 129 |
| Burundi | *2003 | ... | ... | ... | ... | ... | ... | ... | ... | 132 |
| | *2004 | ... | ... | ... | ... | ... | ... | ... | ... | 135 |
| | 2005 | ... | ... | ... | ... | ... | ... | ... | ... | 101 |
| Cameroon | 2002 | ... | 6 439[2] | 232 | 69 | 370 | 317 | 18 | ... | 3 300 |
| Cameroun | 2003 | ... | 6 735[2] | 290 | 69 | 446 | 327 | 21 | ... | 3 684 |
| | 2004 | ... | 6 637[2] | 402 | 69 | 607 | 388 | 28 | ... | 4 110 |
| | 2005 | ... | 6 035[2] | 393 | 62 | 610 | 341 | 26 | ... | 4 145 |
| Cape Verde | 2002 | ... | ... | ... | ... | ... | ... | ... | ... | 182 |
| Cap-Vert | 2003 | ... | ... | ... | ... | ... | ... | ... | ... | 200 |
| | 2004 | ... | ... | ... | ... | ... | ... | ... | ... | 220 |
| | 2005 | ... | ... | ... | ... | ... | ... | ... | ... | 237 |
| Central African Rep.* | 2002 | ... | ... | ... | ... | ... | ... | ... | ... | 108 |
| Rép. centrafricaine* | 2003 | ... | ... | ... | ... | ... | ... | ... | ... | 110 |
| | 2004 | ... | ... | ... | ... | ... | ... | ... | ... | 110 |
| | 2005 | ... | ... | ... | ... | ... | ... | ... | ... | 110 |
| Chad* | 2002 | ... | ... | ... | ... | ... | ... | ... | ... | 98 |
| Tchad* | 2003 | ... | ... | ... | ... | ... | ... | ... | ... | 99 |
| | 2004 | ... | ... | ... | ... | ... | ... | ... | ... | 99 |
| | 2005 | ... | ... | ... | ... | ... | ... | ... | ... | 100 |
| Comoros* | 2002 | ... | ... | ... | ... | ... | ... | ... | ... | 19 |
| Comores* | 2003 | ... | ... | ... | ... | ... | ... | ... | ... | 20 |
| | 2004 | ... | ... | ... | ... | ... | ... | ... | ... | 20 |
| | 2005 | ... | ... | ... | ... | ... | ... | ... | ... | 20 |

| Region, country or area / Région, pays ou zone | Year / Année | Hard coal and lignite / Houille et lignite | Crude petroleum and NGL / Pétrole brut et LGN | Motor gasoline / Essence auto | Jet fuel / Carbu-réacteurs | Gas-diesel oil / Gazole/ carburant diesel | Residual fuel oil / Mazout résiduel | Liquefied petroleum gas / Gaz de pétrole liquéfiés | Natural gas (terajoules) / Gaz naturel (térajoules) | Electricity (million kWh) / Electricité (millions de kWh) |
|---|---|---|---|---|---|---|---|---|---|---|
| | | Thousand metric tons — Milliers de tonnes | | | | | | | | |
| Congo | 2002 | ... | 12 209 | 41 | 43 | 75 | 228 | 2 | 4 940 | 397 |
| Congo | 2003 | ... | 11 142 | 53 | 38 | 119 | 287 | 4 | *4 865 | 343 |
| | 2004 | ... | 11 595 | 49 | 47 | 120 | 295 | 5 | *4 865 | 399 |
| | 2005 | ... | 12 636 | 47 | 45 | 110 | 210 | 5 | *4 775 | 356 |
| Côte d'Ivoire | 2002 | ... | 749[2] | 487 | 92 | 1 084 | 337 | 69 | 60 185 | 5 308 |
| Côte d'Ivoire | 2003 | ... | 1 055[2] | 359 | 104 | 745 | 318 | 49 | 53 012 | 5 093 |
| | 2004 | ... | 1 302[2] | 589 | 88 | 1 313 | 209 | 80 | 57 981 | 5 411 |
| | 2005 | ... | 2 072[2] | 494 | 88 | 1 147 | 506 | 66 | 64 816 | 5 578 |
| Dem. Rep. of the Congo | 2002 | 102[1] | 1 151[2] | ... | ... | ... | ... | ... | ... | 6 075 |
| Rép. dém. du Congo | 2003 | 105[1] | 1 083[2] | ... | ... | ... | ... | ... | ... | 6 258 |
| | 2004 | 108[1] | 1 033[2] | ... | ... | ... | ... | ... | ... | 6 852 |
| | 2005 | 120[1] | 984[2] | ... | ... | ... | ... | ... | ... | 7 419 |
| Djibouti | 2002 | ... | ... | ... | ... | ... | ... | ... | ... | 200 |
| Djibouti | 2003 | ... | ... | ... | ... | ... | ... | ... | ... | 200 |
| | 2004 | ... | ... | ... | ... | ... | ... | ... | ... | 215 |
| | 2005 | ... | ... | ... | ... | ... | ... | ... | ... | 255 |
| Egypt | 2002 | 37[1] | 43 324 | 6 046 | 1 693 | 8 314 | 12 501 | 1 728 | 1 076 806 | 85 946 |
| Egypte | 2003 | 37[1] | *41 112 | *6 306 | 1 469 | 8 703 | 11 661 | 1 739 | 1 214 024 | 91 932 |
| | 2004 | 33[1] | *37 605 | *5 000 | 2 080 | 7 922 | 11 273 | 1 724 | 1 311 413 | 101 299 |
| | 2005 | 33[1] | 36 886 | 2 972 | 2 146 | 8 179 | 11 643 | 1 713 | 1 880 223 | 108 690 |
| Equatorial Guinea | 2002 | ... | 11 597[2] | ... | ... | ... | ... | ... | *18 537 | *26 |
| Guinée équatoriale | 2003 | ... | 10 299[2] | ... | ... | ... | ... | ... | 18 773 | *26 |
| | 2004 | ... | 18 410[2] | ... | ... | ... | ... | ... | *18 730 | *27 |
| | 2005 | ... | 19 807[2] | ... | ... | ... | ... | ... | *18 730 | *27 |
| Eritrea | 2002 | ... | ... | ... | ... | ... | ... | ... | ... | 258 |
| Erythrée | 2003 | ... | ... | ... | ... | ... | ... | ... | ... | 276 |
| | 2004 | ... | ... | ... | ... | ... | ... | ... | ... | 283 |
| | 2005 | ... | ... | ... | ... | ... | ... | ... | ... | 289 |
| Ethiopia | 2002 | ... | ... | ... | ... | ... | ... | 3 | ... | 2 050 |
| Ethiopie | 2003 | ... | ... | ... | ... | ... | ... | *3 | ... | 2 309 |
| | 2004 | ... | ... | ... | ... | ... | ... | *3 | ... | 2 547 |
| | 2005 | ... | ... | ... | ... | ... | ... | *3 | ... | 2 872 |
| Gabon | 2002 | ... | 11 330[2] | 64 | 58 | 219 | 254 | 10 | 4 271 | 1 457 |
| Gabon | 2003 | ... | 11 056[2] | 69 | 54 | 210 | 302 | 9 | 4 421 | 1 504 |
| | 2004 | ... | 10 736[2] | 68 | 45 | 228 | 324 | 9 | 4 912 | 1 537 |
| | 2005 | ... | 10 736[2] | 69 | 45 | 233 | 330 | 9 | 4 912 | 1 569 |
| Gambia | 2002 | ... | ... | ... | ... | ... | ... | ... | ... | 151 |
| Gambie | *2003 | ... | ... | ... | ... | ... | ... | ... | ... | 151 |
| | *2004 | ... | ... | ... | ... | ... | ... | ... | ... | 151 |
| | *2005 | ... | ... | ... | ... | ... | ... | ... | ... | 151 |
| Ghana | 2002 | ... | ... | 346 | 82 | 447 | 196 | 24 | ... | 7 301 |
| Ghana | 2003 | ... | ... | 434 | 91 | 493 | 216 | 53 | ... | 5 908 |
| | 2004 | ... | ... | 580 | 107 | 568 | 199 | 66 | ... | 6 044 |
| | 2005 | ... | ... | 567 | 113 | 520 | 242 | 78 | ... | 6 793 |
| Guinea* | 2002 | ... | ... | ... | ... | ... | ... | ... | ... | 798 |
| Guinée* | 2003 | ... | ... | ... | ... | ... | ... | ... | ... | 801 |
| | 2004 | ... | ... | ... | ... | ... | ... | ... | ... | 801 |
| | 2005 | ... | ... | ... | ... | ... | ... | ... | ... | 802 |
| Guinea-Bissau* | 2002 | ... | ... | ... | ... | ... | ... | ... | ... | 60 |
| Guinée-Bissau* | 2003 | ... | ... | ... | ... | ... | ... | ... | ... | 61 |
| | 2004 | ... | ... | ... | ... | ... | ... | ... | ... | 61 |
| | 2005 | ... | ... | ... | ... | ... | ... | ... | ... | 61 |

| Region, country or area / Région, pays ou zone | Year / Année | Hard coal and lignite / Houille et lignite | Crude petroleum and NGL / Pétrole brut et LGN | Motor gasoline / Essence auto | Jet fuel / Carbu-réacteurs | Gas-diesel oil / Gazole/ carburant diesel | Residual fuel oil / Mazout résiduel | Liquefied petroleum gas / Gaz de pétrole liquéfiés | Natural gas (terajoules) / Gaz naturel (térajoules) | Electricity (million kWh) / Electricité (millions de kWh) |
|---|---|---|---|---|---|---|---|---|---|---|
| | | Thousand metric tons — Milliers de tonnes | | | | | | | | |
| Kenya<br>Kenya | 2002 | ... | ... | 253 | 191 | 405 | 533 | 24 | ... | 4 849 |
| | 2003 | ... | ... | 263 | 204 | 411 | 524 | 24 | ... | 5 185 |
| | 2004 | ... | ... | 275 | 212 | 387 | 620 | 27 | ... | 5 568 |
| | 2005 | ... | ... | 266 | 205 | 374 | 549 | 26 | ... | 6 003 |
| Liberia<br>Libéria | 2002 | ... | ... | ... | ... | ... | ... | ... | ... | 320 |
| | 2003 | ... | ... | ... | ... | ... | ... | ... | ... | 320 |
| | 2004 | ... | ... | ... | ... | ... | ... | ... | ... | 330 |
| | *2005 | ... | ... | ... | ... | ... | ... | ... | ... | 335 |
| Libyan Arab Jamah.<br>Jamah. arabe libyenne | 2002 | ... | 62 629 | 2 020 | 1 525 | 4 843 | 4 659 | 315 | 242 321 | 17 351 |
| | 2003 | ... | 70 781 | 1 972 | 1 491 | 4 737 | 4 556 | 310 | 249 735 | 18 943 |
| | 2004 | ... | 77 420 | 1 991 | 1 504 | 4 782 | 4 597 | 310 | 314 509 | 20 202 |
| | 2005 | ... | 83 016 | 2 020 | 1 525 | 4 849 | 4 665 | 315 | 456 546 | 22 500 |
| Madagascar<br>Madagascar | 2002 | ... | ... | *112 | *1 | *57 | *77 | *6 | ... | 790 |
| | 2003 | ... | ... | *113 | *1 | *57 | *77 | *6 | ... | 900 |
| | 2004 | ... | ... | *113 | *1 | *57 | *77 | *6 | ... | 990 |
| | *2005 | ... | ... | 114 | 1 | 58 | 78 | 6 | ... | 1 035 |
| Malawi<br>Malawi | 2002 | 60[1] | ... | ... | ... | ... | ... | ... | ... | *1 129 |
| | 2003 | 66[1] | ... | ... | ... | ... | ... | ... | ... | *1 177 |
| | *2004 | 70[1] | ... | ... | ... | ... | ... | ... | ... | 1 270 |
| | *2005 | 65[1] | ... | ... | ... | ... | ... | ... | ... | 1 273 |
| Mali*<br>Mali* | 2002 | ... | ... | ... | ... | ... | ... | ... | ... | 417 |
| | 2003 | ... | ... | ... | ... | ... | ... | ... | ... | 449 |
| | 2004 | ... | ... | ... | ... | ... | ... | ... | ... | 455 |
| | 2005 | ... | ... | ... | ... | ... | ... | ... | ... | 459 |
| Mauritania*<br>Mauritanie* | 2002 | ... | ... | ... | ... | ... | ... | ... | ... | 264 |
| | 2003 | ... | ... | ... | ... | ... | ... | ... | ... | 312 |
| | 2004 | ... | ... | ... | ... | ... | ... | ... | ... | 336 |
| | 2005 | ... | ... | ... | ... | ... | ... | ... | ... | 375 |
| Mauritius<br>Maurice | *2002 | ... | ... | ... | ... | ... | ... | ... | ... | 1 949 |
| | 2003 | ... | ... | ... | ... | ... | ... | ... | ... | 2 082 |
| | 2004 | ... | ... | ... | ... | ... | ... | ... | ... | 2 165 |
| | 2005 | ... | ... | ... | ... | ... | ... | ... | ... | 2 271 |
| Morocco<br>Maroc | 2002 | ... | 13[2] | 377 | 137 | 2 323 | 1 999 | 232 | 1 693 | 14 188 |
| | 2003 | ... | 10[2] | 132 | 108 | 1 535 | 1 747 | 67 | 1 633 | 15 385 |
| | 2004 | ... | 11[2] | 257 | 174 | 2 254 | 2 264 | 104 | 1 977 | 16 459 |
| | 2005 | ... | 7[2] | 372 | 264 | 2 295 | 2 545 | 204 | 17 957 | 19 243 |
| Mozambique<br>Mozambique | 2002 | 44[1] | ... | ... | ... | ... | ... | ... | 92 | 12 713 |
| | 2003 | 37[1] | ... | ... | ... | ... | ... | ... | 96 | 10 602 |
| | 2004 | 41[1] | ... | ... | ... | ... | ... | ... | 52 312 | 11 714 |
| | 2005 | 41[1] | ... | ... | ... | ... | ... | ... | 88 029 | 13 289 |
| Niger<br>Niger | 2002 | 183[1] | ... | ... | ... | ... | ... | ... | ... | *243 |
| | 2003 | 189[1] | ... | ... | ... | ... | ... | ... | ... | *245 |
| | 2004 | 200[1] | ... | ... | ... | ... | ... | ... | ... | *247 |
| | 2005 | 182[1] | ... | ... | ... | ... | ... | ... | ... | *250 |
| Nigeria<br>Nigéria | 2002 | 43[1] | 102 189 | 2 603 | 374 | 2 484 | 2 593 | 81 | 623 048 | 21 544 |
| | 2003 | 23[1] | 117 666 | 1 036 | 386 | 1 418 | 1 838 | 17 | 742 296 | 20 183 |
| | 2004 | 3[1] | 128 308 | 534 | 189 | 1 179 | 1 866 | 17 | 873 602 | 20 224 |
| | 2005 | 8[1] | 133 199 | 275 | 480 | 980 | 1 894 | 17 | 850 658 | 20 468 |
| Réunion*<br>Réunion* | 2002 | ... | ... | ... | ... | ... | ... | ... | ... | 1 613 |
| | 2003 | ... | ... | ... | ... | ... | ... | ... | ... | 1 618 |
| | 2004 | ... | ... | ... | ... | ... | ... | ... | ... | 1 620 |
| | 2005 | ... | ... | ... | ... | ... | ... | ... | ... | 1 620 |

| Region, country or area / Région, pays ou zone | Year / Année | Hard coal and lignite / Houille et lignite | Crude petroleum and NGL / Pétrole brut et LGN | Motor gasoline / Essence auto | Jet fuel / Carbu-réacteurs | Gas-diesel oil / Gazole/ carburant diesel | Residual fuel oil / Mazout résiduel | Liquefied petroleum gas / Gaz de pétrole liquéfiés | Natural gas (terajoules) / Gaz naturel (térajoules) | Electricity (million kWh) / Electricité (millions de kWh) |
|---|---|---|---|---|---|---|---|---|---|---|
| | | Thousand metric tons — Milliers de tonnes | | | | | | | | |
| Rwanda | 2002 | ... | ... | ... | ... | ... | ... | ... | 4 | 102 |
| Rwanda | 2003 | ... | ... | ... | ... | ... | ... | ... | 12 | 122 |
| | *2004 | ... | ... | ... | ... | ... | ... | ... | 20 | 130 |
| | *2005 | ... | ... | ... | ... | ... | ... | ... | 23 | 135 |
| Saint Helena | 2002 | ... | ... | ... | ... | ... | ... | ... | ... | 7 |
| Sainte-Hélène | *2003 | ... | ... | ... | ... | ... | ... | ... | ... | 7 |
| | 2004 | ... | ... | ... | ... | ... | ... | ... | ... | 8 |
| | *2005 | ... | ... | ... | ... | ... | ... | ... | ... | 8 |
| Sao Tome and Principe* | 2002 | ... | ... | ... | ... | ... | ... | ... | ... | 18 |
| Sao Tomé-et-Principe* | 2003 | ... | ... | ... | ... | ... | ... | ... | ... | 18 |
| | 2004 | ... | ... | ... | ... | ... | ... | ... | ... | 18 |
| | 2005 | ... | ... | ... | ... | ... | ... | ... | ... | 19 |
| Senegal | 2002 | ... | ... | 140 | 72 | 375 | 255 | 9 | 114 | 2 048 |
| Sénégal | 2003 | ... | ... | 151 | 126 | 463 | 316 | 12 | 423 | 2 157 |
| | 2004 | ... | ... | 148 | 132 | 471 | 327 | 10 | 506 | 2 354 |
| | 2005 | ... | ... | 118 | 88 | 356 | 279 | 3 | 630 | 2 595 |
| Seychelles | 2002 | ... | ... | ... | ... | ... | ... | ... | ... | 219 |
| Seychelles | *2003 | ... | ... | ... | ... | ... | ... | ... | ... | 220 |
| | *2004 | ... | ... | ... | ... | ... | ... | ... | ... | 220 |
| | *2005 | ... | ... | ... | ... | ... | ... | ... | ... | 220 |
| Sierra Leone | *2002 | ... | ... | 31 | 20 | 74 | 55 | ... | ... | 155 |
| Sierra Leone | *2003 | ... | ... | 31 | 20 | 74 | 55 | ... | ... | 139 |
| | 2004 | ... | ... | *32 | *21 | *60 | *55 | ... | ... | 137 |
| | 2005 | ... | ... | *32 | *21 | *60 | *55 | ... | ... | 102 |
| Somalia | 2002 | ... | ... | 5 | ... | 10 | 8 | ... | ... | 274 |
| Somalie | 2003 | ... | ... | 5 | ... | 10 | 8 | ... | ... | 280 |
| | 2004 | ... | ... | 5 | ... | 10 | 10 | ... | ... | 280 |
| | 2005 | ... | ... | 5 | ... | 10 | 10 | ... | ... | 290 |
| South Africa[3] | 2002 | 221 531[1] | 1 026 | 8 085 | 1 637 | 7 383 | 8 026 | 316 | 83 764 | 220 745 |
| Afrique du Sud[3] | 2003 | 239 934[1] | 684 | 8 360 | 1 874 | 7 593 | 5 162 | 307 | 50 218 | 237 183 |
| | 2004 | 244 092[1] | 1 665 | 8 343 | 1 778 | 7 141 | 4 192 | 305 | 77 172 | 247 777 |
| | 2005 | 246 313[1] | 1 541 | 7 858 | 1 840 | 9 201 | 5 040 | 297 | 82 976 | 248 075 |
| Sudan | 2002 | ... | 12 035[2] | 985 | 169 | 1 123 | 290 | 241 | ... | 2 897 |
| Soudan | 2003 | ... | 13 250[2] | 1 111 | 170 | 1 273 | 328 | 284 | ... | 3 354 |
| | 2004 | ... | 15 000[2] | 1 228 | 192 | 1 400 | 361 | 300 | ... | 3 883 |
| | 2005 | ... | 16 100[2] | 1 350 | 206 | 1 547 | 398 | 345 | ... | 4 124 |
| Togo | 2002 | ... | ... | ... | ... | ... | ... | ... | ... | 234 |
| Togo | 2003 | ... | ... | ... | ... | ... | ... | ... | ... | 293 |
| | 2004 | ... | ... | ... | ... | ... | ... | ... | ... | 184 |
| | 2005 | ... | ... | ... | ... | ... | ... | ... | ... | 187 |
| Tunisia | 2002 | ... | 3 589 | 261 | ... | 469 | 604 | 120 | 80 966 | 11 281 |
| Tunisie | 2003 | ... | 3 252 | 234 | ... | 502 | 609 | 103 | 82 331 | 11 829 |
| | 2004 | ... | 3 429 | 226 | ... | 432 | 595 | 108 | 86 816 | 12 455 |
| | 2005 | ... | 3 478 | 216 | ... | 482 | 609 | 109 | 87 857 | 13 007 |
| Uganda | 2002 | ... | ... | ... | ... | ... | ... | ... | ... | 1 674 |
| Ouganda | *2003 | ... | ... | ... | ... | ... | ... | ... | ... | 1 675 |
| | *2004 | ... | ... | ... | ... | ... | ... | ... | ... | 1 896 |
| | 2005 | ... | ... | ... | ... | ... | ... | ... | ... | 1 835 |
| United Rep. of Tanzania | 2002 | 79[1] | ... | ... | ... | ... | ... | ... | 0 | 2 854 |
| Rép.-Unie de Tanzanie | 2003 | 55[1] | ... | ... | ... | ... | ... | ... | 0 | 2 658 |
| | 2004 | 65[1] | ... | ... | ... | ... | ... | ... | 4 975 | 2 478 |
| | 2005 | 75[1] | ... | ... | ... | ... | ... | ... | 5 323 | 3 036 |

| Region, country or area<br>Région, pays ou zone | Year<br>Année | Hard coal and lignite<br>Houille et lignite | Crude petroleum and NGL<br>Pétrole brut et LGN | Motor gasoline<br>Essence auto | Jet fuel<br>Carbu-réacteurs | Gas-diesel oil<br>Gazole/ carburant diesel | Residual fuel oil<br>Mazout résiduel | Liquefied petroleum gas<br>Gaz de pétrole liquéfiés | Natural gas (terajoules)<br>Gaz naturel (térajoules) | Electricity (million kWh)<br>Electricité (millions de kWh) |
|---|---|---|---|---|---|---|---|---|---|---|
| | | Thousand metric tons — Milliers de tonnes | | | | | | | | |
| Western Sahara | 2002 | ... | ... | ... | ... | ... | ... | ... | ... | 90 |
| Sahara occidental | 2003 | ... | ... | ... | ... | ... | ... | ... | ... | 90 |
| | 2004 | ... | ... | ... | ... | ... | ... | ... | ... | 90 |
| | 2005 | ... | ... | ... | ... | ... | ... | ... | ... | 90 |
| Zambia | 2002 | 210[1] | ... | 100 | 27 | 194 | 70 | 3 | ... | 8 152 |
| Zambie | 2003 | 221[1] | ... | 110 | 25 | 208 | 74 | 3 | ... | 8 308 |
| | 2004 | 233[1] | ... | 118 | 27 | 223 | 79 | 3 | ... | 8 512 |
| | 2005 | 244[1] | ... | 126 | 29 | 239 | 85 | 3 | ... | 8 938 |
| Zimbabwe | 2002 | 3 804[1] | ... | ... | ... | ... | ... | ... | ... | 8 587 |
| Zimbabwe | 2003 | 3 450[1] | ... | ... | ... | ... | ... | ... | ... | 8 789 |
| | 2004 | 3 398[1] | ... | ... | ... | ... | ... | ... | ... | 9 908 |
| | 2005 | 3 622[1] | ... | ... | ... | ... | ... | ... | ... | 10 269 |
| **America, North** | **2002** | **1 070 209** | **663 127** | **405 538** | **79 424** | **228 642** | **80 040** | **66 338** | **30 216 784** | **4 969 659** |
| **Amérique du Nord** | **2003** | **1 044 040** | **674 604** | **406 616** | **78 652** | **239 833** | **80 663** | **64 844** | **30 712 555** | **4 998 031** |
| | **2004** | **1 095 008** | **670 679** | **408 903** | **82 411** | **247 008** | **79 518** | **67 463** | **30 262 089** | **5 109 092** |
| | **2005** | **1 114 691** | **650 184** | **407 651** | **82 927** | **253 741** | **76 514** | **64 406** | **29 953 378** | **5 264 253** |
| Anguilla | 2002 | ... | ... | ... | ... | ... | ... | ... | ... | 55 |
| Anguilla | 2003 | ... | ... | ... | ... | ... | ... | ... | ... | 58 |
| | 2004 | ... | ... | ... | ... | ... | ... | ... | ... | 62 |
| | 2005 | ... | ... | ... | ... | ... | ... | ... | ... | 72 |
| Antigua and Barbuda* | 2002 | ... | ... | ... | ... | ... | ... | ... | ... | 105 |
| Antigua-et-Barbuda* | 2003 | ... | ... | ... | ... | ... | ... | ... | ... | 109 |
| | 2004 | ... | ... | ... | ... | ... | ... | ... | ... | 109 |
| | 2005 | ... | ... | ... | ... | ... | ... | ... | ... | 109 |
| Aruba | 2002 | ... | *120[2] | ... | ... | ... | ... | ... | ... | 810 |
| Aruba | 2003 | ... | *120[2] | ... | ... | ... | ... | ... | ... | 816 |
| | 2004 | ... | *120[2] | ... | ... | ... | ... | ... | ... | 816 |
| | *2005 | ... | 120[2] | ... | ... | ... | ... | ... | ... | 830 |
| Bahamas | 2002 | ... | ... | ... | ... | ... | ... | ... | ... | 1 886 |
| Bahamas | 2003 | ... | ... | ... | ... | ... | ... | ... | ... | 1 990 |
| | *2004 | ... | ... | ... | ... | ... | ... | ... | ... | 2 087 |
| | *2005 | ... | ... | ... | ... | ... | ... | ... | ... | 2 090 |
| Barbados | 2002 | ... | 81 | ... | ... | ... | ... | 1 | 1 139 | 859 |
| Barbade | 2003 | ... | 75 | ... | ... | ... | ... | 1 | 1 020 | 871 |
| | 2004 | ... | 85 | ... | ... | ... | ... | 1 | 973 | 895 |
| | 2005 | ... | 88 | ... | ... | ... | ... | 1 | 1 028 | 930 |
| Belize* | 2002 | ... | ... | ... | ... | ... | ... | ... | ... | 159 |
| Belize* | 2003 | ... | ... | ... | ... | ... | ... | ... | ... | 169 |
| | 2004 | ... | ... | ... | ... | ... | ... | ... | ... | 169 |
| | 2005 | ... | ... | ... | ... | ... | ... | ... | ... | 175 |
| Bermuda | 2002 | ... | ... | ... | ... | ... | ... | ... | ... | 644 |
| Bermudes | 2003 | ... | ... | ... | ... | ... | ... | ... | ... | 664 |
| | *2004 | ... | ... | ... | ... | ... | ... | ... | ... | 661 |
| | *2005 | ... | ... | ... | ... | ... | ... | ... | ... | 665 |
| British Virgin Islands | 2002 | ... | ... | ... | ... | ... | ... | ... | ... | 40 |
| Iles Vierges britanniques | *2003 | ... | ... | ... | ... | ... | ... | ... | ... | 45 |
| | *2004 | ... | ... | ... | ... | ... | ... | ... | ... | 45 |
| | *2005 | ... | ... | ... | ... | ... | ... | ... | ... | 45 |
| Canada | 2002 | 66 508 | 133 303 | 33 737 | 3 938 | 29 253 | 6 879 | 1 982 | 7 133 466 | 601 135 |
| Canada | 2003 | 62 163 | 140 928 | 33 689 | 4 200 | 31 136 | 7 989 | 1 991 | 7 032 164 | 589 967 |
| | 2004 | 65 997 | 145 983 | 33 024 | 4 597 | 31 590 | 8 724 | 1 955 | 7 016 682 | 598 514 |
| | 2005 | 65 345 | 144 080 | 32 270 | 4 363 | 30 745 | 8 263 | 1 779 | 7 169 112 | 628 194 |

| Region, country or area / Région, pays ou zone | Year / Année | Hard coal and lignite / Houille et lignite | Crude petroleum and NGL / Pétrole brut et LGN | Motor gasoline / Essence auto | Jet fuel / Carbu-réacteurs | Gas-diesel oil / Gazole/carburant diesel | Residual fuel oil / Mazout résiduel | Liquefied petroleum gas / Gaz de pétrole liquéfiés | Natural gas (terajoules) / Gaz naturel (térajoules) | Electricity (million kWh) / Electricité (millions de kWh) |
|---|---|---|---|---|---|---|---|---|---|---|
| Cayman Islands / Iles Caïmanes | 2002 | ... | ... | ... | ... | ... | ... | ... | ... | 466 |
| | 2003 | ... | ... | ... | ... | ... | ... | ... | ... | 490 |
| | 2004 | ... | ... | ... | ... | ... | ... | ... | ... | 433 |
| | 2005 | ... | ... | ... | ... | ... | ... | ... | ... | 454 |
| Costa Rica / Costa Rica | 2002 | ... | ... | 0 | ... | 143 | 237 | 2 | ... | 7 485 |
| | 2003 | ... | ... | 0 | ... | 173 | 220 | 2 | ... | 7 566 |
| | 2004 | ... | ... | 0 | ... | 162 | 245 | 2 | ... | 8 210 |
| | 2005 | ... | ... | 85 | ... | 152 | 233 | 2 | ... | 8 252 |
| Cuba / Cuba | 2002 | ... | 3 628[2] | 319 | ... | 292 | 774 | 66 | 22 827 | 15 699 |
| | 2003 | ... | 3 680[2] | 412 | ... | 444 | 1 024 | 93 | 25 675 | 15 811 |
| | 2004 | ... | 3 253[2] | 331 | ... | 385 | 858 | 63 | 27 470 | 15 652 |
| | 2005 | ... | 2 876[2] | 340 | ... | 395 | 879 | 65 | 28 637 | 15 638 |
| Dominica / Dominique | 2002 | ... | ... | ... | ... | ... | ... | ... | ... | 80 |
| | 2003 | ... | ... | ... | ... | ... | ... | ... | ... | 79 |
| | 2004 | ... | ... | ... | ... | ... | ... | ... | ... | 79 |
| | 2005 | ... | ... | ... | ... | ... | ... | ... | ... | 84 |
| Dominican Republic / Rép. dominicaine | 2002 | ... | ... | 268 | 61 | 395 | 486 | 38 | ... | 11 510 |
| | 2003 | ... | ... | 284 | 54 | 411 | 449 | 42 | ... | 13 552 |
| | 2004 | ... | ... | 445 | 54 | 417 | 843 | 33 | ... | 13 829 |
| | 2005 | ... | ... | 447 | 56 | 423 | 812 | 35 | ... | 12 961 |
| El Salvador / El Salvador | 2002 | ... | ... | 127 | 39 | 151 | 526 | 14 | ... | 4 100 |
| | 2003 | ... | ... | 135 | 45 | 195 | 485 | 12 | ... | 4 128 |
| | 2004 | ... | ... | 143 | 49 | 199 | 543 | 14 | ... | 4 468 |
| | 2005 | ... | ... | 147 | 51 | 204 | 559 | 15 | ... | 4 788 |
| Greenland* / Groenland* | 2002 | ... | ... | ... | ... | ... | ... | ... | ... | 266 |
| | 2003 | ... | ... | ... | ... | ... | ... | ... | ... | 268 |
| | 2004 | ... | ... | ... | ... | ... | ... | ... | ... | 270 |
| | 2005 | ... | ... | ... | ... | ... | ... | ... | ... | 272 |
| Grenada / Grenade | 2002 | ... | ... | ... | ... | ... | ... | ... | ... | 153 |
| | 2003 | ... | ... | ... | ... | ... | ... | ... | ... | 153 |
| | 2004 | ... | ... | ... | ... | ... | ... | ... | ... | 157 |
| | 2005 | ... | ... | ... | ... | ... | ... | ... | ... | 166 |
| Guadeloupe / Guadeloupe | 2002 | ... | ... | ... | ... | ... | ... | ... | ... | 1 160 |
| | 2003 | ... | ... | ... | ... | ... | ... | ... | ... | 1 165 |
| | *2004 | ... | ... | ... | ... | ... | ... | ... | ... | 1 165 |
| | *2005 | ... | ... | ... | ... | ... | ... | ... | ... | 1 175 |
| Guatemala / Guatemala | 2002 | ... | 1 218[2] | 112 | 13 | 203 | 211 | 6 | ... | 6 191 |
| | 2003 | ... | 1 221[2] | 0 | 0 | 0 | 0 | 0 | ... | 6 561 |
| | 2004 | ... | 999[2] | 0 | 0 | 0 | 0 | 0 | ... | 7 009 |
| | 2005 | ... | 910[2] | 1 | 0 | 25 | 0 | 0 | ... | 7 550 |
| Haiti / Haïti | 2002 | ... | ... | ... | ... | ... | ... | ... | ... | 547 |
| | 2003 | ... | ... | ... | ... | ... | ... | ... | ... | 535 |
| | 2004 | ... | ... | ... | ... | ... | ... | ... | ... | 547 |
| | 2005 | ... | ... | ... | ... | ... | ... | ... | ... | 556 |
| Honduras / Honduras | 2002 | ... | ... | ... | ... | ... | ... | ... | ... | 4 165 |
| | 2003 | ... | ... | ... | ... | ... | ... | ... | ... | 4 530 |
| | 2004 | ... | ... | ... | ... | ... | ... | ... | ... | 4 877 |
| | 2005 | ... | ... | ... | ... | ... | ... | ... | ... | 5 545 |
| Jamaica / Jamaïque | 2002 | ... | ... | 150 | 89 | 242 | 591 | 14 | ... | 6 934 |
| | 2003 | ... | ... | 111 | 62 | 158 | 495 | 7 | ... | 7 146 |
| | 2004 | ... | ... | 95 | 63 | 129 | 370 | 9 | ... | 7 217 |
| | 2005 | ... | ... | 52 | 41 | 87 | 268 | 0 | ... | 7 526 |

| Region, country or area  Région, pays ou zone | Year  Année | Hard coal and lignite  Houille et lignite | Crude petroleum and NGL  Pétrole brut et LGN | Motor gasoline  Essence auto | Jet fuel  Carbu-réacteurs | Gas-diesel oil  Gazole/ carburant diesel | Residual fuel oil  Mazout résiduel | Liquefied petroleum gas  Gaz de pétrole liquéfiés | Natural gas (terajoules)  Gaz naturel (térajoules) | Electricity (million kWh)  Electricité (millions de kWh) |
|---|---|---|---|---|---|---|---|---|---|---|
| | | | | Thousand metric tons — Milliers de tonnes | | | | | | |
| Martinique  Martinique | 2002 | ... | ... | *160 | ... | *176 | *300 | *26 | ... | 1 180 |
| | *2003 | ... | ... | 161 | ... | 177 | 300 | 26 | ... | 1 185 |
| | *2004 | ... | ... | 163 | ... | 178 | 310 | 27 | ... | 1 190 |
| | *2005 | ... | ... | 164 | ... | 179 | 310 | 27 | ... | 1 195 |
| Mexico  Mexique | 2002 | 10 984 | 178 085 | 16 654 | 2 584 | 13 165 | 25 599 | 982 | 1 506 981 | 214 628 |
| | 2003 | 9 599 | 189 016 | 18 587 | 2 717 | 15 182 | 22 581 | 1 059 | 1 579 524 | 217 867 |
| | 2004 | 9 882 | 190 897 | 19 855 | 2 770 | 16 057 | 21 089 | 1 056 | 1 651 290 | 224 077 |
| | 2005 | 10 755 | 187 205 | 20 399 | 3 125 | 17 157 | 20 019 | 1 039 | 1 716 773 | 234 895 |
| Montserrat  Montserrat | 2002 | ... | ... | ... | ... | ... | ... | ... | ... | 20 |
| | 2003 | ... | ... | ... | ... | ... | ... | ... | ... | 21 |
| | 2004 | ... | ... | ... | ... | ... | ... | ... | ... | 21 |
| | *2005 | ... | ... | ... | ... | ... | ... | ... | ... | 21 |
| Netherlands Antilles  Antilles néerlandaises | 2002 | ... | ... | 1 644 | 710 | 2 058 | 4 629 | 119 | ... | 1 090 |
| | 2003 | ... | ... | 1 667 | 770 | 2 087 | 4 253 | 125 | ... | 1 181 |
| | 2004 | ... | ... | 1 697 | 790 | 2 117 | 4 222 | 118 | ... | 1 210 |
| | 2005 | ... | ... | 1 735 | 830 | 2 223 | 4 433 | 124 | ... | 1 248 |
| Nicaragua  Nicaragua | 2002 | ... | ... | 100 | ... | 218 | 410 | 18 | ... | 2 553 |
| | 2003 | ... | ... | 96 | ... | 211 | 400 | 21 | ... | 2 708 |
| | 2004 | ... | ... | 99 | ... | 210 | 427 | 17 | ... | 2 822 |
| | 2005 | ... | ... | 87 | ... | 183 | 378 | 15 | ... | 2 866 |
| Panama  Panama | 2002 | ... | ... | 156 | ... | 289 | 344 | 40 | ... | 5 293 |
| | 2003 | ... | ... | 0 | ... | 0 | 0 | 0 | ... | 5 576 |
| | 2004 | ... | ... | 0 | ... | 0 | 0 | 0 | ... | 5 785 |
| | 2005 | ... | ... | 0 | ... | 0 | 0 | 0 | ... | 5 850 |
| Puerto Rico  Porto Rico | 2002 | ... | ... | ... | ... | ... | ... | ... | ... | 22 340 |
| | 2003 | ... | ... | ... | ... | ... | ... | ... | ... | 23 280 |
| | 2004 | ... | ... | ... | ... | ... | ... | ... | ... | 24 130 |
| | *2005 | ... | ... | ... | ... | ... | ... | ... | ... | 24 995 |
| Saint Kitts and Nevis  Saint-Kitts-et-Nevis | 2002 | ... | ... | ... | ... | ... | ... | ... | ... | 110 |
| | 2003 | ... | ... | ... | ... | ... | ... | ... | ... | 127 |
| | *2004 | ... | ... | ... | ... | ... | ... | ... | ... | 130 |
| | *2005 | ... | ... | ... | ... | ... | ... | ... | ... | 133 |
| Saint Lucia  Sainte-Lucie | 2002 | ... | ... | ... | ... | ... | ... | ... | ... | 288 |
| | 2003 | ... | ... | ... | ... | ... | ... | ... | ... | 299 |
| | 2004 | ... | ... | ... | ... | ... | ... | ... | ... | 309 |
| | *2005 | ... | ... | ... | ... | ... | ... | ... | ... | 310 |
| Saint Pierre and Miquelon*  Saint-Pierre-et-Miquelon* | 2002 | ... | ... | ... | ... | ... | ... | ... | ... | 50 |
| | 2003 | ... | ... | ... | ... | ... | ... | ... | ... | 52 |
| | 2004 | ... | ... | ... | ... | ... | ... | ... | ... | 52 |
| | 2005 | ... | ... | ... | ... | ... | ... | ... | ... | 54 |
| St. Vincent-Grenadines  St. Vincent-Grenadines | 2002 | ... | ... | ... | ... | ... | ... | ... | ... | 102 |
| | 2003 | ... | ... | ... | ... | ... | ... | ... | ... | 108 |
| | 2004 | ... | ... | ... | ... | ... | ... | ... | ... | 121 |
| | *2005 | ... | ... | ... | ... | ... | ... | ... | ... | 124 |
| Trinidad and Tobago  Trinité-et-Tobago | 2002 | ... | 8 082 | 1 313 | 665 | 1 546 | 3 175 | 639 | 638 636 | 5 644 |
| | 2003 | ... | 8 497 | 1 216 | 685 | 1 522 | 3 247 | 726 | 971 764 | 6 437 |
| | 2004 | ... | 7 890 | 1 096 | 615 | 1 421 | 2 971 | 699 | 1 024 185 | 6 430 |
| | 2005 | ... | 8 997 | 1 350 | 827 | 1 764 | 3 180 | 723 | 1 067 201 | 7 058 |
| Turks and Caicos Islands*  Iles Turques et Caïques* | 2002 | ... | ... | ... | ... | ... | ... | ... | ... | 10 |
| | 2003 | ... | ... | ... | ... | ... | ... | ... | ... | 10 |
| | 2004 | ... | ... | ... | ... | ... | ... | ... | ... | 10 |
| | 2005 | ... | ... | ... | ... | ... | ... | ... | ... | 10 |

| Region, country or area / Région, pays ou zone | Year / Année | Hard coal and lignite / Houille et lignite | Crude petroleum and NGL / Pétrole brut et LGN | Motor gasoline / Essence auto | Jet fuel / Carbu-réacteurs | Gas-diesel oil / Gazole/ carburant diesel | Residual fuel oil / Mazout résiduel | Liquefied petroleum gas / Gaz de pétrole liquéfiés | Natural gas (terajoules) / Gaz naturel (térajoules) | Electricity (million kWh) / Electricité (millions de kWh) |
|---|---|---|---|---|---|---|---|---|---|---|
| | | Thousand metric tons — Milliers de tonnes | | | | | | | | |
| United States | 2002 | 992 717 | 338 610 | 350 798 | 71 325 | 180 511 | 35 879 | 62 391 | 20 913 735 | 4 050 862 |
| Etats-Unis | 2003 | 972 278 | 331 067 | 350 258 | 70 119 | 188 137 | 39 219 | 60 739 | 21 102 408 | 4 081 466 |
| | 2004 | 1 019 129 | 321 452 | 351 954 | 73 473 | 194 143 | 38 916 | 63 468 | 20 541 489 | 4 174 484 |
| | 2005 | 1 038 591 | 305 908 | 350 574 | 73 634 | 200 203 | 37 180 | 60 581 | 19 970 627 | 4 286 357 |
| United States Virgin Is.* | 2002 | ... | ... | ... | ... | ... | ... | ... | ... | 1 040 |
| Iles Vierges américaines* | 2003 | ... | ... | ... | ... | ... | ... | ... | ... | 1 040 |
| | 2004 | ... | ... | ... | ... | ... | ... | ... | ... | 1 050 |
| | 2005 | ... | ... | ... | ... | ... | ... | ... | ... | 1 060 |
| America, South | 2002 | 56 915[1] | 341 103 | 45 592 | 10 720 | 63 315 | 44 974 | 14 724 | 3 578 268 | 707 782 |
| Amérique du Sud | 2003 | 62 159[1] | 334 214 | 41 759 | 10 007 | 66 787 | 42 989 | 14 979 | 3 707 728 | 745 702 |
| | 2004 | 66 099[1] | 337 843 | 45 280 | 10 659 | 71 852 | 46 407 | 16 477 | 4 007 394 | 792 341 |
| | 2005 | 73 126[1] | 351 017 | 48 089 | 10 844 | 70 990 | 44 670 | 18 233 | 4 107 792 | 822 596 |
| Argentina | 2002 | 97[1] | 44 144 | 4 884 | 1 305 | 9 402 | 1 803 | 3 450 | 1 496 647 | 85 055 |
| Argentine | 2003 | 89[1] | 44 418 | 4 636 | 1 135 | 9 957 | 1 946 | 4 143 | 1 664 109 | 92 609 |
| | 2004 | 42[1] | 42 765 | 4 018 | 1 209 | 10 590 | 2 368 | 4 431 | 1 713 297 | 100 260 |
| | 2005 | 25[1] | 41 047 | 4 348 | 1 264 | 10 143 | 2 795 | 4 290 | 1 685 308 | 107 053 |
| Bolivia | 2002 | ... | 1 799 | 406 | 117 | 442 | 4 | 253 | 218 691 | 4 188 |
| Bolivie | 2003 | ... | 1 956 | 406 | 121 | 482 | 0 | 301 | 255 726 | 4 269 |
| | 2004 | ... | 2 243 | 455 | 122 | 622 | 0 | 322 | 355 620 | 4 542 |
| | 2005 | ... | 2 416 | 430 | 125 | 601 | 0 | 333 | 442 468 | 5 230 |
| Brazil | 2002 | 5 144[1] | 76 311 | 13 894 | 2 938 | 27 994 | 16 925 | 4 745 | 367 896 | 345 671 |
| Brésil | 2003 | 4 646[1] | 79 081 | 13 477 | 3 073 | 30 608 | 15 779 | 4 934 | 397 527 | 364 339 |
| | 2004 | 5 406[1] | 78 846 | 13 738 | 3 357 | 34 079 | 16 074 | 5 144 | 420 030 | 387 451 |
| | 2005 | 6 255[1] | 87 325 | 14 337 | 3 337 | 33 368 | 15 461 | 5 780 | 429 095 | 402 938 |
| Chile | 2002 | 433[1] | 457 | 2 110 | 606 | 3 793 | 1 368 | 417 | 83 772 | 45 483 |
| Chili | 2003 | 576[1] | 414 | 2 265 | 574 | 3 865 | 1 814 | 533 | 73 681 | 48 780 |
| | 2004 | 188[1] | 413 | 2 383 | 650 | 3 693 | 2 294 | 681 | *73 280 | 51 984 |
| | 2005 | 544[1] | 385 | 2 257 | 574 | 3 534 | 2 306 | 621 | 82 254 | 54 383 |
| Colombia | 2002 | 43 850[1] | 29 959 | 4 676 | 1 031 | 3 275 | 3 136 | 737 | 269 287 | 45 242 |
| Colombie | 2003 | 50 025[1] | 28 200 | 4 756 | 1 254 | 3 308 | 2 932 | 868 | 257 762 | 47 682 |
| | 2004 | 53 693[1] | 26 877 | 4 963 | 861 | 3 689 | 3 330 | 688 | 271 346 | 52 011 |
| | 2005 | 59 064[1] | 26 394 | 4 252 | 858 | 3 660 | 3 056 | 689 | 284 720 | 50 665 |
| Ecuador | 2002 | ... | 20 537 | 1 506 | 260 | 1 822 | 3 544 | 177 | 9 869 | 11 888 |
| Equateur | 2003 | ... | 21 493 | 1 516 | 239 | 1 600 | 3 646 | 231 | 16 234 | 11 546 |
| | 2004 | ... | 27 460 | 895 | 279 | 1 621 | 3 657 | 215 | 25 108 | 12 585 |
| | 2005 | ... | 26 553 | 1 615 | 297 | 1 787 | 3 492 | 228 | 36 632 | 13 404 |
| Falkland Is. (Malvinas)* | 2002 | ... | ... | ... | ... | ... | ... | ... | ... | 16 |
| Iles Falkland (Malvinas)* | 2003 | ... | ... | ... | ... | ... | ... | ... | ... | 16 |
| | 2004 | ... | ... | ... | ... | ... | ... | ... | ... | 16 |
| | 2005 | ... | ... | ... | ... | ... | ... | ... | ... | 16 |
| French Guiana | 2002 | ... | ... | ... | ... | ... | ... | ... | ... | 450 |
| Guyane française | 2003 | ... | ... | ... | ... | ... | ... | ... | ... | 440 |
| | 2004 | ... | ... | ... | ... | ... | ... | ... | ... | 430 |
| | 2005 | ... | ... | ... | ... | ... | ... | ... | ... | 430 |
| Guyana | 2002 | ... | ... | ... | ... | ... | ... | ... | ... | 914 |
| Guyana | 2003 | ... | ... | ... | ... | ... | ... | ... | ... | 820 |
| | 2004 | ... | ... | ... | ... | ... | ... | ... | ... | 835 |
| | 2005 | ... | ... | ... | ... | ... | ... | ... | ... | 862 |
| Paraguay | 2002 | ... | ... | 11 | ... | 48 | 34 | ... | ... | 48 204 |
| Paraguay | 2003 | ... | ... | 10 | ... | 42 | 30 | ... | ... | 51 762 |
| | 2004 | ... | ... | 8 | ... | 33 | 20 | ... | ... | 51 921 |
| | 2005 | ... | ... | 4 | ... | 16 | 11 | ... | ... | 51 156 |

| Region, country or area / Région, pays ou zone | Year / Année | Hard coal and lignite / Houille et lignite | Crude petroleum and NGL / Pétrole brut et LGN | Motor gasoline / Essence auto | Jet fuel / Carbu-réacteurs | Gas-diesel oil / Gazole/carburant diesel | Residual fuel oil / Mazout résiduel | Liquefied petroleum gas / Gaz de pétrole liquéfiés | Natural gas (terajoules) / Gaz naturel (térajoules) | Electricity (million kWh) / Electricité (millions de kWh) |
|---|---|---|---|---|---|---|---|---|---|---|
| | | Thousand metric tons — Milliers de tonnes | | | | | | | | |
| Peru / Pérou | 2002 | 22[1] | 4 927 | 1 407 | 353 | 1 850 | 3 140 | 321 | 23 324 | 22 176 |
| | 2003 | 16[1] | 5 058 | 1 470 | 382 | 1 883 | 3 245 | 319 | 25 802 | 23 128 |
| | 2004 | 22[1] | 5 031 | 1 744 | 418 | 1 999 | 3 324 | 355 | 40 321 | 24 415 |
| | 2005 | 43[1] | 5 267 | 2 220 | 270 | 2 415 | 2 958 | 738 | 68 008 | 25 660 |
| Suriname / Suriname | 2002 | ... | 615[2] | ... | ... | 40 | 334 | ... | ... | 1 482 |
| | 2003 | ... | 588[2] | ... | ... | 39 | 333 | ... | ... | 1 496 |
| | 2004 | ... | 612[2] | ... | ... | 39 | 335 | ... | ... | 1 509 |
| | 2005 | ... | 637[2] | ... | ... | 41 | 349 | ... | ... | 1 571 |
| Uruguay / Uruguay | 2002 | ... | ... | 215 | 40 | 422 | 396 | 63 | ... | 9 607 |
| | 2003 | ... | ... | 320 | 24 | 592 | 452 | 66 | ... | 8 580 |
| | 2004 | ... | ... | 520 | 44 | 772 | 519 | 86 | ... | 5 900 |
| | 2005 | ... | ... | 516 | 41 | 774 | 507 | 90 | ... | 7 684 |
| Venezuela (Bolivar. Rep.of) / Venezuela (Rép. Boliv. du) | 2002 | 7 369[1] | 162 354 | 16 483 | 4 070 | 14 226 | 14 290 | 4 561 | 1 108 782 | 87 406 |
| | 2003 | 6 807[1] | 153 006 | 12 903 | 3 205 | 14 411 | 12 812 | 3 585 | 1 016 887 | 90 235 |
| | 2004 | 6 748[1] | 153 596 | 16 555 | 3 719 | 14 715 | 14 486 | 4 555 | 1 108 392 | 98 482 |
| | 2005 | 7 195[1] | 160 993 | 18 110 | 4 078 | 14 651 | 13 735 | 5 464 | 1 079 307 | 101 544 |
| **Asia / Asie** | **2002** | **2 144 488** | **1 482 944** | **184 500** | **55 674** | **369 470** | **241 789** | **86 987** | **24 501 147** | **5 255 902** |
| | **2003** | **2 451 936** | **1 570 566** | **193 124** | **56 770** | **385 930** | **249 247** | **89 598** | **26 194 194** | **5 654 019** |
| | **2004** | **2 774 868** | **1 643 357** | **203 134** | **63 455** | **413 982** | **247 365** | **96 579** | **28 164 172** | **6 134 192** |
| | **2005** | **3 054 805** | **1 699 250** | **205 982** | **70 115** | **434 034** | **247 597** | **99 749** | **30 308 080** | **6 626 030** |
| Afghanistan / Afghanistan | 2002 | 21[1] | ... | ... | ... | ... | ... | ... | 285 | 846 |
| | 2003 | 35[1] | ... | ... | ... | ... | ... | ... | 242 | 976 |
| | 2004 | 34[1] | ... | ... | ... | ... | ... | ... | 119 | 929 |
| | *2005 | 33[1] | ... | ... | ... | ... | ... | ... | 100 | 960 |
| Armenia / Arménie | 2002 | ... | ... | ... | ... | ... | ... | ... | ... | 5 519 |
| | 2003 | ... | ... | ... | ... | ... | ... | ... | ... | 5 501 |
| | 2004 | ... | ... | ... | ... | ... | ... | ... | ... | 6 030 |
| | 2005 | ... | ... | ... | ... | ... | ... | ... | ... | 6 317 |
| Azerbaijan / Azerbaïdjan | 2002 | ... | 15 333 | 610 | 507 | 1 593 | 2 569 | 94 | 193 928 | 18 701 |
| | 2003 | ... | 15 381 | 720 | 521 | 1 641 | 2 470 | 146 | 193 326 | 21 286 |
| | 2004 | ... | 15 549 | 852 | 536 | 1 789 | 2 521 | 176 | 194 905 | 21 744 |
| | 2005 | ... | 22 435 | 906 | 630 | 2 099 | 3 061 | 182 | 211 786 | 22 872 |
| Bahrain / Bahreïn | 2002 | ... | 9 949 | 746 | 1 980 | 4 233 | 2 835 | 210 | 255 748 | 7 278 |
| | 2003 | ... | 10 130 | 810 | 1 866 | 4 295 | 3 008 | 201 | 263 779 | 7 768 |
| | 2004 | ... | 10 111 | 755 | 2 178 | 4 500 | 2 734 | 204 | 274 330 | 8 448 |
| | 2005 | ... | 10 081 | 789 | 2 276 | 4 702 | 2 857 | 218 | 290 590 | 8 698 |
| Bangladesh / Bangladesh | 2002 | ... | 86[4] | 129 | 3 | 260 | 49 | 21 | 404 256 | 18 665 |
| | 2003 | ... | 100[4] | 150 | 2 | 303 | 58 | 20 | 434 849 | 19 712 |
| | 2004 | ... | 90[4] | 136 | 2 | 274 | 52 | 20 | 467 723 | 21 466 |
| | 2005 | ... | 96[4] | 145 | 1 | 293 | 55 | 20 | 502 829 | 22 643 |
| Bhutan* / Bhoutan* | 2002 | 52[1] | ... | ... | ... | ... | ... | ... | ... | 1 898 |
| | 2003 | 50[1] | ... | ... | ... | ... | ... | ... | ... | 1 900 |
| | 2004 | 51[1] | ... | ... | ... | ... | ... | ... | ... | 1 952 |
| | 2005 | 51[1] | ... | ... | ... | ... | ... | ... | ... | 2 050 |
| Brunei Darussalam / Brunéi Darussalam | 2002 | ... | 10 264 | 198 | 79 | 153 | 70 | 14 | 447 477 | 3 036 |
| | 2003 | ... | 10 452 | 202 | 82 | 165 | 77 | 14 | 482 490 | 3 169 |
| | 2004 | ... | 10 291 | 201 | 80 | 173 | 89 | 15 | 477 318 | 3 236 |
| | 2005 | ... | 10 075 | 196 | 78 | 178 | 92 | 15 | 468 618 | 3 264 |
| Cambodia / Cambodge | *2002 | ... | ... | ... | ... | ... | ... | ... | ... | 574 |
| | 2003 | ... | ... | ... | ... | ... | ... | ... | ... | 637 |
| | 2004 | ... | ... | ... | ... | ... | ... | ... | ... | 744 |
| | *2005 | ... | ... | ... | ... | ... | ... | ... | ... | 764 |

| Region, country or area<br>Région, pays ou zone | Year<br>Année | Hard coal<br>and lignite<br>Houille<br>et lignite | Crude<br>petroleum<br>and NGL<br>Pétrole<br>brut et LGN | Motor<br>gasoline<br>Essence<br>auto | Jet fuel<br>Carbu-<br>réacteurs | Gas-diesel<br>oil<br>Gazole/<br>carburant<br>diesel | Residual<br>fuel oil<br>Mazout<br>résiduel | Liquefied<br>petroleum<br>gas<br>Gaz de<br>pétrole<br>liquéfiés | Natural gas<br>(terajoules)<br>Gaz naturel<br>(térajoules) | Electricity<br>(million kWh)<br>Électricité<br>(millions<br>de kWh) |
|---|---|---|---|---|---|---|---|---|---|---|
| | | Thousand metric tons — Milliers de tonnes | | | | | | | | |
| China[5]<br>Chine[5] | 2002 | 1 455 000[1] | 167 000[2] | 43 208 | ... | 77 061 | 18 455 | 10 368 | 1 571 720 | 1 640 481 |
| | 2003 | 1 722 000[1] | 169 600[2] | 47 909 | ... | 85 328 | 20 048 | 12 117 | 1 685 000 | 1 907 380 |
| | 2004 | 1 992 324[1] | 175 873[2] | 52 236 | ... | 98 436 | 20 293 | 14 170 | 1 544 800 | 2 193 736 |
| | 2005 | 2 204 729[1] | 181 353[2] | 53 884 | ... | 110 902 | 17 674 | 14 327 | 1 898 173 | 2 497 441 |
| China, Hong Kong SAR<br>Chine, Hong Kong RAS | 2002 | ... | ... | ... | ... | ... | ... | ... | ... | 34 312 |
| | 2003 | ... | ... | ... | ... | ... | ... | ... | ... | 35 506 |
| | 2004 | ... | ... | ... | ... | ... | ... | ... | ... | 37 129 |
| | 2005 | ... | ... | ... | ... | ... | ... | ... | ... | 38 451 |
| China, Macao SAR<br>Chine, Macao RAS | 2002 | ... | ... | ... | ... | ... | ... | ... | ... | 1 702 |
| | 2003 | ... | ... | ... | ... | ... | ... | ... | ... | 1 796 |
| | 2004 | ... | ... | ... | ... | ... | ... | ... | ... | 1 973 |
| | 2005 | ... | ... | ... | ... | ... | ... | ... | ... | 2 027 |
| Cyprus<br>Chypre | 2002 | ... | ... | 154 | 8 | 362 | 423 | 33 | ... | 3 785 |
| | 2003 | ... | ... | 146 | 0 | 327 | 362 | 28 | ... | 4 053 |
| | 2004 | ... | ... | 40 | 0 | 88 | 112 | 9 | ... | 4 200 |
| | 2005 | ... | ... | 0 | 0 | 0 | 0 | 0 | ... | 4 377 |
| Georgia<br>Géorgie | 2002 | 6[1] | 74[2] | ... | ... | 2 | 12 | ... | 650 | 7 257 |
| | 2003 | 8[1] | 140[2] | ... | ... | 2 | 13 | ... | 712 | 7 160 |
| | 2004 | 8[1] | 98[2] | ... | ... | 2 | 14 | ... | 461 | 6 924 |
| | 2005 | 5[1] | 67[2] | ... | ... | 1 | 4 | ... | 516 | 7 267 |
| India<br>Inde | 2002 | 366 310 | 37 131 | 10 361 | 2 702 | 39 490 | 12 167 | 7 181 | 958 122 | 596 543 |
| | 2003 | 389 204 | 37 249 | 10 999 | 4 180 | 41 966 | 13 372 | 7 551 | 1 016 146 | 633 275 |
| | 2004 | 412 952 | 37 665 | 11 057 | 5 201 | 47 426 | 14 970 | 7 825 | 1 007 951 | 665 873 |
| | 2005 | 437 079 | 36 323 | 10 502 | 6 196 | 48 495 | 14 305 | 7 710 | 1 025 355 | 697 351 |
| Indonesia<br>Indonésie | 2002 | 103 372[1] | 62 056 | 8 592 | 1 175 | 13 791 | 11 951 | 1 819 | 2 745 127 | 108 206 |
| | 2003 | 115 278[1] | 62 620 | 8 584 | 1 349 | 13 786 | 11 755 | 2 007 | 2 840 729 | 112 944 |
| | 2004 | 132 352[1] | 60 204 | 8 825 | 1 414 | 14 661 | 10 995 | 2 031 | 2 942 183 | 120 160 |
| | 2005 | 152 204[1] | 58 234 | 8 325 | 1 418 | 13 889 | 10 105 | 1 988 | 2 965 596 | 127 362 |
| Iran (Islamic Rep. of)<br>Iran (Rép. islamique d') | 2002 | 1 253[1] | *176 221 | 10 374 | 793 | 22 572 | 27 620 | 3 455 | 2 721 192 | 140 759 |
| | 2003 | 1 232[1] | *195 227 | 10 606 | 868 | 22 958 | 26 566 | 3 750 | 3 079 135 | 152 599 |
| | 2004 | 1 246[1] | *202 527 | 10 836 | 795 | 23 771 | 25 840 | 4 146 | 3 423 814 | 166 016 |
| | 2005 | 1 330[1] | *218 905 | 11 154 | 850 | 24 443 | 26 315 | 4 266 | 3 800 924 | 180 390 |
| Iraq<br>Iraq | 2002 | ... | 100 469 | 3 460 | 640 | 6 884 | 8 221 | 1 546 | 87 400 | 33 863 |
| | 2003 | ... | 65 949 | 3 097 | 573 | 6 610 | 7 404 | 848 | 59 280 | 28 340 |
| | 2004 | ... | 98 951 | 3 278 | 607 | 4 906 | 8 257 | 938 | 101 455 | 32 295 |
| | 2005 | ... | 91 699 | 3 185 | 590 | 4 766 | 8 022 | 951 | 100 674 | 34 000 |
| Israel<br>Israël | 2002 | 458[6] | 5[2] | 2 211 | ... | 2 838 | 3 368 | 482 | 335 | 45 363 |
| | 2003 | 437[6] | 3[2] | 2 231 | ... | 2 977 | 3 440 | 474 | 321 | 47 041 |
| | 2004 | 439[6] | 2[2] | 2 467 | ... | 2 750 | 3 168 | 532 | 43 585 | 48 481 |
| | 2005 | 413[6] | 2[2] | 2 729 | ... | 3 042 | 3 504 | 566 | 59 988 | 49 843 |
| Japan<br>Japon | 2002 | ... | 582 | 42 671 | 8 188 | 57 948 | 32 943 | 4 902 | 117 076 | 1 061 530 |
| | 2003 | ... | 642 | 43 140 | 7 671 | 57 402 | 34 028 | 4 527 | 120 758 | 1 051 210 |
| | 2004 | ... | 663 | 42 711 | 7 902 | 57 059 | 31 008 | 4 448 | 125 356 | 1 080 333 |
| | 2005 | ... | 702 | 43 259 | 8 896 | 57 700 | 31 692 | 4 895 | 133 094 | 1 102 330 |
| Jordan<br>Jordanie | 2002 | ... | 2[2] | 657 | 216 | 1 113 | 1 289 | 136 | 8 748 | 8 130 |
| | 2003 | ... | 2[2] | 667 | 178 | 1 160 | 1 251 | 134 | 9 902 | 8 044 |
| | 2004 | ... | 1[2] | 579 | 291 | 1 223 | 1 516 | 116 | 10 098 | 8 970 |
| | 2005 | ... | 1[2] | 613 | 324 | 1 395 | 1 466 | 118 | 8 315 | 9 651 |
| Kazakhstan<br>Kazakhstan | 2002 | 80 906 | 47 269 | 1 691 | 38 | 2 304 | 2 797 | 1 064 | 550 604 | 58 331 |
| | 2003 | 89 176 | 51 451 | 1 562 | 309 | 2 128 | 2 584 | 1 179 | 647 698 | 63 819 |
| | 2004 | 90 820 | 59 485 | 1 928 | 294 | 2 888 | 2 708 | 1 507 | 862 450 | 66 942 |
| | 2005 | 91 116 | 61 486 | 2 359 | 249 | 3 705 | 3 550 | 1 478 | 974 479 | 67 916 |

| Region, country or area / Région, pays ou zone | Year / Année | Hard coal and lignite / Houille et lignite | Crude petroleum and NGL / Pétrole brut et LGN | Motor gasoline / Essence auto | Jet fuel / Carbu-réacteurs | Gas-diesel oil / Gazole/ carburant diesel | Residual fuel oil / Mazout résiduel | Liquefied petroleum gas / Gaz de pétrole liquéfiés | Natural gas (terajoules) / Gaz naturel (térajoules) | Electricity (million kWh) / Electricité (millions de kWh) |
|---|---|---|---|---|---|---|---|---|---|---|
| | | Thousand metric tons — Milliers de tonnes | | | | | | | | |
| Korea, Dem. P. R. Corée, R. p. dém. de | 2002 | 28 950 | ... | 189 | ... | 207 | 119 | ... | ... | 19 777 |
| | 2003 | 29 479 | ... | 185 | ... | 201 | 116 | ... | ... | 21 035 |
| | 2004 | 30 140 | ... | 188 | ... | 203 | 117 | ... | ... | 21 974 |
| | 2005 | 31 806 | ... | 159 | ... | 171 | 98 | ... | ... | 22 913 |
| Korea, Republic of Corée, République de | 2002 | 3 318[1] | 0[2] | 9 020 | 8 567 | 28 484 | 27 833 | 3 685 | 0 | 331 882 |
| | 2003 | 3 298[1] | 0[2] | 8 564 | 6 944 | 27 801 | 30 095 | 3 613 | 0 | 345 192 |
| | 2004 | 3 191[1] | 0[2] | 8 850 | 9 665 | 29 048 | 29 918 | 3 717 | 0 | 368 162 |
| | 2005 | 2 832[1] | 54[2] | 8 654 | 10 755 | 31 508 | 31 305 | 3 612 | 20 495 | 389 390 |
| Kuwait Koweït | 2002 | ... | 94 765 | 1 384 | 1 716 | 11 644 | 7 491 | 3 732 | 369 003 | 36 892 |
| | 2003 | ... | 113 765 | 1 355 | 2 227 | 12 426 | 9 800 | 4 177 | 429 950 | 39 802 |
| | 2004 | ... | 123 501 | 1 931 | 2 258 | 12 204 | 9 760 | 4 631 | 462 773 | 41 256 |
| | 2005 | ... | 136 982 | 2 812 | 1 586 | 12 397 | 9 166 | 4 510 | 518 914 | 43 734 |
| Kyrgyzstan Kirghizistan | 2002 | 459 | 76[2] | 40 | ... | 27 | 43 | ... | 1 171 | 13 186 |
| | 2003 | 416 | 69[2] | 27 | ... | 22 | 39 | ... | 1 054 | 15 576 |
| | 2004 | 461 | 74[2] | 19 | ... | 27 | 42 | ... | 1 132 | 16 312 |
| | 2005 | 335 | 74[2] | 13 | ... | 21 | 42 | ... | 975 | 16 415 |
| Lao People's Dem. Rep. Rép. dém. pop. lao | 2002 | *555[1] | ... | ... | ... | ... | ... | ... | ... | 3 797 |
| | 2003 | *535[1] | ... | ... | ... | ... | ... | ... | ... | 3 372 |
| | *2004 | 540[1] | ... | ... | ... | ... | ... | ... | ... | 3 513 |
| | *2005 | 550[1] | ... | ... | ... | ... | ... | ... | ... | 3 513 |
| Lebanon Liban | 2002 | ... | ... | ... | ... | ... | ... | ... | ... | 9 660 |
| | 2003 | ... | ... | ... | ... | ... | ... | ... | ... | 10 547 |
| | 2004 | ... | ... | ... | ... | ... | ... | ... | ... | 11 055 |
| | 2005 | ... | ... | ... | ... | ... | ... | ... | ... | 11 125 |
| Malaysia Malaisie | 2002 | 318[1] | 37 436 | 4 245 | 2 489 | 8 271 | 2 351 | 2 206 | *1 787 405 | 74 196 |
| | 2003 | 153[1] | 39 044 | 4 363 | 2 293 | 8 922 | 1 777 | 1 582 | *1 870 708 | 78 427 |
| | 2004 | 382[1] | 37 237 | 4 496 | 2 608 | 9 463 | 1 828 | 1 303 | 2 180 862 | 82 282 |
| | 2005 | 682[1] | 37 468 | 4 040 | 2 472 | 9 020 | 1 792 | 2 470 | 2 402 160 | 87 300 |
| Maldives Maldives | 2002 | ... | ... | ... | ... | ... | ... | ... | ... | 126 |
| | 2003 | ... | ... | ... | ... | ... | ... | ... | ... | 141 |
| | 2004 | ... | ... | ... | ... | ... | ... | ... | ... | 160 |
| | *2005 | ... | ... | ... | ... | ... | ... | ... | ... | 160 |
| Mongolia Mongolie | 2002 | 5 668 | ... | ... | ... | ... | ... | ... | ... | 3 112 |
| | 2003 | 5 666 | ... | ... | ... | ... | ... | ... | ... | 3 138 |
| | 2004 | 6 865 | ... | ... | ... | ... | ... | ... | ... | 3 303 |
| | 2005 | 7 517 | ... | ... | ... | ... | ... | ... | ... | 3 419 |
| Myanmar Myanmar | 2002 | 558 | 871 | 238 | 59 | 364 | 102 | 19 | 252 967 | 5 068 |
| | 2003 | 978 | 976 | 307 | 65 | 249 | 67 | 16 | 306 893 | 5 426 |
| | 2004 | 1 052 | 1 025 | 309 | 61 | 196 | 49 | 20 | 419 860 | 5 608 |
| | 2005 | 1 360 | 1 113 | 302 | 46 | 173 | 48 | 19 | 457 413 | 6 015 |
| Nepal Népal | 2002 | 12[1] | ... | ... | ... | ... | ... | ... | ... | 2 123 |
| | 2003 | 11[1] | ... | ... | ... | ... | ... | ... | ... | 2 267 |
| | 2004 | 11[1] | ... | ... | ... | ... | ... | ... | ... | 2 345 |
| | 2005 | 11[1] | ... | ... | ... | ... | ... | ... | ... | 2 415 |
| Oman Oman | 2002 | ... | 44 921 | 705 | 252 | 889 | 2 257 | *122 | 630 632 | 10 331 |
| | 2003 | ... | 41 058 | 642 | 217 | 878 | 2 259 | 119 | 691 553 | 10 714 |
| | 2004 | ... | 39 226 | 593 | 178 | 864 | 2 121 | 119 | 706 149 | 11 499 |
| | 2005 | ... | 38 878 | 618 | 183 | 894 | 2 167 | *114 | 740 145 | 12 648 |
| Pakistan Pakistan | 2002 | 3 328[1] | 3 262 | 1 316 | 857 | 2 766 | 3 063 | 355 | 829 746 | 72 429 |
| | 2003 | 3 312[1] | 3 302 | 1 075 | 997 | 2 937 | 3 058 | 380 | 1 023 969 | 75 686 |
| | 2004 | 4 587[1] | 3 402 | 1 326 | 1 185 | 3 603 | 3 132 | 412 | 1 115 913 | 85 699 |
| | 2005 | 4 871[1] | 3 474 | 1 195 | 1 258 | 3 419 | 3 358 | 557 | 1 176 498 | 93 699 |

| Region, country or area / Région, pays ou zone | Year / Année | Hard coal and lignite / Houille et lignite | Crude petroleum and NGL / Pétrole brut et LGN | Motor gasoline / Essence auto | Jet fuel / Carbu-réacteurs | Gas-diesel oil / Gazole/ carburant diesel | Residual fuel oil / Mazout résiduel | Liquefied petroleum gas / Gaz de pétrole liquéfiés | Natural gas (terajoules) / Gaz naturel (térajoules) | Electricity (million kWh) / Électricité (millions de kWh) |
|---|---|---|---|---|---|---|---|---|---|---|
| | | | | Thousand metric tons — Milliers de tonnes | | | | | | |
| Philippines Philippines | 2002 | 1 665 | 277[2] | 2 072 | 641 | 4 008 | 5 169 | 462 | 66 367 | 48 484 |
| | 2003 | 4 603 | 20[2] | 1 844 | 634 | 3 851 | 3 899 | 397 | 101 146 | 52 897 |
| | 2004 | 2 726 | 19[2] | 1 501 | 590 | 3 004 | 3 537 | 263 | 96 743 | 55 957 |
| | 2005 | 3 164 | 29[2] | 1 629 | 665 | 3 399 | 3 463 | 322 | 127 566 | 56 549 |
| Qatar Qatar | 2002 | ... | 39 708 | 1 319 | 831 | 889 | 755 | 2 526 | 1 207 536 | 10 940 |
| | 2003 | ... | 40 443 | 1 815 | 921 | 965 | 429 | 2 436 | 1 262 086 | 12 012 |
| | 2004 | ... | 39 013 | 1 709 | 956 | 979 | 618 | 2 606 | 1 619 771 | 13 233 |
| | 2005 | ... | 39 146 | 1 722 | 916 | 924 | 356 | 2 265 | 1 785 772 | 14 396 |
| Saudi Arabia Arabie saoudite | 2002 | ... | 421 406 | 11 195 | 4 100 | 25 834 | 23 676 | 26 359 | 2 236 627 | 141 736 |
| | 2003 | ... | 477 792 | 12 600 | 4 519 | 28 899 | 25 432 | 27 093 | 2 343 541 | 153 000 |
| | 2004 | ... | 491 685 | 13 605 | 4 923 | 31 486 | 25 944 | 29 719 | 2 562 833 | 159 875 |
| | 2005 | ... | 514 624 | 13 400 | 6 627 | 31 685 | 26 722 | 30 979 | 2 779 785 | 176 124 |
| Singapore Singapour | 2002 | ... | ... | 3 632 | 5 361 | 10 775 | 6 614 | 818 | ... | 34 664 |
| | 2003 | ... | ... | 3 350 | 6 322 | 9 938 | 6 400 | 870 | ... | 35 331 |
| | 2004 | ... | ... | 3 948 | 6 481 | 11 711 | 7 523 | 872 | ... | 36 810 |
| | 2005 | ... | ... | 4 879 | 7 610 | 14 474 | 9 798 | 848 | ... | 38 213 |
| Sri Lanka Sri Lanka | 2002 | ... | ... | 226 | 72 | 717 | 800 | 18 | ... | 6 951 |
| | 2003 | ... | ... | 196 | 96 | 622 | 745 | 15 | ... | 7 711 |
| | 2004 | ... | ... | 203 | 126 | 693 | 855 | 15 | ... | 8 158 |
| | 2005 | ... | ... | 161 | 114 | 591 | 762 | 13 | ... | 8 769 |
| Syrian Arab Republic Rép. arabe syrienne | 2002 | ... | 31 150[2] | 1 386 | *222 | 4 035 | 5 126 | 293 | 256 360 | 28 013 |
| | 2003 | ... | 28 000[2] | 1 262 | *204 | 3 906 | 4 793 | 286 | 258 245 | 29 534 |
| | 2004 | ... | 23 300[2] | 1 338 | 245 | 4 123 | 4 536 | 286 | 267 670 | 32 077 |
| | 2005 | ... | 22 828[2] | 1 257 | 221 | 3 665 | 4 646 | 328 | 275 210 | 34 935 |
| Tajikistan Tadjikistan | 2002 | 56 | 16[2] | ... | ... | ... | ... | ... | 1 130 | 15 302 |
| | 2003 | 46 | 18[2] | ... | ... | ... | ... | ... | 1 246 | 16 509 |
| | 2004 | 51 | 18[2] | ... | ... | ... | ... | ... | 1 250 | 16 491 |
| | 2005 | 100 | 22[2] | ... | ... | ... | ... | ... | 1 113 | 17 086 |
| Thailand Thaïlande | 2002 | 19 602[6] | 8 222 | 5 745 | 3 579 | 14 473 | 5 867 | 3 286 | 716 194 | 115 513 |
| | 2003 | 18 843[6] | 9 721 | 6 012 | 3 253 | 15 608 | 5 947 | 3 446 | 707 276 | 116 984 |
| | 2004 | 20 060[6] | 9 903 | 6 674 | 3 774 | 17 511 | 6 335 | 3 917 | 701 157 | 125 727 |
| | 2005 | 20 878[6] | 11 418 | 6 428 | 3 711 | 16 378 | 6 409 | 4 011 | 753 708 | 132 197 |
| Timor-Leste* Timor-Leste* | 2002 | ... | 6 789 | ... | ... | ... | ... | 2 193 | ... | 300 |
| | 2003 | ... | 6 789 | ... | ... | ... | ... | 2 193 | ... | 300 |
| | 2004 | ... | 6 835 | ... | ... | ... | ... | 2 200 | ... | 300 |
| | 2005 | ... | 6 860 | ... | ... | ... | ... | 2 210 | ... | 300 |
| Turkey Turquie | 2002 | 53 984 | 2 420[2] | 3 718 | 1 606 | 7 720 | 7 970 | 741 | 14 477 | 129 400 |
| | 2003 | 48 563 | 2 351[2] | 3 837 | 1 682 | 8 087 | 8 038 | 758 | 21 448 | 140 581 |
| | 2004 | 46 377 | 2 251[2] | 3 479 | 1 767 | 7 665 | 7 845 | 762 | 26 350 | 150 698 |
| | 2005 | 58 340 | 2 258[2] | 3 609 | 1 997 | 7 601 | 7 208 | 766 | 34 355 | 161 955 |
| Turkmenistan Turkménistan | 2002 | ... | 10 117 | 1 292 | 270 | 2 360 | 1 640 | ... | 2 027 062 | 10 700 |
| | 2003 | ... | 10 332 | 1 361 | 270 | 2 478 | 1 831 | ... | 2 241 513 | 10 800 |
| | 2004 | ... | 10 063 | 1 265 | 296 | 2 511 | 1 745 | ... | 2 235 451 | 11 920 |
| | 2005 | ... | 9 794 | 1 313 | 307 | 2 606 | 1 811 | ... | 2 387 007 | 12 820 |
| United Arab Emirates Emirats arabes unis | 2002 | ... | 109 062 | 1 335 | 5 390 | 4 677 | 1 704 | 7 146 | 1 693 142 | 46 856 |
| | 2003 | ... | 131 769 | 1 288 | 5 459 | 4 609 | 1 173 | 7 403 | 1 748 141 | 49 450 |
| | 2004 | ... | 136 157 | 1 746 | 5 400 | 4 754 | 1 291 | 7 671 | 1 806 282 | 52 417 |
| | 2005 | ... | 137 531 | 1 871 | 5 418 | 4 273 | 1 302 | 7 898 | 1 818 379 | 60 698 |
| Uzbekistan Ouzbékistan | 2002 | 2 737 | 7 263 | 1 603 | 274 | 1 735 | 1 675 | 43 | 2 207 973 | 49 310 |
| | 2003 | 1 913 | 7 788 | 1 842 | 314 | 1 993 | 1 925 | 44 | 2 194 105 | 49 400 |
| | 2004 | 2 699 | 7 295 | 1 736 | 296 | 1 879 | 1 814 | 40 | 2 236 391 | 51 030 |
| | 2005 | 3 003 | 6 007 | 1 430 | 244 | 1 547 | 1 494 | 34 | 2 278 677 | 47 707 |

| Region, country or area / Région, pays ou zone | Year / Année | Hard coal and lignite / Houille et lignite | Crude petroleum and NGL / Pétrole brut et LGN | Motor gasoline / Essence auto | Jet fuel / Carbu-réacteurs | Gas-diesel oil / Gazole/carburant diesel | Residual fuel oil / Mazout résiduel | Liquefied petroleum gas / Gaz de pétrole liquéfiés | Natural gas (terajoules) / Gaz naturel (térajoules) | Electricity (million kWh) / Electricité (millions de kWh) |
|---|---|---|---|---|---|---|---|---|---|---|
| | | Thousand metric tons — Milliers de tonnes | | | | | | | | |
| Viet Nam | 2002 | 15 900[1] | 17 125 | ... | ... | ... | ... | 349 | 107 642 | 35 796 |
| Viet Nam | 2003 | 16 700[1] | 17 092 | ... | ... | ... | ... | 307 | 125 993 | *40 925 |
| | 2004 | 25 500[1] | 20 804 | ... | ... | ... | ... | 335 | 214 663 | 46 029 |
| | 2005 | 32 396[1] | 19 399 | ... | ... | ... | ... | 343 | 288 471 | 53 463 |
| Yemen | 2002 | ... | 21 572 | 967 | 339 | 844 | 532 | 95 | ... | 3 769 |
| Yémen | 2003 | ... | 21 251 | 1 059 | 388 | 819 | 586 | 87 | ... | 4 094 |
| | 2004 | ... | 19 999 | 1 138 | 317 | 883 | 268 | 89 | ... | 4 337 |
| | 2005 | ... | 19 802 | 1 195 | 369 | 959 | 399 | 84 | ... | 4 741 |
| Europe | 2002 | 1 012 079 | 698 050 | 192 404 | 47 168 | 328 238 | 187 197 | 38 117 | 35 399 638 | 4 481 922 |
| Europe | 2003 | 1 036 359 | 724 736 | 193 308 | 47 501 | 336 408 | 186 007 | 39 433 | 36 484 965 | 4 591 738 |
| | 2004 | 1 027 782 | 748 931 | 199 833 | 49 011 | 340 572 | 192 117 | 41 167 | 37 311 026 | 4 693 036 |
| | 2005 | 1 023 119 | 741 982 | 199 648 | 48 308 | 352 333 | 193 434 | 41 979 | 37 205 347 | 4 761 233 |
| Albania | 2002 | 77[6] | 393[2] | 21 | 1 | 85 | 80 | 0 | 544 | 3 686 |
| Albanie | 2003 | 81[6] | 375[2] | 6 | 1 | 95 | 45 | 0 | 544 | 5 230 |
| | 2004 | 109[6] | 420[2] | 35 | 16 | 73 | 67 | 1 | 636 | 5 559 |
| | 2005 | 92[6] | 447[2] | 14 | 0 | 72 | 68 | 0 | 670 | 5 443 |
| Austria | 2002 | 1 412[6] | 1 040 | 1 927 | 484 | 3 984 | 1 012 | 23 | 74 295 | 62 488 |
| Autriche | 2003 | 1 152[6] | 1 011 | 1 811 | 446 | 3 849 | 1 062 | 50 | 82 603 | 60 100 |
| | 2004 | 235[6] | 1 061 | 1 738 | 455 | 3 529 | 1 032 | 57 | 77 550 | 64 125 |
| | 2005 | 0[6] | 965 | 1 798 | 592 | 3 894 | 1 009 | 107 | 62 081 | 65 681 |
| Belarus | 2002 | ... | 1 846[2] | 1 756 | ... | 4 606 | 5 099 | 194 | 9 501 | 26 455 |
| Bélarus | 2003 | ... | 1 820[2] | 1 895 | ... | 4 913 | 4 790 | 216 | 9 810 | 26 627 |
| | 2004 | ... | 1 804[2] | 2 842 | ... | 5 845 | 5 501 | 418 | 9 942 | 31 211 |
| | 2005 | ... | 1 785[2] | 3 330 | ... | 6 426 | 6 311 | 459 | 8 806 | 30 961 |
| Belgium | 2002 | 173[6] | ... | 5 775 | 2 067 | 12 464 | 7 603 | 656 | ... | 82 069 |
| Belgique | 2003 | 129[6] | ... | 5 865 | 2 048 | 13 013 | 8 689 | 627 | ... | 84 630 |
| | 2004 | 181[6] | ... | 5 789 | 2 143 | 12 327 | 8 380 | 511 | ... | 85 643 |
| | 2005 | 109[6] | ... | 5 056 | 1 678 | 11 938 | 8 042 | 462 | ... | 86 944 |
| Bosnia and Herzegovina | 2002 | 12 207 | ... | ... | ... | ... | ... | ... | ... | 10 785 |
| Bosnie-Herzégovine | 2003 | 11 492 | ... | ... | ... | ... | ... | ... | ... | 11 250 |
| | 2004 | 11 969 | ... | ... | ... | ... | ... | ... | ... | 12 599 |
| | 2005 | 12 585 | ... | ... | ... | ... | ... | ... | ... | 12 718 |
| Bulgaria | 2002 | 26 053 | 37[2] | 1 030 | 123 | 1 817 | 1 203 | 97 | 752 | 42 679 |
| Bulgarie | 2003 | 27 335 | 30[2] | 967 | 144 | 1 878 | 718 | 85 | 597 | 42 600 |
| | 2004 | 26 485 | 30[2] | 1 401 | 142 | 1 912 | 958 | 103 | 12 432 | 41 621 |
| | 2005 | 24 695 | 30[2] | 1 381 | 144 | 2 265 | 1 217 | 105 | 17 884 | 44 362 |
| Croatia | 2002 | ... | 1 355 | 1 209 | 68 | 1 640 | 1 062 | 432 | 80 572 | 12 240 |
| Croatie | 2003 | ... | 1 291 | 1 261 | 75 | 1 873 | 1 036 | 437 | 83 205 | 12 620 |
| | 2004 | ... | 1 246 | 1 226 | 91 | 1 741 | 1 012 | 443 | 83 528 | 13 295 |
| | 2005 | ... | 1 178 | 1 168 | 99 | 1 603 | 1 160 | 431 | 86 769 | 12 462 |
| Czech Republic | 2002 | 63 356 | 400[2] | 1 246 | 160 | 2 412 | 376 | 157 | 5 338 | 76 348 |
| République tchèque | 2003 | 63 906 | 457[2] | 1 322 | 140 | 2 590 | 445 | 168 | 6 098 | 83 227 |
| | 2004 | 64 076 | 565[2] | 1 289 | 147 | 2 673 | 394 | 181 | 7 555 | 84 333 |
| | 2005 | 62 026 | 569[2] | 1 467 | 132 | 3 067 | 581 | 184 | 7 170 | 82 578 |
| Denmark | 2002 | ... | 18 143[2] | 2 074 | 529 | 3 258 | 1 574 | 163 | 353 693 | 39 283 |
| Danemark | 2003 | ... | 18 143[2] | 2 082 | 611 | 3 451 | 1 519 | 168 | 335 062 | 46 181 |
| | 2004 | ... | 19 262[2] | 1 986 | 606 | 3 329 | 1 557 | 164 | 395 033 | 40 432 |
| | 2005 | ... | 18 517[2] | 1 919 | 507 | 3 224 | 1 405 | 145 | 436 520 | 36 275 |
| Estonia | 2002 | 12 400[6] | ... | ... | ... | ... | ... | ... | ... | 8 520 |
| Estonie | 2003 | 14 892[6] | ... | ... | ... | ... | ... | ... | ... | 10 159 |
| | 2004 | 13 993[6] | ... | ... | ... | ... | ... | ... | ... | 10 128 |
| | 2005 | 14 591[6] | ... | ... | ... | ... | ... | ... | ... | 10 002 |

| Region, country or area / Région, pays ou zone | Year / Année | Hard coal and lignite / Houille et lignite | Crude petroleum and NGL / Pétrole brut et LGN | Motor gasoline / Essence auto | Jet fuel / Carbu-réacteurs | Gas-diesel oil / Gazole/ carburant diesel | Residual fuel oil / Mazout résiduel | Liquefied petroleum gas / Gaz de pétrole liquéfiés | Natural gas (terajoules) / Gaz naturel (térajoules) | Electricity (million kWh) / Electricité (millions de kWh) |
|---|---|---|---|---|---|---|---|---|---|---|
| | | Thousand metric tons — Milliers de tonnes | | | | | | | | |
| Faeroe Islands | 2002 | ... | ... | ... | ... | ... | ... | ... | ... | 240 |
| Iles Féroé | 2003 | ... | ... | ... | ... | ... | ... | ... | ... | 270 |
| | 2004 | ... | ... | ... | ... | ... | ... | ... | ... | 290 |
| | *2005 | ... | ... | ... | ... | ... | ... | ... | ... | 290 |
| Finland | 2002 | ... | ... | 4 350 | 659 | 5 128 | 1 403 | 227 | ... | 74 901 |
| Finlande | 2003 | ... | ... | 4 304 | 614 | 5 038 | 1 267 | 273 | ... | 84 230 |
| | 2004 | ... | ... | 4 321 | 714 | 5 078 | 1 445 | 267 | ... | 85 847 |
| | 2005 | ... | ... | 4 061 | 592 | 4 964 | 1 318 | 315 | ... | 70 550 |
| France[7] | 2002 | 2 068 | 1 519 | 16 920 | 5 238 | 33 110 | 10 626 | 2 692 | 67 438 | 559 186 |
| France[7] | 2003 | 2 243 | 1 405 | 16 804 | 5 169 | 34 979 | 10 919 | 3 071 | 59 621 | 566 949 |
| | 2004 | 872 | 1 364 | 16 926 | 5 616 | 34 421 | 11 887 | 2 979 | 51 530 | 572 241 |
| | 2005 | 617 | 1 227 | 16 305 | 5 478 | 33 590 | 11 823 | 2 868 | 38 509 | 575 351 |
| Germany | 2002 | 210 987 | 3 509[2] | 25 970 | 4 157 | 47 455 | 12 183 | 2 956 | 743 728 | 571 645 |
| Allemagne | 2003 | 207 838 | 3 690[2] | 26 449 | 4 194 | 48 638 | 12 232 | 3 056 | 740 615 | 600 822 |
| | 2004 | 211 077 | 3 463[2] | 26 467 | 4 424 | 49 551 | 14 013 | 2 918 | 685 342 | 616 785 |
| | 2005 | 205 925 | 3 471[2] | 27 240 | 4 252 | 52 137 | 13 340 | 2 951 | 661 721 | 620 300 |
| Gibraltar | 2002 | ... | ... | ... | ... | ... | ... | ... | ... | 129 |
| Gibraltar | 2003 | ... | ... | ... | ... | ... | ... | ... | ... | 134 |
| | 2004 | ... | ... | ... | ... | ... | ... | ... | ... | 136 |
| | 2005 | ... | ... | ... | ... | ... | ... | ... | ... | 145 |
| Greece | 2002 | 70 468[6] | 189 | 3 802 | 1 705 | 5 624 | 7 188 | 694 | 1 973 | 54 608 |
| Grèce | 2003 | 68 299[6] | 137 | 3 653 | 1 630 | 6 053 | 7 456 | 672 | 1 442 | 58 478 |
| | 2004 | 70 041[6] | 133 | 3 629 | 1 720 | 5 369 | 7 095 | 598 | 1 337 | 59 344 |
| | 2005 | 69 398[6] | 100 | 4 058 | 1 737 | 5 653 | 6 956 | 655 | 851 | 60 020 |
| Hungary | 2002 | 13 027[6] | 1 582 | 1 573 | 183 | 3 096 | 358 | 392 | 109 582 | 36 156 |
| Hongrie | 2003 | 13 301[6] | 1 597 | 1 477 | 202 | 3 124 | 367 | 392 | 106 329 | 34 145 |
| | 2004 | 11 242[6] | 1 660 | 1 465 | 239 | 2 989 | 313 | 408 | 110 100 | 33 708 |
| | 2005 | 9 570[6] | 1 723 | 1 317 | 266 | 3 515 | 218 | 393 | 108 422 | 35 756 |
| Iceland | 2002 | ... | ... | ... | ... | ... | ... | ... | ... | 8 416 |
| Islande | 2003 | ... | ... | ... | ... | ... | ... | ... | ... | 8 500 |
| | 2004 | ... | ... | ... | ... | ... | ... | ... | ... | 8 623 |
| | 2005 | ... | ... | ... | ... | ... | ... | ... | ... | 8 683 |
| Ireland | 2002 | ... | ... | 660 | ... | 955 | 1 047 | 60 | 31 519 | 25 170 |
| Irlande | 2003 | ... | ... | 639 | ... | 988 | 1 005 | 59 | 25 293 | 25 235 |
| | 2004 | ... | ... | 552 | ... | 964 | 966 | 53 | 32 025 | 25 627 |
| | 2005 | ... | ... | 683 | ... | 1 097 | 948 | 57 | 21 437 | 26 028 |
| Italy[8] | 2002 | 163[1] | 5 535[2] | 20 804 | 4 023 | 38 993 | 17 190 | 2 472 | 557 137 | 285 276 |
| Italie[8] | 2003 | 250[1] | 5 570[2] | 20 699 | 4 187 | 38 389 | 18 018 | 2 610 | 529 017 | 293 884 |
| | 2004 | 98[1] | 5 445[2] | 20 662 | 3 787 | 39 536 | 17 543 | 2 613 | 493 813 | 303 347 |
| | 2005 | 95[1] | 6 111[2] | 21 189 | 3 910 | 39 844 | 19 032 | 2 517 | 459 905 | 303 699 |
| Latvia | 2002 | ... | ... | ... | ... | ... | ... | ... | ... | 3 977 |
| Lettonie | 2003 | ... | ... | ... | ... | ... | ... | ... | ... | 3 979 |
| | 2004 | ... | ... | ... | ... | ... | ... | ... | ... | 4 683 |
| | 2005 | ... | ... | ... | ... | ... | ... | ... | ... | 4 905 |
| Lithuania | 2002 | ... | 434[2] | 1 719 | 655 | 1 850 | 1 229 | 455 | ... | 17 721 |
| Lituanie | 2003 | ... | 382[2] | 1 882 | 695 | 2 064 | 1 381 | 435 | ... | 19 488 |
| | 2004 | ... | 302[2] | 2 331 | 850 | 2 523 | 1 674 | 525 | ... | 19 274 |
| | 2005 | ... | 216[2] | 2 462 | 832 | 2 781 | 1 799 | 555 | ... | 14 784 |
| Luxembourg | 2002 | ... | ... | ... | ... | ... | ... | ... | ... | 3 675 |
| Luxembourg | 2003 | ... | ... | ... | ... | ... | ... | ... | ... | 3 620 |
| | 2004 | ... | ... | ... | ... | ... | ... | ... | ... | 4 121 |
| | 2005 | ... | ... | ... | ... | ... | ... | ... | ... | 4 135 |

| Region, country or area / Région, pays ou zone | Year / Année | Hard coal and lignite / Houille et lignite | Crude petroleum and NGL / Pétrole brut et LGN | Motor gasoline / Essence auto | Jet fuel / Carbu-réacteurs | Gas-diesel oil / Gazole/carburant diesel | Residual fuel oil / Mazout résiduel | Liquefied petroleum gas / Gaz de pétrole liquéfiés | Natural gas (terajoules) / Gaz naturel (térajoules) | Electricity (million kWh) / Électricité (millions de kWh) |
|---|---|---|---|---|---|---|---|---|---|---|
| | | Thousand metric tons — Milliers de tonnes | | | | | | | | |
| Malta | 2002 | ... | ... | ... | ... | ... | ... | ... | ... | 2 052 |
| Malte | 2003 | ... | ... | ... | ... | ... | ... | ... | ... | 2 236 |
| | 2004 | ... | ... | ... | ... | ... | ... | ... | ... | 2 216 |
| | 2005 | ... | ... | ... | ... | ... | ... | ... | ... | 2 240 |
| Moldova | 2002 | ... | 0[2] | ... | ... | 0 | 0 | ... | ... | *3 233 |
| Moldova | 2003 | ... | 0[2] | ... | ... | 0 | 0 | ... | ... | *3 413 |
| | 2004 | ... | 8[2] | ... | ... | 0 | 0 | ... | ... | 3 617 |
| | 2005 | ... | 5[2] | ... | ... | 1 | 3 | ... | ... | 3 865 |
| Netherlands | 2002 | ... | 3 104 | 15 767 | 6 174 | 19 583 | 12 654 | 4 664 | 2 524 867 | 96 066 |
| Pays-Bas | 2003 | ... | 3 129 | 15 730 | 6 669 | 20 787 | 12 333 | 4 780 | 2 428 905 | 96 763 |
| | 2004 | ... | 2 910 | 15 539 | 6 935 | 20 234 | 13 073 | 5 070 | 2 864 924 | 100 770 |
| | 2005 | ... | 2 530 | 14 234 | 6 990 | 21 346 | 12 394 | 4 579 | 2 617 469 | 100 219 |
| Norway[9] | 2002 | 2 132[1] | 157 698 | 2 920 | 582 | 6 010 | 1 503 | 5 609 | 2 751 407 | 130 705 |
| Norvège[9] | 2003 | 2 944[1] | 153 616 | 3 546 | 415 | 6 635 | 1 702 | 6 167 | 3 081 659 | 107 405 |
| | 2004 | 2 904[1] | 151 779 | 3 261 | 423 | 6 241 | 1 845 | 6 423 | 3 274 692 | 110 598 |
| | 2005 | 1 471[1] | 140 134 | 3 829 | 644 | 6 835 | 1 610 | 6 628 | 3 547 171 | 138 108 |
| Poland | 2002 | 161 915 | 728[2] | 3 932 | 575 | 6 314 | 3 325 | 255 | 166 037 | 144 126 |
| Pologne | 2003 | 163 794 | 765[2] | 3 871 | 647 | 6 722 | 3 253 | 269 | 167 997 | 151 631 |
| | 2004 | 162 428 | 886[2] | 3 978 | 679 | 7 371 | 2 754 | 259 | 182 618 | 154 159 |
| | 2005 | 159 540 | 848[2] | 4 117 | 644 | 7 459 | 2 537 | 284 | 180 700 | 156 936 |
| Portugal | 2002 | ... | ... | 2 518 | 511 | 4 827 | 2 358 | 341 | ... | 46 107 |
| Portugal | 2003 | ... | ... | 2 732 | 703 | 4 955 | 2 388 | 379 | ... | 46 852 |
| | 2004 | ... | ... | 2 551 | 779 | 4 703 | 2 969 | 365 | ... | 45 105 |
| | 2005 | ... | ... | 2 466 | 854 | 4 906 | 3 062 | 391 | ... | 46 575 |
| Romania | 2002 | 30 414 | 6 072 | 3 569 | 105 | 4 689 | 1 700 | 344 | 493 064 | 54 735 |
| Roumanie | 2003 | 33 063 | 5 890 | 3 295 | 158 | 3 988 | 1 562 | 327 | 485 135 | 55 140 |
| | 2004 | 31 792 | 5 705 | 3 419 | 177 | 4 170 | 1 559 | 366 | 482 759 | 56 503 |
| | 2005 | 31 106 | 5 733 | 4 237 | 191 | 4 709 | 1 707 | 658 | 451 305 | 59 413 |
| Russian Federation | 2002 | 237 580 | 373 558 | 28 992 | 9 303 | 52 724 | 58 896 | 7 610 | 22 308 334 | 891 285 |
| Fédération de Russie | 2003 | 256 979 | 414 213 | 29 315 | 9 453 | 53 930 | 56 377 | 8 571 | 23 252 111 | 916 286 |
| | 2004 | 258 944 | 450 251 | 30 505 | 9 592 | 55 389 | 58 330 | 8 760 | 23 693 333 | 931 865 |
| | 2005 | 276 581 | 466 448 | 32 011 | 10 036 | 60 003 | 62 365 | 9 428 | 23 996 973 | 953 115 |
| Serbia and Montenegro | 2002 | 38 398 | 812[2] | 672 | 78 | 1 123 | 839 | 87 | 16 946 | 35 060 |
| Serbie-et-Monténégro | 2003 | 40 279 | 773[2] | 617 | 85 | 1 254 | 919 | 79 | 13 723 | 35 366 |
| | 2004 | 41 157 | 652[2] | 821 | 56 | 1 315 | 853 | 95 | 11 951 | 37 686 |
| | 2005 | 40 456 | 609[2] | 845 | 57 | 1 353 | 879 | 98 | 10 631 | 36 474 |
| Slovakia | 2002 | 3 404[6] | 103 | 1 555 | 42 | 2 341 | 620 | 191 | 6 754 | 32 427 |
| Slovaquie | 2003 | 3 097[6] | 80 | 1 597 | 63 | 2 351 | 635 | 184 | 7 745 | 31 179 |
| | 2004 | 2 952[6] | 42 | 1 670 | 61 | 2 598 | 585 | 206 | 6 603 | 30 567 |
| | 2005 | 2 511[6] | 34 | 1 584 | 36 | 2 455 | 543 | 181 | 5 876 | 31 455 |
| Slovenia | 2002 | 4 686[6] | 1[2] | ... | ... | ... | ... | ... | 222 | 14 690 |
| Slovénie | 2003 | 4 830[6] | 0[2] | ... | ... | ... | ... | ... | 199 | 14 019 |
| | 2004 | 4 809[6] | 0[2] | ... | ... | ... | ... | ... | 201 | 15 271 |
| | 2005 | 4 540[6] | 0[2] | ... | ... | ... | ... | ... | 160 | 15 117 |
| Spain | 2002 | 22 034 | 316[2] | 8 871 | 3 567 | 20 820 | 12 122 | 1 561 | 21 718 | 244 963 |
| Espagne | 2003 | 20 562 | 322[2] | 9 047 | 3 061 | 21 631 | 10 130 | 1 211 | 9 149 | 260 727 |
| | 2004 | 20 487 | 255[2] | 10 434 | 2 713 | 21 563 | 9 125 | 1 058 | 14 398 | 280 007 |
| | 2005 | 19 481 | 166[2] | 10 152 | 2 653 | 23 457 | 9 019 | 1 050 | 6 324 | 294 077 |
| Sweden | 2002 | ... | ... | 3 987 | 57 | 6 964 | 5 069 | 272 | ... | 146 733 |
| Suède | 2003 | ... | ... | 4 309 | 109 | 6 942 | 5 170 | 360 | ... | 135 435 |
| | 2004 | ... | ... | 4 506 | 208 | 7 238 | 5 450 | 423 | ... | 151 726 |
| | 2005 | ... | ... | 4 045 | 70 | 6 951 | 5 576 | 433 | ... | 158 434 |

| Region, country or area / Région, pays ou zone | Year / Année | Hard coal and lignite / Houille et lignite | Crude petroleum and NGL / Pétrole brut et LGN | Motor gasoline / Essence auto | Jet fuel / Carbu-réacteurs | Gas-diesel oil / Gazole/ carburant diesel | Residual fuel oil / Mazout résiduel | Liquefied petroleum gas / Gaz de pétrole liquéfiés | Natural gas (terajoules) / Gaz naturel (térajoules) | Electricity (million kWh) / Electricité (millions de kWh) |
|---|---|---|---|---|---|---|---|---|---|---|
| | | Thousand metric tons — Milliers de tonnes | | | | | | | | |
| Switzerland[10] | 2002 | ... | ... | 1 175 | 406 | 2 011 | 743 | 209 | ... | 66 893 |
| Suisse[10] | 2003 | ... | ... | 1 072 | 344 | 1 893 | 759 | 178 | ... | 67 166 |
| | 2004 | ... | ... | 1 362 | 350 | 2 148 | 701 | 196 | ... | 65 299 |
| | 2005 | ... | ... | 1 268 | 212 | 2 170 | 611 | 197 | ... | 59 612 |
| TFYR of Macedonia | 2002 | 7 580[6] | ... | 78 | 11 | 172 | 254 | 9 | ... | 6 090 |
| L'ex-R.y. Macédoine | 2003 | 7 382[6] | ... | 126 | 0 | 322 | 343 | 21 | ... | 6 737 |
| | 2004 | 7 245[6] | ... | 146 | 0 | 359 | 282 | 20 | ... | 6 665 |
| | 2005 | 6 881[6] | ... | 183 | 23 | 394 | 295 | 24 | ... | 6 942 |
| Ukraine | 2002 | 61 556 | 3 732 | 4 588 | 340 | 5 790 | 7 330 | 627 | 728 882 | 173 740 |
| Ukraine | 2003 | 64 232 | 3 967 | 4 308 | 361 | 6 484 | 7 970 | 581 | 748 794 | 180 354 |
| | 2004 | 59 589 | 4 314 | 4 393 | 473 | 6 544 | 7 766 | 607 | 799 130 | 182 157 |
| | 2005 | 60 351 | 4 414 | 4 609 | 512 | 5 533 | 5 878 | 606 | 811 148 | 186 055 |
| United Kingdom | 2002 | 29 989[1] | 115 944 | 22 944 | 5 365 | 28 393 | 10 551 | 4 668 | 4 345 335 | 387 364 |
| Royaume-Uni | 2003 | 28 279[1] | 106 073 | 22 627 | 5 277 | 27 579 | 11 517 | 4 007 | 4 309 312 | 398 671 |
| | 2004 | 25 097[1] | 95 374 | 24 589 | 5 615 | 28 839 | 12 988 | 5 080 | 4 019 594 | 395 853 |
| | 2005 | 20 498[1] | 84 722 | 22 620 | 5 167 | 28 691 | 11 728 | 5 218 | 3 666 845 | 400 524 |
| **Oceania** | **2002** | **346 300** | **35 479** | **14 789** | **5 159** | **13 170** | **2 123** | **1 712** | **1 652 746** | **275 685** |
| **Océanie** | **2003** | **348 393** | **32 785** | **14 628** | **4 931** | **13 478** | **1 669** | **1 850** | **1 641 590** | **277 952** |
| | **2004** | **359 616** | **29 251** | **15 139** | **5 017** | **13 578** | **1 421** | **1 479** | **1 653 819** | **290 897** |
| | **2005** | **380 853** | **25 823** | **14 931** | **5 253** | **12 782** | **1 524** | **1 427** | **1 802 032** | **303 241** |
| American Samoa | 2002 | ... | ... | ... | ... | ... | ... | ... | ... | 179 |
| Samoa américaines | 2003 | ... | ... | ... | ... | ... | ... | ... | ... | 188 |
| | 2004 | ... | ... | ... | ... | ... | ... | ... | ... | 188 |
| | 2005 | ... | ... | ... | ... | ... | ... | ... | ... | 189 |
| Australia | 2002 | 341 841 | 31 320 | 13 259 | 4 271 | 11 091 | 1 696 | 1 506 | 1 411 424 | 226 359 |
| Australie | 2003 | 343 213 | 29 111 | 13 108 | 4 080 | 11 430 | 1 310 | 1 694 | 1 456 588 | 228 118 |
| | 2004 | 354 461 | 26 218 | 13 453 | 3 937 | 11 590 | 1 071 | 1 312 | 1 488 699 | 239 042 |
| | 2005 | 375 586 | 22 895 | 13 218 | 4 221 | 10 790 | 1 085 | 1 271 | 1 648 435 | 251 120 |
| Cook Islands | 2002 | ... | ... | ... | ... | ... | ... | ... | ... | 28 |
| Iles Cook | 2003 | ... | ... | ... | ... | ... | ... | ... | ... | 29 |
| | 2004 | ... | ... | ... | ... | ... | ... | ... | ... | 30 |
| | 2005 | ... | ... | ... | ... | ... | ... | ... | ... | 30 |
| Fiji* | 2002 | ... | ... | ... | ... | ... | ... | ... | ... | 765 |
| Fidji* | 2003 | ... | ... | ... | ... | ... | ... | ... | ... | 812 |
| | 2004 | ... | ... | ... | ... | ... | ... | ... | ... | 816 |
| | 2005 | ... | ... | ... | ... | ... | ... | ... | ... | 823 |
| French Polynesia | 2002 | ... | ... | ... | ... | ... | ... | ... | ... | 507 |
| Polynésie française | 2003 | ... | ... | ... | ... | ... | ... | ... | ... | 479 |
| | *2004 | ... | ... | ... | ... | ... | ... | ... | ... | 485 |
| | *2005 | ... | ... | ... | ... | ... | ... | ... | ... | 493 |
| Guam | 2002 | ... | ... | ... | ... | ... | ... | ... | ... | 1 720 |
| Guam | 2003 | ... | ... | ... | ... | ... | ... | ... | ... | 1 777 |
| | 2004 | ... | ... | ... | ... | ... | ... | ... | ... | 1 878 |
| | 2005 | ... | ... | ... | ... | ... | ... | ... | ... | 1 897 |
| Kiribati* | 2002 | ... | ... | ... | ... | ... | ... | ... | ... | 10 |
| Kiribati* | 2003 | ... | ... | ... | ... | ... | ... | ... | ... | 10 |
| | 2004 | ... | ... | ... | ... | ... | ... | ... | ... | 10 |
| | 2005 | ... | ... | ... | ... | ... | ... | ... | ... | 10 |
| Mashall Islands | 2002 | ... | ... | ... | ... | ... | ... | ... | ... | 99 |
| Iles Marshall | 2003 | ... | ... | ... | ... | ... | ... | ... | ... | 96 |
| | 2004 | ... | ... | ... | ... | ... | ... | ... | ... | 101 |
| | 2005 | ... | ... | ... | ... | ... | ... | ... | ... | 101 |

| Region, country or area / Région, pays ou zone | Year / Année | Hard coal and lignite / Houille et lignite | Crude petroleum and NGL / Pétrole brut et LGN | Motor gasoline / Essence auto | Jet fuel / Carbu-réacteurs | Gas-diesel oil / Gazole/carburant diesel | Residual fuel oil / Mazout résiduel | Liquefied petroleum gas / Gaz de pétrole liquéfiés | Natural gas (terajoules) / Gaz naturel (térajoules) | Electricity (million kWh) / Électricité (millions de kWh) |
|---|---|---|---|---|---|---|---|---|---|---|
| | | Thousand metric tons — Milliers de tonnes | | | | | | | | |
| Nauru* | 2002 | ... | ... | ... | ... | ... | ... | ... | ... | 30 |
| Nauru* | 2003 | ... | ... | ... | ... | ... | ... | ... | ... | 32 |
| | 2004 | ... | ... | ... | ... | ... | ... | ... | ... | 32 |
| | 2005 | ... | ... | ... | ... | ... | ... | ... | ... | 32 |
| New Caledonia | 2002 | ... | ... | ... | ... | ... | ... | ... | ... | 1 749 |
| Nouvelle-Calédonie | 2003 | ... | ... | ... | ... | ... | ... | ... | ... | 1 758 |
| | 2004 | ... | ... | ... | ... | ... | ... | ... | ... | 1 678 |
| | *2005 | ... | ... | ... | ... | ... | ... | ... | ... | 1 700 |
| New Zealand | 2002 | 4 459 | 1 607 | 1 530 | 869 | 2 049 | 427 | 206 | 235 294 | 41 108 |
| Nouvelle-Zélande | 2003 | 5 180 | 1 247 | 1 520 | 832 | 2 018 | 359 | 156 | 179 476 | 41 249 |
| | 2004 | 5 155 | 1 106 | 1 627 | 930 | 1 763 | 350 | 167 | 160 640 | 42 794 |
| | 2005 | 5 267 | 1 028 | 1 653 | 887 | 1 777 | 439 | 156 | 148 597 | 42 956 |
| Niue* | 2002 | ... | ... | ... | ... | ... | ... | ... | ... | 3 |
| Nioué* | 2003 | ... | ... | ... | ... | ... | ... | ... | ... | 3 |
| | 2004 | ... | ... | ... | ... | ... | ... | ... | ... | 3 |
| | 2005 | ... | ... | ... | ... | ... | ... | ... | ... | 3 |
| Palau | 2002 | ... | ... | ... | ... | ... | ... | ... | ... | 127 |
| Palaos | 2003 | ... | ... | ... | ... | ... | ... | ... | ... | 128 |
| | *2004 | ... | ... | ... | ... | ... | ... | ... | ... | 128 |
| | *2005 | ... | ... | ... | ... | ... | ... | ... | ... | 128 |
| Papua New Guinea | 2002 | ... | 2 552[2] | 0 | *19 | *30 | ... | ... | 6 028 | 2 760 |
| Papouasie-Nvl-Guinée | 2003 | ... | 2 427[2] | 0 | *19 | *30 | ... | ... | 5 526 | 3 030 |
| | 2004 | ... | 1 927[2] | *59 | *150 | *225 | ... | ... | 4 480 | 3 466 |
| | *2005 | ... | 1 900[2] | 60 | 145 | 215 | ... | ... | 5 000 | 3 500 |
| Samoa* | 2002 | ... | ... | ... | ... | ... | ... | ... | ... | 105 |
| Samoa* | 2003 | ... | ... | ... | ... | ... | ... | ... | ... | 106 |
| | 2004 | ... | ... | ... | ... | ... | ... | ... | ... | 110 |
| | 2005 | ... | ... | ... | ... | ... | ... | ... | ... | 111 |
| Solomon Islands* | 2002 | ... | ... | ... | ... | ... | ... | ... | ... | 57 |
| Iles Salomon* | 2003 | ... | ... | ... | ... | ... | ... | ... | ... | 56 |
| | 2004 | ... | ... | ... | ... | ... | ... | ... | ... | 56 |
| | 2005 | ... | ... | ... | ... | ... | ... | ... | ... | 67 |
| Tonga* | 2002 | ... | ... | ... | ... | ... | ... | ... | ... | 36 |
| Tonga* | 2003 | ... | ... | ... | ... | ... | ... | ... | ... | 36 |
| | 2004 | ... | ... | ... | ... | ... | ... | ... | ... | 36 |
| | 2005 | ... | ... | ... | ... | ... | ... | ... | ... | 36 |
| Vanuatu* | 2002 | ... | ... | ... | ... | ... | ... | ... | ... | 43 |
| Vanuatu* | 2003 | ... | ... | ... | ... | ... | ... | ... | ... | 44 |
| | 2004 | ... | ... | ... | ... | ... | ... | ... | ... | 44 |
| | 2005 | ... | ... | ... | ... | ... | ... | ... | ... | 45 |

**Source**

United Nations Statistics Division, New York, the energy statistics database, last accessed January 2008.

**Notes**

1 Hard coal only.
2 Crude petroleum only.
3 Refers to the Southern African Customs Union.
4 Natural gas liquids only.
5 For statistical purposes, the data for China do not include those for the Hong Kong Special Administrative Region (Hong Kong SAR), Macao Special Administrative Region (Macao SAR) and Taiwan Province of China.

**Source**

Organisation des Nations Unies, Division de statistique, New York, la base de données pour les statistiques énergétiques, dernier accès janvier 2008.

**Notes**

1 Houille seulement.
2 Pétrole brut seulement.
3 Se réfèrent à l'Union douanière d'afrique australe.
4 Liquides de gaz naturel seulement.
5 Pour la présentation des statistiques, les données pour la Chine ne comprennent pas la Région Administrative Spéciale de Hong Kong (Hong Kong RAS), la Région Administrative Spéciale de Macao (Macao RAS) et la province de Taiwan.

6  Lignite only.
7  Including Monaco.
8  Including San Marino.
9  Including Svalbard and Jan Mayen Islands.
10  Including Liechtenstein.

6  Lignite seulement.
7  Y compris Monaco.
8  Y compris Saint-Marin.
9  Y compris îles Svalbard et Jan Mayen.
10  Y compris Liechtenstein.

*Tables 49*: Data are presented in metric tons of oil equivalent (TOE), to which the individual energy commodities are converted in the interests of international uniformity and comparability.

To convert from original units to TOE, the data in original units (metric tons, terajoules, kilowatt hours, cubic metres) are multiplied by conversion factors. For a list of the relevant conversion factors and a detailed description of methods, see the United Nations *Energy Statistics Yearbook* and related methodological publications.

Included in the production of commercial primary energy for *solids* are hard coal, lignite, peat and oil shale; *liquids* are comprised of crude petroleum and natural gas liquids; *gas* comprises natural gas; and *electricity* is comprised of primary electricity generation from hydro, nuclear, geothermal, wind, tide, wave and solar sources.

In general, data on stocks refer to changes in stocks of producers, importers and/or industrial consumers at the beginning and end of each year.

International trade of energy commodities is based on the "general trade" system, that is, all goods entering and leaving the national boundary of a country are recorded as imports and exports.

Sea/air bunkers refer to the amounts of fuels delivered to ocean-going ships or aircraft of all flags engaged in international traffic. Consumption by ships engaged in transport in inland and coastal waters, or by aircraft engaged in domestic flights, is not included.

Data on consumption refer to "apparent consumption" and are derived from the formula "production + imports - exports - bunkers +/- stock changes". Accordingly, the series on apparent consumption may in some cases represent only an indication of the magnitude of actual gross inland availability.

Included in the consumption of commercial energy for *solids* are consumption of primary forms of solid fuels, net imports and changes in stocks of secondary fuels; *liquids* are comprised of consumption of energy petroleum products including feedstocks, natural gasoline, condensate, refinery gas and input of crude petroleum to thermal power plants; *gases* include the consumption of natural gas, net imports and changes in stocks of gasworks and coke oven gas; and *electricity* is comprised of production of primary electricity and net imports of electricity.

*Table 50*: The definitions of the energy commodities are as follows:

• Hard coal: Coal that has a high degree of coalification with a gross calorific value above 23,865 KJ/kg (5,700

*Tableau 49* : Les données relatives aux divers produits énergétiques ont été converties en tonnes d'équivalent pétrole (TEP), dans un souci d'uniformité et pour permettre les com-paraisons entre la production de différents pays.

Pour passer des unités de mesure d'origine à l'unité commune, les données en unités d'origine (tonnes, terajoules, kilowatt-heures, mètres cubes) sont multipliées par des facteurs de conversion. Pour une liste des facteurs de conversion appropriée et pour des descriptions détaillées des méthodes appliquées, se reporter à l'*Annuaire des statistiques de l'énergie* des Nations Unies et aux publications méthodologiques apparentées.

Sont compris dans la production d'énergie primaire commer-ciale: pour *les solides*, la houille, le lignite, la tourbe et le schiste bitumineux; pour *les liquides*, le pétrole brut et les liquides de gaz naturel; pour *les gaz*, le gaz naturel; pour *l'électricité*, l'électricité primaire de source hydraulique, nucléaire, géothermique, éolienne, marémotrice, des vagues et solaire.

En général, les variations des stocks se rapportent aux différences entre les stocks des producteurs, des importateurs ou des consommateurs industriels au début et à la fin de chaque année.

Le commerce international des produits énergétiques est fondé sur le système du "commerce général", c'est-à-dire que tous les biens entrant sur le territoire national d'un pays ou en sortant sont respectivement enregistrés comme importations et exportations.

Les soutes maritimes/aériens se rapportent aux quantités de combustibles livrées aux navires de mer et aéronefs assurant des liaisons commerciales internationales, quel que soit leur pavillon. La consommation des navires effectuant des opérations de transport sur les voies navigables intérieures ou dans les eaux côtières n'est pas incluse, tout comme celle des aéronefs effectuant des vols intérieurs.

Les données sur la consommation se rapportent à la "consommation apparente" et sont obtenues par la formule "production + importations - exportations - soutes +/- variations des stocks". En conséquence, les séries relatives à la consommation apparente peuvent occasionnellement ne donner qu'une indication de l'ordre de grandeur des disponibilités intérieures brutes réelles.

Sont compris dans la consommation d'énergie commerciale: pour *les solides*, la consommation de combustibles solides primaires, les importations nettes et les variations de stocks de combustibles solides secondaires; pour *les liquides*, la consommation de produits pétroliers énergétiques y compris les charges d'alimentation des usines de traitement, l'essence naturelle, le condensat et le gaz de raffinerie ainsi

kcal/kg) on an ash free but moist basis, and a mean random reflectance of vitrinite of at least 0.6. Slurries, middlings and other low-grade coal products, which cannot be classified according to the type of coal from which they are obtained, are included under hard coal.

- Lignite: Non-agglomerating coal with a low degree of coalification which retained the anatomical structure of the vegetable matter from which it was formed. Its gross calorific value is less than 17,435 KJ/kg (4,165 kcal/kg), and it contains greater than 31 per cent volatile matter on a dry mineral matter free basis.

- Crude petroleum: A mineral oil consisting of a mixture of hydrocarbons of natural origin, yellow to black in color, of variable density and viscosity. Data in this category also includes lease or field condensate (separator liquids) which is recovered from gaseous hydrocarbons in lease separation facilities, as well as synthetic crude oil, mineral oils extracted from bituminous minerals such as shales and bituminous sand, and oils from coal liquefaction.

- Natural gas liquids (NGL): Liquid or liquefied hydrocarbons produced in the manufacture, purification and stabilization of natural gas. NGLs include, but are not limited to, ethane, propane, butane, pentane, natural gasoline, and plant condensate.

- Motor gasoline: Light hydrocarbon oil for use in internal combustion engines such as motor vehicles, excluding aircraft. It distills between $35^{\circ}C$ and $200^{\circ}C$, and is treated to reach a sufficiently high octane number of generally between 80 and 100 RON. Treatment may be by reforming, blending with an aromatic fraction, or the addition of benzole or other additives (such as tetraethyl lead).

- Jet fuel: Consists of gasoline-type jet fuel and kerosene-type jet fuel. Gasoline-type jet fuel: All light hydrocarbon oils for use in aviation gas-turbine engines. It distills between $100^{\circ}C$ and $250^{\circ}C$ with at least 20% of volume distilling at $143^{\circ}C$. It is obtained by blending kerosene and gasoline or naphtha in such a way that the aromatic content does not exceed 25% in volume. Additives are included to reduce the freezing point to $-58^{\circ}C$ or lower, and to keep the Reid vapour pressure between 0.14 and 0.21 kg/cm2. Kerosene-type jet fuel: Medium oil for use in aviation gas-turbine engines with the same distillation characteristics and flash point as kerosene, with a maximum aromatic content of 20% in volume. It is treated to give a kinematic viscosity of less than 15 cSt at $-34^{\circ}C$ and a freezing point below $-50^{\circ}C$.

- Gas-diesel oil (distillate fuel oil): Heavy oils distilling between $200^{\circ}C$ and $380^{\circ}C$, but distilling less than 65% in volume at $250^{\circ}C$, including losses, and 85% or more at $350^{\circ}C$. Its flash point is always above $50^{\circ}C$ and its spe-

que le pétrole brut consommé dans les centrales thermiques pour la production d'électricité; pour *les gaz*, la consommation de gaz naturel, les importations nettes et les variations de stocks de gaz d'usines à gaz et de gaz de cokerie; pour l'*électricité*, la production d'électricité primaire et les importations nettes d'électricité.

*Tableau 50*: Les définitions des produits énergétiques sont données ciaprès :

- Houille : Charbon à haut degré de houillification et à pouvoir calorifique brut supérieur à 23 865 kJ/kg (5 700 kcal/kg), valeur mesurée pour un combustible exempt de cendres, mais humide et ayant un indice moyen de réflectance de la vitrinite au moins égal à 0,6. Les schlamms, les mixtes et autres produits du charbon de faible qualité qui ne peuvent être classés en fonction du type de charbon dont ils sont dérivés, sont inclus dans cette rubrique.

- Lignite: Le charbon non agglutinant d'un faible degré de houillification qui a gardé la structure anatomique des végétaux dont il est issu. Son pouvoir calorifique supérieur est inférieur à 17 435 kJ/kg (4 165 kcal/kg) et il contient plus de 31% de matières volatiles sur produit sec exempt de matières minérales.

- Pétrole brut : Huile minérale constituée d'un mélange d'hydrocarbures d'origine naturelle, de couleur variant du jaune au noir, d'une densité et d'une viscosité variable. Figurent également dans cette rubrique les condensats directement récupérés sur les sites d'exploitation des hydrocarbures gazeux (dans les installations prévues pour la séparation des phases liquide et gazeuse), le pétrole brut synthétique, les huiles minérales brutes extraites des roches bitumineuses telles que schistes, sables asphaltiques et les huiles issues de la liquéfaction du charbon.

- Liquides de gaz naturel (LGN) : Hydrocarbures liquides ou liquéfiés produits lors de la fabrication, de la purification et de la stabilisation du gaz naturel. Les liquides de gaz naturel comprennent l'éthane, le propane, le butane, le pentane, l'essence naturelle et les condensats d'usine, sans que la liste soit limitative.

- Essence auto : Hydrocarbure léger utilisé dans les moteurs à combustion interne, tels que ceux des véhicules à moteur, à l'exception des aéronefs. Sa température de distillation se situe entre $35^{\circ}C$ et $200^{\circ}C$ et il est traité de façon à atteindre un indice d'octane suffisamment élevé, généralement entre 80 et 100 IOR. Le traitement peut consister en reformage, mélange avec une fraction aromatique, ou adjonction de benzol ou d'autres additifs (tels que du plomb tétraéthyle).

- Carburéacteurs : Comprennent les carburéacteurs du type essence et les carburéacteurs du type kérosène. Carburéacteurs du type essence: Comprennent tous les hydrocarbu-

cific gravity is higher than 0.82. Heavy oils ob-tained by blending are grouped together with gas oils on the condition that their kinematic viscosity does not exceed 27.5 cSt at 38°C. Also included are middle distillates intended for the petrochemical industry. Gas-diesel oils are used as a fuel for internal combustion in diesel engines, as a burner fuel in heating installations, such as furnaces, and for enriching water gas to increase its luminosity. Other names for this product are diesel fuel, diesel oil and gas oil.

- Residual fuel oil: A heavy oil that makes up the distillation residue. It comprises all fuels (including those obtained by blending) with a kinematic viscosity above 27.5 cSt at 38°C. Its flash point is always above 50°C and its specific gravity is higher than 0.90. It is commonly used by ships and industrial large-scale heating installations as a fuel in furnaces or boilers.

- Liquefied petroleum gas (LPG): Hydrocarbons which are gaseous under conditions of normal tempera-ture and pressure but are liquefied by compression or cooling to facilitate storage, handling and transportation. It comprises propane, butane, or a combination of the two. Also included is ethane from petroleum refineries or natural gas producers' separation and stabilization plants.

- Natural gas: Gases consisting mainly of methane occurring naturally in underground deposits. It includes both non associated gas (originating from fields producing only hydrocarbons in gaseous form) and associated gas (originating from fields producing both liquid and gaseous hydrocarbons), as well as methane recovered from coal mines and sewage gas. Production of natural gas refers to dry marketable production, measured after purification and extraction of natural gas liquids and sulphur. Extraction losses and the amounts that have been reinjected, flared, and vented are excluded from the data on production.

- Electricity production refers to gross production, which includes the consumption by station auxiliaries and any losses in the transformers that are considered integral parts of the station. Included also is total electric energy produced by pumping installations without deduction of electric energy absorbed by pumping.

res légers utilisés dans les turboréacteurs d'aviation. Leur température de distillation se situe entre 100°C et 250°C et donne au moins 20% en volume de distillat à 143°C. Ils sont obtenus par mélange de pétrole lampant et d'essence ou de naphta de façon que la teneur en composés aromatiques ne dépasse pas 25% en volume. Des additifs y sont ajoutés afin d'abaisser le point de congélation à -58°C ou audessous, et de maintenir la tension de vapeur Reid entre 0,14 et 0,21 kg/cm2. Carburéacteurs du type kerosene: Huiles moyennement visqueuses utilisées dans les turboréacteurs d'aviation, ayant les mêmes caractéristiques de distillation et le même point d'éclair que le pétrole lampant et une teneur en composés aromatiques ne dépassant pas 20% en volume. Elles sont traitées de façon à atteindre une viscosité cinématique de moins de 15 cSt à -34°C et un point de congélation inférieur à -50°C.

- Gazole/carburant diesel (mazout distillé) : Huiles lourdes dont la température de distillation se situe entre 200oC et 380oC, mais qui donnent moins de 65% en volume de distillat à 250°C (y compris les pertes) et 85% ou davantage à 350°C. Leur point d'éclair est toujours supérieur à 50°C et leur densité supérieure à 0,82. Les huiles lourdes obtenues par mélange sont classées dans la même catégorie que les gazoles à condition que leur viscosité cinématique ne dépasse 27,5 cSt à 38°C. Sont compris dans cette rubrique les distillats moyens destinés à l'industrie pétrochimique. Les gazoles servent de carburant pour la combustion interne dans les moteurs diesel, de combustible dans les installations de chauffage telles que les chaudières, et d'additifs destinés à augmenter la luminosité de la flamme du gaz à l'eau. Ce produit est aussi connu sous les appellations de gazole ou gasoil et carburant ou combustible diesel.

- Gaz de pétrole liquéfiés (GPL) : Hydrocarbures qui sont à l'état gazeux dans des conditions de température et de pression normales mais sont liquéfiés par compression ou refroidissement pour en faciliter l'entreposage, la manipulation et le transport. Dans cette rubrique figurent le propane et le butane ou un mélange de ces deux hydrocarbures. Est également inclus l'éthane produit dans les raffineries ou dans les installations de séparation et de stabilisation des producteurs de gaz naturel.

- Gaz naturel : gaz constitué essentiellement de méthane, extraits de gisements naturels souterrains. Il peut s'agir aussi bien de gaz non associé (provenant de gisements qui produisent uniquement des hydrocarbures gazeux) que de gaz associé (provenant de gisements qui produisent à la fois des hydrocarbures liquides et gazeux) ou de méthane récupéré dans les mines de charbon et le gaz de gadoues. La production de gaz naturel se rapporte à la production

de gaz commercialisable sec, mesurée après purification et extraction des condensats de gaz naturel et du soufre. Les quantités réinjectées, brûlées à la torchère ou éventées et les pertes d'extraction sont exclues des données sur la production.

- La production d'électricité se rapporte à la production brute, qui comprend la consommation des équipements auxiliaires des centrales et les pertes au niveau des transformateurs considérés comme faisant partie intégrante de ces centrales, ainsi que la quantité totale d'énergie électrique produite par les installations de pompage sans déductions de l'énergie électrique absorbée par ces dernières.

# 51

## Land
As of 2005, thousand hectares

## Terres
En 2005, milliers d'hectares

| Country or area — Pays ou zone | Area — Superficie | | | | Net change from 1990 to 2005 Variation nette de 1990 à 2005 | | |
|---|---|---|---|---|---|---|---|
| | Total land Superficie totale | Arable land Terres arables | Permanent crops Cultures permanentes | Forest cover Superficie forestière | Arable land Terres arables | Permanent crops Cultures permanentes | Forest cover Superficie forestière |
| Afghanistan — Afghanistan | 65 209[1] | 7 910[1] | 138[1] | 867[1] | 0 | 8 | -442 |
| Albania — Albanie | 2 740 | 578 | 122 | 794 | -1 | -3 | 5 |
| Algeria — Algérie | 238 174[1] | 7 450[1] | 850[1] | 2 277 | 369 | 296 | 487 |
| American Samoa — Samoa américaines | 20 | 2[1] | 3[1] | 18 | 1 | 0 | -1 |
| Andorra — Andorre | 47 | 1[1] | ... | 16[1] | 0 | ... | 0 |
| Angola — Angola | 124 670 | 3 300[1] | 290[1] | 59 104[1] | 400 | -210 | -1 872 |
| Anguilla — Anguilla | 9 | ... | ... | 6[1] | ... | ... | 0 |
| Antigua and Barbuda — Antigua-et-Barbuda | 44 | 8[1] | 2[1] | 9[1] | 0 | 0 | 0 |
| Argentina — Argentine | 273 669[1] | 28 500[1] | 1 005[1] | 33 021 | 2 100 | -15 | -2 241 |
| Armenia — Arménie | 2 820[1] | 495[1] | 60[1] | 283 | -3[2] | -15[2] | -55[2] |
| Aruba — Aruba | 18 | 2[1] | ... | 0[1] | 0 | ... | 0 |
| Australia — Australie | 768 230 | 49 402[1] | 340[1] | 163 678 | 1 502 | 159 | -4 226 |
| Austria — Autriche | 8 245 | 1 387 | 66 | 3 862 | -39 | -13 | 86 |
| Azerbaijan — Azerbaïdjan | 8 266 | 1 843 | 222 | 936[1] | 139[2] | -89[2] | 0[2] |
| Bahamas — Bahamas | 1 001[1] | 8[1] | 4[1] | 515[1] | 0 | 2 | 0 |
| Bahrain — Bahreïn | 71[1] | 2[1] | 4[1] | 1[1] | 0 | 2 | 0 |
| Bangladesh — Bangladesh | 13 017 | 7 951[1] | 460[1] | 871 | -1 186 | 160 | -11 |
| Barbados — Barbade | 43 | 16[1] | 1[1] | 2[1] | 0 | 0 | 0 |
| Belarus — Bélarus | 20 748[1] | 5 455[1] | 116 | 7 894 | -629[2] | -61[2] | 424[2] |
| Belgium — Belgique | 3 023 | 844 | 23 | 667 | -18[3] | 2[3] | 0[3] |
| Belize — Belize | 2 281 | 70[1] | 32[1] | 1 653 | 18 | 7 | 0 |
| Benin — Bénin | 11 062[1] | 2 750[1] | 267[1] | 2 351[1] | 1 135 | 162 | -971 |
| Bermuda — Bermudes | 5 | 1[1] | ... | 1 | 0 | ... | 0 |
| Bhutan — Bhoutan | 4 700 | 159[1] | 18[1] | 3 195 | 46 | -1 | 160 |
| Bolivia — Bolivie | 108 438[1] | 3 050[1] | 206[1] | 58 740 | 950 | 51 | -4 055 |
| Bosnia and Herzegovina — Bosnie-Herzégovine | 5 120 | 1 000[1] | 97[1] | 2 185 | 150[2] | -53[2] | -20[2] |
| Botswana — Botswana | 56 673[1] | 377[1] | 3[1] | 11 943[1] | -41 | 0 | -1 775 |
| Brazil — Brésil | 845 942[1] | 59 000[1] | 7 600[1] | 477 698 | 8 319 | 873 | -42 329 |
| British Indian Ocean Terr. — Terr. brit. de l'océan Indien | 8[1] | ... | ... | 3 | ... | ... | 0 |
| British Virgin Islands — Iles Vierges britanniques | 15 | 3[1] | 1[1] | 4[1] | 0 | 0 | 0 |
| Brunei Darussalam — Brunéi Darussalam | 527 | 14[1] | 5[1] | 278 | 11 | 1 | -35 |
| Bulgaria — Bulgarie | 10 864 | 3 173 | 201 | 3 625 | -683 | -99 | 298 |
| Burkina Faso — Burkina Faso | 27 360[1] | 4 840[1] | 60[1] | 6 794 | 1 320 | 5 | -360 |
| Burundi — Burundi | 2 568[1] | 971[1] | 365[1] | 152 | 41 | 5 | -137 |
| Cambodia — Cambodge | 17 652 | 3 700[1] | 156 | 10 447 | 5 | 46 | -2 499 |
| Cameroon — Cameroun | 46 540[1] | 5 960[1] | 1 200[1] | 21 245 | 20 | -30 | -3 300 |
| Canada — Canada | 909 351 | 45 660[1] | 6 450[1] | 310 134 | 156 | 89 | 0 |
| Cape Verde — Cap-Vert | 403 | 46[1] | 3[1] | 84 | 5 | 1 | 26 |
| Cayman Islands — Iles Caïmanes | 26 | 1[1] | ... | 12 | 0 | ... | 0 |
| Central African Rep. — Rép. centrafricaine | 62 300 | 1 930[1] | 90[1] | 22 755 | 10 | 4 | -448 |
| Chad — Tchad | 125 920[1] | 4 200[1] | 30[1] | 11 921 | 927 | 3 | -1 189 |
| Channel Islands — Iles Anglo-Normandes | 19[4] | 4[1] | ... | 1 | 0 | ... | 0 |
| Chile — Chili | 74 880[1] | 1 950[1] | 365[1] | 16 121 | -852 | 118 | 858 |
| China — Chine | 932 749 | 143 296 | 13 031 | 197 290 | 19 618 | 5 312 | 40 149 |
| Christmas Is. — Ile Christmas | 14 | ... | ... | ... | ... | ... | ... |
| Cocos (Keeling) Islands — Iles des Cocos (Keeling) | 1 | ... | ... | ... | ... | ... | ... |

| Country or area — Pays ou zone | Area — Superficie | | | | Net change from 1990 to 2005 Variation nette de 1990 à 2005 | | |
|---|---|---|---|---|---|---|---|
| | Total land Superficie totale | Arable land Terres arables | Permanent crops Cultures permanentes | Forest cover Superficie forestière | Arable land Terres arables | Permanent crops Cultures permanentes | Forest cover Superficie forestière |
| Colombia — Colombie | 110 950 | 2 004[1] | 1 609[1] | 60 728 | -1 301 | -86 | -711 |
| Comoros — Comores | 186 | 80[1] | 53[1] | 6 | 2 | 18 | -7 |
| Congo — Congo | 34 150[1] | 495[1] | 50[1] | 22 471 | 16 | 8 | -255 |
| Cook Islands — Iles Cook | 24 | 4[1] | 2[1] | 16[1] | 2 | -2 | 1 |
| Costa Rica — Costa Rica | 5 106[1] | 225[1] | 330[1] | 2 391 | -35 | 80 | -173 |
| Côte d'Ivoire — Côte d'Ivoire | 31 800[1] | 3 500[1] | 3 600[1] | 10 405 | 1 070 | 100 | 183 |
| Croatia — Croatie | 5 592[1] | 1 110[1,5] | 116[1] | 2 135 | -102[2] | 3[2] | 16[2] |
| Cuba — Cuba | 10 982[1] | 3 665[1] | 673[1] | 2 713 | 634 | -137 | 655 |
| Cyprus[6] — Chypre[6] | 924 | 120 | 41 | 174 | 14 | -10 | 13 |
| Czech Republic — République tchèque | 7 726 | 3 047 | 238 | 2 648 | -126[7] | 2[7] | 16[7] |
| Dem. Rep. of the Congo — Rép. dém. du Congo | 226 705[1] | 6 700[1] | 1 100[1] | 133 610 | 30 | -90 | -6 921 |
| Denmark — Danemark | 4 243 | 2 237 | 7 | 500 | -324 | -3 | 55 |
| Djibouti — Djibouti | 2 318[1] | 1[1] | ... | 6[1] | 0 | ... | 0 |
| Dominica — Dominique | 75 | 5[1] | 16[1] | 46 | 0 | 5 | -4 |
| Dominican Republic — Rép. dominicaine | 4 838[1] | 820[1] | 500[1] | 1 376[1] | -80 | 50 | 0 |
| Ecuador — Equateur | 27 684[1] | 1 348[1] | 1 214 | 10 853 | -256 | -107 | -2 964 |
| Egypt — Egypte | 99 545 | 3 000[1] | 520[1] | 67 | 716 | 156 | 23 |
| El Salvador — El Salvador | 2 072[1] | 660[1] | 250[1] | 298 | 110 | -10 | -77 |
| Equatorial Guinea — Guinée équatoriale | 2 805 | 130[1] | 90[1] | 1 632[1] | 0 | -10 | -228 |
| Eritrea — Erythrée | 10 100[1] | 637[1] | 3[1] | 1 554[1] | 139[7] | 1[7] | -54[7] |
| Estonia — Estonie | 4 239 | 591 | 12 | 2 284 | -524[2] | 0[2] | 105[2] |
| Ethiopia — Ethiopie | 100 000[1] | 13 115[1] | 806[1] | 13 000 | 3 115[7] | 246[7] | -1 691[7] |
| Faeroe Islands — Iles Féroé | 140 | 3[1] | ... | 0 | 0 | ... | 0 |
| Falkland Is. (Malvinas) — Iles Falkland (Malvinas) | 1 217 | ... | ... | 0 | ... | ... | 0 |
| Fiji — Fidji | 1 827[1] | 200[1] | 85[1] | 1 000 | 40 | 5 | 21 |
| Finland — Finlande | 30 459 | 2 234 | 6 | 22 500 | -35 | 0 | 306 |
| France — France | 55 010 | 18 507 | 1 128 | 15 554 | 508 | -63 | 1 016 |
| French Guiana — Guyane française | 8 815[1] | 12 | 4 | 8 063 | 2 | 2 | -28 |
| French Polynesia — Polynésie française | 366[1] | 3[1] | 22[1] | 105[1] | 1 | 1 | 0 |
| Gabon — Gabon | 25 767[1] | 325[1] | 170[1] | 21 775[1] | 30 | 8 | -152 |
| Gambia — Gambie | 1 000[1] | 350[1] | 5[1] | 471 | 168 | 0 | 29 |
| Georgia — Géorgie | 6 949 | 802[1] | 264[1] | 2 760 | 7[2] | -70[2] | 0[2] |
| Germany — Allemagne | 34 877 | 11 903 | 198 | 11 076 | -68 | -245 | 335 |
| Ghana — Ghana | 22 754[1] | 4 185[1] | 2 200[1] | 5 517 | 1 485 | 700 | -1 931 |
| Gibraltar — Gibraltar | 1 | ... | ... | 0 | ... | ... | 0 |
| Greece — Grèce | 12 890[1] | 2 627 | 1 132 | 3 752[1] | -272 | 64 | 453 |
| Greenland — Groenland | 41 045[8] | ... | ... | 0 | ... | ... | 0 |
| Grenada — Grenade | 34 | 2[1] | 10[1] | 4[1] | 0 | 0 | 0 |
| Guadeloupe — Guadeloupe | 169[1] | 19[1] | 5[1] | 80 | -2 | -3 | -4 |
| Guam — Guam | 54 | 2[1] | 10[1] | 26 | 0 | 0 | 0 |
| Guatemala — Guatemala | 10 843[1] | 1 440[1] | 610[1] | 3 938 | 140 | 125 | -810 |
| Guinea — Guinée | 24 572[1] | 1 200[1] | 670[1] | 6 724 | 472 | 170 | -684 |
| Guinea-Bissau — Guinée-Bissau | 2 812[1] | 300[1] | 250[1] | 2 072 | 0 | 133 | -145 |
| Guyana — Guyana | 19 685[1] | 480[1] | 30[1] | 15 104 | 0 | 8 | -1 |
| Haiti — Haïti | 2 756[1] | 780[1] | 320[1] | 105[1] | 0 | 0 | -11 |
| Honduras — Honduras | 11 189[1] | 1 068[1] | 360[1] | 4 648 | -394 | 2 | -2 737 |
| Hungary — Hongrie | 8 961 | 4 600 | 207 | 1 976 | -454 | -27 | 175 |
| Iceland — Islande | 10 025 | 7 | ... | 46 | 0 | ... | 21 |
| India — Inde | 297 319 | 159 650[1] | 10 000[1] | 67 701 | -3 138 | 3 350 | 3 762 |
| Indonesia — Indonésie | 181 157 | 23 000[1] | 13 600[1] | 88 495 | 2 747 | 1 880 | -28 072 |
| Iran (Islamic Rep. of) — Iran (Rép. islamique d') | 162 855 | 16 533 | 1 574 | 11 075 | 1 343 | 264 | 0 |
| Iraq — Iraq | 43 737[1] | 5 750[1] | 260[1] | 822 | 450 | -30 | 18 |

| Country or area — Pays ou zone | Total land Superficie totale | Area — Superficie Arable land Terres arables | Permanent crops Cultures permanentes | Forest cover Superficie forestière | Net change from 1990 to 2005 Variation nette de 1990 à 2005 Arable land Terres arables | Permanent crops Cultures permanentes | Forest cover Superficie forestière |
|---|---|---|---|---|---|---|---|
| Ireland — Irlande | 6 889[1] | 1 215[1] | 2[1] | 669[1] | 174 | -1 | 228 |
| Isle of Man — Ile de Man | 57 | 8[1] | ... | 4 | -6 | ... | 0 |
| Israel — Israël | 2 164[9] | 317[1] | 75[1] | 171 | -26 | -13 | 17 |
| Italy — Italie | 29 411 | 7 744[4] | 2 539[1] | 9 979 | -1 268 | -421 | 1 596 |
| Jamaica — Jamaïque | 1 083[1] | 174[1] | 110[1] | 339 | 55 | 10 | -6 |
| Japan — Japon | 36 450[1] | 4 360 | 332 | 24 868 | -408 | -143 | -82 |
| Jordan — Jordanie | 8 824 | 184 | 86 | 83 | 5 | 16 | 0 |
| Kazakhstan — Kazakhstan | 269 970[1] | 22 364[1] | 136[1] | 3 337 | -12 691[2] | -10[2] | -74[2] |
| Kenya — Kenya | 56 914[1] | 5 264[1] | 457 | 3 522 | 274 | -23 | -186 |
| Kiribati — Kiribati | 81 | 2[1] | 35[1] | 2[1] | 0 | -2 | 0 |
| Korea, Dem. P. R. — Corée, R. p. dém. de | 12 041[1] | 2 800[1] | 200[1] | 6 187[1] | 512 | 20 | -2 014 |
| Korea, Republic of — Corée, République de | 9 873[1] | 1 624[1] | 200[1] | 6 265 | -329 | 44 | -106 |
| Kuwait — Koweït | 1 782 | 15[1] | 3[4] | 6[1] | 11 | 2 | 2 |
| Kyrgyzstan — Kirghizistan | 19 180[1] | 1 284 | 72 | 869 | -36[2] | 4[2] | 29[2] |
| Lao People's Dem. Rep. — Rép. dém. pop. lao | 23 080 | 1 000[1] | 81[1] | 16 142 | 201 | 20 | -1 172 |
| Latvia — Lettonie | 6 229 | 1 092 | 13 | 2 941 | -596[2] | -9[2] | 144[2] |
| Lebanon — Liban | 1 023[1] | 186[1] | 142[1] | 137 | 3 | 20 | 16 |
| Lesotho — Lesotho | 3 035 | 330[1] | 4[1] | 8 | 13 | 0 | 3 |
| Liberia — Libéria | 9 632[1] | 382[1] | 220[1] | 3 154 | -18 | 5 | -904 |
| Libyan Arab Jamah. — Jamah. arabe libyenne | 175 954 | 1 750[1] | 335[1] | 217 | -55 | -15 | 0 |
| Liechtenstein — Liechtenstein | 16[1] | 4[1] | ... | 7[1] | 0 | ... | 0 |
| Lithuania — Lituanie | 6 268 | 1 906 | 40 | 2 099 | -979[2] | -4[2] | 139[2] |
| Luxembourg — Luxembourg | 259 | 60 | 2 | 87 | -2[3] | 1[3] | 0[3] |
| Madagascar — Madagascar | 58 154[1] | 2 950[1] | 600[1] | 12 838 | 230 | -5 | -854 |
| Malawi — Malawi | 9 408[1] | 2 600[1] | 140[1] | 3 402[1] | 785 | 25 | -494 |
| Malaysia — Malaisie | 32 855[1] | 1 800[1] | 5 785[1] | 20 890 | 100 | 537 | -1 486 |
| Maldives — Maldives | 30 | 4[1] | 9[1] | 1[1] | 0 | 5 | 0 |
| Mali — Mali | 122 019 | 4 800[1] | 40[1] | 12 572 | 2 747 | 0 | -1 500 |
| Malta — Malte | 32 | 9[4] | 1[4] | 0[1] | -3 | 0 | 0 |
| Marshall Islands — Iles Marshall | 18 | 2 | 8 | ... | 1[10] | 0[10] | ... |
| Martinique — Martinique | 106[1] | 10[1] | 9[1] | 47[1] | 0 | -1 | 0 |
| Mauritania — Mauritanie | 103 070 | 500[1] | 12[1] | 267 | 100 | 6 | -148 |
| Mauritius — Maurice | 203 | 100[1] | 6[1] | 37 | 0 | 0 | -2 |
| Mayotte — Mayotte | 37 | 7[1] | 13[1] | 6[1] | 1 | 1 | 0 |
| Mexico — Mexique | 194 395 | 25 000[1] | 2 600[1] | 64 238 | 700 | 600 | -4 778 |
| Micronesia (Fed. States of) — Micronésie (Etats féd. de) | 70 | 3[1] | 20[1] | 63 | 0[10] | 0[10] | 0[10] |
| Moldova — Moldova | 3 287 | 1 848[1] | 298[1] | 329[1] | 112[2] | -168[2] | 9[2] |
| Mongolia — Mongolie | 156 650 | 1 158[1] | 2[1] | 10 252 | -212 | 1 | -1 240 |
| Montserrat — Montserrat | 10 | 2[1] | ... | 4[1] | 0 | ... | 0 |
| Morocco — Maroc | 44 630[1] | 8 480[1] | 915[1] | 4 364 | -227 | 179 | 75 |
| Mozambique — Mozambique | 78 638 | 4 400[1] | 230[1] | 19 262 | 950 | 0 | -750 |
| Myanmar — Myanmar | 65 755[1] | 10 068[1] | 888[1] | 32 222 | 501 | 386 | -6 997 |
| Namibia — Namibie | 82 329[1] | 815[1] | 5[1] | 7 661 | 155 | 3 | -1 101 |
| Nauru — Nauru | 2 | ... | ... | 0[1] | ... | ... | 0 |
| Nepal — Népal | 14 300 | 2 357 | 130[1] | 3 636 | 70 | 64 | -1 181 |
| Netherlands — Antilles | 3 388 | 908 | 33 | 365 | 29 | 3 | 20 |
| Netherlands Antilles — Antilles néerlandaises | 80 | 8[1] | ... | 1[1] | 0 | ... | 0 |
| New Caledonia — Nouvelle-Calédonie | 1 828[1] | 6[1] | 4[1] | 717[1] | -3 | -2 | 0 |
| New Zealand — Nouvelle-Zélande | 26 771[1,11] | 1 500[1,11] | 1 906[11] | 8 309 | -1 145[11] | 552[11] | 589 |
| Nicaragua — Nicaragua | 12 140[1] | 1 925[1] | 236[1] | 5 189 | 625 | 41 | -1 349 |
| Niger — Niger | 126 670[1] | 14 482[1] | 18[1] | 1 266 | 3 446 | 7 | -679 |
| Nigeria — Nigéria | 91 077[1] | 32 000[1] | 3 000[1] | 11 089 | 2 461 | 465 | -6 145 |

| Country or area — Pays ou zone | Area — Superficie | | | | Net change from 1990 to 2005 Variation nette de 1990 à 2005 | | |
|---|---|---|---|---|---|---|---|
| | Total land Superficie totale | Arable land Terres arables | Permanent crops Cultures permanentes | Forest cover Superficie forestière | Arable land Terres arables | Permanent crops Cultures permanentes | Forest cover Superficie forestière |
| Niue — Nioué | 26 | 3[1] | 4[1] | 14[1] | 0 | 1 | -3 |
| Norfolk Island — Ile Norfolk | 4 | ... | ... | ... | ... | ... | ... |
| Northern Mariana Islands — Iles Mariannes du Nord | 46 | 1[1] | 1[1] | 33 | 0[10] | 0[10] | -1[10] |
| Norway — Norvège | 30 428 | 867 | ... | 9 387 | 3 | ... | 257 |
| Occupied Palestinian Terr. — Terr. palestinien occupé | 602 | 107[1] | 115[1] | 9[1] | -4 | 0 | 0 |
| Oman — Oman | 30 950 | 62[1] | 43[1] | 2 | 27 | -2 | 0 |
| Pakistan — Pakistan | 77 088 | 21 275[1] | 795 | 1 902 | 791 | 339 | -625 |
| Palau — Palaos | 46[1] | 4[1] | 2[1] | 40 | 0[10] | 0[10] | 1[10] |
| Panama — Panama | 7 443[1] | 548[1] | 147[1] | 4 294 | 49 | -8 | -82 |
| Papua New Guinea — Papouasie-Nvl-Guinée | 45 286[1] | 240[1] | 650[1] | 29 437 | 48 | 70 | -2 086 |
| Paraguay — Paraguay | 39 730[1] | 4 200[1] | 98[1] | 18 475 | 2 090 | 9 | -2 682 |
| Peru — Pérou | 128 000[1] | 3 700[1] | 610[1] | 68 742 | 200 | 190 | -1 414 |
| Philippines — Philippines | 29 817 | 5 700[1] | 5 000[1] | 7 162 | 220 | 600 | -3 412 |
| Pitcairn — Pitcairn | 5 | ... | ... | 4 | ... | ... | 0 |
| Poland — Pologne | 30 633 | 12 141 | 378 | 9 192 | -2 247 | 33 | 311 |
| Portugal — Portugal | 9 150 | 1 262 | 649 | 3 783[1] | -1 082 | -132 | 684 |
| Puerto Rico — Porto Rico | 887 | 71[1] | 42[1] | 408 | 6 | -8 | 4 |
| Qatar — Qatar | 1 100[1] | 18[1] | 3[1] | ... | 8 | 2 | ... |
| Réunion — Réunion | 250[1] | 34 | 4 | 84 | -13 | -1 | -3 |
| Romania — Roumanie | 22 998 | 9 288[1] | 540 | 6 370 | -162 | -51 | -1 |
| Russian Federation — Fédération de Russie | 1 638 139 | 121 781 | 1 800 | 808 790 | -10 227[2] | 100[2] | -224[2] |
| Rwanda — Rwanda | 2 467[1] | 1 200[1] | 275[1] | 480 | 320 | -30 | 162 |
| Saint Helena[12] — Sainte-Hélène[12] | 39 | 4[1] | ... | 2[1] | 2 | ... | 0 |
| Saint Kitts and Nevis — Saint-Kitts-et-Nevis | 26 | 7 | 1 | 5[1] | -1 | -1 | 0 |
| Saint Lucia — Sainte-Lucie | 61[1] | 4[1] | 14[1] | 17 | -1 | 1 | 0 |
| Saint Pierre and Miquelon — Saint-Pierre-et-Miquelon | 23[1] | 3[1] | ... | 3[1] | 0 | ... | 0 |
| Saint Vincent-Grenadines — Saint Vincent-Grenadines | 39 | 5[1] | 3[1] | 11[1] | 1 | -3 | 1 |
| Samoa — Samoa | 283[1] | 30[1] | 60[1] | 171 | -6 | 0 | 41 |
| San Marino — Saint-Marin | 6 | 1[1] | ... | 0[1] | 0 | ... | 0 |
| Sao Tome and Principe — Sao Tomé-et-Principe | 96[1] | 9[1] | 47[1] | 27[1] | 7 | 8 | 0 |
| Saudi Arabia — Arabie saoudite | 214 969 | 3 500[1] | 210[1] | 2 728 | 110 | 119 | 0 |
| Senegal — Sénégal | 19 253[1] | 2 550[1] | 48[1] | 8 673 | 225 | 23 | -675 |
| Serbia and Montenegro — Serbie-et-Monténégro | 10 200[1] | 3 505[1] | 317[1] | 2 694 | -215[2] | -39[2] | 117[2] |
| Seychelles — Seychelles | 46 | 1[1] | 5[1] | 40 | 0 | 0 | 0 |
| Sierra Leone — Sierra Leone | 7 162[1] | 600[1] | 80[1] | 2 754[1] | 114 | 26 | -290 |
| Singapore — Singapour | 69[1] | 1[1] | 0[1] | 2 | 0 | -1 | 0 |
| Slovakia — Slovaquie | 4 810 | 1 391 | 26 | 1 929 | -171[7] | -23[7] | 7[7] |
| Slovenia — Slovénie | 2 014 | 176 | 27 | 1 264 | -24[2] | -9[2] | 66[2] |
| Solomon Islands — Iles Salomon | 2 799[1] | 18[1] | 59[1] | 2 172 | 5 | 7 | -596 |
| Somalia — Somalie | 62 734[1] | 1 350[1] | 26[1] | 7 131 | 328 | 6 | -1 151 |
| South Africa — Afrique du Sud | 121 447[1] | 14 753[1] | 959[1] | 9 203 | 1 313 | 99 | 0 |
| Spain — Espagne | 49 919[1] | 13 700[1] | 4 930[1] | 17 915 | -1 635 | 93 | 4 436 |
| Sri Lanka — Sri Lanka | 6 463[1] | 916[1] | 1 000[1] | 1 933 | 41 | -25 | -417 |
| Sudan — Soudan | 237 600 | 19 434[1] | 223 | 67 546 | 6 634 | 113 | -8 836 |
| Suriname — Suriname | 15 600[1] | 60[1] | 10[1] | 14 776 | 3 | -1 | 0 |
| Swaziland — Swaziland | 1 720[1] | 178[1] | 14[1] | 541[1] | -2 | 2 | 69 |
| Sweden — Suède | 41 033 | 2 703 | 3[4] | 27 528 | -142 | -1 | 161 |
| Switzerland — Suisse | 4 000 | 410 | 24 | 1 221 | 19 | 3 | 66 |
| Syrian Arab Republic — Rép. arabe syrienne | 18 378[1] | 4 873 | 869 | 461 | -12 | 128 | 89 |
| Tajikistan — Tadjikistan | 13 996 | 930[1] | 127[1] | 410 | 70[2] | 2[2] | 2[2] |
| TFYR of Macedonia — L'ex-R.y. Macédoine | 51 089[1] | 14 200[1] | 3 600[1] | 14 520 | -3 294 | 491 | -1 445 |
| Thailand — Thaïlande | 2 543 | 566[1] | 46[1] | 906[1] | -40[2] | -10[2] | 0[2] |

| Country or area — Pays ou zone | Area — Superficie | | | | Net change from 1990 to 2005 / Variation nette de 1990 à 2005 | | |
| --- | --- | --- | --- | --- | --- | --- | --- |
| | Total land / Superficie totale | Arable land / Terres arables | Permanent crops / Cultures permanentes | Forest cover / Superficie forestière | Arable land / Terres arables | Permanent crops / Cultures permanentes | Forest cover / Superficie forestière |
| Timor-Leste — Timor-Leste | 1 487 | 122[1] | 68[1] | 798 | 12 | 10 | -168 |
| Togo — Togo | 5 439[1] | 2 490[1] | 140[1] | 386 | 390 | 50 | -299 |
| Tokelau — Tokélaou | 1 | ... | ... | 0[1] | ... | ... | 0 |
| Tonga — Tonga | 72[1] | 15[1] | 11[1] | 4[1] | -1 | -1 | 0 |
| Trinidad and Tobago — Trinité-et-Tobago | 513 | 75[1] | 47[1] | 226 | 1 | 1 | -9 |
| Tunisia — Tunisie | 15 536[1] | 2 729 | 2 155 | 1 056 | -180 | 213 | 413 |
| Turkey — Turquie | 76 963 | 23 830 | 2 776 | 10 175 | -817 | -254 | 495 |
| Turkmenistan — Turkménistan | 46 993[1] | 2 300[1] | 65[1] | 4 127 | 950[2] | 1[2] | 0[2] |
| Turks and Caicos Islands — Iles Turques et Caïques | 43 | 1[1] | ... | 34[1] | 0 | ... | 0 |
| Tuvalu — Tuvalu | 3 | ... | 2[1] | 1[1] | ... | 0 | 0 |
| Uganda — Ouganda | 19 710[1] | 5 400[1] | 2 200[1] | 3 627 | 400 | 350 | -1 297 |
| Ukraine — Ukraine | 57 938 | 32 452 | 901 | 9 575 | -910[2] | -193[2] | 254[2] |
| United Arab Emirates — Emirats arabes unis | 8 360 | 64[1] | 191[1] | 312 | 29 | 171 | 67 |
| United Kingdom — Royaume-Uni | 24 193 | 5 729 | 47 | 2 845 | -891 | -19 | 234 |
| United Rep. of Tanzania — Rép.-Unie de Tanzanie | 88 580 | 9 200[1] | 1 150[1] | 35 257 | 200 | 150 | -6 184 |
| United States — Etats-Unis | 916 192 | 174 448[1] | 2 730[1] | 303 089 | -11 228 | 630 | 4 441 |
| United States Virgin Is. — Iles Vierges américaines | 35 | 2[1] | 1[1] | 10 | -2 | 0 | -2 |
| Uruguay — Uruguay | 17 502 | 1 370[1] | 42[1] | 1 506 | 110 | -3 | 601 |
| Uzbekistan — Ouzbékistan | 42 540 | 4 700[1] | 340[1] | 3 295 | 226[2] | -40[2] | 217[2] |
| Vanuatu — Vanuatu | 1 219[1] | 20[1] | 85[1] | 440 | 0 | 0 | 0 |
| Venezuela (Boliv. Rep. of) — Venezuela (Rép. boliv. du) | 88 205[1] | 2 650[1] | 800[1] | 47 713 | -182 | 22 | -4 313 |
| Viet Nam — Viet Nam | 31 007[1] | 6 600[1] | 2 350[1] | 12 931 | 1 261 | 1 305 | 3 568 |
| Wallis and Futuna Islands — Iles Wallis et Futuna | 14 | 1[1] | 5[1] | 5 | 0 | 0 | -1 |
| Western Sahara — Sahara occidental | 26 600 | 5[1] | ... | 1 011[1] | 1 | ... | 0 |
| Yemen — Yémen | 52 797[1] | 1 515[1] | 135[1] | 549 | -8 | 32 | 0 |
| Zambia — Zambie | 74 339[1] | 5 260[1] | 29[1] | 42 452 | 11 | 10 | -6 672 |
| Zimbabwe — Zimbabwe | 38 685[1] | 3 220[1] | 130[1] | 17 540 | 330 | 10 | -4 694 |

Source

Food and Agriculture Organization of the United Nations (FAO), Rome, FAOSTAT data, last accessed April 2008.

Notes

1  FAO estimate.

2  Net change from 1992 to 2005.

3  Net change from 2000 to 2005.

4  International reliable sources (USDA, WTO, World Bank, IMF).

5  The "Arable land" figures exclude non-cultivated arable land.

6  Data refer to government-controlled areas.

7  Net change from 1993 to 2005.

8  Area free from ice.

9  Data relating to "Land area" include the Golan Heights.

10  Net change from 1995 to 2005.

11  "Land area" category actually refers to the total area of the country, as the area of "Inland waters" is not available; "Arable land" category includes other land in farms; "Permanent crops" category includes area of planted production forest.

12  Including Ascension and Tristan da Cunha.

Source

Organisation des Nations Unies pour l'alimentation et l'agriculture (FAO), Rome, données FAOSTAT, dernier accès avril 2008.

Notes

1  Estimation de la FAO.

2  Variation nette de 1992 à 2005.

3  Variation nette de 2000 à 2005.

4  Sources internationales fiables (Département d'agriculture des États-Unis, OMC, Banque mondiale, FMI).

5  Les chiffres relatifs aux terres arables excluent les terres arables non cultivées.

6  Les données se rapportent aux zones contrôlées par le Gouvernement.

7  Variation nette de 1993 à 2005.

8  Superficie non couverte de glace.

9  Les données relatives aux terres émergées englobent le plateau du Golan.

10  Variation nette de 1995 à 2005.

11  La catégorie portant sur les terres émergées correspond à la superficie totale du pays, puisque les données sur les eaux intérieures ne sont pas disponibles; les "terres arables" comprennent d'autres terres faisant partie des exploitations agricoles; les " récoltes permanentes" comprennent les zones boisées à des fins d'exploitation.

12  Y compris Ascension et Tristan da Cunha.

# Ozone-depleting chlorofluorocarbons (CFCs)
Consumption: ozone-depleting potential (ODP) metric tons

# Chlorofluorocarbones (CFC) qui appauvrissent la couche d'ozone
Consommation : tonnes de potentiel de destruction de l'ozone (PDO)

| Country or area — Pays ou zone | 1997 | 1998 | 1999 | 2000 | 2001 | 2002 | 2003 | 2004 | 2005 | 2006 |
|---|---|---|---|---|---|---|---|---|---|---|
| Afghanistan — Afghanistan | 380.0 | ... | ... | ... | ... | ... | ... | 177.9 | 141.2 | 94.5 |
| Albania — Albanie | 41.9 | 46.5 | 53.1 | 61.9 | 68.8 | 49.9 | 35.0 | 36.6 | 14.3 | 15.2 |
| Algeria — Algérie | 1 774.2 | 1 549.2 | 1 502.2 | 1 474.6 | 1 021.6 | 1 761.8 | 1 761.8 | 1 045.0 | 859.0 | 302.6 |
| Angola — Angola | 114.8 | 115.9 | ... | 107.0 | 114.8 | 105.0 | 104.2 | 75.6 | 52.0 | 42.1 |
| Antigua and Barbuda — Antigua-et-Barbuda | 10.3 | 26.5 | -2.0[1] | 5.0 | 3.1 | 3.7 | 1.5 | 1.9 | 1.1 | 1.1 |
| Argentina — Argentine | 3 523.7 | 3 546.3 | 4 316.3 | 2 396.7 | 3 293.1 | 2 139.2 | 2 255.2 | 2 211.6 | 1 675.5 | 1 654.2 |
| Armenia — Arménie | 191.2 | 185.9 | 9.0 | 25.0 | 162.7 | 172.7 | 172.7 | 110.7 | 84.0 | 59.0 |
| Australia — Australie | 183.9 | 195.1 | 274.1 | 6.5 | 6.0 | 9.8 | 1.1 | -61.8[1] | -51.4[1] | -80.0[1] |
| Azerbaijan — Azerbaïdjan | 201.2 | 152.2 | 99.9 | 87.8 | 52.0 | 12.0 | 10.2 | 15.1 | 21.9 | 0.0 |
| Bahamas — Bahamas | 52.7 | 54.6 | 53.8 | 65.9 | 63.0 | 55.4 | 29.6 | 18.8 | 13.0 | 4.0 |
| Bahrain — Bahreïn | 147.2 | 149.5 | 129.0 | 113.1 | 106.0 | 94.6 | 85.8 | 64.8 | 58.7 | 32.4 |
| Bangladesh — Bangladesh | 832.2 | 830.4 | 800.6 | 805.0 | 807.9 | 328.0 | 333.0 | 294.9 | 263.0 | 196.2 |
| Barbados — Barbade | 17.2 | 22.5 | 16.5 | 8.1 | 12.5 | 9.5 | 8.6 | 14.1 | 6.7 | 7.9 |
| Belarus — Bélarus | 371.8 | 256.2 | 193.7 | 0.0 | 0.0 | 0.0 | 0.0 | 0.0 | 0.0 | 0.0 |
| Belize — Belize | 26.1 | 25.0 | 25.1 | 15.5 | 28.0 | 21.7 | 15.1 | 12.2 | 9.6 | 3.9 |
| Benin — Bénin | 59.6 | 54.2 | 56.6 | 54.6 | 54.0 | 35.5 | 17.3 | 11.5 | 10.0 | ... |
| Bhutan — Bhoutan | 0.2 | 0.0 | 0.0 | 0.0 | ... | ... | ... | 0.1 | 0.1 | 0.1 |
| Bolivia — Bolivie | 58.4 | 74.1 | 72.2 | 78.8 | 76.7 | 65.5 | 32.1 | 42.4 | 26.7 | 33.1 |
| Bosnia and Herzegovina — Bosnie-Herzégovine | 49.0 | 45.1 | 151.0 | 175.9 | 199.7 | 243.6 | 230.0 | 187.9 | 50.8 | 32.6 |
| Botswana — Botswana | 6.8 | 2.6 | 2.6 | 2.5 | 4.0 | 3.6 | 5.1 | 2.7 | 1.9 | 0.7 |
| Brazil — Brésil | 9 809.7 | 9 542.9 | 11 612.0 | 9 275.1 | 6 230.9 | 3 000.6 | 3 224.3 | 1 870.5 | 967.2 | 477.8 |
| Brunei Darussalam — Brunéi Darussalam | 90.0 | 63.5 | 36.7 | 46.6 | 31.4 | 43.4 | 32.3 | 60.2 | 39.0 | 27.8 |
| Bulgaria — Bulgarie | 0.0 | 0.0 | 0.0 | 0.0 | 0.0 | 0.0 | 0.0 | 0.0 | 0.0 | 0.0 |
| Burkina Faso — Burkina Faso | 37.6 | 37.0 | 30.6 | 25.4 | 19.6 | 16.3 | 13.2 | 10.5 | 7.4 | 5.2 |
| Burundi — Burundi | 61.9 | 64.5 | 59.6 | 53.8 | 46.5 | 19.1 | 9.2 | 3.9 | 3.5 | 3.5 |
| Cambodia — Cambodge | 94.2 | 94.2 | 94.2 | 94.2 | 94.2 | 94.2 | 86.7 | 70.4 | 44.5 | 28.3 |
| Cameroon — Cameroun | 259.5 | 311.8 | 361.5 | 368.7 | 364.1 | 226.0 | 220.5 | 148.5 | 120.0 | 103.0 |
| Canada — Canada | 136.2 | 42.2 | -4.8[1] | 10.1 | 0.1 | -12.6[1] | -0.2[1] | 0.0 | 0.0 | 0.0 |
| Cape Verde — Cap-Vert | 2.2 | 2.1 | 2.0 | 1.9 | 1.9 | 1.8 | 1.8 | 1.5 | 0.9 | 0.0 |
| Central African Rep. — Rép. centrafricaine | 0.0 | 7.0 | 1.4 | 4.3 | 4.0 | 4.4 | 4.1 | 3.9 | 2.6 | 2.0 |
| Chad — Tchad | 36.3 | 38.1 | 37.5 | 36.5 | 31.6 | 27.1 | 22.8 | 14.2 | 11.3 | 9.2 |
| Chile — Chili | 674.5 | 737.9 | 657.5 | 576.0 | 470.2 | 370.2 | 424.5 | 230.8 | 221.5 | 181.8 |
| China[2] — Chine[2] | 51 076.4 | 55 414.2 | 42 983.4 | 39 123.6 | 33 922.6 | 30 621.2 | 22 808.8 | 17 902.5 | 13 123.8 | 12 414.9 |
| Colombia — Colombie | 2 166.4 | 1 224.0 | 985.5 | 1 149.3 | 1 164.8 | 907.0 | 1 058.1 | 898.5 | 556.9 | 660.4 |
| Comoros — Comores | 2.9 | 3.6 | 2.5 | 2.7 | 1.9 | 1.8 | 1.2 | 1.1 | 0.9 | 0.8 |
| Congo — Congo | 9.2 | 6.6 | 9.3 | 11.4 | 2.5 | 5.5 | 7.0 | 4.7 | 3.7 | 3.3 |
| Cook Islands — Iles Cook | 1.2 | 0.5 | 0.0 | 0.0 | ... | ... | 0.0 | 0.0 | 0.0 | 0.0 |
| Costa Rica — Costa Rica | 94.8 | -204.2[1] | 152.3 | 105.9 | 144.6 | 137.4 | 142.5 | 111.5 | 96.1 | 55.7 |
| Côte d'Ivoire — Côte d'Ivoire | 144.4 | 267.8 | 166.2 | 206.4 | 148.0 | 106.5 | 93.4 | 79.4 | 70.1 | 85.5 |
| Croatia — Croatie | 280.4 | 85.7 | 141.5 | 171.2 | 113.8 | 140.1 | 88.7 | 78.2 | 43.5 | -31.4[1] |
| Cuba — Cuba | 665.4 | 531.4 | 571.4 | 533.7 | 504.0 | 488.8 | 481.0 | 445.1 | 208.6 | 239.5 |
| Cyprus — Chypre | 143.0 | 81.0 | 114.9 | 165.0 | 137.6 | 131.8 | 62.5 | ... | ... | ... |
| Czech Republic — République tchèque | 11.6 | 7.9 | 11.2 | 5.1 | 2.9 | 3.7 | -4.4[1] | ... | ... | ... |
| Dem. Rep. of the Congo — Rép. dém. du Congo | 469.0 | 688.5 | 368.1 | 386.6 | 639.4 | 569.4 | 566.9 | 329.1 | 268.7 | 170.7 |
| Djibouti — Djibouti | 18.9 | 20.6 | 20.6 | 20.7 | 18.0 | 15.8 | 12.1 | 8.8 | 7.1 | 3.1 |

| Country or area — Pays ou zone | 1997 | 1998 | 1999 | 2000 | 2001 | 2002 | 2003 | 2004 | 2005 | 2006 |
|---|---|---|---|---|---|---|---|---|---|---|
| Dominica — Dominique | 1.7 | 2.1 | 1.1 | 2.1 | 1.6 | 3.0 | 1.4 | 1.0 | 1.4 | 0.5 |
| Dominican Republic — Rép. dominicaine | 426.8 | 311.4 | 752.1 | 401.9 | 485.8 | 329.8 | 266.5 | 310.4 | 204.3 | 156.2 |
| Ecuador — Equateur | 320.4 | 271.7 | 153.0 | 230.5 | 207.0 | 229.6 | 256.3 | 147.4 | 132.5 | 63.0 |
| Egypt — Egypte | 1 632.0 | 1 540.0 | 1 373.6 | 1 267.0 | 1 334.8 | 1 294.0 | 1 102.2 | 1 047.6 | 821.2 | 593.6 |
| El Salvador — El Salvador | 277.8 | 194.6 | 109.5 | 99.1 | 116.9 | 101.6 | 97.5 | 75.6 | 119.2 | 64.4 |
| Equatorial Guinea — Guineé équatoriale | 32.2 | 31.4 | 21.4 | 23.2 | 23.8 | 17.5 | 13.6 | 10.0 | 8.1 | 4.6 |
| Eritrea — Erythrée | 40.3 | 25.5 | 25.2 | 48.8 | ... | ... | ... | ... | 30.2 | 4.2 |
| Estonia — Estonie | 45.2 | 69.8 | 56.3 | 15.7 | -0.4[1] | 0.0 | 0.0 | ... | ... | ... |
| Ethiopia — Ethiopie | 35.1 | 38.2 | 39.2 | 39.2 | 34.6 | 30.0 | 28.0 | 16.0 | 15.0 | ... |
| Fiji — Fidji | 13.7 | 13.1 | 9.4 | 0.0 | 0.0 | 0.0 | 0.0 | 0.0 | 0.0 | 0.0 |
| Gabon — Gabon | 12.0 | 12.0 | 7.8 | 13.7 | 6.4 | 5.0 | 5.0 | 4.5 | 2.1 | 1.2 |
| Gambia — Gambie | 28.0 | 10.9 | 6.9 | 6.1 | 5.8 | 4.7 | 5.1 | 0.2 | 0.7 | 1.0 |
| Georgia — Géorgie | 30.9 | 26.0 | 21.5 | 21.5 | 18.8 | 15.5 | 12.6 | 8.6 | 8.2 | 5.8 |
| Ghana — Ghana | 48.7 | 50.3 | 46.8 | 47.0 | 35.6 | 21.2 | 32.0 | 35.6 | 17.5 | 13.1 |
| Grenada — Grenade | 6.5 | 3.8 | 2.9 | 2.9 | 1.3 | 2.1 | 2.1 | 1.9 | 0.6 | 0.0 |
| Guatemala — Guatemala | 207.3 | 188.7 | 191.1 | 187.9 | 265.0 | 239.6 | 147.1 | 65.4 | 57.5 | 12.7 |
| Guinea — Guinée | 45.9 | 41.8 | 39.9 | 37.5 | 35.4 | 31.3 | 25.9 | 16.7 | 9.3 | 4.9 |
| Guinea-Bissau — Guinée-Bissau | 26.8 | 27.1 | 26.0 | 26.0 | 26.9 | 27.2 | 29.4 | 25.2 | 12.5 | 13.1 |
| Guyana — Guyana | 27.8 | 29.2 | 39.9 | 24.4 | 19.8 | 14.3 | 10.4 | 11.9 | 23.5 | 8.8 |
| Haiti — Haïti | 169.0 | ... | ... | 169.0 | 169.0 | 181.2 | 115.9 | 132.5 | 81.4 | 50.4 |
| Honduras — Honduras | 354.1 | 157.4 | 334.8 | 172.3 | 121.6 | 131.2 | 219.1 | 167.8 | 122.6 | 94.7 |
| Hungary — Hongrie | 3.9 | 1.3 | 0.6 | 0.5 | 0.0 | 0.3 | -1.3[1] | ... | ... | ... |
| Iceland — Islande | 0.0 | 0.0 | 0.0 | 0.0 | 0.0 | 0.0 | 0.0 | 0.0 | 0.0 | 0.0 |
| India — Inde | 6 703.3 | 5 264.7 | 4 142.9 | 5 614.3 | 4 514.3 | 3 917.7 | 2 631.5 | 2 241.6 | 1 957.8 | 3 560.3 |
| Indonesia — Indonésie | 7 634.8 | 6 182.8 | 5 865.8 | 5 411.1 | 5 003.3 | 5 506.3 | 4 829.3 | 3 925.5 | 2 385.3 | 231.0 |
| Iran (Islamic Rep. of) — Iran (Rép. islamique d') | 5 883.0 | 5 571.0 | 4 399.0 | 4 156.5 | 4 204.8 | 4 437.8 | 4 088.8 | 3 471.9 | 2 221.0 | 953.3 |
| Israel — Israël | 0.0 | 0.0 | 0.0 | 0.0 | 0.0 | 0.0 | 0.0 | 0.0 | 0.0 | 0.0 |
| Jamaica — Jamaïque | 106.6 | 199.0 | 210.4 | 59.8 | 48.6 | 31.7 | 16.2 | 16.0 | 5.0 | 0.0 |
| Japan — Japon | -113.0[1] | -208.0[1] | 23.2 | -24.2[1] | -5.5[1] | 19.5 | 4.0 | 0.0 | 0.0 | 0.0 |
| Jordan — Jordanie | 857.4 | 647.2 | 398.0 | 354.0 | 321.0 | 90.0 | 74.4 | 58.4 | 59.6 | 21.8 |
| Kazakhstan — Kazakhstan | 668.8 | 1 025.5 | 730.0 | 523.9 | 290.0 | 112.0 | 30.4 | 11.2 | 0.0 | 0.0 |
| Kenya — Kenya | 250.6 | 245.3 | 241.1 | 203.3 | 168.6 | 152.3 | 168.6 | 131.7 | 160.6 | 57.7 |
| Kiribati — Kiribati | 0.6 | 0.5 | 0.0 | 0.0 | 0.0 | 0.0 | 0.0 | 0.0 | 0.0 | 0.0 |
| Korea, Dem. P. R. — Corée, R. p. dém. de | 233.0 | 112.0 | 106.0 | 77.0 | 320.8 | 299.0 | 587.4 | 7.3 | 91.8 | 24.5 |
| Korea, Republic of — Corée, République de | 9 220.2 | 5 298.8 | 7 402.6 | 7 395.4 | 6 802.2 | 6 646.6 | 5 171.6 | 5 012.2 | 2 730.0 | 3 026.2 |
| Kuwait — Koweït | 484.8 | 399.2 | 450.0 | 419.9 | 354.2 | 349.0 | 247.4 | 233.0 | 152.7 | 106.8 |
| Kyrgyzstan — Kirghizistan | 69.6 | 56.8 | 52.4 | 53.5 | 53.0 | 38.0 | 33.0 | 22.9 | 8.1 | 5.3 |
| Lao People's Dem. Rep. — Rép. dém. pop. lao | 43.3 | 43.3 | 44.1 | 44.6 | 41.2 | 42.3 | 35.3 | 23.1 | 19.5 | 17.8 |
| Latvia — Lettonie | 23.0 | 25.3 | 21.6 | 35.2 | 0.0 | 0.0 | 0.0 | ... | ... | ... |
| Lebanon — Liban | 621.3 | 475.3 | 463.4 | 527.9 | 533.4 | 491.7 | 480.2 | 347.0 | 287.3 | 224.4 |
| Lesotho — Lesotho | 3.5 | 3.4 | 2.8 | 2.4 | 1.8 | 1.6 | 1.4 | 1.2 | 0.0 | 0.0 |
| Liberia — Libéria | 55.7 | 31.1 | 18.2 | 41.4 | 25.1 | 32.8 | 26.3 | 14.2 | 5.0 | 5.0 |
| Libyan Arab Jamah. — Jamah. arabe libyenne | 647.5 | 659.8 | 894.0 | 985.4 | 985.4 | 985.4 | 704.1 | 459.0 | 252.0 | 115.7 |
| Liechtenstein — Liechtenstein | 0.0 | -0.1[1] | 0.0 | 0.0 | 0.0 | 0.0 | 0.0 | -0.1[1] | 0.0 | 0.0 |
| Lithuania — Lituanie | 99.9 | 103.8 | 85.3 | 36.5 | 0.0 | 0.0 | 0.0 | ... | ... | ... |
| Madagascar — Madagascar | 103.6 | 23.9 | 26.3 | 12.4 | 9.9 | 7.8 | 7.2 | 7.1 | 7.0 | 2.3 |
| Malawi — Malawi | 55.6 | 56.9 | 50.4 | 21.5 | 19.0 | 19.0 | 18.7 | 11.4 | 5.6 | 3.6 |

| Country or area — Pays ou zone | 1997 | 1998 | 1999 | 2000 | 2001 | 2002 | 2003 | 2004 | 2005 | 2006 |
|---|---|---|---|---|---|---|---|---|---|---|
| Malaysia — Malaisie | 3 348.4 | 2 333.7 | 2 010.1 | 1 979.8 | 1 946.9 | 1 605.5 | 1 174.4 | 1 128.5 | 668.3 | 565.2 |
| Maldives — Maldives | 7.8 | 0.9 | 1.5 | 4.6 | 14.0 | 2.8 | 0.0 | 0.0 | 0.0 | 1.1 |
| Mali — Mali | 111.1 | 113.1 | 37.1 | 29.2 | 27.0 | 26.0 | 26.0 | 25.0 | 25.0 | 16.2 |
| Malta — Malte | 60.1 | 106.6 | 97.2 | 67.6 | 63.1 | 10.3 | 14.0 | ... | ... | ... |
| Marshall Islands — Iles Marshall | 1.1 | 0.6 | 1.1 | 0.5 | 0.2 | 0.2 | 0.2 | 0.0 | 0.0 | 0.0 |
| Mauritania — Mauritanie | 16.0 | 14.7 | 13.4 | 14.2 | 15.0 | 14.7 | 14.3 | 7.1 | 6.1 | 3.0 |
| Mauritius — Maurice | 27.3 | 39.0 | 18.6 | 19.1 | 14.5 | 7.3 | 4.0 | 3.4 | -0.1[1] | 1.0 |
| Mexico — Mexique | 4 157.2 | 3 482.9 | 2 837.9 | 3 059.5 | 2 223.9 | 1 946.7 | 1 983.2 | 3 208.4 | 1 604.0 | -441.3[1] |
| Micronesia (Fed. States of) — Micronésie (Etats féd. de) | 1.2 | 1.2 | 1.2 | 1.0 | 1.1 | 1.9 | 1.7 | 1.5 | 0.4 | 0.0 |
| Moldova — Moldova | 83.1 | 40.5 | 11.1[*] | 31.7 | 23.5 | 29.6 | 18.9 | 20.0 | 14.4 | 12.0 |
| Monaco — Monaco | 0.0 | 0.0 | 0.0 | 0.0 | 0.0 | 0.0 | 0.0 | 0.0 | 0.0 | 0.0 |
| Mongolia — Mongolie | 12.5 | 13.2 | 12.4 | 11.2 | 9.3 | 6.9 | 5.7 | 4.1 | 3.7 | 2.2 |
| Montenegro — Monténégtp | 104.9 | ... | ... | ... | ... | ... | ... | ... | ... | 14.0 |
| Morocco — Maroc | 886.0 | 923.6 | 870.6 | 564.0 | 435.2 | 668.6 | 474.8 | 329.0 | 38.7 | 40.0 |
| Mozambique — Mozambique | 12.7 | 3.2 | 13.8 | 9.9 | 8.4 | 9.9 | 1.7 | 1.6 | 1.2 | 2.7 |
| Myanmar — Myanmar | 54.8 | 52.3 | 30.7 | 26.3 | 39.4 | 43.5 | 51.6 | 29.6 | 14.8 | 0.0 |
| Namibia — Namibie | 19.3 | 16.4 | 16.8 | 22.1 | 24.0 | 20.0 | 17.2 | 7.7 | 0.0 | 0.0 |
| Nauru — Nauru | 0.5 | 0.5 | 0.4 | 0.4 | 0.4 | 0.0 | 0.0 | 0.0 | 0.0 | 0.0 |
| Nepal — Népal | 29.0 | 32.9 | 25.0 | 94.0 | 0.0 | 0.0 | 0.0 | 0.0 | 0.0 | 0.0 |
| New Zealand — Nouvelle-Zélande | 0.0 | 0.0 | 0.0 | -2.6[1] | 0.0 | -4.7[1] | 0.0 | -1.1[1] | 0.0 | 0.0 |
| Nicaragua — Nicaragua | 55.7 | 37.3 | 52.6 | 44.4 | 35.2 | 54.9 | 29.9 | 48.4 | 36.0 | 27.6 |
| Niger — Niger | 59.4 | 60.7 | 58.3 | 39.9 | 29.1 | 26.6 | 24.5 | 23.0 | 15.1 | 15.9 |
| Nigeria — Nigéria | 4 866.2 | 4 761.5 | 4 286.2 | 4 094.8 | 3 665.5 | 3 286.7 | 2 662.4 | 2 116.1 | 466.1 | 454.0 |
| Niue — Nioué | 0.0 | 0.0 | 0.0 | 0.0 | ... | ... | 0.0 | 0.0 | 0.0 | 0.0 |
| Norway — Norvège | 2.6 | -16.4[1] | -60.2[1] | -39.8[1] | -48.1[1] | -73.5[1] | -65.5[1] | -54.6[1] | -21.8[1] | -26.7[1] |
| Oman — Oman | 250.5 | 261.1 | 259.6 | 282.1 | 207.3 | 179.5 | 134.5 | 98.7 | 54.3 | 25.8 |
| Pakistan — Pakistan | 1 263.8 | 1 196.0 | 1 421.8 | 1 945.3 | 1 666.3 | 1 647.0 | 1 124.0 | 805.0 | 453.0 | 626.0 |
| Palau — Palaos | 2.1 | 2.1 | 0.4 | 0.6 | 0.6 | 0.1 | 1.0 | 0.9 | 0.2 | 0.7 |
| Panama — Panama | 357.9 | 346.0 | 301.1 | 249.9 | 180.4 | 195.3 | 168.5 | 134.7 | 92.8 | 43.7 |
| Papua New Guinea — Papouasie-Nvl-Guinée | 36.4 | 45.2 | 35.5 | 47.9 | 15.0 | 34.6 | 22.7 | 17.2 | 15.1 | 3.1 |
| Paraguay — Paraguay | 240.1 | 113.4 | 345.3 | 153.5 | 116.0 | 96.9 | 91.8 | 141.0 | 250.7 | 102.9 |
| Peru — Pérou | 258.8 | 326.7 | 295.6 | 347.0 | 189.0 | 196.5 | 178.4 | 145.7 | 127.7 | 87.2 |
| Philippines — Philippines | 2 746.8 | 2 130.2 | 2 087.6 | 2 905.2 | 2 049.4 | 1 644.5 | 1 422.4 | 1 389.8 | 1 014.2 | 603.4 |
| Poland — Pologne | 308.3 | 314.1 | 187.0 | 174.8 | 179.0 | 201.5 | 126.3 | ... | ... | ... |
| Qatar — Qatar | 111.0 | 120.8 | 89.0 | 85.8 | 85.4 | 86.7 | 95.1 | 63.7 | 37.0 | 31.4 |
| Romania — Roumanie | 720.5 | 582.0 | 338.1 | 360.6 | 185.7 | 359.4 | 362.1 | 116.7 | 180.2 | 0.0 |
| Russian Federation — Fédération de Russie | 10 986.2 | 11 821.1 | 14 824.4 | 23 820.8 | 0.0 | 0.0 | 258.0 | 373.6 | 349.0 | 394.7 |
| Rwanda — Rwanda | 34.4 | 37.7 | 30.1 | 30.1 | 30.1 | 30.1 | 30.1 | 27.1 | 12.3 | 12.0 |
| Saint Kitts and Nevis — Saint-Kitts-et-Nevis | 3.6 | 1.6 | 2.6 | 7.0 | 6.6 | 5.3 | 2.8 | 3.3 | 1.5 | 0.6 |
| Saint Lucia — Sainte-Lucie | 8.5 | 6.3 | 3.2 | 4.2 | 4.1 | 7.6 | 2.5 | 0.8 | 1.5 | 0.8 |
| Saint Vincent-Grenadines — Saint Vincent-Grenadines | 2.2 | 2.3 | 10.0 | 6.0 | 6.9 | 6.0 | 3.1 | 2.1 | 1.0 | 0.5 |
| Samoa — Samoa | 4.5 | 2.6 | 6.1 | 0.6 | 2.0 | 2.2 | 0.0 | 0.0 | 0.0 | 0.0 |
| Sao Tome and Principe — Sao Tomé-et-Principe | 5.2 | 3.8 | 3.4 | 3.9 | 4.1 | 4.3 | 4.6 | 4.0 | 2.3 | 1.7 |
| Saudi Arabia — Arabie saoudite | 1 899.0 | 1 921.8 | 1 710.4 | 1 593.6 | 1 593.0 | 1 531.0 | 1 300.0 | 1 150.0 | 878.5 | ... |
| Senegal — Sénégal | 138.1 | 128.5 | 121.1 | 116.5 | 98.0 | 71.9 | 51.0 | 40.0 | 30.0 | 25.0 |
| Serbia — Serbie | 832.5 | 519.4 | 548.6 | 309.7 | 263.3 | 371.7 | 412.0 | 282.8 | 52.1 | 233.8 |
| Seychelles — Seychelles | 2.5 | 2.0 | 1.1 | 0.8 | 0.7 | 1.5 | 0.6 | 0.0 | 0.0 | 0.0 |

**Ozone-depleting chlorofluorocarbons (CFCs)** — Consumption: ozone-depleting potential (ODP) metric tons (*continued*)
**Chlorofluorocarbones (CFC) qui appauvrissent la couche d'ozone** — Consommation : tonnes de potentiel de destruction de l'ozone (PDO) (*suite*)

| Country or area — Pays ou zone | 1997 | 1998 | 1999 | 2000 | 2001 | 2002 | 2003 | 2004 | 2005 | 2006 |
|---|---|---|---|---|---|---|---|---|---|---|
| Sierra Leone — Sierra Leone | 81.9 | 81.0 | 75.9 | 75.9 | 92.9 | 80.8 | 66.3 | 64.5 | 26.2 | 18.2 |
| Singapore — Singapour | -178.9[1] | 16.7 | 24.1 | 21.7 | 21.6 | 0.9 | 11.1 | 6.6 | -0.7[1] | 0.0 |
| Slovakia — Slovaquie | 1.2 | 1.4 | 1.4 | 1.7 | 3.3 | 0.8 | 0.6 | ... | ... | ... |
| Slovenia — Slovénie | 0.4 | 0.1 | 0.1 | 0.3 | 2.6 | 0.4 | 0.6 | ... | ... | ... |
| Solomon Islands — Iles Salomon | 2.3 | 0.8 | 6.2 | 0.3 | 0.6 | 0.5 | 0.8 | 1.1 | 0.9 | ... |
| Somalia — Somalie | 241.7 | 246.9 | 48.6 | 65.6 | 86.9 | 98.5 | 108.2 | 97.2 | 88.2 | 84.6 |
| South Africa — Afrique du Sud | 98.3 | 155.1 | 117.3 | 80.5 | 16.0 | 86.6 | 60.8 | 61.8 | 30.0 | 0.0 |
| Sri Lanka — Sri Lanka | 318.5 | 250.4 | 216.4 | 220.3 | 190.4 | 185.0 | 179.9 | 155.7 | 149.2 | 105.3 |
| Sudan — Soudan | 306.0 | 294.5 | 294.5 | 291.5 | 266.0 | 253.0 | 216.0 | 203.0 | 185.0 | 120.0 |
| Suriname — Suriname | 42.0 | 42.0 | 43.0 | 44.0 | 46.0 | 46.0 | 12.3 | 9.2 | 7.5 | 0.1 |
| Swaziland — Swaziland | 16.3 | 2.2 | 2.1 | 0.1 | 1.3 | 1.2 | 1.9 | 3.1 | 1.5 | 0.2 |
| Switzerland[1] — Suisse[1] | -40.9[1] | -28.1[1] | -4.5[1] | -5.8[1] | -1.6[1] | -3.4[1] | -9.1[1] | -19.0[1] | -30.0[1] | 0.0 |
| Syrian Arab Republic — Rép. arabe syrienne | 2 043.7 | 1 245.6 | 1 280.7 | 1 174.7 | 1 392.2 | 1 201.6 | 1 124.6 | 928.3 | 869.7 | 541.2 |
| Tajikistan — Tadjikistan | 48.2 | 56.3 | 50.7 | 28.0 | 28.3 | 11.8 | 4.7 | 0.0 | 0.0 | 0.0 |
| Thailand — Thaïlande | 4 448.0 | 3 783.0 | 3 610.6 | 3 568.3 | 3 375.1 | 2 177.3 | 1 857.0 | 1 358.3 | 1 259.9 | 453.7 |
| TFYR of Macedonia — L'ex-R.y. Macédoine | 487.1 | 62.8 | 191.9 | 49.5 | 46.7 | 34.1 | 49.3 | 8.8 | 11.8 | 7.0 |
| Togo — Togo | 35.2 | 36.7 | 41.7 | 37.5 | 34.7 | 35.3 | 33.7 | 26.4 | 18.6 | 10.1 |
| Tonga — Tonga | 1.2 | 0.0 | 83.4 | 0.5 | 0.7 | 0.8 | 0.3 | 0.0 | 0.0 | 0.0 |
| Trinidad and Tobago — Trinité-et-Tobago | 134.6 | 155.6 | 81.7 | 101.3 | 79.2 | 63.6 | 62.5 | 35.0 | 18.3 | 2.9 |
| Tunisia — Tunisie | 970.2 | 790.6 | 566.0 | 555.0 | 570.0 | 465.8 | 362.5 | 271.0 | 205.0 | 59.0 |
| Turkey — Turquie | 3 869.6 | 3 985.0 | 1 791.1 | 820.2 | 731.2 | 698.9 | 440.9 | 257.6 | 132.8 | 0.2 |
| Turkmenistan — Turkménistan | 26.4 | 25.3 | 18.6 | 21.0 | 57.7 | 10.5 | 43.4 | 58.4 | 17.9 | 16.8 |
| Tuvalu — Tuvalu | 0.3 | 0.3 | 0.2 | 0.0 | 0.0 | 0.0 | 0.0 | 0.0 | 0.0 | ... |
| Uganda — Ouganda | 13.9 | 11.4 | 12.2 | 12.7 | 13.4 | 12.7 | 4.1 | 0.2 | 0.2 | 0.0 |
| Ukraine — Ukraine | 1 404.7 | 1 100.7 | 951.2 | 838.7 | 1 076.5 | 119.7 | 77.8 | 80.0 | 53.1 | 0.0 |
| United Arab Emirates — Emirats arabes unis | 562.8 | 737.4 | 529.2 | 476.2 | 423.4 | 370.4 | 317.5 | 291.0 | 264.6 | 132.3 |
| United Rep. of Tanzania — Rép.-Unie de Tanzanie | 187.7 | 131.5 | 88.9 | 215.5 | 131.2 | 71.5 | 148.2 | 98.8 | 98.9 | 54.0 |
| United States — Etats-Unis | 742.5 | 2 706.0 | 2 903.8 | 2 613.0 | 2 805.2 | 1 357.2 | 1 605.2 | 1 153.6 | 1 496.6 | 752.7 |
| Uruguay — Uruguay | 193.1 | 194.0 | 111.4 | 106.8 | 102.3 | 75.2 | 111.4 | 90.9 | 97.6 | 81.9 |
| Uzbekistan — Ouzbékistan | 53.0 | 119.8 | 52.8 | 41.7 | 15.3 | 0.0 | 0.0 | 0.0 | 0.0 | ... |
| Vanuatu — Vanuatu | 0.0 | 0.0 | 0.0 | 0.0 | 0.0 | 0.0 | 0.0 | 0.0 | 0.0 | ... |
| Venezuela (Boliv. Rep. of) — Venezuela (Rép. boliv. du) | 3 703.9 | 3 213.9 | 1 922.1 | 2 705.9 | 2 546.2 | 1 552.8 | 1 313.5 | 2 944.6 | 1 841.8 | 2 641.8 |
| Viet Nam — Viet Nam | 500.0 | 392.0 | 293.9 | 220.0 | 243.0 | 235.5 | 243.7 | 241.0 | 234.8 | 148.7 |
| Yemen — Yémen | 1 364.4 | 1 060.8 | 1 040.7 | 1 045.0 | 1 023.4 | 959.9 | 758.6 | 746.4 | 710.5 | 394.7 |
| Zambia — Zambie | 28.7 | 26.7 | 24.3 | 23.3 | 11.8 | 10.6 | 10.4 | 10.0 | 9.5 | 6.6 |
| Zimbabwe — Zimbabwe | 435.4 | 390.2 | 229.1 | 145.0 | 259.4 | 129.1 | 117.5 | 112.9 | 49.0 | 63.0 |

Source

United Nations Environment Programme (UNEP), Ozone Secretariat (Nairobi), data access centre, last accessed May 2008.

Notes

1 Negative numbers can occur when destruction and/or exports exceed production plus imports, implying that the destruction and/or exports are from stockpiles.

2 Data include those for Hong Kong Special Administrative Region (Hong Kong SAR) and Taiwan Province of China.

Source

Secrétariat de l'ozone du programme des Nations Unies pour l'environnement (PNUE) (Nairobi), centre de communication de données, dernier accès mai 2008.

Notes

1 Il peut y avoir des chiffres négatifs, lorsque les quantités exportées, ajoutées aux quantités détruites, sont supérieures aux quantités effectivement produites ajoutées aux quantités importées, ce qui est le cas par exemple lorsque les exportations proviennent des stocks reportés d'un exercice précédent.

2 Les données comprennent les chiffres pour la Région Administrative Spéciale de Hong Kong (Hong Kong RAS), et la province de Taiwan.

*Table 51*: The data on land are compiled by the Food and Agriculture Organization of the United Nations (FAO). FAO's definitions of the land categories are as follows:

*Land area*: Total area excluding area under inland water bodies. The definition of inland water bodies generally includes major rivers and lakes.

*Arable land*: Land under temporary crops (double-cropped areas are counted only once); temporary meadows for mowing or pasture; land under market and kitchen gardens; and land temporarily fallow (less than five years). Abandoned land resulting from shifting cultivation is not included in this category. Data for "arable land" are not meant to indicate the amount of land that is potentially cultivable.

*Permanent crops*: Land cultivated with crops that occupy the land for long periods and need not be re-planted after each harvest, such as cocoa, coffee and rubber. This category includes land under flowering shrubs, fruit trees, nut trees and vines, but excludes land under trees grown for wood or timber.

*Forest*: In the *Global Forest Resources Assessment 2005* the following definition is used for forest. Forest includes natural forests and forest plantations and is used to refer to land with a tree crown cover (or equivalent stocking level) of more than 10 per cent and area of more than 0.5 hectares. The trees should be able to reach a minimum height of 5 metres at maturity *in situ*. Forest may consist either of closed forest formations where trees of various storeys and undergrowth cover a high proportion of the ground; or open forest formations with a continuous vegetation cover in which the tree crown cover exceeds 10 per cent. Young natural stands and all plantations established for forestry purposes that have yet to reach a crown density of 10 per cent or tree height of 5 metres are included under forest, as are areas normally forming part of the forest area that are temporarily unstocked as a result of human intervention or natural causes but that are expected to revert to forest.

*Table 52*: Chlorofluorocarbons (CFCs) are synthetic compounds formerly used as refrigerants and aerosol propellants and known to be harmful to the ozone layer of the atmosphere. In the Montreal Protocol on Substances that Deplete the Ozone Layer, CFCs to be measured are found in vehicle air conditioning units, domestic and commercial refrigeration and air conditioning/heat pump equipment, aerosol products, portable fire extinguishers, insulation boards, panels and pipe covers, and pre-polymers.

The Parties to the Montreal Protocol on Substances that Deplete the Ozone Layer report data on CFCs to the Ozone Secretariat of the United Nations Environment Programme. The data on CFCs are shown in ozone depleting potential (ODP) tons that are calculated by multiplying the quanti-

*Tableau 51*: Les données relatives aux terres sont compilées par l'Organisation des Nations Unies pour l'alimentation et l'agriculture (FAO). Les définitions de la FAO en ce qui concerne les terres sont les suivantes:

*Superficie totale des terres*: Superficie totale, à l'exception des eaux intérieures. Les eaux intérieures désignent généralement les principaux fleuves et lacs.

*Terres arables*: Terres affectées aux cultures temporaires (les terres sur lesquelles est pratiquée la double culture ne sont comptabilisées qu'une fois), prairies temporaires à faucher ou à pâturer, jardins maraîchers ou potagers et terres en jachère temporaire (moins de cinq ans). Cette définition ne comprend pas les terres abandonnées du fait de la culture itinérante. Les données relatives aux terres arables ne peuvent être utilisées pour calculer la superficie des terres aptes à l'agriculture.

*Cultures permanentes*: Superficie des terres avec des cultures qui occupent la terre pour de longues périodes et qui ne nécessitent pas d'être replantées après chaque récolte, comme le cacao, le café et le caoutchouc. Cette catégorie comprend les terres plantées d'arbustes à fleurs, d'arbres frui-tiers, d'arbres à noix et de vignes, mais ne comprend pas les terres plantées d'arbres destinés à la coupe.

*Superficie forestière*: Dans *l'Évaluation des ressources forestières mondiales 2005*, la FAO a défini les forêts comme suit : les forêts, qui comprennent les forêts naturelles et les plantations forestières, sont des terres où le couvert arboré (ou la densité de peuplement équivalente) est supérieur à 10 % et représente une superficie de plus de 0,5 hectares. Les arbres doivent être susceptibles d'atteindre sur place, à leur maturité, une hauteur de 5 mètres minimum. Il peut s'agir de forêts denses, où les arbres de différente hauteur et le sousbois couvrent une proportion importante du sol, ou de forêts claires, avec un couvert végétal continu, où le couvert arboré est supérieur à 10 %. Les jeunes peuplements naturels et toutes les plantations d'exploitation forestière n'ayant pas encore atteint une densité de couvert arboré de 10 % ou une hauteur de 5 mètres sont inclus dans les forêts, de même que les aires formant naturellement partie de la superficie forestière mais temporairement déboisées du fait d'une intervention de l'homme ou de causes naturelles, mais devant redevenir boisées.

*Tableau 52*: Les chlorofluorocarbones (CFC) sont des substances de synthèse utilisées comme réfrigérants et propul-seurs d'aérosols, dont on sait qu'elles appauvrissent la couche d'ozone. Aux termes du Protocole de Montréal relatif à des substances qui appauvrissent la couche d'ozone, la production de certains CFC doit être mesurée : ils sont utilisés dans les climatiseurs de véhicules, le matériel do-

ties in metric tons reported by the Parties, by the ODP of that substance, and added together.

Consumption is defined as production plus imports, minus exports of controlled substances. Feedstocks are exempt and are therefore subtracted from the imports and/or production. Similarly, the destroyed amounts are also subtracted. Negative numbers can occur when destruction and/or exports exceed production plus imports, implying that the destruction and/or exports are from stockpiles.

mestique et commercial de réfrigération et de climatisation (pompes à chaleur), les produits sous forme d'aérosols, les extincteurs d'incendie portables, les planches, panneaux et gaines isolants, et les prépolymères.

Les Parties au Protocole de Montréal communiquent leurs données concernant les CFC au secrétariat de l'ozone du Programme des Nations Unies pour l'environnement. Les données sur les CFC, indiquées en tonnes de potentiel de destruction de l'ozone (PDO), sont calculées en multipliant le nombre de tonnes signalé par les Parties par le potentiel de destruction coefficient de la substance considérée, et en faisant la somme de ces PDO.

La consommation est définie comme production de substances contrôlées, plus les importations, moins les exportations. Les produits intermédiaires de l'industrie sont exemptés, et on les soustrait donc des importations et/ou de la production. De même, on soustrait aussi les quantités détruites. On peut obtenir des quantités négatives, lorsque les quantités détruites et/ou exportées sont supérieures à la somme production + importations, ce qui signifie que les quantités détruites ou exportées ont été prélevées sur les stocks accumulés.

# 53

## Human resources in research and development (R & D)
Full-time equivalent (FTE)

## Personnel employé dans la recherche et le développement (R–D)
Equivalent temps plein (ETP)

| Country or area — Pays ou zone | Year Année | Total R & D personnel — Total du personnel de R - D | Researchers — Chercheurs — Total M & W — Total H & F | Women Femmes | Technicians and equivalent staff — Techniciens et personnel assimilé — Total M & W — Total H & F | Women Femmes | Other supporting staff — Autre personnel de soutien — Total M & W — Total H & F | Women Femmes |
|---|---|---|---|---|---|---|---|---|
| Algeria[1] — Algérie[1] | 2005 | 7 331 | 5 593 | 2 043 | 1 134 | ... | 604 | ... |
| American Samoa[1,2] — Samoa américaines[1,2] | 2002 | 5 | 5 | ... | ... | ... | ... | ... |
| Argentina Argentine | 2000[3] | 37 515 | 26 420 | 12 446 | 11 095[5] | ... | ... | ... |
| | 2001[3] | 37 444 | 25 656 | 12 071 | 11 788[5] | ... | ... | ... |
| | 2002[3] | 37 413 | 26 083 | 12 593 | 11 330[5] | ... | ... | ... |
| | 2003[3] | 39 393 | 27 367 | 13 271 | 12 026[5] | ... | ... | ... |
| | 2004[3] | 42 454 | 29 471 | 14 370 | 12 983[5] | ... | ... | ... |
| | 2005[3] | 45 361 | 31 868 | 15 416 | 13 493[5] | ... | ... | ... |
| | 2006[4] | 49 359 | 35 040 | 17 081 | 14 319[5] | ... | ... | ... |
| Armenia[1,2] Arménie[1,2] | 2000 | 7 309 | 4 971 | 2 565 | 373 | ... | 1 965 | ... |
| | 2001 | 6 965 | 5 087 | 2 175 | 415 | ... | 1 463 | ... |
| | 2002 | 6 737 | 4 927 | 2 314 | 451 | ... | 1 359 | ... |
| | 2003 | 6 277 | 4 667 | 2 138 | 313 | ... | 1 297 | ... |
| | 2004 | 6 685 | 4 788 | 2 235 | 423 | ... | 1 474 | ... |
| | 2005 | 6 892 | 5 056 | 2 329 | 345 | ... | 1 491 | ... |
| Australia[4] Australie[4] | 2000 | 95 621 | 66 001 | ... | ... | ... | ... | ... |
| | 2002 | 107 209 | 73 173 | ... | 18 651 | ... | 15 383 | ... |
| | 2004 | 118 145 | 81 384 | ... | 18 146 | ... | 18 615 | ... |
| Austria[4] Autriche[4] | 2002 | 38 893 | 24 124 | 3 811 | 10 194 | 2 683 | 4 575 | 2 068 |
| | 2004 | 42 891 | 25 955 | 4 740 | 12 067 | 2 901 | 4 869 | 2 471 |
| | 2005[6] | 47 584 | 28 795 | ... | ... | ... | ... | ... |
| | 2006[6] | 50 322 | 30 452 | ... | ... | ... | ... | ... |
| Azerbaijan[2] Azerbaïdjan[2] | 2000 | 15 809 | 10 168 | 4 971 | 1 478 | ... | 4 163 | ... |
| | 2001 | 15 929 | 10 139 | 5 069 | 1 552 | ... | 4 238 | ... |
| | 2002 | 16 019 | 10 195 | 5 236 | 1 609 | ... | 4 215 | ... |
| | 2003 | 17 190 | 10 830 | 5 541 | 1 825 | ... | 4 535 | ... |
| | 2004 | 17 712 | 11 531 | 6 110 | 1 749 | ... | 4 432 | ... |
| | 2005 | 18 164 | 11 603 | 6 056 | 1 825 | ... | 4 736 | ... |
| Belarus[2] Bélarus[2] | 2000 | 29 032 | 19 707 | 9 099 | 2 574 | ... | 6 751 | ... |
| | 2001 | 28 186 | 19 133 | 8 648 | 2 332 | ... | 6 721 | ... |
| | 2002 | 26 871 | 18 557 | 8 361 | 2 050 | ... | 6 264 | ... |
| | 2003 | 26 038 | 17 702 | 7 785 | 2 337 | ... | 5 999 | ... |
| | 2004 | 24 946 | 17 034 | 7 556 | 2 068 | ... | 5 844 | ... |
| | 2005 | 26 142 | 18 267 | 7 897 | 2 112 | ... | 5 763 | ... |
| Belgium[2,4] Belgique[2,4] | 2002 | 73 187 | 44 133 | 12 221 | 20 335 | 6 652 | 8 719 | 4 387 |
| | 2003 | 73 629 | 44 500 | 12 522 | 20 396 | 6 711 | 8 733 | 4 486 |
| | 2004 | 76 340 | 47 363 | 13 635 | 20 548 | 6 793 | 8 429 | 4 496 |
| | 2005 | 78 509 | 48 757 | 14 413 | 21 071 | 6 998 | 8 681 | 4 697 |
| Bolivia[2,3] Bolivie[2,3] | 2000 | 1 310 | 1 080 | 419 | 170 | 111 | 60 | 29 |
| | #2001 | 1 650 | 1 250 | 495 | 250 | 150 | 150 | 72 |
| Botswana[1,2] — Botswana[1,2] | 2005 | 2 140 | 1 728 | 529 | 412 | ... | ... | ... |
| Brazil[2,3] Brésil[2,3] | 2000 | 209 386 | 110 885 | 48 679 | 98 501[5] | ... | ... | ... |
| | 2001 | 212 636 | 116 539 | 52 326 | 96 097[5] | ... | ... | ... |
| | 2002 | 216 473 | 122 784 | 56 235 | 93 689[5] | ... | ... | ... |
| | 2003 | 246 782 | 135 080 | 62 677 | 111 702[5] | ... | ... | ... |
| | 2004 | 273 577 | 143 864 | 67 616 | 129 713[5] | ... | ... | ... |

| Country or area<br>Pays ou zone | Year<br>Année | Total R & D<br>personnel<br>Total du<br>personnel<br>de R - D | Researchers<br>Chercheurs | | Technicians and<br>equivalent staff<br>Techniciens et<br>personnel assimilé | | Other<br>supporting staff<br>Autre personnel<br>de soutien | |
|---|---|---|---|---|---|---|---|---|
| | | | Total M & W<br>Total H & F | Women<br>Femmes | Total M & W<br>Total H & F | Women<br>Femmes | Total M & W<br>Total H & F | Women<br>Femmes |
| Brunei Darussalam<br>Brunéi Darussalam | 2002 | 140 | 99 | ... | ... | ... | ... | ... |
| | 2003 | 140 | 98 | ... | ... | ... | ... | ... |
| Bulgaria[2,7]<br>Bulgarie[2,7] | 2000 | 16 853 | 10 527 | 4 797 | 4 192 | 2 683 | 2 134 | 1 426 |
| | 2001 | 16 671 | 10 446 | 4 758 | 4 135 | 2 547 | 2 090 | 1 393 |
| | 2002 | 16 847 | 10 445 | 4 837 | 4 127 | 2 624 | 2 275 | 1 505 |
| | 2003 | 17 400 | 10 876 | 5 070 | 4 206 | 2 567 | 2 318 | 1 518 |
| | 2004 | 18 025 | 11 377 | 5 258 | 4 291 | 2 542 | 2 357 | 1 537 |
| | 2005 | .18 638 | 11 920 | 5 429 | 4 426 | 2 618 | 2 292 | 1 522 |
| Burkina Faso[1]<br>Burkina Faso[1] | 2002 | 828 | 236 | 34 | 244 | ... | 348 | ... |
| | 2003 | 888 | 251 | 32[8] | 260 | ... | 377 | ... |
| | 2004 | 890 | 293 | 34[9] | 227 | ... | 370 | ... |
| | 2005 | 942 | 301 | 37 | 225 | ... | 416 | ... |
| Cambodia[1,6] — Cambodge[1,6] | 2002 | 494 | 223 | 50 | 170 | ... | 102 | ... |
| Cameroon[1] — Cameroun[1] | 2005 | ... | 462 | 88 | ... | ... | ... | ... |
| Canada[4]<br>Canada[4] | 2000 | 167 861 | 108 492 | ... | 38 070 | ... | 21 299 | ... |
| | 2001 | 179 450 | 114 640 | ... | 40 590 | ... | 24 220 | ... |
| | 2002 | 183 240 | 115 860 | ... | 42 660 | ... | 24 720 | ... |
| | *2003[6] | 189 520 | 118 860 | ... | 44 330 | ... | 26 330 | ... |
| | *2004[6] | 199 060 | 125 330 | ... | 46 890 | ... | 26 840 | ... |
| Cape Verde[1,2]<br>Cap-Vert[1,2] | 2001 | 178 | 79 | ... | 16 | ... | 83 | ... |
| | 2002 | 207 | 107 | 56 | 18 | ... | 82 | ... |
| Chile[2,3]<br>Chili[2,3] | 2000 | 13 300 | 7 217 | ... | 6 083[5] | ... | ... | ... |
| | 2001 | 13 838 | 7 778 | ... | 6 060[5] | ... | ... | ... |
| | 2002 | ... | 8 507 | 2 785 | ... | ... | ... | ... |
| | #2003 | 28 220 | 17 212 | 5 168 | 7 273 | ... | 3 735 | ... |
| | 2004 | 30 583 | 18 365 | 5 503 | 7 912 | ... | 4 306 | ... |
| China[4,10]<br>Chine[4,10] | #2000 | 922 131 | 695 062 | ... | ... | ... | ... | ... |
| | 2001 | 956 482 | 742 726 | ... | ... | ... | ... | ... |
| | 2002 | 1 035 197 | 810 525 | ... | ... | ... | ... | ... |
| | 2003 | 1 094 831 | 862 108 | ... | ... | ... | ... | ... |
| | 2004 | 1 152 617 | 926 252 | ... | ... | ... | ... | ... |
| | 2005 | 1 364 799 | 1 118 698 | ... | ... | ... | ... | ... |
| | 2006 | 1 502 472 | 1 223 756 | ... | ... | ... | ... | ... |
| China, Hong Kong SAR<br>Chine, Hong Kong RAS | 2000 | 9 802 | 7 728 | ... | 1 374 | ... | 699 | ... |
| | 2001 | 11 041 | 9 149 | ... | 1 162 | ... | 730 | ... |
| | 2002 | 12 890 | 10 639 | ... | 1 532 | ... | 719 | ... |
| | 2003 | 16 864 | 13 497 | ... | 2 138 | ... | 1 228 | ... |
| | 2004 | 18 846 | 14 594 | ... | 2 904 | ... | 1 348 | ... |
| China, Macao SAR[1,6]<br>Chine, Macao RAS[1,6] | 2001 | 196 | 114 | 20 | 74 | ... | 8 | ... |
| | 2002 | 196 | 105 | 16 | 81 | ... | 10 | ... |
| | 2003 | 249 | 147 | 27 | 94 | ... | 8 | ... |
| | 2004 | 349 | 244 | 48 | 97 | ... | 8 | ... |
| | 2005 | 409 | 298 | 62 | 102 | ... | 9 | ... |
| Colombia[2,3]<br>Colombie[2,3] | 2000 | 9 653 | 6 191 | 2 335 | 3 462[5] | 1 644[5] | ... | ... |
| | 2001 | 9 931 | 6 542 | 2 473 | 3 389[5] | 1 657[5] | ... | ... |
| | 2002 | 13 103 | 7 410 | 2 846 | 5 693[5] | 2 830[5] | ... | ... |
| | #2003 | 19 354 | 10 851 | 4 038 | 8 503[5] | 4 177[5] | ... | ... |
| | 2004 | 23 406 | 12 751 | 4 780 | 10 655[5] | 4 513[5] | ... | ... |
| Congo[1] — Congo[1] | 2000 | 217 | 102 | 13 | 111 | 22 | 4 | ... |

| Country or area<br>Pays ou zone | Year<br>Année | Total R & D<br>personnel<br>Total du<br>personnel<br>de R - D | Researchers<br>Chercheurs<br>Total M & W<br>Total H & F | Women<br>Femmes | Technicians and<br>equivalent staff<br>Techniciens et<br>personnel assimilé<br>Total M & W<br>Total H & F | Women<br>Femmes | Other<br>supporting staff<br>Autre personnel<br>de soutien<br>Total M & W<br>Total H & F | Women<br>Femmes |
|---|---|---|---|---|---|---|---|---|
| Costa Rica[2,3]<br>Costa Rica[2,3] | 2002 | ... | 1 193 | 453 | ... | ... | ... | ... |
| | 2003 | ... | 1 171 | 480 | ... | ... | ... | ... |
| | 2004 | ... | 1 076 | 447 | ... | ... | ... | ... |
| | 2005 | ... | 1 444 | 569 | ... | ... | ... | ... |
| Côte d'ivoire — Côte d'ivoire | 2005 | ... | 1 269 | 210 | ... | ... | ... | ... |
| Croatia[2]<br>Croatie[2] | 2000 | 13 828 | 9 476 | ... | 2 317 | ... | 2 035 | ... |
| | 2001 | 14 117 | 9 660 | ... | 2 342 | ... | 2 115 | ... |
| | 2002 | 16 515 | 11 136 | 4 641 | 2 612 | 1 449 | 2 767 | 2 056 |
| | 2003[7] | 17 216 | 11 464 | 4 843 | 3 278 | 1 715 | 2 474 | 1 920 |
| | 2004[7] | 19 739 | 13 139 | 5 404 | 3 797 | 1 842 | 2 803 | 2 076 |
| Cuba[2,3]<br>Cuba[2,3] | 2000 | 29 568 | 5 378[9] | ... | 24 190[5] | ... | ... | ... |
| | 2001 | 32 721 | 5 849[9] | ... | 26 872[5] | ... | ... | ... |
| | 2002 | 34 326 | 6 057[9] | ... | 28 269[5] | ... | ... | ... |
| | 2003 | 33 855 | 5 075[9] | ... | 28 780[5] | ... | ... | ... |
| | 2004 | 34 094 | 5 115[9] | ... | 28 979[5] | ... | ... | ... |
| | 2005 | 33 988 | 5 526[9] | 2 703 | 28 462[5] | ... | ... | ... |
| Cyprus[2,7]<br>Chypre[2,7] | 2000 | 1 630 | 792 | 208 | 423 | 158 | 415 | 228 |
| | 2001 | 1 733 | 880 | 258 | 431 | 162 | 422 | 236 |
| | 2002 | 1 937 | 1 014 | 298 | 489 | 200 | 434 | 262 |
| | 2003 | 2 102 | 1 089 | 337 | 562 | 210 | 451 | 261 |
| | 2004 | 2 235 | 1 226 | 393 | 575 | 215 | 434 | 261 |
| | 2005 | 2 470 | 1 424 | 464 | 604 | 221 | 442 | 255 |
| Czech Republic[2,4]<br>République tchèque[2,4] | 2000 | 53 506 | 30 165 | 8 395 | 15 236 | 6 576 | 8 105 | 4 351 |
| | 2001 | 51 939 | 29 216 | 8 409 | 15 389 | 6 835 | 7 334 | 3 783 |
| | 2002 | 53 695 | 30 635 | 9 024 | 15 662 | 6 622 | 7 398 | 3 805 |
| | 2003 | 55 699 | 31 421 | 8 905 | 17 059 | 6 938 | 7 219 | 3 735 |
| | 2004 | 60 148 | 34 152 | 9 730 | 18 516 | 7 373 | 7 480 | 3 720 |
| | 2005 | #65 379 | #37 542 | #10 827 | 19 652 | 7 817 | 8 185 | 4 221 |
| | 2006 | 69 162 | 39 676 | 11 295 | 21 338 | 8 099 | 8 147 | 4 000 |
| Dem. Rep. of the Congo[1,2]<br>Rép. dém. du Congo[1,2] | 2004 | 31 923 | 9 072 | ... | 1 444 | ... | 21 407 | ... |
| | 2005 | 33 478 | 10 411 | ... | 1 510 | ... | 21 557 | ... |
| Denmark[2,4]<br>Danemark[2,4] | 2000 | 56 068 | ... | ... | ... | ... | ... | ... |
| | 2001 | 59 811 | 29 791 | 8 355 | ... | ... | ... | ... |
| | 2002 | 61 915 | #37 883 | #9 943 | ... | ... | ... | ... |
| | 2003 | 60 525 | 36 046 | 10 134 | ... | ... | ... | ... |
| | 2004 | 65 994 | 39 533 | ... | ... | ... | ... | ... |
| | 2005 | 67 267 | 43 460 | 12 908 | 15 797 | 8 072 | 8 010 | 4 541 |
| Ecuador[2,3]<br>Equateur[2,3] | #2001 | 1 164 | 648 | 157 | 516[5] | ... | ... | ... |
| | 2002 | 1 271 | 696 | 160 | 575[5] | ... | ... | ... |
| | 2003 | 1 555 | 845 | 241 | 710[5] | ... | ... | ... |
| El Salvador[2,3]<br>El Salvador[2,3] | 2003 | ... | 252 | 78 | ... | ... | ... | ... |
| | 2004 | ... | 258 | 80 | ... | ... | ... | ... |
| | 2005 | ... | 260 | 81 | ... | ... | ... | ... |
| Estonia[2,7]<br>Estonie[2,7] | 2000 | 6 531 | 4 570 | 1 969 | 936 | 619 | 1 025 | 691 |
| | 2001 | 6 818 | 4 803 | 2 078 | 904 | 549 | 1 111 | 756 |
| | 2002 | 6 921 | 5 089 | 2 168 | 902 | 553 | 930 | 665 |
| | 2003 | 7 600 | 5 424 | 2 340 | 1 022 | 629 | 1 154 | 818 |
| | 2004 | 7 882 | 5 678 | 2 412 | 1 178 | 716 | 1 026 | 706 |
| | 2005 | 7 955 | 5 734 | 2 337 | 1 244 | 660 | 977 | 678 |
| | 2006[11] | 8 706 | 6 411 | 2 661 | ... | ... | ... | ... |

## 53

**Human resources in research and development (R & D)** — Full-time equivalent (FTE) (*continued*)
**Personnel employé dans la recherche et le développement (R–D)** — Equivalent temps plein (ETP) (*suite*)

| Country or area<br>Pays ou zone | Year<br>Année | Total R & D<br>personnel<br>Total du<br>personnel<br>de R - D | Researchers<br>Chercheurs<br>Total M & W<br>Total H & F | Women<br>Femmes | Technicians and<br>equivalent staff<br>Techniciens et<br>personnel assimilé<br>Total M & W<br>Total H & F | Women<br>Femmes | Other<br>supporting staff<br>Autre personnel<br>de soutien<br>Total M & W<br>Total H & F | Women<br>Femmes |
|---|---|---|---|---|---|---|---|---|
| Ethiopia[1] — Ethiopie[1] | 2005 | 5 112 | 1 608 | 111 | 779 | ... | 2 725 | ... |
| Finland[2,4]<br>Finlande[2,4] | 2000 | 68 813 | 45 241[12] | 12 904[12] | ... | ... | ... | ... |
| | 2001 | 69 788 | 47 534[12] | 13 814[12] | ... | ... | ... | ... |
| | 2002 | 73 121 | 50 215[12] | 15 025[12] | ... | ... | ... | ... |
| | 2003 | 74 773 | 53 430[12] | 15 931[12] | ... | ... | ... | ... |
| | 2004 | 76 687 | #51 219 | #14 834 | ... | ... | ... | ... |
| | 2005 | 77 275 | 50 773 | 15 349 | ... | ... | ... | ... |
| | 2006 | ... | 53 273 | 16 808 | ... | ... | ... | ... |
| France[2,4]<br>France[2,4] | 2000[9] | 381 609 | 211 365 | 58 124 | ... | ... | ... | ... |
| | 2001[9] | 390 631 | 217 173 | 59 630 | ... | ... | ... | ... |
| | #2002 | 412 938[9] | 231 816 | 64 333 | ... | ... | ... | ... |
| | 2003 | 415 061[9] | 240 186 | 66 713 | ... | ... | ... | ... |
| | 2004 | 421 312[9] | 247 245 | 68 818 | ... | ... | ... | ... |
| | 2005 | 488 949[9] | 252 994 | 70 439 | ... | ... | ... | ... |
| Gabon[1,2]<br>Gabon[1,2] | 2004 | 188 | 80 | 25 | 68 | ... | 40 | ... |
| | 2006 | 322 | 150 | 37 | 42 | 13 | 130 | 40 |
| Gambia[1]<br>Gambie[1] | 2001 | 77 | 40 | 0 | 25 | 0 | 12 | 0 |
| | 2002 | 77 | 40 | 0 | 25 | 0 | 12 | 0 |
| | 2003 | 81 | 44 | 0 | 25 | 0 | 12 | 0 |
| | 2004 | 82 | 44 | 3 | 28 | 0 | 10 | 0 |
| | 2005 | 84 | 46 | 4 | 28 | 0 | 10 | |
| Georgia[2]<br>Géorgie[2] | 2000 | 12 726 | 11 071 | ... | 1 655 | ... | 0[13] | ... |
| | 2001 | 15 100 | 12 400 | 6 400 | 1 180 | ... | 1 520 | ... |
| | 2002 | 16 031 | 11 997 | 6 165 | 1 246 | ... | 2 788 | ... |
| | 2003 | 17 819 | 11 572 | 5 809 | 1 895 | ... | 4 352 | ... |
| | 2004 | 16 698 | 10 910 | 5 664 | 2 262 | ... | 3 526 | ... |
| | 2005 | 13 415 | 8 112 | 4 275 | 1 810 | ... | 3 493 | ... |
| Germany<br>Allemagne | 2000[6] | 484 734 | 257 874 | ... | ... | ... | ... | ... |
| | 2001 | 480 606 | 264 385 | 42 588 | ... | ... | ... | ... |
| | 2002[6] | 480 004 | 265 812 | ... | ... | ... | ... | ... |
| | 2003 | 472 533 | 268 942 | 43 855 | 89 956 | ... | 113 634 | ... |
| | 2004 | 470 729 | 270 215 | ... | 87 873 | ... | 112 640 | ... |
| | 2005 | 480 758 | 277 628 | 48 205 | 94 578 | ... | 108 553 | ... |
| | *2006 | 485 000 | 279 800 | ... | ... | ... | ... | ... |
| Greece[2,4]<br>Grèce[2,4] | 2001 | 55 626 | 26 340 | 9 295 | 15 921 | 5 796 | 13 365 | 6 571 |
| | 2003 | 56 708 | 28 058 | 10 402 | 14 748 | 5 724 | 13 902 | 6 890 |
| | 2005 | 61 569 | 33 033 | 12 065 | 15 680 | 6 749 | 12 857 | 6 807 |
| Greenland<br>Groenland | 2001[6] | 35 | 30 | 10 | 5[5] | ... | ... | ... |
| | 2002 | 34 | 30 | 9 | 3[5] | ... | ... | ... |
| | 2003[6] | 41 | 37 | 12 | 5[5] | ... | ... | ... |
| | 2004 | 48 | 40 | 11 | 8[5] | ... | ... | ... |
| Guatemala[1,2,3] — Guatemala[1,2,3] | | 1 177 | 615 | 262 | 192 | 52 | 370 | 90 |
| Guinea[1,2] — Guinée[1,2] | 2000 | 3 711 | 2 117 | 122 | 768 | ... | 826 | ... |
| Honduras[2,3]<br>Honduras[2,3] | 2000 | 2 167 | 479 | 160 | 1 688[5] | 712[5] | ... | ... |
| | 2001 | 2 262 | 525 | 164 | 1 737[5] | 677[5] | ... | ... |
| | 2002 | 2 321 | 516 | 149 | 1 805[5] | 830[5] | ... | ... |
| | 2003 | 2 280 | 539 | 143 | 1 741[5] | 731[5] | ... | ... |

| Country or area<br>Pays ou zone | Year<br>Année | Total R & D<br>personnel<br>Total du<br>personnel<br>de R - D | Researchers<br>Chercheurs<br>Total M & W<br>Total H & F | Women<br>Femmes | Technicians and<br>equivalent staff<br>Techniciens et<br>personnel assimilé<br>Total M & W<br>Total H & F | Women<br>Femmes | Other<br>supporting staff<br>Autre personnel<br>de soutien<br>Total M & W<br>Total H & F | Women<br>Femmes |
|---|---|---|---|---|---|---|---|---|
| Hungary[2,4]<br>Hongrie[2,4] | 2000[14] | 45 325 | 27 876 | 9 537 | 8 313 | 4 844 | 9 136 | 6 026 |
| | 2001[14] | 45 676 | 28 351 | 9 363 | 8 098 | 4 896 | 9 227 | 6 295 |
| | 2002[14] | 48 727 | 29 764 | 10 039 | 8 965 | 5 590 | 9 998 | 6 617 |
| | 2003[14] | 48 681 | 30 292 | 10 647 | 8 659 | 5 552 | 9 730 | 6 350 |
| | #2004 | 49 615 | 30 420 | 10 484 | 8 873 | 5 910 | 10 322 | 7 138 |
| | 2005 | 49 723 | 31 407 | 10 731 | 8 663 | 5 803 | 9 653 | 6 679 |
| | 2006 | ... | 32 786 | 10 973 | ... | ... | ... | ... |
| Iceland[2,4]<br>Islande[2,4] | 2001 | 5 218 | 3 231 | 1 122 | 1 168 | 530 | 819 | 425 |
| | 2002 | 4 970 | ... | ... | ... | ... | ... | ... |
| | 2003 | 5 466 | 3 517 | 1 384 | 1 147 | 540 | 802 | 416 |
| | 2005 | 5 724 | 3 821 | 1 501 | 1 162 | 533 | 741 | 327 |
| India — Inde | 2000 | 318 443 | 115 936 | 13 912 | 90 045 | ... | 112 462 | ... |
| Indonesia<br>Indonésie | 2000 | 56 356 | 44 984 | ... | ... | ... | ... | ... |
| | 2001 | 51 544 | 42 722 | ... | ... | ... | ... | ... |
| Iran (Islamic Rep. of)[2] — Iran (Rép. islamique d')[2] | 2004 | 91 584 | 51 899 | 10 300 | 22 186 | ... | 17 499 | ... |
| Ireland[2,4]<br>Irlande[2,4] | 2000 | 21 094 | ... | ... | ... | ... | ... | ... |
| | 2001 | 24 220 | ... | ... | ... | ... | ... | ... |
| | 2002 | 24 486 | 15 512 | 4 686 | 4 400 | 1 078 | 4 574 | 2 110 |
| | 2003 | 25 194 | 15 877 | 4 801 | 4 496 | 1 116 | 4 821 | 2 358 |
| | 2004 | 26 584 | 16 641 | 4 985 | 4 656 | 1 140 | 5 287 | 2 669 |
| | 2005 | 28 170 | 17 953 | *5 349 | 4 676 | *1 240 | 5 541 | *2 848 |
| | *2006 | ... | 18 589 | ... | ... | ... | ... | ... |
| Italy[4]<br>Italie[4] | 2000 | 150 066 | 66 110 | ... | ... | ... | ... | ... |
| | 2001 | 153 905 | 66 702 | ... | ... | ... | ... | ... |
| | 2002 | 164 023 | 71 242 | ... | ... | ... | ... | ... |
| | 2003 | 161 828 | 70 332 | 20 105 | ... | ... | ... | ... |
| | 2004 | 164 026 | 72 012 | 20 938 | ... | ... | ... | ... |
| | 2005 | 175 248 | 82 489 | 26 797 | ... | ... | ... | ... |
| Japan[2,4]<br>Japon[2,4] | 2001 | 1 050 414 | 792 699 | 85 207 | 85 257 | 22 433 | 172 458 | 61 731 |
| | 2002 | 1 032 826 | 791 224 | 88 674 | 76 490 | 22 964 | 165 112 | 61 044 |
| | 2003 | 1 081 099 | 830 545 | 96 133 | 82 007 | 24 650 | 168 546 | 62 433 |
| | 2004 | 1 096 078 | 830 474 | 98 690 | 87 886 | 25 696 | 177 719 | 65 308 |
| | 2005 | 1 122 680 | 861 901 | 102 948 | 85 509 | 27 562 | 175 269 | 65 753 |
| | 2006 | ... | 874 690 | 108 547 | ... | ... | ... | ... |
| Jordan[2] — Jordanie[2] | 2003 | 42 153 | 15 891 | 3 385 | 19 322 | 2 073 | 6 940 | 2 101 |
| Kazakhstan<br>Kazakhstan | 2000 | 12 829 | 9 009 | 4 544 | 1 183 | ... | 2 637 | ... |
| | #2001 | 15 339[15] | 9 223 | 4 624 | 1 140 | ... | 4 976[15] | ... |
| | 2002 | 15 998[15] | 9 366 | 4 558 | 1 364 | ... | 5 268[15] | ... |
| | 2003 | 16 578[15] | 9 899 | 4 809 | 1 300 | ... | 5 379[15] | ... |
| | 2004 | 16 715[15] | 10 382 | 5 017 | 1 102 | ... | 5 231[15] | ... |
| | 2005 | 18 912[15] | 11 910 | 6 013 | 1 270 | ... | 5 732[15] | ... |
| Korea, Republic of[1,2,4]<br>Corée, République de[1,2,4] | 2000 | 237 232 | 159 973 | 16 385 | 61 027 | ... | 16 232 | ... |
| | 2001 | 261 802 | 178 937 | 19 930 | 62 738 | 15 243 | 20 127 | 7 167 |
| | 2002 | 279 806 | 189 888 | 22 057 | 69 021 | 17 460 | 20 897 | 7 792 |
| | 2003 | 297 060 | 198 171 | 22 613 | 75 283 | 18 158 | 23 606 | 8 845 |
| | 2004 | 312 314 | 209 979 | 25 198 | 76 730 | 18 908 | 25 605 | 9 401 |
| | 2005 | 335 428 | 234 702 | 30 174 | 75 179 | 19 123 | 25 547 | 9 732 |
| | 2006 | 365 794 | 256 598 | 33 682 | 80 079 | 21 223 | 29 117 | 10 478 |

| Country or area / Pays ou zone | Year / Année | Total R & D personnel / Total du personnel de R-D | Researchers / Chercheurs — Total M & W / Total H & F | Women / Femmes | Technicians and equivalent staff / Techniciens et personnel assimilé — Total M & W / Total H & F | Women / Femmes | Other supporting staff / Autre personnel de soutien — Total M & W / Total H & F | Women / Femmes |
|---|---|---|---|---|---|---|---|---|
| Kuwait[1,2] Koweït[1,2] | 2000 | 744 | 181 | 35 | 383 | ... | 180 | ... |
| | #2001 | 555 | 160 | 37 | 304 | ... | 91 | ... |
| | 2002 | 585 | 163 | 37 | 335 | ... | 87 | ... |
| | 2003 | 631 | 203 | 48 | 381 | ... | 47 | ... |
| | 2004 | 694 | 195 | 43 | 420 | ... | 79 | ... |
| | 2005 | 701 | 200 | 42 | 417 | ... | 84 | ... |
| Kyrgyzstan[2] Kirghizistan[2] | 2000 | 2 886 | 2 121 | 1 028 | 194 | ... | 571 | ... |
| | 2001 | 2 958 | 2 099 | 1 001 | 248 | ... | 611 | ... |
| | 2002 | 2 922 | 2 065 | 1 019 | 257 | ... | 600 | ... |
| | 2003 | 2 699 | 1 979 | 990 | 229 | ... | 491 | ... |
| | 2004 | 2 844 | 2 019 | 971 | 307 | ... | 518 | ... |
| | 2005 | 2 911 | 2 187 | 977 | 226 | ... | 498 | ... |
| Latvia[2] Lettonie[2] | #2000 | 8 229 | 6 117 | 3 033[7] | 931 | 519[7] | 1 181 | 658[7] |
| | 2001 | 8 414 | 5 785 | 3 050[7] | 1 151 | 752[7] | 1 479 | 785[7] |
| | 2002 | 9 153 | 6 101 | 3 159[7] | 1 069 | 630[7] | 1 983 | 1 219[7] |
| | 2003[7] | 8 002 | 5 513 | 2 926 | 1 159 | 662 | 1 330 | 773 |
| | 2004[7] | 8 273 | 5 625 | 2 972 | 1 244 | 700 | 1 404 | 816 |
| | 2005[7] | 9 488 | 5 748 | 2 963 | 2 097 | 1 135 | 1 643 | 806 |
| | 2006[7] | 10 735 | 7 200 | 3 418 | 2 217 | 1 234 | 1 318 | 800 |
| Lesotho[1] Lesotho[1] | 2002 | 26 | 12 | 5[9] | 5 | ... | 9 | ... |
| | 2003 | 26 | 15 | 8[9] | 5 | ... | 6 | ... |
| | 2004 | 51 | 20 | 10[9] | 21 | ... | 10 | ... |
| Lithuania[2,7] Lituanie[2,7] | 2000 | 14 592 | 10 100 | 4 542 | 2 052 | 1 345 | 2 440 | 1 451 |
| | 2001 | 14 980 | 10 213 | 4 801 | 2 052 | 1 448 | 2 715 | 1 805 |
| | 2002 | 13 540 | 9 517 | 4 536 | 1 713 | 1 201 | 2 310 | 1 526 |
| | 2003 | 14 534 | 10 552 | 5 101 | 1 723 | 1 180 | 2 259 | 1 516 |
| | 2004 | 16 436 | 11 636 | 5 658 | 1 888 | 1 208 | 2 912 | 1 962 |
| | 2005 | 16 323 | 11 918 | 5 798 | 1 737 | 1 109 | 2 668 | 1 803 |
| Luxembourg[2,4] Luxembourg[2,4] | 2003 | 4 135 | 2 023 | 353[6] | 1 708[6] | ... | 404[6] | ... |
| | 2005 | 5 015 | 2 443 | 445 | 1 780 | 298 | 792 | 325 |
| Madagascar[1] Madagascar[1] | 2000 | 985 | 240 | ... | 730 | ... | 15 | ... |
| | #2001 | 1 741 | 822 | 253 | 243 | ... | 676 | ... |
| | 2002 | 1 712 | 788 | 241 | 245 | ... | 679 | ... |
| | 2003 | 1 696 | 814 | 259 | 188 | ... | 694 | ... |
| | 2004 | 1 705 | 847 | 410 | 175 | ... | 683 | ... |
| | 2005 | 1 477 | 806 | 246 | 119 | ... | 552 | ... |
| Malaysia Malaisie | 2000 | 10 060 | 6 423 | 2 045 | 921 | ... | 2 716 | ... |
| | 2002 | 10 731 | 7 157 | 2 451 | 1 379 | ... | 2 195 | ... |
| | 2004 | 17 887 | 12 669 | 4 701 | 1 598 | ... | 3 619 | ... |
| Malta[2,7] Malte[2,7] | 2002 | 1 121 | 689 | ... | 83 | ... | 349 | ... |
| | 2003 | 975 | 706 | ... | 100 | ... | 169 | ... |
| | #2004 | 1 329 | 893 | 211 | 200 | 19 | 236 | 139 |
| | *2005 | 1 320 | 901 | 228 | 210 | 20 | 209 | 131 |
| | *2006 | 1 424 | 977 | 241 | 223 | 24 | 224 | 139 |
| Mexico[4] Mexique[4] | 2001 | 43 455 | ... | ... | ... | ... | ... | ... |
| | 2003 | 59 875 | 33 558 | ... | 15 304 | ... | 11 013 | ... |
| | #2004 | 80 685 | 44 614 | ... | 22 597 | ... | 13 474 | ... |
| | 2005 | 89 398 | 48 401 | ... | 27 109 | ... | 13 888 | ... |
| Monaco[1] Monaco[1] | 2004 | 18 | 9 | 4 | 6 | ... | 3 | ... |
| | 2005 | 18 | 10 | 5 | 5 | ... | 3 | ... |

| Country or area<br>Pays ou zone | Year<br>Année | Total R & D personnel<br>Total du personnel de R - D | Researchers<br>Chercheurs<br>Total M & W<br>Total H & F | Women<br>Femmes | Technicians and equivalent staff<br>Techniciens et personnel assimilé<br>Total M & W<br>Total H & F | Women<br>Femmes | Other supporting staff<br>Autre personnel de soutien<br>Total M & W<br>Total H & F | Women<br>Femmes |
|---|---|---|---|---|---|---|---|---|
| Mongolia[1,2]<br>Mongolie[1,2] | 2000 | 2 113 | 1 631 | ... | 294 | 150 | 188 | ... |
| | #2001 | 2 752 | 2 087 | 901 | 215 | ... | 450 | ... |
| | 2002 | 2 879 | 1 973 | 923 | 177 | ... | 729 | ... |
| | 2003 | 2 638 | 1 995 | 909 | 154 | ... | 489 | ... |
| | 2004 | 2 642 | 1 991 | 907 | 146 | ... | 505 | ... |
| | 2005 | 2 283 | 1 731 | 819 | 81 | ... | 471 | ... |
| Morocco[2]<br>Maroc[2] | 2000 | ... | 24 760[1] | 4 957[9] | ... | ... | ... | ... |
| | 2001 | ... | 24 719[1] | 5 061[9] | ... | ... | ... | ... |
| | 2002 | ... | 25 790[1] | 5 133[9] | ... | ... | ... | ... |
| | 2003 | ... | 23 559[1] | 6 049[9] | ... | ... | ... | ... |
| | 2004 | ... | 24 483[1] | 6 872 | ... | ... | ... | ... |
| | 2005 | ... | 24 835[1] | 6 580 | ... | ... | ... | ... |
| Mozambique[1,2,9] — Mozambique[1,2,9] | 2002 | 2 467 | 468 | ... | 1 999[5] | ... | ... | ... |
| Myanmar[1]<br>Myanmar[1] | 2001 | 4 373 | 574 | ... | 3 754 | ... | 46 | ... |
| | 2002 | 7 418 | 837 | ... | 6 499 | ... | 82 | ... |
| Nepal[2,6] — Népal[2,6] | 2002 | 13 500 | 3 000 | 450 | 6 000 | ... | 4 500 | ... |
| Netherlands[2,4]<br>Pays-Bas[2,4] | 2002 | 109 224 | 46 730 | ... | 34 840 | ... | 27 654 | ... |
| | 2003 | 106 980 | 45 554 | 7 852 | 34 893 | 7 767 | 26 533 | 9 593 |
| | *2004[6] | 118 104 | 52 505 | ... | 35 999 | ... | 29 600 | ... |
| | *2005[6] | 113 606 | 49 831 | 8 986 | 36 732 | 8 475 | 27 043 | 10 077 |
| New Zealand[2,4]<br>Nouvelle-Zélande[2,4] | 2001 | 30 183 | 22 045 | 8 657 | 4 200 | 1 617 | 3 938 | 2 789 |
| | 2003 | 36 875 | 25 486 | ... | 5 554 | ... | 5 835 | ... |
| | 2005 | 37 311 | 27 569 | ... | 5 304 | ... | 4 438 | ... |
| Nicaragua[2,3]<br>Nicaragua[2,3] | 2002 | 456 | 256 | 96[9] | 200[5] | ... | ... | ... |
| | 2004 | 371 | 326 | ... | #45 | 15[5] | ... | ... |
| Niger[1]<br>Niger[1] | 2001 | 611 | 109 | ... | 122 | ... | 380 | ... |
| | 2002 | 594 | 104 | ... | 118 | ... | 372 | ... |
| | 2003 | 569 | 100 | ... | 115 | ... | 354 | ... |
| | 2004 | 599 | 106 | ... | 133 | ... | 360 | ... |
| | 2005 | 595 | 101 | ... | 137 | ... | 357 | ... |
| Nigeria[1,2]<br>Nigéria[1,2] | 2001 | 50 229 | 19 447 | 3 691 | 9 261 | ... | 21 521 | ... |
| | 2002 | 50 271 | 18 973 | 3 475 | 8 986 | ... | 22 312 | ... |
| | 2003 | 55 556 | 22 690 | 4 246 | 9 107 | ... | 23 759 | ... |
| | 2004 | ... | 24 727 | 4 286 | 9 847 | ... | ... | ... |
| | 2005 | 66 574 | 28 533 | 4 839 | 10 854 | ... | 27 187 | ... |
| Norway[2,4]<br>Norvège[2,4] | 2001 | 48 691 | 34 864 | 9 883 | ... | ... | ... | ... |
| | 2002 | 51 086 | ... | ... | ... | ... | ... | ... |
| | 2003 | 51 175 | 35 700 | 10 505 | ... | ... | ... | ... |
| | 2005 | 54 341 | 36 998 | 11 740 | ... | ... | ... | ... |
| Pakistan[2]<br>Pakistan[2] | 2002 | ... | 12 820[8] | 1 332[9] | ... | ... | ... | ... |
| | 2005 | 101 789 | 30 982 | 7 261 | 8 659 | ... | 62 148 | ... |
| Panama[2,3]<br>Panama[2,3] | 2000 | 1 196 | 446 | 176 | 750[5] | 285[5] | ... | ... |
| | 2001 | 1 530 | 841 | 297 | 689[5] | 231[5] | ... | ... |
| | 2002 | 1 249 | 416 | 154 | 833[5] | 319[5] | ... | ... |
| | 2003 | 1 319 | 432 | 158 | 887[5] | 347[5] | ... | ... |
| | #2004 | 1 441 | 484 | 199 | 332 | 130 | 625 | 238 |
| | 2005 | 1 802 | 507 | 151 | 386 | 146 | 909 | 365 |
| Paraguay[2,3]<br>Paraguay[2,3] | 2001 | 1 358 | 587 | 294 | 771[5] | 471[5] | ... | ... |
| | 2002 | 1 721 | 794 | 398 | 927[5] | 515[5] | ... | ... |
| | 2003 | 1 734 | 800 | 406 | 934[5] | 504[5] | ... | ... |
| | 2004 | 1 873 | 864 | 444 | 1 009[5] | 525[5] | ... | ... |
| | 2005 | ... | 787 | ... | ... | ... | ... | ... |

| Country or area<br>Pays ou zone | Year<br>Année | Total R & D<br>personnel<br>Total du<br>personnel<br>de R - D | Researchers<br>Chercheurs<br>Total M & W<br>Total H & F | Women<br>Femmes | Technicians and<br>equivalent staff<br>Techniciens et<br>personnel assimilé<br>Total M & W<br>Total H & F | Women<br>Femmes | Other<br>supporting staff<br>Autre personnel<br>de soutien<br>Total M & W<br>Total H & F | Women<br>Femmes |
|---|---|---|---|---|---|---|---|---|
| Peru[2,3] — Pérou[2,3] | 2004 | 8 434 | 4 965 | ... | 1 757 | ... | 1 712 | ... |
| Philippines[2] | 2002 | 9 325 | 7 203 | 3 893 | 956 | ... | 1 166 | ... |
| Philippines[2] | 2003 | 13 488 | 8 866 | 4 674 | 1 245 | ... | 3 377 | ... |
| Poland[2,4] | 2000 | 125 614 | 88 189 | 33 572 | 20 298 | 10 578 | 17 127 | 10 176 |
| Pologne[2,4] | 2001 | 123 840 | 89 596 | ... | 18 279 | ... | 15 965 | ... |
| | 2002 | 122 987 | 90 842 | ... | 17 458 | ... | 14 687 | ... |
| | 2003 | 126 241 | 94 432 | 37 065 | 16 876 | 8 430 | 14 933 | 9 799 |
| | 2004 | 127 356 | 96 531 | 37 594 | 15 686 | 7 844 | 15 139 | 9 865 |
| | 2005 | 123 431 | 97 875 | 38 426 | 13 989 | 6 613 | 11 567 | 7 606 |
| Portugal[2,4] | 2000[6] | 38 018 | 29 761 | 12 914 | 4 360 | ... | 3 897 | ... |
| Portugal[2,4] | 2001 | 39 163 | 31 146 | 13 572 | 4 464 | ... | 3 553 | ... |
| | 2002[6] | 41 601 | 33 501 | 14 734 | 4 623 | ... | 3 477 | ... |
| | 2003 | 44 036 | 35 855 | 15 895 | 4 780 | 1 881 | 3 401 | 1 786 |
| | 2004[6] | 44 311 | 36 812 | 16 326 | 4 500 | 1 780 | 2 999 | 1 576 |
| | 2005 | 44 585 | 37 769 | 16 757 | 4 220 | 1 679 | 2 596 | 1 365 |
| Romania[2,4] | 2000 | 37 241 | 23 179 | 9 841 | 6 754 | 3 982 | 7 308 | 3 291 |
| Roumanie[2,4] | 2001 | 37 696 | 23 597 | 10 107 | 6 243 | 3 565 | 7 856 | 3 839 |
| | 2002 | 38 433 | 24 636 | 10 886 | 6 744 | 3 655 | 7 053 | 3 277 |
| | 2003 | 39 985 | 25 968 | 11 179 | 5 753 | 3 329 | 8 264 | 3 826 |
| | 2004 | 40 725 | 27 253 | 11 632 | 5 734 | 3 305 | 7 738 | 3 415 |
| | 2005 | 41 035 | 29 608 | 13 409 | 5 569 | 3 204 | 5 858 | 2 667 |
| | 2006 | ... | 30 122 | 13 035 | ... | ... | ... | ... |
| Russian Federation[2,4,9] | 2000 | 887 729 | 425 954 | 187 792 | 75 184 | ... | 386 591 | ... |
| Fédération de Russie[2,4,9] | 2001 | 885 568 | 422 176 | 185 609 | 75 416 | ... | 387 976 | ... |
| | 2002 | 870 878 | 414 676 | 179 120 | 74 599 | ... | 381 603 | ... |
| | 2003 | 858 470 | 409 775 | 177 538 | 71 729 | ... | 376 966 | ... |
| | 2004 | 839 338 | 401 425 | 172 177 | 69 963 | ... | 367 950 | ... |
| | 2005 | 813 207 | 391 121 | 165 993 | 65 982 | ... | 356 104 | ... |
| | 2006 | 818 877 | 390 835 | 164 521 | 73 901 | ... | 354 141 | ... |
| Saint Helena[1] — Sainte-Hélène[1] | 2000 | 33 | 2 | ... | 8 | 4 | 23 | |
| Saint Vincent-Grenadines[2] | 2001 | 129 | 20 | ... | 109 | ... | ... | ... |
| Saint Vincent-Grenadines[2] | 2002 | 131 | 21 | ... | 110 | ... | ... | ... |
| Saudi Arabia[1,2] | 2000 | 3 601 | 1 218 | 220 | 1 427 | ... | 956 | ... |
| Arabie saoudite[1,2] | 2001 | 3 708 | 1 239 | 225[9] | 1 498 | ... | 971 | ... |
| | 2002 | 4 182 | 1 513 | 263 | 1 674 | ... | 995 | ... |
| Senegal[1,2] — Sénégal[1,2] | 2005 | 4 200 | 2 349 | ... | 1 751 | ... | 100 | ... |
| Serbia and Montenegro[1,2,16] | 2000 | 23 117 | 11 969 | 4 815 | 5 448 | ... | 5 700 | ... |
| Serbie-et-Monténégro[1,2,16] | 2001 | 19 415 | 10 071 | 4 246 | 4 518 | ... | 4 826 | ... |
| | 2002 | 21 291 | 10 855 | 4 663 | 4 631 | ... | 5 805 | ... |
| | 2003 | 22 054 | 11 353 | 4 968 | 4 732 | ... | 5 969 | ... |
| | 2004 | 22 485 | 11 637 | 5 071 | 4 844 | ... | 6 004 | ... |
| | 2005 | 22 641 | 11 551 | 5 050 | 4 894 | ... | 6 196 | ... |
| Seychelles[1] — Seychelles[1] | 2005 | 180 | 13 | 4 | 53 | ... | 114 | ... |
| Singapore[2,4] | 2000 | 25 220 | 20 800 | ... | 2 262 | ... | 2 158 | ... |
| Singapour[2,4] | 2001 | 25 162 | 20 645 | ... | 2 371 | ... | 2 146 | ... |
| | 2002 | 26 824 | 21 531 | 5 517 | 2 398 | 953 | 2 895 | 1 701 |
| | 2003 | 28 825 | 23 513 | 5 938 | 2 549 | 1 009 | 2 763 | 1 823 |
| | 2004 | 31 006 | 25 251 | 6 506 | 2 823 | 1 121 | 2 932 | 1 901 |
| | 2005 | 34 522 | 27 969 | 7 346 | 3 265 | 1 326 | 3 288 | 2 095 |
| | 2006 | ... | 29 478 | 7 986 | ... | ... | ... | ... |

| Country or area<br>Pays ou zone | Year<br>Année | Total R & D<br>personnel<br>Total du<br>personnel<br>de R - D | Researchers<br>Chercheurs | | Technicians and<br>equivalent staff<br>Techniciens et<br>personnel assimilé | | Other<br>supporting staff<br>Autre personnel<br>de soutien | |
|---|---|---|---|---|---|---|---|---|
| | | | Total M & W<br>Total H & F | Women<br>Femmes | Total M & W<br>Total H & F | Women<br>Femmes | Total M & W<br>Total H & F | Women<br>Femmes |
| Slovakia[2,4]<br>Slovaquie[2,4] | 2000 | 22 256 | 15 747 | ... | 4 406 | ... | 2 103 | ... |
| | 2001 | 21 997 | 15 923 | ... | 4 108 | ... | 1 966 | ... |
| | 2002 | 21 025 | 15 385 | 6 086 | 3 792 | 1 965 | 1 848 | 1 048 |
| | 2003 | 20 928 | 16 108 | 6 543 | 3 229 | 1 836 | 1 591 | 921 |
| | 2004 | 22 217 | 17 354 | 7 152 | 3 108 | 1 659 | 1 755 | 839 |
| | 2005 | 22 294 | 17 526 | 7 268 | 2 986 | 1 557 | 1 782 | 837 |
| | 2006 | ... | 18 816 | 7 856 | ... | ... | ... | ... |
| Slovenia[2,4]<br>Slovénie[2,4] | 2000 | 12 220 | 6 562 | 2 358 | 4 220 | 1 764 | 1 438 | 840 |
| | 2001 | 12 349 | 6 740 | 2 383 | 4 195 | 1 755 | 1 414 | 833 |
| | 2002 | 12 379 | 7 027 | 2 466 | 4 131 | 1 660 | 1 221 | 682 |
| | 2003 | 9 506 | 5 428 | 1 748 | 3 101 | 1 196 | 977 | 557 |
| | 2004 | 10 155 | 5 842 | 1 900 | 3 260 | 1 303 | 1 053 | 595 |
| | 2005 | 12 600 | 7 644 | 2 659 | 3 694 | 1 543 | 1 262 | 714 |
| | 2006 | ... | 8 213 | 2 904 | ... | ... | ... | ... |
| South Africa[2]<br>Afrique du Sud[2] | 2001 | 40 008 | 26 913 | 9 700 | 5 139 | 1 594[4] | 7 956 | 3 488[4] |
| | 2003 | 48 552 | 30 707 | 11 658 | 8 193 | 3 174[4] | 9 652 | 4 167[4] |
| | 2004 | 56 453 | 37 001 | 14 152 | 8 641 | 2 892[4] | 10 811 | 4 797[4] |
| | 2005[4] | 57 275 | 39 266 | 15 598 | 8 325 | 2 831 | 9 684 | 4 683 |
| Spain[2,4]<br>Espagne[2,4] | 2001 | 209 011 | 140 407 | 49 664 | 36 856 | 10 667 | 31 748 | 14 561 |
| | 2002 | 232 019 | 150 098 | 52 850 | 43 420 | 14 197 | 38 501 | 18 051 |
| | 2003 | 249 969 | 158 566 | 57 515 | 49 562 | 16 257 | 41 841 | 19 443 |
| | 2004 | 267 943 | 169 971 | 61 377 | 53 669 | 18 005 | 44 303 | 20 443 |
| | 2005 | 282 804 | 181 023 | 66 418 | 55 833 | 18 892 | 45 948 | 21 385 |
| Sri Lanka[2]<br>Sri Lanka[2] | #2000[1] | 16 851 | 7 807 | 1 294[9] | 1 551 | ... | 7 493 | ... |
| | 2004 | 9 705 | 4 602 | 1 628 | 2 034 | ... | 3 069 | ... |
| Sudan[2]<br>Soudan[2] | 2000 | 15 333 | 7 500 | 1 644[6] | 3 028 | ... | 4 805 | ... |
| | 2001 | 16 050 | 7 850 | 1 664[6] | 3 170 | ... | 5 030 | ... |
| | 2002 | 18 604 | 9 100 | 2 754[6] | 3 674 | ... | 5 830 | ... |
| | 2003 | 18 808 | 9 200 | 2 784[6] | 3 714 | ... | 5 894 | ... |
| | 2004 | 19 772 | 9 340 | 2 830[6] | 4 641 | ... | 5 791 | ... |
| | 2005 | 23 726 | 11 208 | ... | 5 569 | ... | 6 949 | ... |
| Sweden[4]<br>Suède[4] | 2001 | 72 190 | 45 995 | ... | ... | ... | ... | ... |
| | 2003 | 72 978 | 48 186 | ... | ... | ... | ... | ... |
| | 2004[5] | 72 459 | 48 784 | ... | ... | ... | ... | ... |
| | 2005 | #77 704 | #55 090 | 16 002[12] | ... | ... | ... | ... |
| | 2006 | 78 715 | 55 729 | ... | ... | ... | ... | ... |
| Switzerland[2,4]<br>Suisse[2,4] | 2000 | 86 990 | 44 230 | 8 985 | 20 300 | 3 885 | 22 460 | 11 235 |
| | 2004 | 84 090 | 43 220 | 11 555 | 19 775 | 3 590 | 21 095 | 10 960 |
| Tajikistan[2]<br>Tadjikistan[2] | 2001 | 2 799 | 1 845 | 908 | 391 | ... | 563 | ... |
| | 2002 | 2 628 | 1 752 | 701 | 312 | ... | 564 | ... |
| | 2003 | 2 425 | 1 544 | 438 | 270 | ... | 611 | ... |
| | 2004 | 2 487 | 1 548 | 407 | 247 | ... | 692 | ... |
| | 2005 | 3 220 | 1 993 | ... | 324 | ... | 903 | ... |
| Thailand[2]<br>Thaïlande[2] | 2001 | 65 859 | 30 941 | ... | 21 713 | ... | 13 205 | ... |
| | 2003 | 76 184 | 29 850 | 13 607 | 27 467 | ... | 18 867 | ... |
| TFYR of Macedonia<br>L'ex-R.y. Macédoine | 2000 | 1 786 | 1 325 | 635 | 233 | ... | 228 | ... |
| | 2001 | 1 630 | 1 240 | 596 | 199 | ... | 191 | ... |
| | 2002 | 1 518 | 1 164 | 571 | 140 | ... | 214 | ... |
| | 2003 | 1 464 | 1 118 | 557 | 137 | ... | 209 | ... |
| | 2004 | 1 447 | 1 069 | 538 | 195 | ... | 183 | ... |
| | 2005 | 1 434 | 1 113 | 576 | 168 | ... | 153 | ... |

| Country or area<br>Pays ou zone | Year<br>Année | Total R & D personnel<br>Total du personnel de R - D | Researchers<br>Chercheurs | | Technicians and equivalent staff<br>Techniciens et personnel assimilé | | Other supporting staff<br>Autre personnel de soutien | |
|---|---|---|---|---|---|---|---|---|
| | | | Total M & W<br>Total H & F | Women<br>Femmes | Total M & W<br>Total H & F | Women<br>Femmes | Total M & W<br>Total H & F | Women<br>Femmes |
| Trinidad and Tobago[2,3] | 2000 | 1 589 | 447 | 153 | 1 142 | 445 | ... | ... |
| Trinité-et-Tobago[2,3] | 2001 | ... | 509 | 192 | ... | ... | ... | ... |
| | 2003 | ... | 518 | 208 | ... | ... | ... | ... |
| | 2004 | #908 | 550 | 213 | #358 | #132 | ... | ... |
| | 2005 | 1 103 | 603 | 203 | 500 | 229 | ... | ... |
| Tunisia | 2000 | 9 229 | 7 516 | ... | 341 | ... | 1 372 | ... |
| Tunisie | 2001 | 10 090 | 8 515 | ... | 294 | ... | 1 281 | ... |
| | 2002 | 11 510 | 9 910 | ... | 329 | ... | 1 271 | ... |
| | 2003 | 12 857 | 11 265 | 5 471 | 357 | ... | 1 235 | ... |
| | 2004 | 14 556 | 12 950 | 6 145 | 379 | ... | 1 227 | ... |
| | 2005 | 16 289 | 14 650 | 6 995 | 413 | ... | 1 226 | ... |
| Turkey[2,4] | 2000 | 76 074 | 67 512 | 23 173 | 4 345 | 901 | 4 217 | 954 |
| Turquie[2,4] | 2001 | 75 960[9] | 67 190 | 23 663 | 3 851[9] | 688[9] | 4 919[9] | 1 026[9] |
| | 2002 | 79 958[9] | 71 288 | 25 407 | 3 728[9] | 672[9] | 4 942[9] | 1 059[9] |
| | 2003 | 83 281[9] | 74 520 | 26 738 | 4 344[9] | 759[9] | 4 417[9] | 983[9] |
| | 2004 | 86 680[9] | 77 110 | 28 075 | 4 709[9] | 867[9] | 4 861[9] | 1 066[9] |
| | 2005 | 97 355[9] | 83 856 | 30 239 | 6 324[9] | 1 236[9] | 7 175[9] | 1 309[9] |
| | 2006 | ... | 90 118 | 32 686 | ... | ... | ... | ... |
| Uganda[2] | 2000 | 1 187 | 549 | 206 | 330 | ... | 308 | ... |
| Ouganda[2] | 2001 | 1 278 | 568 | 213 | 366 | ... | 344 | ... |
| | 2002 | 1 370 | 630 | 236 | 384 | ... | 356 | ... |
| | 2003 | 1 468 | 675 | 253 | 411 | ... | 382 | ... |
| | 2004 | 1 573 | 724 | 272 | 440 | ... | 409 | ... |
| | 2005 | 1 686 | 776 | 291 | 472 | ... | 438 | ... |
| Ukraine[2] | 2000 | 156 372 | 89 192 | ... | 31 536 | ... | 35 644 | ... |
| Ukraine[2] | 2001 | 147 116 | 86 366 | 36 164 | 26 975 | ... | 33 775 | ... |
| | 2002 | 142 763 | 85 211 | 36 557 | 22 236 | ... | 35 316 | ... |
| | 2003 | 139 470 | 83 890 | 36 174 | 20 951 | ... | 34 629 | ... |
| | 2004 | 140 284 | 85 742 | 37 634 | 20 861 | ... | 33 681 | ... |
| | 2005 | 137 564 | 85 246 | 37 586 | 20 266 | ... | 32 052 | ... |
| United Kingdom[4,17] | 2000 | 298 955 | 161 352 | ... | ... | ... | ... | ... |
| Royaume-Uni[4,17] | 2001 | 311 982 | 167 019 | ... | ... | ... | ... | ... |
| | 2002 | 321 543 | 174 433 | ... | ... | ... | ... | ... |
| | 2003 | 319 239 | 178 035 | ... | ... | ... | ... | ... |
| | 2004 | 315 963 | 176 040 | ... | ... | ... | ... | ... |
| | 2005 | 323 358 | 180 450 | ... | ... | ... | ... | ... |
| | 2006 | 334 686 | 183 535 | ... | ... | ... | ... | ... |
| United States[4,17] | 2000 | ... | 1 289 782 | ... | ... | ... | ... | ... |
| Etats-Unis[4,17] | 2001 | ... | 1 319 705 | ... | ... | ... | ... | ... |
| | 2002 | ... | 1 340 454 | ... | ... | ... | ... | ... |
| | 2003 | ... | 1 390 301 | ... | ... | ... | ... | ... |
| | 2004 | ... | 1 415 873 | ... | ... | ... | ... | ... |
| | 2005 | ... | 1 394 682 | ... | ... | ... | ... | ... |
| United States Virgin Is.[1] | 2000 | 33 | 11 | 2 | 6 | ... | 16 | ... |
| Iles Vierges américaines[1] | #2001 | 36 | 6 | 0 | 15 | ... | 15 | ... |
| | 2002 | 36 | 6 | 0 | 15 | ... | 15 | ... |
| | 2003 | 37 | 6 | 0 | 15 | ... | 16 | ... |
| | 2004 | 38 | 7 | 0 | 15 | ... | 16 | ... |
| | 2005 | 39 | 8 | 0 | 15 | ... | 16 | ... |

| Country or area / Pays ou zone | Year / Année | Total R & D personnel / Total du personnel de R - D | Researchers / Chercheurs Total M & W / Total H & F | Women / Femmes | Technicians and equivalent staff / Techniciens et personnel assimilé Total M & W / Total H & F | Women / Femmes | Other supporting staff / Autre personnel de soutien Total M & W / Total H & F | Women / Femmes |
|---|---|---|---|---|---|---|---|---|
| Uruguay[2,3] | 2000 | 3 602 | 2 892 | 1 261 | 710[5] | 261[5] | ... | ... |
| Uruguay[2,3] | 2002 | 4 323 | 3 839 | 1 813 | 484[5] | 114[5] | ... | ... |
| Venezuela (Bolivarian Rep. of)[2,3,6] | 2000 | 17 525 | 16 692 | 4 645 | 833[5] | 543[5] | ... | ... |
| Venezuela (Rép. bolivarienne du)[2,3,6] | 2001 | 16 336 | 15 568 | 5 063 | 768[5] | 504[5] | ... | ... |
| | 2002 | 21 981 | 20 946 | 6 539 | 1 036[5] | 639[5] | ... | ... |
| | 2003 | 21 506 | 20 495 | 6 353 | 1 011[5] | 631[5] | ... | ... |
| | 2004 | 35 470 | 33 803 | 11 057 | 1 666[5] | 1 087[5] | ... | ... |
| | 2005 | 37 208 | 35 462 | 18 941 | 1 747[5] | 1 134[5] | ... | ... |
| Viet Nam — Viet Nam | 2002 | 11 356 | 9 328 | ... | ... | ... | ... | ... |
| Zambia[1,2] | #2002 | 1 084 | 268 | 31 | 276 | ... | 540 | ... |
| Zambie[1,2] | 2003 | 1 141 | 288 | 36 | 295 | ... | 558 | ... |
| | 2004 | 1 307 | 356 | 79 | 376 | ... | 575 | ... |
| | 2005 | 3 285 | 792 | 116 | 1 240 | ... | 1 253 | ... |

Source

United Nations Educational, Scientific and Cultural Organization (UNESCO) Institute for Statistics, Montreal, the UNESCO Institute of Statistics database, last accessed June 2008.

Notes

1 Partial data.
2 Head count instead of Full-time equivalent.
3 Source : "Red Ibero Americana de Indicadores de Ciencia y Tecnologia (RICYT)".
4 Source: OECD.
5 Including other supporting staff.
6 National estimation.
7 Source: EUROSTAT.
8 UIS estimation.
9 Underestimated or based on underestimated data.
10 For statistical purposes, the data for China do not include those for the Hong Kong Special Administrative Region (Hong Kong SAR) and Macao Special Administrative Region (Macao SAR).
11 EUROSTAT estimation.
12 University graduates instead of researchers.
13 Included elsewhere.
14 Defence excluded (all or mostly).
15 Overestimated or based on overestimated data.
16 Data exclude Montenegro and Kosovo.
17 OECD estimation.

Source

L'Institut de statistique de l'Organisation des Nations Unies pour l'éducation, la science et la culture (UNESCO), Montréal, la base de données de l'Institut de statistique de l'UNESCO, dernier accès juin 2008.

Notes

1 Données partielles.
2 Personnes physiques au lieu d'Equivalent temps plein.
3 Source : "Red IberoAmericana de Indicadores de Ciencia y Tecnologia (RICYT)".
4 Source : OCDE.
5 Y compris autre personnel de soutien.
6 Estimation nationale.
7 Source: EUROSTAT.
8 Estimation de l'ISU.
9 Sous-estimé ou basé sur des données sous-estimées.
10 Pour la présentation des statistiques, les données pour la Chine ne comprennent pas la Région Administrative Spéciale de Hong Kong (Hong Kong RAS) et la Région Administrative Spéciale de Macao (Macao RAS).
11 Estimation de EUROSTAT.
12 Diplômes universitaires au lieu de chercheurs.
13 Inclus ailleurs.
14 A l'exclusion de la défense (en totalité ou en grande partie).
15 Surestimé ou fondé sur des données surestimées.
16 Les données excluent celles de Monténégro et Kosovo.
17 Estimation de l'OCDE.

# 54

## Gross domestic expenditure on R & D by source of funds
National currency and percentage distribution

## Dépenses intérieures brutes de recherche et développement par source de financement
Monnaie nationale et répartition en pourcentage

| Country or area (monetary unit) / Pays ou zone (unité monétaire) | Year / Année | Gross domestic expenditure on R&D (000) / Dépenses int. brutes de R-D (000) | Source of funds (%) / Source de financement (%) | | | | | |
|---|---|---|---|---|---|---|---|---|
| | | | Business enterprises / Entreprises | Govern-ment / Etat | Higher education / Enseigne-ment supérieur | Private non-profit / Institut. privées sans but lucratif | Funds from abroad / Fonds de l'étranger | Not distributed / Non répartis |
| Algeria (Algerian dinar)[1] Algérie (dinar algérien)[1] | 2003 | 10 306 455 | ... | ... | ... | ... | ... | ... |
| | 2004 | 10 058 086 | ... | ... | ... | ... | ... | ... |
| | 2005 | 4 994 000 | ... | ... | ... | ... | ... | ... |
| American Samoa (US dollar)[1] Samoa américaines (dollar des Etats-Unis)[1] | 2001 | 1 117 | ... | ... | ... | ... | ... | ... |
| Argentina (Argentine peso) Argentine (peso argentin) | 2004[2] | 1 958 700 | 30.7 | 64.5 | 2.0 | 1.7 | 1.1 | 0.0 |
| | 2005[2] | 2 451 000 | 31.0 | 65.3 | 1.4 | 1.5 | 0.8 | 0.0 |
| | 2006[3] | 3 237 000 | 29.4 | 66.7 | 1.6 | 1.6 | 0.8 | 0.0 |
| Armenia (dram)[1] Arménie (dram)[1] | 2003 | 3 894 500 | ... | 48.7 | ... | ... | 11.7 | 39.6 |
| | 2004 | 4 045 100 | ... | 51.8 | ... | ... | 9.2 | 39.0 |
| | 2005 | 4 814 400 | ... | 53.8 | ... | ... | 5.7 | 40.5 |
| Australia (Australian dollar)[3] Australie (dollar australien)[3] | 2000 | 10 417 100 | 46.3 | 45.5 | 0.1 | 4.6 | 3.5 | 0.0 |
| | 2002 | 13 211 600 | 50.7 | 41.2 | 0.2 | #1.7 | 3.6 | 2.7[4] |
| | 2004 | 15 974 900 | 53.0 | 40.5 | 0.4 | 1.7 | 2.8 | 1.6[4] |
| Austria (euro)[3,5] Autriche (euro)[3,5] | 2005 | 5 923 790 | 45.5 | 36.5 | ... | 0.4 | 17.6 | ... |
| | 2006 | 6 323 950 | 46.4 | 36.6 | ... | 0.4 | 16.6 | ... |
| | 2007 | 6 833 560 | 46.7 | 37.4 | ... | 0.4 | 15.5 | ... |
| Azerbaijan (manat) Azerbaïdjan (manat) | 2003 | 23 223[6] | 24.7 | 71.4 | 0.0 | 3.8 | 0.0 | 0.0 |
| | 2004 | 25 446[6] | 23.0 | 74.4 | 0.0 | 1.3 | 1.3 | 0.0 |
| | 2005 | 27 542[6] | 18.7 | 77.5 | 0.0 | 1.3 | 2.4 | 0.0 |
| Belarus (Belarussian rouble) Bélarus (rouble bélarussien) | 2003 | 223 582 700 | 21.1 | 69.1 | 2.4 | 0.0 | 7.5 | 0.0 |
| | 2004 | 313 745 800 | 20.3 | 69.7 | 2.4 | 0.0 | 7.6 | 0.0 |
| | 2005 | 441 491 000 | 21.2 | 71.9 | 0.7 | 0.0 | 6.3 | 0.0 |
| Belgium (euro)[3] Belgique (euro)[3] | 2004 | 5 403 617 | 60.2 | 24.4 | 2.6 | 0.5 | 12.3 | 0.0 |
| | 2005 | 5 551 553 | 59.7 | 24.7 | 2.6 | 0.6 | 12.4 | 0.0 |
| | *2006 | 5 797 535 | ... | ... | ... | ... | ... | ... |
| Bermuda (Bermuda dollar) Bermudes (dollar des Bermudes) | 1997 | 1 726 | ... | ... | ... | ... | ... | ... |
| Bolivia (boliviano)[2] Bolivie (boliviano)[2] | 2000 | 149 261 | 22.0 | 22.0 | 32.0 | 15.0 | 9.0 | 0.0 |
| | 2001 | 157 920 | 18.0 | 21.0 | 33.0 | 17.0 | 11.0 | 0.0 |
| | 2002 | 156 801 | 16.0 | 20.0 | 31.0 | 19.0 | 14.0 | 0.0 |
| Botswana (pula)[7] Botswana (pula)[7] | 2005 | 205 567 | ... | ... | ... | ... | ... | ... |
| Brazil (real)[2] Brésil (real)[2] | 2003 | 15 042 200 | 39.2 | 58.7 | 2.1 | ... | ... | ... |
| | 2004 | 16 116 800 | 39.9 | 57.9 | 2.2 | ... | ... | ... |
| | 2005 | 17 715 300 | 39.4 | 58.3 | 2.3 | ... | ... | ... |
| Brunei Darussalam (Brunei dollar)[4] Brunéi Darussalam (dollar du Brunéi)[4] | 2002 | 1 666 | ... | ... | ... | ... | ... | ... |
| | 2003 | 2 104 | ... | ... | ... | ... | ... | ... |
| Bulgaria (lev)[8] Bulgarie (lev)[8] | 2004 | 194 000 | 28.2 | 65.8 | 0.3 | 0.2 | 5.5 | 0.0 |
| | 2005 | 208 142 | 27.8 | 63.9 | 0.4 | 0.3 | 7.6 | 0.0 |
| | 2006 | 237 036 | ... | ... | ... | ... | ... | ... |
| Burkina Faso (CFA franc)[1] Burkina Faso (franc CFA)[1] | 2003 | 6 628 789 | ... | 100.0 | ... | ... | ... | ... |
| | 2004 | 6 185 018 | ... | 100.0 | ... | ... | ... | ... |
| | 2005 | 4 914 954 | ... | 100.0 | ... | ... | ... | ... |
| Cambodia (riel)[1,5] Cambodge (riel)[1,5] | 2002 | 8 357 010 | 0.0 | 17.9 | 0.0 | 43.0 | 28.4 | 10.6 |
| Canada (Canadian dollar)[3] Canada (dollar canadien)[3] | 2004 | 26 003 000 | 49.0 | 32.0[5] | 7.2[5] | 2.8 | 9.0 | 0.0 |
| | 2005 | *27 174 000 | *47.9 | *32.9[5] | *7.5[5] | *2.9 | *8.7 | 0.0 |
| | 2006 | *28 357 000 | *46.7 | *33.7[5] | *7.9[5] | *3.1 | *8.5 | 0.0 |

**54** Gross domestic expenditure on R & D by source of funds—National currency and percentage distribution (*continued*)

Dépenses intérieures brutes de recherche et développement par source de financement—Monnaie nationale et répartition en pourcentage (*suite*)

| Country or area (monetary unit)<br>Pays ou zone (unité monétaire) | Year<br>Année | Gross domestic expenditure on R&D (000)<br>Dépenses int. brutes de R-D (000) | Business enterprises<br>Entreprises | Govern-ment<br>Etat | Higher education<br>Enseigne-ment supérieur | Private non-profit<br>Institut. privées sans but lucratif | Funds from abroad<br>Fonds de l'étranger | Not distributed<br>Non répartis |
|---|---|---|---|---|---|---|---|---|
| Chile (Chilean peso)[2] | #2002 | 315 638 375 | 33.2 | 54.6 | 0.4 | 0.3 | 11.3 | 0.0 |
| Chili (peso chilien)[2] | 2003 | 341 176 371 | 43.5 | 43.3 | 0.8 | 0.4 | 12.0 | 0.0 |
| | 2004 | 392 866 683 | 45.7 | 44.5 | 0.8 | 0.3 | 8.7 | 0.0 |
| China (yuan)[3] | 2004 | 196 633 000 | 65.7 | 26.6 | ... | ... | 1.3 | 6.4[4] |
| Chine (yuan)[3] | 2005 | 244 997 310 | 67.0 | 26.3 | ... | ... | 0.9 | 5.7[4] |
| | 2006 | 300 309 660 | 69.1 | 24.7 | ... | ... | 1.6 | 4.6[4] |
| China, Hong Kong SAR (Hong Kong dollar) | 2002 | 7 543 600 | 35.3[9] | 62.8 | 0.2 | 0.0[10] | 1.7 | 0.0 |
| Chine, Hong Kong RAS (dollar de Hong Kong) | 2003 | 8 548 800 | 42.6[9] | 55.0 | 0.3 | 0.0[10] | 2.1 | 0.0 |
| | 2004 | 9 505 200 | 47.8[9] | 47.0 | 0.1 | 0.0[10] | 5.1 | 0.0 |
| China, Macao SAR (Macao pataca)[1,5] | 2003 | 41 303 | ... | ... | ... | ... | ... | ... |
| Chine, Macao RAS (pataca de Macao)[1,5] | 2004 | 45 629 | ... | ... | ... | ... | ... | ... |
| | 2005 | 97 850 | ... | ... | ... | ... | ... | ... |
| Colombia (Colombian peso)[2] | 1999 | 302 038 500 | 45.0 | 24.0 | 29.0 | 2.0 | ... | ... |
| Colombie (peso colombien)[2] | 2000 | 306 385 210 | 48.4 | 16.6 | 33.6 | 1.4 | ... | ... |
| | 2001 | 313 720 990 | 46.9 | 13.2 | 38.3 | 1.7 | ... | ... |
| Costa Rica (Costa Rican colón)[2] | 2000 | 19 033 194 | ... | ... | ... | ... | ... | ... |
| Costa Rica (colón costa-ricien)[2] | 2003 | 24 918 750 | ... | ... | ... | ... | ... | ... |
| | 2004 | 30 390 300 | ... | ... | ... | ... | ... | ... |
| Croatia (kuna)[8] | 2004 | 2 586 000 | 43.0 | 46.6 | 7.9 | ... | 2.6 | 0.0 |
| Croatie (kuna)[8] | 2005 | 2 312 100 | 34.3 | 58.1 | 4.9 | 0.0 | 2.6 | 0.0 |
| | 2006 | 2 179 000 | 34.6 | 55.8 | 2.5 | 0.3 | 6.8 | 0.0 |
| Cuba (Cuban peso)[2] | 2003 | 209 100 | 35.0 | 60.0 | ... | ... | 5.0 | ... |
| Cuba (peso cubain)[2] | 2004 | 230 100 | 35.0 | 60.0 | ... | ... | 5.0 | ... |
| | 2005 | 234 200 | 35.0 | 60.0 | ... | ... | 5.0 | ... |
| Cyprus (Cyprus pound)[8] | 2004 | 46 508[6] | 18.9 | 64.1 | 3.9 | 1.6 | 11.5 | 0.0 |
| Chypre (livre chypriote)[8] | 2005 | 54 438[6] | 16.8 | 67.0 | 4.2 | 1.2 | 10.9 | 0.0 |
| | 2006[6] | 60 826 | ... | ... | ... | ... | ... | ... |
| Czech Republic (Czech koruna)[3] | 2004 | 35 083 039 | 52.8 | 41.9 | 1.5 | 0.1 | 3.7 | 0.0 |
| République tchèque (couronne tchèque)[3] | 2005 | 42 198 423 | 54.1 | 40.9 | 1.1 | 0.0 | 4.0 | 0.0 |
| | 2006 | 49 900 270 | 56.9 | 39.0 | 1.0 | 0.0 | 3.1 | 0.0 |
| Dem. Rep. of the Congo (Congo franc)[1,7] | 2004 | 11 014 833 | ... | ... | ... | ... | ... | ... |
| Rép. dém. du Congo (franc congolais)[1,7] | 2005 | 16 116 424 | ... | ... | ... | ... | ... | ... |
| Denmark (Danish krone)[3] | 2004 | 36 432 619 | ... | ... | ... | ... | ... | ... |
| Danemark (couronne danoise)[3] | 2005 | 37 958 515 | 59.5 | 27.6 | ... | 2.8 | 10.1 | ... |
| | *2006 | 39 895 400 | ... | ... | ... | ... | ... | ... |
| Ecuador (US dollar)[2] | #2001 | 12 600 | ... | ... | ... | ... | ... | ... |
| Equateur (dollar des Etats-Unis)[2] | 2002 | 15 800 | ... | ... | ... | ... | ... | ... |
| | 2003 | 18 600 | ... | ... | ... | ... | ... | ... |
| Egypt (Egyptian pound)[1] | 1998 | 572 200 | ... | ... | ... | ... | ... | ... |
| Egypte (livre égyptienne)[1] | 1999 | 573 700 | ... | ... | ... | ... | ... | ... |
| | 2000 | 654 600 | ... | ... | ... | ... | ... | ... |
| El Salvador (El Salvadoran colón)[2]<br>El Salvador (cólon salvadorien)[2] | 1998 | 84 437 | 1.2 | 51.9 | 13.2 | 10.4 | 23.4 | 0.0 |
| Estonia (Estonian kroon)[8] | 2004 | 1 294 000 | 36.5 | 44.1 | 1.7 | 0.6 | 17.0 | 0.0 |
| Estonie (couronne estonienne)[8] | 2005 | 1 627 600 | 38.5 | 43.5 | 0.8 | 0.2 | 17.1 | 0.0 |
| | 2006 | *2 362 500 | *38.1 | *44.6 | *0.9 | *0.1 | *16.3 | 0.0 |
| Ethiopia (Ethiopian birr)[1]<br>Ethiopie (birr éthiopien)[1] | 2005 | 192 227 | ... | 69.2 | ... | 0.1 | 30.8 | ... |
| Finland (euro)[3] | 2005 | 5 473 700 | 66.9 | 25.7 | 0.2 | 1.0 | #6.3 | 0.0 |
| Finlande (euro)[3] | 2006 | 5 761 196 | 66.6 | 25.1 | 0.3 | 1.0 | 7.1 | 0.0 |
| | 2007[5] | 6 015 596 | ... | ... | ... | ... | ... | ... |
| France (euro)[3] | 2004 | #35 665 766 | #52.4 | #37.0 | #0.9 | #0.9 | #8.8 | 0.0 |
| France (euro)[3] | 2005 | 36 659 076 | 52.5 | 38.2 | 1.0 | 0.9 | 7.3 | 0.0 |
| | *2006 | 37 982 874 | ... | ... | ... | ... | ... | ... |

54 Gross domestic expenditure on R & D by source of funds—National currency and percentage distribution (*continued*)

Dépenses intérieures brutes de recherche et développement par source de financement—Monnaie nationale et répartition en pourcentage (*suite*)

| Country or area (monetary unit) / Pays ou zone (unité monétaire) | Year / Année | Gross domestic expenditure on R&D (000) / Dépenses int. brutes de R-D (000) | Source of funds (%) / Source de financement (%) | | | | | |
|---|---|---|---|---|---|---|---|---|
| | | | Business enterprises / Entreprises | Govern-ment / Etat | Higher education / Enseigne-ment supérieur | Private non-profit / Institut. privées sans but lucratif | Funds from abroad / Fonds de l'étranger | Not distributed / Non répartis |
| Georgia (lari) | 2003 | 18 635 | ... | ... | ... | ... | ... | ... |
| Géorgie (lari) | 2004 | 23 991 | ... | ... | ... | ... | ... | ... |
| | 2005 | 20 520 | ... | ... | ... | ... | ... | ... |
| Germany (euro)[3] | 2004 | 54 966 900 | 66.6 | 30.5 | ... | 0.4 | 2.5 | ... |
| Allemagne (euro)[3] | 2005 | 55 739 038 | 67.6 | 28.4 | ... | 0.3 | 3.7 | ... |
| | *2006 | 58 231 000 | ... | ... | ... | ... | ... | ... |
| Greece (euro)[3] | 2004[5] | 1 021 470 | ... | ... | ... | ... | ... | ... |
| Grèce (euro)[3] | 2005 | 1 153 170 | 31.0 | 47.0 | 1.7 | 1.5 | 18.8 | 0.0 |
| | 2006[5] | 1 222 600 | ... | ... | ... | ... | ... | ... |
| Greenland (Danish Krone) | 2002 | 54 345 | ... | ... | ... | ... | ... | ... |
| Groenland (couronne danoise) | 2003[5] | 52 169 | ... | ... | ... | ... | ... | ... |
| | 2004 | 70 543 | ... | ... | ... | ... | ... | ... |
| Guam (US dollar)[1] Guam (dollar des Etats-Unis)[1] | 2001 | 3 813 | ... | ... | ... | ... | ... | ... |
| Guatemala (quetzal)[1,2] Guatemala (quetzal)[1,2] | 2005 | 72 700 | ... | 42.1 | 57.9 | ... | ... | ... |
| Honduras (lempira)[2] | 2001 | 45 400 | ... | ... | ... | ... | ... | ... |
| Honduras (lempira)[2] | 2002 | 54 000 | ... | ... | ... | ... | ... | ... |
| | 2003 | 60 200 | ... | ... | ... | ... | ... | ... |
| Hungary (forint)[3] | 2004 | #181 525 400 | 37.1 | #51.8 | ... | 0.6 | 10.4 | 0.2[4] |
| Hongrie (forint)[3] | 2005 | 207 764 000 | 39.4 | 49.4 | ... | 0.3 | 10.7 | 0.1[4] |
| | 2006 | 237 953 200 | 43.3 | #44.8 | ... | 0.6 | 11.3 | ... |
| Iceland (Icelandic króna)[3] | 2002[5] | 24 097 031 | ... | ... | ... | ... | ... | ... |
| Islande (couronne islandaise)[3] | 2003 | 23 720 000 | 43.9 | 40.1 | 0.0 | 1.5 | 14.5 | 0.0 |
| | 2005 | 28 443 011 | 48.0 | 40.5 | 0.0 | 0.3 | 11.2 | 0.0 |
| India (Indian rupee) | 2002 | 180 001 600 | 20.3[9] | 75.6 | 4.2 | 0.0[10] | ... | ... |
| Inde (roupie indienne) | 2003 | 197 269 900[5] | 20.0[5,9] | 75.4[5] | 4.5[5] | 0.0[10] | ... | ... |
| | 2004 | 216 395 800[5] | 19.8[5,9] | 75.3[5] | 4.9[5] | 0.0[10] | ... | ... |
| Indonesia (Indonesian rupiah) | 2000 | 940 776 000[1] | 25.7[1] | 72.7 | 1.1[9] | 0.0[10] | ... | 0.5 |
| Indonésie (roupie indonésien) | 2001 | 783 045 000[1] | 14.7[1] | 84.5 | 0.2[9] | 0.0[10] | ... | 0.7 |
| Iran (Islamic Rep. of) (Iranian rial) | 2002 | 5 072 849 732 | 18.6 | 74.7 | 6.7 | ... | ... | ... |
| Iran (Rép. islamique d') (rial iranien) | 2003 | 7 483 899 781 | 16.5 | 75.8 | 7.7 | ... | ... | ... |
| | 2004 | 8 259 299 100 | 19.6 | 69.0 | 11.4 | ... | ... | ... |
| Ireland (euro)[3] | 2004 | 1 840 400 | 58.6 | 31.1 | 1.7 | 0.0 | 8.6 | 0.0 |
| Irlande (euro)[3] | 2005 | 2 030 000 | 57.4 | 32.0 | 1.7 | 0.2 | 8.6 | 0.0 |
| | 2006 | *2 305 600 | *59.6 | *30.0 | *0.2 | 1.5 | *8.7 | 0.0 |
| Israel (new sheqel)*[3,11] | 2004 | 24 305 000 | ... | ... | ... | ... | ... | ... |
| Israël (nouveau sheqel)*[3,11] | 2005 | 26 130 000 | ... | ... | ... | ... | ... | ... |
| | 2006 | 28 335 000 | ... | ... | ... | ... | ... | ... |
| Italy (euro)[3] | 2003 | 14 769 000 | ... | ... | ... | ... | ... | ... |
| Italie (euro)[3] | 2004 | 15 253 000 | ... | ... | ... | ... | ... | ... |
| | 2005 | 15 598 800 | 39.7 | 50.7 | 0.1 | 1.6 | 8.0 | ... |
| Jamaica (Jamaican dollar)[2] | 2001 | 207 700 | ... | ... | ... | ... | ... | ... |
| Jamaïque (dollar jamaïcain)[2] | 2002 | 286 800 | ... | ... | ... | ... | ... | ... |
| Japan (yen)[3] | 2004 | 15 782 743 000 | 74.8 | 18.1[12] | 6.1[12] | 0.7 | 0.3 | 0.0 |
| Japon (yen)[3] | 2005 | 16 672 632 000 | 76.1 | 16.8[12] | 6.1[12] | 0.7 | 0.3 | 0.0 |
| | 2006 | 17 273 451 000 | 77.1 | 16.2[12] | 6.4[9,12] | 0.0[10] | 0.4 | 0.0 |
| Jordan (Jordan dinar) Jordanie (dinar jordanien) | 2002 | 22 888 | ... | ... | ... | ... | ... | ... |
| Kazakhstan (tenge) | 2003 | 11 643 480 | 38.6 | 41.9 | ... | ... | 5.6 | 13.9 |
| Kazakhstan (tenge) | 2004 | 14 579 835 | 29.0 | 50.0 | ... | ... | 2.4 | 18.7 |
| | 2005 | 21 527 364 | 26.4 | 51.2 | ... | ... | 1.5 | 20.9 |

| Country or area (monetary unit) / Pays ou zone (unité monétaire) | Year / Année | Gross domestic expenditure on R&D (000) / Dépenses int. brutes de R-D (000) | Source of funds (%) / Source de financement (%) | | | | | |
|---|---|---|---|---|---|---|---|---|
| | | | Business enterprises / Entreprises | Govern-ment / Etat | Higher education / Enseigne-ment supérieur | Private non-profit / Institut. privées sans but lucratif | Funds from abroad / Fonds de l'étranger | Not distributed / Non répartis |
| Korea, Republic of (Korean won)[1,3] Corée, République de (won coréen)[1,3] | 2004 | 22 185 344 000 | 75.0 | 23.1 | 1.0 | 0.4 | 0.5 | 0.0 |
| | 2005 | 24 155 413 600 | 75.0 | 23.0 | 0.9 | 0.4 | 0.7 | 0.0 |
| | 2006 | 27 345 704 100 | 75.4 | 23.1 | 0.8 | 0.3 | 0.3 | 0.0 |
| Kuwait (Kuwaiti dinar)[1] Koweït (dinar koweïtien)[1] | 2000 | 14 512 | 20.9 | 79.1 | ... | ... | ... | ... |
| | 2001 | 19 136 | 20.1 | 79.9 | ... | ... | ... | ... |
| | 2002 | 20 864 | 20.0 | 80.0 | ... | ... | ... | ... |
| Kyrgyzstan (Kyrgyz som) Kirghizistan (som kirghize) | 2003 | 186 800 | 53.7 | 45.1 | 0.1 | 0.0 | 1.1 | 0.0 |
| | 2004 | 188 000 | 45.9 | 53.4 | 0.0 | 0.0 | 0.7 | 0.0 |
| | 2005 | 200 400 | 36.4 | 63.6 | 0.0 | 0.0 | 0.0 | 0.0 |
| Latvia (lats)[8] Lettonie (lats)[8] | 2004 | 31 070 | 46.3 | 31.2 | ... | ... | 22.5 | ... |
| | 2005 | 50 609 | 34.3 | 46.0 | 1.2 | ... | 18.5 | ... |
| | 2006 | 78 200 | 32.7 | 58.2 | 1.5 | ... | 7.5 | ... |
| Lesotho (loti)[1] Lesotho (loti)[1] | 2002 | 3 422 | ... | ... | ... | ... | ... | ... |
| | 2003 | 3 762 | ... | ... | ... | ... | ... | ... |
| | 2004 | 5 400 | ... | ... | ... | ... | ... | ... |
| Lithuania (litas)[8] Lituanie (litas)[8] | 2004 | 472 700 | 19.9 | 63.1 | 6.0 | 0.3 | 10.7 | 0.0 |
| | 2005 | 542 000 | 20.8 | 62.7 | 5.7 | 0.2 | 10.5 | 0.0 |
| | 2006 | 657 800 | 26.2 | 53.6 | 5.3 | 0.6 | 14.3 | 0.0 |
| Luxembourg (euro)[3] Luxembourg (euro)[3] | 2004 | 447 700 | ... | ... | ... | ... | ... | ... |
| | 2005 | 472 000 | 79.7 | 16.6 | 0.0 | 0.1 | 3.6 | 0.0 |
| | *2006[5] | 496 800 | ... | ... | ... | ... | ... | ... |
| Madagascar (Malagasy ariary)[1] Madagascar (ariary malgache)[1] | 2003 | 20 962 077[6] | ... | ... | 70.6 | | 29.4 | ... |
| | 2004 | 16 469 769[6] | ... | ... | 73.8 | | 26.2 | ... |
| | 2005 | 15 942 004 | ... | ... | 89.1 | | 10.9 | ... |
| Malaysia (ringgit) Malaisie (ringgit) | 2000 | 1 671 500 | ... | ... | ... | ... | ... | ... |
| | 2002 | 2 500 600 | 51.5 | 32.1 | 4.9 | 0.0 | 11.5 | 0.0 |
| | 2004 | 2 843 800 | 71.2 | 21.5 | 6.9 | 0.0 | 0.4 | 0.0 |
| Malta (euro)[8] Malte (euro)[8] | #2004[6] | 23 974 | ... | ... | ... | ... | ... | ... |
| | 2005 | *25 680[6] | *54.5 | *31.7 | *0.4 | *0.1 | *13.3 | 0.0 |
| | 2006 | *27 560[6] | *52.1 | *34.4 | *0.0 | *0.0 | *13.5 | 0.0 |
| Mauritius (Mauritian rupee)[1] Maurice (roupie mauricienne)[1] | 2003 | 529 139[7] | ... | 100.0 | ... | ... | ... | ... |
| | 2004 | 666 071[7] | ... | 100.0 | ... | ... | ... | ... |
| | 2005 | 690 030[7] | ... | 100.0 | ... | ... | ... | ... |
| Mexico (Nuevo peso)[3] Mexique (nuevo peso)[3] | 2003 | 29 931 528 | 34.7 | 56.1 | 7.7 | 0.8 | 0.8 | 0.0 |
| | 2004 | #36 374 976 | #44.0 | #47.4 | #7.0 | #0.7 | #0.8 | 0.0 |
| | 2005 | 42 183 735 | 46.5 | 45.3 | 6.6 | 0.8 | 0.7 | 0.0 |
| Moldova (Moldovan leu) Moldova (leu moldove) | 1996 | 68 069 | ... | ... | ... | ... | ... | ... |
| | 1997 | 71 941 | 51.4 | 47.8 | 0.2 | ... | 0.6 | ... |
| Monaco (euro)[1] Monaco (euro)[1] | 2005 | 1 291 | ... | ... | ... | ... | ... | ... |
| Mongolia (togrog)[1] Mongolie (togrog)[1] | 2003 | 4 605 600 | 4.8 | 90.5 | 2.2 | ... | 0.9 | 1.6 |
| | 2004 | 6 322 500 | 7.4 | 87.0 | 2.1 | ... | 2.3 | 1.3 |
| | 2005 | 7 231 100 | 10.4 | 77.8 | 0.8 | ... | 4.4 | 6.5 |
| Morocco (Moroccan dirham) Maroc (dirham marocain) | 1998 | 1 097 800 | ... | ... | ... | ... | ... | ... |
| | 2002 | 2 447 850 | 21.6 | 37.1 | 41.2 | ... | ... | ... |
| | 2003 | 3 144 000 | 12.3 | 40.3 | 47.4 | ... | ... | ... |
| Mozambique (new metical)[1,7] Mozambique (nouveau metical)[1,7] | 2002 | 501 580 800 | ... | 34.7 | ... | ... | 65.3 | ... |
| Myanmar (kyat)[1,4] Myanmar (kyat)[1,4] | 2000 | 2 886 055 | ... | ... | ... | ... | ... | ... |
| | 2001 | 2 535 022 | ... | ... | ... | ... | ... | ... |
| | 2002 | 9 122 008 | ... | ... | ... | ... | ... | ... |

**54** Gross domestic expenditure on R & D by source of funds—National currency and percentage distribution (*continued*)

Dépenses intérieures brutes de recherche et développement par source de financement—Monnaie nationale et répartition en pourcentage (*suite*)

| Country or area (monetary unit) / Pays ou zone (unité monétaire) | Year / Année | Gross domestic expenditure on R&D (000) / Dépenses int. brutes de R-D (000) | Business enterprises / Entreprises | Government / Etat | Higher education Enseignement supérieur | Private non-profit Institut. privées sans but lucratif | Funds from abroad / Fonds de l'étranger | Not distributed / Non répartis |
|---|---|---|---|---|---|---|---|---|
| Netherlands (euro)*[3,5] Pays-Bas (euro)*[3,5] | 2004 | 8 722 000 | ... | ... | ... | ... | ... | ... |
| | 2005 | 8 817 000 | ... | ... | ... | ... | ... | ... |
| | 2006 | 8 910 000 | ... | ... | ... | ... | ... | ... |
| New Zealand (New Zealand dollar)[3] Nouvelle-Zélande (dollar néo-zélandais)[3] | 2001 | #1 416 200 | #37.8 | #47.1 | #8.1 | #1.9 | #6.7 | 0.0 |
| | 2003 | 1 660 200 | 38.2 | 43.8 | 8.8 | 2.1 | 7.1 | 0.0 |
| | 2005 | 1 825 600 | 41.2 | 43.0 | 8.9 | 1.7 | 5.2 | 0.0 |
| Nicaragua (córdoba)[2] Nicaragua (córdoba)[2] | 1997 | 27 000 | ... | ... | ... | ... | ... | ... |
| | 2002 | 26 000 | ... | ... | ... | ... | ... | ... |
| Norway (Norwegian krone)[3] Norvège (couronne norvégienne)[3] | 2004 | 27 765 700 | ... | ... | ... | ... | ... | ... |
| | 2005 | 29 627 900 | 46.4 | 44.0 | 0.7 | 0.9 | 8.0 | 0.0 |
| | *2006 | 31 980 000 | ... | ... | ... | ... | ... | ... |
| Pakistan (Pakistan rupee) Pakistan (roupie pakistanaise) | 2001 | 7 017 890[1,5] | ... | 100.0 | ... | ... | ... | ... |
| | 2002 | 9 785 470[1,5] | ... | 100.0 | ... | ... | ... | ... |
| | 2005 | 28 397 000 | ... | 87.0 | 11.9 | ... | 0.3 | 0.8 |
| Panama (balboa)[2] Panama (balboa)[2] | 2003 | 43 970 | 0.6 | 25.5 | 1.8 | 1.0 | 71.0 | 0.0 |
| | 2004 | 34 000 | 0.1 | 35.0 | 2.6 | 2.5 | 59.8 | 0.0 |
| | 2005 | 38 960 | 0.4 | 38.5 | 1.4 | 0.7 | 58.9 | 0.0 |
| Paraguay (guaraní)[2] Paraguay (guaraní)[2] | 2003 | 30 316 461 | 0.0 | 63.2 | 12.7 | 2.3 | 21.8 | 0.0 |
| | 2004 | 34 878 381 | 0.0 | 63.1 | 12.7 | 2.3 | 21.9 | 0.0 |
| | 2005 | 40 402 473 | 0.3 | 74.9 | 8.6 | 2.0 | 14.2 | 0.0 |
| Peru (new sol)[2] Pérou (nouveau sol)[2] | 2002 | 204 530 | ... | ... | ... | ... | ... | ... |
| | 2003 | 220 950 | ... | ... | ... | ... | ... | ... |
| | 2004 | 355 071 | ... | ... | ... | ... | ... | ... |
| Philippines (Philippine peso) Philippines (peso philippin) | 2002 | 5 770 000 | 68.6 | 19.1 | 5.9 | 0.2 | 5.5 | 0.7 |
| | 2003 | 5 910 000 | 68.0 | 21.9 | 4.8 | 0.4 | 3.8 | 1.1 |
| Poland (zloty)[3] Pologne (zloty)[3] | 2004 | 5 155 300 | 30.5 | 61.7 | 2.4 | 0.3 | 5.2 | 0.0 |
| | 2005 | 5 574 500 | 33.4 | 57.7 | 2.9 | 0.3 | 5.7 | 0.0 |
| | 2006 | 5 892 800 | 33.1 | 57.5 | 2.2 | 0.3 | 7.0 | 0.0 |
| Portugal (euro)[3] Portugal (euro)[3] | 2004 | 1 110 346[5] | 34.2[5] | 57.5[5] | 1.1[5] | 2.4[5] | 4.8[5] | 0.0 |
| | 2005 | 1 201 112 | 36.3 | 55.2 | 1.0 | 2.8 | 4.7 | 0.0 |
| | 2006[5] | 1 294 080 | ... | ... | ... | ... | ... | ... |
| Romania (Romanian leu)[3] Roumanie (leu roumain)[3] | 2004 | 952 872[6] | 44.0 | 49.0 | 1.5 | 0.0 | 5.5 | 0.0 |
| | 2005 | 1 183 660[6] | 37.2 | 53.5 | 4.0 | 0.0 | 5.3 | 0.0 |
| | 2006 | 1 565 802[6] | 30.4 | 64.1 | 1.2 | 0.2 | 4.1 | 0.0 |
| Russian Federation (ruble)[3] Fédération de Russie (ruble)[3] | 2004 | 196 039 900 | 31.4 | 60.6 | 0.4 | 0.1 | 7.6 | 0.0 |
| | 2005 | 230 785 200 | 30.0 | 61.9 | 0.4 | 0.0 | 7.6 | 0.0 |
| | 2006 | 288 356 100 | 28.7 | 61.2 | 0.6 | 0.1 | 9.4 | 0.0 |
| Saint Helena (pound sterling)[1] Sainte-Hélène (livre sterling)[1] | 1998 | 30 082 | ... | ... | ... | ... | ... | ... |
| | 1999 | 40 390 | ... | ... | ... | ... | ... | ... |
| | 2000 | 51 156 | ... | ... | ... | ... | ... | ... |
| Saint Lucia (EC dollar)[7] Sainte-Lucie (dollar des Caraïbes orientales)[7] | 1998 | 13 597 | ... | ... | ... | ... | ... | ... |
| | 1999 | 6 814 | ... | ... | ... | ... | ... | ... |
| Saint Vincent-Grenadines (EC dollar) Saint Vincent-Grenadines (dollar des Caraïbes orientales) | 2001 | 500 | ... | ... | ... | ... | ... | ... |
| | 2002 | 1 500 | ... | ... | ... | ... | ... | ... |
| Senegal (CFA franc)[1] Sénégal (franc CFA)[1] | 2005 | 4 090 000[5] | ... | 100.0 | ... | ... | ... | ... |
| Serbia and Montenegro (new dinar)[1,13] Serbie-et-Monténégro (nouveau dinar)[1,13] | 2003 | 14 710 671 | ... | ... | ... | ... | ... | ... |
| | 2004 | 19 466 276 | ... | ... | ... | ... | ... | ... |
| | 2005 | 24 637 550 | ... | ... | ... | ... | ... | ... |

**54** Gross domestic expenditure on R & D by source of funds—National currency and percentage distribution (*continued*)

Dépenses intérieures brutes de recherche et développement par source de financement—Monnaie nationale et répartition en pourcentage (*suite*)

| Country or area (monetary unit) / Pays ou zone (unité monétaire) | Year / Année | Gross domestic expenditure on R&D (000) / Dépenses int. brutes de R-D (000) | Source of funds (%) / Source de financement (%) | | | | | |
|---|---|---|---|---|---|---|---|---|
| | | | Business enterprises / Entreprises | Govern-ment / Etat | Higher education Enseigne-ment supérieur | Private non-profit Institut. privées sans but lucratif | Funds from abroad Fonds de l'étranger | Not distributed Non répartis |
| Seychelles (Seychelles rupee)[1] | 2003 | 15 696 | ... | ... | ... | ... | ... | ... |
| Seychelles (roupie seychelloises)[1] | 2004 | 15 999 | ... | ... | ... | ... | ... | ... |
| | 2005 | 15 271 | ... | ... | ... | ... | ... | ... |
| Singapore (Singapore dollar)[3] | 2004 | 4 061 896 | 55.3 | 37.9 | 1.0 | 0.0 | 5.8 | 0.0 |
| Singapour (dollar singapourien)[3] | 2005 | 4 582 211 | 58.8 | 36.4 | 0.5 | ... | 4.4 | 0.0 |
| | 2006 | 5 009 700 | 58.3 | 36.4 | 0.9 | ... | 4.4 | 0.0 |
| Slovakia (Slovak koruna)[3] | 2004 | 6 965 000 | 38.3 | 57.1[14] | 0.3 | 0.0 | 4.3 | 0.0 |
| Slovaquie (couronne slovaque)[3] | 2005 | 7 503 000 | 36.6 | 57.0[14] | 0.3 | 0.0 | 6.0 | 0.0 |
| | 2006 | 8 063 200 | 35.0 | 55.6[14] | 0.3 | 0.1 | 9.1 | 0.0 |
| Slovenia (euro)[3] | 2004 | 378 579[6] | 58.5 | 30.0 | 0.3 | 0.1 | 11.1 | 0.0 |
| Slovénie (euro)[3] | 2005 | 412 765[6] | 54.8 | 37.2 | 0.7 | 0.0 | 7.3 | 0.0 |
| | 2006 | *485 491[6] | *59.2 | *29.0 | *5.7 | *0.2 | *5.9 | 0.0 |
| South Africa (rand) | 2003 | 10 082 559 | 52.1 | 27.9 | 3.5 | 5.5 | 10.9 | 0.0 |
| Afrique du Sud (rand) | 2004 | 12 009 981 | 44.5 | 23.7 | 9.2 | 6.8 | 15.8 | 0.0 |
| | 2005[3] | 14 149 239 | 43.9 | 38.2 | 3.0 | 1.4 | 13.6 | 0.0 |
| Spain (euro)[3] | 2004 | 8 945 761 | 48.0 | 41.0 | 4.1 | 0.7 | 6.2 | 0.0 |
| Espagne (euro)[3] | 2005 | 10 196 871 | 46.3 | 43.0 | 4.1 | 0.9 | 5.7 | 0.0 |
| | 2006 | 11 815 220 | 47.1 | 42.5 | 3.9[8] | 0.6[8] | 5.9 | ... |
| Sri Lanka (Sri Lanka rupee) | 1996 | 1 410 000 | 1.7 | 52.8 | 21.2 | ... | 24.4 | ... |
| Sri Lanka (roupie sri-lankaise) | #2000[1] | 1 810 000 | 7.7 | 51.7 | 18.5 | 0.0 | 4.5 | 17.5 |
| | #2004 | 3 807 500 | 0.6[9] | 67.5[15] | 0.0[10] | 0.0[10] | 22.6 | 9.3 |
| Sudan (Sudanese pound) | 2003 | 15 650 000 | ... | ... | ... | ... | ... | ... |
| Soudan (livre soudanaise) | 2004 | 16 373 000 | ... | ... | ... | ... | ... | ... |
| | 2005 | 19 284 000 | ... | ... | ... | ... | ... | ... |
| Sweden (Swedish krona)[3] | 2004[14] | 95 131 000 | | | | | | |
| Suède (couronne suédoise)[3] | 2005 | #103 814 000 | #65.7 | #23.5 | #0.6 | #2.5 | #7.7 | 0.0[4] |
| | 2006 | 108 194 000 | | | | | | |
| Switzerland (Swiss franc)[3] | 1996 | 9 990 000 | 67.5 | 26.9 | 1.3 | 1.2 | 3.1 | 0.0 |
| Suisse (franc suisse)[3] | 2000 | 10 675 000 | 69.1 | 23.2 | 2.1 | 1.4 | 4.3 | 0.0 |
| | 2004 | 13 100 000 | 69.7 | 22.7 | 1.5 | 0.8 | 5.2 | 0.0 |
| Tajikistan (somoni) | 2003 | 3 278 | 7.9 | 65.1 | ... | ... | ... | 27.0 |
| Tadjikistan (somoni) | 2004 | 4 130 | 4.8 | 64.7 | 0.1 | ... | ... | 30.4 |
| | 2005 | 6 862 | 2.2 | 91.9 | 0.3 | ... | ... | 5.5 |
| Thailand (baht) | 2002 | 13 302 039[5] | 36.8 | ... | ... | ... | ... | 63.2 |
| Thaïlande (baht) | 2003 | 15 499 201 | 41.8 | 38.6 | 15.1 | 0.6 | 2.6 | 1.3 |
| | 2004 | 16 571 000 | 35.5 | ... | ... | ... | ... | 64.5 |
| TFYR of Macedonia (TFYR Macedonian denar) | 2003 | 565 984 | ... | ... | ... | ... | ... | ... |
| L'ex-R.y. Macédoine | 2004 | 652 470 | ... | ... | ... | ... | ... | ... |
| (denar de l'ex-R.Y. Macédoine) | 2005 | 704 036 | ... | ... | ... | ... | ... | ... |
| Trinidad and Tobago (Trinidad and Tobago dollar)[2] | 2002 | 81 900 | | | | | | |
| | 2003 | 95 700 | | | | | | |
| Trinité-et-Tobago (dollar de la Trinité-et-Tobago)[2] | 2004 | 115 090 | ... | ... | ... | ... | ... | ... |
| Tunisia (Tunisian dinar) | 2003 | 234 000 | 9.6 | 47.0 | 34.2 | 0.0 | 7.5 | 1.7 |
| Tunisie (dinar tunisien) | 2004 | 350 000 | 12.6 | 35.4 | 28.0 | 0.0 | 9.4 | 14.6 |
| | 2005[5] | 384 000 | 14.1 | 45.1 | 30.5 | 0.0 | 10.4 | 0.0 |
| Turkey (new Turkish Lira)[3] | 2004 | 2 897 516[6] | 37.9 | 57.0 | 0.0[10] | 4.8[15] | 0.4 | 0.0 |
| Turquie (nouveau livre turque)[3] | 2005 | 3 835 441[6] | 43.3 | 50.1 | 0.0[10] | 5.8[15] | 0.8 | 0.0 |
| | 2006 | 4 399 880[6] | 46.1 | 48.6 | 0.0[10] | 4.8[15] | 0.5 | ... |
| Uganda (Uganda shilling) | 2003 | 40 027 858 | 2.1 | 24.2 | 0.0 | 0.0 | 73.7 | 0.0 |
| Ouganda (shilling ougandais) | 2004 | 34 531 052 | 1.7 | 41.5 | 0.0 | 0.0 | 56.9 | 0.0 |
| | 2005 | 33 082 120 | ... | ... | ... | ... | ... | ... |

**Gross domestic expenditure on R & D by source of funds**— National currency and percentage distribution (*continued*)

**Dépenses intérieures brutes de recherche et développement par source de financement**— Monnaie nationale et répartition en pourcentage (*suite*)

| Country or area (monetary unit)<br>Pays ou zone (unité monétaire) | Year<br>Année | Gross domestic expenditure on R&D (000)<br>Dépenses int. brutes de R-D (000) | Business enterprises<br>Entreprises | Government<br>Etat | Higher education<br>Enseigne-ment supérieur | Private non-profit<br>Institut. privées sans but lucratif | Funds from abroad<br>Fonds de l'étranger | Not distributed<br>Non répartis |
|---|---|---|---|---|---|---|---|---|
| Ukraine (hryvnia) | 2003 | 2 972 301 | 35.6[4] | 37.5[4] | 0.1[4] | 0.3[4] | 24.3[4] | 2.2[4] |
| Ukraine (hryvnia) | 2004 | 3 732 459 | 32.9[4] | 42.3[4] | 0.2[4] | 0.4[4] | 21.4[4] | 2.9[4] |
| | 2005 | 4 551 153 | 32.3[4] | 40.1[4] | 0.1[4] | 0.4[4] | 24.4[4] | 2.8[4] |
| United Kingdom (pound sterling)[3] | 2004 | 20 396 000 | 44.1 | 32.9 | 1.1 | 4.7 | 17.2 | 0.0 |
| Royaume-Uni (livre sterling)[3] | 2005 | 21 764 000 | 42.1 | 32.8 | 1.2 | 4.7 | 19.2 | 0.0 |
| | 2006 | 23 203 100 | 45.2 | 31.9 | 0.0[10] | 5.9[15] | 17.0 | 0.0 |
| United States (US dollar)[3] | 2002 | 301 015 500[16] | 63.6[16,17] | 30.8[16] | 2.6[16] | 3.0[16] | 0.0[10] | 0.0 |
| Etats-Unis (dollar des Etats-Unis)[3] | 2005 | *324 464 450[16] | *64.0[16,17] | *30.4[16] | *2.6[16] | *3.1[16] | 0.0[10] | 0.0 |
| | 2006 | *343 747 500[16] | *64.9[16,17] | *29.3[16] | *2.6[16] | *3.2[16] | 0.0[10] | 0.0 |
| United States Virgin Is. (US dollar)[1] | 2003 | 2 623 | ... | 81.0 | 18.6 | 0.4 | ... | ... |
| Iles Vierges américaines (dollar des Etats-Unis)[1] | 2004 | 4 562 | ... | 91.2 | 8.8 | ... | ... | ... |
| | 2005 | 1 523 | ... | 76.1 | 23.9 | ... | ... | ... |
| Uruguay (Uruguayan peso)[2] | 1999 | 609 655 | 35.6 | 9.4 | 47.1 | ... | 7.9 | ... |
| Uruguay (peso uruguayen)[2] | 2000 | 577 855 | 39.3 | 20.3 | 35.7 | ... | 4.8 | ... |
| | 2002 | 688 900 | 46.7 | 17.1 | 31.4 | 0.1 | 4.7 | 0.0 |
| Venezuela (Bolivarian Rep. of) (bolívar)[2,5] | 2003 | 390 550 100[7] | #1.0 | #71.6 | #27.4 | ... | ... | ... |
| Venezuela (Rép. bolivarienne du) (bolívar)[2,5] | 2004 | 525 755 900[7] | 14.3 | 62.3 | 23.4 | ... | ... | ... |
| | 2005 | 696 078 700[7] | 16.4 | 62.1 | 21.5 | ... | ... | ... |
| Viet Nam (dong)<br>Viet Nam (dong) | 2002 | 1 032 560 900 | 18.1 | 74.1 | 0.7[9] | 0.0[10] | 6.3 | 0.8 |
| Zambia (Zambia kwacha)[1] | 2003 | 1 965 987 | ... | ... | ... | ... | ... | ... |
| Zambie (kwacha zambie)[1] | 2004 | 6 607 523 | ... | ... | ... | ... | ... | ... |
| | 2005 | 9 272 025 | ... | ... | ... | ... | ... | ... |

Source

United Nations Educational, Scientific and Cultural Organization (UNESCO) Institute for Statistics, Montreal, the UNESCO Institute of Statistics database, last accessed June 2008.

Notes

1 Partial data.
2 Source : "Red Iberoamericana de Indicadores de Ciencia y Tecnologia (RICYT)".
3 Source: OECD.
4 UIS estimation.
5 National estimation.
6 Data have been converted from the former national currency using the appropriate irrevocable conversion rate.
7 Overestimated or based on overestimated data.
8 Source: EUROSTAT.
9 Including private non-profit funds.
10 Included elsewhere.
11 Defence excluded (all or mostly).
12 OECD estimation.
13 Data exclude Montenegro and Kosovo.
14 Underestimated or based on underestimated data.
15 Including higher education.
16 Excluding most or all capital expenditure.

17 Includes funds from abroad.

Source

L'Institut de statistique de l'Organisation des Nations Unies pour l'éducation, la science et la culture (UNESCO), Montréal, la base de données de l'Institut de statistique de l'UNESCO, dernier accès juin 2008.

Notes

1 Données partielles.
2 Source : "Red Iberoamericana de Indicadores de Ciencia y Tecnologia (RICYT)".
3 Source : OCDE.
4 Estimation de l'ISU.
5 Estimation nationale.
6 Les données ont été converties à partir de l'ancienne monnaie nationale et du taux de conversion irrévocable approprié.
7 Surestimé ou fondé sur des données surestimées.
8 Source: EUROSTAT.
9 Y compris les fonds privés à but non lucratif.
10 Inclus ailleurs.
11 A l'exclusion de la défense (en totalité ou en grande partie).
12 Estimation de l'OCDE.
13 Les données excluent celles de Monténégro et Kosovo.
14 Sous-estimé ou basé sur des données sous-estimées.
15 Y compris l'enseignement supérieur.
16 A l'exclusion des dépenses d'équipement (en totalité ou en grande partie).
17 Incluant les fonds de l'étranger.

Research and experimental development (R&D) is defined as any creative work undertaken on a systematic basis in order to increase the stock of knowledge, including knowledge of man, culture and society, and the use of this stock of knowledge to devise new applications.

*Table 53*: The data presented on human resources in research and development (R&D) are compiled by the UNESCO Institute for Statistics. Data for certain countries are provided to UNESCO by OECD, EUROSTAT and the Network on Science and Technology Indicators (RICYT).

The definitions and classifications applied by UNESCO in the table are based on those set out in the *Recommendation concerning the International Standardization of Statistics on Science and Technology* (UNESCO, 1978) and in the *Frascati Manual* (OECD, 2002).

The three categories of personnel shown are defined as follows:

- *Researchers* are professionals engaged in the conception or creation of new knowledge, products, processes, methods and systems, and in the planning and management of R&D projects. Postgraduate students engaged in R&D are considered as researchers.

- *Technicians and equivalent staff* comprise persons whose main tasks require technical knowledge and experience in one or more fields of engineering, physical and life sciences, or social sciences and humanities. They participate in R&D by performing scientific and technical tasks involving the application of concepts and operational methods, normally under the supervision of researchers. As distinguished from technicians participating in the R&D under the supervision of researchers in engineering, physical and life sciences, equivalent staff perform the corresponding R&D tasks in the social sciences and humanities.

- *Other supporting staff* includes skilled and unskilled craftsmen, secretarial and clerical staff participating in or directly associated with R&D projects. Included in this category are all managers and administrators dealing mainly with financial and personnel matters and general administration, insofar as their activities are a direct service to R&D.

Headcount data reflect the total number of persons employed in R&D, independently from their dedication. Full-time equivalent may be thought of as one person-year. Thus, a person who normally spends 30% of his/her time on R&D and the rest on other activities (such as teaching, university administration and student counselling) should be considered as 0.3 FTE. Similarly, if a full-time R&D

La recherche et le développement expérimental (R-D) englobe tous les travaux de création entrepris de façon systématique en vue d'accroître la somme des connaissances, y compris la connaissance de l'homme, de la culture et de la société, ainsi que l'utilisation de cette somme de connaissances pour de nouvelles applications.

*Tableau 53*: Les données présentées sur le personnel employé dans la recherche et le développement (R-D) sont compilées par l'Institut de statistique de l'UNESCO. Les données de certains pays ont été fournies à l'UNESCO par l'OCDE, EUROSTAT et "la Red de Indicadores de Ciencia y Tecnología (RICYT)".

Les définitions et classifications appliquées par l'UNESCO sont basées sur la *Recommandation concernant la normalisation internationale des statistiques relatives à la science et à la technologie* (UNESCO, 1978) et sur le *Manuel de Frascati* (OCDE, 2002).

Les trois catégories du personnel présentées sont définies comme suivant:

- Les *chercheurs* sont des spécialistes travaillant à la conception ou à la création de connaissances, de produits, de procédés, de méthodes et de systèmes, et dans la planification et la gestion de projets de R-D. Les étudiants diplômés ayant des activités de R-D sont considérés comme des chercheurs.

- *Techniciens et personnel assimilé* comprend des personnes dont les tâches principales requièrent des connaissances et une expérience technique dans un ou plusieurs domaines de l'ingénierie, des sciences physiques et de la vie ou des sciences sociales et humaines. Ils participent à la R-D en exécutant des tâches scientifiques et techniques faisant intervenir l'application de principes et de méthodes opérationnelles, généralement sous le contrôle de chercheurs. Pour se distinguer des techniciens qui participent à la R-D sous le contrôle de chercheurs dans les domaines de l'ingénierie, des sciences physiques et de la vie, le personnel assimilé effectue des travaux correspondants dans les sciences sociales et humaines.

- *Autre personnel de soutien* comprend les travailleurs, qualifiés ou non, et le personnel de secrétariat et de bureau qui participent à l'exécution des projets de R-D ou qui sont directement associés à l'exécution de tels projets. Sont inclus dans cette catégorie les gérants et administrateurs qui s'occupent principalement de problèmes financiers, le per-sonnel et l'administration en général, dans la mesure où leurs activités ont une relation directe avec la R-D.

Personnes physiques est le nombre total de personnes qui sont principalement ou partiellement affectées à la R-D. Ce

worker is employed at an R&D unit for only six months, this results in an FTE of 0.5.

More information can be found on the UNESCO Institute for Statistics web site www.uis.unesco.org.

*Table 54*: The data presented on gross domestic expenditure on research and development are compiled by the UNESCO Institute for Statistics. Data for certain countries are provided to UNESCO by OECD, EUROSTAT and the Network on Science and Technology Indicators (RICYT).

Gross domestic expenditure on R&D (GERD) is total intramural expenditure on R&D performed on the national territory during a given period. It includes R&D performed within a country and funded from abroad but excludes payments made abroad for R&D.

The sources of funds for GERD are classified according to the following five categories:

- *Business enterprise funds* include funds allocated to R&D by all firms, organizations and institutions whose primary activity is the market production of goods and services (other than the higher education sector) for sale to the general public at an economically significant price, and those private non-profit institutes mainly serving these firms, organizations and institutions.

- *Government funds* refer to funds allocated to R&D by the central (federal), state or local government authorities. These include all departments, offices and other bodies which furnish, but normally do not sell to the community, those common services, other than higher education, which cannot be conveniently and economically provided, as well as those that administer the state and the economic and social policy of the community. Public enterprises funds are included in the business enterprise funds sector. Government funds also include private non-profit institutes controlled and mainly financed by government.

- *Higher education funds* include funds allocated to R&D by institutions of higher education comprising all universities, colleges of technology, other institutes of post-secondary education, and all research institutes, experimental stations and clinics operating under the direct control of or administered by or associated with higher educational establishments.

- *Private non-profit funds* are funds allocated to R&D by non-market, private non-profit institutions serving the general public, as well as by private individuals and households.

- *Funds from abroad* refer to funds allocated to R&D by in-stitutions and individuals located outside the political frontiers of a country except for vehicles, ships, aircraft and space satellites operated by domestic organizations

dénombrement inclut les employés à 'temps plein' et les employés à 'temps partiel'. Équivalent temps plein (ETP) peut être considéré comme une année-personne. Ainsi, une personne qui consacre 30% de son temps en R&D et le reste à d'autres activités (enseignement, administration universitaire ou direction d'étudiants) compte pour 0.3 ETP en R&D. De façon analogue, si un employé travaille à temps plein dans un centre de R&D pendant six mois seulement, il compte pour 0.5 ETP.

Pour tout renseignement complémentaire, voir le site Web de l'Institut de statistique de l'UNESCO www.uis.unesco.org.

*Tableau 54*: Les données présentées sur les dépenses intérieures brutes de recherche et développement sont compilées par l'Institut de statistique de l'UNESCO. Les données de certains pays ont été fournies à l'UNESCO par l'OCDE, EUROSTAT et "la Red de Indicadores de Ciencia y Tecnología (RICYT)".

La dépense intérieure brute de R-D (DIRD) est la dépense totale intramuros afférente aux travaux de R-D exécutés sur le territoire national pendant une période donnée. Elle comprend la R-D exécutée sur le territoire national et financée par l'étranger mais ne tient pas compte des paiements effectués à l'étranger pour des travaux de R-D.

Les sources de financement pour la DIRD sont classées selon les cinq catégories suivantes:

- *Les fonds des entreprises* incluent les fonds alloués à la R-D par toutes les firmes, organismes et institutions dont l'activité première est la production marchande de biens ou de services (autres que dans le secteur d'enseignement supérieur) en vue de leur vente au public, à un prix qui correspond à la réalité économique, et les institutions privées sans but lucratif principalement au service de ces entreprises, organismes et institutions.

- *Les fonds de l'Etat* sont les fonds fournis à la R-D par le gouvernement central (fédéral), d'état ou par les autorités locales. Ceci inclut tous les ministères, bureaux et autres organismes qui fournissent, sans normalement les vendre, des services collectifs autres que d'enseignement supérieur, qu'il n'est pas possible d'assurer de façon pratique et économique par d'autres moyens et qui, de surcroît, administrent les affaires publiques et appliquent la politique économique et sociale de la collectivité. Les fonds des en-treprises publiques sont compris dans ceux du secteur des entreprises. Les fonds de l'Etat incluent également les institutions privées sans but lucratif contrôlées et principalement financées par l'Etat.

- *Les fonds de l'enseignement supérieur* inclut les fonds fournis à la R-D par les établissements d'enseignement supérieur tels que toutes les universités, grandes écoles, instituts de

and testing grounds acquired by such organizations, and by all international organizations (except business enterprises) including their facilities and operations within the country's borders.

The absolute figures for R&D expenditure should not be compared country by country. Such comparisons would require the conversion of national currencies into a common currency by means of special R&D exchange rates. Official exchange rates do not always reflect the real costs of R&D activities and comparisons are based on such rates can result in misleading conclusions, although they can be used to indicate a gross order of magnitude.

More information can be found on the UNESCO Institute for Statistics web site www.uis.unesco.org.

technologie et autres établissements postsecondaires, ainsi que tous les instituts de recherche, les stations d'essais et les cliniques qui travaillent sous le contrôle direct des établissements d'enseignement supérieur ou qui sont administrés par ces derniers ou leur sont associés.

- *Les fonds d'institutions privées* sans but lucratif sont les fonds destinés à la R-D par les institutions privées sans but lucratif non marchandes au service du public, ainsi que par les simples particuliers ou les ménages.
- *Les fonds étrangers* concernent les fonds destinés à la R-D par les institutions et les individus se trouvant en dehors des frontières politiques d'un pays, à l'exception des véhicules, navires, avions et satellites utilisés par des institutions nationales, ainsi que des terrains d'essai acquis par ces institutions, et par toutes les organisations internationales (à l'exception des entreprises), y compris leurs installations et leurs activités à l'intérieur des frontières d'un pays.

Il faut éviter de comparer les chiffres absolus concernant les dépenses de R-D d'un pays à l'autre. On ne pourrait procéder à des comparaisons détaillées qu'en convertissant en une même monnaie les sommes libellées en monnaie nationale au moyen de taux de change spécialement applicables aux activités de R-D. Les taux de change officiels ne reflètent pas toujours le coût réel des activités de R-D, et les comparaisons établies sur la base de ces taux peuvent conduire à des conclusions trompeuses; toutefois, elles peuvent être utilisées pour donner une idée de l'ordre de grandeur.

Pour tout renseignement complémentaire, voir le site Web de l'Institut de statistique de l'UNESCO www.uis.unesco.org.

Part Four of the *Yearbook* presents statistics on international economic relations in areas of international merchandise trade, international tourism, balance of payments and assistance to developing countries. The series cover all countries or areas of the world for which data have been made available.

La quatrième partie de l'*Annuaire* présente des statistiques sur les relations économiques internationales dans les domaines du commerce international des marchandises, du tourisme international, de la balance des paiements et de l'assistance aux pays en développement. Les séries couvrent tous les pays ou les zones du monde pour lesquels des données sont disponibles.

# Total imports and exports
Imports c.i.f., exports f.o.b. and balance, value in million US dollars

# Importations et exportations totales
Importations c.a.f., exportations f.o.b. et balance, valeur en millions de dollars E.-U.

| Region, country or area[&] | Sys.[t] | 2000 | 2001 | 2002 | 2003 | 2004 | 2005 | 2006 | Région, pays ou zone[&] |
|---|---|---|---|---|---|---|---|---|---|
| **World[1]** | | | | | | | | | **Monde[1]** |
| Imports | | 6 157 088 | 5 937 358 | 6 153 801 | 7 167 501 | 8 752 864 | 9 912 118 | 11 341 309 | Importations |
| Exports | | 5 984 041 | 5 753 630 | 6 027 731 | 7 006 464 | 8 528 159 | 9 697 139 | 11 161 783 | Exportations |
| Balance | | -173 047 | -183 728 | -126 069 | -161 036 | -224 704 | -214 980 | -179 526 | Balance |
| **Developed economies[2,3]** | | | | | | | | | **Economies développées[2,3]** |
| Imports | | 4 380 771 | 4 215 747 | 4 338 259 | 5 036 193 | 5 997 453 | 6 647 410 | 7 508 851 | Importations |
| Exports | | 4 012 321 | 3 897 385 | 4 033 850 | 4 643 854 | 5 469 491 | 5 927 790 | 6 676 090 | Exportations |
| Balance | | -368 450 | -318 362 | -304 408 | -392 339 | -527 962 | -719 620 | -832 762 | Balance |
| **Asia and the Pacific - Developed economies** | | | | | | | | | **Asie et Pacifique - Economies dévelop.** |
| Imports | | 447 181 | 406 269 | 399 695 | 457 240 | 541 373 | 599 179 | 645 972 | Importations |
| Exports | | 538 650 | 460 616 | 470 894 | 526 583 | 626 710 | 655 223 | 696 353 | Exportations |
| Balance | | 91 469 | 54 348 | 71 199 | 69 343 | 85 337 | 56 043 | 50 381 | Balance |
| **Australia** | | | | | | | | | **Australie** |
| Imports | G | 71 537 | 63 890 | 72 693 | 89 089 | 109 383 | 125 283 | 139 279 | Importations |
| Exports | G | 63 878 | 63 389 | 65 036 | 71 551 | 86 420 | 105 833 | 123 316 | Exportations |
| Balance | | -7 659 | -501 | -7 657 | -17 539 | -22 962 | -19 449 | -15 963 | Balance |
| **Japan** | | | | | | | | | **Japon** |
| Imports | G | 379 491 | 349 189 | 337 209 | 383 085 | 454 592 | 514 988 | 579 609 | Importations |
| Exports | G | 479 227 | 403 616 | 416 730 | 471 999 | 565 743 | 594 986 | 649 948 | Exportations |
| Balance | | 99 736 | 54 427 | 79 520 | 88 914 | 111 150 | 79 998 | 70 340 | Balance |
| **New Zealand** | | | | | | | | | **Nouvelle-Zélande** |
| Imports | G | 13 905 | 13 308 | 15 046 | 18 559 | 23 195 | 26 234 | 26 430 | Importations |
| Exports | G | 13 297 | 13 730 | 14 382 | 16 527 | 20 344 | 21 729 | 22 434 | Exportations |
| Balance | | -608 | 422 | -664 | -2 033 | -2 850 | -4 505 | -3 996 | Balance |
| **Europe - Developed economies** | | | | | | | | | **Europe - Economies dévelop.** |
| Imports | | 2 518 590 | 2 487 421 | 2 594 467 | 3 123 975 | 3 764 031 | 4 113 862 | 4 727 613 | Importations |
| Exports | | 2 498 950 | 2 527 417 | 2 696 307 | 3 207 843 | 3 827 428 | 4 128 440 | 4 686 293 | Exportations |
| Balance | | -19 641 | 39 997 | 101 840 | 83 869 | 63 397 | 14 578 | -41 321 | Balance |
| **Andorra** | | | | | | | | | **Andorre** |
| Imports | S | ... | ... | ... | ... | 1 767 | 1 781 | ... | Importations |
| Exports | S | ... | ... | ... | ... | 123 | 141 | ... | Exportations |
| Balance | | ... | ... | ... | ... | -1 644 | -1 641 | ... | Balance |
| **Austria** | | | | | | | | | **Autriche** |
| Imports | S | 68 986 | 70 492 | 72 796 | 91 595 | 113 344 | 119 950 | 134 347 | Importations |
| Exports | S | 64 167 | 66 492 | 73 113 | 89 257 | 111 720 | 117 722 | 134 153 | Exportations |
| Balance | | -4 819 | -3 999 | 316 | -2 339 | -1 623 | -2 228 | -194 | Balance |
| **Belgium** | | | | | | | | | **Belgique** |
| Imports | S | 176 992 | 178 715 | 198 125 | 234 947 | 285 596 | 318 768 | 351 908 | Importations |
| Exports | S | 187 876 | 190 361 | 215 877 | 255 598 | 306 816 | 335 868 | 366 938 | Exportations |
| Balance | | 10 884 | 11 646 | 17 752 | 20 650 | 21 220 | 17 100 | 15 030 | Balance |
| **Croatia** | | | | | | | | | **Croatie** |
| Imports | G | 7 887 | 9 147 | 10 722 | 14 209 | 16 589 | 18 560 | 21 488 | Importations |
| Exports | G | 4 432 | 4 666 | 4 904 | 6 187 | 8 024 | 8 773 | 10 376 | Exportations |
| Balance | | -3 455 | -4 481 | -5 818 | -8 022 | -8 565 | -9 788 | -11 112 | Balance |
| **Czech Republic** | | | | | | | | | **République tchèque** |
| Imports | S | 33 934 | 38 308 | 42 773 | 53 807 | 71 635 | 76 343 | 93 453 | Importations |
| Exports | S | 29 057 | 33 399 | 38 488 | 48 715 | 67 198 | 77 988 | 95 165 | Exportations |
| Balance | | -4 877 | -4 909 | -4 285 | -5 092 | -4 438 | 1 645 | 1 712 | Balance |
| **Denmark** | | | | | | | | | **Danemark** |
| Imports | S | 44 364 | 44 132 | 48 890 | 56 227 | 66 845 | 74 265 | 85 102 | Importations |
| Exports | S | 50 390 | 51 077 | 56 308 | 65 280 | 75 568 | 83 569 | 91 705 | Exportations |
| Balance | | 6 025 | 6 945 | 7 418 | 9 052 | 8 723 | 9 303 | 6 603 | Balance |

55 Total imports and exports—Imports c.i.f., exports f.o.b., and balance, value in million US dollars (*continued*)

Importations et exportations totales—Importations c.a.f., exportations f.o.b. et balance, valeur en millions de dollars E.-U. (*suite*)

| Region, country or area[&] | Sys.[t] | 2000 | 2001 | 2002 | 2003 | 2004 | 2005 | 2006 | Région, pays ou zone[&] |
|---|---|---|---|---|---|---|---|---|---|
| Estonia[4] | | | | | | | | | Estonie[4] |
| Imports | S | 4 236 | 4 280 | 4 810 | 6 480 | 8 334 | 10 189 | 11 883 | Importations |
| Exports | S | 3 166 | 3 298 | 3 448 | 4 539 | 5 934 | 7 676 | 8 759 | Exportations |
| Balance | | -1 070 | -982 | -1 363 | -1 942 | -2 400 | -2 513 | -3 124 | Balance |
| Faeroe Islands | | | | | | | | | Iles Féroé |
| Imports | G | 532 | 498 | ... | ... | ... | ... | ... | Importations |
| Exports | G | 472 | 514 | ... | ... | ... | ... | ... | Exportations |
| Balance | | -60 | 16 | ... | ... | ... | ... | ... | Balance |
| Finland | | | | | | | | | Finlande |
| Imports | G | 33 900 | 32 114 | 33 642 | 41 601 | 50 677 | 58 474 | 69 447 | Importations |
| Exports | G | 45 482 | 42 802 | 44 671 | 52 514 | 60 916 | 65 240 | 77 287 | Exportations |
| Balance | | 11 582 | 10 688 | 11 029 | 10 913 | 10 239 | 6 765 | 7 840 | Balance |
| France[5] | | | | | | | | | France[5] |
| Imports | S | 310 989 | 302 016 | 312 164 | 370 563 | 442 606 | 485 466 | 538 292 | Importations |
| Exports | S | 300 085 | 297 188 | 312 011 | 365 637 | 427 186 | 444 319 | 489 808 | Exportations |
| Balance | | -10 904 | -4 828 | -154 | -4 926 | -15 420 | -41 147 | -48 485 | Balance |
| Germany | | | | | | | | | Allemagne |
| Imports | S | 495 450 | 486 055 | 490 157 | 604 729 | 718 269 | 780 514 | 919 154 | Importations |
| Exports | S | 550 222 | 571 459 | 615 705 | 751 824 | 911 858 | 977 970 | 1 125 877 | Exportations |
| Balance | | 54 772 | 85 404 | 125 548 | 147 095 | 193 589 | 197 456 | 206 724 | Balance |
| Gibraltar | | | | | | | | | Gibraltar |
| Imports | | 480 | 435 | 385 | 468 | 535 | 550 | ... | Importations |
| Exports | | 126 | 120 | 148 | 147 | 199 | 199 | ... | Exportations |
| Balance | | -354 | -315 | -236 | -320 | -336 | -351 | ... | Balance |
| Greece | | | | | | | | | Grèce |
| Imports | S | 29 221 | 29 928 | 31 164 | 44 375 | 51 559 | 49 817 | 59 121 | Importations |
| Exports | S | 10 747 | 9 483 | 10 315 | 13 195 | 14 996 | 15 511 | 20 180 | Exportations |
| Balance | | -18 474 | -20 444 | -20 849 | -31 180 | -36 564 | -34 306 | -38 940 | Balance |
| Greenland | | | | | | | | | Groenland |
| Imports | G | 364 | 324 | 388 | 461 | 547 | 598 | 581 | Importations |
| Exports | G | 271 | 268 | 305 | 348 | 380 | 403 | 408 | Exportations |
| Balance | | -93 | -56 | -82 | -113 | -166 | -196 | -173 | Balance |
| Hungary[4] | | | | | | | | | Hongrie[4] |
| Imports | S | 31 955 | 33 724 | 37 787 | 47 602 | 59 636 | 65 783 | 77 206 | Importations |
| Exports | S | 28 016 | 30 530 | 34 512 | 42 532 | 54 893 | 62 179 | 74 217 | Exportations |
| Balance | | -3 939 | -3 195 | -3 276 | -5 070 | -4 744 | -3 604 | -2 989 | Balance |
| Iceland | | | | | | | | | Islande |
| Imports | G | 2 591 | 2 253 | 2 274 | 2 788 | 3 551 | 4 557 | 5 077 | Importations |
| Exports | G | 1 891 | 2 021 | 2 227 | 2 386 | 2 896 | 2 947 | 3 241 | Exportations |
| Balance | | -700 | -232 | -47 | -403 | -654 | -1 610 | -1 836 | Balance |
| Ireland | | | | | | | | | Irlande |
| Imports | G | 51 444 | 51 305 | 51 508 | 53 315 | 61 413 | 69 177 | 83 884 | Importations |
| Exports | G | 77 097 | 83 020 | 87 497 | 92 431 | 104 204 | 109 605 | 104 638 | Exportations |
| Balance | | 25 653 | 31 715 | 35 990 | 39 117 | 42 791 | 40 428 | 20 753 | Balance |
| Italy | | | | | | | | | Italie |
| Imports | S | 238 071 | 236 128 | 246 613 | 297 405 | 355 269 | 384 837 | 440 770 | Importations |
| Exports | S | 239 934 | 244 253 | 254 219 | 299 468 | 353 544 | 372 962 | 416 145 | Exportations |
| Balance | | 1 863 | 8 125 | 7 606 | 2 063 | -1 726 | -11 875 | -24 626 | Balance |
| Latvia | | | | | | | | | Lettonie |
| Imports | S | 3 187 | 3 504 | 4 053 | 5 242 | 7 048 | 8 592 | 11 430 | Importations |
| Exports | S | 1 867 | 2 001 | 2 284 | 2 893 | 3 983 | 5 108 | 5 896 | Exportations |
| Balance | | -1 320 | -1 504 | -1 769 | -2 350 | -3 066 | -3 483 | -5 535 | Balance |
| Lithuania | | | | | | | | | Lituanie |
| Imports | G | 5 219 | 6 060 | 7 524 | 9 668 | 12 386 | 15 510 | 19 413 | Importations |
| Exports | G | 3 548 | 4 279 | 5 231 | 6 970 | 9 307 | 11 782 | 14 153 | Exportations |
| Balance | | -1 671 | -1 781 | -2 294 | -2 698 | -3 079 | -3 729 | -5 259 | Balance |

| Region, country or area[&] | Sys.[t] | 2000 | 2001 | 2002 | 2003 | 2004 | 2005 | 2006 | Région, pays ou zone[&] |
|---|---|---|---|---|---|---|---|---|---|
| Luxembourg | | | | | | | | | Luxembourg |
| Imports | S | 10 718 | 11 153 | 11 602 | 13 694 | 16 829 | 17 565 | 19 434 | Importations |
| Exports | S | 7 950 | 8 239 | 8 499 | 9 980 | 12 181 | 12 699 | 14 172 | Exportations |
| Balance | | -2 768 | -2 914 | -3 103 | -3 714 | -4 648 | -4 866 | -5 262 | Balance |
| Malta | | | | | | | | | Malte |
| Imports | G | 3 400 | 2 726 | 2 840 | 3 399 | 3 824 | 3 807 | 4 073 | Importations |
| Exports | G | 2 443 | 1 958 | 2 223 | 2 468 | 2 628 | 2 376 | 2 705 | Exportations |
| Balance | | -957 | -768 | -616 | -931 | -1 196 | -1 432 | -1 368 | Balance |
| Netherlands | | | | | | | | | Pays-Bas |
| Imports | S | 198 926 | 195 569 | 194 130 | 234 014 | 284 020 | 310 600 | 357 895 | Importations |
| Exports | S | 213 425 | 216 180 | 219 857 | 264 849 | 318 066 | 349 844 | 399 651 | Exportations |
| Balance | | 14 499 | 20 611 | 25 727 | 30 835 | 34 046 | 39 244 | 41 756 | Balance |
| Norway | | | | | | | | | Norvège |
| Imports | G | 34 351 | 32 954 | 34 889 | 39 284 | 48 062 | 54 786 | 63 347 | Importations |
| Exports | G | 60 063 | 59 193 | 59 576 | 67 103 | 81 709 | 101 917 | 120 541 | Exportations |
| Balance | | 25 712 | 26 239 | 24 687 | 27 818 | 33 646 | 47 131 | 57 193 | Balance |
| Poland | | | | | | | | | Pologne |
| Imports | S | 48 970 | 50 378 | 55 141 | 68 153 | 89 094 | 100 759 | 127 260 | Importations |
| Exports | S | 31 684 | 36 159 | 41 032 | 53 699 | 74 831 | 89 214 | 110 941 | Exportations |
| Balance | | -17 285 | -14 219 | -14 108 | -14 454 | -14 264 | -11 545 | -16 319 | Balance |
| Portugal | | | | | | | | | Portugal |
| Imports | S | 38 192 | 39 422 | 38 326 | 40 843 | 49 225 | 53 407 | 65 605 | Importations |
| Exports | S | 23 279 | 24 449 | 25 536 | 30 714 | 33 023 | 32 137 | 42 890 | Exportations |
| Balance | | -14 913 | -14 973 | -12 791 | -10 129 | -16 201 | -21 270 | -22 716 | Balance |
| Slovakia | | | | | | | | | Slovaquie |
| Imports | S | 13 413 | 15 501 | 17 460 | 23 760 | 30 469 | 36 168 | 47 416 | Importations |
| Exports | S | 11 889 | 12 641 | 14 478 | 21 966 | 27 605 | 31 997 | 41 939 | Exportations |
| Balance | | -1 524 | -2 860 | -2 983 | -1 794 | -2 864 | -4 171 | -5 478 | Balance |
| Slovenia | | | | | | | | | Slovénie |
| Imports | S | 10 116 | 10 148 | 10 933 | 13 853 | 17 571 | 19 626 | 23 014 | Importations |
| Exports | S | 8 732 | 9 252 | 10 357 | 12 767 | 15 879 | 17 896 | 20 985 | Exportations |
| Balance | | -1 384 | -895 | -576 | -1 086 | -1 692 | -1 730 | -2 029 | Balance |
| Spain | | | | | | | | | Espagne |
| Imports | S | 152 901 | 153 634 | 163 575 | 208 553 | 257 672 | 287 610 | 326 046 | Importations |
| Exports | S | 113 348 | 115 175 | 123 563 | 156 024 | 182 156 | 191 021 | 213 350 | Exportations |
| Balance | | -39 553 | -38 459 | -40 012 | -52 529 | -75 516 | -96 589 | -112 697 | Balance |
| Sweden | | | | | | | | | Suède |
| Imports | G | 73 331 | 64 316 | 67 667 | 84 197 | 100 792 | 111 324 | 126 610 | Importations |
| Exports | G | 87 759 | 78 173 | 82 965 | 102 405 | 123 306 | 130 205 | 147 236 | Exportations |
| Balance | | 14 428 | 13 857 | 15 298 | 18 208 | 22 514 | 18 881 | 20 626 | Balance |
| Switzerland | | | | | | | | | Suisse |
| Imports | S | 76 104 | 77 086 | 82 387 | 95 600 | 110 324 | 119 784 | 132 030 | Importations |
| Exports | S | 74 867 | 78 082 | 87 370 | 100 744 | 117 820 | 126 099 | 141 679 | Exportations |
| Balance | | -1 237 | 996 | 4 983 | 5 144 | 7 496 | 6 314 | 9 649 | Balance |
| United Kingdom | | | | | | | | | Royaume-Uni |
| Imports | G | 334 371 | 320 956 | 335 458 | 380 821 | 451 715 | 483 064 | 547 508 | Importations |
| Exports | G | 281 525 | 267 357 | 276 317 | 304 268 | 341 621 | 371 406 | 428 357 | Exportations |
| Balance | | -52 846 | -53 599 | -59 142 | -76 553 | -110 094 | -111 658 | -119 151 | Balance |
| **North America - Developed economies** | | | | | | | | | **Amerique du Nord - Economies dévelop.** |
| **Imports** | | 1 415 000 | 1 322 058 | 1 344 096 | 1 454 978 | 1 692 049 | 1 934 369 | 2 135 266 | **Importations** |
| **Exports** | | 974 722 | 909 351 | 866 649 | 909 427 | 1 015 354 | 1 144 127 | 1 293 444 | **Exportations** |
| **Balance** | | -440 278 | -412 707 | -477 448 | -545 551 | -676 696 | -790 241 | -841 822 | **Balance** |

| Region, country or area[&] | Sys.[t] | 2000 | 2001 | 2002 | 2003 | 2004 | 2005 | 2006 | Région, pays ou zone[&] |
|---|---|---|---|---|---|---|---|---|---|
| **Bermuda** | | | | | | | | | **Bermudes** |
| Imports | G | 720 | 721 | ... | 833 | ... | 937 | ... | Importations |
| Exports | G | ... | ... | ... | 52 | ... | 26 | ... | Exportations |
| Balance | | ... | ... | ... | -781 | ... | -911 | ... | Balance |
| **Canada[6]** | | | | | | | | | **Canada[6]** |
| Imports | G | 238 812 | 221 757 | 221 962 | 239 085 | 273 084 | 323 365 | 348 959 | Importations |
| Exports | G | 276 645 | 259 858 | 252 407 | 272 699 | 304 623 | 359 411 | 389 513 | Exportations |
| Balance | | 37 833 | 38 101 | 30 445 | 33 614 | 31 539 | 36 046 | 40 555 | Balance |
| **United States[7]** | | | | | | | | | **Etats-Unis[7]** |
| Imports | G | 1 259 300 | 1 179 180 | 1 200 230 | 1 303 050 | 1 525 680 | 1 732 350 | 1 919 430 | Importations |
| Exports | G | 781 918 | 729 100 | 693 103 | 724 771 | 818 520 | 907 158 | 1 038 270 | Exportations |
| Balance | | -477 382 | -450 080 | -507 127 | -578 279 | -707 160 | -825 192 | -881 160 | Balance |
| **South-eastern Europe** | | | | | | | | | **Europe du Sud-Est** |
| Imports | | 29 344 | 33 798 | 39 322 | 51 453 | 69 057 | 82 472 | 100 776 | Importations |
| Exports | | 19 353 | 20 679 | 24 112 | 30 661 | 40 949 | 48 751 | 58 815 | Exportations |
| Balance | | -9 992 | -13 119 | -15 210 | -20 793 | -28 108 | -33 721 | -41 961 | Balance |
| **Albania** | | | | | | | | | **Albanie** |
| Imports | G | 1 090 | 1 327 | 1 503 | 1 864 | 2 309 | 2 618 | 3 058 | Importations |
| Exports | G | 258 | 307 | 340 | 448 | 605 | 658 | 793 | Exportations |
| Balance | | -832 | -1 020 | -1 164 | -1 416 | -1 703 | -1 960 | -2 266 | Balance |
| **Bosnia and Herzegovina** | | | | | | | | | **Bosnie-Herzégovine** |
| Imports | S | 3 083 | 3 342 | 3 912 | 4 777 | ... | ... | ... | Importations |
| Exports | S | 1 067 | 1 031 | 1 015 | 1 372 | ... | ... | ... | Exportations |
| Balance | | -2 017 | -2 311 | -2 897 | -3 405 | ... | ... | ... | Balance |
| **Bulgaria** | | | | | | | | | **Bulgarie** |
| Imports | S | 6 505 | 7 263 | 7 987 | 10 887 | 14 467 | 18 162 | 23 270 | Importations |
| Exports | S | 4 809 | 5 115 | 5 749 | 7 540 | 9 931 | 11 739 | 15 101 | Exportations |
| Balance | | -1 696 | -2 148 | -2 238 | -3 346 | -4 536 | -6 423 | -8 168 | Balance |
| **Romania** | | | | | | | | | **Roumanie** |
| Imports | S | 13 055 | 15 561 | 17 862 | 24 003 | 32 664 | 40 463 | 51 106 | Importations |
| Exports | | 10 367 | 11 391 | 13 876 | 17 619 | 23 485 | 27 730 | 32 336 | Exportations |
| Balance | | -2 688 | -4 170 | -3 986 | -6 384 | -9 179 | -12 733 | -18 770 | Balance |
| **Serbia and Montenegro** | | | | | | | | | **Serbie-et-Monténégro** |
| Imports | S | 3 711 | 4 837 | 6 320 | 7 952 | 11 366 | ... | ... | Importations |
| Exports | S | 1 723 | 1 903 | 2 275 | 2 650 | 3 801 | ... | ... | Exportations |
| Balance | | -1 988 | -2 934 | -4 045 | -5 302 | -7 565 | ... | ... | Balance |
| **TFYR of Macedonia** | | | | | | | | | **L'ex-R.y. Macédoine** |
| Imports | S | 2 094 | 1 694 | 1 995 | 2 306 | 2 932 | 3 228 | 3 752 | Importations |
| Exports | S | 1 323 | 1 158 | 1 116 | 1 367 | 1 676 | 2 041 | 2 398 | Exportations |
| Balance | | -771 | -536 | -880 | -939 | -1 256 | -1 187 | -1 355 | Balance |
| **CIS[§]** | | | | | | | | | **CEI[§]** |
| Imports | | 70 813 | 82 758 | 89 194 | 113 360 | 149 403 | 186 920 | 252 354 | Importations |
| Exports | | 143 487 | 142 654 | 152 828 | 190 835 | 261 354 | 333 957 | 417 310 | Exportations |
| Balance | | 72 674 | 59 897 | 63 634 | 77 475 | 111 952 | 147 037 | 164 956 | Balance |
| **Asia** | | | | | | | | | **Asia** |
| Imports | | 13 690 | 16 059 | 16 058 | 20 217 | 26 830 | 33 372 | 44 992 | Importations |
| Exports | | 18 159 | 18 540 | 19 643 | 23 562 | 32 529 | 41 482 | 57 017 | Exportations |
| Balance | | 4 469 | 2 482 | 3 585 | 3 346 | 5 699 | 8 110 | 12 025 | Balance |
| **Armenia** | | | | | | | | | **Arménie** |
| Imports | S | 882 | 874 | 987 | 1 280 | 1 351 | 1 768 | 2 194 | Importations |
| Exports | S | 294 | 343 | 505 | 686 | 715 | 950 | 1 004 | Exportations |
| Balance | | -588 | -532 | -482 | -594 | -636 | -818 | -1 190 | Balance |
| **Azerbaijan** | | | | | | | | | **Azerbaïdjan** |
| Imports | G | 1 172 | 1 431 | 1 666 | 2 626 | 3 516 | 4 211 | 5 268 | Importations |
| Exports | G | 1 745 | 2 314 | 2 167 | 2 590 | 3 615 | 4 347 | 6 372 | Exportations |
| Balance | | 573 | 883 | 502 | -36 | 99 | 136 | 1 105 | Balance |

**55** Total imports and exports—Imports c.i.f., exports f.o.b., and balance, value in million US dollars (*continued*)

Importations et exportations totales—Importations c.a.f., exportations f.o.b. et balance, valeur en millions de dollars E.-U. (*suite*)

| Region, country or area[&] | Sys.[t] | 2000 | 2001 | 2002 | 2003 | 2004 | 2005 | 2006 | Région, pays ou zone[&] |
|---|---|---|---|---|---|---|---|---|---|
| Georgia | | | | | | | | | Géorgie |
| Imports | G | 709 | 752 | 796 | 1 141 | 1 851 | 2 492 | 3 685 | Importations |
| Exports | G | 323 | 317 | 347 | 463 | 656 | 868 | 998 | Exportations |
| Balance | | -386 | -436 | -449 | -679 | -1 195 | -1 623 | -2 687 | Balance |
| Kazakhstan | | | | | | | | | Kazakhstan |
| Imports | G | 5 040 | 6 446 | 6 584 | 8 409 | 12 781 | 17 353 | 24 956 | Importations |
| Exports | G | 8 812 | 8 639 | 9 670 | 12 927 | 20 093 | 27 849 | 40 470 | Exportations |
| Balance | | 3 772 | 2 193 | 3 086 | 4 518 | 7 312 | 10 497 | 15 515 | Balance |
| Kyrgyzstan | | | | | | | | | Kirghizistan |
| Imports | S | 554 | 467 | 587 | 717 | 941 | 1 102 | 1 848 | Importations |
| Exports | S | 505 | 476 | 486 | 582 | 719 | 672 | 796 | Exportations |
| Balance | | -50 | 9 | -101 | -135 | -222 | -430 | -1 052 | Balance |
| Tajikistan | | | | | | | | | Tadjikistan |
| Imports | G | 675 | 688 | 721 | 881 | ... | ... | ... | Importations |
| Exports | G | 784 | 652 | 737 | 797 | ... | ... | ... | Exportations |
| Balance | | 109 | -36 | 17 | -84 | ... | ... | ... | Balance |
| Turkmenistan | | | | | | | | | Turkménistan |
| Imports | G | ... | ... | 2 119 | 2 512 | ... | ... | ... | Importations |
| Exports | G | ... | ... | 2 856 | 2 632 | ... | ... | ... | Exportations |
| Balance | | ... | ... | 736 | 120 | ... | ... | ... | Balance |
| Uzbekistan | | | | | | | | | Ouzbékistan |
| Imports | G | 2 947 | 3 137 | 2 712 | ... | ... | ... | ... | Importations |
| Exports | G | 3 265 | 3 265 | 2 988 | ... | ... | ... | ... | Exportations |
| Balance | | 317 | 128 | 276 | ... | ... | ... | ... | Balance |
| **Europe** | | | | | | | | | **Europe** |
| **Imports** | | 57 122 | 66 699 | 73 136 | 93 143 | 122 572 | 153 548 | 207 362 | **Importations** |
| **Exports** | | 125 327 | 124 114 | 133 185 | 167 273 | 228 825 | 292 475 | 360 293 | **Exportations** |
| **Balance** | | 68 205 | 57 415 | 60 049 | 74 130 | 106 253 | 138 927 | 152 931 | **Balance** |
| Belarus | | | | | | | | | Bélarus |
| Imports | G | 8 646 | 8 286 | 9 092 | 11 558 | 16 491 | 16 708 | 22 351 | Importations |
| Exports | G | 7 326 | 7 451 | 8 021 | 9 946 | 13 774 | 15 979 | 19 734 | Exportations |
| Balance | | -1 320 | -836 | -1 071 | -1 612 | -2 717 | -729 | -2 618 | Balance |
| Moldova | | | | | | | | | Moldova |
| Imports | G | 776 | 893 | 1 039 | 1 403 | 1 773 | 2 293 | 2 585 | Importations |
| Exports | G | 472 | 568 | 644 | 789 | 980 | 1 091 | 1 033 | Exportations |
| Balance | | -305 | -325 | -395 | -614 | -793 | -1 202 | -1 552 | Balance |
| Russian Federation | | | | | | | | | Fédération de Russie |
| Imports | G | 33 880 | 41 883 | 46 177 | 57 347 | 75 569 | 98 708 | 137 744 | Importations |
| Exports | G | 103 093 | 99 969 | 106 712 | 133 656 | 181 663 | 241 473 | 301 515 | Exportations |
| Balance | | 69 213 | 58 086 | 60 535 | 76 309 | 106 093 | 142 766 | 163 771 | Balance |
| Ukraine | | | | | | | | | Ukraine |
| Imports | G | 13 956 | 15 775 | 16 977 | 23 020 | 28 997 | 36 136 | 45 039 | Importations |
| Exports | G | 14 573 | 16 265 | 17 957 | 23 067 | 32 666 | 34 228 | 38 368 | Exportations |
| Balance | | 617 | 490 | 980 | 47 | 3 669 | -1 908 | -6 671 | Balance |
| **Northern Africa** | | | | | | | | | **Afrique du Nord** |
| **Imports** | | 46 790 | 47 433 | 50 108 | 52 778 | 67 401 | 79 405 | 86 773 | **Importations** |
| **Exports** | | 52 419 | 47 731 | 47 886 | 60 616 | 78 684 | 106 783 | 127 379 | **Exportations** |
| **Balance** | | 5 629 | 299 | -2 222 | 7 838 | 11 283 | 27 378 | 40 606 | **Balance** |
| Algeria | | | | | | | | | Algérie |
| Imports | S | 9 169 | 9 941 | 11 969 | 12 392 | 18 166 | 20 356 | 20 984 | Importations |
| Exports | S | 22 030 | 19 139 | 18 801 | 23 206 | 31 300 | 46 000 | 52 784 | Exportations |
| Balance | | 12 861 | 9 198 | 6 832 | 10 814 | 13 133 | 25 644 | 31 800 | Balance |
| Egypt[8] | | | | | | | | | Egypte[8] |
| Imports | S | 14 010 | 12 756 | 12 552 | 11 170 | 12 859 | 19 851 | 20 784 | Importations |
| Exports | S | 4 691 | 4 128 | 4 708 | 6 327 | 7 530 | 10 672 | 13 736 | Exportations |
| Balance | | -9 319 | -8 628 | -7 844 | -4 842 | -5 329 | -9 179 | -7 048 | Balance |

**55**    **Total imports and exports**—Imports c.i.f., exports f.o.b., and balance, value in million US dollars (*continued*)

**Importations et exportations totales**—Importations c.a.f., exportations f.o.b. et balance, valeur en millions de dollars E.-U. (*suite*)

| Region, country or area[&] | Sys.[t] | 2000 | 2001 | 2002 | 2003 | 2004 | 2005 | 2006 | Région, pays ou zone[&] |
|---|---|---|---|---|---|---|---|---|---|
| Libyan Arab Jamah. | | | | | | | | | Jamah. arabe libyenne |
| Imports | G | 3 704 | 4 363 | 4 412 | 4 311 | 6 333 | 6 975 | 8 167 | Importations |
| Exports | G | 12 626 | 10 902 | 9 880 | 14 541 | 20 837 | 30 033 | 38 369 | Exportations |
| Balance | | 8 922 | 6 538 | 5 468 | 10 230 | 14 503 | 23 058 | 30 202 | Balance |
| Morocco | | | | | | | | | Maroc |
| Imports | S | 11 534 | 11 038 | 11 864 | 14 250 | 17 546 | 19 458 | 22 499 | Importations |
| Exports | S | 7 423 | 7 144 | 7 849 | 8 778 | 9 663 | 10 006 | 11 511 | Exportations |
| Balance | | -4 111 | -3 893 | -4 014 | -5 472 | -7 882 | -9 452 | -10 987 | Balance |
| Tunisia | | | | | | | | | Tunisie |
| Imports | G | 8 567 | 9 529 | 9 526 | 10 910 | 12 818 | 13 177 | 14 865 | Importations |
| Exports | G | 5 850 | 6 621 | 6 871 | 8 027 | 9 685 | 10 494 | 11 513 | Exportations |
| Balance | | -2 717 | -2 908 | -2 655 | -2 883 | -3 133 | -2 683 | -3 352 | Balance |
| **Sub-Saharan Africa** | | | | | | | | | **Afrique subsaharienne** |
| **Imports** | | **80 066** | **84 725** | **83 518** | **108 210** | **135 419** | **165 550** | **189 478** | **Importations** |
| **Exports** | | **91 915** | **87 555** | **90 410** | **110 155** | **146 613** | **189 697** | **210 772** | **Exportations** |
| **Balance** | | **11 849** | **2 831** | **6 892** | **1 945** | **11 194** | **24 147** | **21 294** | **Balance** |
| Angola[6] | | | | | | | | | Angola[6] |
| Imports | S | 3 040 | 3 179 | 3 760 | 5 480 | 5 832 | 8 353 | 11 600 | Importations |
| Exports | S | 7 703 | 6 380 | 7 516 | 9 508 | 13 475 | 24 109 | 31 084 | Exportations |
| Balance | | 4 663 | 3 201 | 3 756 | 4 028 | 7 643 | 15 756 | 19 484 | Balance |
| Benin | | | | | | | | | Bénin |
| Imports | S | 567 | 623 | 725 | 892 | 894 | 895 | 990 | Importations |
| Exports | S | 392 | 372 | 450 | 555 | 564 | 564 | 574 | Exportations |
| Balance | | -174 | -251 | -275 | -337 | -330 | -330 | -416 | Balance |
| Botswana | | | | | | | | | Botswana |
| Imports | G | 2 079 | 1 817 | 1 865 | 2 472 | 3 368 | 3 176 | 3 136 | Importations |
| Exports | G | 2 661 | 2 544 | 2 445 | 2 809 | 3 517 | 4 459 | 4 580 | Exportations |
| Balance | | 581 | 726 | 580 | 337 | 148 | 1 284 | 1 444 | Balance |
| Burkina Faso | | | | | | | | | Burkina Faso |
| Imports | G | 608 | 655 | 746 | 932 | 1 273 | 1 275 | 1 454 | Importations |
| Exports | G | 213 | 226 | 248 | 320 | 480 | 346 | 430 | Exportations |
| Balance | | -395 | -429 | -498 | -612 | -793 | -928 | -1 024 | Balance |
| Burundi | | | | | | | | | Burundi |
| Imports | S | 148 | 139 | 129 | 157 | 176 | 267 | 431 | Importations |
| Exports | S | 50 | 39 | 30 | 38 | 47 | 56 | 58 | Exportations |
| Balance | | -98 | -101 | -99 | -119 | -129 | -211 | -372 | Balance |
| Cameroon | | | | | | | | | Cameroun |
| Imports | S | 1 483 | 1 849 | 1 876 | 2 032 | 2 411 | 2 880 | 3 180 | Importations |
| Exports | S | 1 823 | 1 746 | 1 814 | 2 260 | 2 482 | 2 816 | 3 785 | Exportations |
| Balance | | 341 | -104 | -62 | 228 | 71 | -63 | 604 | Balance |
| Cape Verde | | | | | | | | | Cap-Vert |
| Imports | G | 237 | 234 | 276 | 351 | 387 | 438 | 542 | Importations |
| Exports | G | 11 | 10 | 11 | 13 | 15 | 18 | 21 | Exportations |
| Balance | | -227 | -224 | -266 | -338 | -372 | -421 | -521 | Balance |
| Central African Rep. | | | | | | | | | Rép. centrafricaine |
| Imports | S | 118 | 108 | 122 | 119 | 149 | 171 | 210 | Importations |
| Exports | S | 163 | 142 | 150 | 128 | 126 | 127 | 121 | Exportations |
| Balance | | 45 | 35 | 27 | 9 | -23 | -44 | -89 | Balance |
| Chad | | | | | | | | | Tchad |
| Imports | S | 319 | 680 | 1 638 | 788 | 859 | 1 122 | 1 197 | Importations |
| Exports | S | 184 | 189 | 184 | 599 | 2 192 | 3 046 | 3 739 | Exportations |
| Balance | | -135 | -491 | -1 454 | -189 | 1 333 | 1 924 | 2 542 | Balance |

55   **Total imports and exports**—Imports c.i.f., exports f.o.b., and balance, value in million US dollars (*continued*)

**Importations et exportations totales**—Importations c.a.f., exportations f.o.b. et balance, valeur en millions de dollars E.-U. (*suite*)

| Region, country or area[&] | Sys.[t] | 2000 | 2001 | 2002 | 2003 | 2004 | 2005 | 2006 | Région, pays ou zone[&] |
|---|---|---|---|---|---|---|---|---|---|
| Comoros | | | | | | | | | Comores |
| Imports | S | 43 | 51 | 53 | 70 | 86 | 95 | 108 | Importations |
| Exports | S | 14 | 17 | 19 | 27 | 19 | 14 | 11 | Exportations |
| Balance | | -29 | -34 | -34 | -43 | -67 | -81 | -97 | Balance |
| Congo | | | | | | | | | Congo |
| Imports | S | 480 | 703 | 695 | 856 | 879 | 1 459 | 1 853 | Importations |
| Exports | S | 2 482 | 2 053 | 2 290 | 2 686 | 3 410 | 4 788 | 6 796 | Exportations |
| Balance | | 2 003 | 1 350 | 1 596 | 1 830 | 2 531 | 3 329 | 4 943 | Balance |
| Côte d'Ivoire | | | | | | | | | Côte d'Ivoire |
| Imports | S | 2 783 | 2 420 | 2 462 | 3 237 | 4 299 | 5 345 | 5 304 | Importations |
| Exports | S | 3 885 | 3 955 | 5 279 | 5 803 | 6 955 | 7 484 | 8 715 | Exportations |
| Balance | | 1 102 | 1 535 | 2 817 | 2 566 | 2 655 | 2 139 | 3 410 | Balance |
| Dem. Rep. of the Congo | | | | | | | | | Rép. dém. du Congo |
| Imports | S | 697 | 807 | 1 081 | 1 594 | 1 986 | 2 270 | 2 800 | Importations |
| Exports | S | 824 | 901 | 1 132 | 1 374 | 1 850 | 2 190 | 2 300 | Exportations |
| Balance | | 126 | 94 | 51 | -220 | -137 | -80 | -500 | Balance |
| Djibouti | | | | | | | | | Djibouti |
| Imports | S | ... | 196 | 197 | 238 | 261 | 277 | 290 | Importations |
| Exports | S | ... | 32 | 36 | 37 | 38 | 40 | 40 | Exportations |
| Balance | | ... | -164 | -161 | -201 | -223 | -238 | -250 | Balance |
| Equatorial Guinea | | | | | | | | | Guinée équatoriale |
| Imports | G | 451 | 812 | 508 | 1 237 | 1 563 | 2 108 | 2 503 | Importations |
| Exports | G | 1 097 | 1 732 | 2 121 | 2 803 | 4 585 | 7 134 | 8 912 | Exportations |
| Balance | | 646 | 921 | 1 613 | 1 566 | 3 022 | 5 026 | 6 408 | Balance |
| Ethiopia | | | | | | | | | Ethiopie |
| Imports | G | 1 261 | 1 807 | 1 622 | 2 119 | 3 087 | 4 127 | 4 710 | Importations |
| Exports | G | 486 | 456 | 480 | 496 | 678 | 903 | 1 050 | Exportations |
| Balance | | -775 | -1 351 | -1 142 | -1 623 | -2 409 | -3 224 | -3 659 | Balance |
| Gabon | | | | | | | | | Gabon |
| Imports | S | 996 | 858 | 955 | 1 036 | 1 213 | 1 371 | 1 501 | Importations |
| Exports | S | 2 605 | 2 519 | 2 413 | 2 827 | 3 612 | 4 863 | 5 604 | Exportations |
| Balance | | 1 610 | 1 661 | 1 458 | 1 791 | 2 398 | 3 492 | 4 103 | Balance |
| Gambia | | | | | | | | | Gambie |
| Imports | G | 187 | 134 | 159 | 156 | 229 | 237 | 245 | Importations |
| Exports | G | 15 | 10 | 12 | 8 | 10 | 8 | 10 | Exportations |
| Balance | | -172 | -124 | -147 | -148 | -219 | -229 | -235 | Balance |
| Ghana | | | | | | | | | Ghana |
| Imports | G | 2 973 | ... | ... | ... | ... | 5 755 | 5 497 | Importations |
| Exports | G | 1 317 | ... | ... | ... | ... | 2 803 | 3 703 | Exportations |
| Balance | | -1 656 | ... | ... | ... | ... | -2 952 | -1 794 | Balance |
| Guinea-Bissau | | | | | | | | | Guinée-Bissau |
| Imports | G | 59 | 62 | 59 | 66 | 96 | 119 | 111 | Importations |
| Exports | G | 62 | 62 | 54 | 65 | 87 | 80 | 75 | Exportations |
| Balance | | 4 | 1 | -5 | -1 | -9 | -39 | -36 | Balance |
| Kenya | | | | | | | | | Kenya |
| Imports | G | 3 105 | 3 189 | 3 245 | 3 725 | 4 553 | 6 149 | 7 311 | Importations |
| Exports | G | 1 734 | 1 943 | 2 116 | 2 411 | 2 684 | 3 293 | 3 437 | Exportations |
| Balance | | -1 372 | -1 246 | -1 129 | -1 314 | -1 869 | -2 856 | -3 874 | Balance |
| Lesotho | | | | | | | | | Lesotho |
| Imports | G | 809 | 748 | 815 | 1 121 | 1 440 | 1 410 | 1 363 | Importations |
| Exports | G | 221 | 278 | 376 | 485 | 713 | 675 | 695 | Exportations |
| Balance | | -589 | -470 | -438 | -636 | -727 | -735 | -668 | Balance |
| Madagascar | | | | | | | | | Madagascar |
| Imports | S | 999 | 956 | 605 | 1 115 | 1 411 | 1 531 | ... | Importations |
| Exports | S | 828 | 932 | 490 | 863 | 935 | 733 | ... | Exportations |
| Balance | | -171 | -24 | -115 | -252 | -476 | -798 | ... | Balance |

55 Total imports and exports—Imports c.i.f., exports f.o.b., and balance, value in million US dollars (*continued*)

Importations et exportations totales—Importations c.a.f., exportations f.o.b. et balance, valeur en millions de dollars E.-U. (*suite*)

| Region, country or area[&] | Sys.[t] | 2000 | 2001 | 2002 | 2003 | 2004 | 2005 | 2006 | Région, pays ou zone[&] |
|---|---|---|---|---|---|---|---|---|---|
| Malawi | | | | | | | | | Malawi |
| Imports | G | 533 | 563 | 695 | 786 | 933 | 1 095 | ... | Importations |
| Exports | G | 379 | 449 | 407 | 525 | 483 | 496 | ... | Exportations |
| Balance | | -153 | -113 | -288 | -261 | -449 | -599 | ... | Balance |
| Mali | | | | | | | | | Mali |
| Imports | S | 807 | 989 | 927 | 1 247 | 1 300 | 1 623 | 1 599 | Importations |
| Exports | S | 552 | 724 | 873 | 926 | 1 029 | 1 126 | 1 358 | Exportations |
| Balance | | -255 | -265 | -54 | -322 | -271 | -497 | -241 | Balance |
| Mauritius | | | | | | | | | Maurice |
| Imports | G | 2 091 | 1 987 | 2 159 | 2 364 | 2 771 | 3 157 | 3 631 | Importations |
| Exports | G | 1 551 | 1 628 | 1 801 | 1 899 | 1 993 | 2 138 | 2 333 | Exportations |
| Balance | | -540 | -359 | -358 | -465 | -778 | -1 018 | -1 298 | Balance |
| Mozambique | | | | | | | | | Mozambique |
| Imports | S | 1 158 | 1 063 | 1 640 | 1 753 | 1 927 | 2 408 | 2 970 | Importations |
| Exports | S | 364 | 703 | 810 | 1 045 | 1 504 | 1 745 | 2 420 | Exportations |
| Balance | | -794 | -360 | -830 | -708 | -423 | -663 | -550 | Balance |
| Namibia | | | | | | | | | Namibie |
| Imports | G | 1 539 | 1 542 | 1 484 | 1 999 | 2 432 | 2 440 | 2 715 | Importations |
| Exports | G | 1 317 | 1 180 | 1 077 | 1 267 | 1 835 | 1 987 | 2 711 | Exportations |
| Balance | | -222 | -362 | -407 | -732 | -598 | -453 | -4 | Balance |
| Niger | | | | | | | | | Niger |
| Imports | S | 390 | 412 | 474 | 630 | 757 | 797 | 805 | Importations |
| Exports | S | 284 | 273 | 278 | 353 | 439 | 501 | 539 | Exportations |
| Balance | | -107 | -139 | -196 | -277 | -318 | -296 | -266 | Balance |
| Nigeria | | | | | | | | | Nigéria |
| Imports | G | 8 721 | 11 586 | 7 547 | 10 853 | 14 164 | 20 754 | 21 809 | Importations |
| Exports | G | 20 975 | 17 261 | 15 107 | 19 887 | 31 148 | 48 490 | 45 116 | Exportations |
| Balance | | 12 254 | 5 675 | 7 560 | 9 034 | 16 984 | 27 736 | 23 307 | Balance |
| Rwanda | | | | | | | | | Rwanda |
| Imports | G | 211 | 250 | 203 | 245 | 284 | 432 | 484 | Importations |
| Exports | G | 52 | 85 | 56 | 58 | 98 | 125 | 135 | Exportations |
| Balance | | -159 | -165 | -147 | -187 | -186 | -306 | -349 | Balance |
| Senegal | | | | | | | | | Sénégal |
| Imports | G | 1 518 | 1 727 | 2 038 | 2 395 | 2 844 | 3 193 | 3 512 | Importations |
| Exports | G | 919 | 1 002 | 1 070 | 1 259 | 1 506 | 1 534 | 1 513 | Exportations |
| Balance | | -598 | -726 | -968 | -1 136 | -1 337 | -1 659 | -1 999 | Balance |
| Seychelles | | | | | | | | | Seychelles |
| Imports | G | 343 | 478 | 421 | 412 | 497 | 676 | 755 | Importations |
| Exports | G | 193 | 217 | 227 | 274 | 291 | 340 | 430 | Exportations |
| Balance | | -150 | -262 | -194 | -138 | -206 | -336 | -325 | Balance |
| Sierra Leone | | | | | | | | | Sierra Leone |
| Imports | S | 149 | 182 | 264 | 303 | 286 | 345 | 389 | Importations |
| Exports | S | 13 | 29 | 49 | 92 | 139 | 159 | 216 | Exportations |
| Balance | | -136 | -153 | -216 | -211 | -148 | -186 | -173 | Balance |
| South Africa[9,10] | | | | | | | | | Afrique du Sud[9,10] |
| Imports | G | 29 700 | 28 264 | 29 281 | 41 120 | 53 518 | 62 325 | ... | Importations |
| Exports | G | 29 987 | 29 283 | 29 733 | 36 503 | 46 148 | 51 640 | 58 197 | Exportations |
| Balance | | 287 | 1 019 | 452 | -4 617 | -7 370 | -10 685 | ... | Balance |
| Sudan[11] | | | | | | | | | Soudan[11] |
| Imports | G | 1 553 | 2 301 | 2 446 | 2 882 | 4 075 | 6 757 | 8 074 | Importations |
| Exports | G | 1 807 | 1 699 | 1 949 | 2 542 | 3 778 | 4 824 | 5 657 | Exportations |
| Balance | | 254 | -602 | -497 | -340 | -297 | -1 933 | -2 417 | Balance |
| Swaziland | | | | | | | | | Swaziland |
| Imports | G | 1 039 | 1 116 | 946 | 1 523 | 1 931 | 2 237 | 2 495 | Importations |
| Exports | G | 903 | 1 048 | 1 038 | 1 644 | 1 957 | 2 142 | 2 382 | Exportations |
| Balance | | -137 | -68 | 93 | 121 | 25 | -95 | -113 | Balance |

55
Total imports and exports—Imports c.i.f., exports f.o.b., and balance, value in million US dollars (*continued*)

Importations et exportations totales—Importations c.a.f., exportations f.o.b. et balance, valeur en millions de dollars E.-U. (*suite*)

| Region, country or area& | Sys.[t] | 2000 | 2001 | 2002 | 2003 | 2004 | 2005 | 2006 | Région, pays ou zone& |
|---|---|---|---|---|---|---|---|---|---|
| **Togo** | | | | | | | | | **Togo** |
| Imports | S | 562 | 553 | 595 | 775 | 883 | 995 | 1 214 | Importations |
| Exports | S | 362 | 357 | 430 | 600 | 601 | 585 | 638 | Exportations |
| Balance | | -200 | -196 | -165 | -176 | -281 | -410 | -577 | Balance |
| **Uganda** | | | | | | | | | **Ouganda** |
| Imports | G | 1 512 | 1 594 | 1 112 | 1 251 | 2 020 | 1 895 | 2 503 | Importations |
| Exports | G | 469 | 457 | 442 | 563 | 885 | 821 | 970 | Exportations |
| Balance | | -1 043 | -1 137 | -670 | -688 | -1 136 | -1 075 | -1 533 | Balance |
| **United Rep. of Tanzania** | | | | | | | | | **Rép.-Unie de Tanzanie** |
| Imports | G | 1 523 | 1 715 | 1 661 | 2 125 | 2 515 | 2 661 | 4 254 | Importations |
| Exports | G | 663 | 777 | 902 | 1 129 | 1 336 | 1 479 | 1 655 | Exportations |
| Balance | | -860 | -937 | -758 | -996 | -1 179 | -1 182 | -2 598 | Balance |
| **Zambia** | | | | | | | | | **Zambie** |
| Imports | S | 997 | 1 309 | 1 284 | 1 576 | 2 018 | 2 567 | 2 931 | Importations |
| Exports | S | 681 | 993 | 961 | 981 | 1 462 | 1 822 | 3 745 | Exportations |
| Balance | | -316 | -316 | -323 | -595 | -556 | -745 | 814 | Balance |
| **Zimbabwe** | | | | | | | | | **Zimbabwe** |
| Imports | G | 1 863 | 1 715 | 1 751 | 1 710 | 2 204 | 2 330 | 2 100 | Importations |
| Exports | G | 1 925 | 1 207 | 2 012 | 1 670 | 1 887 | 1 820 | 1 920 | Exportations |
| Balance | | 62 | -508 | 261 | -40 | -317 | -510 | -180 | Balance |
| **Latin America and the Carib.** | | | | | | | | | **Amér. latine et Caraïbes** |
| **Imports** | | 374 967 | 366 694 | 342 914 | 354 811 | 433 299 | 511 567 | 607 555 | **Importations** |
| **Exports** | | 353 658 | 339 513 | 343 685 | 374 406 | 460 710 | 556 162 | 666 487 | **Exportations** |
| **Balance** | | -21 309 | -27 182 | 771 | 19 595 | 27 410 | 44 595 | 58 932 | **Balance** |
| **Caribbean** | | | | | | | | | **Caraïbes** |
| **Imports** | | 25 169 | 25 253 | 25 973 | 26 592 | 29 416 | 35 163 | 38 437 | **Importations** |
| **Exports** | | 10 398 | 10 286 | 9 930 | 11 733 | 13 940 | 16 254 | 23 379 | **Exportations** |
| **Balance** | | -14 771 | -14 967 | -16 043 | -14 860 | -15 476 | -18 909 | -15 058 | **Balance** |
| **Anguilla** | | | | | | | | | **Anguilla** |
| Imports | S | 99 | 82 | 74 | 80 | 105 | 133 | 143 | Importations |
| Exports | S | 4 | 4 | 4 | 4 | 6 | 7 | 13 | Exportations |
| Balance | | -95 | -79 | -69 | -76 | -100 | -126 | -130 | Balance |
| **Antigua and Barbuda** | | | | | | | | | **Antigua-et-Barbuda** |
| Imports | G | 407 | 386 | 400 | 422 | 454 | 497 | 550 | Importations |
| Exports | G | 52 | 41 | 39 | 45 | 55 | 58 | 60 | Exportations |
| Balance | | -354 | -345 | -360 | -377 | -399 | -440 | -490 | Balance |
| **Aruba** | | | | | | | | | **Aruba** |
| Imports | S | 835 | 841 | 841 | 848 | 875 | 1 031 | 1 054 | Importations |
| Exports | S | 173 | 149 | 128 | 83 | 80 | 107 | 124 | Exportations |
| Balance | | -662 | -693 | -713 | -764 | -796 | -925 | -930 | Balance |
| **Bahamas[12]** | | | | | | | | | **Bahamas[12]** |
| Imports | G | 2 074 | 1 912 | 1 728 | 1 762 | 1 905 | 2 230 | 2 401 | Importations |
| Exports | G | 576 | 423 | 446 | 425 | 477 | 562 | 674 | Exportations |
| Balance | | -1 498 | -1 489 | -1 282 | -1 337 | -1 428 | -1 668 | -1 726 | Balance |
| **Barbados** | | | | | | | | | **Barbade** |
| Imports | G | 1 156 | 1 069 | 1 071 | 1 195 | 1 413 | 1 604 | 1 586 | Importations |
| Exports | G | 272 | 259 | 242 | 250 | 278 | 359 | 385 | Exportations |
| Balance | | -884 | -809 | -829 | -946 | -1 135 | -1 245 | -1 201 | Balance |
| **Cuba** | | | | | | | | | **Cuba** |
| Imports | S | ... | ... | ... | 4 613 | 5 562 | ... | ... | Importations |
| Exports | S | ... | ... | ... | 1 672 | 2 188 | ... | ... | Exportations |
| Balance | | ... | ... | ... | -2 941 | -3 374 | ... | ... | Balance |
| **Dominica** | | | | | | | | | **Dominique** |
| Imports | S | 148 | 131 | 116 | 128 | 144 | 165 | 165 | Importations |
| Exports | S | 56 | 46 | 46 | 41 | 42 | 43 | ... | Exportations |
| Balance | | -92 | -85 | -70 | -87 | -102 | -122 | ... | Balance |

55 **Total imports and exports**—Imports c.i.f., exports f.o.b., and balance, value in million US dollars (*continued*)

**Importations et exportations totales**—Importations c.a.f., exportations f.o.b. et balance, valeur en millions de dollars E.-U. (*suite*)

| Region, country or area[&] | Sys.[t] | 2000 | 2001 | 2002 | 2003 | 2004 | 2005 | 2006 | Région, pays ou zone[&] |
|---|---|---|---|---|---|---|---|---|---|
| Dominican Republic[6,13] | | | | | | | | | Rép. dominicaine[6,13] |
| Imports | G | 6 416 | 5 937 | 6 037 | 5 266 | 5 368 | 7 207 | 8 745 | Importations |
| Exports | G | 966 | 805 | 834 | 1 041 | 1 251 | 1 398 | 1 933 | Exportations |
| Balance | | -5 450 | -5 132 | -5 204 | -4 225 | -4 117 | -5 809 | -6 812 | Balance |
| Grenada | | | | | | | | | Grenade |
| Imports | S | 246 | 219 | 202 | 254 | 233 | 319 | 280 | Importations |
| Exports | S | 71 | 60 | 58 | 42 | 30 | 39 | 20 | Exportations |
| Balance | | -175 | -160 | -144 | -213 | -203 | -279 | -260 | Balance |
| Haiti | | | | | | | | | Haïti |
| Imports | G | 1 040 | 1 017 | 1 122 | 1 187 | 1 317 | 1 449 | 1 879 | Importations |
| Exports | G | 313 | 275 | 279 | 346 | 394 | 470 | 480 | Exportations |
| Balance | | -727 | -742 | -842 | -841 | -923 | -979 | -1 399 | Balance |
| Jamaica | | | | | | | | | Jamaïque |
| Imports | G | 3 302 | 3 361 | 3 533 | 3 633 | 3 772 | 4 458 | 5 314 | Importations |
| Exports | G | 1 295 | 1 220 | 1 123 | 1 177 | 1 390 | 1 499 | 1 874 | Exportations |
| Balance | | -2 007 | -2 140 | -2 410 | -2 457 | -2 382 | -2 959 | -3 440 | Balance |
| Saint Kitts and Nevis | | | | | | | | | Saint-Kitts-et-Nevis |
| Imports | S | 196 | 189 | 201 | 205 | 182 | 210 | 286 | Importations |
| Exports | S | 33 | 31 | 27 | 48 | 42 | 34 | 31 | Exportations |
| Balance | | -163 | -158 | -174 | -157 | -140 | -176 | -255 | Balance |
| Saint Lucia | | | | | | | | | Sainte-Lucie |
| Imports | S | 355 | 355 | 309 | 403 | 459 | 550 | 600 | Importations |
| Exports | S | 47 | 51 | 49 | 62 | 63 | 64 | 65 | Exportations |
| Balance | | -308 | -304 | -260 | -341 | -397 | -486 | -535 | Balance |
| Saint Vincent-Grenadines | | | | | | | | | Saint Vincent-Grenadines |
| Imports | S | 163 | 172 | 179 | 201 | 226 | 240 | 247 | Importations |
| Exports | S | 47 | 41 | 39 | 38 | 33 | 40 | 25 | Exportations |
| Balance | | -116 | -130 | -139 | -163 | -192 | -200 | -222 | Balance |
| Trinidad and Tobago | | | | | | | | | Trinité-et-Tobago |
| Imports | S | 3 308 | 3 576 | 3 644 | 3 892 | 4 858 | 5 050 | 6 484 | Importations |
| Exports | S | 4 274 | 4 275 | 3 883 | 5 178 | 6 374 | 8 476 | 14 150 | Exportations |
| Balance | | 966 | 698 | 239 | 1 286 | 1 516 | 3 426 | 7 666 | Balance |
| **Latin America** | | | | | | | | | **Amérique latine** |
| **Imports** | | 349 798 | 341 441 | 316 941 | 328 219 | 403 883 | 476 404 | 569 118 | **Importations** |
| **Exports** | | 343 261 | 329 226 | 333 755 | 362 673 | 446 770 | 539 909 | 643 107 | **Exportations** |
| **Balance** | | -6 537 | -12 215 | 16 814 | 34 454 | 42 887 | 63 504 | 73 989 | **Balance** |
| Argentina | | | | | | | | | Argentine |
| Imports | S | 25 280 | 20 320 | 8 990 | 13 834 | 22 445 | 28 688 | 34 158 | Importations |
| Exports | S | 26 341 | 26 543 | 25 650 | 29 566 | 34 576 | 40 351 | 46 569 | Exportations |
| Balance | | 1 061 | 6 223 | 16 660 | 15 732 | 12 131 | 11 664 | 12 411 | Balance |
| Belize | | | | | | | | | Belize |
| Imports | G | 524 | 517 | 525 | 552 | 514 | 593 | 676 | Importations |
| Exports | G | 218 | 169 | 169 | 205 | 213 | 208 | 266 | Exportations |
| Balance | | -306 | -348 | -356 | -347 | -301 | -385 | -410 | Balance |
| Bolivia | | | | | | | | | Bolivie |
| Imports | G | 1 830 | 1 708 | 1 770 | 1 616 | 1 844 | 2 341 | 2 819 | Importations |
| Exports | G | 1 230 | 1 285 | 1 299 | 1 598 | 2 146 | 2 791 | 3 863 | Exportations |
| Balance | | -600 | -423 | -471 | -18 | 302 | 450 | 1 044 | Balance |
| Brazil | | | | | | | | | Brésil |
| Imports | G | 59 066 | 58 672 | 49 723 | 50 881 | 66 433 | 77 628 | 95 853 | Importations |
| Exports | G | 55 119 | 58 287 | 60 439 | 73 203 | 96 678 | 118 529 | 137 807 | Exportations |
| Balance | | -3 947 | -385 | 10 716 | 22 322 | 30 244 | 40 901 | 41 954 | Balance |
| Chile | | | | | | | | | Chili |
| Imports | S | 18 507 | 17 429 | 17 092 | 19 322 | 24 794 | 32 735 | 38 409 | Importations |
| Exports | S | 19 210 | 18 272 | 18 180 | 21 664 | 32 520 | 41 297 | 58 116 | Exportations |
| Balance | | 703 | 843 | 1 088 | 2 342 | 7 727 | 8 562 | 19 707 | Balance |

**Total imports and exports**—Imports c.i.f., exports f.o.b., and balance, value in million US dollars (*continued*)

**Importations et exportations totales**—Importations c.a.f., exportations f.o.b. et balance, valeur en millions de dollars E.-U. (*suite*)

| Region, country or area[&] | Sys.[t] | 2000 | 2001 | 2002 | 2003 | 2004 | 2005 | 2006 | Région, pays ou zone[&] |
|---|---|---|---|---|---|---|---|---|---|
| **Colombia** | | | | | | | | | **Colombie** |
| Imports | G | 11 539 | 12 834 | 12 711 | 13 889 | 16 746 | 21 204 | 26 046 | Importations |
| Exports | G | 13 043 | 12 290 | 11 911 | 13 080 | 16 224 | 21 146 | 24 388 | Exportations |
| Balance | | 1 505 | -544 | -800 | -809 | -522 | -59 | -1 658 | Balance |
| **Costa Rica** | | | | | | | | | **Costa Rica** |
| Imports | S | 6 389 | 6 569 | 7 188 | 7 663 | 8 268 | 9 812 | 11 520 | Importations |
| Exports | S | 5 850 | 5 021 | 5 264 | 6 102 | 6 301 | 7 026 | 8 216 | Exportations |
| Balance | | -539 | -1 547 | -1 924 | -1 561 | -1 967 | -2 786 | -3 305 | Balance |
| **Ecuador** | | | | | | | | | **Equateur** |
| Imports | G | 3 721 | 5 363 | 6 431 | 6 703 | 8 226 | 10 287 | 12 114 | Importations |
| Exports | G | 4 927 | 4 678 | 5 042 | 6 223 | 7 753 | 10 100 | 12 728 | Exportations |
| Balance | | 1 206 | -684 | -1 390 | -480 | -473 | -187 | 615 | Balance |
| **El Salvador** | | | | | | | | | **El Salvador** |
| Imports | S | 4 948 | 5 027 | 5 184 | 5 754 | 6 329 | 6 834 | 7 628 | Importations |
| Exports | S | 2 941 | 2 864 | 2 995 | 3 128 | 3 305 | 3 387 | 3 513 | Exportations |
| Balance | | -2 006 | -2 163 | -2 189 | -2 626 | -3 024 | -3 448 | -4 115 | Balance |
| **Guatemala** | | | | | | | | | **Guatemala** |
| Imports | S | 5 171 | 5 606 | 6 304 | 6 722 | 7 812 | 8 810 | 10 157 | Importations |
| Exports | S | 2 711 | 2 464 | 2 473 | 2 632 | 2 939 | 3 477 | 3 665 | Exportations |
| Balance | | -2 460 | -3 143 | -3 831 | -4 090 | -4 873 | -5 333 | -6 492 | Balance |
| **Guyana** | | | | | | | | | **Guyana** |
| Imports | S | 582 | 583 | 576 | 576 | 652 | 790 | 876 | Importations |
| Exports | S | 502 | 490 | 496 | 513 | 593 | 553 | 569 | Exportations |
| Balance | | -80 | -93 | -81 | -63 | -59 | -237 | -307 | Balance |
| **Honduras** | | | | | | | | | **Honduras** |
| Imports | S | 2 855 | 2 942 | 2 981 | 3 276 | 3 916 | 4 613 | 5 418 | Importations |
| Exports | S | 1 380 | 1 324 | 1 321 | 1 321 | 1 537 | 1 679 | 1 929 | Exportations |
| Balance | | -1 475 | -1 617 | -1 660 | -1 954 | -2 379 | -2 934 | -3 488 | Balance |
| **Mexico[6,14]** | | | | | | | | | **Mexique[6,14]** |
| Imports | G | 174 500 | 168 276 | 168 679 | 170 490 | 197 347 | 221 414 | 256 130 | Importations |
| Exports | G | 166 367 | 158 547 | 160 682 | 165 396 | 189 084 | 213 891 | 250 441 | Exportations |
| Balance | | -8 133 | -9 729 | -7 997 | -5 094 | -8 263 | -7 523 | -5 689 | Balance |
| **Nicaragua** | | | | | | | | | **Nicaragua** |
| Imports | G | 1 805 | 1 775 | 1 754 | 1 879 | 2 212 | 2 595 | 2 977 | Importations |
| Exports | G | 643 | 589 | 561 | 605 | 756 | 858 | 1 035 | Exportations |
| Balance | | -1 163 | -1 186 | -1 193 | -1 275 | -1 457 | -1 737 | -1 941 | Balance |
| **Panama[15]** | | | | | | | | | **Panama[15]** |
| Imports | S | 3 379 | 2 964 | 2 982 | 3 086 | 3 594 | 4 180 | 4 833 | Importations |
| Exports | S | 859 | 911 | 846 | 864 | 944 | 1 018 | 1 039 | Exportations |
| Balance | | -2 519 | -2 053 | -2 136 | -2 222 | -2 651 | -3 162 | -3 793 | Balance |
| **Paraguay** | | | | | | | | | **Paraguay** |
| Imports | S | 2 193 | 2 182 | 1 672 | 2 228 | 3 097 | 3 790 | 6 090 | Importations |
| Exports | S | 869 | 990 | 951 | 1 242 | 1 627 | 1 697 | 1 906 | Exportations |
| Balance | | -1 324 | -1 192 | -721 | -986 | -1 470 | -2 093 | -4 184 | Balance |
| **Peru[6]** | | | | | | | | | **Pérou[6]** |
| Imports | S | 7 407 | 7 273 | 7 440 | 8 244 | 9 812 | 12 084 | 14 897 | Importations |
| Exports | S | 6 955 | 7 026 | 7 714 | 9 091 | 12 617 | 16 587 | 23 749 | Exportations |
| Balance | | -452 | -248 | 274 | 846 | 2 805 | 4 503 | 8 852 | Balance |
| **Suriname** | | | | | | | | | **Suriname** |
| Imports | G | 574 | 136 | 137 | 176 | 217 | 281 | ... | Importations |
| Exports | G | 560 | 201 | 157 | 187 | 232 | 266 | ... | Exportations |
| Balance | | -14 | 64 | 20 | 11 | 15 | -15 | ... | Balance |

| Region, country or area[&] | Sys.[t] | 2000 | 2001 | 2002 | 2003 | 2004 | 2005 | 2006 | Région, pays ou zone[&] |
|---|---|---|---|---|---|---|---|---|---|
| Uruguay | | | | | | | | | Uruguay |
| Imports | G | 3 466 | 3 061 | 1 964 | 2 190 | 3 114 | 3 879 | 4 757 | Importations |
| Exports | G | 2 295 | 2 060 | 1 861 | 2 206 | 2 931 | 3 405 | 3 953 | Exportations |
| Balance | | -1 171 | -1 000 | -103 | 16 | -183 | -474 | -804 | Balance |
| Venezuela (Bolivarian Rep. of) | | | | | | | | | Venezuela (Rép. bolivar. du) |
| Imports | G | 16 213 | 18 323 | 12 963 | 9 256 | 16 679 | 24 027 | 33 616 | Importations |
| Exports | G | 31 413 | 25 353 | 25 890 | 23 990 | 33 994 | 51 859 | 59 208 | Exportations |
| Balance | | 15 200 | 7 030 | 12 927 | 14 734 | 17 315 | 27 832 | 25 592 | Balance |
| **Eastern Asia** | | | | | | | | | **Asie orientale** |
| **Imports** | | 559 236 | 522 820 | 583 412 | 740 940 | 978 656 | 1 128 323 | 1 334 891 | **Importations** |
| **Exports** | | 591 842 | 558 102 | 633 488 | 788 880 | 1 032 705 | 1 256 278 | 1 529 464 | **Exportations** |
| **Balance** | | 32 606 | 35 282 | 50 076 | 47 941 | 54 049 | 127 954 | 194 573 | **Balance** |
| China[16] | | | | | | | | | Chine[16] |
| Imports | S | 225 094 | 243 553 | 295 170 | 412 760 | 561 229 | 659 953 | 791 605 | Importations |
| Exports | S | 249 203 | 266 098 | 325 596 | 438 228 | 593 326 | 761 953 | 969 380 | Exportations |
| Balance | | 24 109 | 22 545 | 30 426 | 25 468 | 32 097 | 102 000 | 177 775 | Balance |
| China, Hong Kong SAR | | | | | | | | | Chine, Hong Kong RAS |
| Imports | G | 212 805 | 201 076 | 207 644 | 231 896 | 271 074 | 299 533 | 334 681 | Importations |
| Exports | G | 201 860 | 189 894 | 200 092 | 223 762 | 259 260 | 289 337 | 316 816 | Exportations |
| Balance | | -10 945 | -11 182 | -7 552 | -8 134 | -11 814 | -10 196 | -17 865 | Balance |
| China, Macao SAR | | | | | | | | | Chine, Macao RAS |
| Imports | G | 2 255 | 2 386 | 2 530 | 2 755 | 3 478 | 3 913 | 4 565 | Importations |
| Exports | G | 2 539 | 2 300 | 2 356 | 2 581 | 2 812 | 2 476 | 2 557 | Exportations |
| Balance | | 284 | -87 | -174 | -174 | -666 | -1 438 | -2 008 | Balance |
| Korea, Republic of | | | | | | | | | Corée, République de |
| Imports | G | 160 481 | 141 098 | 152 126 | 178 827 | 224 463 | 261 238 | 309 383 | Importations |
| Exports | G | 172 267 | 150 439 | 162 471 | 193 817 | 253 845 | 284 419 | 325 465 | Exportations |
| Balance | | 11 786 | 9 341 | 10 345 | 14 990 | 29 382 | 23 181 | 16 082 | Balance |
| Mongolia | | | | | | | | | Mongolie |
| Imports | G | 615 | 638 | 691 | 801 | 1 021 | 1 184 | 1 486 | Importations |
| Exports | G | 536 | 521 | 524 | 616 | 870 | 1 065 | 1 543 | Exportations |
| Balance | | -79 | -116 | -167 | -185 | -151 | -119 | 57 | Balance |
| **Southern Asia** | | | | | | | | | **Asie australe** |
| **Imports** | | 94 593 | 96 152 | 107 240 | 133 879 | 178 529 | 236 602 | 284 913 | **Importations** |
| **Exports** | | 90 957 | 86 989 | 98 494 | 116 167 | 148 108 | 189 053 | 232 130 | **Exportations** |
| **Balance** | | -3 636 | -9 163 | -8 746 | -17 712 | -30 421 | -47 549 | -52 783 | **Balance** |
| Afghanistan | | | | | | | | | Afghanistan |
| Imports | G | 1 176 | 1 696 | 2 452 | 2 101 | 2 177 | ... | ... | Importations |
| Exports | G | 137 | 68 | 100 | 144 | 314 | ... | ... | Exportations |
| Balance | | -1 039 | -1 628 | -2 352 | -1 957 | -1 863 | ... | ... | Balance |
| Bangladesh | | | | | | | | | Bangladesh |
| Imports | G | 8 358 | 8 349 | 7 913 | 9 516 | 12 611 | 12 881 | 14 964 | Importations |
| Exports | G | 4 787 | 4 826 | 4 566 | 5 263 | 6 615 | 7 233 | 9 103 | Exportations |
| Balance | | -3 572 | -3 523 | -3 348 | -4 253 | -5 996 | -5 648 | -5 861 | Balance |
| Bhutan | | | | | | | | | Bhoutan |
| Imports | G | 175 | 191 | 196 | 249 | 411 | 387 | 319 | Importations |
| Exports | G | 103 | 106 | 113 | 133 | 183 | 258 | 350 | Exportations |
| Balance | | -72 | -85 | -84 | -116 | -228 | -129 | 30 | Balance |
| India[17] | | | | | | | | | Inde[17] |
| Imports | G | 51 563 | 50 391 | 56 496 | 72 559 | 99 757 | 142 865 | 175 243 | Importations |
| Exports | G | 42 378 | 43 352 | 50 353 | 58 964 | 76 647 | 99 618 | 120 862 | Exportations |
| Balance | | -9 185 | -7 038 | -6 143 | -13 595 | -23 110 | -43 247 | -54 381 | Balance |
| Iran (Islamic Rep. of)[18,19] | | | | | | | | | Iran (Rép. islamique d')[18,19] |
| Imports | S | 14 347 | 17 627 | 21 180 | 27 676 | 35 207 | 41 561 | ... | Importations |
| Exports | S | 28 345 | 23 904 | 28 237 | 33 991 | 44 403 | 58 400 | ... | Exportations |
| Balance | | 13 998 | 6 277 | 7 057 | 6 315 | 9 196 | 16 840 | ... | Balance |

55    Total imports and exports—Imports c.i.f., exports f.o.b., and balance, value in million US dollars (*continued*)

Importations et exportations totales—Importations c.a.f., exportations f.o.b. et balance, valeur en millions de dollars E.-U. (*suite*)

| Region, country or area& | Sys.t | 2000 | 2001 | 2002 | 2003 | 2004 | 2005 | 2006 | Région, pays ou zone& |
|---|---|---|---|---|---|---|---|---|---|
| **Maldives** | | | | | | | | | **Maldives** |
| Imports | G | 389 | 393 | 392 | 471 | 642 | 745 | 927 | Importations |
| Exports | G | 76 | 76 | 90 | 113 | 122 | 103 | 135 | Exportations |
| Balance | | -313 | -317 | -301 | -358 | -519 | -641 | -791 | Balance |
| **Nepal** | | | | | | | | | **Népal** |
| Imports | G | 1 573 | 1 475 | 1 418 | 1 755 | 1 872 | 1 860 | 2 099 | Importations |
| Exports | G | 803 | 738 | 568 | 662 | 756 | 830 | 760 | Exportations |
| Balance | | -770 | -737 | -850 | -1 093 | -1 115 | -1 031 | -1 338 | Balance |
| **Pakistan** | | | | | | | | | **Pakistan** |
| Imports | G | 10 864 | 10 192 | 11 227 | 13 038 | 17 949 | 25 356 | 29 828 | Importations |
| Exports | G | 9 028 | 9 238 | 9 908 | 11 930 | 13 379 | 16 050 | 16 932 | Exportations |
| Balance | | -1 836 | -953 | -1 319 | -1 107 | -4 570 | -9 306 | -12 896 | Balance |
| **Sri Lanka** | | | | | | | | | **Sri Lanka** |
| Imports | G | 6 281 | 5 973 | 6 105 | 6 672 | 7 973 | 8 833 | 10 259 | Importations |
| Exports | G | 5 433 | 4 815 | 4 699 | 5 125 | 5 757 | 6 347 | 6 886 | Exportations |
| Balance | | -848 | -1 158 | -1 406 | -1 547 | -2 216 | -2 487 | -3 373 | Balance |
| **South-eastern Asia** | | | | | | | | | **Asie du Sud-Est** |
| **Imports** | | 312 923 | 286 918 | 301 208 | 319 031 | 399 364 | 481 274 | 507 053 | **Importations** |
| **Exports** | | 364 590 | 327 776 | 346 406 | 373 894 | 467 526 | 535 691 | 593 070 | **Exportations** |
| **Balance** | | 51 666 | 40 858 | 45 198 | 54 862 | 68 162 | 54 417 | 86 016 | **Balance** |
| **Brunei Darussalam** | | | | | | | | | **Brunéi Darussalam** |
| Imports | S | 1 107 | 1 142 | 1 556 | 1 327 | 1 427 | ... | ... | Importations |
| Exports | S | 3 907 | 3 640 | 3 701 | 4 424 | 5 069 | ... | ... | Exportations |
| Balance | | 2 801 | 2 498 | 2 145 | 3 097 | 3 642 | ... | ... | Balance |
| **Cambodia** | | | | | | | | | **Cambodge** |
| Imports | S | 1 424 | 1 456 | 1 675 | 1 732 | 2 075 | 2 548 | 2 985 | Importations |
| Exports | S | 1 123 | 1 296 | 1 489 | 1 771 | 2 188 | 3 014 | 3 562 | Exportations |
| Balance | | -302 | -160 | -186 | 38 | 113 | 466 | 576 | Balance |
| **Indonesia** | | | | | | | | | **Indonésie** |
| Imports | S | 43 594 | 37 534 | 38 340 | 42 244 | 54 877 | 75 533 | 80 333 | Importations |
| Exports | S | 65 404 | 57 360 | 59 164 | 64 107 | 70 767 | 86 996 | 103 486 | Exportations |
| Balance | | 21 810 | 19 826 | 20 824 | 21 863 | 15 890 | 11 463 | 23 153 | Balance |
| **Lao People's Dem. Rep.** | | | | | | | | | **Rép. dém. pop. lao** |
| Imports | S | 535 | 510 | 447 | 462 | 713 | 882 | 1 060 | Importations |
| Exports | S | 330 | 320 | 301 | 335 | 363 | 553 | 882 | Exportations |
| Balance | | -205 | -191 | -146 | -127 | -349 | -329 | -177 | Balance |
| **Malaysia** | | | | | | | | | **Malaisie** |
| Imports | G | 81 963 | 73 866 | 79 869 | 81 948 | 105 298 | 114 410 | 131 079 | Importations |
| Exports | G | 98 230 | 88 005 | 93 265 | 99 369 | 125 745 | 140 870 | 160 574 | Exportations |
| Balance | | 16 266 | 14 139 | 13 396 | 17 421 | 20 446 | 26 460 | 29 495 | Balance |
| **Myanmar** | | | | | | | | | **Myanmar** |
| Imports | G | 2 401 | 2 877 | 2 348 | 2 092 | 2 196 | 1 927 | 2 108 | Importations |
| Exports | G | 1 647 | 2 382 | 3 046 | 2 485 | 2 380 | 3 813 | 4 506 | Exportations |
| Balance | | -755 | -496 | 698 | 392 | 184 | 1 887 | 2 397 | Balance |
| **Philippines** | | | | | | | | | **Philippines** |
| Imports | G | 36 887 | 34 944 | 37 202 | 39 502 | 42 345 | 46 963 | 54 077 | Importations |
| Exports | G | 39 794 | 32 664 | 36 510 | 36 231 | 39 680 | 39 879 | 47 413 | Exportations |
| Balance | | 2 907 | -2 280 | -692 | -3 271 | -2 664 | -7 084 | -6 665 | Balance |
| **Singapore** | | | | | | | | | **Singapour** |
| Imports | G | 134 546 | 116 004 | 116 441 | 127 935 | 163 851 | 200 050 | 238 711 | Importations |
| Exports | G | 137 806 | 121 755 | 125 177 | 144 183 | 198 633 | 229 652 | 271 809 | Exportations |
| Balance | | 3 259 | 5 752 | 8 736 | 16 248 | 34 782 | 29 602 | 33 098 | Balance |
| **Thailand** | | | | | | | | | **Thaïlande** |
| Imports | S | 61 923 | 61 961 | 64 645 | 75 824 | 94 410 | 118 158 | 128 654 | Importations |
| Exports | S | 68 963 | 64 919 | 68 108 | 80 324 | 96 248 | 110 178 | 130 795 | Exportations |
| Balance | | 7 039 | 2 959 | 3 463 | 4 499 | 1 839 | -7 980 | 2 142 | Balance |
| **Viet Nam** | | | | | | | | | **Viet Nam** |
| Imports | G | 15 638 | 16 218 | 19 746 | 25 256 | 31 969 | 36 978 | 44 410 | Importations |
| Exports | G | 14 483 | 15 029 | 16 706 | 20 149 | 26 485 | 32 442 | 39 605 | Exportations |
| Balance | | -1 155 | -1 189 | -3 040 | -5 107 | -5 484 | -4 536 | -4 805 | Balance |

| Region, country or area[&] | Sys.[t] | 2000 | 2001 | 2002 | 2003 | 2004 | 2005 | 2006 | Région, pays ou zone[&] |
|---|---|---|---|---|---|---|---|---|---|
| **Western Asia** | | | | | | | | | **Asie occidentale** |
| Imports | | 200 600 | 193 278 | 210 952 | 247 535 | 334 114 | 381 586 | 457 499 | Importations |
| Exports | | 258 441 | 240 728 | 252 147 | 311 429 | 415 705 | 545 842 | 642 141 | Exportations |
| Balance | | 57 841 | 47 450 | 41 195 | 63 894 | 81 591 | 164 257 | 184 641 | Balance |
| **Bahrain** | | | | | | | | | **Bahreïn** |
| Imports | G | 4 634 | 4 306 | 4 988 | 5 657 | 7 385 | 8 790 | 8 944 | Importations |
| Exports | G | 6 195 | 5 578 | 5 786 | 6 624 | 7 556 | 10 160 | 11 563 | Exportations |
| Balance | | 1 561 | 1 272 | 798 | 966 | 171 | 1 370 | 2 618 | Balance |
| **Cyprus** | | | | | | | | | **Chypre** |
| Imports | G | 3 846 | 3 922 | 3 863 | 4 288 | 5 659 | 6 282 | 6 951 | Importations |
| Exports | G | 951 | 976 | 770 | 834 | 1 081 | 1 303 | 1 153 | Exportations |
| Balance | | -2 895 | -2 946 | -3 094 | -3 455 | -4 577 | -4 979 | -5 798 | Balance |
| **Israel[20]** | | | | | | | | | **Israël[20]** |
| Imports | S | 37 686 | 35 449 | 35 517 | 36 303 | 42 864 | 47 142 | 50 334 | Importations |
| Exports | S | 31 404 | 29 081 | 29 347 | 31 784 | 38 618 | 42 770 | 46 789 | Exportations |
| Balance | | -6 282 | -6 368 | -6 170 | -4 519 | -4 245 | -4 371 | -3 544 | Balance |
| **Jordan** | | | | | | | | | **Jordanie** |
| Imports | G | 4 597 | 4 871 | 5 076 | 5 743 | 8 128 | 10 506 | 11 447 | Importations |
| Exports | G | 1 899 | 2 294 | 2 770 | 3 082 | 3 922 | 4 302 | 5 175 | Exportations |
| Balance | | -2 698 | -2 577 | -2 306 | -2 662 | -4 206 | -6 204 | -6 272 | Balance |
| **Kuwait** | | | | | | | | | **Koweït** |
| Imports | S | 7 157 | 7 869 | 9 008 | 10 993 | 12 630 | 15 801 | 15 960 | Importations |
| Exports | S | 19 436 | 16 203 | 15 369 | 20 678 | 28 599 | 44 869 | 57 267 | Exportations |
| Balance | | 12 279 | 8 334 | 6 361 | 9 685 | 15 968 | 29 068 | 41 307 | Balance |
| **Lebanon** | | | | | | | | | **Liban** |
| Imports | G | 6 230 | 7 380 | 6 560 | 7 315 | 9 609 | 9 633 | 9 647 | Importations |
| Exports | G | 715 | 1 093 | 1 238 | 1 813 | 2 199 | 2 337 | 2 814 | Exportations |
| Balance | | -5 515 | -6 287 | -5 322 | -5 502 | -7 410 | -7 296 | -6 833 | Balance |
| **Occupied Palestinian Terr.** | | | | | | | | | **Terr. palestinien occupé** |
| Imports | S | 2 383 | ... | 1 516 | ... | 2 373 | 2 667 | ... | Importations |
| Exports | S | 401 | 273 | 241 | ... | 322 | 335 | ... | Exportations |
| Balance | | -1 982 | ... | -1 275 | ... | -2 052 | -2 331 | ... | Balance |
| **Oman** | | | | | | | | | **Oman** |
| Imports | G | 5 040 | 5 798 | 6 005 | 6 572 | 8 865 | 8 827 | 10 915 | Importations |
| Exports | G | 11 319 | 11 074 | 11 172 | 11 669 | 13 341 | 18 692 | 21 585 | Exportations |
| Balance | | 6 279 | 5 276 | 5 166 | 5 096 | 4 476 | 9 865 | 10 670 | Balance |
| **Qatar** | | | | | | | | | **Qatar** |
| Imports | S | 3 252 | 3 758 | 4 052 | 4 897 | 6 004 | 10 061 | 15 861 | Importations |
| Exports | S | 11 594 | 10 871 | 10 978 | 13 383 | 18 685 | 25 763 | 31 278 | Exportations |
| Balance | | 8 342 | 7 114 | 6 926 | 8 485 | 12 681 | 15 702 | 15 418 | Balance |
| **Saudi Arabia** | | | | | | | | | **Arabie saoudite** |
| Imports | S | 30 197 | 31 181 | 32 293 | 36 915 | 44 744 | 59 458 | 69 800 | Importations |
| Exports | S | 77 480 | 67 973 | 72 453 | 93 245 | 125 997 | 180 736 | 211 306 | Exportations |
| Balance | | 47 283 | 36 792 | 40 160 | 56 331 | 81 253 | 121 278 | 141 506 | Balance |
| **Syrian Arab Republic** | | | | | | | | | **Rép. arabe syrienne** |
| Imports | S | 4 055 | 4 773 | 5 097 | 5 119 | 8 411 | 10 862 | ... | Importations |
| Exports | S | 4 674 | 5 257 | 6 520 | 5 731 | 7 485 | 9 174 | ... | Exportations |
| Balance | | 620 | 484 | 1 423 | 611 | -926 | -1 688 | ... | Balance |
| **Turkey** | | | | | | | | | **Turquie** |
| Imports | S | 54 503 | 41 399 | 49 663 | 65 637 | 96 368 | 98 998 | 133 584 | Importations |
| Exports | S | 27 775 | 31 334 | 34 561 | 46 576 | 61 683 | 71 928 | 81 912 | Exportations |
| Balance | | -26 728 | -10 065 | -15 101 | -19 061 | -34 685 | -27 070 | -51 672 | Balance |
| **United Arab Emirates** | | | | | | | | | **Emirats arabes unis** |
| Imports | G | 35 009 | 37 293 | 42 652 | 52 074 | 72 082 | 80 822 | 94 670 | Importations |
| Exports | G | 49 835 | 48 414 | 52 163 | 67 135 | 90 638 | 115 453 | 139 353 | Exportations |
| Balance | | 14 827 | 11 121 | 9 511 | 15 061 | 18 556 | 34 631 | 44 683 | Balance |

**55**

Total imports and exports—Imports c.i.f., exports f.o.b., and balance, value in million US dollars (*continued*)

Importations et exportations totales—Importations c.a.f., exportations f.o.b. et balance, valeur en millions de dollars E.-U. (*suite*)

| Region, country or area[&] | Sys.[t] | 2000 | 2001 | 2002 | 2003 | 2004 | 2005 | 2006 | Région, pays ou zone[&] |
|---|---|---|---|---|---|---|---|---|---|
| Yemen | | | | | | | | | Yémen |
| Imports | S | 2 327 | 2 473 | 2 927 | 3 680 | 3 988 | 4 885 | 5 847 | Importations |
| Exports | S | 4 078 | 3 373 | 3 683 | 3 923 | 4 676 | 6 376 | 8 099 | Exportations |
| Balance | | 1 751 | 900 | 755 | 243 | 688 | 1 491 | 2 252 | Balance |
| Oceania | | | | | | | | | Océanie |
| Imports | | 6 984 | 7 034 | 7 674 | 9 309 | 10 169 | 11 009 | 11 164 | Importations |
| Exports | | 5 060 | 4 516 | 4 426 | 5 568 | 6 314 | 7 134 | 8 126 | Exportations |
| Balance | | -1 925 | -2 518 | -3 248 | -3 741 | -3 855 | -3 875 | -3 038 | Balance |
| American Samoa[21] | | | | | | | | | Samoa américaines[21] |
| Imports | S | 506 | 516 | 499 | 624 | 604 | ... | ... | Importations |
| Exports | S | 346 | 318 | 388 | 460 | 446 | ... | ... | Exportations |
| Balance | | -160 | -198 | -111 | -164 | -158 | ... | ... | Balance |
| Cook Islands | | | | | | | | | Iles Cook |
| Imports | G | 50 | 47 | 47 | 71 | 76 | 81 | ... | Importations |
| Exports | G | 9 | 7 | 5 | 9 | 7 | 5 | ... | Exportations |
| Balance | | -41 | -40 | -42 | -62 | -69 | -76 | ... | Balance |
| Fiji | | | | | | | | | Fidji |
| Imports | G | 857 | 886 | 906 | 1 208 | 1 444 | 1 607 | 1 802 | Importations |
| Exports | G | 538 | 534 | 519 | 674 | 693 | 701 | 679 | Exportations |
| Balance | | -319 | -352 | -386 | -533 | -751 | -906 | -1 123 | Balance |
| French Polynesia | | | | | | | | | Polynésie française |
| Imports | S | 931 | 1 016 | 1 267 | 1 585 | 1 505 | 1 721 | 1 547 | Importations |
| Exports | S | 197 | 175 | 169 | 157 | 200 | 216 | 181 | Exportations |
| Balance | | -733 | -840 | -1 098 | -1 428 | -1 305 | -1 504 | -1 367 | Balance |
| Guam | | | | | | | | | Guam |
| Imports | G | ... | ... | ... | ... | ... | ... | 501 | Importations |
| Exports | G | ... | ... | ... | ... | 53 | 52 | 53 | Exportations |
| Balance | | ... | ... | ... | ... | ... | ... | -448 | Balance |
| Kiribati[6] | | | | | | | | | Kiribati[6] |
| Imports | G | 39 | 41 | ... | ... | ... | ... | ... | Importations |
| Exports | G | 6 | 5 | ... | ... | ... | ... | ... | Exportations |
| Balance | | -33 | -36 | ... | ... | ... | ... | ... | Balance |
| Marshall Islands | | | | | | | | | Iles Marshall |
| Imports | G | 68 | ... | ... | ... | ... | ... | ... | Importations |
| Exports | G | 7 | ... | ... | ... | ... | ... | ... | Exportations |
| Balance | | -61 | ... | ... | ... | ... | ... | ... | Balance |
| New Caledonia | | | | | | | | | Nouvelle-Calédonie |
| Imports | S | 924 | 932 | 1 008 | 1 541 | 1 637 | 1 774 | 1 998 | Importations |
| Exports | S | 605 | 453 | 476 | 785 | 1 034 | 1 086 | 1 189 | Exportations |
| Balance | | -318 | -479 | -532 | -756 | -603 | -688 | -809 | Balance |
| Palau | | | | | | | | | Palaos |
| Imports | S | 123 | ... | ... | ... | ... | ... | ... | Importations |
| Papua New Guinea | | | | | | | | | Papouasie-Nvl-Guinée |
| Imports | G | 1 151 | 1 071 | 1 235 | 1 368 | 1 680 | 1 729 | ... | Importations |
| Exports | G | 2 095 | 1 805 | 1 641 | 2 206 | 2 552 | 3 273 | 4 166 | Exportations |
| Balance | | 944 | 734 | 406 | 838 | 872 | 1 545 | ... | Balance |
| Samoa | | | | | | | | | Samoa |
| Imports | S | 106 | 120 | 127 | 128 | 155 | 187 | 219 | Importations |
| Exports | S | 14 | 16 | 14 | 15 | 11 | 12 | 11 | Exportations |
| Balance | | -92 | -104 | -114 | -113 | -145 | -175 | -208 | Balance |
| Solomon Islands | | | | | | | | | Iles Salomon |
| Imports | S | 98 | 88 | 67 | 83 | 85 | 185 | 210 | Importations |
| Exports | S | 65 | 46 | 58 | 74 | 97 | 105 | 120 | Exportations |
| Balance | | -33 | -42 | -9 | -9 | 12 | -80 | -90 | Balance |

**55** Total imports and exports—Imports c.i.f., exports f.o.b., and balance, value in million US dollars (*continued*)

Importations et exportations totales—Importations c.a.f., exportations f.o.b. et balance, valeur en millions de dollars E.-U. (*suite*)

| Region, country or area& | Sys.[t] | 2000 | 2001 | 2002 | 2003 | 2004 | 2005 | 2006 | Région, pays ou zone& |
|---|---|---|---|---|---|---|---|---|---|
| **Tonga** | | | | | | | | | **Tonga** |
| Imports | G | 69 | 72 | 89 | 94 | 105 | 120 | 130 | Importations |
| Exports | G | 9 | 7 | 14 | 18 | 15 | 10 | 11 | Exportations |
| Balance | | -60 | -66 | -75 | -76 | -90 | -110 | -119 | Balance |
| **Vanuatu** | | | | | | | | | **Vanuatu** |
| Imports | G | 87 | 86 | 90 | 106 | 128 | 140 | 155 | Importations |
| Exports | G | 26 | 19 | 20 | 27 | 38 | 39 | 40 | Exportations |
| Balance | | -61 | -67 | -70 | -79 | -90 | -101 | -115 | Balance |
| **Non Petrol. Exports[22]** | | | | | | | | | **Pétrole non Compris[22]** |
| Exports | | 102 397 | 100 182 | 92 853 | 86 061 | 79 766 | 73 931 | 68 523 | Exportations |
| **Additional country groupings** | | | | | | | | | **Groupements supplémentaires de pays** |
| **ANCOM§** | | | | | | | | | **ANCOM§** |
| Imports | | 40 636 | 45 442 | 41 255 | 39 652 | 53 231 | 69 837 | 89 343 | Importations |
| Exports | | 57 495 | 50 573 | 51 795 | 53 926 | 72 656 | 102 376 | 123 788 | Exportations |
| Balance | | 16 859 | 5 131 | 10 540 | 14 273 | 19 426 | 32 539 | 34 445 | Balance |
| **APEC§** | | | | | | | | | **CEAP§** |
| Imports | | 2 962 081 | 2 765 577 | 2 860 594 | 3 219 734 | 3 909 728 | 4 500 916 | 5 092 013 | Importations |
| Exports | | 2 762 005 | 2 535 270 | 2 605 168 | 2 923 261 | 3 552 612 | 4 100 540 | 4 772 120 | Exportations |
| Balance | | -200 077 | -230 306 | -255 426 | -296 473 | -357 116 | -400 375 | -319 893 | Balance |
| **CARICOM§** | | | | | | | | | **CARICOM§** |
| Imports | | 13 424 | 13 014 | 13 111 | 13 991 | 15 680 | 17 609 | 20 879 | Importations |
| Exports | | 7 645 | 6 954 | 6 402 | 7 938 | 9 528 | 11 821 | 18 194 | Exportations |
| Balance | | -5 778 | -6 060 | -6 709 | -6 053 | -6 152 | -5 788 | -2 685 | Balance |
| **COMESA§** | | | | | | | | | **COMESA§** |
| Imports | | 35 108 | 35 889 | 35 429 | 40 018 | 48 989 | 65 612 | 75 231 | Importations |
| Exports | | 25 230 | 23 385 | 25 847 | 31 720 | 41 035 | 57 139 | 71 224 | Exportations |
| Balance | | -9 878 | -12 504 | -9 582 | -8 298 | -7 954 | -8 473 | -4 007 | Balance |
| **LDC§** | | | | | | | | | **PMA§** |
| Imports | | 40 977 | 45 283 | 47 802 | 56 965 | 68 772 | 77 388 | 61 502 | Importations |
| Exports | | 32 386 | 32 957 | 36 095 | 43 064 | 57 310 | 75 187 | 62 855 | Exportations |
| Balance | | -8 592 | -12 326 | -11 707 | -13 901 | -11 461 | -2 202 | 1 354 | Balance |
| **MERCOSUR§** | | | | | | | | | **MERCOSUR§** |
| Imports | | 90 005 | 84 234 | 62 348 | 69 133 | 95 089 | 113 985 | 140 859 | Importations |
| Exports | | 84 624 | 87 880 | 88 900 | 106 217 | 135 811 | 163 982 | 190 235 | Exportations |
| Balance | | -5 381 | 3 646 | 26 552 | 37 084 | 40 722 | 49 998 | 49 376 | Balance |
| **NAFTA§** | | | | | | | | | **ALENA§** |
| Imports | | 1 588 750 | 1 489 591 | 1 511 991 | 1 624 559 | 1 888 295 | 2 154 652 | 2 390 133 | Importations |
| Exports | | 1 141 068 | 1 067 883 | 1 027 312 | 1 074 800 | 1 204 411 | 1 357 983 | 1 543 838 | Exportations |
| Balance | | -447 682 | -421 708 | -484 679 | -549 759 | -683 884 | -796 669 | -846 294 | Balance |
| **OECD§** | | | | | | | | | **OCDE§** |
| Imports | | 4 732 518 | 4 526 978 | 4 663 765 | 5 393 035 | 6 443 488 | 7 145 819 | 8 108 675 | Importations |
| Exports | | 4 352 942 | 4 210 490 | 4 361 133 | 5 011 263 | 5 925 147 | 6 440 705 | 7 266 368 | Exportations |
| Balance | | -379 576 | -316 489 | -302 632 | -381 773 | -518 341 | -705 114 | -842 308 | Balance |
| **OPEC§** | | | | | | | | | **OPEP§** |
| Imports | | 174 700 | 185 059 | 190 205 | 216 556 | 291 006 | 368 202 | 426 593 | Importations |
| Exports | | 353 476 | 308 368 | 317 194 | 383 239 | 512 385 | 706 244 | 834 413 | Exportations |
| Balance | | 178 776 | 123 309 | 126 989 | 166 682 | 221 379 | 338 042 | 407 820 | Balance |
| **EU-25** | | | | | | | | | **UE-25** |
| Imports | | 2 398 631 | 2 367 132 | 2 465 164 | 2 972 748 | 3 586 910 | 3 917 606 | 4 507 664 | Importations |
| Exports | | 2 357 138 | 2 382 848 | 2 541 434 | 3 030 443 | 3 615 921 | 3 887 305 | 4 408 740 | Exportations |
| Balance | | -41 493 | 15 716 | 76 270 | 57 695 | 29 012 | -30 301 | -98 924 | Balance |
| **Extra-EU-25[23]** | | | | | | | | | **Extra-UE-25[23]** |
| Imports | | 916 360 | 880 948 | 889 542 | 1 063 891 | 1 283 863 | 1 470 417 | 1 702 513 | Importations |
| Exports | | 788 642 | 801 722 | 854 112 | 999 614 | 1 205 484 | 1 331 083 | 1 487 461 | Exportations |
| Balance | | -127 718 | -79 227 | -35 430 | -64 277 | -78 379 | -139 334 | -215 052 | Balance |

## 55

**Total imports and exports**—Imports c.i.f., exports f.o.b., and balance, value in million US dollars (*continued*)

**Importations et exportations totales**—Importations c.a.f., exportations f.o.b. et balance, valeur en millions de dollars E.-U. (*suite*)

Source

United Nations Statistics Division, New York, trade statistics database, last accessed March 2008.

Source

Organisation des Nations Unies, Division de statistique, New York, la base de données pour les statistiques du commerce extérieur, dernier accès mars 2008.

Notes

  **&** The regional totals for imports and exports have been adjusted to exclude the re-exports of countries or areas comprising each region.

  **§** For member states of this grouping, see Annex I – Other groupings. The totals have been calculated for all periods shown according to the current composition.

  **t** Systems of trade: Two systems of recording trade, the General trade system (G) and the Special trade system (S), are in common use. They differ mainly in the way warehoused and re-exported goods are recorded. See the Technical notes for an explanation of the trade systems.

  **1** In April 2006, regional totals have been revised downwards due to the additional identification of re-exports, in particular for Singapore and Italy.

  **2** Developed economies of the Asia-Pacific region, Europe, and North America.

  **3** This classification is intended for statistical convenience and does not, necessarily, express a judgement about the stage reached by a particular country in the development process.

  **4** Data exclude re-exports.

  **5** Trade data for France include the import and export values of French Guiana, Guadeloupe, Martinique, and Réunion.

  **6** Imports FOB.

  **7** Including the trade of the U.S. Virgin Islands and Puerto Rico but excluding shipments of merchandise between the United States and its other possessions (Guam, American Samoa, etc.). Data include imports and exports of non-monetary gold.

  **8** Imports exclude petroleum imported without stated value. Exports cover domestic exports.

  **9** Exports include gold.

  **10** Beginning in January 1998, foreign trade data refer to South Africa only, excluding intra-trade of the Southern African Common Customs Area. Prior to January 1998, trade data refer to the Southern African Common Customs Area, which includes Botswana, Lesotho, Namibia, South Africa and Swaziland.

  **11** Year ending June 30 through 1994. Year ending December 31 thereafter.

  **12** Beginning 1990, trade statistics exclude certain oil and chemical products.

  **13** Export and import values exclude trade in the processing zone.

  **14** Trade data include maquiladoras and exclude goods from customs-bonded warehouses. Total exports include revaluation and exports of silver.

  **15** Exports include re-exports and petroleum products.

  **16** For statistical purposes, the data for China do not include those for the Hong Kong Special Administrative Region (Hong Kong SAR), Macao Special Administrative Region (Macao SAR) and Taiwan Province of China.

  **17** Excluding military goods, fissionable materials, bunkers, ships, and aircraft.

Notes

  **&** Les totaux régionaux pour importations et exportations ont été ajustés pour exclure les re-exportations des pays ou zones qui comprennent la région.

  **§** Pour les Etats membres de ce groupements, voir annexe I – Autres groupements. Les totales ont été calculés pour toutes les périodes données suivant la composition présente.

  **t** Systèmes de commerce : Deux systèmes d'enregistrement du commerce sont couramment utilisés, le Commerce général (G) et le Commerce spécial (S). Ils ne diffèrent que par la façon dont sont enregistrées les merchandises entreposées et les merchandises réexportées. Voir les Notes techniques pour une explication des Systèmes de commerce.

  **1** En avril 2006, les totaux régionaux ont été diminués à cause d'une identification additionelle des re-exportations, en particulier celles du Singapour et de l'Italie.

  **2** Économies développées de la région Asie-Pacifique, de l'Europe, et de l'Amérique de Nord.

  **3** Cette classification est utilisée pour plus de commodité dans la présentation des statistique et n'implique pas nécessairement un jugement quant au stage de développement auquel est parvenu un pays donné.

  **4** Les données non compris les réexportations.

  **5** Les valeurs de commerce pour la France comprennent les valeurs des importations et des exportations de la Guyane française, la Guadeloupe, la Martinique, et la Réunion.

  **6** Importations FOB.

  **7** Y compris le commerce des Iles Vierges américaines et de Porto Rico mais non compris les échanges de marchandises, entre les Etats-Unis et leurs autres possessions (Guam, Samoa americaines, etc.). Les données comprennent les importations et exportations d'or non-monétaire.

  **8** Non compris le petrole brute dont la valeur des importations ne sont pas stipulée. Les exportations sont les exportations d'intérieur.

  **9** Les exportations comprennent l'or.

  **10** A compter de janvier 1998, les données sur le commerce extérieur ne se rapportent qu'à l'Afrique du Sud. et ne tiennent pas compte des échanges commerciaux entre les pays de l'Union douanière de l'Afrique du Sud, qui incluait l'Afrique du Sud, Botswana, Lesotho, Namibie, et Swaziland.

  **11** Année finissant juin 30 à 1994. Année finissant décembre 31 ensuite.

  **12** A compter de 1990, les statistiques commerciales font exclusion de certains produits pétroliers et chimiques.

  **13** Les valeurs à l'exportation et à l'importation excluent le commerce de la zone de transformation.

  **14** Les statistiques du commerce extérieur comprennent maquiladoras et ne comprennent pas les marchandises provenant des entrepôts en douane. Les exportations comprennent la réevaluation et les données sur les exportations d'argent.

  **15** Exportations comprennent re-exportations et produits pétroliers.

  **16** Pour la présentation des statistiques, les données pour la Chine ne comprennent pas la Région Administrative Spéciale de Hong Kong (Hong Kong RAS), la Région Administrative Spéciale de Macao (Macao RAS) et la province de Taiwan.

  **17** A l'exclusion des marchandises militaires, des matières fissibles, des soutes, des bateaux, et de l'avion.

**55**    **Total imports and exports**—Imports c.i.f., exports f.o.b., and balance, value in million US dollars (*continued*)

**Importations et exportations totales**—Importations c.a.f., exportations f.o.b. et balance, valeur en millions de dollars E.-U. (*suite*)

18   Data include oil and gas. Data on the value and volume of oil exports and on the value of total exports are rough estimates based on information published in various petroleum industry journals.

19   Year ending 20 March of the years stated.

20   Imports and exports net of returned goods. The figures also exclude Judea and Samaria and the Gaza area.

21   Year ending 30 September.

22   Data refer to total exports less petroleum exports of Asia Middle East countries where petroleum, in this case, is the sum of SITC groups 333, 334 and 335.

23   Excluding intra-EU trade.

18   Les données comprennent le pétrole et le gaz. La valeur des exportations de pétrole et des exportations totales sont des évaluations grossières basées sur l'information pubilée à divers journaux d'industrie de pétrole.

19   Année finissant le 20 mars de l'année indiquée.

20   Importations et exportations nets, ne comprennant pas les marchandises retournées. Sont également exclues les données de la Judée et de Samaria et ainsi que la zone de Gaza.

21   Année finissant le 30 septembre.

22   Les données se rapportent aux exportations totales moins les exportations pétrolières de moyen-orient d'Asie. Dans ce cas, le pétrole est la somme des groupes CTCI 333, 334 et 335.

23   Non compris le commerce de l'intra-UE.

# 56

## Total imports and exports: index numbers
2000 = 100

## Importations et exportations totales : indices
2000 = 100

| Country or area | 1997 | 1998 | 1999 | 2001 | 2002 | 2003 | 2004 | 2005 | 2006 | Pays ou zone |
|---|---|---|---|---|---|---|---|---|---|---|
| **Argentina** | | | | | | | | | | **Argentine** |
| Imports: volume | 108 | 117 | 101 | 83 | 38 | 58 | 87 | 108 | 125 | Importations : volume |
| Imports: unit value | 112 | 106 | 100 | 97 | 94 | 94 | 102 | 105 | 108 | Importations : valeur unitaire |
| Exports: volume | 88 | 98 | 97 | 104 | 105 | 110 | 118 | 135 | 143 | Exportations : volume |
| Exports: unit value | 114 | 102 | 91 | 97 | 93 | 102 | 111 | 113 | 122 | Exportations : valeur unitaire |
| Terms of trade | 102 | 97 | 91 | 99 | 99 | 108 | 110 | 107 | 114 | Termes de l'échange |
| Purchasing power of exports | 90 | 94 | 89 | 104 | 104 | 120 | 129 | 145 | 163 | Pouvoir d'achat des exportations |
| **Australia** | | | | | | | | | | **Australie** |
| Imports: volume | 77 | 84 | 92 | 96 | 108 | 120 | 137 | 129 | 145 | Importations : volume |
| Imports: unit value[1] | 111 | 102 | 102 | 94 | 95 | 104 | 111 | 117 | 120 | Importations : valeur unitaire[1] |
| Exports: volume | 87 | 87 | 91 | 103 | 104 | 102 | 106 | 119 | 141 | Exportations : volume |
| Exports: unit value[1] | 114 | 101 | 96 | 98 | 100 | 111 | 129 | 153 | 175 | Exportations : valeur unitaire[1] |
| Terms of trade | 103 | 100 | 94 | 104 | 106 | 106 | 116 | 131 | 146 | Termes de l'échange |
| Purchasing power of exports | 90 | 86 | 86 | 107 | 110 | 108 | 123 | 156 | 205 | Pouvoir d'achat des exportations |
| **Austria** | | | | | | | | | | **Autriche** |
| Imports: volume | 84 | 86 | 87 | 103 | 107 | 111 | 118 | 125 | 133 | Importations : volume |
| Imports: unit value | 134 | 124 | 115 | 97 | 100 | 114 | 125 | 123 | 130 | Importations : valeur unitaire |
| Exports: volume | 83 | 91 | 94 | 106 | 112 | 117 | 127 | 132 | 139 | Exportations : volume |
| Exports: unit value | 135 | 126 | 105 | 95 | 101 | 114 | 126 | 126 | 132 | Exportations : valeur unitaire |
| Terms of trade | 101 | 102 | 91 | 98 | 101 | 100 | 101 | 102 | 102 | Termes de l'échange |
| Purchasing power of exports | 84 | 93 | 86 | 104 | 114 | 117 | 128 | 135 | 142 | Pouvoir d'achat des exportations |
| **Belgium** | | | | | | | | | | **Belgique** |
| Imports: volume | 85 | 91 | 91 | 101 | 109 | 111 | 118 | 126 | 132 | Importations : volume |
| Imports: unit value | 110 | 106 | 102 | 100 | 103 | 120 | 136 | 143 | 151 | Importations : valeur unitaire |
| Exports: volume | 84 | 88 | 91 | 102 | 111 | 113 | 121 | 126 | 131 | Exportations : volume |
| Exports: unit value | 112 | 111 | 105 | 99 | 104 | 121 | 135 | 142 | 149 | Exportations : valeur unitaire |
| Terms of trade | 102 | 104 | 102 | 100 | 101 | 100 | 99 | 99 | 99 | Termes de l'échange |
| Purchasing power of exports | 86 | 92 | 93 | 102 | 112 | 113 | 120 | 125 | 130 | Pouvoir d'achat des exportations |
| **Bolivia** | | | | | | | | | | **Bolivie** |
| Exports: volume | 101 | 96 | 88 | 107 | 129 | 145 | 173 | 195 | 214 | Exportations : volume |
| Exports: unit value | 90 | 79 | 78 | 92 | 81 | 90 | 122 | 146 | 242 | Exportations : valeur unitaire |
| **Brazil** | | | | | | | | | | **Brésil** |
| Imports: volume | 94 | 98 | 92 | 101 | 99 | 136 | 111 | 101 | 110 | Importations : volume |
| Imports: unit value | 125 | 105 | 96 | 99 | 86 | 64 | 102 | 131 | 148 | Importations : valeur unitaire |
| Exports: volume | 85 | 94 | 93 | 111 | 121 | 131 | 154 | 162 | 173 | Exportations : volume |
| Exports: unit value | 113 | 100 | 94 | 95 | 91 | 101 | 114 | 133 | 144 | Exportations : valeur unitaire |
| Terms of trade | 90 | 95 | 98 | 96 | 106 | 158 | 112 | 101 | 97 | Termes de l'échange |
| Purchasing power of exports | 77 | 89 | 91 | 107 | 128 | 208 | 173 | 165 | 168 | Pouvoir d'achat des exportations |
| **Bulgaria** | | | | | | | | | | **Bulgarie** |
| Imports: unit value | ... | ... | ... | 96 | 98 | 112 | 130 | 140 | 156 | Importations : valeur unitaire |
| Exports: unit value | ... | ... | ... | 95 | 95 | 114 | 133 | 142 | 161 | Exportations : valeur unitaire |
| Terms of trade | ... | ... | ... | 99 | 98 | 102 | 102 | 102 | 103 | Termes de l'échange |
| **Canada** | | | | | | | | | | **Canada** |
| Imports: volume | 79 | 86 | 96 | 94 | 96 | 100 | 109 | 119 | 127 | Importations : volume |
| Imports: unit value | 98 | 92 | 93 | 96 | 95 | 99 | 105 | 113 | 121 | Importations : valeur unitaire |
| Exports: volume | 76 | 82 | 91 | 96 | 97 | 95 | 102 | 105 | 107 | Exportations : volume |
| Exports: unit value | 101 | 98 | 98 | 101 | 96 | 107 | 119 | 133 | 142 | Exportations : valeur unitaire |
| Terms of trade | 103 | 107 | 105 | 105 | 101 | 108 | 113 | 118 | 118 | Termes de l'échange |
| Purchasing power of exports | 78 | 88 | 96 | 101 | 97 | 103 | 115 | 125 | 126 | Pouvoir d'achat des exportations |

| Country or area | 1997 | 1998 | 1999 | 2001 | 2002 | 2003 | 2004 | 2005 | 2006 | Pays ou zone |
|---|---|---|---|---|---|---|---|---|---|---|
| China, Hong Kong SAR | | | | | | | | | | Chine, Hong Kong RAS |
| Imports: volume | 91 | 85 | 85 | 98 | 106 | 119 | 136 | 148 | 163 | Importations : volume |
| Imports: unit value | 107 | 102 | 100 | 97 | 93 | 93 | 96 | 98 | 101 | Importations : valeur unitaire |
| Exports: volume | 86 | 82 | 85 | 97 | 105 | 120 | 138 | 154 | 169 | Exportations : volume |
| Exports: unit value | 108 | 104 | 101 | 98 | 95 | 94 | 95 | 96 | 97 | Exportations : valeur unitaire |
| Terms of trade | 100 | 102 | 101 | 101 | 102 | 101 | 99 | 98 | 97 | Termes de l'échange |
| Purchasing power of exports | 86 | 84 | 86 | 97 | 107 | 121 | 137 | 151 | 164 | Pouvoir d'achat des exportations |
| Colombia | | | | | | | | | | Colombie |
| Imports: unit value | 120 | 110 | 103 | 98 | 95 | 95 | 103 | 114 | 114 | Importations : valeur unitaire |
| Exports: unit value | 115 | 103 | 96 | 89 | 84 | 87 | 96 | 111 | 119 | Exportations : valeur unitaire |
| Terms of trade | 96 | 93 | 93 | 91 | 89 | 92 | 93 | 97 | 104 | Termes de l'échange |
| Czech Republic | | | | | | | | | | République tchèque |
| Imports: unit value | 110 | 105 | 99 | 101 | 107 | 123 | 137 | 148 | 158 | Importations : valeur unitaire |
| Exports: unit value | 111 | 114 | 105 | 102 | 111 | 130 | 147 | 155 | 164 | Exportations : valeur unitaire |
| Terms of trade | 101 | 108 | 105 | 101 | 104 | 105 | 107 | 105 | 104 | Termes de l'échange |
| Denmark | | | | | | | | | | Danemark |
| Imports: volume | 88 | 93 | 93 | 102 | 108 | 106 | 113 | 122 | 136 | Importations : volume |
| Imports: unit value | 114 | 113 | 108 | 98 | 102 | 119 | 133 | 138 | 142 | Importations : valeur unitaire |
| Exports: volume | 84 | 86 | 92 | 103 | 109 | 107 | 110 | 116 | 122 | Exportations : volume |
| Exports: unit value | 115 | 112 | 108 | 99 | 103 | 122 | 136 | 143 | 150 | Exportations : valeur unitaire |
| Terms of trade | 101 | 99 | 100 | 101 | 101 | 102 | 102 | 104 | 105 | Termes de l'échange |
| Purchasing power of exports | 85 | 85 | 92 | 104 | 110 | 109 | 113 | 121 | 129 | Pouvoir d'achat des exportations |
| Dominica | | | | | | | | | | Dominique |
| Imports: volume | 90 | 94 | 97 | 98 | 82 | ... | ... | ... | ... | Importations : volume |
| Imports: unit value | 97 | 116 | 95 | 95 | 91 | ... | ... | ... | ... | Importations : valeur unitaire |
| Exports: volume | 101 | 94 | 92 | 78 | 72 | ... | ... | ... | ... | Exportations : volume |
| Exports: unit value | 134 | 113 | 113 | 101 | 101 | ... | ... | ... | ... | Exportations : valeur unitaire |
| Terms of trade | 137 | 98 | 119 | 106 | 111 | ... | ... | ... | ... | Termes de l'échange |
| Purchasing power of exports | 139 | 91 | 110 | 82 | 80 | ... | ... | ... | ... | Pouvoir d'achat des exportations |
| Ecuador | | | | | | | | | | Equateur |
| Imports: volume | 133 | 166 | 96 | 119 | 148 | 161 | 168 | 204 | 229 | Importations : volume |
| Exports: volume | 102 | 96 | 93 | 101 | 99 | 107 | 133 | 117 | 143 | Exportations : volume |
| Exports: unit value | 85 | 64 | 77 | 88 | 94 | 107 | 118 | 150 | 182 | Exportations : valeur unitaire |
| Estonia | | | | | | | | | | Estonie |
| Imports: unit value | ... | 113 | 109 | 98 | 103 | 121 | 135 | 140 | 147 | Importations : valeur unitaire |
| Exports: unit value | 111 | 113 | 107 | 129 | 136 | 173 | 194 | 199 | 210 | Exportations : valeur unitaire |
| Terms of trade | ... | 99 | 98 | 132 | 132 | 143 | 144 | 143 | 143 | Termes de l'échange |
| Finland | | | | | | | | | | Finlande |
| Imports: volume | 88 | 95 | 96 | 97 | 104 | 103 | 108 | 114 | 127 | Importations : volume |
| Imports: unit value | 105 | 102 | 101 | 98 | 97 | 115 | 131 | 146 | 152 | Importations : valeur unitaire |
| Exports: volume | 85 | 89 | 92 | 99 | 104 | 106 | 112 | 111 | 124 | Exportations : volume |
| Exports: unit value | 106 | 105 | 102 | 96 | 94 | 107 | 117 | 127 | 126 | Exportations : valeur unitaire |
| Terms of trade | 101 | 103 | 101 | 97 | 97 | 93 | 89 | 87 | 83 | Termes de l'échange |
| Purchasing power of exports | 85 | 92 | 93 | 97 | 101 | 98 | 99 | 96 | 103 | Pouvoir d'achat des exportations |
| France | | | | | | | | | | France |
| Imports: volume | 71 | 79 | 87 | 116 | 112 | 112 | 125 | 136 | 148 | Importations : volume |
| Imports: unit value | 130 | 129 | 108 | 100 | 99 | 119 | 128 | 127 | 124 | Importations : valeur unitaire |
| Exports: volume | 75 | 83 | 89 | 119 | 112 | 110 | 118 | 125 | 138 | Exportations : volume |
| Exports: unit value | 137 | 137 | 114 | 108 | 109 | 131 | 142 | 140 | 127 | Exportations : valeur unitaire |
| Terms of trade | 106 | 106 | 105 | 108 | 110 | 110 | 111 | 111 | 102 | Termes de l'échange |
| Purchasing power of exports | 79 | 87 | 93 | 129 | 123 | 121 | 131 | 138 | 141 | Pouvoir d'achat des exportations |
| Germany | | | | | | | | | | Allemagne |
| Imports: volume | 77 | 85 | 89 | 101 | 100 | 110 | 121 | 126 | 133 | Importations : volume |
| Imports: unit value | 115 | 111 | 104 | 97 | 98 | 111 | 121 | 123 | 140 | Importations : valeur unitaire |
| Exports: volume | 77 | 83 | 87 | 103 | 104 | 115 | 129 | 136 | 151 | Exportations : volume |
| Exports: unit value | 121 | 118 | 111 | 99 | 102 | 119 | 129 | 130 | 135 | Exportations : valeur unitaire |
| Terms of trade | 105 | 107 | 107 | 102 | 104 | 107 | 107 | 105 | 97 | Termes de l'échange |
| Purchasing power of exports | 81 | 89 | 93 | 105 | 109 | 123 | 139 | 143 | 146 | Pouvoir d'achat des exportations |

| Country or area | 1997 | 1998 | 1999 | 2001 | 2002 | 2003 | 2004 | 2005 | 2006 | Pays ou zone |
|---|---|---|---|---|---|---|---|---|---|---|
| Greece | | | | | | | | | | Grèce |
| Imports: volume | 70 | 85 | 90 | ... | ... | ... | ... | ... | ... | Importations : volume |
| Imports: unit value[1] | 122 | 119 | 115 | 100 | 106 | 127 | 144 | 158 | 166 | Importations : valeur unitaire[1] |
| Exports: volume | 80 | 90 | 96 | ... | ... | ... | ... | ... | ... | Exportations : volume |
| Exports: unit value[1] | 117 | 111 | 107 | 98 | 104 | 124 | 143 | 149 | 157 | Exportations : valeur unitaire[1] |
| Terms of trade | 96 | 93 | 93 | 98 | 98 | 98 | 99 | 95 | 94 | Termes de l'échange |
| Purchasing power of exports | 77 | 84 | 90 | ... | ... | ... | ... | ... | ... | Pouvoir d'achat des exportations |
| Honduras | | | | | | | | | | Honduras |
| Exports: volume | 60 | 77 | 70 | 104 | 105 | 95 | 111 | 101 | 110 | Exportations : volume |
| Exports: unit value | 133 | 134 | 101 | 96 | 91 | 79 | 98 | 135 | 142 | Exportations : valeur unitaire |
| Hungary | | | | | | | | | | Hongrie |
| Imports: volume | 58 | 72 | 83 | 104 | 109 | 120 | 139 | 147 | 166 | Importations : volume |
| Imports: unit value | 114 | 111 | 106 | 101 | 107 | 123 | 135 | 138 | 142 | Importations : valeur unitaire |
| Exports: volume | 58 | 71 | 82 | 108 | 114 | 125 | 147 | 164 | 194 | Exportations : volume |
| Exports: unit value | 117 | 116 | 108 | 101 | 107 | 122 | 134 | 134 | 136 | Exportations : valeur unitaire |
| Terms of trade | 103 | 104 | 103 | 100 | 100 | 100 | 99 | 97 | 95 | Termes de l'échange |
| Purchasing power of exports | 60 | 74 | 84 | 107 | 114 | 124 | 146 | 159 | 185 | Pouvoir d'achat des exportations |
| Iceland | | | | | | | | | | Islande |
| Imports: volume | 74 | 92 | 96 | 90 | ... | ... | ... | ... | ... | Importations : volume |
| Imports: unit value | 105 | 104 | 101 | 97 | ... | ... | ... | ... | ... | Importations : valeur unitaire |
| Exports: volume | 96 | 93 | 100 | 107 | ... | ... | ... | ... | ... | Exportations : volume |
| Exports: unit value | 102 | 110 | 106 | 99 | ... | ... | ... | ... | ... | Exportations : valeur unitaire |
| Terms of trade | 97 | 105 | 104 | 102 | ... | ... | ... | ... | ... | Termes de l'échange |
| Purchasing power of exports | 92 | 97 | 104 | 109 | ... | ... | ... | ... | ... | Pouvoir d'achat des exportations |
| India | | | | | | | | | | Inde |
| Imports: volume | 81 | 92 | 101 | 105 | 115 | 139 | 155 | 151 | ... | Importations : volume |
| Imports: unit value | 103 | 91 | 96 | 96 | 104 | 113 | 134 | 124 | ... | Importations : valeur unitaire |
| Exports: volume | 68 | 70 | 81 | 104 | 126 | 134 | 152 | 184 | ... | Exportations : volume |
| Exports: unit value | 117 | 107 | 101 | 94 | 92 | 107 | 122 | 130 | ... | Exportations : valeur unitaire |
| Terms of trade | 114 | 117 | 105 | 98 | 89 | 95 | 91 | 105 | ... | Termes de l'échange |
| Purchasing power of exports | 77 | 82 | 85 | 102 | 112 | 127 | 138 | 194 | ... | Pouvoir d'achat des exportations |
| Indonesia | | | | | | | | | | Indonésie |
| Exports: volume | 110 | 102 | 84 | 121 | 100 | 97 | 101 | 64 | ... | Exportations : volume |
| Exports: unit value | 104 | 81 | 65 | 90 | 96 | 103 | 120 | 81 | ... | Exportations : valeur unitaire |
| Ireland | | | | | | | | | | Irlande |
| Imports: volume | 67 | 79 | 86 | 99 | 97 | 90 | 98 | 112 | 117 | Importations : volume |
| Imports: unit value | 114 | 109 | 107 | 100 | 101 | 112 | 120 | 121 | 126 | Importations : valeur unitaire |
| Exports: volume | 58 | 72 | 84 | 105 | 104 | 99 | 110 | 113 | 117 | Exportations : volume |
| Exports: unit value | 114 | 110 | 110 | 99 | 104 | 115 | 116 | 119 | 118 | Exportations : valeur unitaire |
| Terms of trade | 100 | 101 | 103 | 98 | 102 | 103 | 97 | 99 | 94 | Termes de l'échange |
| Purchasing power of exports | 58 | 73 | 86 | 103 | 107 | 103 | 107 | 111 | 110 | Pouvoir d'achat des exportations |
| Israel | | | | | | | | | | Israël |
| Imports: volume | 77 | 77 | 88 | 93 | 93 | 92 | 103 | 105 | 105 | Importations : volume |
| Imports: unit value | 106 | 100 | 97 | 99 | 99 | 104 | 112 | 120 | 127 | Importations : valeur unitaire |
| Exports: volume | 69 | 74 | 80 | 96 | 97 | 101 | 116 | 119 | 125 | Exportations : volume |
| Exports: unit value | 102 | 99 | 100 | 96 | 96 | 100 | 106 | 115 | 120 | Exportations : valeur unitaire |
| Terms of trade | 96 | 99 | 103 | 98 | 98 | 96 | 95 | 95 | 94 | Termes de l'échange |
| Purchasing power of exports | 67 | 73 | 82 | 94 | 95 | 97 | 110 | 114 | 117 | Pouvoir d'achat des exportations |
| Italy | | | | | | | | | | Italie |
| Imports: volume | 83 | 90 | 93 | 99 | 99 | 100 | 103 | 103 | 105 | Importations : volume |
| Imports: unit value | 106 | 103 | 99 | 100 | 105 | 125 | 144 | 157 | 175 | Importations : valeur unitaire |
| Exports: volume | 94 | 94 | 92 | 101 | 99 | 96 | 99 | 98 | 101 | Exportations : volume |
| Exports: unit value | 108 | 109 | 107 | 101 | 108 | 130 | 149 | 158 | 171 | Exportations : valeur unitaire |
| Terms of trade | 101 | 107 | 108 | 101 | 103 | 104 | 103 | 101 | 98 | Termes de l'échange |
| Purchasing power of exports | 95 | 100 | 99 | 102 | 101 | 100 | 102 | 99 | 98 | Pouvoir d'achat des exportations |

| Country or area | 1997 | 1998 | 1999 | 2001 | 2002 | 2003 | 2004 | 2005 | 2006 | Pays ou zone |
|---|---|---|---|---|---|---|---|---|---|---|
| **Japan** | | | | | | | | | | **Japon** |
| Imports: volume | 87 | 82 | 90 | 99 | 100 | 107 | 115 | 118 | 123 | Importations : volume |
| Imports: unit value | 103 | 90 | 91 | 87 | 86 | 91 | 101 | 112 | 120 | Importations : valeur unitaire |
| Exports: volume | 91 | 90 | 91 | 90 | 97 | 102 | 113 | 114 | 123 | Exportations : volume |
| Exports: unit value | 97 | 91 | 95 | 94 | 89 | 96 | 104 | 109 | 110 | Exportations : valeur unitaire |
| Terms of trade | 94 | 101 | 105 | 107 | 104 | 105 | 103 | 98 | 92 | Termes de l'échange |
| Purchasing power of exports | 85 | 90 | 96 | 97 | 101 | 108 | 116 | 111 | 113 | Pouvoir d'achat des exportations |
| **Jordan** | | | | | | | | | | **Jordanie** |
| Imports: volume | 90 | 85 | 84 | 103 | 104 | 109 | 136 | 155 | ... | Importations : volume |
| Imports: unit value | 101 | 100 | 97 | 102 | 105 | 115 | 130 | 148 | ... | Importations : valeur unitaire |
| Exports: volume | 88 | 90 | 93 | 123 | 142 | 152 | 190 | 182 | ... | Exportations : volume |
| Exports: unit value | 114 | 107 | 105 | 101 | 102 | 102 | 114 | 131 | ... | Exportations : valeur unitaire |
| Terms of trade | 113 | 107 | 107 | 99 | 97 | 88 | 87 | 88 | ... | Termes de l'échange |
| Purchasing power of exports | 99 | 97 | 100 | 122 | 137 | 135 | 166 | 161 | ... | Pouvoir d'achat des exportations |
| **Kenya** | | | | | | | | | | **Kenya** |
| Imports: volume | 95 | 96 | 87 | ... | ... | ... | ... | ... | ... | Importations : volume |
| Imports: unit value | 107 | 105 | 98 | ... | ... | ... | ... | ... | ... | Importations : valeur unitaire |
| Exports: unit value | 128 | 125 | 101 | ... | ... | ... | ... | ... | ... | Exportations : valeur unitaire |
| Terms of trade | 120 | 119 | 103 | ... | ... | ... | ... | ... | ... | Termes de l'échange |
| **Korea, Republic of** | | | | | | | | | | **Corée, République de** |
| Imports: volume | 87 | 65 | 84 | 98 | 110 | 118 | 132 | 140 | 155 | Importations : volume |
| Imports: unit value | 107 | 88 | 87 | 91 | 88 | 96 | 107 | 117 | 126 | Importations : valeur unitaire |
| Exports: volume | 62 | 74 | 83 | 101 | 114 | 133 | 163 | 178 | 204 | Exportations : volume |
| Exports: unit value | 131 | 103 | 100 | 87 | 83 | 85 | 92 | 93 | 92 | Exportations : valeur unitaire |
| Terms of trade | 122 | 117 | 114 | 95 | 95 | 89 | 85 | 79 | 73 | Termes de l'échange |
| Purchasing power of exports | 76 | 86 | 95 | 96 | 108 | 119 | 139 | 141 | 149 | Pouvoir d'achat des exportations |
| **Latvia** | | | | | | | | | | **Lettonie** |
| Imports: unit value | ... | 102 | 97 | 98 | 106 | 122 | 140 | 150 | 166 | Importations : valeur unitaire |
| Exports: unit value | 110 | 108 | 105 | 99 | 104 | 121 | 145 | 153 | 169 | Exportations : valeur unitaire |
| Terms of trade | ... | 106 | 108 | 101 | 98 | 99 | 104 | 102 | 102 | Termes de l'échange |
| **Libyan Arab Jamah.** | | | | | | | | | | **Jamah. arabe libyenne** |
| Imports: volume | 208 | 156 | 147 | 173 | 214 | ... | ... | ... | ... | Importations : volume |
| Imports: unit value | 93 | 96 | 115 | 83 | 48 | ... | ... | ... | ... | Importations : valeur unitaire |
| Exports: volume | 129 | 94 | 108 | 110 | 95 | ... | ... | ... | ... | Exportations : volume |
| Exports: unit value | 64 | 53 | 72 | 87 | 88 | ... | ... | ... | ... | Exportations : valeur unitaire |
| Terms of trade | 69 | 55 | 63 | 104 | 185 | ... | ... | ... | ... | Termes de l'échange |
| Purchasing power of exports | 89 | 52 | 68 | 115 | 175 | ... | ... | ... | ... | Pouvoir d'achat des exportations |
| **Lithuania** | | | | | | | | | | **Lituanie** |
| Imports: volume | ... | ... | ... | 120 | 143 | 155 | 182 | 209 | 233 | Importations : volume |
| Imports: unit value | 105 | 99 | 95 | 97 | 101 | 117 | 127 | 138 | 151 | Importations : valeur unitaire |
| Exports: volume | ... | ... | ... | 125 | 145 | 161 | 185 | 214 | 234 | Exportations : volume |
| Exports: unit value | 103 | 97 | 94 | 97 | 101 | 120 | 137 | 151 | 160 | Exportations : valeur unitaire |
| Terms of trade | 97 | 98 | 99 | 101 | 100 | 102 | 108 | 109 | 106 | Termes de l'échange |
| Purchasing power of exports | ... | ... | ... | 126 | 146 | 164 | 199 | 233 | 247 | Pouvoir d'achat des exportations |
| **Malaysia** | | | | | | | | | | **Malaisie** |
| Imports: volume | ... | ... | ... | 92 | 97 | ... | ... | ... | ... | Importations : volume |
| Imports: unit value | ... | ... | ... | 98 | 99 | ... | ... | ... | ... | Importations : valeur unitaire |
| Exports: volume | ... | ... | ... | 96 | 102 | ... | ... | ... | ... | Exportations : volume |
| Exports: unit value | ... | ... | ... | 94 | 93 | ... | ... | ... | ... | Exportations : valeur unitaire |
| Terms of trade | ... | ... | ... | 96 | 94 | ... | ... | ... | ... | Termes de l'échange |
| Purchasing power of exports | ... | ... | ... | 92 | 96 | ... | ... | ... | ... | Pouvoir d'achat des exportations |
| **Mauritius** | | | | | | | | | | **Maurice** |
| Imports: volume | ... | 99 | 107 | 98 | 103 | 96 | 100 | 106 | 110 | Importations : volume |
| Imports: unit value | 106 | 99 | 100 | 97 | 99 | 80 | 90 | 98 | 102 | Importations : valeur unitaire |

| Country or area | 1997 | 1998 | 1999 | 2001 | 2002 | 2003 | 2004 | 2005 | 2006 | Pays ou zone |
|---|---|---|---|---|---|---|---|---|---|---|
| Exports: volume | ... | 95 | 98 | 116 | 121 | 92 | 89 | 96 | 107 | Exportations : volume |
| Exports: unit value | 111 | 111 | 106 | 92 | 98 | 84 | 92 | 90 | 89 | Exportations : valeur unitaire |
| Terms of trade | 105 | 112 | 106 | 95 | 98 | 105 | 101 | 92 | 87 | Termes de l'échange |
| Purchasing power of exports | ... | 107 | 103 | 110 | 119 | 96 | 90 | 89 | 93 | Pouvoir d'achat des exportations |
| **Mexico** | | | | | | | | | | **Mexique** |
| Imports: unit value | 99 | 98 | 97 | 101 | 100 | 103 | 108 | 114 | 119 | Importations : valeur unitaire |
| Exports: unit value | 95 | 90 | 93 | 98 | 100 | 105 | 117 | 127 | 137 | Exportations : valeur unitaire |
| Terms of trade | 96 | 91 | 96 | 97 | 100 | 102 | 108 | 112 | 115 | Termes de l'échange |
| **Moldova** | | | | | | | | | | **Moldova** |
| Imports: volume | ... | ... | ... | 118 | 139 | 180 | 205 | 248 | ... | Importations : volume |
| Imports: unit value | ... | ... | ... | 97 | 92 | 95 | 119 | 124 | ... | Importations : valeur unitaire |
| Exports: volume | ... | ... | ... | 122 | 142 | 170 | 199 | 215 | ... | Exportations : volume |
| Exports: unit value | ... | ... | ... | 93 | 87 | 88 | 107 | 107 | ... | Exportations : valeur unitaire |
| Terms of trade | ... | ... | ... | 96 | 95 | 93 | 90 | 86 | ... | Termes de l'échange |
| Purchasing power of exports | ... | ... | ... | 117 | 134 | 158 | 178 | 186 | ... | Pouvoir d'achat des exportations |
| **Morocco** | | | | | | | | | | **Maroc** |
| Imports: volume | ... | ... | 89 | 98 | 105 | 113 | 127 | 136 | ... | Importations : volume |
| Imports: unit value | 126 | 109 | 107 | 97 | 98 | 110 | 121 | 129 | ... | Importations : valeur unitaire |
| Exports: volume | ... | ... | 92 | 102 | 107 | 104 | 103 | 108 | ... | Exportations : volume |
| Exports: unit value | 118 | 115 | 110 | 94 | 99 | 116 | 127 | 129 | ... | Exportations : valeur unitaire |
| Terms of trade | 94 | 105 | 103 | 97 | 101 | 105 | 105 | 100 | ... | Termes de l'échange |
| Purchasing power of exports | ... | ... | 95 | 99 | 107 | 110 | 108 | 107 | ... | Pouvoir d'achat des exportations |
| **Netherlands** | | | | | | | | | | **Pays-Bas** |
| Imports: volume | 81 | 89 | 96 | 97 | 95 | 98 | 106 | 115 | 126 | Importations : volume |
| Imports: unit value | 113 | 108 | 103 | 101 | 101 | 118 | 131 | 133 | 139 | Importations : valeur unitaire |
| Exports: volume | 82 | 88 | 92 | 102 | 103 | 106 | 116 | 122 | 133 | Exportations : volume |
| Exports: unit value | 114 | 109 | 101 | 100 | 100 | 116 | 127 | 133 | 140 | Exportations : valeur unitaire |
| Terms of trade | 101 | 101 | 98 | 99 | 98 | 99 | 96 | 100 | 101 | Termes de l'échange |
| Purchasing power of exports | 83 | 88 | 90 | 100 | 101 | 104 | 112 | 122 | 133 | Pouvoir d'achat des exportations |
| **New Zealand** | | | | | | | | | | **Nouvelle-Zélande** |
| Imports: volume | 88 | 91 | 103 | 102 | 111 | 124 | 142 | 151 | 152 | Importations : volume |
| Imports: unit value | 118 | 99 | 100 | 94 | 98 | 109 | 118 | 125 | 126 | Importations : valeur unitaire |
| Exports: volume | 93 | 92 | 95 | 103 | 109 | 112 | 119 | 118 | 120 | Exportations : volume |
| Exports: unit value | 117 | 99 | 99 | 101 | 99 | 111 | 129 | 138 | 138 | Exportations : valeur unitaire |
| Terms of trade | 99 | 99 | 99 | 107 | 102 | 102 | 109 | 111 | 110 | Termes de l'échange |
| Purchasing power of exports | 92 | 92 | 93 | 110 | 111 | 115 | 130 | 130 | 131 | Pouvoir d'achat des exportations |
| **Norway** | | | | | | | | | | **Norvège** |
| Imports: volume[2] | 83 | 94 | 94 | 101 | 103 | 106 | 118 | 129 | 142 | Importations : volume[2] |
| Imports: unit value[2] | 127 | 118 | 109 | 98 | 104 | 116 | 127 | 133 | 139 | Importations : valeur unitaire[2] |
| Exports: volume[2] | 93 | 93 | 95 | 105 | 107 | 107 | 108 | 108 | 105 | Exportations : volume[2] |
| Exports: unit value[2] | 86 | 71 | 78 | 93 | 94 | 104 | 127 | 161 | 194 | Exportations : valeur unitaire[2] |
| Terms of trade | 68 | 61 | 71 | 95 | 91 | 90 | 100 | 122 | 139 | Termes de l'échange |
| Purchasing power of exports | 63 | 56 | 68 | 99 | 97 | 97 | 109 | 131 | 147 | Pouvoir d'achat des exportations |
| **Pakistan** | | | | | | | | | | **Pakistan** |
| Imports: volume | 94 | 90 | 101 | 112 | 123 | 123 | 142 | 165 | 153 | Importations : volume |
| Imports: unit value | 97 | 86 | 93 | 94 | 95 | 109 | 122 | 138 | 151 | Importations : valeur unitaire |
| Exports: volume | 82 | 79 | 89 | 102 | 109 | 110 | 103 | 126 | 127 | Exportations : volume |
| Exports: unit value | 115 | 118 | 109 | 94 | 90 | 96 | 103 | 103 | 106 | Exportations : valeur unitaire |
| Terms of trade | 118 | 137 | 118 | 100 | 95 | 89 | 85 | 75 | 70 | Termes de l'échange |
| Purchasing power of exports | 97 | 109 | 105 | 102 | 104 | 98 | 87 | 95 | 89 | Pouvoir d'achat des exportations |
| **Panama** | | | | | | | | | | **Panama** |
| Exports: volume | ... | 143 | 105 | ... | 81 | 84 | 83 | 98 | ... | Exportations : volume |

| Country or area | 1997 | 1998 | 1999 | 2001 | 2002 | 2003 | 2004 | 2005 | 2006 | Pays ou zone |
|---|---|---|---|---|---|---|---|---|---|---|
| Papua New Guinea | | | | | | | | | | Papouasie-Nvl-Guinée |
| Exports: unit value | 98 | 80 | 79 | 90 | 85 | 101 | 126 | 156 | 247 | Exportations : valeur unitaire |
| Peru | | | | | | | | | | Pérou |
| Exports: volume | 91 | 78 | 88 | 114 | 126 | 122 | 135 | 150 | 144 | Exportations : volume |
| Exports: unit value | 90 | 70 | 75 | 84 | 87 | 97 | 100 | 170 | 264 | Exportations : valeur unitaire |
| Philippines | | | | | | | | | | Philippines |
| Imports: volume | 106 | 85 | 95 | 98 | 116 | 118 | 137 | 127 | ... | Importations : volume |
| Imports: unit value[1] | 162 | 121 | 118 | 84 | 83 | 82 | 81 | 94 | ... | Importations : valeur unitaire[1] |
| Exports: volume | 74 | 80 | 87 | 89 | 104 | 98 | 110 | 104 | ... | Exportations : volume |
| Exports: unit value[1] | 134 | 105 | 121 | 84 | 77 | 79 | 75 | 84 | ... | Exportations : valeur unitaire[1] |
| Terms of trade | 83 | 87 | 103 | 100 | 93 | 96 | 93 | 89 | ... | Termes de l'échange |
| Purchasing power of exports | 61 | 70 | 89 | 88 | 97 | 94 | 102 | 93 | ... | Pouvoir d'achat des exportations |
| Poland | | | | | | | | | | Pologne |
| Imports: volume | 75 | 87 | 90 | 104 | 111 | 119 | 140 | 148 | 173 | Importations : volume |
| Imports: unit value[1] | 114 | 111 | 103 | 100 | 101 | 116 | 131 | 141 | 151 | Importations : valeur unitaire[1] |
| Exports: volume | 72 | 79 | 80 | 114 | 122 | 143 | 170 | 189 | 220 | Exportations : volume |
| Exports: unit value[1] | 113 | 115 | 108 | 102 | 107 | 118 | 139 | 150 | 160 | Exportations : valeur unitaire[1] |
| Terms of trade | 99 | 103 | 105 | 102 | 105 | 102 | 107 | 107 | 107 | Termes de l'échange |
| Purchasing power of exports | 71 | 82 | 83 | 116 | 129 | 146 | 182 | 201 | 235 | Pouvoir d'achat des exportations |
| Portugal | | | | | | | | | | Portugal |
| Imports: volume | ... | ... | ... | 97 | 94 | 94 | ... | ... | ... | Importations : volume |
| Imports: unit value[1] | 115 | 110 | 106 | 89 | 91 | 110 | ... | ... | ... | Importations : valeur unitaire[1] |
| Exports: volume | ... | ... | ... | 95 | 95 | 97 | ... | ... | ... | Exportations : volume |
| Exports: unit value[1] | 119 | 116 | 109 | 93 | 96 | 112 | ... | ... | ... | Exportations : valeur unitaire[1] |
| Terms of trade | 104 | 106 | 103 | 105 | 106 | 102 | ... | ... | ... | Termes de l'échange |
| Purchasing power of exports | ... | ... | ... | 99 | 101 | 99 | ... | ... | ... | Pouvoir d'achat des exportations |
| Romania | | | | | | | | | | Roumanie |
| Imports: volume | ... | ... | ... | 124 | 143 | 169 | 207 | 244 | 293 | Importations : volume |
| Imports: unit value | 133 | 117 | 105 | 96 | 96 | 106 | 106 | 112 | 116 | Importations : valeur unitaire |
| Exports: volume | ... | ... | ... | 112 | 132 | 144 | 166 | 179 | 191 | Exportations : volume |
| Exports: unit value | 118 | 109 | 102 | 98 | 102 | 119 | 125 | 137 | 148 | Exportations : valeur unitaire |
| Terms of trade | 89 | 93 | 97 | 102 | 106 | 112 | 118 | 122 | 127 | Termes de l'échange |
| Purchasing power of exports | ... | ... | ... | 114 | 139 | 161 | 195 | 218 | 244 | Pouvoir d'achat des exportations |
| Russian Federation | | | | | | | | | | Fédération de Russie |
| Imports: volume | ... | ... | ... | 123 | 136 | 168 | 222 | 288 | 398 | Importations : volume |
| Exports: volume | ... | ... | ... | 99 | 105 | 133 | 180 | 240 | 303 | Exportations : volume |
| Seychelles | | | | | | | | | | Seychelles |
| Imports: volume | 68 | 83 | 105 | ... | ... | ... | ... | ... | ... | Importations : volume |
| Imports: unit value | 146 | 136 | 120 | ... | ... | ... | ... | ... | ... | Importations : valeur unitaire |
| Exports: volume | 51 | 51 | 78 | ... | ... | ... | ... | ... | ... | Exportations : volume |
| Exports: unit value | 110 | 143 | 114 | ... | ... | ... | ... | ... | ... | Exportations : valeur unitaire |
| Terms of trade | 75 | 105 | 94 | ... | ... | ... | ... | ... | ... | Termes de l'échange |
| Purchasing power of exports | 38 | 54 | 73 | ... | ... | ... | ... | ... | ... | Pouvoir d'achat des exportations |
| Singapore | | | | | | | | | | Singapour |
| Imports: volume | 92 | 83 | 88 | 89 | 90 | 96 | 117 | 134 | 149 | Importations : volume |
| Imports: unit value[1] | 107 | 93 | 93 | 97 | 96 | 99 | 104 | 111 | 120 | Importations : valeur unitaire[1] |
| Exports: volume | 81 | 82 | 86 | 95 | 100 | 116 | 155 | 173 | 192 | Exportations : volume |
| Exports: unit value[1] | 112 | 97 | 96 | 93 | 91 | 90 | 93 | 96 | 103 | Exportations : valeur unitaire[1] |
| Terms of trade | 105 | 104 | 103 | 96 | 94 | 91 | 89 | 87 | 86 | Termes de l'échange |
| Purchasing power of exports | 85 | 86 | 89 | 91 | 95 | 106 | 139 | 151 | 165 | Pouvoir d'achat des exportations |
| Slovakia | | | | | | | | | | Slovaquie |
| Imports: unit value | ... | ... | ... | ... | 106 | 129 | 147 | 157 | 177 | Importations : valeur unitaire |
| Exports: unit value | ... | ... | ... | ... | 105 | 139 | 174 | 191 | 204 | Exportations : valeur unitaire |
| Terms of trade | ... | ... | ... | ... | 99 | 108 | 118 | 121 | 115 | Termes de l'échange |

| Country or area | 1997 | 1998 | 1999 | 2001 | 2002 | 2003 | 2004 | 2005 | 2006 | Pays ou zone |
|---|---|---|---|---|---|---|---|---|---|---|
| Slovenia | | | | | | | | | | Slovénie |
| Imports: volume | ... | 88 | 96 | 101 | 105 | 111 | ... | ... | ... | Importations : volume |
| Imports: unit value | ... | 113 | 104 | 100 | 104 | 124 | 141 | 152 | 164 | Importations : valeur unitaire |
| Exports: volume | ... | 86 | 89 | 105 | 110 | 115 | ... | ... | ... | Exportations : volume |
| Exports: unit value | ... | 119 | 109 | 100 | 106 | 126 | 142 | 149 | 159 | Exportations : valeur unitaire |
| Terms of trade | ... | 105 | 105 | 100 | 102 | 102 | 101 | 98 | 97 | Termes de l'échange |
| Purchasing power of exports | ... | 90 | 94 | 105 | 112 | 117 | ... | ... | ... | Pouvoir d'achat des exportations |
| South Africa | | | | | | | | | | Afrique du Sud |
| Imports: volume | 99 | 101 | 93 | 100 | 105 | 115 | 131 | 144 | ... | Importations : volume |
| Imports: unit value | 107 | 99 | 98 | 94 | 93 | 116 | 136 | 144 | ... | Importations : valeur unitaire |
| Exports: volume | 88 | 90 | 91 | 102 | 102 | 103 | 105 | 112 | ... | Exportations : volume |
| Exports: unit value | 113 | 104 | 100 | 96 | 96 | 123 | 148 | 156 | ... | Exportations : valeur unitaire |
| Terms of trade | 106 | 105 | 102 | 101 | 104 | 107 | 109 | 109 | ... | Termes de l'échange |
| Purchasing power of exports | 93 | 94 | 92 | 103 | 106 | 109 | 114 | 122 | ... | Pouvoir d'achat des exportations |
| Spain | | | | | | | | | | Espagne |
| Imports: volume | ... | ... | 92 | 104 | 109 | 117 | 129 | ... | ... | Importations : volume |
| Imports: unit value[1] | 112 | 108 | 102 | 96 | 99 | 116 | 131 | 138 | 143 | Importations : valeur unitaire[1] |
| Exports: volume | ... | ... | 89 | 104 | 107 | 114 | 120 | ... | ... | Exportations : volume |
| Exports: unit value[1] | 117 | 115 | 109 | 98 | 102 | 121 | 134 | 140 | 148 | Exportations : valeur unitaire[1] |
| Terms of trade | 105 | 107 | 106 | 101 | 103 | 104 | 102 | 102 | 103 | Termes de l'échange |
| Purchasing power of exports | ... | ... | 94 | 106 | 111 | 118 | 123 | ... | ... | Pouvoir d'achat des exportations |
| Sri Lanka | | | | | | | | | | Sri Lanka |
| Imports: volume | 82 | 89 | 90 | 91 | 101 | 111 | 122 | 126 | 135 | Importations : volume |
| Imports: unit value | ... | ... | ... | 98 | 90 | ... | ... | ... | ... | Importations : valeur unitaire |
| Exports: volume | 82 | 81 | 84 | 92 | 93 | 98 | 106 | 113 | 97 | Exportations : volume |
| Exports: unit value | 105 | 110 | 101 | 97 | 91 | 97 | 101 | 104 | 109 | Exportations : valeur unitaire |
| Terms of trade | ... | ... | ... | 98 | 101 | ... | ... | ... | ... | Termes de l'échange |
| Purchasing power of exports | ... | ... | ... | 90 | 94 | ... | ... | ... | ... | Pouvoir d'achat des exportations |
| Sweden | | | | | | | | | | Suède |
| Imports: volume | 78 | 86 | 89 | 95 | 94 | 100 | 108 | 116 | 126 | Importations : volume |
| Imports: unit value[1] | 110 | 104 | 103 | 93 | 99 | 117 | 132 | 139 | 149 | Importations : valeur unitaire[1] |
| Exports: volume | 78 | 85 | 90 | 98 | 101 | 106 | 117 | 122 | 133 | Exportations : volume |
| Exports: unit value[1] | 117 | 112 | 106 | 90 | 94 | 111 | 121 | 124 | 131 | Exportations : valeur unitaire[1] |
| Terms of trade | 107 | 107 | 104 | 97 | 95 | 95 | 92 | 90 | 88 | Termes de l'échange |
| Purchasing power of exports | 83 | 91 | 93 | 96 | 96 | 101 | 108 | 109 | 117 | Pouvoir d'achat des exportations |
| Switzerland | | | | | | | | | | Suisse |
| Imports: volume | 80 | 87 | 93 | 101 | 99 | 100 | 104 | 106 | 117 | Importations : volume |
| Imports: unit value | 116 | 112 | 107 | 100 | 105 | 121 | 135 | 143 | 149 | Importations : valeur unitaire |
| Exports: volume | 87 | 91 | 93 | 103 | 105 | 105 | 111 | 115 | 132 | Exportations : volume |
| Exports: unit value | 111 | 110 | 109 | 101 | 107 | 124 | 137 | 141 | 143 | Exportations : valeur unitaire |
| Terms of trade | 96 | 99 | 103 | 101 | 102 | 102 | 102 | 99 | 96 | Termes de l'échange |
| Purchasing power of exports | 83 | 90 | 95 | 104 | 106 | 107 | 113 | 114 | 127 | Pouvoir d'achat des exportations |
| Thailand | | | | | | | | | | Thaïlande |
| Imports: volume | 91 | 67 | 82 | 89 | 100 | 112 | 124 | 135 | 195 | Importations : volume |
| Imports: unit value | 109 | 98 | 95 | 109 | 102 | 107 | 121 | 140 | 151 | Importations : valeur unitaire |
| Exports: volume | 68 | 73 | 82 | 92 | 101 | 109 | 119 | 124 | 135 | Exportations : volume |
| Exports: unit value | 122 | 107 | 102 | 102 | 97 | 105 | 118 | 130 | 140 | Exportations : valeur unitaire |
| Terms of trade | 112 | 109 | 107 | 93 | 95 | 99 | 98 | 93 | 92 | Termes de l'échange |
| Purchasing power of exports | 76 | 80 | 88 | 85 | 96 | 108 | 116 | 115 | 125 | Pouvoir d'achat des exportations |
| Turkey | | | | | | | | | | Turquie |
| Imports: volume | 78 | 76 | 75 | 75 | 91 | 121 | 153 | 172 | 186 | Importations : volume |
| Imports: unit value | 106 | 101 | 96 | 100 | 98 | 106 | 120 | 128 | 139 | Importations : valeur unitaire |
| Exports: volume | 79 | 87 | 90 | 122 | 142 | 173 | 199 | 219 | 246 | Exportations : volume |
| Exports: unit value | 117 | 112 | 104 | 97 | 96 | 105 | 122 | 129 | 134 | Exportations : valeur unitaire |
| Terms of trade | 111 | 111 | 109 | 98 | 97 | 99 | 102 | 101 | 96 | Termes de l'échange |
| Purchasing power of exports | 88 | 96 | 98 | 119 | 137 | 171 | 203 | 222 | 237 | Pouvoir d'achat des exportations |

| Country or area | 1997 | 1998 | 1999 | 2001 | 2002 | 2003 | 2004 | 2005 | 2006 | Pays ou zone |
|---|---|---|---|---|---|---|---|---|---|---|
| United Kingdom | | | | | | | | | | Royaume-Uni |
| Imports: volume | 79 | 86 | 91 | 105 | 110 | 112 | 120 | 128 | 143 | Importations : volume |
| Imports: unit value[1] | 112 | 106 | 104 | 94 | 96 | 104 | 116 | 120 | 126 | Importations : valeur unitaire[1] |
| Exports: volume | 85 | 86 | 89 | 102 | 101 | 101 | 102 | 111 | 123 | Exportations : volume |
| Exports: unit value[1] | 115 | 111 | 106 | 94 | 98 | 108 | 122 | 125 | 131 | Exportations : valeur unitaire[1] |
| Terms of trade | 103 | 104 | 102 | 99 | 102 | 104 | 105 | 105 | 104 | Termes de l'échange |
| Purchasing power of exports | 88 | 90 | 91 | 101 | 103 | 105 | 108 | 117 | 128 | Pouvoir d'achat des exportations |
| United States | | | | | | | | | | Etats-Unis |
| Imports: volume | 72 | 81 | 90 | 97 | 101 | 107 | 118 | 125 | 132 | Importations : volume |
| Imports: unit value[1] | 99 | 93 | 94 | 96 | 94 | 97 | 102 | 110 | 115 | Importations : valeur unitaire[1] |
| Exports: volume[3] | 86 | 88 | 90 | 94 | 90 | 93 | 101 | 109 | 120 | Exportations : volume[3] |
| Exports: unit value[1,3] | 103 | 100 | 98 | 99 | 98 | 100 | 104 | 107 | 111 | Exportations : valeur unitaire[1,3] |
| Terms of trade | 104 | 107 | 105 | 103 | 104 | 103 | 101 | 97 | 96 | Termes de l'échange |
| Purchasing power of exports | 89 | 94 | 95 | 97 | 94 | 96 | 102 | 105 | 115 | Pouvoir d'achat des exportations |
| Uruguay | | | | | | | | | | Uruguay |
| Imports: unit value | 108 | 101 | 96 | 94 | 87 | ... | ... | ... | ... | Importations : valeur unitaire |
| Exports: unit value | 119 | 118 | 101 | 98 | 93 | ... | ... | ... | ... | Exportations : valeur unitaire |
| Terms of trade | 110 | 117 | 106 | 104 | 106 | ... | ... | ... | ... | Termes de l'échange |
| Venezuela (Bolivarian Rep. of)[1] | | | | | | | | | | Venezuela (Rép. bolivarienne du)[1] |
| Imports: unit value | 98 | 102 | 102 | 105 | 105 | 112 | 123 | 126 | 132 | Importations : valeur unitaire |

Source

United Nations Statistics Division, New York, trade statistics database, last accessed March 2008.

Notes

1 Price index numbers.
2 Index numbers exclude ships.
3 Excluding military goods.

Source

Organisation des Nations Unies, Division de statistique, New York, la base de données pour les statistiques du commerce extérieur, dernier accès mars 2008.

Notes

1 Les indices des prix.
2 Les indices excluent les navires.
3 Non compris les biens militaires.

# Manufactured goods exports
Unit value and volume indices: 2000 = 100; value: thousand million US dollars

# Exportations des produits manufacturés
Indices de valeur unitaire et de volume : 2000 = 100; valeur : milliards de dollars E.-U.

| Region, country or area — Région, pays ou zone | 1997 | 1998 | 1999 | 2000 | 2001 | 2002 | 2003 | 2004 | 2005 | 2006 |
|---|---|---|---|---|---|---|---|---|---|---|
| **Total — Total** | | | | | | | | | | |
| Unit value indices, US $[1] <br> Indices de valeur unitaire, $ E.-U.[1] | 110 | 108 | 103 | 100 | 98 | 98 | 104 | 111 | 112 | ... |
| Unit value indices, SDRs <br> Indices de valeur unitaire, DTS | 105 | 106 | 99 | 100 | 102 | 99 | 99 | 98 | 100 | ... |
| Volume indices <br> Indices de volume | 80 | 82 | 88 | 100 | 100 | 103 | 111 | 116 | 126 | ... |
| Value, thousand million US $ <br> Valeur, millards de $ E.-U. | 4 064.2 | 4 094.8 | 4 194.4 | 4 620.8 | 4 548.3 | 4 648.6 | 5 356.1 | 5 944.9 | 6 546.0 | ... |
| **Developed economies — Économies développées** | | | | | | | | | | |
| Unit value indices, US $ <br> Indices de valeur unitaire, $ E.-U. | 111 | 110 | 105 | 100 | 98 | 99 | 108 | 117 | 120 | 123 |
| Unit value indices, SDRs <br> Indices de valeur unitaire, DTS | 106 | 107 | 101 | 100 | 102 | 100 | 102 | 103 | 107 | ... |
| Volume indices <br> Indices de volume | 83 | 84 | 89 | 100 | 102 | 101 | 105 | 115 | 119 | 129 |
| Value, thousand million US $ <br> Valeur, millards de $ E.-U. | 2 955.5 | 2 983.8 | 3 021.0 | 3 209.4 | 3 215.6 | 3 196.4 | 3 653.2 | 4 312.7 | 4 572.7 | 5 095.1 |
| **Americas — Amériques** | | | | | | | | | | |
| Unit value indices, US $ <br> Indices de valeur unitaire, $ E.-U. | 101 | 100 | 99 | 100 | 99 | 100 | 103 | 106 | 108 | 111 |
| Volume indices <br> Indices de volume | 85 | 87 | 91 | 100 | 101 | 88 | 88 | 97 | 104 | 114 |
| Value, thousand million US $ <br> Valeur, millards de $ E.-U. | 667.7 | 675.6 | 703.7 | 780.3 | 781.7 | 685.3 | 704.0 | 803.2 | 872.2 | 983.2 |
| Canada — Canada | | | | | | | | | | |
| Unit value indices, US $ <br> Indices de valeur unitaire, $ E.-U. | 106 | 101 | 99 | 100 | 98 | 96 | 103 | 112 | 119 | ... |
| Unit value indices, national currency <br> Indices de val. unitaire, monnaie nationale | 99 | 101 | 99 | 100 | 102 | 102 | 98 | 98 | 97 | ... |
| Volume indices <br> Indices de volume | 73 | 80 | 90 | 100 | 94 | 94 | 92 | 97 | 100 | ... |
| Value, thousand million US $ <br> Valeur, millards de $ E.-U. | 142.9 | 148.7 | 165.6 | 184.0 | 169.1 | 166.6 | 173.6 | 200.2 | 219.2 | 234.6 |
| United States — Etats-Unis | | | | | | | | | | |
| Unit value indices, US $[2] <br> Indices de valeur unitaire, $ E.-U.[2] | 99 | 100 | 99 | 100 | 100 | 102 | 103 | 104 | 104 | 107 |
| Unit value indices, national currency[2] <br> Indices de val. unitaire, monnaie nationale[2] | 99 | 100 | 99 | 100 | 100 | 102 | 103 | 104 | 104 | 107 |
| Volume indices <br> Indices de volume | 89 | 89 | 91 | 100 | 103 | 86 | 87 | 97 | 105 | 118 |
| Value, thousand million US $ <br> Valeur, millards de $ E.-U. | 524.8 | 527.0 | 538.1 | 596.3 | 612.6 | 518.8 | 530.4 | 603.0 | 653.1 | 748.6 |
| **Europe — Europe** | | | | | | | | | | |
| Unit value indices, US $ <br> Indices de valeur unitaire, $ E.-U. | 117 | 118 | 110 | 100 | 99 | 100 | 112 | 122 | 125 | 130 |
| Volume indices <br> Indices de volume | 82 | 84 | 89 | 100 | 106 | 108 | 113 | 124 | 127 | 138 |
| Value, thousand million US $ <br> Valeur, millards de $ E.-U. | 1 826.5 | 1 884.5 | 1 856.3 | 1 903.5 | 1 986.4 | 2 051.3 | 2 426.2 | 2 877.4 | 3 037.3 | 3 393.2 |
| Austria — Autriche | | | | | | | | | | |
| Unit value indices, US $ <br> Indices de valeur unitaire, $ E.-U | 152 | 141 | 118 | 100 | 94 | 100 | ... | ... | ... | ... |
| Unit value indices, national currency <br> Indices de val. unitaire, monnaie nationale | 125 | 117 | 102 | 100 | 98 | 98 | ... | ... | ... | ... |

**57** Manufactured goods exports—Unit value and volume indices: 2000 = 100; value: thousand million US dollars (*continued*)

**Exportations des produits manufacturés**—Indices de valeur unitaire et de volume : 2000 = 100; valeur : milliards de dollars E.-U. (*suite*)

| Region, country or area — Région, pays ou zone | 1997 | 1998 | 1999 | 2000 | 2001 | 2002 | 2003 | 2004 | 2005 | 2006 |
|---|---|---|---|---|---|---|---|---|---|---|
| Volume indices<br>Indices de volume | 70 | 74 | 86 | 100 | 124 | 118 | ... | ... | ... | ... |
| Value, thousand million US $<br>Valeur, millards de $ E.-U. | 53.1 | 51.7 | 50.4 | 49.8 | 58.3 | 59.0 | 76.8 | 96.7 | 100.2 | 114.0 |
| **Belgium — Belgique** | | | | | | | | | | |
| Unit value indices, US $<br>Indices de valeur unitaire, $ E.-U. | 115 | 114 | 108 | 100 | 99 | 106 | 125 | 141 | 148 | 156 |
| Unit value indices, national currency<br>Indices de val. unitaire, monnaie nationale | 94 | 95 | 94 | 100 | 102 | 103 | 103 | 105 | 110 | 115 |
| Volume indices<br>Indices de volume | 84 | 87 | 92 | 100 | 100 | 100 | 100 | 106 | 107 | 107 |
| Value, thousand million US $<br>Valeur, millards de $ E.-U. | 127.0 | 132.2 | 131.8 | 132.5 | 131.6 | 139.5 | 166.3 | 198.7 | 209.9 | 222.3 |
| **Denmark — Danemark** | | | | | | | | | | |
| Unit value indices, US $<br>Indices de valeur unitaire, $ E.-U. | 118 | 116 | 112 | 100 | 100 | 103 | 122 | 136 | 138 | 141 |
| Unit value indices, national currency<br>Indices de val. unitaire, monnaie nationale | 96 | 96 | 97 | 100 | 102 | 100 | 101 | 101 | 102 | 103 |
| Volume indices<br>Indices de volume | 81 | 84 | 95 | 100 | 105 | 114 | 119 | 119 | 129 | 137 |
| Value, thousand million US $<br>Valeur, millards de $ E.-U. | 30.2 | 31.2 | 33.8 | 31.8 | 33.5 | 37.2 | 46.4 | 51.4 | 56.6 | 61.1 |
| **Finland — Finlande** | | | | | | | | | | |
| Unit value indices, US $<br>Indices de valeur unitaire, $ E.-U. | 109 | 107 | 104 | 100 | 95 | 100 | 117 | 120 | 131 | 141 |
| Unit value indices, national currency<br>Indices de val. unitaire, monnaie nationale | 88 | 89 | 90 | 100 | 98 | 98 | 96 | 89 | 97 | 104 |
| Volume indices<br>Indices de volume | 81 | 89 | 89 | 100 | 103 | 98 | 98 | 109 | 108 | 116 |
| Value, thousand million US $<br>Valeur, millards de $ E.-U. | 35.1 | 38.0 | 36.7 | 39.7 | 38.9 | 38.9 | 45.4 | 51.8 | 56.1 | 65.1 |
| **France — France** | | | | | | | | | | |
| Unit value indices, US $<br>Indices de valeur unitaire, $ E.-U. | 120 | 120 | 113 | 100 | 98 | 84 | 101 | 111 | 111 | 109 |
| Unit value indices, national currency<br>Indices de val. unitaire, monnaie nationale | 98 | 100 | 98 | 100 | 101 | 83 | 83 | 82 | 82 | 81 |
| Volume indices<br>Indices de volume | 76 | 82 | 86 | 100 | 119 | 120 | 118 | 127 | 132 | 148 |
| Value, thousand million US $<br>Valeur, millards de $ E.-U. | 225.8 | 244.3 | 242.5 | 249.2 | 290.2 | 251.9 | 298.5 | 351.8 | 365.3 | 404.9 |
| **Germany — Allemagne** | | | | | | | | | | |
| Unit value indices, US $<br>Indices de valeur unitaire, $ E.-U. | 121 | 124 | 111 | 100 | 99 | 104 | 118 | 128 | 128 | 132 |
| Unit value indices, national currency<br>Indices de val. unitaire, monnaie nationale | 99 | 103 | 97 | 100 | 102 | 102 | 96 | 95 | 95 | 97 |
| Volume indices<br>Indices de volume | 79 | 80 | 86 | 100 | 105 | 107 | 114 | 128 | 138 | 152 |
| Value, thousand million US $<br>Valeur, millards de $ E.-U. | 455.3 | 477.9 | 461.1 | 481.0 | 499.2 | 534.8 | 644.3 | 790.3 | 849.0 | 970.0 |
| **Greece — Grèce** | | | | | | | | | | |
| Unit value indices, US $<br>Indices de valeur unitaire, $ E.-U. | 122 | 113 | 107 | 100 | ... | ... | ... | ... | ... | ... |
| Unit value indices, national currency<br>Indices de val. unitaire, monnaie nationale | 91 | 91 | 90 | 100 | ... | ... | ... | ... | ... | ... |
| Volume indices<br>Indices de volume | 84 | 93 | 86 | 100 | ... | ... | ... | ... | ... | ... |
| Value, thousand million US $<br>Valeur, millards de $ E.-U. | 6.2 | 6.3 | 5.6 | 6.1 | 6.0 | 5.7 | 8.7 | 8.5 | 10.7 | ... |

**57** **Manufactured goods exports** — Unit value and volume indices: 2000 = 100; value: thousand million US dollars (*continued*)

**Exportations des produits manufacturés** — Indices de valeur unitaire et de volume : 2000 = 100; valeur : milliards de dollars E.-U. (*suite*)

| Region, country or area — Région, pays ou zone | 1997 | 1998 | 1999 | 2000 | 2001 | 2002 | 2003 | 2004 | 2005 | 2006 |
|---|---|---|---|---|---|---|---|---|---|---|
| **Iceland — Islande** | | | | | | | | | | |
| Unit value indices, US $[3] Indices de valeur unitaire, $ E.-U.[3] | 113 | 100 | ... | ... | ... | ... | ... | ... | ... | ... |
| Volume indices Indices de volume | 64 | 72 | ... | 100 | ... | ... | ... | ... | ... | ... |
| Value, thousand million US $ Valeur, millards de $ E.-U. | 0.4 | 0.4 | 0.6 | 0.6 | 0.7 | 0.7 | 0.8 | 1.0 | 1.1 | 1.3 |
| **Ireland — Irlande** | | | | | | | | | | |
| Unit value indices, US $[3] Indices de valeur unitaire, $ E.-U.[3] | 104 | 96 | ... | ... | ... | ... | ... | ... | ... | ... |
| Volume indices Indices de volume | 63 | 86 | ... | ... | ... | ... | ... | ... | ... | ... |
| Value, thousand million US $ Valeur, millards de $ E.-U. | 42.8 | 53.6 | 59.6 | 65.6 | 75.1 | 77.7 | 79.4 | 88.7 | 94.0 | 96.5 |
| **Italy — Italie** | | | | | | | | | | |
| Unit value indices, US $[3] Indices de valeur unitaire, $ E.-U.[3] | 112 | 119 | 113 | 100 | 100 | ... | 104 | ... | 118 | 125 |
| Volume indices Indices de volume | 90 | 87 | 86 | 100 | 105 | ... | 119 | ... | 128 | 135 |
| Value, thousand million US $ Valeur, millards de $ E.-U. | 215.0 | 219.7 | 206.7 | 212.6 | 223.2 | 226.1 | 262.5 | 309.7 | 320.2 | 357.9 |
| **Netherlands — Pays-Bas** | | | | | | | | | | |
| Unit value indices, US $[3] Indices de valeur unitaire, $ E.-U.[3] | 117 | 115 | 109 | 100 | 104 | 104 | 120 | 130 | 139 | ... |
| Unit value indices, national currency[3] Indices de val. unitaire, monnaie nationale[3] | 96 | 95 | 95 | 100 | 107 | 102 | 98 | 97 | 103 | ... |
| Volume indices Indices de volume | 89 | 83 | 88 | 100 | 115 | 117 | 122 | 135 | 136 | ... |
| Value, thousand million US $ Valeur, millards de $ E.-U. | 133.5 | 121.7 | 122.2 | 127.5 | 152.8 | 154.6 | 186.1 | 224.7 | 240.4 | 271.0 |
| **Norway — Norvège** | | | | | | | | | | |
| Unit value indices, US $ Indices de valeur unitaire, $ E.-U. | 116 | 112 | 106 | 100 | 97 | 100 | 110 | 126 | 131 | 145 |
| Unit value indices, national currency Indices de val. unitaire, monnaie nationale | 93 | 96 | 94 | 100 | 99 | 91 | 89 | 96 | 96 | 106 |
| Volume indices Indices de volume | 88 | 95 | 96 | 100 | 92 | 110 | 110 | 112 | 119 | 129 |
| Value, thousand million US $ Valeur, millards de $ E.-U. | 17.0 | 17.7 | 16.8 | 16.6 | 14.8 | 18.3 | 20.3 | 23.5 | 25.9 | 31.1 |
| **Portugal — Portugal** | | | | | | | | | | |
| Unit value indices, US $[3] Indices de valeur unitaire, $ E.-U.[3] | 117 | 115 | 110 | 100 | 99 | ... | ... | ... | ... | ... |
| Volume indices Indices de volume | 79 | 88 | 93 | 100 | 103 | ... | ... | ... | ... | ... |
| Value, thousand million US $ Valeur, millards de $ E.-U. | 19.5 | 21.1 | 21.3 | 21.0 | 21.4 | 22.4 | 27.5 | 30.5 | 28.8 | 32.1 |
| **Spain — Espagne** | | | | | | | | | | |
| Unit value indices, US $[3] Indices de valeur unitaire, $ E.-U.[3] | 117 | 115 | ... | ... | ... | ... | ... | ... | ... | ... |
| Volume indices Indices de volume | 79 | 84 | ... | ... | ... | ... | ... | ... | ... | ... |
| Value, thousand million US $ Valeur, millards de $ E.-U. | 82.3 | 86.3 | 88.7 | 89.4 | 91.4 | 99.0 | 124.0 | 142.8 | 150.1 | ... |
| **Sweden — Suède** | | | | | | | | | | |
| Unit value indices, US $ Indices de valeur unitaire, $ E.-U. | 117 | 112 | 106 | 100 | ... | ... | ... | ... | ... | ... |
| Unit value indices, national currency Indices de val. unitaire, monnaie nationale | 97 | 97 | 96 | 100 | ... | ... | ... | ... | ... | ... |

*57* **Manufactured goods exports**—Unit value and volume indices: 2000 = 100; value: thousand million US dollars (*continued*)

**Exportations des produits manufacturés**—Indices de valeur unitaire et de volume : 2000 = 100; valeur : milliards de dollars E.-U. (*suite*)

| Region, country or area — Région, pays ou zone | 1997 | 1998 | 1999 | 2000 | 2001 | 2002 | 2003 | 2004 | 2005 | 2006 |
|---|---|---|---|---|---|---|---|---|---|---|
| Volume indices<br>Indices de volume | 91 | 91 | 100 | 100 | ... | ... | ... | ... | ... | ... |
| Value, thousand million US $<br>Valeur, millards de $ E.-U. | 71.4 | 68.7 | 71.1 | 67.2 | 58.7 | 66.9 | 82.4 | 101.0 | 111.0 | 124.1 |
| **Switzerland — Suisse** | | | | | | | | | | |
| Unit value indices, US $<br>Indices de valeur unitaire, $ E.-U. | 112 | 111 | 109 | 100 | 104 | 109 | | ... | ... | ... |
| Volume indices<br>Indices de volume | 83 | 87 | 94 | 100 | 97 | 99 | ... | ... | ... | ... |
| Value, thousand million US $<br>Valeur, millards de $ E.-U. | 72.9 | 75.7 | 80.0 | 78.2 | 78.8 | 84.5 | 96.8 | 113.7 | ... | ... |
| **United Kingdom — Royaume-Uni** | | | | | | | | | | |
| Unit value indices, US $<br>Indices de valeur unitaire, $ E.-U. | 115 | 114 | 108 | 100 | 95 | 98 | 108 | 120 | 120 | 123 |
| Unit value indices, national currency<br>Indices de val. unitaire, monnaie nationale | 106 | 104 | 101 | 100 | 99 | 99 | 100 | 99 | 100 | 101 |
| Volume indices<br>Indices de volume | 89 | 89 | 90 | 100 | 96 | 102 | 103 | 104 | 111 | 124 |
| Value, thousand million US $<br>Valeur, millards de $ E.-U. | 237.7 | 236.4 | 225.6 | 232.5 | 210.2 | 232.6 | 258.1 | 290.2 | 310.5 | 355.4 |
| **Other developed economies — Autres économies développées** | | | | | | | | | | |
| **Unit value indices, US $<br>Indices de valeur unitaire, $ E.-U.** | **104** | **99** | **98** | **100** | **93** | **91** | **97** | **107** | **113** | **114** |
| **Volume indices<br>Indices de volume** | **85** | **82** | **90** | **100** | **91** | **96** | **103** | **112** | **112** | **120** |
| **Value, thousand million US $<br>Valeur, millards de $ E.-U.** | **461.3** | **423.7** | **461.0** | **525.6** | **447.5** | **459.8** | **523.1** | **632.1** | **663.2** | **718.6** |
| **Australia — Australie** | | | | | | | | | | |
| Unit value indices, US $<br>Indices de valeur unitaire, $ E.-U. | 112 | 98 | 97 | 100 | 93 | 92 | 101 | 133 | 151 | 203 |
| Unit value indices, national currency<br>Indices de val. unitaire, monnaie nationale | 87 | 90 | 87 | 100 | 104 | 97 | 89 | 104 | 114 | 156 |
| Volume indices<br>Indices de volume | 86 | 83 | 91 | 100 | 99 | 104 | 103 | 88 | 88 | 73 |
| Value, thousand million US $<br>Valeur, millards de $ E.-U. | 20.4 | 17.3 | 18.7 | 21.2 | 19.5 | 20.2 | 22.0 | 25.0 | 28.2 | 31.6 |
| **Israel — Israël** | | | | | | | | | | |
| Unit value indices, US $<br>Indices de valeur unitaire, $ E.-U. | 75 | 77 | 83 | 100 | 98 | 95 | 95 | 99 | 109 | 118 |
| Volume indices<br>Indices de volume | 94 | 95 | 98 | 100 | 95 | 98 | 105 | 124 | 125 | 123 |
| Value, thousand million US $<br>Valeur, millards de $ E.-U. | 20.8 | 21.7 | 24.2 | 29.7 | 27.6 | 27.5 | 29.5 | 36.5 | 40.5 | 43.3 |
| **Japan — Japon** | | | | | | | | | | |
| Unit value indices, US $<br>Indices de valeur unitaire, $ E.-U. | 104 | 100 | 98 | 100 | 94 | 92 | 97 | 107 | 112 | 112 |
| Unit value indices, national currency<br>Indices de val. unitaire, monnaie nationale | 117 | 121 | 104 | 100 | 110 | 106 | 105 | 107 | 114 | 121 |
| Volume indices<br>Indices de volume | 85 | 81 | 89 | 100 | 89 | 94 | 100 | 110 | 109 | 117 |
| Value, thousand million US $<br>Valeur, millards de $ E.-U. | 402.1 | 369.6 | 397.5 | 454.8 | 378.0 | 391.8 | 443.3 | 534.1 | 553.7 | 597.3 |
| **New Zealand — Nouvelle-Zélande** | | | | | | | | | | |
| Unit value indices, US $<br>Indices de valeur unitaire, $ E.-U. | 122 | 101 | 96 | 100 | 98 | 99 | 112 | 125 | 136 | 140 |
| Unit value indices, national currency<br>Indices de val. unitaire, monnaie nationale | 84 | 85 | 83 | 100 | 105 | 97 | 88 | 86 | 88 | 98 |
| Volume indices<br>Indices de volume | 80 | 92 | 99 | 100 | 108 | 105 | 109 | 116 | 115 | 117 |
| Value, thousand million US $<br>Valeur, millards de $ E.-U. | 4.6 | 4.3 | 4.5 | 4.7 | 5.0 | 4.9 | 5.7 | 6.8 | 7.3 | 7.7 |

**Manufactured goods exports**—Unit value and volume indices: 2000 = 100; value: thousand million US dollars (*continued*)

**Exportations des produits manufacturés**—Indices de valeur unitaire et de volume : 2000 = 100; valeur : milliards de dollars E.-U. (*suite*)

| Region, country or area — Région, pays ou zone | 1997 | 1998 | 1999 | 2000 | 2001 | 2002 | 2003 | 2004 | 2005 | 2006 |
|---|---|---|---|---|---|---|---|---|---|---|
| **South Africa — Afrique du Sud** | | | | | | | | | | |
| Value, thousand million US $<br>Valeur, millards de $ E.-U. | 13.3 | 10.8 | 16.1 | 15.2 | 17.5 | 15.3 | 22.5 | 29.7 | 33.5 | 38.7 |
| **Developing economies — Économies en développement** | | | | | | | | | | |
| Unit value indices, US $<br>Indices de valeur unitaire, $ E.-U. | 108 | 104 | 97 | 100 | 98 | 96 | 97 | 98 | 98 | ... |
| Unit value indices, SDRs<br>Indices de valeur unitaire, DTS | 103 | 101 | 93 | 100 | 102 | 98 | 92 | 87 | 88 | ... |
| Volume indices<br>Indices de volume | 73 | 76 | 86 | 100 | 96 | 107 | 124 | 118 | 142 | ... |
| Value, thousand million US $<br>Valeur, millards de $ E.-U. | 1 108.7 | 1 111.0 | 1 173.3 | 1 411.4 | 1 332.7 | 1 452.2 | 1 702.8 | 1 632.3 | 1 973.4 | ... |
| **China, Hong Kong SAR — Chine, Hong Kong RAS** | | | | | | | | | | |
| Unit value indices, US $<br>Indices de valeur unitaire, $ E.-U. | 107 | 104 | 102 | 100 | 95 | 93 | 93 | 94 | 96 | 93 |
| Unit value indices, national currency<br>Indices de val. unitaire, monnaie nationale | 106 | 103 | 101 | 100 | 96 | 93 | 93 | 94 | 96 | 93 |
| Volume indices<br>Indices de volume | 107 | 100 | 93 | 100 | 88 | 93 | 70 | 71 | 75 | 77 |
| Value, thousand million US $<br>Valeur, millards de $ E.-U. | 25.7 | 23.3 | 21.2 | 22.4 | 18.9 | 19.4 | 14.7 | 15.1 | 16.3 | 16.0 |
| **India — Inde** | | | | | | | | | | |
| Unit value indices, US $<br>Indices de valeur unitaire, $ E.-U. | 113 | 107 | 121 | 100 | 92 | 99 | ... | ... | ... | ... |
| Unit value indices, national currency<br>Indices de val. unitaire, monnaie nationale | 92 | 98 | 116 | 100 | 95 | 107 | ... | ... | ... | ... |
| Volume indices<br>Indices de volume | 65 | 67 | 69 | 100 | 105 | 115 | ... | ... | ... | ... |
| Value, thousand million US $<br>Valeur, millards de $ E.-U. | 26.0 | 25.3 | 29.3 | 35.0 | 33.6 | 39.9 | 48.8 | ... | ... | ... |
| **Korea, Republic of — Corée, République de** | | | | | | | | | | |
| Unit value indices, US $<br>Indices de valeur unitaire, $ E.-U. | 115 | 101 | 96 | 100 | 92 | 82 | 83 | 92 | 96 | 101 |
| Unit value indices, national currency<br>Indices de val. unitaire, monnaie nationale | 95 | 125 | 101 | 100 | 105 | 91 | 87 | 93 | 87 | 85 |
| Volume indices<br>Indices de volume | 66 | 73 | 87 | 100 | 95 | 97 | 118 | 145 | 175 | 188 |
| Value, thousand million US $<br>Valeur, millards de $ E.-U. | 120.0 | 116.3 | 130.6 | 156.9 | 137.3 | 125.4 | 153.0 | 207.9 | 262.8 | 297.5 |
| **Pakistan — Pakistan** | | | | | | | | | | |
| Unit value indices, US $<br>Indices de valeur unitaire, $ E.-U. | 117 | 115 | 106 | 100 | 100 | 96 | 101 | 108 | ... | ... |
| Unit value indices, national currency<br>Indices de val. unitaire, monnaie nationale | 91 | 99 | 100 | 100 | 117 | 109 | 111 | 119 | ... | ... |
| Volume indices<br>Indices de volume | 82 | 79 | 90 | 100 | 101 | 113 | 140 | 137 | ... | ... |
| Value, thousand million US $<br>Valeur, millards de $ E.-U. | 7.4 | 7.1 | 7.4 | 7.7 | 7.8 | 8.4 | 10.9 | 11.4 | ... | ... |
| **Singapore — Singapour** | | | | | | | | | | |
| Unit value indices, US $<br>Indices de valeur unitaire, $ E.-U. | 116 | 105 | 101 | 100 | 98 | 100 | 99 | 98 | 78 | ... |
| Unit value indices, national currency<br>Indices de val. unitaire, monnaie nationale | ... | ... | ... | ... | ... | ... | ... | ... | 76 | ... |
| Volume indices<br>Indices de volume | 77 | 75 | 82 | 100 | 89 | 90 | 104 | 129 | 188 | ... |
| Value, thousand million US $<br>Valeur, millards de $ E.-U. | 106.6 | 94.2 | 99.7 | 119.3 | 103.7 | 106.7 | 122.8 | 151.7 | 175.7 | 217.4 |

**Manufactured goods exports**—Unit value and volume indices: 2000 = 100; value: thousand million US dollars (*continued*)

**Exportations des produits manufacturés**—Indices de valeur unitaire et de volume : 2000 = 100; valeur : milliards de dollars E.-U. (*suite*)

| Region, country or area — Région, pays ou zone | 1997 | 1998 | 1999 | 2000 | 2001 | 2002 | 2003 | 2004 | 2005 | 2006 |
|---|---|---|---|---|---|---|---|---|---|---|
| **Turkey — Turquie** | | | | | | | | | | |
| Unit value indices, US $[4] Indices de valeur unitaire, $ E.-U.[4] | 116 | 109 | 105 | 100 | 99 | 96 | 108 | 124 | 130 | 127 |
| Volume indices Indices de volume | 75 | 83 | 88 | 100 | 114 | 138 | 162 | 189 | 204 | 240 |
| Value, thousand million US $ Valeur, millards de $ E.-U. | 20.0 | 21.0 | 21.2 | 23.1 | 26.1 | 30.8 | 40.3 | 54.2 | 61.1 | 70.9 |

Source

United Nations Statistics Division, New York, trade statistics database, last accessed March 2008.

Notes

1 Excluding trade of the countries of Eastern Europe and the former USSR.
2 Derived from price indices; national unit value index is discontinued.
3 Calculated by the United Nations Statistics Division.
4 Industrial products.

Source

Organisation des Nations Unies, Division de statistique, New York, la base de données pour les statistiques du commerce extérieur, dernier accès mars 2008.

Notes

1 Non compris le commerce des pays de l'Europe de l'Est et l'ex-URSS.
2 Calculés à partir des indices des prix; l'indice de la valeur unitaire nationale est discontinué.
3 Calculés par la Division de statistique des Nations Unies.
4 Produits industriels.

Current data (annual, monthly and/or quarterly) for most of the series are published regularly by the Statistics Division in the United Nations *Monthly Bulletin of Statistics*. More detailed descriptions of the tables and notes on methodology appear in the United Nations publications *International Trade Statistics: Concepts and Definitions* and the *International Trade Statistics Yearbook*. More detailed data including series for individual countries showing the value in national currencies for imports and exports and notes on these series can be found in the *International Trade Statistics Yearbook* and in the *Monthly Bulletin of Statistics*.

Data are obtained from national published sources, from data supplied by the governments for dissemination in United Nations publications and from publications of other United Nations agencies.

## Territory

The statistics reported by each country refer to its customs area, which in most cases coincides with its geographical area.

## Systems of trade

Two systems of recording trade are in common use, differing mainly in the way warehoused and re-exported goods are recorded:

(a) Special trade (S): special imports are the combined total of imports for direct domestic consumption (including transformation and repair) and withdrawals from bonded warehouses or free zones for domestic consumption. Special exports comprise exports of national merchandise, namely, goods wholly or partly produced or manufactured in the country, together with exports of nationalized goods. (Nationalized goods are goods which, having been included in special imports, are then exported without transformation);

(b) General trade (G): general imports are the combined total of imports for direct domestic consumption and imports into bonded warehouses or free zones. General exports are the combined total of national exports and re-exports. Re-exports, in the general trade system, consist of the outward movement of nationalized goods plus goods which, after importation, move outward from bonded warehouses or free zones without having been transformed.

## Valuation

Goods are, in general, valued according to the transaction value. In the case of imports, the transaction value is the val-

La Division de statistique des Na-tions Unies publie régulièrement dans le *Bulletin mensuel de statistique* des données courantes (annuelles, mensuelles et/ou trimestrielles) pour la plupart des séries de ces tableaux. Des descriptions plus détaillées des tableaux et des notes méthodologiques figurent dans les publications des Nations Unies *Statistiques du commerce international, Concepts et définitions* et l'*Annuaire statistique du Commerce international*. Des données plus détaillées, comprenant des séries indiquant la valeur en monnaie nationale des importations et des exportations des divers pays et les notes accompagnant ces séries figurent dans l'*Annuaire statistique du Commerce international* et dans le *Bulletin mensuel de statistique*.

Les données proviennent de publications nationales et des informations fournies par les gouvernements pour les publications des Nations Unies ainsi que de publications d'autres institutions des Nations Unies.

## Territoire

Les statistiques fournies par chaque pays se rapportent au territoire douanier de ce pays. Le plus souvent, ce territoire coïncide avec l'étendue géographique du pays.

## Systèmes de commerce

Deux systèmes d'enregistrement du commerce sont couramment utilisés, et ne diffèrent que par la façon dont sont enregistrées les marchandises entreposées et les marchandises réexportées :

(a) Commerce spécial (S) : les importations spéciales représentent le total combiné des importations destinées directement à la consommation intérieure (transformations et réparations comprises) et les marchandises retirées des entrepôts douaniers ou des zones franches pour la consommation intérieure. Les exportations spéciales comprennent les exportations de marchandises nationales, c'est-à-dire des biens produits ou fabriqués en totalité ou en partie dans le pays, ainsi que les exportations de biens nationalisés. (Les biens nationalisés sont des biens qui, ayant été inclus dans les importations spéciales, sont ensuite réexportés tels quels).

(b) Commerce général (G) : les importations générales sont le total combiné des importations destinées directement à la consommation intérieure et des importations placées en entrepôt douanier ou destinées aux zones franches. Les exportations générales sont le total combiné des exportations de biens nationaux et des réexportations. Ces dernières, dans le système du

ue at which the goods were purchased by the importer plus the cost of transportation and insurance to the frontier of the importing country (c.i.f. valuation). In the case of exports, the transaction value is the value at which the goods were sold by the exporter, including the cost of transportation and insurance to bring the goods onto the transporting vehicle at the frontier of the exporting country (f.o.b. valuation).

### Currency conversion

Conversion of values from national currencies into United States dollars is done by means of external trade conversion factors which are generally weighted averages of exchange rates, the weight being the corresponding monthly or quarterly value of imports or exports.

### Coverage

The statistics relate to merchandise trade. Merchandise trade is defined to include, as far as possible, all goods which add to or subtract from the material resources of a country as a result of their movement into or out of the country. Thus, ordinary commercial transactions, government trade (including foreign aid, war reparations and trade in military goods), postal trade and all kinds of silver (except silver coins after their issue), are included in the statistics. Since their movement affects monetary rather than material resources, monetary gold, together with currency and titles of ownership after their issue into circulation, are excluded.

### Commodity classification

The commodity classification of trade is in accordance with the United Nations *Standard International Trade Classification (SITC)*.

### World and regional totals

The regional, economic and world totals have been adjusted: (a) to include estimates for countries or areas for which full data are not available; (b) to include insurance and freight for imports valued f.o.b.; (c) to include countries or areas not listed separately; (d) to approximate special trade; (e) to approximate calendar years; and (f) where possible, to eliminate incomparabilities owing to geographical changes, by adjusting the figures for periods before the change to be comparable to those for periods after the change.

### Volume and unit value index numbers

These index numbers show the changes in the volume of imports or exports (volume index) and the average price of imports or exports (unit value index).

commerce général, comprennent les exportations de biens nationalisés et de biens qui, après avoir été importés, sortent des entrepôts de douane ou des zones franches sans avoir été transformés.

### Evaluation

En général, les marchandises sont évaluées à la valeur de la transaction. Dans le cas des importations, cette valeur est celle à laquelle les marchandises ont été achetées par l'importateur plus le coût de leur transport et de leur assurance jusqu'à la frontière du pays importateur (valeur c.a.f.). Dans le cas des exportations, la valeur de la transaction est celle à laquelle les marchandises ont été vendues par l'exportateur, y compris le coût de transport et d'assurance des marchandises jusqu'à leur chargement sur le véhicule de transport à la frontière du pays exportateur (valeur f.à.b.).

### Conversion des monnaies

La conversion en dollars des Etats-Unis de valeurs exprimées en monnaie nationale se fait par application de coefficients de conversion du commerce extérieur, qui sont généralement les moyennes pondérées des taux de change, le poids étant la valeur mensuelle ou trimestrielle correspondante des importations ou des exportations.

### Couverture

Les statistiques se rapportent au commerce des marchandises. Le commerce des marchandises se définit comme comprenant, dans toute la mesure du possible, toutes les marchandises que l'ajoute ou retranche aux ressources matérielles d'un pays suite à leur importation ou à leur exportation par ce pays. Ainsi, les transactions commerciales ordinaires, le commerce pour le compte de l'Etat (y compris l'aide extérieure, les réparations pour dommages de guerre et le commerce des fournitures militaires), le commerce par voie postale et les transactions de toutes sortes sur l'argent (à l'exception des transac-tions sur les pièces d'argent après leur émission) sont inclus dans ces statistiques. La monnaie or ainsi que la monnaie et les titres de propriété après leur mise en circulation sont exclus, car leurs mouvements influent sur les ressources monétaires plutôt que sur les ressources matérielles.

### Classification par marchandise

La classification par marchandise du commerce extérieur est celle adoptée dans la *Classification type pour le commerce international* des Nations Unies (CTCI).

## Description of tables

*Table 55*: World imports and exports are the sum of imports and exports of Developed economies, Developing economies and other. The regional totals for imports and exports and have been adjusted to exclude the re-exports of countries or areas comprising each region. Estimates for certain countries or areas not shown separately as well as for those shown separately but for which no data are yet available are included in the regional and world totals. Export and import values in terms of U.S. dollars are derived by the United Nations Statistics Division from data published in national publications, from data in the replies to the *Monthly Bulletin of Statistics* questionnaires and from data published by the International Monetary Fund (IMF) in the publication *International Financial Statistics*.

*Table 56*: These index numbers show the changes in the volume (quantum index) and the average price (unit value index) of total imports and exports. The terms of trade figures are calculated by dividing export unit value indices by the corresponding import unit value indices. The product of the net terms of trade and the volume index of exports is called the index of the purchasing power of exports. The footnotes to countries appearing in table 55 also apply to the index numbers in this table.

*Table 57*: Manufactured goods are defined here to comprise sections 5 through 8 of the *Standard International Trade Classification* (SITC). These sections are: chemicals and related products, manufactured goods classified chiefly by material, machinery and transport equipment and miscellaneous manufactured articles. The economic and geographic groupings in this table are in accordance with those of table 55, although table 55 includes more detailed geographical sub-groups which make up the groupings "other developed economies" and "developing economies" of this table.

The unit value indices are obtained from national sources, except those of a few countries which the United Nations Statistics Division compiles using their quantity and value figures. For countries that do not compile indices for manufactured goods exports conforming to the above definition, sub-indices are aggregated to approximate an index of SITC sections 5-8. Unit value indices obtained from national indices are rebased, where necessary, so that 2000=100. Indices in national currency are converted into US dollars using conversion factors obtained by dividing the weighted average exchange rate of a given currency in the current period by the weighted average exchange rate in the base period. All aggregate unit value indices are current period weighted.

## Totaux mondiaux et régionaux

Les totaux économiques, régionaux et mondiaux ont été ajustés de manière: (a) à inclure les estimations pour les pays ou régions pour lesquels on ne disposait pas de données complètes; (b) à inclure l'assurance et le fret dans la valeur f.o.b. des importations; (c) à inclure les pays ou régions non indiqués séparément; (d) à donner une approximation du commerce spécial; (e) à les ramener à des années civiles; et (f) à éliminer, dans la mesure du possible, les données non comparables par suite de changements géographiques, en ajustant les chiffres correspondant aux périodes avant le changement de manière à les rendre comparables à ceux des périodes après le changement.

## Indices de volume et de valeur unitaire

Ces indices indiquent les variations du volume des importations ou des exportations (indice de volume) et du prix moyen des importations ou des exportations (in-dice de valeur unitaire).

## Description des tableaux

*Tableau 55*: Les importations et les exportations totales pour le monde se composent des importations et exportations des Economies développées, des Economies en développement et des autres. Les totaux régionaux pour importations et exportations ont été ajustés pour exclure les re-exportations des pays ou zones que comprennent une région donnée. Les totaux régionaux et mondiaux comprennent des estimations pour certains pays ou zones ne figurant pas séparément mais pour lesquels les données ne sont pas encore disponibles. Les valeurs en dollars des E.-U. des exportations et des importations ont été obtenues par la Division de statistique des Nations Unies à partir des réponses aux questionnaires du *Bulletin Mensuel de Statistique*, des données publiées par le Fonds Monétaire International dans la publication *Statistiques financières internationales*.

*Tableau 56*: Ces indices indiquent les variations du volume (indice de quantum) et du prix moyen (indice de valeur unitaire) des importations et des exportations totales. Les chiffres relatifs aux termes de l'échange se calculent en divisant les indices de valeur unitaire des exportations par les indices correspondants de valeur unitaire des importations. Le produit de la valeur nette des termes de l'échange et de l'indice du volume des exportations est appelé indice du pouvoir d'achat des exportations. Les notes figurant au bas du tableau 55 concernant certains pays s'appliquent également aux indices du présent tableau.

The indices in Special Drawing Rights (SDRs) are calculated by multiplying the equivalent aggregate indices in United States dollars by conversion factors obtained by dividing the SDR/US$ exchange rate in the current period by the rate in the base period.

The volume indices are derived from the value data and the unit value indices. All aggregate volume indices are base period weighted.

*Tableau 57*: Les produits manufacturés se définissent comme correspondant aux sections 5 à 8 de la *Classification type pour le commerce international* (CTCI). Ces sections sont: produits chimiques et produits liés connexes, biens manufacturés classés principalement par matière première, machines et équipements de transport et articles divers manufacturés. Les groupements économiques et géographiques de ce tableau sont conformes à ceux du tableau 55; toutefois, le tableau 55 comprend des subdivisions géographiques plus détaillées qui composent les groupements "autres pays développés" et "pays en développement" du présent tableau.

Les indices de valeur unitaire sont obtenus de sources nationales, à l'exception de ceux de certains pays que la Division de statistique des Nations Unies compile en utilisant les chiffres de ces pays relatifs aux quantités et aux valeurs. Pour les pays qui n'établissent pas d'indices conformes à la définition ci-dessus pour leurs exportations de produits manufacturés, on fait la synthèse de sous-indices de manière à établir un indice proche de celui des sections 5 à 8 de la CTCI. Le cas échéant, les indices de valeur unitaire obtenus à partir des indices nationaux sont ajustés sur la base 2000=100. On convertit les indices en monnaie nationale en indices en dollars des Etats-Unis en utilisant des facteurs de conversion obtenus en divisant la moyenne pondérée des taux de change d'une monnaie donnée pendant la période courante par la moyenne pondérée des taux de change de la période de base. Tous les indices globaux de valeur unitaire sont pondérés pour la période courante.

On calcule les indices en droits de tirages spéciaux (DTS) en multipliant les indices globaux équivalents en dollars des Etats-Unis par les facteurs de conversion obtenus en divisant le taux de change DTS/dollars E.-U. de la période courante par le taux correspondant de la période de base.

On détermine les indices de volume à partir des données de valeur et des indices de valeur unitaire. Tous les indices globaux de volume sont pondérés par rapport à la période de base.

| Country or area of destination and region of origin& | Series Série | 2002 | 2003 | 2004 | 2005 | 2006 | Pays ou zone de destination et région de provenance& |
|---|---|---|---|---|---|---|---|
| Albania | VFN | | | | | | Albanie |
| Total | | 469 691 | 557 210 | 645 409 | 747 837 | 937 038 | Total |
| Africa | | 75 | 233 | 174 | 174 | 220 | Afrique |
| Americas | | 15 790 | 18 895 | 25 519 | 34 816 | 42 241 | Amériques |
| Europe | | 439 151 | 531 927 | 609 821 | 703 205 | 857 358 | Europe |
| Asia, East/S.East/Oceania | | 2 901 | 3 805 | 4 288 | 5 444 | 7 592 | Asie, Est/S.-Est/Océanie |
| Southern Asia | | 351 | 424 | 410 | 354 | 376 | Asie du Sud |
| Western Asia | | 752 | 896 | 775 | 837 | 1 068 | Asie occidentale |
| Region not specified | | 10 671 | 1 030 | 4 422 | 3 007 | 28 183 | Région non spécifiée |
| Algeria | VFN | | | | | | Algérie |
| Total[1] | | 988 060 | 1 166 287 | 1 233 719 | 1 443 090 | 1 637 582 | Total[1] |
| Africa | | 72 041 | 111 941 | 131 066 | 161 182 | 159 869 | Afrique |
| Americas | | 4 626 | 4 949 | 6 830 | 8 117 | 9 724 | Amériques |
| Europe | | 140 844 | 157 093 | 198 230 | 227 618 | 252 553 | Europe |
| Asia, East/S.East/Oceania | | 9 491 | 8 260 | 9 401 | 15 157 | 19 207 | Asie, Est/S.-Est/Océanie |
| Western Asia | | 24 143 | 22 671 | 23 035 | 29 132 | 37 005 | Asie occidentale |
| Region not specified | | 736 915 | 861 373 | 865 157 | 1 001 884 | 1 159 224 | Région non spécifiée |
| American Samoa | TFN | | | | | | Samoa américaines |
| Total | | ... | ... | ... | 24 496 | 25 347 | Total |
| Africa | | ... | ... | ... | 11 | 7 | Afrique |
| Americas | | ... | ... | ... | 6 899 | 7 205 | Amériques |
| Europe | | ... | ... | ... | 382 | 358 | Europe |
| Asia, East/S.East/Oceania | | ... | ... | ... | 16 933 | 17 640 | Asie, Est/S.-Est/Océanie |
| Southern Asia | | ... | ... | ... | 37 | 49 | Asie du Sud |
| Western Asia | | ... | ... | ... | 8 | 5 | Asie occidentale |
| Region not specified | | ... | ... | ... | 226 | 83 | Région non spécifiée |
| Andorra | TFR | | | | | | Andorre |
| Total | | 3 387 586 | 3 137 738 | 2 791 116 | 2 418 409 | 2 226 922 | Total |
| Europe | | 3 387 586 | 3 137 738 | 2 791 116 | 2 418 409 | 2 226 922 | Europe |
| Angola | TFR | | | | | | Angola |
| Total | | 90 532 | 106 625 | 194 329 | 209 956 | 121 426 | Total |
| Africa | | 16 618 | 30 915 | 41 873 | 43 138 | 18 921 | Afrique |
| Americas | | 15 044 | 14 770 | 34 045 | 36 140 | 20 847 | Amériques |
| Europe | | 52 169 | 55 190 | 101 180 | 110 025 | 63 459 | Europe |
| Asia, East/S.East/Oceania | | 4 746 | 5 396 | 16 061 | 15 358 | 15 248 | Asie, Est/S.-Est/Océanie |
| Southern Asia | | 828 | ... | ... | 2 144 | 2 055 | Asie du Sud |
| Western Asia | | 1 127 | 354 | 1 170 | 3 151 | 896 | Asie occidentale |
| Anguilla | TFR | | | | | | Anguilla |
| Total[2] | | 43 969 | 46 915 | 53 987 | 62 084 | 72 962 | Total[2] |
| Americas | | 37 479 | 39 295 | 44 799 | 52 054 | 61 746 | Amériques |
| Europe | | 5 415 | 6 308 | 7 667 | 8 113 | 9 218 | Europe |
| Region not specified | | 1 075 | 1 312 | 1 521 | 1 917 | 1 998 | Région non spécifiée |
| Antigua and Barbuda | TFR | | | | | | Antigua-et-Barbuda |
| Total[2,3] | | 198 085 | 224 032 | 245 797 | 238 804 | 253 669 | Total[2,3] |
| Americas | | 108 235 | 121 563 | 129 316 | 126 096 | 138 547 | Amériques |
| Western Asia | | 81 907 | 98 665 | 113 033 | 105 735 | 106 538 | Asie occidentale |
| Region not specified | | 7 943 | 3 804 | 3 448 | 6 973 | 8 584 | Région non spécifiée |
| Argentina | TFN | | | | | | Argentine |
| Total[2] | | 2 820 039 | 2 995 271 | 3 456 526 | *3 822 666 | *4 155 921 | Total[2] |
| Americas | | 2 419 591 | 2 424 735 | 2 721 888 | 2 983 895 | 3 271 292 | Amériques |
| Europe | | 323 729 | 455 998 | 546 184 | 630 888 | 658 160 | Europe |
| Region not specified | | 76 719 | 114 538 | 188 454 | 207 883 | 226 469 | Région non spécifiée |

| Country or area of destination and region of origin& | Series Série | 2002 | 2003 | 2004 | 2005 | 2006 | Pays ou zone de destination et région de provenance& |
|---|---|---|---|---|---|---|---|
| Armenia | TFR | | | | | | Arménie |
| Total | | 162 089 | 206 094 | 262 959 | 318 563 | 381 136 | Total |
| Africa | | 89 | 133 | 184 | 335 | 396 | Afrique |
| Americas | | 46 088 | 58 258 | 75 496 | 85 994 | 96 525 | Amériques |
| Europe | | 79 761 | 98 884 | 127 242 | 160 479 | 203 539 | Europe |
| Asia, East/S.East/Oceania | | 3 369 | 5 669 | 9 355 | 13 592 | 15 557 | Asie, Est/S.-Est/Océanie |
| Southern Asia | | 19 090 | 23 995 | 27 551 | 29 981 | 32 498 | Asie du Sud |
| Western Asia | | 13 692 | 19 155 | 23 131 | 28 182 | 32 621 | Asie occidentale |
| Aruba | TFR | | | | | | Aruba |
| Total | | 642 627 | 641 906 | 728 157 | 732 514 | 694 372 | Total |
| Americas | | 595 350 | 584 651 | 665 489 | 666 454 | 629 925 | Amériques |
| Europe | | 43 970 | 54 711 | 60 428 | 63 181 | 61 993 | Europe |
| Asia, East/S.East/Oceania | | 209 | 162 | 211 | 191 | 199 | Asie, Est/S.-Est/Océanie |
| Region not specified | | 3 098 | 2 382 | 2 029 | 2 688 | 2 255 | Région non spécifiée |
| Australia | VFR | | | | | | Australie |
| Total[4] | | 4 841 152 | 4 745 855 | 5 214 981 | 5 499 050 | 5 532 435 | Total[4] |
| Africa | | 68 244 | 69 535 | 67 711 | 70 877 | 77 615 | Afrique |
| Americas | | 556 186 | 537 494 | 561 454 | 584 395 | 611 140 | Amériques |
| Europe | | 1 198 361 | 1 228 033 | 1 261 477 | 1 330 233 | 1 367 738 | Europe |
| Asia, East/S.East/Oceania | | 2 924 158 | 2 811 834 | 3 205 477 | 3 374 765 | 3 314 747 | Asie, Est/S.-Est/Océanie |
| Southern Asia | | 60 687 | 63 264 | 75 233 | 89 356 | 108 324 | Asie du Sud |
| Western Asia | | 30 962 | 34 432 | 43 484 | 49 195 | 52 401 | Asie occidentale |
| Region not specified | | 2 554 | 1 263 | 145 | 229 | 470 | Région non spécifiée |
| Austria | TCER | | | | | | Autriche |
| Total[5] | | 18 610 925 | 19 077 630 | 19 372 816 | 19 952 350 | 20 261 292 | Total[5] |
| Africa | | 25 779 | 27 206 | 32 114 | 42 259 | 42 501 | Afrique |
| Americas | | 646 863 | 599 474 | 673 695 | 691 644 | 780 218 | Amériques |
| Europe | | 16 983 956 | 17 386 722 | 17 445 939 | 18 030 663 | 18 257 289 | Europe |
| Asia, East/S.East/Oceania | | 593 583 | 618 852 | 755 406 | 792 197 | 797 479 | Asie, Est/S.-Est/Océanie |
| Southern Asia | | 39 011 | 29 619 | 39 882 | 39 204 | 49 684 | Asie du Sud |
| Western Asia | | 28 524 | 37 667 | 43 202 | 67 833 | 75 217 | Asie occidentale |
| Region not specified | | 293 209 | 378 090 | 382 578 | 288 550 | 258 904 | Région non spécifiée |
| Azerbaijan | TFR | | | | | | Azerbaïdjan |
| Total | | 834 351 | 1 013 811 | 1 348 655 | 1 177 277 | 1 193 742 | Total |
| Africa | | 108 | 320 | 661 | 544 | 807 | Afrique |
| Americas | | 6 532 | 7 951 | 12 358 | 11 272 | 10 133 | Amériques |
| Europe | | 581 633 | 746 916 | 1 050 943 | 945 662 | 1 007 670 | Europe |
| Asia, East/S.East/Oceania | | 2 748 | 4 271 | 6 051 | 6 825 | 7 205 | Asie, Est/S.-Est/Océanie |
| Southern Asia | | 241 352 | 252 669 | 275 147 | 211 032 | 165 144 | Asie du Sud |
| Western Asia | | 1 978 | 1 684 | 2 143 | 1 942 | 1 888 | Asie occidentale |
| Region not specified | | ... | ... | 1 352 | ... | 895 | Région non spécifiée |
| Bahamas | TFR | | | | | | Bahamas |
| Total | | 1 513 151 | 1 510 169 | 1 561 312 | 1 608 153 | 1 600 112 | Total |
| Africa | | 1 166 | 1 409 | 1 427 | 1 302 | 1 397 | Afrique |
| Americas | | 1 406 458 | 1 392 578 | 1 455 375 | 1 484 921 | 1 484 485 | Amériques |
| Europe | | 80 140 | 93 714 | 84 121 | 85 857 | 82 740 | Europe |
| Asia, East/S.East/Oceania | | 8 080 | 6 285 | 6 890 | 7 145 | 6 907 | Asie, Est/S.-Est/Océanie |
| Southern Asia | | 377 | 381 | 347 | 285 | 438 | Asie du Sud |
| Western Asia | | 347 | 346 | 616 | 361 | 452 | Asie occidentale |
| Region not specified | | 16 583 | 15 456 | 12 536 | 28 282 | 23 693 | Région non spécifiée |
| Bahrain | VFN | | | | | | Bahreïn |
| Total[2] | | 4 830 943 | 4 844 497 | 5 667 331 | 6 313 232 | 7 288 716 | Total[2] |
| Africa | | 46 663 | 59 989 | 76 325 | 82 121 | 98 749 | Afrique |
| Americas | | 177 089 | 192 206 | 200 481 | 189 778 | 234 467 | Amériques |
| Europe | | 256 437 | 260 698 | 333 920 | 357 623 | 429 750 | Europe |
| Asia, East/S.East/Oceania | | 187 058 | 211 749 | 267 978 | 287 257 | 374 335 | Asie, Est/S.-Est/Océanie |
| Southern Asia | | 521 796 | 561 050 | 648 003 | 720 007 | 941 590 | Asie du Sud |
| Western Asia | | 3 641 900 | 3 558 805 | 4 140 624 | 4 676 446 | 5 209 825 | Asie occidentale |

| Country or area of destination and region of origin& | Series Série | 2002 | 2003 | 2004 | 2005 | 2006 | Pays ou zone de destination et région de provenance& |
|---|---|---|---|---|---|---|---|
| Bangladesh | TFN | | | | | | Bangladesh |
| Total | | 207 246 | 244 509 | 271 270 | 207 662 | 200 311 | Total |
| Africa | | 1 297 | 2 012 | 2 147 | 1 730 | 1 953 | Afrique |
| Americas | | 17 538 | 30 795 | 37 404 | 18 673 | 25 129 | Amériques |
| Europe | | 46 641 | 63 749 | 77 307 | 48 961 | 56 709 | Europe |
| Asia, East/S.East/Oceania | | 41 019 | 42 824 | 51 230 | 35 887 | 37 032 | Asie, Est/S.-Est/Océanie |
| Southern Asia | | 97 623 | 102 503 | 99 939 | 99 458 | 75 467 | Asie du Sud |
| Western Asia | | 3 128 | 2 626 | 3 243 | 2 861 | 4 021 | Asie occidentale |
| Region not specified | | ... | ... | ... | 92 | ... | Région non spécifiée |
| Barbados | TFR | | | | | | Barbade |
| Total | | 497 899 | 531 211 | 551 502 | 547 534 | *562 558 | Total |
| Africa | | 626 | 668 | 753 | 1 117 | 988 | Afrique |
| Americas | | 275 144 | 291 623 | 301 268 | 311 222 | 312 317 | Amériques |
| Europe | | 219 006 | 233 791 | 245 919 | 230 167 | 241 141 | Europe |
| Asia, East/S.East/Oceania | | 2 103 | 4 027 | 2 679 | 2 710 | 2 758 | Asie, Est/S.-Est/Océanie |
| Southern Asia | | 503 | 466 | 627 | 756 | 784 | Asie du Sud |
| Western Asia | | 101 | 160 | 145 | 154 | 230 | Asie occidentale |
| Region not specified | | 416 | 476 | 111 | 1 408 | 4 340 | Région non spécifiée |
| Belarus | TFN | | | | | | Bélarus |
| Total[6] | | 63 336 | 64 190 | 67 297 | 90 588 | 89 101 | Total[6] |
| Africa | | 58 | 65 | 47 | 399 | 148 | Afrique |
| Americas | | 2 999 | 3 522 | 5 892 | 4 663 | 4 292 | Amériques |
| Europe | | 56 833 | 57 916 | 58 524 | 82 247 | 80 956 | Europe |
| Asia, East/S.East/Oceania | | 2 766 | 1 833 | 2 150 | 1 860 | 1 815 | Asie, Est/S.-Est/Océanie |
| Southern Asia | | 279 | 472 | 269 | 594 | 572 | Asie du Sud |
| Western Asia | | 401 | 382 | 415 | 825 | 1 318 | Asie occidentale |
| Belgium | TCER | | | | | | Belgique |
| Total[7] | | 6 719 653 | 6 689 998 | 6 709 740 | 6 747 123 | 6 994 819 | Total[7] |
| Africa | | 60 026 | 62 755 | 60 872 | 62 455 | 65 438 | Afrique |
| Americas | | 399 576 | 368 814 | 382 249 | 390 160 | 407 403 | Amériques |
| Europe | | 5 798 298 | 5 846 966 | 5 800 440 | 5 835 628 | 6 035 866 | Europe |
| Asia, East/S.East/Oceania | | 347 725 | 294 364 | 318 231 | 298 360 | 304 773 | Asie, Est/S.-Est/Océanie |
| Southern Asia | | 38 542 | 32 362 | 33 152 | 34 844 | 32 673 | Asie du Sud |
| Western Asia | | 17 724 | 17 502 | 17 664 | 19 793 | 20 978 | Asie occidentale |
| Region not specified | | 57 762 | 67 235 | 97 132 | 105 883 | 127 688 | Région non spécifiée |
| Belize | TFN | | | | | | Belize |
| Total[1] | | 199 521 | 220 574 | 230 835 | 236 573 | 247 309 | Total[1] |
| Africa | | 374 | 337 | 349 | 348 | 359 | Afrique |
| Americas | | 154 321 | 174 784 | 185 254 | 190 301 | 199 315 | Amériques |
| Europe | | 29 115 | 33 530 | 32 768 | 33 466 | 34 373 | Europe |
| Asia, East/S.East/Oceania | | 3 411 | 3 754 | 4 285 | 4 384 | 4 516 | Asie, Est/S.-Est/Océanie |
| Western Asia | | 405 | 370 | 481 | 369 | 381 | Asie occidentale |
| Region not specified | | 11 895 | 7 799 | 7 698 | 7 705 | 8 365 | Région non spécifiée |
| Benin | TFR | | | | | | Bénin |
| Total | | 72 288 | *175 000 | *173 500 | *176 000 | *180 006 | Total |
| Africa | | 49 387 | 148 646 | 147 536 | 140 185 | 152 000 | Afrique |
| Americas | | 1 281 | 471 | 360 | 500 | 972 | Amériques |
| Europe | | 21 090 | 25 403 | 25 157 | 31 500 | 22 257 | Europe |
| Asia, East/S.East/Oceania | | 220 | 225 | 261 | 321 | 633 | Asie, Est/S.-Est/Océanie |
| Southern Asia | | 115 | 137 | 125 | 2 956 | 3 500 | Asie du Sud |
| Western Asia | | 185 | 112 | 61 | 518 | 644 | Asie occidentale |
| Region not specified | | 10 | 6 | ... | 20 | ... | Région non spécifiée |
| Bermuda | TFR | | | | | | Bermudes |
| Total[3] | | 284 024 | 256 579 | 271 620 | 269 591 | 298 973 | Total[3] |
| Americas | | 243 793 | 222 396 | 235 546 | 232 661 | 255 400 | Amériques |
| Europe | | 30 669 | 25 938 | 25 873 | 26 678 | 32 347 | Europe |
| Asia, East/S.East/Oceania | | 861 | 503 | 834 | 639 | 647 | Asie, Est/S.-Est/Océanie |
| Region not specified | | 8 701 | 7 742 | 9 367 | 9 613 | 10 579 | Région non spécifiée |

| Country or area of destination and region of origin& | Series Série | 2002 | 2003 | 2004 | 2005 | 2006 | Pays ou zone de destination et région de provenance& |
|---|---|---|---|---|---|---|---|
| Bhutan | TFN | | | | | | Bhoutan |
| Total | | 5 599 | 6 261 | 9 249 | 13 626 | 17 348 | Total |
| Africa | | 17 | 14 | 14 | 45 | 88 | Afrique |
| Americas | | 2 154 | 2 034 | 3 607 | 5 168 | 5 627 | Amériques |
| Europe | | 2 094 | 2 774 | 3 905 | 5 619 | 7 267 | Europe |
| Asia, East/S.East/Oceania | | 1 310 | 1 415 | 1 680 | 2 759 | 4 317 | Asie, Est/S.-Est/Océanie |
| Southern Asia | | 18 | 12 | 19 | 17 | 30 | Asie du Sud |
| Western Asia | | 3 | ... | ... | 7 | 12 | Asie occidentale |
| Region not specified | | 3 | 12 | 24 | 11 | 7 | Région non spécifiée |
| Bolivia | THSN | | | | | | Bolivie |
| Total[8] | | 380 202 | 367 036 | 390 888 | 413 267 | ... | Total[8] |
| Africa | | 977 | 1 117 | 1 278 | 1 661 | ... | Afrique |
| Americas | | 216 960 | 209 715 | 227 280 | 250 107 | ... | Amériques |
| Europe | | 145 972 | 140 913 | 143 413 | 141 621 | ... | Europe |
| Asia, East/S.East/Oceania | | 16 293 | 15 291 | 18 917 | 19 878 | ... | Asie, Est/S.-Est/Océanie |
| Bonaire | TFR | | | | | | Bonaire |
| Total | | 52 085 | 62 179 | 63 156 | 62 550 | 63 552 | Total |
| Americas | | 33 548 | 32 771 | 34 576 | 32 244 | 35 093 | Amériques |
| Europe | | 18 152 | 29 079 | 27 973 | 30 066 | 28 202 | Europe |
| Region not specified | | 385 | 329 | 607 | 240 | 257 | Région non spécifiée |
| Bosnia and Herzegovina | TCER | | | | | | Bosnie-Herzégovine |
| Total | | 159 763 | 165 465 | 190 300 | 217 273 | 255 764 | Total |
| Americas | | 8 286 | 7 339 | 8 442 | 8 030 | 10 195 | Amériques |
| Europe | | 145 883 | 152 246 | 176 588 | 203 564 | 238 976 | Europe |
| Asia, East/S.East/Oceania | | 1 496 | 1 870 | 2 177 | 2 355 | 2 869 | Asie, Est/S.-Est/Océanie |
| Southern Asia | | 122 | 189 | 116 | 265 | 51 | Asie du Sud |
| Western Asia | | 93 | 94 | 132 | 46 | 175 | Asie occidentale |
| Region not specified | | 3 883 | 3 727 | 2 845 | 3 013 | 3 498 | Région non spécifiée |
| Botswana | TFR | | | | | | Botswana |
| Total | | 1 273 784 | 1 405 535 | 1 522 807 | ... | ... | Total |
| Africa | | 1 095 572 | 1 235 404 | 1 353 125 | ... | ... | Afrique |
| Americas | | 19 014 | 18 025 | 21 023 | ... | ... | Amériques |
| Europe | | 56 917 | 55 054 | 58 432 | ... | ... | Europe |
| Asia, East/S.East/Oceania | | 11 972 | 12 442 | 11 848 | ... | ... | Asie, Est/S.-Est/Océanie |
| Southern Asia | | 4 542 | 1 889 | 2 223 | ... | ... | Asie du Sud |
| Western Asia | | 20 | ... | ... | ... | ... | Asie occidentale |
| Region not specified | | 85 747 | 82 721 | 76 156 | ... | ... | Région non spécifiée |
| Brazil | TFR | | | | | | Brésil |
| Total | | 3 784 898 | 4 132 847 | 4 793 703 | 5 358 170 | 5 018 991 | Total |
| Africa | | 40 259 | 52 489 | 64 678 | 75 676 | 83 721 | Afrique |
| Americas | | 2 205 618 | 2 396 832 | 2 703 442 | 2 998 060 | 2 703 123 | Amériques |
| Europe | | 1 414 962 | 1 543 559 | 1 860 259 | 2 097 357 | 1 997 127 | Europe |
| Asia, East/S.East/Oceania | | 108 201 | 128 640 | 155 605 | 177 381 | 219 936 | Asie, Est/S.-Est/Océanie |
| Western Asia | | 7 118 | 5 595 | 6 064 | 7 002 | 13 172 | Asie occidentale |
| Region not specified | | 8 740 | 5 732 | 3 655 | 2 694 | 1 912 | Région non spécifiée |
| British Virgin Islands | TFR | | | | | | Iles Vierges britanniques |
| Total | | 281 696 | 317 758 | ... | ... | ... | Total |
| Americas | | 250 013 | 261 201 | ... | ... | ... | Amériques |
| Europe | | 28 511 | 49 952 | ... | ... | ... | Europe |
| Region not specified | | 3 172 | 6 605 | ... | ... | ... | Région non spécifiée |
| Brunei Darussalam | TFN | | | | | | Brunéi Darussalam |
| Total | | ... | ... | ... | 126 217 | 158 095 | Total |
| Americas | | ... | ... | ... | 3 313 | 3 943 | Amériques |
| Europe | | ... | ... | ... | 14 428 | 20 847 | Europe |
| Asia, East/S.East/Oceania | | ... | ... | ... | 75 781 | 100 160 | Asie, Est/S.-Est/Océanie |
| Southern Asia | | ... | ... | ... | 210 | 654 | Asie du Sud |
| Western Asia | | ... | ... | ... | 32 485 | 32 491 | Asie occidentale |

| Country or area of destination and region of origin& | Series Série | 2002 | 2003 | 2004 | 2005 | 2006 | Pays ou zone de destination et région de provenance& |
|---|---|---|---|---|---|---|---|
| **Bulgaria** | VFR | | | | | | **Bulgarie** |
| Total | | 5 562 917 | 6 240 932 | 6 981 597 | 7 282 455 | 7 499 117 | Total |
| Africa | | 3 778 | 3 848 | 2 937 | 2 774 | 2 668 | Afrique |
| Americas | | 46 934 | 54 701 | 67 605 | 76 514 | 85 158 | Amériques |
| Europe | | 5 426 164 | 6 088 039 | 6 806 650 | 7 087 954 | 7 286 509 | Europe |
| Asia, East/S.East/Oceania | | 21 957 | 26 521 | 32 067 | 35 127 | 38 186 | Asie, Est/S.-Est/Océanie |
| Southern Asia | | 9 498 | 11 613 | 12 199 | 11 396 | 13 267 | Asie du Sud |
| Western Asia | | 14 144 | 15 132 | 16 124 | 17 569 | 14 284 | Asie occidentale |
| Region not specified | | 40 442 | 41 078 | 44 015 | 51 121 | 59 045 | Région non spécifiée |
| **Burkina Faso** | THSN | | | | | | **Burkina Faso** |
| Total[1] | | 150 204 | 163 123 | 222 201 | 244 728 | 263 978 | Total[1] |
| Africa | | 55 144 | 65 459 | 96 385 | 100 674 | 108 019 | Afrique |
| Americas | | 9 840 | 10 025 | 12 991 | 14 724 | 15 814 | Amériques |
| Europe | | 73 076 | 76 743 | 99 742 | 113 496 | 123 426 | Europe |
| Asia, East/S.East/Oceania | | 3 760 | 3 271 | 4 550 | 6 582 | 6 387 | Asie, Est/S.-Est/Océanie |
| Western Asia | | 876 | 1 447 | 1 982 | 2 220 | 2 022 | Asie occidentale |
| Region not specified | | 7 508 | 6 178 | 6 551 | 7 032 | 8 310 | Région non spécifiée |
| **Burundi** | TFN | | | | | | **Burundi** |
| Total[9] | | 74 406 | 74 116 | 133 228 | 148 418 | 201 241 | Total[9] |
| Africa | | 24 802 | 24 706 | 1 333 | 49 473 | 140 868 | Afrique |
| Americas | | 2 090 | 2 308 | 5 908 | 9 956 | 4 025 | Amériques |
| Europe | | 6 156 | 7 620 | 29 409 | 29 486 | 32 199 | Europe |
| Asia, East/S.East/Oceania | | 1 054 | 1 162 | 4 528 | 4 023 | 10 062 | Asie, Est/S.-Est/Océanie |
| Region not specified | | 40 304 | 38 320 | 92 050 | 55 480 | 14 087 | Région non spécifiée |
| **Cambodia** | TFR | | | | | | **Cambodge** |
| Total | | 786 526 | 701 014 | 1 055 202[10] | 1 421 615[11] | 1 700 041[12] | Total |
| Americas | | 113 144 | 88 662 | 122 169 | 152 328 | 159 429 | Amériques |
| Europe | | 218 950 | 183 353 | 242 811 | 310 006 | 314 194 | Europe |
| Asia, East/S.East/Oceania | | 409 489 | 412 245 | 589 230 | 786 506 | 1 022 181 | Asie, Est/S.-Est/Océanie |
| Southern Asia | | 4 459 | 5 286 | 7 132 | 7 516 | 9 245 | Asie du Sud |
| Region not specified | | 40 484 | 11 468 | 93 860 | 165 259 | 194 992 | Région non spécifiée |
| **Cameroon** | THSN | | | | | | **Cameroun** |
| Total | | 226 019 | ... | 189 856 | 176 372 | ... | Total |
| Africa | | 104 695 | ... | 80 013 | 88 739 | ... | Afrique |
| Americas | | 13 506 | ... | 11 593 | 10 002 | ... | Amériques |
| Europe | | 98 570 | ... | 83 272 | 68 058 | ... | Europe |
| Asia, East/S.East/Oceania | | 4 882 | ... | 4 248 | 4 580 | ... | Asie, Est/S.-Est/Océanie |
| Western Asia | | 1 153 | ... | 4 583 | 2 007 | ... | Asie occidentale |
| Region not specified | | 3 213 | ... | 6 147 | 2 986 | ... | Région non spécifiée |
| **Canada** | TFR | | | | | | **Canada** |
| Total | | 20 057 024 | 17 534 329 | 19 144 810 | 18 770 444 | 18 265 071 | Total |
| Africa | | 54 111 | 52 437 | 58 210 | 61 842 | 72 388 | Afrique |
| Americas | | 16 576 480 | 14 588 822 | 15 518 243 | 14 867 460 | 14 372 244 | Amériques |
| Europe | | 2 095 148 | 1 872 693 | 2 202 397 | 2 397 323 | 2 359 997 | Europe |
| Asia, East/S.East/Oceania | | 1 209 706 | 900 328 | 1 221 981 | 1 282 007 | 1 282 444 | Asie, Est/S.-Est/Océanie |
| Southern Asia | | 79 073 | 79 792 | 96 342 | 109 681 | 118 728 | Asie du Sud |
| Western Asia | | 42 506 | 40 257 | 47 637 | 52 131 | 59 270 | Asie occidentale |
| **Cape verde** | THSR | | | | | | **Cap-Vert** |
| Total | | 125 852 | 150 048 | 157 052 | 197 844 | 241 742 | Total |
| Africa | | 10 003 | 5 225 | 10 034 | 9 432 | 4 659 | Afrique |
| Americas | | 1 665 | 1 740 | 1 472 | 2 102 | 5 949 | Amériques |
| Europe | | 105 790 | 134 749 | 136 304 | 173 318 | 207 964 | Europe |
| Region not specified | | 8 394 | 8 334 | 9 242 | 12 992 | 23 170 | Région non spécifiée |
| **Cayman Islands** | TFR | | | | | | **Iles Caïmanes** |
| Total[3] | | 302 797 | 293 513 | 259 929 | 167 802 | 267 257 | Total[3] |
| Africa | | 353 | 373 | 321 | 325 | 435 | Afrique |

| Country or area of destination and region of origin& | Series Série | 2002 | 2003 | 2004 | 2005 | 2006 | Pays ou zone de destination et région de provenance& |
|---|---|---|---|---|---|---|---|
| Americas | | 281 796 | 272 381 | 242 012 | 152 735 | 247 420 | Amériques |
| Europe | | 18 705 | 19 001 | 15 938 | 13 221 | 17 516 | Europe |
| Asia, East/S.East/Oceania | | 1 382 | 1 201 | 1 216 | 1 129 | 1 370 | Asie, Est/S.-Est/Océanie |
| Southern Asia | | 238 | 274 | 176 | 97 | 158 | Asie du Sud |
| Western Asia | | 100 | 65 | 72 | 24 | 53 | Asie occidentale |
| Region not specified | | 223 | 218 | 194 | 271 | 305 | Région non spécifiée |
| Central African Rep. | TFN | | | | | | Rép. centrafricaine |
| Total[3] | | 2 910 | 5 687 | 8 156 | 11 969 | *13 764 | Total[3] |
| Africa | | 1 455 | 3 111 | 3 501 | 6 156 | 7 079 | Afrique |
| Americas | | 176 | 374 | 449 | 639 | 735 | Amériques |
| Europe | | 1 025 | 1 881 | 3 674 | 4 349 | 5 001 | Europe |
| Asia, East/S.East/Oceania | | 170 | 288 | 317 | 373 | 429 | Asie, Est/S.-Est/Océanie |
| Western Asia | | 15 | 18 | 192 | 397 | 457 | Asie occidentale |
| Region not specified | | 69 | 15 | 23 | 55 | 63 | Région non spécifiée |
| Chad | THSN | | | | | | Tchad |
| Total | | 32 334 | 20 974 | 25 899 | 29 356 | ... | Total |
| Africa | | 7 514 | 5 141 | 5 855 | 6 695 | ... | Afrique |
| Americas | | 6 485 | 4 368 | 5 609 | 5 976 | ... | Amériques |
| Europe | | 15 225 | 10 029 | 12 690 | 14 805 | ... | Europe |
| Asia, East/S.East/Oceania | | 1 000 | 297 | 398 | 550 | ... | Asie, Est/S.-Est/Océanie |
| Western Asia | | 2 110 | 1 139 | 1 347 | 1 330 | ... | Asie occidentale |
| Chile | TFN | | | | | | Chili |
| Total | | 1 412 315 | 1 613 523 | 1 785 024 | 2 027 082 | 2 252 952 | Total |
| Africa | | 2 476 | 2 872 | 3 653 | 3 544 | 4 150 | Afrique |
| Americas | | 1 119 232 | 1 242 956 | 1 360 342 | 1 553 381 | 1 754 599 | Amériques |
| Europe | | 245 494 | 309 008 | 344 774 | 384 886 | 401 775 | Europe |
| Asia, East/S.East/Oceania | | 40 786 | 54 476 | 69 883 | 74 927 | 83 683 | Asie, Est/S.-Est/Océanie |
| Southern Asia | | 1 697 | 2 039 | 3 605 | 4 257 | 4 100 | Asie du Sud |
| Western Asia | | 728 | 637 | 812 | 682 | 2 015 | Asie occidentale |
| Region not specified | | 1 902 | 1 535 | 1 955 | 5 405 | 2 630 | Région non spécifiée |
| China[13] | VFN | | | | | | Chine[13] |
| Total | | 97 908 252 | 91 662 082 | 109 038 218 | 120 292 255 | 124 942 096 | Total |
| Africa | | 84 541 | 91 949 | 154 223 | 210 533 | 255 288 | Afrique |
| Americas | | 1 509 574 | 1 132 937 | 1 789 500 | 2 145 758 | 2 405 829 | Amériques |
| Europe | | 3 007 483 | 2 789 888 | 4 096 999 | 5 165 588 | 5 769 346 | Europe |
| Asia, East/S.East/Oceania | | 92 865 905 | 87 214 341 | 102 393 763 | 112 053 459 | 115 700 406 | Asie, Est/S.-Est/Océanie |
| Southern Asia | | 380 512 | 383 121 | 514 163 | 599 435 | 670 505 | Asie du Sud |
| Western Asia | | 52 122 | 46 856 | 84 376 | 110 966 | 136 429 | Asie occidentale |
| Region not specified | | 8 115 | 2 990 | 5 194 | 6 516 | 4 293 | Région non spécifiée |
| China, Hong Kong SAR | TFR | | | | | | Chine, Hong Kong RAS |
| Total | | 10 688 700 | 9 676 300 | 13 655 100 | 14 773 200 | 15 821 400 | Total |
| Africa | | 63 600 | 68 100 | 91 100 | 116 600 | 123 400 | Afrique |
| Americas | | 1 094 900 | 713 400 | 1 091 600 | 1 196 700 | 1 229 500 | Amériques |
| Europe | | 855 000 | 588 000 | 888 700 | 1 083 900 | 1 198 700 | Europe |
| Asia, East/S.East/Oceania | | 8 486 600 | 8 154 000 | 11 368 600 | 12 124 500 | 12 989 900 | Asie, Est/S.-Est/Océanie |
| Southern Asia | | 131 400 | 113 700 | 159 500 | 180 500 | 191 800 | Asie du Sud |
| Western Asia | | 57 200 | 39 100 | 55 600 | 71 000 | 88 100 | Asie occidentale |
| China, Hong Kong SAR | VFR | | | | | | Chine, Hong Kong RAS |
| Total | | 16 566 382 | 15 536 839 | 21 810 630 | 23 359 417 | 25 251 124 | Total |
| Africa | | 91 670 | 98 862 | 146 130 | 206 487 | 218 315 | Afrique |
| Americas | | 1 346 840 | 925 907 | 1 399 572 | 1 565 350 | 1 630 637 | Amériques |
| Europe | | 1 135 044 | 822 146 | 1 201 751 | 1 471 602 | 1 634 925 | Europe |
| Asia, East/S.East/Oceania | | 13 654 656 | 13 410 004 | 18 705 602 | 19 706 889 | 21 330 293 | Asie, Est/S.-Est/Océanie |
| Southern Asia | | 302 794 | 255 104 | 326 183 | 363 080 | 375 205 | Asie du Sud |
| Western Asia | | 35 378 | 24 816 | 31 392 | 45 951 | 61 659 | Asie occidentale |
| Region not specified | | ... | ... | ... | 58 | 90 | Région non spécifiée |

| Country or area of destination and region of origin& | Series Série | 2002 | 2003 | 2004 | 2005 | 2006 | Pays ou zone de destination et région de provenance& |
|---|---|---|---|---|---|---|---|
| China, Macao SAR | VFN | | | | | | Chine, Macao RAS |
| Total[14,15] | | 11 530 841 | 11 887 876 | 16 672 556 | 18 711 187 | 21 998 122 | Total[14,15] |
| Africa | | 4 439 | 4 668 | 6 042 | 8 082 | 13 693 | Afrique |
| Americas | | 128 219 | 95 502 | 147 953 | 182 830 | 218 277 | Amériques |
| Europe | | 127 614 | 94 078 | 128 887 | 161 204 | 188 189 | Europe |
| Asia, East/S.East/Oceania | | 11 249 556 | 11 673 256 | 16 361 807 | 18 321 056 | 21 525 911 | Asie, Est/S.-Est/Océanie |
| Southern Asia | | 17 719 | 17 324 | 23 771 | 32 335 | 42 604 | Asie du Sud |
| Western Asia | | 943 | 1 171 | 1 905 | 2 679 | 3 747 | Asie occidentale |
| Region not specified | | 2 351 | 1 877 | 2 191 | 3 001 | 5 701 | Région non spécifiée |
| Colombia | VFN | | | | | | Colombie |
| Total[16] | | 563 761 | 624 909 | 790 940 | 933 243 | *1 053 348 | Total[16] |
| Africa | | 976 | 897 | 935 | 1 380 | 1 695 | Afrique |
| Americas | | 428 403 | 484 379 | 617 896 | 730 495 | 825 335 | Amériques |
| Europe | | 117 500 | 125 073 | 155 657 | 182 822 | 204 298 | Europe |
| Asia, East/S.East/Oceania | | 11 854 | 11 271 | 13 294 | 15 395 | 17 141 | Asie, Est/S.-Est/Océanie |
| Southern Asia | | 1 226 | 1 119 | 1 404 | 1 618 | 1 841 | Asie du Sud |
| Western Asia | | 1 062 | 1 004 | 1 399 | 1 167 | 1 348 | Asie occidentale |
| Region not specified | | 2 740 | 1 166 | 355 | 366 | 1 690 | Région non spécifiée |
| Comoros | TFN | | | | | | Comores |
| Total[3] | | 18 936 | 14 229 | 17 603 | 19 551 | 17 060 | Total[3] |
| Africa | | 8 715 | 5 590 | 6 344 | 8 793 | 6 123 | Afrique |
| Americas | | 60 | 26 | 162 | 83 | 358 | Amériques |
| Europe | | 9 490 | 8 003 | 10 562 | 9 625 | 9 470 | Europe |
| Asia, East/S.East/Oceania | | 64 | 610 | 165 | 543 | 582 | Asie, Est/S.-Est/Océanie |
| Region not specified | | 607 | ... | 370 | 507 | 527 | Région non spécifiée |
| Congo | THSR | | | | | | Congo |
| Total | | 21 611 | ... | ... | ... | ... | Total |
| Africa | | 11 006 | ... | ... | ... | ... | Afrique |
| Americas | | 694 | ... | ... | ... | ... | Amériques |
| Europe | | 8 752 | ... | ... | ... | ... | Europe |
| Region not specified | | 1 159 | ... | ... | ... | ... | Région non spécifiée |
| Cook Islands | TFR | | | | | | Iles Cook |
| Total[17] | | 72 781 | 78 328 | 83 333 | 88 405 | 92 251 | Total[17] |
| Americas | | 11 505 | 11 390 | 8 445 | 6 463 | 7 677 | Amériques |
| Europe | | 19 630 | 21 559 | 20 410 | 18 162 | 18 112 | Europe |
| Asia, East/S.East/Oceania | | 41 277 | 45 008 | 53 962 | 63 319 | 65 972 | Asie, Est/S.-Est/Océanie |
| Region not specified | | 369 | 371 | 516 | 461 | 490 | Région non spécifiée |
| Costa Rica | TFN | | | | | | Costa Rica |
| Total | | 1 113 359 | 1 238 692 | 1 452 926 | 1 679 051 | 1 725 261 | Total |
| Africa | | 900 | 1 048 | 1 194 | 1 164 | 1 204 | Afrique |
| Americas | | 927 509 | 1 017 831 | 1 213 784 | 1 411 640 | 1 456 947 | Amériques |
| Europe | | 164 263 | 198 242 | 215 072 | 241 751 | 243 100 | Europe |
| Asia, East/S.East/Oceania | | 16 140 | 16 403 | 16 043 | 23 687 | 23 425 | Asie, Est/S.-Est/Océanie |
| Region not specified | | 4 547 | 5 168 | 6 833 | 809 | 585 | Région non spécifiée |
| Croatia | TCER | | | | | | Croatie |
| Total[18] | | 6 944 345 | 7 408 590 | 7 911 874 | 8 466 886 | 8 658 876 | Total[18] |
| Americas | | 74 938 | 84 470 | 119 485 | 140 031 | 182 916 | Amériques |
| Europe | | 6 806 518 | 7 244 346 | 7 692 506 | 8 192 055 | 8 281 634 | Europe |
| Asia, East/S.East/Oceania | | 36 068 | 43 173 | 58 370 | 83 273 | 132 824 | Asie, Est/S.-Est/Océanie |
| Region not specified | | 26 821 | 36 601 | 41 513 | 51 527 | 61 502 | Région non spécifiée |
| Cuba | VFR | | | | | | Cuba |
| Total | | 1 686 162 | 1 905 682 | 2 048 572 | 2 319 334 | 2 220 567 | Total |
| Africa | | 5 641 | 6 679 | 5 868 | 6 619 | 6 636 | Afrique |
| Americas | | 787 729 | 916 818 | 1 025 756 | 1 215 857 | 1 149 135 | Amériques |
| Europe | | 859 129 | 942 052 | 976 727 | 1 047 669 | 1 013 273 | Europe |
| Asia, East/S.East/Oceania | | 27 354 | 32 463 | 33 861 | 41 858 | 43 819 | Asie, Est/S.-Est/Océanie |
| Southern Asia | | 4 096 | 5 559 | 4 176 | 5 149 | 5 248 | Asie du Sud |

| Country or area of destination and region of origin[&] | Series Série | 2002 | 2003 | 2004 | 2005 | 2006 | Pays ou zone de destination et région de provenance[&] |
|---|---|---|---|---|---|---|---|
| Western Asia | | 1 737 | 1 514 | 1 517 | 1 622 | 1 643 | Asie occidentale |
| Region not specified | | 476 | 597 | 667 | 560 | 813 | Région non spécifiée |
| **Curaçao** | TFR | | | | | | **Curaçao** |
| Total[3] | | 217 963 | 221 395 | 223 439 | 222 061 | 234 383 | Total[3] |
| Americas | | 141 006 | 125 794 | 128 873 | 123 353 | 126 521 | Amériques |
| Europe | | 70 390 | 91 384 | 89 752 | 94 957 | 104 232 | Europe |
| Region not specified | | 6 567 | 4 217 | 4 814 | 3 751 | 3 630 | Région non spécifiée |
| **Cyprus** | TFR | | | | | | **Chypre** |
| Total | | 2 418 238 | 2 303 246 | 2 349 012 | 2 470 063 | 2 400 924 | Total |
| Africa | | 6 890 | 6 752 | 4 936 | 7 097 | 6 641 | Afrique |
| Americas | | 26 734 | 23 246 | 22 924 | 28 984 | 26 353 | Amériques |
| Europe | | 2 323 568 | 2 207 434 | 2 263 145 | 2 375 402 | 2 307 885 | Europe |
| Asia, East/S.East/Oceania | | 11 697 | 12 266 | 13 042 | 15 043 | 16 262 | Asie, Est/S.-Est/Océanie |
| Southern Asia | | 3 383 | 3 130 | 1 992 | 2 777 | 3 808 | Asie du Sud |
| Western Asia | | 45 170 | 49 413 | 41 379 | 40 233 | 39 291 | Asie occidentale |
| Region not specified | | 796 | 1 005 | 1 594 | 527 | 684 | Région non spécifiée |
| **Czech Republic** | TCEN | | | | | | **République tchèque** |
| Total | | 4 742 773 | 5 075 756 | 6 061 225 | 6 336 128 | 6 435 474 | Total |
| Africa | | 12 842 | 14 097 | 15 394 | 18 539 | 19 411 | Afrique |
| Americas | | 238 767 | 282 239 | 380 056 | 400 840 | 435 280 | Amériques |
| Europe | | 4 248 907 | 4 528 009 | 5 314 123 | 5 495 760 | 5 487 941 | Europe |
| Asia, East/S.East/Oceania | | 242 257 | 251 411 | 351 652 | 420 989 | 492 842 | Asie, Est/S.-Est/Océanie |
| **Dem. Rep. of the Congo** | TFN | | | | | | **Rép. dém. du Congo** |
| Total | | 28 179[3] | 35 141[3] | 36 238[3] | *61 007 | *55 148 | Total |
| Africa | | 9 088 | 20 380 | 14 531 | 36 489 | 33 089 | Afrique |
| Americas | | 3 678 | 2 568 | 4 592 | 3 824 | 3 309 | Amériques |
| Europe | | 11 273 | 9 037 | 13 117 | 14 751 | 13 235 | Europe |
| Asia, East/S.East/Oceania | | 4 140 | 3 156 | 3 998 | 5 943 | 5 515 | Asie, Est/S.-Est/Océanie |
| **Denmark** | TCER | | | | | | **Danemark** |
| Total | | 3 435 563 | 3 473 808 | 4 421 442[19] | 4 698 668 | 4 716 257 | Total |
| Americas | | 79 513 | 78 382 | 126 276 | 147 289 | 185 668 | Amériques |
| Europe | | 3 220 983 | 3 253 489 | 4 065 043 | 4 357 752 | 4 364 147 | Europe |
| Asia, East/S.East/Oceania | | 49 299 | 46 850 | 82 957 | 110 098 | 90 776 | Asie, Est/S.-Est/Océanie |
| Region not specified | | 85 768 | 95 087 | 147 166 | 83 529 | 75 666 | Région non spécifiée |
| **Dominica** | TFR | | | | | | **Dominique** |
| Total | | 69 193 | 73 190 | 80 087 | 79 257 | 84 041 | Total |
| Americas | | 58 153 | 61 536 | 69 115 | 68 164 | 71 832 | Amériques |
| Europe | | 10 131 | 10 772 | 10 208 | 10 258 | 11 303 | Europe |
| Asia, East/S.East/Oceania | | 455 | 486 | 387 | 529 | 495 | Asie, Est/S.-Est/Océanie |
| Region not specified | | 454 | 396 | 377 | 306 | 411 | Région non spécifiée |
| **Dominican Republic** | TFR | | | | | | **Rép. dominicaine** |
| Total[1,3] | | 2 793 209[20] | 3 282 138 | 3 450 180 | 3 690 692 | *3 965 055 | Total[1,3] |
| Americas | | 1 260 558 | 1 503 896 | 1 597 342 | 1 711 341 | 1 947 796 | Amériques |
| Europe | | 1 031 456 | 1 250 608 | 1 271 299 | 1 371 663 | 1 388 757 | Europe |
| Asia, East/S.East/Oceania | | 3 106 | 3 417 | 3 511 | 4 280 | 4 631 | Asie, Est/S.-Est/Océanie |
| Southern Asia | | 75 | 236 | 249 | 337 | 279 | Asie du Sud |
| Region not specified | | 498 014 | 523 981 | 577 779 | 603 071 | 623 592 | Région non spécifiée |
| **Ecuador** | VFN | | | | | | **Equateur** |
| Total[2] | | 682 962 | 760 776 | 818 927 | 859 888 | 840 555 | Total[2] |
| Africa | | 2 107 | 1 720 | 2 191 | 1 919 | 1 240 | Afrique |
| Americas | | 549 927 | 617 088 | 662 019 | 690 743 | 642 075 | Amériques |
| Europe | | 113 435 | 124 137 | 133 495 | 146 537 | 144 682 | Europe |
| Asia, East/S.East/Oceania | | 17 493 | 17 831 | 21 195 | 20 222 | 19 488 | Asie, Est/S.-Est/Océanie |
| Region not specified | | ... | ... | 27 | 467 | 33 070 | Région non spécifiée |
| **Egypt** | VFN | | | | | | **Egypte** |
| Total[2] | | 5 191 678 | 6 044 160 | 8 020 327 | 8 607 807 | 9 082 777 | Total[2] |

| Country or area of destination and region of origin& | Series Série | 2002 | 2003 | 2004 | 2005 | 2006 | Pays ou zone de destination et région de provenance& |
|---|---|---|---|---|---|---|---|
| Africa | | 161 497 | 183 035 | 244 662 | 263 847 | 301 866 | Afrique |
| Americas | | 171 458 | 187 828 | 257 418 | 297 675 | 340 530 | Amériques |
| Europe | | 3 583 791 | 4 203 687 | 5 836 293 | 6 047 194 | 6 259 732 | Europe |
| Asia, East/S.East/Oceania | | 213 771 | 226 756 | 296 189 | 411 048 | 389 304 | Asie, Est/S.-Est/Océanie |
| Southern Asia | | 46 110 | 51 042 | 63 310 | 73 000 | 80 501 | Asie du Sud |
| Western Asia | | 1 012 613 | 1 188 994 | 1 317 883 | 1 511 285 | 1 706 423 | Asie occidentale |
| Region not specified | | 2 438 | 2 818 | 4 572 | 3 758 | 4 421 | Région non spécifiée |
| El Salvador | TFN | | | | | | El Salvador |
| Total | | 798 243 | 719 963 | 811 527 | 969 372 | 1 138 378 | Total |
| Africa | | ... | 368 | 499 | 537 | 674 | Afrique |
| Americas | | 732 738 | 681 953 | 775 117 | 934 002 | 1 103 716 | Amériques |
| Europe | | 22 272 | 30 144 | 27 785 | 26 451 | 25 357 | Europe |
| Asia, East/S.East/Oceania | | 3 127 | 7 474 | 8 115 | 8 360 | 8 616 | Asie, Est/S.-Est/Océanie |
| Western Asia | | ... | 24 | 11 | 22 | 15 | Asie occidentale |
| Region not specified | | 40 106 | ... | ... | ... | ... | Région non spécifiée |
| Eritrea | VFN | | | | | | Erythrée |
| Total[1] | | 100 828 | 80 029 | 87 298 | 83 307 | 78 451 | Total[1] |
| Africa | | 8 185 | 3 147 | 4 503 | 3 182 | 3 645 | Afrique |
| Americas | | 2 094 | 2 321 | 2 559 | 2 263 | 1 474 | Amériques |
| Europe | | 8 378 | 8 367 | 10 142 | 8 364 | 5 983 | Europe |
| Asia, East/S.East/Oceania | | 1 700 | 1 953 | 2 484 | 2 267 | 2 275 | Asie, Est/S.-Est/Océanie |
| Southern Asia | | 2 549 | 2 580 | 2 420 | 2 985 | 2 895 | Asie du Sud |
| Western Asia | | 3 565 | 2 857 | 4 196 | 3 862 | 3 241 | Asie occidentale |
| Region not specified | | 74 357 | 58 804 | 60 994 | 60 384 | 58 938 | Région non spécifiée |
| Estonia | TCER | | | | | | Estonie |
| Total | | 1 003 383 | 1 112 746 | 1 374 414 | 1 453 418 | 1 427 583 | Total |
| Africa | | ... | 542 | 641 | 1 033 | 723 | Afrique |
| Americas | | 15 601 | 14 823 | 23 448 | 24 037 | 24 359 | Amériques |
| Europe | | 967 167 | 1 080 977 | 1 333 979 | 1 411 062 | 1 382 143 | Europe |
| Asia, East/S.East/Oceania | | 6 587 | 10 663 | 13 456 | 15 130 | 17 663 | Asie, Est/S.-Est/Océanie |
| Region not specified | | 14 028 | 5 741 | 2 890 | 2 156 | 2 695 | Région non spécifiée |
| Ethiopia | TFN | | | | | | Ethiopie |
| Total[9,21] | | 156 327 | 179 910 | 184 079 | 227 398 | 290 458 | Total[9,21] |
| Africa | | 59 640 | 82 152 | 65 744 | 85 501 | 89 923 | Afrique |
| Americas | | 19 433 | 27 456 | 33 895 | 41 380 | 61 353 | Amériques |
| Europe | | 34 280 | 43 647 | 47 955 | 57 103 | 76 466 | Europe |
| Asia, East/S.East/Oceania | | 7 916 | 7 645 | 9 825 | 12 188 | 20 058 | Asie, Est/S.-Est/Océanie |
| Southern Asia | | 3 778 | 3 602 | 4 641 | 7 125 | 7 975 | Asie du Sud |
| Western Asia | | 9 189 | 14 366 | 20 618 | 22 162 | 30 556 | Asie occidentale |
| Region not specified | | 22 091 | 1 042 | 1 401 | 1 939 | 4 127 | Région non spécifiée |
| Fiji | TFR | | | | | | Fidji |
| Total[2] | | 397 859 | 430 800 | 502 765 | 549 911 | ... | Total[2] |
| Americas | | 68 617 | 69 313 | 77 605 | 85 536 | ... | Amériques |
| Europe | | 65 047 | 71 641 | 71 372 | 78 507 | ... | Europe |
| Asia, East/S.East/Oceania | | 261 690 | 288 321 | 351 819 | 383 691 | ... | Asie, Est/S.-Est/Océanie |
| Region not specified | | 2 505 | 1 525 | 1 969 | 2 177 | ... | Région non spécifiée |
| Finland | TCER | | | | | | Finlande |
| Total | | 2 042 540 | 2 047 444 | 2 083 487[22] | 2 080 194 | 2 325 330 | Total |
| Africa | | 3 646 | 3 370 | 3 185 | 4 123 | 5 147 | Afrique |
| Americas | | 108 446 | 102 034 | 111 245 | 105 992 | 110 530 | Amériques |
| Europe | | 1 659 534 | 1 683 624 | 1 698 936 | 1 712 228 | 1 884 448 | Europe |
| Asia, East/S.East/Oceania | | 157 635 | 146 652 | 167 808 | 158 128 | 188 447 | Asie, Est/S.-Est/Océanie |
| Southern Asia | | 5 285 | 5 361 | 5 965 | 7 445 | 10 707 | Asie du Sud |
| Western Asia | | 3 857 | 3 463 | 3 168 | 3 613 | 3 824 | Asie occidentale |
| Region not specified | | 104 137 | 102 940 | 93 180 | 88 665 | 122 227 | Région non spécifiée |

| Country or area of destination and region of origin[&] | Series Série | 2002 | 2003 | 2004 | 2005 | 2006 | Pays ou zone de destination et région de provenance[&] |
|---|---|---|---|---|---|---|---|
| France | TFR | | | | | | France |
| Total | | 77 012 000 | 75 048 000 | 75 121 000 | #75 908 000 | *79 083 000 | Total |
| Africa | | 924 000 | 889 000 | 895 000 | 1 252 000 | 1 213 000 | Afrique |
| Americas | | 4 639 000 | 3 954 000 | 4 206 000 | 5 086 000 | 5 562 000 | Amériques |
| Europe | | 69 078 000 | 68 072 000 | 67 711 000 | 66 029 000 | 68 590 000 | Europe |
| Asia, East/S.East/Oceania | | 2 080 000 | 1 890 000 | 2 058 000 | 3 192 000 | 3 338 000 | Asie, Est/S.-Est/Océanie |
| Western Asia | | 249 000 | 210 000 | 237 000 | 349 000 | 380 000 | Asie occidentale |
| Region not specified | | 42 000 | 33 000 | 14 000 | ... | ... | Région non spécifiée |
| French Guiana | TFR | | | | | | Guyane française |
| Total | | 65 000 | ... | ... | ... | ... | Total |
| Americas | | 17 550 | ... | ... | ... | ... | Amériques |
| Europe | | 44 850 | ... | ... | ... | ... | Europe |
| Region not specified | | 2 600 | ... | ... | ... | ... | Région non spécifiée |
| French Polynesia | TFR | | | | | | Polynésie française |
| Total[2,3] | | 188 998 | 212 692 | 211 828 | 208 045 | 221 549 | Total[2,3] |
| Africa | | 253 | 294 | 257 | 235 | 255 | Afrique |
| Americas | | 72 468 | 89 454 | 86 032 | 80 067 | 88 991 | Amériques |
| Europe | | 76 100 | 80 182 | 79 944 | 81 643 | 82 580 | Europe |
| Asia, East/S.East/Oceania | | 39 697 | 42 235 | 45 083 | 45 655 | 48 344 | Asie, Est/S.-Est/Océanie |
| Southern Asia | | 46 | 62 | 75 | 69 | 116 | Asie du Sud |
| Western Asia | | 182 | 163 | 172 | 165 | 226 | Asie occidentale |
| Region not specified | | 252 | 302 | 265 | 211 | 1 037 | Région non spécifiée |
| Gabon | TFN | | | | | | Gabon |
| Total[23] | | 208 348 | 222 257 | ... | ... | ... | Total[23] |
| Africa | | 52 408 | 55 487 | ... | ... | ... | Afrique |
| Region not specified | | 155 940 | 166 770 | ... | ... | ... | Région non spécifiée |
| Gambia | TFN | | | | | | Gambie |
| Total[24] | | 81 005 | 73 485 | 90 095 | 107 904 | 124 800 | Total[24] |
| Africa | | 726 | 4 542 | 1 330 | 11 497 | 18 135 | Afrique |
| Americas | | 1 075 | 643 | 3 248 | 1 387 | 2 189 | Amériques |
| Europe | | 77 155 | 63 625 | 81 955 | 86 181 | 91 194 | Europe |
| Region not specified | | 2 049 | 4 675 | 3 562 | 8 839 | 13 282 | Région non spécifiée |
| Georgia | VFR | | | | | | Géorgie |
| Total | | 298 469 | 313 442 | 368 312 | 560 021 | 983 114 | Total |
| Africa | | 586 | 306 | 788 | 431 | 777 | Afrique |
| Americas | | 8 156 | 8 731 | 11 209 | 14 842 | 19 417 | Amériques |
| Europe | | 275 332 | 288 648 | 342 596 | 533 129 | 935 747 | Europe |
| Asia, East/S.East/Oceania | | 6 865 | 6 756 | 4 952 | 3 244 | 13 732 | Asie, Est/S.-Est/Océanie |
| Southern Asia | | 5 822 | 6 683 | 6 635 | 6 641 | 9 977 | Asie du Sud |
| Western Asia | | 1 250 | 1 835 | 1 563 | 973 | 2 105 | Asie occidentale |
| Region not specified | | 458 | 483 | 569 | 761 | 1 359 | Région non spécifiée |
| Germany | TCER | | | | | | Allemagne |
| Total | | 17 969 396 | 18 399 093 | 20 136 979 | 21 500 067 | 23 569 145 | Total |
| Africa | | 143 714 | 143 156 | 146 454 | 144 391 | 167 005 | Afrique |
| Americas | | 2 150 961 | 2 048 770 | 2 337 209 | 2 397 527 | 2 782 911 | Amériques |
| Europe | | 13 288 813 | 13 877 895 | 14 918 028 | 16 099 891 | 17 504 005 | Europe |
| Asia, East/S.East/Oceania | | 1 715 992 | 1 605 064 | 1 931 265 | 2 000 752 | 2 176 143 | Asie, Est/S.-Est/Océanie |
| Southern Asia | | ... | ... | ... | ... | 736 712 | Southern Asia |
| Western Asia | | 128 054 | 142 732 | 160 110 | 185 497 | 202 369 | Asie occidentale |
| Region not specified | | 541 862 | 581 476 | 643 913 | 672 009 | ... | Région non spécifiée |
| Ghana | TFN | | | | | | Ghana |
| Total[1] | | 482 637 | 530 827 | 583 819 | 428 533 | ... | Total[1] |
| Africa | | 164 210 | 180 609 | 198 638 | 172 913 | ... | Afrique |
| Americas | | 40 534 | 44 581 | 49 031 | 62 572 | ... | Amériques |
| Europe | | 119 642 | 131 587 | 144 724 | 100 509 | ... | Europe |

| Country or area of destination and region of origin& | Series Série | 2002 | 2003 | 2004 | 2005 | 2006 | Pays ou zone de destination et région de provenance& |
|---|---|---|---|---|---|---|---|
| Asia, East/S.East/Oceania | | 23 214 | 25 532 | 28 081 | 16 812 | ... | Asie, Est/S.-Est/Océanie |
| Western Asia | | 3 661 | 4 026 | 4 428 | 10 632 | ... | Asie occidentale |
| Region not specified | | 131 376 | 144 492 | 158 917 | 65 095 | ... | Région non spécifiée |
| Greece | TFN | | | | | | Grèce |
| Total[25] | | 14 179 999 | 13 969 393 | 13 312 629 | 14 765 463 | 16 039 216 | Total[25] |
| Africa | | 22 265 | 19 184 | 23 073 | 22 961 | 30 296 | Afrique |
| Americas | | 217 369 | 219 391 | 236 274 | 416 746 | 513 402 | Amériques |
| Europe | | 13 630 328 | 13 459 272 | 12 766 224 | 13 996 356 | 15 104 338 | Europe |
| Asia, East/S.East/Oceania | | 242 040 | 212 791 | 226 973 | 253 686 | 315 691 | Asie, Est/S.-Est/Océanie |
| Southern Asia | | 4 252 | 3 919 | 4 828 | 3 657 | 174 | Asie du Sud |
| Western Asia | | 63 745 | 54 836 | 55 257 | 72 057 | 75 315 | Asie occidentale |
| Grenada | TFN | | | | | | Grenade |
| Total[1] | | 132 416 | 142 355 | 133 865 | 98 548 | 118 654 | Total[1] |
| Africa | | 494 | 522 | 562 | 325 | 461 | Afrique |
| Americas | | 76 572 | 80 126 | 77 126 | 58 629 | 65 292 | Amériques |
| Europe | | 38 976 | 43 167 | 36 222 | 22 423 | 32 556 | Europe |
| Asia, East/S.East/Oceania | | 980 | 1 062 | 722 | 1 054 | 1 515 | Asie, Est/S.-Est/Océanie |
| Western Asia | | 115 | 109 | 132 | 121 | 110 | Asie occidentale |
| Region not specified | | 15 279 | 17 369 | 19 101 | 15 996 | 18 720 | Région non spécifiée |
| Guadeloupe | THSR | | | | | | Guadeloupe |
| Total | | ... | 438 819[26] | 455 981[26] | 371 985[27] | ... | Total |
| Europe | | ... | 386 737 | 406 204 | 369 800 | ... | Europe |
| Region not specified | | ... | 52 082 | 49 777 | 2 185 | ... | Région non spécifiée |
| Guam | TFR | | | | | | Guam |
| Total[17] | | 1 058 704 | 909 506 | 1 159 881 | 1 227 587 | 1 211 674 | Total[17] |
| Americas | | 42 975 | 41 160 | 46 754 | 46 362 | 44 811 | Amériques |
| Europe | | 1 436 | ... | 1 511 | 1 750 | 1 382 | Europe |
| Asia, East/S.East/Oceania | | 984 373 | 808 623 | 1 068 997 | 1 133 807 | 1 134 264 | Asie, Est/S.-Est/Océanie |
| Region not specified | | 29 920 | 59 723 | 42 619 | 45 668 | 31 217 | Région non spécifiée |
| Guatemala | TFN | | | | | | Guatemala |
| Total | | 884 190 | 880 223 | 1 181 526 | 1 315 646 | 1 502 069 | Total |
| Americas | | 712 261 | 703 841 | 1 006 614 | 1 148 318 | 1 325 209 | Amériques |
| Europe | | 144 846 | 150 920 | 149 871 | 139 996 | 147 227 | Europe |
| Asia, East/S.East/Oceania | | 24 370 | 21 999 | 23 167 | 24 921 | 26 802 | Asie, Est/S.-Est/Océanie |
| Western Asia | | 590 | 603 | 365 | 1 182 | 446 | Asie occidentale |
| Region not specified | | 2 123 | 2 860 | 1 509 | 1 229 | 2 385 | Région non spécifiée |
| Guinea | TFR | | | | | | Guinée |
| Total[28] | | ... | 43 966 | 42 041 | 45 334 | 46 096 | Total[28] |
| Africa | | ... | 19 227 | 17 915 | 17 008 | 6 562 | Afrique |
| Americas | | ... | 4 064 | 4 377 | 5 336 | 2 260 | Amériques |
| Europe | | ... | 17 114 | 15 564 | 18 007 | 13 717 | Europe |
| Asia, East/S.East/Oceania | | ... | 1 833 | 2 160 | 2 545 | 2 002 | Asie, Est/S.-Est/Océanie |
| Southern Asia | | ... | 641 | 985 | 1 251 | 20 800 | Asie du Sud |
| Western Asia | | ... | 938 | 1 040 | 628 | 755 | Asie occidentale |
| Region not specified | | ... | 149 | ... | 559 | ... | Région non spécifiée |
| Guinea-Bissau | TFN | | | | | | Guinée-Bissau |
| Total[29] | | ... | ... | ... | 4 978 | 11 617 | Total[29] |
| Africa | | ... | ... | ... | 1 224 | 2 705 | Afrique |
| Americas | | ... | ... | ... | 451 | 1 992 | Amériques |
| Europe | | ... | ... | ... | 3 123 | 5 063 | Europe |
| Asia, East/S.East/Oceania | | ... | ... | ... | 102 | 1 601 | Asie, Est/S.-Est/Océanie |
| Southern Asia | | ... | ... | ... | 66 | 162 | Asie du Sud |
| Western Asia | | ... | ... | ... | 12 | 94 | Asie occidentale |
| Guyana | TFR | | | | | | Guyana |
| Total[30] | | 104 341 | 100 911 | 121 989 | 116 596 | 113 474 | Total[30] |
| Americas | | 94 620 | 91 022 | 111 078 | 105 468 | 102 627 | Amériques |

| Country or area of destination and region of origin[&] | Series Série | 2002 | 2003 | 2004 | 2005 | 2006 | Pays ou zone de destination et région de provenance[&] |
|---|---|---|---|---|---|---|---|
| Europe | | 8 190 | 8 136 | 9 056 | 8 704 | 8 390 | Europe |
| Region not specified | | 1 531 | 1 753 | 1 855 | 2 424 | 2 457 | Région non spécifiée |
| **Haiti** | TFR | | | | | | **Haïti** |
| Total | | 140 112 | 136 031 | 96 439 | 112 267 | ... | Total |
| Americas | | 126 683 | 125 214 | 90 615 | 103 595 | ... | Amériques |
| Europe | | 11 312 | 7 659 | 4 246 | 6 720 | ... | Europe |
| Region not specified | | 2 117 | 3 158 | 1 578 | 1 952 | ... | Région non spécifiée |
| **Honduras** | TFN | | | | | | **Honduras** |
| Total | | 549 500 | 610 535 | 640 981 | 673 035 | 738 667 | Total |
| Africa | | 297 | 206 | 251 | 231 | 330 | Afrique |
| Americas | | 493 330 | 557 262 | 584 831 | 610 179 | 666 017 | Amériques |
| Europe | | 48 681 | 45 152 | 47 504 | 53 482 | 60 324 | Europe |
| Asia, East/S.East/Oceania | | 6 727 | 7 115 | 7 542 | 8 437 | 11 069 | Asie, Est/S.-Est/Océanie |
| Southern Asia | | 209 | 260 | 278 | 321 | 396 | Asie du Sud |
| Western Asia | | 96 | 102 | 109 | 90 | 135 | Asie occidentale |
| Region not specified | | 160 | 438 | 466 | 295 | 396 | Région non spécifiée |
| **Hungary** | TCEN | | | | | | **Hongrie** |
| Total[31] | | 3 013 116 | 2 948 224 | 3 269 868 | 3 446 362 | 3 309 753 | Total[31] |
| Africa | | 5 739 | 5 756 | 12 379 | 10 310 | 7 557 | Afrique |
| Americas | | 169 967 | 173 862 | 202 180 | 218 304 | 244 890 | Amériques |
| Europe | | 2 688 940 | 2 626 677 | 2 860 588 | 2 985 842 | 2 827 586 | Europe |
| Asia, East/S.East/Oceania | | 82 781 | 77 189 | 104 805 | 132 564 | 122 687 | Asie, Est/S.-Est/Océanie |
| Region not specified | | 65 689 | 64 740 | 89 916 | 99 342 | 107 033 | Région non spécifiée |
| **Hungary** | VFN | | | | | | **Hongrie** |
| Total[32] | | 31 739 243 | 31 412 483 | 36 635 132 | 38 554 561 | 40 962 830 | Total[32] |
| Africa | | 11 026 | 14 300 | 15 833 | 13 502 | 16 675 | Afrique |
| Americas | | 427 547 | 385 191 | 515 112 | 490 440 | 521 151 | Amériques |
| Europe | | 31 081 931 | 30 817 730 | 35 781 644 | 37 744 758 | 40 100 380 | Europe |
| Asia, East/S.East/Oceania | | 183 789 | 167 361 | 247 520 | 272 207 | 290 992 | Asie, Est/S.-Est/Océanie |
| Southern Asia | | 9 899 | 10 858 | 15 641 | 15 179 | 15 500 | Asie du Sud |
| Western Asia | | 8 775 | 8 478 | 26 037 | 9 538 | 9 477 | Asie occidentale |
| Region not specified | | 16 276 | 8 565 | 33 345 | 8 937 | 8 655 | Région non spécifiée |
| **Iceland** | TCEN | | | | | | **Islande** |
| Total | | 704 633 | 771 323 | 836 230 | 871 401 | 970 821 | Total |
| Africa | | ... | ... | ... | 1 104 | 1 508 | Afrique |
| Americas | | 69 342 | 72 174 | 74 857 | 84 839 | 86 650 | Amériques |
| Europe | | 593 315 | 642 762 | 706 580 | 714 982 | 785 148 | Europe |
| Asia, East/S.East/Oceania | | 7 048 | 9 013 | 10 520 | 29 723 | 32 943 | Asie, Est/S.-Est/Océanie |
| Region not specified | | 34 928 | 47 374 | 44 273 | 40 753 | 64 572 | Région non spécifiée |
| **India** | TFN | | | | | | **Inde** |
| Total[2] | | 2 384 364 | 2 726 214 | 3 457 477 | 3 918 610 | 4 447 167 | Total[2] |
| Africa | | 80 317 | 89 201 | 111 711 | 130 753 | 137 285 | Afrique |
| Americas | | 459 462 | 540 128 | 690 169 | 804 394 | 912 051 | Amériques |
| Europe | | 796 613 | 942 061 | 1 257 239 | 1 434 983 | 1 662 362 | Europe |
| Asia, East/S.East/Oceania | | 327 976 | 393 281 | 511 681 | 584 753 | 702 147 | Asie, Est/S.-Est/Océanie |
| Southern Asia | | 630 653 | 666 889 | 790 698 | 841 969 | 908 916 | Asie du Sud |
| Western Asia | | 66 051 | 68 917 | 80 073 | 86 450 | 98 439 | Asie occidentale |
| Region not specified | | 23 292 | 25 737 | 15 906 | 35 308 | 25 967 | Région non spécifiée |
| **Indonesia** | TFR | | | | | | **Indonésie** |
| Total | | 5 033 400 | 4 467 021 | 5 321 165 | 5 002 101 | 4 871 351 | Total |
| Africa | | 36 503 | 30 244 | 35 507 | 27 450 | 22 655 | Afrique |
| Americas | | 222 052 | 175 546 | 209 779 | 209 511 | 184 525 | Amériques |
| Europe | | 808 067 | 605 904 | 720 706 | 798 408 | 730 398 | Europe |
| Asia, East/S.East/Oceania | | 3 877 195 | 3 575 842 | 4 265 551 | 3 837 107 | 3 795 481 | Asie, Est/S.-Est/Océanie |
| Southern Asia | | 51 596 | 48 114 | 53 839 | 69 024 | 83 259 | Asie du Sud |
| Western Asia | | 37 987 | 31 371 | 35 783 | 60 601 | 55 033 | Asie occidentale |

| Country or area of destination and region of origin& | Series Série | 2002 | 2003 | 2004 | 2005 | 2006 | Pays ou zone de destination et région de provenance& |
|---|---|---|---|---|---|---|---|
| Ireland | TFR | | | | | | Irlande |
| Total | | 6 477 000 | 6 764 000 | 6 953 000 | 7 334 000 | 8 001 000 | Total |
| Africa | | 29 000 | 32 000 | 42 000 | 39 000 | 48 000 | Afrique |
| Americas | | 860 000 | 913 000 | 975 000 | 956 000 | 1 058 000 | Amériques |
| Europe | | 5 387 000 | 5 623 000 | 5 677 000 | 6 113 000 | 6 658 000 | Europe |
| Asia, East/S.East/Oceania | | 201 000 | 196 000 | 259 000 | 226 000 | 237 000 | Asie, Est/S.-Est/Océanie |
| Israel | TFR | | | | | | Israël |
| Total[2] | | 861 859 | 1 063 381 | 1 505 606 | 1 902 787 | 1 825 207 | Total[2] |
| Africa | | 29 323 | 29 547 | 40 122 | 41 450 | 54 337 | Afrique |
| Americas | | 260 912 | 347 622 | 486 508 | 602 578 | 606 771 | Amériques |
| Europe | | 484 353 | 598 231 | 857 133 | 1 107 142 | 1 015 624 | Europe |
| Asia, East/S.East/Oceania | | 35 885 | 42 384 | 65 953 | 87 572 | 94 407 | Asie, Est/S.-Est/Océanie |
| Southern Asia | | 10 745 | 10 172 | 15 155 | 22 911 | 23 219 | Asie du Sud |
| Western Asia | | 28 356 | 23 159 | 28 561 | 29 946 | 20 613 | Asie occidentale |
| Region not specified | | 12 285 | 12 266 | 12 174 | 11 188 | 10 236 | Région non spécifiée |
| Italy | TFN | | | | | | Italie |
| Total[33] | | 39 798 969 | 39 604 118 | 37 070 775 | 36 512 500 | 41 057 834 | Total[33] |
| Africa | | 179 251 | 122 472 | 205 617 | 250 705 | 253 863 | Afrique |
| Americas | | 2 064 520 | 1 680 228 | 2 988 244 | 3 250 284 | 3 579 393 | Amériques |
| Europe | | 36 001 041 | 36 583 819 | 32 521 819 | 31 571 338 | 35 594 161 | Europe |
| Asia, East/S.East/Oceania | | 1 382 734 | 1 074 563 | 1 088 281 | 1 111 603 | 1 188 781 | Asie, Est/S.-Est/Océanie |
| Southern Asia | | 89 329 | 67 001 | 135 290 | 115 193 | 189 745 | Asie du Sud |
| Western Asia | | 82 093 | 76 035 | 129 760 | 212 716 | 246 956 | Asie occidentale |
| Region not specified | | 1 | ... | 1 764 | 661 | 4 935 | Région non spécifiée |
| Jamaica | TFR | | | | | | Jamaïque |
| Total[3,9] | | 1 266 366 | 1 350 285 | 1 414 786 | 1 478 663 | 1 678 905 | Total[3,9] |
| Africa | | 1 131 | 1 084 | 1 139 | 889 | 1 032 | Afrique |
| Americas | | 1 076 044 | 1 119 679 | 1 161 840 | 1 233 846 | 1 411 339 | Amériques |
| Europe | | 179 902 | 219 406 | 242 904 | 234 952 | 257 224 | Europe |
| Asia, East/S.East/Oceania | | 8 292 | 9 051 | 7 971 | 8 129 | 8 240 | Asie, Est/S.-Est/Océanie |
| Southern Asia | | 530 | 643 | 554 | 464 | 600 | Asie du Sud |
| Western Asia | | 392 | 363 | 350 | 347 | 394 | Asie occidentale |
| Region not specified | | 75 | 59 | 28 | 36 | 76 | Région non spécifiée |
| Japan | VFN | | | | | | Japon |
| Total[2] | | 5 238 963 | 5 211 725 | 6 137 905 | 6 727 926 | 7 334 077 | Total[2] |
| Africa | | 16 698 | 16 434 | 16 946 | 20 583 | 18 678 | Afrique |
| Americas | | 927 598 | 824 345 | 951 074 | 1 032 140 | 1 035 300 | Amériques |
| Europe | | 688 250 | 665 187 | 744 142 | 817 092 | 817 670 | Europe |
| Asia, East/S.East/Oceania | | 3 528 489 | 3 625 013 | 4 337 788 | 4 761 395 | 5 362 608 | Asie, Est/S.-Est/Océanie |
| Southern Asia | | 72 580 | 76 217 | 83 856 | 92 676 | 95 555 | Asie du Sud |
| Western Asia | | 3 394 | 3 166 | 3 285 | 3 072 | 3 218 | Asie occidentale |
| Region not specified | | 1 954 | 1 363 | 814 | 968 | 1 048 | Région non spécifiée |
| Jordan | TFN | | | | | | Jordanie |
| Total[1] | | 2 384 472 | 2 353 087 | 2 852 803 | 2 986 589 | 3 225 409 | Total[1] |
| Africa | | 19 582 | 17 537 | 19 938 | 30 234 | 50 670 | Afrique |
| Americas | | 51 908 | 64 545 | 93 477 | 111 975 | 163 918 | Amériques |
| Europe | | 313 467 | 314 858 | 374 428 | 391 846 | 424 583 | Europe |
| Asia, East/S.East/Oceania | | 43 251 | 43 883 | 60 121 | 64 191 | 82 943 | Asie, Est/S.-Est/Océanie |
| Southern Asia | | 36 421 | 27 034 | 37 885 | 42 947 | 41 884 | Asie du Sud |
| Western Asia | | 1 497 960 | 1 464 910 | 1 780 755 | 1 828 735 | 1 879 541 | Asie occidentale |
| Region not specified | | 421 883 | 420 320 | 486 199 | 516 661 | 581 870 | Région non spécifiée |
| Kazakhstan | VFR | | | | | | Kazakhstan |
| Total | | 3 677 921 | 3 236 788 | 4 291 040 | 4 364 949 | 4 706 742 | Total |
| Africa | | 1 159 | 1 064 | 1 506 | 1 703 | 5 023 | Afrique |
| Americas | | 24 699 | 23 203 | 32 345 | 30 768 | 31 978 | Amériques |
| Europe | | 3 569 412 | 3 114 377 | 4 125 909 | 4 194 081 | 4 486 983 | Europe |

| Country or area of destination and region of origin[&] | Series Série | 2002 | 2003 | 2004 | 2005 | 2006 | Pays ou zone de destination et région de provenance[&] |
|---|---|---|---|---|---|---|---|
| Asia, East/S.East/Oceania | | 65 929 | 72 359 | 96 660 | 113 842 | 152 929 | Asie, Est/S.-Est/Océanie |
| Southern Asia | | 12 437 | 17 733 | 20 849 | 19 036 | 21 811 | Asie du Sud |
| Western Asia | | 3 330 | 2 917 | 1 984 | 2 276 | 3 212 | Asie occidentale |
| Region not specified | | 955 | 5 135 | 11 787 | 3 243 | 4 806 | Région non spécifiée |
| Kenya | VFR | | | | | | Kenya |
| Total[2,34] | | 1 001 297 | 1 146 099 | ... | ... | ... | Total[2,34] |
| Africa | | 272 429 | 311 819 | ... | ... | ... | Afrique |
| Americas | | 85 083 | 97 389 | ... | ... | ... | Amériques |
| Europe | | 575 197 | 658 384 | ... | ... | ... | Europe |
| Asia, East/S.East/Oceania | | 44 278 | 50 681 | ... | ... | ... | Asie, Est/S.-Est/Océanie |
| Southern Asia | | 24 007 | 27 479 | ... | ... | ... | Asie du Sud |
| Region not specified | | 303 | 347 | ... | ... | ... | Région non spécifiée |
| Kiribati | TFN | | | | | | Kiribati |
| Total[3] | | 4 935[35] | 4 905[35] | 3 616[36] | 3 037[36] | 4 406[35] | Total[3] |
| Americas | | 1 112 | 786 | 123 | 300 | 760 | Amériques |
| Europe | | 504 | 388 | 387 | 133 | 232 | Europe |
| Asia, East/S.East/Oceania | | 2 722 | 2 875 | 2 463 | 2 185 | 2 744 | Asie, Est/S.-Est/Océanie |
| Region not specified | | 597 | 856 | 643 | 419 | 670 | Région non spécifiée |
| Korea, Republic of | VFN | | | | | | Corée, République de |
| Total[37] | | 5 347 468 | 4 753 604 | 5 818 138 | 6 022 752 | 6 155 046 | Total[37] |
| Africa | | 16 322 | 14 834 | 14 649 | 14 464 | 16 071 | Afrique |
| Americas | | 556 440 | 505 067 | 610 562 | 640 050 | 673 118 | Amériques |
| Europe | | 536 261 | 514 403 | 531 257 | 540 694 | 571 612 | Europe |
| Asia, East/S.East/Oceania | | 3 829 548 | 3 334 633 | 4 252 976 | 4 441 757 | 4 557 030 | Asie, Est/S.-Est/Océanie |
| Southern Asia | | 81 648 | 86 000 | 95 398 | 92 189 | 95 430 | Asie du Sud |
| Western Asia | | 10 715 | 8 045 | 11 155 | 13 050 | 15 000 | Asie occidentale |
| Region not specified | | 316 534 | 290 622 | 302 141 | 280 548 | 226 785 | Région non spécifiée |
| Kuwait | VFN | | | | | | Koweït |
| Total | | 2 315 568 | 2 602 300 | 3 056 093 | ... | ... | Total |
| Africa | | 24 407 | 26 167 | 29 144 | ... | ... | Afrique |
| Americas | | 50 267 | 103 447 | 115 260 | ... | ... | Amériques |
| Europe | | 80 650 | 94 168 | 125 509 | ... | ... | Europe |
| Asia, East/S.East/Oceania | | 117 923 | 124 868 | 158 006 | ... | ... | Asie, Est/S.-Est/Océanie |
| Southern Asia | | 648 075 | 745 679 | 855 730 | ... | ... | Asie du Sud |
| Western Asia | | 1 391 296 | 1 505 733 | 1 769 220 | ... | ... | Asie occidentale |
| Region not specified | | 2 950 | 2 238 | 3 224 | ... | ... | Région non spécifiée |
| Kyrgyzstan | TFR | | | | | | Kirghizistan |
| Total | | 139 589 | 341 990[38] | 398 078[38] | 315 290[38] | 765 850[38] | Total |
| Americas | | 11 936 | 12 744 | 12 266 | 13 023 | 14 140 | Amériques |
| Europe | | 88 148 | 269 575 | 356 982 | 273 696 | 715 435 | Europe |
| Asia, East/S.East/Oceania | | 11 333 | 14 005 | 16 766 | 22 099 | 26 288 | Asie, Est/S.-Est/Océanie |
| Southern Asia | | 3 400 | 5 395 | 5 864 | 6 364 | 5 142 | Asie du Sud |
| Western Asia | | 45 | ... | ... | 80 | 134 | Asie occidentale |
| Region not specified | | 24 727 | 40 271 | 6 200 | 28 | 4 711 | Région non spécifiée |
| Lao People's Dem. Rep. | VFN | | | | | | Rép. dém. pop. lao |
| Total | | 735 662 | 636 361 | 894 806 | 1 095 315 | 1 215 107 | Total |
| Americas | | 46 704 | 39 453 | 47 153 | 60 061 | 60 883 | Amériques |
| Europe | | 107 439 | 97 314 | 116 180 | 134 472 | 143 716 | Europe |
| Asia, East/S.East/Oceania | | 575 268 | 495 253 | 728 262 | 897 177 | 1 006 564 | Asie, Est/S.-Est/Océanie |
| Southern Asia | | 3 763 | 2 932 | 1 845 | 2 096 | 2 100 | Asie du Sud |
| Region not specified | | 2 488 | 1 409 | 1 366 | 1 509 | 1 844 | Région non spécifiée |
| Latvia | TCER | | | | | | Lettonie |
| Total | | 360 927 | 414 924 | 545 366 | 730 146 | 816 297 | Total |
| Africa | | 87 | 151 | 83 | 71 | 137 | Afrique |
| Americas | | 15 014 | 14 128 | 21 091 | 20 423 | 22 517 | Amériques |
| Europe | | 332 107 | 386 070 | 500 979 | 680 362 | 757 385 | Europe |

| Country or area of destination and region of origin& | Series / Série | 2002 | 2003 | 2004 | 2005 | 2006 | Pays ou zone de destination et région de provenance& |
|---|---|---|---|---|---|---|---|
| Asia, East/S.East/Oceania | | 7 611 | 7 603 | 9 511 | 9 941 | 10 131 | Asie, Est/S.-Est/Océanie |
| Southern Asia | | 403 | 294 | 308 | 570 | 620 | Asie du Sud |
| Western Asia | | 158 | 131 | 196 | 524 | 233 | Asie occidentale |
| Region not specified | | 5 547 | 6 547 | 13 198 | 18 255 | 25 274 | Région non spécifiée |
| Lebanon | TFN | | | | | | Liban |
| Total[39] | | 956 464 | 1 015 793 | 1 278 469 | 1 139 524 | 1 062 625 | Total[39] |
| Africa | | 37 240 | 39 453 | 45 095 | 31 073 | 39 021 | Afrique |
| Americas | | 108 329 | 120 239 | 152 175 | 136 904 | 130 117 | Amériques |
| Europe | | 250 817 | 267 077 | 337 337 | 316 561 | 269 263 | Europe |
| Asia, East/S.East/Oceania | | 60 543 | 65 581 | 92 285 | 87 813 | 74 461 | Asie, Est/S.-Est/Océanie |
| Southern Asia | | 95 647 | 102 035 | 128 120 | 129 315 | 115 243 | Asie du Sud |
| Western Asia | | 403 000 | 421 148 | 520 230 | 436 549 | 433 323 | Asie occidentale |
| Region not specified | | 888 | 260 | 3 227 | 1 309 | 1 197 | Région non spécifiée |
| Lesotho | VFR | | | | | | Lesotho |
| Total | | 287 280 | 329 301 | 303 530 | 303 578 | 356 913 | Total |
| Africa | | 278 662 | 302 924 | 290 295 | 289 342 | 329 838 | Afrique |
| Americas | | 861 | 2 842 | 1 375 | 1 490 | 3 412 | Amériques |
| Europe | | 5 746 | 12 569 | 7 568 | 7 930 | 19 641 | Europe |
| Asia, East/S.East/Oceania | | 2 011 | 4 009 | 2 551 | 2 657 | 3 456 | Asie, Est/S.-Est/Océanie |
| Southern Asia | | ... | ... | ... | ... | 318 | Asie du Sud |
| Western Asia | | ... | ... | ... | ... | 117 | Asie occidentale |
| Region not specified | | ... | 6 957 | 1 741 | 2 159 | 131 | Région non spécifiée |
| Libyan Arab Jamah. | VFN | | | | | | Jamah. arabe libyenne |
| Total *[40] | | 857 952 | 957 896 | 999 343 | ... | ... | Total *[40] |
| Africa | | 438 881 | 457 721 | 482 704 | ... | ... | Afrique |
| Americas | | 1 943 | 1 926 | 2 201 | ... | ... | Amériques |
| Europe | | 36 418 | 42 056 | 45 657 | ... | ... | Europe |
| Asia, East/S.East/Oceania | | 6 611 | 6 601 | 6 942 | ... | ... | Asie, Est/S.-Est/Océanie |
| Southern Asia | | 4 325 | 4 031 | 3 704 | ... | ... | Asie du Sud |
| Western Asia | | 369 774 | 445 561 | 458 124 | ... | ... | Asie occidentale |
| Region not specified | | ... | ... | 11 | ... | ... | Région non spécifiée |
| Liechtenstein | THSR | | | | | | Liechtenstein |
| Total | | 48 727 | 49 002 | 48 501 | 49 767 | 54 856 | Total |
| Africa | | 223 | 214 | 198 | 170 | 189 | Afrique |
| Americas | | 2 852 | 2 414 | 2 739 | 2 888 | 2 999 | Amériques |
| Europe | | 43 990 | 44 740 | 43 836 | 44 944 | 49 818 | Europe |
| Asia, East/S.East/Oceania | | 1 662 | 1 634 | 1 728 | 1 635 | 1 740 | Asie, Est/S.-Est/Océanie |
| Southern Asia | | ... | ... | ... | 47 | 59 | Asie du Sud |
| Region not specified | | ... | ... | ... | 83 | 51 | Région non spécifiée |
| Lithuania | TCER | | | | | | Lituanie |
| Total | | 393 126 | 438 299 | 590 043 | 681 487 | 756 855 | Total |
| Africa | | 271 | 400 | 525 | 1 159 | 1 360 | Afrique |
| Americas | | 15 673 | 16 324 | 22 385 | 23 626 | 25 955 | Amériques |
| Europe | | 357 990 | 400 338 | 538 078 | 623 045 | 694 241 | Europe |
| Asia, East/S.East/Oceania | | 9 808 | 11 003 | 15 472 | 15 032 | 16 260 | Asie, Est/S.-Est/Océanie |
| Region not specified | | 9 384 | 10 234 | 13 583 | 18 625 | 19 039 | Région non spécifiée |
| Luxembourg | TCER | | | | | | Luxembourg |
| Total | | 884 674 | 867 048 | 877 712 | 912 798 | 908 171 | Total |
| Americas | | 33 136 | 28 562 | 29 777 | 32 249 | 34 516 | Amériques |
| Europe | | 809 403 | 801 138 | 806 575 | 840 259 | 831 114 | Europe |
| Region not specified | | 42 135 | 37 348 | 41 360 | 40 290 | 42 541 | Région non spécifiée |
| Madagascar | TFN | | | | | | Madagascar |
| Total[3] | | 61 674 | 139 230 | 228 785 | 277 422 | 311 730 | Total[3] |
| Africa | | 6 218 | 21 725 | 39 302 | 52 277 | 58 520 | Afrique |
| Americas | | 1 880 | 4 177 | 9 180 | 13 853 | 15 587 | Amériques |
| Europe | | 43 172 | 99 271 | 175 727 | 202 530 | 228 452 | Europe |
| Asia, East/S.East/Oceania | | 617 | 4 872 | 3 432 | 6 404 | 7 206 | Asie, Est/S.-Est/Océanie |

| Country or area of destination and region of origin& | Series Série | 2002 | 2003 | 2004 | 2005 | 2006 | Pays ou zone de destination et région de provenance& |
|---|---|---|---|---|---|---|---|
| Region not specified | | 9 787 | 9 185 | 1 144 | 2 358 | 1 965 | Région non spécifiée |
| **Malawi** | TFR | | | | | | **Malawi** |
| Total[32] | | 382 647 | 424 000 | 427 360 | 437 718 | ... | Total[32] |
| Africa | | 299 973 | 320 360 | 335 651 | 336 856 | ... | Afrique |
| Americas | | 15 251 | 18 070 | 20 828 | 18 725 | ... | Amériques |
| Europe | | 55 222 | 67 500 | 48 929 | 60 437 | ... | Europe |
| Asia, East/S.East/Oceania | | 5 542 | 9 940 | 11 313 | 8 698 | ... | Asie, Est/S.-Est/Océanie |
| Southern Asia | | 1 659 | 3 620 | 6 815 | 9 549 | ... | Asie du Sud |
| Region not specified | | 5 000 | 4 510 | 3 824 | 3 453 | ... | Région non spécifiée |
| **Malaysia** | TFR | | | | | | **Malaisie** |
| Total[41] | | 13 292 010 | 10 576 915 | 15 703 406 | 16 431 055 | 17 546 863 | Total[41] |
| Africa | | 148 102 | 133 762 | 136 587 | 128 208 | 157 342 | Afrique |
| Americas | | 283 216 | 270 157 | 271 901 | 274 915 | 312 478 | Amériques |
| Europe | | 636 972 | 456 351 | 540 306 | 618 188 | 673 118 | Europe |
| Asia, East/S.East/Oceania | | 11 456 003 | 9 073 882 | 13 983 381 | 14 685 975 | 15 475 553 | Asie, Est/S.-Est/Océanie |
| Southern Asia | | 244 351 | 209 120 | 248 673 | 321 246 | 390 189 | Asie du Sud |
| Western Asia | | 126 239 | 78 324 | 124 331 | 145 448 | 173 750 | Asie occidentale |
| Region not specified | | 397 127 | 355 319 | 398 227 | 257 075 | 364 433 | Région non spécifiée |
| **Maldives** | TFN | | | | | | **Maldives** |
| Total[3] | | 484 680 | 563 593 | 616 716 | 395 320 | 601 923 | Total[3] |
| Africa | | 3 002 | 3 984 | 5 325 | 3 460 | 4 169 | Afrique |
| Americas | | 7 487 | 7 660 | 9 385 | 7 238 | 10 813 | Amériques |
| Europe | | 373 428 | 443 093 | 475 707 | 306 856 | 457 535 | Europe |
| Asia, East/S.East/Oceania | | 77 289 | 83 640 | 99 735 | 55 985 | 102 277 | Asie, Est/S.-Est/Océanie |
| Southern Asia | | 20 533 | 21 580 | 22 047 | 19 377 | 22 757 | Asie du Sud |
| Western Asia | | 2 941 | 3 636 | 4 517 | 2 404 | 4 372 | Asie occidentale |
| **Mali** | THSN | | | | | | **Mali** |
| Total | | 95 851 | 110 365 | 112 654 | 142 814 | 152 660 | Total |
| Africa | | 21 165 | 27 816 | 29 256 | 35 985 | 38 892 | Afrique |
| Americas | | 9 232 | 9 393 | 12 494 | 13 287 | 18 507 | Amériques |
| Europe | | 55 763 | 62 744 | 64 252 | 80 968 | 86 443 | Europe |
| Asia, East/S.East/Oceania | | 1 189 | 1 200 | 3 117 | 2 090 | 1 636 | Asie, Est/S.-Est/Océanie |
| Western Asia | | 2 567 | 2 712 | 1 524 | 1 064 | 1 128 | Asie occidentale |
| Region not specified | | 5 935 | 6 500 | 2 011 | 9 420 | 6 054 | Région non spécifiée |
| **Malta** | TFN | | | | | | **Malte** |
| Total | | 1 133 814 | 1 126 601 | 1 156 028[42] | 1 170 610[42] | 1 124 233[42] | Total |
| Africa | | 9 086 | ... | ... | ... | ... | Afrique |
| Americas | | 27 005 | 20 657 | 18 720 | 18 136 | 16 970 | Amériques |
| Europe | | 1 039 904 | 939 793 | 982 623 | 989 283 | 939 798 | Europe |
| Asia, East/S.East/Oceania | | 25 020 | ... | ... | ... | ... | Asie, Est/S.-Est/Océanie |
| Southern Asia | | 1 549 | ... | ... | ... | ... | Asie du Sud |
| Western Asia | | 25 484 | 20 218 | 12 831 | 10 662 | 9 198 | Asie occidentale |
| Region not specified | | 5 766 | 145 933 | 141 854 | 152 529 | 158 267 | Région non spécifiée |
| **Marshall Islands** | TFR | | | | | | **Iles Marshall** |
| Total | | 6 002[3] | 7 195[3] | 9 007[17] | 9 173[17] | 5 780[3] | Total |
| Americas | | 2 156 | 2 189 | 2 099 | 1 721 | 1 472 | Amériques |
| Europe | | 147 | 196 | 160 | 160 | 180 | Europe |
| Asia, East/S.East/Oceania | | 3 397 | 4 422 | 4 466 | 5 577 | 3 850 | Asie, Est/S.-Est/Océanie |
| Region not specified | | 302 | 388 | 2 282 | 1 715 | 278 | Région non spécifiée |
| **Martinique** | TFR | | | | | | **Martinique** |
| Total | | 446 689 | 453 159 | 470 890 | 484 127 | 503 475 | Total |
| Americas | | 70 378 | 71 559 | 73 011 | 81 247 | 79 335 | Amériques |
| Europe | | 371 978 | 379 922 | 396 138 | 399 083 | 422 453 | Europe |
| Region not specified | | 4 333 | 1 678 | 1 741 | 3 797 | 1 687 | Région non spécifiée |
| **Mauritius** | TFR | | | | | | **Maurice** |
| Total | | 681 648 | 702 018 | 718 861 | 761 063 | 788 276 | Total |
| Africa | | 172 351 | 173 996 | 175 295 | 184 821 | 189 026 | Afrique |

| Country or area of destination and region of origin& | Series Série | 2002 | 2003 | 2004 | 2005 | 2006 | Pays ou zone de destination et région de provenance& |
|---|---|---|---|---|---|---|---|
| Americas | | 7 451 | 8 106 | 8 380 | 8 791 | 9 759 | Amériques |
| Europe | | 451 791 | 465 620 | 477 347 | 503 037 | 510 872 | Europe |
| Asia, East/S.East/Oceania | | 24 694 | 21 934 | 27 026 | 28 924 | 34 103 | Asie, Est/S.-Est/Océanie |
| Southern Asia | | 22 869 | 27 277 | 26 558 | 31 087 | 39 070 | Asie du Sud |
| Western Asia | | 2 287 | 4 800 | 3 883 | 3 737 | 4 715 | Asie occidentale |
| Region not specified | | 205 | 285 | 372 | 666 | 731 | Région non spécifiée |
| Mexico | TFR | | | | | | Mexique |
| Total[9] | | 19 666 677 | 18 665 384 | 20 617 746 | 21 914 917 | *21 352 605 | Total[9] |
| Americas | | 19 133 397 | 18 155 315 | 19 705 636 | 20 691 415 | 20 094 345 | Amériques |
| Europe | | 479 174 | 443 366 | ... | ... | ... | Europe |
| Region not specified | | 54 106 | 66 703 | 912 110 | 1 223 502 | 1 258 260 | Région non spécifiée |
| Mexico | TFN | | | | | | Mexique |
| Total[9] | | ... | ... | ... | 21 914 917 | *21 352 605 | Total[9] |
| Americas | | ... | ... | ... | 19 045 615 | 18 711 456 | Amériques |
| Europe | | ... | ... | ... | 1 149 162 | 1 310 318 | Europe |
| Asia, East/S.East/Oceania | | ... | ... | ... | 91 595 | 99 726 | Asie, Est/S.-Est/Océanie |
| Region not specified | | ... | ... | ... | 1 628 545 | 1 231 105 | Région non spécifiée |
| Micronesia (Fed. States of) | TFR | | | | | | Micronésie (Etats féd. de) |
| Total[43] | | 19 056 | 18 211 | 19 260 | 18 958 | 19 136 | Total[43] |
| Americas | | 8 439 | 7 671 | 7 744 | 7 955 | 8 256 | Amériques |
| Europe | | 1 483 | 1 568 | 1 408 | 2 019 | 2 398 | Europe |
| Asia, East/S.East/Oceania | | 9 044 | 8 884 | 9 982 | 8 895 | 8 361 | Asie, Est/S.-Est/Océanie |
| Region not specified | | 90 | 88 | 126 | 89 | 121 | Région non spécifiée |
| Moldova | VFN | | | | | | Moldova |
| Total[44] | | 20 161 | 23 598 | 26 045 | 25 073 | 14 240 | Total[44] |
| Africa | | 40 | 45 | 71 | 15 | 10 | Afrique |
| Americas | | 1 788 | 2 556 | 2 564 | 3 161 | 1 123 | Amériques |
| Europe | | 17 631 | 20 152 | 22 686 | 21 223 | 12 741 | Europe |
| Asia, East/S.East/Oceania | | 411 | 295 | 307 | 277 | 243 | Asie, Est/S.-Est/Océanie |
| Southern Asia | | 10 | 25 | 25 | 35 | 9 | Asie du Sud |
| Western Asia | | 281 | 525 | 392 | 362 | 114 | Asie occidentale |
| Monaco | THSN | | | | | | Monaco |
| Total | | 262 520 | 234 638 | 250 159 | 285 675 | 313 070 | Total |
| Africa | | 2 440 | 2 228 | 2 230 | 2 601 | 2 826 | Afrique |
| Americas | | 32 499 | 23 660 | 25 132 | 28 626 | 34 071 | Amériques |
| Europe | | 205 062 | 186 972 | 190 326 | 214 131 | 239 872 | Europe |
| Asia, East/S.East/Oceania | | 12 143 | 9 781 | 12 653 | 11 746 | 10 632 | Asie, Est/S.-Est/Océanie |
| Western Asia | | 4 024 | 3 320 | 3 367 | 3 190 | 3 694 | Asie occidentale |
| Region not specified | | 6 352 | 8 677 | 16 451 | 25 381 | 21 975 | Région non spécifiée |
| Mongolia | TFN | | | | | | Mongolie |
| Total | | 228 719 | 201 153 | 300 537 | 337 790 | 385 989 | Total |
| Africa | | 143 | 209 | 263 | 297 | 502 | Afrique |
| Americas | | 7 973 | 6 863 | 12 198 | 12 913 | 14 433 | Amériques |
| Europe | | 97 674 | 72 345 | 98 592 | 100 123 | 124 002 | Europe |
| Asia, East/S.East/Oceania | | 122 106 | 120 691 | 188 250 | 223 411 | 245 760 | Asie, Est/S.-Est/Océanie |
| Southern Asia | | 655 | 803 | 966 | 792 | 1 129 | Asie du Sud |
| Western Asia | | 155 | 229 | 249 | 232 | 159 | Asie occidentale |
| Region not specified | | 13 | 13 | 19 | 22 | 4 | Région non spécifiée |
| Montenegro | TCEN | | | | | | Monténégro |
| Total | | 136 160 | 141 787 | 188 060 | 272 005 | 377 798 | Total |
| Americas | | 3 006 | 2 657 | 3 354 | 4 302 | 7 324 | Amériques |
| Europe | | 129 491 | 135 329 | 180 286 | 259 596 | 359 937 | Europe |
| Asia, East/S.East/Oceania | | 441 | 427 | 682 | 973 | 1 488 | Asie, Est/S.-Est/Océanie |
| Region not specified | | 3 222 | 3 374 | 3 738 | 7 134 | 9 049 | Région non spécifiée |
| Montserrat | TFR | | | | | | Montserrat |
| Total | | 9 836 | 8 390 | 10 138 | 9 690 | 7 991 | Total |

| Country or area of destination and region of origin[&] | Series Série | 2002 | 2003 | 2004 | 2005 | 2006 | Pays ou zone de destination et région de provenance[&] |
|---|---|---|---|---|---|---|---|
| Americas | | 7 014 | 5 932 | 6 822 | 6 448 | 5 427 | Amériques |
| Europe | | 2 759 | 2 414 | 3 197 | 3 196 | 2 501 | Europe |
| Region not specified | | 63 | 44 | 119 | 46 | 63 | Région non spécifiée |
| Morocco | TFN | | | | | | Maroc |
| Total[1] | | 4 453 259 | 4 761 271 | 5 476 712 | 5 843 360 | 6 558 269 | Total[1] |
| Africa | | 91 698 | 103 194 | 123 070 | 143 855 | 165 307 | Afrique |
| Americas | | 119 229 | 107 877 | 127 974 | 140 194 | 173 258 | Amériques |
| Europe | | 1 868 540 | 1 880 177 | 2 309 477 | 2 607 239 | 3 024 876 | Europe |
| Asia, East/S.East/Oceania | | 44 242 | 41 651 | 48 874 | 51 745 | 65 234 | Asie, Est/S.-Est/Océanie |
| Southern Asia | | 6 053 | 5 383 | 6 486 | 7 723 | 8 795 | Asie du Sud |
| Western Asia | | 85 996 | 78 639 | 84 298 | 91 029 | 105 632 | Asie occidentale |
| Region not specified | | 2 237 501 | 2 544 350 | 2 776 533 | 2 801 575 | 3 015 167 | Région non spécifiée |
| Mozambique | VFR | | | | | | Mozambique |
| Total | | 942 885 | 726 099 | 711 060 | 954 433 | 1 095 000 | Total |
| Africa | | 848 259 | 591 647 | 623 240 | 851 999 | 977 468 | Afrique |
| Americas | | 10 401 | 5 035 | 5 647 | 12 399 | 14 226 | Amériques |
| Europe | | 53 691 | 42 698 | 56 508 | 47 999 | 55 074 | Europe |
| Asia, East/S.East/Oceania | | 5 721 | ... | ... | 8 036 | 9 220 | Asie, Est/S.-Est/Océanie |
| Region not specified | | 24 813 | 86 719 | 25 665 | 34 000 | 39 012 | Région non spécifiée |
| Myanmar | TFN | | | | | | Myanmar |
| Total[45] | | 217 212 | 205 610 | 241 938 | 232 218 | 263 514 | Total[45] |
| Africa | | 430 | 390 | 395 | 488 | 502 | Afrique |
| Americas | | 17 824 | 16 426 | 20 451 | 20 701 | 22 880 | Amériques |
| Europe | | 65 477 | 60 364 | 65 411 | 67 933 | 80 791 | Europe |
| Asia, East/S.East/Oceania | | 124 280 | 115 614 | 141 683 | 129 922 | 148 282 | Asie, Est/S.-Est/Océanie |
| Southern Asia | | 7 179 | 11 668 | 12 167 | 11 254 | 8 882 | Asie du Sud |
| Western Asia | | 2 022 | 1 148 | 1 831 | 1 920 | 2 177 | Asie occidentale |
| Namibia | TFR | | | | | | Namibie |
| Total | | 757 201 | 695 221 | ... | 777 890 | 833 345 | Total |
| Africa | | 591 612 | 525 885 | ... | 601 737 | 628 588 | Afrique |
| Americas | | 9 625 | 11 775 | ... | 14 685 | 16 324 | Amériques |
| Europe | | 140 781 | 141 834 | ... | 146 362 | 166 974 | Europe |
| Asia, East/S.East/Oceania | | 3 430 | 4 280 | ... | 4 607 | 4 644 | Asie, Est/S.-Est/Océanie |
| Region not specified | | 11 753 | 11 447 | ... | 10 499 | 16 815 | Région non spécifiée |
| Nepal | TFR | | | | | | Népal |
| Total | | 275 468 | 338 132 | 385 297 | 375 398 | 383 926 | Total |
| Africa | | 1 117 | 1 501 | 1 346 | 1 285 | 1 571 | Afrique |
| Americas | | 25 110 | 25 156 | 29 791 | 26 385 | 27 991 | Amériques |
| Europe | | 97 026 | 111 822 | 131 999 | 112 341 | 108 166 | Europe |
| Asia, East/S.East/Oceania | | 67 985 | 91 582 | 96 565 | 92 733 | 95 407 | Asie, Est/S.-Est/Océanie |
| Southern Asia | | 84 230 | 108 071 | 124 804 | 139 288 | 137 059 | Asie du Sud |
| Region not specified | | ... | ... | 792 | 3 366 | 13 732 | Région non spécifiée |
| Netherlands | TCER | | | | | | Pays-Bas |
| Total | | 9 595 300 | 9 180 600 | 9 646 500 | 10 011 900 | 10 738 700 | Total |
| Africa | | 172 800 | 130 600 | 117 300 | 101 100 | 92 700 | Afrique |
| Americas | | 1 099 700 | 996 100 | 1 131 500 | 1 222 200 | 1 325 000 | Amériques |
| Europe | | 7 591 600 | 7 431 800 | 7 644 000 | 7 939 900 | 8 598 400 | Europe |
| Asia, East/S.East/Oceania | | 731 200 | 622 100 | 753 700 | 748 700 | 722 600 | Asie, Est/S.-Est/Océanie |
| New Caledonia | TFR | | | | | | Nouvelle-Calédonie |
| Total[9] | | 103 933 | 101 983 | 99 515 | 100 651 | 100 491 | Total[9] |
| Africa | | 520 | 489 | 615 | 637 | 705 | Afrique |
| Americas | | 2 141 | 1 753 | 1 676 | 1 785 | 1 854 | Amériques |
| Europe | | 32 683 | 32 492 | 29 992 | 30 268 | 31 850 | Europe |
| Asia, East/S.East/Oceania | | 67 998 | 65 382 | 65 892 | 67 753 | 66 074 | Asie, Est/S.-Est/Océanie |
| Region not specified | | 591 | 1 867 | 1 340 | 208 | 8 | Région non spécifiée |
| New Zealand | VFR | | | | | | Nouvelle-Zélande |
| Total[9,46] | | 2 045 064 | 2 104 420 | 2 334 153 | 2 365 529 | 2 408 888 | Total[9,46] |

| Country or area of destination and region of origin& | Series Série | 2002 | 2003 | 2004 | 2005 | 2006 | Pays ou zone de destination et région de provenance& |
|---|---|---|---|---|---|---|---|
| Africa | | 20 679 | 19 395 | 18 673 | 19 709 | 20 643 | Afrique |
| Americas | | 261 273 | 266 245 | 275 699 | 275 616 | 294 450 | Amériques |
| Europe | | 423 200 | 460 938 | 488 674 | 521 267 | 515 716 | Europe |
| Asia, East/S.East/Oceania | | 1 240 381 | 1 271 657 | 1 468 307 | 1 484 424 | 1 512 292 | Asie, Est/S.-Est/Océanie |
| Southern Asia | | 19 410 | 17 028 | 17 830 | 19 833 | 22 507 | Asie du Sud |
| Western Asia | | 5 922 | 7 048 | 8 122 | 8 871 | 9 607 | Asie occidentale |
| Region not specified | | 74 199 | 62 109 | 56 848 | 35 809 | 33 673 | Région non spécifiée |
| Nicaragua | TFN | | | | | | Nicaragua |
| Total | | 471 622[2] | 525 775[2] | 614 782[2] | 712 444[1] | *773 398[1] | Total |
| Africa | | 287 | 378 | 515 | 621 | ... | Afrique |
| Americas | | 417 226 | 464 176 | 552 846 | 619 305 | 660 405 | Amériques |
| Europe | | 44 730 | 49 147 | 52 564 | 58 964 | 55 026 | Europe |
| Asia, East/S.East/Oceania | | 8 732 | 10 674 | 8 326 | 11 235 | ... | Asie, Est/S.-Est/Océanie |
| Southern Asia | | 549 | 1 254 | 437 | 1 522 | ... | Asie du Sud |
| Western Asia | | 64 | 89 | 76 | 82 | ... | Asie occidentale |
| Region not specified | | 34 | 57 | 18 | 20 715 | 57 967 | Région non spécifiée |
| Niger | TFN | | | | | | Niger |
| Total | | 39 337 | 55 344 | 57 004 | 59 920 | 60 332 | Total |
| Africa | | 26 198 | 37 344 | 38 000 | 35 952 | 36 199 | Afrique |
| Americas | | 1 574 | 2 000 | 2 500 | 4 194 | 4 223 | Amériques |
| Europe | | 10 110 | 14 344 | 14 500 | 16 778 | 16 893 | Europe |
| Asia, East/S.East/Oceania | | 983 | 1 400 | 1 500 | 2 996 | 3 017 | Asie, Est/S.-Est/Océanie |
| Region not specified | | 472 | 256 | 504 | ... | ... | Région non spécifiée |
| Nigeria | VFN | | | | | | Nigéria |
| Total | | 2 045 543 | 2 253 115 | 2 646 411 | 2 778 365 | 3 055 800 | Total |
| Africa | | 1 450 814 | 1 554 308 | 1 825 312 | 1 916 246 | 2 107 870 | Afrique |
| Americas | | 80 412 | 94 486 | 111 020 | 116 563 | 129 219 | Amériques |
| Europe | | 317 317 | 372 846 | 438 093 | 459 985 | 506 000 | Europe |
| Asia, East/S.East/Oceania | | 110 832 | 130 228 | 153 020 | 160 666 | 177 001 | Asie, Est/S.-Est/Océanie |
| Southern Asia | | 44 701 | 52 523 | 61 714 | 64 796 | 72 000 | Asie du Sud |
| Western Asia | | 34 560 | 40 608 | 47 714 | 50 095 | 55 104 | Asie occidentale |
| Region not specified | | 6 907 | 8 116 | 9 538 | 10 014 | 8 606 | Région non spécifiée |
| Niue | TFR | | | | | | Nioué |
| Total[3,47] | | 2 084 | 2 706 | 2 550 | 2 793 | 3 008 | Total[3,47] |
| Americas | | 252 | 178 | 138 | 181 | 161 | Amériques |
| Europe | | 275 | 235 | 168 | 295 | 237 | Europe |
| Asia, East/S.East/Oceania | | 1 387 | 2 247 | 2 217 | 2 272 | 2 588 | Asie, Est/S.-Est/Océanie |
| Region not specified | | 170 | 46 | 27 | 45 | 22 | Région non spécifiée |
| Northern Mariana Islands | VFN | | | | | | Iles Mariannes du Nord |
| Total | | 475 547 | 459 458 | 535 873 | 506 846 | 435 494 | Total |
| Americas | | 36 451 | 34 670 | 37 334 | 37 989 | 32 582 | Amériques |
| Europe | | 598 | 439 | 666 | 1 300 | 2 324 | Europe |
| Asia, East/S.East/Oceania | | 437 322 | 422 811 | 494 826 | 465 360 | 398 952 | Asie, Est/S.-Est/Océanie |
| Region not specified | | 1 176 | 1 538 | 3 047 | 2 197 | 1 636 | Région non spécifiée |
| Norway | TFN | | | | | | Norvège |
| Total[48] | | 3 111 000 | 3 269 000 | 3 628 000 | 3 824 000 | 3 945 000 | Total[48] |
| Americas | | 126 000 | 144 000 | 176 000 | 146 000 | 163 000 | Amériques |
| Europe | | 2 865 000 | 3 009 000 | 3 307 000 | 3 508 000 | 3 591 000 | Europe |
| Asia, East/S.East/Oceania | | 35 000 | 35 000 | 35 000 | 41 000 | 37 000 | Asie, Est/S.-Est/Océanie |
| Region not specified | | 85 000 | 81 000 | 110 000 | 129 000 | 154 000 | Région non spécifiée |
| Occupied Palestinian Terr. | THSN | | | | | | Terr. palestinien occupé |
| Total | | 33 424 | 36 722 | 56 011 | 88 360 | 122 616 | Total |
| Africa | | 1 209 | 604 | 641 | 971 | 1 643 | Afrique |
| Americas | | 6 480 | 6 407 | 10 649 | 13 735 | 18 728 | Amériques |
| Europe | | 18 352 | 23 701 | 35 210 | 55 324 | 83 178 | Europe |
| Asia, East/S.East/Oceania | | 6 487 | 4 872 | 8 399 | 16 490 | 16 595 | Asie, Est/S.-Est/Océanie |
| Western Asia | | 896 | 1 138 | 1 112 | 1 840 | 2 472 | Asie occidentale |

| Country or area of destination and region of origin[&] | Series Série | 2002 | 2003 | 2004 | 2005 | 2006 | Pays ou zone de destination et région de provenance[&] |
|---|---|---|---|---|---|---|---|
| Oman | THSN | | | | | | Oman |
| Total | | 643 326 | 629 525 | 908 466 | 989 390 | 1 306 128 | Total |
| Africa | | 17 277 | 19 035 | 28 266 | 14 598 | 15 161 | Afrique |
| Americas | | 36 022 | 36 356 | 40 154 | 17 938 | 47 639 | Amériques |
| Europe | | 197 015 | 163 855 | 280 727 | 403 962 | 577 546 | Europe |
| Asia, East/S.East/Oceania | | 66 416 | 51 026 | 54 971 | 56 245 | 82 616 | Asie, Est/S.-Est/Océanie |
| Southern Asia | | 85 238 | 101 971 | 130 565 | 140 832 | 133 180 | Asie du Sud |
| Western Asia | | 192 817 | 204 586 | 249 285 | 240 506 | 230 777 | Asie occidentale |
| Region not specified | | 48 541 | 52 696 | 124 498 | 115 309 | 219 209 | Région non spécifiée |
| Pakistan | TFN | | | | | | Pakistan |
| Total | | 498 059 | 500 918 | 647 993 | 798 260 | 898 389 | Total |
| Africa | | 11 620 | 11 721 | 12 521 | 14 691 | 18 970 | Afrique |
| Americas | | 87 884 | 85 910 | 103 104 | 146 548 | 160 713 | Amériques |
| Europe | | 215 280 | 192 854 | 280 877 | 356 804 | 393 919 | Europe |
| Asia, East/S.East/Oceania | | 43 920 | 43 521 | 59 503 | 83 607 | 99 063 | Asie, Est/S.-Est/Océanie |
| Southern Asia | | 116 449 | 146 655 | 160 345 | 158 549 | 182 144 | Asie du Sud |
| Western Asia | | 22 329 | 19 593 | 28 365 | 31 920 | 37 661 | Asie occidentale |
| Region not specified | | 577 | 664 | 3 278 | 6 141 | 5 919 | Région non spécifiée |
| Palau | TFR | | | | | | Palaos |
| Total[49] | | 58 560 | 68 296 | 94 894 | 86 126 | 86 375 | Total[49] |
| Americas | | 4 774 | 4 511 | 6 507 | 5 910 | 7 019 | Amériques |
| Europe | | 834 | 818 | 1 837 | 2 390 | 2 493 | Europe |
| Asia, East/S.East/Oceania | | 51 504 | 61 400 | 84 449 | 75 503 | 75 542 | Asie, Est/S.-Est/Océanie |
| Region not specified | | 1 448 | 1 567 | 2 101 | 2 323 | 1 321 | Région non spécifiée |
| Panama | VFR | | | | | | Panama |
| Total[50] | | 426 154 | 468 686 | 498 415 | 576 050 | 703 745 | Total[50] |
| Africa | | 334 | 354 | 335 | 390 | 477 | Afrique |
| Americas | | 375 518 | 410 957 | 438 872 | 507 185 | 619 526 | Amériques |
| Europe | | 38 417 | 43 355 | 45 254 | 52 339 | 63 451 | Europe |
| Asia, East/S.East/Oceania | | 11 864 | 13 968 | 13 919 | 16 095 | 20 241 | Asie, Est/S.-Est/Océanie |
| Western Asia | | 21 | 52 | 35 | 41 | 50 | Asie occidentale |
| Papua New Guinea | TFR | | | | | | Papouasie-Nvl-Guinée |
| Total | | 53 761 | 56 282 | 59 013 | 69 251 | 77 731 | Total |
| Africa | | 271 | 193 | 241 | 353 | 500 | Afrique |
| Americas | | 6 990 | 5 215 | 5 440 | 6 491 | 7 348 | Amériques |
| Europe | | 4 733 | 4 218 | 4 739 | 4 155 | 5 498 | Europe |
| Asia, East/S.East/Oceania | | 39 316 | 45 999 | 47 963 | 57 516 | 63 383 | Asie, Est/S.-Est/Océanie |
| Southern Asia | | 2 451 | 657 | 630 | 736 | 1 002 | Asie du Sud |
| Paraguay | TFN | | | | | | Paraguay |
| Total[4,51] | | 250 423 | 268 175 | 309 287 | 340 845 | 388 465 | Total[4,51] |
| Africa | | 161 | 185 | 211 | 253 | 358 | Afrique |
| Americas | | 231 727 | 248 364 | 284 325 | 311 628 | 349 105 | Amériques |
| Europe | | 13 915 | 15 375 | 19 788 | 23 201 | 30 531 | Europe |
| Asia, East/S.East/Oceania | | 4 620 | 4 251 | 4 718 | 5 466 | 8 058 | Asie, Est/S.-Est/Océanie |
| Southern Asia | | ... | ... | 148 | 200 | 229 | Asie du Sud |
| Western Asia | | ... | ... | 96 | 97 | 184 | Asie occidentale |
| Region not specified | | ... | ... | 1 | ... | ... | Région non spécifiée |
| Peru | TFN | | | | | | Pérou |
| Total | | 997 628[52] | 1 069 517 | 1 276 639[53] | 1 486 502[53] | 1 634 745[53] | Total |
| Africa | | 1 889 | 2 127 | 2 703 | 3 347 | 3 025 | Afrique |
| Americas | | 713 555 | 762 290 | 928 818 | 1 066 044 | 1 190 018 | Amériques |
| Europe | | 236 157 | 252 435 | 281 039 | 340 095 | 353 533 | Europe |
| Asia, East/S.East/Oceania | | 44 454 | 49 918 | 61 781 | 73 618 | 81 627 | Asie, Est/S.-Est/Océanie |
| Southern Asia | | 1 320 | 1 294 | 1 237 | 1 825 | 1 931 | Asie du Sud |
| Western Asia | | 119 | 117 | 140 | 204 | 156 | Asie occidentale |
| Region not specified | | 134 | 1 336 | 921 | 1 369 | 4 455 | Région non spécifiée |

| Country or area of destination and region of origin[&] | Series Série | 2002 | 2003 | 2004 | 2005 | 2006 | Pays ou zone de destination et région de provenance[&] |
|---|---|---|---|---|---|---|---|
| Philippines | TFR | | | | | | Philippines |
| Total[1] | | 1 932 677 | 1 907 226 | 2 291 352 | 2 623 084 | 2 843 345 | Total[1] |
| Africa | | 1 465 | 1 442 | 1 700 | 2 294 | 2 246 | Afrique |
| Americas | | 453 667 | 444 264 | 545 867 | 604 793 | 651 705 | Amériques |
| Europe | | 183 910 | 177 338 | 212 305 | 246 449 | 264 353 | Europe |
| Asia, East/S.East/Oceania | | 1 154 439 | 1 128 540 | 1 359 256 | 1 565 359 | 1 690 939 | Asie, Est/S.-Est/Océanie |
| Southern Asia | | 20 822 | 21 543 | 24 997 | 28 485 | 31 975 | Asie du Sud |
| Western Asia | | 18 500 | 16 736 | 20 683 | 24 532 | 27 544 | Asie occidentale |
| Region not specified | | 99 874 | 117 363 | 126 544 | 151 172 | 174 583 | Région non spécifiée |
| Poland | TCER | | | | | | Pologne |
| Total | | 3 145 439 | 3 331 870 | 3 934 064 | 4 310 401 | 4 313 578 | Total |
| Africa | | 5 051 | 6 009 | 5 483 | 5 637 | 6 969 | Afrique |
| Americas | | 189 177 | 182 309 | 232 723 | 242 264 | 250 413 | Amériques |
| Europe | | 2 818 036 | 3 022 645 | 3 521 865 | 3 882 651 | 3 870 392 | Europe |
| Asia, East/S.East/Oceania | | 64 206 | 66 951 | 98 239 | 110 944 | 117 857 | Asie, Est/S.-Est/Océanie |
| Southern Asia | | 6 238 | 4 843 | 8 659 | 8 293 | 7 093 | Asie du Sud |
| Western Asia | | 2 621 | 3 780 | 4 403 | 3 648 | 5 742 | Asie occidentale |
| Region not specified | | 60 110 | 45 333 | 62 692 | 56 964 | 55 112 | Région non spécifiée |
| Poland | VFN | | | | | | Pologne |
| Total | | 50 734 623 | 52 129 778 | 61 917 759 | 64 606 085 | 65 114 865 | Total |
| Africa | | 8 699 | 9 538 | 11 114 | 13 217 | 14 914 | Afrique |
| Americas | | 272 329 | 294 313 | 345 181 | 439 417 | 466 299 | Amériques |
| Europe | | 50 315 365 | 51 691 151 | 61 385 787 | 63 926 773 | 64 366 590 | Europe |
| Asia, East/S.East/Oceania | | 87 430 | 88 693 | 123 114 | 163 414 | 193 899 | Asie, Est/S.-Est/Océanie |
| Southern Asia | | 8 875 | 9 483 | 11 710 | 13 219 | 15 246 | Asie du Sud |
| Western Asia | | 6 277 | 6 065 | 6 471 | 7 636 | 8 265 | Asie occidentale |
| Region not specified | | 35 648 | 30 535 | 34 382 | 42 409 | 49 652 | Région non spécifiée |
| Portugal | TFR | | | | | | Portugal |
| Total | | 11 644 231[2] | 11 707 228[2] | 10 639 000[9,54] | 10 612 000[9] | 11 282 000[9] | Total |
| Americas | | 463 847 | 480 544 | 367 000 | 413 000 | 499 000 | Amériques |
| Europe | | 10 849 103 | 10 887 861 | 9 343 000 | 9 271 000 | 9 831 000 | Europe |
| Asia, East/S.East/Oceania | | 43 964 | 40 055 | 43 000 | 37 000 | 32 000 | Asie, Est/S.-Est/Océanie |
| Region not specified | | 287 317 | 298 768 | 886 000 | 891 000 | 920 000 | Région non spécifiée |
| Puerto Rico | TFR | | | | | | Porto Rico |
| Total[3,55] | | 3 087 100 | 3 238 300 | 3 541 000 | 3 685 900 | 3 722 000 | Total[3,55] |
| Americas | | 2 230 400 | 2 470 500 | 2 754 400 | 2 847 400 | 2 929 900 | Amériques |
| Region not specified | | 856 700 | 767 800 | 786 600 | 838 500 | 792 100 | Région non spécifiée |
| Qatar | THSR | | | | | | Qatar |
| Total[56] | | 586 645 | 556 965 | 732 454 | 912 997 | 945 970 | Total[56] |
| Europe | | 102 983 | 88 620 | 195 732 | 233 315 | 201 187 | Europe |
| Asia, East/S.East/Oceania | | 107 832 | 127 348 | 145 974 | 159 279 | 180 543 | Asie, Est/S.-Est/Océanie |
| Western Asia | | 312 063 | 282 538 | 295 335 | 364 977 | 413 523 | Asie occidentale |
| Region not specified | | 63 767 | 58 459 | 95 413 | 155 426 | 150 717 | Région non spécifiée |
| Réunion | TFR | | | | | | Réunion |
| Total | | 426 000 | 432 000 | 430 000 | 409 000 | 278 800 | Total |
| Africa | | 30 625 | 27 367 | 26 222 | 24 815 | 20 109 | Afrique |
| Europe | | 356 828 | 366 725 | 370 474 | 349 113 | 224 065 | Europe |
| Region not specified | | 38 547 | 37 908 | 33 304 | 35 072 | 34 626 | Région non spécifiée |
| Romania | VFR | | | | | | Roumanie |
| Total | | 4 793 722 | 5 594 828 | 6 600 115 | 5 839 374 | 6 036 999 | Total |
| Africa | | 4 984 | 5 461 | 6 585 | 6 992 | 9 274 | Afrique |
| Americas | | 102 481 | 115 373 | 139 463 | 154 244 | 171 930 | Amériques |
| Europe | | 4 603 867 | 5 391 609 | 6 360 587 | 5 580 091 | 5 751 503 | Europe |
| Asia, East/S.East/Oceania | | 41 703 | 41 610 | 49 309 | 57 028 | 61 921 | Asie, Est/S.-Est/Océanie |
| Southern Asia | | 12 423 | 12 856 | 15 344 | 15 566 | 15 774 | Asie du Sud |
| Western Asia | | 27 105 | 26 867 | 27 760 | 24 090 | 25 049 | Asie occidentale |
| Region not specified | | 1 159 | 1 052 | 1 067 | 1 363 | 1 548 | Région non spécifiée |

| Country or area of destination and region of origin[&] | Series Série | 2002 | 2003 | 2004 | 2005 | 2006 | Pays ou zone de destination et région de provenance[&] |
|---|---|---|---|---|---|---|---|
| Russian Federation | VFN | | | | | | Fédération de Russie |
| Total | | 23 308 711 | 22 521 059 | 22 064 213 | 22 200 649 | 22 486 043 | Total |
| Africa | | 31 473 | 28 985 | 29 217 | 26 909 | 28 288 | Afrique |
| Americas | | 342 594 | 420 857 | 477 338 | 457 301 | 532 991 | Amériques |
| Europe | | 21 097 290 | 20 236 821 | 19 607 077 | 19 690 628 | 19 872 873 | Europe |
| Asia, East/S.East/Oceania | | 1 150 430 | 1 106 605 | 1 313 669 | 1 315 480 | 1 345 870 | Asie, Est/S.-Est/Océanie |
| Southern Asia | | 57 708 | 58 804 | 62 927 | 68 421 | 71 917 | Asie du Sud |
| Western Asia | | 28 312 | 31 792 | 31 765 | 33 405 | 33 029 | Asie occidentale |
| Region not specified | | 600 904 | 637 195 | 542 220 | 608 505 | 601 075 | Région non spécifiée |
| Saba | TFR | | | | | | Saba |
| Total | | 10 778 | 10 260 | 11 012 | 11 462 | ... | Total |
| Americas | | 4 380 | 4 106 | 4 764 | 4 933 | ... | Amériques |
| Europe | | 4 565 | 4 732 | 5 043 | 5 484 | ... | Europe |
| Region not specified | | 1 833 | 1 422 | 1 205 | 1 045 | ... | Région non spécifiée |
| Saint Eustatius | TFR | | | | | | Saint-Eustache |
| Total[57] | | 9 781 | 10 451 | 11 056 | 10 355 | 9 584 | Total[57] |
| Americas | | 3 403 | 3 483 | 3 732 | 3 457 | 3 177 | Amériques |
| Europe | | 4 600 | 5 272 | 5 505 | 5 400 | 4 851 | Europe |
| Region not specified | | 1 778 | 1 696 | 1 819 | 1 498 | 1 556 | Région non spécifiée |
| Saint Kitts and Nevis | TFR | | | | | | Saint-Kitts-et-Nevis |
| Total[3] | | 68 998 | 90 599 | 117 638 | 127 728 | 132 970 | Total[3] |
| Americas | | 60 023 | ... | 103 093 | 112 153 | 118 963 | Amériques |
| Europe | | 5 464 | ... | 13 181 | 11 553 | 12 030 | Europe |
| Region not specified | | 3 511 | 90 599 | 1 364 | 4 022 | 1 977 | Région non spécifiée |
| Saint Lucia | TFR | | | | | | Sainte-Lucie |
| Total[2] | | 253 463 | 276 948 | 298 431 | 317 939 | 302 510 | Total[2] |
| Americas | | 175 390 | 183 349 | 197 433 | 214 621 | 213 405 | Amériques |
| Europe | | 76 199 | 90 193 | 96 793 | 101 790 | 85 565 | Europe |
| Asia, East/S.East/Oceania | | 278 | 373 | 282 | 260 | ... | Asie, Est/S.-Est/Océanie |
| Region not specified | | 1 596 | 3 033 | 3 923 | 1 268 | 3 540 | Région non spécifiée |
| Saint Maarten | TFN | | | | | | Saint-Martin |
| Total[58] | | 380 801 | 427 587 | 475 032 | 467 861 | 467 804 | Total[58] |
| Americas | | 259 506 | 301 018 | 338 241 | 331 841 | 328 450 | Amériques |
| Europe | | 87 147 | 88 259 | 96 404 | 93 821 | 97 058 | Europe |
| Region not specified | | 34 148 | 38 310 | 40 387 | 42 199 | 42 296 | Région non spécifiée |
| St. Vincent-Grenadines | TFR | | | | | | St. Vincent-Grenadines |
| Total[3] | | 77 631 | 78 535 | 86 722 | 95 506 | 97 432 | Total[3] |
| Americas | | 58 465 | 60 315 | 66 871 | 74 173 | 74 193 | Amériques |
| Europe | | 17 997 | 17 201 | 18 652 | 19 928 | 21 961 | Europe |
| Region not specified | | 1 169 | 1 019 | 1 199 | 1 405 | 1 278 | Région non spécifiée |
| Samoa | TFR | | | | | | Samoa |
| Total | | 88 971 | 92 486 | 98 155 | 101 807 | 115 882 | Total |
| Americas | | 9 095 | 8 959 | 8 311 | 9 682 | 9 067 | Amériques |
| Europe | | 4 762 | 5 136 | 4 756 | 4 632 | 4 581 | Europe |
| Asia, East/S.East/Oceania | | 74 833 | 78 155 | 84 882 | 87 217 | 101 915 | Asie, Est/S.-Est/Océanie |
| Region not specified | | 281 | 236 | 206 | 276 | 319 | Région non spécifiée |
| San Marino | VFN | | | | | | Saint-Marin |
| Total[59] | | 3 102 453 | 2 882 207 | 2 812 488 | 2 107 092[19] | 2 135 589 | Total[59] |
| Africa | | ... | ... | ... | 111 | 140 | Afrique |
| Americas | | ... | ... | ... | 17 479 | 22 131 | Amériques |
| Europe | | ... | ... | ... | 2 035 386 | 2 075 681 | Europe |
| Asia, East/S.East/Oceania | | ... | ... | ... | 53 328 | 36 340 | Asie, Est/S.-Est/Océanie |
| Southern Asia | | ... | ... | ... | 436 | ... | Asie du Sud |
| Western Asia | | ... | ... | ... | 270 | 88 | Asie occidentale |
| Region not specified | | 3 102 453 | 2 882 207 | 2 812 488 | 82 | 1 209 | Région non spécifiée |

| Country or area of destination and region of origin& | Series Série | 2002 | 2003 | 2004 | 2005 | 2006 | Pays ou zone de destination et région de provenance& |
|---|---|---|---|---|---|---|---|
| Sao Tome and Principe | TFN | | | | | | Sao Tomé-et-Principe |
| Total | | 9 189 | 10 039 | 10 576 | . 15 746 | 12 266 | Total |
| Africa | | 1 938 | 2 550 | 2 076 | 4 361 | 2 751 | Afrique |
| Americas | | 251 | 638 | 710 | 580 | 525 | Amériques |
| Europe | | 5 429 | 6 742 | 6 803 | 10 299 | 7 568 | Europe |
| Asia, East/S.East/Oceania | | ... | ... | ... | 156 | ... | Asie, Est/S.-Est/Océanie |
| Southern Asia | | ... | ... | ... | 23 | ... | Asie du Sud |
| Western Asia | | ... | ... | ... | 35 | ... | Asie occidentale |
| Region not specified | | 1 571 | 109 | 987 | 292 | 1 422 | Région non spécifiée |
| Saudi Arabia | TFN | | | | | | Arabie saoudite |
| Total | | 7 511 299 | 7 332 233 | 8 599 430 | 8 036 613 | 8 620 465 | Total |
| Africa | | 606 791 | 525 045 | 675 441 | 436 292 | 488 751 | Afrique |
| Americas | | 51 981 | 46 496 | 53 190 | 70 196 | 66 464 | Amériques |
| Europe | | 338 580 | 334 159 | 424 297 | 340 310 | 484 575 | Europe |
| Asia, East/S.East/Oceania | | 660 329 | 612 340 | 752 905 | 439 021 | 595 438 | Asie, Est/S.-Est/Océanie |
| Southern Asia | | 1 618 928 | 1 868 897 | 1 932 990 | 1 142 202 | 1 469 257 | Asie du Sud |
| Western Asia | | 4 212 598 | 3 923 873 | 4 752 257 | 5 607 356 | 5 515 980 | Asie occidentale |
| Region not specified | | 22 092 | 21 423 | 8 350 | 1 236 | ... | Région non spécifiée |
| Senegal | TFN | | | | | | Sénégal |
| Total | | ... | ... | 666 616 | 769 489 | 866 154 | Total |
| Africa | | ... | ... | 209 226 | 265 113 | 429 955 | Afrique |
| Americas | | ... | ... | 24 686 | 26 274 | 25 921 | Amériques |
| Europe | | ... | ... | 348 852 | 392 767 | 323 721 | Europe |
| Region not specified | | ... | ... | 83 852 | 85 335 | 86 557 | Région non spécifiée |
| Senegal | THSN | | | | | | Sénégal |
| Total | | 426 825 | 353 539 | 363 490 | 386 565 | 405 827 | Total |
| Africa | | 86 037 | 85 664 | 89 660 | 87 565 | 106 396 | Afrique |
| Americas | | 9 536 | 10 025 | 12 431 | 13 989 | 14 684 | Amériques |
| Europe | | 322 631 | 252 568 | 242 944 | 274 439 | 271 231 | Europe |
| Asia, East/S.East/Oceania | | 1 864 | 2 273 | 3 705 | 3 837 | 3 846 | Asie, Est/S.-Est/Océanie |
| Western Asia | | 994 | 1 253 | 1 672 | 1 467 | 1 882 | Asie occidentale |
| Region not specified | | 5 763 | 1 756 | 13 078 | 5 268 | 7 788 | Région non spécifiée |
| Serbia | TCEN | | | | | | Serbie-et-Monténégro |
| Total | | 312 063 | 339 283 | 391 826 | 452 679 | 468 842 | Total |
| Americas | | 11 587 | 14 155 | 13 483 | 15 789 | 17 038 | Amériques |
| Europe | | 288 380 | 312 666 | 363 345 | 419 058 | 435 400 | Europe |
| Asia, East/S.East/Oceania | | 2 966 | 3 680 | 4 879 | 5 675 | 6 402 | Asie, Est/S.-Est/Océanie |
| Region not specified | | 9 130 | 8 782 | 10 119 | 12 157 | 10 002 | Région non spécifiée |
| Seychelles | TFR | | | | | | Seychelles |
| Total | | 132 246 | 122 038 | 120 765 | 128 654 | 140 627 | Total |
| Africa | | 13 819 | 13 578 | 12 598 | 12 478 | 13 408 | Afrique |
| Americas | | 3 670 | 3 477 | 4 030 | 3 867 | 3 398 | Amériques |
| Europe | | 108 246 | 99 961 | 98 654 | 103 581 | 114 211 | Europe |
| Asia, East/S.East/Oceania | | 2 678 | 1 977 | 2 135 | 2 647 | 2 996 | Asie, Est/S.-Est/Océanie |
| Southern Asia | | 1 810 | 1 275 | 1 437 | 1 623 | 1 883 | Asie du Sud |
| Western Asia | | 2 023 | 1 770 | 1 911 | 4 458 | 4 731 | Asie occidentale |
| Sierra Leone | TFR | | | | | | Sierra Leone |
| Total[3] | | 28 463 | 38 107 | 43 560 | 40 023 | 33 704 | Total[3] |
| Africa | | 13 519 | 23 341 | 24 446 | 21 798 | 10 122 | Afrique |
| Americas | | 3 785 | 4 699 | 4 790 | 4 713 | 6 669 | Amériques |
| Europe | | 7 403 | 6 460 | 9 476 | 9 879 | 10 470 | Europe |
| Asia, East/S.East/Oceania | | 2 134 | 1 995 | 2 257 | 2 343 | 4 898 | Asie, Est/S.-Est/Océanie |
| Western Asia | | 1 622 | 1 612 | 2 591 | 1 290 | 1 545 | Asie occidentale |
| Singapore | VFR | | | | | | Singapour |
| Total[60] | | 7 567 110 | 6 127 288 | 8 328 658 | 8 943 029 | 9 750 967 | Total[60] |
| Africa | | 70 117 | 55 997 | 70 626 | 78 803 | 87 132 | Afrique |

| Country or area of destination and region of origin[&] | Series Série | 2002 | 2003 | 2004 | 2005 | 2006 | Pays ou zone de destination et région de provenance[&] |
|---|---|---|---|---|---|---|---|
| Americas | | 416 375 | 314 728 | 422 167 | 470 493 | 509 771 | Amériques |
| Europe | | 1 112 156 | 885 146 | 1 081 336 | 1 136 024 | 1 220 159 | Europe |
| Asia, East/S.East/Oceania | | 5 426 216 | 4 426 234 | 6 072 654 | 6 445 012 | 7 012 090 | Asie, Est/S.-Est/Océanie |
| Southern Asia | | 490 262 | 415 151 | 626 153 | 751 437 | 849 798 | Asie du Sud |
| Western Asia | | 46 770 | 29 844 | 55 449 | 56 165 | 65 923 | Asie occidentale |
| Region not specified | | 5 214 | 188 | 273 | 5 095 | 6 094 | Région non spécifiée |
| Slovakia | TCEN | | | | | | Slovaquie |
| Total | | 1 398 740 | 1 386 791 | 1 401 189 | 1 514 980 | 1 611 808 | Total |
| Africa | | 2 960 | 2 581 | 2 482 | 2 252 | 2 726 | Afrique |
| Americas | | 33 352 | 33 981 | 38 712 | 42 100 | 39 118 | Amériques |
| Europe | | 1 326 492 | 1 316 120 | 1 316 705 | 1 412 628 | 1 499 394 | Europe |
| Asia, East/S.East/Oceania | | 34 130 | 32 258 | 42 249 | 55 992 | 69 102 | Asie, Est/S.-Est/Océanie |
| Southern Asia | | 1 437 | 1 305 | 384 | 603 | 443 | Asie du Sud |
| Western Asia | | 224 | 241 | 314 | 328 | 272 | Asie occidentale |
| Region not specified | | 145 | 305 | 343 | 1 077 | 753 | Région non spécifiée |
| Slovenia | TCEN | | | | | | Slovénie |
| Total | | 1 302 019 | 1 373 137 | 1 498 852 | 1 554 969 | 1 616 650 | Total |
| Africa | | ... | ... | ... | 1 546 | 1 409 | Afrique |
| Americas | | 36 232 | 35 945 | 45 880 | 59 303 | 67 159 | Amériques |
| Europe | | 1 235 856 | 1 307 775 | 1 410 671 | 1 454 494 | 1 495 711 | Europe |
| Asia, East/S.East/Oceania | | 17 430 | 17 141 | 24 237 | 39 626 | 52 371 | Asie, Est/S.-Est/Océanie |
| Region not specified | | 12 501 | 12 276 | 18 064 | ... | ... | Région non spécifiée |
| Solomon Islands | TFR | | | | | | Iles Salomon |
| Total | | ... | 6 595 | ... | 9 400[61] | 11 482 | Total |
| Americas | | ... | 600 | ... | 642 | 879 | Amériques |
| Europe | | ... | 464 | ... | 545 | 708 | Europe |
| Asia, East/S.East/Oceania | | ... | 5 406 | ... | 8 128 | 9 755 | Asie, Est/S.-Est/Océanie |
| Region not specified | | ... | 125 | ... | 85 | 140 | Région non spécifiée |
| South Africa | TFR | | | | | | Afrique du Sud |
| Total[62] | | 6 429 583 | 6 504 890 | 6 677 844 | 7 368 742 | 8 395 833 | Total[62] |
| Africa | | 4 452 762 | 4 450 212 | 4 638 371 | 5 370 137 | 6 280 500 | Afrique |
| Americas | | 254 586 | 262 496 | 290 625 | 322 099 | 358 096 | Amériques |
| Europe | | 1 274 365 | 1 338 976 | 1 306 389 | 1 328 521 | 1 402 643 | Europe |
| Asia, East/S.East/Oceania | | 229 128 | 224 610 | 238 829 | 238 885 | 257 666 | Asie, Est/S.-Est/Océanie |
| Southern Asia | | 34 062 | 41 018 | 36 172 | 36 045 | 44 337 | Asie du Sud |
| Western Asia | | 14 955 | 15 048 | 16 037 | 17 194 | 19 806 | Asie occidentale |
| Region not specified | | 169 725 | 172 530 | 151 421 | 55 861 | 32 785 | Région non spécifiée |
| Spain | TFR | | | | | | Espagne |
| Total | | 52 326 766 | 50 853 822 | 52 429 836 | 55 913 780 | 58 190 469 | Total |
| Americas | | 2 079 643 | 1 893 950 | 2 079 065 | 2 232 851 | 2 383 760 | Amériques |
| Europe | | 49 303 582 | 47 835 345 | 49 238 605 | 52 189 873 | 54 361 593 | Europe |
| Asia, East/S.East/Oceania | | 240 637 | 237 392 | 150 583 | 181 050 | 257 200 | Asie, Est/S.-Est/Océanie |
| Region not specified | | 702 904 | 887 135 | 961 583 | 1 310 006 | 1 187 916 | Région non spécifiée |
| Sri Lanka | TFR | | | | | | Sri Lanka |
| Total[2] | | 393 171 | 500 642 | 566 202 | 549 308 | 559 603 | Total[2] |
| Africa | | 1 611 | 1 991 | 1 855 | 2 340 | 3 235 | Afrique |
| Americas | | 20 421 | 25 744 | 30 500 | 47 162 | 36 098 | Amériques |
| Europe | | 208 374 | 265 802 | 298 776 | 236 481 | 242 666 | Europe |
| Asia, East/S.East/Oceania | | 66 084 | 84 145 | 91 076 | 99 736 | 98 476 | Asie, Est/S.-Est/Océanie |
| Southern Asia | | 90 189 | 116 171 | 133 532 | 153 353 | 168 783 | Asie du Sud |
| Western Asia | | 6 492 | 6 789 | 10 463 | 10 236 | 10 345 | Asie occidentale |
| Sudan | TFN | | | | | | Soudan |
| Total | | 51 580 | 52 291 | 60 577 | 245 798[9] | 328 148[9] | Total |
| Africa | | 7 000 | 7 000 | 9 000 | 58 991 | 50 665 | Afrique |
| Americas | | ... | ... | ... | 20 751 | 11 607 | Amériques |
| Europe | | 12 000 | 14 000 | 17 000 | 55 796 | 43 719 | Europe |
| Asia, East/S.East/Oceania | | 13 000 | 14 000 | 17 000 | 109 380 | 222 157 | Asie, Est/S.-Est/Océanie |

| Country or area of destination and region of origin& | Series Série | 2002 | 2003 | 2004 | 2005 | 2006 | Pays ou zone de destination et région de provenance& |
|---|---|---|---|---|---|---|---|
| Region not specified | | 19 580 | 17 291 | 17 577 | 880 | ... | Région non spécifiée |
| Suriname | TFR | | | | | | Suriname |
| Total | | ... | ... | 137 808 | 160 022 | ... | Total |
| Africa | | ... | ... | ... | 279 | ... | Afrique |
| Americas | | ... | ... | 44 802 | 56 338 | ... | Amériques |
| Europe | | ... | ... | 86 913 | 99 265 | ... | Europe |
| Asia, East/S.East/Oceania | | ... | ... | ... | 3 247 | ... | Asie, Est/S.-Est/Océanie |
| Southern Asia | | ... | ... | ... | 498 | ... | Asie du Sud |
| Region not specified | | ... | ... | 6 093 | 395 | ... | Région non spécifiée |
| Suriname | TFN | | | | | | Suriname |
| Total[63] | | 60 223 | 82 298 | 74 887 | ... | ... | Total[63] |
| Africa | | 32 | 187 | 177 | ... | ... | Afrique |
| Americas | | 4 307 | 6 903 | 7 986 | ... | ... | Amériques |
| Europe | | 54 477 | 74 153 | 64 011 | ... | ... | Europe |
| Asia, East/S.East/Oceania | | 1 306 | 998 | 2 522 | ... | ... | Asie, Est/S.-Est/Océanie |
| Southern Asia | | 68 | 55 | 165 | ... | ... | Asie du Sud |
| Region not specified | | 33 | 2 | 26 | ... | ... | Région non spécifiée |
| Swaziland | THSR | | | | | | Swaziland |
| Total[56] | | 255 927 | 218 813 | 352 040 | 311 656 | 316 082 | Total[56] |
| Africa | | 173 420 | 110 054 | 151 879 | 134 456 | 167 347 | Afrique |
| Americas | | 10 380 | 11 092 | 4 968 | 4 398 | 3 576 | Amériques |
| Europe | | 40 483 | 87 999 | 110 709 | 98 009 | 114 249 | Europe |
| Asia, East/S.East/Oceania | | 5 244 | 2 343 | 3 485 | 3 085 | 5 423 | Asie, Est/S.-Est/Océanie |
| Region not specified | | 26 400 | 7 325 | 80 999 | 71 708 | 25 487 | Région non spécifiée |
| Sweden | TFR | | | | | | Suède |
| Total[64] | | 7 459 000 | 7 627 000 | ... | ... | ... | Total[64] |
| Africa | | 42 000 | 46 000 | ... | ... | ... | Afrique |
| Americas | | 413 000 | 467 000 | ... | ... | ... | Amériques |
| Europe | | 6 656 000 | 6 696 000 | ... | ... | ... | Europe |
| Asia, East/S.East/Oceania | | 348 000 | 380 000 | ... | ... | ... | Asie, Est/S.-Est/Océanie |
| Region not specified | | ... | 38 000 | ... | ... | ... | Région non spécifiée |
| Switzerland | THSR | | | | | | Suisse |
| Total | | 6 867 696[65] | 6 530 108[65] | ... | 7 228 851[66] | 7 862 957[66] | Total |
| Africa | | 74 195 | 72 786 | ... | 78 143 | 85 460 | Afrique |
| Americas | | 871 279 | 757 015 | ... | 829 551 | 933 715 | Amériques |
| Europe | | 4 906 368 | 4 821 157 | ... | 5 304 949 | 5 747 455 | Europe |
| Asia, East/S.East/Oceania | | 865 244 | 727 005 | ... | 846 703 | 896 031 | Asie, Est/S.-Est/Océanie |
| Southern Asia | | 80 430 | 84 685 | ... | 93 472 | 115 055 | Asie du Sud |
| Western Asia | | 70 180 | 67 460 | ... | 76 033 | 85 241 | Asie occidentale |
| Syrian Arab Republic | TCEN | | | | | | Rép. arabe syrienne |
| Total[67,68] | | 1 657 779 | 2 084 956 | 3 029 964 | 3 367 935 | 4 422 482 | Total[67,68] |
| Africa | | 63 008 | 73 487 | 89 664 | 92 585 | 71 796 | Afrique |
| Americas | | 16 577 | 43 901 | 57 032 | 57 795 | 54 583 | Amériques |
| Europe | | 113 436 | 204 445 | 313 956 | 430 120 | 467 151 | Europe |
| Asia, East/S.East/Oceania | | 6 228 | 25 897 | 36 852 | 35 088 | 32 378 | Asie, Est/S.-Est/Océanie |
| Southern Asia | | 293 628 | 228 357 | 217 947 | 268 952 | 264 998 | Asie du Sud |
| Western Asia | | 1 055 832 | 1 470 289 | 2 259 703 | 2 416 358 | 3 458 290 | Asie occidentale |
| Region not specified | | 109 070 | 38 580 | 54 810 | 67 037 | 73 286 | Région non spécifiée |
| Syrian Arab Republic | VFN | | | | | | Rép. arabe syrienne |
| Total[2,67] | | 4 272 911 | 4 388 119 | 6 153 653 | 5 837 980 | 6 009 483 | Total[2,67] |
| Africa | | 71 089 | 73 487 | 89 664 | 92 585 | 81 136 | Afrique |
| Americas | | 44 588 | 43 901 | 58 032 | 57 795 | 59 408 | Amériques |
| Europe | | 645 942 | 651 800 | 933 239 | 946 853 | 709 697 | Europe |
| Asia, East/S.East/Oceania | | 27 767 | 25 897 | 36 852 | 35 088 | 35 155 | Asie, Est/S.-Est/Océanie |
| Southern Asia | | 340 457 | 228 357 | 217 947 | 268 952 | 289 658 | Asie du Sud |
| Western Asia | | 3 093 856 | 3 325 490 | 4 760 773 | 4 369 669 | 4 734 283 | Asie occidentale |
| Region not specified | | 49 212 | 39 187 | 57 146 | 67 038 | 100 146 | Région non spécifiée |

| Country or area of destination and region of origin& | Series Série | 2002 | 2003 | 2004 | 2005 | 2006 | Pays ou zone de destination et région de provenance& |
|---|---|---|---|---|---|---|---|
| Thailand | TFR | | | | | | Thaïlande |
| Total | | 10 872 976[1] | 10 082 109[1] | 11 737 413[1] | 11 567 341[1] | 13 821 802[2] | Total |
| Africa | | 89 153 | 67 121 | 82 711 | 72 875 | 96 117 | Afrique |
| Americas | | 640 142 | 576 587 | 692 792 | 739 703 | 825 079 | Amériques |
| Europe | | 2 549 488 | 2 320 807 | 2 706 062 | 2 778 693 | 3 439 010 | Europe |
| Asia, East/S.East/Oceania | | 6 955 363 | 6 510 375 | 7 500 966 | 7 194 866 | 8 568 558 | Asie, Est/S.-Est/Océanie |
| Southern Asia | | 413 741 | 411 224 | 495 473 | 552 081 | 653 867 | Asie du Sud |
| Western Asia | | 151 180 | 118 339 | 172 699 | 178 718 | 239 171 | Asie occidentale |
| Region not specified | | 73 909 | 77 656 | 86 710 | 50 405 | ... | Région non spécifiée |
| TFYR of Macedonia | TCEN | | | | | | L'ex-R.y. Macédoine |
| Total | | 122 861 | 157 692 | 165 306 | 197 216 | 202 357 | Total |
| Americas | | 7 773 | 8 373 | 8 362 | 8 439 | 9 181 | Amériques |
| Europe | | 110 878 | 143 387 | 151 215 | 182 534 | 186 519 | Europe |
| Asia, East/S.East/Oceania | | 1 566 | 2 362 | 2 143 | 2 747 | 3 490 | Asie, Est/S.-Est/Océanie |
| Region not specified | | 2 644 | 3 570 | 3 586 | 3 496 | 3 167 | Région non spécifiée |
| Togo | THSR | | | | | | Togo |
| Total | | 57 539 | 60 592 | 82 686 | 80 763 | 94 096 | Total |
| Africa | | 28 636 | 31 334 | 43 842 | 45 967 | 52 549 | Afrique |
| Americas | | 1 975 | 1 785 | 2 738 | 2 633 | 3 314 | Amériques |
| Europe | | 24 097 | 24 484 | 30 018 | 27 092 | 33 266 | Europe |
| Asia, East/S.East/Oceania | | 1 125 | 1 452 | 3 492 | 2 627 | 3 205 | Asie, Est/S.-Est/Océanie |
| Western Asia | | 1 680 | 1 495 | 2 500 | 2 371 | 1 635 | Asie occidentale |
| Region not specified | | 26 | 42 | 96 | 73 | 127 | Région non spécifiée |
| Tonga | TFR | | | | | | Tonga |
| Total[3] | | 36 588 | 40 110 | 41 208 | 41 862 | 39 451 | Total[3] |
| Africa | | 92 | ... | ... | ... | ... | Afrique |
| Americas | | 7 860 | 7 930 | 8 202 | 8 147 | 6 345 | Amériques |
| Europe | | 4 082 | 4 131 | 3 408 | 2 908 | 2 875 | Europe |
| Asia, East/S.East/Oceania | | 24 477 | 27 932 | 28 972 | 30 424 | 29 720 | Asie, Est/S.-Est/Océanie |
| Southern Asia | | 77 | ... | ... | ... | ... | Asie du Sud |
| Region not specified | | ... | 117 | 626 | 383 | 511 | Région non spécifiée |
| Trinidad and Tobago | TFR | | | | | | Trinité-et-Tobago |
| Total[3] | | 384 212 | 409 069 | 442 596 | 463 191 | 457 434 | Total[3] |
| Africa | | 997 | 935 | 1 017 | 1 299 | 1 389 | Afrique |
| Americas | | 308 018 | 324 175 | 347 181 | 365 311 | 364 888 | Amériques |
| Europe | | 71 133 | 79 236 | 89 512 | 91 424 | 84 243 | Europe |
| Asia, East/S.East/Oceania | | 2 670 | 3 313 | 2 925 | 3 046 | 4 082 | Asie, Est/S.-Est/Océanie |
| Southern Asia | | 1 164 | 1 136 | 1 411 | 1 632 | 2 365 | Asie du Sud |
| Western Asia | | 219 | 239 | 221 | 338 | 363 | Asie occidentale |
| Region not specified | | 11 | 35 | 329 | 141 | 104 | Région non spécifiée |
| Tunisia | TFN | | | | | | Tunisie |
| Total[2] | | 5 063 538 | 5 114 304 | 5 997 918 | 6 378 430 | 6 549 549 | Total[2] |
| Africa | | 786 053 | 872 251 | 984 538 | 993 378 | 1 010 195 | Afrique |
| Americas | | 21 920 | 23 217 | 30 347 | 35 202 | 33 947 | Amériques |
| Europe | | 2 918 526 | 2 840 307 | 3 482 041 | 3 869 030 | 3 956 274 | Europe |
| Asia, East/S.East/Oceania | | 7 167 | 9 389 | 10 784 | 13 710 | 15 442 | Asie, Est/S.-Est/Océanie |
| Western Asia | | 1 310 607 | 1 355 878 | 1 471 752 | 1 440 387 | 1 507 155 | Asie occidentale |
| Region not specified | | 19 265 | 13 262 | 18 456 | 26 723 | 26 536 | Région non spécifiée |
| Turkey | TFN | | | | | | Turquie |
| Total | | 12 789 827 | 13 340 956 | 16 826 062 | 20 272 877 | 18 916 436 | Total |
| Africa | | 130 758 | 119 122 | 131 148 | 154 489 | 152 983 | Afrique |
| Americas | | 253 804 | 213 136 | 282 586 | 390 884 | 458 898 | Amériques |
| Europe | | 11 359 447 | 11 871 694 | 14 946 162 | 17 663 077 | 16 268 842 | Europe |
| Asia, East/S.East/Oceania | | 280 607 | 241 996 | 288 326 | 421 643 | 471 280 | Asie, Est/S.-Est/Océanie |
| Southern Asia | | 450 787 | 522 054 | 660 787 | 994 620 | 917 360 | Asie du Sud |
| Western Asia | | 303 860 | 359 281 | 498 095 | 625 686 | 630 140 | Asie occidentale |
| Region not specified | | 10 564 | 13 673 | 18 958 | 22 478 | 16 933 | Région non spécifiée |

| Country or area of destination and region of origin& | Series Série | 2002 | 2003 | 2004 | 2005 | 2006 | Pays ou zone de destination et région de provenance& |
|---|---|---|---|---|---|---|---|
| Turkmenistan | TFN | | | | | | Turkménistan |
| Total | | 10 791 | 8 214 | 14 799 | 11 611 | ... | Total |
| Africa | | ... | ... | ... | 1 | ... | Afrique |
| Americas | | 249 | 207 | 374 | 384 | ... | Amériques |
| Europe | | 2 344 | 1 855 | 3 915 | 3 284 | ... | Europe |
| Asia, East/S.East/Oceania | | 545 | 466 | 1 053 | 753 | ... | Asie, Est/S.-Est/Océanie |
| Southern Asia | | 7 631 | 5 649 | 9 425 | 7 185 | ... | Asie du Sud |
| Western Asia | | 22 | 37 | 32 | 4 | ... | Asie occidentale |
| Turks and Caicos Islands | TFR | | | | | | Iles Turques et Caïques |
| Total | | 154 961 | 164 100 | 173 081 | 176 130 | 248 343 | Total |
| Americas | | 139 901 | 149 072 | 148 711 | 156 674 | 221 372 | Amériques |
| Europe | | 10 548 | 12 626 | 13 807 | 17 613 | 24 834 | Europe |
| Asia, East/S.East/Oceania | | 35 | ... | ... | ... | ... | Asie, Est/S.-Est/Océanie |
| Region not specified | | 4 477 | 2 402 | 10 563 | 1 843 | 2 137 | Région non spécifiée |
| Tuvalu | TFN | | | | | | Tuvalu |
| Total | | 1 313 | 1 377 | 1 290 | 1 085 | 1 135 | Total |
| Americas | | 92 | 130 | 79 | 101 | 63 | Amériques |
| Europe | | 108 | 97 | 108 | 104 | 120 | Europe |
| Asia, East/S.East/Oceania | | 1 075 | 1 101 | 1 043 | 828 | 858 | Asie, Est/S.-Est/Océanie |
| Region not specified | | 38 | 49 | 60 | 52 | 94 | Région non spécifiée |
| Uganda | TFR | | | | | | Ouganda |
| Total | | 254 212 | 304 656 | 512 379 | 467 728 | 538 586 | Total |
| Africa | | 192 278 | 233 043 | 405 706 | 337 188 | 397 031 | Afrique |
| Americas | | 14 785 | 16 409 | 23 438 | 28 557 | 35 749 | Amériques |
| Europe | | 33 850 | 39 207 | 48 847 | 62 312 | 71 131 | Europe |
| Asia, East/S.East/Oceania | | 4 188 | 4 845 | 8 150 | 10 046 | 12 003 | Asie, Est/S.-Est/Océanie |
| Southern Asia | | 6 439 | 7 647 | 12 139 | 13 879 | 14 339 | Asie du Sud |
| Western Asia | | 1 836 | 1 976 | 3 133 | 3 766 | 4 111 | Asie occidentale |
| Region not specified | | 836 | 1 529 | 10 966 | 11 980 | 4 222 | Région non spécifiée |
| Ukraine | TFR | | | | | | Ukraine |
| Total | | 10 516 665 | 12 513 883 | 15 629 213 | 17 630 760 | 18 900 263 | Total |
| Africa | | 4 748 | 12 367 | 6 586 | 7 259 | 10 696 | Afrique |
| Americas | | 52 632 | 83 451 | 99 135 | 95 540 | 140 633 | Amériques |
| Europe | | 10 408 714 | 12 345 396 | 15 450 129 | 17 442 407 | 18 655 155 | Europe |
| Asia, East/S.East/Oceania | | 21 900 | 26 362 | 32 494 | 34 946 | 40 956 | Asie, Est/S.-Est/Océanie |
| Southern Asia | | 9 866 | 13 978 | 13 434 | 14 544 | 14 490 | Asie du Sud |
| Western Asia | | 14 777 | 18 720 | 20 130 | 25 501 | 22 209 | Asie occidentale |
| Region not specified | | 4 028 | 13 609 | 7 305 | 10 563 | 16 124 | Région non spécifiée |
| United Arab Emirates | THSN | | | | | | Emirats arabes unis |
| Total[69] | | 5 445 367 | 5 871 023 | 6 195 006 | ... | ... | Total[69] |
| Africa | | 310 722 | 306 872 | 315 418 | ... | ... | Afrique |
| Americas | | 238 749 | 254 362 | 285 627 | ... | ... | Amériques |
| Europe | | 1 468 015 | 1 584 792 | 2 007 600 | ... | ... | Europe |
| Asia, East/S.East/Oceania | | 395 061 | 427 506 | 444 575 | ... | ... | Asie, Est/S.-Est/Océanie |
| Southern Asia | | 807 094 | 921 698 | 909 339 | ... | ... | Asie du Sud |
| Western Asia | | 1 556 533 | 1 583 258 | 1 544 557 | ... | ... | Asie occidentale |
| Region not specified | | 669 193 | 792 535 | 687 890 | ... | ... | Région non spécifiée |
| United Kingdom | VFR | | | | | | Royaume-Uni |
| Total | | 24 181 000 | 24 715 000 | 27 754 000 | 29 970 000 | 32 712 919 | Total |
| Africa | | 631 000 | 569 000 | 639 000 | 654 000 | 701 468 | Afrique |
| Americas | | 4 619 000 | 4 326 000 | 4 692 000 | 4 597 000 | 5 166 674 | Amériques |
| Europe | | 16 409 000 | 17 371 000 | 19 582 000 | 21 742 000 | 23 541 245 | Europe |
| Asia, East/S.East/Oceania | | 1 854 000 | 1 809 000 | 2 086 000 | 2 190 000 | 2 310 449 | Asie, Est/S.-Est/Océanie |
| Southern Asia | | 308 000 | 294 000 | 371 000 | 407 000 | 521 228 | Asie du Sud |
| Western Asia | | 360 000 | 346 000 | 384 000 | 380 000 | 471 855 | Asie occidentale |
| United Rep. of Tanzania | VFR | | | | | | Rép.-Unie de Tanzanie |
| Total | | 575 296 | 576 198 | 582 807 | 612 754 | 644 124 | Total |
| Africa | | 249 601 | 267 940 | 256 455 | 275 718 | 293 440 | Afrique |

| Country or area of destination and region of origin[&] | Series Série | 2002 | 2003 | 2004 | 2005 | 2006 | Pays ou zone de destination et région de provenance[&] |
|---|---|---|---|---|---|---|---|
| Americas | | 59 077 | 49 781 | 53 437 | 61 604 | 71 278 | Amériques |
| Europe | | 191 982 | 191 025 | 221 865 | 220 255 | 229 048 | Europe |
| Asia, East/S.East/Oceania | | 30 087 | 27 208 | 22 928 | 24 714 | 28 222 | Asie, Est/S.-Est/Océanie |
| Southern Asia | | 27 867 | 26 502 | 16 528 | 19 935 | 15 321 | Asie du Sud |
| Western Asia | | 16 682 | 13 742 | 11 594 | 10 528 | 6 815 | Asie occidentale |
| United States | TFR | | | | | | Etats-Unis |
| Total | | 43 580 707 | 41 218 213 | 46 086 257 | 49 205 528 | 50 977 532 | Total |
| Africa | | 241 011 | 236 067 | 240 488 | 251 654 | 251 841 | Afrique |
| Americas | | 28 035 856 | 26 368 298 | 29 195 830 | 31 178 408 | 33 128 737 | Amériques |
| Europe | | 8 964 202 | 8 981 711 | 10 055 657 | 10 701 847 | 10 530 566 | Europe |
| Asia, East/S.East/Oceania | | 5 888 710 | 5 192 366 | 6 086 708 | 6 518 211 | 6 427 817 | Asie, Est/S.-Est/Océanie |
| Southern Asia | | 324 315 | 329 660 | 370 315 | 411 277 | 474 288 | Asie du Sud |
| Western Asia | | 126 613 | 110 111 | 137 259 | 144 131 | 164 283 | Asie occidentale |
| United States Virgin Is. | THSN | | | | | | Iles Vierges américaines |
| Total | | 585 684 | 623 394 | 603 944 | 617 603 | 701 023 | Total |
| Africa | | 828 | 134 | 289 | 162 | 59 | Afrique |
| Americas | | 494 324 | 531 270 | 560 581 | 568 908 | 648 824 | Amériques |
| Europe | | 6 144 | 7 747 | 15 819 | 18 821 | 15 076 | Europe |
| Asia, East/S.East/Oceania | | 333 | 363 | 379 | 501 | 350 | Asie, Est/S.-Est/Océanie |
| Region not specified | | 84 055 | 83 880 | 26 876 | 29 211 | 36 714 | Région non spécifiée |
| Uruguay | VFN | | | | | | Uruguay |
| Total[1] | | 1 353 872 | 1 508 055 | 1 870 858 | 1 917 049 | 1 824 340 | Total[1] |
| Americas | | 1 030 738 | 1 159 580 | 1 457 944 | 1 497 756 | 1 402 957 | Amériques |
| Europe | | 56 159 | 73 230 | 97 223 | 119 553 | 124 215 | Europe |
| Asia, East/S.East/Oceania | | 5 618 | 6 230 | 7 221 | 11 686 | 12 877 | Asie, Est/S.-Est/Océanie |
| Western Asia | | 170 | 131 | 489 | 182 | 172 | Asie occidentale |
| Region not specified | | 261 187 | 268 884 | 307 981 | 287 872 | 284 119 | Région non spécifiée |
| Uzbekistan | TFR | | | | | | Ouzbékistan |
| Total | | 331 500 | 231 000 | 261 600 | ... | ... | Total |
| Africa | | 1 000 | 1 000 | 1 000 | ... | ... | Afrique |
| Americas | | 4 100 | 2 000 | 12 000 | ... | ... | Amériques |
| Europe | | 99 800 | 51 000 | 68 600 | ... | ... | Europe |
| Asia, East/S.East/Oceania | | 195 100 | 145 000 | 140 000 | ... | ... | Asie, Est/S.-Est/Océanie |
| Southern Asia | | 8 000 | 8 000 | 10 000 | ... | ... | Asie du Sud |
| Western Asia | | 23 500 | 24 000 | 30 000 | ... | ... | Asie occidentale |
| Vanuatu | TFR | | | | | | Vanuatu |
| Total | | 49 462 | 50 400 | 61 453 | 62 123 | 68 179 | Total |
| Americas | | 1 438 | 1 625 | 1 954 | 1 625 | 1 896 | Amériques |
| Europe | | 2 948 | 3 003 | 3 388 | 3 504 | 4 021 | Europe |
| Asia, East/S.East/Oceania | | 44 256 | 44 876 | 55 027 | 55 894 | 61 023 | Asie, Est/S.-Est/Océanie |
| Region not specified | | 820 | 896 | 1 084 | 1 100 | 1 239 | Région non spécifiée |
| Venezuela (Bolivarian Rep. of) | TFN | | | | | | Venezuela (Rép. bolivar. du) |
| Total | | 431 677 | 336 974 | 486 401 | 706 103 | 747 930 | Total |
| Africa | | 518 | 438 | 640 | 787 | 914 | Afrique |
| Americas | | 185 276 | 154 334 | 217 699 | 374 460 | 411 772 | Amériques |
| Europe | | 237 250 | 175 159 | 258 178 | 296 310 | 297 601 | Europe |
| Asia, East/S.East/Oceania | | 3 756 | 3 201 | 4 475 | 16 360 | 17 106 | Asie, Est/S.-Est/Océanie |
| Southern Asia | | 302 | 270 | 344 | 1 801 | 1 931 | Asie du Sud |
| Western Asia | | 432 | 371 | 492 | 9 957 | 10 324 | Asie occidentale |
| Region not specified | | 4 143 | 3 201 | 4 573 | 6 428 | 8 282 | Région non spécifiée |
| Viet Nam | VFR | | | | | | Viet Nam |
| Total[9] | | 2 627 988 | 2 428 735 | 2 927 873 | 3 467 757 | 3 583 488 | Total[9] |
| Americas | | 303 519 | 258 991 | 326 286 | 396 997 | 459 398 | Amériques |
| Europe | | 343 360 | 293 636 | 354 735 | 425 774 | 480 585 | Europe |
| Asia, East/S.East/Oceania | | 1 694 624 | 1 669 541 | 2 008 366 | 2 365 222 | 2 361 258 | Asie, Est/S.-Est/Océanie |
| Region not specified | | 286 485 | 206 567 | 238 486 | 279 764 | 282 247 | Région non spécifiée |

| Country or area of destination and region of origin& | Series Série | 2002 | 2003 | 2004 | 2005 | 2006 | Pays ou zone de destination et région de provenance& |
|---|---|---|---|---|---|---|---|
| Yemen | THSN | | | | | | Yémen |
| Total | | 98 020 | 154 667 | 273 732 | 336 070 | 382 332 | Total |
| Africa | | 3 045 | 8 627 | 10 853 | 12 628 | 13 025 | Afrique |
| Americas | | 4 429 | 12 932 | 17 099 | 18 253 | 18 771 | Amériques |
| Europe | | 15 828 | 13 733 | 28 608 | 26 456 | 32 788 | Europe |
| Asia, East/S.East/Oceania | | 11 303 | 15 966 | 22 512 | 24 437 | 18 839 | Asie, Est/S.-Est/Océanie |
| Southern Asia | | ... | ... | 18 981 | 15 772 | 20 524 | Asie du Sud |
| Western Asia | | 63 415 | 103 409 | 175 679 | 238 524 | 278 385 | Asie occidentale |
| Zambia | TFR | | | | | | Zambie |
| Total | | *565 073 | 412 675 | 515 000 | 668 862 | 756 860 | Total |
| Africa | | 363 783 | 298 485 | 366 918 | 461 000 | 510 270 | Afrique |
| Americas | | 33 935 | 22 667 | 29 053 | 37 580 | 52 457 | Amériques |
| Europe | | 130 218 | 71 363 | 91 863 | 121 712 | 143 304 | Europe |
| Asia, East/S.East/Oceania | | 34 230 | 17 297 | 23 107 | 39 912 | 38 171 | Asie, Est/S.-Est/Océanie |
| Southern Asia | | 2 907 | 2 863 | 4 059 | 8 658 | 12 658 | Asie du Sud |
| Zimbabwe | VFR | | | | | | Zimbabwe |
| Total | | 2 041 202 | 2 256 205 | 1 854 488 | 1 558 501 | 2 286 572 | Total |
| Africa | | 1 760 097 | 1 942 052 | 1 523 090 | 1 356 384 | 2 082 724 | Afrique |
| Americas | | 65 194 | 61 181 | 75 161 | 43 976 | 44 746 | Amériques |
| Europe | | 149 995 | 169 938 | 155 767 | 112 608 | 96 849 | Europe |
| Asia, East/S.East/Oceania | | 65 916 | 68 414 | 90 405 | 38 767 | 53 908 | Asie, Est/S.-Est/Océanie |
| Southern Asia | | ... | 12 411 | 6 316 | 4 777 | 4 200 | Asie du Sud |
| Western Asia | | ... | 2 209 | 3 749 | 1 989 | 4 145 | Asie occidentale |

Source

World Tourism Organization (UNWTO), Madrid, UNWTO statistics database and the "Yearbook of Tourism Statistics", 2007 edition.

Notes

& For a listing of the Member States of the regions of origin, see Annex I, with the following exceptions:

Africa includes the countries and territories listed under Africa in Annex I but excludes Egypt, Guinea-Bissau, Liberia, Libyan Arab Jamahiriya, and Western Sahara.

Americas is as shown in Annex I, but excludes Falkland Islands (Malvinas), Greenland and Saint Pierre and Miquelon.

Europe is as shown in Annex I, but excludes Channel Islands, Faeroe Islands, Holy See, Isle of Man and Svalbard and Jan Mayen Islands. The Europe group also includes Armenia, Azerbaijan, Cyprus, Israel, Kazakhstan, Kyrgyzstan, Tajikistan, Turkey, Turkmenistan and Uzbekistan.

Asia, East and South East/Oceania includes the countries and territories listed under Eastern Asia and South-eastern Asia in Annex I (except for Timor-Leste), and under Oceania except for Christmas Island, Cocos Island, Norfolk Island, Nauru, Wake Island, Johnston Island, Midway Islands, Pitcairn, Tokelau and Wallis and Futuna Islands. The Asia, East and South East/Oceania group also includes Taiwan Province of China.

Southern Asia is as shown in Annex I under South-central Asia, but excludes Kazakhstan, Kyrgyzstan, Tajikistan, Turkmenistan and Uzbekistan.

Western Asia is as shown in Annex I but excludes Armenia, Azerbaijan, Cyprus, Georgia, Israel, Occupied Palestinian Territory, and Turkey. The Western Asia group also includes Egypt and the Libyan Arab Jamahiriya.

Source

Organisation mondiale du tourisme (OMT), Madrid, la base de données de l'OMT, et "l'Annuaire des statistiques du tourisme", 2007 édition.

Notes

& On se reportera à l'Annexe I pour les États Membres classés dans les différentes régions de provenance, avec les exceptions ci-après ;

Afrique – Comprend les États et territoires énumérés à l'Annexe I, sauf l'Égypte, la Guinée-Bissau, le Libéria, la Jamahiriya arabe libyenne, et le Sahara occidental.

Amériques – Comprend les États et territoires énumérés à l'Annexe I, sauf les îles Falkland (Malvinas), le Groënland, et Saint-Pierre-et-Miquelon.

Europe – Comprend les États et territoires énumérés à l'Annexe I, sauf les îles Anglo-normandes, les îles Féroé, l'île de Man, le Saint-Siège et les îles Svalbard et Jan Mayen. Le Groupe comprend en revanche l'Arménie, l'Azerbaïdjan, Chypre, Israël, le Kazakhstan, le Kirghizistan, la Turquie, le Tadjikistan, le Turkménistan, et l'Ouzbékistan.

L'Asie de l'Est et du Sud-Est/Océanie – Comprend les États et territoires énumérés à l'Annexe I dans les Groupes Asie de l'Est et Asie de Sud-Est sauf le Timor-Leste, et les États et territoires énumérés dans le Groupe Océanie sauf les îles Christmas, les îles Cocos, l'île Johnston, les îles Midway, Nauru, l'îles Norfolk, Pitcairn, Tokélou, l'île Wake et Wallis-et-Futuna. Le Groupe Asie de l'Est et du Sud-Est/Océanie comprend en revanche la Province chinoise de Taiwan.

Asie du Sud – Comprend les États et territoires énumérés à l'Annexe I, sauf le Kazakhstan, le Kirghizistan, l'Ouzbékistan, le Tadjikistan et le Turkménistan.

Asie occidentale – Comprend les États et territoires énumérés à l'Annexe I, sauf l'Arménie, l'Azerbaïdjan, Chypre, la Géorgie, Israël, le territoire Palestinien Occupé et la Turquie. Le Groupe comprend en revanche l'Égypte et la Jamahiriya arabe libyenne.

TFN: Arrivals of non-resident tourists at national borders (excluding same-day visitors), by nationality.

TFR: Arrivals of non-resident tourists at national borders (excluding same- day visitors), by country of residence.

TCEN: Arrivals of non-resident tourists in all types of accommodation establishments, by nationality.

TCER: Arrivals of non-resident tourists in all types of accommodation establishments, by country of residence.

THSN: Arrivals of non-resident tourists in hotels and similar establishments, by nationality.

THSR: Arrivals of non-resident tourists in hotels and similar establishments, by country of residence.

VFN: Arrivals of non-resident visitors at national borders (including tourists and same-day visitors), by nationality.

VFR: Arrivals of non-resident visitors at national borders (including tourists and same-day visitors), by country of residence.

Footnotes on the totals also apply to the other regions.

1 Arrivals of nationals residing abroad are included in the total and are all accounted for in "region not specified" only.

2 Excluding nationals of the country residing abroad.

3 Air arrivals.

4 Excluding nationals residing abroad and crew members.

5 Including private accommodation.

6 Organized tourism.

7 Hotels establishments, campings, holiday centres, holiday villages and specific categories of accommodation.

8 International tourist arrivals in hotels of regional capitals.

9 Arrivals of nationals residing abroad are included in the total and are also accounted for in the individual regions.

10 Arrivals in the Phreah Vihear Province are included in the total and are all accounted for in "Region not specified": 67 843.

11 Arrivals in the Phreah Vihear Province are included in the total and are all accounted for in "region not specified": 88 615.

12 Arrivals in the Phreah Vihear Province are included in the total and are all accounted for in "region not specified": 108 691.

13 For statistical purposes, the data for China do not include those for the Hong Kong Special Administrative Region (Hong Kong SAR), Macao Special Administrative Region (Macao SAR) and Taiwan Province of China.

14 Including stateless and Chinese people who do not have permanent residency in Hong Kong SAR, China.

15 Including arrivals by sea, land and by air.

16 Source: "Departamento Administrativo de Seguridad (DAS)".

17 Air and sea arrivals.

18 Including arrivals in ports of nautical tourism.

19 New methodology.

20 Excluding the passengers at Herrera airport.

21 Arrivals through all ports of entry.

22 Due to a change in the methodology, data are not comparable to previous years.

23 Arrivals of non-resident tourists at Libreville airport.

24 Charter tourists only.

25 Information based on administrative data.

TFN : Arrivées de touristes non résidents aux frontières nationales (a l'exclusion de visiteurs de la journée), par nationalité.

TFR : Arrivées de touristes non résidents aux frontières nationales (a l'exclusion de visiteurs de la journée), par pays de résidence.

TCEN : Arrivées de touristes non résidents dans tous les types d'établissements d'hébergement, par nationalité.

TCER : Arrivées de touristes non résidents dans tous les types d'établissements d'hébergement, par pays de résidence.

THSN : Arrivées de touristes non résidents dans les hôtels et établissements assimilés, par nationalité.

THSR : Arrivées de touristes non résidents dans les hôtels et établissements assimilés, par pays de résidence.

VFN : Arrivées de visiteurs non résidents aux frontières nationales (y compris touristes et visiteurs de la journée), par nationalité.

VFR : Arrivées de visiteurs non résidents aux frontières nationales (y compris touristes et visiteurs de la journée), par pays de résidence.

Les notes sur les totaux s'appliquent aussi aux autres régions.

1 Les arrivées de nationaux résidant à l'étranger sont comprises dans le total, et sont toutes comptabilisées uniquement dans la catégorie Région non spécifiée.

2 A l'exclusion des nationaux du pays résidant à l'étranger.

3 Arrivées par voie aérienne.

4 A l'exclusion des nationaux du pays résidant à l'étranger et des membres des équipages.

5 Y compris l'hébergement privé.

6 Tourisme organisé.

7 Établissements hôteliers, terrains de camping, centres de vacances, villages de vacances et catégories spécifiques d'hébergement.

8 Arrivées de touristes internationaux dans les hôtels des capitales de département.

9 Les arrivées de nationaux résidant à l'étranger sont comprises dans le total, et comptabilisées aussi dans chacune des régions.

10 Les arrivées dans la province de Phreah Vihear sont comprises dans le total, et sont toutes prises en compte dans "Région non spécifiée" : 67 843.

11 Les arrivées dans la province de Phreah Vihear sont comprises dans le total, et sont toutes prises en compte dans "Région non spécifiée": 88 615.

12 Les arrivées dans la province de Phreah Vihear sont comprises dans le total, et sont toutes prises en compte dans "Région non spécifiée": 108 691.

13 Pour la présentation des statistiques, les données pour la Chine ne comprennent pas la Région Administrative Spéciale de Hong Kong (Hong Kong RAS), la Région Administrative Spéciale de Macao (Macao RAS) et la province de Taiwan.

14 Y compris les chinois qui ne résident pas de manière permanente à Hong Kong SAR, Chine.

15 Y compris les arrivées par mer, terre et air.

16 Source: "Departamento Administrativo de Seguridad (DAS)".

17 Arrivées par voie aérienne et maritime.

18 Y compris les arrivées dans des ports à tourisme nautique.

19 Nouvelle méthodologie.

20 A l'exclusion des passagers à l'aéroport de Herrera.

21 Arrivées à travers tous les ports d'entrée.

22 Dû à un changement dans la méthodologie, l'information n'est pas comparable à celle des années précédentes.

23 Arrivées de touristes non résidents à l'aéroport de Libreville.

24 Arrivées en vols à la demande seulement.

25 Information tirée de données administratives.

| | |
|---|---|
| 26 Estimates for continental Guadeloupe (without Saint-Martin and Saint-Barthelemy). | 26 Estimations pour la Guadeloupe continentale (sans Saint-Martin et Saint-Barthélemy). |
| 27 Data based on a survey conducted at Guadeloupe airport. | 27 Données tirées d'une enquête réalisée à l'aéroport de Guadeloupe. |
| 28 Air arrivals at Conakry airport. | 28 Arrivées par voie aérienne à l'aéroport de Conakry. |
| 29 Arrivals at "Osvaldo Vieira" Airport. | 29 Arrivées à l'aéroport "Osvaldo Vieira". |
| 30 Arrivals to Timehri airport only. | 30 Arrivées à l'aéroport de Timehri seulement. |
| 31 Collective accommodation establishments. | 31 Etablissements d'hébergement collectif. |
| 32 Departures. | 32 Départs. |
| 33 Excluding seasonal and border workers. | 33 A l'exclusion des travailleurs saisoniers et frontaliers. |
| 34 All data are estimates, projected using 1989 market shares. Source: Economic survey various years. | 34 Toutes les données représentent des estimations, dont la projection a été faite sur la base des taux de marché de l'année 1989. Source: Enquête économique de diverses années. |
| 35 Tarawa and Christmas Island. | 35 Tarawa et Ile Christmas. |
| 36 Tarawa only. | 36 Tarawa uniquement. |
| 37 Including nationals residing abroad and crew members. | 37 Y compris les nationaux résidant à l'étranger et membres des équipages. |
| 38 New data source: Department of Customs Control. | 38 Nouvelle source d'information: Département du Contrôle douanier. |
| 39 Excluding Syrian nationals, Palestinians and students. | 39 A l'exclusion des ressortissants syriens, palestiniens et sous-études. |
| 40 Travellers. | 40 Voyaeurs. |
| 41 Including Singapore residents crossing the frontier by road through Johore Causeway. | 41 Y compris les résidents de Singapour traversant la frontière par voie terrestre à travers le Johore Causeway. |
| 42 Departures by air and by sea. | 42 Départs par voies aérienne et maritime. |
| 43 Arrivals in the States of Kosrae, Chuuk, Pohnpei and Yap. | 43 Arrivées dans les États de Kosrae, Chuuk, Pohnpei et Yap. |
| 44 Visitors who enjoyed the services of the economic agents officially registered under tourism activity and accommodation (excluding the regions of the left bank of the Dniestr and the municipality of Bender). | 44 Visiteurs qui ont bénéficié des services des agents économiques officiellement enregistrés avec le type d'activité tourisme et des unités d'hébergement qui leur appartiennent (à l'exception des régions de la partie gauche du Dniestr et de la municipalité de Bender). |
| 45 Including tourist arrivals through border entry points to Yangon. | 45 Comprenant les arrivées de touristes aux postes-frontières de Yangon. |
| 46 Data regarding to short term movements are compiled from a random sample of passenger declarations. Source: Statistics New Zealand, External Migration. | 46 Les données relatives aux mouvements de courte durée sont obtenues à partir d'un échantillon aléatoire de déclarations des passagers. Source : Statistiques de la Nouvelle Zélande, Immigration. |
| 47 Including Niuans residing usually in New Zealand. | 47 Y compris les nationaux de Niue résidant habituellement en Nouvelle-Zélande. |
| 48 Figures are based on "The Guest survey" carried out by "Institute of Transport Economics". | 48 Les chiffres se fondent sur "l'enquête auprès de la clientèle" de l'Institut d'économie des transports. |
| 49 Air arrivals (Palau International Airport). | 49 Arrivées par voie aérienne (Aéroport international de Palau). |
| 50 Total number of visitors broken down by permanent residence who arrived in Panama at Tocumen International Airport. | 50 Nombre total de visiteurs arrivées au Panama par l'aéroport international de Tocúmen. |
| 51 E/D cards in the "Silvio Petirossi" airport and passenger counts at the national border crossings - National Police and SENATUR. | 51 Cartes d'embarquement et de débarquement à l'aéroport Silvio Petirossi et comptages des passagers lors du franchissement des frontières nationales – Police Nationale et SENATUR. |
| 52 From 2002, new estimated series including tourists with identity document other than a passport. | 52 À partir de 2002, nouvelle série estimée comprenant les touristes avec une pièce d'identité autre qu'un passeport. |
| 53 Preliminary estimates. | 53 Estimations préliminaires. |
| 54 Due to a change in the methodology, from 2004 the data are not comparable with those of previous years. | 54 La méthodologie a été modifiée et pour cela, à partir de 2004 les données ne sont pas comparables avec celles des années précédentes. |
| 55 Fiscal year July to June. | 55 Année fiscale de juillet à juin. |
| 56 Arrivals in hotels only. | 56 Arrivées dans les hôtels uniquement. |
| 57 Excluding Netherlands Antillean residents. | 57 A l'exclusion des résidents des Antilles Néerlandaises. |
| 58 Arrivals at Princess Juliana International airport. Including visitors to St. Maarten (the French side of the island). | 58 Arrivées à l'aéroport international "Princess Juliana". Y compris les visiteurs à Saint-Martin (partie française de l'île). |
| 59 Including Italian visitors. | 59 Y compris les visiteurs italiens. |
| 60 Excluding Malaysian citizens arriving by land. | 60 Non compris les arrivées de malaysiens par voie terrestre. |
| 61 Without 1st quarter. | 61 À l'exclusion du 1er trimestre. |
| 62 Excluding arrivals by work and contract workers. | 62 À l'exclusion des arrivées par travail et les travailleurs contractuels. |
| 63 Arrivals at Zanderij Airport. | 63 Arrivées à l'aéroport de Zanderij. |

64 Data according to IBIS-Survey (Incoming Visitors to Sweden) during the years 2001 to 2003, (no data collected before 2001 or after 2003). Source: Swedish Tourist Authority and Statistics Sweden.

65 Hotels, motels and inns.

66 Hotels and health establishments.

67 Data source: The survey of Incoming Tourism in 2002 and 2004.

68 Excluding private accommodation.

69 Domestic tourism and arrivals of nationals residing abroad are included in the total and are all accounted for in "Region not specified" only.

64 Données reposant sur l'enquête IBIS (auprès des visiteurs du tourisme récepteur) portant sur les années 2001 à 2003 (aucune donnée n'a été collectée avant 2001 ni après 2003). Source: "Swedish Tourist Authority" et "Statistics Sweden".

65 Hôtels, motels et auberges.

66 Hôtels et établissements de cure.

67 Source des données: enquête du tourisme récepteur en 2002 et 2004.

68 À l'exclusion de l'hébergement chez des particuliers.

69 Les touristes nationaux et les arrivées de nationaux résidant à l'étranger sont compris dans le total, et sont tous pris en compte uniquement dans "Région non spécifiée" seulement.

# Tourist/visitor arrivals and tourism expenditure
Thousands arrivals and millions of US dollars

# Arrivées de touristes/visiteurs et dépenses touristiques
Milliers d'arrivées et millions de dollars E.-U.

| Country or area of destination | Category&<br>Catégorie& | 2001 | 2002 | 2003 | 2004 | 2005 | 2006 | Pays ou zone de destination |
|---|---|---|---|---|---|---|---|---|
| Albanie | | | | | | | | Albanie |
| Tourist/visitor arrivals[1] | THS | 34 | 36 | 41 | 32 | 48 | 60 | Arrivées de touristes/visiteurs[1] |
| Tourism expenditure | | 451 | 492 | 537 | 756 | 880 | 1 057 | Dépenses touristiques |
| Algeria | | | | | | | | Algérie |
| Tourist/visitor arrivals[2] | VF | 901 | 988 | 1 166 | 1 234 | 1 443 | 1 638 | Arrivées de touristes/visiteurs[2] |
| Tourism expenditure[3] | | 100 | 111 | 112 | 178 | 184 | 215 | Dépenses touristiques[3] |
| American Samoa | | | | | | | | Samoa américaines |
| Tourist/visitor arrivals | TF | 36 | ... | ... | ... | 24 | 25 | Arrivées de touristes/visiteurs |
| Andorra | | | | | | | | Andorre |
| Tourist/visitor arrivals | TF | 3 516 | 3 387 | 3 138 | 2 791 | 2 418 | 2 227 | Arrivées de touristes/visiteurs |
| Angola | | | | | | | | Angola |
| Tourist/visitor arrivals | TF | 67 | 91 | 107 | 194 | 210 | 121 | Arrivées de touristes/visiteurs |
| Tourism expenditure | | 36 | 51 | 63 | 82 | 103 | 91 | Dépenses touristiques |
| Anguilla | | | | | | | | Anguilla |
| Tourist/visitor arrivals[4] | TF | 48 | 44 | 47 | 54 | 62 | 73 | Arrivées de touristes/visiteurs[4] |
| Tourism expenditure[5] | | 62 | 57 | 60 | 69 | 86 | 107 | Dépenses touristiques[5] |
| Antigua and Barbuda | | | | | | | | Antigua-et-Barbuda |
| Tourist/visitor arrivals[4] | TF | 215 | 218 | 239 | 268 | 267 | 273 | Arrivées de touristes/visiteurs[4] |
| Tourism expenditure[5] | | 272 | 274 | 300 | 338 | 335 | 347 | Dépenses touristiques[5] |
| Argentina[6] | | | | | | | | Argentine[6] |
| Tourist/visitor arrivals | TF | 2 620 | 2 820 | 2 995 | 3 457 | 3 823 | 4 156 | Arrivées de touristes/visiteurs |
| Tourism expenditure | | 2 756 | 1 716 | 2 306 | 2 660 | 3 209 | 3 863 | Dépenses touristiques |
| Armenia | | | | | | | | Arménie |
| Tourist/visitor arrivals | TF | 123 | 162 | 206 | 263 | 319 | 381 | Arrivées de touristes/visiteurs |
| Tourism expenditure | | 81 | 81 | 90 | 188 | 240 | 307 | Dépenses touristiques |
| Aruba | | | | | | | | Aruba |
| Tourist/visitor arrivals | TF | 691 | 643 | 642 | 728 | 733 | 694 | Arrivées de touristes/visiteurs |
| Tourism expenditure | | 826 | 835 | 859 | 1 056[5] | 1 094[5] | 1 076 | Dépenses touristiques |
| Australia | | | | | | | | Australie |
| Tourist/visitor arrivals[7] | TF | 4 435 | 4 420 | 4 354 | 4 774 | 5 020 | 5 064 | Arrivées de touristes/visiteurs[7] |
| Tourism expenditure | | 12 804 | 13 624 | 16 647 | 20 453 | 22 566 | 23 729 | Dépenses touristiques |
| Austria | | | | | | | | Autriche |
| Tourist/visitor arrivals | TCE | 18 180 | 18 611 | 19 078 | 19 373 | 19 952 | 20 261 | Arrivées de touristes/visiteurs |
| Tourism expenditure | | 12 033 | 13 046 | 16 342 | 18 385 | 19 310 | 18 890 | Dépenses touristiques |
| Azerbaijan | | | | | | | | Azerbaïdjan |
| Tourist/visitor arrivals | TF | 767 | 834 | 1 014 | 1 349 | 1 177 | 1 194 | Arrivées de touristes/visiteurs |
| Tourism expenditure | | 57 | 63 | 70 | 79 | 100 | 201 | Dépenses touristiques |
| Bahamas | | | | | | | | Bahamas |
| Tourist/visitor arrivals | TF | 1 538 | 1 513 | 1 510 | 1 561 | 1 608 | 1 601 | Arrivées de touristes/visiteurs |
| Tourism expenditure | | 1 665 | 1 773 | 1 770 | 1 897 | 2 082 | 2 079 | Dépenses touristiques |
| Bahrain | | | | | | | | Bahreïn |
| Tourist/visitor arrivals | TF | 2 789 | 3 167 | 2 955 | 3 514 | 3 914 | 4 519 | Arrivées de touristes/visiteurs |
| Tourism expenditure | | 886 | 985 | 1 206 | 1 504 | 1 603 | 1 786 | Dépenses touristiques |
| Bangladesh | | | | | | | | Bangladesh |
| Tourist/visitor arrivals | TF | 207 | 207 | 245 | 271 | 208 | 200 | Arrivées de touristes/visiteurs |
| Tourism expenditure | | 48[5] | 59 | 59 | 76 | 79 | 80 | Dépenses touristiques |

| Country or area of destination | Category[&] Catégorie[&] | 2001 | 2002 | 2003 | 2004 | 2005 | 2006 | Pays ou zone de destination |
|---|---|---|---|---|---|---|---|---|
| Barbados | | | | | | | | Barbade |
| Tourist/visitor arrivals | TF | 507 | 498 | 531 | 552 | 548 | 563 | Arrivées de touristes/visiteurs |
| Tourism expenditure | | 706 | 666 | 767 | 785 | 905 | 978[5] | Dépenses touristiques |
| Belarus | | | | | | | | Bélarus |
| Tourist/visitor arrivals[8] | TF | 61 | 63 | 64 | 67 | 91 | 89 | Arrivées de touristes/visiteurs[8] |
| Tourism expenditure | | 273 | 295 | 339 | 362 | 346 | 386 | Dépenses touristiques |
| Belgium | | | | | | | | Belgique |
| Tourist/visitor arrivals | TCE | 6 452 | 6 720 | 6 690 | 6 710 | 6 747 | 6 995 | Arrivées de touristes/visiteurs |
| Tourism expenditure | | 8 304 | 7 598 | 8 848 | 10 089 | 10 881 | 11 556 | Dépenses touristiques |
| Belize | | | | | | | | Belize |
| Tourist/visitor arrivals | TF | 196 | 200 | 221 | 231 | 237 | 247 | Arrivées de touristes/visiteurs |
| Tourism expenditure[5] | | 111 | 121 | 150 | 168 | 204 | 253 | Dépenses touristiques[5] |
| Benin | | | | | | | | Bénin |
| Tourist/visitor arrivals | TF | 88 | 72 | 175[9] | 174[9] | 176[9] | 180[9] | Arrivées de touristes/visiteurs |
| Tourism expenditure | | 86 | 95 | 108 | 121 | 108 | ... | Dépenses touristiques |
| Bermuda | | | | | | | | Bermudes |
| Tourist/visitor arrivals[7] | TF | 278 | 284 | 257 | 272 | 270 | 299 | Arrivées de touristes/visiteurs[7] |
| Tourism expenditure[3] | | 351 | 378 | 348 | 426 | 429 | 508 | Dépenses touristiques[3] |
| Bhutan | | | | | | | | Bhoutan |
| Tourist/visitor arrivals | TF | 6 | 6 | 6 | 9 | 14 | 17 | Arrivées de touristes/visiteurs |
| Tourism expenditure[3] | | 9 | 8 | 8 | 13 | 19 | 24 | Dépenses touristiques[3] |
| Bolivia | | | | | | | | Bolivie |
| Tourist/visitor arrivals | TF | 316 | 334 | 427 | 480 | 524 | 515 | Arrivées de touristes/visiteurs |
| Tourism expenditure | | 119 | 143 | 243 | 283 | 345 | 287 | Dépenses touristiques |
| Bonaire | | | | | | | | Bonaire |
| Tourist/visitor arrivals | TF | 50 | 52 | 62 | 63 | 63 | 64 | Arrivées de touristes/visiteurs |
| Tourism expenditure[5,10] | | 64 | 65 | 84 | 87 | 87 | 91 | Dépenses touristiques[5,10] |
| Bosnia and Herzegovina | | | | | | | | Bosnie-Herzégovine |
| Tourist/visitor arrivals | TCE | 139 | 160 | 165 | 190 | 217 | 256 | Arrivées de touristes/visiteurs |
| Tourism expenditure | | 279 | 307 | 404 | 507 | 550 | 643 | Dépenses touristiques |
| Botswana | | | | | | | | Botswana |
| Tourist/visitor arrivals | TF | 1 193 | 1 274 | 1 406 | 1 523 | 1 675 | ... | Arrivées de touristes/visiteurs |
| Tourism expenditure | | 235 | 324 | 459 | 582 | 561 | 539 | Dépenses touristiques |
| Brazil | | | | | | | | Brésil |
| Tourist/visitor arrivals | TF | 4 773 | 3 785 | 4 133 | 4 794 | 5 358 | 5 019 | Arrivées de touristes/visiteurs |
| Tourism expenditure | | 1 844 | 2 142 | 2 673 | 3 389 | 4 168 | 4 577 | Dépenses touristiques |
| British Virgin Islands | | | | | | | | Iles Vierges britanniques |
| Tourist/visitor arrivals | TF | 296 | 282 | 318 | 304 | 337 | ... | Arrivées de touristes/visiteurs |
| Tourism expenditure[3] | | 401 | 345 | 342 | 393 | 437 | ... | Dépenses touristiques[3] |
| Brunei Darussalam | | | | | | | | Brunéi Darussalam |
| Tourist/visitor arrivals[7] | VF | 840 | ... | ... | ... | 815 | 836 | Arrivées de touristes/visiteurs[7] |
| Tourism expenditure[5] | | 155 | 114 | 124 | 181 | 191 | 224 | Dépenses touristiques[5] |
| Bulgaria | | | | | | | | Bulgarie |
| Tourist/visitor arrivals | TF | 3 186 | 3 433 | 4 048 | 4 630 | 4 837 | 5 158 | Arrivées de touristes/visiteurs |
| Tourism expenditure | | 1 262 | 1 392 | 2 051 | 2 796 | 3 063 | 3 315 | Dépenses touristiques |
| Burkina Faso | | | | | | | | Burkina Faso |
| Tourist/visitor arrivals | THS | 128 | 150 | 163 | 222 | 245 | 264 | Arrivées de touristes/visiteurs |
| Tourism expenditure[11] | | 25 | ... | ... | 40[5] | 45 | ... | Dépenses touristiques[11] |
| Burundi | | | | | | | | Burundi |
| Tourist/visitor arrivals[2] | TF | 36 | 74 | 74 | 133 | 148 | 201 | Arrivées de touristes/visiteurs[2] |
| Tourism expenditure | | 1 | 2 | 1 | 2 | 2 | 2 | Dépenses touristiques |
| Cambodia | | | | | | | | Cambodge |
| Tourist/visitor arrivals | TF | 605[12] | 787[12] | 701[12] | 1 055[4] | 1 422[12] | 1 700[12] | Arrivées de touristes/visiteurs |
| Tourism expenditure | | 429 | 509 | 441 | 673 | 929 | 1 080 | Dépenses touristiques |

| Country or area of destination | Category&<br>Catégorie& | 2001 | 2002 | 2003 | 2004 | 2005 | 2006 | Pays ou zone de destination |
|---|---|---|---|---|---|---|---|---|
| Cameroon | | | | | | | | Cameroun |
| Tourist/visitor arrivals | THS | 221 | 226 | ... | 190 | 176 | ... | Arrivées de touristes/visiteurs |
| Tourism expenditure | | 182 | 124 | 266 | 212 | ... | ... | Dépenses touristiques |
| Canada | | | | | | | | Canada |
| Tourist/visitor arrivals[13] | TF | 19 679 | 20 057 | 17 534 | 19 145 | 18 770 | 18 265 | Arrivées de touristes/visiteurs[13] |
| Tourism expenditure | | 12 680 | 12 744 | 12 236 | 14 953 | 16 006 | 16 976 | Dépenses touristiques |
| Cape Verde | | | | | | | | Cap-Vert |
| Tourist/visitor arrivals | TF | 134 | 126 | 150 | 157 | 198 | 242 | Arrivées de touristes/visiteurs |
| Tourism expenditure | | 77 | 100 | 135 | 153 | 177 | 286 | Dépenses touristiques |
| Cayman Islands | | | | | | | | Iles Caïmanes |
| Tourist/visitor arrivals[7] | TF | 334 | 303 | 294 | 260 | 168 | 267 | Arrivées de touristes/visiteurs[7] |
| Tourism expenditure[3] | | 585 | 607 | 518 | 523 | 356 | 509 | Dépenses touristiques[3] |
| Central African Rep. | | | | | | | | Rép. centrafricaine |
| Tourist/visitor arrivals[14] | TF | 10 | 3 | 6 | 8 | 12 | 14 | Arrivées de touristes/visiteurs[14] |
| Tourism expenditure[15] | | 5 | 3 | 4 | 4 | ... | ... | Dépenses touristiques[15] |
| Chad | | | | | | | | Tchad |
| Tourist/visitor arrivals | THS | 57 | 32 | 21 | 26 | 29 | ... | Arrivées de touristes/visiteurs |
| Tourism expenditure[15] | | 23 | 25 | ... | ... | ... | ... | Dépenses touristiques[15] |
| Chile | | | | | | | | Chili |
| Tourist/visitor arrivals | TF | 1 723 | 1 412 | 1 614 | 1 785 | 2 027 | 2 253 | Arrivées de touristes/visiteurs |
| Tourism expenditure | | 1 184 | 1 221 | 1 309 | 1 571 | 1 652 | 1 816 | Dépenses touristiques |
| China[16] | | | | | | | | Chine[16] |
| Tourist/visitor arrivals | TF | 33 167 | 36 803 | 32 970 | 41 761 | 46 809 | 49 913 | Arrivées de touristes/visiteurs |
| Tourism expenditure | | 19 006 | 21 742 | 18 707 | 27 755 | 31 842 | 37 132 | Dépenses touristiques |
| China· Hong Kong SAR | | | | | | | | Chine· Hong Kong RAS |
| Tourist/visitor arrivals | TF | 8 878 | 10 689 | 9 676 | 13 655 | 14 773 | 15 821 | Arrivées de touristes/visiteurs |
| Tourism expenditure[17] | | 7 924 | 9 849 | 9 004 | 11 874 | 13 588 | 15 311 | Dépenses touristiques[17] |
| China· Macao SAR | | | | | | | | Chine· Macao RAS |
| Tourist/visitor arrivals[9] | TF | 5 842 | 6 565 | 6 309 | 8 324 | 9 014 | 10 683 | Arrivées de touristes/visiteurs[9] |
| Tourism expenditure[17] | | 3 745 | 4 440 | 5 303 | 7 344 | 7 757 | 9 337 | Dépenses touristiques[17] |
| Colombia | | | | | | | | Colombie |
| Tourist/visitor arrivals | VF | 616 | 567 | 625 | 791 | 933 | 1 053 | Arrivées de touristes/visiteurs |
| Tourism expenditure | | 1 483 | 1 237 | 1 191 | 1 366 | 1 570 | 2 005 | Dépenses touristiques |
| Comoros | | | | | | | | Comores |
| Tourist/visitor arrivals | TF | 19 | 19 | 21 | 23 | 26 | 29 | Arrivées de touristes/visiteurs |
| Tourism expenditure[18] | | 9 | 11 | 16 | 21 | 24 | 27 | Dépenses touristiques[18] |
| Congo | | | | | | | | Congo |
| Tourist/visitor arrivals | THS | 27 | 22 | ... | ... | ... | ... | Arrivées de touristes/visiteurs |
| Tourism expenditure | | 23 | 26 | 30 | 23 | 34[5] | ... | Dépenses touristiques |
| Cook Islands | | | | | | | | Iles Cook |
| Tourist/visitor arrivals | TF | 75 | 73 | 78 | 83 | 88 | 92 | Arrivées de touristes/visiteurs |
| Tourism expenditure[3] | | 38 | 46 | 69 | 72 | 91 | 90 | Dépenses touristiques[3] |
| Costa Rica | | | | | | | | Costa Rica |
| Tourist/visitor arrivals | TF | 1 131 | 1 113 | 1 239 | 1 453 | 1 679 | 1 725 | Arrivées de touristes/visiteurs |
| Tourism expenditure | | 1 339 | 1 292 | 1 424 | 1 586 | 1 810 | 1 890 | Dépenses touristiques |
| Côte d'Ivoire | | | | | | | | Côte d'Ivoire |
| Tourism expenditure | | 58 | 56 | 76 | 91 | 93 | 84[5] | Dépenses touristiques |
| Croatia | | | | | | | | Croatie |
| Tourist/visitor arrivals | TCE | 6 544 | 6 944 | 7 409 | 7 912 | 8 467 | 8 659 | Arrivées de touristes/visiteurs |
| Tourism expenditure | | 3 463 | 3 952 | 6 513 | 6 945 | 7 625 | 8 296 | Dépenses touristiques |
| Cuba | | | | | | | | Cuba |
| Tourist/visitor arrivals[7] | TF | 1 736 | 1 656 | 1 847 | 2 017 | 2 261 | 2 150 | Arrivées de touristes/visiteurs[7] |
| Tourism expenditure[3] | | 1 840 | 1 769 | 1 999 | 2 114 | 2 399 | 2 404 | Dépenses touristiques[3] |

| Country or area of destination | Category&<br>Catégorie& | 2001 | 2002 | 2003 | 2004 | 2005 | 2006 | Pays ou zone de destination |
|---|---|---|---|---|---|---|---|---|
| Curaçao | | | | | | | | Curaçao |
| Tourist/visitor arrivals[7] | TF | 205 | 218 | 221 | 223 | 222 | 234 | Arrivées de touristes/visiteurs[7] |
| Tourism expenditure[3] | | 271 | 290 | 286 | 296 | 284 | ... | Dépenses touristiques[3] |
| Cyprus | | | | | | | | Chypre |
| Tourist/visitor arrivals | TF | 2 697 | 2 418 | 2 303 | 2 349 | 2 470 | 2 401 | Arrivées de touristes/visiteurs |
| Tourism expenditure | | 2 203 | 2 178 | 2 325 | 2 552 | 2 644 | 2 735 | Dépenses touristiques |
| Czech Republic | | | | | | | | République tchèque |
| Tourist/visitor arrivals | TCE | 5 405 | 4 743 | 5 076 | 6 061 | 6 336 | 6 435 | Arrivées de touristes/visiteurs |
| Tourism expenditure | | 3 106[5] | 3 376 | 4 069 | 4 931 | 5 618 | 5 844 | Dépenses touristiques |
| Dem. Rep. of the Congo[7] | | | | | | | | Rép. dém. du Congo[7] |
| Tourist/visitor arrivals | TF | 55 | 28 | 35 | 36 | 61 | 55 | Arrivées de touristes/visiteurs |
| Denmark | | | | | | | | Danemark |
| Tourist/visitor arrivals[19] | TCE | 3 684 | 3 436 | 3 474 | #4 421 | 4 699 | 4 716 | Arrivées de touristes/visiteurs[19] |
| Tourism expenditure[5] | | 4 003 | 4 791 | 5 271 | 5 652 | 5 293 | 5 587 | Dépenses touristiques[5] |
| Djibouti | | | | | | | | Djibouti |
| Tourist/visitor arrivals | THS | 22 | 23 | 23 | 26 | 30 | 40 | Arrivées de touristes/visiteurs |
| Tourism expenditure[5] | | 9 | 9 | 7 | 7 | 7 | 9 | Dépenses touristiques[5] |
| Dominica | | | | | | | | Dominique |
| Tourist/visitor arrivals | TF | 66 | 69 | 73 | 80 | 79 | 84 | Arrivées de touristes/visiteurs |
| Tourism expenditure[5] | | 46 | 46 | 52 | 61 | 56 | 68 | Dépenses touristiques[5] |
| Dominican Republic | | | | | | | | Rép. dominicaine |
| Tourist/visitor arrivals[2,7] | TF | 2 882 | 2 811 | 3 282 | 3 450 | 3 691 | 3 965 | Arrivées de touristes/visiteurs[2,7] |
| Tourism expenditure[5] | | 2 798 | 2 730 | 3 128 | 3 152 | 3 518 | 3 792 | Dépenses touristiques[5] |
| Ecuador | | | | | | | | Equateur |
| Tourist/visitor arrivals[4] | VF | 641 | 683 | 761 | 819 | 860 | 841 | Arrivées de touristes/visiteurs[4] |
| Tourism expenditure | | 438 | 449 | 408 | 464 | 488 | 492 | Dépenses touristiques |
| Egypt | | | | | | | | Egypte |
| Tourist/visitor arrivals | TF | 4 357 | 4 906 | 5 746 | 7 795 | 8 244 | 8 646 | Arrivées de touristes/visiteurs |
| Tourism expenditure | | 4 119 | 4 133 | 4 704 | 6 328 | 7 206 | 8 133 | Dépenses touristiques |
| El Salvador | | | | | | | | El Salvador |
| Tourist/visitor arrivals | TF | 735 | 798 | 720 | 812 | 969 | 1 138 | Arrivées de touristes/visiteurs |
| Tourism expenditure | | 452 | 521 | 664 | 748 | 838 | 1 175 | Dépenses touristiques |
| Equatorial Guinea[11] | | | | | | | | Guinée équatoriale[11] |
| Tourism expenditure | | 14 | ... | ... | ... | ... | ... | Dépenses touristiques |
| Eritrea | | | | | | | | Erythrée |
| Tourist/visitor arrivals[2] | VF | 113 | 101 | 80 | 87 | 83 | 78 | Arrivées de touristes/visiteurs[2] |
| Tourism expenditure[17] | | 74 | 73 | 74 | 73 | 66 | 60 | Dépenses touristiques[17] |
| Estonia | | | | | | | | Estonie |
| Tourist/visitor arrivals | TF | 1 320 | 1 362 | 1 462 | 1 750[20,21] | 1 917[20,21] | 1 940[20,21] | Arrivées de touristes/visiteurs |
| Tourism expenditure | | 661 | 737 | 883 | 1 111 | 1 207 | 1 372 | Dépenses touristiques |
| Ethiopia | | | | | | | | Ethiopie |
| Tourist/visitor arrivals[22] | TF | 148 | 156 | 180 | 184 | 227 | 290 | Arrivées de touristes/visiteurs[22] |
| Tourism expenditure | | 218 | 261 | 336 | 458 | 533 | 639 | Dépenses touristiques |
| Fiji | | | | | | | | Fidji |
| Tourist/visitor arrivals[4] | TF | 348 | 398 | 431 | 499 | 550 | 545 | Arrivées de touristes/visiteurs[4] |
| Tourism expenditure | | 309 | 379 | 490 | 585 | 676 | 636 | Dépenses touristiques |
| Finland | | | | | | | | Finlande |
| Tourist/visitor arrivals | TF | 2 826 | 2 875 | 2 601 | 2 840 | 3 140 | 3 375 | Arrivées de touristes/visiteurs |
| Tourism expenditure | | 2 066 | 2 236 | 2 678 | 2 975 | 3 070 | 3 509 | Dépenses touristiques |
| France | | | | | | | | France |
| Tourist/visitor arrivals | TF | 75 202[23] | 77 012[23] | 75 048[23] | 75 121[23] | 75 908[24] | *79 083 | Arrivées de touristes/visiteurs |
| Tourism expenditure | | 35 316 | 38 110 | 43 406 | 52 607 | 52 153 | 54 033 | Dépenses touristiques |
| French Guiana | | | | | | | | Guyane française |
| Tourist/visitor arrivals | TF | 65 | 65 | ... | ... | 95[25] | ... | Arrivées de touristes/visiteurs |
| Tourism expenditure[3] | | 42 | 45 | ... | ... | 45 | ... | Dépenses touristiques[3] |

| Country or area of destination | Category&<br>Catégorie& | 2001 | 2002 | 2003 | 2004 | 2005 | 2006 | Pays ou zone de destination |
|---|---|---|---|---|---|---|---|---|
| French Polynesia | | | | | | | | Polynésie française |
| Tourist/visitor arrivals[4] | TF | 228 | 189 | 213 | 212 | 208 | 222 | Arrivées de touristes/visiteurs[4] |
| Tourism expenditure | | ... | 471 | 651 | 737 | 751 | 785 | Dépenses touristiques |
| Gabon | | | | | | | | Gabon |
| Tourist/visitor arrivals[26] | TF | 169 | 208 | 222 | ... | ... | ... | Arrivées de touristes/visiteurs[26] |
| Tourism expenditure | | 46 | 77 | 84 | 74 | ... | ... | Dépenses touristiques |
| Gambia | | | | | | | | Gambie |
| Tourist/visitor arrivals[27] | TF | 57 | 81 | 73 | 90 | 108 | 125 | Arrivées de touristes/visiteurs[27] |
| Tourism expenditure | | ... | ... | 58 | 51 | 57 | 69 | Dépenses touristiques |
| Georgia | | | | | | | | Géorgie |
| Tourist/visitor arrivals | VF | 302 | 298 | 313 | 368 | 560 | 983 | Arrivées de touristes/visiteurs |
| Tourism expenditure | | 136 | 144 | 172 | 209 | 287 | 361 | Dépenses touristiques |
| Germany | | | | | | | | Allemagne |
| Tourist/visitor arrivals | TCE | 17 861 | 17 969 | 18 399 | 20 137 | 21 500 | 23 569 | Arrivées de touristes/visiteurs |
| Tourism expenditure | | 24 175 | 26 690 | 30 104 | 35 569 | 38 220 | 42 792 | Dépenses touristiques |
| Ghana | | | | | | | | Ghana |
| Tourist/visitor arrivals[2] | TF | 439 | 483 | 531 | 584 | 429 | ... | Arrivées de touristes/visiteurs[2] |
| Tourism expenditure | | 374 | 383 | 441 | 495 | 867 | 910 | Dépenses touristiques |
| Greece | | | | | | | | Grèce |
| Tourist/visitor arrivals[28] | TF | 14 057 | 14 180 | 13 969 | 13 313 | 14 765 | 16 039 | Arrivées de touristes/visiteurs[28] |
| Tourism expenditure | | 9 216 | 10 005 | 10 842 | 12 809 | 13 453 | 14 495 | Dépenses touristiques |
| Grenada | | | | | | | | Grenade |
| Tourist/visitor arrivals | TF | 123 | 132 | 142 | 134 | 99 | 119 | Arrivées de touristes/visiteurs |
| Tourism expenditure[5] | | 83 | 91 | 104 | 83 | 71 | 93 | Dépenses touristiques[5] |
| Guadeloupe | | | | | | | | Guadeloupe |
| Tourist/visitor arrivals[7,29,30] | TCE | 521 | ... | 439[31] | 456[31] | 372[32] | 375 | Arrivées de touristes/visiteurs[7,29,30] |
| Tourism expenditure[3] | | ... | ... | ... | ... | 306 | 299 | Dépenses touristiques[3] |
| Guam | | | | | | | | Guam |
| Tourist/visitor arrivals | TF | 1 159 | 1 059 | 910 | 1 160 | 1 228 | 1 212 | Arrivées de touristes/visiteurs |
| Guatemala | | | | | | | | Guatemala |
| Tourist/visitor arrivals | TF | 835 | 884 | 880 | 1 182 | 1 316 | 1 502 | Arrivées de touristes/visiteurs |
| Tourism expenditure | | 588 | 647 | 646 | 806 | 883 | 1 008 | Dépenses touristiques |
| Guinea | | | | | | | | Guinée |
| Tourist/visitor arrivals | TF | 38[33] | 43[33] | 44[33,34] | 45[33] | 45[34] | 46[33,34] | Arrivées de touristes/visiteurs |
| Tourism expenditure | | 22 | 43[5] | 32 | 30[5] | ... | 70[5] | Dépenses touristiques |
| Guinea-Bissau | | | | | | | | Guinée-Bissau |
| Tourist/visitor arrivals[7] | TF | 8 | ... | ... | ... | 5 | 12 | Arrivées de touristes/visiteurs[7] |
| Tourism expenditure | | 3[5] | 2[5] | 2 | 2 | 2[5] | ... | Dépenses touristiques |
| Guyana | | | | | | | | Guyana |
| Tourist/visitor arrivals[35] | TF | 99 | 104 | 101 | 122 | 117 | 113 | Arrivées de touristes/visiteurs[35] |
| Tourism expenditure | | 65 | 53 | 28 | 29 | 37 | 40 | Dépenses touristiques |
| Haiti | | | | | | | | Haïti |
| Tourist/visitor arrivals | TF | 142 | 140 | 136 | 96 | 112 | ... | Arrivées de touristes/visiteurs |
| Tourism expenditure[5] | | 105 | 108 | 96 | 87 | 80 | 135 | Dépenses touristiques[5] |
| Honduras | | | | | | | | Honduras |
| Tourist/visitor arrivals | TF | 518 | 550 | 611 | 641 | 673 | 739 | Arrivées de touristes/visiteurs |
| Tourism expenditure | | 260 | 305 | 364 | 420 | 466 | 490 | Dépenses touristiques |
| Hungary | | | | | | | | Hongrie |
| Tourist/visitor arrivals | TCE | 3 070 | 3 013 | 2 948 | 3 270 | 3 446 | 3 310 | Arrivées de touristes/visiteurs |
| Tourism expenditure | | 4 191 | 3 774 | 4 119 | 4 129 | 4 717 | 4 943 | Dépenses touristiques |
| Iceland | | | | | | | | Islande |
| Tourist/visitor arrivals | TCE | 672 | 705 | 771 | 836 | 871 | 971 | Arrivées de touristes/visiteurs |
| Tourism expenditure | | 383 | 415 | 486 | 558 | 630 | 663 | Dépenses touristiques |

| Country or area of destination | Category&<br>Catégorie& | 2001 | 2002 | 2003 | 2004 | 2005 | 2006 | Pays ou zone de destination |
|---|---|---|---|---|---|---|---|---|
| India | | | | | | | | Inde |
| Tourist/visitor arrivals[4] | TF | 2 537 | 2 384 | 2 726 | 3 457 | 3 919 | 4 447 | Arrivées de touristes/visiteurs[4] |
| Tourism expenditure | | 3 342 | 3 300 | 4 560 | 6 307 | 7 652 | 9 227 | Dépenses touristiques |
| Indonesia | | | | | | | | Indonésie |
| Tourist/visitor arrivals | TF | 5 153 | 5 033 | 4 467 | 5 321 | 5 002 | 4 871 | Arrivées de touristes/visiteurs |
| Tourism expenditure | | 5 277[5] | 5 797 | 4 461 | 5 226 | 5 094 | 4 890 | Dépenses touristiques |
| Iran (Islamic Rep. of) | | | | | | | | Iran (Rép. islamique d') |
| Tourist/visitor arrivals | TF | 1 402 | 1 585 | 1 546 | 1 659 | ... | ... | Arrivées de touristes/visiteurs |
| Tourism expenditure[36] | | 1 122 | 1 607 | 1 266 | 1 305 | 1 364 | 1 513 | Dépenses touristiques[36] |
| Iraq | | | | | | | | Iraq |
| Tourist/visitor arrivals | VF | 127 | ... | ... | ... | ... | ... | Arrivées de touristes/visiteurs |
| Tourism expenditure[5,37] | | 15 | 45 | ... | ... | ... | ... | Dépenses touristiques[5,37] |
| Ireland | | | | | | | | Irlande |
| Tourist/visitor arrivals[38] | TF | 6 353 | 6 476 | 6 764 | 6 953 | 7 333 | 8 001 | Arrivées de touristes/visiteurs[38] |
| Tourism expenditure | | 3 789 | 4 228 | 5 206 | 6 075 | 6 780 | 7 664 | Dépenses touristiques |
| Israel | | | | | | | | Israël |
| Tourist/visitor arrivals[4] | TF | 1 196 | 862 | 1 063 | 1 506 | 1 903 | 1 825 | Arrivées de touristes/visiteurs[4] |
| Tourism expenditure | | 2 855 | 2 426 | 2 473 | 2 863 | 3 358 | 3 319 | Dépenses touristiques |
| Italy | | | | | | | | Italie |
| Tourist/visitor arrivals[39] | TF | 39 563 | 39 799 | 39 604 | 37 071 | 36 513 | 41 058 | Arrivées de touristes/visiteurs[39] |
| Tourism expenditure | | 26 916 | 28 192 | 32 591 | 37 870 | 38 374 | 41 644 | Dépenses touristiques |
| Jamaica | | | | | | | | Jamaïque |
| Tourist/visitor arrivals[2,40] | TF | 1 277 | 1 266 | 1 350 | 1 415 | 1 479 | 1 679 | Arrivées de touristes/visiteurs[2,40] |
| Tourism expenditure | | 1 494 | 1 482 | 1 621 | 1 733 | 1 783 | 2 094 | Dépenses touristiques |
| Japan | | | | | | | | Japon |
| Tourist/visitor arrivals[4] | VF | 4 772 | 5 239 | 5 212 | 6 138 | 6 728 | 7 334 | Arrivées de touristes/visiteurs[4] |
| Tourism expenditure | | 5 750 | 6 069 | 11 475 | 14 343 | 15 555 | 11 490 | Dépenses touristiques |
| Jordan | | | | | | | | Jordanie |
| Tourist/visitor arrivals[2,41] | TF | 1 672 | 2 384 | 2 353 | 2 853 | 2 987 | 3 225 | Arrivées de touristes/visiteurs[2,41] |
| Tourism expenditure | | 884 | 1 254 | 1 266 | 1 621 | 1 759 | 2 008 | Dépenses touristiques |
| Kazakhstan | | | | | | | | Kazakhstan |
| Tourist/visitor arrivals | TF | 1 845 | 2 832 | 2 410 | 3 073 | 3 143 | 3 468 | Arrivées de touristes/visiteurs |
| Tourism expenditure | | 502 | 680 | 638 | 803 | 801 | 973 | Dépenses touristiques |
| Kenya | | | | | | | | Kenya |
| Tourist/visitor arrivals | TF | 828 | 825 | 927 | 1 193 | 1 536 | 1 644 | Arrivées de touristes/visiteurs |
| Tourism expenditure | | 536 | 513 | 619 | 799 | 969 | 1 182 | Dépenses touristiques |
| Kiribati | | | | | | | | Kiribati |
| Tourist/visitor arrivals[7] | TF | 5 | 5 | 5 | 4 | 3 | 4 | Arrivées de touristes/visiteurs[7] |
| Tourism expenditure[3] | | 3 | ... | ... | ... | ... | ... | Dépenses touristiques[3] |
| Korea Republic of | | | | | | | | Corée République de |
| Tourist/visitor arrivals[2,42] | VF | 5 147 | 5 347 | 4 753 | 5 818 | 6 023 | 6 155 | Arrivées de touristes/visiteurs[2,42] |
| Tourism expenditure | | 7 919 | 7 621 | 7 005 | 8 226 | 8 290 | 8 069 | Dépenses touristiques |
| Kuwait | | | | | | | | Koweït |
| Tourist/visitor arrivals | VF | 2 072 | 2 316 | 2 602 | 3 056 | 3 474 | ... | Arrivées de touristes/visiteurs |
| Tourism expenditure | | 286 | 320 | 328 | 412 | 410 | 470 | Dépenses touristiques |
| Kyrgyzstan | | | | | | | | Kirghizistan |
| Tourist/visitor arrivals | TF | 99 | 140 | 342[43] | 398[43] | 315[43] | 766[43] | Arrivées de touristes/visiteurs |
| Tourism expenditure | | 32 | 48 | 62 | 92 | 94 | 189 | Dépenses touristiques |
| Lao People's Dem. Rep. | | | | | | | | Rép. dém. pop. lao |
| Tourist/visitor arrivals | TF | 173 | 215 | 196 | 407 | 672 | 842 | Arrivées de touristes/visiteurs |
| Tourism expenditure[5] | | 104 | 113 | 87 | 119 | 147 | 173 | Dépenses touristiques[5] |
| Latvia | | | | | | | | Lettonie |
| Tourist/visitor arrivals[44] | TF | 591 | 848 | 971 | 1 079 | 1 116 | 1 535 | Arrivées de touristes/visiteurs[44] |
| Tourism expenditure | | 153 | 201 | 271 | 343 | 446 | 622 | Dépenses touristiques |

| Country or area of destination | Category&<br>Catégorie& | 2001 | 2002 | 2003 | 2004 | 2005 | 2006 | Pays ou zone de destination |
|---|---|---|---|---|---|---|---|---|
| Lebanon | | | | | | | | Liban |
| Tourist/visitor arrivals[45] | TF | 837 | 956 | 1 016 | 1 278 | 1 140 | 1 063 | Arrivées de touristes/visiteurs[45] |
| Tourism expenditure | | 837[3,46] | 4 284[5] | 6 782 | 5 931 | 5 969 | 5 491 | Dépenses touristiques |
| Lesotho | | | | | | | | Lesotho |
| Tourist/visitor arrivals | VF | 295 | 287 | 329 | 304 | 304 | 357 | Arrivées de touristes/visiteurs |
| Tourism expenditure[5] | | 23 | 20 | 28 | 34 | 30 | 28 | Dépenses touristiques[5] |
| Libyan Arab Jamah. | | | | | | | | Jamah. arabe libyenne |
| Tourist/visitor arrivals | TF | 169 | 135 | 142 | 149 | ... | ... | Arrivées de touristes/visiteurs |
| Tourism expenditure | | 90 | 202 | 243 | 261 | 301 | 244 | Dépenses touristiques |
| Liechtenstein | | | | | | | | Liechtenstein |
| Tourist/visitor arrivals | THS | 56 | 49 | 49 | 49 | 50 | 55 | Arrivées de touristes/visiteurs |
| Lithuania | | | | | | | | Lituanie |
| Tourist/visitor arrivals | TF | 1 271 | 1 428 | 1 491 | 1 800 | 2 000 | 2 180 | Arrivées de touristes/visiteurs |
| Tourism expenditure | | 425 | 556 | 700 | 834 | 975 | 1 077 | Dépenses touristiques |
| Luxembourg | | | | | | | | Luxembourg |
| Tourist/visitor arrivals | TCE | 836 | 885 | 867 | 878 | 913 | 908 | Arrivées de touristes/visiteurs |
| Tourism expenditure | | 1 780[5] | 2 547 | 3 149 | 3 880 | 3 614[5] | 3 626[5] | Dépenses touristiques |
| Madagascar | | | | | | | | Madagascar |
| Tourist/visitor arrivals[40] | TF | 170 | 62 | 139 | 229 | 277 | 312 | Arrivées de touristes/visiteurs[40] |
| Tourism expenditure | | 149 | 109 | 119 | 239 | 290 | 386 | Dépenses touristiques |
| Malawi | | | | | | | | Malawi |
| Tourist/visitor arrivals[47] | TF | 266 | 383 | 424 | 427 | 438 | ... | Arrivées de touristes/visiteurs[47] |
| Tourism expenditure[48] | | 40 | 45 | 35 | 36 | 43 | 43 | Dépenses touristiques[48] |
| Malaysia | | | | | | | | Malaisie |
| Tourist/visitor arrivals[49] | TF | 12 775 | 13 292 | 10 577 | 15 703 | 16 431 | 17 547 | Arrivées de touristes/visiteurs[49] |
| Tourism expenditure | | 7 627 | 8 084 | 6 799 | 9 183 | 10 389 | 12 355 | Dépenses touristiques |
| Maldives | | | | | | | | Maldives |
| Tourist/visitor arrivals[7] | TF | 461 | 485 | 564 | 617 | 395 | 602 | Arrivées de touristes/visiteurs[7] |
| Tourism expenditure[5] | | 327 | 337 | 402 | 471 | 287 | 434 | Dépenses touristiques[5] |
| Mali | | | | | | | | Mali |
| Tourist/visitor arrivals[7] | THS | 89 | 96 | 110 | 113 | 143 | 153 | Arrivées de touristes/visiteurs[7] |
| Tourism expenditure | | 91 | 105 | 136 | 142 | 149 | 167[5] | Dépenses touristiques |
| Malta | | | | | | | | Malte |
| Tourist/visitor arrivals | TF | 1 180 | 1 134 | 1 127 | 1 156[50] | 1 171[50] | 1 124[50] | Arrivées de touristes/visiteurs |
| Tourism expenditure | | 704 | 757 | 869 | 953 | 923 | 970 | Dépenses touristiques |
| Marshall Islands | | | | | | | | Iles Marshall |
| Tourist/visitor arrivals | TF | 5[7] | 6[7] | 7[7] | 9[52] | 9[52] | 6[7] | Arrivées de touristes/visiteurs |
| Tourism expenditure[3,51] | | 3 | 3 | 4 | 5 | 6 | 7 | Dépenses touristiques[3,51] |
| Martinique | | | | | | | | Martinique |
| Tourist/visitor arrivals | TF | 460 | 447 | 453 | 471 | 484 | 503 | Arrivées de touristes/visiteurs |
| Tourism expenditure[3] | | 245 | 237 | 247 | 291 | 280 | 306 | Dépenses touristiques[3] |
| Mauritius | | | | | | | | Maurice |
| Tourist/visitor arrivals | TF | 660 | 682 | 702 | 719 | 761 | 788 | Arrivées de touristes/visiteurs |
| Tourism expenditure | | 820 | 829 | 960 | 1 156 | 1 189 | 1 302 | Dépenses touristiques |
| Mexico | | | | | | | | Mexique |
| Tourist/visitor arrivals[2] | TF | 19 810 | 19 667 | 18 665 | 20 618 | 21 915 | 21 353 | Arrivées de touristes/visiteurs[2] |
| Tourism expenditure | | 9 190 | 9 547 | 10 058 | 11 609 | 12 801 | 13 329 | Dépenses touristiques |
| Micronesia (Fed. States of) | | | | | | | | Micronésie (Etats féd. de) |
| Tourist/visitor arrivals[53] | TF | 15 | 19 | 18 | 19 | 19 | 19 | Arrivées de touristes/visiteurs[53] |
| Tourism expenditure[3,51] | | 15 | 17 | 17 | 17 | 17 | ... | Dépenses touristiques[3,51] |

| Country or area of destination | Category[&] Catégorie[&] | 2001 | 2002 | 2003 | 2004 | 2005 | 2006 | Pays ou zone de destination |
|---|---|---|---|---|---|---|---|---|
| Moldova | | | | | | | | Moldova |
| Tourist/visitor arrivals[54] | THS | 16 | 18 | 21 | 24 | 23 | 13 | Arrivées de touristes/visiteurs[54] |
| Tourism expenditure | | 58 | 72 | 79 | 112 | 138 | 145 | Dépenses touristiques |
| Monaco | | | | | | | | Monaco |
| Tourist/visitor arrivals | THS | 270 | 263 | 235 | 250 | 286 | 313 | Arrivées de touristes/visiteurs |
| Mongolia | | | | | | | | Mongolie |
| Tourist/visitor arrivals[55] | TF | 166 | 229 | 201 | 301 | 338 | 386 | Arrivées de touristes/visiteurs[55] |
| Tourism expenditure | | 49 | 143 | 154 | 205 | 203 | 261 | Dépenses touristiques |
| Montenegro | | | | | | | | Monténégro |
| Tourist/visitor arrivals | TCE | ... | 136 | 142 | 188 | 272 | 378 | Arrivées de touristes/visiteurs |
| Montserrat | | | | | | | | Montserrat |
| Tourist/visitor arrivals | TF | 10 | 10 | 8 | 10 | 10 | 8 | Arrivées de touristes/visiteurs |
| Tourism expenditure[5] | | 8 | 9 | 7 | 9 | 9 | 8 | Dépenses touristiques[5] |
| Morocco | | | | | | | | Maroc |
| Tourist/visitor arrivals[2] | TF | 4 380 | 4 453 | 4 761 | 5 477 | 5 843 | 6 558 | Arrivées de touristes/visiteurs[2] |
| Tourism expenditure | | 2 966 | 3 157 | 3 802 | 4 540 | 5 426 | 6 899 | Dépenses touristiques |
| Mozambique | | | | | | | | Mozambique |
| Tourist/visitor arrivals | TF | 323 | 541 | 441 | 470 | 578 | 664 | Arrivées de touristes/visiteurs |
| Tourism expenditure | | 64[5] | 65 | 106 | 96 | 138 | 145 | Dépenses touristiques |
| Myanmar | | | | | | | | Myanmar |
| Tourist/visitor arrivals[56] | TF | 205 | 217 | 206 | 242 | 232 | 264 | Arrivées de touristes/visiteurs[56] |
| Tourism expenditure | | 132 | 136 | 70 | 97 | 85 | 59 | Dépenses touristiques |
| Namibia | | | | | | | | Namibie |
| Tourist/visitor arrivals | TF | 670 | 757 | 695 | ... | 778 | 833 | Arrivées de touristes/visiteurs |
| Tourism expenditure | | 264 | 251 | 383 | 426 | 363 | 473 | Dépenses touristiques |
| Nepal | | | | | | | | Népal |
| Tourist/visitor arrivals[57] | TF | 361 | 275 | 338 | 385 | 375 | 284 | Arrivées de touristes/visiteurs[57] |
| Tourism expenditure | | 191 | 134 | 232 | 260 | 160 | 157 | Dépenses touristiques |
| Netherlands | | | | | | | | Pays-Bas |
| Tourist/visitor arrivals | TCE | 9 500 | 9 595 | 9 181 | 9 646 | 10 012 | 10 739 | Arrivées de touristes/visiteurs |
| Tourism expenditure | | 11 147 | 11 745 | 9 163[5] | 10 308[5] | 10 446[5] | 11 381[5] | Dépenses touristiques |
| New Caledonia | | | | | | | | Nouvelle-Calédonie |
| Tourist/visitor arrivals[2] | TF | 101 | 104 | 102 | 100 | 101 | 100 | Arrivées de touristes/visiteurs[2] |
| Tourism expenditure[5] | | 94 | 156 | 196 | 241 | 253 | 258 | Dépenses touristiques[5] |
| New Zealand | | | | | | | | Nouvelle-Zélande |
| Tourist/visitor arrivals | VF | 1 909 | 2 045 | 2 104 | 2 334 | 2 365 | 2 409 | Arrivées de touristes/visiteurs |
| Tourism expenditure[5] | | 2 350 | 3 077 | 4 028 | 4 782 | 4 873 | 4 563 | Dépenses touristiques[5] |
| Nicaragua | | | | | | | | Nicaragua |
| Tourist/visitor arrivals | TF | 483 | 472 | 526 | 615 | 712[2] | 773[2] | Arrivées de touristes/visiteurs |
| Tourism expenditure | | 138 | 138 | 164 | 196 | 210 | 237 | Dépenses touristiques |
| Niger | | | | | | | | Niger |
| Tourist/visitor arrivals | TF | 52 | 39 | 55 | 57 | 60 | 60 | Arrivées de touristes/visiteurs |
| Tourism expenditure | | 30 | 20 | 28 | 32 | 44 | 35[5] | Dépenses touristiques |
| Nigeria | | | | | | | | Nigéria |
| Tourist/visitor arrivals | TF | 850 | 887 | 924 | 962 | 1 010 | 1 111 | Arrivées de touristes/visiteurs |
| Tourism expenditure | | 168 | 256 | 58 | 49 | 46 | 51 | Dépenses touristiques |
| Niue | | | | | | | | Nioué |
| Tourist/visitor arrivals[58] | TF | 1 | 2 | 3 | 3 | 3 | 3 | Arrivées de touristes/visiteurs[58] |
| Tourism expenditure[3] | | ... | ... | 1 | 1 | 1 | 1 | Dépenses touristiques[3] |
| Northern Mariana Islands[7] | | | | | | | | Iles Mariannes du Nord[7] |
| Tourist/visitor arrivals | TF | 438 | 466 | 452 | 525 | 498 | 429 | Arrivées de touristes/visiteurs |
| Norway | | | | | | | | Norvège |
| Tourist/visitor arrivals[59] | TF | 3 073 | 3 111 | 3 269 | 3 628 | 3 824 | 3 945 | Arrivées de touristes/visiteurs[59] |
| Tourism expenditure | | 2 380 | 2 581 | 2 989 | 3 531 | 3 959 | 4 251 | Dépenses touristiques |

| Country or area of destination | Category&<br>Catégorie& | 2001 | 2002 | 2003 | 2004 | 2005 | 2006 | Pays ou zone de destination |
|---|---|---|---|---|---|---|---|---|
| Occupied Palestinian Terr. | | | | | | | | Terr. palestinien occupé |
| Tourist/visitor arrivals | THS | 43 | 33 | 37 | 56 | 88 | 123 | Arrivées de touristes/visiteurs |
| Tourism expenditure[5] | | 35 | 33 | 107 | 56 | 121 | ... | Dépenses touristiques[5] |
| Oman | | | | | | | | Oman |
| Tourist/visitor arrivals | THS | 647 | 643 | 630 | 908 | 989 | 1 306 | Arrivées de touristes/visiteurs |
| Tourism expenditure | | 539 | 539 | 546 | 604 | 599 | 743 | Dépenses touristiques |
| Pakistan | | | | | | | | Pakistan |
| Tourist/visitor arrivals | TF | 500 | 498 | 501 | 648 | 798 | 898 | Arrivées de touristes/visiteurs |
| Tourism expenditure | | 533 | 562 | 620 | 765 | 828 | 899 | Dépenses touristiques |
| Palau | | | | | | | | Palaos |
| Tourist/visitor arrivals[60] | TF | 54 | 59 | 68 | 95 | 86 | 86 | Arrivées de touristes/visiteurs[60] |
| Tourism expenditure[3] | | 59 | 57 | 76 | 97 | 97 | 90 | Dépenses touristiques[3] |
| Panama | | | | | | | | Panama |
| Tourist/visitor arrivals | TF | 519 | 534 | 566 | 621 | 702 | 843 | Arrivées de touristes/visiteurs |
| Tourism expenditure | | 665 | 710 | 804 | 903 | 1 108 | 1 450 | Dépenses touristiques |
| Papua New Guinea | | | | | | | | Papouasie-Nvl-Guinée |
| Tourist/visitor arrivals | TF | 54 | 54 | 56 | 59 | 69 | 78 | Arrivées de touristes/visiteurs |
| Tourism expenditure | | 5 | 3[5] | 4[5] | 6 | 4 | ... | Dépenses touristiques |
| Paraguay | | | | | | | | Paraguay |
| Tourist/visitor arrivals[61,62] | TF | 279 | 250 | 268 | 309 | 341 | 388 | Arrivées de touristes/visiteurs[61,62] |
| Tourism expenditure | | 91 | 76 | 81 | 87 | 96 | 111 | Dépenses touristiques |
| Peru | | | | | | | | Pérou |
| Tourist/visitor arrivals | TF | 901 | 998[63] | 1 070[63] | 1 277[63] | 1 487[63] | 1 635[63] | Arrivées de touristes/visiteurs |
| Tourism expenditure | | 763 | 836 | 1 023 | 1 232 | 1 438 | 1 586 | Dépenses touristiques |
| Philippines | | | | | | | | Philippines |
| Tourist/visitor arrivals[2] | TF | 1 797 | 1 933 | 1 907 | 2 291 | 2 623 | 2 843 | Arrivées de touristes/visiteurs[2] |
| Tourism expenditure | | 2 011 | 2 018 | 1 821 | 2 390 | 2 755 | 4 019 | Dépenses touristiques |
| Poland | | | | | | | | Pologne |
| Tourist/visitor arrivals | TF | 15 000 | 13 980 | 13 720 | 14 290 | 15 200 | 15 670 | Arrivées de touristes/visiteurs |
| Tourism expenditure | | 5 121 | 4 971 | 4 733 | 6 499 | 7 128 | 8 122 | Dépenses touristiques |
| Portugal | | | | | | | | Portugal |
| Tourist/visitor arrivals | TF | 12 167[4] | 11 644[4] | 11 707[4] | 10 639[2,64] | 10 612[2,64] | 11 282[2,64] | Arrivées de touristes/visiteurs |
| Tourism expenditure | | 6 236 | 6 595 | 7 634 | 8 863 | 9 009 | 10 036 | Dépenses touristiques |
| Puerto Rico | | | | | | | | Porto Rico |
| Tourist/visitor arrivals[65] | TF | 3 551 | 3 087 | 3 238 | 3 541 | 3 686 | 3 722 | Arrivées de touristes/visiteurs[65] |
| Tourism expenditure[3] | | 2 728 | 2 486 | 2 677 | 3 024 | 3 239 | 3 369 | Dépenses touristiques[3] |
| Qatar | | | | | | | | Qatar |
| Tourist/visitor arrivals[1] | THS | 376 | 587 | 557 | 732 | 913 | 946 | Arrivées de touristes/visiteurs[1] |
| Tourism expenditure[5,66] | | 272 | 285 | 369 | 498 | 760 | 374 | Dépenses touristiques[5,66] |
| Réunion | | | | | | | | Réunion |
| Tourist/visitor arrivals | TF | 424 | 426 | 432 | 430 | 409 | 279 | Arrivées de touristes/visiteurs |
| Tourism expenditure[3] | | 281 | 329 | 413 | 448 | 442 | 308 | Dépenses touristiques[3] |
| Romania | | | | | | | | Roumanie |
| Tourist/visitor arrivals | VF | 4 938 | 4 794 | 5 595 | 6 600 | 5 839 | 6 037 | Arrivées de touristes/visiteurs |
| Tourism expenditure | | 419 | 400 | 523 | 607 | 1 325 | 1 676 | Dépenses touristiques |
| Russian Federation | | | | | | | | Fédération de Russie |
| Tourist/visitor arrivals | VF | 21 595 | 23 309 | 22 521 | 22 064 | 22 201 | 22 486 | Arrivées de touristes/visiteurs |
| Tourism expenditure | | 4 726 | 5 428 | 5 879 | 7 262 | 7 806 | 9 720 | Dépenses touristiques |
| Rwanda | | | | | | | | Rwanda |
| Tourist/visitor arrivals[67] | TF | 113 | ... | ... | ... | ... | ... | Arrivées de touristes/visiteurs[67] |
| Tourism expenditure | | 29 | 31[5] | 30[5] | 44[5] | 49[5] | 31[5] | Dépenses touristiques |
| Saba | | | | | | | | Saba |
| Tourist/visitor arrivals | TF | 9 | 11 | 10 | 11 | 11 | 11 | Arrivées de touristes/visiteurs |
| Saint Eustatius[68] | | | | | | | | Saint-Eustache[68] |
| Tourist/visitor arrivals | TF | 10 | 10 | 10 | 11 | 10 | 10 | Arrivées de touristes/visiteurs |

| Country or area of destination | Category&<br>Catégorie& | 2001 | 2002 | 2003 | 2004 | 2005 | 2006 | Pays ou zone de destination |
|---|---|---|---|---|---|---|---|---|
| Saint Kitts and Nevis | | | | | | | | Saint-Kitts-et-Nevis |
| Tourist/visitor arrivals[40] | TF | 71 | 69 | 91 | 118 | 128 | 133 | Arrivées de touristes/visiteurs[40] |
| Tourism expenditure[5] | | 62 | 57 | 75 | 103 | 115 | 116 | Dépenses touristiques[5] |
| Saint Lucia | | | | | | | | Sainte-Lucie |
| Tourist/visitor arrivals[4] | TF | 250 | 253 | 277 | 298 | 318 | 303 | Arrivées de touristes/visiteurs[4] |
| Tourism expenditure[5] | | 233 | 207 | 282 | 326 | 356 | 347 | Dépenses touristiques[5] |
| Saint Maarten | | | | | | | | Saint-Martin |
| Tourist/visitor arrivals[69] | TF | 403 | 381 | 428 | 475 | 468 | 468 | Arrivées de touristes/visiteurs[69] |
| Tourism expenditure[5,70] | | 484 | 489 | 538 | 626 | 659 | 652 | Dépenses touristiques[5,70] |
| Saint Vincent-Grenadines | | | | | | | | Saint Vincent-Grenadines |
| Tourist/visitor arrivals[40] | TF | 71 | 78 | 79 | 87 | 96 | 97 | Arrivées de touristes/visiteurs[40] |
| Tourism expenditure[5] | | 89 | 91 | 91 | 96 | 104 | 113 | Dépenses touristiques[5] |
| Samoa | | | | | | | | Samoa |
| Tourist/visitor arrivals | TF | 88 | 89 | 92 | 98 | 102 | 116 | Arrivées de touristes/visiteurs |
| Tourism expenditure | | 39[5,33] | 45[5,33] | 54[5,33] | 70 | 78 | 91 | Dépenses touristiques |
| San Marino[71] | | | | | | | | Saint-Marin[71] |
| Tourist/visitor arrivals | THS | 49 | 46 | 41 | 42 | 50 | 50 | Arrivées de touristes/visiteurs |
| Sao Tome and Principe | | | | | | | | Sao Tomé-et-Principe |
| Tourist/visitor arrivals | TF | 8 | 9 | 10 | 11 | 16 | 12 | Arrivées de touristes/visiteurs |
| Tourism expenditure[5] | | 10 | 10 | 11 | 13 | 14 | ... | Dépenses touristiques[5] |
| Saudi Arabia | | | | | | | | Arabie saoudite |
| Tourist/visitor arrivals | TF | 6 727 | 7 511 | 7 332 | 8 599 | 8 037 | 8 620 | Arrivées de touristes/visiteurs |
| Tourism expenditure[3] | | ... | ... | 3 418 | 6 916 | 5 626 | 5 391 | Dépenses touristiques[3] |
| Senegal | | | | | | | | Sénégal |
| Tourist/visitor arrivals | THS | 396 | 427 | 354 | 363 | 387 | 406 | Arrivées de touristes/visiteurs |
| Tourism expenditure | | 175 | 210 | 269 | 287 | 334 | ... | Dépenses touristiques |
| Serbia | | | | | | | | Serbie |
| Tourist/visitor arrivals | TCE | ... | 312 | 339 | 392 | 453 | 469 | Arrivées de touristes/visiteurs |
| Tourism expenditure[3] | | ... | 77 | 159 | 220 | 308 | 398 | Dépenses touristiques[3] |
| Serbia and Montenegro | | | | | | | | Serbie-et-Monténégro |
| Tourist/visitor arrivals | TCE | 351 | ... | ... | ... | ... | ... | Arrivées de touristes/visiteurs |
| Tourism expenditure[3,5,72] | | 54 | ... | ... | ... | ... | ... | Dépenses touristiques[3,5,72] |
| Seychelles | | | | | | | | Seychelles |
| Tourist/visitor arrivals | TF | 130 | 132 | 122 | 121 | 129 | 141 | Arrivées de touristes/visiteurs |
| Tourism expenditure | | 221 | 247 | 258 | 256 | 269 | 323 | Dépenses touristiques |
| Sierra Leone | | | | | | | | Sierra Leone |
| Tourist/visitor arrivals[7] | TF | 24 | 28 | 38 | 44 | 40 | 34 | Arrivées de touristes/visiteurs[7] |
| Tourism expenditure[5] | | 14 | 38 | 60 | 58 | 64 | 23 | Dépenses touristiques[5] |
| Singapore | | | | | | | | Singapour |
| Tourist/visitor arrivals | TF | 5 857 | 5 855 | 4 703 | 6 553 | 7 080 | 7 588 | Arrivées de touristes/visiteurs |
| Tourism expenditure[5] | | 4 619 | 4 428 | 3 783 | 5 226 | 5 903 | 7 069 | Dépenses touristiques[5] |
| Slovakia | | | | | | | | Slovaquie |
| Tourist/visitor arrivals | TCE | 1 219 | 1 399 | 1 387 | 1 401 | 1 515 | 1 612 | Arrivées de touristes/visiteurs |
| Tourism expenditure | | 649[33] | 742 | 876 | 932[33] | 1 210[5,33] | 1 513[5,33] | Dépenses touristiques |
| Slovenia | | | | | | | | Slovénie |
| Tourist/visitor arrivals | TCE | 1 219 | 1 302 | 1 373 | 1 499 | 1 555 | 1 617 | Arrivées de touristes/visiteurs |
| Tourism expenditure | | 1 059 | 1 152 | 1 427 | 1 725 | 1 894 | 1 911 | Dépenses touristiques |
| Solomon Islands | | | | | | | | Iles Salomon |
| Tourist/visitor arrivals | TF | ... | ... | 7 | ... | 9[73] | 11 | Arrivées de touristes/visiteurs |
| Tourism expenditure | | 9 | 1 | 2 | 4 | 7 | 8 | Dépenses touristiques |
| South Africa | | | | | | | | Afrique du Sud |
| Tourist/visitor arrivals[74] | TF | 5 787 | 6 430 | 6 505 | 6 678 | 7 369 | 8 396 | Arrivées de touristes/visiteurs[74] |
| Tourism expenditure | | 3 256 | 3 695 | 6 533 | 7 380 | 8 448 | 8 967 | Dépenses touristiques |

# 59

**Tourism/visitor arrivals and tourism expenditure** — Thousands arrivals and millions of US dollars (*continued*)
**Arrivées de touristes/visiteurs et dépenses touristiques** — Milliers d'arrivées et millions de dollars E.-U. (*suite*)

| Country or area of destination | Category&<br>Catégorie& | 2001 | 2002 | 2003 | 2004 | 2005 | 2006 | Pays ou zone de destination |
|---|---|---|---|---|---|---|---|---|
| Spain | | | | | | | | Espagne |
| Tourist/visitor arrivals | TF | 50 094 | 52 327 | 50 854 | 52 430 | 55 914 | 58 190 | Arrivées de touristes/visiteurs |
| Tourism expenditure | | 33 829 | 35 468 | 43 863 | 49 996 | 53 066 | 57 537 | Dépenses touristiques |
| Sri Lanka | | | | | | | | Sri Lanka |
| Tourist/visitor arrivals[4] | TF | 337 | 393 | 501 | 566 | 549 | 560 | Arrivées de touristes/visiteurs[4] |
| Tourism expenditure | | 347 | 594 | 709 | 808 | 729 | 733 | Dépenses touristiques |
| Sudan | | | | | | | | Soudan |
| Tourist/visitor arrivals | TF | 50 | 52 | 52 | 61 | 246[2] | 328[2] | Arrivées de touristes/visiteurs |
| Tourism expenditure | | 3 | 108 | 17 | 21 | 89 | 126 | Dépenses touristiques |
| Suriname | | | | | | | | Suriname |
| Tourist/visitor arrivals | TF | 54[75] | 60[75] | 82[75] | 138 | 160 | ... | Arrivées de touristes/visiteurs |
| Tourism expenditure | | 26 | 17 | 18 | 52 | 96 | 109 | Dépenses touristiques |
| Swaziland | | | | | | | | Swaziland |
| Tourist/visitor arrivals | THS | 283[1] | 256[1] | 461 | 459 | 839 | 873 | Arrivées de touristes/visiteurs |
| Tourism expenditure | | 23 | 45 | 70 | 75 | 78 | 74 | Dépenses touristiques |
| Sweden | | | | | | | | Suède |
| Tourist/visitor arrivals[76] | TCE | 2 894 | 2 989 | 2 952 | 3 003 | 3 133 | 3 270 | Arrivées de touristes/visiteurs[76] |
| Tourism expenditure | | 5 200 | 5 671 | 6 548 | 7 686 | 8 580 | 10 437 | Dépenses touristiques |
| Switzerland | | | | | | | | Suisse |
| Tourist/visitor arrivals | THS | 7 455 | 6 868 | 6 530 | ... | 7 229 | 7 863 | Arrivées de touristes/visiteurs |
| Tourism expenditure | | 9 290 | 9 117 | 10 496 | 11 409 | 11 991 | 12 755 | Dépenses touristiques |
| Syrian Arab Republic | | | | | | | | Rép. arabe syrienne |
| Tourist/visitor arrivals | TF | 1 801 | 2 186 | 2 085 | 3 033 | 3 368 | 4 422 | Arrivées de touristes/visiteurs |
| Tourism expenditure | | 1 150 | 970[5] | 877 | 1 883 | 2 035 | 2 113 | Dépenses touristiques |
| Tajikistan | | | | | | | | Tadjikistan |
| Tourist/visitor arrivals | TF | 4 | ... | ... | ... | ... | ... | Arrivées de touristes/visiteurs |
| Tourism expenditure | | ... | 5 | 7 | 9 | 10 | 11 | Dépenses touristiques |
| Thailand | | | | | | | | Thaïlande |
| Tourist/visitor arrivals[2] | TF | 10 133 | 10 873 | 10 082 | 11 737 | 11 567 | 13 822 | Arrivées de touristes/visiteurs[2] |
| Tourism expenditure | | 9 380 | 10 388 | 10 456 | 13 054 | 12 102 | 15 653 | Dépenses touristiques |
| TFYR of Macedonia | | | | | | | | Ex-R.Y. Macédoine |
| Tourist/visitor arrivals | TCE | 99 | 123 | 158 | 165 | 197 | 202 | Arrivées de touristes/visiteurs |
| Tourism expenditure | | 49 | 55 | 65 | 77 | 92 | 156 | Dépenses touristiques |
| Togo | | | | | | | | Togo |
| Tourist/visitor arrivals | THS | 57 | 58 | 61 | 83 | 81 | 94 | Arrivées de touristes/visiteurs |
| Tourism expenditure | | 14 | 16 | 26 | 25 | 27 | 26 | Dépenses touristiques |
| Tonga | | | | | | | | Tonga |
| Tourist/visitor arrivals[7] | TF | 32 | 37 | 40 | 41 | 42 | 39 | Arrivées de touristes/visiteurs[7] |
| Tourism expenditure[5] | | 7 | 6 | 10 | 13 | 15 | 16 | Dépenses touristiques[5] |
| Trinidad and Tobago | | | | | | | | Trinité-et-Tobago |
| Tourist/visitor arrivals[7] | TF | 383 | 384 | 409 | 443 | 463 | 457 | Arrivées de touristes/visiteurs[7] |
| Tourism expenditure | | 361 | 402 | 437 | 568 | 593 | 357 | Dépenses touristiques |
| Tunisia | | | | | | | | Tunisie |
| Tourist/visitor arrivals[4] | TF | 5 387 | 5 064 | 5 114 | 5 998 | 6 378 | 6 550 | Arrivées de touristes/visiteurs[4] |
| Tourism expenditure | | 2 061 | 1 831 | 1 935 | 2 432 | 2 800 | 2 999 | Dépenses touristiques |
| Turkey | | | | | | | | Turquie |
| Tourist/visitor arrivals | TF | 10 783 | 12 790 | 13 341 | 16 826 | 20 273 | 18 916 | Arrivées de touristes/visiteurs |
| Tourism expenditure | | 10 067[5,33,77] | 11 901[5,33,77] | 13 203[5,77] | 15 888[5,77] | 19 720 | 18 520 | Dépenses touristiques |
| Turkmenistan | | | | | | | | Turkménistan |
| Tourist/visitor arrivals | TF | 5 | 11 | 8 | 15 | 12 | ... | Arrivées de touristes/visiteurs |
| Turks and Caicos Islands | | | | | | | | Iles Turques et Caïques |
| Tourist/visitor arrivals | TF | 166 | 155 | 164 | 173 | 176 | 248 | Arrivées de touristes/visiteurs |
| Tourism expenditure[3] | | 311 | 292 | ... | ... | ... | ... | Dépenses touristiques[3] |
| Tuvalu | | | | | | | | Tuvalu |
| Tourist/visitor arrivals | TF | 1 | 1 | 1 | 1 | 1 | 1 | Arrivées de touristes/visiteurs |

| Country or area of destination | Category[&] Catégorie[&] | 2001 | 2002 | 2003 | 2004 | 2005 | 2006 | Pays ou zone de destination |
|---|---|---|---|---|---|---|---|---|
| Uganda | | | | | | | | Ouganda |
| Tourist/visitor arrivals | TF | 205 | 254 | 305 | 512 | 468 | 539 | Arrivées de touristes/visiteurs |
| Tourism expenditure | | 187 | 194 | 185 | 257 | 383 | 356 | Dépenses touristiques |
| Ukraine | | | | | | | | Ukraine |
| Tourist/visitor arrivals | TF | 9 174 | 10 517 | 12 514 | 15 629 | 17 631 | 18 900 | Arrivées de touristes/visiteurs |
| Tourism expenditure | | 759 | 1 001 | 1 204 | 2 931 | 3 542 | 4 018 | Dépenses touristiques |
| United Arab Emirates | | | | | | | | Emirats arabes unis |
| Tourist/visitor arrivals[1,78] | THS | 4 134 | 5 445 | 5 871 | 6 195 | 7 126 | ... | Arrivées de touristes/visiteurs[1,78] |
| Tourism expenditure[3] | | 1 200 | 1 332 | 1 438 | 1 593 | 3 218 | 4 972 | Dépenses touristiques[3] |
| United Kingdom | | | | | | | | Royaume-Uni |
| Tourist/visitor arrivals | TF | 20 982 | 22 307 | 22 787 | 25 678 | 28 039 | 30 654 | Arrivées de touristes/visiteurs |
| Tourism expenditure | | 26 137 | 27 819 | 30 736 | 37 166 | 39 569 | 43 041 | Dépenses touristiques |
| United Rep. of Tanzania | | | | | | | | Rép.-Unie de Tanzanie |
| Tourist/visitor arrivals | TF | 501 | 550 | 552 | 566 | 590 | 622 | Arrivées de touristes/visiteurs |
| Tourism expenditure | | 626 | 639 | 654 | 762 | 835 | 950 | Dépenses touristiques |
| United States | | | | | | | | Etats-Unis |
| Tourist/visitor arrivals[79] | TF | 46 927 | 43 581 | 41 218 | 46 086 | 49 206 | 50 978 | Arrivées de touristes/visiteurs[79] |
| Tourism expenditure | | 106 705 | 101 798 | 99 207 | 113 387 | 123 093 | 128 922 | Dépenses touristiques |
| United States Virgin Is. | | | | | | | | Iles Vierges américaines |
| Tourist/visitor arrivals | TF | 527 | 520 | 538 | 544 | 582 | 570 | Arrivées de touristes/visiteurs |
| Tourism expenditure[3] | | 1 234 | 1 195 | 1 257 | 1 356 | 1 491 | 1 466 | Dépenses touristiques[3] |
| Uruguay | | | | | | | | Uruguay |
| Tourist/visitor arrivals | TF | 1 892 | 1 258 | 1 420 | 1 756 | 1 808 | 1 749 | Arrivées de touristes/visiteurs |
| Tourism expenditure | | 700 | 409 | 419 | 591 | 699 | 706 | Dépenses touristiques |
| Uzbekistan | | | | | | | | Ouzbékistan |
| Tourist/visitor arrivals | TF | 345 | 332 | 231 | 262 | 242 | 281 | Arrivées de touristes/visiteurs |
| Tourism expenditure[3] | | 72 | 68 | 48 | 57 | 28[5] | 43[5] | Dépenses touristiques[3] |
| Vanuatu | | | | | | | | Vanuatu |
| Tourist/visitor arrivals | TF | 53 | 49 | 50 | 61 | 62 | 68 | Arrivées de touristes/visiteurs |
| Tourism expenditure | | 58 | 72 | 83 | 93 | 104 | 109 | Dépenses touristiques |
| Venezuela (Bolivarian Rep. of) | | | | | | | | Venezuela (Rép. bolivarienne du) |
| Tourist/visitor arrivals | TF | 584 | 432 | 337 | 486 | 706 | 748 | Arrivées de touristes/visiteurs |
| Tourism expenditure | | 677 | 484 | 378 | 554 | 722 | 843 | Dépenses touristiques |
| Viet Nam | | | | | | | | Viet Nam |
| Tourist/visitor arrivals | VF | 2 330 | 2 628 | 2 429 | 2 928 | 3 468 | 3 583 | Arrivées de touristes/visiteurs |
| Tourism expenditure[3] | | ... | ... | 1 400 | 1 700 | 1 880 | 3 200 | Dépenses touristiques[3] |
| Yemen | | | | | | | | Yémen |
| Tourist/visitor arrivals | THS | 76 | 98 | 155 | 274 | 336 | 382 | Arrivées de touristes/visiteurs |
| Tourism expenditure[5] | | 38 | 38 | 139 | 139 | 181 | 181 | Dépenses touristiques[5] |
| Zambia | | | | | | | | Zambie |
| Tourist/visitor arrivals | TF | 492 | 565 | 413 | 515 | 669 | 757 | Arrivées de touristes/visiteurs |
| Tourism expenditure[5] | | 80 | 64 | 88 | 92 | 98 | 110 | Dépenses touristiques[5] |
| Zimbabwe | | | | | | | | Zimbabwe |
| Tourist/visitor arrivals | VF | 2 217 | 2 041 | 2 256 | 1 854 | 1 559 | 2 287 | Arrivées de touristes/visiteurs |
| Tourism expenditure[3] | | 81 | 76 | 61 | 194 | 99 | 338 | Dépenses touristiques[3] |

Source

World Tourism Organization (UNWTO), Madrid, UNWTO statistics database and the "Yearbook of Tourism Statistics", 2007 edition.

The majority of the expenditure data have been provided to the UNWTO by the International Monetary Fund. Exceptions are footnoted.

Source

Organisation mondiale du tourisme (OMT), Madrid, la base de données de l'OMT, et "l'Annuaire des statistiques du tourisme", 2007 édition.

La majorité des données sur les déspenses touristique sont celles que le Fonds monétaire international a fournis à l'OMT. Les exceptions sont signalées par une note.

& Categories:

TF: Arrivals of non-resident tourists at national borders.

VF: Arrivals of non-resident visitors at national borders.

THS: Arrivals of non-resident tourists in hotels and similar establishments.

TCE: Arrivals of non-resident tourists in all types of accommodation establishments.

Notes

1 Arrivals in hotels only.

2 Including nationals of the country residing abroad.

3 The expenditure figures are those provided by the country to UNWTO, which do not appear in the International Monetary Fund data.

4 Excluding nationals of the country residing abroad.

5 Excluding passenger transport.

6 Starting 2004, as a result of the importance of the "Survey on International Tourism", the estimates of the series of the "Travel" item of the Balance of Payments were modified. For this reason, the data are not rigorously comparable with those of previous years.

7 Air arrivals.

8 Organized tourism.

9 Country estimates.

10 Source: Central Bank of the Netherlands Antilles.

11 Source: "Banque Centrale des Etats de l'Afrique de l'Ouest".

12 International tourist arrivals by all means of transport.

13 Different types of methodological changes that affect the estimates for 2000 and 2001 for expenditures and characteristics of International Tourists to Canada, have been introduced in 2002. Therefore, Statistics Canada advises not to compare the estimates for 2000 and 2001 with the years prior because of these methodological changes for the non-count estimates (one of the reasons ALS numbers are not provided).

14 Arrivals by air to Bangui only.

15 Source: "Banque des Etats de l'Afrique Centrale (B.E.A.C.)".

16 For statistical purposes, the data for China do not include those for the Hong Kong Special Administrative Region (Hong Kong SAR), Macao Special Administrative Region (Macao SAR) and Taiwan Province of China.

17 The expenditure figures used were the ones provided by the country to UNWTO, as this data series is more complete than that provided by the International Monetary Fund (IMF).

18 Source: "Banque centrale des Comores".

19 New accommodation coverage from 2000.

20 Calculated on the basis of accommodation statistics and "Foreign Visitor Survey" carried out by the Statistical Office of Estonia.

21 Starting from 2004, border statistics are not collected any more.

22 Arrivals through all ports of entry. Including nationals residing abroad.

23 Estimates based on the 1996 survey at national borders. Data revised from 1996.

24 Break in the series, data not comparable with previous years. Revised data.

25 2005 survey at Cayenne-Rochambeau airport on departure.

26 Arrivals of non-resident tourists at Libreville airport.

27 Charter tourists only.

& Catégories :

TF : Arrivées de touristes non résidents aux frontières nationales.

VF : Arrivées de visiteurs non résidents aux frontières nationales.

THS: Arrivées de touristes non résidents dans les hôtels et établissements assimilés.

TCE: Arrivées de touristes non résidents dans tous les types d'établissements d'hébergement touristique.

Notes

1 Arrivées dans les hôtels uniquement.

2 Y compris les nationaux du pays résidant à l'étranger.

3 Les chiffres de dépense sont ceux que le pays a fournis à l'OMT mais ils ne figurent pas dans les données du Fonds monétaire international.

4 A l'exclusion des nationaux du pays résidant à l'étranger.

5 Non compris le transport de passagers.

6 À partir de 2004, vu l'importance de l'« Enquête sur le tourisme international », des modifications ont été apportées aux estimations de la série du poste « Voyages » de la balance des paiements. C'est la raison pour laquelle les données ne sont pas rigoureusement comparables avec celles des années précédentes.

7 Arrivées par voie aérienne.

8 Tourisme organisé.

9 Estimations du pays.

10 Source: "Central Bank of the Netherlands Antilles".

11 Source: Banque Centrale des Etats de l'Afrique de l'Ouest.

12 Touristes étrangers, tous moyens de transport confondus.

13 En 2002, il a été adopté différents types de changements méthodologiques qui ont eu des effets sur les estimations des dépenses et des caractéristiques des touristes internationaux ayant visité le Canada en 2000 et 2001. Pour 2000 et 2001, Statistique Canada conseille par conséquent de ne pas comparer les estimations ne reposant pas sur des comptages aux données des années précédentes (c'est une des raisons pour lesquelles les données DMS ne sont pas fournies).

14 Arrivées par voie aérienne à Bangui uniquement.

15 Source: Banque des Etats de l'Afrique Centrale (B.E.A.C.).

16 Pour la présentation des statistiques, les données pour la Chine ne comprennent pas la Région Administrative Spéciale de Hong Kong (Hong Kong RAS), la Région Administrative Spéciale de Macao (Macao RAS) et la province de Taiwan.

17 Les données de dépense sont celles que le pays a fournies à l'OMT car il s'agit d'une série plus complète que celle obtenue du Fonds monétaire international (FMI).

18 Source: Banque centrale des Comores.

19 Porte sur les nouveaux logements depuis 2000.

20 Calculé sur la base des statistiques d'hébergement et de la "Foreign Visitor Survey" menée par la "Statistical Office of Estonia".

21 À partir de 2004, les statistiques de frontière ne sont plus collectées.

22 Arrivées à travers tous les ports d'entrée. Y compris les nationaux résidant à l'étranger.

23 Estimation à partir de l'enquête aux frontières 1996. Données révisées depuis 1996.

24 La série ayant été interrompue, les données ne sont pas comparables avec celles des années précédentes. Données révisées.

25 Enquête 2005 au départ de l'aéroport de Cayenne-Rochambeau.

26 Arrivées de touristes non résidents à l'aéroport de Libreville.

27 Arrivées en vols à la demande seulement.

| | |
|---|---|
| 28 Data based on surveys. | 28 Données obtenues au moyen d'enquêtes. |
| 29 Excluding the north islands (Saint Maarten and Saint Bartholemy). | 29 Excluant les îles du Nord (Saint Martin et Saint Barthélemy). |
| 30 Non-resident tourists staying in all types of accommodation establishments. | 30 Arrivées de touristes non résidents dans tous les types d'établissements d'hébergement touristique. |
| 31 Arrivals of non-resident tourists in hotels only. | 31 Arrivées de touristes non résidents dans les hôtels seulement. |
| 32 Data based on a survey conducted at Guadeloupe airport. | 32 Données tirées d'une enquête réalisée à l'aéroport de Guadeloupe. |
| 33 Country data. | 33 Données du pays. |
| 34 Air arrivals at Conakry airport. | 34 Arrivées par voie aérienne à l'aéroport de Conakry. |
| 35 Arrivals to Timehri airport only. | 35 Arrivées à l'aéroport de Timehri seulement. |
| 36 Source: Central Bank of Islamic Republic of Iran. | 36 Source: "Central Bank of Islamic Republic of Iran". |
| 37 Source: Central Bank of Iraq. | 37 Source: "Central Bank of Iraq". |
| 38 Including tourists from Northern Ireland. | 38 Y compris touristes à Irlande du Nord. |
| 39 Excluding seasonal and border workers. | 39 A l'exclusion des travailleurs saisoniers et frontaliers. |
| 40 Arrivals of non-resident tourists by air. E/D cards. | 40 Arrivées de touristes non résidents par voie aérienne. Cartes d'embarquement |
| 41 Change in methodology. | 41 Changement de méthode. |
| 42 Including crew members | 42 Y compris les membres d'équipage. |
| 43 New data source: Department of Customs Control. | 43 Nouvelle source d'information: Département du Contrôle douanier. |
| 44 Non-resident departures. Survey of persons crossing the state border. | 44 Départs de non-résidents. Enquête menée auprès de personnes franchissant la frontière de l'État. |
| 45 Excluding Syrian nationals. | 45 A l'exclusion des ressortissants syriens. |
| 46 Due to the lack of data on international tourism receipts concerning statistics on inbound tourism, the Department of "Internet and Statistics Service of the Ministry of Tourism" considers that a tourist spends an average of US$ 1,000. | 46 Du fait d'un manque de données sur les recettes du tourisme international concernant les statistiques sur le tourisme récepteur, le Département "Internet et Service Statistique du Ministère du Tourisme" considère qu'un touriste dépense en moyenne 1 000 $É.-U. |
| 47 Departures. | 47 Départs. |
| 48 Source: Reserve Bank of Malawi. | 48 Source: "Reserve Bank of Malawi". |
| 49 Including Singapore residents crossing the frontier by road through Johore Causeway. | 49 Y compris les résidents de Singapour traversant la frontière par voie terrestre à travers le Johore Causeway. |
| 50 Departures by air and by sea. | 50 Départs par voies aérienne et maritime. |
| 51 Fiscal years (October 1 to September 30). | 51 Années fiscales (du 1er octobre au 30 septembre). |
| 52 Air and sea arrivals. | 52 Arrivées par voie aérienne et maritime. |
| 53 Arrivals in the States of Kosrae, Chuuk, Pohnpei and Yap. Excluding FSM citizens. | 53 Arrivées dans les États de Kosrae, Chuuk, Pohnpei et Yap. Excluant les citoyens de EFM. |
| 54 Visitors who enjoyed the services of the economic agents officially registered under tourism activity and accommodation (excluding the regions of the left bank of the Dniestr and the municipality of Bender). | 54 Visiteurs qui ont bénéficié des services des agents économiques officiellement enregistrés avec le type d'activité tourisme et des unités d'hébergement qui leur appartiennent (à l'exception des régions de la partie gauche du Dniestr et de la municipalité de Bender). |
| 55 Excluding diplomats and foreign residents in Mongolia. | 55 Sont exclus les diplomates et les étrangers qui résident en Mongolie. |
| 56 Including tourist arrivals through border entry points to Yangon. | 56 Comprenant les arrivées de touristes aux postes-frontières de Yangon. |
| 57 Including arrivals from India. | 57 Y compris les arrivées à Inde. |
| 58 Arrivals by air, including Niueans residing usually in New Zealand. | 58 Arrivées par voie aérienne et y compris les nationaux de Niue résidant habituellement en Nouvelle-Zélande. |
| 59 Figures are based on "The Guest survey" carried out by "Institute of Transport Economics". | 59 Les chiffres se fondent sur "l'enquête auprès de la clientèle" de l'Institut d'économie des transports. |
| 60 Air arrivals (Palau International Airport). | 60 Arrivées par voie aérienne (Aéroport international de Palau). |
| 61 Excluding nationals residing abroad and crew members. | 61 A l'exclusion des nationaux du pays résidant à l'étranger et des membres des équipages. |
| 62 E/D cards in the "Silvio Petirossi" airport and passenger counts at the national border crossings - National Police and SENATUR. | 62 Cartes d'embarquement et de débarquement à l'aéroport Silvio Petirossi et comptages des passagers lors du franchissement des frontières nationales – Police Nationale et SENATUR. |
| 63 From 2002, new estimated series including tourists with identity document other than a passport. | 63 À partir de 2002, nouvelle série estimée comprenant les touristes avec une pièce d'identité autre qu'un passeport. |
| 64 Due to a change in the methodology, data are not comparable to previous years. | 64 Dû à un changement dans la méthodologie, l'information n'est pas comparable à celle des années précédentes. |

65 Arrivals by air. Source: "Junta de Planificación de Puerto Rico".

66 Source: Qatar Central Bank.

67 January-November.

68 Excluding Netherlands Antillean residents.

69 Including air arrivals to Saint Maarten (the French side of the island).

70 Source: Central Bank of the Netherlands Antilles - Including the estimates for Saba and Saint Eustatius.

71 Including Italian visitors.

72 Starting 1997 data are presented according to the IMF's Fifth issue of instructions on balance of payments.

73 Without 1st quarter.

74 Excluding arrivals by work and contract workers.

75 Arrivals at Zanderij Airport.

76 Excluding camping.

77 Including expenditure of the nationals residing abroad.

78 Including domestic tourism and nationals of the country residing abroad.

79 Including Mexicans staying one or more nights in the United States.

65 Arrivées par voie aérienne. Source: "Junta de Planificación de Puerto Rico".

66 Source: "Qatar Central Bank".

67 Janvier-novembre.

68 A l'exclusion des résidents des Antilles Néerlandaises.

69 Y compris les arrivées par voie aérienne à Saint-Martin (côté français de l'île).

70 Source: "Central Bank of the Netherlands Antilles". Y compris estimations pour Saba et Saint-Eustache.

71 Y compris les visiteurs italiens.

72 Depuis 1997, les données sont présentées conformément à la cinquième édition du manuel du FMI sur la balance des paiements.

73 À l'exclusion du 1er trimestre.

74 À l'exclusion des arrivées par travail et les travailleurs contractuels.

75 Arrivées à l'aéroport de Zanderij.

76 Camping exclu.

77 Y compris dépenses des nationaux résidant à l'étranger.

78 Y compris le tourisme interne et les nationaux résidant à l'étranger.

79 Incluyant Mexicains passant 1 nuit ou plus aux EU.

# Tourism expenditure in other countries
Total, travel and passenger transport: million US dollars

# Dépenses touristiques dans d'autres pays
Total, voyage et transport de passagers : millions de dollars E.-U.

| Country or area | 2002 | 2003 | 2004 | 2005 | 2006 | Pays ou zone |
|---|---|---|---|---|---|---|
| Albania | | | | | | Albanie |
| Total | 387 | 507 | 669 | 808 | 989 | Total |
| Travel | 366 | 489 | 642 | 786 | 965 | Voyage |
| Passenger transport | 21 | 18 | 27 | 22 | 24 | Transport de passagers |
| Algeria[1] | | | | | | Algérie[1] |
| Total | 248 | 255 | 341 | 370 | 381 | Total |
| Angola | | | | | | Angola |
| Total | 52 | 49 | 86 | 135 | 393 | Total |
| Travel | 19 | 12 | 39 | 74 | 148 | Voyage |
| Passenger transport | 33 | 37 | 47 | 61 | 245 | Transport de passagers |
| Anguilla | | | | | | Anguilla |
| Travel | 8 | 9 | 9 | 10 | ... | Voyage |
| Antigua and Barbuda | | | | | | Antigua-et-Barbuda. |
| Travel | 33 | 35 | 38 | 40 | 46 | Voyage |
| Argentina | | | | | | Argentine |
| Total | 2 744 | 2 997 | 3 208 | 3 564 | 4 078 | Total |
| Travel | 2 328 | 2 511 | 2 604[2] | 2 790[2,3] | 3 131[2,3] | Voyage |
| Passenger transport | 416 | 486 | 604 | 774 | 947 | Transport de passagers |
| Armenia | | | | | | Arménie |
| Total | 85 | 97 | 216 | 284 | 321 | Total |
| Travel | 54 | 67 | 179 | 236 | 286 | Voyage |
| Passenger transport | 31 | 30 | 37 | 48 | 35 | Transport de passagers |
| Aruba | | | | | | Aruba |
| Total | 172 | 214 | 248 | 241 | 256 | Total |
| Travel | 159 | 189 | 218 | 217 | 233 | Voyage |
| Passenger transport | 13 | 25 | 30 | 24 | 23 | Transport de passagers |
| Australia | | | | | | Australie |
| Total | 8 494 | 10 135 | 14 224 | 15 593 | 16 393 | Total |
| Travel | 6 072 | 7 270 | 10 242 | 11 253 | 11 690 | Voyage |
| Passenger transport | 2 422 | 2 865 | 3 982 | 4 340 | 4 703 | Transport de passagers |
| Austria | | | | | | Autriche |
| Total | 10 300 | 12 894 | 13 411 | 12 755 | 11 035 | Total |
| Travel | 9 460 | 11 757 | 11 834 | 10 994 | 9 348 | Voyage |
| Passenger transport | 840 | 1 137 | 1 577 | 1 761 | 1 687 | Transport de passagers |
| Azerbaijan | | | | | | Azerbaïdjan |
| Total | 110 | 120 | 140 | 188 | 256 | Total |
| Travel | 105 | 111 | 126 | 164 | 201 | Voyage |
| Passenger transport | 5 | 9 | 14 | 24 | 55 | Transport de passagers |
| Bahamas | | | | | | Bahamas |
| Total | 338 | 404 | 469 | 528 | 541 | Total |
| Travel | 244 | 305 | 316 | 344 | 385 | Voyage |
| Passenger transport | 94 | 99 | 153 | 184 | 156 | Transport de passagers |
| Bahrain | | | | | | Bahreïn |
| Total | 550 | 492 | 528 | 574 | 639 | Total |
| Travel | 380 | 372 | 387 | 414 | 455 | Voyage |
| Passenger transport | 170 | 120 | 141 | 160 | 184 | Transport de passagers |
| Bangladesh | | | | | | Bangladesh |
| Total | 309 | 389 | 442 | 375 | 444 | Total |
| Travel | 113 | 165 | 161 | 136 | 140 | Voyage |
| Passenger transport | 196 | 224 | 281 | 239 | 304 | Transport de passagers |
| Barbados | | | | | | Barbade |
| Total | 146 | 154 | 163 | 153 | ... | Total |
| Travel | 99 | 105 | 108 | 96 | ... | Voyage |
| Passenger transport | 47 | 49 | 55 | 57 | ... | Transport de passagers |

| Country or area | 2002 | 2003 | 2004 | 2005 | 2006 | Pays ou zone |
|---|---|---|---|---|---|---|
| Belarus | | | | | | Bélarus |
| Total | 593 | 510 | 588 | 672 | 823 | Total |
| Travel | 559 | 473 | 538 | 604 | 735 | Voyage |
| Passenger transport | 34 | 37 | 50 | 68 | 88 | Transport de passagers |
| Belgium | | | | | | Belgique |
| Total | 11 270 | 13 402 | 15 456 | 16 771 | 17 799 | Total |
| Travel | 10 185 | 12 210 | 13 956 | 14 948 | 15 482 | Voyage |
| Passenger transport | 1 085 | 1 192 | 1 500 | 1 823 | 2 317 | Transport de passagers |
| Belize | | | | | | Belize |
| Total | 48 | 50 | 47 | 45 | 43 | Total |
| Travel | 44 | 46 | 43 | 42 | 41 | Voyage |
| Passenger transport | 4 | 4 | 4 | 3 | 2 | Transport de passagers |
| Benin | | | | | | Bénin |
| Total | 49 | 53 | 59 | 58 | ... | Total |
| Travel | 20 | 21 | 29 | 27 | ... | Voyage |
| Passenger transport | 29 | 32 | 30 | 31 | ... | Transport de passagers |
| Bermuda[1] | | | | | | Bermudes[1] |
| Total | 243 | 248 | 217 | 239 | 277 | Total |
| Bolivia | | | | | | Bolivie |
| Total | 114 | 197 | 232 | 257 | 328 | Total |
| Travel | 80 | 138 | 164 | 186 | 226 | Voyage |
| Passenger transport | 34 | 59 | 68 | 71 | 102 | Transport de passagers |
| Bonaire[4] | | | | | | Bonaire[4] |
| Travel | 2 | 3 | 6 | 5 | 5 | Voyage |
| Bosnia and Herzegovina | | | | | | Bosnie-Herzégovine |
| Total | 112 | 145 | 162 | 158 | 198 | Total |
| Travel | 85 | 106 | 117 | 122 | 158 | Voyage |
| Passenger transport | 27 | 39 | 45 | 36 | 40 | Transport de passagers |
| Botswana | | | | | | Botswana |
| Total | 197 | 235 | 280 | 301 | 285 | Total |
| Travel | 184 | 230 | 276 | 282 | 277 | Voyage |
| Passenger transport | 13 | 5 | 4 | 19 | 8 | Transport de passagers |
| Brazil | | | | | | Brésil |
| Total | 2 929 | 2 874 | 3 752 | 5 905 | 7 501 | Total |
| Travel | 2 396 | 2 261 | 2 871 | 4 720 | 5 764 | Voyage |
| Passenger transport | 533 | 613 | 881 | 1 185 | 1 737 | Transport de passagers |
| Brunei Darussalam | | | | | | Brunéi Darussalam |
| Travel | 398 | 468 | 382 | 374 | 408 | Voyage |
| Bulgaria | | | | | | Bulgarie |
| Total | 1 018 | 1 467 | 1 935 | 1 858 | 2 092 | Total |
| Travel | 717 | 1 033 | 1 363 | 1 309 | 1 474 | Voyage |
| Passenger transport | 301 | 434 | 572 | 549 | 618 | Transport de passagers |
| Burkina Faso[5] | | | | | | Burkina Faso[5] |
| Total | ... | ... | ... | 53 | ... | Total |
| Travel | ... | ... | 39 | 46 | ... | Voyage |
| Passenger transport | ... | ... | ... | 7 | ... | Transport de passagers |
| Burundi | | | | | | Burundi |
| Total | ... | ... | 29 | 62 | 126 | Total |
| Travel | 14 | 15 | 23 | 60 | 125 | Voyage |
| Passenger transport | ... | ... | 6 | 2 | 1 | Transport de passagers |
| Cambodia | | | | | | Cambodge |
| Total | 64 | 60 | 80 | 138 | 176 | Total |
| Travel | 38 | 36 | 48 | 97 | 122 | Voyage |
| Passenger transport | 26 | 24 | 32 | 41 | 54 | Transport de passagers |

| Country or area | 2002 | 2003 | 2004 | 2005 | 2006 | Pays ou zone |
|---|---|---|---|---|---|---|
| Cameroon | | | | | | Cameroun |
| Total | 205 | 272 | 394 | ... | ... | Total |
| Travel | 171 | 171 | 323 | ... | ... | Voyage |
| Passenger transport | 34 | 101 | 71 | ... | ... | Transport de passagers |
| Canada | | | | | | Canada |
| Total | 14 257 | 16 309 | 19 657 | 22 891 | 25 994 | Total |
| Travel | 11 722 | 13 337 | 15 914 | 18 174 | 20 538 | Voyage |
| Passenger transport | 2 535 | 2 972 | 3 743 | 4 717 | 5 456 | Transport de passagers |
| Cape Verde | | | | | | Cap-Vert |
| Total | 63 | 89 | 93 | 82 | 104 | Total |
| Travel | 56 | 73 | 78 | 67 | 82 | Voyage |
| Passenger transport | 7 | 16 | 15 | 15 | 22 | Transport de passagers |
| Central African Rep.[6] | | | | | | Rép. centrafricaine[6] |
| Total | 29 | 31[7] | 32[7] | ... | | Total |
| Chad[6] | | | | | | Tchad[6] |
| Total | 80 | ... | ... | ... | ... | Total |
| Chile | | | | | | Chili |
| Total | 932 | 1 109 | 1 251 | 1 349 | 1 581 | Total |
| Travel | 673 | 850 | 977 | 1 051 | 1 252 | Voyage |
| Passenger transport | 259 | 259 | 274 | 298 | 329 | Transport de passagers |
| China[8] | | | | | | Chine[8] |
| Total | 16 759 | 16 716 | 21 360 | 24 715 | 28 242 | Total |
| Travel | 15 398 | 15 187 | 19 149 | 21 759 | 24 322 | Voyage |
| Passenger transport | 1 361 | 1 529 | 2 211 | 2 956 | 3 920 | Transport de passagers |
| China, Hong Kong SAR[9] | | | | | | Chine, Hong Kong RAS[9] |
| Travel | 12 418 | 11 447 | 13 270 | 13 305 | 13 974 | Voyage |
| Colombia | | | | | | Colombie |
| Total | 1 355 | 1 349 | 1 466 | 1 562 | 1 796 | Total |
| Travel | 1 075 | 1 062 | 1 108 | 1 127 | 1 329 | Voyage |
| Passenger transport | 280 | 287 | 358 | 435 | 467 | Transport de passagers |
| Comoros[10] | | | | | | Comores[10] |
| Total | ... | 8 | 9 | 10 | 11 | Total |
| Congo | | | | | | Congo |
| Total | 85 | 118 | 176 | ... | ... | Total |
| Travel | 70 | 78 | 103 | 103 | ... | Voyage |
| Passenger transport | 15 | 40 | 73 | ... | ... | Transport de passagers |
| Costa Rica | | | | | | Costa Rica |
| Total | 430 | 434 | 481 | 556 | 577 | Total |
| Travel | 345 | 353 | 406 | 470 | 485 | Voyage |
| Passenger transport | 85 | 81 | 75 | 86 | 92 | Transport de passagers |
| Côte d'Ivoire | | | | | | Côte d'Ivoire |
| Total | 490 | 551 | 571 | 549 | ... | Total |
| Travel | 358 | 387 | 381 | 354 | 361 | Voyage |
| Passenger transport | 132 | 164 | 190 | 195 | ... | Transport de passagers |
| Croatia | | | | | | Croatie |
| Total | 852 | 709 | 881 | 786 | 770 | Total |
| Travel | 781 | 672 | 848 | 754 | 737 | Voyage |
| Passenger transport | 71 | 37 | 33 | 32 | 33 | Transport de passagers |
| Cyprus | | | | | | Chypre |
| Total | 582 | 700 | 907 | 1 001 | 1 047 | Total |
| Travel | 512 | 611 | 811 | 932 | 982 | Voyage |
| Passenger transport | 70 | 89 | 96 | 69 | 65 | Transport de passagers |
| Czech Republic | | | | | | République tchèque |
| Total | 1 797 | 2 177 | 2 682 | 2 603 | 2 779 | Total |
| Travel | 1 597 | 1 934 | 2 280 | 2 405 | 2 670 | Voyage |
| Passenger transport | 200 | 243 | 402 | 198 | 109 | Transport de passagers |

**60**

**Tourism expenditure in other countries**—Total, travel and passenger transport: million US dollars (*continued*)

**Dépenses touristiques dans d'autres pays**—Total, voyage et transport de passagers : millions de dollars E.-U. (*suite*)

| Country or area | 2002 | 2003 | 2004 | 2005 | 2006 | Pays ou zone |
|---|---|---|---|---|---|---|
| Denmark | | | | | | Danemark |
| Travel | 5 838 | 6 659 | 7 279 | 6 850 | 7 428 | Voyage |
| Djibouti | | | | | | Djibouti |
| Total | 8 | 10 | 14 | 14 | 15 | Total |
| Travel | 3 | 3 | 3 | 3 | 4 | Voyage |
| Passenger transport | 5 | 7 | 11 | 12 | 12 | Transport de passagers |
| Dominica | | | | | | Dominique |
| Travel | 9 | 9 | 9 | 10 | 10 | Voyage |
| Dominican Republic | | | | | | Rép. dominicaine |
| Total | 429 | 408 | 448 | 511 | 499 | Total |
| Travel | 295 | 272 | 310 | 352 | 333 | Voyage |
| Passenger transport | 134 | 136 | 138 | 159 | 166 | Transport de passagers |
| Ecuador | | | | | | Equateur |
| Total | 507 | 500 | 577 | 644 | 706 | Total |
| Travel | 364 | 354 | 391 | 429 | 466 | Voyage |
| Passenger transport | 143 | 146 | 186 | 215 | 240 | Transport de passagers |
| Egypt | | | | | | Egypte |
| Total | 1 309 | 1 465 | 1 543 | 1 932 | 2 156 | Total |
| Travel | 1 266 | 1 321 | 1 257 | 1 629 | 1 784 | Voyage |
| Passenger transport | 43 | 144 | 286 | 303 | 372 | Transport de passagers |
| El Salvador | | | | | | El Salvador |
| Total | 266 | 311 | 373 | 429 | 601 | Total |
| Travel | 191 | 230 | 292 | 347 | 518 | Voyage |
| Passenger transport | 75 | 81 | 81 | 82 | 83 | Transport de passagers |
| Estonia | | | | | | Estonie |
| Total | 305 | 404 | 481 | 538 | 705 | Total |
| Travel | 231 | 319 | 400 | 448 | 592 | Voyage |
| Passenger transport | 74 | 85 | 81 | 90 | 113 | Transport de passagers |
| Ethiopia | | | | | | Ethiopie |
| Total | 55 | 63 | 59 | ... | ... | Total |
| Travel | 45 | 50 | 58 | 77 | 97 | Voyage |
| Passenger transport | 10 | 13 | 1 | ... | ... | Transport de passagers |
| Fiji | | | | | | Fidji |
| Total | 79 | 87 | 118 | 132 | 123 | Total |
| Travel | 55 | 69 | 94 | 106 | 101 | Voyage |
| Passenger transport | 24 | 18 | 24 | 26 | 22 | Transport de passagers |
| Finland | | | | | | Finlande |
| Total | 2 438 | 2 954 | 3 383 | 3 622 | 4 094 | Total |
| Travel | 2 006 | 2 433 | 2 821 | 3 057 | 3 424 | Voyage |
| Passenger transport | 432 | 521 | 562 | 565 | 670 | Transport de passagers |
| France | | | | | | France |
| Total | 23 773 | 28 143 | 34 674 | 37 549 | 37 793 | Total |
| Travel | 19 518 | 23 392 | 28 703 | 30 458 | 31 264 | Voyage |
| Passenger transport | 4 255 | 4 751 | 5 971 | 7 091 | 6 529 | Transport de passagers |
| French Polynesia | | | | | | Polynésie française |
| Total | 264 | 335 | 425 | 421 | 428 | Total |
| Travel | 180 | 236 | 311 | 303 | 298 | Voyage |
| Passenger transport | 84 | 99 | 114 | 118 | 130 | Transport de passagers |
| Gabon | | | | | | Gabon |
| Total | 234 | 239 | 275 | ... | ... | Total |
| Travel | 194 | 194 | 214 | ... | ... | Voyage |
| Passenger transport | 40 | 45 | 61 | ... | ... | Transport de passagers |
| Gambia | | | | | | Gambie |
| Total | ... | 8 | 6 | 7 | 8 | Total |
| Travel | ... | 4 | 4 | 5 | 6 | Voyage |
| Passenger transport | ... | 4 | 2 | 2 | 2 | Transport de passagers |

| Country or area | 2002 | 2003 | 2004 | 2005 | 2006 | Pays ou zone |
|---|---|---|---|---|---|---|
| Georgia | | | | | | Géorgie |
| Total | 189 | 170 | 196 | 237 | 257 | Total |
| Travel | 149 | 130 | 147 | 169 | 167 | Voyage |
| Passenger transport | 40 | 40 | 49 | 68 | 90 | Transport de passagers |
| Germany | | | | | | Allemagne |
| Total | 59 832 | 72 777 | 79 434 | 82 228 | 83 006 | Total |
| Travel | 53 006 | 65 234 | 71 187 | 74 189 | 74 123 | Voyage |
| Passenger transport | 6 826 | 7 543 | 8 247 | 8 039 | 8 883 | Transport de passagers |
| Ghana | | | | | | Ghana |
| Total | 184 | 216 | 270 | 472 | 575 | Total |
| Travel | 119 | 138 | 186 | 303 | 345 | Voyage |
| Passenger transport | 65 | 78 | 84 | 169 | 230 | Transport de passagers |
| Greece | | | | | | Grèce |
| Total | 2 453 | 2 439 | 2 880 | 3 045 | 3 004 | Total |
| Travel | 2 436 | 2 431 | 2 872 | 3 039 | 2 997 | Voyage |
| Passenger transport | 17 | 8 | 8 | 6 | 7 | Transport de passagers |
| Grenada | | | | | | Grenade |
| Travel | 8 | 8 | 8 | 10 | 11 | Voyage |
| Guatemala | | | | | | Guatemala |
| Total | 329 | 373 | 456 | 500 | 572 | Total |
| Travel | 276 | 312 | 391 | 444 | 494 | Voyage |
| Passenger transport | 53 | 61 | 65 | 56 | 78 | Transport de passagers |
| Guinea | | | | | | Guinée |
| Total | 38 | 36 | 29 | 41 | ... | Total |
| Travel | 31 | 26 | 25 | 28 | ... | Voyage |
| Passenger transport | 7 | 10 | 4 | 13 | ... | Transport de passagers |
| Guinea-Bissau | | | | | | Guinée-Bissau |
| Total | 10 | 21 | 22 | 18 | ... | Total |
| Travel | 5 | 13 | 13 | 10 | ... | Voyage |
| Passenger transport | 5 | 8 | 9 | 8 | ... | Transport de passagers |
| Guyana | | | | | | Guyana |
| Total | 44 | 30 | 35 | 45 | 54 | Total |
| Travel | 38 | 26 | 30 | 40 | 49 | Voyage |
| Passenger transport | 6 | 4 | 5 | 5 | 5 | Transport de passagers |
| Haiti | | | | | | Haïti |
| Total | 172 | 202 | 206 | 173 | 233 | Total |
| Travel | 18 | 42 | 72 | 54 | 56 | Voyage |
| Passenger transport | 154 | 160 | 134 | 119 | 177 | Transport de passagers |
| Honduras | | | | | | Honduras |
| Total | 217 | 271 | 307 | 327 | 353 | Total |
| Travel | 149 | 211 | 245 | 262 | 283 | Voyage |
| Passenger transport | 68 | 60 | 62 | 65 | 70 | Transport de passagers |
| Hungary | | | | | | Hongrie |
| Total | 2 211 | 2 700 | 2 909 | 2 826 | 2 568 | Total |
| Travel | 2 133 | 2 594 | 2 848 | 2 382 | 2 126 | Voyage |
| Passenger transport | 78 | 106 | 61 | 444 | 442 | Transport de passagers |
| Iceland | | | | | | Islande |
| Total | 373 | 524 | 699 | 991 | 1 084 | Total |
| Travel | 371 | 523 | 697 | 980 | 1 076 | Voyage |
| Passenger transport | 2 | 1 | 2 | 11 | 8 | Transport de passagers |
| India | | | | | | Inde |
| Total | 4 350 | 4 385 | 5 783 | 7 798 | 9 296 | Total |
| Travel | 2 988 | 3 585 | 4 816 | 6 013 | 7 352 | Voyage |
| Passenger transport | 1 362 | 800 | 967 | 1 785 | 1 944 | Transport de passagers |

**Tourism expenditure in other countries** — Total, travel and passenger transport: million US dollars (*continued*)

**Dépenses touristiques dans d'autres pays** — Total, voyage et transport de passagers : millions de dollars E.-U. (*suite*)

| Country or area | 2002 | 2003 | 2004 | 2005 | 2006 | Pays ou zone |
|---|---|---|---|---|---|---|
| Indonesia | | | | | | Indonésie |
| Total | 5 042 | 4 427 | 4 569 | 4 740 | 5 028 | Total |
| Travel | 3 289 | 3 082 | 3 507 | 3 584 | 3 600 | Voyage |
| Passenger transport | 1 753 | 1 345 | 1 062 | 1 156 | 1 428 | Transport de passagers |
| Iran (Islamic Rep. of)[11] | | | | | | Iran (Rép. islamique d')[11] |
| Total | 3 990 | 4 120 | 4 402 | 4 560 | 5 004 | Total |
| Travel | 3 750 | 3 842 | 4 093 | 4 202 | 4 597 | Voyage |
| Passenger transport | 240 | 278 | 309 | 358 | 407 | Transport de passagers |
| Iraq[12] | | | | | | Iraq[12] |
| Travel | 26 | ... | ... | ... | ... | Voyage |
| Ireland | | | | | | Irlande |
| Total | 3 835 | 4 832 | 5 291 | 6 186 | 6 978 | Total |
| Travel | 3 755 | 4 736 | 5 177 | 6 074 | 6 862 | Voyage |
| Passenger transport | 80 | 96 | 114 | 112 | 116 | Transport de passagers |
| Israel | | | | | | Israël |
| Total | 3 323 | 3 342 | 3 663 | 3 780 | 3 870 | Total |
| Travel | 2 543 | 2 550 | 2 796 | 2 895 | 2 983 | Voyage |
| Passenger transport | 780 | 792 | 867 | 885 | 887 | Transport de passagers |
| Italy | | | | | | Italie |
| Total | 19 636 | 23 731 | 24 064 | 26 774 | 27 437 | Total |
| Travel | 16 924 | 20 589 | 20 460 | 22 370 | 23 152 | Voyage |
| Passenger transport | 2 712 | 3 142 | 3 604 | 4 404 | 4 285 | Transport de passagers |
| Jamaica | | | | | | Jamaïque |
| Total | 274 | 269 | 318 | 290 | 315 | Total |
| Travel | 258 | 252 | 286 | 249 | 273 | Voyage |
| Passenger transport | 16 | 17 | 32 | 41 | 42 | Transport de passagers |
| Japan | | | | | | Japon |
| Total | 34 977 | 36 505 | 48 175 | 48 102 | 37 659 | Total |
| Travel | 26 656 | #28 958 | 38 252 | 37 565 | #26 876 | Voyage |
| Passenger transport | 8 321 | 7 547 | 9 923 | 10 537 | 10 783 | Transport de passagers |
| Jordan | | | | | | Jordanie |
| Total | 504 | 503 | 585 | 653 | 698 | Total |
| Travel | 453 | 452 | 524 | 585 | 625 | Voyage |
| Passenger transport | 51 | 51 | 61 | 68 | 73 | Transport de passagers |
| Kazakhstan | | | | | | Kazakhstan |
| Total | 863 | 783 | 997 | 940 | 1 060 | Total |
| Travel | 757 | 669 | 844 | 753 | 821 | Voyage |
| Passenger transport | 106 | 114 | 153 | 187 | 239 | Transport de passagers |
| Kenya | | | | | | Kenya |
| Travel | 126 | 127 | 108 | 124 | 178 | Voyage |
| Korea, Republic of | | | | | | Corée, République de |
| Total | 11 440 | 11 063 | 13 507 | 16 924 | 20 386 | Total |
| Travel | 10 465 | 10 103 | 12 350 | 15 406 | 18 241 | Voyage |
| Passenger transport | 975 | 960 | 1 157 | 1 518 | 2 145 | Transport de passagers |
| Kuwait | | | | | | Koweït |
| Total | 3 412 | 3 750 | 4 148 | 4 741 | 5 753 | Total |
| Travel | 3 021 | 3 348 | 3 701 | 4 277 | 5 253 | Voyage |
| Passenger transport | 391 | 402 | 447 | 464 | 500 | Transport de passagers |
| Kyrgyzstan | | | | | | Kirghizistan |
| Total | 27 | 35 | 73 | 94 | 142 | Total |
| Travel | 10 | 17 | 50 | 58 | 92 | Voyage |
| Passenger transport | 17 | 18 | 23 | 36 | 50 | Transport de passagers |
| Latvia | | | | | | Lettonie |
| Total | 267 | 365 | 428 | 655 | 788 | Total |
| Travel | 230 | 328 | 377 | 584 | 704 | Voyage |
| Passenger transport | 37 | 37 | 51 | 71 | 84 | Transport de passagers |

60 **Tourism expenditure in other countries** — Total, travel and passenger transport: million US dollars (*continued*)

**Dépenses touristiques dans d'autres pays** — Total, voyage et transport de passagers : millions de dollars E.-U. (*suite*)

| Country or area | 2002 | 2003 | 2004 | 2005 | 2006 | Pays ou zone |
|---|---|---|---|---|---|---|
| Lebanon | | | | | | Liban |
| Total | ... | 3 319 | 3 719 | 3 565 | 3 783 | Total |
| Travel | 2 683 | 2 943 | 3 170 | 2 908 | 3 006 | Voyage |
| Passenger transport | ... | 376 | 549 | 657 | 777 | Transport de passagers |
| Lesotho | | | | | | Lesotho |
| Total | 16 | 30 | 37 | 36 | 22 | Total |
| Travel | 14 | 26 | 30 | 27 | 19 | Voyage |
| Passenger transport | 2 | 4 | 7 | 9 | 3 | Transport de passagers |
| Libyan Arab Jamah. | | | | | | Jamah. arabe libyenne |
| Total | 654 | 689 | 789 | 920 | 915 | Total |
| Travel | 586 | 557 | 603 | 680 | 668 | Voyage |
| Passenger transport | 68 | 132 | 186 | 240 | 247 | Transport de passagers |
| Lithuania | | | | | | Lituanie |
| Total | 334 | 476 | 643 | 757 | 931 | Total |
| Travel | 326 | 471 | 636 | 744 | 909 | Voyage |
| Passenger transport | 8 | 5 | 7 | 13 | 22 | Transport de passagers |
| Luxembourg | | | | | | Luxembourg |
| Total | 1 963 | 2 445 | 2 950 | ... | ... | Total |
| Travel | 1 942 | 2 423 | 2 911 | 2 976 | 3 136 | Voyage |
| Passenger transport | 21 | 22 | 39 | ... | ... | Transport de passagers |
| Madagascar | | | | | | Madagascar |
| Total | 192 | 67 | 108 | 80 | ... | Total |
| Travel | 160 | 64 | 93 | 74 | 86 | Voyage |
| Passenger transport | 32 | 3 | 15 | 6 | ... | Transport de passagers |
| Malawi[13] | | | | | | Malawi[13] |
| Total | 86 | 61 | 59 | 75 | 75 | Total |
| Travel | 78 | 48 | 50 | 65 | 65 | Voyage |
| Passenger transport | 8 | 13 | 9 | 10 | 10 | Transport de passagers |
| Malaysia | | | | | | Malaisie |
| Total | 3 330 | 3 401 | 3 822 | 4 339 | 4 847 | Total |
| Travel | 2 618 | 2 846 | 3 178 | 3 711 | 4 020 | Voyage |
| Passenger transport | 712 | 555 | 644 | 628 | 827 | Transport de passagers |
| Maldives | | | | | | Maldives |
| Total | 60 | 60 | 75 | 94 | 106 | Total |
| Travel | 46 | 46 | 56 | 70 | 78 | Voyage |
| Passenger transport | 14 | 14 | 19 | 24 | 28 | Transport de passagers |
| Mali | | | | | | Mali |
| Total | 62 | 94 | 125 | 133 | ... | Total |
| Travel | 36 | 48 | 66 | 77 | ... | Voyage |
| Passenger transport | 26 | 46 | 59 | 56 | ... | Transport de passagers |
| Malta | | | | | | Malte |
| Total | 180 | 238 | 292 | 311 | 363 | Total |
| Travel | 154 | 215 | 256 | 268 | 321 | Voyage |
| Passenger transport | 26 | 23 | 36 | 43 | 42 | Transport de passagers |
| Mauritius | | | | | | Maurice |
| Total | 224 | 236 | 277 | 295 | 347 | Total |
| Travel | 204 | 216 | 255 | 275 | 327 | Voyage |
| Passenger transport | 20 | 20 | 22 | 20 | 20 | Transport de passagers |
| Mexico | | | | | | Mexique |
| Total | 7 087 | 7 252 | 8 034 | 8 951 | 9 387 | Total |
| Travel | 6 060 | 6 253 | 6 959 | 7 600 | 8 108 | Voyage |
| Passenger transport | 1 027 | 999 | 1 075 | 1 351 | 1 279 | Transport de passagers |
| Micronesia (Fed. States of)[1,14] | | | | | | Micronésie (Etats féd. de)[1,14] |
| Total | 5 | 6 | 5 | 6 | ... | Total |

| Country or area | 2002 | 2003 | 2004 | 2005 | 2006 | Pays ou zone |
|---|---|---|---|---|---|---|
| Moldova | | | | | | Moldova |
| Total | 109 | 118 | 135 | 170 | 220 | Total |
| Travel | 95 | 99 | 113 | 141 | 187 | Voyage |
| Passenger transport | 14 | 19 | 22 | 29 | 33 | Transport de passagers |
| Mongolia | | | | | | Mongolie |
| Total | 125 | 144 | 207 | 173 | 212 | Total |
| Travel | 119 | 138 | 193 | 157 | 188 | Voyage |
| Passenger transport | 6 | 6 | 14 | 16 | 24 | Transport de passagers |
| Montserrat | | | | | | Montserrat |
| Travel | 2 | 2 | 2 | 3 | 3 | Voyage |
| Morocco | | | | | | Maroc |
| Total | 669 | 845 | 912 | 999 | 1 123 | Total |
| Travel | 444 | 548 | 574 | 612 | 703 | Voyage |
| Passenger transport | 225 | 297 | 338 | 387 | 420 | Transport de passagers |
| Mozambique | | | | | | Mozambique |
| Total | 115 | 141 | 140 | 187 | 205 | Total |
| Travel | 113 | 140 | 134 | 176 | 179 | Voyage |
| Passenger transport | 2 | 1 | 6 | 11 | 26 | Transport de passagers |
| Myanmar | | | | | | Myanmar |
| Total | 34 | 36 | 32 | 34 | 40 | Total |
| Travel | 29 | 32 | 29 | 31 | 37 | Voyage |
| Passenger transport | 5 | 4 | 3 | 3 | 3 | Transport de passagers |
| Namibia | | | | | | Namibie |
| Travel | 65 | 101 | 123 | 108 | 118 | Voyage |
| Nepal | | | | | | Népal |
| Total | 108 | 119 | 205 | 221 | 261 | Total |
| Travel | 69 | 81 | 154 | 163 | 185 | Voyage |
| Passenger transport | 39 | 38 | 51 | 58 | 76 | Transport de passagers |
| Netherlands | | | | | | Pays-Bas |
| Total | 14 201 | ... | ... | ... | ... | Total |
| Travel | 12 976 | 15 265 | 16 348 | 16 140 | 17 087 | Voyage |
| Passenger transport | 1 225 | ... | ... | ... | ... | Transport de passagers |
| New Caledonia | | | | | | Nouvelle-Calédonie |
| Travel | 104 | 128 | 167 | 171 | 186 | Voyage |
| New Zealand | | | | | | Nouvelle-Zélande |
| Travel | 1 386 | 1 649 | 2 217 | 2 657 | 2 526 | Voyage |
| Nicaragua | | | | | | Nicaragua |
| Total | 125 | 139 | 154 | 162 | 177 | Total |
| Travel | 69 | 75 | 89 | 91 | 97 | Voyage |
| Passenger transport | 56 | 64 | 65 | 71 | 80 | Transport de passagers |
| Niger | | | | | | Niger |
| Total | 29 | 39 | 42 | 42 | 54[7] | Total |
| Travel | 17 | 22 | 22 | 30 | 31[7] | Voyage |
| Passenger transport | 12 | 17 | 20 | 12 | 23[7] | Transport de passagers |
| Nigeria | | | | | | Nigéria |
| Total | * 910 | 2 076 | 1 469 | 1 385 | 2 078 | Total |
| Travel | 881 | 1 795 | 1 161 | 1 109 | 1 664 | Voyage |
| Passenger transport | 29 | 281 | 308 | 276 | 414 | Transport de passagers |
| Norway | | | | | | Norvège |
| Total | 5 610 | 7 089 | 8 894 | ... | 12 072 | Total |
| Travel | 5 189 | 6 716 | 8 489 | 10 182 | 11 586 | Voyage |
| Passenger transport | 421 | 373 | 405 | ... | 486 | Transport de passagers |
| Occupied Palestinian Terr.[15] | | | | | | Terr. palestinien occupé[15] |
| Travel | 388 | 317 | 286 | 265 | ... | Voyage |

| Country or area | 2002 | 2003 | 2004 | 2005 | 2006 | Pays ou zone |
|---|---|---|---|---|---|---|
| Oman | | | | | | Oman |
| Total | 702 | 752 | 795 | 838 | 868 | Total |
| Travel | 530 | 578 | 616 | 643 | 686 | Voyage |
| Passenger transport | 172 | 174 | 179 | 195 | 182 | Transport de passagers |
| Pakistan | | | | | | Pakistan |
| Total | 491 | 1 163 | 1 612 | 1 753 | 2 029 | Total |
| Travel | 255 | 925 | 1 268 | 1 280 | 1 545 | Voyage |
| Passenger transport | 236 | 238 | 344 | 473 | 484 | Transport de passagers |
| Palau[1] | | | | | | Palaos[1] |
| Total | 1 | 1 | 2 | 2 | 1 | Total |
| Panama | | | | | | Panama |
| Total | 252 | 267 | 294 | 388 | 403 | Total |
| Travel | 179 | 208 | 239 | 271 | 271 | Voyage |
| Passenger transport | 73 | 59 | 55 | 117 | 132 | Transport de passagers |
| Papua New Guinea | | | | | | Papouasie-Nvl-Guinée |
| Total | ... | ... | 72 | 56 | ... | Total |
| Travel | 60 | 52 | 71 | 56 | ... | Voyage |
| Passenger transport | ... | ... | 1 | 1 | ... | Transport de passagers |
| Paraguay | | | | | | Paraguay |
| Total | 117 | 115 | 121 | 130 | 143 | Total |
| Travel | 65 | 67 | 71 | 79 | 91 | Voyage |
| Passenger transport | 52 | 48 | 50 | 51 | 52 | Transport de passagers |
| Peru | | | | | | Pérou |
| Total | 806 | 847 | 852 | 970 | 1 005 | Total |
| Travel | 606 | 641 | 643 | 752 | 760 | Voyage |
| Passenger transport | 200 | 206 | 209 | 218 | 245 | Transport de passagers |
| Philippines | | | | | | Philippines |
| Total | 1 874 | 1 649 | 1 526 | 1 547 | 1 558 | Total |
| Travel | 1 626 | 1 413 | 1 275 | 1 279 | 1 232 | Voyage |
| Passenger transport | 248 | 236 | 251 | 268 | 326 | Transport de passagers |
| Poland | | | | | | Pologne |
| Total | 3 364 | 3 002 | 4 157 | 4 687 | 6 190 | Total |
| Travel | 3 202 | 2 801 | 3 841 | 4 341 | 5 760 | Voyage |
| Passenger transport | 162 | 201 | 316 | 346 | 430 | Transport de passagers |
| Portugal | | | | | | Portugal |
| Total | 2 631 | 2 982 | 3 369 | 3 744 | 4 050 | Total |
| Travel | 2 125 | 2 409 | 2 763 | 3 050 | 3 298 | Voyage |
| Passenger transport | 506 | 573 | 606 | 694 | 752 | Transport de passagers |
| Puerto Rico[1,16] | | | | | | Porto Rico[1,16] |
| Total | 1 319 | 1 420 | 1 584 | 1 663 | 1 752 | Total |
| Travel | 928 | 985 | 1 085 | 1 143 | 1 205 | Voyage |
| Passenger transport | 391 | 435 | 499 | 520 | 547 | Transport de passagers |
| Qatar[17] | | | | | | Qatar[17] |
| Travel | 423 | 471 | 691 | 1 759 | 3 993 | Voyage |
| Romania | | | | | | Roumanie |
| Total | 448 | 572 | 672 | 1 073 | 1 459 | Total |
| Travel | 396 | 479 | 539 | 925 | 1 310 | Voyage |
| Passenger transport | 52 | 93 | 133 | 148 | 149 | Transport de passagers |
| Russian Federation | | | | | | Fédération de Russie |
| Total | 11 713 | 13 427 | 16 082 | 18 425 | 19 601 | Total |
| Travel | 11 284 | 12 880 | 15 285 | 17 434 | 18 235 | Voyage |
| Passenger transport | 429 | 547 | 797 | 991 | 1 366 | Transport de passagers |
| Rwanda | | | | | | Rwanda |
| Travel | 24 | 26 | 31 | 37 | 35 | Voyage |
| Saint Kitts and Nevis | | | | | | Saint-Kitts-et-Nevis |
| Travel | 8 | 8 | 10 | 10 | 12 | Voyage |
| Saint Lucia | | | | | | Sainte-Lucie |
| Travel | 34 | 36 | 37 | 39 | 43 | Voyage |

**Tourism expenditure in other countries**—Total, travel and passenger transport: million US dollars (*continued*)

**Dépenses touristiques dans d'autres pays**—Total, voyage et transport de passagers : millions de dollars E.-U. (*suite*)

| Country or area | 2002 | 2003 | 2004 | 2005 | 2006 | Pays ou zone |
|---|---|---|---|---|---|---|
| Saint Maarten[18] | | | | | | Saint-Martin[18] |
| Travel | 140 | 144 | 80 | 94 | 86 | Voyage |
| Saint Vincent-Grenadines | | | | | | Saint Vincent-Grenadines |
| Travel | 10 | 13 | 14 | 15 | 15 | Voyage |
| Samoa | | | | | | Samoa |
| Total | ... | ... | 12 | 13 | 16 | Total |
| Travel | ... | ... | 5 | 9 | 6 | Voyage |
| Passenger transport | ... | ... | 7 | 4 | 10 | Transport de passagers |
| Sao Tome and Principe | | | | | | Sao Tomé-et-Principe |
| Total | 2 | ... | ... | ... | ... | Total |
| Travel | 1 | ... | ... | ... | ... | Voyage |
| Passenger transport | 1 | ... | ... | ... | ... | Transport de passagers |
| Saudi Arabia[1] | | | | | | Arabie saoudite[1] |
| Total | 7 370 | 4 165 | 4 600 | 4 178 | 2 316 | Total |
| Travel | ... | ... | 4 428 | 3 975 | 1 804 | Voyage |
| Passenger transport | ... | ... | 172 | 203 | 512 | Transport de passagers |
| Senegal | | | | | | Sénégal |
| Total | 112 | 129 | 138 | 144 | ... | Total |
| Travel | 43 | 55 | 57 | 65 | ... | Voyage |
| Passenger transport | 69 | 74 | 81 | 79 | ... | Transport de passagers |
| Serbia[1] | | | | | | Serbie[1] |
| Total | 105 | 144 | 208 | 260 | 322 | Total |
| Seychelles | | | | | | Seychelles |
| Total | 53 | 54 | 53 | 59 | 56 | Total |
| Travel | 33 | 36 | 34 | 39 | 36 | Voyage |
| Passenger transport | 20 | 18 | 19 | 20 | 20 | Transport de passagers |
| Sierra Leone | | | | | | Sierra Leone |
| Total | 39 | 38 | 30 | 34 | 15 | Total |
| Travel | 39 | 37 | 30 | 32 | 12 | Voyage |
| Passenger transport | ^0 | 1 | ^0 | 2 | 3 | Transport de passagers |
| Singapore | | | | | | Singapour |
| Travel | 7 861 | 7 916 | 9 242 | 9 947 | 10 384 | Voyage |
| Slovakia | | | | | | Slovaquie |
| Total | 506 | 662 | 903[7] | ... | ... | Total |
| Travel | 442 | 573 | 745[7] | 846[7] | 1 055[7] | Voyage |
| Passenger transport | 64 | 89 | 158[7] | ... | ... | Transport de passagers |
| Slovenia | | | | | | Slovénie |
| Total | 647 | 805 | 937 | 1 019 | 1 058 | Total |
| Travel | 608 | 753 | 868 | 950 | 974 | Voyage |
| Passenger transport | 39 | 52 | 69 | 69 | 84 | Transport de passagers |
| Solomon Islands | | | | | | Iles Salomon |
| Total | 9 | 6 | 12 | 11 | 15 | Total |
| Travel | 6 | 4 | 9 | 5 | 8 | Voyage |
| Passenger transport | 3 | 2 | 3 | 6 | 7 | Transport de passagers |
| South Africa | | | | | | Afrique du Sud |
| Total | 2 251 | 3 654 | 4 237 | 4 811 | 5 230 | Total |
| Travel | 1 811 | 2 889 | 3 157 | 3 373 | 3 384 | Voyage |
| Passenger transport | 440 | 765 | 1 080 | 1 438 | 1 846 | Transport de passagers |
| Spain | | | | | | Espagne |
| Total | 9 366 | 11 330 | 14 864 | 18 441 | 20 348 | Total |
| Travel | 7 295 | 9 071 | 12 153 | 15 046 | 16 697 | Voyage |
| Passenger transport | 2 071 | 2 259 | 2 711 | 3 395 | 3 651 | Transport de passagers |
| Sri Lanka | | | | | | Sri Lanka |
| Total | 438 | 462 | 499 | 552 | 666 | Total |
| Travel | 263 | 279 | 296 | 314 | 373 | Voyage |
| Passenger transport | 175 | 183 | 203 | 238 | 293 | Transport de passagers |

| Country or area | 2002 | 2003 | 2004 | 2005 | 2006 | Pays ou zone |
|---|---|---|---|---|---|---|
| Sudan | | | | | | Soudan |
| Travel | 91 | 119 | 176 | 667 | 1 403 | Voyage |
| Suriname | | | | | | Suriname |
| Total | 54 | 68 | 85 | 94 | 33 | Total |
| Travel | 10 | 6 | 14 | 17 | 18 | Voyage |
| Passenger transport | 44 | 62 | 71 | 77 | 15 | Transport de passagers |
| Swaziland | | | | | | Swaziland |
| Total | 27 | 23 | 54 | 60 | 53 | Total |
| Travel | 26 | 22 | 48 | 49 | 48 | Voyage |
| Passenger transport | 1 | 1 | 6 | 11 | 5 | Transport de passagers |
| Sweden | | | | | | Suède |
| Total | 8 221 | 9 375 | 11 088 | 11 844 | 12 844 | Total |
| Travel | 7 301 | 8 296 | 10 165 | 10 771 | 11 543 | Voyage |
| Passenger transport | 920 | 1 079 | 923 | 1 073 | 1 301 | Transport de passagers |
| Switzerland | | | | | | Suisse |
| Total | 7 210 | 8 614 | 9 924 | 10 634 | 11 866 | Total |
| Travel | 5 537 | 6 883 | 8 104 | 8 837 | 9 919 | Voyage |
| Passenger transport | 1 673 | 1 731 | 1 820 | 1 797 | 1 947 | Transport de passagers |
| Syrian Arab Republic | | | | | | Rép. arabe syrienne |
| Total | ... | 734 | 688 | 584 | 585 | Total |
| Travel | 760 | 700 | 650 | 550 | 540 | Voyage |
| Passenger transport | ... | 34 | 38 | 34 | 45 | Transport de passagers |
| Tajikistan | | | | | | Tadjikistan |
| Travel | 2 | 2 | 3 | 4 | 6 | Voyage |
| Thailand | | | | | | Thaïlande |
| Total | 3 888 | 3 538 | 5 343 | 4 917 | 6 140 | Total |
| Travel | 3 303 | 2 921 | 4 514 | 3 800 | 4 632 | Voyage |
| Passenger transport | 585 | 617 | 829 | 1 117 | 1 508 | Transport de passagers |
| TFYR of Macedonia | | | | | | Ex-R.Y. Macédoine |
| Total | 61 | 71 | 83 | 94 | 110 | Total |
| Travel | 45 | 48 | 54 | 60 | 71 | Voyage |
| Passenger transport | 16 | 23 | 29 | 34 | 39 | Transport de passagers |
| Togo | | | | | | Togo |
| Total | 26 | 37 | 38 | 42 | 24 | Total |
| Travel | 5 | 7 | 8 | 8 | 3 | Voyage |
| Passenger transport | 21 | 30 | 30 | 34 | 21 | Transport de passagers |
| Tonga | | | | | | Tonga |
| Travel | 3 | 3 | 6 | 4 | 8 | Voyage |
| Trinidad and Tobago | | | | | | Trinité-et-Tobago |
| Total | 208 | 143 | 141 | 234 | 147 | Total |
| Travel | 186 | 107 | 96 | 180 | 82 | Voyage |
| Passenger transport | 22 | 36 | 45 | 54 | 65 | Transport de passagers |
| Tunisia | | | | | | Tunisie |
| Total | 303 | 355 | 427 | 452 | 498 | Total |
| Travel | 260 | 300 | 340 | 374 | 410 | Voyage |
| Passenger transport | 43 | 55 | 87 | 78 | 88 | Transport de passagers |
| Turkey | | | | | | Turquie |
| Total | ... | ... | ... | 3 210 | 3 155 | Total |
| Travel | 1 880 | 2 113 | 2 524 | 2 872 | 2 743 | Voyage |
| Passenger transport | ... | ... | ... | 338 | 412 | Transport de passagers |
| Uganda | | | | | | Ouganda |
| Total | ... | ... | 136 | 133 | 210 | Total |
| Travel | ... | ... | 133 | 129 | 137 | Voyage |
| Passenger transport | 2 | 2 | 3 | 4 | 73 | Transport de passagers |

**Tourism expenditure in other countries** — Total, travel and passenger transport: million US dollars (*continued*)

**Dépenses touristiques dans d'autres pays** — Total, voyage et transport de passagers : millions de dollars E.-U. (*suite*)

| Country or area | 2002 | 2003 | 2004 | 2005 | 2006 | Pays ou zone |
|---|---|---|---|---|---|---|
| Ukraine | | | | | | Ukraine |
| Total | 794 | 953 | 2 660 | 3 078 | 3 202 | Total |
| Travel | 657 | 789 | 2 463 | 2 805 | 2 834 | Voyage |
| Passenger transport | 137 | 164 | 197 | 273 | 368 | Transport de passagers |
| United Arab Emirates[1] | | | | | | Emirats arabes unis[1] |
| Total | 3 651 | 3 956 | 4 472 | 6 186 | 8 827 | Total |
| United Kingdom | | | | | | Royaume-Uni |
| Total | 51 125 | 58 627 | 69 463 | 73 672 | 78 325 | Total |
| Travel | 41 744 | 47 853 | 56 444 | 59 532 | 63 319 | Voyage |
| Passenger transport | 9 381 | 10 774 | 13 019 | 14 140 | 15 006 | Transport de passagers |
| United Rep. of Tanzania | | | | | | Rép.-Unie de Tanzanie |
| Total | 361 | 375 | 470 | 577 | 571 | Total |
| Travel | 337 | 353 | 445 | 554 | 534 | Voyage |
| Passenger transport | 24 | 22 | 25 | 23 | 37 | Transport de passagers |
| United States | | | | | | Etats-Unis |
| Total | 81 707 | 81 924 | 94 345 | 99 439 | 104 310 | Total |
| Travel | 61 738 | 60 935 | 69 627 | 73 290 | 76 807 | Voyage |
| Passenger transport | 19 969 | 20 989 | 24 718 | 26 149 | 27 503 | Transport de passagers |
| Uruguay | | | | | | Uruguay |
| Total | 243 | 236 | 267 | 331 | 306 | Total |
| Travel | 178 | 169 | 194 | 252 | 213 | Voyage |
| Passenger transport | 65 | 67 | 73 | 79 | 93 | Transport de passagers |
| Vanuatu | | | | | | Vanuatu |
| Total | 11 | 14 | 15 | 13 | 11 | Total |
| Travel | 9 | 12 | 13 | 11 | 9 | Voyage |
| Passenger transport | 2 | 2 | 2 | 2 | 2 | Transport de passagers |
| Venezuela (Bolivarian Rep. of) | | | | | | Venezuela (Rép. bolivarienne du) |
| Total | 1 546 | 1 311 | 1 604 | 1 843 | 1 807 | Total |
| Travel | 981 | 859 | 1 077 | 1 276 | 1 229 | Voyage |
| Passenger transport | 565 | 452 | 527 | 567 | 578 | Transport de passagers |
| Yemen | | | | | | Yémen |
| Total | 135 | 134 | 183 | 224 | 225 | Total |
| Travel | 78 | 77 | 126 | 167 | 162 | Voyage |
| Passenger transport | 57 | 57 | 57 | 57 | 63 | Transport de passagers |
| Zambia | | | | | | Zambie |
| Total | 109 | 115 | 68 | 79 | 96 | Total |
| Travel | 47 | 49 | 37 | 43 | 53 | Voyage |
| Passenger transport | 62 | 66 | 31 | 36 | 43 | Transport de passagers |

Source

World Tourism Organization (UNWTO), Madrid, UNWTO statistics database and the "Yearbook of Tourism Statistics", 2007 edition. The majority of the data have been provided to the UNWTO by the International Monetary Fund (IMF). Exceptions are footnoted.

Notes

1 The expenditure figures are those provided by the country to UNWTO, which do not appear in the International Monetary Fund data.

2 Starting 2004, as a result of the importance of the "Survey on International Tourism", the estimates of the series of the "Travel" item of the Balance of Payments were modified. For this reason, the data are not rigorously comparable with those of previous years.

3 Provisional data.

4 Source: Central Bank of the Netherlands Antilles.

Source

Organisation mondiale du tourisme (OMT), Madrid, la base de données de l'OMT, et "l'Annuaire des statistiques du tourisme", 2007 édition. La majorité des données sont celles que le Fonds monétaire international (FMI) a fournies à l'Organisation mondiale du tourisme (OMT). Les exceptions sont signalées par une note.

Notes

1 Les chiffres de dépense sont ceux que le pays a fournis à l'OMT mais ils ne figurent pas dans les données du Fonds monétaire international.

2 À partir de 2004, vu l'importance de l'"Enquête sur le tourisme international", des modifications ont été apportées aux estimations de la série du poste "Voyages" de la balance des paiements. C'est la raison pour laquelle les données ne sont pas rigoureusement comparables avec celles des années précédentes.

3 Données provisoires.

4 Source: "Central Bank of the Netherlands Antilles".

5   The Central Bank of Western African States.

6   Source: "Banque des Etats de l'Afrique Centrale (B.E.A.C.)".

7   Country data.

8   For statistical purposes, the data for China do not include those for the Hong Kong Special Administrative Region (Hong Kong SAR), Macao Special Administrative Region (Macao SAR) and Taiwan Province of China.

9   Source: Census and Statistics Department.

10  The Central Bank of Comoros.

11  Source: Central Bank of Islamic Republic of Iran.

12  Source: Central Bank of Iraq.

13  Source: Reserve Bank of Malawi.

14  Fiscal years (October 1 to September 30).

15  West Bank and Gaza.

16  Fiscal years (July-June).

17  Source: Qatar Central Bank.

18  Source: Central Bank of the Netherlands Antilles - Including the estimates for Saba and Saint Eustatius.

5   Banque Centrale des Etats de l'Afrique de l'Ouest.

6   Source: Banque des Etats de l'Afrique Centrale (B.E.A.C.).

7   Données du pays.

8   Pour la présentation des statistiques, les données pour la Chine ne comprennent pas la Région Administrative Spéciale de Hong Kong (Hong Kong RAS), la Région Administrative Spéciale de Macao (Macao RAS) et la province de Taiwan.

9   Source: "Census and Statistics Department".

10  Banque centrale des Comores.

11  Source: "Central Bank of Islamic Republic of Iran".

12  Source: "Central Bank of Iraq".

13  Source: "Reserve Bank of Malawi".

14  Années fiscales (du 1 er octobre au 30 septembre).

15  Cisjordanie et Gaza.

16  Années fiscales (juillet-juin).

17  Source: "Qatar Central Bank".

18  Source : Banque centrale des Antilles néerlandaises. Comprend des estimations concernant Saint-Eustache et Saba.

# Civil aviation: scheduled airline traffic
Passengers carried (thousands); kilometres (millions)

# Aviation civile : trafic aérien régulier
Passagers transportés (milliers) ; kilomètres (millions)

| Country or area and traffic | Total traffic (domestic and international) Trafic total (intérieur et international) | | | | International traffic Trafic international | | | | Pays ou zone et trafic |
|---|---|---|---|---|---|---|---|---|---|
| | 2002 | 2003 | 2004 | 2005 | 2002 | 2003 | 2004 | 2005 | |
| **Albania** | | | | | | | | | **Albanie** |
| Kilometres flown | 2 | 2 | 3 | 3 | 2 | 2 | 3 | 3 | Kilomètres parcourus |
| Passengers carried | 138 | 159 | 180 | 196 | 138 | 159 | 180 | 196 | Passagers transportés |
| Passenger-kilometres | 96 | 121 | 136 | 149 | 96 | 121 | 136 | 149 | Passagers-kilomètres |
| Total tonne-kilometres | 9 | 11 | 12 | 13 | 9 | 11 | 12 | 13 | Tonnes-kilomètres totales |
| **Algeria** | | | | | | | | | **Algérie** |
| Kilometres flown | 42 | 41 | 44 | 40 | 27 | 27 | 30 | 27 | Kilomètres parcourus |
| Passengers carried | 3 002 | 3 293 | 3 236 | 3 037 | 1 876 | 2 019 | 1 913 | 1 842 | Passagers transportés |
| Passenger-kilometres | 3 257 | 3 415 | 3 353 | 3 101 | 2 605 | 2 672 | 2 652 | 2 505 | Passagers-kilomètres |
| Total tonne-kilometres | 313 | 328 | 323 | 311 | 251 | 258 | 258 | 255 | Tonnes-kilomètres totales |
| **Angola** | | | | | | | | | **Angola** |
| Kilometres flown | 5 | 5 | 6 | 6 | 3 | 4 | 4 | 5 | Kilomètres parcourus |
| Passengers carried | 190 | 198 | 222 | 240 | 101 | 99 | 113 | 122 | Passagers transportés |
| Passenger-kilometres | 470 | 479 | 548 | 605 | 417 | 417 | 479 | 532 | Passagers-kilomètres |
| Total tonne-kilometres | 92 | 98 | 111 | 121 | 87 | 92 | 105 | 115 | Tonnes-kilomètres totales |
| **Antigua and Barbuda** | | | | | | | | | **Antigua-et-Barbuda** |
| Kilometres flown | 11 | 12 | 5 | 5 | 11 | 12 | 5 | 5 | Kilomètres parcourus |
| Passengers carried | 1 287 | 1 428 | 714 | 778 | 1 287 | 1 428 | 714 | 778 | Passagers transportés |
| Passenger-kilometres | 301 | 325 | 114 | 123 | 301 | 325 | 114 | 123 | Passagers-kilomètres |
| Total tonne-kilometres | 30 | 32 | 10 | 11 | 30 | 32 | 10 | 11 | Tonnes-kilomètres totales |
| **Argentina** | | | | | | | | | **Argentine** |
| Kilometres flown | 102 | 104 | 111 | 110 | 38 | 48 | 50 | 51 | Kilomètres parcourus |
| Passengers carried | 5 257 | 5 946 | 6 795 | 6 938 | 1 248 | 1 709 | 1 872 | 1 860 | Passagers transportés |
| Passenger-kilometres | 9 844 | 12 381 | 14 450 | 15 025 | 5 568 | 7 764 | 9 036 | 9 224 | Passagers-kilomètres |
| Total tonne-kilometres | 956 | 1 218 | 1 413 | 1 481 | 556 | 787 | 918 | 948 | Tonnes-kilomètres totales |
| **Armenia** | | | | | | | | | **Arménie** |
| Kilometres flown | 8 | 8 | 12 | 12 | 8 | 8 | 12 | 12 | Kilomètres parcourus |
| Passengers carried | 408 | 370 | 510 | 556 | 408 | 370 | 510 | 556 | Passagers transportés |
| Passenger-kilometres | 747 | 716 | 974 | 1 071 | 747 | 716 | 974 | 1 071 | Passagers-kilomètres |
| Total tonne-kilometres | 73 | 70 | 97 | 106 | 73 | 70 | 97 | 106 | Tonnes-kilomètres totales |
| **Australia** | | | | | | | | | **Australie** |
| Kilometres flown | 640 | 482 | 547 | 579 | 212 | 204 | 235 | 249 | Kilomètres parcourus |
| Passengers carried | 39 022 | 36 400 | 41 597 | 44 657 | 7 961 | 7 452 | 8 464 | 8 762 | Passagers transportés |
| Passenger-kilometres | 86 138 | 83 886 | 94 811 | 99 614 | 52 583 | 49 244 | 54 712 | 56 275 | Passagers-kilomètres |
| Total tonne-kilometres | 9 726 | 9 524 | 11 075 | 12 081 | 6 694 | 6 212 | 7 273 | 7 984 | Tonnes-kilomètres totales |
| **Austria** | | | | | | | | | **Autriche** |
| Kilometres flown | 130 | 130 | 149 | 159 | 126 | 126 | 145 | 155 | Kilomètres parcourus |
| Passengers carried | 7 070 | 6 903 | 7 619 | 8 038 | 6 646 | 6 461 | 7 166 | 7 583 | Passagers transportés |
| Passenger-kilometres | 13 794 | 14 558 | 17 530 | 18 835 | 13 682 | 14 440 | 17 407 | 18 713 | Passagers-kilomètres |
| Total tonne-kilometres | 1 859 | 1 983 | 2 366 | 2 542 | 1 847 | 1 971 | 2 353 | 2 529 | Tonnes-kilomètres totales |
| **Azerbaijan** | | | | | | | | | **Azerbaïdjan** |
| Kilometres flown | 11 | 12 | 14 | 15 | 8 | 9 | 11 | 12 | Kilomètres parcourus |
| Passengers carried | 575 | 684 | 1 007 | 1 134 | 171 | 245 | 501 | 570 | Passagers transportés |
| Passenger-kilometres | 579 | 751 | 1 276 | 1 431 | 347 | 497 | 983 | 1 107 | Passagers-kilomètres |
| Total tonne-kilometres | 128 | 135 | 149 | 141 | 105 | 111 | 121 | 109 | Tonnes-kilomètres totales |
| **Bahamas** | | | | | | | | | **Bahamas** |
| Kilometres flown | 6 | 6 | 7 | 8 | 4 | 4 | 3 | 4 | Kilomètres parcourus |
| Passengers carried | 1 543 | 1 601 | 900 | 1 020 | 886 | 984 | 398 | 470 | Passagers transportés |
| Passenger-kilometres | 369 | 388 | 219 | 277 | 266 | 287 | 129 | 184 | Passagers-kilomètres |
| Total tonne-kilometres | 47 | 48 | 20 | 26 | 33 | 35 | 12 | 17 | Tonnes-kilomètres totales |

| Country or area and traffic | Total traffic (domestic and international) Trafic total (intérieur et international) | | | | International traffic Trafic international | | | | Pays ou zone et trafic |
|---|---|---|---|---|---|---|---|---|---|
| | 2002 | 2003 | 2004 | 2005 | 2002 | 2003 | 2004 | 2005 | |
| **Bahrain[1]** | | | | | | | | | **Bahreïn[1]** |
| Kilometres flown | 27 | 40 | 50 | 48 | 27 | 40 | 50 | 48 | Kilomètres parcourus |
| Passengers carried | 1 256 | 1 850 | 2 285 | 2 234 | 1 256 | 1 850 | 2 285 | 2 234 | Passagers transportés |
| Passenger-kilometres | 2 944 | 4 494 | 5 954 | 5 822 | 2 944 | 4 494 | 5 954 | 5 822 | Passagers-kilomètres |
| Total tonne-kilometres | 523 | 769 | 981 | 933 | 523 | 769 | 981 | 933 | Tonnes-kilomètres totales |
| **Bangladesh** | | | | | | | | | **Bangladesh** |
| Kilometres flown | 27 | 29 | 30 | 31 | 26 | 27 | 29 | 30 | Kilomètres parcourus |
| Passengers carried | 1 536 | 1 579 | 1 650 | 1 634 | 1 172 | 1 205 | 1 324 | 1 338 | Passagers transportés |
| Passenger-kilometres | 4 580 | 4 662 | 5 042 | 5 381 | 4 503 | 4 583 | 4 972 | 5 317 | Passagers-kilomètres |
| Total tonne-kilometres | 684 | 704 | 747 | 796 | 677 | 697 | 740 | 789 | Tonnes-kilomètres totales |
| **Belarus** | | | | | | | | | **Bélarus** |
| Kilometres flown | 7 | 7 | 7 | 6 | 7 | 7 | 7 | 6 | Kilomètres parcourus |
| Passengers carried | 205 | 234 | 274 | 282 | 203 | 232 | 274 | 282 | Passagers transportés |
| Passenger-kilometres | 308 | 338 | 399 | 383 | 308 | 337 | 399 | 383 | Passagers-kilomètres |
| Total tonne-kilometres | 30 | 32 | 38 | 36 | 29 | 32 | 38 | 36 | Tonnes-kilomètres totales |
| **Belgium** | | | | | | | | | **Belgique** |
| Kilometres flown | 115 | 103 | 125 | 124 | 115 | 103 | 125 | 124 | Kilomètres parcourus |
| Passengers carried | 2 342 | 2 904 | 3 265 | 3 341 | 2 342 | 2 904 | 3 265 | 3 341 | Passagers transportés |
| Passenger-kilometres | 2 606 | 3 958 | 4 738 | 4 918 | 2 606 | 3 958 | 4 738 | 4 918 | Passagers-kilomètres |
| Total tonne-kilometres | 890 | 961 | 1 130 | 1 126 | 890 | 961 | 1 130 | 1 126 | Tonnes-kilomètres totales |
| **Bhutan** | | | | | | | | | **Bhoutan** |
| Kilometres flown | 2 | 2 | 2 | 2 | 2 | 2 | 2 | 2 | Kilomètres parcourus |
| Passengers carried | 41 | 36 | 45 | 49 | 41 | 36 | 45 | 49 | Passagers transportés |
| Passenger-kilometres | 61 | 56 | 69 | 74 | 61 | 56 | 69 | 74 | Passagers-kilomètres |
| Total tonne-kilometres | 6 | 5 | 6 | 7 | 6 | 5 | 6 | 7 | Tonnes-kilomètres totales |
| **Bolivia** | | | | | | | | | **Bolivie** |
| Kilometres flown | 18 | 22 | 22 | 22 | 12 | 14 | 15 | 15 | Kilomètres parcourus |
| Passengers carried | 1 509 | 1 771 | 1 844 | 1 892 | 446 | 568 | 586 | 614 | Passagers transportés |
| Passenger-kilometres | 1 432 | 1 744 | 1 787 | 1 903 | 982 | 1 311 | 1 341 | 1 434 | Passagers-kilomètres |
| Total tonne-kilometres | 148 | 187 | 186 | 196 | 106 | 145 | 145 | 151 | Tonnes-kilomètres totales |
| **Bosnia and Herzegovina** | | | | | | | | | **Bosnie-Herzégovine** |
| Kilometres flown | 1 | 1 | ... | ... | 1 | 1 | ... | ... | Kilomètres parcourus |
| Passengers carried | 66 | 73 | ... | ... | 66 | 73 | ... | ... | Passagers transportés |
| Passenger-kilometres | 43 | 47 | ... | ... | 43 | 47 | ... | ... | Passagers-kilomètres |
| Total tonne-kilometres | 5 | 6 | ... | ... | 5 | 6 | ... | ... | Tonnes-kilomètres totales |
| **Botswana** | | | | | | | | | **Botswana** |
| Kilometres flown | 3 | 3 | 3 | 4 | 2 | 2 | 2 | 2 | Kilomètres parcourus |
| Passengers carried | 179 | 189 | 213 | 230 | 124 | 131 | 149 | 161 | Passagers transportés |
| Passenger-kilometres | 80 | 83 | 95 | 104 | 54 | 55 | 63 | 70 | Passagers-kilomètres |
| Total tonne-kilometres | 8 | 8 | 9 | 10 | 5 | 5 | 6 | 7 | Tonnes-kilomètres totales |
| **Brazil** | | | | | | | | | **Brésil** |
| Kilometres flown | 529 | 443 | 441 | 467 | 137 | 123 | 129 | 136 | Kilomètres parcourus |
| Passengers carried | 35 890 | 32 293 | 35 264 | 37 662 | 3 387 | 3 448 | 3 727 | 3 980 | Passagers transportés |
| Passenger-kilometres | 46 092 | 44 192 | 47 462 | 50 689 | 20 761 | 20 252 | 21 286 | 22 733 | Passagers-kilomètres |
| Total tonne-kilometres | 5 763 | 5 447 | 5 844 | 6 173 | 2 950 | 2 875 | 3 013 | 3 174 | Tonnes-kilomètres totales |
| **Brunei Darussalam** | | | | | | | | | **Brunéi Darussalam** |
| Kilometres flown | 27 | 28 | 30 | 29 | 27 | 28 | 30 | 29 | Kilomètres parcourus |
| Passengers carried | 1 036 | 956 | 1 080 | 978 | 1 036 | 956 | 1 080 | 978 | Passagers transportés |
| Passenger-kilometres | 3 715 | 3 591 | 3 852 | 3 762 | 3 715 | 3 591 | 3 852 | 3 762 | Passagers-kilomètres |
| Total tonne-kilometres | 496 | 473 | 478 | 473 | 496 | 473 | 478 | 473 | Tonnes-kilomètres totales |
| **Bulgaria** | | | | | | | | | **Bulgarie** |
| Kilometres flown | 1 | 7 | 11 | 14 | 1 | 7 | 10 | 14 | Kilomètres parcourus |
| Passengers carried | 63 | 311 | 476 | 654 | 38 | 270 | 431 | 603 | Passagers transportés |
| Passenger-kilometres | 57 | 457 | 747 | 1 123 | 47 | 442 | 731 | 1 104 | Passagers-kilomètres |
| Total tonne-kilometres | 5 | 42 | 71 | 105 | 4 | 41 | 69 | 104 | Tonnes-kilomètres totales |

| Country or area and traffic | Total traffic (domestic and international) Trafic total (intérieur et international) | | | | International traffic Trafic international | | | | Pays ou zone et trafic |
|---|---|---|---|---|---|---|---|---|---|
| | 2002 | 2003 | 2004 | 2005 | 2002 | 2003 | 2004 | 2005 | |
| Burkina Faso[2] | | | | | | | | | Burkina Faso[2] |
| Kilometres flown | 1 | 1 | 1 | 1 | 1 | 1 | 1 | 1 | Kilomètres parcourus |
| Passengers carried | 53 | 54 | 61 | 66 | 37 | 36 | 41 | 44 | Passagers transportés |
| Passenger-kilometres | 29 | 29 | 33 | 37 | 24 | 24 | 28 | 31 | Passagers-kilomètres |
| Total tonne-kilometres | 3 | 3 | 3 | 3 | 2 | 2 | 3 | 3 | Tonnes-kilomètres totales |
| Cambodia | | | | | | | | | Cambodge |
| Kilometres flown | 2 | 2 | 2 | 2 | 1 | 1 | 1 | 2 | Kilomètres parcourus |
| Passengers carried | 125 | 165 | 162 | 169 | 13 | 70 | 74 | 101 | Passagers transportés |
| Passenger-kilometres | 61 | 106 | 98 | 165 | 14 | 82 | 77 | 148 | Passagers-kilomètres |
| Total tonne-kilometres | 9 | 12 | 12 | 16 | 5 | 11 | 10 | 14 | Tonnes-kilomètres totales |
| Cameroon | | | | | | | | | Cameroun |
| Kilometres flown | 11 | 9 | 11 | 12 | 9 | 8 | 9 | 10 | Kilomètres parcourus |
| Passengers carried | 322 | 315 | 356 | 384 | 235 | 225 | 257 | 277 | Passagers transportés |
| Passenger-kilometres | · 646 | 629 | 720 | 797 | 585 | 562 | 646 | 717 | Passagers-kilomètres |
| Total tonne-kilometres | 79 | 77 | 88 | 97 | 73 | 70 | 81 | 89 | Tonnes-kilomètres totales |
| Canada | | | | | | | | | Canada |
| Kilometres flown | 885 | 870 | 936 | 974 | 387 | 338 | 373 | 388 | Kilomètres parcourus |
| Passengers carried | 36 202 | 36 264 | 40 701 | 45 230 | 13 370 | 12 191 | 12 936 | 14 376 | Passagers transportés |
| Passenger-kilometres | 80 426 | 76 328 | 87 025 | 94 680 | 49 540 | 45 875 | 51 151 | 55 650 | Passagers-kilomètres |
| Total tonne-kilometres | 9 942 | 8 816 | 9 886 | 10 590 | 6 422 | 5 406 | 5 978 | 6 335 | Tonnes-kilomètres totales |
| Cape Verde | | | | | | | | | Cap-Vert |
| Kilometres flown | 4 | 5 | 9 | 11 | 3 | 3 | 7 | 8 | Kilomètres parcourus |
| Passengers carried | 237 | 253 | 560 | 690 | 87 | 86 | 224 | 304 | Passagers transportés |
| Passenger-kilometres | 279 | 285 | 804 | 1 078 | 242 | 242 | 725 | 986 | Passagers-kilomètres |
| Total tonne-kilometres | 26 | 27 | 74 | 99 | 23 | 23 | 66 | 90 | Tonnes-kilomètres totales |
| Chile | | | | | | | | | Chili |
| Kilometres flown | 108 | 107 | 110 | 119 | 70 | 71 | 72 | 76 | Kilomètres parcourus |
| Passengers carried | 4 987 | 5 247 | 5 464 | 5 939 | 2 120 | 2 387 | 2 479 | 2 742 | Passagers transportés |
| Passenger-kilometres | 11 094 | 12 187 | 12 874 | 14 067 | 8 110 | 9 140 | 9 648 | 10 529 | Passagers-kilomètres |
| Total tonne-kilometres | 2 110 | 2 237 | 2 260 | 2 336 | 1 785 | 1 913 | 1 922 | 1 961 | Tonnes-kilomètres totales |
| China[3] | | | | | | | | | Chine[3] |
| Kilometres flown | 1 149 | 1 195 | 1 542 | 1 731 | 199 | 209 | 287 | 315 | Kilomètres parcourus |
| Passengers carried | 83 672 | 86 041 | 119 789 | 136 722 | 8 050 | 6 641 | 10 553 | 11 991 | Passagers transportés |
| Passenger-kilometres | 123 908 | 124 591 | 176 268 | 201 961 | 28 821 | 24 346 | 39 179 | 44 603 | Passagers-kilomètres |
| Total tonne-kilometres | 16 200 | 17 641 | 22 912 | 25 765 | 5 400 | 6 246 | 7 679 | 8 387 | Tonnes-kilomètres totales |
| China, Hong Kong SAR | | | | | | | | | Chine, Hong Kong RAS |
| Kilometres flown | 231 | 272 | 338 | 383 | 231 | 272 | 338 | 383 | Kilomètres parcourus |
| Passengers carried | 15 636 | 13 025 | 17 893 | 20 230 | 15 636 | 13 025 | 17 893 | 20 230 | Passagers transportés |
| Passenger-kilometres | 53 148 | 46 402 | 62 094 | 70 603 | 53 148 | 46 402 | 62 094 | 70 603 | Passagers-kilomètres |
| Total tonne-kilometres | 10 821 | 10 278 | 12 939 | 14 606 | 10 821 | 10 278 | 12 939 | 14 606 | Tonnes-kilomètres totales |
| China, Macao SAR | | | | | | | | | Chine, Macao RAS |
| Kilometres flown | 18 | 15 | 23 | 27 | 18 | 15 | 23 | 27 | Kilomètres parcourus |
| Passengers carried | 1 728 | 1 212 | 1 800 | 2 041 | 1 728 | 1 212 | 1 800 | 2 041 | Passagers transportés |
| Passenger-kilometres | 2 056 | 1 566 | 2 127 | 2 406 | 2 056 | 1 566 | 2 127 | 2 406 | Passagers-kilomètres |
| Total tonne-kilometres | 236 | 198 | 320 | 410 | 236 | 198 | 320 | 410 | Tonnes-kilomètres totales |
| Colombia | | | | | | | | | Colombie |
| Kilometres flown | 114 | 110 | 118 | 127 | 57 | 54 | 69 | 75 | Kilomètres parcourus |
| Passengers carried | 9 425 | 8 665 | 8 829 | 9 984 | 1 842 | 1 714 | 1 781 | 2 120 | Passagers transportés |
| Passenger-kilometres | 8 271 | 8 299 | 9 045 | 9 688 | 4 272 | 4 210 | 4 382 | 4 782 | Passagers-kilomètres |
| Total tonne-kilometres | 1 281 | 1 390 | 1 926 | 1 982 | 871 | 953 | 1 442 | 1 455 | Tonnes-kilomètres totales |
| Congo[2] | | | | | | | | | Congo[2] |
| Kilometres flown | 1 | 1 | ... | ... | ^0 | ^0 | ... | ... | Kilomètres parcourus |
| Passengers carried | 47 | 52 | ... | ... | 2 | 2 | ... | ... | Passagers transportés |
| Passenger-kilometres | 27 | 31 | ... | ... | 4 | 4 | ... | ... | Passagers-kilomètres |
| Total tonne-kilometres | 3 | 3 | ... | ... | ^0 | ^0 | ... | ... | Tonnes-kilomètres totales |

| Country or area and traffic | Total traffic (domestic and international) Trafic total (intérieur et international) | | | | International traffic Trafic international | | | | Pays ou zone et trafic |
|---|---|---|---|---|---|---|---|---|---|
| | 2002 | 2003 | 2004 | 2005 | 2002 | 2003 | 2004 | 2005 | |
| Costa Rica | | | | | | | | | Costa Rica |
| Kilometres flown | 22 | 20 | 24 | 27 | 18 | 16 | 19 | 21 | Kilomètres parcourus |
| Passengers carried | 680 | 750 | 901 | 953 | 512 | 584 | 706 | 748 | Passagers transportés |
| Passenger-kilometres | 1 784 | 1 671 | 2 173 | 2 306 | 1 766 | 1 654 | 2 152 | 2 284 | Passagers-kilomètres |
| Total tonne-kilometres | 107 | 122 | 157 | 156 | 105 | 120 | 155 | 154 | Tonnes-kilomètres totales |
| Croatia | | | | | | | | | Croatie |
| Kilometres flown | 11 | 12 | 12 | 14 | 10 | 10 | 10 | 11 | Kilomètres parcourus |
| Passengers carried | 1 127 | 1 267 | 1 336 | 1 361 | 736 | 795 | 866 | 897 | Passagers transportés |
| Passenger-kilometres | 783 | 869 | 941 | 974 | 665 | 726 | 796 | 827 | Passagers-kilomètres |
| Total tonne-kilometres | 74 | 81 | 88 | 91 | 63 | 68 | 74 | 77 | Tonnes-kilomètres totales |
| Cuba | | | | | | | | | Cuba |
| Kilometres flown | 15 | 19 | 21 | 22 | 12 | 16 | 18 | 19 | Kilomètres parcourus |
| Passengers carried | 589 | 664 | 743 | 813 | 339 | 429 | 480 | 523 | Passagers transportés |
| Passenger-kilometres | 1 887 | 2 036 | 2 241 | 2 422 | 1 795 | 1 945 | 2 140 | 2 311 | Passagers-kilomètres |
| Total tonne-kilometres | 223 | 224 | 246 | 263 | 210 | 211 | 232 | 247 | Tonnes-kilomètres totales |
| Cyprus | | | | | | | | | Chypre |
| Kilometres flown | 25 | 30 | 32 | 32 | 25 | 30 | 32 | 32 | Kilomètres parcourus |
| Passengers carried | 1 705 | 1 883 | 2 013 | 1 921 | 1 705 | 1 883 | 2 013 | 1 921 | Passagers transportés |
| Passenger-kilometres | 3 436 | 3 935 | 4 230 | 4 184 | 3 436 | 3 935 | 4 230 | 4 184 | Passagers-kilomètres |
| Total tonne-kilometres | 355 | 408 | 442 | 428 | 355 | 408 | 442 | 428 | Tonnes-kilomètres totales |
| Czech Republic | | | | | | | | | République tchèque |
| Kilometres flown | 44 | 53 | 67 | 75 | 44 | 52 | 66 | 74 | Kilomètres parcourus |
| Passengers carried | 2 809 | 3 391 | 4 219 | 4 706 | 2 760 | 3 339 | 4 157 | 4 626 | Passagers transportés |
| Passenger-kilometres | 3 855 | 4 938 | 5 988 | 6 605 | 3 842 | 4 923 | 5 970 | 6 583 | Passagers-kilomètres |
| Total tonne-kilometres | 378 | 485 | 584 | 638 | 377 | 483 | 582 | 636 | Tonnes-kilomètres totales |
| Denmark[4] | | | | | | | | | Danemark[4] |
| Kilometres flown | 81 | 78 | 82 | 102 | 72 | 73 | 78 | 76 | Kilomètres parcourus |
| Passengers carried | 6 322 | 5 886 | 5 923 | 9 721 | 5 013 | 4 855 | 5 088 | 5 389 | Passagers transportés |
| Passenger-kilometres | 7 453 | 7 202 | 7 857 | 9 904 | 6 956 | 6 968 | 7 685 | 7 955 | Passagers-kilomètres |
| Total tonne-kilometres | 925 | 885 | 952 | 1 175 | 870 | 863 | 935 | 980 | Tonnes-kilomètres totales |
| Ecuador | | | | | | | | | Equateur |
| Kilometres flown | 7 | 9 | 11 | 11 | 2 | ^0 | ^0 | ^0 | Kilomètres parcourus |
| Passengers carried | 1 184 | 1 521 | 1 828 | 2 011 | 61 | 16 | 13 | 14 | Passagers transportés |
| Passenger-kilometres | 626 | 674 | 788 | 867 | 112 | 9 | 3 | 3 | Passagers-kilomètres |
| Total tonne-kilometres | 64 | 64 | 75 | 83 | 13 | 1 | ^0 | ^0 | Tonnes-kilomètres totales |
| Egypt | | | | | | | | | Egypte |
| Kilometres flown | 64 | 63 | 69 | 76 | 59 | 58 | 63 | 70 | Kilomètres parcourus |
| Passengers carried | 4 527 | 4 181 | 4 621 | 4 888 | 3 141 | 2 916 | 3 260 | 3 402 | Passagers transportés |
| Passenger-kilometres | 9 000 | 8 103 | 8 918 | 9 401 | 8 357 | 7 517 | 8 298 | 8 720 | Passagers-kilomètres |
| Total tonne-kilometres | 1 068 | 975 | 1 053 | 1 194 | 1 009 | 921 | 997 | 1 129 | Tonnes-kilomètres totales |
| El Salvador | | | | | | | | | El Salvador |
| Kilometres flown | 26 | 34 | 40 | 40 | 26 | 34 | 40 | 40 | Kilomètres parcourus |
| Passengers carried | 1 804 | 2 271 | 2 391 | 2 541 | 1 804 | 2 182 | 2 391 | 2 541 | Passagers transportés |
| Passenger-kilometres | 3 300 | 3 644 | 4 236 | 4 419 | 3 300 | 3 616 | 4 236 | 4 419 | Passagers-kilomètres |
| Total tonne-kilometres | 309 | 339 | 407 | 417 | 309 | 336 | 407 | 417 | Tonnes-kilomètres totales |
| Estonia | | | | | | | | | Estonie |
| Kilometres flown | 6 | 7 | 8 | 9 | 6 | 7 | 8 | 9 | Kilomètres parcourus |
| Passengers carried | 304 | 395 | 510 | 578 | 298 | 389 | 510 | 578 | Passagers transportés |
| Passenger-kilometres | 283 | 415 | 547 | 660 | 280 | 413 | 547 | 660 | Passagers-kilomètres |
| Total tonne-kilometres | 27 | 39 | 51 | 61 | 27 | 39 | 51 | 61 | Tonnes-kilomètres totales |
| Ethiopia | | | | | | | | | Ethiopie |
| Kilometres flown | 34 | 35 | 42 | 49 | 31 | 32 | 38 | 46 | Kilomètres parcourus |
| Passengers carried | 1 103 | 1 147 | 1 403 | 1 667 | 831 | 881 | 1 110 | 1 358 | Passagers transportés |
| Passenger-kilometres | 3 287 | 3 573 | 4 394 | 5 418 | 3 170 | 3 460 | 4 270 | 5 286 | Passagers-kilomètres |
| Total tonne-kilometres | 442 | 484 | 595 | 725 | 432 | 474 | 584 | 713 | Tonnes-kilomètres totales |

| Country or area and traffic | Total traffic (domestic and international)<br>Trafic total (intérieur et international) | | | | International traffic<br>Trafic international | | | | Pays ou zone et trafic |
|---|---|---|---|---|---|---|---|---|---|
| | 2002 | 2003 | 2004 | 2005 | 2002 | 2003 | 2004 | 2005 | |
| **Fiji** | | | | | | | | | **Fidji** |
| Kilometres flown | 20 | 21 | 22 | 23 | 16 | 17 | 18 | 18 | Kilomètres parcourus |
| Passengers carried | 715 | 766 | 837 | 871 | 450 | 516 | 587 | 601 | Passagers transportés |
| Passenger-kilometres | 2 906 | 2 233 | 2 430 | 2 403 | 2 872 | 2 190 | 2 389 | 2 360 | Passagers-kilomètres |
| Total tonne-kilometres | 368 | 298 | 318 | 332 | 365 | 294 | 314 | 329 | Tonnes-kilomètres totales |
| **Finland** | | | | | | | | | **Finlande** |
| Kilometres flown | 91 | 97 | 108 | 109 | 73 | 80 | 92 | 95 | Kilomètres parcourus |
| Passengers carried | 6 416 | 6 184 | 7 049 | 7 075 | 4 012 | 3 971 | 4 796 | 5 019 | Passagers transportés |
| Passenger-kilometres | 8 807 | 9 056 | 11 142 | 11 900 | 7 649 | 7 981 | 10 009 | 10 870 | Passagers-kilomètres |
| Total tonne-kilometres | 1 025 | 1 086 | 1 342 | 1 439 | 924 | 991 | 1 242 | 1 348 | Tonnes-kilomètres totales |
| **France**[5] | | | | | | | | | **France**[5] |
| Kilometres flown | 856 | 860 | 867 | 886 | 602 | 620 | 663 | 677 | Kilomètres parcourus |
| Passengers carried | 47 834 | 47 641 | 46 507 | 50 246 | 23 894 | 23 904 | 24 863 | 28 732 | Passagers transportés |
| Passenger-kilometres | 114 698 | 112 260 | 116 850 | 126 702 | 79 164 | 79 027 | 86 476 | 99 670 | Passagers-kilomètres |
| Total tonne-kilometres | 15 507 | 15 293 | 16 147 | 17 347 | 12 049 | 12 029 | 13 158 | 14 675 | Tonnes-kilomètres totales |
| **Gabon** | | | | | | | | | **Gabon** |
| Kilometres flown | 7 | 8 | 9 | 9 | 5 | 5 | 6 | 7 | Kilomètres parcourus |
| Passengers carried | 366 | 386 | 431 | 465 | 173 | 170 | 194 | 209 | Passagers transportés |
| Passenger-kilometres | 643 | 655 | 750 | 829 | 571 | 571 | 656 | 728 | Passagers-kilomètres |
| Total tonne-kilometres | 106 | 112 | 128 | 140 | 100 | 104 | 119 | 130 | Tonnes-kilomètres totales |
| **Georgia** | | | | | | | | | **Géorgie** |
| Kilometres flown | 4 | 6 | 7 | 8 | 4 | 6 | 7 | 8 | Kilomètres parcourus |
| Passengers carried | 112 | 180 | 229 | 249 | 112 | 180 | 229 | 249 | Passagers transportés |
| Passenger-kilometres | 230 | 384 | 473 | 520 | 230 | 384 | 473 | 520 | Passagers-kilomètres |
| Total tonne-kilometres | 23 | 37 | 46 | 50 | 23 | 37 | 46 | 50 | Tonnes-kilomètres totales |
| **Germany** | | | | | | | | | **Allemagne** |
| Kilometres flown | 927 | 1 070 | 1 198 | 1 285 | 801 | 952 | 1 082 | 1 149 | Kilomètres parcourus |
| Passengers carried | 61 890 | 72 693 | 82 100 | 90 789 | 42 818 | 53 645 | 63 493 | 69 144 | Passagers transportés |
| Passenger-kilometres | 124 246 | 149 672 | 170 628 | 182 508 | 116 020 | 141 313 | 162 427 | 172 799 | Passagers-kilomètres |
| Total tonne-kilometres | 19 425 | 21 937 | 24 736 | 25 457 | 18 594 | 21 097 | 23 911 | 24 509 | Tonnes-kilomètres totales |
| **Ghana** | | | | | | | | | **Ghana** |
| Kilometres flown | 12 | 12 | 5 | ... | 12 | 12 | 5 | ... | Kilomètres parcourus |
| Passengers carried | 256 | 241 | 96 | ... | 256 | 241 | 96 | ... | Passagers transportés |
| Passenger-kilometres | 912 | 906 | 363 | ... | 912 | 906 | 363 | ... | Passagers-kilomètres |
| Total tonne-kilometres | 107 | 101 | 41 | ... | 107 | 101 | 41 | ... | Tonnes-kilomètres totales |
| **Greece** | | | | | | | | | **Grèce** |
| Kilometres flown | 82 | 80 | 96 | 88 | 58 | 55 | 67 | 61 | Kilomètres parcourus |
| Passengers carried | 7 579 | 7 657 | 9 277 | 9 452 | 3 015 | 2 855 | 3 587 | 3 722 | Passagers transportés |
| Passenger-kilometres | 8 587 | 7 650 | 9 166 | 9 410 | 7 194 | 6 177 | 7 421 | 7 656 | Passagers-kilomètres |
| Total tonne-kilometres | 891 | 785 | 927 | 956 | 760 | 640 | 759 | 787 | Tonnes-kilomètres totales |
| **Hungary** | | | | | | | | | **Hongrie** |
| Kilometres flown | 39 | 46 | 52 | 54 | 39 | 46 | 52 | 54 | Kilomètres parcourus |
| Passengers carried | 2 134 | 2 362 | 2 546 | 2 735 | 2 134 | 2 362 | 2 546 | 2 735 | Passagers transportés |
| Passenger-kilometres | 3 116 | 3 130 | 3 510 | 3 806 | 3 116 | 3 130 | 3 510 | 3 806 | Passagers-kilomètres |
| Total tonne-kilometres | 312 | 314 | 344 | 368 | 312 | 314 | 344 | 368 | Tonnes-kilomètres totales |
| **Iceland** | | | | | | | | | **Islande** |
| Kilometres flown | 26 | 25 | 29 | 32 | 26 | 25 | 29 | 32 | Kilomètres parcourus |
| Passengers carried | 1 199 | 1 134 | 1 333 | 1 529 | 1 199 | 1 134 | 1 333 | 1 529 | Passagers transportés |
| Passenger-kilometres | 3 188 | 2 998 | 3 635 | 4 308 | 3 188 | 2 998 | 3 635 | 4 308 | Passagers-kilomètres |
| Total tonne-kilometres | 413 | 378 | 481 | 551 | 413 | 378 | 481 | 551 | Tonnes-kilomètres totales |
| **India** | | | | | | | | | **Inde** |
| Kilometres flown | 244 | 277 | 327 | 372 | 81 | 94 | 115 | 147 | Kilomètres parcourus |
| Passengers carried | 17 633 | 19 455 | 23 934 | 27 879 | 4 049 | 4 348 | 5 250 | 6 103 | Passagers transportés |
| Passenger-kilometres | 27 478 | 31 196 | 38 888 | 47 023 | 15 052 | 17 221 | 21 617 | 26 495 | Passagers-kilomètres |
| Total tonne-kilometres | 3 035 | 3 410 | 4 238 | 5 046 | 1 797 | 2 011 | 2 497 | 2 997 | Tonnes-kilomètres totales |

| Country or area and traffic | Total traffic (domestic and international) Trafic total (intérieur et international) | | | | International traffic Trafic international | | | | Pays ou zone et trafic |
|---|---|---|---|---|---|---|---|---|---|
| | 2002 | 2003 | 2004 | 2005 | 2002 | 2003 | 2004 | 2005 | |
| Indonesia | | | | | | | | | Indonésie |
| Kilometres flown | 159 | 211 | 263 | 266 | 62 | 40 | 55 | 49 | Kilomètres parcourus |
| Passengers carried | 12 113 | 20 358 | 26 781 | 26 836 | 2 513 | 1 984 | 2 823 | 2 713 | Passagers transportés |
| Passenger-kilometres | 18 419 | 21 274 | 28 447 | 28 243 | 10 298 | 6 487 | 8 800 | 7 589 | Passagers-kilomètres |
| Total tonne-kilometres | 1 879 | 2 164 | 2 963 | 2 924 | 1 093 | 776 | 1 080 | 928 | Tonnes-kilomètres totales |
| Iran (Islamic Rep. of) | | | | | | | | | Iran (Rép. islamique d') |
| Kilometres flown | 75 | 89 | 91 | 99 | 28 | 34 | 37 | 39 | Kilomètres parcourus |
| Passengers carried | 9 892 | 11 664 | 11 878 | 12 708 | 1 942 | 2 282 | 2 554 | 2 887 | Passagers transportés |
| Passenger-kilometres | 8 616 | 10 231 | 11 657 | 12 194 | 3 022 | 3 761 | 4 925 | 5 250 | Passagers-kilomètres |
| Total tonne-kilometres | 835 | 1 002 | 1 136 | 1 169 | 329 | 401 | 509 | 539 | Tonnes-kilomètres totales |
| Ireland | | | | | | | | | Irlande |
| Kilometres flown | 138 | 197 | 236 | 292 | 138 | 197 | 236 | 292 | Kilomètres parcourus |
| Passengers carried | 19 729 | 28 923 | 34 749 | 42 873 | 19 630 | 28 890 | 34 749 | 42 873 | Passagers transportés |
| Passenger-kilometres | 18 575 | 27 441 | 34 597 | 44 792 | 18 552 | 27 433 | 34 597 | 44 792 | Passagers-kilomètres |
| Total tonne-kilometres | 1 756 | 2 573 | 3 216 | 4 156 | 1 754 | 2 572 | 3 216 | 4 156 | Tonnes-kilomètres totales |
| Israel | | | | | | | | | Israël |
| Kilometres flown | 90 | 89 | 99 | 101 | 81 | 83 | 93 | 96 | Kilomètres parcourus |
| Passengers carried | 3 708 | 3 678 | 4 969 | 4 392 | 2 482 | 2 581 | 3 970 | 3 352 | Passagers transportés |
| Passenger-kilometres | 12 234 | 12 465 | 14 674 | 16 362 | 11 862 | 12 157 | 14 381 | 16 057 | Passagers-kilomètres |
| Total tonne-kilometres | 2 437 | 2 535 | 2 695 | 2 710 | 2 404 | 2 507 | 2 669 | 2 683 | Tonnes-kilomètres totales |
| Italy | | | | | | | | | Italie |
| Kilometres flown | 351 | 398 | 407 | 448 | 235 | 265 | 284 | 313 | Kilomètres parcourus |
| Passengers carried | 28 245 | 36 077 | 35 922 | 36 116 | 10 989 | 13 613 | 14 729 | 15 129 | Passagers transportés |
| Passenger-kilometres | 34 328 | 40 823 | 43 237 | 51 127 | 24 735 | 28 559 | 32 136 | 39 141 | Passagers-kilomètres |
| Total tonne-kilometres | 4 798 | 5 343 | 5 626 | 6 426 | 3 859 | 4 171 | 4 572 | 5 278 | Tonnes-kilomètres totales |
| Jamaica | | | | | | | | | Jamaïque |
| Kilometres flown | 41 | 48 | 53 | 53 | 41 | 48 | 53 | 53 | Kilomètres parcourus |
| Passengers carried | 2 016 | 1 838 | 2 008 | 1 574 | 2 016 | 1 838 | 2 008 | 1 574 | Passagers transportés |
| Passenger-kilometres | 4 912 | 5 005 | 5 060 | 3 855 | 4 912 | 5 005 | 5 060 | 3 855 | Passagers-kilomètres |
| Total tonne-kilometres | 589 | 484 | 499 | 369 | 589 | 484 | 499 | 369 | Tonnes-kilomètres totales |
| Japan | | | | | | | | | Japon |
| Kilometres flown | 853 | 834 | 838 | 863 | 443 | 420 | 432 | 449 | Kilomètres parcourus |
| Passengers carried | 109 038 | 103 650 | 101 741 | 102 279 | 18 839 | 14 411 | 16 259 | 16 484 | Passagers transportés |
| Passenger-kilometres | 164 134 | 146 856 | 151 810 | 153 289 | 90 595 | 73 610 | 81 674 | 82 227 | Passagers-kilomètres |
| Total tonne-kilometres | 22 470 | 21 071 | 22 027 | 21 992 | 16 075 | 14 643 | 15 803 | 15 691 | Tonnes-kilomètres totales |
| Jordan | | | | | | | | | Jordanie |
| Kilometres flown | 37 | 36 | 42 | 44 | 37 | 36 | 42 | 44 | Kilomètres parcourus |
| Passengers carried | 1 300 | 1 353 | 1 660 | 1 737 | 1 300 | 1 353 | 1 660 | 1 732 | Passagers transportés |
| Passenger-kilometres | 4 146 | 4 498 | 5 327 | 5 390 | 4 146 | 4 498 | 5 327 | 5 389 | Passagers-kilomètres |
| Total tonne-kilometres | 577 | 602 | 740 | 716 | 577 | 602 | 740 | 716 | Tonnes-kilomètres totales |
| Kazakhstan | | | | | | | | | Kazakhstan |
| Kilometres flown | 25 | 31 | 22 | 35 | 13 | 17 | 13 | 18 | Kilomètres parcourus |
| Passengers carried | 757 | 1 010 | 835 | 1 160 | 305 | 405 | 308 | 395 | Passagers transportés |
| Passenger-kilometres | 1 730 | 2 149 | 1 898 | 2 470 | 1 141 | 1 404 | 1 197 | 1 515 | Passagers-kilomètres |
| Total tonne-kilometres | 184 | 222 | 185 | 241 | 127 | 151 | 118 | 151 | Tonnes-kilomètres totales |
| Kenya | | | | | | | | | Kenya |
| Kilometres flown | 36 | 41 | 43 | 48 | 31 | 35 | 40 | 43 | Kilomètres parcourus |
| Passengers carried | 1 600 | 1 732 | 2 005 | 2 424 | 1 148 | 1 250 | 1 513 | 1 821 | Passagers transportés |
| Passenger-kilometres | 3 939 | 4 245 | 5 310 | 6 540 | 3 754 | 4 050 | 5 105 | 6 292 | Passagers-kilomètres |
| Total tonne-kilometres | 465 | 527 | 674 | 850 | 448 | 509 | 655 | 826 | Tonnes-kilomètres totales |
| Korea, Dem. P. R. | | | | | | | | | Corée, R. p. dém. de |
| Kilometres flown | 1 | 1 | 1 | 1 | 1 | 1 | 1 | 1 | Kilomètres parcourus |
| Passengers carried | 84 | 75 | 94 | 101 | 84 | 75 | 94 | 101 | Passagers transportés |
| Passenger-kilometres | 35 | 32 | 39 | 42 | 35 | 32 | 39 | 42 | Passagers-kilomètres |
| Total tonne-kilometres | 5 | 5 | 6 | 6 | 5 | 5 | 6 | 6 | Tonnes-kilomètres totales |

| Country or area and traffic | Total traffic (domestic and international) Trafic total (intérieur et international) | | | | International traffic Trafic international | | | | Pays ou zone et trafic |
|---|---|---|---|---|---|---|---|---|---|
| | 2002 | 2003 | 2004 | 2005 | 2002 | 2003 | 2004 | 2005 | |
| **Korea, Republic of** | | | | | | | | | **Corée, République de** |
| Kilometres flown | 400 | 370 | 407 | 398 | 343 | 311 | 355 | 351 | Kilomètres parcourus |
| Passengers carried | 34 832 | 33 373 | 34 511 | 33 888 | 14 077 | 13 051 | 15 917 | 17 198 | Passagers transportés |
| Passenger-kilometres | 65 852 | 57 624 | 67 131 | 69 292 | 58 249 | 50 104 | 60 103 | 62 896 | Passagers-kilomètres |
| Total tonne-kilometres | 13 875 | 12 134 | 14 140 | 13 687 | 13 123 | 11 402 | 13 443 | 13 053 | Tonnes-kilomètres totales |
| **Kuwait** | | | | | | | | | **Koweït** |
| Kilometres flown | 41 | 39 | 44 | 43 | 41 | 39 | 44 | 43 | Kilomètres parcourus |
| Passengers carried | 2 299 | 2 186 | 2 496 | 2 433 | 2 299 | 2 186 | 2 496 | 2 433 | Passagers transportés |
| Passenger-kilometres | 6 706 | 6 311 | 7 285 | 7 282 | 6 706 | 6 311 | 7 285 | 7 282 | Passagers-kilomètres |
| Total tonne-kilometres | 867 | 795 | 892 | 905 | 867 | 795 | 892 | 905 | Tonnes-kilomètres totales |
| **Kyrgyzstan** | | | | | | | | | **Kirghizistan** |
| Kilometres flown | 5 | 6 | 6 | 6 | 4 | 5 | 5 | 4 | Kilomètres parcourus |
| Passengers carried | 174 | 206 | 246 | 226 | 85 | 103 | 125 | 116 | Passagers transportés |
| Passenger-kilometres | 315 | 372 | 418 | 368 | 280 | 332 | 370 | 324 | Passagers-kilomètres |
| Total tonne-kilometres | 35 | 39 | 40 | 35 | 32 | 35 | 36 | 31 | Tonnes-kilomètres totales |
| **Lao People's Dem. Rep.** | | | | | | | | | **Rép. dém. pop. lao** |
| Kilometres flown | 2 | 3 | 3 | 3 | 1 | 1 | 1 | 1 | Kilomètres parcourus |
| Passengers carried | 220 | 219 | 272 | 293 | 65 | 58 | 72 | 78 | Passagers transportés |
| Passenger-kilometres | 91 | 90 | 113 | 124 | 40 | 37 | 45 | 48 | Passagers-kilomètres |
| Total tonne-kilometres | 9 | 9 | 12 | 13 | 5 | 4 | 5 | 6 | Tonnes-kilomètres totales |
| **Latvia** | | | | | | | | | **Lettonie** |
| Kilometres flown | 6 | 7 | 13 | 21 | 6 | 7 | 13 | 21 | Kilomètres parcourus |
| Passengers carried | 265 | 340 | 594 | 1 032 | 265 | 340 | 594 | 1 032 | Passagers transportés |
| Passenger-kilometres | 184 | 245 | 581 | 1 161 | 184 | 245 | 581 | 1 161 | Passagers-kilomètres |
| Total tonne-kilometres | 18 | 23 | 53 | 106 | 18 | 23 | 53 | 106 | Tonnes-kilomètres totales |
| **Lebanon** | | | | | | | | | **Liban** |
| Kilometres flown | 20 | 20 | 22 | 22 | 20 | 20 | 22 | 22 | Kilomètres parcourus |
| Passengers carried | 874 | 935 | 1 087 | 1 076 | 874 | 935 | 1 087 | 1 076 | Passagers transportés |
| Passenger-kilometres | 1 749 | 1 905 | 2 197 | 2 168 | 1 749 | 1 905 | 2 197 | 2 168 | Passagers-kilomètres |
| Total tonne-kilometres | 244 | 253 | 292 | 291 | 244 | 253 | 292 | 291 | Tonnes-kilomètres totales |
| **Libyan Arab Jamah.** | | | | | | | | | **Jamah. arabe libyenne** |
| Kilometres flown | 4 | 8 | 9 | 18 | ... | 4 | 5 | 13 | Kilomètres parcourus |
| Passengers carried | 559 | 742 | 850 | ... | ... | 115 | 161 | ... | Passagers transportés |
| Passenger-kilometres | 409 | 825 | 985 | 1 572 | ... | 346 | 454 | 918 | Passagers-kilomètres |
| Total tonne-kilometres | 33 | 69 | 82 | 142 | ... | 31 | 41 | 92 | Tonnes-kilomètres totales |
| **Lithuania** | | | | | | | | | **Lituanie** |
| Kilometres flown | 10 | 10 | 12 | 14 | 10 | 10 | 12 | 14 | Kilomètres parcourus |
| Passengers carried | 304 | 329 | 448 | 505 | 303 | 329 | 447 | 505 | Passagers transportés |
| Passenger-kilometres | 355 | 395 | 557 | 700 | 355 | 395 | 557 | 700 | Passagers-kilomètres |
| Total tonne-kilometres | 34 | 37 | 52 | 65 | 34 | 37 | 52 | 65 | Tonnes-kilomètres totales |
| **Luxembourg** | | | | | | | | | **Luxembourg** |
| Kilometres flown | 70 | 74 | 78 | 91 | 70 | 74 | 78 | 91 | Kilomètres parcourus |
| Passengers carried | 823 | 854 | 856 | 851 | 823 | 854 | 856 | 851 | Passagers transportés |
| Passenger-kilometres | 437 | 548 | 573 | 566 | 437 | 548 | 573 | 566 | Passagers-kilomètres |
| Total tonne-kilometres | 4 197 | 4 397 | 4 722 | 5 201 | 4 197 | 4 397 | 4 722 | 5 201 | Tonnes-kilomètres totales |
| **Madagascar** | | | | | | | | | **Madagascar** |
| Kilometres flown | 5 | 9 | 11 | 13 | 2 | 4 | 6 | 8 | Kilomètres parcourus |
| Passengers carried | 391 | 452 | 514 | 575 | 241 | 140 | 167 | 207 | Passagers transportés |
| Passenger-kilometres | 319 | 715 | 911 | 1 174 | 266 | 562 | 736 | 982 | Passagers-kilomètres |
| Total tonne-kilometres | 48 | 74 | 95 | 121 | 42 | 60 | 78 | 103 | Tonnes-kilomètres totales |
| **Malawi** | | | | | | | | | **Malawi** |
| Kilometres flown | 3 | 4 | 5 | 5 | 2 | 2 | 3 | 3 | Kilomètres parcourus |
| Passengers carried | 105 | 109 | 122 | 132 | 67 | 68 | 78 | 84 | Passagers transportés |
| Passenger-kilometres | 140 | 147 | 167 | 182 | 80 | 86 | 99 | 110 | Passagers-kilomètres |
| Total tonne-kilometres | 14 | 16 | 18 | 20 | 8 | 11 | 12 | 14 | Tonnes-kilomètres totales |

| Country or area and traffic | Total traffic (domestic and international) Trafic total (intérieur et international) | | | | International traffic Trafic international | | | | Pays ou zone et trafic |
|---|---|---|---|---|---|---|---|---|---|
| | 2002 | 2003 | 2004 | 2005 | 2002 | 2003 | 2004 | 2005 | |
| Malaysia | | | | | | | | | Malaisie |
| Kilometres flown | 232 | 247 | 278 | 291 | 176 | 179 | 207 | 218 | Kilomètres parcourus |
| Passengers carried | 16 275 | 16 710 | 19 227 | 20 369 | 7 527 | 6 949 | 8 369 | 9 353 | Passagers transportés |
| Passenger-kilometres | 36 923 | 38 415 | 44 642 | 49 578 | 32 191 | 32 309 | 37 823 | 42 416 | Passagers-kilomètres |
| Total tonne-kilometres | 5 345 | 5 689 | 6 672 | 7 103 | 4 920 | 5 126 | 6 047 | 6 445 | Tonnes-kilomètres totales |
| Maldives | | | | | | | | | Maldives |
| Kilometres flown | 1 | 2 | 2 | 2 | ... | ... | ... | ... | Kilomètres parcourus |
| Passengers carried | 58 | 60 | 76 | 82 | ... | ... | ... | ... | Passagers transportés |
| Passenger-kilometres | 26 | 28 | 35 | 39 | ... | ... | ... | ... | Passagers-kilomètres |
| Total tonne-kilometres | 2 | 3 | 3 | 4 | ... | ... | ... | ... | Tonnes-kilomètres totales |
| Malta | | | | | | | | | Malte |
| Kilometres flown | 22 | 22 | 22 | 24 | 22 | 22 | 22 | 24 | Kilomètres parcourus |
| Passengers carried | 1 399 | 1 309 | 1 365 | 1 372 | 1 399 | 1 309 | 1 365 | 1 372 | Passagers transportés |
| Passenger-kilometres | 2 305 | 2 174 | 2 282 | 2 292 | 2 305 | 2 174 | 2 282 | 2 292 | Passagers-kilomètres |
| Total tonne-kilometres | 221 | 209 | 212 | 218 | 221 | 209 | 212 | 218 | Tonnes-kilomètres totales |
| Marshall Islands | | | | | | | | | Iles Marshall |
| Kilometres flown | 1 | 1 | 1 | 1 | ^0 | ^0 | ^0 | ... | Kilomètres parcourus |
| Passengers carried | 25 | 27 | 29 | 26 | 1 | 1 | 1 | ... | Passagers transportés |
| Passenger-kilometres | 32 | 36 | 38 | 34 | 2 | 1 | 1 | ... | Passagers-kilomètres |
| Total tonne-kilometres | 3 | 4 | 4 | 4 | ^0 | ^0 | ^0 | ... | Tonnes-kilomètres totales |
| Mauritania[2] | | | | | | | | | Mauritanie[2] |
| Kilometres flown | 1 | 1 | 1 | 1 | ^0 | ^0 | ^0 | ^0 | Kilomètres parcourus |
| Passengers carried | 106 | 116 | 128 | 139 | 15 | 14 | 17 | 18 | Passagers transportés |
| Passenger-kilometres | 45 | 49 | 56 | 60 | 17 | 17 | 19 | 22 | Passagers-kilomètres |
| Total tonne-kilometres | 4 | 5 | 5 | 6 | 2 | 2 | 2 | 2 | Tonnes-kilomètres totales |
| Mauritius | | | | | | | | | Maurice |
| Kilometres flown | 30 | 33 | 44 | 47 | 29 | 32 | 43 | 46 | Kilomètres parcourus |
| Passengers carried | 1 006 | 1 043 | 1 089 | 1 146 | 909 | 929 | 991 | 1 064 | Passagers transportés |
| Passenger-kilometres | 5 084 | 5 243 | 5 739 | 6 266 | 5 026 | 5 175 | 5 680 | 6 217 | Passagers-kilomètres |
| Total tonne-kilometres | 667 | 687 | 739 | 778 | 661 | 680 | 733 | 774 | Tonnes-kilomètres totales |
| Mexico | | | | | | | | | Mexique |
| Kilometres flown | 337 | 344 | 366 | 386 | 144 | 149 | 163 | 185 | Kilomètres parcourus |
| Passengers carried | 19 619 | 19 642 | 21 168 | 21 858 | 5 312 | 5 383 | 6 071 | 6 905 | Passagers transportés |
| Passenger-kilometres | 28 264 | 28 927 | 31 924 | 34 123 | 13 347 | 13 517 | 15 499 | 17 713 | Passagers-kilomètres |
| Total tonne-kilometres | 3 216 | 3 300 | 3 645 | 3 869 | 1 689 | 1 739 | 1 979 | 2 206 | Tonnes-kilomètres totales |
| Moldova | | | | | | | | | Moldova |
| Kilometres flown | 5 | 5 | 6 | 6 | 5 | 5 | 6 | 6 | Kilomètres parcourus |
| Passengers carried | 129 | 179 | 201 | 232 | 129 | 179 | 201 | 232 | Passagers transportés |
| Passenger-kilometres | 161 | 223 | 257 | 325 | 161 | 223 | 257 | 325 | Passagers-kilomètres |
| Total tonne-kilometres | 15 | 22 | 26 | 35 | 15 | 22 | 26 | 35 | Tonnes-kilomètres totales |
| Monaco | | | | | | | | | Monaco |
| Kilometres flown | 1 | 1 | 1 | 1 | 1 | 1 | 1 | 1 | Kilomètres parcourus |
| Passengers carried | 104 | 95 | 84 | 88 | 104 | 95 | 84 | 88 | Passagers transportés |
| Passenger-kilometres | 7 | 6 | 4 | 5 | 7 | 6 | 4 | 5 | Passagers-kilomètres |
| Total tonne-kilometres | 1 | 1 | ^0 | ^0 | 1 | 1 | ^0 | ^0 | Tonnes-kilomètres totales |
| Mongolia | | | | | | | | | Mongolie |
| Kilometres flown | 7 | 9 | 9 | 9 | 5 | 5 | 5 | 6 | Kilomètres parcourus |
| Passengers carried | 270 | 289 | 310 | 295 | 153 | 139 | 162 | 178 | Passagers transportés |
| Passenger-kilometres | 661 | 691 | 735 | 753 | 560 | 552 | 611 | 657 | Passagers-kilomètres |
| Total tonne-kilometres | 69 | 71 | 74 | 76 | 59 | 58 | 63 | 66 | Tonnes-kilomètres totales |
| Morocco | | | | | | | | | Maroc |
| Kilometres flown | 58 | 59 | 70 | 76 | 55 | 56 | 67 | 71 | Kilomètres parcourus |
| Passengers carried | 3 146 | 2 638 | 3 004 | 3 493 | 2 501 | 2 049 | 2 363 | 2 738 | Passagers transportés |
| Passenger-kilometres | 6 045 | 4 905 | 5 551 | 6 434 | 5 834 | 4 710 | 5 341 | 6 181 | Passagers-kilomètres |
| Total tonne-kilometres | 626 | 528 | 642 | 714 | 605 | 507 | 617 | 687 | Tonnes-kilomètres totales |

| Country or area and traffic | Total traffic (domestic and international) Trafic total (intérieur et international) | | | | International traffic Trafic international | | | | Pays ou zone et trafic |
|---|---|---|---|---|---|---|---|---|---|
| | 2002 | 2003 | 2004 | 2005 | 2002 | 2003 | 2004 | 2005 | |
| Mozambique | | | | | | | | | Mozambique |
| Kilometres flown | 7 | 6 | 7 | 8 | 3 | 3 | 3 | 3 | Kilomètres parcourus |
| Passengers carried | 282 | 281 | 294 | 347 | 98 | 103 | 100 | 126 | Passagers transportés |
| Passenger-kilometres | 397 | 405 | 372 | 445 | 201 | 214 | 133 | 211 | Passagers-kilomètres |
| Total tonne-kilometres | 43 | 43 | 37 | 45 | 23 | 23 | 14 | 21 | Tonnes-kilomètres totales |
| Myanmar | | | | | | | | | Myanmar |
| Kilometres flown | 15 | 16 | 19 | 20 | 11 | 11 | 13 | 14 | Kilomètres parcourus |
| Passengers carried | 1 186 | 1 117 | 1 392 | 1 504 | 776 | 691 | 863 | 932 | Passagers transportés |
| Passenger-kilometres | 1 154 | 1 083 | 1 339 | 1 448 | 932 | 848 | 1 043 | 1 116 | Passagers-kilomètres |
| Total tonne-kilometres | 106 | 100 | 122 | 132 | 85 | 78 | 94 | 100 | Tonnes-kilomètres totales |
| Namibia | | | | | | | | | Namibie |
| Kilometres flown | 9 | 11 | 11 | 11 | 6 | 8 | 8 | 10 | Kilomètres parcourus |
| Passengers carried | 222 | 266 | 283 | 399 | 179 | 222 | 235 | 354 | Passagers transportés |
| Passenger-kilometres | 760 | 930 | 913 | 1 569 | 734 | 904 | 885 | 1 540 | Passagers-kilomètres |
| Total tonne-kilometres | 98 | 139 | 147 | 157 | 95 | 136 | 144 | 154 | Tonnes-kilomètres totales |
| Nauru | | | | | | | | | Nauru |
| Kilometres flown | 3 | 3 | 3 | 3 | 3 | 3 | 3 | 3 | Kilomètres parcourus |
| Passengers carried | 175 | 156 | 195 | 211 | 175 | 156 | 195 | 211 | Passagers transportés |
| Passenger-kilometres | 302 | 275 | 338 | 361 | 302 | 275 | 338 | 361 | Passagers-kilomètres |
| Total tonne-kilometres | 30 | 28 | 34 | 36 | 30 | 28 | 34 | 36 | Tonnes-kilomètres totales |
| Nepal | | | | | | | | | Népal |
| Kilometres flown | 10 | 8 | 9 | 10 | 9 | 6 | 8 | 8 | Kilomètres parcourus |
| Passengers carried | 681 | 356 | 445 | 480 | 553 | 279 | 349 | 377 | Passagers transportés |
| Passenger-kilometres | 1 211 | 663 | 816 | 873 | 1 191 | 652 | 802 | 858 | Passagers-kilomètres |
| Total tonne-kilometres | 127 | 64 | 77 | 82 | 125 | 63 | 76 | 81 | Tonnes-kilomètres totales |
| Netherlands[6] | | | | | | | | | Pays-Bas[6] |
| Kilometres flown | 424 | 429 | 460 | 481 | 423 | 428 | 459 | 481 | Kilomètres parcourus |
| Passengers carried | 22 119 | 22 590 | 24 627 | 26 133 | 22 000 | 22 482 | 24 526 | 26 057 | Passagers transportés |
| Passenger-kilometres | 68 979 | 68 688 | 75 706 | 82 269 | 68 962 | 68 673 | 75 692 | 82 258 | Passagers-kilomètres |
| Total tonne-kilometres | 11 244 | 11 331 | 12 487 | 13 235 | 11 243 | 11 329 | 12 486 | 13 234 | Tonnes-kilomètres totales |
| New Zealand | | | | | | | | | Nouvelle-Zélande |
| Kilometres flown | 180 | 164 | 176 | 185 | 96 | 109 | 116 | 122 | Kilomètres parcourus |
| Passengers carried | 11 285 | 10 334 | 11 305 | 11 952 | 3 746 | 4 042 | 4 338 | 4 623 | Passagers transportés |
| Passenger-kilometres | 23 323 | 23 280 | 24 710 | 26 093 | 19 802 | 20 440 | 21 536 | 22 766 | Passagers-kilomètres |
| Total tonne-kilometres | 2 787 | 3 203 | 3 307 | 3 486 | 2 463 | 2 902 | 2 970 | 3 133 | Tonnes-kilomètres totales |
| Nigeria | | | | | | | | | Nigéria |
| Kilometres flown | 6 | 12 | 12 | 14 | 1 | 4 | 5 | 6 | Kilomètres parcourus |
| Passengers carried | 512 | 520 | 540 | 748 | 41 | 51 | 51 | 100 | Passagers transportés |
| Passenger-kilometres | 522 | 638 | 683 | 935 | 27 | 15 | 10 | 153 | Passagers-kilomètres |
| Total tonne-kilometres | 57 | 61 | 64 | 89 | 3 | 2 | 2 | 16 | Tonnes-kilomètres totales |
| Norway[4] | | | | | | | | | Norvège[4] |
| Kilometres flown | 129 | 127 | 128 | 110 | 64 | 66 | 68 | 68 | Kilomètres parcourus |
| Passengers carried | 13 699 | 12 806 | 12 277 | 10 398 | 4 474 | 4 407 | 4 410 | 4 849 | Passagers transportés |
| Passenger-kilometres | 10 546 | 10 506 | 10 321 | 9 408 | 6 444 | 6 726 | 6 958 | 7 152 | Passagers-kilomètres |
| Total tonne-kilometres | 1 231 | 1 211 | 1 199 | 1 125 | 822 | 834 | 864 | 904 | Tonnes-kilomètres totales |
| Oman[1] | | | | | | | | | Oman[1] |
| Kilometres flown | 32 | 45 | 52 | 52 | 31 | 43 | 50 | 51 | Kilomètres parcourus |
| Passengers carried | 2 104 | 2 777 | 3 267 | 3 369 | 1 931 | 2 617 | 3 094 | 3 167 | Passagers transportés |
| Passenger-kilometres | 4 133 | 5 899 | 7 455 | 7 538 | 3 989 | 5 765 | 7 313 | 7 369 | Passagers-kilomètres |
| Total tonne-kilometres | 485 | 746 | 945 | 951 | 468 | 731 | 931 | 934 | Tonnes-kilomètres totales |
| Pakistan | | | | | | | | | Pakistan |
| Kilometres flown | 61 | 68 | 79 | 79 | 47 | 52 | 63 | 64 | Kilomètres parcourus |
| Passengers carried | 4 141 | 4 522 | 5 097 | 5 364 | 2 205 | 2 433 | 2 985 | 3 171 | Passagers transportés |
| Passenger-kilometres | 10 680 | 11 880 | 13 459 | 14 304 | 9 089 | 10 154 | 11 713 | 12 496 | Passagers-kilomètres |
| Total tonne-kilometres | 1 322 | 1 432 | 1 629 | 1 708 | 1 141 | 1 239 | 1 433 | 1 504 | Tonnes-kilomètres totales |

**Civil aviation: scheduled airline traffic**—Passengers carried (thousands); kilometres (millions) (*continued*)

**Aviation civile : trafic aérien régulier**—Passagers transportés (milliers) ; kilomètres (millions) (*suite*)

| Country or area and traffic | Total traffic (domestic and international) Trafic total (intérieur et international) | | | | International traffic Trafic international | | | | Pays ou zone et trafic |
|---|---|---|---|---|---|---|---|---|---|
| | 2002 | 2003 | 2004 | 2005 | 2002 | 2003 | 2004 | 2005 | |
| Panama | | | | | | | | | Panama |
| Kilometres flown | 38 | 43 | 46 | 55 | 38 | 43 | 46 | 55 | Kilomètres parcourus |
| Passengers carried | 1 048 | 1 313 | 1 501 | 1 796 | 1 048 | 1 313 | 1 501 | 1 796 | Passagers transportés |
| Passenger-kilometres | 2 974 | 3 529 | 4 100 | 5 206 | 2 974 | 3 529 | 4 100 | 5 206 | Passagers-kilomètres |
| Total tonne-kilometres | 317 | 375 | 442 | 553 | 317 | 375 | 442 | 553 | Tonnes-kilomètres totales |
| Papua New Guinea | | | | | | | | | Papouasie-Nvl-Guinée |
| Kilometres flown | 18 | 11 | 12 | 12 | 6 | 5 | 5 | 5 | Kilomètres parcourus |
| Passengers carried | 1 235 | 691 | 763 | 819 | 296 | 127 | 146 | 148 | Passagers transportés |
| Passenger-kilometres | 1 175 | 576 | 667 | 695 | 660 | 334 | 389 | 394 | Passagers-kilomètres |
| Total tonne-kilometres | 133 | 76 | 84 | 92 | 82 | 50 | 57 | 59 | Tonnes-kilomètres totales |
| Paraguay | | | | | | | | | Paraguay |
| Kilometres flown | 6 | 6 | 7 | 7 | 5 | 5 | 7 | 7 | Kilomètres parcourus |
| Passengers carried | 269 | 299 | 373 | 446 | 254 | 288 | 366 | 442 | Passagers transportés |
| Passenger-kilometres | 279 | 320 | 433 | 501 | 274 | 318 | 431 | 500 | Passagers-kilomètres |
| Total tonne-kilometres | 25 | 29 | 39 | 45 | 25 | 29 | 39 | 45 | Tonnes-kilomètres totales |
| Peru | | | | | | | | | Pérou |
| Kilometres flown | 38 | 44 | 50 | 66 | 22 | 29 | 31 | 39 | Kilomètres parcourus |
| Passengers carried | 2 092 | 2 226 | 3 225 | 4 332 | 500 | 547 | 741 | 922 | Passagers transportés |
| Passenger-kilometres | 2 340 | 2 796 | 3 901 | 5 298 | 1 279 | 1 727 | 2 296 | 2 959 | Passagers-kilomètres |
| Total tonne-kilometres | 317 | 382 | 594 | 602 | 208 | 265 | 417 | 386 | Tonnes-kilomètres totales |
| Philippines | | | | | | | | | Philippines |
| Kilometres flown | 79 | 75 | 82 | 87 | 53 | 53 | 57 | 61 | Kilomètres parcourus |
| Passengers carried | 6 449 | 6 435 | 7 388 | 8 057 | 2 547 | 2 416 | 2 765 | 3 110 | Passagers transportés |
| Passenger-kilometres | 14 216 | 13 904 | 15 739 | 17 123 | 11 753 | 11 387 | 12 845 | 14 022 | Passagers-kilomètres |
| Total tonne-kilometres | 1 755 | 1 729 | 1 929 | 2 085 | 1 497 | 1 468 | 1 630 | 1 773 | Tonnes-kilomètres totales |
| Poland | | | | | | | | | Pologne |
| Kilometres flown | 66 | 68 | 73 | 77 | 59 | 61 | 66 | 70 | Kilomètres parcourus |
| Passengers carried | 2 846 | 3 252 | 3 493 | 3 554 | 2 196 | 2 495 | 2 678 | 2 749 | Passagers transportés |
| Passenger-kilometres | 5 111 | 5 434 | 5 861 | 6 223 | 4 921 | 5 213 | 5 622 | 5 988 | Passagers-kilomètres |
| Total tonne-kilometres | 581 | 608 | 654 | 687 | 565 | 589 | 634 | 667 | Tonnes-kilomètres totales |
| Portugal[7] | | | | | | | | | Portugal[7] |
| Kilometres flown | 117 | 128 | 149 | 158 | 100 | 110 | 124 | 133 | Kilomètres parcourus |
| Passengers carried | 6 796 | 7 590 | 9 052 | 10 140 | 4 403 | 4 994 | 5 756 | 5 900 | Passagers transportés |
| Passenger-kilometres | 12 109 | 13 562 | 16 093 | 16 834 | 10 674 | 11 904 | 13 634 | 14 519 | Passagers-kilomètres |
| Total tonne-kilometres | 1 314 | 1 455 | 1 723 | 1 789 | 1 169 | 1 289 | 1 467 | 1 547 | Tonnes-kilomètres totales |
| Qatar[1] | | | | | | | | | Qatar[1] |
| Kilometres flown | 65 | 59 | 87 | 118 | 65 | 59 | 87 | 118 | Kilomètres parcourus |
| Passengers carried | 3 571 | 3 184 | 4 453 | 6 041 | 3 571 | 3 184 | 4 453 | 6 041 | Passagers transportés |
| Passenger-kilometres | 8 608 | 8 003 | 12 172 | 17 890 | 8 608 | 8 003 | 12 172 | 17 890 | Passagers-kilomètres |
| Total tonne-kilometres | 1 095 | 1 003 | 1 579 | 2 494 | 1 095 | 1 003 | 1 579 | 2 494 | Tonnes-kilomètres totales |
| Romania | | | | | | | | | Roumanie |
| Kilometres flown | 21 | 26 | 28 | 36 | 19 | 24 | 26 | 33 | Kilomètres parcourus |
| Passengers carried | 959 | 1 255 | 1 338 | 1 708 | 858 | 1 034 | 1 150 | 1 484 | Passagers transportés |
| Passenger-kilometres | 1 593 | 1 696 | 1 532 | 1 967 | 1 555 | 1 634 | 1 463 | 1 886 | Passagers-kilomètres |
| Total tonne-kilometres | 153 | 160 | 144 | 188 | 150 | 155 | 137 | 181 | Tonnes-kilomètres totales |
| Russian Federation | | | | | | | | | Fédération de Russie |
| Kilometres flown | 653 | 602 | 694 | 680 | 196 | 199 | 250 | 245 | Kilomètres parcourus |
| Passengers carried | 20 892 | 22 723 | 25 949 | 26 522 | 6 667 | 6 972 | 8 404 | 8 560 | Passagers transportés |
| Passenger-kilometres | 49 890 | 53 894 | 62 010 | 63 192 | 19 552 | 20 478 | 25 151 | 25 413 | Passagers-kilomètres |
| Total tonne-kilometres | 5 580 | 6 018 | 7 064 | 7 285 | 2 395 | 2 513 | 3 224 | 3 339 | Tonnes-kilomètres totales |
| Samoa | | | | | | | | | Samoa |
| Kilometres flown | 2 | 4 | 5 | 5 | 1 | 3 | 4 | 4 | Kilomètres parcourus |
| Passengers carried | 182 | 198 | 247 | 267 | 97 | 121 | 151 | 164 | Passagers transportés |
| Passenger-kilometres | 306 | 279 | 343 | 368 | 295 | 270 | 332 | 355 | Passagers-kilomètres |
| Total tonne-kilometres | 31 | 27 | 32 | 35 | 29 | 26 | 31 | 33 | Tonnes-kilomètres totales |

| Country or area and traffic | Total traffic (domestic and international) Trafic total (intérieur et international) | | | | International traffic Trafic international | | | | Pays ou zone et trafic |
|---|---|---|---|---|---|---|---|---|---|
| | 2002 | 2003 | 2004 | 2005 | 2002 | 2003 | 2004 | 2005 | |
| Sao Tome and Principe | | | | | | | | | Sao Tomé-et-Principe |
| Kilometres flown | ^0 | ^0 | 1 | 1 | ^0 | ^0 | ^0 | ^0 | Kilomètres parcourus |
| Passengers carried | 34 | 36 | 40 | 43 | 21 | 21 | 24 | 25 | Passagers transportés |
| Passenger-kilometres | 14 | 15 | 17 | 18 | 7 | 7 | 8 | 9 | Passagers-kilomètres |
| Total tonne-kilometres | 1 | 1 | 2 | 2 | 1 | 1 | 1 | 1 | Tonnes-kilomètres totales |
| Saudi Arabia | | | | | | | | | Arabie saoudite |
| Kilometres flown | 124 | 125 | 135 | 141 | 71 | 72 | 81 | 85 | Kilomètres parcourus |
| Passengers carried | 13 564 | 13 822 | 14 943 | 15 933 | 4 622 | 4 801 | 5 251 | 5 538 | Passagers transportés |
| Passenger-kilometres | 20 804 | 20 801 | 22 557 | 23 793 | 13 818 | 13 693 | 14 897 | 15 534 | Passagers-kilomètres |
| Total tonne-kilometres | 2 748 | 2 739 | 3 000 | 3 174 | 2 031 | 2 014 | 2 229 | 2 351 | Tonnes-kilomètres totales |
| Senegal[2] | | | | | | | | | Sénégal[2] |
| Kilometres flown | 7 | 6 | 8 | 9 | 7 | 6 | 8 | 9 | Kilomètres parcourus |
| Passengers carried | 231 | 130 | 416 | 450 | 199 | 96 | 379 | 409 | Passagers transportés |
| Passenger-kilometres | 572 | 388 | 767 | 851 | 554 | 378 | 756 | 839 | Passagers-kilomètres |
| Total tonne-kilometres | 20 | 35 | 69 | 77 | 18 | 34 | 68 | 76 | Tonnes-kilomètres totales |
| Serbia and Montenegro | | | | | | | | | Serbie-et-Monténégro |
| Kilometres flown | 17 | 18 | 20 | 18 | 14 | 16 | 17 | 16 | Kilomètres parcourus |
| Passengers carried | 1 185 | 1 298 | 1 414 | 1 302 | 767 | 871 | 943 | 877 | Passagers transportés |
| Passenger-kilometres | 1 081 | 1 199 | 1 286 | 1 169 | 949 | 1 061 | 1 137 | 1 032 | Passagers-kilomètres |
| Total tonne-kilometres | 98 | 156 | 122 | 109 | 87 | 137 | 108 | 97 | Tonnes-kilomètres totales |
| Seychelles | | | | | | | | | Seychelles |
| Kilometres flown | 12 | 12 | 14 | 15 | 11 | 11 | 13 | 14 | Kilomètres parcourus |
| Passengers carried | 518 | 413 | 462 | 499 | 250 | 187 | 213 | 230 | Passagers transportés |
| Passenger-kilometres | 1 397 | 986 | 1 134 | 1 258 | 1 387 | 976 | 1 123 | 1 246 | Passagers-kilomètres |
| Total tonne-kilometres | 153 | 114 | 131 | 145 | 152 | 113 | 130 | 144 | Tonnes-kilomètres totales |
| Sierra Leone | | | | | | | | | Sierra Leone |
| Kilometres flown | 1 | 1 | 1 | 2 | 1 | 1 | 1 | 2 | Kilomètres parcourus |
| Passengers carried | 14 | 14 | 16 | 17 | 14 | 14 | 16 | 17 | Passagers transportés |
| Passenger-kilometres | 74 | 74 | 85 | 94 | 74 | 74 | 85 | 94 | Passagers-kilomètres |
| Total tonne-kilometres | 13 | 13 | 15 | 17 | 13 | 13 | 15 | 17 | Tonnes-kilomètres totales |
| Singapore | | | | | | | | | Singapour |
| Kilometres flown | 361 | 341 | 397 | 425 | 361 | 341 | 397 | 425 | Kilomètres parcourus |
| Passengers carried | 17 257 | 14 737 | 16 996 | 17 744 | 17 257 | 14 737 | 16 996 | 17 744 | Passagers transportés |
| Passenger-kilometres | 75 620 | 65 387 | 79 085 | 82 904 | 75 620 | 65 387 | 79 085 | 82 904 | Passagers-kilomètres |
| Total tonne-kilometres | 14 140 | 13 062 | 14 206 | 14 913 | 14 140 | 13 062 | 14 206 | 14 913 | Tonnes-kilomètres totales |
| Slovakia | | | | | | | | | Slovaquie |
| Kilometres flown | 3 | 5 | 12 | 13 | 2 | 4 | 11 | 12 | Kilomètres parcourus |
| Passengers carried | 83 | 190 | 636 | 712 | 53 | 159 | 601 | 674 | Passagers transportés |
| Passenger-kilometres | 94 | 220 | 848 | 949 | 85 | 211 | 837 | 938 | Passagers-kilomètres |
| Total tonne-kilometres | 9 | 20 | 65 | 73 | 8 | 19 | 64 | 72 | Tonnes-kilomètres totales |
| Slovenia | | | | | | | | | Slovénie |
| Kilometres flown | 12 | 13 | 14 | 15 | 12 | 13 | 14 | 15 | Kilomètres parcourus |
| Passengers carried | 721 | 758 | 765 | 758 | 721 | 758 | 765 | 758 | Passagers transportés |
| Passenger-kilometres | 678 | 700 | 711 | 707 | 678 | 700 | 711 | 707 | Passagers-kilomètres |
| Total tonne-kilometres | 66 | 67 | 67 | 66 | 66 | 67 | 67 | 66 | Tonnes-kilomètres totales |
| Solomon Islands | | | | | | | | | Iles Salomon |
| Kilometres flown | 4 | 2 | 3 | 3 | 1 | 1 | 1 | 1 | Kilomètres parcourus |
| Passengers carried | 85 | 68 | 85 | 91 | 19 | 23 | 28 | 31 | Passagers transportés |
| Passenger-kilometres | 55 | 59 | 73 | 79 | 39 | 47 | 58 | 62 | Passagers-kilomètres |
| Total tonne-kilometres | 6 | 6 | 7 | 8 | 5 | 5 | 6 | 6 | Tonnes-kilomètres totales |
| South Africa | | | | | | | | | Afrique du Sud |
| Kilometres flown | 170 | 188 | 194 | 218 | 94 | 104 | 109 | 122 | Kilomètres parcourus |
| Passengers carried | 8 167 | 9 160 | 9 879 | 11 845 | 2 834 | 2 996 | 3 156 | 3 397 | Passagers transportés |
| Passenger-kilometres | 22 914 | 24 666 | 26 048 | 29 191 | 17 953 | 18 852 | 19 684 | 21 289 | Passagers-kilomètres |
| Total tonne-kilometres | 2 853 | 3 125 | 3 270 | 3 580 | 2 330 | 2 505 | 2 618 | 2 760 | Tonnes-kilomètres totales |

| Country or area and traffic | Total traffic (domestic and international) Trafic total (intérieur et international) | | | | International traffic Trafic international | | | | Pays ou zone et trafic |
|---|---|---|---|---|---|---|---|---|---|
| | 2002 | 2003 | 2004 | 2005 | 2002 | 2003 | 2004 | 2005 | |
| Spain | | | | | | | | | Espagne |
| Kilometres flown | 442 | 473 | 520 | 561 | 261 | 279 | 308 | 323 | Kilomètres parcourus |
| Passengers carried | 40 381 | 42 507 | 45 540 | 49 855 | 12 858 | 13 515 | 14 704 | 15 911 | Passagers transportés |
| Passenger-kilometres | 54 044 | 57 594 | 64 141 | 70 975 | 36 511 | 38 723 | 43 509 | 48 008 | Passagers-kilomètres |
| Total tonne-kilometres | 5 715 | 6 096 | 6 859 | 7 459 | 4 040 | 4 268 | 4 858 | 5 265 | Tonnes-kilomètres totales |
| Sri Lanka | | | | | | | | | Sri Lanka |
| Kilometres flown | 29 | 34 | 43 | 42 | 29 | 34 | 43 | 42 | Kilomètres parcourus |
| Passengers carried | 1 741 | 1 958 | 2 413 | 2 818 | 1 741 | 1 958 | 2 413 | 2 818 | Passagers transportés |
| Passenger-kilometres | 6 327 | 6 910 | 8 310 | 8 599 | 6 327 | 6 910 | 8 310 | 8 599 | Passagers-kilomètres |
| Total tonne-kilometres | 778 | 864 | 1 068 | 1 089 | 778 | 864 | 1 068 | 1 089 | Tonnes-kilomètres totales |
| Sudan | | | | | | | | | Soudan |
| Kilometres flown | 6 | 7 | 8 | 8 | 5 | 5 | 6 | 7 | Kilomètres parcourus |
| Passengers carried | 409 | 420 | 473 | 511 | 270 | 264 | 301 | 326 | Passagers transportés |
| Passenger-kilometres | 767 | 786 | 898 | 992 | 659 | 659 | 758 | 841 | Passagers-kilomètres |
| Total tonne-kilometres | 98 | 103 | 116 | 128 | 85 | 88 | 100 | 110 | Tonnes-kilomètres totales |
| Suriname | | | | | | | | | Suriname |
| Kilometres flown | 5 | 5 | 5 | 6 | 5 | 4 | 5 | 5 | Kilomètres parcourus |
| Passengers carried | 191 | 258 | 289 | 315 | 186 | 253 | 283 | 308 | Passagers transportés |
| Passenger-kilometres | 889 | 1 470 | 1 616 | 1 746 | 887 | 1 469 | 1 616 | 1 745 | Passagers-kilomètres |
| Total tonne-kilometres | 101 | 183 | 201 | 214 | 101 | 183 | 201 | 214 | Tonnes-kilomètres totales |
| Sweden[4] | | | | | | | | | Suède[4] |
| Kilometres flown | 130 | 129 | 133 | 119 | 81 | 86 | 89 | 76 | Kilomètres parcourus |
| Passengers carried | 12 421 | 11 873 | 11 624 | 10 808 | 5 958 | 5 900 | 5 976 | 5 030 | Passagers transportés |
| Passenger-kilometres | 11 663 | 11 638 | 11 976 | 11 389 | 8 643 | 8 846 | 9 304 | 8 774 | Passagers-kilomètres |
| Total tonne-kilometres | 1 427 | 1 410 | 1 452 | 1 410 | 1 137 | 1 142 | 1 197 | 1 157 | Tonnes-kilomètres totales |
| Switzerland | | | | | | | | | Suisse |
| Kilometres flown | 256 | 218 | 172 | 166 | 252 | 216 | 170 | 164 | Kilomètres parcourus |
| Passengers carried | 13 292 | 10 118 | 9 287 | 9 663 | 12 311 | 9 642 | 8 624 | 9 013 | Passagers transportés |
| Passenger-kilometres | 26 704 | 23 295 | 20 602 | 20 476 | 26 501 | 23 186 | 20 456 | 20 334 | Passagers-kilomètres |
| Total tonne-kilometres | 3 720 | 3 617 | 2 986 | 2 994 | 3 699 | 3 605 | 2 971 | 2 979 | Tonnes-kilomètres totales |
| Syrian Arab Republic | | | | | | | | | Rép. arabe syrienne |
| Kilometres flown | 16 | 9 | 11 | 12 | 15 | 9 | 11 | 12 | Kilomètres parcourus |
| Passengers carried | 824 | 940 | 1 170 | 1 240 | 705 | 908 | 1 135 | 1 203 | Passagers transportés |
| Passenger-kilometres | 1 609 | 1 744 | 2 212 | 2 520 | 1 565 | 1 727 | 2 193 | 2 500 | Passagers-kilomètres |
| Total tonne-kilometres | 169 | 173 | 219 | 249 | 165 | 171 | 217 | 247 | Tonnes-kilomètres totales |
| Tajikistan | | | | | | | | | Tadjikistan |
| Kilometres flown | 9 | 10 | 11 | 9 | 8 | 8 | 9 | 8 | Kilomètres parcourus |
| Passengers carried | 397 | 413 | 498 | 479 | 316 | 291 | 342 | 313 | Passagers transportés |
| Passenger-kilometres | 864 | 854 | 1 000 | 942 | 829 | 803 | 937 | 877 | Passagers-kilomètres |
| Total tonne-kilometres | 82 | 84 | 96 | 91 | 79 | 79 | 90 | 85 | Tonnes-kilomètres totales |
| Thailand | | | | | | | | | Thaïlande |
| Kilometres flown | 194 | 204 | 223 | 229 | 173 | 175 | 193 | 200 | Kilomètres parcourus |
| Passengers carried | 18 112 | 17 892 | 20 343 | 18 903 | 12 537 | 11 774 | 13 671 | 12 946 | Passagers transportés |
| Passenger-kilometres | 48 337 | 45 449 | 51 564 | 50 809 | 45 084 | 41 910 | 47 699 | 47 385 | Passagers-kilomètres |
| Total tonne-kilometres | 6 241 | 5 920 | 6 579 | 6 646 | 5 913 | 5 579 | 6 209 | 6 317 | Tonnes-kilomètres totales |
| TFYR of Macedonia | | | | | | | | | L'ex-R.y. Macédoine |
| Kilometres flown | 3 | 3 | 3 | 3 | 3 | 3 | 3 | 3 | Kilomètres parcourus |
| Passengers carried | 166 | 201 | 211 | 192 | 166 | 201 | 211 | 192 | Passagers transportés |
| Passenger-kilometres | 236 | 280 | 276 | 249 | 236 | 280 | 276 | 249 | Passagers-kilomètres |
| Total tonne-kilometres | 21 | 25 | 25 | 22 | 21 | 25 | 25 | 22 | Tonnes-kilomètres totales |
| Tonga | | | | | | | | | Tonga |
| Kilometres flown | 1 | 1 | 1 | ... | ... | ... | ... | ... | Kilomètres parcourus |
| Passengers carried | 58 | 61 | 75 | ... | ... | ... | ... | ... | Passagers transportés |
| Passenger-kilometres | 14 | 15 | 19 | ... | ... | ... | ... | ... | Passagers-kilomètres |
| Total tonne-kilometres | 1 | 1 | 2 | ... | ... | ... | ... | ... | Tonnes-kilomètres totales |

| Country or area and traffic | Total traffic (domestic and international) Trafic total (intérieur et international) | | | | International traffic Trafic international | | | | Pays ou zone et trafic |
|---|---|---|---|---|---|---|---|---|---|
| | 2002 | 2003 | 2004 | 2005 | 2002 | 2003 | 2004 | 2005 | |
| Trinidad and Tobago | | | | | | | | | Trinité-et-Tobago |
| Kilometres flown | 28 | 31 | 28 | 27 | 28 | 31 | 28 | 27 | Kilomètres parcourus |
| Passengers carried | 1 269 | 1 084 | 1 132 | 1 055 | 1 164 | 972 | 1 088 | 1 044 | Passagers transportés |
| Passenger-kilometres | 2 875 | 2 671 | 3 013 | 3 100 | 2 866 | 2 662 | 3 009 | 3 100 | Passagers-kilomètres |
| Total tonne-kilometres | 295 | 276 | 314 | 328 | 294 | 275 | 314 | 328 | Tonnes-kilomètres totales |
| Tunisia | | | | | | | | | Tunisie |
| Kilometres flown | 24 | 25 | 28 | 30 | 24 | 25 | 28 | 30 | Kilomètres parcourus |
| Passengers carried | 1 789 | 1 720 | 1 940 | 1 997 | 1 789 | 1 720 | 1 940 | 1 997 | Passagers transportés |
| Passenger-kilometres | 2 511 | 2 459 | 2 853 | 2 995 | 2 511 | 2 459 | 2 853 | 2 995 | Passagers-kilomètres |
| Total tonne-kilometres | 266 | 261 | 299 | 312 | 266 | 261 | 299 | 312 | Tonnes-kilomètres totales |
| Turkey | | | | | | | | | Turquie |
| Kilometres flown | 140 | 142 | 161 | 186 | 108 | 111 | 119 | 136 | Kilomètres parcourus |
| Passengers carried | 10 640 | 10 745 | 14 276 | 16 944 | 5 276 | 5 239 | 6 094 | 7 194 | Passagers transportés |
| Passenger-kilometres | 16 818 | 16 451 | 20 500 | 24 297 | 13 822 | 13 343 | 15 422 | 18 259 | Passagers-kilomètres |
| Total tonne-kilometres | 2 117 | 2 071 | 2 448 | 2 814 | 1 813 | 1 756 | 1 959 | 2 247 | Tonnes-kilomètres totales |
| Turkmenistan | | | | | | | | | Turkménistan |
| Kilometres flown | 22 | 22 | 17 | 16 | 11 | 12 | 11 | 11 | Kilomètres parcourus |
| Passengers carried | 1 407 | 1 412 | 1 612 | 1 654 | 345 | 307 | 436 | 420 | Passagers transportés |
| Passenger-kilometres | 1 608 | 1 538 | 1 916 | 1 905 | 1 104 | 1 005 | 1 363 | 1 337 | Passagers-kilomètres |
| Total tonne-kilometres | 156 | 150 | 182 | 182 | 110 | 102 | 131 | 129 | Tonnes-kilomètres totales |
| Uganda | | | | | | | | | Ouganda |
| Kilometres flown | 2 | 2 | 3 | 3 | 2 | 2 | 3 | 3 | Kilomètres parcourus |
| Passengers carried | 41 | 40 | 46 | 49 | 41 | 40 | 46 | 49 | Passagers transportés |
| Passenger-kilometres | 237 | 237 | 272 | 302 | 237 | 237 | 272 | 302 | Passagers-kilomètres |
| Total tonne-kilometres | 42 | 44 | 50 | 55 | 42 | 44 | 50 | 55 | Tonnes-kilomètres totales |
| Ukraine | | | | | | | | | Ukraine |
| Kilometres flown | 32 | 38 | 54 | 56 | 27 | 30 | 44 | 44 | Kilomètres parcourus |
| Passengers carried | 1 120 | 1 476 | 2 200 | 2 513 | 882 | 1 054 | 1 610 | 1 802 | Passagers transportés |
| Passenger-kilometres | 1 578 | 2 351 | 3 826 | 4 087 | 1 443 | 2 115 | 3 282 | 3 549 | Passagers-kilomètres |
| Total tonne-kilometres | 156 | 231 | 372 | 405 | 144 | 211 | 325 | 352 | Tonnes-kilomètres totales |
| United Arab Emirates[1] | | | | | | | | | Emirats arabes unis[1] |
| Kilometres flown | 159 | 207 | 277 | 321 | 159 | 207 | 277 | 321 | Kilomètres parcourus |
| Passengers carried | 9 667 | 11 610 | 14 314 | 16 210 | 9 667 | 11 610 | 14 314 | 16 210 | Passagers transportés |
| Passenger-kilometres | 33 125 | 41 504 | 54 703 | 65 121 | 33 125 | 41 504 | 54 703 | 65 121 | Passagers-kilomètres |
| Total tonne-kilometres | 5 261 | 6 760 | 8 979 | 10 669 | 5 261 | 6 760 | 8 979 | 10 669 | Tonnes-kilomètres totales |
| United Kingdom[8,9] | | | | | | | | | Royaume-Uni[8,9] |
| Kilometres flown | 1 048 | 1 087 | 1 205 | 1 324 | 925 | 965 | 1 066 | 1 177 | Kilomètres parcourus |
| Passengers carried | 72 381 | 76 389 | 86 055 | 93 603 | 52 802 | 55 604 | 63 515 | 70 475 | Passagers transportés |
| Passenger-kilometres | 156 594 | 166 518 | 182 736 | 200 333 | 148 305 | 157 503 | 173 205 | 190 543 | Passagers-kilomètres |
| Total tonne-kilometres | 20 041 | 20 689 | 22 260 | 24 008 | 19 335 | 19 942 | 21 474 | 23 173 | Tonnes-kilomètres totales |
| United Rep. of Tanzania | | | | | | | | | Rép.-Unie de Tanzanie |
| Kilometres flown | 3 | 4 | 5 | 8 | 2 | 3 | 3 | 5 | Kilomètres parcourus |
| Passengers carried | 134 | 150 | 243 | 257 | 67 | 61 | 82 | 74 | Passagers transportés |
| Passenger-kilometres | 136 | 151 | 216 | 246 | 93 | 102 | 135 | 148 | Passagers-kilomètres |
| Total tonne-kilometres | 14 | 16 | 22 | 24 | 9 | 10 | 14 | 14 | Tonnes-kilomètres totales |
| United States[10] | | | | | | | | | Etats-Unis[10] |
| Kilometres flown | 9 946 | 10 526 | 11 634 | 12 197 | 1 901 | 1 937 | 2 161 | 2 352 | Kilomètres parcourus |
| Passengers carried | 595 561 | 615 944 | 676 655 | 719 023 | 63 008 | 61 639 | 70 458 | 79 064 | Passagers transportés |
| Passenger-kilometres | 1 014 132 | 1 035 277 | 1 160 236 | 1 239 844 | 270 076 | 261 070 | 303 202 | 333 554 | Passagers-kilomètres |
| Total tonne-kilometres | 125 555 | 130 979 | 144 508 | 151 465 | 44 496 | 42 991 | 48 560 | 51 386 | Tonnes-kilomètres totales |
| Uruguay | | | | | | | | | Uruguay |
| Kilometres flown | 7 | 8 | 9 | 8 | 7 | 8 | 9 | 8 | Kilomètres parcourus |
| Passengers carried | 525 | 464 | 564 | 586 | 525 | 464 | 564 | 586 | Passagers transportés |
| Passenger-kilometres | 577 | 1 029 | 1 076 | 980 | 577 | 1 029 | 1 076 | 980 | Passagers-kilomètres |
| Total tonne-kilometres | 64 | 118 | 101 | 92 | 64 | 118 | 101 | 92 | Tonnes-kilomètres totales |

| Country or area and traffic | Total traffic (domestic and international) Trafic total (intérieur et international) | | | | International traffic Trafic international | | | | Pays ou zone et trafic |
|---|---|---|---|---|---|---|---|---|---|
| | 2002 | 2003 | 2004 | 2005 | 2002 | 2003 | 2004 | 2005 | |
| **Uzbekistan** | | | | | | | | | **Ouzbékistan** |
| Kilometres flown | 39 | 40 | 44 | 42 | 32 | 33 | 37 | 36 | Kilomètres parcourus |
| Passengers carried | 1 451 | 1 466 | 1 588 | 1 639 | 1 036 | 1 048 | 1 183 | 1 220 | Passagers transportés |
| Passenger-kilometres | 3 835 | 3 889 | 4 454 | 4 409 | 3 600 | 3 646 | 4 215 | 4 171 | Passagers-kilomètres |
| Total tonne-kilometres | 417 | 424 | 486 | 479 | 396 | 401 | 464 | 457 | Tonnes-kilomètres totales |
| **Vanuatu** | | | | | | | | | **Vanuatu** |
| Kilometres flown | 3 | 3 | 3 | 3 | 3 | 3 | 3 | 3 | Kilomètres parcourus |
| Passengers carried | 104 | 83 | 104 | 112 | 104 | 83 | 104 | 112 | Passagers transportés |
| Passenger-kilometres | 223 | 176 | 217 | 232 | 223 | 176 | 217 | 232 | Passagers-kilomètres |
| Total tonne-kilometres | 23 | 18 | 21 | 23 | 23 | 18 | 21 | 23 | Tonnes-kilomètres totales |
| **Venezuela (Bolivarian Rep. of)** | | | | | | | | | **Venezuela (Rép. bolivar. du)** |
| Kilometres flown | 79 | 50 | 57 | 59 | 28 | 17 | 21 | 20 | Kilomètres parcourus |
| Passengers carried | 6 369 | 3 887 | 4 944 | 5 043 | 1 361 | 726 | 1 018 | 870 | Passagers transportés |
| Passenger-kilometres | 4 103 | 2 048 | 2 469 | 2 579 | 2 162 | 841 | 991 | 985 | Passagers-kilomètres |
| Total tonne-kilometres | 405 | 187 | 218 | 234 | 227 | 78 | 88 | 91 | Tonnes-kilomètres totales |
| **Viet Nam** | | | | | | | | | **Viet Nam** |
| Kilometres flown | 50 | 48 | 60 | 65 | 34 | 32 | 43 | 46 | Kilomètres parcourus |
| Passengers carried | 4 082 | 3 969 | 5 050 | 5 454 | 1 790 | 1 644 | 2 298 | 2 482 | Passagers transportés |
| Passenger-kilometres | 6 676 | 6 246 | 8 518 | 9 219 | 4 895 | 4 459 | 6 428 | 6 878 | Passagers-kilomètres |
| Total tonne-kilometres | 756 | 726 | 983 | 1 060 | 562 | 523 | 745 | 790 | Tonnes-kilomètres totales |
| **Yemen** | | | | | | | | | **Yémen** |
| Kilometres flown | 16 | 18 | 22 | 24 | 15 | 17 | 21 | 23 | Kilomètres parcourus |
| Passengers carried | 869 | 844 | 1 022 | 1 083 | 632 | 622 | 778 | 825 | Passagers transportés |
| Passenger-kilometres | 1 598 | 1 956 | 2 473 | 2 812 | 1 518 | 1 876 | 2 382 | 2 716 | Passagers-kilomètres |
| Total tonne-kilometres | 180 | 225 | 282 | 320 | 172 | 217 | 274 | 311 | Tonnes-kilomètres totales |
| **Zambia** | | | | | | | | | **Zambie** |
| Kilometres flown | 2 | 2 | 2 | 2 | ^0 | 1 | 1 | 1 | Kilomètres parcourus |
| Passengers carried | 47 | 45 | 50 | 54 | 12 | 17 | 19 | 21 | Passagers transportés |
| Passenger-kilometres | 16 | 14 | 16 | 17 | 5 | 6 | 7 | 8 | Passagers-kilomètres |
| Total tonne-kilometres | 1 | 1 | 1 | 2 | ^0 | 1 | 1 | 1 | Tonnes-kilomètres totales |
| **Zimbabwe** | | | | | | | | | **Zimbabwe** |
| Kilometres flown | 8 | 6 | 6 | 7 | 7 | 5 | 6 | 6 | Kilomètres parcourus |
| Passengers carried | 251 | 201 | 225 | 243 | 155 | 102 | 116 | 126 | Passagers transportés |
| Passenger-kilometres | 674 | 437 | 500 | 553 | 635 | 391 | 450 | 499 | Passagers-kilomètres |
| Total tonne-kilometres | 87 | 58 | 67 | 74 | 83 | 54 | 62 | 68 | Tonnes-kilomètres totales |

Source

International Civil Aviation Organization (ICAO), Montreal, the ICAO Integrated Statistical Database (ISDB), last accessed March 2008.

Source

Organisation de l'aviation civile internationale (OACI), Montréal, la base de données statistiques intégrée (ISDB), dernier accès mars 2008

Notes

1 Includes apportionment (1/4) of the traffic of Gulf Air, a multinational airline with headquarters in Bahrain and operated by four Gulf States.

2 Includes apportionment (1/10) of the traffic of Air Afrique, a multi-national airline with headquarters in Côte d'Ivoire and operated by 10 African states until 1991. From 1992 includes apportionment (1/11) of the traffic of Air Afrique and operated by 11 African states.

3 For statistical purposes, the data for China do not include those for the Hong Kong Special Administrative Region (Hong Kong SAR), Macao Special Administrative Region (Macao SAR) and Taiwan Province of China.

Notes

1 Ces chiffres comprennent une partie du trafic (1/4) assurée par Gulf Air, compagnie aérienne multinationale dont le siège est situé en Bahreïn et est exploitée conjointement par 4 Etats Gulf.

2 Ces chiffres comprennent une partie du trafic (1/10) assurée par Air Afrique, compagnie aérienne multinationale dont le siège est situé en Côte d'Ivoire et est exploitée conjointement par 10 Etats Africains jusqu'à 1991. A partir de 1992 ces chiffres comprennent une partie du trafic (1/11) assurée par Air Afrique et exploitée conjointement par 11 Etats Africains.

3 Pour la présentation des statistiques, les données pour la Chine ne comprennent pas la Région Administrative Spéciale de Hong Kong (Hong Kong RAS), la Région Administrative Spéciale de Macao (Macao RAS) et la province de Taiwan.

4   Includes the apportionment of international operations performed by Scandinavian Airlines System (SAS): Denmark (2/7), Norway (2/7) and Sweden (3/7).

5   Includes data for airlines based in the territories and dependencies of France.

6   Including data for airlines based in the territories and dependencies of the Netherlands.

7   Beginning in 2000, data exclude those for China, Macao SAR.

8   Beginning the second half of 1997, data exclude those for Hong Kong Special Administrative Region (SAR) of China.

9   Including data for airlines based in the territories and dependencies of the United Kingdom (2001 and 2002).

10   Including data for airlines based in the territories and dependencies of the United States.

4   Y compris une partie des vols internationaux effectués par le SAS; Danemark (2/7), Norvège (2/7) et Suède (3/7).

5   Y compris les données relatives aux compagnies aériennes ayant des bases d'opérations dans les territoires et dépendances de France.

6   Y compris les données relatives aux compagnies aériennes ayant des bases d'opérations dans les territoires et dépendances des Pays-Bas.

7   A partir de 2000, non compris la RAS de Macao de la Chine.

8   A partir du second semestre de 1997, les données ne comprennent pas celles relatives à la RAS de Hong Kong de la Chine.

9   Y compris les données relatives aux compagnies aériennes ayant des bases d'opération dans les territoires et dépendances du Royaume-Uni (2001 et 2002).

10   Y compris les données relatives aux compagnies aériennes ayant des bases d'opérations dans les territoires et dépendances des Etats-Unis.

The data on international tourism have been supplied by the United Nations World Tourism Organization (UNWTO) from detailed tourism information published in the *Compendium of Tourism Statistics* and in the *Tourism Factbook* online available from http://www.unwto.org/statistics/index.htm.

For statistical purposes, the term "international visitor" describes "any person who travels to a country other than that in which he/she has his/her usual residence but outside his/her usual environment for a period not exceeding 12 months and whose main purpose of visit is other than the exercise of an activity remunerated from within the country visited".

International visitors include: (a) *tourists* (overnight visitors): "visitors who stay at least one night in a collective or private accommodation in the country visited"; and (b) *same-day visitors*: "visitors who do not spend the night in a collective or private accommodation in the country visited". The figures do not include immigrants, residents in a frontier zone, persons domiciled in one country or area and working in an adjoining country or area, members of the armed forces and diplomats and consular representatives when they travel from their country of origin to the country in which they are stationed and vice-versa. The figures also exclude persons in transit who do not formally enter the country through passport control, such as air transit passengers who remain for a short period in a designated area of the air terminal or ship passengers who are not permitted to disembark. This category includes passengers transferred directly between airports or other terminals. Other passengers in transit through a country are classified as visitors.

*Tables 58 and 59*: Data on arrivals of non-resident (or international) visitors may be obtained from different sources. In some cases data are obtained from border statistics derived from administrative records (police, immigration, traffic counts and other types of controls), border surveys and registrations at accommodation establishments.

Unless otherwise stated, table 58 shows the number of non-resident tourist/visitor arrivals at national borders classified by their region of origin. Totals correspond to the total number of arrivals from the regions indicated in the table. However, these totals may not correspond to the number of tourist arrivals shown in table 59. The latter excludes same day visitors except when indicated whereas they may be included in table 58.

When a person visits the same country several times a year, an equal number of arrivals is recorded. Likewise, if a person visits several countries during the course of a single trip, his/her arrival in each country is recorded separately.

Les données sur le tourisme international ont été fournies par l'Organisation mondiale du tourisme (l'OMT) qui publie des renseignements détaillés sur le tourisme dans *le Compendium de statistiques du tourisme* et dans le "*Tourism Factbook*" en ligne au http://www.unwto.org/statistics/index.htm.

A des fins statistiques, l'expression "visiteur international" désigne "toute personne qui se rend dans un pays autre que celui où elle a son lieu de résidence habituelle, mais différent de son environnement habituel, pour une période de 12 mois au maximum, dans un but principal autre que celui d'y exercer une profession rémunérée".

Entrent dans cette catégorie: (a) *les touristes* (visiteurs passant la nuit), c'est à dire "les visiteurs qui passent une nuit au moins en logement collectif ou privé dans le pays visité"; et (b) *les visiteurs ne restant que la journée*, c'est à dire "les visiteurs qui ne passent pas la nuit en logement collectif ou privé dans le pays visité". Ces chiffres ne comprennent pas les immigrants, les résidents frontaliers, les personnes domiciliées dans une zone ou un pays donné et travaillant dans une zone ou pays limitrophe, les membres des forces armées et les membres des corps diplomatique et consulaire lorsqu'ils se rendent de leur pays d'origine au pays où ils sont en poste, et vice versa. Ne sont pas non plus inclus les voyageurs en transit, qui ne pénètrent pas officiellement dans le pays en faisant contrôler leurs passeports, tels que les passagers d'un vol en escale, qui demeurent pendant un court laps de temps dans une aire distincte de l'aérogare, ou les passagers d'un navire qui ne sont pas autorisés à débarquer. Cette catégorie comprend également les passagers transportés directement d'une aérogare à l'autre ou à un autre terminal. Les autres passagers en transit dans un pays sont classés parmi les visiteurs.

*Tableaux 58 et 59*: Les données relatives aux arrivées des visiteurs non résidents (ou internationaux) peuvent être obtenues de différentes sources. Dans certains cas, elles proviennent des statistiques des frontières tirées des registres administratifs (contrôles de police, de l'immigration, de la circulation et autres effectués aux frontières nationales), des enquêtes statistiques aux frontières et des enregistrements d'établissements d'hébergement touristique.

Sauf indication contraire, le tableau 58 indique le nombre d'arrivées de touristes/visiteurs non résidents aux frontières nationales par région de provenance. Les totaux correspondent au nombre total d'arrivées de touristes des régions indiquées sur le tableau. Les chiffres totaux peuvent, néanmoins, ne pas coïncider avec le nombre des arrivées de touristes indiqué dans le tableau 59, qui sauf indication contraire ne comprend pas les visiteurs ne restant que la journée, lesquels peuvent au contraire être inclus dans les chiffres du tableau 58.

Consequently, arrivals cannot be assumed to be equal to the number of persons travelling.

Expenditure associated with tourism activity of visitors has been traditionally identified with the travel item of the Balance of Payments (BOP): in the case of inbound tourism, those expenditures in the country of reference associated with non-resident visitors are registered as "credits" in the BOP and refer to "travel receipts".

The new conceptual framework approved by the United Nations Statistical Commission in relation to the measurement of tourism macroeconomic activity (the so-called Tourism Satellite Account) considers that "tourism industries and products" includes transport of passengers. Consequently, a better estimate of tourism-related expenditures by resident and non-resident visitors in an international scenario would be, in terms of the BOP, the value of the travel item plus that of the passenger transport item.

Nevertheless, users should be aware that BOP estimates include, in addition to expenditures associated with visitors, those related to other types of individuals.

The data published should allow international comparability and therefore correspond to those published by the International Monetary Fund (and provided by the Central Banks). Exceptions are footnoted.

*Table 60*: Indicators on expenditure (in other countries) are equivalent to those for inbound tourism but are registered as "debits" in the BOP's *travel* and *passenger transport* items. The data published are also provided by the International Monetary Fund and the same previous warning is applicable.

More detailed tourism information from the United Nations World Tourism Organization is available in the *Compendium of Tourism Statistics* and from http://www.unwto.org/statistics/index.htm; information on the balance of payments is published by the International Monetary Fund in the *Balance of Payments Statistics Yearbook*.

*Table 61*: Data for total traffic cover both domestic and international scheduled services operated by airlines registered in each country. Scheduled services include supplementary services occasioned by overflow traffic on regularly scheduled trips and preparatory flights for newly scheduled services. The data are prepared by the International Civil Aviation Organization (see also www.icao.int).

The following terms have been used in the table:

- Kilometres flown - aircraft kilometres performed, which is the sum of the products obtained by multiplying the number of revenue flight stages flown by the corresponding stage distance.

Lorsqu'une personne visite le même pays plusieurs fois dans l'année, il est enregistré un nombre égal d'arrivées. En outre, si une personne visite plusieurs pays au cours d'un seul et même voyage, son arrivée dans chaque pays est enregistrée séparément. Par conséquent, on ne peut pas partir du postulat que les arrivées sont égales au nombre de personnes qui voyagent.

Les dépenses associées à l'activité touristique des visiteurs sont traditionnellement identifiées au poste Voyages de la balance des paiements. Dans le cas du tourisme récepteur, ces dépenses associées aux visiteurs non résidents sont enregistrées dans la balance des paiements comme des "crédits" et il s'agit de "recettes au titre des voyages".

Le cadre conceptuel approuvé par la Commission de statistique de l'Organisation des Nations Unies concernant l'évaluation de l'activité touristique à l'échelle macroéconomique (cadre qu'il est convenu d'appeler compte satellite du tourisme) considère que la notion "industries et produits touristiques" englobe le transport de passagers. Par conséquent, une meilleure estimation des dépenses liées au tourisme international que font les visiteurs résidents et non résidents serait, sous l'angle de la balance des paiements, la somme des valeurs des postes Voyages et Transport de passagers.

Néanmoins, les utilisateurs doivent être conscients que les estimations de la balance des paiements comprennent, outre les dépenses associées aux visiteurs, celles liées à d'autres types d'individus.

Les données publiées doivent permettre la comparabilité internationale et donc correspondre à celles publiées par le Fonds monétaire international (FMI) qui viennent des banques centrales. Les exceptions sont signalées par une note de pied.

*Tableau 60*: Les indicateurs relatifs aux dépenses touristiques dans d'autres pays sont équivalents à ceux du tourisme récepteur mais ils sont enregistrés comme "débits" aux postes *Voyages* et *Transport de passagers* de la balance des paiements.

Les données publiées sont également fournies par le FMI. Il y a lieu de faire la même mise en garde que plus haut. On trouvera plus de renseignements publiés par l'Organisation mondiale du tourisme dans le *Compendium des statistiques du tourisme* et au http://www.unwto.org/statistics/index.htm; des renseignements sur la balance des paiements sont publiés par le Fonds monétaire international dans "*Balance of Payments Statistics Yearbook*".

*Tableau 61*: Les données relatives au trafic total se rapportent aux services réguliers, intérieurs ou internationaux des compagnies de transport aérien enregistrées dans chaque pays. Les services réguliers comprennent aussi les vols supplémentaires nécessités par un surcroît d'activité des services réguliers et les vols préparatoires en vue de nouveaux services réguliers.

- Passengers carried - the number of passengers carried is obtained by counting each passenger on a particular flight (with one flight number) once only and not repeatedly on each individual stage of that flight, with a single exception that a passenger flying on both the international and domestic stages of the same flight should be counted as both a domestic and an international passenger.

- Passenger-kilometres performed a passenger-kilometre is performed when a passenger is carried one kilometre. Calculation of passenger-kilometres equals the sum of the products obtained by multiplying the number of revenue passengers carried on each flight stage by the stage distance. The resultant figure is equal to the number of kilometres travelled by all passengers.

- Tonne-kilometres performed - a metric tonne of revenue load carried one kilometre. Tonne-kilometres performed equals the sum of the product obtained by multiplying the number of total tonnes of revenue load (passengers, freight and mail) carried on each flight stage by the stage distance. See http://www.icaodata.com/Terms.aspx for more information.

Les données sont préparées par l'Organisation de l'aviation civile internationale (voir aussi www.icao.int).

Les termes ci-après ont été utilisés dans le tableau:

- Kilomètres parcourus – le nombre de kilomètres parcourus équivaut à la somme des produits du nombre de vols payants effectués sur chaque étapepar la longueur de l'étape.

- Passagers transportés – pour calculer le nombre de passagers transportés, on compte chaque passager d'un vol donné (correspondant à un numéro de vol) une seule fois et non pour chacune des étapes de ce vol; toutefois, les passagers qui voyagent sur une étape internationale et sur une étape intérieure d'un même vol doivent être comptés à la fois comme passagers d'un vol intérieur et comme passagers d'un vol international.

- Passager-kilomètre réalisé – un passager-kilomètre est réalisé lorsqu'un passager est transporté sur une distance d'un kilomètre. Le nombre de passagers-kilomètres réalisés équivaut à la somme des produits du nombre de passagers payants transportés sur chaque étape par la longueur de l'étape. Le total obtenu est égal au nombre de kilomètres parcourus par l'ensemble des passagers.

- Tonnes-kilomètres réalisées – la tonne-kilomètre est une unité de mesure qui correspond au déplacement d'une tonne métrique de charge payante sur un kilomètre. Les tonnes-kilomètres réalisées sont la somme des produits du nombre de tonnes de charge payante (passagers, fret, envois postaux) transportées sur chaque étape par la longueur de l'étape. Pour plus de détails, voir http://www.icaodata.com/Terms.aspx.

# Balance of payments summary
Millions of US dollars

# Résumé de la balance des paiements
Millions de dollars E.-U

| Country or area | 2000 | 2001 | 2002 | 2003 | 2004 | 2005 | 2006 | Pays ou zone |
|---|---|---|---|---|---|---|---|---|
| Albania | | | | | | | | Albanie |
| Current account | -156 | -217 | -408 | -407 | -358 | -571 | -671 | Compte des transactions courantes |
| Goods: exports f.o.b. | 256 | 305 | 330 | 447 | 603 | 656 | 793 | Biens : exportations f.à.b. |
| Goods: imports f.o.b. | -1 070 | -1 332 | -1 485 | -1 783 | -2 195 | -2 478 | -2 916 | Biens : importations f.à.b. |
| Services: credit | 448 | 534 | 585 | 720 | 1 003 | 1 165 | 1 504 | Services : crédit |
| Services: debit | -429 | -444 | -590 | -803 | -1 055 | -1 383 | -1 585 | Services : débit |
| Income: credit | 116 | 163 | 148 | 195 | 204 | 227 | 332 | Revenus : crédit |
| Income: debit | -9 | -14 | -21 | -24 | -28 | -53 | -69 | Revenus : débit |
| Current transfers, n.i.e.: credit | 629 | 648 | 684 | 924 | 1 200 | 1 519 | 1 426 | Transferts courants, n.i.a. : crédit |
| Current transfers: debit | -96 | -77 | -59 | -82 | -91 | -225 | -157 | Transferts courants : débit |
| Capital account, n.i.e. | 78 | 118 | 121 | 157 | 132 | 123 | 180 | Compte de capital, n.i.a. |
| Financial account, n.i.e. | 188 | 110 | 213 | 201 | 396 | 393 | 523 | Compte financier, n.i.a. |
| Net errors and omissions | 10 | 136 | 108 | 147 | 115 | 204 | 237 | Erreurs et omissions nettes |
| Reserves and related items | -120 | -147 | -36 | -98 | -286 | -148 | -269 | Réserves et postes apparentés |
| Angola | | | | | | | | Angola |
| Current account | 796 | -1 431 | -150 | -720 | 686 | 5 138 | 10 690 | Compte des transactions courantes |
| Goods: exports f.o.b. | 7 921 | 6 534 | 8 328 | 9 508 | 13 475 | 24 109 | 31 862 | Biens : exportations f.à.b. |
| Goods: imports f.o.b. | -3 040 | -3 179 | -3 760 | -5 480 | -5 832 | -8 353 | -8 778 | Biens : importations f.à.b. |
| Services: credit | 267 | 203 | 207 | 201 | 323 | 177 | 1 484 | Services : crédit |
| Services: debit | -2 699 | -3 518 | -3 322 | -3 321 | -4 803 | -6 791 | -7 511 | Services : débit |
| Income: credit | 34 | 23 | 18 | 12 | 33 | 26 | 145 | Revenus : crédit |
| Income: debit | -1 715 | -1 584 | -1 652 | -1 739 | -2 517 | -4 057 | -6 323 | Revenus : débit |
| Current transfers, n.i.e.: credit | 123 | 208 | 142 | 186 | 124 | 173 | 60 | Transferts courants, n.i.a. : crédit |
| Current transfers: debit | -96 | -118 | -110 | -87 | -118 | -146 | -250 | Transferts courants : débit |
| Capital account, n.i.e. | 18 | 4 | 0 | 0 | 0 | 0 | 0 | Compte de capital, n.i.a. |
| Financial account, n.i.e. | -446 | 950 | -357 | 1 371 | -623 | -3 115 | -5 601 | Compte financier, n.i.a. |
| Net errors and omissions | -51 | -309 | 150 | -388 | 277 | -378 | 290 | Erreurs et omissions nettes |
| Reserves and related items | -318 | 786 | 356 | -263 | -340 | -1 645 | -5 378 | Réserves et postes apparentés |
| Anguilla | | | | | | | | Anguilla |
| Current account | -61 | -40 | -36 | -44 | -48 | -53 | ... | Compte des transactions courantes |
| Goods: exports f.o.b. | 4 | 4 | 4 | 4 | 6 | 15 | ... | Biens : exportations f.à.b. |
| Goods: imports f.o.b. | -83 | -68 | -62 | -68 | -90 | -114 | ... | Biens : importations f.à.b. |
| Services: credit | 65 | 70 | 66 | 69 | 78 | 99 | ... | Services : crédit |
| Services: debit | -41 | -39 | -39 | -44 | -47 | -56 | ... | Services : débit |
| Income: credit | 4 | 2 | 2 | 2 | 8 | 12 | ... | Revenus : crédit |
| Income: debit | -13 | -9 | -8 | -8 | -7 | -9 | ... | Revenus : débit |
| Current transfers, n.i.e.: credit | 11 | 10 | 9 | 10 | 14 | 11 | ... | Transferts courants, n.i.a. : crédit |
| Current transfers: debit | -8 | -9 | -8 | -10 | -10 | -10 | ... | Transferts courants : débit |
| Capital account, n.i.e. | 10 | 9 | 8 | 8 | 8 | 13 | ... | Compte de capital, n.i.a. |
| Financial account, n.i.e. | 45 | 20 | 18 | 46 | 42 | 42 | ... | Compte financier, n.i.a. |
| Net errors and omissions | 7 | 15 | 12 | -3 | -2 | 4 | ... | Erreurs et omissions nettes |
| Reserves and related items | ^0 | -4 | -2 | -7 | -1 | -5 | ... | Réserves et postes apparentés |
| Antigua and Barbuda | | | | | | | | Antigua-et-Barbuda |
| Current account | -67 | -57 | -82 | -98 | -68 | -62 | ... | Compte des transactions courantes |
| Goods: exports f.o.b. | 52 | 45 | 34 | 45 | 57 | 82 | ... | Biens : exportations f.à.b. |
| Goods: imports f.o.b. | -342 | -317 | -303 | -352 | -375 | -390 | ... | Biens : importations f.à.b. |
| Services: credit | 415 | 401 | 394 | 418 | 477 | 488 | ... | Services : crédit |
| Services: debit | -156 | -169 | -171 | -182 | -190 | -208 | ... | Services : débit |
| Income: credit | 16 | 19 | 8 | 9 | 12 | 18 | ... | Revenus : crédit |
| Income: debit | -60 | -43 | -50 | -47 | -57 | -60 | ... | Revenus : débit |
| Current transfers, n.i.e.: credit | 18 | 23 | 23 | 29 | 25 | 26 | ... | Transferts courants, n.i.a. : crédit |
| Current transfers: debit | -9 | -13 | -17 | -16 | -17 | -18 | ... | Transferts courants : débit |
| Capital account, n.i.e. | 39 | 12 | 14 | 10 | 21 | 214 | ... | Compte de capital, n.i.a. |
| Financial account, n.i.e. | 42 | 60 | 102 | 91 | 58 | -126 | ... | Compte financier, n.i.a. |

| Country or area | 2000 | 2001 | 2002 | 2003 | 2004 | 2005 | 2006 | Pays ou zone |
|---|---|---|---|---|---|---|---|---|
| Net errors and omissions | -21 | 1 | -25 | 23 | -5 | -19 | ... | Erreurs et omissions nettes |
| Reserves and related items | 6 | -16 | -8 | -26 | -6 | -7 | ... | Réserves et postes apparentés |
| **Argentina** | | | | | | | | **Argentine** |
| Current account | -8 981 | -3 780 | 8 767 | 8 140 | 3 217 | 5 691 | 8 092 | Compte des transactions courantes |
| Goods: exports f.o.b. | 26 341 | 26 543 | 25 651 | 29 939 | 34 576 | 40 387 | 46 456 | Biens : exportations f.à.b. |
| Goods: imports f.o.b. | -23 889 | -19 158 | -8 473 | -13 134 | -21 311 | -27 300 | -32 585 | Biens : importations f.à.b. |
| Services: credit | 4 936 | 4 627 | 3 495 | 4 500 | 5 289 | 6 453 | 7 666 | Services : crédit |
| Services: debit | -9 219 | -8 490 | -4 956 | -5 693 | -6 618 | -7 640 | -8 503 | Services : débit |
| Income: credit | 7 420 | 5 358 | 3 039 | 3 104 | 3 721 | 4 279 | 5 411 | Revenus : crédit |
| Income: debit | -14 968 | -13 085 | -10 530 | -11 080 | -13 003 | -11 016 | -10 851 | Revenus : débit |
| Current transfers, n.i.e.: credit | 792 | 856 | 818 | 942 | 1 114 | 1 235 | 1 391 | Transferts courants, n.i.a. : crédit |
| Current transfers: debit | -393 | -431 | -278 | -438 | -550 | -706 | -894 | Transferts courants : débit |
| Capital account, n.i.e. | 106 | 157 | 406 | 39 | 196 | 89 | 97 | Compte de capital, n.i.a. |
| Financial account, n.i.e. | 7 853 | -14 971 | -20 681 | -15 860 | -10 997 | 1 865 | 4 187 | Compte financier, n.i.a. |
| Net errors and omissions | -154 | -2 810 | -1 894 | -1 397 | 590 | -1 | 919 | Erreurs et omissions nettes |
| Reserves and related items | 1 176 | 21 405 | 13 402 | 9 077 | 6 993 | -7 644 | -13 295 | Réserves et postes apparentés |
| **Armenia** | | | | | | | | **Arménie** |
| Current account | -278 | -200 | -148 | -189 | -20 | -52 | -117 | Compte des transactions courantes |
| Goods: exports f.o.b. | 310 | 353 | 514 | 696 | 738 | 1 005 | 1 025 | Biens : exportations f.à.b. |
| Goods: imports f.o.b. | -773 | -773 | -883 | -1 130 | -1 196 | -1 593 | -1 921 | Biens : importations f.à.b. |
| Services: credit | 137 | 187 | 184 | 207 | 333 | 411 | 485 | Services : crédit |
| Services: debit | -193 | -204 | -225 | -276 | -432 | -531 | -615 | Services : débit |
| Income: credit | 104 | 104 | 137 | 166 | 397 | 458 | 624 | Revenus : crédit |
| Income: debit | -51 | -39 | -48 | -71 | -290 | -325 | -409 | Revenus : débit |
| Current transfers, n.i.e.: credit | 209 | 201 | 200 | 245 | 515 | 604 | 792 | Transferts courants, n.i.a. : crédit |
| Current transfers: debit | -20 | -27 | -26 | -27 | -85 | -80 | -98 | Transferts courants : débit |
| Capital account, n.i.e. | 28 | 30 | 68 | 90 | 41 | 73 | 86 | Compte de capital, n.i.a. |
| Financial account, n.i.e. | 250 | 175 | 147 | 174 | 17 | 163 | 434 | Compte financier, n.i.a. |
| Net errors and omissions | 17 | 11 | -4 | -2 | -6 | 2 | -16 | Erreurs et omissions nettes |
| Reserves and related items | -17 | -17 | -63 | -73 | -33 | -187 | -387 | Réserves et postes apparentés |
| **Aruba** | | | | | | | | **Aruba** |
| Current account | 211 | 320 | -335 | -157 | 3 | -203 | 213 | Compte des transactions courantes |
| Goods: exports f.o.b. | 2 525 | 2 423 | 1 488 | 2 052 | 2 723 | 3 483 | 3 951 | Biens : exportations f.à.b. |
| Goods: imports f.o.b. | -2 583 | -2 371 | -2 024 | -2 400 | -3 005 | -3 494 | -3 838 | Biens : importations f.à.b. |
| Services: credit | 1 009 | 988 | 1 001 | 1 046 | 1 248 | 1 304 | 1 314 | Services : crédit |
| Services: debit | -644 | -614 | -607 | -727 | -794 | -904 | -985 | Services : débit |
| Income: credit | 53 | 50 | 32 | 32 | 35 | 41 | 58 | Revenus : crédit |
| Income: debit | -73 | -98 | -157 | -74 | -100 | -503 | -162 | Revenus : débit |
| Current transfers, n.i.e.: credit | 39 | 42 | 36 | 41 | 45 | 51 | 57 | Transferts courants, n.i.a. : crédit |
| Current transfers: debit | -115 | -100 | -105 | -126 | -149 | -182 | -182 | Transferts courants : débit |
| Capital account, n.i.e. | 11 | -1 | 21 | 100 | 20 | 18 | 21 | Compte de capital, n.i.a. |
| Financial account, n.i.e. | -202 | -230 | 342 | -4 | -26 | 154 | -181 | Compte financier, n.i.a. |
| Net errors and omissions | -35 | -6 | 13 | 24 | 4 | 8 | 2 | Erreurs et omissions nettes |
| Reserves and related items | 15 | -83 | -40 | 36 | -2 | 22 | -55 | Réserves et postes apparentés |
| **Australia** | | | | | | | | **Australie** |
| Current account | -14 763 | -7 433 | -15 824 | -28 666 | -38 810 | -40 954 | -41 046 | Compte des transactions courantes |
| Goods: exports f.o.b. | 64 004 | 63 626 | 65 014 | 70 517 | 87 161 | 107 011 | 124 913 | Biens : exportations f.à.b. |
| Goods: imports f.o.b. | -68 866 | -61 890 | -70 528 | -85 862 | -105 230 | -120 383 | -134 509 | Biens : importations f.à.b. |
| Services: credit | 19 894 | 18 092 | 19 594 | 23 747 | 28 485 | 31 047 | 33 089 | Services : crédit |
| Services: debit | -18 934 | -17 351 | -18 388 | -21 941 | -27 943 | -30 505 | -32 251 | Services : débit |
| Income: credit | 8 977 | 8 200 | 8 522 | 10 487 | 14 311 | 16 445 | 21 942 | Revenus : crédit |
| Income: debit | -19 791 | -18 132 | -19 974 | -25 456 | -35 327 | -44 166 | -54 018 | Revenus : débit |
| Current transfers, n.i.e.: credit | 2 622 | 2 242 | 2 310 | 2 767 | 3 145 | 3 277 | 3 573 | Transferts courants, n.i.a. : crédit |
| Current transfers: debit | -2 669 | -2 221 | -2 373 | -2 927 | -3 414 | -3 680 | -3 786 | Transferts courants : débit |
| Capital account, n.i.e. | 615 | 591 | 443 | 736 | 816 | 963 | 1 603 | Compte de capital, n.i.a. |
| Financial account, n.i.e. | 12 954 | 8 155 | 16 249 | 34 694 | 39 374 | 47 617 | 49 630 | Compte financier, n.i.a. |
| Net errors and omissions | -171 | -218 | -746 | 114 | -214 | -369 | -465 | Erreurs et omissions nettes |
| Reserves and related items | 1 365 | -1 096 | -122 | -6 877 | -1 166 | -7 256 | -9 722 | Réserves et postes apparentés |

| Country or area | 2000 | 2001 | 2002 | 2003 | 2004 | 2005 | 2006 | Pays ou zone |
|---|---|---|---|---|---|---|---|---|
| **Austria** | | | | | | | | **Autriche** |
| Current account | -4 864 | -3 636 | 565 | -638 | 1 382 | 4 252 | 10 259 | Compte des transactions courantes |
| Goods: exports f.o.b. | 64 684 | 66 900 | 73 668 | 89 622 | 112 070 | 117 233 | 134 302 | Biens : exportations f.à.b. |
| Goods: imports f.o.b. | -67 421 | -68 169 | -70 080 | -88 480 | -109 020 | -113 806 | -133 661 | Biens : importations f.à.b. |
| Services: credit | 31 342 | 33 352 | 35 386 | 42 964 | 49 153 | 53 921 | 45 202 | Services : crédit |
| Services: debit | -29 653 | -31 437 | -34 996 | -41 261 | -46 737 | -49 107 | -32 398 | Services : débit |
| Income: credit | 11 992 | 12 031 | 13 816 | 16 169 | 19 891 | 24 151 | 27 506 | Revenus : crédit |
| Income: debit | -14 456 | -15 111 | -15 406 | -17 357 | -21 216 | -25 488 | -29 337 | Revenus : débit |
| Current transfers, n.i.e.: credit | 2 914 | 3 267 | 3 815 | 4 388 | 5 314 | 6 257 | 4 368 | Transferts courants, n.i.a. : crédit |
| Current transfers: debit | -4 267 | -4 468 | -5 639 | -6 683 | -8 073 | -8 908 | -5 724 | Transferts courants : débit |
| Capital account, n.i.e. | -432 | -529 | -378 | 8 | -341 | -237 | -930 | Compte de capital, n.i.a. |
| Financial account, n.i.e. | 3 407 | 1 795 | -4 713 | -2 483 | -2 618 | -1 627 | -9 049 | Compte financier, n.i.a. |
| Net errors and omissions | 1 143 | 482 | 2 803 | 1 089 | -272 | -3 138 | -1 142 | Erreurs et omissions nettes |
| Reserves and related items | 746 | 1 888 | 1 723 | 2 023 | 1 849 | 750 | 862 | Réserves et postes apparentés |
| **Azerbaijan** | | | | | | | | **Azerbaïdjan** |
| Current account | -168 | -52 | -768 | -2 021 | -2 589 | 167 | 3 708 | Compte des transactions courantes |
| Goods: exports f.o.b. | 1 858 | 2 079 | 2 305 | 2 625 | 3 743 | 7 649 | 13 015 | Biens : exportations f.à.b. |
| Goods: imports f.o.b. | -1 539 | -1 465 | -1 823 | -2 723 | -3 582 | -4 350 | -5 269 | Biens : importations f.à.b. |
| Services: credit | 260 | 290 | 362 | 432 | 492 | 683 | 940 | Services : crédit |
| Services: debit | -485 | -665 | -1 298 | -2 047 | -2 730 | -2 653 | -2 863 | Services : débit |
| Income: credit | 56 | 41 | 37 | 53 | 65 | 202 | 280 | Revenus : crédit |
| Income: debit | -391 | -409 | -422 | -495 | -766 | -1 847 | -2 961 | Revenus : débit |
| Current transfers, n.i.e.: credit | 135 | 176 | 228 | 225 | 263 | 626 | 748 | Transferts courants, n.i.a. : crédit |
| Current transfers: debit | -62 | -100 | -158 | -91 | -74 | -142 | -182 | Transferts courants : débit |
| Capital account, n.i.e. | 0 | 0 | -29 | -23 | -4 | 41 | -4 | Compte de capital, n.i.a. |
| Financial account, n.i.e. | 493 | 126 | 918 | 2 280 | 2 960 | 78 | -2 105 | Compte financier, n.i.a. |
| Net errors and omissions | ^0 | -1 | -87 | -112 | -50 | -126 | -256 | Erreurs et omissions nettes |
| Reserves and related items | -326 | -73 | -34 | -124 | -317 | -161 | -1 343 | Réserves et postes apparentés |
| **Bahamas** | | | | | | | | **Bahamas** |
| Current account | -633 | -645 | -423 | -474 | -307 | -819 | -1 567 | Compte des transactions courantes |
| Goods: exports f.o.b. | 465 | 417 | 422 | 427 | 477 | 549 | 692 | Biens : exportations f.à.b. |
| Goods: imports f.o.b. | -1 983 | -1 804 | -1 749 | -1 759 | -1 907 | -2 401 | -2 626 | Biens : importations f.à.b. |
| Services: credit | 1 973 | 1 804 | 2 062 | 2 055 | 2 244 | 2 485 | 2 449 | Services : crédit |
| Services: debit | -1 026 | -973 | -1 016 | -1 092 | -1 231 | -1 373 | -1 916 | Services : débit |
| Income: credit | 317 | 185 | 108 | 79 | 80 | 116 | 119 | Revenus : crédit |
| Income: debit | -457 | -383 | -292 | -232 | -221 | -279 | -337 | Revenus : débit |
| Current transfers, n.i.e.: credit | 88 | 121 | 55 | 60 | 265 | 103 | 66 | Transferts courants, n.i.a. : crédit |
| Current transfers: debit | -10 | -11 | -13 | -11 | -14 | -18 | -14 | Transferts courants : débit |
| Capital account, n.i.e. | -16 | -21 | -25 | -37 | -48 | -60 | -64 | Compte de capital, n.i.a. |
| Financial account, n.i.e. | 430 | 265 | 405 | 535 | 358 | 694 | 1 203 | Compte financier, n.i.a. |
| Net errors and omissions | 158 | 371 | 103 | 85 | 180 | 97 | 348 | Erreurs et omissions nettes |
| Reserves and related items | 61 | 31 | -60 | -110 | -183 | 88 | 80 | Réserves et postes apparentés |
| **Bahrain** | | | | | | | | **Bahreïn** |
| Current account | 830 | 227 | -50 | 201 | 415 | 1 575 | 1 918 | Compte des transactions courantes |
| Goods: exports f.o.b. | 6 243 | 5 657 | 5 887 | 6 721 | 7 621 | 10 131 | 11 703 | Biens : exportations f.à.b. |
| Goods: imports f.o.b. | -4 394 | -4 047 | -4 697 | -5 319 | -6 135 | -7 606 | -8 565 | Biens : importations f.à.b. |
| Services: credit | 933 | 950 | 1 068 | 1 260 | 1 558 | 1 662 | 1 849 | Services : crédit |
| Services: debit | -738 | -748 | -927 | -886 | -933 | -977 | -1 153 | Services : débit |
| Income: credit | 6 328 | 3 794 | 1 679 | 1 267 | 2 544 | 5 016 | 7 634 | Revenus : crédit |
| Income: debit | -6 552 | -4 116 | -2 204 | -1 760 | -3 119 | -5 428 | -8 019 | Revenus : débit |
| Current transfers, n.i.e.: credit | 22 | 23 | 15 | 0 | 0 | 0 | 0 | Transferts courants, n.i.a. : crédit |
| Current transfers: debit | -1 013 | -1 287 | -872 | -1 082 | -1 120 | -1 223 | -1 531 | Transferts courants : débit |
| Capital account, n.i.e. | 50 | 100 | 102 | 50 | 50 | 50 | 75 | Compte de capital, n.i.a. |
| Financial account, n.i.e. | -30 | -417 | -1 234 | 493 | -391 | -1 368 | -1 179 | Compte financier, n.i.a. |
| Net errors and omissions | -650 | 214 | 1 218 | -700 | 83 | 37 | 8 | Erreurs et omissions nettes |
| Reserves and related items | -200 | -123 | -35 | -44 | -158 | -294 | -822 | Réserves et postes apparentés |

| Country or area | 2000 | 2001 | 2002 | 2003 | 2004 | 2005 | 2006 | Pays ou zone |
|---|---|---|---|---|---|---|---|---|
| **Bangladesh** | | | | | | | | **Bangladesh** |
| Current account | -306 | -535 | 739 | 132 | -279 | -176 | 1 196 | Compte des transactions courantes |
| Goods: exports f.o.b. | 6 399 | 6 085 | 6 102 | 7 050 | 8 151 | 9 302 | 11 554 | Biens : exportations f.à.b. |
| Goods: imports f.o.b. | -8 053 | -8 133 | -7 780 | -9 492 | -11 157 | -12 502 | -14 443 | Biens : importations f.à.b. |
| Services: credit | 815 | 752 | 849 | 1 012 | 1 083 | 1 249 | 1 334 | Services : crédit |
| Services: debit | -1 620 | -1 522 | -1 406 | -1 711 | -1 931 | -2 207 | -2 340 | Services : débit |
| Income: credit | 78 | 77 | 57 | 57 | 103 | 117 | 177 | Revenus : crédit |
| Income: debit | -345 | -362 | -322 | -361 | -474 | -910 | -1 018 | Revenus : débit |
| Current transfers, n.i.e.: credit | 2 426 | 2 573 | 3 245 | 3 586 | 3 960 | 4 785 | 5 941 | Transferts courants, n.i.a. : crédit |
| Current transfers: debit | -7 | -5 | -6 | -8 | -13 | -11 | -8 | Transferts courants : débit |
| Capital account, n.i.e. | 249 | 235 | 364 | 387 | 142 | 262 | 153 | Compte de capital, n.i.a. |
| Financial account, n.i.e. | -256 | 262 | -256 | 289 | 665 | 142 | 120 | Compte financier, n.i.a. |
| Net errors and omissions | 282 | -106 | -349 | 81 | -25 | -644 | -604 | Erreurs et omissions nettes |
| Reserves and related items | 31 | 144 | -497 | -889 | -503 | 416 | -865 | Réserves et postes apparentés |
| **Barbados** | | | | | | | | **Barbade** |
| Current account | -146 | -111 | -168 | -170 | -337 | -387 | ... | Compte des transactions courantes |
| Goods: exports f.o.b. | 286 | 271 | 253 | 264 | 293 | 379 | ... | Biens : exportations f.à.b. |
| Goods: imports f.o.b. | -1 030 | -952 | -955 | -1 066 | -1 264 | -1 464 | ... | Biens : importations f.à.b. |
| Services: credit | 1 090 | 1 069 | 1 041 | 1 165 | 1 224 | 1 457 | ... | Services : crédit |
| Services: debit | -487 | -499 | -491 | -519 | -556 | -680 | ... | Services : débit |
| Income: credit | 70 | 73 | 72 | 75 | 75 | 85 | ... | Revenus : crédit |
| Income: debit | -152 | -166 | -174 | -182 | -197 | -257 | ... | Revenus : débit |
| Current transfers, n.i.e.: credit | 109 | 126 | 120 | 127 | 126 | 160 | ... | Transferts courants, n.i.a. : crédit |
| Current transfers: debit | -31 | -32 | -34 | -34 | -38 | -67 | ... | Transferts courants : débit |
| Capital account, n.i.e. | 2 | 1 | 0 | 0 | 0 | 0 | ... | Compte de capital, n.i.a. |
| Financial account, n.i.e. | 289 | 285 | 119 | 203 | 135 | 391 | ... | Compte financier, n.i.a. |
| Net errors and omissions | 32 | 47 | 25 | 34 | 45 | 18 | ... | Erreurs et omissions nettes |
| Reserves and related items | -178 | -222 | 24 | -67 | 157 | -22 | ... | Réserves et postes apparentés |
| **Belarus** | | | | | | | | **Bélarus** |
| Current account | -338 | -411 | -326 | -434 | -1 194 | 434 | -1 512 | Compte des transactions courantes |
| Goods: exports f.o.b. | 6 640 | 7 334 | 7 965 | 10 076 | 13 942 | 16 109 | 19 838 | Biens : exportations f.à.b. |
| Goods: imports f.o.b. | -7 525 | -8 141 | -8 879 | -11 324 | -16 126 | -16 610 | -22 237 | Biens : importations f.à.b. |
| Services: credit | 1 000 | 1 143 | 1 341 | 1 500 | 1 747 | 1 959 | 2 299 | Services : crédit |
| Services: debit | -563 | -841 | -908 | -915 | -1 058 | -1 250 | -1 487 | Services : débit |
| Income: credit | 26 | 27 | 45 | 126 | 158 | 283 | 245 | Revenus : crédit |
| Income: debit | -72 | -78 | -83 | -113 | -159 | -228 | -352 | Revenus : débit |
| Current transfers, n.i.e.: credit | 177 | 202 | 260 | 292 | 391 | 281 | 302 | Transferts courants, n.i.a. : crédit |
| Current transfers: debit | -22 | -57 | -67 | -77 | -88 | -111 | -120 | Transferts courants : débit |
| Capital account, n.i.e. | 69 | 56 | 53 | 69 | 49 | 41 | 71 | Compte de capital, n.i.a. |
| Financial account, n.i.e. | 140 | 265 | 666 | 279 | 1 046 | -61 | 1 707 | Compte financier, n.i.a. |
| Net errors and omissions | 254 | 11 | -294 | -3 | 274 | 112 | -250 | Erreurs et omissions nettes |
| Reserves and related items | -125 | 79 | -98 | 90 | -175 | -525 | -16 | Réserves et postes apparentés |
| **Belgium** | | | | | | | | **Belgique** |
| Current account | ... | ... | 11 611 | 12 906 | 12 537 | 9 945 | 10 671 | Compte des transactions courantes |
| Goods: exports f.o.b. | ... | ... | 169 166 | 204 962 | 245 426 | 263 056 | 281 135 | Biens : exportations f.à.b. |
| Goods: imports f.o.b. | ... | ... | -159 648 | -194 003 | -235 718 | -257 137 | -277 778 | Biens : importations f.à.b. |
| Services: credit | ... | ... | 37 822 | 44 708 | 52 708 | 56 144 | 59 592 | Services : crédit |
| Services: debit | ... | ... | -35 863 | -42 862 | -49 023 | -51 172 | -53 148 | Services : débit |
| Income: credit | ... | ... | 36 372 | 40 213 | 48 891 | 59 028 | 70 267 | Revenus : crédit |
| Income: debit | ... | ... | -31 897 | -33 732 | -43 269 | -53 604 | -62 736 | Revenus : débit |
| Current transfers, n.i.e.: credit | ... | ... | 5 275 | 6 515 | 7 949 | 9 355 | 8 808 | Transferts courants, n.i.a. : crédit |
| Current transfers: debit | ... | ... | -9 616 | -12 894 | -14 427 | -15 724 | -15 469 | Transferts courants : débit |
| Capital account, n.i.e. | ... | ... | -585 | -1 021 | -497 | -894 | -401 | Compte de capital, n.i.a. |
| Financial account, n.i.e. | ... | ... | -6 483 | -12 518 | -10 660 | -8 929 | -11 943 | Compte financier, n.i.a. |
| Net errors and omissions | ... | ... | -4 579 | -1 093 | -2 103 | -2 298 | 1 829 | Erreurs et omissions nettes |
| Reserves and related items | ... | ... | 35 | 1 725 | 723 | 2 176 | -156 | Réserves et postes apparentés |
| **Belgium-Luxembourg**[1] | | | | | | | | **Belgique-Luxembourg**[1] |
| Current account | 11 381 | 9 392 | ... | ... | ... | ... | ... | Compte des transactions courantes |
| Goods: exports f.o.b. | 164 677 | 163 498 | ... | ... | ... | ... | ... | Biens : exportations f.à.b. |

| Country or area | 2000 | 2001 | 2002 | 2003 | 2004 | 2005 | 2006 | Pays ou zone |
|---|---|---|---|---|---|---|---|---|
| Goods: imports f.o.b. | -162 086 | -159 790 | ... | ... | ... | ... | ... | Biens : importations f.à.b. |
| Services: credit | 49 789 | 50 314 | ... | ... | ... | ... | ... | Services : crédit |
| Services: debit | -41 868 | -43 316 | ... | ... | ... | ... | ... | Services : débit |
| Income: credit | 75 673 | 78 906 | ... | ... | ... | ... | ... | Revenus : crédit |
| Income: debit | -70 625 | -75 999 | ... | ... | ... | ... | ... | Revenus : débit |
| Current transfers, n.i.e.: credit | 7 014 | 7 316 | ... | ... | ... | ... | ... | Transferts courants, n.i.a. : crédit |
| Current transfers: debit | -11 193 | -11 535 | ... | ... | ... | ... | ... | Transferts courants : débit |
| Capital account, n.i.e. | -213 | 26 | ... | ... | ... | ... | ... | Compte de capital, n.i.a. |
| Financial account, n.i.e. | -9 233 | -7 978 | ... | ... | ... | ... | ... | Compte financier, n.i.a. |
| Net errors and omissions | -2 894 | 3 | ... | ... | ... | ... | ... | Erreurs et omissions nettes |
| Reserves and related items | 959 | -1 442 | ... | ... | ... | ... | ... | Réserves et postes apparentés |
| **Belize** | | | | | | | | **Belize** |
| Current account | -162 | -190 | -165 | -184 | -155 | -161 | -26 | Compte des transactions courantes |
| Goods: exports f.o.b. | 282 | 269 | 310 | 316 | 308 | 325 | 427 | Biens : exportations f.à.b. |
| Goods: imports f.o.b. | -478 | -478 | -497 | -522 | -481 | -556 | -612 | Biens : importations f.à.b. |
| Services: credit | 153 | 166 | 176 | 212 | 235 | 292 | 355 | Services : crédit |
| Services: debit | -123 | -120 | -130 | -141 | -147 | -159 | -151 | Services : débit |
| Income: credit | 7 | 9 | 4 | 5 | 4 | 7 | 10 | Revenus : crédit |
| Income: debit | -60 | -76 | -72 | -95 | -121 | -121 | -129 | Revenus : débit |
| Current transfers, n.i.e.: credit | 61 | 54 | 59 | 59 | 61 | 68 | 92 | Transferts courants, n.i.a. : crédit |
| Current transfers: debit | -3 | -14 | -16 | -18 | -15 | -17 | -18 | Transferts courants : débit |
| Capital account, n.i.e. | -3 | 6 | 14 | 4 | 10 | 3 | 9 | Compte de capital, n.i.a. |
| Financial account, n.i.e. | 205 | 165 | 151 | 204 | 117 | 175 | 61 | Compte financier, n.i.a. |
| Net errors and omissions | 11 | 9 | -9 | -35 | -4 | 2 | 6 | Erreurs et omissions nettes |
| Reserves and related items | -52 | 11 | 8 | 11 | 31 | -19 | -49 | Réserves et postes apparentés |
| **Benin** | | | | | | | | **Bénin** |
| Current account | -111 | -160 | -239 | -349 | -317 | -270 | ... | Compte des transactions courantes |
| Goods: exports f.o.b. | 392 | 373 | 448 | 541 | 569 | 578 | ... | Biens : exportations f.à.b. |
| Goods: imports f.o.b. | -516 | -553 | -679 | -819 | -842 | -866 | ... | Biens : importations f.à.b. |
| Services: credit | 136 | 147 | 152 | 172 | 216 | 194 | ... | Services : crédit |
| Services: debit | -192 | -192 | -209 | -254 | -287 | -279 | ... | Services : débit |
| Income: credit | 23 | 22 | 21 | 23 | 23 | 25 | ... | Revenus : crédit |
| Income: debit | -36 | -36 | -47 | -61 | -60 | -43 | ... | Revenus : débit |
| Current transfers, n.i.e.: credit | 91 | 87 | 93 | 57 | 73 | 153 | ... | Transferts courants, n.i.a. : crédit |
| Current transfers: debit | -11 | -10 | -19 | -8 | -8 | -33 | ... | Transferts courants : débit |
| Capital account, n.i.e. | 73 | 49 | 38 | 34 | 52 | 99 | ... | Compte de capital, n.i.a. |
| Financial account, n.i.e. | 11 | 40 | -61 | 32 | -34 | 105 | ... | Compte financier, n.i.a. |
| Net errors and omissions | 7 | 4 | 2 | 182 | -10 | 9 | ... | Erreurs et omissions nettes |
| Reserves and related items | 20 | 69 | 261 | 100 | 310 | 57 | ... | Réserves et postes apparentés |
| **Bolivia** | | | | | | | | **Bolivie** |
| Current account | -446 | -274 | -352 | 76 | 337 | 622 | 1 319 | Compte des transactions courantes |
| Goods: exports f.o.b. | 1 246 | 1 285 | 1 299 | 1 598 | 2 146 | 2 791 | 3 863 | Biens : exportations f.à.b. |
| Goods: imports f.o.b. | -1 610 | -1 580 | -1 639 | -1 497 | -1 725 | -2 183 | -2 631 | Biens : importations f.à.b. |
| Services: credit | 224 | 236 | 257 | 364 | 416 | 489 | 434 | Services : crédit |
| Services: debit | -468 | -399 | -433 | -551 | -607 | -683 | -805 | Services : débit |
| Income: credit | 140 | 121 | 103 | 71 | 76 | 121 | 215 | Revenus : crédit |
| Income: debit | -365 | -333 | -308 | -374 | -461 | -498 | -578 | Revenus : débit |
| Current transfers, n.i.e.: credit | 420 | 432 | 408 | 511 | 543 | 649 | 895 | Transferts courants, n.i.a. : crédit |
| Current transfers: debit | -33 | -35 | -38 | -46 | -52 | -65 | -73 | Transferts courants : débit |
| Capital account, n.i.e. | 0 | 0 | 0 | 0 | 0 | 9 | 1 813 | Compte de capital, n.i.a. |
| Financial account, n.i.e. | 462 | 441 | 649 | 36 | 361 | 181 | -1 622 | Compte financier, n.i.a. |
| Net errors and omissions | -55 | -203 | -640 | -174 | -625 | -374 | -71 | Erreurs et omissions nettes |
| Reserves and related items | 39 | 36 | 343 | 62 | -73 | -437 | -1 439 | Réserves et postes apparentés |
| **Bosnia and Herzegovina** | | | | | | | | **Bosnie-Herzégovine** |
| Current account | -396 | -743 | -1 191 | -1 631 | -1 639 | -1 976 | -1 233 | Compte des transactions courantes |
| Goods: exports f.o.b. | 1 130 | 1 134 | 1 110 | 1 477 | 2 087 | 2 590 | 3 381 | Biens : exportations f.à.b. |
| Goods: imports f.o.b. | -3 894 | -4 092 | -4 449 | -5 637 | -6 656 | -7 543 | -7 680 | Biens : importations f.à.b. |
| Services: credit | 450 | 497 | 524 | 721 | 864 | 950 | 1 115 | Services : crédit |
| Services: debit | -263 | -269 | -305 | -384 | -432 | -459 | -508 | Services : débit |

| Country or area | 2000 | 2001 | 2002 | 2003 | 2004 | 2005 | 2006 | Pays ou zone |
|---|---|---|---|---|---|---|---|---|
| Income: credit | 667 | 625 | 605 | 654 | 675 | 682 | 733 | Revenus : crédit |
| Income: debit | -76 | -93 | -97 | -121 | -170 | -212 | -324 | Revenus : débit |
| Current transfers, n.i.e.: credit | 1 667 | 1 528 | 1 524 | 1 781 | 2 204 | 2 215 | 2 275 | Transferts courants, n.i.a. : crédit |
| Current transfers: debit | -75 | -73 | -102 | -123 | -210 | -199 | -226 | Transferts courants : débit |
| Capital account, n.i.e. | 546 | 400 | 412 | 466 | 301 | 289 | 231 | Compte de capital, n.i.a. |
| Financial account, n.i.e. | 84 | 995 | 552 | 1 056 | 1 389 | 1 763 | 1 445 | Compte financier, n.i.a. |
| Net errors and omissions | -173 | 100 | 98 | 323 | 409 | 415 | 321 | Erreurs et omissions nettes |
| Reserves and related items | -61 | -752 | 129 | -214 | -459 | -491 | -764 | Réserves et postes apparentés |
| **Botswana** | | | | | | | | **Botswana** |
| Current account | 545 | 598 | 157 | 462 | 309 | 1 597 | 1 940 | Compte des transactions courantes |
| Goods: exports f.o.b. | 2 675 | 2 315 | 2 319 | 3 024 | 3 696 | 4 444 | 4 521 | Biens : exportations f.à.b. |
| Goods: imports f.o.b. | -1 773 | -1 604 | -1 642 | -2 127 | -2 864 | -2 686 | -2 617 | Biens : importations f.à.b. |
| Services: credit | 325 | 340 | 490 | 643 | 780 | 854 | 771 | Services : crédit |
| Services: debit | -547 | -513 | -510 | -652 | -793 | -857 | -835 | Services : débit |
| Income: credit | 378 | 358 | 268 | 383 | 217 | 456 | 529 | Revenus : crédit |
| Income: debit | -729 | -495 | -980 | -1 098 | -1 254 | -1 292 | -1 301 | Revenus : débit |
| Current transfers, n.i.e.: credit | 426 | 383 | 400 | 538 | 743 | 896 | 1 073 | Transferts courants, n.i.a. : crédit |
| Current transfers: debit | -209 | -185 | -188 | -248 | -217 | -218 | -202 | Transferts courants : débit |
| Capital account, n.i.e. | 38 | 6 | 16 | 22 | 32 | 31 | 24 | Compte de capital, n.i.a. |
| Financial account, n.i.e. | -214 | -509 | -217 | -379 | -276 | 54 | -67 | Compte financier, n.i.a. |
| Net errors and omissions | -2 | 76 | 106 | 66 | -122 | -319 | -142 | Erreurs et omissions nettes |
| Reserves and related items | -367 | -170 | -61 | -171 | 57 | -1 364 | -1 756 | Réserves et postes apparentés |
| **Brazil** | | | | | | | | **Brésil** |
| Current account | -24 225 | -23 215 | -7 637 | 4 177 | 11 738 | 13 984 | 13 620 | Compte des transactions courantes |
| Goods: exports f.o.b. | 55 086 | 58 223 | 60 362 | 73 084 | 96 475 | 118 308 | 137 807 | Biens : exportations f.à.b. |
| Goods: imports f.o.b. | -55 783 | -55 572 | -47 241 | -48 290 | -62 809 | -73 606 | -91 350 | Biens : importations f.à.b. |
| Services: credit | 9 498 | 9 322 | 9 551 | 10 447 | 12 584 | 16 048 | 19 462 | Services : crédit |
| Services: debit | -16 660 | -17 081 | -14 509 | -15 378 | -17 260 | -24 356 | -29 116 | Services : débit |
| Income: credit | 3 621 | 3 280 | 3 295 | 3 339 | 3 199 | 3 194 | 6 438 | Revenus : crédit |
| Income: debit | -21 507 | -23 023 | -21 486 | -21 891 | -23 719 | -29 162 | -33 927 | Revenus : débit |
| Current transfers, n.i.e.: credit | 1 828 | 1 934 | 2 627 | 3 132 | 3 582 | 4 050 | 4 846 | Transferts courants, n.i.a. : crédit |
| Current transfers: debit | -307 | -296 | -237 | -265 | -314 | -493 | -541 | Transferts courants : débit |
| Capital account, n.i.e. | 273 | -36 | 433 | 498 | 339 | 663 | 869 | Compte de capital, n.i.a. |
| Financial account, n.i.e. | 29 376 | 20 331 | -3 909 | -157 | -3 333 | 13 144 | 15 113 | Compte financier, n.i.a. |
| Net errors and omissions | 2 557 | -498 | -154 | -933 | -2 145 | -225 | 967 | Erreurs et omissions nettes |
| Reserves and related items | -7 981 | 3 418 | 11 266 | -3 586 | -6 599 | -27 566 | -30 569 | Réserves et postes apparentés |
| **Bulgaria** | | | | | | | | **Bulgarie** |
| Current account | -703 | -805 | -319 | -1 022 | -1 671 | -3 244 | -5 010 | Compte des transactions courantes |
| Goods: exports f.o.b. | 4 825 | 5 113 | 5 354 | 7 081 | 9 931 | 11 754 | 15 064 | Biens : exportations f.à.b. |
| Goods: imports f.o.b. | -6 000 | -6 693 | -7 013 | -9 657 | -13 619 | -17 204 | -21 874 | Biens : importations f.à.b. |
| Services: credit | 2 175 | 2 163 | 2 203 | 2 961 | 4 029 | 4 404 | 5 044 | Services : crédit |
| Services: debit | -1 670 | -1 910 | -1 755 | -2 447 | -3 238 | -3 404 | -4 112 | Services : débit |
| Income: credit | 321 | 706 | 924 | 1 298 | 1 539 | 1 516 | 1 602 | Revenus : crédit |
| Income: debit | -644 | -681 | -581 | -954 | -1 236 | -1 323 | -1 555 | Revenus : débit |
| Current transfers, n.i.e.: credit | 355 | 599 | 654 | 865 | 1 121 | 1 238 | 1 040 | Transferts courants, n.i.a. : crédit |
| Current transfers: debit | -64 | -100 | -106 | -170 | -199 | -225 | -219 | Transferts courants : débit |
| Capital account, n.i.e. | 25 | ^0 | ^0 | ^0 | 204 | 256 | 228 | Compte de capital, n.i.a. |
| Financial account, n.i.e. | 781 | 663 | 3 513 | 2 738 | 3 428 | 6 387 | 6 816 | Compte financier, n.i.a. |
| Net errors and omissions | 34 | 515 | -716 | -889 | 371 | -772 | 254 | Erreurs et omissions nettes |
| Reserves and related items | -137 | -373 | -2 478 | -827 | -2 332 | -2 627 | -2 288 | Réserves et postes apparentés |
| **Burkina Faso** | | | | | | | | **Burkina Faso** |
| Current account | -392 | -381 | ... | ... | ... | ... | ... | Compte des transactions courantes |
| Goods: exports f.o.b. | 206 | 223 | ... | ... | ... | ... | ... | Biens : exportations f.à.b. |
| Goods: imports f.o.b. | -518 | -509 | ... | ... | ... | ... | ... | Biens : importations f.à.b. |
| Services: credit | 31 | 37 | ... | ... | ... | ... | ... | Services : crédit |
| Services: debit | -140 | -141 | ... | ... | ... | ... | ... | Services : débit |
| Income: credit | 14 | 15 | ... | ... | ... | ... | ... | Revenus : crédit |
| Income: debit | -34 | -40 | ... | ... | ... | ... | ... | Revenus : débit |
| Current transfers, n.i.e.: credit | 88 | 72 | ... | ... | ... | ... | ... | Transferts courants, n.i.a. : crédit |

**62** Balance of payments summary—Millions of US dollars (*continued*)
Résumé de la balance des paiements—Millions de dollars E.-U (*suite*)

| Country or area | 2000 | 2001 | 2002 | 2003 | 2004 | 2005 | 2006 | Pays ou zone |
|---|---|---|---|---|---|---|---|---|
| Current transfers: debit | -39 | -38 | ... | ... | ... | ... | ... | Transferts courants : débit |
| Capital account, n.i.e. | 176 | 165 | ... | ... | ... | ... | ... | Compte de capital, n.i.a. |
| Financial account, n.i.e. | 19 | 25 | ... | ... | ... | ... | ... | Compte financier, n.i.a. |
| Net errors and omissions | 5 | 3 | ... | ... | ... | ... | ... | Erreurs et omissions nettes |
| Reserves and related items | 192 | 187 | ... | ... | ... | ... | ... | Réserves et postes apparentés |
| **Burundi** | | | | | | | | **Burundi** |
| Current account | -103 | -109 | -111 | -131 | -166 | -227 | -325 | Compte des transactions courantes |
| Goods: exports f.o.b. | 49 | 39 | 31 | 38 | 48 | 57 | 59 | Biens : exportations f.à.b. |
| Goods: imports f.o.b. | -108 | -108 | -105 | -130 | -158 | -211 | -249 | Biens : importations f.à.b. |
| Services: credit | 4 | 5 | 8 | 7 | 16 | 35 | 34 | Services : crédit |
| Services: debit | -43 | -38 | -43 | -45 | -74 | -113 | -199 | Services : débit |
| Income: credit | 2 | 2 | 1 | 1 | 1 | 3 | 5 | Revenus : crédit |
| Income: debit | -14 | -16 | -13 | -19 | -20 | -21 | -13 | Revenus : débit |
| Current transfers, n.i.e.: credit | 8 | 10 | 13 | 20 | 24 | 27 | 41 | Transferts courants, n.i.a. : crédit |
| Current transfers: debit | -2 | -3 | -3 | -3 | -3 | -3 | -3 | Transferts courants : débit |
| Capital account, n.i.e. | ^0 | ^0 | ^0 | -1 | 18 | 24 | 46 | Compte de capital, n.i.a. |
| Financial account, n.i.e. | -7 | -4 | -41 | -50 | -40 | -17 | -17 | Compte financier, n.i.a. |
| Net errors and omissions | -34 | -31 | 2 | -14 | -21 | -80 | 5 | Erreurs et omissions nettes |
| Reserves and related items | 145 | 144 | 150 | 196 | 209 | 300 | 291 | Réserves et postes apparentés |
| **Cambodia** | | | | | | | | **Cambodge** |
| Current account | -136 | -88 | -107 | -233 | -183 | -360 | -337 | Compte des transactions courantes |
| Goods: exports f.o.b. | 1 397 | 1 571 | 1 770 | 2 087 | 2 589 | 2 910 | 3 693 | Biens : exportations f.à.b. |
| Goods: imports f.o.b. | -1 936 | -2 094 | -2 361 | -2 668 | -3 269 | -3 928 | -4 749 | Biens : importations f.à.b. |
| Services: credit | 428 | 525 | 604 | 548 | 805 | 1 118 | 1 296 | Services : crédit |
| Services: debit | -328 | -347 | -376 | -434 | -514 | -647 | -790 | Services : débit |
| Income: credit | 67 | 58 | 51 | 44 | 49 | 68 | 90 | Revenus : crédit |
| Income: debit | -190 | -195 | -234 | -223 | -270 | -322 | -380 | Revenus : débit |
| Current transfers, n.i.e.: credit | 432 | 404 | 448 | 425 | 444 | 461 | 527 | Transferts courants, n.i.a. : crédit |
| Current transfers: debit | -7 | -8 | -9 | -12 | -15 | -21 | -25 | Transferts courants : débit |
| Capital account, n.i.e. | 36 | 45 | 8 | 66 | 68 | 95 | 268 | Compte de capital, n.i.a. |
| Financial account, n.i.e. | 184 | -41 | 165 | 244 | 219 | 335 | 324 | Compte financier, n.i.a. |
| Net errors and omissions | 9 | ^0 | 2 | -40 | -46 | 5 | -46 | Erreurs et omissions nettes |
| Reserves and related items | -92 | 85 | -67 | -36 | -58 | -74 | -208 | Réserves et postes apparentés |
| **Cameroon** | | | | | | | | **Cameroun** |
| Current account | -249 | -376 | -445 | -596 | -608 | ... | ... | Compte des transactions courantes |
| Goods: exports f.o.b. | 1 986 | 1 891 | 1 964 | 2 483 | 2 708 | ... | ... | Biens : exportations f.à.b. |
| Goods: imports f.o.b. | -1 484 | -1 797 | -1 812 | -2 214 | -2 473 | ... | ... | Biens : importations f.à.b. |
| Services: credit | 590 | 858 | 939 | 645 | 921 | ... | ... | Services : crédit |
| Services: debit | -957 | -1 082 | -1 212 | -1 222 | -1 497 | ... | ... | Services : débit |
| Income: credit | 26 | 47 | 43 | 108 | 105 | ... | ... | Revenus : crédit |
| Income: debit | -519 | -380 | -420 | -518 | -549 | ... | ... | Revenus : débit |
| Current transfers, n.i.e.: credit | 173 | 147 | 127 | 205 | 225 | ... | ... | Transferts courants, n.i.a. : crédit |
| Current transfers: debit | -64 | -61 | -75 | -83 | -49 | ... | ... | Transferts courants : débit |
| Capital account, n.i.e. | 17 | 56 | 61 | 112 | 42 | ... | ... | Compte de capital, n.i.a. |
| Financial account, n.i.e. | -15 | 679 | 678 | -198 | 143 | ... | ... | Compte financier, n.i.a. |
| Net errors and omissions | 112 | -124 | -130 | 467 | 201 | ... | ... | Erreurs et omissions nettes |
| Reserves and related items | 135 | -234 | -164 | 216 | 222 | ... | ... | Réserves et postes apparentés |
| **Canada** | | | | | | | | **Canada** |
| Current account | 19 622 | 16 281 | 12 604 | 10 696 | 22 321 | 23 408 | 20 797 | Compte des transactions courantes |
| Goods: exports f.o.b. | 289 022 | 271 849 | 263 908 | 285 186 | 330 057 | 373 254 | 401 786 | Biens : exportations f.à.b. |
| Goods: imports f.o.b. | -243 975 | -226 132 | -227 410 | -244 904 | -279 623 | -320 575 | -356 641 | Biens : importations f.à.b. |
| Services: credit | 40 230 | 38 804 | 40 481 | 44 242 | 49 747 | 55 313 | 59 332 | Services : crédit |
| Services: debit | -44 118 | -43 843 | -45 070 | -52 454 | -58 990 | -65 333 | -72 649 | Services : débit |
| Income: credit | 24 746 | 16 823 | 19 444 | 21 050 | 29 431 | 39 860 | 54 344 | Revenus : crédit |
| Income: debit | -47 036 | -42 238 | -38 745 | -42 295 | -47 980 | -58 397 | -64 760 | Revenus : débit |
| Current transfers, n.i.e.: credit | 4 122 | 4 500 | 4 387 | 4 814 | 5 518 | 6 754 | 8 517 | Transferts courants, n.i.a. : crédit |
| Current transfers: debit | -3 368 | -3 480 | -4 391 | -4 943 | -5 839 | -7 467 | -9 133 | Transferts courants : débit |
| Capital account, n.i.e. | 3 581 | 3 721 | 3 145 | 3 020 | 3 437 | 4 889 | 3 702 | Compte de capital, n.i.a. |
| Financial account, n.i.e. | -14 500 | -11 609 | -14 360 | -18 070 | -31 565 | -30 150 | -19 215 | Compte financier, n.i.a. |

| Country or area | 2000 | 2001 | 2002 | 2003 | 2004 | 2005 | 2006 | Pays ou zone |
|---|---|---|---|---|---|---|---|---|
| Net errors and omissions | -4 984 | -6 220 | -1 574 | 1 098 | 2 972 | 3 189 | -4 458 | Erreurs et omissions nettes |
| Reserves and related items | -3 720 | -2 172 | 185 | 3 255 | 2 836 | -1 335 | -826 | Réserves et postes apparentés |
| Cape Verde | | | | | | | | Cap-Vert |
| Current account | -58 | -56 | -72 | -91 | -130 | -35 | -40 | Compte des transactions courantes |
| Goods: exports f.o.b. | 38 | 37 | 42 | 53 | 57 | 89 | 122 | Biens : exportations f.à.b. |
| Goods: imports f.o.b. | -226 | -232 | -278 | -361 | -435 | -438 | -563 | Biens : importations f.à.b. |
| Services: credit | 108 | 130 | 153 | 202 | 239 | 277 | 397 | Services : crédit |
| Services: debit | -100 | -119 | -142 | -189 | -207 | -208 | -245 | Services : débit |
| Income: credit | 5 | 8 | 6 | 16 | 18 | 19 | 19 | Revenus : crédit |
| Income: debit | -18 | -13 | -18 | -29 | -36 | -52 | -64 | Revenus : débit |
| Current transfers, n.i.e.: credit | 146 | 156 | 182 | 235 | 278 | 310 | 336 | Transferts courants, n.i.a. : crédit |
| Current transfers: debit | -12 | -22 | -16 | -18 | -43 | -31 | -41 | Transferts courants : débit |
| Capital account, n.i.e. | 11 | 24 | 9 | 25 | 24 | 20 | 27 | Compte de capital, n.i.a. |
| Financial account, n.i.e. | 32 | 39 | 81 | 82 | 124 | 4 | 111 | Compte financier, n.i.a. |
| Net errors and omissions | -12 | -24 | -8 | -12 | 10 | 63 | -41 | Erreurs et omissions nettes |
| Reserves and related items | 28 | 17 | -10 | -4 | -28 | -52 | -58 | Réserves et postes apparentés |
| Chile | | | | | | | | Chili |
| Current account | -898 | -1 100 | -580 | -779 | 2 074 | 1 315 | 5 256 | Compte des transactions courantes |
| Goods: exports f.o.b. | 19 210 | 18 272 | 18 180 | 21 664 | 32 520 | 41 297 | 58 116 | Biens : exportations f.à.b. |
| Goods: imports f.o.b. | -17 091 | -16 428 | -15 794 | -17 941 | -22 935 | -30 492 | -35 903 | Biens : importations f.à.b. |
| Services: credit | 4 083 | 4 138 | 4 386 | 5 070 | 6 034 | 7 020 | 7 504 | Services : crédit |
| Services: debit | -4 802 | -4 983 | -5 087 | -5 688 | -6 780 | -7 656 | -8 426 | Services : débit |
| Income: credit | 1 598 | 1 458 | 1 114 | 1 552 | 1 983 | 2 452 | 3 342 | Revenus : crédit |
| Income: debit | -4 453 | -3 985 | -3 960 | -6 041 | -9 820 | -13 097 | -22 734 | Revenus : débit |
| Current transfers, n.i.e.: credit | 765 | 713 | 954 | 901 | 1 411 | 2 236 | 3 889 | Transferts courants, n.i.a. : crédit |
| Current transfers: debit | -207 | -286 | -372 | -296 | -339 | -445 | -532 | Transferts courants : débit |
| Capital account, n.i.e. | 0 | 0 | 83 | 0 | 5 | 41 | 13 | Compte de capital, n.i.a. |
| Financial account, n.i.e. | 787 | 1 362 | 1 634 | 1 145 | -2 001 | 1 623 | -4 808 | Compte financier, n.i.a. |
| Net errors and omissions | 427 | -861 | -952 | -724 | -270 | -1 268 | 1 537 | Erreurs et omissions nettes |
| Reserves and related items | -317 | 599 | -185 | 357 | 191 | -1 711 | -1 998 | Réserves et postes apparentés |
| China[2] | | | | | | | | Chine[2] |
| Current account | 20 518 | 17 401 | 35 422 | 45 875 | 68 659 | 160 818 | 249 866 | Compte des transactions courantes |
| Goods: exports f.o.b. | 249 131 | 266 075 | 325 651 | 438 270 | 593 393 | 762 484 | 969 682 | Biens : exportations f.à.b. |
| Goods: imports f.o.b. | -214 657 | -232 058 | -281 484 | -393 618 | -534 410 | -628 295 | -751 936 | Biens : importations f.à.b. |
| Services: credit | 30 431 | 33 334 | 39 745 | 46 734 | 62 434 | 74 404 | 91 999 | Services : crédit |
| Services: debit | -36 031 | -39 267 | -46 528 | -55 306 | -72 133 | -83 796 | -100 833 | Services : débit |
| Income: credit | 12 550 | 9 388 | 8 344 | 16 095 | 20 544 | 38 959 | 51 240 | Revenus : crédit |
| Income: debit | -27 216 | -28 563 | -23 290 | -23 933 | -24 067 | -28 324 | -39 485 | Revenus : débit |
| Current transfers, n.i.e.: credit | 6 861 | 9 125 | 13 795 | 18 483 | 24 326 | 27 735 | 31 578 | Transferts courants, n.i.a. : crédit |
| Current transfers: debit | -550 | -633 | -811 | -848 | -1 428 | -2 349 | -2 378 | Transferts courants : débit |
| Capital account, n.i.e. | -35 | -54 | -50 | -48 | -69 | 4 102 | 4 020 | Compte de capital, n.i.a. |
| Financial account, n.i.e. | 1 958 | 34 832 | 32 341 | 52 774 | 110 729 | 58 862 | 6 017 | Compte financier, n.i.a. |
| Net errors and omissions | -11 748 | -4 732 | 7 504 | 17 985 | 26 834 | -16 441 | -13 048 | Erreurs et omissions nettes |
| Reserves and related items | -10 693 | -47 447 | -75 217 | -116 586 | -206 153 | -207 342 | -246 855 | Réserves et postes apparentés |
| China, Hong Kong SAR | | | | | | | | China, Hong Kong RAS |
| Current account | 6 993 | 9 786 | 12 412 | 16 470 | 15 728 | 20 233 | 20 151 | Compte des transactions courantes |
| Goods: exports f.o.b. | 202 698 | 190 926 | 200 300 | 224 656 | 260 263 | 289 579 | 317 600 | Biens : exportations f.à.b. |
| Goods: imports f.o.b. | -210 891 | -199 257 | -205 353 | -230 435 | -269 575 | -297 206 | -331 634 | Biens : importations f.à.b. |
| Services: credit | 40 430 | 41 135 | 44 601 | 46 555 | 55 157 | 63 761 | 72 283 | Services : crédit |
| Services: debit | -24 698 | -24 899 | -25 964 | -26 126 | -31 138 | -33 979 | -36 533 | Services : débit |
| Income: credit | 54 483 | 48 058 | 41 511 | 43 181 | 52 003 | 64 806 | 82 792 | Revenus : crédit |
| Income: debit | -53 359 | -44 398 | -40 787 | -39 525 | -48 997 | -64 604 | -82 135 | Revenus : débit |
| Current transfers, n.i.e.: credit | 538 | 605 | 777 | 529 | 626 | 943 | 940 | Transferts courants, n.i.a. : crédit |
| Current transfers: debit | -2 208 | -2 385 | -2 673 | -2 366 | -2 611 | -3 067 | -3 161 | Transferts courants : débit |
| Capital account, n.i.e. | -1 546 | -1 174 | -2 011 | -1 065 | -329 | -634 | -286 | Compte de capital, n.i.a. |
| Financial account, n.i.e. | 4 165 | -6 626 | -19 751 | -20 953 | -20 094 | -21 448 | -19 659 | Compte financier, n.i.a. |
| Net errors and omissions | 431 | 2 699 | 6 973 | 6 542 | 7 980 | 3 227 | 5 809 | Erreurs et omissions nettes |
| Reserves and related items | -10 044 | -4 684 | 2 377 | -994 | -3 286 | -1 378 | -6 016 | Réserves et postes apparentés |

**Balance of payments summary**—Millions of US dollars (*continued*)
**Résumé de la balance des paiements**—Millions de dollars E.-U (*suite*)

| Country or area | 2000 | 2001 | 2002 | 2003 | 2004 | 2005 | 2006 | Pays ou zone |
|---|---|---|---|---|---|---|---|---|
| **China, Macao SAR** | | | | | | | | **China, Macao RAS** |
| Current account | ... | ... | 2 719 | 3 160 | 4 240 | 3 367 | 2 946 | Compte des transactions courantes |
| Goods: exports f.o.b. | ... | ... | 2 358 | 2 585 | 2 816 | 2 478 | 2 559 | Biens : exportations f.à.b. |
| Goods: imports f.o.b. | ... | ... | -3 277 | -3 678 | -4 658 | -5 271 | -6 496 | Biens : importations f.à.b. |
| Services: credit | ... | ... | 4 758 | 5 605 | 8 063 | 8 612 | 10 538 | Services : crédit |
| Services: debit | ... | ... | -1 071 | -1 175 | -1 364 | -1 576 | -1 866 | Services : débit |
| Income: credit | ... | ... | 450 | 395 | 387 | 806 | 1 426 | Revenus : crédit |
| Income: debit | ... | ... | -468 | -547 | -959 | -1 582 | -2 981 | Revenus : débit |
| Current transfers, n.i.e.: credit | ... | ... | 69 | 83 | 79 | 83 | 108 | Transferts courants, n.i.a. : crédit |
| Current transfers: debit | ... | ... | -99 | -108 | -124 | -184 | -343 | Transferts courants : débit |
| Capital account, n.i.e. | ... | ... | 139 | 88 | 274 | 515 | 438 | Compte de capital, n.i.a. |
| Financial account, n.i.e. | ... | ... | -1 084 | -1 680 | -1 558 | -262 | -806 | Compte financier, n.i.a. |
| Net errors and omissions | ... | ... | -1 572 | -1 077 | -1 932 | -2 494 | -520 | Erreurs et omissions nettes |
| Reserves and related items | ... | ... | -202 | -491 | -1 024 | -1 126 | -2 058 | Réserves et postes apparentés |
| **Colombia** | | | | | | | | **Colombie** |
| Current account | 770 | -1 088 | -1 357 | -974 | -906 | -1 881 | -3 057 | Compte des transactions courantes |
| Goods: exports f.o.b. | 13 722 | 12 848 | 12 316 | 13 812 | 17 224 | 21 730 | 25 181 | Biens : exportations f.à.b. |
| Goods: imports f.o.b. | -11 090 | -12 269 | -12 078 | -13 258 | -15 878 | -20 134 | -24 859 | Biens : importations f.à.b. |
| Services: credit | 2 049 | 2 190 | 1 867 | 1 921 | 2 255 | 2 664 | 3 373 | Services : crédit |
| Services: debit | -3 307 | -3 602 | -3 302 | -3 360 | -3 935 | -4 766 | -5 493 | Services : débit |
| Income: credit | 1 054 | 919 | 717 | 553 | 671 | 1 074 | 1 525 | Revenus : crédit |
| Income: debit | -3 331 | -3 528 | -3 584 | -3 951 | -4 967 | -6 531 | -7 528 | Revenus : débit |
| Current transfers, n.i.e.: credit | 1 911 | 2 656 | 3 010 | 3 565 | 3 994 | 4 342 | 5 037 | Transferts courants, n.i.a. : crédit |
| Current transfers: debit | -238 | -302 | -304 | -256 | -270 | -260 | -293 | Transferts courants : débit |
| Capital account, n.i.e. | 0 | 0 | 0 | 0 | 0 | 0 | 0 | Compte de capital, n.i.a. |
| Financial account, n.i.e. | 50 | 2 453 | 1 305 | 652 | 3 134 | 3 228 | 2 801 | Compte financier, n.i.a. |
| Net errors and omissions | 41 | -140 | 191 | 134 | 241 | 379 | 288 | Erreurs et omissions nettes |
| Reserves and related items | -862 | -1 225 | -139 | 188 | -2 470 | -1 726 | -32 | Réserves et postes apparentés |
| **Congo** | | | | | | | | **Congo** |
| Current account | 648 | -28 | -34 | 520 | 674 | 903 | ... | Compte des transactions courantes |
| Goods: exports f.o.b. | 2 492 | 2 055 | 2 289 | 2 637 | 3 433 | 4 730 | ... | Biens : exportations f.à.b. |
| Goods: imports f.o.b. | -455 | -681 | -691 | -831 | -969 | -1 356 | ... | Biens : importations f.à.b. |
| Services: credit | 137 | 144 | 165 | 194 | 197 | 235 | ... | Services : crédit |
| Services: debit | -738 | -852 | -927 | -875 | -1 016 | -1 560 | ... | Services : débit |
| Income: credit | 14 | 15 | 6 | 10 | 13 | 15 | ... | Revenus : crédit |
| Income: debit | -819 | -694 | -866 | -596 | -962 | -1 138 | ... | Revenus : débit |
| Current transfers, n.i.e.: credit | 39 | 18 | 13 | 26 | 34 | 31 | ... | Transferts courants, n.i.a. : crédit |
| Current transfers: debit | -20 | -34 | -23 | -44 | -56 | -54 | ... | Transferts courants : débit |
| Capital account, n.i.e. | 8 | 13 | 5 | 17 | 13 | 6 | ... | Compte de capital, n.i.a. |
| Financial account, n.i.e. | -822 | -653 | -464 | -701 | -775 | -823 | ... | Compte financier, n.i.a. |
| Net errors and omissions | -78 | -12 | -220 | -116 | -93 | 326 | ... | Erreurs et omissions nettes |
| Reserves and related items | 243 | 681 | 713 | 280 | 181 | -412 | ... | Réserves et postes apparentés |
| **Costa Rica** | | | | | | | | **Costa Rica** |
| Current account | -707 | -603 | -857 | -880 | -796 | -971 | -1 118 | Compte des transactions courantes |
| Goods: exports f.o.b. | 5 813 | 4 923 | 5 270 | 6 163 | 6 370 | 7 100 | 8 068 | Biens : exportations f.à.b. |
| Goods: imports f.o.b. | -6 024 | -5 743 | -6 548 | -7 252 | -7 791 | -9 242 | -10 811 | Biens : importations f.à.b. |
| Services: credit | 1 936 | 1 926 | 1 868 | 2 021 | 2 242 | 2 621 | 2 955 | Services : crédit |
| Services: debit | -1 273 | -1 180 | -1 183 | -1 245 | -1 384 | -1 505 | -1 612 | Services : débit |
| Income: credit | 243 | 193 | 158 | 146 | 144 | 234 | 340 | Revenus : crédit |
| Income: debit | -1 495 | -872 | -598 | -922 | -589 | -449 | -408 | Revenus : débit |
| Current transfers, n.i.e.: credit | 204 | 266 | 297 | 369 | 371 | 471 | 586 | Transferts courants, n.i.a. : crédit |
| Current transfers: debit | -110 | -116 | -121 | -160 | -159 | -200 | -237 | Transferts courants : débit |
| Capital account, n.i.e. | 9 | 18 | 12 | 24 | 11 | 0 | ^0 | Compte de capital, n.i.a. |
| Financial account, n.i.e. | -35 | 271 | 857 | 595 | 472 | 873 | 1 839 | Compte financier, n.i.a. |
| Net errors and omissions | 391 | 168 | -51 | 35 | 64 | 156 | 293 | Erreurs et omissions nettes |
| Reserves and related items | 341 | 146 | 38 | 226 | 249 | -57 | -1 015 | Réserves et postes apparentés |
| **Côte d'Ivoire** | | | | | | | | **Côte d'Ivoire** |
| Current account | -241 | -61 | 768 | 294 | 241 | 40 | 529 | Compte des transactions courantes |
| Goods: exports f.o.b. | 3 888 | 3 946 | 5 275 | 5 788 | 6 919 | 7 697 | 8 191 | Biens : exportations f.à.b. |

62

**Balance of payments summary**—Millions of US dollars (*continued*)
**Résumé de la balance des paiements**—Millions de dollars E.-U (*suite*)

| Country or area | 2000 | 2001 | 2002 | 2003 | 2004 | 2005 | 2006 | Pays ou zone |
|---|---|---|---|---|---|---|---|---|
| Goods: imports f.o.b. | -2 402 | -2 418 | -2 456 | -3 231 | -4 291 | -5 251 | -5 039 | Biens : importations f.à.b. |
| Services: credit | 482 | 578 | 585 | 664 | 763 | 832 | 819 | Services : crédit |
| Services: debit | -1 227 | -1 271 | -1 545 | -1 780 | -2 033 | -2 124 | -2 217 | Services : débit |
| Income: credit | 142 | 137 | 141 | 171 | 190 | 194 | 198 | Revenus : crédit |
| Income: debit | -794 | -723 | -771 | -830 | -841 | -847 | -926 | Revenus : débit |
| Current transfers, n.i.e.: credit | 79 | 89 | 132 | 196 | 187 | 195 | 204 | Transferts courants, n.i.a. : crédit |
| Current transfers: debit | -409 | -399 | -594 | -683 | -653 | -657 | -700 | Transferts courants : débit |
| Capital account, n.i.e. | 8 | 10 | 8 | 14 | 146 | 185 | 28 | Compte de capital, n.i.a. |
| Financial account, n.i.e. | -363 | -66 | -1 029 | -1 035 | -263 | -469 | -441 | Compte financier, n.i.a. |
| Net errors and omissions | -13 | 31 | -26 | -888 | 27 | -58 | 52 | Erreurs et omissions nettes |
| Reserves and related items | 608 | 86 | 278 | 1 615 | -150 | 302 | -168 | Réserves et postes apparentés |
| Croatia | | | | | | | | Croatie |
| Current account | -533 | -729 | -1 925 | -2 162 | -1 898 | -2 571 | -3 220 | Compte des transactions courantes |
| Goods: exports f.o.b. | 4 574 | 4 767 | 5 006 | 6 311 | 8 214 | 8 960 | 10 644 | Biens : exportations f.à.b. |
| Goods: imports f.o.b. | -7 770 | -8 860 | -10 652 | -14 216 | -16 560 | -18 301 | -21 131 | Biens : importations f.à.b. |
| Services: credit | 4 071 | 4 884 | 5 582 | 8 569 | 9 373 | 9 921 | 10 809 | Services : crédit |
| Services: debit | -1 822 | -1 949 | -2 414 | -2 982 | -3 565 | -3 400 | -3 548 | Services : débit |
| Income: credit | 346 | 434 | 437 | 508 | 756 | 756 | 1 036 | Revenus : crédit |
| Income: debit | -812 | -988 | -975 | -1 760 | -1 602 | -1 982 | -2 420 | Revenus : débit |
| Current transfers, n.i.e.: credit | 1 098 | 1 193 | 1 375 | 1 741 | 1 974 | 2 027 | 2 059 | Transferts courants, n.i.a. : crédit |
| Current transfers: debit | -218 | -209 | -285 | -334 | -488 | -552 | -670 | Transferts courants : débit |
| Capital account, n.i.e. | 9 | 134 | 443 | 82 | 28 | 59 | -175 | Compte de capital, n.i.a. |
| Financial account, n.i.e. | 1 953 | 2 431 | 2 725 | 4 363 | 3 173 | 4 811 | 6 504 | Compte financier, n.i.a. |
| Net errors and omissions | -773 | -438 | -428 | -881 | -1 234 | -1 277 | -1 382 | Erreurs et omissions nettes |
| Reserves and related items | -656 | -1 398 | -815 | -1 401 | -68 | -1 022 | -1 727 | Réserves et postes apparentés |
| Cyprus | | | | | | | | Chypre |
| Current account | -488 | -322 | -379 | -292 | -827 | -971 | -1 091 | Compte des transactions courantes |
| Goods: exports f.o.b. | 951 | 975 | 852 | 925 | 1 173 | 1 545 | 1 417 | Biens : exportations f.à.b. |
| Goods: imports f.o.b. | -3 557 | -3 553 | -3 735 | -4 108 | -5 222 | -5 792 | -6 440 | Biens : importations f.à.b. |
| Services: credit | 4 068 | 4 340 | 4 531 | 5 372 | 6 235 | 6 502 | 7 274 | Services : crédit |
| Services: debit | -1 585 | -1 615 | -1 742 | -2 237 | -2 644 | -2 706 | -2 987 | Services : débit |
| Income: credit | 572 | 559 | 757 | 905 | 1 160 | 1 635 | 2 175 | Revenus : crédit |
| Income: debit | -1 115 | -1 083 | -1 158 | -1 295 | -1 697 | -2 247 | -2 739 | Revenus : débit |
| Current transfers, n.i.e.: credit | 237 | 147 | 270 | 386 | 585 | 631 | 836 | Transferts courants, n.i.a. : crédit |
| Current transfers: debit | -60 | -93 | -153 | -242 | -417 | -539 | -627 | Transferts courants : débit |
| Capital account, n.i.e. | 5 | 6 | 20 | 38 | 134 | 87 | 34 | Compte de capital, n.i.a. |
| Financial account, n.i.e. | 530 | 965 | 826 | 46 | 912 | 1 421 | 2 264 | Compte financier, n.i.a. |
| Net errors and omissions | -55 | -38 | -77 | 21 | 152 | 165 | -182 | Erreurs et omissions nettes |
| Reserves and related items | 8 | -611 | -389 | 188 | -371 | -703 | -1 026 | Réserves et postes apparentés |
| Czech Republic | | | | | | | | République tchèque |
| Current account | -2 690 | -3 273 | -4 265 | -5 785 | -5 749 | -1 939 | -4 586 | Compte des transactions courantes |
| Goods: exports f.o.b. | 29 019 | 33 404 | 38 480 | 48 705 | 67 220 | 77 951 | 95 119 | Biens : exportations f.à.b. |
| Goods: imports f.o.b. | -32 115 | -36 482 | -40 720 | -51 224 | -67 749 | -75 430 | -92 139 | Biens : importations f.à.b. |
| Services: credit | 6 839 | 7 092 | 7 083 | 7 789 | 9 643 | 11 748 | 13 331 | Services : crédit |
| Services: debit | -5 436 | -5 567 | -6 439 | -7 320 | -9 008 | -10 217 | -11 801 | Services : débit |
| Income: credit | 1 952 | 2 233 | 2 052 | 2 681 | 3 405 | 4 390 | 5 381 | Revenus : crédit |
| Income: debit | -3 323 | -4 422 | -5 632 | -6 966 | -9 497 | -10 874 | -13 585 | Revenus : débit |
| Current transfers, n.i.e.: credit | 948 | 959 | 1 465 | 1 663 | 2 081 | 3 296 | 2 911 | Transferts courants, n.i.a. : crédit |
| Current transfers: debit | -575 | -489 | -553 | -1 114 | -1 845 | -2 805 | -3 802 | Transferts courants : débit |
| Capital account, n.i.e. | -5 | -9 | -4 | -3 | -602 | 196 | 380 | Compte de capital, n.i.a. |
| Financial account, n.i.e. | 3 835 | 4 569 | 10 621 | 5 620 | 7 036 | 6 379 | 5 073 | Compte financier, n.i.a. |
| Net errors and omissions | -296 | 499 | 266 | 611 | -422 | -757 | -775 | Erreurs et omissions nettes |
| Reserves and related items | -844 | -1 787 | -6 618 | -442 | -263 | -3 879 | -92 | Réserves et postes apparentés |
| Denmark | | | | | | | | Danemark |
| Current account | 2 262 | 4 848 | 3 460 | 6 963 | 5 941 | 11 253 | 7 339 | Compte des transactions courantes |
| Goods: exports f.o.b. | 50 084 | 50 466 | 55 473 | 64 537 | 75 050 | 82 660 | 90 615 | Biens : exportations f.à.b. |
| Goods: imports f.o.b. | -43 443 | -43 048 | -47 810 | -54 840 | -65 524 | -75 193 | -87 923 | Biens : importations f.à.b. |
| Services: credit | 23 721 | 25 134 | 26 667 | 31 672 | 36 304 | 43 956 | 52 679 | Services : crédit |
| Services: debit | -21 063 | -22 121 | -24 305 | -28 254 | -33 401 | -37 624 | -46 138 | Services : débit |

| Country or area | 2000 | 2001 | 2002 | 2003 | 2004 | 2005 | 2006 | Pays ou zone |
|---|---|---|---|---|---|---|---|---|
| Income: credit | 11 883 | 10 737 | 9 265 | 11 180 | 12 784 | 24 928 | 27 463 | Revenus : crédit |
| Income: debit | -15 907 | -13 748 | -12 805 | -13 796 | -15 114 | -23 327 | -24 852 | Revenus : débit |
| Current transfers, n.i.e.: credit | 3 395 | 3 719 | 3 466 | 4 615 | 5 120 | 3 931 | 3 567 | Transferts courants, n.i.a. : crédit |
| Current transfers: debit | -6 410 | -6 291 | -6 489 | -8 151 | -9 279 | -8 078 | -8 073 | Transferts courants : débit |
| Capital account, n.i.e. | -11 | 14 | 152 | -7 | 13 | 307 | -44 | Compte de capital, n.i.a. |
| Financial account, n.i.e. | -3 311 | -5 712 | 3 819 | -5 129 | -19 023 | -10 222 | -9 226 | Compte financier, n.i.a. |
| Net errors and omissions | -4 460 | 4 167 | -1 887 | 2 846 | 11 644 | -2 844 | -4 057 | Erreurs et omissions nettes |
| Reserves and related items | 5 521 | -3 317 | -5 546 | -4 674 | 1 426 | 1 506 | 5 988 | Réserves et postes apparentés |
| **Djibouti** | | | | | | | | **Djibouti** |
| Current account | -71 | -38 | -17 | -34 | -68 | -55 | -99 | Compte des transactions courantes |
| Goods: exports f.o.b. | 32 | 32 | 36 | 37 | 38 | 40 | 55 | Biens : exportations f.à.b. |
| Goods: imports f.o.b. | -207 | -196 | -197 | -238 | -261 | -277 | -336 | Biens : importations f.à.b. |
| Services: credit | 162 | 182 | 192 | 216 | 213 | 248 | 257 | Services : crédit |
| Services: debit | -71 | -66 | -62 | -67 | -77 | -84 | -96 | Services : débit |
| Income: credit | 25 | 21 | 24 | 31 | 33 | 32 | 35 | Revenus : crédit |
| Income: debit | -9 | -9 | -9 | -10 | -11 | -11 | -12 | Revenus : débit |
| Current transfers, n.i.e.: credit | 1 | 1 | 1 | 3 | 3 | 3 | 4 | Transferts courants, n.i.a. : crédit |
| Current transfers: debit | -3 | -2 | -2 | -6 | -6 | -6 | -7 | Transferts courants : débit |
| Capital account, n.i.e. | 9 | 5 | 10 | -7 | 20 | 27 | 17 | Compte de capital, n.i.a. |
| Financial account, n.i.e. | 30 | -65 | -58 | -37 | -36 | -33 | 65 | Compte financier, n.i.a. |
| Net errors and omissions | -31 | 34 | 9 | 1 | -16 | -45 | -58 | Erreurs et omissions nettes |
| Reserves and related items | 63 | 64 | 56 | 77 | 100 | 107 | 75 | Réserves et postes apparentés |
| **Dominica** | | | | | | | | **Dominique** |
| Current account | -70 | -61 | -51 | -48 | -62 | -98 | ... | Compte des transactions courantes |
| Goods: exports f.o.b. | 55 | 44 | 44 | 41 | 43 | 43 | ... | Biens : exportations f.à.b. |
| Goods: imports f.o.b. | -130 | -116 | -102 | -105 | -128 | -146 | ... | Biens : importations f.à.b. |
| Services: credit | 90 | 77 | 80 | 77 | 88 | 83 | ... | Services : crédit |
| Services: debit | -53 | -50 | -54 | -44 | -46 | -52 | ... | Services : débit |
| Income: credit | 5 | 4 | 3 | 2 | 4 | 6 | ... | Revenus : crédit |
| Income: debit | -44 | -29 | -31 | -29 | -37 | -48 | ... | Revenus : débit |
| Current transfers, n.i.e.: credit | 15 | 16 | 17 | 17 | 22 | 24 | ... | Transferts courants, n.i.a. : crédit |
| Current transfers: debit | -7 | -7 | -7 | -8 | -6 | -9 | ... | Transferts courants : débit |
| Capital account, n.i.e. | 11 | 18 | 20 | 19 | 27 | 18 | ... | Compte de capital, n.i.a. |
| Financial account, n.i.e. | 55 | 30 | 20 | 22 | 16 | 76 | ... | Compte financier, n.i.a. |
| Net errors and omissions | -6 | 7 | 16 | 1 | 11 | 11 | ... | Erreurs et omissions nettes |
| Reserves and related items | 10 | 5 | -6 | 5 | 8 | -7 | ... | Réserves et postes apparentés |
| **Dominican Republic** | | | | | | | | **Rép. dominicaine** |
| Current account | -1 027 | -741 | -798 | 1 036 | 1 047 | -478 | -786 | Compte des transactions courantes |
| Goods: exports f.o.b. | 5 737 | 5 276 | 5 165 | 5 471 | 5 936 | 6 145 | 6 440 | Biens : exportations f.à.b. |
| Goods: imports f.o.b. | -9 479 | -8 779 | -8 838 | -7 627 | -7 888 | -9 869 | -11 190 | Biens : importations f.à.b. |
| Services: credit | 3 228 | 3 110 | 3 071 | 3 469 | 3 504 | 3 913 | 4 224 | Services : crédit |
| Services: debit | -1 373 | -1 284 | -1 314 | -1 219 | -1 213 | -1 467 | -1 558 | Services : débit |
| Income: credit | 300 | 271 | 300 | 341 | 336 | 418 | 557 | Revenus : crédit |
| Income: debit | -1 341 | -1 363 | -1 452 | -1 734 | -2 155 | -2 315 | -2 292 | Revenus : débit |
| Current transfers, n.i.e.: credit | 2 096 | 2 232 | 2 452 | 2 512 | 2 701 | 2 908 | 3 245 | Transferts courants, n.i.a. : crédit |
| Current transfers: debit | -193 | -205 | -183 | -176 | -174 | -211 | -212 | Transferts courants : débit |
| Capital account, n.i.e. | 0 | 0 | 0 | 0 | 0 | 0 | 0 | Compte de capital, n.i.a. |
| Financial account, n.i.e. | 1 597 | 1 707 | 383 | -16 | 117 | 1 563 | 1 556 | Compte financier, n.i.a. |
| Net errors and omissions | -618 | -452 | -139 | -1 568 | -987 | -379 | -500 | Erreurs et omissions nettes |
| Reserves and related items | 48 | -515 | 554 | 548 | -178 | -707 | -271 | Réserves et postes apparentés |
| **Ecuador** | | | | | | | | **Equateur** |
| Current account | 926 | -654 | -1 272 | -422 | -542 | 295 | 1 503 | Compte des transactions courantes |
| Goods: exports f.o.b. | 5 057 | 4 821 | 5 258 | 6 446 | 7 968 | 10 427 | 13 125 | Biens : exportations f.à.b. |
| Goods: imports f.o.b. | -3 657 | -5 178 | -6 160 | -6 366 | -7 684 | -9 695 | -11 396 | Biens : importations f.à.b. |
| Services: credit | 849 | 862 | 884 | 881 | 1 014 | 1 012 | 1 016 | Services : crédit |
| Services: debit | -1 269 | -1 434 | -1 600 | -1 624 | -1 968 | -2 142 | -2 341 | Services : débit |
| Income: credit | 70 | 48 | 30 | 27 | 37 | 86 | 165 | Revenus : crédit |
| Income: debit | -1 476 | -1 412 | -1 335 | -1 555 | -1 940 | -2 029 | -2 115 | Revenus : débit |
| Current transfers, n.i.e.: credit | 1 437 | 1 686 | 1 710 | 1 791 | 2 049 | 2 756 | 3 179 | Transferts courants, n.i.a. : crédit |

**62** Balance of payments summary—Millions of US dollars (*continued*)
Résumé de la balance des paiements—Millions de dollars E.-U (*suite*)

| Country or area | 2000 | 2001 | 2002 | 2003 | 2004 | 2005 | 2006 | Pays ou zone |
|---|---|---|---|---|---|---|---|---|
| Current transfers: debit | -85 | -47 | -58 | -22 | -18 | -120 | -130 | Transferts courants : débit |
| Capital account, n.i.e. | -1 | 15 | 16 | 8 | 8 | 13 | 14 | Compte de capital, n.i.a. |
| Financial account, n.i.e. | -6 360 | 626 | 1 193 | 322 | 244 | -515 | -2 015 | Compte financier, n.i.a. |
| Net errors and omissions | -262 | -301 | -157 | 163 | 681 | 477 | 424 | Erreurs et omissions nettes |
| Reserves and related items | 5 697 | 313 | 221 | -70 | -391 | -269 | 74 | Réserves et postes apparentés |
| **Egypt** | | | | | | | | **Egypte** |
| Current account | -971 | -388 | 622 | 3 743 | 3 922 | 2 103 | 2 635 | Compte des transactions courantes |
| Goods: exports f.o.b. | 7 061 | 7 025 | 7 118 | 8 987 | 12 320 | 16 073 | 20 546 | Biens : exportations f.à.b. |
| Goods: imports f.o.b. | -15 382 | -13 960 | -12 879 | -13 189 | -18 895 | -23 818 | -28 984 | Biens : importations f.à.b. |
| Services: credit | 9 803 | 9 042 | 9 320 | 11 073 | 14 197 | 14 643 | 16 135 | Services : crédit |
| Services: debit | -7 513 | -7 037 | -6 629 | -6 474 | -8 020 | -10 508 | -11 569 | Services : débit |
| Income: credit | 1 871 | 1 468 | 698 | 578 | 572 | 1 425 | 2 560 | Revenus : crédit |
| Income: debit | -983 | -885 | -965 | -832 | -818 | -1 460 | -1 822 | Revenus : débit |
| Current transfers, n.i.e.: credit | 4 224 | 4 056 | 4 002 | 3 708 | 4 615 | 5 831 | 5 933 | Transferts courants, n.i.a. : crédit |
| Current transfers: debit | -52 | -98 | -42 | -109 | -48 | -82 | -163 | Transferts courants : débit |
| Capital account, n.i.e. | 0 | 0 | 0 | 0 | 0 | -40 | -36 | Compte de capital, n.i.a. |
| Financial account, n.i.e. | -1 646 | 190 | -3 333 | -5 725 | -4 461 | 5 591 | -297 | Compte financier, n.i.a. |
| Net errors and omissions | 587 | -1 146 | 1 906 | 1 575 | -45 | -2 427 | 634 | Erreurs et omissions nettes |
| Reserves and related items | 2 030 | 1 345 | 804 | 407 | 584 | -5 226 | -2 937 | Réserves et postes apparentés |
| **El Salvador** | | | | | | | | **El Salvador** |
| Current account | -431 | -150 | -405 | -702 | -628 | -911 | -855 | Compte des transactions courantes |
| Goods: exports f.o.b. | 2 963 | 2 892 | 3 020 | 3 153 | 3 339 | 3 429 | 3 567 | Biens : exportations f.à.b. |
| Goods: imports f.o.b. | -4 703 | -4 824 | -4 885 | -5 439 | -6 000 | -6 534 | -7 257 | Biens : importations f.à.b. |
| Services: credit | 698 | 704 | 783 | 948 | 1 090 | 1 128 | 1 503 | Services : crédit |
| Services: debit | -933 | -954 | -1 023 | -1 055 | -1 154 | -1 210 | -1 484 | Services : débit |
| Income: credit | 141 | 169 | 159 | 140 | 144 | 183 | 238 | Revenus : crédit |
| Income: debit | -394 | -435 | -483 | -563 | -602 | -754 | -757 | Revenus : débit |
| Current transfers, n.i.e.: credit | 1 830 | 2 374 | 2 111 | 2 200 | 2 615 | 2 919 | 3 397 | Transferts courants, n.i.a. : crédit |
| Current transfers: debit | -33 | -75 | -88 | -86 | -60 | -71 | -62 | Transferts courants : débit |
| Capital account, n.i.e. | 109 | 199 | 209 | 113 | 100 | 94 | 96 | Compte de capital, n.i.a. |
| Financial account, n.i.e. | 288 | 230 | 688 | 1 049 | 123 | 811 | 1 018 | Compte financier, n.i.a. |
| Net errors and omissions | -12 | -457 | -615 | -143 | 352 | -52 | -187 | Erreurs et omissions nettes |
| Reserves and related items | 46 | 178 | 124 | -316 | 53 | 59 | -72 | Réserves et postes apparentés |
| **Eritrea** | | | | | | | | **Erythrée** |
| Current account | -105 | ... | ... | ... | ... | ... | ... | Compte des transactions courantes |
| Goods: exports f.o.b. | 37 | ... | ... | ... | ... | ... | ... | Biens : exportations f.à.b. |
| Goods: imports f.o.b. | -471 | ... | ... | ... | ... | ... | ... | Biens : importations f.à.b. |
| Services: credit | 61 | ... | ... | ... | ... | ... | ... | Services : crédit |
| Services: debit | -28 | ... | ... | ... | ... | ... | ... | Services : débit |
| Income: credit | 9 | ... | ... | ... | ... | ... | ... | Revenus : crédit |
| Income: debit | -11 | ... | ... | ... | ... | ... | ... | Revenus : débit |
| Current transfers, n.i.e.: credit | 306 | ... | ... | ... | ... | ... | ... | Transferts courants, n.i.a. : crédit |
| Current transfers: debit | -7 | ... | ... | ... | ... | ... | ... | Transferts courants : débit |
| Capital account, n.i.e. | 0 | ... | ... | ... | ... | ... | ... | Compte de capital, n.i.a. |
| Financial account, n.i.e. | 63 | ... | ... | ... | ... | ... | ... | Compte financier, n.i.a. |
| Net errors and omissions | -23 | ... | ... | ... | ... | ... | ... | Erreurs et omissions nettes |
| Reserves and related items | 64 | ... | ... | ... | ... | ... | ... | Réserves et postes apparentés |
| **Estonia** | | | | | | | | **Estonie** |
| Current account | -299 | -325 | -779 | -1 115 | -1 458 | -1 445 | -2 446 | Compte des transactions courantes |
| Goods: exports f.o.b. | 3 298 | 3 367 | 3 508 | 4 597 | 5 983 | 7 783 | 9 635 | Biens : exportations f.à.b. |
| Goods: imports f.o.b. | -4 080 | -4 142 | -4 626 | -6 164 | -8 002 | -9 628 | -12 374 | Biens : importations f.à.b. |
| Services: credit | 1 486 | 1 607 | 1 706 | 2 224 | 2 830 | 3 156 | 3 493 | Services : crédit |
| Services: debit | -886 | -963 | -1 106 | -1 393 | -1 756 | -2 156 | -2 460 | Services : débit |
| Income: credit | 119 | 173 | 205 | 249 | 436 | 669 | 979 | Revenus : crédit |
| Income: debit | -322 | -454 | -530 | -785 | -1 073 | -1 369 | -1 730 | Revenus : débit |
| Current transfers, n.i.e.: credit | 115 | 115 | 126 | 266 | 424 | 497 | 474 | Transferts courants, n.i.a. : crédit |
| Current transfers: debit | -29 | -29 | -61 | -110 | -300 | -398 | -463 | Transferts courants : débit |
| Capital account, n.i.e. | 26 | 14 | 38 | 50 | 93 | 140 | 412 | Compte de capital, n.i.a. |

**62** Balance of payments summary—Millions of US dollars (*continued*)
Résumé de la balance des paiements—Millions de dollars E.-U (*suite*)

| Country or area | 2000 | 2001 | 2002 | 2003 | 2004 | 2005 | 2006 | Pays ou zone |
|---|---|---|---|---|---|---|---|---|
| Financial account, n.i.e. | 393 | 269 | 752 | 1 275 | 1 622 | 1 702 | 2 732 | Compte financier, n.i.a. |
| Net errors and omissions | 8 | -1 | 59 | -39 | 14 | -11 | -78 | Erreurs et omissions nettes |
| Reserves and related items | -128 | 42 | -69 | -169 | -271 | -386 | -620 | Réserves et postes apparentés |
| **Ethiopia** | | | | | | | | **Ethiopie** |
| Current account | 13 | -373 | -137 | -136 | -668 | -1 568 | -1 786 | Compte des transactions courantes |
| Goods: exports f.o.b. | 486 | 456 | 480 | 496 | 678 | 917 | 1 025 | Biens : exportations f.à.b. |
| Goods: imports f.o.b. | -1 131 | -1 626 | -1 455 | -1 895 | -2 768 | -3 701 | -4 106 | Biens : importations f.à.b. |
| Services: credit | 506 | 523 | 585 | 762 | 1 005 | 1 012 | 1 174 | Services : crédit |
| Services: debit | -490 | -524 | -580 | -709 | -958 | -1 194 | -1 171 | Services : débit |
| Income: credit | 16 | 16 | 14 | 19 | 32 | 43 | 56 | Revenus : crédit |
| Income: debit | -52 | -48 | -37 | -43 | -60 | -48 | -38 | Revenus : débit |
| Current transfers, n.i.e.: credit | 698 | 854 | 876 | 1 267 | 1 421 | 1 426 | 1 297 | Transferts courants, n.i.a. : crédit |
| Current transfers: debit | -20 | -24 | -21 | -33 | -17 | -24 | -23 | Transferts courants : débit |
| Capital account, n.i.e. | 0 | 0 | 0 | 0 | 0 | 0 | 0 | Compte de capital, n.i.a. |
| Financial account, n.i.e. | 28 | -178 | -83 | 247 | 73 | 759 | 976 | Compte financier, n.i.a. |
| Net errors and omissions | -231 | -229 | -915 | -390 | -354 | 486 | 1 161 | Erreurs et omissions nettes |
| Reserves and related items | 190 | 781 | 1 134 | 280 | 949 | 323 | -352 | Réserves et postes apparentés |
| **Euro Area** | | | | | | | | **Zone euro** |
| Current account | -81 836 | #-19 745 | 54 782 | 38 775 | 79 764 | 12 561 | -12 488 | Compte des transactions courantes |
| Goods: exports f.o.b. | 907 876 | #920 862 | 998 201 | 1 172 750 | 1 406 250 | 1 523 290 | 1 753 860 | Biens : exportations f.à.b. |
| Goods: imports f.o.b. | -879 079 | #-855 641 | -876 731 | -1 053 440 | -1 276 970 | -1 461 120 | -1 721 780 | Biens : importations f.à.b. |
| Services: credit | 258 844 | #287 120 | 316 488 | 378 515 | 452 270 | 496 334 | 535 621 | Services : crédit |
| Services: debit | -278 424 | #-290 550 | -299 880 | -353 270 | -416 897 | -457 765 | -491 555 | Services : débit |
| Income: credit | 258 076 | #244 245 | 232 377 | 275 925 | 362 753 | 452 642 | 583 741 | Revenus : crédit |
| Income: debit | -299 568 | #-279 964 | -269 596 | -317 877 | -373 622 | -450 188 | -575 717 | Revenus : débit |
| Current transfers, n.i.e.: credit | 62 625 | #71 185 | 81 081 | 93 237 | 101 777 | 105 992 | 108 372 | Transferts courants, n.i.a. : crédit |
| Current transfers: debit | -112 186 | #-117 001 | -127 158 | -157 059 | -175 801 | -196 631 | -205 030 | Transferts courants : débit |
| Capital account, n.i.e. | 8 409 | #5 619 | 9 697 | 14 315 | 20 558 | 13 975 | 11 713 | Compte de capital, n.i.a. |
| Financial account, n.i.e. | 50 856 | #-41 164 | -16 937 | -49 001 | -38 966 | 8 798 | 143 807 | Compte financier, n.i.a. |
| Net errors and omissions | 6 420 | #38 841 | -44 566 | -36 892 | -76 915 | -58 246 | -140 470 | Erreurs et omissions nettes |
| Reserves and related items | 16 152 | #16 449 | -2 977 | 32 802 | 15 560 | 22 912 | -2 562 | Réserves et postes apparentés |
| **Faeroe Islands** | | | | | | | | **Iles Féroé** |
| Current account | 99 | 146 | 126 | -7 | ... | ... | ... | Compte des transactions courantes |
| Goods: exports f.o.b. | 477 | 516 | 537 | 594 | ... | ... | ... | Biens : exportations f.à.b. |
| Goods: imports f.o.b. | -515 | -479 | -472 | -684 | ... | ... | ... | Biens : importations f.à.b. |
| Services: credit | 54 | 57 | 71 | 78 | ... | ... | ... | Services : crédit |
| Services: debit | -97 | -105 | -132 | -147 | ... | ... | ... | Services : débit |
| Income: credit | 102 | 91 | 92 | 106 | ... | ... | ... | Revenus : crédit |
| Income: debit | -67 | -76 | -73 | -76 | ... | ... | ... | Revenus : débit |
| Current transfers, n.i.e.: credit | 148 | 147 | 109 | 128 | ... | ... | ... | Transferts courants, n.i.a. : crédit |
| Current transfers: debit | -2 | -4 | -7 | -6 | ... | ... | ... | Transferts courants : débit |
| Capital account, n.i.e. | 0 | 0 | 0 | 0 | ... | ... | ... | Compte de capital, n.i.a. |
| Financial account, n.i.e. | 0 | 0 | 0 | 0 | ... | ... | ... | Compte financier, n.i.a. |
| Net errors and omissions | 0 | 0 | 0 | 0 | ... | ... | ... | Erreurs et omissions nettes |
| Reserves and related items | 0 | 0 | 0 | 0 | ... | ... | ... | Réserves et postes apparentés |
| **Fiji** | | | | | | | | **Fidji** |
| Current account | -68 | -113 | -21 | -96 | -372 | -399 | -714 | Compte des transactions courantes |
| Goods: exports f.o.b. | 547 | 507 | 484 | 679 | 653 | 698 | 713 | Biens : exportations f.à.b. |
| Goods: imports f.o.b. | -774 | -777 | -800 | -1 064 | -1 286 | -1 462 | -1 640 | Biens : importations f.à.b. |
| Services: credit | 423 | 404 | 502 | 614 | 688 | 810 | 774 | Services : crédit |
| Services: debit | -333 | -297 | -290 | -397 | -486 | -525 | -542 | Services : débit |
| Income: credit | 53 | 67 | 72 | 92 | 145 | 80 | 66 | Revenus : crédit |
| Income: debit | -36 | -84 | -68 | -103 | -156 | -126 | -184 | Revenus : débit |
| Current transfers, n.i.e.: credit | 111 | 122 | 133 | 164 | 165 | 229 | 211 | Transferts courants, n.i.a. : crédit |
| Current transfers: debit | -59 | -55 | -55 | -81 | -96 | -102 | -111 | Transferts courants : débit |
| Capital account, n.i.e. | -29 | -10 | -10 | -6 | -12 | -18 | -6 | Compte de capital, n.i.a. |
| Financial account, n.i.e. | 13 | 41 | 91 | 27 | 158 | -39 | 201 | Compte financier, n.i.a. |
| Net errors and omissions | 112 | 98 | -90 | 10 | 308 | 305 | 370 | Erreurs et omissions nettes |
| Reserves and related items | -29 | -15 | 29 | 64 | -82 | 150 | 149 | Réserves et postes apparentés |

| Country or area | 2000 | 2001 | 2002 | 2003 | 2004 | 2005 | 2006 | Pays ou zone |
|---|---|---|---|---|---|---|---|---|
| Finland | | | | | | | | Finlande |
| Current account | 10 526 | 12 077 | 13 929 | 10 727 | 14 822 | 9 480 | 10 878 | Compte des transactions courantes |
| Goods: exports f.o.b. | 45 703 | 42 980 | 44 862 | 52 740 | 61 139 | 65 451 | 77 529 | Biens : exportations f.à.b. |
| Goods: imports f.o.b. | -32 019 | -30 321 | -32 022 | -39 792 | -48 369 | -55 887 | -66 352 | Biens : importations f.à.b. |
| Services: credit | 7 728 | 9 205 | 10 441 | 11 471 | 15 169 | 17 010 | 16 102 | Services : crédit |
| Services: debit | -8 440 | -8 105 | -8 073 | -10 007 | -12 284 | -15 202 | -15 604 | Services : débit |
| Income: credit | 7 265 | 8 568 | 8 606 | 9 349 | 13 129 | 14 406 | 18 275 | Revenus : crédit |
| Income: debit | -8 989 | -9 573 | -9 210 | -11 980 | -12 884 | -14 754 | -17 390 | Revenus : débit |
| Current transfers, n.i.e.: credit | 1 611 | 1 562 | 1 674 | 1 963 | 2 040 | 1 904 | 1 946 | Transferts courants, n.i.a. : crédit |
| Current transfers: debit | -2 334 | -2 239 | -2 350 | -3 018 | -3 118 | -3 448 | -3 628 | Transferts courants : débit |
| Capital account, n.i.e. | 103 | 83 | 125 | 150 | 188 | 336 | 223 | Compte de capital, n.i.a. |
| Financial account, n.i.e. | -8 841 | -10 942 | -7 312 | -11 978 | -9 476 | -4 347 | -15 609 | Compte financier, n.i.a. |
| Net errors and omissions | -1 438 | -808 | -6 857 | 594 | -4 719 | -5 649 | 188 | Erreurs et omissions nettes |
| Reserves and related items | -351 | -410 | 115 | 508 | -814 | 180 | 4 321 | Réserves et postes apparentés |
| France | | | | | | | | France |
| Current account | 22 307 | 26 191 | 19 703 | 14 757 | 10 425 | -19 522 | -28 315 | Compte des transactions courantes |
| Goods: exports f.o.b. | 297 557 | 294 181 | 307 201 | 361 930 | 421 106 | 439 899 | 483 112 | Biens : exportations f.à.b. |
| Goods: imports f.o.b. | -300 730 | -290 666 | -299 576 | -358 499 | -425 953 | -468 392 | -520 806 | Biens : importations f.à.b. |
| Services: credit | 80 489 | 80 125 | 86 160 | 98 814 | 112 706 | 118 762 | 118 478 | Services : crédit |
| Services: debit | -60 691 | -62 372 | -68 960 | -82 898 | -98 384 | -105 582 | -107 995 | Services : débit |
| Income: credit | 73 995 | 75 927 | 66 875 | 89 357 | 119 722 | 144 850 | 186 163 | Revenus : crédit |
| Income: debit | -54 542 | -56 357 | -57 507 | -74 489 | -97 080 | -121 764 | -159 712 | Revenus : débit |
| Current transfers, n.i.e.: credit | 17 340 | 17 180 | 19 767 | 24 050 | 25 443 | 25 443 | 26 956 | Transferts courants, n.i.a. : crédit |
| Current transfers: debit | -31 112 | -31 826 | -34 257 | -43 508 | -47 135 | -52 739 | -54 511 | Transferts courants : débit |
| Capital account, n.i.e. | 1 350 | -333 | -215 | -8 260 | 1 810 | 662 | -259 | Compte de capital, n.i.a. |
| Financial account, n.i.e. | -31 964 | -33 089 | -20 294 | 13 512 | -6 260 | -20 059 | 88 100 | Compte financier, n.i.a. |
| Net errors and omissions | 5 870 | 1 660 | -3 164 | -18 717 | -1 868 | 29 871 | -47 742 | Erreurs et omissions nettes |
| Reserves and related items | 2 437 | 5 570 | 3 970 | -1 291 | -4 108 | 9 047 | -11 783 | Réserves et postes apparentés |
| Gabon | | | | | | | | Gabon |
| Current account | 1 001 | 517 | 338 | 766 | 924 | ... | ... | Compte des transactions courantes |
| Goods: exports f.o.b. | 3 321 | 2 614 | 2 556 | 3 178 | 4 072 | ... | ... | Biens : exportations f.à.b. |
| Goods: imports f.o.b. | -798 | -847 | -935 | -1 043 | -1 216 | ... | ... | Biens : importations f.à.b. |
| Services: credit | 178 | 168 | 86 | 172 | 156 | ... | ... | Services : crédit |
| Services: debit | -858 | -710 | -759 | -840 | -939 | ... | ... | Services : débit |
| Income: credit | 48 | 30 | 18 | 48 | 13 | ... | ... | Revenus : crédit |
| Income: debit | -827 | -659 | -496 | -570 | -978 | ... | ... | Revenus : débit |
| Current transfers, n.i.e.: credit | 16 | 34 | 5 | 7 | 10 | ... | ... | Transferts courants, n.i.a. : crédit |
| Current transfers: debit | -79 | -113 | -136 | -188 | -194 | ... | ... | Transferts courants : débit |
| Capital account, n.i.e. | ^0 | 3 | 3 | 43 | 0 | ... | ... | Compte de capital, n.i.a. |
| Financial account, n.i.e. | -568 | -674 | -437 | -650 | -499 | ... | ... | Compte financier, n.i.a. |
| Net errors and omissions | -152 | -104 | -125 | -260 | -357 | ... | ... | Erreurs et omissions nettes |
| Reserves and related items | -280 | 258 | 222 | 101 | -68 | ... | ... | Réserves et postes apparentés |
| Gambia | | | | | | | | Gambie |
| Current account | ... | ... | ... | -2 | -44 | -50 | -72 | Compte des transactions courantes |
| Goods: exports f.o.b. | ... | ... | ... | 78 | 109 | 101 | 109 | Biens : exportations f.à.b. |
| Goods: imports f.o.b. | ... | ... | ... | -156 | -207 | -215 | -222 | Biens : importations f.à.b. |
| Services: credit | ... | ... | ... | 84 | 73 | 80 | 92 | Services : crédit |
| Services: debit | ... | ... | ... | -36 | -46 | -45 | -94 | Services : débit |
| Income: credit | ... | ... | ... | 5 | 2 | 3 | 4 | Revenus : crédit |
| Income: debit | ... | ... | ... | -32 | -30 | -35 | -42 | Revenus : débit |
| Current transfers, n.i.e.: credit | ... | ... | ... | 89 | 78 | 88 | 107 | Transferts courants, n.i.a. : crédit |
| Current transfers: debit | ... | ... | ... | -33 | -24 | -26 | -27 | Transferts courants : débit |
| Capital account, n.i.e. | ... | ... | ... | 5 | 5 | 1 | 0 | Compte de capital, n.i.a. |
| Financial account, n.i.e. | ... | ... | ... | -10 | 47 | 68 | 78 | Compte financier, n.i.a. |
| Net errors and omissions | ... | ... | ... | 3 | -9 | -54 | -6 | Erreurs et omissions nettes |
| Reserves and related items | ... | ... | ... | 5 | 1 | 36 | ^0 | Réserves et postes apparentés |
| Georgia | | | | | | | | Géorgie |
| Current account | -269 | -212 | -231 | -384 | -421 | -763 | -1 235 | Compte des transactions courantes |
| Goods: exports f.o.b. | 459 | 496 | 603 | 831 | 1 092 | 1 472 | 1 667 | Biens : exportations f.à.b. |

| Country or area | 2000 | 2001 | 2002 | 2003 | 2004 | 2005 | 2006 | Pays ou zone |
|---|---|---|---|---|---|---|---|---|
| Goods: imports f.o.b. | -971 | -1 046 | -1 092 | -1 469 | -2 008 | -2 687 | -3 686 | Biens : importations f.à.b. |
| Services: credit | 206 | 314 | 406 | 456 | 552 | 711 | 901 | Services : crédit |
| Services: debit | -216 | -237 | -363 | -397 | -485 | -632 | -727 | Services : débit |
| Income: credit | 179 | 98 | 161 | 177 | 252 | 263 | 339 | Revenus : crédit |
| Income: debit | -61 | -65 | -138 | -154 | -162 | -188 | -171 | Revenus : débit |
| Current transfers, n.i.e.: credit | 163 | 246 | 222 | 208 | 389 | 351 | 504 | Transferts courants, n.i.a. : crédit |
| Current transfers: debit | -28 | -18 | -29 | -36 | -51 | -54 | -63 | Transferts courants : débit |
| Capital account, n.i.e. | -5 | -5 | 18 | 20 | 41 | 59 | 169 | Compte de capital, n.i.a. |
| Financial account, n.i.e. | 93 | 210 | 14 | 314 | 446 | 666 | 1 339 | Compte financier, n.i.a. |
| Net errors and omissions | 187 | 35 | 7 | -14 | 1 | 19 | 58 | Erreurs et omissions nettes |
| Reserves and related items | -6 | -28 | 191 | 64 | -68 | 19 | -331 | Réserves et postes apparentés |
| **Germany** | | | | | | | | **Allemagne** |
| Current account | -31 955 | 482 | 40 710 | 49 170 | 120 325 | 131 811 | 150 745 | Compte des transactions courantes |
| Goods: exports f.o.b. | 543 285 | 563 670 | 609 779 | 744 806 | 903 447 | 978 181 | 1 131 300 | Biens : exportations f.à.b. |
| Goods: imports f.o.b. | -487 821 | -476 256 | -484 024 | -600 061 | -718 051 | -789 773 | -934 088 | Biens : importations f.à.b. |
| Services: credit | 83 150 | 88 714 | 103 144 | 122 560 | 144 345 | 155 894 | 173 115 | Services : crédit |
| Services: debit | -137 254 | -141 916 | -145 158 | -169 162 | -191 257 | -202 684 | -215 020 | Services : débit |
| Income: credit | 106 635 | 91 209 | 97 983 | 118 531 | 164 443 | 192 808 | 236 026 | Revenus : crédit |
| Income: debit | -114 297 | -100 956 | -115 005 | -135 518 | -148 016 | -167 120 | -207 221 | Revenus : débit |
| Current transfers, n.i.e.: credit | 15 348 | 15 337 | 15 923 | 18 983 | 20 172 | 22 149 | 25 152 | Transferts courants, n.i.a. : crédit |
| Current transfers: debit | -41 002 | -39 319 | -41 933 | -50 970 | -54 757 | -57 644 | -58 522 | Transferts courants : débit |
| Capital account, n.i.e. | 6 188 | -327 | -225 | 353 | 513 | -1 691 | -260 | Compte de capital, n.i.a. |
| Financial account, n.i.e. | 28 987 | -16 131 | -40 754 | -71 601 | -146 895 | -151 165 | -179 844 | Compte financier, n.i.a. |
| Net errors and omissions | -8 442 | 10 509 | -1 709 | 21 394 | 24 249 | 18 443 | 25 707 | Erreurs et omissions nettes |
| Reserves and related items | 5 222 | 5 466 | 1 979 | 684 | 1 807 | 2 601 | 3 652 | Réserves et postes apparentés |
| **Ghana** | | | | | | | | **Ghana** |
| Current account | -487 | -428 | -105 | 124 | -567 | -1 105 | -1 040 | Compte des transactions courantes |
| Goods: exports f.o.b. | 1 936 | 1 867 | 2 015 | 2 562 | 2 704 | 2 802 | 3 727 | Biens : exportations f.à.b. |
| Goods: imports f.o.b. | -2 767 | -2 969 | -2 707 | -3 233 | -4 297 | -5 347 | -6 754 | Biens : importations f.à.b. |
| Services: credit | 504 | 532 | 555 | 630 | 702 | 1 106 | 1 399 | Services : crédit |
| Services: debit | -584 | -606 | -621 | -900 | -1 058 | -1 273 | -1 533 | Services : débit |
| Income: credit | 16 | 16 | 15 | 21 | 45 | 43 | 73 | Revenus : crédit |
| Income: debit | -123 | -124 | -189 | -202 | -242 | -230 | -201 | Revenus : débit |
| Current transfers, n.i.e.: credit | 548 | 875 | 839 | 1 254 | 1 580 | 1 794 | 2 248 | Transferts courants, n.i.a. : crédit |
| Current transfers: debit | -18 | -19 | -12 | -9 | 0 | 0 | 0 | Transferts courants : débit |
| Capital account, n.i.e. | 101 | 103 | 73 | 154 | 251 | 331 | 230 | Compte de capital, n.i.a. |
| Financial account, n.i.e. | 369 | 392 | -39 | 340 | 202 | 834 | 1 053 | Compte financier, n.i.a. |
| Net errors and omissions | -97 | -60 | 57 | -47 | 115 | 26 | 174 | Erreurs et omissions nettes |
| Reserves and related items | 114 | -8 | 14 | -571 | -1 | -87 | -417 | Réserves et postes apparentés |
| **Greece** | | | | | | | | **Grèce** |
| Current account | -9 820 | -9 400 | -9 582 | -12 804 | -13 476 | -18 233 | -29 565 | Compte des transactions courantes |
| Goods: exports f.o.b. | 10 202 | 10 615 | 9 865 | 12 578 | 15 739 | 17 631 | 20 300 | Biens : exportations f.à.b. |
| Goods: imports f.o.b. | -30 440 | -29 702 | -31 321 | -38 184 | -47 360 | -51 900 | -64 585 | Biens : importations f.à.b. |
| Services: credit | 19 239 | 19 456 | 20 142 | 24 283 | 33 085 | 33 914 | 35 762 | Services : crédit |
| Services: debit | -11 286 | -11 589 | -9 819 | -11 250 | -14 020 | -14 742 | -16 367 | Services : débit |
| Income: credit | 2 807 | 1 885 | 1 532 | 2 911 | 3 495 | 4 072 | 4 566 | Revenus : crédit |
| Income: debit | -3 692 | -3 652 | -3 488 | -7 414 | -8 920 | -11 102 | -13 524 | Revenus : débit |
| Current transfers, n.i.e.: credit | 4 116 | 4 592 | 5 536 | 7 202 | 7 901 | 8 615 | 8 587 | Transferts courants, n.i.a. : crédit |
| Current transfers: debit | -764 | -1 005 | -2 029 | -2 930 | -3 396 | -4 722 | -4 305 | Transferts courants : débit |
| Capital account, n.i.e. | 2 112 | 2 153 | 1 530 | 1 411 | 2 990 | 2 563 | 3 822 | Compte de capital, n.i.a. |
| Financial account, n.i.e. | 10 830 | 537 | 11 578 | 6 417 | 6 836 | 15 633 | 25 661 | Compte financier, n.i.a. |
| Net errors and omissions | -550 | 1 011 | -1 663 | 253 | 373 | -67 | 361 | Erreurs et omissions nettes |
| Reserves and related items | -2 573 | 5 699 | -1 863 | 4 723 | 3 277 | 104 | -279 | Réserves et postes apparentés |
| **Grenada** | | | | | | | | **Grenade** |
| Current account | -88 | -105 | -126 | -144 | -64 | -187 | ... | Compte des transactions courantes |
| Goods: exports f.o.b. | 83 | 64 | 41 | 46 | 38 | 33 | ... | Biens : exportations f.à.b. |
| Goods: imports f.o.b. | -221 | -197 | -181 | -226 | -236 | -288 | ... | Biens : importations f.à.b. |
| Services: credit | 153 | 133 | 131 | 134 | 157 | 117 | ... | Services : crédit |
| Services: debit | -89 | -85 | -91 | -83 | -93 | -93 | ... | Services : débit |

| Country or area | 2000 | 2001 | 2002 | 2003 | 2004 | 2005 | 2006 | Pays ou zone |
|---|---|---|---|---|---|---|---|---|
| Income: credit | 5 | 4 | 4 | 4 | 6 | 11 | ... | Revenus : crédit |
| Income: debit | -39 | -45 | -52 | -54 | -56 | -46 | ... | Revenus : débit |
| Current transfers, n.i.e.: credit | 30 | 31 | 32 | 48 | 126 | 84 | ... | Transferts courants, n.i.a. : crédit |
| Current transfers: debit | -10 | -9 | -10 | -12 | -5 | -5 | ... | Transferts courants : débit |
| Capital account, n.i.e. | 32 | 43 | 32 | 43 | 40 | 54 | ... | Compte de capital, n.i.a. |
| Financial account, n.i.e. | 64 | 47 | 100 | 90 | 58 | 120 | ... | Compte financier, n.i.a. |
| Net errors and omissions | -1 | 21 | 24 | -6 | 8 | -14 | ... | Erreurs et omissions nettes |
| Reserves and related items | -7 | -6 | -31 | 17 | -42 | 27 | ... | Réserves et postes apparentés |
| Guatemala | | | | | | | | Guatemala |
| Current account | -1 050 | -1 253 | -1 235 | -1 039 | -1 211 | -1 432 | -1 592 | Compte des transactions courantes |
| Goods: exports f.o.b. | 3 085 | 2 860 | 2 819 | 3 060 | 3 368 | 5 381 | 6 025 | Biens : exportations f.à.b. |
| Goods: imports f.o.b. | -4 742 | -5 142 | -5 791 | -6 176 | -7 175 | -9 755 | -11 069 | Biens : importations f.à.b. |
| Services: credit | 777 | 1 045 | 1 145 | 1 059 | 1 178 | 1 230 | 1 395 | Services : crédit |
| Services: debit | -825 | -928 | -1 066 | -1 126 | -1 308 | -1 479 | -1 681 | Services : débit |
| Income: credit | 214 | 317 | 161 | 179 | 173 | 253 | 355 | Revenus : crédit |
| Income: debit | -424 | -402 | -479 | -497 | -492 | -585 | -734 | Revenus : débit |
| Current transfers, n.i.e.: credit | 908 | 1 024 | 2 078 | 2 559 | 3 088 | 3 570 | 4 182 | Transferts courants, n.i.a. : crédit |
| Current transfers: debit | -43 | -28 | -101 | -97 | -43 | -47 | -65 | Transferts courants : débit |
| Capital account, n.i.e. | 86 | 93 | 124 | 134 | 135 | 113 | 259 | Compte de capital, n.i.a. |
| Financial account, n.i.e. | 1 521 | 1 547 | 1 197 | 1 516 | 1 709 | 1 487 | 1 699 | Compte financier, n.i.a. |
| Net errors and omissions | 86 | 87 | -65 | -61 | -25 | 87 | -88 | Erreurs et omissions nettes |
| Reserves and related items | -643 | -474 | -21 | -550 | -608 | -255 | -278 | Réserves et postes apparentés |
| Guinea | | | | | | | | Guinée |
| Current account | -155 | -102 | -200 | -188 | -175 | ... | ... | Compte des transactions courantes |
| Goods: exports f.o.b. | 666 | 731 | 709 | 609 | 726 | ... | ... | Biens : exportations f.à.b. |
| Goods: imports f.o.b. | -587 | -562 | -669 | -644 | -688 | ... | ... | Biens : importations f.à.b. |
| Services: credit | 68 | 103 | 90 | 134 | 85 | ... | ... | Services : crédit |
| Services: debit | -285 | -319 | -331 | -307 | -275 | ... | ... | Services : débit |
| Income: credit | 23 | 11 | 6 | 13 | 10 | ... | ... | Revenus : crédit |
| Income: debit | -101 | -114 | -52 | -124 | -37 | ... | ... | Revenus : débit |
| Current transfers, n.i.e.: credit | 89 | 92 | 71 | 195 | 55 | ... | ... | Transferts courants, n.i.a. : crédit |
| Current transfers: debit | -29 | -44 | -25 | -62 | -50 | ... | ... | Transferts courants : débit |
| Capital account, n.i.e. | 0 | 0 | 92 | 58 | -30 | ... | ... | Compte de capital, n.i.a. |
| Financial account, n.i.e. | 8 | -12 | -115 | 59 | 78 | ... | ... | Compte financier, n.i.a. |
| Net errors and omissions | 84 | -2 | 143 | -157 | 69 | ... | ... | Erreurs et omissions nettes |
| Reserves and related items | 63 | 117 | 80 | 229 | 59 | ... | ... | Réserves et postes apparentés |
| Guinea-Bissau | | | | | | | | Guinée-Bissau |
| Current account | ... | -27 | -9 | -7 | -13 | ... | ... | Compte des transactions courantes |
| Goods: exports f.o.b. | ... | 63 | 54 | 65 | 76 | ... | ... | Biens : exportations f.à.b. |
| Goods: imports f.o.b. | ... | -62 | -59 | -65 | -83 | ... | ... | Biens : importations f.à.b. |
| Services: credit | ... | 4 | 6 | 6 | 8 | ... | ... | Services : crédit |
| Services: debit | ... | -30 | -27 | -36 | -44 | ... | ... | Services : débit |
| Income: credit | ... | 1 | 1 | 2 | 1 | ... | ... | Revenus : crédit |
| Income: debit | ... | -13 | -10 | -11 | -11 | ... | ... | Revenus : débit |
| Current transfers, n.i.e.: credit | ... | 10 | 30 | 40 | 47 | ... | ... | Transferts courants, n.i.a. : crédit |
| Current transfers: debit | ... | ^0 | -5 | -7 | -7 | ... | ... | Transferts courants : débit |
| Capital account, n.i.e. | ... | 25 | 39 | 43 | 27 | ... | ... | Compte de capital, n.i.a. |
| Financial account, n.i.e. | ... | -17 | -21 | -13 | 1 | ... | ... | Compte financier, n.i.a. |
| Net errors and omissions | ... | 6 | -3 | 6 | -4 | ... | ... | Erreurs et omissions nettes |
| Reserves and related items | ... | 13 | -6 | -29 | -11 | ... | ... | Réserves et postes apparentés |
| Guyana | | | | | | | | Guyane |
| Current account | -82 | -91 | -62 | -45 | -20 | -96 | -112 | Compte des transactions courantes |
| Goods: exports f.o.b. | 503 | 485 | 490 | 508 | 584 | 546 | 595 | Biens : exportations f.à.b. |
| Goods: imports f.o.b. | -550 | -541 | -514 | -525 | -592 | -717 | -792 | Biens : importations f.à.b. |
| Services: credit | 169 | 172 | 172 | 157 | 161 | 148 | 148 | Services : crédit |
| Services: debit | -193 | -192 | -196 | -172 | -208 | -201 | -218 | Services : débit |
| Income: credit | 12 | 10 | 8 | 5 | 4 | 3 | 3 | Revenus : crédit |
| Income: debit | -70 | -69 | -63 | -60 | -43 | -42 | -46 | Revenus : débit |
| Current transfers, n.i.e.: credit | 101 | 98 | 129 | 127 | 194 | 262 | 294 | Transferts courants, n.i.a. : crédit |

| Country or area | 2000 | 2001 | 2002 | 2003 | 2004 | 2005 | 2006 | Pays ou zone |
|---|---|---|---|---|---|---|---|---|
| Current transfers: debit | -54 | -54 | -89 | -84 | -120 | -95 | -95 | Transferts courants : débit |
| Capital account, n.i.e. | 16 | 32 | 31 | 44 | 46 | 52 | 351 | Compte de capital, n.i.a. |
| Financial account, n.i.e. | 111 | 84 | 54 | 35 | 39 | 127 | -80 | Compte financier, n.i.a. |
| Net errors and omissions | -4 | -45 | -1 | -20 | -43 | -68 | -119 | Erreurs et omissions nettes |
| Reserves and related items | -40 | 19 | -22 | -14 | -21 | -14 | -40 | Réserves et postes apparentés |
| **Haiti** | | | | | | | | **Haïti** |
| Current account | -114 | -132 | -189 | -182 | -156 | -274 | -379 | Compte des transactions courantes |
| Goods: exports f.o.b. | 332 | 305 | 274 | 334 | 377 | 459 | 494 | Biens : exportations f.à.b. |
| Goods: imports f.o.b. | -1 087 | -1 055 | -980 | -1 116 | -1 210 | -1 308 | -1 548 | Biens : importations f.à.b. |
| Services: credit | 172 | 139 | 147 | 136 | 133 | 138 | 204 | Services : crédit |
| Services: debit | -282 | -260 | -270 | -301 | -336 | -452 | -538 | Services : débit |
| Income: credit | 0 | 0 | 0 | 0 | 0 | 2 | 19 | Revenus : crédit |
| Income: debit | -9 | -9 | -14 | -14 | -12 | -39 | -12 | Revenus : débit |
| Current transfers, n.i.e.: credit | 771 | 769 | 676 | 811 | 932 | 985 | 1 070 | Transferts courants, n.i.a. : crédit |
| Current transfers: debit | -11 | -19 | -22 | -31 | -39 | -59 | -68 | Transferts courants : débit |
| Capital account, n.i.e. | 0 | 0 | 0 | 0 | 0 | 0 | 0 | Compte de capital, n.i.a. |
| Financial account, n.i.e. | -16 | 82 | -33 | -129 | 24 | -86 | 61 | Compte financier, n.i.a. |
| Net errors and omissions | 73 | 44 | 41 | 121 | 48 | -59 | -42 | Erreurs et omissions nettes |
| Reserves and related items | 57 | 5 | 181 | 190 | 83 | 418 | 360 | Réserves et postes apparentés |
| **Honduras** | | | | | | | | **Honduras** |
| Current account | -273 | -339 | -260 | -304 | -478 | -132 | -195 | Compte des transactions courantes |
| Goods: exports f.o.b. | 2 012 | 1 935 | 1 977 | 2 090 | 2 421 | 2 749 | 3 043 | Biens : exportations f.à.b. |
| Goods: imports f.o.b. | -2 680 | -2 769 | -2 806 | -3 035 | -3 677 | -4 239 | -5 037 | Biens : importations f.à.b. |
| Services: credit | 479 | 487 | 530 | 589 | 683 | 744 | 753 | Services : crédit |
| Services: debit | -597 | -627 | -617 | -686 | -784 | -875 | -1 019 | Services : débit |
| Income: credit | 118 | 92 | 58 | 47 | 51 | 105 | 178 | Revenus : crédit |
| Income: debit | -252 | -262 | -251 | -305 | -410 | -445 | -465 | Revenus : débit |
| Current transfers, n.i.e.: credit | 718 | 894 | 947 | 1 085 | 1 369 | 1 985 | 2 531 | Transferts courants, n.i.a. : crédit |
| Current transfers: debit | -70 | -90 | -99 | -89 | -130 | -155 | -180 | Transferts courants : débit |
| Capital account, n.i.e. | 30 | 37 | 24 | 22 | 22 | 582 | 1 467 | Compte de capital, n.i.a. |
| Financial account, n.i.e. | -29 | 124 | 157 | 139 | 786 | -192 | -879 | Compte financier, n.i.a. |
| Net errors and omissions | 115 | 105 | 61 | -55 | 42 | -53 | -93 | Erreurs et omissions nettes |
| Reserves and related items | 157 | 74 | 19 | 198 | -373 | -206 | -301 | Réserves et postes apparentés |
| **Hungary** | | | | | | | | **Hongrie** |
| Current account | -4 004 | -3 205 | -4 693 | -6 721 | -8 561 | -7 463 | -7 421 | Compte des transactions courantes |
| Goods: exports f.o.b. | 28 762 | 31 081 | 34 792 | 42 943 | 55 689 | 62 245 | 74 348 | Biens : exportations f.à.b. |
| Goods: imports f.o.b. | -31 675 | -33 318 | -36 911 | -46 221 | -58 695 | -64 077 | -75 494 | Biens : importations f.à.b. |
| Services: credit | 5 901 | 7 029 | 7 417 | 9 211 | 10 890 | 12 778 | 13 295 | Services : crédit |
| Services: debit | -4 775 | -5 550 | -6 849 | -9 150 | -10 605 | -11 466 | -11 674 | Services : débit |
| Income: credit | 1 165 | 1 302 | 1 236 | 1 371 | 1 877 | 1 931 | 5 567 | Revenus : crédit |
| Income: debit | -3 740 | -4 152 | -4 870 | -5 541 | -8 013 | -9 089 | -13 911 | Revenus : débit |
| Current transfers, n.i.e.: credit | 674 | 781 | 1 070 | 1 283 | 1 633 | 2 592 | 3 117 | Transferts courants, n.i.a. : crédit |
| Current transfers: debit | -316 | -377 | -579 | -616 | -1 338 | -2 377 | -2 668 | Transferts courants : débit |
| Capital account, n.i.e. | 270 | 317 | 191 | -27 | 328 | 885 | 732 | Compte de capital, n.i.a. |
| Financial account, n.i.e. | 4 960 | 2 775 | 2 565 | 6 858 | 11 988 | 14 529 | 12 103 | Compte financier, n.i.a. |
| Net errors and omissions | -174 | 29 | 145 | 226 | -1 773 | -3 047 | -4 311 | Erreurs et omissions nettes |
| Reserves and related items | -1 052 | 84 | 1 792 | -336 | -1 981 | -4 904 | -1 102 | Réserves et postes apparentés |
| **Iceland** | | | | | | | | **Islande** |
| Current account | -847 | -336 | 145 | -534 | -1 317 | -2 645 | -4 234 | Compte des transactions courantes |
| Goods: exports f.o.b. | 1 902 | 2 016 | 2 240 | 2 386 | 2 896 | 3 107 | 3 477 | Biens : exportations f.à.b. |
| Goods: imports f.o.b. | -2 376 | -2 091 | -2 090 | -2 596 | -3 415 | -4 590 | -5 716 | Biens : importations f.à.b. |
| Services: credit | 1 044 | 1 086 | 1 118 | 1 378 | 1 623 | 2 041 | 1 834 | Services : crédit |
| Services: debit | -1 164 | -1 074 | -1 123 | -1 503 | -1 838 | -2 560 | -2 553 | Services : débit |
| Income: credit | 147 | 171 | 305 | 376 | 470 | 1 456 | 2 587 | Revenus : crédit |
| Income: debit | -390 | -435 | -318 | -559 | -1 035 | -2 072 | -3 827 | Revenus : débit |
| Current transfers, n.i.e.: credit | 6 | 8 | 36 | 12 | 10 | 11 | 8 | Transferts courants, n.i.a. : crédit |
| Current transfers: debit | -16 | -17 | -22 | -28 | -27 | -38 | -42 | Transferts courants : débit |
| Capital account, n.i.e. | -3 | 4 | -1 | -5 | -3 | -27 | -26 | Compte de capital, n.i.a. |
| Financial account, n.i.e. | 846 | 172 | -64 | 444 | 1 925 | 2 354 | 7 417 | Compte financier, n.i.a. |

| Country or area | 2000 | 2001 | 2002 | 2003 | 2004 | 2005 | 2006 | Pays ou zone |
|---|---|---|---|---|---|---|---|---|
| Net errors and omissions | -70 | 111 | -19 | 401 | -404 | 389 | -1 906 | Erreurs et omissions nettes |
| Reserves and related items | 74 | 48 | -61 | -307 | -202 | -71 | -1 252 | Réserves et postes apparentés |
| **India** | | | | | | | | **Inde** |
| Current account | -4 601 | 1 410 | 7 060 | 8 773 | 780 | -7 835 | -9 415 | Compte des transactions courantes |
|    Goods: exports f.o.b. | 43 247 | 44 793 | 51 141 | 60 893 | 77 939 | 102 176 | 123 617 | Biens : exportations f.à.b. |
|    Goods: imports f.o.b. | -53 887 | -51 212 | -54 702 | -68 081 | -95 539 | -134 702 | -166 695 | Biens : importations f.à.b. |
|    Services: credit | 16 684 | 17 337 | 19 478 | 23 902 | 38 281 | 55 831 | 75 354 | Services : crédit |
|    Services: debit | -19 187 | -20 099 | -21 039 | -24 878 | -35 641 | -47 989 | -63 537 | Services : débit |
|    Income: credit | 2 521 | 3 524 | 3 188 | 3 491 | 4 690 | 5 082 | 7 795 | Revenus : crédit |
|    Income: debit | -7 414 | -7 666 | -7 097 | -8 386 | -8 742 | -11 475 | -12 059 | Revenus : débit |
|    Current transfers, n.i.e.: credit | 13 548 | 15 140 | 16 789 | 22 401 | 20 615 | 24 120 | 27 449 | Transferts courants, n.i.a. : crédit |
|    Current transfers: debit | -114 | -407 | -698 | -570 | -822 | -877 | -1 340 | Transferts courants : débit |
| Capital account, n.i.e. | 716 | 0 | 0 | 0 | 0 | 0 | 0 | Compte de capital, n.i.a. |
| Financial account, n.i.e. | 9 623 | 7 995 | 11 985 | 16 421 | 22 229 | 21 622 | 37 776 | Compte financier, n.i.a. |
| Net errors and omissions | 331 | -715 | -190 | 471 | 637 | 769 | -4 623 | Erreurs et omissions nettes |
| Reserves and related items | -6 069 | -8 690 | -18 854 | -25 665 | -23 646 | -14 555 | -23 737 | Réserves et postes apparentés |
| **Indonesia** | | | | | | | | **Indonésie** |
| Current account | 7 992 | 6 901 | 7 824 | 8 107 | 1 563 | 278 | 9 937 | Compte des transactions courantes |
|    Goods: exports f.o.b. | 65 407 | 57 365 | 59 165 | 64 109 | 70 767 | 86 995 | 103 514 | Biens : exportations f.à.b. |
|    Goods: imports f.o.b. | -40 365 | -34 669 | -35 652 | -39 546 | -50 615 | -69 462 | -73 868 | Biens : importations f.à.b. |
|    Services: credit | 5 214 | 5 500 | 6 663 | 5 293 | 12 045 | 12 927 | 11 518 | Services : crédit |
|    Services: debit | -15 637 | -15 880 | -17 045 | -17 400 | -20 856 | -22 049 | -21 625 | Services : débit |
|    Income: credit | 2 458 | 2 004 | 1 318 | 1 054 | 1 995 | 2 338 | 2 577 | Revenus : crédit |
|    Income: debit | -10 901 | -8 940 | -8 365 | -7 272 | -12 912 | -15 264 | -17 042 | Revenus : débit |
|    Current transfers, n.i.e.: credit | 1 816 | 1 520 | 2 210 | 2 053 | 2 433 | 5 993 | 6 079 | Transferts courants, n.i.a. : crédit |
|    Current transfers: debit | 0 | 0 | -470 | -184 | -1 294 | -1 200 | -1 216 | Transferts courants : débit |
| Capital account, n.i.e. | 0 | 0 | 0 | 0 | 0 | 334 | 350 | Compte de capital, n.i.a. |
| Financial account, n.i.e. | -7 896 | -7 617 | -1 103 | -949 | -667 | -2 587 | -1 378 | Compte financier, n.i.a. |
| Net errors and omissions | 3 829 | 701 | -1 763 | -3 510 | -3 094 | -136 | 2 460 | Erreurs et omissions nettes |
| Reserves and related items | -3 926 | 15 | -4 958 | -3 647 | 2 198 | 2 111 | -11 370 | Réserves et postes apparentés |
| **Iran (Islamic Rep. of)** | | | | | | | | **Iran (Rép. islamique d')** |
| Current account | 12 481 | ... | ... | ... | ... | ... | ... | Compte des transactions courantes |
|    Goods: exports f.o.b. | 28 345 | ... | ... | ... | ... | ... | ... | Biens : exportations f.à.b. |
|    Goods: imports f.o.b. | -15 207 | ... | ... | ... | ... | ... | ... | Biens : importations f.à.b. |
|    Services: credit | 1 382 | ... | ... | ... | ... | ... | ... | Services : crédit |
|    Services: debit | -2 296 | ... | ... | ... | ... | ... | ... | Services : débit |
|    Income: credit | 404 | ... | ... | ... | ... | ... | ... | Revenus : crédit |
|    Income: debit | -604 | ... | ... | ... | ... | ... | ... | Revenus : débit |
|    Current transfers, n.i.e.: credit | 539 | ... | ... | ... | ... | ... | ... | Transferts courants, n.i.a. : crédit |
|    Current transfers: debit | -82 | ... | ... | ... | ... | ... | ... | Transferts courants : débit |
| Capital account, n.i.e. | 0 | ... | ... | ... | ... | ... | ... | Compte de capital, n.i.a. |
| Financial account, n.i.e. | -10 189 | ... | ... | ... | ... | ... | ... | Compte financier, n.i.a. |
| Net errors and omissions | -1 209 | ... | ... | ... | ... | ... | ... | Erreurs et omissions nettes |
| Reserves and related items | -1 083 | ... | ... | ... | ... | ... | ... | Réserves et postes apparentés |
| **Ireland** | | | | | | | | **Irlande** |
| Current account | -516 | -690 | -1 101 | 89 | -1 081 | -7 150 | -9 095 | Compte des transactions courantes |
|    Goods: exports f.o.b. | 73 530 | 77 623 | 84 216 | 88 590 | 100 116 | 102 825 | 104 667 | Biens : exportations f.à.b. |
|    Goods: imports f.o.b. | -48 520 | -50 360 | -50 769 | -51 709 | -61 102 | -67 730 | -72 779 | Biens : importations f.à.b. |
|    Services: credit | 18 538 | 23 465 | 29 901 | 42 061 | 52 718 | 59 920 | 69 191 | Services : crédit |
|    Services: debit | -31 272 | -35 339 | -42 829 | -54 597 | -65 384 | -71 437 | -78 528 | Services : débit |
|    Income: credit | 27 613 | 28 850 | 27 200 | 34 095 | 43 457 | 53 862 | 75 321 | Revenus : crédit |
|    Income: debit | -41 160 | -45 202 | -49 515 | -58 879 | -71 388 | -84 876 | -106 422 | Revenus : débit |
|    Current transfers, n.i.e.: credit | 4 143 | 7 400 | 7 538 | 7 027 | 6 626 | 6 963 | 6 648 | Transferts courants, n.i.a. : crédit |
|    Current transfers: debit | -3 388 | -7 128 | -6 842 | -6 500 | -6 123 | -6 679 | -7 192 | Transferts courants : débit |
| Capital account, n.i.e. | 1 074 | 635 | 512 | 126 | 368 | 323 | 283 | Compte de capital, n.i.a. |
| Financial account, n.i.e. | 7 912 | 16 | 468 | -3 481 | 3 301 | -2 501 | 10 732 | Compte financier, n.i.a. |
| Net errors and omissions | -8 509 | 434 | -171 | 1 375 | -4 023 | 7 552 | -2 032 | Erreurs et omissions nettes |
| Reserves and related items | 39 | -395 | 292 | 1 890 | 1 435 | 1 776 | 112 | Réserves et postes apparentés |

| Country or area | 2000 | 2001 | 2002 | 2003 | 2004 | 2005 | 2006 | Pays ou zone |
|---|---|---|---|---|---|---|---|---|
| Israel | | | | | | | | Israël |
| Current account | -980 | -1 262 | -875 | 1 440 | 2 980 | 4 334 | 7 990 | Compte des transactions courantes |
| Goods: exports f.o.b. | 31 188 | 27 967 | 27 535 | 30 187 | 36 658 | 40 101 | 43 725 | Biens : exportations f.à.b. |
| Goods: imports f.o.b. | -34 728 | -31 714 | -31 971 | -33 294 | -39 488 | -43 868 | -46 958 | Biens : importations f.à.b. |
| Services: credit | 15 082 | 12 552 | 11 898 | 13 394 | 16 029 | 17 447 | 19 267 | Services : crédit |
| Services: debit | -11 905 | -11 848 | -10 904 | -11 205 | -12 825 | -13 711 | -14 934 | Services : débit |
| Income: credit | 3 632 | 2 734 | 2 459 | 2 814 | 2 999 | 5 579 | 7 921 | Revenus : crédit |
| Income: debit | -10 719 | -7 612 | -6 678 | -6 867 | -6 670 | -7 187 | -8 497 | Revenus : débit |
| Current transfers, n.i.e.: credit | 7 466 | 7 791 | 8 165 | 7 556 | 7 358 | 7 010 | 8 577 | Transferts courants, n.i.a. : crédit |
| Current transfers: debit | -997 | -1 133 | -1 380 | -1 146 | -1 081 | -1 038 | -1 111 | Transferts courants : débit |
| Capital account, n.i.e. | 466 | 721 | 207 | 535 | 667 | 727 | 904 | Compte de capital, n.i.a. |
| Financial account, n.i.e. | 1 223 | -307 | -3 118 | -2 514 | -7 391 | -7 081 | -13 189 | Compte financier, n.i.a. |
| Net errors and omissions | -387 | 1 237 | 2 717 | 344 | 724 | 3 730 | -140 | Erreurs et omissions nettes |
| Reserves and related items | -321 | -388 | 1 068 | 195 | 3 020 | -1 710 | 4 435 | Réserves et postes apparentés |
| Italy | | | | | | | | Italie |
| Current account | -5 781 | -652 | -9 369 | -19 407 | -16 456 | -29 441 | -47 312 | Compte des transactions courantes |
| Goods: exports f.o.b. | 240 473 | 244 931 | 252 618 | 298 118 | 352 171 | 372 378 | 417 054 | Biens : exportations f.à.b. |
| Goods: imports f.o.b. | -230 925 | -229 392 | -239 206 | -286 641 | -341 278 | -371 814 | -428 744 | Biens : importations f.à.b. |
| Services: credit | 56 556 | 57 676 | 60 439 | 71 767 | 84 524 | 89 205 | 98 581 | Services : crédit |
| Services: debit | -55 601 | -57 753 | -63 166 | -74 332 | -83 246 | -90 046 | -100 409 | Services : débit |
| Income: credit | 38 671 | 38 574 | 43 303 | 48 780 | 53 118 | 61 288 | 72 350 | Revenus : crédit |
| Income: debit | -50 680 | -48 911 | -57 854 | -69 003 | -71 457 | -78 423 | -89 468 | Revenus : débit |
| Current transfers, n.i.e.: credit | 15 797 | 16 137 | 20 871 | 20 650 | 21 833 | 24 017 | 22 021 | Transferts courants, n.i.a. : crédit |
| Current transfers: debit | -20 073 | -21 915 | -26 375 | -28 745 | -32 120 | -36 044 | -38 696 | Transferts courants : débit |
| Capital account, n.i.e. | 2 879 | 846 | -80 | 2 667 | 2 172 | 1 239 | 2 393 | Compte de capital, n.i.a. |
| Financial account, n.i.e. | 7 504 | -3 570 | 11 224 | 20 437 | 8 426 | 25 049 | 43 598 | Compte financier, n.i.a. |
| Net errors and omissions | -1 355 | 2 787 | 1 395 | -2 583 | 3 014 | 2 123 | 754 | Erreurs et omissions nettes |
| Reserves and related items | -3 247 | 588 | -3 169 | -1 115 | 2 844 | 1 030 | 567 | Réserves et postes apparentés |
| Jamaica | | | | | | | | Jamaïque |
| Current account | -367 | -759 | -1 074 | -773 | -509 | -1 071 | -1 170 | Compte des transactions courantes |
| Goods: exports f.o.b. | 1 563 | 1 454 | 1 309 | 1 386 | 1 602 | 1 664 | 2 134 | Biens : exportations f.à.b. |
| Goods: imports f.o.b. | -3 004 | -3 073 | -3 180 | -3 328 | -3 546 | -4 246 | -5 077 | Biens : importations f.à.b. |
| Services: credit | 2 026 | 1 897 | 1 912 | 2 138 | 2 297 | 2 330 | 2 649 | Services : crédit |
| Services: debit | -1 423 | -1 514 | -1 597 | -1 586 | -1 725 | -1 722 | -2 021 | Services : débit |
| Income: credit | 193 | 218 | 221 | 218 | 270 | 328 | 378 | Revenus : crédit |
| Income: debit | -543 | -656 | -826 | -789 | -852 | -1 004 | -981 | Revenus : débit |
| Current transfers, n.i.e.: credit | 969 | 1 091 | 1 338 | 1 524 | 1 892 | 1 935 | 2 088 | Transferts courants, n.i.a. : crédit |
| Current transfers: debit | -149 | -177 | -251 | -334 | -446 | -357 | -340 | Transferts courants : débit |
| Capital account, n.i.e. | 2 | -22 | -17 | ^0 | 2 | -3 | ^0 | Compte de capital, n.i.a. |
| Financial account, n.i.e. | 854 | 1 661 | 911 | 314 | 1 216 | 1 258 | 1 381 | Compte financier, n.i.a. |
| Net errors and omissions | 30 | -14 | -61 | 28 | -14 | 46 | 20 | Erreurs et omissions nettes |
| Reserves and related items | -518 | -865 | 241 | 431 | -695 | -230 | -230 | Réserves et postes apparentés |
| Japan | | | | | | | | Japon |
| Current account | 119 660 | 87 798 | 112 447 | 136 216 | 172 059 | 165 783 | 170 517 | Compte des transactions courantes |
| Goods: exports f.o.b. | 459 513 | 383 592 | 395 581 | 449 119 | 538 999 | 567 572 | 615 813 | Biens : exportations f.à.b. |
| Goods: imports f.o.b. | -342 797 | -313 378 | -301 751 | -342 723 | -406 866 | -473 614 | -534 509 | Biens : importations f.à.b. |
| Services: credit | 69 238 | 64 516 | 65 712 | 77 621 | 97 611 | 110 210 | 117 298 | Services : crédit |
| Services: debit | -116 864 | -108 249 | -107 940 | -111 528 | -135 514 | -134 256 | -135 556 | Services : débit |
| Income: credit | 97 199 | 103 095 | 91 478 | 95 211 | 113 331 | 141 062 | 165 802 | Revenus : crédit |
| Income: debit | -36 799 | -33 874 | -25 709 | -23 971 | -27 628 | -37 618 | -47 647 | Revenus : débit |
| Current transfers, n.i.e.: credit | 7 380 | 6 152 | 10 038 | 6 508 | 6 907 | 9 738 | 6 184 | Transferts courants, n.i.a. : crédit |
| Current transfers: debit | -17 211 | -14 056 | -14 960 | -14 020 | -14 782 | -17 311 | -16 868 | Transferts courants : débit |
| Capital account, n.i.e. | -9 259 | -2 869 | -3 321 | -3 998 | -4 787 | -4 878 | -4 757 | Compte de capital, n.i.a. |
| Financial account, n.i.e. | -78 313 | -48 160 | -63 381 | 71 924 | 22 500 | -122 682 | -102 343 | Compte financier, n.i.a. |
| Net errors and omissions | 16 866 | 3 718 | 388 | -16 990 | -28 918 | -15 898 | -31 437 | Erreurs et omissions nettes |
| Reserves and related items | -48 955 | -40 487 | -46 134 | -187 153 | -160 854 | -22 325 | -31 982 | Réserves et postes apparentés |
| Jordan | | | | | | | | Jordanie |
| Current account | 60 | 5 | 544 | 1 245 | 89 | -2 228 | -1 909 | Compte des transactions courantes |
| Goods: exports f.o.b. | 1 899 | 2 294 | 2 770 | 3 082 | 3 883 | 4 301 | 5 204 | Biens : exportations f.à.b. |

| Country or area | 2000 | 2001 | 2002 | 2003 | 2004 | 2005 | 2006 | Pays ou zone |
|---|---|---|---|---|---|---|---|---|
| Goods: imports f.o.b. | -4 074 | -4 301 | -4 501 | -5 078 | -7 261 | -9 317 | -10 260 | Biens : importations f.à.b. |
| Services: credit | 1 640 | 1 487 | 1 774 | 1 748 | 2 073 | 2 334 | 2 489 | Services : crédit |
| Services: debit | -1 722 | -1 726 | -1 883 | -1 889 | -2 146 | -2 542 | -2 712 | Services : débit |
| Income: credit | 668 | 652 | 492 | 550 | 649 | 791 | 1 032 | Revenus : crédit |
| Income: debit | -535 | -461 | -372 | -374 | -326 | -383 | -451 | Revenus : débit |
| Current transfers, n.i.e.: credit | 2 611 | 2 366 | 2 524 | 3 501 | 3 562 | 3 030 | 3 379 | Transferts courants, n.i.a. : crédit |
| Current transfers: debit | -427 | -307 | -260 | -295 | -346 | -441 | -589 | Transferts courants : débit |
| Capital account, n.i.e. | 65 | 22 | 69 | 94 | 2 | 8 | 63 | Compte de capital, n.i.a. |
| Financial account, n.i.e. | 285 | -191 | 337 | -211 | -103 | 1 638 | 2 994 | Compte financier, n.i.a. |
| Net errors and omissions | 288 | -90 | -56 | 149 | 192 | 842 | 294 | Erreurs et omissions nettes |
| Reserves and related items | -697 | 255 | -894 | -1 277 | -180 | -261 | -1 442 | Réserves et postes apparentés |
| Kazakhstan | | | | | | | | Kazakhstan |
| Current account | 366 | -1 390 | -1 024 | -273 | 335 | -1 056 | -1 795 | Compte des transactions courantes |
| Goods: exports f.o.b. | 9 288 | 8 928 | 10 027 | 13 233 | 20 603 | 28 301 | 38 762 | Biens : exportations f.à.b. |
| Goods: imports f.o.b. | -7 120 | -7 944 | -8 040 | -9 554 | -13 818 | -17 979 | -24 120 | Biens : importations f.à.b. |
| Services: credit | 1 053 | 1 260 | 1 540 | 1 712 | 2 009 | 2 228 | 2 808 | Services : crédit |
| Services: debit | -1 850 | -2 635 | -3 538 | -3 753 | -5 108 | -7 496 | -8 720 | Services : débit |
| Income: credit | 139 | 225 | 234 | 255 | 423 | 680 | 1 441 | Revenus : crédit |
| Income: debit | -1 393 | -1 462 | -1 361 | -2 002 | -3 286 | -6 377 | -10 758 | Revenus : débit |
| Current transfers, n.i.e.: credit | 352 | 394 | 426 | 279 | 353 | 810 | 904 | Transferts courants, n.i.a. : crédit |
| Current transfers: debit | -103 | -156 | -312 | -443 | -841 | -1 223 | -2 112 | Transferts courants : débit |
| Capital account, n.i.e. | -291 | -185 | -120 | -28 | -21 | 14 | 33 | Compte de capital, n.i.a. |
| Financial account, n.i.e. | 1 307 | 2 614 | 1 359 | 2 766 | 4 701 | 898 | 16 091 | Compte financier, n.i.a. |
| Net errors and omissions | -813 | -654 | 320 | -932 | -1 016 | -1 800 | -3 255 | Erreurs et omissions nettes |
| Reserves and related items | -570 | -385 | -535 | -1 534 | -3 999 | 1 944 | -11 075 | Réserves et postes apparentés |
| Kenya | | | | | | | | Kenya |
| Current account | -199 | -320 | -118 | 132 | -137 | -261 | -526 | Compte des transactions courantes |
| Goods: exports f.o.b. | 1 782 | 1 891 | 2 162 | 2 412 | 2 721 | 3 455 | 3 502 | Biens : exportations f.à.b. |
| Goods: imports f.o.b. | -3 044 | -3 238 | -3 159 | -3 569 | -4 351 | -5 602 | -6 768 | Biens : importations f.à.b. |
| Services: credit | 993 | 1 120 | 1 054 | 1 198 | 1 557 | 1 880 | 2 461 | Services : crédit |
| Services: debit | -719 | -810 | -708 | -691 | -939 | -1 138 | -1 431 | Services : débit |
| Income: credit | 45 | 46 | 35 | 60 | 45 | 73 | 99 | Revenus : crédit |
| Income: debit | -178 | -168 | -179 | -148 | -172 | -182 | -170 | Revenus : débit |
| Current transfers, n.i.e.: credit | 927 | 854 | 689 | 884 | 1 045 | 1 319 | 1 829 | Transferts courants, n.i.a. : crédit |
| Current transfers: debit | -6 | -16 | -12 | -14 | -43 | -67 | -48 | Transferts courants : débit |
| Capital account, n.i.e. | 50 | 51 | 82 | 163 | 145 | 103 | 168 | Compte de capital, n.i.a. |
| Financial account, n.i.e. | 270 | 148 | -174 | 406 | 40 | 511 | 674 | Compte financier, n.i.a. |
| Net errors and omissions | -127 | 131 | 193 | -277 | -62 | -237 | 265 | Erreurs et omissions nettes |
| Reserves and related items | 7 | -10 | 16 | -425 | 13 | -117 | -581 | Réserves et postes apparentés |
| Korea, Republic of | | | | | | | | Corée, République de |
| Current account | 12 251 | 8 033 | 5 394 | 11 950 | 28 174 | 14 981 | 6 092 | Compte des transactions courantes |
| Goods: exports f.o.b. | 176 221 | 151 478 | 163 414 | 197 289 | 257 710 | 288 971 | 331 845 | Biens : exportations f.à.b. |
| Goods: imports f.o.b. | -159 267 | -137 990 | -148 637 | -175 337 | -220 141 | -256 288 | -302 631 | Biens : importations f.à.b. |
| Services: credit | 30 534 | 29 055 | 28 388 | 32 957 | 41 882 | 45 129 | 51 873 | Services : crédit |
| Services: debit | -33 381 | -32 927 | -36 585 | -40 381 | -49 928 | -58 788 | -70 637 | Services : débit |
| Income: credit | 6 375 | 6 650 | 6 900 | 7 176 | 9 410 | 10 432 | 13 596 | Revenus : crédit |
| Income: debit | -8 797 | -7 848 | -6 467 | -6 850 | -8 328 | -11 994 | -14 134 | Revenus : débit |
| Current transfers, n.i.e.: credit | 6 500 | 6 687 | 7 314 | 7 859 | 9 151 | 10 004 | 9 337 | Transferts courants, n.i.a. : crédit |
| Current transfers: debit | -5 934 | -7 072 | -8 932 | -10 764 | -11 583 | -12 486 | -13 157 | Transferts courants : débit |
| Capital account, n.i.e. | -615 | -731 | -1 087 | -1 398 | -1 753 | -2 340 | -3 033 | Compte de capital, n.i.a. |
| Financial account, n.i.e. | 12 725 | 3 025 | 7 338 | 15 308 | 9 359 | 7 104 | 21 654 | Compte financier, n.i.a. |
| Net errors and omissions | -571 | 2 951 | 124 | -68 | 2 895 | 119 | -2 624 | Erreurs et omissions nettes |
| Reserves and related items | -23 790 | -13 278 | -11 769 | -25 791 | -38 675 | -19 864 | -22 089 | Réserves et postes apparentés |
| Kuwait | | | | | | | | Koweït |
| Current account | 14 672 | 8 324 | 4 265 | 9 424 | 18 162 | 34 308 | 50 996 | Compte des transactions courantes |
| Goods: exports f.o.b. | 19 478 | 16 237 | 15 367 | 21 795 | 30 089 | 46 971 | 58 638 | Biens : exportations f.à.b. |
| Goods: imports f.o.b. | -6 451 | -7 047 | -8 117 | -9 880 | -11 663 | -14 238 | -14 350 | Biens : importations f.à.b. |
| Services: credit | 1 823 | 1 664 | 1 648 | 3 144 | 3 743 | 4 723 | 6 972 | Services : crédit |
| Services: debit | -4 921 | -5 355 | -5 838 | -6 615 | -7 586 | -8 604 | -10 192 | Services : débit |

62 Balance of payments summary—Millions of US dollars (*continued*)
Résumé de la balance des paiements—Millions de dollars E.-U (*suite*)

| Country or area | 2000 | 2001 | 2002 | 2003 | 2004 | 2005 | 2006 | Pays ou zone |
|---|---|---|---|---|---|---|---|---|
| Income: credit | 7 315 | 5 427 | 3 716 | 3 733 | 6 584 | 9 413 | 14 659 | Revenus : crédit |
| Income: debit | -616 | -524 | -369 | -372 | -456 | -556 | -1 274 | Revenus : débit |
| Current transfers, n.i.e.: credit | 85 | 53 | 50 | 66 | 88 | 86 | 113 | Transferts courants, n.i.a. : crédit |
| Current transfers: debit | -2 041 | -2 132 | -2 192 | -2 446 | -2 638 | -3 487 | -3 571 | Transferts courants : débit |
| Capital account, n.i.e. | 2 217 | 2 931 | 1 672 | 1 431 | 433 | 797 | 882 | Compte de capital, n.i.a. |
| Financial account, n.i.e. | -13 779 | -5 478 | -5 038 | -12 101 | -16 830 | -31 145 | -48 001 | Compte financier, n.i.a. |
| Net errors and omissions | -842 | -2 869 | -1 869 | -579 | -1 136 | -3 341 | -293 | Erreurs et omissions nettes |
| Reserves and related items | -2 268 | -2 908 | 970 | 1 824 | -629 | -619 | -3 584 | Réserves et postes apparentés |
| **Kyrgyzstan** | | | | | | | | **Kirghizistan** |
| Current account | -123 | -52 | -61 | -61 | 3 | -54 | -403 | Compte des transactions courantes |
| Goods: exports f.o.b. | 511 | 480 | 498 | 590 | 733 | 687 | 811 | Biens : exportations f.à.b. |
| Goods: imports f.o.b. | -506 | -449 | -571 | -723 | -904 | -1 106 | -1 792 | Biens : importations f.à.b. |
| Services: credit | 62 | 83 | 142 | 158 | 210 | 256 | 374 | Services : crédit |
| Services: debit | -148 | -125 | -148 | -160 | -223 | -291 | -461 | Services : débit |
| Income: credit | 17 | 12 | 6 | 5 | 8 | 17 | 36 | Revenus : crédit |
| Income: debit | -99 | -71 | -64 | -67 | -109 | -92 | -70 | Revenus : débit |
| Current transfers, n.i.e.: credit | 43 | 23 | 79 | 143 | 307 | 514 | 749 | Transferts courants, n.i.a. : crédit |
| Current transfers: debit | -2 | -4 | -3 | -7 | -18 | -38 | -50 | Transferts courants : débit |
| Capital account, n.i.e. | -11 | -32 | -8 | -1 | -20 | -21 | -44 | Compte de capital, n.i.a. |
| Financial account, n.i.e. | 83 | 46 | 97 | 28 | 180 | 85 | 334 | Compte financier, n.i.a. |
| Net errors and omissions | 18 | 24 | -8 | 81 | -19 | 58 | 290 | Erreurs et omissions nettes |
| Reserves and related items | 33 | 13 | -20 | -47 | -145 | -68 | -177 | Réserves et postes apparentés |
| **Lao People's Dem. Rep.** | | | | | | | | **Rép. dém. pop. lao** |
| Current account | -8 | -82 | ... | ... | ... | ... | ... | Compte des transactions courantes |
| Goods: exports f.o.b. | 330 | 311 | ... | ... | ... | ... | ... | Biens : exportations f.à.b. |
| Goods: imports f.o.b. | -535 | -528 | ... | ... | ... | ... | ... | Biens : importations f.à.b. |
| Services: credit | 176 | 166 | ... | ... | ... | ... | ... | Services : crédit |
| Services: debit | -43 | -32 | ... | ... | ... | ... | ... | Services : débit |
| Income: credit | 7 | 6 | ... | ... | ... | ... | ... | Revenus : crédit |
| Income: debit | -60 | -40 | ... | ... | ... | ... | ... | Revenus : débit |
| Current transfers, n.i.e.: credit | 116 | 34 | ... | ... | ... | ... | ... | Transferts courants, n.i.a. : crédit |
| Current transfers: debit | 0 | 0 | ... | ... | ... | ... | ... | Transferts courants : débit |
| Capital account, n.i.e. | 0 | 0 | ... | ... | ... | ... | ... | Compte de capital, n.i.a. |
| Financial account, n.i.e. | 126 | 136 | ... | ... | ... | ... | ... | Compte financier, n.i.a. |
| Net errors and omissions | -74 | -57 | ... | ... | ... | ... | ... | Erreurs et omissions nettes |
| Reserves and related items | -43 | 4 | ... | ... | ... | ... | ... | Réserves et postes apparentés |
| **Latvia** | | | | | | | | **Lettonie** |
| Current account | -371 | -626 | -625 | -921 | -1 762 | -1 992 | -4 522 | Compte des transactions courantes |
| Goods: exports f.o.b. | 2 079 | 2 243 | 2 545 | 3 171 | 4 221 | 5 361 | 6 140 | Biens : exportations f.à.b. |
| Goods: imports f.o.b. | -3 123 | -3 578 | -4 024 | -5 173 | -7 002 | -8 379 | -11 271 | Biens : importations f.à.b. |
| Services: credit | 1 150 | 1 179 | 1 238 | 1 506 | 1 779 | 2 163 | 2 642 | Services : crédit |
| Services: debit | -690 | -671 | -701 | -929 | -1 178 | -1 557 | -1 980 | Services : débit |
| Income: credit | 215 | 278 | 289 | 368 | 500 | 772 | 1 078 | Revenus : crédit |
| Income: debit | -198 | -221 | -235 | -393 | -775 | -948 | -1 610 | Revenus : débit |
| Current transfers, n.i.e.: credit | 406 | 373 | 538 | 924 | 1 289 | 1 373 | 1 789 | Transferts courants, n.i.a. : crédit |
| Current transfers: debit | -211 | -229 | -275 | -394 | -595 | -776 | -1 310 | Transferts courants : débit |
| Capital account, n.i.e. | 36 | 41 | 21 | 76 | 144 | 212 | 239 | Compte de capital, n.i.a. |
| Financial account, n.i.e. | 413 | 900 | 687 | 937 | 2 013 | 2 600 | 6 141 | Compte financier, n.i.a. |
| Net errors and omissions | -75 | ^0 | -71 | -13 | 8 | -296 | 120 | Erreurs et omissions nettes |
| Reserves and related items | -3 | -314 | -12 | -79 | -403 | -524 | -1 979 | Réserves et postes apparentés |
| **Lebanon** | | | | | | | | **Liban** |
| Current account | ... | ... | -4 415 | -4 930 | -4 080 | -2 279 | -1 451 | Compte des transactions courantes |
| Goods: exports f.o.b. | ... | ... | 1 210 | 1 733 | 2 050 | 2 278 | 2 792 | Biens : exportations f.à.b. |
| Goods: imports f.o.b. | ... | ... | -5 910 | -6 528 | -8 502 | -8 397 | -8 547 | Biens : importations f.à.b. |
| Services: credit | ... | ... | 4 429 | 9 462 | 9 704 | 10 858 | 11 625 | Services : crédit |
| Services: debit | ... | ... | -3 354 | -6 488 | -8 230 | -7 895 | -8 706 | Services : débit |
| Income: credit | ... | ... | 395 | 1 399 | 1 060 | 1 733 | 2 059 | Revenus : crédit |
| Income: debit | ... | ... | -1 263 | -4 836 | -1 878 | -1 919 | -1 849 | Revenus : débit |

| Country or area | 2000 | 2001 | 2002 | 2003 | 2004 | 2005 | 2006 | Pays ou zone |
|---|---|---|---|---|---|---|---|---|
| Current transfers, n.i.e.: credit | ... | ... | 2 591 | 4 079 | 5 325 | 4 399 | 5 053 | Transferts courants, n.i.a. : crédit |
| Current transfers: debit | ... | ... | -2 513 | -3 751 | -3 609 | -3 337 | -3 878 | Transferts courants : débit |
| Capital account, n.i.e. | ... | ... | 13 | 29 | 50 | 27 | 1 940 | Compte de capital, n.i.a. |
| Financial account, n.i.e. | ... | ... | 348 | 9 963 | 6 148 | 6 857 | 3 154 | Compte financier, n.i.a. |
| Net errors and omissions | ... | ... | 4 719 | -25 | -2 898 | -4 148 | -3 497 | Erreurs et omissions nettes |
| Reserves and related items | ... | ... | -664 | -5 037 | 780 | -458 | -146 | Réserves et postes apparentés |
| **Lesotho** | | | | | | | | **Lesotho** |
| Current account | -151 | -95 | -143 | -135 | -76 | -98 | 67 | Compte des transactions courantes |
| Goods: exports f.o.b. | 211 | 279 | 357 | 475 | 707 | 650 | 694 | Biens : exportations f.à.b. |
| Goods: imports f.o.b. | -728 | -679 | -763 | -994 | -1 302 | -1 306 | -1 361 | Biens : importations f.à.b. |
| Services: credit | 43 | 40 | 35 | 50 | 64 | 56 | 60 | Services : crédit |
| Services: debit | -43 | -49 | -55 | -85 | -96 | -103 | -95 | Services : débit |
| Income: credit | 289 | 235 | 207 | 304 | 379 | 370 | 412 | Revenus : crédit |
| Income: debit | -63 | -57 | -45 | -54 | -76 | -65 | -33 | Revenus : débit |
| Current transfers, n.i.e.: credit | 140 | 137 | 123 | 172 | 251 | 304 | 392 | Transferts courants, n.i.a. : crédit |
| Current transfers: debit | -1 | -3 | -2 | -2 | -3 | -3 | -3 | Transferts courants : débit |
| Capital account, n.i.e. | 22 | 17 | 24 | 27 | 33 | 21 | 11 | Compte de capital, n.i.a. |
| Financial account, n.i.e. | 85 | 89 | 89 | 98 | 63 | 39 | -29 | Compte financier, n.i.a. |
| Net errors and omissions | 62 | 155 | -98 | -57 | -17 | 81 | 142 | Erreurs et omissions nettes |
| Reserves and related items | -18 | -166 | 128 | 66 | -4 | -44 | -191 | Réserves et postes apparentés |
| **Libyan Arab Jamah.** | | | | | | | | **Jamah. arabe libyenne** |
| Current account | 6 270 | 3 332 | 694 | 3 402 | 4 616 | 14 945 | 22 170 | Compte des transactions courantes |
| Goods: exports f.o.b. | 12 038 | 10 634 | 9 851 | 12 878 | 17 425 | 28 849 | 37 473 | Biens : exportations f.à.b. |
| Goods: imports f.o.b. | -4 129 | -4 825 | -7 408 | -7 200 | -8 768 | -11 174 | -13 219 | Biens : importations f.à.b. |
| Services: credit | 172 | 184 | 401 | 442 | 437 | 534 | 489 | Services : crédit |
| Services: debit | -895 | -1 034 | -1 544 | -1 597 | -1 914 | -2 349 | -2 564 | Services : débit |
| Income: credit | 723 | 684 | 1 773 | 1 689 | 1 339 | 1 837 | 2 180 | Revenus : crédit |
| Income: debit | -1 152 | -1 583 | -1 508 | -1 149 | -1 394 | -2 118 | -2 775 | Revenus : débit |
| Current transfers, n.i.e.: credit | 16 | 20 | 13 | 255 | 254 | 418 | 1 646 | Transferts courants, n.i.a. : crédit |
| Current transfers: debit | -503 | -748 | -884 | -1 916 | -2 763 | -1 052 | -1 060 | Transferts courants : débit |
| Capital account, n.i.e. | 0 | 0 | 0 | 0 | 0 | 0 | 0 | Compte de capital, n.i.a. |
| Financial account, n.i.e. | -149 | -977 | 89 | -166 | -238 | 392 | -4 731 | Compte financier, n.i.a. |
| Net errors and omissions | -764 | -1 206 | 362 | 1 890 | 1 733 | -1 497 | 2 008 | Erreurs et omissions nettes |
| Reserves and related items | -5 357 | -1 149 | -1 145 | -5 126 | -6 111 | -13 840 | -19 447 | Réserves et postes apparentés |
| **Lithuania** | | | | | | | | **Lituanie** |
| Current account | -675 | -574 | -721 | -1 278 | -1 725 | -1 831 | -3 218 | Compte des transactions courantes |
| Goods: exports f.o.b. | 4 050 | 4 889 | 6 028 | 7 658 | 9 306 | 11 774 | 14 151 | Biens : exportations f.à.b. |
| Goods: imports f.o.b. | -5 154 | -5 997 | -7 343 | -9 362 | -11 689 | -14 690 | -18 360 | Biens : importations f.à.b. |
| Services: credit | 1 059 | 1 157 | 1 464 | 1 878 | 2 444 | 3 104 | 3 623 | Services : crédit |
| Services: debit | -679 | -700 | -915 | -1 264 | -1 632 | -2 055 | -2 540 | Services : débit |
| Income: credit | 186 | 206 | 192 | 235 | 355 | 448 | 590 | Revenus : crédit |
| Income: debit | -379 | -385 | -375 | -717 | -967 | -1 075 | -1 407 | Revenus : débit |
| Current transfers, n.i.e.: credit | 247 | 262 | 232 | 302 | 612 | 951 | 1 425 | Transferts courants, n.i.a. : crédit |
| Current transfers: debit | -4 | -4 | -3 | -8 | -154 | -289 | -700 | Transferts courants : débit |
| Capital account, n.i.e. | 2 | 1 | 56 | 68 | 287 | 331 | 351 | Compte de capital, n.i.a. |
| Financial account, n.i.e. | 702 | 778 | 1 048 | 1 642 | 1 141 | 2 262 | 4 663 | Compte financier, n.i.a. |
| Net errors and omissions | 128 | 154 | 79 | 181 | 192 | -49 | -289 | Erreurs et omissions nettes |
| Reserves and related items | -158 | -359 | -463 | -613 | 104 | -712 | -1 507 | Réserves et postes apparentés |
| **Luxembourg** | | | | | | | | **Luxembourg** |
| Current account | 2 562 | 1 674 | 2 568 | 2 345 | 3 991 | 4 088 | 4 370 | Compte des transactions courantes |
| Goods: exports f.o.b. | 8 635 | 8 996 | 9 535 | 10 942 | 13 527 | 14 545 | 16 371 | Biens : exportations f.à.b. |
| Goods: imports f.o.b. | -11 056 | -11 395 | -11 599 | -13 938 | -17 079 | -18 662 | -20 798 | Biens : importations f.à.b. |
| Services: credit | 20 301 | 19 945 | 20 280 | 25 283 | 33 684 | 40 833 | 51 007 | Services : crédit |
| Services: debit | -13 581 | -13 708 | -12 254 | -15 377 | -20 789 | -24 572 | -30 207 | Services : débit |
| Income: credit | 50 400 | 52 302 | 49 009 | 51 205 | 63 874 | 75 216 | 99 947 | Revenus : crédit |
| Income: debit | -51 678 | -53 941 | -52 123 | -55 220 | -68 136 | -82 141 | -110 322 | Revenus : débit |
| Current transfers, n.i.e.: credit | 2 750 | 2 269 | 3 604 | 3 782 | 4 039 | 4 753 | 5 295 | Transferts courants, n.i.a. : crédit |
| Current transfers: debit | -3 211 | -2 794 | -3 884 | -4 332 | -5 130 | -5 882 | -6 922 | Transferts courants : débit |

| Country or area | 2000 | 2001 | 2002 | 2003 | 2004 | 2005 | 2006 | Pays ou zone |
|---|---|---|---|---|---|---|---|---|
| Capital account, n.i.e. | 0 | 0 | -89 | -142 | -695 | 1 305 | -243 | Compte de capital, n.i.a. |
| Financial account, n.i.e. | 0 | 0 | -2 702 | -2 086 | -3 516 | -5 228 | -3 382 | Compte financier, n.i.a. |
| Net errors and omissions | 0 | 0 | 258 | -9 | 228 | -214 | -774 | Erreurs et omissions nettes |
| Reserves and related items | 0 | 0 | -35 | -108 | -8 | 48 | 28 | Réserves et postes apparentés |
| **Madagascar** | | | | | | | | **Madagascar** |
| Current account | -283 | -170 | -528 | -458 | -541 | -626 | ... | Compte des transactions courantes |
| Goods: exports f.o.b. | 824 | 928 | 859 | 854 | 990 | 834 | ... | Biens : exportations f.à.b. |
| Goods: imports f.o.b. | -997 | -955 | -1 066 | -1 111 | -1 427 | -1 427 | ... | Biens : importations f.à.b. |
| Services: credit | 364 | 351 | 397 | 322 | 425 | 498 | ... | Services : crédit |
| Services: debit | -522 | -511 | -704 | -619 | -637 | -615 | ... | Services : débit |
| Income: credit | 22 | 24 | 46 | 16 | 15 | 24 | ... | Revenus : crédit |
| Income: debit | -64 | -106 | -178 | -94 | -89 | -104 | ... | Revenus : débit |
| Current transfers, n.i.e.: credit | 122 | 114 | 156 | 357 | 245 | 208 | ... | Transferts courants, n.i.a. : crédit |
| Current transfers: debit | -31 | -15 | -36 | -183 | -62 | -45 | ... | Transferts courants : débit |
| Capital account, n.i.e. | 115 | 113 | 102 | 143 | 182 | 192 | ... | Compte de capital, n.i.a. |
| Financial account, n.i.e. | -31 | -139 | -96 | -126 | 251 | -6 | ... | Compte financier, n.i.a. |
| Net errors and omissions | 39 | -57 | 29 | 67 | -35 | 91 | ... | Erreurs et omissions nettes |
| Reserves and related items | 160 | 253 | 493 | 374 | 143 | 349 | ... | Réserves et postes apparentés |
| **Malawi** | | | | | | | | **Malawi** |
| Current account | -73 | -60 | -201 | ... | ... | ... | ... | Compte des transactions courantes |
| Goods: exports f.o.b. | 403 | 428 | 422 | ... | ... | ... | ... | Biens : exportations f.à.b. |
| Goods: imports f.o.b. | -462 | -472 | -573 | ... | ... | ... | ... | Biens : importations f.à.b. |
| Services: credit | 34 | 44 | 49 | ... | ... | ... | ... | Services : crédit |
| Services: debit | -167 | -171 | -222 | ... | ... | ... | ... | Services : débit |
| Income: credit | 33 | 12 | 6 | ... | ... | ... | ... | Revenus : crédit |
| Income: debit | -51 | -43 | -45 | ... | ... | ... | ... | Revenus : débit |
| Current transfers, n.i.e.: credit | 143 | 149 | 170 | ... | ... | ... | ... | Transferts courants, n.i.a. : crédit |
| Current transfers: debit | -8 | -6 | -9 | ... | ... | ... | ... | Transferts courants : débit |
| Capital account, n.i.e. | 0 | 0 | 0 | ... | ... | ... | ... | Compte de capital, n.i.a. |
| Financial account, n.i.e. | 189 | 213 | 134 | ... | ... | ... | ... | Compte financier, n.i.a. |
| Net errors and omissions | -24 | -221 | 157 | ... | ... | ... | ... | Erreurs et omissions nettes |
| Reserves and related items | -91 | 68 | -90 | ... | ... | ... | ... | Réserves et postes apparentés |
| **Malaysia** | | | | | | | | **Malaisie** |
| Current account | 8 488 | 7 287 | 7 190 | 13 381 | 15 079 | 19 980 | 25 488 | Compte des transactions courantes |
| Goods: exports f.o.b. | 98 429 | 87 981 | 93 383 | 104 999 | 126 817 | 141 808 | 160 842 | Biens : exportations f.à.b. |
| Goods: imports f.o.b. | -77 602 | -69 597 | -75 248 | -79 289 | -99 244 | -108 653 | -124 144 | Biens : importations f.à.b. |
| Services: credit | 13 941 | 14 455 | 14 878 | 13 578 | 17 111 | 19 576 | 21 831 | Services : crédit |
| Services: debit | -16 747 | -16 657 | -16 448 | -17 532 | -19 269 | -21 956 | -23 720 | Services : débit |
| Income: credit | 1 986 | 1 847 | 2 139 | 3 448 | 4 329 | 5 373 | 8 463 | Revenus : crédit |
| Income: debit | -9 594 | -8 590 | -8 734 | -9 376 | -10 751 | -11 691 | -13 192 | Revenus : débit |
| Current transfers, n.i.e.: credit | 756 | 537 | 661 | 508 | 422 | 299 | 313 | Transferts courants, n.i.a. : crédit |
| Current transfers: debit | -2 680 | -2 689 | -3 442 | -2 955 | -4 335 | -4 776 | -4 904 | Transferts courants : débit |
| Capital account, n.i.e. | 0 | 0 | 0 | 0 | 0 | 0 | 0 | Compte de capital, n.i.a. |
| Financial account, n.i.e. | -6 276 | -3 892 | -3 142 | -3 196 | 5 091 | -9 806 | -11 894 | Compte financier, n.i.a. |
| Net errors and omissions | -3 221 | -2 394 | -391 | -4 | 1 880 | -6 555 | -6 731 | Erreurs et omissions nettes |
| Reserves and related items | 1 009 | -1 000 | -3 657 | -10 181 | -22 050 | -3 620 | -6 864 | Réserves et postes apparentés |
| **Maldives** | | | | | | | | **Maldives** |
| Current account | -56 | -65 | -45 | -37 | -128 | -279 | -379 | Compte des transactions courantes |
| Goods: exports f.o.b. | 104 | 104 | 123 | 146 | 175 | 152 | 216 | Biens : exportations f.à.b. |
| Goods: imports f.o.b. | -342 | -346 | -345 | -414 | -565 | -655 | -815 | Biens : importations f.à.b. |
| Services: credit | 348 | 354 | 363 | 432 | 508 | 323 | 473 | Services : crédit |
| Services: debit | -110 | -110 | -111 | -120 | -157 | -204 | -233 | Services : débit |
| Income: credit | 10 | 8 | 6 | 6 | 10 | 11 | 15 | Revenus : crédit |
| Income: debit | -40 | -45 | -41 | -45 | -45 | -42 | -56 | Revenus : débit |
| Current transfers, n.i.e.: credit | 19 | 20 | 11 | 13 | 8 | 206 | 105 | Transferts courants, n.i.a. : crédit |
| Current transfers: debit | -46 | -50 | -50 | -55 | -61 | -70 | -83 | Transferts courants : débit |
| Capital account, n.i.e. | 0 | 0 | 0 | 0 | 0 | 0 | 0 | Compte de capital, n.i.a. |
| Financial account, n.i.e. | 40 | 34 | 74 | 51 | 153 | 263 | 290 | Compte financier, n.i.a. |

a

| Country or area | 2000 | 2001 | 2002 | 2003 | 2004 | 2005 | 2006 | Pays ou zone |
|---|---|---|---|---|---|---|---|---|
| Net errors and omissions | 12 | 1 | 11 | 12 | 19 | -8 | 133 | Erreurs et omissions nettes |
| Reserves and related items | 4 | 30 | -40 | -26 | -44 | 23 | -45 | Réserves et postes apparentés |
| **Mali** | | | | | | | | **Mali** |
| Current account | -255 | -310 | -149 | -271 | -409 | -438 | ... | Compte des transactions courantes |
| Goods: exports f.o.b. | 545 | 725 | 875 | 928 | 976 | 1 101 | ... | Biens : exportations f.à.b. |
| Goods: imports f.o.b. | -592 | -735 | -712 | -988 | -1 093 | -1 245 | ... | Biens : importations f.à.b. |
| Services: credit | 99 | 151 | 169 | 224 | 241 | 274 | ... | Services : crédit |
| Services: debit | -335 | -421 | -387 | -482 | -532 | -588 | ... | Services : débit |
| Income: credit | 21 | 22 | 36 | 21 | 24 | 32 | ... | Revenus : crédit |
| Income: debit | -119 | -188 | -276 | -181 | -219 | -239 | ... | Revenus : débit |
| Current transfers, n.i.e.: credit | 157 | 161 | 182 | 266 | 251 | 286 | ... | Transferts courants, n.i.a. : crédit |
| Current transfers: debit | -31 | -25 | -36 | -58 | -58 | -58 | ... | Transferts courants : débit |
| Capital account, n.i.e. | 102 | 107 | 104 | 114 | 151 | 149 | ... | Compte de capital, n.i.a. |
| Financial account, n.i.e. | 220 | 146 | 189 | 289 | 100 | 333 | ... | Compte financier, n.i.a. |
| Net errors and omissions | -5 | 9 | -6 | 45 | -26 | -29 | ... | Erreurs et omissions nettes |
| Reserves and related items | -63 | 47 | -138 | -177 | 184 | -16 | ... | Réserves et postes apparentés |
| **Malta** | | | | | | | | **Malte** |
| Current account | -480 | -150 | 106 | -156 | -337 | -518 | -435 | Compte des transactions courantes |
| Goods: exports f.o.b. | 2 479 | 2 023 | 2 342 | 2 592 | 2 728 | 2 583 | 2 966 | Biens : exportations f.à.b. |
| Goods: imports f.o.b. | -3 233 | -2 575 | -2 681 | -3 232 | -3 601 | -3 692 | -4 156 | Biens : importations f.à.b. |
| Services: credit | 1 092 | 1 099 | 1 201 | 1 379 | 1 701 | 2 004 | 2 660 | Services : crédit |
| Services: debit | -761 | -759 | -798 | -894 | -1 045 | -1 211 | -1 696 | Services : débit |
| Income: credit | 917 | 839 | 857 | 905 | 976 | 1 206 | 1 853 | Revenus : crédit |
| Income: debit | -1 009 | -800 | -833 | -934 | -1 024 | -1 450 | -2 049 | Revenus : débit |
| Current transfers, n.i.e.: credit | 93 | 201 | 281 | 276 | 221 | 343 | 530 | Transferts courants, n.i.a. : crédit |
| Current transfers: debit | -60 | -178 | -263 | -248 | -292 | -299 | -542 | Transferts courants : débit |
| Capital account, n.i.e. | 19 | 1 | 7 | 17 | 83 | 193 | 190 | Compte de capital, n.i.a. |
| Financial account, n.i.e. | 232 | 143 | 231 | 259 | -27 | 592 | 417 | Compte financier, n.i.a. |
| Net errors and omissions | 8 | 261 | -56 | 24 | 74 | -49 | -60 | Erreurs et omissions nettes |
| Reserves and related items | 222 | -255 | -288 | -144 | 206 | -218 | -112 | Réserves et postes apparentés |
| **Mauritius** | | | | | | | | **Maurice** |
| Current account | -37 | 276 | 249 | 93 | -112 | -324 | -611 | Compte des transactions courantes |
| Goods: exports f.o.b. | 1 552 | 1 628 | 1 801 | 1 898 | 1 993 | 2 138 | 2 333 | Biens : exportations f.à.b. |
| Goods: imports f.o.b. | -1 944 | -1 846 | -2 013 | -2 201 | -2 573 | -2 935 | -3 412 | Biens : importations f.à.b. |
| Services: credit | 1 070 | 1 222 | 1 149 | 1 280 | 1 456 | 1 618 | 1 671 | Services : crédit |
| Services: debit | -763 | -810 | -793 | -906 | -1 023 | -1 198 | -1 324 | Services : débit |
| Income: credit | 49 | 75 | 80 | 47 | 52 | 143 | 374 | Revenus : crédit |
| Income: debit | -65 | -61 | -67 | -77 | -66 | -151 | -324 | Revenus : débit |
| Current transfers, n.i.e.: credit | 168 | 193 | 195 | 163 | 168 | 162 | 179 | Transferts courants, n.i.a. : crédit |
| Current transfers: debit | -104 | -125 | -104 | -111 | -119 | -101 | -108 | Transferts courants : débit |
| Capital account, n.i.e. | -1 | -1 | -2 | -1 | -2 | -2 | -3 | Compte de capital, n.i.a. |
| Financial account, n.i.e. | 258 | -240 | 84 | 90 | 8 | 142 | 60 | Compte financier, n.i.a. |
| Net errors and omissions | 10 | -86 | 9 | 40 | 78 | 19 | 413 | Erreurs et omissions nettes |
| Reserves and related items | -231 | 52 | -341 | -222 | 27 | 165 | 140 | Réserves et postes apparentés |
| **Mexico** | | | | | | | | **Mexique** |
| Current account | -18 708 | -17 720 | -14 131 | -8 585 | -6 592 | -5 191 | -2 008 | Compte des transactions courantes |
| Goods: exports f.o.b. | 166 121 | 158 780 | 161 046 | 164 766 | 187 999 | 214 233 | 249 997 | Biens : exportations f.à.b. |
| Goods: imports f.o.b. | -174 458 | -168 397 | -168 679 | -170 546 | -196 810 | -221 820 | -256 130 | Biens : importations f.à.b. |
| Services: credit | 13 756 | 12 701 | 12 740 | 12 617 | 14 047 | 16 137 | 16 393 | Services : crédit |
| Services: debit | -17 360 | -17 194 | -17 660 | -18 141 | -19 779 | -21 440 | -22 833 | Services : débit |
| Income: credit | 5 977 | 5 326 | 4 051 | 3 858 | 5 617 | 5 359 | 6 406 | Revenus : crédit |
| Income: debit | -19 712 | -18 250 | -15 881 | -15 235 | -14 811 | -18 378 | -19 950 | Revenus : débit |
| Current transfers, n.i.e.: credit | 6 999 | 9 336 | 10 287 | 14 134 | 17 226 | 20 774 | 24 197 | Transferts courants, n.i.a. : crédit |
| Current transfers: debit | -30 | -22 | -35 | -37 | -80 | -57 | -88 | Transferts courants : débit |
| Capital account, n.i.e. | 0 | 0 | 0 | 0 | 0 | 0 | 0 | Compte de capital, n.i.a. |
| Financial account, n.i.e. | 23 994 | 28 020 | 28 829 | 23 498 | 12 311 | 14 009 | -2 163 | Compte financier, n.i.a. |
| Net errors and omissions | 1 839 | -2 986 | -7 339 | -5 096 | -1 615 | -1 854 | 2 868 | Erreurs et omissions nettes |
| Reserves and related items | -7 126 | -7 314 | -7 359 | -9 817 | -4 104 | -6 965 | 1 303 | Réserves et postes apparentés |

| Country or area | 2000 | 2001 | 2002 | 2003 | 2004 | 2005 | 2006 | Pays ou zone |
|---|---|---|---|---|---|---|---|---|
| **Moldova** | | | | | | | | **Moldova** |
| Current account | -108 | -37 | -25 | -130 | -47 | -248 | -392 | Compte des transactions courantes |
| Goods: exports f.o.b. | 477 | 565 | 660 | 805 | 994 | 1 105 | 1 053 | Biens : exportations f.à.b. |
| Goods: imports f.o.b. | -770 | -880 | -1 038 | -1 428 | -1 748 | -2 296 | -2 644 | Biens : importations f.à.b. |
| Services: credit | 165 | 171 | 217 | 250 | 332 | 399 | 489 | Services : crédit |
| Services: debit | -202 | -209 | -257 | -294 | -353 | -420 | -484 | Services : débit |
| Income: credit | 139 | 174 | 229 | 341 | 490 | 539 | 606 | Revenus : crédit |
| Income: debit | -118 | -78 | -73 | -110 | -133 | -129 | -205 | Revenus : débit |
| Current transfers, n.i.e.: credit | 214 | 236 | 256 | 334 | 407 | 597 | 855 | Transferts courants, n.i.a. : crédit |
| Current transfers: debit | -13 | -16 | -19 | -28 | -36 | -43 | -60 | Transferts courants : débit |
| Capital account, n.i.e. | -14 | -21 | -19 | -19 | -18 | -17 | -23 | Compte de capital, n.i.a. |
| Financial account, n.i.e. | 126 | 19 | 21 | 84 | 113 | 202 | 318 | Compte financier, n.i.a. |
| Net errors and omissions | -9 | 16 | -24 | 47 | 101 | 178 | 105 | Erreurs et omissions nettes |
| Reserves and related items | 5 | 23 | 48 | 18 | -148 | -115 | -9 | Réserves et postes apparentés |
| **Mongolia** | | | | | | | | **Mongolie** |
| Current account | -156 | -154 | -158 | -148 | -25 | -5 | 109 | Compte des transactions courantes |
| Goods: exports f.o.b. | 536 | 523 | 524 | 627 | 872 | 1 069 | 1 545 | Biens : exportations f.à.b. |
| Goods: imports f.o.b. | -608 | -624 | -680 | -827 | -901 | -1 097 | -1 357 | Biens : importations f.à.b. |
| Services: credit | 78 | 114 | 184 | 208 | 338 | 414 | 486 | Services : crédit |
| Services: debit | -163 | -205 | -266 | -257 | -504 | -476 | -523 | Services : débit |
| Income: credit | 13 | 15 | 14 | 14 | 17 | 11 | 17 | Revenus : crédit |
| Income: debit | -20 | -17 | -19 | -25 | -28 | -61 | -162 | Revenus : débit |
| Current transfers, n.i.e.: credit | 25 | 40 | 127 | 167 | 231 | 178 | 180 | Transferts courants, n.i.a. : crédit |
| Current transfers: debit | -17 | 0 | -42 | -55 | -50 | -41 | -77 | Transferts courants : débit |
| Capital account, n.i.e. | 0 | 0 | 0 | 0 | 0 | 0 | 0 | Compte de capital, n.i.a. |
| Financial account, n.i.e. | 90 | 107 | 157 | 5 | -23 | 46 | 181 | Compte financier, n.i.a. |
| Net errors and omissions | -19 | -32 | 14 | -6 | 1 | -75 | -8 | Erreurs et omissions nettes |
| Reserves and related items | 86 | 79 | -13 | 149 | 46 | 34 | -283 | Réserves et postes apparentés |
| **Montserrat** | | | | | | | | **Montserrat** |
| Current account | -8 | -6 | -10 | -8 | -9 | -16 | ... | Compte des transactions courantes |
| Goods: exports f.o.b. | 1 | 1 | 2 | 2 | 5 | 2 | ... | Biens : exportations f.à.b. |
| Goods: imports f.o.b. | -19 | -17 | -22 | -25 | -25 | -26 | ... | Biens : importations f.à.b. |
| Services: credit | 16 | 15 | 14 | 12 | 15 | 15 | ... | Services : crédit |
| Services: debit | -23 | -22 | -16 | -18 | -23 | -26 | ... | Services : débit |
| Income: credit | 1 | 1 | 1 | 1 | 1 | 2 | ... | Revenus : crédit |
| Income: debit | -4 | -2 | -4 | -2 | -5 | -5 | ... | Revenus : débit |
| Current transfers, n.i.e.: credit | 22 | 22 | 21 | 27 | 28 | 28 | ... | Transferts courants, n.i.a. : crédit |
| Current transfers: debit | -3 | -4 | -5 | -5 | -5 | -6 | ... | Transferts courants : débit |
| Capital account, n.i.e. | 4 | 8 | 13 | 14 | 12 | 10 | ... | Compte de capital, n.i.a. |
| Financial account, n.i.e. | 2 | -4 | -2 | -8 | -2 | 6 | ... | Compte financier, n.i.a. |
| Net errors and omissions | -3 | 4 | 1 | 3 | ^0 | 1 | ... | Erreurs et omissions nettes |
| Reserves and related items | 4 | -2 | -2 | -1 | -1 | -1 | ... | Réserves et postes apparentés |
| **Morocco** | | | | | | | | **Maroc** |
| Current account | -501 | 1 606 | 1 472 | 1 552 | 922 | 1 018 | 1 778 | Compte des transactions courantes |
| Goods: exports f.o.b. | 7 419 | 7 142 | 7 839 | 8 771 | 9 922 | 10 690 | 11 916 | Biens : exportations f.à.b. |
| Goods: imports f.o.b. | -10 654 | -10 164 | -10 900 | -13 117 | -16 408 | -18 894 | -21 332 | Biens : importations f.à.b. |
| Services: credit | 3 034 | 4 029 | 4 360 | 5 478 | 6 710 | 8 098 | 9 835 | Services : crédit |
| Services: debit | -1 892 | -2 118 | -2 413 | -2 861 | -3 451 | -3 845 | -4 479 | Services : débit |
| Income: credit | 276 | 326 | 377 | 370 | 505 | 689 | 747 | Revenus : crédit |
| Income: debit | -1 140 | -1 159 | -1 115 | -1 162 | -1 176 | -1 003 | -1 169 | Revenus : débit |
| Current transfers, n.i.e.: credit | 2 574 | 3 670 | 3 441 | 4 214 | 4 974 | 5 441 | 6 439 | Transferts courants, n.i.a. : crédit |
| Current transfers: debit | -118 | -120 | -115 | -141 | -154 | -158 | -179 | Transferts courants : débit |
| Capital account, n.i.e. | -6 | -9 | -6 | -10 | -8 | -5 | -3 | Compte de capital, n.i.a. |
| Financial account, n.i.e. | -774 | -966 | -1 336 | -1 091 | 102 | -155 | -561 | Compte financier, n.i.a. |
| Net errors and omissions | 114 | 230 | -182 | -297 | -282 | -414 | -498 | Erreurs et omissions nettes |
| Reserves and related items | 1 166 | -861 | 52 | -154 | -733 | -445 | -717 | Réserves et postes apparentés |
| **Mozambique** | | | | | | | | **Mozambique** |
| Current account | -764 | -657 | -869 | -816 | -607 | -761 | -634 | Compte des transactions courantes |
| Goods: exports f.o.b. | 364 | 726 | 810 | 1 044 | 1 504 | 1 745 | 2 381 | Biens : exportations f.à.b. |

62

Balance of payments summary—Millions of US dollars (*continued*)
Résumé de la balance des paiements—Millions de dollars E.-U (*suite*)

| Country or area | 2000 | 2001 | 2002 | 2003 | 2004 | 2005 | 2006 | Pays ou zone |
|---|---|---|---|---|---|---|---|---|
| Goods: imports f.o.b. | -1 046 | -997 | -1 476 | -1 648 | -1 850 | -2 242 | -2 649 | Biens : importations f.à.b. |
| Services: credit | 325 | 250 | 339 | 304 | 256 | 342 | 386 | Services : crédit |
| Services: debit | -446 | -618 | -577 | -574 | -531 | -649 | -758 | Services : débit |
| Income: credit | 79 | 56 | 52 | 56 | 75 | 99 | 160 | Revenus : crédit |
| Income: debit | -271 | -291 | -655 | -221 | -374 | -459 | -655 | Revenus : débit |
| Current transfers, n.i.e.: credit | 337 | 255 | 827 | 293 | 371 | 479 | 574 | Transferts courants, n.i.a. : crédit |
| Current transfers: debit | -106 | -37 | -189 | -70 | -57 | -76 | -74 | Transferts courants : débit |
| Capital account, n.i.e. | 227 | 257 | 222 | 271 | 578 | 188 | 489 | Compte de capital, n.i.a. |
| Financial account, n.i.e. | 83 | -25 | -732 | 373 | -47 | 95 | -1 641 | Compte financier, n.i.a. |
| Net errors and omissions | 37 | -60 | -60 | 208 | 216 | 281 | 144 | Erreurs et omissions nettes |
| Reserves and related items | 416 | 485 | 1 439 | -35 | -141 | 197 | 1 643 | Réserves et postes apparentés |
| **Myanmar** | | | | | | | | **Myanmar** |
| Current account | -212 | -154 | 97 | -19 | 112 | 588 | 802 | Compte des transactions courantes |
| Goods: exports f.o.b. | 1 662 | 2 522 | 2 421 | 2 710 | 2 927 | 3 788 | 4 555 | Biens : exportations f.à.b. |
| Goods: imports f.o.b. | -2 165 | -2 444 | -2 022 | -1 912 | -1 999 | -1 759 | -2 343 | Biens : importations f.à.b. |
| Services: credit | 478 | 408 | 426 | 249 | 255 | 259 | 280 | Services : crédit |
| Services: debit | -328 | -361 | -309 | -420 | -460 | -502 | -563 | Services : débit |
| Income: credit | 35 | 37 | 37 | 29 | 40 | 56 | 98 | Revenus : crédit |
| Income: debit | -169 | -549 | -620 | -771 | -786 | -1 427 | -1 346 | Revenus : débit |
| Current transfers, n.i.e.: credit | 290 | 249 | 188 | 118 | 161 | 198 | 161 | Transferts courants, n.i.a. : crédit |
| Current transfers: debit | -14 | -14 | -23 | -23 | -27 | -24 | -39 | Transferts courants : débit |
| Capital account, n.i.e. | 0 | 0 | 0 | 0 | 0 | 0 | 0 | Compte de capital, n.i.a. |
| Financial account, n.i.e. | 213 | 348 | -32 | 137 | 125 | 166 | 253 | Compte financier, n.i.a. |
| Net errors and omissions | -24 | -14 | -19 | -79 | -143 | -610 | -632 | Erreurs et omissions nettes |
| Reserves and related items | 23 | -180 | -45 | -39 | -94 | -144 | -423 | Réserves et postes apparentés |
| **Namibia** | | | | | | | | **Namibie** |
| Current account | 173 | -20 | 57 | 204 | 384 | 268 | 999 | Compte des transactions courantes |
| Goods: exports f.o.b. | 1 309 | 1 147 | 1 072 | 1 262 | 1 827 | 2 070 | 2 648 | Biens : exportations f.à.b. |
| Goods: imports f.o.b. | -1 310 | -1 349 | -1 283 | -1 726 | -2 110 | -2 326 | -2 544 | Biens : importations f.à.b. |
| Services: credit | 222 | 294 | 272 | 414 | 475 | 414 | 529 | Services : crédit |
| Services: debit | -333 | -276 | -234 | -276 | -420 | -369 | -430 | Services : débit |
| Income: credit | 128 | 121 | 110 | 185 | 216 | 225 | 234 | Revenus : crédit |
| Income: debit | -226 | -269 | -122 | -54 | -212 | -353 | -319 | Revenus : débit |
| Current transfers, n.i.e.: credit | 419 | 347 | 270 | 426 | 642 | 651 | 926 | Transferts courants, n.i.a. : crédit |
| Current transfers: debit | -37 | -36 | -30 | -27 | -35 | -45 | -45 | Transferts courants : débit |
| Capital account, n.i.e. | 113 | 96 | 41 | 68 | 77 | 80 | 83 | Compte de capital, n.i.a. |
| Financial account, n.i.e. | -494 | -435 | -366 | -582 | -778 | -875 | -1 459 | Compte financier, n.i.a. |
| Net errors and omissions | -4 | -28 | 16 | -89 | 115 | 164 | 134 | Erreurs et omissions nettes |
| Reserves and related items | 212 | 388 | 252 | 398 | 202 | 364 | 243 | Réserves et postes apparentés |
| **Nepal** | | | | | | | | **Népal** |
| Current account | -299 | -339 | 56 | 120 | -45 | 1 | -10 | Compte des transactions courantes |
| Goods: exports f.o.b. | 776 | 721 | 632 | 703 | 773 | 903 | 849 | Biens : exportations f.à.b. |
| Goods: imports f.o.b. | -1 590 | -1 486 | -1 425 | -1 666 | -1 908 | -2 276 | -2 441 | Biens : importations f.à.b. |
| Services: credit | 506 | 413 | 305 | 372 | 461 | 380 | 386 | Services : crédit |
| Services: debit | -200 | -215 | -237 | -266 | -385 | -435 | -493 | Services : débit |
| Income: credit | 72 | 70 | 57 | 49 | 63 | 140 | 158 | Revenus : crédit |
| Income: debit | -35 | -59 | -71 | -69 | -78 | -92 | -96 | Revenus : débit |
| Current transfers, n.i.e.: credit | 189 | 240 | 828 | 1 022 | 1 092 | 1 441 | 1 696 | Transferts courants, n.i.a. : crédit |
| Current transfers: debit | -17 | -24 | -33 | -25 | -63 | -61 | -69 | Transferts courants : débit |
| Capital account, n.i.e. | 0 | 0 | 102 | 25 | 16 | 40 | 46 | Compte de capital, n.i.a. |
| Financial account, n.i.e. | 76 | -217 | -405 | -354 | -488 | -277 | 3 | Compte financier, n.i.a. |
| Net errors and omissions | 146 | 257 | -67 | 310 | 416 | 139 | 109 | Erreurs et omissions nettes |
| Reserves and related items | 77 | 300 | 313 | -101 | 102 | 96 | -147 | Réserves et postes apparentés |
| **Netherlands** | | | | | | | | **Pays-bas** |
| Current account | 7 264 | 9 810 | 11 018 | 29 867 | 46 100 | 45 723 | 55 795 | Compte des transactions courantes |
| Goods: exports f.o.b. | 205 271 | 203 201 | 209 516 | 264 966 | 313 429 | 343 726 | 386 923 | Biens : exportations f.à.b. |
| Goods: imports f.o.b. | -187 471 | -184 015 | -190 950 | -228 447 | -272 590 | -298 684 | -341 728 | Biens : importations f.à.b. |
| Services: credit | 49 319 | 51 248 | 56 138 | 63 227 | 73 772 | 80 092 | 82 271 | Services : crédit |
| Services: debit | -51 339 | -53 713 | -57 204 | -63 897 | -69 444 | -73 313 | -79 539 | Services : débit |

| Country or area | 2000 | 2001 | 2002 | 2003 | 2004 | 2005 | 2006 | Pays ou zone |
|---|---|---|---|---|---|---|---|---|
| Income: credit | 45 506 | 43 458 | 40 304 | 59 006 | 80 671 | 98 837 | 131 087 | Revenus : crédit |
| Income: debit | -47 803 | -43 631 | -40 245 | -57 773 | -69 306 | -93 529 | -110 715 | Revenus : débit |
| Current transfers, n.i.e.: credit | 4 399 | 4 475 | 4 961 | 8 444 | 9 764 | 11 145 | 12 392 | Transferts courants, n.i.a. : crédit |
| Current transfers: debit | -10 618 | -11 214 | -11 501 | -15 660 | -20 197 | -22 550 | -24 897 | Transferts courants : débit |
| Capital account, n.i.e. | -97 | -3 200 | -545 | -3 069 | -1 614 | -1 764 | -2 792 | Compte de capital, n.i.a. |
| Financial account, n.i.e. | -7 604 | -3 852 | -4 527 | -23 964 | -46 181 | -35 746 | -53 792 | Compte financier, n.i.a. |
| Net errors and omissions | 657 | -3 110 | -6 077 | -3 272 | 785 | -10 003 | 1 567 | Erreurs et omissions nettes |
| Reserves and related items | -219 | 351 | 132 | 437 | 911 | 1 790 | -778 | Réserves et postes apparentés |
| **Netherlands Antilles** | | | | | | | | **Antilles néerlandaises** |
| Current account | -37 | -210 | -59 | 5 | -113 | -148 | ... | Compte des transactions courantes |
| Goods: exports f.o.b. | 675 | 637 | 577 | 654 | 776 | 971 | ... | Biens : exportations f.à.b. |
| Goods: imports f.o.b. | -1 656 | -1 747 | -1 598 | -1 672 | -1 956 | -2 285 | ... | Biens : importations f.à.b. |
| Services: credit | 1 614 | 1 651 | 1 626 | 1 701 | 1 799 | 1 847 | ... | Services : crédit |
| Services: debit | -732 | -790 | -793 | -812 | -801 | -813 | ... | Services : débit |
| Income: credit | 126 | 104 | 91 | 90 | 95 | 103 | ... | Revenus : crédit |
| Income: debit | -103 | -84 | -90 | -97 | -105 | -108 | ... | Revenus : débit |
| Current transfers, n.i.e.: credit | 243 | 212 | 361 | 395 | 311 | 401 | ... | Transferts courants, n.i.a. : crédit |
| Current transfers: debit | -204 | -193 | -233 | -254 | -233 | -265 | ... | Transferts courants : débit |
| Capital account, n.i.e. | 30 | 37 | 28 | 26 | 79 | 96 | ... | Compte de capital, n.i.a. |
| Financial account, n.i.e. | -135 | 298 | 90 | -36 | ^0 | 21 | ... | Compte financier, n.i.a. |
| Net errors and omissions | 13 | 92 | -6 | 32 | 42 | 80 | ... | Erreurs et omissions nettes |
| Reserves and related items | 130 | -218 | -52 | -27 | -8 | -49 | ... | Réserves et postes apparentés |
| **New Zealand** | | | | | | | | **Nouvelle-Zélande** |
| Current account | -2 683 | -1 421 | -2 454 | -3 580 | -6 499 | -9 756 | -9 381 | Compte des transactions courantes |
| Goods: exports f.o.b. | 13 459 | 13 871 | 14 495 | 16 804 | 20 466 | 21 956 | 22 491 | Biens : exportations f.à.b. |
| Goods: imports f.o.b. | -12 850 | -12 449 | -14 351 | -17 315 | -21 894 | -24 615 | -24 602 | Biens : importations f.à.b. |
| Services: credit | 4 403 | 4 452 | 5 325 | 6 687 | 7 898 | 8 306 | 7 874 | Services : crédit |
| Services: debit | -4 490 | -4 327 | -4 788 | -5 759 | -7 215 | -8 209 | -7 774 | Services : débit |
| Income: credit | 694 | 610 | 1 138 | 1 435 | 1 530 | 1 451 | 1 430 | Revenus : crédit |
| Income: debit | -4 137 | -3 731 | -4 347 | -5 586 | -7 404 | -9 021 | -9 308 | Revenus : débit |
| Current transfers, n.i.e.: credit | 635 | 585 | 642 | 856 | 901 | 1 243 | 1 291 | Transferts courants, n.i.a. : crédit |
| Current transfers: debit | -397 | -432 | -568 | -702 | -781 | -867 | -782 | Transferts courants : débit |
| Capital account, n.i.e. | -180 | 480 | 813 | 502 | 156 | -197 | -217 | Compte de capital, n.i.a. |
| Financial account, n.i.e. | 3 135 | 854 | 2 383 | 3 422 | 8 519 | 11 213 | 13 613 | Compte financier, n.i.a. |
| Net errors and omissions | -416 | -100 | 344 | 439 | -1 555 | 1 149 | 242 | Erreurs et omissions nettes |
| Reserves and related items | 143 | 187 | -1 086 | -783 | -620 | -2 410 | -4 258 | Réserves et postes apparentés |
| **Nicaragua** | | | | | | | | **Nicaragua** |
| Current account | -842 | -805 | -744 | -663 | -657 | -745 | -855 | Compte des transactions courantes |
| Goods: exports f.o.b. | 881 | 895 | 914 | 1 056 | 1 369 | 1 654 | 1 978 | Biens : exportations f.à.b. |
| Goods: imports f.o.b. | -1 802 | -1 805 | -1 853 | -2 027 | -2 457 | -2 956 | -3 422 | Biens : importations f.à.b. |
| Services: credit | 221 | 223 | 226 | 258 | 286 | 309 | 342 | Services : crédit |
| Services: debit | -351 | -364 | -355 | -377 | -409 | -448 | -483 | Services : débit |
| Income: credit | 31 | 15 | 9 | 7 | 9 | 23 | 41 | Revenus : crédit |
| Income: debit | -233 | -255 | -215 | -205 | -210 | -150 | -166 | Revenus : débit |
| Current transfers, n.i.e.: credit | 410 | 486 | 530 | 625 | 755 | 824 | 856 | Transferts courants, n.i.a. : crédit |
| Current transfers: debit | 0 | 0 | 0 | 0 | 0 | 0 | 0 | Transferts courants : débit |
| Capital account, n.i.e. | 296 | 298 | 312 | 284 | 307 | 289 | 282 | Compte de capital, n.i.a. |
| Financial account, n.i.e. | -44 | -171 | 360 | 37 | 361 | 252 | 424 | Compte financier, n.i.a. |
| Net errors and omissions | 206 | 215 | -332 | -119 | -416 | -37 | 127 | Erreurs et omissions nettes |
| Reserves and related items | 384 | 464 | 404 | 462 | 404 | 241 | 21 | Réserves et postes apparentés |
| **Niger** | | | | | | | | **Niger** |
| Current account | -104 | -92 | -165 | -219 | -231 | -312 | ... | Compte des transactions courantes |
| Goods: exports f.o.b. | 283 | 272 | 279 | 352 | 437 | 478 | ... | Biens : exportations f.à.b. |
| Goods: imports f.o.b. | -324 | -331 | -371 | -488 | -590 | -769 | ... | Biens : importations f.à.b. |
| Services: credit | 38 | 57 | 51 | 63 | 93 | 88 | ... | Services : crédit |
| Services: debit | -132 | -147 | -152 | -193 | -262 | -279 | ... | Services : débit |
| Income: credit | 13 | 12 | 13 | 17 | 26 | 37 | ... | Revenus : crédit |
| Income: debit | -30 | -27 | -37 | -43 | -39 | -47 | ... | Revenus : débit |
| Current transfers, n.i.e.: credit | 64 | 88 | 65 | 83 | 129 | 217 | ... | Transferts courants, n.i.a. : crédit |

| Country or area | 2000 | 2001 | 2002 | 2003 | 2004 | 2005 | 2006 | Pays ou zone |
|---|---|---|---|---|---|---|---|---|
| Current transfers: debit | -17 | -16 | -12 | -10 | -25 | -35 | ... | Transferts courants : débit |
| Capital account, n.i.e. | 55 | 40 | 92 | 92 | 249 | 49 | ... | Compte de capital, n.i.a. |
| Financial account, n.i.e. | 98 | 61 | 69 | 97 | -173 | 174 | ... | Compte financier, n.i.a. |
| Net errors and omissions | -14 | 14 | -9 | -15 | 116 | 121 | ... | Erreurs et omissions nettes |
| Reserves and related items | -35 | -22 | 12 | 44 | 39 | -33 | ... | Réserves et postes apparentés |
| **Nigeria** | | | | | | | | **Nigéria** |
| Current account | 7 429 | 2 478 | 1 083 | 3 391 | 16 840 | 24 202 | ... | Compte des transactions courantes |
| Goods: exports f.o.b. | 19 132 | 17 992 | 15 613 | 23 976 | 34 766 | 48 069 | ... | Biens : exportations f.à.b. |
| Goods: imports f.o.b. | -8 717 | -11 097 | -10 876 | -16 152 | -15 009 | -17 288 | ... | Biens : importations f.à.b. |
| Services: credit | 1 833 | 1 653 | 2 524 | 3 473 | 3 336 | 4 164 | ... | Services : crédit |
| Services: debit | -3 300 | -4 640 | -4 922 | -5 715 | -5 973 | -7 321 | ... | Services : débit |
| Income: credit | 218 | 199 | 184 | 82 | 157 | 705 | ... | Revenus : crédit |
| Income: debit | -3 365 | -2 997 | -2 854 | -3 325 | -2 689 | -7 437 | ... | Revenus : débit |
| Current transfers, n.i.e.: credit | 1 637 | 1 373 | 1 422 | 1 063 | 2 273 | 3 329 | ... | Transferts courants, n.i.a. : crédit |
| Current transfers: debit | -8 | -6 | -9 | -12 | -21 | -18 | ... | Transferts courants : débit |
| Capital account, n.i.e. | 33 | 0 | 55 | 20 | 36 | 23 | ... | Compte de capital, n.i.a. |
| Financial account, n.i.e. | -6 219 | -3 035 | -6 609 | -10 285 | -13 061 | -23 586 | ... | Compte financier, n.i.a. |
| Net errors and omissions | 1 847 | 779 | 782 | 5 614 | 4 676 | 9 758 | ... | Erreurs et omissions nettes |
| Reserves and related items | -3 089 | -223 | 4 689 | 1 260 | -8 491 | -10 397 | ... | Réserves et postes apparentés |
| **Norway** | | | | | | | | **Norvège** |
| Current account | 25 079 | 27 546 | 24 269 | 27 698 | 33 000 | 46 560 | 58 323 | Compte des transactions courantes |
| Goods: exports f.o.b. | 60 393 | 59 448 | 59 555 | 68 666 | 83 164 | 104 179 | 122 789 | Biens : exportations f.à.b. |
| Goods: imports f.o.b. | -34 485 | -33 046 | -35 263 | -40 504 | -49 035 | -54 490 | -62 933 | Biens : importations f.à.b. |
| Services: credit | 17 718 | 18 355 | 19 488 | 21 663 | 25 263 | 29 305 | 33 328 | Services : crédit |
| Services: debit | -14 991 | -15 798 | -17 972 | -20 569 | -24 304 | -29 549 | -31 957 | Services : débit |
| Income: credit | 7 546 | 9 671 | 10 351 | 14 077 | 17 117 | 18 764 | 30 988 | Revenus : crédit |
| Income: debit | -9 851 | -9 502 | -9 654 | -12 712 | -16 570 | -18 819 | -31 610 | Revenus : débit |
| Current transfers, n.i.e.: credit | 1 657 | 1 815 | 1 877 | 2 049 | 2 553 | 2 983 | 3 304 | Transferts courants, n.i.a. : crédit |
| Current transfers: debit | -2 908 | -3 398 | -4 112 | -4 972 | -5 188 | -5 814 | -5 587 | Transferts courants : débit |
| Capital account, n.i.e. | -91 | -90 | -191 | 678 | -154 | -290 | -97 | Compte de capital, n.i.a. |
| Financial account, n.i.e. | -14 805 | -28 720 | -10 534 | -21 745 | -22 300 | -36 584 | -40 088 | Compte financier, n.i.a. |
| Net errors and omissions | -6 498 | -1 216 | -6 814 | -6 303 | -5 319 | -5 174 | -12 662 | Erreurs et omissions nettes |
| Reserves and related items | -3 686 | 2 481 | -6 730 | -328 | -5 227 | -4 511 | -5 475 | Réserves et postes apparentés |
| **Occupied Palestinian Terr.[3]** | | | | | | | | **Terr. palestinien occupé[3]** |
| Current account | -1 047 | -741 | -458 | -979 | -1 417 | -1 107 | ... | Compte des transactions courantes |
| Goods: exports f.o.b. | 526 | 448 | 365 | 384 | 410 | 412 | ... | Biens : exportations f.à.b. |
| Goods: imports f.o.b. | -2 934 | -2 117 | -1 836 | -2 280 | -2 710 | -3 050 | ... | Biens : importations f.à.b. |
| Services: credit | 462 | 178 | 192 | 214 | 181 | 265 | ... | Services : crédit |
| Services: debit | -566 | -702 | -651 | -516 | -489 | -487 | ... | Services : débit |
| Income: credit | 867 | 504 | 392 | 458 | 459 | 610 | ... | Revenus : crédit |
| Income: debit | -42 | -19 | -11 | -2 | -33 | -36 | ... | Revenus : débit |
| Current transfers, n.i.e.: credit | 764 | 1 068 | 1 187 | 917 | 904 | 1 309 | ... | Transferts courants, n.i.a. : crédit |
| Current transfers: debit | -123 | -101 | -97 | -153 | -139 | -129 | ... | Transferts courants : débit |
| Capital account, n.i.e. | 198 | 226 | 301 | 305 | 670 | 422 | ... | Compte de capital, n.i.a. |
| Financial account, n.i.e. | 890 | 367 | 11 | 888 | 728 | 657 | ... | Compte financier, n.i.a. |
| Net errors and omissions | 50 | 133 | 161 | -113 | 46 | 3 | ... | Erreurs et omissions nettes |
| Reserves and related items | -91 | 16 | -15 | -100 | -27 | 26 | ... | Réserves et postes apparentés |
| **Oman** | | | | | | | | **Oman** |
| Current account | 3 129 | 2 082 | 1 696 | 1 263 | 802 | 4 176 | 4 377 | Compte des transactions courantes |
| Goods: exports f.o.b. | 11 318 | 11 074 | 11 170 | 11 670 | 13 381 | 18 692 | 21 587 | Biens : exportations f.à.b. |
| Goods: imports f.o.b. | -4 593 | -5 308 | -5 633 | -6 086 | -7 873 | -8 029 | -9 896 | Biens : importations f.à.b. |
| Services: credit | 452 | 606 | 606 | 645 | 726 | 741 | 913 | Services : crédit |
| Services: debit | -1 759 | -1 899 | -1 880 | -2 180 | -2 756 | -3 052 | -3 740 | Services : débit |
| Income: credit | 291 | 307 | 242 | 244 | 658 | 676 | 1 202 | Revenus : crédit |
| Income: debit | -1 129 | -1 165 | -1 207 | -1 358 | -1 508 | -2 596 | -2 900 | Revenus : débit |
| Current transfers, n.i.e.: credit | 0 | 0 | 0 | 0 | 0 | 0 | 0 | Transferts courants, n.i.a. : crédit |
| Current transfers: debit | -1 451 | -1 532 | -1 602 | -1 672 | -1 826 | -2 257 | -2 788 | Transferts courants : débit |

**62** Balance of payments summary—Millions of US dollars (*continued*)
Résumé de la balance des paiements—Millions de dollars E.-U (*suite*)

| Country or area | 2000 | 2001 | 2002 | 2003 | 2004 | 2005 | 2006 | Pays ou zone |
|---|---|---|---|---|---|---|---|---|
| Capital account, n.i.e. | 8 | -10 | 5 | 10 | 21 | -16 | -96 | Compte de capital, n.i.a. |
| Financial account, n.i.e. | -370 | -502 | -718 | 140 | 1 012 | -749 | -1 004 | Compte financier, n.i.a. |
| Net errors and omissions | -504 | -557 | -656 | -739 | -987 | -666 | -1 077 | Erreurs et omissions nettes |
| Reserves and related items | -2 263 | -1 013 | -328 | -675 | -847 | -2 746 | -2 200 | Réserves et postes apparentés |
| Pakistan | | | | | | | | Pakistan |
| Current account | -85 | 1 878 | 3 854 | 3 573 | -817 | -3 608 | -6 795 | Compte des transactions courantes |
| Goods: exports f.o.b. | 8 739 | 9 131 | 9 832 | 11 869 | 13 297 | 15 432 | 16 999 | Biens : exportations f.à.b. |
| Goods: imports f.o.b. | -9 896 | -9 741 | -10 428 | -11 978 | -16 693 | -21 773 | -26 701 | Biens : importations f.à.b. |
| Services: credit | 1 380 | 1 459 | 2 429 | 2 968 | 2 749 | 3 678 | 3 508 | Services : crédit |
| Services: debit | -2 252 | -2 330 | -2 241 | -3 294 | -5 333 | -7 510 | -8 411 | Services : débit |
| Income: credit | 118 | 113 | 128 | 180 | 221 | 658 | 867 | Revenus : crédit |
| Income: debit | -2 336 | -2 189 | -2 414 | -2 404 | -2 584 | -3 172 | -3 996 | Revenus : débit |
| Current transfers, n.i.e.: credit | 4 200 | 5 496 | 6 593 | 6 300 | 7 666 | 9 169 | 11 030 | Transferts courants, n.i.a. : crédit |
| Current transfers: debit | -38 | -61 | -45 | -68 | -140 | -90 | -90 | Transferts courants : débit |
| Capital account, n.i.e. | 0 | 0 | 40 | 1 138 | 591 | 202 | 347 | Compte de capital, n.i.a. |
| Financial account, n.i.e. | -3 099 | -389 | -784 | -1 751 | -1 810 | 4 079 | 7 257 | Compte financier, n.i.a. |
| Net errors and omissions | 557 | 708 | 974 | -52 | 685 | -198 | 742 | Erreurs et omissions nettes |
| Reserves and related items | 2 627 | -2 197 | -4 084 | -2 908 | 1 351 | -475 | -1 551 | Réserves et postes apparentés |
| Panama | | | | | | | | Panama |
| Current account | -673 | -170 | -96 | -580 | -1 012 | -759 | -552 | Compte des transactions courantes |
| Goods: exports f.o.b. | 5 839 | 5 992 | 5 315 | 5 072 | 6 078 | 7 591 | 8 476 | Biens : exportations f.à.b. |
| Goods: imports f.o.b. | -6 981 | -6 689 | -6 350 | -6 274 | -7 617 | -8 907 | -10 201 | Biens : importations f.à.b. |
| Services: credit | 1 994 | 1 993 | 2 278 | 2 510 | 2 788 | 3 217 | 3 940 | Services : crédit |
| Services: debit | -1 141 | -1 103 | -1 310 | -1 312 | -1 457 | -1 781 | -1 726 | Services : débit |
| Income: credit | 1 575 | 1 384 | 953 | 793 | 787 | 1 056 | 1 422 | Revenus : crédit |
| Income: debit | -2 136 | -1 974 | -1 226 | -1 614 | -1 811 | -2 181 | -2 719 | Revenus : débit |
| Current transfers, n.i.e.: credit | 209 | 278 | 299 | 311 | 300 | 342 | 394 | Transferts courants, n.i.a. : crédit |
| Current transfers: debit | -32 | -52 | -55 | -64 | -81 | -97 | -136 | Transferts courants : débit |
| Capital account, n.i.e. | 2 | 2 | 0 | 0 | 0 | 0 | 0 | Compte de capital, n.i.a. |
| Financial account, n.i.e. | 332 | 1 301 | 194 | 178 | 497 | 1 989 | 671 | Compte financier, n.i.a. |
| Net errors and omissions | 262 | -499 | 45 | 133 | 119 | -554 | 56 | Erreurs et omissions nettes |
| Reserves and related items | 77 | -634 | -144 | 269 | 396 | -676 | -176 | Réserves et postes apparentés |
| Papua New Guinea | | | | | | | | Papouasie-Nvl-Guinée |
| Current account | 345 | 282 | -129 | -35 | -82 | 423 | ... | Compte des transactions courantes |
| Goods: exports f.o.b. | 2 094 | 1 813 | 1 640 | 2 201 | 2 555 | 3 278 | ... | Biens : exportations f.à.b. |
| Goods: imports f.o.b. | -999 | -932 | -1 077 | -1 187 | -1 459 | -1 525 | ... | Biens : importations f.à.b. |
| Services: credit | 243 | 285 | 162 | 233 | 203 | 302 | ... | Services : crédit |
| Services: debit | -772 | -662 | -678 | -868 | -998 | -1 167 | ... | Services : débit |
| Income: credit | 32 | 20 | 27 | 16 | 20 | 26 | ... | Revenus : crédit |
| Income: debit | -242 | -250 | -229 | -493 | -456 | -565 | ... | Revenus : débit |
| Current transfers, n.i.e.: credit | 62 | 76 | 86 | 144 | 130 | 167 | ... | Transferts courants, n.i.a. : crédit |
| Current transfers: debit | -73 | -67 | -59 | -81 | -77 | -94 | ... | Transferts courants : débit |
| Capital account, n.i.e. | 0 | 0 | 0 | 0 | 0 | 0 | ... | Compte de capital, n.i.a. |
| Financial account, n.i.e. | -254 | -152 | 56 | -282 | -42 | -752 | ... | Compte financier, n.i.a. |
| Net errors and omissions | 13 | -2 | 91 | 40 | 26 | 47 | ... | Erreurs et omissions nettes |
| Reserves and related items | -104 | -129 | -19 | 277 | 98 | 282 | ... | Réserves et postes apparentés |
| Paraguay | | | | | | | | Paraguay |
| Current account | -163 | -266 | 93 | 129 | 143 | 37 | -217 | Compte des transactions courantes |
| Goods: exports f.o.b. | 2 329 | 1 890 | 1 858 | 2 170 | 2 861 | 3 352 | 4 838 | Biens : exportations f.à.b. |
| Goods: imports f.o.b. | -2 866 | -2 504 | -2 138 | -2 446 | -3 105 | -3 814 | -5 772 | Biens : importations f.à.b. |
| Services: credit | 595 | 555 | 568 | 574 | 628 | 693 | 807 | Services : crédit |
| Services: debit | -420 | -390 | -355 | -329 | -301 | -344 | -425 | Services : débit |
| Income: credit | 261 | 256 | 196 | 166 | 165 | 193 | 258 | Revenus : crédit |
| Income: debit | -238 | -240 | -153 | -171 | -299 | -266 | -309 | Revenus : débit |
| Current transfers, n.i.e.: credit | 178 | 168 | 118 | 166 | 196 | 225 | 390 | Transferts courants, n.i.a. : crédit |
| Current transfers: debit | -2 | -2 | -2 | -2 | -2 | -2 | -4 | Transferts courants : débit |
| Capital account, n.i.e. | 3 | 15 | 4 | 15 | 16 | 20 | 30 | Compte de capital, n.i.a. |
| Financial account, n.i.e. | 64 | 151 | 44 | 132 | 19 | 314 | 359 | Compte financier, n.i.a. |

| Country or area | 2000 | 2001 | 2002 | 2003 | 2004 | 2005 | 2006 | Pays ou zone |
|---|---|---|---|---|---|---|---|---|
| Net errors and omissions | -243 | 53 | -263 | -41 | 95 | -208 | 212 | Erreurs et omissions nettes |
| Reserves and related items | 339 | 47 | 123 | -236 | -273 | -163 | -383 | Réserves et postes apparentés |
| **Peru** | | | | | | | | **Pérou** |
| Current account | -1 546 | -1 203 | -1 110 | -949 | 19 | 1 148 | 2 589 | Compte des transactions courantes |
| Goods: exports f.o.b. | 6 955 | 7 026 | 7 714 | 9 091 | 12 809 | 17 368 | 23 800 | Biens : exportations f.à.b. |
| Goods: imports f.o.b. | -7 358 | -7 204 | -7 393 | -8 205 | -9 805 | -12 082 | -14 866 | Biens : importations f.à.b. |
| Services: credit | 1 555 | 1 437 | 1 455 | 1 716 | 1 993 | 2 289 | 2 451 | Services : crédit |
| Services: debit | -2 290 | -2 400 | -2 449 | -2 616 | -2 725 | -3 123 | -3 400 | Services : débit |
| Income: credit | 737 | 670 | 370 | 322 | 332 | 625 | 1 033 | Revenus : crédit |
| Income: debit | -2 146 | -1 771 | -1 827 | -2 466 | -4 017 | -5 701 | -8 614 | Revenus : débit |
| Current transfers, n.i.e.: credit | 1 010 | 1 048 | 1 028 | 1 215 | 1 439 | 1 781 | 2 194 | Transferts courants, n.i.a. : crédit |
| Current transfers: debit | -9 | -8 | -8 | -6 | -6 | -10 | -10 | Transferts courants : débit |
| Capital account, n.i.e. | -259 | -155 | -112 | -112 | -86 | -123 | -127 | Compte de capital, n.i.a. |
| Financial account, n.i.e. | 1 015 | 1 534 | 1 983 | 820 | 2 286 | 24 | 1 204 | Compte financier, n.i.a. |
| Net errors and omissions | 659 | 255 | 249 | 801 | 236 | 362 | -445 | Erreurs et omissions nettes |
| Reserves and related items | 130 | -432 | -1 010 | -561 | -2 456 | -1 411 | -3 221 | Réserves et postes apparentés |
| **Philippines** | | | | | | | | **Philippines** |
| Current account | -2 225 | -1 744 | -279 | 288 | 1 633 | 1 984 | 5 897 | Compte des transactions courantes |
| Goods: exports f.o.b. | 37 347 | 31 313 | 34 403 | 35 339 | 38 794 | 40 263 | 46 526 | Biens : exportations f.à.b. |
| Goods: imports f.o.b. | -43 318 | -37 578 | -39 933 | -41 190 | -44 478 | -48 036 | -53 343 | Biens : importations f.à.b. |
| Services: credit | 3 377 | 3 072 | 3 428 | 3 389 | 4 043 | 4 525 | 6 453 | Services : crédit |
| Services: debit | -5 247 | -5 360 | -5 430 | -5 352 | -5 815 | -5 865 | -6 120 | Services : débit |
| Income: credit | 3 336 | 3 553 | 3 306 | 3 330 | 3 725 | 3 937 | 4 390 | Revenus : crédit |
| Income: debit | -3 363 | -3 604 | -3 733 | -3 614 | -3 796 | -4 231 | -5 189 | Revenus : débit |
| Current transfers, n.i.e.: credit | 5 909 | 7 119 | 7 948 | 8 626 | 9 420 | 11 711 | 13 511 | Transferts courants, n.i.a. : crédit |
| Current transfers: debit | -266 | -259 | -268 | -240 | -260 | -320 | -331 | Transferts courants : débit |
| Capital account, n.i.e. | 138 | 62 | 27 | 54 | 17 | 40 | 138 | Compte de capital, n.i.a. |
| Financial account, n.i.e. | 3 234 | 366 | 394 | 481 | -1 671 | 1 441 | -663 | Compte financier, n.i.a. |
| Net errors and omissions | -1 624 | 629 | 33 | -902 | -282 | -1 803 | -657 | Erreurs et omissions nettes |
| Reserves and related items | 477 | 687 | -175 | 79 | 303 | -1 662 | -4 715 | Réserves et postes apparentés |
| **Poland** | | | | | | | | **Pologne** |
| Current account | -9 981 | -5 375 | -5 009 | -4 599 | -10 693 | -4 775 | -11 084 | Compte des transactions courantes |
| Goods: exports f.o.b. | 35 902 | 41 663 | 46 742 | 61 007 | 81 862 | 96 395 | 117 468 | Biens : exportations f.à.b. |
| Goods: imports f.o.b. | -48 209 | -49 324 | -53 991 | -66 732 | -87 484 | -99 161 | -124 472 | Biens : importations f.à.b. |
| Services: credit | 10 398 | 9 753 | 10 037 | 11 174 | 13 471 | 16 258 | 20 584 | Services : crédit |
| Services: debit | -8 993 | -8 966 | -9 186 | -10 647 | -12 457 | -14 312 | -18 367 | Services : débit |
| Income: credit | 2 250 | 2 625 | 1 948 | 2 108 | 2 016 | 2 795 | 4 147 | Revenus : crédit |
| Income: debit | -3 709 | -4 015 | -3 837 | -5 745 | -13 552 | -13 684 | -18 647 | Revenus : débit |
| Current transfers, n.i.e.: credit | 3 008 | 3 737 | 4 181 | 5 316 | 8 101 | 11 036 | 12 785 | Transferts courants, n.i.a. : crédit |
| Current transfers: debit | -628 | -848 | -903 | -1 080 | -2 650 | -4 102 | -4 582 | Transferts courants : débit |
| Capital account, n.i.e. | 34 | 76 | -7 | -46 | 1 180 | 995 | 2 105 | Compte de capital, n.i.a. |
| Financial account, n.i.e. | 10 221 | 3 173 | 7 180 | 8 686 | 8 532 | 15 295 | 12 111 | Compte financier, n.i.a. |
| Net errors and omissions | 350 | 1 699 | -1 516 | -2 835 | 1 782 | -3 369 | -643 | Erreurs et omissions nettes |
| Reserves and related items | -624 | 427 | -648 | -1 206 | -801 | -8 146 | -2 489 | Réserves et postes apparentés |
| **Portugal** | | | | | | | | **Portugal** |
| Current account | -11 595 | -11 445 | -10 264 | -9 593 | -13 851 | -18 048 | -18 281 | Compte des transactions courantes |
| Goods: exports f.o.b. | 24 663 | 24 456 | 25 975 | 32 055 | 36 957 | 38 238 | 43 579 | Biens : exportations f.à.b. |
| Goods: imports f.o.b. | -39 195 | -38 362 | -39 286 | -46 337 | -55 673 | -59 073 | -64 451 | Biens : importations f.à.b. |
| Services: credit | 9 016 | 9 379 | 10 357 | 12 354 | 14 701 | 15 193 | 17 809 | Services : crédit |
| Services: debit | -7 053 | -6 826 | -7 146 | -8 293 | -9 746 | -10 463 | -11 612 | Services : débit |
| Income: credit | 4 806 | 5 669 | 4 900 | 6 622 | 8 025 | 9 297 | 12 308 | Revenus : crédit |
| Income: debit | -7 177 | -9 127 | -7 891 | -9 260 | -11 652 | -14 066 | -19 062 | Revenus : débit |
| Current transfers, n.i.e.: credit | 5 495 | 5 677 | 5 544 | 6 544 | 7 297 | 7 226 | 8 039 | Transferts courants, n.i.a. : crédit |
| Current transfers: debit | -2 150 | -2 312 | -2 717 | -3 278 | -3 761 | -4 399 | -4 892 | Transferts courants : débit |
| Capital account, n.i.e. | 1 512 | 1 069 | 1 906 | 3 010 | 2 808 | 2 139 | 1 578 | Compte de capital, n.i.a. |
| Financial account, n.i.e. | 10 749 | 10 606 | 8 796 | -838 | 9 989 | 15 275 | 12 672 | Compte financier, n.i.a. |
| Net errors and omissions | -295 | 623 | 580 | 967 | -809 | -1 106 | 1 675 | Erreurs et omissions nettes |
| Reserves and related items | -371 | -852 | -1 017 | 6 455 | 1 863 | 1 741 | 2 357 | Réserves et postes apparentés |

**62** Balance of payments summary—Millions of US dollars (*continued*)
Résumé de la balance des paiements—Millions de dollars E.-U (*suite*)

| Country or area | 2000 | 2001 | 2002 | 2003 | 2004 | 2005 | 2006 | Pays ou zone |
|---|---|---|---|---|---|---|---|---|
| Romania | | | | | | | | Roumanie |
| Current account | -1 355 | -2 229 | -1 525 | -3 311 | -6 382 | -8 621 | -12 785 | Compte des transactions courantes |
| Goods: exports f.o.b. | 10 366 | 11 385 | 13 876 | 17 618 | 23 485 | 27 730 | 32 336 | Biens : exportations f.à.b. |
| Goods: imports f.o.b. | -12 050 | -14 354 | -16 487 | -22 155 | -30 150 | -37 348 | -47 172 | Biens : importations f.à.b. |
| Services: credit | 1 747 | 2 032 | 2 347 | 3 028 | 3 614 | 5 083 | 7 032 | Services : crédit |
| Services: debit | -1 993 | -2 153 | -2 338 | -2 958 | -3 879 | -5 518 | -7 027 | Services : débit |
| Income: credit | 325 | 455 | 413 | 372 | 433 | 1 533 | 2 176 | Revenus : crédit |
| Income: debit | -610 | -737 | -872 | -1 077 | -3 582 | -4 432 | -6 255 | Revenus : débit |
| Current transfers, n.i.e.: credit | 1 079 | 1 417 | 1 808 | 2 200 | 4 188 | 4 939 | 6 995 | Transferts courants, n.i.a. : crédit |
| Current transfers: debit | -219 | -274 | -272 | -339 | -491 | -607 | -870 | Transferts courants : débit |
| Capital account, n.i.e. | 36 | 95 | 93 | 213 | 643 | 731 | -34 | Compte de capital, n.i.a. |
| Financial account, n.i.e. | 2 102 | 2 938 | 4 079 | 4 400 | 10 761 | 14 089 | 18 899 | Compte financier, n.i.a. |
| Net errors and omissions | 125 | 731 | -856 | -289 | 1 167 | 612 | 521 | Erreurs et omissions nettes |
| Reserves and related items | -908 | -1 535 | -1 791 | -1 013 | -6 189 | -6 811 | -6 602 | Réserves et postes apparentés |
| Russian Federation | | | | | | | | Fédération de Russie |
| Current account | 46 839 | 33 935 | 29 116 | 35 410 | 59 514 | 84 444 | 94 257 | Compte des transactions courantes |
| Goods: exports f.o.b. | 105 033 | 101 884 | 107 301 | 135 929 | 183 207 | 243 798 | 303 926 | Biens : exportations f.à.b. |
| Goods: imports f.o.b. | -44 862 | -53 764 | -60 966 | -76 070 | -97 382 | -125 434 | -164 692 | Biens : importations f.à.b. |
| Services: credit | 9 565 | 11 442 | 13 611 | 16 229 | 20 595 | 24 970 | 30 927 | Services : crédit |
| Services: debit | -16 230 | -20 572 | -23 497 | -27 122 | -33 287 | -38 865 | -44 739 | Services : débit |
| Income: credit | 4 753 | 6 800 | 5 677 | 11 057 | 11 998 | 17 382 | 29 505 | Revenus : crédit |
| Income: debit | -11 489 | -11 038 | -12 260 | -24 228 | -24 767 | -36 371 | -59 133 | Revenus : débit |
| Current transfers, n.i.e.: credit | 807 | 744 | 1 352 | 2 537 | 3 467 | 4 490 | 6 403 | Transferts courants, n.i.a. : crédit |
| Current transfers: debit | -738 | -1 561 | -2 103 | -2 922 | -4 317 | -5 528 | -7 940 | Transferts courants : débit |
| Capital account, n.i.e. | 10 676 | -9 378 | -12 396 | -993 | -1 624 | -12 764 | 191 | Compte de capital, n.i.a. |
| Financial account, n.i.e. | -33 855 | -3 308 | 1 345 | 3 558 | -4 564 | 1 614 | 5 568 | Compte financier, n.i.a. |
| Net errors and omissions | -9 737 | -9 982 | -6 502 | -9 713 | -6 436 | -8 326 | 7 450 | Erreurs et omissions nettes |
| Reserves and related items | -13 923 | -11 266 | -11 563 | -28 262 | -46 890 | -64 968 | -107 466 | Réserves et postes apparentés |
| Rwanda | | | | | | | | Rwanda |
| Current account | -94 | -102 | -126 | -121 | -198 | -84 | -180 | Compte des transactions courantes |
| Goods: exports f.o.b. | 68 | 93 | 67 | 63 | 98 | 128 | 145 | Biens : exportations f.à.b. |
| Goods: imports f.o.b. | -223 | -245 | -233 | -229 | -276 | -355 | -488 | Biens : importations f.à.b. |
| Services: credit | 59 | 66 | 65 | 76 | 103 | 129 | 131 | Services : crédit |
| Services: debit | -200 | -189 | -202 | -204 | -240 | -304 | -243 | Services : débit |
| Income: credit | 14 | 14 | 8 | 6 | 6 | 27 | 27 | Revenus : crédit |
| Income: debit | -28 | -34 | -27 | -37 | -39 | -44 | -48 | Revenus : débit |
| Current transfers, n.i.e.: credit | 233 | 210 | 215 | 223 | 169 | 352 | 319 | Transferts courants, n.i.a. : crédit |
| Current transfers: debit | -17 | -18 | -20 | -20 | -18 | -18 | -23 | Transferts courants : débit |
| Capital account, n.i.e. | 62 | 50 | 66 | 41 | 61 | 93 | 1 323 | Compte de capital, n.i.a. |
| Financial account, n.i.e. | 11 | -44 | 81 | -21 | -21 | -59 | -1 204 | Compte financier, n.i.a. |
| Net errors and omissions | 21 | 71 | -8 | 23 | -9 | 26 | 87 | Erreurs et omissions nettes |
| Reserves and related items | ^0 | 26 | -13 | 78 | 168 | 23 | -26 | Réserves et postes apparentés |
| Saint Kitts and Nevis | | | | | | | | Saint-Kitts-et-Nevis |
| Current account | -66 | -107 | -125 | -116 | -86 | -80 | ... | Compte des transactions courantes |
| Goods: exports f.o.b. | 51 | 55 | 63 | 57 | 57 | 62 | ... | Biens : exportations f.à.b. |
| Goods: imports f.o.b. | -173 | -167 | -178 | -176 | -175 | -185 | ... | Biens : importations f.à.b. |
| Services: credit | 99 | 98 | 90 | 108 | 135 | 148 | ... | Services : crédit |
| Services: debit | -76 | -75 | -79 | -80 | -83 | -92 | ... | Services : débit |
| Income: credit | 6 | 5 | 6 | 6 | 8 | 11 | ... | Revenus : crédit |
| Income: debit | -36 | -39 | -44 | -49 | -46 | -45 | ... | Revenus : débit |
| Current transfers, n.i.e.: credit | 70 | 27 | 28 | 30 | 31 | 33 | ... | Transferts courants, n.i.a. : crédit |
| Current transfers: debit | -7 | -11 | -12 | -11 | -13 | -13 | ... | Transferts courants : débit |
| Capital account, n.i.e. | 6 | 11 | 15 | 5 | 5 | 15 | ... | Compte de capital, n.i.a. |
| Financial account, n.i.e. | 77 | 114 | 116 | 105 | 80 | 52 | ... | Compte financier, n.i.a. |
| Net errors and omissions | -21 | -6 | 2 | 5 | 14 | 6 | ... | Erreurs et omissions nettes |
| Reserves and related items | 4 | -12 | -9 | 1 | -14 | 7 | ... | Réserves et postes apparentés |

| Country or area | 2000 | 2001 | 2002 | 2003 | 2004 | 2005 | 2006 | Pays ou zone |
|---|---|---|---|---|---|---|---|---|
| Saint Lucia | | | | | | | | Sainte-Lucie |
| Current account | -95 | -108 | -106 | -144 | -115 | -154 | ... | Compte des transactions courantes |
| Goods: exports f.o.b. | 53 | 54 | 69 | 72 | 96 | 83 | ... | Biens : exportations f.à.b. |
| Goods: imports f.o.b. | -312 | -272 | -272 | -355 | -371 | -418 | ... | Biens : importations f.à.b. |
| Services: credit | 324 | 274 | 250 | 318 | 367 | 410 | ... | Services : crédit |
| Services: debit | -133 | -131 | -129 | -145 | -154 | -171 | ... | Services : débit |
| Income: credit | 4 | 3 | 4 | 5 | 6 | 8 | ... | Revenus : crédit |
| Income: debit | -48 | -50 | -40 | -52 | -74 | -79 | ... | Revenus : débit |
| Current transfers, n.i.e.: credit | 29 | 29 | 28 | 29 | 30 | 30 | ... | Transferts courants, n.i.a. : crédit |
| Current transfers: debit | -10 | -15 | -16 | -16 | -16 | -17 | ... | Transferts courants : débit |
| Capital account, n.i.e. | 14 | 25 | 20 | 17 | 3 | 5 | ... | Compte de capital, n.i.a. |
| Financial account, n.i.e. | 86 | 87 | 94 | 136 | 129 | 151 | ... | Compte financier, n.i.a. |
| Net errors and omissions | 8 | 8 | -2 | 10 | 9 | -17 | ... | Erreurs et omissions nettes |
| Reserves and related items | -13 | -13 | -6 | -18 | -27 | 15 | ... | Réserves et postes apparentés |
| Saint Vincent-Grenadines | | | | | | | | Saint Vincent-Grenadines |
| Current account | -24 | -37 | -42 | -79 | -103 | -101 | ... | Compte des transactions courantes |
| Goods: exports f.o.b. | 52 | 43 | 41 | 40 | 39 | 44 | ... | Biens : exportations f.à.b. |
| Goods: imports f.o.b. | -144 | -152 | -158 | -177 | -199 | -212 | ... | Biens : importations f.à.b. |
| Services: credit | 128 | 133 | 137 | 133 | 145 | 159 | ... | Services : crédit |
| Services: debit | -56 | -57 | -57 | -65 | -73 | -85 | ... | Services : débit |
| Income: credit | 3 | 2 | 3 | 4 | 5 | 12 | ... | Revenus : crédit |
| Income: debit | -22 | -19 | -21 | -28 | -34 | -37 | ... | Revenus : débit |
| Current transfers, n.i.e.: credit | 25 | 23 | 24 | 24 | 25 | 27 | ... | Transferts courants, n.i.a. : crédit |
| Current transfers: debit | -8 | -11 | -12 | -11 | -11 | -8 | ... | Transferts courants : débit |
| Capital account, n.i.e. | 6 | 9 | 11 | 14 | 19 | 14 | ... | Compte de capital, n.i.a. |
| Financial account, n.i.e. | 25 | 49 | 15 | 49 | 82 | 79 | ... | Compte financier, n.i.a. |
| Net errors and omissions | 8 | -11 | 9 | 16 | 27 | 6 | ... | Erreurs et omissions nettes |
| Reserves and related items | -14 | -9 | 7 | 1 | -25 | 3 | ... | Réserves et postes apparentés |
| Samoa | | | | | | | | Samoa |
| Current account | ... | ... | ... | ... | -17 | -24 | -51 | Compte des transactions courantes |
| Goods: exports f.o.b. | ... | ... | ... | ... | 12 | 12 | 10 | Biens : exportations f.à.b. |
| Goods: imports f.o.b. | ... | ... | ... | ... | -155 | -187 | -219 | Biens : importations f.à.b. |
| Services: credit | ... | ... | ... | ... | 95 | 112 | 134 | Services : crédit |
| Services: debit | ... | ... | ... | ... | -42 | -53 | -57 | Services : débit |
| Income: credit | ... | ... | ... | ... | 4 | 6 | 4 | Revenus : crédit |
| Income: debit | ... | ... | ... | ... | -21 | -20 | -18 | Revenus : débit |
| Current transfers, n.i.e.: credit | ... | ... | ... | ... | 105 | 114 | 107 | Transferts courants, n.i.a. : crédit |
| Current transfers: debit | ... | ... | ... | ... | -15 | -8 | -13 | Transferts courants : débit |
| Capital account, n.i.e. | ... | ... | ... | ... | 44 | 41 | 42 | Compte de capital, n.i.a. |
| Financial account, n.i.e. | ... | ... | ... | ... | -7 | -10 | 8 | Compte financier, n.i.a. |
| Net errors and omissions | ... | ... | ... | ... | -12 | -7 | -3 | Erreurs et omissions nettes |
| Reserves and related items | ... | ... | ... | ... | -8 | 1 | 5 | Réserves et postes apparentés |
| Sao Tome and Principe | | | | | | | | Sao Tomé-et-Principé |
| Current account | -19 | -27 | -27 | -28 | ... | ... | ... | Compte des transactions courantes |
| Goods: exports f.o.b. | 3 | 3 | 6 | 7 | ... | ... | ... | Biens : exportations f.à.b. |
| Goods: imports f.o.b. | -25 | -27 | -28 | -34 | ... | ... | ... | Biens : importations f.à.b. |
| Services: credit | 14 | 8 | 9 | 9 | ... | ... | ... | Services : crédit |
| Services: debit | -11 | -12 | -12 | -14 | ... | ... | ... | Services : débit |
| Income: credit | 0 | 1 | 1 | 1 | ... | ... | ... | Revenus : crédit |
| Income: debit | -4 | -4 | -4 | -4 | ... | ... | ... | Revenus : débit |
| Current transfers, n.i.e.: credit | 4 | 5 | 4 | 7 | ... | ... | ... | Transferts courants, n.i.a. : crédit |
| Current transfers: debit | 0 | -1 | -1 | -1 | ... | ... | ... | Transferts courants : débit |
| Capital account, n.i.e. | 12 | 17 | 15 | 19 | ... | ... | ... | Compte de capital, n.i.a. |
| Financial account, n.i.e. | 3 | 10 | 7 | 9 | ... | ... | ... | Compte financier, n.i.a. |
| Net errors and omissions | -2 | 1 | 1 | 2 | ... | ... | ... | Erreurs et omissions nettes |
| Reserves and related items | 5 | -1 | 4 | -2 | ... | ... | ... | Réserves et postes apparentés |
| Saudi Arabia | | | | | | | | Arabie saoudite |
| Current account | 14 317 | 9 353 | 11 873 | 28 048 | 51 926 | 90 060 | 99 066 | Compte des transactions courantes |
| Goods: exports f.o.b. | 77 481 | 67 973 | 72 464 | 93 244 | 125 998 | 180 712 | 211 305 | Biens : exportations f.à.b. |

| Country or area | 2000 | 2001 | 2002 | 2003 | 2004 | 2005 | 2006 | Pays ou zone |
|---|---|---|---|---|---|---|---|---|
| Goods: imports f.o.b. | -27 704 | -28 607 | -29 624 | -33 868 | -41 050 | -54 595 | -63 914 | Biens : importations f.à.b. |
| Services: credit | 4 779 | 5 008 | 5 177 | 5 713 | 5 852 | 6 677 | 7 297 | Services : crédit |
| Services: debit | -25 228 | -19 281 | -19 980 | -20 857 | -25 696 | -28 639 | -40 552 | Services : débit |
| Income: credit | 3 345 | 4 125 | 3 714 | 2 977 | 4 278 | 4 964 | 10 376 | Revenus : crédit |
| Income: debit | -2 865 | -4 644 | -3 925 | -4 277 | -3 800 | -4 963 | -9 734 | Revenus : débit |
| Current transfers, n.i.e.: credit | 0 | 0 | 0 | 0 | 0 | 0 | 0 | Transferts courants, n.i.a. : crédit |
| Current transfers: debit | -15 490 | -15 220 | -15 954 | -14 883 | -13 655 | -14 096 | -15 711 | Transferts courants : débit |
| Capital account, n.i.e. | 0 | 0 | 0 | 0 | 0 | 0 | 0 | Compte de capital, n.i.a. |
| Financial account, n.i.e. | -11 652 | -11 262 | -9 137 | -26 440 | -47 428 | -90 525 | -98 172 | Compte financier, n.i.a. |
| Net errors and omissions^ | 0 | 0 | 0 | 0 | 0 | 0 | 0 | Erreurs et omissions nettes^ |
| Reserves and related items | -2 665 | 1 909 | -2 736 | -1 608 | -4 498 | 465 | -894 | Réserves et postes apparentés |
| **Senegal** | | | | | | | | **Sénégal** |
| Current account | -332 | -245 | -317 | -437 | -513 | ... | ... | Compte des transactions courantes |
| Goods: exports f.o.b. | 920 | 1 003 | 1 067 | 1 257 | 1 509 | ... | ... | Biens : exportations f.à.b. |
| Goods: imports f.o.b. | -1 337 | -1 428 | -1 604 | -2 066 | -2 496 | ... | ... | Biens : importations f.à.b. |
| Services: credit | 387 | 398 | 456 | 569 | 670 | ... | ... | Services : crédit |
| Services: debit | -405 | -414 | -474 | -591 | -698 | ... | ... | Services : débit |
| Income: credit | 76 | 62 | 65 | 86 | 95 | ... | ... | Revenus : crédit |
| Income: debit | -188 | -166 | -195 | -223 | -226 | ... | ... | Revenus : débit |
| Current transfers, n.i.e.: credit | 275 | 354 | 414 | 596 | 715 | ... | ... | Transferts courants, n.i.a. : crédit |
| Current transfers: debit | -61 | -53 | -46 | -65 | -83 | ... | ... | Transferts courants : débit |
| Capital account, n.i.e. | 83 | 146 | 127 | 150 | 750 | ... | ... | Compte de capital, n.i.a. |
| Financial account, n.i.e. | 27 | -103 | -88 | 3 | -54 | ... | ... | Compte financier, n.i.a. |
| Net errors and omissions | -9 | 8 | 31 | 11 | 16 | ... | ... | Erreurs et omissions nettes |
| Reserves and related items | 231 | 194 | 247 | 273 | -199 | ... | ... | Réserves et postes apparentés |
| **Seychelles** | | | | | | | | **Seychelles** |
| Current account | -54 | -158 | -108 | -12 | -64 | -210 | -175 | Compte des transactions courantes |
| Goods: exports f.o.b. | 195 | 216 | 237 | 286 | 301 | 351 | 423 | Biens : exportations f.à.b. |
| Goods: imports f.o.b. | -312 | -429 | -380 | -376 | -456 | -650 | -710 | Biens : importations f.à.b. |
| Services: credit | 287 | 294 | 313 | 330 | 327 | 369 | 431 | Services : crédit |
| Services: debit | -190 | -216 | -217 | -220 | -216 | -256 | -312 | Services : débit |
| Income: credit | 10 | 8 | 7 | 12 | 9 | 10 | 10 | Revenus : crédit |
| Income: debit | -43 | -37 | -75 | -55 | -43 | -50 | -54 | Revenus : débit |
| Current transfers, n.i.e.: credit | 7 | 8 | 8 | 13 | 17 | 21 | 47 | Transferts courants, n.i.a. : crédit |
| Current transfers: debit | -8 | -4 | -2 | -3 | -3 | -4 | -10 | Transferts courants : débit |
| Capital account, n.i.e. | 1 | 9 | 5 | 7 | 1 | 30 | 13 | Compte de capital, n.i.a. |
| Financial account, n.i.e. | 76 | 94 | 131 | -31 | -30 | 148 | 253 | Compte financier, n.i.a. |
| Net errors and omissions | 3 | 1 | -10 | -5 | 1 | 2 | 2 | Erreurs et omissions nettes |
| Reserves and related items | -26 | 54 | -17 | 41 | 93 | 29 | -93 | Réserves et postes apparentés |
| **Sierra Leone** | | | | | | | | **Sierra Leone** |
| Current account | -112 | -98 | -125 | -99 | -141 | -170 | -146 | Compte des transactions courantes |
| Goods: exports f.o.b. | 13 | 29 | 60 | 111 | 154 | 184 | 273 | Biens : exportations f.à.b. |
| Goods: imports f.o.b. | -137 | -165 | -255 | -311 | -274 | -362 | -351 | Biens : importations f.à.b. |
| Services: credit | 42 | 52 | 38 | 66 | 61 | 78 | 40 | Services : crédit |
| Services: debit | -113 | -111 | -81 | -94 | -92 | -91 | -83 | Services : débit |
| Income: credit | 7 | 4 | 18 | 2 | 4 | 5 | 11 | Revenus : crédit |
| Income: debit | -13 | -15 | -21 | -17 | -71 | -56 | -52 | Revenus : débit |
| Current transfers, n.i.e.: credit | 92 | 121 | 119 | 149 | 80 | 74 | 53 | Transferts courants, n.i.a. : crédit |
| Current transfers: debit | -5 | -13 | -4 | -5 | -3 | -2 | -36 | Transferts courants : débit |
| Capital account, n.i.e. | 0 | ^0 | 8 | 16 | 18 | 37 | 50 | Compte de capital, n.i.a. |
| Financial account, n.i.e. | 125 | 30 | 19 | 34 | 76 | 63 | 36 | Compte financier, n.i.a. |
| Net errors and omissions | -3 | 97 | -16 | -50 | -54 | -59 | 119 | Erreurs et omissions nettes |
| Reserves and related items | -10 | -30 | 114 | 100 | 100 | 130 | -59 | Réserves et postes apparentés |
| **Singapore** | | | | | | | | **Singapour** |
| Current account | 10 728 | 11 974 | 12 126 | 22 331 | 21 559 | 28 569 | 36 326 | Compte des transactions courantes |
| Goods: exports f.o.b. | 153 095 | 136 609 | 140 776 | 161 724 | 201 059 | 232 123 | 274 980 | Biens : exportations f.à.b. |
| Goods: imports f.o.b. | -139 138 | -119 358 | -121 972 | -132 152 | -168 179 | -195 436 | -230 233 | Biens : importations f.à.b. |
| Services: credit | 28 171 | 27 406 | 29 524 | 36 288 | 46 688 | 52 742 | 59 076 | Services : crédit |
| Services: debit | -29 506 | -31 524 | -33 172 | -39 926 | -50 206 | -55 083 | -61 929 | Services : débit |

| Country or area | 2000 | 2001 | 2002 | 2003 | 2004 | 2005 | 2006 | Pays ou zone |
|---|---|---|---|---|---|---|---|---|
| Income: credit | 15 623 | 13 863 | 13 554 | 16 640 | 20 780 | 25 680 | 30 340 | Revenus : crédit |
| Income: debit | -16 357 | -13 856 | -15 450 | -19 112 | -27 432 | -30 244 | -34 524 | Revenus : débit |
| Current transfers, n.i.e.: credit | 128 | 124 | 127 | 131 | 136 | 138 | 144 | Transferts courants, n.i.a. : crédit |
| Current transfers: debit | -1 288 | -1 291 | -1 263 | -1 263 | -1 286 | -1 351 | -1 527 | Transferts courants : débit |
| Capital account, n.i.e. | -163 | -161 | -160 | -168 | -184 | -202 | -226 | Compte de capital, n.i.a. |
| Financial account, n.i.e. | -5 760 | -11 765 | -10 392 | -17 476 | -7 393 | -18 950 | -20 754 | Compte financier, n.i.a. |
| Net errors and omissions | 2 017 | -964 | -317 | 2 017 | -1 789 | 2 897 | 1 662 | Erreurs et omissions nettes |
| Reserves and related items | -6 822 | 917 | -1 256 | -6 703 | -12 193 | -12 315 | -17 008 | Réserves et postes apparentés |
| **Slovakia** | | | | | | | | **Slovaquie** |
| Current account | -694 | ... | -1 955 | -282 | ... | ... | ... | Compte des transactions courantes |
| Goods: exports f.o.b. | 11 896 | ... | 14 460 | 21 944 | ... | ... | ... | Biens : exportations f.à.b. |
| Goods: imports f.o.b. | -12 791 | ... | -16 626 | -22 593 | ... | ... | ... | Biens : importations f.à.b. |
| Services: credit | 2 241 | ... | 2 812 | 3 297 | ... | ... | ... | Services : crédit |
| Services: debit | -1 805 | ... | -2 351 | -3 056 | ... | ... | ... | Services : débit |
| Income: credit | 268 | ... | 342 | 907 | ... | ... | ... | Revenus : crédit |
| Income: debit | -623 | ... | -791 | -1 026 | ... | ... | ... | Revenus : débit |
| Current transfers, n.i.e.: credit | 344 | ... | 480 | 537 | ... | ... | ... | Transferts courants, n.i.a. : crédit |
| Current transfers: debit | -224 | ... | -282 | -292 | ... | ... | ... | Transferts courants : débit |
| Capital account, n.i.e. | 91 | ... | 110 | 102 | ... | ... | ... | Compte de capital, n.i.a. |
| Financial account, n.i.e. | 1 472 | ... | 5 230 | 1 661 | ... | ... | ... | Compte financier, n.i.a. |
| Net errors and omissions | 51 | ... | 298 | 27 | ... | ... | ... | Erreurs et omissions nettes |
| Reserves and related items | -920 | ... | -3 684 | -1 508 | ... | ... | ... | Réserves et postes apparentés |
| **Slovenia** | | | | | | | | **Slovénie** |
| Current account | -548 | 31 | 244 | -216 | -893 | -681 | -1 088 | Compte des transactions courantes |
| Goods: exports f.o.b. | 8 808 | 9 343 | 10 471 | 12 916 | 16 065 | 18 146 | 21 397 | Biens : exportations f.à.b. |
| Goods: imports f.o.b. | -9 947 | -9 962 | -10 719 | -13 539 | -17 322 | -19 404 | -22 856 | Biens : importations f.à.b. |
| Services: credit | 1 888 | 1 961 | 2 316 | 2 791 | 3 455 | 3 976 | 4 344 | Services : crédit |
| Services: debit | -1 438 | -1 458 | -1 732 | -2 183 | -2 603 | -2 915 | -3 254 | Services : débit |
| Income: credit | 434 | 463 | 468 | 589 | 667 | 781 | 1 135 | Revenus : crédit |
| Income: debit | -408 | -444 | -617 | -821 | -1 060 | -1 143 | -1 642 | Revenus : débit |
| Current transfers, n.i.e.: credit | 341 | 390 | 473 | 538 | 698 | 878 | 988 | Transferts courants, n.i.a. : crédit |
| Current transfers: debit | -225 | -261 | -416 | -508 | -792 | -998 | -1 202 | Transferts courants : débit |
| Capital account, n.i.e. | 3 | -3 | -159 | -191 | -123 | -138 | -169 | Compte de capital, n.i.a. |
| Financial account, n.i.e. | 680 | 1 204 | 1 987 | 567 | 702 | 844 | -129 | Compte financier, n.i.a. |
| Net errors and omissions | 42 | 53 | -255 | 150 | 17 | 181 | -270 | Erreurs et omissions nettes |
| Reserves and related items | -178 | -1 285 | -1 817 | -310 | 296 | -206 | 1 656 | Réserves et postes apparentés |
| **Solomon Islands** | | | | | | | | **Iles Salomon** |
| Current account | -41 | -65 | -68 | -40 | -19 | -90 | -97 | Compte des transactions courantes |
| Goods: exports f.o.b. | 69 | 40 | 33 | 67 | 86 | 105 | 122 | Biens : exportations f.à.b. |
| Goods: imports f.o.b. | -92 | -85 | -69 | -94 | -121 | -185 | -217 | Biens : importations f.à.b. |
| Services: credit | 52 | 52 | 16 | 25 | 31 | 41 | 60 | Services : crédit |
| Services: debit | -73 | -81 | -49 | -62 | -41 | -58 | -95 | Services : débit |
| Income: credit | 7 | 7 | 3 | 4 | 11 | 9 | 19 | Revenus : crédit |
| Income: debit | -11 | -7 | -10 | -7 | -8 | -7 | -13 | Revenus : débit |
| Current transfers, n.i.e.: credit | 35 | 31 | 29 | 46 | 50 | 41 | 69 | Transferts courants, n.i.a. : crédit |
| Current transfers: debit | -29 | -21 | -20 | -19 | -25 | -36 | -42 | Transferts courants : débit |
| Capital account, n.i.e. | 8 | 4 | 8 | 12 | 1 | 28 | 29 | Compte de capital, n.i.a. |
| Financial account, n.i.e. | 40 | 15 | -4 | -29 | -19 | -9 | -32 | Compte financier, n.i.a. |
| Net errors and omissions | 5 | 49 | 55 | 35 | -6 | 54 | 74 | Erreurs et omissions nettes |
| Reserves and related items | -12 | -3 | 9 | 22 | 43 | 18 | 25 | Réserves et postes apparentés |
| **South Africa** | | | | | | | | **Afrique du Sud** |
| Current account | -191 | 343 | 884 | -1 902 | -7 003 | -9 723 | -16 488 | Compte des transactions courantes |
| Goods: exports f.o.b. | 31 950 | 31 064 | 31 772 | 38 700 | 48 237 | 55 284 | 63 841 | Biens : exportations f.à.b. |
| Goods: imports f.o.b. | -27 252 | -25 809 | -27 016 | -35 270 | -48 518 | -56 279 | -69 942 | Biens : importations f.à.b. |
| Services: credit | 5 046 | 4 845 | 4 985 | 8 298 | 9 682 | 11 157 | 12 014 | Services : crédit |
| Services: debit | -5 823 | -5 232 | -5 504 | -8 045 | -10 328 | -12 155 | -14 291 | Services : débit |
| Income: credit | 2 511 | 2 480 | 2 179 | 2 857 | 3 259 | 4 640 | 5 944 | Revenus : crédit |
| Income: debit | -5 696 | -6 267 | -4 975 | -7 447 | -7 576 | -9 569 | -11 238 | Revenus : débit |

| Country or area | 2000 | 2001 | 2002 | 2003 | 2004 | 2005 | 2006 | Pays ou zone |
|---|---|---|---|---|---|---|---|---|
| Current transfers, n.i.e.: credit | 106 | 126 | 139 | 252 | 257 | 240 | 261 | Transferts courants, n.i.a. : crédit |
| Current transfers: debit | -1 033 | -865 | -695 | -1 248 | -2 015 | -3 041 | -3 078 | Transferts courants : débit |
| Capital account, n.i.e. | -52 | -31 | -15 | 44 | 52 | 30 | 30 | Compte de capital, n.i.a. |
| Financial account, n.i.e. | 73 | -1 188 | -707 | -1 961 | 7 651 | 12 583 | 14 684 | Compte financier, n.i.a. |
| Net errors and omissions | 649 | 855 | -485 | 3 466 | 5 623 | 2 875 | 5 484 | Erreurs et omissions nettes |
| Reserves and related items | -480 | 22 | 322 | 354 | -6 324 | -5 766 | -3 711 | Réserves et postes apparentés |
| **Spain** | | | | | | | | **Espagne** |
| Current account | -23 185 | -24 065 | -22 239 | -30 886 | -54 865 | -83 388 | -106 344 | Compte des transactions courantes |
| Goods: exports f.o.b. | 115 769 | 117 522 | 127 162 | 158 049 | 185 209 | 196 580 | 216 483 | Biens : exportations f.à.b. |
| Goods: imports f.o.b. | -152 856 | -152 039 | -161 794 | -203 205 | -251 939 | -281 784 | -317 212 | Biens : importations f.à.b. |
| Services: credit | 52 453 | 55 651 | 60 247 | 74 308 | 86 078 | 94 663 | 106 278 | Services : crédit |
| Services: debit | -33 171 | -35 182 | -38 712 | -47 951 | -59 188 | -67 129 | -78 315 | Services : débit |
| Income: credit | 18 904 | 20 243 | 21 536 | 27 209 | 33 948 | 39 445 | 49 143 | Revenus : crédit |
| Income: debit | -25 753 | -31 509 | -33 194 | -38 910 | -48 986 | -60 701 | -75 597 | Revenus : débit |
| Current transfers, n.i.e.: credit | 11 380 | 12 143 | 14 575 | 17 048 | 20 366 | 20 194 | 21 465 | Transferts courants, n.i.a. : crédit |
| Current transfers: debit | -9 911 | -10 893 | -12 059 | -17 434 | -20 353 | -24 656 | -28 590 | Transferts courants : débit |
| Capital account, n.i.e. | 4 797 | 4 811 | 7 236 | 9 274 | 10 450 | 10 107 | 7 831 | Compte de capital, n.i.a. |
| Financial account, n.i.e. | 15 261 | 18 169 | 17 782 | 4 353 | 36 964 | 73 885 | 102 582 | Compte financier, n.i.a. |
| Net errors and omissions | 247 | -257 | 912 | 1 769 | 1 039 | -2 524 | -3 490 | Erreurs et omissions nettes |
| Reserves and related items | 2 880 | 1 341 | -3 690 | 15 490 | 6 412 | 1 920 | -578 | Réserves et postes apparentés |
| **Sri Lanka** | | | | | | | | **Sri Lanka** |
| Current account | -1 044 | -237 | -268 | -106 | -677 | -743 | -1 434 | Compte des transactions courantes |
| Goods: exports f.o.b. | 5 440 | 4 817 | 4 699 | 5 133 | 5 757 | 6 347 | 6 883 | Biens : exportations f.à.b. |
| Goods: imports f.o.b. | -6 484 | -5 377 | -5 495 | -6 005 | -7 200 | -7 977 | -9 228 | Biens : importations f.à.b. |
| Services: credit | 939 | 1 355 | 1 268 | 1 411 | 1 527 | 1 540 | 1 625 | Services : crédit |
| Services: debit | -1 621 | -1 749 | -1 584 | -1 679 | -1 908 | -2 089 | -2 394 | Services : débit |
| Income: credit | 149 | 108 | 75 | 170 | 157 | 76 | 312 | Revenus : crédit |
| Income: debit | -449 | -375 | -328 | -341 | -360 | -375 | -700 | Revenus : débit |
| Current transfers, n.i.e.: credit | 1 166 | 1 155 | 1 287 | 1 414 | 1 564 | 1 968 | 2 326 | Transferts courants, n.i.a. : crédit |
| Current transfers: debit | -183 | -172 | -190 | -209 | -214 | -233 | -258 | Transferts courants : débit |
| Capital account, n.i.e. | 49 | 50 | 65 | 74 | 64 | 250 | 291 | Compte de capital, n.i.a. |
| Financial account, n.i.e. | 447 | -136 | -196 | -219 | -133 | 67 | 687 | Compte financier, n.i.a. |
| Net errors and omissions | 186 | 15 | 136 | -114 | -189 | -73 | -261 | Erreurs et omissions nettes |
| Reserves and related items | 361 | 308 | 262 | 365 | 935 | 498 | 717 | Réserves et postes apparentés |
| **Sudan** | | | | | | | | **Soudan** |
| Current account | -557 | -618 | -1 008 | -955 | -871 | -3 013 | -5 110 | Compte des transactions courantes |
| Goods: exports f.o.b. | 1 807 | 1 699 | 1 949 | 2 542 | 3 778 | 4 824 | 5 657 | Biens : exportations f.à.b. |
| Goods: imports f.o.b. | -1 366 | -1 395 | -2 294 | -2 536 | -3 586 | -5 946 | -7 105 | Biens : importations f.à.b. |
| Services: credit | 27 | 15 | 132 | 36 | 44 | 114 | 206 | Services : crédit |
| Services: debit | -648 | -660 | -818 | -830 | -1 065 | -1 844 | -2 789 | Services : débit |
| Income: credit | 5 | 18 | 29 | 10 | 22 | 44 | 89 | Revenus : crédit |
| Income: debit | -580 | -572 | -638 | -879 | -1 135 | -1 406 | -2 103 | Revenus : débit |
| Current transfers, n.i.e.: credit | 651 | 730 | 1 086 | 1 218 | 1 580 | 1 681 | 1 877 | Transferts courants, n.i.a. : crédit |
| Current transfers: debit | -453 | -453 | -454 | -517 | -510 | -480 | -941 | Transferts courants : débit |
| Capital account, n.i.e. | -119 | -93 | #0 | 0 | 0 | 0 | 0 | Compte de capital, n.i.a. |
| Financial account, n.i.e. | 432 | 561 | 761 | 1 284 | 1 428 | 2 885 | 4 739 | Compte financier, n.i.a. |
| Net errors and omissions | 338 | -24 | 479 | -14 | 212 | 727 | -220 | Erreurs et omissions nettes |
| Reserves and related items | -94 | 175 | -232 | -315 | -769 | -598 | 591 | Réserves et postes apparentés |
| **Suriname** | | | | | | | | **Suriname** |
| Current account | 32 | -84 | -131 | -159 | -138 | -144 | 110 | Compte des transactions courantes |
| Goods: exports f.o.b. | 399 | 437 | 369 | 488 | 782 | 1 212 | 1 174 | Biens : exportations f.à.b. |
| Goods: imports f.o.b. | -246 | -297 | -322 | -458 | -740 | -1 189 | -1 013 | Biens : importations f.à.b. |
| Services: credit | 91 | 59 | 39 | 59 | 141 | 204 | 234 | Services : crédit |
| Services: debit | -216 | -174 | -166 | -195 | -271 | -352 | -269 | Services : débit |
| Income: credit | 13 | 5 | 8 | 12 | 16 | 24 | 28 | Revenus : crédit |
| Income: debit | -7 | -113 | -51 | -60 | -79 | -64 | -80 | Revenus : débit |
| Current transfers, n.i.e.: credit | 1 | 2 | 13 | 25 | 76 | 52 | 74 | Transferts courants, n.i.a. : crédit |
| Current transfers: debit | -3 | -3 | -21 | -30 | -63 | -30 | -38 | Transferts courants : débit |

| Country or area | 2000 | 2001 | 2002 | 2003 | 2004 | 2005 | 2006 | Pays ou zone |
|---|---|---|---|---|---|---|---|---|
| Capital account, n.i.e. | 2 | 2 | 6 | 9 | 19 | 15 | 19 | Compte de capital, n.i.a. |
| Financial account, n.i.e. | -139 | 104 | -38 | -37 | -24 | -21 | -181 | Compte financier, n.i.a. |
| Net errors and omissions | 114 | 56 | 144 | 194 | 218 | 169 | 145 | Erreurs et omissions nettes |
| Reserves and related items | -10 | -78 | 19 | -7 | -76 | -20 | -94 | Réserves et postes apparentés |
| **Swaziland** | | | | | | | | **Swaziland** |
| Current account | -46 | 9 | 33 | 89 | 52 | 86 | 98 | Compte des transactions courantes |
| Goods: exports f.o.b. | 967 | 1 039 | 1 079 | 1 667 | 1 806 | 1 965 | 1 976 | Biens : exportations f.à.b. |
| Goods: imports f.o.b. | -1 128 | -1 120 | -1 027 | -1 540 | -1 715 | -1 949 | -1 961 | Biens : importations f.à.b. |
| Services: credit | 273 | 114 | 93 | 205 | 250 | 284 | 283 | Services : crédit |
| Services: debit | -310 | -208 | -210 | -349 | -402 | -407 | -368 | Services : débit |
| Income: credit | 136 | 136 | 127 | 61 | 132 | 158 | 168 | Revenus : crédit |
| Income: debit | -85 | -43 | -124 | -105 | -125 | -96 | -167 | Revenus : débit |
| Current transfers, n.i.e.: credit | 248 | 230 | 216 | 337 | 371 | 412 | 457 | Transferts courants, n.i.a. : crédit |
| Current transfers: debit | -147 | -138 | -120 | -186 | -265 | -282 | -290 | Transferts courants : débit |
| Capital account, n.i.e. | ^0 | ^0 | ^0 | 0 | -1 | ^0 | 53 | Compte de capital, n.i.a. |
| Financial account, n.i.e. | -70 | -144 | -166 | -89 | -190 | -76 | 18 | Compte financier, n.i.a. |
| Net errors and omissions | 162 | 210 | 62 | -92 | 97 | -12 | -28 | Erreurs et omissions nettes |
| Reserves and related items | -46 | -75 | 70 | 92 | 42 | 2 | -141 | Réserves et postes apparentés |
| **Sweden** | | | | | | | | **Suède** |
| Current account | 6 617 | 6 696 | 12 784 | 22 844 | 24 127 | 25 230 | 28 413 | Compte des transactions courantes |
| Goods: exports f.o.b. | 87 431 | 76 200 | 84 172 | 102 080 | 123 187 | 131 319 | 148 756 | Biens : exportations f.à.b. |
| Goods: imports f.o.b. | -72 216 | -62 368 | -67 541 | -83 147 | -100 217 | -111 971 | -127 341 | Biens : importations f.à.b. |
| Services: credit | 20 252 | 21 997 | 24 009 | 30 654 | 39 023 | 42 946 | 50 374 | Services : crédit |
| Services: debit | -23 440 | -23 020 | -23 958 | -28 771 | -33 138 | -35 273 | -39 774 | Services : débit |
| Income: credit | 20 074 | 17 934 | 18 018 | 22 934 | 31 332 | 38 490 | 45 310 | Revenus : crédit |
| Income: debit | -22 137 | -20 786 | -19 044 | -22 638 | -31 310 | -35 708 | -44 215 | Revenus : débit |
| Current transfers, n.i.e.: credit | 2 602 | 2 578 | 3 345 | 3 577 | 4 067 | 5 027 | 4 894 | Transferts courants, n.i.a. : crédit |
| Current transfers: debit | -5 950 | -5 839 | -6 218 | -1 845 | -8 817 | -9 600 | -9 590 | Transferts courants : débit |
| Capital account, n.i.e. | 384 | 509 | -79 | -46 | 34 | 308 | -2 585 | Compte de capital, n.i.a. |
| Financial account, n.i.e. | -3 297 | 1 824 | -10 704 | -20 163 | -26 010 | -24 251 | -32 882 | Compte financier, n.i.a. |
| Net errors and omissions | -3 534 | -10 078 | -1 336 | -558 | 750 | -1 038 | 8 343 | Erreurs et omissions nettes |
| Reserves and related items | -170 | 1 048 | -665 | -2 076 | 1 100 | -250 | -1 289 | Réserves et postes apparentés |
| **Switzerland** | | | | | | | | **Suisse** |
| Current account | 32 830 | 22 223 | 24 914 | 43 454 | 54 798 | 51 692 | 54 849 | Compte des transactions courantes |
| Goods: exports f.o.b. | 94 810 | 95 897 | 104 281 | 118 837 | 141 874 | 151 309 | 167 251 | Biens : exportations f.à.b. |
| Goods: imports f.o.b. | -92 746 | -94 264 | -97 584 | -111 831 | -126 089 | -145 442 | -162 213 | Biens : importations f.à.b. |
| Services: credit | 28 727 | 27 690 | 29 616 | 34 600 | 41 900 | 47 225 | 51 968 | Services : crédit |
| Services: debit | -14 646 | -15 366 | -16 150 | -18 533 | -23 760 | -27 384 | -28 774 | Services : débit |
| Income: credit | 61 844 | 53 074 | 42 150 | 63 636 | 72 418 | 103 467 | 110 277 | Revenus : crédit |
| Income: debit | -40 676 | -39 305 | -31 468 | -37 736 | -45 195 | -65 565 | -73 339 | Revenus : débit |
| Current transfers, n.i.e.: credit | 6 580 | 9 721 | 10 635 | 13 202 | 14 306 | 12 286 | 13 703 | Transferts courants, n.i.a. : crédit |
| Current transfers: debit | -11 063 | -15 225 | -16 567 | -18 722 | -20 656 | -24 205 | -24 024 | Transferts courants : débit |
| Capital account, n.i.e. | -3 541 | 1 523 | -1 159 | -667 | -1 409 | -665 | -2 712 | Compte de capital, n.i.a. |
| Financial account, n.i.e. | -29 948 | -36 679 | -22 789 | -24 306 | -63 107 | -87 279 | -70 167 | Compte financier, n.i.a. |
| Net errors and omissions | -3 555 | 13 555 | 1 584 | -15 077 | 11 336 | 18 037 | 18 399 | Erreurs et omissions nettes |
| Reserves and related items | 4 214 | -622 | -2 549 | -3 405 | -1 618 | 18 215 | -370 | Réserves et postes apparentés |
| **Syrian Arab Republic** | | | | | | | | **Rép. arabe syrienne** |
| Current account | 1 061 | 1 221 | 1 440 | 728 | 587 | 295 | 890 | Compte des transactions courantes |
| Goods: exports f.o.b. | 5 146 | 5 706 | 6 668 | 5 762 | 7 220 | 8 602 | 10 245 | Biens : exportations f.à.b. |
| Goods: imports f.o.b. | -3 723 | -4 282 | -4 458 | -4 430 | -6 957 | -8 742 | -9 359 | Biens : importations f.à.b. |
| Services: credit | 1 699 | 1 781 | 1 559 | 1 331 | 2 613 | 2 910 | 2 924 | Services : crédit |
| Services: debit | -1 667 | -1 694 | -1 883 | -1 806 | -2 235 | -2 359 | -2 520 | Services : débit |
| Income: credit | 345 | 379 | 250 | 282 | 385 | 395 | 428 | Revenus : crédit |
| Income: debit | -1 224 | -1 162 | -1 175 | -1 139 | -1 114 | -1 258 | -1 363 | Revenus : débit |
| Current transfers, n.i.e.: credit | 495 | 512 | 499 | 743 | 690 | 763 | 770 | Transferts courants, n.i.a. : crédit |
| Current transfers: debit | -10 | -19 | -20 | -15 | -16 | -16 | -235 | Transferts courants : débit |
| Capital account, n.i.e. | 63 | 17 | 20 | 20 | 18 | 18 | 18 | Compte de capital, n.i.a. |
| Financial account, n.i.e. | -139 | -244 | -250 | -436 | -97 | -162 | -1 052 | Compte financier, n.i.a. |

| Country or area | 2000 | 2001 | 2002 | 2003 | 2004 | 2005 | 2006 | Pays ou zone |
|---|---|---|---|---|---|---|---|---|
| Net errors and omissions | -171 | 26 | -160 | 383 | -256 | -137 | -588 | Erreurs et omissions nettes |
| Reserves and related items | -814 | -1 020 | -1 050 | -695 | -251 | -14 | 732 | Réserves et postes apparentés |
| **Tajikistan** | | | | | | | | **Tadjikistan** |
| Current account | ... | ... | -15 | -5 | -57 | -19 | -21 | Compte des transactions courantes |
| Goods: exports f.o.b. | ... | ... | 699 | 906 | 1 097 | 1 108 | 1 512 | Biens : exportations f.à.b. |
| Goods: imports f.o.b. | ... | ... | -823 | -1 026 | -1 232 | -1 431 | -1 955 | Biens : importations f.à.b. |
| Services: credit | ... | ... | 69 | 89 | 123 | 146 | 134 | Services : crédit |
| Services: debit | ... | ... | -105 | -122 | -213 | -252 | -394 | Services : débit |
| Income: credit | ... | ... | 1 | 1 | 2 | 10 | 12 | Revenus : crédit |
| Income: debit | ... | ... | -42 | -71 | -59 | -50 | -76 | Revenus : débit |
| Current transfers, n.i.e.: credit | ... | ... | 202 | 285 | 348 | 600 | 1 146 | Transferts courants, n.i.a. : crédit |
| Current transfers: debit | ... | ... | -16 | -67 | -123 | -150 | -400 | Transferts courants : débit |
| Capital account, n.i.e. | ... | ... | 0 | 0 | 0 | 0 | ^0 | Compte de capital, n.i.a. |
| Financial account, n.i.e. | ... | ... | 72 | 63 | 93 | 101 | 276 | Compte financier, n.i.a. |
| Net errors and omissions | ... | ... | -56 | -30 | -33 | -76 | -265 | Erreurs et omissions nettes |
| Reserves and related items | ... | ... | -2 | -28 | -4 | -6 | 10 | Réserves et postes apparentés |
| **Thailand** | | | | | | | | **Thaïlande** |
| Current account | 9 313 | 5 101 | 4 654 | 4 772 | 2 759 | -7 923 | 2 175 | Compte des transactions courantes |
| Goods: exports f.o.b. | 67 894 | 63 082 | 66 052 | 78 083 | 94 979 | 109 199 | 127 929 | Biens : exportations f.à.b. |
| Goods: imports f.o.b. | -56 193 | -54 539 | -57 008 | -66 909 | -84 194 | -105 995 | -113 993 | Biens : importations f.à.b. |
| Services: credit | 13 868 | 13 024 | 15 391 | 15 798 | 19 040 | 20 163 | 24 130 | Services : crédit |
| Services: debit | -15 460 | -14 610 | -16 720 | -18 169 | -23 077 | -27 120 | -32 415 | Services : débit |
| Income: credit | 4 235 | 3 917 | 3 421 | 3 150 | 3 244 | 3 640 | 4 659 | Revenus : crédit |
| Income: debit | -5 616 | -6 375 | -7 084 | -8 123 | -9 364 | -10 813 | -11 502 | Revenus : débit |
| Current transfers, n.i.e.: credit | 952 | 990 | 979 | 1 326 | 2 479 | 3 351 | 3 764 | Transferts courants, n.i.a. : crédit |
| Current transfers: debit | -366 | -389 | -375 | -385 | -348 | -348 | -396 | Transferts courants : débit |
| Capital account, n.i.e. | 0 | 0 | 0 | 0 | 0 | 0 | 0 | Compte de capital, n.i.a. |
| Financial account, n.i.e. | -10 026 | -2 105 | -295 | -4 111 | 3 647 | 11 082 | 5 649 | Compte financier, n.i.a. |
| Net errors and omissions | -1 094 | -720 | 1 178 | -143 | -696 | 2 257 | 4 845 | Erreurs et omissions nettes |
| Reserves and related items | 1 806 | -2 276 | -5 537 | -518 | -5 710 | -5 417 | -12 669 | Réserves et postes apparentés |
| **TFYR of Macedonia** | | | | | | | | **Ex-R.Y. Macédoine** |
| Current account | -72 | -244 | -358 | -149 | -415 | -81 | -24 | Compte des transactions courantes |
| Goods: exports f.o.b. | 1 321 | 1 155 | 1 112 | 1 363 | 1 672 | 2 040 | 2 396 | Biens : exportations f.à.b. |
| Goods: imports f.o.b. | -2 011 | -1 682 | -1 916 | -2 211 | -2 784 | -3 097 | -3 681 | Biens : importations f.à.b. |
| Services: credit | 317 | 245 | 253 | 327 | 408 | 472 | 601 | Services : crédit |
| Services: debit | -268 | -264 | -275 | -337 | -462 | -505 | -576 | Services : débit |
| Income: credit | 42 | 53 | 51 | 60 | 85 | 98 | 135 | Revenus : crédit |
| Income: debit | -87 | -93 | -81 | -92 | -124 | -153 | -138 | Revenus : débit |
| Current transfers, n.i.e.: credit | 788 | 726 | 536 | 779 | 837 | 1 110 | 1 283 | Transferts courants, n.i.a. : crédit |
| Current transfers: debit | -173 | -383 | -37 | -38 | -46 | -45 | -43 | Transferts courants : débit |
| Capital account, n.i.e. | ^0 | 1 | 8 | -7 | -5 | -2 | -1 | Compte de capital, n.i.a. |
| Financial account, n.i.e. | 290 | 326 | 257 | 237 | 440 | 507 | 400 | Compte financier, n.i.a. |
| Net errors and omissions | 61 | 2 | -30 | -26 | 8 | -13 | 10 | Erreurs et omissions nettes |
| Reserves and related items | -279 | -86 | 122 | -55 | -28 | -411 | -385 | Réserves et postes apparentés |
| **Togo** | | | | | | | | **Togo** |
| Current account | -140 | -169 | -140 | -162 | -206 | -461 | ... | Compte des transactions courantes |
| Goods: exports f.o.b. | 362 | 357 | 424 | 598 | 601 | 660 | ... | Biens : exportations f.à.b. |
| Goods: imports f.o.b. | -485 | -516 | -576 | -755 | -853 | -1 172 | ... | Biens : importations f.à.b. |
| Services: credit | 62 | 72 | 90 | 95 | 150 | 177 | ... | Services : crédit |
| Services: debit | -118 | -130 | -148 | -204 | -239 | -279 | ... | Services : débit |
| Income: credit | 33 | 26 | 26 | 27 | 40 | 46 | ... | Revenus : crédit |
| Income: debit | -62 | -55 | -48 | -50 | -73 | -80 | ... | Revenus : débit |
| Current transfers, n.i.e.: credit | 73 | 88 | 113 | 161 | 207 | 229 | ... | Transferts courants, n.i.a. : crédit |
| Current transfers: debit | -5 | -11 | -22 | -34 | -37 | -42 | ... | Transferts courants : débit |
| Capital account, n.i.e. | 9 | 21 | 14 | 21 | 40 | 51 | ... | Compte de capital, n.i.a. |
| Financial account, n.i.e. | 163 | 151 | 151 | 143 | 292 | 287 | ... | Compte financier, n.i.a. |
| Net errors and omissions | 5 | -5 | 5 | -10 | 14 | 9 | ... | Erreurs et omissions nettes |
| Reserves and related items | -37 | 2 | -30 | 9 | -141 | 113 | ... | Réserves et postes apparentés |

**62** Balance of payments summary—Millions of US dollars (*continued*)
Résumé de la balance des paiements—Millions de dollars E.-U (*suite*)

| Country or area | 2000 | 2001 | 2002 | 2003 | 2004 | 2005 | 2006 | Pays ou zone |
|---|---|---|---|---|---|---|---|---|
| **Tonga** | | | | | | | | **Tonga** |
| Current account | ... | -11 | -3 | -10 | -15 | -14 | -15 | Compte des transactions courantes |
| Goods: exports f.o.b. | ... | 7 | 18 | 21 | 19 | 18 | 10 | Biens : exportations f.à.b. |
| Goods: imports f.o.b. | ... | -64 | -73 | -75 | -86 | -100 | -86 | Biens : importations f.à.b. |
| Services: credit | ... | 20 | 23 | 26 | 27 | 37 | 31 | Services : crédit |
| Services: debit | ... | -28 | -32 | -44 | -52 | -50 | -58 | Services : débit |
| Income: credit | ... | 6 | 7 | 8 | 5 | 8 | 11 | Revenus : crédit |
| Income: debit | ... | -2 | -4 | -4 | -7 | -2 | -3 | Revenus : débit |
| Current transfers, n.i.e.: credit | ... | 63 | 75 | 67 | 92 | 87 | 93 | Transferts courants, n.i.a. : crédit |
| Current transfers: debit | ... | -12 | -16 | -8 | -13 | -12 | -13 | Transferts courants : débit |
| Capital account, n.i.e. | ... | 10 | 13 | 10 | 11 | 13 | 7 | Compte de capital, n.i.a. |
| Financial account, n.i.e. | ... | 1 | -3 | 8 | 28 | 3 | 12 | Compte financier, n.i.a. |
| Net errors and omissions | ... | 2 | ^0 | -2 | -6 | -6 | -4 | Erreurs et omissions nettes |
| Reserves and related items | ... | -2 | -7 | -6 | -19 | 4 | 1 | Réserves et postes apparentés |
| **Trinidad and Tobago** | | | | | | | | **Trinité-et-Tobago** |
| Current account | 544 | 416 | 76 | 985 | 1 447 | 3 594 | ... | Compte des transactions courantes |
| Goods: exports f.o.b. | 4 290 | 4 304 | 3 920 | 5 205 | 6 403 | 9 672 | ... | Biens : exportations f.à.b. |
| Goods: imports f.o.b. | -3 322 | -3 586 | -3 682 | -3 912 | -4 894 | -5 725 | ... | Biens : importations f.à.b. |
| Services: credit | 554 | 574 | 637 | 685 | 851 | 897 | ... | Services : crédit |
| Services: debit | -388 | -370 | -373 | -371 | -371 | -541 | ... | Services : débit |
| Income: credit | 81 | 109 | 64 | 78 | 66 | 84 | ... | Revenus : crédit |
| Income: debit | -709 | -648 | -544 | -759 | -664 | -844 | ... | Revenus : débit |
| Current transfers, n.i.e.: credit | 64 | 64 | 96 | 101 | 99 | 102 | ... | Transferts courants, n.i.a. : crédit |
| Current transfers: debit | -26 | -31 | -42 | -42 | -42 | -52 | ... | Transferts courants : débit |
| Capital account, n.i.e. | 0 | 0 | 0 | 0 | 0 | 0 | ... | Compte de capital, n.i.a. |
| Financial account, n.i.e. | 174 | 322 | 397 | 34 | -200 | -454 | ... | Compte financier, n.i.a. |
| Net errors and omissions | -277 | -235 | -358 | -610 | -537 | -1 335 | ... | Erreurs et omissions nettes |
| Reserves and related items | -441 | -502 | -116 | -409 | -710 | -1 805 | ... | Réserves et postes apparentés |
| **Tunisia** | | | | | | | | **Tunisie** |
| Current account | -821 | -840 | -746 | -730 | -551 | -304 | -634 | Compte des transactions courantes |
| Goods: exports f.o.b. | 5 840 | 6 628 | 6 857 | 8 027 | 9 679 | 10 488 | 11 507 | Biens : exportations f.à.b. |
| Goods: imports f.o.b. | -8 093 | -8 997 | -8 981 | -10 297 | -12 110 | -12 456 | -14 035 | Biens : importations f.à.b. |
| Services: credit | 2 767 | 2 912 | 2 681 | 2 937 | 3 629 | 4 021 | 4 295 | Services : crédit |
| Services: debit | -1 218 | -1 425 | -1 450 | -1 612 | -1 986 | -2 191 | -2 455 | Services : débit |
| Income: credit | 94 | 95 | 72 | 81 | 114 | 118 | 160 | Revenus : crédit |
| Income: debit | -1 036 | -1 036 | -1 056 | -1 174 | -1 412 | -1 786 | -1 746 | Revenus : débit |
| Current transfers, n.i.e.: credit | 854 | 1 016 | 1 156 | 1 343 | 1 564 | 1 537 | 1 676 | Transferts courants, n.i.a. : crédit |
| Current transfers: debit | -29 | -34 | -25 | -36 | -31 | -36 | -37 | Transferts courants : débit |
| Capital account, n.i.e. | 3 | 53 | 75 | 59 | 108 | 127 | 145 | Compte de capital, n.i.a. |
| Financial account, n.i.e. | 646 | 1 063 | 845 | 1 101 | 1 439 | 1 136 | 2 595 | Compte financier, n.i.a. |
| Net errors and omissions | -33 | 13 | -35 | -47 | -18 | -23 | -24 | Erreurs et omissions nettes |
| Reserves and related items | 205 | -288 | -140 | -383 | -977 | -936 | -2 082 | Réserves et postes apparentés |
| **Turkey** | | | | | | | | **Turquie** |
| Current account | -9 824 | 3 393 | -1 521 | -8 036 | -15 601 | -22 603 | -32 774 | Compte des transactions courantes |
| Goods: exports f.o.b. | 30 721 | 34 373 | 40 124 | 51 206 | 67 047 | 76 949 | 91 937 | Biens : exportations f.à.b. |
| Goods: imports f.o.b. | -52 681 | -38 103 | -47 407 | -65 216 | -90 925 | -110 479 | -133 175 | Biens : importations f.à.b. |
| Services: credit | 19 528 | 15 234 | 14 046 | 18 013 | 22 960 | 26 648 | 24 547 | Services : crédit |
| Services: debit | -8 153 | -6 098 | -6 161 | -7 502 | -10 163 | -11 376 | -11 186 | Services : débit |
| Income: credit | 2 836 | 2 753 | 2 486 | 2 246 | 2 651 | 3 684 | 4 473 | Revenus : crédit |
| Income: debit | -6 839 | -7 753 | -7 042 | -7 803 | -8 288 | -9 483 | -11 057 | Revenus : débit |
| Current transfers, n.i.e.: credit | 4 856 | 3 045 | 2 478 | 1 081 | 1 155 | 1 475 | 1 764 | Transferts courants, n.i.a. : crédit |
| Current transfers: debit | -92 | -58 | -45 | -61 | -38 | -21 | -77 | Transferts courants : débit |
| Capital account, n.i.e. | 0 | 0 | 0 | 0 | 0 | 0 | 0 | Compte de capital, n.i.a. |
| Financial account, n.i.e. | 8 584 | -14 557 | 1 194 | 7 192 | 17 752 | 43 687 | 45 794 | Compte financier, n.i.a. |
| Net errors and omissions | -2 694 | -1 724 | 113 | 4 931 | 2 109 | 2 092 | -2 399 | Erreurs et omissions nettes |
| Reserves and related items | 3 934 | 12 888 | 214 | -4 087 | -4 260 | -23 176 | -10 621 | Réserves et postes apparentés |
| **Uganda** | | | | | | | | **Ouganda** |
| Current account | -825 | -370 | -362 | -354 | -288 | -386 | -240 | Compte des transactions courantes |
| Goods: exports f.o.b. | 450 | 476 | 481 | 563 | 709 | 864 | 1 004 | Biens : exportations f.à.b. |

**62** Balance of payments summary—Millions of US dollars (*continued*)
Résumé de la balance des paiements—Millions de dollars E.-U (*suite*)

| Country or area | 2000 | 2001 | 2002 | 2003 | 2004 | 2005 | 2006 | Pays ou zone |
|---|---|---|---|---|---|---|---|---|
| Goods: imports f.o.b. | -950 | -975 | -1 052 | -1 246 | -1 461 | -1 780 | -2 239 | Biens : importations f.à.b. |
| Services: credit | 213 | 217 | 225 | 266 | 358 | 508 | 490 | Services : crédit |
| Services: debit | -459 | -506 | -558 | -502 | -651 | -787 | -990 | Services : débit |
| Income: credit | 53 | 37 | 24 | 28 | 36 | 50 | 72 | Revenus : crédit |
| Income: debit | -166 | -203 | -148 | -171 | -329 | -299 | -297 | Revenus : débit |
| Current transfers, n.i.e.: credit | 340 | 889 | 1 023 | 923 | 1 233 | 1 365 | 2 022 | Transferts courants, n.i.a. : crédit |
| Current transfers: debit | -308 | -304 | -357 | -214 | -183 | -307 | -302 | Transferts courants : débit |
| Capital account, n.i.e. | 0 | 0 | 0 | 0 | 0 | 0 | 0 | Compte de capital, n.i.a. |
| Financial account, n.i.e. | 321 | 441 | 178 | 359 | 415 | 465 | 532 | Compte financier, n.i.a. |
| Net errors and omissions | 41 | 19 | 9 | -8 | -4 | 2 | 41 | Erreurs et omissions nettes |
| Reserves and related items | 464 | -91 | 175 | 3 | -123 | -82 | -333 | Réserves et postes apparentés |
| **Ukraine** | | | | | | | | **Ukraine** |
| Current account | 1 481 | 1 402 | 3 174 | 2 891 | 6 909 | 2 531 | -1 617 | Compte des transactions courantes |
| Goods: exports f.o.b. | 15 722 | 17 091 | 18 669 | 23 739 | 33 432 | 35 024 | 38 949 | Biens : exportations f.à.b. |
| Goods: imports f.o.b. | -14 943 | -16 893 | -17 959 | -23 221 | -29 691 | -36 159 | -44 143 | Biens : importations f.à.b. |
| Services: credit | 3 800 | 3 995 | 4 682 | 5 214 | 7 859 | 9 354 | 11 290 | Services : crédit |
| Services: debit | -3 004 | -3 580 | -3 535 | -4 444 | -6 622 | -7 548 | -9 164 | Services : débit |
| Income: credit | 143 | 167 | 165 | 254 | 389 | 758 | 1 332 | Revenus : crédit |
| Income: debit | -1 085 | -834 | -769 | -835 | -1 034 | -1 743 | -3 054 | Revenus : débit |
| Current transfers, n.i.e.: credit | 967 | 1 516 | 1 967 | 2 270 | 2 671 | 3 111 | 3 533 | Transferts courants, n.i.a. : crédit |
| Current transfers: debit | -119 | -60 | -46 | -86 | -95 | -266 | -360 | Transferts courants : débit |
| Capital account, n.i.e. | -8 | 3 | 17 | -17 | 7 | -65 | 3 | Compte de capital, n.i.a. |
| Financial account, n.i.e. | -752 | -191 | -1 065 | 264 | -4 339 | 8 103 | 4 085 | Compte financier, n.i.a. |
| Net errors and omissions | -148 | -221 | -895 | -965 | -54 | 156 | -62 | Erreurs et omissions nettes |
| Reserves and related items | -573 | -993 | -1 231 | -2 173 | -2 523 | -10 725 | -2 409 | Réserves et postes apparentés |
| **United Kingdom** | | | | | | | | **Royaume-Uni** |
| Current account | -37 357 | -31 416 | -24 606 | -24 468 | -35 184 | -54 996 | -77 548 | Compte des transactions courantes |
| Goods: exports f.o.b. | 284 378 | 272 279 | 279 866 | 307 799 | 349 657 | 384 318 | 449 483 | Biens : exportations f.à.b. |
| Goods: imports f.o.b. | -334 228 | -331 567 | -351 636 | -387 254 | -461 133 | -509 394 | -592 385 | Biens : importations f.à.b. |
| Services: credit | 120 397 | 120 978 | 135 308 | 158 615 | 197 431 | 209 435 | 229 681 | Services : crédit |
| Services: debit | -99 747 | -100 193 | -110 023 | -127 250 | -149 916 | -164 584 | -175 894 | Services : débit |
| Income: credit | 204 239 | 202 931 | 187 292 | 205 803 | 260 540 | 340 528 | 445 524 | Revenus : crédit |
| Income: debit | -197 289 | -186 115 | -151 837 | -165 703 | -211 709 | -293 369 | -412 014 | Revenus : débit |
| Current transfers, n.i.e.: credit | 16 031 | 20 794 | 18 414 | 19 953 | 23 663 | 31 381 | 29 672 | Transferts courants, n.i.a. : crédit |
| Current transfers: debit | -31 137 | -30 523 | -31 991 | -36 431 | -43 716 | -53 311 | -51 616 | Transferts courants : débit |
| Capital account, n.i.e. | 2 569 | 1 890 | 1 420 | 2 425 | 3 777 | 2 801 | 1 259 | Compte de capital, n.i.a. |
| Financial account, n.i.e. | 24 388 | 20 627 | 12 053 | 31 754 | 10 441 | 73 804 | 49 012 | Compte financier, n.i.a. |
| Net errors and omissions | 15 699 | 4 442 | 10 499 | -12 303 | 21 372 | -19 877 | 25 976 | Erreurs et omissions nettes |
| Reserves and related items | -5 300 | 4 456 | 635 | 2 592 | -407 | -1 732 | 1 301 | Réserves et postes apparentés |
| **United Rep. of Tanzania** | | | | | | | | **Rép.-Unie de Tanzanie** |
| Current account | -499 | -200 | 84 | -88 | -383 | -881 | -1 442 | Compte des transactions courantes |
| Goods: exports f.o.b. | 663 | 851 | 980 | 1 216 | 1 473 | 1 676 | 1 723 | Biens : exportations f.à.b. |
| Goods: imports f.o.b. | -1 368 | -1 560 | -1 511 | -1 933 | -2 483 | -2 998 | -3 864 | Biens : importations f.à.b. |
| Services: credit | 627 | 915 | 920 | 948 | 1 134 | 1 269 | 1 483 | Services : crédit |
| Services: debit | -682 | -649 | -633 | -726 | -975 | -1 207 | -1 249 | Services : débit |
| Income: credit | 50 | 55 | 68 | 87 | 82 | 81 | 80 | Revenus : crédit |
| Income: debit | -180 | -208 | -157 | -236 | -201 | -198 | -165 | Revenus : débit |
| Current transfers, n.i.e.: credit | 464 | 475 | 478 | 620 | 652 | 563 | 616 | Transferts courants, n.i.a. : crédit |
| Current transfers: debit | -73 | -80 | -61 | -63 | -65 | -67 | -66 | Transferts courants : débit |
| Capital account, n.i.e. | 420 | 1 004 | 786 | 693 | 460 | 633 | 5 293 | Compte de capital, n.i.a. |
| Financial account, n.i.e. | 493 | -374 | 265 | 148 | 276 | 665 | -4 287 | Compte financier, n.i.a. |
| Net errors and omissions | -416 | -479 | -811 | -281 | -148 | -672 | 874 | Erreurs et omissions nettes |
| Reserves and related items | 1 | 49 | -323 | -472 | -204 | 254 | -437 | Réserves et postes apparentés |
| **United States** | | | | | | | | **Etats-Unis** |
| Current account | -417 324 | -384 597 | -459 441 | -522 101 | -640 149 | -754 848 | -811 486 | Compte des transactions courantes |
| Goods: exports f.o.b. | 774 632 | 721 842 | 685 933 | 716 704 | 811 010 | 898 457 | 1 026 850 | Biens : exportations f.à.b. |
| Goods: imports f.o.b. | -1 226 590 | -1 148 160 | -1 167 200 | -1 264 340 | -1 477 130 | -1 681 810 | -1 861 410 | Biens : importations f.à.b. |
| Services: credit | 295 965 | 283 054 | 288 788 | 301 053 | 346 240 | 384 612 | 418 848 | Services : crédit |
| Services: debit | -223 739 | -221 764 | -231 049 | -250 328 | -292 214 | -315 632 | -342 817 | Services : débit |

| Country or area | 2000 | 2001 | 2002 | 2003 | 2004 | 2005 | 2006 | Pays ou zone |
|---|---|---|---|---|---|---|---|---|
| Income: credit | 350 919 | 290 799 | 281 215 | 320 569 | 401 941 | 505 487 | 650 453 | Revenus : crédit |
| Income: debit | -329 863 | -259 076 | -253 544 | -275 148 | -345 585 | -457 428 | -613 820 | Revenus : débit |
| Current transfers, n.i.e.: credit | 10 828 | 9 011 | 12 321 | 14 959 | 20 281 | 18 607 | 24 415 | Transfers courants, n.i.a. : crédit |
| Current transfers: debit | -69 473 | -60 306 | -75 908 | -85 566 | -104 695 | -107 142 | -114 010 | Transfers courants : débit |
| Capital account, n.i.e. | -1 010 | -1 271 | -1 470 | -3 481 | -2 368 | -4 057 | -3 915 | Compte de capital, n.i.a. |
| Financial account, n.i.e. | 486 663 | 405 152 | 506 849 | 537 405 | 553 935 | 763 260 | 830 808 | Compte financier, n.i.a. |
| Net errors and omissions | -68 034 | -14 357 | -42 246 | -13 352 | 85 779 | -18 456 | -17 800 | Erreurs et omissions nettes |
| Reserves and related items | -295 | -4 927 | -3 693 | 1 529 | 2 804 | 14 100 | 2 392 | Réserves et postes apparentés |
| **Uruguay** | | | | | | | | **Uruguay** |
| Current account | -566 | -488 | 322 | -56 | 3 | 24 | -436 | Compte des transactions courantes |
| Goods: exports f.o.b. | 2 384 | 2 139 | 1 922 | 2 281 | 3 145 | 3 774 | 4 375 | Biens : exportations f.à.b. |
| Goods: imports f.o.b. | -3 311 | -2 915 | -1 874 | -2 098 | -2 992 | -3 753 | -4 859 | Biens : importations f.à.b. |
| Services: credit | 1 276 | 1 123 | 754 | 803 | 1 112 | 1 311 | 1 285 | Services : crédit |
| Services: debit | -882 | -801 | -600 | -636 | -786 | -939 | -902 | Services : débit |
| Income: credit | 782 | 832 | 453 | 242 | 372 | 563 | 734 | Revenus : crédit |
| Income: debit | -842 | -895 | -405 | -730 | -960 | -1 057 | -1 203 | Revenus : débit |
| Current transfers, n.i.e.: credit | 48 | 48 | 84 | 95 | 127 | 143 | 153 | Transfers courants, n.i.a. : crédit |
| Current transfers: debit | -21 | -18 | -12 | -12 | -14 | -17 | -19 | Transfers courants : débit |
| Capital account, n.i.e. | 0 | 0 | 0 | 0 | 5 | 4 | 7 | Compte de capital, n.i.a. |
| Financial account, n.i.e. | 779 | 457 | -1 928 | 4 | -82 | 924 | 2 775 | Compte financier, n.i.a. |
| Net errors and omissions | -47 | 334 | -2 292 | 1 009 | 378 | -173 | 22 | Erreurs et omissions nettes |
| Reserves and related items | -166 | -304 | 3 897 | -958 | -304 | -778 | -2 367 | Réserves et postes apparentés |
| **Vanuatu** | | | | | | | | **Vanuatu** |
| Current account | -14 | -15 | -31 | -34 | -42 | -53 | -50 | Compte des transactions courantes |
| Goods: exports f.o.b. | 27 | 20 | 20 | 27 | 38 | 38 | 38 | Biens : exportations f.à.b. |
| Goods: imports f.o.b. | -77 | -78 | -78 | -92 | -113 | -131 | -148 | Biens : importations f.à.b. |
| Services: credit | 130 | 119 | 94 | 111 | 122 | 139 | 146 | Services : crédit |
| Services: debit | -70 | -73 | -52 | -61 | -66 | -74 | -71 | Services : débit |
| Income: credit | 19 | 17 | 22 | 24 | 27 | 28 | 32 | Revenus : crédit |
| Income: debit | -32 | -21 | -34 | -39 | -46 | -54 | -52 | Revenus : débit |
| Current transfers, n.i.e.: credit | 27 | 40 | 6 | 5 | 5 | 7 | 10 | Transfers courants, n.i.a. : crédit |
| Current transfers: debit | -38 | -38 | -9 | -10 | -10 | -6 | -5 | Transfers courants : débit |
| Capital account, n.i.e. | -24 | -16 | -1 | -2 | 3 | 11 | 25 | Compte de capital, n.i.a. |
| Financial account, n.i.e. | 19 | 13 | 26 | 38 | 48 | 38 | 33 | Compte financier, n.i.a. |
| Net errors and omissions | -1 | 8 | -13 | -12 | -15 | -7 | 5 | Erreurs et omissions nettes |
| Reserves and related items | 19 | 10 | 18 | 11 | 5 | 11 | -13 | Réserves et postes apparentés |
| **Venezuela (Bolivarian Rep. of)** | | | | | | | | **Venezuela (Rép. bolivarienne du)** |
| Current account | 11 853 | 1 983 | 7 599 | 11 796 | 15 519 | 25 110 | 27 149 | Compte des transactions courantes |
| Goods: exports f.o.b. | 33 529 | 26 667 | 26 781 | 27 230 | 39 668 | 55 647 | 65 210 | Biens : exportations f.à.b. |
| Goods: imports f.o.b. | -16 865 | -19 211 | -13 360 | -10 483 | -17 021 | -24 195 | -32 498 | Biens : importations f.à.b. |
| Services: credit | 1 182 | 1 376 | 1 013 | 878 | 1 114 | 1 341 | 1 572 | Services : crédit |
| Services: debit | -4 435 | -4 681 | -3 922 | -3 512 | -4 497 | -5 349 | -6 005 | Services : débit |
| Income: credit | 3 049 | 2 603 | 1 474 | 1 729 | 2 050 | 4 146 | 7 934 | Revenus : crédit |
| Income: debit | -4 437 | -4 623 | -4 230 | -4 066 | -5 723 | -6 411 | -9 026 | Revenus : débit |
| Current transfers, n.i.e.: credit | 261 | 356 | 288 | 257 | 227 | 249 | 296 | Transfers courants, n.i.a. : crédit |
| Current transfers: debit | -431 | -504 | -445 | -237 | -299 | -318 | -334 | Transfers courants : débit |
| Capital account, n.i.e. | 0 | 0 | 0 | 0 | 0 | 0 | 0 | Compte de capital, n.i.a. |
| Financial account, n.i.e. | -2 969 | -211 | -9 246 | -5 547 | -10 861 | -16 480 | -19 244 | Compte financier, n.i.a. |
| Net errors and omissions | -2 926 | -3 601 | -2 781 | -795 | -2 503 | -3 205 | -2 828 | Erreurs et omissions nettes |
| Reserves and related items | -5 958 | 1 829 | 4 428 | -5 454 | -2 155 | -5 425 | -5 077 | Réserves et postes apparentés |
| **Viet Nam** | | | | | | | | **Viet Nam** |
| Current account | 1 106 | 682 | -604 | -1 931 | -957 | 217 | ... | Compte des transactions courantes |
| Goods: exports f.o.b. | 14 448 | 15 027 | 16 706 | 20 149 | 26 485 | 32 442 | ... | Biens : exportations f.à.b. |
| Goods: imports f.o.b. | -14 073 | -14 546 | -17 760 | -22 730 | -28 772 | -33 280 | ... | Biens : importations f.à.b. |
| Services: credit | 2 702 | 2 810 | 2 948 | 3 272 | 3 867 | 4 176 | ... | Services : crédit |
| Services: debit | -3 252 | -3 382 | -3 698 | -4 050 | -4 739 | -5 282 | ... | Services : débit |
| Income: credit | 331 | 318 | 167 | 125 | 188 | 364 | ... | Revenus : crédit |

| Country or area | 2000 | 2001 | 2002 | 2003 | 2004 | 2005 | 2006 | Pays ou zone |
|---|---|---|---|---|---|---|---|---|
| Income: debit | -782 | -795 | -888 | -936 | -1 079 | -1 583 | ... | Revenus : débit |
| Current transfers, n.i.e.: credit | 1 732 | 1 250 | 1 921 | 2 239 | 3 093 | 3 380 | ... | Transferts courants, n.i.a. : crédit |
| Current transfers: debit | 0 | 0 | 0 | 0 | 0 | 0 | ... | Transferts courants : débit |
| Capital account, n.i.e. | 0 | 0 | 0 | 0 | 0 | 0 | ... | Compte de capital, n.i.a. |
| Financial account, n.i.e. | -316 | 371 | 2 090 | 3 279 | 2 807 | 2 926 | ... | Compte financier, n.i.a. |
| Net errors and omissions | -680 | -847 | -1 038 | 798 | -915 | -1 059 | ... | Erreurs et omissions nettes |
| Reserves and related items | -110 | -206 | -448 | -2 146 | -935 | -2 084 | ... | Réserves et postes apparentés |
| **Yemen** | | | | | | | | **Yémen** |
| Current account | 1 337 | 667 | 538 | 149 | 225 | 624 | 206 | Compte des transactions courantes |
| Goods: exports f.o.b. | 3 797 | 3 367 | 3 621 | 3 934 | 4 676 | 6 413 | 7 316 | Biens : exportations f.à.b. |
| Goods: imports f.o.b. | -2 484 | -2 600 | -2 932 | -3 557 | -3 859 | -4 713 | -5 926 | Biens : importations f.à.b. |
| Services: credit | 211 | 166 | 166 | 318 | 370 | 372 | 549 | Services : crédit |
| Services: debit | -809 | -848 | -935 | -1 004 | -1 059 | -1 241 | -1 855 | Services : débit |
| Income: credit | 150 | 179 | 135 | 99 | 104 | 178 | 316 | Revenus : crédit |
| Income: debit | -927 | -869 | -901 | -1 008 | -1 450 | -1 791 | -1 551 | Revenus : débit |
| Current transfers, n.i.e.: credit | 1 472 | 1 344 | 1 457 | 1 442 | 1 493 | 1 458 | 1 402 | Transferts courants, n.i.a. : crédit |
| Current transfers: debit | -72 | -71 | -73 | -75 | -49 | -53 | -46 | Transferts courants : débit |
| Capital account, n.i.e. | 339 | 50 | 0 | 5 | 163 | 202 | 94 | Compte de capital, n.i.a. |
| Financial account, n.i.e. | -376 | -53 | -157 | 20 | -69 | -606 | 632 | Compte financier, n.i.a. |
| Net errors and omissions | 295 | -110 | 43 | 156 | 53 | 213 | 180 | Erreurs et omissions nettes |
| Reserves and related items | -1 594 | -553 | -425 | -330 | -373 | -434 | -1 112 | Réserves et postes apparentés |
| **Zambia** | | | | | | | | **Zambie** |
| Current account | -623 | -724 | -700 | -716 | -208 | -344 | 743 | Compte des transactions courantes |
| Goods: exports f.o.b. | 757 | 911 | 931 | 1 083 | 1 837 | 2 210 | 3 819 | Biens : exportations f.à.b. |
| Goods: imports f.o.b. | -978 | -1 253 | -1 204 | -1 393 | -1 727 | -2 161 | -2 636 | Biens : importations f.à.b. |
| Services: credit | 115 | 144 | 115 | 165 | 232 | 272 | 305 | Services : crédit |
| Services: debit | -335 | -367 | -375 | -408 | -384 | -471 | -587 | Services : débit |
| Income: credit | 19 | 21 | 42 | 32 | 32 | 37 | 43 | Revenus : crédit |
| Income: debit | -184 | -161 | -190 | -177 | -183 | -207 | -166 | Revenus : débit |
| Current transfers, n.i.e.: credit | 0 | 0 | 0 | 36 | 48 | 53 | 58 | Transferts courants, n.i.a. : crédit |
| Current transfers: debit | -18 | -20 | -20 | -54 | -64 | -77 | -93 | Transferts courants : débit |
| Capital account, n.i.e. | 153 | 222 | 236 | 240 | 239 | 287 | 255 | Compte de capital, n.i.a. |
| Financial account, n.i.e. | -208 | -209 | -79 | -40 | -554 | -2 189 | -2 859 | Compte financier, n.i.a. |
| Net errors and omissions | 165 | -407 | -363 | -178 | -44 | -112 | -87 | Erreurs et omissions nettes |
| Reserves and related items | 513 | 1 118 | 907 | 693 | 568 | 2 359 | 1 948 | Réserves et postes apparentés |

Source

International Monetary Fund (IMF), Washington, D.C., "International Financial Statistics," February 2008 and the IMF database.

Notes

1　Balance of payments data for the Belgium-Luxembourg Economic Union (BLEU) were available until December 31, 2001. From January 1, 2002, Belgium and Luxembourg have separate balance of payments data.

2　For statistical purposes, the data for China do not include those for the Hong Kong Special Administrative Region (Hong Kong SAR), Macao Special Administrative Region (Macao SAR) and Taiwan Province of China.

3　West Bank and Gaza.

Source

Fonds monétaire international (FMI), Washington, D.C.,"Statistiques Financières Internationales," fevrier 2008 et la base de données du FMI.

Notes

1　Les données sur la balance des paiements pour l'Union économique belgo-luxembourgeoise (UEBL) sont disponibles jusqu'au 31 décembre 2001. À partir du 1er janvier 2002, les données sur la balance des paiements de la Belgique et du Luxembourg sont séparées.

2　Pour la présentation des statistiques, les données pour la Chine ne comprennent pas la Région Administrative Spéciale de Hong Kong (Hong Kong RAS), la Région Administrative Spéciale de Macao (Macao RAS) et la province de Taiwan.

3　Cisjordanie et Gaza.

A balance of payments can be broadly described as the record of an economy's international economic transactions. It shows (a) transactions in goods, services and income between an economy and the rest of the world, (b) changes of ownership and other changes in that economy's monetary gold, special drawing rights (SDRs) and claims on and liabilities to the rest of the world, and (c) unrequited transfers and counterpart entries needed to balance in the accounting sense any entries for the foregoing transactions and changes which are not mutually offsetting.

The balance of payments data are presented on the basis of the methodology and presentation of the fifth edition of the *Balance of Payments Manual* (BPM5), published by the International Monetary Fund in September 1993. The BPM5 incorporates several major changes to take account of developments in international trade and finance over the years, and to better harmonize the Fund's balance of payments methodology with the methodology of the 1993 *System of National Accounts* (SNA). The Fund's balance of payments has been converted for all periods from the BPM4 basis to the BPM5 basis; thus the time series conform to the BPM5 methodology with no methodological breaks.

The detailed definitions concerning the content of the basic categories of the balance of payments are given in the BMP5. Brief explanatory notes are given below to clarify the scope of the major items.

*Goods: exports f.o.b.* and *Goods: imports f.o.b.* are both measured on the "free-on-board" (f.o.b.) basis—that is, by the value of the goods at the border of the exporting country; in the case of imports, this excludes the cost of freight and insurance incurred beyond the border of the exporting country.

*Services* and *income* cover transactions in real resources between residents and non residents other than those classified as merchandise, including (a) shipment and other transportation services, including freight, insurance and other distributive services in connection with the movement of commodities, (b) travel, i.e. goods and services acquired by non resident travellers in a given country and similar acquisitions by resident travellers abroad, and (c) investment income which covers income of non residents from their financial assets invested in the compiling economy (debit) and similar income of residents from their financial assets invested abroad (credit).

*Current transfers, n.i.e.: credit* comprises all current transfers received by the reporting country, except those made to the country to finance its "overall balance", hence, the label "n.i.e." (not included elsewhere). (Note: some of the capital and financial accounts labelled "n.i.e." denote that Exceptional financing items and *Liabilities constituting foreign authorities' reserves* (LCFARs) have been excluded.)

La balance des paiements peut se définir d'une façon gé-né-rale comme le relevé des transactions économiques in-ternationales d'une économie. Elle indique (a) les transac-tions sur biens, services et revenus entre une économie et le reste du monde, (b) les transferts de propriété et autres variations intervenues au niveau des avoirs en or monétaire de cette économie, de ses avoirs en droits de tirages spéciaux (DTS) ainsi que de ses créances financières sur le reste du monde ou de ses engagements financiers envers lui et (c) les "in-scriptions de transferts sans contrepartie" et de "contrepar-tie" destinées à équilibrer, d'un point de vue comptable, les transactions et changements précités qui ne se compensent pas réciproquement.

Les données de la balance des paiements sont présentées conformément à la méthodologie et à la classification re-commandées dans la cinquième édition du *Manuel de la bal-ance des paiements*, publiée en septembre 1993 par le Fonds monétaire international. La cinquième édition fait état de plusieurs changements importants qui ont été opérés de manière à rendre compte de l'évolution des finances et des changes internationaux pendant les années et à harmoniser davantage la méthodologie de la balance des paiements du FMI avec celle du *Système de comptabilité nationale* (SCN) de 1993. Les statistiques incluses dans la balance des paie-ments du FMI ont été converties et sont désormais établies, pour toutes les périodes, sur la base de la cinquième et non plus de la quatrième édition; en conséquence, les séries chronologiques sont conformes aux principes de la cin-quième édition, sans rupture due à des différences d'ordre méthodologique.

Les définitions détaillées relatives au contenu des postes fondamentaux de la balance des paiements figurent dans le *Manuel de la balance des paiements (cinquième édition)*. De brèves notes explicatives sont présentées ci-après pour clari-fier la portée de ces principales rubriques.

*Les Biens: exportations, f.à.b.* et *Biens: importations, f.à.b.* sont évalués sur la base f.à.b. (franco à bord) - c'est-à-dire à la frontière du pays exportateur; dans le cas des importations, cette valeur exclut le coût du fret et de l'assurance audelà de la frontière du pays exportateur.

*Services* et *revenus*: transactions en ressources effectuées entre résidents et non résidents, autres que celles qui sont considérées comme des marchandises, notamment: (a) ex-péditions et autres services de transport, y compris le fret, l'assurance et les autres services de distribution liés aux mou-vements de marchandises; (b) voyages, à savoir les biens et services acquis par des voyageurs non résidents dans un pays donné et achats similaires faits par des résidents voyageant à l'étranger; et (c) revenus des investissements, qui corre-

*Capital account, n.i.e.* refers mainly to capital transfers linked to the acquisition of a fixed asset other than transactions relating to debt forgiveness plus the disposal of nonproduced, nonfinancial assets, and to capital transfers linked to the disposal of fixed assets by the donor or to the financing of capital formation by the recipient, plus the acquisition of nonproduced, nonfinancial assets.

*Financial account, n.i.e.* is the net sum of the balance of direct investment, portfolio investment, and other investment transactions.

*Net errors and omissions* is a residual category needed to ensure that all debit and credit entries in the balance of payments statement sum to zero and reflects statistical inconsistencies in the recording of the credit and debit entries.

*Reserves and related items* is the sum of transactions in reserve assets, LCFARs, exceptional financing, and use of Fund credit and loans.

For further information see *International Financial Statistics* and www.imf.org.

spondent aux revenus que les non résidents tirent de leurs avoirs financiers placés dans l'économie déclarante (débit) et les revenus similaires que les résidents tirent de leurs avoirs financiers placés à l'étranger (crédit).

*Les transferts courants, n.i.a: crédit* englobent tous les transferts courants reçus par l'économie qui établit sa bal-ance des paiements, à l'exception de ceux qui sont destinés à financer sa "balance globale"—c'est ce qui explique la mention "n.i.a." (non inclus ailleurs). (Note: comptes de capital et d'opérations financières portent la mention "n.i.a.", ce qui signifie que les postes de Financement exceptionnel et les *Engagements constituant des réserves pour les autorités étrangères* ont été exclus de ces composantes du compte de capital et d'opérations financières.)

*Le Compte de capital, n.i.a* retrace principalement les trans-ferts de capital liés à l'acquisition d'un actif fixe autres que les transactions ayant trait à des remises de dettes plus les cessions d'actifs non financiers non produits, et les transferts de capital liés à la cession d'actifs fixes par le donateur ou au financement de la formation de capital par le bénéficiaire, plus les acquisitions d'actifs non financiers non produits.

*Le Compte financier, n.i.a* est la somme des soldes des investissements directs, des investissements de portefeuille et des autres investissements.

Le poste des *Erreurs et omissions nettes* est une catégorie résiduelle qui est nécessaire pour assurer que la somme de toutes les inscriptions effectuées au débit et au crédit est égal à zéro et qui laisse apparaître les écarts entre les mon-tants portés au débit et ceux qui sont inscrits au crédit.

Le montant de *Réserves et postes apparentés* est égal à la somme de transactions afférentes aux avoirs de réserve, aux engagements constituant des réserves pour les autorités étrangères, au financement exceptionnel et à l'utilisation des crédits et des prêts du FMI.

Pour plus de renseignements, voir *Statistiques financières internationales* et www.imf.org.

# Exchange rates
National currency per US dollar

# Cours des changes
Valeur du dollar E.-U. en monnaie nationale

| Country or area Pays ou zone | 1998 | 1999 | 2000 | 2001 | 2002 | 2003 | 2004 | 2005 | 2006 | 2007 |
|---|---|---|---|---|---|---|---|---|---|---|
| **Afghanistan[1,2] (afghani) — Afghanistan[1,2] (afghani)** | | | | | | | | | | |
| End of period Fin de période | 47.500 | #46.791 | ... | 47.259 | 47.263 | #48.865 | 48.220 | 50.410 | 49.850 | 49.720 |
| Period average Moyenne sur période | 3.000 | 45.106 | 61.629 | 65.690 | 41.459 | 48.763 | 47.845 | 49.495 | 49.925 | 49.962 |
| **Albania (lek) — Albanie (lek)** | | | | | | | | | | |
| End of period Fin de période | 140.580 | 135.120 | 142.640 | 136.550 | 133.740 | 106.580 | 92.640 | 103.580 | 94.140 | 82.890 |
| Period average Moyenne sur période | 150.633 | 137.691 | 143.709 | 143.485 | 140.155 | 121.863 | 102.780 | 99.870 | 98.103 | 90.428 |
| **Algeria (Algerian dinar) — Algérie (dinar algérien)** | | | | | | | | | | |
| End of period Fin de période | 60.353 | 69.314 | 75.343 | 77.820 | 79.723 | 72.613 | 72.614 | 73.380 | 71.158 | 66.830 |
| Period average Moyenne sur période | 58.739 | 66.574 | 75.260 | 77.215 | 79.682 | 77.395 | 72.061 | 73.276 | 72.647 | 69.292 |
| **Angola (readjusted kwanza) — Angola (réajusté kwanza)** | | | | | | | | | | |
| End of period Fin de période | 0.697 | #5.580 | 16.818 | 31.949 | 58.666 | 79.082 | 85.988 | 80.780 | 80.264 | 75.023 |
| Period average Moyenne sur période | 0.393 | #2.791 | 10.041 | 22.058 | 43.530 | 74.606 | 83.541 | 87.159 | 80.368 | 76.706 |
| **Anguilla (EC dollar) — Anguilla (dollar des Caraïbes orientales)** | | | | | | | | | | |
| End of period Fin de période | 2.700 | 2.700 | 2.700 | 2.700 | 2.700 | 2.700 | 2.700 | 2.700 | 2.700 | 2.700 |
| Period average Moyenne sur période | 2.700 | 2.700 | 2.700 | 2.700 | 2.700 | 2.700 | 2.700 | 2.700 | 2.700 | 2.700 |
| **Antigua and Barbuda (EC dollar) — Antigua-et-Barbuda (dollar des Caraïbes orientales)** | | | | | | | | | | |
| End of period Fin de période | 2.700 | 2.700 | 2.700 | 2.700 | 2.700 | 2.700 | 2.700 | 2.700 | 2.700 | 2.700 |
| Period average Moyenne sur période | 2.700 | 2.700 | 2.700 | 2.700 | 2.700 | 2.700 | 2.700 | 2.700 | 2.700 | 2.700 |
| **Argentina[3] (Argentine peso) — Argentine[3] (peso argentin)** | | | | | | | | | | |
| End of period Fin de période | 1.000 | 1.000 | 1.000 | 1.000 | 3.320 | 2.905 | 2.959 | 3.012 | 3.042 | 3.129 |
| Period average Moyenne sur période | 1.000 | 1.000 | 1.000 | 1.000 | 3.063 | 2.901 | 2.923 | 2.904 | 3.054 | 3.096 |
| **Armenia (dram) — Arménie (dram)** | | | | | | | | | | |
| End of period Fin de période | 522.030 | 523.770 | 552.180 | 561.810 | 584.890 | 566.000 | 485.840 | 450.190 | 363.500 | 304.220 |
| Period average Moyenne sur période | 504.915 | 535.062 | 539.526 | 555.078 | 573.353 | 578.763 | 533.451 | 457.687 | 416.040 | 342.079 |
| **Aruba (Aruban florin) — Aruba (florin de Aruba)** | | | | | | | | | | |
| End of period Fin de période | 1.790 | 1.790 | 1.790 | 1.790 | 1.790 | 1.790 | 1.790 | 1.790 | 1.790 | 1.790 |
| Period average Moyenne sur période | 1.790 | 1.790 | 1.790 | 1.790 | 1.790 | 1.790 | 1.790 | 1.790 | 1.790 | 1.790 |
| **Australia (Australian dollar) — Australie (dollar australien)** | | | | | | | | | | |
| End of period Fin de période | 1.629 | 1.530 | 1.805 | 1.959 | 1.766 | 1.333 | 1.284 | 1.363 | 1.264 | 1.134 |
| Period average Moyenne sur période | 1.592 | 1.550 | 1.725 | 1.933 | 1.841 | 1.542 | 1.360 | 1.310 | 1.328 | 1.195 |
| **Austria[4] (Austrian schilling, euro) — Autriche[4] (schilling autrichien, euro)** | | | | | | | | | | |
| End of period Fin de période | 11.747 | #0.995 | 1.075 | 1.135 | 0.954 | 0.792 | 0.734 | 0.848 | 0.759 | 0.679 |
| Period average Moyenne sur période | 12.379 | #0.939 | 1.085 | 1.118 | 1.063 | 0.886 | 0.805 | 0.804 | 0.797 | 0.731 |

| Country or area<br>Pays ou zone | 1998 | 1999 | 2000 | 2001 | 2002 | 2003 | 2004 | 2005 | 2006 | 2007 |
|---|---|---|---|---|---|---|---|---|---|---|
| **Azerbaijan[5] (manat) — Azerbaïdjan[5] (manat)** | | | | | | | | | | |
| End of period<br>Fin de période | 0.778 | 0.876 | 0.913 | 0.955 | 0.979 | 0.985 | 0.981 | 0.919 | #0.871 | 0.845 |
| Period average<br>Moyenne sur période | 0.774 | 0.824 | 0.895 | 0.931 | 0.972 | 0.982 | 0.983 | 0.945 | #0.893 | 0.858 |
| **Bahamas[1] (Bahamian dollar) — Bahamas[1] (dollar des Bahamas)** | | | | | | | | | | |
| End of period<br>Fin de période | 1.000 | 1.000 | 1.000 | 1.000 | 1.000 | 1.000 | 1.000 | 1.000 | 1.000 | 1.000 |
| Period average<br>Moyenne sur période | 1.000 | 1.000 | 1.000 | 1.000 | 1.000 | 1.000 | 1.000 | 1.000 | 1.000 | 1.000 |
| **Bahrain (Bahrain dinar) — Bahreïn (dinar de Bahreïn)** | | | | | | | | | | |
| End of period<br>Fin de période | 0.376 | 0.376 | 0.376 | 0.376 | 0.376 | 0.376 | 0.376 | 0.376 | 0.376 | 0.376 |
| Period average<br>Moyenne sur période | 0.376 | 0.376 | 0.376 | 0.376 | 0.376 | 0.376 | 0.376 | 0.376 | 0.376 | 0.376 |
| **Bangladesh[1] (taka) — Bangladesh[1] (taka)** | | | | | | | | | | |
| End of period<br>Fin de période | 48.500 | 51.000 | 54.000 | 57.000 | 57.900 | 58.782 | 60.742 | 66.210 | 69.065 | 68.576 |
| Period average<br>Moyenne sur période | 46.906 | 49.085 | 52.142 | 55.807 | 57.888 | 58.150 | 59.513 | 64.328 | 68.933 | 68.875 |
| **Barbados (Barbados dollar) — Barbade (dollar de la Barbade)** | | | | | | | | | | |
| End of period<br>Fin de période | 2.000 | 2.000 | 2.000 | 2.000 | 2.000 | 2.000 | 2.000 | 2.000 | 2.000 | 2.000 |
| Period average<br>Moyenne sur période | 2.000 | 2.000 | 2.000 | 2.000 | 2.000 | 2.000 | 2.000 | 2.000 | 2.000 | 2.000 |
| **Belarus (Belarussian rouble) — Bélarus (rouble bélarussien)** | | | | | | | | | | |
| End of period<br>Fin de période | 106.000 | #320.000 | 1 180.000 | 1 580.000 | 1 920.000 | 2 156.000 | 2 170.000 | 2 152.000 | 2 140.000 | 2 150.000 |
| Period average<br>Moyenne sur période | 46.128 | 249.295 | 876.750 | 1 390.000 | 1 790.920 | 2 051.270 | 2 160.260 | 2 153.820 | 2 144.560 | 2 146.080 |
| **Belgium[4] (Belgian franc, euro) — Belgique[4] (franc belge, euro)** | | | | | | | | | | |
| End of period<br>Fin de période | 34.575 | #0.995 | 1.075 | 1.135 | 0.954 | 0.792 | 0.734 | 0.848 | 0.759 | 0.679 |
| Period average<br>Moyenne sur période | 36.299 | #0.939 | 1.085 | 1.118 | 1.063 | 0.886 | 0.805 | 0.804 | 0.797 | 0.731 |
| **Belize (Belize dollar) — Belize (dollar du Belize)** | | | | | | | | | | |
| End of period<br>Fin de période | 2.000 | 2.000 | 2.000 | 2.000 | 2.000 | 2.000 | 2.000 | 2.000 | 2.000 | 2.000 |
| Period average<br>Moyenne sur période | 2.000 | 2.000 | 2.000 | 2.000 | 2.000 | 2.000 | 2.000 | 2.000 | 2.000 | 2.000 |
| **Benin[6] (CFA franc) — Bénin[6] (franc CFA)** | | | | | | | | | | |
| End of period<br>Fin de période | 562.210 | #652.953 | 704.951 | 744.306 | 625.495 | 519.364 | 481.578 | 556.037 | 498.069 | 445.593 |
| Period average<br>Moyenne sur période | 589.952 | #615.699 | 711.976 | 733.039 | 696.988 | 581.200 | 528.285 | 527.468 | 522.890 | 479.267 |
| **Bhutan (ngultrum) — Bhoutan (ngultrum)** | | | | | | | | | | |
| End of period<br>Fin de période | 42.480 | 43.490 | 46.750 | 48.180 | 48.030 | 45.605 | 43.585 | 45.065 | 44.245 | 39.415 |
| Period average<br>Moyenne sur période | 41.259 | 43.055 | 44.942 | 47.186 | 48.610 | 46.583 | 45.317 | 44.100 | 45.307 | 41.349 |
| **Bolivia (boliviano) — Bolivie (boliviano)** | | | | | | | | | | |
| End of period<br>Fin de période | 5.645 | 5.990 | 6.390 | 6.820 | 7.490 | 7.830 | 8.050 | 8.040 | 7.980 | 7.620 |
| Period average<br>Moyenne sur période | 5.510 | 5.812 | 6.184 | 6.607 | 7.170 | 7.659 | 7.936 | 8.066 | 8.012 | 7.851 |
| **Bosnia and Herzegovina (convertible marka) — Bosnie-Herzégovine (marka convertible)** | | | | | | | | | | |
| End of period<br>Fin de période | 1.673 | 1.947 | 2.102 | 2.219 | 1.865 | 1.549 | 1.436 | 1.658 | 1.485 | 1.329 |
| Period average<br>Moyenne sur période | 1.760 | 1.836 | 2.123 | 2.186 | 2.078 | 1.733 | 1.575 | 1.573 | 1.559 | 1.429 |

| Country or area<br>Pays ou zone | 1998 | 1999 | 2000 | 2001 | 2002 | 2003 | 2004 | 2005 | 2006 | 2007 |
|---|---|---|---|---|---|---|---|---|---|---|
| **Botswana (pula) — Botswana (pula)** | | | | | | | | | | |
| End of period<br>Fin de période | 4.458 | 4.632 | 5.362 | 6.983 | 5.468 | 4.443 | 4.281 | 5.513 | 6.031 | 6.006 |
| Period average<br>Moyenne sur période | 4.226 | 4.624 | 5.102 | 5.841 | 6.328 | 4.950 | 4.693 | 5.110 | 5.837 | 6.139 |
| **Brazil (real) — Brésil (real)** | | | | | | | | | | |
| End of period<br>Fin de période | 1.209 | 1.788 | 1.955 | 2.320 | 3.533 | 2.888 | 2.654 | 2.340 | 2.137 | 1.771 |
| Period average<br>Moyenne sur période | 1.161 | 1.814 | 1.829 | 2.350 | 2.920 | 3.078 | 2.925 | 2.434 | 2.175 | 1.947 |
| **Brunei Darussalam (Brunei dollar) — Brunéi Darussalam (dollar du Brunéi)** | | | | | | | | | | |
| End of period<br>Fin de période | 1.661 | 1.666 | 1.732 | 1.851 | 1.737 | 1.701 | 1.634 | 1.664 | 1.534 | 1.441 |
| Period average<br>Moyenne sur période | 1.674 | 1.695 | 1.724 | 1.792 | 1.791 | 1.742 | 1.690 | 1.664 | 1.589 | 1.507 |
| **Bulgaria (lev) — Bulgarie (lev)** | | | | | | | | | | |
| End of period<br>Fin de période | 1.675 | 1.947 | 2.102 | 2.219 | 1.885 | 1.549 | 1.436 | 1.658 | 1.485 | 1.331 |
| Period average<br>Moyenne sur période | 1.760 | 1.836 | 2.123 | 2.185 | 2.077 | 1.733 | 1.575 | 1.574 | 1.559 | 1.429 |
| **Burkina Faso[6] (CFA franc) — Burkina Faso[6] (franc CFA)** | | | | | | | | | | |
| End of period<br>Fin de période | 562.210 | #652.953 | 704.951 | 744.306 | 625.495 | 519.364 | 481.578 | 556.037 | 498.069 | 445.593 |
| Period average<br>Moyenne sur période | 589.952 | #615.699 | 711.976 | 733.039 | 696.988 | 581.200 | 528.285 | 527.468 | 522.890 | 479.267 |
| **Burundi (Burundi franc) — Burundi (franc burundais)** | | | | | | | | | | |
| End of period<br>Fin de période | 505.160 | 628.580 | 778.200 | 864.200 | 1 071.230 | 1 093.000 | 1 109.510 | 997.780 | 1 002.470 | 1 119.540 |
| Period average<br>Moyenne sur période | 447.766 | 563.563 | 720.673 | 830.353 | 930.749 | 1 082.620 | 1 100.900 | 1 081.580 | 1 028.680 | 1 081.870 |
| **Cambodia (riel) — Cambodge (riel)** | | | | | | | | | | |
| End of period<br>Fin de période | 3 770.000 | 3 770.000 | 3 905.000 | 3 895.000 | 3 930.000 | 3 984.000 | 4 027.000 | 4 112.000 | 4 057.000 | 3 999.000 |
| Period average<br>Moyenne sur période | 3 744.420 | 3 807.830 | 3 840.750 | 3 916.330 | 3 912.080 | 3 973.330 | 4 016.250 | 4 092.500 | 4 103.250 | 4 056.170 |
| **Cameroon[6] (CFA franc) — Cameroun[6] (franc CFA)** | | | | | | | | | | |
| End of period<br>Fin de période | 562.210 | #652.953 | 704.951 | 744.306 | 625.495 | 519.364 | 481.578 | 556.037 | 498.069 | 445.593 |
| Period average<br>Moyenne sur période | 589.952 | #615.699 | 711.976 | 733.039 | 696.988 | 581.200 | 528.285 | 527.468 | 522.890 | 479.267 |
| **Canada (Canadian dollar) — Canada (dollar canadien)** | | | | | | | | | | |
| End of period<br>Fin de période | 1.531 | 1.443 | 1.500 | 1.593 | 1.580 | 1.292 | 1.204 | 1.165 | 1.165 | 0.988 |
| Period average<br>Moyenne sur période | 1.484 | 1.486 | 1.485 | 1.549 | 1.569 | 1.401 | 1.301 | 1.212 | 1.134 | 1.074 |
| **Cape Verde (Cape Verde escudo) — Cap-Vert (escudo du Cap-Vert)** | | | | | | | | | | |
| End of period<br>Fin de période | 94.255 | 109.765 | 118.506 | 125.122 | 105.149 | 87.308 | 80.956 | 93.473 | 83.728 | 74.907 |
| Period average<br>Moyenne sur période | 98.158 | 103.502 | 119.687 | 123.228 | 117.168 | 97.703 | 88.808 | 88.670 | 87.901 | 80.567 |
| **Central African Rep.[6] (CFA franc) — Rép. centrafricaine[6] (franc CFA)** | | | | | | | | | | |
| End of period<br>Fin de période | 562.210 | #652.953 | 704.951 | 744.306 | 625.495 | 519.364 | 481.578 | 556.037 | 498.069 | 445.593 |
| Period average<br>Moyenne sur période | 589.952 | #615.699 | 711.976 | 733.039 | 696.988 | 581.200 | 528.285 | 527.468 | 522.890 | 479.267 |
| **Chad[6] (CFA franc) — Tchad[6] (franc CFA)** | | | | | | | | | | |
| End of period<br>Fin de période | 562.210 | #652.953 | 704.951 | 744.306 | 625.495 | 519.364 | 481.578 | 556.037 | 498.069 | 445.593 |
| Period average<br>Moyenne sur période | 589.952 | #615.699 | 711.976 | 733.039 | 696.988 | 581.200 | 528.285 | 527.468 | 522.890 | 479.267 |

| Country or area / Pays ou zone | 1998 | 1999 | 2000 | 2001 | 2002 | 2003 | 2004 | 2005 | 2006 | 2007 |
|---|---|---|---|---|---|---|---|---|---|---|
| **Chile[1] (Chilean peso) — Chili[1] (peso chilien)** | | | | | | | | | | |
| End of period / Fin de période | 473.770 | 530.070 | 572.680 | 656.200 | 712.380 | 599.420 | 559.830 | 514.210 | 534.430 | 495.820 |
| Period average / Moyenne sur période | 460.288 | 508.777 | 539.588 | 634.938 | 688.937 | 691.398 | 609.529 | 559.768 | 530.275 | 522.464 |
| **China[1] (yuan) — Chine[1] (yuan)** | | | | | | | | | | |
| End of period / Fin de période | 8.279 | 8.280 | 8.277 | 8.277 | 8.277 | 8.277 | 8.277 | 8.070 | 7.809 | 7.305 |
| Period average / Moyenne sur période | 8.279 | 8.278 | 8.279 | 8.277 | 8.277 | 8.277 | 8.277 | 8.194 | 7.973 | 7.608 |
| **China, Hong Kong SAR (Hong Kong dollar) — Chine, Hong Kong RAS (dollar de Hong Kong)** | | | | | | | | | | |
| End of period / Fin de période | 7.746 | 7.771 | 7.796 | 7.797 | 7.798 | 7.763 | 7.774 | 7.753 | 7.775 | 7.802 |
| Period average / Moyenne sur période | 7.745 | 7.758 | 7.791 | 7.799 | 7.799 | 7.787 | 7.788 | 7.777 | 7.768 | 7.801 |
| **China, Macao SAR (Macao pataca) — Chine, Macao RAS (pataca de Macao)** | | | | | | | | | | |
| End of period / Fin de période | 7.980 | 8.005 | 8.034 | 8.031 | 8.033 | 7.997 | 8.010 | 7.987 | 8.006 | 8.034 |
| Period average / Moyenne sur période | 7.979 | 7.992 | 8.026 | 8.034 | 8.033 | 8.021 | 8.022 | 8.011 | 8.001 | 8.036 |
| **Colombia (Colombian peso) — Colombie (peso colombien)** | | | | | | | | | | |
| End of period / Fin de période | 1 507.520 | 1 873.770 | 2 187.020 | 2 301.330 | 2 864.790 | 2 780.820 | 2 412.100 | 2 284.220 | 2 225.440 | 1 987.810 |
| Period average / Moyenne sur période | 1 426.040 | 1 756.230 | 2 087.900 | 2 299.630 | 2 504.240 | 2 877.650 | 2 628.610 | 2 320.830 | 2 361.140 | 2 078.290 |
| **Comoros[7] (Comorian franc) — Comores[7] (franc comorien)** | | | | | | | | | | |
| End of period / Fin de période | 421.657 | 489.715 | 528.714 | 558.230 | 469.122 | 389.523 | 361.183 | 417.028 | 373.552 | 334.195 |
| Period average / Moyenne sur période | 442.459 | 461.775 | 533.982 | 549.779 | 522.741 | 435.900 | 396.214 | 395.601 | 392.168 | 359.450 |
| **Congo[6] (CFA franc) — Congo[6] (franc CFA)** | | | | | | | | | | |
| End of period / Fin de période | 562.210 | #652.953 | 704.951 | 744.306 | 625.495 | 519.364 | 481.578 | 556.037 | 498.069 | 445.593 |
| Period average / Moyenne sur période | 589.952 | #615.699 | 711.976 | 733.039 | 696.988 | 581.200 | 528.285 | 527.468 | 522.890 | 479.267 |
| **Costa Rica (Costa Rican colón) — Costa Rica (colón costa-ricien)** | | | | | | | | | | |
| End of period / Fin de période | 271.420 | 298.190 | 318.020 | 341.670 | 378.720 | 418.530 | 458.610 | 496.680 | 517.895 | 498.100 |
| Period average / Moyenne sur période | 257.229 | 285.685 | 308.187 | 328.871 | 359.818 | 398.662 | 437.935 | 477.787 | 511.302 | 516.617 |
| **Côte d'Ivoire[6] (CFA franc) — Côte d'Ivoire[6] (franc CFA)** | | | | | | | | | | |
| End of period / Fin de période | 562.210 | #652.953 | 704.951 | 744.306 | 625.495 | 519.364 | 481.578 | 556.037 | 498.069 | 445.593 |
| Period average / Moyenne sur période | 589.952 | #615.699 | 711.976 | 733.039 | 696.988 | 581.200 | 528.285 | 527.468 | 522.890 | 479.267 |
| **Croatia (kuna) — Croatie (kuna)** | | | | | | | | | | |
| End of period / Fin de période | 6.248 | 7.648 | 8.155 | 8.356 | 7.146 | 6.119 | 5.637 | 6.234 | 5.578 | 4.986 |
| Period average / Moyenne sur période | 6.363 | 7.112 | 8.278 | 8.342 | 7.872 | 6.705 | 6.034 | 5.949 | 5.838 | 5.365 |
| **Cyprus (Cyprus pound) — Chypre (livre chypriote)** | | | | | | | | | | |
| End of period / Fin de période | 0.498 | 0.575 | 0.617 | 0.650 | 0.547 | 0.465 | 0.425 | 0.484 | 0.439 | 0.398 |
| Period average / Moyenne sur période | 0.518 | 0.543 | 0.622 | 0.643 | 0.611 | 0.517 | 0.469 | 0.464 | 0.459 | 0.426 |
| **Czech Republic (Czech koruna) — République tchèque (couronne tchèque)** | | | | | | | | | | |
| End of period / Fin de période | 29.855 | 35.979 | 37.813 | 36.259 | 30.141 | 25.654 | 22.365 | 24.588 | 20.876 | 18.078 |
| Period average[1] / Moyenne sur période[1] | 32.281 | 34.569 | 38.598 | 38.035 | 32.739 | 28.209 | 25.700 | 23.957 | 22.596 | 20.294 |

| Country or area<br>Pays ou zone | 1998 | 1999 | 2000 | 2001 | 2002 | 2003 | 2004 | 2005 | 2006 | 2007 |
|---|---|---|---|---|---|---|---|---|---|---|
| **Dem. Rep. of the Congo (Congo franc) — Rép. dém. du Congo (franc congolais)** | | | | | | | | | | |
| End of period<br>Fin de période | #2.453 | 4.505 | 50.059 | 313.968 | 382.588 | #372.520 | 444.088 | 431.279 | 503.430 | ... |
| Period average<br>Moyenne sur période | 1.605 | 4.012 | 21.786 | 206.306 | 345.963 | #404.614 | 395.930 | 473.908 | 468.279 | ... |
| **Denmark (Danish krone) — Danemark (couronne danoise)** | | | | | | | | | | |
| End of period<br>Fin de période | 6.387 | 7.399 | 8.021 | 8.410 | 7.082 | 5.958 | 5.468 | 6.324 | 5.661 | 5.075 |
| Period average<br>Moyenne sur période | 6.701 | 6.976 | 8.083 | 8.323 | 7.895 | 6.588 | 5.991 | 5.997 | 5.947 | 5.444 |
| **Djibouti (Djibouti franc) — Djibouti (franc djiboutien)** | | | | | | | | | | |
| End of period<br>Fin de période | 177.721 | 177.721 | 177.721 | 177.721 | 177.721 | 177.721 | 177.721 | 177.721 | 177.721 | 177.721 |
| Period average<br>Moyenne sur période | 177.721 | 177.721 | 177.721 | 177.721 | 177.721 | 177.721 | 177.721 | 177.721 | 177.721 | 177.721 |
| **Dominica (EC dollar) — Dominique (dollar des Caraïbes orientales)** | | | | | | | | | | |
| End of period<br>Fin de période | 2.700 | 2.700 | 2.700 | 2.700 | 2.700 | 2.700 | 2.700 | 2.700 | 2.700 | 2.700 |
| Period average<br>Moyenne sur période | 2.700 | 2.700 | 2.700 | 2.700 | 2.700 | 2.700 | 2.700 | 2.700 | 2.700 | 2.700 |
| **Dominican Republic[1] (Dominican peso) — Rép. dominicaine[1] (peso dominicain)** | | | | | | | | | | |
| End of period<br>Fin de période | 15.788 | 16.039 | 16.674 | 17.149 | 21.194 | 37.250 | 31.109 | 34.879 | 33.797 | 34.342 |
| Period average<br>Moyenne sur période | 15.267 | 16.033 | 16.415 | 16.952 | 18.610 | 30.831 | 42.120 | 30.409 | 33.365 | 33.263 |
| **Egypt[1] (Egyptian pound) — Egypte[1] (livre égyptienne)** | | | | | | | | | | |
| End of period<br>Fin de période | 3.388 | 3.405 | 3.690 | 4.490 | 4.500 | 6.153 | 6.131 | 5.732 | 5.704 | ... |
| Period average<br>Moyenne sur période | 3.388 | 3.395 | 3.472 | 3.973 | 4.500 | 5.851 | 6.196 | 5.779 | 5.733 | ... |
| **El Salvador[1] (El Salvadoran colón) — El Salvador[1] (cólon salvadorien)** | | | | | | | | | | |
| End of period<br>Fin de période | 8.755 | 8.755 | 8.755 | 8.750 | 8.750 | 8.750 | 8.750 | 8.750 | 8.750 | 8.750 |
| Period average<br>Moyenne sur période | 8.755 | 8.755 | 8.755 | 8.750 | 8.750 | 8.750 | 8.750 | 8.750 | 8.750 | 8.750 |
| **Equatorial Guinea[6] (CFA franc) — Guinée équatoriale[6] (franc CFA)** | | | | | | | | | | |
| End of period<br>Fin de période | 562.210 | #652.953 | 704.951 | 744.306 | 625.495 | 519.364 | 481.578 | 556.037 | 498.069 | 445.593 |
| Period average<br>Moyenne sur période | 589.952 | #615.699 | 711.976 | 733.039 | 696.988 | 581.200 | 528.285 | 527.468 | 522.890 | 479.267 |
| **Eritrea (nakfa) — Erythrée (nakfa)** | | | | | | | | | | |
| End of period<br>Fin de période | 7.597 | 9.600 | 10.200 | 13.798 | 14.309 | 13.788 | 13.788 | 15.375 | 15.375 | 15.375 |
| Period average<br>Moyenne sur période | 7.362 | 8.153 | 9.625 | 11.310 | 13.958 | 13.878 | 13.788 | 15.368 | 15.375 | 15.375 |
| **Estonia (Estonian kroon) — Estonie (couronne estonienne)** | | | | | | | | | | |
| End of period<br>Fin de période | 13.410 | 15.562 | 16.820 | 17.692 | 14.936 | 12.410 | 11.471 | 13.221 | 11.882 | 10.638 |
| Period average<br>Moyenne sur période | 14.075 | 14.678 | 16.969 | 17.478 | 16.612 | 13.856 | 12.596 | 12.584 | 12.466 | 11.434 |
| **Ethiopia (Ethiopian birr) — Ethiopie (birr éthiopien)** | | | | | | | | | | |
| End of period<br>Fin de période | 7.503 | 8.134 | 8.314 | 8.558 | 8.581 | 8.621 | 8.652 | 8.681 | 8.776 | 9.201 |
| Period average<br>Moyenne sur période | 7.116 | 7.942 | 8.217 | 8.458 | 8.568 | 8.600 | 8.636 | 8.666 | 8.699 | 8.949 |
| **Euro Area[8] (euro) — Zone euro[8] (euro)** | | | | | | | | | | |
| End of period<br>Fin de période | ... | 0.995 | 1.075 | 1.135 | 0.954 | 0.792 | 0.734 | 0.848 | 0.759 | 0.679 |
| Period average<br>Moyenne sur période | ... | 0.939 | 1.085 | 1.118 | 1.063 | 0.886 | 0.805 | 0.804 | 0.797 | 0.731 |

| Country or area<br>Pays ou zone | 1998 | 1999 | 2000 | 2001 | 2002 | 2003 | 2004 | 2005 | 2006 | 2007 |
|---|---|---|---|---|---|---|---|---|---|---|
| **Fiji (Fiji dollar) — Fidji (dollar des Fidji)** | | | | | | | | | | |
| End of period<br>Fin de période | 1.986 | 1.966 | 2.186 | 2.309 | 2.065 | 1.722 | 1.645 | 1.745 | 1.664 | 1.551 |
| Period average<br>Moyenne sur période | 1.987 | 1.970 | 2.129 | 2.277 | 2.187 | 1.896 | 1.733 | 1.691 | 1.731 | 1.610 |
| **Finland[4] (Finnish markka, euro) — Finlande[4] (markka finlandais, euro)** | | | | | | | | | | |
| End of period<br>Fin de période | 5.096 | #0.995 | 1.075 | 1.135 | 0.954 | 0.792 | 0.734 | 0.848 | 0.759 | 0.679 |
| Period average<br>Moyenne sur période | 5.344 | #0.939 | 1.085 | 1.118 | 1.063 | 0.886 | 0.805 | 0.804 | 0.797 | 0.731 |
| **France[4] (French franc, euro) — France[4] (franc français, euro)** | | | | | | | | | | |
| End of period<br>Fin de période | 5.622 | #0.995 | 1.075 | 1.135 | 0.954 | 0.792 | 0.734 | 0.848 | 0.759 | 0.679 |
| Period average<br>Moyenne sur période | 5.900 | #0.939 | 1.085 | 1.118 | 1.063 | 0.886 | 0.805 | 0.804 | 0.797 | 0.731 |
| **Gabon[6] (CFA franc) — Gabon[6] (franc CFA)** | | | | | | | | | | |
| End of period<br>Fin de période | 562.210 | #652.953 | 704.951 | 744.306 | 625.495 | 519.364 | 481.578 | 556.037 | 498.069 | 445.593 |
| Period average<br>Moyenne sur période | 589.952 | #615.699 | 711.976 | 733.039 | 696.988 | 581.200 | 528.285 | 527.468 | 522.890 | 479.267 |
| **Gambia (dalasi) — Gambie (dalasi)** | | | | | | | | | | |
| End of period<br>Fin de période | 10.991 | 11.547 | 14.888 | 16.932 | 23.392 | 30.960 | 29.674 | 28.135 | 28.047 | 22.539 |
| Period average<br>Moyenne sur période | 10.643 | 11.395 | 12.788 | 15.687 | 19.918 | 27.306 | 30.030 | 28.575 | 28.066 | 24.875 |
| **Georgia (lari) — Géorgie (lari)** | | | | | | | | | | |
| End of period<br>Fin de période | 1.800 | 1.930 | 1.975 | 2.060 | 2.090 | 2.075 | 1.825 | 1.793 | 1.714 | 1.592 |
| Period average<br>Moyenne sur période | 1.390 | 2.025 | 1.976 | 2.073 | 2.196 | 2.146 | 1.917 | 1.813 | 1.780 | 1.671 |
| **Germany[4] (deutsche mark, euro) — Allemagne[4] (deutsche mark, euro)** | | | | | | | | | | |
| End of period<br>Fin de période | 1.673 | #0.995 | 1.075 | 1.135 | 0.954 | 0.792 | 0.734 | 0.848 | 0.759 | 0.679 |
| Period average<br>Moyenne sur période | 1.760 | #0.939 | 1.085 | 1.118 | 1.063 | 0.886 | 0.805 | 0.804 | 0.797 | 0.731 |
| **Ghana[1] (cedi) — Ghana[1] (cedi)** | | | | | | | | | | |
| End of period<br>Fin de période | 0.233 | 0.354 | 0.705 | 0.732 | 0.844 | 0.885 | 0.905 | 0.913 | 0.924 | ... |
| Period average<br>Moyenne sur période | 0.231 | 0.267 | 0.545 | 0.717 | 0.793 | 0.867 | 0.900 | 0.907 | 0.917 | 0.936 |
| **Greece[4] (drachma, euro) — Grèce[4] (drachma, euro)** | | | | | | | | | | |
| End of period<br>Fin de période | 282.570 | 328.440 | 365.620 | #1.135 | 0.954 | 0.792 | 0.734 | 0.848 | 0.759 | 0.679 |
| Period average<br>Moyenne sur période | 295.529 | 305.647 | 365.399 | #1.118 | 1.063 | 0.886 | 0.805 | 0.804 | 0.797 | 0.731 |
| **Grenada (EC dollar) — Grenade (dollar des Caraïbes orientales)** | | | | | | | | | | |
| End of period<br>Fin de période | 2.700 | 2.700 | 2.700 | 2.700 | 2.700 | 2.700 | 2.700 | 2.700 | 2.700 | 2.700 |
| Period average<br>Moyenne sur période | 2.700 | 2.700 | 2.700 | 2.700 | 2.700 | 2.700 | 2.700 | 2.700 | 2.700 | 2.700 |
| **Guatemala (quetzal) — Guatemala (quetzal)** | | | | | | | | | | |
| End of period<br>Fin de période | 6.848 | 7.821 | 7.731 | 8.001 | 7.807 | 8.041 | 7.748 | 7.610 | 7.625 | 7.631 |
| Period average<br>Moyenne sur période | 6.395 | 7.386 | 7.763 | 7.859 | 7.822 | 7.941 | 7.947 | 7.634 | 7.603 | 7.673 |
| **Guinea (Guinean franc) — Guinée (franc guinéen)** | | | | | | | | | | |
| End of period<br>Fin de période | 1 298.030 | 1 736.000 | 1 882.270 | 1 988.330 | 1 976.000 | 2 000.000 | 2 550.000 | 4 500.000 | ... | ... |
| Period average<br>Moyenne sur période | 1 236.830 | 1 387.400 | 1 746.870 | 1 950.560 | 1 975.840 | 1 984.930 | 2 225.030 | 3 644.330 | ... | ... |

| Country or area<br>Pays ou zone | 1998 | 1999 | 2000 | 2001 | 2002 | 2003 | 2004 | 2005 | 2006 | 2007 |
|---|---|---|---|---|---|---|---|---|---|---|
| **Guinea-Bissau[9] (CFA franc) — Guinée-Bissau[9] (franc CFA)** | | | | | | | | | | |
| End of period<br>Fin de période | 562.210 | 652.953 | 704.951 | 744.306 | 625.495 | 519.364 | 481.578 | 556.037 | 498.069 | 445.593 |
| Period average<br>Moyenne sur période | 589.952 | #615.699 | 711.976 | 733.039 | 696.988 | 581.200 | 528.285 | 527.468 | 522.890 | 479.267 |
| **Guyana[1] (Guyana dollar) — Guyana[1] (dollar guyanais)** | | | | | | | | | | |
| End of period<br>Fin de période | 162.250 | 180.500 | 184.750 | 189.500 | 191.750 | 194.250 | 199.750 | 200.250 | 201.000 | 203.500 |
| Period average<br>Moyenne sur période | 150.519 | 177.995 | 182.430 | 187.321 | 190.665 | 193.878 | 198.307 | 199.875 | 200.188 | 202.347 |
| **Haiti[1] (gourde) — Haïti[1] (gourde)** | | | | | | | | | | |
| End of period<br>Fin de période | 16.505 | 17.965 | 22.524 | 26.339 | 37.609 | 42.085 | 37.232 | 43.000 | 37.591 | 36.784 |
| Period average<br>Moyenne sur période | 16.766 | 16.938 | 21.171 | 24.429 | 29.251 | 42.367 | 38.352 | 40.449 | 40.409 | 36.861 |
| **Honduras[1] (lempira) — Honduras[1] (lempira)** | | | | | | | | | | |
| End of period<br>Fin de période | 13.808 | 14.504 | 15.141 | 15.920 | 16.923 | 17.748 | 18.633 | 18.895 | 18.895 | 18.895 |
| Period average<br>Moyenne sur période | 13.385 | 14.213 | 14.839 | 15.474 | 16.433 | 17.345 | 18.206 | 18.832 | 18.895 | 18.895 |
| **Hungary (forint) — Hongrie (forint)** | | | | | | | | | | |
| End of period<br>Fin de période | 219.030 | 252.520 | 284.730 | 279.030 | 225.160 | 207.920 | 180.290 | 213.580 | 191.620 | 172.610 |
| Period average<br>Moyenne sur période | 214.402 | 237.146 | 282.179 | 286.490 | 257.887 | 224.307 | 202.746 | 199.582 | 210.390 | 183.626 |
| **Iceland (Icelandic króna) — Islande (couronne islandaise)** | | | | | | | | | | |
| End of period<br>Fin de période | 69.320 | 72.550 | 84.700 | 102.950 | 80.580 | 70.990 | 61.040 | 62.980 | 71.660 | 61.850 |
| Period average<br>Moyenne sur période | 70.958 | 72.335 | 78.616 | 97.425 | 91.662 | 76.709 | 70.192 | 62.982 | 70.195 | 64.088 |
| **India (Indian rupee) — Inde (roupie indienne)** | | | | | | | | | | |
| End of period<br>Fin de période | 42.480 | 43.490 | 46.750 | 48.180 | 48.030 | 45.605 | 43.585 | 45.065 | 44.245 | 39.415 |
| Period average<br>Moyenne sur période | 41.259 | 43.055 | 44.942 | 47.186 | 48.610 | 46.583 | 45.317 | 44.100 | 45.307 | 41.349 |
| **Indonesia (Indonesian rupiah) — Indonésie (roupie indonésien)** | | | | | | | | | | |
| End of period<br>Fin de période | 8 025.000 | 7 085.000 | 9 595.000 | 10 400.000 | 8 940.000 | 8 465.000 | 9 290.000 | 9 830.000 | 9 020.000 | 9 419.000 |
| Period average<br>Moyenne sur période | 10 013.600 | 7 855.150 | 8 421.780 | 10 260.900 | 9 311.190 | 8 577.130 | 8 938.850 | 9 704.740 | 9 159.320 | 9 143.360 |
| **Iran (Islamic Rep. of) (Iranian rial) — Iran (Rép. islamique d') (rial iranien)** | | | | | | | | | | |
| End of period<br>Fin de période | 1 750.930 | 1 752.290 | 2 262.930 | 1 750.950 | #7 951.980 | 8 272.110 | 8 793.000 | 9 091.000 | 9 223.000 | 9 282.000 |
| Period average<br>Moyenne sur période | 1 751.860 | 1 752.930 | 1 764.430 | 1 753.560 | #6 906.960 | 8 193.890 | 8 613.990 | 8 963.960 | 9 170.940 | 9 281.150 |
| **Iraq[1] (Iraqi dinar) — Iraq[1] (dinar iraquien)** | | | | | | | | | | |
| End of period<br>Fin de période | 0.310 | 0.310 | 0.310 | 0.310 | 0.310 | ... | #1 469.000 | 1 487.000 | 1 325.000 | 1 215.000 |
| Period average<br>Moyenne sur période | 0.311 | 0.311 | 0.311 | 0.311 | 0.311 | ... | 1 453.420 | 1 472.000 | 1 467.420 | 1 254.570 |
| **Ireland[4] (Irish pound, euro) — Irlande[4] (livre irlandaise, euro)** | | | | | | | | | | |
| End of period<br>Fin de période | 0.672 | #0.995 | 1.075 | 1.135 | 0.954 | 0.792 | 0.734 | 0.848 | 0.759 | 0.679 |
| Period average<br>Moyenne sur période | 0.702 | #0.939 | 1.085 | 1.118 | 1.063 | 0.886 | 0.805 | 0.804 | 0.797 | 0.731 |
| **Israel (new sheqel) — Israël (nouveau sheqel)** | | | | | | | | | | |
| End of period<br>Fin de période | 4.161 | 4.153 | 4.041 | 4.416 | 4.737 | 4.379 | 4.308 | 4.603 | 4.225 | 3.846 |
| Period average<br>Moyenne sur période | 3.800 | 4.140 | 4.077 | 4.206 | 4.738 | 4.554 | 4.482 | 4.488 | 4.456 | 4.108 |

| Country or area / Pays ou zone | 1998 | 1999 | 2000 | 2001 | 2002 | 2003 | 2004 | 2005 | 2006 | 2007 |
|---|---|---|---|---|---|---|---|---|---|---|
| **Italy[4] (Italian lira, euro) — Italie[4] (lire italienne, euro)** | | | | | | | | | | |
| End of period / Fin de période | 1 653.100 | #0.995 | 1.075 | 1.135 | 0.954 | 0.792 | 0.734 | 0.848 | 0.759 | 0.679 |
| Period average / Moyenne sur période | 1 736.210 | #0.939 | 1.085 | 1.118 | 1.063 | 0.886 | 0.805 | 0.804 | 0.797 | 0.731 |
| **Jamaica (Jamaican dollar) — Jamaïque (dollar jamaïcain)** | | | | | | | | | | |
| End of period / Fin de période | 37.055 | 41.291 | 45.415 | 47.286 | 50.762 | 60.517 | 61.450 | 64.381 | 67.032 | ... |
| Period average / Moyenne sur période | 36.550 | 39.044 | 42.986 | 45.996 | 48.416 | 57.741 | 61.197 | 62.281 | 65.744 | ... |
| **Japan (yen) — Japon (yen)** | | | | | | | | | | |
| End of period / Fin de période | 115.600 | 102.200 | 114.900 | 131.800 | 119.900 | 107.100 | 104.120 | 117.970 | 118.950 | 114.000 |
| Period average / Moyenne sur période | 130.905 | 113.907 | 107.765 | 121.529 | 125.388 | 115.933 | 108.193 | 110.218 | 116.299 | 117.754 |
| **Jordan (Jordan dinar) — Jordanie (dinar jordanien)** | | | | | | | | | | |
| End of period / Fin de période | 0.709 | 0.709 | 0.709 | 0.709 | 0.709 | 0.709 | 0.709 | 0.709 | 0.709 | 0.709 |
| Period average / Moyenne sur période | 0.709 | 0.709 | 0.709 | 0.709 | 0.709 | 0.709 | 0.709 | 0.709 | 0.709 | 0.709 |
| **Kazakhstan (tenge) — Kazakhstan (tenge)** | | | | | | | | | | |
| End of period / Fin de période | 83.800 | 138.200 | 144.500 | 150.200 | 154.600 | 144.220 | 130.000 | 133.980 | 127.000 | 120.300 |
| Period average / Moyenne sur période | 78.303 | 119.523 | 142.133 | 146.736 | 153.279 | 149.576 | 136.035 | 132.880 | 126.089 | 122.554 |
| **Kenya (Kenya shilling) — Kenya (shilling kényen)** | | | | | | | | | | |
| End of period / Fin de période | 61.906 | 72.931 | 78.036 | 78.600 | 77.072 | 76.139 | 77.344 | 72.367 | 69.397 | 62.675 |
| Period average / Moyenne sur période | 60.367 | 70.326 | 76.176 | 78.563 | 78.749 | 75.936 | 79.174 | 75.554 | 72.101 | 67.318 |
| **Kiribati (Australian dollar) — Kiribati (dollar australien)** | | | | | | | | | | |
| End of period / Fin de période | 1.629 | 1.530 | 1.805 | 1.959 | 1.766 | 1.333 | 1.284 | 1.363 | 1.264 | 1.134 |
| Period average / Moyenne sur période | 1.592 | 1.550 | 1.725 | 1.933 | 1.841 | 1.542 | 1.360 | 1.310 | 1.328 | 1.195 |
| **Korea, Republic of (Korean won) — Corée, République de (won coréen)** | | | | | | | | | | |
| End of period / Fin de période | 1 204.000 | 1 138.000 | 1 264.500 | 1 313.500 | 1 186.200 | 1 192.600 | 1 035.100 | 1 011.600 | 929.800 | 936.100 |
| Period average / Moyenne sur période | 1 401.440 | 1 188.820 | 1 130.960 | 1 290.990 | 1 251.090 | 1 191.610 | 1 145.320 | 1 024.120 | 954.791 | 929.257 |
| **Kuwait (Kuwaiti dinar) — Koweït (dinar koweïtien)** | | | | | | | | | | |
| End of period / Fin de période | 0.302 | 0.304 | 0.305 | 0.308 | 0.300 | 0.295 | 0.295 | 0.292 | 0.289 | 0.273 |
| Period average / Moyenne sur période | 0.305 | 0.304 | 0.307 | 0.307 | 0.304 | 0.298 | 0.295 | 0.292 | 0.290 | 0.284 |
| **Kyrgyzstan (Kyrgyz som) — Kirghizistan (som kirghize)** | | | | | | | | | | |
| End of period / Fin de période | 29.376 | 45.429 | 48.304 | 47.719 | 46.095 | 44.190 | 41.625 | 41.301 | 38.124 | 35.499 |
| Period average / Moyenne sur période | 20.838 | 39.008 | 47.704 | 48.378 | 46.937 | 43.648 | 42.650 | 41.012 | 40.153 | 37.316 |
| **Lao People's Dem. Rep. (kip) — Rép. dém. pop. lao (kip)** | | | | | | | | | | |
| End of period / Fin de période | 4 274.000 | 7 600.000 | 8 218.000 | 9 490.000 | 10 680.000 | 10 467.000 | 10 376.500 | 10 743.000 | 9 696.480 | ... |
| Period average / Moyenne sur période | 3 298.330 | 7 102.020 | 7 887.640 | 8 954.580 | 10 056.300 | 10 569.000 | 10 585.500 | 10 655.200 | 10 159.900 | ... |
| **Latvia (lats) — Lettonie (lats)** | | | | | | | | | | |
| End of period / Fin de période | 0.569 | 0.583 | 0.613 | 0.638 | 0.594 | 0.541 | 0.516 | 0.593 | 0.536 | 0.484 |
| Period average / Moyenne sur période | 0.590 | 0.585 | 0.607 | 0.628 | 0.618 | 0.572 | 0.540 | 0.565 | 0.560 | 0.514 |

| Country or area<br>Pays ou zone | 1998 | 1999 | 2000 | 2001 | 2002 | 2003 | 2004 | 2005 | 2006 | 2007 |
|---|---|---|---|---|---|---|---|---|---|---|
| **Lebanon (Lebanese pound) — Liban (livre libanaise)** | | | | | | | | | | |
| End of period<br>Fin de période | 1 508.000 | 1 507.500 | 1 507.500 | 1 507.500 | 1 507.500 | 1 507.500 | 1 507.500 | 1 507.500 | 1 507.500 | 1 507.500 |
| Period average<br>Moyenne sur période | 1 516.130 | 1 507.840 | 1 507.500 | 1 507.500 | 1 507.500 | 1 507.500 | 1 507.500 | 1 507.500 | 1 507.500 | 1 507.500 |
| **Lesotho[1] (loti) — Lesotho[1] (loti)** | | | | | | | | | | |
| End of period<br>Fin de période | 5.860 | 6.155 | 7.569 | 12.127 | 8.640 | 6.640 | 5.630 | 6.325 | 6.970 | 6.810 |
| Period average<br>Moyenne sur période | 5.528 | 6.110 | 6.940 | 8.609 | 10.541 | 7.565 | 6.460 | 6.359 | 6.772 | 7.045 |
| **Liberia[1] (Liberian dollar) — Libéria[1] (dollar libérien)** | | | | | | | | | | |
| End of period<br>Fin de période | #43.250 | 39.500 | 42.750 | 49.500 | 65.000 | 50.500 | 54.500 | 56.500 | 59.500 | 62.500 |
| Period average<br>Moyenne sur période | #41.508 | 41.903 | 40.953 | 48.583 | 61.754 | 59.379 | 54.906 | 57.096 | 58.013 | 61.272 |
| **Libyan Arab Jamah. (Libyan dinar) — Jamah. arabe libyenne (dinar libyen)** | | | | | | | | | | |
| End of period<br>Fin de période | 0.450 | 0.462 | 0.540 | 0.650 | 1.210 | 1.300 | 1.244 | 1.352 | 1.285 | 1.223 |
| Period average<br>Moyenne sur période | 0.468 | 0.464 | 0.512 | 0.605 | 1.271 | 1.293 | 1.305 | 1.308 | 1.314 | 1.263 |
| **Lithuania (litas) — Lituanie (litas)** | | | | | | | | | | |
| End of period<br>Fin de période | 4.000 | 4.000 | 4.000 | 4.000 | 3.311 | 2.762 | 2.535 | 2.910 | 2.630 | 2.357 |
| Period average<br>Moyenne sur période | 4.000 | 4.000 | 4.000 | 4.000 | 3.677 | 3.061 | 2.781 | 2.774 | 2.752 | 2.524 |
| **Luxembourg[4] (Luxembourg franc, euro) — Luxembourg[4] (franc luxembourgeois, euro)** | | | | | | | | | | |
| End of period<br>Fin de période | 34.575 | #0.995 | 1.075 | 1.135 | 0.954 | 0.792 | 0.734 | 0.848 | 0.759 | 0.679 |
| Period average<br>Moyenne sur période | 36.299 | #0.939 | 1.085 | 1.118 | 1.063 | 0.886 | 0.805 | 0.804 | 0.797 | 0.731 |
| **Madagascar[10] (Malagasy ariary) — Madagascar[10] (ariary malgache)** | | | | | | | | | | |
| End of period<br>Fin de période | 1 080.440 | 1 308.640 | 1 310.090 | 1 326.240 | 1 286.950 | 1 219.620 | 1 869.400 | #2 159.820 | 2 013.950 | 1 786.690 |
| Period average<br>Moyenne sur période | 1 088.280 | 1 256.760 | 1 353.500 | 1 317.700 | 1 366.390 | 1 238.330 | 1 868.860 | 2 003.030 | 2 142.300 | 1 873.880 |
| **Malawi (Malawi kwacha) — Malawi (kwacha malawien)** | | | | | | | | | | |
| End of period<br>Fin de période | 43.884 | 46.438 | 80.076 | 67.294 | 87.139 | 108.566 | 108.943 | 123.781 | 139.343 | 140.316 |
| Period average<br>Moyenne sur période | 31.073 | 44.088 | 59.544 | 72.197 | 76.687 | 97.433 | 108.898 | 118.420 | 136.014 | 139.957 |
| **Malaysia (ringgit) — Malaisie (ringgit)** | | | | | | | | | | |
| End of period<br>Fin de période | 3.800 | 3.800 | 3.800 | 3.800 | 3.800 | 3.800 | 3.800 | 3.780 | 3.532 | 3.307 |
| Period average<br>Moyenne sur période | 3.924 | 3.800 | 3.800 | 3.800 | 3.800 | 3.800 | 3.800 | 3.787 | 3.668 | 3.438 |
| **Maldives[11] (rufiyaa) — Maldives[11] (rufiyaa)** | | | | | | | | | | |
| End of period<br>Fin de période | 11.770 | 11.770 | 11.770 | 12.800 | 12.800 | 12.800 | 12.800 | 12.800 | 12.800 | 12.800 |
| Period average<br>Moyenne sur période | 11.770 | 11.770 | 11.770 | 12.242 | 12.800 | 12.800 | 12.800 | 12.800 | 12.800 | 12.800 |
| **Mali[6] (CFA franc) — Mali[6] (franc CFA)** | | | | | | | | | | |
| End of period<br>Fin de période | 562.210 | #652.953 | 704.951 | 744.306 | 625.495 | 519.364 | 481.578 | 556.037 | 498.069 | 445.593 |
| Period average<br>Moyenne sur période | 589.952 | #615.699 | 711.976 | 733.039 | 696.988 | 581.200 | 528.285 | 527.468 | 522.890 | 479.267 |
| **Malta (Maltese lira) — Malte (lire maltaise)** | | | | | | | | | | |
| End of period<br>Fin de période | 0.377 | 0.412 | 0.438 | 0.452 | 0.399 | 0.343 | 0.319 | 0.363 | 0.326 | 0.292 |
| Period average<br>Moyenne sur période | 0.389 | 0.399 | 0.438 | 0.450 | 0.434 | 0.377 | 0.345 | 0.346 | 0.341 | 0.312 |

63

Exchange rates — National currency per US dollar (*continued*)
Cours des changes — Valeur du dollar E.-U. en monnaie nationale (*suite*)

| Country or area<br>Pays ou zone | 1998 | 1999 | 2000 | 2001 | 2002 | 2003 | 2004 | 2005 | 2006 | 2007 |
|---|---|---|---|---|---|---|---|---|---|---|
| **Mauritania (ouguiya) — Mauritanie (ouguiya)** | | | | | | | | | | |
| End of period<br>Fin de période | 205.780 | 225.000 | 252.300 | 264.120 | 268.710 | 265.600 | 257.190 | 270.610 | ... | ... |
| Period average<br>Moyenne sur période | 188.476 | 209.514 | 238.923 | 255.629 | 271.739 | 263.030 | ... | 265.528 | ... | ... |
| **Mauritius (Mauritian rupee) — Maurice (roupie mauricienne)** | | | | | | | | | | |
| End of period<br>Fin de période | 24.784 | 25.468 | 27.882 | 30.394 | 29.197 | 26.088 | 28.204 | 30.667 | 34.337 | 28.216 |
| Period average<br>Moyenne sur période | 23.993 | 25.186 | 26.250 | 29.129 | 29.962 | 27.902 | 27.499 | 29.496 | 31.708 | 31.314 |
| **Mexico[1] (Mexican peso) — Mexique[1] (peso mexicain)** | | | | | | | | | | |
| End of period<br>Fin de période | 9.865 | 9.514 | 9.572 | 9.142 | 10.313 | 11.236 | 11.265 | 10.778 | 10.881 | 10.866 |
| Period average<br>Moyenne sur période | 9.136 | 9.560 | 9.456 | 9.342 | 9.656 | 10.789 | 11.286 | 10.898 | 10.899 | 10.928 |
| **Micronesia (Fed. States of) (US dollar) — Micronésie (Etats féd. de) (dollar des Etats-Unis)** | | | | | | | | | | |
| End of period<br>Fin de période | 1.000 | 1.000 | 1.000 | 1.000 | 1.000 | 1.000 | 1.000 | 1.000 | 1.000 | 1.000 |
| Period average<br>Moyenne sur période | 1.000 | 1.000 | 1.000 | 1.000 | 1.000 | 1.000 | 1.000 | 1.000 | 1.000 | 1.000 |
| **Moldova (Moldovan leu) — Moldova (leu moldove)** | | | | | | | | | | |
| End of period<br>Fin de période | 8.323 | 11.590 | 12.383 | 13.091 | 13.822 | 13.220 | 12.461 | 12.832 | 12.905 | 11.319 |
| Period average<br>Moyenne sur période | 5.371 | 10.516 | 12.434 | 12.865 | 13.571 | 13.945 | 12.330 | 12.600 | 13.131 | 12.140 |
| **Mongolia (togrog) — Mongolie (togrog)** | | | | | | | | | | |
| End of period<br>Fin de période | 902.000 | 1 072.370 | 1 097.000 | 1 102.000 | 1 125.000 | 1 168.000 | 1 209.000 | 1 221.000 | 1 165.000 | 1 170.000 |
| Period average<br>Moyenne sur période | 840.828 | 1 021.870 | 1 076.670 | 1 097.700 | 1 110.310 | 1 146.540 | 1 185.280 | 1 205.220 | 1 165.370 | 1 170.960 |
| **Montenegro (euro) — Monténégro (euro)** | | | | | | | | | | |
| End of period<br>Fin de période | ... | ... | ... | ... | ... | ... | ... | ... | 0.759 | 0.679 |
| Period average<br>Moyenne sur période | ... | ... | ... | ... | ... | ... | ... | ... | 0.797 | 0.731 |
| **Montserrat (EC dollar) — Montserrat (dollar des Caraïbes orientales)** | | | | | | | | | | |
| End of period<br>Fin de période | 2.700 | 2.700 | 2.700 | 2.700 | 2.700 | 2.700 | 2.700 | 2.700 | 2.700 | 2.700 |
| Period average<br>Moyenne sur période | 2.700 | 2.700 | 2.700 | 2.700 | 2.700 | 2.700 | 2.700 | 2.700 | 2.700 | 2.700 |
| **Morocco (Moroccan dirham) — Maroc (dirham marocain)** | | | | | | | | | | |
| End of period<br>Fin de période | 9.255 | 10.087 | 10.619 | 11.560 | 10.167 | 8.750 | 8.218 | 9.249 | 8.457 | 7.713 |
| Period average<br>Moyenne sur période | 9.604 | 9.804 | 10.626 | 11.303 | 11.021 | 9.574 | 8.868 | 8.865 | 8.796 | 8.192 |
| **Mozambique[1,12] (new metical) — Mozambique[1,12] (nouveau metical)** | | | | | | | | | | |
| End of period<br>Fin de période | 12.366 | 13.300 | 17.141 | 23.320 | 23.854 | 23.857 | 18.899 | 24.183 | #25.970 | 23.820 |
| Period average<br>Moyenne sur période | 11.875 | 12.775 | 15.227 | 20.704 | 23.678 | 23.782 | 22.581 | 23.061 | 25.401 | 25.840 |
| **Myanmar (kyat) — Myanmar (kyat)** | | | | | | | | | | |
| End of period<br>Fin de période | 6.043 | 6.199 | 6.530 | 6.770 | 6.258 | 5.726 | 5.479 | 5.953 | 5.656 | 5.384 |
| Period average<br>Moyenne sur période | 6.274 | 6.223 | 6.426 | 6.684 | 6.573 | 6.076 | 5.746 | 5.761 | 5.784 | 5.608 |
| **Namibia (Namibia dollar) — Namibie (dollar namibien)** | | | | | | | | | | |
| End of period<br>Fin de période | 5.860 | 6.155 | 7.569 | 12.127 | 8.640 | 6.640 | 5.630 | 6.325 | 6.970 | 6.810 |
| Period average<br>Moyenne sur période | 5.528 | 6.110 | 6.940 | 8.609 | 10.541 | 7.565 | 6.460 | 6.359 | 6.772 | 7.045 |

| Country or area / Pays ou zone | 1998 | 1999 | 2000 | 2001 | 2002 | 2003 | 2004 | 2005 | 2006 | 2007 |
|---|---|---|---|---|---|---|---|---|---|---|
| **Nepal (Nepalese rupee) — Népal (roupie népalaise)** | | | | | | | | | | |
| End of period / Fin de période | 67.675 | 68.725 | 74.300 | 76.475 | 78.300 | 74.040 | 71.800 | 74.050 | 71.100 | 63.550 |
| Period average / Moyenne sur période | 65.976 | 68.239 | 71.094 | 74.949 | 77.877 | 76.141 | 73.674 | 71.368 | 72.756 | 66.415 |
| **Netherlands[4] (Netherlands guilder, euro) — Pays-Bas[4] (florin néerlandais, euro)** | | | | | | | | | | |
| End of period / Fin de période | 1.889 | #0.995 | 1.075 | 1.135 | 0.954 | 0.792 | 0.734 | 0.848 | 0.759 | 0.679 |
| Period average / Moyenne sur période | 1.984 | #0.939 | 1.085 | 1.118 | 1.063 | 0.886 | 0.805 | 0.804 | 0.797 | 0.731 |
| **Netherlands Antilles (Netherlands Antillean guilder) — Antilles néerlandaises (florin des Antilles néerlandaises)** | | | | | | | | | | |
| End of period / Fin de période | 1.790 | 1.790 | 1.790 | 1.790 | 1.790 | 1.790 | 1.790 | 1.790 | 1.790 | 1.790 |
| Period average / Moyenne sur période | 1.790 | 1.790 | 1.790 | 1.790 | 1.790 | 1.790 | 1.790 | 1.790 | 1.790 | 1.790 |
| **New Zealand (New Zealand dollar) — Nouvelle-Zélande (dollar néo-zélandais)** | | | | | | | | | | |
| End of period / Fin de période | 1.898 | 1.921 | 2.272 | 2.407 | 1.899 | 1.539 | 1.392 | 1.468 | 1.417 | 1.292 |
| Period average / Moyenne sur période | 1.868 | 1.890 | 2.201 | 2.379 | 2.162 | 1.722 | 1.509 | 1.420 | 1.542 | 1.361 |
| **Nicaragua[1] (córdoba) — Nicaragua[1] (córdoba)** | | | | | | | | | | |
| End of period / Fin de période | 11.194 | 12.318 | 13.057 | 13.841 | 14.671 | 15.552 | 16.329 | 17.146 | 18.003 | 18.903 |
| Period average / Moyenne sur période | 10.582 | 11.809 | 12.684 | 13.372 | 14.251 | 15.105 | 15.937 | 16.733 | 17.570 | 18.449 |
| **Niger[6] (CFA franc) — Niger[6] (franc CFA)** | | | | | | | | | | |
| End of period / Fin de période | 562.210 | #652.953 | 704.951 | 744.306 | 625.495 | 519.364 | 481.578 | 556.037 | 498.069 | 445.593 |
| Period average / Moyenne sur période | 589.952 | #615.699 | 711.976 | 733.039 | 696.988 | 581.200 | 528.285 | 527.468 | 522.890 | 479.267 |
| **Nigeria[1] (naira) — Nigéria[1] (naira)** | | | | | | | | | | |
| End of period / Fin de période | #21.886 | 97.950 | 109.550 | 112.950 | 126.400 | 136.500 | 132.350 | 129.000 | 128.270 | 117.968 |
| Period average / Moyenne sur période | #21.886 | 92.338 | 101.697 | 111.231 | 120.578 | 129.222 | 132.888 | 131.274 | 128.652 | 125.808 |
| **Norway (Norwegian krone) — Norvège (couronne norvégienne)** | | | | | | | | | | |
| End of period / Fin de période | 7.600 | 8.040 | 8.849 | 9.012 | 6.966 | 6.680 | 6.040 | 6.770 | 6.260 | 5.410 |
| Period average / Moyenne sur période | 7.545 | 7.799 | 8.802 | 8.992 | 7.984 | 7.080 | 6.741 | 6.443 | 6.413 | 5.862 |
| **Oman (rial Omani) — Oman (rial omani)** | | | | | | | | | | |
| End of period / Fin de période | 0.385 | 0.385 | 0.385 | 0.385 | 0.385 | 0.385 | 0.385 | 0.385 | 0.385 | 0.385 |
| Period average / Moyenne sur période | 0.385 | 0.385 | 0.385 | 0.385 | 0.385 | 0.385 | 0.385 | 0.385 | 0.385 | 0.385 |
| **Pakistan (Pakistan rupee) — Pakistan (roupie pakistanaise)** | | | | | | | | | | |
| End of period / Fin de période | 45.885 | #51.785 | 58.029 | 60.864 | 58.534 | 57.215 | 59.124 | 59.830 | 60.918 | 61.221 |
| Period average / Moyenne sur période | 45.047 | #49.501 | 53.648 | 61.927 | 59.724 | 57.752 | 58.258 | 59.515 | 60.271 | 60.739 |
| **Panama (balboa) — Panama (balboa)** | | | | | | | | | | |
| End of period / Fin de période | 1.000 | 1.000 | 1.000 | 1.000 | 1.000 | 1.000 | 1.000 | 1.000 | 1.000 | 1.000 |
| Period average / Moyenne sur période | 1.000 | 1.000 | 1.000 | 1.000 | 1.000 | 1.000 | 1.000 | 1.000 | 1.000 | 1.000 |
| **Papua New Guinea (kina) — Papouasie-Nvl-Guinée (kina)** | | | | | | | | | | |
| End of period / Fin de période | 2.096 | 2.695 | 3.072 | 3.762 | 4.019 | 3.333 | 3.125 | 3.096 | 3.030 | 2.837 |
| Period average / Moyenne sur période | 2.074 | 2.571 | 2.782 | 3.389 | 3.895 | 3.564 | 3.223 | 3.102 | 3.057 | 2.965 |

**63**

**Exchange rates**—National currency per US dollar (*continued*)
**Cours des changes**—Valeur du dollar E.-U. en monnaie nationale (*suite*)

| Country or area<br>Pays ou zone | 1998 | 1999 | 2000 | 2001 | 2002 | 2003 | 2004 | 2005 | 2006 | 2007 |
|---|---|---|---|---|---|---|---|---|---|---|
| **Paraguay (guaraní) — Paraguay (guaraní)** | | | | | | | | | | |
| End of period<br>Fin de période | 2 840.190 | 3 328.860 | 3 526.900 | 4 682.000 | 7 103.590 | 6 114.960 | 6 250.000 | 6 120.000 | 5 190.000 | 4 875.000 |
| Period average<br>Moyenne sur période | 2 726.490 | 3 119.070 | 3 486.350 | 4 105.930 | 5 716.260 | 6 424.340 | 5 974.580 | 6 177.960 | 5 635.460 | 5 032.720 |
| **Peru (new sol) — Pérou (nouveau sol)** | | | | | | | | | | |
| End of period<br>Fin de période | 3.160 | 3.510 | 3.527 | 3.444 | 3.514 | 3.463 | 3.282 | 3.430 | 3.196 | 2.996 |
| Period average<br>Moyenne sur période | 2.930 | 3.383 | 3.490 | 3.507 | 3.517 | 3.479 | 3.413 | 3.296 | 3.274 | 3.128 |
| **Philippines (Philippine peso) — Philippines (peso philippin)** | | | | | | | | | | |
| End of period<br>Fin de période | 39.059 | 40.313 | 49.998 | 51.404 | 53.096 | 55.569 | 56.267 | 53.067 | 49.132 | 41.401 |
| Period average<br>Moyenne sur période | 40.893 | 39.089 | 44.192 | 50.993 | 51.604 | 54.203 | 56.040 | 55.086 | 51.314 | 46.148 |
| **Poland (zloty) — Pologne (zloty)** | | | | | | | | | | |
| End of period<br>Fin de période | 3.504 | 4.148 | 4.143 | 3.986 | 3.839 | 3.741 | 2.990 | 3.261 | 2.911 | 2.435 |
| Period average<br>Moyenne sur période | 3.475 | 3.967 | 4.346 | 4.094 | 4.080 | 3.889 | 3.658 | 3.236 | 3.103 | 2.768 |
| **Portugal[4] (Portuguese escudo, euro) — Portugal[4] (escudo portugais, euro)** | | | | | | | | | | |
| End of period<br>Fin de période | 171.829 | #0.995 | 1.075 | 1.135 | 0.954 | 0.792 | 0.734 | 0.848 | 0.759 | 0.679 |
| Period average<br>Moyenne sur période | 180.104 | #0.939 | 1.085 | 1.118 | 1.063 | 0.886 | 0.805 | 0.804 | 0.797 | 0.731 |
| **Qatar (Qatar riyal) — Qatar (riyal qatarien)** | | | | | | | | | | |
| End of period<br>Fin de période | 3.640 | 3.640 | 3.640 | 3.640 | 3.640 | 3.640 | 3.640 | 3.640 | 3.640 | 3.640 |
| Period average<br>Moyenne sur période | 3.640 | 3.640 | 3.640 | 3.640 | 3.640 | 3.640 | 3.640 | 3.640 | 3.640 | 3.640 |
| **Romania[1,13] (Romanian leu) — Roumanie[1,13] (leu roumain)** | | | | | | | | | | |
| End of period<br>Fin de période | 1.095 | 1.826 | 2.593 | 3.160 | 3.350 | 3.260 | 2.907 | #3.108 | 2.568 | 2.456 |
| Period average<br>Moyenne sur période | 0.888 | 1.533 | 2.171 | 2.906 | 3.306 | 3.320 | 3.264 | 2.914 | 2.809 | 2.438 |
| **Russian Federation[14] (ruble) — Fédération de Russie[14] (ruble)** | | | | | | | | | | |
| End of period<br>Fin de période | #20.650 | 27.000 | 28.160 | 30.140 | 31.784 | 29.455 | 27.749 | 28.783 | 26.331 | 24.546 |
| Period average<br>Moyenne sur période | #9.705 | 24.620 | 28.129 | 29.169 | 31.349 | 30.692 | 28.814 | 28.284 | 27.191 | 25.581 |
| **Rwanda (Rwanda franc) — Rwanda (franc rwandais)** | | | | | | | | | | |
| End of period<br>Fin de période | 320.338 | 349.530 | 430.486 | 457.900 | 511.854 | 580.280 | 566.860 | 553.719 | 548.650 | 544.220 |
| Period average<br>Moyenne sur période | 312.314 | 333.942 | 389.696 | 442.992 | 475.365 | 537.655 | 577.449 | 557.823 | 551.710 | 546.955 |
| **Saint Kitts and Nevis (EC dollar) — Saint-Kitts-et-Nevis (dollar des Caraïbes orientales)** | | | | | | | | | | |
| End of period<br>Fin de période | 2.700 | 2.700 | 2.700 | 2.700 | 2.700 | 2.700 | 2.700 | 2.700 | 2.700 | 2.700 |
| Period average<br>Moyenne sur période | 2.700 | 2.700 | 2.700 | 2.700 | 2.700 | 2.700 | 2.700 | 2.700 | 2.700 | 2.700 |
| **Saint Lucia (EC dollar) — Sainte-Lucie (dollar des Caraïbes orientales)** | | | | | | | | | | |
| End of period<br>Fin de période | 2.700 | 2.700 | 2.700 | 2.700 | 2.700 | 2.700 | 2.700 | 2.700 | 2.700 | 2.700 |
| Period average<br>Moyenne sur période | 2.700 | 2.700 | 2.700 | 2.700 | 2.700 | 2.700 | 2.700 | 2.700 | 2.700 | 2.700 |
| **St. Vincent-Grenadines (EC dollar) — St. Vincent-Grenadines (dollar des Caraïbes orientales)** | | | | | | | | | | |
| End of period<br>Fin de période | 2.700 | 2.700 | 2.700 | 2.700 | 2.700 | 2.700 | 2.700 | 2.700 | 2.700 | 2.700 |
| Period average<br>Moyenne sur période | 2.700 | 2.700 | 2.700 | 2.700 | 2.700 | 2.700 | 2.700 | 2.700 | 2.700 | 2.700 |

| Country or area<br>Pays ou zone | 1998 | 1999 | 2000 | 2001 | 2002 | 2003 | 2004 | 2005 | 2006 | 2007 |
|---|---|---|---|---|---|---|---|---|---|---|
| **Samoa (tala) — Samoa (tala)** | | | | | | | | | | |
| End of period<br>Fin de période | 3.010 | 3.018 | 3.341 | 3.551 | 3.217 | 2.778 | 2.673 | 2.764 | 2.685 | 2.558 |
| Period average<br>Moyenne sur période | 2.948 | 3.013 | 3.286 | 3.478 | 3.376 | 2.973 | 2.781 | 2.710 | 2.779 | 2.617 |
| **San Marino[4] (Italian lira, euro) — Saint-Marin[4] (lire italienne, euro)** | | | | | | | | | | |
| End of period<br>Fin de période | 1 653.100 | #0.995 | 1.075 | 1.135 | 0.954 | 0.792 | 0.734 | 0.848 | 0.759 | 0.679 |
| Period average<br>Moyenne sur période | 1 736.210 | #0.939 | 1.085 | 1.118 | 1.063 | 0.886 | 0.805 | 0.804 | 0.797 | 0.731 |
| **Sao Tome and Principe (dobra) — Sao Tomé-et-Principe (dobra)** | | | | | | | | | | |
| End of period<br>Fin de période | 6 885.000 | 7 300.000 | 8 610.650 | 9 019.710 | 9 191.840 | 9 455.900 | 10 104.000 | 11 929.700 | 13 073.900 | 14 362.300 |
| Period average<br>Moyenne sur période | 6 883.240 | 7 118.960 | 7 978.170 | 8 842.110 | 9 088.330 | 9 347.580 | 9 902.320 | 10 558.000 | 12 448.600 | 13 536.800 |
| **Saudi Arabia (Saudi Arabian riyal) — Arabie saoudite (riyal saoudien)** | | | | | | | | | | |
| End of period<br>Fin de période | 3.750 | 3.750 | 3.750 | 3.750 | 3.750 | 3.750 | 3.750 | 3.745 | 3.745 | 3.750 |
| Period average<br>Moyenne sur période | 3.750 | 3.750 | 3.750 | 3.750 | 3.750 | 3.750 | 3.750 | 3.747 | 3.745 | 3.748 |
| **Senegal[6] (CFA franc) — Sénégal[6] (franc CFA)** | | | | | | | | | | |
| End of period<br>Fin de période | 562.210 | #652.953 | 704.951 | 744.306 | 625.495 | 519.364 | 481.578 | 556.037 | 498.069 | 445.593 |
| Period average<br>Moyenne sur période | 589.952 | #615.699 | 711.976 | 733.039 | 696.988 | 581.200 | 528.285 | 527.468 | 522.890 | 479.267 |
| **Serbia (dinar) — Serbie (dinar)** | | | | | | | | | | |
| End of period<br>Fin de période | 10.031 | 11.662 | 63.166 | 67.670 | 58.985 | 54.637 | 57.936 | 72.219 | 59.976 | 53.727 |
| Period average<br>Moyenne sur période | 10.031 | 11.662 | 63.166 | 66.914 | 64.398 | 57.585 | 58.381 | 66.714 | 67.146 | 58.454 |
| **Seychelles (Seychelles rupee) — Seychelles (roupie seychelloises)** | | | | | | | | | | |
| End of period<br>Fin de période | 5.452 | 5.368 | 6.269 | 5.752 | 5.055 | 5.500 | 5.500 | 5.500 | 5.796 | 7.998 |
| Period average<br>Moyenne sur période | 5.262 | 5.343 | 5.714 | 5.858 | 5.480 | 5.401 | 5.500 | 5.500 | 5.520 | 6.701 |
| **Sierra Leone (leone) — Sierra Leone (leone)** | | | | | | | | | | |
| End of period<br>Fin de période | 1 590.760 | 2 276.050 | 1 666.670 | 2 161.270 | 2 191.730 | 2 562.180 | 2 860.490 | 2 932.520 | 2 973.940 | 2 977.600 |
| Period average<br>Moyenne sur période | 1 563.620 | 1 804.200 | 2 092.120 | 1 986.150 | 2 099.030 | 2 347.940 | 2 701.300 | 2 889.590 | 2 961.910 | 2 985.190 |
| **Singapore (Singapore dollar) — Singapour (dollar singapourien)** | | | | | | | | | | |
| End of period<br>Fin de période | 1.661 | 1.666 | 1.732 | 1.851 | 1.737 | 1.701 | 1.634 | 1.664 | 1.534 | 1.441 |
| Period average<br>Moyenne sur période | 1.674 | 1.695 | 1.724 | 1.792 | 1.791 | 1.742 | 1.690 | 1.664 | 1.589 | 1.507 |
| **Slovakia (Slovak koruna) — Slovaquie (couronne slovaque)** | | | | | | | | | | |
| End of period<br>Fin de période | 36.913 | 42.266 | 47.389 | 48.467 | 40.036 | 32.920 | 28.496 | 31.948 | 26.246 | 22.870 |
| Period average[1]<br>Moyenne sur période[1] | 35.233 | 41.363 | 46.035 | 48.355 | 45.327 | 36.773 | 32.257 | 31.018 | 29.697 | 24.694 |
| **Slovenia[4] (tolar, euro) — Slovénie[4] (tolar, euro)** | | | | | | | | | | |
| End of period<br>Fin de période | 161.200 | 196.771 | 227.377 | 250.946 | 221.071 | 189.367 | 176.243 | 202.430 | 181.931 | #0.679 |
| Period average<br>Moyenne sur période | 166.134 | 181.769 | 222.656 | 242.749 | 240.248 | 207.114 | 192.381 | 192.705 | 191.028 | #0.731 |
| **Solomon Islands (Solomon Islands dollar) — Iles Salomon (dollar des Iles Salomon)** | | | | | | | | | | |
| End of period<br>Fin de période | 4.859 | 5.076 | 5.099 | 5.565 | 7.457 | 7.491 | 7.508 | 7.576 | 7.616 | 7.663 |
| Period average<br>Moyenne sur période | 4.816 | 4.838 | 5.089 | 5.278 | 6.749 | 7.506 | 7.485 | 7.530 | 7.610 | 7.652 |

| Country or area<br>Pays ou zone | 1998 | 1999 | 2000 | 2001 | 2002 | 2003 | 2004 | 2005 | 2006 | 2007 |
|---|---|---|---|---|---|---|---|---|---|---|
| **South Africa[1] (rand) — Afrique du Sud[1] (rand)** | | | | | | | | | | |
| End of period<br>Fin de période | 5.860 | 6.155 | 7.569 | 12.127 | 8.640 | 6.640 | 5.630 | 6.325 | 6.970 | 6.810 |
| Period average<br>Moyenne sur période | 5.528 | 6.110 | 6.940 | 8.609 | 10.541 | 7.565 | 6.460 | 6.359 | 6.772 | 7.045 |
| **Spain[4] (peseta, euro) — Espagne[4] (peseta, euro)** | | | | | | | | | | |
| End of period<br>Fin de période | 142.607 | #0.995 | 1.075 | 1.135 | 0.954 | 0.792 | 0.734 | 0.848 | 0.759 | 0.679 |
| Period average<br>Moyenne sur période | 149.395 | #0.939 | 1.085 | 1.118 | 1.063 | 0.886 | 0.805 | 0.804 | 0.797 | 0.731 |
| **Sri Lanka (Sri Lanka rupee) — Sri Lanka (roupie sri-lankaise)** | | | | | | | | | | |
| End of period<br>Fin de période | 68.297 | 68.297 | 72.170 | 82.580 | 93.159 | 96.725 | 96.738 | 104.605 | 102.117 | 107.706 |
| Period average<br>Moyenne sur période | 58.995 | 64.450 | 70.635 | 77.005 | 89.383 | 95.662 | 96.521 | 101.194 | 100.498 | 103.914 |
| **Sudan[1] (Sudanese dinar) — Soudan[1] (dinar soudanaise)** | | | | | | | | | | |
| End of period<br>Fin de période | 2.378 | #2.577 | 2.574 | 2.614 | 2.617 | 2.602 | 2.506 | 2.305 | 2.013 | #2.053 |
| Period average<br>Moyenne sur période | 2.008 | 2.526 | 2.571 | 2.587 | 2.633 | 2.610 | 2.579 | 2.436 | 2.172 | 2.016 |
| **Suriname[15] (Surinamese dollar) — Suriname[15] (dollar surinamais)** | | | | | | | | | | |
| End of period<br>Fin de période | 0.401 | 0.988 | 2.179 | 2.179 | 2.515 | #2.625 | #2.715 | 2.740 | 2.745 | 2.745 |
| Period average<br>Moyenne sur période | 0.402 | 0.834 | 1.323 | 2.178 | 2.347 | #2.601 | 2.734 | 2.732 | 2.744 | 2.745 |
| **Swaziland (lilangeni) — Swaziland (lilangeni)** | | | | | | | | | | |
| End of period<br>Fin de période | 5.860 | 6.155 | 7.569 | 12.127 | 8.640 | 6.640 | 5.630 | 6.325 | 6.970 | 6.810 |
| Period average<br>Moyenne sur période | 5.528 | 6.110 | 6.940 | 8.609 | 10.541 | 7.565 | 6.460 | 6.359 | 6.772 | 7.045 |
| **Sweden (Swedish krona) — Suède (couronne suédoise)** | | | | | | | | | | |
| End of period<br>Fin de période | 8.061 | 8.525 | 9.535 | 10.668 | 8.825 | 7.189 | 6.615 | 7.958 | 6.864 | 6.414 |
| Period average<br>Moyenne sur période | 7.950 | 8.262 | 9.162 | 10.329 | 9.737 | 8.086 | 7.349 | 7.473 | 7.378 | 6.759 |
| **Switzerland (Swiss franc) — Suisse (franc suisse)** | | | | | | | | | | |
| End of period<br>Fin de période | 1.377 | 1.600 | 1.637 | 1.677 | 1.387 | 1.237 | 1.132 | 1.314 | 1.220 | 1.126 |
| Period average<br>Moyenne sur période | 1.450 | 1.502 | 1.689 | 1.688 | 1.559 | 1.347 | 1.244 | 1.245 | 1.254 | 1.200 |
| **Syrian Arab Republic[1] (Syrian pound) — Rép. arabe syrienne[1] (livre syrienne)** | | | | | | | | | | |
| End of period<br>Fin de période | 11.225 | 11.225 | 11.225 | 11.225 | 11.225 | 11.225 | 11.225 | 11.225 | 11.225 | 11.225 |
| Period average<br>Moyenne sur période | 11.225 | 11.225 | 11.225 | 11.225 | 11.225 | 11.225 | 11.225 | 11.225 | 11.225 | 11.225 |
| **Tajikistan (somoni) — Tadjikistan (somoni)** | | | | | | | | | | |
| End of period<br>Fin de période | 0.978 | 1.436 | #2.200 | 2.550 | 3.000 | 2.957 | 3.037 | 3.199 | 3.427 | 3.465 |
| Period average<br>Moyenne sur période | 0.777 | 1.238 | #2.076 | 2.372 | 2.764 | 3.061 | 2.971 | 3.117 | 3.298 | 3.443 |
| **Thailand (baht) — Thaïlande (baht)** | | | | | | | | | | |
| End of period<br>Fin de période | 36.691 | 37.470 | 43.268 | 44.222 | 43.152 | 39.591 | 39.061 | 41.030 | 36.046 | 33.718 |
| Period average<br>Moyenne sur période | 41.359 | 37.814 | 40.112 | 44.432 | 42.960 | 41.485 | 40.222 | 40.220 | 37.882 | 34.518 |
| **TFYR of Macedonia (TFYR Macedonian denar) — L'ex-R.y. Macédoine (denar de l'ex-R.Y. Macédoine)** | | | | | | | | | | |
| End of period<br>Fin de période | 51.836 | 60.339 | 66.328 | 69.172 | 58.598 | 49.050 | 45.068 | 51.859 | 46.450 | 41.656 |
| Period average<br>Moyenne sur période | 54.462 | 56.902 | 65.904 | 68.037 | 64.350 | 54.322 | 49.410 | 49.284 | 48.802 | 44.730 |

**63**

**Exchange rates**—National currency per US dollar (*continued*)
**Cours des changes**—Valeur du dollar E.-U. en monnaie nationale (*suite*)

| Country or area / Pays ou zone | 1998 | 1999 | 2000 | 2001 | 2002 | 2003 | 2004 | 2005 | 2006 | 2007 |
|---|---|---|---|---|---|---|---|---|---|---|
| **Togo[6] (CFA franc) — Togo[6] (franc CFA)** | | | | | | | | | | |
| End of period / Fin de période | 562.210 | #652.953 | 704.951 | 744.306 | 625.495 | 519.364 | 481.578 | 556.037 | 498.069 | 445.593 |
| Period average / Moyenne sur période | 589.952 | #615.699 | 711.976 | 733.039 | 696.988 | 581.200 | 528.285 | 527.468 | 522.890 | 479.267 |
| **Tonga (pa'anga) — Tonga (pa'anga)** | | | | | | | | | | |
| End of period / Fin de période | 1.616 | 1.608 | 1.977 | 2.207 | 2.229 | 2.020 | 1.912 | 2.060 | 2.000 | 1.887 |
| Period average / Moyenne sur période | 1.492 | 1.599 | 1.759 | 2.124 | 2.195 | 2.146 | 1.972 | 1.943 | 2.026 | 1.971 |
| **Trinidad and Tobago (Trinidad and Tobago dollar) — Trinité-et-Tobago (dollar de la Trinité-et-Tobago)** | | | | | | | | | | |
| End of period / Fin de période | 6.597 | 6.300 | 6.300 | 6.290 | 6.300 | 6.300 | 6.300 | 6.310 | 6.312 | 6.341 |
| Period average / Moyenne sur période | 6.298 | 6.299 | 6.300 | 6.233 | 6.249 | 6.295 | 6.299 | 6.300 | 6.312 | 6.328 |
| **Tunisia (Tunisian dinar) — Tunisie (dinar tunisien)** | | | | | | | | | | |
| End of period / Fin de période | 1.101 | 1.253 | 1.385 | 1.468 | 1.334 | 1.208 | 1.199 | 1.363 | 1.297 | 1.221 |
| Period average / Moyenne sur période | 1.139 | 1.186 | 1.371 | 1.439 | 1.422 | 1.289 | 1.246 | 1.297 | 1.331 | 1.281 |
| **Turkey[16] (new Turkish Lira) — Turquie[16] (nouvelle livre turque)** | | | | | | | | | | |
| End of period / Fin de période | 0.315 | 0.541 | 0.673 | 1.450 | 1.644 | 1.397 | 1.340 | #1.345 | 1.409 | 1.162 |
| Period average / Moyenne sur période | 0.261 | 0.419 | 0.625 | 1.226 | 1.507 | 1.501 | 1.426 | 1.344 | 1.429 | 1.303 |
| **Turkmenistan (Turkmen manat) — Turkménistan (manat turkmène)** | | | | | | | | | | |
| End of period / Fin de période | 5 200.000 | 5 200.000 | 5 200.000 | 5 200.000 | ... | ... | ... | ... | ... | ... |
| Period average / Moyenne sur période | 4 890.170 | 5 200.000 | 5 200.000 | 5 200.000 | ... | ... | ... | ... | ... | ... |
| **Uganda[1] (Uganda shilling) — Ouganda[1] (shilling ougandais)** | | | | | | | | | | |
| End of period / Fin de période | 1 362.690 | 1 506.040 | 1 766.680 | 1 727.400 | 1 852.570 | 1 935.320 | 1 738.590 | 1 816.860 | 1 741.440 | 1 697.340 |
| Period average / Moyenne sur période | 1 240.310 | 1 454.830 | 1 644.480 | 1 755.660 | 1 797.550 | 1 963.720 | 1 810.300 | 1 780.670 | 1 831.450 | 1 723.490 |
| **Ukraine (hryvnia) — Ukraine (hryvnia)** | | | | | | | | | | |
| End of period / Fin de période | 3.427 | 5.216 | 5.435 | 5.299 | 5.332 | 5.332 | 5.305 | 5.050 | 5.050 | 5.050 |
| Period average / Moyenne sur période | 2.450 | 4.130 | 5.440 | 5.372 | 5.327 | 5.333 | 5.319 | 5.125 | 5.050 | 5.050 |
| **United Arab Emirates (UAE dirham) — Emirats arabes unis (dirham des EAU)** | | | | | | | | | | |
| End of period / Fin de période | 3.673 | 3.673 | 3.673 | 3.673 | 3.673 | 3.673 | 3.673 | 3.673 | 3.673 | 3.673 |
| Period average / Moyenne sur période | 3.673 | 3.673 | 3.673 | 3.673 | 3.673 | 3.673 | 3.673 | 3.673 | 3.673 | 3.673 |
| **United Kingdom (pound sterling) — Royaume-Uni (livre sterling)** | | | | | | | | | | |
| End of period / Fin de période | 0.601 | 0.619 | 0.670 | 0.690 | 0.620 | 0.560 | 0.518 | 0.581 | 0.509 | 0.499 |
| Period average / Moyenne sur période | 0.604 | 0.618 | 0.661 | 0.695 | 0.667 | 0.613 | 0.546 | 0.550 | 0.544 | 0.500 |
| **United Rep. of Tanzania (Tanzania shilling) — Rép.-Unie de Tanzanie (shilling tanzanien)** | | | | | | | | | | |
| End of period / Fin de période | 681.000 | 797.330 | 803.260 | 916.300 | 976.300 | 1 063.620 | 1 042.960 | 1 165.510 | 1 261.640 | 1 132.090 |
| Period average / Moyenne sur période | 664.671 | 744.759 | 800.409 | 876.412 | 966.583 | 1 038.420 | 1 089.330 | 1 128.930 | 1 251.900 | 1 245.040 |
| **United States (US dollar) — Etats-Unis (dollar des Etats-Unis)** | | | | | | | | | | |
| End of period / Fin de période | 1.000 | 1.000 | 1.000 | 1.000 | 1.000 | 1.000 | 1.000 | 1.000 | 1.000 | 1.000 |
| Period average / Moyenne sur période | 1.000 | 1.000 | 1.000 | 1.000 | 1.000 | 1.000 | 1.000 | 1.000 | 1.000 | 1.000 |

| Country or area<br>Pays ou zone | 1998 | 1999 | 2000 | 2001 | 2002 | 2003 | 2004 | 2005 | 2006 | 2007 |
|---|---|---|---|---|---|---|---|---|---|---|
| **Uruguay (Uruguayan peso) — Uruguay (peso uruguayen)** | | | | | | | | | | |
| End of period<br>Fin de période | 10.817 | 11.615 | 12.515 | 14.768 | 27.200 | 29.300 | 26.350 | 24.100 | 24.400 | 21.500 |
| Period average<br>Moyenne sur période | 10.472 | 11.339 | 12.100 | 13.319 | 21.257 | 28.209 | 28.704 | 24.479 | 24.073 | 23.471 |
| **Uzbekistan (Uzbek sum) — Ouzbékistan (sum ouzbek)** | | | | | | | | | | |
| End of period<br>Fin de période | ... | 140.000 | ... | ... | ... | ... | ... | ... | ... | ... |
| Period average<br>Moyenne sur période | 94.492 | 124.625 | 236.608 | ... | ... | ... | ... | ... | ... | ... |
| **Vanuatu (vatu) — Vanuatu (vatu)** | | | | | | | | | | |
| End of period<br>Fin de période | 129.780 | 128.890 | 142.810 | 146.740 | 133.170 | 111.810 | 106.530 | 112.330 | 106.480 | 99.860 |
| Period average<br>Moyenne sur période | 127.517 | 129.075 | 137.643 | 145.313 | 139.198 | 122.189 | 111.790 | 109.246 | 110.641 | 102.438 |
| **Venezuela (Bolivarian Republic of) (bolívar) — Venezuela (République bolivarienne du) (bolívar)** | | | | | | | | | | |
| End of period<br>Fin de période | 0.565 | 0.648 | 0.700 | 0.763 | 1.401 | 1.598 | 1.918 | 2.147 | 2.147 | 2.147 |
| Period average<br>Moyenne sur période | 0.548 | 0.606 | 0.680 | 0.724 | 1.161 | 1.607 | 1.891 | 2.090 | 2.147 | 2.147 |
| **Viet Nam (dong) — Viet Nam (dong)** | | | | | | | | | | |
| End of period<br>Fin de période | 13 890.000 | 14 028.000 | 14 514.000 | 15 084.000 | 15 403.000 | 15 646.000 | 15 777.000 | 15 916.000 | 16 054.000 | ... |
| Period average<br>Moyenne sur période | 13 268.000 | 13 943.200 | 14 167.700 | 14 725.200 | 15 279.500 | 15 509.600 | ... | 15 858.900 | 15 994.300 | ... |
| **Yemen (Yemeni rial) — Yémen (rial yéménite)** | | | | | | | | | | |
| End of period<br>Fin de période | 141.650 | 159.100 | 165.590 | 173.270 | 179.010 | 184.310 | 185.870 | 195.080 | 198.500 | 199.540 |
| Period average<br>Moyenne sur période | 135.882 | 155.718 | 161.718 | 168.672 | 175.625 | 183.448 | 184.776 | 191.509 | 197.049 | 198.953 |
| **Zambia (Zambia kwacha) — Zambie (kwacha zambie)** | | | | | | | | | | |
| End of period<br>Fin de période | 2 298.920 | 2 632.190 | 4 157.830 | 3 830.400 | 4 334.400 | 4 645.480 | 4 771.310 | 3 508.980 | 4 406.670 | 3 844.810 |
| Period average<br>Moyenne sur période | 1 862.070 | 2 388.020 | 3 110.840 | 3 610.940 | 4 398.590 | 4 733.270 | 4 778.880 | 4 463.500 | 3 603.070 | 4 002.520 |
| **Zimbabwe (Zimbabwe dollar) — Zimbabwe (dollar zimbabwéen)** | | | | | | | | | | |
| End of period<br>Fin de période | 0.039 | 0.040 | 0.057 | 0.057 | 0.057 | 0.853 | 5.936 | 80.774 | #258.920 | ... |
| Period average<br>Moyenne sur période | 0.024 | 0.038 | 0.044 | 0.055 | 0.055 | 0.697 | 5.069 | 22.364 | 164.361 | ... |

Source

International Monetary Fund (IMF), Washington, D.C., "International Financial Statistics," May 2008 and the IMF database.

Notes

1  Principal rate.
2  In October 2002, Afghanistan redenominated its currency. One afghani is equal to 1,000 old afghanis.
3  Pesos per million US dollars through 1983, per thousand US dollars through 1988 and per US dollar up to 2001. A unified floating exchange rate regime was introduced on 11 Feb. 2002, with the exchange rate determined by market conditions.
4  Beginning 1999 - euro (Greece, beginning 2001; Slovenia, beginning 2007).
5  The manat, which was first introduced on 15 August 1992 and circulated alongside the Russian ruble at a fixed rate of 10 rubles per manat, became the sole legal tender in Azerbaijan on 1 January 1994. On 1 January 2006, the new manat, equivalent to 5,000 old manats, was introduced.

Source

Fonds monétaire international (FMI), Washington, D.C.,"Statistiques Financières Internationales," mai 2008 et la base de données du FMI.

Notes

1  Taux principal.
2  L'Afghanistan a changé en octobre 2002 la valeur de sa monnaie : un afghani vaut 1 000 afghanis anciens.
3  Pesos par million de dollars des États-Unis jusqu'en 1983, par millier de dollars des États-Unis jusqu'en 1988 et par dollar des États-Unis apres 2001. Un régime de taux de change flottant unifié a été introduit le 11 février 2002, le taux de change étant déterminé par le marché.
4  A partir de 1999 - euro (Grèce, à partir de 2001 ; Slovénie, à partir de 2007).
5  Le manat, introduit d'abord le 15 août 1992 et circulant parallèlement au rouble russe, au taux fixe de 10 roubles pour un manat, est la seule monnaie ayant cours légal en Azerbaïdjan depuis le 1er janvier 1994. Le nouveau manat, valant 5 000 manats anciens, a été introduit le 1er janvier 2006.

6 Prior to January 1999, the official rate was pegged to the French franc. On 12 January 1994, the CFA franc was devalued to CFAF 100 per French franc from CFAF 50 at which it had been fixed since 1948. From 1 January 1999, the CFAF is pegged to the euro at a rate of CFA francs 655.957 per euro.

7 Prior to January 1999, the official rate was pegged to the French franc Beginning 12 January 1994, the CFA franc was devalued to CFAF 75 per French franc from CFAF 50 at which it had been fixed since 1948. From January 1, 1999, the CFAF is pegged to the euro at a rate of CFA franc 491.9677 per euro.

8 "Euro Area" is an official descriptor for the European Economic and Monetary Union (EMU). The participating member states of the EMU are Austria, Belgium, Cyprus (beginining 2008), Finland, France, Germany, Greece (beginning 2001), Ireland, Italy, Luxembourg, Malta (beginining 2008), Netherlands, Portugal, Slovenia (beginning 2007), and Spain.

9 Prior to January 1999, the official rate was pegged to the French franc at CFAF 100 per French franc. The CFA franc was adopted as national currency as of May 2, 1997. The Guinean peso and the CFA franc were set at PG65 per CFA franc. From January 1, 1999, the CFAF is pegged to the euro at a rate of CFA franc 655.957 per euro.

10 Effective 1 January 2005, Madagascar announced a new currency, the ariary. One ariary is equal to 5 Malagasy francs.

11 Effective 19 October 1994, the official rate of the rufiyaa was pegged to the US dollar at a rate of Rf 11.77 per US dollar. Effective 25 July 2001, the rufiyaa was devalued and fixed at Rf 12.80 per US dollar.

12 On July 1, 2006, the new metical (MTn), equivalent to 1,000 of the old metical (MT) was introduced.

13 Effective 1 July 2005, Romania redenominated its currency. One new leu is equal to 10,000 old lei.

14 The post-1 January 1998 ruble is equal to 1,000 pre-January 1998 rubles.

15 On 1 January 2004, the Surinamese dollar, equal to 1 000 Surinamese guilders, replaced the guilder as the currency unit.

16 Effective 1 January 2005, Turkey adopted a new currency, the new Turkish lira. One new Turkish lira (yeni Türk lirasi) is equal to 1,000,000 Turkish lira (Türk lirasi).

6 Avant janvier 1999, le taux officiel était établi par référence au franc français. Le 12 janvier 1994, le franc CFA a été dévalué; son taux par rapport au franc français, auquel il est rattaché depuis 1948, est passé de 50 à 100 francs CFA pour 1 franc français. A compter du 1er janvier 1999, le taux officiel est établi par référence à l'euro à un taux de 655.957 francs CFA pour un euro.

7 Avant janvier 1999, le taux de change officiel est raccroché au taux de change du franc français. Le 12 janvier 1994, le CFA a été dévalué de 50 par franc français, valeur qu'il avait conservée depuis 1948, à 75 par franc français. A compter du 1er janvier 1999, le taux officiel est établi par référence à l'euro : 491.9677 francs CFA pour un euro.

8 L'expression "zone euro" est un intitulé officiel pour l'Union économique et monétaire (UEM) européenne. L'UEM est composée des pays membres suivants : Allemagne, Autriche, Belgique, Chypre (à partir de 2008), Espagne, Finlande, France, Grèce (à partir de 2001), Irlande, Italie, Luxembourg, Malte (à partir de 2008), Pays-Bas, Portugal et Slovénie (à partir de 2007).

9 Avant janvier 1999, le taux de change officiel était fixé à 100 francs CFA pour un franc français. Le franc CFA avait été adopté comme monnaie nationale à compter du 2 mai 1997. Le taux de change du peso guinéen par rapport au franc CFA a été établi à 65 pesos guinéens pour 1 franc CFA. A compter du 1er janvier 1999, le taux officiel est établi par référence à l'euro : 655.957 francs CFA pour un euro.

10 À compter du 1er janvier 2005, Madagascar a adopté une nouvelle monnaie, l'ariary, qui vaut 5 francs malgaches.

11 À compter du 19 octobre 1994, le taux de change officiel du rufiyaa est indexé sur le dollar des États-Unis, et établi à 11.77 Rf pour 1 dollar. À compter du 25 juillet 2001, le rufiyaa a été dévalué et le taux de change fixe est de 12.80 Rf pour 1 dollar.

12 En 1er juillet 2006, le nouveau metical (MTn), valant 1 000 metical anciens, a été introduit.

13 À compter du 1er juillet 2005, la Roumanie a changé la valeur de sa monnaie : un nouveau leu vaut 10 000 lei anciens.

14 Le rouble ayant cours après le 1er janvier 1998 vaut 1 000 roubles de la période antérieure à cette date.

15 Le 1er janvier 2004, le dollar de Suriname, égal à 1 000 florins de Suriname, a remplacé le florin comme unité monétaire.

16 À compter du 1er janvier 2005, la Turquie a adopté une nouvelle monnaie, la nouvelle livre turque (yeni Türk lirasi), qui vaut 1 000 000 de livres turques (Türk lirasi).

# International reserves minus gold
Millions of US dollars, end of period

# Réserves internationales, moins l'or
Millions de dollars E.-U., fin de période

| Country or area<br>Pays ou zone | 1998 | 1999 | 2000 | 2001 | 2002 | 2003 | 2004 | 2005 | 2006 | 2007 |
|---|---|---|---|---|---|---|---|---|---|---|
| **Albania — Albanie** | | | | | | | | | | |
| Total reserves minus gold<br>Rés. totale, moins l'or | 384.2 | 488.3 | 615.6 | 739.9 | 838.8 | 1 009.4 | 1 357.6 | 1 404.1 | 1 768.8 | 2 104.2 |
| Foreign exchange<br>Devises étrangères | 323.1 | 406.7 | 535.3 | 654.2 | 752.6 | 913.8 | 1 251.6 | 1 386.8 | 1 754.8 | 2 097.0 |
| **Algeria — Algérie** | | | | | | | | | | |
| Total reserves minus gold<br>Rés. totale, moins l'or | 6 845.5 | 4 525.7 | 12 023.9 | 18 081.4 | 23 237.5 | 33 125.2 | 43 246.4 | 56 303.1 | 77 913.7 | 110 318.0 |
| Foreign exchange<br>Devises étrangères | 6 844.0 | 4 407.0 | 11 910.0 | 17 963.0 | 23 108.0 | 32 942.0 | 43 113.0 | 56 178.0 | 77 781.0 | 110 180.0 |
| **Angola — Angola** | | | | | | | | | | |
| Total reserves minus gold<br>Rés. totale, moins l'or | 203.5 | 496.1 | 1 198.2 | 731.9 | 375.5 | 634.2 | 1 374.1 | 3 196.9 | 8 598.6 | 11 329.7 |
| Foreign exchange<br>Devises étrangères | 203.3 | 495.9 | 1 198.0 | 731.7 | 375.4 | 634.0 | 1 373.8 | 3 196.6 | 8 598.4 | 11 329.4 |
| **Anguilla — Anguilla** | | | | | | | | | | |
| Total reserves minus gold<br>Rés. totale, moins l'or | 18.1 | 19.9 | 20.3 | 24.2 | 26.2 | 33.3 | 34.3 | 39.7 | 41.8 | 44.9 |
| Foreign exchange<br>Devises étrangères | 18.1 | 19.9 | 20.3 | 24.2 | 26.2 | 33.3 | 34.3 | 39.7 | 41.8 | 44.9 |
| **Antigua and Barbuda — Antigua-et-Barbuda** | | | | | | | | | | |
| Total reserves minus gold<br>Rés. totale, moins l'or | 59.4 | 69.7 | 63.6 | 79.7 | 87.6 | 113.8 | 120.1 | 127.3 | 142.6 | 143.8 |
| Foreign exchange<br>Devises étrangères | 59.4 | 69.7 | 63.6 | 79.7 | 87.6 | 113.7 | 120.1 | 127.3 | 142.6 | 143.8 |
| **Argentina — Argentine** | | | | | | | | | | |
| Total reserves minus gold<br>Rés. totale, moins l'or | 24 752.1 | 26 252.1 | 25 146.9 | 14 553.1 | 10 489.3 | 14 153.4 | 18 884.3 | 27 178.9 | 30 903.5 | 44 682.1 |
| Foreign exchange<br>Devises étrangères | 24 487.8 | 26 114.3 | 24 414.4 | 14 542.4 | 10 395.1 | 13 144.8 | 18 007.5 | 22 742.0 | 30 420.9 | 44 175.1 |
| **Armenia — Arménie** | | | | | | | | | | |
| Total reserves minus gold<br>Rés. totale, moins l'or | 280.7 | 290.9 | 302.0 | 317.2 | 415.6 | 502.0 | 547.8 | 669.5 | 1 071.9 | 1 656.8 |
| Foreign exchange<br>Devises étrangères | 252.7 | 250.2 | 280.4 | 307.0 | 385.5 | 483.1 | 535.8 | 659.3 | 1 058.0 | 1 647.2 |
| **Aruba — Aruba** | | | | | | | | | | |
| Total reserves minus gold<br>Rés. totale, moins l'or | 222.2 | 219.9 | 208.0 | 293.7 | 339.7 | 295.2 | 295.4 | 273.5 | 337.8 | 372.1 |
| Foreign exchange<br>Devises étrangères | 222.2 | 219.9 | 208.0 | 293.7 | 339.7 | 295.2 | 295.4 | 273.5 | 337.8 | 372.1 |
| **Australia — Australie** | | | | | | | | | | |
| Total reserves minus gold<br>Rés. totale, moins l'or | 14 640.5 | 21 212.2 | 18 118.1 | 17 955.3 | 20 688.5 | 32 188.7 | 35 802.5 | 41 941.2 | 53 448.1 | 24 768.5 |
| Foreign exchange<br>Devises étrangères | 13 366.4 | 19 507.4 | 16 781.8 | 16 434.2 | 18 617.8 | 29 966.2 | 33 901.3 | 40 972.0 | 52 820.9 | 24 236.9 |
| **Austria — Autriche** | | | | | | | | | | |
| Total reserves minus gold<br>Rés. totale, moins l'or | 22 432.4 | #15 120.5 | 14 318.6 | 12 509.1 | 9 683.2 | 8 470.0 | 7 858.4 | 6 839.1 | 7 010.0 | 10 688.5 |
| Foreign exchange<br>Devises étrangères | 20 918.0 | 14 016.2 | 13 492.2 | 11 443.7 | 8 539.6 | 7 143.5 | 6 762.8 | 6 298.4 | 6 573.2 | 10 260.5 |
| **Azerbaijan — Azerbaïdjan** | | | | | | | | | | |
| Total reserves minus gold<br>Rés. totale, moins l'or | 447.3 | 672.6 | 679.6 | 725.0 | 720.5 | 802.8 | 1 075.1 | 1 177.7 | 2 500.4 | 4 273.1 |
| Foreign exchange<br>Devises étrangères | 447.2 | 665.5 | 673.0 | 722.5 | 719.8 | 784.8 | 1 060.5 | 1 163.8 | 2 484.9 | 4 262.9 |

| Country or area<br>Pays ou zone | 1998 | 1999 | 2000 | 2001 | 2002 | 2003 | 2004 | 2005 | 2006 | 2007 |
|---|---|---|---|---|---|---|---|---|---|---|
| **Bahamas—Bahamas** | | | | | | | | | | |
| Total reserves minus gold<br>Rés. totale, moins l'or | 346.5 | 410.5 | 349.6 | 319.3 | 380.6 | 491.1 | 674.4 | 586.3 | 461.3 | 464.5 |
| Foreign exchange<br>Devises étrangères | 337.7 | 401.9 | 341.4 | 311.3 | 372.1 | 481.8 | 664.7 | 577.3 | 451.9 | 454.5 |
| **Bahrain—Bahreïn** | | | | | | | | | | |
| Total reserves minus gold<br>Rés. totale, moins l'or | 1 079.2 | 1 369.0 | 1 564.1 | 1 684.0 | 1 725.8 | 1 778.4 | 1 940.5 | ... | ... | ... |
| Foreign exchange<br>Devises étrangères | 993.8 | 1 283.4 | 1 478.3 | 1 598.5 | 1 631.4 | 1 673.8 | 1 829.6 | ... | ... | ... |
| **Bangladesh—Bangladesh** | | | | | | | | | | |
| Total reserves minus gold<br>Rés. totale, moins l'or | 1 905.4 | 1 603.6 | 1 486.0 | 1 275.0 | 1 683.2 | 2 577.9 | 3 172.4 | 2 767.2 | 3 805.6 | 5 420.4 |
| Foreign exchange<br>Devises étrangères | 1 892.3 | 1 602.5 | 1 485.3 | 1 273.6 | 1 680.7 | 2 574.4 | 3 170.9 | 2 766.0 | 3 803.9 | 5 419.2 |
| **Barbados—Barbade** | | | | | | | | | | |
| Total reserves minus gold<br>Rés. totale, moins l'or | 365.9 | 301.9 | 472.7 | 690.4 | 668.5 | 737.9 | 579.9 | 603.5 | 636.1 | 839.3 |
| Foreign exchange<br>Devises étrangères | 365.9 | 295.5 | 466.6 | 684.4 | 661.9 | 730.5 | 571.8 | 595.9 | 627.9 | 830.3 |
| **Belarus—Bélarus** | | | | | | | | | | |
| Total reserves minus gold<br>Rés. totale, moins l'or | 702.8 | 294.3 | 350.5 | 390.7 | 618.8 | 594.8 | 749.4 | 1 136.6 | 1 163.0 | 4 266.3 |
| Foreign exchange<br>Devises étrangères | 702.3 | 293.8 | 350.3 | 390.3 | 618.5 | 594.8 | 749.3 | 1 136.6 | 1 163.0 | 4 266.2 |
| **Belgium—Belgique** | | | | | | | | | | |
| Total reserves minus gold<br>Rés. totale, moins l'or | 18 271.6 | #10 937.7 | 9 994.4 | 11 266.2 | 11 855.1 | 10 989.4 | 10 361.1 | 8 241.2 | 8 783.4 | 10 383.9 |
| Foreign exchange<br>Devises étrangères | 15 763.0 | #8 377.4 | 7 988.3 | 8 743.4 | 8 908.7 | 7 651.3 | 7 714.9 | 6 815.1 | 7 618.9 | 9 297.8 |
| **Belize—Belize** | | | | | | | | | | |
| Total reserves minus gold<br>Rés. totale, moins l'or | 44.1 | 71.3 | 122.9 | 112.0 | 114.5 | 84.7 | 48.3 | 71.4 | 113.7 | 108.5 |
| Foreign exchange<br>Devises étrangères | 38.8 | 64.1 | 115.8 | 105.0 | 106.7 | 76.1 | 39.1 | 62.8 | 104.4 | 98.4 |
| **Benin—Bénin** | | | | | | | | | | |
| Total reserves minus gold<br>Rés. totale, moins l'or | 261.5 | 400.1 | 458.1 | 578.1 | 615.7 | 717.9 | 640.0 | 656.8 | 912.2 | 1 209.2 |
| Foreign exchange<br>Devises étrangères | 258.4 | 396.9 | 455.2 | 574.9 | 612.6 | 714.4 | 636.5 | 653.5 | 908.9 | 1 205.6 |
| **Bhutan—Bhoutan** | | | | | | | | | | |
| Total reserves minus gold<br>Rés. totale, moins l'or | 256.8 | 292.3 | 317.6 | 323.4 | 354.9 | 366.6 | 398.6 | 467.4 | 545.3 | ... |
| Foreign exchange<br>Devises étrangères | 255.2 | 290.7 | 316.1 | 321.8 | 353.2 | 364.7 | 396.6 | 465.5 | 543.3 | ... |
| **Bolivia—Bolivie** | | | | | | | | | | |
| Total reserves minus gold<br>Rés. totale, moins l'or | 948.5 | 974.9 | 926.4 | 886.4 | 580.5 | 716.8 | 872.4 | 1 327.6 | 2 614.8 | 4 542.9 |
| Foreign exchange<br>Devises étrangères | 898.3 | 925.3 | 879.3 | 840.9 | 531.2 | 663.3 | 817.3 | 1 276.7 | 2 561.2 | 4 486.5 |
| **Bosnia and Herzegovina—Bosnie-Herzégovine** | | | | | | | | | | |
| Total reserves minus gold<br>Rés. totale, moins l'or | 174.5 | 452.3 | 496.6 | 1 221.2 | 1 321.4 | 1 795.6 | 2 407.9 | 2 530.9 | 3 371.6 | 4 524.8 |
| Foreign exchange<br>Devises étrangères | 169.3 | 444.7 | 485.9 | 1 215.1 | 1 318.2 | 1 792.2 | 2 407.4 | 2 530.5 | 3 371.3 | 4 524.5 |
| **Botswana—Botswana** | | | | | | | | | | |
| Total reserves minus gold<br>Rés. totale, moins l'or | 5 940.7 | 6 228.8 | 6 318.2 | 5 897.3 | 5 473.9 | 5 339.8 | 5 661.4 | 6 309.1 | 7 992.4 | ... |
| Foreign exchange<br>Devises étrangères | 5 856.2 | 6 159.3 | 6 256.2 | 5 829.6 | 5 397.2 | 5 244.9 | 5 576.1 | 6 247.6 | 7 927.5 | ... |

| Country or area / Pays ou zone | 1998 | 1999 | 2000 | 2001 | 2002 | 2003 | 2004 | 2005 | 2006 | 2007 |
|---|---|---|---|---|---|---|---|---|---|---|
| **Brazil—Brésil** | | | | | | | | | | |
| Total reserves minus gold / Rés. totale, moins l'or | 42 579.8 | 35 279.3 | 32 434.0 | 35 563.0 | 37 462.0 | 48 846.6 | 52 461.8 | 53 245.2 | 85 156.2 | 179 433.0 |
| Foreign exchange / Devises étrangères | 42 578.0 | 35 269.3 | 32 433.6 | 35 552.5 | 37 187.3 | 48 844.3 | 52 457.6 | 53 216.4 | 85 147.8 | 179 431.0 |
| **Brunei Darussalam—Brunéi Darussalam** | | | | | | | | | | |
| Total reserves minus gold / Rés. totale, moins l'or | ... | 516.8 | 408.3 | 391.4 | 437.8 | 481.5 | 505.1 | 494.2 | 523.3 | ... |
| Foreign exchange / Devises étrangères | ... | 463.3 | 355.8 | 339.2 | 357.9 | 383.3 | 400.9 | 433.5 | 469.5 | ... |
| **Bulgaria—Bulgarie** | | | | | | | | | | |
| Total reserves minus gold / Rés. totale, moins l'or | 2 684.7 | 2 892.1 | 3 154.9 | 3 290.8 | 4 407.1 | 6 291.0 | 8 776.3 | 8 040.5 | 10 943.0 | 16 477.9 |
| Foreign exchange / Devises étrangères | 2 608.7 | 2 765.5 | 3 027.6 | 3 247.3 | 4 361.8 | 6 174.6 | 8 712.1 | 7 992.4 | 10 892.1 | 16 424.2 |
| **Burkina Faso—Burkina Faso** | | | | | | | | | | |
| Total reserves minus gold / Rés. totale, moins l'or | 373.3 | 295.0 | 243.6 | 260.5 | 313.4 | 752.2 | 669.1 | 438.4 | 554.9 | 1 029.2 |
| Foreign exchange / Devises étrangères | 362.4 | 284.4 | 233.8 | 250.9 | 303.1 | 741.1 | 657.6 | 427.7 | 543.7 | 1 017.4 |
| **Burundi—Burundi** | | | | | | | | | | |
| Total reserves minus gold / Rés. totale, moins l'or | 65.5 | 48.0 | 32.9 | 17.7 | 58.8 | 67.0 | 65.8 | 100.1 | 130.5 | 176.3 |
| Foreign exchange / Devises étrangères | 57.2 | 39.8 | 25.2 | 17.2 | 58.1 | 66.3 | 64.8 | 99.3 | 129.7 | 175.4 |
| **Cambodia—Cambodge** | | | | | | | | | | |
| Total reserves minus gold / Rés. totale, moins l'or | 324.4 | 393.2 | 501.7 | 586.8 | 776.1 | 815.5 | 943.2 | 953.0 | 1 157.3 | 1 806.9 |
| Foreign exchange / Devises étrangères | 314.6 | 388.0 | 501.5 | 586.3 | 775.6 | 815.3 | 943.1 | 952.7 | 1 157.1 | 1 806.7 |
| **Cameroon—Cameroun** | | | | | | | | | | |
| Total reserves minus gold / Rés. totale, moins l'or | 1.3 | 4.4 | 212.0 | 331.8 | 629.7 | 639.6 | 829.3 | 949.4 | 1 716.2 | 2 908.8 |
| Foreign exchange / Devises étrangères | 0.6 | 1.1 | 203.6 | 331.1 | 627.7 | 637.2 | 827.6 | 946.2 | 1 710.5 | 2 902.8 |
| **Canada—Canada** | | | | | | | | | | |
| Total reserves minus gold / Rés. totale, moins l'or | 23 307.5 | 28 126.4 | 32 102.3 | 33 961.8 | 36 984.1 | 36 222.1 | 34 428.7 | 32 962.1 | 34 993.8 | 40 991.2 |
| Foreign exchange / Devises étrangères | 19 911.0 | 24 432.0 | 29 019.0 | 30 484.0 | 32 685.0 | 31 537.0 | 30 166.0 | 30 664.0 | 33 198.0 | 39 314.0 |
| **Cape Verde—Cap-Vert** | | | | | | | | | | |
| Total reserves minus gold / Rés. totale, moins l'or | 8.3 | 42.6 | 28.3 | 45.4 | 79.8 | 93.6 | 139.5 | 174.0 | 254.5 | ... |
| Foreign exchange / Devises étrangères | 8.3 | 42.6 | 28.2 | 45.4 | 79.8 | 93.6 | 139.5 | 173.9 | 254.4 | ... |
| **Central African Rep.—Rép. centrafricaine** | | | | | | | | | | |
| Total reserves minus gold / Rés. totale, moins l'or | 145.7 | 136.3 | 133.3 | 118.8 | 123.2 | 132.4 | 148.3 | 139.2 | 125.3 | 82.1 |
| Foreign exchange / Devises étrangères | 145.6 | 136.1 | 133.1 | 118.6 | 123.1 | 132.2 | 145.6 | 138.9 | 124.4 | 81.1 |
| **Chad—Tchad** | | | | | | | | | | |
| Total reserves minus gold / Rés. totale, moins l'or | 120.1 | 95.0 | 110.7 | 122.4 | 218.7 | 187.1 | 221.7 | 225.6 | 625.1 | 959.9 |
| Foreign exchange / Devises étrangères | 119.7 | 94.6 | 110.3 | 122.0 | 218.3 | 186.7 | 221.2 | 225.1 | 624.6 | 959.4 |
| **Chile—Chili** | | | | | | | | | | |
| Total reserves minus gold / Rés. totale, moins l'or | 15 869.3 | 14 616.6 | 15 034.9 | 14 379.0 | 15 341.1 | 15 839.6 | 15 993.8 | 16 929.2 | 19 392.0 | 16 836.8 |
| Foreign exchange / Devises étrangères | 15 256.1 | 14 187.1 | 14 686.1 | 14 041.3 | 14 813.9 | 15 211.0 | 15 495.4 | 16 689.1 | 19 224.9 | 16 695.3 |

| Country or area<br>Pays ou zone | 1998 | 1999 | 2000 | 2001 | 2002 | 2003 | 2004 | 2005 | 2006 | 2007 |
|---|---|---|---|---|---|---|---|---|---|---|
| **China[1] — Chine[1]** | | | | | | | | | | |
| Total reserves minus gold<br>Rés. totale, moins l'or | 149 188.0 | 157 728.0 | 168 278.0 | 215 605.0 | 291 128.0 | 408 151.0 | 614 500.0 | 821 514.0 | 1 068 490.0 | 1 530 280.0 |
| Foreign exchange<br>Devises étrangères | 144 959.0 | 154 675.0 | 165 574.0 | 212 165.0 | 286 407.0 | 403 251.0 | 609 932.0 | 818 872.0 | 1 066 340.0 | 1 528 250.0 |
| **China, Hong Kong SAR — Chine, Hong Kong RAS** | | | | | | | | | | |
| Total reserves minus gold<br>Rés. totale, moins l'or | 89 650.1 | 96 236.0 | 107 542.0 | 111 155.0 | 111 896.0 | 118 360.0 | 123 540.0 | 124 244.0 | 133 168.0 | 152 646.0 |
| Foreign exchange<br>Devises étrangères | #89 606.0 | 96 236.0 | 107 542.0 | 111 155.0 | 111 896.0 | 118 360.0 | 123 540.0 | 124 244.0 | 133 168.0 | 152 646.0 |
| **China, Macao SAR — Chine, Macao RAS** | | | | | | | | | | |
| Total reserves minus gold<br>Rés. totale, moins l'or | 2 462.6 | 2 857.4 | 3 323.0 | 3 508.4 | 3 800.3 | 4 343.4 | 5 436.1 | 6 689.4 | 9 132.1 | 13 229.9 |
| Foreign exchange<br>Devises étrangères | 2 462.6 | 2 857.4 | 3 323.0 | 3 508.4 | 3 800.3 | 4 343.4 | 5 436.1 | 6 689.4 | 9 132.1 | 13 229.9 |
| **Colombia — Colombie** | | | | | | | | | | |
| Total reserves minus gold<br>Rés. totale, moins l'or | 8 651.1 | 8 007.9 | 8 916.0 | 10 153.7 | 10 732.4 | 10 783.9 | 13 393.8 | 14 787.0 | 15 296.2 | 20 767.3 |
| Foreign exchange<br>Devises étrangères | 7 880.0 | 7 485.0 | 8 409.0 | 9 659.0 | 10 190.0 | 10 188.0 | 12 769.0 | 14 206.0 | 14 673.0 | 20 096.0 |
| **Comoros — Comores** | | | | | | | | | | |
| Total reserves minus gold<br>Rés. totale, moins l'or | 39.1 | 37.1 | 43.2 | 62.3 | 79.9 | 94.3 | 103.7 | 85.8 | 93.5 | ... |
| Foreign exchange<br>Devises étrangères | 38.4 | 36.2 | 42.3 | 61.6 | 79.2 | 93.5 | 102.9 | 85.0 | 92.7 | ... |
| **Congo — Congo** | | | | | | | | | | |
| Total reserves minus gold<br>Rés. totale, moins l'or | 0.8 | 39.4 | 222.0 | 68.9 | 31.6 | 34.8 | 119.6 | 731.8 | 1 840.9 | 2 196.9 |
| Foreign exchange<br>Devises étrangères | 0.1 | 38.5 | 221.3 | 68.0 | 27.7 | 33.4 | 111.5 | 728.6 | 1 839.9 | 2 195.8 |
| **Costa Rica — Costa Rica** | | | | | | | | | | |
| Total reserves minus gold<br>Rés. totale, moins l'or | 1 063.4 | 1 460.4 | 1 317.8 | 1 329.8 | 1 501.7 | 1 839.2 | 1 921.8 | 2 312.7 | 3 114.6 | 4 113.6 |
| Foreign exchange<br>Devises étrangères | 1 051.0 | 1 432.1 | 1 291.3 | 1 304.6 | 1 474.4 | 1 809.4 | 1 890.6 | 2 284.0 | 3 084.5 | 4 081.9 |
| **Côte d'Ivoire — Côte d'Ivoire** | | | | | | | | | | |
| Total reserves minus gold<br>Rés. totale, moins l'or | 855.5 | 630.4 | 667.9 | 1 019.0 | 1 863.3 | 1 303.9 | 1 693.6 | 1 321.6 | 1 797.7 | 2 519.0 |
| Foreign exchange<br>Devises étrangères | 855.0 | 626.6 | 666.2 | 1 017.9 | 1 861.5 | 1 302.7 | 1 692.5 | 1 320.0 | 1 795.7 | 2 517.3 |
| **Croatia — Croatie** | | | | | | | | | | |
| Total reserves minus gold<br>Rés. totale, moins l'or | 2 815.7 | 3 025.0 | 3 524.4 | 4 703.2 | 5 884.9 | 8 190.5 | 8 758.2 | 8 800.3 | 11 487.8 | 13 674.5 |
| Foreign exchange<br>Devises étrangères | 2 584.4 | 2 835.3 | 3 376.9 | 4 595.6 | 5 883.2 | 8 190.2 | 8 757.9 | 8 799.8 | 11 487.4 | 13 674.0 |
| **Cyprus — Chypre** | | | | | | | | | | |
| Total reserves minus gold<br>Rés. totale, moins l'or | 1 379.7 | 1 832.9 | 1 741.1 | 2 267.8 | 3 022.1 | 3 256.7 | 3 910.0 | 4 191.1 | 5 646.8 | 6 118.6 |
| Foreign exchange<br>Devises étrangères | 1 343.6 | 1 783.8 | 1 694.0 | 2 221.9 | 2 953.2 | 3 154.5 | 3 832.7 | 4 155.9 | 5 621.5 | 6 100.1 |
| **Czech Republic — République tchèque** | | | | | | | | | | |
| Total reserves minus gold<br>Rés. totale, moins l'or | 12 542.1 | 12 806.1 | 13 019.2 | 14 341.2 | 23 555.6 | 26 770.6 | 28 259.3 | 29 330.4 | 31 181.7 | 34 549.6 |
| Foreign exchange<br>Devises étrangères | 12 542.1 | 12 806.1 | 13 015.9 | 14 189.0 | 23 315.2 | 26 293.8 | 27 844.1 | 29 137.7 | 31 053.7 | 34 445.2 |
| **Denmark — Danemark** | | | | | | | | | | |
| Total reserves minus gold<br>Rés. totale, moins l'or | 15 264.2 | 22 286.9 | 15 108.2 | 17 110.2 | 26 985.7 | 37 105.0 | 39 083.7 | #32 930.4 | 29 723.7 | 32 534.4 |
| Foreign exchange<br>Devises étrangères | 13 752.8 | 21 145.0 | 14 469.0 | 16 117.0 | 25 901.0 | 36 004.0 | 38 196.0 | #32 510.0 | 29 160.0 | 32 029.0 |

| Country or area<br>Pays ou zone | 1998 | 1999 | 2000 | 2001 | 2002 | 2003 | 2004 | 2005 | 2006 | 2007 |
|---|---|---|---|---|---|---|---|---|---|---|
| **Djibouti — Djibouti** | | | | | | | | | | |
| Total reserves minus gold<br>Rés. totale, moins l'or | 66.5 | 70.6 | 67.8 | 70.3 | 73.7 | 100.1 | 93.9 | 89.3 | 120.3 | ... |
| Foreign exchange<br>Devises étrangères | 66.1 | 69.0 | 66.0 | 68.8 | 71.2 | 98.4 | 91.2 | 87.7 | 117.8 | ... |
| **Dominica — Dominique** | | | | | | | | | | |
| Total reserves minus gold<br>Rés. totale, moins l'or | 27.7 | 31.6 | 29.4 | 31.2 | 45.5 | 47.7 | 42.3 | 49.2 | 63.0 | 60.5 |
| Foreign exchange<br>Devises étrangères | 27.7 | 31.6 | 29.4 | 31.2 | 45.5 | 47.7 | 42.3 | 49.1 | 63.0 | 60.4 |
| **Dominican Republic — Rép. dominicaine** | | | | | | | | | | |
| Total reserves minus gold<br>Rés. totale, moins l'or | 501.9 | 694.0 | 627.2 | 1 099.5 | 468.4 | 253.1 | 798.3 | 1 843.2 | 2 115.6 | 2 546.4 |
| Foreign exchange<br>Devises étrangères | 501.6 | 693.7 | 626.8 | 1 099.0 | 468.1 | 253.0 | 796.7 | 1 842.6 | 2 091.2 | 2 447.8 |
| **Ecuador — Equateur** | | | | | | | | | | |
| Total reserves minus gold<br>Rés. totale, moins l'or | 1 619.7 | 1 642.4 | 946.9 | 839.8 | 714.6 | 812.6 | 1 069.6 | 1 714.2 | 1 489.5 | 2 816.4 |
| Foreign exchange<br>Devises étrangères | 1 595.3 | 1 616.5 | 924.3 | 815.9 | 689.4 | 786.1 | 986.9 | 1 667.9 | 1 456.1 | 2 764.9 |
| **Egypt — Egypte** | | | | | | | | | | |
| Total reserves minus gold<br>Rés. totale, moins l'or | 18 123.9 | 14 484.1 | 13 117.6 | 12 925.8 | 13 242.4 | 13 588.7 | 14 273.2 | 20 609.1 | 24 461.6 | 30 187.7 |
| Foreign exchange<br>Devises étrangères | 17 888.0 | 14 278.0 | 12 913.0 | 12 891.0 | 13 151.0 | 13 400.0 | 14 108.0 | 20 508.0 | 24 341.0 | 30 054.0 |
| **El Salvador — El Salvador** | | | | | | | | | | |
| Total reserves minus gold<br>Rés. totale, moins l'or | 1 613.1 | 1 819.8 | 1 772.6 | 1 593.7 | 1 472.8 | 1 792.3 | 1 754.0 | 1 722.8 | 1 814.9 | 2 110.0 |
| Foreign exchange<br>Devises étrangères | 1 577.9 | 1 785.5 | 1 740.0 | 1 562.3 | 1 438.9 | 1 755.2 | 1 715.2 | 1 687.1 | 1 777.3 | 2 070.5 |
| **Equatorial Guinea — Guinée équatoriale** | | | | | | | | | | |
| Total reserves minus gold<br>Rés. totale, moins l'or | 0.8 | 3.4 | 23.0 | 70.9 | 88.5 | 237.7 | 945.0 | 2 102.5 | 3 066.7 | 3 837.4 |
| Foreign exchange<br>Devises étrangères | 0.8 | 3.4 | 22.9 | 69.9 | 87.9 | 237.7 | 944.3 | 2 101.9 | 3 066.1 | 3 836.7 |
| **Eritrea — Erythrée** | | | | | | | | | | |
| Total reserves minus gold<br>Rés. totale, moins l'or | 23.1 | 34.2 | 25.5 | 39.8 | 30.3 | 24.7 | 34.7 | 27.9 | 25.4 | ... |
| Foreign exchange<br>Devises étrangères | 23.1 | 34.2 | 25.5 | 39.7 | 30.3 | 24.7 | 34.7 | 27.9 | 25.3 | ... |
| **Estonia — Estonie** | | | | | | | | | | |
| Total reserves minus gold<br>Rés. totale, moins l'or | 810.6 | 853.5 | 920.6 | 820.2 | 1 000.4 | 1 373.4 | 1 788.2 | 1 943.2 | 2 781.2 | 3 262.7 |
| Foreign exchange<br>Devises étrangères | 810.5 | 852.1 | 920.6 | 820.2 | 1 000.3 | 1 373.3 | 1 788.1 | 1 943.1 | 2 781.1 | 3 262.6 |
| **Ethiopia — Ethiopie** | | | | | | | | | | |
| Total reserves minus gold<br>Rés. totale, moins l'or | 511.1 | 458.5 | 306.3 | 433.2 | 881.7 | 955.6 | 1 496.8 | 1 121.5 | 832.7 | ... |
| Foreign exchange<br>Devises étrangères | 501.0 | 448.7 | 297.1 | 424.1 | 871.9 | 944.8 | 1 485.1 | 1 111.0 | 821.6 | ... |
| **Euro Area — Zone euro** | | | | | | | | | | |
| Total reserves minus gold<br>Rés. totale, moins l'or | ... | 256 780.0 | 242 327.0 | 234 931.0 | 247 168.0 | 223 145.0 | 211 971.0 | 184 714.0 | 197 006.0 | 215 557.0 |
| Foreign exchange<br>Devises étrangères | ... | 227 989.0 | 218 633.0 | 207 817.0 | 215 812.0 | 188 173.0 | 181 196.0 | 167 150.0 | 184 034.0 | 203 450.0 |
| **Fiji — Fidji** | | | | | | | | | | |
| Total reserves minus gold<br>Rés. totale, moins l'or | 385.7 | 428.7 | 411.8 | 366.4 | 358.8 | 423.6 | 478.1 | 314.7 | ... | ... |
| Foreign exchange<br>Devises étrangères | 359.3 | 402.6 | 386.5 | 341.5 | 331.5 | 393.3 | 446.1 | 284.9 | ... | ... |

| Country or area Pays ou zone | 1998 | 1999 | 2000 | 2001 | 2002 | 2003 | 2004 | 2005 | 2006 | 2007 |
|---|---|---|---|---|---|---|---|---|---|---|
| **Finland — Finlande** | | | | | | | | | | |
| Total reserves minus gold Rés. totale, moins l'or | 9 694.5 | #8 219.7 | 7 976.9 | 7 983.4 | 9 285.0 | 10 514.9 | 12 221.5 | 10 521.1 | 6 494.2 | 7 063.2 |
| Foreign exchange Devises étrangères | 8 508.2 | 7 292.4 | 7 340.7 | 7 197.6 | 8 436.8 | 9 544.5 | 11 425.3 | 10 075.8 | 6 134.6 | 6 689.2 |
| **France — France** | | | | | | | | | | |
| Total reserves minus gold Rés. totale, moins l'or | 44 311.7 | #39 701.5 | 37 039.2 | 31 749.1 | 28 365.3 | 30 186.5 | 35 314.0 | 27 752.9 | 42 651.6 | 45 709.7 |
| Foreign exchange Devises étrangères | 38 752.8 | 33 933.4 | 32 114.3 | 26 363.2 | 21 965.0 | 23 121.7 | 29 076.7 | 23 996.3 | 40 287.0 | 43 587.4 |
| **Gabon — Gabon** | | | | | | | | | | |
| Total reserves minus gold Rés. totale, moins l'or | 15.4 | 17.9 | 190.1 | 9.9 | 139.7 | 196.6 | 443.4 | 668.6 | 1 113.4 | 1 225.4 |
| Foreign exchange Devises étrangères | 15.3 | 17.8 | 189.8 | 9.6 | 139.4 | 196.3 | 436.9 | 668.1 | 1 112.2 | 1 224.2 |
| **Gambia — Gambie** | | | | | | | | | | |
| Total reserves minus gold Rés. totale, moins l'or | 106.4 | 111.2 | 109.4 | 106.0 | 106.9 | 59.3 | 83.8 | 98.3 | 120.6 | 142.8 |
| Foreign exchange Devises étrangères | 103.9 | 108.5 | 107.3 | 104.1 | 104.8 | 57.1 | 80.7 | 96.0 | 116.9 | 140.2 |
| **Georgia — Géorgie** | | | | | | | | | | |
| Total reserves minus gold Rés. totale, moins l'or | 132.9 | 144.4 | 116.0 | 161.9 | 202.2 | 196.2 | 386.7 | 478.6 | 930.8 | 1 361.2 |
| Foreign exchange Devises étrangères | 127.7 | 135.9 | 112.7 | 158.0 | 199.3 | 191.3 | 375.4 | 477.6 | 929.9 | 1 346.3 |
| **Germany — Allemagne** | | | | | | | | | | |
| Total reserves minus gold Rés. totale, moins l'or | 74 024.2 | #61 038.8 | 56 890.5 | 51 403.9 | 51 170.6 | 50 694.0 | 48 822.7 | 45 139.7 | 41 686.5 | 44 326.5 |
| Foreign exchange Devises étrangères | 64 133.0 | #52 661.1 | 49 667.3 | 43 709.8 | 42 495.4 | 41 095.5 | 39 898.6 | 39 765.3 | 37 718.9 | 40 768.3 |
| **Ghana — Ghana** | | | | | | | | | | |
| Total reserves minus gold Rés. totale, moins l'or | 377.0 | 453.8 | 232.1 | 298.2 | 539.7 | 1 352.8 | 1 626.7 | 1 752.9 | 2 090.3 | ... |
| Foreign exchange Devises étrangères | 292.8 | 379.1 | 231.5 | 294.2 | 536.1 | 1 306.0 | 1 605.9 | 1 751.8 | 2 089.1 | ... |
| **Greece — Grèce** | | | | | | | | | | |
| Total reserves minus gold Rés. totale, moins l'or | 17 458.4 | 18 122.3 | 13 424.3 | #5 154.2 | 8 082.8 | 4 361.5 | 1 191.0 | 506.4 | 565.9 | 631.1 |
| Foreign exchange Devises étrangères | 17 188.3 | 17 726.0 | 13 115.5 | #4 787.2 | 7 629.3 | 3 843.3 | 743.7 | 309.1 | 408.3 | 518.2 |
| **Grenada — Grenade** | | | | | | | | | | |
| Total reserves minus gold Rés. totale, moins l'or | 46.8 | 50.8 | 57.7 | 63.9 | 87.8 | 83.2 | 121.7 | 94.3 | 100.0 | 110.6 |
| Foreign exchange Devises étrangères | 46.8 | 50.8 | 57.7 | 63.9 | 87.8 | 83.2 | 121.7 | 94.2 | 99.8 | 110.4 |
| **Guatemala — Guatemala** | | | | | | | | | | |
| Total reserves minus gold Rés. totale, moins l'or | 1 335.1 | 1 189.2 | 1 746.4 | 2 292.2 | 2 299.1 | 2 833.2 | 3 426.3 | 3 663.8 | 3 915.0 | 4 129.9 |
| Foreign exchange Devises étrangères | 1 322.9 | 1 177.7 | 1 736.6 | 2 283.7 | 2 290.9 | 2 825.0 | 3 418.3 | 3 657.3 | 3 909.3 | 4 125.6 |
| **Guinea — Guinée** | | | | | | | | | | |
| Total reserves minus gold Rés. totale, moins l'or | 236.7 | 199.7 | 147.9 | 200.2 | 171.4 | ... | 110.5 | 95.1 | ... | ... |
| Foreign exchange Devises étrangères | 235.2 | 198.3 | 147.6 | 199.3 | 169.6 | ... | 110.4 | 94.9 | ... | ... |
| **Guinea-Bissau — Guinée-Bissau** | | | | | | | | | | |
| Total reserves minus gold Rés. totale, moins l'or | 35.8 | 35.3 | 66.7 | 69.5 | 102.7 | 32.9 | 73.1 | 79.8 | 82.0 | 112.9 |
| Foreign exchange Devises étrangères | 35.7 | 35.2 | 66.7 | 69.3 | 102.3 | 31.7 | 72.4 | 79.2 | 81.5 | 112.8 |

**International reserves minus gold**—Millions of US dollars, end of period (*continued*)
**Réserves internationales, moins l'or**—Millions de dollars E.-U., fin de période (*suite*)

| Country or area<br>Pays ou zone | 1998 | 1999 | 2000 | 2001 | 2002 | 2003 | 2004 | 2005 | 2006 | 2007 |
|---|---|---|---|---|---|---|---|---|---|---|
| Guyana — Guyana | | | | | | | | | | |
| Total reserves minus gold<br>Rés. totale, moins l'or | 276.6 | 268.3 | 305.0 | 287.3 | 284.5 | 276.4 | 231.8 | 251.9 | 279.6 | 313.0 |
| Foreign exchange<br>Devises étrangères | 276.4 | 267.0 | 295.8 | 284.8 | 279.8 | 271.5 | 224.7 | 251.4 | 278.0 | 312.5 |
| Haiti — Haïti | | | | | | | | | | |
| Total reserves minus gold<br>Rés. totale, moins l'or | 258.2 | 264.0 | 182.1 | 141.4 | 81.7 | 62.0 | 114.4 | 133.1 | 253.1 | 443.2 |
| Foreign exchange<br>Devises étrangères | 257.6 | 263.1 | 182.0 | 140.8 | 81.1 | 61.6 | 114.1 | 120.7 | 245.1 | 435.6 |
| Honduras — Honduras | | | | | | | | | | |
| Total reserves minus gold<br>Rés. totale, moins l'or | 818.1 | 1 257.6 | 1 313.0 | 1 415.6 | 1 524.1 | 1 430.0 | 1 970.4 | 2 327.2 | 2 628.5 | 2 526.8 |
| Foreign exchange<br>Devises étrangères | 818.0 | 1 244.8 | 1 301.7 | 1 404.4 | 1 511.9 | 1 417.1 | 1 956.9 | 2 314.6 | 2 615.5 | 2 513.1 |
| Hungary — Hongrie | | | | | | | | | | |
| Total reserves minus gold<br>Rés. totale, moins l'or | 9 318.7 | 10 954.0 | 11 189.6 | 10 727.2 | 10 348.5 | 12 751.4 | 15 922.1 | 18 552.1 | 21 527.0 | 23 969.8 |
| Foreign exchange<br>Devises étrangères | 9 239.0 | 10 707.0 | 10 915.0 | 10 302.0 | 9 721.0 | 12 029.0 | 15 326.0 | 18 296.0 | 21 316.0 | 23 773.0 |
| Iceland — Islande | | | | | | | | | | |
| Total reserves minus gold<br>Rés. totale, moins l'or | 426.4 | 478.4 | 388.9 | 338.2 | 440.1 | 792.3 | 1 046.2 | 1 035.7 | 2 301.3 | 2 578.7 |
| Foreign exchange<br>Devises étrangères | 411.6 | 452.9 | 364.6 | 314.8 | 414.7 | 764.6 | 1 017.3 | 1 009.1 | 2 273.2 | 2 549.1 |
| India — Inde | | | | | | | | | | |
| Total reserves minus gold<br>Rés. totale, moins l'or | 27 340.7 | 32 666.7 | 37 902.2 | 45 870.5 | 67 665.5 | 98 937.9 | 126 593.0 | 131 924.0 | 170 738.0 | 266 988.0 |
| Foreign exchange<br>Devises étrangères | 26 958.0 | 31 992.0 | 37 264.0 | 45 251.0 | 66 994.0 | 97 617.0 | 125 164.0 | 131 018.0 | 170 187.0 | 266 553.0 |
| Indonesia — Indonésie | | | | | | | | | | |
| Total reserves minus gold<br>Rés. totale, moins l'or | 22 713.4 | 26 445.0 | 28 501.9 | 27 246.2 | 30 970.7 | 34 962.3 | 34 952.5 | 33 140.5 | 41 103.1 | 54 976.4 |
| Foreign exchange<br>Devises étrangères | 22 401.4 | 26 245.0 | 28 280.4 | 27 047.5 | 30 754.3 | 34 742.4 | 34 724.1 | 32 925.5 | 40 866.0 | 54 737.3 |
| Iraq — Iraq | | | | | | | | | | |
| Total reserves minus gold<br>Rés. totale, moins l'or | ... | ... | ... | ... | ... | ... | 7 824.1 | 12 104.1 | 19 535.4 | ... |
| Foreign exchange<br>Devises étrangères | ... | ... | ... | ... | ... | ... | 7 098.5 | 11 439.9 | 18 839.2 | ... |
| Ireland — Irlande | | | | | | | | | | |
| Total reserves minus gold<br>Rés. totale, moins l'or | 9 397.3 | #5 325.0 | 5 359.7 | 5 586.5 | 5 414.8 | 4 078.5 | 2 830.9 | 778.7 | 720.0 | 778.7 |
| Foreign exchange<br>Devises étrangères | 8 621.9 | 4 869.1 | 4 982.7 | 5 195.5 | 4 879.4 | 3 425.2 | 2 323.7 | 514.4 | 493.8 | 590.8 |
| Israel — Israël | | | | | | | | | | |
| Total reserves minus gold<br>Rés. totale, moins l'or | 22 674.3 | 22 604.9 | 23 281.2 | 23 378.6 | 24 082.9 | 26 315.1 | 27 094.4 | 28 059.4 | 29 153.2 | 28 518.5 |
| Foreign exchange<br>Devises étrangères | 22 674.0 | 22 514.8 | 23 163.0 | 23 179.1 | 23 665.0 | 25 778.4 | 26 616.0 | 27 839.0 | 29 011.0 | 28 406.0 |
| Italy — Italie | | | | | | | | | | |
| Total reserves minus gold<br>Rés. totale, moins l'or | 29 887.8 | #22 421.8 | 25 566.5 | 24 419.4 | 28 603.1 | 30 372.2 | 27 859.0 | 25 514.7 | 25 661.7 | 28 385.0 |
| Foreign exchange<br>Devises étrangères | 25 447.0 | #18 707.7 | 22 423.2 | 20 905.3 | 24 587.8 | 26 062.0 | 24 011.1 | 23 527.9 | 24 413.2 | 27 319.2 |
| Jamaica — Jamaïque | | | | | | | | | | |
| Total reserves minus gold<br>Rés. totale, moins l'or | 709.5 | 554.5 | 1 053.7 | 1 900.5 | 1 645.1 | 1 194.9 | 1 846.5 | 2 169.8 | 2 318.4 | ... |
| Foreign exchange<br>Devises étrangères | 708.8 | 553.8 | 1 053.6 | 1 899.0 | 1 644.2 | 1 194.8 | 1 846.4 | 2 169.8 | 2 318.2 | ... |

| Country or area<br>Pays ou zone | 1998 | 1999 | 2000 | 2001 | 2002 | 2003 | 2004 | 2005 | 2006 | 2007 |
|---|---|---|---|---|---|---|---|---|---|---|
| **Japan — Japon** | | | | | | | | | | |
| Total reserves minus gold<br>Rés. totale, moins l'or | 215 471.0 | 286 916.0 | 354 902.0 | 395 155.0 | 461 186.0 | 663 289.0 | 833 891.0 | 834 275.0 | 879 682.0 | 952 784.0 |
| Foreign exchange<br>Devises étrangères | 203 215.0 | 277 708.0 | 347 212.0 | 387 727.0 | 451 458.0 | 652 790.0 | 824 264.0 | 828 813.0 | 874 936.0 | 948 356.0 |
| **Jordan — Jordanie** | | | | | | | | | | |
| Total reserves minus gold<br>Rés. totale, moins l'or | 1 750.4 | 2 629.1 | 3 331.3 | 3 062.2 | 3 975.9 | 5 194.3 | 5 266.6 | 5 250.3 | 6 722.0 | 7 542.0 |
| Foreign exchange<br>Devises étrangères | 1 749.6 | 2 628.8 | 3 330.6 | 3 061.0 | 3 975.0 | 5 193.1 | 5 264.8 | 5 249.5 | 6 720.4 | 7 539.4 |
| **Kazakhstan — Kazakhstan** | | | | | | | | | | |
| Total reserves minus gold<br>Rés. totale, moins l'or | 1 461.2 | 1 479.2 | 1 594.1 | 1 997.2 | 2 555.3 | 4 236.2 | 8 473.1 | 6 084.2 | 17 750.8 | 15 539.9 |
| Foreign exchange<br>Devises étrangères | 1 073.9 | 1 253.8 | 1 594.1 | 1 997.2 | 2 554.3 | 4 235.0 | 8 471.9 | 6 083.0 | 17 749.5 | 15 538.5 |
| **Kenya — Kenya** | | | | | | | | | | |
| Total reserves minus gold<br>Rés. totale, moins l'or | 783.1 | 791.6 | 897.7 | 1 064.9 | 1 068.0 | 1 481.9 | 1 519.3 | 1 798.8 | 2 415.8 | 3 354.9 |
| Foreign exchange<br>Devises étrangères | 765.0 | 772.2 | 881.2 | 1 048.1 | 1 050.0 | 1 461.0 | 1 499.0 | 1 780.6 | 2 396.0 | 3 334.5 |
| **Korea, Republic of — Corée, République de** | | | | | | | | | | |
| Total reserves minus gold<br>Rés. totale, moins l'or | 51 974.5 | 73 987.3 | 96 130.5 | 102 753.0 | 121 345.0 | 155 284.0 | 198 997.0 | 210 317.0 | 238 882.0 | 262 150.0 |
| Foreign exchange<br>Devises étrangères | 51 963.0 | 73 700.3 | 95 855.1 | 102 487.0 | 120 811.0 | 154 509.0 | 198 175.0 | 209 968.0 | 238 388.0 | 261 771.0 |
| **Kuwait — Koweït** | | | | | | | | | | |
| Total reserves minus gold<br>Rés. totale, moins l'or | 3 947.1 | 4 823.7 | 7 082.4 | 9 897.3 | 9 208.1 | 7 577.0 | 8 241.9 | 8 862.8 | 12 566.0 | 16 660.0 |
| Foreign exchange<br>Devises étrangères | 3 486.3 | 4 244.5 | 6 504.4 | 9 191.1 | 8 357.0 | 6 640.5 | 7 347.4 | 8 380.4 | 12 177.6 | 16 285.6 |
| **Kyrgyzstan — Kirghizistan** | | | | | | | | | | |
| Total reserves minus gold<br>Rés. totale, moins l'or | 163.8 | 229.7 | 239.0 | 263.5 | 288.8 | 364.6 | 528.2 | 569.7 | 764.4 | 1 107.2 |
| Foreign exchange<br>Devises étrangères | 163.4 | 224.6 | 238.3 | 262.2 | 288.2 | 354.3 | 508.3 | 564.5 | 731.1 | 1 093.4 |
| **Lao People's Dem. Rep. — Rép. dém. pop. lao** | | | | | | | | | | |
| Total reserves minus gold<br>Rés. totale, moins l'or | 112.2 | 101.2 | 139.0 | 130.9 | 191.6 | 208.6 | 223.2 | 234.3 | 326.9 | ... |
| Foreign exchange<br>Devises étrangères | 106.1 | 101.1 | 138.9 | 127.5 | 185.5 | 189.5 | 207.9 | 220.2 | 312.2 | ... |
| **Latvia — Lettonie** | | | | | | | | | | |
| Total reserves minus gold<br>Rés. totale, moins l'or | 801.2 | 872.0 | 850.9 | 1 148.7 | 1 241.4 | 1 432.4 | 1 912.0 | 2 232.1 | 4 353.4 | 5 553.4 |
| Foreign exchange<br>Devises étrangères | 800.9 | 868.9 | 850.8 | 1 148.6 | 1 241.3 | 1 432.2 | 1 911.7 | 2 231.9 | 4 353.1 | 5 553.1 |
| **Lebanon — Liban** | | | | | | | | | | |
| Total reserves minus gold<br>Rés. totale, moins l'or | 6 556.3 | 7 775.6 | 5 943.7 | 5 013.8 | 7 243.8 | 12 519.4 | 11 734.6 | 11 887.1 | 13 376.4 | 12 909.9 |
| Foreign exchange<br>Devises étrangères | 6 508.0 | 7 727.3 | 5 895.4 | 4 965.8 | 7 190.9 | 12 460.8 | 11 672.4 | 11 828.7 | 13 313.3 | 12 844.1 |
| **Lesotho — Lesotho** | | | | | | | | | | |
| Total reserves minus gold<br>Rés. totale, moins l'or | 575.1 | 499.6 | 417.9 | 386.5 | 406.4 | 460.3 | 501.5 | 519.1 | 658.4 | ... |
| Foreign exchange<br>Devises étrangères | 568.9 | 493.5 | 412.6 | 381.5 | 401.0 | 454.4 | 495.3 | 513.5 | 652.7 | ... |
| **Liberia — Libéria** | | | | | | | | | | |
| Total reserves minus gold<br>Rés. totale, moins l'or | 0.6 | 0.4 | 0.3 | 0.5 | 3.3 | 7.4 | 18.7 | 25.4 | 72.0 | 119.4 |
| Foreign exchange<br>Devises étrangères | 0.6 | 0.4 | 0.2 | 0.4 | 3.3 | 7.3 | 18.7 | 25.4 | 71.9 | 119.3 |

**64** International reserves minus gold—Millions of US dollars, end of period (*continued*)
Réserves internationales, moins l'or—Millions de dollars E.-U., fin de période (*suite*)

| Country or area<br>Pays ou zone | 1998 | 1999 | 2000 | 2001 | 2002 | 2003 | 2004 | 2005 | 2006 | 2007 |
|---|---|---|---|---|---|---|---|---|---|---|
| **Libyan Arab Jamah.—Jamah. arabe libyenne** | | | | | | | | | | |
| Total reserves minus gold<br>Rés. totale, moins l'or | 7 269.7 | 7 279.7 | 12 460.8 | 14 800.5 | 14 307.4 | 19 584.0 | 25 688.8 | 39 507.8 | 59 289.2 | 79 404.7 |
| Foreign exchange<br>Devises étrangères | 6 221.0 | 6 225.5 | 11 407.7 | 13 749.0 | 13 159.4 | 18 309.8 | 24 336.3 | 38 235.2 | 57 907.3 | 77 897.5 |
| **Lithuania—Lituanie** | | | | | | | | | | |
| Total reserves minus gold<br>Rés. totale, moins l'or | 1 409.1 | 1 195.0 | 1 311.6 | 1 617.7 | 2 349.3 | 3 372.0 | 3 512.6 | 3 720.2 | 5 654.4 | 7 565.8 |
| Foreign exchange<br>Devises étrangères | 1 392.9 | 1 190.6 | 1 310.2 | 1 599.3 | 2 295.9 | 3 371.9 | 3 512.5 | 3 720.1 | 5 654.3 | 7 565.6 |
| **Luxembourg—Luxembourg** | | | | | | | | | | |
| Total reserves minus gold<br>Rés. totale, moins l'or | ... | #77.4 | 76.6 | 105.6 | 151.7 | 279.9 | 298.4 | 241.1 | 218.1 | 143.6 |
| Foreign exchange<br>Devises étrangères | ... | 0.3 | 0.1 | 0.1 | 0.2 | 88.9 | 143.9 | 166.7 | 156.0 | 93.8 |
| **Madagascar—Madagascar** | | | | | | | | | | |
| Total reserves minus gold<br>Rés. totale, moins l'or | 171.4 | 227.2 | 285.2 | 398.4 | 363.3 | 414.3 | 503.5 | 481.3 | 583.2 | 846.7 |
| Foreign exchange<br>Devises étrangères | 171.3 | 227.0 | 285.1 | 398.2 | 363.2 | 414.2 | 503.3 | 481.2 | 583.1 | 846.6 |
| **Malawi—Malawi** | | | | | | | | | | |
| Total reserves minus gold<br>Rés. totale, moins l'or | 255.4 | 246.4 | 243.0 | 202.5 | 161.5 | 122.0 | 128.1 | 158.9 | 133.8 | 216.4 |
| Foreign exchange<br>Devises étrangères | 245.5 | 243.0 | 239.6 | 198.8 | 158.3 | 118.2 | 123.3 | 154.6 | 129.6 | 212.8 |
| **Malaysia—Malaisie** | | | | | | | | | | |
| Total reserves minus gold<br>Rés. totale, moins l'or | 25 559.4 | 30 588.2 | 28 329.8 | 29 522.3 | 33 360.7 | 43 821.7 | 65 881.1 | 69 858.0 | 82 132.3 | 101 024.0 |
| Foreign exchange<br>Devises étrangères | 24 728.0 | 29 670.0 | 27 432.2 | 28 632.9 | 32 419.1 | 42 772.4 | 64 905.9 | 69 376.9 | 81 723.6 | 100 640.0 |
| **Maldives—Maldives** | | | | | | | | | | |
| Total reserves minus gold<br>Rés. totale, moins l'or | 118.5 | 127.1 | 122.8 | 93.1 | 133.1 | 159.5 | 203.6 | 186.3 | 231.4 | 308.3 |
| Foreign exchange<br>Devises étrangères | 117.2 | 124.8 | 120.5 | 90.8 | 130.6 | 156.7 | 200.7 | 183.6 | 228.5 | 305.3 |
| **Mali—Mali** | | | | | | | | | | |
| Total reserves minus gold<br>Rés. totale, moins l'or | 402.9 | 349.7 | 381.3 | 348.9 | 594.5 | 952.5 | 860.7 | 854.6 | 969.5 | 1 087.1 |
| Foreign exchange<br>Devises étrangères | 390.4 | 337.1 | 369.7 | 337.4 | 582.4 | 938.4 | 846.2 | 841.2 | 955.4 | 1 071.9 |
| **Malta—Malte** | | | | | | | | | | |
| Total reserves minus gold<br>Rés. totale, moins l'or | 1 662.7 | 1 788.0 | 1 470.2 | 1 666.2 | 2 209.3 | 2 728.7 | 2 732.0 | 2 576.4 | 2 976.8 | 3 785.4 |
| Foreign exchange<br>Devises étrangères | 1 555.7 | 1 701.9 | 1 385.8 | 1 582.4 | 2 115.3 | 2 624.5 | 2 621.7 | 2 473.0 | 2 865.0 | 3 662.0 |
| **Mauritania—Mauritanie** | | | | | | | | | | |
| Total reserves minus gold<br>Rés. totale, moins l'or | 202.9 | 224.3 | 279.9 | 284.5 | 396.2 | 415.3 | ... | ... | ... | ... |
| Foreign exchange<br>Devises étrangères | 202.8 | 224.3 | 279.5 | 284.3 | 396.0 | 415.2 | ... | ... | ... | ... |
| **Mauritius—Maurice** | | | | | | | | | | |
| Total reserves minus gold<br>Rés. totale, moins l'or | 559.0 | 731.0 | 897.4 | 835.6 | 1 227.4 | 1 577.3 | 1 605.9 | 1 339.9 | 1 269.6 | 1 780.3 |
| Foreign exchange<br>Devises étrangères | 516.5 | 689.1 | 857.1 | 796.3 | 1 184.5 | 1 519.2 | 1 544.7 | 1 289.2 | 1 226.3 | 1 739.9 |
| **Mexico—Mexique** | | | | | | | | | | |
| Total reserves minus gold<br>Rés. totale, moins l'or | 31 799.0 | 31 782.2 | 35 508.8 | 44 740.7 | 50 594.4 | 58 955.6 | 64 140.7 | 74 054.1 | 76 270.5 | 87 109.2 |
| Foreign exchange<br>Devises étrangères | 31 461.3 | 30 992.0 | 35 142.0 | 44 384.0 | 49 895.0 | 57 739.9 | 62 777.9 | 73 014.6 | 75 447.7 | 86 309.4 |

**64** International reserves minus gold—Millions of US dollars, end of period *(continued)*
Réserves internationales, moins l'or—Millions de dollars E.-U., fin de période *(suite)*

| Country or area<br>Pays ou zone | 1998 | 1999 | 2000 | 2001 | 2002 | 2003 | 2004 | 2005 | 2006 | 2007 |
|---|---|---|---|---|---|---|---|---|---|---|
| **Micronesia (Fed. States of) (US dollar) — Micronésie** | | | | | | | | | | |
| Total reserves minus gold<br>Rés. totale, moins l'or | 101.6 | 92.7 | 113.0 | 98.3 | 117.4 | 89.6 | 54.8 | 50.0 | 46.6 | ... |
| Foreign exchange<br>Devises étrangères | 100.2 | 91.2 | 111.6 | 96.9 | 115.8 | 87.8 | 52.9 | 48.2 | 44.7 | ... |
| **Moldova — Moldova** | | | | | | | | | | |
| Total reserves minus gold<br>Rés. totale, moins l'or | 143.6 | 185.7 | 222.5 | 228.5 | 268.9 | 302.3 | 470.3 | 597.4 | 775.5 | 1 333.7 |
| Foreign exchange<br>Devises étrangères | 142.9 | 185.4 | 222.1 | 227.8 | 268.6 | 302.2 | 470.2 | 597.4 | 775.3 | 1 333.5 |
| **Mongolia — Mongolie** | | | | | | | | | | |
| Total reserves minus gold<br>Rés. totale, moins l'or | 94.1 | 136.5 | 178.8 | 205.7 | 349.7 | 236.1 | 236.3 | 430.3 | 926.0 | 1 195.6 |
| Foreign exchange<br>Devises étrangères | 93.6 | 136.3 | 178.7 | 205.6 | 349.5 | 235.9 | 236.1 | 430.1 | 925.8 | 1 195.4 |
| **Montenegro — Monténégro** | | | | | | | | | | |
| Total reserves minus gold<br>Rés. totale, moins l'or | ... | ... | ... | ... | 58.2 | 63.7 | 81.8 | 204.0 | 432.7 | ... |
| Foreign exchange<br>Devises étrangères | ... | ... | ... | ... | 58.2 | 63.7 | 81.8 | 204.0 | 432.7 | ... |
| **Montserrat — Montserrat** | | | | | | | | | | |
| Total reserves minus gold<br>Rés. totale, moins l'or | 24.8 | 14.0 | 10.4 | 12.5 | 14.4 | 15.2 | 14.1 | 13.9 | 14.6 | 14.5 |
| Foreign exchange<br>Devises étrangères | 24.8 | 14.0 | 10.4 | 12.5 | 14.4 | 15.2 | 14.1 | 13.9 | 14.6 | 14.5 |
| **Morocco — Maroc** | | | | | | | | | | |
| Total reserves minus gold<br>Rés. totale, moins l'or | 4 435.0 | 5 689.4 | 4 823.2 | 8 473.9 | 10 132.7 | 13 851.1 | 16 336.6 | 16 187.4 | 20 340.7 | ... |
| Foreign exchange<br>Devises étrangères | 4 389.1 | 5 507.5 | 4 612.0 | 8 262.0 | 9 914.5 | 13 634.1 | 16 107.0 | 16 008.0 | 20 182.1 | ... |
| **Mozambique — Mozambique** | | | | | | | | | | |
| Total reserves minus gold<br>Rés. totale, moins l'or | 608.5 | 654.0 | 723.2 | 713.2 | 802.5 | 937.5 | 1 131.0 | 1 053.8 | 1 155.7 | 1 444.7 |
| Foreign exchange<br>Devises étrangères | 608.4 | 653.9 | 723.1 | 713.2 | 802.4 | 937.4 | 1 130.9 | 1 053.6 | 1 155.5 | 1 444.5 |
| **Myanmar — Myanmar** | | | | | | | | | | |
| Total reserves minus gold<br>Rés. totale, moins l'or | 314.9 | 265.5 | 223.0 | 400.5 | 470.0 | 550.2 | 672.1 | 770.7 | 1 235.6 | ... |
| Foreign exchange<br>Devises étrangères | 314.6 | 265.3 | 222.8 | 399.9 | 469.9 | 550.1 | 672.1 | 770.5 | 1 235.4 | ... |
| **Namibia — Namibie** | | | | | | | | | | |
| Total reserves minus gold<br>Rés. totale, moins l'or | 260.3 | 305.5 | 259.8 | 234.3 | 323.1 | 325.2 | 345.1 | 312.1 | 449.6 | 896.0 |
| Foreign exchange<br>Devises étrangères | 260.2 | 305.4 | 259.8 | 234.2 | 323.0 | 325.1 | 344.9 | 312.0 | 449.4 | 895.9 |
| **Nepal — Népal** | | | | | | | | | | |
| Total reserves minus gold<br>Rés. totale, moins l'or | 756.3 | 845.1 | 945.4 | 1 037.7 | 1 017.6 | 1 222.5 | 1 462.2 | 1 499.0 | ... | ... |
| Foreign exchange<br>Devises étrangères | 748.2 | 836.9 | 937.9 | 1 030.4 | 1 009.8 | 1 213.1 | 1 452.5 | 1 490.2 | ... | ... |
| **Netherlands — Pays-Bas** | | | | | | | | | | |
| Total reserves minus gold<br>Rés. totale, moins l'or | 21 417.8 | #9 885.7 | 9 642.5 | 9 034.3 | 9 563.3 | 11 167.0 | 10 654.8 | 8 986.0 | 10 802.4 | 10 269.7 |
| Foreign exchange<br>Devises étrangères | 17 536.4 | 6 286.8 | 7 003.9 | 5 930.3 | 6 017.4 | 7 335.5 | 7 209.6 | 7 078.2 | 9 327.0 | 8 748.7 |
| **Netherlands Antilles — Antilles néerlandaises** | | | | | | | | | | |
| Total reserves minus gold<br>Rés. totale, moins l'or | 248.0 | 265.0 | 260.7 | 301.1 | 398.9 | 372.9 | 415.4 | 545.4 | 495.0 | 660.9 |
| Foreign exchange<br>Devises étrangères | 248.0 | 265.0 | 260.7 | 301.1 | 398.9 | 372.9 | 415.4 | 545.4 | 495.0 | 660.9 |

| Country or area<br>Pays ou zone | 1998 | 1999 | 2000 | 2001 | 2002 | 2003 | 2004 | 2005 | 2006 | 2007 |
|---|---|---|---|---|---|---|---|---|---|---|
| **New Zealand — Nouvelle-Zélande** | | | | | | | | | | |
| Total reserves minus gold<br>Rés. totale, moins l'or | 4 203.7 | 4 455.3 | 3 952.1 | 3 564.7 | 4 962.8 | 6 085.4 | 6 947.4 | 8 892.7 | 14 068.5 | 17 247.2 |
| Foreign exchange<br>Devises étrangères | 3 846.0 | 4 025.0 | 3 618.9 | 3 161.2 | 4 481.8 | 5 413.7 | 6 438.8 | 8 693.6 | 13 916.0 | 17 124.1 |
| **Nicaragua — Nicaragua** | | | | | | | | | | |
| Total reserves minus gold<br>Rés. totale, moins l'or | 350.4 | 509.7 | 488.5 | 379.9 | 448.1 | 502.1 | 668.2 | 727.8 | 921.9 | 1 103.3 |
| Foreign exchange<br>Devises étrangères | 350.2 | 509.5 | 488.4 | 379.6 | 448.1 | 502.0 | 667.7 | 727.5 | 921.5 | 1 103.2 |
| **Niger — Niger** | | | | | | | | | | |
| Total reserves minus gold<br>Rés. totale, moins l'or | 53.1 | 39.2 | 80.4 | 107.0 | 133.9 | 260.1 | 258.0 | 249.5 | 370.9 | 593.0 |
| Foreign exchange<br>Devises étrangères | 40.8 | 26.1 | 69.2 | 95.9 | 121.6 | 244.7 | 243.7 | 236.9 | 357.8 | 579.3 |
| **Nigeria — Nigéria** | | | | | | | | | | |
| Total reserves minus gold<br>Rés. totale, moins l'or | 7 100.8 | 5 450.3 | 9 910.9 | 10 456.6 | 7 331.3 | 7 128.4 | 16 955.6 | 28 279.6 | 42 298.7 | 51 334.2 |
| Foreign exchange<br>Devises étrangères | 7 100.0 | 5 450.0 | 9 910.4 | 10 455.8 | 7 331.0 | 7 128.0 | 16 955.0 | 28 279.0 | 42 298.1 | 51 333.1 |
| **Norway — Norvège** | | | | | | | | | | |
| Total reserves minus gold<br>Rés. totale, moins l'or | 19 048.1 | 23 807.3 | 27 597.4 | 23 277.5 | 31 999.8 | 37 220.0 | 44 307.5 | 46 985.9 | 56 841.6 | 60 839.6 |
| Foreign exchange<br>Devises étrangères | 17 368.0 | 22 545.7 | 26 706.9 | 22 197.5 | 30 692.1 | 35 890.2 | 43 078.2 | 46 377.4 | 56 181.4 | 60 294.1 |
| **Oman — Oman** | | | | | | | | | | |
| Total reserves minus gold<br>Rés. totale, moins l'or | 1 937.7 | 2 767.5 | 2 379.9 | 2 364.9 | 3 173.5 | 3 593.5 | 3 597.3 | 4 358.1 | 5 014.1 | 9 523.5 |
| Foreign exchange<br>Devises étrangères | 1 877.7 | 2 697.3 | 2 310.9 | 2 277.0 | 3 064.8 | 3 466.6 | 3 484.5 | 4 308.7 | 4 970.2 | 9 485.1 |
| **Pakistan — Pakistan** | | | | | | | | | | |
| Total reserves minus gold<br>Rés. totale, moins l'or | 1 028.0 | 1 511.4 | 1 513.4 | 3 640.0 | 8 078.3 | 10 941.0 | 9 799.0 | 10 032.8 | 11 543.1 | 14 044.0 |
| Foreign exchange<br>Devises étrangères | 1 027.0 | 1 511.0 | 1 499.0 | 3 636.0 | 8 076.0 | 10 693.0 | 9 554.0 | 9 817.0 | 11 327.6 | 13 829.0 |
| **Panama — Panama** | | | | | | | | | | |
| Total reserves minus gold<br>Rés. totale, moins l'or | 954.5 | 822.9 | 722.6 | 1 091.8 | 1 182.8 | 1 011.0 | 630.6 | 1 210.5 | 1 335.0 | 1 935.1 |
| Foreign exchange<br>Devises étrangères | 937.7 | 805.0 | 706.8 | 1 075.5 | 1 165.7 | 992.5 | 611.4 | 1 192.5 | 1 315.9 | 1 915.4 |
| **Papua New Guinea — Papouasie-Nvl-Guinée** | | | | | | | | | | |
| Total reserves minus gold<br>Rés. totale, moins l'or | 192.9 | 205.1 | 286.9 | 422.6 | 321.5 | 494.2 | 632.6 | 718.1 | 1 400.7 | ... |
| Foreign exchange<br>Devises étrangères | 192.8 | 204.3 | 274.5 | 413.6 | 315.0 | 489.9 | 631.2 | 717.4 | 1 400.0 | ... |
| **Paraguay — Paraguay** | | | | | | | | | | |
| Total reserves minus gold<br>Rés. totale, moins l'or | 864.7 | 978.1 | 762.8 | 713.5 | 629.2 | 968.9 | 1 168.1 | 1 297.1 | 1 701.7 | 2 463.0 |
| Foreign exchange<br>Devises étrangères | 732.9 | 845.9 | 632.6 | 584.3 | 486.8 | 811.2 | 1 001.1 | 1 140.3 | 1 531.5 | 2 385.5 |
| **Peru — Pérou** | | | | | | | | | | |
| Total reserves minus gold<br>Rés. totale, moins l'or | 9 565.5 | 8 730.5 | 8 374.0 | 8 671.9 | 9 339.1 | 9 776.8 | 12 176.4 | 13 599.4 | 16 733.3 | 26 856.5 |
| Foreign exchange<br>Devises étrangères | 9 563.4 | 8 730.1 | 8 372.5 | 8 670.1 | 9 338.3 | 9 776.4 | 12 176.1 | 13 598.9 | 16 732.4 | 26 852.7 |
| **Philippines — Philippines** | | | | | | | | | | |
| Total reserves minus gold<br>Rés. totale, moins l'or | 9 274.2 | 13 269.7 | 13 090.2 | 13 476.3 | 13 329.3 | 13 654.9 | 13 116.3 | 15 926.0 | 20 025.4 | 30 210.6 |
| Foreign exchange<br>Devises étrangères | 9 149.6 | 13 143.2 | 12 974.8 | 13 352.7 | 13 200.5 | 13 523.3 | 12 979.5 | 15 800.1 | 19 891.4 | 30 071.4 |

**64** International reserves minus gold — Millions of US dollars, end of period (*continued*)
Réserves internationales, moins l'or — Millions de dollars E.-U., fin de période (*suite*)

| Country or area<br>Pays ou zone | 1998 | 1999 | 2000 | 2001 | 2002 | 2003 | 2004 | 2005 | 2006 | 2007 |
|---|---|---|---|---|---|---|---|---|---|---|
| **Poland — Pologne** | | | | | | | | | | |
| Total reserves minus gold<br>Rés. totale, moins l'or | 27 325.2 | 26 354.7 | 26 562.0 | 25 648.4 | 28 649.7 | 32 579.1 | 35 323.9 | 40 863.7 | 46 371.1 | 62 966.8 |
| Foreign exchange<br>Devises étrangères | 27 209.5 | 26 107.1 | 26 319.9 | 25 161.6 | 27 959.2 | 31 724.9 | 34 552.8 | 40 486.9 | 46 107.0 | 62 720.3 |
| **Portugal — Portugal** | | | | | | | | | | |
| Total reserves minus gold<br>Rés. totale, moins l'or | 15 824.6 | #8 427.1 | 8 908.7 | 9 666.6 | 11 179.1 | 5 875.9 | 5 174.1 | 3 478.7 | 2 063.6 | 1 257.8 |
| Foreign exchange<br>Devises étrangères | 15 067.0 | #8 005.7 | 8 539.2 | 9 228.2 | 10 655.8 | 5 248.8 | 4 631.2 | 3 173.4 | 1 835.3 | 1 044.4 |
| **Qatar — Qatar** | | | | | | | | | | |
| Total reserves minus gold<br>Rés. totale, moins l'or | 1 043.4 | 1 304.2 | 1 158.0 | 1 312.7 | 1 566.8 | 2 944.2 | 3 395.9 | 4 542.4 | 5 382.7 | 9 452.7 |
| Foreign exchange<br>Devises étrangères | 970.8 | 1 228.2 | 1 079.1 | 1 190.8 | 1 404.2 | 2 758.1 | 3 225.4 | 4 456.5 | 5 307.1 | 9 381.3 |
| **Romania — Roumanie** | | | | | | | | | | |
| Total reserves minus gold<br>Rés. totale, moins l'or | 2 867.4 | 1 526.3 | 2 469.7 | 3 922.5 | 6 125.3 | 8 040.0 | 14 616.4 | 19 872.1 | 28 066.2 | 37 194.6 |
| Foreign exchange<br>Devises étrangères | 2 866.2 | 1 516.2 | 2 468.7 | 3 915.7 | 6 123.0 | 8 039.7 | 14 615.8 | 19 871.5 | 28 065.9 | 37 194.1 |
| **Russian Federation — Fédération de Russie** | | | | | | | | | | |
| Total reserves minus gold<br>Rés. totale, moins l'or | 7 801.4 | 8 457.2 | 24 264.3 | 32 542.4 | 44 053.6 | 73 174.9 | 120 809.0 | 175 891.0 | 295 568.0 | 464 379.0 |
| Foreign exchange<br>Devises étrangères | 7 800.0 | 8 455.4 | 24 262.6 | 32 538.1 | 44 050.8 | 73 172.1 | 120 805.0 | 175 690.0 | 295 277.0 | 464 004.0 |
| **Rwanda — Rwanda** | | | | | | | | | | |
| Total reserves minus gold<br>Rés. totale, moins l'or | 168.8 | 174.2 | 190.6 | 212.1 | 243.7 | 214.7 | 314.6 | 405.8 | 439.7 | ... |
| Foreign exchange<br>Devises étrangères | 144.3 | 159.7 | 189.5 | 199.8 | 233.6 | 184.9 | 284.4 | 379.8 | 416.8 | ... |
| **Saint Kitts and Nevis — Saint-Kitts-et-Nevis** | | | | | | | | | | |
| Total reserves minus gold<br>Rés. totale, moins l'or | 46.8 | 49.6 | 45.2 | 56.4 | 65.8 | 64.8 | 78.5 | 71.6 | 88.7 | 95.8 |
| Foreign exchange<br>Devises étrangères | 46.8 | 49.5 | 45.1 | 56.3 | 65.6 | 64.7 | 78.3 | 71.5 | 88.6 | 95.7 |
| **Saint Lucia — Sainte-Lucie** | | | | | | | | | | |
| Total reserves minus gold<br>Rés. totale, moins l'or | 70.6 | 74.5 | 78.8 | 88.9 | 93.9 | 106.9 | 132.5 | 116.4 | 134.5 | 153.7 |
| Foreign exchange<br>Devises étrangères | 68.5 | 72.5 | 77.0 | 87.1 | 91.9 | 104.7 | 130.2 | 114.2 | 132.2 | 151.2 |
| **St. Vincent-Grenadines — St. Vincent-Grenadines** | | | | | | | | | | |
| Total reserves minus gold<br>Rés. totale, moins l'or | 38.8 | 42.6 | 55.2 | 61.4 | 53.2 | 51.2 | 75.0 | 69.5 | 78.7 | 87.0 |
| Foreign exchange<br>Devises étrangères | 38.0 | 41.8 | 54.5 | 60.8 | 52.5 | 50.4 | 74.2 | 68.8 | 77.9 | 86.2 |
| **Samoa — Samoa** | | | | | | | | | | |
| Total reserves minus gold<br>Rés. totale, moins l'or | 61.4 | 68.2 | 63.7 | 56.6 | 62.5 | 83.9 | 95.5 | 92.2 | 91.1 | 111.7 |
| Foreign exchange<br>Devises étrangères | 57.4 | 64.2 | 59.8 | 52.8 | 58.3 | 79.3 | 90.7 | 87.7 | 86.3 | 106.5 |
| **San Marino — Saint-Marin** | | | | | | | | | | |
| Total reserves minus gold<br>Rés. totale, moins l'or | 170.7 | 144.1 | 135.2 | 133.5 | 183.4 | 252.7 | 355.6 | 354.0 | 479.1 | ... |
| Foreign exchange<br>Devises étrangères | 166.8 | 138.4 | 129.6 | 127.9 | 177.3 | 245.9 | 348.3 | 347.2 | 471.8 | ... |
| **Sao Tome and Principe — Sao Tomé-et-Principe** | | | | | | | | | | |
| Total reserves minus gold<br>Rés. totale, moins l'or | 9.7 | 10.9 | 11.6 | 15.5 | 17.4 | 25.5 | 19.5 | 26.7 | 34.2 | ... |
| Foreign exchange<br>Devises étrangères | 9.7 | 10.9 | 11.6 | 15.5 | 17.3 | 25.4 | 19.5 | 26.7 | 34.1 | ... |

| Country or area / Pays ou zone | 1998 | 1999 | 2000 | 2001 | 2002 | 2003 | 2004 | 2005 | 2006 | 2007 |
|---|---|---|---|---|---|---|---|---|---|---|
| **Saudi Arabia — Arabie saoudite** | | | | | | | | | | |
| Total reserves minus gold Rés. totale, moins l'or | 14 220.2 | 16 996.9 | 19 585.5 | 17 595.7 | 20 610.4 | 22 620.0 | 27 290.9 | 26 530.0 | 27 522.9 | 33 760.2 |
| Foreign exchange Devises étrangères | 12 714.0 | 15 490.0 | 18 036.0 | 14 796.0 | 16 715.0 | 17 662.0 | 23 273.0 | 24 074.0 | 25 971.0 | 32 308.0 |
| **Senegal — Sénégal** | | | | | | | | | | |
| Total reserves minus gold Rés. totale, moins l'or | 430.8 | 403.0 | 384.0 | 447.3 | 637.4 | 1 110.9 | 1 386.4 | 1 191.0 | 1 334.3 | 1 660.0 |
| Foreign exchange Devises étrangères | 428.4 | 398.6 | 381.2 | 438.0 | 626.3 | 1 098.2 | 1 376.7 | 1 187.4 | 1 331.8 | 1 657.3 |
| **Serbia — Serbie** | | | | | | | | | | |
| Total reserves minus gold Rés. totale, moins l'or | ... | 154.4 | 391.5 | 1 004.7 | 2 166.0 | 3 410.8 | 4 095.9 | 5 627.9 | 11 647.7 | 13 892.6 |
| Foreign exchange Devises étrangères | ... | 154.4 | 371.7 | 996.1 | 2 165.0 | 3 410.4 | 4 095.8 | 5 597.7 | 11 638.9 | 13 891.8 |
| **Seychelles — Seychelles** | | | | | | | | | | |
| Total reserves minus gold Rés. totale, moins l'or | 21.6 | 30.3 | 43.8 | 37.1 | 69.8 | 67.4 | 34.6 | 56.2 | 112.9 | 40.8 |
| Foreign exchange Devises étrangères | 21.6 | 30.3 | 43.7 | 37.1 | 69.8 | 67.4 | 34.6 | 56.2 | 112.9 | 40.7 |
| **Sierra Leone — Sierra Leone** | | | | | | | | | | |
| Total reserves minus gold Rés. totale, moins l'or | 43.9 | 39.5 | 49.2 | 51.3 | 84.7 | 66.6 | 125.1 | 170.5 | 183.9 | 216.6 |
| Foreign exchange Devises étrangères | 33.5 | 18.6 | 43.9 | 50.9 | 60.6 | 32.1 | 74.1 | 137.7 | 154.7 | 185.8 |
| **Singapore — Singapour** | | | | | | | | | | |
| Total reserves minus gold Rés. totale, moins l'or | 75 077.2 | 77 047.1 | 80 170.3 | 75 677.0 | 82 221.2 | 96 245.5 | 112 579.0 | 116 172.0 | 136 259.0 | 162 957.0 |
| Foreign exchange Devises étrangères | 74 566.7 | 76 508.2 | 79 723.4 | 75 152.9 | 81 566.6 | 95 474.4 | 111 845.0 | 115 712.0 | 135 813.0 | 162 517.0 |
| **Slovakia — Slovaquie** | | | | | | | | | | |
| Total reserves minus gold Rés. totale, moins l'or | 2 868.8 | 3 370.7 | 4 022.3 | 4 141.0 | 8 808.7 | 11 678.1 | 14 417.5 | 14 900.7 | 12 646.6 | 18 032.1 |
| Foreign exchange Devises étrangères | 2 867.1 | 3 369.9 | 4 021.8 | 4 140.3 | 8 807.5 | 11 676.8 | 14 416.1 | 14 899.4 | 12 645.2 | 18 025.8 |
| **Slovenia — Slovénie** | | | | | | | | | | |
| Total reserves minus gold Rés. totale, moins l'or | 3 638.5 | 3 168.0 | 3 196.0 | 4 330.0 | 6 980.2 | 8 496.9 | 8 793.4 | 8 076.4 | 7 036.1 | #979.8 |
| Foreign exchange Devises étrangères | 3 572.9 | 3 058.8 | 3 110.0 | 4 244.3 | 6 852.6 | 8 343.1 | 8 662.3 | 8 013.1 | 6 987.1 | #942.0 |
| **Solomon Islands — Iles Salomon** | | | | | | | | | | |
| Total reserves minus gold Rés. totale, moins l'or | 49.0 | 51.1 | 32.0 | 19.3 | 18.2 | 37.2 | 80.6 | 95.4 | 104.4 | 119.1 |
| Foreign exchange Devises étrangères | 48.3 | 50.4 | 31.3 | 18.7 | 17.5 | 36.4 | 79.7 | 94.6 | 103.6 | 118.2 |
| **South Africa — Afrique du Sud** | | | | | | | | | | |
| Total reserves minus gold Rés. totale, moins l'or | 4 356.9 | 6 353.1 | 6 082.8 | 6 045.3 | 5 904.2 | 6 495.5 | 13 141.3 | 18 579.1 | 23 056.9 | 29 588.6 |
| Foreign exchange Devises étrangères | 4 171.3 | 6 065.3 | 5 792.7 | 5 765.1 | 5 600.8 | 6 163.7 | 12 794.3 | 18 259.6 | 22 720.1 | 29 234.2 |
| **Spain — Espagne** | | | | | | | | | | |
| Total reserves minus gold Rés. totale, moins l'or | 55 258.0 | #33 115.0 | 30 988.9 | 29 582.3 | 34 535.7 | 19 788.4 | 12 388.8 | 9 677.6 | 10 822.2 | 11 480.2 |
| Foreign exchange Devises étrangères | 52 490.0 | 31 329.5 | 29 516.4 | 27 905.5 | 32 590.4 | 17 512.8 | 10 481.4 | 8 594.1 | 10 088.2 | 10 792.0 |
| **Sri Lanka — Sri Lanka** | | | | | | | | | | |
| Total reserves minus gold Rés. totale, moins l'or | 1 979.8 | 1 635.6 | 1 039.0 | 1 286.8 | 1 631.0 | 2 264.9 | 2 132.1 | 2 650.9 | 2 836.7 | ... |
| Foreign exchange Devises étrangères | 1 950.0 | 1 569.1 | 976.4 | 1 225.9 | 1 563.6 | 2 193.2 | 2 057.6 | 2 581.0 | 2 762.0 | ... |

**64** International reserves minus gold — Millions of US dollars, end of period *(continued)*
Réserves internationales, moins l'or — Millions de dollars E.-U., fin de période *(suite)*

| Country or area / Pays ou zone | 1998 | 1999 | 2000 | 2001 | 2002 | 2003 | 2004 | 2005 | 2006 | 2007 |
|---|---|---|---|---|---|---|---|---|---|---|
| **Sudan — Soudan** | | | | | | | | | | |
| Total reserves minus gold / Rés. totale, moins l'or | 90.6 | 188.7 | #137.8 | 49.7 | 248.9 | 529.4 | 1 338.0 | 1 868.6 | 1 659.9 | 1 377.9 |
| Foreign exchange / Devises étrangères | 90.6 | 188.7 | #137.8 | 49.7 | 248.8 | 529.1 | 1 338.0 | 1 868.5 | 1 659.9 | 1 377.9 |
| **Suriname — Suriname** | | | | | | | | | | |
| Total reserves minus gold / Rés. totale, moins l'or | 106.1 | 38.5 | 63.0 | 119.3 | 106.2 | 105.8 | 129.4 | 125.8 | 215.4 | 400.9 |
| Foreign exchange / Devises étrangères | 94.5 | 27.3 | 52.7 | 109.6 | 95.9 | 94.7 | 118.0 | 115.5 | 204.9 | 390.4 |
| **Swaziland — Swaziland** | | | | | | | | | | |
| Total reserves minus gold / Rés. totale, moins l'or | 358.6 | 375.9 | 351.8 | 271.8 | 275.8 | 277.5 | 323.6 | 243.9 | 372.5 | 762.7 |
| Foreign exchange / Devises étrangères | 346.0 | 363.6 | 340.1 | 260.5 | 263.6 | 264.1 | 309.5 | 231.0 | 358.9 | 748.3 |
| **Sweden — Suède** | | | | | | | | | | |
| Total reserves minus gold / Rés. totale, moins l'or | 14 098.2 | 15 019.0 | 14 862.6 | 13 976.9 | 17 127.4 | 19 681.1 | 22 157.7 | 22 090.1 | 24 777.8 | 27 044.4 |
| Foreign exchange / Devises étrangères | 12 419.5 | 13 522.0 | 13 757.0 | 12 740.0 | 15 520.0 | 18 015.0 | 20 640.0 | 21 382.0 | 24 074.0 | 26 382.0 |
| **Switzerland — Suisse** | | | | | | | | | | |
| Total reserves minus gold / Rés. totale, moins l'or | 41 190.7 | 36 321.0 | 32 272.1 | 32 005.6 | 40 154.7 | 47 652.5 | 55 496.6 | 36 297.3 | 38 093.7 | 44 474.2 |
| Foreign exchange / Devises étrangères | 38 346.0 | 34 176.0 | 30 854.0 | 30 141.0 | 38 164.0 | 45 560.0 | 53 634.0 | 35 421.0 | 37 364.0 | 43 867.0 |
| **Tajikistan — Tadjikistan** | | | | | | | | | | |
| Total reserves minus gold / Rés. totale, moins l'or | 53.6 | 55.2 | 92.9 | 92.6 | 89.5 | 111.9 | 157.5 | 168.2 | 175.1 | ... |
| Foreign exchange / Devises étrangères | 50.7 | 55.1 | 85.0 | 87.7 | 87.7 | 111.0 | 156.2 | 162.8 | 171.6 | ... |
| **Thailand — Thaïlande** | | | | | | | | | | |
| Total reserves minus gold / Rés. totale, moins l'or | 28 825.1 | 34 062.8 | 32 015.9 | 32 354.8 | 38 046.4 | 41 076.9 | 48 664.0 | 50 690.7 | 65 291.4 | 85 221.3 |
| Foreign exchange / Devises étrangères | 28 433.8 | 33 804.7 | 31 933.2 | 32 349.5 | 38 042.2 | 40 965.1 | 48 497.5 | 50 502.0 | 65 147.1 | 85 110.1 |
| **TFYR of Macedonia — L'ex-R.y. Macédoine** | | | | | | | | | | |
| Total reserves minus gold / Rés. totale, moins l'or | 306.1 | 429.9 | 429.4 | 745.2 | 722.0 | 897.7 | 905.0 | 1 228.5 | 1 750.6 | 2 082.3 |
| Foreign exchange / Devises étrangères | 305.0 | 428.7 | 428.7 | 742.9 | 715.9 | 897.4 | 904.2 | 1 227.7 | 1 747.6 | 2 080.8 |
| **Timo-Leste — Timor-Leste** | | | | | | | | | | |
| Total reserves minus gold / Rés. totale, moins l'or | ... | ... | ... | ... | 43.5 | 61.3 | 182.4 | 153.3 | 83.8 | 230.3 |
| Foreign exchange / Devises étrangères | ... | ... | ... | ... | 43.5 | 61.3 | 182.4 | 153.3 | 83.8 | 230.3 |
| **Togo — Togo** | | | | | | | | | | |
| Total reserves minus gold / Rés. totale, moins l'or | 117.7 | 122.1 | 152.3 | 126.4 | 205.1 | 204.9 | 359.7 | 194.6 | 374.5 | 438.1 |
| Foreign exchange / Devises étrangères | 117.3 | 121.5 | 151.9 | 125.8 | 204.4 | 204.2 | 359.2 | 194.1 | 373.9 | 437.5 |
| **Tonga — Tonga** | | | | | | | | | | |
| Total reserves minus gold / Rés. totale, moins l'or | 28.7 | 24.5 | 24.6 | 23.8 | 25.1 | 39.8 | 55.3 | 46.9 | 48.0 | 65.2 |
| Foreign exchange / Devises étrangères | 26.7 | 22.1 | 22.3 | 21.4 | 22.5 | 36.9 | 52.2 | 44.0 | 44.9 | 61.9 |
| **Trinidad and Tobago — Trinité-et-Tobago** | | | | | | | | | | |
| Total reserves minus gold / Rés. totale, moins l'or | 783.1 | 945.4 | 1 386.3 | 1 907.1 | 2 027.7 | 2 451.1 | 3 168.2 | 4 856.4 | 6 569.5 | ... |
| Foreign exchange / Devises étrangères | 783.0 | 945.4 | 1 386.2 | 1 876.0 | 1 923.5 | 2 257.8 | 2 993.0 | 4 781.4 | 6 514.7 | ... |

| Country or area<br>Pays ou zone | 1998 | 1999 | 2000 | 2001 | 2002 | 2003 | 2004 | 2005 | 2006 | 2007 |
|---|---|---|---|---|---|---|---|---|---|---|
| **Tunisia — Tunisie** | | | | | | | | | | |
| Total reserves minus gold<br>Rés. totale, moins l'or | 1 850.1 | 2 261.5 | 1 811.1 | 1 989.2 | 2 290.3 | 2 945.4 | 3 935.7 | 4 436.7 | 6 773.2 | 7 850.8 |
| Foreign exchange<br>Devises étrangères | 1 847.1 | 2 207.3 | 1 780.9 | 1 962.2 | 2 260.2 | 2 912.9 | 3 895.0 | 4 405.6 | 6 741.4 | 7 816.8 |
| **Turkey — Turquie** | | | | | | | | | | |
| Total reserves minus gold<br>Rés. totale, moins l'or | 19 488.8 | 23 345.9 | 22 488.4 | 18 879.2 | 27 068.6 | 33 991.0 | 35 669.1 | 50 579.0 | 60 891.9 | 73 383.9 |
| Foreign exchange<br>Devises étrangères | 19 442.0 | 23 191.0 | 22 313.0 | 18 733.0 | 26 884.0 | 33 793.0 | 35 480.0 | 50 402.0 | 60 710.0 | 73 155.8 |
| **Uganda1 — Ouganda1** | | | | | | | | | | |
| Total reserves minus gold<br>Rés. totale, moins l'or | 725.4 | 763.1 | 808.0 | 983.4 | 934.0 | 1 080.3 | 1 308.1 | 1 344.2 | 1 810.9 | ... |
| Foreign exchange<br>Devises étrangères | 720.4 | 760.8 | 804.5 | 981.5 | 931.1 | 1 075.5 | 1 307.4 | 1 343.1 | 1 810.8 | ... |
| **Ukraine — Ukraine** | | | | | | | | | | |
| Total reserves minus gold<br>Rés. totale, moins l'or | 761.3 | 1 046.4 | 1 352.7 | 2 955.3 | 4 205.3 | 6 683.2 | 9 490.7 | 18 988.0 | 21 844.6 | 31 786.0 |
| Foreign exchange<br>Devises étrangères | 578.9 | 980.7 | 1 103.6 | 2 704.3 | 4 177.0 | 6 662.0 | 9 489.5 | 18 987.0 | 21 843.2 | 31 783.2 |
| **United Arab Emirates — Emirats arabes unis** | | | | | | | | | | |
| Total reserves minus gold<br>Rés. totale, moins l'or | 9 077.1 | 10 675.1 | 13 522.7 | 14 146.4 | 15 219.4 | 15 087.8 | 18 529.9 | 21 010.3 | 27 617.4 | ... |
| Foreign exchange<br>Devises étrangères | 8 664.4 | 10 377.1 | 13 303.9 | 13 918.2 | 14 897.2 | 14 731.5 | 18 209.0 | 20 867.7 | 27 511.9 | ... |
| **United Kingdom — Royaume-Uni** | | | | | | | | | | |
| Total reserves minus gold<br>Rés. totale, moins l'or | 32 211.6 | #33 297.4 | 38 773.6 | 34 188.7 | 37 549.9 | 35 348.5 | 39 942.3 | 38 467.2 | 40 697.8 | 48 958.1 |
| Foreign exchange<br>Devises étrangères | 27 363.0 | #27 504.7 | 34 163.4 | 28 843.1 | 30 979.8 | 28 645.4 | 34 081.7 | 35 853.9 | 38 888.6 | 47 497.8 |
| **United Rep. of Tanzania — Rép.-Unie de Tanzanie** | | | | | | | | | | |
| Total reserves minus gold<br>Rés. totale, moins l'or | 599.2 | 775.5 | 974.2 | 1 156.6 | 1 528.8 | 2 038.4 | 2 295.7 | 2 048.8 | 2 259.4 | 2 886.4 |
| Foreign exchange<br>Devises étrangères | 584.8 | 761.5 | 961.1 | 1 143.6 | 1 515.2 | 2 023.1 | 2 280.1 | 2 033.8 | 2 244.2 | 2 870.4 |
| **United States — Etats-Unis** | | | | | | | | | | |
| Total reserves minus gold<br>Rés. totale, moins l'or | 70 714.9 | 60 499.6 | 56 600.4 | 57 633.7 | 67 962.3 | 74 894.1 | 75 890.0 | 54 083.8 | 54 853.9 | 59 524.3 |
| Foreign exchange<br>Devises étrangères | 36 000.9 | 32 182.1 | 31 238.3 | 28 981.0 | 33 818.0 | 39 721.8 | 42 718.3 | 37 838.1 | 40 943.5 | 45 803.8 |
| **Uruguay — Uruguay** | | | | | | | | | | |
| Total reserves minus gold<br>Rés. totale, moins l'or | 2 073.2 | 2 081.2 | 2 478.9 | 3 097.1 | 769.1 | 2 083.2 | 2 508.5 | 3 074.1 | 3 085.3 | 4 104.7 |
| Foreign exchange<br>Devises étrangères | 2 050.8 | 2 031.3 | 2 431.9 | 3 050.4 | 763.5 | 2 079.4 | 2 507.3 | 3 067.8 | 3 084.2 | 4 104.3 |
| **Vanuatu — Vanuatu** | | | | | | | | | | |
| Total reserves minus gold<br>Rés. totale, moins l'or | 44.7 | 41.4 | 38.9 | 37.7 | 36.5 | 43.8 | 61.8 | 67.2 | 104.7 | 119.6 |
| Foreign exchange<br>Devises étrangères | 40.4 | 37.1 | 34.8 | 33.5 | 32.0 | 38.8 | 56.5 | 62.2 | 99.3 | 113.8 |
| **Venezuela (Bolivarian Republic of) — Venezuela** | | | | | | | | | | |
| Total reserves minus gold<br>Rés. totale, moins l'or | 11 919.9 | 12 277.3 | 13 088.5 | 9 239.5 | 8 487.1 | 16 034.7 | 18 375.4 | 23 918.8 | 29 417.3 | 24 196.1 |
| Foreign exchange<br>Devises étrangères | 11 612.0 | 11 708.0 | 12 633.0 | 8 825.0 | 8 038.0 | 15 546.0 | 17 867.0 | 23 454.0 | 28 933.0 | 23 686.0 |
| **Viet Nam — Viet Nam** | | | | | | | | | | |
| Total reserves minus gold<br>Rés. totale, moins l'or | 2 002.3 | 3 326.2 | 3 416.5 | 3 674.6 | 4 121.1 | 6 224.2 | 7 041.5 | 9 050.6 | 13 384.1 | ... |
| Foreign exchange<br>Devises étrangères | 1 999.7 | 3 324.7 | 3 416.2 | 3 660.0 | 4 121.0 | 6 222.0 | 7 041.0 | 9 049.7 | 13 382.5 | ... |

| Country or area<br>Pays ou zone | 1998 | 1999 | 2000 | 2001 | 2002 | 2003 | 2004 | 2005 | 2006 | 2007 |
|---|---|---|---|---|---|---|---|---|---|---|
| **Yemen — Yémen** | | | | | | | | | | |
| Total reserves minus gold<br>Rés. totale, moins l'or | 995.5 | 1 471.5 | 2 900.3 | 3 658.1 | 4 410.5 | 4 987.0 | 5 664.8 | 6 115.4 | 7 511.5 | 7 715.4 |
| Foreign exchange<br>Devises étrangères | 810.3 | 1 295.1 | 2 815.6 | 3 639.6 | 4 365.6 | 4 982.0 | 5 613.5 | 6 096.6 | 7 504.4 | 7 715.4 |
| **Zambia — Zambie** | | | | | | | | | | |
| Total reserves minus gold<br>Rés. totale, moins l'or | 69.4 | 45.4 | 244.8 | 183.4 | 535.1 | 247.7 | 337.1 | 559.8 | 719.7 | 1 090.0 |
| Foreign exchange<br>Devises étrangères | 68.6 | 45.3 | 222.5 | 116.5 | 464.8 | 247.2 | 312.2 | 544.0 | 706.4 | 1 080.2 |
| **Zimbabwe — Zimbabwe** | | | | | | | | | | |
| Total reserves minus gold<br>Rés. totale, moins l'or | 130.8 | 268.0 | 193.1 | 64.7 | 83.4 | ... | ... | ... | ... | ... |
| Foreign exchange<br>Devises étrangères | 130.1 | 266.5 | 192.5 | 64.3 | 82.9 | ... | ... | ... | ... | ... |

## Source

International Monetary Fund (IMF), Washington, D.C., "International Financial Statistics," April 2008 and the IMF database.

## Notes

1 For statistical purposes, the data for China do not include those for the Hong Kong Special Administrative Region (Hong Kong SAR) and Macao Special Administrative Region (Macao SAR).

## Source

Fonds monétaire international (FMI), Washington, D.C.,"Statistiques Financières Internationales," avril 2008 et la base de données du FMI.

## Notes

1 Pour la présentation des statistiques, les données pour la Chine ne comprennent pas la Région Administrative Spéciale de Hong Kong (Hong Kong RAS) et la Région Administrative Spéciale de Macao (Macao RAS).

# 65

## Total external and public/publicly guaranteed long-term debt of developing countries
Millions of US dollars
### A.   Total external debt&

## Total de la dette extérieure et dette publique extérieure à long terme garantie par l'Etat des pays en développement
Millions de dollars des E.-U.
### A.   Total de la dette extérieure&

| Developing economies | 2000 | 2001 | 2002 | 2003 | 2004 | 2005 | 2006 | Economies en développement |
|---|---|---|---|---|---|---|---|---|
| **Total long-term debt** | **1 888 478** | **1 865 139** | **1 924 032** | **2 051 333** | **2 171 445** | **2 128 222** | **2 283 848** | **Total de la dette à long terme** |
| Public and publicly guaranteed | 1 350 242 | 1 329 623 | 1 386 330 | 1 467 487 | 1 516 097 | 1 365 492 | 1 288 545 | Dette publique ou garantie par l'Etat |
| Official creditors | 779 759 | 749 954 | 777 733 | 817 699 | 832 289 | 726 527 | 648 594 | Créanciers publics |
| Multilateral | 331 612 | 337 011 | 356 544 | 379 618 | 392 267 | 379 565 | 353 275 | Multilatéraux |
| IBRD | 111 711 | 112 159 | 110 679 | 108 631 | 105 652 | 99 718 | 96 188 | BIRD |
| IDA | 86 843 | 89 220 | 100 613 | 113 973 | 124 347 | 121 471 | 98 306 | IDA |
| Bilateral | 448 147 | 412 943 | 421 189 | 438 082 | 440 022 | 346 962 | 295 319 | Bilatéraux |
| Private creditors | 570 483 | 579 669 | 608 597 | 649 787 | 683 808 | 638 965 | 639 951 | Créanciers privées |
| Bonds | 366 955 | 367 140 | 390 836 | 428 492 | 459 483 | 422 534 | 427 003 | Obligations |
| Commercial banks | 131 851 | 145 380 | 155 692 | 162 025 | 170 237 | 169 696 | 170 478 | Banques commerciales |
| Other private | 71 676 | 67 149 | 62 069 | 59 271 | 54 088 | 46 735 | 42 470 | Autres institutions privées |
| Private non-guaranteed | 538 236 | 535 516 | 537 701 | 583 846 | 655 348 | 762 729 | 995 303 | Dette privée non garantie |
| **Undisbursed debt** | **240 388** | **216 599** | **220 296** | **240 346** | **232 979** | **222 363** | **208 950** | **Dette (montants non versés)** |
| Official creditors | 184 753 | 172 594 | 177 377 | 181 738 | 185 551 | 186 377 | 173 348 | Créanciers publics |
| Private creditors | 55 635 | 44 005 | 42 919 | 58 608 | 47 427 | 35 986 | 35 603 | Créanciers privées |
| **Commitments** | **150 333** | **150 865** | **118 114** | **149 479** | **146 597** | **160 356** | **124 248** | **Engagements** |
| Official creditors | 51 393 | 66 424 | 52 672 | 52 395 | 52 002 | 64 219 | 54 175 | Créanciers publics |
| Private creditors | 98 941 | 84 441 | 65 442 | 97 083 | 94 595 | 96 137 | 70 074 | Créanciers privées |
| **Disbursements** | **248 572** | **250 628** | **246 051** | **300 638** | **390 194** | **450 811** | **562 484** | **Versements** |
| Public and publicly guaranteed | 140 147 | 126 690 | 115 049 | 135 198 | 153 938 | 146 469 | 131 886 | Dette publique ou garantie par l'Etat |
| Official creditors | 53 724 | 51 666 | 45 702 | 49 901 | 47 490 | 46 085 | 53 943 | Créanciers publics |
| Multilateral | 34 984 | 34 240 | 31 706 | 37 731 | 34 032 | 34 802 | 39 885 | Mutilatéraux |
| IBRD | 13 412 | 12 288 | 9 971 | 11 500 | 10 463 | 9 620 | 12 291 | BIRD |
| IDA | 5 219 | 6 091 | 6 768 | 6 528 | 7 699 | 7 030 | 6 593 | IDA |
| Bilateral | 18 740 | 17 425 | 13 996 | 12 169 | 13 458 | 11 283 | 14 057 | Bilatéraux |
| Private creditors | 86 423 | 75 025 | 69 347 | 85 297 | 106 448 | 100 384 | 77 943 | Créanciers privées |
| Bonds | 57 753 | 43 672 | 39 297 | 50 037 | 67 060 | 63 551 | 51 612 | Obligations |
| Commercial banks | 19 701 | 24 640 | 24 925 | 28 062 | 34 660 | 32 693 | 20 740 | Banques commerciales |
| Other private | 8 969 | 6 713 | 5 125 | 7 198 | 4 729 | 4 140 | 5 591 | Autres institutions privées |
| Private non-guaranteed | 108 425 | 123 938 | 131 002 | 165 440 | 236 256 | 304 342 | 430 598 | Dette privée non garantie |
| **Principal repayments** | **231 587** | **241 381** | **254 521** | **283 913** | **313 989** | **349 138** | **412 033** | **Remboursements du principal** |
| Public and publicly guaranteed | 120 499 | 119 208 | 122 660 | 144 073 | 136 984 | 158 644 | 193 674 | Dette publique ou garantie par l'Etat |
| Official creditors | 48 916 | 44 338 | 54 819 | 64 062 | 58 941 | 77 601 | 97 372 | Créanciers publics |
| Multilateral | 23 062 | 18 755 | 30 656 | 36 192 | 31 114 | 27 522 | 37 098 | Multilatéraux |
| IBRD | 9 758 | 9 744 | 15 928 | 17 474 | 15 216 | 12 512 | 17 546 | BIRD |
| IDA | 949 | 1 085 | 1 243 | 1 322 | 1 546 | 1 634 | 2 066 | IDA |
| Bilateral | 25 855 | 25 583 | 24 163 | 27 870 | 27 827 | 50 078 | 60 275 | Bilatéraux |
| Private creditors | 71 582 | 74 871 | 67 840 | 80 011 | 78 043 | 81 044 | 96 301 | Créanciers privées |
| Bonds | 34 854 | 34 150 | 28 214 | 38 564 | 37 480 | 45 890 | 61 950 | Obligations |
| Commercial banks | 24 328 | 27 749 | 28 125 | 30 356 | 31 993 | 26 226 | 24 885 | Banques commerciales |
| Other private | 12 400 | 12 972 | 11 502 | 11 091 | 8 569 | 8 927 | 9 466 | Autres institutions privées |
| Private non-guaranteed | 111 088 | 122 173 | 131 861 | 139 840 | 177 005 | 190 494 | 218 359 | Dette privée non garantie |

**Total external and public/publicly guaranteed long-term debt of developing countries**—Millions of US dollars (*continued*)
A. Total external debt[&]

**Total de la dette extérieure et dette publique extérieure à long terme garantie par l'Etat de pays en développement**—Millions de dollars des E.-U. (*suite*)
A. Total de la dette extérieure[&]

| Developing economies | 2000 | 2001 | 2002 | 2003 | 2004 | 2005 | 2006 | Economies en développement |
|---|---|---|---|---|---|---|---|---|
| **Net flows** | **16 986** | **9 247** | **-8 470** | **16 725** | **76 205** | **101 672** | **150 451** | **Apports nets** |
| Public and publicly guaranteed | 19 649 | 7 482 | -7 611 | -8 875 | 16 954 | -12 175 | -61 788 | Dette publique ou garantie par l'Etat |
| Official creditors | 4 808 | 7 328 | -9 117 | -14 161 | -11 452 | -31 516 | -43 429 | Créanciers publics |
| Multilateral | 11 922 | 15 486 | 1 050 | 1 539 | 2 918 | 7 280 | 2 788 | Multilatéraux |
| IBRD | 3 654 | 2 545 | -5 956 | -5 974 | -4 753 | -2 892 | -5 255 | BIRD |
| IDA | 4 271 | 5 007 | 5 525 | 5 205 | 6 154 | 5 397 | 4 526 | IDA |
| Bilateral | -7 114 | -8 158 | -10 167 | -15 701 | -14 369 | -38 796 | -46 217 | Bilatéraux |
| Private creditors | 14 840 | 154 | 1 506 | 5 286 | 28 406 | 19 340 | -18 358 | Créanciers privées |
| Bonds | 22 899 | 9 522 | 11 084 | 11 473 | 29 580 | 17 661 | -10 338 | Obligations |
| Commercial banks | -4 627 | -3 109 | -3 200 | -2 294 | 2 667 | 6 467 | -4 146 | Banques commerciales |
| Other private | -3 431 | -6 259 | -6 377 | -3 893 | -3 841 | -4 788 | -3 875 | Autres institutions privées |
| Private non-guaranteed | -2 663 | 1 765 | -860 | 25 601 | 59 251 | 113 847 | 212 239 | Dette privée non garantie |
| **Interest payments** | **98 912** | **94 787** | **82 355** | **86 996** | **84 056** | **92 891** | **99 595** | **Paiements d'intérets** |
| Public and publicly guaranteed | 66 164 | 63 399 | 56 773 | 59 987 | 57 594 | 64 589 | 59 978 | Dette publique ou garantie par l'Etat |
| Official creditors | 26 908 | 27 965 | 23 974 | 23 647 | 21 999 | 24 123 | 19 884 | Créanciers publics |
| Multilateral | 15 503 | 15 193 | 13 570 | 12 107 | 10 954 | 10 814 | 11 923 | Multilatéraux |
| IBRD | 7 652 | 7 443 | 6 366 | 5 108 | 4 121 | 4 156 | 4 938 | BIRD |
| IDA | 578 | 576 | 695 | 698 | 896 | 898 | 841 | IDA |
| Bilateral | 11 405 | 12 772 | 10 404 | 11 540 | 11 046 | 13 309 | 7 961 | Bilatéraux |
| Private creditors | 39 256 | 35 435 | 32 799 | 36 340 | 35 595 | 40 466 | 40 095 | Créanciers privées |
| Bonds | 26 185 | 23 004 | 22 535 | 25 754 | 26 486 | 31 029 | 29 125 | Obligations |
| Commercial banks | 9 334 | 9 004 | 7 858 | 8 122 | 7 061 | 7 805 | 9 373 | Banques commerciales |
| Other private | 3 737 | 3 426 | 2 407 | 2 464 | 2 048 | 1 632 | 1 596 | Autres institutions privées |
| Private non-guaranteed | 32 748 | 31 388 | 25 582 | 27 009 | 26 462 | 28 301 | 39 616 | Dette privée non garantie |
| **Net transfers** | **-118 695** | **-106 299** | **-86 224** | **-28 517** | **27 164** | **37 691** | **92 249** | **Transferts nets** |
| Public and publicly guaranteed | -46 516 | -55 917 | -64 383 | -68 862 | -40 640 | -76 764 | -121 766 | Dette publique ou garantie par l'Etat |
| Official creditors | -22 100 | -20 637 | -33 091 | -37 808 | -33 451 | -55 639 | -63 313 | Créanciers publics |
| Multilateral | -3 581 | 293 | -12 520 | -10 567 | -8 036 | -3 534 | -9 135 | Multilatéraux |
| IBRD | -3 997 | -4 898 | -12 322 | -11 082 | -8 875 | -7 048 | -10 192 | BIRD |
| IDA | 3 693 | 4 430 | 4 830 | 4 508 | 5 258 | 4 499 | 3 685 | IDA |
| Bilateral | -18 519 | -20 929 | -20 571 | -27 241 | -25 415 | -52 104 | -54 178 | Bilatéraux |
| Private creditors | -24 416 | -35 281 | -31 293 | -31 054 | -7 189 | -21 126 | -58 453 | Créanciers privées |
| Bonds | -3 286 | -13 482 | -11 451 | -14 281 | 3 094 | -13 367 | -39 463 | Obligations |
| Commercial banks | -13 961 | -12 113 | -11 058 | -10 416 | -4 395 | -1 338 | -13 519 | Banques commerciales |
| Other private | -7 169 | -9 685 | -8 784 | -6 357 | -5 889 | -6 420 | -5 471 | Autres institutions privées |
| Private non-guaranteed | -35 411 | -29 623 | -26 442 | -1 409 | 32 789 | 85 546 | 172 622 | Dette privée non garantie |
| **Total debt service** | **330 499** | **336 168** | **336 876** | **370 909** | **398 045** | **442 029** | **511 628** | **Total du service de la dette** |
| Public and publicly guaranteed | 186 663 | 182 608 | 179 432 | 204 060 | 194 578 | 223 233 | 253 652 | Dette publique ou garantie par l'Etat |
| Official creditors | 75 824 | 72 302 | 78 793 | 87 709 | 80 940 | 101 724 | 117 256 | Créanciers publics |
| Multilateral | 38 565 | 33 948 | 44 225 | 48 298 | 42 068 | 38 337 | 49 020 | Multilatéraux |
| IBRD | 17 410 | 17 187 | 22 294 | 22 582 | 19 337 | 16 668 | 22 484 | BIRD |
| IDA | 1 527 | 1 661 | 1 938 | 2 020 | 2 442 | 2 531 | 2 908 | IDA |
| Bilateral | 37 259 | 38 355 | 34 567 | 39 410 | 38 872 | 63 387 | 68 236 | Bilatéraux |
| Private creditors | 110 839 | 110 305 | 100 639 | 116 351 | 113 638 | 121 510 | 136 396 | Créanciers publics |
| Bonds | 61 039 | 57 154 | 50 748 | 64 318 | 63 966 | 76 918 | 91 075 | Obligations |
| Commercial banks | 33 662 | 36 753 | 35 982 | 38 478 | 39 054 | 34 032 | 34 259 | Banques commerciales |
| Other private | 16 138 | 16 398 | 13 909 | 13 555 | 10 618 | 10 560 | 11 063 | Autres institutions privées |
| Private non-guaranteed | 143 836 | 153 561 | 157 443 | 166 849 | 203 467 | 218 796 | 257 975 | Dette privée non garantie |

# Total external and public/publicly guaranteed long-term debt of developing countries

Millions of US dollars

**B. Public and publicly guaranteed long-term debt**

# Total de la dette extérieure et dette publique extérieure à long terme garantie par l'Etat des pays en développement

Millions de dollars E.-U.

**B. Dette publique extérieure à long terme garantie par l'Etat**

| Country or area — Pays ou zone | 1997 | 1998 | 1999 | 2000 | 2001 | 2002 | 2003 | 2004 | 2005 | 2006 |
|---|---|---|---|---|---|---|---|---|---|---|
| Albania<br>Albanie | 412.1 | 506.1 | 583.4 | 921.3 | 970.9 | 994.8 | 1 231.9 | 1 402.6 | 1 378.0 | 1 588.5 |
| Algeria<br>Algérie | 28 714.5 | 28 484.2 | 25 897.3 | 23 331.6 | 20 849.4 | 21 283.4 | 21 830.7 | 20 374.1 | 15 457.3 | 3 737.9 |
| Angola<br>Angola | 8 681.6 | 9 099.6 | 8 713.0 | 8 084.8 | 6 982.7 | 7 530.9 | 7 620.0 | 8 144.7 | 9 461.5 | 7 351.0 |
| Argentina<br>Argentine | 66 888.7 | 77 147.7 | 81 223.4 | 84 845.4 | 86 106.5 | 90 126.1 | 96 547.8 | 100 502.0 | 60 674.0 | 64 710.8 |
| Armenia<br>Arménie | 484.4 | 568.6 | 651.4 | 675.1 | 715.6 | 818.5 | 877.2 | 960.7 | 922.5 | 1 037.3 |
| Azerbaijan<br>Azerbaïdjan | 237.3 | 314.2 | 528.4 | 737.4 | 784.5 | 1 046.0 | 1 288.4 | 1 372.2 | 1 278.0 | 1 359.5 |
| Bangladesh<br>Bangladesh | 13 876.7 | 15 098.7 | 15 995.2 | 15 167.7 | 14 741.0 | 16 403.5 | 18 083.0 | 19 186.4 | 17 931.3 | 18 866.3 |
| Belarus<br>Bélarus | 681.4 | 796.4 | 709.1 | 688.9 | 664.3 | 748.6 | 710.0 | 744.4 | 788.3 | 845.8 |
| Belize<br>Belize | 266.2 | 279.8 | 337.5 | 553.2 | 645.4 | 775.6 | 945.2 | 923.2 | 972.5 | 993.5 |
| Benin<br>Bénin | 1 396.4 | 1 472.0 | 1 472.9 | 1 441.9 | 1 505.4 | 1 689.2 | 1 726.2 | 1 827.1 | 1 762.4 | 782.1 |
| Bhutan<br>Bhoutan | 117.6 | 171.0 | 181.8 | 202.2 | 265.2 | 376.9 | 481.5 | 593.3 | 636.7 | 697.3 |
| Bolivia<br>Bolivie | 4 131.4 | 4 294.1 | 4 245.3 | 4 136.5 | 3 123.9 | 3 514.5 | 4 153.7 | 4 550.8 | 4 595.6 | 3 202.7 |
| Bosnia and Herzegovina<br>Bosnie-Herzégovine | ... | ... | 2 240.1 | 1 956.5 | 1 780.3 | 2 030.8 | 2 316.4 | 2 686.3 | 2 555.8 | 2 829.6 |
| Botswana<br>Botswana | 534.7 | 524.7 | 484.5 | 437.8 | 378.9 | 472.4 | 484.6 | 488.0 | 437.6 | 384.5 |
| Brazil<br>Brésil | 87 738.2 | 98 636.6 | 92 514.5 | 96 129.7 | 96 129.0 | 99 148.4 | 99 503.3 | 96 818.2 | 93 803.2 | 82 839.0 |
| Bulgaria<br>Bulgarie | 7 736.8 | 7 972.8 | 7 777.6 | 7 671.3 | 7 386.6 | 7 479.9 | 7 676.2 | 7 413.7 | 5 075.2 | 5 001.3 |
| Burkina Faso<br>Burkina Faso | 1 143.0 | 1 287.1 | 1 359.1 | 1 225.7 | 1 312.8 | 1 406.6 | 1 595.9 | 1 900.9 | 1 917.0 | 1 022.0 |
| Burundi<br>Burundi | 1 025.6 | 1 082.1 | 1 053.1 | 1 036.0 | 985.6 | 1 104.3 | 1 251.9 | 1 326.8 | 1 229.6 | 1 290.8 |
| Cambodia<br>Cambodge | 2 192.7 | 2 261.4 | 2 292.9 | 2 328.1 | 2 392.8 | 2 587.3 | 2 868.4 | 3 079.7 | 3 154.7 | 3 317.7 |
| Cameroon<br>Cameroun | 8 832.3 | 9 199.9 | 8 574.1 | 8 326.5 | 7 917.5 | 8 387.6 | 9 380.2 | 8 604.6 | 5 924.0 | 2 077.7 |
| Cape Verde<br>Cap-Vert | 198.9 | 240.2 | 307.2 | 313.8 | 340.6 | 383.4 | 439.6 | 466.1 | 480.0 | 530.5 |
| Central African Rep.<br>Rép. centrafricaine | 801.5 | 841.0 | 826.1 | 795.7 | 756.8 | 980.0 | 900.4 | 929.5 | 870.8 | 862.8 |

# 65

**Total external and public/publicly guaranteed long-term debt of developing countries** — Millions of US dollars (*continued*)

B. Public and publicly guaranteed long term debt

**Total de la dette extérieure et dette publique extérieure à long terme garantie par l'Etat de pays en développement** — Millions de dollars E.-U. (*suite*)

B. Dette publique extérieure à long terme garantie par l'Etat

| Country or area — Pays ou zone | 1997 | 1998 | 1999 | 2000 | 2001 | 2002 | 2003 | 2004 | 2005 | 2006 |
|---|---|---|---|---|---|---|---|---|---|---|
| Chad<br>Tchad | 928.2 | 1 001.5 | 1 054.0 | 1 031.2 | 1 023.9 | 1 190.9 | 1 461.7 | 1 582.3 | 1 537.1 | 1 685.7 |
| Chile<br>Chili | 4 367.1 | 5 004.8 | 5 654.6 | 5 255.2 | 5 581.2 | 6 799.5 | 8 046.3 | 9 426.0 | 9 096.5 | 9 454.2 |
| China<br>Chine | 112 821.4 | 99 424.1 | 99 217.3 | 94 860.0 | 91 775.7 | 88 613.2 | 85 329.2 | 89 773.2 | 82 853.1 | 85 802.3 |
| Colombia<br>Colombie | 15 432.5 | 16 745.3 | 20 216.5 | 20 799.6 | 21 773.6 | 20 668.8 | 22 783.5 | 23 771.4 | 22 491.4 | 25 764.0 |
| Comoros<br>Comores | 211.0 | 219.8 | 213.9 | 206.9 | 222.2 | 244.6 | 265.4 | 273.2 | 257.3 | 259.8 |
| Congo<br>Congo | 4 270.4 | 4 237.2 | 3 920.4 | 3 744.1 | 3 617.6 | 3 960.7 | 4 412.5 | 5 609.2 | 5 161.4 | 5 327.8 |
| Costa Rica<br>Costa Rica | 2 768.7 | 3 032.5 | 3 194.8 | 3 264.0 | 3 272.8 | 3 139.1 | 3 619.5 | 3 778.8 | 3 470.0 | 3 668.7 |
| Côte d'Ivoire<br>Côte d'Ivoire | 10 427.1 | 10 799.7 | 9 699.1 | 9 063.4 | 8 602.7 | 9 110.3 | 9 700.5 | 11 091.5 | 9 973.1 | 10 830.3 |
| Croatia<br>Croatie | 4 273.8 | 4 924.8 | 5 523.2 | 6 111.3 | 6 424.5 | 7 679.3 | 10 083.3 | 11 618.0 | 9 836.6 | 10 235.0 |
| Dem. Rep. of the Congo<br>Rép. dém. du Congo | 8 628.3 | 9 214.3 | 8 262.3 | 7 880.2 | 7 586.5 | 8 845.4 | 10 161.3 | 10 125.0 | 9 411.8 | 9 847.8 |
| Djibouti<br>Djibouti | 253.0 | 263.8 | 248.4 | 237.9 | 235.7 | 296.1 | 355.5 | 382.1 | 376.9 | 426.4 |
| Dominica<br>Dominique | 94.6 | 98.1 | 99.0 | 147.8 | 193.4 | 200.4 | 206.3 | 226.4 | 233.6 | 232.8 |
| Dominican Republic<br>Rép. dominicaine | 3 461.1 | 3 482.4 | 3 584.0 | 3 311.3 | 3 790.3 | 4 029.9 | 5 427.5 | 6 156.0 | 6 451.8 | 6 570.7 |
| Ecuador<br>Equateur | 12 876.2 | 13 089.0 | 13 555.8 | 11 337.3 | 11 250.0 | 11 240.1 | 11 368.3 | 10 626.6 | 10 660.2 | 10 107.6 |
| Egypt<br>Egypte | 26 978.8 | 27 793.9 | 26 269.5 | 24 510.0 | 25 342.0 | 25 874.9 | 27 265.8 | 27 241.5 | 26 385.1 | 26 071.6 |
| El Salvador<br>El Salvador | 2 301.7 | 2 336.9 | 2 542.5 | 2 710.1 | 2 976.0 | 4 414.8 | 4 814.8 | 4 858.0 | 4 775.3 | 5 504.4 |
| Equatorial Guinea<br>Guinée équatoriale | 208.6 | 216.5 | 207.9 | 198.9 | 192.1 | 209.1 | 227.7 | 244.4 | 223.9 | 224.6 |
| Eritrea<br>Erythrée | 75.5 | 146.1 | 252.6 | 298.0 | 394.8 | 489.2 | 605.1 | 704.0 | 723.0 | 781.4 |
| Ethiopia<br>Ethiopie | 9 424.7 | 9 613.6 | 5 361.7 | 5 326.8 | 5 561.3 | 6 318.7 | 7 031.3 | 6 332.0 | 5 898.6 | 2 211.6 |
| Fiji<br>Fidji | 125.8 | 136.7 | 118.5 | 99.5 | 86.3 | 96.0 | 110.5 | 119.6 | 116.0 | 122.8 |
| Gabon<br>Gabon | 3 664.8 | 3 835.4 | 3 293.0 | 3 453.5 | 3 041.3 | 3 240.9 | 3 394.8 | 3 800.1 | 3 582.4 | 3 859.6 |
| Gambia<br>Gambie | 401.2 | 433.6 | 431.1 | 437.9 | 435.3 | 507.3 | 566.6 | 620.3 | 625.0 | 688.9 |
| Georgia<br>Géorgie | 1 173.4 | 1 284.8 | 1 292.9 | 1 257.7 | 1 294.4 | 1 431.9 | 1 551.1 | 1 580.1 | 1 481.5 | 1 457.5 |
| Ghana<br>Ghana | 4 429.2 | 5 004.0 | 5 144.2 | 4 994.4 | 5 253.5 | 5 755.7 | 6 422.5 | 5 892.6 | 5 738.6 | 1 890.7 |

**65** Total external and public/publicly guaranteed long-term debt of developing countries — Millions of US dollars (*continued*)
B.   Public and publicly guaranteed long term debt

Total de la dette extérieure et dette publique extérieure à long terme garantie par l'Etat de pays en développement — Millions de dollars E.-U. (*suite*)
B.   Dette publique extérieure à long terme garantie par l'Etat

| Country or area — Pays ou zone | 1997 | 1998 | 1999 | 2000 | 2001 | 2002 | 2003 | 2004 | 2005 | 2006 |
|---|---|---|---|---|---|---|---|---|---|---|
| Grenada<br>Grenade | 107.7 | 107.2 | 112.1 | 179.8 | 183.9 | 294.1 | 300.1 | 346.7 | 391.5 | 447.9 |
| Guatemala<br>Guatemala | 2 323.9 | 2 428.6 | 2 531.9 | 2 539.7 | 2 928.4 | 3 097.7 | 3 426.6 | 3 794.5 | 3 687.5 | 3 920.8 |
| Guinea<br>Guinée | 3 008.7 | 3 126.4 | 3 061.0 | 2 940.4 | 2 843.8 | 2 972.5 | 3 154.0 | 3 187.7 | 2 930.5 | 2 980.4 |
| Guinea-Bissau<br>Guinée-Bissau | 838.4 | 874.3 | 834.2 | 715.5 | 627.2 | 662.3 | 712.5 | 737.9 | 671.3 | 695.0 |
| Guyana<br>Guyana | 1 328.9 | 1 197.9 | 1 129.8 | 1 123.8 | 1 094.9 | 1 144.8 | 1 216.6 | 1 141.2 | 1 041.2 | 1 084.0 |
| Haiti<br>Haïti | 906.4 | 986.5 | 1 045.0 | 1 043.0 | 1 031.3 | 1 065.9 | 1 210.1 | 1 224.4 | 1 280.5 | 1 345.7 |
| Honduras<br>Honduras | 4 058.9 | 3 949.2 | 4 121.3 | 4 210.8 | 3 860.7 | 4 058.7 | 4 423.3 | 4 831.8 | 4 092.3 | 2 985.8 |
| Hungary<br>Hongrie | 15 128.7 | 15 904.3 | 16 869.3 | 14 354.5 | 12 696.5 | 13 551.3 | 16 473.4 | 21 093.4 | 21 215.9 | 28 017.0 |
| India<br>Inde | 79 398.1 | 84 611.3 | 86 410.3 | 80 050.9 | 78 818.4 | 82 256.5 | 84 640.1 | 89 004.4 | 80 285.9 | 84 477.0 |
| Indonesia<br>Indonésie | 55 968.5 | 67 416.4 | 73 790.1 | 69 519.9 | 68 503.9 | 71 145.1 | 73 722.3 | 71 669.9 | 69 643.6 | 67 272.8 |
| Iran (Islamic Rep. of)<br>Iran (Rép. islamique d') | 8 285.1 | 7 712.0 | 5 731.9 | 4 706.6 | 5 291.5 | 6 604.0 | 8 933.4 | 9 984.9 | 10 492.5 | 11 089.9 |
| Jamaica<br>Jamaïque | 2 778.9 | 2 979.8 | 2 888.3 | 3 763.9 | 4 312.7 | 4 604.7 | 4 576.2 | 5 284.5 | 5 550.5 | 6 009.8 |
| Jordan<br>Jordanie | 6 143.4 | 6 498.3 | 6 714.2 | 6 182.8 | 6 632.3 | 7 071.7 | 7 172.6 | 7 227.2 | 6 877.7 | 7 142.9 |
| Kazakhstan<br>Kazakhstan | 2 621.6 | 3 037.8 | 3 360.1 | 3 622.5 | 3 450.2 | 3 210.4 | 3 469.4 | 3 232.9 | 2 176.8 | 2 136.2 |
| Kenya<br>Kenya | 5 093.1 | 5 513.2 | 5 344.1 | 5 045.5 | 4 710.7 | 5 244.7 | 5 823.9 | 6 071.0 | 5 770.3 | 5 807.3 |
| Kyrgyzstan<br>Kirghizistan | 750.6 | 933.9 | 1 134.4 | 1 220.3 | 1 256.8 | 1 397.3 | 1 584.5 | 1 742.4 | 1 664.8 | 1 860.2 |
| Lao People's Dem. Rep.<br>Rép. dém. pop. lao | 2 246.8 | 2 373.1 | 2 471.3 | 2 452.6 | 2 455.9 | 2 620.2 | 1 894.9 | 2 036.6 | 1 970.9 | 2 190.9 |
| Latvia<br>Lettonie | 313.7 | 404.2 | 864.8 | 827.1 | 978.2 | 1 123.6 | 1 238.1 | 1 580.2 | 1 318.2 | 1 555.4 |
| Lebanon<br>Liban | 2 349.1 | 4 047.8 | 5 332.4 | 6 579.9 | 8 957.0 | 13 833.3 | 14 784.9 | 17 455.9 | 17 901.4 | 18 957.9 |
| Lesotho<br>Lesotho | 641.9 | 660.5 | 661.0 | 656.7 | 578.5 | 631.8 | 676.0 | 724.1 | 620.6 | 633.4 |
| Liberia<br>Libéria | 1 061.3 | 1 092.3 | 1 062.2 | 1 040.1 | 1 011.8 | 1 064.6 | 1 126.8 | 1 176.9 | 1 114.7 | 1 115.3 |
| Lithuania<br>Lituanie | 1 049.9 | 1 217.1 | 2 119.1 | 2 191.4 | 2 365.9 | 2 482.4 | 2 118.9 | 3 057.5 | 1 983.1 | 3 244.3 |
| Madagascar<br>Madagascar | 3 865.1 | 4 096.1 | 4 358.2 | 4 285.8 | 3 786.7 | 4 130.1 | 4 615.8 | 3 486.7 | 3 178.8 | 1 235.7 |
| Malawi<br>Malawi | 2 096.3 | 2 304.8 | 2 587.0 | 2 544.6 | 2 469.1 | 2 670.6 | 2 935.0 | 3 295.8 | 3 061.6 | 766.7 |
| Malaysia<br>Malaisie | 16 807.5 | 18 154.5 | 18 930.1 | 19 233.7 | 24 156.3 | 26 414.7 | 25 399.6 | 25 570.3 | 22 449.3 | 21 898.8 |

**65** Total external and public/publicly guaranteed long-term debt of developing countries—Millions of US dollars (*continued*)
B. Public and publicly guaranteed long term debt

Total de la dette extérieure et dette publique extérieure à long terme garantie par l'Etat de pays en développement—Millions de dollars E.-U. (*suite*)
B. Dette publique extérieure à long terme garantie par l'Etat

| Country or area — Pays ou zone | 1997 | 1998 | 1999 | 2000 | 2001 | 2002 | 2003 | 2004 | 2005 | 2006 |
|---|---|---|---|---|---|---|---|---|---|---|
| Maldives<br>Maldives | 164.3 | 183.4 | 194.1 | 184.7 | 180.7 | 223.0 | 258.5 | 313.0 | 307.0 | 359.9 |
| Mali<br>Mali | 2 701.9 | 2 833.1 | 2 813.6 | 2 671.0 | 2 642.5 | 2 517.8 | 2 910.1 | 3 135.5 | 2 898.8 | 1 411.4 |
| Mauritania<br>Mauritanie | 2 077.1 | 2 048.9 | 2 147.8 | 2 028.5 | 1 936.3 | 1 938.0 | 2 076.3 | 2 081.7 | 2 079.3 | 1 401.1 |
| Mauritius<br>Maurice | 1 151.1 | 1 124.4 | 1 135.2 | 827.8 | 761.0 | 830.6 | 921.7 | 853.8 | 723.5 | 585.5 |
| Mexico<br>Mexique | 83 302.2 | 87 044.7 | 87 910.7 | 81 488.2 | 94 230.4 | 99 517.9 | 106 659.8 | 108 507.0 | 108 481.9 | 96 304.0 |
| Moldova<br>Moldova | 795.8 | 796.5 | 719.1 | 852.8 | 792.0 | 825.8 | 848.2 | 754.3 | 699.7 | 735.1 |
| Mongolia<br>Mongolie | 533.3 | 650.0 | 841.1 | 833.4 | 823.7 | 949.0 | 1 137.5 | 1 306.6 | 1 266.7 | 1 361.0 |
| Montenegro<br>Monténégro | ... | ... | ... | ... | ... | ... | ... | ... | ... | 911.6 |
| Morocco<br>Maroc | 20 413.9 | 20 730.7 | 18 850.9 | 17 277.9 | 15 722.6 | 14 783.9 | 14 955.7 | 14 642.9 | 12 924.5 | 14 108.1 |
| Mozambique<br>Mozambique | 5 211.0 | 6 030.8 | 4 880.2 | 4 742.4 | 2 595.7 | 2 912.2 | 3 219.3 | 3 768.0 | 3 773.1 | 2 511.4 |
| Myanmar<br>Myanmar | 5 068.7 | 5 052.7 | 5 337.1 | 5 241.6 | 5 006.5 | 5 390.8 | 5 857.4 | 5 646.6 | 5 195.7 | 5 233.6 |
| Nepal<br>Népal | 2 355.4 | 2 615.5 | 2 960.8 | 2 827.2 | 2 672.8 | 2 947.8 | 3 139.3 | 3 299.9 | 3 130.1 | 3 285.2 |
| Nicaragua<br>Nicaragua | 5 364.4 | 5 635.6 | 5 778.8 | 5 492.3 | 5 437.2 | 5 573.2 | 5 893.5 | 4 125.1 | 4 113.2 | 3 424.9 |
| Niger<br>Niger | 1 308.6 | 1 440.5 | 1 454.6 | 1 462.6 | 1 412.9 | 1 598.8 | 1 883.3 | 1 789.6 | 1 778.3 | 703.2 |
| Nigeria<br>Nigéria | 22 631.2 | 23 445.0 | 22 357.7 | 30 019.9 | 29 218.1 | 28 057.1 | 31 350.2 | 32 637.3 | 20 342.2 | 3 799.8 |
| Oman<br>Oman | 2 567.1 | 2 235.0 | 2 595.8 | 2 970.0 | 2 687.5 | 2 048.7 | 1 573.3 | 1 224.0 | 847.5 | 819.4 |
| Pakistan<br>Pakistan | 23 973.4 | 26 140.2 | 28 134.7 | 27 173.2 | 26 436.2 | 28 015.7 | 30 768.5 | 30 889.2 | 29 487.4 | 32 309.2 |
| Panama<br>Panama | 5 073.2 | 5 417.4 | 5 676.3 | 5 703.8 | 6 326.8 | 6 404.7 | 6 481.5 | 7 215.0 | 7 492.0 | 7 774.2 |
| Papua New Guinea<br>Papouasie-Nvl-Guinée | 1 338.4 | 1 430.0 | 1 466.7 | 1 454.0 | 1 370.2 | 1 438.8 | 1 504.5 | 1 445.1 | 1 266.4 | 1 225.5 |
| Paraguay<br>Paraguay | 1 463.8 | 1 590.6 | 2 074.5 | 2 059.8 | 1 981.0 | 2 045.4 | 2 200.6 | 2 430.5 | 2 265.2 | 2 234.6 |
| Peru<br>Pérou | 19 215.8 | 19 309.8 | 19 491.5 | 19 236.9 | 18 898.9 | 20 410.5 | 22 530.8 | 24 199.1 | 22 225.0 | 21 825.4 |
| Philippines<br>Philippines | 26 394.8 | 29 172.9 | 34 770.6 | 33 744.5 | 29 210.2 | 32 318.6 | 36 146.7 | 36 108.4 | 35 424.1 | 36 792.5 |
| Poland<br>Pologne | 33 996.7 | 34 160.6 | 32 180.3 | 29 775.3 | 24 040.9 | 27 543.7 | 33 251.0 | 34 737.8 | 35 093.9 | 39 247.8 |
| Romania<br>Roumanie | 6 346.5 | 6 636.7 | 5 632.6 | 6 583.0 | 7 028.7 | 9 028.7 | 11 723.6 | 13 661.9 | 13 329.9 | 14 204.5 |
| Russian Federation<br>Fédération de Russie | 106 541.6 | 121 574.3 | 121 188.3 | 110 988.5 | 103 765.3 | 96 059.2 | 99 051.4 | 102 910.4 | 75 390.3 | 50 254.2 |

**Total external and public/publicly guaranteed long-term debt of developing countries**—Millions of US dollars (*continued*)

B.   Public and publicly guaranteed long term debt

**Total de la dette extérieure et dette publique extérieure à long terme garantie par l'Etat de pays en développement**—Millions de dollars E.-U. (*suite*)

B.   Dette publique extérieure à long terme garantie par l'Etat

| Country or area — Pays ou zone | 1997 | 1998 | 1999 | 2000 | 2001 | 2002 | 2003 | 2004 | 2005 | 2006 |
|---|---|---|---|---|---|---|---|---|---|---|
| Rwanda<br>Rwanda | 994.3 | 1 120.5 | 1 162.5 | 1 147.3 | 1 163.6 | 1 305.3 | 1 416.5 | 1 543.4 | 1 419.6 | 389.6 |
| Saint Kitts and Nevis<br>Saint-Kitts-et-Nevis | 112.0 | 124.4 | 133.8 | 152.7 | 214.7 | 260.9 | 314.9 | 313.5 | 293.2 | 290.7 |
| Saint Lucia<br>Sainte-Lucie | 119.9 | 133.6 | 140.9 | 167.6 | 166.0 | 210.7 | 235.0 | 256.6 | 248.9 | 256.5 |
| Saint Vincent-Grenadines<br>Saint Vincent-Grenadines | 94.2 | 109.8 | 163.2 | 164.9 | 163.8 | 174.1 | 195.2 | 223.9 | 247.4 | 242.1 |
| Samoa<br>Samoa | 148.3 | 154.3 | 156.6 | 147.3 | 143.3 | 156.8 | 177.7 | 185.7 | 177.3 | 205.9 |
| Sao Tome and Principe<br>Sao Tomé-et-Principe | 226.8 | 245.3 | 295.2 | 284.4 | 290.6 | 309.7 | 332.0 | 346.6 | 323.1 | 336.4 |
| Senegal<br>Sénégal | 3 235.4 | 3 499.4 | 3 356.9 | 3 193.9 | 3 157.9 | 3 523.1 | 3 939.7 | 3 555.7 | 3 557.3 | 1 712.3 |
| Serbia<br>Serbie | 6 108.9 | 6 461.1 | 6 194.6 | 6 177.9 | 6 177.5 | 7 814.9 | 8 475.1 | 8 519.7 | 7 972.1 | 7 685.9 |
| Seychelles<br>Seychelles | 169.3 | 199.6 | 210.8 | 219.5 | 220.6 | 283.6 | 328.5 | 344.6 | 401.1 | 299.4 |
| Sierra Leone<br>Sierra Leone | 1 023.5 | 1 093.4 | 1 066.0 | 1 005.8 | 1 120.9 | 1 260.0 | 1 417.7 | 1 509.6 | 1 420.4 | 1 323.2 |
| Slovakia<br>Slovaquie | 4 449.5 | 5 417.4 | 5 957.7 | 6 304.2 | 5 531.2 | 4 295.9 | 4 510.4 | 5 166.6 | 3 315.3 | 4 507.6 |
| Solomon Islands<br>Iles Salomon | 96.5 | 113.7 | 125.3 | 120.7 | 130.9 | 150.2 | 151.3 | 155.3 | 144.1 | 150.8 |
| Somalia<br>Somalie | 1 852.5 | 1 886.4 | 1 859.4 | 1 825.1 | 1 794.7 | 1 859.9 | 1 936.1 | 1 949.0 | 1 881.5 | 1 922.6 |
| South Africa<br>Afrique du Sud | 11 516.9 | 10 667.8 | 8 173.3 | 9 087.7 | 7 941.0 | 12 427.1 | 14 120.1 | 13 793.4 | 15 661.6 | 13 939.8 |
| Sri Lanka<br>Sri Lanka | 7 077.5 | 8 063.6 | 8 412.9 | 7 944.1 | 7 499.7 | 8 400.4 | 9 158.8 | 9 847.5 | 9 655.2 | 10 140.4 |
| Sudan<br>Soudan | 8 998.2 | 9 225.9 | 8 852.0 | 10 447.9 | 10 641.8 | 10 938.9 | 11 391.4 | 11 741.0 | 11 163.8 | 11 608.6 |
| Swaziland<br>Swaziland | 283.6 | 307.1 | 308.1 | 286.7 | 283.2 | 335.8 | 386.8 | 411.1 | 449.2 | 493.7 |
| Syrian Arab Republic<br>Rép. arabe syrienne | 16 326.4 | 16 352.6 | 16 142.4 | 15 929.8 | 15 809.2 | 15 848.7 | 15 847.6 | 15 742.4 | 5 640.2 | 5 576.5 |
| Tajikistan<br>Tadjikistan | 669.0 | 702.5 | 741.3 | 755.1 | 761.6 | 901.1 | 911.8 | 758.3 | 796.8 | 982.4 |
| Thailand<br>Thaïlande | 22 292.0 | 28 087.6 | 31 305.8 | 29 462.5 | 26 218.0 | 22 533.8 | 17 711.6 | 15 307.5 | 13 841.7 | 11 914.4 |
| TFYR of Macedonia<br>Ex-R.Y. Macédoine | 941.7 | 1 053.8 | 1 138.3 | 1 192.1 | 1 145.2 | 1 264.6 | 1 437.7 | 1 536.8 | 1 613.2 | 1 497.7 |
| Togo<br>Togo | 1 214.1 | 1 325.3 | 1 286.6 | 1 227.6 | 1 191.9 | 1 323.4 | 1 484.9 | 1 608.7 | 1 468.7 | 1 564.9 |
| Tonga<br>Tonga | 57.7 | 64.1 | 68.5 | 64.7 | 62.3 | 71.6 | 84.7 | 85.1 | 81.1 | 84.0 |
| Tunisia<br>Tunisie | 9 516.2 | 9 675.3 | 10 246.5 | 9 684.3 | 10 227.4 | 12 384.7 | 14 870.0 | 16 262.0 | 14 596.1 | 15 144.2 |
| Turkey<br>Turquie | 47 513.3 | 50 197.3 | 50 505.6 | 56 191.4 | 54 046.8 | 59 986.6 | 63 446.7 | 67 669.3 | 61 918.2 | 67 214.1 |

**65**

Total external and public/publicly guaranteed long-term debt of developing countries—Millions of US dollars (*continued*)

B.  Public and publicly guaranteed long term debt

Total de la dette extérieure et dette publique extérieure à long terme garantie par l'Etat de pays en développement—Millions de dollars E.-U. (*suite*)

B.  Dette publique extérieure à long terme garantie par l'Etat

| Country or area—Pays ou zone | 1997 | 1998 | 1999 | 2000 | 2001 | 2002 | 2003 | 2004 | 2005 | 2006 |
|---|---|---|---|---|---|---|---|---|---|---|
| Turkmenistan Turkménistan | 1 338.2 | 1 869.8 | 2 311.2 | 2 271.3 | 1 855.9 | 1 583.0 | 1 402.4 | 1 226.6 | 877.8 | 725.3 |
| Uganda Ouganda | 3 391.1 | 3 401.0 | 2 994.2 | 3 051.3 | 3 304.9 | 3 564.5 | 4 158.3 | 4 425.6 | 4 216.5 | 1 106.5 |
| Ukraine Ukraine | 7 015.2 | 8 971.9 | 9 590.4 | 8 141.8 | 8 098.5 | 8 272.1 | 8 890.9 | 10 589.5 | 10 458.4 | 9 537.8 |
| United Rep. of Tanzania Rép.-Unie de Tanzanie | 5 775.6 | 6 086.9 | 6 316.3 | 5 732.0 | 5 276.1 | 5 720.7 | 5 723.8 | 6 226.7 | 6 203.6 | 2 886.4 |
| Uruguay Uruguay | 4 549.7 | 5 108.2 | 5 079.6 | 5 512.6 | 6 030.6 | 6 683.7 | 7 468.2 | 7 813.3 | 7 867.5 | 7 210.7 |
| Uzbekistan Ouzbékistan | 2 107.6 | 2 660.7 | 3 565.2 | 3 763.5 | 3 905.4 | 4 005.5 | 4 149.0 | 4 117.4 | 3 638.5 | 3 322.2 |
| Vanuatu Vanuatu | 39.7 | 55.2 | 64.5 | 73.1 | 70.2 | 76.5 | 82.0 | 83.6 | 71.9 | 72.0 |
| Venezuela (Bolivarian Rep. of) Venezuela (Rép. bolivarienne du) | 27 053.4 | 28 034.9 | 27 653.9 | 27 432.5 | 24 915.3 | 23 063.8 | 24 155.6 | 26 140.4 | 30 942.9 | 27 180.1 |
| Viet Nam Viet Nam | 18 982.4 | 19 873.7 | 20 479.4 | 11 586.1 | 11 436.3 | 12 178.6 | 14 363.3 | 15 630.7 | 16 433.4 | 17 517.5 |
| Yemen Yémen | 3 433.8 | 5 231.8 | 5 372.3 | 4 059.2 | 4 276.8 | 4 497.4 | 4 744.5 | 4 799.3 | 4 717.1 | 4 999.6 |
| Zambia Zambie | 5 251.5 | 5 326.3 | 4 505.4 | 4 443.7 | 4 826.6 | 5 264.5 | 5 582.3 | 5 847.6 | 3 946.2 | 1 002.6 |
| Zimbabwe Zimbabwe | 3 065.6 | 3 194.6 | 2 982.3 | 2 774.1 | 2 678.8 | 3 020.7 | 3 388.1 | 3 594.4 | 3 258.1 | 3 451.7 |

Source

World Bank, Washington, D.C., "Global Development Finance 2007", volumes 1 and 2.

Notes

&  The following abbreviations have been used in the table:

  IBRD: International Bank for Reconstruction and Development
  IDA: International Development Association

Source

Banque mondiale, Washington, D.C., "Global Development Finance 2007", volumes 1 et 2.

Notes

&  Les abbréviations ci-après ont été utilisées dans le tableau :

  BIRD : Banque internationale pour la réconstruction et la développement
  IDA : Association internationale de développement

*Table 63*: Foreign exchange rates are shown in units of national currency per US dollar. The exchange rates are classified into three broad categories, reflecting both the role of the authorities in the determination of the exchange and/or the multiplicity of exchange rates in a country. The *market rate* is used to describe exchange rates determined largely by market forces; the *official rate* is an exchange rate determined by the authorities, sometimes in a flexible manner. For countries maintaining multiple exchange arrangements, the rates are labelled *principal rate, secondary rate*, and *tertiary rate*. Unless otherwise stated, the table refers to end of period and period averages of market exchange rates or official exchange rates. For further information see *International Financial Statistics* and www.imf.org.

*Table 64*: Total Reserves Minus Gold is the sum of the items Foreign Exchange, shown in this table, as well as Reserve Position in the Fund, and the U.S. dollar value of SDR holdings by monetary authorities.

Foreign Exchange includes monetary authorities' claims on non-residents in the form of foreign banknotes, bank deposits, treasury bills, short- and long-term government securities, ECUs (for periods before January 1999), and other claims usable in the event of balance of payments need.

*Table 65*: The data on external debt for developing countries were extracted from *Global Development Finance 2007*, published by the World Bank. In this table, developing countries are those in which 2004 GNI per capita was below $11,456.

The World Bank Debtor Reporting System (DRS) maintains statistics on the external debt of developing countries on a loan-by-loan basis. The estimated total external in-debtedness of developing countries is a combination of DRS data and other information obtained from creditors through the debt data collection systems of other agencies such as the Bank for International Settlements (BIS) and the Organization for Economic Co-operation and Development (OECD), supplemented by market sources and estimates made by country economists of the World Bank and desk officers of the International Monetary Fund (IMF).

Long-term external debt is defined as debt that has an original or extended maturity of more than one year and that is owed to non-residents and is repayable in foreign currency, goods, or services. Long-term debt has three components: a) public debt, which is an external obligation of a public debtor, including the national government, a political subdivision (or an agency of either), and autonomous public bodies; b) publicly guaranteed debt, which is an external obligation of a private debtor that is guaranteed for repayment by a public entity; and c) private non-guaranteed external debt, which is an

*Tableau 63:* Les taux des changes sont exprimés par le nombre d'unités de monnaie nationale pour un dollar des Etats-Unis. Les taux de change sont classés en trois catégories, qui dénotent le rôle des autorités dans l'établissement des taux de change et/ou la multiplicité des taux de change dans un pays. Par taux du marché, on entend les taux de change déterminés essentiellement par les forces du marché; le taux officiel est un taux de change établi par les autorités, parfois selon des dispositions souples. Pour les pays qui continuent à mettre en œuvre des régimes de taux de change multiples, les taux sont désignés par les appellations suivantes: "taux principal", "taux secondaire" et "taux tertiaire". Sauf indication contraire, le tableau indique des taux de fin de période et les moyennes sur la période, des taux de change du marché ou des taux de change officiels. Pour plus de renseignements, voir *Statistiques financières internationales* et www.imf.org.

*Tableau 64* : Le total des réserves, déduction faite de l'or, correspond à la somme de tous les éléments de change figurant dans ce tableau, ainsi qu'à la situation des réserves du fonds, et à la valeur en dollars des États-Unis des droits de tirage spéciaux détenus par les autorités monétaires.

Les éléments de change comprennent les créances détenues par les autorités monétaires sur des non-résidents sous forme de billets de banque étrangers, de dépôts bancaires, de bons du Trésor, d'effets publics à court et à long terme, d'unités monétaires européennes (pour les périodes antérieures à 1999) et d'autres éléments utilisables si la situation de la balance des paiements l'exige.

*Tableau 65*: Les données concernant la dette extérieure des pays en développement sont tirées de "*Global Development Finance 2007*", publié par la Banque. Les pays en développement sont dans ce tableau ceux où le RNB par habitant était en 2004 inférieur à 11 456 dollars.

Le Système de notification de la dette de la Banque mondiale sert à tenir à jour prêt par prêt les statistiques de la dette extérieure des pays en développement. Le total estimatif de la dette extérieure des pays en développement a été calculé en combinant les données du Système de notification avec d'autres informations obtenues auprès des créanciers par le biais des systèmes de collecte de données d'autres organismes, tels que la Banque des règlements internationaux (BRI) et l'Organisation de coopération et développement économiques, ou de sources du marché, et avec des estimations des économistes chargés des pays à la Banque mondiale et au Fonds monétaire international (FMI).

La dette extérieure à long terme s'entend de celle dont la maturité d'origine (ou la maturité après prorogation) est à plus d'un an, contractée auprès de non-résidents et remboursable en devises, en biens ou en services. La dette à long terme comporte trois éléments : a) la dette publique, dette (ou administration relevant de l'un ou de l'autre), et administrations

external obligation of a private debtor that is not guaranteed for repayment by a public entity. Public and publicly guaranteed long-term debt are aggregated.

All data related to public and publicly guaranteed debt are from debtors except for those on lending by some multilateral agencies, in which case the data are taken from the creditors' records. These creditors include the African Development Bank, the Asian Development Bank, the Central Bank for Economic Integration, the Inter-American Development Bank, the International Bank for Reconstruction and Development (IBRD) and the International Development Association (IDA). (The IBRD and IDA are components of the World Bank.)

The data referring to public and publicly guaranteed debt do not include data for (a) transactions with the International Monetary Fund, (b) debt repayable in local currency, (c) direct investment and (d) short term debt (that is, debt with an original maturity of less than a year).

The data referring to private non guaranteed debt also exclude the above items but include contractual obligations on loans to direct investment enterprises by foreign parent companies or their affiliates.

Data are aggregated by type of creditor. The breakdown is as follows:

### Official creditors:

(a) Loans from international organizations (multilateral loans), excluding loans from funds administered by an international organization on behalf of a single donor government. The latter are classified as loans from govern-ments;

(b) Loans from governments (bilateral loans) and from autonomous public bodies;

### Private creditors:

(a) Suppliers: Credits from manufacturers, exporters, or other suppliers of goods;

(b) Financial markets: Loans from private banks and other private financial institutions as well as publicly issued and privately placed bonds;

(c) Other: External liabilities on account of nationalized properties and unclassified debts to private creditors.

A distinction is made between the following categories of external public debt:

- Debt outstanding (including undisbursed) is the sum of disbursed and undisbursed debt and represents the total outstanding external obligations of the borrower at year end;

publiques autonomes; b) la dette garantie par une administration publique, obligation extérieure d'un débiteur privé dont le remboursement est garanti par une entité publique; c) la dette extérieure privée non garantie, obligation extérieure d'un débiteur privé dont le remboursement n'est pas garanti par une entité publique. La dette extérieure publique et la dette extérieure garantie à long terme sont agrégées.

Toutes les données concernant la dette publique et la dette garantie par une entité publique proviennent des débiteurs, sauf celles concernant les prêts consentis par certains organismes multilatéraux, pour lesquels les données proviennent des dossiers des créanciers : il s'agit notamment de la Banque africaine de développement, de la Banque asiatique de développement, de la Banque centrale d'intégration économique, de la Banque interaméricaine de développement, de la Banque internationale de reconstruction et de développement (BIRD) et de l'Association inter-nationale de développement (IDA) (la BIRD et l'IDA font partie du groupe de la Banque mondiale).

Les statistiques relatives à la dette publique ou à la dette garantie par l'Etat ne comprennent pas les données concernant: (a) les transactions avec le Fonds monétaire international; (b) la dette remboursable en monnaie nationale; (c) les investissements directs; et (d) la dette à court terme (c'est-à-dire la dette dont l'échéance initiale est inférieure à un an).

Les statistiques relatives à la dette privée non garantie ne comprennent pas non plus les éléments précités, mais comprennent les obligations contractuelles au titre des prêts consentis par des sociétés mères étrangères ou leurs filiales à des entreprises créées dans le cadre d'investissements directs.

Les données sont groupées par type de créancier, comme suit:

### Créanciers publics:

(a) Les prêts obtenus auprès d'organisations internationales (prêts multi-latéraux), à l'exclusion des prêts au titre de fonds administrés par une organisation internationale pour le compte d'un gouvernement donateur précis, qui sont classés comme prêts consentis par des gouvernements;

(b) Les prêts consentis par des gouvernements (prêts bilatéraux) et par des organisations publiques autonomes.

### Créanciers privés:

(a) Fournisseurs: Crédits consentis par des fabricants exportateurs et autres fournisseurs de biens;

(b) Marchés financiers: prêts consentis par des banques privées et autres institutions financières privées, et émissions publiques d'obligations placées auprès d'investisseurs privés;

(c) Autres créanciers: engagements vis-à-vis de l'extérieur au titre des biens nationalisés et dettes diverses à l'égard de créanciers privés.

- Debt outstanding (disbursed only) is total outstanding debt drawn by the borrower at year-end;
- Commitments are the total of loans for which contracts are signed in the year specified;
- Disbursements are drawings on outstanding loan commitments during the year specified;
- Service payments are actual repayments of principal amortization and interest payments made in foreign currencies, goods or services in the year specified;
- Net flows (or net lending) are disbursements minus principal repayments;
- Net transfers are net flows minus interest payments or disbursements minus total debt service payments.

The countries included in the table are those for which data are sufficiently reliable to provide a meaningful presentation of debt outstanding and future service payments.

On fait une distinction entre les catégories suivantes de dette publique extérieure:

- L'encours de la dette (y compris les fonds non décaissés) est la somme des fonds décaissés et non décaissés et représente le total des obligations extérieures en cours de l'emprunteur à la fin de l'année;
- L'encours de la dette (fonds décaissés seulement) est le montant total des tirages effectués par l'emprunteur sur sa dette en cours à la fin de l'année;
- Les engagements représentent le total des prêts dont les contrats ont été signés au cours de l'année considérée;
- Les décaissements sont les sommes tirées sur l'encours des prêts pendant l'année considérée;
- Les paiements au titre du service de la dette sont les remboursements effectifs du principal et les paiements d'intérêts effectués en devises, biens ou services pendant l'année considérée;
- Les flux nets (ou prêts nets) sont les décaissements moins les remboursements de principal;
- Les transferts nets désignent les flux nets moins les paiements d'intérêts, ou les décaissements moins le total des paiements au titre du service de la dette.

Les pays figurant sur ce tableau sont ceux pour lesquels les données sont suffisamment fiables pour permettre une présentation significative de l'encours de la dette et des paiements futurs au titre du service de la dette.

## 66

Disbursements of bilateral and multilateral official development assistance and official aid to individual recipients

Versements d'aide publique au développement et d'aide publique bilatérales et multilatérales aux bénéficiaires

| Country or area<br>Pays ou zone | Year<br>Année | Net disbursements (US $) — Versements nets ($E.-U.) | | | |
|---|---|---|---|---|---|
| | | Bilateral<br>(millions)<br>Bilatérale<br>(millions) | Multilateral[1]<br>(millions)<br>Multilatérale[1]<br>(millions) | Total<br>(millions)<br>Total<br>(millions) | Per capita<br>Par habitant |
| Developing Countries, total<br>Pays en développement, total | 2002 | 40 756.9 | 16 749.0 | 57 505.9 | ... |
| | 2003 | 49 735.0 | 17 451.9 | 67 186.8 | ... |
| | 2004 | 54 304.2 | 21 257.1 | 75 561.3 | ... |
| | 2005 | 82 445.3 | 21 837.8 | 104 283.1 | ... |
| | 2006 | 76 960.1 | 23 847.4 | 100 807.5 | ... |
| Afghanistan<br>Afghanistan | 2002 | 985.9 | 290.5 | 1 276.4 | 57.5 |
| | 2003 | 1 199.7 | 362.8 | 1 562.5 | 67.6 |
| | 2004 | 1 701.1 | 418.4 | 2 119.5 | 88.0 |
| | 2005 | 2 168.2 | 536.4 | 2 704.6 | 107.9 |
| | 2006 | 2 404.6 | 487.2 | 2 891.8 | 110.8 |
| Albania<br>Albanie | 2002 | 177.2 | 122.6 | 299.8 | 96.8 |
| | 2003 | 230.3 | 109.7 | 340.0 | 109.1 |
| | 2004 | 165.0 | 121.9 | 286.9 | 91.5 |
| | 2005 | 183.4 | 127.4 | 310.8 | 98.5 |
| | 2006 | 176.9 | 118.6 | 295.4 | 93.1 |
| Algeria<br>Algérie | 2002 | 122.8 | 62.9 | 185.6 | 5.9 |
| | 2003 | 168.8 | 68.2 | 237.0 | 7.4 |
| | 2004 | 234.7 | 79.7 | 314.4 | 9.7 |
| | 2005 | 289.4 | 70.4 | 359.8 | 11.0 |
| | 2006 | 204.6 | -3.5 | 201.0 | 6.0 |
| Angola<br>Angola | 2002 | 286.4 | 129.1 | 415.5 | 28.2 |
| | 2003 | 372.2 | 122.3 | 494.5 | 32.6 |
| | 2004 | 1 015.7 | 131.2 | 1 146.9 | 73.3 |
| | 2005 | 261.4 | 176.0 | 437.4 | 27.2 |
| | 2006 | -55.2 | 123.8 | 68.6 | 4.1 |
| Anguilla<br>Anguilla | 2002 | 1.8 | -1.1 | 0.7 | 62.7 |
| | 2003 | 1.8 | 2.1 | 3.9 | 332.5 |
| | 2004 | 1.4 | 1.3 | 2.7 | 223.1 |
| | 2005 | 4.3 | -0.3 | 4.0 | 327.2 |
| | 2006 | 0.3 | 4.1 | 4.4 | 355.2 |
| Antigua and Barbuda<br>Antigua-et-Barbuda | 2002 | 11.1 | 4.1 | 15.2 | 190.4 |
| | 2003 | 3.0 | 2.0 | 5.0 | 62.2 |
| | 2004 | 1.2 | 1.4 | 2.6 | 31.6 |
| | 2005 | 6.9 | 0.2 | 7.1 | 85.9 |
| | 2006 | 1.9 | 1.1 | 3.1 | 36.5 |
| Argentina<br>Argentine | 2002 | 51.9 | -1.5 | 50.4 | 1.3 |
| | 2003 | 98.2 | 2.9 | 101.1 | 2.7 |
| | 2004 | 78.5 | 13.9 | 92.4 | 2.4 |
| | 2005 | 77.8 | 20.0 | 97.8 | 2.5 |
| | 2006 | 81.0 | 33.8 | 114.8 | 2.9 |
| Armenia<br>Arménie | 2002 | 171.4 | 120.8 | 292.2 | 95.8 |
| | 2003 | 127.4 | 120.8 | 248.2 | 81.7 |
| | 2004 | 133.1 | 119.9 | 253.1 | 83.6 |
| | 2005 | 147.8 | 44.2 | 192.0 | 63.6 |
| | 2006 | 135.0 | 76.4 | 211.4 | 70.2 |
| Azerbaijan<br>Azerbaïdjan | 2002 | 232.2 | 104.9 | 337.0 | 41.0 |
| | 2003 | 158.5 | 131.7 | 290.2 | 35.1 |
| | 2004 | 92.3 | 57.5 | 149.8 | 18.0 |
| | 2005 | 108.3 | 87.0 | 195.3 | 23.4 |
| | 2006 | 95.2 | 73.5 | 168.7 | 20.1 |

| Country or area<br>Pays ou zone | Year<br>Année | Bilateral<br>(millions)<br>Bilatérale<br>(millions) | Multilateral[1]<br>(millions)<br>Multilatérale[1]<br>(millions) | Total<br>(millions)<br>Total<br>(millions) | Per capita<br>Par habitant |
|---|---|---|---|---|---|
| Bahrain<br>Bahreïn | 2002 | 1.1 | 2.6 | 3.7 | 5.5 |
| | 2003 | 1.1 | -0.1 | 1.1 | 1.5 |
| | 2004 | 1.4 | -0.8 | 0.6 | 0.9 |
| Bangladesh<br>Bangladesh | 2002 | 520.8 | 375.9 | 896.7 | 6.2 |
| | 2003 | 695.0 | 687.1 | 1 382.1 | 9.4 |
| | 2004 | 632.7 | 754.2 | 1 386.9 | 9.2 |
| | 2005 | 562.3 | 739.7 | 1 302.0 | 8.5 |
| | 2006 | 456.5 | 743.0 | 1 199.4 | 7.7 |
| Barbados<br>Barbade | 2002 | 2.8 | 0.4 | 3.2 | 11.1 |
| | 2003 | 2.4 | 17.3 | 19.7 | 68.1 |
| | 2004 | 2.6 | 26.3 | 28.8 | 99.0 |
| | 2005 | 6.0 | -8.2 | -2.2 | -7.6 |
| | 2006 | 3.1 | -3.7 | -0.6 | -2.0 |
| Belarus<br>Bélarus | 2005 | 33.8 | 9.3 | 43.0 | 4.4 |
| | 2006 | 38.2 | 22.8 | 61.0 | 6.3 |
| Belize<br>Belize | 2002 | 9.0 | 9.3 | 18.3 | 71.1 |
| | 2003 | 4.2 | 7.8 | 12.0 | 45.5 |
| | 2004 | 3.8 | 4.5 | 8.3 | 30.9 |
| | 2005 | 7.5 | 5.4 | 12.9 | 46.7 |
| | 2006 | 3.7 | 4.6 | 8.3 | 29.4 |
| Benin<br>Bénin | 2002 | 140.1 | 73.5 | 213.5 | 27.7 |
| | 2003 | 196.1 | 99.8 | 295.9 | 37.2 |
| | 2004 | 210.0 | 176.5 | 386.5 | 47.0 |
| | 2005 | 207.7 | 138.9 | 346.7 | 40.8 |
| | 2006 | 228.4 | 146.7 | 375.1 | 42.8 |
| Bhutan<br>Bhoutan | 2002 | 42.9 | 31.7 | 74.5 | 126.1 |
| | 2003 | 52.1 | 24.7 | 76.8 | 126.3 |
| | 2004 | 53.1 | 25.5 | 78.6 | 126.2 |
| | 2005 | 57.0 | 32.8 | 89.8 | 140.9 |
| | 2006 | 51.1 | 42.8 | 93.9 | 144.7 |
| Bolivia<br>Bolivie | 2002 | 482.2 | 197.1 | 679.2 | 78.4 |
| | 2003 | 552.9 | 375.5 | 928.4 | 105.1 |
| | 2004 | 557.3 | 211.6 | 768.9 | 85.3 |
| | 2005 | 437.3 | 190.1 | 627.4 | 68.3 |
| | 2006 | 569.7 | 6.3 | 576.0 | 61.6 |
| Bosnia and Herzegovina<br>Bosnie-Herzégovine | 2002 | 292.3 | 250.6 | 542.9 | 139.9 |
| | 2003 | 331.2 | 202.0 | 533.2 | 136.8 |
| | 2004 | 298.8 | 351.4 | 650.2 | 166.5 |
| | 2005 | 291.0 | 236.4 | 527.4 | 134.7 |
| | 2006 | 320.2 | 134.8 | 455.0 | 115.9 |
| Botswana<br>Botswana | 2002 | 36.7 | 2.2 | 38.9 | 21.9 |
| | 2003 | 27.4 | 2.1 | 29.5 | 16.4 |
| | 2004 | 31.8 | 16.9 | 48.7 | 26.8 |
| | 2005 | 30.0 | 19.4 | 49.4 | 26.9 |
| | 2006 | 36.3 | 30.5 | 66.7 | 35.9 |
| Brazil<br>Brésil | 2002 | 197.6 | 3.8 | 201.4 | 1.1 |
| | 2003 | 184.3 | 8.4 | 192.6 | 1.1 |
| | 2004 | 147.2 | 8.4 | 155.6 | 0.8 |
| | 2005 | 174.6 | 19.7 | 194.2 | 1.0 |
| | 2006 | 74.8 | 6.4 | 81.1 | 0.4 |

**66** Disbursements of bilateral and multilateral official development assistance and official aid to individual recipients (*continued*)
Versements d'aide publique au développement et d'aide publique bilatérales et multilatérales aux bénéficiaires (*suite*)

| Country or area / Pays ou zone | Year / Année | Net disbursements (US $) — Versements nets ($E.-U.) | | | |
|---|---|---|---|---|---|
| | | Bilateral (millions) / Bilatérale (millions) | Multilateral[1] (millions) / Multilatérale[1] (millions) | Total (millions) / Total (millions) | Per capita / Par habitant |
| Burkina Faso | 2002 | 229.9 | 196.3 | 426.2 | 33.7 |
| Burkina Faso | 2003 | 265.7 | 238.3 | 504.0 | 38.5 |
| | 2004 | 331.4 | 288.0 | 619.4 | 45.9 |
| | 2005 | 338.6 | 334.2 | 672.8 | 48.3 |
| | 2006 | 385.8 | 474.8 | 860.6 | 59.9 |
| Burundi | 2002 | 84.7 | 86.8 | 171.5 | 24.3 |
| Burundi | 2003 | 121.2 | 106.2 | 227.4 | 31.2 |
| | 2004 | 185.8 | 175.8 | 361.6 | 47.8 |
| | 2005 | 180.8 | 184.2 | 365.0 | 46.4 |
| | 2006 | 222.5 | 192.2 | 414.7 | 50.7 |
| Cambodia | 2002 | 272.8 | 188.7 | 461.4 | 34.8 |
| Cambodge | 2003 | 319.2 | 184.3 | 503.5 | 37.3 |
| | 2004 | 297.4 | 161.3 | 458.8 | 33.4 |
| | 2005 | 347.3 | 175.5 | 522.8 | 37.5 |
| | 2006 | 347.5 | 150.1 | 497.6 | 35.0 |
| Cameroon | 2002 | 436.0 | 219.8 | 655.7 | 39.4 |
| Cameroun | 2003 | 751.6 | 142.9 | 894.5 | 52.6 |
| | 2004 | 572.1 | 199.6 | 771.7 | 44.3 |
| | 2005 | 336.2 | 79.3 | 415.5 | 23.3 |
| | 2006 | 1 505.3 | 173.5 | 1 678.7 | 92.4 |
| Cape Verde | 2002 | 43.2 | 49.9 | 93.2 | 197.2 |
| Cap-Vert | 2003 | 90.2 | 53.3 | 143.5 | 296.7 |
| | 2004 | 90.8 | 51.6 | 142.4 | 287.5 |
| | 2005 | 104.2 | 55.5 | 159.7 | 315.1 |
| | 2006 | 98.7 | 37.7 | 136.4 | 263.0 |
| Central African Rep. | 2002 | 39.6 | 20.1 | 59.7 | 14.9 |
| Rép. centrafricaine | 2003 | 32.4 | 18.8 | 51.2 | 12.6 |
| | 2004 | 54.8 | 55.1 | 109.9 | 26.7 |
| | 2005 | 62.4 | 33.2 | 95.6 | 22.8 |
| | 2006 | 65.3 | 68.6 | 133.9 | 31.4 |
| Chad | 2002 | 67.0 | 159.1 | 226.2 | 24.8 |
| Tchad | 2003 | 95.5 | 151.0 | 246.5 | 26.0 |
| | 2004 | 163.1 | 163.1 | 326.2 | 33.3 |
| | 2005 | 165.6 | 212.2 | 377.8 | 37.2 |
| | 2006 | 152.5 | 127.8 | 280.3 | 26.8 |
| Chile | 2002 | -13.8 | 4.9 | -8.9 | -0.6 |
| Chili | 2003 | 61.4 | 16.6 | 78.0 | 4.9 |
| | 2004 | 25.9 | 29.7 | 55.6 | 3.4 |
| | 2005 | 75.6 | 75.0 | 150.6 | 9.2 |
| | 2006 | 64.3 | 17.8 | 82.1 | 5.0 |
| China[2] | 2002 | 1 211.5 | 227.4 | 1 438.9 | 1.1 |
| Chine[2] | 2003 | 1 139.5 | 174.7 | 1 314.2 | 1.0 |
| | 2004 | 1 584.9 | 63.0 | 1 647.8 | 1.3 |
| | 2005 | 1 692.9 | 39.2 | 1 732.1 | 1.3 |
| | 2006 | 1 173.7 | 12.0 | 1 185.6 | 0.9 |
| Colombia | 2002 | 426.1 | 12.4 | 438.5 | 10.2 |
| Colombie | 2003 | 767.1 | 32.8 | 799.8 | 18.3 |
| | 2004 | 481.7 | 36.6 | 518.3 | 11.7 |
| | 2005 | 572.6 | 51.9 | 624.6 | 13.9 |
| | 2006 | 917.1 | 69.7 | 986.8 | 21.7 |
| Comoros | 2002 | 11.0 | 16.6 | 27.6 | 37.4 |
| Comores | 2003 | 11.1 | 13.3 | 24.4 | 32.2 |
| | 2004 | 13.9 | 11.6 | 25.5 | 32.8 |
| | 2005 | 17.2 | 7.7 | 24.9 | 31.2 |
| | 2006 | 19.9 | 9.9 | 29.9 | 36.5 |

| Country or area<br>Pays ou zone | Year<br>Année | Net disbursements (US $) — Versements nets ($E.-U.) | | | |
| | | Bilateral<br>(millions)<br>Bilatérale<br>(millions) | Multilateral[1]<br>(millions)<br>Multilatérale[1]<br>(millions) | Total<br>(millions)<br>Total<br>(millions) | Per capita<br>Par habitant |
|---|---|---|---|---|---|
| Congo<br>Congo | 2002 | 41.4 | 15.4 | 56.8 | 16.9 |
| | 2003 | 33.9 | 35.0 | 68.9 | 20.0 |
| | 2004 | 47.8 | 67.6 | 115.4 | 32.7 |
| | 2005 | 1 359.5 | 84.6 | 1 444.2 | 400.1 |
| | 2006 | 169.1 | 84.4 | 253.5 | 68.7 |
| Cook Islands<br>Iles Cook | 2002 | 3.5 | 0.3 | 3.8 | 249.4 |
| | 2003 | 4.6 | 1.2 | 5.8 | 393.3 |
| | 2004 | 5.9 | 2.9 | 8.8 | 610.6 |
| | 2005 | 7.0 | 0.8 | 7.8 | 554.2 |
| | 2006 | 31.0 | 1.3 | 32.3 | 2 365.7 |
| Costa Rica<br>Costa Rica | 2002 | 4.5 | -0.2 | 4.3 | 1.0 |
| | 2003 | 31.0 | -3.7 | 27.3 | 6.5 |
| | 2004 | 11.4 | 2.6 | 14.0 | 3.3 |
| | 2005 | 25.0 | 3.9 | 28.9 | 6.7 |
| | 2006 | 20.1 | 2.7 | 22.8 | 5.2 |
| Côte d'Ivoire<br>Côte d'Ivoire | 2002 | 831.1 | 236.4 | 1 067.5 | 60.3 |
| | 2003 | 281.2 | -27.7 | 253.5 | 14.1 |
| | 2004 | 196.6 | -36.0 | 160.6 | 8.8 |
| | 2005 | 142.1 | -32.3 | 109.8 | 5.9 |
| | 2006 | 198.8 | 51.7 | 250.5 | 13.2 |
| Croatia<br>Croatie | 2002 | 82.1 | 29.8 | 111.9 | 24.8 |
| | 2003 | 80.3 | 37.9 | 118.2 | 26.1 |
| | 2004 | 87.4 | 32.7 | 120.1 | 26.4 |
| | 2005 | 63.0 | 60.8 | 123.8 | 27.2 |
| | 2006 | 68.2 | 130.5 | 198.7 | 43.6 |
| Cuba<br>Cuba | 2002 | 49.6 | 10.8 | 60.5 | 5.4 |
| | 2003 | 59.3 | 15.2 | 74.5 | 6.6 |
| | 2004 | 69.8 | 26.8 | 96.6 | 8.6 |
| | 2005 | 68.4 | 18.9 | 87.3 | 7.8 |
| | 2006 | 56.9 | 20.6 | 77.4 | 6.9 |
| Dem. Rep. of the Congo<br>Rép. dém. du Congo | 2002 | 351.0 | 823.7 | 1 174.7 | 21.9 |
| | 2003 | 5 009.5 | 406.4 | 5 415.9 | 98.2 |
| | 2004 | 1 165.0 | 658.9 | 1 823.9 | 32.0 |
| | 2005 | 1 036.6 | 792.8 | 1 829.4 | 31.1 |
| | 2006 | 1 500.4 | 556.0 | 2 056.3 | 33.9 |
| Djibouti<br>Djibouti | 2002 | 36.9 | 38.7 | 75.6 | 99.1 |
| | 2003 | 37.0 | 39.4 | 76.4 | 98.3 |
| | 2004 | 39.4 | 27.2 | 66.7 | 84.3 |
| | 2005 | 53.9 | 23.5 | 77.3 | 96.2 |
| | 2006 | 89.5 | 26.0 | 115.5 | 141.1 |
| Dominica<br>Dominique | 2002 | 14.0 | 15.9 | 29.9 | 438.1 |
| | 2003 | 3.4 | 7.5 | 10.8 | 158.9 |
| | 2004 | 10.7 | 18.3 | 29.0 | 425.7 |
| | 2005 | 4.5 | 10.5 | 15.0 | 221.4 |
| | 2006 | 1.8 | 17.3 | 19.2 | 283.3 |
| Dominican Republic<br>Rép. dominicaine | 2002 | 138.2 | 6.5 | 144.7 | 16.0 |
| | 2003 | 60.4 | 8.2 | 68.6 | 7.5 |
| | 2004 | 84.5 | -0.1 | 84.4 | 9.1 |
| | 2005 | 56.6 | 19.9 | 76.5 | 8.1 |
| | 2006 | 13.0 | 38.4 | 51.4 | 5.3 |
| Ecuador<br>Equateur | 2002 | 205.1 | 10.0 | 215.1 | 17.0 |
| | 2003 | 173.6 | 1.2 | 174.9 | 13.7 |
| | 2004 | 158.5 | -0.2 | 158.3 | 12.3 |
| | 2005 | 192.9 | 35.0 | 227.9 | 17.5 |
| | 2006 | 170.5 | 17.6 | 188.1 | 14.3 |

# 66

Disbursements of bilateral and multilateral official development assistance and official aid to individual recipients (*continued*)

Versements d'aide publique au développement et d'aide publique bilatérales et multilatérales aux bénéficiaires (*suite*)

| Country or area<br>Pays ou zone | Year<br>Année | Net disbursements (US $) — Versements nets ($E.-U.) | | | |
|---|---|---|---|---|---|
| | | Bilateral (millions)<br>Bilatérale (millions) | Multilateral[1] (millions)<br>Multilatérale[1] (millions) | Total (millions)<br>Total (millions) | Per capita<br>Par habitant |
| Egypt<br>Egypte | 2002 | 1 123.9 | 82.5 | 1 206.4 | 17.5 |
| | 2003 | 775.1 | 84.1 | 859.2 | 12.2 |
| | 2004 | 1 175.6 | 260.4 | 1 436.0 | 20.1 |
| | 2005 | 663.2 | 241.4 | 904.5 | 12.4 |
| | 2006 | 536.8 | 286.5 | 823.3 | 11.1 |
| El Salvador<br>El Salvador | 2002 | 217.9 | 14.4 | 232.3 | 36.3 |
| | 2003 | 170.4 | 21.1 | 191.4 | 29.5 |
| | 2004 | 201.7 | 14.1 | 215.9 | 32.8 |
| | 2005 | 162.6 | 34.3 | 196.9 | 29.5 |
| | 2006 | 150.6 | 6.1 | 156.7 | 23.2 |
| Equatorial Guinea<br>Guinée équatoriale | 2002 | 13.7 | 6.6 | 20.2 | 44.8 |
| | 2003 | 17.6 | 3.4 | 21.0 | 45.4 |
| | 2004 | 23.1 | 6.4 | 29.5 | 62.4 |
| | 2005 | 29.8 | 9.5 | 39.2 | 81.1 |
| | 2006 | 18.9 | 8.1 | 27.0 | 54.5 |
| Eritrea<br>Erythrée | 2002 | 120.7 | 96.5 | 217.2 | 54.3 |
| | 2003 | 185.5 | 130.7 | 316.1 | 75.7 |
| | 2004 | 177.5 | 90.6 | 268.1 | 61.6 |
| | 2005 | 226.4 | 132.3 | 358.7 | 79.2 |
| | 2006 | 63.2 | 67.4 | 130.6 | 27.8 |
| Ethiopia<br>Ethiopie | 2002 | 489.2 | 774.3 | 1 263.5 | 17.3 |
| | 2003 | 1 033.3 | 528.1 | 1 561.5 | 20.8 |
| | 2004 | 1 024.7 | 744.0 | 1 768.7 | 23.0 |
| | 2005 | 1 185.1 | 695.8 | 1 880.9 | 23.8 |
| | 2006 | 1 024.1 | 897.6 | 1 921.7 | 23.7 |
| Fiji<br>Fidji | 2002 | 31.3 | 2.5 | 33.8 | 41.5 |
| | 2003 | 42.9 | 7.9 | 50.8 | 62.1 |
| | 2004 | 36.4 | 27.1 | 63.5 | 77.2 |
| | 2005 | 38.8 | 24.8 | 63.6 | 76.8 |
| | 2006 | 39.1 | 15.7 | 54.8 | 65.7 |
| Gabon<br>Gabon | 2002 | 49.5 | 22.2 | 71.6 | 58.3 |
| | 2003 | -41.2 | 30.1 | -11.1 | -8.9 |
| | 2004 | 23.5 | 16.3 | 39.9 | 31.4 |
| | 2005 | 29.8 | 22.5 | 52.3 | 40.5 |
| | 2006 | 31.9 | -1.3 | 30.6 | 23.3 |
| Gambia<br>Gambie | 2002 | 17.5 | 40.3 | 57.9 | 39.2 |
| | 2003 | 19.7 | 40.0 | 59.6 | 39.1 |
| | 2004 | 11.6 | 43.4 | 55.0 | 35.0 |
| | 2005 | 15.1 | 46.0 | 61.1 | 37.8 |
| | 2006 | 25.1 | 43.4 | 68.5 | 41.2 |
| Georgia<br>Géorgie | 2002 | 209.6 | 92.3 | 301.9 | 65.4 |
| | 2003 | 163.9 | 53.0 | 216.9 | 47.5 |
| | 2004 | 209.1 | 95.4 | 304.5 | 67.4 |
| | 2005 | 197.2 | 102.8 | 300.0 | 67.1 |
| | 2006 | 210.4 | 137.0 | 347.4 | 78.4 |
| Ghana<br>Ghana | 2002 | 405.0 | 238.0 | 643.0 | 30.5 |
| | 2003 | 471.4 | 464.8 | 936.2 | 43.4 |
| | 2004 | 913.3 | 452.3 | 1 365.5 | 61.9 |
| | 2005 | 602.8 | 504.1 | 1 106.9 | 49.1 |
| | 2006 | 594.7 | 580.1 | 1 174.7 | 51.1 |
| Grenada<br>Grenade | 2002 | 2.2 | 9.1 | 11.3 | 110.2 |
| | 2003 | 8.3 | 3.4 | 11.7 | 112.7 |
| | 2004 | 10.5 | 5.3 | 15.8 | 151.1 |
| | 2005 | 26.0 | 24.8 | 50.8 | 482.6 |
| | 2006 | 3.4 | 23.6 | 27.0 | 255.6 |

| Country or area<br><br>Pays ou zone | Year<br><br>Année | Net disbursements (US $) — Versements nets ($E.-U.) | | | |
|---|---|---|---|---|---|
| | | Bilateral<br>(millions)<br>Bilatérale<br>(millions) | Multilateral[1]<br>(millions)<br>Multilatérale[1]<br>(millions) | Total<br>(millions)<br>Total<br>(millions) | Per capita<br><br>Par habitant |
| Guatemala | 2002 | 199.6 | 48.2 | 247.8 | 21.0 |
| Guatemala | 2003 | 216.0 | 29.3 | 245.4 | 20.3 |
| | 2004 | 203.7 | 15.5 | 219.1 | 17.7 |
| | 2005 | 219.1 | 33.3 | 252.4 | 19.9 |
| | 2006 | 445.1 | 39.6 | 484.7 | 37.2 |
| Guinea | 2002 | 125.6 | 117.0 | 242.5 | 28.5 |
| Guinée | 2003 | 134.6 | 104.6 | 239.1 | 27.6 |
| | 2004 | 178.3 | 93.5 | 271.8 | 30.8 |
| | 2005 | 128.6 | 58.6 | 187.2 | 20.8 |
| | 2006 | 102.9 | 57.7 | 160.6 | 17.5 |
| Guinea-Bissau | 2002 | 25.8 | 33.5 | 59.3 | 40.8 |
| Guinée-Bissau | 2003 | 97.6 | 47.6 | 145.2 | 96.7 |
| | 2004 | 28.6 | 48.4 | 77.0 | 49.7 |
| | 2005 | 39.4 | 39.6 | 79.0 | 49.5 |
| | 2006 | 39.4 | 42.9 | 82.3 | 50.0 |
| Guyana | 2002 | 34.0 | 30.6 | 64.6 | 87.7 |
| Guyana | 2003 | 28.7 | 57.9 | 86.5 | 117.3 |
| | 2004 | 70.3 | 63.7 | 134.0 | 181.3 |
| | 2005 | 40.1 | 98.0 | 138.0 | 186.6 |
| | 2006 | 46.6 | 126.3 | 172.9 | 233.9 |
| Haiti | 2002 | 125.4 | 29.9 | 155.4 | 17.5 |
| Haïti | 2003 | 153.2 | 59.0 | 212.2 | 23.6 |
| | 2004 | 209.1 | 50.5 | 259.5 | 28.4 |
| | 2005 | 340.9 | 160.5 | 501.4 | 53.9 |
| | 2006 | 363.3 | 218.1 | 581.4 | 61.5 |
| Honduras | 2002 | 297.9 | 172.5 | 470.4 | 73.0 |
| Honduras | 2003 | 231.4 | 155.3 | 386.7 | 58.8 |
| | 2004 | 328.4 | 316.8 | 645.2 | 96.3 |
| | 2005 | 456.4 | 223.0 | 679.4 | 99.4 |
| | 2006 | 384.7 | 204.0 | 588.7 | 84.5 |
| India | 2002 | 785.3 | 657.8 | 1 443.1 | 1.3 |
| Inde | 2003 | 384.3 | 541.7 | 926.1 | 0.8 |
| | 2004 | 14.6 | 676.2 | 690.8 | 0.6 |
| | 2005 | 850.1 | 874.6 | 1 724.7 | 1.5 |
| | 2006 | 653.1 | 723.3 | 1 376.4 | 1.2 |
| Indonesia | 2002 | 1 162.0 | 123.2 | 1 285.2 | 5.9 |
| Indonésie | 2003 | 1 580.5 | 164.9 | 1 745.4 | 7.9 |
| | 2004 | -117.4 | 226.8 | 109.4 | 0.5 |
| | 2005 | 2 242.1 | 227.5 | 2 469.6 | 10.9 |
| | 2006 | 688.4 | 657.0 | 1 345.4 | 5.9 |
| Iran (Islamic Rep. of) | 2002 | 81.5 | 31.6 | 113.1 | 1.7 |
| Iran (Rép. islamique d') | 2003 | 102.1 | 25.8 | 127.9 | 1.9 |
| | 2004 | 138.9 | 32.9 | 171.8 | 2.5 |
| | 2005 | 78.2 | 21.3 | 99.4 | 1.4 |
| | 2006 | 70.8 | -44.2 | 115.0 | 1.6 |
| Iraq | 2002 | 85.1 | 20.8 | 105.8 | 4.0 |
| Iraq | 2003 | 2 095.0 | 70.4 | 2 165.4 | 80.5 |
| | 2004 | 4 393.8 | 142.0 | 4 535.8 | 165.2 |
| | 2005 | 21 824.7 | 53.2 | 21 877.9 | 781.5 |
| | 2006 | 8 487.8 | 17.9 | 8 505.7 | 298.4 |
| Jamaica | 2002 | -3.8 | 28.3 | 24.5 | 9.3 |
| Jamaïque | 2003 | 1.1 | 2.1 | 3.1 | 1.2 |
| | 2004 | 13.3 | 67.2 | 80.6 | 30.2 |
| | 2005 | 11.5 | 24.3 | 35.8 | 13.3 |
| | 2006 | -0.6 | 37.8 | 37.2 | 13.8 |

| Country or area<br>Pays ou zone | Year<br>Année | Net disbursements (US $) — Versements nets ($E.-U.) | | | |
|---|---|---|---|---|---|
| | | Bilateral<br>(millions)<br>Bilatérale<br>(millions) | Multilateral[1]<br>(millions)<br>Multilatérale[1]<br>(millions) | Total<br>(millions)<br>Total<br>(millions) | Per capita<br>Par habitant |
| Jordan<br>Jordanie | 2002 | 370.9 | 148.5 | 519.4 | 102.7 |
| | 2003 | 1 092.2 | 134.6 | 1 226.7 | 235.6 |
| | 2004 | 433.8 | 147.2 | 581.0 | 108.2 |
| | 2005 | 440.2 | 149.4 | 589.6 | 106.4 |
| | 2006 | 361.8 | 156.5 | 518.3 | 90.5 |
| Kazakhstan<br>Kazakhstan | 2002 | 143.9 | 18.4 | 162.3 | 10.9 |
| | 2003 | 228.0 | 15.3 | 243.3 | 16.2 |
| | 2004 | 203.3 | 21.7 | 224.9 | 14.9 |
| | 2005 | 147.7 | 20.8 | 168.6 | 11.1 |
| | 2006 | 96.0 | 23.2 | 119.2 | 7.8 |
| Kenya<br>Kenya | 2002 | 288.1 | 93.0 | 381.1 | 11.6 |
| | 2003 | 320.3 | 198.9 | 519.2 | 15.4 |
| | 2004 | 470.8 | 184.5 | 655.3 | 18.9 |
| | 2005 | 510.1 | 244.3 | 754.4 | 21.2 |
| | 2006 | 761.2 | 166.4 | 927.5 | 25.4 |
| Kiribati<br>Kiribati | 2002 | 18.7 | 2.1 | 20.8 | 238.8 |
| | 2003 | 12.8 | 5.5 | 18.4 | 206.9 |
| | 2004 | 10.1 | 6.6 | 16.7 | 184.6 |
| | 2005 | 21.3 | 6.5 | 27.8 | 302.2 |
| | 2006 | -50.6 | 5.6 | -45.1 | -481.5 |
| Korea, Dem. P. R.<br>Corée, R. p. dém. de | 2002 | 187.8 | 75.5 | 263.4 | 11.3 |
| | 2003 | 77.9 | 51.7 | 129.6 | 5.5 |
| | 2004 | 102.2 | 47.5 | 149.7 | 6.4 |
| | 2005 | 39.4 | 41.5 | 80.9 | 3.4 |
| | 2006 | 28.9 | 23.3 | 52.2 | 2.2 |
| Kyrgyzstan<br>Kirghizistan | 2002 | 95.2 | 83.1 | 178.2 | 35.2 |
| | 2003 | 112.6 | 80.8 | 193.4 | 37.9 |
| | 2004 | 109.6 | 114.5 | 224.0 | 43.5 |
| | 2005 | 125.8 | 83.8 | 209.6 | 40.3 |
| | 2006 | 123.6 | 72.2 | 195.8 | 37.2 |
| Lao People's Dem. Rep.<br>Rép. dém. pop. lao | 2002 | 177.8 | 98.5 | 276.3 | 51.1 |
| | 2003 | 189.0 | 109.8 | 298.8 | 54.5 |
| | 2004 | 176.1 | 89.9 | 266.0 | 47.7 |
| | 2005 | 159.0 | 126.3 | 285.3 | 50.4 |
| | 2006 | 187.6 | 124.1 | 311.7 | 54.1 |
| Lebanon<br>Liban | 2002 | 102.4 | 77.6 | 180.0 | 46.5 |
| | 2003 | 118.8 | 111.1 | 229.9 | 58.7 |
| | 2004 | 128.5 | 138.8 | 267.3 | 67.4 |
| | 2005 | 129.8 | 117.7 | 247.5 | 61.7 |
| | 2006 | 388.6 | 284.0 | 672.6 | 165.9 |
| Lesotho<br>Lesotho | 2002 | 29.7 | 47.7 | 77.5 | 40.1 |
| | 2003 | 32.9 | 47.4 | 80.3 | 41.2 |
| | 2004 | 35.1 | 61.5 | 96.5 | 49.1 |
| | 2005 | 39.9 | 29.7 | 69.6 | 35.1 |
| | 2006 | 38.5 | 34.1 | 72.5 | 36.3 |
| Liberia<br>Libéria | 2002 | 27.0 | 24.8 | 51.8 | 15.9 |
| | 2003 | 70.3 | 36.2 | 106.5 | 32.4 |
| | 2004 | 163.0 | 49.9 | 212.9 | 63.6 |
| | 2005 | 145.0 | 87.5 | 232.5 | 67.5 |
| | 2006 | 187.4 | 80.8 | 268.2 | 74.9 |
| Libyan Arab Jamah.<br>Jamah. arabe libyenne | 2005 | 16.8 | 3.4 | 20.2 | 3.4 |
| | 2006 | 33.4 | 2.7 | 36.2 | 6.0 |

| Country or area<br>Pays ou zone | Year<br>Année | Net disbursements (US $) — Versements nets ($E.-U.) | | | |
| | | Bilateral<br>(millions)<br>Bilatérale<br>(millions) | Multilateral[1]<br>(millions)<br>Multilatérale[1]<br>(millions) | Total<br>(millions)<br>Total<br>(millions) | Per capita<br>Par habitant |
| Madagascar<br>Madagascar | 2002 | 125.9 | 244.6 | 370.5 | 21.6 |
| | 2003 | 224.9 | 314.9 | 539.9 | 30.6 |
| | 2004 | 684.6 | 564.1 | 1 248.7 | 68.9 |
| | 2005 | 500.6 | 413.7 | 914.4 | 49.0 |
| | 2006 | 265.6 | 484.8 | 750.4 | 39.2 |
| Malawi<br>Malawi | 2002 | 224.9 | 141.6 | 366.5 | 29.9 |
| | 2003 | 308.9 | 201.3 | 510.3 | 40.6 |
| | 2004 | 308.2 | 191.6 | 499.8 | 38.8 |
| | 2005 | 325.3 | 250.8 | 576.0 | 43.6 |
| | 2006 | 397.9 | 258.7 | 656.6 | 48.4 |
| Malaysia<br>Malaisie | 2002 | 85.4 | 1.8 | 87.2 | 3.6 |
| | 2003 | 103.6 | 4.4 | 108.0 | 4.4 |
| | 2004 | 293.8 | 3.2 | 297.0 | 11.8 |
| | 2005 | 17.9 | 7.0 | 24.9 | 1.0 |
| | 2006 | 230.2 | 8.9 | 239.2 | 9.2 |
| Maldives<br>Maldives | 2002 | 12.9 | 15.3 | 28.2 | 99.9 |
| | 2003 | 8.7 | 9.2 | 17.9 | 62.5 |
| | 2004 | 8.8 | 13.5 | 22.4 | 77.0 |
| | 2005 | 39.7 | 23.7 | 63.3 | 214.5 |
| | 2006 | 16.0 | 20.3 | 36.3 | 120.8 |
| Mali<br>Mali | 2002 | 256.8 | 155.4 | 412.2 | 38.9 |
| | 2003 | 271.9 | 272.4 | 544.3 | 49.8 |
| | 2004 | 327.5 | 240.8 | 568.4 | 50.5 |
| | 2005 | 377.1 | 314.8 | 691.9 | 59.6 |
| | 2006 | 398.4 | 418.2 | 816.7 | 68.2 |
| Malta<br>Malte | 2002 | 0.2 | 11.3 | 11.5 | 29.2 |
| Marshall Islands<br>Iles Marshall | 2002 | 55.4 | 7.0 | 62.4 | 1 165.5 |
| | 2003 | 51.5 | 5.0 | 56.5 | 1 036.3 |
| | 2004 | 49.5 | 1.6 | 51.1 | 919.4 |
| | 2005 | 55.8 | 0.7 | 56.5 | 996.1 |
| | 2006 | 55.0 | ^0.0 | 55.0 | 949.6 |
| Mauritania<br>Mauritanie | 2002 | 146.6 | 199.3 | 345.9 | 127.1 |
| | 2003 | 136.1 | 104.9 | 241.0 | 86.0 |
| | 2004 | 83.1 | 96.6 | 179.7 | 62.4 |
| | 2005 | 123.1 | 72.4 | 195.4 | 66.0 |
| | 2006 | 93.7 | 93.3 | 186.9 | 61.4 |
| Mauritius<br>Maurice | 2002 | 3.5 | 19.6 | 23.1 | 19.1 |
| | 2003 | -17.7 | 2.5 | -15.2 | -12.4 |
| | 2004 | 14.7 | 19.9 | 34.7 | 28.2 |
| | 2005 | 21.7 | 10.5 | 32.2 | 26.0 |
| | 2006 | 8.5 | 12.0 | 20.5 | 16.4 |
| Mayotte<br>Mayotte | 2002 | 125.2 | -0.3 | 124.9 | ... |
| | 2003 | 166.1 | ^0.0 | 166.0 | ... |
| | 2004 | 208.6 | -0.2 | 208.5 | ... |
| | 2005 | 201.9 | -0.5 | 201.3 | ... |
| | 2006 | 337.5 | 0.1 | 337.6 | ... |
| Mexico<br>Mexique | 2002 | 92.6 | 39.8 | 132.4 | 1.3 |
| | 2003 | 73.6 | 24.1 | 97.7 | 1.0 |
| | 2004 | 78.9 | 34.6 | 113.5 | 1.1 |
| | 2005 | 160.4 | 27.5 | 187.8 | 1.8 |
| | 2006 | 208.9 | 37.0 | 245.9 | 2.3 |

| Country or area<br>Pays ou zone | Year<br>Année | Net disbursements (US $) — Versements nets ($E.-U.) | | | |
| | | Bilateral<br>(millions)<br>Bilatérale<br>(millions) | Multilateral[1]<br>(millions)<br>Multilatérale[1]<br>(millions) | Total<br>(millions)<br>Total<br>(millions) | Per capita<br>Par habitant |
|---|---|---|---|---|---|
| Micronesia (Fed. States of)<br>Micronésie (Etats féd. de) | 2002 | 110.1 | 1.6 | 111.6 | 1 034.6 |
| | 2003 | 109.3 | 3.0 | 112.4 | 1 034.3 |
| | 2004 | 85.2 | 1.1 | 86.3 | 788.9 |
| | 2005 | 104.4 | 1.9 | 106.4 | 966.3 |
| | 2006 | 105.9 | 2.5 | 108.5 | 980.5 |
| Moldova<br>Moldova | 2002 | 86.3 | 50.5 | 136.9 | 33.9 |
| | 2003 | 80.4 | 32.8 | 113.2 | 28.5 |
| | 2004 | 76.6 | 37.0 | 113.6 | 28.9 |
| | 2005 | 105.7 | 77.4 | 183.1 | 47.2 |
| | 2006 | 83.5 | 131.0 | 214.5 | 56.0 |
| Mongolia<br>Mongolie | 2002 | 141.3 | 44.8 | 186.1 | 74.1 |
| | 2003 | 148.9 | 86.6 | 235.5 | 93.0 |
| | 2004 | 147.4 | 95.7 | 243.1 | 95.1 |
| | 2005 | 132.3 | 54.0 | 186.2 | 72.2 |
| | 2006 | 126.7 | 46.2 | 172.9 | 66.4 |
| Montenegro<br>Monténégro | 2006 | 60.3 | 33.8 | 94.1 | 156.5 |
| Montserrat<br>Montserrat | 2002 | 45.3 | -1.8 | 43.5 | 9 285.4 |
| | 2003 | 36.3 | 0.2 | 36.5 | 7 312.6 |
| | 2004 | 37.4 | 7.1 | 44.5 | 8 308.7 |
| | 2005 | 27.0 | 0.9 | 27.8 | 4 939.6 |
| | 2006 | 24.9 | 7.4 | 32.4 | 5 591.6 |
| Morocco<br>Maroc | 2002 | 216.6 | 135.0 | 351.6 | 11.9 |
| | 2003 | 335.7 | 157.3 | 492.9 | 16.5 |
| | 2004 | 393.5 | 243.8 | 637.3 | 21.1 |
| | 2005 | 287.5 | 315.9 | 603.4 | 19.8 |
| | 2006 | 566.7 | 362.5 | 929.2 | 30.1 |
| Mozambique<br>Mozambique | 2002 | 1 661.0 | 537.4 | 2 198.4 | 114.9 |
| | 2003 | 697.1 | 336.8 | 1 033.9 | 52.7 |
| | 2004 | 731.3 | 499.8 | 1 231.1 | 61.3 |
| | 2005 | 760.2 | 514.9 | 1 275.1 | 62.1 |
| | 2006 | 938.3 | 669.4 | 1 607.7 | 76.7 |
| Myanmar<br>Myanmar | 2002 | 79.1 | 32.6 | 111.7 | 2.4 |
| | 2003 | 83.4 | 34.9 | 118.3 | 2.5 |
| | 2004 | 81.5 | 39.3 | 120.8 | 2.5 |
| | 2005 | 77.8 | 58.7 | 136.5 | 2.8 |
| | 2006 | 92.0 | 41.4 | 133.5 | 2.8 |
| Namibia<br>Namibie | 2002 | 84.8 | 47.4 | 132.2 | 68.1 |
| | 2003 | 110.3 | 33.5 | 143.8 | 73.0 |
| | 2004 | 124.0 | 33.8 | 157.8 | 79.1 |
| | 2005 | 88.1 | 23.0 | 111.1 | 55.0 |
| | 2006 | 105.7 | 37.8 | 143.5 | 70.1 |
| Nauru<br>Nauru | 2002 | 11.6 | ... | 11.6 | 1 154.6 |
| | 2003 | 16.0 | 0.1 | 16.1 | 1 602.5 |
| | 2004 | 13.6 | 0.1 | 13.7 | 1 355.5 |
| | 2005 | 8.9 | 0.1 | 9.0 | 889.1 |
| | 2006 | 17.3 | 0.1 | 17.4 | 1 717.7 |
| Nepal<br>Népal | 2002 | 279.4 | 60.9 | 340.3 | 13.3 |
| | 2003 | 320.4 | 142.1 | 462.5 | 17.8 |
| | 2004 | 318.5 | 106.0 | 424.5 | 16.0 |
| | 2005 | 346.0 | 77.4 | 423.3 | 15.6 |
| | 2006 | 317.6 | 195.3 | 512.9 | 18.6 |

# 66

**Disbursements of bilateral and multilateral official development assistance and official aid to individual recipients** (*continued*)
**Versements d'aide publique au développement et d'aide publique bilatérales et multilatérales aux bénéficiaires** (*suite*)

| Country or area<br>Pays ou zone | Year<br>Année | Net disbursements (US $) — Versements nets ($E.-U.) | | | |
| | | Bilateral<br>(millions)<br>Bilatérale<br>(millions) | Multilateral[1]<br>(millions)<br>Multilatérale[1]<br>(millions) | Total<br>(millions)<br>Total<br>(millions) | Per capita<br>Par habitant |
|---|---|---|---|---|---|
| Nicaragua<br>Nicaragua | 2002 | 287.2 | 227.6 | 514.8 | 97.9 |
| | 2003 | 521.8 | 306.8 | 828.5 | 155.6 |
| | 2004 | 856.3 | 376.9 | 1 233.2 | 228.6 |
| | 2005 | 509.7 | 229.6 | 739.3 | 135.3 |
| | 2006 | 385.5 | 340.1 | 725.6 | 131.2 |
| Niger<br>Niger | 2002 | 114.5 | 179.5 | 294.0 | 24.6 |
| | 2003 | 244.5 | 212.2 | 456.7 | 36.9 |
| | 2004 | 305.7 | 234.9 | 540.6 | 42.2 |
| | 2005 | 254.3 | 256.4 | 510.6 | 38.5 |
| | 2006 | 235.2 | 165.9 | 401.1 | 29.2 |
| Nigeria<br>Nigéria | 2002 | 215.0 | 80.7 | 295.7 | 2.3 |
| | 2003 | 199.8 | 108.8 | 308.6 | 2.3 |
| | 2004 | 314.6 | 263.9 | 578.5 | 4.2 |
| | 2005 | 5 944.7 | 471.2 | 6 416.0 | 45.4 |
| | 2006 | 10 819.6 | 612.7 | 11 432.3 | 79.0 |
| Niue<br>Nioué | 2002 | 4.2 | 0.2 | 4.4 | 2 508.5 |
| | 2003 | 8.8 | 0.1 | 8.9 | 5 201.6 |
| | 2004 | 13.8 | 0.2 | 14.0 | 8 402.2 |
| | 2005 | 20.1 | 1.0 | 21.1 | 12 922.8 |
| | 2006 | 8.6 | 0.4 | 9.0 | 5 610.5 |
| Occupied Palestinian Terr.<br>Terr. palestinien occupé | 2002 | 410.2 | 429.3 | 839.5 | 247.8 |
| | 2003 | 490.8 | 455.4 | 946.2 | 269.6 |
| | 2004 | 605.3 | 481.4 | 1 086.7 | 298.9 |
| | 2005 | 569.7 | 525.3 | 1 095.0 | 291.1 |
| | 2006 | 754.4 | 671.6 | 1 426.0 | 366.7 |
| Oman<br>Oman | 2002 | -0.4 | 0.3 | -0.1 | ^0.0 |
| | 2003 | 10.5 | 1.1 | 11.5 | 4.7 |
| | 2004 | 2.0 | -0.3 | 1.7 | 0.7 |
| | 2005 | 3.6 | 0.6 | 4.3 | 1.7 |
| | 2006 | -14.5 | 4.7 | -9.9 | -3.9 |
| Pakistan<br>Pakistan | 2002 | 702.5 | 1 381.4 | 2 083.9 | 13.9 |
| | 2003 | 536.3 | 527.0 | 1 063.2 | 7.0 |
| | 2004 | 382.2 | 1 027.9 | 1 410.1 | 9.1 |
| | 2005 | 792.8 | 698.7 | 1 491.5 | 9.4 |
| | 2006 | 1 144.9 | 933.6 | 2 078.5 | 12.9 |
| Palau<br>Palaos | 2002 | 30.9 | 0.2 | 31.1 | 1 575.6 |
| | 2003 | 25.3 | 0.1 | 25.4 | 1 274.5 |
| | 2004 | 19.4 | 0.1 | 19.5 | 971.9 |
| | 2005 | 23.4 | 0.1 | 23.4 | 1 164.1 |
| | 2006 | 37.2 | 0.1 | 37.3 | 1 843.3 |
| Panama<br>Panama | 2002 | 23.3 | -2.2 | 21.1 | 6.9 |
| | 2003 | 31.3 | -3.0 | 28.3 | 9.1 |
| | 2004 | 25.3 | -1.6 | 23.7 | 7.5 |
| | 2005 | 17.3 | 1.6 | 18.9 | 5.9 |
| | 2006 | 19.3 | 10.6 | 29.9 | 9.1 |
| Papua New Guinea<br>Papouasie-Nvl-Guinée | 2002 | 197.1 | 5.9 | 203.0 | 35.9 |
| | 2003 | 218.8 | 2.1 | 220.9 | 38.1 |
| | 2004 | 249.7 | 19.3 | 269.1 | 45.3 |
| | 2005 | 245.3 | 21.2 | 266.5 | 43.9 |
| | 2006 | 248.3 | 26.9 | 275.2 | 44.4 |
| Paraguay<br>Paraguay | 2002 | 50.8 | 5.1 | 55.9 | 10.0 |
| | 2003 | 55.4 | -5.7 | 49.8 | 8.8 |
| | 2004 | 26.4 | -6.0 | 20.5 | 3.5 |
| | 2005 | 55.0 | -6.7 | 48.3 | 8.2 |
| | 2006 | 62.1 | -8.2 | 54.0 | 9.0 |

| Country or area / Pays ou zone | Year / Année | Net disbursements (US $) — Versements nets ($E.-U.) | | | |
|---|---|---|---|---|---|
| | | Bilateral (millions) / Bilatérale (millions) | Multilateral[1] (millions) / Multilatérale[1] (millions) | Total (millions) / Total (millions) | Per capita / Par habitant |
| Peru / Pérou | 2002 | 463.0 | 23.3 | 486.2 | 18.5 |
| | 2003 | 447.7 | 45.7 | 493.4 | 18.5 |
| | 2004 | 439.3 | 29.4 | 468.8 | 17.4 |
| | 2005 | 389.0 | 82.8 | 471.8 | 17.3 |
| | 2006 | 374.9 | 87.0 | 461.9 | 16.7 |
| Philippines / Philippines | 2002 | 509.1 | 34.4 | 543.6 | 6.8 |
| | 2003 | 675.4 | 28.2 | 703.6 | 8.7 |
| | 2004 | 413.1 | 21.7 | 434.9 | 5.2 |
| | 2005 | 524.7 | 27.4 | 552.1 | 6.5 |
| | 2006 | 519.5 | 34.1 | 553.6 | 6.4 |
| Rwanda / Rwanda | 2002 | 199.1 | 154.7 | 353.8 | 40.4 |
| | 2003 | 213.4 | 121.4 | 334.8 | 37.6 |
| | 2004 | 216.9 | 269.2 | 486.1 | 53.7 |
| | 2005 | 285.9 | 285.1 | 571.0 | 61.8 |
| | 2006 | 321.1 | 263.3 | 584.4 | 61.7 |
| Saint Helena / Sainte-Hélène | 2002 | 13.4 | 0.5 | 13.9 | 2 255.7 |
| | 2003 | 17.6 | 0.4 | 18.0 | 2 877.3 |
| | 2004 | 26.1 | 0.2 | 26.2 | 4 145.8 |
| | 2005 | 22.5 | 0.1 | 22.6 | 3 524.0 |
| | 2006 | 23.1 | 5.0 | 28.1 | 4 340.4 |
| Saint Kitts and Nevis / Saint-Kitts-et-Nevis | 2002 | 6.1 | 20.1 | 26.2 | 554.0 |
| | 2003 | -0.3 | 0.3 | ^0.0 | -0.4 |
| | 2004 | -0.2 | 0.9 | 0.8 | 16.1 |
| | 2005 | 1.6 | 1.8 | 3.4 | 69.2 |
| | 2006 | 3.6 | 3.2 | 6.8 | 136.6 |
| Saint Lucia / Sainte-Lucie | 2002 | 12.5 | 21.2 | 33.7 | 215.9 |
| | 2003 | 4.8 | 10.0 | 14.8 | 93.8 |
| | 2004 | -23.7 | 2.3 | -21.4 | -134.2 |
| | 2005 | 6.5 | 4.5 | 11.0 | 68.0 |
| | 2006 | 2.4 | 14.2 | 16.7 | 102.2 |
| Saint Vincent-Grenadines / Saint Vincent-Grenadines | 2002 | 1.1 | 4.3 | 5.3 | 45.2 |
| | 2003 | 3.7 | 2.6 | 6.3 | 53.3 |
| | 2004 | 7.3 | 3.8 | 11.1 | 93.4 |
| | 2005 | 5.7 | -0.9 | 4.8 | 40.6 |
| | 2006 | 2.3 | 3.0 | 5.3 | 44.1 |
| Samoa / Samoa | 2002 | 30.8 | 6.4 | 37.2 | 206.4 |
| | 2003 | 27.0 | 6.0 | 33.0 | 181.7 |
| | 2004 | 24.6 | 6.0 | 30.6 | 167.9 |
| | 2005 | 29.9 | 13.9 | 43.8 | 238.4 |
| | 2006 | 38.3 | 8.7 | 47.0 | 253.5 |
| Sao Tome and Principe / Sao Tomé-et-Principe | 2002 | 19.2 | 6.8 | 26.0 | 179.0 |
| | 2003 | 25.5 | 12.2 | 37.6 | 254.9 |
| | 2004 | 21.7 | 11.7 | 33.4 | 222.2 |
| | 2005 | 18.4 | 13.5 | 31.9 | 208.7 |
| | 2006 | 18.3 | 3.3 | 21.5 | 138.9 |
| Saudi Arabia / Arabie saoudite | 2002 | 13.4 | 3.0 | 16.4 | 0.8 |
| | 2003 | 9.9 | 1.7 | 11.6 | 0.5 |
| | 2004 | 8.5 | 1.7 | 10.2 | 0.4 |
| | 2005 | 13.0 | 2.0 | 15.1 | 0.6 |
| | 2006 | 11.2 | 2.8 | 13.9 | 0.6 |
| Senegal / Sénégal | 2002 | 242.8 | 191.3 | 434.0 | 39.9 |
| | 2003 | 314.4 | 135.8 | 450.2 | 40.3 |
| | 2004 | 755.5 | 283.6 | 1 039.0 | 90.6 |
| | 2005 | 445.0 | 227.2 | 672.3 | 57.1 |
| | 2006 | 509.1 | 304.0 | 813.1 | 67.4 |

| Country or area<br>Pays ou zone | Year<br>Année | Net disbursements (US $) — Versements nets ($E.-U.) | | | |
| | | Bilateral<br>(millions)<br>Bilatérale<br>(millions) | Multilateral[1]<br>(millions)<br>Multilatérale[1]<br>(millions) | Total<br>(millions)<br>Total<br>(millions) | Per capita<br>Par habitant |
|---|---|---|---|---|---|
| Serbia<br>Serbie | 2002 | 1 921.3 | 3.4 | 1 924.7 | 192.3 |
| | 2003 | 853.0 | 444.2 | 1 297.2 | 130.4 |
| | 2004 | 583.7 | 564.6 | 1 148.3 | 116.0 |
| | 2005 | 812.4 | 280.9 | 1 093.4 | 110.9 |
| | 2006 | 1 169.2 | 409.0 | 1 578.3 | 160.2 |
| Seychelles<br>Seychelles | 2002 | 3.7 | 4.2 | 7.9 | 95.0 |
| | 2003 | 4.9 | 3.2 | 8.1 | 96.6 |
| | 2004 | 6.1 | 2.9 | 9.0 | 106.6 |
| | 2005 | 7.9 | 6.9 | 14.8 | 173.0 |
| | 2006 | 7.1 | 7.5 | 14.6 | 169.6 |
| Sierra Leone<br>Sierra Leone | 2002 | 225.3 | 124.6 | 349.9 | 71.1 |
| | 2003 | 208.3 | 92.0 | 300.3 | 58.2 |
| | 2004 | 162.6 | 190.4 | 353.1 | 65.5 |
| | 2005 | 131.3 | 213.6 | 345.0 | 61.7 |
| | 2006 | 199.1 | 164.3 | 363.4 | 63.3 |
| Slovenia<br>Slovénie | 2002 | 2.4 | 50.3 | 52.7 | 26.5 |
| Solomon Islands<br>Iles Salomon | 2002 | 21.3 | 4.9 | 26.2 | 59.8 |
| | 2003 | 56.5 | 3.7 | 60.1 | 133.8 |
| | 2004 | 116.8 | 4.5 | 121.3 | 263.2 |
| | 2005 | 172.3 | 25.9 | 198.2 | 419.5 |
| | 2006 | 178.9 | 25.5 | 204.4 | 422.2 |
| Somalia<br>Somalie | 2002 | 102.4 | 44.4 | 146.8 | 19.6 |
| | 2003 | 113.6 | 60.1 | 173.7 | 22.5 |
| | 2004 | 139.7 | 60.0 | 199.7 | 25.1 |
| | 2005 | 146.1 | 90.8 | 236.9 | 28.9 |
| | 2006 | 263.1 | 125.3 | 388.5 | 46.0 |
| South Africa<br>Afrique du Sud | 2002 | 375.3 | 128.5 | 503.8 | 10.8 |
| | 2003 | 477.3 | 163.2 | 640.5 | 13.6 |
| | 2004 | 459.2 | 168.4 | 627.6 | 13.2 |
| | 2005 | 466.0 | 213.5 | 679.5 | 14.2 |
| | 2006 | 560.6 | 156.6 | 717.2 | 14.9 |
| Sri Lanka<br>Sri Lanka | 2002 | 188.5 | 135.2 | 323.6 | 17.1 |
| | 2003 | 271.0 | 388.5 | 659.4 | 34.8 |
| | 2004 | 337.2 | 162.0 | 499.1 | 26.2 |
| | 2005 | 857.3 | 284.7 | 1 142.0 | 59.7 |
| | 2006 | 485.3 | 272.8 | 758.1 | 39.5 |
| Sudan<br>Soudan | 2002 | 232.3 | 59.9 | 292.2 | 8.4 |
| | 2003 | 332.0 | 277.8 | 609.8 | 17.2 |
| | 2004 | 847.9 | 118.8 | 966.7 | 26.7 |
| | 2005 | 1 459.6 | 323.0 | 1 782.5 | 48.3 |
| | 2006 | 1 518.1 | 453.5 | 1 971.6 | 52.3 |
| Suriname<br>Suriname | 2002 | 7.7 | 3.9 | 11.6 | 26.1 |
| | 2003 | 4.0 | 6.8 | 10.9 | 24.3 |
| | 2004 | 15.8 | 8.1 | 23.9 | 53.0 |
| | 2005 | 33.5 | 10.3 | 43.9 | 97.0 |
| | 2006 | 55.6 | 8.1 | 63.7 | 139.9 |
| Swaziland<br>Swaziland | 2002 | 6.6 | 11.7 | 18.3 | 16.8 |
| | 2003 | 12.7 | 20.3 | 33.0 | 29.9 |
| | 2004 | 7.3 | 14.4 | 21.7 | 19.4 |
| | 2005 | 20.9 | 26.0 | 46.9 | 41.7 |
| | 2006 | 12.3 | 22.8 | 35.1 | 31.0 |

| Country or area<br>Pays ou zone | Year<br>Année | Net disbursements (US $) — Versements nets ($E.-U.) | | | |
|---|---|---|---|---|---|
| | | Bilateral<br>(millions)<br>Bilatérale<br>(millions) | Multilateral[1]<br>(millions)<br>Multilatérale[1]<br>(millions) | Total<br>(millions)<br>Total<br>(millions) | Per capita<br>Par habitant |
| Syrian Arab Republic<br>Rép. arabe syrienne | 2002 | 25.0 | 47.2 | 72.2 | 4.1 |
| | 2003 | 28.8 | 91.9 | 120.7 | 6.7 |
| | 2004 | 15.7 | 111.3 | 127.0 | 6.9 |
| | 2005 | 5.9 | 73.7 | 79.6 | 4.2 |
| | 2006 | -11.4 | 64.2 | 52.8 | 2.7 |
| Tajikistan<br>Tadjikistan | 2002 | 128.8 | 38.0 | 166.8 | 26.4 |
| | 2003 | 80.3 | 63.5 | 143.7 | 22.5 |
| | 2004 | 91.9 | 139.1 | 230.9 | 35.7 |
| | 2005 | 104.8 | 134.2 | 238.9 | 36.5 |
| | 2006 | 91.8 | 142.0 | 233.9 | 35.2 |
| Thailand<br>Thaïlande | 2002 | 279.6 | 17.4 | 296.9 | 4.8 |
| | 2003 | -969.3 | 24.1 | -945.2 | -15.2 |
| | 2004 | -3.6 | 48.1 | 44.5 | 0.7 |
| | 2005 | -214.2 | 40.3 | -173.9 | -2.8 |
| | 2006 | -292.7 | 74.5 | -218.3 | -3.4 |
| TFYR of Macedonia<br>L'ex-R.y. Macédoine | 2002 | 179.8 | 93.0 | 272.8 | 134.9 |
| | 2003 | 179.3 | 85.2 | 264.5 | 130.5 |
| | 2004 | 162.2 | 83.3 | 245.5 | 120.9 |
| | 2005 | 165.4 | 56.1 | 221.5 | 108.9 |
| | 2006 | 131.0 | 63.0 | 194.1 | 95.3 |
| Timor-Leste<br>Timor-Leste | 2002 | 187.0 | 30.7 | 217.7 | 243.0 |
| | 2003 | 147.4 | 27.3 | 174.7 | 183.1 |
| | 2004 | 141.3 | 20.0 | 161.2 | 159.1 |
| | 2005 | 160.1 | 24.3 | 184.4 | 172.8 |
| | 2006 | 173.7 | 35.4 | 209.1 | 187.8 |
| Togo<br>Togo | 2002 | 39.2 | 9.0 | 48.2 | 8.4 |
| | 2003 | 46.3 | 1.9 | 48.1 | 8.1 |
| | 2004 | 52.3 | 12.0 | 64.4 | 10.6 |
| | 2005 | 59.4 | 23.2 | 82.6 | 13.2 |
| | 2006 | 54.8 | 23.9 | 78.6 | 12.3 |
| Tokelau<br>Tokélaou | 2002 | 4.6 | 0.2 | 4.8 | 3 231.9 |
| | 2003 | 6.2 | 0.2 | 6.4 | 4 430.6 |
| | 2004 | 8.4 | 0.1 | 8.4 | 5 932.4 |
| | 2005 | 15.9 | 0.1 | 16.0 | 11 406.1 |
| | 2006 | 10.7 | 0.2 | 10.9 | 7 857.7 |
| Tonga<br>Tonga | 2002 | 16.7 | 5.5 | 22.2 | 225.6 |
| | 2003 | 15.0 | 10.8 | 25.8 | 261.5 |
| | 2004 | 14.9 | 4.3 | 19.2 | 193.8 |
| | 2005 | 24.7 | 7.0 | 31.7 | 319.0 |
| | 2006 | 18.6 | 2.8 | 21.4 | 214.7 |
| Trinidad and Tobago<br>Trinité-et-Tobago | 2002 | 5.7 | -14.4 | -8.7 | -6.7 |
| | 2003 | 5.1 | -8.2 | -3.1 | -2.4 |
| | 2004 | 7.2 | -9.3 | -2.0 | -1.5 |
| | 2005 | 6.1 | -8.2 | -2.1 | -1.6 |
| | 2006 | 4.0 | 8.9 | 12.9 | 9.7 |
| Tunisia<br>Tunisie | 2002 | 144.6 | 77.3 | 221.9 | 22.7 |
| | 2003 | 207.7 | 94.8 | 302.5 | 30.6 |
| | 2004 | 230.8 | 95.5 | 326.3 | 32.6 |
| | 2005 | 269.1 | 103.3 | 372.5 | 36.9 |
| | 2006 | 287.0 | 154.4 | 441.4 | 43.2 |

| Country or area<br>Pays ou zone | Year<br>Année | Net disbursements (US $) — Versements nets ($E.-U.) | | | |
| | | Bilateral (millions)<br>Bilatérale (millions) | Multilateral[1] (millions)<br>Multilatérale[1] (millions) | Total (millions)<br>Total (millions) | Per capita<br>Par habitant |
|---|---|---|---|---|---|
| Turkey<br>Turquie | 2002 | 99.0 | 161.1 | 260.1 | 3.7 |
| | 2003 | 19.5 | 145.9 | 165.4 | 2.3 |
| | 2004 | -16.5 | 308.3 | 291.8 | 4.1 |
| | 2005 | 51.1 | 410.2 | 461.3 | 6.3 |
| | 2006 | 147.2 | 401.4 | 548.6 | 7.4 |
| Turkmenistan<br>Turkménistan | 2002 | 26.0 | 5.7 | 31.7 | 6.9 |
| | 2003 | 16.7 | 6.7 | 23.4 | 5.0 |
| | 2004 | 11.4 | 7.2 | 18.5 | 3.9 |
| | 2005 | 11.9 | 5.9 | 17.7 | 3.7 |
| | 2006 | 5.4 | 6.0 | 11.4 | 2.3 |
| Turks and Caicos Islands<br>Iles Turques et Caïques | 2002 | 2.6 | 1.5 | 4.1 | 193.8 |
| | 2003 | 1.2 | 1.0 | 2.2 | 97.7 |
| | 2004 | 1.2 | 1.9 | 3.2 | 133.8 |
| | 2005 | 3.1 | 2.1 | 5.2 | 212.6 |
| | 2006 | 0.1 | -0.5 | -0.4 | -16.7 |
| Tuvalu<br>Tuvalu | 2002 | 11.2 | 0.6 | 11.7 | 1 137.0 |
| | 2003 | 5.5 | 0.4 | 5.8 | 564.3 |
| | 2004 | 5.4 | 2.6 | 8.0 | 769.5 |
| | 2005 | 5.9 | 3.1 | 8.9 | 856.2 |
| | 2006 | 12.7 | 2.6 | 15.3 | 1 462.9 |
| Uganda<br>Ouganda | 2002 | 466.1 | 238.3 | 704.4 | 26.8 |
| | 2003 | 587.3 | 387.6 | 974.9 | 35.9 |
| | 2004 | 683.9 | 508.4 | 1 192.3 | 42.5 |
| | 2005 | 690.7 | 484.8 | 1 175.5 | 40.6 |
| | 2006 | 938.2 | 609.5 | 1 547.7 | 51.8 |
| Ukraine<br>Ukraine | 2005 | 238.2 | 116.8 | 355.0 | 7.6 |
| | 2006 | 280.6 | 170.7 | 451.3 | 9.7 |
| United Rep. of Tanzania<br>Rép.-Unie de Tanzanie | 2002 | 908.9 | 330.6 | 1 239.4 | 34.8 |
| | 2003 | 965.6 | 738.1 | 1 703.7 | 46.6 |
| | 2004 | 1 028.7 | 720.2 | 1 748.9 | 46.6 |
| | 2005 | 860.3 | 609.2 | 1 469.5 | 38.2 |
| | 2006 | 991.7 | 832.2 | 1 823.9 | 46.2 |
| Uruguay<br>Uruguay | 2002 | 6.8 | 3.0 | 9.8 | 2.9 |
| | 2003 | 7.7 | 6.2 | 14.0 | 4.2 |
| | 2004 | 9.9 | 11.6 | 21.5 | 6.5 |
| | 2005 | 2.8 | 11.2 | 14.0 | 4.2 |
| | 2006 | 10.8 | 9.6 | 20.4 | 6.1 |
| Uzbekistan<br>Ouzbékistan | 2002 | 152.9 | 20.5 | 173.4 | 6.8 |
| | 2003 | 167.5 | 16.6 | 184.1 | 7.1 |
| | 2004 | 205.8 | 25.4 | 231.2 | 8.8 |
| | 2005 | 121.5 | 31.6 | 153.1 | 5.8 |
| | 2006 | 92.5 | 41.2 | 133.7 | 5.0 |
| Vanuatu<br>Vanuatu | 2002 | 22.4 | 5.1 | 27.5 | 138.0 |
| | 2003 | 28.2 | 4.2 | 32.4 | 158.6 |
| | 2004 | 34.6 | 3.1 | 37.7 | 179.7 |
| | 2005 | 33.4 | 6.1 | 39.4 | 183.1 |
| | 2006 | 41.4 | 7.4 | 48.8 | 221.0 |
| Venezuela (Bolivarian Rep. of)<br>Venezuela (Rép. bolivarienne du) | 2002 | 42.0 | 14.1 | 56.1 | 2.2 |
| | 2003 | 64.2 | 16.1 | 80.2 | 3.1 |
| | 2004 | 28.4 | 15.9 | 44.2 | 1.7 |
| | 2005 | 20.8 | 27.1 | 47.8 | 1.8 |
| | 2006 | 32.9 | 24.7 | 57.6 | 2.1 |

**66** Disbursements of bilateral and multilateral official development assistance and official aid to individual recipients (*continued*)

Versements d'aide publique au développement et d'aide publique bilatérales et multilatérales aux bénéficiaires (*suite*)

| Country or area / Pays ou zone | Year / Année | Net disbursements (US $) — Versements nets ($E.-U.) | | | |
|---|---|---|---|---|---|
| | | Bilateral (millions) / Bilatérale (millions) | Multilateral[1] (millions) / Multilatérale[1] (millions) | Total (millions) / Total (millions) | Per capita / Par habitant |
| Viet Nam Viet Nam | 2002 | 746.0 | 508.6 | 1 254.7 | 15.4 |
| | 2003 | 967.7 | 785.6 | 1 753.3 | 21.2 |
| | 2004 | 1 184.8 | 617.8 | 1 802.6 | 21.5 |
| | 2005 | 1 253.2 | 634.1 | 1 887.3 | 22.2 |
| | 2006 | 1 306.5 | 527.2 | 1 833.7 | 21.3 |
| Wallis and Futuna Islands Iles Wallis et Futuna | 2002 | 52.7 | 0.1 | 52.7 | 3 519.1 |
| | 2003 | 53.6 | 1.9 | 55.5 | 3 699.0 |
| | 2004 | 71.5 | 1.3 | 72.8 | 4 843.6 |
| | 2005 | 71.7 | 0.4 | 72.0 | 4 776.8 |
| | 2006 | 102.0 | 0.4 | 102.4 | 6 756.4 |
| Yemen Yémen | 2002 | 119.4 | 106.0 | 225.4 | 11.7 |
| | 2003 | 126.6 | 109.3 | 235.9 | 11.9 |
| | 2004 | 152.7 | 100.0 | 252.7 | 12.3 |
| | 2005 | 132.9 | 178.5 | 311.4 | 14.8 |
| | 2006 | 134.8 | 149.0 | 283.9 | 13.1 |
| Zambia Zambie | 2002 | 359.5 | 277.4 | 636.9 | 58.6 |
| | 2003 | 591.9 | -8.2 | 583.7 | 52.7 |
| | 2004 | 745.8 | 376.8 | 1 122.6 | 99.6 |
| | 2005 | 822.5 | 110.4 | 932.9 | 81.3 |
| | 2006 | 1 115.2 | 307.6 | 1 422.8 | 121.6 |
| Zimbabwe Zimbabwe | 2002 | 177.8 | 20.7 | 198.5 | 15.4 |
| | 2003 | 160.7 | 25.3 | 186.0 | 14.4 |
| | 2004 | 166.4 | 19.7 | 186.1 | 14.3 |
| | 2005 | 187.0 | 188.8 | 375.8 | 28.6 |
| | 2006 | 199.8 | 79.9 | 279.7 | 21.1 |

Source

Organization for Economic Co-operation and Development (OECD), Paris, the OECD Development Assistance Committee database, last accessed January 2008. Per capita calculated by the United Nations Statistics Division from the World Population Prospects: The 2006 Revision, mid-year population data.

Notes

1 As reported by OECD/DAC, covers agencies of the United Nations family, the European Commission, IDA and the concessional lending facilities of regional development banks. Excludes non-concessional flows (i.e., less than 25% grant elements).

2 For statistical purposes, the data for China do not include those for the Hong Kong Special Administrative Region (Hong Kong SAR), Macao Special Administrative Region (Macao SAR) and Taiwan Province of China.

Source

Organisation de coopération et de développement économiques (OCDE), Paris, la base de données du comité d'aide au développement de l'OCDE, dernier accès janvier 2008. Les données par habitant ont été calculées par la Division de statistiques de l'ONU de "World Population Prospects: The 2006 Revision," d'après les données de la population au milieu de l'année.

Notes

1 Communiqué par le Comité d'aide au développement de l'OCDE, comprend les institutions et organismes du système des Nations Unies, la commission européenne, l'Association internationale de développement, et les mécanismes de prêt à des conditions privilégiées des banques régionales de développement. Les apports aux conditions du marché (élément de libéralité inférieur à 25) en sont exclus.

2 Pour la présentation des statistiques, les données pour la Chine ne comprennent pas la Région Administrative Spéciale de Hong Kong (Hong Kong RAS), la Région Administrative Spéciale de Macao (Macao RAS) et la province de Taiwan.

# Net official development assistance from DAC countries to developing countries and multilateral organizations

Net disbursements: millions of US dollars and as a percentage of gross national income (GNI)

# Aide publique au développement nette des pays du CAD aux pays en développement et aux organisations multilatérales

Versements nets : millions de dollars E.-U. et en pourcentage du revenu national brut (RNB)

| Country or area<br>Pays ou zone | 2001<br>US$/$ E.-U.<br>(millions) | 2001<br>As % of GNI<br>En %<br>du RNB | 2002<br>US$/$ E.-U.<br>(millions) | 2002<br>As % of GNI<br>En %<br>du RNB | 2003<br>US$/$ E.-U.<br>(millions) | 2003<br>As % of GNI<br>En %<br>du RNB | 2004<br>US$/$ E.-U.<br>(millions) | 2004<br>As % of GNI<br>En %<br>du RNB | 2005<br>US$/$ E.-U.<br>(millions) | 2005<br>As % of GNI<br>En %<br>du RNB | 2006<br>US$/$ E.-U.<br>(millions) | 2006<br>As % of GNI<br>En %<br>du RNB |
|---|---|---|---|---|---|---|---|---|---|---|---|---|
| Total<br>Total | 52 423 | 0.22 | 58 297 | 0.23 | 69 065 | 0.25 | 79 432 | 0.26 | 107 099 | 0.33 | 104 421 | 0.31 |
| Australia<br>Australie | 873 | 0.25 | 989 | 0.26 | 1 219 | 0.25 | 1 460 | 0.25 | 1 680 | 0.25 | 2 123 | 0.30 |
| Austria<br>Autriche | 633 | 0.34 | 520 | 0.26 | 505 | 0.20 | 678 | 0.23 | 1 573 | 0.52 | 1 498 | 0.47 |
| Belgium<br>Belgique | 867 | 0.37 | 1 072 | 0.43 | 1 853 | 0.60 | 1 463 | 0.41 | 1 963 | 0.53 | 1 978 | 0.50 |
| Canada<br>Canada | 1 533 | 0.22 | 2 004 | 0.28 | 2 031 | 0.24 | 2 599 | 0.27 | 3 756 | 0.34 | 3 684 | 0.29 |
| Denmark<br>Danemark | 1 634 | 1.03 | 1 643 | 0.96 | 1 748 | 0.84 | 2 037 | 0.85 | 2 109 | 0.81 | 2 236 | 0.80 |
| Finland<br>Finlande | 389 | 0.32 | 462 | 0.35 | 558 | 0.35 | 680 | 0.37 | 902 | 0.46 | 834 | 0.40 |
| France<br>France | 4 198 | 0.31 | 5 486 | 0.37 | 7 253 | 0.40 | 8 473 | 0.41 | 10 026 | 0.47 | 10 601 | 0.47 |
| Germany<br>Allemagne | 4 990 | 0.27 | 5 324 | 0.27 | 6 784 | 0.28 | 7 534 | 0.28 | 10 082 | 0.36 | 10 435 | 0.36 |
| Greece<br>Grèce | 202 | 0.17 | 276 | 0.21 | 362 | 0.21 | 321 | 0.16 | 384 | 0.17 | 424 | 0.17 |
| Ireland<br>Irlande | 287 | 0.33 | 398 | 0.40 | 504 | 0.39 | 607 | 0.39 | 719 | 0.42 | 1 022 | 0.54 |
| Italy<br>Italie | 1 627 | 0.15 | 2 332 | 0.20 | 2 433 | 0.17 | 2 462 | 0.15 | 5 091 | 0.29 | 3 641 | 0.20 |
| Japan<br>Japon | 9 847 | 0.23 | 9 283 | 0.23 | 8 880 | 0.20 | 8 922 | 0.19 | 13 147 | 0.28 | 11 187 | 0.25 |
| Luxembourg<br>Luxembourg | 139 | 0.76 | 147 | 0.77 | 194 | 0.81 | 236 | 0.83 | 256 | 0.86 | 291 | 0.89 |
| Netherlands<br>Pays-Bas | 3 172 | 0.82 | 3 338 | 0.81 | 3 972 | 0.80 | 4 204 | 0.73 | 5 115 | 0.82 | 5 452 | 0.81 |
| New Zealand<br>Nouvelle-Zélande | 112 | 0.25 | 122 | 0.22 | 165 | 0.23 | 212 | 0.23 | 274 | 0.27 | 259 | 0.27 |
| Norway<br>Norvège | 1 346 | 0.80 | 1 696 | 0.89 | 2 042 | 0.92 | 2 199 | 0.87 | 2 786 | 0.94 | 2 954 | 0.89 |
| Portugal<br>Portugal | 268 | 0.25 | 323 | 0.27 | 320 | 0.22 | 1 031 | 0.63 | 377 | 0.21 | 396 | 0.21 |
| Spain<br>Espagne | 1 737 | 0.30 | 1 712 | 0.26 | 1 961 | 0.23 | 2 437 | 0.24 | 3 018 | 0.27 | 3 814 | 0.32 |
| Sweden<br>Suède | 1 666 | 0.77 | 2 012 | 0.84 | 2 400 | 0.79 | 2 722 | 0.78 | 3 362 | 0.94 | 3 955 | 1.02 |
| Switzerland<br>Suisse | 908 | 0.34 | 939 | 0.32 | 1 299 | 0.39 | 1 545 | 0.41 | 1 772 | 0.44 | 1 646 | 0.39 |
| United Kingdom<br>Royaume-Uni | 4 566 | 0.32 | 4 929 | 0.31 | 6 262 | 0.34 | 7 905 | 0.36 | 10 772 | 0.47 | 12 459 | 0.51 |
| United States<br>Etats-Unis | 11 429 | 0.11 | 13 290 | 0.13 | 16 320 | 0.15 | 19 705 | 0.17 | 27 935 | 0.23 | 23 532 | 0.18 |

Source

Organisation for Economic Co-operation and Development (OECD), Paris, the OECD Development Assistance Committee database, last accessed January 2008.

Source

Organisation de coopération et de développement économiques (OCDE), Paris, la base de données du Comité d'aide au développement de l'OCDE, dernier accès janvier 2008.

# 68

## Socio-economic development assistance through the United Nations system
Development grants: thousands of US dollars, 2006

## Assistance en matière de développement socioéconomique fournie par le système des Nations Unies
Subventions au développement : en milliers de dollars des E.-U., 2006

| Region, country or area / Région, pays ou zone | UNDP[a] / PNUD[a] | UNFPA / FNUAP | UNHCR / HCR | UNICEF | WFP[b] / PAM[b] | IFAD / FIDA | Specialized agencies[c] / Institutions spécialisées[c] | Other UN funds and programmes / Autres fonds et programmes des NU | Total develop. grants / Total subventions au développ. |
|---|---|---|---|---|---|---|---|---|---|
| Total / Total | 4 040 687 | 392 117 | 1 090 890 | 2 070 325 | 2 664 994 | 386 716 | 2 301 690 | 1 485 505 | 14 527 116 |
| Regional programmes / Totaux régionaux | 387 141 | 99 670 | 245 784 | 105 486 | 14 692 | 0 | 920 793 | 666 886 | 2 526 055 |
| Africa / Afrique | 4 288 | 9 214 | 13 528 | 17 331 | 7 444 | 0 | 210 252 | 61 085 | 336 664 |
| Americas / Amériques | 2 527 | 7 083 | 3 416 | 7 563 | 1 478 | 0 | 58 830 | 19 714 | 108 287 |
| Asia and the Pacific / Asie et le Pacifique | 1 701 | 12 073 | 1 697 | 15 718 | 5 659 | 0 | 103 771 | 40 323 | 192 766 |
| Europe / Europe | 12 820 | 0 | 857 | 4 229 | 0 | 0 | 81 787 | 23 754 | 132 517 |
| Western Asia / Asie occidentale | -240 | 5 038 | 9 097 | 2 333 | 111 | 0 | 73 632 | 11 024 | 107 058 |
| Global/Interregional / Global/Interrégional | 146 049 | 66 262 | 217 188 | 58 311 | 0 | 0 | 391 278 | 501 438 | 1 417 976 |
| Other countries [1] / Autres pays [1] | 219 996 | 0 | 0 | 0 | 0 | 0 | 1 243 | 9 548 | 230 787 |
| Not elsewhere classified [2] / Non-classé ailleurs [2] | 0 | 0 | 0 | 0 | 223 694 | 0 | 0 | 0 | 223 694 |
| Total all countries / Total, tous pays | 3 653 546 | 292 447 | 845 107 | 1 964 839 | 2 426 608 | 386 716 | 1 380 898 | 818 620 | 11 777 368 |
| Afghanistan / Afghanistan | 204 034 | 4 056 | 47 533 | 55 567 | 94 872 | 0 | 42 363 | 33 702 | 482 127 |
| Albania / Albanie | 11 299 | 584 | 1 427 | 3 456 | 8 | 224 | 3 989 | 7 632 | 28 619 |
| Algeria / Algérie | 3 169 | 829 | 5 983 | 1 656 | 10 411 | 0 | 3 804 | 296 | 26 148 |
| Angola / Angola | 31 786 | 2 362 | 17 798 | 43 359 | 28 054 | 1 865 | 10 288 | 3 311 | 138 794 |
| Antigua and Barbuda / Antigua-et-Barbuda | 179 | 0 | 0 | 0 | 0 | 0 | 6 697 | 595 | 7 471 |
| Argentina / Argentine | 271 397 | 546 | 821 | 3 089 | 0 | 5 759 | 6 270 | 1 886 | 290 716 |
| Armenia / Arménie | 4 603 | 500 | 1 733 | 1 460 | 2 725 | 6 673 | 1 796 | 448 | 19 939 |
| Australia[3] / Australie[3] | 0 | 0 | 978 | 0 | 0 | 0 | 47 | 0 | 1 025 |
| Austria / Autriche | 0 | 0 | 1 117 | 0 | 0 | 0 | 119 | 0 | 1 236 |
| Azerbaijan / Azerbaïdjan | 16 048 | 813 | 3 477 | 2 578 | 5 084 | 2 747 | 2 189 | 510 | 33 446 |
| Bahamas / Bahamas | 0 | 0 | 0 | 0 | 0 | 0 | 309 | 433 | 742 |
| Bahrain / Bahreïn | 1 787 | 0 | 0 | 0 | 0 | 0 | 186 | 18 | 1 992 |

Assistance en matière de développement socioéconomique fournie par le système des Nations Unies — Subventions au développement : en milliers de dollars des E.-U., 2006 (*suite*)

| Region, country or area / Région, pays ou zone | UNDP[a] PNUD[a] | UNFPA FNUAP | UNHCR HCR | UNICEF | WFP[b] PAM[b] | IFAD FIDA | Specialized agencies[c] Institutions spécialisées[c] | Other UN funds and programmes Autres fonds et programmes des NU | Total develop. grants Total subventions au développ. |
|---|---|---|---|---|---|---|---|---|---|
| Bangladesh / Bangladesh | 24 315 | 7 175 | 2 655 | 29 262 | 49 521 | 8 951 | 20 170 | 1 749 | 143 798 |
| Barbados / Barbade | 2 129 | 0 | 0 | 0 | 184 | 0 | 172 | 71 | 2 556 |
| Belarus / Bélarus | 9 956 | 280 | 1 291 | 944 | 0 | 0 | 1 090 | 205 | 13 766 |
| Belgium / Belgique | 0 | 0 | 3 298 | 0 | 0 | 0 | 305 | 0 | 3 603 |
| Belize / Belize | 458 | 0 | 0 | 774 | 0 | 0 | 185 | 1 413 | 2 830 |
| Benin / Bénin | 17 586 | 1 738 | 2 002 | 11 393 | 3 141 | 4 372 | 2 352 | 31 | 42 614 |
| Bhutan / Bhoutan | 3 019 | 1 356 | 0 | 2 469 | 1 694 | 2 519 | 2 166 | 94 | 13 318 |
| Bolivia / Bolivie | 34 554 | 1 627 | 0 | 11 922 | 4 952 | 2 103 | 4 002 | 2 362 | 61 624 |
| Bosnia and Herzegovina / Bosnie-Herzégovine | 16 436 | 426 | 8 722 | 3 138 | 0 | 4 050 | 2 307 | 530 | 35 615 |
| Botswana / Botswana | 5 318 | 895 | 1 743 | 2 328 | 0 | 0 | 2 430 | 103 | 12 817 |
| Brazil / Brésil | 235 959 | 1 275 | 2 238 | 12 345 | 0 | 4 454 | 235 230 | 11 614 | 503 380 |
| Brunei Darussalam / Brunéi Darussalam | 0 | 0 | 0 | 0 | 0 | 0 | 22 | 0 | 22 |
| Bulgaria / Bulgarie | 24 930 | 369 | 886 | 806 | 0 | 0 | 1 836 | 155 | 28 982 |
| Burkina Faso / Burkina Faso | 15 672 | 2 511 | 0 | 12 825 | 6 199 | 10 511 | 4 792 | 3 546 | 56 056 |
| Burundi / Burundi | 10 080 | 1 119 | 30 509 | 25 499 | 46 970 | 3 231 | 10 128 | 691 | 128 228 |
| Cambodia / Cambodge | 29 055 | 2 612 | 1 125 | 22 714 | 13 940 | 4 331 | 15 071 | 3 447 | 98 674 |
| Cameroon / Cameroun | 4 503 | 3 087 | 1 926 | 7 215 | 2 740 | 3 134 | 4 511 | 908 | 28 022 |
| Canada / Canada | 2 437 | 0 | 1 669 | 0 | 0 | 0 | 54 | 0 | 4 160 |
| Cape Verde / Cap-Vert | 0 | 990 | 0 | 654 | 932 | 607 | 1 862 | 1 379 | 6 424 |
| Central African Rep. / Rép. centrafricaine | 22 262 | 3 306 | 3 696 | 7 339 | 7 228 | 0 | 3 854 | 228 | 47 914 |
| Chad / Tchad | 11 455 | 1 707 | 65 214 | 21 228 | 55 308 | 1 529 | 5 859 | 4 808 | 167 107 |
| Chile / Chili | 26 497 | 154 | 0 | 1 021 | 0 | 0 | 1 866 | 104 | 29 660 |
| China / Chine | 52 787 | 3 695 | 3 534 | 18 267 | 181 | 22 344 | 23 540 | 3 756 | 128 104 |
| China, Macao SAR / Chine, Macao RAS | 0 | 0 | 0 | 0 | 0 | 0 | 3 | 0 | 3 |
| Colombia / Colombie | 89 320 | 1 569 | 9 812 | 6 536 | 12 544 | 4 356 | 5 526 | 6 314 | 136 088 |
| Comoros / Comores | 3 502 | 411 | 0 | 2 273 | 0 | 0 | 1 413 | 702 | 8 300 |

**68** Socio-economic development assistance through the United Nations system — Development grants: thousands of US dollars, 2006 (*continued*)

**Assistance en matière de développement socioéconomique fournie par le système des Nations Unies** — Subventions au développement : en milliers de dollars des E.-U., 2006 (*suite*)

| Region, country or area<br>Région, pays ou zone | UNDP[a]<br>PNUD[a] | UNFPA<br>FNUAP | UNHCR<br>HCR | UNICEF | WFP[b]<br>PAM[b] | IFAD<br>FIDA | Specialized agencies[c]<br>Institutions spécialisées[c] | Other UN funds and programmes<br>Autres fonds et programmes des NU | Total develop. grants<br>Total subventions au développ. |
|---|---|---|---|---|---|---|---|---|---|
| Congo<br>Congo | 5 957 | 1 207 | 7 617 | 5 361 | 2 748 | 1 017 | 2 739 | 193 | 26 838 |
| Cook Islands<br>Iles Cook | 92 | 0 | 0 | 0 | 0 | 0 | 407 | 0 | 499 |
| Costa Rica<br>Costa Rica | 2 890 | 564 | 1 505 | 819 | 0 | 0 | 1 792 | 108 | 7 678 |
| Côte d'Ivoire<br>Côte d'Ivoire | 12 874 | 2 935 | 7 929 | 18 636 | 23 791 | 1 766 | 5 917 | 776 | 74 624 |
| Croatia<br>Croatie | 2 959 | 0 | 4 210 | 784 | 0 | 0 | 789 | 185 | 8 927 |
| Cuba<br>Cuba | 11 445 | 648 | 282 | 1 417 | 5 106 | 0 | 3 072 | 486 | 22 496 |
| Cyprus<br>Chypre | 15 841 | 0 | 708 | 0 | 0 | 0 | 231 | 0 | 16 780 |
| Czech Republic<br>République tchèque | 0 | 0 | 908 | 0 | 0 | 0 | 274 | 506 | 1 688 |
| Dem. Rep. of the Congo<br>Rép. dém. du Congo | 230 130 | 9 458 | 40 207 | 88 689 | 47 874 | 500 | 28 715 | 59 | 445 631 |
| Djibouti<br>Djibouti | 2 071 | 659 | 2 676 | 3 925 | 5 297 | 337 | 2 496 | 209 | 17 670 |
| Dominica<br>Dominique | 69 | 0 | 0 | 0 | 0 | 0 | 33 | 615 | 717 |
| Dominican Republic<br>Rép. dominicaine | 6 778 | 917 | 0 | 1 398 | 2 | 2 160 | 3 473 | 91 | 14 818 |
| Ecuador<br>Equateur | 43 482 | 889 | 3 692 | 4 352 | 1 146 | 0 | 4 305 | 390 | 58 255 |
| Egypt<br>Egypte | 48 570 | 3 028 | 4 500 | 9 363 | 1 501 | 9 112 | 8 046 | 750 | 84 869 |
| El Salvador<br>El Salvador | 15 979 | 1 375 | 0 | 2 945 | 2 293 | 4 727 | 3 941 | 40 | 31 300 |
| Equatorial Guinea<br>Guinée équatoriale | 2 764 | 1 922 | 0 | 1 242 | 0 | 0 | 1 650 | 0 | 7 578 |
| Eritrea<br>Erythrée | 12 795 | 1 769 | 6 546 | 19 273 | 0 | 2 441 | 4 967 | 448 | 48 239 |
| Estonia<br>Estonie | 0 | 0 | 0 | 0 | 0 | 0 | 1 877 | 295 | 2 172 |
| Ethiopia<br>Ethiopie | 25 079 | 4 059 | 16 508 | 90 968 | 194 380 | 18 274 | 28 814 | 1 528 | 379 610 |
| Fiji<br>Fidji | 8 069 | 0 | 0 | 0 | 0 | 0 | 1 581 | 0 | 9 650 |
| Finland<br>Finlande | 0 | 0 | 0 | 0 | 0 | 0 | 73 | 0 | 73 |
| France<br>France | 0 | 0 | 2 429 | 0 | 0 | 0 | 1 384 | 0 | 3 813 |
| French Guiana<br>Guyane française | 0 | 0 | 0 | 0 | 0 | 0 | 33 | 0 | 33 |
| Gabon<br>Gabon | 8 832 | 398 | 2 612 | 1 756 | 0 | 0 | 1 751 | 132 | 15 482 |
| Gambia<br>Gambie | 2 280 | 839 | 655 | 2 066 | 2 129 | 1 209 | 2 357 | 270 | 11 803 |
| Georgia<br>Géorgie | 13 461 | 1 270 | 4 158 | 2 066 | 4 589 | 632 | 987 | 32 | 27 195 |

68 Socio-economic development assistance through the United Nations system—Development grants: thousands of US dollars, 2006 (*continued*)

Assistance en matière de développement socioéconomique fournie par le système des Nations Unies—Subventions au développement : en milliers de dollars des E.-U., 2006 (*suite*)

| Region, country or area<br>Région, pays ou zone | UNDP[a]<br>PNUD[a] | UNFPA<br>FNUAP | UNHCR<br>HCR | UNICEF | WFP[b]<br>PAM[b] | IFAD<br>FIDA | Specialized agencies[c]<br>Institutions spécialisées[c] | Other UN funds and programmes<br>Autres fonds et programmes des NU | Total develop. grants<br>Total subventions au développ. |
|---|---|---|---|---|---|---|---|---|---|
| Germany<br>Allemagne | 0 | 0 | 2 047 | 0 | 0 | 0 | 396 | 0 | 2 443 |
| Ghana<br>Ghana | 14 641 | 1 523 | 8 993 | 26 966 | 3 261 | 5 760 | 5 829 | 469 | 67 442 |
| Greece<br>Grèce | 0 | 0 | 1 337 | 0 | 0 | 0 | 530 | 0 | 1 867 |
| Grenada<br>Grenade | 292 | 0 | 0 | 0 | 0 | 300 | 502 | 13 | 1 107 |
| Guam<br>Guam | 0 | 0 | 0 | 0 | 0 | 0 | 15 | 0 | 15 |
| Guatemala<br>Guatemala | 102 403 | 3 909 | 0 | 7 034 | 15 048 | 5 093 | 48 718 | 2 | 182 207 |
| Guinea<br>Guinée | 6 431 | 2 360 | 11 610 | 8 503 | 10 662 | 2 992 | 2 443 | 664 | 45 665 |
| Guinea-Bissau<br>Guinée-Bissau | 7 099 | 1 114 | 0 | 6 124 | 3 844 | 0 | 1 980 | 47 | 20 208 |
| Guyana<br>Guyana | 5 595 | 0 | 0 | 1 678 | 0 | 1 919 | 1 161 | 0 | 10 352 |
| Haiti<br>Haïti | 38 555 | 3 887 | 0 | 11 170 | 14 687 | 3 454 | 6 605 | 687 | 79 047 |
| Honduras<br>Honduras | 106 932 | 1 914 | 0 | 2 221 | 1 922 | 2 145 | 5 432 | 186 | 120 752 |
| Hungary<br>Hongrie | 0 | 0 | 1 902 | 0 | 0 | 0 | 709 | 0 | 2 611 |
| India<br>Inde | 39 969 | 13 911 | 2 966 | 116 256 | 14 990 | 25 126 | 51 170 | 3 838 | 268 226 |
| Indonesia<br>Indonésie | 95 624 | 10 347 | 18 545 | 98 387 | 92 026 | 2 679 | 49 102 | 19 177 | 385 888 |
| Iran (Islamic Rep. of)<br>Iran (Rép. islamique d') | 6 951 | 1 750 | 13 000 | 8 746 | 384 | 0 | 5 488 | 778 | 37 097 |
| Iraq<br>Iraq | 69 674 | 2 793 | 16 993 | 63 994 | 7 271 | 0 | 60 510 | 23 470 | 244 705 |
| Ireland<br>Irlande | 0 | 0 | 594 | 0 | 0 | 0 | 0 | 0 | 594 |
| Israel<br>Israël | 0 | 0 | 220 | 0 | 0 | 0 | 209 | 0 | 428 |
| Italy<br>Italie | 0 | 0 | 2 800 | 0 | 0 | 0 | 6 069 | 0 | 8 869 |
| Jamaica<br>Jamaïque | 1 582 | 0 | 0 | 1 760 | 0 | 0 | 833 | 5 | 4 180 |
| Japan<br>Japon | 0 | 0 | 2 709 | 0 | 0 | 0 | 2 696 | -2 | 5 403 |
| Jordan<br>Jordanie | 10 276 | 728 | 3 357 | 1 377 | 500 | 1 495 | 4 275 | 101 590 | 123 598 |
| Kazakhstan<br>Kazakhstan | 6 437 | 614 | 1 594 | 1 829 | 0 | 0 | 1 031 | 1 302 | 12 807 |
| Kenya<br>Kenya | 21 928 | 3 658 | 37 213 | 31 541 | 153 134 | 5 407 | 13 562 | 1 801 | 268 243 |
| Kiribati<br>Kiribati | 0 | 0 | 0 | 0 | 0 | 0 | 402 | 79 | 481 |

**68** Socio-economic development assistance through the United Nations system — Development grants: thousands of US dollars, 2006 (*continued*)

**Assistance en matière de développement socioéconomique fournie par le système des Nations Unies** — Subventions au développement : en milliers de dollars des E.-U., 2006 (*suite*)

| Region, country or area<br>Région, pays ou zone | UNDP[a]<br>PNUD[a] | UNFPA<br>FNUAP | UNHCR<br>HCR | UNICEF | WFP[b]<br>PAM[b] | IFAD<br>FIDA | Specialized agencies[c]<br>Institutions spécialisées[c] | Other UN funds and programmes<br>Autres fonds et programmes des NU | Total develop. grants<br>Total subventions au développ. |
|---|---|---|---|---|---|---|---|---|---|
| Korea, Dem. P. R.<br>Corée, R. p. dém. de | 4 451 | 1 012 | 0 | 8 732 | 9 964 | 4 569 | 9 586 | 115 | 38 429 |
| Korea, Republic of<br>Corée, République de | 4 404 | 0 | 701 | 0 | 0 | 0 | 1 644 | 13 | 6 808 |
| Kosovo<br>kossovo | 14 405 | 1 218 | 0 | 0 | 0 | 0 | -752 | 1 626 | 16 497 |
| Kuwait<br>Koweït | 2 392 | 0 | 0 | 0 | 0 | 0 | 296 | 0 | 2 688 |
| Kyrgyzstan<br>Kirghizistan | 12 180 | 704 | 1 373 | 1 468 | 0 | 658 | 1 946 | 1 276 | 19 605 |
| Lao People's Dem. Rep.<br>Rép. dém. pop. lao | 11 837 | 1 679 | 0 | 8 827 | 4 397 | 5 094 | 5 978 | 1 344 | 39 433 |
| Latvia<br>Lettonie | 887 | 0 | 0 | 0 | 0 | 0 | 503 | 0 | 1 390 |
| Lebanon<br>Liban | 17 447 | 1 441 | 5 970 | 13 882 | 24 339 | 0 | 5 634 | 62 813 | 131 526 |
| Lesotho<br>Lesotho | 3 669 | 544 | 0 | 5 085 | 10 638 | 1 870 | 2 875 | 236 | 24 917 |
| Liberia<br>Libéria | 51 218 | 2 930 | 38 543 | 26 608 | 34 282 | 0 | 4 190 | 765 | 158 535 |
| Libyan Arab Jamah.<br>Jamah. arabe libyenne | 3 169 | 0 | 799 | 0 | 1 265 | 0 | 6 308 | 1 286 | 12 826 |
| Lithuania<br>Lituanie | 1 533 | 0 | 0 | 0 | 0 | 0 | 912 | 12 | 2 458 |
| Madagascar<br>Madagascar | 15 432 | 1 486 | 0 | 11 770 | 4 014 | 4 466 | 6 438 | 1 011 | 44 645 |
| Malawi<br>Malawi | 13 088 | 4 270 | 2 148 | 25 939 | 48 664 | 2 738 | 3 696 | 373 | 100 916 |
| Malaysia<br>Malaisie | 7 489 | 413 | 3 153 | 2 069 | 0 | 0 | 1 193 | 173 | 14 490 |
| Maldives<br>Maldives | 23 884 | 1 413 | 0 | 16 361 | 3 309 | 400 | 2 052 | 620 | 48 039 |
| Mali<br>Mali | 15 213 | 2 548 | 0 | 15 015 | 16 897 | 5 586 | 5 184 | 252 | 60 695 |
| Malta<br>Malte | 0 | 0 | 22 | 0 | 0 | 0 | 1 127 | 0 | 1 149 |
| Marshall Islands<br>Iles Marshall | 0 | 0 | 0 | 0 | 0 | 0 | 201 | 70 | 271 |
| Mauritania<br>Mauritanie | 11 667 | 2 380 | 837 | 5 243 | 13 521 | 2 784 | 3 135 | 327 | 39 893 |
| Mauritius<br>Maurice | 3 038 | 121 | 0 | 0 | 0 | 2 132 | 1 207 | 95 | 6 592 |
| Mexico<br>Mexique | 23 594 | 2 248 | 1 584 | 5 127 | 0 | 3 387 | 21 711 | 595 | 58 251 |
| Micronesia (Fed. States of)<br>Micronésie (Etats féd. de) | 0 | 0 | 0 | 0 | 0 | 0 | 133 | 0 | 133 |
| Moldova<br>Moldova | 6 803 | 398 | 726 | 4 291 | 0 | 3 482 | 1 404 | 505 | 17 608 |
| Mongolia<br>Mongolie | 4 713 | 1 710 | 69 | 2 712 | 0 | 2 146 | 3 801 | 141 | 15 291 |

Assistance en matière de développement socioéconomique fournie par le système des Nations Unies—Subventions au développement : en milliers de dollars des E.-U., 2006 (*suite*)

| Region, country or area / Région, pays ou zone | UNDP[a] PNUD[a] | UNFPA FNUAP | UNHCR HCR | UNICEF | WFP[b] PAM[b] | IFAD FIDA | Specialized agencies[c] Institutions spécialisées[c] | Other UN funds and programmes Autres fonds et programmes des NU | Total develop. grants Total subventions au développ. |
|---|---|---|---|---|---|---|---|---|---|
| Montserrat / Montserrat | 60 | 0 | 0 | 0 | 0 | 0 | 0 | 0 | 60 |
| Morocco / Maroc | 10 267 | 3 516 | 766 | 3 191 | 0 | 1 977 | 6 154 | 267 | 26 137 |
| Mozambique / Mozambique | 15 884 | 10 105 | 2 833 | 26 223 | 36 871 | 9 836 | 11 378 | 866 | 113 995 |
| Myanmar / Myanmar | 33 010 | 3 794 | 4 203 | 26 716 | 9 527 | 0 | 9 372 | 1 201 | 87 823 |
| Namibia / Namibie | 8 966 | 670 | 2 791 | 4 354 | 2 488 | 0 | 2 718 | 299 | 22 286 |
| Nauru / Nauru | 0 | 0 | 0 | 0 | 0 | 0 | 137 | 24 | 161 |
| Nepal / Népal | 18 415 | 6 508 | 6 289 | 18 713 | 25 345 | 2 107 | 12 017 | 56 | 89 449 |
| Netherlands / Pays-Bas | 0 | 0 | 0 | 0 | 0 | 0 | 2 080 | 0 | 2 080 |
| Netherlands Antilles / Antilles néerlandaises | 0 | 0 | 0 | 0 | 0 | 0 | 24 | 24 | 48 |
| Nicaragua / Nicaragua | 23 925 | 2 554 | 0 | 5 261 | 10 416 | 2 304 | 3 925 | 21 | 48 406 |
| Niger / Niger | 12 793 | 3 680 | 0 | 29 052 | 38 157 | 1 142 | 13 272 | 619 | 98 714 |
| Nigeria / Nigéria | 151 607 | 8 531 | 3 317 | 98 730 | 0 | 5 439 | 43 122 | 4 841 | 315 587 |
| Niue / Nioué | 74 | 0 | 0 | 0 | 0 | 0 | 247 | 41 | 362 |
| Norway / Norvège | 0 | 0 | 0 | 0 | 0 | 0 | 33 | 0 | 33 |
| Occupied Palestinian Terr. / Terr. palestinien occupé | 0 | 0 | 0 | 22 875 | 36 625 | 0 | 425 | 402 618 | 462 543 |
| Oman / Oman | 0 | 532 | 0 | 468 | 0 | 0 | 1 223 | -4 | 2 219 |
| Pakistan / Pakistan | 45 088 | 9 415 | 43 110 | 97 423 | 113 281 | 30 427 | 50 077 | 4 479 | 393 299 |
| Palau / Palaos | 0 | 0 | 0 | 0 | 0 | 0 | 118 | 179 | 297 |
| Panama / Panama | 154 549 | 564 | 816 | 793 | 856 | 3 806 | 11 220 | 182 | 172 797 |
| Papua New Guinea / Papouasie-Nvl-Guinée | 5 185 | 987 | 431 | 4 558 | 0 | 0 | 4 722 | 232 | 16 115 |
| Paraguay / Paraguay | 35 537 | 1 171 | 0 | 1 658 | 0 | -34 | 760 | 155 | 39 247 |
| Peru / Pérou | 111 920 | 12 690 | 0 | 5 239 | 1 352 | 7 432 | 7 631 | 3 181 | 149 444 |
| Philippines / Philippines | 23 066 | 5 584 | 201 | 13 953 | 4 551 | 5 669 | 8 444 | 444 | 61 913 |
| Poland / Pologne | 8 223 | 52 | 807 | 0 | 0 | 0 | 720 | 460 | 10 263 |
| Portugal / Portugal | 0 | 0 | 43 | 0 | 0 | 0 | 216 | 0 | 260 |

**68**

Socio-economic development assistance through the United Nations system — Development grants: thousands of US dollars, 2006 (*continued*)

Assistance en matière de développement socioéconomique fournie par le système des Nations Unies — Subventions au développement : en milliers de dollars des E.-U., 2006 (*suite*)

| Region, country or area<br>Région, pays ou zone | UNDP[a]<br>PNUD[a] | UNFPA<br>FNUAP | UNHCR<br>HCR | UNICEF | WFP[b]<br>PAM[b] | IFAD<br>FIDA | Specialized agencies[c]<br>Institutions spécialisées[c] | Other UN funds and programmes<br>Autres fonds et programmes des NU | Total develop. grants<br>Total subventions au développ. |
|---|---|---|---|---|---|---|---|---|---|
| Qatar<br>Qatar | 0 | 0 | 0 | 0 | 0 | 0 | 1 371 | 37 | 1 408 |
| Romania<br>Roumanie | 5 806 | 845 | 1 323 | 2 824 | 0 | 4 530 | 7 056 | 515 | 22 898 |
| Russian Federation<br>Fédération de Russie | 16 442 | 616 | 12 974 | 11 040 | 5 931 | 0 | 9 792 | 1 872 | 58 667 |
| Rwanda<br>Rwanda | 13 159 | 1 944 | 6 225 | 10 785 | 22 592 | 12 690 | 5 106 | 1 789 | 74 292 |
| Saint Helena<br>Sainte-Hélène | -38 | 0 | 0 | 0 | 0 | 0 | 0 | 0 | -38 |
| Saint Kitts and Nevis<br>Saint-Kitts-et-Nevis | 153 | 0 | 0 | 0 | 0 | 0 | 223 | 5 | 381 |
| Saint Lucia<br>Sainte-Lucie | 137 | 0 | 0 | 0 | 0 | 0 | 290 | 286 | 713 |
| Saint Vincent-Grenadines<br>Saint Vincent-Grenadines | 241 | 0 | 0 | 0 | 0 | 0 | 74 | 8 | 322 |
| Samoa<br>Samoa | 3 452 | 0 | 0 | 0 | 0 | 0 | 958 | 0 | 4 410 |
| Sao Tome and Principe<br>Sao Tomé-et-Principe | 1 706 | 444 | 0 | 1 093 | 816 | 410 | 1 413 | 7 | 5 890 |
| Saudi Arabia<br>Arabie saoudite | 15 823 | 0 | 1 941 | 741 | 0 | 0 | 15 697 | 0 | 34 202 |
| Senegal<br>Sénégal | 11 119 | 2 879 | 1 456 | 9 984 | 6 167 | 8 971 | 5 416 | 626 | 46 619 |
| Serbia and Montenegro<br>Serbie-et-Monténégro | 14 168 | 46 | 20 583 | 3 019 | 0 | 0 | 3 131 | 4 735 | 45 682 |
| Seychelles<br>Seychelles | 0 | 43 | 0 | 0 | 0 | 0 | 1 065 | 50 | 1 158 |
| Sierra Leone<br>Sierra Leone | 11 775 | 2 469 | 14 073 | 16 066 | 10 118 | 77 | 4 078 | 227 | 58 883 |
| Singapore<br>Singapour | 0 | 0 | 37 | 0 | 0 | 0 | 146 | 0 | 183 |
| Slovakia<br>Slovaquie | 0 | 0 | 756 | 0 | 0 | 0 | 493 | 39 | 1 289 |
| Slovenia<br>Slovénie | 0 | 0 | 334 | 0 | 0 | 0 | 301 | 19 | 654 |
| Solomon Islands<br>Iles Salomon | 0 | 0 | 0 | 0 | 0 | 0 | 1 586 | 0 | 1 586 |
| Somalia<br>Somalie | 40 188 | 943 | 7 094 | 59 525 | 53 465 | 0 | 30 518 | 4 852 | 196 584 |
| South Africa<br>Afrique du Sud | 6 462 | 719 | 3 048 | 7 304 | 893 | 0 | 4 735 | 329 | 23 490 |
| Spain<br>Espagne | 0 | 0 | 1 213 | 0 | 0 | 0 | 566 | 0 | 1 778 |
| Sri Lanka<br>Sri Lanka | 11 652 | 6 201 | 16 946 | 53 032 | 23 591 | 3 694 | 22 522 | 7 205 | 144 842 |
| Sudan<br>Soudan | 116 089 | 11 306 | 68 571 | 127 144 | 557 631 | 7 709 | 45 873 | 1 188 | 935 511 |
| Suriname<br>Suriname | 0 | 0 | 0 | 0 | 0 | 0 | 379 | 4 | 383 |

Assistance en matière de développement socioéconomique fournie par le système des Nations Unies — Subventions au développement : en milliers de dollars des E.-U., 2006 (*suite*)

| Region, country or area<br>Région, pays ou zone | UNDP[a]<br>PNUD[a] | UNFPA<br>FNUAP | UNHCR<br>HCR | UNICEF | WFP[b]<br>PAM[b] | IFAD<br>FIDA | Specialized agencies[c]<br>Institutions spécialisées[c] | Other UN funds and programmes<br>Autres fonds et programmes des NU | Total develop. grants<br>Total subventions au développ. |
|---|---|---|---|---|---|---|---|---|---|
| Swaziland<br>Swaziland | 1 156 | 640 | 0 | 4 892 | 8 136 | 2 654 | 1 488 | 102 | 19 069 |
| Sweden<br>Suède | 0 | 0 | 1 739 | 0 | 0 | 0 | 953 | 0 | 2 692 |
| Switzerland<br>Suisse | 0 | 0 | 509 | 0 | 0 | 0 | 84 | 0 | 593 |
| Syrian Arab Republic<br>Rép. arabe syrienne | 8 088 | 2 530 | 2 762 | 2 315 | 1 036 | 248 | 3 397 | 36 035 | 56 410 |
| Tajikistan<br>Tadjikistan | 16 214 | 688 | 1 053 | 3 883 | 13 709 | 0 | 4 466 | 3 246 | 43 259 |
| Thailand<br>Thaïlande | 11 351 | 1 986 | 10 560 | 12 704 | 0 | 0 | 7 497 | 213 | 44 310 |
| TFYR of Macedonia<br>L'ex-R.y. Macédoine | 6 250 | 3 | 3 088 | 1 680 | 0 | 2 892 | 1 335 | 0 | 15 247 |
| Timor-Leste<br>Timor-Leste | 19 070 | 1 816 | 4 767 | 11 120 | 7 275 | 0 | 2 959 | 51 | 47 059 |
| Togo<br>Togo | 8 006 | 991 | 64 | 3 702 | 465 | 0 | 1 580 | 61 | 14 868 |
| Tokelau<br>Tokélaou | 134 | 0 | 0 | 0 | 0 | 0 | 78 | 0 | 212 |
| Tonga<br>Tonga | 0 | 0 | 0 | 0 | 0 | 0 | 748 | 128 | 876 |
| Trinidad and Tobago<br>Trinité-et-Tobago | 6 444 | 0 | 0 | 0 | 0 | 0 | 633 | 194 | 7 271 |
| Tunisia<br>Tunisie | 4 221 | 517 | 308 | 1 091 | 0 | 5 505 | 3 252 | 317 | 15 211 |
| Turkey<br>Turquie | 13 828 | 1 382 | 6 594 | 6 177 | 0 | 450 | 5 340 | 311 | 34 082 |
| Turkmenistan<br>Turkménistan | 2 314 | 612 | 859 | 1 576 | 0 | 0 | 182 | 918 | 6 461 |
| Turks and Caicos Islands<br>Iles Turques et Caïques | 0 | 0 | 0 | 0 | 0 | 0 | 5 | 0 | 5 |
| Tuvalu<br>Tuvalu | 0 | 0 | 0 | 0 | 0 | 0 | 176 | 20 | 196 |
| Uganda<br>Ouganda | 9 506 | 5 688 | 20 956 | 55 730 | 103 253 | 6 750 | 16 270 | 674 | 218 827 |
| Ukraine<br>Ukraine | 23 602 | 827 | 3 113 | 2 582 | 0 | 0 | 4 505 | 83 | 34 712 |
| United Arab Emirates<br>Emirats arabes unis | 3 216 | 0 | 149 | 0 | 0 | 0 | 53 | 10 | 3 428 |
| United Kingdom<br>Royaume-Uni | 0 | 0 | 1 533 | 0 | 0 | 0 | 91 | 0 | 1 624 |
| United Rep. of Tanzania<br>Rép.-Unie de Tanzanie | 17 708 | 3 611 | 27 399 | 22 238 | 38 608 | 7 514 | 15 310 | 1 298 | 133 685 |
| United States<br>Etats-Unis | 0 | 0 | 5 864 | 0 | 0 | 0 | 318 | 0 | 6 182 |
| Uruguay<br>Uruguay | 12 373 | 550 | 0 | 842 | 0 | 1 590 | 3 011 | 367 | 18 801 |
| Uzbekistan<br>Ouzbékistan | 18 439 | 963 | 592 | 3 323 | 0 | 0 | 2 126 | 133 | 25 576 |

**68** Socio-economic development assistance through the United Nations system—Development grants: thousands of US dollars, 2006 (*continued*)

**Assistance en matière de développement socioéconomique fournie par le système des Nations Unies**—Subventions au développement : en milliers de dollars des E.-U., 2006 (*suite*)

| Region, country or area / Région, pays ou zone | UNDPa / PNUDa | UNFPA / FNUAP | UNHCR / HCR | UNICEF | WFPb / PAMb | IFAD / FIDA | Specialized agenciesc / Institutions spécialiséesc | Other UN funds and programmes / Autres fonds et programmes des NU | Total develop. grants / Total subventions au développ. |
|---|---|---|---|---|---|---|---|---|---|
| Vanuatu / Vanuatu | 37 | 0 | 0 | 0 | 0 | 0 | 1 405 | 138 | 1 580 |
| Venezuela (Bolivarian Rep. of) / Venezuela (Rép. bolivar. du) | 37 462 | 2 861 | 1 710 | 1 696 | 0 | 2 429 | 5 596 | 141 | 51 894 |
| Viet Nam / Viet Nam | 14 075 | 4 332 | 521 | 12 441 | 0 | 6 469 | 14 943 | 1 107 | 53 980 |
| Yemen / Yémen | 17 402 | 4 359 | 4 394 | 13 689 | 7 891 | 3 834 | 7 968 | 205 | 59 741 |
| Zambia / Zambie | 16 899 | 1 268 | 12 444 | 10 401 | 60 135 | 6 578 | 5 783 | 239 | 113 746 |
| Zimbabwe / Zimbabwe | 12 941 | 3 483 | 1 821 | 19 515 | 98 870 | 0 | 7 928 | 127 | 144 684 |

## Source

United Nations, "Operational activities of the United Nations for international development cooperation, Report of the Secretary-General, Addendum, Comprehensive statistical data on operational activities for development for the year 2006" (A/62/326).

The following abbreviations have been used in the table:
IFAD: International Fund for Agricultural Development
UNDP: United Nations Development Programme
UNFPA: United Nations Population Fund
UNHCR: United Nations High Commissioner for Refugees
UNICEF: United Nations Children's Fund
WFP: World Food Programme

## Notes

a  Total of central resources and UNDP-administered funds.

b  Includes extra-budgetary expenditures and WFP project expenditures for development activities and emergency operations. Of the latter, most was financed from the International Emergency Food Reserve and the remainder from WFP general resources.

c  Total of regular budget and extra-budgetary. Regular budget includes grants financed by specialized agencies and other organizations; the major share of such expenditures is financed by WHO. Extra-budgetary includes grants financed by specialized agencies and other organizations; i.e., from funds not elsewhere specified in the table. Starting in 1998 it includes UNEP extra-budgetary expenditures. Also included are expenditures financed from government "self-supporting" contributions.

1  Expenditures reported with no further breakdown.

2  Direct expenditures such as general fund, special accounts, insurance and trust funds that cannot be apportioned by project/operation.

3  UNHCR figure for Australia includes expenditures in New Zealand.

## Source

Nations Unies, "Activités opérationnelles du système des Nations Unies au service de la coopération internationale pour le développement, Rapport du Secrétaire général, Additif, Données statistiques globales sur les activités opérationnelles au service du développement pour 2006" (A/62/326).

Les abréviations ci-après ont été utilisées dans le tableau :
FIDA : Fonds international de développement agricole
PNUD : Programme des Nations Unies pour le développement
FNUAP : Fonds des Nations Unies pour la population
HCR : Haut Commissariat des Nations Unies
UNICEF : Fonds des Nations Unies pour l'enfance
PAM : Programme alimentaire mondial

## Notes

a  Y compris ressources centrales et fonds gérés.

b  Y compris les dépenses extrabudgétaires et celles afférentes aux projets du PAM relatifs aux activités de développement et aux opérations de secours d'urgence. Les dépenses au titre des opérations de secours d'urgence ont été financées pour la plus grande partie au moyen de la réserve alimentaire internationale d'urgence, le reste étant imputé sur les ressources générales du PAM.

c  Y compris budget ordinaire et extrabudgétaire. Budget ordinaire compris subventions financées par les institutions spécialisées et autres organisations sur les budgets ordinaires; la plus grande part est financée par l'OMS. Extrabudgétaire compris subventions financées par les institutions spécialisées et autres organisations sur les budgets ordinaires; fonds ne figurant pas ailleurs dans le tableau, y compris les dépenses financées au moyen des contributions "d'auto-assistance" versées par les gouvernements, comme indiqué dans la rubrique explicative, et, à partir de 1998, les dépenses du PNUE financées à l'aide de fonds extrabudgétaires.

1  Dépenses communiquées sans autre ventilation.

2  Dépenses directes telles que le fonds général, les comptes spéciaux, les frais d'assurance et les fonds d'affectation spéciale qui ne peuvent être ventilées par programmes ou activités.

3  Les données de l'UNHCR pour Australie compris les dépenses en Nouvelle Zélande.

*Table 66* presents estimates of flows of financial resources to individual recipients either directly (bilaterally) or through multilateral institutions (multilaterally).

The multilateral institutions include the World Bank Group, regional banks, financial institutions of the European Union and a number of United Nations institutions, programmes and trust funds.

The source of data is the Development Assistance Committee of OECD to which member countries reported data on their flow of resources to developing countries and territories, countries and territories in transition, and multilateral institutions.

Additional information on definitions, methods and sources can be found in OECD's *Geographical Distribution of Financial Flows to Aid Recipients* and www.oecd.org.

*Table 67* presents the development assistance expenditures of donor countries. This table includes donors' contributions to multilateral agencies; therefore, the overall totals differ from those in table 66, which include disbursements by multilateral agencies.

*Table 68* includes data on expenditures on operational activities for development undertaken by the organizations of the United Nations system. Operational activities encompass, in general, those activities of a development cooperation character that seek to mobilize or increase the potential and capacity of countries to promote economic and social development and welfare, including the transfer of resources to developing countries or regions in a tangible or intangible form.

Expenditures on operational activities for development are financed from contributions from governments and other official and non official sources to a variety of funding channels in the United Nations system. These include United Nations funds and programmes such as contributions to the United Nations Development Programme, contributions to funds administered by the United Nations Development Programme, and regular (assessed) and other extra budgetary contributions to specialized agencies.

Data are taken from the latest report of the Secretary-General to the General Assembly on operational activities for development.

Le *tableau 66* présente les estimations des flux de ressources financières mises à la disposition des pays soit directement (aide bilatérale) soit par l'intermédiaire d'institutions multilatérales (aide multilatérale).

Les institutions multilatérales comprennent le Groupe de la Banque mondiale, les banques régionales, les institutions financières de l'Union européenne et un certain nombre d'institutions, de programmes et de fonds d'affectation spéciale des Nations Unies.

La source de données est le Comité d'aide au développement de l'OCDE, auquel les pays membres ont communiqué des données sur les flux de ressources qu'ils mettent à la disposition des pays et territoires en développement et en transition et des institutions multilatérales.

Pour plus de renseignements sur les définitions, méthodes et sources, se reporter à la publication de l'OCDE, *la Répartition géographique des ressources financières de aux pays bénéficiaires de l'Aide* et www.oecd.org.

Le *tableau 67* présente les dépenses que les pays donateurs consacrent à l'aide publique au développement (APD). Ces chiffres incluent les contributions des donateurs à des agences multilatérales, de sorte que les totaux diffèrent de ceux du tableau 66, qui incluent les dépenses des agences multilatérales.

Le *tableau 68* présente des données sur les dépenses consacrées à des activités opérationnelles pour le développement par les organisations du système des Nations Unies. Par "activités opérationnelles", on entend en général les activités ayant trait à la coopération au développement, qui visent à mobiliser ou à accroître les potentialités et aptitudes que présentent les pays pour promouvoir le développement et le bien-être économiques et sociaux, y compris les transferts de ressources vers les pays ou régions en développement sous forme tangible ou non.

Les dépenses consacrées aux activités opérationnelles pour le développement sont financées au moyen de contributions que les gouvernements et d'autres sources officielles et non officielles apportent à divers organes de financement, tels que fonds et programmes du système des Nations Unies. On peut citer notamment les contributions au Programme des Nations Unies pour le développement, les contributions aux fonds gérés par le Programme des Nations Unies pour le développement, les contributions régulières (budgétaires) et les contributions extrabudgétaires aux institutions spécialisées.

Les données sont extraites du dernier rapport annuel du Secrétaire général à la session de l'Assemblée générale sur les activités opérationnelles pour le développement.

# Annex I

## Country and area nomenclature, regional and other groupings

### A. Changes in country or area names

In the periods covered by the statistics in the *Statistical Yearbook*, the following changes in designation have taken place:

*Brunei Darussalam* was formerly listed as Brunei;

*Burkina Faso* was formerly listed as Upper Volta;

*Cambodia* was formerly listed as Democratic Kampuchea;

*Cameroon* was formerly listed as United Republic of Cameroon;

*Côte d'Ivoire* was formerly listed as Ivory Coast;

*Czech Republic, Slovakia*: Since 1 January 1993, data for the Czech Republic and Slovakia, where available, are shown separately under the appropriate country name. For periods prior to 1 January 1993, where no separate data are available for the Czech Republic and Slovakia, unless otherwise indicated, data for the former Czechoslovakia are shown under the country name "former Czechoslovakia";

*Democratic Republic of the Congo* was formerly listed as Zaire;

*Germany*: Through the accession of the German Democratic Republic to the Federal Republic of Germany with effect from 3 October 1990, the two German States have united to form one sovereign State. As from the date of unification, the Federal Republic of Germany acts in the United Nations under the designation "Germany". All data shown which pertain to Germany prior to 3 October 1990 are indicated separately for the Federal Republic of Germany and the former German Democratic Republic based on their respective territories at the time indicated;

*Hong Kong Special Administrative Region of China:* Pursuant to a Joint Declaration signed on 19 December 1984, the United Kingdom restored Hong Kong to the People's Republic of China with effect from 1 July 1997; the People's Republic of China resumed the exercise of sovereignty over the territory with effect from that date;

*Macao Special Administrative Region of China*: Pursuant to the joint declaration signed on 13 April 1987, Portugal restored Macao to the People's Republic of China with effect from 20 December 1999; the People's Republic of China resumed the exercise of sovereignty over the territory with effect from that date;

*Myanmar* was formerly listed as Burma;

*Palau* was formerly listed as Pacific Islands and includes data for Federated States of Micronesia, Marshall Islands and Northern Mariana Islands;

*Saint Kitts and Nevis* was formerly listed as Saint Christopher and Nevis;

*Serbia, Montenegro*: As of 1992, data provided for Yugoslavia refer to the Federal Republic of Yugoslavia which was

# Annexe I

## Nomenclature des pays ou zones, groupements régionaux et autres groupements

### A. Changements dans le nom des pays ou zones

Au cours des périodes sur lesquelles portent les statistiques, dans l'*Annuaire Statistique* les changements de désignation suivants ont eu lieu:

Le *Brunei Darussalam* apparaissait antérieurement sous le nom de Brunei;

Le *Burkina Faso* apparaissait antérieurement sous le nom de la Haute-Volta;

Le *Cambodge* apparaissait antérieurement sous le nom de la Kampuchéa démocratique;

Le *Cameroun* apparaissait antérieurement sous le nom de République-Unie du Cameroun;

*République tchèque, Slovaquie*: Depuis le 1er janvier 1993, les données relatives à la République tchèque, et à la Slovaquie, lorsqu'elles sont disponibles, sont présentées séparément sous le nom de chacun des pays. En ce qui concerne la période précédant le 1er janvier 1993, pour laquelle on ne possède pas de données séparées pour les deux Républiques, les données relatives à l'ex-Tchécoslovaquie sont, sauf indication contraire, présentées sous le titre "l'ex-Tchécoslovaquie";

La *République démocratique du Congo* apparaissait antérieurement sous le nom de Zaïre;

*Allemagne:* En vertu de l'adhésion de la République démocratique allemande à la République fédérale d'Allemagne, prenant effet le 3 octobre 1990, les deux Etats allemands se sont unis pour former un seul Etat souverain. A compter de la date de l'unification, la République fédérale d'Allemagne est désigné à l'ONU sous le nom d'"Allemagne". Toutes les données se rapportant à l'Allemagne avant le 3 octobre figurent dans deux rubriques séparées basées sur les territoires respectifs de la République fédérale d'Allemagne et l'ex-République démocratique allemande selon la période indiquée;

*Hong Kong, région administrative spéciale de Chine*: Conformément à une Déclaration commune signée le 19 décembre 1984, le Royaume-Uni a rétrocédé Hong Kong à la République populaire de Chine, avec effet au 1er juillet 1997; la souveraineté de la République populaire de Chine s'exerce à nouveau sur le territoire à compter de cette date;

*Macao, région administrative spéciale de Chine:* Conformément à une Déclaration commune signée le 13 avril 1987, le Portugal a rétrocédé Macao à la République populaire de Chine, avec effet au 20 décembre 1999; la souveraineté de la République populaire de Chine s'exerce à nouveau sur le territoire à compter de cette date;

Le *Myanmar* apparaissait antérieurement sous le nom de Birmanie;

Les *Palaos* apparaissait antérieurement sous le nom de Iles du Pacifique y compris les données pour les Etats fédérés de

composed of the two republics of Serbia and Montenegro. On 4 February 2003, the official name of the "Federal Republic of Yugoslavia" was changed to "Serbia and Montenegro". On 3 June 2006, Serbia and Montenegro formally dissolved into two independent countries. When data are available separately for Montenegro and/or Serbia, they are shown under the respective heading.

*Timor-Leste*: Formerly East Timor;

*Former USSR*: In 1991, the Union of Soviet Socialist Republics formally dissolved into fifteen independent countries (Armenia, Azerbaijan, Belarus, Estonia, Georgia, Kazakhstan, Kyrgyzstan, Latvia, Lithuania, Republic of Moldova, Russian Federation, Tajikistan, Turkmenistan, Ukraine and Uzbekistan). Whenever possible, data are shown for the individual countries. Otherwise, data are shown for the former USSR;

*Yemen*: On 22 May 1990 Democratic Yemen and Yemen merged to form a single State. Since that date they have been represented as one Member with the name 'Yemen'.

It should be noted that unless otherwise indicated, for statistical purposes, the data for China exclude those for Hong Kong Special Administrative Region of China, Macao Special Administrative Region of China and Taiwan province of China.

## B. Regional groupings

The scheme of regional groupings given below presents seven regions based mainly on continents. Five of the seven continental regions are further subdivided into 21 regions that are so drawn as to obtain greater homogeneity in sizes of population, demographic circumstances and accuracy of demographic statistics. This nomenclature is widely used in international statistics and is followed to the greatest extent possible in the present *Yearbook* in order to promote consistency and facilitate comparability and analysis. However, it is by no means universal in international statistical compilation, even at the level of continental regions, and variations in international statistical sources and methods dictate many unavoidable differences in particular fields in the present *Yearbook*. General differences are indicated in the footnotes to the classification presented below. More detailed differences are given in the footnotes and technical notes to individual tables.

Neither is there international standardization in the use of the terms "developed" and "developing" countries, areas or regions. These terms are used in the present publication to refer to regional groupings generally considered as "developed": these are Europe and the former USSR, the United States of America and Canada in Northern America, and Australia, Japan and New Zealand in Asia and Oceania. These designations are intended for statistical convenience and do not necessarily express a judgement about the stage reached by a particular

Micronésie, les îles Marshall et îles Mariannes du Nord;

*Saint-Kitts-Et-Nevis* apparaissait antérieurement sous le nom de Saint-Christophe-et-Nevis;

*Serbie, Monténégro* : Les données fournies pour la Yougoslavie à partir de 1992 se rapportent à la République fédérale de Yougoslavie, qui était composée des deux républiques de la Serbie et du Monténégro. Le 4 février 2003, la "République fédérale de Yougoslavie", ayant changé de nom officiel, est devenu la "Serbie-et-Monténégro". Le 3 juin 2006, la Serbie-et-Monténégro s'est officiellement dissoute pour former deux États indépendants. Lorsque des données sont disponibles séparément pour la Serbie et le Monténégro, elles sont présentées dans leurs catégories respectives.

*Timor-Leste*: Ex Timor oriental;

L'*ex-URSS*: En 1991, l'Union des républiques socialistes soviétiques s'est séparé en 15 pays distincts (Arménie, Azerbaïdjan, Belarus, Estonie, Géorgie, Kazakhstan, Kirghizistan, Lettonie, Lituanie, République de Moldova, Fédération de Russie, Tadjikistan, Turkménistan, Ukraine, Ouzbékistan). Les données sont présentées pour ces pays pris séparément quand cela est possible. Autrement, les données sont présentées pour l'ex-URSS;

*Yémen*: Le Yémen et le Yémen démocratique ont fusionné le 22 mai 1990 pour ne plus former qu'un seul Etat, qui est depuis lors représenté comme tel à l'Organisation, sous le nom 'Yémen'.

Il convient de noter que sauf indication contraire, les données statistiques relatives à la Chine ne comprennent pas celles qui concernent la région administrative spéciale de Hong Kong, la région administrative spéciale de Macao et la province chinoise de Taiwan.

## B. Groupements régionaux

Le système de groupements régionaux présenté ci-dessous comporte sept régions basées principalement sur les continents. Cinq des sept régions continentales sont elles-mêmes subdivisées, formant ainsi 21 régions délimitées de manière à obtenir une homogénéité accrue dans les effectifs de population, les situations démographiques et la précision des statistiques démographiques. Cette nomenclature est couramment utilisée aux fins des statistiques internationales et a été appliquée autant qu'il a été possible dans le présent *Annuaire* en vue de renforcer la cohérence et de faciliter la comparaison et l'analyse. Son utilisation pour l'établissement des statistiques internationales n'est cependant rien moins qu'universelle, même au niveau des régions continentales, et les variations que présentent les sources et méthodes statistiques internationales entraînent inévitablement de nombreuses différences dans certains domaines de cet *Annuaire*. Les différences d'ordre général sont indiquées dans les notes figurant au bas de la classifica-

country or area in the development process. Differences from this usage are indicated in the notes to individual tables

tion présentée ci-dessous. Les différences plus spécifiques sont mentionnées dans les notes techniques et notes de bas de page accompagnant les divers tableaux.

L'application des expressions "développés" et "en développement" aux pays, zones ou régions n'est pas non plus normalisée à l'échelle internationale. Ces expressions sont utilisées dans la présente publication en référence aux groupements régionaux généralement considérés comme "développés", à savoir l'Europe et l'ex-URSS, les Etats-Unis d'Amérique et le Canada en Amérique septentrionale, et l'Australie, le Japon et la Nouvelle-Zélande dans la région de l'Asie et du Pacifique. Ces appellations sont employées pour des raisons de commodité statistique et n'expriment pas nécessairement un jugement sur le stade de développement atteint par tel ou tel pays ou zone. Les cas différant de cet usage sont signalés dans les notes accompagnant les tableaux concernés.

## Africa

### *Sub-Saharan Africa*

#### *Eastern Africa*

| | |
|---|---|
| Burundi | Mozambique |
| Comoros | Réunion |
| Djibouti | Rwanda |
| Eritrea | Seychelles |
| Ethiopia | Somalia |
| Kenya | Uganda |
| Madagascar | United Republic of Tanzania |
| Malawi | Zambia |
| Mauritius | Zimbabwe |

#### *Middle Africa*

| | |
|---|---|
| Angola | Democratic Republic of the Congo |
| Cameroon | |
| Central African Republic | Equatorial Guinea |
| Chad | Gabon |
| Congo | Sao Tome and Principe |

#### *Southern Africa*

| | |
|---|---|
| Botswana | South Africa |
| Lesotho | Swaziland |
| Namibia | |

#### *Western Africa*

| | |
|---|---|
| Benin | Guinea |
| Burkina Faso | Guinea-Bissau |
| Cape Verde | Liberia |
| Côte d'Ivoire | Mali |
| Gambia | Mauritania |
| Ghana | Niger |

## Afrique

### *Afrique subsaharienne*

#### *Afrique orientale*

| | |
|---|---|
| Burundi | Mozambique |
| Comores | Ouganda |
| Djibouti | République-Unie de Tanzanie |
| Erythrée | Réunion |
| Ethiopie | Rwanda |
| Kenya | Seychelles |
| Madagascar | Somalie |
| Malawi | Zambie |
| Maurice | Zimbabwe |

#### *Afrique centrale*

| | |
|---|---|
| Angola | République centrafricaine |
| Cameroun | République démocratique du Congo |
| Congo | |
| Gabon | Sao Tomé-et-Principe |
| Guinée équatoriale | Tchad |

#### *Afrique australe*

| | |
|---|---|
| Afrique du Sud | Namibie |
| Botswana | Swaziland |
| Lesotho | |

#### *Afrique occidentale*

| | |
|---|---|
| Bénin | Guinée |
| Burkina Faso | Guinée-Bissau |
| Cap-Vert | Libéria |
| Côte d'Ivoir | Mali |
| Gambie | Mauritanie |
| Ghana | Niger |

| | | | |
|---|---|---|---|
| Nigeria | Sierra Leone | Nigéria | Sierra Leone |
| Saint Helena | Togo | Sainte-Hélène | Togo |
| Senegal | | Sénégal | |

### Northern Africa

| | |
|---|---|
| Algeria | Sudan |
| Egypt | Tunisia |
| Libyan Arab Jamahiriya | Western Sahara |
| Morocco | |

### Afrique septentrionale

| | |
|---|---|
| Algérie | Sahara occidental |
| Egypte | Soudan |
| Jamahiriya arabe libyenne | Tunisie |
| Maroc | |

## Americas

### Latin America and the Caribbean

*Caribbean*

| | |
|---|---|
| Anguilla | Jamaica |
| Antigua and Barbuda | Martinique |
| Aruba | Montserrat |
| Bahamas | Netherlands Antilles |
| Barbados | Puerto Rico |
| British Virgin Islands | Saint Kitts and Nevis |
| Cayman Islands | Saint Lucia |
| Cuba | Saint Vincent and the |
| Dominica | Grenadines |
| Dominican Republic | Trinidad and Tobago |
| Grenada | Turks and Caicos Islands |
| Guadeloupe | United States Virgin Islands |
| Haiti | |

## Amériques

### Amérique latine et Caraïbes

*Caraïbes*

| | |
|---|---|
| Anguilla | Iles Vierges américaines |
| Antigua-et-Barbuda | Iles Vierges britanniques |
| Antilles néerlandaises | Jamaïque |
| Aruba | Martinique |
| Bahamas | Montserrat |
| Barbade | Porto Rico |
| Cuba | République dominicaine |
| Dominique | Sainte-Lucie |
| Grenade | Saint-Kitts-et-Nevis |
| Guadeloupe | Saint-Vincent-et-les |
| Haïti | Grenadines |
| Iles Caïmanes | Trinité-et-Tobago |
| Iles Turques et Caïques | |

*Central America*

| | |
|---|---|
| Belize | Honduras |
| Costa Rica | Mexico |
| El Salvador | Nicaragua |
| Guatemala | Panama |

*Amérique centrale*

| | |
|---|---|
| Belize | Honduras |
| Costa Rica | Mexique |
| El Salvador | Nicaragua |
| Guatemala | Panama |

*South America*

| | |
|---|---|
| Argentina | French Guiana |
| Bolivia | Guyana |
| Brazil | Paraguay |
| Chile | Peru |
| Colombia | Suriname |
| Ecuador | Uruguay |
| Falkland Islands (Malvinas) | Venezuela |

*Amérique du Sud*

| | |
|---|---|
| Argentine | Guyane française |
| Bolivie | Iles Falkland (Malvinas) |
| Brésil | Paraguay |
| Chili | Pérou |
| Colombie | Suriname |
| Equateur | Uruguay |
| Guyana | Venezuela |

### Northern America[a]

| | |
|---|---|
| Bermuda | Saint Pierre and Miquelon |
| Canada | United States of America |
| Greenland | |

### Amérique septentrionale[a]

| | |
|---|---|
| Bermudes | Groenland |
| Canada | Saint-Pierre-et-Miquelon |
| Etats-Unis d'Amérique | |

## Asia

### Eastern Asia

| | |
|---|---|
| China | Democratic People's Republic |
| China, Hong Kong Special | of Korea |
| Administrative Region | Japan |
| China, Macao Special | Mongolia |
| Administrative Region | Republic of Korea |

## Asie

### Asie orientale

| | |
|---|---|
| Chine | Japon |
| Chine, Hong Kong, région | Mongolie |
| administrative spéciale | République de Corée |
| Chine, Macao, région | République populaire |
| administrative spéciale | démocratique de Corée |

## South-central Asia

Afghanistan
Bangladesh
Bhutan
India
Iran (Islamic Republic of)
Kazakhstan
Kyrgyzstan
Maldives
Nepal
Pakistan
Sri Lanka
Tajikistan
Turkmenistan
Uzbekistan

## South-eastern Asia

Brunei Darussalam
Cambodia
Indonesia
Lao People's Democratic Republic
Malaysia
Myanmar
Philippines
Singapore
Thailand
Timor-Leste
Viet Nam

## Western Asia

Armenia
Azerbaijan
Bahrain
Cyprus
Georgia
Iraq
Israel
Jordan
Kuwait
Lebanon
Occupied Palestinian Territory
Oman
Qatar
Saudi Arabia
Syrian Arab Republic
Turkey
United Arab Emirates
Yemen

## Europe

### Eastern Europe

Belarus
Bulgaria
Czech Republic
Hungary
Poland
Republic of Moldova
Romania
Russian Federation
Slovakia
Ukraine

### Northern Europe

Channel Islands
Denmark
Estonia
Faeroe Islands
Finland
Iceland
Ireland
Isle of Man
Latvia
Lithuania
Norway
Svalbard and Jan Mayen Islands
Sweden
United Kingdom

### Southern Europe

Albania
Andorra
Bosnia and Herzegovina
Croatia
Gibraltar
Greece
Holy See
Italy
Malta
Portugal
San Marino
Serbia and Montenegro
Slovenia
Spain
The former Yugoslav Republic of Macedonia

## Asie centrale et du Sud

Afghanistan
Bangladesh
Bhoutan
Inde
Iran (République islamique d')
Kazakhstan
Kirghizistan
Maldives
Népal
Ouzbékistan
Pakistan
Sri Lanka
Tadjikistan
Turkménistan

## Asie du Sud-Est

Brunéi Darussalam
Cambodge
Indonésie
Malaisie
Myanmar
Philippines
République démocratique populaire lao
Singapour
Thaïlande
Timor-Leste
Viet Nam

## Asie occidentale

Arabie saoudite
Arménie
Azerbaïdjan
Bahreïn
Chypre
Emirats arabes unis
Géorgie
Iraq
Israël
Jordanie
Koweït
Liban
Oman
Qatar
République arabe syrienne
Territoire palestinien occupé
Turquie
Yémen

## Europe

### Europe orientale

Bélarus
Bulgarie
Fédération de Russie
Hongrie
Pologne
République de Moldova
République tchèque
Roumanie
Slovaquie
Ukraine

### Europe septentrionale

Danemark
Estonie
Finlande
Ile de Man
Iles Anglo-Normandes
Iles Féroé
Iles Svalbard et Jan Mayen
Irlande
Islande
Lettonie
Lituanie
Norvège
Royaume-Uni
Suède

### Europe méridionale

Albanie
Andorre
Bosnie-Herzégovine
Croatie
Espagne
Ex-République yougoslave de Macédoine
Gibraltar
Grèce
Italie
Malte
Portugal
Saint-Marin
Saint-Siège
Serbie-et-Monténégro
Slovénie

## Western Europe

| | |
|---|---|
| Austria | Luxembourg |
| Belgium | Monaco |
| France | Netherlands |
| Germany | Switzerland |
| Liechtenstein | |

## Oceania

### Australia and New Zealand

| | |
|---|---|
| Australia | Norfolk Island |
| New Zealand | |

### Melanesia

| | |
|---|---|
| Fiji | Solomon Islands |
| New Caledonia | Vanuatu |
| Papua New Guinea | |

### Micronesia-Polynesia

*Micronesia*

| | |
|---|---|
| Guam | Nauru |
| Kiribati | Northern Mariana Islands |
| Marshall Islands | Palau |
| Micronesia | |
| (Federated States of) | |

*Polynesia*

| | |
|---|---|
| American Samoa | Samoa |
| Cook Islands | Tokelau |
| French Polynesia | Tonga |
| Niue | Tuvalu |
| Pitcairn | Wallis and Futuna Islands |

## C. Other groupings

Following is a list of other groupings and their compositions presented in the *Yearbook*. These groupings are organized mainly around economic and trade interests in regional associations.

### Andean Common Market (ANCOM)

| | |
|---|---|
| Bolivia | Peru |
| Colombia | Venezuela |
| Ecuador | |

### Asia-Pacific Economic Cooperation (APEC)

| | |
|---|---|
| Australia | Japan |
| Brunei Darussalam | Malaysia |
| Canada | Mexico |
| Chile | New Zealand |
| China | Papua New Guinea |
| China, Hong Kong Special | Peru |
| Administrative Region | Philippines |
| Indonesia | Republic of Korea |

## Europe occidentale

| | |
|---|---|
| Allemagne | Luxembourg |
| Autriche | Monaco |
| Belgique | Pays-Bas |
| France | Suisse |
| Liechtenstein | |

## Océanie

### Australie et Nouvelle-Zélande

| | |
|---|---|
| Australie | Nouvelle-Zélande |
| Ile Norfolk | |

### Mélanésie

| | |
|---|---|
| Fidji | Papouasie-Nouvelle-Guinée |
| Iles Salomon | Vanuatu |
| Nouvelle-Calédonie | |

### Micronésie-Polynésie

*Micronésie*

| | |
|---|---|
| Guam | Micronésie |
| Iles Mariannes | (Etats fédérés de) |
| septentrionales | Nauru |
| Iles Marshall | Palaos |
| Kiribati | |

*Polynésie*

| | |
|---|---|
| Iles Cook | Samoa |
| Iles Wallis-et-Futuna | Samoa américaines |
| Nioué | Tokélaou |
| Pitcairn | Tonga |
| Polynésie française | Tuvalu |

## C. Autres groupements

On trouvera ci-après une liste des autres groupements et de leur composition, présentée dans l'*Annuaire*. Ces groupements correspondent essentiellement à des intérêts économiques et commerciaux d'après les associations régionales.

### Marché commun andin (ANCOM)

| | |
|---|---|
| Bolivie | Pérou |
| Colombie | Venezuela |
| Equateur | |

### Coopération économique Asie-Pacifique (CEAP)

| | |
|---|---|
| Australie | Fédération de Russie |
| Brunéi Darussalam | Indonésie |
| Canada | Japon |
| Chili | Malaisie |
| Chine | Mexique |
| Chine, Hong Kong, région | Nouvelle-Zélande |
| administrative spéciale | Papouasie-Nouvelle-Guinée |
| Etats-Unis d'Amérique | Pérou |

Russian Federation
Singapore
Taiwan Province of China
Thailand
United States of America
Viet Nam

### Caribbean Community and Common Market (CARICOM)

Antigua and Barbuda
Bahamas (member of the Community only)
Barbados
Belize
Dominica
Grenada
Guyana
Haiti
Jamaica
Montserrat
Saint Kitts and Nevis
Saint Lucia
Saint Vincent and the Grenadines
Suriname
Trinidad and Tobago

### Common Market for Eastern and Southern Africa (COMESA)

Angola
Burundi
Comoros
Democratic Republic of the Congo
Djibouti
Egypt
Eritrea
Ethiopia
Kenya
Madagascar
Malawi
Mauritius
Namibia
Rwanda
Seychelles
Sudan
Swaziland
Uganda
Zambia
Zimbabwe

### Commonwealth of Independent States (CIS)

Armenia
Azerbaijan
Belarus
Georgia
Kazakhstan
Kyrgyzstan
Republic of Moldova
Russian Federation
Tajikistan
Turkmenistan
Ukraine
Uzbekistan

### European Union (EU)

Austria
Belgium
Bulgaria
Cyprus
Czech Republic
Denmark
Estonia
Finland
France
Germany
Greece
Hungary
Ireland
Italy
Latvia
Lithuania
Luxembourg
Malta
Netherlands
Poland
Portugal
Romania
Slovakia
Slovenia
Spain
Sweden
United Kingdom

Philippines
Province chinoise de Taiwan
République de Corée
Singapour
Thaïlande
Viet Nam

### Communauté des Caraïbes et Marché commun des Caraïbes (CARICOM)

Antigua-et-Barbuda
Bahamas (membre de la communauté seulement)
Barbade
Belize
Dominique
Grenade
Guyana
Haïti
Jamaïque
Montserrat
Sainte-Lucie
Saint-Kitts-et-Nevis
Saint-Vincent-et-les Grenadines
Suriname
Trinité-et-Tobago

### Marché commun de l'Afrique de l'Est et de l'Afrique australe (COMESA)

Angola
Burundi
Comores
Djibouti
Egypte
Erythrée
Ethiopie
Kenya
Madagascar
Malawi
Maurice
Namibie
Ouganda
République démocratique du Congo
Rwanda
Seychelles
Soudan
Swaziland
Zambie
Zimbabwe

### Communauté d'Etats indépendants (CEI)

Arménie
Azerbaïdjan
Belarus
Fédération de Russie
Géorgie
Kazakhstan
Kirghizistan
Ouzbékistan
République de Moldova
Tadjikistan
Turkménistan
Ukraine

### Union européenne (UE)

Allemagne
Autriche
Belgique
Bulgarie
Chypre
Danemark
Espagne
Estonie
Finlande
France
Grèce
Hongrie
Irlande
Italie
Lettonie
Lituanie
Luxembourg
Malte
Pays-Bas
Pologne
Portugal
République tchèque
Roumanie
Royaume-Uni
Slovaquie
Slovénie
Suède

## Least deveveloped countries (LDCs)

| | |
|---|---|
| Afghanistan | Madagascar |
| Angola | Malawi |
| Bangladesh | Maldives |
| Benin | Mali |
| Bhutan | Mauritania |
| Burkina Faso | Mozambique |
| Burundi | Myanmar |
| Cambodia | Nepal |
| Cape Verde | Niger |
| Central African Republic | Rwanda |
| Chad | Samoa |
| Comoros | Sao Tome and Principe |
| Democratic Republic of the Congo | Senegal |
| Djibouti | Sierra Leone |
| Equatorial Guinea | Solomon Islands |
| Eritrea | Somalia |
| Ethiopia | Sudan |
| Gambia | Timor-Leste |
| Guinea | Togo |
| Guinea-Bissau | Tuvalu |
| Haiti | Uganda |
| Kiribati | United Republic of Tanzania |
| Lao People's Democratic Republic | Vanuatu |
| Lesotho | Yemen |
| Liberia | Zambia |

## Mercado Común Sudamericano (MERCOSUR)

| | |
|---|---|
| Argentina | Paraguay |
| Brazil | Uruguay |

## North American Free Trade Agreement (NAFTA)

| | |
|---|---|
| Canada | United States of America |
| Mexico | |

## Organisation for Economic Cooperation and Development (OECD)

| | |
|---|---|
| Australia | Luxembourg |
| Austria | Mexico |
| Belgium | Netherlands |
| Canada | New Zealand |
| Czech Republic | Norway |
| Denmark | Poland |
| Finland | Portugal |
| France | Republic of Korea |
| Germany | Slovakia |
| Greece | Spain |
| Hungary | Sweden |
| Iceland | Switzerland |
| Ireland | Turkey |
| Italy | United Kingdom |
| Japan | United States of America |

## Pays les moins avancés (PMA)

| | |
|---|---|
| Afghanistan | Mozambique |
| Angola | Myanmar |
| Bangladesh | Népal |
| Bénin | Niger |
| Bhoutan | Ouganda |
| Burkina Faso | République centrafricaine |
| Burundi | République démocratique du Congo |
| Cambodge | République démocratique populaire lao |
| Cap-Vert | |
| Comores | République-Unie de Tanzanie |
| Djibouti | |
| Erythrée | Rwanda |
| Ethiopie | Samoa |
| Gambie | Sao Tomé-et-Principe |
| Guinée | Sénégal |
| Guinée équatoriale | Sierra Leone |
| Guinée-Bissau | Somalie |
| Haïti | Soudan |
| Iles Salomon | Tchad |
| Kiribati | Timor-Leste |
| Lesotho | Togo |
| Libéria | Tuvalu |
| Madagascar | Vanuatu |
| Malawi | Yémen |
| Maldives | Zambie |
| Mali | |
| Mauritanie | |

## Marché commun sud-américain (Mercosur)

| | |
|---|---|
| Argentine | Paraguay |
| Brésil | Uruguay |

## Accord de libre-échange nord-américain (ALENA)

| | |
|---|---|
| Canada | Mexique |
| Etats-Unis d'Amérique | |

## Organisation de coopération et de développement économiques (OCDE)

| | |
|---|---|
| Allemagne | Japon |
| Australie | Luxembourg |
| Autriche | Mexique |
| Belgique | Norvège |
| Canada | Nouvelle-Zélande |
| Danemark | Pays-Bas |
| Espagne | Pologne |
| Etats-Unis d'Amérique | Portugal |
| Finlande | République de Corée |
| France | République tchèque |
| Grèce | Royaume-Uni |
| Hongrie | Slovaquie |
| Irlande | Suède |
| Islande | Suisse |
| Italie | Turquie |

## Organization of Petroleum Exporting Countries (OPEC)

| | |
|---|---|
| Algeria | Libyan Arab Jamahiriya |
| Angola | Nigeria |
| Ecuador | Qatar |
| Indonesia | Saudi Arabia |
| Iran (Islamic Republic of) | United Arab Emirates |
| Iraq | Venezuela |
| Kuwait | |

## Southern African Customs Union (SACU)

| | |
|---|---|
| Botswana | South Africa |
| Lesotho | Swaziland |
| Namibia | |

Notes

a  The continent of North America comprises Northern America, Caribbean and Central America.

## Organisation des pays exportateurs de pétrole (OPEP)

| | |
|---|---|
| Algérie | Iraq |
| Angola | Jamahiriya arabe libyenne |
| Arabie saoudite | Koweït |
| Emirats arabes unis | Nigéria |
| Equater | Qatar |
| Indonésie | Venezuela |
| Iran (République islamique d') | |

## Union douanière d'Afrique australe

| | |
|---|---|
| Afrique du Sud | Namibie |
| Botswana | Swaziland |
| Lesotho | |

Notes

a  Le continent de l'Amérique du Nord comprend l'Amérique septentrionale, les Caraïbes et l'Amérique centrale.

# Annex II

# Annexe II

## Conversion coefficients and factors

The metric system of weights and measures is employed in the *Statistical Yearbook*. In this system, the relationship between units of volume and capacity is: 1 litre = 1 cubic decimetre (dm³) exactly (as decided by the 12th International Conference of Weights and Measures, New Delhi, November 1964).

Section A shows the equivalents of the basic metric, British imperial and United States units of measurements. According to an agreement between the national standards institutions of English-speaking nations, the British and United States units of length, area and volume are now identical, and based on the yard = 0.9144 metre exactly. The weight measures in both systems are based on the pound = 0.45359237 kilogram exactly (Weights and Measures Act 1963 (London), and *Federal Register announcement of 1 July 1959: Refinement of Values for the Yard and Pound* (Washington D.C.)).

Section B shows various derived or conventional conversion coefficients and equivalents.

Section C shows other conversion coefficients or factors which have been utilized in the compilation of certain tables in the *Statistical Yearbook*. Some of these are only of an approximate character and have been employed solely to obtain a reasonable measure of international comparability in the tables.

For a comprehensive survey of international and national systems of weights and measures and of units' weights for a large number of commodities in different countries, see *World Weights and Measures*.

## A. Equivalents of metric, British imperial and United States units of measure

## Coefficients et facteurs de conversion

L'*Annuaire statistique* utilise le système métrique pour les poids et mesures. La relation entre unités métriques de volume et de capacité est: 1 litre = 1 décimètre cube (dm³) exactement (comme fut décidé à la Conférence internationale des poids et mesures, New Delhi, novembre 1964).

La section A fournit les équivalents principaux des systèmes de mesure métrique, britannique et américain. Suivant un accord entre les institutions de normalisation nationales des pays de langue anglaise, les mesures britanniques et américaines de longueur, superficie et volume sont désormais identiques, et sont basées sur le yard = 0.9144 mètre exactement. Les mesures de poids se rapportent, dans les deux systèmes, à la livre (pound) = 0.45359237 kilogramme exactement (*Weights and Measures Act 1963* (Londres), et *Federal Register Announcement of 1 July 1959: Refinement of Values for the Yard and Pound* (Washington, D.C.)).

La section B fournit divers coefficients et facteurs de conversion conventionnels ou dérivés.

La section C fournit d'autres coefficients ou facteurs de conversion utilisés dans l'élaboration de certains tableaux de l'*Annuaire statistique*. D'aucuns ne sont que des approximations et n'ont été utilisés que pour obtenir un degré raisonnable de comparabilité sur le plan international.

Pour une étude d'ensemble des systèmes internationaux et nationaux de poids et mesures, et d'unités de poids pour un grand nombre de produits dans différents pays, voir *World Weights and Measures*.

## A. Equivalents des unités métriques, britanniques et des États-Unis

| Metric units / Unités métriques | British imperial and US equivalents / Equivalents en mesures britanniques et des Etats-Unis | British imperial and US units / Unités britanniques et des Etats-Unis | Metric equivalents / Equivalents en mesures métriques |
|---|---|---|---|
| **Length — Longueur** | | | |
| 1 centimetre – centimètre (cm) | 0.3937008 inch | 1 inch | 2.540 cm |
| 1 metre – mètre (m) | 3.280840 feet | 1 foot | 30.480 cm |
| | 1.093613 yard | 1 yard | 0.9144 m |
| 1 kilometre – kilomètre (km) | 0.6213712 mile | 1 mile | 1609.344 m |
| | 0.5399568 international nautical mile | 1 international nautical mile | 1852.000 m |
| **Area — Superficie** | | | |
| 1 square centimetre – (cm²) | 0.1550003 square inch | 1 square inch | 6.45160 cm² |
| 1 square metre – (m²) | 10.763910 square feet | 1 square foot | 9.290304 dm² |
| | 1.195990 square yards | 1 square yard | 0.83612736 m² |
| 1 hectare – (ha) | 2.471054 acres | 1 acre | 0.4046856 ha |
| 1 square kilometre – (km²) | 0.3861022 square mile | 1 square mile | 2.589988 km² |
| **Volume** | | | |
| 1 cubic centimetre – (cm³) | 0.06102374 cubic inch | 1 cubic inch | 16.38706 cm³ |
| 1 cubic metre – (m³) | 35.31467 cubic feet | 1 cubic foot | 28.316847 dm³ |
| | 1.307951 cubic yards | 1 cubic yard | 0.76455486 m³ |

| Metric units Unités métriques | British imperial and US equivalents Equivalents en mesures britanniques et des Etats-Unis | | British imperial and US units Unités britanniques et des Etats-Unis | Metric equivalents Equivalents en mesures métriques |
|---|---|---|---|---|
| Capacity — Capacité | | | | |
| 1 litre (l) | 0.8798766 | British imperial quart | 1 British imperial quart | 1.136523 l |
| | 1.056688 | U.S. liquid quart | 1 U.S. liquid quart | 0.9463529 l |
| | 0.908083 | U.S. dry quart | 1 U.S. dry quart | 1.1012208 l |
| 1 hectolitre (hl) | 21.99692 | British imperial gallons | 1 British imperial gallon | 4.546092 l |
| | 26.417200 | U.S. gallons | 1 U.S. gallon | 3.785412 l |
| | 2.749614 | British imperial bushels | 1 imperial bushel | 36.368735 l |
| | 2.837760 | U.S. bushels | 1 U.S. bushel | 35.239067 l |
| Weight or mass — Poids | | | | |
| 1 kilogram (kg) | 35.27396 | av. ounce | 1 av. ounce | 28.349523 g |
| | 32.15075 | troy ounces | 1 troy ounce | 31.10348 g |
| | 2.204623 | av. pounds | 1 av. pound | 453.59237 g |
| | | | 1 cental (100 lb.) | 45.359237 kg |
| | | | 1 hundredweight (112 lb.) | 50.802345 kg |
| 1 ton – tonne (t) | 1.1023113 | short tons | 1 short ton (2 000 lb.) | 0.9071847 t |
| | 0.9842065 | long tons | 1 long ton (2 240 lb.) | 1.0160469 t |

## B. Various conventional or derived coefficients

### *Air transport*

- 1 passenger-mile = 1.609344 passenger kilometre
- 1 short ton-mile = 1.459972 tonne-kilometre
- 1 long ton-mile = 1.635169 tonne kilometre

### *Electric energy*

- 1 Kilowatt (kW) = 1.34102 British horsepower (hp)
- 1.35962 cheval vapeur (cv)

## C. Other coefficients or conversion factors employed in *Statistical Yearbook* tables

### *Roundwood*

- Equivalent in solid volume without bark.

### *Sugar*

- 1 metric ton raw sugar = 0.9 metric ton refined sugar
  For the United States and its possessions:
- 1 metric ton refined sugar = 1.07 metric tons raw sugar

## B. Divers coefficients conventionnels ou dérivés

### *Transport aérien*

- 1 voyageur (passager)-kilomètre = 0.621371 passenger-mile
- 1 tonne-kilomètre = 0.684945 short ton-mile
- 0.611558 long ton-mile

### *Energie électrique*

- 1 British horsepower (hp) = 0.7457 kW
- 1 cheval vapeur (cv) = 0.735499 kW

## C. Autres coefficients ou facteurs de conversion utilisés dans les tableaux de l'*Annuaire statistique*

### *Bois rond*

- Equivalences en volume solide sans écorce.

### *Sucre*

- 1 tonne métrique de sucre brut = 0.9 tonne métrique de sucre raffiné
  Pour les États-Unis et leurs possessions:
- 1 tonne métrique de sucre raffiné = 1.07 tonne métrique de sucre brut

# Annex III

## Tables added and omitted

### A. Tables added

The present issue of the *Statistical Yearbook* features a brand new chapter on gender (Chapter III), which includes three tables:

- Table 12: Women in national parliaments;
- Table 13: Share of women in wage employment in the non-agricultural sector;
- Table 14: Ratio of girls to boys in primary, secondary and tertiary education.

The current issue also includes the following five tables which were not presented in the previous issue:

- Table 9: Selected indicators of life expectancy, childbearing and mortality;
- Table 15: Daily newspapers;
- Table 20: Implicit price deflators of gross domestic product;
- Table 36: Oil crops;
- Table 64: International reserves minus gold.

### B. Tables omitted

The following tables which were presented in previous issues are not presented in the present issue. They will be updated in future issues of the Yearbook when new data become available:

- Population in urban and rural areas, rates of growth and largest urban agglomeration population;
- Livestock;
- Fertilizers;
- Threatened species;
- $CO_2$ emission estimates.

### C. The following tables have been discontinued:

- Railways: traffic;
- Motor vehicles in use;
- International maritime transport.

# Annexe III

## Tableaux ajoutés et supprimés

### A. Tableaux ajoutés

Un nouveau chapitre, le chapitre 3, a été ajouté. Il est consacré à la situation des femmes et comprend trois tableaux fondés sur les indicateurs des objectifs du Millénaire pour le développement :

- Tableau 12 : Femmes élues à l'assemblée nationale;
- Tableau 13 : Proportion de femmes salariées dans le secteur non agricole;
- Tableau 14 : Proportion de filles inscrites dans l'enseignement primaire, secondaire et tertiaire par rapport aux garçons.

En plus, les cinq tableaux suivants qui n'ont pas été présentés dans le numéro antérieur, ont été ajoutés:

- Tableau 9 : Choix d'indicateurs de l'espérance de vie, de la maternité et de la mortalité;
- Tableau 15 : Journaux quotidiens;
- Tableau 20 : Déflateurs implicites des prix de produit intérieur brut;
- Tableau 36 : Culture oléagineuses;
- Tableau 64 : Réserves internationales, moins l'or.

### B. Tableaux supprimés

Les tableaux suivants qui ont été repris dans les éditions antérieures n'ont pas été repris dans la présente édition. Ils seront actualisés dans les futures livraisons de l'Annuaire à mesure que des données nouvelles deviendront disponibles:

- Population urbaine, population rurale, taux d'accroissement et population de l'agglomération urbaine la plus peuplée;
- Cheptel;
- Engrais;
- Espèces menaces;
- Estimations des émissions de $CO_2$.

### C. Les tableaux suivant ont été discontinués :

- Chemins de fer : trafic;
- Véhicules automobiles en circulation;
- Transports maritimes internationaux.

# Statistical sources and references

## A. Statistical sources

1. Food and Agriculture Organization of the United Nations, *FAO Statistical Yearbook* (Rome); web site http://faostat.fao.org.
2. _____, *FAO Yearbook of Fishery Statistics, Aquaculture production* (Rome).
3. _____, *FAO Yearbook of Fishery Statistics, Capture production* (Rome).
4. _____, *Global Forest Resources Assessment 2005* (Rome); web site www.fao.org/forestry/fra2005.
5. International Civil Aviation Organization (Montreal); web site www.icao.int.
6. International Labour Office, *Yearbook of Labour Statistics* (Geneva); web site http://laborsta.ilo.org.
7. International Monetary Fund, *Balance of Payments Statistics Yearbook* (Washington, D.C.); web site www.imf.org.
8. _____, *International Financial Statistics* (Washington, D.C.).
9. International Sugar Organization, *Sugar Yearbook* (London).
10. International Telecommunication Union, *World Telecommunication Development Report* (Geneva); web site www.itu.int.
11. _____, *Yearbook of Statistics, Telecommunication Services, Chronological Time Series* (Geneva).
12. Organisation for Economic Co-operation and Development, *Development Co-operation Report* (Paris); web site www.oecd.org.
13. _____, *Geographical Distribution of Financial Flows to Aid Recipients* (Paris).
14. United Nations, *Demographic Yearbook 2006* (United Nations publication, Sales No. E/F.09.XIII.1).
15. _____, *Energy Statistics Yearbook 2005* (United Nations publication, Sales No. E/F.08.XVII.4).
16. _____, *Industrial Commodity Statistics Yearbook 2005* (United Nations publications, Sales No. E/F.07.XVII.10).
17. _____, *International Trade Statistics Yearbook 2006*, (United Nations publication, Sales No. E/F.08.XVII.24, Vols.I&II).
18. _____, *Monthly Bulletin of Statistics*, various issues up to March 2008 (United Nations publication, Series Q).

# Sources statistiques et références

## A. Sources statistiques

1. Organisation des Nations Unies pour l'alimentation et l'agriculture, *Annuaire Statistique de la FAO* (Rome); site Web http://faostat.fao.org.
2. _____, *Annuaire statistique des pêches, production de l'aquaculture* (Rome).
3. _____, *Annuaire statistique des pêches, captures* (Rome).
4. _____, *Evaluation des ressources forestières mondiales 2005* (Rome); site Web www.fao.org/forestry/fra2005.
5. Organisation de l'aviation civile internationale (Montréal); site Web www.icao.int.
6. Bureau international du Travail, *Annuaire des statistiques du Travail* (Genève); site Web http://laborsta.ilo.org.
7. Fonds monétaire international, "*Balance of Payments Statistics Yearbook*", (Washington, D.C.); site Web www.imf.org.
8. _____, *Statistiques financières internationales*, (Washington, D.C.).
9. Organisation internationale du sucre, *Annuaire du sucre* (Londres).
10. Union internationale des télécommunications, "*World Telecommunication Development Report*" (Genève); site Web www.itu.int.
11. _____, "*Yearbook of Statistics, Telecommunication Services, Chronological Time Series*" (Genève).
12. Organisation de Coopération et de Développement Economiques, *Coopération pour le développement, Rapport* (Paris); site Web www.oecd.org.
13. _____, *Répartition géographique des ressources financières allouées aux pays bénéficiaires de l'aide,* (Paris).
14. Nations Unies, *Annuaire démographique 2006* (publication des Nations Unies, No de vente E/F.09.XIII.1).
15. _____, *Annuaire des statistiques de l'énergie 2005* (publication des Nations Unies, No de vente E/F.08.XVII.4).
16. _____, *Annuaire des statistiques industrielles par produit 2005* (publications des Nations Unies, No de vente E/F.07.XVII.10).
17. _____, *Annuaire statistique du commerce international 2005*, PDF (publication des Nations Unies, No de vente E/F.08.XVII.24, Vols.I&II).
18. _____, *Bulletin mensuel de statistique*, différentes éditions, jusqu'à mars 2008 (publication des Nations Unies, Série Q).

## Statistical sources and references (*continued*)

19. _____, *National Accounts Statistics: Main Aggregates and Detailed Tables, 2006* (United Nations publication, Sales No. 08.XVII.3)

20. _____, *Operational activities of the United Nations for international development cooperation, Report of the Secretary-General, Addendum, Comprehensive statistical data on operational activities for development for the year 2006*" (A/62/326).

21. _____, *World Population Prospects: The 2006 Revision - Comprehensive Dataset* (CD-ROM) (United Nations publication, Sales No. E.07.XIII.8).

22. United Nations Educational, Scientific and Cultural Organization Institute for Statistics (Montreal); web site www.uis.unesco.org.

23. World Bank, *Global Development Finance*, vols. I and II, (Washington, D.C.); web site www.worldbank.org.

24. World Tourism Organization, *Yearbook of Tourism Statistics, 2007 edition* (Madrid); web site www.world-tourism.org.

### B. References

37. International Labour Office, *International Standard Classification of Occupations, Revised Edition 1968* (Geneva, 1969); revised edition, 1988, *ISCO-88* (Geneva, 1990).

38. International Monetary Fund, *Balance of Payments Manual, Fifth Edition* (Washington, D.C., 1993).

39. United Nations, *Classifications of Expenditure According to Purpose: Classification of the Functions of Government (COFOG), Classification of Individual Consumption According to Purpose (COICOP), Classification of the Purposes of Non-Profit Institutions Serving Households (COPNI), Classification of the Outlays of Producers According to Purpose (COPP)*, Series M, No. 84 (United Nations publication, Sales No. E.00.XVII.6).

40. _____, *Energy Statistics: Definitions, Units of Measure and Conversion Factors*, Series F, No. 44 (United Nations publication, Sales No. E.86.XVII.21).

41. _____, *Energy Statistics: Manual for Developing Countries*, Series F, No. 56 (United Nations publication, Sales No. E.91.XVII.10).

42. _____, *Handbook of Vital Statistics Systems and Methods*, vol. I, *Legal, Organization and Technical Aspects*, Series F, No. 35, vol. I (United Nations publication, Sales No. E.91.XVII.5).

43. _____, *Handbook on Social Indicators*, Studies in Methods, Series F, No. 49 (United Nations publication, Sales No. E.89.XVII.6).

## Sources statistiques et références (*suite*)

19. _____, "*National Accounts Statistics: Main Aggregates and Detailed Tables, 2006*" (publication des Nations Unies, No de vente 08.XVII.3.

20. _____, *Activités opérationnelles du système des Nations Unies au service de la coopération internationale pour le développement, Rapport du Secrétaire général, Additif, Données statistiques globales sur les activités opérationnelles au service du développement pour 2006 (A/62/74).*

21. _____, "*World Population Prospects: The 2006 Revision - Comprehensive Dataset* "(CD-ROM) (publication des Nations Unies, No de vente F.07.XIII.8).

22. Institut de statistique de l'Organisation des Nations Unies pour l'éducation, la science et la culture (Montréal); site Web www.uis.unesco.org.

23. Banque mondiale, "*Global Development Finance*, Vols. I et II," (Washington, D.C.).

24. Organisation mondiale du tourisme, *l'Annuaire des statistiques du tourisme, 2007* (Madrid); site Web www.world-tourism.org.

### B. Références

37. Organisation internationale du Travail, *Classification internationale type des professions, édition révisée* 1968 (Genève, 1969); édition révisée 1988, *CITP-88* (Genève, 1990).

38. Fonds monétaire international, *Manuel de la balance des paiements, cinquième édition* (Washington, D.C., 1993).

39. Nations Unies, "*Classifications of Expenditure According to Purpose: Classification of the Functions of Government (COFOG), Classification of Individual Consumption According to Purpose (COICOP), Classification of the Purposes of Non-Profit Institutions Serving Households (COPNI), Classification of the Outlays of Producers According to Purpose (COPP)*", Série M, No 84 (publication des Nations Unies, No de vente E. 00.XVII.6).

40. _____, *Statistiques de l'énergie: définitions, unités de mesures et facteurs de conversion*, Série F, No 44 (publication des Nations Unies, No de vente F.86.XVII.21).

41. _____, *Statistiques de l'énergie: Manuel pour les pays en développement*, Série F, No 56 (publication des Nations Unies, No de vente F.91.XVII.10).

42. _____, "*Handbook of Vital Statistics System and Methods*, Vol. 1, *Legal, Organization and Technical Aspects*", Série F, No 35, Vol. 1 (publication des Nations Unies, No de vente E.91.XVII.5).

44. _____, *International Recommendations for Industrial Statistics*, Series M, No. 48, Rev. 1 (United Nations publication, Sales No. E.83.XVII.8).

45. _____, *International Standard Industrial Classification of All Economic Activities*, Statistical Papers, Series M, No. 4, Rev. 2 (United Nations publication, Sales No. E.68.XVII.8); Rev. 3 (United Nations publication, Sales No. E.90.XVII.11).

46. _____, *International Trade Statistics: Concepts and Definitions*, Series M, No. 52, Rev. 1 (United Nations publication, Sales No. E.82.XVII.14).

47. _____, *Methods Used in Compiling the United Nations Price Indexes for External Trade*, volume 1, Statistical Papers, Series M, No. 82 (United Nations Publication, Sales No. E.87.XVII.4).

48. _____, *Principles and Recommendations for Population and Housing Censuses*, Statistical Papers, Series M, No. 67 (United Nations publication, Sales No. E.80.XVII.8).

49. _____, *Provisional Guidelines on Statistics of International Tourism*, Statistical Papers, Series M, No. 62 (United Nations publication, Sales No. E.78.XVII.6).

50. _____ and World Tourism Organization, *Recommendations on Tourism Statistics*, Statistical Papers, Series M, No. 83 (United Nations publication, Sales No. E.94.XVII.6).

51. _____, *Standard International Trade Classification, Revision 3*, Statistical Papers, Series M, No. 34, Rev. 3 (United Nations publication, Sales No. E.86.XVII.12), *Revision 2*, Series M, No. 34, Rev. 2 (United Nations publication), *Revision*, Series M, No. 34, Revision (United Nations publication, Sales No. E.61.XVII.6).

52. _____, *Supplement to the Statistical Yearbook and the Monthly Bulletin of Statistics, 1977*, Series S and Series Q, Supplement 2 (United Nations publication, Sales No. E.78.XVII.10).

53. _____, *System of National Accounts, Studies in Methods*, Series F, No. 2, Rev. 3 (United Nations publication, Sales No. E.69.XVII.3).

54. _____, *System of National Accounts 1993*, Studies in Methods, Series F, No. 2, Rev. 4 (United Nations publication, Sales No. E.94.XVII.4).

55. _____, *Towards a System of Social and Demographic Statistics, Studies in Methods*, Series F, No. 18 (United Nations publication, Sales No. E.74.XVII.8).

56. _____, *World Weights and Measures* (United Nations publication, Sales No. E.66.XVII.3).

57. World Health Organization, *Manual of the International Statistical Classification of Diseases, Injuries and Causes of Death*, vol. 1 (Geneva, 1977).

43. _____, *Manuel des indicateurs sociaux*, Série F, No 49 (publication des Nations Unies, No de vente F.89.XVII.6).

44. _____, *Recommandations internationales concernant les statistiques industrielles*, Série M, No 48, Rev. 1 (publication des Nations Unies, No de vente F.83.XVII.8).

45. _____, *Classification internationale type, par industrie, de toutes les branches d'activité économique*, Série M, No 4, Rev. 2 (publication des Nations Unies, No de vente F.68.XVII.8); Rev. 3 (publication des Nations Unies, No de vente F.90.XVII.11).

46. _____, *Statistiques du commerce international: Concepts et définitions*, Série M, No 52, Rev. 1 (publication des Nations Unies, No de vente F.82.XVII.14).

47. _____, *Méthodes utilisées par les Nations Unies pour établir les indices des prix des produits de base entrant dans le commerce international*, Série M, No 82, Vol. 1 (publication des Nations Unies, No de vente F.87.XVII.4).

48. _____, *Principes et recommandations concernant les recensements de la population et de l'habitation*, Série M, No 67 (publication des Nations Unies, No de vente F.80.XVII.8).

49. _____, *Directives provisoires pour l'établissement des statistiques du tourisme international*, Série M, No 62 (publication des Nations Unies, No de vente 78.XVII.6).

50. _____ et l'Organisation mondiale du tourisme, "*Recommendations on Tourism Statistics*, Statistical Papers", Série M, No. 83 (publication des Nations Unies, No. de vente E.94.XVII.6).

51. _____, *Classification type pour le commerce international (troisième version révisée)*, Série M, No 34, Rev. 3 (publication des Nations Unies, No de vente F.86.XVII.12), *Révision 2*, Série M, No 34, Rev. 2 (publication des Nations Unies), *Révision*, Série M, No. 34, Révision (publication des Nations Unies, No de vente F.61.XVII.6).

52. _____, *Supplément à l'Annuaire statistique et au bulletin mensuel de statistique, 1977*, Série S et Série Q, supplément 2 (publication des Nations Unies, No de vente F.78.XVII.10).

53. _____, *Système de comptabilité nationale*, Série F, No 2, Rev. 3 (publication des Nations Unies, No de vente F.69.XVII.3).

54. _____, *Système de comptabilité nationale 1993*, Série F, No 2, Rev. 4 (publication des Nations Unies, No de vente F.94.XVII.4).

# Index

*Note*: References to tables are indicated by **boldface** type.

## A

aggregates, national accounting, relationships among, **235–246**, 291–292

agricultural production, **15**, **16**, **401–404**

    method of calculating series, 26, 430

    per capita, **16**

    sources of information, 26, 430

agricultural products (non–food), 378–385, 398–399

    defined, 430

    prices, 378–385

    production, **401–404**

    *See also* food

agriculture, hunting, forestry, fishing, 3, 291

production, 11, **401–432**

    value added by, **220–234**

aid. *See* development assistance

airline traffic. *See* civil aviation

aluminium

    defined, 490

    production, **484–485**

apparel industry. *See* textile, wearing apparel, leather and footwear

arable land, as percentage of total land area, 549–553, 558

aviation. *See* civil aviation

## B

balance of payments, 3, 697

    by category of payment, **699–739**

    definition of terms, 740–741

*Balance of Payments Manual* (IMF), 740

*Balance of Payments Statistics Yearbook* (IMF), 697

beer

    defined, 489

    production, **463–467**

beverage industry. *See* food, beverages, tobacco industries

beverages, 292

    as percentage of household consumption expenditure, **255–260**

    production, **17–21**, **261–288**

beverages, alcoholic. *See* beer

birth, rate of, **13–14**, 26

brown coal. *See* lignite

buffalo

    meat production, **444–462**, 489

business enterprises, research and development expenditures by, **572–578**, 580

## C

call money rates. *See* money market rate

capital account

    defined, 741

    in balance of payments, **699–739**

capital goods, 398

    prices, **378–385**

cattle

    meat production, **444–462**

cellular mobile telephones,

    defined, 166

    subscribers and per 100 inhabitants, **138–151**

cement, **480–483**, 490

central banks, discount rates, **295–298**

cereals (grain),

    defined, 430

    production, **11**, **405–411**

chemical industry production, **17–21**, **261–288**, 546, 619

chicken

    meat production, **444–462**

chlorofluorocarbon (CFC) consumption, **554–557**

    method of calculating series, 558–559

cigarettes, production, **468–472**, 489

civil aviation

    definition of terms, 697–698

    passengers and freight carried, **681–695**

Classification of the Functions of Government (COFOG), **247–254**

clothing and footwear

    as percentage of household consumption expenditure, **255–260**, 292

    *See also* textile, wearing apparel, leather and footwear

coal

    defined, 544–546

    production, **11**, **17–21**, **526–542**

coke, 544

commodities, 3, **11–12**, 26, 430, 544, 740, 823

    classification of, 618

    conversion tables for, 824

commodities, primary. *See* raw materials

communication, **124–165**. *See also* transport and communications

communication industry. *See* transport, storage and communication industries

*Compendium of Tourism Statistics* (UNWTO), 696, 697

compensation of employees to and from the rest of the world, as percentage of GDP, **235–246**

construction industry, value added by, **220–234**

consumer price index, **386–397**, 399

consumption. *See* government final consumption; household final consumption

conversion factors, 544, 824

    currency, 618–620

conversion tables

    for selected commodities, 824

    for units of measure and weight, 823–824

countries and areas

    boundaries and legal status of, not implied by this publication, ii

    coverage of, in *Statistical Yearbook*, 2–3

    economic and regional associations, **818–821**

    recent name changes, **813–814**

    regional groupings for statistical purposes, 3, **814–821**

    statistics reported for, 617, 618

    surface area, **13–14**, 26, **31–43**, 54

    *See also* developed countries, economies or areas; developing countries, economies or areas

    croplands, permanent, as percentage of total land area, **549–553**

crops, 26, **412–418**, 430–431, **549–553**, 558

crude oil. *See* petroleum, crude

culture, **117–123**, 166

currency

    conversion factors, 4, 289–291, 581, 618–620

    exchange rates, 4, **189–206**, 289–291, 618–620, **743–759**, 784

    method of calculating series, 289–291, 618–620

current account

    defined, 740

    in balance of payments, **699–739**

current transfers, **235–246**, 291

    defined, 740

    in balance of payments, **699–739**

customs area, 601, 617

## D

daily newspapers, **117-123**, 166

death, rate of, **13–14**, 26

defence, national, as percentage of government final consumption expenditure, **247–253**, 291–292

*Demographic Yearbook* (UN), 14, 39, 54

developed countries, economies or areas, ii, 3, **17**, **24**, 166, **585**, **587**, **611**, **614**, 619, 814

    defined, ii, 3, 814–815

    development assistance from, **802**

developing countries, economies or areas, ii, 2–3, **18**, 27, 54, 166, **615**, 619, **776–783**, 784, **787**, **802–812**, 814

    defined, ii, 3, 814–815

    development assistance to, 3, **787–811**, 812

    external debt of, **776–783**, 784–786

development assistance, **787–811**, 812

    bilateral and multilateral, to individuals, 785, **787–801**

    to developing countries and multilateral organizations, **802**

    United Nations system, **803–811**, 812

*Development Assistance Committee (DAC)* countries, development assistance from, **802**, 812

discount rates, **295–298**

    defined, 308

domestic production, prices, **378–385**, 398

domestic supply, prices, **378–385**, 398

## E

earnings. *See* wages

economic activity (industry), iii, 2, 291, **336–362**, 363–364

    employment by, **336–362**

    value added by kind of, **220–234**

economic affairs, as percentage of government final consumption expenditure, **247–254**, 292

economic associations, country lists, 818–821

economic relations, international. *See* international economic relations

economic statistics, **171–581**

education

    as percentage of government final consumption expenditure, **247–253**, 291

    as percentage of household consumption expenditure, **255–260**, 292

    definition of terms, 114–115

    levels of, primary, secondary and tertiary, number of students, **91–108**

    method of calculating series, 114–115

    public expenditures on, **109–113**

    sources of information, 114–115

education sector, research and development expenditures by, **572–578**

electrical products. *See* office and related electrical products

electricity, 27, 88, **220–232**, 291–292, 489

    consumption, **22**, **492–525**, **255–260**

    defined, 544, 546

    production, **11**, **17–21**, **22–23**, **261–287**, **492–524**, **526–542**

electricity, gas, water utilities

    production, **17–21**

    value added by, **220–232**

employment, 2, 4, 5, **65–72**, 88–89, 374, 375, 398

    by economic activity, **336–362**

    definition, 363–364

    *See also* unemployment; labour force

energy, iii, 2, 3, **22–23**,

energy commodities (solid, liquid, gas, and electrical)

    consumption, **22–23**, **492–525**

    definition of terms, 544–547

    method of calculating series, 544–547

    production, **22–23**, **526–543**

    stocks, **492–525**

    trade, **22–23**, **492–525**

*Energy Statistics Yearbook* (UN), 544

environment, **549–559**

environmental protection, as percentage of government final consumption expenditure, **247–254**

exchange rates. *See* currency

exports

    as percentage of GDP, **207–219**

    defined, 617–620

    in balance of payments, **699–739**, 740

    index numbers, **24–25**, **603–616**

    purchasing power of, **603–610**

    value of, **12**, **585–616**, 617–620, 740

    volume of, **12**, 601, **603–616**, 618–620

    *See also* external trade

external debt

    definition of terms, 784–786

    of developing countries or areas, **776–783**

external trade (international trade), **12**, **24–25**, **585–616**

    as percentage of GDP, **207–219**

    method of calculating series, 617–620

    sources of information, 617

    systems for recording of, 617

    value of, **12**, **585–616**, 617–620, 740

    volume of, **12**, 601, **603–616**, 617–620

    *See also* exports; imports

**F**

fabrics. *See* textile, wearing apparel, leather and footwear

*Factbook of Tourism Statistics*, 696

factor income, 291

*FAO Yearbook of Fishery Statistics, Aquaculture Production*, 431

*FAO Yearbook of Fishery Statistics, Capture Production*, 431

*FAO Global Forest Resources Assessment. See Global Forest Resources Assessment* (FAO)

finance, international. *See* international finance

financial account

    defined, 741

    in balance of payments, **699–739**

financial statistics, **12**, **295–307**

    sources of information, 308

fishing

    aquaculture, **422–429**, 431

    captures, **422–429**

    definition of terms, 431

    production, **11**

    sources of information, 429, 431

    *See also* agriculture, hunting, forestry, fishing

fixed capital. *See* gross fixed capital formation

food

    defined, 430

    prices, **386–397**, 399

    production, **11**, **15**, **17–21**, **401–404**

    production per capita, **16**

food, beverages, tobacco, as percentage of household consumption expenditure, **255–260**

food, beverages, tobacco industries, production, **17–21**, **261–288**

foreign exchange reserves, **12**, **760–775**

forest cover, **549–553**, 558

forestry. *See* agriculture, hunting, forestry, fishing

*Frascati Manual*, 579

free–on–board (f.o.b.), defined, 618, 740

fuel, 27, 115, 292, **526–543**, 544–546. *See also* housing and utilities

furniture, household equipment, maintenance, ss percentage of household consumption expenditure, **255–260**

furniture industry. *See* wood and wood products

**G**

gas. *See* liquefied petroleum gas; natural gas; natural gas liquids; refinery gas

gas utilities. *See* electricity, gas, water utilities

international trade. *See* external trade

*International Trade Statistics: Concepts and Definitions* (UN), 617

*International Trade Statistics Yearbook* (UN), 617

Internet users

    method of calculating series, 166–167

    number and per 100 inhabitants, **152–165**

inventories (stocks), changes in, as percentage of GDP, **207–219**

investment income. *See* property income to and from the rest of the world

ISCED. *See International Standard Classification of Education Statistics* (ISCED)

ISIC. *See International Standard Industrial Classification of All Economic Activities* (ISIC)


## L

labour force, **309–364**

    sources of information, 363–364

    wages, **365–377**

land

    area and categories of, arable, forest and permanent cropland, **549–553**

    definition of terms, 558

lignite

    defined, 544–545

    production, **11**, **526–543**

liquefied petroleum gas (LPG), 546

    production, **526–543**


## M

manufactured goods

    defined, 617–620

    external trade in, **611–616**

    value of, **12**

manufacturing industries

    production, **11–12**, **17–21**, **433–488**

    sources of information, 489–490

    value added by, **220–234**

    wages, **365–377**

market exchange rates (MERs), 188, 289–290

meat

    defined, 489

    production, **444–462**

metal ores, production, **17–21**

metal products industries, production, **17–21**, **261–288**

metals, basic, **17–21**, **261–288**

mineral products, non–metallic, production, **17–21**, **261–288**

mining and quarrying, 88, 234, 291–292, 489

    employment by, **336–362**

    production, **11**, **17–21**, **261–288**

    value added by, **220–234**

monetary gold and silver, 618, 740

money market rate, **299–307**

    defined, 308

*Monthly Bulletin of Statistics* (UN), 308, 399, 617, 619

multilateral institutions, 812

    debt to, **776–777**

    defined, 784–786, 812

    development assistance from, **787–801**

    development contributions to, **802**


## N

national accounts, **171–260**

    definition of terms, 289–292

    relationships between principal aggregates of, **235–246**

*National Accounts Statistics: Main Aggregates and Detailed Tables* (UN), 289

national income, as percentage of GDP, **235–246**

natural gas,

    defined, 544–546

    production, **11**, **17–21**, **526–543**

natural gas liquids (NGL), 544

    defined, 545

    production, **526–543**

net current transfers to and from the rest of the world, as percentage of GDP, **235–246**

net errors and omissions

    defined, 741

    in balance of payments, **699–739**

newspapers. *See* daily newspapers


## O

office and related electrical products, **17–21**

online databases, 6

"other" economic activities, value added by, **220–234**, 291

ozone–depleting chlorofluorocarbons (CFC), consumption, **554–557**, 558–559


## P

paper, printing, publishing, recorded media industries, production, **17–21**, **477–479**, 490

paper and paperboard

    defined, 490

water utilities. *See* electricity, gas, water utilities

welfare services. *See* social protection

wholesale prices, **378–385**

    defined, 399

wholesale trade. *See* trade (wholesale/retail), restaurants, hotel industries

wood and wood products, **17–21**. *See* also roundwood; sawnwood

woodpulp, production, **12**

*World Debt Tables. See Global Development Finance*

*World Population Prospects* (UN), 26, 53–54, 123, 801

world statistics

    selected series, **11–12**

    summary, **9–28**

*World Weights and Measures*, 823

## Y

*Yearbook of Labour Statistics* (ILO), 360, 363, 398

*Yearbook of Statistics, Telecommunication Services* (ITU), 166

# Related Products

## World Statistics Pocketbook

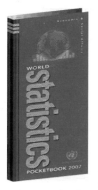

The United Nations World Statistics Pocketbook is an authoritative and comprehensive compilation of key statistical indicators in convenient country profile format. The 2007 edition presents available data for 215 countries and areas for 55 indicators, generally for the years 2000 and 2006, in the areas of population, economic activity, agriculture, industry, energy, international trade, transport, communications, gender, education and environment, based on over 20 international statistical sources. The notes on the sources and definitions of the indicators are provided to help users perform further research on the statistics.

## Monthly Bulletin of Statistics (MBS)

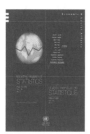

MBS presents current economic and social statistics for more than 200 countries and territories of the world. It contains over 50 tables of monthly and/or annual and quarterly data on a variety of subjects illustrating important economic long-term trends and developments, including population, prices, employment and earnings, energy, manufacturing, transport, construction, international merchandise trade and finance. A subscription to the printed version of MBS includes access to the MBS Online.

*To order any of these products, visit the United Nations Sales Section website at* https://unp.un.org:

## UNdata

The United Nations Statistics Division has launched a new internet-based data service for the global user community. It brings UN statistical databases within easy reach of users through a single entry point. Users can search and download a variety of statistical resources of the UN system.

*To use UNdata, visit* http://data.un.org

# Autres produits

## World Statistics Pocketbook

Le "World Statistics Pocketbook" de l'Organization des Nations Unies présente, dans un format commode, pays par pays, un ensemble complet d'indicateurs statistiques de base. Sauf exception, l'édition 2007 comprend les donnees disponibles sur 55 indicateurs pour 215 pays et zones géographiques pour les années 2000 et 2006 dans les domaines suivants : population, activité économique, agriculture, industrie, énergie, commerce international, transports, communications, situation des femmes, éducation et environnement. Des explications sur les sources et les définitions des indicateurs sont fournies afin de permettre aux utilisateurs de faire des recherches plus approfondies sur les statistiques.

## Bulletin mensuel de statistique

Le Bulletin mensuel de statistique présente les statistiques économiques et sociales de plus de 200 pays et régions du monde. On y trouve une cinquantaine de tableaux regroupant des données mensuelles, annuelles ou trimestrielles sur de nombreux sujets qui illustrent d'importantes tendances économiques à long terme touchant la population, les prix, l'emploi et les salaires, l'énergie, les industries manufacturières, les transports, le bâtiment, le commerce international de marchandies et les finances. L'abonnement à la version papier du Bulletin permet également de consulter la version en ligne.

*Pour commander ces ouvrages, consultez le site Web de la Section des ventes de l'ONU, à l'adresse* https://unp.un.org

## UNdata

Le département de statistique des Nations Unies lance un nouveau service sur internet destiné à l'ensemble des utilisateurs à travers le monde. Les bases de données statistiques des Nations unies seront désormais accessibles aisément sur le site où les utilisateurs pourront rechercher ou télécharger une variété de ressources statistiques du système.

*Pour utiliser UNdata, consultez* http://data.un.org